London 2012
Olympic Games
and Paralympic Games

Lee Valley White Water Centre

Hadleigh Farm

Wembley Arena
Wembley Stadium

Lord's Cricket Ground

Olympic Park

ExCeL

Hyde Park

The Mall

Hampton Court Palace

Earls Court

Horse Guards Parade

North Greenwich Arena

Eton Dorney

Greenwich Park

The Royal Artillery Barracks

Brands Hatch

Wimbledon

Olympic Park Map —II-III.
Olympic Park
  Aquatics Centre —V. (7E 68)
  Basketball Arena —V. (5D 68)
  BMX Track —VI. (5D 68)
  Copper Box —VI. (6C 68)
  Eton Manor —VII. (4D 68)
  Olympic Stadium —V. (7D 68)
  Riverbank Arena —X. (5C 68)
  Velodrome —XI. (5D 68)
  Water Polo Arena —XII. (7D 68)
 Brands Hatch —VI.
 Earls Court —VI. (5J 99)
 Eton Dorney —VI.
 ExCeL —VII. (7K 87)
 Greenwich Park —VIII. (6F 105)
 Hadleigh Farm —IX.
 Hampton Court Palace —IX. (3K 149)
 Horse Guards Parade —IX. (5D 12)
 Hyde Park —IX. (4C 10)
 Lee Valley White Water
   Centre —IX.

Lord's Cricket Ground —X. (1B 4)
The Mall —X. (6C 12)
North Greenwich Arena —X. (1G 105)
The Royal Artillery Barracks —XI. (6D 106)
Wembley Arena —XII. (4G 61)
Wembley Stadium —XII. (4G 61)
Weymouth and Portland—XII
Wimbledon —XII. (3G 135)

London 2012 Shops —XIII
Live sites —XIII
Transport —XIII
Journey Planner —XVI

Olympic Park Map
Olympic sport
Paralympic sport
Venue entrance
Spectator route
Step-free station
London 2012 shop
0 100 m
P+R
Eton Manor Transport Hub
HACKNEY MARSH RECREATION GROUND
RIVER LEA
RUCKHOLT ROAD A106
Perimeter
A12
HIGH ROAD LEYTON MAJOR ROAD
CHOBHAM ROAD
LEYTON
A112
ANGEL ROAD
LANE
Eton Manor
Eton Manor Gate
Eton Manor Walk
HOMERTON ROAD B112
LEA INTERCHANGE
Temple Mills Bridge
EAST CROSS ROUTE
EAST WAY A106
WICK WOODLAND HACKNEY MARSH
Athletes Transport Hub
BMX Track
Riverbank Arena
Velodrome
River Lawns
The Street Market
Park Live East
Park Live West
Warm-up Pitch
Basketball Arena
Olympic and Paralympic Village
International Broadcast Centre
Main Press Centre
LS
Wetlands Walk
London
Britannia Row
Copper Box
STRATFORD INTERNATIONAL
DLR
High Speed 1
WESTFIELD STRATFORD CITY SHOPPING CENTRE
Bus Sta.

HACKNEY WICK
Way
World Square
Art Installation
Hospitality Centre
Stratford Gate
STRATFORD
Jubilee
Central
DLR
THE STRATFORD CENTRE
A118 EASTERN
GT. EASTERN RD.
BROADWAY
Hertford Union Canal
Water Polo Arena
Stratford Walk
Aquatics Centre
The Orbit
Orbit Circus
Olympic Stadium
Perimeter
Old Ford Locks
Victoria Walk
Victoria Gate
Mitford Bri.
A12
EAST CROSS ROUTE
Warm-up Field
OLD FORD
PARNELL ROAD
B142
TREDEGAR ROAD
Marketing Transport Hub
Greenway Walk
Greenway Gate
Greenway Transport Hub
P+R
HIGH A118 STREET
A118
Three Mills Wall River
Stratford Bri.
STRATFORD HIGH STREET
WEST HAM
District
Hammersmith
Jubilee

This summer London and the UK will come alive with the world's largest sporting events when the Games begin.

The London 2012 Olympic and Paralympic Games will encompass 30 days of competition with 14,723 athletes and millions of people gathered here to enjoy the sporting and cultural action.

Olympic Heritage

The first ancient Olympic Games can be traced back to 776 BC. They were dedicated to the Olympian gods and staged on the plains of Olympia in Greece. The modern Olympic Games were founded by French-born athlete, poet and educator Pierre de Coubertin (1863–1937).

Olympic Games

In 2012 London will host a Games like never before, drawing on the UK's proud Olympic heritage. In 1908, London stood in as Host City for Rome after an eruption of Mount Vesuvius. It was the first time that the athletes paraded under national flags at the start of the Games and the Marathon was fixed at 42.195km (26.2 miles). In 1948, London again stepped in at the last minute to host the first Games after World War II. It was the first time that the Games were shown on home television.

Paralympic Games

The London 2012 Paralympic Games are being organised together with the Olympic Games. In 1948, Dr Ludwig Guttmann organised a sports competition that involved World War II soldiers with spinal cord injuries based at Stoke Mandeville Hospital. The competition took place between sports clubs and other hospitals on the same day as the Opening Ceremony of the London 1948 Olympic Games. Four years later, athletes from Holland joined in, creating the forerunner of the Paralympic Games. The first official Paralympic Games was that held in Rome in 1960.

Olympic Torch Relay

An important element of the Olympic Games of Ancient Greece, the Flame is lit from the sun's rays at the Temple of Hera in Olympia. The Olympic Torch Relay route has been planned so that the Flame will come within 10 miles of 95% of people in the UK. The last Torchbearer lights the cauldron at the Olympic Games Opening Ceremony.

Cultural Olympiad

The London 2012 Festival will bring leading artists from all over the world to create the UK's biggest ever festival; a chance for everyone to celebrate London 2012 through dance, music, theatre, the visual arts, film and digital innovation and leave a lasting legacy for the arts in the UK.

Legacy

For the first time, the Games are being planned hand-in-hand with the long-term improvement of the area. A new sustainable community will be integrated with the area surrounding the Olympic Park, with local people benefiting from a new park, homes and world-class sporting facilities.

Olympic Stadium

The Olympic Stadium will host the Athletics and Paralympic Athletics events at the London 2012 Games, as well as the Opening and Closing Ceremonies.

Athletics

One of the most popular sports is also the biggest, with 2,000 athletes competing in 47 events. There are four main strands to the Athletics competition: track events, such as the 100m; field events, which include the High Jump and the Shot Put; combined events such as the Decathlon, a mix of track and field elements; and road events, among them the Marathon.

Paralympic Athletics

Athletics will also be the largest sport at the Paralympic Games with 1,100 athletes competing. Some athletes compete in wheelchairs or throwing frames, others with prostheses, and others with the guidance of a sighted companion.

Aquatics Centre

The Aquatics Centre will be the venue for Swimming, Paralympic Swimming, Diving, Synchronised Swimming and the swimming element of the Modern Pentathlon. The venue features a spectacular wave-like roof that is 160m long and up to 80m wide.

Diving

Diving requires acrobatic excellence and supreme coordination skills, as athletes dive from heights of up to 10m.

Swimming

There are four strokes used in Olympic competition: Freestyle, Backstroke, Breaststroke and Butterfly. The 10km Marathon Swimming will be held in the Serpentine within Hyde Park.

Synchronised Swimming

Synchronised Swimmers use pinpoint precision and immense stamina to deliver beautiful routines in the pool.

Modern Pentathlon

The venue for the swimming element of Modern Pentathlon. The fencing element takes place in Copper Box, riding and the combined event will be staged in Greenwich Park.

Paralympic Swimming

Swimmers are classified according to their functional ability to perform each stroke, and compete against athletes in their own classification.

Basketball Arena

The fourth-largest venue on the Olympic Park and one of the largest ever temporary venues built for any Games.

Basketball

Preliminaries and women's quarter-finals are held here at the Basketball Arena. All other rounds take place in the North Greenwich Arena.

Handball

Venue for the Handball men's quarter-finals, all semi-finals and all medal matches. All other rounds take place in the Copper Box.

 ## Wheelchair Basketball

Preliminary games will be split between the Basketball Arena and North Greenwich Arena. All quarter-finals, semi-finals and medal games will take place at North Greenwich Arena.

 ## Wheelchair Rugby

Played indoors on a regulation-size basketball court by teams of four, contact between wheelchairs is permitted, but physical contact is outlawed.

BMX Track

The purpose built BMX Track will be re-configured after the Games to form part of a new VeloPark with a mountain bike track and road-cycle circuit.

 ## BMX Racing

Inspired by motocross, BMX Racing is the most recent discipline to have been added to the Olympic programme.

Brands Hatch

Brands Hatch motor racing circuit in Kent is approximately 20 miles south-east of the Olympic Park.

Paralympic Cycling - Road

Athletes with a visual impairment, cerebral palsy, amputations or other physical disabilities compete on bicycles, tricycles, tandems and hand cycles.

Copper Box

This Olympic Park venue will be adapted after the Games to become a multi-use sports centre for community use, athlete training and small- to medium-sized events.

 ## Handball

Preliminary rounds of both the men's and women's competitions, as well as the women's quarter-finals, will take place here. The competition will then move to the Basketball Arena, also in the Olympic Park.

 ## Modern Pentathlon

Fencing, the first element of Modern Pentathlon takes place here. Swimming takes place in the Aquatics Centre, riding and the combined event in Greenwich Park.

 ## Goalball

Goalball is played by visually impaired athletes using a ball with bells inside. Athletes wear blackout masks on the playing court, which allows persons with varying degrees of vision to participate together.

Earls Court

A major west London venue for exhibitions, conferences and events.

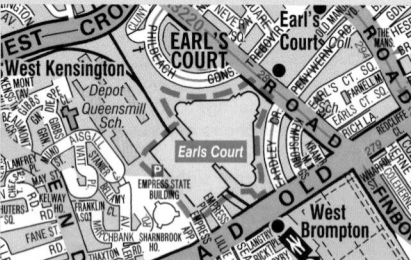

 ## Volleyball

The dynamic, competitive sport of Volleyball made its Olympic debut in 1964.

Eton Dorney

Eton Dorney is located near Windsor Castle, about 25 miles west of London.

 ## Canoe Sprint

Races will be held over three distances

with the fastest races taking just 30 seconds to complete. Canoe Slalom takes place at Lee Valley White Water Centre.

 ## Rowing

The 14 Olympic Rowing events range from the Single Sculls, featuring solo rowers, to the Eights, contested by teams of eight rowers plus a cox.

 ## Paralympic Rowing

Appearing at the Paralympic Games for only the second time. Adaptive rowing boats are equipped with special seats, which vary according to the disability of the athlete.

Eton Manor

Eton Manor will be transformed after the Games into sporting facilities for local and regional communities.

 ## Wheelchair Tennis

First played in 1976, Wheelchair Tennis is one of the fastest-growing wheelchair sports in the world.

ExCeL

A London Docklands exhibition and conference centre, its arenas will host a range of Olympic and Paralympic sports.

Boxing

Men's Boxing events will be joined on the Olympic programme by a women's competition for the first time. Boxing

featured at the original Olympic Games in the 7th century BC.

 ## Fencing

Although sword fighting dates back thousands of years, Fencing really came of age as a sport in the 19th century.

 ## Judo

Developed from jujitsu and established as a sport in the late 19th century, contests will be a five-minute whirlwind of combat, with athletes attempting a combination of throws and holds in a bid to defeat their opponents.

 ## Table Tennis

Table Tennis, based on the same basic principles as Tennis, is a spectacle that blends power, speed, skill and subtlety.

 ## Taekwondo

'Taekwondo' translates into English as 'the way of foot and fist' – an accurate description of this martial art - with the aim being to land powerful kicks and punches on your opponent.

Weightlifting

The aim of Weightlifting is simple, to lift more weight than anyone else - resulting in pure sporting theatre. The strongest competitors may lift more than three times their body weight.

Wrestling

Recognised as one of the world's oldest sports, Wrestling was first held at the ancient Olympic Games in 708 BC.

Boccia

Boccia is a target sport that tests muscle control and accuracy, demanding extreme skill and concentration. Players must be in a seated position within a throwing box at one end of the playing court.

Paralympic Judo

Contested by visually impaired athletes, the mats have different textures to indicate the competition area and zones.

Paralympic Table Tennis

A permanent part of the Paralympic programme since the first Games in 1960, it is also one of the largest with 29 medal events and 300 athletes.

Powerlifting

Paralympic Powerlifting is a bench-press competition – competitors are classified by bodyweight alone.

Sitting Volleyball

Sitting Volleyball emerged in the Netherlands in the 1950s, a combination of Volleyball and a German game called Sitzbal.

Wheelchair Fencing

Athletes compete in wheelchairs fastened to the floor, resulting in a fierce, fast-moving battle of tactics and technique.

Greenwich Park

Greenwich Park will host the Olympic and Paralympic Equestrian competitions, plus the combined running and shooting element of the Modern Pentathlon. Situated on the south bank of the River Thames in south-east London.

Equestrian - Dressage

Dressage events will be a test of both athletic prowess and supreme elegance.

Equestrian - Eventing

Featuring dressage, cross-country and a dramatic jumping finale, the Eventing competition showcases an all-encompassing test of Equestrian skill.

Equestrian - Jumping

Known as 'show jumping' in the UK, the Jumping competition will require horse and rider to navigate a short course with precision, speed and perfect technique.

Modern Pentathlon

Riding and combined running/shooting will be staged here in Greenwich Park. Fencing will be in the Copper Box, swimming in the Aquatics Centre - both venues in the Olympic Park.

Paralympic Equestrian

Athletes with a disability have long taken part in Equestrian activities, originally as a means of rehabilitation and recreation. Classified across five grades to ensure that the tests can be judged on the skill of the rider, regardless of their disability.

Hadleigh Farm

Hadleigh Farm, with its ideal mountain biking terrain, is to the east of London in Essex.

 ## Cycling - Mountain Bike

Rocky paths, tricky climbs and technical descents will provide plenty of challenges for riders in the competition.

Hampton Court Palace

Hampton Court Palace is one of London's historic Royal Palaces. It is located in the London Borough of Richmond upon Thames in south-west London.

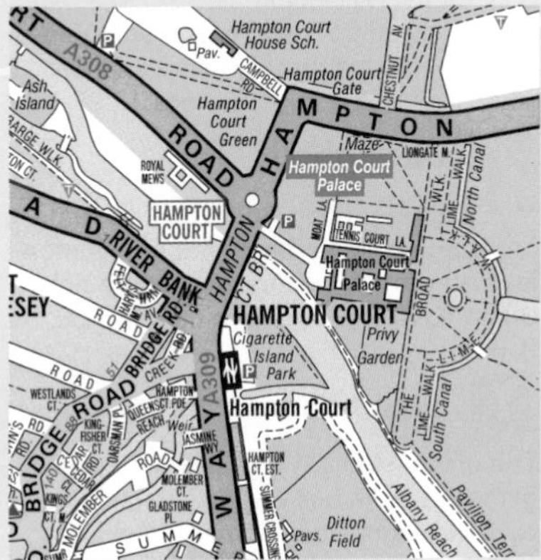

 ## Cycling - Road

The Olympic Road Cycling programme includes two events. Time Trials begin and finish at Hampton Court Palace, Road Racing will begin and end on The Mall.

Horse Guards Parade

Horse Guards Parade is situated between Whitehall and St James's Park. A temporary beach will be created with 3,000 tonnes of imported sand.

 ## Beach Volleyball

Beach Volleyball is similar to the indoor game, although it is played by teams of two, instead of teams of six.

Hyde Park

Within London's West End this extensive park abuts Mayfair and Knightsbridge.

 ## Marathon Swimming 10km

This event takes place in the Serpentine lake. All other Swimming events are held in the Olympic Park Aquatics Centre.

Triathlon

Triathlon races combine swimming, cycling and running, in that order. Events are conducted over a variety of distances: for the Olympic Games, the men's and women's Triathlons will consist of a 1,500m swim, a 40km bike ride and a 10km run.

Lee Valley White Water Centre

Lee Valley White Water Centre is located in the River Lee Country Park 30km north of the Olympic Park. After the Games this new centre will become a venue for canoeing, kayaking and white water rafting.

 ## Canoe Slalom

Modelled on slalom skiing, the sport was first staged on flat water, but was later switched to white water rapids. The competitions consist of timed runs down a white water course with up to 25 gates. Canoe Sprint takes place at Eton Dorney.

Lord's Cricket Ground

Lord's is the home of cricket. It is located in St John's Wood, north-west London, near Regent's Park.

 ### Archery

Archery dates back around 10,000 years; developed as a competitive activity in medieval England, it is now practised in more than 140 countries around the world.

The Mall

This famous wide tree lined ceremonial route connecting Buckingham Palace and Trafalgar Square was laid out in 1910 as part of the national memorial to Queen Victoria.

 ### Athletics - Marathon and Race Walk

The start and finish points for the Olympic Marathon and Race Walk. At London 1908, the marathon distance was extended from around 25 miles to 26.2 miles (42.195 kilometres) so that it finished in front of the Royal Box. This distance became standard for the Marathon and is still used today.

 ### Cycling - Road Racing

The start and finish point for Cycling Road Racing events. There are two Road Cycling events for both men and women. Time Trials take place at Hampton Court Palace.

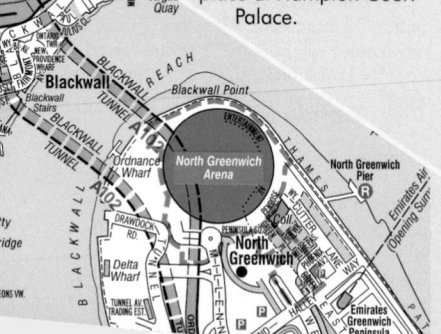

 ### Paralympic Athletics - Marathon

Men's and women's Marathons will be held on the streets of central London, starting and finishing on The Mall.

North Greenwich Arena

Built for the Millennium celebrations, and transformed into a sports and entertainment venue, the arena is sited on the south side of the River Thames.

 ### Basketball

Men's quarter-finals and women's semi-finals onwards are held here, preliminaries and women's quarter-finals are held at the Basketball Arena in the Olympic Park.

 ### Gymnastics - Artistic

The grace, strength and skill of Olympic gymnasts have been astonishing audiences since the Games in Ancient Greece.

 ### Gymnastics - Trampoline

Trampoline is the newest of the three Gymnastics disciplines making its Olympic debut at Sydney in 2000.

 ### Wheelchair Basketball

Preliminary games will be split between the Olympic Park Basketball Arena and North Greenwich Arena. All quarter-finals, semi-finals and medal games will take place here.

Riverbank Arena

The Riverbank Arena is located in the Olympic Park.

 Hockey

Until the 1970s, hockey was always played on grass. However, top-level matches now take place on water-based synthetic-turf pitches.

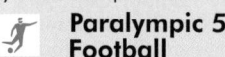 Paralympic 5-a-side Football

Played by visually impaired athletes using a ball with a noise-making device inside, the pitch is surrounded by a rebound wall. The sport is played with no throw-ins and no offside rule.

Paralympic 7-a-side Football

Follows modified FIFA rules; the playing field is smaller, as are the goals. Teams are made up of ambulant cerebral palsy athletes, featuring players with varying levels of disability.

The Royal Artillery Barracks

Located south of the River Thames in Woolwich, the Barracks are a historic military site dating from 1776 when a Royal Warrant authorised the formation of two artillery companies.

Shooting

Olympic Shooting events fall broadly into three types: Pistol, Rifle and Shotgun events. Having been practised competitively for centuries, the sport of Shooting is now popular all over the world.

Paralympic Archery

Paralympic Archery consists of both standing and wheelchair events for individuals and teams.

Paralympic Shooting

Athletes with different disabilities compete together in two classes – for athletes who can support the weight of their firearm themselves, and for athletes who use a shooting stand to support their arm.

Velodrome

Purpose built within the Olympic Park, the Velodrome features a distinctive sweeping roof design reflecting the geometry of the cycling track. The track has been laid with 5-metre lengths of Siberian pine, and is banked to an angle of 42 degrees at its steepest point.

After the Games a new mountain bike course and road-cycle circuit will be added to create a VeloPark for the local community, sports clubs and elite athletes.

Cycling - Track

Cycling has a long history in the UK. As early as 1870, large crowds were drawn to races held on indoor wooden tracks. Track Cycling has featured at every Games but one since the first modern Olympic Games in 1896.

There are ten Olympic Track Cycling events (five for men, five for women): Sprint, Keirin, Team Sprint, Team Pursuit and Omnium.

Paralympic Cycling - Track

The competition is for athletes with a visual impairment, cerebral palsy, amputations or other physical disabilities competing on bicycles, tricycles, tandems and hand cycles.

Water Polo Arena

A temporary Olympic Park venue adjacent to the Aquatics Centre.

 ### Water Polo

Water Polo developed during the 19th century as an aquatic version of rugby, played informally in rivers and lakes. The version of the game that survives today is closer to handball.

Wembley Arena

A flagship live music and sport venue, in north-west London.

 ### Badminton

One of the most dynamic Olympic sports, Badminton made its full Olympic debut at Barcelona 1992.

 ### Gymnastics - Rhythmic

Rhythmic Gymnastics is a combination of gymnastics and dance. Scores are awarded for difficulty, artistry and execution.

Wembley Stadium

England's national stadium is situated in north-west London. Opened in 2007 to replace the 1923 structure with its famous twin towers, the illuminated arch of the new stadium soars over 130m into the sky, more than four times the height of the towers of the old Wembley Stadium. This is the biggest of the six stadiums staging the London 2012 Olympic

Games Football competition, each seat has an unrestricted view of the pitch.

 ### Football

The five other co-Host City stadia are: **City of Coventry Stadium**, Glasgow's **Hampden Park**, Cardiff's **Millennium Stadium**, Manchester's **Old Trafford** and Newcastle upon Tyne's **St. James' Park**. The finals for both the men's and women's competitions will be played at Wembley.

Weymouth and Portland

This beautiful bay setting has some of the best natural sailing waters in the UK.

 ### Sailing

The competition will host 10 Sailing events featuring a variety of craft from dinghies and keelboats, to windsurfing boards.

 ### Paralympic Sailing

Paralympic Sailing will consist of three mixed events.

Wimbledon

The home of the All England Lawn Tennis and Croquet Club. Wimbledon staged the tennis competition for London's first Olympic Games in 1908.

 ### Tennis

The Tennis competition will feature five medal events including Mixed Doubles, making its first apperance since 1924. Situated in south-west London about 12 miles from the Olympic Park.

London 2012 Shops

Canary Wharf, Jubilee Place........1D 104
(Off Bank Street)
Heathrow Airport
 Terminal 3 (airside) 3C 110
 Terminal 5 (airside)...................6D 174
John Lewis
 Brent Cross Shopping Centre.......7E 44
 Kingston, Wood Street...............2D 150
 Oxford Street (fifth floor)............ 1K 11
 Stratford City Shopping Centre.... 6E 68
Paddington Station...........................7A 4
Peter Jones, Sloane Square.............4F 17
Royal Opera House........................1F 13
St Pancras International....................1E 6
Stansted Airport, Essex
Team GB and ParalympicsGB Shop
 Stratford City Shopping Centre.... 6E 68

http://shop.london2012.com

Live Sites

Live Sites are big screen and event spaces in urban centres providing a unique combination of free sports screenings, cultural entertainment and ticketed concerts. With the exception of the Hyde Park Opening and Closing Ceremony Celebrations (27 July and 12 August), entry will be free though ticketed to control numbers, with daily guaranteed entry tickets available in advance.
■ All tickets via btlondonlive.com

■ **BT London Live Sites:**
Hyde Park (Olympic Games).......... 4F 11
Trafalgar Square (Paralympic
 Games)...................................... 4D 12
Victoria Park (Olympic Games)...... 7B 68

■ Additional Live Sites include:
 London Park (Olympic Games &
 Paralympic Games)....................5H 15

Transport

Scan for up-to-date travel details and bookings

www.london2012.com/getting-to-the-games

London 2012 is aiming for a 'public transport' Games, so please do not drive as there will be no parking at or around venues. You can travel to each competition venue using different types of public transport, or by walking or cycling.

Venues in London
London's transport system will be very busy, so you should allow plenty of time to travel to, from and between venues. Check the information on travelling to your event to find out where your venue is, the best way to get there and how long your journey will take between the recommended stations serving venues. London is well-served by public transport with travel options including the London Underground, London Overground, Docklands Light Railway, National Rail, buses and river services.

Outer London venues
Some sporting events are being held in venues on the outskirts of London, including Eton Dorney, the Lee Valley White Water Centre and Hadleigh Farm. All of these venues are linked to London by National Rail services.

Co-Host Cities and Towns
The co-Host Cities are Cardiff, Coventry, Glasgow, Manchester, Newcastle upon Tyne (all for Football) and Weymouth and Portland (Sailing). They all have National

Rail stations with direct links to London, although some of these venues are significant distances from the capital.

Travel tickets

London 2012 ticket holders can benefit from a range of special travel tickets for the Games. Spectators with a ticket for a Games event in London will receive a one-day Games Travelcard for the day of that event, valid within zones 1 to 9. This includes London Underground (Tube), London Overground, Docklands Light Railway (DLR), buses, trams and National Rail services, including the Javelin® service between St Pancras and Stratford International stations, but excluding the Heathrow, Stansted or Gatwick Express trains, or taxis and private hire vehicles.

Travel to outer London venues

Spectators with tickets for Games events at Eton Dorney, the Lee Valley White Water Centre and Hadleigh Farm will receive a Games Travelcard for use on public transport in London and National Rail between London and the recommended stations for those venues.

London Underground

The Underground is one of the main ways to travel around London. All of the London 2012 venues within London can be reached by London Underground, with the exception of ExCeL, Greenwich Park and The Royal Artillery Barracks. Travel within zones 1 to 9 on London Underground for the day of your event is included with the Games Travelcard. Many of London Underground's stations have been improved to make them more accessible, details on www.tfl.gov.uk

London Buses

London has an extensive bus network and there are routes and stops close to all London 2012 venues. London's buses are a good travel option for people with accessibility needs. Most of London's 8,000 buses are low-floor with clearly marked priority seating next to doors for disabled people. There is room for one wheelchair space and assistance dogs are allowed on all buses.

Travel on London's buses on the day of your event is included with the Games Travelcard. There are 24-hour bus routes providing travel options all night in London.

Docklands Light Railway (DLR)

The DLR serves London 2012 venues at the Olympic Park, ExCeL, Greenwich Park and The Royal Artillery Barracks. The DLR is a step-free network and all DLR stations have lift or ramp access to all platforms. Travel on the DLR for the day of your event is included with the Games Travelcard.

London Overground

London Overground is a suburban network of rail services in London, managed by Transport for London. Travel on London Overground on the day of your event is included with the Games Travelcard. Passengers requiring assistance are recommended to give at least 24 hours notice by calling London Overground Customer Services on 0845 601 4867, 9am–5pm on weekdays.

Rail

The National Rail network connects London and all the co-Host Cities for the

London 2012 venues. Extra Rail services will be provided to Games venues, and trains will run later from London to key destinations up to approximately two hours away, such as Birmingham, Manchester, Leeds and Cardiff.

Cycling

Cycling in London is an easy and convenient alternative to public transport. Free, secure, managed cycle parking will be provided at all London 2012 venues. Bicycle locks are not supplied. TfL cycle hire docking stations may be within walking distance of London 2012 venues, but you will not be able to dock your cycle hire bike at venues.

Shuttle Buses

Shuttle buses will be provided from some recommended stations to London 2012 and co-Host City venues, particularly where these stations are more than a short walk away from the venue entrance. These shuttles will be low-floor accessible buses and the service will be available for all spectators.

River services

Venues accessible by river include Greenwich Park, North Greenwich Arena, The Royal Artillery Barracks, Horse Guards Parade, The Mall and Eton Dorney. All passengers on boat services will have a seat or wheelchair space. Travel by scheduled river services on the Thames in London is not included with the Games Travelcard provided with your event tickets, but it does entitle spectators to a one third discount on the price of river service tickets.

Taxis

Taxis and private hire vehicles do not accept Oyster cards or travelcards and are not covered by the Games Travelcard that you will receive with your event ticket. Only licensed taxis can pick up passengers on the street or at ranks without a booking. Minicabs and other private hire vehicles must be booked through a licensed operator (in person, over the phone or online) before the journey starts.

Unbooked minicabs are illegal. You may be approached by touts or minicab drivers seeking passengers or offering a service; these are unsafe, unlicensed and uninsured. You put yourself in danger if you use these services.

2012 Games coach services

- During the Olympic Games coach services will be provided to the Olympic Park, ExCeL, Greenwich Park (30 July only) and Weymouth and Portland from a range of locations outside the M25. Coaches will pick up from bus stops and bus stations throughout Great Britain.
- During the Paralympic Games, 2012 Games coach services will be provided to the Olympic Park and ExCeL.
- All passengers on the coach services will have a dedicated seat or wheelchair space.
- All seats and wheelchair spaces on 2012 Games coach services must be booked in advance: www.first-groupgamestravel.com/direct-coaching

2012 Games park-and-ride

- Secure park-and-ride sites with limited space will be provided at convenient locations.
- Park-and-ride services must be booked in advance:

www.firstgroupgamestravel.com
- Venues with park-and-ride facilities during the Olympic Games include: the Olympic Park, ExCeL, Greenwich Park (30 July only), Eton Dorney, Hadleigh Farm, the Lee Valley White Water Centre and Weymouth and Portland.
- Venues with park-and-ride facilities during the Paralympic Games include: the Olympic Park, ExCeL and Eton Dorney.

Blue Badge Parking

Blue Badge parking spaces are available for spectators who hold a valid Blue Badge or recognised national disability permit.
- Blue Badge parking spaces must be booked in advance: www.firstgroupgamestravel.com

Scan for 2012 Games spectator journey planner

Plan your journey using the 2012 Games spectator journey planner. It will provide you with:
- Estimated journey times to and from Games venues from anywhere in Great Britain.
- Estimated walking and cycling times to and from recommended stations to Games venues.
- Timetable information to allow Games ticket holders to plan their travel.
- Links to travel booking sites (such as 2012 Games Rail services and 2012 Games coach services) to enable Games ticket holders to purchase travel tickets in advance of travel.
- Recommended routes to make your journey as easy as possible.

Useful websites

London 2012 Information
www.london2012.com

2012 Games Travel Services
Rail:
■ www.nationalrailgamestravel.co.uk
Eurostar:
■ www.eurostar.com
Coach, park-and-ride & Blue Badge:
■ www.firstgroupgamestravel.co.uk
River:
■ www.citycruisesgamestravel.co.uk
■ https://booking.thamesclippers.com/gamestravel
■ www.frenchbrothers.co.uk/gamestravel
■ www.water-chariots.co.uk/gamestravel

London Travel Information
■ www.tfl.gov.uk
London Tourist Information
■ www.visitlondon.com
  Hotels, places to visit, events, travel and other important information.
Accessibility Information
■ www.london2012.com/accessibility
■ www.inclusivelondon.com

Every possible care has been taken to ensure that, to the best of our knowledge, the information contained in this atlas is accurate at the date of publication 03.2012.

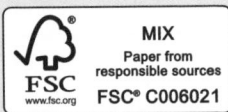

MIX
Paper from responsible sources
FSC® C006021
www.fsc.org

LONDON

A-Z ®

Geographers' A-Z Map Company Ltd.

Geographers' A-Z Map Company Ltd.

Fairfield Road, Borough Green, Sevenoaks, Kent TN15 8PP
Telephone : 01732 781000 (Enquiries & Trade Sales)
            01732 783422 (Retail Sales)

www.a-zmaps.co.uk

Edition 9 2011
© Copyright of Geographers' A-Z Map Company Limited

The publishers are deeply grateful for the ready co-operation and valuable help given to them in the production of this atlas. They would like to record their obligation to: The Engineers and Surveyors Departments and Planning Offices of all the Local Authorities covered in this atlas, The Department for Transport, Highways Agency, Transport for London, The Post Office, Police Authorities, Fire Brigades, London 2012, Taxi Drivers, Members of the Public.

Printed and bound in the United Kingdom by Polestar Wheatons Ltd., Exeter.

An AtoZ Publication

CONTENTS

Congestion Charging Overview and Information	Inside Front Cover
Key to Map Pages	2-3
Super Scale Map Pages @ 5¾" to 1 mile	4-19
Map Pages @ approx. 3" to 1 mile	20-174
Index to Streets, Areas & selected Places of Interest	175-432
Index to Hospitals etc.	433-438
Index to Stations	439-441
Railway Connections Map	442-443
Underground Railway Map	444-445
West End Theatres Map	446

REFERENCE

Motorway **M1**	
A Road A2	
Under Construction	
Proposed	
B Road B408	
Dual Carriageway	
One-way Street Traffic flow on A Roads is also indicated by a heavy line on the driver's left.	
Junction Name MARBLE ARCH	
Restricted Access	
Pedestrianized Road	
Track & Footpath	
Residential Walkway	
Congestion Charging Zone	
Railway Tunnel / Level Crossing	
Stations:	
National Rail Network & Overground	⇥
Docklands Light Railway	DLR
Underground	●⊖ Super Scale Map Pages
London Tramlink Tunnel / Stop The boarding of Tramlink trams at stops may be limited to a single direction, indicated by the arrow.	
Postcode Boundary	
Built-up Area BANK STREET	
Map Continuation 62	Super Scale Map Pages 12

Airport	✈
Car Park (Selected)	P
Church or Chapel	†
Fire Station	■
Hospital	H
House Numbers (A & B Roads only)	51 19 22 48
Information Centre	i
National Grid Reference	530
Park & Ride	Bromley P+🚍
Police Station	▲
Post Office	★
River Bus Stop	R
Safety Camera with Speed Limit ㉚ Ⓥ Fixed and long term road works cameras only Symbols do not indicate camera direction	Fixed Speed Limit Variable Speed Limit
Toilet:	
without facilities for the Disabled	▼
with facilities for the Disabled	▼
Disabled facilities only	▼
Educational Establishment	▭
Hospital or Healthcare Building	▭
Industrial Building	▭
Leisure or Recreational Facility	▭
Place of Interest	▭
Public Building	▭
Shopping Centre or Market	▭
Other Selected Buildings	▭

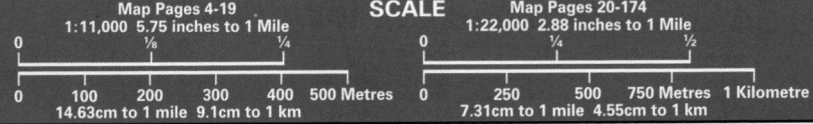

SCALE

Map Pages 4-19
1:11,000 5.75 inches to 1 Mile
0   ⅛   ¼
0   100   200   300   400   500 Metres
14.63cm to 1 mile 9.1cm to 1 km

Map Pages 20-174
1:22,000 2.88 inches to 1 Mile
0   ¼   ½
0   250   500   750 Metres   1 Kilometre
7.31cm to 1 mile 4.55cm to 1 km

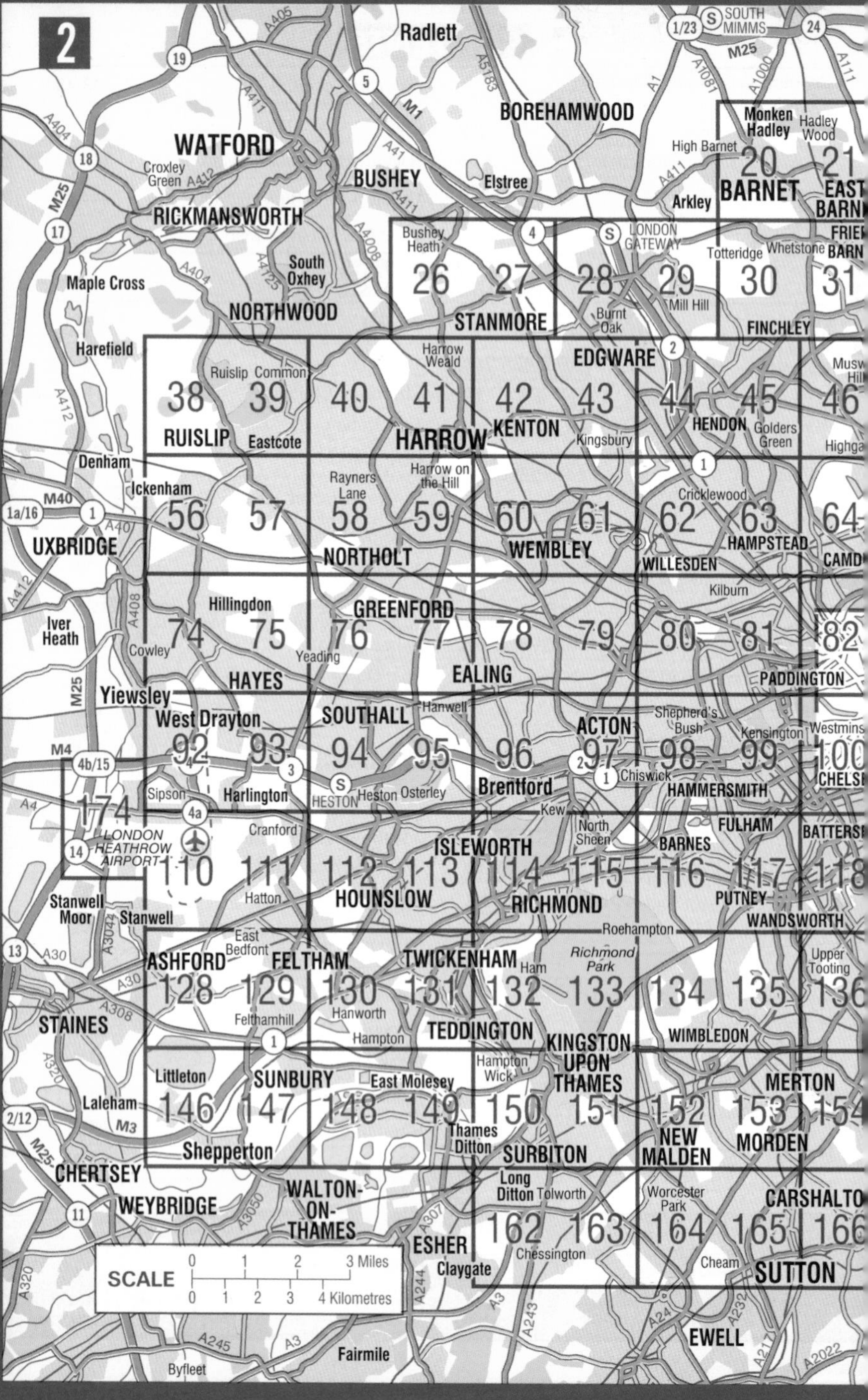

2

Radlett

1/23 SOUTH MIMMS · M25 · 24

BOREHAMWOOD

19 · A405 · A5183 · M1 · 5 · A1 · A1081

WATFORD · Monken Hadley · Hadley Wood

High Barnet · 20 · 21 EAST BARN

BUSHEY · Elstree · Arkley · BARNET

18 · Croxley Green A412 · A411 · A411

RICKMANSWORTH · A411 · FRIE BARN

17 · M25 · Bushey Heath · 4 · LONDON GATEWAY · Totteridge · Whetstone · 30 · 31

South Oxhey · 26 · 27 · 28 · 29 · Mill Hill

Maple Cross · NORTHWOOD · STANMORE · Burnt Oak · FINCHLEY

Harefield · A412 · Harrow Weald · EDGWARE · 2 · Musw Hill

38 · 39 · 40 · 41 · 42 · 43 · 44 · 45 · 46

Ruislip Common · HENDON · Golders Green

RUISLIP · Eastcote · HARROW · KENTON · Kingsbury · Highga

Denham · Ickenham · Rayners Lane · Harrow on the Hill · 1 · Cricklewood

1a/16 · A40 · 56 · 57 · 58 · 59 · 60 · 61 · 62 · 63 · 64

UXBRIDGE · NORTHOLT · WEMBLEY · WILLESDEN · HAMPSTEAD · CAMD

A412 · Hillingdon · Kilburn

Iver Heath · 74 · 75 · 76 · 77 · 78 · 79 · 80 · 81 · 82

Cowley · Yeading · GREENFORD · PADDINGTON

M25 · Yiewsley · HAYES · EALING · Shepherd's Bush · Kensington · Westmins

West Drayton · SOUTHALL · Hanwell · ACTON · 97 · 98 · 99 · 100

92 · 93 · 94 · 95 · 96 · Chiswick · CHELSI

M4 · 3 · Sipson · Harlington · HESTON · Heston Osterley · Brentford · HAMMERSMITH

4b/15 · A4 · 4a · Cranford · Kew · North Sheen · FULHAM · BATTERS

174 · LONDON HEATHROW AIRPORT · ISLEWORTH · BARNES

14 · 110 · 111 · 112 · 113 · 114 · 115 · 116 · 117 · 118

Stanwell Moor · Stanwell · Hatton · HOUNSLOW · RICHMOND · PUTNEY

East Bedfont · Roehampton · WANDSWORTH

13 · A30 · ASHFORD · FELTHAM · TWICKENHAM · Ham · Richmond Park · Upper Tooting

128 · 129 · 130 · 131 · 132 · 133 · 134 · 135 · 136

STAINES · Felthamhill · Hanworth · TEDDINGTON · WIMBLEDON

A308 · Hampton · KINGSTON UPON THAMES

2/12 · M25 · Littleton · SUNBURY · East Molesey · Hampton Wick · MERTON

146 · 147 · 148 · 149 · 150 · 151 · 152 · 153 · 154

Laleham · M3 · Thames Ditton · NEW MALDEN · MORDEN

CHERTSEY · Shepperton · SURBITON

11 · WEYBRIDGE · WALTON-ON-THAMES · Long Ditton · Tolworth · Worcester Park · CARSHALTO

162 · 163 · 164 · 165 · 166

ESHER · Chessington · Cheam · SUTTON

Claygate

SCALE 0 1 2 3 Miles · 0 1 2 3 4 Kilometres

Byfleet · Fairmile · EWELL

SUPER SCALE SECTION
4 5 6 7 8 9
Shoreditch
Marylebone
Holborn
10 11 12 13 14 15
West End
City
16 17 18 19
Westminster
Chelsea
Theydon Bois
Crews Hill
Enfield Wash
Sewardstone
Epping Forest
ENFIELD
LOUGHTON
22 23 24 25
Winchmore Hill
Ponders End
SOUTHGATE
EDMONTON
CHINGFORD
Buckhurst Hill
32 33 34 35 36 37
Woodford Green
WOODFORD
Barkingside
Collier Row
Harold Hill
WOOD GREEN
TOTTENHAM
WALTHAMSTOW
47 48 49 50 51 52 53 54 55
HORNSEY
WANSTEAD
Chadwell Heath
ROMFORD
Leytonstone
Goodmayes
STOKE NEWINGTON
LEYTON
ILFORD
Becontree
HORNCHURCH
65 66 67 68 69 70 71 72 73
STRATFORD
Manor Park
Elm Park
ISLINGTON
HACKNEY
OLYMPIC PARK
BARKING
DAGENHAM
FINSBURY
Bethnal Green
WEST HAM
EAST HAM
Creekmouth
South Hornchurch
83 84 85 86 87 88 89 90 91
Holborn
City
Stepney
POPLAR
London City Airport
Beckton
River Thames
Thamesmead
SUPER SCALE SECTION 4-19
Wennington
Bermondsey
Blackwall Tunnel
Woolwich Ferry
Abbey Wood
Belvedere
101 102 103 104 105 106 107 108 109
LAMBETH
DEPTFORD
GREENWICH
WOOLWICH
Charlton
Plumstead
ERITH
BRIXTON
CAMBERWELL
Blackheath
Kidbrooke
Welling
Bexleyheath
Crayford
119 120 121 122 123 124 125 126 127
LEWISHAM
Lee
ELTHAM
DARTFORD
Blackfen
BEXLEY
CATFORD
Mottingham
New Eltham
Old Bexley
West Norwood
Dulwich
Grove Park
SIDCUP
137 138 139 140 141 142 143 144 145
Crystal Palace
Sydenham
Wilmington
Foots Cray
TREATHAM
Swanley
ITCHAM
South Norwood
Penge
BECKENHAM
CHISLEHURST
St. Paul's Cray
155 156 157 158 159 160 161
Thornton Heath
BROMLEY
Hayes
Petts Wood
St. Mary Cray
Crockenhill
Farningham
Addiscombe
West Wickham
Farnborough
ORPINGTON
Eynsford
Beddington
167 168 169 170 171 172 173
ALLINGTON
CROYDON
Addington
Keston
New Addington
Pratt's Bottom
PURLEY
M25
M11
M20
A10
A1010
A121
A112
A104
A1069
A113
A123
A12
A118
A127
A124
A125
A1306
A13
A206
A2
A20
A224
A21
A233
A2022
A23
A22
A225
A1005
25 26 6/27 5 4 1/3

4
82
ST. JOHN'S WOOD
The Wellington Hosp.
St. John's Wood Church Gardens
Winfield House
PRINCE ALBERT RD.
(Regent's Canal)
WELLINGTON RD.
Middlesex CCC & Marylebone CC (Lord's)
Media Centre
MCC Cricket Mus.& Tours
London Central Mosque
Playground
Children's Boating Pond
ST. JOHN'S WOOD ROAD
GROVE END ROAD
PARK ROAD
LISSON GROVE
NW8
Grand Union Canal
Royal Coll. of Obstetricians & Gynaecologists
MARYLEBONE
LISSON GROVE
EDGWARE ROAD
Little Venice Sports Cen.
St. Mary's Gdns.
City of Westminster College
EDGWARE RD.
MARYLEBONE RD.
WESTWAY A40 MARYLEBONE FLY-OVER
HARROW ROAD
City of Westminster College
Paddington Basin
St. Mary's Hosp.
Imperial Coll.
Mus.
PADDINGTON
Seymour Leisure Cen.
THE WATER GARDENS
THE QUADRANGLE
SUSSEX GARDENS
PRAED ST.
OLD MARYLEBONE RD.
EDGWARE ROAD
BISHOP'S BRI. RD
MAIDA VALE
MAIDA AVENUE
CHAPEL ST.
BRYANSTON SQUARE
10

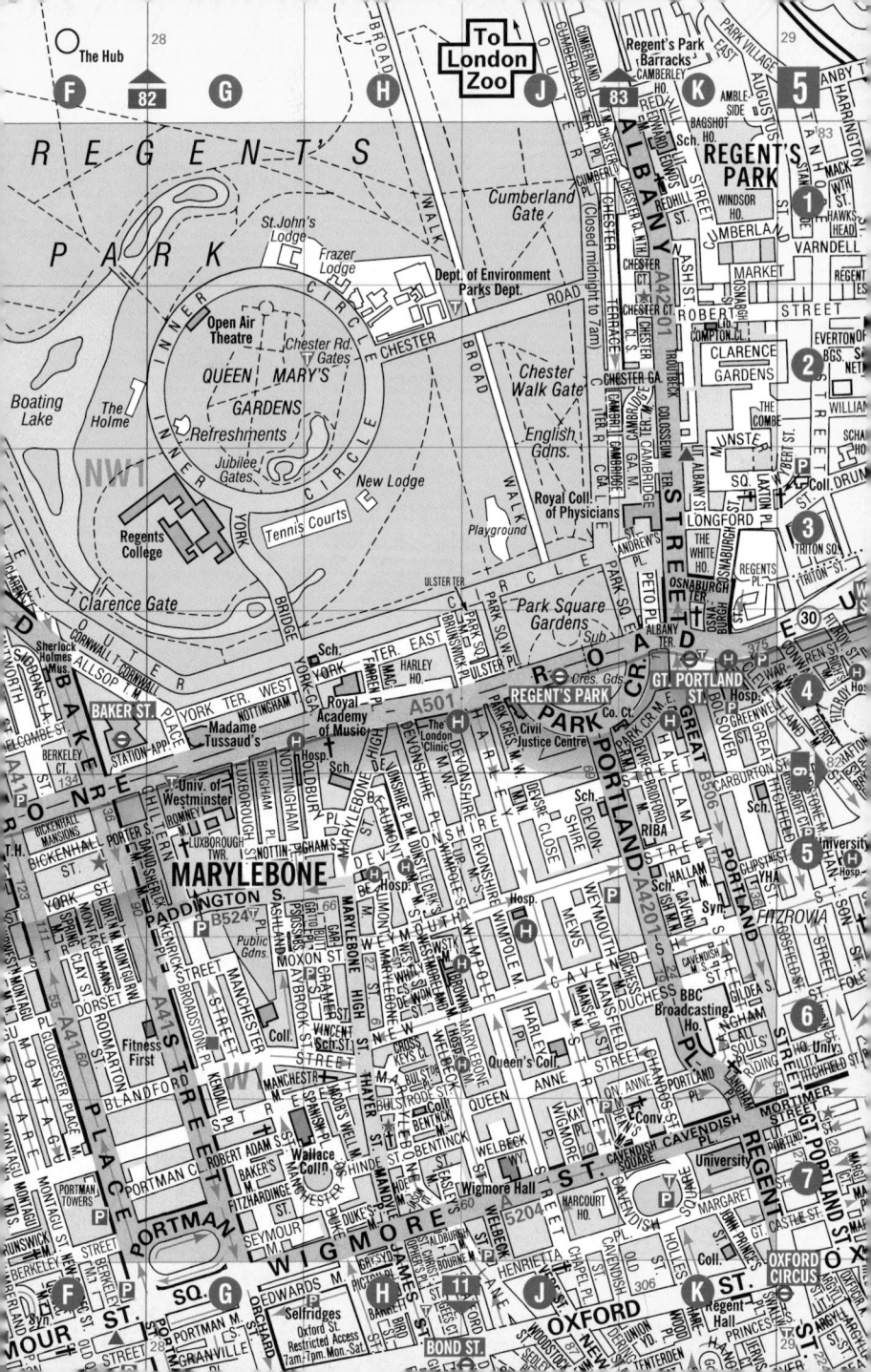
The Hub
28
82
83
29
5
F
G
H
J
K
To London Zoo
REGENT'S PARK
Regent's Park Barracks
CAMBERLEY HO.
REDHILL
AMBLESIDE
BAGSHOT HO.
AUGUSTUS
PARK VILLAGE EAST
HARRINGTON
CUMBERLAND TER.
CUMBERLAND
OUTER
BROAD WALK
Cumberland Gate
(Closed midnight to 7am)
CHESTER TER.
ALBANY STREET
A4201
WINDSOR HO.
CUMBERLAND MARKET
VARNDELL
ROBERT
COMPTON CL.
CLARENCE GARDENS
EVERTON BGS.
St. John's Lodge
Frazer Lodge
Dept. of Environment Parks Dept.
INNER CIRCLE
CHESTER ROAD
Open Air Theatre
Chester Rd. Gates
QUEEN MARY'S GARDENS
Refreshments
Jubilee Gates
New Lodge
Tennis Courts
Boating Lake
The Holme
NW1
Regents College
Clarence Gate
YORK BRIDGE
Chester Walk Gate
English Gdns.
CHESTER GA.
CAMBRIDGE TER.
CAMBRIDGE GA.
COLOSSEUM TER.
MUNSTER SQ.
THE COMBE
LAXTON PL.
Royal Coll. of Physicians
Playground
ST. ANDREW'S PL.
LONGFORD
THE WHITE HO.
OSNABURGH ST.
REGENTS PL.
TRITON SQ.
ULSTER TER.
PARK SQUARE GARDENS
PARK SQ. EAST
PETO PL.
OSNABURGH TER.
Sub.
ALBANY TER.
Sherlock Holmes Mus.
BAKER ST.
BAKER STREET
ALLSOP PL.
CORNWALL T.
YORK TER. WEST
YORK TER. EAST
HARLEY HO.
Sch.
NOTTINGHAM T.
Madame Tussaud's
Royal Academy of Music
The London Clinic
A501
MARYLEBONE ROAD
REGENT'S PARK
Cres. Gds.
PARK CRESCENT
GT. PORTLAND ST.
Hosp.
Civil Justice Centre
Co. Ct.
375
30
4
STATION APP.
BERKELEY CT.
134
A41
Univ. of Westminster
ROMNEY
LUXBOROUGH TWR.
BINGHAM
OLDBURY
DEVONSHIRE PL.
DEVONSHIRE ST.
HARLEY ST.
PORTLAND PL.
GREAT PORTLAND ST.
BOLSOVER
GREENWELL
CARBURTON ST.
B506
Sch.
RIBA
HALLAM
BICKENHALL MANSIONS
BICKENHALL ST.
MARYLEBONE
PADDINGTON S.
B524
YORK ST.
MONTAGU
DURWEN
Public Gdns.
ASHLAND
MOXON ST.
CRAMER
MARYLEBONE HIGH ST.
WEYMOUTH
WIMPOLE ST.
WIMPOLE M.
WEYMOUTH MEWS
DEVONSHIRE CLOSE
Syn.
HALLAM M.
CAVENDISH
FITZROVIA
5
University
YHA
CLIPSTONE
Hosp.
DORSET
RODMARTON ST.
GLOUCESTER PL.
BROADSTONE PL.
MANCHESTER STREET
Coll.
Fitness First
VINCENT ST.
NEW CAVENDISH STREET
DUCHESS
BBC Broadcasting Ho.
LANGHAM
ALL SOULS'
6
MANSFIELD ST.
HARLEY ST.
Queen's Coll.
CHANDOS ST.
QUEEN ANNE STREET
RIDING
TITCHFIELD ST.
Univ.
W1
BLANDFORD
BAKER STREET
KENDALL PL.
MANCHESTER M.
SPANISH PL.
JACOB'S WELL M.
THAYER ST.
BULSTRODE ST.
BENTINCK
MARYLEBONE LANE
WELBECK
QUEEN ANNE ST.
WIGMORE PL.
PORTLAND PL.
Conv.
MORTIMER STREET
GT. PORTLAND ST.
CAVENDISH PL.
CAVENDISH SQUARE
University
REGENT ST.
7
ROBERT ADAM ST.
PORTMAN CL.
BAKER'S M.
FITZHARDINGE ST.
Wallace Colln.
HINDE ST.
MANCHESTER SQ.
DUKE
DUKE'S M.
MANDEVILLE
Wigmore Hall
WELBECK WY.
HARCOURT HO.
HOLLES
MARGARET
JOHN PRINCE'S
CASTLE ST.
PORTMAN TOWERS
MONTAGU SQUARE
PORTMAN
SEYMOUR M.
WIGMORE ST.
A5204
HENRIETTA
CHAPEL PL.
OLD
306
Coll.
OXFORD CIRCUS
BERKELEY
BERKELEY ST.
PORTMAN SQ.
EDWARDS M.
JAMES ST.
PICTON PL.
11
Selfridges
Oxford St. Restricted Access 7am-7pm. Mon.-Sat.
BOND ST.
ORCHARD
OXFORD ST.
Regent Hall
PRINCES
ARGYLL
SEYMOUR ST.
PORTMAN M.
GRANVILLE
WOODSTOCK
NEW
UNION YD.
TENTERDEN
29

REGENT'S PARK
HAMPSTEAD ROAD
A400
NW1
SOMERS TOWN
ST. PANCRAS INTERNATIONAL
King's Cross St. Pancras
British Library
EUSTON
EUSTON STATION
Euston Sq.
St. James's Gardens
Euston Tower
EUSTON SQ.
WARREN STREET
University Coll. Hosp.
University College
Wellcome Collection
Friends Ho.
Shaw Theatre
Town Hall
Lib.
British Med. Ass.
Gordon Sq. Garden
Univ. of London Union
Halls of Residence
Sch. of Oriental & African Studies
Russell Sq. Gdns.
BLOOMSBURY
RADA
Birkbeck Coll.
Sch. of Hygiene & Tropical Med.
University of London Senate House
British Museum
Great Court
Telecom Tower
GOODGE STREET
TOTTENHAM COURT ROAD
FITZROVIA
W1
A5204
OXFORD STREET
A40
OXFORD CIRCUS
NEW OXFORD ST.
SOHO
The Plaza
YMCA Central
Regent Hall
BBC Broadcasting Ho.
A501
A4200
A5202
B506
B504
A B C D E
1 2 3 4 5 6 7

PENTONVILLE ROAD
A501
83
84
7
The Angel Centre
Sadler's Wells
KING'S CROSS
GRAY'S INN ROAD
A5200
SWINTON ST.
ACTON ST.
ST. PANCRAS
Westminster Kingsway Coll.
The Foundling Museum
The Wolfson Assessment Cen.
Coram's Fields
Mecklenburgh Sq. Gds.
The Eastman Dental Hosp. & Institute
St. Andrew's Gds.
The Charles Dickens Mus.
Mount Pleasant Sorting Office
The British Postal Mus.
FARRINGDON ROAD
A201
ROSEBERY AVENUE
CLERKENWELL
CLERKENWELL RD.
A5201
London Metropolitan Archives
Spa Fields Open Space
NEW RIVER HEAD
THE HYDRA BUILDING
MYDDELTON SQUARE
ST. JOHN ST.
SKINNER ST.
Great Ormond Street Hosp. for Children
The National Hosp.
WC1
THEOBALD'S ROAD
A401
Gray's Inn Gdns.
Gray's Inn
BOURNE ESTATE
Islamic Cen.
SOUTHAMPTON ROW
HIGH HOLBORN
HOLBORN
HOLBORN CIR.
HOLBORN VIADUCT
A40
CHANCERY LA.
CHANCERY LANE
HOLBORN
Lincoln's Inn Fields
Lincoln's Inn Liby.
Lincoln's Inn Hall
Land Registry Off.
Royal Coll. of Surgeons
KINGSWAY
A4200
WC2
Freemasons' Hall
King's Coll. Maughan Library
NEW FETTER LA.
FETTER LA.
A4
SHOE LA.
FARRINGDON ST.
FLEET ST.
13
Royal Courts of Justice
F
G
H
J
K
1
2
3
4
5
6
7
8

8
The Angel Centre
CITY ROAD
GOSWELL ROAD
Fitness First
ELIA MEWS
ELIA ST.
A
B
C
D
E
84
City Road Basin
Wenlock Basin
WHARF
SHEPHERDESS WALK
MURRAY
College
Sadler's Wells
ROSEBERY AV.
1
2
3
4
5
6
7
A501
30
CITY FORUM
PEREGRINE HO.
Moreland Prim. Sch.
City University
SPENCER
NORTHAMPTON SQ.
LLOYD'S RW.
B501
B502
EC1
FINSBURY
Baths
Leisure Cen.
ST. LUKE'S
OLD STREET
A5201
Moorfields Eye Hosp.
ST. LUKE'S ESTATE
BUNHILL ROW
Bunhill Flds. Burial Grd.
Virgin Active
HAC Ground
The College of Law
SKINNER ST.
Spa Fields Open Space
London Metropolitan Archives
ST. JOHN STREET
PERCIVAL
CLERKENWELL
CLERKENWELL ROAD
OLD ROAD
A1
Queen Mary University of London
Charterhouse
St. John's Ga.
St. John's Gardens
FARRINGDON
FARRINGDON RD.
COWCROSS
A201
GOLDEN LANE ESTATE
Leis. Cen.
FORTUNE ST.
CHISWELL STREET
THE BREWERY
BARBICAN
BEECH ST.
ALDERSGATE
Arts Cen.
Lib.
LAKESIDE TER.
CITYPOINT
MOORGATE
ROPEMAKER
Central Markets
SMITHFIELD
WEST SMITHFIELD
CHARTERHOUSE SQUARE
CLOTH FAIR
LONG LA.
Ironmongers Hall
Museum
LONDON WALL
A1211
ST. ALBANS CT.
St. Bartholomew's Hospital
HOLBORN
HOLBORN CIR.
CITY THAMESLINK
VIADUCT
NEWGATE ST.
A40
KING EDWARD ST.
British Telecom Cen.
Old Bailey
Cen. Crim. Ct.
Fitness First
Stock Ex.
ST. PAUL'S
PATERNOSTER
St. Paul's Cathedral
One New Change
CHEAPSIDE
GRESHAM ST.
Guildhall
Clock Mus.
POULTRY
LUDGATE HILL
FLEET BUILDING
NEW BRIDGE ST.
WATLING
Bank of England
LOTHBURY
COLEMAN ST.
14

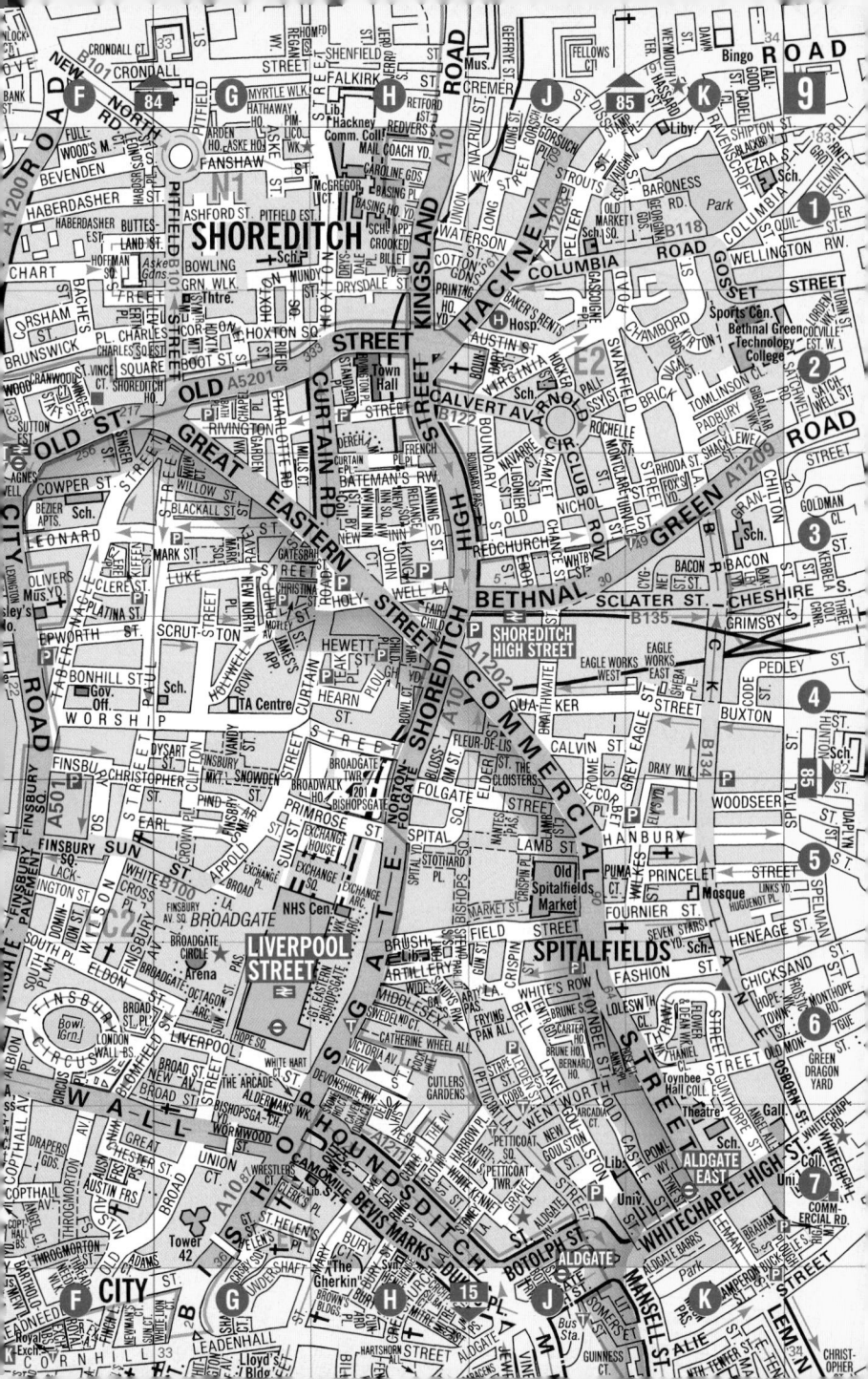
9
84
85
15
F
G
H
J
K
1
2
3
4
5
6
7
SHOREDITCH
N1
E2
E1
EC2
SPITALFIELDS
CITY
SHOREDITCH HIGH STREET
LIVERPOOL STREET
ALDGATE EAST
ALDGATE
OLD STREET
NEW NORTH ROAD
A1200
B101
CRONDALL
FANSHAW
PITFIELD STREET
BEVENDEN
HABERDASHER
CHART
CORSHAM
BRUNSWICK PL.
CHARLES SQUARE
ASHFORD ST.
PITFIELD EST.
BOWLING GRN. WLK.
HOXTON SQ.
OLD ST.
A5201
HOXTON
KINGSLAND ROAD
A10
HACKNEY ROAD
A1208
COLUMBIA ROAD
B118
GOSSET STREET
BARONESS RD.
Park
FALKIRK STREET
CREMER
GEFFRYE ST.
Mus.
Hackney Comm. Coll.
MAIL COACH YD.
CAROLINE GDS.
DRYSDALE ST.
Town Hall
CURTAIN RD.
GREAT EASTERN STREET
CALVERT AV.
ARNOLD CIR.
BOUNDARY
B122
CLUB ROW
REDCHURCH
BETHNAL GREEN ROAD
A1209
SCLATER ST.
CHESHIRE
B135
BRICK LANE
B134
Bethnal Green Technology College
Sports Cen.
CHAMBORD
SWANFIELD
VIRGINIA
Hosp.
COWPER ST.
LEONARD
CITY ROAD
EPWORTH
BONHILL ST.
WORSHIP
FINSBURY SQ.
A501
TABERNACLE
PAUL STREET
LUKE STREET
SCRUTTON
HOLYWELL ROW
TA Centre
HEWETT ST.
HEARN
PLOUGH
SHOREDITCH
A1202
COMMERCIAL STREET
QUAKER STREET
BUXTON
PEDLEY
FLEUR-DE-LIS
CALVIN ST.
FOLGATE STREET
SPITAL SQ.
LAMB ST.
HANBURY
PRINCELET STREET
Mosque
FOURNIER ST.
Old Spitalfields Market
FASHION
WHITE'S ROW
BROADGATE
BROADGATE CIRCLE
Arena
NHS Cen.
EXCHANGE SQ.
PRIMROSE ST.
SUN ST.
APPOLD ST.
EARL
CHRISTOPHER
FINSBURY PAVEMENT
WILSON
ELDON
FINSBURY CIRCUS
LONDON WALL
WALL
BISHOPSGATE
HOUNDSDITCH
BEVIS MARKS
CAMOMILE ST.
ST. HELEN'S PL.
Tower 42
"The Gherkin"
LIVERPOOL ST.
OLD BROAD ST.
THROGMORTON
AUSTIN FRS.
ARTILLERY
MIDDLESEX
WENTWORTH
PETTICOAT LA.
CUTLERS GARDENS
TOYNBEE ST.
BELL LANE
WHITECHAPEL HIGH ST.
Theatre
Gall.
Toynbee Hall COLL.
MANSELL ST.
LEMAN STREET
ALIE ST.
Bus Sta.
LEADENHALL
CORNHILL
Royal Exch.
Lloyd's Bldg.
ALDGATE
DUKE'S PL.
BOTOLPH ST.
OSBORN ST.
SPELMAN
HENEAGE ST.
CHICKSAND
WOODSEER
GREEN DRAGON YARD
COMMERCIAL RD.
Bingo
ROAD
33
34

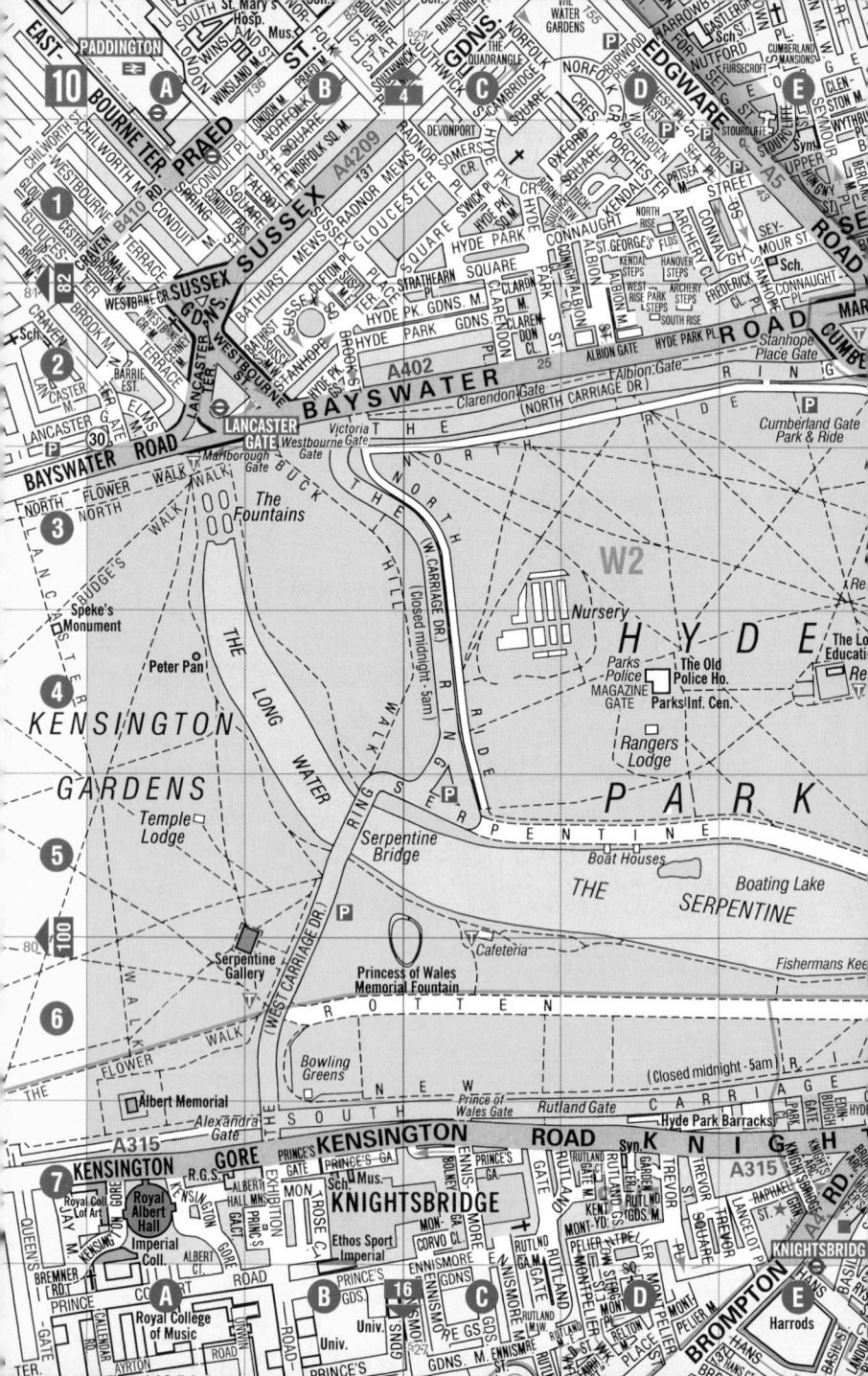

10
PADDINGTON
A
B
C
D
E
4
82
100
16
1
2
3
4
5
6
7
St. Mary's Hosp.
Mus.
THE WATER GARDENS
THE QUADRANGLE
EDGWARE ROAD
A5
PRAED ST.
A4209
SUSSEX GDNS.
SUSSEX SQUARE
BAYSWATER ROAD
A402
LANCASTER GATE
Victoria Gate
Westbourne Gate
Marlborough Gate
Clarendon Gate
Albion Gate
Stanhope Place Gate
Cumberland Gate Park & Ride
THE NORTH RIDE
The Fountains
THE LONG WATER
Speke's Monument
Peter Pan
KENSINGTON GARDENS
Temple Lodge
W2
Nursery
HYDE PARK
Parks Police
The Old Police Ho.
MAGAZINE GATE
Parks Inf. Cen.
Rangers Lodge
SERPENTINE
Serpentine Bridge
Boat Houses
THE SERPENTINE
Boating Lake
Cafeteria
Fishermans Keep
Serpentine Gallery
Princess of Wales Memorial Fountain
ROTTEN ROW
(Closed midnight - 5am)
Bowling Greens
Albert Memorial
Alexandra Gate
Prince of Wales Gate
Rutland Gate
Hyde Park Barracks
SOUTH CARRIAGE DR.
KENSINGTON ROAD
A315
KENSINGTON GORE
KNIGHTSBRIDGE
Royal Albert Hall
Royal Coll. of Art
Imperial Coll.
Royal College of Music
Ethos Sport Imperial
Univ.
Harrods
BROMPTON ROAD
KNIGHTSBRIDGE

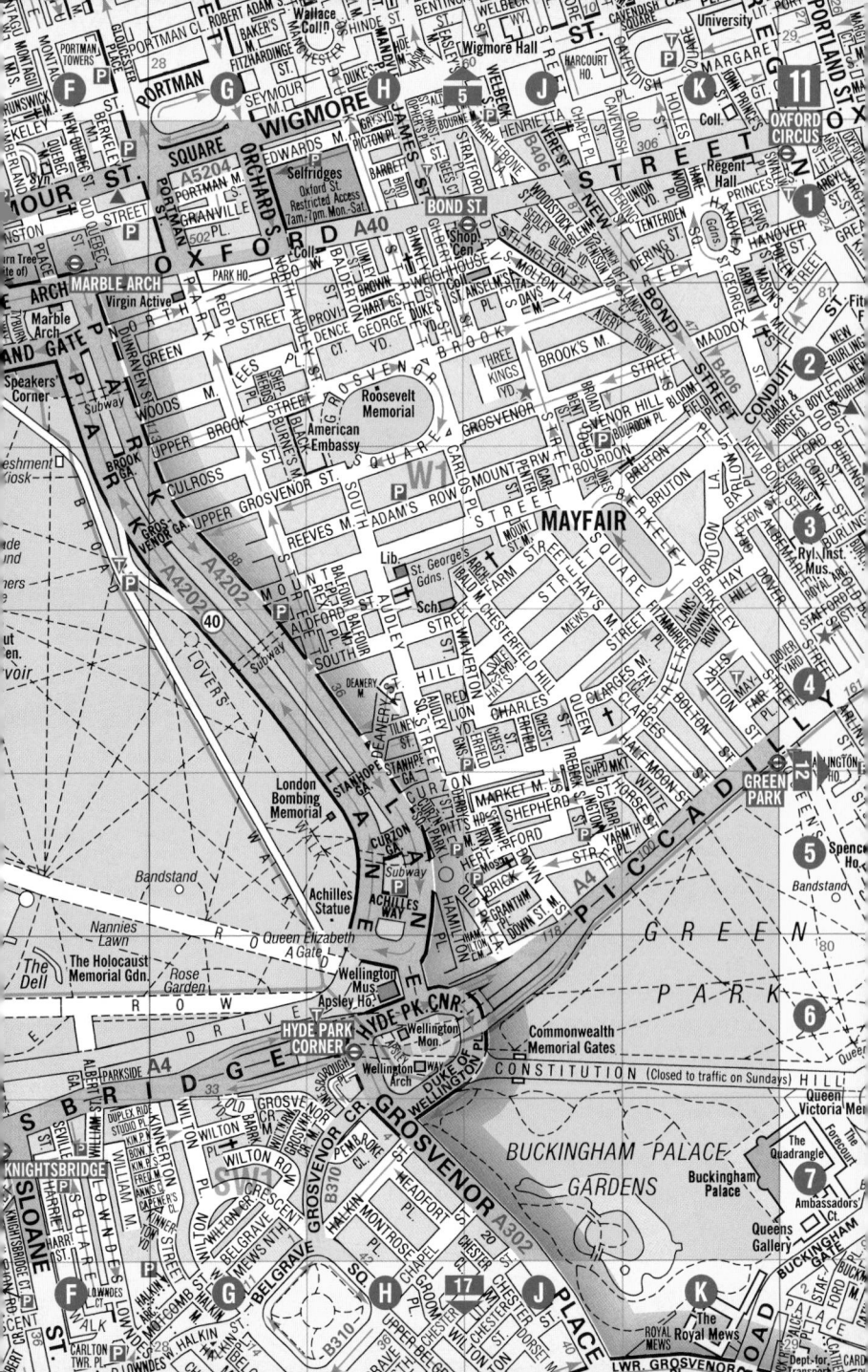

OXFORD STREET
WIGMORE
PORTMAN SQUARE
MARBLE ARCH
OXFORD CIRCUS
BOND ST.
MAYFAIR
GROSVENOR SQUARE
Roosevelt Memorial
American Embassy
Selfridges
Oxford St. Restricted Access 7am.-7pm. Mon.-Sat.
Wigmore Hall
Wallace Coll.
Regent Hall
PICCADILLY
GREEN PARK
HYDE PARK CORNER
KNIGHTSBRIDGE
PARK LANE
London Bombing Memorial
Achilles Statue
Queen Elizabeth Gate
The Holocaust Memorial Gdn.
Rose Garden
The Dell
Nannies Lawn
Bandstand
Wellington Mus.
Apsley Ho.
Wellington Arch
Commonwealth Memorial Gates
CONSTITUTION HILL (Closed to traffic on Sundays)
BUCKINGHAM PALACE GARDENS
Buckingham Palace
Queens Gallery
The Royal Mews
Speakers' Corner
BELGRAVE SQ.
GROSVENOR PLACE

12
OXFORD CIRCUS
OXFORD STREET
TOTTENHAM COURT ROAD
NEW OXFORD ST.
A
B
C
D
E
6
1
2
3
4
5
6
7
Regent Hall
Coll.
University
The Plaza
Fitness First
Leis Cen.
Syn
SOHO
SOHO SQUARE
CHARING CROSS ROAD
SHAFTESBURY AVENUE
REGENT STREET
CONDUIT STREET
GREAT MARLBOROUGH ST.
BROADWICK ST.
WARDOUR ST.
OLD COMPTON ST.
CAMBRIDGE CIRCUS
SEVEN DIALS
Thomas Neal's
Sports Cen.
COVENT GARDEN
LONG ACRE
GARRICK ST.
LEICESTER SQ.
London Trocadero
PICCADILLY CIRCUS
PICCADILLY
COVENTRY ST.
Royal Academy of Arts
Royal Academy Schs.
Ryl. Inst. Mus.
National Portrait Gallery
National Gallery
Cent. Lending Lib.
Shop. Cen.
WILLIAM IV ST.
TRAFALGAR SQ.
Nelson's Column
CHARING CROSS
Canada Ho.
HAYMARKET
JERMYN ST.
ST. JAMES'S SQUARE
London Lib.
ST. JAMES'S ST.
PALL MALL
COCKSPUR ST.
NORTHUMBERLAND AVE.
King Charles I Island
Admiralty Arch
Old Admiralty Offices
Mall Galls.
Inst. of Contemp. Arts
Duke of York Mem.
RAC
SW1
Marlborough Ho.
King George VI Memorial
(Commonwealth Conference Centre)
Spencer Ho.
Bandstand
GREEN PARK
St. James's Palace
Clarence Ho.
Lancaster Ho.
Chap.
Stable Yard Gate
(Closed to traffic on Sundays)
THE MALL
HORSE GUARDS RD.
Horse Guards
The Household Cavalry Mus.
Horse Guards Parade
Guards Memorial
Banqueting Ho.
Scotland Off.
Old War Office
WHITEHALL
DOWNING ST.
Foreign Office
Cenotaph
Government Offices
KING CHARLES ST.
Churchill Mus.
ST. JAMES'S PARK
Duck Island
Lake
Clive Steps
Parks Police
Queen Victoria Mem.
CONSTITUTION HILL
Buckingham Palace
The Quadrangle
The Forecourt
Ambassadors' Ct.
Queens Gallery
BIRDCAGE WALK
Queen Anne's Gate
Guards' Mus.
Wellington Barracks
OLD QUEEN ST.
GREAT GEORGE ST.
PARLIAMENT ST.
PARLIAMENT SQ.
QEII Conf. Cen.
Guildhall
Westminster Abbey
BROAD SANCTUARY
The Cloisters
The Close
Abbey Garden
TOTHILL ST.
ST. JAMES'S PARK
New Scotland Yard
Caxton Hall
BUCKINGHAM GATE
VICTORIA ST.
Dept. of Trade & Industry
11
GREEN PARK
18

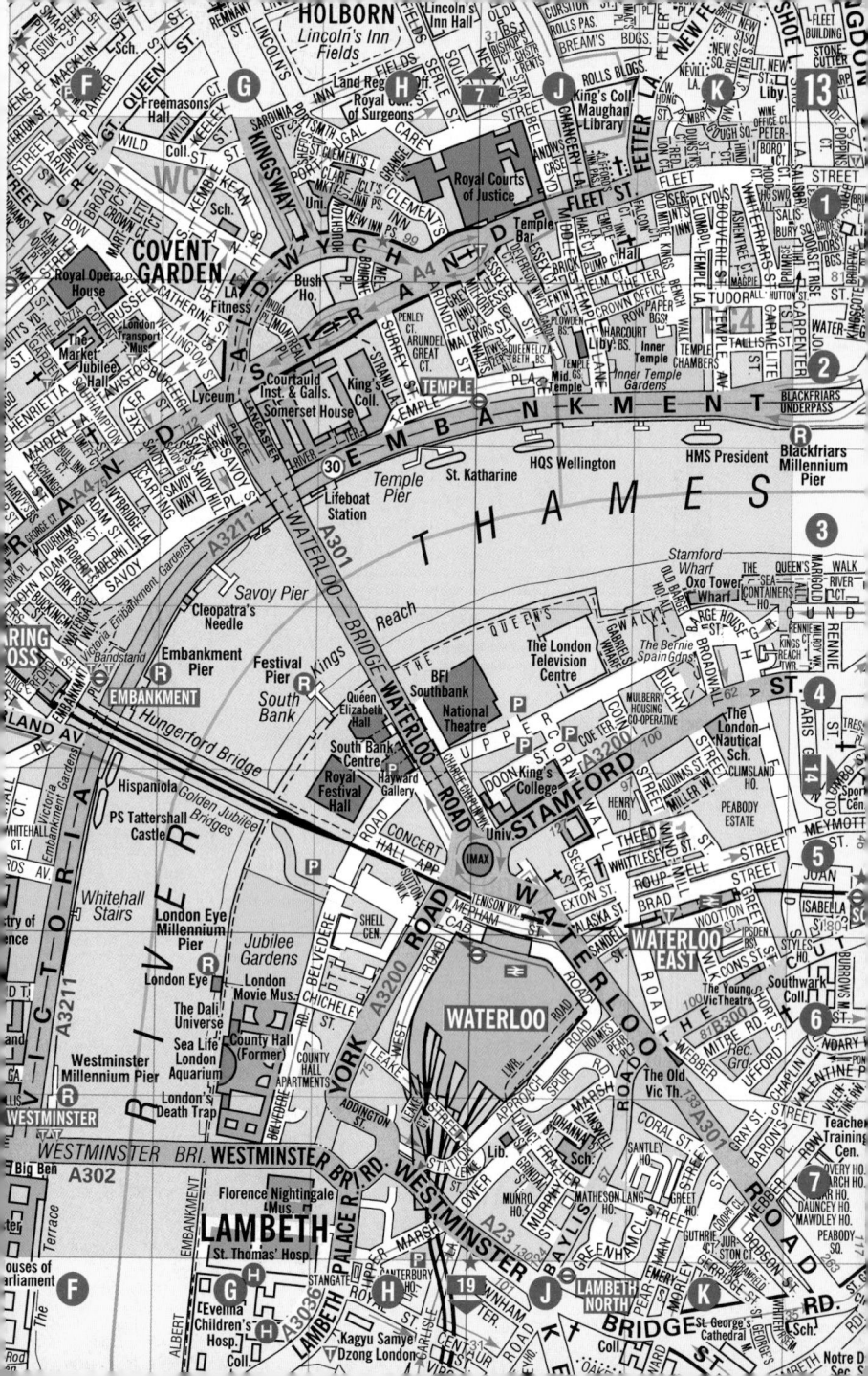

HOLBORN
Lincoln's Inn Fields
Lincoln's Inn Hall
Land Regy. Off.
Royal Coll. of Surgeons
King's Coll. Maughan Library
F
G
H
J
K
7
13
Freemasons Hall
KINGSWAY
Royal Courts of Justice
FLEET ST.
FETTER LA.
CHANCERY LA.
COVENT GARDEN
Royal Opera House
The Market
Jubilee Hall
London Transport Mus.
Lyceum
LA Fitness
Bush Ho.
Temple Bar
ALDWYCH
STRAND
A4
Courtauld Inst. & Galls.
Somerset House
King's Coll.
TEMPLE
Inner Temple
Inner Temple Gardens
Mid. Temple
TEMPLE CHAMBERS
BLACKFRIARS UNDERPASS
EMBANKMENT
Blackfriars Millennium Pier
HMS President
HQS Wellington
St. Katharine
Temple Pier
Lifeboat Station
30
THAMES
1
2
3
4
5
6
7
Stamford Wharf
Oxo Tower Wharf
SEA CONTAINERS HO.
WATERLOO BRIDGE
A301
A3211
Savoy Pier
Cleopatra's Needle
Victoria Embankment Gardens
Reach
Kings
QUEEN'S WALK
The London Television Centre
The Bernie Spain Gdns.
MULBERRY HOUSING CO-OPERATIVE
BFI Southbank
National Theatre
Festival Pier
South Bank
Embankment Pier
EMBANKMENT
Bandstand
Hungerford Bridge
Queen Elizabeth Hall
South Bank Centre
Royal Festival Hall
Hayward Gallery
King's College
STAMFORD ST.
A3200
The London Nautical Sch.
PEABODY ESTATE
14
Hispaniola
Golden Jubilee Bridges
PS Tattershall Castle
IMAX
Univ.
CONCERT HALL APP.
Whitehall Stairs
London Eye Millennium Pier
Jubilee Gardens
London Eye
London Movie Mus.
The Dali Universe
Sea Life London Aquarium
County Hall (Former)
COUNTY HALL APARTMENTS
London's Death Trap
Westminster Millennium Pier
WESTMINSTER
SHELL CEN.
YORK ROAD
WATERLOO
WATERLOO EAST
WATERLOO ROAD
The Young Vic Theatre
Southwark Coll.
The Old Vic Th.
VICTORIA EMBANKMENT
RIVER
WESTMINSTER BRI.
A302
Big Ben
Houses of Parliament
Florence Nightingale Mus.
LAMBETH
St. Thomas' Hosp.
Evelina Children's Hosp.
Kagyu Samye Dzong London
LAMBETH PALACE RD.
WESTMINSTER BRI. RD.
A23
19
LAMBETH NORTH
Lib.
Sch.
St. George's Cathedral
Teacher Training Cen.
BRIDGE RD.
A3036

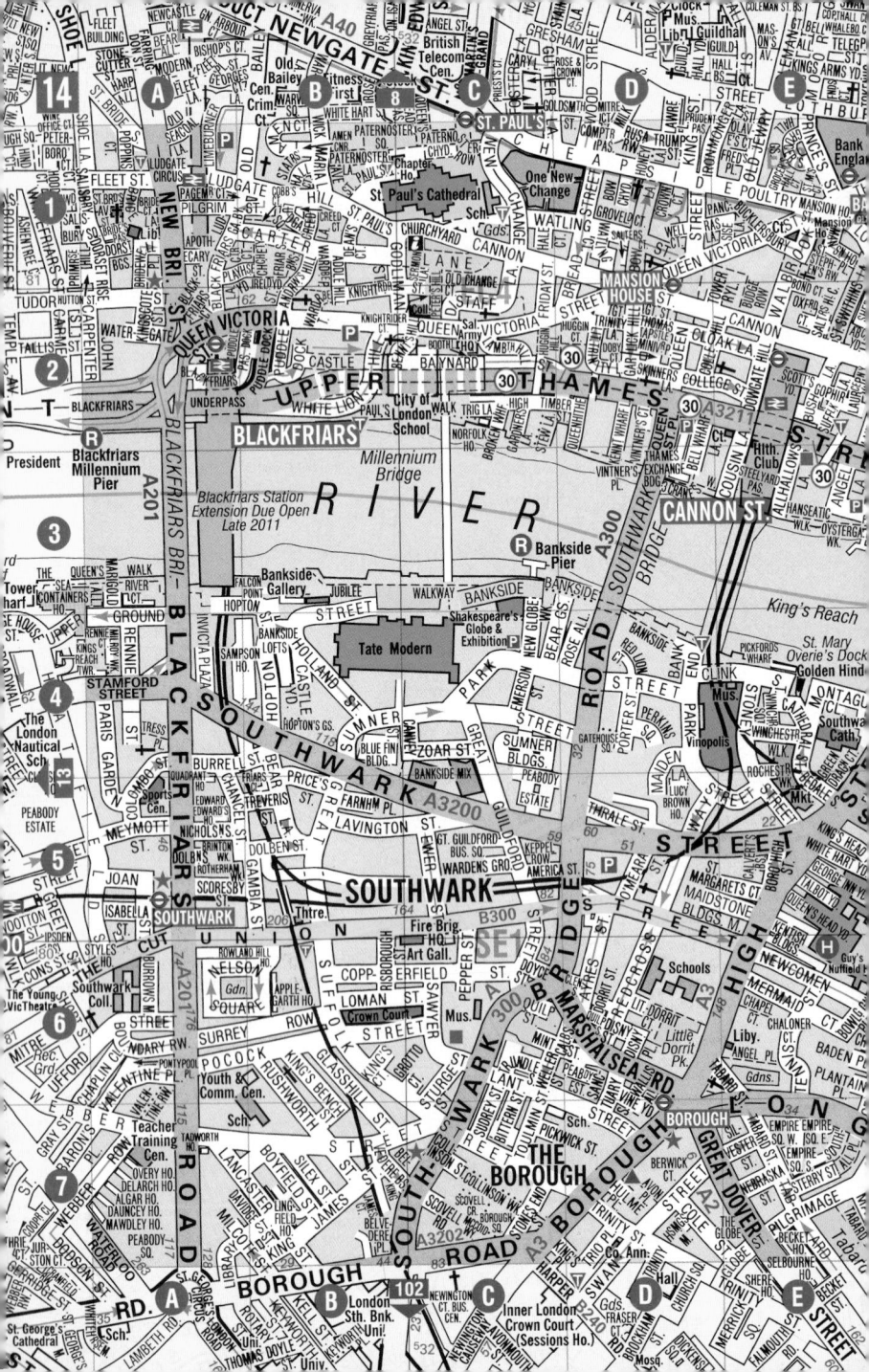
14
A
B
C
D
E
1
2
3
4
5
6
7
NEWGATE ST.
A40
ST. PAUL'S
St. Paul's Cathedral
One New Change
CHEAPSIDE
POULTRY
Bank of England
MANSION HOUSE
QUEEN VICTORIA ST.
CANNON ST.
LUDGATE HILL
LUDGATE CIRCUS
FLEET ST.
NEW BRI. ST.
FARRINGDON ST.
Old Bailey
Cen. Crim. Ct.
British Telecom Cen.
Fitness First
8
UPPER THAMES ST.
30
A3211
BLACKFRIARS
BLACKFRIARS UNDERPASS
City of London School
Blackfriars Millennium Pier
President
Millennium Bridge
RIVER
Blackfriars Station Extension Due Open Late 2011
Bankside Pier
Bankside Gallery
Tate Modern
Shakespeare's Globe & Exhibition
King's Reach
St. Mary Overie's Dock
Golden Hinde
Southwark Cath.
Clink Mus.
Vinopolis
CANNON ST.
Hllth. Club
BLACKFRIARS BRI.
A201
BLACKFRIARS ROAD
SOUTHWARK BRIDGE
SOUTHWARK BRIDGE ROAD
A300
SOUTHWARK ST.
A3200
STAMFORD STREET
UPPER GROUND
HOPTON STREET
BANKSIDE
PARK STREET
SUMNER ST.
ZOAR ST.
Bankside Mix
The London Nautical Sch
13
PEABODY ESTATE
Sports Cen.
SOUTHWARK
UNION STREET
B300
SE1
Fire Brig. HQ
Art Gall.
Thtre.
NELSON SQUARE
Southwark Coll.
The Young Vic Theatre
Crown Court
Little Dorrit Pk.
Schools
MARSHALSEA RD.
BOROUGH HIGH ST.
A3
LONG LANE
BOROUGH
THE BOROUGH
GREAT DOVER ST.
A2
BOROUGH ROAD
A3202
Teacher Training Cen.
Youth & Comm. Cen.
ST. GEORGE'S CIRCUS
LAMBETH RD.
London Sth. Bnk. Uni.
102
Inner London Crown Court (Sessions Ho.)
NEWINGTON CAUSEWAY
B240
St. George's Cathedral
Guy's Nuffield Ho.
Liby.
WATERLOO ROAD
SOUTH-WARK BRIDGE RD.

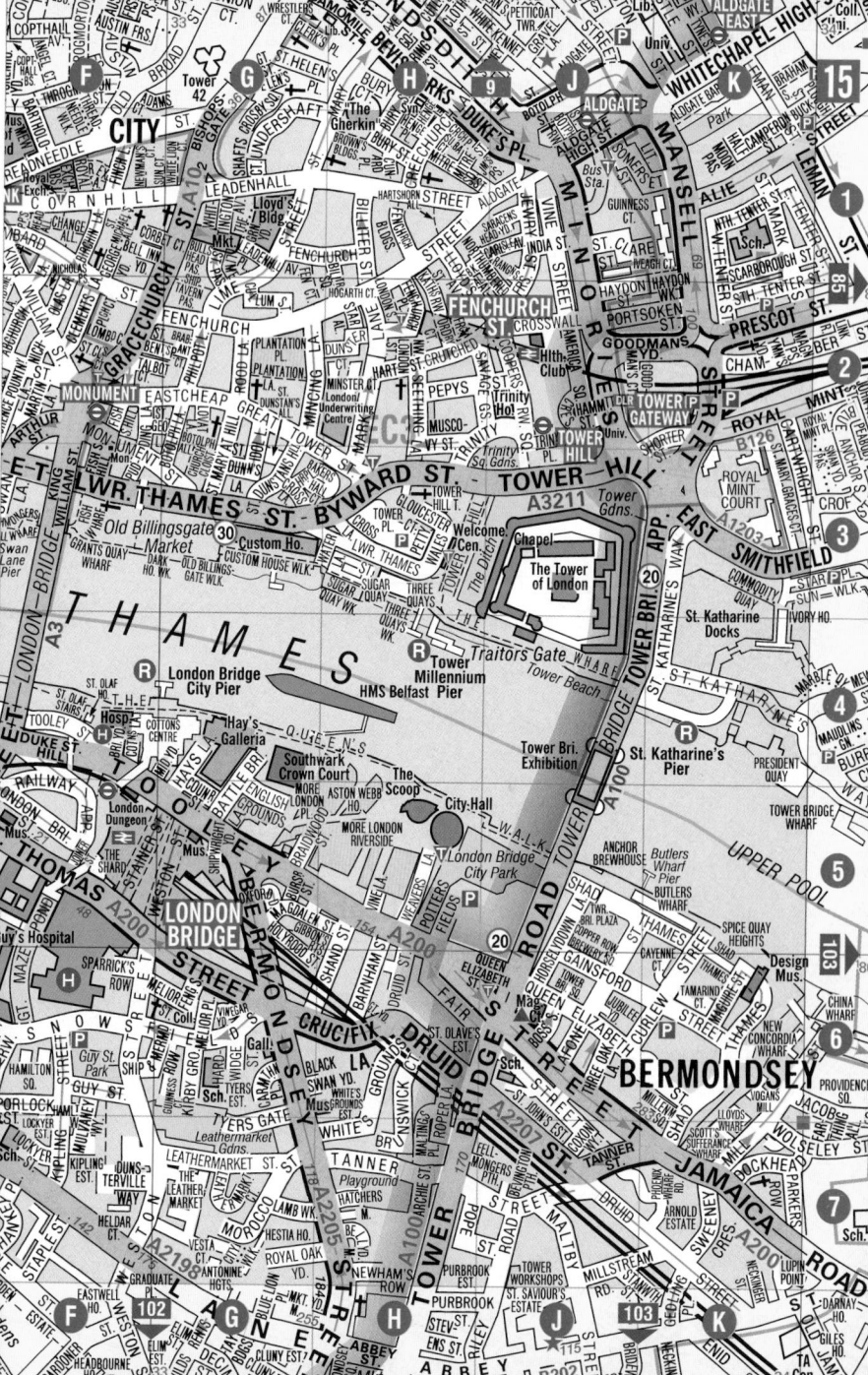
15
CITY
Tower 42
"The Gherkin"
Lloyd's Bldg
FENCHURCH ST.
ALDGATE
ALDGATE EAST
WHITECHAPEL HIGH ST.
MINORIES
MANSELL STREET
LEMAN ST.
PRESCOT ST.
ROYAL MINT ST.
ROYAL MINT COURT
EAST SMITHFIELD
MONUMENT
EASTCHEAP
GRACECHURCH ST.
LEADENHALL
CORNHILL
BISHOPSGATE
GREAT TOWER ST.
LWR. THAMES ST.
BYWARD ST.
TOWER HILL
TOWER GATEWAY
Trinity Ho!
Old Billingsgate Market
Custom Ho.
The Tower of London
Chapel
Traitors Gate
Tower Beach
Tower Gdns.
TOWER BRI. APP.
St. Katharine Docks
St. Katharine's Pier
THAMES
HMS Belfast
London Bridge City Pier
Tower Millennium Pier
Hay's Galleria
Southwark Crown Court
City Hall
The Scoop
Tower Bri. Exhibition
TOWER BRIDGE
TOWER BRIDGE ROAD
TOOLEY ST.
LONDON BRIDGE
London Dungeon
THE SHARD
ST. THOMAS ST.
Guy's Hospital
BERMONDSEY ST.
CRUCIFIX LA.
DRUID ST.
Leathermarket Gdns.
UPPER POOL
Butlers Wharf Pier
Design Mus.
BERMONDSEY
JAMAICA ROAD
TANNER ST.
ABBEY ST.
LONG LANE
WESTON ST.
103
102
85
1
2
3
4
5
6
7
F
G
H
J
K

16
KENSINGTON
Royal Geographical Society
GORE
KNIGHTSBRIDGE
Royal Coll. of Art
Royal Albert Hall
Imperial Coll.
Royal College of Music
Imperial Coll. London (South Kensington Campus)
Science Mus.
Natural History Museum
Victoria & Albert Museum
Brompton Oratory
Harrods
KNIGHTSBRIDGE
CROMWELL RD.
THURLOE PLACE
Ismaili Cen.
Institut Francais
SOUTH KENSINGTON
BROMPTON
LA Fitness
OLD BROMPTON RD.
BROMPTON ROAD
The Royal Marsden Hosp. (Fulham)
Ryl. Brompton Hosp. (Fulham)
CHELSEA
Royal Brompton Hospital
Thamesbrook
Chelsea Old Town Hall
Sports Cen.
Chelsea Cin.
THE SUTTON ESTATE
CHELSEA CLOISTERS
SAMUEL LEWIS TRUST DWELLINGS
KINGS WALK SHOP. CEN.
FULHAM ROAD
KING'S ROAD
Carlyle's House
Chelsea Physic Garden
CHELSEA EMBANKMENT
Cadogan Pier
A B C D E
1 2 3 4 5 6 7
10
100

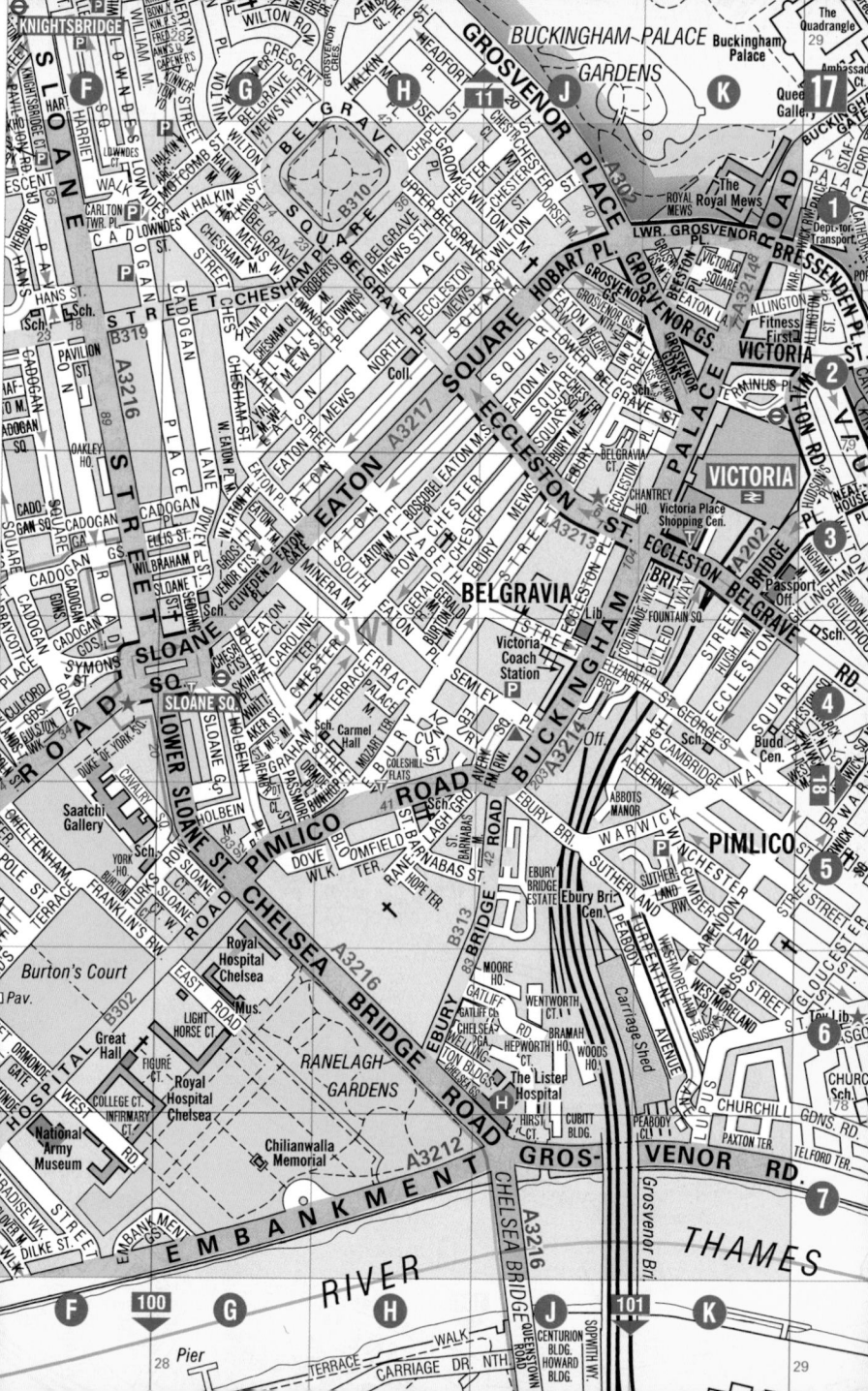

KNIGHTSBRIDGE
BUCKINGHAM PALACE GARDENS
Buckingham Palace
The Quadrangle
The Royal Mews
Queen's Gallery
17
11
GROSVENOR PLACE
A302
BELGRAVE SQUARE
B310
SLOANE STREET
A3216
B319
CADOGAN PLACE
LOWNDES SQ.
CHESHAM PLACE
EATON SQUARE
A3217
ECCLESTON ST.
BUCKINGHAM PALACE ROAD
A3213
A3214
LWR. GROSVENOR PL.
BRESSENDEN PL.
VICTORIA ST.
VICTORIA
Victoria Place Shopping Cen.
A202
VAUXHALL BRIDGE ROAD
BELGRAVE RD.
ECCLESTON SQUARE
Passport Off.
BELGRAVIA
SW1
Victoria Coach Station
Lib.
Coll.
Carmel Hall
SLOANE SQ.
SLOANE SQUARE
LOWER SLOANE ST.
PIMLICO ROAD
PIMLICO
WARWICK WAY
ST. GEORGE'S DR.
EBURY BRIDGE ROAD
B313
Ebury Bridge Estate
Ebury Bri. Cen.
Carriage Shed
Saatchi Gallery
KING'S ROAD
Burton's Court
Royal Hospital Chelsea
Mus.
Great Hall
National Army Museum
B302
ROYAL HOSPITAL ROAD
CHELSEA BRIDGE ROAD
A3216
RANELAGH GARDENS
Chilianwalla Memorial
The Lister Hospital
GROSVENOR RD.
CHELSEA EMBANKMENT
A3212
CHELSEA BRIDGE
Grosvenor Bri.
RIVER THAMES
100
101
Pier
CARRIAGE DR. NTH.
QUEENSTOWN ROAD
1
2
3
4
5
6
7
F
G
H
J
K
28
29

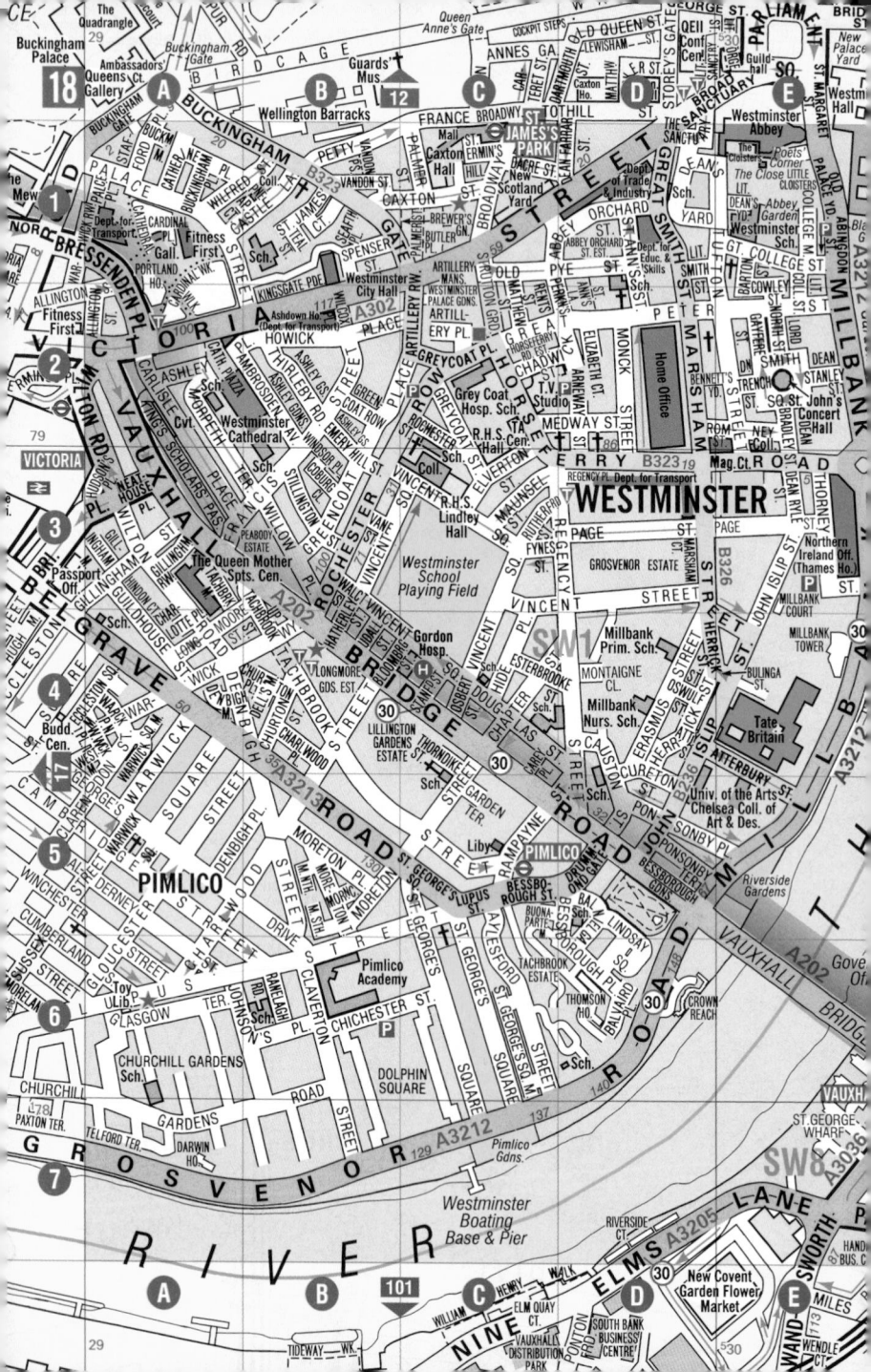

18
12
17
101
A
B
C
D
E
1
2
3
4
5
6
7
Buckingham Palace
The Quadrangle
Queens Gallery
Ambassadors' Ct.
Buckingham Gate
BIRDCAGE
Guards' Mus
Wellington Barracks
Queen Anne's Gate
COCKPIT STEPS
OLD QUEEN ST.
ANNES GA.
GEORGE ST.
QEII Conf. Cen.
PARLIAMENT SQ.
New Palace Yard
Guild-hall
BROAD SANCTUARY
THE SANCTUARY
Westminster Abbey
Westminster Hall
ST. MARGARET ST.
BUCKINGHAM
PALACE
PETTY FRANCE
BROADWY
ST. JAMES'S PARK
TOTHILL ST.
Caxton Hall
CAXTON ST.
New Scotland Yard
Dept. of Trade & Industry
DEAN'S YARD
The Cloisters
Poets' Corner
The Close
Abbey Garden
Westminster Sch.
GT. COLLEGE ST.
OLD PALACE YD.
ABINGDON ST.
MILLBANK
A3212
B323
A302
VICTORIA
STREET
Westminster City Hall
Ashdown Ho. (Dept. for Transport)
Dept. for Transport
Fitness First
BRESSENDEN PL.
Westminster Cathedral
VAUXHALL BRIDGE ROAD
HOWICK PLACE
GREYCOAT PL.
Grey Coat Hosp. Sch.
HORSEFERRY ROAD
B323
Home Office
MARSHAM STREET
Dept. for Educ. & Skills
SMITH SQ.
St. John's Concert Hall
T.V. Studio
R.H.S. Hall
R.H.S. Lindley Hall
WESTMINSTER
Westminster School Playing Field
VINCENT SQ.
VINCENT STREET
GROSVENOR ESTATE
Northern Ireland Off. (Thames Ho.)
MILLBANK COURT
MILLBANK TOWER
SW1
Millbank Prim. Sch.
Millbank Nurs. Sch.
Tate Britain
ATTERBURY ST.
Univ. of the Arts Chelsea Coll. of Art & Des.
JOHN ISLIP ST.
B326
VICTORIA
Passport Off.
The Queen Mother Spts. Cen.
PEABODY ESTATE
ROCHESTER ROW
Gordon Hosp.
A202
BELGRAVE ROAD
A3213
LILLINGTON GARDENS ESTATE
Budd. Cen.
WARWICK SQUARE
PIMLICO
ST. GEORGE'S SQ.
LUPUS ST.
RAMPAYNE ST.
BESSBOROUGH ST.
PIMLICO
Liby.
Riverside Gardens
VAUXHALL BRIDGE
Pimlico Academy
CHICHESTER ST.
DOLPHIN SQUARE
TACHBROOK ESTATE
CROWN REACH
CHURCHILL GARDENS
CHURCHILL GARDENS ROAD
GROSVENOR ROAD
A3212
Pimlico Gdns.
Westminster Boating Base & Pier
RIVER
SW8
A3036
NINE ELMS LANE
A3205
RIVERSIDE CT.
New Covent Garden Flower Market
WANDSWORTH RD.
MILES ST.
SOUTH BANK BUSINESS CENTRE
VAUXHALL DISTRIBUTION PARK
ELM QUAY CT.
TIDEWAY WK.
30
29
79

WESTMINSTER BRI. WESTMINSTER BRI. RD.
Big Ben
Houses of Parliament
Florence Nightingale Mus.
St. Thomas' Hosp.
Evelina Children's Hosp.
Kagyu Samye Dzong London
LAMBETH
King's College London (St. Thomas' Campus)
ARCHBISHOP'S PARK
Lambeth Palace
Marine Institute
The Garden Mus.
Lambeth Pier
LAMBETH BRI.
Police H.Q.
LAMBETH NORTH
St. George's Cathedral
Imperial War Museum
Geraldine Mary Harmsworth Park
SE1
SE11
Millbank Millennium Pier
Victoria Tower
VAUXHALL
Spring Gardens
All Nations Centre
Superstore
Gas Works
Westminster Business Sq.
Surrey County Cricket Club (The Oval Cricket Grd.)
KENNINGTON
KENNINGTON PARK
Vauxhall Park
St. Peter's Residence
Referral Unit
KENNINGTON ROAD
KENNINGTON LANE
KENNINGTON OVAL
HARLEYFORD RD.
ALBERT EMBANKMENT
ST. GEORGE'S ROAD
LAMBETH ROAD
A3036
A3203
A3204
A23
A202
A3
13
19
101
102

20
A
B
C
D
E
1
2
3
4
5
6
7
ST. ALBANS ROAD
A1081
OLD FOLD MANOR GOLF COURSE
BRIDGEDOWN GOLF COURSE
Club House
Club Ho.
Electricity Transformer Sta.
Playing Field
HIGH BARNET
Burial Ground
Play. Fld.
Christ Church Primary School
GT. NORTH RD.
(HADLEY HIGHSTONE)
A1000
KITTS END ROAD
Hadley Green
HADLEY GREEN
MONKEN HADLEY
Rectory Farm
St. Martha's Senior School
Monken Hadley C of E Prim. Sch.
CAMLET WAY
Bournwell Hill
HADLEY ROAD
MONKEN HADLEY COMMON
Priddeon's Hill
COMMON
HADLEY
King George's Field
BARNET
Queen Elizabeth's School
WOOD STREET
A411
HIGH STREET
A1000
Whalebone Park
BARNET HOSPITAL
Psychiatric Unit
Cemy.
CHIPPING BARNET
EN5
Queen Elizabeth's Girls' Sch.
High Barnet
BARNET HILL
GREAT NORTH ROAD
STATION ROAD
Barnet Vale
Whitings Hill Prim. Sch.
Schools
Barnet FC (Underhill Stadium)
Underhill Playing Fields
Odeon Cin.
The Rainbow Cen.
Ducks Island
Recreation Ground
Dollis Brook
RIVERSIDE WALK
KING GEORGE V PLAYING FIELDS
Grasvenor Avenue Inf. Sch.
Greenhill Gdns.
East Barnet Old Grammarians Playing Field
Grange Playing Fields
Grange Avenue Open Space
Totteridge Park Open Space
Sports Centre
Tennis Courts
The Ravenscroft School Playing Field
N20
Wyatts Farm Open Space
Recreation Ground
SOUTH HERTS GOLF COURSE
Pavilion
Brook Farm Open Space
Hall
Hillsborough Cottage
Fairlight Cottage
Totteridge Park
TOTTERIDGE COMMON
A5109
TOTTERIDGE VILLAGE
30
Redings
Hillsdown
TOTTERIDGE
Club House
Sports Grd.
24
525
98
97
195

Hadley Wood
Lawn Tennis Club
HADLEY WOOD
The Beale Arboretum
Ash Wood
ENFIELD CHASE
21
Ferny Hill Cottage
Ferny Hill Farm
Moat Wood
Club House
Great Broadgates Hill
BEECH HILL PARK
HADLEY WOOD GOLF COURSE
Fernyhill Wood
Rough Lot
TRENT PARK
(COUNTRY PARK)
Seedfield Spinney
Green Brook
Fish Pond
Monken Mead Brook
Hadley Wood Nature Reserve
Sewits Hill
Newmans Hill
Beech Hill Lake
Water Tower
Oak Wood
Trent Park
Reservoir (covered)
Picnic Area
EAST BARNET GOLF COURSE
Playing Field
Artificial Pitches
Livingstone Prim. Sch.
Monument
Church Wood
Playing Fields
Cemetery
EN4
Recreation Ground
NEW BARNET
Cockfosters
COCKFOSTERS
COCKFOSTERS
A111
Pymmes Brook
Pleasure Ground
New Barnet
Lyonsdown
EAST BARNET
A110
CAT HILL
BRAMLEY RD.
Chicken Shed Theatre
Middlesex Uni. (Cat Hill Campus)
Bramley Sports Grd.
Saracens Amateur Rugby Football Club
Oaktree Sch.
East Barnet Sch.
Oak Hill Woods Nature Reserve
Oak Hill College
LONGMORE AV.
B193
Bandstand
Playground
OAK HILL PARK
N14
Pavilion
Miniature Golf Course
Monkfrith Prim. Sch.
Bowling Green
Oakleigh Park
OAKLEIGH PARK
A1000
WHETSTONE
Oak Hill Campus
Pool
Study Centre
Pupil Referral Unit
31
South Barnet
Southgate Sch. & Sports Cen.
22
F
G
H
J
K
1
2
3
4
5
6
7

22
HADLEY ROAD
Park Farm
Park Farm Cottages
Reservoir
ENFIELD CHASE
Camlet Moat
Obelisk
Moat Wood
Picnic Area
Ferny Hill Cottage
Parkside Farm
Pumping Station
Vicarage Farm
Wolverton
RIDGE ROAD
THE
Camlet Hill
Ride Wood
TRENT PARK (COUNTRY PARK)
Leeging Beech Gutter
Salmon's Brook
Fish Pond
Icehouse Wood
Seedfield Spinney
Hog Hill
Williams Wood
Middlesex University (Trent Park Campus)
Noddins Well
College Ho.
Shaws Wood Cottages
Shaws Wood
Trent Park
Lodge
The Rookery
Rookery Cotts.
Miniature Rifle Range
Merryhills Brook
Trent Park Sports Cen.
Sports Ground
Hockey Pitches
TRENT PARK GOLF COURSE
SNAKES LANE
Church Wood
EN4
Triangular Wood
Trent Park Stables
ENFIELD ROAD
A110
Driving Range
EAST POLE COTTAGES
Club Ho.
Lodge
Depot
WESTPOLE AVENUE
21
Play. Fld.
Southgate Sch. & Sports Cen.
Oakwood
BRAMLEY ROAD
SUSSEX WAY
Highlands Village
Boxer's Lake
Nursing Home
Prim. Sch.
Superstore
Chicken Shed Theatre
Bramley Sports Grd.
De Bohun Prim. Sch.
Saracens Amateur Rugby Football Club
Oaktree Sch.
Addison
The Ho. (PRU)
N14
CHASEVILLE PARK RD.
OAKWOOD PARK
OAKWOOD
Yacht Pond
Oak Hill College
CHASE SIDE
A111
Monkfrith Prim. Sch.
B1453
OSIDGE LA.
Osidge Prim. Sch.
Superstore
32
Leisure Cen.
Southgate
SOUTHGATE CIRCUS
WINCHMORE HILL ROAD
NORTH LONDON PRIORY HOSP.
GROVELANDS PARK
Bowling Green
Tennis Courts
Boating Lake
South Barnet
A B C D E
1 2 3 4 5 6 7

23
FORTY HILL
CHASE FARM HOSPITAL
CEMETERY
Gordon Hill
Chase Side
ENFIELD TOWN
ENFIELD
EN1
EN2
N21
N9
SLADES HILL
WINDMILL HILL
A110
RIDGEWAY
A1005
CHURCH ST.
SOUTHBURY ROAD
SILVER ST.
BAKER ST.
LONDON ROAD
A105
Enfield Chase
Enfield Town
World's End
Moat
Club House
ENFIELD GOLF COURSE
GRANGE PARK
Grange Park
BUSH HILL PARK GOLF COURSE
Bush Hill
BUSH HILL PARK
Bush Hill Park
LONDON PARK AV.
VILLAGE RD.
RIDGE AV.
A105
WINCHMORE HILL
Winchmore Hill
GREEN LANES
CHURCH ST.
B154
GT. CAMBRIDGE RD.
A10
Enfield Grammar School (Lower)
Chace Com. Sch. & Spts. Cen.
Lavender Prim. Sch.
Highlands School
Grange Park Prim. Sch.
Cricket Ground
Town Park
Tennis Courts
New River (old course)
Salmon's Brook
Playing Fields
24
33
1
2
3
4
5
6
7
F
G
H
J
K

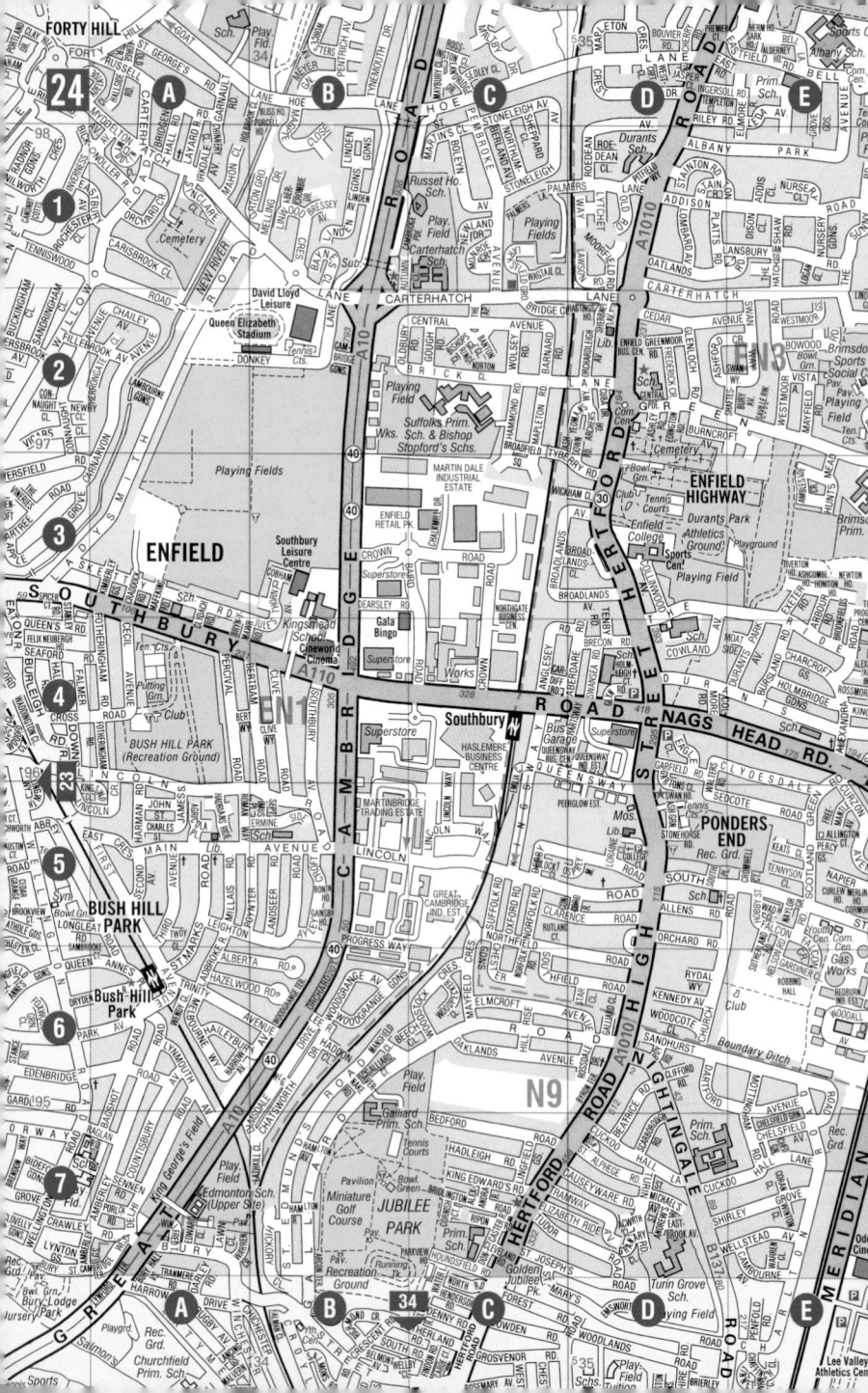

24
23
34
A
B
C
D
E
1
2
3
4
5
6
7
FORTY HILL
ENFIELD
EN1
EN3
N9
ENFIELD HIGHWAY
PONDERS END
BUSH HILL PARK
Bush Hill Park
Southbury
David Lloyd Leisure
Queen Elizabeth Stadium
Southbury Leisure Centre
Kingsmead School
Cineworld Cinema
Gala Bingo
Superstore
Playing Fields
Cemetery
MARTIN DALE INDUSTRIAL ESTATE
ENFIELD RETAIL PK.
NORTHGATE BUSINESS CEN.
HASLEMERE BUSINESS CENTRE
MARTINBRIDGE TRADING ESTATE
GREAT CAMBRIDGE IND. EST.
Suffolks Prim. Sch. & Bishop Stopford's Schs.
Carterhatch Sch.
Russet Ho. Sch.
Durants Sch.
Enfield College
Durants Park Athletics Ground
Brimsdown Sports Social Cen.
BUSH HILL PARK (Recreation Ground)
JUBILEE PARK
Miniature Golf Course
Galliard Prim. Sch.
Edmonton Sch. (Upper Site)
Turin Grove Sch.
Golden Jubilee Pk.
Recreation Ground
Churchfield Prim. Sch.
Bury Lodge Park
Lee Valley Athletics Cent
Albany Sch.
Boundary Ditch
Gas Works
King George's Field
SOUTHBURY ROAD
GREAT CAMBRIDGE ROAD
HERTFORD ROAD
HIGH STREET
NAGS HEAD RD.
CARTERHATCH LANE
NIGHTINGALE ROAD
GREAT CAMBRIDGE ROAD
LADYSMITH ROAD
NEW RIVER
A10
A110
A1010
B137
MERIDIAN

ALBANY PARK
NFIELD WASH
Enfield Island Village
ENFIELD LOCK
Depot
WATERWAYS BUSINESS CENTRE
HERON MEAD
ENFIELD LOCK
Sewardstone Hall
BUTLERS DR.
Beechside Nursy.
25
Kingsfield Nurseries
Barnfield Riding Stables
GODWIN CL.
Netherhouse Nursery
Netherhouse Farm
F
G
H
J
K
Power Station
Overflow Channel
Pumping Station
Cattlegate Flood Relief Channel
Hannah Nursery
Fouracres Nursery
Northfield Nursery
Northcroft Nursery
Marshfield Nursery
Luthers Farm
Amesbury Mead Farm
Playing Field
SEWARDSTONE
Chapelfield Nursery
Barn Hill
1
2
3
4
5
6
7
Woodlands Nursery
Santa Maria Nursery
Caravan Park
Sewardstone Lodge
MILL LANE
Hall
DAWS HILL
Gilwellbury
Picks Farm
SEWARDSTONE ROAD
A112
AVENUE
A1055
BRANCROFT WAY
LOCKFIELD AV.
BRIMSDOWN INDUSTRIAL ESTATE
WATERMILL BUSINESS CENTRE
EDISON RD.
WALCOT RD.
MILLMARSH LANE
BRIMSDOWN
PLAZA BUSINESS CENTRE
LEASIDE BUSINESS CENTRE
DELTA PK. IND. EST.
SOVEREIGN BUSINESS CENTRE
STOCKINGSWATER LA.
BRAITHWAITE RD.
Depot
Brimsdown
GOLDSDOWN CL.
CELADON CL.
WESTFIELD CL.
ENSTONE RD.
CORNELL CT.
AVONDALE CRES.
DUNDEE RD.
JUTE LA.
THE DENCORA CEN.
MILL RIVER TRADING ESTATE
CENTENARY TRADING ESTATE
RIVER WALK RD.
TRAFALGAR TRAD. EST.
CENTENARY RD.
JEFFREYS RD.
SUEZ RD.
KING GEORGE'S
RESERVOIR
River Lee Navigation
River Lea (or Lee) Diversion
GILWELL PARK
Gilwell Park
The White Cottage
E4
Kennels
ALBION TER.
GILWELL LANE
Yardley Hill
Pitch & Putt
Club Ho.
The Hawk Wood
YARDLEY LANE
Yardley Prim. Sch.
Nursery
HAWKWOOD CRESCENT
HAWKDENE
EPPING GLADE
ROYAL EPPING FOREST & CHINGFORD GOLF COURSE
King George's Sailing Club
DUCK LEES LA.
ALPHA ROAD
NORTHFIELD RD.
LEES LA.
Warehouses
PONDERS END INDUSTRIAL ESTATE
MOLLISON
Weir
South Marsh
Overflow Channel
Ponders End
WAY
A110
LEA VALLEY ROAD
River Lea
Mill
WHARF ROAD
VALLEYLINK ESTATE
COLUMBIA WHARF
WHARF RD. IND. EST.
MORSON ROAD
RIVERSIDE IND. EST.
WILLIAM GIRLING RESERVOIR
LEE VALLEY GOLF COURSE
EPPING WAY
MARK AV.
MARGARET AV.
SOUTH AV.
Drysdale Pk.
DELLS CL.
HARFORD RD.
ALBANY CT.
RIVERSIDE CT.
REDWOOD GDS.
Depot
WINGROVE
Playing Field
LOW HALL CL.
MAIDA AV.
MAIDA WAY
LAUREL GS.
MERRYHILL CL.
KINGS HEAD HILL
Obelisk
Pole Hill
CHINGFORD
The Hawk Wood
CHINGFORD GREEN
FOREST VW.
CONNAUGHT AV.
MORNINGTON RD.
ARABIA CL.
EGLINTON RD.
HERITAGE PL.
MOUNT VIEW R.
SUNNYSIDE DR.
WOODBERRY WAY
PARKHILL RD.
POLE HILL RD.
ENTERPRISE HO.
BLANDFORD CRES.
HAWKSMOUTH
COLLEGE
SEYMOUR
MANSFIELD HILL
35
WALTHAM WAY
Pav.
Playing Field
SUNSET AV.
Nursy. Sch.
Play. Fld.
Chingford Pav.
Council Offs.
GARDENS
THE RIDGEWAY
THE GREEN WK.
THE GN.
STATION ROAD
Lib.
37
38
98
97
96

26
Bushey Golf Course
Tennis Courts
Play. Fld.
Ashfield Jun. Sch.
Tennis Ct.
St. Margaret's Sch.
Merry Hill Fm.
St. Margaret's Sports Centre
Merry Hill
SPARROWS
A411
HERNE
ELSTREE
BUSHEY
Heath Ho.
Caldecote Hill
BUSHEY SPIRE HOSP.
BUSHEY HEATH
WD23
HIGH ROAD
A4140
A409
HEATHBOURNE
Belswood Cottage
Stanmore Common Local Nature Reserve
Hartsbourne Prim. Sch.
Hartsbourne Country Club (Club House)
Tennis Courts
Kestrel Grove (Offices)
The Cedars
Peterborough & St. Margaret's School
Bentley Priory
Tennis Court
HARTSBOURNE GOLF COURSE
Levels Wood
HARROW WEALD COMMON
COMMON ROAD
Lodge
The Princess Alexandra Home
Bentley Priory Local Nature Reserve
Deer Park
Heriot's Wood
Grim's Ditch
Grim's Dyke
Harrow Weald Common
Grimsdyke Open Space
Nurseries
The City
The Old Barn
GRIM'S DYKE GOLF COURSE
Weald Wood
REDDING
Scout Hall
Priory House
Club House
Hertfordshire & Middlesex Country Club
Copse Farm
Lower Priory Farm
Nursery
Bentley Wood High Sch.
Stony Wood
Grimswood Lodge
Grimswood House
Highcroft
The Lodge
Hermitage Cottages
Hermitage Gate
Woodland Hall
BROOKSHILL
HA3
Harrow Weald Cemetery
OXHEY LANE
A4008
Saddlers Mead
Hatch End Ten. Club
Harrow Coll. (Harrow Weald Campus)
Brockhurst Cnr.
Playing Fields
The Roger Bannister Sports Centre
Play. Fld.
Grave Yard
HA5
Playing Fields
UXBRIDGE ROAD
A410
Harrow Arts Cen.
Hatch End Play. Flds.
Liby.
Swim. Pool
Superstore
HATCH END
Hatch End High Sch.
The Cedars
Cedars Manor Sch.
41
HARROW WEALD
Bus Depot
Superstore
Recreation Ground
Tennis Club
Weald Schs.
Bedford Coll. Sports Grd.
High Sch.
First & Mid. Sch.
COLLEGE AV.
A B C D E
1 2 3 4 5 6 7

WATFORD BY-PASS
A41
M1
Junction 4
M1-MOTORWAY
A5183
Elstree Open Space
WD6
Norwegian Barn
Penniwells Fm.
27
CENTENNIAL PARK
Brockley Hill Farm
Sports Ground
Brockley Grange
BROCKLEY
EDGWARE
ROYAL NATIONAL ORTHOPAEDIC HOSPITAL
Brockley Hill Ho.
ASPIRE
Pear Wood Cottages
Limes House
Wood Farm
Pear Wood
Fish Pond
HA8
Newlands
(WATFORD BY-PASS)
A5 (WATLING STREET)
Driving Range
Club House
Brockley Hill Golf Course
Edgwarebury Golf Course
Club Ho.
Cricket Ground
Grove Field Pavilion
Islamic Centre
Tennis Cts.
Cloisters Wood
Stanmore Hall
STANMORE COUNTRY PARK & (Local Nature Reserve)
HA7
COMMON
STANMORE HILL
A4140
Playing Field
London Academy
Stonegrove
CANONS CORNER
SPUR
A410
STONEGROVE
28
St. John's C of E Sch.
Bowling Green
Stanmore Rec. Grd.
Lib.
THE BROADWAY
LONDON ROAD
Stanmore
MARSH
Boot Pond
CHURCH RD.
BROADWAY
Aylward First & Mid. Sch.
Lake Grove Rec. Grd.
The Lake
North London Collegiate School
Tennis Courts
STANMORE
Stanmore College
Comm. Cen.
Temple Pond
King George V Memorial Gdns.
CANONS PARK
Gas Works
Stanmore Marsh
Club House
STANMORE GOLF COURSE
Sports Ground
Whitchurch First & Mid. Schs.
Bowling Green
Stanburn Schs.
WHITCHURCH LANE
B461
Canons Park
Playing Field
Offices
Works
HONEYPOT LANE
42
Sports Ground
LITTLE STANMORE
Little Stanmore First & Middle Sch.
Prince Edward Playing Field
F
G
H
J
K
1
2
3
4
5
6
7
17
18

28
WD6
M1 MOTORWAY
M1
Penniwells Farm
The Dower Ho.
Boys Hill Wood
Thistle Wood
Scratchwood Open Space
Depot
Clump of Trees Wood
Bury Farm
Edgware Bury
Gate Cottages
Nursery Cottage
London Gateway Service Area
MILL HILL GOLF COURSE
Edgwarebury Cemetery
Play. Fld.
Broadfields Prim. Sch.
Sports. Grd.
Tennis Courts
Hemmings Wood
Stoney Wood Lake
Stoney Wood
Northway Sch.
Fairway Prim. Sch.
EDGWAREBURY PARK
Club Ho.
Edgwarebury Golf Course
Tennis Courts
Pav.
Playground
EDGWARE WAY
A41
SPUR ROAD
A410
London Academy
CANONS CORNER
EDGWARE WAY (WATFORD BY-PASS)
A41
Stonegrove
HA8
St. Mary's Convent
Stoneyfields Park
A5100
A5109
SELVAGE LA
HALE LANE
The Hale
STONEGROVE
HIGH STREET
Stonegrove Park
Lake Grove Rec. Grd.
The Lake
The Basin
Edgware Bus Sta.
Broadwalk Shopping Centre
Bus Depot
EDGWARE
STATION RD.
Sch. & Syn.
Lib.
Schools
Mill Hill Old Railway Nature Reserve
CANONS PARK
Tennis Courts
Playing Field
WHITCHURCH LANE
B461
DEANSBROOK RD.
DEANS LANE
BURNT OAK
EDGWARE COMM. HOSP.
NHS Walk-in Cen.
Chandos Recreation Grd.
LITTLE STANMORE
Woodlands Sch.
Little Stanmore First & Mid. Sch.
Prince Edward Playing Field
Watling
WATLING PARK
Sports Ground
BURNT OAK BROADWAY
Burnt Oak
43
27
A B C D E
1 2 3 4 5 6 7

29
Hyver Manor
Gravel Pit Wood
Tanglewood
Barnet Gate Wood
HENDON WOOD LANE
B552
BARNET GATE LANE
MAYS LA.
AUTHORS CL.
Allendale
Brent Lodge Farm
EN5
Dollis Brook
Totteridge Park Open Space
F
G
H
J
K
Hendon Wood Lane Open Space
Sports Ground
Pav.
Fairlight Cottage
HORSESHOE LA.
Totteridge Park
N20
1
The Shrubbery
MOAT MOUNT OPEN SPACE
Leg of Mutton Pond
Totteridge Fields Local Nature Reserve
Abattoir
St. Edward's
TOTTERIDGE COMMON
A5109
Burnhams
Mote End Farm
Farmleigh
Boundary House
Oak Lodge
Ellern Mede Centre
Mote Mount
Nut Wood
White Lodge
Tennis Courts
Mill Hill High Sch.
Playing Field
Beech Wood
Highwood Park
The Barn
Highwood Ho.
CLARK'S LANE
Hendon Park
CROWN CL.
HIGHWOOD HILL
TOTTERIDGE
Totteridge Common
Ellern Mede Farm
The Lynch House
Fairlawn
Highwood
Highwood Hill
2
RAMILLIES RD.
BEDFORD RD.
HANKINS LANE
WORCESTER
NORBURY GRO.
GLENWOOD RD.
BRAMLEY CL.
Highwood Hill Cottage
Holcombe Dale
THE LINCOLNS
ABBEY VIEW
LAWRENCE GDS.
HIGHWOOD HILL
HOLCOMBE HILL
Holcombe Hill
Folly Brook
3
MARSH LANE
A5109
BRABOURNE HGTS.
AUSTELL GDS.
HORNBEAM CL.
THE REDDINGS
REDDINGS CL.
Pool
Playing Field
Riding School
Folly Farm
School
THE RIDGEWAY
B552
Sports Ground Cricket Club
Pav.
Burtonhole Farm
UPHILL RD.
RETAWN PK.
LAWRENCE GARDENS
SUNNYFIELD
St. Mary's Abbey
The Mill Field
Belmont Farm
MILLERS
Cemetery
Sports Ground
Nursery
APEX CORNER
Lawrence Green
St. Joseph's College
Tennis Courts
LANE
St. Paul's C of E Prim. Sch.
Burtonhole Farm
4
NW7
DRAPERS' COTTAGE HOMES
CHALET ESTATE
BUCKLAND CL.
Leisure Cen.
Spts. Grd.
KINGSHEAD HO.
ST. VINCENT'S LA.
National Centre for Medical Research
Works
WATFORD WAY
FOXWOOD CL.
RUSSELL GRO.
LAWRENCE GROVE
SHAKESPEARE RD.
B1461
DRAPERS' COTTAGE HOMES
MARSHALL ESTATE
Mill Hill School
RIDGEWAY
30
MILL HILL CIRCUS
MILTON RD.
TAYLORSMEAD
Sch.
TENNYSON RD.
Ten. Cts.
Pav.
THE RIDGEWAY
B552
BURTONHOLE
Oakfield House
WEYMOUTH AV.
LAWRENCE CT.
NEWCOMBE
UPHILL DR.
CLARENCE CT.
VICTORIA RD.
BIRKBECK
BYRON RD.
MARION RD.
HAMMERS
MILL HILL
Playing Field
GROVE
HIGH ST.
HOLLIES END
Convent
St. Vincent's Catholic Prim. Sch.
Wentworth Hall
5
A1
M1 MOTORWAY
Hall
Sch.
GOODWYN AV.
THE BROADWAY
MILL HILL CIRCUS
WILTSHIRE CL.
ALBERT RD.
Lib.
HARTLEY AV.
DAWS LANE
Sub.
P
STOKE GDS.
WILLS GRO.
Tennis Court
Ridgeway Ho.
VINERIES BANK
Play. Fld.
The Mount Sch.
Drivers Hill
Pavilion
Burton Bank
School Park
Watch Tower House
LANE
BUNNS
FLOWER LANE
HARTLEY CL.
Garden Centre
WISE
WINTER
Arrandene Open Space
AVENUE
Featherstone Hill
Playground
Univ.
OAKLODGE WY.
WISTERIA CL.
SYLVAN AV.
STANHOPE GDNS.
Bus Sta.
LANGLEY PK.
Mill Hill Broadway
COURTGATE CL.
PARK MEAD GDS.
Pav.
Cricket Ground
Tennis Courts
MILL HILL PARK
(BARNET BY-PASS)
Sub.
MELDEX CL.
Mill Hill Cemetery
RUSHDEN GDNS.
WOODCOTE GS.
BITTACY RISE
PARK
6
Bittacy Hill Park
Ten. Cts.
GRANARD BUS. CEN.
Lyndhurst Park
LYNDHURST AV.
WOODLAND WAY
MILL HILL PARK
50
ROAD
WOODCROFT AV.
Woodcroft Park
Sports Ground
Pavilion
GRAHAME PARK
MILL HILL IND. EST.
BUNNS LANE
THE RISE
HOLMDENE AV.
GLENMERE AV.
PARKSIDE
LANE WISE
GRENFELL CL.
Playing Field
FEATHERSTONE RD.
MOORLANDS AV.
BROOKFIELD CRES.
BROOKFIELD AV.
MORETON CL.
SALCOMBE
ENGEL PARK
BITTACY
TUDOR CL.
HOLLAND CT.
Copthall Sch. & Sports Cen.
HILLSIDE GRO.
COPTHALL GDNS.
PAGE MDW.
PURSLEY
Dollis Jun. & Inf. Schs.
SANDERS LA.
ROAD
GRANTS CL.
TAVISTOCK AV.
7
STORKSMEAD RD.
MAPLE GDNS.
M1
PENTAVIA RETAIL PK.
ROWLANDS CL.
CALDEW CT.
SANDWICK CL.
PAGE CT.
Chase Lodge
Chase Lodge Playing Fields
Powerleague Soccer Cen.
METRO PLAYGOLF
Club House
ASHLEY LA.
ABERDARE GDNS.
CLAYTON FIELD
VANGUARD
LONG FIELD
CORNER MEAD
PARK
COLENSO DR.
LONGFIELD AVENUE
BAMPTON DR.
Tennis Courts
Copthall Leisure Centre
Metro Playgolf Driving Range
NW4
BIRCH GRN.
HIGHLEA CL.
WILLOW GN.
BROOKLEA CL.
LARCH GN.
PARKLEA CL.
SATCHELL MEAD
SASSOON
ORDE
WITHERS MEAD
Play. Field
TITHE WLK.
Play. Fld.
Pav. Rugby Club
CHAMPIONS WAY
91
Hendon Crematorium
F
G
H
J
K
Tennis Cts.
Barnet Coll.
Sub.
Grahame Park
44
Junc. 2
FIVEWAYS CORNER
BARNET COPTHALL SPORTS CENTRE
Pavilion
Barnet Copthall Stadium
HENDON GOLF COURSE
GREENLANDS
MEAD WAY
SOUTH MEAD

30
A
B
C
D
E
1
2
3
4
5
6
7
20
29
45
TOTTERIDGE COMMON
TOTTERIDGE
TOTTERIDGE VILLAGE
A5109
Park Open Space
Avenue Open Space
Ravenscroft School Playing Field
OAKLANDS RD.
LANE
Recreation Ground
Pavilion
Brook Farm Open Space
SOUTH HERTS GOLF COURSE
Club House
Sports Grd.
Ten. Cts.
GRANGE
AVENUE
BADGERS CFT.
Hall
LIME GRO.
PRIORY CL.
WHITE ORCHARDS
BARNET
THE PASTURES
Fairlight Cottage
Hillsborough Cottage
HORSESHOE LA.
Totteridge Park
Redings
CHESTNUT LA.
WYKEHAM RISE
Hillsdown
Montebello
Burnhams
Chestnut Cottages
The Warren
Ellern Mede Centre
NORTHCLIFFE DRIVE
BARNWOOD CL.
PINE GROVE
HARMSWORTH WAY
LINKS DR.
HADAR CL.
BELMONT CL.
ROWBEN CL.
WEST HILL WAY
GREAT BUSHEY DR.
OAK TREE DR.
HILL CRESCENT
EDER
N20
THE CLOSE
Prim. Sch.
Waverley
Windyridge
Dell House
The Croft
TOTTERIDGE GREEN
GREENWAY
WILLOW END
ELM-STEAD CL.
Cricket Ground
GREEN WAY
COPPICE WLK
SOUTHWAY
LYNTON
VENTNOR
MEAD
LONGLAND DRIVE
HOLDEN
Dollis Brook
RIVERSIDE
Folly Brook & Darland's Lake Nature Reserve
Laurel Farmhouse
LAUREL WAY
Woodridge Prim. Sch.
SOUTHOVER
CHIDDINGFOLD
NORTHIAM
ARLINGTON
FRAMFIELD CL.
MICHLEHAM DOWN
SHORTGATE
Sports Ground
Woodside Park Club
Tennis Courts
Club Ho.
TILLINGHAM WAY
Pav.
GRN.
Woodside Park
Woodside Park
CHANCTONBURY WAY
PYECOMBE CORNER
RODMELL SLOPE
CISSBURY RING NORTH
SINGLETON SCARP
OFFHAM SLOPE
CISSBURY RING
WOLSTONBURY
SOUTH GARTH
SUSSEX RING
SADDLESCOMBE WAY
POYNINGS WAY
FOLKINGTON CORNER
STEYNINGS WAY
Frith Br.
Tennis Courts
ARGYLE RD.
ALEXANDRA
Folly Farm
Sports Ground
Cricket Club
Pav.
Sports Ground
Nursery
Burtonhole Lane Farm Estate
Burtonhole Farm
BURTONHOLE LANE
Sports Ground
HILLVIEW RD.
ELEANOR CRES.
Mill Hill Sub. Sta.
London Equestrian Centre
Frith Manor Ho.
LULLINGTON
Frith Manor Prim. Sch.
NW7
Oakfield House
Partingdale Manor
THE RIDGEWAY
Wentworth Hall
PARTINGDALE LANE
WAY
Works
READING
CHARLE
HENRY
DARLOT DRIVE
Tennis Courts
ROBERTS RD.
KELLY RD.
SEVRIGHT DR.
BRAY RD.
HOLMES AV.
PEACOCK
CLOSE
ROAD
LANE
Watch Tower House
BITTACY PK. AV.
BITTACY RISE
PARK
BITTACY
CURRY RISE
LIDBURY
DREW AV.
MORPHOU
Depot
WESTLINTON CL.
FINCHLEY GOLF COURSE
LOVERS WALK
Nether Court (Club House)
Dollis Brook
WALDEN
Pav.
Bittacy Hill Park
Playgrd.
Ten. Cts.
Depot
B552
Mill Hill East
Virgin Active Superstore
BITTACY BUSINESS CENTRE
HILL
ENGEL
BITTACY
RUSHDEN GDNS.
WOODCOTE
AVENUE
SANDERS LA.
GRANTS CL.
WOODBERRY
TAVISTOCK
ONE WAY
DEVONSHIRE
DEVONSHIRE CR.
LEE RD.
VINEYARD AV.
DOLLISCROFT
ROAD
ABERCORN
FRITH
MALLOW
HOLDERS HILL CIRCUS
DOLLIS
ASHLEY
ABERDARE GDNS.
OAKHAMPTON RD.
Club House
Hendon Crematorium
HENDON GOLF COURSE
HENDON CEMETERY
HOLDERS HILL RD.
THORNFIELD
Playing Fields
Pav.
Swim. Pool
Finchley Manor Club
B1462
Sikh Cen.
LINKS ROAD
Prim. Sch.
CRESCENT
GORDON
ELM PARK RD.
EVERSLEIGH RD.
GROSVENOR RD.
LANSDOWNE RD.
FINCHLEY WAY
HAMILTON
BRENT
WEST AV.
WEST WAY
Ten. Cts.
LINKSIDE
WALMINGTON
BROOKSIDE
FURSBY
CHESTERFIELD RD.
NETHERCOURT AV.
WESTBURY GRO.
COURTHOUSE GDS.
COURTHOUSE
West Finchley
NETHER STREET
NETHER CL.
SELLERS HALL CL.
CORNWALL AV.
WENTWORTH AVENUE
WENTWORTH PK.
N3
BALLARDS
A598
FINCHLEY CT.
Jun. & Inf. Schs.
MOSS HALL
GREENLAWNS
THE RIDGEWAY
WILLOW WAY
PARKSIDE
Bowling Green
Tennis Courts
Putting Green
Victoria Park
SEYMOUR
HILLCOURT AV.
ROAD
AVONDALE
GAINSBOROUGH CT.
HUTTON
Woodside Park
STATION APP.
HOLMDENE
HOLDEN AV.
ROAD
WORCESTER CT.
North London Hosp.
BROOKFIELD CT.
HENDERSON CT.
GRANGE
FOUR ACRES
SYLVAN CT.
GUILDOWN AV.
BUDD CL.
WILLOW CT.
BEECHCROFT CL.
Sch.
DOLLIS RD.
PRINCES AV.
DORSET MEWS
REDBOURNE
FAIRCHILD HO.
DUKES
VINES
FINCHLEY
FALKLAND AV.
GROVE AV.
Syn.
CLIFTON AV.
BRUNSWICK HO.
NETHER ST.
91
92
93
94
24
5 25

31
21
32
46
Oakleigh Park
OAKLEIGH PARK
South Barnet
BRUNSWICK PARK
NEW SOUTHGATE CEMETERY
New Southgate Crematorium
WHETSTONE
NORTH MIDDLESEX GOLF COURSE
FRIERN BARNET
Bethune Park
Friary Park
NORTH FINCHLEY
COLNEY HATCH
Coppetts Wood & Glebelands Local Nature Reserve
NEW SOUTHGATE
New Southgate
Fallow Corner
FINCHLEY MEM. HOSP.
Finchley Lido
GREAT NORTH LEISURE PARK
ST. PANCRAS & ISLINGTON CEMETERY
Islington Crematorium
EN4
N14
N11
N12
N2
N10
NORTH CIRCULAR ROAD
A406
A1000
A109
A1003
B550
B1453

32
A
B
C
D
E
22
47
31
1
2
3
4
5
6
7
South Barnet
OSIDGE
SOUTHGATE
NEW SOUTHGATE
N14
N11
N22
Southgate
Arnos Grove
Bounds Green
Bowes Park
New Southgate
Monkfrith Prim. Sch.
Brunswick Park Prim. Sch.
Osidge Prim. Sch.
Southgate Circus
Southgate Coll.
Southgate Lib.
Ashmole Sch. & Sports Cen.
Playing Fields
Southgate Cricket Club Ground
Cemetery
NEW SOUTHGATE CEMETERY
New Southgate Crematorium
War Mem.
Recreation Gd
Cricket Ground
Curtis Family Centre
Esporta Hlth. & Fitness
Friern Bridge Retail Park
Superstore
Depot
Hollickwood Park
MUSWELL HILL GOLF COURSE
Alexandra Park School
Albert Road Rec. Grd.
Club House
Bounds Green Ind. Est.
Scout Park
ARNOS PARK
Putting Green
Tennis Court
Playground
Pymme's Play. Fld.
Broomfield Sch.
Broomfield Park
The Avenue
Bowling Greens
Tennis Courts
Sports Ground
GROVELANDS PARK
Boating Lake
NORTH LONDON PRIORY HOSPITAL
Sports Grd.
Pitch & Putt Course Club Ho.
Bowling Green
Leisure Cen.
Prim. Sch.
Syn.
CLOCKHOUSE JUNCTION
Pymme's Brook
CHASE SIDE
THE BOURNE
BOURNE
HIGH STREET
CANNON HILL
ALDERMANS HILL
BOWES RD.
WATERFALL RD.
WATERFALL WALK
HAMPDEN WAY
OSIDGE LANE
CHASE ROAD
WINCHMORE HILL RD.
POWYS LA.
WILMER WY.
TELFORD RD.
BOUNDS GREEN RD.
BROWNLOW RD.
STATION RD.
FRIERN BARNET RD.
OAKLEIGH RD. STH.
PINKHAM WAY
NORTH CIRCULAR ROAD
DURNSFORD RD.
ALBERT RD.
COLNEY HATCH LA.
ALEXANDRA PARK RD.
GREEN LANES
MORTON WAY
BROOKDALE
CHANDOS AV.
A111
A1004
A1003
A1110
A109
A406
A105
B1453
B1452
B106

33
23
WINCHMORE HILL
Winchmore Hill
F
G
H
J
K
1
2
3
4
5
6
7
34
48
N21
N9
N13
N18
N17
N22
A105
A10
A111
A406
A1080
B154
GREEN LANES
RIDGE AV.
CHURCH STREET
GREAT CAMBRIDGE ROAD
HEDGE LANE
NORTH CIRCULAR ROAD
SILVER STREET
STIRLING WAY
THE ROUNDWAY
WHITE HART LANE
The Paulin Ground
Highfield Sch.
Winchmore Sch.
Sports Cen.
City Amenity Site
Clowes Sports Grd.
EDMONTON CEMETERY
Firs Farm Playing Fields
Firs Farm Prim. Sch.
Recreation Ground
Playing Field
The Latymer School
West Lea Sch.
Hazelbury Jun. & Inf. Schs.
Starks Field Prim. Sch.
Churchfield Prim. Sch.
Salmon's Brook
Bury Lodge Park
PALMERS GREEN
Sports Ground
Superstore
Tatem Rec. Grd.
Hollywood Gardens
The Gladys Aylward Sch.
GREAT CAMBRIDGE JUNCTION
NORTH MIDDLESEX UNIVERSITY HOSPITAL
Pymme's Sports Grd.
Wilbury Prim. Sch.
Playing Fields
White Hart Lane Community Sports Centre (New River Stadium)
Sports Centre Play. Fld.
Woodside High Sch.
Wood Gn. Cemy.
Football Ground
Garden of Peace
TOTTENHAM
TOTTENHAM CEMETERY
BRUCE CASTLE PARK
Bruce Castle & Haringey Mus.
White Hart Lane
The Selby Cen.
PYMMES PARK

34
A
B
C
D
E
24
Edmonton (Upper Site)
Miniature Golf Course
JUBILEE PARK
Recreation Ground
Running Track
Golden Jubilee Pk.
Turin Grove Sch.
Playing Field
NIGHTINGALE
GT. CAMBRIDGE ROAD
A10
Bury Lodge Park
Salmon's Brook
Churchfield Prim. Sch.
Rec. Grd.
Starks Field Prim. Sch.
Playing Field
Play Field
Tuition Cen.
Lee Valley Athletics
Warehouse
1
2
3
4
5
6
7
CHURCH STREET
B154
LOWER EDMONTON
Tower Gym
HERTFORD ROAD
A1010
Edmonton Green
Bus Station
Leis. Cen.
Superstore
N9
Tottenham Park Cemetery
Federation Cemetery (Jewish)
Montagu Rec. Grd.
Playground
EDMONTON
MONTAGU ROAD
B137
MERIDIAN WAY
A1055
DOMINION BUSINESS PARK
Sewage Works
Works
Teamsport Karting
Refuse Incineration Plant
PYMMES PARK
Silver Street
33
FORE ST.
Craig Park
N18
STERLING WAY
ANGEL ROAD
A406
CONDUIT LANE
Angel Rd.
MONTAGU IND. ESTATE
ELEYS ESTATE
LEA VALLEY ROAD
NORTH MIDDLESEX UNIVERSITY HOSP.
UPPER EDMONTON
KENNINGHALL
Gas Works
Superstore
Works
N17
TRIUMPH TRADING EST.
Powerleague Soccer Cen.
Sports Cen.
Tottenham Hotspur FC (White Hart Lane)
White Hart Lane
LEE VALLEY PARK
Chalk Bridge
RIVER LEA or LEE
Pymme's Brook
Recreation Ground
Northumberland Park
WATERMEAD WAY
49
TOTTENHAM
Bruce Castle Park
Bruce Castle & Haringey Mus.
HIGH ROAD
River Lee Navigation
Diversion

35
F
G
H
J
K
37
38
25
36
50
1
2
3
4
5
6
7
LEE VALLEY GOLF COURSE
WILLIAM GIRLING RESERVOIR
BANBURY RESERVOIR
CHINGFORD
SOUTH CHINGFORD
CHINGFORD HATCH
CHINGFORD MOUNT
HIGHAMS PARK
E4
E17
Pickett's Lock
Pumping Station
River Lee Diversion
Chingford Mount Cemetery
Old People's Centre
Mansfield Park
Playground
Ridgeway Putting Park Green
Chase Lane Park
Larkswood Playing Fields
Larks Wood
Larkswood Park
Larkswood Club
Larkswood Leisure Centre
Greens Health & Fitness
Suffield Hatch
Ainslie Wood Nature Reserve
Rolls Sports Grd.
Walthamstow Stadium (Closed)
The Peter May Centre
Playing Field
Sports Ground
Golf Driving Range
Rec. Ground
Walthamstow Academy
City Learning Centre
William Morris Sch.
Goals Soccer Cen.
River Ching
Crooked Billet
The Cottage
Superstore
Higham Park Ind. Est.
Highams Park
KINGS HEAD HILL
A110
MANSFIELD HILL
A112
WALTHAM WAY
A1037
OLD CHURCH ROAD
CHINGFORD MOUNT RD.
NEW ROAD
A1009
HALL LANE
LARKSHALL RD.
B160
WINCHESTER ROAD
NORTH CIRCULAR ROAD
A406
SOUTHEND ROAD
VIADUCT
RIDGEWAY
THE RIDGEWAY
B169
ENDLEBURY
WADHAM
BILLET ROAD
B179

36
35
51
A
B
C
D
E
1
2
3
4
5
6
7
RANGER'S RD.
Queen Elizabeth's Hunting Lodge
The Warren
Club
Tennis Courts
Bowl. Grn.
Warren Pond
Barn Hoppet
Albany Ho.
Oak Hall
CHINGFORD
Chingford
STATION ROAD
A1069
KINGS HEAD HILL
THE GN.
CHINGFORD GREEN
KINGS RD.
WHITEHALL RD.
A110
Cricket Ground
Club
Whitehall Plain
St.John's C of E Prim. School
NEW ROAD
A104
A121
Pimp Hall Nurseries
Pimp Hall Park
Friday Hill
FRIDAY HILL
B146
B160
LARKSHALL RD.
Bluehouse Grove
Playing Field
Hatch Grove
Hatch Forest
River Ching
Football Ground
WOODFORD GOLF COURSE
The Lops
HATCH LA.
E4
Sch.
Play. Fld.
Reed's Forest
HOLLY HOUSE HOSP.
Bancroft's Sch. & Prep. Sch.
EPPING NEW RD.
HIGH RD.
Knighton Wood
WOODFORD WELLS
NEW RD.
Suffield Hatch
Greens Health Fitness
CHINGFORD HATCH
CHINGFORD LANE
A1009
Sports Ground
The Ching
Highams Park
The Highams Park
Boating Lake
Woodford Side
Woodford Green Prim. Sch.
WOODFORD GREEN
IG8
Sports Grd.
Club & Pav.
HIGHAMS PARK
Highams Park
Lib.
Schools
Football Ground
HALE END
Rugby Football Grd.
HAVEN HO. FOUNDATION
Sports Grd.
Woodford High Sch. for Girls
HIGH LANE
The Green
BROADMEAD RD.
A1009
HIGH RD. WOODFORD GREEN
A1199
WOODFORD NEW RD.
A104
EPPING FOREST
Hotel
St. Aubyn's Sch.
HAMS PARK INDUSTRIAL ESTATE
B160
WINCHESTER RD.
SOUTHEND RD.
A406
Fullers Day Cen.
CHELMSFORD ROAD
CHURCHFIELDS
Woodbridge High Sch.
Woodford

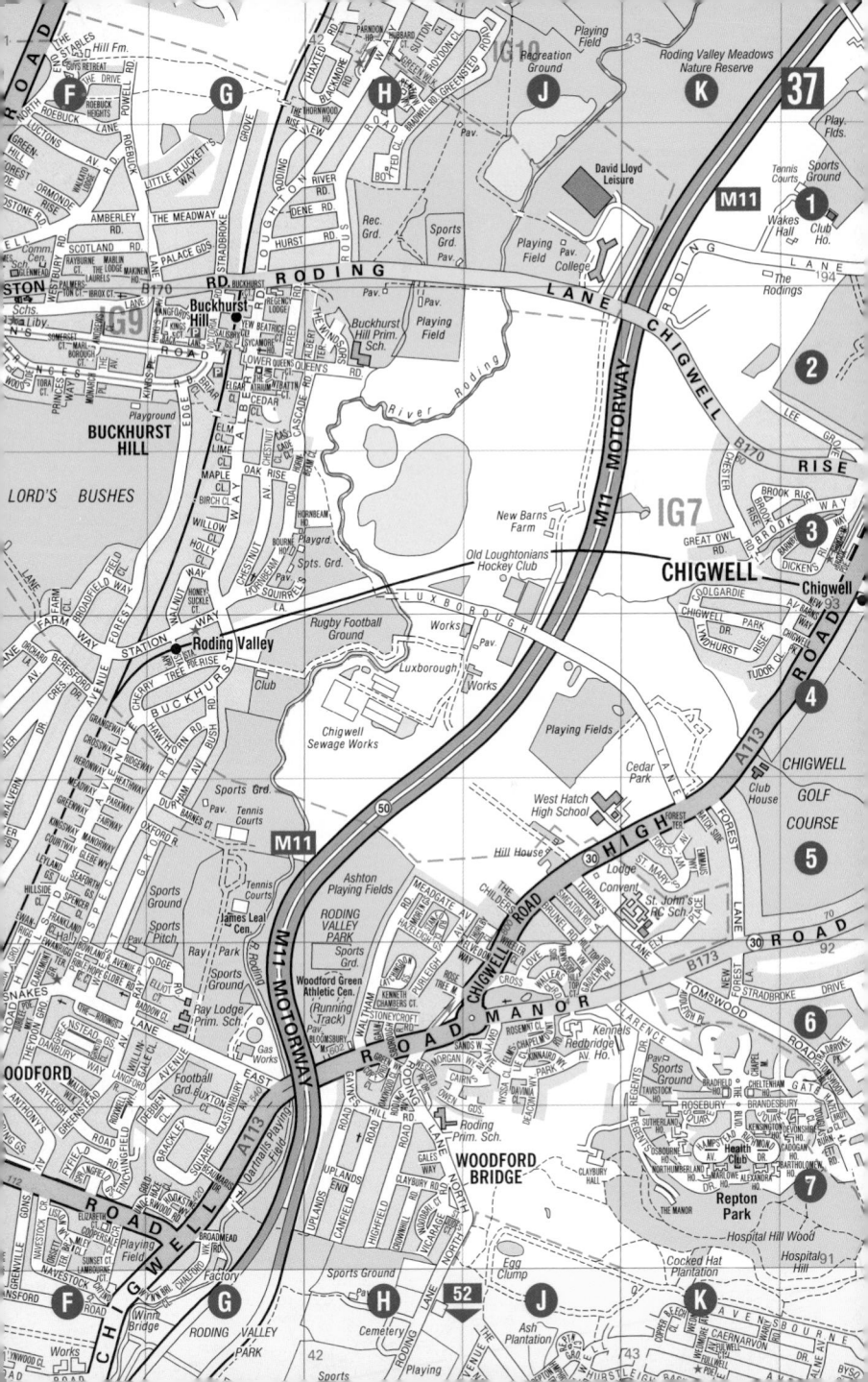

37
F
G
H
J
K
1
2
3
4
5
6
7
IG10
IG9
IG7
Hill Fm.
Recreation Ground
Playing Field
Roding Valley Meadows Nature Reserve
Play. Flds.
Tennis Courts
Sports Ground
David Lloyd Leisure
M11
Wakes Hall
Club Ho.
Roding Lane
The Rodings
College
Pav.
Rec. Grd.
Sports Grd.
Buckhurst Hill Prim. Sch.
Playing Field
Buckhurst Hill
BUCKHURST HILL
LORD'S BUSHES
Playground
River Roding
RODING RD.
RODING LANE
CHIGWELL
Chigwell
M11 MOTORWAY
New Barns Farm
Old Loughtonians Hockey Club
LUXBOROUGH LANE
Luxborough
Works
Rugby Football Ground
Roding Valley
STATION WAY
Chigwell Sewage Works
Playing Fields
Cedar Park
West Hatch High School
CHIGWELL GOLF COURSE
Club House
Hill House
HIGH ROAD
Lodge
Convent
St. John's RC Sch.
Ashton Playing Fields
RODING VALLEY PARK
Sports Grd.
Woodford Green Athletic Cen. (Running Track)
James Leal Cen.
Ray Park
Sports Ground
Sports Pitch
Ray Lodge Prim. Sch.
Gas Works
Football Grd.
MANOR ROAD
CHIGWELL ROAD
Kennels
Redbridge Ho.
Roding Prim. Sch.
WOODFORD BRIDGE
WOODFORD
Repton Park
Health Club
Hospital Hill Wood
Hospital Hill
Cocked Hat Plantation
Egg Clump
Ash Plantation
Cemetery
Sports Ground
Playing Field
Factory
Winn Bridge
RODING VALLEY PARK
Darnalls Playing Field
A113
B170
B173
52
CLAYBURY HALL
THE MANOR
TOMSWOOD ROAD
STRADBROKE DRIVE
CLARENCE
RAVENSBOURNE

38
Shepherds Hill Farm
Battlers Wells Wood
Shepherds Hill House
HAREFIELD
Furzefield
Deadman's Grove
Ashain Spring
Scarlet Spring
Kiln Pond
Claypits
Knightscote Farm
Dell
Raveners Spring
Badminton Shooting Ground
Duck's Hill Farm
Ducks Hill Grange
Duck's Hill
Ashby Cottages
Ashby Farm
COPSE
RUISLIP
Bourne Farm
UB9
Youngwood Farm
Breakspear House
Middle Lodge
YOUNG WOOD
MAD BESS WOOD
NORTH RIDING WOOD
Warren Farm
Mad Bess Wood Cottage
RUISLIP COMMON
Breakspear Crematorium (Ruislip)
BAYHURST WOOD COUNTRY PARK
Willow Tree Farm
Football Ground
The Lodge
Lower Lodge
The Bungalow
Dews Fm. Sand Pits Nature Reserve
Oak Cottage
St. Leonard's Farm
Pylon Farm
Elm Tree Farm
High View Farm
Highway Farm
Dewes Farm Cottages
Newyears Green
Braemar Farm
Crows Nest Farm
Newyears Green Covert
Old Clack Farm
The Corner
Tile Kiln
Grays Cottages
Dunster Cottage
Works
Depot
Gatemead Farm
RUISLIP GOLF COURSE
Playground
Whiteheath Jun. & Inf. Schs
56

39
40
57
NORTHWOOD
NORTHWOOD HILLS
Northwood Hills
HA6
HA5
HA4
EASTCOTE VILLAGE
EASTCOTE
RUISLIP
Ruislip Manor
RICKMANSWORTH ROAD
PINNER ROAD
A404
HIGH ST.
A4125
JOEL STREET
B472
HIGH ROAD
EASTCOTE ROAD
B466
HIGH STREET
A4180
FIELD END ROAD
CUCKOO HILL
NORTHWOOD GOLF COURSE
HASTE HILL GOLF COURSE
Haste Hill
Eleanor's
Ruislip Lido Railway
Lakeside
RUISLIP LIDO
Ruislip Lido Woodlands Centre
Woody Bay
PARK WOOD
RUISLIP WOODS (National Nature Reserve)
Cannons Bridge Farm
Hillingdon Athletic Club
Poor's Field
Miniature Rifle Range
Club House
LA Fitness
Northwood FC (Northwood Pk.)
Cemetery
Haydon School
Playing Field
Joel Street Farm
White Cottage
Harlyn Primary Sch.
Northwood Schs.
Northwood Sports Centre
Pinnerwood Park
Pinner Wood Sch.
Cuckoo Hill
Grangewood School
Coteford Junior Sch.
Coteford Sch.
Haydon Hall Pk.
Cricket Grd.
Eastcote Ho. Gs.
Kings College Playing Fields
King's Coll. Play. Flds. Track
Eastcote Hockey & Badminton Club
Winston Churchill Hall
High Grove
Highgrove Swim. Pool
Bishop Ramsey C of E Sch.
Warrender Park
Warrender Sch.
Church Field Gdns.
Nurseries
Superstore
Offices
River Pinn
Cavendish Recreation

40
PINNER HILL GOLF COURSE
A
B
C
D
E
Pinnerwood Park
Hatch End
HATCH END
A410
Superstore
Harrow Arts
Lib.
Rugby Football Ground
UXBRIDGE ROAD
A404
ST. THOMAS' DR.
GEORGE V
AVENUE
1
2
3
4
5
6
7
Pinner Wood Sch.
PINNER GREEN
Montesole Play. Flds.
RICKMANSWORTH ROAD
CUCKOO HILL
B466
Superstore
Little Common
Woodridings
PINNER
Pinner Park Farm
Pinner Lawn Tennis Club
Ten. Cts.
Paine's Br.
Cemetery
River Pinn
Pinner Village Hall
Pinner Memorial Park
West Lodge First & Middle Sch.
Superstore
Pinner
PINNER
Reddiford Sch.
Nower Hill
Pinner New Cemetery
Nower Hill High Sch.
HA5
39
Pinner Village Gardens
Tennis Cts.
Woodlands Open Space
North Harrow
Yeading Brook Open Space
The Croft
Play. Fld.
Cannon Lane First & Mid. Schs.
Play. Fld.
Heathfield Sch.
Streamside Rec. Grd.
Longfield Schs.
EASTCOTE
Eastcote
HA4
Roxborough Rough
Playground
Roxbourne Park
58
Rayners Lane
RAYNERS LANE
ALEXANDRA AV.
IMPERIAL
Sports Ground
Rayners La. Junc.
Cavendish Recreation Ground
Comm. Cen.
HIGH RD.
EASTCOTE ROAD
VILLAGE WAY
WHITTINGTON WAY
CANNON LANE
MARSH ROAD
RAYNERS LANE
NORTH VIEW
EASTERN AVENUE
30

41
26
42
59
HARROW WEALD
HA3
HA2
HA1
WEALDSTONE
HEADSTONE
GREENHILL
HARROW
WEST HARROW
NORTH HARROW
HARROW ON THE HILL
Headstone Lane
Harrow & Wealdstone
Harrow-on-the-Hill
West Harrow
Hatch End High Sch.
Cedars Manor Sch.
Headstone Lane Sports Grd.
Headstone Manor Recreation Ground
Headstone Manor
Harrow Museum & Heritage Cen.
Harrow Crown Court
Salvatorian Coll.
Harrow Leisure Centre
Recreation Ground
Harrow Recreation Ground
Harrow Cemetery
Civic Centre
St. Ann's Shopping Cen.
The Grove Open Space
Harrow Sch.
Harrow School Playing Fields
Whitmore High Sch.
Whitmore Sports Cen.
Cricket Ground
Harrow Hill Golf Course
Miniature Rifle Range
Playing Fields
Belmont Sch.
Works
Sports Ground
Open Air Theatre
Running Track
Yeading Brook
Superstore
Cin. Gala Bingo
A409
A404
A4005
A312
HIGH ROAD
ELMES COLLEGE AV.
LONG ELMES
HARROW VIEW
PINNER VIEW
HEADSTONE DRIVE
HEADSTONE GS.
STATION ROAD
ST. GEORGE GANGE WAY
GREENHILL WAY
SHEEPCOTE ROAD
KENTON RD.
LOWLANDS RD.
BESSBOROUGH RD.
PINNER RD.
WATFORD RD.
MOUNTSIDE
CHRISTCHURCH AVENUE
WHITMORE RD.
COLLEGE ROAD

42
27
41
60
A
B
C
D
E
1
2
3
4
5
6
7
16
17
18
91
90
89
88
STANMORE GOLF COURSE
Stanburn Schs.
Whitchurch First & Mid. Schs.
Sports Ground
Bowling Green
WHITCHURCH
Canons Park
B461
Offices
Works
Tennis Courts
Sports Ground
HONEYPOT BUS. CEN.
Little Fir Prince
Edware Playing Field
HONEYPOT LA.
A4140
HA7
BELMONT
Belmont Sch.
Kenton Lane Farm
Priestmead Rec. Grd.
Play. Field Schs.
Centenary Park
Park High Sch.
Bowl. Grn.
Putting Green
Pitch & Putt
Sports Ground
Byron Recreation Ground
Cemetery
WEALDSTONE
Harrow Leisure Centre
Harrow Driving, Cycling and Road Safety Centre
Liby.
Hall
Schs. Comm. Cen.
Glebe Sch.
HA3
Sports Ground
Club
Tennis Cts.
Hindu Tem.
Elmgrove First & Middle Schools
Kenton Recreation Ground
KENTON
Bowling Green
Tennis Courts
Hospice
Wealdstone Brook
School
WOODCOCK PARK
Tennis Courts
Bowling Green
School
School Play. Fld.
KENTON ROAD
A4006
HA1
Super-store
Kenton
Sports Cen.
Sch.
Mt. Stewart Jun. & Inf. Sch.
Halls of Residence
Northwick Park
University of Westminster (Harrow Campus)
Univ. of Westminster Sports Hall
NORTHWICK PARK HOSPITAL
ST.MARK'S HOSP.
NORTHWICK PARK
HA9
John Billam Playing Fields
Ten. Cts.
Sports Grd.
PRESTON
Preston Road
HARROW
HARROW HILL GOLF COURSE
Club Ho.
WATFORD ROAD
A404
Playing Fields
Driving Range
Club Ho.
Northwick Park
Harrow School Playing Fields
Ind. Est.
THE HAWTHORN CENTRE
NORTHWICK ROUNDABOUT
KENTON RD.
QUEENSBURY CIRCLE PDE.
Tennis Courts
Pav.

43
F
G
H
J
K
28
44
61
1
2
3
4
5
6
7
BURNT OAK
EDGWARE COMM. HOSP.
NHS Walk-in Cen.
Watling
WATLING
Tennis Courts PARK
Leisure Cen.
Chandos Recreation Grd.
LITTLE STANMORE
Canons High Sch.
QUEENSBURY
Queensbury
Burnt Oak
Comm. Cen.
Sports Ground
Prim. Sch.
Schools
Lib.
HA8
BROADWAY
EDGWARE
WATLING
Silk Stream Park
Montrose Recreation Ground
National Blood Service
Elysian House
Silkstream Unit East
Colindale
COLINDALE
Offices
Superstore
ORIENTAL CITY
Mecca Burnt Oak
COLINDALE BUSINESS PARK
EUROPEAN BUSINESS CENTRE
Sikh Tem.
Spts. Grd.
Roe Green
COLINDEEP LA.
NW9
Eton Grove Open Space
Kingsbury High Sch. Play. Fld.
Roe Grn. Jun. & Inf. Sch.
Kingsbury Manor
Roe Green Park
Kingsbury Manor Studio
Playground
Pupil Referal Unit
Comm. Cen.
Kingswood Centre
Queensbury Park Rec. Grd.
Factory
A4140
A5
A4006
B454
KINGSBURY ROAD
Kingsbury
Health Club
TA Centre
Buddhist Cen.
Recreation Ground
Kingsbury Grn. Prim. Sch.
St. Robert Southwell RC Prim. Sch.
Sports Ground
JFS School
Spts. Grd.
KINGSBURY
FRYENT COUNTRY PARK
Fryent Country Park Local Nature Reserve
Barn Hill Open Space
Barn Hill
Kingsbury Green Rec. Grd.
Pupil Referal Unit
Silver Jubilee Park
Kingsbury Town FC Grd.
HA9
FRYENT WAY
CHURCH LANE
Field Study Centre
Nursery
Woodfield Sch.
Tennis Courts
Welsh Harp

44
A
B
C
D
E
29
43
62
1
2
3
4
5
6
7
Grahame Park
COLINDALE
Colindale
Colindale Park
Newspaper Library
RAF Museum Hendon
Battle of Britain Hall
Barnet Coll.
Peel Centre (Metropolitan Police Training Establishment)
Sports Ground
Junction 2
FIVEWAYS CORNER
BARNET COPTHALL SPORTS CENTRE
Barnet Copthall Stadium
Copthall Leisure Centre
METRO PLAYGOLF
Metro Playgolf Driving Range
Powerleague Soccer Cen.
Hasmonean High Sch. for Girls
Rugby Club
Chase Lodge Playing Fields
SUNNY HILL PARK
THE GARDEN BMI HOSP.
Museum
The Burroughs
Middlesex University
HENDON
Hendon Central
Virgin Active
HENDON PARK
NW9
NW4
THE HYDE
Hendon
BRENT CROSS INTERCHANGE
BRENT CROSS SHOPPING CENTRE
Brent Cross
Junc. 1
STAPLES CORNER
WEST HENDON
WEST HENDON PLAYING FIELDS
Silver Jubilee Park
Kingsbury Town FC Grd.
Youth Sailing Base
Cool Oak Bridge
BRENT RESERVOIR
Brent Reservoir (Welsh Harp) Nature Reserve
Woodfield Sch.
Malcolm Park
M1 MOTORWAY
A41 WATFORD WAY
GREAT (BARNET BY-PASS)
COLINDEEP LANE
A5150
EDGWARE ROAD
THE HYDE
WEST HENDON BROADWAY
A5
KINGSBURY RD.
A4006
STATION ROAD
A504
QUEENS ROAD
B551
HENDON WAY
A406 NORTH CIRCULAR ROAD
AERODROME ROAD
GRAHAME PARK WAY
COOL OAK LANE
THE BURROUGHS
CHURCH RD.
PARSON STREET

F
G
H
J
K
30
FINCHLEY
1
2
3
4
5
6
7
46
63
Hendon Crematorium
HENDON CEMETERY
HENDON GOLF COURSE
Holders Hill
DOLLIS ROAD
NETHER
BALLARDS
LANE
A598
B552
B1462
Finchley Manor Club
Swim. Pool
Playing Fields
Finchley Central
Courts
CHURCH END
Victoria Park
Pentland Centre
Windsor Open Space
College
Avenue House Grounds
Sports Ground
EAST END ROAD
Play. Fld.
Cricket Sch.
The Sternberg Centre
LA Fitness
A504
HENDON LANE
REGENTS PARK ROAD
HOLDERS HILL ROAD
HOLDERS HILL
N3
College Farm
St. Marylebone Crematorium
EAST FINCHLEY CEMETERY
Christ's College Finchley
NORTH CIRCULAR ROAD
A406
A1
HENDON WAY
NORTH CIRCULAR
FALLODEN WAY
HENLYS CORNER
Playing Field
Mutton Brook
Little Wood
Big Wood
Willifred Green
Bowl Grn.
Monastery
The Decoy
Brent Park
Temple Fortune
Princes Park
FINCHLEY ROAD
NW11
Jewish Cemetery
Golders Green Crematorium
HAMPSTEAD
HEATH
GOLDERS GREEN
GOLDERS GREEN RD.
A502
Brent Cross
NW2
Superstores
Leisure Cen.
Works
Golders Green
NORTH END RD.
A41
HENDON WAY
Tennis Courts
Yth. Hostel
Temple
Bunkers Hill

46
31
45
64
A
B
C
D
E
1
2
3
4
5
6
7
N12
N3
N2
N6
NW11
Fallow Corner
FINCHLEY MEM. HOSP.
Finchley Rugby FC Grd. Football Ground
Cricket & Football Grounds
Finchley Lido
Glebe Open Space
GT. NORTH LEISURE PARK
Bowl. Alley
Cinema
NORTH CIRCULAR ROAD
A406
HIGH RD. NTH. FINCHLEY
A1000
HIGH ROAD
EAST FINCHLEY
BOBBY MOORE WAY
Powerleague Soccer Cen.
COLNEY HATCH
Islington Crematorium
ST. PANCRAS & ISLINGTON CEM.
Strawberry Vale Brook
Muswell Hill Spts. Grd.
COLDFALL WOOD
Coldfall Prim. Sch.
Recreation Ground
Playing Field
Sports Ground
Martin Prim. Sch.
Fortismere Sch. (North Wing)
Fortismere Sch. (South Wing)
St. Marylebone Crem.
EAST FINCHLEY CEMETERY
EAST END ROAD
A504
FORTIS GREEN
FORTIS GREEN ROAD
Oak Lodge Sch.
EAST FINCHLEY
East Finchley
ABBOTS GARDENS
ST. LUKE'S WOODSIDE HOSP.
Reservoir
Cherry Tree Wood
Rec. Grd.
GREAT NORTH RD.
St. James C of E Prim. Sch.
THE MKT. PL.
LYTTELTON ROAD
A1
AYLMER ROAD
Brook
HAMPSTEAD GARDEN SUBURB
Playing Fields
Stormont Lawn Tennis & Squash Club
HIGHGATE WOOD
Sports Ground
Depot
ARCHWAY ROAD
HIGHGATE GOLF COURSE
Club House
HIGHGATE
HIGHGATE HOSPITAL
HAMPSTEAD GOLF COURSE
Bunkers Hill
HAMPSTEAD HEATH
Turners Wood
Club House
HAMPSTEAD LANE
B519
North Wood
Kenwood House
Athlone House
Mallinson Sports Centre
Sports Ground
Highgate School Playing Field
Spts. Grd.
Nursery
The Spaniards
Yth. Hostel
SOUTHWOOD LANE
B550
NORTH HILL
NORTH ROAD
B519
Bowling

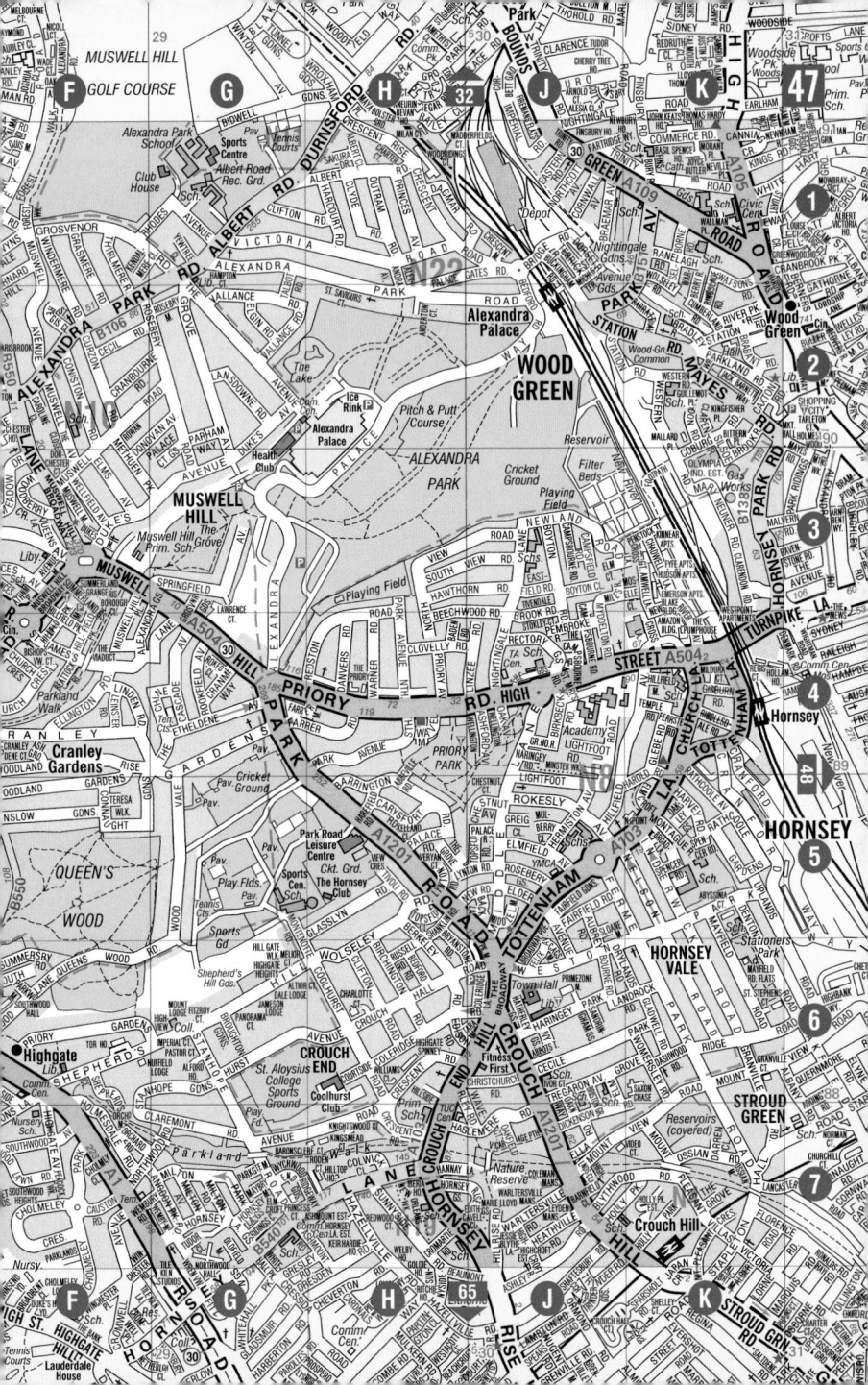
47
32
48
65
F
G
H
J
K
1
2
3
4
5
6
7
MUSWELL HILL GOLF COURSE
Alexandra Park School
Sports Centre
Albert Road Rec. Grd.
Club House
ALEXANDRA PARK RD.
ALBERT RD.
DURNSFORD RD.
BOUNDS GREEN RD.
GREEN LANES
N22
N10
N8
Alexandra Palace
WOOD GREEN
ALEXANDRA PARK
Pitch & Putt Course
The Lake
Ice Rink
Cricket Ground
Playing Field
Filter Beds
Reservoir
Depot
Wood Green
SHOPPING CITY
Wood Gn. Common
Olympia Ind. Est.
Gas Works
MUSWELL HILL
The Grove
Muswell Hill Prim. Sch.
MUSWELL HILL BROADWAY
PRIORY RD.
HIGH STREET
PARK RD.
PRIORY PARK
TURNPIKE LA.
Hornsey
HORNSEY
TOTTENHAM LA.
CHURCH LA.
Cranley Gardens
QUEEN'S WOOD
Park Road Leisure Centre
The Hornsey Club
Parkland Walk
Shepherd's Hill Gds.
CROUCH END
St. Aloysius College Sports Ground
Coolhurst Club
Town Hall
Fitness First
Nature Reserve
HORNSEY VALE
Stationers Park
STROUD GREEN
Reservoirs (covered)
Crouch Hill
Highgate
HIGHGATE HILL
Lauderdale House
CROUCH HILL
HORNSEY RISE
HORNSEY RD.
STROUD GRN. RD.
A1
A103
A105
A109
A504
A1201
B106
B138
B151
B540
B550
30

48
33
47
66
A
B
C
D
E
1
2
3
4
5
6
7
TOTTENHAM
TOTTENHAM CEMETERY
WOOD GREEN
Wood Green
NOEL PARK
N22
LORDSHIP RECREATION GROUND
Open Air Theatre
Comm. Cen.
The Moselle
Playing Field
Broadwater Farm Estate
Belmont Rec. Grd.
DOWNHILLS PARK
WEST GREEN
Park View Academy Spts. Cen.
Turnpike La.
TURNPIKE LANE
HORNSEY
Hornsey
HARRINGAY
Harringay
Harringay Green Lanes
Railway Fields Local Nature Reserve
N8
N4
N15
N16
N17
ST. ANN'S HOSPITAL
Chestnuts Rec. Ground
STROUD GREEN
FINSBURY PARK
Track & Gym
Cricket Ground
American Gds.
Manor House
MANOR HO.
EAST RESERVOIR
WEST RESERVOIR
Reservoir (covered)
Sir Thomas Abney Prim. Sch.
Stamford Hill
SOUTH TOTTENHAM
Stationers Park
Woodside Pk.
Wood Gn. Cemy.
Woodside High Sch.
Sports Centre
Garden of Peace
Seven Sisters Bri.
LORDSHIP LANE
A109
A1080
WESTBURY AVENUE
DOWNHILLS WAY
B155
PHILIP LA.
WEST GREEN ROAD
A504
GREEN LANES
A105
ST. ANN'S ROAD
B152
SEVEN SISTERS ROAD
A503
AMHURST
A107
WIGHTMAN ROAD
B138
HIGH ROAD
ENDYMION
B150
LORDSHIP
ROUNDWAY
A10
HERMITAGE ROAD
HARRINGAY
GRAND PARADE
STROUD GRN. RD.
HIGH STREET

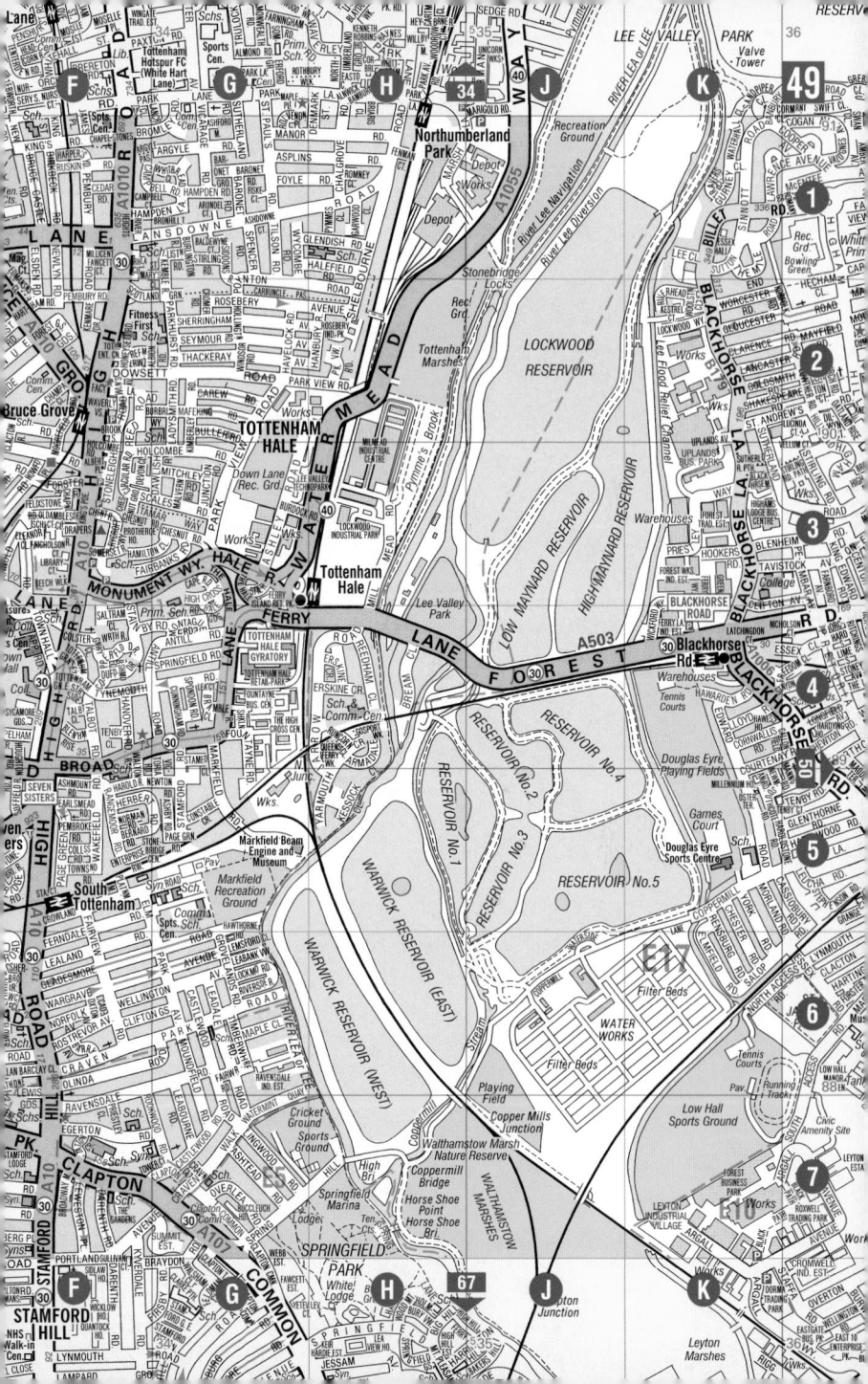

LEE VALLEY PARK
Valve Tower
49
36
34
Tottenham Hotspur FC (White Hart Lane)
Northumberland Park
Recreation Ground
River Lee Navigation
River Lee Diversion
RIVER LEA or LEE
Stonebridge Locks
LOCKWOOD RESERVOIR
Tottenham Marshes
TOTTENHAM HALE
Bruce Grove
Down Lane Rec. Grd.
MILMEAD INDUSTRIAL CENTRE
LOCKWOOD INDUSTRIAL PARK
Pymme's Brook
Tottenham Hale
LOW MAYNARD RESERVOIR
HIGH MAYNARD RESERVOIR
Lee Flood Relief Channel
Warehouses
BLACKHORSE ROAD
Blackhorse Rd.
TOTTENHAM HALE GYRATORY
Lee Valley Park
FERRY LANE
FOREST ROAD
A503
A1055
A1006
A10
A107
MONUMENT WY.
HALE RD.
WATERMEAD WAY
BLACKHORSE LA.
HIGH RD.
BROAD LANE
RESERVOIR No.1
RESERVOIR No.2
RESERVOIR No.3
RESERVOIR No.4
RESERVOIR No.5
Douglas Eyre Playing Fields
Douglas Eyre Sports Centre
Games Court
50
WARWICK RESERVOIR (EAST)
WARWICK RESERVOIR (WEST)
Markfield Beam Engine and Museum
Markfield Recreation Ground
South Tottenham
SEVEN SISTERS
E17
E5
E10
Filter Beds
WATER WORKS
Playing Field
Copper Mills Junction
Walthamstow Marsh Nature Reserve
WALTHAMSTOW MARSHES
Coppermill Bridge
Horse Shoe Point
Horse Shoe Bri.
Springfield Marina
SPRINGFIELD PARK
White Lodge
Low Hall Sports Ground
Running Track
Civic Amenity Site
FOREST BUSINESS PARK
LEYTON INDUSTRIAL VILLAGE
ROXWELL TRADING PARK
Leyton Marshes
67
Clapton Junction
CLAPTON COMMON
STAMFORD HILL
STAMFORD HILL
F G H J K
1 2 3 4 5 6 7

50
35
49
68
A
B
C
D
E
1
2
3
4
5
6
7
36
37
38
88
89
90
91
BANBURY RESERVOIR
Golf Driving Range
Playing Field
Sports Ground
Walthamstow Stadium (Closed)
The Peter May Centre
Walthamstow Academy
City Learning Centre
CROOKED BILLET
SOUTHEND ROAD
A406
BILLET ROAD
B179
HIGHAM HILL
Whittingham Prim. Sch.
William Morris Sch.
Chapel End
CHINGFORD ROAD
A112
LLOYD PARK
Waltham Forest Pool & Track
Chestnuts Sports Ground
WALTHAMSTOW
Town Hall
Civic Cen.
College
FOREST ROAD
A503
THE BELL
THORPE COOMBE HOSP.
WOOD ROAD
FULBOURNE ROAD
B160
HOE ST.
E17
BLACKHORSE RD.
BLACKHORSE LANE
Blackhorse
Walthamstow Central
Walthamstow Queens Rd.
St. James St.
Queens Road Cemetery
MARKHOUSE ROAD
A1006
Kelmscott Leisure Cen.
ST. JAMES'S PARK
HIGH STREET
HIGH ST.
BRIDGE
LEA BRIDGE ROAD
A104
CHURCH RD.
LEYTON RD.
B159
Leyton Midland Rd.
LEYTON
E10
Brooks Farm
Leyton FC Grd.
Bingo
Superstore
Leisure Pool
Bus Depot
Civic Amenity Site
LEYTON LINK ESTATE
ROXWELL TRADING PARK
CROMWELL IND. EST.
DORMA TRADING PARK
Playground
Works
Tennis Courts
Running Track
Eyre Centre

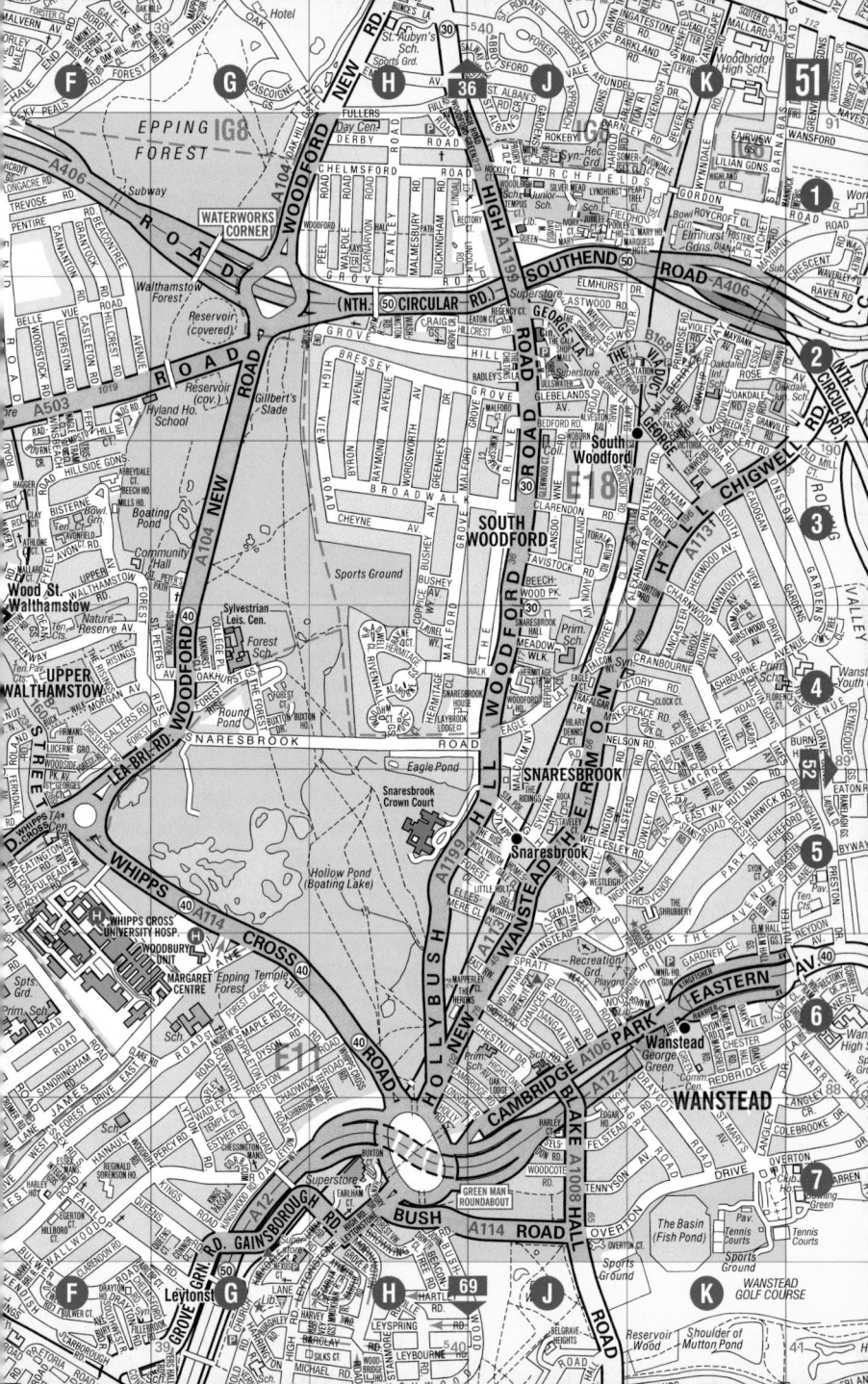

51
F
G
H
J
K
36
EPPING FOREST
IG8
A406
ROAD
WATERWORKS CORNER
Walthamstow Forest
Reservoir (covered)
Reservoir (cov.)
A503
Hyland Ho. School
Gillbert's Slade
A104
NEW ROAD
WOODFORD
CHELMSFORD ROAD
DERBY ROAD
FULLERS Day Cen.
HIGH ROAD WOODFORD GREEN
St. Aubyn's Sch.
Sports Grd.
(NTH. CIRCULAR RD.)
SOUTHEND ROAD
A1199
CHURCHFIELDS
Superstore
GEORGE LA.
SOUTH WOODFORD
South Woodford
E18
BROADWALK
CHEYNE AV.
BRESSEY GROVE
Sports Ground
Sylvestrian Leis. Cen.
Forest Sch.
Boating Pond
Community Hall
Wood St. Walthamstow
UPPER WALTHAMSTOW
Nature Reserve
Round Pond
SNARESBROOK ROAD
Eagle Pond
Snaresbrook Crown Court
Hollow Pond (Boating Lake)
SNARESBROOK
Snaresbrook
HOLLYBUSH HILL
WOODFORD ROAD
HERMON HILL
WANSTEAD
CHIGWELL
A113
WHIPPS CROSS ROAD
A114
WHIPPS CROSS UNIVERSITY HOSP.
WOODBURY UNIT
MARGARET CENTRE
Epping Forest
Temple
E11
Recreation Grd.
CAMBRIDGE PARK
A106
EASTERN AV.
Wanstead
George Green
A12
BLAKE HALL ROAD
A1008
GREEN MAN ROUNDABOUT
BUSH ROAD
Superstore
GAINSBOROUGH RD.
Leytonstone
69
The Basin (Fish Pond)
Tennis Courts
Sports Ground
WANSTEAD GOLF COURSE
Reservoir Wood
Shoulder of Mutton Pond
Bowling Green
52
1
2
3
4
5
6
7

52
37
51
70
A
B
C
D
E
1
2
3
4
5
6
7
WOODFORD BRIDGE
Repton Park
BROADMEAD RD.
ROAD
CHIGWELL
M11
Junction 4
RODING VALLEY PARK
A406
A113
Egg Clump
Cocked Hat Plantation
Ash Plantation
Sports Ground
Cemetery
Playing Field
IG8
IG5
IG4
IG1
E18
E11
SOUTHEND RD.
WOODFORD
A1400
CHARLIE BROWN'S ROUNDABOUT
WOODFORD TRADING ESTATE
THE ORBITAL CENTRE
(NORTH CIRCULAR ROAD)
CLAYHALL
CLAYHALL PARK
Hatton School
PDSA (Veterinary Centre)
Beal High Sch.
RODING SPIRE HOSPITAL
River Roding
Recreation Ground
WOODFORD AVENUE
BEEHIVE
GANTS HILL
Gants Hill
Nightingale Prim. Sch.
Wanstead Youth Cen.
VALLEY PARK
REDBRIDGE ROUNDABOUT
Redbridge
EASTERN AVENUE
A12
SOUTH WOODFORD TO BARKING RELIEF ROAD
REDBRIDGE
Leisure Cen.
Wanstead High School
Golf Course
WANSTEAD
The Heronry
Lincoln Island
Rook Island
WANSTEAD PARK
WANSTEAD GOLF COURSE
The Temple
Heronry Pond
Perch Pond
Cranbrook Prim. Sch.
CRANBROOK RD.
A123
B192
Valentines Mansion & Gardens
Ilford Cricket Club
ILFO

53
54
71
FAIRLOP
FULLWELL CROSS
BARKINGSIDE
ALDBOROUGH HATCH
NEWBURY PARK
SEVEN KINGS
Fairlop
Barkingside
Newbury Park
Fairlop Lake
FAIRLOP WATERS COUNTRY PARK
FAIRLOP WATERS GOLF COURSE
Fairlop Sailing Centre
Hainault Recreation Grd.
Fairlop Oak Recreation Ground
Powerleague Soccer Cen.
Redbridge Sports & Leisure Cen.
Oakfield Playing Field
Old Parkonians Association
King Solomon High Sch.
Ilford Jewish Primary School
Ilford High Sch.
Fairlop Prim. Sch.
Fullwood Prim. Sch.
Barnardos
Redbridge FC (Oakside Stadium)
Oaks Park High Sch.
William Torbitt Prim. Sch.
Aldborough Hall Equestrian Centre
Aldborough Hall Farm
Aldborough Ho. Farm
Aldborough House
SEVEN KINGS PARK
VALENTINES PARK
Barkingside Rec. Grd.
Cemetery
Golf Driving Range
Lagoon
Forest Farm
Fairlop Lodge
FENCEPIECE A123
HIGH ROAD
FOREST ROAD
EASTERN AVENUE A12
PAINTERS ROAD

54
53
72
IG6
IG2
IG3
RM6
RM8
Marks Gate
ALDBOROUGH HATCH
LITTLE HEATH
CHADWELL HEATH
FAIRLOP WATERS COUNTRY PARK
Fairlop Sailing Centre
Hainault Works
Hainault Farm
Farm Cottages
Red House Farm
Hainault House
Willow Farm
Furze Cottage
Furze House Farm
Aldborough Hall Farm
KING GEORGE HOSPITAL
GOODMAYES HOSPITAL
Redbridge College
ST. CHAD'S PARK
Chadwell Heath Cemetery
Goodmayes
Chadwell Heath
CHADWELL HEATH INDUSTRIAL PARK
EASTERN AVENUE
A12
A118
A1112
WHALEBONE LANE
HIGH ROAD
PAINTERS ROAD
HAINAULT ROAD
BARLEY LANE
CHADWELL HEATH LANE

55
73
RM5
RM1
RM7
COLLIER ROW
RISE PARK
Mawney
ROMFORD
Crowlands
RUSH GREEN
BEACONTREE HEATH
Cold Blow Farm
Gobions Farm
Works
Football Grd.
NORTHGATE INDUSTRIAL PARK
City Limits
Whites Farm
Mill Farm
Moat
Crownfield Jun. & Inf. Schs.
King Georges Field
MAWNEY PARK
Warehouse
HUBBINET IND. EST.
EASTERN AV. RETAIL PK.
Bus Depot
Rise Park Jun. & Inf Schs.
Lawns Rec. Grd.
Tennis Courts
Prim. Sch.
Prim. Schs.
Schs.
Comm. Cen.
Comm. Cens.
Mus.
THE BREWERY
Esporta
Bowl. Cin. Alley
ROGER REEDE'S ALMS-HOUSES
MOBY DICK
Warren Park Centre
Rec. Grd.
Club House
Warren Sports Centre
Warren Jun. Sch.
Playing Field
Sports Ground
Crown Farm
Crown Cottages
Pavilion
St. Edward's C of E Comp. School
Westlands Playing Field
West Ham FC Training Grd.
TA Cen.
Romford Stadium (Greyhound)
Gas Works
Jutsums Rec. Grd.
Romford Cemetery
Crowlands Sports Ground
CROWLANDS HEATH GOLF COURSE
Fords Sports Ground
Football Ground
Wood Lane Sports Centre
QUEEN'S HOSPITAL
Helipad
Oldchurch Park
Robert Clack Sch.
All Saints
COLLIER ROW RD.
HOG HILL RD.
CHASE CROSS RD.
COLLIER ROW
EASTERN AVENUE
A12
WEST
NORTH ST.
ST. EDWARDS WAY
WATERLOO RD.
A125
A118
LONDON ROAD
CROW LANE
HAVERING LANE
MAWNEY ROAD
WHITE HART LANE
MARKS ROAD
OLDCHURCH RD.
RUSH GREEN ROAD
A124
WHALEBONE LA. STH.
A1112
B174
B175
B1459

56
A
B
C
D
E
38
74
06
07
08
1
2
3
4
5
6
7
87
86
85
Braemar Farm
Crows Nest Farm
Old Clack Farm
Newyears Green Covert
The Corner
Kiln
Grays Cottages
Research Farm
UB9
Dunster Cottage
Works
Depot
Gatemead Farm
Brackenbury Barn
Moat
Copthall Covert
RUISLIP GOLF COURSE
WEST RUISLIP
Golf Driving Range
Playground
Club Ho.
Playing Field
Cricket Ground
Pav.
Club House
Harvil Farm
UXBRIDGE GOLF COURSE
Copthall Farm
Schs.
Harefield Place
HIGH ROAD
ICKENHAM
Compass Theatre
Ickenham
Lib.
Playing Field
Weatherlys Covert
SWAKELEYS ROUNDABOUT
WESTERN AVENUE
A40
B467
B466
B483
A437
Fray's Farm
Common Plantation
Vyners School
The Clump
Tennis Cts.
UB10
Swakeleys
Sports Ground
Bowl. Grn.
Ten. Cts.
River Pinn
Adult Learning Centre
Park Wood
Moat
Tennis Courts
Ickenham Manor
Play. Flds.
Long Lane Farm
Clare House
Sports Ground
UB8
Uxbridge Common
Hillingdon Athletics Stadium
Hillingdon Sports & Leisure Complex
Games Court
Playing Fields
Playing Field
Cricket Ground
Uxbridge Lido
Learning Cen.
Uxbridge College (Uxbridge Campus)
UXBRIDGE
Prim. Sch.
Superstore
Hillingdon
Motel
HILLINGDON CIRCUS
Freezeland Covert
Canal
TA Centre
RAF Uxbridge Track
Cin.
HILLINGDON COURT PARK
Bowling Green
Tennis Courts
Coll.
Play. Fld.
Playgrd.
Halls
Rec. Grd.
Sports Ground
RAF UXBRIDGE
Gate
Tennis Courts
YMCA
Sch.
ACS Hillingdon International Sch.
Convent
Playground
Schs.
LONG LANE
SWAKELEYS ROAD
HARVIL ROAD
PARK ROAD
HILLINGDON ROAD
BREAKSPEAR ROAD SOUTH
HERCIES ROAD
SWAKELEYS DRIVE
GIBSON ROAD
FREEZELAND WAY
GRANVILLE ROAD
RICHMOND AVENUE
MERTON AVENUE
GROSVENOR AVENUE
SWEETCROFT LANE
HONEYCROFT HILL
HARTSHILL CL.
TUDOR WAY
HIGHFIELD DRIVE
HAREFIELD RD.
NORTH COMMON RD.
WEST COMMON RD.
GATTING WAY
THE GREENWAY
PARKFIELD AV.
GLEBE AV.

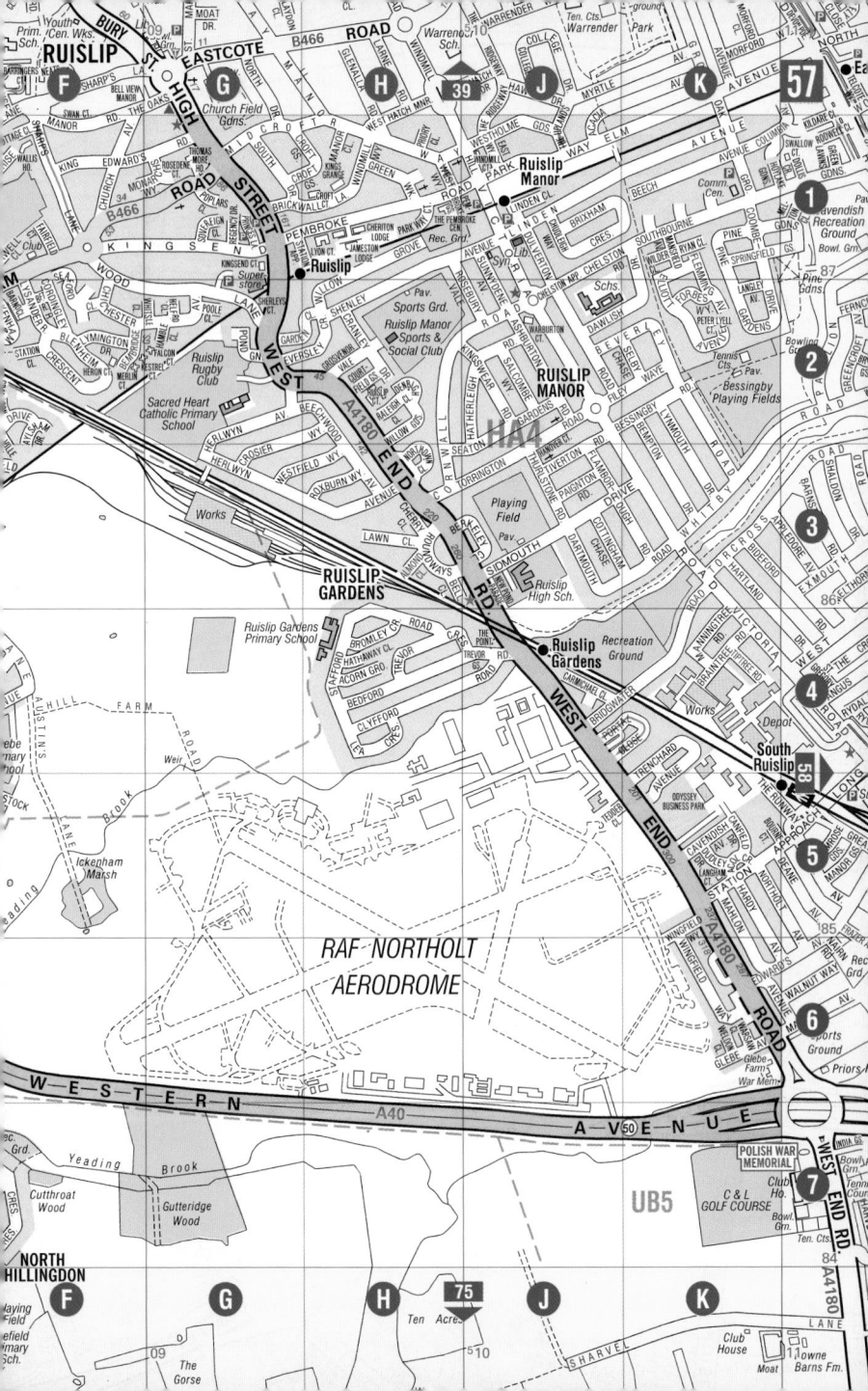

RUISLIP
EASTCOTE
ROAD
B466
BURY ST.
HIGH STREET
Church Field Gdns.
Warrender Sch.
Warrender Park
39
57
F
G
H
J
K
MANOR RD.
KING EDWARD'S RD.
MIDCROFT
WESTHOLME GDS.
MYRTLE AV.
OAK AV.
ELM AVENUE
Ruislip Manor
PARK WAY
LINDEN CL.
BEECH AVENUE
BRIXHAM CRES.
PEMBROKE RD.
Rec. Grd.
Comm. Cen.
1
Cavendish Recreation Ground
Bowl. Grn.
Pine Gdns.
87
KINGSEND
Ruislip
Super-store
WOOD LANE
Lib.
Syn.
Schs.
SOUTHBOURNE
CHELSTON RD.
PINE GDNS.
SPRINGFIELD GDNS.
Sports Grd.
Ruislip Manor Sports & Social Club
Pav.
Ruislip Rugby Club
Sacred Heart Catholic Primary School
WEST END
A4180
RUISLIP MANOR
HA4
BEVERLEY RD.
Tennis Cts.
Bessingby Playing Fields
2
HERLWYN AV.
WESTFIELD WY.
ROXBURN WY.
TORRINGTON
Playing Field
WHITBY ROAD
3
Works
LAWN CL.
SIDMOUTH
Ruislip High Sch.
RUISLIP GARDENS
Ruislip Gardens Primary School
Ruislip Gardens
Recreation Ground
VICTORIA
4
Depot
South Ruislip
58
WEST END ROAD
FARM ROAD
Weir
Brook
Ickenham Marsh
ODYSSEY BUSINESS PARK
TRENCHARD AVENUE
5
RAF NORTHOLT AERODROME
STATION APPROACH
85
6
Sports Ground
Glebe Farm
War Mem.
WESTERN AVENUE
A40
50
POLISH WAR MEMORIAL
7
C & L GOLF COURSE
Club Ho.
UB5
Yeading Brook
Cutthroat Wood
Gutteridge Wood
NORTH HILLINGDON
84
75
Ten Acres
09
510
11
SHARVEL LANE
Club House
Towne Barns Fm.
Moat
The Gorse

58
Eastcote
Roxbourne Park
Rayners Lane
RAYNERS LANE
HA5
40
Cavendish Recreation Ground
Pine Gdns.
Bessingby Playing Fields
Miniature Railway
Roxbourne First & Mid. Schs.
Recreation Ground
Newton Farm First & Mid. Sch.
Newton Park West
Newton Ecology Park
Alexandra Sch.
Field End Jun. & Inf. Schs.
HA4
SOUTH RUISLIP
Rec. Grd.
Deane Park
Heathland Sch.
Rooks Heath Coll.
Harrow Borough FC (Earlsmead Stadium)
Deanesfield Prim. Sch.
Queensmead Sch.
Queensmead Sports Cen.
Goals Soccer Centre
South Ruislip
57
Superstore
Warehouses
Victoria Retail Park
Chancerygate Bus. Cen.
Solid Waste Transfer Station
Northolt Park
Northolt High Sch.
Bourne Prim. School
Sports Ground
Polish War Memorial
Lord Halsbury Memorial Playing Flds.
Willow Tree Prim. Sch.
NORTHOLT
Islip Manor Park
UB5
Northolt
Lime Trees Park Golf Course
Northolt Prim. Sch.
John Chilton Sch.
West London Academy
76
Target Roundabout
Belvue Park
Health Club
Ealing Driving Range
Western Avenue
A40
A4180
A4090
A312
Alexandra Av.
Mandeville Road
Church Avenue
Eastcote Road
Long Dr.
Victoria Road
West End Rd.
A
B
C
D
E
1
2
3
4
5
6
7

59
60
41
77
F
G
H
J
K
1
2
3
4
5
6
7
WEST HARROW
HARROW
The Grove Open Space
Miniature Rifle Range
Playing Fields
Harrow School
Harrow Sch.
Sports Cen.
Parade Grd.
Harrow School Playing Fields
Tennis Cts.
HARROW ON THE HILL
School Lake
Harrow School Farm
HA1
Kennet End
HARROW CYGNET HOSPITAL
THE CLEMENTINE CHURCHILL BMI HOSPITAL
Burial Ground
St. George's Catholic Prim. Sch.
Elmwood Pk.
Whitmore High Sch.
Whitmore Sports Cen.
Cricket Ground
Grange Schs.
ROXETH
Superstore
ROXETH HILL
LOWER RD.
BESSBOROUGH RD.
A312
HA2
South Harrow
Orley Farm Sch.
Playing Fld.
Toll Gate
Harrow Ckt. Club
Playing Fields
SUDBURY HILL
A4005
A4127
HARROW RD.
Sudbury Hill Harrow
HA0
Sudbury Hill Play. Flds.
SOUTH HARROW
Welldon Park First Sch.
Bowling Green
Roxeth Rec. Grd.
Tennis Courts
Cemetery
NORTHOLT RD.
Northolt Pk.
Sudbury Hill
David Lloyd Leisure
Ealing Northern Sports Centre
Kellogg Tower
Wood End
WHITTON AV.
WEST WHITTON AVENUE
A4090
EAST
PETT'S HILL
HORSENDEN LA. NORTH
Greenford Green
Horsenden Primary Sch.
UB6
Tennis Courts
Bowling Green
Pavilion
BERKELEY FIELDS
HORSENDEN HILL GOLF COURSE
Horsenden Hill Rec. Grd.
Nature Reserve
GREENFORD RD.
Factory
Warehouses
GRAND UNION CANAL
Lyon's Dock
Youth & Comm. Cen.
Works
Greenford
GREENFORD INDUSTRIAL ESTATE
Depot
Perivale Wood Local Nature Reserve
Comm. Centre
Oldfield Rec. Grd.
Sports Ground
Tennis Courts
Radio Station
Sch.
Liby.

HARROW
60
42
59
78
A
B
C
D
E
1
2
3
4
5
6
7
HA1
HA3
HA0
UB6
NORTH WEMBLEY
SUDBURY
PERIVALE
Northwick Park Hospital
St. Mark's Hosp.
Westminster (Harrow Campus)
Westminster Sports Hall
Northwick Park
Driving Range
Club Ho.
Northwick Park Playgolf
Playing Fields
Harrow School Playing Fields
Harrow School Farm
South Kenton
Preston Road
North Wembley
Wembley Central
Sudbury & Harrow Road
Sudbury Town
Alperton
Byron Ct. Prim. Sch.
Tennis Courts
Pav.
Playground
Preston Park Recreation Ground
John Billam Playing Fields
Sports Ground
Play. Fld.
Wembley High Tech. Coll.
Train. Cen.
Wembley Commercial Centre
East Lane Business Park
Sports Grd.
Vale Farm Sports Ground
Vale Farm Sports Centre
East Lane Pavilion
Rugby Football Grd.
Wembley FC (Vale Farm)
East La. Theatre Club
Pavilion
Rec. Grd.
Elmwood Pk.
Sudbury Hill Play. Flds.
Butler's Grn.
Maybank Open Space
Barham Park
Library
NHS Walk-in Centre
King Edward VII Park
Bowl. Grns.
Prim. Sch.
Wembley Prim. Sch.
Fitness First
Horsenden Wood
Club House
Horsenden Hill Golf Course
Horsenden Hill
Horsenden Farm
Sudbury Golf Course
Alperton Cemetery
One Tree Hill Rec. Grd.
Hindu Tem.
Alperton Sch. (Lower)
Bus Garage
Perivale Wood Local Nature Reserve
Grand Union Canal (Paddington Branch)
Moat
Comm. Centre
Lib.
Govt. Training Cen.
WATFORD ROAD
A404
A4127
SUDBURY COURT DRIVE
HARROW ROAD
A4005
EAST LANE
A4088
WHITTON AVENUE EAST
A4090
BRIDGEWATER ROAD
HIGH ROAD
EALING ROAD
A4089
NORVAL ROAD
ABBOTTS DRIVE
CARLTON AVENUE
PAXFORD ROAD
BLOCKLEY ROAD
FAIRWAY AVENUE
WINDERMERE AVENUE
GRASMERE AVENUE
WOODCOCK HILL
PRESTON ROAD
COLLEGE AVENUE
SUDBURY AVENUE
HARROWDENE ROAD
ST. JOHN'S ROAD
CASTLETON AVENUE
CHAPLIN ROAD
HORSENDEN LANE NORTH
ALPERTON
BILTON ROAD
CLIFFORD ROAD

61
43
79
62
FRYENT COUNTRY PARK
Fryent Country Park Local Nature Reserve
Barn Hill Open Space
Barn Hill
FRYENT WAY
A4140
SALMON STREET
NW9
PRESTON
Stanmore Junction
Wealdstone Brook
Preston Manor High Sch.
FORTY AVENUE
FORTY LANE
A4088
BARN HILL
WEST HILL
WENTWORTH HILL
WYKEHAM HILL
UXENDON HILL
ALVERSTONE RD.
Tennis Courts
Town Hall
Liby.
Wembley Park
Ark Academy
Carriage Shed
BRIDGE RD.
Superstore
CHALK HILL
Chalkhill Prim. Sch.
Ind. Est.
EMPIRE WAY
A479
WEMBLEY PARK DR.
A4089
HA9
WEMBLEY PARK
Wembley Arena
Wembley Stadium
Market
Works
FULTON ROAD
ENGINEERS WAY
OLYMPIC WAY
RUTHERFORD WAY
FIFTH WY.
FOURTH WY.
FIRST WY.
Wembley Retail Park
WEMBLEY HILL RD.
SOUTH WAY
B4557
GREAT CENTRAL WAY
Depot
Railway Works
Neasden Depot
NEASDEN JUNCTION
NEASDEN LA.
BLACKBIRD HILL
Kingsbury Bridge Comm. Cen.
Sports Ground
Play. Fld.
St. Margaret Clitherow RC Prim. Sch.
Welsh Harp Nature Reserve
Field Study Centre
Nursery
Wembley Sailing Club
Seahorse Sailing Club
BRENT RESERVOIR
River Brent
Sports Grd.
Superstores
DRURY WAY
Vernon Ho. Sch.
HARROW ROAD
A404
WEMBLEY
Schools
Playing Fld.
Youth & Comm. Cen.
Elsley Prim. Sch.
TOKYNGTON
Sherrans Farm Open Space
Oakington Mnr. Prim. Sch.
Bowling Grn.
Recreation Ground
NORTH CIRCULAR ROAD
A406
Wembley Brook Depot
Carriage Shed
Stonebridge Park
Brent Junction
Bridge Park
HILLSIDE
NW10
Hindu Temple
Power Station
CHURCH END
Gibbons Recreation Ground
School
Sch.
ALPERTON
Sports Ground
NORTHFIELDS INDUSTRIAL ESTATE
STONEBRIDGE
CRAVEN PK.
BRENTFIELD RD.
BRENT TRADING CENTRE

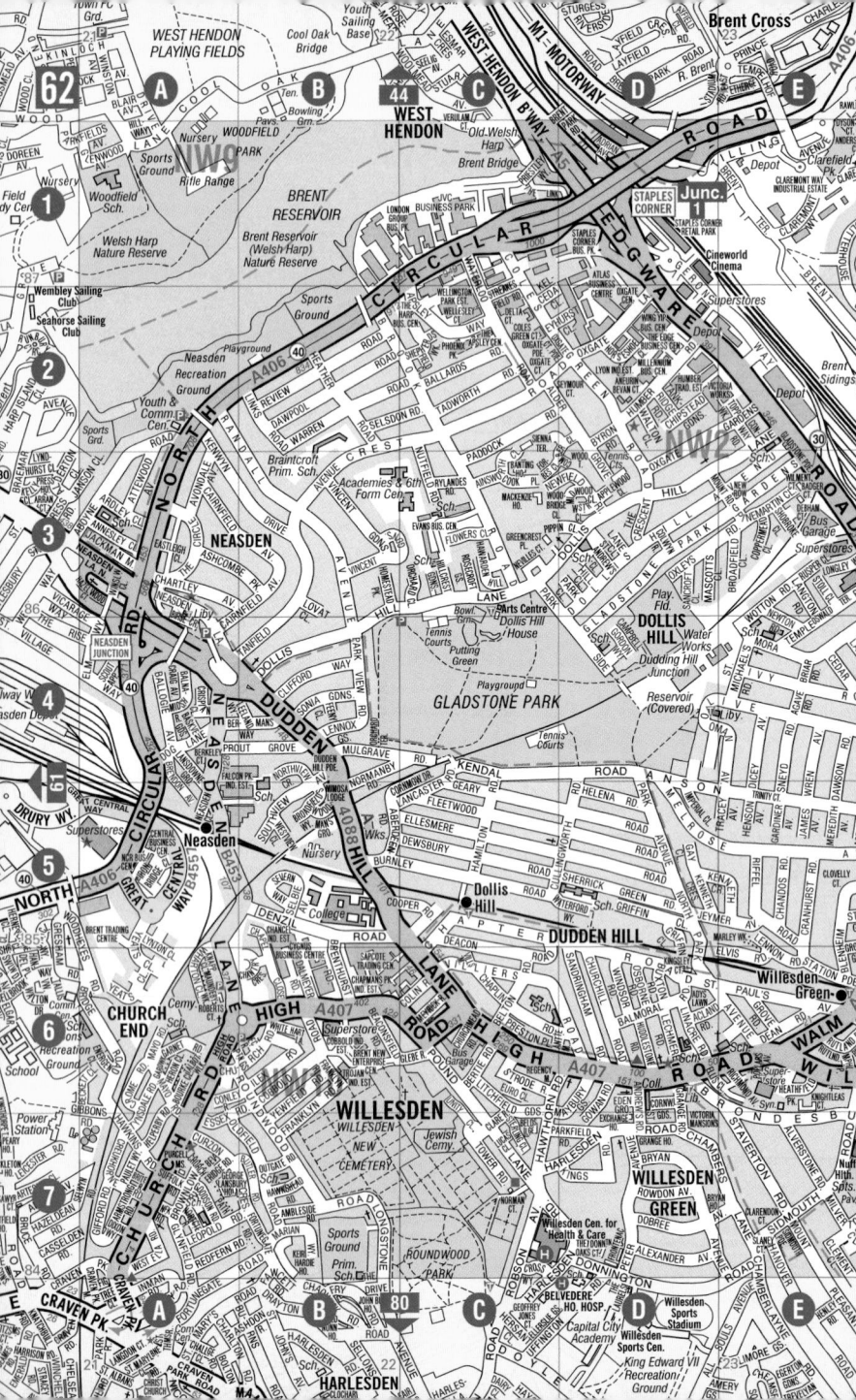

63
45
64
81
F
G
H
J
K
1
2
3
4
5
6
7
24
25
26
HAMPSTEAD HEATH
GOLDERS GREEN
NW11
Golders Green
NORTH END ROAD
A502
GOLDERS HILL PARK
Leg of Mutton Pond
West Heath
Jack Straw's Castle
The Hill
Clitterhouse Recreation Ground
Hendon FC (Claremont Rd.)
Tennis Courts
HENDON WAY
A41
FINCHLEY ROAD
A598
Basing Hill Park
Childs Hill Park
CHILD'S HILL
CRICKLEWOOD
RICKLEWOOD
Cricklewood
A407
CRICKLEWOOD BROADWAY
A5
CHICHELE RD.
SHOOT UP HILL
NW3
Kings Coll. (Hampstead Campus)
Sports Ground
Hampstead Cemetery
Hampstead School
Fortune Green
FORTUNE GREEN RD.
WEST END LANE
B510
WEST HAMPSTEAD
West Hampstead Thameslink
West Hampstead
Finchley Rd. & Frognal
Camden Arts Cen.
SOUTH HAMPSTEAD
Kilburn
Brondesbury
BRONDESBURY
Brondesbury Park
KILBURN HIGH RD.
B520
IVERSON RD.
WILLESDEN LANE
A4003
Kilburn Grange Park
Paddington Old Cemetery (Willesden Lane Cemetery)
ABBEY RD.
BELSIZE ROAD
B509
The Hope Cen.
Mosque
Hindu Temple
Superstore
Res. (cov.)

64
A
B
C
D
E
46
63
82
1
2
3
4
5
6
7
HAMPSTEAD HEATH
HAMPSTEAD
HIGHGATE
NW11
NW3
NW6
N6
Bunkers Hill
Turners Wood
Club House
North Wood
Kenwood House
Caen Wood
Athlone House
Highgate School
Sports Ground
Highgate Ponds
Men's Bathing Pond
Ladies' Bathing Pond
Open Air Stage
KEN WOOD
Mount Tyndal
Sandy Heath
The Spaniards
North End
VALE OF HEALTH
The Hill
West Heath
Jack Straw's Castle
Whitestone Pond
East Heath
Sports Ground
Bathing Pond
PARLIAMENT HILL
Parliament Hill Fields
William Ellis School
Parliament Hill School
Parliament Hill Fields Athletics Track
GOSPEL OAK
Gospel Oak
Hampstead Ponds
Hampstead Heath
Hampstead
Burgh Ho.
Keats Ho.
2 Willow Rd.
THE ROYAL FREE HOSPITAL
University College School
Camden Arts Cen.
Finchley Rd. & Frognal
Finchley Rd.
Sigmund Freud Statue
Hospice
Belsize Pk.
SOUTH HAMPSTEAD
Swiss Cottage
South Hampstead
Chalk Farm
PRIMROSE HILL
Reservoir (covered)
NORTH END RD.
SPANIARDS ROAD
HAMPSTEAD LANE
HEATH ST.
FITZJOHN'S AVENUE
ROSSLYN HILL
HAVERSTOCK HILL
FINCHLEY ROAD
BELSIZE RD.
ADELAIDE ROAD
AGINCOURT RD.
MANSFIELD ROAD
MALDEN ROAD
CHALK FARM ROAD
FLEET ROAD
POND ST.
MILLFIELD LA.
HIGHGATE WEST HILL
WILLOW ROAD
A502
A41
B519
B518
B511
B509
B517
B525

65
F
G
H
J
K
1
2
3
4
5
6
7
47
83
Crouch Hill
HIGHGATE
CEMETERY
Lauderdale House
WATERLOW PARK
Waterlow Park Cen.
Highgate Mental Health Centre
WHITTINGTON HOSPITAL
Middlesex Uni.
Archway
N19
Upper Holloway
UPPER HOLLOWAY
Whittington Park
DARTMOUTH PARK
HOLLOWAY
TUFNELL PARK
Tufnell Pk.
Elthorne Park
Convent
Fitness First
Sobell Leisure Cen.
Odeon Cinema
Hlth.Club
NAG'S HEAD
NAGS HEAD SHOPPING CENTRE
HMP HOLLOWAY
HILLDROP ESTATE
Holloway Rd.
University
LOWER HOLLOWAY
Arsenal F.C. (Emirates Stadium)
Finsbury Pa
Isle
Kentish Town Forum
KENTISH TOWN
KENTISH TOWN INDUSTRIAL EST.
Kentish Town
Caledonian Rd.
Caledonian Park
Islington Ten. Cen.
HMP PENTONVILLE
Paradise Park
City Farm
BARNSBURY
Caledonian Rd. & Barnsbury
Camden Rd.
CAMDEN TOWN
Camden Town
BRITANNIA JUNC.
Warehouse
Oblique Bridge
High Speed 1
HIGHGATE RD.
FORTRESS RD.
JUNCTION RD.
HOLLOWAY RD.
HORNSEY RD.
SEVEN SISTERS RD.
CAMDEN RD.
CALEDONIAN RD.
YORK WAY
BRECKNOCK RD.
TUFNELL PARK RD.
HORNSEY LANE
HORNSEY RISE
STROUD GREEN RD.
TOLLINGTON RD.
HILLMARTON RD.
KENTISH TOWN RD.
CAMDEN PARK RD.
ST. PANCRAS WAY
AGAR GROVE
CAMDEN ST.
COLLEGE ST.
LIVERPOOL RD.

66
A
B
C
D
E
1
2
3
4
5
6
7
48
65
84
FINSBURY PARK
Finsbury Park
Manor House
EAST RESERVOIR
WEST RESERVOIR
Reservoir (covered)
West Reservoir Centre
The Castle Climbing Cen.
Abney Park Cemetery (Local Nature Reserve)
STOKE NEWINGTON
Sir Thomas Abney Prim. Sch.
BROWNSWOOD PARK
N4
CLISSOLD PARK
Clissold Ho.
Council Offices
Paddling Pool
Tennis Courts
Isledon Village
Gillespie Park Nature Res.
Arsenal
Ecology Cen.
Ashburton Grove
Arsenal FC (Emirates Stadium)
N7
Drayton Pk.
Holloway Rd.
LOWER HOLLOWAY
University
HIGHBURY
N5
Highbury Pool
City Farm
Highbury & Islington
Canonbury
CANONBURY
N16
N1
KINGSLAND
Dalston Kingsland
Essex Rd.
BARNSBURY
ISLINGTON
DE BEAUVOIR TOWN
SEVEN SISTERS ROAD
GREEN LANES
BLACKSTOCK ROAD
HIGHBURY PARK
HIGHBURY GROVE
ST. PAUL'S ROAD
BALLS POND ROAD
HOLLOWAY ROAD
LIVERPOOL ROAD
UPPER STREET
NEW NORTH ROAD
ESSEX ROAD
CANONBURY ROAD
NEWINGTON GRN. RD.
ALBION ROAD
STOKE NEWINGTON CHURCH ST.
LORDSHIP PARK
MANOR ROAD
SEVEN SISTERS RD.
ISLEDON RD.
HORNSEY RD.
TOLLINGTON RD.
STROUD GREEN RD.
WOODSTOCK RD.
ENDYMION RD.
A503
A1201
A105
A1199
A104
A103
A1
B150
B105
B104
B515
30

67
68
49
85
F
G
H
J
K
1
2
3
4
5
6
7
CLAPTON
STAMFORD HILL
Stoke Newington
UPPER CLAPTON
SPRINGFIELD PARK
Walthamstow Marsh Nature Reserve
Coppermill Bridge
Springfield Marina
Horse Shoe Point
WALTHAMSTOW
Clapton Junction
E17
MARSHES
RIVER LEA or LEE
LEYTON INDUSTRIAL VILLAGE
FOREST BUSINESS PARK
Leyton Marshes
Lea Valley Riding Centre
E10
Playing Field
Lee Valley Ice Centre
LEA BRIDGE ROAD
A104
North Millfields Recreation Ground
Middlesex Filter Beds Nature Reserve
LEA BRIDGE
SOUTH MILL FIELDS
South Millfields Rec. Grd.
Clapton
E5
NORTHWOLD ROAD
Rectory Road
RECTORY ROAD
STOKE NEWINGTON HIGH ST.
A10
UPPER CLAPTON ROAD
A107
LOWER CLAPTON
HACKNEY DOWNS
Stormont House Sch.
Mossbourne Community Academy
SHACKLEWELL
EVERING RD.
AMHURST ROAD
HOMERTON
HOMERTON UNIVERSITY HOSPITAL
HOMERTON HIGH ST.
Homerton
CLAPTON PARK
DALSTON LA.
LWR.CLAPTON R.
URSWICK RD.
Hackney Downs
Hackney Cen.
GRAHAM ROAD
A1207
DALSTON
QUEENSBRIDGE RD.
E8
E9
HACKNEY
London Fields Lido
London Fields
LONDON FIELDS
MARE STREET
MORNING LANE
WICK RD.
B113
KENTON RD.
CASSLAND RD.
WELL STREET COMMON
SOUTH HACKNEY
VICTORIA PARK
A106
Haggerston
Victoria Fountain
Royal Gate East

68
50
67
86
A
B
C
D
E
1
2
3
4
5
6
7
LEYTON
E10
E20
E3
HACKNEY MARSH
RECREATION GROUND
CLAPTON PARK
HOMERTON
HACKNEY WICK
OLD FORD
STRATFORD
Leyton Midland Rd.
Temple Mills
Eton Manor
Eton Manor Transport Hub
Market Pavilion
New Spitalfields Market
Lea Interchange
Waterworks Vis. Cen.
Waterworks Golf Course (Nature Reserve)
River Lea or Lee
Middlesex Filter Beds Nature Reserve
Cow Bridge
Changing Rooms
Leyton FC Grd.
Gala Bingo
The Lammas Sch.
Playing Fields
Manor Lodge
Marsh Lane Cottage
Running Track
Dagenham Brook
Leyton Orient FC
The Score Complex
Waste Management Centre
Football Pitch
Superstore
Fitness First
Leyton Mills
Brooks Farm
The Davis Cen.
Sidmouth Park
Velodrome
BMX Track
Riverbank Arena
Basketball Arena
Olympic & Paralympic Village
Stratford International
Westfield Stratford City Shopping Centre
Main Press Centre
International Broadcast Centre
Copper Box
Olympic Park
Water Polo Arena
Aquatics Centre
Olympic Stadium
The Orbit
Wick Woodland
Marshgate Bri.
Hackney Cut
Football Ground
Mabley Green
Recreation Ground
Homerton
Hackney Wick
VICTORIA PARK
Victoria Park Athletics Arena
Victoria Fountain
Royal Gate East
Three Colt Bridge
Cadogan Gate
Mitford Bri.
Bowling Green
Tennis Courts
Well Street Common
LEA BRIDGE ROAD
CHURCH ROAD
HIGH ROAD LEYTON
RUCKHOLT ROAD
EAST CROSS ROUTE
EASTWAY
ORIENT WAY
HOMERTON ROAD
WICK ROAD
VICTORIA PARK ROAD
HOMERTON HIGH ST.
KENWORTHY RD.
CASSLAND RD.
A104
A106
A12
A102
A1006
A112
B112
B113
B161

69
GREEN MAN ROUNDABOUT
BUSH RD.
51
Leytonstone
LEYTONSTONE
Leytonstone High Rd.
E11
WANSTEAD GOLF COURSE
Reservoir Wood
Shoulder of Mutton Pond
Bush Wood
The Basin (Fish Pond)
Sports Ground
ALDERSBROOK ROAD
A116
E12
WANSTEAD FLATS
HARROW ROAD
DAMES ROAD
WOODFORD ROAD
CENTRE ROAD
BLAKE HALL ROAD
A114
GREEN
GROVE
CATHALL
St. Patrick's RC Cemetery
Langthorne Park
Cann Hall
West Ham Cemetery
CANN HALL
Wanstead Pk.
70
E7
E15
Forest Gate
FOREST GATE
Maryland
Stratford New Town
ROMFORD ROAD
A118
WOODGRANGE
Stratford
BROADWAY
WEST HAM LA.
GREAT EASTERN
A112
VICARAGE
WEST HAM PARK
UPTON
UPTON LANE
Stratford High St.
PORTWAY
87
PLASHET
WEST HAM
Upton Park
ROAD
F
G
H
J
K
1
2
3
4
5
6
7

52
69
88
A
B
C
D
E
1
2
3
4
5
6
7
WANSTEAD PARK
WANSTEAD GOLF COURSE
The Temple
Keepers Lodge
E11
Heronry Pond
Perch Pond
Riding Sch.
Lincoln Island
Rook Island
River Roding
Bowling Green
Tennis Courts
Sports Ground
Aldersbrook Prim. Sch.
ALDERSBROOK
A116
WANSTEAD FLATS
NORTHUMBERLAND AVENUE
CITY OF LONDON CEMETERY
City of London Crematorium
Lodge
FOREST DRIVE
A116 ROAD
ILFORD GOLF COURSE
Alders Brook
SOUTH WOODFORD TO BARKING RELIEF ROAD
A406
CRANBROOK
Cranbrook Coll.
Ilford Cricket Club
NHS Walk-Cen.
MANOR PARK
THE MANOR PARK CEMETERY
Manor Park Crem.
Manor Park
E12
A117
A118
ROMFORD ROAD
Woodgrange Park
Woodgrange Park Cemetery
E7
LITTLE ILFORD
Little Ilford Park
LITTLE ILFORD LA.
CHURCH RD.
HIGH STREET NORTH
PLASHET
Jewish Cemetery
PLASHET PARK
GREEN STREET
KATHERINE ROAD
B167
B165
B109
PLASHET RD.
EAST AV.
GROVE
East Ham
E6
HOSP
The Shrewsbury Cen.
Sports Ground
Gasholder
Running Track
Playing Field
Depot
Wallend
Upton Park
UPTON PARK
BARKING
RON LEIGHTON WAY
NORTH CIRCULAR
SOUTH WOODFORD

VALENTINES PARK
F
G
H
J
K
53
71
72
89
SEVEN KINGS
IG2
IG3
IG1
IG11
1
2
3
4
5
6
7
Council Depot
Sports Ground
Playing Field
LADYSMITH AV.
KIMBERLEY
BENTON RD.
KINGS GS.
VICARAGE LANE
Depot
Seven Kings
CAMERON RD.
ALDBOROUGH RD. STH.
A118
HIGH ROAD
Repair Shed
REDBRIDGE ENTERPRISE CEN.
Court
Cemetery
Ilford FC (Cricklefield Stadium)
Youth Cen.
Fitness First
HIGH RD.
GREEN LANE
A1083
WINSTON WY.
EASTERN RDBT.
Town Hall
Lib.
Thtre.
ILFORD
Gordon Fields Prim. Sch.
TA Centre
School
SOUTH PARK
The Lake
Pav.
Bowl. Grn.
SOUTH PARK DRIVE
SOUTH PARK TER.
WATER LA.
Pav. Sports Fld.
PARKWAY
EGERTON GARDENS
MEADWAY
DAWLISH DR.
LEVETT RD.
ASHBURTON AV.
ILFORD LANE
A123
Woodlands Jun. & Inf. Schs.
Loxford Sch. of Science & Technology
Hyleford (Home for the Elderly)
LOXFORD PARK
LOXFORD
Loxford Water
Playing Field
Barking Abbey Sch. (Lwr. Sch.)
Bus Depot
FAIR CROSS
A124
LONGBRIDGE RD.
BARKING PARK
The Lake
Tennis Courts
Putting Green
Indoor Bowls Centre
Miniature Railway
Barking Abbey Sch.
Leisure Centre
Play. Fld.
Manor Jun. & Inf. Schs.
FANSHAWE AV.
FAIRCROSS AV.
Eastbury Comp. Sch.
Playing Field
NHS Cen.
BARKING HOSPITAL
Upney
Upney Sidings
BARKING NORTHERN RELIEF RD.
Barking
RODING TRADING ESTATE
Comm. Cen.
VICARAGE FIELD SHOPPING CEN.
BARKING
LONDON RD.
ABBEY RD.
ABBEY RETAIL PARK
Superstore
Barking Abbey
Thtre
Lib.
Spts. Cen.
HIGHBRIDGE RD.
BARKING RELIEF RD.
RIPPLE RD.
A123
Eastbury Manor Ho.
DAWSON AVENUE
Prim. Sch.

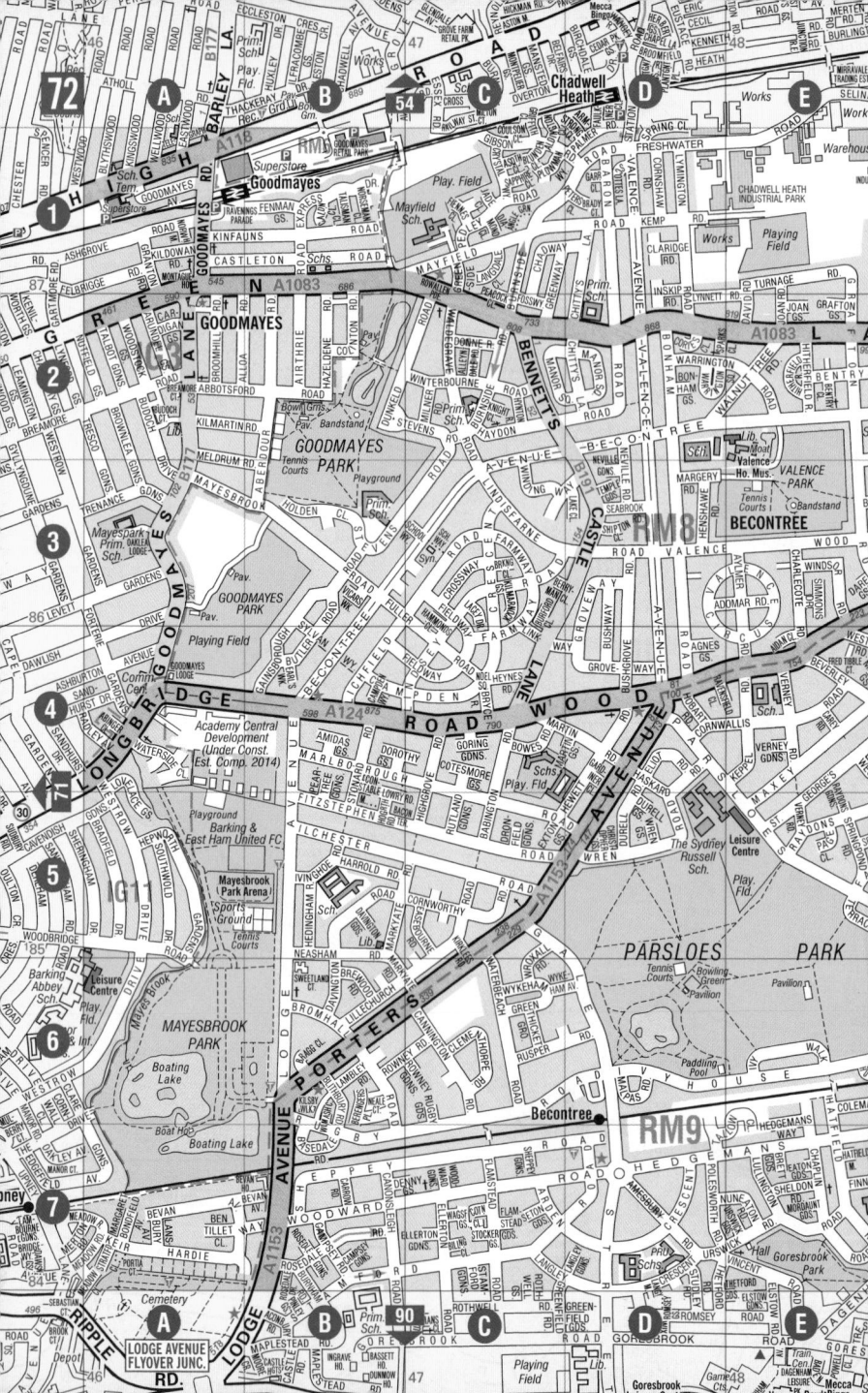

72
54
71
90
A
B
C
D
E
1
2
3
4
5
6
7
HIGH ROAD
A118
RM6
RM8
RM9
IG3
IG11
Chadwell Heath
Goodmayes
GOODMAYES
GOODMAYES LANE
GREEN LANE
A1083
BARLEY LA.
B177
Superstore
GOODMAYES RETAIL PARK
Prim. Sch.
Play. Fld.
Rec. Grd.
Bowl. Grn.
Works
GROVE FARM RETAIL PARK
Mecca Bingo
CHADWELL HEATH INDUSTRIAL PARK
Warehouse
Play. Field
Mayfield Sch.
Playing Field
FRESHWATER ROAD
VALENCE AVENUE
KEMP RD.
CLARIDGE RD.
INSKIP RD.
TURNAGE RD.
GRAFTON GS.
LYNNETT RD.
DAVID RD.
BENNETT'S CASTLE LANE
B191
Chitty's Prim. Sch.
GOODMAYES PARK
Bowl. Grns.
Bandstand
Tennis Courts
Playground
Pav.
Mayespark Prim. Sch.
MAYESBROOK
HOLDEN CL.
STEVENS ROAD
BECONTREE AVENUE
VALENCE PARK
Valence Ho. Mus.
BECONTREE
Lib.
Moat
Sch.
WOOD LANE
VALENCE CIRCUS
ADDMAR RD.
LONGBRIDGE ROAD
A124
ROAD WOOD
Academy Central Development (Under Const. Est. Comp. 2014)
Barking & East Ham United FC
Mayesbrook Park Arena
Sports Ground
MAYESBROOK PARK
Mayes Brook
Boating Lake
Boat Ho.
Barking Abbey Sch.
Leisure Centre
PORTERS AVENUE
A1153
LODGE AVENUE
PARSLOES PARK
The Sydney Russell Sch.
Leisure Centre
Play. Fld.
Tennis Courts
Bowling Green
Pavilion
Paddling Pool
IVYHOUSE ROAD
Becontree
HEDGEMANS ROAD
Goresbrook Park
Hall
Cemetery
RIPPLE RD.
LODGE AVENUE FLYOVER JUNC.
GORESBROOK ROAD
Playing Field
Lib.
Depot
Train. Cen.
DAGENHAM LEISURE PK
Mecca Road Bingo
Goresbrook Leisure Centre
Game Cts.
46
47
48

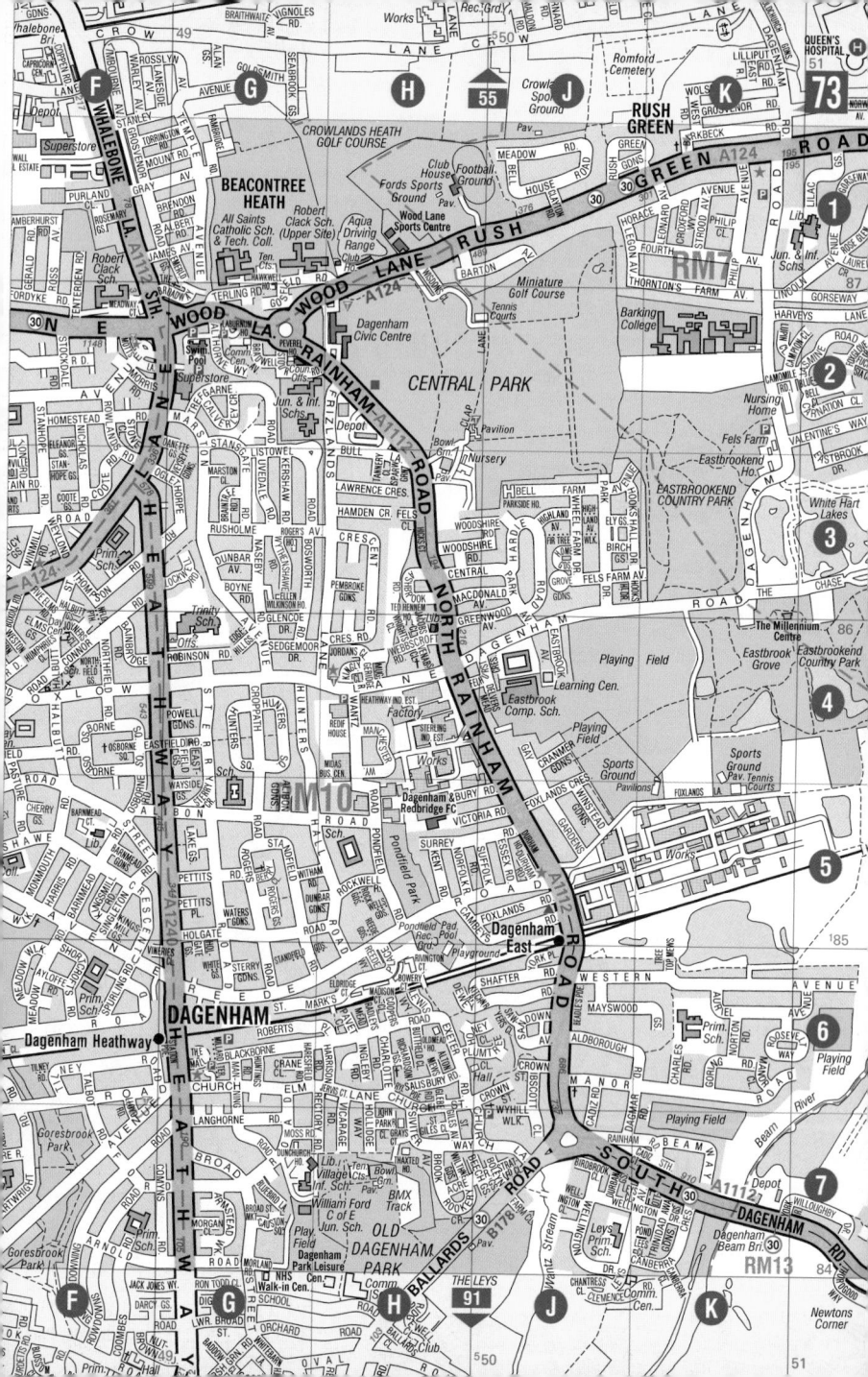

55
73
91
RUSH GREEN
BEACONTREE HEATH
CROWLANDS HEATH GOLF COURSE
Fords Sports Ground
Football Ground
Club House
Wood Lane Sports Centre
Aqua Driving Range
All Saints Catholic Sch. & Tech. Coll.
Robert Clack Sch. (Upper Site)
Romford Cemetery
Crowlands Sports Ground
QUEEN'S HOSPITAL
RM7
RM10
RM13
Dagenham Civic Centre
CENTRAL PARK
Miniature Golf Course
Tennis Courts
Barking College
Nursing Home
Fels Farm
Eastbrookend Ho.
EASTBROOKEND COUNTRY PARK
White Hart Lakes
The Millennium Centre
Eastbrook Grove
Eastbrookend Country Park
Playing Field
Learning Cen.
Eastbrook Comp. Sch.
Sports Ground
Pavilions
Works
Dagenham & Redbridge FC
Pondfield Park
Dagenham East
DAGENHAM
Dagenham Heathway
Goresbrook Park
OLD DAGENHAM PARK
Dagenham Park Leisure Cen.
BMX Track
William Ford C of E Jun. Sch.
Village Inf. Sch.
NHS Walk-in Cen.
THE LEYS
Leys Prim. Sch.
Dagenham Beam Bri.
Beam River
Wantz Stream
Newtons Corner
RUSH GREEN ROAD
WOOD LANE
RAINHAM ROAD
NORTH RAINHAM ROAD
SOUTH ROAD
DAGENHAM ROAD
BALLARDS ROAD
HEATHWAY
WHALEBONE LA.
CROW LANE
A124
A1112
A1240
B178

74
56
92
A
B
C
D
E
1
2
3
4
5
6
7
UXBRIDGE
RAF UXBRIDGE
TA Centre
RAF Uxbridge Track
Sports Ground
HILLINGDON COURT PARK (Recreation Ground)
Bowling Green
Tennis Courts
Playground
TACS Hillingdon International Sch.
Convent
HILLINGDON GOLF COURSE
Club Ho.
UB10
Weir
Rifle Ranges
Sports Grd.
Uxbridge High Sch.
Playing Field
Stratford Bri.
HILLINGDON HILL
A4020
Hillingdon Cem.
Uxbridge Cem.
Halls of Residence
Athletics Centre
Brunel University (Uxbridge Campus)
BRUNEL SCIENCE PK.
Bishopshalt School
Coney Green
Tennis Courts
Playing Field
Tudor Cott.
Running Track
Brunel Uni. Sports Park
Games Ct.
The Grove Nature Reserve
Nursing Home
Pield Heath House RC Sch.
Convent
Garden Centre
COWLEY
UB8
COLHAM GREEN
HILLINGDON HEATH
HILLINGDON
Swakeleys School
Abbotsfield School
Playing Field
Home Covert
Tennis Courts
Playing Fld.
Prim. Sch.
Liby.
Mellow Lane Farm
Hillingdon Heath
PIELD HEATH
Playing Fields
River Pinn
COWLEY PEACHEY
Manor Fm.
Meadow High Sch.
HILLINGDON HOSPITAL
Colham Manor Prim. Sch.
Moorcroft Sch.
Stockley Academy
Hillingdon Manor Prim. School
Moorcroft
Moorcroft Fm.
Middlesex Lodge
Parkview Day Cen.
Goulds Green
Rabbsfarm Prim. Sch.
Chantry Sch.
Philpot's Bri.
Airport Parking
STOCKLEY COUNTRY PARK
STILWELL ROUNDABOUT
UB7
YIEWSLEY
Library
Bowls
Yiewsley Swim. Pool
Recreation Ground
Uxbridge FC
STOCKLEY PARK GOLF COURSE
UB11
Club House
The Arena
Virgin Active
Stockley Park
HILLINGDON ROAD
UXBRIDGE ROAD
HARLINGTON ROAD
LONG LANE
STOCKLEY ROAD
FALLING LANE
WEST DRAYTON ROAD
A437
A408
A408
B465
B483

75
57
93
76
NORTH HILLINGDON
HAYES END
WOOD END GREEN
WOOD END
HAYES
YEADING
UB5
UB4
UB3
POLISH WAR MEMORIAL
C & L GOLF COURSE
Club Ho.
WEST END RD.
Yeading Brook
Cutthroat Wood
Gutteridge Wood
Ten Acres
The Gorse
Recreation Ground
Westways Fm.
Lane Covert
SHARVEL LANE
Club House
Moat
Barns Fm.
West London Shooting Grounds
Rugby Ground
Hare Plantation
Children's Cen.
Comm. Cen.
Charville Prim. Sch.
Hedgewood School
Canal Feeder
Grosvenor Playing Field
Hayes Shrub
Hayes Park
Home Farm
The Paddocks Farm
Hostel
Nursery
Grange Park Jun. & Inf. Schs.
Yeading Brook Meadows Nature Reserve
Belmore Playing Fields
Comm. Cen.
Belmore Prim. Sch.
Barnhill High Sch. Playing Fields
Prim. Sch.
Rosedale Park
Rosedale College
Hayes Stadium & Sports Cen.
All Weather Pitch
County Court
Nurs. Home
Thtre
Norman Leddy Mem. Gdns.
Day Cen.
Hayes Botanical Gdns.
Cricket Grd.
Barra Hall
Open Air Theatre
Town Hall Park
Mecca Bingo
Uxbridge Coll. (Hayes Comm. Campus)
Hayes & Yeading United FC (Church Rd.)
Convent
Lombardy Retail Park
Lake Farm Country Park
BMX Track
Minet Jun. & Inf. Schs.
Hillingdon Cycling Circuit
Goals Soccer Centre (Hayes)
UXBRIDGE ROAD
A4020
A312
A437
THE PARKWAY
OSSIE GARVIN ROUNDABOUT
KINGSHILL DRIVE
LANSBURY DRIVE
BALMORAL DRIVE
YEADING LANE
GLEDWOOD AV.
CHURCH RD.
BOTWELL LA.
BOTWELL COMMON ROAD
COMPTON ROAD
FREEMANS LA.
HEATH LANE
HEMMEN LA.
HARBOUR AVENUE
HUGHES RD.
CHAUCER AV.
SPENCER AV.
WARLEY AV.
SHAKESPEARE AV.
HAYES END ROAD
WOOD END GREEN RD.
F G H J K
1 2 3 4 5 6 7

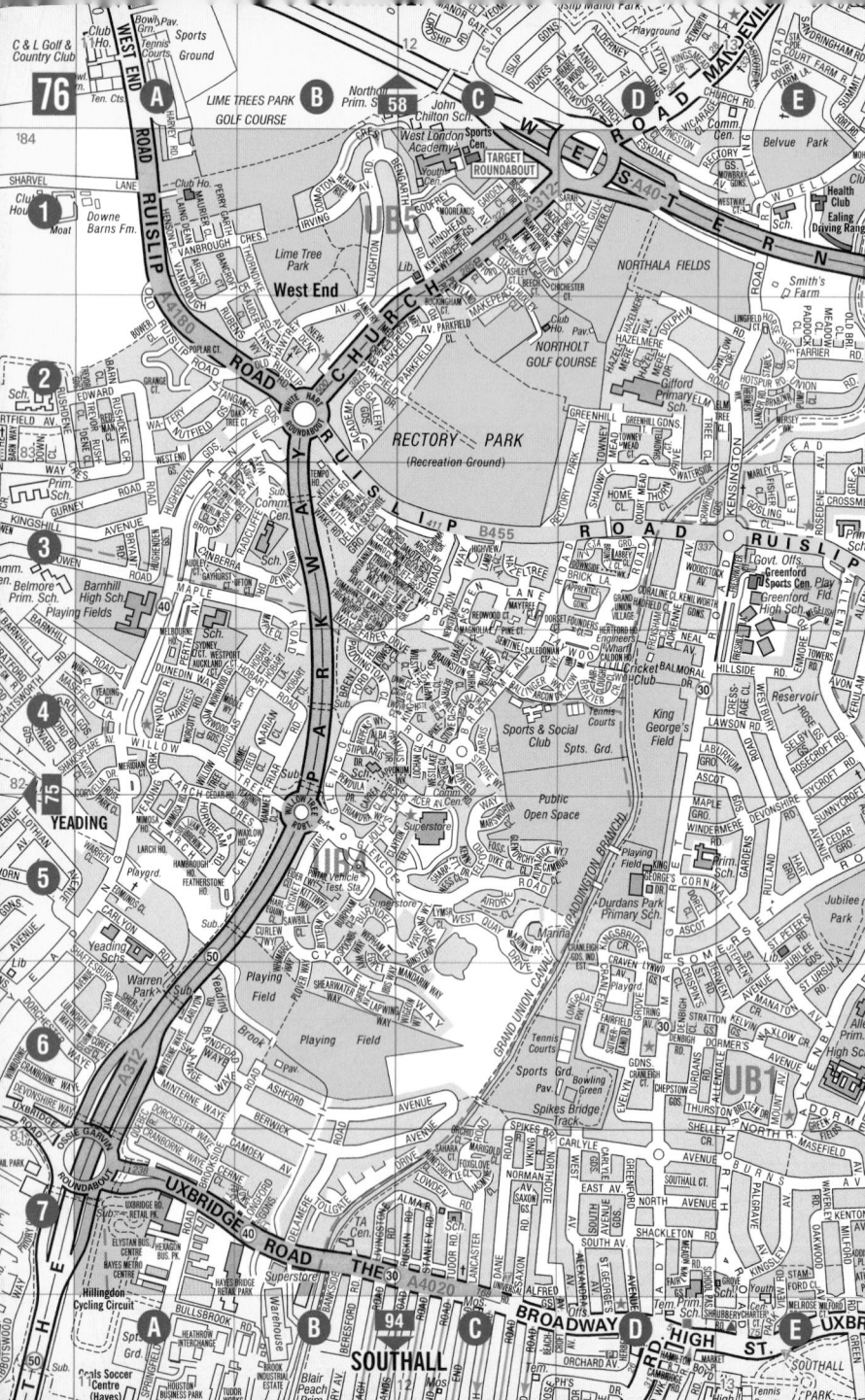
76
58
75
94
A
B
C
D
E
1
2
3
4
5
6
7
C & L Golf & Country Club
LIME TREES PARK GOLF COURSE
Northolt Prim. Sch.
John Chilton Sch.
West London Academy
TARGET ROUNDABOUT
WESTERN AV. A40
UB5
Lime Tree Park
West End
NORTHALA FIELDS
NORTHOLT GOLF COURSE
Downe Barns Fm.
Moat
RUISLIP ROAD A4180
CHURCH RD. A312
WHITE HART ROUNDABOUT
RECTORY PARK
(Recreation Ground)
RUISLIP ROAD B455
Gifford Primary Sch.
Belvue Park
Health Club
Ealing Driving Range
Smith's Farm
Greenford Sports Cen.
Greenford High Sch.
Govt. Offs.
Barnhill High Sch.
Playing Fields
Belmore Prim. Sch.
PARKWAY
YEADING
WILLOW TREE RDBT.
Superstore
UB4
Vehicle Test. Sta.
Sports & Social Club
Public Open Space
King George's Field
Reservoir
Jubilee Park
Durdans Park Primary Sch.
GRAND UNION CANAL (PADDINGTON BRANCH)
Marina
Yeading Schs.
Warren Park
Playing Field
Yeading Brook
Tennis Courts
Sports Grd.
Bowling Green
Spikes Bridge Track
UB1
OSSIE GARVIN ROUNDABOUT
UXBRIDGE ROAD A4020
UXBRIDGE RD. RETAIL PK.
HAYES BRIDGE RETAIL PARK
Hillingdon Cycling Circuit
THE BROADWAY
HIGH ST.
SOUTHALL
Brook Industrial Estate
Blair Peach Prim. Sch.
Goals Soccer Centre (Hayes)
Heathrow Interchange
Houston Business Park

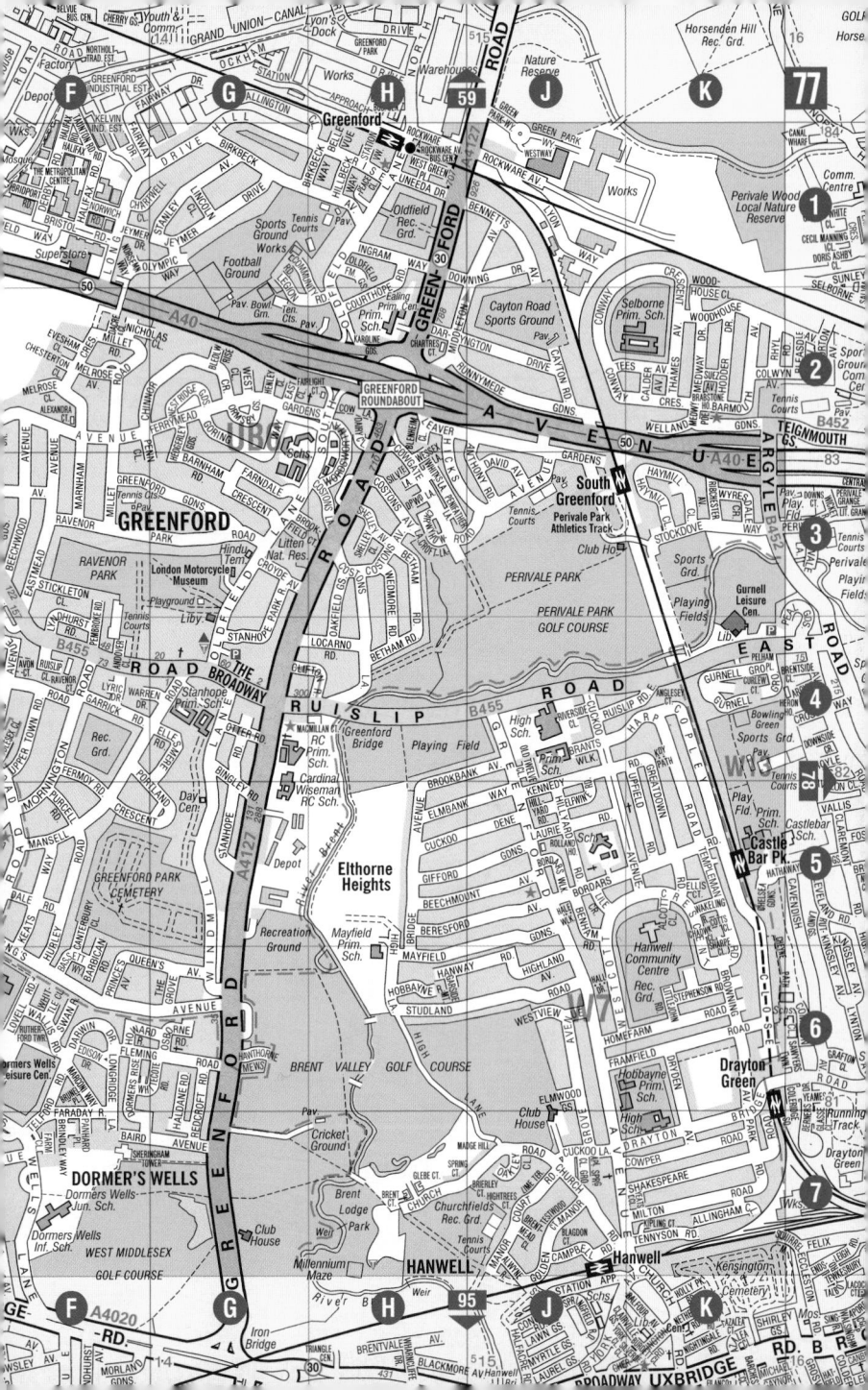
77
59
95
78
GREENFORD
Greenford
South Greenford
GREENFORD ROUNDABOUT
PERIVALE PARK
PERIVALE PARK GOLF COURSE
Elthorne Heights
BRENT VALLEY GOLF COURSE
HANWELL
Hanwell
DORMER'S WELLS
WEST MIDDLESEX GOLF COURSE
Drayton Green
Castle Bar Pk.
Gurnell Leisure Cen.
Horsenden Hill Rec. Grd.
Perivale Wood Local Nature Reserve
Kensington Cemetery
GRAND UNION CANAL
RUISLIP ROAD
GREENFORD ROAD
A40
A4127
A4020
B455
B452
UB6
W7
W13

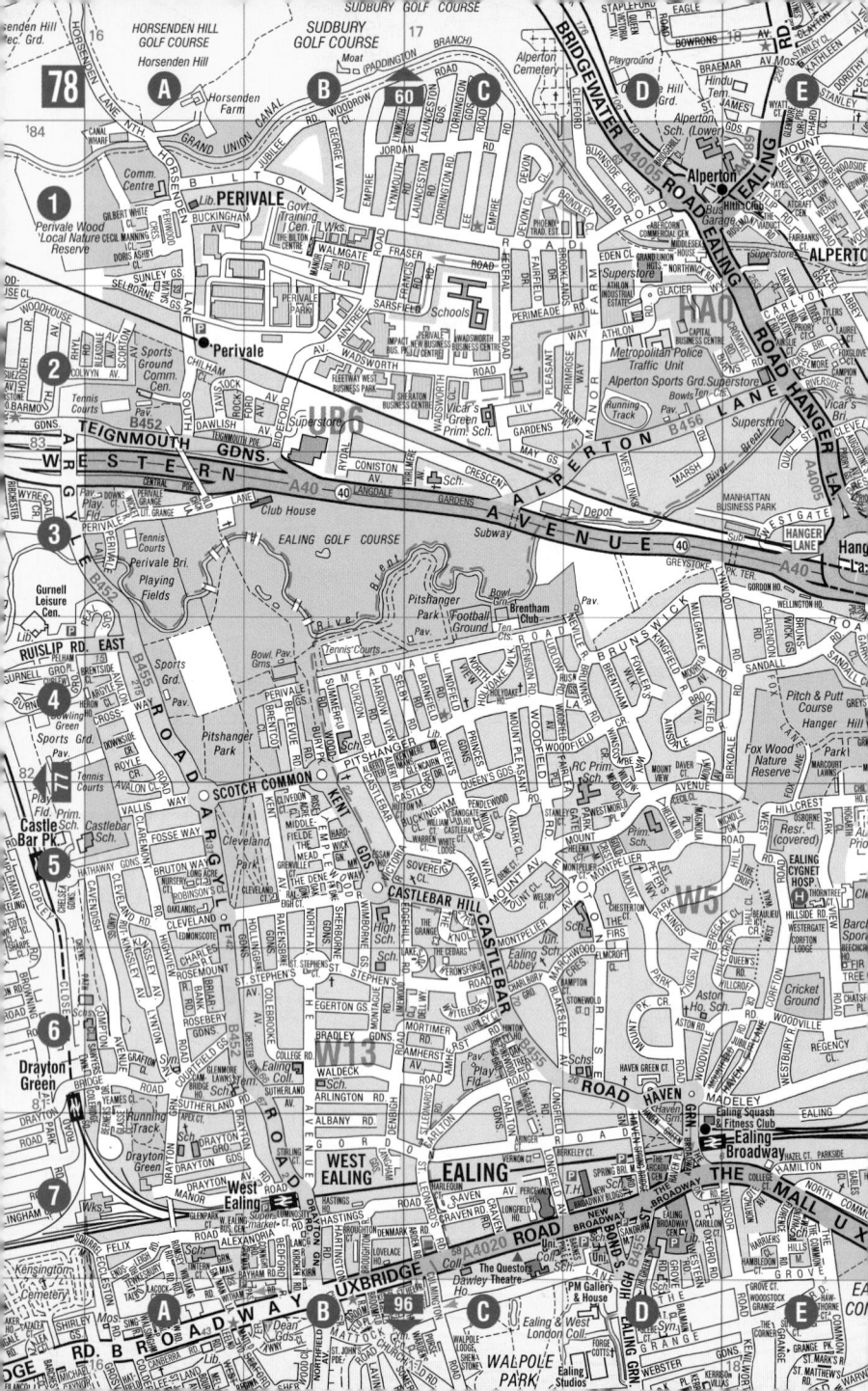

78
60
96
77
A
B
C
D
E
1
2
3
4
5
6
7
HORSENDEN HILL GOLF COURSE
Horsenden Hill
Horsenden Farm
SUDBURY GOLF COURSE
Alperton Cemetery
GRAND UNION CANAL
(PADDINGTON BRANCH)
Perivale Wood Local Nature Reserve
PERIVALE
Perivale
Sports Ground Comm. Cen.
UB6
HA0
W5
W13
Alperton
Metropolitan Police Traffic Unit
Alperton Sports Grd.
Running Track
MANHATTAN BUSINESS PARK
WESTERN AVENUE
A40
ALPERTON LANE
HANGER LANE
EALING ROAD
BRIDGEWATER ROAD
EALING GOLF COURSE
Perivale Bri. Playing Fields
Gurnell Leisure Cen.
RUISLIP RD. EAST
Pitshanger Park
Football Ground
Brentham Club
River Brent
SCOTCH COMMON
ARGYLE ROAD
Cleveland Park
Castle Bar Pk.
CASTLEBAR HILL
CASTLEBAR ROAD
Pitch & Putt Course
Fox Wood Nature Reserve
Hanger Hill Park
EALING CYGNET HOSP.
Cricket Ground
Ealing Abbey
Drayton Green
West Ealing
WEST EALING
EALING
Ealing Broadway
Ealing Squash & Fitness Club
HAVEN GRN.
THE MALL
UXBRIDGE ROAD
A4020
BROADWAY
The Questors Theatre
PM Gallery & House
Ealing & West London Coll.
WALPOLE PARK
Ealing Studios
EALING GRN.
HIGH ST.
Kensington Cemetery

79
Stonebridge Park
STONEBRIDGE PARK
61
Brent Junction
Royal Mail Depot
Stonebridge Rec.Grd.
STONEBRIDGE
HILLSIDE
CRAVEN PK.
NORTHFIELDS INDUSTRIAL ESTATE
NORTH CIRCULAR ROAD
A406
PARK ROYAL JUNCTION
PREMIER PARK
Works
NW10
TOWNSEND INDUSTRIAL ESTATE
Harlesden
Lower Place
GRAND UNION CANAL (Paddington Branch)
Twyford Abbey
PARK ROYAL CEN.
CENTRAL MIDDLESEX HOSPITAL
PARK ROYAL
ACTON LANE
B4492
Power Station
Playing Field
WESTERN AVENUE
A40
Park Royal
Hanger Hill
Tenpin Cinema
NORTH ACTON
North Acton
Cemetery
VICTORIA RD.
A4000
80
82
83
GYPSY CORNER
NORTH ACTON PLAYING FIELDS
West Acton
Sports Ground
Nth. Ealing
Acton Main Line
W3
HORN LANE
WALES FARM RD.
EAST ACTON
Japanese Sch. London
ACTON
97
Twyford Spts. Cen.
Ealing Common
GUNNERSBURY AV.
Acton Central
ACTON PARK
Maples Children's Cen.
The Park Club
Cricket Grd.
Football Pitch
HIGH ST.
ROAD
F
G
H
J
K
1
2
3
4
5
6
7
19
20
21

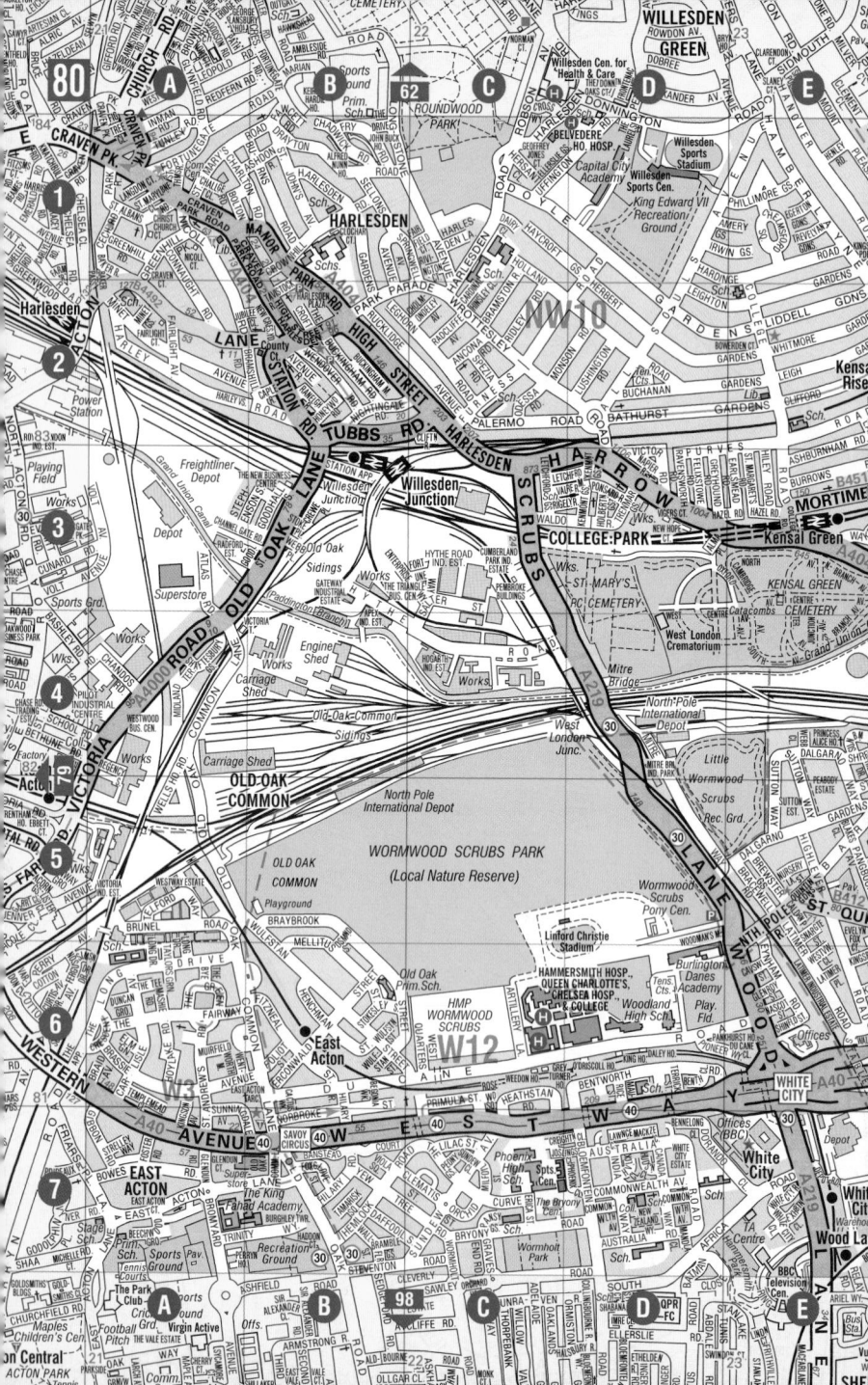

80
62
98
WILLESDEN GREEN
HARLESDEN
NW10
Harlesden
Willesden Junction
COLLEGE PARK
Kensal Green
KENSAL GREEN CEMETERY
OLD OAK COMMON
WORMWOOD SCRUBS PARK
(Local Nature Reserve)
Little Wormwood Scrubs Rec. Grd.
HMP WORMWOOD SCRUBS
W12
W3
EAST ACTON
East Acton
White City
WESTERN AVENUE
WESTWAY
WOOD LANE
SCRUBS LANE
OLD OAK LANE
VICTORIA ROAD
HARROW ROAD
HIGH STREET
TUBBS RD.
Willesden Sports Stadium
King Edward VII Recreation Ground
Linford Christie Stadium
HAMMERSMITH HOSP., QUEEN CHARLOTTE'S, CHELSEA HOSP., & COLLEGE
BBC Television Cen.

81
63
82
99
F
G
H
J
K
1
2
3
4
5
6
7
BRONDESBURY
WILLESDEN
KILBURN
Brondesbury Park
BRONDESBURY PARK
Paddington Old Cemetery
(Willesden Lane Cemetery)
QUEENS PARK
KENSAL RISE
Queens Park
Kilburn High Road
Kilburn Park
NW6
BELSIZE
ABBEY ROAD
MAIDA VALE
Maida Vale
Paddington Rec. Grd.
Cricket Ground
W9
WEST KILBURN
KENSAL GREEN
HARROW ROAD
KENSAL TOWN
MAIDA HILL
SHIRLAND ROAD
Paddington Bowl. & Spts. Club
BBC Studios
WESTBOURNE GREEN
Westbourne Park
WESTWAY
A40
Royal Oak
ST. CHARLES HOSPITAL
Carmelite Monastery
NORTH KENSINGTON
Ladbroke Gro.
W11
NOTTING HILL
Latimer Rd.
WESTBOURNE GRO.
BAYSWATER
Bayswater
Queensway
W2
BAYSWATER ROAD
Notting Hill Gate
Holland Park
KENSINGTON GARDENS
The Orangery
Ladbroke Square Gardens
Little Venice

82
A
B
C
D
E
1
2
3
4
5
6
7
64
4
5
81
10
100
Swiss Cottage
South Hampstead
Hilgrove Rd.
Adelaide Rd.
Avenue Rd.
Belsize Rd.
Finchley Rd.
NW3
NW8
W9
Primrose Hill
Reservoir (covered)
Barrow Hill
Primrose Hill
Albert Rd.
Prince Albert Rd.
Regent's Park
The Hub
Winfield House
London Central Mosque
London Zoo
Main Entrance
Running Track
Macclesfield Bridge
Boating Lake
Open Air Theatre
Queen Mary's Gardens
Regent's College
Marylebone
Baker St.
Madame Tussaud's
Abbey Rd.
Maida Vale
St. John's Wood
St. John's Wood Rd.
Wellington Rd.
The Wellington Hosp.
Middlesex CC Club
Lord's Cricket Ground
Lisson Green
Lisson Grove
Grove End Rd.
Edgware Rd.
Marylebone Rd.
Marylebone Flyover
Westway
Warwick Av.
Little Venice
Royal Oak
Paddington
Paddington Basin
St. Mary's Hosp.
Bishop's Bridge Rd.
Eastbourne Ter.
Praed St.
Sussex Gdns.
Bayswater
Bayswater Rd.
Queensway
Lancaster Gate
Marble Arch
Oxford St.
Park Lane
Speakers Corner
Hyde Park
Kensington Gardens
The Long Water
Peter Pan Statue
Speke's Monument
Temple Lodge
The Orangery
Parks Police
The Old Police House & Parks Information Centre
Rangers Lodge
The Look Out
Reformers Tree
Parade Ground
Refreshment Kiosk
St. George's Field
Wigmore St.
Seymour St.
Portman Square
Wallace Collection
Mayfair

F
G
H
J
K
F
G
H
J
K
83
65
84
101
6
7
1
2
3
4
5
6
7
CAMDEN TOWN
Camden Town
Camden Rd
Caledonian Rd. & Barnsbury
PENTONVILLE
KING'S CROSS
ST. PANCRAS INTERNATIONAL
SOMERS TOWN
EUSTON
Euston Sq.
British Library
The Granary Complex & Goods Yard
REGENT'S PARK
Regent's Park
Mornington Cres
Warren St.
Great Portland St.
Goodge St.
Tottenham Ct. R.
Oxford Circus
Piccadilly Circus
Leicester Sq.
Covent Gdn.
Holborn
Russell Sq.
Temple
Embankment
Charing Cross
BLOOMSBURY
British Museum
University College London
ST. PANCRAS
HOLBORN
SOHO
STRAND
Royal Courts of Justice
National Gallery
Somerset Ho.
RIVER THAMES
The London Television Centre
National Theatre
Southbank Cen.
Royal Festival Hall
PARKWAY
DELANCEY ST.
ALBANY STREET
HAMPSTEAD RD.
EUSTON RD.
PENTONVILLE ROAD
YORK WAY
CALEDONIAN RD.
PANCRAS WAY
GOWER ST.
TOTTENHAM COURT RD.
CHARING CROSS RD.
SHAFTESBURY AV.
REGENT ST.
PICCADILLY
KINGSWAY
ALDWYCH
VICTORIA EMBANKMENT
GRAY'S INN RD.
FARRINGDON RD.
THEOBALDS RD.
SOUTHAMPTON ROW
GUILFORD ST.
HIGH HOLBORN
NEW OXFORD ST.
CHANCERY LA.

84
A
B
C
D
E
66
1
2
3
4
5
6
7
7
8
9
83
102
ISLINGTON
Essex Rd.
DE BEAUVOIR TOWN
HOXTON
SHOREDITCH
FINSBURY
CLERKENWELL
HOLBORN
CITY
SOUTHWARK
Angel
Old Street
Farringdon
Barbican
Moorgate
Liverpool St.
St. Paul's
Bank
Mansion Ho.
Monument
Temple
Blackfriars
Cannon Street
City Thameslink
PENTONVILLE RD.
CITY RD.
GOSWELL RD.
ST. JOHN ST.
UPPER ST.
NEW NORTH RD.
OLD ST.
GREAT EASTERN ST.
LIVERPOOL RD.
ESSEX RD.
FARRINGDON RD.
ROSEBERY AV.
CLERKENWELL RD.
HOLBORN
HOLBORN VIADUCT
NEWGATE ST.
CHEAPSIDE
LONDON WALL
BISHOPSGATE
MOORGATE
CORNHILL
LEADENHALL ST.
FENCHURCH ST.
GRACECHURCH ST.
UPPER THAMES ST.
LOWER THAMES ST.
VICTORIA EMB.
STRAND
FLEET ST.
QUEEN VICTORIA ST.
CANNON ST.
SOUTHWARK BRI.
LONDON BR.
BLACKFRIARS BRI.
RIVER THAMES
Barnard Park
Shoreditch Park
Royal Courts of Justice
The Temple
St. Paul's Cath.
St. Bart's Hosp.
Barbican Arts Centre
Tate Modern
National Theatre
Royal Festival Hall
Queen Elizabeth Hall
Millennium Bridge

85
DALSTON
London Fields
SOUTH HACKNEY
67
F
G
H
J
K
Haggerston
HAGGERSTON
Victoria Fountain
Royal Gate East
1
2
3
4
5
6
7
E8
E9
VICTORIA PARK
REGENT'S ROW
Regent's Canal
Hackney City Farm
Cambridge Heath
BISHOP'S WAY
SEWARDSTONE RD.
LONDON CHEST HOSP.
Hoxton
COLUMBIA RD.
HACKNEY RD.
A1208
E2
BETHNAL GREEN
BETHNAL GREEN RD.
A1209
OLD FORD RD.
B118
GLOBE TOWN
ROMAN RD.
Bethnal Grn.
York Hall
MILE END
MILE END HOSPITAL
Queen Mary University of London
Shoreditch High St.
SPITALFIELDS
CHESHIRE ST.
CAMBRIDGE HEATH RD.
A107
Stepney Green
MILE END RD.
A11
Whitechapel
THE ROYAL LONDON HOSP.
WHITECHAPEL RD.
COMMERCIAL ST.
Aldgate East
Aldgate
WHITECHAPEL
COMMERCIAL RD.
E1
STEPNEY
RATCLIFF
A13
Tower Gateway
Tower Hill
CABLE ST.
Shadwell
THE HIGHWAY
A1203
SHADWELL
King Edward Mem. Park
Shadwell Basin
THAMES
RIVER
ROTHERHITHE TUNNEL
The Tower of London
St. Katharine's Pier
Wapping
103
15
98
Limehouse

SOUTH HACKNEY
86
A
B
68
C
D
E
Water Polo Arena
STRATFORD
Aquatics Centre
Olympic Stadium
The Orbit
Olympic Park
Victoria Park Athletics Arena
OLD FORD
E9
VICTORIA PARK
Victoria Fountain
Three Colt Bridge
Skew Bridge
Crown Gate East
Crown Gate West
E20
Warm up Facilities
Pudding Mill Lane
BOW INTERCHANGE
1
2
3
4
5
6
7
EAST CROSS ROUTE
BLACKWALL
A12
ROMAN ROAD
GROVE ROAD
BOW ROAD
Bow Church
Bow Rd.
Grove Hall Park
HIGH STREET
Three-Mills-Wall-River
The House Mill
THREE MILL LA.
BLACKWALL TUNNEL NORTHERN APPROACH
MILE END
MILE END HOSPITAL
Queen Mary University of London
Mile End
E3
BURDETT ROAD
A1205
MILE END ROAD
A11
TOWER HAMLETS CEMETERY PARK
BOW COMMON
BROMLEY
Bromley-by-Bow
DEVAS ROAD
Devons Rd.
DEVONS WAY
B140
85
Mile End Park Leisure Centre
Mile End Stadium
BEN JONSON RD.
ST. PAUL'S WAY
RATCLIFF
LIMEHOUSE
Langdon Pk.
E14
COMMERCIAL ROAD
Limehouse
LIMEHOUSE LINK
EAST INDIA DOCK ROAD
A13
All Saints
POPLAR
Poplar
Westferry
WESTFERRY RD.
WEST INDIA DOCK RD.
ASPEN WAY
A1261
NARROW ST.
RIVER THAMES
LIMEHOUSE REACH
Ratcliff Cross Stairs
West India Quay
Canary Wharf
Billingsgate Market
WEST INDIA DOCKS
Canary Wharf Pier
Hilton Docklands Pier
104
SALTER RD.
B205
BLACKWALL BASIN

WEST HAM PARK
WEST HAM
UPTON
PLASHET
PLAISTOW
CANNING TOWN
LEAMOUTH
Stratford High St.
Abbey Road
West Ham
Star La.
Canning Town
East India
Blackwall
Royal Victoria
Custom House for ExCeL
Prince Regent
Upton Park
Plaistow
East London Crematorium
EAST LONDON CEMETERY
Memorial Recreation Ground
ROYAL VICTORIA DOCK
RIVER THAMES
BOW CREEK
Bow Creek Ecology Park
East India Dock Basin Nature Reserve
Emirates Royal Docks
Royal Victoria Docks Watersports Cen.
London City Airport Pier
Millennium Mill
Newham College
E13
E15
E16
87
88
105
69

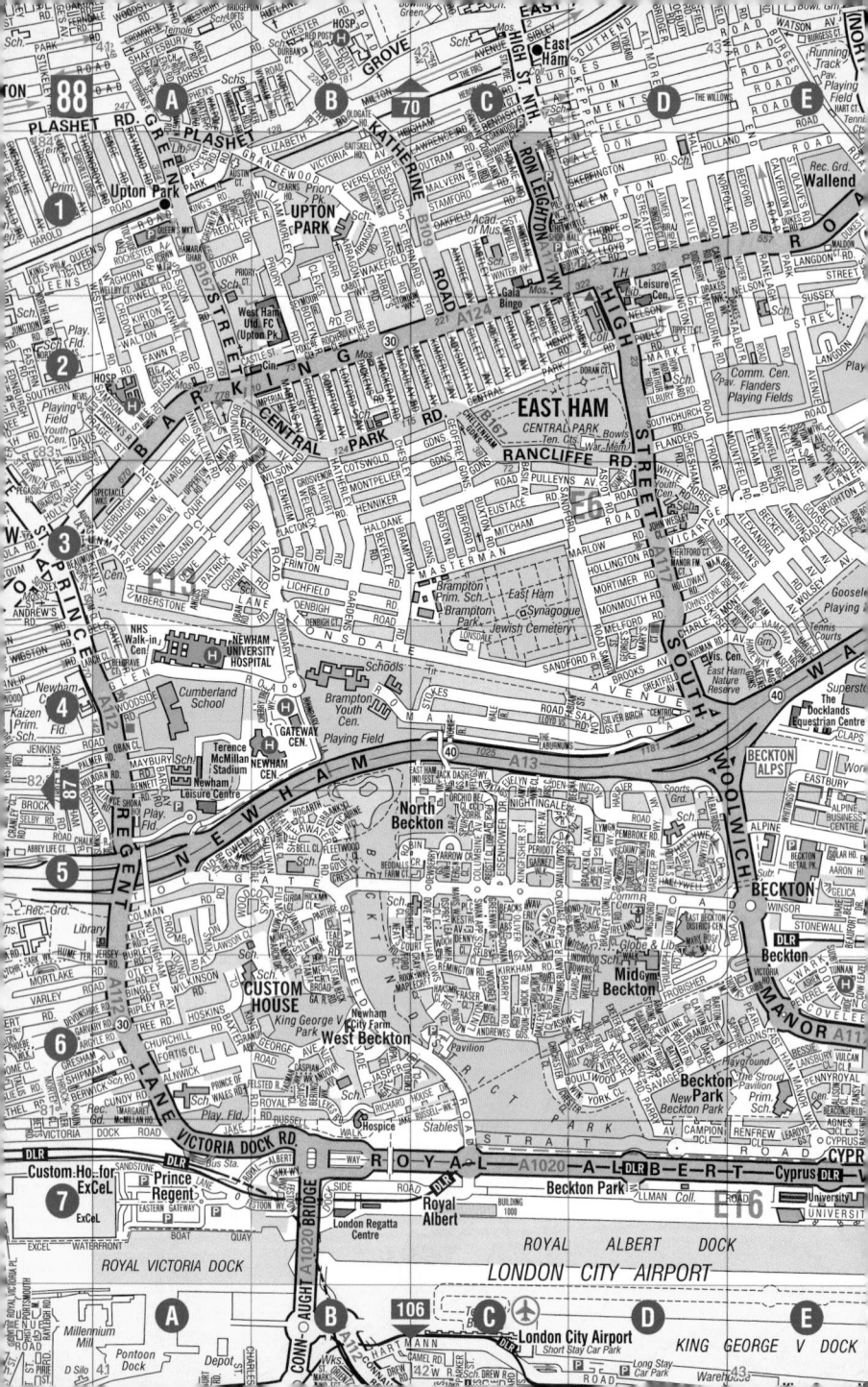

88
70
87
106
A
B
C
D
E
1
2
3
4
5
6
7
Upton Park
UPTON PARK
East Ham
EAST HAM
Wallend
North Beckton
Mid Beckton
West Beckton
BECKTON
Beckton
CUSTOM HOUSE
Prince Regent
Royal Albert
Beckton Park
Cyprus
Custom Ho. for ExCeL
ExCeL
E13
E6
E16
PLASHET RD.
PLASHET GROVE
KATHERINE ROAD
HIGH ST. NTH.
HIGH STREET SOUTH
BARKING ROAD
NEWHAM WAY
REGENT LANE
VICTORIA DOCK RD.
ROYAL ALBERT WAY
WOOLWICH MANOR WAY
CENTRAL PARK RD.
RANCLIFFE RD.
TOLLGATE ROAD
CONNAUGHT BRIDGE
GREEN STREET
RON LEIGHTON WAY
West Ham Utd. FC (Upton Pk.)
NEWHAM UNIVERSITY HOSPITAL
NHS Walk-in Cen.
Cumberland School
Terence McMillan Stadium
Newham Leisure Centre
Brampton Youth Cen.
East Ham Jewish Cemetery
East Ham Nature Reserve
The Docklands Equestrian Centre
BECKTON ALPS
BECKTON RETAIL PK.
King George V Park
Newham City Farm
Beckton Park
New Beckton Park
London Regatta Centre
ROYAL ALBERT DOCK
ROYAL VICTORIA DOCK
LONDON CITY AIRPORT
London City Airport
KING GEORGE V DOCK
Millennium Mill
Pontoon Dock
Comm. Cen. Flanders Playing Fields
Rec. Grd.
Gala Bingo
Leisure Cen.

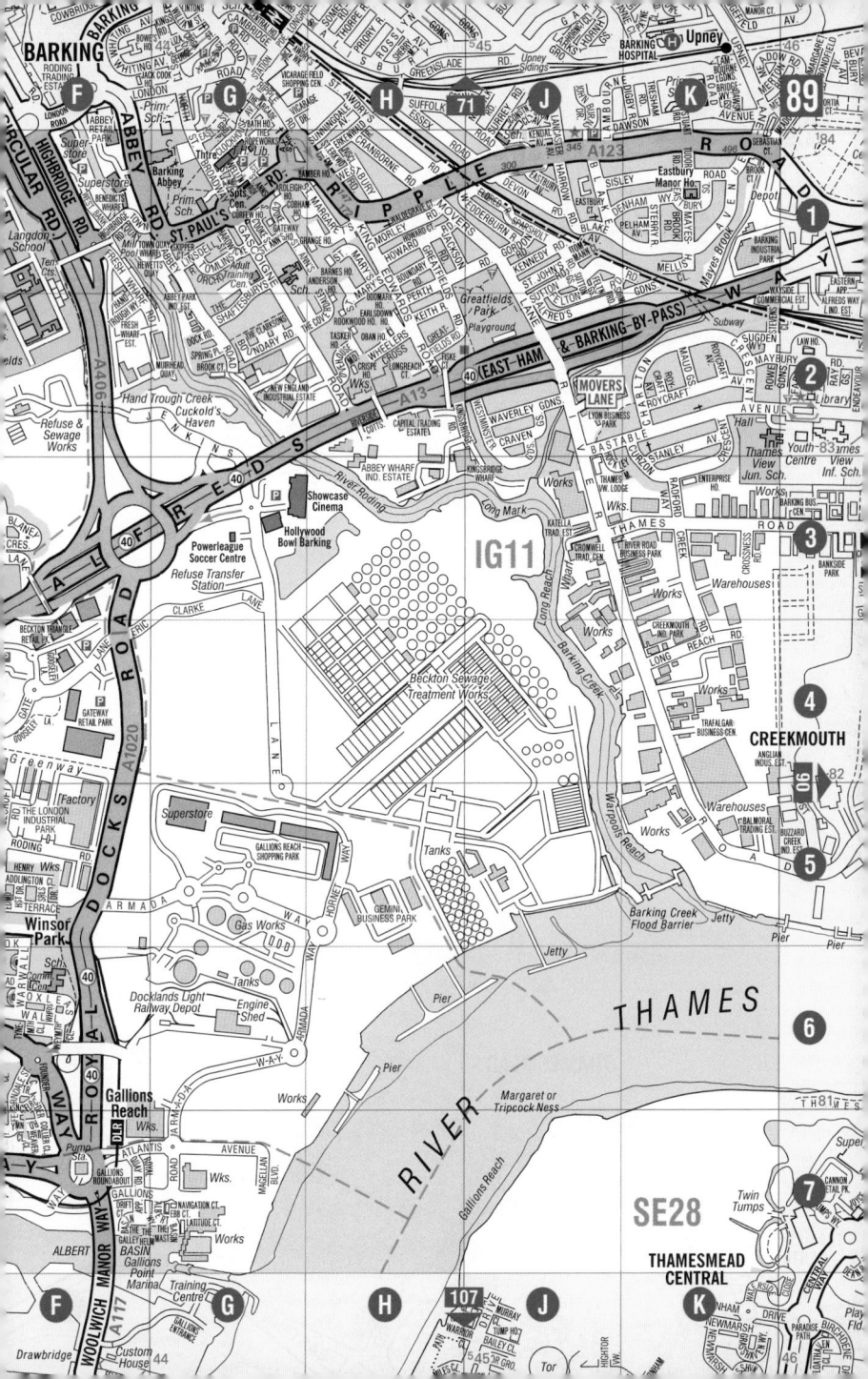

BARKING
89
F
G
H
J
K
71
Upney
BARKING HOSPITAL
RODING TRADING ESTATE
ABBEY RETAIL PARK
Superstore
Barking Abbey
ST. PAUL'S RD.
RIPPLE RD.
A123
Eastbury Manor Ho.
BARKING INDUSTRIAL PARK
Langdon School
Greatfields Park
Playground
EAST HAM & BARKING BY-PASS
A13
MOVERS LANE
LYON BUSINESS PARK
NEW ENGLAND INDUSTRIAL ESTATE
Hand Trough Creek
Cuckold's Haven
Refuse & Sewage Works
ALFREDS WAY
A406
Showcase Cinema
Hollywood Bowl Barking
Powerleague Soccer Centre
Refuse Transfer Station
River Roding
ABBEY WHARF IND. ESTATE
KINGSBRIDGE WHARF
CAPITAL TRADING ESTATE
Long Mark
IG11
THAMES ROAD
RIVER ROAD BUSINESS PARK
CREEKMOUTH IND. PARK
Long Reach
Barking Creek
Beckton Sewage Treatment Works
CREEKMOUTH
ANGLIAN INDUS. EST.
90
82
Warpools Reach
BECKTON TRIANGLE RETAIL PK.
GATEWAY RETAIL PARK
DOCKS ROAD
A1020
Greenway
THE LONDON INDUSTRIAL PARK
Superstore
GALLIONS REACH SHOPPING PARK
Tanks
GEMINI BUSINESS PARK
Gas Works
ARMADA WAY
Winsor Park
Docklands Light Railway Depot
Engine Shed
Barking Creek Flood Barrier
Jetty
Pier
THAMES
RIVER
Margaret or Tripcock Ness
Gallions Reach
Works
SE28
Twin Tumps
THAMESMEAD CENTRAL
Gallions Reach
DLR
ROYAL DOCKS RD.
WOOLWICH MANOR WAY
A117
ALBERT BASIN
Gallions Point Marina
Training Centre
Drawbridge
Custom House
107
1
2
3
4
5
6
7

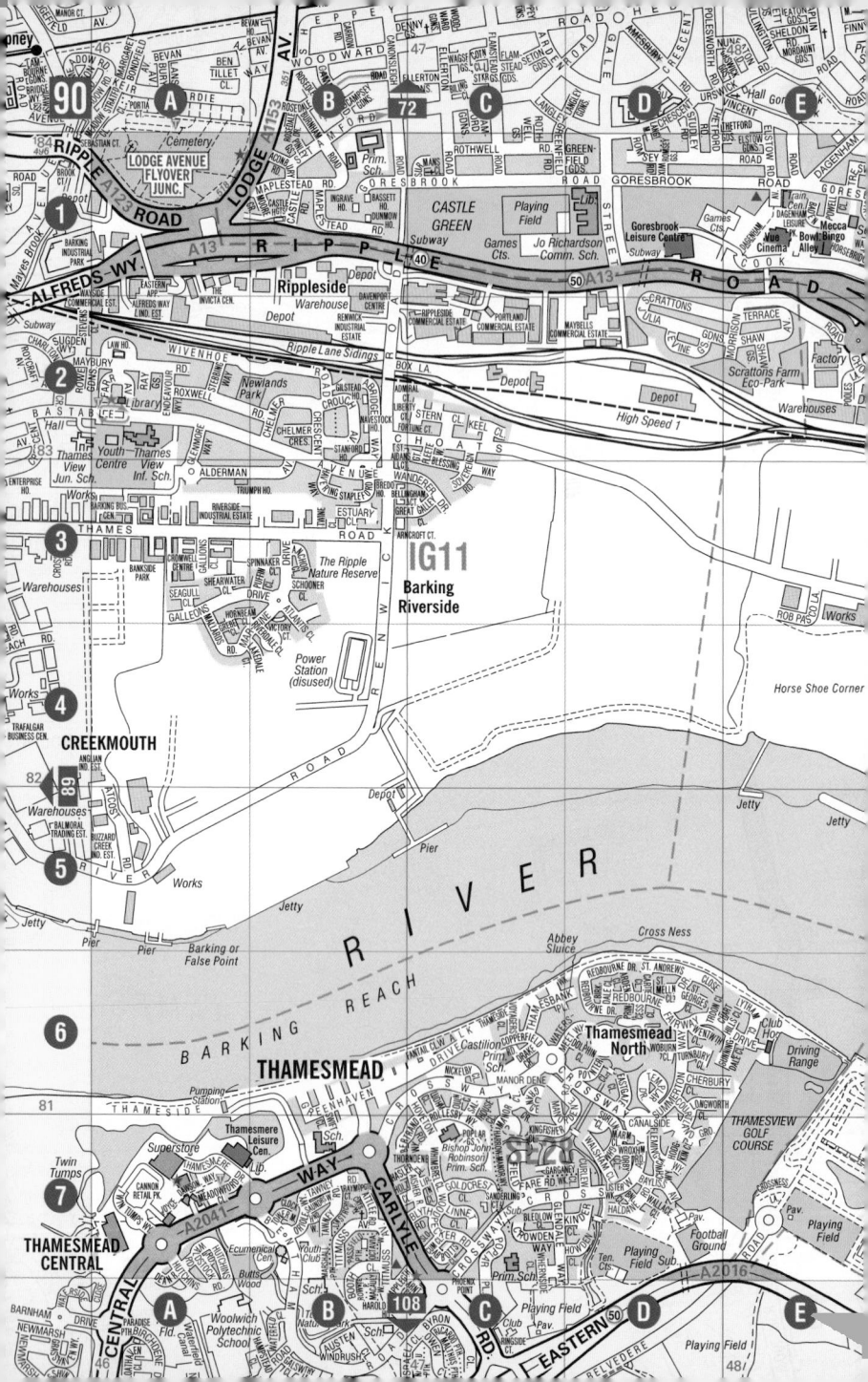
90
72
68
108
A
B
C
D
E
1
2
3
4
5
6
7
LODGE AVENUE FLYOVER JUNC.
Cemetery
RIPPLE ROAD
LODGE AV.
ALFREDS WY.
RIPPLE ROAD
GORESBROOK ROAD
CASTLE GREEN
Playing Field
Jo Richardson Comm. Sch.
Games Cts.
Goresbrook Leisure Centre
Vue Cinema
Bowl. Alley
Mecca Bingo
Rippleside
Warehouse
Depot
Ripple Lane Sidings
High Speed 1
Scrattons Farm Eco-Park
Factory
Warehouses
Newlands Park
Library
Youth Centre
Thames View Jun. Sch.
Thames View Inf. Sch.
THAMES ROAD
RENWICK ROAD
IG11
Barking Riverside
The Ripple Nature Reserve
Power Station (disused)
Horse Shoe Corner
CREEKMOUTH
Works
Jetty
Pier
RIVER
Barking or False Point
BARKING REACH
Abbey Sluice
Cross Ness
THAMESMEAD
Thamesmead North
Driving Range
THAMESVIEW GOLF COURSE
Pumping Station
Thamesmere Leisure Cen.
Superstore
Twin Tumps
THAMESMEAD CENTRAL
WAY CARLYLE
A2041
Woolwich Polytechnic School
Playing Field
Football Ground
SE28
EASTERN WAY
A2016
BELVEDERE

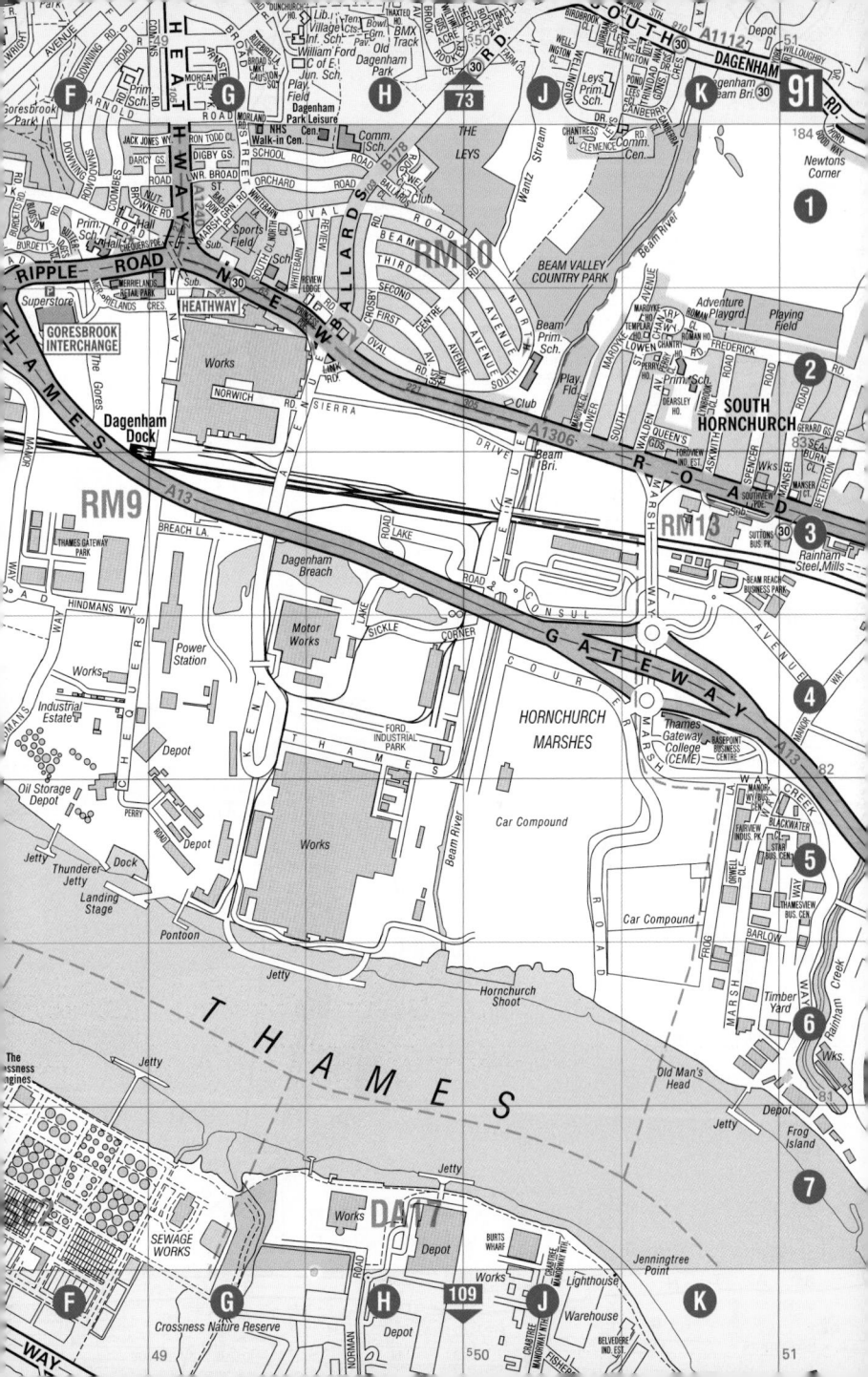
91
73
109
RM10
RM9
RM13
DA17
THE LEYS
BEAM VALLEY COUNTRY PARK
SOUTH HORNCHURCH
HORNCHURCH MARSHES
THAMES
Dagenham Dock
GORESBROOK INTERCHANGE
Dagenham Breach
Motor Works
Power Station
Works
Depot
Car Compound
Oil Storage Depot
Industrial Estate
Thunderer Jetty
Landing Stage
Pontoon
Jetty
Hornchurch Shoot
Old Man's Head
Frog Island
Rainham Creek
Rainham Steel Mills
Timber Yard
Thames Gateway College (CEME)
FORD INDUSTRIAL PARK
THAMES GATEWAY PARK
Adventure Playgrd.
Playing Field
Newtons Corner
Beam Prim. Sch.
Beam River
Wantz Stream
Dagenham Park Leisure Cen.
Comm. Sch.
Old Dagenham Park
BMX Track
William Ford C of E Jun. Sch.
NHS Walk-in Cen.
Leys Prim. Sch.
SEWAGE WORKS
Crossness Nature Reserve
Jenningtree Point
Lighthouse
Warehouse
BURTS WHARF
BELVEDERE IND. EST.
RIPPLE ROAD
HEATHWAY
NEW ROAD
BALLARDS ROAD
SOUTH DAGENHAM RD.
A13
A1306
A1240
A1112
B178
GATEWAY
CONSUL AVENUE
KENT AVENUE
MARSH WAY
FROG ISLAND
FERRY LANE
CHEQUERS LA.
BREACH LA.
HINDMANS WY.
MANOR ROAD
SIERRA DRIVE
THAMES AVENUE
NORWICH RD.
COURIER ROAD
NORMAN ROAD
CRABTREE MANORWAY NTH.
F
G
H
J
K
1
2
3
4
5
6
7
49
550
51
184
83
82
81

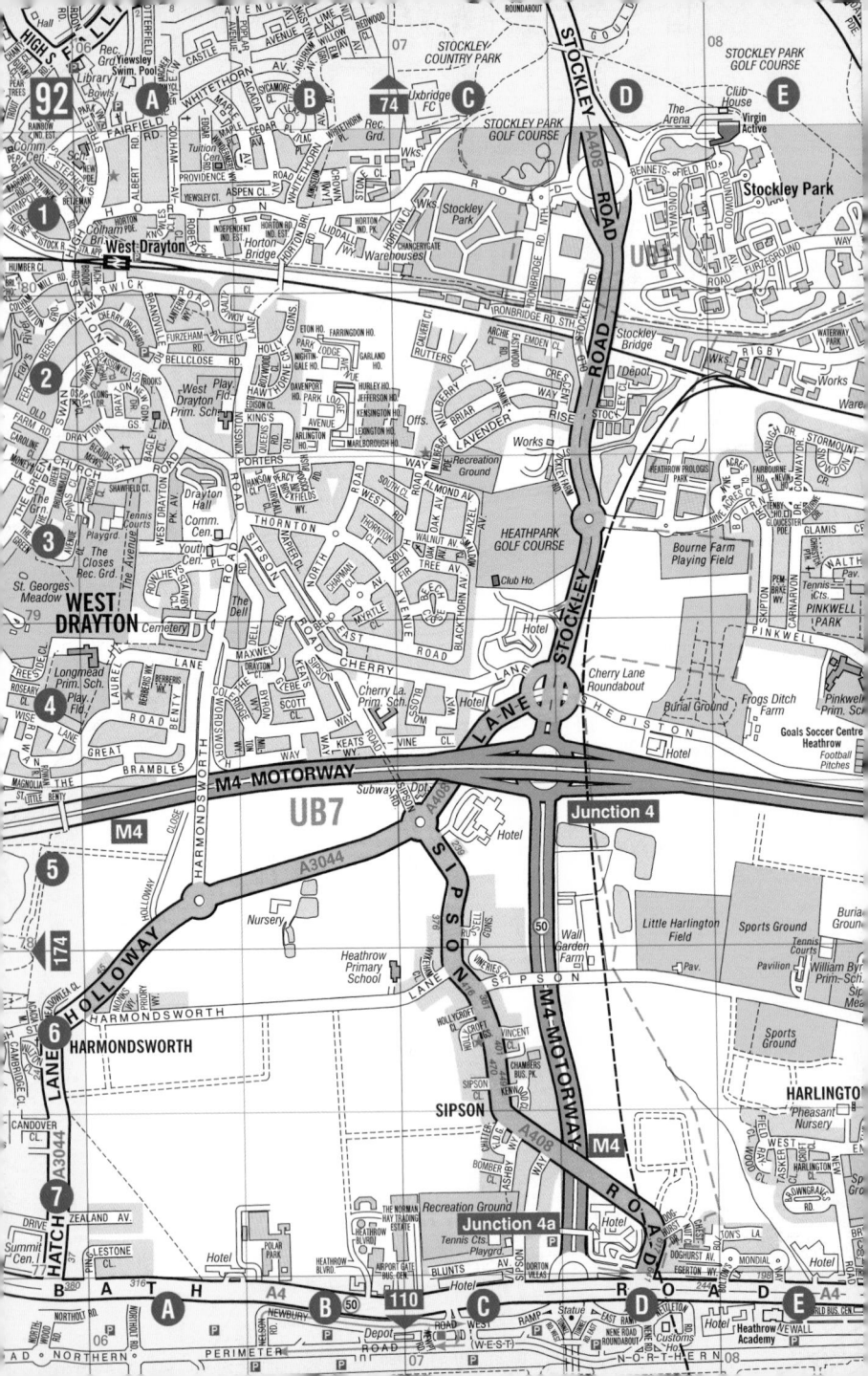
92
74
174
110
A
B
C
D
E
1
2
3
4
5
6
7
06
07
08
79
78
77
80
STOCKLEY COUNTRY PARK
STOCKLEY PARK GOLF COURSE
Club House
The Arena
Virgin Active
Uxbridge FC
Rec. Grd.
Yiewsley Swim. Pool
Library
Bowls
Rec. Grd
FAIRFIELD RD.
WHITETHORN AV.
CASTLE AVENUE
POPLAR AVENUE
LIME AV.
REDWOOD CL.
WILLOW AV.
ELM AV.
SYCAMORE CL.
ACACIA AV.
MAPLE AV.
CEDAR AV.
LILAC PL.
WHITETHORN PL.
ALBERT RD.
COLHAM AV.
PROVIDENCE RD.
YIEWSLEY CT.
ASPEN CL.
STONE CL.
CROWN WY.
KINGSTON WY.
RAINBOW IND. EST.
Comm. Cen.
Sch.
NEW PDE.
WIMPOLE RD.
BETJEMAN CL.
STEPHEN'S RD.
HIGH ST.
HORTON RD.
Colham Bri.
HORTON PDE.
STA. APP.
West Drayton
INDEPENDENT IND. EST.
HORTON RD. IND. EST.
Horton Bridge
HORTON BRI. RD.
LIDDALL WY.
HORTON IND. PK.
HORTON CL.
Wks.
CHANCERYGATE
Warehouses
Stockley Park
STOCKLEY ROAD
A408
IRONBRIDGE RD. NTH.
IRONBRIDGE RD. STH.
BENNETS-FIELD RD.
LONGWALK RD.
ROUNDWOOD
Stockley Park
FURZEGROUND WAY
UB11
Stockley Bridge
RIGBY LANE
WATERWAY PARK
Works
HUMBER CL.
WARWICK ROAD
STATION RD.
COLHAM MILL RD.
HILTON GRO.
BRANDVILLE RD.
LANTERN WY.
FURZEHAM RD.
CHERRY ORCHARD
BELLCLOSE RD.
Frays River
SWAN RD.
OSPREY CL.
LONG DR.
DRAYTON GS.
Lib.
West Drayton Prim. Sch.
Play. Fld.
HOLLY GDNS.
ETON HO.
FARRINGDON HO.
PARK LODGE AVENUE
GARLAND HO.
HUBLEY HO.
JEFFERSON HO.
KENSINGTON HO.
LEXINGTON HO.
MARLBOROUGH HO.
DAVENPORT HO.
ARLINGTON HO.
HAWTHORNE CR.
BOXWOOD WY.
EDISON CL.
KING'S
QUEENS RD.
PORTERS WAY
Offs.
CALVERT CT.
RUTTERS CL.
ARCHIE CL.
EASTWOOD RD.
EMDEN CL.
CRESCENT WAY
MULBERRY CRES.
BRIAR WAY
JASMINE
LAVENDER RISE
Depot
STOCKLEY CL.
Works
Recreation Ground
MULBERRY PDE.
HEATHROW PROLOGIS PARK
OLD FARM RD.
CAROLINE CL.
CHURCH RD.
THE GREEN
The Grn.
BEAUDESERT MEWS
SHAWFIELD CT.
WEST DRAYTON ROAD
PK. AV.
Drayton Hall
Comm. Cen.
Youth Cen.
Tennis Courts
Playgrd.
The Closes Rec. Grd.
The Avenue
THORNTON AV.
ALMOND AV.
OAK AV.
HAZEL AV.
WALNUT AV.
TREE AV.
FIR TREE AV.
BEECH CL.
BLACKTHORN AV.
NORTH AVENUE
SOUTH CL.
WEST RD.
THORNTON CL.
CHAPMAN CL.
MYRTLE CL.
EAST ROAD
HEATHPARK GOLF COURSE
Club Ho.
Hotel
DENBIGH DR.
STORMOUNT DR.
SNOWDON CR.
CONWAY DR.
FAIRBOURNE HO.
NEVIN HO.
WYNE ACRES
NINE ACRES CL.
BOURNE AV.
TENBY HO.
GLOUCESTER PDE.
GLAMIS CR.
Bourne Farm Playing Field
SKIPTON DR.
PEMBROKE WY.
CARNARVON DR.
Tennis Cts.
PINKWELL PARK
PINKWELL LA.
St. Georges Meadow
WEST DRAYTON
Cemetery
ROWLHEYS PL.
STAINBY CL.
The Dell
DELL RD.
NAPIER CL.
SIPSON ROAD
MAXWELL RD.
DRAYTON CT.
GLEBE RD.
KEATS WY.
SCOTT CL.
BYRON WY.
COLERIDGE WY.
WORDSWORTH RD.
CHERRY LANE
Cherry La. Prim. Sch.
BLOSSOM WAY
Cherry Lane Roundabout
SHEPISTON LANE
Burial Ground
Frogs Ditch Farm
Hotel
Pinkwell Prim. Sch.
Goals Soccer Centre Heathrow
Football Pitches
Longmead Prim. Sch.
Play. Fld.
TREESIDE CL.
ROSEARY CL.
WISE LANE
ROWAN RD.
LAUREL LANE
BERBERIS WK.
BENTY ROAD
GREAT BRAMBLES
VINE CL.
MAGNOLIA ST.
THE LITTLE BENTY
M4 MOTORWAY
M4
Subway
Dpt.
UB7
Junction 4
HARMONDSWORTH LANE
CLOSE
HOLLOWAY CLOSE
A3044
HOLLOWAY LANE
Nursery
Hotel
SIPSON ROAD
RUSSELL GDNS.
VINERIES CL.
Heathrow Primary School
SIPSON LANE
Wall Garden Farm
Little Harlington Field
Pav.
Sports Ground
Tennis Courts
Pavilion
William Byrd Prim. Sch.
Sports Ground
MONKS WY.
PRIORY WY.
MEADOWLEA CL.
HARMONDSWORTH
HOLLYCROFT CL.
HOLLYCROFT GDNS.
VINCENT CL.
CHAMBERS BUS. PK.
SIPSON CL.
KENWOOD DR.
SIPSON
CHITTERFIELD
BOMBER CL.
ASHBY WY.
M4 MOTORWAY
HARLINGTON
Pheasant Nursery
FIELD RD.
WEST END
WOOD CL.
TASKER CL.
HARLINGTON CL.
BROWNGRAVES RD.
CAMBRIDGE CL.
CANDOVER CL.
HATCH LANE
A3044
ZEALAND AV.
DRIVE
Summit Cen.
PINGLESTONE CL.
Hotel
POLAR PARK
THE NORMAN HAY TRADING ESTATE
HEATHROW BLVRD.
AIRPORT GATE BUS. CEN.
Recreation Ground
Junction 4a
Tennis Cts.
Playgrd.
BLUNTS AV.
SIPSON DORTON VILLAS
Hotel
DOGHURST DR.
DOGHURST AV.
EGERTON WY.
BOLTON'S LA.
MONDIAL WAY
Hotel
BATH ROAD
A4
NORTHOLT RD.
NEWBURY RD.
NELSON RD.
Depot
ROAD WEST
RAMP
Statue
EAST RAMP
NENE ROAD ROUNDABOUT
NETTLETON RD.
Customs Ho.
Hotel
Heathrow Academy
NEWALL RD.
NORTHERN PERIMETER ROAD (WEST)
NORTHERN

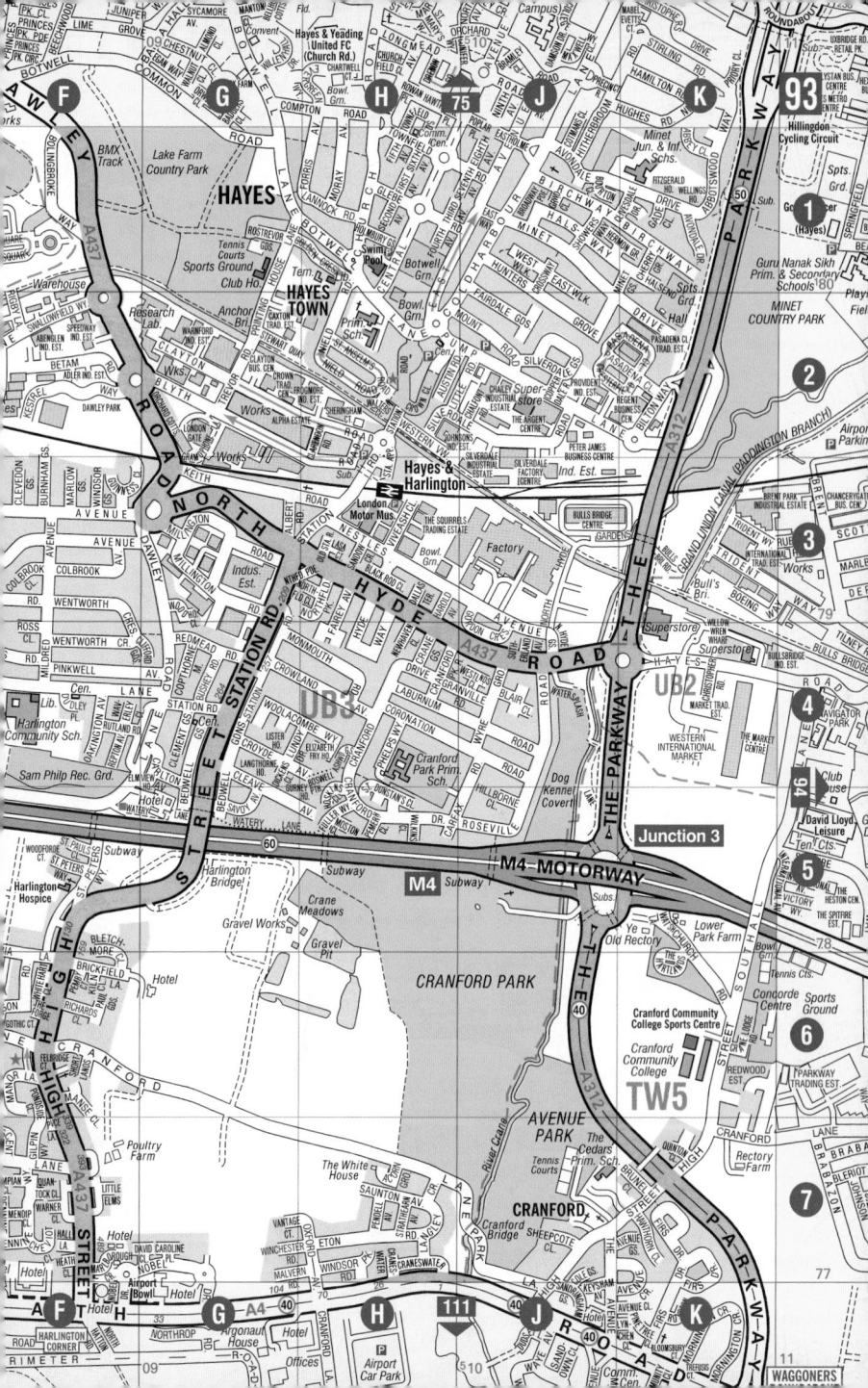

93
75
94
111
F
G
H
J
K
1
2
3
4
5
6
7
09
510
11
77
78
79
80
HAYES
HAYES TOWN
CRANFORD
UB3
UB2
TW5
Hayes & Yeading United FC (Church Rd.)
Lake Farm Country Park
BMX Track
Hillingdon Cycling Circuit
MINET COUNTRY PARK
Minet Jun. & Inf. Schs.
Guru Nanak Sikh Prim. & Secondary Schools
Hayes & Harlington
London Motor Mus.
Swim. Pool
Botwell Grn.
Superstore
Factory
Indus. Est.
Research Lab.
Sports Ground
Tennis Courts
Club Ho.
Warehouse
Works
Anchor Bri.
Harlington Community Sch.
Sam Philp Rec. Grd.
Cranford Park Prim. Sch.
Dog Kennel Covert
Junction 3
M4 MOTORWAY
M4
Subway
Harlington Bridge
Harlington Hospice
Crane Meadows
Gravel Works
Gravel Pit
CRANFORD PARK
WESTERN INTERNATIONAL MARKET
THE MARKET CENTRE
GRAND UNION CANAL (PADDINGTON BRANCH)
BRENT PARK INDUSTRIAL ESTATE
Bull's Bri.
David Lloyd Leisure
Ye Old Rectory
Lower Park Farm
Cranford Community College Sports Centre
Cranford Community College
Concorde Centre
Sports Ground
REDWOOD EST.
PARKWAY TRADING EST.
Rectory Farm
AVENUE PARK
The Cedars Prim. Sch.
River Crane
Cranford Bridge
The White House
Poultry Farm
Airport Bowl
Argonaut House
HARLINGTON CORNER
Airport Car Park
Offices
THE PARKWAY
NORTH HYDE ROAD
STATION RD.
HIGH STREET
DAWLEY ROAD
BOTWELL COMMON ROAD
BATH ROAD
A437
A312
A4

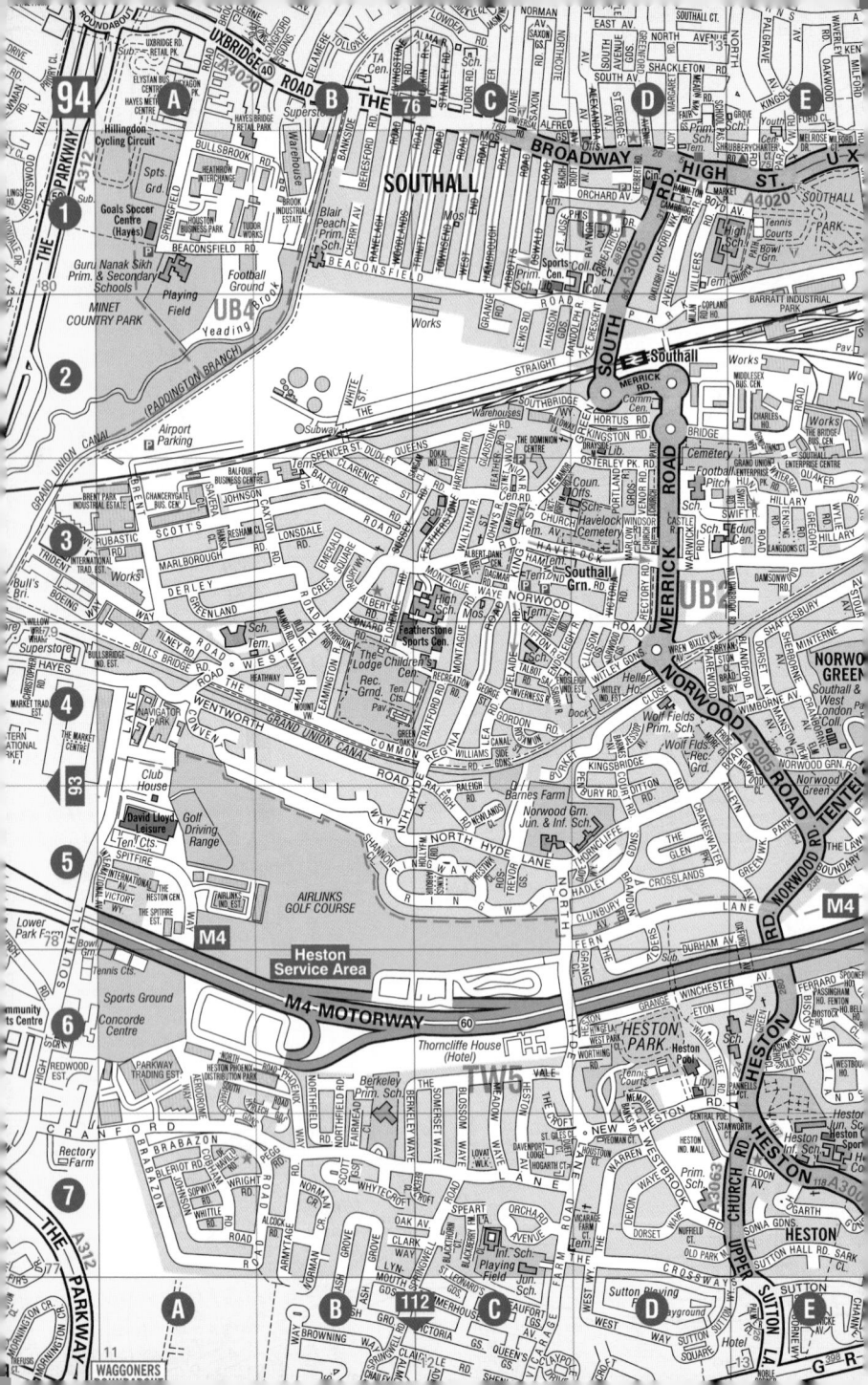

94
93
76
112
A
B
C
D
E
1
2
3
4
5
6
7
SOUTHALL
UB4
UB1
UB2
TW5
UXBRIDGE ROAD
BROADWAY
HIGH ST.
A4020
A3005
A3063
A312
THE PARKWAY
SOUTH RD.
MERRICK ROAD
NORWOOD ROAD
GRAND UNION CANAL
M4
M4 MOTORWAY
Heston Service Area
AIRLINKS GOLF COURSE
MINET COUNTRY PARK
Hillingdon Cycling Circuit
Goals Soccer Centre (Hayes)
Guru Nanak Sikh Prim. & Secondary Schools
Football Ground
Playing Field
Airport Parking
Southall
Havelock Cemetery
Southall Grn.
Featherstone Sports Cen.
The Lodge Rec. Grnd.
Wolf Fields Prim. Sch.
Norwood Grn. Jun. & Inf. Sch.
Barnes Farm
David Lloyd Leisure
Golf Driving Range
Sports Ground
Concorde Centre
Thorncliffe House (Hotel)
HESTON PARK
Heston Pool
Berkeley Prim. Sch.
Rectory Farm
HESTON
NORWOOD GREEN
Sutton Playing Fields
NORTH HYDE LANE
CRANFORD LANE
HESTON RD.
WAGGONERS ROUNDABOUT

DORMER'S WELLS
WEST MIDDLESEX GOLF COURSE
Brent Lodge Park
Millennium Maze
River Brent
Churchfields Rec. Grd.
Hanwell
Kensington Cemetery
UXBRIDGE RD.
BROADWAY
A4020
City of Westminster Cemetery
HANWELL
Oaklands Primary Sch.
ST. BERNARD'S HOSPITAL
EALING HOSP.
Meadow Ho. Hospice
GREAT WESTERN INDUSTRIAL PARK
Hanwell Locks
Windmill Bridge
Glade Lane Canalside Park
GRAND UNION CANAL
BOSTON RD.
A3002
W7
Osterley Sports Club
Sports Ground
Games Courts
Warren Farm Sports Centre
WINDMILL LANE
B454
The Aviary
Elthorne Park
Elthorne Park High Sch.
Elthorne Sports Cen.
Playing Field
Osterley Lock
Wincott Farm
OSTERLEY
M4 MOTORWAY
M4
Long Wood
Trumpers Wood
OSTERLEY LANE
Osterley Park Farm
Bothy Cottage
Osterley Park House
PARK
TW7
WYKE GREEN GOLF COURSE
Garden Cen.
SYON LANE
Club House
Sports Ground
OSTERLEY
JERSEY ROAD
Playing Field
A4
GREAT WEST ROAD
Osterley
Isleworth Crown Court
Education Service
SPRING GROVE
95
96
77
113

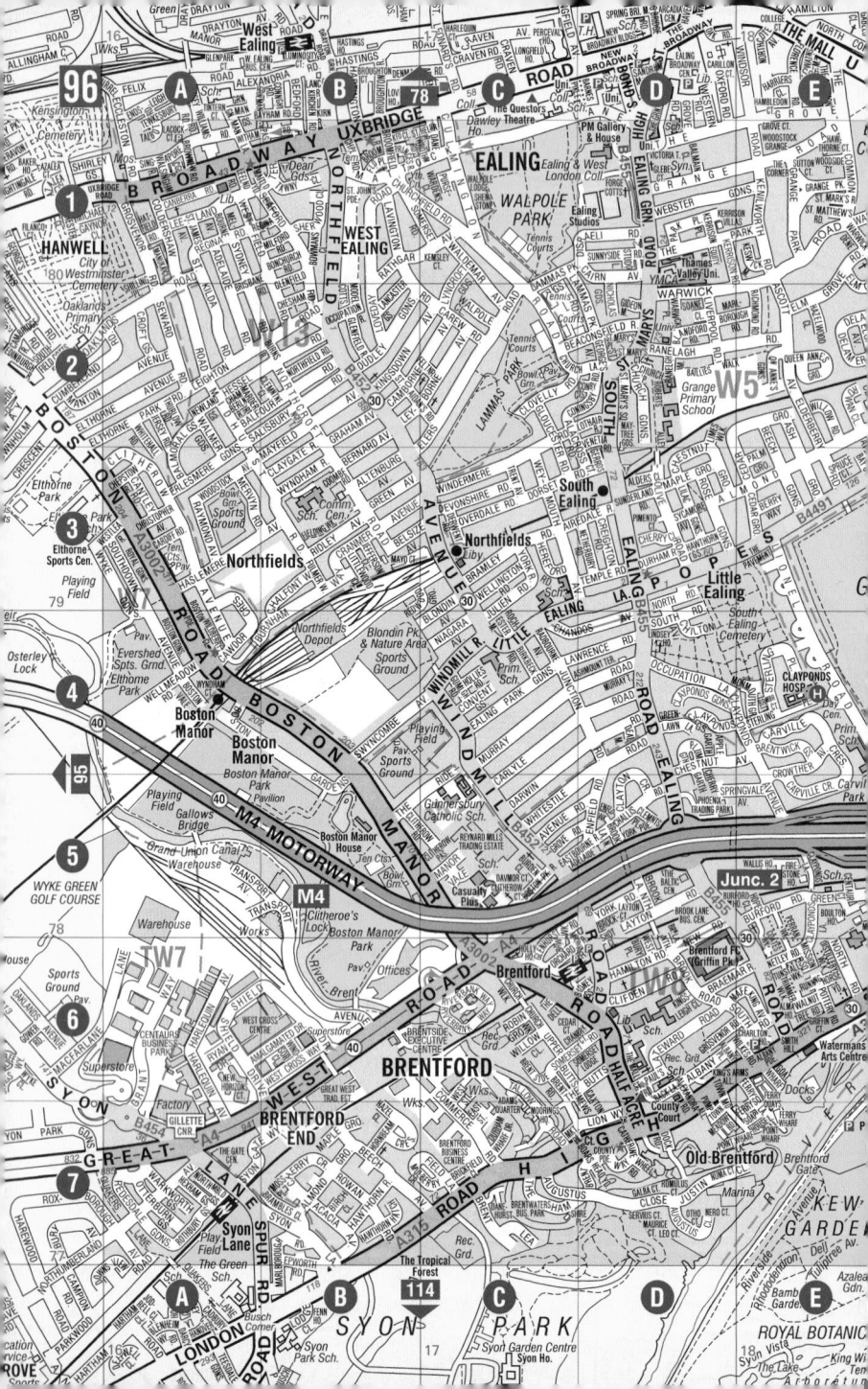

96
78
95
114
A
B
C
D
E
1
2
3
4
5
6
7
West Ealing
EALING
Ealing & West London Coll.
PM Gallery & House
WALPOLE PARK
Ealing Studios
Thames Valley Uni.
The Questors Theatre
Dawley Ho.
HANWELL
City of Westminster Cemetery
Kensington Cemetery
Oaklands Primary Sch.
WEST EALING
W13
W5
W7
TW7
TW8
Grange Primary School
LAMMAS PARK
South Ealing
Northfields
Northfields Depot
Blondin Pk. & Nature Area
Sports Ground
Little Ealing
South Ealing Cemetery
CLAYPONDS HOSP.
Elthorne Park
Elthorne Sports Cen.
Playing Field
Osterley Lock
Evershed Spts. Grnd.
Boston Manor
Boston Manor Park
Boston Manor House
Gunnersbury Catholic Sch.
Reynard Mills Trading Estate
Casualty Plus
Pavilion
Gallows Bridge
Grand Union Canal
Warehouse
WYKE GREEN GOLF COURSE
M4 MOTORWAY
M4
Junc. 2
Clitheroe's Lock
River Brent
Brentford
Brentford FC (Griffin Pk.)
BRENTFORD
BRENTFORD END
Old Brentford
Watermans Arts Centre
Brentside Executive Centre
Great West Trad. Est.
West Cross Centre
Centaurs Business Park
Superstore
Factory
GILLETTE CNR.
County Court
Syon Lane
The Green Sch.
Busch Corner
Syon Park Sch.
SYON PARK
Syon Garden Centre
Syon Ho.
The Tropical Forest
Rec. Grd.
Marina
KEW GARDE
ROYAL BOTANIC
Brentford Gate
Riverside Avenue
Rhododendron Dell
Tulip Tree Av.
Azalea Gdn.
Bamboo Garden
Syon Vista
The Lake
UXBRIDGE ROAD
BROADWAY
NORTHFIELD AVENUE
BOSTON ROAD
BOSTON MANOR ROAD
WINDMILL ROAD
SOUTH EALING ROAD
POPES LA.
GREAT WEST ROAD
HIGH ROAD
HALF ACRE
LONDON ROAD
SYON LANE
SPUR RD.
A3002
A4
A315
B452
B454
B455
B4491

97
EAST ACTON
ACTON
Ealing Common
GUNNERSBURY
A406
A4020
A4000
HIGH ST.
THE VALE
Acton Central
ACTON PARK
SOUTH ACTON
Acton Town
GUNNERSBURY LANE
South Acton
ACTON GREEN
SOUTHFIELD
BEDFORD PARK
Southfields Rec. Grd.
London Transport Mus. Depot
Reynolds Sports Cen.
Gunnersbury Park Mus.
Boating Lake
Miniature Golf Course
PARK
International Sch. of London
Kensington Cemetery
Acton Sports Club
Esporta Health Club Chiswick Park
CHISWICK PARK
Chiswick Pk.
SOUTH PARADE
CHISWICK HIGH RD.
M4 MOTORWAY
M4
Junc.1
Gunnersbury
Kew Bridge
Steam Mus.
Brentford Fountain Leis. Cen.
KEW BRIDGE
WELLESLEY RD.
CEDARS RD.
ELLESMERE RD.
A4
A315
A3000
A205
A307
A316
TURNHAM GREEN
W3
W4
TW9
CHISWICK
Chiswick House
Chiswick Ho. Grds.
Cricket Ground
Strand on the Green
Oliver's Island
The National Archives
Kew Green
KEW
Kew Gardens Gallery
Kew Gds.
Chiswick
Chiswick Cemetery
GROVE PARK
BURLINGTON LANE
HEATHFIELD TER.
79
98
115

98
EAST ACTON
White City
80
97
116
A
B
C
D
E
1
2
3
4
5
6
7
The Park Club
Sports Cricket Ground Grd.
Football Pitch
Virgin Active
Recreation Ground
The King Fahad Academy
Wormholt Park
QPR FC (Loftus Rd.)
BBC Television Centre
Shepherd's Bush Mkt.
UXBRIDGE ROAD
THE VALE
A4020
W12
ASKEW RD.
Wendell Park
Cathnor Park
Goldhawk Rd.
SOUTHFIELD RD.
BEDFORD PARK
THE AVENUE
BATH RD.
Turnham Green
Stamford Brook
GOLDHAWK RD.
Ravenscourt Park
Adventure Playground
PADDENSWICK RD.
W6
Hammersmith
KING ST.
GLENTHORNE ROAD
CHISWICK HIGH RD.
A315
CHISWICK LA.
A316
W4
Health Club
Homefield Recreation Ground
GREAT WEST ROAD
A4
HAMMERSMITH ROAD
TURNHAM GREEN
HOGARTH LA.
Hammersmith Pier
Chiswick Eyot
Brewery
St. Pauls School
Playing Field
Riverside Studios
CHISWICK
Chiswick House
BURLINGTON LA.
ALEXANDRA AV.
LONSDALE ROAD
The Harrodian Sch.
Lonsdale Road Reservoir Local Nature Reserve
Riverside Recreation Ground
SW13
CASTELNAU
Castelnau
A306
HAMMERSMITH BRI.
LONDON WETLAND CENTRE
The Wetland Centre
RIVER THAMES
Sports Ground

NOTTING HILL
KENSINGTON
HOLLAND PARK
Holland Park
King George VI Memorial Youth Hostel
Theatre
Holland Ho.
Cricket Field
Notting Hill Gate
Holland Park
Shepherd's Bush
Kensington Olympia
Olympia
High St. Kensington
Kensington Palace
The Orangery
KENSINGTON GARDENS
Round Pond
Gloucester Rd.
SOUTH KENSINGTON
WEST KENSINGTON
West Kensington
Barons Court
Earl's Court
EARL'S COURT
Earls Court Exhibition Building
West Brompton
WEST BROMPTON
Brompton Cemetery
SW10
Brompton Park
Chelsea FC (Stamford Bridge)
Fulham Broadway
The London Oratory Sch.
Brook Green
HAMMERSMITH
CHARING CROSS HOSP.
Hammersmith Cemetery
The Queen's Club
Fulham Pools
Fulham Cross Girls' Sch. & Coll.
Fulham Cemetery
FULHAM
WALHAM GREEN
Eel Brook Common
SANDS END
Imperial Wharf
Gas Works
Bayswater
Queensway
BAYSWATER RD.
HOLLAND PARK AVENUE
HOLLAND ROAD
KENSINGTON HIGH STREET
KENSINGTON RD.
CROMWELL ROAD
WEST CROMWELL RD.
TALGARTH RD.
NORTH END ROAD
EARLS COURT ROAD
OLD BROMPTON ROAD
BROMPTON RD.
FINBOROUGH RD.
REDCLIFFE GDNS.
LILLIE ROAD
DAWES ROAD
FULHAM ROAD
FULHAM PALACE ROAD
KING'S RD.
WARWICK RD.
ADDISON RD.
CHURCH ST.
KENSINGTON CHURCH
A4
A315
A3220
A402
A3218
A3219
A304
A308
A219
B405
B450
B317
B325
F
G
H
J
K
1
2
3
4
5
6
7
24
25
26
81
99
100
117

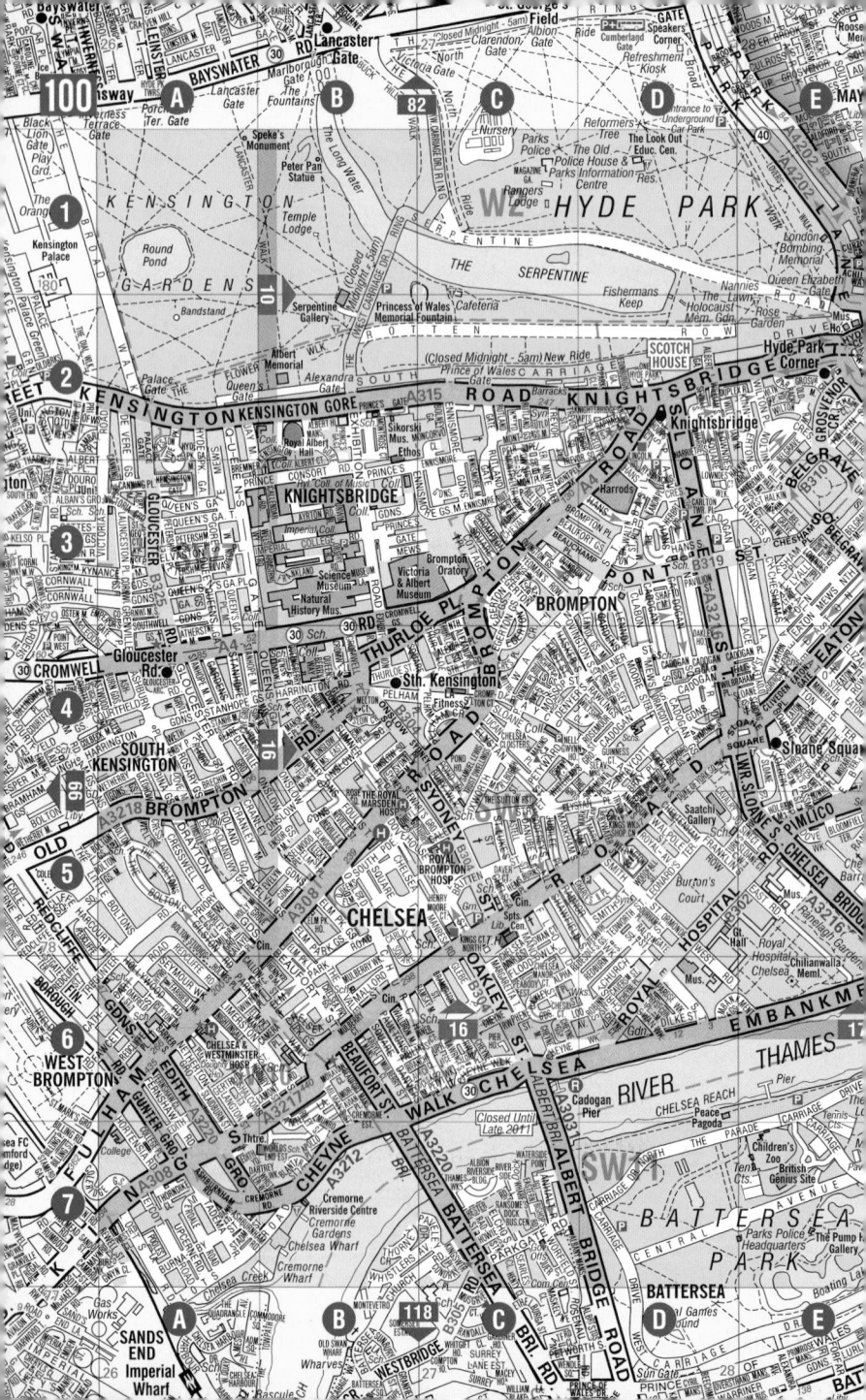

100
A
B
C
D
E
1
2
3
4
5
6
7
82
10
16
99
118
KENSINGTON GARDENS
HYDE PARK
W2
THE SERPENTINE
Round Pond
Kensington Palace
Speke's Monument
Peter Pan Statue
The Long Water
Serpentine Gallery
Princess of Wales Memorial Fountain
Albert Memorial
Royal Albert Hall
KENSINGTON GORE
KENSINGTON ROAD
KNIGHTSBRIDGE
Knightsbridge
Harrods
Hyde Park Corner
BAYSWATER RD
Lancaster Gate
Speakers' Corner
Science Museum
Natural History Mus.
Victoria & Albert Museum
Brompton Oratory
Imperial College
CROMWELL RD
Gloucester Rd.
Sth. Kensington
SOUTH KENSINGTON
BROMPTON
BROMPTON ROAD
FULHAM ROAD
THE ROYAL MARSDEN HOSP
ROYAL BROMPTON HOSP
CHELSEA & WESTMINSTER HOSP
CHELSEA
KINGS RD.
Sloane Square
SLOANE ST.
Saatchi Gallery
Royal Hospital Chelsea
CHELSEA EMBANKMENT
CHEYNE WALK
THAMES
RIVER
CHELSEA REACH
Cadogan Pier
Peace Pagoda
Children's Zoo
BATTERSEA PARK
BATTERSEA
ALBERT BRIDGE ROAD
BATTERSEA BRI. RD.
Cremorne Riverside Centre
Cremorne Gardens
Chelsea Wharf
Chelsea Creek
Gas Works
SANDS END
Imperial Wharf
WEST BROMPTON
OLD BROMPTON ROAD
REDCLIFFE
BELGRAVIA
EATON
PIMLICO RD.

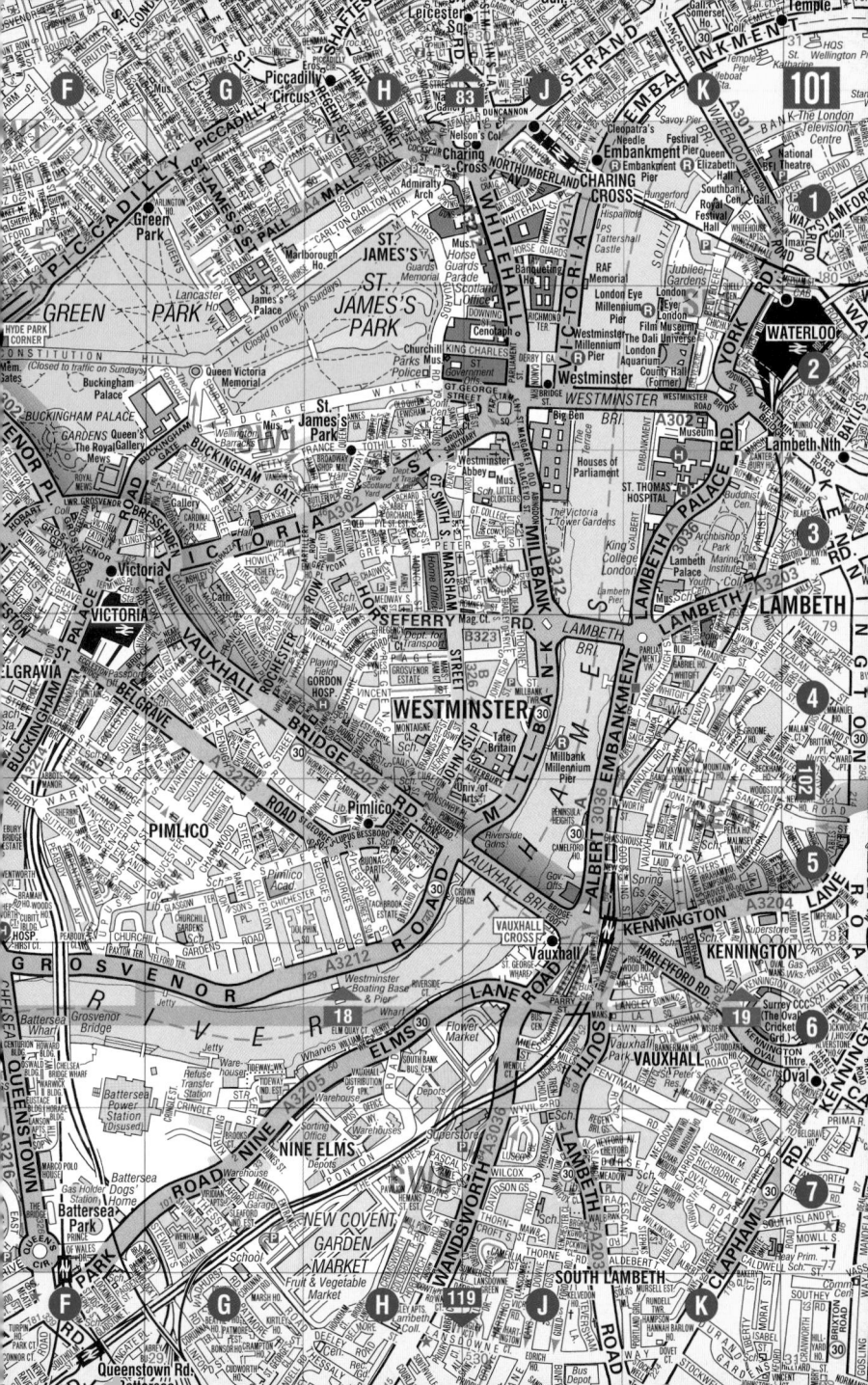
F
G
H
J
K
83
Leicester Sq.
Temple
Piccadilly Circus
STRAND
EMBANKMENT
WATERLOO
The London Television Centre
National Theatre
Savoy Pier
Festival Pier
Queen Elizabeth Hall
Cleopatra's Needle
Embankment
Embankment Pier
CHARING CROSS
Charing Cross
Nelson's Col.
Admiralty Arch
NORTHUMBERLAND AV.
Hungerford Bri.
Royal Festival Hall
Southbank Cen.
PICCADILLY
Green Park
GREEN PARK
ST. JAMES'S ST.
PALL MALL
Marlborough Ho.
Lancaster Ho.
St. James's Palace
ST. JAMES'S PARK
Guards Memorial
Horse Guards Parade
Scotland Office
WHITEHALL
Banqueting Ho.
Hispaniola
PS Tattershall Castle
RAF Memorial
London Eye Millennium Pier
London Eye
Film Museum
The Dali Universe
London Aquarium
County Hall (Former)
Jubilee Gardens
YORK RD.
Imax
1
2
3
4
5
6
7
HYDE PARK CORNER
CONSTITUTION HILL
(Closed to traffic on Sundays)
Queen Victoria Memorial
Buckingham Palace
BUCKINGHAM PALACE GARDENS
Queen's Gallery
The Royal Mews
Wellington Barracks
BIRDCAGE WALK
Cenotaph
Churchill Mus.
Parks Police
Westminster Millennium Pier
Westminster
WESTMINSTER BRI.
Big Ben
Houses of Parliament
The Victoria Tower Gardens
Museum
ST. THOMAS' HOSPITAL
Lambeth Nth.
Archbishop's Park
Lambeth Palace
King's College London
St. James's Park
TOTHILL ST.
Westminster Abbey
BUCKINGHAM GATE
VICTORIA ST.
Victoria
VICTORIA
Home Office
HORSEFERRY RD.
Dept. for Transport
LAMBETH BRI.
LAMBETH
MILLBANK
VAUXHALL BRIDGE RD.
BELGRAVIA
WESTMINSTER
Tate Britain
Millbank Millennium Pier
Univ. of Arts
PIMLICO
Pimlico
Riverside Gdns.
ALBERT EMBANKMENT
KENNINGTON
VAUXHALL BRI.
Vauxhall
VAUXHALL CROSS
GROSVENOR ROAD
RIVER THAMES
Westminster Boating Base & Pier
18
19
102
Battersea Power Station (Disused)
Grosvenor Bridge
NINE ELMS
NINE ELMS LANE
Flower Market
SOUTH LAMBETH RD.
Vauxhall Park
VAUXHALL
Surrey CCC (The Oval Cricket Grd.)
Oval
KENNINGTON OVAL
NEW COVENT GARDEN MARKET
Fruit & Vegetable Market
WANDSWORTH RD.
SOUTH LAMBETH
CLAPHAM RD.
QUEENSTOWN RD.
Battersea Park
Battersea Dogs' Home
Queenstown Rd.
119
Lambeth Coll.
BATTERSEA PARK ROAD

102
84
14
15
19
101
120
A
B
C
D
E
1
2
3
4
5
6
7
Temple
EMBANKMENT
UNDERPASS
BLACKFRIARS
Millennium Bridge
THAMES
RIVER
Blackfriars Millennium Pier
HQS Wellington
HMS President
Bankside Pier
CANNON STREET
LOWER THAMES ST.
BYWARD ST.
LONDON BRIDGE HOSP.
London Bri. City Pier
HMS Belfast
Tower Millennium Pier
The Scoop
Golden Hinde
Tate Modern
The London Television Centre
National Theatre
South Bank
BFI
Imax
STAMFORD ST.
SOUTHWARK
SOUTHWARK ST.
LONDON BRI
TOOLEY
BERMONDSEY
THE BOROUGH
GUY'S HOSP.
Southwark
UNION
Waterloo East
WATERLOO
YORK RD.
WATERLOO RD.
BLACKFRIARS RD.
SOUTHWARK BRIDGE RD.
BOROUGH HIGH ST.
Borough
LONG LA.
GREAT DOVER ST.
BOROUGH RD.
Lambeth Nth.
ST. GEORGE'S CIRCUS
Crown Ct.
NEWINGTON
Elephant & Castle
ELEPHANT & CASTLE
NEW KENT RD.
BRICKLAYER'S ARMS
TOWER BRIDGE RD.
Imperial War Mus.
Geraldine Mary Harmsworth Park
LAMBETH
LAMBETH RD.
ST. GEORGE'S RD.
KENNINGTON RD.
WALWORTH RD.
WALWORTH
Kennington
KENNINGTON PARK RD.
KENNINGTON LANE
Buddhist Cen.
SE17
KENNINGTON
Surrey CCC (The Oval Cricket Grd.)
Oval
KENNINGTON OVAL
Kennington Park
CAMBERWELL NEW RD.
CAMBERWELL RD.
ALBANY RD.
Burgess Park
Burgess Pk. Kart Track
Playing Fields
SOUTHAMPTON WAY
PECKHAM
SE5
SW9
CLAPHAM RD.
BRIXTON RD.
CAMBERWELL GREEN
Camberwell Green
St. Gabriel's Manor

103
F
G
H
J
K
1
2
3
4
5
6
7
THAMES
RIVER
THE POOL
UPPER POOL
LOWER POOL
WAPPING
BERMONDSEY
ROTHERHITHE
SHADWELL
SE16
SE15
SE14
Tower Hill
Tower Gateway
Wapping
Rotherhithe
Bermondsey
Canada Water
Surrey Quays
South Bermondsey
New Cross Gate
Queens Rd. (Peckham)
JAMAICA ROAD
BRUNEL TUNNEL APP.
LOWER ROAD
SALTER RD.
REDRIFF RD.
PLOUGH WY.
SOUTHWARK PARK RD.
RAYMOUTH RD.
ROTHERHITHE NEW RD.
ROLLS ROAD
DUNTON RD.
CATLIN ST.
TRAFALGAR AV.
OLD KENT ROAD
NEW CROSS RD.
QUEEN'S ROAD
PECKHAM HIGH ST.
PECKHAM HILL ST.
PECKHAM PARK ROAD
ASYLUM ROAD
ROTHERHITHE TUNNEL
SOUTHWARK PARK
Millwall FC (The Den)
Surrey Quays Shopping Centre
Greenland Dock
St. Katharine's Pier
Cherry Garden Pier
The Tower of London
15
85
104
121

POPLAR
Westferry
Poplar
West India Quay
Canary Wharf
Billingsgate Market
WEST INDIA DOCKS
Heron Quays
South Quay
ISLE OF DOGS
Crossharbour
MILLWALL
CUBITT TOWN
Mudchute
Mudchute Park & Farm
Island Gds.
MILLWALL PARK
MILLWALL OUTER DOCK
Docklands Sailing Cen.
Canary Wharf Pier
Hilton Docklands Pier
Greenland Pier
Masthouse Terrace Pier
Greenwich Pier
LIMEHOUSE REACH
RIVER THAMES
GREENWICH REACH
SALTER ROAD
Stave Hill Ecological Park
Surrey Docks Farm
Russia Dock Woodland
Redriff Prim. Sch.
GREENLAND DOCK
SOUTH DOCK
Watersports Cen.
PLOUGH WAY
GROVE
EVELYN
DEPTFORD PARK
Pepys Park
SE8
CONVOY'S WHARF
DEPTFORD
Deptford
Cutty Sark for Maritime Greenwich
Cutty Sark
CREEK ROAD
DEPTFORD CHURCH ST.
Greenwich
GREENWICH HIGH RD.
NORMAN RD.
SOUTH ST.
New Cross
New Cross Gate
NEW CROSS RD.
NEW CROSS GATE
NEW CROSS
Goldsmiths' College
Deptford Bri.
BLACKHEATH RD.
BLACKHEATH HILL
SANFORD ST.
Silwood Triangle
Odeon Cinema
Bowl. Alley & Gala Bingo
Printing Works
A B C D E
1 2 3 4 5 6 7
86
103
122

F
G
H
J
K
1
2
3
4
5
6
7
87
106
123
East India
Blackwall
LEAMOUTH
East India Dock Basin Nature Reserve
Virginia Quay
Blackwall Pier
Wharves
Works
Watersports Centre
Tidal Basin
ROYAL VICTORIA DOCK
Custom House for ExCeL
ExCeL
Millennium Mill
D Silo
BLACKWALL REACH
Blackwall Point
Blackwall Stairs
BLACKWALL TUNNEL
A102
Ordnance Wharf
The O2 (Millennium Dome)
RIVER THAMES
Thames Wharf
London City Airport Pier
Brewery
Wharf
Queen Elizabeth II Pier
SILVERTOWN WY.
NORTH WOOLWICH RD.
A1020
E16
West Silvertown
SILVERTOWN
Lyle Park
Manhattan Wharf
KIERBECK BUSINESS COMPLEX
DEANSTON WHARF
CRESCENT WHARF
PLAISTOW WHARF
North Greenwich
College
Delta Wharf
Victoria Deep Water Terminal
TUNNEL AVENUE TRADING ESTATE
Central Park
Thames Barrier Yacht Club Marina
Gas Works
Lorry Park
TUNNEL APPROACH
MILLENNIUM WAY
Greenwich Peninsula Ecology Park
Greenwich Yacht Club
Christie's Wharf
Jetty
Slipway
Swan Lake
Southern Park
Greenwich Millennium Village
SE7
MERIDIAN TRADING ESTATE
BROCKLEBANK INDUSTRIAL ESTATE
Depot
New Charlton
Superstore
Superstores
Cinema
Nature Res.
GREENWICH SHOP. PK.
PENINSULAR PK.
BLACKWALL TUNNEL SOUTHERN APPROACH
A2203
Primrose Wharf
Morden Wharf
Enderby's Wharf
Pipers Wharf
Granite Wharf
Lovell's Wharf
Cubitt Town Wharf
Newcastle Drawdock
Pier
Jetty
Works
A206
WOOLWICH RD.
ROAD
Charlton
Warehouse
Westcombe Park
SE10
TRAFALGAR RD.
Trident Hall
Leisure Cen.
Maze Hill
National Maritime Museum
GREENWICH
GREENWICH PARK
St. Mary's Gate
Circus Gate
Prime Meridian Line
Planetarium
Royal Observatory Greenwich
Open Mon.-Fri. Dawn-10am and 4pm-Dusk
Bandstand
Reservoir (covered)
The Gardens
The Wilderness (Deer Park)
Tennis Courts
Parks Police
Ranger's House
Playground
SE3
Woodland Dell
Liby.
Sch.
A102
Tennis Courts
Blackheath RUFC (Rectory Fld.)
CHARLTON RD.
B210
OLD DOVER ROAD
B211
A207
ROAD
SUN-IN-THE-SANDS
SHOOTERS HILL
A2
KIDBROOKE PK. RD.
Blackheath Nursy. & Prep. Sch.
Bowls
Sports Ground
50
30

106
Prince Regent
ExCeL
ROYAL VICTORIA DOCK
Royal Albert
London Regatta Centre
88
Beckton Park
Cyprus
University
ROYAL ALBERT DOCK
A
B
C
D
E
LONDON CITY AIRPORT
E16
Terminal Building
London City Airport
Short Stay Car Park
KING GEORGE V DOCK
Long Stay Car Park
Warehouse
King George V
Millennium Mill
Pontoon Dock
Depot
1
A1020
NORTH WOOLWICH RD.
CONNAUGHT BRIDGE
CONNAUGHT ROAD
HARTMANN
Pontoon Dock
SILVERTOWN
Thames Barrier Park
FACTORY ROAD
ALBERT
A112
THAMES ROAD IND. EST.
THAMESIDE INDUSTRIAL ESTATE
Sugar Refinery
Works
STANDARD INDUSTRIAL ESTATE
CRESCENT WHARF
2
Jetty
WOOLWICH REACH
THAMES FLOOD BARRIER
RIVER
NORTH WOOLWICH
PIER
A117
North Woolwich Pier
Subway
WOOLWICH FREE FERRY
Barrier Gardens Pier
Thames Barrier Info. Cen.
Waterfront Leisure Cen.
3
HARRINGTON WY.
BOWATER
WESTMINSTER IND. EST.
FARADAY
WESTFIELD
ANCHORAGE POINT IND. EST.
Works
NEW LYDENBURG COMMERCIAL ESTATE
ASHLEIGH COMMERCIAL ESTATE
WOOLWICH DOCKYARD IND. EST.
WOOLWICH
CHURCH ST.
30
WOOLWICH HIGH ST.
MERIDIAN TRADING ESTATE
LOMBARD TRAD. EST.
New Charlton
STONE LAKE RETAIL PK.
CHARLTON GATE BUSINESS PK.
4
WOOLWICH ROAD
A206
Tennis Courts
Maryon Park
Woolwich Dockyard
WOOLWICH
JOHN WILSON ST.
Mulgrave Pond
Super-store
105
Charlton
Charlton Athletic FC (The Valley)
HARVEY GDNS.
MARYON WILSON PARK
ARTILLERY PL.
WELLINGTON
HILL REACH
B210
Gun Park
Royal Artillery Barracks
5
SE7
LITTLE HEATH
Rifle Range
Repository Woods
Playground
White Gate
Barrack Field
Tennis Courts
A205
GRAND DEPOT RD.
ST. ALFEGE RD.
CHARLTON PARK RD.
CEMETERY
Depots
Blue Gate
6
CHARLTON
THE VILLAGE
Charlton Ho.
Library
Charlton School
CHARLTON CEMETERY
CHARLTON PARK
Cricket Ground
HA HA
CIRCULAR
CHARLTON
CHARLTON ROAD
Blackheath RUFC (Rectory Fld.)
QUEEN ELIZABETH HOSPITAL
WOOLWICH COMMON
Sports Ground
Playing Field
7
Hornfair Park
Charlton Lido
Old Royal Military Academy
SHOOTERS HILL ROAD
A207
124
Recreation Ground
Reservoir (covered)
Shooters Hill Post 16 Campus
ACADEMY ROAD
Bowls
Sports Ground
50

107
89
125
108
F
G
H
J
K
1
2
3
4
5
6
7
44
45
46
77
78
79
ALBERT BASIN
Gallions Point Marina
Training Centre
GALLIONS ENTRANCE
Custom House
Drawbridge
WOOLWICH MANOR WAY
A117
SUNDERLAND POINT
Gallions Point
GALLIONS REACH
THAMES
Hoba Wharf
WOOLWICH REACH
Royal Arsenal Woolwich Pier
Firepower (The Royal Artillery Mus.)
Greenwich Heritage Cen.
British Liby.
Royal Arsenal West
Royal Brass Foundry
THAMESMEAD WEST
THAMESMEAD
THAMESMEAD CENTRAL
Twin Tumps
Tor
Prim. Sch.
Gallions Park
Gallions Lake
Broadwater
Broadwater Green
WESTERN WAY
A2016
HARTS LANE
PLUMSTEAD MARSHES
SE28
HMP BELMARSH
Crown Ct. & Magistrates Ct.
WHITE HART TRIANGLE
Thamesmead South West
WEST THAMESMEAD BUSINESS PK.
WEST THAMESMEAD BUSINESS PARK
Southern Outflow Sewers
Comm. Cen.
Works
Recreation Ground
Bowling Green
Ten. Cts.
PETTMAN CRES
Bus. Depot
WOOLWICH TRADE PK.
PLUMSTEAD RD.
A206
Plumstead
DLR
Woolwich Arsenal
PLUMSTEAD HIGH STREET
Plumstead Gdns.
WICKHAM LA.
A209
PLUMSTEAD
WINN'S COMMON
PLUMSTEAD COMMON
SE18
KING'S HIGHWAY
BLEAK HILL LANE
Bleak Hill
Woolwich Cemetery
Rockliffe Gds.
The William Barefoot Gdn.
Playing Field
Tennis Courts
Play. Field
Super-store
Plumstead Common
SHREWSBURY PARK
Clothworkers Wood
SHOOTERS HILL GOLF COURSE
Club House
SHOOTERS HILL
Willow Dene School
East Wickham Open Space
Pav.
Playing Field

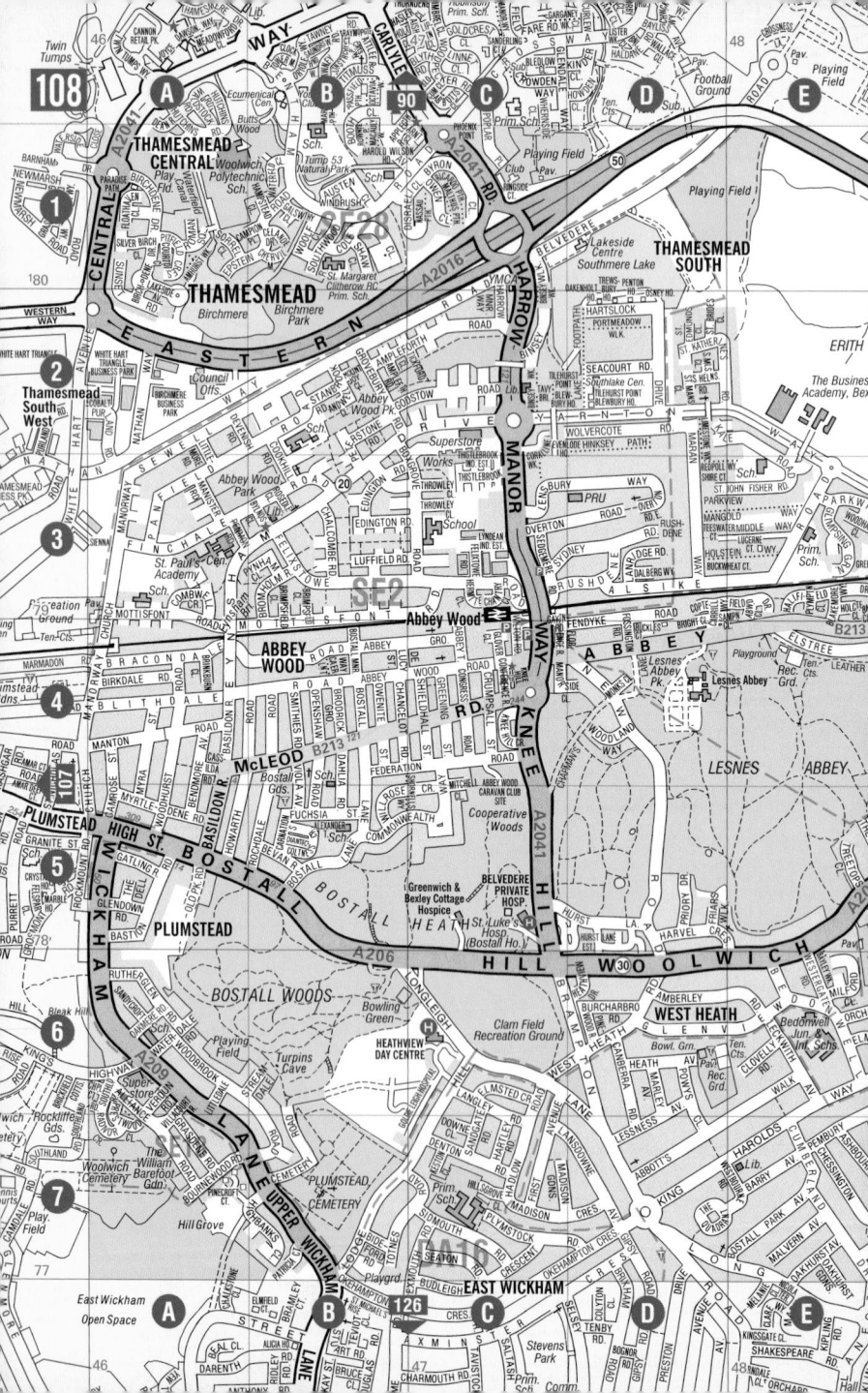

108
90
107
126
A
B
C
D
E
1
2
3
4
5
6
7
46
47
48
180
79
78
77
Twin Tumps
THAMESMEAD CENTRAL
THAMESMEAD
THAMESMEAD SOUTH
Thamesmead South West
SE28
SE2
SE18
DA16
ERITH
ABBEY WOOD
PLUMSTEAD
WEST HEATH
EAST WICKHAM
Abbey Wood
LESNES ABBEY
Lesnes Abbey
Lesnes Abbey Pk.
BOSTALL WOODS
BOSTALL HEATH
Plumstead Cemetery
Woolwich Cemetery
Clam Field Recreation Ground
Cooperative Woods
Greenwich & Bexley Cottage Hospice
BELVEDERE PRIVATE HOSP.
St. Luke's Hosp. (Bostall Ho.)
HEATHVIEW DAY CENTRE
Turpins Cave
Bowling Green
Playing Field
Football Ground
Lakeside Centre
Southmere Lake
The Business Academy, Bexley
Woolwich Polytechnic Sch.
St. Margaret Clitherow RC Prim. Sch.
St. Paul's Academy
Abbey Wood Park
Abbey Wood Pk.
Superstore
Council Offs.
WHITE HART TRIANGLE BUSINESS PARK
BIRCHMERE BUSINESS PARK
Birchmere
Birchmere Park
Tump 53 Natural Park
Ecumenical Cen.
Butts Wood
The William Barefoot Gdn.
Hill Grove
East Wickham Open Space
Stevens Park
Bedonwell Jun. & Inf. Schs.
ABBEY WOOD CARAVAN CLUB SITE
Recreation Ground
Bleak Hill
Rockliffe Gds.
A2041
A2016
A206
A209
B213
EASTERN WAY
WESTERN WAY
HARROW MANOR WAY
KNEE HILL
BOSTALL HILL
WOOLWICH ROAD
WICKHAM LANE
UPPER WICKHAM LANE
PLUMSTEAD HIGH ST.
McLEOD RD.
ABBEY ROAD
YARNTON WAY
SEWELL ROAD
CENTRAL WAY
CARLYLE RD.
BOSTALL LANE
LONGLEIGH LANE
KING HAROLDS WAY
LONG LANE
AXMINSTER CRES.
BRAMPTON RD.

Jetty
Works
SEWAGE WORKS
Depot
91
BURTS WHARF
Jenningtree Point
RIVER THAMES
ERITH REACH
Crossness Nature Reserve
Lighthouse
Warehouse
BELVEDERE IND. EST.
Depot
A2016
Works
Wharf
RIVER WHARF BUSINESS PARK
FORDGATE BUSINESS PARK
EURO TRADE CEN.
THAMESMEAD EAST
DA18
MARSHES
THAMES INNOVATION CENTRE
EASTERN INDUSTRIAL ESTATE
HAILEY RD. BUS. PK.
EAST THAMESMEAD BUS. PK.
BRONZE WAY
MANORWAY
CLAYTONVILLE TER.
CALLENDERS COTTS.
Pier
BELVEDERE BUS. PK.
Warehouse
CAPITAL INDUSTRIAL ESTATE
Indoor Bowls Club
ELBOURNE TRADING ESTATE
BELVEDERE LINK BUS. PK.
Mill
Pier (disused)
Belvedere
Super-store
Belvedere Youth Cen.
Belvedere Jun. & Inf. Schs.
Sikh Temple
New Bri.
LOWER ROAD
PICARDY ST.
B253
B213
Woodside Sch.
BELVEDERE
HILLSIDE
FRANK'S PARK
Bexley College
Trinity Sch. Belvedere
B250
DA17
Play. Fld.
ERITH ROAD
PICARDY ROAD
HAMLET INTERNATIONAL IND. EST.
EUROPA TRAD. EST.
Erith
A206
LESSNESS HEATH
Open Space
Bexley Coll.
ERITH
Sand and Gravel Pit
ATLAS TRADE PARK
Cemetery
Lime Wood
A220
ERITH & DIST. HOSP.
Spts. Grd.
Prim. Sch.
Monastery Prim. Sch.
Playing Field
DA8
DA7
Belmont Prim. Sch.
NORTHUMBERLAND HEATH
Erith Sch.
LESNEY FARM ESTATE
127
Reservoir (covered)
BEXLEY ROAD
PARSONAGE MANORWAY
STREAMWAY
COLYERS LANE
NORTHUMBERLAND AVENUE
1
2
3
4
5
6
7
F
G
H
J
K

110
Junction 4a
92
LONDON-HEATHROW AIRPORT
D'Albiac House
TERMINAL 1
TERMINAL 3
Heathrow Cen.
Heathrow Terminals 1, 2, 3
Control Twr.
Vehicle Tunnel
Airside Road Tunnel
Heathrow Express Rail Link
Cargo Tunnel
TW6
TERMINAL 4
Heathrow Terminal 4
Cargo Terminal
174
BATH A4
NORTHERN PERIMETER ROAD
SOUTHERN PERIMETER ROAD
Heathrow Academy
Customs Ho.
WEST BEDFONT
STANWELL
TW19
Stanwell Fields C of E Prim. Sch.
Recreation Ground
Ashford Town FC
Westview Cotts.
Sports Ground
CLOCKHOUSE ROUNDABOUT
Longford River
STANWELL ROAD
Airport Car Park
Heathrow Corporate Cen.
HM Customs & Excise
Warehouses
GREAT SOUTH-WEST ROAD A30
STAINES ROAD
128
Nursery
Playing Field
Hotel
Depot
Works
Statue
SIPSON RD.
M4

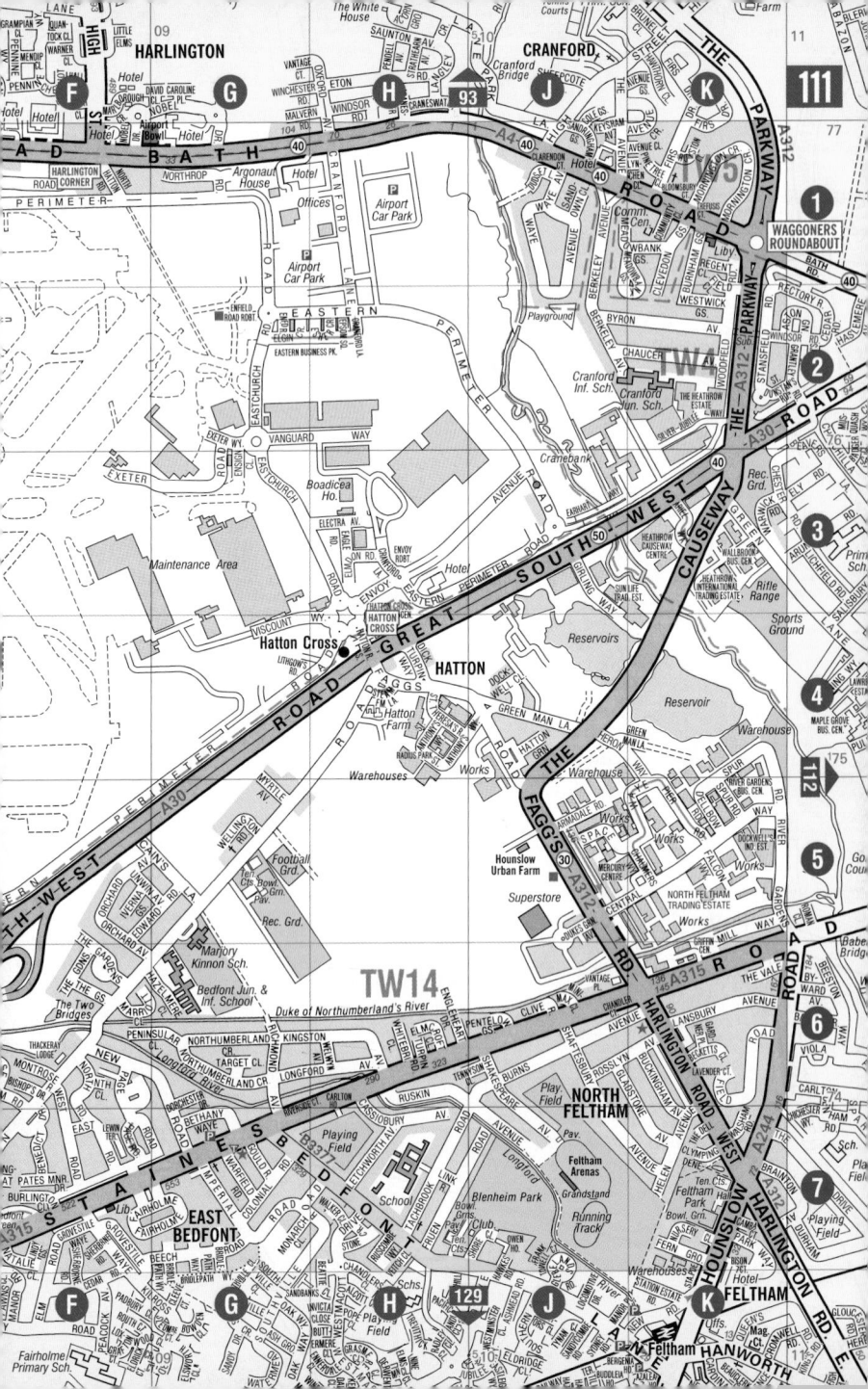
111
HARLINGTON
CRANFORD
Cranford Bridge
93
WAGGONERS ROUNDABOUT
BATH ROAD
THE PARKWAY
A312
A4
TW5
TW4
Airport Car Park
Airport Bowl
Argonaut House
Offices
Maintenance Area
Boadicea Ho.
EASTERN PERIMETER ROAD
EASTERN BUSINESS PK.
VANGUARD WAY
Hatton Cross
HATTON
GREAT SOUTH WEST ROAD
A30
HEATHROW CAUSEWAY CENTRE
HEATHROW INTERNATIONAL TRADING ESTATE
Cranebank
Cranford Inf. Sch.
Cranford Jun. Sch.
Reservoirs
Reservoir
Rifle Range
Sports Ground
THE CAUSEWAY
THE FAGG'S RD.
A312
112
Hounslow Urban Farm
Superstore
NORTH FELTHAM TRADING ESTATE
Hatton Farm
Warehouses
Works
Football Grd.
Rec. Grd.
Marjory Kinnon Sch.
Bedfont Jun. & Inf. School
TW14
Duke of Northumberland's River
Longford River
The Two Bridges
STAINES ROAD
A315
BEDFONT LANE
B3377
EAST BEDFONT
NORTH FELTHAM
Playing Field
Blenheim Park
Feltham Arenas
Grandstand
Running Track
Feltham Park
HOUNSLOW ROAD
HARLINGTON ROAD WEST
HARLINGTON RD. E.
A244
FELTHAM
HANWORTH
Feltham
129
Fairholme Primary Sch.
F
G
H
J
K
1
2
3
4
5
6
7

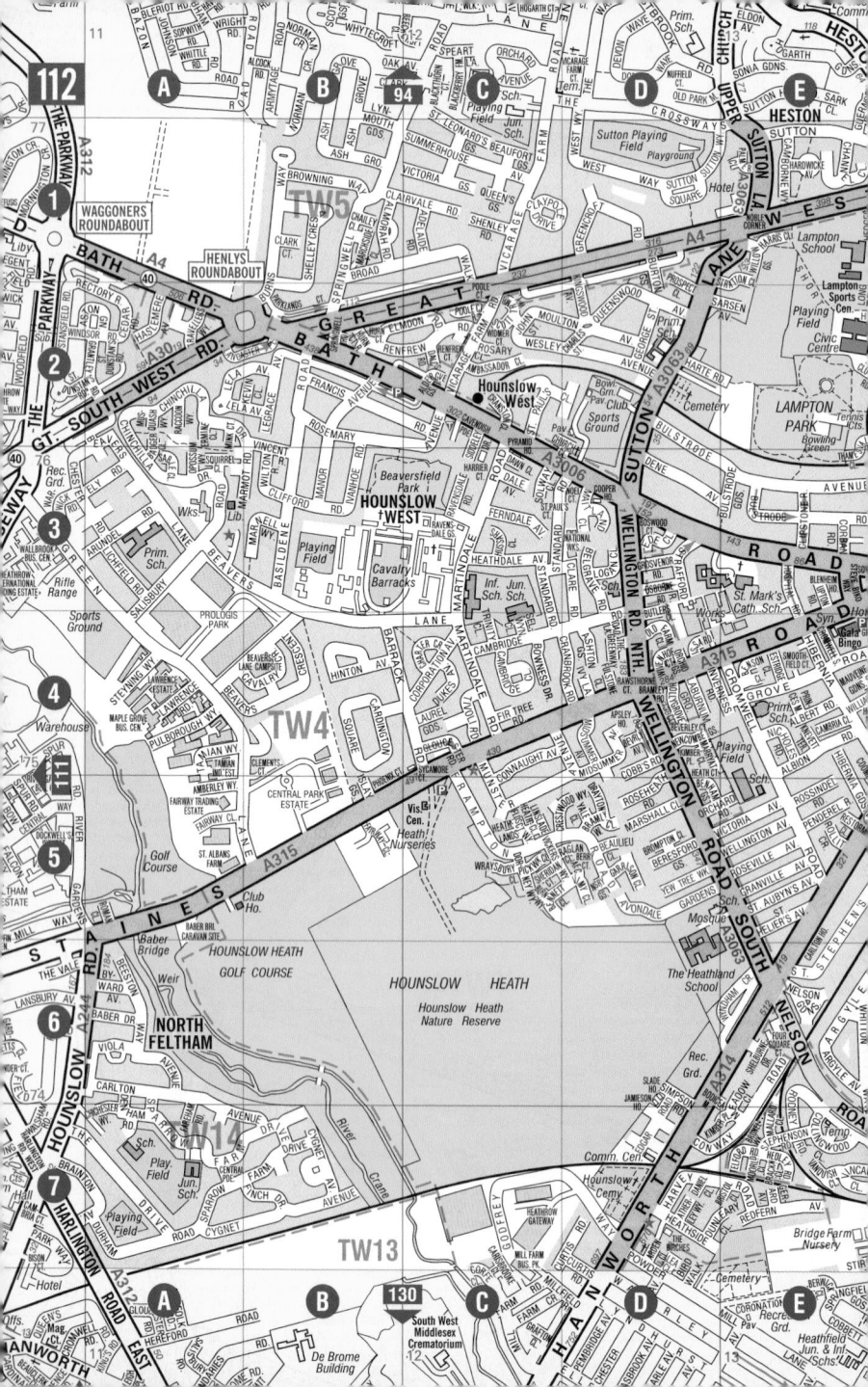

112
A
B
C
D
E
1
2
3
4
5
6
7
94
111
130
TW5
TW4
TW14
TW13
WAGGONERS ROUNDABOUT
HENLYS ROUNDABOUT
THE PARKWAY
A312
A4
BATH RD.
GT. SOUTH WEST RD.
A30
GREAT WEST ROAD
BATH ROAD
A3006
A3063
SUTTON LANE
WELLINGTON RD. NTH
WELLINGTON ROAD SOUTH
A315
STAINES RD.
A244
HOUNSLOW ROAD
HARLINGTON ROAD EAST
HANWORTH ROAD
A314
NELSON ROAD
HESTON
Sutton Playing Field
Playground
Hotel
Lampton School
Lampton Sports Cen.
Playing Field
Civic Centre
LAMPTON PARK
Tennis Cts.
Bowling Green
Hounslow West
Cemetery
Sports Ground
Beaversfield Park
HOUNSLOW WEST
Cavalry Barracks
Prim. Sch.
Inf. Sch.
Jun. Sch.
St. Mark's Cath. Sch.
Gala Bingo
PROLOGIS PARK
BEAVERS LANE CAMPSITE
Rifle Range
Sports Ground
Warehouse
MAPLE GROVE BUS. CEN.
TAMIAN IND. EST.
FAIRWAY TRADING ESTATE
CENTRAL PARK ESTATE
ST. ALBANS FARM
Golf Course
Club Ho.
Vis. Cen.
Heath Nurseries
HOUNSLOW HEATH GOLF COURSE
BABER BRI. CARAVAN SITE
Baber Bridge
Weir
NORTH FELTHAM
HOUNSLOW HEATH
Hounslow Heath Nature Reserve
The Heathland School
Mosque
Rec. Grd.
River Crane
Comm. Cen.
Hounslow Cemy.
HEATHROW GATEWAY
MILL FARM BUS. PK.
Bridge Farm Nursery
Cemetery
Recreation Grd.
Heathfield Jun. & Inf. Schs.
South West Middlesex Crematorium
De Brome Building
Play. Field
Sch.
Jun. Sch.
Hotel
HANWORTH

113
95
114
131
F
G
H
J
K
1
2
3
4
5
6
7
Osterley
GREAT WEST ROAD
LAMPTON
SPRING GROVE
Isleworth
ISLEWORTH
WOODLANDS
HOUNSLOW
TW3
TW7
TW2
Hounslow East
Hounslow Central
Hounslow
Whitton
TWICKENHAM
Maswell Park
Inwood Park
Redlees Park
West Middlesex Drainage Works
Twickenham Stadium
World Rugby Museum
Twickenham Trading Estate
Royal Military Sch. of Music (Kneller Hall)
Richmond upon Thames College
Harlequins RUFC & Harlequins RLFC (The Twickenham Stoop)
Isleworth Crown Court
West Thames College
Indian Gymkhana Club
Alexandra Jun. & Inf. Schs.
Hounslow Manor Sch.
Treaty Centre
Isleworth Rec. Cen.
Education Service
Gov. Offices
Bus Depot
Playing Field
Sports Ground
Murray Park
Queen's Bri.
Duke of Northumberland's River
Chase Bridge
London Rd. Roundabout
Whitton Rd. R'bout
Clock Tower Ind. Est.
Worton Hall Industrial Estate
Victory Business Centre
Superstore
A4
A315
A316
A310
A3005
A314
B363
B361
B358
LONDON ROAD
GROVE ROAD
KNELLER ROAD
WHITTON ROAD
WHITTON DENE
CHERTSEY ROAD
HOSPITAL BRIDGE RD.
TWICKENHAM ROAD

114
96
113
132
A
B
C
D
E
1
2
3
4
5
6
7
Old Brentford
Syon Lane
TW8
SYON PARK
Syon Garden Centre
Syon House
The Tropical Forest
DUKE OF NORTHUMBERLAND ESTATE
West Middlesex University Hosp.
Syon Park Sch.
Busch Corner
LONDON ROAD
TWICKENHAM ROAD
RIVER THAMES
Syon Reach
Isleworth Ferry Gate (Closed)
ROYAL BOTANIC GARDENS
KEW
Syon Vista
The Lake
Arboretum
King William's Temple
Bamboo Garden
Azalea Gdn.
Evolution House
Temperate House
Waterlilly Pond
Conservation Area
Queen Charlotte's Cottage
Cedar Vista
Pavilion Restaurant
Japanese Gateway & Landscape
Pagoda
OLD DEER PARK
ROYAL MID-SURREY GOLF COURSE
King's Observatory
London Welsh RUFC
Cricket Grd.
Bowling Green
Richmond Athletic Ground
London Scottish RUFC
Club House
Grandstand
Tennis Courts
Pools on the Park
Obelisk
Old Deer Park Recreation Ground
Old Isleworth
Isleworth Ait Nature Reserve
Nazareth Ho.
ISLEWORTH
REDLEES PARK
Isleworth Rec. Cen.
Richmond Lock
RICHMOND
Richmond Green
Richmond Circus
TWICKENHAM ROAD
Corporation Island
Asgill Ho.
ST. MARGARETS
St. Margarets
Pleasure Gdns.
ST. MARGARETS ROAD
RICHMOND ROAD
THE AVENUE
PETERSHAM ROAD
RICHMOND HILL
Cole Park
Moor Mead Gd.
Moor Mead Bridge
London Rd. Roundabout
CHERTSEY
Twickenham
TWICKENHAM
Marble Hill Park
Marble Hill House
Orleans Ho. Gallery
Orleans Gdns.
Glover's Island
Petersham Meadows
Petersham Farm
Terrace Gardens
Terrace Fld.
Buccleugh Gdns.
Royal Star & Garter Home
Petersham Common
PETERSHAM
The German Sch. London
Sports Grd.
Foot Ferry
Petersham Gate
Theatre
WARREN FOOTPATH
Playing Field
Tennis Courts
A310
A315
A316
A3004
A305
A307
B321
B363
B454

KEW
The National Archives
Princess of Wales Conservatory
Davies Alpine Ho.
Plants Exhibition
The Pond
Palm House
Rose Garden
Visitor Centre
Victoria Ga.
Temple of Bellona
Berberis Dell
Gallery
Marianne North Gallery
Kew Gds.
Chiswick
GROVE PARK
University of Westminster Sports Ground
Esporta Health Club Chiswick
W4
RIVER
Thames Village
Yacht Basin
Sports Ground
Westminster Boathouse
Riverside Lands
Playing Fields
DUKE'S MEADOWS
Duke's Meadow Golf Course
Driving Range
Pavilion
Boat Houses
CHISWICK BRI.
GREAT CHERTSEY RD.
A316
THAMES
A3003
MORTLAKE
MORTLAKE HIGH ST
Mortlake
Brewery
Sports Ground
Mortlake Crematorium
Hammersmith Cemetery
FULHAM (NORTH SHEEN) CEMETERY
CHALKER'S CORNER
NORTH SHEEN
A205
LOWER RICHMOND ROAD
CLIFFORD AV.
MORTLAKE ROAD
SANDYCOMBE ROAD
KEW GARDENS RD.
B353
A307
TW9
MANOR CIRCUS
North Sheen
Holy Trinity C of E Prim. Sch.
UPPER RICHMOND ROAD
A305
MANOR ROAD
SHEEN LANE
B351
SW14
EAST SHEEN
WEST
Sports Cen.
Pesthouse Common
Christ's Sch.
East Sheen Cemetery
Richmond Cemetery
SHEEN COMMON
Football Ground
Bowling Green
Tennis Courts
Sheen Mt. Prim. Sch.
Palewell Common
Palewell Fields
Playing Fields
Pitch and Putt Course
East Sheen Gate
Adam's Pond
Horse Ride
Roehampton Gate
Bog Gate
Teck Plantation
Sheen Wood
The Bog
Riding Ring
RICHMOND PARK
(Open during daylight hours only)
Sheen Cross Wood
Polo Field
Playing Field
Barn Wood Pond
Holly Lodge
Cambrian Gate
Bishop's Pond
Conduit Wood
Richmond Gate
SAWYER'S HILL
Saw Pit Plantation
Kidney Wood
Jubilee Plantation
Queen's Ride
Deer Pen
White Lodge Plantation
Duchess' Wood
The Royal Ballet School
Queen Mothers Copse
SIDMOUTH WOOD
King Henry VIII
TW10
97
116
133
F G H J K
1 2 3 4 5 6 7

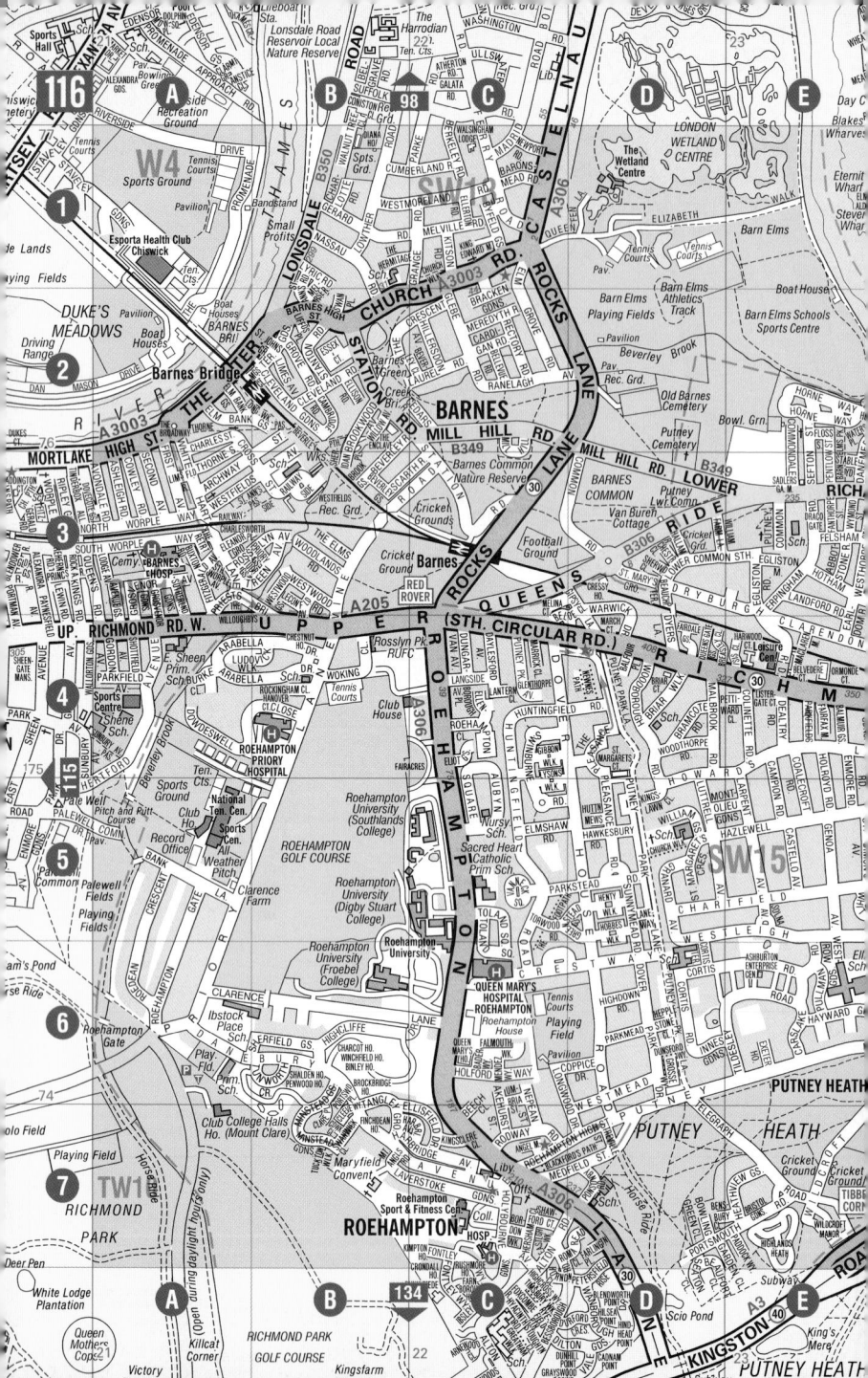

116
98
134
115
A
B
C
D
E
1
2
3
4
5
6
7
W4
SW13
SW15
TW10
BARNES
ROEHAMPTON
MORTLAKE
PUTNEY HEATH
RICHMOND PARK
The Harrodian
Lonsdale Road Reservoir Local Nature Reserve
Riverside Recreation Ground
Sports Ground
Esporta Health Club Chiswick
DUKE'S MEADOWS
Driving Range
Barnes Bridge
RIVER THAMES
LONDON WETLAND CENTRE
The Wetland Centre
Barn Elms
Barn Elms Playing Fields
Barn Elms Athletics Track
Barn Elms Schools Sports Centre
Beverley Brook
Old Barnes Cemetery
Putney Cemetery
Barnes Common Nature Reserve
BARNES COMMON
Putney Lwr. Comn.
Van Buren Cottage
Football Ground
Cricket Grounds
Cricket Ground
Barnes
RED ROVER
BARNES HOSP.
Rosslyn Pk. RUFC
Club House
ROEHAMPTON PRIORY HOSPITAL
National Ten. Cen.
Sports Cen.
All Weather Pitch
Record Office
Clarence Farm
ROEHAMPTON GOLF COURSE
Roehampton University (Southlands College)
Roehampton University (Digby Stuart College)
Roehampton University
Roehampton University (Froebel College)
Sacred Heart Catholic Prim Sch.
QUEEN MARY'S HOSPITAL ROEHAMPTON
Roehampton House
Playing Field
Ibstock Place Sch.
Roehampton Gate
Palewell Fields
Palewell Common
Pale Well Pitch and Putt Course
Club College Halls Ho. (Mount Clare)
Maryfield Convent
Roehampton Sport & Fitness Cen.
PUTNEY
HEATH
Scio Pond
King's Mere
White Lodge Plantation
Queen Mothers Copse
Killcat Corner
RICHMOND PARK GOLF COURSE
Kingsfarm
Deer Pen
Horse Ride
(Open during daylight hours only)
UPPER RICHMOND RD. (STH. CIRCULAR RD.)
UP. RICHMOND RD. W.
ROEHAMPTON LANE
ROCKS LANE
CASTELNAU
LONSDALE RD.
CHURCH RD.
MILL HILL RD.
LOWER RICHMOND RD.
QUEENS RIDE
STATION RD.
HIGH ST.
KINGSTON RD.
A3003
A306
A205
B349
B350
B306
A3

F
G
H
J
K
99
FULHAM
WALHAM GREEN
SANDS END
1
2
3
4
5
6
7
Parsons Grn.
PARSONS GRN
SW6
SOUTH PARK
HURLINGHAM PARK
Hurlingham
The Hurlingham Club
Fulham Palace
Fulham FC
Putney Bri.
Putney Pier
THAMES
RIVER
Wandsworth Riverside Quarter Pier
Wandsworth Town
118
WANDSWORTH
Putney
PUTNEY
East Putney
West Hill
SW18
SW15
SOUTHFIELDS
Southfields
135
King George's Park
Broadway
Eel Brook Common
Hurlingham Wharf
Solid Waste Transfer Station
ROYAL HOSP FOR NEURO-DISABILITY
Nuffield Health Fitness & Wellbeing Centre
A219
A304
A308
A217
A3209
A205
A3
A218

118
100
117
136
A
B
C
D
E
1
2
3
4
5
6
7
BATTERSEA PARK
SANDS END
Imperial Wharf
Cremorne Riverside Centre
Cremorne Gardens
Cremorne Wharf
Chelsea Creek
Gas Works
RIVER THAMES
Chelsea Harbour Pier
Bascule Bri.
Lensbury Wharf
Shell Wharf
THE LONDON HELIPORT
Fulham Wharf
Trinidad Wharf
Warehouse
Superstore
Leisure Cen.
SW6
SW11
SW18
SW12
WESTBRIDGE RD.
VICARAGE CR.
LOMBARD RD.
BATTERSEA BRIDGE RD.
ALBERT BRIDGE RD.
BATTERSEA PARK RD.
BATTERSEA
LATCHMERE RD.
FALCON RD.
Falcon Park
CLAPHAM JUNCTION
LAVENDER HILL
ELSPETH RD.
YORK RD.
WANDSWORTH BRI. RD.
Wandsworth Town
ST. JOHN'S HILL
EAST HILL
HUGUENOT PL.
NORTH SIDE WANDSWORTH COMMON
BATTERSEA RISE
NORTHCOTE RD.
CLAPHAM COMMON NORTH SIDE
CLAPHAM COMM. W. SIDE
THE CLAPHAM COMMON
Spencer Park
Emanuel School
St. Mary's Cemy.
Tennis Courts
Bowling Green
Cricket Ground
WANDSWORTH COMMON
Wandsworth Common
HMP WANDSWORTH
TRINITY RD.
WINDMILL RD.
BOLINGBROKE GRO.
NIGHTINGALE LA.
EARLSFIELD RD.
WANDSWORTH CEMETERY
EARLSFIELD
GARRATT LANE
The Chelsea Group of Children
Beatrix Potter Prim. Sch.
BALHAM
General Games Ground
Boating Lake
Parks Police Headquarters
The Pump Ho. Gallery
British Genius Site
Sun Gate

119
101
120
137
F
G
H
J
K
1
2
3
4
5
6
7
29
30
31
NINE ELMS
Battersea Pk.
Battersea Dogs' Home
NEW COVENT GARDEN MARKET
Fruit & Vegetable Market
SOUTH LAMBETH
Queenstown Rd. (Battersea)
SW8
Larkhall Park
Heathbrook Park
Stockwell
Angell Town
Wandsworth Rd.
STOCKWELL
Clapham High St.
SW9
Clapham North
LAMBETH HOSPITAL
CLAPHAM
Clapham Comn.
CLAPHAM COMMON
BRIXTON
SW4
Lambeth Academy
CLAPHAM COMMON
Mount Pond
Eagle Pond
CLAPHAM PARK
SW2
Windmill Gdns
Sports Ground
HMP BRIXTON
Clapham Sth.
QUEENSTOWN RD.
WANDSWORTH RD.
CLAPHAM RD.
STOCKWELL RD.
BRIXTON RD.
CLAPHAM HIGH ST.
CLAPHAM PARK RD.
ACRE LANE
BEDFORD RD.
LONG RD.
SOUTH SIDE
CLAPHAM COMMON NORTH SIDE
KING'S AVENUE
BRIXTON HILL
POYNDERS RD.
CAVENDISH RD.
BALHAM HIGH RD.
ATKINS RD.
STREATHAM PL.
CHRISTCHURCH RD.
A3
A23
A24
A205
A2217

120
102
119
138
A
B
C
D
E
1
2
3
4
5
6
7
CAMBERWELL
STOCKWELL
BRIXTON
HERNE HILL
North Dulwich
East Dulwich
DULWICH VILLAGE
Angell Town
Brixton
Loughborough Junc.
Herne Hill
Denmark Hill
SE5
SE24
SW9
SW2
SE21
CAMBERWELL GREEN
CAMBERWELL NEW RD.
SOUTHAMPTON WAY
PECKHAM RD.
DENMARK HILL
COLDHARBOUR LANE
BRIXTON RD.
EFFRA RD.
TULSE HILL
DULWICH ROAD
HALF MOON LA.
VILLAGE WAY
EAST DULWICH GROVE
NORWOOD ROAD
CROXTED ROAD
MILKWOOD RD.
RAILTON RD.
HERNE HILL
FERNDENE RD.
CHAMPION PK.
GROVE LA.
DOG KENNEL HILL
LOUGHBOROUGH RD.
BROCKWELL PARK
RUSKIN PARK
MYATTS FIELDS
KINGS COLLEGE HOSPITAL
THE MAUDSLEY HOSP
Brockwell Park Lido
Herne Hill Stadium
Dulwich Picture Gallery
Dulwich Old College
The Charter School
Knight's Hill
TULSE

121
103
139
122
F
G
H
J
K
1
2
3
4
5
6
7
PECKHAM
PECKHAM HIGH ST.
QUEEN'S ROAD
A202
NEW CROSS ROAD
NEW CROSS GATE
Queens Rd. (Peckham)
Peckham Rye
SE15
SE14
SE4
SE22
SE23
NUNHEAD
Nunhead
NUNHEAD CEMETERY
Nunhead Cemetery Nature Reserve
BROCKLEY
PECKHAM RYE COMMON
PECKHAM RYE PARK
EAST DULWICH
EAST DULWICH ROAD
LORDSHIP LANE
AQUARIUS GOLF COURSE
Telegraph Hill Park
One Tree Hill Local Nature Reserve
HONOR OAK
Honor Oak Park
Honor Oak Crematorium
Camberwell Old Cemetery
Newlands
FOREST HILL
DULWICH PARK
Horniman Gardens
THE GROVE
STANSTEAD RD.
DRAKEFELL

122
104
121
140
A
B
C
D
E
1
2
3
4
5
6
7
New Cross Gate
NEW CROSS GATE
NEW CROSS
New Cross
Deptford
Deptford Bri.
Goldsmiths College
NEW CROSS ROAD
LEWISHAM WAY
BROOKMILL ROAD
BLACKHEATH RD.
BLACKHEATH HILL
GREENWICH HIGH RD.
ST. JOHNS
St. Johns
Elverson Rd.
LOAMPIT HILL
LOAMPIT VALE
THURSTON RD.
Lewisham
LEWISHAM
Lewisham College
DRAKEFELL RD.
Brockley
BROCKLEY
BROCKLEY ROAD
MALPAS
SE4
HILLY FIELDS PARK
Cricket Ground
Bowling Green
ADELAIDE AV.
IVY ROAD
LADYWELL RD.
Ladywell
LADYWELL
LEWISHAM UNIVERSITY HOSPITAL
Brockley Cemetery
Ladywell Cemetery
Crofton Park
Crofton Pk.
Honor Oak Crematorium
Honor Oak Pk.
HONOR OAK PARK
STONDON PARK
Blythe Hill Fields
Blythe Hill
Catford Bridge
Catford
CATFORD
CATFORD RD.
Powerleague Soccer Centre
RUSHEY GRN.
LEWISHAM HIGH STREET
Lewisham Park
STANSTEAD ROAD
BROWNHILL ROAD
SE6
SE23

123
124
141
105
F
G
H
J
K
1
2
3
4
5
6
7
GREENWICH PARK
Planetarium
Royal Observatory Greenwich
Bandstand
Reservoir (covered)
The Gardens
The Wilderness (Deer Park)
Tennis Courts
Parks Police
Ranger's House
SHOOTERS HILL ROAD
A2
B210
B212
BLACK HEATH
Hollyhedge Ho.
Blackheath Vale
PRINCE CHARLES RD.
PRINCE OF WALES RD.
VANBRUGH PARK
OLD DOVER ROAD
SUN-IN-THE-SANDS
KIDBROOKE PARK RD.
ROCHESTER WAY RELIEF ROAD
A2213
Blackheath Nursy. & Prep. Sch.
Morden College (Almshouses)
SE3
THE PARAGON
BLACKHEATH
Blackheath
College
Academy
Age Cen.
Concert Halls
LEE TERRACE
LEE HIGH ROAD
B220
A20
BLACKHEATH PARK
Sports Ground
Sports Grounds
The Priory
Kidbrooke
Kidbrooke Nature Reserve
Thomas Tallis Sch.
Warehouse
Superstore
David Lloyd Leis.
Quaggy River
Roan School Playing Fields
SUTCLIFFE PARK
Sutcliffe Pk. Athletics Track
ELTHAM ROAD
SIDCUP ROAD
Horn Park
Colfes Senior Sch.
Colfes Prep. Sch.
Colfes Leisure Cen.
Lee
LEE
SE12
Brindishe Prim. Sch.
BURNT ASH RD.
A2212
BURNT ASH HILL
WESTHORNE AVENUE
A205
Euro Cen.
Manor House Gdns.
Manor Park
Hither Green
HITHER GREEN
Depot
CHILTONIAN IND. EST.
ST. MILDREDS ROAD
BARING ROAD
Horn Park Prim. Sch.
Comm. Cen.
Hadlow Coll. (Mottingham Campus)
MOTTINGHAM LA.
Grove Park
Hither Green Sidings

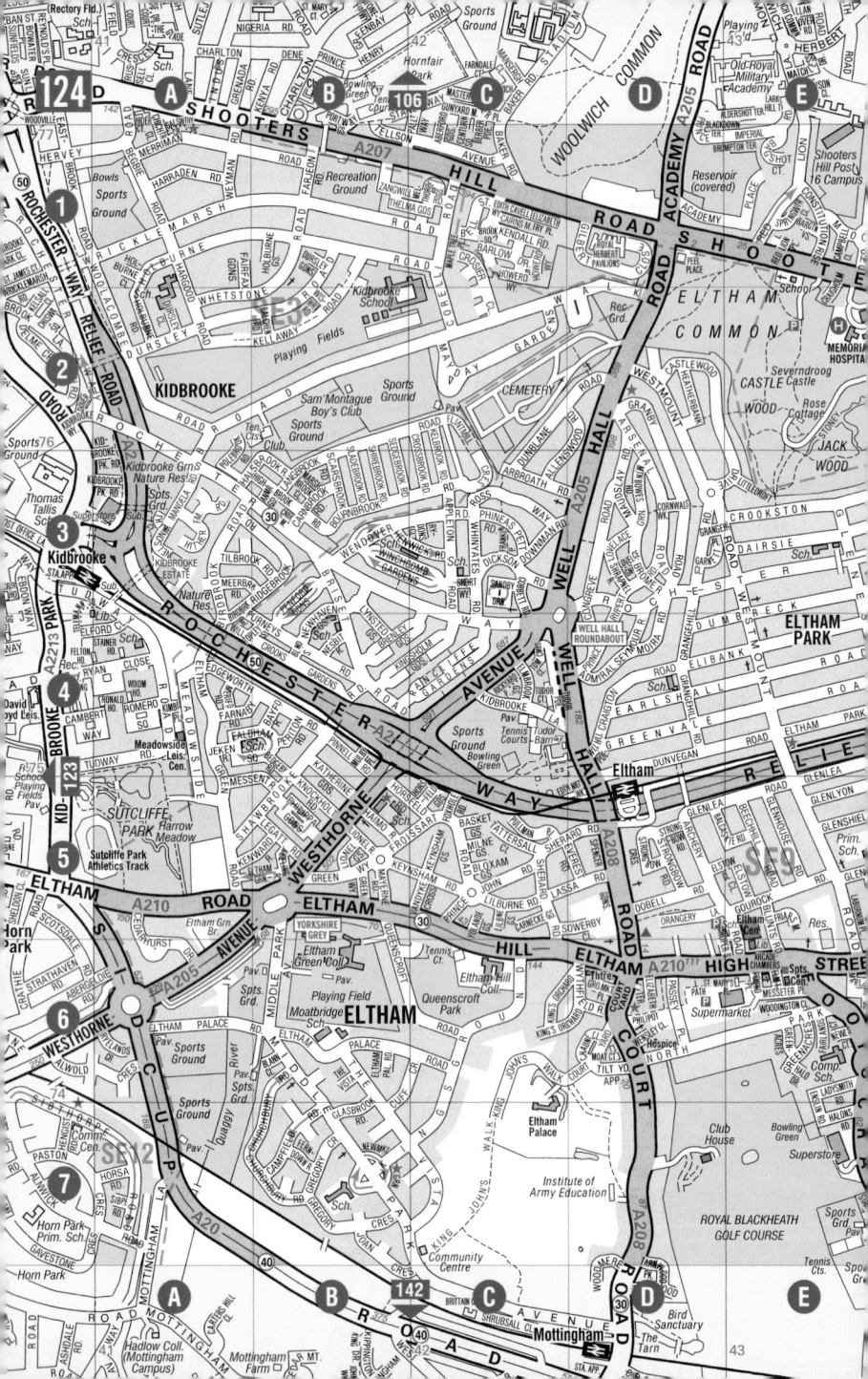

124
106
123
142
A
B
C
D
E
1
2
3
4
5
6
7
SHOOTERS HILL ROAD
A207
A205
ACADEMY ROAD
WOOLWICH COMMON
Hornfair Park
Old Royal Military Academy
Reservoir (covered)
Shooters Hill Post 16 Campus
ELTHAM COMMON
MEMORIAL HOSPITAL
Severndroog Castle
CASTLE WOOD
Rose Cottage
JACK WOOD
KIDBROOKE
SE3
Kidbrooke School
Playing Fields
Recreation Ground
Sports Ground
Sam Montague Boy's Club
CEMETERY
ROCHESTER WAY RELIEF ROAD
A2
ROCHESTER WAY
WELL HALL ROAD
WELL HALL ROUNDABOUT
Kidbrooke Grn. Nature Res.
Thomas Tallis Sch.
Kidbrooke
KIDBROOKE ESTATE
A2213
KIDBROOKE PARK ROAD
David Lloyd Leis.
Meadowside Leis. Cen.
SUTCLIFFE PARK
Harrow Meadow
Sutcliffe Park Athletics Track
ELTHAM ROAD
A210
WESTHORNE AVENUE
ELTHAM HILL
ELTHAM PARK
Eltham
SE9
ELTHAM HIGH STREET
YORKSHIRE GREY
Eltham Green Coll.
Eltham Hill Coll.
Queenscroft Park
Playing Field
Moatbridge Sch.
ELTHAM
Eltham Palace
Institute of Army Education
COURT ROAD
A208
Supermarket
Hospice
Club House
ROYAL BLACKHEATH GOLF COURSE
Bowling Green
Superstore
SE12
Horn Park
Horn Park Prim. Sch.
SIDCUP ROAD
A20
Community Centre
Mottingham
MOTTINGHAM ROAD
Hadlow Coll. (Mottingham Campus)
Mottingham Farm
Bird Sanctuary
The Tarn

125
SHREWSBURY PARK
SHOOTERS HILL GOLF COURSE
SHOOTERS HILL
Club House
Eaglesfield Rec. Grd.
Clothworkers Wood
Willow Dene School
East Wickham Open Space
Hillview Cemetery
Council Offices
Woodlands Farm
Garden Centre
SHOOTERS HILL
BELLEGROVE
A207
Welling
Jackwood Ho.
Oxleas Meadows
OXLEAS WOOD
Eastcote Prim. Sch.
DA16
Falconwood Field
Playing Field
SHEPHERDLEAS WOOD
ELTHAM PARK NORTH
Falconwood
FALCONWOOD
ROCHESTER WAY
EAST ROCHESTER WAY
A2
Eltham Cemetery
Eltham Crematorium
ELTHAM PARK SOUTH
ELTHAM WARREN GOLF COURSE
Crown Woods School
Nature Study Centre
BEXLEY ROAD
BLACKFEN ROAD
A210
University of Greenwich (Avery Hill Campus)
AVERY HILL
AVERY HILL PARK
Alderwood Prim. Sch.
(Halls of Residence)
Sports Ground
All Weather Pitches
Sparrow's Farm Leisure Centre
Parish Wood
BLACKFEN
Hollyoak Wood Park
DA15
HALFWAY STREET
Lamorbey
Marlborough Sch.
Willersley Pk.
107
126
143
F
G
H
J
K
1
2
3
4
5
6
7

126
108
125
144
A
B
C
D
E
1
2
3
4
5
6
7
Woolwich Cemetery
William Barefoot Gdn.
Plumstead Cemetery
Hill Grove
East Wickham Open Space
EAST WICKHAM
Stevens Park
Prim. Sch.
Comm. Cen.
Wrotham Offs.
Jun. & Inf. Schs
Welling Sch.
Playing Field
Games Court
Ten. Cts.
Brampton Prim. Sch.
DA16
WELLING
Welling
Warehouse
Bexleyheath Station
BELLEGROVE RD.
WELLING HIGH ST.
PARK VIEW RD.
A207
CROOK LOG
Welling Corner
Hook La. Prim. Sch.
Westbrooke Sch.
The Danson Cen.
Crook Log Sports Cen.
Welling United FC
Bexleyheath Sports Club
Sports Grd.
Tennis Courts
Pitch & Putt Pav.
Bowl. Grns.
Playground
War Mem.
Crook Log Prim. Sch.
UPTON CENTRE
Bexley Grammar Sch.
Playing Field
Danson Ho.
Danson Park Watersports Centre
DANSON PARK
THE LAKE
Upton
Red House
Club Ho.
BEXLEYHEATH GOLF COURSE
EAST ROCHESTER WAY
A2
DANSON INTERCHANGE
BLACKFEN ROAD
A210
BLACKFEN
Blackfen Sch. for Girls
Sherwood Park Prim. Sch.
Days Lane Prim. Sch.
DA15
PENHILL PARK
PENHILL RD.
A221
DANSON ROAD
UPPER WICKHAM LANE
A209
BLENDON RD.
B2210
Blendon
THE SANCTUARY
Riverside Wlk.
Hurst Prim. Sch.
Play. Fld.
Bexley Park Wood
Bridgen
Hollyoak Wood Park
Lib.
Willersley Pk.
Marlborough Park
Marlborough Sch.
SIDCUP GOLF COURSE
Chatsworth Inf. Sch.
Rose Theatre
Lamorbey Park
Rose Bruford
Lamorbey
Club House
Penhill Bri.
Play. Fld.
Haysmere Foundation Sch.
Rec. Grd.
Hurst Pl. Com. Cen.
HURST RD.
A222

127
109
145
NORTHUMBERLAND HEATH
BARNEHURST
BEXLEYHEATH
BEXLEY
OLD BEXLEY
CRAYFORD
DA8
DA7
DA6
DA5
DA1
F
G
H
J
K
1
2
3
4
5
6
7
Barnehurst
Bexley
A220
A207
A221
A222
A223
A2
A2000
COLYERS LANE
NORTHUMBERLAND AVENUE
MAYPLACE ROAD
BROADWAY
WATLING ST.
LONDON RD. (WATLING ST.)
GRAVEL HILL
BOURNE ROAD
ROCHESTER WAY
DARTFORD-BY-PASS
ARNSBERG WAY
ALBION ROAD
BELMONT ROAD
LONG LANE
Bursted Wood
Bursted Wood Prim. Sch.
Russell Park
Bexleyheath School
Martens Grove Park
BARNEHURST GOLF COURSE
Mayplace (Club Ho.)
Crayford Manor House (Adult Ed. Cen.)
VCD Athletic FC Ground
SHENSTONE PARK
Bigs Hill Wood
St. Columba's Catholic Boys Sch.
Gravel Hill Prim. Sch.
St. Catherine's Catholic School for Girls
Hall Place House & Gardens
Hall Place Gardens
BLACK PRINCE INTERCHANGE
SPORTS FIELD
Pumping Station
The Old Orchard
Churchfield Wood
Grammar Sch.
Old Bexley C of E Prim. Sch.
Cricket Ground
Erith Sch.
Normandy Prim. Sch.

128
110
146
A
B
C
D
E
1
2
3
4
5
6
7
STANWELL
ASHFORD
CHATTERN HILL
Littleton Common
TW19
TW15
TW17
TW18
QUEEN MARY RESERVOIR
STAINES RESERVOIRS
CLOCKHOUSE ROUNDABOUT
FORDBRIDGE ROUNDABOUT
SCHOOL ROAD JUNCTION
LONDON ROAD
STAINES ROAD
KINGSTON ROAD
STAINES-BY-PASS
FELTHAM ROAD
CHURCH ROAD
CLOCKHOUSE LANE
CONVENT RD.
SCHOOL ROAD
STANWELL ROAD
TOWN LANE
LONG LANE
SHORT LANE
GT. SOUTH-WEST RD.
FORDBRIDGE ROAD
ASHFORD ROAD
WOODTHORPE ROAD
A30
A315
A308
B378
B377
B3003
Ashford Town FC
Recreation Ground
Sports Ground
Playing Field
Nurseries
Club
Nursery
Homers Farm
Warehouse
Warehouses
WESTGATE ESTATE
Superstore
ASHFORD HOSP.
Ashford Cemetery
Thomas Knyvett College
Fordway Cen.
St. James Independent Schools (Senior Boys)
Waterski & Wakeboard Centre
Princes Club
Information Centre
Bridge Farm
BEDFONT LAKES COUNTRY PARK
Bedfont Cemetery
Offices
Ashford
Clarendon Prim. Sch.
Echelforde Play. Field
Brooklands College
Piggeries
ASHFORD INDUSTRIAL EST.
ASHFORD BUSINESS COMPLEX
The Echelford Prim. Sch.
Depot
Club House
ASHFORD MANOR GOLF COURSE
Ford Bridge
Fordbridge Park
Staines Reservoirs Aqueduct
Works
Tennis Cts.
Spts. Cen.
Spts. Grd.

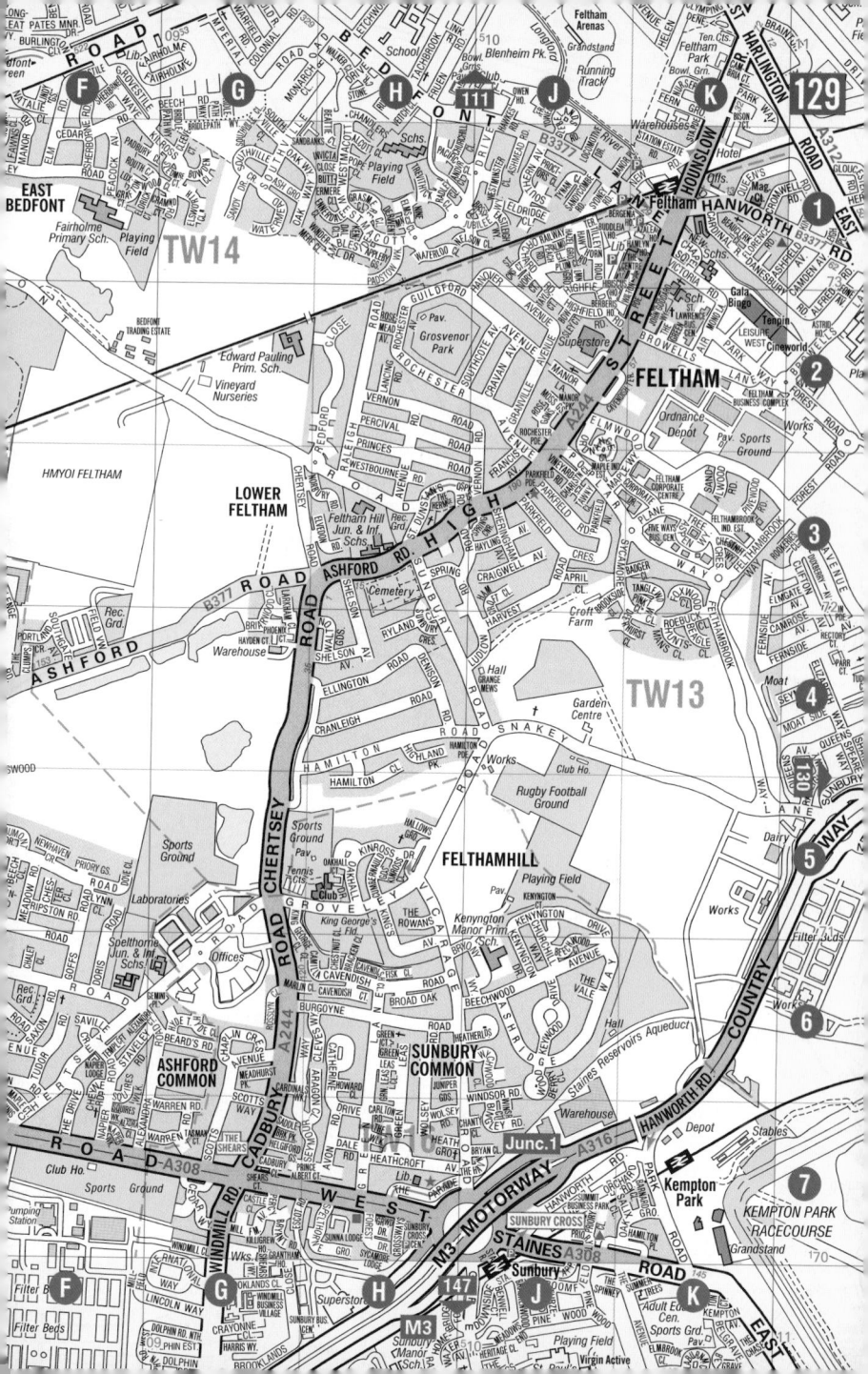
129
F
G
H
J
K
1
2
3
4
5
6
7
EAST BEDFONT
Fairholme Primary Sch.
Playing Field
TW14
BEDFONT TRADING ESTATE
Edward Pauling Prim. Sch.
Vineyard Nurseries
HMYOI FELTHAM
LOWER FELTHAM
Feltham Arenas
Grandstand
Running Track
Blenheim Pk.
Bowl. Grns.
Club
School
Schs.
Playing Field
111
B3377
Feltham Park
Warehouses
Hotel
Offs.
Feltham
HANWORTH RD.
HIGH STREET
HOUNSLOW RD.
HARLINGTON ROAD
A312
EAST
FELTHAM
Grosvenor Park
Pav.
Superstore
Lib.
Gala Bingo
Tenpin
Cineworld
LEISURE WEST
FELTHAM BUSINESS COMPLEX
Ordnance Depot
Pav. Sports Ground
Works
FOREST ROAD
FELTHAM CORPORATE CENTRE
FELTHAMBROOK IND. EST.
FIVE WAYS BUS. CEN.
Feltham Hill Jun. & Inf. Schs.
Rec. Grd.
ASHFORD ROAD
B377
A244
Cemetery
Warehouse
Rec. Grd.
Croft Farm
TW13
Hall
GRANGE MEWS
Garden Centre
SNAKEY LANE
Works
Club Ho.
Rugby Football Ground
Moat
130
SUNBURY WAY
Dairy
Works
Filter Beds
CHERTSEY ROAD
Sports Ground
Pav.
Tennis Cts.
Club
FELTHAMHILL
Playing Field
Pav.
King George's Fld.
Kenyngton Manor Prim. Sch.
Sports Ground
Laboratories
Spelthorne Jun. & Inf. Schs.
Offices
Rec. Grd.
ASHFORD COMMON
SUNBURY COMMON
Hall
Staines Reservoirs Aqueduct
COUNTRY WAY
HANWORTH RD.
Warehouse
Depot
Stables
Junc.1
A316
M3 MOTORWAY
Kempton Park
KEMPTON PARK RACECOURSE
Grandstand
Club Ho.
Sports Ground
A308
ROAD WEST
STAINES ROAD
SUNBURY CROSS
Sunbury
Pumping Station
Filter Beds
WINDMILL RD.
CADBURY RD.
Wks.
WINDMILL BUSINESS VILLAGE
Superstore
SUNBURY BUS. CEN.
147
M3
Sunbury Manor Sch.
Playing Field
Virgin Active
Adult Edu. Cen.
Sports Grd.
Pav.
LINCOLN WAY
DOLPHIN

130
112
129
148
A
B
C
D
E
1
2
3
4
5
6
7
FELTHAM
HANWORTH
HANWORTH PARK
Hanworth Park House
TW13
TW16
HARLINGTON ROAD EAST
A312
UXBRIDGE ROAD
HAMPTON RD. WEST
HAMPTON RD. EAST
HOUNSLOW ROAD
HANWORTH ROAD
A314
A316
COUNTRY WAY
GREAT CHERTSEY
TWICKENHAM RD.
APEX CORNER
STAINES RD. EAST
Feltham Community College
Playing Field
De Brome Building
South West Middlesex Crematorium
Tennis Courts
Feltham Airparcs Leisure Centre
Mount Corner
Cineworld
Gala Bingo
Tenpin
Hounslow Cemy.
Heathrow Gateway
Mill Farm Bus. Pk.
Recreation Grd.
Heathfield Jun. & Inf. Schs.
Nature Reserve
School
Hampton Farm Ind. Est.
Hanworth Trad. Est.
Air Links Ind. Est.
Apex Retail Pk.
Amida Racquets & Fitness Spa.
Superstore
Longford River
Hampton Comm. Coll.
Hampton Sports & Fitness Cen.
Hospice
Marling Hall
Marling Park
Hatherop Park
Rectory Meadow
Rec. Grd.
Lindon Bennett Sch.
Reservoir
Filter Beds
Works
Dairy
Staines Reservoirs Aqueduct
Half Moon Covert
Sports Ground
Football Ground
Hydes Field
Portlane Bridge
KEMPTON PARK RACECOURSE
Grandstand
Stables
Depot
Kempton Gate
Kingsway Bus. Pk.
Feltham Business Complex
Moat
SNAKEY LA.
Pav. Sports Ground

WHITTON
Whitton
TWICKENHAM
Twickenham
131
113
132
149
TW2
TW1
TW11
Harlequins RUFC & Harlequins RLFC (The Twickenham Stoop)
Twickenham Cemetery
Kneller Gdns.
HOSPITAL BRIDGE ROUNDABOUT
Hospital Bridge
Sports Ground
River Crane
Twickenham Green
THE GREEN
HEATH ROAD
CHERTSEY ROAD
STAINES ROAD
SIXTH CROSS ROAD
CROSS DEEP
Radnor Gardens
Swan Island
Strawberry Hill
STRAWBERRY HILL
St. Mary's University College
Playing Field
Waldegrave Sch. for Girls
St. James's Catholic Primary School
STRAWBERRY HILL GOLF COURSE
Fulwell Park
FULWELL GOLF COURSE
Fulwell
Bus Garage
Stanley Jun.& Inf. Schs.
Cemetery
WALDEGRAVE ROAD
WELLINGTON ROAD
HAMPTON ROAD
STANLEY ROAD
PARK ROAD
HAMPTON HILL
TEDDINGTON
Teddington
HIGH ST.
BROAD ST.
National Phy. Lab.
Clarendon Sch.
Carlisle Park
Cricket Grd.
Upper Lodge
Canal Plantation
Pantile Bridge
The Brew House
Bartons Cottage
Cricket Ground
Bushy House
Sports Ground
Round Plantation
Longford River
Hampton Open Air Pool
BUSHY PARK
Broom Clumps
Willow Plantation
The Pheasantry Welcome Centre
River Lodge
Hawthorn Lodge
Deer Pen
Teddington Lodge
HAMPTON
Hampton & Richmond Borough FC (Beveree Stadium)
HIGH STREET
F
G
H
J
K
1
2
3
4
5
6
7

132
114
131
150
A
B
C
D
E
1
2
3
4
5
6
7
16
17
18
TWICKENHAM
Twickenham
TEDDINGTON
Teddington
STRAWBERRY HILL
HAM
PETERSHAM
KINGSTON UPON THAMES
HAMPTON WICK
Hampton Wick
BUSHY PARK
MARBLE HILL PARK
Marble Hill House
Orleans Ho. Gallery
Orleans Gdns.
Ham House
Polo Ground
Ham Lands Nature Reserve
Ham Riverside Lands
Ham Fields
Thames Young Mariners Base
Radnor Gardens
St. Mary's University College
Grey Court School
Meadlands Prim. Sch.
The German Sch. London
The Russell Sch. (Juniors)
The Russell Sch. (Infants)
Strathmore Sch.
The Copse
SUDBROOK PARK
Sudbrook Park (Club Ho.)
The Wilderness
RICHMOND GOLF COURSE
Petersham Meadows
Petersham Farm
Petersham Gate
Royal Star & Garter Home
Glover's Island
Eel Pie Island
Swan Island
Thames Eyot
Teddington Lock
Teddington Weir
Teddington Studios
Lensbury Club
Sports Ground
Athletic Ground
Collis Prim. Sch.
YMCA Sports Grd.
Trowlock Island
Sports Cen.
Recreation Ground
The Avenue Centre
Steven's Eyot
Canbury Gds.
The Tiffin Girls' Sch.
Tiffins Girls Comm. Spts. Cen.
Fern Hill Prim. Sch.
St. George's Industrial Estate
Cassel Hosp.
Teddington Lodge
Warren Plantation
Hawthorn Lodge
Half Moon Plantation
Deer Pen
Leg-of-Mutton Pond
Thatched Cottage
Foot Ferry
RIVER THAMES
TW1
TW10
TW11
A305
A310
A313
A307
B352
B353
B358
RICHMOND RD.
LONDON RD.
HEATH RD.
CROSS DEEP
STRAWBERRY VALE
TWICKENHAM RD.
KINGSTON RD.
HIGH STREET
PETERSHAM RD.
UPPER HAM RD.
RICHMOND RD.
HAM GATE AV.
SANDY LA.
PARK RD.
SANDY LANE
UP. TEDDINGTON RD.

133
115
134
151
RICHMOND PARK
SIDMOUTH WOOD
DEER PARK
Pen Ponds
Queen Elizabeth's Plantation
Leg of Mutton Pond
Jubilee Plantation
Saw Pit Plantation
Queen's Ride
Duchess' Wood
The Royal Ballet School
White Lodge Plantation
Deer Pen
Queen Mothers Copse
Victory Plantation
Treebox Wood
SPANKERS HILL WOOD
Lawn Plantation
King George V Jubilee Plantation
Pond Plantation
Tercentenary Plantation
Oak Lodge
White Ash Lodge
Kidney Wood
King Henry VIII Mound
Richmond Gate
Conduit Wood
Barn Wood Pond
Playing Field
Playing Fields
Pond Slade
Ham Cross Plantation
Isabella Plantation Garden
Peg's Pond
Thomson's Pond
ISABELLA PLANTATION
Ham Cross
Ham Gate
Ham Bottom
Ham Dip
High Wood
Still Pond
Deer Fold
Coronation Plantation
The Flat
Dann's Pond
Gallows Pond
King's Clump
Prince Charles's Spinney
Gibbet Wood
Broomfield Hill
Broomfield Hill Wood
Robin Hood Gate
Ladderstile Gate
Kingston Gate
Kingston University (Kingston Hill Campus)
Walkden Hall
Robin Hood Prim. Sch.
COOMBE HILL GOLF COURSE
COOMBE WOOD GOLF COURSE
COOMBE
Warren House
Club House
Holy Cross Preparatory RC Sch.
Rokeby Sch.
Marymount International School
KINGSTON HOSPITAL
Park Hill Sch.
Coombe Hill Jun. & Inf. Schools
Latchmere Sch.
RC Prim. Sch.
Sports Ground
Canbury Sch.
KINGSTON HILL
KINGSTON VALE
A308
A238
B351
B283
SW15
KT2
COOMBE LANE WEST
TRAPS LA.
QUEENS RD.
GEORGE RD.
LIVERPOOL ROAD
WARREN RD.
COOMBE PARK
PARK ROAD
HAM RIDINGS
KING'S ROAD
ROBIN HOOD LANE
Tennis Cts.
Club Ho.

134
116
133
152
ROEHAMPTON
RICHMOND PARK
RICHMOND PARK GOLF COURSE
SW15
PUTNEY VALE
KINGSTON VALE
WIMBLEDON COMMON
WIMBLEDON COMMON GOLF COURSE
ROYAL WIMBLEDON GOLF COURSE
COOMBE HILL GOLF COURSE
KT2
SW20
COPSE HILL
KINGSTON VALE
ROEHAMPTON VALE
KINGSTON ROAD
ROBIN HOOD WAY (KINGSTON BY-PASS)
COOMBE LANE WEST
PUTNEY HEATH
Putney Vale Crematorium
PUTNEY VALE CEMETERY
Wimbledon Windmill Museum
Kingston University (Roehampton Vale Centre)
NEW VICTORIA HOSPITAL
Wolfson Neurorehab. Centre
Caesar's Camp
Beverley Meads & Fishpond Woods Nature Reserve
Cannizaro Park
Queen's Mere
King's Mere
Scio Pond
Stag Bog
Silent Pools
Fishpond Wood
Shadwell Wood
Warren Farm
Mill Corner
Robin Hood Gate
Killcat Corner
Victory Plantation
Kingsfarm Plantation
White Lodge Plantation
Treebox Wood
Hyde Park Nursery
Chohole Gate
Silver Hill
Jerry's Hill
STAG LANE
ROBIN HOOD
ROEHAMPTON LANE
COOMBE LANE
Horse Ride
Stag Ride
Gravelly Ride
Inner Park Ride
Ladies Mile
Beverley Brook
The Rowans Sch.
Robin Hood Prim. Sch.
Cottenham Park
Lady Jane's Wood
A3
A306
A308
A238
B281
A
B
C
D
E
1
2
3
4
5
6
7
21
22
23
70
71
72
73

135
117
136
153
F
G
H
J
K
1
2
3
4
5
6
7
SOUTHFIELDS
Southfields
Earlsfield
SW18
SW17
SW19
WIMBLEDON PARK
Wimbledon Park
Wimbledon Park Athletics Track
Wimbledon Park Sailing Club
Golf Course
Cricket Ground
Club House
Tennis Courts
Aorangi Park
Museum
Wimbledon All England Lawn Tennis & Croquet Club
Indoor Ten. Cts.
Buddhist Temple
Parkside Hosp.
WIMBLEDON PARK GOLF COURSE
Ricards Lodge High Sch.
Bishop Gilpin C of E Prim Sch.
Wimbledon Cemetery
SUMMERSTOWN
Wimbledon Stadium
Superstore
Carriage Cleaning Shed
Recreation Ground
Depot
Works
King George's Park
Nuffield Health Fitness & Wellbeing Centre
Southfields Comm. Coll.
Westfield House Sports Grd.
Play. Fields
Garratt Park
River Wandle
Haydons Road
The Priory C of E Sch.
South Park Gardens
SOUTH WIMBLEDON
South Wimbledon
MERTON
Merton Park
WIMBLEDON
Wimbledon
Wimbledon High Sch.
Wimbledon Coll.
Ursuline Prep. Sch.
Wimbledon Mag. Ct.
Centre Court
Esporta
Dundonald Rd.
Dundonald Prim. Sch.
Recreation Ground
Fitness Cen.
YMCA
Leisure Cen.
Theatre-rites
A219
A218
A217
A238
A24
B235
B285
PARKSIDE
WIMBLEDON PARK ROAD
HOME PARK ROAD
DURNSFORD ROAD
MERTON ROAD
GARRATT LANE
HAYDONS ROAD
PLOUGH LANE
GAP ROAD
HIGH ST.
WIMBLEDON HILL
ALEXANDRA RD.
THE BROADWAY
HARTFIELD ROAD
KINGSTON ROAD
MERTON HIGH ST.
MERANTUN WAY
WORPLE ROAD
ARTHUR ROAD
QUEENSMERE ROAD
AUGUSTUS ROAD
VICTORIA DRIVE
REPLINGHAM ROAD
CHURCH ROAD
SOUTH PARK ROAD
QUEENS ROAD
HIGH ST.

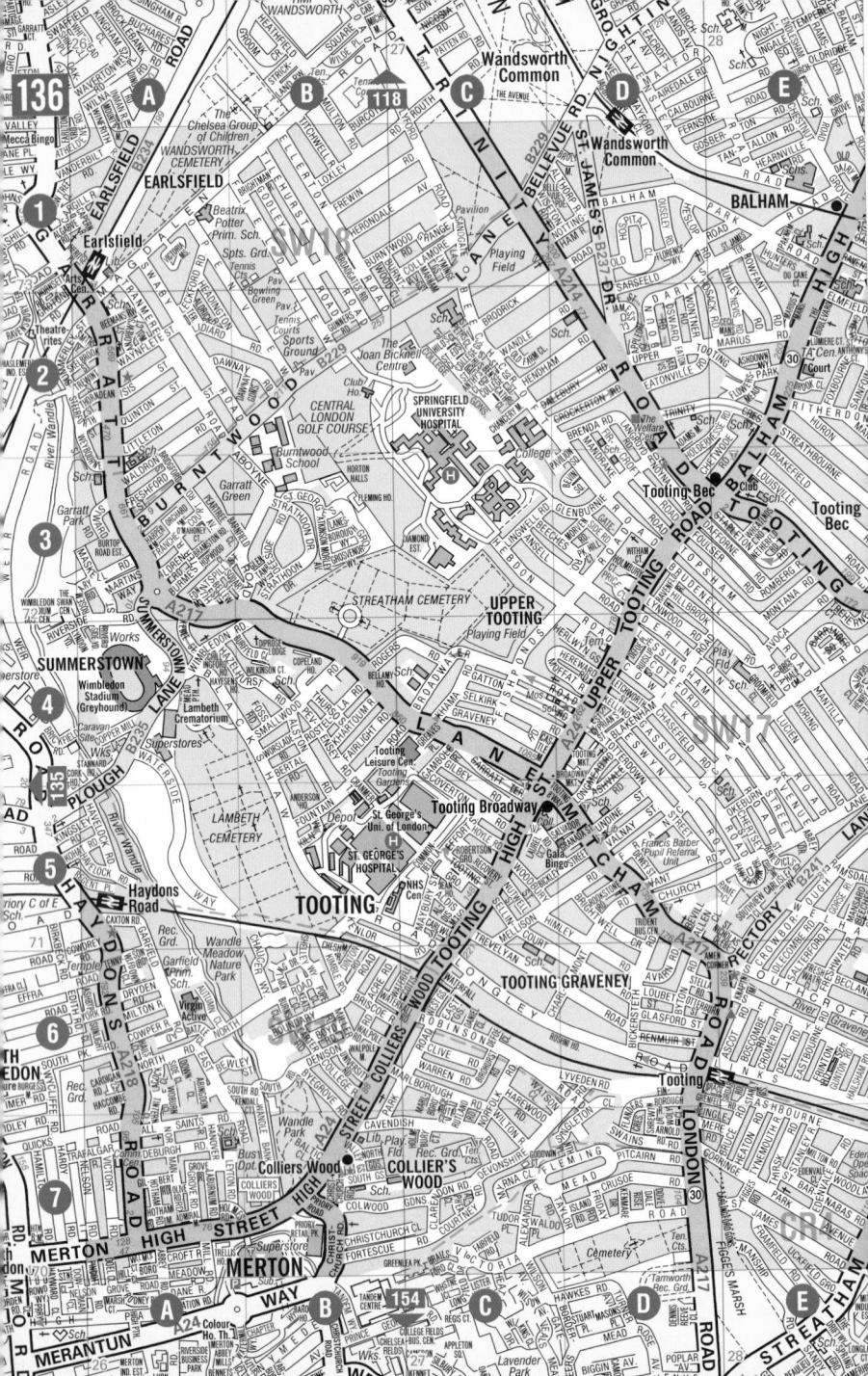
136
A
B
C
D
E
118
Wandsworth Common
EARLSFIELD
Earlsfield
WANDSWORTH CEMETERY
The Chelsea Group of Children
Beatrix Potter Prim. Sch.
SW18
Playing Field
Pavilion
Sports Ground
The Joan Bicknell Centre
CENTRAL LONDON GOLF COURSE
SPRINGFIELD UNIVERSITY HOSPITAL
Burntwood School
Garratt Green
Garratt Park
BALHAM
Tooting Bec
STREATHAM CEMETERY
UPPER TOOTING
SUMMERSTOWN
Wimbledon Stadium (Greyhound)
Lambeth Crematorium
Superstores
LAMBETH CEMETERY
Tooting Leisure Cen.
Tooting Gardens
St. George's Uni. of London
ST. GEORGE'S HOSPITAL
Tooting Broadway
Gala Bingo
Francis Barber Pupil Referral Unit
SW17
Haydons Road
TOOTING
Wandle Meadow Nature Park
Garfield Prim. Sch.
Virgin Active
TOOTING GRAVENEY
Tooting
Wandle Park
Colliers Wood
COLLIER'S WOOD
MERTON
Superstore
Cemetery
Tamworth Rec. Grd.
Lavender Park
154
135
1
2
3
4
5
6
7
A24
A217
A214
A218
B229
B234
B235
B237
B241
30
BURNTWOOD LANE
GARRATT LANE
TRINITY ROAD
UPPER TOOTING ROAD
TOOTING HIGH ST.
MITCHAM ROAD
BALHAM HIGH ROAD
TOOTING BEC ROAD
HAYDONS ROAD
MERTON HIGH STREET
MERANTUN WAY
LONDON ROAD
STREATHAM ROAD
RECTORY LANE
PLOUGH LANE
SUMMERSTOWN
COLLIERS WOOD
STREET
26
27
28

137
119
138
155
SW12
SW2
SW16
Balham
STREATHAM HILL
Streatham Hill
STREATHAM
Streatham
STREATHAM PARK
FURZEDOWN
STREATHAM VALE
Streatham Common
STREATHAM COMMON
NORBURY
Norbury
TOOTING BEC COMMON
Tooting Bec Lido
Tooting Graveney Common
Tooting Bec Athletic Track
Streatham Vale Park
Bishop Thomas Grant Sch.
Hitherfield Prim. Sch.
Norwood Recreation Gd
NORBURY PARK
The Rookery
Paddling Pool
Football Pitch
Leisure Cen.
Odeon Cin.
Riva Bingo
Superstore
Ice Arena
Karting Track
Sports Ground
School Playing Fields
Beecholme Prim. Sch.
Lonesome
CHRISTCHURCH ROAD
A205
BEDFORD HILL
BEC ROAD
A214
TOOTING BEC ROAD
STREATHAM HIGH ROAD
A23
BRIXTON HILL
THORNTON AV.
STERNHOLD AV.
B221
MITCHAM LANE
A216
MITCHAM ROAD
STREATHAM COMMON NORTH
GREEN LANE
B273
GREYHOUND LA.
STREATHAM VALE
B272
GARRAD'S RD.
CHURCH LANE
ATKINS RD.
B242

138
120
156
137
BROCKWELL PARK
TULSE HILL
WEST DULWICH
WEST NORWOOD
SE27
NORWOOD NEW TOWN
STREATHAM COMMON
SW16
NORWOOD
UPPER NORWOOD
NORBURY
Gipsy Hill
West Norwood
Tulse Hill
West Dulwich
West Norwood Crematorium
Dulwich College
Dulwich Picture Gallery
Norwood Grove Recreation Ground
NORWOOD PARK
DULWICH VILLAGE

139
140
121
157
F
G
H
J
K
1
2
3
4
5
6
7
34
35
36
DULWICH PARK
COMMON
A205
LORDSHIP LA.
THE GROVE
LONDON
ROAD
Horniman Gardens
Horniman Museum
SE23
FOREST HILL
Forest Hill
WALDRAM PK.
STANSTEAD RD.
DEVONSHIRE
PERRY
B227
DULWICH & SYDENHAM HILL GOLF COURSE
DULWICH
Sydenham Hill Wood & Cox's Walk Nature Reserve
Dulwich Wood
Sydenham Hill
UPPER SYDENHAM
Sydenham Wells Park
DARTMOUTH
A2216
KIRKDALE
SE26
A212
HILL
Sydenham
SYDENHAM
ROAD
Mayow Park
LOWER SYDENHAM
WESTWOOD
CRYSTAL PALACE PARK
CRYSTAL PALACE
Crystal Palace National Sports Centre
Crystal Palace Athletics Stadium
Crystal Palace Museum
Crystal Palace
Crystal Palace Dinosaurs
Crystal Palace Park Farm
A234
PALACE
PARK
RD.
A213
NEWLANDS
PARISH
LANE
Penge East
Penge West
HIGH
ST.
PENGE
SE20
ANERLEY
HILL
A214
Anerley
A2199
COLLEGE RD.
Alexandra Rec. Grd.
Alexandra Jun. Sch.
Kent House
Harris City Academy
James Dixon Prim. Sch.
Orchard Lodge (Remand Centre)
CROYDON
ROAD
St. Christopher's Hospice
TV Transmitter
Intermediate Lake
Lower Lake
Bus Terminal
Site of Crystal Palace
The Kentwood Cen.

140
139
122
158
A
B
C
D
E
1
2
3
4
5
6
7
Blythe Hill
Catford Bridge
Catford
CATFORD
SE23
SE6
SE26
BR3
STANSTEAD ROAD
A205
CATFORD HILL
A212
BROMLEY ROAD
A21
BROWNHILL RD.
PERRY VALE
PERRY RISE
PERRY HILL
B227
BELL GREEN
SOUTHEND LA.
SOUTHEND LANE
A2218
SYDENHAM RD.
LWR. SYDENHAM
Lwr. Sydenham
Bellingham
BELLINGHAM
Bellingham Leisure & Lifestyle Cen.
Powerleague Soccer Centre
Private Banks Sports Ground
Catford Trading Estate
Bus Garage
Sports Ground
Playing Fields
Gasholder Station
Superstore
Southend Park
Sedgehill School
Beckenham Hill
BECKENHAM HILL ROAD
NEW BECKENHAM
New Beckenham
Fitness First Health Club
Gambado
Cricket Ground
Athletics Ground
Stumpshill Wood
Ash Plantation
Beckenham Place Park Nature Reserve
BECKENHAM PLACE PARK
Beckenham Place Club House
BECKENHAM PLACE PARK GOLF COURSE
Cator Park Sports Cen.
Cator Pk. Sch.
CATOR PARK
SOUTHEND ROAD
A2015
Kent House
Beckenham Road
Beckenham Junc.
RECTORY RD.
ALBEMARLE
BECKENHAM

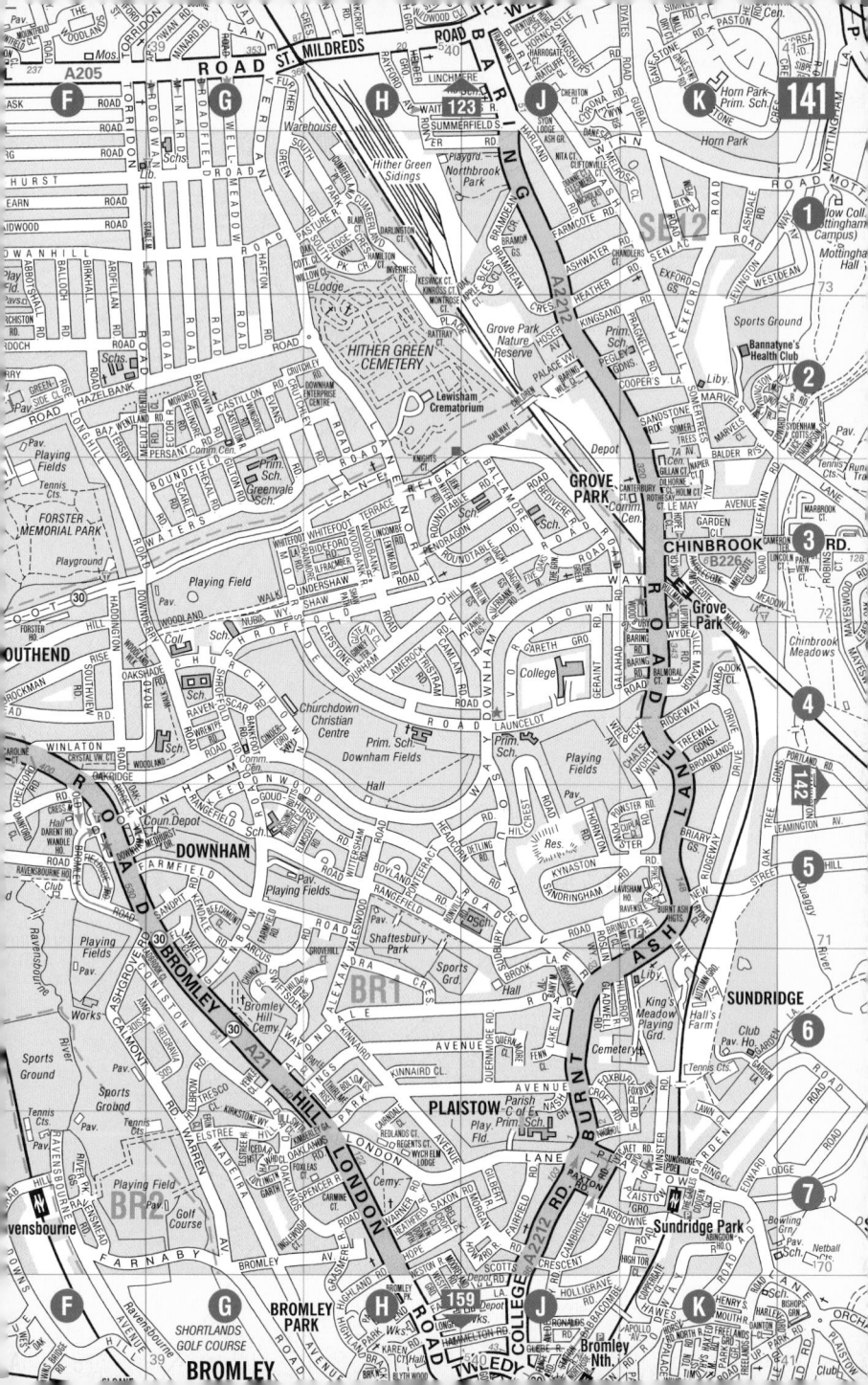

141
142
123
159
A205
ST. MILDREDS ROAD
Hither Green Sidings
Northbrook Park
HITHER GREEN CEMETERY
Lewisham Crematorium
Grove Park Nature Reserve
SE12
Horn Park
Horn Park Prim. Sch.
Sports Ground
Bannatyne's Health Club
Mottingham Hall
GROVE PARK
Grove Park
CHINBROOK RD.
B226
Chinbrook Meadows
BURNT ASH LANE
A2212
BARING ROAD
FORSTER MEMORIAL PARK
Playing Fields
Playing Field
SOUTHEND
Churchdown Christian Centre
Downham Fields
DOWNHAM
DOWNHAM WAY
Shaftesbury Park
BR1
Bromley Hill Cemy.
BROMLEY ROAD
A21
LONDON ROAD
PLAISTOW
Parish C of E Prim. Sch.
King's Meadow Playing Grd.
SUNDRIDGE
Hall's Farm
Sundridge Park
BR2
Golf Course
Ravensbourne
Ravensbourne River
SHORTLANDS GOLF COURSE
BROMLEY PARK
BROMLEY
Bromley Nth.
COLLEGE RD.
Quaggy River
F
G
H
J
K
1
2
3
4
5
6
7

142
124
160
141
A
B
C
D
E
1
2
3
4
5
6
7
MOTTINGHAM
SIDCUP ROAD
A20
A208
B226
GROVE PARK
CHINBROOK RD.
Mottingham
Hadlow Coll. (Mottingham Campus)
Mottingham Hall
Eltham College Jun. Sch.
Eltham Coll.
Eric Liddell Spts. Cen.
Institute of Army Education
ROYAL BLACKHEATH GOLF COURSE
Coldharbour Leisure Centre
SE9
SE12
BR1
ELMSTEAD WOOD
Grove Park Cemetery
Chinbrook Meadows
ELMSTEAD
SUNDRIDGE
Sundridge Park Manor Conference Centre
SUNDRIDGE PARK GOLF COURSE
Elmstead Woods
Sundridge Park
CHISLEHURST WEST
WHITE HORSE ROAD
Castlecombe Prim. Sch.
Bullers Wood Sch.
Scotts Park Prim. Sch.

143
125
144
161
F
G
H
J
K
1
2
3
4
5
6
7
Lamorbey
DA15
DA14
BR7
New Eltham
NEW ELTHAM
LONGLANDS
SIDCUP
CHISLEHURST
CHISLEHURST COMMON
FIVEWAYS
FROGNAL CORNER
SCADBURY PARK
(Nature Reserve)
Sparrow's Farm Leisure Centre
Sports Ground
Playing Fields
Spts. Grd.
Cricket Ground
St. Olave's Prep. School
Dulverton Sch.
Old Farm Park
Playground
King George's Rec. Grd.
Marlowe Ho. Offs.
World of Golf at Sidcup
Flamingo Park Sports Grd.
Pitch & Putt Course
Kemnal Manor
Ashen Grove
Edgebury Prim. Sch.
Partridge Shaw
Esporta Health & Fitness
Beavers Wood
Chislehurst Cemetery
Hoblands Wood
Playing Field
Garden Centre
Old Elthamians Sports Club
Beaverwood Sch. for Girls
Athletic Ground
Darul Uloom London Islamic Institute
Foxbury
Mead Rd. Inf. Sch.
Farringtons School
Icehouse Wood
Square Clump
Bushy Clump
Bank's Shaw
Christ The King (St Mary's) Sixth Form College
Resource Centre
Camden Place (Club House)
Midfield Prim. Sch.
PARK WOOD
Hadresham
The Fantails
Holbrook Wood
Archway
Moat
FOOTSCRAY ROAD
A211
A20
A222
A208
B2214
B263
B264
SIDCUP ROAD
MAIN ROAD
SIDCUP BY-PASS
HALFWAY STREET
STATION RD.
PERRY STREET
BROMLEY LANE
BROMLEY RD.
ROYAL PDE.
ST. PAUL'S CRAY RD.
HIGH ST.
CENTRE COMN. RD.
IMPERIAL WAY
LONGLANDS RD.
FARM AVENUE
WATTS LA.
MANOR PARK RD.

144
126
143
A
B
C
D
E
1
2
3
4
5
6
7
Bridgen
Bexley Park Wood
Lamorbey
HALFWAY
Willersley Pk.
Marlborough Park
Marlborough Sch.
Comm. Cen.
Chatsworth Inf. Sch.
Rose Theatre
Lamorbey Park
Rose Bruford College
SIDCUP GOLF COURSE
River Shuttle
Play. Fld.
Hurtsmere Foundation Sch.
Club House
Penhill Bri.
Rec. Grd.
Hurst Prim. Sch.
Hurst Pl. (Com. Cen.)
HURST ROAD
Prim. Sch.
Sidcup Leisure Centre
The Glade
Chislehurst & Sidcup Grammar Sch.
Abbeyhill Park
Rutland Shaw
Sidcup Cemy.
Albany Park
Sidcup
King George's Rec. Grd.
Marlowe Ho. Offs.
Birkbeck Prim. Sch.
WARING PARK
Tennis Cts.
Playgrd.
DA14
Royal Park Prim. Sch.
Playing Field
The Alders
Stable Meadow
Cleeve Pk. Sch.
North Cray Woods
Five Arch Bri.
Playing Field
SIDCUP
FOOTS CRAY MEADOWS
(Nature Reserve)
Foots Cray Place
Dower House
Playing Fields
David Lloyd Leisure
Cray Youth & Community Centre
Catholic Prim. Sch.
Sidcup Place
Sidcup Place Park
Sidcup Green
Bowling Grn.
Sixth Form College
QUEEN MARY'S HOSPITAL
FROGNAL CORNER
Frognal Cen.
Frognal Ho.
Chestnut Ho.
Orchard Prim. Sch.
Football Grd.
Warehouse
FIVE ARCHES BUSINESS PARK
SIDCUP TECHNOLOGY CENTRE
FOOTS CRAY
Foots Cray Bri.
Works
Factory
Rec. Grd.
Spring Shaw
The Lodge
Black Clump
Little Wood
SCADBURY PARK
(Nature Reserve)
BR7
BR5
Irish Plantation
Kemnal Tech. College
CRITTALLS CORNER
Superstores
Superstore
RUXLEY
RUXLEY WOOD
Ruxley Corner
Midfield Prim. Sch.
Youth Club
Playing Field
ST. PAUL'S CRAY
Grays Farm Cottages
Bromley Ski Centre
LA Fitness
Driving Range
RUXLEY PARK GOLF COURSE
CRAY VALLEY GOLF COURSE
A20
A222
A223
A224
A211
A2001
B2173
B2214
SIDCUP HIGH ST.
MAIN RD.
STATION RD.
CHISLEHURST RD.
SIDCUP HILL
MAIDSTONE RD.
NORTH CRAY RD.
EDGINGTON WY.
SEVENOAKS WY.
SIDCUP BY-PASS
LONGMEAD DRIVE
FARADAY AVENUE
BEXLEY LANE
RECTORY LANE
CRAY RD.
WATERY LANE

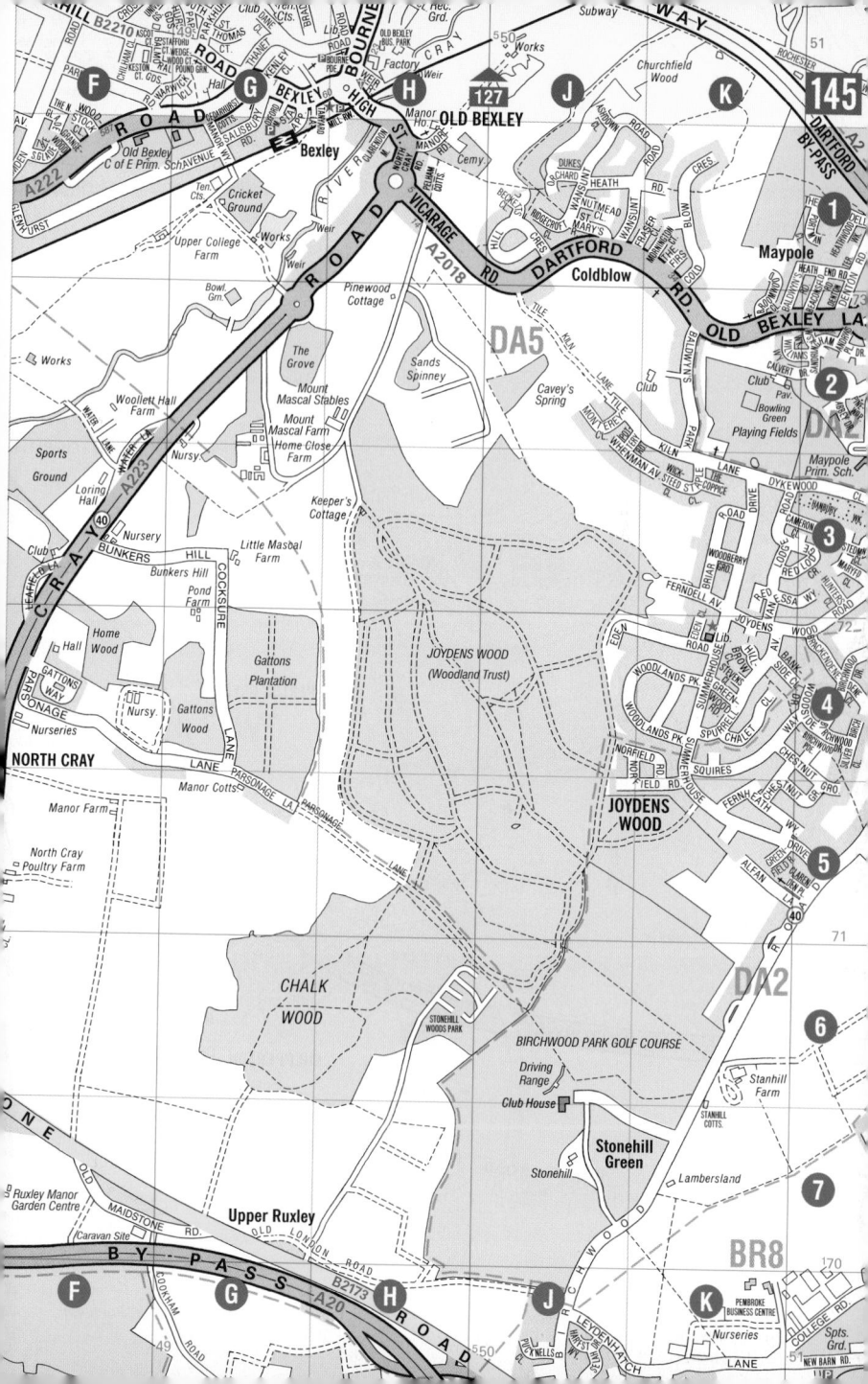
145
127
OLD BEXLEY
Bexley
Old Bexley C of E Prim. Sch.
Cricket Ground
Upper College Farm
Coldblow
Maypole
DA5
DA2
BR8
Churchfield Wood
Pinewood Cottage
The Grove
Sands Spinney
Mount Mascal Stables
Mount Mascal Farm
Home Close Farm
Woollett Hall Farm
Sports Ground
Loring Hall
Cavey's Spring
Playing Fields
Bowling Green
Maypole Prim. Sch.
Keeper's Cottage
Little Mascal Farm
Bunkers Hill
Pond Farm
Home Wood
Gattons Plantation
Gattons Wood
JOYDENS WOOD (Woodland Trust)
JOYDENS WOOD
NORTH CRAY
Manor Cotts.
Manor Farm
North Cray Poultry Farm
CHALK WOOD
STONEHILL WOODS PARK
BIRCHWOOD PARK GOLF COURSE
Driving Range
Club House
Stonehill Green
Stonehill
Stanhill Farm
Lambersland
Ruxley Manor Garden Centre
Caravan Site
Upper Ruxley
PEMBROKE BUSINESS CENTRE
Nurseries
DARTFORD BY-PASS
VICARAGE RD.
DARTFORD RD.
OLD BEXLEY LA.
CRAY ROAD
BY-PASS
A20
A2018
A223
A222
B2173
ROAD
BIRCHWOOD ROAD
LEYDENHATCH LANE
MAIDSTONE RD.
OLD LONDON ROAD
COOKHAM ROAD
COLLEGE RD.
NEW BARN RD.
PARSONAGE LA.
BUNKERS HILL
COCKSURE LANE
TILE KILN LANE
SUMMERHOUSE DRIVE
SQUIRES WAY
JOYDENS WOOD RD.
WOODLANDS PK.
FERNDELL AV.
DYKEWOOD CL.
HEATH RD.
BLOW CRES.
WANSUNT RD.
ASHDOWN RD.
Spts. Grd.

146
128
QUEEN MARY RESERVOIR
Pumping Station
Round Copse
TW18
TW17
KT16
KT13
SHEPPERTON RD
LALEHAM ROAD
M3-MOTORWAY
CHERTSEY ROAD
RENFREE WAY
RUSSELL ROAD
NEW ROAD
CHARLTON ROAD
HIGH ST.
LITTLETON
SHEPPERTON GREEN
SHEPPERTON
CHARLTON
Shepperton Film Studios
Laleham Nurseries
Squire's Bridge
Staines Road Farm
Pool End
Sheepwalk Lake
Gravel Pit
Halliford Mere Lake
Cemetery
Cricket Ground
Las Palmas Estate
Desborough Sailing Club
DESBOROUGH
Chertsey Meads Local Nature Reserve
Chertsey Meads
RIVER THAMES
River Ash
Riversleigh Farm
Mead Farm
The Range
Manor Farm
Driving Range
SUNBURY GOLF
Saxon Prim. Sch.
Playing Field
DOCKETT EDDY LA.
FERRY LANE
CHURCH ROAD
SPELTHORNE ROAD

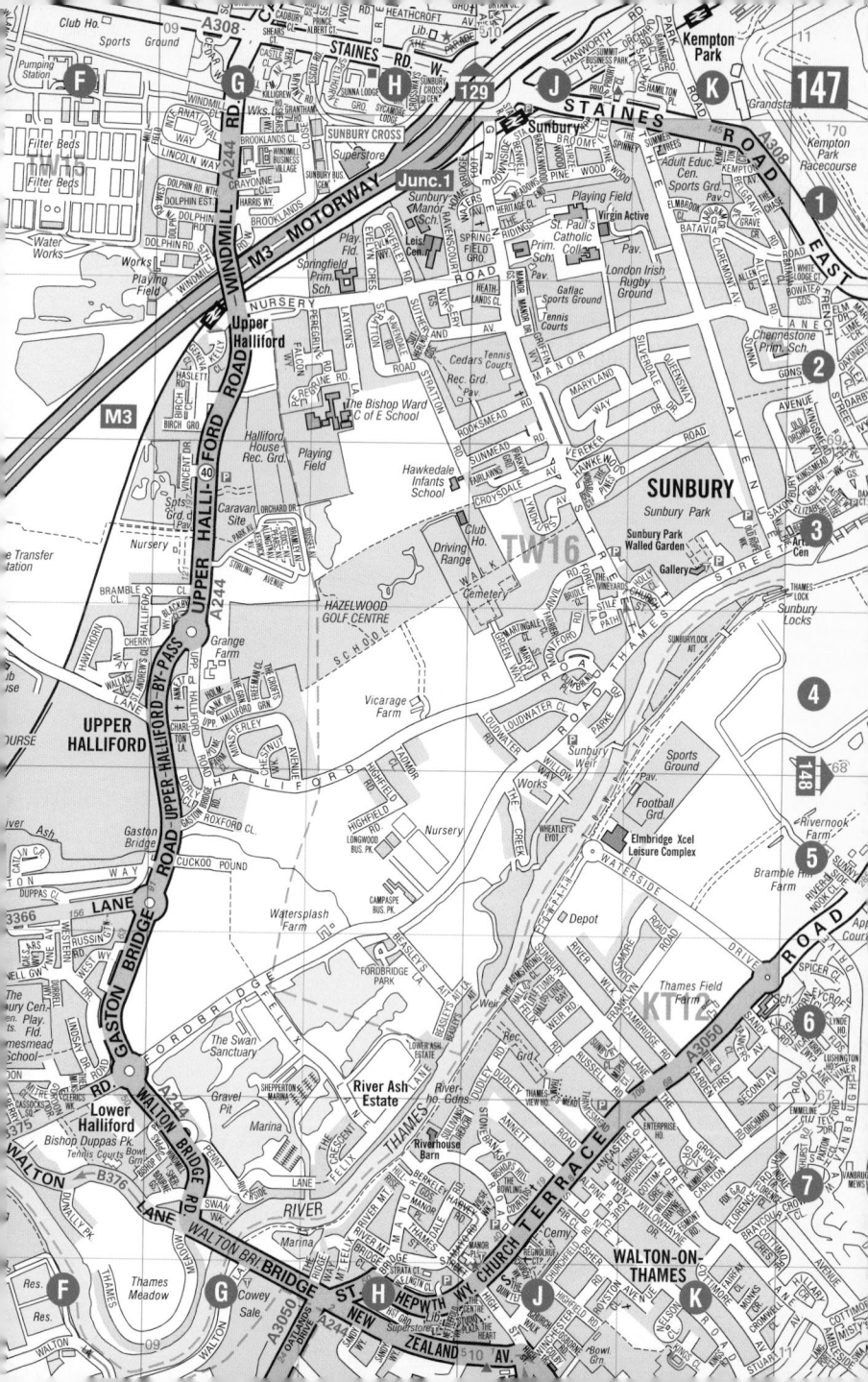
147
F
G
H
J
K
1
2
3
4
5
6
7
148
129
Club Ho.
Sports Ground
Pumping Station
A308
STAINES RD. W.
HEATHCROFT AV.
CADBURY
SHEARS CT.
PRINCE ALBERT CT.
Lib.
THE PARADE
KILLIGREW HO.
SUNNA LODGE
GRANTHAM HO.
SYCAMORE LODGE
CROSSWAYS
SUNBURY CROSS CEN.
Kempton Park
HANWORTH
SUMMIT BUSINESS PARK
ORCHARD
PRIORY
HAMILTON PL.
PARK ROAD
Grandstand
Kempton Park Racecourse
STAINES ROAD EAST
A308
WINDMILL CL.
INTERNATIONAL WAY
Wks.
BROOKLANDS CL.
WINDMILL BUSINESS VILLAGE
SUNBURY CROSS
Superstore
SUNBURY BUS. CEN.
Sunbury
BROOMFIELD
PINE WOOD
THE SPINNEY
SUMMER TREES
Adult Educ. Cen.
Sports Grd.
Pav.
KEMPTON AV.
Filter Beds
TW15
LINCOLN WAY
CRAYONNE CL.
HARRIS WY.
BROOKLANDS
DOLPHIN RD. NTH.
DOLPHIN EST.
DOLPHIN RD.
M3 MOTORWAY
Junc.1
Sunbury Manor Sch.
Leis. Cen.
RAVENSCOURT
HOME BRIDGE
WATERS AV.
MEADOWS END
HERITAGE CL.
THE RIDINGS
Playing Field
St. Paul's Catholic Coll.
Virgin Active
ELMBROOK CL.
BATAVIA
CLAREMONT AV.
BELGRAVE
GRAVE CR.
THE CHASE
Water Works
Works
Playing Field
WINDMILL RD.
A244
Play. Fld.
EVELYN CRES.
BEVERLEY RD.
Springfield Prim. Sch.
SPRINGFIELD GRO.
SPRINGFIELD ROAD
Prim. Sch.
Pav.
London Irish Rugby Ground
ALLEN RD.
WHITE LODGE CT.
BOWATER GDS.
FRENCH
NURSERY
Upper Halliford
PEREGRINE RD.
LAYTON'S LA.
STRATTON ROAD
RAVENDALE RD.
SUTHERLAND AV.
NURSERY GDS.
HEATHLANDS CL.
MANOR LA.
MANOR DR.
GRIFFIN WY.
Gaflac Sports Ground
Tennis Courts
LANE
Chennestone Prim. Sch.
SUNNA GDNS.
GENEVA
KELLY
HASLETT
BIRCH GRO.
FALCON WY.
Cedars Rec. Grd.
Tennis Courts
Pav.
MANOR
SILVERDALE DR.
QUEENSWAY DR.
MARYLAND WAY
AVENUE
KINGSMEAD
OLD ORCHARD
M3
The Bishop Ward C of E School
ROOKSMEAD RD.
VEREKER RD.
ROAD
Halliford House Rec. Grd.
Playing Field
SUNMEAD RD.
FAIRLAWNS GRO.
PARKWOOD GRO.
HAWKEWOOD RD.
THE PINES
40
VINCENT DR.
UPPER HALLIFORD ROAD
A244
Hawkedale Infants School
CROYSDALE AV.
LYNDHURST AV.
SUNBURY
Sunbury Park
SAXONBURY
ELIZABETH
Arts Cen.
Spts. Grd.
Pav.
Caravan Site
ORCHARD DR.
PARK AV.
BRAMLEY AV.
RUSSELL RD.
Club Ho.
Driving Range
TW16
Sunbury Park Walled Garden
Gallery
OLD ROPE WK.
Nursery
Transfer Station
STIRLING AVENUE
WALK
Cemetery
FORGE
THE VINEYARDS
HOLLY CL.
CHURCH ST.
STREET
THAMES LOCK
Sunbury Locks
BRAMBLE CL.
HALLIFORD CL.
BLACKBY
CHERRY WAY
HAWTHORN WAY
WALLACE CL.
ST. ANDREW'S CL.
HAZELWOOD GOLF CENTRE
SCHOOL
Grange Farm
MARTINGALE CL.
ANVIL RD.
BRIDLE CL.
STILE PATH
MONTFORD RD.
GREEN WAY
ST. MARY'S
THAMES ST.
SUNBURYLOCK AIT
UPPER HALLIFORD
UPPER HALLIFORD BY-PASS
HOLMBANK DR.
THE GRN.
FREEMAN CL.
THE CROFTS
HALLIFORD GRN.
CHARLTON LA.
MINSTERLEY
CHESTNUT WK.
AVENUE
Vicarage Farm
CUMBERLAND CL.
LOUDWATER CL.
LOUDWATER RD.
ROAD
PARKE
Sunbury Weir
WILLOW WAY
Works
Sports Ground
Pav.
Football Grd.
DORLY CL.
GASTON BRIDGE RD.
ROXFORD CL.
HALLIFORD
TADMOR CL.
HIGHFIELD RD.
Nursery
LONGWOOD BUS. PK.
THE CREEK
WHEATLEY'S EYOT
Elmbridge Xcel Leisure Complex
Rivernook Farm
Bramble Hill Farm
River Ash
Gaston Bridge
CUCKOO POUND
WAY
DUPPAS CL.
LANE
CAMPASPE BUS. PK.
WATERSIDE DRIVE
Depot
RIVER NOOK CL.
Watersplash Farm
ROAD
SPICER CL.
B3366
156
RUSSINGTON
WESTERN AV.
WEST WY.
NELL GWYNNE AV.
BEASLEY'S LA.
FORDBRIDGE PARK
BEASLEY'S AIT
Weir
SUNBURY LA.
RIVER WLK.
DUNSMORE RD.
Thames Field Farm
KT12
FELIX
FORDBRIDGE
LINDSAY DR.
DURRELL
The Swan Sanctuary
Gravel Pit
Marina
LOWER ASH ESTATE
River Ash Estate
HALLIWELL
WEIR RD.
Rec. Grd.
DUDLEY RD.
RUSSELL RD.
FRANKLYN
CAMBRIDGE RD.
A3050
SANDY LA.
FIRST AV.
SECOND AV.
LUSHINGTON
GASTON BRIDGE
ROAD
RD.
WALTON BRIDGE RD.
A244
Lower Halliford
Bishop Duppas Pk.
Tennis Courts
Bowl. Grn.
SHEPPERTON MARINA
THE CRESCENT
THAMES
River-ho. Gdns.
Riverhouse Barn
DUDLEY
THAMES VIEW HO.
THAMESMEAD
ANNETT RD.
STONEBANKS
EMMELINE CT.
TELFORD
WALTON
B376
B375
DUNALLY PK.
PENNY LANE
SWAN WK.
RIVER
LANE
RIVERSIDE
BERKELEY GDS.
MANOR PL.
HARVEY
RIVER MT.
DALE
BISHOPS HILL
THE BOWLING
TERRACE
CHURCH
SIDNEY RD.
LANCASTER CT.
KINGS BRIDGE
COTTIMORE
ENTERPRISE HO.
GROVE CR.
CARLTON
FOX GRO.
FLORENCE
BRAYCOURT
COTTIMORE CRES.
AVENUE
VANBRUGH MEWS
MEADOW
Marina
THAMES ST.
MT. FELIX
BRIDGE CL.
STRATA CT.
MANOR
Cemy.
FIR CL.
CHURCHFIELD RD.
ESHER
ALPINE
WILLOWHAYNE DR.
EGMONT RD.
WALTON-ON-THAMES
Thames Meadow
Res.
Res.
Cowey Sale
WALTON BRI.
BRIDGE ST.
HEPWORTH WY.
Lib.
THE CENTRE
THE HEART
Superstore
A3050
OATLANDS DRIVE
A244
NEW ZEALAND AV.
WINCHESTER
HIGHFIELD RD.
ROYSTON AV.
NELSON CL.
FAIRFAX
MONKS
CROMWELL CL.
HILLARY CR.
AMBLESIDE
COTTIMORE LA.
STUART AV.
KINGS
ROAD
Bowl. Grn.
CHURCH WALK
WALTON LA.
WALTON
09
10
11
69
68
67
170

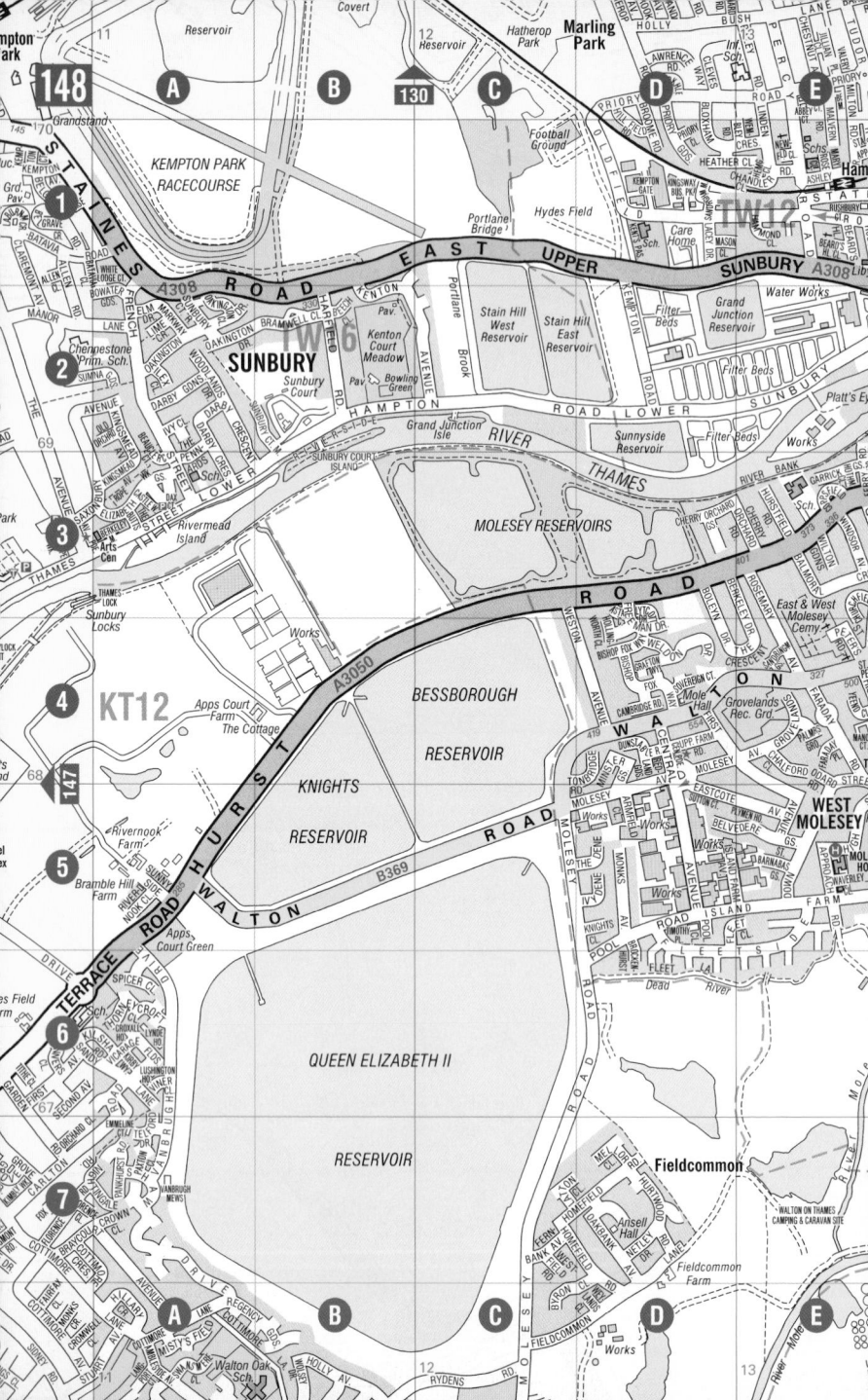

148
130
147
A
B
C
D
E
1
2
3
4
5
6
7
11
12
13
Marling Park
Hatherop Park
Kempton Park
Reservoir
Covert
Grandstand
KEMPTON PARK RACECOURSE
Football Ground
Hydes Field
Portlane Bridge
STAINES ROAD
EAST
UPPER
SUNBURY
A308
ROAD
TW12
TW16
SUNBURY
Chennestone Prim. Sch.
Kenton Court Meadow
Sunbury Court
Bowling Green
Stain Hill West Reservoir
Stain Hill East Reservoir
Portlane Brook
Filter Beds
Grand Junction Reservoir
Water Works
Sunnyside Reservoir
HAMPTON
ROAD
LOWER
Grand Junction Isle
RIVER
THAMES
Sunbury Court Island
Rivermead Island
Arts Cen
Thames Lock
Sunbury Locks
MOLESEY RESERVOIRS
East & West Molesey Cemy.
Works
KT12
Apps Court Farm
The Cottage
A3050
BESSBOROUGH
RESERVOIR
KNIGHTS
RESERVOIR
HURST
WALTON
B369
Rivernook Farm
Bramble Hill Farm
Apps Court Green
TERRACE ROAD
Mole Hall
Grovelands Rec. Grd.
WEST MOLESEY
Dead River
QUEEN ELIZABETH II
RESERVOIR
Fieldcommon
Ansell Hall
Fieldcommon Farm
WALTON ON THAMES CAMPING & CARAVAN SITE
River Mole
Walton Oak Sch.
RYDENS RD.
MOLESEY ROAD

149
131
150
F
G
H
J
K
1
2
3
4
5
6
7
HAMPTON
BUSHY PARK
TW11
HURST PARK
EAST MOLESEY
HAMPTON COURT
THAMES DITTON
KT8
KT7
KT10
ISLAND BARN
RESERVOIR
WESTON GREEN
Giggshill
Hampton Open Air Pool
Hampton & Richmond Borough FC (Beveree Stadium)
Round Plantation
Willow Plantation
River Lodge
Waterhouse Woodland Garden
Waterhouse Pond
Fisher's Pond
Red Brick Bridge
White Lodge
Broom Clumps
The Pheasantry Welcome Centre
Bushy House
Teddington Lodge
Hawthorn Lodge
Deer Pen
Heron Pond
Diana Fountain
Hampton Court House Sch.
Hampton Court Gate
Hampton Court Green
Royal Mews
Maze
Hampton Court Gardens
Hampton Court Palace
Privy Garden
Cigarette Island Park
Hampton Court
Ditton Field
Albany Reach
Pavilion Terrace
Thames Ditton Island
Garrick's Ait
Garrick Lawn
Foot Ferry
Filter Beds
St. Alban's Lodge
Hurst Park Open Space
Terrace Gardens
Taggs Island
Ash Island
Cricket Ground
Hurst Pool
Molesey Hurst Rec. Grd.
The Pav. Sports & Fitness Club
Vine Play. Fld.
Nielson Playing Field
Sports Ground
Sailing Club
Tanners Bridge
Grist Memorial Sports Ground
Imber Court Trading Estate
Imber Court
Football Grd.
Recreation Grd.
Esher College
Playing Field
Thames Ditton Jun. Sch.
Cranmere Primary School
Water Pollution Control Works
Golf Course
A311
A308
A3050
A309
B369
B3379
B364
A307
HAMPTON COURT ROAD
HAMPTON COURT WAY
HURST ROAD
THAMES STREET
HIGH STREET
BRIDGE ROAD
WALTON ROAD
EMBER LANE
ESHER ROAD
EMBER COURT RD.
STATION RD.
PORTSMOUTH RD.
CHESTNUT AVENUE
RIVER EMBER
RIVER THAMES
River Mole

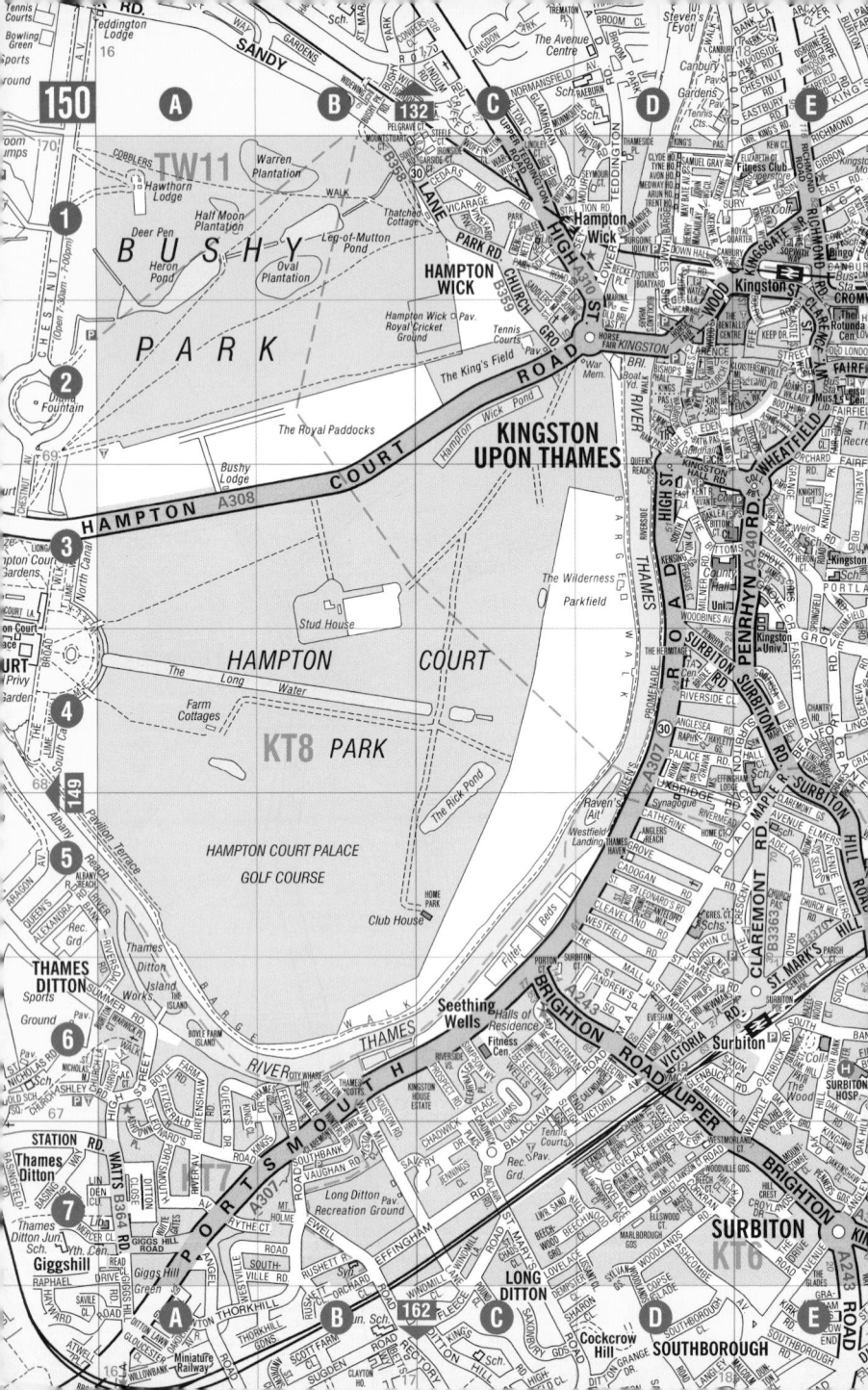
150
132
149
162
A
B
C
D
E
1
2
3
4
5
6
7
TW11
KT8
KT7
KT6
BUSHY PARK
Teddington Lodge
Warren Plantation
Hawthorn Lodge
Half Moon Plantation
Deer Pen
Heron Pond
Leg-of-Mutton Pond
Oval Plantation
Thatched Cottage
Diana Fountain
CHESTNUT AV.
(Open 7-30am - 7-00pm)
COBBLERS WALK
SANDY LANE
HAMPTON WICK
Hampton Wick
Hampton Wick Royal Cricket Ground
Tennis Courts
The King's Field
The Royal Paddocks
Bushy Lodge
HAMPTON COURT ROAD
A308
Hampton Wick Pond
KINGSTON UPON THAMES
Kingston
KINGSTON BRI.
Stud House
HAMPTON COURT PARK
The Long Water
Farm Cottages
The Rick Pond
HAMPTON COURT PALACE GOLF COURSE
Club House
The Wilderness
Parkfield
RIVER THAMES
BARGE WALK
QUEEN'S PROMENADE
Raven's Ait
Westfield Landing
Seething Wells
Halls of Residence
Filter Beds
PORTSMOUTH ROAD
A307
BRIGHTON ROAD
A243
UPPER BRIGHTON ROAD
VICTORIA RD.
Surbiton
SURBITON
SURBITON HOSP.
PENRHYN RD.
A240
CLAREMONT RD.
B3363
SURBITON HILL ROAD
The Bentalls Centre
The Rotunda Cen.
County Hall
Kingston Univ.
Fitness Club
Synagogue
THAMES DITTON
Thames Ditton
Thames Ditton Island
Giggshill
Giggs Hill Green
Long Ditton Recreation Ground
LONG DITTON
Kingston House Estate
Cockcrow Hill
SOUTHBOROUGH
Miniature Railway
Albany Reach
Pavilion Terrace
HIGH STREET
WAITS B364
STATION RD.
Steven's Eyot
Canbury Gardens
The Avenue Centre

151
133
152
163
F
G
H
J
K
1
2
3
4
5
6
7
COOMBE
KT2
KT3
KT5
NORBITON
BERRYLANDS
Norbiton
Berrylands
Kingston Hospital
Coombe Wood Golf Course
Holy Cross Preparatory RC Sch.
Marymount International School
Coombe Hill Jun. & Inf. Schools
Coombe Girls' Sch.
Corpus Christi Catholic Prim. School
Kingston Cemetery
Kingston Crematorium
Athletics Centre
AFC Wimbledon & Kingstonian FC (Kingsmeadow)
Hogsmill River
Sewage Works
Surbiton Cemetery
Recreation Ground
Grand Avenue Prim. Sch.
Richard Challoner School
Malden Manor Prim. Sch.
Alexandra Millennium Green
COOMBE LANE WEST
COOMBE ROAD
KINGSTON ROAD
CAMBRIDGE RD.
LONDON RD.
MALDEN WAY
KINGSTON BY-PASS
A238
A308
A2043
A3
A240
B351
B283

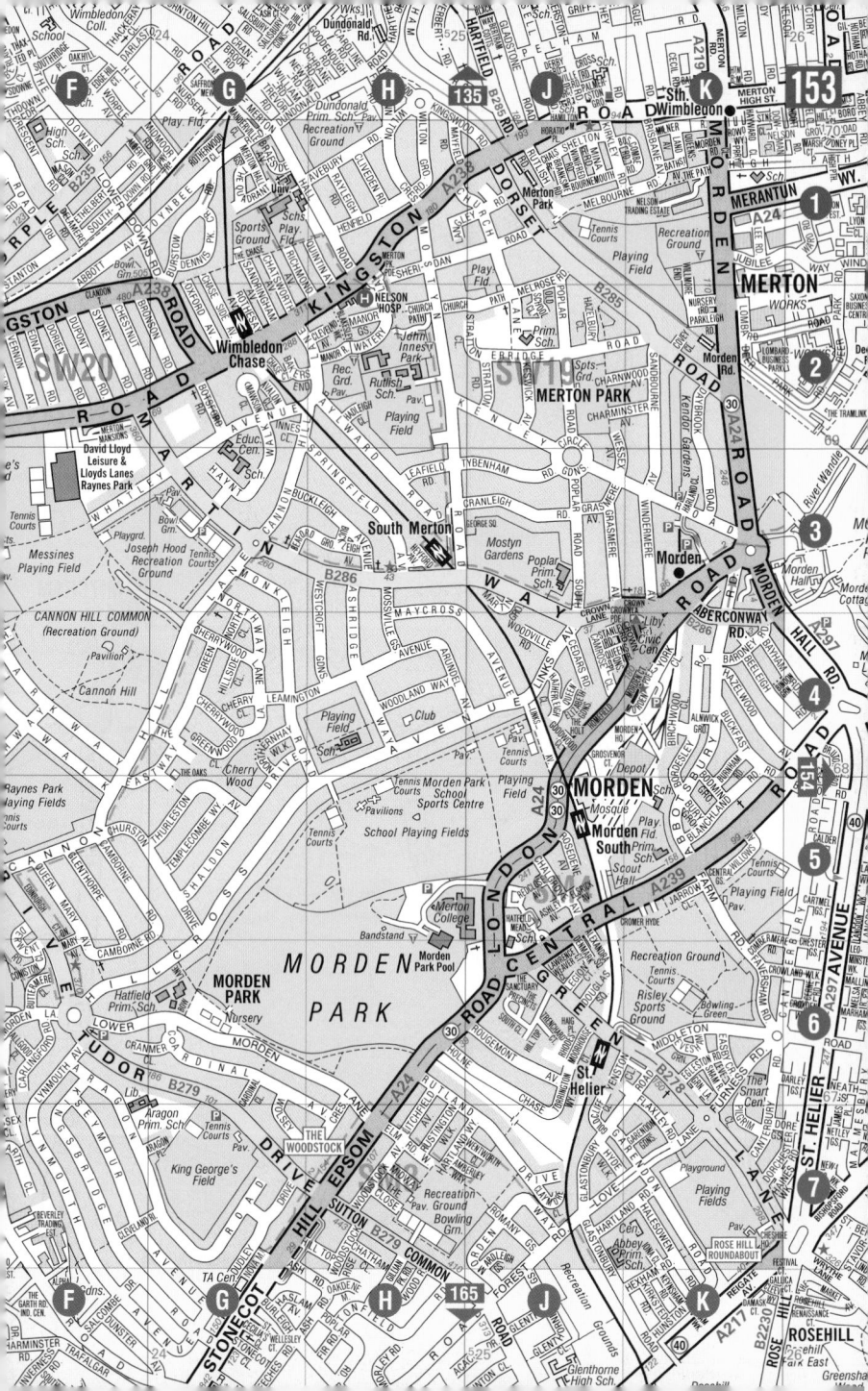

153
135
154
165
F
G
H
J
K
1
2
3
4
5
6
7
24
25
26
Wimbledon Coll.
Dundonald Rd.
Dundonald Prim. Sch.
Recreation Ground
Sth. Wimbledon
MERTON HIGH ST.
MERANTUN WY.
A24
MERTON
WORKS
Merton Park
NELSON TRADING ESTATE
Recreation Ground
Tennis Courts
Playing Field
KINGSTON ROAD
A238
Wimbledon Chase
NELSON HOSP.
John Innes Park
Rutlish Sch.
Playing Field
SW20
SW19
MERTON PARK
Morden Rd.
Kendor Gardens
David Lloyd Leisure & Lloyds Lanes Raynes Park
Educ. Cen.
Joseph Hood Recreation Ground
Messines Playing Field
CANNON HILL COMMON (Recreation Ground)
Pavilion
Cannon Hill
South Merton
Mostyn Gardens
Poplar Prim. Sch.
Morden
MORDEN HALL RD.
A297
River Wandle
Morden Hall
ABERCONWAY RD.
B286
LEAMINGTON AVENUE
WOODLAND WAY
Playing Field
Club
Cherry Wood
Raynes Park Playing Fields
Morden Park School Sports Centre
Pavilions
School Playing Fields
MORDEN
Mosque
Morden South
Play. Fld.
Scout Hall
Depot
LONDON ROAD
A24
CENTRAL ROAD
A239
Merton College
Bandstand
Morden Park Pool
MORDEN PARK
Hatfield Prim. Sch.
MORDEN PARK
Nursery
LOWER MORDEN LANE
TUDOR DRIVE
B279
Lib.
Aragon Prim. Sch.
King George's Field
Tennis Courts
THE WOODSTOCK
EPSOM ROAD
STONECOT HILL
SUTTON COMMON ROAD
Recreation Ground
Bowling Grn.
St. Helier
B278
Recreation Ground
Tennis Courts
Risley Sports Ground
Bowling Green
The Smart Cen.
Playing Field
Playground
Playing Fields
Abbey Prim. Sch.
ROSE HILL ROUNDABOUT
ST. HELIER AVENUE
A217
B2230
ROSEHILL
Rosehill Park East
Glenthorne High Sch.
Recreation Grounds
THE GARTH RD. IND. CEN.
BEVERLEY TRADING EST.
TA Cen.

154
136
153
166
A
B
C
D
E
1
2
3
4
5
6
7
Colliers Wood
COLLIER'S WOOD
MERTON
HIGH ST.
A238
MERANTUN WAY
A24
Superstore
Colour Ho. Th.
Merton Abbey Mills
Riverside Business Park
Merton Ind. Est.
SW19
Saxon Business Centre
Deen City Farm
The Tramlink
Tandem Centre
Christchurch Rd.
Western Road
A236
Lavender Park
Play. Liberty Prim. Sch.
Cemetery
Tamworth Rec. Grd.
London Rd.
A217
Streatham Road
A216
Figges Marsh
Gas Works
Holborn Way
Upr. Green West
Upr. Green East
CR4
Morden Road
Morden Hall Park
Phipps Bridge
Morden Hall
Morden Cottage
Morden Lodge
River Wandle
Morden Hall Rd.
A297
B286
Belgrave Wlk.
Melrose Sch.
Playing Field
Lower Green W.
Mus.
Cricket Green
Cricket Grn.
Canons Leisure Centre
Sports Ground
Running Track
MITCHAM
Commonside West
Beehive Bridge
Blue Houses Bridge
Madeira Rd.
A239
Cranmer Rd.
Cranmer Bri.
Carshalton Road
Mitcham
Tramway Path
Ravensbury Park
Liongate Enterprise Park
St. Helier Avenue
Central Road
SM4
Watermeads
Tooting & Mitcham United FC (Imperial Fields)
Bennett's Hole
Poulter Park
Bishopsford House
Bishopsford Comm. Sch.
Bishopsford Road
Playing Fields
Willow Lane
Willow Lane Business Park
Willow Lane Industrial Estate
Mitcham Golf Course
Mitcham Junction
A237
Mill Green
Wandle Trad. Est.
Comm. Hall
Nature Reserves
Open Space
ST. HELIER
Hill Ho. Comm. Cen.
Bingo
Shaftesbury
SM5
Running Track
Sutton Arena Leisure Centre
St. Helier Open Space
BEDDINGTON CORNER
Rose Hill Roundabout
Reigate Av.
A217
Wrythe
ROSEHILL
Rose Hill
B2230
B278
St. Helier Hospital
Greenshaw Wood
Rosehill Park East

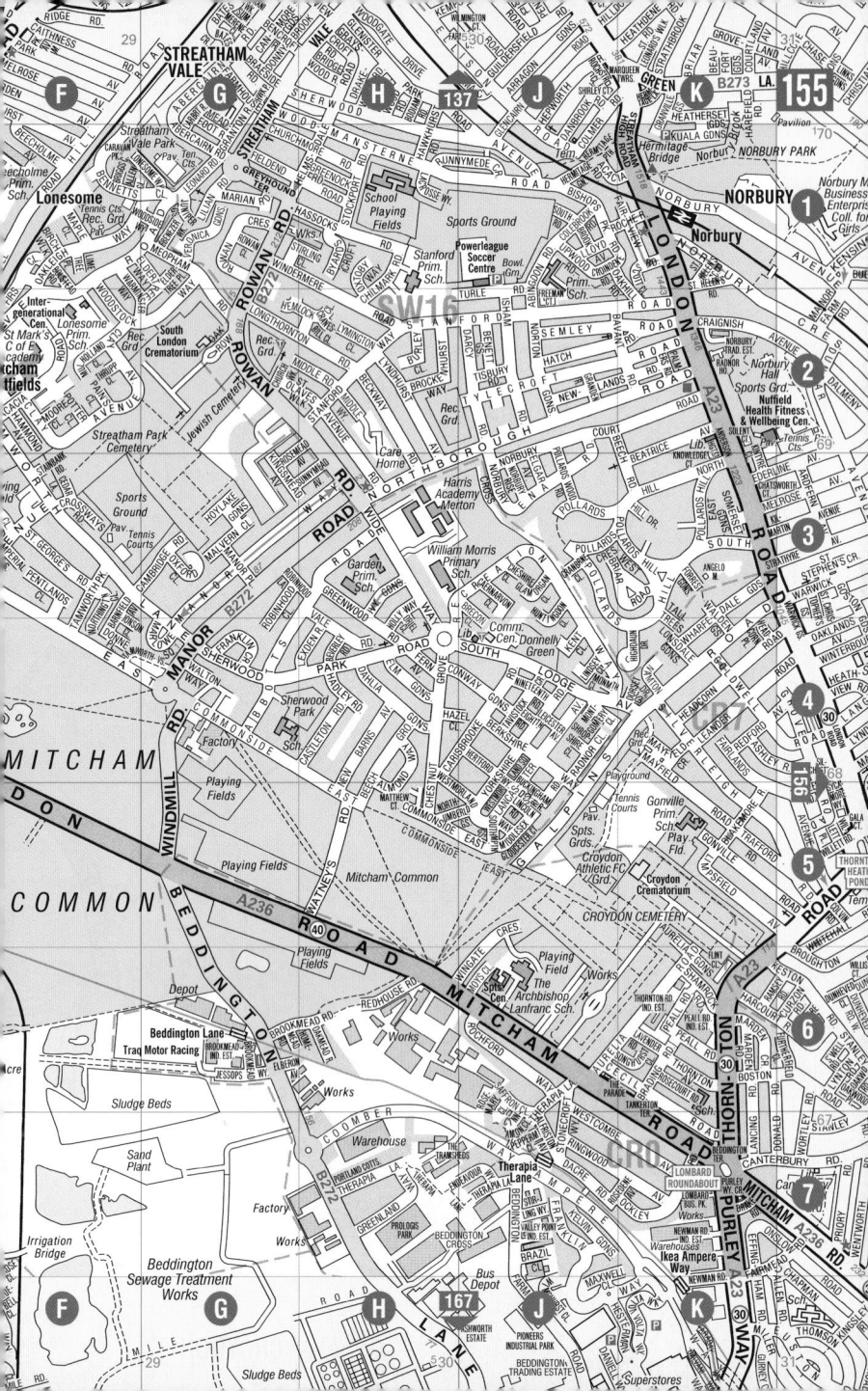
155
137
156
167
STREATHAM VALE
Streatham Vale Park
Lonesome
Lonesome Prim. Sch.
Intergenerational Cen.
St Mark's C of E Academy
South London Crematorium
Jewish Cemetery
Streatham Park Cemetery
Sports Ground
School Playing Fields
Powerleague Soccer Centre
Stanford Prim. Sch.
SW16
NORBURY
Norbury
NORBURY PARK
Norbury Hall
Nuffield Health Fitness & Wellbeing Cen.
Harris Academy Merton
William Morris Primary Sch.
Garden Prim. Sch.
Sherwood Park Sch.
Donnelly Green
Comm. Cen.
Gonville Prim. Sch.
Croydon Athletic FC Grd.
Croydon Crematorium
CROYDON CEMETERY
CR7
MITCHAM
COMMON
Mitcham Common
Playing Fields
Factory
The Archbishop Lanfranc Sch.
Beddington Lane
Traq Motor Racing
Sludge Beds
Sand Plant
Irrigation Bridge
Beddington Sewage Treatment Works
Warehouse
Therapia Lane
PROLOGIS PARK
BEDDINGTON CROSS
Bus Depot
PIONEERS INDUSTRIAL PARK
BEDDINGTON TRADING ESTATE
Superstores
Ikea Ampere Way
LOMBARD ROUNDABOUT
CR0
LONDON ROAD
A23
MITCHAM ROAD
A236
ROWAN RD.
B272
MANOR RD.
WINDMILL
BEDDINGTON LANE
NORTHBOROUGH ROAD
STREATHAM HIGH ROAD
THORNTON ROAD
PURLEY WAY
F
G
H
J
K
1
2
3
4
5
6
7

156
138
155
168
A
B
C
D
E
1
2
3
4
5
6
7
NORBURY
Norbury
NORBURY PARK
Biggin Wood
Downsview Prim. Sch.
Westwood Girls' College for Languages & Arts
UPPER NORWOOD
The Lawns
Norbury Manor Business & Enterprise Coll. for Girls
Kensington Avenue Prim. School
David Livingstone Prim. Sch.
Sports Ground
Comm. Cen.
Norbury Hall
Nuffield Health Fitness & Wellbeing Cen.
SW16
RC Prim. Sch.
Spurgeon's College
Coun. Offs.
Grangewood Park
TV Station
Cypress Inf. Sch.
Rec. Ground
Thornton Heath
THORNTON HEATH
CR7
Crystal Palace FC (Selhurst Park)
THORNTON HEATH POND
Ecclesbourne Prim. Sch.
Queen's Rd. Cemy.
MAYDAY UNIVERSITY HOSP.
Selhurst
SELHURST
The BRIT Sch.
St. Chad's Prim. Sch.
Heavers Farm Centre
Works
Lupin Bri.
Gloucester Rd. Junc.
Cottage Bri.
Cottage Junc.
Broad Green
Canterbury Rec. Grd.
Ampere
West Croydon
CROYDON
Council Offices
High Sch.
Super store
Gym
GREEN LANE
LONDON ROAD
BRIGSTOCK ROAD
MELFORT AVENUE
CRESCENT
PARCHMORE ROAD
BEULAH HILL
BEULAH ROAD
CHURCH ROAD
SOUTH NORWOOD HILL
GRANGE ROAD
HIGH STREET
WHITEHORSE ROAD
WHITEHORSE LANE
SELHURST ROAD
MITCHAM ROAD
PURLEY WAY
ST. JAMES'S RD.
WINDMILL RD.
NORTHCOTE RD.
LOWER ADDISCOMBE ROAD
SUMNER ROAD
WELLESLEY RD.
QUEENS ROAD
A23
A212
A213
A222
A235
A236
B266
B273

157
139
158
169
F
G
H
J
K
1
2
3
4
5
6
7
34
35
36
ANERLEY
PENGE
SE20
SE19
SE25
BR3
CRO
SOUTH NORWOOD
WOODSIDE
ELMERS END
Anerley
Kent House
Birkbeck
Elmers End
Norwood Junc.
Woodside
Blackhorse La.
Addiscombe
Shirley Oaks
Harrington Rd.
Avenue Road
ANERLEY ROAD
CROYDON RD.
PENGE RD.
ELMERS END ROAD
CROYDON ROAD
LONG LANE
SPRING LANE
PORTLAND ROAD
WOODSIDE GREEN
WOODSIDE ROAD
HIGH ROAD
HIGH STREET
ST. BECKENHAM RD.
LOWER ADDISCOMBE RD.
SHIRLEY RD.
UPPER ELMERS END RD.
CLOCK HOUSE RD.
A213
A214
A215
A222
A234
B243
30
South Norwood Lake
South Norwood Country Park
Pitch & Putt Course
South Norwood Country Park Visitors Cen.
Croydon Sports Arena
Croydon FC Grd.
Ryelands Prim. Sch.
Croydon Golf Driving Range
Beckenham Crematorium
Orchard School Sports Centre
Orchard Lodge (Remand Centre)
James Dixon Prim. Sch.
Phil Edwards Cen.
Harris City Academy
Harris Academy
Athletic Grounds
Recreation Ground
Betts Park
Ashburton Park
Ashburton Playing Fields
Oasis Academy Shirley Park (Seniors)
SHIRLEY OAKS BMI HOSPITAL
Monks Orchard Prim. Sch.
Brickfields Mdw.
Bromley Junction
Blind Corner
Chaffinch Brook
Glade Wood
Long Lane Wood Bird Sanctuary
Davidson Prim. Sch.
Swim. Pools
Playing Field

158
A
B
C
D
E
1
2
3
4
5
6
7
140
157
170
36
37
38
CATOR PARK
Cator Pk. Sch.
Kent House
Beckenham Road
Beckenham Junc.
Clock Ho.
BECKENHAM
BR3
BECKENHAM BEACON
Recreation Ground
Kelsey Park
Elgood Playing Field
Kelsey Park Sports College
Crease Park
ELMERS END
EDEN PARK
Eden Park
PARK LANGLE
Langley Court (Research Labs)
Langley Park Schools
Langley Park Sports Centre
Unicorn Prim. Sch.
David Lloyd Leisure
UPPER ELMERS END
Crouch Oak Wood
MONKS ORCHARD
Edenham High Sch.
BETHLEM ROYAL HOSPITAL
High Broom Wood
Blake Recreation Ground
West Wickham
WEST WICKHAM
CR0
CROYDON RD.
UPPER ELMERS END RD.
ELMERS END ROAD
SOUTH EDEN PARK RD.
BECKENHAM RD.
HIGH ST.
BROMLEY RD.
SOUTHEND RD.
HAYES RD.
A222
A234
A214
A2015
B230

159
141
160
171
F
G
H
J
K
1
2
3
4
5
6
7
Ravensbourne
Sundridge Park
Bromley Nth.
Shortlands
Bromley South
SHORTLANDS GOLF COURSE
BROMLEY PARK
BROMLEY
SHORTLANDS
HAYES
NORMAN PARK
BR1
BR2
BR4
SLOANE BMI HOSP.
BECKENHAM LANE
TWEEDY RD.
WIDMORE RD.
KENTISH WAY
MASONS HILL
WESTMORELAND ROAD
HAYES ROAD
HAYES LANE
PICKHURST LANE
WEST WICKHAM
Bromley Civic Centre
Churchill Theatre
Leisure Cen.
Queens Gdn.
THE GLADES SHOPPING CENTRE
Queen's Mead
Martin's Hill
Rec. Grd.
Cricket Ground
Playing Field
Nuffield Health Fitness & Wellbeing Centre
Bromley FC
Fishers Wood
Norman Park Athletics Track
Scrogginhall Wood
Brook Wood
Hayes Street Farm
Hayes Prim. Sch.
Cupola Wood
Recreation Ground
Pickhurst Jun. & Inf. Schs.
Pickhurst Green
Sports Grounds
Tennis Courts
The Ravensbourne Sch.
Bromley PRU at Kingswood
Hayesford
Highfield Jun. Sch.
Highfield Inf. Sch.
South Hill Wood Rec. Grnd
Bishop Challoner Sch.
Golf Course
Bromley Common
A21
A222
A2212
B228
B2212
B251
B265

160
Sundridge Park
142
A
B
C
D
E
1
2
3
4
5
6
7
Scotts Park Prim. Sch.
Widmore Green
Cricket Grd.
Club
WIDMORE ROAD
A222
ORCHARD RD.
PLAISTOW LANE
HOMEFIELD RD.
FREELANDS GRO.
HENVILLE RD.
SUNDRIDGE AV.
MAVELSTONE RD.
MAVELSTONE CL.
WOOD LODGE GDS.
ROMNEY DR.
SERVIDEN DR.
EDGEBOROUGH WY.
HOLMBURY PK.
LOGS HILL
YESTER DR.
YESTER RD.
Bullers Wood Sch.
LUBBOCK RD.
CAMDEN RD.
CAMDEN PK.
LOWER CAMDEN
BROOK CL.
OLD ROAD
St. Cecilia's
WESTBURY RD.
FARM LANE
SIMONE CL.
DUNORAN HOME
ST. NICOLAS LA.
NORTHFIELD CL.
WESTLEIGH DR.
B264
ST. GEORGE'S RD. W.
BEECH COPSE
CEDAR COPSE
ASPEN COPSE
SPINNEYS
SPINNEY OAK
WELLS RD.
DENBRIDGE RD.
BOSCOBEL CL.
PRIORY CL.
MERLEWOOD DR.
OAKHURST CL.
TUDOR CL.
Caves Chalkpit Wood
Chislehurst
CHISLEHURST ROAD
BICKLEY RD.
Tennis Cts.
Pav.
Play. Fld.
PINES RD.
WOODLANDS RD.
WOODLANDS CL.
HARTLEY CL.
INGLEWOOD COPSE
EASTMEAD CL.
Hadlow
BICKLEY
Ckt. Gd.
BICKLEY PARK
A222
BR1
HEVER GDNS.
WELLSMOOR GS.
REYNARD CL.
COATES HILL RD.
SYCAMORE PL.
OTFORD CL.
BARFIELD
GOLF RD.
THORNET WOOD RD.
ROSHESTER AV.
NIGHTINGALE LANE
Moat
Bromley Civic Centre
CHASE
MURRAY AV.
FORDE AV.
BISHOPS AV.
WANSTEAD RD.
WANSTEAD CL.
BEECHFIELD RD.
CEDAR RD.
Rec. Grd
TYLNEY RD.
BIRD IN HAND LA.
WESTWOOD LA.
School
The Widmore Cen.
Bickley Prim. Sch.
WIDMORE
Playing Field
Gas Works
PALACE VW.
CANON RD.
LIDDON RD.
PAGE HEATH LA.
Sch.
CHARLOTTE PARK AV.
Bickley
ST. GEORGE'S RD.
ST. MATTHEW'S DR.
NEWNHAMS CL.
HAWTHORNE ROAD
South
LANGDON RD.
SIWARD ROAD
GODWIN RD.
GLANVILLE ROAD
WALDO RD.
WALDO IND. EST.
BEACONSFIELD RD.
AVENUE
LINDSEY CL.
Depot
Recreation Ground
B265
HOMESDALE RD.
Virgin Active Health Club
SOUTHLANDS GROVE
CHADD DR.
FALCON AV.
WYNCROFT CL.
SOUTHWARK PL.
ROSEMOUNT DR.
HURSTWOOD DR.
OLDFIELD ROAD
AYCLIFFE CL.
Tennis Cts.
Hall
Playing Field
Tennis Courts
HAYES LA.
159
Bromley PRU at Kingswood
Playing Field
Hayesford
BROMLEY COMMON
Whitehall Pleasure Ground
COWPER ROAD
TREDWELL CL.
BLENHEIM RD.
CLAREMONT RD.
BURFORD RD.
WALDEGRAVE RD.
MAYFIELD RD.
WOODSIDE RD.
SOUTHBOROUGH ROAD
SPRINGFIELD GDNS.
TANGLEBERRY CL.
PARK HILL
HIGHFIELD RD.
HOMEMEAD
BLACKBROOK LANE
Bromley High Sch.
SOUTHBOROUGH
30
Southborough Prim. Sch.
Playing Field
Youth Cen.
Parkfield Recreation Ground
Cemetery
SOUTHBOROUGH LANE
CROWN LANE
HOLBROOK WAY
A21
Sports Ground
Field Health & Wellbeing Centre
Cricket Ground
Bromley FC
Pavilion
Fishers Wood
Ravens Bourne
NORMAN PARK
Norman Park Athletics Track
Scrogginhall Wood
Playground
ROOKERY LA.
Bromley College of Further & Higher Education
BR2
MONS WAY
MOSUL WAY
TURPINGTON LANE
BROMLEY GOLF COURSE
BROMLEY COMMON
Club Ho.
Driving Range
Bishop Justus C of E School
Rookery Lake
Lord's Wood
Brook Wood
Playing Field
Princes Plain Prim. Sch.
Play. Fld.
Prince's Plain
Oakley House
Mazzards Wood
Woodcock Grove
GEORGE LA.
Hayes Prim. Sch.
172
Ravens Bourne
OAKLEY RD.
A233
HASTINGS ROAD
CHURCH LA.
COTTAGE AV.
BREWERY RD.
Playing Field
Scrubs Farm
LOVELACE
HAZEL WK.
LARCH WAY
ALMOND WY.
WHITEBEAM AV.
67
68
69
170
41
42
43

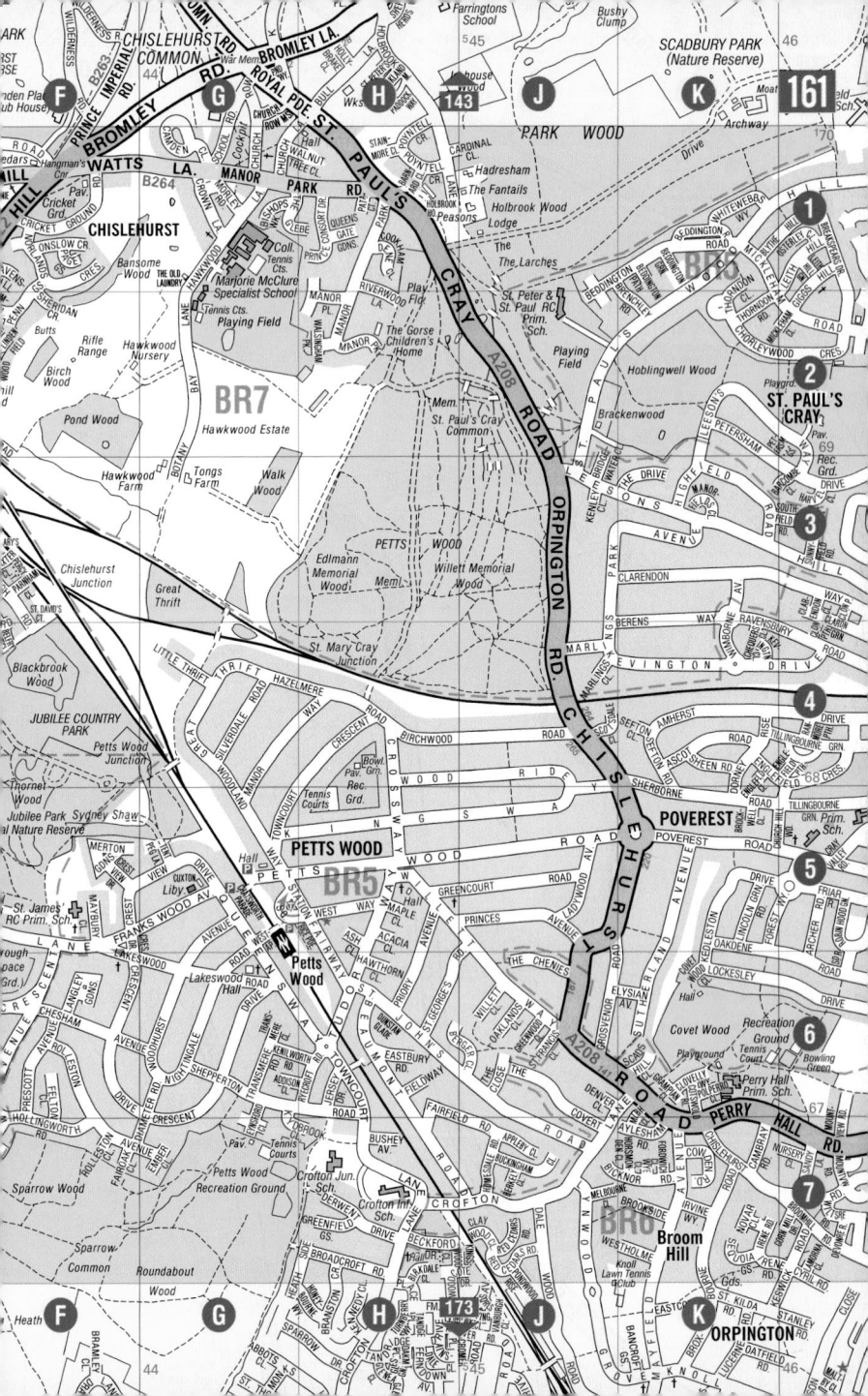
161
143
173
F
G
H
J
K
1
2
3
4
5
6
7
44
545
46
70
69
68
67
Farringtons School
Bushy Clump
SCADBURY PARK (Nature Reserve)
Moat
Archway
PARK WOOD
CHISLEHURST COMMON
PRINCE IMPERIAL RD.
BROMLEY RD.
BROMLEY LA.
ROYAL PDE.
War Mem.
WATTS LA.
MANOR PARK RD.
B263
B264
CHISLEHURST
Cricket Grd.
Pav.
CRICKET GROUND RD.
Hangman's Cnr.
Bansome Wood
Coll.
Tennis Cts.
Marjorie McClure Specialist School
THE OLD LAUNDRY
Playing Field
Rifle Range
Hawkwood Nursery
Birch Wood
Butts
Pond Wood
BR7
Hawkwood Estate
Hawkwood Farm
Tongs Farm
Walk Wood
BOTANY BAY LANE
ST. PAUL'S CRAY ROAD
A208
CARDINAL CL.
Hadresham
The Fantails
Holbrook Wood Lodge
Peasons
The Larches
St. Peter & St. Paul RC Prim. Sch.
Play Fld.
The Gorse Children's Home
Mem.
St. Paul's Cray Common
Playing Field
Hoblingwell Wood
Brackenwood
BR5
ST. PAUL'S CRAY
Playgrd.
Pav.
Rec. Grd.
CHORLEYWOOD CRES.
BEDDINGTON RD.
MICKLEHAM RD.
THORNDON RD.
PETERSHAM DRIVE
HIGHFIELD RD.
THE DRIVE
SOUTHFIELD RD.
AVENUE
PARK AV.
CLARENDON WAY
BERENS WAY
RAVENSBURY ROAD
KEVINGTON DRIVE
MARLINGS CL.
PETTS WOOD
Edlmann Memorial Wood
Meml.
Willett Memorial Wood
ORPINGTON RD.
Chislehurst Junction
Great Thrift
St. Mary Cray Junction
Blackbrook Wood
JUBILEE COUNTRY PARK
Petts Wood Junction
Thornet Wood
Jubilee Park Sydney Shaw Local Nature Reserve
LITTLE THRIFT
HAZELMERE WAY
CRESCENT ROAD
BIRCHWOOD ROAD
WOOD RIDE
KINGSWAY
CROSSWAY
Bowl. Grn.
Pav.
Rec. Grd.
Tennis Courts
PETTS WOOD
BR5
CHISLEHURST RD.
POVEREST
POVEREST ROAD
SHERBORNE ROAD
AMHERST DRIVE
TILLINGBOURNE GRN.
Prim. Sch.
CRAY VALLEY RD.
GREENCOURT ROAD
PRINCES AVENUE
WEST WAY
Hall
Liby.
St. James' RC Prim. Sch.
FRANKS WOOD AV.
QUEENSWAY
Petts Wood
Lakeswood Hall
LAKESWOOD ROAD
TUDOR WAY
TOWNCOURT LANE
ST. JOHN'S RD.
BEAUMONT RD.
EASTBURY RD.
FAIRFIELD RD.
THE CHENIES
OAKLANDS WAY
SUTHERLAND AVENUE
Covet Wood
Recreation Ground
Tennis Court
Bowling Green
Playground
Perry Hall Prim. Sch.
PERRY HALL RD.
ROAD
LOCKESLEY DRIVE
OAKDENE ROAD
Hall
SHEPPERTON
CRESCENT
HOLLINGWORTH
Pav.
Tennis Courts
Petts Wood Recreation Ground
Sparrow Wood
Crofton Jun. Sch.
Crofton Inf. Sch.
CROFTON LANE
CROFTON ROAD
BR6
Broom Hill
Knoll Lawn Tennis Club
WESTHOLME
Sparrow Common
Roundabout Wood
Heath
ORPINGTON
GROVE
KNOLL

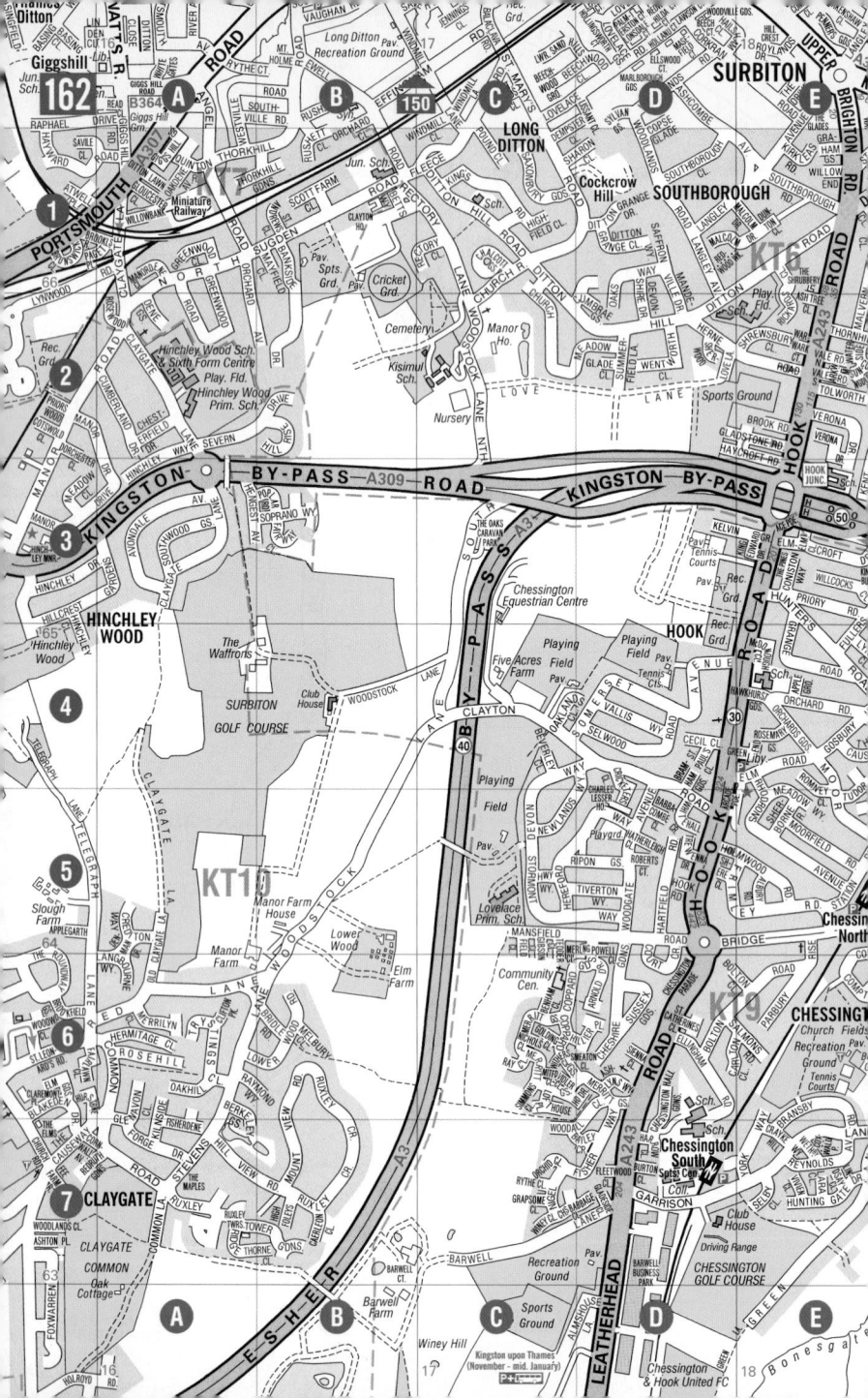

162
150
A
B
C
D
E
1
2
3
4
5
6
7
16
17
18
66
65
64
63
Giggshill
Long Ditton Recreation Ground
LONG DITTON
Cockcrow Hill
SURBITON
SOUTHBOROUGH
KT7
KT6
KT10
KT9
PORTSMOUTH ROAD
A307
Miniature Railway
Hinchley Wood Sch. & Sixth Form Centre
Hinchley Wood Prim. Sch.
Cricket Grd.
Cemetery
Kisimul Sch.
Manor Ho.
Nursery
LOVE LANE
Sports Ground
KINGSTON BY-PASS
A309
ROAD
A3
HINCHLEY WOOD
Hinchley Wood
The Waffrons
SURBITON GOLF COURSE
Club House
Chessington Equestrian Centre
Five Acres Farm
Playing Field
HOOK
HOOK ROAD
A243
Slough Farm
Manor Farm House
Lower Wood
Manor Farm
Elm Farm
Lovelace Prim. Sch.
Community Cen.
CHESSINGTON
Church Fields Recreation Ground
Tennis Courts
Chessington North
Chessington South
CLAYGATE
CLAYGATE COMMON
Oak Cottage
ESHER BY-PASS
Barwell Farm
Winey Hill
Recreation Ground
Sports Ground
LEATHERHEAD ROAD
BARWELL BUSINESS PARK
Driving Range
CHESSINGTON GOLF COURSE
Chessington & Hook United FC
Kingston upon Thames (November - mid. January)
Bonesgate

163
151
164
F
G
H
J
K
1
2
3
4
5
6
7
19
20
21
TOLWORTH
Tolworth
TOLWORTH JUNCTION
KT5
KT4
KT19
Malden Manor
WEST EWELL
ALEXANDRA RD.
Alexandra Millennium Green
Recreation Ground
A240 ROAD
KINGSTON ROAD
KINGSTON-BY-PASS
A3
TOLWORTH BROADWAY
TOLWORTH RISE NORTH
TOLWORTH RISE SOUTH
WARREN DRIVE NORTH
WARREN DRIVE SOUTH
KNOLLMEAD
ELMDENE
Playing Field
Tennis Courts
Community Centre
Knollmead Prim. Sch.
Maori Sports Ground
Riverhill
Sports Grd.
Crkt. Grd.
Surbiton Raceway
Sports Ground
Government Offices
King George's Field Playing Field
Bowling Green
Corinthian Casuals FC Grd.
Club
King George's Field
Tolworth Court Bridge
TOLWORTH HOSP.
Play. Fld.
Tolworth Rec. Cen.
Playing Field
Depot
Works
Castle Hill Prim. Sch.
Hogsmill Local Nature Reserve
Comm. Cen.
Youth Cen.
Riverview C of E Prim. Sch.
Play. Fld.
LA Fitness
Sports Ground
WORCESTER PARK RD.
CHESSINGTON RD.
RUXLEY LANE
Epsom & Ewell High Sch.
Playing Field
West Ewell Inf. Sch.
Hogsmill Local Nature Reserve
King George's Field
The Harrier Cen.
Running Track
Jun. Sch.
Linden Bridge School
Dancer Dick Wood
MALDEN LANE
CHURCH RD.
Nursery
Butcher's Grove
Castle Hill
HORTON COUNTRY PARK
HORTON PARK GOLF COURSE
Club Ho.
Driving Range
Hook Road Arena
Gt. Wood
St. Ebba's Farm Cottage
Cemetery
Horton Country Park Local Nature Reserve
HOOK ROAD
Playing Field
Rec. Grd.
Stream
Hogsmill

164
152
163
A
B
C
D
E
1
2
3
4
5
6
7
OLD MALDEN
Malden Manor
Malden Green
Worcester Park
WORCESTER PARK
KT4
STONELEIGH
Stoneleigh
KT17
KT19
WEST EWELL
EWELL
NONSUCH PARK
BEGGAR'S HILL
ORGAN CROSSROADS
CENTRAL ROAD
CHEAM COMMON ROAD
MALDEN ROAD
OLD MALDEN LANE
KINGSTON ROAD
LONDON ROAD
EWELL BY-PASS
Cuddington Recreation Ground
King George's Field
Auriol Park
Shadbolt Park
Oak Plantation
London Road Plantation
Hogsmill River
Chamber Mead
Playing Fields
Linden Bridge School
Wandgas Athletics Ground
Cuddington Prim. Sch.
Meadow Prim. Sch.
Dorchester Prim. Sch.
Mayflower Park
Maori Sports Ground
Ewell West
Bourne Hall Mus.
Ewell Castle Jun. Sch.
Ewell Castle Senior Sch.

165
166
153
F
G
H
J
K
1
2
3
4
5
6
7
24
25
26
SM1
SM2
SM3
SM4
ROSEHILL
BENHILTON
NORTH CHEAM
SUTTON
CHEAM
BELMONT
CHEAM PARK
Sutton Common
West Sutton
Sutton
Cheam
ROSE HILL ROUNDABOUT
ST. DUNSTAN'S
CHEAM VILLAGE
QUEEN VICTORIA
King George's Field
Recreation Ground
Playing Fields
Rosehill Recreation Ground
Rosehill Park East
Greenshaw Wood
Sutton Junior Tennis Centre
Sutton Cemetery
Recycling Cen.
Kimpton Ind. Est.
Superstore
Glenthorne High Sch.
St. Anthony's Hosp.
St. Raphael's Hospice
Sports Club
All Weather Pitch
Fairlands Pk.
Cheam Leisure Cen.
Cheam High Sch.
Sports Hall
Prim. School
Collingwood Road Recreation Ground
Sutton United FC
Perrett's Field
Water Wks.
Seears Park
Sutton Ckt. Grd.
Fitness Cen.
Secombe Thtre.
Civic Cen.
St. Nicholas Cen.
Cheam Recreation Ground
Nursery
Nonsuch High Sch.
Harefield Bri. Playing Field
Sports Grd.
Cricket Grd.
Overton Grange Sch.
Sports Ground
STONECOT HILL
SUTTON COMMON ROAD
ROSE HILL
ST. HELIER AVENUE
REIGATE AVENUE
OLDFIELDS ROAD
ST. DUNSTAN'S HILL
MALDEN ROAD
CHEAM ROAD
HIGH ST.
EWELL RD.
MULGRAVE RD.
BELMONT RISE
BRIGHTON ROAD
ANGEL HILL
ST. NICHOLAS WAY
THROWLEY WAY
CARSHALTON RD.
A24
A217
A2043
A232
A217
B279
B2230
B283

166
154
165
A
B
C
D
E
1
2
3
4
5
6
7
ST. HELIER
ROSEHILL
Rosehill Park East
Greenshaw Wood
St. Helier Open Space
Sutton Arena Leisure Centre
Running Track
ST. HELIER HOSPITAL
QUEEN MARY'S HOSPITAL FOR CHILDREN
BENHILTON
Royston Park
Benhill Rec. Grd.
THE WRYTHE
Muschamp Prim. Sch.
Sports Cen.
Rushy Meadow Prim. Sch.
Limes Grn.
Wrythe Rec. Grd.
Carshalton Athletic FC
Carshalton Coll.
Carshalton
CARSHALTON
St. Philomena's School
Heritage Cen.
Westcroft Leisure Cen.
The Grove
Council Offices
Studio Thtre.
Wilderness Island
Wandle Bri.
HACKBRIDGE
Hack Bri.
Comm Hall
Nature Reserves
The Frying Pan
CARSHALTON PARK
SUTTON
Sutton
Rec. Grd.
Super-store
Carshalton Beeches
Stanley Pk. Rec. Grd.
CARSHALTON BEECHES
CARSHALTON ON THE HILL
Resrs (covered)
SUTTON HEIGHTS
SM1
SM2
SM5
CR4
CARSHALTON ROAD
WRYTHE LANE
WEST ST.
NORTH ST.
HIGH ST.
RUSKIN RD.
POUND ST.
NIGHTINGALE RD.
HACKBRIDGE RD.
BRIGHTON ROAD
REIGATE AV.
ROSE HILL
ST. ANGEL HILL
BEECHES AV.
STANLEY PARK RD.
GROSVENOR AV.
BANSTEAD RD.
THE CROSSWAYS
A217
A232
B2230
B278
B277
B271

167
168
155
Hackbridge
Mile Road Bridge
Beddington Sewage Treatment Works
Sludge Beds
Sludge Beds
Factory
Works
Therapia Lane
Lombard Roundabout
Canterbury
Mitcham Road
Prologis Park
Beddington Cross
Bus Depot
Ashworth Estate
Pioneers Industrial Park
Beddington Trading Estate
Ikea Ampere Way
Superstores
Valley Leisure Park
Vue Cinema
Tenpin
Waddon Marsh
Superstore
Warehouse
CR0
The Orion Centre
Electricity Switching Station
Beddington
Waddon
Waddon Ponds
Waddon
Beddington Park
River Wandle
Carew Manor & Dovecote
Carew Manor Sch.
Sports Ground
Tennis Courts
Pavilions
The Grange
Boating Lake
Manor Gdn.
Grammar Sch.
Church Paddock
The Warren
Croydon Road
London Road
A232 Road
A237
A23
B272
B271
Bandon Hill Cemetery
SM6
Bandonhill
Fiveways Corner
Retail Park
Playing Field
Purley Way
Stafford Road
Red Gates Sch.
Wallington
Mellows Park
Tennis Courts
Bowling Green
Woodcote Road
Manor Road
Stafford Road
South Beddington
Sandy Lane
Foresters Drive
Foresters Prim. Sch.
Powerleague Soccer Cen.
Wilson's Sch.
Croydon Airport Ind. Est.
Connaught Business Cen.
Esporta Health & Racquets Club
Visitor Cen.
Roundshaw
Phoenix Cen.
Amy Johnson Prim. Sch.
Roundshaw Park (Playing Fields)
Roundshaw Park
Nature Reserve
Sports Ground
Wallington Cen.
Hostel
Sutton Mag. Ct.
Stanley Pk. Rd.
Plough Lane
Plough Lane
Beddington Lane
Demesne Road
Mollison Drive
Woodcote Road
Dragons Health Club
Works
F
G
H
J
K
1
2
3
4
5
6
7
29
30
31
63
64
65
66

168
156
167
CROYDON
WEST CROYDON
East Croydon
South Croydon
SOUTH CROYDON
Sanderstead
WADDON
Waddon
Waddon Marsh
WANDLE PARK
Wandle Park
Duppas Hill
Recreation Ground
Sports Ground
FIVEWAYS CORNER
HALING PARK
HALING GROVE
Purley Way Playing Fields
Roundshaw Park (Playing Fields)
Nature Reserve
Russell Hill Resr. (covered)
Harris Academy Purley
St. Giles' School
Whitgift Sch.
Cumnor House Sch.
Fairfield Halls
Croydon Coll.
Centrale
George St.
Wellesley Rd.
Church St.
Reeves Cnr.
Lebanon Rd.
Sandilands
Esporta Health & Racquets Club
Dragons Health Club
Bowl. Alley Health Club
Visitor Cen.
Retail Park
Superstores
Warehouses
MITCHAM ROAD
ST. JAMES'S ROAD
ROMAN WAY
OLD TOWN
DUPPAS HILL RD.
THE CROYDON FLYOVER
WELLESLEY ROAD
PARK LANE
COOMBE ROAD
LOWER ADDISCOMBE ROAD
FAIRFIELD RD.
BRIGHTON ROAD
SOUTH END
SELSDON RD.
DENNING AV.
WARHAM ROAD
WADDON WAY
PURLEY WAY
CROHAM ROAD
CHERRY ORCHARD ROAD
PARK HILL RD.
SANDERSTEAD ROAD
A23
A212
A232
A235
A236
A222
A213
B243
B269
B271
B274
B275
CR0
CR2
A
B
C
D
E
1
2
3
4
5
6
7

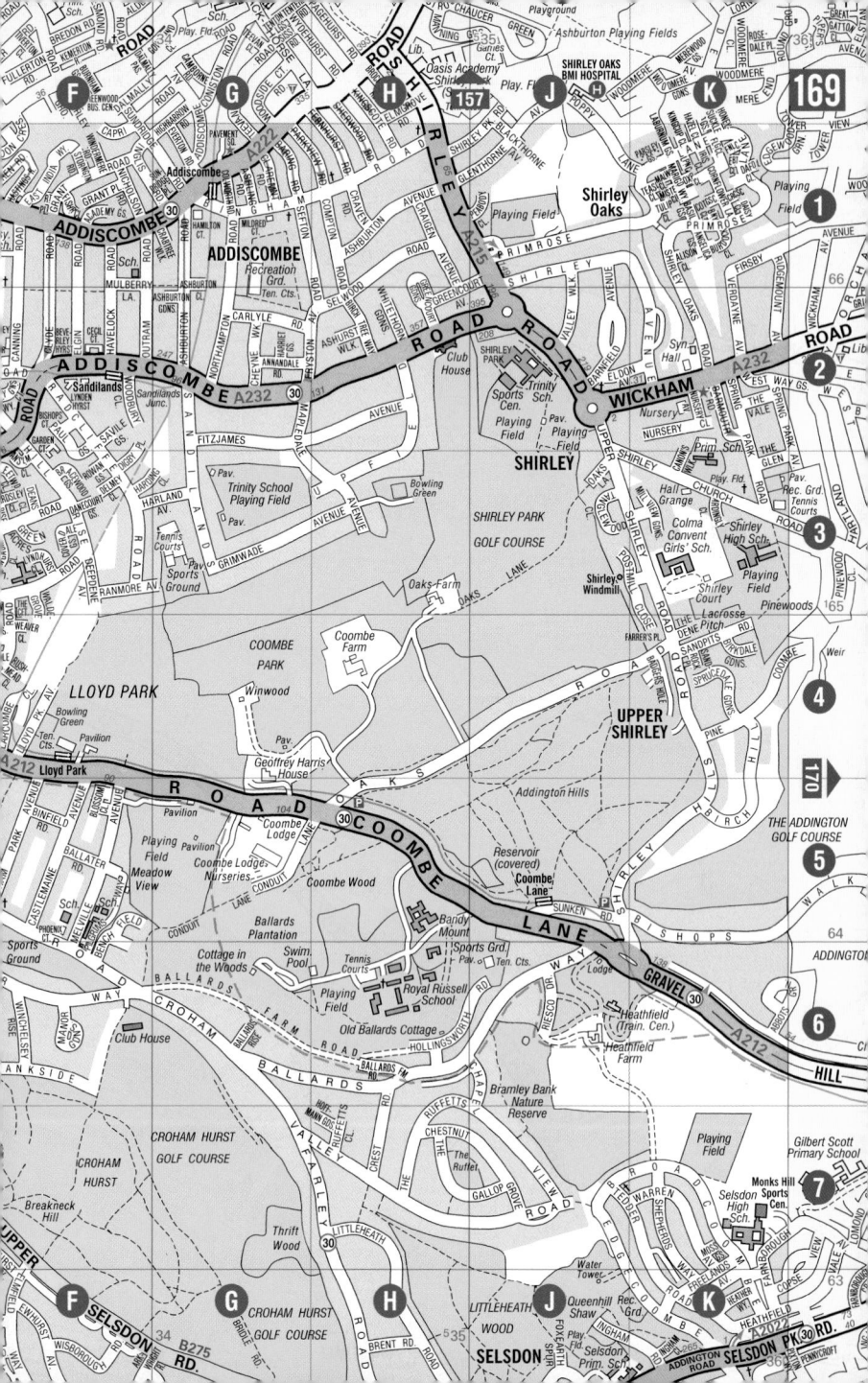
169
157
170
F
G
H
J
K
1
2
3
4
5
6
7
ADDISCOMBE
ADDISCOMBE ROAD
A232
A222
A215
A212
A2022
B275
Addiscombe
Recreation Grd.
Ten. Cts.
Sch.
Sandilands
Sandilands Junc.
Lloyd Park
LLOYD PARK
Bowling Green
Pavilion
Ten. Cts.
Trinity School Playing Field
Pav.
Tennis Courts
Sports Ground
COOMBE PARK
Coombe Farm
Winwood
Geoffrey Harris House
Oaks Farm
SHIRLEY PARK GOLF COURSE
Bowling Green
Club House
SHIRLEY PARK
Trinity Sch.
Sports Cen.
Playing Field
SHIRLEY
Shirley Oaks
Playing Field
SHIRLEY OAKS BMI HOSPITAL
Oasis Academy Shirley Park
Ashburton Playing Fields
Playground
Playing Field
WICKHAM ROAD
Syn. Hall
Nursery
Prim. Sch.
Hall Grange
Colma Convent Girls' Sch.
Shirley High Sch.
Shirley Windmill
Shirley Court
Lacrosse Pitch
Pinewoods
Rec. Grd.
Tennis Courts
Weir
UPPER SHIRLEY
Addington Hills
Reservoir (covered)
Coombe Lane
THE ADDINGTON GOLF COURSE
ADDINGTON
COOMBE ROAD
COOMBE LANE
GRAVEL HILL
SUNKEN RD.
BISHOPS WALK
Coombe Lodge
Coombe Lodge Nurseries
Playing Field
Meadow View
Coombe Wood
Ballards Plantation
Cottage in the Woods
Swim. Pool
Tennis Courts
Bandy Mount
Sports Grd.
Royal Russell School
Old Ballards Cottage
Heathfield (Train. Cen.)
Heathfield Farm
Lodge
Sports Ground
Club House
CROHAM HURST GOLF COURSE
CROHAM HURST
Breakneck Hill
Thrift Wood
Bramley Bank Nature Reserve
The Ruffett
Playing Field
Gilbert Scott Primary School
Monks Hill Sports Cen.
Selsdon High Sch.
Water Tower
Queenhill Shaw
Rec. Grd.
LITTLEHEATH WOOD
SELSDON
Selsdon Prim. Sch.
CROHAM HURST GOLF COURSE
SELSDON RD.
SELSDON PK. RD.
ADDINGTON ROAD
BALLARDS WAY
CROHAM ROAD
BALLARDS FARM ROAD
FARLEY ROAD
VALLEY
GALLOP
VIEW ROAD
BROADCOOMBE
EDGECOOMBE
PRIMROSE
SHIRLEY ROAD
SHIRLEY CHURCH ROAD
SHIRLEY HILLS ROAD
OAKS ROAD
UPPER SHIRLEY ROAD
FITZJAMES AVENUE
GRIMWADE AVENUE
HARLAND AV.
RANMORE AV.

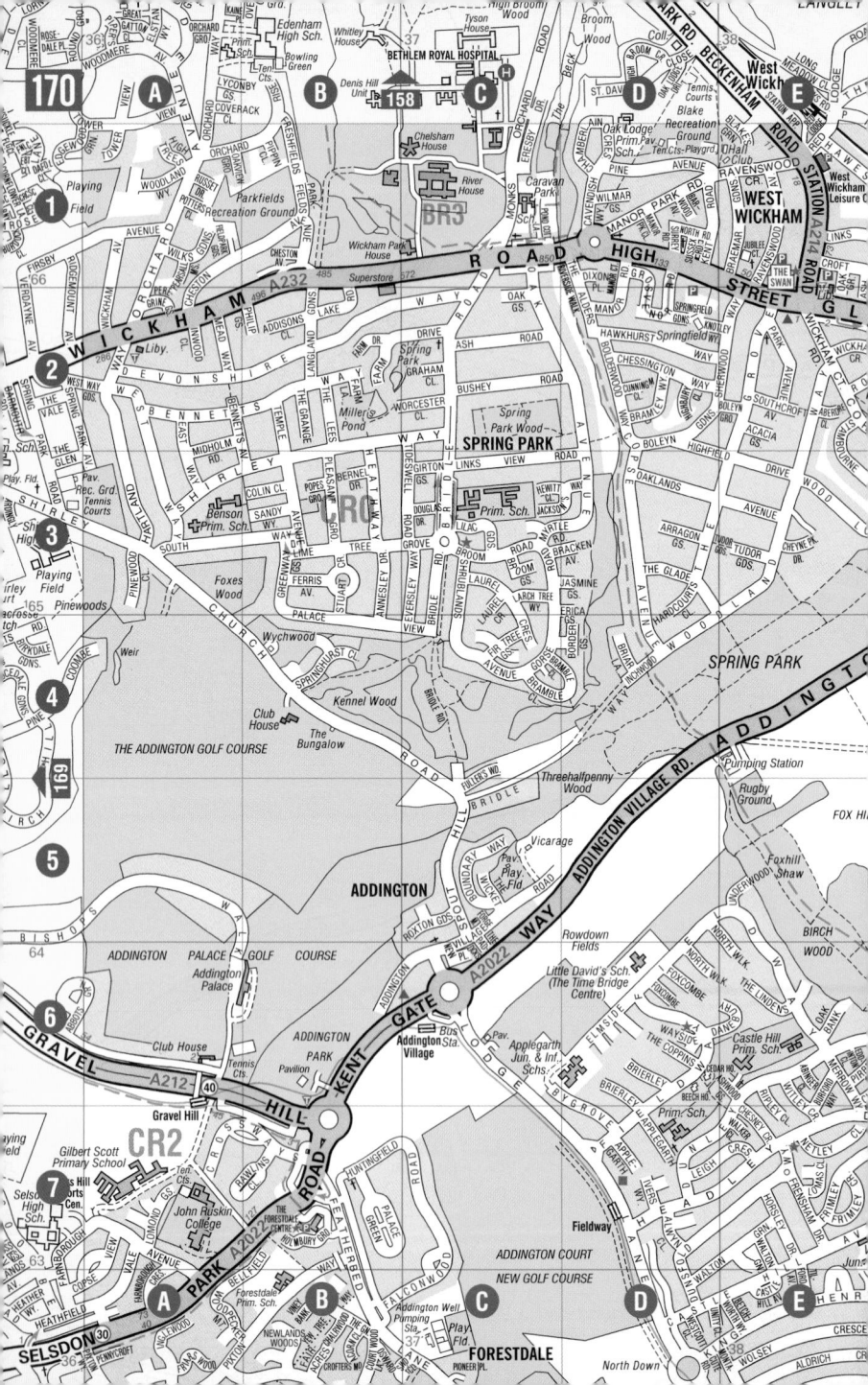
170
158
169
A
B
C
D
E
1
2
3
4
5
6
7
Edenham High Sch.
Bowling Green
High Broom Wood
Whitley House
Tyson House
BETHLEM ROYAL HOSPITAL
Denis Hill Unit
Broom Wood
LANGLEY
West Wickham
Chelsham House
River House
BR3
Parkfields Recreation Ground
Playing Field
Caravan Park
Wickham Park House
Oak Lodge Prim. Sch.
Blake Recreation Ground
WEST WICKHAM
West Wickham Leisure C
THE SWAN
WICKHAM ROAD
HIGH STREET
A232
A214
STATION ROAD
BECKENHAM
Superstore
Liby.
Spring Park
Miller's Pond
Spring Park Wood
SPRING PARK
CR0
Benson Prim. Sch.
Prim. Sch.
Foxes Wood
Pinewoods
Wychwood
Kennel Wood
Club House
The Bungalow
THE ADDINGTON GOLF COURSE
Threehalfpenny Wood
Pumping Station
Rugby Ground
FOX HI
Foxhill Shaw
BIRCH WOOD
ADDINGTON VILLAGE RD.
ADDINGTON
Vicarage
Pav. Play. Fld
Rowdown Fields
Little David's Sch. (The Time Bridge Centre)
ADDINGTON PALACE GOLF COURSE
Addington Palace
Club House
ADDINGTON PARK
Pavilion
Addington Village
Bus Sta.
A2022
KENT GATE WAY
GRAVEL HILL
A212
Gravel Hill
CR2
Gilbert Scott Primary School
John Ruskin College
Selsdon High Sch.
THE FORESTDALE CENTRE
Forestdale Prim. Sch.
PARK ROAD
Applegarth Jun. & Inf. Schs
Castle Hill Prim. Sch.
Fieldway
ADDINGTON COURT NEW GOLF COURSE
Addington Well Pumping Sta.
Play. Fld.
FORESTDALE
NEWLANDS WOODS
SELSDON
North Down
BISHOPS WALK
SHIRLEY CHURCH ROAD
SPOUT HILL
LODGE LANE
FIELDWAY
KING HENRY'S DRIVE
WOODLAND WAY
FEATHERBED LANE
FALCONWOOD

171
159
172
HAYES
CONEY HALL
NASH
NEW ADDINGTON
HAYES COMMON
BR2
BR4
Hayes
Hayes Street Farm
Brook Wood
Bolds Wood
Hayes Prim. Sch.
Playing Field
Hayes Sch.
HAYES GROVE PRIORY HOSP.
Nash College
West Wickham Common
The Warren Bowl. Grn.
Hayes Court
Baston Manor
Keston Court Riding School
Rouse Farm
Arlington Orchard
Well Wood
Cooper's Wood
Long Shaw
Elm Farm
Nash Farm
James's Wood
Fuller's Wood
North Pole Farm
Five Oaks
Baldwin Shaw
Bradmanshill Wood
Broomfieldbank Shaw
Rushfield Shaw
Metropolitan Police Dog Training Establishment
Wickham Court Farm
The Cottages
The Bungalows
Electricity Sub Station
Castlehill Ruffs
Rowdown Wood
Court Sch.
The Emmaus Centre
Lodge Coney Hall Rec. Grd.
Recreation Ground
Hawes Down Jun.& Inf. Schs.
Glebe Sch.
Fox Hill Nursery
Milchden
Gorsewood
Hast Hill
CROYDON ROAD
A232
A2022
B251
B265

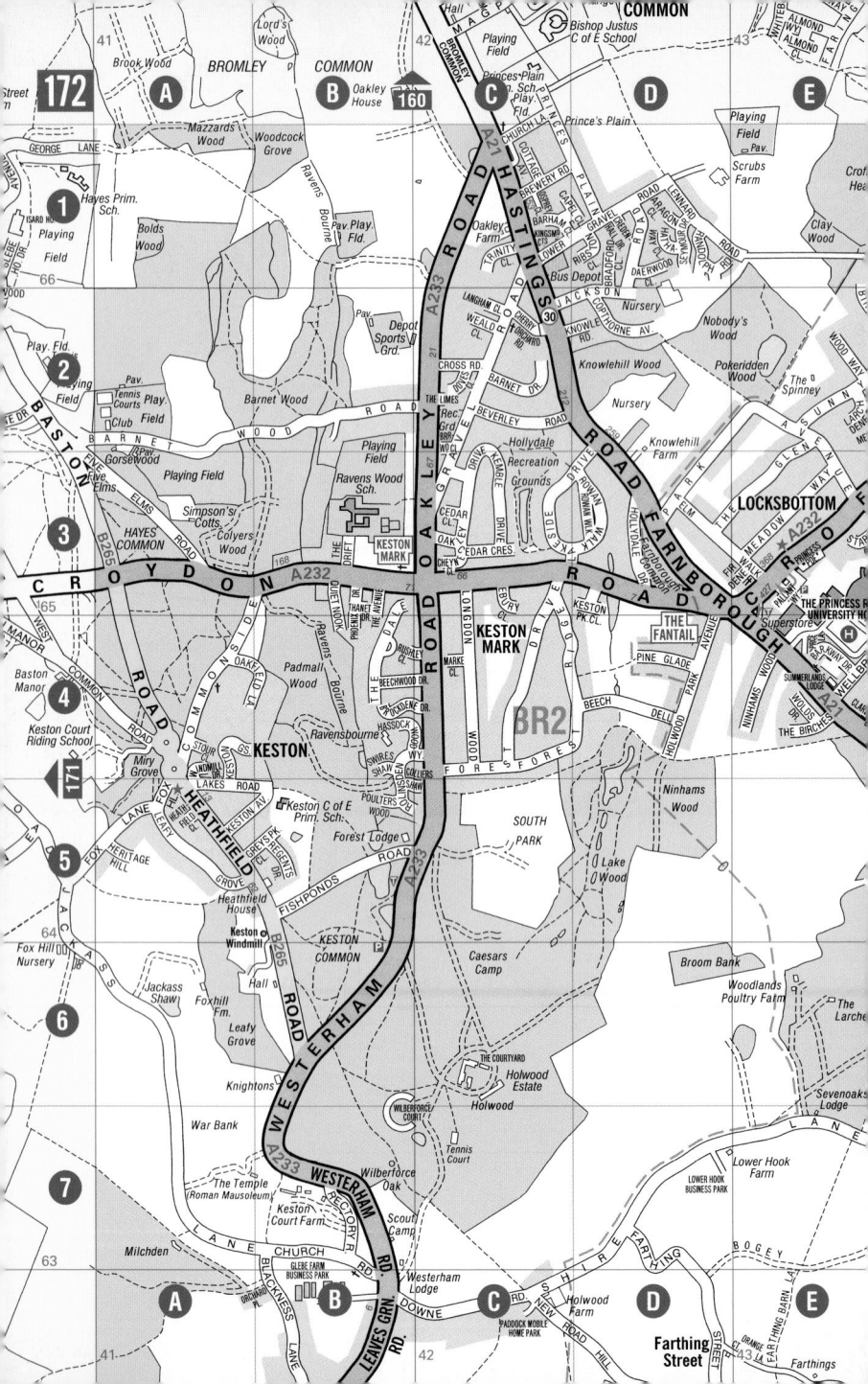

172
160
171
BROMLEY
COMMON
KESTON
KESTON MARK
LOCKSBOTTOM
Farthing Street
BR2
CROYDON ROAD
FARNBOROUGH ROAD
HASTINGS ROAD
OAKLEY ROAD
WESTERHAM ROAD
HEATHFIELD ROAD
BASTON
A21
A232
A233
B265
Brook Wood
Lord's Wood
Mazzards Wood
Woodcock Grove
Hayes Prim. Sch.
Playing Field
Bolds Wood
Ravens Bourne
Depot Sports Grd.
Barnet Wood
Playing Field
Ravens Wood Sch.
Gorsewood
Five Elms
Simpson's Cotts.
Colyers Wood
HAYES COMMON
Padmall Wood
Ravensbourne
Baston Manor
Keston Court Riding School
Miry Grove
Keston C of E Prim. Sch.
Forest Lodge
Heathfield House
Keston Windmill
KESTON COMMON
Jackass Shaw
Foxhill Fm.
Leafy Grove
Knightons
War Bank
The Temple (Roman Mausoleum)
Keston Court Farm
Milchden
GLEBE FARM BUSINESS PARK
Westerham Lodge
Scout Camp
Wilberforce Oak
Tennis Court
WILBERFORCE COURT
Holwood
Holwood Estate
THE COURTYARD
Caesars Camp
SOUTH PARK
Lake Wood
Ninhams Wood
Broom Bank
Woodlands Poultry Farm
Sevenoaks Lodge
Lower Hook Farm
LOWER HOOK BUSINESS PARK
Holwood Farm
PADDOCK MOBILE HOME PARK
Farthings
Fox Hill Nursery
Oakley Farm
Bus Depot
Nursery
Nobody's Wood
Pokeridden Wood
Knowlehill Wood
Knowlehill Farm
The Spinney
Hollydale Recreation Grounds
Farnborough Common
THE FANTAIL
Superstore
THE PRINCESS ROYAL UNIVERSITY HOSPITAL
SUMMERLANDS LODGE
Scrubs Farm
Clay Wood
Prince's Plain
Bishop Justus C of E School
Oakley House
KESTON MARK
DOWNE RD.
SHIRE LANE
CHURCH RD.
BLACKNESS LANE
LEAVES GRN. RD.
FISHPONDS ROAD
FOREST DRIVE
JACKASS LANE
COMMONSIDE
BARNET WOOD ROAD
CROSS RD.
BEVERLEY ROAD
BARNET DR.
CEDAR CRES.
LONGDON WOOD
BEECH DELL
HOLWOOD PARK AVENUE
PINE GLADE
MEADOW WALK

173
161
ORPINGTON
CROFTON
FARNBOROUGH
GREEN STREET GREEN
BR5
BR6
Broom Hill
Orpington
A232
A223
A21
B2158
STATION ROAD
SEVENOAKS ROAD
SEVENOAKS WAY
FARNBOROUGH COMMON
HIGH STREET FARNBOROUGH
HIGH ST.
Petts Wood Recreation Ground
Sparrow Wood
Sparrow Common
Roundabout Wood
Crofton Jun. Sch.
Crofton Inf. Sch.
Knoll Lawn Tennis Club
Gumping Common
Civic Halls
Villa
Super store
Darrick Wood Swimming Pool
Darrick Wood School
Darrick Wood Sports Cen.
Darrick Wood
Darrick Wood Jun. & Inf. Schs.
Farnborough Recreation Ground
Tennis Courts
Newstead Wood
Newstead Wood Sch. for Girls
Bromley Ten. Cen.
Playing Field
Tubbenden Prim. Sch.
Ontario Centre
HOSPICE
ORPINGTON HOSPITAL
Prim. Sch.
Play. Fld.
Bassetts Cen.
Scouts Hall
Club Sports Ground
Farnborough Prim. Sch.
The Manse
Mill Hill
Church Field Plantation
Ramus Wood
Cocksett Plantation
Cocksett Hill
Glentrammon Rec. Grd.
Chelsfield Hall
The Lodge
Bromley Environmental Education Centre at High Elms (BEECHE)
Woodpiece
HIGH ELMS COUNTRY PARK (Local Nature Reserve)
Whitelands Wood
Club House
The Rookery
High Elms Clockhouse
HIGH ELMS GOLF COURSE
North End Farm
Blacklands
Rounds Wood
Rec. Grd.
SHIRE LANE
HIGH ELMS ROAD
CUDHAM LANE
NORTH END LANE

174
92
110
M4 MOTORWAY
M25 MOTORWAY
Junction 4b (M4)
Junction 15 (M25)
Junction 14
COLNBROOK BY-PASS
HARMONDSWORTH
HARMONDSWORTH MOOR WATERSIDE
LONGFORD
Longfordmoor
POYLE
STANWELL MOOR
LONDON HEATHROW AIRPORT
TERMINAL 5A
TERMINAL 5B
Heathrow Terminal 5
MOOR JUNCTION
Longford Roundabout
AIRPORT WAY
A3113
A3044
A4
SL0
SL3
UB7
TW19
TW6
Old Slade Lake
Orlitts Lake
Sewage Works
Sludge Beds
LAKESIDE IND. EST.
Warehouses
Works
Depot
New Wood
Visitor Centre
Harmondsworth Immigration Detention Centre
Computer Centre
Harmondsworth Prim. Sch.
The Great Barn
Manor Court
Bedfont Court Estate
Nurseries
Airport Parking
The Mill
Recreation Ground
POYLE INDUSTRIAL ESTATE
POLYGON BUSINESS CENTRE
BLACKTHORNE IND. EST.
POYLE TRADING ESTATE
POYLE TECHNICAL CENTRE
COLN TRADING EST.
ARGONAUT PARK
HATCH LANE
PERIMETER ROAD
SOUTHERN PERIMETER ROAD
STANWELL MOOR ROAD
BATH ROAD
HORTON ROAD
Airside Road Tunnel

INDEX

Including Streets, Places & Areas, Industrial Estates, Selected Flats & Walkways,
Junction Names & Service Areas and Selected Places of Interest.

HOW TO USE THIS INDEX

1. Each street name is followed by its Postcode District (or, if outside the London Postcodes, by its Locality Abbreviation(s)) then by its map reference;
   e.g. **Abbey Av.** HA0: Wemb . . . .2E **78** is in the HA0 Postcode District and the Wembley Locality and is to be found in square 2E on page **78**. The page number being shown in bold type.

2. A strict alphabetical order is followed in which Av., Rd., St., etc. (though abbreviated) are read in full and as part of the street name;
   e.g. **Alder M.** appears after **Aldermary Rd.** but before **Aldermoor Rd.**

3. Streets and a selection of flats and walkways that cannot be shown on the mapping, appear in the index with the thoroughfare to which they are connected shown in brackets;
   e.g. **Abady Ho.** SW1 . . . .3D **18** (off Page St.)

4. Addresses that are in more than one part are referred to as not continuous.

5. Places and areas are shown in the index in BLUE TYPE and the map reference is to the actual map square in which the town centre or area is located and not to the place name shown on the map;
   e.g. ABBEY WOOD 4C **108**

6. An example of a selected place of interest is Barnet Mus. 4B **20**

7. An example of a Park & Ride is Bromley (Park & Ride) 6K **159**

8. Junction names and Service Areas are shown in the index in **BOLD CAPITAL TYPE**; e.g. **ALDGATE** 6F **85**

9. Map references for entries that appear on large scale pages **4-19** are shown first, with small scale map references shown in brackets; e.g. **Abbey Orchard St.** SW1 . . . .1D **18** (3H **101**)

GENERAL ABBREVIATIONS

All. : Alley	**Cotts.** : Cottages	**Info.** : Information	**Prom.** : Promenade
App. : Approach	**Ct.** : Court	**Intl.** : International	**Quad.** : Quadrant
Arc. : Arcade	**Cres.** : Crescent	**Junc.** : Junction	**Ri.** : Rise
Av. : Avenue	**Cft.** : Croft	**La.** : Lane	**Rd.** : Road
Bk. : Back	**Dpt.** : Depot	**Lit.** : Little	**Rdbt.** : Roundabout
Blvd. : Boulevard	**Dr.** : Drive	**Lwr.** : Lower	**Shop.** : Shopping
Bri. : Bridge	**E.** : East	**Mnr.** : Manor	**Sth.** : South
B'way. : Broadway	**Emb.** : Embankment	**Mans.** : Mansions	**Sq.** : Square
Bldg. : Building	**Ent.** : Enterprise	**Mkt.** : Market	**Sta.** : Station
Bldgs. : Buildings	**Est.** : Estate	**Mdw.** : Meadow	**St.** : Street
Bus. : Business	**Fld.** : Field	**Mdws.** : Meadows	**Ter.** : Terrace
Cvn. : Caravan	**Flds.** : Fields	**M.** : Mews	**Twr.** : Tower
C'way. : Causeway	**Gdn.** : Garden	**Mt.** : Mount	**Trad.** : Trading
Cen. : Centre	**Gdns.** : Gardens	**Mus.** : Museum	**Up.** : Upper
Chu. : Church	**Gth.** : Garth	**Nth.** : North	**Va.** : Vale
Chyd. : Churchyard	**Ga.** : Gate	**No.** : Number	**Vw.** : View
Circ. : Circle	**Gt.** : Great	**Pal.** : Palace	**Vs.** : Villas
Cir. : Circus	**Grn.** : Green	**Pde.** : Parade	**Vis.** : Visitors
Cl. : Close	**Gro.** : Grove	**Pk.** : Park	**Wlk.** : Walk
Coll. : College	**Hgts.** : Heights	**Pas.** : Passage	**W.** : West
Comn. : Common	**Ho.** : House	**Pav.** : Pavilion	**Yd.** : Yard
Cnr. : Corner	**Ho's.** : Houses	**Pl.** : Place	
Cott. : Cottage	**Ind.** : Industrial	**Pct.** : Precinct	

LOCALITY ABBREVIATIONS

Addtn : **Addington**	Chess : **Chessington**	Erith : **Erith**	Hin W : **Hinchley Wood**
Ark : **Arkley**	Chig : **Chigwell**	Esh : **Esher**	Houn : **Hounslow**
Ashf : **Ashford**	Chst : **Chislehurst**	Ewe : **Ewell**	Ick : **Ickenham**
Avel : **Aveley**	Clay : **Claygate**	Farnb : **Farnborough**	Ilf : **Ilford**
Bans : **Banstead**	Cockf : **Cockfosters**	Felt : **Feltham**	Isle : **Isleworth**
Bark : **Barking**	Col R : **Collier Row**	G'frd : **Greenford**	Kenton : **Kenton**
Barn : **Barnet**	Coln : **Colnbrook**	Had W : **Hadley Wood**	Kes : **Keston**
Beck : **Beckenham**	Cowl : **Cowley**	Ham : **Ham**	Kew : **Kew**
Bedd : **Beddington**	Cran : **Cranford**	Hamp : **Hampton**	King T : **Kingston Upon Thames**
Bedf : **Bedfont**	Cray : **Crayford**	Ham H : **Hampton Hill**	Lale : **Laleham**
Belv : **Belvedere**	C'don : **Croydon**	Ham W : **Hampton Wick**	L'ly : **Langley**
Bexl : **Bexley**	Dag : **Dagenham**	Hanw : **Hanworth**	H'row A : **London Heathrow Airport**
Bex : **Bexleyheath**	Dart : **Dartford**	Hare : **Harefield**	Lford : **Longford**
Bford : **Brentford**	Downe : **Downe**	Harl : **Harlington**	Lough : **Loughton**
Brim : **Brimsdown**	E Barn : **East Barnet**	Harm : **Harmondsworth**	Mawney : **Mawney**
Brom : **Bromley**	E Mos : **East Molesey**	Harr : **Harrow**	Mitc : **Mitcham**
Buck H : **Buckhurst Hill**	Eastc : **Eastcote**	Hrw W : **Harrow Weald**	Mord : **Morden**
Bush : **Bushey**	Edg : **Edgware**	Hat E : **Hatch End**	New Ad : **New Addington**
B Hea : **Bushy Heath**	E'tree : **Elstree**	Have B : **Havering-Atte-Bower**	New Bar : **New Barnet**
Cars : **Carshalton**	Enf : **Enfield**	Hayes : **Hayes**	N Mald : **New Malden**
Chad H : **Chadwell Heath**	Enf H : **Enfield Highway**	Hers : **Hersham**	N'olt : **Northolt**
Cheam : **Cheam**	Enf L : **Enfield Lock**	Hest : **Heston**	Nwood : **Northwood**
Chels : **Chelsfield**	Enf W : **Enfield Wash**	Hext : **Hextable**	Orp : **Orpington**
Chert : **Chertsey**	Eps : **Epsom**	Hil : **Hillingdon**	Pet W : **Petts Wood**

1st Bowl—Abingdon Mans.

Pinn : **Pinner**
Pond E : **Ponders End**
Poyle : **Poyle**
Prat B : **Pratts Bottom**
Purl : **Purley**
Rain : **Rainham**
Rich P : **Richings Park**
Rich : **Richmond**
Rom : **Romford**
Ruis : **Ruislip**
Rush G : **Rush Green**
St M Cry : **St Mary Cray**
St P : **St Pauls Cray**
Sande : **Sanderstead**
Sels : **Selsdon**
Shep : **Shepperton**
Sidc : **Sidcup**
Sip : **Sipson**
S'hall : **Southall**
S Croy : **South Croydon**
Staines : **Staines**
Stan : **Stanmore**
Stanw : **Stanwell**
Stan M : **Stanwell Moor**
Stock P : **Stockley Park**
Sun : **Sunbury**
Surb : **Surbiton**
Sutt : **Sutton**
Swan : **Swanley**
Tedd : **Teddington**
T Ditt : **Thames Ditton**
Thor H : **Thornton Heath**
Twick : **Twickenham**
Uxb : **Uxbridge**
Wadd : **Waddon**
Wall : **Wallington**
Walt C : **Waltham Cross**
Walt T : **Walton-on-Thames**
W'stone : **Wealdstone**
Well : **Welling**
Wemb : **Wembley**
Wenn : **Wennington**
W Dray : **West Drayton**
W Mole : **West Molesey**
W W'ck : **West Wickham**
Weyb : **Weybridge**
Whitt : **Whitton**
Wfd G : **Woodford Green**
Wor Pk : **Worcester Park**
Yead : **Yeading**
Yiew : **Yiewsley**

1st Bowl . . . 3E 122
2 Willow Road . . . 4C 64
60 St Martins La. *WC2* . . . *2E 12*
(off St Martin's La.)
198 Contemporary Arts and Learning . . . *6B 120*
(off Railton Rd.)
201 Bishopsgate EC2 . . . 5H 9

A

Aaron Hill Rd. E6 . . . 5E 88
Abady Ho. *SW1* . . . *3D 18*
(off Page St.)
Abberley M. SW4 . . . 3F 119
Abbess Cl. E6 . . . 5C 88
SW2 . . . 1B 138
Abbeville M. SW4 . . . 4H 119
Abbeville Rd. N8 . . . 5H 47
SW4 . . . 6G 119
Abbey Av. HA0: Wemb . . . 2E 78
Abbey Bus. Cen. SW8 . . . 1G 119
Abbey Cl. E5 . . . 4G 67
HA5: Pinn . . . 3K 39
SW8 . . . 1H 119
UB3: Hayes . . . 1K 93
UB5: N'olt . . . 3D 76
Abbey Ct. *NW8* . . . *2A 82*
(off Abbey Rd.)
SE17 . . . *5C 102*
(off Macleod St.)
TW12: Hamp . . . 7E 130
Abbey Cres. DA17: Belv . . . 4G 109
Abbeydale Ct. E17 . . . 3F 51
Abbeydale Rd. HA0: Wemb . . . 1F 79
Abbey Dr. DA2: Dart . . . 2K 145
SW17 . . . 5E 136
Abbey Est. NW8 . . . 1K 81
Abbeyfield Cl. CR4: Mitc . . . 2C 154
Abbeyfield Est. SE16 . . . 4J 103
Abbeyfield Rd. SE16 . . . 4J 103
(not continuous)
Abbeyfields Cl. NW10 . . . 3G 79
Abbey Gdns. BR7: Chst . . . 1E 160
NW8 . . . 2A 82
SE16 . . . 4G 103
W6 . . . 6G 99
Abbey Gro. SE2 . . . 4B 108
Abbeyhill Rd. DA15: Sidc . . . 2C 144
Abbey Ho. *E15* . . . *2G 87*
(off Baker's Row)
NW8 . . . 1A 4
Abbey Ind. Est. CR4: Mitc . . . 5D 154
HA0: Wemb . . . 1F 79
Abbey La. BR3: Beck . . . 7C 140
E15 . . . 2E 86
Abbey La. Commercial Est.
E15 . . . 2G 87
Abbey Life Ct. E16 . . . 5K 87
Abbey Lodge NW8 . . . 2D 4
Abbey M. E17 . . . 5C 50
TW7: Isle . . . 1B 114
Abbey Mt. DA17: Belv . . . 5F 109
Abbey Orchard St. SW1 . . . 1D **18** (3H **101**)
Abbey Orchard St. Est.
SW1 . . . 1D **18** (3H **101**)
(not continuous)
Abbey Pde. *SW19* . . . *7A 136*
(off Merton High St.)
W5 . . . 3F 79
Abbey Pk. BR3: Beck . . . 7C 140
Abbey Pk. Ind. Est. IG11: Bark . . . 2G 89
Abbey Retail Pk. IG11: Bark . . . 7F 71
Abbey Rd. CR0: C'don . . . 3B 168
DA7: Bex . . . 4E 126
DA17: Belv . . . 4D 108
E15 . . . 2F 87
EN1: Enf . . . 5K 23
IG2: Ilf . . . 5H 53
IG11: Bark . . . 1F 89
NW6 . . . 7K 63
NW8 . . . 1A **4** (7K **63**)
NW10 . . . 1H 79
SE2 . . . 4D 108
SW19 . . . 7A 136
Abbey Rd. Apartments *NW8* . . . *2A 82*
(off Abbey Rd.)
Abbey Sports Cen. . . . 1G 89
Abbey St. E13 . . . 4J 87
SE1 . . . 7H **15** (3F **103**)
Abbey Ter. SE2 . . . 4C 108
Abbey Trad. Est. SE26 . . . 5B 140
Abbey Vw. NW7 . . . 3G 29
Abbey Wlk. KT8: W Mole . . . 3F 149
Abbey Wharf Ind. Est. IG11: Bark . . . 3H 89
ABBEY WOOD . . . 4C 108
Abbey Wood Cvn. Club Site SE2 . . . 4C 108
Abbey Wood Rd. SE2 . . . 4B 108
Abbot Cl. HA4: Ruis . . . 3B 58
Abbot Ct. *SW8* . . . *7J 101*
(off Hartington Rd.)
Abbot Ho. *E14* . . . *7D 86*
(off Smythe St.)
Abbotsbury *NW1* . . . *7H 65*
(off Camley St.)
Abbotsbury Cl. E15 . . . 2E 86
W14 . . . 2G 99
Abbotsbury Gdns. HA5: Eastc . . . 7A 40
Abbotsbury Ho. W14 . . . 2G 99
Abbotsbury M. SE15 . . . 3J 121
Abbotsbury Rd. BR2: Hayes . . . 2H 171
SM4: Mord . . . 5K 153
W14 . . . 2G 99
Abbots Cl. BR5: Farnb . . . 1G 173
Abbots Ct. *W8* . . . *2K 99*
(off Thackeray St.)
Abbots Dr. HA2: Harr . . . 2E 58
Abbotsford Av. N15 . . . 4C 48
Abbotsford Gdns. IG8: Wfd G . . . 7D 36
Abbotsford Rd. IG3: Ilf . . . 2A 72
Abbots Gdns. N2 . . . 4B 46
Abbots Grn. CR0: Addtn . . . 6K 169
Abbotshade Rd. SE16 . . . 1K 103
Abbotshall Av. N14 . . . 3B 32
Abbotshall Rd. SE6 . . . 1F 141
Abbot's Ho. *W14* . . . *3H 99*
(off St Mary Abbots Ter.)
Abbotsleigh Cl. SM2: Sutt . . . 7K 165
Abbotsleigh Rd. SW16 . . . 4G 137
Abbots Mnr. SW1 . . . 5J **17** (4F **101**)
Abbotsmede Cl. TW1: Twick . . . 2K 131
Abbots Pk. SW2 . . . 1A 138
Abbot's Pl. NW6 . . . 1K 81
Abbots Rd. E6 . . . 1B 88
HA8: Edg . . . 7D 28
Abbots Ter. N8 . . . 6J 47
Abbotstone Rd. SW15 . . . 3E 116
Abbot St. E8 . . . 6F 67
Abbots Wlk. W8 . . . 3K 99
Abbots Way BR3: Beck . . . 5A 158
Abbotswell Rd. SE4 . . . 5B 122
Abbotswood Cl. DA17: Belv . . . 3E 108
Abbotswood Gdns. IG5: Ilf . . . 3D 52
Abbotswood Rd. SE22 . . . 4E 120
SW16 . . . 3H 137
Abbotswood Way UB3: Hayes . . . 1K 93
Abbott Av. SW20 . . . 1F 153
Abbott Cl. TW12: Hamp . . . 6C 130
UB5: N'olt . . . 6D 58
Abbott Rd. E14 . . . 5E 86
(not continuous)
Abbotts Cl. N1 . . . 6C 66
RM7: Mawney . . . 3H 55
SE28 . . . 7C 90
UB8: Cowl . . . 5A 74
Abbotts Cres. E4 . . . 4A 36
EN2: Enf . . . 2G 23
Abbotts Dr. HA0: Wemb . . . 2B 60
Abbotts Ho. *SW1* . . . *6C 18*
(off Aylesford St.)
Abbotts Mead TW10: Ham . . . 4D 132
Abbotts Pk. Rd. E10 . . . 7E 50
Abbotts Rd. CR4: Mitc . . . 4G 155
(not continuous)
EN5: New Bar . . . 4E 20
SM3: Cheam . . . 4G 165
UB1: S'hall . . . 1C 94
Abbott's Wlk. DA7: Bex . . . 7D 108
Abbott's Wharf *E14* . . . *6C 86*
(off Stainsby Pl.)
Abchor Ho. *SW1* . . . *5J 17*
(off Warwick Way)
Abchurch La. EC4 . . . 2F **15** (7D **84**)
(not continuous)
Abchurch Yd. EC4 . . . 2E **14** (7D **84**)
Abdale Rd. W12 . . . 1D 98
Abel Ho. *SE11* . . . *7K 19*
(off Kennington Rd.)
Abenglen Ind. Est. UB3: Hayes . . . 2F 93
Aberavon Rd. E3 . . . 3A 86
Abercairn Rd. SW16 . . . 7G 137
Aberconway Rd. SM4: Mord . . . 4K 153
Abercorn Cl. NW7 . . . 7B 30
NW8 . . . 3A 82
Abercorn Commercial Cen.
HA0: Wemb . . . 1D 78
Abercorn Cotts. *NW8* . . . *3A 82*
(off Abercorn Pl.)
Abercorn Cres. HA2: Harr . . . 1F 59
Abercorn Dell WD23: B Hea . . . 2B 26
Abercorn Gdns. HA3: Kenton . . . 7D 42
RM6: Chad H . . . 6B 54
Abercorn Gro. HA4: Ruis . . . 4F 39
Abercorn Mans. *NW8* . . . *2A 82*
(off Abercorn Pl.)
Abercorn M. TW10: Rich . . . 4F 115
Abercorn Pl. NW8 . . . 3A 82
Abercorn Rd. HA7: Stan . . . 7H 27
NW7 . . . 7B 30
Abercorn Wlk. NW8 . . . 3A 82
Abercorn Way SE1 . . . 5G 103
Abercrombie Dr. EN1: Enf . . . 1B 24
Abercrombie St. SW11 . . . 2C 118
Aberdale Ct. *SE16* . . . *2K 103*
(off Garter Way)
Aberdare Cl. BR4: W W'ck . . . 2E 170
Aberdare Gdns. NW6 . . . 7K 63
NW7 . . . 7A 30
Aberdare Rd. EN3: Pond E . . . 4D 24
Aberdeen Cotts. HA7: Stan . . . 7H 27
Aberdeen Ct. *W9* . . . *4A 4*
(off Maida Va.)
Aberdeen La. N5 . . . 5C 66
Aberdeen Mans. *WC1* . . . *3E 6*
(off Kenton St.)
Aberdeen Pde. *N18* . . . *5C 34*
(off Aberdeen Rd.)
Aberdeen Pk. N5 . . . 5C 66
Aberdeen Pl. NW8 . . . 4A **4** (4B **82**)
Aberdeen Rd. CR0: C'don . . . 4C 168
HA3: W'stone . . . 2K 41
N5 . . . 4C 66
N18 . . . 5B 34
(not continuous)
NW10 . . . 5B 62
Aberdeen Sq. E14 . . . 1B 104
Aberdeen Ter. SE3 . . . 2F 123
Aberdeen Wharf *E1* . . . *1H 103*
(off Wapping High St.)
Aberdour Rd. IG3: Ilf . . . 3B 72
Aberdour St. SE1 . . . 4E 102
Aberfeldy Ho. SE5 . . . 7B 102
(not continuous)
Aberfeldy St. E14 . . . 5E 86
(not continuous)
Aberford Gdns. SE18 . . . 1C 124
Aberfoyle Rd. SW16 . . . 6H 137
(not continuous)
Abergeldie Rd. SE12 . . . 6K 123
Abernethy Rd. SE13 . . . 4G 123
Abersham Rd. E8 . . . 5F 67
Abery St. SE18 . . . 4J 107
Ability Pl. E14 . . . 2D 104
Ability Towers *EC1* . . . *1C 8*
(off Macclesfield Rd.)
Abingdon *W14* . . . *4H 99*
(off Kensington Village)
Abingdon Cl. KT4: Wor Pk . . . 3D 164
NW1 . . . 6H 65
SE1 . . . *4F 103*
(off Bushwood Dr.)
SW19 . . . 6A 136
UB10: Hil . . . 1B 74
Abingdon Ct. *W8* . . . *3J 99*
(off Abingdon Vs.)
Abingdon Gdns. W8 . . . 3J 99
Abingdon Ho. BR1: Brom . . . 7K 141
E2 . . . *3J 9*
(off Boundary St.)
Abingdon Lodge *BR2: Brom* . . . *2H 159*
(off Beckenham La.)
W8 . . . 3J 99
Abingdon Mans. *W8* . . . *3J 99*
(off Pater St.)

Abingdon Rd. N3 2A 46
SW16 2J 155
W8 3J 99
Abingdon St. SW1 1E 18 (3J 101)
Abingdon Vs. W8 3J 99
Abinger Cl. BR1: Brom 3C 160
CR0: New Ad 6E 170
IG11: Bark 4A 72
SM6: Wall 5J 167
Abinger Ct. SM6: Wall 5J 167
(off Abinger Cl.)
W5 7C 78
Abinger Gdns. TW7: Isle 3J 113
Abinger Gro. SE8 6B 104
Abinger Ho. SE1 7E 14
(off Gt. Dover St.)
Abinger M. W9 4J 81
Abinger Rd. W4 3A 98
Ablett St. SE16 5J 103
Abney Gdns. N16 2F 67
Abney Pk. Cemetery (Local Nature Reserve) 2E 66
Abney Pk. Ter. N16 2F 67
(off Cazenov Rd.)
Aborfield NW5 5G 65
Aboyne Dr. SW20 2C 152
Aboyne Rd. NW10 3A 62
SW17 3B 136
Abraham Fisher Ho.
E12 5E 70
Abridge Way IG11: Bark 2B 90
Abyssinia Cl. SW11 4C 118
Abyssinia Ct. N8 5K 47
Abyssinia Rd. SW11 4C 118
Acacia Av. HA4: Ruis 1J 57
HA9: Wemb 5E 60
N17 7J 33
TW8: Bford 7B 96
TW17: Shep 5C 146
UB3: Hayes 6H 75
UB7: Yiew 7B 74
Acacia Bus. Cen. E11 3G 69
Acacia Cl. BR5: Pet W 5H 161
HA7: Stan 6D 26
SE8 4A 104
SE20 2G 157
Acacia Ct. HA1: Harr 5F 41
Acacia Dr. SM3: Sutt 1H 165
Acacia Gdns. BR4: W W'ck 2E 170
NW8 2B 82
Acacia Gro. KT3: N Mald 3K 151
SE21 2D 138
Acacia Ho. N22 1A 48
(off Douglas Rd.)
Acacia M. UB7: Harm 2E 174
Acacia Pl. NW8 2B 82
Acacia Rd. BR3: Beck 3B 158
CR4: Mitc 2E 154
E11 2G 69
E17 6A 50
EN2: Enf 1J 23
N22 1A 48
NW8 2B 82
SW16 1J 155
TW12: Hamp 6E 130
W3 7J 79
Acacias, The EN4: E Barn 5G 21
Acacia Wlk. SW10 7A 100
(off Tadema Rd.)
Acacia Way DA15: Sidc 1K 143
Academia Way N17 6K 33
Academy Apartments E8 5H 67
(off Dalston La.)
E8 5H 67
(off Institute Pl.)
Academy Bldgs. N1 1G 9
(off Fanshaw St.)
Academy Ct. DA5: Bexl 2K 145
(off Beaconsfield Rd.)
E2 3J 85
(off Kirkwall Pl.)
NW6 1J 81
Academy Gdns. CR0: C'don 1F 169
UB5: N'olt 2B 76
W8 2J 99
Academy Ho. E3 5D 86
(off Violet Rd.)
Academy Pl. SE18 1D 124
TW7: Isle 1J 113
Academy Rd. SE18 1D 124
Acanthus Dr. SE1 5G 103
Acanthus Rd. SW11 3E 118
Accommodation La.
UB7: Harm 2D 174
UB7: Lford 4B 174
Accommodation Rd. E4 3A 36
(off Ashwood Rd.)
KT17: Ewe 5C 164
NW11 1H 63
AC Court KT7: T Ditt 6A 150
Ace Pde. KT9: Chess 3E 162
Acer Av. UB4: Yead 5C 76
Acer Ct. EN3: Enf H 3F 25
(off Enstone Rd.)
Acer Rd. E8 7F 67
Acers BR7: Chst 7C 142
Acfold Rd. SW6 1K 117
Achilles Cl. SE1 5G 103
Achilles Ho. E2 2H 85
(off Old Bethnal Grn. Rd.)
Achilles Rd. NW6 5J 63
Achilles Statue 5H 11 (1E 100)
Achilles St. SE14 7A 104
Achilles Way W1 5H 11 (1E 100)
Acklam Rd. W10 5G 81
(not continuous)
Acklington Dr. NW9 1A 44
Ackmar Rd. SW6 1J 117
Ackroyd Dr. E3 5B 86
Ackroyd Rd. SE23 7K 121
Acland Cl. SE18 7H 107
Acland Cres. SE5 3D 120
Acland Ho. SW9 1K 119
Acland Rd. NW2 6D 62
Acle Cl. IG6: Ilf 1F 53
Acme Ho. E14 5E 86
Acock Gro. UB5: N'olt 4F 59
Acol Ct. NW6 7J 63
Acol Cres. HA4: Ruis 5K 57
Acol Rd. NW6 7J 63
Aconbury Rd. RM9: Dag 1B 90
Acorn Cl. BR7: Chst 5G 143
E4 5J 35
EN2: Enf 1G 23
HA7: Stan 7G 27
TW12: Hamp 6F 131
Acorn Ct. E3 2C 86
(off Morville St.)
E6 7C 70
IG2: Ilf 6J 53
Acorn Gdns. SE19 1F 157
W3 5K 79
Acorn Gro. HA4: Ruis 4H 57
UB3: Harl 7H 93
Acorn Pde. SE15 7H 103
Acorn Production Cen.
N7 7J 65
Acorn Wlk. SE16 1A 104
Acorn Way BR3: Beck 5E 158
BR6: Farnb 4F 173
SE23 3K 139
Acqua Ho. TW9: Kew 7H 97
Acre Dr. SE22 4G 121
Acrefield Ho. NW4 4F 45
(off Belle Vue Est.)
Acre La. SM5: Cars 4E 166
SM6: Wall 4E 166
SW2 4J 119
Acre Path UB5: N'olt 6C 58
(off Arnold Rd.)
Acre Rd. KT2: King T 1E 150
RM10: Dag 7H 73
SW19 6B 136
Acre Way HA6: Nwood 1H 39
Acris St. SW18 5A 118
Acropolis Ho. KT1: King T 3F 151
(off Winery La.)
Active Sports and Fitness Cen. 7A 34
ACTON 1J 97
Acton Central Ind. Est. W3 1H 97
Acton Cl. N9 2B 34
ACTON GREEN 3J 97
Acton Hill M. W3 1H 97
Acton Ho. E8 1F 85
(off Lee St.)
W3 6J 79
Acton La. NW10 3J 79
W3 2J 97
W4 2J 97
Acton M. E8 1F 85
Acton Pk. Est. W3 2K 97
Acton Sports Club 4G 97
Acton St. WC1 2G 7 (3K 83)
Acton Swimming Baths 1J 97
(off Salisbury St.)
Acton Tenpin Bowling 4G 79
Acton Va. Ind. Pk. W3 2B 98
Acuba Rd. SW18 2K 135
Acworth Cl. N9 7D 24
Acworth Ho. SE18 6F 107
(off Barnfield Rd.)
Ada Cl. N11 3J 31
Ada Ct. N1 1C 84
(off Packington St.)
W9 2A 4 (3A 82)
Ada Gdns. E14 6F 87
E15 1H 87
Ada Ho. E2 1G 85
(off Ada Pl.)
Adair Cl. SE25 3H 157
Adair Ho. SW3 7D 16
Adair Rd. W10 4G 81
Adair Twr. W10 4G 81
(off Appleford Rd.)
Ada Kennedy Ct. SE10 7E 104
(off Greenwich Sth. St.)
Ada Lewis Ho. HA9: Wemb 4F 61
Adam & Eve Ct. W1 7B 6
Adam & Eve M. W8 3J 99
Ada Maria Ct. E1 6H 85
(off James Voller Way)
Adam Cl. SE6 4B 140
Adam Ct. SE11 4K 19
SW7 4A 100
(off Gloucester Rd.)
Adam Rd. E4 6G 35
Adams Bri. Bus. Cen.
HA9: Wemb 5H 61
Adams Cl. KT5: Surb 6F 151
N3 7D 30
NW9 2H 61
Adams Ct. E17 6A 50
EC2 7F 9 (6E 84)
Adams Gdns. Est. SE16 2J 103
Adams Ho. E14 6F 87
(off Aberfeldy St.)
Adams M. N22 7E 32
SW17 2D 136
Adamson Ct. N2 3C 46
Adamson Rd. E16 6J 87
NW3 7B 64
Adamson Way BR3: Beck 5E 158
Adams Pl. E14 1D 104
(off The Nth. Colonnade)
N7 5K 65
Adams Quarter TW8: Bford 6C 96
Adamsrill Cl. EN1: Enf 6J 23
Adamsrill Rd. SE26 4K 139
Adams Rd. BR3: Beck 5A 158
N17 2D 48
Adam's Row W1 3H 11 (7E 82)
Adams Sq. DA6: Bex 3E 126
Adams Ter. E3 3C 86
(off Rainhill Way)
Adam St. WC2 3F 13 (7J 83)
Adams Wlk. KT1: King T 2E 150
Adams Way CR0: C'don 6F 157
SE25 5H 157
Adam Wlk. SW6 7E 98
Adana SE13 2E 122
Ada Pl. E2 1G 85
Adare Wlk. SW16 3K 137
Ada Rd. HA0: Wemb 3D 60
SE5 7E 102
Adastral Ho. WC1 5G 7
(off Harpur St.)
Adastra Way SM6: Wall 6J 167
Ada St. E8 1H 85
Ada Workshops E8 1H 85
Adcock Wlk. BR6: Orp 4K 173
Adderley Gdns. SE9 4E 142
Adderley Gro. SW11 5E 118
Adderley Rd. HA3: W'stone 1K 41
Adderley St. E14 6E 86
Addey Ho. SE8 7B 104
ADDINGTON 5C 170
Addington Ct. SW14 3K 115
Addington Dr. N12 6G 31
Addington Gro. SE26 4A 140
Addington Ho. SW9 2K 119
(off Stockwell Rd.)
Addington Lofts SE5 7C 102
(off Wyndham Est.)
Addington Rd. BR4: W W'ck 4E 170
CR0: C'don 1A 168
CR2: Sande, Sels 7K 169
E3 3C 86
E16 4G 87
N4 6A 48
Addington Sq. SE5 6D 102
Addington St. SE1 7H 13 (2K 101)
Addington Village Rd.
CR0: Addtn 6B 170
(not continuous)
Addis Cl. EN3: Enf H 1E 24
ADDISCOMBE 1G 169
Addiscombe Av. CR0: C'don 1G 169
Addiscombe Cl. HA3: Kenton 5C 42
Addiscombe Ct. Rd.
CR0: C'don 1E 168
Addiscombe Gro. CR0: C'don 2E 168
Addiscombe Rd. CR0: C'don 2D 168
(not continuous)
Addis Ho. E1 5J 85
(off Lindley St.)
Addisland Ct. W14 2G 99
(off Holland Vs. Rd.)
Addison Av. N14 6A 22
TW3: Houn 1G 113
W11 1G 99
Addison Bri. Pl. W14 4H 99
Addison Cl. BR5: Pet W 6G 161
HA6: Nwood 1J 39
Addison Ct. NW6 1J 81
(off Brondesbury Rd.)
Addison Cres. W14 3G 99
(not continuous)
Addison Dr. SE12 5K 123
Addison Gdns. KT5: Surb 4F 151
W14 3F 99
Addison Gro. W4 3A 98
Addison Ho. NW8 1A 4
Addison Pk. Mans. W14 3F 99
(off Richmond Way)
Addison Pl. SE25 4G 157
UB1: S'hall 7E 76
W11 1G 99
Addison Rd. BR2: Brom 5A 160
E11 6J 51
E17 5D 50
EN3: Enf H 1D 24
IG6: Ilf 1G 53
SE25 4G 157
TW11: Tedd 6B 132
W14 2G 99
Addisons Cl. CR0: C'don 2B 170
Addison Ter. W4 4J 97
(off Chiswick Rd.)

Addison Way HA6: Nwood 1H 39
NW11 4H 45
UB3: Hayes 6J 75
Addle Hill EC4 1B 14 (6B 84)
Addlestone Ho. *W10* *5E 80*
(off Sutton Way)
Addle St. EC2 7D 8 (6C 84)
Addy Ho. SE16 4J 103
Adecroft Way KT8: W Mole 3G 149
Adela Av. KT3: N Mald 5D 152
Adela Ho. *W6* *5E 98*
(off Queen Caroline St.)
Adelaide Av. SE4 4B 122
Adelaide Cl. EN1: Enf 1K 23
HA7: Stan 4F 27
SW9 4A 120
Adelaide Ct. BR3: Beck 7B 140
NW8 1A 4
W7 2K 95
Adelaide Gdns. RM6: Chad H 5E 54
Adelaide Gro. W12 1C 98
Adelaide Ho. E15 2H 87
E17 2B 50
SE5 2E 120
W11 *6H 81*
(off Portobello Rd.)
Adelaide Rd. BR7: Chst 5F 143
E10 3D 68
IG1: Ilf 2F 71
KT6: Surb 5E 150
NW3 7B 64
SW18 5J 117
TW5: Hest 1C 112
TW9: Rich 4F 115
TW11: Tedd 6K 131
TW15: Ashf 5A 128
UB2: S'hall 4C 94
W13 1A 96
Adelaide St. WC2 3E 12 (7J 83)
Adelaide Ter. TW8: Bford 5D 96
Adela St. W10 4G 81
Adelina Gro. E1 5J 85
Adelina M. SW12 1H 137
Adelina Yd. *E1* *5J 85*
(off Adelina Gro.)
Adeline Pl. WC1 6D 6 (5H 83)
Adeliza Cl. IG11: Bark 7G 71
Adelphi Ct. *E8* *7F 67*
(off Celandine Dr.)
SE16 *2K 103*
(off Garter Way)
W4 6K 97
Adelphi Cres. UB4: Hayes 3G 75
Adelphi Ter. WC2 3F 13 (7J 83)
Adelphi Theatre *3F 13*
(off Strand)
Adelphi Way UB4: Hayes 3H 75
Adeney Cl. W6 6F 99
Aden Gro. N16 4D 66
Aden Ho. *E1* *5K 85*
(off Duckett St.)
Adenmore Rd. SE6 7C 122
Aden Rd. EN3: Brim 4F 25
IG1: Ilf 7G 53
Aden Ter. N16 4D 66
Adeyfield Ho. *EC1* *2F 9*
(off Cranwood St.)
Adie Rd. W6 3E 98
Adine Rd. E13 4K 87
Adler Ind. Est. UB3: Hayes 2F 93
Adler St. E1 6G 85
Adley St. E5 5A 68
Adlington Cl. N18 5J 33
Admaston Rd. SE18 7G 107
Admiral Ct. IG11: Bark 2B 90
SE5 *1E 120*
(off Havil St.)
SM5: Cars 1C 166
SW10 *1A 118*
(off Admiral Sq.)
W1 *6G 5*
(off Blandford St.)
Admiral Ho. *SW1* *3B 18*
(off Willow Pl.)
TW11: Tedd 4A 132
Admiral Hyson Ind. Est. SE16 5H 103
Admiral M. SW19 7A 136
W10 4F 81
Admiral Pl. N8 4B 48
SE16 1A 104
Admirals Cl. E18 4K 51
Admirals Ct. *E6* *6F 89*
(off Trader Rd.)
SE1 *5J 15*
(off Horselydown La.)
Admiral Seymour Rd. SE9 4D 124
Admiral's Ga. SE10 1D 122
Admiral Sq. SW10 1A 118
Admiral St. SE8 2C 122
Admirals Wlk. NW3 3A 64
Admirals Way E14 2C 104
Admiralty Arch 4D 12 (1H 101)
Admiralty Cl. SE8 7C 104
UB7: W Dray 2A 92
Admiralty Rd. TW11: Tedd 6K 131
Admiralty Way TW11: Tedd 6K 131
Admiral Wlk. W9 5J 81
Adolf St. SE6 4D 140
Adolphus Rd. N4 2B 66
Adolphus St. SE8 7B 104
Adomar Rd. RM8: Dag 3D 72
Adpar St. W2 5A 4 (5B 82)
Adrian Av. NW2 1D 62
Adrian Boult Ho. *E2* *3H 85*
(off Mansford St.)
Adrian Cl. EN5: Barn 6A 20
Adrian Ho. *N1* *1K 83*
(off Barnsbury Est.)
SW8 *7J 101*
(off Wyvil Rd.)
Adrian M. SW10 6K 99
Adriatic Apartments *E16* *7J 87*
(off Western Gateway)
Adriatic Bldg. *E14* *7A 86*
(off Horseferry Rd.)
Adriatic Ho. *E1* *4K 85*
(off Ernest St.)
Adrienne Av. UB1: S'hall 4D 76
Adron Ho. *SE16* *4J 103*
(off Millender Wlk.)
Adstock Ho. *N1* *7B 66*
(off The Sutton Est.)
Advance Rd. SE27 4C 138
Adventure Kingdom *2K 159*
(off Stockwell Cl.)
Adventurers Ct. *E14* *7F 87*
(off Newport Av.)
Advent Way N18 5D 34
Adys Lawn NW2 6D 62
Ady's Rd. SE15 3F 121
Aegean Apartments *E16* *7J 87*
(off Western Gateway)
Aegon Ho. *E14* *3D 104*
(off Lanark Sq.)
Aerodrome Rd. NW4 2B 44
NW9 2B 44
Aerodrome Way TW5: Hest 6A 94
Aeroville NW9 2A 44
Affleck St. N1 1G 7 (2K 83)
Afghan Rd. SW11 2C 118
Afsil Ho. *EC1* *6K 7*
(off Viaduct Bldgs.)
Aftab Ter. *E1* *4H 85*
(off Tent St.)
Agamemnon Rd. NW6 4H 63
Agar Cl. KT6: Surb 2F 163
Agar Gro. NW1 7G 65
Agar Gro. Est. NW1 7H 65
Agar Ho. *KT1: King T* *3E 150*
(off Denmark Rd.)
Agar Pl. NW1 7G 65
Agar St. WC2 3E 12 (7J 83)
Agate Cl. E16 6B 88
NW10 3G 79
Agate Rd. W6 3E 98
Agatha Cl. E1 1H 103
Agaton Path SE9 2G 143
Agaton Rd. SE9 2G 143
Agave Rd. NW2 4E 62
Agdon St. EC1 3A 8 (4B 84)
Age Exchange Reminiscence Cen. 3H 123
Agincourt Rd. NW3 4D 64
Agnes Av. IG1: Ilf 4E 70
Agnes Cl. E6 7E 88
Agnesfield Cl. N12 6H 31
Agnes Gdns. RM8: Dag 4D 72
Agnes Ho. *W11* *7F 81*
(off St Ann's Rd.)
Agnes Rd. W3 1B 98
Agnes St. E14 6B 86
Agnew Rd. SE23 7K 121
Agricola Ct. *E3* *1B 86*
(off Parnell Rd.)
Agricola Pl. EN1: Enf 5A 24
Ahoy Sailing Cen. *5C 104*
(off Stretton Mans.)
Aidan Cl. RM8: Dag 4E 72
Aigburth Mans. *SW9* *7A 102*
(off Mowll St.)
Ailantus Ct. HA8: Edg 5A 28
Aileen Wlk. E15 7H 69
Ailsa Av. TW1: Twick 5A 114
Ailsa Ho. *E16* *7E 88*
(off University Way)
Ailsa Rd. TW1: Twick 5B 114
Ailsa St. E14 5E 86
Ailsa Wlk. *E14* *2C 104*
(off Alpha Gro.)
Ainger M. *NW3* *7D 64*
(off Ainger Rd.)
Ainger Rd. NW3 7D 64
Ainsdale *NW1* *1A 6*
(off Harrington St.)
Ainsdale Cl. BR6: Orp 1H 173
Ainsdale Cres. HA5: Pinn 3E 40
Ainsdale Dr. SE1 5G 103
Ainsdale Rd. W5 4D 78
Ainsley Av. RM7: Rom 6H 55
Ainsley Cl. N9 1K 33
Ainsley St. E2 3H 85
Ainslie Ct. HA0: Wemb 2E 78
Ainslie Wlk. SW12 7F 119
Ainslie Wood Cres. E4 5J 35
Ainslie Wood Gdns. E4 4J 35
Ainslie Wood Nature Reserve 5J 35
Ainslie Wood Rd. E4 5H 35
Ainsty Est. SE16 2K 103
Ainsty St. SE16 2J 103
Ainsworth Cl. NW2 3C 62
SE15 2E 120
Ainsworth Ho. *NW8* *1K 81*
(off Ainsworth Way)
W10 *3G 81*
(off Kilburn La.)
Ainsworth Rd. CR0: C'don 1B 168
E9 7J 67
Ainsworth Way NW8 1A 82
Aintree Av. E6 1C 88
Aintree Cl. UB8: Hil 6D 74
Aintree Cres. IG6: Ilf 2G 53
Aintree Est. *SW6* *7G 99*
(off Aintree St.)
Aintree Rd. UB6: G'frd 2B 78
Aintree St. SW6 7G 99
Airbourne Ho. *SM6: Wall* *4G 167*
(off Maldon Rd.)
Air Call Bus. Cen. NW9 3K 43
Airco Cl. NW9 3K 43
Aird Ho. *SE1* *3C 102*
(off Rockingham St.)
Airdrie Cl. N1 7K 65
UB4: Yead 5C 76
Airedale Av. W4 4B 98
Airedale Av. Sth. W4 5B 98
Airedale Rd. SW12 7D 118
W5 3C 96
Airlie Gdns. IG1: Ilf 1F 71
W8 1J 99
Air Links Ind. Est.
TW13: Hanw 3C 130
Airlinks Ind. Est. TW5: Cran 5A 94
Air Pk. Way TW13: Felt 2K 129
Airport Bowl 1G 111
Airport Ga. Bus. Cen.
UB7: Sip 7B 92
Airport Way TW19: Stan M 7A 174
Air St. W1 3B 12 (7G 83)
Airthrie Rd. IG3: Ilf 2B 72
Aisgill Av. W14 5H 99
(not continuous)
Aisher Rd. SE28 7C 90
Aislibie Rd. SE12 4G 123
Aiten Pl. W6 4C 98
Aithan Ho. *E14* *6B 86*
(off Copenhagen Pl.)
Aitken Cl. CR4: Mitc 7D 154
E8 1G 85
Aitken Rd. SE6 2D 140
Aitman Dr. TW8: Bford 5G 97
Aits Vw. KT8: W Mole 3F 149
Ajax Av. NW9 3A 44
Ajax Ho. *E2* *2H 85*
(off Old Bethnal Grn. Rd.)
Ajax Rd. NW6 4H 63
Akabusi Cl. CR0: C'don 6G 157
Akbar Ho. *E14* *4D 104*
(off Cahir St.)
Akehurst St. SW15 6C 116
Akenside Rd. NW3 5B 64
Akerman Rd. KT6: Surb 6C 150
SW9 2B 120
Akintaro Ho. *SE8* *6B 104*
(off Alverton St.)
Alabama St. SE18 7H 107
Alacross Rd. W5 2C 96
Alamaro Lodge *SE10* *3H 105*
(off Teal St.)
Alandale Dr. HA5: Pinn 1K 39
Aland Ct. SE16 3A 104
Alander M. E17 4E 50
Alan Dr. EN5: Barn 6B 20
Alan Gdns. RM7: Rush G 7G 55
Alan Hocken Way E15 2G 87
Alan Preece Ct. NW6 7F 63
Alan Rd. SW19 5G 135
Alanthus Cl. SE12 6J 123
Alaska Apartments *E16* *7J 87*
(off Western Gateway)
Alaska Bldg. *SE10* *1D 122*
(off Deal's Gateway)
Alaska Bldgs. SE1 3E 102
Alaska St. SE1 5J 13 (1A 102)
Alastor Ho. *E14* *3E 104*
(off Strattondale Ho.)
Alba Cl. UB4: Yead 4B 76
Albacore Cres. SE13 6D 122
Alba Gdns. NW11 6G 45
Albain Cres. TW15: Ashf 2A 128
Alba M. SW18 2J 135
Alban Highwalk EC2 7D 8
(not continuous)
EC2 *6D 8*
(off Wood St.)
Albany N12 6E 30
W1 3A 12 (7G 83)
Albany, The IG8: Wfd G 4C 36
Albany Cl. DA5: Bexl 7C 126
N15 4B 48
SW14 4H 115
UB10: Ick 5C 56
Albany Ct. E4 6H 25
(Chelwood Cl.)
E4 5G 35
(Westward Rd.)
E10 7C 50
HA8: Edg 1K 43
NW8 *1A 4*
(off Abbey Rd.)

Albany Ct. *NW10* *3D 80*
(off Trenmar Gdns.)
TW15: Ashf 7E 128
Albany Courtyard W1 3B 12 (7G 83)
Albany Cres. HA8: Edg 7B 28
Albany Mans. SW11 7C 100
Albany M. BR1: Brom 6J 141
KT2: King T 6D 132
N1 7A 66
SE5 6C 102
SM1: Sutt 5K 165
Albany Pde. TW8: Bford 6E 96
Albany Pk. Av. EN3: Enf W 1D 24
Albany Pk. Rd. KT2: King T 6D 132
Albany Pas. TW10: Rich 5E 114
Albany Pl. TW8: Bford 6D 96
Albany Reach KT7: T Ditt 5K 149
Albany Rd. BR7: Chst 5F 143
DA5: Bexl 7C 126
DA17: Belv 6F 109
E10 7C 50
E12 4B 70
E17 6A 50
KT3: N Mald 4K 151
N4 6A 48
N18 5D 34
RM6: Chad H 6F 55
SE5 6D 102
SW19 5K 135
TW8: Bford 6D 96
TW10: Rich 5F 115
W13 7B 78
Albany St. NW1 1K 5 (2F 83)
Albany Ter. NW1 4K 5
TW10: Rich *5F 115*
(off Albany Pas.)
Albany Vw. IG9: Buck H 1D 36
Albany Works *E3* *1A 86*
(off Gunmakers La.)
Alba Pl. W11 6H 81
Albatross NW9 2B 44
Albatross Cl. E6 5D 88
Albatross St. SE18 7J 107
Albatross Way SE16 2K 103
Albemarle SW19 2F 135
Albemarle App. IG2: Ilf 6F 53
Albemarle Av. TW2: Whitt 1D 130
Albemarle Gdns. IG2: Ilf 6F 53
KT3: N Mald 4K 151
Albemarle Ho. *SE8* *4B 104*
(off Foreshore)
SW9 3A 120
Albemarle Pk. BR3: Beck 1D 158
HA7: Stan 5H 27
Albemarle Rd. BR3: Beck 1D 158
EN4: E Barn 7H 21
Albemarle St. W1 3K 11 (7F 83)
Albemarle Way EC1 4A 8 (4B 84)
Alberon Gdns. NW11 4H 45
Alberta Av. SM1: Sutt 4G 165
Alberta Est. *SE17* *5B 102*
(off Alberta St.)
Alberta Ho. *E14* *1E 104*
(off Gaselee St.)
Alberta Rd. DA8: Erith 1J 127
EN1: Enf 6A 24
Alberta St. SE17 5B 102
Albert Av. E4 4H 35
SW8 7K 101
Albert Barnes Ho. *SE1* *3C 102*
(off New Kent Rd.)
Albert Basin Way E16 7G 89
Albert Bigg Point *E15* *2E 86*
(off Godfrey St.)
Albert Bri. SW3 6C 100
Albert Bri. Rd. SW11 7C 100
Albert Carr Gdns.
SW16 5J 137
Albert Cl. E9 1H 85
N22 1H 47
Albert Cotts. *E1* *5G 85*
(off Deal St.)

Albert Ct. E7 4J 69
SW7 7A 10 (3B 100)
Albert Ct. Ga. *SW1* *7E 10*
(off Knightsbridge)
Albert Cres. E4 4H 35
Albert Dane Cen.
UB2: S'hall 3C 94
Albert Dr. SW19 2G 135
Albert Emb. SE1 1G 19 (3K 101)
(Lambeth Pal. Rd.)
SE1 6F 19 (5J 101)
(Vauxhall Bri.)
Albert Gdns. E1 6K 85
Albert Ga. SW1 6F 11 (2D 100)
Albert Gray Ho. *SW10* *7B 100*
(off Worlds End Est.)
Albert Gro. SW20 1F 153
Albert Hall Mans. SW7 7A 10 (2B 100)
Albert Ho. *E18* *3K 51*
(off Albert Rd.)
SE28 3G 107
Albert Mans. *CR0: C'don* *1D 168*
(off Lansdowne Rd.)
SW11 *1D 118*
(off Albert Bri. Rd.)
Albert Memorial
Knightsbridge 7A 10 (2B 100)
Albert M. *E14* *7A 86*
(off Northey St.)
N4 1K 65
SE4 4A 122
W8 3A 100
Albert Pal. Mans. *SW11* *1F 119*
(off Lurline Gdns.)
Albert Pl. N3 1J 45
N17 3F 49
W8 3K 99
Albert Rd. BR2: Brom 5B 160
CR4: Mitc 3D 154
DA5: Bexl 6G 127
DA17: Belv 5F 109
E10 2E 68
E16 1C 106
E17 5C 50
E18 3K 51
EN4: E Barn 4F 21
HA2: Harr 3G 41
IG1: Ilf 3F 71
IG9: Buck H 2G 37
KT1: King T 2F 151
KT3: N Mald 4B 152
N4 1K 65
N15 6E 48
N22 1G 47
NW4 4F 45
NW6 2H 81
NW7 5G 29
RM8: Dag 1G 73
SE9 3C 142
SE20 6K 139
SE25 4G 157
SM1: Sutt 5B 166
TW1: Twick 1K 131
TW3: Houn 4E 112
TW10: Rich 5E 114
TW11: Tedd 6K 131
TW12: Ham H 5G 131
TW15: Ashf 5B 128
UB2: S'hall 3B 94
UB3: Hayes 3G 93
UB7: Yiew 1A 92
W5 4B 78
Albert Rd. Cen. *NW6* *2H 81*
(off Albert Rd.)
Albert Rd. Est. DA17: Belv 5F 109
Alberts Ct. NW1 3D 4
Albert Sleet Ct. *N9* *3C 34*
(off Colthurst Dr.)
Albert Sq. E15 5G 69
SW8 7K 101
Albert Starr Ho. *SE8* *4K 103*
(off Haddonfield)

Albert St. N12 5F 31
NW1 1F 83
Albert Studios SW11 1D 118
Albert Ter. IG9: Buck H 2H 37
NW1 1E 82
NW10 1J 79
W5 4B 78
W6 *5C 98*
(off Beavor La.)
Albert Ter. M. NW1 1E 82
Albert Victoria Ho. N22 1A 48
Albert Wlk. E16 2E 106
Albert Way SE15 7H 103
Albert Westcott Ho.
SE17 5B 102
Albert Whicher Ho. E17 4E 50
Albert Yd. SE19 6F 139
Albery Ct. *E8* *7F 67*
(off Middleton Rd.)
Albion Av. N10 1E 46
SW8 2H 119
Albion Bldgs. *N1* *2J 83*
(off Albion Yd.)
Albion Cl. RM7: Rom 6K 55
W2 2D 10 (7C 82)
Albion Ct. *SE10* *4G 105*
(off Azof St.)
SM2: Sutt 7B 166
W6 *4D 98*
(off Albion Pl.)
Albion Dr. E8 7F 67
Albion Est. SE16 2K 103
Albion Gdns. W6 4D 98
Albion Ga. W2 2D 10
(not continuous)
Albion Gro. N16 4E 66
Albion Ho. *E16* *1F 107*
(off Church St.)
SE8 *7C 104*
(off Watsons St.)
Albion M. N1 1A 84
NW6 7H 63
W2 2D 10 (7C 82)
W6 4D 98
Albion Pde. N16 4D 66
Albion Pl. EC1 5A 8 (5B 84)
EC2 6F 9 (5D 84)
SE25 3G 157
W6 4D 98
Albion Riverside Bldg.
SW11 7C 100
Albion Rd. DA6: Bex 4F 127
E17 3E 50
KT2: King T 1J 151
N16 4D 66
N17 2G 49
SM2: Sutt 6B 166
TW2: Twick 1J 131
TW3: Houn 4E 112
UB3: Hayes 6G 75
Albion Sq. E8 7F 67
(not continuous)
Albion St. CR0: C'don 1B 168
SE16 2J 103
W2 1D 10 (6C 82)
Albion Ter. E4 4J 25
E8 7F 67
Albion Vs. Rd. SE26 3J 139
Albion Wlk. *N1* *1F 7*
(off York Way)
Albion Way EC1 6C 8 (5C 84)
HA9: Wemb 3G 61
SE13 4E 122
Albion Yd. E1 5H 85
N1 2J 83
Albon Ho. *SW18* *6K 117*
(off Neville Gill Cl.)
Albrighton Rd. SE22 3E 120
Albuhera Cl. EN2: Enf 1F 23
Albury Av. DA7: Bex 2E 126
TW7: Isle 7K 95
Albury Cl. TW12: Hamp 6F 131

Albury Ct. *CR2: S Croy* *4C 168*
(off Tanfield Rd.)
CR4: Mitc 2B 154
SE8 *6C 104*
(off Albury St.)
SM1: Sutt 4A 166
UB5: N'olt *3A 76*
(off Canberra Dr.)
Albury Dr. HA5: Pinn 1A 40 & 1C 40
Albury Ho. *SE1* *7B 14*
(off Boyfield St.)
Albury M. E12 2A 70
Albury Rd. KT9: Chess 5E 162
Albury St. SE8 6C 104
Albyfield BR1: Brom 4D 160
Albyn Rd. SE8 1C 122
Alcester Ct. SM6: Wall 4F 167
Alcester Cres. E5 2H 67
Alcester Rd. SM6: Wall 4F 167
Alcock Cl. SM6: Wall 7H 167
Alcock Rd. TW5: Hest 7B 94
Alconbury DA6: Bex 5H 127
Alconbury Rd. E5 2G 67
Alcorn Cl. SM3: Sutt 2J 165
Alcott Cl. TW14: Felt 1H 129
W7 5K 77
Alcuin Ct. HA7: Stan 7H 27
Aldam Pl. N16 2F 67
Aldborough Ct. *IG2: Ilf* *5K 53*
(off Aldborough Rd. Nth.)
ALDBOROUGH HATCH 4K 53
Aldborough Rd. RM10: Dag 6J 73
Aldborough Rd. Nth. IG2: Ilf 5K 53
Aldborough Rd. Sth. IG3: Ilf 1J 71
Aldbourne Rd. W12 1B 98
(not continuous)
Aldbridge St. SE17 5E 102
Aldburgh M. W1 7H 5 (6E 82)
Aldbury Av. HA9: Wemb 7H 61
Aldbury Ho. *SW3* *5C 16*
(off Cale St.)
Aldbury M. N9 7J 23
Aldebert Ter. SW8 7J 101
Aldeburgh Cl. E5 2H 67
Aldeburgh Pl. IG8: Wfd G 4D 36
SE10 *4J 105*
(off Aldeburgh St.)
Aldeburgh St. SE10 5J 105
Alden Av. E15 3H 87
Alden Ct. CR0: C'don 3E 168
Aldenham Dr. UB8: Hil 4D 74
Aldenham Ho. *NW1* *1B 6*
(off Aldenham St.)
Aldenham St. NW1 1C 6 (2G 83)
Alden Ho. *E8* *1H 85*
(off Duncan Rd.)
Aldensley Rd. W6 3D 98
Alderbrook Rd. SW12 6F 119
Alderbury Rd. SW13 6C 98
Alder Cl. DA18: Erith 2F 109
SE15 6F 103
Alder Ct. E7 5J 69
N11 6B 32
Alder Gro. NW2 2C 62
Aldergrove Gdns. TW3: Houn 2C 112
Alder Ho. *E3* *1B 86*
(off Hornbeam Sq.)
NW3 6D 64
SE4 3C 122
SE15 *6F 103*
(off Alder Cl.)
Alder Lodge SW6 1E 116
Alderman Av. IG11: Bark 3A 90
Aldermanbury EC2 7D 8 (6C 84)
Aldermanbury Sq. EC2 6D 8 (5C 84)
Alderman Judge Mall
KT1: King T *2E 150*
(off Eden St.)
Aldermans Hill N13 4D 32
Aldermans Wlk. EC2 6G 9 (5E 84)
Aldermary Rd. BR1: Brom 1J 159
Alder M. N19 2G 65

Aldermoor Rd. SE6 . . . . .3B 140
Alderney Av. TW5: Hest, Isle 7F 95
Alderney Ct. SE10 . . . . .6F 105
    (off Trafalgar Rd.)
Alderney Gdns. UB5: N'olt 7D 58
Alderney Ho. EN3: Enf W 1E 24
  N1 . . . . .6C 66
    (off Arran Wlk.)
Alderney M. SE1 . . . . .3D 102
Alderney Rd. E1 . . . . .4K 85
Alderney St. SW1 . . . .4K 17 (4F 101)
Alder Rd. DA14: Sidc 3K 143
  SW14 . . . . .3K 115
Alders, The BR4: W W'ck 1D 170
  N21 . . . . .6F 23
  SW16 . . . . .4G 137
  TW5: Hest 6D 94
  TW13: Hanw 4C 130
Alders Av. IG8: Wfd G 6B 36
ALDERSBROOK 2K 69
Aldersbrook Av. EN1: Enf 2K 23
Aldersbrook Dr. KT2: King T 6F 133
Aldersbrook La. E12 . . . . .3D 70
Aldersbrook Rd. E11 . . . . .2K 69
  E12 . . . . .2K 69
Alders Cl. E11 . . . . .2K 69
  HA8: Edg 5D 28
  W5 . . . . .3D 96
Aldersey Gdns. IG11: Bark 6H 71
Aldersford Cl. SE4 . . . . .5K 121
Aldersgate Ct. EC1 . . . . .6C 8
    (off Bartholomew Cl.)
Aldersgate St. EC1 . . . . .5C 8 (5C 84)
Alders Gro. KT8: E Mos 5H 149
Aldersgrove Av. SE9 . . . . .3B 142
Aldershot Rd. NW6 . . . . .1H 81
Aldershot Ter. SE18 . . . . .7E 106
Aldersmead Av. CRO: C'don 6K 157
Aldersmead Rd. BR3: Beck 7A 140
Alderson Pl. UB2: S'hall 1G 95
Alderson St. W10 . . . . .4G 81
Alders Rd. HA8: Edg 5D 28
Alderton Cl. NW10 . . . . .3K 61
Alderton Ct. KT8: W Mole 4D 148
    (off Walton Rd.)
Alderton Cres. NW4 . . . . .5D 44
Alderton Rd. CRO: C'don 7F 157
  SE24 .3C 120
Alderton Way NW4 . . . . .5D 44
Alderville Rd. SW6 . . . . .2H 117
Alder Wlk. IG1: Ilf 5G 71
Alderwick Ct. N7 . . . . .6K 65
    (off Cornelia St.)
Alderwick Dr. TW3: Houn 3H 113
Alderwood M. EN4: Had W 1F 21
Alderwood Rd. SE9 . . . . .6H 125
Aldford Ho. W1 . . . . .4G 11
    (off Park St.)
Aldford St. W1 . . . . .4H 11 (1E 100)
ALDGATE .6F 85
Aldgate E1 . . . . .6F 85
    (off Whitechapel High Street)
  EC3 . . . . .1J 15 (6E 84)
Aldgate Av. E1 . . . . .7J 9 (6F 85)
Aldgate Barrs E1 . . . . .7K 9
Aldgate High St. EC3 . . . .1J 15 (6F 85)
Aldgate Twr. E1 . . . . .6F 85
Aldham Ho. SE4 . . . . .2B 122
    (off Malpas Rd.)
Aldine Ct. W12 . . . . .2E 98
    (off Aldine St.)
Aldine Pl. W12 . . . . .2E 98
Aldine St. W12 . . . . .2E 98
Aldington Cl. RM8: Dag 1C 72
Aldington Ct. E8 . . . . .7G 67
    (off London Flds. W. Side)
Aldington Rd. SE18 . . . . .3B 106
Aldis M. SW17 . . . . .5C 136
Aldis St. SW17 . . . . .5C 136
Aldred Rd. NW6 . . . . .5J 63
Aldren Rd. SW17 . . . . .3A 136
Aldrich Cres. CRO: New Ad 7E 170

Aldriche Way E4 . . . . .6K 35
Aldrich Gdns. SM3: Cheam 3H 165
Aldrich Ter. SW18 . . . . .2A 136
Aldrick Ho. N1 . . . . .1K 83
    (off Barnsbury Est.)
Aldridge Av. HA4: Ruis 5K 39
  HA7: Stan 1E 42
  HA8: Edg 3C 28
Aldridge Ct. W11 . . . . .5H 81
    (off Aldridge Rd. Vs.)
Aldridge Ri. KT3: N Mald 7A 152
Aldridge Rd. Vs. W11 . . . . .5H 81
Aldridge Wlk. N14 . . . . .7D 22
Aldrington Rd. SW16 . . . . .5G 137
Aldsworth Cl. W9 . . . . .4K 81
Aldwick Cl. SE9 . . . . .3H 143
Aldwick Rd. CRO: Bedd 3K 167
Aldworth Gro. SE13 . . . . .6E 122
Aldworth Rd. E15 . . . . .7G 69
Aldwych WC2 . . . . .2G 13 (6K 83)
Aldwych Av. IG6: Ilf 4G 53
Aldwych Bldgs. WC2 . . . . .7F 7
    (off Parker St.)
Aldwych Ct. E8 . . . . .7F 67
    (off Middleton Rd.)
Aldwych Theatre 1G 13
    (off Aldwych)
Aldwyn Ho. SW8 . . . . .7J 101
    (off Davidson Gdns.)
Alers Rd. DA6: Bex 5D 126
Alesia Cl. N22 . . . . .7D 32
Alestan Beck Rd. E16 . . . . .6B 88
Alexa Cl. SM2: Sutt 6J 165
  W8 . . . . .4J 99
Alexander Av. NW10 . . . . .7D 62
Alexander Cl. BR2: Hayes 1J 171
  DA15: Sidc 6J 125
  EN4: E Barn 4G 21
  TW2: Twick 2J 131
  UB2: S'hall 1G 95
Alexander Ct. BR3: Beck 1F 159
  HA7: Stan 3F 43
Alexander Evans M. SE23 . . . . . . .2K 139
Alexander Fleming Laboratory Mus.
  .7B 4 (6B 82)
Alexander Ho. E14 . . . . .3C 104
    (off Tiller Rd.)
  KT2: King T 1E 150
    (off Seven Kings Way)
  SE15 .2H 121
    (off Godman Rd.)
Alexander M. SW16 . . . . .5G 137
  W2 . . . . .6K 81
Alexander Pl. SW7 . . . . .3C 16 (4C 100)
Alexander Rd. BR7: Chst 6F 143
  DA7: Bex 2D 126
  N19 . . . . .3J 65
Alexander Sq. SW3 . . . .3C 16 (4C 100)
Alexander St. W2 . . . . .6J 81
Alexander Studios SW11 . . . . .4B 118
    (off Haydon Way)
Alexander Ter. SE2 . . . . .5B 108
Alexandra Av. HA2: Harr 1D 58
  N22 . . . . .1H 47
  SM1: Sutt 3J 165
  SW11 . . . . .1E 118
  UB1: S'hall 7D 76
  W4 . . . . .7K 97
Alexandra Cl. HA2: Harr 3E 58
  SE8 . . . . .6B 104
  TW15: Ashf 7F 129
Alexandra Cotts. SE14 . . . . .1B 122
Alexandra Ct. HA9: Wemb 4F 61
  N14 . . . . .5B 22
  SE5 . . . . .6C 102
    (off Urlwin St.)
  SW7 . . . . .1A 16
  TW3: Houn 2F 113
  TW15: Ashf 6F 129
  UB6: G'frd 2F 77
  W2 . . . . .7K 81
    (off Moscow Rd.)

Alexandra Ct. W9 . . . . .4A 82
    (off Maida Va.)
Alexandra Cres. BR1: Brom 6H 141
Alexandra Dr. KT5: Surb 7G 151
  SE19 .5E 138
Alexandra Gdns. N10 . . . . .4F 47
  SM5: Cars 7E 166
  TW3: Houn 2F 113
  W4 . . . . .7A 98
Alexandra Gro. N4 . . . . .1B 66
  N12 . . . . .5E 30
Alexandra Ho. E16 . . . . .1K 105
    (off Wesley Av.)
  IG8: Wfd G 7K 37
  W6 . . . . .5E 98
    (off Queen Caroline St.)
Alexandra Mans. SW3 . . . . .7A 16
    (off King's Rd.)
Alexandra M. N2 . . . . .3D 46
  SW19 . . . . .6H 135
Alexandra National Ho. N4 . . . . . . .1B 66
Alexandra Pde. HA2: Harr 4F 59
Alexandra Palace 2H 47
Alexandra Pal. Way N22 . . . . .4G 47
Alexandra Pde. HA2: Harr 4F 59
  N22 . . . . .1G 47
Alexandra Pk. Rd. N10 . . . . .2F 47
  N22 . . . . .1G 47
Alexandra Pk. Sports Cen. 1G 47
Alexandra Pl. CRO: C'don 1E 168
  NW8 . . . . .1A 82
  SE25 .5D 156
Alexandra Rd. CRO: C'don 1E 168
  CR4: Mitc 7C 136
  E6 . . . . .3E 88
  E10 . . . . .3E 68
  E17 . . . . .6B 50
  E18 . . . . .3K 51
  EN3: Pond E 4E 24
  KT2: King T 7G 133
  KT7: T Ditt 5K 149
  N8 . . . . .3A 48
  N9 . . . . .7C 24
  N10 . . . . .7A 32
  N15 . . . . .5D 48
  NW4 . . . . .4F 45
  NW8 . . . . .1A 82
  RM6: Chad H 6E 54
  SE26 .6K 139
  SW14 . . . . .3K 115
  SW19 . . . . .6H 135
  TW1: Twick 6C 114
  TW3: Houn 2F 113
  TW8: Bford 6D 96
  TW9: Kew 2F 115
  TW15: Ashf 7F 129
  W4 . . . . .2K 97
Alexandra Rd. Ind. Est. EN3: Pond E . .4E 24
Alexandra Sq. SM4: Mord 5J 153
Alexandra St. E16 . . . . .5J 87
  SE14 .7A 104
Alexandra Ter. E14 . . . . .5D 104
    (off Westferry Rd.)
Alexandra Wlk. SE19 . . . . .5E 138
Alexandra Wharf E2 . . . . .1H 85
    (off Darwen Pl.)
Alexandra Yd. E9 . . . . .1K 85
Alexandria Apartments
  SE17 .4E 102
    (off Townsend St.)
Alexandria Rd. W13 . . . . .7A 78
Alexia Sq. E14 . . . . .3D 104
Alexis St. SE16 . . . . .4G 103
Alfan La. DA2: Dart 5K 145
Alfearn Rd. E5 . . . . .4J 67
Alford Cl. N1 . . . . .2J 67
    (off Shepherdess Wlk.)
Alford Gdn. CRO: New Ad 6F 171
Alford Ho. N6 . . . . .6G 47
Alford Pl. N1 . . . . .1D 8 (2C 84)
Alford Rd. DA8: Erith 5J 109
Alloxton Av. N15 . . . . .4B 48
Alfreda St. SW11 . . . . .1F 119
Alfred Cl. W4 . . . . .4K 97

Alfred Dickens Ho. E16 . . . . .6H 87
    (off Hallsville Rd.)
Alfred Finlay Ho. N22 . . . . .2B 48
Alfred Gdns. UB1: S'hall 7C 76
Alfred Ho. E9 . . . . .5A 68
    (off Homerton Rd.)
  E12 . . . . .7C 70
    (off Tennyson Av.)
Alfred M. W1 . . . . .5C 6 (5H 83)
Alfred Nunn Ho. NW10 . . . . .1B 80
Alfred Pl. WC1 . . . . .5C 6 (5H 83)
Alfred Prior Ho. E12 . . . . .4E 70
Alfred Rd. DA17: Belv 5F 109
  E15 . . . . .5H 69
  IG9: Buck H 2G 37
  KT1: King T 3E 150
  SE25 .5G 157
  SM1: Sutt 5A 166
  TW13: Felt 2A 130
  W2 . . . . .5J 81
  W3 . . . . .1J 97
Alfred Salter Ho. SE1 . . . . .4F 103
    (off Fort Rd.)
Alfred's Gdns. IG11: Bark 2J 89
Alfred St. E3 . . . . .3B 86
Alfreds Way IG11: Bark 3F 89
Alfreds Way Ind. Est. IG11: Bark . . .2A 90
Alfred Vs. E17 . . . . .4E 50
Alfreton Cl. SW19 . . . . .3F 135
Alfriston KT5: Surb 6F 151
Alfriston Av. CRO: C'don 7J 155
  HA2: Harr 6E 40
Alfriston Cl. KT5: Surb 5F 151
Alfriston Rd. SW11 . . . . .5D 118
Algar Cl. HA7: Stan 5E 26
  TW7: Isle 3A 114
Algar Ho. SE1 . . . . .7A 14
Algar Rd. TW7: Isle 3A 114
Algarve Rd. SW18 . . . . .1K 135
Algernon Rd. NW4 . . . . .6C 44
  NW6 . . . . .1J 81
  SE13 .4D 122
Algiers Rd. SE13 . . . . .4C 122
Alibon Gdns. RM10: Dag 5G 73
Alibon Rd. RM9: Dag 5F 73
  RM10: Dag 5G 73
Alice Cl. EN5: New Bar 4F 21
    (off Station App.)
Alice Gilliatt Ct. W14 . . . . .6H 99
    (off Star Rd.)
Alice La. E3 . . . . .1B 86
Alice M. TW11: Tedd 5K 131
Alice Owen Technology Cen. EC1 . . . .1A 8
    (off Goswell Rd.)
Alice Shepherd Ho. E14 . . . . .2E 104
    (off Manchester Rd.)
Alice St. SE1 . . . . .3E 102
    (not continuous)
Alice Thompson Cl. SE12 . . . . . . .2A 142
Alice Walker Cl. SE24 . . . . .4B 120
Alice Way TW3: Houn 4F 113
Alicia Av. HA3: Kenton 4B 42
Alicia Cl. HA3: Kenton 4C 42
Alicia Gdns. HA3: Kenton 4B 42
Alicia Ho. DA16: Well 1B 126
Alie St. E1 . . . . .1K 15 (6F 85)
Alington Cres. NW9 . . . . .7J 43
Alington Gro. SM6: Wall 7G 167
Alison Cl. CRO: C'don 1K 169
  E6 . . . . .6E 88
  HA5: Eastc 6K 39
Aliwal M. SW11 . . . . .4C 118
Aliwal Rd. SW11 . . . . .4C 118
Alkerden Rd. W4 . . . . .5A 98
Alkham Rd. N16 . . . . .2F 67
Allan Barclay Cl. N15 . . . . .6F 49
Allan Cl. KT3: N Mald 5K 151
Allandale Av. N3 . . . . .3G 45
Allanson Ct. E10 . . . . .2C 68
    (off Leyton Grange Est.)
Allan Way W3 . . . . .5J 79
Allard Cres. WD23: B Hea 1B 26

Allard Gdns.—Alwyn Gdns.

Allard Gdns. SW4 5H **119**
Allard Ho. *NW9* *2B* ***44***
(off Boulevard Dr.)
Allardyce St. SW4 4K **119**
Allbrook Cl. TW11: Tedd 5J **131**
Allcott Ho. *W12* *6D* ***80***
(off Du Cane Rd.)
Allcroft Rd. NW5 5E **64**
Allder Way CR2: S Croy 7B **168**
Allenby Cl. UB6: G'frd 3E **76**
Allenby Rd. SE23 3A **140**
SE28 3G **107**
UB1: S'hall 3E **76**
Allen Cl. CR4: Mitc 1F **155**
TW16: Sun 1K **147**
Allen Ct. *E17* *6C* ***50***
(off Yunus Khan Cl.)
UB6: G'frd 5K **59**
Allendale Av. UB1: S'hall 6E **76**
Allendale Cl. SE5 2D **120**
SE26 5K **139**
Allendale Rd. UB6: G'frd 6B **60**
Allen Edwards Dr.
SW8 1J **119**
Allenford Ho. *SW15* *6B* ***116***
(off Tunworth Cres.)
Allen Ho. *W8* *3J* ***99***
(off Allen St.)
Allen Mans. *W8* *3J* ***99***
(off Allen St.)
Allen Rd. BR3: Beck 2K **157**
CR0: C'don 1A **168**
E3 2B **86**
N16 4E **66**
TW16: Sun 1K **147**
Allensbury Pl. NW1 7H **65**
Allens Rd. EN3: Pond E 5D **24**
Allen St. W8 3J **99**
Allenswood SW19 1G **135**
Allenswood Rd. SE9 3C **124**
Allerford Ct. HA2: Harr 5G **41**
Allerford Rd. SE6 3D **140**
Allerton Ho. *N1* *1E* ***8***
(off Provost Est.)
Allerton Rd. N16 2C **66**
Allerton St. N1 1E **8** (3D **84**)
Allerton Wlk. N7 2K **65**
Allestree Rd. SW6 7G **99**
Alleyn Cres. SE21 2D **138**
Alleyndale Rd. RM8: Dag 2C **72**
Alleyn Ho. *SE1* *3D* ***102***
(off Burbage Cl.)
Alleyn Pk. SE21 2D **138**
UB2: S'hall 5E **94**
Alleyn Rd. SE21 3D **138**
Alley Way UB8: Uxb 7A **56**
Allfarthing La. SW18 6K **117**
Allgood Cl. SM4: Mord 6F **153**
Allgood St. E2 1K **9** (2F **85**)
Allhallows La. EC4 3E **14** (7D **84**)
All Hallows Rd. N17 1E **48**
Allhallows Rd. E6 5C **88**
Alliance Cl. HA0: Wemb 4D **60**
TW4: Houn 5D **112**
Alliance Ct. TW15: Ashf 4E **128**
W3 5H **79**
Alliance Rd. E13 5A **88**
SE18 6A **108**
W3 4H **79**
Allied Ct. *N1* *7E* ***66***
(off Enfield Rd.)
Allied Ind. Est. W3 2A **98**
Allied Way W3 2A **98**
Allingham Cl. W7 7K **77**
Allingham Ct. BR2: Brom 4H **159**
Allingham M. *N1* *2C* ***84***
(off Allingham St.)
Allingham St. N1 2C **84**
Allington Av. N17 6K **33**
TW17: Shep 3G **147**
Allington Cl. SW19 5F **135**
UB6: G'frd 7G **59**
Allington Ct. *CR0: C'don* *6J* ***157***
(off Chart Cl.)
EN3: Pond E 5E **24**
SW1 *2K* ***17***
(off Allington St.)
SW8 2G **119**
Allington Rd. BR6: Orp 2H **173**
HA2: Harr 5G **41**
NW4 5D **44**
W10 3G **81**
Allington St. SW1 2K **17** (3F **101**)
Allison Cl. SE10 1E **122**
Allison Gro. SE21 1E **138**
Allison Rd. N8 5A **48**
W3 6J **79**
Alliston Ho. *E2* *2K* ***9***
(off Gibraltar Wlk.)
Allitsen Rd. NW8 2C **82**
(not continuous)
All Nations Ho. *E8* *7H* ***67***
(off Martello St.)
Allnutt Way SW4 5H **119**
Alloa Rd. IG3: Ilf 2A **72**
SE8 5K **103**
Allom Ho. *W11* *7G* ***81***
(off Clarendon Rd.)
Allonby Dr. HA4: Ruis 7D **38**
Allonby Gdns. HA9: Wemb 1C **60**
Allonby Ho. *E14* *5A* ***86***
(off Aston St.)
Allotment Way NW2 3F **63**
Alloway Rd. E3 3A **86**
Allport Ho. *SE5* *3D* ***120***
(off Champion Pk.)
Allport M. *E1* *4J* ***85***
(off Hayfield Pas.)
All Saints Cl. N9 2B **34**
SW8 1J **119**
All Saints Ct. *E1* *7J* ***85***
(off Johnson St.)
SW11 *7F* ***101***
(off Prince of Wales Dr.)
TW5: Hest *1B* ***112***
(off Springwell Rd.)
All Saints Dr. SE3 2G **123**
(not continuous)
All Saints Ho. *W11* *5H* ***81***
(off All Saints Rd.)
All Saints M. HA3: Hrw W 6D **26**
All Saints Pas.
SW18 5J **117**
All Saints Rd. SM1: Sutt 3K **165**
SW19 7A **136**
(not continuous)
W3 3J **97**
W11 5H **81**
All Saints St. N1 2K **83**
All Saints Twr. E10 7D **50**
Allsop Pl. NW1 4F **5** (4D **82**)
All Souls Av. NW10 2D **80**
All Souls' Pl. W1 6K **5** (5F **83**)
Allum Way N20 1F **31**
Alluvium Ct. *SE1* *7G* ***15***
(off Long La.)
Allwood Cl. SE26 4K **139**
Alma Av. E4 7K **35**
Alma Birk Ho. NW6 7G **63**
Almack Rd. E5 4J **67**
Alma Cl. N10 1F **47**
Alma Ct. HA2: Harr 2H **59**
Alma Cres. SM1: Sutt 5G **165**
Alma Gro. SE1 4F **103**
Alma Ho. N9 4B **34**
TW8: Bford 6E **96**
Alma Pl. CR7: Thor H 5A **156**
NW10 3D **80**
SE19 7F **139**
Alma Rd. DA14: Sidc 3A **144**
EN3: Pond E 5F **25**
KT10: Esh 7J **149**
N10 7A **32**
SM5: Cars 5C **166**
Alma Rd. SW18 4A **118**
UB1: S'hall 7C **76**
Alma Rd. Ind. Est. EN3: Pond E 4E **24**
Alma Row HA3: Hrw W 1H **41**
Alma Sq. NW8 2A **82**
Alma St. E15 6F **69**
NW5 6F **65**
Alma Ter. *E3* *1B* ***86***
(off Beale Rd.)
SW18 7B **118**
W8 3J **99**
Almeida St. N1 1B **84**
Almeida Theatre *1B* ***84***
(off Almeida St.)
Almeric Rd. SW11 4D **118**
Almer Rd. SW20 7C **134**
Almington St. N4 1K **65**
Almond Av. SM5: Cars 2D **166**
UB7: W Dray 3C **92**
UB10: Ick 3D **56**
W5 3D **96**
Almond Cl. BR2: Brom 7E **160**
HA4: Ruis 3H **57**
SE15 2G **121**
TW13: Felt 1J **129**
TW17: Shep 2E **146**
UB3: Hayes 7G **75**
Almond Gro. TW8: Bford 7B **96**
Almond Rd. N17 7B **34**
SE16 4H **103**
Almonds Av. IG9: Buck H 2D **36**
Almond Way BR2: Brom 7E **160**
CR4: Mitc 5H **155**
HA2: Harr 2F **41**
Almorah Rd. N1 7D **66**
TW5: Hest 1B **112**
Almshouse La. KT9: Chess 7C **162**
Alms Houses, The
IG11: Bark 6G **71**
Alnmouth Ct. *UB1: S'hall* *6G* ***77***
(off Fleming Rd.)
Alnwick N17 7C **34**
Alnwick Gro. SM4: Mord 4K **153**
Alnwick Rd. E16 6A **88**
SE12 6K **123**
ALPERTON 2E **78**
Alperton La. HA0: Wemb 3C **78**
UB6: G'frd 3C **78**
Alperton St. W10 4H **81**
Alphabet Gdns. SM5: Cars 6B **154**
Alphabet Sq. E3 5C **86**
Alpha Bus. Cen. E17 5B **50**
Alpha Cl. NW1 2D **4** (4C **82**)
Alpha Est. UB3: Hayes 2G **93**
Alpha Gro. E14 2C **104**
Alpha Ho. NW6 2J **81**
NW8 4D **4**
SW4 4K **119**
Alpha Pl. NW6 2J **81**
SM4: Mord 1F **165**
SW3 7D **16** (6C **100**)
Alpha Rd. CR0: C'don 1E **168**
E4 3H **35**
EN3: Pond E 4F **25**
KT5: Surb 6F **151**
N18 6B **34**
SE14 1B **122**
TW11: Tedd 5H **131**
UB10: Hil 4D **74**
Alpha St. SE15 2G **121**
Alphea Cl. SW19 7C **136**
Alpine Av. KT5: Surb 2J **163**
Alpine Bus. Cen. E6 5E **88**
Alpine Cl. CR0: C'don 3E **168**
Alpine Copse BR1: Brom 2E **160**
Alpine Gro. E9 7J **67**
Alpine Rd. E10 2D **68**
KT12: Walt T 7J **147**
SE16 5K **103**
Alpine Vw. SM5: Cars 5C **166**
Alpine Wlk. HA7: Stan 2D **26**
Alpine Way E6 5E **88**
Alric Av. KT3: N Mald 3A **152**
NW10 7K **61**
Alroy Rd. N4 7A **48**
Alsace Rd. SE17 5E **102**
Alscot Rd. SE1 4F **103**
Alscot Rd. Ind. Est. SE1 3F **103**
Alscot Way SE1 4F **103**
Alsike Rd. DA18: Erith 3D **108**
SE2 3D **108**
Alsom Av. KT4: Wor Pk 4C **164**
Alston Cl. KT6: Surb 7B **150**
Alston Rd. EN5: Barn 3B **20**
N18 5C **34**
SW17 4B **136**
Alston Works EN5: Barn 2B **20**
Altair Cl. N17 6A **34**
Altash Way SE9 2D **142**
Altenburg Av. W13 3B **96**
Altenburg Gdns. SW11 4D **118**
Alt Gro. SW19 7H **135**
Altham Ct. HA2: Harr 1F **41**
Altham Rd. HA5: Pinn 1C **40**
Althea St. SW6 2K **117**
Althorne Gdns. E18 4H **51**
Althorne Way RM10: Dag 2G **73**
Althorp Cl. EN5: Ark 1H **29**
Althorpe M. SW11 1B **118**
Althorpe Rd. HA1: Harr 5G **41**
Althorp Rd. SW17 1D **136**
Altima Ct. *SE22* *4G* ***121***
(off E. Dulwich Rd.)
Altior Ct. N6 6G **47**
Altius Apartments *E3* *2C* ***86***
(off Wick La.)
Altmore Av. E6 7D **70**
Alton Av. HA7: Stan 7E **26**
Alton Cl. DA5: Bexl 1E **144**
TW7: Isle 2K **113**
Alton Gdns. BR3: Beck 7C **140**
TW2: Whitt 7H **113**
Alton Ho. *E3* *3D* ***86***
(off Bromley High St.)
Alton Rd. CR0: Wadd 3A **168**
N17 3D **48**
SW15 1C **134**
TW9: Rich 4E **114**
Alton St. E14 5D **86**
Altura Twr. SW11 2B **118**
Altyre Cl. BR3: Beck 5B **158**
Altyre Rd. CR0: C'don 2D **168**
Altyre Way BR3: Beck 5B **158**
Aluna Ct. SE15 3J **121**
Alvanley Gdns. NW6 5K **63**
Alverstone Av. EN4: E Barn 7H **21**
SW19 2J **135**
Alverstone Gdns. SE9 1G **143**
Alverstone Ho. SE11 7J **19** (6A **102**)
Alverstone Rd. E12 4E **70**
HA9: Wemb 1F **61**
KT3: N Mald 4B **152**
NW2 7E **62**
Alverston Gdns. SE25 5E **156**
Alverton St. SE8 5B **104**
(not continuous)
Alveston Av. HA3: Kenton 3B **42**
Alveston Sq. E18 2J **51**
Alvey St. SE17 5E **102**
Alvia Gdns. SM1: Sutt 4A **166**
Alvington Cres. E8 5F **67**
Alway Av. KT19: Ewe 5K **163**
Alwold Cres. SE12 6K **123**
Alwyn Av. W4 5K **97**
Alwyn Cl. CR0: New Ad 7D **170**
Alwyne La. N1 7B **66**
Alwyne Pl. N1 6C **66**
Alwyne Rd. N1 7C **66**
SW19 6H **135**
W7 7J **77**
Alwyne Sq. N1 6C **66**
Alwyne Vs. N1 7B **66**
Alwyn Gdns. NW4 4C **44**
W3 6H **79**

Alyth Gdns.—Anerley Sta. Rd.

Alyth Gdns. NW11 . . . 6J **45**
Alzette Ho. *E2* . . . *2K 85*
(off Mace St.)
Amadeus Ho. *BR1: Brom* . . . *3K 159*
(off Elmfield Rd.)
Amalgamated Dr. TW8: Bford . . . 6B **96**
Amanda Ct. *TW15: Ashf* . . . *2B 128*
(off Edward Way)
Amanda M. RM7: Rom . . . 5J **55**
Amar Ct. SE18 . . . 4K **107**
Amar Deep Ct. SE18 . . . 5K **107**
Amazon Bldg. N8 . . . 4K **47**
Amazon St. E1 . . . 6G **85**
Ambassador Cl. TW3: Houn . . . 2C **112**
Ambassador Gdns. E6 . . . 5D **88**
Ambassadors Ct. *E8* . . . *7F 67*
(off Holly St.)
SW1 . . . 5B **12**
Ambassador Sq. E14 . . . 4D **104**
Ambassadors Theatre . . . *2D 12*
(off West St.)
Amber Av. E17 . . . 1A **50**
Amber Cl. EN5: New Bar . . . 6E **20**
Amber Ct. CR0: C'don . . . 1E **168**
KT5: Surb . . . 7F **151**
N7 . . . *6A 66*
(off Bride St.)
Amberden Av. N3 . . . 3J **45**
Ambergate St. SE17 . . . 5B **102**
Amber Gro. NW2 . . . 1F **63**
Amberley Cl. BR6: Chels . . . 5K **173**
HA5: Pinn . . . 3D **40**
Amberley Ct. BR3: Beck . . . 7B **140**
DA14: Sidc . . . 5C **144**
Amberley Gdns. EN1: Enf . . . 7K **23**
KT19: Ewe . . . 4B **164**
Amberley Gro. CR0: C'don . . . 7F **157**
SE26 . . . 5H **139**
Amberley Rd. E10 . . . 7C **50**
EN1: Enf . . . 7A **24**
IG9: Buck H . . . 1F **37**
N13 . . . 2E **32**
SE2 . . . 6D **108**
W9 . . . 5J **81**
Amberley Way RM7: Mawney . . . 4H **55**
SM4: Mord . . . 7H **153**
TW4: Houn . . . 5A **112**
UB10: Uxb . . . 2A **74**
Amber M. *N22* . . . *3A 48*
(off High Rd.)
Amberside Cl. TW7: Isle . . . 6H **113**
Amber Wharf *E2* . . . *1F 85*
(off Nursery La.)
Amberwood Cl. SM6: Wall . . . 5J **167**
Amberwood Ri. KT3: N Mald . . . 6A **152**
Amblecote Cl. SE12 . . . 3K **141**
Amblecote Mdws. SE12 . . . 3K **141**
Amblecote Rd. SE12 . . . 3K **141**
Ambler Rd. N4 . . . 3B **66**
Ambleside BR1: Brom . . . 6F **141**
NW1 . . . 1K **5**
SW19 . . . 1G **135**
Ambleside Av. BR3: Beck . . . 5A **158**
KT12: Walt T . . . 7A **148**
SW16 . . . 4H **137**
Ambleside Cl. E9 . . . 5J **67**
E10 . . . 7D **50**
N17 . . . 3F **49**
Ambleside Cres. EN3: Enf H . . . 3E **24**
Ambleside Dr. TW14: Felt . . . 1H **129**
Ambleside Gdns. HA9: Wemb . . . 1D **60**
IG4: Ilf . . . 4C **52**
SM2: Sutt . . . 6A **166**
SW16 . . . 5H **137**
Ambleside Point *SE15* . . . *7J 103*
(off Tustin Est.)
Ambleside Rd. DA7: Bex . . . 2G **127**
NW10 . . . 7B **62**
Ambleside Wlk. UB8: Uxb . . . 1A **74**
Ambrooke Rd. DA17: Belv . . . 3G **109**
Ambrosden Av. SW1 . . . 2B **18** (3G **101**)
Ambrose Av. NW11 . . . 7G **45**
Ambrose Cl. BR6: Orp . . . 3K **173**
E6 . . . 5D **88**
Ambrose Ho. *E14* . . . *5C 86*
(off Selsey St.)
Ambrose M. SW11 . . . 2D **118**
Ambrose St. SE16 . . . 4H **103**
Ambrose Wlk. E3 . . . 2C **86**
AMC Bus. Cen. *NW10* . . . *3H 79*
(off Cumberland Av.)
Amelia Cl. W3 . . . 1H **97**
Amelia Ho. *NW9* . . . *2B 44*
(off Boulevard Dr.)
TW9: Kew . . . 7H **97**
W6 . . . *5E 98*
(off Queen Caroline St.)
Amelia St. SE17 . . . 5C **102**
Amen Cnr. EC4 . . . 1B **14** (6B **84**)
SW17 . . . 6D **136**
Amen Ct. EC4 . . . 1B **14** (6B **84**)
Amenity Way SM4: Mord . . . 7E **152**
American International University in London, The
Richmond Hill Campus . . . 7E 114
Kensington Campus -
Ansdell Street . . . 3K 99
St Albans Grove . . . 3K 99
Young Street . . . 2K 99
American University of London, The . . . 3K 65
America Sq. EC3 . . . 2J **15** (7F **85**)
America St. SE1 . . . 5C **14** (1C **102**)
Amerland Rd. SW18 . . . 5H **117**
Amersham Av. N18 . . . 6J **33**
Amersham Gro. SE14 . . . 7B **104**
Amersham Rd. CR0: C'don . . . 6C **156**
SE14 . . . 1B **122**
Amersham Va. SE14 . . . 7B **104**
Amery Gdns. NW10 . . . 1E **80**
Amery Ho. *SE17* . . . *5E 102*
(off Kinglake St.)
Amery Rd. HA1: Harr . . . 2A **60**
Amesbury Av. SW2 . . . 2J **137**
Amesbury Cl. KT4: Wor Pk . . . 1E **164**
Amesbury Ct. EN2: Enf . . . 2F **23**
Amesbury Dr. E4 . . . 6J **25**
Amesbury Rd. BR1: Brom . . . 3B **160**
RM9: Dag . . . 7D **72**
TW13: Felt . . . 2B **130**
Amesbury Twr. SW8 . . . 2G **119**
Ames Cotts. *E14* . . . *5A 86*
(off Maroon St.)
Ames Ho. *E2* . . . *2K 85*
(off Mace St.)
Amethyst Cl. N11 . . . 7C **32**
Amethyst Ct. *BR6: Chels* . . . *5J 173*
(off Farnborough Hill)
EN3: Enf H . . . *3F 25*
(off Enstone Rd.)
Amethyst Rd. E15 . . . 4F **69**
Amherst Av. W13 . . . 6C **78**
Amherst Dr. BR5: St M Cry . . . 4K **161**
Amherst Gdns. *W13* . . . *6C 78*
(off Amherst Rd.)
Amherst Ho. *SE16* . . . *2K 103*
(off Wolfe Cres.)
Amherst Rd. W13 . . . 6C **78**
Amhurst Gdns. TW7: Isle . . . 2A **114**
Amhurst Pde. *N16* . . . *7F 49*
(off Amhurst Pk.)
Amhurst Pk. N16 . . . 7D **48**
Amhurst Pas. E8 . . . 4G **67**
Amhurst Rd. E8 . . . 5H **67**
N16 . . . 4F **67**
Amhurst Ter. E8 . . . 4G **67**
Amhurst Wlk. SE28 . . . 1A **108**
Amias Ho. *EC1* . . . *3C 8*
(off Central St.)
Amida Racquets & Fitness Spa . . . 3E 130
Amidas Gdns. RM8: Dag . . . 4B **72**
Amiel St. E1 . . . 4J **85**
Amies St. SW11 . . . 3D **118**
Amigo Ho. *SE1* . . . *1K 19*
(off Morley St.)
Amina Way SE16 . . . 3G **103**
Amiot Ho. *NW9* . . . *2B 44*
(off Heritage Av.)
Amis Av. KT19: Ewe . . . 6H **163**
Amisha Ct. *SE1* . . . *3F 103*
(off Spa Rd.)
Amity Gro. SW20 . . . 1D **152**
Amity Rd. E15 . . . 7H **69**
Ammanford Grn. NW9 . . . 6A **44**
Ammonite Ho. E15 . . . 7H **69**
Amner Rd. SW11 . . . 6E **118**
Amor Rd. W6 . . . 3E **98**
Amory Ho. *N1* . . . *1K 83*
(off Barnsbury Est.)
Amott Rd. SE15 . . . 3G **121**
Amoy Pl. E14 . . . 7C **86**
(not continuous)
Ampere Way CR0: Wadd . . . 7J **155**
Ampleforth Rd. SE2 . . . 2B **108**
Ampthill Est. NW1 . . . 1B **6** (2G **83**)
Ampthill Sq. NW1 . . . 1B **6** (2G **83**)
Ampton Pl. WC1 . . . 2G **7** (3K **83**)
Ampton St. WC1 . . . 2G **7** (3K **83**)
Amroth Cl. SE23 . . . 1H **139**
Amroth Grn. NW9 . . . 6A **44**
Amstel Ct. SE15 . . . 7F **103**
Amsterdam Rd. E14 . . . 3E **104**
Amundsen Ct. *E14* . . . *5C 104*
(off Napier Av.)
Amunsden Ho. *NW10* . . . *7K 61*
(off Stonebridge Pk.)
Amwell Cl. EN2: Enf . . . 5J **23**
Amwell Ct. Est. N4 . . . 2C **66**
Amwell St. EC1 . . . 1J **7** (3A **84**)
Amyand Cotts. TW1: Twick . . . 6B **114**
Amyand La. TW1: Twick . . . 7B **114**
Amyand Pk. Gdns. TW1: Twick . . . 7B **114**
Amyand Pk. Rd. TW1: Twick . . . 7A **114**
Amy Cl. SM6: Wall . . . 7J **167**
Amy Johnson Ct. HA8: Edg . . . 2H **43**
Amyruth Rd. SE4 . . . 5C **122**
Amy Warne Cl. E6 . . . 4C **88**
Anaesthesia Heritage Cen. . . . *6K 5*
(off Portland Pl.)
Anatola Rd. N19 . . . 2G **65**
Ancaster Cres. KT3: N Mald . . . 6C **152**
Ancaster M. BR3: Beck . . . 3K **157**
Ancaster Rd. BR3: Beck . . . 3K **157**
Ancaster St. SE18 . . . 7J **107**
Anchor SW18 . . . 4K **117**
Anchorage Cl. SW19 . . . 5J **135**
Anchorage Ho. *E14* . . . *7F 87*
(off Clove Cres.)
Anchorage Point *E14* . . . *2B 104*
(off Cuba St.)
Anchorage Point Ind. Est. SE7 . . . 3A **106**
Anchor & Hope La. SE7 . . . 3K **105**
Anchor Brewhouse SE1 . . . 5J **15** (1F **103**)
Anchor Bus. Cen. CR0: Bedd . . . 3J **167**
Anchor Cl. IG11: Bark . . . 3B **90**
Anchor Ct. EN1: Enf . . . 5K **23**
SW1 . . . *4C 18*
(off Vauxhall Bri. Rd.)
Anchor Ho. *E16* . . . *5H 87*
(off Barking Rd.)
E16 . . . *6A 88*
(off Prince Regent La.)
EC1 . . . *3C 8*
(off Old St.)
SW10 . . . *6B 100*
(off Cremorne Est.)
Anchor M. N1 . . . 6E **66**
SW12 . . . 6F **119**
Anchor Retail Pk. E1 . . . 4J **85**
Anchor Rd. E12 . . . 2B **70**
Anchor St. SE16 . . . 4H **103**
Anchor Ter. E1 . . . 4J **85**
SE1 . . . *4D 14*
(off Southwark Bri. Rd.)
Anchor Wharf *E3* . . . *5D 86*
(off Yeo St.)
Anchor Yd. EC1 . . . 3D **8** (4C **84**)
Ancill Cl. W6 . . . 6G **99**
Ancona Rd. NW10 . . . 2C **80**
SE18 . . . 5H **107**
Andace Pk. Gdns. BR1: Brom . . . 2A **160**
Andalus Rd. SW9 . . . 3J **119**
Andaman Ho. *E1* . . . *5A 86*
(off Duckett St.)
Ander Cl. HA0: Wemb . . . 4D **60**
Anderson Cl. N21 . . . 5E **22**
SM3: Sutt . . . 1J **165**
W3 . . . 6K **79**
Anderson Ct. NW2 . . . 1E **62**
Anderson Dr. TW15: Ashf . . . 4E **128**
Anderson Hgts. SW16 . . . 2K **155**
Anderson Ho. *E14* . . . *7E 86*
(off Woolmore St.)
IG11: Bark . . . 1H **89**
SW17 . . . 5B **136**
W12 . . . *6D 80*
(off Du Cane Rd.)
Anderson Pl. TW3: Houn . . . 4F **113**
Anderson Rd. E9 . . . 6K **67**
IG8: Wfd G . . . 3B **52**
Anderson Sq. *N1* . . . *1B 84*
(off Gaskin St.)
Anderson St. SW3 . . . 5E **16** (5D **100**)
Anderson Way DA17: Belv . . . 2H **109**
Anderton Cl. SE5 . . . 3D **120**
Anderton Ct. N22 . . . 2H **47**
Andora Ct. *NW6* . . . *7G 63*
(off Brondesbury Pk.)
Andorra Ct. BR1: Brom . . . 1A **160**
Andover Av. E16 . . . 6B **88**
Andover Cl. TW14: Felt . . . 1H **129**
UB6: G'frd . . . 4F **77**
Andover Ct. TW19: Stanw . . . 7A **110**
Andover Pl. NW6 . . . 2K **81**
Andover Rd. BR6: Orp . . . 1H **173**
N7 . . . 2K **65**
TW2: Twick . . . 1H **131**
Andoversford Ct. *SE15* . . . *6E 102*
(off Bibury Cl.)
Andover Ter. *W6* . . . *4D 98*
(off Raynham Rd.)
Andreck Ct. *BR3: Beck* . . . *2E 158*
(off Crescent Rd.)
Andre St. E8 . . . 5G **67**
Andrew Borde St. WC2 . . . 7D **6** (6H **83**)
Andrew Cl. DA1: Cray . . . 5K **127**
Andrew Ct. SE23 . . . 2K **139**
Andrewes Gdns. E6 . . . 6C **88**
Andrewes Highwalk EC2 . . . 6D **8**
Andrewes Ho. EC2 . . . 6D **8**
SM1: Sutt . . . 4J **165**
Andrew Gibb Memorial, The . . . 1H 123
Andrew Pl. SW8 . . . 7H **101**
Andrew Reed Ho. *SW18* . . . *7G 117*
(off Linstead Way)
Andrews Cl. HA1: Harr . . . 7H **41**
IG9: Buck H . . . 2F **37**
KT4: Wor Pk . . . 2E **164**
Andrews Crosse WC2 . . . 1J **13**
Andrews Ho. CR2: S Croy . . . 6C **168**
NW3 . . . *7D 64*
(off Fellows Rd.)
Andrews Pl. DA2: Dart . . . 2K **145**
SE9 . . . 6F **125**
Andrew's Rd. E8 . . . 1H **85**
Andrew St. E14 . . . 6E **86**
Andrews Wlk. SE17 . . . 6B **102**
Andringham Lodge *BR1: Brom* . . . *1K 159*
(off Palace Gro.)
Andrula Ct. N22 . . . 1B **48**
Andwell Cl. SE2 . . . 2B **108**
ANERLEY . . . 1H **157**
Anerley Gro. SE19 . . . 7F **139**
Anerley Hill SE19 . . . 6F **139**
Anerley Pk. SE20 . . . 7G **139**
Anerley Pk. Rd. SE20 . . . 7H **139**
Anerley Rd. SE19 . . . 7G **139**
SE20 . . . 7G **139**
Anerley Sta. Rd. SE20 . . . 1H **157**

182 A-Z London

Anerley Va. SE19 . . . . .7F **139**
Aneurin Bevan Ct. NW2 . . . . .2D **62**
Aneurin Bevan Ho. N11 . . . . .7C **32**
Anfield Cl. SW12 . . . . .7G **119**
ANGEL 2A **84**
Angela Carter Cl. SW9 . . . . .3A **120**
Angela Davies Ind. Est.
SE24 . . . . .4B **120**
Angel All. E1 . . . . .7K **9**
Angel Cen., The N1 . . . . .1K **7**
Angel Cl. N18 . . . . .5A **34**
TW12: Ham H 5G **131**
Angel Cnr. Pde. N18 . . . . .4B **34**
Angel Ct. EC2 . . . . .7F **9** (6D **84**)
SW1 . . . . .5B **12** (1G **101**)
ANGEL EDMONTON JUNC. 5B **34**
Angelfield TW3: Houn 4F **113**
Angel Ga. EC1 . . . . .1B **8** (3B **84**)
(not continuous)
Angel Hill SM1: Sutt 3K **165**
Angel Hill Dr. SM1: Sutt 3K **165**
Angelica Cl. UB7: Yiew 6A **74**
Angelica Dr. E6 . . . . .5E **88**
Angelica Gdns. CR0: C'don 1K **169**
Angelica Ho. E3 . . . . .1B **86**
(off Sycamore Av.)
Angelina Ho. SE15 . . . . .1G **121**
(off Goldsmith Rd.)
Angelis Apartments N1 . . . . .1B **8**
(off Graham St.)
Angel La. E15 . . . . .6F **69**
EC4 . . . . .3E **14** (7D **84**)
UB3: Hayes 5F **75**
Angel Pk. Gdns. SW9 . . . . .3A **120**
Angell Rd. SW9 . . . . .3A **120**
ANGELL TOWN 1A **120**
Angell Town Est. SW9 . . . . .2A **120**
Angel M. E1 . . . . .7H **85**
N1 . . . . .2A **84**
SW15 . . . . .7C **116**
Angelo M. SW16 . . . . .3K **155**
Angel Pl. N18 . . . . .4B **34**
SE1 . . . . .6E **14** (2D **102**)
Angel Rd. HA1: Harr 6J **41**
KT7: T Ditt 7A **150**
N18 . . . . .5B **34**
Angel Rd. Works N18 . . . . .5D **34**
Angel Sq. EC1 . . . . .2B **84**
Angel St. EC1 . . . . .7C **8** (6C **84**)
Angel Wlk. W6 . . . . .4E **98**
Angel Way RM1: Rom 5K **55**
Angel Wharf N1 . . . . .2C **84**
Angel Yd. N6 . . . . .1E **64**
Angerstein Bus. Pk. SE10 . . . . .4J **105**
Angerstein La. SE3 . . . . .1H **123**
Anglebury W2 . . . . .6J **81**
(off Talbot Rd.)
Angle Cl. UB10: Hil 1C **74**
Angle Grn. RM8: Dag 1G **72**
Anglers, The KT1: King T 3D **150**
(off High St.)
Anglers Cl. TW10: Ham 4C **132**
Angler's La. NW5 . . . . .6F **65**
Anglers Reach KT6: Surb 5D **150**
Anglesea Av. SE18 . . . . .4F **107**
Anglesea Ho. KT1: King T 4D **150**
(off Anglesea Rd.)
Anglesea M. SE18 . . . . .4F **107**
Anglesea Rd. KT1: King T 4D **150**
SE18 . . . . .4F **107**
Anglesea Ter. W6 . . . . .3D **98**
Anglesey Cl. TW15: Ashf 3C **128**
Anglesey Ct. W7 . . . . .4K **77**
Anglesey Ct. Rd. SM5: Cars 6E **166**
Anglesey Gdns. SM5: Cars 6E **166**
Anglesey Ho. E14 . . . . .6C **86**
(off Lindfield St.)
Anglesey Rd. EN3: Pond E 4C **24**
Anglesmede Cres. HA5: Pinn 3E **40**
Anglesmede Way HA5: Pinn 3E **40**
Anglia Rd. SW16 . . . . .4J **137**
Anglia Cl. N17 . . . . .7C **34**

Anglia Ct. RM8: Dag 1D **72**
(off Spring Cl.)
Anglia Ho. E14 . . . . .6A **86**
(off Salmon La.)
Anglian Ind. Est. IG11: Bark 4K **89**
Anglian Rd. E11 . . . . .3F **69**
Anglia Wlk. E6 . . . . .1E **88**
(off Napier Rd.)
Anglo Rd. E3 . . . . .2B **86**
Angrave Ct. E8 . . . . .1F **85**
(off Scriven St.)
Angrave Pas. E8 . . . . .1F **85**
Angus Cl. KT9: Chess 5G **163**
Angus Dr. HA4: Ruis 4A **58**
Angus Gdns. NW9 . . . . .1K **43**
Angus Ho. SW2 . . . . .7H **119**
Angus Rd. E13 . . . . .3A **88**
Angus St. SE14 . . . . .7A **104**
Anhalt Rd. SW11 . . . . .7C **100**
Ankerdine Cres. SE18 . . . . .7F **107**
Anlaby Rd. TW11: Tedd 5J **131**
Anley Rd. W14 . . . . .2F **99**
Anmersh Gro. HA7: Stan 1D **42**
Annabel Cl. E14 . . . . .6D **86**
Anna Cl. E8 .1F **85**
Annandale Gro. UB10: Ick 3E **56**
Annandale Rd. CR0: C'don 2G **169**
DA15: Sidc 7J **125**
SE10 . . . . .6H **105**
W4 . . . . .5A **98**
Anna Neagle Cl. E7 . . . . .4J **69**
Annan Way RM1: Rom 1K **55**
Anne Boleyn Ct. SE9 . . . . .6G **125**
Anne Boleyn's Wlk.
KT2: King T 5E **132**
SM3: Cheam 7F **165**
Anne Case M. KT3: N Mald 3K **151**
Anne Compton M. SE12 . . . . .7H **123**
Anne Goodman Ho. E1 . . . . .6J **85**
(off Jubilee St.)
Anne of Cleeves Ct. SE9 . . . . .6H **125**
Annes Ct. NW1 . . . . .3D **4**
Annesley Av. NW9 . . . . .3K **43**
Annesley Cl. NW10 . . . . .3A **62**
Annesley Dr. CR0: C'don 3B **170**
Annesley Ho. SW9 . . . . .1A **120**
Annesley Rd. SE3 . . . . .1K **123**
Annesley Wlk. N19 . . . . .2G **65**
Annesmere Gdns. SE3 . . . . .3B **124**
Anne St. E13 . . . . .4J **87**
Anne Sutherland Ho. BR3: Beck 7A **140**
Annett Cl. TW17: Shep 4G **147**
Annette Cl. HA3: W'stone 2J **41**
Annette Cres. N1 . . . . .7C **66**
Annette Rd. N7 . . . . .3K **65**
(not continuous)
Annett Rd. KT12: Walt T 7J **147**
Anne Way KT8: W Mole 4F **149**
Annexe Mkt. E1 . . . . .5J **9**
(off Spital Sq.)
Annie Besant Cl. E3 . . . . .1B **86**
Annie Taylor Ho. E12 . . . . .4E **70**
(off Walton Rd.)
Anning St. EC2 . . . . .3H **9** (4E **84**)
Annington Rd. N2 . . . . .3D **46**
Annis Rd. E9 . . . . .6A **68**
Ann La. SW10 . . . . .6B **100**
Ann Moss Way SE16 . . . . .3J **103**
Ann's Cl. SW1 . . . . .7F **11**
Ann's Pl. E1 .6J **9**
Ann St. SE18 . . . . .5G **107**
(not continuous)
Ann Stroud Ct. SE12 . . . . .5J **123**
Annsworthy Av. CR7: Thor H 3D **156**
Annsworthy Cres. SE25 . . . . .2D **156**
Ansar Gdns. E17 . . . . .5B **50**
Ansdell Rd. SE15 . . . . .2J **121**
Ansdell St. W8 . . . . .3K **99**
Ansdell Ter. W8 . . . . .3K **99**
Ansell Gro. SM5: Cars 1E **166**
Ansell Ho. E1 . . . . .5J **85**
(off Mile End Rd.)

Ansell Rd. SW17 . . . . .3C **136**
Anselm Cl. CR0: C'don 3F **169**
Anselm Rd. HA5: Hat E 1D **40**
SW6 .6J **99**
Ansford Rd. BR1: Brom 5E **140**
Ansleigh Pl. W11 . . . . .7F **81**
Anson Cl. RM7: Mawney 2H **55**
Anson Ho. E1 . . . . .4A **86**
(off Shandy St.)
SW1 .7A **18**
(off Churchill Gdns.)
Anson Pl. SE28 . . . . .2H **107**
Anson Rd. N7 . . . . .4G **65**
NW2 .4D **62**
Anson Ter. UB5: N'olt 6F **59**
Anstey Cl. W3 . . . . .2H **97**
Anstey Ho. E9 . . . . .1J **85**
(off Templecombe Rd.)
Anstey Rd. SE15 . . . . .3G **121**
Anstey Wlk. N15 . . . . .4B **48**
Anstice Cl. W4 . . . . .7A **98**
Anstridge Path SE9 . . . . .6H **125**
Anstridge Rd. SE9 . . . . .6H **125**
Antelope Rd. SE18 . . . . .3D **106**
Antelope Wlk. KT6: Surb 5D **150**
Antenor Ho. E2 . . . . .2H **85**
(off Old Bethnal Grn. Rd.)
Anthony Cl. NW7 . . . . .4F **29**
Anthony Cope Ct. N1 . . . . .1F **9**
(off Chart St.)
Anthony Ho. NW8 . . . . .4C **4**
(off Ashbridge St.)
Anthony Rd. DA16: Well 1A **126**
SE25 . . . . .6G **157**
UB6: G'frd 3J **77**
Anthony St. E1 . . . . .6H **85**
Anthony Way N18 . . . . .6E **34**
Antigua Wlk. SE19 . . . . .5D **138**
Antilles Bay E14 . . . . .2E **104**
Antill Rd. E3 . . . . .3A **86**
N15 .4G **49**
Antill Ter. E1 . . . . .6K **85**
Antlers Hill E4 . . . . .5J **25**
Antoinette M. NW2 . . . . .6C **62**
Anton Cres. SM1: Sutt 3J **165**
Antoneys Cl. HA5: Pinn 2B **40**
Antonine Hgts.
SE1 .7G **15**
Anton Pl. HA9: Wemb 3H **61**
Anton St. E8 . . . . .5G **67**
Antony Ho. SE14 . . . . .7K **103**
(off Barlborough St.)
SE16 . . . . .4J **103**
(off Raymouth Rd.)
Antrim Gro. NW3 . . . . .6D **64**
Antrim Ho. E3 . . . . .1B **86**
(off Birdsfield La.)
Antrim Rd. NW3 . . . . .6D **64**
Antrobus Cl. SM1: Sutt 5H **165**
Antrobus Rd. W4 . . . . .4J **97**
Anvil Cl. SW16 . . . . .7G **137**
Anvil Rd. TW16: Sun 3J **147**
Anworth Cl. IG8: Wfd G 6E **36**
AOP Gallery .3G **9**
(off Leonard St.)
Apeldoorn Dr. SM6: Wall 7J **167**
Apex Cl. BR3: Beck 1D **158**
APEX CORNER
Feltham 3D **130**
Mill Hill 4F **29**
Apex Ct. W13 . . . . .7A **78**
Apex Ho. E16 . . . . .4B **80**
Apex Pde. NW7 . . . . .4E **28**
(off Selvage La.)
Apex Retail Pk. TW13: Hanw 3D **130**
Aphrodite Ct. E14 . . . . .4C **104**
(off Homer Dr.)
E15 . . . . .1E **86**
Aplin Way TW7: Isle 1J **113**
Apollo Av. BR1: Brom 1K **159**
Apollo Bldg. E14 . . . . .4C **104**
Apollo Bus. Cen. SE8 . . . . .5K **103**

Apollo Ct. E1 . . . . .7G **85**
(off Thomas More St.)
E15 . . . . .1E **86**
SW9 . . . . .1A **120**
(off Southey Rd.)
Apollo Ho. E2 . . . . .2H **85**
(off St Jude's Rd.)
E3 . . . . .2C **86**
(off Garrison Rd.)
N6 . . . . .7D **46**
SW10 . . . . .7B **100**
(off Milman's St.)
Apollo Pl. E11 . . . . .3G **69**
SW10 . . . . .7B **100**
Apollo Theatre
Soho 2C **12**
(off Shaftesbury Av.)
Victoria 2A **18**
(off Wilton Rd.)
Apollo Way DA8: Erith 4K **109**
SE28 . . . . .3H **107**
Apollo West End Cinema 3C **12**
(off Regent St.)
Apostles, The SE23 . . . . .2K **139**
(off Church Ri.)
Apostle Way CR7: Thor H 2B **156**
Apothecary St. EC4 . . . . .1A **14** (6B **84**)
Appach Rd. SW2 . . . . .5A **120**
Appian Cl. E3 . . . . .2B **86**
(off Parnell Rd.)
Apple Blossom Ct. SW8 . . . . .7H **101**
(off Pascal St.)
Appleby Cl. BR5: Pet W 7J **161**
E4 . . . . .6K **35**
N15 .5D **48**
TW2: Twick 2H **131**
UB8: Hil 6E **74**
Appleby Ct. W3 . . . . .2J **97**
(off Newport Rd.)
Appleby Gdns. TW14: Felt 1H **129**
Appleby Rd. E8 . . . . .7G **67**
E16 .6H **87**
Appleby St. E2 . . . . .2F **85**
Appledore Av. DA7: Bex 1J **127**
HA4: Ruis 3K **57**
Appledore Cl. BR2: Brom 5H **159**
HA8: Edg 1G **43**
SW17 . . . . .2D **136**
Appledore Cres. DA14: Sidc 3J **143**
Appledore Way NW7 . . . . .7A **30**
Appleford Ho. W10 . . . . .4G **81**
(off Bosworth Rd.)
Appleford Rd. W10 . . . . .4G **81**
Apple Gth. TW8: Bford 4D **96**
Applegarth CR0: New Ad 7D **170**
(not continuous)
KT10: Clay 5A **162**
Applegarth Dr. IG2: Ilf 4G **53**
Applegarth Ho. SE1 . . . . .6B **14**
SE15 . . . . .7G **103**
(off Bird in Bush Rd.)
Applegarth Rd. SE28 . . . . .1B **108**
W14 .3F **99**
Apple Gro. EN1: Enf 3K **23**
KT9: Chess 4E **162**
Apple Mkt. KT1: King T 2D **150**
(off Market Pl.)
Apple Rd. E11 . . . . .3G **69**
Appleshaw Ho. SE5 . . . . .3E **120**
Appleton Cl. DA7: Bex 2J **127**
Appleton Gdns. KT3: N Mald 6C **152**
Appleton Rd. SE9 . . . . .3C **124**
Appleton Sq. CR4: Mitc 1C **154**
Appletree Av. UB8: Hil 5B **74**
Appletree Cl. SE20 . . . . .1H **157**
Appletree Gdns. EN4: E Barn 4H **21**
Apple Tree Rdbt. UB7: Yiew 6B **74**
Apple Tree Yd. SW1 . . . .4B **12** (1G **101**)
Applewood Cl. N20 . . . . .1H **31**
NW2 .3D **62**
UB10: Ick 4A **56**
Applewood Dr. E13 . . . . .4K **87**

Appold St. EC2 5G 9 (5E 84)
Apprentice Gdns. UB5: N'olt 3D 76
Apprentice Way E5 4H 67
Approach, The BR6: Orp 2K 173
EN1: Enf 2C 24
NW4 5F 45
W3 6K 79
Approach Cl. N16 4E 66
Approach Rd. E2 2J 85
EN4: E Barn 4G 21
HA8: Edg 6B 28
KT8: W Mole 5E 148
SW20 2E 152
TW15: Ashf 6E 128
Aprey Gdns. NW4 4E 44
April Cl. BR6: Chels 5K 173
TW13: Felt 3J 129
W7 7J 77
April Ct. *E2* *2G 85*
(off Teale St.)
April Glen SE23 3K 139
April St. E8 4F 67
Apsley Cen., The
NW2 2C 62
Apsley Cl. HA2: Harr 5G 41
Apsley House 6H 11 (2E 100)
Apsley Ho. *E1* *5J 85*
(off Stepney Way)
NW8 *2B 82*
(off Finchley Rd.)
TW4: Houn 4D 112
Apsley Rd. KT3: N Mald 3J 151
SE25 4H 157
Apsley Way NW2 2C 62
W1 6H 11 (2E 100)
(not continuous)
Aqua Ho. NW10 3G 79
Aquarius TW1: Twick 1B 132
Aquarius Bus. Pk. *NW2* *1C 62*
(off Priestley Way)
Aquila St. NW8 2B 82
Aquinas St. SE1 5K 13 (1A 102)
Arabella Ct. *NW8* *2A 82*
(off Marlborough Pl.)
Arabella Dr. SW15 4A 116
Arabia Cl. E4 7K 25
Arabian Ho. *E1* *4A 86*
(off Ernest St.)
Arabin Rd. SE4 4A 122
Arado Ho. *NW9* *2B 44*
(off Boulevard Dr.)
Aragon Av. KT7: T Ditt 5K 149
Aragon Cl. BR2: Brom 1D 172
EN2: Enf 1E 22
TW16: Sun 6H 129
Aragon Ct. KT8: E Mos 4G 149
SE11 *5J 19*
(off Hotspur St.)
Aragon Dr. HA4: Ruis 1B 58
Aragon Ho. *E16* *1J 105*
(off Capulet M.)
Aragon Pl. SM4: Mord 7G 153
Aragon Rd. KT2: King T 5E 132
SM4: Mord 6F 153
Aragon Twr. SE8 4B 104
Aral Ho. *E1* *4K 85*
(off Ernest St.)
Arandora Cres. RM6: Chad H 7B 54
Aran Dr. HA7: Stan 4H 27
Aran Lodge *NW6* *7J 63*
(off Woodchurch Rd.)
Aran M. *N7* *7A 66*
(off St Clements St.)
Arapiles Ho. *E14* *6F 87*
(off Blair St.)
Arbery Rd. E3 3A 86
Arbon Ct. *N1* *1C 84*
(off Linton St.)
Arbor Cl. BR3: Beck 2D 158
Arbor Ct. N16 2D 66
Arboretum Ct. *N1* *6D 66*
(off Dove Rd.)
Arboretum Pl. *IG11: Bark* *7G 71*
(off Clockhouse Av.)
Arborfield Cl. SW2 1K 137
Arborfield Ho. *E14* *7C 86*
(off E. India Dock Rd.)
Arbor Ho. *BR6: Orp* *2K 173*
(off Orchard Gro.)
Arbor Rd. E4 3A 36
Arbour Ho. *E1* *6K 85*
(off Arbour Sq.)
Arbour Rd. EN3: Pond E 3E 24
Arbour Sq. E1 6K 85
Arbroath Rd. SE9 3C 124
Arbury Ter. SE26 3G 139
Arbuthnot La. DA5: Bexl 6E 126
Arbuthnot Rd. SE14 2K 121
Arbutus St. E8 1F 85
Arcade CR0: C'don 2C 168
Arcade, The *CR0: C'don* *3C 168*
(off High St.)
E17 4C 50
EC2 6G 9
IG11: Bark 7G 71
N7 *4J 65*
(off Macready Pl.)
SE9 *6E 124*
(off High St.)
Arcade Chambers SE9 6E 124
Arcade Ct. N11 4A 32
Arcade Pde. KT9: Chess 5D 162
Arcadia Av. N3 2J 45
Arcadia Cen., The W5 7D 78
Arcadia Cl. SM5: Cars 4E 166
Arcadia Ct. E1 7J 9
Arcadia M. KT3: N Mald 3A 152
Arcadian Av. DA5: Bexl 6E 126
Arcadian Cl. DA5: Bexl 6E 126
Arcadian Gdns. N22 7E 32
Arcadian Pl. SW18 7H 117
Arcadian Rd. DA5: Bexl 6E 126
Arcadia St. E14 6C 86
Archangel St. SE16 2K 103
Archbishop Lanfranc School Sports Cen.
6J 155
Archbishop's Pl. SW2 7K 119
Archdale Bus. Cen.
HA2: Harr 2G 59
Archdale Ct. W12 1D 98
Archdale Ho. *SE1* *7G 15*
(off Long La.)
Archdale Pl. KT3: N Mald 3H 151
Archdale Rd. SE22 5F 121
Archel Rd. W14 6H 99
Archer Apartments *N1* *2E 84*
(off Fern Cl.)
Archer Cl. EN5: Barn 6C 20
KT2: King T 7E 132
Archer Ho. *N1* *1E 84*
(off Whitmore Est.)
SE14 1A 122
SW11 1B 118
W11 *7H 81*
(off Westbourne Gro.)
W13 *1B 96*
(off Sherwood Cl.)
Archer M. SW9 3J 119
TW12: Ham H 6G 131
Archer Rd. BR5: St M Cry 5K 161
SE25 4H 157
Archers Ct. BR2: Brom 4K 159
CR2: S Croy *5C 168*
(off Nottingham Rd.)
Archers Dr. EN3: Enf H 2D 24
Archers Lodge *SE16* *5G 103*
(off Culloden Cl.)
Archer Sq. SE14 6A 104
Archer St. W1 2C 12 (7H 83)
Archer Ter. UB7: Yiew 7A 74
Archery Cl. HA3: W'stone 3K 41
W2 1D 10 (6C 82)
Archery Flds. Ho. *WC1* *1H 7*
(off Wharton St.)
Archery Rd. SE9 5D 124
Archery Steps W2 2D 10
Arches SW8 7F 19 (6J 101)
Arches, The E16 4G 87
HA2: Harr 2F 59
NW1 7F 65
SE8 6A 104
SW8 7H 101
WC2 *4F 13*
(off Villiers St.)
Arches Bus. Cen., The *UB2: S'hall* *2D 94*
(off Merrick Rd.)
Arches Leisure Cen. 6G 105
Archgate Bus. Cen. N12 5F 31
Archibald M. W1 3J 11 (7F 83)
Archibald Rd. N7 4H 65
Archibald St. E3 3C 86
Archie Cl. UB7: W Dray 2C 92
Archie St. SE1 7H 15 (2E 102)
Arch St. SE1 3C 102
ARCHWAY 2G 65
Archway Bus. Cen. N19 3H 65
Archway Cl. N19 2G 65
SM6: Bedd 3H 167
SW19 3K 135
W10 5F 81
Archway Leisure Cen. 2G 65
Archway Mall N19 2G 65
Archway M. *SW15* *4G 117*
(off Putney Bri. Rd.)
Archway Rd. N6 6E 46
N19 6E 46
Archway St. SW13 3A 116
Arcola St. E8 5F 67
Arcola Theatre 5F 67
Arcon Dr. UB5: N'olt 4C 76
Arcon Ter. N9 7B 24
Arctic Ho. *NW9* *2B 44*
(off Heritage Av.)
Arctic St. NW5 5F 65
Arcus Rd. BR1: Brom 6G 141
Ardbeg Rd. SE24 5D 120
Arden Cl. HA1: Harr 3H 59
SE28 6D 90
TW4: Houn 7D 112
Arden Ct. Gdns. N2 6B 46
Arden Cres. E14 4C 104
RM9: Dag 7C 72
Arden Est. N1 2E 84
Arden Grange N12 4F 31
Arden Gro. BR6: Farnb 4F 173
Arden Ho. N1 1G 9
SE11 4G 19
SW9 *2J 119*
(off Grantham Rd.)
Arden M. E17 5D 50
Arden Mhor HA5: Eastc 4K 39
Arden Rd. N3 3H 45
W13 7C 78
Ardent Cl. SE25 3E 156
Ardent Ho. *E3* *2A 86*
(off Roman Rd.)
Ardfern Av. SW16 3A 156
Ardfillan Rd. SE6 1F 141
Ardgowan Rd. SE6 7G 123
Ardilaun Rd. N5 4C 66
Ardingly Cl. CR0: C'don 3K 169
Ardleigh Ct. *BR1: Brom* *7H 141*
(off London Rd.)
Ardleigh Gdns. SM3: Sutt 7J 153
Ardleigh Ho. IG11: Bark 1G 89
Ardleigh M. IG1: Ilf 3F 71
Ardleigh Rd. E17 1B 50
N1 6E 66
Ardleigh Ter. E17 1B 50
Ardley Cl. HA4: Ruis 7E 38
NW10 3A 62
SE6 3A 140
Ardlui Rd. SE27 2C 138
Ardmay Gdns. KT6: Surb 5E 150
Ardmere Rd. SE13 6F 123
Ardmore La. IG9: Buck H 1E 36
Ardmore Pl. IG9: Buck H 1E 36
Ardoch Rd. SE6 2F 141
Ardra Rd. N9 3E 34
Ardrossan Gdns. KT4: Wor Pk 3C 164
Ardshiel Cl. SW15 3F 117
Ardwell Av. IG6: Ilf 5G 53
Ardwell Rd. SW2 2J 137
Ardwick Rd. NW2 4J 63
Arena, The EN3: Enf L 1G 25
Arena Bus. Cen. N4 6C 48
Arena Ho. *E3* *2C 86*
(off Lefevre Wlk.)
Arena Shop. Pk. N4 6B 48
Arena Sq. HA9: Wemb 4G 61
Ares Ct. *E14* *4C 104*
(off Homer Dr.)
Arethusa Ho. *E14* *4C 104*
(off Cahir St.)
Argali Ho. *DA18: Erith* *3E 108*
(off Kale Rd.)
Argall Av. E10 7K 49
Argall Way E10 1K 67
Argenta Way HA9: Wemb 6G 61
NW10 7H 61
Argent Cen., The UB3: Hayes 2J 93
Argent Ct. *EN5: New Bar* *4F 21*
(off Leicester Rd.)
KT6: Surb 3G 163
Argenton Twr. *SW18* *6K 117*
(off Mapleton Cres.)
Argo Bus. Cen. NW6 3J 81
Argonaut Pk. SL3: Poyle 4A 174
Argon M. SW6 7J 99
Argon Rd. N18 5D 34
Argos Ct. *SW9* *1A 120*
(off Caldwell St.)
Argos Ho. *E2* *2H 85*
(off Old Bethnal Grn. Rd.)
Argosy Ho. SE8 4A 104
Argosy La. TW19: Stanw 7A 110
Argus Cl. RM7: Mawney 1H 55
Argus Way UB5: N'olt 3C 76
Argyle Av. TW3: Houn 6E 112
(not continuous)
Argyle Cl. W13 4A 78
Argyle Ho. E14 3E 104
Argyle Pas. N17 1F 49
Argyle Pl. W6 4D 98
Argyle Rd. E1 4K 85
E15 4G 69
E16 6K 87
EN5: Barn 4A 20
HA2: Harr 6F 41
IG1: Ilf 2E 70
N12 5E 30
N17 1G 49
N18 4B 34
Argyle Rd. TW3: Houn 5F 113
UB6: G'frd, Lon 3K 77
W13 5A 78
Argyle Sq. WC1 1F 7 (3J 83)
Argyle St. WC1 1E 6 (3J 83)
Argyle Wlk. WC1 2F 7 (3J 83)
Argyle Way SE16 5G 103
Argyll Av. UB1: S'hall 1F 95
Argyll Cl. SW9 3K 119
Argyll Ct. *SW2* *7J 119*
(off New Pk. Rd.)
Argyll Gdns. HA8: Edg 2H 43
Argyll Mans. SW3 7B 16 (6B 100)
W14 *4G 99*
(off Hammersmith Rd.)
Argyll Rd. SE18 3G 107
W8 2J 99
Argyll St. W1 1A 12 (6G 83)
Aria Ct. IG2: Ilf 6G 53
Arica Ho. *SE16* *3H 103*
(off Slippers Pl.)
Arica Rd. SE4 4A 122
Ariel Apartments E16 6J 87
Ariel Ct. SE11 4K 19 (4B 102)
Ariel Rd. NW6 6J 63

Ariel Way TW4: Houn 3K 111
   W12 . . . . .1E 98
Aristotle Rd. SW4 . . . . .3H 119
Arizona Bldg. SE10 . . . . .1D 122
   (off Deal's Gateway)
Ark, The W6 . . . . .5F 99
   (off Talgarth Rd.)
Arkell Gro. SE19 . . . . .7B 138
Arkindale Rd. SE6 . . . . .3E 140
Arklay Cl. UB8: Hil 4B 74
Arkley Cres. E17 . . . . .5B 50
Arkley Rd. E17 . . . . .5B 50
Arklow Ho. SE17 . . . . .6D 102
Arklow M. KT6: Surb 2E 162
Arklow Rd. SE14 . . . . .6B 104
Arklow Rd. Trad. Est.
   SE14 . . . . .6A 104
Arkwright Rd. CR2: Sande 7F 169
   NW3 . . . . .5A 64
Arlesey Cl. SW15 . . . . .5G 117
Arlesford Rd. SW9 . . . . .3J 119
Arlidge Ho. EC1 . . . . .5K 7
   (off Kirby St.)
Arlingford Rd. SW2 . . . . .5A 120
Arlington N12 .3D 30
Arlington Av. N1 . . . . .1C 84
   (not continuous)
Arlington Bldg. E3 . . . . .2C 86
Arlington Cl. DA15: Sidc 7J 125
   SE13 . . . . .5F 123
   SM1: Sutt .2J 165
   TW1: Twick 6C 114
Arlington Ct. UB3: Harl 5G 93
   W3 . . . . .2H 97
   (off Mill Hill Rd.)
Arlington Dr. HA4: Ruis 6F 39
   SM5: Cars 2D 166
Arlington Gdns. IG1: Ilf 1E 70
   W4 . . . . .5J 97
Arlington Grn. NW7 . . . . .7A 30
Arlington Ho. EC1 . . . . .1K 7
   (off Arlington Way)
   SE8 . . . . .6B 104
   (off Evelyn St.)
   SW1 . . . . .4A 12 (1G 101)
   TW9: Kew .7H 97
   UB7: W Dray 2B 92
   W12 . . . . .1D 98
   (off Tunis Rd.)
Arlington Lodge SW2 . . . . .4K 119
Arlington Pk. Mans. W4 . . . . .5J 97
   (off Sutton La. Nth.)
Arlington Pas.
   TW11: Tedd 4K 131
Arlington Pl. SE10 . . . . .7E 104
Arlington Rd. IG8: Wfd G 1J 51
   KT6: Surb .6D 150
   N14 . . . . .2A 32
   NW1 . . . . .1F 83
   TW1: Twick 6C 114
   TW10: Ham 2D 132
   TW11: Tedd 4K 131
   TW15: Ashf 5B 128
   W13 . . . . .6B 78
Arlington Sq. N1 . . . . .1C 84
Arlington St. SW1 . . . . . .4A 12 (1G 101)
Arlington Way EC1 . . . . .1K 7 (3A 84)
Arliss Ho. HA1: Harr 5K 41
Arliss Way UB5: N'olt 1A 76
Arlow Rd. N21 . . . . .1F 33
Armada Ct. SE8 . . . . .6C 104
Armadale Cl. N17 . . . . .4H 49
Armadale Rd. SW6 . . . . .7J 99
   TW14: Felt 5J 111
Armada St. SE8 . . . . .6C 104
Armada Way E6 . . . . .7G 89
Armagh Rd. E3 . . . . .1B 86
Armfield Cl. KT8: W Mole 5D 148
Armfield Cres. CR4: Mitc 2D 154
Armfield Rd. EN2: Enf 1J 23
Arminger Rd. W12 . . . . .1D 98
Armistice Gdns. SE25 . . . . .3G 157

Armitage Ho. NW1 . . . . .5D 4
   (off Lisson Gro.)
Armitage Rd. NW11 . . . . .1G 63
   SE10 . . . . .5H 105
Armour Cl. N7 . . . . .6K 65
Armoury Ho. E3 . . . . .1A 86
   (off Gunmakers La.)
Armoury Rd. SE8 . . . . .2D 122
Armoury Way SW18 . . . . .5J 117
Armsby Ho. E1 . . . . .5J 85
   (off Stepney Way)
Armstead Wlk. RM10: Dag 7G 73
Armstrong Av. IG8: Wfd G 6B 36
Armstrong Cl. BR1: Brom 3C 160
   E6 . . . . .6D 88
   HA5: Eastc .6J 39
   KT12: Walt T 6J 147
   RM8: Dag 7D 54
Armstrong Cres. EN4: Cockf 3G 21
Armstrong Rd. NW10 . . . . .7A 62
   SE18 . . . . .3G 107
Armstrong Rd. SW7 . . .2A 16 (3B 100)
   TW13: Hanw 5C 130
   W3 . . . . .1B 98
Armstrong Way UB2: S'hall 2F 95
Armytage Rd. TW5: Hest 7B 94
Arnal Cres. SW18 . . . . .7G 117
Arncliffe NW6 .2K 81
Arncliffe Cl. N11 . . . . .6K 31
Arncroft Ct. IG11: Bark 3B 90
Arndale Wlk. SW18 . . . . .5K 117
Arne Gro. BR6: Orp 3K 173
Arne Ho. SE11 . . . . .5G 19
Arne St. WC2 . . . . .1E 13 (6J 83)
Arnett Sq. E4 .6G 35
Arne Wlk. SE3 . . . . .4H 123
Arneways Av. RM6: Chad H 3D 54
Arneway St. SW1 . . . . . .2D 18 (3H 101)
Arnewood Cl. SW15 . . . . .1C 134
Arneys La. CR4: Mitc 6E 154
Arngask Rd. SE6 . . . . .7F 123
Arnhem Pl. E14 . . . . .3C 104
Arnhem Way SE22 . . . . .5E 120
Arnhem Wharf E14 . . . . .3B 104
Arnison Rd. KT8: E Mos 4H 149
Arnold Bennett Way N8 . . . . .3A 48
Arnold Cir. E2 . . . . .2J 9 (3F 85)
Arnold Cl. HA3: Kenton 7F 43
Arnold Ct. N22 . . . . .7D 32
Arnold Cres. TW7: Isle 5H 113
Arnold Dr. KT9: Chess 6D 162
Arnold Est. SE1 . . . . .7K 15 (2F 103)
Arnold Gdns. N13 . . . . .5G 33
Arnold Ho. SE3 . . . . .7A 106
   (off Shooters Hill Rd.)
   SE17 . . . . .5B 102
   (off Doddington Gro.)
Arnold Mans. W14 . . . . .6H 99
   (off Queen's Club Gdns.)
Arnold Rd. E3 .3C 86
   N15 . . . . .3F 49
   RM9: Dag 7F 73
   RM10: Dag .7G 73
   SW17 . . . . .7D 136
   UB5: N'olt 6B 58
Arnold Ter. HA7: Stan 5E 26
Arnos Gro. N14 . . . . .4C 32
Arnos Gro. Ct. N11 . . . . .5B 32
   (off Palmer's Rd.)
Arnos Rd. N11 . . . . .5B 32
Arnos Swimming Pool 5C 32
Arnot Ho. SE5 . . . . .7C 102
   (off Comber Gro.)
Arnott Cl. SE28 . . . . .1C 108
   W4 . . . . .4K 97
Arnould Av. SE5 . . . . .4D 120
Arnsberg Way DA6: Bex 4G 127
   DA7: Bex .4G 127
Arnside Gdns. HA9: Wemb 1D 60
Arnside Ho. SE17 . . . . .6D 102
   (off Arnside St.)
Arnside Rd. DA7: Bex 1G 127

Arnside St. SE17 . . . . .6D 102
Arnulf St. SE6 . . . . .4D 140
Arnulls Rd. SW16 . . . . .6B 138
Arodene Rd. SW2 . . . . .6K 119
Arona Ho. BR3: Beck 2E 158
Arosa Rd. TW1: Twick 6D 114
   (not continuous)
Arpley Sq. SE20 . . . . .7J 139
   (off High St.)
Arragon Gdns. BR4: W W'ck 3D 170
   SW16 . . . . .7J 137
Arragon Rd. E6 . . . . .1B 88
   SW18 . . . . .1J 135
   TW1: Twick 7A 114
Arran Cl. DA8: Erith 6K 109
   SM6: Wall .4F 167
Arran Ct. NW9 . . . . .2B 44
   NW10 . . . . .3K 61
Arran Dr. E12 .1B 70
Arran Ho. E14 . . . . .1E 104
   (off Raleana Rd.)
Arran M. W5 . . . . .1F 97
Arran Rd. SE6 . . . . .2D 140
Arran Wlk. N1 .7C 66
Arras Av. SM4: Mord 5A 154
Arrol Ho. SE1 . . . . .3C 102
Arrol Rd. BR3: Beck 3J 157
Arrow Ct. SW5 . . . . .4J 99
   (off W. Cromwell Rd.)
Arrow Ho. N1 .1E 84
   (off Wilmer Gdns.)
Arrow Rd. E3 .3D 86
Arrowscout Wlk. UB5: N'olt 3C 76
   (off Argus Way)
Arrows Ho. SE15 . . . . .7J 103
   (off Clifton Way)
Arrowsmith Ho. SE11 . . . . .5G 19
Arsenal FC 4A 66
Arsenal Rd. SE9 . . . . .2D 124
Arsenal Way SE18 . . . . .3G 107
Arta Ho. E1 . . . . .6J 85
   (off Devonport St.)
Artbrand Ho. SE1 . . . . .7G 15
   (off Leathermarket St.)
Artemis Ct. E14 . . . . .4C 104
   (off Homer Dr.)
Artemis Pl. SW18 . . . . .7H 117
Arterberry Rd. SW20 . . . . .7E 134
Artesian Cl. NW10 . . . . .7K 61
Artesian Gro. EN5: New Bar 4F 21
Artesian Ho. SE1 . . . . .3F 103
   (off Grange Rd.)
Artesian Rd. W2 . . . . .6J 81
Artesian Wlk. E11 . . . . .3G 69
Arthingworth St. E15 . . . . .1G 87
Arthur Ct. CR0: C'don 3E 168
   (off Fairfield Path)
   SW11 . . . . .1E 118
   W2 . . . . .6K 81
   (off Queensway)
   W10 . . . . .6F 81
   (off Silchester Rd.)
Arthur Deakin Ho. E1 . . . . .5K 9
   (off Hunton St.)
Arthurdon Rd. SE4 . . . . .5C 122
Arthur Gro. SE18 . . . . .4G 107
Arthur Henderson Ho. SW6 . . . . .2H 117
   (off Fulham Rd.)
Arthur Horsley Wlk. E7 . . . . .5H 69
   (off Twr. Hamlets Rd.)
Arthur Ho. N1 .1E 84
   (off New Era Est.)
Arthur Newton Ho. SW11 . . . . .3B 118
   (off Winstanley Est.)
Arthur Rd. E6 .2D 88
   KT2: King T 7G 133
   KT3: N Mald 5D 152
   N7 . . . . .4K 65
   N9 . . . . .2A 34
   RM6: Chad H 6C 54
   SW19 . . . . .5H 135

Arthur St. EC4 . . . . .2F 15 (7D 84)
Arthur Wade Ho. E2 . . . . .1K 9
   (off Baroness Rd.)
Arthur Wallis Ho. E12 . . . . .3E 70
   (off Grantham Rd.)
Artichoke Hill E1 . . . . .7H 85
Artichoke M. SE5 . . . . .1D 120
   (off Artichoke Pl.)
Artichoke Pl. SE5 . . . . .1D 120
Artillery Bldg., The E1 . . . . .6H 9
   (off Artillery La.)
Artillery Cl. IG2: Ilf 6G 53
Artillery Ho. E3 . . . . .1A 86
   (off Barge La.)
   E15 . . . . .6G 69
   SE18 . . . . .5E 106
   (off Connaught M.)
Artillery La. E1 . . . . .6H 9 (5E 84)
   W12 . . . . .6C 80
Artillery Mans. SW1 . . . . .1C 18
   SW1 . . . . .3H 101
   (off Victoria St.)
Artillery Pas. E1 . . . . .6J 9
Artillery Pl. HA3: Hrw W 7B 26
   SE18 . . . . .5D 106
   SW1 . . . . .2C 18 (3H 101)
Artillery Row SW1 . . . . . .2C 18 (3G 101)
Artillery Sq. SE18 . . . . .3F 107
   (off No. 1 St.)
Artington Cl. BR6: Farnb 4G 173
Artisan Cl. E6 .6F 89
Artisan Ct. E8 .6G 67
Artisan M. NW10 . . . . .3F 81
   (off Warfield Rd.)
Artisan Quarter NW10 . . . . .3F 81
   (off Wellington Rd.)
Artizan St. E1 .7J 9
Arts Depot 5F 31
Arts Theatre .2E 12
   (off St. Newport St.)
Arun Ct. SE25 . . . . .5G 157
Arundale KT1: King T 4D 150
   (off Anglesea Rd.)
Arundel Av. SM4: Mord 4H 153
Arundel Bldgs. SE1 . . . . .3E 102
   (off Swan Mead)
Arundel Cl. CR0: Wadd 3B 168
   DA5: Bexl .6F 127
   E15 . . . . .4G 69
   SW11 . . . . .5C 118
   TW12: Ham H 5F 131
Arundel Ct. BR2: Brom 2G 159
   HA2: Harr 4E 58
   N12 . . . . .6H 31
   N17 . . . . .1G 49
   SE16 . . . . .5H 103
   (off Verney Rd.)
   SW3 . . . . .5D 16
   (off Jubilee Pl.)
   SW13 . . . . .6D 98
   (off Arundel Ter.)
   W11 . . . . .7H 81
   (off Arundel Gdns.)
Arundel Dr. HA2: Harr 4D 58
   IG8: Wfd G .7D 36
Arundel Gdns. HA8: Edg 7E 28
   IG3: Ilf 2A 72
   N21 . . . . .1F 33
   W11 . . . . .7H 81
Arundel Gt. Ct.
   WC2 . . . . .2H 13 (7K 83)
Arundel Gro. N16 . . . . .5E 66
Arundel Ho. CR0: C'don 5D 168
   (off Heathfield Rd.)
   W3 . . . . .2H 97
   (off Park Rd. Nth.)
Arundel Mans. SW6 . . . . .1H 117
   (off Kelvedon Rd.)
Arundel Pl. N1 . . . . .6A 66
Arundel Rd. CR0: C'don 6D 156
   EN4: Cockf .3H 21
   KT1: King T 3H 151

Arundel Rd. SM2: Cheam, Sutt 7H 165
TW4: Houn 3A 112
Arundel Sq. N1 6A 66
N7 6A 66
Arundel St. WC2 2H 13 (7K 83)
Arundel Ter. SW13 6D 98
Arun Ho. KT2: King T 1D 150
Arvon Rd. N5 5A 66
(not continuous)
Asa Ct. UB3: Harl 3H 93
Asbaston Ter. IG1: Ilf 5G 71
Asbridge Ct. *W6* *3D 98*
(off Dalling Rd.)
Asbury Ct. *N21* *5D 22*
(off Pennington Dr.)
Ascalon Ho. *SW8* *7G 101*
(off Thessaly Rd.)
Ascalon St. SW8 7G 101
Ascensis Twr. SW18 4A 118
Ascent Ho. *NW9* *2C 44*
(off Boulevard Dr.)
Ascham Dr. E4 7J 35
Ascham End E17 1A 50
Ascham St. NW5 5G 65
Aschurch Rd. CR0: C'don 7F 157
Ascot Cl. UB5: N'olt 5E 58
Ascot Ct. DA5: Bexl 7F 127
NW8 2A 4
Ascot Gdns. UB1: S'hall 4D 76
Ascot Ho. NW1 1K 5
W9 *4J 81*
(off Harrow Rd.)
Ascot Lodge NW6 1K 81
Ascot Pl. HA7: Stan 5H 27
Ascot Rd. BR5: St M Cry 4K 161
E6 3D 88
N15 5D 48
N18 4B 34
SW17 6E 136
TW14: Bedf 1C 128
Ascott Av. W5 2E 96
Ascott Cl. HA5: Eastc 4J 39
Ashanti M. E8 5J 67
Ashbee Ho. *E2* *3J 85*
(off Portman Pl.)
Ashbourne Av. DA7: Bex 7E 108
E18 4K 51
HA2: Harr 2H 59
N20 2J 31
NW11 5H 45
Ashbourne Cl. N12 4E 30
W5 5G 79
Ashbourne Ct. E5 4A 68
N12 *4E 30*
(off Ashbourne Cl.)
Ashbourne Gro. NW7 5E 28
SE22 4F 121
W4 5A 98
Ashbourne Pde. NW11 4H 45
W5 4F 79
Ashbourne Ri. BR6: Orp 4J 173
Ashbourne Rd. CR4: Mitc 7E 136
W5 4F 79
Ashbourne Ter. SW19 7H 135
Ashbourne Way NW11 4H 45
Ashbridge Rd. E11 7G 51
Ashbridge St. NW8 4C 4 (4C 82)
Ashbrook HA8: Edg 6A 28
Ashbrook Rd. N19 1H 65
RM10: Dag 3H 73
Ashburn Gdns. SW7 4A 100
Ashburnham Av. HA1: Harr 6K 41
Ashburnham Cl. N2 3B 46
Ashburnham Ct. BR3: Beck 2E 158
Ashburnham Gdns. HA1: Harr 6K 41
Ashburnham Gro. SE10 7D 104
Ashburnham Mans. *SW10* *7A 100*
(off Ashburnham Rd.)
Ashburnham Pl. SE10 7D 104
Ashburnham Retreat SE10 7D 104
Ashburnham Rd. DA17: Belv 4J 109
NW10 3E 80

Ashburnham Rd. SW10 7A 100
TW10: Ham 3B 132
Ashburnham Twr. *SW10* *7B 100*
(off Worlds End Est.)
Ashburn Pl. SW7 4A 100
Ashburton Av. CR0: C'don 1H 169
IG3: Ilf 5J 71
Ashburton Cl. CR0: C'don 1G 169
Ashburton Ent. Cen. SW15 6E 116
Ashburton Gdns. CR0: C'don 2G 169
ASHBURTON GROVE 4A 66
Ashburton Ho. *W9* *4H 81*
(off Fernhead Rd.)
Ashburton Memorial Homes
CR0: C'don 7H 157
Ashburton Rd. CR0: C'don 2G 169
E16 6J 87
HA4: Ruis 2J 57
Ashburton Ter. E13 2J 87
Ashburton Triangle N7 4A 66
Ashbury Dr. UB10: Ick 3D 56
Ashbury Gdns. RM6: Chad H 5D 54
Ashbury Pl. SW19 6A 136
Ashbury Rd. SW11 3D 118
Ashby Av. KT9: Chess 6G 163
Ashby Cl. BR4: W W'ck 3F 171
Ashby Ct. *NW8* *3B 4*
(off Pollitt Dr.)
Ashby Gro. N1 7C 66
(not continuous)
Ashby Ho. *N1* *7C 66*
(off Essex Rd.)
SW9 2B 120
UB5: N'olt 4D 76
Ashby M. SE4 2B 122
SW2 *5J 119*
(off Prague Pl.)
Ashby Rd. N15 5G 49
SE4 2B 122
Ashbys Ct. *E3* *2B 86*
(off Centurion La.)
Ashby St. EC1 2B 8 (3B 84)
Ashby Wlk. CR0: C'don 6C 156
Ashby Way UB7: Sip 7C 92
Ashchurch Gro. W12 3C 98
Ashchurch Pk. Vs. W12 3C 98
Ashchurch Ter. W12 3C 98
Ash Cl. BR5: Pet W 5H 161
DA14: Sidc 3B 144
HA7: Stan 6F 27
HA8: Edg 4D 28
KT3: N Mald 2K 151
RM5: Col R 1H 55
SE20 2J 157
SM5: Cars 2D 166
UB9: Hare 1A 38
Ashcombe Av. KT6: Surb 7D 150
Ashcombe Cl. TW15: Ashf 3A 128
Ashcombe Ct. TW15: Ashf 2B 128
Ashcombe Gdns. HA8: Edg 4B 28
Ashcombe Ho. *E3* *3D 86*
(off Bruce Rd.)
EN3: Pond E 3E 24
Ashcombe Pk. NW2 3A 62
Ashcombe Rd. SM5: Cars 6E 166
SW19 5J 135
Ashcombe Sq. KT3: N Mald 3J 151
Ashcombe St. SW6 2K 117
Ash Ct. KT19: Ewe 4J 163
N11 6B 32
SW19 7G 135
Ashcroft HA5: Hat E 6A 26
N14 2C 32
Ashcroft Av. DA15: Sidc 6A 126
Ashcroft Ct. N20 2G 31
Ashcroft Cres. DA15: Sidc 6A 126
Ashcroft Ho. *SW8* *1G 119*
(off Wadhurst Rd.)
Ashcroft Rd. KT9: Chess 3F 163
Ashcroft Sq. W6 4E 98
Ashcroft Theatre *3D 168*
(in Fairfield Halls)

Ashdale Cl. TW2: Whitt 7G 113
TW19: Stanw 2A 128
Ashdale Gro. HA7: Stan 6E 26
Ashdale Ho. N4 7D 48
Ashdale Rd. SE12 1K 141
Ashdale Way TW2: Whitt 7F 113
Ashdene HA5: Pinn 3A 40
SE15 7H 103
Ashdene Cl. TW15: Ashf 7E 128
Ashdon Cl. IG8: Wfd G 6E 36
Ashdon Rd. NW10 1B 80
Ashdown *W13* *5B 78*
(off Clivedon Ct.)
Ashdown Cl. BR3: Beck 2D 158
DA5: Bexl 7J 127
Ashdown Ct. E17 2E 50
IG11: Bark 6F 71
SM2: Sutt 6A 166
Ashdown Cres. NW5 5E 64
Ashdowne Ct. N17 1G 49
Ashdown Ho. (Department for Transport)
SW1 2B 18
Ashdown Pl. KT7: T Ditt 7A 150
KT17: Ewe 7B 164
Ashdown Rd. EN3: Enf H 2D 24
KT1: King T 2E 150
UB10: Hil 2C 74
Ashdown Wlk. E14 4C 104
RM7: Mawney 1H 55
Ashdown Way SW17 2E 136
Ashe Ho. TW1: Twick 6D 114
Ashen E6 6E 88
Ashenden *SE17* *4C 102*
(off Deacon Way)
Ashenden Rd. E5 5A 68
Ashen Gro. SW19 3J 135
Ashentree Ct. EC4 1K 13
Asher Loftus Way N11 6J 31
Asher Way E1 7G 85
Ashfield Av. TW13: Felt 1K 129
WD23: Bush 1B 26
Ashfield Cl. BR3: Beck 7C 140
TW10: Ham 1E 132
Ashfield Ct. *SW9* *2J 119*
(off Clapham Rd.)
Ashfield Ho. *W14* *5H 99*
(off W. Cromwell Rd.)
Ashfield La. BR7: Chst 6F 143
(not continuous)
Ashfield Pde. N14 1C 32
Ashfield Rd. N4 6C 48
N14 3B 32
W3 1B 98
Ashfield St. E1 5H 85
Ashfield Yd. E1 5J 85
ASHFORD 4B 128
Ashford Av. N8 4J 47
TW15: Ashf 6D 128
UB4: Yead 6B 76
Ashford Bus. Complex
TW15: Ashf 5E 128
Ashford Cl. E17 6B 50
TW15: Ashf 4A 128
ASHFORD COMMON 7F 129
Ashford Ct. HA8: Edg 3C 28
NW2 4F 63
Ashford Cres. EN3: Enf H 2D 24
TW15: Ashf 3A 128
Ashford Ho. SE8 6B 104
SW9 4B 120
Ashford Ind. Est.
TW15: Ashf 4E 128
Ashford M. N17 1G 49
Ashford Pas. NW2 4F 63
Ashford Rd. E6 7E 70
E18 2K 51
NW2 4F 63
TW13: Felt 4F 129
TW15: Ashf 7E 128
TW18: Lale, Staines 7A 128
Ashford Sports Cen. 4A 128
Ashford St. N1 1G 9 (3E 84)

Ash Gro. BR4: W W'ck 2E 170
E8 1H 85
(not continuous)
EN1: Enf 7K 23
HA0: Wemb 4A 60
N10 4F 47
N13 3H 33
NW2 4F 63
SE12 1J 141
SE20 2J 157
TW5: Hest 1B 112
TW14: Felt 1G 129
UB1: S'hall 5E 76
UB3: Hayes 7F 75
UB7: Yiew 7B 74
UB9: Hare 1A 38
W5 2E 96
Ashgrove Ct. *W9* *5J 81*
(off Elmfield Way)
Ashgrove Ho. *SW1* *5D 18*
(off Lindsay Sq.)
Ashgrove Rd. BR1: Brom 6F 141
IG3: Ilf 1K 71
TW15: Ashf 5E 128
Ash Hill Cl. WD23: Bush 1A 26
Ash Hill Dr. HA5: Pinn 3A 40
Ash Ho. *E14* *2E 104*
(off E. Ferry Rd.)
SE1 *4F 103*
(off Longfield Est.)
TW15: Ashf *4B 128*
(off Station Rd.)
W10 *4G 81*
(off Heather Wlk.)
Ashingdon Cl. E4 3K 35
Ashington Ho. *E1* *4H 85*
(off Barnsley St.)
Ashington Rd. SW6 2H 117
Ash Island KT8: E Mos 3H 149
Ashlake Rd. SW16 4J 137
Ashland Pl. W1 5G 5 (5E 82)
Ashlar Pl. SE18 4F 107
Ashleigh Commercial Est. SE7 3A 106
Ashleigh Ct. N14 7B 22
W5 *4D 96*
(off Murray Rd.)
Ashleigh Gdns. SM1: Sutt 2K 165
Ashleigh M. *SE15* *3F 121*
(off Oglander Rd.)
Ashleigh Point SE23 3K 139
Ashleigh Rd. SE20 3H 157
SW14 3A 116
Ashley Av. IG6: Ilf 2F 53
SM4: Mord 5J 153
Ashley Cl. HA5: Pinn 2K 39
NW4 2E 44
Ashley Ct. EN5: New Bar 5F 21
NW4 2E 44
NW9 *2B 44*
(off Guilfoyle)
SW1 *2A 18*
(off Morpeth Ter.)
UB5: N'olt 1C 76
Ashley Cres. N22 2A 48
SW11 3E 118
Ashley Dr. TW2: Whitt 7F 113
TW7: Isle 6J 95
Ashley Gdns. BR6: Orp 5J 173
HA9: Wemb 2E 60
N13 4H 33
SW1 2B 18 (3G 101)
(not continuous)
TW10: Ham 2D 132
Ashley La. CR0: Wadd 4B 168
NW4 7K 29
Ashley Pl. SW1 2A 18 (3G 101)
(not continuous)
Ashley Rd. CR7: Thor H 4K 155
E4 6H 35
E7 7A 70
EN3: Enf H 2D 24
KT7: T Ditt 6K 149

Ashley Rd. N17 ....3G 49
  N19 ....1J 65
  SW19 ....6K 135
  TW9: Rich 3E 114
  TW12: Hamp 1E 148
Ashley Wlk. NW7 ....7A 30
Ashling Rd. CRO: C'don 1G 169
Ashlin Rd. E15 ....4F 69
Ash Lodge TW16: Sun 7H 129
  (off Forest Dr.)
Ashlone Rd. SW15 ....3E 116
Ashlyns Way KT9: Chess 6D 162
Ashmead N14 ....5B 22
Ashmead Bus. Cen. E16 ....4F 87
Ashmead Ga. BR1: Brom 1A 160
Ashmead Ho. E9 ....5A 68
  (off Homerton Rd.)
Ashmead M. SE8 ....2C 122
Ashmead Rd. SE8 ....2C 122
  TW14: Felt 1J 129
Ashmere Av. BR3: Beck 2F 159
Ashmere Ct. SM3: Cheam 5F 165
Ashmere Gro. SW2 ....4J 119
Ash M. NW5 ....5G 65
Ashmill St. NW1 ....5C 4 (5C 82)
Ashmole Pl. SW8 ....6K 101
Ashmole St. SW8 ....6K 101
Ashmore NW1 ....7H 65
  (off Agar Gro.)
Ashmore Cl. SE15 ....7F 103
Ashmore Ct. N11 ....6J 31
  TW5: Hest 6E 94
Ashmore Gro. DA16: Well 3H 125
Ashmore Ho. W14 ....3G 99
  (off Russell Rd.)
Ashmount Est. N19 ....7H 47
Ashmount Rd. N15 ....5F 49
  N19 ....7G 47
Ashmount Ter. W5 ....4D 96
Ashmour Gdns. RM1: Rom 2K 55
Ashneal Gdns. HA1: Harr 3H 59
Ashness Gdns. UB6: G'frd 6B 60
Ashness Rd. SW11 ....5D 118
Ashpark Ho. E14 ....6B 86
  (off Norbiton Rd.)
Ashridge Cl. HA3: Kenton 6C 42
Ashridge Ct. N14 ....5B 22
  UB1: S'hall 6G 77
  (off Redcroft Rd.)
Ashridge Cres. SE18 ....7G 107
Ashridge Gdns. HA5: Pinn 4C 40
  N13 ....5C 32
Ashridge Way SM4: Mord 3H 153
  TW16: Sun 6J 129
Ash Rd. BR6: Chels 7K 173
  CRO: C'don 2C 170
  E15 ....5G 69
  SM3: Sutt 7G 153
  TW17: Shep 4C 146
Ash Row BR2: Brom 7E 160
Ashtead Rd. E5 ....7G 49
Ashton Cl. SM1: Sutt 4J 165
  HA1: Harr 3K 59
Ashton Ct. E4 ....3B 36
  HA1: Harr 3K 59
Ashton Gdns. RM6: Chad H 6E 54
  TW4: Houn 4D 112
Ashton Hgts. SE23 ....1J 139
Ashton Ho. SE11 ....5K 19
  SW9 ....7A 102
Ashton Pl. KT10: Clay 7A 162
Ashton Rd. E15 ....5F 69
Ashton St. E14 ....7E 86
Ashtree Av. CR4: Mitc 2B 154
Ash Tree Cl. CRO: C'don 6A 158
  KT6: Surb 1E 162
Ashtree Cl. BR6: Farnb 4F 173
Ash Tree Ct. TW15: Ashf 5D 128
  (off Feltham Hill Rd.)
Ash Tree Dell NW9 ....5J 43
Ash Tree Ho. SE5 ....7C 102
  (off Pitman St.)

Ash Tree Way CRO: C'don 5K 157
Ashurst Cl. SE20 ....1H 157
Ashurst Dr. IG2: Ilf 6F 53
  IG6: Ilf 5G 53
  (Aldwych Av.)
  IG6: Ilf 4G 53
  (Walnut Cl.)
  TW17: Shep 5A 146
Ashurst Gdns. SW2 ....1A 138
Ashurst Rd. EN4: Cockf 5J 21
  N12 ....5H 31
Ashurst Wlk. CRO: C'don 2H 169
Ashvale Ct. E3 ....2C 86
  (off Matilda Gdns.)
Ashvale Rd. SW17 ....5D 136
Ashview Cl. TW15: Ashf 5A 128
Ashview Gdns. TW15: Ashf 5A 128
Ashville Rd. E11 ....2F 69
Ash Wlk. HAO: Wemb 4C 60
Ashwater Rd. SE12 ....1J 141
Ashway Cen., The KT2: King T 1E 150
Ashwell Cl. E6 ....6C 88
Ashwell Ct. TW15: Ashf 2A 128
Ashwin St. E8 ....6F 67
Ashwood Av. UB8: Hil 6C 74
Ashwood Gdns. CRO: New Ad 6E 170
  UB3: Harl 4H 93
Ashwood Ho. NW4 ....4E 44
  (off Harmony Way)
Ashwood Rd. E4 ....3A 36
Ashworth Cl. SE5 ....2D 120
Ashworth Est. CRO: Bedd 1J 167
Ashworth Mans. W9 ....3K 81
  (off Elgin Av.)
Ashworth Rd. W9 ....3K 81
Aske Ho. N1 ....1G 9
Asker Ho. N7 ....4J 65
Askern Cl. DA6: Bex 4D 126
Aske St. N1 ....1G 9 (3E 84)
Askew Cres. W12 ....2B 98
Askew Est. W12 ....1B 98
  (off Uxbridge Rd.)
Askew Rd. W12 ....2B 98
Askham Ct. W12 ....1C 98
Askham Rd. W12 ....1C 98
Askill Dr. SW15 ....5G 117
Askwith Rd. RM13: Rain 3K 91
Asland Rd. E15 ....1G 87
Aslett St. SW18 ....7K 117
Asman Ho. N1 ....2B 84
  (off Colebrooke Rd.)
Asmara Rd. NW2 ....5G 63
Asmuns Hill NW11 ....5J 45
Asmuns Pl. NW11 ....5H 45
Asolando Dr. SE17 ....4C 102
Aspect Ct. E14 ....2E 104
  (off Manchester Rd.)
  SW6 ....2A 118
Aspects SM1: Sutt 5K 165
Aspen Cl. N19 ....2G 65
  UB7: Yiew 1B 92
  W5 ....2F 97
Aspen Copse BR1: Brom 2D 160
Aspen Ct. NW4 ....2G 45
Aspen Dr. HAO: Wemb 3A 60
Aspen Gdns. CR4: Mitc 5E 154
  TW15: Ashf 5E 128
  W6 ....5D 98
Aspen Grn. DA18: Erith 3F 109
Aspen Gro. HA5: Eastc 3H 39
Aspen Ho. DA15: Sidc 2A 144
  SE15 ....6J 103
  (off Sharratt St.)
Aspen La. UB5: N'olt 3C 76
Aspenlea Rd. W6 ....6F 99
Aspen Lodge W8 ....3K 99
  (off Abbots Wlk.)
Aspen Way E14 ....7D 86
  TW13: Felt 3K 129
Aspern Gro. NW3 ....5C 64
Aspinall Rd. SE4 ....3K 121
  (not continuous)

Aspinden Rd. SE16 ....4H 103
Aspire National Training Cen. 2G 27
Aspley Rd. SW18 ....5K 117
Asplins Rd. N17 ....1G 49
Asprey M. BR3: Beck 5B 158
Asprey Pl. BR1: Brom 2C 160
Asquith Cl. RM8: Dag 1C 72
Asquith Ho. SW1 ....2D 18
  (off Monck St.)
Assam St. E1 ....6G 85
  (off White Church La.)
Assata M. N1 ....6B 66
Assembly Apartments SE15 ....1J 121
  (off York Gro.)
Assembly Pas. E1 ....5J 85
Assembly Wlk. SM5: Cars 7C 154
Ass Ho. La. HA3: Hrw W 4A 26
Astall Cl. HA3: Hrw W 1J 41
Astbury Bus. Pk. SE15 ....1J 121
Astbury Ho. SE11 ....2J 19
Astbury Rd. SE15 ....1J 121
Astell Ho. SW3 ....5D 16
  (off Astell St.)
Astell St. SW3 ....5D 16 (5C 100)
Aster Ct. E5 ....2J 67
  (off Woodmill Rd.)
Aste St. E14 ....2E 104
Astey's Row N1 ....7C 66
Asthall Gdns. IG6: Ilf 4G 53
Astins Ho. E17 ....4D 50
Astleham Rd. TW17: Shep 3A 146
Astle St. SW11 ....2E 118
Astley Av. NW2 ....5E 62
Astley Ho. SE1 ....5F 103
  (off Rowcross St.)
  SW13 ....6D 98
  (off Wyatt Dr.)
  W2 ....5J 81
  (off Alfred Rd.)
Aston Av. HA3: Kenton 7C 42
Aston Cl. DA14: Sidc 3A 144
Aston Ct. IG8: Wfd G 6D 36
Aston Grn. TW4: Cran 2A 112
Aston Ho. SW8 ....1H 119
  W11 ....7H 81
  (off Westbourne Gro.)
Aston M. RM6: Chad H 7C 54
  W10 ....3F 81
Aston Pl. SW16 ....6B 138
Aston Rd. SW20 ....2E 152
  W5 ....6D 78
Aston St. E14 ....5A 86
Aston Ter. SW12 ....6F 119
Astonville St. SW18 ....1J 135
Aston Webb Ho. SE1 ....5H 15
Astor Av. RM7: Rom 6J 55
Astor Cl. KT2: King T 6H 133
Astor Ct. E16 ....6A 88
  (off Ripley Rd.)
  SW6 ....7A 100
  (off Maynard Cl.)
Astoria Ct. E8 ....7F 67
  (off Queensbridge Rd.)
Astoria Ho. NW9 ....2B 44
  (off Boulevard Dr.)
Astoria Mans. SW16 ....3J 137
Astoria Wlk. SW9 ....3A 120
Astra Ho. E3 ....3B 86
  (off Alfred St.)
  SE14 ....6B 104
  (off Arklow Rd.)
Astral Ho. E1 ....6H 9
  (off Middlesex St.)
Astrid Ho. TW13: Felt 2A 130
Astrop M. W6 ....3E 98
Astrop Ter. W6 ....2E 98
Astwood M. SW7 ....4A 100
Asylum Rd. SE15 ....7H 103
Atalanta St. SW6 ....7F 99
Atbara Rd. TW11: Tedd 6B 132
Atcham Rd. TW3: Houn 4G 113
Atcost Rd. IG11: Bark 5A 90

Atcraft Cen. HAO: Wemb 1E 78
Atheldene Rd. SW18 ....1K 135
Athelney St. SE6 ....3C 140
Athelstane Gro. E3 ....2B 86
Athelstane M. N4 ....1A 66
Athelstan Gdns. NW6 ....7G 63
Athelstan Ho. KT1: King T 4F 151
  (off Athelstan Rd.)
Athelstan Rd. KT1: King T 4F 151
Athelstone Rd. HA3: W'stone 2H 41
Athena Cl. HA2: Harr 2H 59
  KT1: King T 3F 151
Athena Ct. E15 ....1E 86
  SE1 ....7G 15
  (off City Wlk.)
Athenaeum Ct. N5 ....4C 66
Athenaeum Pl. N10 ....3F 47
Athenaeum Rd. N20 ....1F 31
Athena Pl. HA6: Nwood 1H 39
Athene Pl. EC4 ....7K 7
  (off Thavie's Inn)
Athenia Ho. E14 ....6F 87
  (off Blair St.)
Athenlay Rd. SE15 ....5K 121
Athens Gdns. W9 ....4J 81
  (off Harrow Rd.)
Atherden Rd. E5 ....4J 67
Atherfold Rd. SW9 ....3J 119
Atherley Way TW4: Houn 7D 112
Atherstone Ct. W2 ....5K 81
  (off Delamere Ter.)
Atherstone M. SW7 ....4A 100
Atherton Dr. SW19 ....4F 135
Atherton Hgts. HAO: Wemb 7C 60
Atherton Leisure Cen. 6H 69
Atherton M. E7 ....6H 69
Atherton Pl. HA2: Harr 3H 41
  UB1: S'hall 7E 76
Atherton Rd. E7 ....6H 69
  IG5: Ilf 2C 52
  SW13 ....7C 98
Atherton St. SW11 ....2C 118
Athlone Cl. E5 ....5H 67
  E17 ....3F 51
Athlone Ho. E1 ....6J 85
  (off Sidney St.)
Athlone Rd. SW2 ....7K 119
Athlone St. NW5 ....6E 64
Athlon Ind. Est.
  HAO: Wemb 1D 78
  HAO: Wemb 2D 78
Athol Cl. HA5: Pinn 1K 39
Athole Gdns. EN1: Enf 5K 23
Athol Gdns. HA5: Pinn 1K 39
Atholl Ho. W9 ....3A 82
  (off Maida Va.)
Atholl Rd. IG3: Ilf 7A 54
Athol Rd. DA8: Erith 5J 109
Athol Sq. E14 ....6E 86
Athol Way UB10: Hil 3C 74
Atkin Bldg. WC1 ....5H 7
  (off Raymond Bldgs.)
Atkins Ct. E3 ....1B 86
  (off Willow Tree Cl.)
Atkins Dr. BR4: W W'ck 2F 171
Atkins Lodge W8 ....2J 99
  (off Thornwood Gdns.)
Atkinson Cl. BR6: Chels 5K 173
Atkinson Ct. E10 ....7D 50
  (off Kings Cl.)
Atkinson Ho. E2 ....2G 85
  (off Pritchards Rd.)
  E13 ....4H 87
  (off Sutton Rd.)
  SE17 ....4D 102
  (off Catesby St.)
  SW11 ....1E 118
  (off Austin Rd.)
Atkinson Morley Av. SW17 ....3B 136
Atkinson Rd. E16 ....5A 88
Atkins Rd. E10 ....6D 50
  SW12 ....7G 119

Atlanta Bldg. *SE10* 1D *122*
   (off Deal's Gateway)
Atlanta Ct. CR7: Thor H 3C 156
Atlanta Ho. *SE16* 3A *104*
   (off Brunswick Quay)
Atlantic Apartments *E16* 7J *87*
   (off Seagull La.)
Atlantic Ct. *E14* 7F *87*
   (off Jamestown Way)
Atlantic Ho. *E1* 5K *86*
   (off Harford St.)
Atlantic Rd. SW9 . . . . .4A 120
Atlantic Wharf E1 . . . . .7K 85
Atlantis Av. E16 . . . . .7F 89
Atlantis Cl. IG11: Bark 3B 90
Atlas Bus. Cen. NW2 . . . . .1D 62
Atlas Cres. HA8: Edg 2C 28
Atlas Gdns. SE7 . . . . .4A 106
Atlas M. E8 . . . . .6F 67
   N7 . . . . .6K 65
Atlas Rd. E13 .2J 87
   HA9: Wemb 4J 61
   N11 . . . . .7K 31
   NW10 . . . . .3A 80
Atlas Trade Pk. DA8: Erith 5K 109
Atlas Wharf E9 . . . . .6C 68
Atley Rd. E3 . . . . .1C 86
Atlip Rd. HA0: Wemb 1E 78
Atney Rd. SW15 . . . . .4G 117
Atrium, The IG9: Buck H 2G 37
Atrium Apartments *N1* 1D *84*
   (off Felton St.)
Atrium Ho. SE8 . . . . .7B 104
Atterbury Rd. N4 . . . . .6A 48
Atterbury St. SW1 . . . . . .4D 18 (4J 101)
Attewood Av. NW10 . . . . .3A 62
Attewood Rd. UB5: N'olt 6C 58
Attfield Cl. N20 . . . . .2G 31
Attfield Ct. *KT1: King T* 2F *151*
   (off Albert Rd.)
Attilburgh Ho. *SE1* 7J *15*
   (off St Saviour's Est.)
Attleborough Ct. SE23 . . . . .2G 139
Attle Cl. UB10: Hil 2C 74
Attlee Cl. CR7: Thor H 5C 156
   UB4: Yead 3K 75
   UB5: N'olt 3K 75
Attlee Rd. SE28 . . . . .7B 90
   UB4: Yead 3J 75
Attlee Ter. E17 . . . . .4D 50
Attneave St. WC1 . . . . .2J 7 (3A 84)
Atunbi Ct. *NW1* 7G *65*
   (off Farrier St.)
Atwater Cl. SW2 . . . . .1A 138
Atwell Cl. E10 . . . . .6D 50
Atwell Pl. KT7: T Ditt 7K 149
Atwell Rd. SE15 . . . . .2G 121
Atwood Av. TW9: Kew 2G 115
Atwood Ho. *W14* 4H *99*
   (off Beckford Cl.)
Atwood Rd. W6 . . . . .4D 98
Atwoods All. TW9: Kew 1G 115
Aubert Ct. N5 .4B 66
Aubert Pk. N5 . . . . .4B 66
Aubert Rd. N5 . . . . .4B 66
Aubrey Beardsley Ho. *SW1* 4B *18*
   (off Vauxhall Bri. Rd.)
Aubrey Mans. *NW1* 5C *4*
   (off Lisson St.)
Aubrey Moore Point *E15* 2E *86*
   (off Abbey La.)
Aubrey Pl. NW8 . . . . .2A 82
Aubrey Rd. E17 . . . . .3C 50
   N8 . . . . .5J 47
   W8 . . . . .1H 99
Aubrey Wlk. W8 . . . . .1H 99
Auburn Cl. SE14 . . . . .7A 104
Aubyn Hill SE27 . . . . .4C 138
Aubyn Sq. SW15 . . . . .5C 116
Auckland Cl. SE19 . . . . .1F 157
Auckland Ct. UB4: Yead 4A 76
Auckland Gdns. SE19 . . . . .1E 156

Auckland Hill SE27 . . . . .4C 138
Auckland Ho. *W12* 7D *80*
   (off White City Est.)
Auckland Ri. SE19 . . . . .1E 156
Auckland Rd. E10 . . . . .3D 68
   IG1: Ilf 1F 71
   KT1: King T 4F 151
   SE19 . . . . .1F 157
   SW11 . . . . .4C 118
Auckland St. SE11 . . . . . . .6G 19 (5K 101)
Audax NW9 . . . . .2B 44
Auden Pl. NW1 . . . . .1E 82
   SM3: Cheam 4E 164
Audleigh Pl. IG7: Chig 6K 37
Audley Cl. N10 . . . . .7A 32
   SW11 . . . . .3E 118
Audley Ct. E18 . . . . .4H 51
   HA5: Pinn .2A 40
   TW2: Twick 3H 131
   UB5: N'olt 3A 76
Audley Dr. E16 . . . . .1K 105
Audley Gdns. IG3: Ilf 2K 71
Audley Pl. SM2: Sutt 7K 165
Audley Rd. EN2: Enf 2G 23
   NW4 . . . . .5C 44
   TW10: Rich 5F 115
   W5 . . . . .5F 79
Audley Sq. W1 . . . . .4H 11 (1E 100)
Audrey Cl. BR3: Beck 6D 158
Audrey Gdns. HA0: Wemb 2B 60
Audrey Rd. IG1: Ilf 3F 71
Audrey St. E2 . . . . .2G 85
Audric Cl. KT2: King T 1G 151
Augurs La. E13 . . . . .3K 87
Augusta Cl. KT8: W Mole 3D 148
Augusta Rd. TW2: Twick 2G 131
Augusta St. E14 . . . . .6D 86
Augustine Bell Twr. *E3* 2C *86*
   (off Pancras Way)
Augustine Rd. HA3: Hrw W 1F 41
   W14 . . . . .3F 99
Augustus Bldg. *E1* 6H *85*
   (off Tarling St.)
Augustus Cl. HA7: Stan 3J 27
   TW8: Bford 7C 96
   W12 . . . . .2D 98
Augustus Ct. *SE1* 4E *102*
   (off Old Kent Rd.)
   SW16 . . . . .2H 137
   TW13: Hanw 4D 130
Augustus Ho. *NW1* 1A *6*
   (off Augustus St.)
Augustus La. BR6: Orp 2K 173
Augustus Rd. SW19 . . . . .1F 135
Augustus St. NW1 . . . . . . .1K 5 (2F 83)
Aulay Ho. SE16 . . . . .3F 103
Aultone Way SM1: Sutt 2K 165
   SM5: Cars 3D 166
Aultone Yd. Ind. Est. SM5: Cars 3D 166
Aulton Pl. SE11 . . . . .6K 19 (5A 102)
Aura Ct. SE15 . . . . .4H 121
Aura Ho. TW9: Kew 1H 115
Aurelia Gdns. CR0: C'don 5K 155
Aurelia Rd. CR0: C'don 6J 155
Auriel Av. RM10: Dag 6K 73
Auriga M. N1 .5D 66
Auriol Cl. KT4: Wor Pk 3A 164
Auriol Dr. UB6: G'frd 7H 59
   UB10: Hil .6C 56
Auriol Ho. *W12* 1D *98*
   (off Ellerslie Rd.)
Auriol Mans. *W14* 4G *99*
   (off Edith Rd.)
Auriol Pk. Rd. KT4: Wor Pk 3A 164
Auriol Rd. W14 . . . . .4G 99
Aurora Bldg. *E14* 1E *104*
   (off Blackwall Way)
Aurora Ho. *E14* 6D *86*
   (off Kerbey St.)
Austell Gdns. NW7 . . . . .3F 29
Austell Hgts. *NW7* 3F *29*
   (off Austell Gdns.)

Austen Apartments SE20 . . . . .2H 157
Austen Cl. SE28 . . . . .1B 108
Austen Ho. *NW6* 3J *81*
   (off Cambridge Rd.)
   SW17 . . . . .3B *136*
   (off St George's Gro.)
Austen Rd. DA8: Erith 7H 109
   HA2: Harr .2F 59
Austin Av. BR2: Brom 5C 160
Austin Cl. SE23 . . . . .7A 122
   TW1: Twick 5C 114
Austin Ct. E6 .1A 88
   EN1: Enf 5K 23
   SE15 . . . . .3G *121*
   (off Peckham Rye)
Austin Friars EC2 . . . . .7F 9 (6D 84)
Austin Friars Pas. EC2 . . . . .7F 9
Austin Friars Sq. *EC2* 7F *9*
   (off Austin Friars)
Austin Ho. *SE14* 7B *104*
   (off Achilles St.)
Austin Rd. SW11 . . . . .1E 118
   UB3: Hayes 2H 93
Austin's La. HA4: Ruis 4F 57
Austin St. E2 . . . . .2J 9 (3F 85)
Austin Ter. *SE1* 1K *19*
   (off Morley St.)
Austral Cl. DA15: Sidc 3K 143
Australian War Memorial 6H 11
   (off Duke of Wellington Pl.)
Australia Rd. W12 . . . . .7D 80
Austral St. SE11 . . . . .3K 19 (4B 102)
Austyn Gdns. KT5: Surb 1H 163
Austyns Pl. KT17: Ewe 7C 164
Autumn Cl. EN1: Enf 1B 24
   SW19 . . . . .6A 136
Autumn Gro. BR1: Brom 6K 141
Autumn Lodge *CR0: C'don* 4E *168*
   (off South Pk. Hill Rd.)
Autumn St. E3 . . . . .1C 86
Avalon Cl. EN2: Enf 2F 23
   SW20 . . . . .2G 153
   W13 . . . . .5A 78
Avalon Rd. SW6 . . . . .1K 117
   W13 . . . . .4A 78
Avante KT1: King T 3D 150
Avard Gdns. BR6: Farnb 4G 173
Avarn Rd. SW17 . . . . .6D 136
Avebury Ct. *N1* 1D *84*
   (off Imber St.)
Avebury Pk. KT6: Surb 7D 150
Avebury Rd. BR6: Orp 3H 173
   E11 . . . . .1F 69
   SW19 . . . . .1H 153
Avebury St. N1 . . . . .1D 84
Aveley Mans. *IG11: Bark* 7F *71*
   (off Whiting Av.)
Aveley Rd. RM1: Rom 4K 55
Aveline St. SE11 . . . . .5H 19 (5A 102)
Aveling Pk. Rd. E17 . . . . .2C 50
Ave Maria La. EC4 . . . . . . .1B 14 (6B 84)
Avenell Mans. N5 . . . . .4B 66
Avenell Rd. N5 . . . . .3B 66
Avenfield Ho. *W1* 2F 11
   (off Park La.)
Avening Rd. SW18 . . . . .7J 117
Avening Ter. SW18 . . . . .7J 117
Avenons Rd. E13 . . . . .4J 87
Avenue, The BR1: Brom 3B 160
   BR2: Kes .4B 172
   BR3: Beck 1D 158
   (not continuous)
   BR4: W W'ck 7E 158
   BR5: St P .7B 144
   BR6: Orp .2K 173
   CR0: C'don 3E 168
   DA5: Bexl .7D 126
   E1 . . . . .7H 9 (6E 84)
   E4 . . . . .6A 36
   E11 . . . . .6K 51
   EN5: Barn 3B 20

Avenue, The HA3: Hrw W 1K 41
   HA5: Pinn .6D 40
   HA9: Wemb 1E 60
   IG9: Buck H 2F 37
   KT4: Wor Pk 2B 164
   KT5: Surb 6F 151
   KT17: Ewe 7D 164
   N3 . . . . .2J 45
   N8 . . . . .3A 48
   N10 . . . . .2G 47
   N11 . . . . .5A 32
   N17 . . . . .3D 48
   NW6 . . . . .1F 81
   RM1: Rom 4K 55
   SE10 . . . . .7F 105
   SM2: Cheam 7G 165
   SM3: Cheam 7G 165
   SM5: Cars 7E 166
   SW4 . . . . .4E 118
   SW18 . . . . .7C 118
   TW1: Twick 5B 114
   TW3: Houn 5F 113
   TW5: Cran 7J 93
   TW9: Kew 2F 115
   TW12: Hamp 6D 130
   TW16: Sun 1K 147
   UB10: Ick .4C 56
   W4 . . . . .3A 98
   W13 . . . . .6B 78
Avenue Cl. N14 . . . . .6B 22
   NW8 . . . . .1C 82
   (not continuous)
   TW5: Cran 1K 111
   UB7: W Dray 3A 92
Avenue Cl. IG5: Ilf 3C 52
   N14 . . . . .6B 22
   NW2 . . . . .3H 63
   SW3 . . . . .4E *16*
   (off Draycott Av.)
Avenue Cres. TW5: Cran 1K 111
   W3 . . . . .2H 97
Avenue Elmers KT6: Surb 5E 150
Avenue Gdns. SE25 . . . . .2G 157
   SW14 . . . . .3A 116
   TW5: Cran 7K 93
   TW11: Tedd 7K 131
   W3 . . . . .2H 97
Avenue Ho. *NW6* 7G *63*
   (off The Avenue)
   NW8 . . . . .2C *82*
   (off Allitsen Rd.)
   NW10 . . . . .2D *80*
   (off All Souls Av.)
Avenue Ind. Est. E4 . . . . .6H 35
Avenue Lodge *NW8* 7B *64*
   (off Avenue Rd.)
Avenue Mans. *NW3* 5K *63*
   (off Finchley Rd.)
Avenue M. N10 . . . . .3F 47
Avenue Pde. N21 . . . . .7J 23
   TW16: Sun 3K 147
Avenue Pk. Rd. SE27 . . . . .2B 138
Avenue Rd. BR3: Beck 2K 157
   DA7: Bex .3E 126
   DA8: Erith .7J 109
   DA17: Belv, Erith 4J 109
   E7 . . . . .4K 69
   HA5: Pinn .3C 40
   IG8: Wfd G 6F 37
   KT1: King T 3E 150
   KT3: N Mald 4A 152
   N6 . . . . .7G 47
   N12 . . . . .4F 31
   N14 . . . . .7B 22
   N15 . . . . .5D 48
   NW3 . . . . .7B 64
   NW8 . . . . .7B 64
   NW10 . . . . .2B 80
   RM6: Chad H 7B 54
   SE20 . . . . .1J 157
   SE25 . . . . .2F 157
   SM6: Wall .7G 167

Avenue Rd. SW16 2H 155
SW20 2D 152
TW7: Isle 1K 113
TW8: Bford 5C 96
TW11: Tedd 7A 132
TW12: Hamp 1F 149
TW13: Felt 3H 129
UB1: S'hall 1D 94
W3 2H 97
Avenue Sth. KT5: Surb 7G 151
Avenue Ter. KT3: N Mald 3J 151
Averil Gro. SW16 6B 138
Averill St. W6 6F 99
Avern Gdns. KT8: W Mole 4F 149
Avern Rd. KT8: W Mole 4F 149
Avery Farm Row SW1 4J 17 (4E 100)
Avery Gdns. IG2: Ilf 5D 52
AVERY HILL 6H 125
Avery Hill Rd. SE9 6H 125
Avery Row W1 2J 11 (7F 83)
Aviary Cl. E16 5H 87
Aviation Dr. NW9 2C 44
Aviemore Cl. BR3: Beck 5B 158
Aviemore Way BR3: Beck 5A 158
Avignon Rd. SE4 3K 121
Avingdor Ct. *W3* *1J 97*
(off Horn La.)
Avington Ct. *SE1* *4E 102*
(off Old Kent Rd.)
Avington Gro. SE20 7J 139
Avion Cres. NW9 1C 44
Avis Sq. E1 6K 85
Avoca Rd. SW17 4E 136
Avocet Cl. SE1 5G 103
Avocet M. SE28 3H 107
Avon Cl. KT4: Wor Pk 2C 164
SM1: Sutt 4A 166
UB4: Yead 4A 76
Avon Ct. E4 1K 35
IG9: Buck H 1E 36
N12 5E 30
SW15 5G 117
UB6: G'frd 4F 77
W9 *5J 81*
(off Elmfield Way)
Avondale Av. EN4: E Barn 1J 31
KT4: Wor Pk 1B 164
KT10: Hin W 3A 162
N12 5E 30
NW2 3A 62
Avondale Ct. E11 1G 69
E16 5G 87
E18 1K 51
SM2: Sutt *7A 166*
(off Brighton Rd.)
Avondale Cres. EN3: Enf H 3F 25
IG4: Ilf 5B 52
Avondale Dr. UB3: Hayes 1J 93
Avondale Gdns. TW4: Houn 5D 112
Avondale Ho. *SE1* *5G 103*
(off Avondale Sq.)
Avondale Mans. *SW6* *1H 117*
(off Rostrevor Rd.)
Avondale Pk. Gdns. W11 7G 81
Avondale Pk. Rd. W11 7G 81
Avondale Pavement SE1 5G 103
Avondale Ri. SE15 3F 121
Avondale Rd. BR1: Brom 6G 141
CR2: S Croy 6C 168
DA16: Well 2C 126
E16 5G 87
E17 7C 50
HA3: W'stone 3K 41
N3 1A 46
N13 2F 33
N15 5B 48
SE9 2C 142
SW14 3A 116
SW19 5K 135
TW15: Ashf 3A 128
Avondale Sq. SE1 5G 103
Avonfield Ct. E17 3F 51

Avon Ho. KT2: King T 1D 150
W8 *3J 99*
(off Allen St.)
W14 *4H 99*
(off Kensington Village)
Avonhurst Ho. NW2 7G 63
Avonley Rd. SE14 7J 103
Avon M. HA5: Hat E 1D 40
Avonmore Gdns. W14 4H 99
Avonmore Mans. *W14* *4G 99*
(off Avonmore Rd.)
Avonmore Pl. W14 4G 99
Avonmore Rd. W14 4G 99
Avonmouth St. SE1 7C 14 (3C 102)
Avon Path CR2: S Croy 6C 168
Avon Pl. SE1 7D 14 (2C 102)
Avon Rd. E17 3F 51
SE4 3C 122
TW16: Sun 7H 129
UB6: G'frd 4E 76
Avonstowe Cl. BR6: Farnb 3G 173
Avon Way E18 3J 51
Avonwick Rd. TW3: Houn 2F 113
Avril Way E4 5K 35
Avro Ho. *NW9* *2B 44*
(off Boulevard Dr.)
SW8 *7F 101*
(off Havelock Ter.)
Avro Way SM6: Wall 7J 167
Awlfield Av. N17 1D 48
Awliscombe Rd. DA16: Well 2K 125
Axe St. IG11: Bark 1G 89
(not continuous)
Axholme Av. HA8: Edg 1G 43
Axiom Apartments *BR2: Brom* *4K 159*
(off Masons Hill)
Axis Ct. *SE10* *6G 105*
(off Woodland Cres.)
SE16 *2G 103*
(off East La.)
Axis Ho. *SE13* *4E 122*
(off Lewisham High St.)
Axminster Cres. DA16: Well 1C 126
Axminster Rd. N7 3J 65
Axon Pl. IG1: Ilf 2G 71
Aybrook St. W1 6G 5 (5E 82)
Aycliffe Cl. BR1: Brom 4D 160
Aycliffe Ho. *SE17* *6D 102*
(off Portland St.)
Aycliffe Rd. W12 1C 98
Ayerst Ct. E10 7E 50
Aylands Cl. HA9: Wemb 2E 60
Aylesbury Cl. E7 6H 69
Aylesbury Ct. SM1: Sutt 3A 166
Aylesbury Ho. *SE15* *6G 103*
(off Friary Est.)
Aylesbury Rd. BR2: Brom 3J 159
SE17 5D 102
Aylesbury St. EC1 4A 8 (4B 84)
NW10 3K 61
Aylesford Av. BR3: Beck 5A 158
Aylesford Ho. *SE1* *7F 15*
(off Long La.)
Aylesford St. SW1 5C 18 (5H 101)
Aylesham Cen. SE15 1G 121
Aylesham Cl. NW7 7H 29
Aylesham Rd. BR6: Orp 7K 161
Ayles Rd. UB4: Yead 3K 75
Aylestone Av. NW6 7F 63
Aylett Rd. SE25 4H 157
TW7: Isle 2J 113
Ayley Cft. EN1: Enf 5B 24
Ayliffe Cl. KT1: King T 2G 151
Aylmer Cl. HA7: Stan 4F 27
Aylmer Ct. N2 5D 46
Aylmer Dr. HA7: Stan 4F 27
Aylmer Ho. SE10 5F 105
Aylmer Pde. N2 5D 46
Aylmer Rd. E11 1H 69
N2 5C 46
RM8: Dag 3E 72
W12 2B 98

Ayloffe Rd. RM9: Dag 6F 73
Aylsham Dr. UB10: Ick 2E 56
Aylton Est. SE16 2J 103
Aylward Rd. SE23 2K 139
SW20 2H 153
Aylwards Ri. HA7: Stan 4F 27
Aylward St. E1 6J 85
(Jamaica St.)
E1 6J 85
(Jubilee St.)
Aylwin Est. SE1 3E 102
Aynhoe Mans. *W14* *4F 99*
(off Aynhoe Rd.)
Aynhoe Rd. W14 4F 99
Aynscombe Path SW14 2J 115
Ayr Ct. W3 5G 79
Ayres Cl. E13 3J 87
Ayres St. SE1 6D 14 (2C 102)
Ayr Grn. RM1: Rom 1K 55
Ayrsome Rd. N16 3E 66
Ayrton Gould Ho. *E2* *3K 85*
(off Roman Rd.)
Ayrton Rd. SW7 1A 16 (3B 100)
Ayr Way RM1: Rom 1K 55
Aysgarth Ct. SM1: Sutt 3K 165
Aysgarth Rd. SE21 7E 120
Ayshford Ho. *E2* *3H 85*
(off Viaduct St.)
Ayston Ho. *SE16* *4K 103*
(off Plough Way)
Aytoun Pl. SW9 2K 119
Aytoun Rd. SW9 2K 119
Azalea Cl. IG1: Ilf 5F 71
W7 1K 95
Azalea Ct. IG8: Wfd G 6B 36
W7 1K 95
Azalea Ho. *SE14* *7B 104*
(off Achilles St.)
TW13: Felt 1K 129
Azalea Wlk. HA5: Eastc 5K 39
Azania M. NW5 6F 65
Azenby Rd. SE15 2F 121
Azof St. SE10 4G 105
Azov Ho. *E1* *4A 86*
(off Commodore St.)
Aztec Ho. IG1: Ilf 2H 71
IG6: Ilf 1G 53
Azura Ct. *E15* *1E 86*
(off Warton Rd.)
Azure W2 6B 4
Azure Ct. *NW9* *5G 43*
(off Kingsbury Cir.)
Azure Ho. *E2* *3G 85*
(off Buckfast St.)
Azure Pl. TW3: Houn 4F 113

B

Baalbec Rd. N5 5B 66
Babbacombe Cl. KT9: Chess 5D 162
Babbacombe Gdns. IG4: Ilf 4C 52
Babbacombe Rd. BR1: Brom 1J 159
Baber Bri. Cvn. Site TW14: Felt 5A 112
Baber Dr. TW14: Felt 6A 112
Babington Ct. WC1 5G 7
Babington Ho. *SE1* *6D 14*
(off Disney St.)
Babington Ri. HA9: Wemb 6G 61
Babington Rd. NW4 4D 44
RM8: Dag 5C 72
SW16 5H 137
Babmaes St. SW1 3C 12 (7H 83)
Bacchus Wlk. *N1* *2E 84*
(off Regan Way)
Bache's St. N1 1F 9 (3D 84)
Back All. EC3 1H 15
Bk. Church La. E1 6G 85
Back Hill EC1 4K 7 (4A 84)
Backhouse Pl. SE17 4E 102
Back La. DA5: Bexl 7G 127
HA8: Edg 1J 43

Back La. IG9: Buck H 2G 37
N8 5J 47
NW3 4A 64
RM6: Chad H 7D 54
TW8: Bford 6D 96
TW10: Ham 3C 132
Backley Gdns. SE25 6G 157
Back Pas. *EC1* *5B 8*
(off Long La.)
Back Rd. DA14: Sidc 4A 144
TW11: Tedd 7J 131
Bacon Gro. SE1 3F 103
Bacon La. HA8: Edg 1G 43
NW9 4H 43
(not continuous)
Bacon's College Sports Cen. 1A 104
Bacons La. N6 1E 64
Bacon St. E1 3K 9 (4F 85)
E2 3K 9 (4F 85)
Bacon Ter. RM8: Dag 5B 72
Bacton NW5 5E 64
Bacton St. E2 3J 85
Baddeley Ho. *KT8: W Mole* *5E 148*
(off Down St.)
Baddesley Ho. SE11 5H 19
Baddow Cl. IG8: Wfd G 6F 37
RM10: Dag 1G 91
Baddow Wlk. *N1* *1C 84*
(off New North Rd.)
Baden Pl. SE1 6E 14 (2D 102)
Baden Powell Cl. KT6: Surb 2F 163
RM9: Dag 1E 90
Baden Powell Ho. *DA17: Belv* *3G 109*
(off Ambrooke Rd.)
SW7 2A 16
Baden Rd. IG1: Ilf 5F 71
N8 4H 47
Bader Ct. *NW9* *2B 44*
(off Runway Cl.)
Bader Way SW15 6C 116
Badger Cl. IG2: Ilf 6G 53
TW4: Houn 3A 112
TW13: Felt 3K 129
Badger Ct. NW2 3E 62
Badgers Cl. EN2: Enf 3G 23
HA1: Harr 6H 41
TW15: Ashf 5B 128
UB3: Hayes 7G 75
Badgers Copse BR6: Orp 2K 173
KT4: Wor Pk 2B 164
Badgers Cft. N20 7B 20
SE9 3E 142
Badgers Hole CR0: C'don 4K 169
Badgers Wlk. KT3: N Mald 2A 152
Badlis Rd. E17 3C 50
Badma Cl. N9 3D 34
Badminton Cl. HA1: Harr 4J 41
UB5: N'olt 6E 58
Badminton M. E16 1J 105
Badminton Rd. SW12 6E 118
Badric Ct. SW11 2B 118
Badsworth Rd. SE5 1C 120
Baffin Way E14 1E 104
Bafton Ga. BR2: Hayes 1K 171
Bagley Cl. UB7: W Dray 2A 92
Bagley's La. SW6 1K 117
Bagleys Spring RM6: Chad H 4E 54
Bagnigge Ho. *WC1* *2J 7*
(off Margery St.)
Bagshot Ct. SE18 1E 124
Bagshot Ho. NW1 1K 5
Bagshot Rd. EN1: Enf 7A 24
Bagshot St. SE17 5E 102
Baildon *E2* *2J 85*
(off Cyprus St.)
Baildon St. SE8 7B 104
Bailey Cl. E4 4K 35
N11 7C 32
SE28 1J 107
Bailey Cotts. *E14* *5A 86*
(off Maroon St.)
Bailey Cres. KT9: Chess 7D 162

Bailey Ho. *E3* *3D 86*
(off Talwin St.)
SW10 .... *7K 99*
(off Coleridge Gdns.)
Bailey M. SW2 .... 5A **120**
W4 .... *6H 97*
(off Hervert Gdns.)
Bailey Pl. SE26 .... 6K **139**
Baileys Pl. N16 .... 5E **66**
Baillies Wlk. W5 .... 2D **96**
Bainbridge Cl. TW10: Ham 5E **132**
Bainbridge Rd. RM9: Dag 4F **73**
Bainbridge St. WC1 .... 7D **6** (6H **83**)
Baines Cl. CR2: S Croy 5D **168**
Baird Av. UB1: S'hall 7F **77**
Baird Cl. E10 .... 1C **68**
NW9 .... 6J **43**
Baird Gdns. SE19 .... 4E **138**
Baird Ho. *W12* *7D 80*
(off White City Est.)
Baird Memorial Cotts. *N14* *2C 32*
(off Balaams La.)
Baird Rd. EN1: Enf 3C **24**
Baird St. EC1 .... 3D **8** (4C **84**)
Bairny Wood App. IG8: Wfd G 6E **36**
Baizdon Rd. SE3 .... 2G **123**
Bakehouse M. TW12: Hamp 7E **130**
Baker Beal Ct. DA7: Bex 3H **127**
Baker Ho. *E3* *3D 86*
(off Bromley High St.)
W7 .... 1K **95**
WC1 .... *4F 7*
(off Colonnade)
Baker La. CR4: Mitc 2E **154**
Baker Pas. NW10 .... 1A **80**
Baker Pl. KT19: Ewe 6J **163**
Baker Rd. NW10 .... 1A **80**
SE18 .... 7C **106**
Bakers Av. E17 .... 6D **50**
Bakers Ct. SE25 .... 3E **156**
Bakers End SW20 .... 2G **153**
Baker's Fld. N7 .... 4J **65**
Bakers Gdns. SM5: Cars 2C **166**
Bakers Hall Ct. EC3 .... 3G **15**
Bakers Hill E5 .... 1J **67**
EN5: New Bar 2E **20**
Bakers Ho. *W5* *7D 78*
(off The Grove)
Bakers La. N6 .... 6D **46**
Bakers M. BR6: Chels 6K **173**
W1 .... 7G **5** (6E **82**)
Bakers Pas. *NW3* *4A 64*
(off Heath St.)
Baker's Rents E2 .... 2J **9** (3F **85**)
Baker's Row E15 .... 2G **87**
EC1 .... 4J **7** (4A **84**)
BAKER STREET **5D 82**
Baker St. EN1: Enf 3J **23**
NW1 .... 4F **5** (4D **82**)
W1 .... 4F **5** (4D **82**)
Baker's Yd. EC1 .... 4J **7**
Bakery Cl. SW9 .... 7K **101**
Bakery M. KT6: Surb 1G **163**
Bakery Path *HA8: Edg* *6C 28*
(off St Margaret's Rd.)
Bakery Pl. SW11 .... 4D **118**
Bakewell Way KT3: N Mald 2A **152**
Balaam Ho. SM1: Sutt 4J **165**
Balaam Leisure Cen. 4J **87**
Balaams La. N14 .... 2C **32**
Balaam St. E13 .... 4J **87**
Balaclava Rd. KT6: Surb 7C **150**
SE1 .... 4F **103**
Bala Grn. *NW9* *6A 44*
(off Ruthin Cl.)
Balcaskie Rd. SE9 .... 5D **124**
Balchen Rd. SE3 .... 2B **124**
Balchier Rd. SE22 .... 6H **121**
Balcombe Cl. DA6: Bex 4D **126**
Balcombe Ho. *NW1* *3E 4*
(off Taunton Pl.)
Balcombe St. NW1 .... 3E **4** (4D **82**)
Balcon Ct. W5 .... 6F **79**
Balcorne St. E9 .... 7J **67**
Balder Ri. SE12 .... 2K **141**
Balderton Flats *W1* *1H 11*
(off Balderton St.)
Balderton St. W1 .... 1H **11** (6E **82**)
Baldewyne Ct. N17 .... 1G **49**
Baldock St. E3 .... 2D **86**
Baldrey Ho. *SE10* *5H 105*
(off Blackwall La.)
Baldry Gdns. SW16 .... 6J **137**
Baldwin Cres. SE5 .... 1C **120**
Baldwin Gdns. TW3: Houn 1G **113**
Baldwin Ho. SW2 .... 1A **138**
Baldwin Rd. SW11 .... 6E **118**
Baldwins Gdns. EC1 .... 5J **7** (5A **84**)
Baldwin St. EC1 .... 2E **8** (3D **84**)
Baldwin Ter. N1 .... 2C **84**
Baldwyn Gdns. W3 .... 7K **79**
Baldwyn's Pk. DA5: Bexl 2K **145**
Baldwyn's Rd. DA5: Bexl 2K **145**
Balearic Apartments *E16* *7J 87*
(off Western Gateway)
Bale Rd. E1 .... 5A **86**
Bales Ter. N9 .... 3A **34**
Balfern Gro. W4 .... 5A **98**
Balfern St. SW11 .... 2C **118**
Balfe St. N1 .... 2J **83**
Balfour Av. W7 .... 1K **95**
Balfour Bus. Cen. UB2: S'hall 3A **94**
Balfour Gro. N20 .... 3J **31**
Balfour Ho. *SW11* *1E 118*
(off Forfar Rd.)
W10 .... *5F 81*
(off St Charles Sq.)
Balfour M. N9 .... 3B **34**
W1 .... 4H **11** (1E **100**)
Balfour Pl. SW15 .... 4D **116**
W1 .... 3H **11** (7E **82**)
Balfour Rd. BR2: Brom 5B **160**
HA1: Harr 5H **41**
IG1: Ilf 2F **71**
N5 .... 4C **66**
SE25 .... 5G **157**
SM5: Cars 7D **166**
SW19 .... 7K **135**
TW3: Houn 3F **113**
UB2: S'hall 3B **94**
W3 .... 5J **79**
W13 .... 2A **96**
Balfour St. SE17 .... 4D **102**
Balfour Ter. N3 .... 2K **45**
Balfron Twr. E14 .... 6E **86**
Balgonie Rd. E4 .... 1A **36**
Balgove Ct. *NW10* *6D 62*
(off Eden Gro.)
Balgowan Cl. KT3: N Mald 5A **152**
Balgowan Rd. BR3: Beck 3A **158**
Balgowan St. SE18 .... 4K **107**
BALHAM 1E **136**
Balham Continental Mkt.
SW12 .... *1F 137*
(off Shipka Rd.)
Balham Gro. SW12 .... 7E **118**
Balham High Rd. SW12 .... 3E **136**
SW17 .... 3E **136**
Balham Hill SW12 .... 7F **119**
Balham Leisure Cen. 2F **137**
Balham New Rd. SW12 .... 7F **119**
Balham Pk. Rd. SW12 .... 1D **136**
Balham Rd. N9 .... 2B **34**
Balham Sta. Rd. SW12 .... 1F **137**
Balin Ho. *SE1* *6E 14*
(off Long La.)
Balkan Wlk. E1 .... 7H **85**
Balladier Wlk. E14 .... 5D **86**
Ballamore Rd. BR1: Brom 3J **141**
Ballance Rd. E9 .... 6K **67**
Ballantine St. SW18 .... 4A **118**
Ballantrae Ho. NW2 .... 4H **63**
Ballantyne Cl. SE9 .... 4C **142**
Ballard Cl. KT2: King T 7K **133**
Ballard Ho. *SE10* *6D 104*
(off Thames St.)
Ballards Cl. RM10: Dag 1H **91**
Ballards Farm Rd. CR0: C'don 6G **169**
CR2: C'don, S Croy 6G **169**
Ballards La. N3 .... 1J **45**
N12 .... 1J **45**
Ballards M. HA8: Edg 6B **28**
Ballards Ri. CR2: Sels 6G **169**
Ballards Rd. NW2 .... 2C **62**
RM10: Dag 2H **91**
Ballards Way CR0: C'don 6G **169**
CR2: Sels 6G **169**
Ballast Quay SE10 .... 5F **105**
Ballater Rd. CR2: S Croy 5F **169**
SW2 .... 4J **119**
Ball Ct. *EC3* *1F 15*
(off Cornhill)
Balletica Apartments *WC2* *1F 13*
(off Long Acre)
Ball Ho. *NW9* *3B 44*
(off Aerodrome Rd.)
Ballina St. SE23 .... 7K **121**
Ballin Ct. *E14* *2E 104*
(off Stewart St.)
Ballingdon Rd. SW11 .... 6E **118**
Ballinger Point *E3* *3D 86*
(off Bromley High St.)
Ballinger Way UB5: N'olt 4C **76**
Balliol Av. E4 .... 4B **36**
Balliol Rd. DA16: Well 2B **126**
N17 .... 1E **48**
W10 .... 6E **80**
Balloch Rd. SE6 .... 1F **141**
Ballogie Av. NW10 .... 4A **62**
Ballow Cl. SE5 .... 7E **102**
Balls Pond Pl. N1 .... 6D **66**
Balls Pond Rd. N1 .... 6D **66**
Balmain Cl. W5 .... 1D **96**
Balmain Ct. TW3: Houn 1F **113**
Balmain Lodge *KT5: Surb* *4E 150*
(off Cranes Pk. Av.)
Balman Ho. *SE16* *4K 103*
(off Rotherhithe New Rd.)
Balmer Rd. E3 .... 2B **86**
Balmes Rd. N1 .... 1D **84**
Balmoral Apartments *W2* *6C 4*
(off Praed St.)
Balmoral Av. BR3: Beck 4A **158**
N11 .... 6K **31**
Balmoral Cl. SW15 .... 6F **117**
Balmoral Ct. *BR3: Beck* *1E 158*
(off The Avenue)
HA9: Wemb 3F **61**
KT4: Wor Pk 2D **164**
NW8 .... *2B 82*
(off Queen's Ter.)
SE12 .... 4K **141**
SE16 .... *1K 103*
(off King & Queen Wharf)
SE17 .... *5D 102*
(off Lytham St.)
SE27 .... 4C **138**
SM2: Sutt 7J **165**
Balmoral Cres. KT8: W Mole 3E **148**
Balmoral Dr. UB1: S'hall 4D **76**
UB4: Hayes 4G **75**
Balmoral Gdns. DA5: Bexl 7F **127**
IG3: Ilf 1K **71**
W13 .... 3A **96**
Balmoral Gro. N7 .... 6K **65**
Balmoral Ho. *E14* *3D 104*
(off Lanark Sq.)
E16 .... *1K 105*
(off Keats Av.)
W14 .... *4G 99*
(off Windsor Way)
Balmoral M. W12 .... 3B **98**
Balmoral Rd. E7 .... 4A **70**
E10 .... 2D **68**
HA2: Harr 4E **58**
KT1: King T 4F **151**
Balmoral Rd. KT4: Wor Pk 3D **164**
NW2 .... 6D **62**
Balmoral Trad. Est. IG11: Bark 5K **89**
Balmore Cl. E14 .... 6E **86**
Balmore Cres. EN4: Cockf 5K **21**
Balmore St. N19 .... 2F **65**
Balmuir Gdns. SW15 .... 4E **116**
Balnacraig Av. NW10 .... 4A **62**
Balniel Ga. SW1 .... 5D **18** (5H **101**)
Balsam Ho. *E14* *7D 86*
(off E. India Dock Rd.)
Baltic Apartments *E16* *7J 87*
(off Western Gateway)
Baltic Cen., The TW8: Bford 5D **96**
Baltic Cl. SW19 .... 7B **136**
Baltic Ct. *E1* *1J 103*
(off Clave Ct.)
SE16 .... 2K **103**
Baltic Ho. SE5 .... 2C **120**
Baltic Pl. N1 .... 1E **84**
Baltic St. E. EC1 .... 4C **8** (4C **84**)
Baltic St. W. EC1 .... 4C **8** (4C **84**)
Baltimore Ct. *SW1* *4C 18*
(off Chapter St.)
Baltimore Ho. SE11 .... 5J **19**
SW18 .... 3A **118**
Baltimore Pl. DA16: Well 2K **125**
Baltimore Wharf E14 .... 3D **104**
Balvaird Pl. SW1 .... 6D **18** (5H **101**)
Balvernie Gro. SW18 .... 7H **117**
Balvernie M. SW18 .... 7J **117**
Bamber Ho. IG11: Bark 1G **89**
Bamber Rd. SE15 .... 1F **121**
Bamborough Gdns. W12 .... 2E **98**
Bamburgh N17 .... 7C **34**
Bamford Av. HA0: Wemb 1F **79**
Bamford Rd. BR1: Brom 5E **140**
IG11: Bark 6G **71**
Bampfylde Cl. SM6: Wall 3G **167**
Bampton Ct. W5 .... 6D **78**
Bampton Dr. NW7 .... 7H **29**
Bampton Rd. SE23 .... 3K **139**
Banavie Gdns. BR3: Beck 1E **158**
Banbury Cl. EN2: Enf 1G **23**
Banbury Ct. SM2: Sutt 7J **165**
WC2 .... 2E **12**
Banbury Ho. E9 .... 7K **67**
Banbury Rd. E9 .... 7K **67**
E17 .... 7E **34**
Banbury St. SW11 .... 2C **118**
Banbury Wlk. *UB5: N'olt* *2E 76*
(off Brabazon Rd.)
Banchory Rd. SE3 .... 7K **105**
Bancroft Av. IG9: Buck H 2D **36**
N2 .... 5C **46**
Bancroft Cl. TW15: Ashf 5C **128**
Bancroft Ct. *SW8* *7J 101*
(off Allen Edwards Dr.)
UB5: N'olt 1A **76**
Bancroft Gdns. BR6: Orp 1K **173**
HA3: Hrw W 1G **41**
Bancroft Ho. *E1* *4J 85*
(off Cephas St.)
Bancroft Rd. E1 .... 3J **85**
HA3: Hrw W 2G **41**
Bandon Cl. UB10: Uxb 2B **74**
BANDONHILL 5H **167**
Bandon Ri. SM6: Wall 5H **167**
Banfield Rd. SE15 .... 3H **121**
Banfor Ct. SM6: Wall 5G **167**
Bangalore St. SW15 .... 3E **116**
Bangor Cl. UB5: N'olt 5F **59**
Banim St. W6 .... 4D **98**
Banister Ho. E9 .... 5K **67**
SW8 .... *1G 119*
(off Wadhurst Rd.)
W10 .... *3G 81*
(off Bruckner St.)
Banister M. NW6 .... 7K **63**
Banister Rd. W10 .... 3F **81**
Bank, The N6 .... 1F **65**
Bank Av. CR4: Mitc 2B **154**

Bank Bldgs. E4 . . . . 6A 36
(off The Avenue)
Bank End SE1 . . . . 4D 14 (1C 102)
Bankfoot Rd. BR1: Brom 4G 141
Bankhurst Rd. SE6 . . . . 7B 122
Bank La. KT2: King T 7E 132
SW15 . . . . 5A 116
Bank M. SM1: Sutt 6A 166
Bank of England 1E 14 (6D 84)
Bank of England Mus. 1F 15
Bank of England Sports Cen. 5A 116
(off Priory La.)
Banks Ho. SE1 . . . . 3C 102
(off Rockingham St.)
Banksian Wlk. TW7: Isle 1J 113
Banksia Rd. N18 . . . . 5E 34
Bankside CR2: S Croy 6F 169
EN2: Enf 1G 23
SE1 . . . . 3C 14 (7C 84)
(not continuous)
UB1: S'hall 1B 94
Bankside Av. SE13 . . . . 3E 122
UB5: N'olt 2J 75
Bankside Cl. DA5: Bexl 4K 145
SM5: Cars 6C 166
TW7: Isle 4K 113
Bankside Dr. KT7: T Ditt 1B 162
Bankside Gallery 3B 14 (7B 84)
Bankside Lofts SE1 . . . . 4B 14
SE1 . . . . 1B 102
(off Hopton St.)
Bankside Mix SE1 . . . . 4C 14
SE1 . . . . 1C 102
Bankside Pk. IG11: Bark 3A 90
Bankside Pl. N4 . . . . 6C 48
Bankside Rd. IG1: Ilf 5G 71
Bankside Way SE19 . . . . 6E 138
Banks La. DA6: Bex 4F 127
Bank St. E14 . . . . 1D 104
Banks Way E12 . . . . 4E 70
Banks Yd. TW5: Hest 6D 94
Bankton Rd. SW2 . . . . 4A 120
Bankwell Rd. SE13 . . . . 4G 123
Bannatyne's Health Club
Chingford 6H 35
Grove Park 2K 141
Banner Ct. SE16 . . . . 4J 103
(off Rotherhithe New Rd.)
Banner Ho. EC1 . . . . 4D 8
(off Banner St.)
Bannerman Ho. SW8 . . . . 7G 19 (6K 101)
Banner St. EC1 . . . . 4D 8 (4C 84)
Banning St. SE10 . . . . 5G 105
Bannister Cl. SW2 . . . . 1A 138
UB6: G'frd 5H 59
Bannister Ho. HA3: W'stone 3J 41
(off Headstone Dr.)
SE14 . . . . 6K 103
(off John Williams Cl.)
Bannockburn Rd. SE18 . . . . 4J 107
Bannon Ct. SW6 . . . . 1K 117
(off Michael Rd.)
Bannow Cl. KT19: Ewe 4A 164
Banqueting House 5E 12 (1J 101)
Banstead Ct. W12 . . . . 7B 80
Banstead Gdns. N9 . . . . 3K 33
Banstead Rd. SM5: Cars 7B 166
Banstead Rd. Sth. SM2: Sutt 7B 166
Banstead St. SE15 . . . . 3J 121
Banstead Way SM6: Wall 5J 167
Banstock Rd. HA8: Edg 6C 28
Bantam Ho. NW9 . . . . 2B 44
(off Heritage Av.)
Banting Dr. N21 . . . . 5E 22
Banting Ho. NW2 . . . . 3C 62
Bantock Ho. W10 . . . . 3G 81
(off Third Av.)
Banton Cl. EN1: Enf 2C 24
Bantry Ho. E1 . . . . 4K 85
(off Ernest St.)
Bantry St. SE5 . . . . 7D 102
Banwell Rd. DA5: Bexl 6D 126
Banyard Rd. SE16 . . . . 3H 103
Baptist Gdns. NW5 . . . . 6E 64
Baquba SE13 . . . . 2D 122
Barandon Rd. W11 . . . . 7F 81
(off Grenfell Rd.)
Barandon Wlk. W11 . . . . 7F 81
Barbanel Ho. E1 . . . . 4J 85
(off Cephas St.)
Barbara Brosnan Ct. NW8 . . . . 1A 4 (2B 82)
Barbara Castle Cl. SW6 . . . . 6H 99
Barbara Cl. TW17: Shep 5D 146
Barbara Hucklesby Cl. N22 . . . . 2B 48
Barbauld Rd. N16 . . . . 3E 66
Barber Beaumont Ho. E1 . . . . 3K 85
(off Bancroft Rd.)
Barber Cl. N21 . . . . 7F 23
Barberry Ct. E15 . . . . 6GK 69
Barbers All. E13 . . . . 3K 87
Barbers Rd. E15 . . . . 2D 86
Barbican EC2 . . . . 5D 8
Barbican Arts Cen. 5D 8 (5C 84)
Barbican Cinema 5D 8
(in Barbican Arts Cen.)
Barbican Rd. UB6: G'frd 6F 77
Barbican Theatre 5D 8
(in Barbican Arts Cen.)
Barbican Trade Cen. EC1 . . . . 5D 8
(off Beech St.)
Barb M. W6 . . . . 3E 98
Barbon All. EC2 . . . . 7H 9
(off Devonshire Sq.)
Barbon Cl. WC1 . . . . 5F 7 (5K 83)
Barbot Cl. N9 . . . . 3B 34
Barchard St. SW18 . . . . 5K 117
Barchester Cl. W7 . . . . 1K 95
Barchester Rd. HA3: Hrw W 2H 41
Barchester St. E14 . . . . 5D 86
Barclay Cl. SW6 . . . . 7J 99
Barclay Ho. E9 . . . . 7J 67
(off Well St.)
Barclay Oval IG8: Wfd G 4D 36
Barclay Path E17 . . . . 5E 50
Barclay Rd. CR0: C'don 3D 168
E11 . . . . 1H 69
E13 . . . . 4A 88
E17 . . . . 5E 50
N18 . . . . 6J 33
SW6 . . . . 7J 99
Barcombe Av. SW2 . . . . 2J 137
Barcombe Cl. BR5: St P 3K 161
Bardell Ho. SE1 . . . . 7K 15
(off Parkers Row)
Barden St. SE18 . . . . 7J 107
Bardfield Av. RM6: Chad H 3D 54
Bardney Rd. SM4: Mord 4K 153
Bardolph Rd. N7 . . . . 4J 65
TW9: Rich 3F 115
Bard Rd. W10 . . . . 7F 81
Bardsey Pl. E1 . . . . 4J 85
Bardsey Wlk. N1 . . . . 6C 66
(off Douglas Rd. Nth.)
Bardsley Cl. CR0: C'don 3F 169
Bardsley Ho. SE10 . . . . 6E 104
(off Bardsley La.)
Bardsley La. SE10 . . . . 6E 104
Barents Ho. E1 . . . . 4K 85
(off White Horse La.)
Barfett St. W10 . . . . 4H 81
Barfield Av. N20 . . . . 2J 31
Barfield Rd. BR1: Brom 3E 160
E11 . . . . 1H 69
Barfleur La. SE8 . . . . 4B 104
Barford Cl. NW4 . . . . 2C 44
Barford Ho. E3 . . . . 2B 86
(off Tredegar Rd.)
Barford St. N1 . . . . 1A 84
Barforth Rd. SE15 . . . . 3H 121
Barfreston Way SE20 . . . . 1H 157
Bargate Cl. KT3: N Mald 7C 152
SE18 . . . . 5K 107
Barge Ho. Rd. E16 . . . . 2F 107
Barge Ho. St. SE1 . . . . 4K 13 (1A 102)
Barge La. E3 . . . . 1A 86
Bargery Rd. SE6 . . . . 1D 140
Barge Wlk. KT1: Ham W 3D 150
KT8: E Mos 3H 149
(Hampton Ct. Cres.)
KT8: E Mos 6A 150
(The Island)
Bargrove Cl. SE20 . . . . 7G 139
Bargrove Cres. SE6 . . . . 2B 140
Barham Cl. BR2: Brom 1C 172
BR7: Chst 5F 143
HA0: Wemb 6B 60
RM7: Mawney 2H 55
Barham Ct. CR2: S Croy 4C 168
(off Barham Rd.)
Barham Ho. SE17 . . . . 5E 102
(off Kinglake Est.)
Barham Rd. BR7: Chst 5F 143
CR2: S Croy 4C 168
SW20 . . . . 7C 134
Baring Cl. SE12 . . . . 2J 141
Baring Ct. N1 . . . . 1D 84
(off Baring St.)
Baring Ho. E14 . . . . 6C 86
(off Canton St.)
Baring Rd. CR0: C'don 1G 169
EN4: Cockf 4G 21
SE12 . . . . 7J 123
Baring St. N1 . . . . 1D 84
Baritone Ct. E15 . . . . 1H 87
(off Church St.)
Barker Cl. HA6: Nwood 1H 39
KT3: N Mald 4H 151
TW9: Kew 2H 115
Barker Dr. NW1 . . . . 7G 65
Barker Ho. SE17 . . . . 4E 102
(off Congreve St.)
Barker M. SW4 . . . . 4F 119
Barkers Arc. W8 . . . . 2K 99
Barker St. SW10 . . . . 6A 100
Barker Wlk. SW16 . . . . 3H 137
Barkham Rd. N17 . . . . 7J 33
Barkham Ter. SE1 . . . . 1K 19
BARKING 7G 71
Barking Abbey 1G 89
Barking Abbey School Leisure Cen. . . . 6A 72
Barking Bus. Cen. IG11: Bark 3A 90
Barking Ind. Pk. IG11: Bark 1K 89
Barking Northern Relief Rd.
IG11: Bark 7F 71
BARKING RIVERSIDE 3C 90
Barking Rd. E6 . . . . 2A 88
E13 . . . . 5H 87
E16 . . . . 5H 87
BARKINGSIDE 3G 53
Bark Pl. W2 . . . . 7K 81
Barkston Gdns. SW5 . . . . 4K 99
Barkway Ct. N4 . . . . 2C 66
Barkway Dr. BR6: Farnb 4E 172
Barkwith Ho. SE14 . . . . 6K 103
(off Cold Blow La.)
Barkwood Cl. RM7: Rom 5J 55
Barkworth Rd. SE16 . . . . 5H 103
Barlborough St. SE14 . . . . 7K 103
Barlby Gdns. W10 . . . . 4F 81
Barlby Rd. W10 . . . . 5E 80
Barley Cl. HA0: Wemb 4D 60
Barleycorn Way E14 . . . . 7B 86
(not continuous)
Barleyfields Cl. RM6: Chad H 6B 54
Barley La. IG3: Ilf 7A 54
RM6: Chad H 7A 54
Barley Mow Pas. EC1 . . . . 5B 8
W4 . . . . 5K 97
Barley Mow Way TW17: Shep 4C 146
Barley Shotts Bus. Pk. W10 . . . . 5H 81
Barling NW1 . . . . 6F 65
(off Castlehaven Rd.)
Barlow Cl. SM6: Wall 6J 167
Barlow Dr. SE18 . . . . 1C 124
Barlow Ho. N1 . . . . 1E 8
(off Provost Est.)
Barlow Ho. SE16 . . . . 4H 103
(off Rennie Est.)
W11 . . . . 7G 81
(off Walmer Rd.)
Barlow Pl. W1 . . . . 3K 11 (7F 83)
Barlow Rd. NW6 . . . . 6H 63
TW12: Hamp 7E 130
W3 . . . . 1H 97
Barlow St. SE17 . . . . 4D 102
Barlow Way RM13: Rain 5K 91
Barmeston Rd. SE6 . . . . 2D 140
Barmor Cl. HA2: Harr 2F 41
Barmouth Av. UB6: G'frd 2K 77
Barmouth Rd. CR0: C'don 2K 169
SW18 . . . . 6A 118
Barnabas Ct. EN2: Enf 4F 23
Barnabas Ho. EC1 . . . . 2C 8
Barnabas Lodge SW8 . . . . 1J 119
(off Guildford Rd.)
Barnabas Rd. E9 . . . . 5K 67
Barnaby Cl. HA2: Harr 2G 59
Barnaby Ct. NW9 . . . . 3A 44
SE16 . . . . 2G 103
(off Scott Lidgett Cres.)
Barnaby Pl. SW7 . . . . 4A 16
Barnaby Way IG7: Chig 3K 37
Barnard Cl. BR7: Chst 1H 161
SE18 . . . . 3E 106
SM6: Wall 7H 167
TW16: Sun 7K 129
Barnard Gdns. KT3: N Mald 4C 152
UB4: Yead 4K 75
Barnard Gro. E15 . . . . 7H 69
Barnard Hill N10 . . . . 1F 47
Barnard Ho. E2 . . . . 3H 85
(off Ellsworth St.)
Barnard Lodge EN5: New Bar 4F 21
W9 . . . . 5J 81
(off Admiral Wlk.)
Barnard M. SW11 . . . . 4C 118
Barnardo Dr. IG6: Ilf 4G 53
Barnardo Gdns. E1 . . . . 7K 85
Barnardo St. E1 . . . . 6K 85
Barnardos Village IG6: Ilf 4G 53
Barnard Rd. CR4: Mitc 3E 154
EN1: Enf 2C 24
SW11 . . . . 4C 118
Barnards Ho. SE16 . . . . 2B 104
(off Wyatt Cl.)
Barnard's Inn EC1 . . . . 6J 7
Barnbrough NW1 . . . . 1G 83
(off Camden St.)
Barnby Sq. E15 . . . . 1G 87
Barnby St. E15 . . . . 1G 87
NW1 . . . . 1B 6 (2G 83)
Barn Cl. NW5 . . . . 5H 65
(off Torriano Av.)
TW15: Ashf 5D 128
UB5: N'olt 2A 76
Barn Cres. HA7: Stan 6H 27
Barncroft Cl. UB8: Hil 5D 74
Barneby Cl. TW2: Twick 1J 131
BARNEHURST 3J 127
Barnehurst Av. DA7: Bex 1J 127
DA8: Erith 1J 127
Barnehurst Cl. DA8: Erith 1J 127
Barnehurst Rd. DA7: Bex 2J 127
Barn Elms Athletic Track 1D 116
Barn Elms Pk. SW15 . . . . 3E 116
BARNES 2B 116
Barnes All. TW12: Hamp 2G 149
Barnes Av. SW13 . . . . 7C 98
UB2: S'hall 4D 94
Barnes Bri W4 . . . . 2A 116
Barnes Cl. E12 . . . . 4B 70
Barnes Common Nature Reserve 3C 116
Barnes Ct. CR7: Thor H 3C 156
E16 . . . . 5A 88
EN5: New Bar 4E 20
IG8: Buck H, Wfd G 5G 37
N1 . . . . 7A 66
Barnes End KT3: N Mald 5C 152

Barnes High St.—Basil Spence Ho.

Barnes High St. SW13 2B **116**
Barnes Ho. *E2* *2J 85*
(off Wadeson St.)
IG11: Bark 1H **89**
NW1 *7G 65*
(off Camden Rd.)
SE14 *6K 103*
(off John Williams Cl.)
Barnes Pikle W5 7D **78**
Barnes Rd. IG1: Ilf 5G **71**
N18 4D **34**
Barnes St. E14 6A **86**
Barnes Ter. SE8 5B **104**
Barnes Wallis Ct. HA9: Wemb 3J **61**
BARNET 3B **20**
Barnet Burnt Oak Leisure Cen. 1K **43**
Barnet Bus. Cen. EN5: Barn 3B **20**
Barnet By-Pass NW7 6G **29**
Barnet Civil and Family Courts 1J **45**
Barnet Copthall Stadium 1E **44**
Barnet Dr. BR2: Brom 2C **172**
Barnet FC 5D **20**
Barnet Ga. La. EN5: Ark 1H **29**
Barnet Gro. E2 1K **9** (3G **85**)
Barnet Hill EN5: Barn 4C **20**
Barnet Ho. N20 2F **31**
Barnet La. EN5: Barn 1C **30**
N20: Barn, Lon 1C **30**
Barnet Mus. 4B **20**
Barnet Trad. Est. EN5: Barn 3C **20**
Barnetts Ct. HA2: Harr 3F **59**
Barnett St. E1 6H **85**
BARNET VALE 5E **20**
Barnet Way NW7 3E **28**
Barnet Wood Rd. BR2: Brom 2A **172**
Barney Cl. SE7 5A **106**
Barn Fld. NW3 5D **64**
Barnfield KT3: N Mald 6A **152**
Barnfield Av. CR0: C'don 2J **169**
CR4: Mitc 4F **155**
KT2: King T 4D **132**
Barnfield Cl. N4 7J **47**
SW17 3B **136**
Barnfield Gdns. KT2: King T 4E **132**
SE18 6F **107**
Barnfield Pl. E14 4C **104**
Barnfield Rd. CR2: Sande 7E **168**
DA17: Belv 6F **109**
HA8: Edg 1J **43**
SE18 6F **107**
(not continuous)
W5 4C **78**
Barnfield Wood Cl. BR3: Beck 6F **159**
Barnfield Wood Rd. BR3: Beck 6F **159**
Barnham Dr. SE28 1K **107**
(not continuous)
Barnham Rd. UB6: G'frd 3G **77**
Barnham St. SE1 6H **15** (2E **102**)
Barn Hill HA9: Wemb 1G **61**
Barnhill HA5: Eastc 5A **40**
Barnhill Av. BR2: Brom 5H **159**
Barnhill La. UB4: Yead 3K **75**
Barnhill Rd. HA9: Wemb 3J **61**
UB4: Yead 3K **75**
Barningham Way NW9 6K **43**
Barnlea Cl. TW13: Hanw 2C **130**
Barnmead Ct. RM9: Dag 5F **73**
Barnmead Gdns. RM9: Dag 5F **73**
Barnmead Rd. BR3: Beck 1K **157**
RM9: Dag 5F **73**
Barn M. HA2: Harr 3E **58**
Barn Ri. HA9: Wemb 1G **61**
BARNSBURY 7K **65**
Barnsbury Cl. KT3: N Mald 4J **151**
Barnsbury Cres. KT5: Surb 1J **163**
Barnsbury Est. N1 1K **83**
(not continuous)
Barnsbury Gro. N7 7K **65**
Barnsbury Ho. SW4 6H **119**
Barnsbury La. KT5: Surb 2H **163**
Barnsbury Pk. N1 7A **66**
Barnsbury Rd. N1 2A **84**
Barnsbury Sq. N1 7A **66**
Barnsbury St. N1 7A **66**
Barnsbury Ter. N1 7K **65**
Barnscroft SW20 3D **152**
Barnsdale Av. E14 4D **104**
Barnsdale Rd. W9 4H **81**
Barnsley St. E1 4H **85**
Barnstable La. SE13 4E **122**
Barnstaple Ho. *SE10* *7D 104*
(off Devonshire Dr.)
SE12 *5H 123*
(off Taunton Rd.)
Barnstaple Rd. HA4: Ruis 3A **58**
Barnston Wlk. *N1* *1C 84*
(off Popham St.)
Barn St. N16 2E **66**
Barn Theatre, The
West Molesey 4E **148**
Barn Way HA9: Wemb 1G **61**
Barnwell Ho. *SE5* *1E 120*
(off St Giles Rd.)
Barnwell Rd. SW2 5A **120**
Barnwood Cl. HA4: Ruis 2F **57**
N20 1C **30**
W9 4K **81**
Baron Cl. N1 2A **84**
N11 5K **31**
Baroness Rd. E2 1K **9** (3F **85**)
Baronet Gro. N17 1G **49**
Baronet Rd. N17 1G **49**
Baron Gdns. IG6: Ilf 3G **53**
Baron Gro. CR4: Mitc 4C **154**
Baron Ho. SW19 1B **154**
Baron Rd. RM8: Dag 1D **72**
Barons, The TW1: Twick 6B **114**
Baronsclere Ct. N6 7G **47**
BARONS COURT 5G **99**
Barons Ct. IG1: Ilf 2H **71**
NW9 6K **43**
SM6: Bedd 3H **167**
Baron's Ct. Rd. W14 5G **99**
Barons Court Theatre *5G 99*
(off Comeragh Rd.)
Baronsfield Rd. TW1: Twick 6B **114**
Barons Ga. EN4: E Barn 6H **21**
W4 3J **97**
Barons Keep W14 5G **99**
Barons Mead HA1: Harr 4J **41**
Baronsmead Rd. SW13 1C **116**
Baronsmede W5 2F **97**
Baronsmere Ct. EN5: Barn 4B **20**
Baronsmere Rd. N2 4C **46**
Baron's Pl. SE1 7K **13** (2A **102**)
Baron St. N1 2A **84**
Baron's Wlk. CR0: C'don 6A **158**
Baron Wlk. CR4: Mitc 4C **154**
E16 5H **87**
Baroque Ct. TW3: Houn 3F **113**
Barque M. SE8 6C **104**
Barrack Rd. TW4: Houn 4B **112**
Barracks La. EN5: Barn 3B **20**
Barra Hall Cir. UB3: Hayes 7G **75**
Barra Hall Rd. UB3: Hayes 7G **75**
Barratt Av. N22 2K **47**
Barratt Ho. *N1* *7B 66*
(off Sable St.)
Barratt Ind. Pk. E3 4E **86**
UB1: S'hall 2E **94**
Barratt Way HA3: W'stone 2H **41**
Barrenger Rd. N10 1D **46**
Barret Ho. NW6 1J **81**
SW9 *3K 119*
(off Benedict Rd.)
Barrett Ho. *SE17* *5C 102*
(off Browning St.)
Barrett Rd. E17 4E **50**
Barrett's Grn. Rd. NW10 3J **79**
Barrett's Gro. N16 5E **66**
Barrett St. W1 1H **11** (6E **82**)
Barrhill Rd. SW2 2J **137**
Barrie Ct. *EN5: New Bar* *5F 21*
(off Lyonsdown Rd.)
Barriedale SE14 2A **122**
Barrie Est. W2 2A **10** (7B **82**)
Barrie Ho. *NW8* *1C 82*
(off St Edmund's Ter.)
W2 *7A 82*
(off Lancaster Ga.)
Barrier App. SE7 3B **106**
Barrier Point Rd. E16 1A **106**
Barringers Ct. HA4: Ruis 7F **39**
Barringer Sq. SW17 4E **136**
Barrington Cl. IG5: Ilf 1D **52**
NW5 5E **64**
Barrington Ct. N10 2E **46**
SW4 2J **119**
W3 *2H 97*
(off Cheltenham Pl.)
Barrington Rd. DA7: Bex 2D **126**
E12 6E **70**
N8 5H **47**
SM3: Sutt 2J **165**
SW9 3B **120**
Barrington Vs. SE18 1E **124**
Barrington Wlk. SE19 6E **138**
Barrow Av. SM5: Cars 7D **166**
Barrow Cl. N21 3G **33**
Barrow Ct. *SE6* *1H 141*
(off Cumberland Pl.)
Barrowdene Cl. HA5: Pinn 2C **40**
Barrowell Grn. N21 2G **33**
Barrowfield Cl. N9 3C **34**
Barrowgate Rd. W4 5J **97**
Barrow Hedges Cl. SM5: Cars 7C **166**
Barrow Hedges Way SM5: Cars 7C **166**
Barrow Hill KT4: Wor Pk 2A **164**
Barrow Hill Cl. KT4: Wor Pk 2A **164**
Barrow Hill Est. *NW8* *2C 82*
(off Barrow Hill Rd.)
Barrow Hill Rd. NW8 1C **4** (2C **82**)
Barrow Point Av. HA5: Pinn 2C **40**
Barrow Point La. HA5: Pinn 2C **40**
Barrow Rd. CR0: Wadd 5A **168**
SW16 6H **137**
Barrow Store Ct. *SE1* *7G 15*
(off Decima St.)
Barrow Wlk. TW8: Bford 6C **96**
Barrs Rd. NW10 7K **61**
Barry Av. DA7: Bex 7E **108**
N15 6F **49**
Barry Cl. BR6: Orp 3J **173**
Barrydene N20 1G **31**
Barry Ho. *SE16* *4H 103*
(off Rennie Est.)
Barry Pde. SE22 5G **121**
Barry Rd. E6 6C **88**
NW10 7J **61**
SE22 6G **121**
Barset Rd. SE15 3J **121**
(not continuous)
Barson Cl. SE20 7J **139**
Barston Rd. SE27 3C **138**
Barstow Cres. SW2 1K **137**
Barter St. WC1 6F **7** (5J **83**)
Barters Wlk. HA5: Pinn 3C **40**
Barth M. SE18 4J **107**
Bartholomew Cl. EC1 6B **8** (5C **84**)
(not continuous)
SW18 4A **118**
Bartholomew Ct. *E14* *7F 87*
(off Newport Av.)
EC1 *3D 8*
(off Old St.)
HA8: Edg 7J **27**
Bartholomew Ho. IG8: Wfd G 7K **37**
W10 *4G 81*
(off Appleford Rd.)
Bartholomew La. EC2 1F **15** (6D **84**)
Bartholomew Pl. EC1 6C **8**
Bartholomew Rd. NW5 6G **65**
Bartholomew Sq. E1 4H **85**
EC1 3D **8** (4C **84**)
Bartholomew St. SE1 3D **102**
Bartholomew Vs. NW5 6G **65**
Barth Rd. SE18 4J **107**
(not continuous)
Bartle Av. E6 2C **88**
Bartle Rd. W11 6G **81**
Bartlett Cl. E14 6C **86**
Bartlett Ct. EC4 7K **7** (6A **84**)
Bartlett Ho's. *RM10: Dag* *7H 73*
(off Vicarage Rd.)
Bartlett M. E14 5D **104**
Bartletts Pas. *EC4* *7K 7*
(off Fetter La.)
Bartlett St. CR2: S Croy 5D **168**
Bartlow Gdns. RM5: Col R 1K **55**
Bartok Ho. *W11* *1H 99*
(off Lansdowne Wlk.)
Barton Av. RM7: Rush G 1H **73**
Barton Cl. DA6: Bex 5E **126**
E6 6D **88**
E9 5J **67**
NW4 5C **44**
SE15 3H **121**
TW17: Shep 6D **146**
Barton Ct. *W14* *5G 99*
(off Baron's Ct. Rd.)
Barton Grn. KT3: N Mald 2K **151**
Barton Green Theatre 2K **151**
Barton Ho. *E3* *3D 86*
(off Bow Rd.)
N1 *7B 66*
(off Sable St.)
SW6 *3K 117*
(off Wandsworth Bri. Rd.)
Barton Mdws. IG6: Ilf 4F **53**
Barton Rd. DA14: Sidc 6E **144**
W14 5G **99**
Barton St. SW1 1E **18** (3J **101**)
Bartonway *NW8* *1B 82*
(off Queen's Ter.)
Bartram Cl. UB8: Hil 4D **74**
Bartram Rd. SE4 5A **122**
Bartrams La. EN4: Had W 1F **21**
Bartrip St. E9 6B **68**
Barts Cl. BR3: Beck 5C **158**
Barville Cl. SE4 4A **122**
Barwell Bus. Pk. KT9: Chess 7D **162**
Barwell Ct. KT9: Chess 7B **162**
Barwell Ho. *E2* *4G 85*
(off Menotti St.)
Barwell La. KT9: Chess 7C **162**
Barwick Dr. UB8: Hil 5D **74**
Barwick Ho. *W3* *2J 97*
(off Strafford Rd.)
Barwick Rd. E7 4K **69**
Barwood Av. BR4: W W'ck 1D **170**
Bascombe Gro. DA1: Bexl, Cray 7K **127**
Bascombe St. SW2 6A **120**
Basden Gro. TW13: Hanw 2E **130**
Basden Ho. TW13: Hanw 2E **130**
Basedale Rd. RM9: Dag 7B **72**
Baseing Cl. E6 7E **88**
Baseline Bus. Studios *W11* *7F 81*
(off Barandon Wlk.)
Basepoint Bus. Cen. RM13: Rain 4K **91**
Basevi Way SE8 6D **104**
Bashley Rd. NW10 4K **79**
Basil Av. E6 3C **88**
Basildene Rd. TW4: Houn 3B **112**
Basildon Av. IG5: Ilf 1E **52**
Basildon Cl. SM2: Sutt 7K **165**
Basildon Ct. *W1* *5H 5*
(off Devonshire Rd.)
Basildon Rd. SE2 5A **108**
Basil Gdns. CR0: C'don 1K **169**
SE27 5C **138**
Basil Ho. *E1* *6G 85*
(off Henriques St.)
SW8 *7J 101*
(off Wyvil Rd.)
Basil Mans. *SW3* *7E 10*
(off Basil St.)
Basilon Rd. DA7: Bex 2E **126**
Basil Spence Ho. N22 1K **47**

Basil St.—Beacontree Rd.

Basil St. SW3 1E 16 (3D 100)
Basin App. E14 6A 86
E16 7F 89
Basing Cl. KT7: T Ditt 7K 149
Basing Ct. SE15 1F 121
Basingdon Way SE5 4D 120
Basing Dr. DA5: Bexl 6F 127
Basingfield Rd. KT7: T Ditt 7K 149
Basinghall Av. EC2 7E 8 (6D 84)
Basinghall Gdns. SM2: Sutt 7K 165
Basinghall St. EC2 7E 8 (6D 84)
Basing Hill HA9: Wemb 2F 61
NW11 1H 63
Basing Ho. *IG11: Bark* *1H 89*
(off St Margarets)
Basing Ho. Yd. E2 1H 9
Basing Pl. E2 1H 9 (3E 84)
Basing St. W11 6H 81
Basing Way KT7: T Ditt 7K 149
N3 3J 45
Basire St. N1 1C 84
Baskerville Gdns. NW10 4A 62
Baskerville Rd. SW18 7C 118
Basket Gdns. SE9 5C 124
Baslow Cl. HA3: Hrw W 1H 41
Baslow Wlk. E5 4K 67
Basnett Rd. SW11 3E 118
Basque Ct. *SE16* *2K 103*
(off Garter Way)
Bassano St. SE22 5F 121
Bassant Rd. SE18 6K 107
Bass Ct. *E15* *1H 87*
(off Plaistow Rd.)
Bassein Pk. Rd. W12 2B 98
Bassett Gdns. TW7: Isle 7G 95
Bassett Ho. RM9: Dag 1B 90
Bassett Rd. E7 4B 70
W10 6F 81
Bassett's Cl. BR6: Farnb 4F 173
Bassett St. NW5 6E 64
Bassett's Way BR6: Farnb 4F 173
Bassett Way UB6: G'frd 6F 77
Bassingbourn Ho. *N1* *7A 66*
(off The Sutton Est.)
Bassingham Rd. HA0: Wemb 6D 60
SW18 7A 118
Bassishaw Highwalk
EC2 6E 8
Basswood Cl. SE15 3H 121
Bastable Av. IG11: Bark 2J 89
Basterfield Ho. *EC1* *4C 8*
(off Golden La. Est.)
Bastion Highwalk EC2 6C 8
Bastion Ho. *EC2* *6D 8*
(off London Wall)
Bastion Rd. SE2 5A 108
Baston Mnr. Rd. BR2: Hayes, Kes 3K 171
Baston Rd. BR2: Hayes 2K 171
Bastwick St. EC1 3C 8 (4C 84)
Basuto Rd. SW6 1J 117
Batavia Cl. TW16: Sun 1K 147
Batavia Ho. *SE14* *7A 104*
(off Batavia Rd.)
Batavia M. SE14 7A 104
Batavia Rd. SE14 7A 104
TW16: Sun 1K 147
Batchelor St. N1 1A 84
Bateman Cl. IG11: Bark 6G 71
Bateman Ho. *SE17* *6B 102*
(off Otto St.)
Bateman M. SW4 6H 119
Bateman Rd. E4 6H 35
Bateman's Bldgs. W1 1C 12
Bateman's Row EC2 3H 9 (4E 84)
Bateman St. W1 1C 12 (6H 83)
Bates Cres. CR0: Wadd 5A 168
SW16 7G 137
Bateson St. SE18 4J 107
Bates Point *E13* *1J 87*
(off Pelly Rd.)
Bate St. E14 7B 86
Bath Cl. SE15 7H 103
Bath Ct. EC1 2E 8
EC1 4J 7
EC1 *3D 84*
(off St Luke's Est.)
SE26 *3G 139*
(off Droitwich Cl.)
Bathgate Ho. *SW9* *1B 120*
(off Lothian Rd.)
Bathgate Rd. SW19 3F 135
Bath Gro. *E2* *2G 85*
(off Horatio St.)
Bath Ho. *E2* *4G 85*
(off Ramsey St.)
IG11: Bark 7G 71
SE1 *3C 102*
(off Bath Ter.)
Bath Ho. Rd. CR0: Bedd 1J 167
Bath Pas. KT1: King T 2D 150
Bath Pl. EC2 2G 9 (3E 84)
EN5: Barn 3C 20
W6 *5E 98*
(off Peabody Est.)
Bath Rd. E7 6B 70
N9 2C 34
RM6: Chad H 6E 54
SL3: Coln, Poyle 4A 174
TW3: Houn 2B 112
TW4: Houn 2B 112
TW5: Cran 1G 111
TW6: H'row A 1G 111
UB3: Harl 1G 111
UB7: Harm, Sip 1A 110
UB7: Lford 4C 174
W4 4A 98
Baths Rd. BR2: Brom 4B 160
Bath St. EC1 2D 8 (3C 84)
Bath Ter. SE1 3C 102
Bathurst Av. SW19 1K 153
Bathurst Gdns. NW10 2D 80
Bathurst Ho. *W12* *7D 80*
(off White City Est.)
Bathurst M. W2 2B 10 (6B 82)
Bathurst Rd. IG1: Ilf 1F 71
Bathurst St. W2 2B 10 (7B 82)
Bathway SE18 4E 106
Batley Cl. CR4: Mitc 7D 154
Batley Pl. N16 3F 67
Batley Rd. EN2: Enf 1H 23
N16 3F 67
Batman Cl. W12 1D 98
Batoum Gdns. W6 3E 98
Batson Ho. *E1* *6G 85*
(off Fairclough St.)
Batson St. W12 2C 98
Batsworth Rd. CR4: Mitc 3B 154
Battenberg Wlk. SE19 6E 138
Batten Cl. E6 6D 88
Batten Cotts. *E14* *5A 86*
(off Maroon St.)
Batten Ho. SW4 5G 119
W10 *3G 81*
(off Third Av.)
Batten St. SW11 3C 118
Battersby Rd. SE6 2F 141
BATTERSEA 1E 118
Battersea Arts Cen. 3D 118
Battersea Bri. SW3 7B 100
Battersea Bri. Rd. SW11 7C 100
Battersea Bus. Cen. SW11 3E 118
Battersea Church Rd. SW11 1B 118
Battersea High St. SW11 1B 118
(not continuous)
BATTERSEA PARK 7F 101
Battersea Pk. 7D 100
Battersea Pk. Children's Zoo 7E 100
Battersea Pk. Equestrian Cen. 2C 118
Battersea Pk. Rd. SW8 1E 118
SW11 2C 118
Battersea Ri. SW11 5C 118
Battersea Sports Cen. 3B 118
Battersea Sq. SW11 1B 118
Battery Rd. SE28 2J 107
Battilion Ho. *NW9* *2B 44*
(off Heritage Av.)
Battishill St. N1 7B 66
Battlebridge Ct. *N1* *2J 83*
(off Wharfdale Rd.)
Battle Bri. La. SE1 5G 15 (1E 102)
Battle Cl. SW19 6A 136
Battledean Rd. N5 5B 66
Battle Ho. *SE15* *6G 103*
(off Haymerle Rd.)
Battle Rd. DA8: Erith 4J 109
DA17: Belv, Erith 4J 109
Batty St. E1 6G 85
Batwa Ho. SE16 5H 103
Baudwin Rd. SE6 2G 141
Baugh Rd. DA14: Sidc 5C 144
Baulk, The SW18 7J 117
Bavant Rd. SW16 2J 155
Bavaria Rd. N19 2J 65
Bavdene M. *NW4* *4D 44*
(off The Burroughs)
Bavent Rd. SE5 2C 120
Bawdale Rd. SE22 5F 121
Bawdsey Av. IG2: Ilf 4K 53
Bawtree Rd. SE14 7A 104
Bawtry Rd. N20 3J 31
Baxendale N20 2F 31
Baxendale St. E2 3G 85
Baxter Cl. BR1: Brom 3F 161
UB2: S'hall 3F 95
UB10: Hil 3D 74
Baxter Ho. *E3* *3D 86*
(off Bromley High St.)
Baxter Rd. E16 6A 88
IG1: Ilf 5F 71
N1 6D 66
N18 4C 34
Bayard Ct. DA6: Bex 4H 127
Bay Ct. *E1* *4K 85*
(off Frimley Way)
W5 3E 96
Baycroft Cl. HA5: Eastc 3A 40
Baydon Ct. BR2: Brom 3H 159
Bayer Ho. *EC1* *4C 8*
(off Golden La. Est.)
Bayes Cl. SE26 5J 139
Bayes Ct. *NW3* *7D 64*
(off Primrose Hill Rd.)
Bayfield Ho. *SE4* *4K 121*
(off Coston Wlk.)
Bayfield Rd. SE9 4B 124
Bayford M. *E8* *7H 67*
(off Bayford St.)
Bayford Rd. NW10 3F 81
Bayford St. E8 7H 67
Bayford St. Bus. Cen. *E8* *7H 67*
(off Sidworth St.)
Baygrove M. KT1: Ham W 1C 150
Bayham Pl. NW1 1G 83
Bayham Rd. SM4: Mord 4K 153
W4 3K 97
W13 7B 78
Bayham St. NW1 1G 83
Bayhurst Wood Country Pk. 5B 38
Bayleaf Cl. TW12: Ham H 5H 131
Bayley St. WC1 6C 6 (5H 83)
Bayley Wlk. SE2 6E 108
Baylis Pl. BR1: Brom 3C 160
Baylis Rd. SE1 7J 13 (2A 102)
Bayliss Av. SE28 7D 90
Bayliss Cl. N21 5D 22
UB1: S'hall *6F 77*
(off Whitecote Rd.)
Bayne Cl. E6 6D 88
Baynes Cl. EN1: Enf 1B 24
Baynes M. NW3 6B 64
Baynes St. NW1 7G 65
Baynham Cl. DA5: Bexl 6F 127
Bayonne Rd. W6 6G 99
Bays Ct. HA8: Edg 5C 28
Bays Farm Ct. UB7: Lford 4D 174
Bayshill Ri. UB5: N'olt 6F 59
Bayston Rd. N16 3F 67
BAYSWATER 7A 82
Bayswater Rd. W2 3A 10 (7K 81)
Baythorne Ho. *E16* *6H 87*
(off Turner St.)
Baythorne St. E3 5B 86
Bayton Ct. *E8* *7G 67*
(off Lansdowne Dr.)
Bay Tree Cl. BR1: Brom 1B 160
Baytree Cl. DA15: Sidc 1K 143
Baytree Ct. SW2 4K 119
Baytree Ho. E4 7J 25
Baytree M. SE17 4D 102
Baytree Rd. SW2 4K 119
Bazalgette Cl. KT3: N Mald 5K 151
Bazalgette Gdns. KT3: N Mald 5K 151
Bazalgette Ho. *NW8* *3B 4*
(off Orchardson St.)
Bazeley Ho. *SE1* *7A 14*
(off Library St.)
Bazely St. E14 7E 86
Bazile Rd. N21 6F 23
BBC Broadcasting House 6K 5 (5F 83)
BBC Maida Vale Studios 4K 81
(off Delaware Rd.)
BBC Television Cen. 7E 80
Beacham Cl. SE7 5B 106
Beachborough Rd. BR1: Brom 4E 140
Beachcroft Av. UB1: S'hall 1C 94
Beachcroft Rd. E11 3G 69
Beachcroft Way N19 1H 65
Beach Gro. TW13: Hanw 2E 130
Beach Ho. *SW5* *5J 99*
(off Philbeach Gdns.)
TW13: Hanw 2E 130
Beachy Rd. E3 7C 68
Beacon Bingo Hall 4F 63
Beacon Cl. UB8: Uxb 5A 56
Beacon Ga. SE14 3K 121
Beacon Gro. SM5: Cars 4E 166
Beacon Hill N7 5J 65
Beacon Ho. *E14* *5D 104*
(off Burrells Wharf Sq.)
SE5 *7E 102*
(off Southampton Way)
Beacon Pl. CR0: Bedd 3J 167
Beacon Rd. SE13 6F 123
TW6: H'row A 6C 110
Beacons Cl. E6 5C 88
Beaconsfield *WC1* *6G 7*
(off Red Lion St.)
Beaconsfield Cl. N11 5K 31
SE3 6J 105
W4 5J 97
Beaconsfield Pde. SE9 4C 142
Beaconsfield Rd. BR1: Brom 3B 160
CR0: C'don 6D 156
DA5: Bexl 2K 145
E10 2E 68
E16 4H 87
E17 6B 50
KT3: N Mald 2K 151
KT5: Surb 7F 151
N9 3B 34
N11 3K 31
N15 4E 48
NW10 6B 62
SE3 7H 105
SE9 2C 142
SE17 5D 102
TW1: Twick 6B 114
UB1: S'hall 1B 94
UB4: Yead 1A 94
W4 3K 97
W5 2C 96
Beaconsfield Ter. RM6: Chad H 6D 54
Beaconsfield Ter. Rd. W14 3G 99
Beaconsfield Wlk. E6 6E 88
SW6 1H 117
Beacontree Av. E17 1F 51
BEACONTREE HEATH 1G 73
Beacontree Rd. E11 1H 69

A-Z London 193

Beadle's Pde.—Beckwith Ho.

Beadle's Pde. RM10: Dag 6J **73**
Beadlow Cl. SM5: Cars 6B **154**
Beadman Pl. SE27 4B **138**
Beadman St. SE27 4B **138**
Beadnell Rd. SE23 1K **139**
Beadon Rd. BR2: Brom 4J **159**
W6 4E **98**
Beaford Gro. SW20 3G **153**
Beagle Cl. TW13: Felt 4K **129**
Beak St. W1 2B **12** (7G **83**)
Beal Cl. DA16: Well 1A **126**
Beale Arboretum, The 1J **21**
Beale Cl. N13 5G **33**
Beale Pl. E3 2B **86**
Beale Rd. E3 1B **86**
Beal Rd. IG1: Ilf 2E **70**
Beam Av. RM10: Dag 1H **91**
Beames Rd. NW10 1K **79**
Beaminster Gdns. IG6: Ilf 2F **53**
Beaminster Ho. *SW8* *7K 101*
(off Dorset Rd.)
Beamish Dr. WD23: B Hea 1B **26**
Beamish Ho. *SE16* *4H 103*
(off Rennie Est.)
Beamish Rd. N9 1B **34**
Beam Reach Bus. Pk
RM13: Rain 3K **91**
Beam Valley Country Pk. 1J **91**
Beamway RM10: Dag 7K **73**
Beanacre Cl. E9 6B **68**
Bean Rd. DA6: Bex 4D **126**
Beanshaw SE9 4E **142**
Beansland Gro. RM6: Chad H 2E **54**
Bear All. EC4 7A **8** (6B **84**)
Bear Cl. RM7: Rom 6H **55**
Beardell St. SE19 6F **139**
Beardow Gro. N14 6B **22**
Beard Rd. KT2: King T 5F **133**
Beardsfield E13 2J **87**
Beard's Hill TW12: Hamp 1E **148**
Beard's Hill Cl. TW12: Hamp 1E **148**
Beardsley Ter. *RM8: Dag* *5B 72*
(off Stonard Rd.)
Beardsley Way W3 2K **97**
Beard's Rd. TW15: Ashf 6G **129**
Bearfield Rd. KT2: King T 7E **132**
Bear Gdns. SE1 4C **14** (1C **102**)
Bear La. SE1 4B **14** (1B **102**)
Bear Rd. TW13: Hanw 4B **130**
Bearstead Ri. SE4 5B **122**
Bearsted Ter. BR3: Beck 1C **158**
Bear St. WC2 2D **12** (7H **83**)
Beasley's Ait TW16: Sun 6H **147**
Beasley's Ait La. TW16: Sun 6H **147**
Beaton Cl. SE15 1F **121**
Beatrice Av. HA9: Wemb 5E **60**
SW16 3K **155**
Beatrice Cl. E13 4J **87**
HA5: Eastc 4J **39**
Beatrice Ct. IG9: Buck H 2G **37**
Beatrice Ho. *W6* *5E 98*
(off Queen Caroline St.)
Beatrice Pl. W8 3K **99**
Beatrice Rd. E17 5C **50**
N4 7A **48**
N9 7D **24**
SE1 4G **103**
TW10: Rich 5F **115**
UB1: S'hall 1D **94**
Beatrice Webb Ho. *E3* *2A 86*
(off Chisenhale Rd.)
Beatrix Ho. *SW5* *5K 99*
(off Old Brompton Rd.)
Beatson Wlk. SE16 1A **104**
(not continuous)
Beattie Cl. TW14: Felt 7H **111**
Beattie Ho. SW8 1G **119**
Beattock Ri. N10 4F **47**
Beatty Ho. *E14* *2C 104*
(off Admirals Way)
SW1 *6B 18*
(off Dolphin Sq.)
Beatty Rd. HA7: Stan 6H **27**
N16 4E **66**
Beatty St. NW1 2G **83**
Beattyville Gdns. IG6: Ilf 4E **52**
Beauchamp Cl. W4 3J **97**
Beauchamp Ct. *EN5: Barn* *4C 20*
(off Victors Way)
HA7: Stan 5H **27**
Beauchamp Pl. SW3 1D **16** (3C **100**)
Beauchamp Rd. E7 7K **69**
KT8: W Mole, E Mos 5F **149**
SE19 1D **156**
SM1: Sutt 4J **165**
SW11 4C **118**
TW1: Twick 7A **114**
Beauchamp St. EC1 6J **7** (5A **84**)
Beauchamp Ter. SW15 3D **116**
Beauclerc Ct. TW16: Sun 2A **148**
Beauclerc Rd. W6 3D **98**
Beauclere Ho. SM2: Sutt 6A **166**
Beauclerk Cl. TW13: Felt 1K **129**
Beauclerk Ho. SW16 3J **137**
Beaudesert M.
UB7: W Dray 2A **92**
Beaufort E6 5E **88**
Beaufort Av. HA3: Kenton 4A **42**
Beaufort Cl. E4 6J **35**
RM7: Mawney 4J **55**
SW15 7D **116**
W5 5F **79**
Beaufort Ct. *E14* *2C 104*
(off Admirals Way)
EN5: New Bar 5F **21**
N11 *5A 32*
(off The Limes Av.)
SW6 6J **99**
TW10: Ham 4C **132**
Beaufort Dr. NW11 4J **45**
Beaufort Gdns. IG1: Ilf 1E **70**
NW4 6E **44**
SW3 1D **16** (3C **100**)
SW16 7K **137**
TW5: Hest 1C **112**
Beaufort Ho. *E16* *1K 105*
(off Fairfax M.)
SW1 *6C 18*
(off Aylesford St.)
SW1 *5K 17*
(off Sutherland Row)
SW3 *7B 16*
(off Beaufort St.)
Beaufort Mans. SW3 7B **16** (6B **100**)
Beaufort M. SW6 6H **99**
Beaufort Pk. NW11 4J **45**
Beaufort Rd. HA4: Ruis 2F **57**
KT1: King T 4E **150**
TW1: Twick 7C **114**
TW10: Ham 4C **132**
W5 5F **79**
Beaufort St. SW3 7A **16** (6B **100**)
Beaufort Ter. *E14* *5E 104*
(off Ferry St.)
Beaufort Way KT17: Ewe 7C **164**
Beaufoy Ho. SE27 3B **138**
SW8 *7K 101*
(off Rita Rd.)
Beaufoy Rd. N17 7K **33**
Beaufoy Wlk. SE11 4H **19** (4K **101**)
Beaulieu Av. E16 1K **105**
SE26 4H **139**
Beaulieu Cl. CR4: Mitc 1E **154**
NW9 4A **44**
SE5 3D **120**
TW1: Twick 6D **114**
TW4: Houn 5D **112**
Beaulieu Ct. W5 5E **78**
Beaulieu Dr. HA5: Pinn 6B **40**
Beaulieu Gdns. N21 7H **23**
Beaulieu Lodge *E14* *3F 105*
(off Schooner Cl.)
Beaulieu Pl. W4 3J **97**
Beaumanor Gdns. SE9 4E **142**
Beaumanor Mans. *W2* *7K 81*
(off Queensway)
Beaumaris Dr. IG8: Wfd G 7G **37**
Beaumaris Grn. NW9 6A **44**
Beaumaris Twr. *W3* *2H 97*
(off Park Rd. Nth.)
Beaumont *W14* *4H 99*
(off Kensington Village)
Beaumont Av. HA0: Wemb 5C **60**
HA2: Harr 6F **41**
TW9: Rich 3F **115**
W14 5H **99**
Beaumont Bldgs. *WC2* *1F 13*
(off Martlett Ct.)
Beaumont Cl. KT2: King T 7G **133**
N2 4C **46**
Beaumont Ct. E1 3A **86**
E5 3H **67**
HA0: Wemb 5C **60**
NW1 1H **83**
NW9 *2B 44*
(off Cherry Cl.)
W1 *5H 5*
(off Beaumont St.)
W4 5J **97**
Beaumont Cres. W14 5H **99**
Beaumont Dr. KT4: Wor Pk 7D **152**
TW15: Ashf 5F **129**
Beaumont Gdns. NW3 3J **63**
Beaumont Gro. E1 4K **85**
Beaumont Ho. *E10* *7D 50*
(off Skelton's La.)
W9 *3H 81*
(off Fernhead Rd.)
Beaumont Lodge *E8* *6G 67*
(off Greenwood Rd.)
Beaumont M. HA5: Pinn 3C **40**
W1 5H **5** (5E **82**)
Beaumont Pl. EN5: Barn 1C **20**
TW7: Isle 5K **113**
W1 3B **6** (4G **83**)
Beaumont Ri. N19 1H **65**
Beaumont Rd. BR5: Pet W 6H **161**
E10 7D **50**
(not continuous)
E13 3K **87**
SE19 6C **138**
SW19 7G **117**
W4 3J **97**
Beaumont Sq. E1 5K **85**
Beaumont St. W1 5H **5** (5E **82**)
Beaumont Ter. *SE13* *7G 123*
(off Wellmeadow Rd.)
Beaumont Wlk. NW3 7D **64**
Beauvais Ter. UB5: N'olt 3B **76**
Beauvale *NW1* *7E 64*
(off Ferdinand St.)
Beauval Rd. SE22 6F **121**
Beaux Arts Bldg., The
N7 3J **65**
Beaverbank Rd. SE9 1H **143**
Beaver Cl. SE20 7G **139**
SM4: Mord 7E **152**
TW12: Hamp 1F **149**
Beaver Ct. BR3: Beck 7D **140**
Beaver Gro. UB5: N'olt 3C **76**
Beavers Cres. TW4: Houn 4A **112**
Beavers La. TW4: Houn 2A **112**
(not continuous)
Beavers La. Campsite TW4: Houn 4B **112**
Beavers Lodge DA14: Sidc 4K **143**
Beaverwood Rd. BR7: Chst 5J **143**
Beavor Gro. *W6* *5C 98*
(off Beavor La.)
Beavor La. W6 5C **98**
Bebbington Rd. SE18 4J **107**
Beblets Cl. BR6: Chels 5K **173**
Beccles Dr. IG11: Bark 6J **71**
Beccles St. E14 6B **86**
Bec Cl. HA4: Ruis 3B **58**
Bechervaise Ct. *E10* *1D 68*
(off Leyton Grange Est.)
Bechtel Ho. *W6* *4F 99*
(off Hammersmith Rd.)
Beck Cl. SE13 1D **122**
Beck Ct. BR3: Beck 3K **157**
BECKENHAM 1C **158**
Beckenham Bus. Cen. BR3: Beck 6A **140**
Beckenham Crematorium BR3: Beck 3J **157**
Beckenham Gdns. N9 3K **33**
Beckenham Gro. BR2: Brom 2F **159**
Beckenham Hill Est. BR3: Beck 5D **140**
Beckenham Hill Rd. BR3: Beck 6D **140**
SE6 6D **140**
Beckenham La. BR2: Brom 2G **159**
Beckenham Pl. Pk. BR3: Beck 7D **140**
Beckenham Place Pk. Nature Reserve
6E **140**
Beckenham Rd. BR3: Beck 1K **157**
BR4: W W'ck 7D **158**
Beckenham Theatre Cen., The 2D **158**
Beckers, The N16 4G **67**
Becket Av. E6 3E **88**
Becket Cl. SE25 6G **157**
SW19 *1K 153*
(off High Path)
Becket Fold HA1: Harr 5K **41**
Becket Ho. *E16* *1K 105*
(off Constable Av.)
SE1 7E **14**
Becket Rd. N18 4D **34**
Becket St. SE1 7E **14** (3D **102**)
Beckett Cl. DA17: Belv 3F **109**
NW10 6A **62**
SW16 2H **137**
Beckett Ho. *E1* *5J 85*
(off Jubilee St.)
SW9 2J **119**
Becketts Cl. BR6: Orp 3K **173**
DA5: Bexl 1J **145**
TW14: Felt 6K **111**
Becketts Ho. IG1: Ilf 3E **70**
Becketts Pl. KT1: Ham W 1D **150**
Becketts Wharf *KT1: Ham W* *1D 150*
(off Lwr. Teddington Rd.)
Beckett Wlk. BR3: Beck 6A **140**
Beckfoot *NW1* *1B 6*
(off Ampthill Est.)
Beckford Cl. W14 4H **99**
Beckford Dr. BR5: Orp 7H **161**
Beckford Ho. N16 5E **66**
Beckford Pl. SE17 5C **102**
Beckford Rd. CR0: C'don 6F **157**
Beckham Ho. SE11 4H **19** (4K **101**)
Beckhaven Ho. *SE11* *4A 102*
(off Gilbert Rd.)
Beck Ho. *N18* *5C 34*
(off Upton Rd.)
Beck La. BR3: Beck 3K **157**
Beckley Ho. *E3* *4B 86*
(off Hamlets Way)
Becklow Gdns. *W12* *2C 98*
(off Becklow Rd.)
Becklow M. *W12* *2C 98*
(off Becklow Rd.)
Becklow Rd. W12 2B **98**
(not continuous)
Beck River Pk. BR3: Beck 1C **158**
Beck Rd. CR4: Mitc 6D **154**
E8 1H **85**
Becks Rd. DA14: Sidc 3A **144**
Beck Theatre, The 6H **75**
BECKTON 5E **88**
BECKTON ALPS 4D **88**
BECKTON PARK 6D **88**
Beckton Retail Pk. E6 5E **88**
Beckton Rd. E16 5H **87**
Beckton Triangle Retail Pk. E6 4F **89**
Beck Way BR3: Beck 3B **158**
Beckway Rd. SW16 2H **155**
Beckway St. SE17 4E **102**
(not continuous)
Beckwith Ho. *E2* *2H 85*
(off Wadeson St.)

194 A-Z London

Beckwith Rd. SE24 5D 120
Beclands Rd. SW17 6E 136
Becmead Av. HA3: Kenton 5B 42
SW16 4H 137
Becondale Rd. SE19 5E 138
BECONTREE 4D 72
Becontree Av. RM8: Dag 4B 72
Becquerel Ct. *SE10* *3H 105*
(off West Parkside)
Bective Pl. SW15 4H 117
Bective Rd. E7 4J 69
SW15 4H 117
Becton Pl. DA8: Erith 7H 109
Bedale Rd. EN2: Enf 1H 23
Bedale St. SE1 5E 14 (1D 102)
Beddalls Farm Ct. E6 5B 88
BEDDINGTON 4J 167
BEDDINGTON CORNER 7E 154
Beddington Cross CR0: Bedd 7H 155
Beddington Farm Rd. CR0: Bedd 7J 155
Beddington Gdns. SM5: Cars 6E 166
SM6: Wall 6E 166
Beddington Grn. BR5: St P 1K 161
Beddington Gro. SM6: Wall 5H 167
Beddington La. CR0: C'don 5G 155
Beddington Pk. 3F 167
Beddington Pk. Cotts.
SM6: Bedd 3H 167
Beddington Path BR5: St P 1K 161
Beddington Rd. BR5: St P 2J 161
IG3: Ilf 7K 53
Beddington Ter. CR0: C'don 7K 155
Beddington Trad. Est. CR0: Bedd 1J 167
Bede Cl. HA5: Pinn 1B 40
Bedefield WC1 2F 7 (3J 83)
Bede Ho. *SE14* *1B 122*
(off Clare Rd.)
Bedens Rd. DA14: Sidc 6E 144
Bede Rd. RM6: Chad H 6C 54
Bedevere Rd. N9 3B 34
Bedfont Cl. CR4: Mitc 2E 154
TW14: Bedf 6E 110
Bedfont Ct. TW19: Stan M 6B 174
Bedfont Ct. Est. TW19: Stan M 7C 174
Bedfont Grn. Cl. TW14: Bedf 1E 128
Bedfont Ind. Pk. TW15: Ashf 3E 128
Bedfont Ind. Pk. Nth. TW15: Ashf 3E 128
Bedfont Lakes Country Pk. 2E 128
Bedfont Lakes Country Pk. Info. Cen.
3D 128
Bedfont La. TW13: Felt 7G 111
TW14: Felt 7G 111
Bedfont Rd. TW13: Felt 1E 128
TW14: Bedf 1E 128
TW19: Stanw 6A 110
Bedfont Trad. Est. TW14: Bedf 2F 129
Bedford Av. EN5: Barn 5C 20
UB4: Yead 6K 75
WC1 6D 6 (5H 83)
Bedfordbury WC2 2E 12 (7J 83)
(not continuous)
Bedford Cl. N10 7K 31
W4 6A 98
Bedford Cnr. *W4* *4A 98*
(off South Pde.)
Bedford Ct. *CR0: C'don* *1C 168*
(off Tavistock Rd.)
WC2 3E 12 (7J 83)
Bedford Ct. Mans. WC1 6D 6
Bedford Gdns. W8 1J 99
Bedford Gdns. Ho. *W8* *1J 99*
(off Bedford Gdns.)
Bedford Hill SW12 1F 137
SW16 1F 137
Bedford Ho. *SW4* *4J 119*
(off Solon New Rd. Est.)
Bedford M. N2 3C 46
SE6 2D 140
BEDFORD PARK 3K 97
Bedford Pk. CR0: C'don 1C 168
Bedford Pk. Cnr. W4 4A 98
Bedford Pk. Mans. W4 4K 97
Bedford Pas. *SW6* *7G 99*
(off Dawes Rd.)
W1 5B 6 (5G 83)
Bedford Pl. CR0: C'don 1D 168
WC1 5E 6 (5J 83)
Bedford Rd. DA15: Sidc 3J 143
E6 1E 88
E17 2C 50
E18 2J 51
HA1: Harr 6G 41
HA4: Ruis 4H 57
IG1: Ilf 3F 71
KT4: Wor Pk 2E 164
N2 3C 46
N8 6H 47
N9 7C 24
N15 4E 48
N22 2J 47
NW7 2F 29
SW4 4J 119
TW2: Twick 3H 131
W4 3K 97
W13 7B 78
Bedford Row WC1 5H 7 (5K 83)
Bedford Sq. WC1 6D 6 (5H 83)
Bedford St. WC2 2E 12 (7J 83)
Bedford Ter. SM2: Sutt 6A 166
SW2 5J 119
Bedford Way WC1 4D 6 (4H 83)
Bedgebury Ct. E17 2E 50
Bedgebury Gdns. SW19 2G 135
Bedgebury Rd. SE9 4B 124
Bedivere Rd. BR1: Brom 3J 141
Bedlam M. SE11 3J 19
Bedlow Way CR0: Bedd 4K 167
Bedmond Ho. *SW3* *5C 16*
(off Cale St.)
Bedonwell Rd. DA7: Belv, Bex, Erith 6F 109
DA17: Belv 6E 108
SE2 6E 108
Bedser Cl. CR7: Thor H 3C 156
SE11 7H 19 (6K 101)
Bedser Dr. UB6: G'frd 5H 59
Bedster Gdns. KT8: W Mole 2F 149
Bedwardine Rd. SE19 7E 138
Bedwell Ct. *RM6: Chad H* *7D 54*
(off Chapel La.)
Bedwell Gdns. UB3: Harl 5G 93
(not continuous)
Bedwell Ho. SW9 2A 120
Bedwell Rd. DA17: Belv 5G 109
N17 1E 48
Beeby Rd. E16 5K 87
Beech Av. DA15: Sidc 7A 126
HA4: Ruis 1K 57
IG9: Buck H 2E 36
N20 1H 31
TW8: Bford 7B 96
W3 1A 98
Beech Cl. N9 6B 24
SE8 6C 104
SM5: Cars 2D 166
SW15 7C 116
SW19 6E 134
TW15: Ashf 5F 129
TW16: Sun 2B 148
UB7: W Dray 3C 92
Beech Copse BR1: Brom 1D 160
CR2: S Croy 5E 168
Beech Ct. *BR1: Brom* *1H 159*
(off Blyth Rd.)
BR3: Beck 7B 140
IG1: Ilf *3E 70*
(off Riverdene Rd.)
KT6: Surb 7D 150
UB5: N'olt 1C 76
W9 *5J 81*
(off Elmfield Way)
Beech Cres. Ct. N5 4B 66
Beechcroft BR7: Chst 7E 142
Beechcroft Av. DA7: Bex 1K 127
HA2: Harr 7E 40
Beechcroft Av. KT3: N Mald 1J 151
NW11 7H 45
Beechcroft Cl. BR6: Orp 4H 173
SW16 5K 137
TW5: Hest 7C 94
Beechcroft Ct. N12 4E 30
NW11 *7H 45*
(off Beechcroft Av.)
Beechcroft Gdns. HA9: Wemb 3F 61
Beechcroft Ho. W5 5E 78
Beechcroft Lodge SM2: Sutt 7A 166
Beechcroft Rd. BR6: Orp 4H 173
E18 2K 51
KT9: Chess 3F 163
SW14 3J 115
SW17 2C 136
Beechdale N21 2E 32
Beechdale Rd. SW2 6K 119
Beech Dell BR2: Kes 4D 172
Beechdene *SE15* *1H 121*
(off Carlton Gro.)
Beech Dr. N2 2D 46
Beechen Cliff Way TW7: Isle 2K 113
Beechen Gro. HA5: Pinn 3D 40
Beechen Pl. SE23 2K 139
Beeches, The *CR2: S Croy* *5D 168*
(off Blunt Rd.)
E12 7C 70
TW3: Houn 1F 113
Beeches Av. SM5: Cars 7C 166
Beeches Cl. SE20 1J 157
Beeches Rd. SM3: Sutt 1G 165
SW17 3C 136
Beeches Wlk. SM5: Cars 7B 166
Beechey Ho. *E1* *1H 103*
(off Watts St.)
Beechfield Cotts. BR1: Brom 1A 160
Beechfield Ct. *CR2: S Croy* *4C 168*
(off Bramley Hill)
Beechfield Gdns. RM7: Rush G 7J 55
Beechfield Rd. BR1: Brom 2A 160
DA8: Erith 7K 109
N4 6C 48
SE6 1B 140
Beech Gdns. *EC2* *5C 8*
(off Beech St.)
RM10: Dag 7J 73
W5 2E 96
Beech Gro. CR4: Mitc 5H 155
(not continuous)
KT3: N Mald 3K 151
Beech Hall Cres. E4 7A 36
Beech Hall Rd. E4 7K 35
Beech Haven Ct. *DA1: Cray* *5K 127*
(off London Rd.)
Beech Hill EN4: Had W 1G 21
Beech Hill Av. EN4: Had W 1F 21
Beechhill Rd. SE9 5E 124
Beech Ho. CR0: New Ad 6D 170
E17 3F 51
SE16 *2J 103*
(off Ainsty Est.)
Beech Ho. Rd. CR0: C'don 3D 168
Beech La. IG9: Buck H 2E 36
Beech Lawns N12 5G 31
Beechmont Cl. BR1: Brom 5G 141
Beechmore Gdns. SM3: Cheam 2F 165
Beechmore Rd. SW11 1D 118
Beechmount Av. W7 5H 77
Beecholme N12 5E 30
Beecholme Av. CR4: Mitc 1F 155
Beecholme Est. E5 3H 67
Beech Rd. N11 6D 32
SW16 2J 155
TW14: Bedf 7G 111
Beechrow TW10: Ham 4E 132
Beech St. EC2 5C 8 (5C 84)
RM7: Rom 4J 55
Beech Tree Cl. HA7: Stan 5H 27
N1 7A 66
Beech Tree Glade E4 1C 36
Beech Tree Pl. SM1: Sutt 5K 165
Beechvale Cl. N12 5H 31
Beech Wlk. N17 3F 49
NW7 6F 29
Beech Way NW10 7K 61
TW2: Twick 3E 130
Beechway DA5: Bexl 6D 126
Beechwood Av. BR6: Chels 5J 173
CR7: Thor H 4B 156
HA2: Harr 3F 59
HA4: Ruis 2H 57
N3 3H 45
TW9: Kew 1G 115
TW16: Sun 6J 129
UB3: Hayes 7F 75
UB6: G'frd 3F 77
UB8: Hil 6C 74
Beechwood Cen., The *BR2: Brom* *1D 172*
(off Lwr. Gravel Rd.)
Beechwood Circ. HA2: Harr 3F 59
Beechwood Cl. KT6: Surb 7C 150
N2 *4D 46*
(off Western Rd.)
NW7 5F 29
Beechwood Ct. SM5: Cars 4D 166
TW16: Sun 6J 129
W4 6K 97
Beechwood Cres. DA7: Bex 3D 126
Beechwood Dr. BR2: Kes 4B 172
IG8: Wfd G 5C 36
Beechwood Gdns. HA2: Harr 3F 59
IG5: Ilf 5D 52
NW10 3F 79
Beechwood Gro. KT6: Surb 7C 150
W3 7A 80
Beechwood Hall N3 3H 45
Beechwood Ho. *E2* *2G 85*
(off Teale St.)
Beechwood M. N9 2B 34
Beechwood Pk. E18 3J 51
Beechwood Ri. BR7: Chst 4F 143
Beechwood Rd. CR2: Sande 7E 168
E8 6F 67
N8 4H 47
Beechwoods Ct. SE19 5F 139
Beechworth NW6 7G 63
Beechworth Cl. NW3 2J 63
Beecroft La. SE4 5A 122
Beecroft M. SE4 5A 122
Beecroft Rd. SE4 5A 122
Beehive Cl. E8 7F 67
UB10: Uxb 7B 56
Beehive Ct. IG1: Ilf 6D 52
Beehive La. IG1: Ilf 5D 52
IG4: Ilf 5D 52
Beehive Pas. *EC3* *1G 15*
(off Lime St.)
Beehive Pl. SW9 3A 120
Beeken Dene BR6: Farnb 4G 173
Beeleigh Rd. SM4: Mord 4K 153
Beemans Row SW18 2A 136
Beeston Cl. E8 5G 67
Beeston Ho. *SE1* *3D 102*
(off Burbage Cl.)
Beeston Pl. SW1 1K 17 (3F 101)
Beeston Rd. EN4: E Barn 6G 21
Beeston Way TW14: Felt 6A 112
Beethoven St. W10 3G 81
Beeton Cl. HA5: Hat E 1E 40
Beeton Way SE27 4D 138
Begbie Rd. SE3 1A 124
BEGGAR'S HILL 6B 164
Beggar's Hill KT17: Ewe 7B 164
Beggars Roost La. SM1: Sutt 6J 165
Begonia Cl. E6 5D 88
Begonia Pl. TW12: Hamp 6E 130
Begonia Wlk. W12 6B 80
Beira St. SW12 7F 119
Bejun Ct. EN5: New Bar 4F 21
Bekesbourne St. E14 6A 86
Belcroft Cl. BR1: Brom 7H 141
Beldanes Lodge NW10 7C 62
Beldham Gdns. KT8: W Mole 2F 149

Belfairs Dr.—Benbow St.

Belfairs Dr. RM6: Chad H 7C 54
Belfast Rd. N16 2F 67
SE25 4H 157
Belfield Rd. KT19: Ewe 7K 163
Belfont Wlk. N7 4J 65
(not continuous)
Belford Gro. SE18 4E 106
Belford Ho. E8 1F 85
Belfort Rd. SE15 2J 121
Belfry Cl. BR1: Brom 4F 161
SE16 5H 103
Belfry Rd. E12 2B 70
Belgrade Rd. N16 4E 66
TW12: Hamp 1F 149
Belgrave Cl. N14 5B 22
NW7 5E 28
W3 2H 97
Belgrave Ct. E2 2H 85
(off Temple St.)
E13 4A 88
E14 7B 86
(off Westferry Cir.)
SW8 7G 101
(off Ascalon St.)
W4 5J 97
Belgrave Cres. TW16: Sun 1K 147
Belgrave Gdns. HA7: Stan 5H 27
N14 5C 22
NW8 1K 81
Belgrave Hgts. E11 1J 69
Belgrave Ho. SW9 7A 102
Belgrave Mans. NW8 1K 81
(off Belgrave Gdns.)
Belgrave M. Nth. SW1 7G 11 (2E 100)
Belgrave M. Sth. SW1 1H 17 (3E 100)
Belgrave M. W. SW1 1G 17 (3E 100)
Belgrave Pl. SW1 1H 17 (3E 100)
Belgrave Rd. CR4: Mitc 3B 154
E10 1E 68
E11 2J 69
E13 4A 88
E17 5C 50
IG1: Ilf 1D 70
SE25 4F 157
SW1 3K 17 (4F 101)
SW13 7B 98
TW4: Houn 3D 112
TW16: Sun 1K 147
Belgrave Sq. SW1 1G 17 (3E 100)
Belgrave St. E1 5K 85
Belgrave Ter. IG8: Wfd G 3D 36
Belgrave Wlk. CR4: Mitc 3B 154
Belgrave Yd. SW1 2J 17
BELGRAVIA 2H 17 (3E 100)
Belgravia Cl. EN5: Barn 3C 20
Belgravia Ct. SW1 2J 17
Belgravia Gdns. BR1: Brom 6G 141
Belgravia Ho. SW1 1G 17
(off Halkin Pl.)
SW4 6H 119
Belgravia M. KT1: King T 4D 150
Belgravia Workshops N19 2J 65
(off Marlborough Rd.)
Belgrove St. WC1 1F 7 (3J 83)
Belham Wlk. SE5 1D 120
Belinda Rd. SW9 3B 120
Belitha Vs. N1 7K 65
BELL, THE 3C 50
Bella Best Ho. SW1 5K 17
(off Westmoreland Ter.)
Bellamy Cl. E14 2C 104
HA8: Edg 2D 28
UB10: Ick 3C 56
W14 5H 99
Bellamy Ct. HA7: Stan 1B 42
Bellamy Dr. HA7: Stan 1B 42
Bellamy Ho. SW17 4B 136
TW5: Hest 6E 94
Bellamy Rd. E4 6J 35
EN2: Enf 2J 23
Bellamy's Ct. SE16 1K 103
(off Abbotshade Rd.)
Bellamy St. SW12 7F 119
Bel La. TW13: Hanw 3C 130
Bellarmine Cl. SE28 1K 107
Bellasis Av. SW2 2J 137
Bell Av. UB7: W Dray 4B 92
Bell Cl. HA4: Ruis 3H 57
HA5: Pinn 2A 40
Bellclose Rd. UB7: W Dray 2A 92
Bell Ct. NW4 4E 44
Bell Dr. SW18 7G 117
Bellefields Rd. SW9 3K 119
Bellegrove Cl. DA16: Well 2K 125
Bellegrove Pde. DA16: Well 3K 125
Bellegrove Rd. DA16: Well 2H 125
Bellenden Rd. SE15 1F 121
Bellenden Rd. Retail Pk.
SE15 1G 121
Bellestaines Pleasaunce
E4 2H 35
Belleville Rd. SW11 5C 118
Belle Vue UB6: G'frd 1H 77
Belle Vue Est. NW4 4F 45
Belle Vue La. WD23: B Hea 1C 26
Bellevue M. N11 5K 31
Bellevue Pde. SW17 1D 136
Belle Vue Pk. CR7: Thor H 3C 156
Bellevue Pl. E1 4J 85
Belle Vue Rd. E17 2F 51
NW4 4E 44
Bellevue Rd. DA6: Bex 5F 127
KT1: King T 3E 150
(not continuous)
N11 4K 31
SW13 2C 116
SW17 1C 136
W13 4B 78
Bellew St. SW17 3A 136
Bell Farm Av. RM10: Dag 3J 73
Bellfield CR0: Sels 7A 170
Bellfield Av. HA3: Hrw W 6C 26
Bellfield Cl. SE3 7K 105
Bellflower Cl. E6 5C 88
Bell Gdns. E10 1C 68
(off Church Rd.)
Bellgate M. NW5 4F 65
BELL GREEN 4A 140
Bell Grn. SE26 4B 140
Bell Grn. La. SE26 5B 140
Bellhaven E15 6F 69
Bell Hill CR0: C'don 2C 168
Bell Ho. HA9: Wemb 3E 60
SE10 6E 104
(off Haddo St.)
Bellhouse Cotts. UB3: Hayes 7G 75
Bell Ho. Rd. RM7: Rush G 1J 73
Bellina M. NW5 4F 65
Bell Ind. Est. W4 4J 97
BELLINGHAM 3C 140
Bellingham N17 7C 34
(off Park La.)
Bellingham Ct. IG11: Bark 3B 90
Bellingham Grn. SE6 3C 140
Bellingham Leisure & Lifestyle Cen.
3D 140
Bellingham Rd. SE6 3D 140
Bellingham Trad. Est. SE6 3D 140
Bell Inn Yd. EC3 1F 15 (6D 84)
Bell Junc. TW3: Houn 3F 113
Bell La. E1 6J 9 (5F 85)
E16 1H 105
EN3: Enf H, Enf W 1E 24
HA9: Wemb 2D 60
NW4 4F 45
TW1: Twick 1A 132
Bellmaker Ct. E3 5C 86
Bell Mdw. SE19 5E 138
Bell Moor NW3 3A 64
Bello Cl. SE24 7B 120
Bellot Gdns. SE10 5G 105
(off Bellot St.)
Bellot St. SE10 5G 105
Bellring Cl. DA17: Belv 6G 109
Bell Rd. EN1: Enf 1J 23
KT8: E Mos 5H 149
TW3: Houn 3F 113
Bells All. SW6 2J 117
Bells Hill EN5: Barn 5A 20
Bellsize Ct. NW3 5B 64
Bell St. NW1 5C 4 (5C 82)
SE18 1C 124
Belltrees Gro. SW16 5K 137
Bell Vw. Mnr. HA4: Ruis 7F 39
Bell Water Ga. SE18 3E 106
Bell Wharf La. EC4 3D 14 (7C 84)
Bellwood Rd. SE15 4K 121
Bell Yd. WC2 1J 13 (6A 84)
Bell Yd. M. SE1 7H 15
Belmarsh Rd. SE28 2J 107
BELMONT
HA3 2A 42
SM2 7J 165
Belmont Av. DA16: Well 2J 125
EN4: Cockf 5J 21
HA0: Wemb 1F 79
KT3: N Mald 5C 152
N9 1B 34
N13 5E 32
N17 3C 48
UB2: S'hall 3C 94
Belmont Circ. HA3: Kenton 1B 42
Belmont Cl. E4 5A 36
EN4: Cockf 4J 21
IG8: Wfd G 4E 36
N20 1E 30
SW4 3G 119
UB8: Uxb 6A 56
Belmont Ct. N5 4C 66
NW11 5H 45
Belmont Gro. SE13 3F 123
W4 4K 97
Belmont Hall Ct. SE13 3F 123
Belmont Hill SE13 3E 122
Belmont La. BR7: Chst 5G 143
HA7: Stan 1C 42
Belmont Lodge HA3: Hrw W 7C 26
Belmont M. SW19 2F 135
Belmont Pde. BR7: Chst 5G 143
NW11 5H 45
Belmont Pk. SE13 4F 123
Belmont Pk. Cl. SE13 4G 123
Belmont Pk. Rd. E10 6D 50
Belmont Ri. SM2: Sutt 6H 165
Belmont Rd. BR3: Beck 2A 158
BR7: Chst 5F 143
DA8: Erith 7G 109
HA3: W'stone 3K 41
IG1: Ilf 3G 71
N15 4C 48
N17 4C 48
SE25 5H 157
SM6: Wall 5F 167
SW4 3G 119
TW2: Twick 2H 131
UB8: Uxb 7A 56
W4 4K 97
Belmont St. NW1 7E 64
Belmont Ter. W4 4K 97
Belmore Av. UB4: Hayes 6J 75
Belmore Ho. N7 5H 65
Belmore La. N7 5H 65
Belmore St. SW8 1H 119
Beloe Cl. SW15 4C 116
Belsham St. E9 6J 67
Belsize Av. N13 6E 32
NW3 6B 64
W13 3B 96
Belsize Ct. SM1: Sutt 4K 165
Belsize Ct. Garages NW3 5B 64
(off Belsize La.)
Belsize Cres. NW3 5B 64
Belsize Gdns. SM1: Sutt 4K 165
Belsize Gro. NW3 6C 64
Belsize La. NW3 6B 64
Belsize M. NW3 6B 64
Belsize Pk. NW3 6B 64
Belsize Pk. Gdns. NW3 6B 64
Belsize Pk. M. NW3 6B 64
Belsize Pl. NW3 5B 64
Belsize Rd. HA3: Hrw W 7C 26
NW6 1K 81
Belsize Sq. NW3 6B 64
Belsize Ter. NW3 6B 64
Belson Rd. SE18 4D 106
Beltane Dr. SW19 3F 135
Belthorn Cres. SW12 7G 119
Belton Rd. DA14: Sidc 4A 144
E7 7K 69
E11 4G 69
N17 3E 48
NW2 6C 62
Belton Way E3 5C 86
Beltran Rd. SW6 2K 117
Beltwood Rd. DA17: Belv 4J 109
BELVEDERE 3G 109
Belvedere, The SW10 1A 118
(off Chelsea Harbour)
Belvedere Av. IG5: Ilf 2F 53
SW19 5G 135
Belvedere Bldgs. SE1 7B 14 (2B 102)
Belvedere Bus. Pk. DA17: Belv 2H 109
Belvedere Cl. TW11: Tedd 5J 131
Belvedere Ct. DA17: Belv 3F 109
N1 1E 84
(off De Beauvoir Cres.)
N2 5B 46
NW2 6F 63
(off Willesden La.)
SW15 4E 116
Belvedere Dr. SW19 5G 135
Belvedere Gdns. KT8: W Mole 5D 148
Belvedere Gro. SW19 5G 135
Belvedere Ho. TW13: Felt 1J 129
(off Lemon Gro.)
Belvedere Ind. Est. DA17: Belv 1J 109
Belvedere Link Bus. Pk. DA8: Erith 3J 109
Belvedere M. SE3 7K 105
SE15 3J 121
Belvedere Pl. SE1 7B 14 (2B 102)
SW2 4K 119
Belvedere Rd. DA7: Bex 3F 127
E10 1A 68
SE1 7G 13 (2K 101)
SE2 1C 108
SE19 7F 139
W7 3K 95
Belvedere Sq. SW19 5G 135
Belvedere Strand NW9 2B 44
Belvedere Way HA3: Kenton 6E 42
Belvoir Cl. SE9 3C 142
Belvoir Ho. SW1 4G 101
Belvoir Rd. SE22 7G 121
Belvue Bus. Cen. UB5: N'olt 7F 59
Belvue Cl. UB5: N'olt 7E 58
Belvue Rd. UB5: N'olt 7E 58
Bembridge Cl. NW6 7G 63
Bembridge Gdns. HA4: Ruis 2F 57
Bembridge Ho. KT2: King T 2G 151
(off Coombe Rd.)
SE8 4B 104
(off Longshore)
SW18 6K 117
(off Iron Mill Rd.)
Bemersyde Point E13 3K 87
(off Dongola Rd. W.)
Bemerton Est. N1 7J 65
Bemerton St. N1 1K 83
Bemish Rd. SW15 3F 117
Bempton Dr. HA4: Ruis 2K 57
Bemsted Rd. E17 3B 50
Benares Rd. SE18 4K 107
Benbow Ct. W6 3E 98
(off Benbow Rd.)
Benbow Ho. SE8 6C 104
(off Benbow St.)
Benbow Rd. W6 3D 98
Benbow St. SE8 6C 104

Benbury Cl.—Berkshire Rd.

Benbury Cl. BR1: Brom 5E **140**
Bence Ho. *SE8* *4A* ***104***
(off Rainsborough Av.)
Bench, The TW10: Ham 3C **132**
Bench Fld. CR2: S Croy 6F **169**
Bencroft Rd. SW16 ....7G **137**
Bencurtis Pk. BR4: W W'ck 3F **171**
Bendall Ho. *NW1* *5D* ***4***
(off Bell St.)
Bendall M. NW1 ....5D **4**
Bendemeer Rd. SW15 ....3F **117**
Benden Ho. *SE13* *5E* ***122***
(off Monument Gdns.)
Bendish Point SE28 ....2G **107**
Bendish Rd. E6 ....7C **70**
Bendmore Av. SE2 ....5A **108**
Bendon Valley SW18 ....7K **117**
Benedict Cl. BR6: Orp 3J **173**
DA17: Belv 3E **108**
Benedict Ct. RM6: Chad H 6F **55**
Benedict Dr. TW14: Bedf 7F **111**
Benedict Rd. CR4: Mitc 3B **154**
SW9 ....3K **119**
Benedicts Wharf IG11: Bark 1F **89**
Benedict Way N2 ....3A **46**
Benedict Wharf CR4: Mitc 3C **154**
Benenden Grn. BR2: Brom 5J **159**
Benenden Ho. *SE17* *5E* ***102***
(off Mina Rd.)
Benett Gdns. SW16 ....2J **155**
Ben Ezra Ct. *SE17* *4C* ***102***
(off Asolando Dr.)
Benfleet Cl. SM1: Sutt 3A **166**
Benfleet Ct. E8 ....1F **85**
Benfleet Way N11 ....2K **31**
Bengal Ct. *EC3* *1F* ***15***
(off Birchin La.)
Bengal Ho. *E1* *5K* ***85***
(off Duckett St.)
Bengal Rd. IG1: Ilf 4F **71**
Bengarth Dr. HA3: Hrw W 2H **41**
Bengarth Rd. UB5: N'olt 1C **76**
Bengeo Gdns. RM6: Chad H 6C **54**
Bengeworth Rd. HA1: Harr 2A **60**
SE5 ....3C **120**
Ben Hale Cl. HA7: Stan 5G **27**
Benham Cl. KT9: Chess 6C **162**
SW11 ....3B **118**
Benham Gdns. TW4: Houn 5D **112**
Benham Ho. *SW10* *7K* ***99***
(off Coleridge Gdns.)
Benham Rd. W7 ....5J **77**
Benham's Pl. NW3 ....4A **64**
Benhill Av. SM1: Sutt 4K **165**
(not continuous)
Benhill Rd. SE5 ....7D **102**
SM1: Sutt 3A **166**
Benhill Wood Rd. SM1: Sutt 3A **166**
BENHILTON **2K 165**
Benhilton Gdns. SM1: Sutt 3K **165**
Benhurst Ct. SW16 ....5A **138**
Benhurst La. SW16 ....5A **138**
Benin Ho. *WC1* *6G* ***7***
(off Procter St.)
Benin St. SE13 ....7F **123**
Benjafield Cl. N18 ....4C **34**
Benjamin Cl. E8 ....1G **85**
Benjamin Ct. DA17: Belv 6F **109**
TW15: Ashf 7E **128**
Benjamin Franklin House *4E* ***12***
(off Craven St.)
Benjamin M. SW12 ....7G **119**
Benjamin St. EC1 ....5A **8** (5B **84**)
Ben Jonson Ct. N1 ....2E **84**
Ben Jonson Ho. EC2 ....5D **8**
Ben Jonson Pl. EC2 ....5D **8**
Ben Jonson Rd. E1 ....5K **85**
Benledi Rd. E14 ....6F **87**
Benlow Works *UB3: Hayes* *2H* ***93***
(off Silverdale Rd.)
Bennelong Cl. W12 ....7D **80**
Bennerley Rd. SW11 ....5C **118**
Bennet M. *N19* *3H* ***65***
(off Wedmore St.)
Bennets Courtyard SW19 ....1A **154**
Bennets Fld. Rd. UB11: Stock P 1D **92**
Bennet's Hill EC4 ....2B **14** (7C **84**)
Bennets Lodge EN2: Enf 3G **23**
Bennet St. SW1 ....4A **12** (1G **101**)
Bennett Cl. DA16: Well 2A **126**
HA6: Nwood 1H **39**
KT1: Ham W 1C **150**
TW4: Houn 5C **112**
Bennett Ct. N7 ....3K **65**
Bennett Gro. SE13 ....1D **122**
Bennett Ho. *SW1* *3D* ***18***
(off Page St.)
Bennett Pk. SE3 ....3H **123**
Bennett Rd. E13 ....4A **88**
N16 ....4E **66**
RM6: Chad H 6E **54**
SW9 ....2A **120**
Bennetts Av. CR0: C'don 2A **170**
UB6: G'frd 1J **77**
Bennett's Castle La. RM8: Dag 2C **72**
Bennetts Cl. CR4: Mitc 1F **155**
N17 ....6A **34**
Bennetts Copse BR7: Chst 6C **142**
Bennett St. W4 ....6A **98**
Bennetts Way CR0: C'don 2A **170**
Bennett's Yd. SW1 ....2D **18** (3H **101**)
Benningholme Rd. HA8: Edg 6F **29**
Bennington Rd. IG8: Wfd G 7B **36**
N17 ....1E **48**
Benn's All. TW12: Hamp 2F **149**
Benn St. E9 ....6A **68**
Benns Wlk. *TW9: Rich* *4E* ***114***
(off Michelsdale Dr.)
Benrek Cl. IG6: Ilf 1G **53**
Bensbury Cl. SW15 ....7D **116**
Bensham Cl. CR7: Thor H 4C **156**
Bensham Gro. CR7: Thor H 2C **156**
Bensham La. CR0: C'don 7B **156**
CR7: Thor H 5B **156**
Bensham Mnr. Rd. CR7: Thor H 4C **156**
Bensham Mnr. Rd. Pas.
CR7: Thor H 4C **156**
Bensley Cl. N11 ....5J **31**
Ben Smith Way SE16 ....3G **103**
Benson Av. E6 ....2A **88**
Benson Cl. TW3: Houn 4E **112**
UB8: Hil 5A **74**
Benson Ct. *SW8* *1J* ***119***
(off Hartington Rd.)
Benson Ho. *E2* *3J* ***9***
(off Ligonier St.)
SE1 ....*5K* ***13***
(off Hatfields)
Benson Quay E1 ....7J **85**
Benson Rd. CR0: Wadd 3A **168**
SE23 ....1J **139**
Bentalls Cen., The KT1: King T 2D **150**
Bentfield Gdns. SE9 ....3B **142**
Bentfield Ho. *NW9* *3B* ***44***
(off Heritage Way)
Benthal Rd. N16 ....2G **67**
Bentham Ct. *N1* *7C* ***66***
(off Ecclesbourne Rd.)
Bentham Ho. *SE1* *3D* ***102***
(off Falmouth Rd.)
Bentham Rd. E9 ....6K **67**
SE28 ....7B **90**
Bentham Wlk. NW10 ....5J **61**
Ben Tillet Cl. E16 ....1D **106**
IG11: Bark 7A **72**
Ben Tillet Ho. N15 ....3B **48**
Bentinck Cl. NW8 ....2C **82**
Bentinck Ho. *SW1* *2D* ***18***
(off Monck St.)
W12 ....*7D* ***80***
(off White City Est.)
Bentinck Mans. *W1* *7H* ***5***
(off Bentinck St.)
Bentinck M. W1 ....7H **5** (6E **82**)
Bentinck Rd. UB7: Yiew 1A **92**
Bentinck St. W1 ....7H **5** (6E **82**)
Bentley Cl. SW19 ....3J **135**
Bentley Ct. *SE13* *4E* ***122***
(off Whitburn Rd.)
Bentley Dr. IG2: Ilf 6G **53**
NW2 ....3H **63**
Bentley Ho. *E3* *4C* ***86***
(off Wellington Way)
SE5 ....*1E* ***120***
(off Peckham Rd.)
Bentley Lodge WD23: B Hea 2D **26**
Bentley M. EN1: Enf 6J **23**
Bentley Priory Local Nature Reserve
....4D **26**
Bentley Rd. N1 ....6E **66**
Bentley Way HA7: Stan 5F **27**
IG8: Buck H, Wfd G 2D **36**
Benton Rd. IG1: Ilf 1H **71**
Bentons La. SE27 ....4C **138**
Benton's Ri. SE27 ....5D **138**
Bentry Cl. RM8: Dag 2E **72**
Bentry Rd. RM8: Dag 2E **72**
Bentworth Ct. *E2* *3K* ***9***
(off Granby St.)
Bentworth Rd. W12 ....6D **80**
Benville Ho. *SW8* *7K* ***101***
(off Dorset Rd.)
Benwell Ct. TW16: Sun 1J **147**
Benwell Rd. N7 ....4A **66**
Benwick Cl. SE16 ....4H **103**
Benwood Ct. SM1: Sutt 3A **166**
Benworth St. E3 ....3B **86**
Benyon Ct. *N1* *1E* ***84***
(off De Beauvoir Est.)
Benyon Ho. *EC1* *1K* ***7***
(off Myddelton Pas.)
Benyon Rd. N1 ....1D **84**
Benyon Wharf *N1* *1E* ***84***
(off Kingsland Rd.)
Berberis Ct. IG1: Ilf 6F **71**
Berberis Ho. *E3* *5C* ***86***
(off Gale St.)
TW13: Felt 2J **129**
Berberis Wlk. UB7: W Dray 4A **92**
Berber Pde. SE18 ....1C **124**
Berber Pl. E14 ....7C **86**
Berber Rd. SW11 ....5D **118**
Berberry Cl. HA8: Edg 4D **28**
Bercta Rd. SE9 ....2G **143**
Berebinder Ho. *E3* *2B* ***86***
(off Tredegar Rd.)
Beregaria Ct. *SE11* *7K* ***19***
(off Kennington Pk. Rd.)
Berengers Ct. *RM6: Chad H* *7F* ***55***
(off Whalebone La. Sth.)
Berengers Pl. RM9: Dag 6B **72**
Berenger Twr. *SW10* *7B* ***100***
(off Worlds End Est.)
Berenger Wlk. *SW10* *7B* ***100***
(off Worlds End Est.)
Berens Ct. DA14: Sidc 4K **143**
Berens Rd. NW10 ....3F **81**
Berens Way BR7: Chst 3K **161**
Beresford Av. HA0: Wemb 1F **79**
KT5: Surb 1H **163**
N20 ....2J **31**
TW1: Twick 6C **114**
W7 ....5H **77**
Beresford Dr. BR1: Brom 3C **160**
IG8: Wfd G 4F **37**
Beresford Gdns. EN1: Enf 4K **23**
RM6: Chad H 5E **54**
TW4: Houn 5D **112**
Beresford Rd. E4 ....1B **36**
E17 ....1D **50**
HA1: Harr 5H **41**
KT2: King T 1F **151**
KT3: N Mald 4J **151**
N2 ....3C **46**
N5 ....5D **66**
N8 ....5A **48**
Beresford Rd. SM2: Sutt 7H **165**
UB1: S'hall 1B **94**
Beresford Sq. SE18 ....4F **107**
Beresford St. SE18 ....3F **107**
Beresford Ter. N5 ....5C **66**
Berestede Rd. W6 ....5B **98**
Bere St. E1 ....7K **85**
Bergen Ho. *SE5* *2C* ***120***
(off Carew St.)
Bergenia Ho. TW13: Felt 1K **129**
Bergen Sq. SE16 ....3A **104**
Berger Cl. BR5: Pet W 6H **161**
Berger Rd. E9 ....6K **67**
Berghem M. W14 ....3F **99**
Bergholt Av. IG4: Ilf 5C **52**
Bergholt Cres. N16 ....7E **48**
Bergholt M. NW1 ....7H **65**
Berglen Ct. E14 ....6A **86**
Bering Sq. E14 ....5C **104**
Bering Wlk. E16 ....6B **88**
Berisford M. SW18 ....6A **118**
Berkeley Av. DA7: Bex 1D **126**
IG5: Ilf 2E **52**
RM5: Col R 1J **55**
TW4: Cran 1J **111**
UB6: G'frd 6H **59**
(not continuous)
Berkeley Cl. BR5: Pet W 7J **161**
HA4: Ruis 3J **57**
KT2: King T 7E **132**
Berkeley Ct. *CR0: C'don* *4D* ***168***
(off Coombe Rd.)
KT6: Surb 7D **150**
N3 ....1K **45**
N14 ....6B **22**
NW1 ....4F **5**
NW10 ....4A **62**
NW11 ....*7H* ***45***
(off Ravenscroft Av.)
SM6: Wall 3G **167**
W5 ....7C **78**
Berkeley Cres. EN4: E Barn 5G **21**
Berkeley Dr. KT8: W Mole 3D **148**
Berkeley Gdns. KT10: Clay 6A **162**
KT12: Walt T 7H **147**
N21 ....7J **23**
W8 ....1J **99**
Berkeley Ho. *E3* *3C* ***86***
(off Wellington Way)
SE8 ....*5B* ***104***
(off Grove St.)
TW8: Bford *6D* ***96***
(off Albany Rd.)
Berkeley M. TW16: Sun 3A **148**
W1 ....1F **11** (6D **82**)
Berkeley Pl. SW19 ....6F **135**
Berkeley Rd. E12 ....5C **70**
N8 ....5H **47**
N15 ....6D **48**
NW9 ....4G **43**
SW13 ....1C **116**
UB10: Hil 7E **56**
Berkeleys, The SE25 ....4G **157**
Berkeley Sq. W1 ....3K **11** (7F **83**)
Berkeley St. W1 ....3K **11** (7F **83**)
Berkeley Twr. *E14* *1B* ***104***
(off Westferry Cir.)
Berkeley Wlk. *N7* *2K* ***65***
(off Durham Rd.)
Berkeley Waye TW5: Hest 6B **94**
Berkhampstead Rd. DA17: Belv 5G **109**
Berkhamsted Av. HA9: Wemb 6F **61**
Berkley Cl. *TW2: Twick* *3J* ***131***
(off Wellesley Rd.)
Berkley Gro. NW1 ....7E **64**
Berkley Rd. NW1 ....7D **64**
Berkshire Ct. *W7* *4K* ***77***
(off Copley Cl.)
Berkshire Gdns. N13 ....6F **33**
N18 ....5C **34**
Berkshire Ho. SE6 ....4C **140**
Berkshire Rd. E9 ....6B **68**

Berkshire Way CR4: Mitc 4J **155**
Bermans Way NW10 4A **62**
BERMONDSEY 7K **15** (2G **103**)
Bermondsey Exchange *SE1* *7H* ***15***
(off Bermondsey St.)
Bermondsey Sq. SE1 7H **15** (3E **102**)
Bermondsey St. SE1 5G **15** (1E **102**)
Bermondsey Trad. Est.
SE16 5J **103**
Bermondsey Wall E. SE16 2G **103**
Bermondsey Wall W. SE16 2G **103**
Bernal Cl. SE28 7D **90**
Bernard Angell Ho. *SE10* *6F* ***105***
(off Trafalgar Rd.)
Bernard Ashley Dr. SE7 5K **105**
Bernard Av. W13 3B **96**
Bernard Cassidy St. E16 5H **87**
Bernard Gdns. SW19 5H **135**
Bernard Hegarty Lodge *E8* *7G* ***67***
(off Lansdowne Dr.)
Bernard Ho. E1 6J **9**
E1 *5F* ***85***
(off Toynbee St.)
Bernard Mans. *WC1* *4E* ***6***
(off Bernard St.)
Bernard Myers Ho. *SE5* *7E* ***102***
(off Harris St.)
Bernard Rd. N15 5F **49**
RM7: Rush G 7J **55**
SM6: Wall 4F **167**
Bernard Shaw Ct. *NW1* *7G* ***65***
(off St Pancras Way)
Bernard Shaw Ho. *NW10* *1K* ***79***
(off Knatchbull Rd.)
Bernard St. WC1 4E **6** (4J **83**)
Bernard Sunley Ho. *SW9* *7A* ***102***
(off Sth. Island Pl.)
Bernays Cl. HA7: Stan 6H **27**
Bernays Gro. SW9 4K **119**
Bernel Dr. CR0: C'don 3B **170**
Berne Rd. CR7: Thor H 5C **156**
Berners Dr. W13 7A **78**
Berners Ho. *N1* *2A* ***84***
(off Barnsbury Est.)
Berners M. W1 6B **6** (5G **83**)
Berners Pl. W1 7B **6** (6G **83**)
Berners Rd. N1 1B **84**
N22 1A **48**
Berners St. W1 6B **6** (5G **83**)
Berner Ter. *E1* *6G* ***85***
(off Fairclough St.)
Berney Ho. BR3: Beck 5A **158**
Berney Rd. CR0: C'don 7D **156**
Bernhard Baron Ho. *E1* *6G* ***85***
(off Henriques St.)
Bernhardt Cres. NW8 3C **4** (4C **82**)
Bernhart Cl. HA8: Edg 7D **28**
Bernie Grant Arts Cen. 4F **49**
Bernville Way HA3: Kenton 5F **43**
Bernwell Rd. E4 3B **36**
Berridge Grn. HA8: Edg 7B **28**
Berridge M. NW6 5J **63**
Berridge Rd. SE19 5D **138**
Berriman Rd. N7 3K **65**
Berrington Ho. *W2* *7J* ***81***
(off Herrington Rd.)
Berriton Rd. HA2: Harr 1D **58**
Berrybank Cl. E4 2K **35**
Berry Cl. N21 1G **33**
RM10: Dag 5G **73**
Berry Cotts. *E14* *6A* ***86***
(off Maroon St.)
Berry Ct. TW4: Houn 5D **112**
Berrydale Rd. UB4: Yead 4C **76**
Berryfield Cl. BR1: Brom 1C **160**
E17 4D **50**
Berryfield Rd. SE17 5B **102**
Berry Hill HA7: Stan 4J **27**
Berryhill SE9 4F **125**
Berryhill Gdns. SE9 4F **125**
Berry Ho. *E1* *4H* ***85***
(off Headlam St.)
Berry Ho. *SW11* *2D* ***118***
(off Culvert Rd.)
BERRYLANDS 6G **151**
Berrylands KT5: Surb 6F **151**
SW20 3E **152**
Berrylands Rd. KT5: Surb 6F **151**
Berry La. SE21 4D **138**
Berryman Cl. RM8: Dag 3C **72**
Berryman's La. SE26 4K **139**
Berrymead Gdns. W3 1J **97**
Berrymede Rd. W4 3K **97**
Berry Pl. EC1 2B **8** (3B **84**)
Berry St. EC1 3B **8** (4B **84**)
Berry Way W5 3E **96**
Bertal Rd. SW17 4B **136**
Bertha Hollamby Ct. *DA14: Sidc* *5C* ***144***
(off Sidcup Hill)
Bertha James Ct. BR2: Brom 4K **159**
Berthons Gdns. *E17* *5F* ***51***
(off Wood St.)
Berthon St. SE8 7C **104**
Bertie Rd. NW10 6C **62**
SE26 6K **139**
Bertram Cotts. SW19 7J **135**
Bertram Rd. EN1: Enf 4B **24**
KT2: King T 7G **133**
NW4 6C **44**
Bertram St. N19 2F **65**
Bertrand Ho. *E16* *6K* ***87***
(off Russell Rd.)
SW16 *3J* ***137***
(off Leigham Av.)
Bertrand St. SE13 3D **122**
Bertrand Way SE28 7B **90**
Bert Rd. CR7: Thor H 5C **156**
Bert Way EN1: Enf 4A **24**
Berwick Av. UB4: Yead 6B **76**
Berwick Cl. HA7: Stan 6E **26**
TW2: Whitt 1E **130**
Berwick Ct. SE1 7D **14**
Berwick Cres. DA15: Sidc 7J **125**
Berwick Gdns. SM1: Sutt 3A **166**
Berwick Ho. N2 2B **46**
Berwick Rd. DA16: Well 1B **126**
E16 6K **87**
N22 1B **48**
Berwick St. W1 7B **6** (6G **83**)
Berwick Way BR6: Orp 1K **173**
Berwyn Av. TW3: Houn 1F **113**
Berwyn Rd. SE24 1B **138**
TW10: Rich 4H **115**
Beryl Av. E6 5C **88**
Beryl Ho. *SE18* *5K* ***107***
(off Spinel Cl.)
Beryl Rd. W6 5F **99**
Berystede KT2: King T 7H **133**
Besant Cl. NW2 3G **63**
Besant Ct. N1 5D **66**
SE28 *1B* ***108***
(off Titmuss Av.)
Besant Ho. *NW8* *1A* ***82***
(off Boundary Rd.)
Besant Pl. SE22 4F **121**
Besant Rd. NW2 4G **63**
Besant Wlk. N7 2K **65**
Besant Way NW10 5J **61**
Besford Ho. *E2* *2G* ***85***
(off Pritchard's Rd.)
Besley St. SW16 6G **137**
Bessant Dr. TW9: Kew 1G **115**
Bessborough Gdns.
SW1 5D **18** (5H **101**)
Bessborough Pl. SW1 5D **18** (5H **101**)
Bessborough Rd. HA1: Harr 1H **59**
SW15 1C **134**
Bessborough St. SW1 5C **18** (5H **101**)
Bessemer Ct. *NW1* *7G* ***65***
(off Rochester Sq.)
Bessemer Pk. Ind. Est. SE24 4B **120**
Bessemer Rd. SE5 2C **120**
Bessie Lansbury Cl. E6 6E **88**
Bessingby Rd. HA4: Ruis 2K **57**
Bessingham Wlk. *SE4* *4K* ***121***
(off Aldersford Cl.)
Besson St. SE14 1J **121**
Bessy St. E2 3J **85**
Bestwood St. SE8 4K **103**
Beswick M. NW6 6K **63**
Beta Ct. *CR0: C'don* *1D* ***168***
(off Sydenham Rd.)
Betam Rd. UB3: Hayes 2F **93**
Beta Pl. SW4 4K **119**
Betchworth Cl. SM1: Sutt 5B **166**
Betchworth Rd. IG3: Ilf 2J **71**
Betchworth Way CR0: New Ad 7E **170**
Betham Rd. UB6: G'frd 3H **77**
Bethany Waye TW14: Bedf 7G **111**
Bethecar Rd. HA1: Harr 5J **41**
Bethel Cl. NW4 5F **45**
Bethell Av. E16 4H **87**
IG1: Ilf 7E **52**
Bethel Rd. DA16: Well 3C **126**
Bethersden Cl. BR3: Beck 7B **140**
Bethersden Ho. *SE17* *5E* ***102***
(off Kinglake Est.)
Bethlehem Ho. *E14* *7B* ***86***
(off Limehouse C'way.)
BETHNAL GREEN 3H **85**
Bethnal Green Cen. for
Sports & Performing Arts 3F **85**
Bethnal Grn. Rd. E1 3J **9** (4F **85**)
E2 3J **9** (4F **85**)
Bethune Av. N11 4J **31**
Bethune Cl. N16 1E **66**
Bethune Rd. N16 7D **48**
NW10 4K **79**
Bethwin Rd. SE5 7B **102**
Betjeman Cl. HA5: Pinn 4E **40**
Betjeman Ct. UB7: Yiew 1A **92**
Betony Cl. CR0: C'don 1K **169**
Betoyne Av. E4 4B **36**
Betsham Ho. *SE1* *6E* ***14***
(off Newcomen St.)
Betstyle Cir. N11 4A **32**
Betstyle Ho. N10 7K **31**
Betstyle Rd. N11 4A **32**
Betterton Dr. DA14: Sidc 2E **144**
Betterton Ho. *WC2* *1F* ***13***
(off Betterton St.)
Betterton Rd. RM13: Rain 3K **91**
Betterton St. WC2 1E **12** (6J **83**)
Bettons Pk. E15 1G **87**
Bettridge Rd. SW6 2H **117**
Betts Cl. BR3: Beck 2A **158**
Betts Ho. *E1* *7H* ***85***
(off Betts St.)
Betts M. E17 6B **50**
Betts Rd. E16 7K **87**
Betts St. E1 7H **85**
Betts Way KT6: Surb 1B **162**
SE20 1H **157**
Betty Brooks Ho. E11 3F **69**
Betty May Gray Ho. *E14* *4E* ***104***
(off Pier St.)
Beulah Av. CR7: Thor H 2C **156**
Beulah Cl. HA8: Edg 3C **28**
Beulah Cres. CR7: Thor H 2C **156**
Beulah Gro. CR0: C'don 6C **156**
Beulah Hill SE19 6B **138**
Beulah Path E17 5E **50**
Beulah Rd. CR7: Thor H 3C **156**
E17 5D **50**
SM1: Sutt 4J **165**
SW19 7H **135**
Bevan Av. IG11: Bark 7A **72**
Bevan Ct. CR0: Wadd 5A **168**
E3 *2C* ***86***
(off Tredegar Rd.)
Bevan Ho. IG11: Bark 7B **72**
N1 *1E* ***84***
(off New Era Est.)
TW1: Twick 6D **114**
WC1 *5F* ***7***
(off Boswell St.)
Bevan Rd. EN4: Cockf 4J **21**
SE2 5B **108**
Bevan St. N1 1C **84**
Bev Callender Cl. SW8 3F **119**
Bevenden St. N1 1F **9** (3D **84**)
Bevercote Wlk. *DA17: Belv* *6F* ***109***
(off Osborne Rd.)
Beveree Stadium 1F **149**
Beveridge Ct. *N21* *5D* ***22***
(off Pennington Dr.)
SE28 *7B* ***90***
(off Saunders Way)
Beveridge Rd. NW10 7A **62**
Beverley Av. DA15: Sidc 7K **125**
SW20 1B **152**
TW4: Houn 4D **112**
Beverley Cl. EN1: Enf 4K **23**
KT9: Chess 4C **162**
N21 1H **33**
SW11 4B **118**
SW13 2C **116**
Beverley Cotts. SW15 3A **134**
Beverley Ct. HA2: Harr 3H **41**
HA3: Kenton 4C **42**
N2 *4D* ***46***
(off Western Rd.)
N14 7B **22**
NW6 *7A* ***64***
(off Fairfax Rd.)
SE4 3B **122**
(not continuous)
TW4: Houn 4D **112**
W4 5J **97**
Beverley Cres. IG8: Wfd G 1K **51**
Beverley Dr. HA8: Edg 3G **43**
Beverley Gdns. HA7: Stan 1A **42**
HA9: Wemb 1F **61**
KT4: Wor Pk 1C **164**
NW11 7G **45**
SW13 3B **116**
Beverley Ho. *BR1: Brom* *5F* ***141***
(off Brangbourne Rd.)
Beverley Hyrst CR0: C'don 2F **169**
Beverley La. KT2: King T 7A **134**
SW15 3B **134**
Beverley Meads & Fishpond Woods
Nature Reserve 6B **134**
Beverley M. E4 6A **36**
Beverley Path SW13 2B **116**
Beverley Rd. BR2: Brom 2C **172**
CR4: Mitc 4H **155**
DA7: Bex 2J **127**
E4 6A **36**
E6 3B **88**
HA4: Ruis 2J **57**
KT1: Ham W 1C **150**
KT3: N Mald 4C **152**
KT4: Wor Pk 2E **164**
RM9: Dag 4E **72**
SE20 2H **157**
SW13 3B **116**
TW16: Sun 1H **147**
UB2: S'hall 4C **94**
W4 5B **98**
Beverley Trad. Est.
SM4: Mord 7F **153**
Beverley Way KT3: N Mald 1B **152**
SW20 1B **152**
Beversbrook Rd. N19 3H **65**
Beverstone Rd. CR7: Thor H 4A **156**
SW2 5K **119**
Beverston M. W1 6E **4**
Bevill Allen Cl. SW17 5D **136**
Bevill Cl. SE25 3G **157**
Bevin Cl. SE16 1A **104**
Bevin Ct. WC1 1H **7** (3K **83**)
Bevington Path SE1 7J **15**
Bevington Rd. BR3: Beck 2D **158**
W10 5G **81**
Bevington St. SE16 2G **103**
Bevin Ho. *E2* *3J* ***85***
(off Butler St.)

Bevin Ho. *E3* 3C *86*
(off Alfred St.)
Bevin Rd. UB4: Yead 3J 75
Bevin Sq. SW17 . . . . .3D 136
Bevin Way WC1 . . . . .1J 7 (2A 84)
Bevis Marks EC3 . . . . .7H 9 (6E 84)
Bewcastle Gdns.
EN2: Enf 4D 22
Bew Ct. SE22 . . . . .7G 121
Bewdley St. N1 . . . . .7A 66
Bewick M. SE15 . . . . .7H 103
Bewick St. SW8 . . . . .2F 119
Bewley Ho. *E1* 7H 85
(off Bewley St.)
Bewley St. E1 . . . . .7J 85
SW19 . . . . .6A 136
Bewlys Rd. SE27 . . . . .5B 138
Bexhill Cl. TW13: Felt 2C 130
Bexhill Rd. N11 . . . . .5C 32
SE4 . . . . .6B 122
SW14 . . . . .3J 115
Bexhill Wlk. E15 . . . . .1G 87
BEXLEY 7G 127
Bexley Gdns. N9 . . . . .3J 33
RM6: Chad H 5B 54
BEXLEYHEATH 4F 127
Bexleyheath Sports Club 3C 126
Bexley High St. DA5: Bexl 7G 127
Bexley Ho. SE4 . . . . .4A 122
Bexley La. DA1: Cray 5K 127
DA1: Sidc 4C 144
Bexley Mus. Collection, The . .6J 127
Bexley Music & Dance Cen. 4A 144
(off Station Rd.)
Bexley Rd. DA8: Erith 7J 109
SE9 .5F 125
Beynon Rd. SM5: Cars 5D 166
Bezier Apartments EC2 . .3F 9 (4D 84)
BFI Southbank 4H 13
Bianca Ho. *N1* 1C 9
(off Arden Est.)
Bianca Rd. SE15 . . . . .6G 103
Bibsworth Rd. N3 . . . . .2H 45
Bibury Cl. SE15 . . . . .6E 102
Bicester Rd. TW9: Rich 3G 115
Bickels Yd. SE1 . . . . .7H 15
Bickenhall Mans. W1 . . . . .5F 5
(not continuous)
Bickenhall St. W1 . . . . .5F 5 (5D 82)
Bickersteth Rd. SW17 . . . . .6D 136
Bickerton Rd. N19 . . . . .2G 65
BICKLEY 3C 160
Bickley Cres. BR1: Brom 4C 160
Bickley Pk. Rd. BR1: Brom 3C 160
Bickley Rd. BR1: Brom 2B 160
E10 . . . . .7D 50
Bickley St. SW17 . . . . .5C 136
Bicknell Ho. *E1* 6G 85
(off Ellen St.)
Bicknell Rd. SE5 . . . . .3C 120
Bicknoller Rd. EN1: Enf 1K 23
Bicknor Rd. BR6: Orp 7J 161
Bidborough Cl. BR2: Brom 5H 159
Bidborough St. WC1 . . . .2E 6 (3J 83)
Biddenden Way SE9 . . . . .4E 142
Biddenham Ho. *SE16* 4K 103
(off Plough Way)
Bidder St. E16 . . . . .5G 87
(not continuous)
Biddesden Ho. *SW3* 4E 16
(off Cadogan St.)
Biddestone Rd. N7 . . . . .4K 65
Biddulph Ho. SE18 . . . . .4D 106
Biddulph Mans. *W9* 3K 81
(off Elgin Av.)
Biddulph Rd. W9 . . . . .3K 81
Bideford Av. UB6: G'frd 2B 78
Bideford Cl. HA8: Edg 1G 43
TW13: Hanw 3D 130
Bideford Gdns. EN1: Enf 7K 23
Bideford Rd. BR1: Brom 3H 141
DA16: Well 7B 108

Bideford Rd. EN3: Enf L 1G 25
HA4: Ruis 3K 57
Bidwell Gdns. N11 . . . . .7B 32
Bidwell St. SE15 . . . . .1H 121
Big Ben 7F 13 (2J 101)
Bigbury Cl. N17 . . . . .7J 33
Biggerstaff Rd. E15 . . . . .1E 86
Biggerstaff St. N4 . . . . .2A 66
Biggin Av. CR4: Mitc 1D 154
Biggin Hill SE19 . . . . .1B 156
Biggin Hill Cl. KT2: King T 5C 132
Biggin Way SE19 . . . . .7B 138
Bigginwood Rd.
SW16 . . . . .7B 138
Biggs Row SW15 . . . . .3F 117
Biggs Sq. E9 . . . . .6B 68
Big Hill E5 . . . . .1H 67
Bigland St. E1 . . . . .6H 85
Bignell Rd. SE18 . . . . .5F 107
Bignold Rd. E7 . . . . .4J 69
Bigwood Ct. NW11 . . . . .5K 45
Bigwood Rd. NW11 . . . . .5K 45
Bike Shed, The *IG11: Bark* 7G 71
(off Ripple Rd.)
Bilberry Ho. *E3* 5C 86
(off Watts Gro.)
Billet Cl. RM6: Chad H 3D 54
Billet Rd. E17 . . . . .1K 49
RM6: Chad H 3B 54
Billets Hart Cl. W7 . . . . .2J 95
Bill Hamling Cl. SE9 . . . . .2D 142
Billing Cl. RM9: Dag 7C 72
Billingford Cl. SE4 . . . . .4K 121
Billing Ho. *E1* 6K 85
(off Bower St.)
Billingley *NW1* 1G 83
(off Pratt St.)
Billing Pl. SW10 . . . . .7K 99
Billing Rd. SW10 . . . . .7K 99
Billingsgate Market 1D 104
Billing St. SW10 . . . . .7K 99
Billington M. *W3* 1H 97
(off High St.)
Billington Rd. SE14 . . . . .7K 103
Billinton Hill CR0: C'don 2D 168
Billiter Sq. EC3 . . . . .1H 15
Billiter St. EC3 . . . . .1H 15 (6E 84)
Bill Nicholson Way *N17* 7A 34
(off High Rd.)
Billockby Cl. KT9: Chess 6F 163
Billson St. E14 . . . . .4E 104
Bilsby Gro. SE9 . . . . .4B 142
Bilsby Lodge *HA9: Wemb* 3J 61
(off Chalklands)
Bilton Cen., The UB6: G'frd 1B 78
Bilton Rd. UB6: G'frd 1A 78
Bilton Towers *W1* 1F 11
(off Gt. Cumberland Pl.)
Bilton Way EN3: Enf L 1F 25
UB3: Hayes 2K 93
Bina Gdns. SW5 . . . . .4A 100
Binbrook Ho. *W10* 5E 80
(off Sutton Way)
Bincote Rd. EN2: Enf 3E 22
Binden Rd. W12 . . . . .3B 98
Bindon Grn. SM4: Mord 4K 153
Binfield Rd. CR2: S Croy 5F 169
SW4 . . . . .1J 119
Bingfield St. N1 . . . . .1J 83
(not continuous)
Bingham Ct. *N1* 7B 66
(off Halton Rd.)
Bingham Pl. W1 . . . . .5G 5 (5E 82)
Bingham Point *SE18* 4F 107
(off Wilmount St.)
Bingham Rd. CR0: C'don 1G 169
Bingham St. N1 . . . . .6D 66
Bingley Rd. E16 . . . . .6A 88
TW16: Sun 7J 129
UB6: G'frd 4G 77
Binley Ho. SW15 . . . . .6B 116
Binney St. W1 . . . . .1H 11 (6E 82)

Binnie Ct. SE10 . . . . .7D 104
(off Greenwich High Rd.)
Binnie Ho. *SE1* 3C 102
(off Bath Ter.)
Binnington Twr. BR2: Brom 6C 160
Binns Rd. W4 . . . . .5A 98
Binns Ter. W4 . . . . .5A 98
Binsey Wlk. SE2 . . . . .2C 108
(not continuous)
Binstead Cl. UB4: Yead 5C 76
Binyon Cres. HA7: Stan 5E 26
Biraj Ho. E6 .1D 88
Birbetts Rd. SE9 . . . . .2D 142
Bircham Path *SE4* 4K 121
(off Aldersford Cl.)
Birchanger Rd. SE25 . . . . .5G 157
Birch Av. N13 . . . . .3H 33
UB7: Yiew 6B 74
Birch Cl. E16 . . . . .5G 87
IG9: Buck H 3G 37
N19 . . . . .2G 65
RM7: Mawney 3H 55
SE15 . . . . .2G 121
TW3: Houn 2H 113
TW8: Bford 7B 96
TW11: Tedd 5A 132
TW17: Shep 2G 147
Birch Ct. N12 . . . . .4E 30
RM6: Chad H 6C 54
SM1: Sutt 4A 166
SM6: Wall 4F 167
Birch Cres. UB10: Uxb 1B 74
Birchdale Gdns.
RM6: Chad H 7D 54
Birchdale Rd. E7 . . . . .5A 70
Birchdene Dr. SE28 . . . . .1A 108
Birchdown Ho. *E3* 3D 86
(off Rainhill Way)
Birchen Cl. NW9 . . . . .2K 61
Birchend Cl. CR2: S Croy 6D 168
Birchen Gro. NW9 . . . . .2K 61
Birches, The *BR2: Brom* 4H 159
(off Durham Rd.)
BR6: Farnb 4E 172
E12 . . . . .4C 70
N21 . . . . .6E 22
SE5 .2E 120
SE7 .6K 105
TW4: Houn 7D 112
Birches Cl. CR4: Mitc 3D 154
HA5: Pinn 5C 40
Birchfield Cl. *KT12: Walt T* 7K 147
(off Grove Cres.)
Birchfield Ho. *E14* 7C 86
(off Birchfield St.)
Birchfield St. E14 . . . . .7C 86
Birch Gdns. RM10: Dag 3J 73
Birch Grn. NW9 . . . . .7F 29
Birch Gro. DA16: Well 4A 126
E11 . . . . .4G 69
SE12 . . . . .7H 123
TW17: Shep 2G 147
W3 . . . . .1H 97
Birchgrove Ho. TW9: Kew 7H 97
Birch Hill CR0: C'don 5K 169
Birch Ho. *N22* 1A 48
(off Acacia Rd.)
SE14 . . . . .1B 122
SW2 . . . . .6A 120
(off Tulse Hill)
UB7: W Dray 2B 92
(off Park Lodge Av.)
W10 .4G 81
(off Droop St.)
Birchington Cl. DA7: Bex 1H 127
Birchington Ct. *NW6* 1K 81
(off West End La.)
Birchington Ho. E5 . . . . .5H 67
Birchington Rd. KT5: Surb 7F 151
N8 . . . . .6H 47
NW6 .1J 81
Birchin La. EC3 . . . . .1F 15 (6D 84)

Birchlands Av. SW12 . . . . .7D 118
Birchmead BR6: Farnb 2E 172
Birchmead Av. HA5: Pinn 4A 40
Birchmere Bus. Pk. SE28 . . . . . . .2A 108
Birchmere Lodge *SE16* 5H 103
(off Sherwood Gdns.)
Birchmere Row SE3 . . . . .2H 123
Birchmore Hall N5 . . . . .3C 66
Birchmore Wlk. N5 . . . . .3C 66
(not continuous)
Birch Pk. HA3: Hrw W 7B 26
Birch Rd. RM7: Mawney 3H 55
TW13: Hanw 5B 130
Birch Row BR2: Brom 7E 160
Birch Tree Av. BR4: W W'ck 5H 171
Birch Tree Way CR0: C'don 2H 169
Birch Va. Ct. *NW8* 3B 4
(off Pollitt Dr.)
Birchville Ct. WD23: B Hea 1D 26
Birch Wlk. CR4: Mitc 1F 155
DA8: Erith 6J 109
IG1: Ilf 4J 71
(off Loxford La.)
Birchway UB3: Hayes 1J 93
Birchwood Av. BR3: Beck 4B 158
DA14: Sidc 2B 144
N10 . . . . .3E 46
SM6: Wall 3E 166
Birchwood Cl. SM4: Mord 4K 153
Birchwood Ct. HA8: Edg 2J 43
N13 . . . . .5G 33
Birchwood Dr. DA2: Dart 4K 145
NW3 .3K 63
Birchwood Gro. TW12: Hamp 6E 130
Birchwood Pde. DA2: Dart 4K 145
Birchwood Rd. BR5: Pet W 4H 161
BR8: Swan 7J 145
DA2: Dart 7J 145
SW17 . . . . .5F 137
Birdbrook Ho. *N1* 7C 66
(off Popham Rd.)
Birdbrook Rd. SE3 . . . . .4A 124
Birdcage Wlk. SW1 . . . .7A 12 (2G 101)
Birdham Cl. BR1: Brom 5C 160
Birdhurst Av. CR2: S Croy 4D 168
Birdhurst Ct. *SM6: Wall* 7H 167
(off Woodcote Av.)
Birdhurst Gdns. CR2: S Croy 4D 168
Birdhurst Ri. CR2: S Croy 5E 168
Birdhurst Rd. CR2: S Croy 5E 168
SW18 . . . . .5A 118
SW19 . . . . .6C 136
Bird in Bush BMX Track 7H 103
(off Bird in Bush Rd.)
Bird in Bush Rd. SE15 . . . . .7G 103
Bird in Hand La. BR1: Brom 2B 160
Bird-in-Hand M. *SE23* 2J 139
(off Bird-in-Hands Pas.)
Bird-in-Hand Pas. SE23 . . . . .2J 139
Bird in Hand Path *CR0: C'don* 7D 156
(off Sydenham Rd.)
Bird in Hand Yd. *NW3* 4A 64
(off Holly Bush Va.)
NW3 .4A 64
(Perrin's Ct.)
Birdsall Ho. SE5 . . . . .3E 120
Birds Farm Av. RM5: Col R 1H 55
Birdsfield La. E3 . . . . .1B 86
Bird St. W1 . . . . .1H 11 (6E 82)
Birdwood Av. SE13 . . . . .6F 123
Birdwood Cl. TW11: Tedd 4J 131
Birkbeck Av. UB6: G'frd 1G 77
W3 . . . . .7J 79
Birkbeck Cl. W3 . . . . .1K 97
Birkbeck Gdns. IG8: Wfd G 2D 36
Birkbeck Gro. W3 . . . . .2K 97
Birkbeck Hill SE21 . . . . .1B 138
Birkbeck M. E8 . . . . .5F 67
W3 . . . . .1K 97
Birkbeck Pl. SE21 . . . . .2C 138

Birkbeck Rd.—Blairgowrie Ct.

Birkbeck Rd. BR3: Beck 2J **157**
DA14: Sidc 3A **144**
E8 5F **67**
EN2: Enf 1J **23**
IG2: Ilf 5H **53**
N8 4J **47**
N12 5F **31**
N17 1F **49**
NW7 5G **29**
RM7: Rush G 1K **73**
SW19 5K **135**
W3 1K **97**
W5 4C **96**
Birkbeck St. E2 3H **85**
Birkbeck Way UB6: G'frd 1H **77**
Birkdale Av. HA5: Pinn 3E **40**
Birkdale Cl. BR6: Orp 7H **161**
SE16 5H **103**
SE28 6D **90**
Birkdale Ct. *UB1: S'hall 6G **77***
(off Redcroft Rd.)
Birkdale Gdns. CR0: C'don 4K **169**
Birkdale Rd. SE2 4A **108**
W5 4E **78**
Birkenhead Av. KT2: King T 2F **151**
Birkenhead St. WC1 1F **7** (3J **83**)
Birkhall Rd. SE6 1F **141**
Birkwood Cl. SW12 7H **119**
Birley Lodge *NW8 2B **82***
(off Acacia Rd.)
Birley Rd. N20 2F **31**
Birley St. SW11 2E **118**
Birling Rd. DA8: Erith 7K **109**
Birnam Rd. N4 2K **65**
Birnbeck Ct. EN5: Barn 4A **20**
NW11 5H **45**
Birrell Ho. *SW9 2K **119***
(off Stockwell Rd.)
Birse Cres. NW10 3A **62**
Birstall Rd. N15 5E **48**
Birtwhistle Ho. *E3 1B **86***
(off Parnell Rd.)
Biscay Ho. *E1 4K **85***
(off Mile End Rd.)
Biscayne Av. E14 1F **105**
Biscay Rd. W6 5F **99**
Biscoe Cl. TW5: Hest 6E **94**
Biscoe Way SE13 3F **123**
Biscott Ho. E3 4D **86**
Bisenden Rd. CR0: C'don 2E **168**
Bisham Cl. SM5: Cars 1D **166**
Bisham Gdns. N6 1E **64**
Bishop Butt Cl. BR6: Orp 3K **173**
Bishop Ct. TW9: Rich 3E **114**
Bishop Duppas Pk. TW17: Shep 7G **147**
Bishop Fox Way KT8: W Mole 4D **148**
Bishopgate Churchyard
EC2 7G **9** (5E **84**)
Bishop Ken Rd. HA3: W'stone 2K **41**
Bishop King's Rd. W14 4G **99**
Bishop Rd. N14 7A **22**
Bishops Av. BR1: Brom 2A **160**
E13 1K **87**
RM6: Chad H 6C **54**
SW6 2F **117**
Bishops Avenue, The N2 7B **46**
Bishop's Bri. Rd. W2 6A **4** (6K **81**)
Bishops Cl. E17 4D **50**
EN1: Enf 2C **24**
EN5: Barn 6A **20**
N19 3G **65**
SE9 2G **143**
SM1: Sutt 3J **165**
TW10: Ham 3D **132**
UB10: Hil 2C **74**
W4 5J **97**
Bishops Ct. CR0: C'don 2F **169**
EC4 7A **8**
HA0: Wemb 4B **60**
*W2 6K **81***
(off Bishop's Bri. Rd.)
WC2 7J **7**
Bishopsdale Ho. *NW6 1J **81***
(off Kilburn Va.)
Bishops Dr. TW14: Bedf 6F **111**
UB5: N'olt 1C **76**
Bishopsford Rd. SM4: Mord 7A **154**
Bishopsgate EC2 1G **15** (6E **84**)
Bishopsgate Arc. EC2 6H **9**
Bishopsgate Institute & Libraries *6H **9***
(off Bishopsgate)
Bishops Grn. BR1: Brom 1A **160**
Bishops Gro. N2 6C **46**
TW12: Hamp 4D **130**
Bishops Gro. Cvn. Site
TW12: Hamp 4E **130**
Bishop's Hall KT1: King T 2D **150**
Bishops Hill KT12: Walt T 7J **147**
Bishops Ho. *SW8 7J **101***
(off Sth. Lambeth Rd.)
Bishop's Mans. SW6 2F **117**
(not continuous)
Bishops Mead *SE5 7C **102***
(off Camberwell Rd.)
Bishops Pk. Rd. SW6 2F **117**
SW16 1J **155**
Bishops Pl. SM1: Sutt 5A **166**
Bishops Rd. CR0: C'don 7B **156**
N6 6E **46**
SW6 1G **117**
SW11 7C **100**
UB3: Hayes 6E **74**
W7 2J **95**
Bishops Sq. E1 5H **9** (5E **84**)
Bishop's Ter. SE11 3K **19** (4A **102**)
Bishopsthorpe Rd. SE26 4K **139**
Bishop St. N1 1C **84**
Bishops Vw. Ct. N10 4F **47**
Bishops Wlk. BR7: Chst 1G **161**
CR0: Addtn 5K **169**
HA5: Pinn 3C **40**
Bishop's Way E2 2H **85**
Bishops Wood Almshouses *E5 4H **67***
(off Lwr. Clapton Rd.)
Bishopswood Rd. N6 7D **46**
Bishop Wilfred Wood Cl. SE15 2G **121**
Bishop Wilfred Wood Ct. *E13 2A **88***
(off Pragel St.)
Bisley Cl. KT4: Wor Pk 1E **164**
Bison Ct. TW14: Felt 7K **111**
Bispham Rd. NW10 3F **79**
Bissextile Ho. SE13 2D **122**
Bisson Rd. E15 2E **86**
Bisterne Av. E17 3F **51**
Bittacy Bus. Cen. NW7 7B **30**
Bittacy Cl. NW7 6A **30**
Bittacy Ct. NW7 7B **30**
Bittacy Hill NW7 6A **30**
Bittacy Pk. Av. NW7 5A **30**
Bittacy Ri. NW7 6K **29**
Bittacy Rd. NW7 6A **30**
Bittern Cl. UB4: Yead 5B **76**
Bittern Ct. NW9 2A **44**
SE8 6C **104**
Bittern Ho. *SE1 7C **14***
(off Gt. Suffolk St.)
Bittern Pl. N22 2K **47**
Bittern St. SE1 7C **14** (2C **102**)
Bittoms, The KT1: King T 3D **150**
(not continuous)
Bittoms Ct. KT1: King T 3D **150**
Bixley Cl. UB2: S'hall 4D **94**
Blackall St. EC2 3G **9** (4E **84**)
Blackberry Cl. TW17: Shep 4G **147**
Blackberry Ct. HA9: Wemb 7E **42**
Blackberry Farm Cl. TW5: Hest 7C **94**
Blackberry Fld. BR5: St P 7A **144**
Blackbird Ct. NW9 3K **61**
Blackbird Hill NW9 2J **61**
Blackbird Yd. E2 1K **9** (3F **85**)
Blackborne Rd. RM10: Dag 6G **73**
Blackborough Ho. *IG9: Buck H 2G **37***
(off Beatrice Ct.)
Black Boy La. N15 5C **48**
Blackbrook La. BR1: Brom 5D **160**
BR2: Brom 5E **160**
Black Bull Yd. *EC1 5K **7***
(off Hatton Wall)
Blackburn NW9 2B **44**
Blackburne's M. W1 2G **11** (7E **82**)
Blackburn Rd. NW6 6K **63**
Blackburn Trad. Est. TW19: Stanw 6B **110**
Blackburn Way TW4: Houn 5C **112**
Blackbush Av. RM6: Chad H 5D **54**
Blackbush Cl. SM2: Sutt 7K **165**
Blackdown Cl. N2 2A **46**
Blackdown Ter. SE18 1D **124**
Blackett St. SW15 3F **117**
Black Fan Cl. EN2: Enf 1H **23**
BLACKFEN 7A **126**
Blackfen Pde. DA15: Sidc 6A **126**
Blackfen Rd. DA15: Sidc 5J **125**
Blackford Cl. CR2: S Croy 7B **168**
Blackford's Path SW15 7C **116**
Blackfriars Bri. EC4 2A **14** (7B **84**)
Blackfriars Ct. EC4 2A **14**
Black Friars La. EC4 2A **14** (6B **84**)
(not continuous)
Blackfriars Pas. EC4 2A **14** (7B **84**)
Blackfriars Rd. SE1 4A **14** (2B **102**)
Blackfriars Underpass EC4 2A **14** (7A **84**)
Black Gates HA5: Pinn 3D **40**
BLACKHEATH 2H **123**
Blackheath Av. SE10 7F **105**
Blackheath Bus. Est. *SE10 1E **122***
(off Blackheath Hill)
Blackheath Concert Halls 3H **123**
Blackheath Gro. SE3 2H **123**
Blackheath Hill SE10 1E **122**
BLACKHEATH PARK 3J **123**
Blackheath Pk. SE3 3H **123**
Blackheath Ri. SE13 2E **122**
(not continuous)
Blackheath Rd. SE10 1D **122**
Blackheath RUFC 7K **105**
BLACKHEATH VALE 2H **123**
Blackheath Va. SE3 2G **123**
Blackheath Village SE3 2H **123**
Black Horse Ct. SE1 3D **102**
Blackhorse La. CR0: C'don 7G **157**
E17 2K **49**
Blackhorse M. E17 3K **49**
Black Horse Pde. HA5: Eastc 5K **39**
BLACKHORSE ROAD 4K **49**
Blackhorse Rd. DA14: Sidc 4A **144**
E17 4K **49**
SE8 6A **104**
Blacklands Dr. UB4: Hayes 4E **74**
Blacklands Rd. SE6 4E **140**
Blacklands Ter. SW3 4E **16** (4D **100**)
Black Lion La. W6 4C **98**
Black Lion M. W6 4C **98**
Blackmans Yd. E2 4G **85**
Blackmore Av. UB1: S'hall 1H **95**
Blackmore Dr. NW10 7H **61**
Blackmore Gdns. SW13 6D **98**
Blackmore Ho. *N1 1K **83***
(off Barnsbury Est.)
Blackmore Rd. IG9: Buck H 1H **37**
Blackmore's Gro. TW11: Tedd 6A **132**
Blackmore Twr. *W3 3J **97***
(off Stanley Rd.)
Blackness La. BR2: Kes 7B **172**
Black Path E10 7A **50**
Blackpool Gdns. UB4: Hayes 4G **75**
Blackpool Rd. SE15 2H **121**
BLACK PRINCE INTERCHANGE 6H **127**
Black Prince Rd. SE1 4G **19** (4K **101**)
SE11 4G **19** (4K **101**)
Black Rod Cl. UB3: Hayes 3H **93**
Blackshaw Rd. SW17 4A **136**
Blacksmiths Cl. RM6: Chad H 6C **54**
Blacksmiths Ho. *E17 4C **50***
(off Gillards M.)
Blacks Rd. W6 5E **98**
Blackstock M. N4 2B **66**
Blackstock Rd. N4 2B **66**
N5 2B **66**
Blackstone Est. E8 7G **67**
Blackstone Ho. *SW1 6A **18***
(off Churchill Gdns.)
Blackstone Rd. NW2 5E **62**
Black Swan Yd. SE1 6H **15** (2E **102**)
Blackthorn Av. UB7: W Dray 4C **92**
Blackthorn Ct. *E15 4F **69***
(off Hall Rd.)
TW5: Hest 7C **94**
Blackthorne Av. CR0: C'don 1J **169**
Blackthorne Ct. *SE15 7F **103***
(off Cator St.)
TW15: Ashf 7E **128**
*UB1: S'hall 1F **95***
(off Dormer's Wells La.)
Blackthorne Cres. SL3: Poyle 5A **174**
Blackthorne Dr. E4 4A **36**
Blackthorne Ind. Est. SL3: Poyle 6A **174**
Blackthorne Rd. SL3: Poyle 5A **174**
Blackthorn Gro. DA7: Bex 3E **126**
Blackthorn Rd. IG1: Ilf 5H **71**
Blackthorn St. E3 4C **86**
Blacktree M. SW9 3A **120**
BLACKWALL 1E **104**
Blackwall La. SE10 5G **105**
Blackwall Trad. Est. E14 5F **87**
Blackwall Tunnel E14 1F **105**
(not continuous)
Blackwall Tunnel App. E14 6E **86**
Blackwall Tunnel Northern App. E3 2C **86**
E14 2C **86**
Blackwall Tunnel Southern App.
SE10 3G **105**
Blackwall Way E14 1E **104**
Blackwater Cl. E7 4H **69**
RM13: Rain 5K **91**
Blackwater Ho. *NW8 5B **4***
(off Church St.)
Blackwater St. SE22 5F **121**
Blackwell Cl. E5 4K **67**
HA3: Hrw W 7C **26**
N21 5D **22**
Blackwell Gdns. HA8: Edg 4B **28**
Blackwell Ho. SW4 6H **119**
Blackwood Av. N18 5E **34**
Blackwood Ho. *E1 4H **85***
(off Collingwood St.)
Blackwood St. SE17 5D **102**
Blade, The W2 6B **4**
*W2 5B **82***
(off Nth. Wharf Rd.)
Blade M. SW15 4H **117**
Bladen Ho. *E1 6K **85***
(off Dunelm St.)
Blades Ct. SW15 4H **117**
*W6 5D **98***
(off Lower Mall)
Blades Ho. *SE11 7J **19***
(off Kennington Oval)
Bladindon Dr. DA5: Bexl 7C **126**
Bladon Ct. SW16 6J **137**
Bladon Gdns. HA2: Harr 6F **41**
Blagdens Cl. N14 2C **32**
Blagdens La. N14 2B **32**
Blagdon Ct. W7 7J **77**
Blagdon Rd. KT3: N Mald 4B **152**
(not continuous)
SE13 6D **122**
Blagdon Wlk. TW11: Tedd 6C **132**
Blagrove Rd. W10 5G **81**
Blair Av. NW9 7A **44**
Blair Cl. DA15: Sidc 5J **125**
N1 6C **66**
UB3: Harl 4J **93**
Blair Ct. BR3: Beck 1D **158**
NW8 1B **82**
SE6 1H **141**
Blairderry Rd. SW2 2J **137**
Blairgowrie Ct. *E14 6F **87***
(off Blair St.)

Blair Ho.—Blydon Ct.

Blair Ho. SW9 2K 119
Blair St. E14 6E 86
Blake Av. IG11: Bark 1J 89
Blake Bldg. N8 3K 47
Blake Cl. DA16: Well 1J 125
SM5: Cars 1C 166
UB4: Hayes 2F 75
Blake Ct. N21 5E 22
NW6 *3J 81*
(off Malvern Rd.)
SE16 *5H 103*
(off Stubbs Dr.)
Blakeden Dr. KT10: Clay 6A 162
Blake Gdns. SW6 1K 117
Blake Hall Cres. E11 1J 69
Blake Hall Rd. E11 7J 51
Blakehall Rd. SM5: Cars 6D 166
Blake Ho. *E14* *2C 104*
(off Admirals Way)
SE1 1J 19 (3A 102)
SE8 *6C 104*
(off New King St.)
Blakeley Cotts. SE10 2F 105
Blake M. TW9: Kew 1G 115
Blakemore Rd. CR7: Thor H 5K 155
SW16 3J 137
Blakemore Way DA17: Belv 3E 108
Blakeney Av. BR3: Beck 1B 158
Blakeney Cl. E8 5G 67
N20 1F 31
NW1 7H 65
Blakeney Rd. BR3: Beck 7B 140
Blakenham Rd. SW17 4D 136
Blaker Ct. SE7 7A 106
(not continuous)
Blake Rd. CR0: C'don 2E 168
CR4: Mitc 3C 154
E16 4H 87
N11 7B 32
Blaker Rd. E15 2E 86
Blakes Av. KT3: N Mald 5B 152
Blakes Cl. W10 5E 80
Blake's Grn. BR4: W W'ck 1E 170
Blakes La. KT3: N Mald 5B 152
Blakesley Av. W5 6C 78
Blakesley Ho. *E12* *3E 70*
(off Grantham Rd.)
Blakesley Wlk. SW20 2H 153
Blake's Rd. SE15 7E 102
Blakes Ter. KT3: N Mald 5C 152
Blakesware Gdns. N9 7J 23
Blakewood Cl. TW13: Hanw 4A 130
Blakewood Ct. *SE20* *7H 139*
(off Anerley Pk.)
Blanchard Cl. SE9 3C 142
Blanchard Ho. *TW1: Twick* *6D 114*
(off Clevedon Rd.)
Blanchard Way E8 6G 67
Blanch Cl. SE15 7J 103
Blanchedowne SE5 4D 120
Blanche St. E16 4H 87
Blanchland Rd. SM4: Mord 5K 153
Blandfield Rd. SW12 7E 118
Blandford Av. BR3: Beck 2A 158
TW2: Whitt 1F 131
Blandford Cl. CR0: Bedd 3J 167
N2 4A 46
RM7: Mawney 4H 55
Blandford Ct. *N1* *7E 66*
(off St Peter's Way)
NW6 7F 63
Blandford Cres. E4 7K 25
Blandford Ho. *SW8* *7K 101*
(off Richborne Ter.)
Blandford Rd. BR3: Beck 2J 157
TW11: Tedd 5H 131
UB2: S'hall 4E 94
W4 3A 98
W5 2D 96
Blandford Sq. NW1 4D 4 (4C 82)
Blandford St. W1 7F 5 (6D 82)
Blandford Waye UB4: Yead 6A 76
Bland Ho. SE11 5H 19
Bland St. SE9 4B 124
Blaney Cres. E6 3F 89
Blanmerle Rd. SE9 1F 143
Blann Cl. SE9 6B 124
Blantyre St. SW10 7B 100
Blantyre Twr. *SW10* *7B 100*
(off Blantyre St.)
Blantyre Wlk. *SW10* *7B 100*
(off Worlds End Est.)
Blashford *NW3* *7D 64*
(off Adelaide Rd.)
Blashford St. SE13 7F 123
Blasker Wlk. E14 5D 104
Blawith Rd. HA1: Harr 4J 41
Blaxland Ho. *W12* *7D 80*
(off White City Est.)
Blaydon Cl. HA4: Ruis 7G 39
N17 7C 34
Blaydon Ct. UB5: N'olt 6E 58
Blaydon Wlk. N17 7C 34
Blazer Ct. NW8 2B 4
Bleak Hill La. SE18 6K 107
Blean Gro. SE20 7J 139
Bleasdale Av. UB6: G'frd 2A 78
Blechynden Ho. *W10* *6F 81*
(off Kingsdown Cl.)
Blechynden St. W10 7F 81
Bledlow Cl. NW8 4B 4 (4B 82)
SE28 7C 90
Bledlow Ri. UB6: G'frd 2G 77
Bleeding Heart Yd. EC1 6K 7
Blegborough Rd. SW16 6G 137
Blemundsbury *WC1* *5G 7*
(off Dombey St.)
BLENDON 6D 126
Blendon Dr. DA5: Bexl 6D 126
Blendon Path BR1: Brom 7H 141
Blendon Rd. DA5: Bexl 6D 126
Blendon Row *SE17* *4D 102*
(off Orb St.)
Blendon Ter. SE18 5G 107
Blendworth Point SW15 1D 134
Blenheim Av. IG2: Ilf 6E 52
Blenheim Bus. Cen. *CR4: Mitc* *2D 154*
(off London Rd.)
Blenheim Cen., The
TW3: Houn 3F 113
Blenheim Cl. N21 1H 33
RM7: Mawney 4J 55
SE12 1K 141
SM6: Wall 7G 167
SW20 3E 152
UB6: G'frd 2H 77
Blenheim Ct. BR2: Brom 4H 159
DA14: Sidc 3H 143
HA3: Kenton 6A 42
IG8: Wfd G 7E 36
N7 6J 65
N19 2J 65
SE10 *5J 105*
(off Denham St.)
SE16 *1K 103*
(off King & Queen Wharf)
SM2: Sutt 6A 166
Blenheim Cres. CR2: S Croy 7C 168
HA4: Ruis 2F 57
W11 7G 81
Blenheim Dr. DA16: Well 1K 125
Blenheim Gdns. HA9: Wemb 3E 60
KT2: King T 7H 133
NW2 6E 62
SM6: Wall 6G 167
SW2 6K 119
Blenheim Gro. SE15 2G 121
Blenheim Ho. *E16* *1K 105*
(off Constable Av.)
SE18 3G 107
SW3 *6D 16*
(off Kings Rd.)
TW3: Houn 3E 112
Blenheim Pde. UB10: Hil 4D 74
Blenheim Pk. Rd. CR2: S Croy 7C 168
Blenheim Pas. NW8 2A 82
Blenheim Pl. TW11: Tedd 5K 131
Blenheim Ri. N15 4F 49
Blenheim Rd. BR1: Brom 4C 160
DA15: Sidc 1C 144
E6 3B 88
E15 4G 69
E17 3K 49
EN5: Barn 3A 20
HA2: Harr 6F 41
NW8 2A 82
SE20 7J 139
SM1: Sutt 3J 165
SW20 3E 152
UB5: N'olt 6F 59
W4 3A 98
Blenheim Shop. Cen. SE20 7J 139
Blenheim St. W1 1J 11 (6F 83)
Blenheim Ter. NW8 2A 82
Blenheim Way TW7: Isle 1A 114
Blenkarne Rd. SW11 6D 118
Bleriot *NW9* *2B 44*
(off Belvedere Strand)
Bleriot Rd. TW5: Hest 7A 94
Blessbury Rd. HA8: Edg 1J 43
Blessington Cl. SE13 3F 123
Blessington Rd. SE13 3F 123
Blessing Way IG11: Bark 3C 90
Bletchingley Cl. CR7: Thor H 4B 156
Bletchley Ct. N1 1E 8
Bletchley St. N1 1D 8 (2D 84)
Bletchmore Cl. UB3: Harl 5F 93
Bletsoe Wlk. N1 2C 84
Blewbury Ho. SE2 2C 108
(not continuous)
Blick Ho. *SE16* *3J 103*
(off Neptune St.)
Blincoe Cl. SW19 2F 135
Bliss Cres. SE13 2D 122
Blissett St. SE10 1E 122
Bliss Ho. EN1: Enf 1B 24
Bliss M. W10 3G 81
Blisworth Cl. UB4: Yead 4C 76
Blisworth Ho. *E2* *1G 85*
(off Whiston Rd.)
Blithbury Rd. RM9: Dag 6B 72
Blithdale Rd. SE2 4A 108
Blithehale Ct. *E2* *3H 85*
(off Withan St.)
Blithfield St. W8 3K 99
Blockley Rd. HA0: Wemb 2B 60
Block Wharf *E14* *2C 104*
(off Cuba St.)
Bloemfontein Av. W12 1D 98
Bloemfontein Rd. W12 7D 80
Bloemfontein Way W12 1D 98
Blomfield Ct. *W9* *3A 4*
(off Maida Va.)
Blomfield Mans. *W12* *1E 98*
(off Stanlake Rd.)
Blomfield Rd. W9 4A 4 (5K 81)
Blomfield St. EC2 6F 9 (5D 84)
Blomfield Vs. W2 5K 81
Blomville Rd. RM8: Dag 3E 72
Blondell Cl. UB7: Harm 2E 174
Blondel St. SW11 2E 118
Blondin Av. W5 4C 96
Blondin Pk. & Nature Area 4B 96
Blondin St. E3 2C 86
Bloomburg St. SW1 4B 18 (4H 101)
Bloomfield Ct. *E10* *3D 68*
(off Brisbane Rd.)
N6 6E 46
Bloomfield Cres. IG2: Ilf 6F 53
Bloomfield Ho. *E1* *5G 85*
(off Old Montague St.)
Bloomfield Pl. W1 2K 11
Bloomfield Rd. BR2: Brom 5B 160
KT1: King T 4E 150
N6 6E 46
SE18 6F 107
Bloomfield Ter. SW1 5H 17 (5E 100)
Bloom Gro. SE27 3B 138
Bloomhall Rd. SE19 5D 138
Bloom Pk. Rd. SW6 7H 99
BLOOMSBURY 5E 6 (5J 83)
Bloomsbury Cl. NW7 7H 29
W5 7F 79
Bloomsbury Ct. HA5: Pinn 3D 40
TW5: Cran 1K 111
WC1 6F 7
Bloomsbury Ho. SW4 6H 119
Bloomsbury Mans. *BR1: Brom* *1K 159*
(off Widmore Rd.)
Bloomsbury M. IG8: Wfd G 6H 37
Bloomsbury Pl. SW18 5A 118
WC1 5F 7 (5J 83)
Bloomsbury Sq. WC1 6F 7 (5J 83)
Bloomsbury St. WC1 6D 6 (5H 83)
Bloomsbury Theatre 3C 6
Bloomsbury Way WC1 6E 6 (5J 83)
Blore Cl. SW8 1H 119
Blore Ct. W1 1C 12
Blore Ho. *SW10* *7K 99*
(off Coleridge Gdns.)
Blossom Cl. CR2: S Croy 5F 169
RM9: Dag 1F 91
W5 2E 96
Blossom Dr. BR6: Orp 2K 173
Blossom La. EN2: Enf 1H 23
Blossom Pl. SE28 3G 107
Blossom St. E1 4H 9 (4E 84)
Blossom Way UB7: W Dray 4C 92
UB10: Hil 7B 56
Blossom Waye TW5: Hest 6C 94
Blount St. E14 6A 86
Bloxam Gdns. SE9 5C 124
Bloxhall Rd. E10 1B 68
Bloxham Cres. TW12: Hamp 7D 130
Bloxworth Cl. SM6: Wall 3G 167
Blucher Rd. SE5 7C 102
Blue Anchor All. TW9: Rich 4E 114
Blue Anchor La. SE16 4G 103
Blue Anchor Yd. E1 2K 15 (7G 85)
Blue Ball Yd. SW1 5A 12 (1G 101)
Bluebell Av. E12 5B 70
Bluebell Cl. BR6: Farnb 2G 173
E9 1J 85
RM7: Rush G 2K 73
SE26 4F 139
SM6: Wall 1F 167
UB5: N'olt 6D 58
Bluebell Way IG1: Ilf 6F 71
Blueberry Cl. IG8: Wfd G 6D 36
Bluebird La. RM10: Dag 7G 73
Bluebird Way SE28 2H 107
Blue Bldg. *SE10* *5H 105*
(off Glenforth St.)
Blue Ct. *N1* *1D 84*
(off Sherborne St.)
Blue Elephant Theatre *7C 102*
(off Bethwin Rd.)
Bluefield Cl. TW12: Hamp 5E 130
Blue Fin Bldg. SE1 4B 14
Bluegate M. E1 7H 85
Bluegates KT17: Ewe 7C 164
Bluehouse Rd. E4 2B 36
Blue Lion Pl. SE1 7G 15 (3E 102)
Blueprint Apartments
SW12 *7F 119*
(off Balham Gro.)
Blue Riband Ind. Est. CR0: C'don 2B 168
Blue Water SW18 4K 117
Blundell Cl. E8 5G 67
Blundell Rd. HA8: Edg 1K 43
Blundell St. N7 7J 65
Blunden Cl. RM8: Dag 1C 72
Blunt Rd. CR2: S Croy 5D 168
Blunts Av. UB7: Sip 7C 92
Blunts Rd. SE9 5E 124
Blurton Rd. E5 4J 67
Blydon Ct. *N21* *5E 22*
(off Chaseville Pk. Rd.)

A-Z London 201

Blyth Cl. E14 . . . . .4F 105
  TW1: Twick 6K 113
Blyth Ct. BR1: Brom 1H 159
             (off Blyth Rd.)
Blythe Cl. SE6 . . . . .7B 122
BLYTHE HILL 7B 122
Blythe Hill BR5: St P 1K 161
  SE6 . . . . .7B 122
Blythe Hill La. SE6 . . . . .7B 122
Blythe Hill Pl. SE23 . . . . .7A 122
Blythe Ho. SE11 . . . .7J 19 (6A 102)
Blythe M. W14 . . . . .3F 99
Blythendale Ho. E2 . . . . .2G 85
           (off Mansford St.)
Blythe Rd. W14 . . . . .3F 99
Blythe St. E2 . . . . .3H 85
Blytheswood Pl. SW16 . . . . .4K 137
Blythe Va. SE6 . . . . .1B 140
Blyth Hill Pl. SE23 . . . . .7A 122
          (off Brockley Pk.)
Blyth Ho. DA8: Erith 5K 109
Blyth Rd. BR1: Brom 1H 159
  E17 . . . . .7B 50
  SE28 . . . . .7C 90
  UB3: Hayes 2G 93
Blyth's Wharf E14 . . . . .7A 86
Blythswood Rd. IG3: Ilf 1A 72
Blyth Wood Pk. BR1: Brom 1H 159
Blythwood Rd. HA5: Pinn 1B 40
  N4 . . . . .7J 47
Boades M. NW3 . . . . .4B 64
Boadicea St. N1 . . . . .1K 83
Boakes Cl. NW9 . . . . .4J 43
Boardman Av. E4 . . . . .5J 25
Boardman Cl. EN5: Barn 5B 20
Boardwalk Pl. E14 . . . . .1E 104
Boarhound NW9 . . . . .2B 44
       (off Further Acre)
Boarley Ho. SE17 . . . . .4E 102
      (off Massinger St.)
Boars Head Yd. TW8: Bford 7D 96
Boatemah Wlk. SW9 . . . . .2A 120
       (off Peckford Pl.)
Boathouse Cen., The W10 . . . . .4F 81
          (off Canal Cl.)
Boathouse Wlk. SE15 . . . . .7F 103
        (not continuous)
Boat Lifter Way SE16 . . . . .4A 104
Boat Quay E16 . . . . .7A 88
Boatyard Apartments E14 . . . . .5D 104
Bob Anker Cl. E13 . . . . .3J 87
Bobbin Cl. SW4 . . . . .3G 119
Bobby Moore Way N10 . . . . .7J 31
Bob Hope Theatre, The 6D 124
Bob Marley Way SE24 . . . . .4A 120
Bockhampton Rd. KT2: King T 7F 133
Bocking St. E8 . . . . .1H 85
Boddicott Cl. SW19 . . . . .2G 135
Boddington Gdns. W3 . . . . .2G 97
Boddington Ho. SE14 . . . . .1J 121
        (off Pomeroy St.)
  SW13 . . . . .6D 98
           (off Wyatt Dr.)
Bodeney Ho. SE5 . . . . .1E 120
         (off Peckham Rd.)
Boden Ho. E1 . . . . .5K 9
        (off Woodseer St.)
Bodiam Cl. EN1: Enf 2K 23
Bodiam Rd. SW16 . . . . .7H 137
Bodiam Way NW10 . . . . .3F 79
Bodicea M. TW4: Houn 6D 112
Bodington Cl. W12 . . . . .2F 99
Bodley Cl. KT3: N Mald 5A 152
Bodley Mnr. Way SW2 . . . . .7A 120
Bodley Rd. KT3: N Mald 6K 151
Bodmin NW9 . . . . .2B 44
       (off Further Acre)
Bodmin Cl. HA2: Harr 3D 58
Bodmin Gro. SM4: Mord 5K 153
Bodmin St. SW18 . . . . .1J 135
Bodnant Gdns. SW20 . . . . .3C 152
Bodney Rd. E8 . . . . .5H 67

Boeing Way UB2: S'hall 3K 93
Boevey Path DA17: Belv 5F 109
Bogart Ct. E14 . . . . .7C 86
         (off Premiere Pl.)
Bogey La. BR6: Downe 7E 172
Bognor Rd. DA16: Well 1D 126
Bohemia Pl. E8 . . . . .6J 67
Bohn Rd. E1 . . . . .5A 86
Bohun Gro. EN4: E Barn 6H 21
Boileau Pde. W5 . . . . .6F 79
        (off Boileau Rd.)
Boileau Rd. SW13 . . . . .7C 98
  W5 . . . . .6F 79
Boisseau Ho. E1 . . . . .5J 85
        (off Stepney Way)
Bolanachi Bldg. SE16 . . . . .3F 103
Bolden St. SE8 . . . . .2D 122
Boldero Pl. NW8 . . . . .4C 4
Bolderwood Way BR4: W W'ck 2D 170
Boldmere Rd. HA5: Eastc 7A 40
Boleyn Av. EN1: Enf 1C 24
Boleyn Cl. E17 . . . . .4C 50
Boleyn Ct. IG9: Buck H 1D 36
  KT8: E Mos 4H 149
        (off Bridge Rd.)
Boleyn Dr. HA4: Ruis 2B 58
  KT8: W Mole 3D 148
Boleyn Gdns. BR4: W W'ck 2D 170
  RM10: Dag 7J 73
Boleyn Gro. BR4: W W'ck 2E 170
Boleyn Ho. E16 . . . . .1J 105
        (off Southey M.)
Boleyn Rd. E6 . . . . .2B 88
  E7 . . . . .7J 69
  N16 . . . . .5E 66
Boleyn Way EN5: New Bar 3F 21
Bolina Rd. SE16 . . . . .5J 103
Bolingbroke Gro. SW11 . . . . .4C 118
Bolingbroke Rd. W14 . . . . .3F 99
Bolingbroke Wlk. SW11 . . . . .1B 118
Bolingbroke Way UB3: Hayes 1F 93
Bolliger Ct. NW10 . . . . .4J 79
Bollo Bri. Rd. W3 . . . . .3H 97
Bollo Ct. W3 . . . . .3J 97
       (off Bollo Bri. Rd.)
Bollo La. W3 . . . . .2H 97
  W4 . . . . .4J 97
Bolney Ga. SW7 . . . . . .7C 10 (2C 100)
Bolney St. SW8 . . . . .7K 101
Bolney Way TW13: Hanw 3C 130
Bolsover St. W1 . . . . .4K 5 (4F 83)
Bolstead Rd. CR4: Mitc 1F 155
Bolster Gro. N22 . . . . .7C 32
Bolt Cl. EC4 . . . . .1K 13
Bolt Ho. N1 . . . . .1E 84
        (off Phillipp St.)
Boltmore Cl. NW4 . . . . .3F 45
Bolton Cl. KT9: Chess 6D 162
  SE20 . . . . .2G 157
Bolton Cres. SE5 . . . . .7B 102
Bolton Dr. SM4: Mord 7A 154
Bolton Gdns. BR1: Brom 6H 141
  NW10 . . . . .2F 81
  SW5 . . . . .5K 99
  TW11: Tedd 6A 132
Bolton Gdns. M. SW10 . . . . .5A 100
Bolton Ho. SE10 . . . . .5G 105
       (off Trafalgar Rd.)
Bolton Pl. NW8 . . . . .1K 81
        (off Bolton Rd.)
Bolton Rd. E15 . . . . .6H 69
  HA1: Harr 4G 41
  KT9: Chess 6D 162
  N18 . . . . .5A 34
  NW8 . . . . .1K 81
  NW10 . . . . .1A 80
  W4 . . . . .7J 97
Boltons, The HA0: Wemb 4K 59
  IG8: Wfd G 4D 36
  SW10 . . . . .5A 100
Boltons Ct. SW5 . . . . .5K 99
      (off Old Brompton Rd.)

Bolton's La. UB3: Harl 1E 110
        (not continuous)
Boltons Pl. SW5 . . . . .5A 100
Bolton St. W1 . . . . .4K 11 (1F 101)
Bolton Studios SW10 . . . . .5A 100
Bolton Wlk. N7 . . . . .2K 65
        (off Durham Rd.)
Bombay Ct. SE16 . . . . .2J 103
     (off St Marychurch St.)
Bombay St. SE16 . . . . .4H 103
Bomer Cl. UB7: Sip 7C 92
Bomore Rd. W11 . . . . .7G 81
Bonar Pl. BR7: Chst 7C 142
Bonar Rd. SE15 . . . . .7G 103
Bonchester Cl. BR7: Chst 7E 142
Bonchurch Cl. SM2: Sutt 7K 165
Bonchurch Rd. W10 . . . . .5G 81
  W13 . . . . .1B 96
Bond Cl. UB7: View 6B 74
Bond Ct. EC4 . . . . .2E 14 (7D 84)
Bondfield Av. UB4: Yead 3J 75
Bondfield Rd. E6 . . . . .5D 88
Bond Gdns. SM6: Wall 4G 167
Bond Ho. NW6 . . . . .2H 81
        (off Rupert Rd.)
  SE14 . . . . .7A 104
       (off Goodwood Rd.)
Bonding Yd. Wlk. SE16 . . . . .3A 104
Bond Rd. CR4: Mitc 2C 154
  KT6: Surb 2F 163
Bond St. E15 . . . . .5G 69
  W4 . . . . .4K 97
  W5 . . . . .7D 78
Bondway SW8 . . . . .7F 19 (6J 101)
Boneta Rd. SE18 . . . . .3D 106
Bonfield Rd. SE13 . . . . .4E 122
Bonham Cl. DA17: Belv 5F 109
        (not continuous)
Bonham Gdns. RM8: Dag 2D 72
Bonham Ga. KT12: Walt T 7J 147
     (off New Zealand Av.)
Bonham Ho. W11 . . . . .1H 99
       (off Boyne Ter. M.)
Bonham Rd. RM8: Dag 2D 72
  SW2 . . . . .5K 119
Bonheur Rd. W4 . . . . .2K 97
Bonhill St. EC2 . . . . .4F 9 (4D 84)
Boniface Gdns. HA3: Hrw W 7A 26
Boniface Rd. UB10: Ick 3D 56
Boniface Wlk. HA3: Hrw W 7A 26
Bonington Ho. EN1: Enf 5B 24
Bonita M. SE4 . . . . .3K 121
Bon Marche Ter. M. SE27 . . . . .4E 138
        (off Gypsy Rd.)
Bonner Hill Rd. KT1: King T 2F 151
        (not continuous)
Bonner Rd. E2 . . . . .2J 85
Bonnersfield Cl. HA1: Harr 6K 41
Bonnersfield La. HA1: Harr 6K 41
        (not continuous)
Bonner St. E2 . . . . .2J 85
Bonneville Gdns. SW4 . . . . .6G 119
Bonnington Ct. UB5: N'olt 2B 76
        (off Gallery Gdns.)
Bonnington Ho. N1 . . . . .2K 83
Bonnington Sq. SW8 . . . .7G 19 (6K 101)
Bonny St. NW1 . . . . .7G 65
Bonser Rd. TW1: Twick 2K 131
Bonsor Ho. SW8 . . . . .1G 119
Bonsor St. SE5 . . . . .7E 102
Bonville Gdns. NW4 . . . . .4D 44
Bonville Rd. BR1: Brom 5H 141
Bookbinders Cott. Homes N20 . . . . .3J 31
Booker Cl. E14 . . . . .5B 86
Booker Rd. N18 . . . . .5B 34
Bookham Ct. CR4: Mitc 3B 154
Boone Ct. N9 . . . . .3D 34
Boones Rd. SE13 . . . . .4G 123
Boone St. SE13 . . . . .4G 123
Boord St. SE10 . . . . .3G 105
Boothby Ct. E4 . . . . .3K 35
Boothby Rd. N19 . . . . .2H 65

Booth Cl. E9 . . . . .1H 85
  SE28 . . . . .1B 108
Booth Dr. TW18: Staines 6A 128
Booth Ho. TW8: Bford 7C 96
        (off High St.)
Booth La. EC4 . . . . .2C 14
Boothman Ho. HA3: Kenton 3D 42
Booth Rd. CR0: C'don 2B 168
  NW9 . . . . .2K 43
Booth's Pl. W1 . . . . .6B 6 (5G 83)
Boot Pde. HA8: Edg 6B 28
        (off High St.)
Boot St. N1 . . . . .2G 9 (3E 84)
Bordars Rd. W7 . . . . .5J 77
Bordars Wlk. W7 . . . . .5J 77
Borden Av. EN1: Enf 6J 23
Border Cres. SE26 . . . . .5H 139
Border Gdns. CR0: C'don 4D 170
Bordergate CR4: Mitc 1C 154
Border Rd. SE26 . . . . .5H 139
Bordesley Rd. SM4: Mord 5K 153
Bordeston Ct. TW8: Bford 7C 96
        (off The Ham)
Bordon Wlk. SW15 . . . . .7C 116
Boreas Wlk. N1 . . . . .1B 8
Boreham Av. E16 . . . . .6J 87
Boreham Cl. E11 . . . . .1E 68
Boreham Rd. N22 . . . . .2C 48
Boreman Ho. SE10 . . . . .6E 104
      (off Thames St.)
Borgard Rd. SE18 . . . . .4D 106
Borkwood Pk. BR6: Orp 4K 173
Borkwood Way BR6: Orp 4J 173
Borland Rd. SE15 . . . . .4J 121
  TW11: Tedd 7B 132
Borley Ct. TW19: Stanw 1A 128
Borneo St. SW15 . . . . .3E 116
BOROUGH, THE 7D 14 (2D 102)
Borough High St. SE1 . . .7D 14 (2C 102)
Borough Hill CR0: Wadd 3B 168
Borough Mkt. SE1 . . . . .5E 14
Borough Rd. CR4: Mitc 2C 154
  KT2: King T 1G 151
  SE1 . . . . .7B 14 (3B 102)
  TW7: Isle 1J 113
Borough Sq. SE1 . . . . .7C 14
Borough Way WS17 . . . . .3B 136
Borrett Cl. SE17 . . . . .5C 102
Borrodaile Rd. SW18 . . . . .6K 117
Borrowdale NW1 . . . . .2A 6
        (off Robert St.)
Borrowdale Av. HA3: W'stone 2A 42
Borrowdale Cl. IG4: Ilf 4C 52
  N2 . . . . .2A 46
Borrowdale Ct. EN2: Enf 1H 23
Borthwick M. E15 . . . . .4G 69
Borthwick Rd. E15 . . . . .4G 69
  NW9 . . . . .6B 44
Borthwick St. SE8 . . . . .5C 104
Borwick Av. E17 . . . . .3B 50
Bosanquet Cl. UB8: Cowl 4A 74
Bosbury Rd. SE6 . . . . .3E 140
Boscastle Rd. NW5 . . . . .3F 65
Boscobel Cl. BR1: Brom 2D 160
Boscobel Ho. E8 . . . . .6H 67
Boscobel Pl. SW1 . . . . . . .3H 17 (4E 100)
Boscobel St. NW8 . . . . . . .4B 4 (4B 82)
Bosco Cl. BR6: Orp 4K 173
Boscombe Av. E10 . . . . .7F 51
Boscombe Cir. NW9 . . . . .1K 43
Boscombe Cl. E5 . . . . .5A 68
Boscombe Gdns. SW16 . . . . .6J 137
Boscombe Ho. CR0: C'don 1D 168
      (off Sydenham Rd.)
Boscombe Rd. KT4: Wor Pk 1E 164
  SW17 . . . . .6E 136
  SW19 . . . . .1K 153
  W12 . . . . .1C 98
Bose Cl. N3 . . . . .1G 45
Bosgrove E4 . . . . .2K 35
Boss Ho. SE1 . . . . .6J 15
        (off Boss St.)

Boss St.—Bow Rd.

Boss St. SE1 6J 15 (2F 103)
Bostall Hill SE2 5A 108
Bostall La. SE2 4B 108
Bostall Mnr. Way SE2 4B 108
Bostall Pk. Av. DA7: Bex 7E 108
Bostall Rd. BR5: St P 7B 144
Bostock Ho. TW5: Hest 6E 94
Boston Bus. Pk. W7 3J 95
Boston Ct. SE25 4F 157
SM2: Sutt 7A 166
Boston Gdns. TW8: Bford 4A 96
W4 6A 98
W7 4A 96
Boston Gro. HA4: Ruis 6E 38
Boston Ho. SW5 4K 99
(off Collingham Rd.)
BOSTON MANOR 4A 96
Boston Manor House 5B 96
Boston Mnr. Rd. TW8: Bford 4B 96
Boston Pde. W7 3A 96
Boston Pk. Rd. TW8: Bford 5C 96
Boston Pl. NW1 4E 4 (4D 82)
Boston Rd. CR0: C'don 6K 155
E6 3C 88
E17 6C 50
HA8: Edg 7D 28
W7 1J 95
Bostonthorpe Rd. W7 2J 95
Boston Va. W7 4A 96
Bosun Cl. E14 2C 104
Boswell Ct. KT2: King T 1F 151
(off Clifton Rd.)
W14 3F 99
(off Blythe Rd.)
WC1 5F 7 (5J 83)
Boswell Ho. WC1 5F 7
(off Boswell St.)
Boswell Path UB3: Harl 4H 93
Boswell Rd. CR7: Thor H 4C 156
Boswell St. WC1 5F 7 (5J 83)
Boswood Ct. TW3: Houn 3D 112
Bosworth Cl. E17 1B 50
Bosworth Ho. W10 4G 81
(off Bosworth Rd.)
Bosworth Rd. EN5: New Bar 3D 20
N11 6C 32
RM10: Dag 3G 73
W10 4G 81
Botany Bay La. BR7: Chst 3G 161
Botany Cl. EN4: E Barn 4H 21
Boteley Cl. E4 2A 36
Botham Cl. HA8: Edg 7D 28
Botha Rd. E13 5K 87
Bothwell Cl. E16 5H 87
Bothwell St. W6 6F 99
Botolph All. EC3 2G 15
Botolph La. EC3 3G 15 (7E 84)
Botsford Rd. SW20 2G 153
Botts M. W2 6J 81
Botwell Comn. Rd. UB3: Hayes 7F 75
Botwell Cres. UB3: Hayes 6G 75
Botwell La. UB3: Hayes 7G 75
Boucher Cl. TW11: Tedd 5K 131
Bouchier Ho. N2 2B 46
Boughton Av. BR2: Hayes 7H 159
Boughton Ho. SE1 6E 14
(off Tennis St.)
Boughton Rd. SE28 3J 107
Boulcott St. E1 6K 85
Boulevard, The IG8: Wfd G 6K 37
SW6 1A 118
SW17 2E 136
SW18 4K 117
Boulevard Dr. NW9 2B 44
Boulogne Ho. SE1 7J 15
(off St Saviour's Est.)
Boulogne Rd. CR0: C'don 6C 156
Boulter Cl. BR1: Brom 3E 160
Boulter Ho. SE14 1J 121
(off Kender St.)
Boulton Ho. TW8: Bford 5E 96
Boulton Rd. RM8: Dag 2E 72
Boultwood Rd. E6 6D 88
Bounces La. N9 2C 34
Bounces Rd. N9 2C 34
Boundaries Rd. SW12 2D 136
TW13: Felt 1A 130
Boundary Av. E17 7B 50
Boundary Bus. Ct. CR4: Mitc 3B 154
Boundary Cl. EN5: Barn 1C 20
IG3: Ilf 4J 71
KT1: King T 3H 151
SE20 2G 157
UB2: S'hall 5E 94
Boundary Ct. N18 6A 34
(off Snells Pk.)
Boundary Ho. SE5 7C 102
W11 1F 99
(off Queensdale Cres.)
Boundary La. E13 3B 88
SE17 6C 102
Boundary Pas. E2 3J 9 (4F 85)
Boundary Rd. DA15: Sidc 5J 125
E13 2A 88
E17 7B 50
HA5: Eastc 7B 40
HA9: Wemb 3E 60
IG11: Bark 1H 89
(King Edwards Rd.)
IG11: Bark 2G 89
(The Clarksons)
N2 1B 46
N9 6D 24
N22 3B 48
NW8 1K 81
SM5: Cars 6F 167
SM6: Wall 6F 167
SW19 6B 136
Boundary Row SE1 6A 14 (2B 102)
Boundary St. E2 2J 9 (3F 85)
Boundary Way CR0: Addtn 5C 170
Boundfield Rd. SE6 3G 141
BOUNDS GREEN 6C 32
Bounds Grn. Ct. N11 6C 32
(off Bounds Grn. Rd.)
Bounds Grn. Ind. Est. N11 6B 32
Bounds Grn. Rd. N11 6B 32
N22 6B 32
Bourbon Ho. SE6 5E 140
Bourbon La. W12 1F 99
Bourchier St. W1 2C 12 (7H 83)
Bourdon Pl. W1 2K 11
Bourdon Rd. SE20 2J 157
Bourdon St. W1 3J 11 (7F 83)
Bourke Cl. NW10 6A 62
SW4 6J 119
Bourlet Cl. W1 6A 6 (5G 83)
Bourn Av. EN4: E Barn 5G 21
N15 4D 48
UB8: Hil 4C 74
Bournbrook Rd. SE3 3B 124
Bourne, The N14 1C 32
Bourne Av. HA4: Ruis 5A 58
N14 2D 32
UB3: Harl 3E 92
Bourne Cir. UB3: Harl 3E 92
Bourne Cl. TW7: Isle 3J 113
Bourne Ct. HA4: Ruis 5K 57
IG8: Wfd G 3B 52
W4 6J 97
Bourne Dr. CR4: Mitc 2B 154
Bourne Est. EC1 5J 7 (5A 84)
Bourne Gdns. E4 4J 35
Bourne Hall Mus. 7B 164
Bourne Hill N13 2D 32
Bourne Hill Cl. N13 2E 32
Bourne Ho. IG9: Buck H 3G 37
TW15: Ashf 5C 128
Bourne Ind. Pk., The DA1: Cray 5K 127
Bourne Mead DA5: Bexl 5K 127
Bournemead Av. UB5: N'olt 2J 75
Bournemead Cl. UB5: N'olt 3J 75
Bournemead Way UB5: N'olt 2K 75
Bourne M. W1 1H 11 (6E 82)
Bournemouth Cl. SE15 2G 121
Bournemouth Rd. SE15 2G 121
SW19 1J 153
Bourne Pde. DA5: Bexl 7H 127
Bourne Pl. W4 5K 97
Bourne Rd. BR2: Brom 4B 160
DA1: Cray 6J 127
DA5: Bexl, Dart 7H 127
E7 3H 69
N8 6J 47
Bournes Ho. N15 6E 48
(off Chisley Rd.)
Bourneside Cres. N14 1C 32
Bourneside Gdns. SE6 5E 140
Bourne St. CR0: C'don 2B 168
SW1 4G 17 (4E 100)
Bourne Ter. W2 5K 81
Bourne Va. BR2: Hayes 1H 171
Bournevale Rd. SW16 4J 137
Bourne Vw. UB6: G'frd 6K 59
Bourneville Rd. SE6 7C 122
Bourne Way BR2: Hayes 2H 171
KT19: Ewe 4J 163
SM1: Sutt 5H 165
Bournewood Rd. SE18 7A 108
Bournwell Cl. EN4: Cockf 3J 21
Bourton Cl. UB3: Hayes 1J 93
Bousfield Rd. SE14 2K 121
Boutflower Rd. SW11 4C 118
Boutique Hall SE13 4E 122
Bouton Pl. N1 7B 66
(off Waterloo Ter.)
Bouverie Gdns. HA3: Kenton 6D 42
Bouverie M. N16 2E 66
Bouverie Pl. W2 7B 4 (6B 82)
Bouverie Rd. HA1: Harr 6G 41
N16 1E 66
Bouverie St. EC4 1K 13 (6A 84)
Bouvier Rd. EN3: Enf W 1D 24
Boveney Rd. SE23 7K 121
Bovill Rd. SE23 7K 121
Bovingdon Av. HA9: Wemb 6G 61
Bovingdon Cl. N19 2G 65
Bovingdon La. NW9 1A 44
Bovingdon Rd. SW6 1K 117
Bovril Ct. SW6 7K 99
(off Fulham Rd.)
BOW 3B 86
Bowater Cl. NW9 5K 43
SW2 6J 119
Bowater Gdns. TW16: Sun 2A 148
Bowater Ho. EC1 4C 8
(off Golden La. Est.)
Bowater Pl. SE3 7K 105
Bowater Rd. HA9: Wemb 3H 61
SE18 3B 106
Bow Bell Twr. E3 1C 86
(off Pancras Way)
Bow Bri. Est. E3 3D 86
Bow Brook, The E2 2K 85
(off Mace St.)
Bow Central Sports Cen. 3B 86
(off Harley Gro.)
Bow Chyd. EC4 1D 14
BOW COMMON 5C 86
Bow Comn. La. E3 4B 86
Bow Creek Ecology Pk. 6G 87
Bowden Cl. TW14: Bedf 1G 129
Bowden Ho. E3 3D 86
(off Rainhill Way)
Bowden St. SE11 6K 19 (5A 102)
Bowditch SE8 4B 104
Bowdon Rd. E17 7C 50
Bowen Dr. SE21 3E 138
Bowen Rd. HA1: Harr 7G 41
Bowen St. E14 6D 86
Bower Av. SE10 1G 123
Bower Cl. RM5: Col R 1K 55
UB5: N'olt 2A 76
Bower Ct. E4 1K 35
(off The Ridgeway)
Bowerdean St. SW6 1K 117
Bowerden Ct. NW10 2D 80
Bowerman Av. SE14 6A 104
Bowerman Ct. N19 2H 65
(off St John's Way)
Bower St. E1 6K 85
Bowers Wlk. E6 6D 88
Bowery Ct. RM10: Dag 6H 73
Bowes Cl. DA15: Sidc 6B 126
Bowe's Ho. IG11: Bark 7F 71
Bowes-Lyon Hall E16 1J 105
(off Wesley Av.)
BOWES PARK 6D 32
Bowes Rd. N11 5B 32
N13 5B 32
RM8: Dag 4C 72
W3 7A 80
Bow Exchange E3 5D 86
(off Yeo St.)
Bow Fair E3 2C 86
(off Fairfield Rd.)
Bowfell Rd. W6 6E 98
Bowford Av. DA7: Bex 1E 126
Bowhill Cl. SW9 7A 102
Bow Ho. E3 3C 86
(off Bow Rd.)
N1 1E 84
(off Whitmore Est.)
Bowie Cl. SW4 7H 119
BOW INTERCHANGE 2D 86
Bowland Rd. IG8: Wfd G 6F 37
SW4 4H 119
Bowland Yd. SW1 7F 11
Bow La. EC4 1D 14 (6C 84)
N12 7F 31
SM4: Mord 6G 153
Bowlby Ho. SE4 4K 121
(off Frendbury Rd.)
Bowl Ct. EC2 4H 9 (4E 84)
Bowles Ct. N12 7H 31
Bowles Rd. SE1 6G 103
Bowley Cl. SE19 6F 139
Bowley Ho. SE16 3G 103
Bowley La. SE19 5F 139
Bowling, The KT12: Walt T 7J 147
Bowling Cl. UB10: Uxb 1B 74
Bowling Grn. Cl. SW15 7D 116
Bowling Grn. Ct. HA9: Wemb 2F 61
Bowling Grn. Ho. SW10 7B 100
(off Riley St.)
Bowling Grn. La. EC1 3K 7 (4A 84)
Bowling Grn. Pl. SE1 6E 14 (2D 102)
Bowling Grn. Row SE18 3D 106
Bowling Grn. St. SE11 7J 19 (6A 102)
Bowling Grn. Wlk. N1 1G 9 (3E 84)
Bow Locks E3 4E 86
Bowls Cl. HA7: Stan 5G 27
Bowman Av. E16 7H 87
Bowman Ho. N1 1E 84
(off Nuttall St.)
Bowman M. SW18 1H 135
Bowman's Bldgs. NW1 5C 4
(off Penfold Pl.)
Bowmans Cl. W13 1B 96
Bowmans Lea SE23 7J 121
Bowmans Mdw. SM6: Wall 3F 167
Bowman's M. E1 7G 85
N7 3J 65
Bowman's Pl. N7 3J 65
Bowman Trad. Est. NW9 3G 43
Bowmead SE9 2D 142
Bowmore Wlk. NW1 7H 65
Bowness Cl. E8 6F 67
(off Beechwood Rd.)
Bowness Cres. SW15 5A 134
Bowness Dr. TW4: Houn 4C 112
Bowness Ho. SE15 7J 103
(off Hillbeck Cl.)
Bowness Rd. DA7: Bex 2H 127
SE6 7D 122
Bowood Rd. EN3: Enf H 2E 24
SW11 5E 118
Bow Rd. E3 3B 86

Bowrons Av. HA0: Wemb 7D 60
Bowry Ho. E14 .5B 86
    (off Wallwood St.)
Bowsley Ct. TW13: Felt 2J 129
Bowsprit Point E14 . . . . .3C 104
    (off Westferry Rd.)
Bow St. E15 . . . . .5G 69
  WC2 . . . . .1F 13 (6J 83)
Bow Triangle Bus. Cen. E3 . . . . .4C 86
Bowyer Cl. E6 .5D 88
Bowyer Ho. N1 . . . . .1E 84
    (off Mill Row)
Bowyer Pl. SE5 . . . . .7C 102
Bowyers Ct. TW1: Isle 4B 114
Bowyer St. SE5 . . . . .7C 102
Boxall Rd. SE21 . . . . .6E 120
Boxelder Cl. HA8: Edg 5D 28
Boxgrove Rd. SE2 . . . . .3C 108
Box La. IG11: Bark 2B 90
Boxley Rd. SM4: Mord 4A 154
Boxley St. E16 . . . . .1K 105
Boxmoor Ho. E2 . . . . .1G 85
    (off Whiston Rd.)
  W11 . . . . .1F 99
    (off Queensdale Cres.)
Boxmoor Rd. HA3: Kenton 4B 42
Boxoll Rd. RM9: Dag 4F 73
Boxted Cl. IG9: Buck H 1H 37
Box Tree Ho. SE8 . . . . .6A 104
Boxtree La. HA3: Hrw W 1G 41
Boxtree Rd. HA3: Hrw W 7C 26
Boxwood Cl. UB7: W Dray 2B 92
Boxworth Cl. N12 . . . . .5G 31
Boxworth Gro. N1 . . . . .1K 83
Boyard Rd. SE18 . . . . .5F 107
Boyce Ho. SW16 . . . . .5G 137
  W10 . . . . .3H 81
    (off Bruckner St.)
Boyce Way E13 . . . . .4J 87
Boycroft Av. NW9 . . . . .6J 43
Boyd Av. UB1: S'hall 1D 94
Boyd Cl. KT2: King T 7G 133
Boydell Ct. NW8 . . . . .7B 64
    (not continuous)
Boyden Ho. E17 . . . . .3E 50
Boyd Rd. SW19 . . . . .6B 136
Boyd St. E1 . . . . .6G 85
Boyfield St. SE1 . . . . .7B 14 (2B 102)
Boyland Rd. BR1: Brom 5H 141
Boyle Av. HA7: Stan 6F 27
Boyle Cl. UB10: Uxb 2B 74
Boyle Farm Island KT7: T Ditt 6A 150
Boyle Farm Rd. KT7: T Ditt 6A 150
Boyle St. W1 . . . . .2A 12 (7G 83)
Boyne Av. NW4 . . . . .4F 45
Boyne Rd. RM10: Dag 3G 73
  SE13 .3E 122
Boyne Ter. M. W11 . . . . .1H 99
Boyseland Ct. HA8: Edg 2D 28
Boyson Rd. SE17 . . . . .6C 102
    (not continuous)
Boyson Wlk. SE17 . . . . .6D 102
Boyton Cl. E1 .4J 85
  N8 . . . . .3J 47
Boyton Ho. NW8 . . . . .2B 82
    (off Wellington Rd.)
Boyton Rd. N8 . . . . .3J 47
Brabant Ct. EC3 . . . . .2G 15
Brabant Rd. N22 . . . . .2K 47
Brabazon Av. SM6: Wall 7J 167
Brabazon Ct. SW1 . . . . .5H 101
    (off Moreton Ct.)
  SW1 . . . . .5C 18
    (off Moreton St.)
Brabazon Rd. TW5: Hest 7A 94
  UB5: N'olt 2E 76
Brabazon St. E14 . . . . .6D 86
Brabner Ho. E2 . . . . .1K 9
    (off Wellington Row)
Brabourne Cl. SE19 . . . . .5E 138
Brabourne Cres. DA7: Bex 6F 109
Brabourne Hgts. NW7 . . . . .3F 29

Brabourne Ri. BR3: Beck 5E 158
Brabourn Gro. SE15 . . . . .2J 121
Brabrook Ct. SM6: Wall 4F 167
Brabstone Ho. UB6: G'frd 2K 77
Bracer Ho. N1 .2E 84
    (off Whitmore Rd.)
Bracewell Av. UB6: G'frd 5K 59
Bracewell Rd. W10 . . . . .5E 80
Bracewood Gdns. CR0: C'don 3F 169
Bracey M. N4 .2J 65
Bracey St. N4 .2J 65
Bracken, The E4 . . . . .2K 35
Bracken Av. CR0: C'don 3C 170
  SW12 .6E 118
Brackenbridge Dr. HA4: Ruis 3B 58
Brackenbury N4 . . . . .1A 66
    (off Osborne Rd.)
Brackenbury Gdns. W6 . . . . .3D 98
Brackenbury Rd. N2 . . . . .3A 46
  W6 . . . . .3D 98
Bracken Cl. E6 . . . . .5D 88
  TW2: Whitt 7E 112
  TW16: Sun 6H 129
Brackendale N21 . . . . .2E 32
Brackendale Cl. TW3: Houn 1F 113
Brackendene DA2: Dart 4K 145
Bracken End TW7: Isle 5H 113
Brackenfield Cl. E5 . . . . .3H 67
Bracken Gdns. SW13 . . . . .2C 116
Brackenhill HA4: Ruis 4C 58
Bracken Hill Cl. BR1: Brom 1H 159
Bracken Hill La. BR1: Brom 1H 159
Bracken Ho. E3 . . . . .5C 86
    (off Devons Rd.)
Bracken Ind. Est. IG6: Ilf 1J 53
Bracken M. E4 . . . . .1K 35
  RM7: Rom 6H 55
Brackens BR3: Beck 7C 140
Brackens, The EN1: Enf 7K 23
Brackenwood TW16: Sun 1J 147
Brackenwood Lodge EN5: New Bar . . .4D 20
    (off Prospect Rd.)
Brackley Av. SE15 . . . . .3J 121
Brackley Cl. SM6: Wall 7J 167
Brackley Ct. NW8 . . . . .3B 4
    (off Pollitt Dr.)
Brackley Rd. BR3: Beck 7B 140
  W4 . . . . .5A 98
Brackley Sq. IG8: Wfd G 7G 37
Brackley St. EC1 . . . . .5D 8 (4C 84)
Brackley Ter. W4 . . . . .5A 98
Bracklyn Cl. N1 . . . . .2D 84
Bracklyn St. N1 . . . . .2D 84
Bracknell Cl. N22 . . . . .1A 48
Bracknell Gdns. NW3 . . . . .4K 63
Bracknell Ga. NW3 . . . . .5K 63
Bracknell Way NW3 . . . . .4K 63
Bracondale Rd. SE2 . . . . .4A 108
Bradbeer Ho. E2 . . . . .3J 85
    (off Cornwall Rd.)
Bradbourne Rd. DA5: Bexl 7G 127
Bradbourne St. SW6 . . . . .2J 117
Bradbury Cl. UB2: S'hall 4D 94
Bradbury M. N16 . . . . .5E 66
Bradbury St. N16 . . . . .5E 66
Bradby Ho. NW8 . . . . .2K 81
    (off Hamilton Ter.)
Bradby's HA1: Harr 1J 59
    (off High St.)
Braddock Cl. TW7: Isle 2K 113
Braddon Ct. EN5: Barn 3B 20
Braddon Rd. TW9: Rich 3F 115
Braddyll St. SE10 . . . . .5G 105
Bradenham SE17 . . . . .6D 102
    (off Bradenham Cl.)
Bradenham Av. DA16: Well 4A 126
Bradenham Cl. SE17 . . . . .6D 102
Bradenham Rd. HA3: Kenton 4B 42
  UB4: Hayes 3G 75
Braden St. W9 . . . . .4K 81
Bradfield Ct. NW1 . . . . .7F 65
    (off Hawley Rd.)

Bradfield Dr. IG11: Bark 5A 72
Bradfield Ho. IG8: Wfd G 6K 37
Bradfield Rd. E16 . . . . .2J 105
  HA4: Ruis 5C 58
Bradford Cl. BR2: Brom 1D 172
  N17 . . . . .6A 34
  SE26 .4H 139
Bradford Dr. KT19: Ewe 6B 164
Bradford Ho. W14 . . . . .3F 99
    (off Spring Va. Ter.)
Bradford Rd. IG1: Ilf 1H 71
  W3 . . . . .2A 98
Bradgate Rd. SE6 . . . . .6D 122
Brading Cres. E11 . . . . .2K 69
Brading Rd. CR0: C'don 6K 155
  SW2 . . . . .7K 119
Brading Ter. W12 . . . . .3C 98
Bradiston Rd. W9 . . . . .3H 81
Bradley Cl. N7 .6J 65
Bradley Gdns. W13 . . . . .6B 78
Bradley Ho. E3 . . . . .3D 86
    (off Bromley High St.)
  IG8: Wfd G 7D 36
  SE16 . . . . .4J 103
    (off Raymouth Rd.)
Bradley M. SW17 . . . . .1D 136
Bradley Rd. N22 . . . . .2A 47
  SE19 . . . . .6C 138
Bradley's Cl. N1 . . . . .2A 84
Bradley Stone Rd. E6 . . . . .5D 88
Bradman Row HA8: Edg 7D 28
Bradmead SW8 . . . . .7F 101
Bradmore Ct. EN3: Enf H 3F 25
    (off Enstone Rd.)
Bradmore Pk. Rd. W6 . . . . .4D 98
Bradon NW9 . . . . .2B 44
    (off Further Acre)
Brad Rd. NW7 .6A 30
Bradshaw Cl. SW19 . . . . .6J 135
Bradshaw Cotts. E14 . . . . .6A 86
    (off Repton St.)
Bradshaw Dr. NW7 . . . . .7A 30
Bradshawe Waye
  UB8: Hil 5B 74
Bradshaws Cl. SE25 . . . . .3G 157
Bradstock Ho. E9 . . . . .7K 67
Bradstock Rd. E9 . . . . .6K 67
  KT17: Ewe 5C 164
Brad St. SE1 . . . . .5K 13 (1A 102)
Bradwell Av. RM10: Dag 2G 73
Bradwell Cl. E18 . . . . .4H 51
Bradwell Ho. NW6 . . . . .1K 81
    (off Mortimer Cres.)
Bradwell M. N18 . . . . .4B 34
Bradwell Rd. IG9: Buck H 1H 37
Brady Ct. RM8: Dag 1D 72
Brady Dr. BR1: Brom 3E 160
Brady Ho. SW8 . . . . .1G 119
    (off Corunna Rd.)
Bradymead E6 . . . . .6E 88
Brady St. E1 . . . . .4H 85
Braeburn Ct. BR6: Orp 2K 173
    (off Blossom Dr.)
  EN4: E Barn 4G 21
Brae Ct. KT2: King T 1G 151
Braemar SW15 . . . . .6F 117
Braemar Av. CR2: S Croy 7C 168
  CR7: Thor H 3A 156
  DA7: Bex 4J 127
  HA0: Wemb 7D 60
  N22 . . . . .1J 47
  NW10 . . . . .3K 61
  SW19 .2J 135
Braemar Cl. SE16 . . . . .5H 103
    (off Masters Dr.)
Braemar Ct. SE6 . . . . .1H 141
    (off Cumberland Pl.)
Braemar Gdns. BR4: W W'ck 1E 170
  DA15: Sidc 3H 143
  NW9 . . . . .1K 43
Braemar Ho. W9 . . . . .3A 82
    (off Maida Va.)

Braemar Mans. SW7 . . . . .3K 99
    (off Cornwall Gdns.)
Braemar Rd. E13 . . . . .4H 87
  KT4: Wor Pk 3D 164
  N15 . . . . .5E 48
  TW8: Bford 6D 96
Braeside BR3: Beck 5C 140
Braeside Av. SW19 . . . . .1G 153
Braeside Cres. DA7: Bex 4J 127
Braeside Rd. SW16 . . . . .7G 137
Braes St. N1 . . . . .7B 66
Braesyde Cl. DA17: Belv 4F 109
Brafferton Rd. CR0: C'don 4C 168
Braganza St. SE17 . . . . .5B 102
Bragg Cl. RM8: Dag 6B 72
Bragg Rd. TW11: Tedd 6J 131
Braham Ho. SE11 . . . . .6H 19 (5K 101)
Braham St. E1 . . . . .6F 85
  E1 . . . . .7K 9
Braid Av. W3 . . . . .6A 80
Braid Cl. TW13: Hanw 2D 130
Braid Ho. SE10 . . . . .1E 122
    (off Blackheath Hill)
Braidwood Pas. EC1 . . . . .5C 8
    (off Aldersgate St.)
Braidwood Rd. SE6 . . . . .1F 141
Braidwood St. SE1 . . . . .5G 15 (1E 102)
Brailsford Cl. CR4: Mitc 7C 136
Brailsford Rd. SW2 . . . . .5A 120
Brainton Av. TW14: Felt 7K 111
Braintree Av. IG4: Ilf 4C 52
Braintree Ho. E1 . . . . .4J 85
    (off Malcolm Rd.)
Braintree Rd. HA4: Ruis 4K 57
  RM10: Dag 3G 73
Braintree St. E2 . . . . .3J 85
Braithwaite Av. RM7: Rush G 7G 55
Braithwaite Gdns. HA7: Stan 1C 42
Braithwaite Ho. EC1 . . . . .3E 8
    (off Bunhill Row)
Braithwaite Rd. EN3: Brim 3G 25
Braithwaite St. EN1 . . . . .4J 9 (4F 85)
Braithwaite Twr. W2 . . . . .5B 4
Bramah Grn. SW9 . . . . .1A 120
Bramah Ho. SW1 . . . . .6J 17
  SW1 . . . . .5F 101
Bramalea Cl. N6 . . . . .6E 46
Bramall Cl. E15 . . . . .5H 69
Bramall Ct. N7 . . . . .5K 65
    (off George's Rd.)
Bramber WC1 .2E 6
Bramber Ct. TW8: Bford 4E 96
  W14 . . . . .6H 99
    (off North End Rd.)
Bramber Ho. KT2: King T 1E 150
    (off Seven Kings Way)
Bramber Rd. N12 . . . . .5H 31
  W14 . . . . .6H 99
Brambleacres Cl. SM2: Sutt 7J 165
Brambledown Rd. SE18 . . . . .5G 107
Brambledown BR3: Beck 5E 158
  CR0: C'don 4C 170
  HA7: Stan 7J 27
  N15 . . . . .4G 49
  SE19 . . . . .1D 156
  TW17: Shep 3F 147
  UB8: Hil 6B 74
Bramble Cft. DA8: Erith 4J 109
Brambledown Cl. BR4: W W'ck 5G 159
Brambledown Rd. CR2: Sande 7E 168
  SM5: Cars 7E 166
  SM6: Wall 7E 166
Bramble Gdns. W12 . . . . .7B 80
Bramble Ho. E3 . . . . .5C 86
    (off Devons Rd.)
Bramble La. TW12: Hamp 6D 130
Brambles, The SW19 . . . . .5H 135
    (off Woodside)
  UB7: W Dray 4A 92
Brambles Cl. TW7: Isle 7B 96
Brambles Farm Dr. UB10: Hil 3C 74
Bramblewood Cl. SM5: Cars 1C 166

Brambling Ct.—Brent Cross

Brambling Ct. SE8 6B 104
(off Abinger Gro.)
Bramblings, The E4 4A 36
Bramcote Av. CR4: Mitc 4D 154
Bramcote Ct. CR4: Mitc 4D 154
(off Bramcote Av.)
Bramcote Gro. SE16 5J 103
Bramcote Rd. SW15 4D 116
Bramdean Cres. SE12 1J 141
Bramdean Gdns. SE12 1J 141
Bramerton NW6 7F 63
(off Willesden La.)
Bramerton Rd. BR3: Beck 3B 158
Bramerton St. SW3 7C 16 (6C 100)
Bramfield Ct. N4 2C 66
(off Queens Dr.)
Bramfield Rd. SW11 6C 118
Bramford Ct. N14 2C 32
Bramford Rd. SW18 4A 118
Bramham Gdns. KT9: Chess 4D 162
SW5 5K 99
Bramhope La. SE7 6K 105
Bramlands Cl. SW11 3C 118
Bramley Av. TW17: Shep 3G 147
Bramley Bank Nature Reserve 6J 169
Bramley Cl. BR6: Farnb 1F 173
CR2: S Croy 5C 168
E17 2A 50
HA5: Eastc 3H 39
IG8: Wfd G 7F 37
N14 5A 22
NW7 3F 29
TW2: Whitt 6G 113
UB3: Hayes 7J 75
Bramley Ct. BR6: Orp 2K 173
(off Blossom Dr.)
CR4: Mitc 2B 154
DA16: Well 1B 126
E4 1K 35
(off The Ridgeway)
EN4: E Barn 4H 21
UB1: S'hall 7G 77
(off Haldane Rd.)
Bramley Cres. IG2: Ilf 6E 52
SW8 7H 101
Bramley Hill CR2: S Croy 5B 168
Bramley Ho. SW15 6B 116
(off Tunworth Cres.)
TW4: Houn 4D 112
W10 6F 81
Bramley Hyrst CR2: S Croy 5C 168
Bramley Lodge HA0: Wemb 4D 60
Bramley Pde. N14 4C 22
Bramley Rd. N14 5K 21
SM1: Sutt 5B 166
SM2: Cheam 7F 165
W5 3C 96
W10 6F 81
Bramley Sports Ground 5K 21
Bramley Way BR4: W W'ck 2D 170
TW4: Houn 5D 112
Brampton WC1 6G 7
(off Red Lion Sq.)
Brampton Cl. E5 2H 67
Brampton Ct. NW4 4D 44
RM7: Rush G 6K 55
(off Union Rd.)
Brampton Gdns. N15 5C 48
Brampton Gro. HA3: Kenton 4A 42
HA9: Wemb 1G 61
NW4 4D 44
Brampton La. NW4 4E 44
Brampton Pk. Rd. N22 3A 48
Brampton Rd. CR0: C'don 7F 157
DA7: Bex 3D 126
E6 3B 88
N15 5C 48
NW9 4G 43
SE2 6C 108
UB10: Hil 2D 74
Bramshaw Ri. KT3: N Mald 6A 152
Bramshaw Rd. E9 6K 67
Bramshill Gdns. NW5 3F 65
Bramshill Rd. NW10 2B 80
Bramshot Av. SE7 6J 105
Bramshurst NW8 1K 81
(off Abbey Rd.)
Bramston Rd. NW10 2C 80
SW17 3A 136
Bramwell Cl. TW16: Sun 2B 148
Bramwell Ho. SE1 3C 102
SW1 6A 18
(off Churchill Gdns.)
Bramwell M. N1 1K 83
Brancaster Dr. NW7 7H 29
Brancaster Ho. E1 3K 85
(off Moody St.)
Brancaster Rd. E12 4D 70
IG2: Ilf 6J 53
SW16 3J 137
Brancepeth Gdns. IG9: Buck H 2D 36
Branch Hill NW3 3A 64
Branch Hill Ho. NW3 3K 63
Branch Pl. N1 1D 84
Branch Rd. E14 7A 86
Branch St. SE15 7E 102
Brancker Rd. HA3: Kenton 3D 42
Brancroft Way EN3: Brim 1F 25
Brand Cl. N4 1B 66
Brandesbury Sq. IG8: Wfd G 7K 37
Brandlehow Rd. SW15 4H 117
Brandon Est. SE17 6B 102
Brandon Ho. BR3: Beck 5D 140
(off Beckenham Hill Rd.)
Brandon Mans. W14 6G 99
(off Queen's Club Gdns.)
Brandon M. EC2 6E 8
SE17 4C 102
(off Brandon St.)
Brandon Rd. E17 4E 50
N7 7J 65
SM1: Sutt 4K 165
UB2: S'hall 5D 94
Brandon St. SE17 4C 102
(not continuous)
Brandram M. SE13 4G 123
(off Brandram Rd.)
Brandram Rd. SE13 3G 123
Brandrams Wharf SE16 2J 103
Brandreth Ct. HA1: Harr 6K 41
Brandreth Rd. E6 6D 88
SW17 2F 137
Brandries, The SM6: Bedd 3H 167
Brands Ho. NW6 1H 81
(off Lincoln M.)
Brand St. SE10 7E 104
Brandville Gdns. IG6: Ilf 4F 53
Brandville Rd. UB7: W Dray 2A 92
Brandy Way SM2: Sutt 7J 165
Brangbourne Rd. BR1: Brom 5E 140
Brangton Rd. SE11 6H 19 (5K 101)
Brangwyn Ct. W14 3G 99
(off Blythe Rd.)
Brangwyn Cres. SW19 1A 154
Branham Ho. SE18 5F 107
Branksea St. SW6 7G 99
Branksome Av. N18 6A 34
Branksome Cl. TW11: Tedd 4H 131
Branksome Ho. SW8 7K 101
(off Meadow Rd.)
Branksome Rd. SW2 5J 119
SW19 1J 153
Branksome Way HA3: Kenton 6F 43
KT3: N Mald 1J 151
Branksone Ct. N2 3A 46
Bransby Rd. KT9: Chess 6E 162
Branscombe NW1 1G 83
(off Plender St.)
Branscombe Ct. BR2: Brom 5H 159
Branscombe Gdns. N21 7F 23
Branscombe St. SE13 3D 122
Bransdale Cl. NW6 1J 81
Bransgrove Rd. HA8: Edg 1F 43
Branston Cres. BR5: Pet W 1H 173
Branstone Rd. TW9: Kew 1F 115
Brants Wlk. W7 4J 77
Brantwood Av. DA8: Erith 7J 109
TW7: Isle 4A 114
Brantwood Cl. E17 3D 50
Brantwood Gdns. EN2: Enf 4D 22
IG4: Ilf 4C 52
Brantwood Ho. SE5 7C 102
(off Wyndam Est.)
Brantwood Rd. CR2: S Croy 7C 168
DA7: Bex 2H 127
N17 6B 34
SE24 5C 120
Branxholme Ct. BR1: Brom 1H 159
(off Highland Rd.)
Brasenose Dr. SW13 6E 98
Brasher Cl. UB6: G'frd 5H 59
Brassett Point E15 1G 87
(off Abbey Rd.)
Brassey Cl. TW14: Felt 1J 129
Brassey Ho. E14 4D 104
(off Cahir St.)
Brassey Rd. NW6 6H 63
Brassey Sq. SW11 3E 118
Brassie Av. W3 6A 80
Brass Talley All. SE16 2K 103
Brasted Cl. BR6: Orp 2K 173
DA6: Bex 5D 126
SE26 4J 139
Brasted Lodge BR3: Beck 7C 140
Brathay NW1 1B 6
(off Ampthill Est.)
Brathway Rd. SW18 7J 117
Bratley St. E1 4G 85
Bratten Ct. CR0: C'don 6D 156
Braund Av. UB6: G'frd 4F 77
Braundton Av. DA15: Sidc 1K 143
Braunston Dr. UB4: Yead 4C 76
Bravington Cl. TW17: Shep 5B 146
Bravington Pl. W9 4H 81
Bravington Rd. W9 2H 81
Bravingtons Wlk. N1 1F 7
(off York Way)
Brawne Ho. SE17 6B 102
(off Brandon Est.)
Braxfield Rd. SE4 4A 122
Braxted Pk. SW16 6K 137
Bray NW3 7C 64
Brayards Rd. SE15 2H 121
Brayards Rd. Est. SE15 2H 121
(off Caulfield Rd.)
Braybourne Dr. TW7: Isle 7K 95
Braybrooke Gdns. SE19 7E 138
Braybrook St. W12 5B 80
Brayburne Av. SW4 2G 119
Bray Ct. E2 3K 85
(off Meath Cres.)
SW16 5J 137
Braycourt Av. KT12: Walt T 7K 147
Bray Cres. SE16 2K 103
Braydon Rd. N16 1G 67
Bray Dr. E16 7H 87
Brayfield Ter. N1 7A 66
Brayford Sq. E1 6J 85
Bray Pas. E16 7J 87
Bray Pl. SW3 4E 16 (4D 100)
Bray Rd. NW7 6A 30
Brayton Gdns. EN2: Enf 4C 22
Braywood Rd. SE9 4H 125
Brazier Cres. UB5: N'olt 4D 76
Brazil Cl. CR0: Bedd 7J 155
Breach La. RM9: Dag 3G 91
Bread St. EC4 1D 14 (6C 84)
(not continuous)
Breakspear Crematorium (Ruislip)
HA4: Ruis 5E 38
Breakspear M. UB9: Hare 3A 38
Breakspear Rd. HA4: Ruis 7D 38
Breakspear Rd. Nth. UB9: Hare 3A 38
Breakspear Rd. Sth. UB9: Hare 3B 56
UB10: Ick 3B 56
Breakspears Dr. BR5: St P 7A 144
Breakspears M. SE4 2B 122
Breakspears Rd. SE4 4B 122
(not continuous)
Breakwell Ct. W10 4G 81
(off Wornington Rd.)
Bream Cl. N17 4H 49
Bream Gdns. E6 3E 88
Breamore Cl. SW15 1C 134
Breamore Ct. IG3: Ilf 2A 72
Breamore Ho. SE15 7G 103
(off Friary Est.)
Breamore Rd. IG3: Ilf 2K 71
Bream's Bldgs. EC4 7J 7 (6A 84)
Bream St. E3 7C 68
Breamwater Gdns.
TW10: Ham 3B 132
Brearley Cl. HA8: Edg 7D 28
UB8: Uxb 6A 56
Breasley Cl. SW15 4D 116
Breasy Pl. NW4 4D 44
(off Burroughs Gdns.)
Brechin Pl. SW7 4A 100
Brecknock Rd. N7 5H 65
N19 4G 65
Brecknock Rd. Est. N19 4G 65
Breckonmead BR1: Brom 2A 160
Brecon Cl. CR4: Mitc 3J 155
KT4: Wor Pk 2E 164
Brecon Grn. NW9 6A 44
Brecon Ho. E3 2B 86
(off Ordell Rd.)
W2 6A 82
(off Hallfield Est.)
Brecon M. N7 5H 65
Brecon Rd. EN3: Pond E 4D 24
W6 6G 99
Brede Cl. E6 3E 88
Bredel Ho. E14 5C 86
(off St Paul's Way)
Bredgar SE13 5D 122
Bredgar Rd. N19 2G 65
Bredhurst Cl. SE20 6J 139
Bredinghurst SE22 7G 121
Bredin Ho. SW10 7K 99
(off Coleridge Gdns.)
Bredo Ho. IG11: Bark 3B 90
Bredon Rd. CR0: C'don 7F 157
Breer St. SW6 3K 117
Breezers Ct. E1 7G 85
(off The Highway)
Breezer's Hill E1 7G 85
Brember Rd. HA2: Harr 2G 59
Bremer M. E17 4D 50
Bremner Rd. SW7 1A 16 (3A 100)
Brenchley Cl. BR2: Brom 6H 159
BR7: Chst 1E 160
Brenchley Gdns. SE23 6J 121
Brenchley Rd. BR5: St P 2K 161
Brenda Rd. SW17 2D 136
Brende Gdns. KT8: W Mole 4F 149
Brendon Av. NW10 4A 62
Brendon Cl. UB3: Harl 7E 92
Brendon Ct. UB2: S'hall 4F 95
Brendon Gdns. HA2: Harr 4F 59
IG2: Ilf 5J 53
Brendon Gro. N2 2A 46
Brendon Rd. RM8: Dag 1F 73
SE9 2H 143
Brendon St. W1 7D 4 (6C 82)
Brendon Vs. N21 1H 33
Brendon Way EN1: Enf 7K 23
Brenley Cl. CR4: Mitc 3E 154
Brenley Gdns. SE9 4B 124
Brenley Ho. SE1 6E 14
(off Tennis St.)
Brennand Ct. N19 3G 65
Brent Cl. DA5: Bexl 1E 144
Brentcot Cl. W13 4B 78
Brent Ct. NW11 7F 45
W7 7H 77
Brent Cres. NW10 2F 79
BRENT CROSS 7E 44

Brent Cross Fly-Over NW2 . . . . .7F 45
  NW4 . . . . .7F 45
Brent Cross Gdns. NW4 . . . . .6F 45
BRENT CROSS INTERCHANGE 6E 44
Brent Cross Shop. Cen. NW4 . . . . .7F 44
Brentfield NW10 . . . . .7H 61
Brentfield Cl. NW10 . . . . .6K 61
Brentfield Gdns. NW2 . . . . .7F 45
Brentfield Ho. NW10 . . . . .7K 61
Brentfield Rd. NW10 . . . . .6K 61
BRENTFORD 6D 96
Brentford Bus. Cen. TW8: Bford 7C 96
Brentford Cl. UB4: Yead 4B 76
BRENTFORD END 7B 96
Brentford FC 6D 96
Brentford Fountain Leisure Cen. 5G 97
Brentford Ho. TW1: Twick 7B 114
Brentford Musical Mus. 6F 97
Brent Grn. NW4 . . . . .5E 44
Brent Grn. Wlk. HA9: Wemb 3J 61
Brentham Club .3C 78
Brentham Way W5 . . . . .4D 78
Brent Ho. E9 . . . . .6J 67
                (off Brenthouse Rd.)
Brenthouse Rd. E9 . . . . .7J 67
Brenthurst Rd. NW10 . . . . .6B 62
Brent Lea TW8: Bford 7C 96
Brentmead Cl. W7 . . . . .7J 77
Brentmead Gdns. NW10 . . . . .2F 79
Brentmead Pl. NW11 . . . . .6F 45
Brent Mus. 6D 62
                    (off High Rd.)
Brent New Ent. Cen. NW10 . . . . .6B 62
Brenton St. E14 . . . . .6A 86
Brent Pk. Ind. Est. UB2: S'hall 3K 93
Brent Pk. Rd. NW4 . . . . .7D 44
  NW9 . . . . .7D 44
Brent Pl. EN5: Barn 5C 20
Brent Reservoir (Welsh Harp) Nature Reserve
                     . . . . .1B 62
Brent Rd. CR2: Sels 7H 169
  E16 . . . . .6J 87
  SE18 . . . . .7F 107
  TW8: Bford 6C 96
  UB2: S'hall 3A 94
Brent Side TW8: Bford 6C 96
Brentside Cl. W13 . . . . .4A 78
Brentside Executive Cen.
  TW8: Bford 6B 96
Brent St. NW4 . . . . .4E 44
Brent Ter. NW2 .1E 62
               (not continuous)
Brent Trad. Cen. NW10 . . . . .5A 62
Brentvale Av. HA0: Wemb 1F 79
  UB1: S'hall 1H 95
Brent Vw. Rd. NW9 . . . . .6C 44
Brentwaters Bus. Pk. TW8: Bford 7C 96
Brent Way HA9: Wemb 6H 61
  N3 . . . . .6D 30
  TW8: Bford 7D 96
Brentwick Gdns. TW8: Bford 4E 96
Brentwood Cl. SE9 . . . . .1G 143
Brentwood Ho. SE18 . . . . .7B 106
             (off Portway Gdns.)
Brentwood Lodge NW4 . . . . .5F 45
          (off Holmdale Gdns.)
Brereton Rd. N17 . . . . .7H 34
Bressay Dr. NW7 . . . . .7H 29
Bressenden Pl. SW1 . . . . . .1K 17 (3F 101)
Bressey Av. EN1: Enf 1B 24
Bressey Gro. E18 . . . . .2H 51
Breton Highwalk EC2 . . . . .5D 8
               (off Golden La.)
Breton Ho. EC2 .5D 8
  SE1 . . . . .7J 15
           (off St Saviour's Est.)
Brett Cl. N16 . . . . .2E 66
  UB5: N'olt 3B 76
Brett Ct. N9 . . . . .2D 34
Brett Cres. NW10 . . . . .1K 79
Brettell St. SE17 . . . . .5D 102
Brettenham Av. E17 . . . . .1C 50

Brettenham Rd. E17 . . . . .2C 50
  N18 . . . . .4B 34
Brett Gdns. RM9: Dag 7E 72
Brett Ho. Cl. SW15 . . . . .7F 117
Brettinghurst SE1 . . . . .5G 103
             (off Avondale La.)
Brett Pas. E8 . . . . .5H 67
Brett Rd. E8 . . . . .5H 67
Brewers Bldgs. EC1 . . . . .1A 8
           (off Rawstorne St.)
Brewer's Grn. SW1 . . . . .1C 18
Brewer's Hall Gdn. EC2 . . . . .6D 8
         (off Aldermanbury Sq.)
Brewers La. TW9: Rich 5D 114
Brewer St. W1 . . . . .2B 12 (7G 83)
Brewery, The EC2 . . . . .5E 8 (5C 84)
  RM1: Rom 5K 55
Brewery Cl. HA0: Wemb 5A 60
Brewery Ind. Est., The N1 . . . . .1D 8
           (off Wenlock Rd.)
Brewery La. TW1: Twick 7K 113
Brewery M. Cen. TW7: Isle 3A 114
Brewery Rd. BR2: Brom 2C 172
  N7 . . . . .7J 65
  SE18 . . . . .5H 107
Brewery Sq. EC1 . . . . .3A 8 (4B 84)
  SE1 . . . . .5J 15
Brewery Wlk. RM1: Rom 5K 55
Brewhouse La. E1 . . . . .1H 103
  SW15 . . . . .3G 117
Brewhouse Rd. SE18 . . . . .4D 106
Brewhouse Wlk. SE16 . . . . .1A 104
Brewhouse Yd. EC1 . . . . . . .3A 8 (4B 84)
Brewin Ter. UB4: Yead 5A 76
Brewood Rd. RM8: Dag 6B 72
Brewster Gdns. W10 . . . . .5E 80
Brewster Ho. E14 . . . . .7B 86
          (off Three Colt St.)
  SE1 . . . . .4F 103
             (off Dunton Rd.)
Brewster Rd. E10 . . . . .1D 68
Brian Rd. RM6: Chad H 5C 54
Briant Ho. SE1 .2J 19
Briants Cl. HA5: Pinn 2D 40
Briant St. SE14 . . . . .1K 121
Briar Av. SW16 . . . . .7K 137
Briarbank Rd. W13 . . . . .6A 78
Briar Cl. IG9: Buck H 2G 37
  N2 . . . . .3K 45
  N13 . . . . .3H 33
  TW7: Isle 5K 113
  TW12: Hamp .5D 130
Briar Ct. E3 . . . . .2C 86
            (off Morville St.)
  SM3: Cheam 4E 164
  SW15 . . . . .4D 116
Briar Cres. UB5: N'olt 6F 59
Briardale HA8: Edg 4E 28
Briardale Gdns. NW3 . . . . .3J 63
Briarfield Av. N3 . . . . .3K 45
            (not continuous)
Briarfield Cl. DA7: Bex 2G 127
Briar Gdns. BR2: Hayes 1H 171
Briaris Cl. N17 . . . . .7C 34
Briar La. CR0: Addtn 4D 170
Briar Rd. DA5: Bexl 3K 145
  HA3: Kenton 5C 42
  NW2 . . . . .4E 62
  SW16 . . . . .3J 155
  TW2: Twick 1J 131
  TW17: Shep 5B 146
Briars, The TW19: Stan M 7B 174
  WD23: B Hea .1D 26
Briarswood Way
  BR6: Chels 5K 173
Briar Wlk. HA8: Edg 7D 28
  SW15 . . . . .4D 116
  W10 . . . . .4G 81
Briar Way UB7: W Dray 2C 92
Briar Wood Cl. BR2: Brom 2C 172
Briarwood Cl. NW9 . . . . .6J 43
  TW13: Felt 4G 129

Briarwood Ct. KT4: Wor Pk 1C 164
              (off The Avenue)
Briarwood Dr. HA6: Nwood 2J 39
Briarwood Rd. KT17: Ewe 6C 164
  SW4 . . . . .5H 119
Briary Cl. NW3 .7C 64
Briary Ct. DA14: Sidc 5B 144
  E16 . . . . .6H 87
Briary Gdns. BR1: Brom 5K 141
Briary Gro. HA8: Edg 2H 43
Briary La. N9 . . . . .3A 34
Brickbarn Cl. SW10 . . . . .7A 100
             (off King's Barn)
Brick Ct. EC4 . . . . .1J 13 (6A 84)
Brickett Cl. HA4: Ruis 5E 38
Brick Farm Cl. TW9: Kew 1H 115
Brickfield Cl. E3 . . . . .6J 67
  TW8: Bford 7C 96
Brickfield Cotts. BR7: Chst 5E 142
  SE18 . . . . .6K 107
Brickfield Farm Gdns. BR6: Farnb 4G 173
Brickfield La. UB3: Harl 6F 93
Brickfield Rd. CR7: Thor H 1B 156
  SW19 . . . . .4K 135
             (not continuous)
Brickfields HA2: Harr 2H 59
Brickfields Way UB7: W Dray 3B 92
Brick La. E1 . . . . .3K 9 (4F 85)
  E2 .2K 9 (3F 85)
  EN1: Enf 2C 24
  EN3: Enf H 2C 24
  HA7: Stan 7J 27
  UB5: N'olt 3D 76
Brick Lane Music Hall 1B 106
BRICKLAYER'S ARMS 4D 102
Bricklayers Arms Distribution Cen.
  SE1 . . . . .4E 102
Brick St. W1 . . . . .5J 11 (1F 101)
Brickwall La. HA4: Ruis 1G 57
Brickwood Cl. SE26 . . . . .3H 139
Brickwood Rd. CR0: C'don 2E 168
Brideale Cl. SE15 . . . . .6F 103
Bride Cl. EC4 . . . . .1A 14
Bride La. EC4 . . . . .1A 14 (6B 84)
Bridel M. N1 . . . . .1B 84
           (off Colebrook Row)
Brides Pl. N1 . . . . .7E 66
Bride St. N7 . . . . .6K 65
Bridewain St. SE1 . . . . .7J 15 (3F 103)
Bridewell Pl. E1 . . . . .1H 103
  EC4 . . . . .1A 14 (6B 84)
Bridford M. W1 . . . . .5K 5 (5F 83)
Bridge, The HA3: W'stone 4K 41
  SW8 . . . . .7F 101
Bridge Academy 1F 85
           (off Laburnum St.)
Bridge App. NW1 . . . . .7E 64
Bridge Av. W6 . . . . .4E 98
  W7 . . . . .5H 77
Bridge Av. Mans. W6 . . . . .5E 98
             (off Bridge Av.)
Bridge Bus. Cen., The UB2: S'hall 2E 94
Bridge Cl. EN1: Enf 2C 24
  KT12: Walt T 7H 147
  TW11: Tedd 4K 131
  W10 . . . . .6F 81
Bridge Ct. E10 .1B 68
  E14 . . . . .7F 87
           (off Newport Av.)
  KT12: Walt T 7H 147
            (off Bridge Rd.)
Bridge Dr. N13 .4E 32
Bridge End E17 .1E 50
Bridge End Cl. KT2: King T 1G 151
Bridgefield Rd. SM1: Sutt 6J 165
Bridgefoot SE1 . . . . .6F 19 (5J 101)
  TW16: Sun 1H 147
Bridge Gdns. KT8: E Mos 4H 149
  N16 . . . . .4D 66
  TW15: Ashf 7E 128
Bridge Ga. N21 .7H 23

Bridgehill Cl. HA0: Wemb 1D 78
Bridge Ho. E9 . . . . .6K 67
          (off Shepherds La.)
  NW3 . . . . .7E 64
          (off Adelaide Rd.)
  NW10 . . . . .2F 81
         (off Chamberlayne Rd.)
  SE4 . . . . .4B 122
  SM2: Sutt 6K 165
           (off Bridge Rd.)
  SW1 . . . . .5J 17
          (off Ebury Bri.)
  UB7: W Dray 1A 92
  W2 . . . . .6A 4
Bridgehouse Ct. SE1 . . . . .7A 14
          (off Blackfriars Rd.)
Bridge Ho. Quay E14 . . . . .1E 104
Bridgeland Rd. E16 . . . . .7J 87
Bridgelands Cl. BR3: Beck 7B 140
Bridge La. NW11 . . . . .4G 45
  SW11 . . . . .1C 118
Bridge Leisure Cen., The 4B 140
Bridgeman Ho. E9 . . . . .7J 67
         (off Frampton Pk. Rd.)
Bridgeman Rd. N1 . . . . .7K 65
  TW11: Tedd 6A 132
Bridgeman St. NW8 . . . . .2C 82
Bridge Mdws. SE14 . . . . .6K 103
BRIDGEN 7E 126
Bridgend Rd. SW18 . . . . .4A 118
Bridgenhall Rd. EN1: Enf 1A 24
Bridgen Ho. E1 .6H 85
           (off Nelson St.)
Bridgen Rd. DA5: Bexl 7E 126
Bridge Pde. N21 . . . . .7H 23
           (off Ridge Av.)
Bridge Pk. 7H 61
Bridgepark SW18 . . . . .5J 117
Bridge Pl. CR0: C'don 1D 168
  SW1 . . . . .3K 17 (4F 101)
Bridgepoint Lofts E7 . . . . .7A 70
Bridgepoint Pl. N6 . . . . .1G 65
           (off Hornsey La.)
Bridgeport Pl. E1 . . . . .1G 103
Bridge Rd. BR3: Beck 7B 140
  DA7: Bex 2E 126
  E6 . . . . .7D 70
  E15 . . . . .7F 69
  E17 . . . . .7B 50
  HA9: Wemb 3G 61
  KT8: E Mos 4H 149
  KT9: Chess 5E 162
  N9 . . . . .3B 34
  N22 . . . . .1J 47
  NW10 . . . . .6A 62
  SM2: Sutt 6K 165
  SM6: Wall 5F 167
  TW1: Twick 6B 114
  TW3: Houn, Isle 3H 113
  TW7: Isle 3H 113
  UB2: S'hall 2D 94
Bridge Row CR0: C'don 1D 168
Bridges Cl. SW11 . . . . .3B 118
          (not continuous)
Bridges Ho. SE5 . . . . .7D 102
          (off Elmington Est.)
Bridgeside Lodge N1 . . . . .2C 84
           (off Wharf Rd.)
Bridges La. CR0: Bedd 4J 167
Bridges Pl. SW6 . . . . .1H 117
Bridges Rd. HA7: Stan 5E 26
  SW19 . . . . .6K 135
Bridges Rd. M. SW19 . . . . .6K 135
Bridge St. HA5: Pinn 3C 40
  KT12: Walt T 7G 147
  SW1 . . . . .7E 12 (2J 101)
  TW9: Rich 5D 114
  W4 . . . . .4K 97
Bridges Wharf SW11 . . . . .3B 118
Bridge Ter. E15 .7F 69
Bridgetown Cl. SE19 . . . . .5E 138
Bridge Vw. W6 .5E 98

Bridge Vw. Ct. *SE1* *3E 102*
(off Grange Rd.)
Bridge Wlk. *IG1: Ilf* *2F 71*
(in The Exchange)
Bridgewalk Hgts. *SE1* *6F 15*
(off Weston St.)
Bridgewater Cl. BR7: Chst 3J 161
Bridgewater Gdns. HA8: Edg 2F 43
Bridgewater Highwalk EC2 . . . . . 5C 8
Bridgewater Rd. HA0: Wemb 6C 60
Bridgewater Sq. EC2 . . . . . 5C 8 (5C 84)
Bridgewater St. EC2 . . . . . 5C 8 (5C 84)
Bridge Way N11 . . . . . 3B 32
NW11 . . . . . 5H 45
TW2: Whitt 7G 113
UB10: Ick 5D 56
Bridgeway HA0: Wemb 7E 60
IG11: Bark 7K 71
Bridgeway St. NW1 . . . . . 2G 83
Bridge Wharf E2 . . . . . 2K 85
N1 . . . . . *2K 83*
(off Calshot St.)
Bridge Wharf Rd. TW7: Isle 3B 114
Bridgewood Cl. SE20 . . . . . 7H 139
Bridgewood Rd. KT4: Wor Pk 4C 164
SW16 . . . . . 7H 137
Bridge Yd. SE1 . . . . . 4F 15 (1D 102)
Bridgford St. SW18 . . . . . 3A 136
Bridgman Rd. W4 . . . . . 3J 97
Bridgnorth Ho. *SE15* *6G 103*
(off Friary Est.)
Bridgwater Ho. *W2* *6A 82*
(off Hallfield Est.)
Bridgwater Rd. HA4: Ruis 4J 57
Bridle Cl. KT1: King T 4D 150
KT19: Ewe 5K 163
TW16: Sun 3J 147
Bridle La. TW1: Twick 6B 114
W1 . . . . . 2B 12 (7G 83)
Bridle M. EN5: Barn 4C 20
Bridle Path CR0: Bedd 3J 167
(not continuous)
Bridle Path, The IG8: Wfd G 7B 36
Bridlepath Way TW14: Bedf 7G 111
Bridle Rd. CR0: C'don 3C 170
(not continuous)
CR2: Sande 7G 169
HA5: Eastc 6K 39
KT10: Clay 6B 162
Bridle Way BR6: Farnb 4G 173
CR0: C'don 5C 170
Bridleway, The SM6: Wall 5G 167
Bridlington Rd. N9 . . . . . 7C 24
Bridport *SE17* *5D 102*
(off Cadiz St.)
Bridport Av. RM7: Rom 6H 55
Bridport Ho. *N1* *1D 84*
(off Bridport Pl.)
N18 . . . . . *5A 34*
(off College Gdns.)
Bridport Pl. N1 . . . . . 1D 84
(not continuous)
Bridport Rd. CR7: Thor H 3A 156
N18 . . . . . 5K 33
UB6: G'frd 1F 77
Bridstow Pl. W2 . . . . . 6J 81
Brief St. SE5 . . . . . 1B 120
Brierfield *NW1* *1G 83*
(off Arlington Rd.)
Brierley CR0: New Ad 6D 170
(not continuous)
Brierley Av. N9 . . . . . 1D 34
Brierley Cl. SE25 . . . . . 4G 157
Brierley Ct. W7 . . . . . 7J 77
Brierley Rd. E11 . . . . . 4F 69
SW12 . . . . . 2G 137
Brierly Gdns. E2 . . . . . 2J 85
Brigade Cl. HA2: Harr 2H 59
Brigade St. *SE3* *2H 123*
(off Tranquil Va.)
Brigadier Av. EN2: Enf 1H 23
Brigadier Hill EN2: Enf 1H 23
Brigadier Ho. *NW9* *2B 44*
(off Heritage Av.)
Briggeford Cl. E5 . . . . . 2G 67
Briggs Cl. CR4: Mitc 1F 155
Briggs Ho. *E2* *1K 9*
(off Chambord St.)
Bright Cl. DA17: Belv 4D 108
Brightfield Rd. SE12 . . . . . 5G 123
Brightling Rd. SE4 . . . . . 6B 122
Brightlingsea Pl. E14 . . . . . 7B 86
Brightman Rd. SW18 . . . . . 1B 136
Brighton Av. E17 . . . . . 5B 50
Brighton Bldgs. *SE1* *3E 102*
(off Tower Bri. Rd.)
Brighton Cl. UB10: Hil 7D 56
Brighton Dr. UB5: N'olt 6E 58
Brighton Gro. SE14 . . . . . 1A 122
Brighton Ho. *SE5* *1D 120*
(off Camberwell Grn.)
Brighton Rd. CR2: S Croy 5C 168
E6 . . . . . 3E 88
(not continuous)
KT6: Surb 6C 150
N2 . . . . . 2A 46
N16 . . . . . 4E 66
SM2: Bans, Sutt 7K 165
Brighton Ter. SW9 . . . . . 4K 119
Brightside, The EN3: Enf H 1E 24
Brightside Rd. SE13 . . . . . 6F 123
Bright St. E14 . . . . . 5D 86
Brightwell Cl. CR0: C'don 1A 168
Brightwell Ct. *N7* *5K 65*
(off Mackenzie Rd.)
Brightwell Cres. SW17 . . . . . 5D 136
Brightwen Gro. HA7: Stan 2F 27
Brig M. SE8 . . . . . 6C 104
Brigstock Ho. SE5 . . . . . 2C 120
Brigstock Rd. CR7: Thor H 5A 156
DA17: Belv 4H 109
Brill Pl. NW1 . . . . . 1D 6 (2H 83)
Brim Hill N2 . . . . . 4A 46
Brimpsfield Cl. SE2 . . . . . 3B 108
(not continuous)
BRIMSDOWN 2G 25
Brimsdown Av. EN3: Enf H 2F 25
Brimsdown Ho. E3 . . . . . 4D 86
Brimsdown Ind. Est. EN3: Brim 1G 25
(Lockfield Av.)
EN3: Brim 2G 25
(Stockingswater La.)
Brimstone Ho. *E15* *7G 69*
(off Victoria St.)
Brindle Ga. DA15: Sidc 1J 143
Brindley Cl. DA7: Bex 3H 127
HA0: Wemb 1D 78
Brindley Ho. *W2* *5J 81*
(off Alfred Rd.)
Brindley St. SE14 . . . . . 1B 122
Brindley Way BR1: Brom 5J 141
UB1: S'hall 7F 77
Brindwood Rd. E4 . . . . . 3G 35
Brine Ho. *E3* *2A 86*
(off St Stephen's Rd.)
Brinkburn Cl. HA8: Edg 3H 43
SE2 . . . . . 4A 108
Brinkburn Gdns. HA8: Edg 3G 43
Brinkley KT1: King T 2G 151
Brinkley Rd. KT4: Wor Pk 2D 164
Brinklow Cres. SE18 . . . . . 7F 107
Brinklow Ho. *W2* *5K 81*
(off Torquay St.)
Brinkworth Rd. IG5: Ilf 3C 52
Brinkworth Way E9 . . . . . 6B 68
Brinsdale Rd. NW4 . . . . . 3F 45
Brinsley Ho. *E1* *6J 85*
(off Tarling St.)
Brinsley Rd. HA3: Hrw W 2H 41
Brinsworth Cl. TW2: Twick 1H 131
Brinsworth Ho. TW2: Twick 2H 131
Brinton Wlk. SE1 . . . . . 5A 14
Brion Pl. E14 . . . . . 5E 86
Brisbane Av. SW19 . . . . . 1K 153
Brisbane Ho. *W12* *7D 80*
(off White City Est.)
Brisbane Rd. E10 . . . . . 2D 68
IG1: Ilf 7F 53
W13 . . . . . 2A 96
Brisbane Road Stadium 3D 68
Brisbane St. SE5 . . . . . 7D 102
Briscoe Cl. E11 . . . . . 2H 69
Briscoe Rd. SW19 . . . . . 6B 136
Briset Rd. SE9 . . . . . 3B 124
Briset St. EC1 . . . . . 5A 8 (5B 84)
Briset Way N7 . . . . . 2K 65
Bristol Cl. SM6: Wall 7J 167
TW4: Houn 7E 112
TW19: Stanw 6A 110
Bristol Ct. TW19: Stanw 6A 110
Bristol Gdns. SW15 . . . . . 7E 116
W9 . . . . . 4K 81
Bristol Ho. *IG11: Bark* *7A 72*
(off Margaret Bondfield Av.)
SE11 . . . . . 2J 19
SW1 . . . . . *5G 17*
(off Lwr. Sloane St.)
WC1 . . . . . *5F 7*
(off Southampton Row)
Bristol M. W9 . . . . . 4K 81
Bristol Pk. Rd. E17 . . . . . 4A 50
Bristol Rd. E7 . . . . . 6A 70
SM4: Mord 5A 154
UB6: G'frd 1F 77
Briston Gro. N8 . . . . . 6J 47
Briston M. NW7 . . . . . 7H 29
Bristow Ct. *E8* *1H 85*
(off Triangle Rd.)
Bristowe Cl. SW2 . . . . . 6A 120
Bristow Rd. CR0: Bedd 4J 167
DA7: Bex 1E 126
SE19 . . . . . 5E 138
TW3: Houn 3G 113
Britain & London Vis. Cen. *4C 12*
(off Regent St.)
Britannia Bri. *E14* *6B 86*
(off Commercial Rd.)
Britannia Bldg. *N1* *1E 8*
(off Ebenezer St.)
Britannia Bus. Cen. NW2 . . . . . 4F 63
Britannia Cl. SW4 . . . . . 4H 119
UB5: N'olt 3B 76
Britannia Ct. *KT2: King T* *1D 150*
(off Skerne Wlk.)
UB7: W Dray 3A 92
Britannia Ga. E16 . . . . . 1J 105
BRITANNIA JUNC. 1F 83
Britannia La. TW2: Whitt 7G 113
Britannia Leisure Cen. 1D 84
Britannia Rd. E14 . . . . . 4C 104
IG1: Ilf 3F 71
KT5: Surb 7F 151
N12 . . . . . 3F 31
SW6 . . . . . 7K 99
(not continuous)
Britannia Row N1 . . . . . 1B 84
Britannia St. WC1 . . . . . 1G 7 (3K 83)
Britannia Wlk. N1 . . . . . 1E 8 (2D 84)
(not continuous)
Britannia Way NW10 . . . . . 4H 79
SW6 . . . . . *7K 99*
(off Britannia Rd.)
TW19: Stanw 7A 110
Britannic Highwalk *EC2* *6E 8*
(off Moor La.)
British Genius Site 7E 100
British Gro. W4 . . . . . 5B 98
British Gro. Pas. W4 . . . . . 5B 98
British Gro. Sth. *W4* *5B 98*
(off British Gro. Pas.)
British Legion Rd. E4 . . . . . 2C 36
British Library 1D 6 (3H 83)
British Mus. 6D 6 (5J 83)
British Postal Mus. and Archive, The
. . . . . 3J 7 (4A 84)
British St. E3 . . . . . 3B 86
British Telecom Cen. EC1 . . . . . 7C 8
British Wharf Ind. Est. SE14 . . . . . 5K 103
Britley Ho. *E14* *6B 86*
(off Copenhagen Pl.)
Brit Oval, The 7H 19 (6K 101)
Brittain Ct. SE9 . . . . . 1C 142
Brittain Rd. RM8: Dag 3E 72
Brittany Ho. EN2: Enf 1H 23
Brittany Point SE11 . . . . . 4J 19 (4A 102)
Britten Cl. NW11 . . . . . 1K 63
Britten Ct. E15 . . . . . 2F 87
Brittenden Cl. BR6: Chels 6K 173
Brittenden Pde. BR6: Chels 6K 173
Britten Dr. UB1: S'hall 6E 76
Britten Ho. *SW3* *5D 16*
(off Britten St.)
Britten St. SW3 . . . . . 6C 16 (5C 100)
Brittidge Rd. NW10 . . . . . 7A 62
Britton Cl. SE6 . . . . . 7F 123
Britton St. EC1 . . . . . 4A 8 (4B 84)
Brixham Cres. HA4: Ruis 1J 57
Brixham Gdns. IG3: Ilf 5J 71
Brixham Rd. DA16: Well 1D 126
Brixham St. E16 . . . . . 1E 106
BRIXTON 4K 119
Brixton Academy 3A 120
Brixton Hill SW2 . . . . . 7J 119
Brixton Hill Ct. SW2 . . . . . 5K 119
Brixton Hill Pl. SW2 . . . . . 7J 119
Brixton Oval SW2 . . . . . 4A 120
Brixton Recreation Cen. *3A 120*
(off Brixton Sta. Rd.)
Brixton Rd. SE11 . . . . . 7J 19 (6A 102)
SW9 . . . . . 4A 120
Brixton Sta. Rd. SW9 . . . . . 3A 120
Brixton Water La. SW2 . . . . . 5K 119
Broadacre Cl. UB10: Ick 3D 56
Broadbent Cl. N6 . . . . . 1F 65
Broadbent St. W1 . . . . . 2J 11 (7F 83)
Broadberry Ct. N18 . . . . . 6C 34
Broadbridge Cl. SE3 . . . . . 7J 105
Broad Comn. Est.
N16 . . . . . *1G 67*
(off Osbaldeston Rd.)
Broadcoombe CR2: Sels 7J 169
Broad Ct. WC2 . . . . . 1F 13 (6J 83)
Broadcroft Av. HA7: Stan 2D 42
Broadcroft Rd. BR5: Pet W 7H 161
Broadeaves Cl. CR2: S Croy 5E 168
Broadfield NW6 . . . . . 6K 63
Broadfield Cl. CR0: Wadd 2K 167
NW2 . . . . . 3E 62
Broadfield Ct. *HA2: Harr* *1F 41*
(off Broadfields)
WD23: B Hea 2D 26
Broadfield La. NW1 . . . . . 7J 65
Broadfield Pde. *HA8: Edg* *3C 28*
(off Glengall Rd.)
Broadfield Rd. SE6 . . . . . 7G 123
Broadfields HA2: Harr 2F 41
KT8: E Mos 6J 149
Broadfields Av. HA8: Edg 4C 28
N21 . . . . . 6F 23
Broadfields Hgts. HA8: Edg 4C 28
Broadfield Sq. EN1: Enf 2C 24
Broadfields Way NW10 . . . . . 5B 62
Broadfield Way IG9: Buck H 3F 37
Broadford Ho. *E1* *4A 86*
(off Commodore St.)
Broadgate EC2 . . . . . 6F 9
Broadgate Arena 6G 9
Broadgate Circ. EC2 . . . . . 5G 9 (5E 84)
Broadgate Ice Rink 6G 9
Broadgate Plaza EC2 . . . . . 5E 84
Broadgate Rd. E16 . . . . . 6B 88
Broadgates Av. EN4: Had W 1E 20
Broadgates Ct. *SE11* *6K 19*
(off Cleaver St.)
Broadgates Rd. SW18 . . . . . 1B 136
Broadgate Twr. EC2 . . . . . 4H 9 (4E 84)
BROAD GREEN 7B 156
Broad Grn. Av. CR0: C'don 7B 156

Broadhead Strand NW9 1B **44**
Broadheath Dr. BR7: Chst 5D **142**
Broadhinton Rd. SW4 3F **119**
Broadhurst Av. HA8: Edg 4C **28**
IG3: Ilf 4K **71**
Broadhurst Cl. NW6 6A **64**
TW10: Rich 5F **115**
Broadhurst Gdns. HA4: Ruis 2A **58**
NW6 6K **63**
Broadlands E17 3A **50**
TW13: Hanw 3E **130**
Broadlands Av. EN3: Enf H 3C **24**
SW16 2J **137**
TW17: Shep 6E **146**
Broadlands Cl. EN3: Enf H 3D **24**
N6 7E **46**
SW16 2J **137**
Broadlands Ct. *TW9: Kew 7G* ***97***
(off Kew Gdns. Rd.)
Broadlands Lodge N6 7D **46**
Broadlands Rd. BR1: Brom 4K **141**
N6 7D **46**
Broadlands Way
KT3: N Mald 6B **152**
Broad La. EC2 5G **9** (5E **84**)
N8 5K **47**
N15 4F **49**
TW12: Hamp 7D **130**
Broad Lawn SE9 2E **142**
Broadlawns Ct. HA3: Hrw W 1K **41**
Broadley St. NW8 5B **4** (5B **82**)
Broadley Ter. NW1 4D **4** (4C **82**)
Broadmayne *SE17 5D* ***102***
(off Portland St.)
Broadmead SE6 3C **140**
W14 4G **99**
Broadmead Av. KT4: Wor Pk 7C **152**
Broadmead Cen. *IG8: Wfd G 7F* ***37***
(off Navestock Cres.)
Broadmead Cl. HA5: Hat E 1C **40**
TW12: Hamp 6E **130**
Broadmead Ct. IG8: Wfd G 6D **36**
Broadmead Rd. IG8: Wfd G 6D **36**
(not continuous)
UB4: Yead 4C **76**
UB5: N'olt 4C **76**
Broad Oak IG8: Wfd G 5E **36**
TW16: Sun 6H **129**
Broad Oak Cl. E4 5H **35**
Broadoak Ct. *SW9 3A* ***120***
(off Gresham Rd.)
Broadoak Ho. *NW6 1K* ***81***
(off Mortimer Cres.)
Broadoak Rd. DA8: Erith 7K **109**
Broadoaks KT6: Surb 2H **163**
Broadoaks Way BR2: Brom 5H **159**
Broad Sanctuary SW1 7D **12** (2H **101**)
Broadstone *NW1 7H* ***65***
(off Agar Gro.)
Broadstone Ho. *SW8 7K* ***101***
(off Dorset Rd.)
Broadstone Pl. W1 6G **5** (5E **82**)
Broad St. RM10: Dag 7G **73**
TW11: Tedd 6K **131**
Broad St. Av. EC2 6G **9** (5E **84**)
Broad St. Mkt. RM10: Dag 7G **73**
Broad St. Pl. EC2 6F **9**
Broadview NW9 6G **43**
Broadview Rd. SW16 7H **137**
Broad Wlk. N21 2E **32**
NW1 1H **5** (1E **82**)
SE3 2A **124**
TW5: Hest 1B **112**
TW9: Kew 7F **97**
W1 3F **11** (7D **82**)
Broad Wlk., The KT8: E Mos 4K **149**
W8 1K **99**
Broadwalk E18 3H **51**
HA2: Harr 5E **40**
Broadwalk, The HA6: Nwood 2E **38**
Broadwalk Ct. *W8 1J* ***99***
(off Palace Gdns. Ter.)
Broadwalk Ho. EC2 5G **9**
SW7 2A ***100***
(off Hyde Pk. Ga.)
Broad Wlk. La. NW11 7H **45**
Broadwalk Shop. Cen.
HA8: Edg 6C **28**
Broadwall SE1 4K **13** (1A **102**)
Broadwater Farm Est. N17 2D **48**
Broadwater Gdns. BR6: Farnb 4F **173**
Broadwater Rd. N17 1E **48**
SE28 3H **107**
SW17 4C **136**
Broadway DA6: Bex 4E **126**
(not continuous)
E13 2K **87**
E15 7F **69**
IG11: Bark 1G **89**
SW1 7C **12** (3H **101**)
W7 1J **95**
W13 1A **96**
Broadway, The CR0: Bedd 4J **167**
E4 6A **36**
HA3: W'stone 2J **41**
HA6: Nwood 2J **39**
HA7: Stan 5H **27**
HA9: Wemb 3E **60**
IG8: Wfd G 6E **36**
KT7: T Ditt 7J **149**
N8 6J **47**
N9 3B **34**
N11 5J **31**
N14 1C ***32***
(off The Bourne)
N22 2A **48**
NW7 5F **29**
RM8: Dag 1F **73**
SM1: Sutt 5A **166**
SM3: Cheam 6G **165**
SW13 2A **116**
SW19 6H **135**
UB1: S'hall 7B **76**
UB6: G'frd 4G **77**
W3 2G ***97***
(off Ridgeway Dr.)
W5 7D **78**
Broadway Arc. *W6 4E* ***98***
(off Hammersmith B'way.)
Broadway Av. CR0: C'don 5D **156**
TW1: Twick 6B **114**
Broadway Cen., The W6 4E **98**
Broadway Chambers *W6 4E* ***98***
(off Hammersmith B'way.)
Broadway Cl. IG8: Wfd G 6E **36**
Broadway Ct. BR3: Beck 3E **158**
SW19 6J **135**
Broadway Gdns. CR4: Mitc 4C **154**
IG8: Wfd G 6E **36**
Broadway Ho. *BR1: Brom 5F* ***141***
(off Bromley Rd.)
E8 1H ***85***
(off Ada St.)
Broadway Mans. *SW6 7J* ***99***
(off Fulham Rd.)
Broadway Mkt. E8 1H **85**
IG6: Ilf 1H **53**
(not continuous)
SW17 4D **136**
Broadway Mkt. M. E8 1G **85**
Broadway M. E5 7F **49**
N13 5E **32**
N21 1G **33**
Broadway Pde. E4 6K **35**
HA2: Harr 5F **41**
N8 6J **47**
UB3: Hayes 1J **93**
Broadway Pl. SW19 6H **135**
Broadway Retail Pk. NW2 4F **63**
Broadway Shop. Cen.
DA6: Bex 4G **127**
Broadway Shop. Mall
SW1 1C **18** (3H **101**)
Broadway Sq. DA6: Bex 4G **127**
Broadway Theatre, The
Barking 1G **89**
Catford ***7D 122***
(off Rushey Grn.)
Broadway Wlk. E14 2C **104**
Broadwell Ct. *TW5: Hest 1B* ***112***
(off Springwell Rd.)
Broadwell Pde. *NW6 6K* ***63***
(off Broadhurst Gdns.)
Broadwick St. W1 2B **12** (7G **83**)
Broadwood Av. HA4: Ruis 6F **39**
Broadwood Ter. W8 4H **99**
Broad Yd. EC1 4A **8** (4B **84**)
Brocas Cl. NW3 7C **64**
Brockbridge Ho. SW15 6B **116**
Brockdene Dr. BR2: Kes 4B **172**
Brockdish Av. IG11: Bark 5K **71**
Brockenhurst KT8: W Mole 5D **148**
Brockenhurst Av. KT4: Wor Pk 1A **164**
Brockenhurst Gdns. IG1: Ilf 5G **71**
NW7 5F **29**
Brockenhurst M. N18 4B **34**
Brockenhurst Rd. CR0: C'don 7H **157**
Brockenhurst Way SW16 2H **155**
Brocket Ho. SW8 2H **119**
Brockham Cl. SW19 5H **135**
Brockham Cres. CR0: New Ad 7F **171**
Brockham Dr. IG2: Ilf 6F **53**
SW2 7K **119**
Brockham Ho. *NW1 1G* ***83***
(off Bayham Pl.)
SW2 7K ***119***
(off Brockham Dr.)
Brockham St. SE1 7D **14** (3C **102**)
Brockhurst Cl. HA7: Stan 6E **26**
Brockill Cres. SE4 4A **122**
Brocklebank Ho. *E16 1E* ***106***
(off Glenister St.)
Brocklebank Ind. Est. SE7 4J **105**
Brocklebank Rd. SE7 4K **105**
SW18 7A **118**
Brocklehurst St. SE14 7K **103**
Brocklesby Rd. SE25 4H **157**
BROCKLEY **4K 121**
Brockley Av. HA7: Stan 3K **27**
Brockley Cl. HA7: Stan 4K **27**
Brockley Cres. RM5: Col R 1J **55**
Brockley Cross SE4 3A **122**
Brockley Cross Bus. Cen. SE4 3A **122**
Brockley Footpath SE4 5A **122**
(not continuous)
SE15 3J **121**
Brockley Gdns. SE4 2B **122**
Brockley Gro. SE4 5B **122**
Brockley Hall Rd. SE4 5A **122**
Brockley Hill HA7: Stan 1H **27**
Brockley Jack Theatre **5A 122**
Brockley M. SE4 5A **122**
Brockley Pk. SE23 7A **122**
Brockley Ri. SE23 1A **140**
Brockley Rd. SE4 3B **122**
Brockleyside HA7: Stan 4K **27**
Brockley Vw. SE23 7A **122**
Brockley Way SE4 5K **121**
Brockman Ri. BR1: Brom 4F **141**
Brockmer Ho. *E1 7H* ***85***
(off Crowder St.)
Brock Pl. E3 4D **86**
Brock Rd. E13 5K **87**
Brocks Dr. SM3: Cheam 3G **165**
Brockshot Cl. TW8: Bford 5D **96**
Brock St. SE15 3J **121**
Brockway Cl. E11 2G **69**
Brockweir *E2 2J* ***85***
(off Cyprus St.)
Brockwell Av. BR3: Beck 5D **158**
Brockwell Cl. BR5: St M Cry 5K **161**
Brockwell Ct. SW2 5A **120**
Brockwell Ho. *SE11 7H* ***19***
(off Vauxhall St.)
Brockwell Pk. **6B 120**
Brockwell Pk. Gdns. SE24 7A **120**
Brockwell Pk. Lido **6B 120**
Brockwell Pk. Row SW2 7A **120**
Brodia Rd. N16 3E **66**
Brodick Ho. *E3 2B* ***86***
(off Saxon Rd.)
Brodie Ho. *SE1 5F* ***103***
(off Cooper's Rd.)
Brodie Rd. E4 1K **35**
EN2: Enf 1H **23**
Brodie St. SE1 5F **103**
Brodlove La. E1 7K **85**
Brodrick Gro. SE2 4B **108**
Brodrick Rd. SW17 2C **136**
Brody Ho. *E1 6J* ***9***
(off Strype St.)
Brograve Gdns. BR3: Beck 2D **158**
Broken Wharf EC4 2C **14** (7C **84**)
Brokesley St. E3 3B **86**
Broke Wlk. E8 1F **85**
Bromar Rd. SE5 3E **120**
Bromefield HA7: Stan 1C **42**
Bromehead St. E1 6J **85**
Bromell's Rd. SW4 4G **119**
Brome Rd. SE9 3D **124**
Bromfelde Rd. SW4 3H **119**
Bromfelde Wlk. SW4 2H **119**
Bromfield Ct. *SE16 3G* ***103***
(off Ben Smith Way)
Bromfield St. N1 1A **84**
Bromhall Rd. RM8: Dag 6B **72**
Bromhead Rd. *E1 6J* ***85***
(off Jubilee St.)
Bromhedge SE9 3D **142**
Bromholm Rd. SE2 3B **108**
Bromleigh Ct. SE23 2G **139**
Bromleigh Ho. *SE1 7J* ***15***
(off St Saviour's Est.)
BROMLEY
BR1 **2J 159**
E3 **3D 86**
Bromley Av. BR1: Brom 7G **141**
Bromley Coll. BR1: Brom 1J **159**
BROMLEY COMMON **1C 172**
Bromley Comn. BR2: Brom 4A **160**
Bromley Cres. BR2: Brom 3H **159**
HA4: Ruis 4H **57**
Bromley Environmental Education Cen. at
High Elms (Beeche) **6H 173**
Bromley FC **5K 159**
Bromley Gdns. BR2: Brom 3H **159**
Bromley Gro. BR2: Brom 2F **159**
Bromley Hall Rd. E14 5E **86**
Bromley High St. E3 3D **86**
Bromley Hill BR1: Brom 6G **141**
Bromley Ho. *BR1: Brom 1J* ***159***
(off North St.)
Bromley Ind. Cen. BR1: Brom 3B **160**
Bromley La. BR7: Chst 7G **143**
Bromley Little Theatre **1J 159**
BROMLEY PARK **1G 159**
Bromley Pk. BR1: Brom 1H **159**
Bromley (Park & Ride) **6K 159**
Bromley Pl. W1 5A **6** (5G **83**)
Bromley Rd. BR1: Brom 1D **140**
BR2: Brom 2D **158**
BR3: Beck 1D **158**
BR7: Chst 1F **161**
E10 6D **50**
E17 3C **50**
N17 1F **49**
N18 3J **33**
SE6 1D **140**
Bromley Ski Cen. **7E 144**
Bromley St. E1 5K **85**
BROMPTON **2D 16 (3C 100)**
Brompton Arc. SW3 7E **10**
Brompton Cl. SE20 2G **157**
TW4: Houn 5D **112**
Brompton Cotts. *SW10 6A* ***100***
(off Hollywood Rd.)
Brompton Ct. *BR1: Brom 1J* ***159***
(off Tweedy Rd.)

Brompton Gro.—Broomwood Cl.

Brompton Gro. N2 4C 46
Brompton Oratory 2C 16 (3C 100)
Brompton Pk. Cres. SW6 6K 99
Brompton Pl. SW3 1D 16 (3C 100)
Brompton Rd. SW1 3C 16 (4C 100)
SW3 3C 16 (4C 100)
Brompton Sq. SW3 1C 16 (3C 100)
Brompton Ter. SE18 1D 124
Brompton Vs. *SW6* *6J 99*
(off Lillie Rd.)
Bromwich Av. N6 2E 64
Bromyard Av. W3 7A 80
Bromyard Ho. *SE15* *7H 103*
(off Commercial Way)
Bron Ct. NW6 1J 81
BRONDESBURY 7H 63
Brondesbury Ct. NW2 6F 63
Brondesbury M. NW6 7J 63
BRONDESBURY PARK 1E 80
Brondesbury Pk. NW2 6E 62
NW6 6E 62
Brondesbury Pk. Mans.
NW6 *1G 81*
(off Salusbury Rd.)
Brondesbury Rd. NW6 2H 81
Brondesbury Vs. NW6 2H 81
Bronhill Ter. N17 1G 49
Bronsart Rd. SW6 7G 99
Bronson Rd. SW20 2F 153
Bronte Cl. DA8: Erith 7H 109
E7 4J 69
IG2: Ilf 4E 52
Bronte Ct. W3 2G 97
W14 *3F 99*
(off Girdler's Rd.)
Bronte Ho. N16 5E 66
NW6 3J 81
SW4 7G 119
SW17 *3B 136*
(off Grosvenor Way)
Bronti Cl. SE17 5C 102
Bronwen Ct. *NW8* *2A 4*
(off Grove End Rd.)
Bronze Age Way DA8: Erith 2H 109
DA17: Belv 2H 109
Bronze St. SE8 7C 104
Brook Av. HA8: Edg 6C 28
HA9: Wemb 2F 61
RM10: Dag 7H 73
Brookbank Av. W7 5H 77
Brookbank Rd. SE13 3C 122
Brook Cl. HA4: Ruis 7G 39
NW7 7B 30
SW17 2E 136
SW20 3D 152
TW19: Stanw 7B 110
W3 1G 97
Brook Ct. BR3: Beck 1B 158
E11 3G 69
E17 3A 50
HA8: Edg 5C 28
IG11: Bark 1K 89
(Sebastian Ct.)
IG11: Bark 2G 89
(Spring Pl.)
SE12 3A 142
Brook Cres. E4 4H 35
N9 4C 34
Brookdale N11 4B 32
Brookdale Rd. DA5: Bexl 6E 126
E17 3C 50
SE6 6D 122
(Medusa Rd.)
SE6 7D 122
(Catford B'way)
Brookdales NW11 4G 45
Brookdene Rd. SE18 4J 107
Brook Dr. HA1: Harr 4G 41
HA4: Ruis 7G 39
SE11 2K 19 (3A 102)
Brooke Av. HA2: Harr 3G 59
Brooke Cl. WD23: Bush 1B 26
Brooke Ct. *W10* *2G 81*
(off Kilburn La.)
Brooke Ho. SE14 1A 122
WD23: Bush 1B 26
Brookehowse Rd. SE6 2C 140
Brookend Rd. DA15: Sidc 1J 143
Brooke Rd. E5 3G 67
E17 4E 50
N16 3F 67
Brooke's Ct. EC1 6J 7 (5A 84)
Brooke's Mkt. EC1 5K 7
Brooke St. EC1 6J 7 (5A 84)
Brooke Way WD23: Bush 1B 26
Brookfield N6 3E 64
Brookfield Av. E17 4E 50
NW7 6J 29
SM1: Sutt 4B 166
W5 4D 78
Brookfield Cl. NW7 6J 29
Brookfield Ct. N12 4E 30
UB6: G'frd 3G 77
Brookfield Cres. HA3: Kenton 5E 42
NW7 6J 29
Brookfield Gdns. KT10: Clay 6A 162
Brookfield Pk. NW5 3F 65
Brookfield Path IG8: Wfd G 6B 36
Brookfield Rd. E9 6A 68
N9 3B 34
W4 2K 97
Brookfields EN3: Pond E 4E 24
Brookfields Av. CR4: Mitc 5C 154
Brook Gdns. E4 4J 35
KT2: King T 1J 151
SW13 3B 116
Brook Ga. W1 3F 11 (7D 82)
BROOK GREEN 4F 99
Brook Grn. W6 3F 99
Brook Grn. Flats *W14* *3F 99*
(off Dunsany Rd.)
Brookhill Cl. EN4: E Barn 5H 21
SE18 5F 107
Brookhill Rd. EN4: E Barn 5H 21
SE18 6F 107
Brook Ho. *W6* *4E 98*
(off Shepherd's Bush Rd.)
Brookhouse Gdns. E4 4B 36
Brook Ho's. *NW1* *2G 83*
(off Cranleigh St.)
Brook Ind. Est. UB4: Yead 1B 94
Brooking Cl. RM8: Dag 3C 72
Brooking Rd. E7 5J 69
Brookland Cl. NW11 4J 45
Brookland Gth. NW11 4J 45
Brookland Hill NW11 4K 45
Brookland Ri. NW11 4J 45
Brooklands, The TW7: Isle 1H 113
Brooklands App. RM1: Rom 4K 55
Brooklands Av. DA15: Sidc 2H 143
SW19 2K 135
Brooklands Cl. RM7: Rom 4K 55
TW16: Sun 1G 147
Brooklands Ct. CR4: Mitc 2B 154
KT1: King T *4D 150*
(off Surbiton Rd.)
N21 5J 23
NW6 7H 63
Brooklands Dr. UB6: G'frd 1C 78
Brooklands La. RM7: Rom 4K 55
(not continuous)
Brooklands Pk. SE3 3J 123
Brooklands Pas. SW8 1H 119
Brooklands Pl. TW12: Ham H 5F 131
Brooklands Rd. KT7: T Ditt 1A 162
RM7: Rom 4K 55
Brook La. BR1: Brom 6J 141
DA5: Bexl, Bex 6D 126
SE3 2K 123
Brook La. Bus. Cen.
TW8: Bford 5D 96
Brook La. Nth. TW8: Bford 5D 96
(not continuous)
Brooklea Cl. NW9 1A 44
Brook Lodge *NW11* *5F 45*
(off Nth. Circular Rd.)
RM7: Rom *4K 55*
(off Brooklands Rd.)
Brooklyn SE20 7G 139
Brooklyn Av. SE25 4H 157
Brooklyn Cl. SM5: Cars 2C 166
Brooklyn Ct. *W12* *1E 98*
(off Frithville Gdns.)
Brooklyn Gro. SE25 4H 157
Brooklyn Pas. *W12* *2E 98*
(off Lime Gro.)
Brooklyn Rd. BR2: Brom 5B 160
SE25 4H 157
Brookman Ho. *E3* *2B 86*
(off Mostyn Gro.)
Brookmarsh Ind. Est. SE10 7D 104
Brook Mead KT19: Ewe 6A 164
Brookmead CR0: Bedd 6G 155
Brookmead Av. BR1: Brom 5D 160
Brookmead Ind. Est.
CR0: Bedd 6G 155
Brook Mdw. N12 3E 30
Brook Mdw. Cl. IG8: Wfd G 6B 36
Brookmead Rd. CR0: C'don 6G 155
Brook M. IG7: Chig 3K 37
WC2 1D 12
Brook M. Nth. W2 2A 10 (7A 82)
Brookmill Rd. SE8 1C 122
Brook Pde. IG7: Chig 3K 37
Brook Pk. Cl. N21 5G 23
Brook Pl. EN5: Barn 5D 20
Brook Ri. IG7: Chig 3K 37
Brook Rd. CR7: Thor H 4C 156
IG2: Ilf 6J 53
IG9: Buck H, Wfd G 2D 36
KT6: Surb 2E 162
N2 7H 31
N8 4J 47
N22 3K 47
NW2 2B 62
TW1: Twick 6A 114
Brook Rd. Sth. TW8: Bford 6D 96
Brooks Av. E6 4D 88
Brooksbank Ho. *E9* *6J 67*
(off Retreat Pl.)
Brooksbank St. E9 6J 67
Brooksby Ho. *N1* *7A 66*
(off Liverpool Rd.)
Brooksby M. N1 7A 66
Brooksby St. N1 7A 66
Brooksby's Wlk. E9 5K 67
Brooks Cl. SE9 2E 142
Brooks Ct. SW8 7G 101
Brookscroft E17 3D 50
Brookscroft Rd. E17 1D 50
(not continuous)
Brooks Farm 7D 50
Brookshill HA3: Hrw W 5C 26
Brookshill Av. HA3: Hrw W 5C 26
Brookshill Dr. HA3: Hrw W 5C 26
Brookshill Ga. HA3: Hrw W 5C 26
Brookside BR6: Orp 7K 161
EN4: E Barn 6H 21
N21 6E 22
SM5: Cars 5E 166
UB10: Uxb 7B 56
Brookside Cl. EN5: Barn 6B 20
HA2: Harr 4C 58
HA3: Kenton 5D 42
TW13: Felt 3J 129
Brookside Cres. KT4: Wor Pk 1C 164
Brookside Rd. N9 4C 34
(not continuous)
N19 2G 65
NW11 6G 45
UB4: Yead 7A 76
Brookside Sth. EN4: E Barn 7K 21
Brookside Wlk. N12 6D 30
NW11 4G 45
Brookside Way CR0: C'don 6K 157
Brooks La. W4 6G 97
Brooks Lodge *N1* *2E 84*
(off Hoxton St.)
Brook's M. W1 2J 11 (7F 83)
Brook Sq. SE18 1C 124
Brooks Rd. E13 1J 87
W4 5G 97
Brook St. DA8: Erith 5H 109
DA17: Belv, Erith 5H 109
KT1: King T 2E 150
N17 2F 49
W1 2J 11 (7F 83)
W2 2B 10 (7B 82)
Brooksville Av. NW6 1G 81
Brooks Wlk. N3 3G 45
Brook Va. DA8: Erith 1H 127
Brookview Ct. EN1: Enf 5K 23
Brookview Rd. SW16 5G 137
Brookville Rd. SW6 7H 99
Brook Wlk. HA8: Edg 6E 28
N2 1B 46
Brook Way IG7: Chig 3K 37
Brookway SE3 3J 123
Brookwood Av. SW13 2B 116
Brookwood Cl. BR2: Brom 4H 159
Brookwood Ho. *SE1* *7B 14*
(off Webber St.)
Brookwood Rd. SW18 1H 135
TW3: Houn 2F 113
Broom Cl. BR2: Brom 6C 160
TW11: Tedd 7D 132
Broomcroft Av. UB5: N'olt 3A 76
Broome Rd. TW12: Hamp 7D 130
Broome Way SE5 7D 102
Broomfield E17 7B 50
NW1 *7E 64*
(off Ferdinand St.)
TW16: Sun 1J 147
Broomfield Av. N13 5E 32
Broomfield Ho. *HA7: Stan* *3F 27*
(off Stanmore Hill)
SE17 *4E 102*
(off Massinger St.)
Broomfield La. N13 4D 32
Broomfield Pl. W13 1B 96
Broomfield Rd. BR3: Beck 3A 158
DA6: Bex 5G 127
KT5: Surb 1F 163
N13 5D 32
RM6: Chad H 7D 54
TW9: Kew 1F 115
TW11: Tedd 6C 132
W13 1B 96
Broomfield St. E14 5C 86
Broom Gdns. CR0: C'don 3C 170
Broomgrove Gdns. HA8: Edg 1G 43
Broomgrove Rd. SW9 2K 119
Broomhall Rd. CR2: Sande 7D 168
RM9: Dag 6B 72
BROOM HILL 7K 161
Broomhill Ct. IG8: Wfd G 6D 36
Broomhill Ri. DA6: Bex 5G 127
Broomhill Rd. BR6: Orp 7K 161
IG3: Ilf 2A 72
IG8: Wfd G 6D 36
(not continuous)
SW18 5J 117
Broomhill Wlk. IG8: Wfd G 6C 36
Broomhouse La. SW6 2J 117
(not continuous)
Broomhouse Rd. SW6 2J 117
Broomloan La. SM1: Sutt 2J 165
Broom Lock TW11: Tedd 6C 132
Broom Mead DA6: Bex 6G 127
Broom Pk. TW11: Tedd 7D 132
Broom Rd. CR0: C'don 3C 170
TW11: Tedd 5B 132
Broomsleigh Bus. Pk. SE26 5B 140
Broomsleigh St. NW6 5H 63
Broom Water TW11: Tedd 6C 132
Broom Water W. TW11: Tedd 5C 132
Broomwood Cl. CR0: C'don 5K 157
DA5: Bexl 2K 145

Broomwood Rd.—Buckingham La.

Broomwood Rd. SW11 6D 118
Broseley Gro. SE26 5A 140
Broster Gdns. SE25 3F 157
Brougham Rd. E8 1G 85
W3 6J 79
Brougham St. SW11 2D 118
Brough Cl. KT2: King T 5D 132
SW8 7J 101
Broughton Av. N3 3G 45
TW10: Ham 3B 132
Broughton Ct. W13 7B 78
Broughton Dr. SW9 4A 120
Broughton Gdns. N6 6G 47
Broughton Rd. BR6: Orp 2H 173
CR7: Thor H 6A 156
SW6 2K 117
W13 7B 78
Broughton St. SW8 2E 118
Broughton St. Ind. Est. SW11 2E 118
Brouncker Rd. W3 2J 97
Browells La. TW13: Felt 2K 129
(not continuous)
Brown Bear Ct. TW13: Hanw 4B 130
Brown Cl. SM6: Wall 7J 167
Browne Ho. *SE8* *7C 104*
(off Deptford Church St.)
Brownfield Area E14 6D 86
Brownfield St. E14 6D 86
Browngraves Rd. UB3: Harl 7E 92
Brown Hart Gdns. W1 2H 11 (7E 82)
Brownhill Rd. SE6 7D 122
Browning Av. KT4: Wor Pk 1D 164
SM1: Sutt 4C 166
W7 6K 77
Browning Cl. DA16: Well 1J 125
E17 4E 50
RM5: Col R 1F 55
TW12: Hamp 4D 130
W9 4A 4 (4A 82)
Browning Ct. *W14* *6H 99*
(off Turneville Rd.)
Browning Ho. *N16* *4E 66*
(off Shakspeare Wlk.)
SE14 *1A 122*
(off Loring Rd.)
W12 *6E 80*
(off Wood La.)
Browning M. W1 6H 5 (5F 83)
Browning Rd. E11 7H 51
E12 5D 70
EN2: Enf 1J 23
Browning St. SE17 5C 102
Browning Way TW5: Hest 1B 112
Brownlea Gdns. IG3: Ilf 2A 72
Brownlow Cl. EN4: E Barn 5G 21
Brownlow Ct. N2 5A 46
N11 *6D 32*
(off Brownlow Rd.)
Brownlow Ho. *SE16* *2G 103*
(off George Row)
Brownlow M. WC1 4H 7 (4K 83)
Brownlow Rd. CR0: C'don 4E 168
E7 4J 69
E8 1F 85
N3 7E 30
N11 6D 32
NW10 7A 62
W13 1A 96
Brownlow St. WC1 6H 7 (5K 83)
Brownrigg Rd. TW15: Ashf 4C 128
Brown's Bldgs. EC3 1H 15 (6E 84)
Brownsea Wlk. NW7 6A 30
Browns La. NW5 5F 65
Brownspring Dr. SE9 4F 143
Browns Rd. E17 3C 50
KT5: Surb 7F 151
Brown St. W1 7E 4 (6D 82)
Brownswell Rd. N2 2B 46
BROWNSWOOD PARK 2B 66
Brownswood Rd. N4 3B 66
Broxash Rd. SW11 6E 118
Broxbourne Av. E18 4K 51
Broxbourne Ho. *E3* *4D 86*
(off Empson St.)
Broxbourne Rd. BR6: Orp 1K 173
E7 3J 69
Broxholme Cl. SE25 4D 156
Broxholme Ho. *SW6* *1K 117*
(off Harwood Rd.)
Broxholm Rd. SE27 3A 138
Broxted Rd. SE6 2B 140
Broxwood Way NW8 1C 82
Bruce Av. TW17: Shep 6E 146
Bruce Castle 1E 48
Bruce Castle Ct. *N17* *1F 49*
(off Lordship La.)
Bruce Castle Rd. N17 1F 49
Bruce Cl. DA16: Well 1B 126
W10 5F 81
Bruce Ct. DA15: Sidc 4K 143
Bruce Gdns. N20 3J 31
Bruce Gro. N17 1E 48
Bruce Hall M. SW17 4E 136
Bruce Ho. W10 5F 81
Bruce Rd. CR4: Mitc 7E 136
E3 3D 86
EN5: Barn 3B 20
HA3: W'stone 2J 41
NW10 7K 61
SE25 4D 156
Bruckner St. W10 3G 81
Brudenell Rd. SW17 3D 136
Bruffs Mdw. UB5: N'olt 6C 58
Bruford Ct. SE8 6C 104
Bruges Pl. *NW1* *7G 65*
(off Randolph St.)
Brumfield Rd. KT19: Ewe 5J 163
Brummel Cl. DA7: Bex 3J 127
Brune Ho. E1 6J 9
Brunei Gallery 5D 6 (5H 83)
Brunel Cl. SE19 6F 139
TW5: Cran 7K 93
UB5: N'olt 3D 76
Brunel Ct. *SE16* *2J 103*
(off Canon Beck Rd.)
SW13 *2B 116*
(off Westfields Av.)
Brunel Est. W2 5J 81
Brunel Ho. *E14* *5D 104*
(off Ship Yd.)
Brunel M. *W10* *3F 81*
(off Kilburn La.)
Brunel Mus. 2J 103
Brunel Pl. UB1: S'hall 6F 77
Brunel Rd. E17 6A 50
IG8: Wfd G 5J 37
SE16 2J 103
W3 5A 80
Brunel Science Pk.
UB8: Cowl 3A 74
Brunel St. E16 6H 87
Brunel University
Uxbridge Campus 3A 74
Brunel University Indoor Athletics Cen.
3A 74
Brunel University Sports Pk. 4B 74
Brunel Wlk. N15 5E 48
SW10 *7B 100*
(off Cheyne Rd.)
TW2: Whitt 7E 112
Brune St. E1 6J 9 (5F 85)
Brunlees Ho. *SE1* *3C 102*
(off Bath Ter.)
Brunner Cl. NW11 5K 45
Brunner Ho. SE6 4E 140
Brunner Rd. E17 5A 50
W5 4D 78
Bruno Pl. NW9 2J 61
Brunswick Av. N11 3K 31
Brunswick Cen. WC1 3E 6 (4J 83)
Brunswick Cl. DA6: Bex 4D 126
HA5: Pinn 6C 40
KT7: T Ditt 1A 162
TW2: Twick 3H 131
Brunswick Cl. Est. EC1 2A 8 (3B 84)
Brunswick Ct. *EC1* *2A 8*
(off Tompion St.)
EN4: E Barn 5G 21
SE1 7H 15 (2E 102)
SM1: Sutt 4K 165
SW1 *4D 18*
(off Regency St.)
Brunswick Cres. N11 3K 31
Brunswick Fitness Cen. 1C 32
Brunswick Flats *W11* *6J 81*
(off Westbourne Gro.)
Brunswick Gdns. IG6: Ilf 1G 53
W5 4E 78
W8 1J 99
Brunswick Gro. N11 3K 31
Brunswick Ho. *E2* *2F 85*
(off Thurtle Rd.)
N3 1H 45
SE16 *3A 104*
(off Brunswick Quay)
Brunswick Ind. Pk. N11 4A 32
Brunswick Mans. *WC1* *3F 7*
(off Handel St.)
Brunswick M. SW16 6H 137
W1 7F 5 (6D 82)
BRUNSWICK PARK 3J 31
Brunswick Pk. SE5 1E 120
Brunswick Pk. Gdns. N11 2K 31
Brunswick Pk. Rd. N11 2K 31
Brunswick Pl. N1 2F 9 (3D 84)
NW1 4H 5 (4E 82)
(not continuous)
SE19 7G 139
Brunswick Quay SE16 3K 103
Brunswick Rd. DA6: Bex 4D 126
E10 1E 68
E14 6E 86
EN3: Enf L 1H 25
KT2: King T 1G 151
N15 4E 48
(not continuous)
SM1: Sutt 4K 165
W5 4D 78
Brunswick Sq. N17 6A 34
WC1 3F 7 (4J 83)
Brunswick St. E17 5E 50
Brunswick Ter. BR3: Beck 1D 158
Brunswick Vs. SE5 1E 120
Brunswick Way N11 4A 32
Brunton Pl. E14 6A 86
Brushfield St. E1 5H 9 (5E 84)
Brushwood Cl. E14 5D 86
Brussels Rd. SW11 4B 118
Bruton Cl. BR7: Chst 7D 142
Bruton La. W1 3K 11 (7F 83)
Bruton Pl. W1 3K 11 (7F 83)
Bruton Rd. SM4: Mord 4A 154
Bruton St. W1 3K 11 (7F 83)
Bruton Way W13 5A 78
Brutus Ct. *SE11* *4B 102*
(off Kennington La.)
Bryan Av. NW10 7D 62
Bryan Cl. TW16: Sun 7J 129
Bryan Ho. NW10 7D 62
SE16 2B 104
Bryan Rd. SE16 2B 104
Bryan's All. SW6 2K 117
Bryanston Av. TW2: Whitt 1F 131
Bryanston Cl. UB2: S'hall 4D 94
Bryanston Ct. W1 7E 4
(not continuous)
Bryanstone Ct. SM1: Sutt 3A 166
Bryanstone Rd. N8 5H 47
Bryanston Mans. *W1* *5E 4*
(off York St.)
Bryanston M. E. W1 6E 4 (5D 82)
Bryanston M. W. W1 6E 4 (5D 82)
Bryanston Pl. W1 6E 4 (5D 82)
Bryanston Sq. W1 6E 4 (6D 82)
Bryanston St. W1 1E 10 (6D 82)
Bryant Cl. EN5: Barn 5C 20
Bryant Ct. *E2* *2F 85*
(off Whiston Rd., not continuous)
W3 1K 97
Bryant Ho. *E3* *2C 86*
(off Thomas Frye Dr.)
Bryant Rd. UB5: N'olt 3A 76
Bryant St. E15 7F 69
Bryantwood Rd. N7 5A 66
Brycedale Cres. N14 4C 32
Bryce Ho. *SE14* *6K 103*
(off John Williams Cl.)
Bryce Rd. RM8: Dag 4C 72
Brydale Ho. *SE16* *4K 103*
(off Rotherhithe New Rd.)
Bryden Cl. SE26 5A 140
Brydges Pl. WC2 3E 12 (7J 83)
Brydges Rd. E15 5F 69
Brydon Wlk. N1 1J 83
Bryer Ct. EC2 5C 8
Bryett Rd. N7 3J 65
Bryher Ct. SE11 5J 19
Brymay Cl. E3 2C 86
Brynmaer Rd. SW11 1D 118
Bryn-y-mawr Rd. EN1: Enf 4A 24
Bryony Cl. UB8: Hil 5B 74
Bryony Rd. W12 7C 80
Bryony Way TW16: Sun 6J 129
Buccleugh Ho. E5 7G 49
Buchanan Cl. N21 5E 22
Buchanan Ct. *SE16* *4K 103*
(off Worgan St.)
Buchanan Gdns. NW10 2D 80
Buchan Ho. *W3* *2H 97*
(off Hanbury Rd.)
Buchan Rd. SE15 3J 121
Bucharest Rd. SW18 7A 118
Buckden Cl. N2 4D 46
SE12 6J 123
Buckfast Ct. *W13* *7A 78*
(off Romsey Rd.)
Buckfast Ho. N14 5B 22
Buckfast Rd. SM4: Mord 4K 153
Buckfast St. E2 3G 85
Buck Hill Wlk. W2 3B 10 (7B 82)
Buckhold Rd. SW18 6J 117
Buckhurst Av. SM5: Cars 1C 166
Buckhurst Ct. *IG9: Buck H* *2G 37*
(off Albert Rd.)
IG9: Buck H 1G 37
(Roding La.)
BUCKHURST HILL 2G 37
Buckhurst Hill Ho. IG9: Buck H 2E 36
Buckhurst Ho. N7 5H 65
Buckhurst St. E1 4H 85
Buckhurst Way IG9: Buck H 4G 37
Buckingham Arc. WC2 3E 12
Buckingham Av. CR7: Thor H 1A 156
DA16: Well 4J 125
KT8: W Mole 2F 149
N20 7F 21
TW14: Felt 6K 111
UB6: G'frd 1A 78
Buckingham Chambers *SW1* *3B 18*
(off Greencoat Pl.)
Buckingham Cl. BR5: Pet W 7J 161
EN1: Enf 2K 23
TW12: Hamp 5D 130
W5 5C 78
Buckingham Ct. NW4 3C 44
UB5: N'olt 2C 76
W7 *4K 77*
(off Copley Cl.)
W11 *7J 81*
(off Kensington Pk.)
Buckingham Dr. BR7: Chst 4G 143
Buckingham Gdns.
CR7: Thor H 2A 156
HA8: Edg 7K 27
KT8: W Mole 2F 149
Buckingham Ga. SW1 1A 18 (3G 101)
Buckingham Gro. UB10: Hil 2C 74
Buckingham La. SE23 7A 122

Buckingham Mans. *NW6* 5K *63*
  (off West End La.)
Buckingham M. N1 . . . . .6E *66*
  NW10 .2B *80*
  SW1 . . . . .1A *18*
Buckingham Palace 7K 11 (2F *101*)
Buckingham Pal. Rd. SW1 . .4J 17 (4F *101*)
Buckingham Pde. HA7: Stan 5H *27*
Buckingham Pl. SW1 . . . . .1A 18 (3G *101*)
Buckingham Rd. CR4: Mitc 4J *155*
  E10 . . . . .3D *68*
  E11 . . . . .5A *52*
  E15 . . . . .5H *69*
  E18 . . . . .1H *51*
  HA1: Harr 5H *41*
  HA8: Edg 7A *28*
  IG1: Ilf 2H *71*
  KT1: King T 4F *151*
  N1 . . . . .6E *66*
  N22 . . . . .1J *47*
  NW10 .2B *80*
  TW10: Ham 2D *132*
  TW12: Hamp 4D *130*
Buckingham St. WC2 . . . . . .4F 13 (7J *83*)
Buckingham Way SM6: Wall 7G *167*
Buckland Cl. NW7 . . . . .4H *29*
Buckland Ct. *N1* 2E *84*
  (off St John's Est.)
  UB10: Ick 2E *56*
Buckland Cres. NW3 . . . . .7B *64*
Buckland Ho. *SW1* 5F *101*
  (off Abbots Mnr.)
Buckland Ri. HA5: Pinn 1A *40*
Buckland Rd. BR6: Orp 4J *173*
  E10 . . . . .2E *68*
  KT9: Chess 5F *163*
Bucklands Rd. TW11: Tedd 6C *132*
Buckland St. N1 . . . . .2D *84*
Buckland's Wharf KT1: King T 2D *150*
Buckland Wlk. SM4: Mord 4A *154*
  W3 . . . . .2J *97*
Buckland Way KT4: Wor Pk 1E *164*
Buck La. NW9 . . . . .5K *43*
Bucklebury *NW1* 3A *6*
  (off Stanhope St.)
Buckleigh Av. SW20 . . . . .3G *153*
Buckleigh Rd. SW16 . . . . .6H *137*
Buckleigh Way SW19 . . . . .7F *139*
Buckler Ct. N7 . . . . .5K *65*
Buckler Gdns. SE9 . . . . .3D *142*
Bucklers All. SW6 . . . . .6H *99*
  (not continuous)
Bucklersbury EC4 . . . . .1E 14 (6D *84*)
Bucklersbury Pas. EC4 . . . . .6D *84*
Buckler's Way SM5: Cars 3D *166*
Buckles Ct. DA17: Belv 4D *108*
Buckle St. E1 . . . . .7K 9 (6F *85*)
Buckley Cl. SE23 . . . . .7H *121*
Buckley Ct. NW6 . . . . .7H *63*
Buckley Ho. *W14* 2G *99*
  (off Holland Pk. Av.)
Buckley Rd. NW6 . . . . .7H *63*
Buckmaster Cl. *SW9* 3A *120*
  (off Stockwell Pk. Rd.)
Buckmaster Ho. N7 . . . . .4K *65*
Buckmaster Rd. SW11 . . . . .4C *118*
Bucknall St. WC2 . . . . .7D 6 (6J *83*)
Bucknall Way BR3: Beck 4D *158*
Bucknell Cl. SW2 . . . . .4K *119*
Buckner Rd. SW2 . . . . .4K *119*
Bucknill Ho. *SW1* 5J *17*
  (off Ebury Bri. Rd.)
Buckrell Rd. E4 . . . . .2A *36*
Buckridge Ho. *EC1* 5J *7*
  (off Portpool La.)
Buckshead Ho. *W2* 5J *81*
  (off Gt. Western Rd.)
Buckstone Cl. SE23 . . . . .6J *121*
Buckstone Rd. N18 . . . . .5B *34*
Buck St. NW1 . . . . .7F *65*
Buckters Rents SE16 . . . . .1A *104*
Buckthorne Rd. SE4 . . . . .5A *122*

Buckthorn Ho. DA15: Sidc 3K *143*
  (off Longlands Rd.)
Buck Wlk. E17 . . . . .4F *51*
Buckwheat Ct. DA18: Erith 3D *108*
Budd Cl. N12 . . . . .4E *30*
Buddings Circ. HA9: Wemb 3J *61*
Buddleia Ho. TW13: Felt 1J *129*
Budd's All. TW1: Twick 5C *114*
Bude Cl. E17 . . . . .5B *50*
Budge La. CR4: Mitc 7D *154*
Budge Row EC4 . . . . .2E 14 (7D *84*)
Budge's Wlk. W2 . . . . .3A *10*
Budleigh Cres. DA16: Well 1C *126*
Budleigh Ho. *SE15* 7G *103*
  (off Bird in Bush Rd.)
Budoch Ct. IG3: Ilf 2A *72*
Budoch Dr. IG3: Ilf 2A *72*
Buer Rd. SW6 . . . . .2G *117*
Bugsby's Way SE7 . . . . .4H *105*
  SE10 . . . . .4H *105*
Buick Ho. *E3* 4C *86*
  (off Wellington Way)
  KT1: King T 2G *151*
Building 50 SE18 . . . . .3G *107*
Building 1000 E16 . . . . .7C *88*
Bulbarrow *NW8* 1K *81*
  (off Abbey Rd.)
Bulganak Rd. CR7: Thor H 4C *156*
Bulinga St. SW1 . . . . .4E *18*
Bullace Row SE5 . . . . .1D *120*
Bull All. DA16: Well 3B *126*
Bullard Rd. TW11: Tedd 6J *131*
Bullard's Pl. E2 . . . . .3K *85*
Bullbanks Rd. DA17: Belv 4J *109*
Bulleid Way SW1 . . . . .4K 17 (4F *101*)
Bullen Ho. *E1* 4H *85*
  (off Collingwood St.)
Bullen St. SW11 . . . . .2C *118*
Buller Cl. SE15 . . . . .7G *103*
Buller Rd. CR7: Thor H 2D *156*
  IG11: Bark 7J *71*
  N17 . . . . .2G *49*
  N22 . . . . .2A *48*
  NW10 .3F *81*
Bullers Cl. DA14: Sidc 5E *144*
Bullers Wood Dr. BR7: Chst 7D *142*
Bullescroft Rd. HA8: Edg 3B *28*
Bullingham Mans. *W8* 2J *99*
  (off Pitt St.)
Bull Inn Ct. WC2 . . . . .3F *13*
Bullivant St. E14 . . . . .7E *86*
Bull La. BR7: Chst 7H *143*
  N18 . . . . .5K *33*
  RM10: Dag 3H *73*
Bull Rd. E15 . . . . .2H *87*
Bullrush Cl. CR0: C'don 6E *156*
  SM5: Cars 2C *166*
Bull's All. SW14 . . . . .2K *115*
Bulls Bri. Cen. UB3: Hayes 3J *93*
Bullsbridge Ind. Est. UB2: S'hall 4A *94*
Bulls Bri. Rd. UB2: S'hall 4A *94*
  UB3: Hayes 3K *93*
Bullsbrook Rd. UB4: Yead 1A *94*
Bulls Gdns. SW3 . . . . .3D 16 (4C *100*)
  (not continuous)
Bulls Head Pas. EC3 . . . . .1G *15*
Bull Theatre, The 4C *20*
Bull Yd. SE15 . . . . .1G *121*
Bulmer Gdns. HA3: Kenton 7D *42*
Bulmer M. W11 . . . . .7J *81*
Bulmer Pl. W11 . . . . .1J *99*
Bulow Est. SW6 . . . . .1K *117*
  (off Pearscroft Rd.)
Bulringion Cnr. *NW1* 7G *65*
  (off Camden Rd.)
Bulstrode Av. TW3: Houn 2D *112*
Bulstrode Gdns. TW3: Houn 3E *112*
Bulstrode Pl. W1 . . . . .6H 5 (5E *82*)
Bulstrode Rd. TW3: Houn 3E *112*
Bulstrode St. W1 . . . . .7H 5 (6E *82*)
Bulwer Cl. E11 . . . . .1F *69*
Bulwer Ct. Rd. E11 . . . . .1F *69*

Bulwer Gdns. EN5: New Bar 4F *21*
Bulwer Rd. E11 . . . . .7F *51*
  EN5: New Bar 4E *20*
  N18 . . . . .4K *33*
Bulwer St. W12 . . . . .1E *98*
Bunbury Ho. *SE15* 7G *103*
  (off Fenham Rd.)
Bunce's La. IG8: Wfd G 7C *36*
Bungalow Rd. SE25 . . . . .4E *156*
Bungalows, The E10 . . . . .6E *50*
  HA2: Harr 4D *58*
  IG6: Ilf 1J *53*
  SM6: Wall 5F *167*
  SW16 . . . . .7F *137*
Bunhill Row EC1 . . . . .3E 8 (4D *84*)
Bunhouse Pl. SW1 . . . . . . .5H 17 (5E *100*)
Bunkers Hill DA14: Sidc 3F *145*
  DA17: Belv 4G *109*
  NW11 .7A *46*
Bunning Way N7 . . . . .7J *65*
Bunns La. NW7 . . . . .6F *29*
  (not continuous)
Bunsen Ho. *E3* 2A *86*
  (off Grove Rd.)
Bunsen St. E3 . . . . .2A *86*
Buntingbridge Rd. IG2: Ilf 5H *53*
Bunting Cl. CR4: Mitc 5D *154*
  N9 . . . . .1E *34*
Bunting Ct. NW9 . . . . .2A *44*
Bunton St. SE18 . . . . .3E *106*
Bunyan Cl. EC2 . . . . .5C *8*
Bunyan Rd. E17 . . . . .3A *50*
Buonaparte M. SW1 . . . . . .5C 18 (5H *101*)
Burbage Cl. SE1 . . . . .3D *102*
  UB3: Hayes 6F *75*
Burbage Ho. *N1* 1D *84*
  (off Poole St.)
  SE14 . . . . .6K *103*
  (off Samuel Cl.)
Burbage Rd. SE21 . . . . .6C *120*
  SE24 . . . . .6C *120*
Burberry Cl. KT3: N Mald 2A *152*
Burbidge Rd. TW17: Shep 4C *146*
Burbridge Way N17 . . . . .2G *49*
Burcham St. E14 . . . . .6D *86*
Burcharbro Rd. SE2 . . . . .6D *108*
Burchell Ct. WD23: Bush 1B *26*
Burchell Ho. *SE11* 5H *19*
  (off Jonathan St.)
Burchell Rd. E10 . . . . .1D *68*
  SE15 . . . . .1H *121*
Burcher Gale Gro. SE15 . . . . .7F *103*
Burchetts Way TW17: Shep 6D *146*
Burchett Way RM6: Chad H 6F *55*
Burchwall Cl. RM5: Col R 1J *55*
Burcote Rd. SW18 . . . . .7B *118*
Burden Cl. TW8: Bford 5C *96*
Burden Ho. *SW8* 7J *101*
  (off Thorncroft St.)
Burdenshott Av. TW10: Rich 4H *115*
Burden Way E11 . . . . .2K *69*
Burder Cl. N1 . . . . .6E *66*
Burder Rd. N1 . . . . .6E *66*
Burdett Av. SW20 . . . . .1C *152*
Burdett Cl. DA14: Sidc 5E *144*
  W7 . . . . .1K *95*
Burdett M. NW3 . . . . .6B *64*
  W2 . . . . .6K *81*
Burdett Rd. CR0: C'don 6D *156*
  E3 . . . . .4B *86*
  E14 . . . . .4A *86*
  TW9: Rich 2F *115*
Burdetts Rd. RM9: Dag 1F *91*
Burdock Cl. CR0: C'don 1K *169*
Burdock Rd. N17 . . . . .3G *49*
Burdon La. SM2: Cheam 7G *165*
Burdon Pk. SM2: Cheam 7H *165*
Bure Ct. EN5: New Bar 5E *20*
Burfield Cl. SW17 . . . . .4B *136*
Burford Cl. IG6: Ilf 4G *53*
  RM8: Dag 3C *72*
  UB10: Ick 4A *56*

Burford Gdns. N13 . . . . .3E *32*
Burford Ho. TW8: Bford 5D *96*
Burford Rd. BR1: Brom 4C *160*
  E6 . . . . .3C *88*
  E15 . . . . .1F *87*
  KT4: Wor Pk 7B *152*
  SE6 . . . . .2B *140*
  SM1: Sutt 2J *165*
  TW8: Bford 5E *96*
Burford Wlk. SW6 . . . . .7A *100*
Burford Way CR0: New Ad 6E *170*
Burford Wharf Apartments E15 . . . . .1F *87*
  (off Cam Rd.)
Burge Rd. E7 . . . . .4B *70*
Burges Gro. SW13 . . . . .7D *98*
Burges Rd. E6 . . . . .7C *70*
Burgess M. SW19 . . . . .6K *43*
Burgess Bus. Pk. SE5 . . . . .7D *102*
Burgess Cl. TW13: Hanw 4C *130*
Burgess Ct. E6 . . . . .7E *70*
  UB1: S'hall 6F *77*
  (off Fleming Rd.)
Burgess Hill NW2 . . . . .4J *63*
Burgess Ho. SE5 . . . . .7C *102*
  (off Bethwin Rd.)
Burgess Lofts SE5 . . . . .7C *102*
  (off Wyndham Est.)
Burgess M. SW19 . . . . .6K *135*
Burgess Pk. 6D *102*
  (off Albany Rd.)
Burgess Pk. Kart Track 5G *87*
Burgess Rd. E6 . . . . .7E *70*
  E15 . . . . .4G *69*
  SM1: Sutt 4K *165*
Burgess St. E14 . . . . .5C *86*
Burge St. SE1 . . . . .3D *102*
Burgh House 4B *64*
Burghill Rd. SE26 . . . . .4A *140*
Burghley Av. KT3: N Mald 1K *151*
Burghley Hall Cl. SW19 . . . . .1G *135*
Burghley Ho. SW19 . . . . .3G *135*
Burghley Pas. E11 . . . . .1G *69*
  (off Burghley Rd.)
Burghley Pl. CR4: Mitc 5D *154*
Burghley Rd. E11 . . . . .1G *69*
  N8 . . . . .3A *48*
  NW5 . . . . .4F *65*
  SW19 . . . . .4F *135*
Burghley Twr. W3 . . . . .7B *80*
Burgh St. N1 . . . . .2B *84*
Burgoine Quay KT1: Ham W 1D *150*
Burgon St. EC4 . . . . .1B 14 (6B *84*)
Burgos Cl. CR0: Wadd 6A *168*
Burgos Gro. SE10 . . . . .1D *122*
Burgoyne Rd. N4 . . . . .6B *48*
  SE25 . . . . .4F *157*
  SW9 . . . . .3K *119*
  TW16: Sun 6H *129*
Burgundy Ho. EN2: Enf 1H *23*
  (off Bedale Rd.)
Burgundy Pl. W12 . . . . .1F *99*
Burham Cl. SE20 . . . . .7J *139*
Burhill Gro. HA5: Pinn 2C *40*
Burke Cl. SW15 . . . . .4A *116*
Burke Lodge E13 . . . . .3K *87*
Burke St. E16 . . . . .5H *87*
  (not continuous)
Burket Cl. UB2: S'hall 4C *94*
Burland Rd. SW11 . . . . .5D *118*
Burleigh Av. DA15: Sidc 5K *125*
  SM6: Wall 3E *166*
Burleigh Cl. RM7: Mawney 4H *55*
Burleigh Gdns. N14 . . . . .1B *32*
  TW15: Ashf 5E *128*
Burleigh Ho. SW3 . . . . .7B *16*
  W10 . . . . .5F *81*
  (off St Charles Sq.)
Burleigh Pde. N14 . . . . .1C *32*
Burleigh Pl. SW15 . . . . .5F *117*
Burleigh Rd. EN1: Enf 4K *23*
  SM3: Sutt 1G *165*
  UB10: Hil 1D *74*

Burleigh St.—Bushnell Rd.

Burleigh St. WC2 2G 13 (7K 83)
Burleigh Wlk. SE6 1E 140
Burleigh Way EN2: Enf 3J 23
Burley Cl. E4 5H 35
SW16 2H 155
Burley Ho. *E1 6K 85*
(off Chudleigh St.)
Burley Rd. E16 6A 88
Burlington Arc. W1 3A 12 (7G 83)
Burlington Av. RM7: Rom 6H 55
TW9: Kew 1G 115
Burlington Cl. BR6: Farnb 2F 173
E6 6C 88
HA5: Eastc 3K 39
TW14: Bedf 7F 111
W9 4J 81
Burlington Gdns.
RM6: Chad H 7E 54
SW6 2G 117
W1 3A 12 (7G 83)
W3 1J 97
W4 5J 97
Burlington Ho. *N15 6D 48*
(off Tewkesbury Rd.)
UB7: W Dray 2B 92
(off Park Lodge Av.)
Burlington La. W4 7J 97
Burlington M. SW15 5H 117
W3 1J 97
Burlington Pl. IG8: Wfd G 3E 36
SW6 2G 117
Burlington Ri. EN4: E Barn 1H 31
Burlington Rd.
CR7: Thor H 2C 156
EN2: Enf 1J 23
KT3: N Mald 4B 152
N10 3E 46
N17 1G 49
SW6 2G 117
TW7: Isle 1H 113
W4 5J 97
Burma M. N16 4D 66
Burma Rd. N16 4D 66
Burmarsh NW5 6E 64
Burmarsh Ct. SE20 1J 157
Burma Ter. SE19 5E 138
Burmester Rd. SW17 3A 136
Burnaby Cres. W4 6J 97
Burnaby Gdns. W4 6H 97
Burnaby St. SW10 7A 100
Burnand Ho. *W14 3F 99*
(off Redan St.)
Burnbrae Cl. N12 6E 30
Burnbury Rd. SW12 1G 137
Burncroft Av. EN3: Enf H 2D 24
Burndell Way UB4: Yead 5B 76
Burne Jones Ho.
W14 4G 99
Burnell Av. DA16: Well 2A 126
TW10: Ham 5C 132
Burnell Gdns. HA7: Stan 2D 42
Burnelli Bldg. *SW8 7F 101*
(off Sopwith Way)
Burnell Rd. SM1: Sutt 4K 165
Burnell Wlk. *SE1 5F 103*
(off Cadet Dr.)
Burnels Av. E6 3E 88
Burness Cl. N7 6K 65
Burne St. NW1 5C 4 (5C 82)
Burnett Cl. E9 5J 67
Burnett Ho. *SE13 2E 122*
(off Lewisham Hill)
Burnett Rd. IG6: Ilf 7K 37
Burney Av. KT5: Surb 5F 151
Burney St. SE10 7E 104
Burnfoot Av. SW6 1G 117
Burnham NW3 7C 64
Burnham Av. UB10: Ick 4E 56
Burnham Cl. EN1: Enf 1K 23
HA3: W'stone 4A 42
NW7 7H 29
SE1 4F 103
Burnham Ct. *NW4 4E 44*
(off Brent St.)
NW6 7A 64
(off Fairhazel Gdns.)
W2 7K 81
(off Moscow Rd.)
Burnham Cres. E11 4A 52
Burnham Dr. KT4: Wor Pk 2F 165
Burnham Est. *E2 3J 85*
(off Burnham St.)
Burnham Gdns. CR0: C'don 7F 157
TW4: Cran 1K 111
UB3: Harl 3F 93
Burnham Rd. DA14: Sidc 2E 144
E4 5G 35
RM7: Rom 3K 55
RM9: Dag 7B 72
SM4: Mord 4K 153
Burnham St. E2 3J 85
KT2: King T 1G 151
Burnham Way SE26 5B 140
W13 4B 96
Burnhill Cl. SE15 7H 103
Burnhill Ho. *EC1 2C 8*
(off Norman St.)
Burnhill Rd. BR3: Beck 2C 158
Burnley Rd. NW10 5B 62
SW9 2K 119
Burnsall St. SW3 6D 16 (5C 100)
Burns Av. DA15: Sidc 6B 126
RM6: Chad H 7C 54
TW14: Felt 6J 111
UB1: S'hall 7E 76
Burns Cl. DA16: Well 1K 125
E17 4E 50
SW19 6B 136
UB4: Hayes 5H 75
Burns Ho. *E2 3J 85*
(off Cornwall Av.)
SE17 5B 102
(off Doddington Gro.)
Burnside Av. E4 6G 35
Burnside Cl. EN5: New Bar 3D 20
SE16 1K 103
TW1: Twick 6A 114
Burnside Ct. SM5: Cars 3E 166
Burnside Cres. HA0: Wemb 1D 78
Burnside Rd. RM8: Dag 2C 72
Burns Rd. HA0: Wemb 2E 78
NW10 1B 80
SW11 2D 118
W13 2B 96
Burns Way TW5: Hest 2B 112
Burnt Ash Hgts. BR1: Brom 5K 141
Burnt Ash Hill SE12 6H 123
Burnt Ash La. BR1: Brom 7J 141
Burnt Ash Rd. SE12 5H 123
Burnthwaite Rd. SW6 7H 99
BURNT OAK 1H 43
Burnt Oak HA8: Edg 7B 28
Burnt Oak Apartments *E16 6J 87*
(off Pacific Rd.)
Burnt Oak B'way. HA8: Edg 7B 28
Burnt Oak Flds. HA8: Edg 1J 43
Burnt Oak La. DA15: Sidc 6A 126
(Elmcroft Av.)
DA15: Sidc 2A 144
(Halfway St.)
Burntwood Cl. SW18 1C 136
Burntwood Grange Rd.
SW18 1B 136
Burntwood La. SW17 3A 136
Burntwood Vw. SE19 5F 139
Buross St. E1 6H 85
Burpham Cl. UB4: Yead 5B 76
Burrage Ct. *SE16 4K 103*
(off Worgan St.)
Burrage Gro. SE18 4G 107
Burrage Pl. SE18 5F 107
Burrage Rd. SE18 5G 107
Burrard Ho. *E2 2J 85*
(off Bishop's Way)
Burrard Rd. E16 6K 87
NW6 5J 63
Burr Cl. DA7: Bex 3F 127
E1 4K 15 (1G 103)
Burrell Cl. CR0: C'don 6A 158
HA8: Edg 2C 28
Burrell Row BR3: Beck 2C 158
Burrell St. SE1 4A 14 (1B 102)
Burrells Wharf Sq. E14 5D 104
Burrell Towers E10 7C 50
Burrhill Ct. *SE16 3K 103*
(off Worgan St.)
Burritt Rd. KT1: King T 2G 151
Burroughs, The NW4 4D 44
Burroughs Club, The 4D 44
Burroughs Cotts. *E14 5A 86*
(off Halley St.)
Burroughs Gdns. NW4 4D 44
Burroughs Pde. NW4 4D 44
Burrow Ho. *SW9 2A 120*
(off Stockwell Pk. Rd.)
Burrow Rd. SE22 4E 120
Burrows M. SE1 6A 14 (2B 102)
Burrows Rd. NW10 3E 80
Burrow Wlk. SE21 7C 120
Burr Rd. SW18 1J 135
Bursar St. SE1 5G 15 (1E 102)
Bursdon Cl. DA15: Sidc 2K 143
Bursland Rd. EN3: Pond E 4E 24
Burslem St. E1 6G 85
Burstock Rd. SW15 4G 117
Burston Rd. SW15 5F 117
Burston Vs. *SW15 5F 117*
(off St John's Av.)
Burstow Rd. SW20 1G 153
Burtenshaw Rd. KT7: T Ditt 7A 150
Burtley Cl. N4 1C 66
Burton Bank *N1 7D 66*
(off Yeate St.)
Burton Cl. CR7: Thor H 3D 156
KT9: Chess 7D 162
Burton Ct. KT7: T Ditt 6A 150
SE20 2J 157
SW3 5F 17
(not continuous)
Burton Gdns. TW5: Hest 1D 112
Burton Gro. SE17 5D 102
Burtonhole Cl. NW7 4A 30
Burtonhole La. N12 4B 30
NW7 5K 29
Burton Ho. *SE16 2H 103*
(off Cherry Gdn. St.)
Burton La. SW9 2A 120
(not continuous)
Burton M. SW1 4H 17 (4E 100)
Burton Pl. WC1 2D 6 (3H 83)
Burton Rd. E18 3K 51
KT2: King T 7E 132
NW6 7H 63
SW9 2B 120
(Akerman Rd.)
SW9 2A 120
(Evesham Wlk.)
Burtons Ct. E15 7F 69
Burton's Rd. TW12: Ham H 4F 131
Burton St. WC1 2D 6 (3H 83)
Burtonwood Ho. N4 7D 48
Burtop Rd. Est.
SW17 3A 136
Burt Rd. E16 1A 106
Burts Wharf DA17: Belv 7J 91
Burtt Ho. *N1 1G 9*
(off Aske St.)
Burtwell La. SE27 4D 138
Burwash Ho. *SE1 7F 15*
(off Kipling Est.)
Burwash Rd. SE18 5H 107
Burway Cl. CR2: S Croy 6E 168
Burwell *KT1: King T 2G 151*
(off Excelsior Rd.)
Burwell Av. UB6: G'frd 6J 59
Burwell Cl. E1 6H 85
Burwell Rd. E10 1A 68
Burwell Rd. Ind. Est. E10 1A 68
Burwell Wlk. E3 4C 86
Burwood Av. BR2: Hayes 2K 171
HA5: Eastc 5K 39
Burwood Cl. KT6: Surb 1G 163
Burwood Ho. SW9 4B 120
Burwood Pl. EN4: Had W 1F 21
W2 7D 4 (6C 82)
Bury Av. HA4: Ruis 6E 38
UB4: Hayes 2G 75
Bury Cl. SE16 1K 103
Bury Ct. EC3 7H 9 (6E 84)
Buryfield Ct. *SE8 4K 103*
(off Lower Rd.)
Bury Gro. SM4: Mord 5K 153
Bury Hall Vs. N9 7A 24
Bury Pl. WC1 6E 6 (5J 83)
Bury Rd. E4 1B 36
N22 2A 48
RM10: Dag 5H 73
Buryside Cl. IG2: Ilf 4K 53
Bury St. EC3 1H 15 (6E 84)
HA4: Ruis 5E 38
N9 7A 24
SW1 4B 12 (1G 101)
Bury St. W. N9 7J 23
Bury Wlk. SW3 4C 16 (4C 100)
Busbridge Ho. *E14 5C 86*
(off Brabazon St.)
Busby Ho. SW16 4G 137
Busby M. NW5 6H 65
Busby Pl. NW5 6H 65
Busch Cl. TW7: Isle 1B 114
Bushbaby Cl. SE1 3E 102
Bushberry Rd. E9 6A 68
Bush Cl. IG2: Ilf 5H 53
Bush Cotts. SW18 5J 117
Bush Ct. N14 1C 32
W12 2F 99
Bushell Cl. SW2 2K 137
Bushell Grn. WD23: B Hea 2C 26
Bushell St. E1 1G 103
Bushell Way BR7: Chst 5E 142
BUSHEY 1C 26
Bushey Av. BR5: Pet W 7H 161
E18 3H 51
Bushey Cl. E4 3K 35
UB10: Ick 2C 56
Bushey Ct. SW20 3D 152
Bushey Down SW12 2F 137
BUSHEY HEATH 1C 26
Bushey Hill Rd. SE5 1E 120
Bushey La. SM1: Sutt 4J 165
Bushey Lees DA15: Sidc 6K 125
BUSHEY MEAD 2F 153
Bushey Rd. CR0: C'don 2C 170
E13 2A 88
N15 6E 48
SM1: Sutt 4J 165
SW20 3D 152
UB3: Harl 4G 93
UB10: Ick 2C 56
Bushey Way BR3: Beck 6F 159
Bush Fair Ct. N14 6A 22
Bushfield Cl. HA8: Edg 2C 28
Bushfield Cres. HA8: Edg 2C 28
Bush Gro. HA7: Stan 1D 42
NW9 7J 43
Bushgrove Rd. RM8: Dag 4D 72
Bush Hill N21 7H 23
Bush Hill Pde. EN1: Enf 7J 23
N9 7J 23
BUSH HILL PARK 6A 24
Bush Hill Rd. HA3: Kenton 6F 43
N21 6J 23
Bush Ind. Est. N19 3G 65
NW10 4K 79
Bush La. EC4 2E 14 (7D 84)
Bushmead Cl. N15 4F 49
Bushmoor Cres. SE18 7F 107
Bushnell Rd. SW17 2F 137

Bush Rd. E8 . . . . 1H 85
E11 . . . . 7H 51
IG9: Buck H 4G 37
SE8 . . . . *4K 103*
(off Rotherhithe New Rd.)
TW9: Kew 6F 97
TW17: Shep 5B 146
Bush Theatre 2E 98
Bushway RM8: Dag 4D 72
Bushwood E11 . . . . 1H 69
Bushwood Dr. SE1 . . . . 4F 103
Bushwood Rd. TW9: Kew 6G 97
Bushy Ct. *KT1: Ham W* *1C 150*
(off Beverley Rd.)
Bushy Pk. 7H 131
Bushy Pk. Gdns. TW11: Tedd 5H 131
Bushy Pk. Rd. TW11: Tedd 7B 132
(not continuous)
Bushy Rd. TW11: Tedd 6K 131
Business Design Cen. *N1* *1A 84*
(off Upper St.)
Business Village, The SW18 . . . . 5J 117
Buspace Studios *W10* *4G 81*
(off Conlan St.)
Butcher Row E14 . . . . 7K 85
Butchers M. *UB3: Hayes* *7H 75*
(off Hemmen La.)
Butchers Rd. E16 . . . . 6J 87
Bute Av. TW10: Ham 2E 132
Bute Ct. SM6: Wall 5G 167
Bute Gdns. SM6: Wall 5G 167
TW10: Ham 1E 132
W6 . . . . 4F 99
Bute Gdns. W. SM6: Wall 5G 167
Bute M. NW11 . . . . 5A 46
Bute Rd. CR0: C'don 1A 168
IG6: Ilf 5F 53
SM6: Wall 4G 167
Bute St. SW7 . . . . 3A **16** (4B 100)
Bute Wlk. N1 . . . . 6D 66
Butfield Ho. *E9* *6J 67*
(off Stevens Av.)
Butler Av. HA1: Harr 7H 41
Butler Cl. HA8: Edg 2H 43
Butler Ct. HA0: Wemb 4A 60
RM8: Dag *2G 73*
(off Gosfield Rd.)
Butler Farm Cl. TW10: Ham 4D 132
Butler Ho. *E2* *3J 85*
(off Bacton St.)
E14 . . . . *6B 86*
(off Burdett St.)
SW9 . . . . *1B 120*
(off Lothian Rd.)
Butler Pl. SW1 . . . . 1C **18** (3H 101)
Butler Rd. HA1: Harr 7G 41
NW10 . . . . 7B 62
RM8: Dag 4B 72
Butlers & Colonial Wharf
SE1 . . . . *6K 15*
(off Shad Thames)
Butlers Cl. TW4: Houn 3D 112
Butlers Dr. E4 . . . . 1K 25
Butler St. E2 . . . . 3J 85
UB10: Hil 4D 74
Butlers Wharf SE1 . . . . 1F 103
Butlers Wharf W. *SE1* *5J 15*
(off Shad Thames)
Butley Ct. *E3* *2A 86*
(off Ford St.)
Buttercup Cl. UB5: N'olt 6D 58
Butterfield Cl. N17 . . . . 6H 33
SE16 . . . . 2H 103
TW1: Twick 6K 113
Butterfields E17 . . . . 5E 50
Butterfield Sq. E6 . . . . 6D 88
Butterfly La. SE9 . . . . 6F 125
Butterfly Wlk. *SE5* *1D 120*
(off Denmark Hill)
Butter Hill SM5: Cars 3E 166
SM6: Wall 3E 166
Butteridges Cl. RM9: Dag 1F 91
Buttermere *NW1* *1K 5*
(off Augustus St.)
Buttermere Cl. E15 . . . . 4F 69
SE1 . . . . 4F 103
SM4: Mord 6F 153
TW14: Felt 1H 129
Buttermere Ct. *NW8* *1B 82*
(off Boundary Rd.)
Buttermere Dr. SW15 . . . . 5G 117
Buttermere Ho. *E3* *3B 86*
(off Mile End Rd.)
Buttermere Wlk. E8 . . . . 6F 67
Butterwick W6 . . . . 4F 99
Butterworth Gdns.
IG8: Wfd G 6D 36
Butterworth Ter. *SE17* *5C 102*
(off Sutherland Wlk.)
Buttery M. N14 . . . . 3D 32
Buttesland St. N1 . . . . 1F **9** (3D **84**)
Buttfield Cl. RM10: Dag 6H 73
Buttmarsh Cl. SE18 . . . . 5F 107
Buttonscroft Cl.
CR7: Thor H 3C 156
Butts, The TW8: Bford 6C 96
TW16: Sun 3A 148
Buttsbury Rd. IG1: Ilf 5G 71
Butts Cotts TW13: Hanw 3C 130
Butts Cres. TW13: Hanw 3E 130
Buttsmead HA6: Nwood 1E 38
Butts Piece UB5: N'olt 2K 75
Butts Rd. BR1: Brom 5G 141
Buxhall Cres. E9 . . . . 6B 68
Buxted Rd. E8 . . . . 7F 67
N12 . . . . 5H 31
SE22 . . . . 4E 120
Buxton Cl. IG8: Wfd G 6G 37
N9 . . . . 2D 34
Buxton Ct. E11 . . . . 7H 51
N1 . . . . 1D 8
Buxton Cres. SM3: Cheam 4G 165
Buxton Dr. E11 . . . . 4G 51
KT3: N Mald 2K 151
Buxton Gdns. W3 . . . . 7H 79
Buxton Ho. E11 . . . . 4G 51
Buxton M. SW4 . . . . 2H 119
Buxton Rd. CR7: Thor H 5B 156
DA8: Erith 7K 109
E4 . . . . 1A 36
E6 . . . . 3C 88
E15 . . . . 5G 69
E17 . . . . 4A 50
(not continuous)
IG2: Ilf 6J 53
N19 . . . . 1H 65
NW2 . . . . 6D 62
SW14 . . . . 3A 116
TW15: Ashf 5A 128
Buxton St. E1 . . . . 4K **9** (4G **85**)
Buzzard Creek Ind. Est.
IG11: Bark 5A 90
Byam St. SW6 . . . . 2A 118
Byards Ct. *SE16* *4K 103*
(off Worgan St.)
Byards Cft. SW16 . . . . 1H 155
Byas Ho. *E3* *3B 86*
(off Benworth St.)
Byatt Wlk. TW12: Hamp 6C 130
Bychurch End TW11: Tedd 5K 131
Bycroft Rd. UB1: S'hall 4E 76
Bycroft St. SE20 . . . . 7K 139
Bycullah Av. EN2: Enf 3G 23
Bycullah Rd. EN2: Enf 2G 23
Bye, The W3 . . . . 6A 80
Byegrove Rd. SW19 . . . . 6B 136
Byelands Cl. SE16 . . . . 1K 103
Bye Way, The HA3: W'stone 1J 41
Byeway, The SW14 . . . . 3J 115
Byeways TW2: Twick 3F 131
Byeways, The KT5: Surb 5G 151
Byfeld Gdns. SW13 . . . . 1C 116
Byfield Cl. SE16 . . . . 2B 104
Byfield Rd. TW7: Isle 3A 114
Byford Cl. E15 . . . . 7G 69
Byford Ho. EN5: Barn 4A 20
Bygrove CR0: New Ad 6D 170
Bygrove St. E14 . . . . 6D 86
(not continuous)
Byland Cl. N21 . . . . 7E 22
SM4: Mord 7A 154
Bylands Cl. SE2 . . . . 3B 108
Byne Rd. SE26 . . . . 6J 139
SM5: Cars 2C 166
Bynes Rd. CR2: S Croy 7D 168
Byng Pl. WC1 . . . . 4D **6** (4H **83**)
Byng Rd. EN5: Barn 2A 20
Byng St. E14 . . . . 2C 104
Bynon Av. DA7: Bex 3F 127
Byre Rd. N14 . . . . 6A 22
Byrne Cl. CR0: C'don 6C 156
Byrne Rd. SW12 . . . . 1F 137
Byron Av. E12 . . . . 6C 70
E18 . . . . 3H 51
KT3: N Mald 5C 152
NW9 . . . . 4H 43
SM1: Sutt 4B 166
TW4: Cran 2J 111
Byron Av. E. SM1: Sutt 4B 166
Byron Cl. E8 . . . . 1G 85
KT12: Walt T 7C 148
SE20 . . . . 3H 157
SE26 . . . . 4A 140
SE28 . . . . 1C 108
SW16 . . . . 6J 137
TW12: Hamp 4D 130
Byron Ct. *E11* *4K 51*
(off Makepeace Rd.)
EN2: Enf 2G 23
HA1: Harr 6J 41
NW6 . . . . *7A 64*
(off Fairfax Rd.)
SE22 . . . . 1G 139
SW3 . . . . *4D 16*
(off Elystan St.)
W7 . . . . *4A 96*
(off Boston Rd.)
W9 . . . . *4J 81*
(off Lanhill Rd.)
WC1 . . . . *3G 7*
(off Mecklenburgh Sq.)
Byron Dr. DA8: Erith 7H 109
N2 . . . . 6B 46
Byron Gdns. SM1: Sutt 4B 166
Byron Hill Rd.
HA2: Harr 1H 59
Byron Ho. DA1: Cray 5K 127
Byron M. NW3 . . . . 4C 64
W9 . . . . 4J 81
Byron Pde. UB10: Hil 4E 74
Byron Rd. E10 . . . . 1D 68
E17 . . . . 3C 50
HA0: Wemb 2C 60
HA1: Harr 6J 41
HA3: W'stone 2K 41
NW2 . . . . 2D 62
NW7 . . . . 5H 29
W5 . . . . 1F 97
Byron St. E14 . . . . 6E 86
Byron Ter. N9 . . . . 6D 24
Byron Way UB4: Hayes 4H 75
UB5: N'olt 3C 76
UB7: W Dray 4B 92
Bysouth Cl. IG5: Ilf 1F 53
N15 . . . . 4D 48
Bythorn St. SW9 . . . . 3K 119
Byton Rd. SW17 . . . . 6D 136
Byward Av. TW14: Felt 6A 112
Byward St. EC3 . . . . 3H **15** (7E **84**)
Bywater Ho. SE18 . . . . 3C 106
Bywater Pl. SE16 . . . . 1A 104
Bywater St. SW3 . . . . 5E **16** (5D **100**)
Byway E11 . . . . 5A 52
Byway, The KT19: Ewe 4B 164
SM2: Sutt 7B 166
Bywell Pl. W1 . . . . 6A 6
Bywood Av. CR0: C'don 6J 157
Byworth Wlk. N19 . . . . 1J 65

C

Cabbell St. NW1 . . . . 6C **4** (5C **82**)
Cabinet Way E4 . . . . 6G 35
Cable Ho. *WC1* *1J 7*
(off Gt. Percy St.)
Cable Pl. SE10 . . . . 1E 122
Cable St. E1 . . . . 7G 85
Cable Trade Pk. SE7 . . . . 4A 106
Cabot Ct. *SE16* *4K 103*
(off Worgan St.)
Cabot Sq. E14 . . . . 1C 104
Cabot Way E6 . . . . 1B 88
Cab Rd. *SE1* *2A 102*
(off West Rd.)
Cabul Rd. SW11 . . . . 2C 118
Caci Ho. *W14* *4H 99*
(off Kensington Village)
Cactus Cl. SE15 . . . . 2E 120
Cactus Wlk. W12 . . . . 6B 80
Cadbury Cl. TW7: Isle 1A 114
TW16: Sun 7G 129
Cadbury Rd. TW16: Sun 7G 129
Cadbury Way SE16 . . . . 3F 103
Caddington Cl. EN4: E Barn 5H 21
Caddington Rd. NW2 . . . . 3G 63
Caddis Cl. HA7: Stan 7E 26
Cadell Cl. E2 . . . . 1K **9** (2F **85**)
Cade Rd. SE10 . . . . 1F 123
Cader Rd. SW18 . . . . 6A 118
Cadet Dr. SE1 . . . . 4F 103
Cadet Pl. SE10 . . . . 5G 105
Cadiz Ct. RM10: Dag 7K 73
Cadiz Rd. RM10: Dag 7J 73
Cadiz St. SE17 . . . . 5C 102
Cadley Ter. SE23 . . . . 2J 139
Cadman Cl. SW9 . . . . 7B 102
Cadman Ct. *W4* *5H 97*
(off Chaseley Dr.)
Cadmer Cl. KT3: N Mald 4A 152
Cadmore Ho. *N1* *7B 66*
(off The Sutton Est.)
Cadmus Cl. SW4 . . . . 3H 119
Cadmus Ct. *SW9* *1A 120*
(off Southey Rd.)
Cadnam Lodge *E14* *3E 104*
(off Schooner Cl.)
Cadnam Point SW15 . . . . 1D 134
Cadogan Cl. BR3: Beck 1F 159
E9 . . . . 7B 68
HA2: Harr 4F 59
TW11: Tedd 5J 131
Cadogan Ct. SM2: Sutt 6K 165
SW3 . . . . *4E 16*
(off Draycott Av.)
Cadogan Ct. Gdns. *SW1* *3G 17*
(off D'Oyley St.)
Cadogan Gdns. E18 . . . . 3K 51
N3 . . . . 1K 45
N21 . . . . 5F 23
SW3 . . . . 3F **17** (4D **100**)
Cadogan Ga. SW1 . . . . 3F **17** (4D **100**)
Cadogan Hall *3G 17*
(off Sloane Ter.)
Cadogan Ho. IG8: Wfd G 7K 37
SW3 . . . . 7B 16
Cadogan La. SW1 . . . . 2G **17** (3E **100**)
Cadogan Mans. *SW3* *4F 17*
(off Cadogan Gdns.)
Cadogan Pl. SW1 . . . . 1F **17** (3D **100**)
Cadogan Rd. KT6: Surb 5D 150
SE18 . . . . 3G 107
Cadogan Sq. SW1 . . . . 2E **16** (3D **100**)
Cadogan St. SW3 . . . . 4E **16** (4D **100**)
Cadogan Ter. E9 . . . . 6B 68
Cadoxton Av. N15 . . . . 6F 49
Cadwallon Rd. SE9 . . . . 2F 143
Caedmon Rd. N7 . . . . 4K 65

Caerleon Cl. DA14: Sidc 5C 144
  KT10: Clay 7B 162
Caerleon Ter. SE2 . . . . .4B 108
Caernafon Ho. HA7: Stan 5F 27
Caernarvon Cl. CR4: Mitc 3J 155
Caernarvon Dr. IG5: Ilf 1E 52
Caernarvon Ho. E16 . . . . .1K 105
  (off Audley Dr.)
  W2 . . . . .6A 82
  (off Hallfield Est.)
Caesar Ct. E2 .2K 85
  (off Palmer's Rd.)
Caesars Wlk. CR4: Mitc 5D 154
Caesars Way TW17: Shep 6F 147
Café Gallery 3J 103
Cahill St. EC1 . . . . .4D 8 (4E 84)
Cahir St. E14 .4D 104
Cain Cl. W5 . . . . .5C 78
  (off Castlebar M.)
Caine Ho. W3 .2H 97
  (off Hanbury Rd.)
Cain's La. TW14: Felt 5G 111
Caird St. W10 .3G 81
Cairn Av. W5 .1D 96
Cairncross M. N8 . . . . .6J 47
  (off Felix Av.)
Cairndale Cl. BR1: Brom 7H 141
Cairnfield Av. NW2 . . . . .3A 62
Cairngorm Cl. TW11: Tedd 5A 132
Cairns Av. IG8: Wfd G 6H 37
Cairns M. SE18 . . . . .1C 124
Cairns Rd. SW11 . . . . .5C 118
Cairn Way HA7: Stan 6E 26
Cairo New Rd. CR0: C'don 2B 168
Cairo Rd. E17 .4C 50
Caister Ho. N7 .6K 65
Caistor Ho. E15 . . . . .1H 87
  (off Caistor Pk. Rd.)
Caistor M. SW12 . . . . .7F 119
Caistor Pk. Rd. E15 . . . . .1H 87
Caistor Rd. SW12 . . . . .7F 119
Caithness Gdns. DA15: Sidc 6K 125
Caithness Ho. N1 . . . . .1K 83
  (off Twyford St.)
Caithness Rd. CR4: Mitc 7F 137
  W14 . . . . .3F 99
Calabria Rd. N5 . . . . .6B 66
Calais Ga. SE5 . . . . .1B 120
Calais St. SE5 . . . . .1B 120
Calbourne Rd. SW12 . . . . .7D 118
Calcott Ct. W14 . . . . .3G 99
  (off Blythe Rd.)
Calcott Wlk. SE9 . . . . .4C 142
Calcraft Ho. E2 .2J 85
  (off Bonner Rd.)
Caldbeck Av. KT4: Wor Pk 2C 164
Caldecote KT1: King T 2G 151
  (off Excelsior Cl.)
Caldecote Gdns. WD23: Bush 1D 26
CALDECOTE HILL 1E 26
Caldecot Rd. SE5 . . . . .2C 120
Caldecott Way E5 . . . . .3K 67
Calder Av. UB6: G'frd 2K 77
Calder Cl. EN1: Enf 3K 23
Calder Ct. SE16 . . . . .1B 104
Calder Gdns. HA8: Edg 3G 43
Calderon Ho. NW8 . . . . .2C 82
  (off Townshend Est.)
Calderon Pl. W10 . . . . .5E 80
Calderon Rd. E11 . . . . .4E 68
Calder Rd. SM4: Mord 5A 154
Caldervale Rd. SW4 . . . . .5H 119
Calder Way SL3: Poyle 6A 174
Calderwood Pl. EN4: Had W 1E 20
Calderwood St. SE18 . . . . .4E 106
Caldew Ct. NW7 . . . . .7H 29
Caldew St. SE5 . . . . .7D 102
Caldicot Grn. NW9 . . . . .6A 44
Caldon Ho. UB5: N'olt 4D 76
Caldwell Ho. SW13 . . . . .7E 98
  (off Trinity Chu. Rd.)
Caldwell St. SW9 . . . . .7K 101

Caldy Rd. DA17: Belv 3H 109
Caldy Wlk. N1 .7C 66
Caleb St. SE1 . . . . .6C 14 (2C 102)
Caledonia Ct. IG11: Bark 2C 90
  (off Keel Cl.)
Caledonia Ho. E14 . . . . .6A 86
  (off Salmon La.)
Caledonian Cl. IG3: Ilf 1B 72
Caledonian Ct. UB5: N'olt 4C 76
Caledonian Rd. N1 . . . . .1F 7 (2J 83)
  N7 . . . . .4K 65
Caledonian Sq. NW1 . . . . .6H 65
Caledonian Wharf E14 . . . . .4F 105
Caledonia Rd. TW19: Stanw 1A 128
Caledonia St. N1 . . . . .1F 7 (2J 83)
Caledon Rd. E6 . . . . .1D 88
  SM6: Wall 4E 166
Calendar M. KT6: Surb 6D 150
Cale St. SW3 . . . . .5C 16 (5C 100)
Caletock Way SE10 . . . . .5H 105
Calgarth NW1 . . . . .1B 6
  (off Ampthill Est.)
Calgary Ct. RM7: Mawney 4H 55
  SE16 . . . . .2J 103
  (off Canada Est.)
Caliban Twr. N1 . . . . .2E 84
  (off Arden Est.)
Calico Ho. EC4 . . . . .1D 14
  (off Well Ct.)
Calico Row SW11 . . . . .3A 118
Calidore Cl. SW2 . . . . .6K 119
Californian Bldg. SE10 . . . . .1D 122
  (off Deal's Gateway)
California La. WD23: B Hea 1C 26
California Pl. WD23: B Hea 1C 26
  (off High Rd.)
California Rd. KT3: N Mald 4H 151
Callaby Ter. N1 . . . . .6D 66
Callaghan Cl. SE13 . . . . .4G 123
Callahan Cotts. E1 . . . . .5J 85
  (off Lindley St.)
Callander Rd. SE6 . . . . .2D 140
Callanders, The WD23: B Hea 1D 26
Callard Av. N13 . . . . .4G 33
Callcott Ct. NW6 . . . . .7H 63
Callcott Rd. NW6 . . . . .7H 63
Callcott St. W8 .1J 99
Callendar Rd. SW7 . . . . . .1A 16 (3B 100)
Callender Ct. CR0: C'don 6C 156
  (off Harry Cl.)
Callenders Cotts. DA17: Belv 2K 109
Callingham Cl. E14 . . . . .5B 86
Callis Farm Cl. TW19: Stanw 6A 110
Callisons Pl. SE10 . . . . .5G 105
Callis Rd. E17 .6B 50
Callonfield E17 . . . . .4K 49
Callow St. SW3 . . . . .7A 16 (6B 100)
Cally Swimming Pool 1K 83
Calmington Rd. SE5 . . . . .6E 102
Calmont Rd. BR1: Brom 6F 141
Calne Av. IG5: Ilf 1F 53
Calonne Rd. SW19 . . . . .4F 135
Calshot Ho. N1 .2K 83
  (off Calshot St.)
Calshot Rd. TW6: H'row A 2C 110
Calshot St. N1 . . . . .1G 7 (2K 83)
Calshot Way EN2: Enf 3G 23
  TW6: H'row A 2C 110
  (not continuous)
Calstock NW1 . . . . .1G 83
  (off Royal Coll. St.)
Calstock Ho. SE11 . . . . .5K 19
Calthorpe Gdns. HA8: Edg 5K 27
  (not continuous)
  SM1: Sutt .3A 166
Calthorpe St. WC1 . . . . .3H 7 (4K 83)
Calton Av. SE21 . . . . .6E 120
Calton Rd. EN5: New Bar 6F 21
Calverley Cl. BR3: Beck 6D 140
Calverley Ct. KT19: Ewe 4K 163
Calverley Cres. RM10: Dag 2G 73
Calverley Gdns. HA3: Kenton 7D 42

Calverley Gro. N19 . . . . .1H 65
Calverley Rd. KT17: Ewe 6C 164
Calvert Av. E2 . . . . .2H 9 (3E 84)
Calvert Cl. DA14: Sidc 6E 144
  DA17: Belv 4G 109
Calvert Ct. TW9: Rich 4F 115
Calvert Dr. DA2: Dart 2K 145
Calvert Ho. W12 . . . . .7D 80
  (off White City Est.)
Calverton SE5 .6E 102
  (off Albany Rd.)
Calverton Rd. E6 . . . . .1E 88
Calvert Rd. EN5: Barn 2A 20
  SE10 . . . . .5H 105
Calvert's Bldgs. SE1 . . . . .5E 14 (1D 102)
Calvert St. NW1 . . . . .1E 82
Calvin St. E1 . . . . .4J 9 (4F 85)
Calydon Rd. SE7 . . . . .5K 105
Calypso Cres. SE15 . . . . .7F 103
Calypso Way SE16 . . . . .3B 104
Camac Rd. TW2: Twick 1H 131
Camarthen Grn. NW9 . . . . .5A 44
Cambalt Rd. SW15 . . . . .5F 117
Cambay Ho. E1 . . . . .4A 86
  (off Harford St.)
Camber Ho. SE15 . . . . .6J 103
Camberley Av. EN1: Enf 4K 23
  SW20 . . . . .2D 152
Camberley Cl. SM3: Cheam 3F 165
Camberley Ho. NW1 . . . . .1K 5
Camberley Rd. TW6: H'row A 3C 110
Cambert Way SE3 . . . . .4K 123
CAMBERWELL 1D 120
Camberwell Bus. Cen. SE5 . . . . .7D 102
Camberwell Chu. St. SE5 . . . . .1D 120
Camberwell Glebe SE5 . . . . .1E 120
CAMBERWELL GREEN 1C 120
Camberwell Grn. SE5 . . . . .1D 120
Camberwell Gro. SE5 . . . . .1D 120
Camberwell Leisure Cen. 1D 120
Camberwell New Rd. SE5 . . . . .6A 102
Camberwell Pl. SE5 . . . . .1C 120
Camberwell Rd. SE5 . . . . .6C 102
Camberwell Sta. Rd. SE5 . . . . .1C 120
Camberwell Trad. Est. SE5 . . . . .1B 120
Cambeys Rd. RM10: Dag 5H 73
Camborne Av. W13 . . . . .2B 96
Camborne Cl. TW6: H'row A 3C 110
Camborne Cres. TW6: H'row A 3C 110
Camborne M. SW18 . . . . .7J 117
  W11 . . . . .6G 81
Camborne Rd. CR0: C'don 7G 157
  DA14: Sidc 3C 144
  DA16: Well 2K 125
  SM2: Sutt .7J 165
  SM4: Mord 5F 153
  SW18 . . . . .7J 117
  TW6: H'row A 3C 110
Camborne Way TW5: Hest 1E 112
  TW6: H'row A 3C 110
Cambourne Av. N9 . . . . .7E 24
Cambourne Wlk. TW10: Rich 6D 114
Cambrai Ct. N13 . . . . .3D 32
Cambray Rd. BR6: Orp 7K 161
  SW12 . . . . .1G 137
Cambria Cl. DA15: Sidc 1H 143
  TW3: Houn 4E 112
Cambria Ct. TW14: Felt 7K 111
  (not continuous)
Cambria Gdns. TW19: Stanw 7A 110
Cambria Ho. E14 . . . . .6A 86
  (off Salmon La.)
  SE26 . . . . .4G 139
  (off High Level Dr.)
Cambrian Av. IG2: Ilf 5J 53
Cambrian Cl. SE27 . . . . .3B 138
Cambrian Grn. NW9 . . . . .5A 44
  (off Snowden Dr.)
Cambrian Rd. E10 . . . . .7C 50
  TW10: Rich 6F 115
Cambria Rd. SE5 . . . . .3C 120
Cambria St. SW6 . . . . .7K 99

Cambridge Arc. E9 . . . . .7J 67
  (off Elsdale St.)
Cambridge Av. DA16: Well 4K 125
  KT3: N Mald 3A 152
  (not continuous)
  NW6 . . . . .2J 81
  NW10 . . . . .3E 80
  UB6: G'frd 5K 59
Cambridge Barracks Rd.
  SE18 . . . . .4D 106
Cambridge Cir. WC2 . . . . . .1D 12 (6H 83)
Cambridge Cl. E17 . . . . .6B 50
  EN4: E Barn 1K 31
  N22 . . . . .1A 48
  NW10 . . . . .3J 61
  SW20 . . . . .1D 152
  TW4: Houn 4C 112
  UB7: Harm 2E 174
Cambridge Cotts. TW9: Kew 6G 97
Cambridge Ct. E2 . . . . .2H 85
  (off Cambridge Heath Rd.)
  N16 . . . . .7F 48
  (off Amhurst Pk.)
  NW6 . . . . .2J 81
  (not continuous)
  W2 . . . . .6C 4
  (off Edgware Rd.)
  W6 . . . . .4E 98
  (off Shepherd's Bush Rd.)
Cambridge Cres. E2 . . . . .2H 85
  TW11: Tedd 5A 132
Cambridge Dr. HA4: Ruis 2A 58
  SE12 . . . . .5J 123
Cambridge Gdns. EN1: Enf 2B 24
  KT1: King T 2G 151
  N10 . . . . .1E 46
  N17 . . . . .7J 33
  N21 . . . . .7J 23
  NW6 . . . . .2J 81
  W10 . . . . .6F 81
Cambridge Ga. NW1 . . . . .3J 5 (4F 83)
Cambridge Ga. M. NW1 . . . . .3K 5 (4F 83)
Cambridge Grn. SE9 . . . . .1F 143
Cambridge Gro. SE20 . . . . .1H 157
  W6 . . . . .4D 98
Cambridge Gro. Rd. KT1: King T 3G 151
  (not continuous)
Cambridge Heath Rd. E1 . . . . .5H 85
  E2 . . . . .5H 85
Cambridge Ho. W6 . . . . .4D 98
  (off Cambridge Gro.)
  W13 . . . . .6A 78
Cambridge Pde. EN1: Enf 1B 24
Cambridge Pk. E11 . . . . .7J 51
  TW1: Twick 6C 114
Cambridge Pk. Ct. TW1: Twick 7D 114
Cambridge Pk. Rd. E11 . . . . .7J 51
  (off Lonsdale Rd.)
Cambridge Pl. W8 . . . . .2K 99
Cambridge Rd. BR1: Brom 7J 141
  CR4: Mitc .3G 155
  DA14: Sidc 4J 143
  E4 . . . . .1A 36
  E11 . . . . .6H 51
  HA2: Harr .5E 40
  IG3: Ilf 1J 71
  IG11: Bark 7G 71
  KT1: King T 2F 151
  KT2: King T 2F 151
  KT3: N Mald 4K 151
  KT8: W Mole 4D 148
  KT12: Walt T 6K 147
  NW6 . . . . .2J 81
  (not continuous)
  SE20 . . . . .3H 157
  SM5: Cars 6C 166
  SW11 . . . . .1D 118
  SW13 . . . . .2B 116
  SW20 . . . . .1C 152
  TW1: Twick 6D 114
  TW4: Houn 4C 112
  TW9: Kew .7G 97

Cambridge Rd. TW11: Tedd 4K **131**
TW12: Hamp 7D **130**
TW15: Ashf 7E **128**
UB1: S'hall 1D **94**
W7 ....2K **95**
Cambridge Rd. Nth. W4 ....5H **97**
Cambridge Rd. Sth. W4 ....5H **97**
Cambridge Row SE18 ....5F **107**
Cambridge Sq. W2 ....7C **4** (6C **82**)
Cambridge St. SW1 ....4K **17** (4F **101**)
Cambridge Ter. N9 ....7K **23**
NW1 ....2J **5** (3F **83**)
Cambridge Ter. M. NW1 ......2K **5** (3F **83**)
Cambridge Theatre *1E 12*
(off Earlham St.)
Cambridge Yd. W7 ....2K **95**
Cambstone Cl. N11 ....2K **31**
Cambus Cl. UB4: Yead 5C **76**
Cambus Rd. E16 ....5J **87**
Cam Ct. SE15 ....6F **103**
Camdale Rd. SE18 ....7K **107**
Camden Arts Cen. 5K **63**
Camden Av. TW13: Felt 1A **130**
UB4: Yead 7B **76**
Camden Cl. BR7: Chst 1G **161**
Camden Ct. DA17: Belv 5G **109**
NW1 ....*7G 65*
(off Rousden St.)
Camden Gdns. CR7: Thor H 3B **156**
NW1 ....7F **65**
SM1: Sutt 5K **165**
Camden Gro. BR7: Chst 6F **143**
Camden High St. NW1 ....7F **65**
Camden Hill Rd. SE19 ....6E **138**
Camden Ho. SE8 ....5B **104**
Camdenhurst St. E14 ....6A **86**
Camden La. N7 ....5H **65**
Camden Lock Market *7F 65*
(off Camden Lock Pl.)
Camden Lock Pl. NW1 ....7F **65**
Camden Markets *7F 65*
(off Camden Lock Pl.)
Camden M. NW1 ....7G **65**
Camden Pk. Rd. BR7: Chst 7D **142**
NW1 ....6H **65**
Camden Pas. N1 ....2B **84**
Camden Peoples Theatre *3A 6*
(off Hampstead Rd.)
Camden Rd. DA5: Bexl 1E **144**
E11 ....6K **51**
E17 ....6B **50**
N7 ....4J **65**
NW1 ....7G **65**
SM1: Sutt 5K **165**
SM5: Cars 4D **166**
Camden Row HA5: Pinn 3A **40**
SE3 ....2G **123**
Camden Sq. NW1 ....7H **65**
(not continuous)
SE15 ....1F **121**
Camden St. NW1 ....7G **65**
Camden Studios *NW1* *1G 83*
(off Camden St.)
Camden Ter. NW1 ....6H **65**
CAMDEN TOWN 1F **83**
Camden Wlk. N1 ....1B **84**
Camden Way BR7: Chst 7D **142**
CR7: Thor H 3B **156**
Cameford Ct. SW2 ....7J **119**
Camelford *NW1* *1G 83*
(off Royal Coll. St.)
Camelford Ct. W11 ....6G **81**
Camelford Ho. SE1 ....5F **19** (5J **101**)
Camelford Wlk. W11 ....6G **81**
Camel Gro. KT2: King T 5D **132**
Camellia Ho. *SE8* *7B 104*
(off Idonia St.)
TW13: Felt *1J 129*
(off Tilley Rd.)
Camellia Pl. TW2: Whitt 7F **113**
Camellia St. SW8 ....7J **101**
(not continuous)
Camelot Cl. SE28 ....2H **107**
SW19 ....4H **135**
Camelot Ho. NW1 ....6H **65**
Camel Rd. E16 ....1C **106**
Camera Pl. SW10 ....7A **16** (6B **100**)
Camera Press Gallery, The *6J 15*
(off Queen Elizabeth St.)
Cameret Ct. *W11* *2F 99*
(off Holland Rd.)
Cameron Cl. DA5: Bexl 3K **145**
N18 ....4C **34**
N20 ....2G **31**
N22 ....7E **32**
Cameron Cres. HA8: Edg 1H **43**
Cameron Ho. *NW8* *2C 82*
(off St John's Wood Ter.)
SE5 ....7C **102**
Cameron Pl. E1 ....6H **85**
SW16 ....2A **138**
Cameron Rd. BR2: Brom 5J **159**
CR0: C'don 6B **156**
IG3: Ilf 1J **71**
SE6 ....2B **140**
Cameron Sq. CR4: Mitc 1C **154**
Cameron Ter. SE12 ....3K **141**
Camerton Cl. E8 ....6F **67**
Camgate Cen., The TW19: Stanw 6B **110**
Camgate Mans. *SE5* *6C 102*
(off Camberwell Rd.)
Camilla Cl. TW16: Sun 6H **129**
Camilla Rd. SE16 ....4H **103**
Camille Cl. SE25 ....3G **157**
Camlan Rd. BR1: Brom 4H **141**
Camlet St. E2 ....3J **9** (4F **85**)
Camlet Way EN4: Barn, Had W 2D **20**
Camley St. NW1 ....7H **65**
Camley Street Natural Pk. Vis. Cen.
......................2H **83**
Camm Gdns. KT1: King T 2F **151**
KT7: T Ditt 7K **149**
Camomile Av. CR4: Mitc 1D **154**
Camomile Rd. RM7: Rush G 2K **73**
Camomile St. EC3 ....7H **9** (6E **84**)
Camomile Way UB7: Yiew 6A **74**
Campana Rd. SW6 ....1J **117**
Campania Bldg. *E1* *7K 85*
(off Jardine Rd.)
Campaspe Bus. Pk. TW16: Sun 5H **147**
Campbell Av. IG6: Ilf 4F **53**
Campbell Cl. HA4: Ruis 6J **39**
SE18 ....1E **124**
SW16 ....4H **137**
TW2: Twick 1H **131**
Campbell Ct. N17 ....1F **49**
NW9 ....6J **43**
SE22 ....1G **139**
SW7 ....*3A 100*
(off Gloucester Rd.)
Campbell Cft. HA8: Edg 5B **28**
Campbell Gordon Way NW2 ....4D **62**
Campbell Ho. *SW1* *6A 18*
(off Churchill Gdns.)
W2 ....*4A 4*
(off Hall Pl.)
W12 ....*7D 80*
(off White City Est.)
Campbell Rd. CR0: C'don 7B **156**
E3 ....3C **86**
E6 ....1C **88**
E15 ....4H **69**
E17 ....4B **50**
KT8: E Mos 3J **149**
N17 ....1F **49**
TW2: Twick 2H **131**
W7 ....7J **77**
Campbell Wlk. *N1* *1J 83*
(off Outram Pl.)
Campdale Rd. N7 ....3H **65**
Campden Cres. HA0: Wemb 3B **60**
RM8: Dag 4B **72**
Campden Gro. W8 ....2J **99**
Campden Hill W8 ....2J **99**
Campden Hill Ct. W8 ....2J **99**
Campden Hill Gdns. W8 ....1J **99**
Campden Hill Ga. W8 ....2J **99**
Campden Hill Mans. *W8* *1J 99*
(off Edge St.)
Campden Hill Pl. W11 ....1H **99**
Campden Hill Rd. W8 ....1J **99**
Campden Hill Sq. W8 ....1H **99**
Campden Hill Towers W11 ....1J **99**
Campden Ho. *NW6* *7B 64*
(off Harben Rd.)
W8 ....*1J 99*
(off Sheffield Ter.)
Campden Ho. Cl. W8 ....2J **99**
Campden Houses W8 ....1J **99**
Campden Ho. Ter. *W8* *1J 99*
(off Kensington Chu. St.)
Campden Mans. *W8* *1J 99*
(off Kensington Chu. St.)
Campden Rd. CR2: S Croy 5E **168**
UB10: Ick 3B **56**
Campden St. W8 ....1J **99**
Campden Way RM8: Dag 4B **72**
Campe Ho. N10 ....7K **31**
Campen Cl. SW19 ....2G **135**
Camperdown St. E1 ....1K **15** (6F **85**)
Campfield Rd. SE9 ....7B **124**
Campion Cl. CR0: C'don 4E **168**
E6 ....7D **88**
HA3: Kenton 6F **43**
RM7: Rush G 2K **73**
UB8: Hil 5B **74**
Campion Ct. HA0: Wemb 2E **78**
Campion Gdns. IG8: Wfd G 5D **36**
Campion Ho. *E14* *6B 86*
(off Frances Wharf)
Campion Pl. SE28 ....1A **108**
Campion Rd. SW15 ....4E **116**
TW7: Isle 1K **113**
Campion Ter. NW2 ....3F **63**
Campion Way HA8: Edg 4D **28**
Camplin Rd. HA3: Kenton 5E **42**
Camplin St. SE14 ....7K **103**
Camp Rd. SW19 ....5D **134**
(not continuous)
Campsbourne, The N8 ....4J **47**
Campsbourne Ho. *N8* *4J 47*
(off Pembroke Rd.)
Campsbourne Pde. *N8* *4J 47*
(off High St.)
Campsbourne Rd. N8 ....3J **47**
(not continuous)
Campsey Gdns. RM9: Dag 7B **72**
Campsey Rd. RM9: Dag 7B **72**
Campsfield Ho. *N8* *3J 47*
(off Campsfield Rd.)
Campsfield Rd. N8 ....3J **47**
Campshill Pl. SE13 ....5E **122**
Campshill Rd. SE13 ....5E **122**
Campus Ho. TW7: Isle 7J **95**
Campus Rd. E17 ....6B **50**
Campus Way NW4 ....3D **44**
Camp Vw. SW19 ....5D **134**
Cam Rd. E15 ....1F **87**
Camrose Av. DA8: Erith 6H **109**
HA8: Edg 2F **43**
TW13: Felt 4A **130**
Camrose Cl. CR0: C'don 7A **158**
SM4: Mord 4J **153**
Camrose St. SE2 ....5A **108**
Canada Av. N18 ....6H **33**
Canada Cres. W3 ....5J **79**
Canada Est. SE16 ....3J **103**
Canada Gdns. SE13 ....5E **122**
Canada Ho. *SE16* *3A 104*
(off Brunswick Quay)
SW1 ....*1H 101*
(off Trafalgar Sq.)
Canada Memorial *6A 12*
(off Green Pk.)
Canada Pl. *E14* *1D 104*
(off Up. Bank St.)
Canada Rd. W3 ....5J **79**
Canada Sq. E14 ....1D **104**
Canada St. SE16 ....2K **103**
Canada Way W12 ....7D **80**
Canada Wharf SE16 ....1B **104**
Canadian Av. SE6 ....1D **140**
Canal App. SE8 ....5A **104**
Canal Blvd. NW1 ....6H **65**
CANAL BRIDGE 6G **103**
Canal Bldg. N1 ....2C **84**
Canal Cl. E1 ....4A **86**
W10 ....4F **81**
Canal Cotts. *E3* *1B 86*
(off Parnell Rd.)
Canal Gro. SE15 ....6H **103**
Canal Market *7F 65*
(off Castlehaven Rd.)
Canal Path E2 ....1F **85**
Canalside SE28 ....7D **90**
Canalside Activity Cen. 4F **81**
Canalside Gdns. UB2: S'hall 4C **94**
Canal Side Studios *NW1* *1H 83*
(off St Pancras Way)
Canalside Studios *N1* *1E 84*
(off Orsman Rd.)
Canal St. SE5 ....6D **102**
Canal Wlk. CR0: C'don 6E **156**
N1 ....1D **84**
NW10 ....*7J 61*
(off Westend Cl.)
SE26 ....5J **139**
Canal Way W10 ....4F **81**
Canal Wharf UB6: G'frd 1A **78**
Canberra Cl. NW4 ....3C **44**
RM10: Dag 1K **91**
Canberra Cres. RM10: Dag 7K **73**
Canberra Dr. UB5: N'olt 3A **76**
Canberra Rd. DA7: Bex 6D **108**
E6 ....1D **88**
SE7 ....6A **106**
TW6: H'row A 3C **110**
W13 ....1A **96**
Canbury Av. KT2: King T 1F **151**
Canbury Bus. Cen. KT2: King T 1E **150**
Canbury Bus. Pk. *KT2: King T* *1E 150*
(off Canbury Pk. Rd.)
Canbury Ct. KT2: King T 7D **132**
Canbury M. SE26 ....3G **139**
Canbury Pk. Rd. KT2: King T 1E **150**
Canbury Pas. KT2: King T 1D **150**
Cancell Rd. SW9 ....1A **120**
Candahar Rd. SW11 ....2C **118**
Candida Ct. NW1 ....7F **65**
Candid Ho. *NW10* *3D 80*
(off Trenmar Gdns.)
Candle Gro. SE15 ....3H **121**
Candlelight Ct. *E15* *6H 69*
(off Romford Rd.)
Candler M. TW1: Twick 7A **114**
Candler St. N15 ....6D **48**
Candle St. E1 ....5A **86**
Candover Cl. UB7: Harm 3E **174**
Candover St. W1 ....6A **6** (5G **83**)
Candy St. E3 ....1B **86**
Candy Wharf E3 ....4A **86**
Caney M. NW2 ....2F **63**
Canfield Dr. HA4: Ruis 5K **57**
Canfield Gdns. NW6 ....7K **63**
Canfield Ho. *N15* *6E 48*
(off Albert Rd.)
Canfield Pl. NW6 ....6A **64**
Canfield Rd. IG8: Wfd G 7H **37**
Canford Av. UB5: N'olt 1D **76**
Canford Cl. EN2: Enf 2F **23**
Canford Gdns. KT3: N Mald 6A **152**
Canford Pl. TW11: Tedd 6C **132**
Canford Rd. SW11 ....5E **118**
Canham Rd. SE25 ....3E **156**
W3 ....2A **98**
Canmore Gdns. SW16 ....7G **137**
CANN HALL 4G **69**
Cann Hall Rd. E11 ....4G **69**

Cann Ho. *W14* 3G *99*
      (off Russell Rd.)
Canning Cres. N22 . . . . .1K 47
Canning Cross SE5 . . . . .2E 120
Canning Ho. *W12* 7D *80*
      (off Australia Rd.)
Canning Pas. W8 . . . . .3A 100
Canning Pl. W8 . . . . .3A 100
Canning Pl. M. *W8* 3A *100*
      (off Canning Pl.)
Canning Rd. CR0: C'don 2F *169*
  E15 .2G 87
  E17 .4A 50
  HA3: W'stone 3J 41
  N5 .3B 66
Cannington Rd. RM9: Dag 6C 72
CANNING TOWN 6H 87
CANNING TOWN 5G 87
Cannizaro Rd. SW19 . . . . .6E 134
Cannock Cl. E17 . . . . .2E 50
Cannock Ho. N4 . . . . .7C 48
Cannonbury Av. HA5: Pinn 6B 40
Cannon Cl. SW20 . . . . .3E 152
  TW12: Hamp 6F 131
Cannon Ct. *EC1* 3B *8*
      (off Brewhouse Yd.)
Cannon Dr. E14 . . . . .7C 86
Cannon Hill N14 . . . . .3D 32
  NW6 . . . . .5J 63
Cannon Hill La. SW20 . . . . .5F 153
Cannon Hill M. N14 . . . . .3D 32
Cannon Ho. SE11 . . . . .4H 19
Cannon La. HA5: Pinn 5C 40
  NW3 . . . . .3B 64
Cannon Pl. NW3 . . . . .3B 64
  SE7 . . . . .5C 106
Cannon Retail Pk. SE28 . . . . .7A 90
Cannon Rd. DA7: Bex 1E 126
  N14 . . . . .3D 32
Cannon St. EC4 . . . . .1C 14 (6C 84)
Cannon St. Rd. E1 . . . . .6H 85
Cannon Trad. Est. HA9: Wemb . . .4H 61
Cannon Way KT8: W Mole 4E 148
Cannon Wharf Bus. Cen.
  SE8 . . . . .4A 104
Cannon Workshops *E14* 7C *86*
      (off Cannon Dr.)
Canon All. *EC4* 1C *14*
      (off Queen's Head Pas.)
Canon Av. RM6: Chad H 5C 54
Canon Beck Rd. SE16 . . . . .2J 103
Canonbie Rd. SE23 . . . . .7J 121
CANONBURY 6C 66
Canonbury Bus. Cen. N1 . . . . . . .1C 84
Canonbury Cotts. EN1: Enf 1K 23
Canonbury Ct. *N1* 7B *66*
      (off Hawes St.)
Canonbury Cres. N1 . . . . .7C 66
Canonbury Gro. N1 . . . . .7C 66
Canonbury Hgts. *N1* 6D *66*
      (off Dove St.)
Canonbury La. N1 . . . . .7B 66
Canonbury Pk. Nth. N1 . . . . .6C 66
Canonbury Pk. Sth. N1 . . . . .6C 66
Canonbury Pl. N1 . . . . .6B 66
      (not continuous)
Canonbury Rd. EN1: Enf 1K 23
  N1 .6B 66
Canonbury Sq. N1 . . . . .7B 66
Canonbury St. N1 . . . . .7C 66
Canonbury Vs. N1 . . . . .7B 66
Canon Mohan Cl. N14 . . . . .6K 21
Canon Rd. BR1: Brom 3A 160
Canon Row SW1 . . . . . . .7E 12 (2J 101)
      (not continuous)
Canons Cl. HA8: Edg 6A 28
  N2 .7B 46
Canons Cnr. HA8: Edg 4K 27
Canons Ct. E15 . . . . .4G 69
  HA8: Edg 6A 28
Canons Dr. HA8: Edg 6K 27
Canonsleigh Rd. RM9: Dag 7B 72

Canons Leisure Cen. 4D 154
CANONS PARK 7J 27
Canons Pk. HA7: Stan 6J 27
Canons Pk. Cl. HA8: Edg 7K 27
Canon St. N1 . . . . .1C 84
Canon's Wlk. CR0: C'don 3K 169
Canopus Way TW19: Stanw 7A 110
Canrobert St. E2 . . . . .2H 85
Cantelowes Rd. NW1 . . . . .6H 65
Canterbury Av. DA15: Sidc 2B 144
  IG1: Ilf 7C 52
Canterbury Cl. BR3: Beck 1D 158
  E6 .6D 88
  KT4: Wor Pk 2F 165
  SE5 . . . . .2C 120
      (off Lilford Rd.)
  UB6: G'frd 5F 77
Canterbury Ct. CR2: S Croy 7C *168*
      (off St Augustines Av.)
  NW6 . . . . .2J *81*
      (off Canterbury Rd.)
  NW9 . . . . .2A 44
  SE5 . . . . .7A 102
  SE12 . . . . .3K 141
  TW15: Ashf 4B 128
Canterbury Cres. SW9 . . . . .3A 120
Canterbury Gro. SE27 . . . . .4A 138
Canterbury Hall KT4: Wor Pk 7D 152
Canterbury Ho. CR0: C'don 1D *168*
      (off Sydenham Rd.)
  E3 .3D *86*
      (off Bow Rd.)
  IG11: Bark 7A *72*
      (off Margaret Bondfield Av.)
  SE1 . . . . .1H 19 (3K 101)
Canterbury Ind. Pk. SE15 . . . . . . .6J 103
Canterbury Pl. SE17 . . . . .5B 102
Canterbury Rd. CR0: C'don 7K 155
  E10 . . . . .7E 50
  HA1: Harr 5F 41
  HA2: Harr 5F 41
  NW6 . . . . .2H 81
      (not continuous)
  SM4: Mord 7K 153
  TW13: Hanw 2C 130
Canterbury Ter. NW6 . . . . .2J 81
Cantium Retail Pk. SE1 . . . . .6G 103
Cantley Gdns. IG2: Ilf 6G 53
  SE19 . . . . .1F 157
Cantley Rd. W7 . . . . .3A 96
Canto Ct. *EC1* 3D *8*
      (off Old St.)
Canton St. E14 . . . . .6C 86
Cantrell Rd. E3 . . . . .4B 86
Cantwell Rd. SE18 . . . . .7F 107
Canute Gdns. SE16 . . . . .4K 103
Canvey St. SE1 . . . . . . .4C 14 (1C 102)
Cape Cl. IG11: Bark 7F 71
Cape Henry Ct. *E14* 7F *87*
      (off Jamestown Way)
Cape Ho. *E8* 6F *67*
      (off Dalston La.)
Capel Av. SM6: Wall 5K 167
Capel Cl. BR2: Brom 1C 172
  N20 . . . . .3F 31
Capel Ct. *EC2* 1F *15*
      (off Bartholomew La.)
  SE20 . . . . .1J 157
Capel Cres. HA7: Stan 2F 27
Capel Gdns. HA5: Pinn 4D 40
  IG3: Bark, Ilf 4K 71
Capel Ho. *E9* 7J *67*
      (off Loddiges Rd.)
Capel Rd. E7 . . . . .4K 69
  EN4: E Barn 6H 21
Capel St. E12 . . . . .4K 69
Capener's Cl. SW1 . . . . .7F 11
Capern Rd. SW18 . . . . .1A 136
Cape Rd. N17 . . . . .3G 49
Cape Yd. E1 . . . . .7G 85
Capital Bus. Cen. CR2: S Croy 7D *168*
  HA0: Wemb 2D 78

Capital E. Apartments *E16* 7J *87*
      (off Western Gateway)
Capital Ind. Est. CR4: Mitc 5D *154*
  DA17: Belv 3H 109
Capital Interchange Way TW8: Bford . . .5G 97
Capital Trad. Est. IG11: Bark 2H 89
Capital Wharf *E1* 1G 103
Capitol Ind. Pk. NW9 . . . . .3J 43
Capitol Way NW9 . . . . .3J 43
Capland Ho. *NW8* 3B *4*
      (off Capland St.)
Capland St. NW8 . . . . . . .3B 4 (4B 82)
Caple Ho. *SW10* 7A *100*
      (off King's Rd.)
Caple Rd. NW10 . . . . .2B 80
Capper St. WC1 . . . . .4B 6 (4G 83)
Caprea Cl. UB4: Yead 5B 76
Capricorn Cen. RM8: Dag 7F 55
Capri Ho. E17 . . . . .2B 50
Capri Rd. CR0: C'don 1F 169
Capstan Cl. RM6: Chad H 6B 54
Capstan Ct. *E1* 7J *85*
      (off Wapping Wall)
Capstan Ho. *E14* 7F *87*
      (off Clove Cres.)
  E14 . . . . .4E *104*
      (off Stebondale St.)
Capstan Ride EN2: Enf 2F 23
Capstan Rd. SE8 . . . . .4B 104
Capstan Sq. E14 . . . . .2E 104
Capstan Way SE16 . . . . .1A 104
Capstone Rd. BR1: Brom 4H 141
Capthorne Av. HA2: Harr 1C 58
Capuchin Cl. HA7: Stan 6G 27
Capulet M. E16 . . . . .1J 105
Capulet Sq. *E3* 3D *86*
      (off Talwin St.)
Capworth St. E10 . . . . .1C 68
Caradoc Cl. W2 . . . . .6J 81
Caradoc Evans Cl. *N11* 5A *32*
      (off Springfield Rd.)
Caradoc St. SE10 . . . . .5G 105
Caradon Cl. E11 . . . . .1G 69
Caradon Way N15 . . . . .4D 48
Cara Ho. *N1* 7A *66*
      (off Liverpool Rd.)
Caranday Vs. *W11* 1F *99*
      (off Norland Rd.)
Caravel Cl. E14 . . . . .3C 104
Caravelle Gdns. UB5: N'olt 3B 76
Caravel M. SE8 . . . . .6C 104
Caraway Apartments *SE1* 6K *15*
      (off Cayenne Ct.)
Caraway Cl. E13 . . . . .5K 87
Caraway Hgts. *E14* 7E *86*
      (off Poplar High St.)
Caraway Pl. SM6: Wall 3F 167
Carberry Rd. SE19 . . . . .6E 138
Carbery Av. W3 . . . . .2F 97
Carbis Cl. E4 . . . . .1A 36
Carbis Rd. E14 . . . . .6B 86
Carbrooke Ho. *E9* 1J *85*
      (off Templecombe Rd.)
Carbuncle Pas. N17 . . . . .2G 49
Carburton St. W1 . . . . . . .5K 5 (5F 83)
Cardale St. E14 . . . . .2E 104
Cardamon Bldg. *SE1* 5K *15*
      (off Shad Thames)
Carden Rd. SE15 . . . . .3H 121
Cardiff Ho. *SE15* 6G *103*
      (off Friary Est.)
Cardiff Rd. EN3: Pond E 4C 24
  W7 .3A 96
Cardiff St. SE18 . . . . .7J 107
Cardigan Cl. *W7* 4K *77*
      (off Copley Cl.)
Cardigan Gdns. IG3: Ilf 2A 72
Cardigan Pl. SE3 . . . . .2F 123
Cardigan Rd. E3 . . . . .2B 86
  SW13 . . . . .2C 116
  SW19 . . . . .6A 136
  TW10: Rich 6E 114

Cardigan St. SE11 . . . . . .5J 19 (5A 102)
Cardigan Wlk. *N1* 7C *66*
      (off Ashby Gro.)
Cardinal Av. KT2: King T 5E 132
  SM4: Mord 6G 153
Cardinal Bourne St. SE1 . . . . .3D 102
Cardinal Cap All. SE1 . . . . .1C 102
Cardinal Cl. BR7: Chst 1J 161
  HA8: Edg 7D 28
  KT4: Wor Pk 4C 164
  SM4: Mord 6G 153
Cardinal Ct. *E1* 7G *85*
      (off Thomas More St.)
Cardinal Cres. KT3: N Mald 2J 151
Cardinal Hinsley Cl. NW10 . . . . . .2C 80
Cardinal Mans. *SW1* 3A *18*
      (off Carlisle Pl.)
Cardinal Pl. SW1 . . . . .1A 18 (3G 101)
  SW15 . . . . .4F 117
Cardinal Rd. HA4: Ruis 1B 58
  TW13: Felt 1K 129
Cardinals Wlk. TW12: Hamp 7G 131
  TW16: Sun 6G 129
Cardinals Way N19 . . . . .1H 65
Cardinal Wlk. SW1 . . . . .2A 18
Cardinal HA3: W'stone 3J 41
Cardine M. SE15 . . . . .7H 103
Cardington Sq. TW4: Houn 4B 112
Cardington St. NW1 . . . . .1B 6 (3G 83)
Cardinham Rd. BR6: Chels 4K 173
Cardozo Rd. N7 . . . . .5J 65
Cardrew Av. N12 . . . . .5G 31
Cardrew Cl. N12 . . . . .5H 31
Cardrew Ct. N12 . . . . .5G 31
Cardross Ho. *W6* 3D *98*
      (off Cardross St.)
Cardross St. W6 . . . . .3D 98
Cardwell Rd. N7 . . . . .4J 65
Cardwell Ter. *N7* 4J *65*
      (off Cardwell Rd.)
Career Ct. SE16 . . . . .2K *103*
      (off Christopher Cl.)
Carew Cl. N7 . . . . .2K 65
Carew Ct. RM6: Chad H 6B *54*
      (off Quarles Pk. Rd.)
  SE14 . . . . .6K *103*
      (off Samuel Cl.)
  SM2: Sutt 7K 165
Carew Manor & Dovecote 3G 167
Carew Mnr. Cotts. SM6: Bedd 3H 167
Carew Rd. CR4: Mitc 2E 154
  CR7: Thor H 4B 156
  N17 . . . . .2G 49
  SM6: Wall 6G 167
  TW15: Ashf 6E 128
  W13 . . . . .2C 96
Carew St. SE5 . . . . .2C 120
Carey Cl. DA6: Bex 5H 127
  SE5 . . . . .7C 102
Carey Gdns. SW8 . . . . .1G 119
Carey La. EC2 . . . . .7C 8 (6C 84)
Carey Mans. *SW1* 3C *18*
      (off Rutherford St.)
Carey Pl. SW1 . . . . .4C 18 (4H 101)
Carey Rd. RM9: Dag 4E 72
Carey St. WC2 . . . . .1H 13 (6K 83)
Carey Way HA9: Wemb 4H 61
Carfax Pl. SW4 . . . . .4H 119
Carfax Rd. UB3: Harl 5H 93
Carfree Cl. N1 . . . . .7A 66
Cargill Rd. SW18 . . . . .1K 135
Cargo Point TW19: Stanw 6B 110
Cargreen Pl. SE25 . . . . .4F 157
Cargreen Rd. SE25 . . . . .4F 157
Cargrey Ho. HA7: Stan 5H 27
Carholme Rd. SE23 . . . . .1B 140
Carillon Ct. *E1* 5G *85*
      (off Greatorex St.)
  W5 .7D 78
Carinthia Ct. SE16 . . . . .4A *104*
      (off Plough Way)
Carisbrook N10 . . . . .2F 47

Carisbrook Cl. EN1: Enf 1A 24
Carisbrooke Av. DA5: Bexl 1D 144
Carisbrooke Cl. HA7: Stan 2D 42
TW4: Houn 7C 112
Carisbrooke Ct. SM2: Cheam 7H 165
UB5: N'olt 1D 76
(off Eskdale Av.)
W1 6H 5
(off Weymouth St.)
W3 2J 97
(off Brouncker Rd.)
Carisbrooke Gdns. SE15 7F 103
Carisbrooke Ho. *KT2: King T 1E 150*
(off Seven Kings Way)
TW10: Rich 5G 115
UB7: W Dray 2B 92
(off Park Lodge Av.)
Carisbrooke Rd. BR2: Brom 4A 160
CR4: Mitc 4H 155
E17 4A 50
Carker's La. NW5 5F 65
Carleton Av. SM6: Wall 7H 167
Carleton Cl. KT10: Esh 7H 149
Carleton Gdns. N19 5G 65
Carleton Rd. N7 5H 65
Carleton Vs. NW5 5G 65
Carlile Cl. E3 2B 86
Carlile Ho. *SE1 3D 102*
(off Tabard St.)
Carlina Gdns. IG8: Wfd G 5E 36
Carlingford Gdns. CR4: Mitc 7D 136
Carlingford Rd. N15 3B 48
NW3 4B 64
SM4: Mord 6F 153
Carlisle Av. EC3 1J 15 (6F 85)
W3 6A 80
Carlisle Cl. HA5: Pinn 7C 40
KT2: King T 1G 151
Carlisle Gdns. HA3: Kenton 7D 42
IG1: Ilf 6C 52
Carlisle Ho. IG1: Ilf 6C 52
Carlisle La. SE1 2H 19 (3K 101)
Carlisle Mans. *SW1 3A 18*
(off Carlisle Pl.)
Carlisle M. KT2: King T 1G 151
Carlisle Pl. N11 4A 32
SW1 2A 18 (3G 101)
Carlisle Rd. E10 1C 68
N4 7A 48
NW6 1G 81
NW9 3J 43
SM1: Sutt 6H 165
TW12: Hamp 7F 131
Carlisle St. W1 1C 12 (6H 83)
Carlisle Wlk. E8 6F 67
Carlisle Way SW17 5E 136
Carlos Pl. W1 3H 11 (7E 82)
Carlow St. NW1 2G 83
Carlson Ct. SW15 4H 117
Carlton Av. CR2: S Croy 7E 168
HA3: Kenton 5B 42
N14 5C 22
TW14: Felt 6A 112
UB3: Harl 4G 93
Carlton Av. E. HA9: Wemb 2D 60
Carlton Av. W. HA0: Wemb 2B 60
Carlton Cl. HA8: Edg 5B 28
KT9: Chess 6D 162
NW3 2J 63
UB5: N'olt 5G 59
Carlton Ct. IG6: Ilf 3H 53
N3 7D 30
SE20 1H 157
SW9 1B 120
UB8: Cowl 5A 74
W9 2K 81
(off Maida Va.)
Carlton Cres. SM3: Cheam 4G 165
Carlton Dr. IG6: Ilf 3H 53
SW15 5F 117
Carlton Gdns. SW1 5C 12 (1H 101)
W5 6C 78
Carlton Grn. DA14: Sidc 4K 143
Carlton Gro. SE15 1H 121
Carlton Hill NW8 2K 81
Carlton Ho. *NW6 2J 81*
(off Canterbury Ter.)
SE16 2K 103
(off Wolfe Cres.)
TW3: Houn 6E 112
TW14: Felt 6H 111
Carlton Ho. Ter. SW1 5C 12 (1H 101)
Carlton Lodge *N4 7A 48*
(off Carlton Rd.)
Carlton Mans. N16 1F 67
NW6 7J 63
(off West End La.)
W9 3K 81
W14 2G 99
(off Holland Pk. Gdns.)
Carlton M. *NW6 5J 63*
(off West Cotts.)
Carlton Pde. HA9: Wemb 2E 60
Carlton Pk. Av. SW20 2F 153
Carlton Rd. CR2: S Croy 6D 168
DA8: Erith 6H 109
DA14: Sidc 5K 143
DA16: Well 3B 126
E11 1H 69
E12 4B 70
E17 1A 50
KT3: N Mald 2A 152
KT12: Walt T 7K 147
N4 7A 48
N11 5K 31
SW14 3J 115
TW16: Sun 7H 129
W4 2K 97
W5 7C 78
Carlton Sq. E1 4K 85
(not continuous)
Carlton St. SW1 3C 12 (7H 83)
Carlton Ter. E7 7A 70
E11 5K 51
(not continuous)
N18 3J 33
SE26 3J 139
Carlton Twr. Pl. SW1 1F 17 (3D 100)
Carlton Towers SM5: Cars 3D 166
Carlton Va. NW6 2H 81
Carlton Vs. SW15 5G 117
Carlton Works, The
SE15 7H 103
(off Asylum Rd.)
Carlwell St. SW17 5C 136
Carlyle Av. BR1: Brom 3B 160
UB1: S'hall 7D 76
Carlyle Cl. KT8: W Mole 2F 149
N2 6A 46
Carlyle Ct. *SW6 1K 117*
(off Imperial Rd.)
SW10 1A 118
(off Chelsea Harbour Dr.)
Carlyle Gdns. UB1: S'hall 7D 76
Carlyle Ho. *KT8: W Mole 5E 148*
(off Down St.)
N16 3E 66
SE5 7C 102
(off Bethwin Rd.)
SW3 7B 16
(off Old Church St.)
Carlyle Mans. *SW3 7C 16*
(off Cheyne Wlk.)
W8 1J 99
(off Kensington Mall)
Carlyle M. E1 4K 85
Carlyle Pl. SW15 4F 117
Carlyle Rd. CR0: C'don 2G 169
E12 4C 70
NW10 1K 79
SE28 7B 90
W5 4C 96
Carlyle's House 7C 16
Carlyle Sq. SW3 6B 16 (5B 100)
Carly M. *E2 3G 85*
(off Barnet Gro.)
Carlyon Av. HA2: Harr 4D 58
Carlyon Cl. HA0: Wemb 1E 78
Carlyon Rd. HA0: Wemb 2E 78
UB4: Yead 5A 76
(not continuous)
Carlys Cl. BR3: Beck 2K 157
Carmalt Gdns. SW15 4E 116
Carmarthen Ct. *W7 4K 77*
(off Copley Cl.)
Carmarthen Pl. SE1 6G 15 (2E 102)
Carmel Ct. HA9: Wemb 2H 61
W8 2K 99
(off Holland St.)
Carmelite Cl. HA3: Hrw W 1G 41
Carmelite Rd. HA3: Hrw W 1G 41
Carmelite St. EC4 2K 13 (7A 84)
Carmelite Wlk. HA3: Hrw W 1G 41
Carmelite Way HA3: Hrw W 2G 41
Carmel Lodge *SW6 6J 99*
(off Lillie Rd.)
Carmel Way TW9: Rich 2H 115
Carmen St. E14 6D 86
Carmichael Cl. HA4: Ruis 4J 57
SW11 3B 118
Carmichael Ct. *SW13 2B 116*
(off Grove Rd.)
Carmichael Ho. *E14 7E 86*
(off Poplar High St.)
Carmichael M. SW18 7B 118
Carmichael Rd. SE25 5F 157
Carmine W2 6B 4
Carmine Ct. BR1: Brom 7H 141
Carmine Wharf E14 6B 86
Carminia Rd. SW17 2F 137
Carnaby St. W1 1A 12 (6G 83)
Carnac St. SE27 4D 138
Carnanton Rd. E17 1F 51
Carnarvon Av. EN1: Enf 3A 24
Carnarvon Dr. UB3: Harl 3E 92
Carnarvon Rd. E10 5E 50
E15 6H 69
E18 1H 51
EN5: Barn 3B 20
Carnation Cl. RM7: Rush G 2K 73
Carnation St. SE2 5B 108
Carnbrook M. SE3 3B 124
Carnbrook Rd. SE3 3B 124
Carnecke Gdns. SE9 5C 124
Carnegie Cl. KT6: Surb 2F 163
Carnegie Pl. SW19 3F 135
Carnegie Rd. HA1: Harr 7K 41
Carnegie St. N1 1K 83
Carnell Apartments
E14 6B 86
(off St Anne's Row)
Carnforth Cl. KT19: Ewe 6H 163
Carnforth Rd. SW16 7H 137
(not continuous)
Carnie Lodge SW17 3F 137
Carnival Ho. *SE1 6K 15*
(off Gainsford St.)
Carnoustie Cl. SE28 6D 90
Carnoustie Dr. N1 7K 65
(not continuous)
Carnwath Rd. SW6 3J 117
Caroe Ct. N9 1C 34
Carol Cl. NW4 4F 45
Carole Ho. *NW1 1D 82*
(off Regent's Pk. Rd.)
Carolina Cl. E15 5G 69
Carolina Rd. CR7: Thor H 2B 156
Caroline Cl. CR0: C'don 4E 168
N10 2F 47
SW16 3K 137
TW7: Isle 7H 95
UB7: W Dray 2A 92
W2 7K 81
Caroline Ct. HA7: Stan 6F 27
SE6 4F 141
TW15: Ashf 6D 128
Caroline Gdns. E2 1H 9 (3E 84)
SE15 7H 103
(not continuous)
Caroline Ho. *W2 7K 81*
(off Bayswater Rd.)
W6 5E 98
(off Queen Caroline St.)
Caroline Pl. SW11 2E 118
UB3: Harl 7G 93
W2 7K 81
Caroline Pl. M. W2 7K 81
Caroline Rd. SW19 7H 135
Caroline St. E1 6K 85
Caroline Ter. SW1 4G 17 (4E 100)
Caroline Wlk. *W6 6G 99*
(off Lillie Rd.)
Carol St. NW1 1G 83
Caronia Ct. *SE16 4A 104*
(off Plough Way)
Carpenter Gdns. N21 2G 33
Carpenter Ho. *E14 5C 86*
(off Burgess St.)
NW11 6A 46
Carpenters Arms Path *SE9 6D 124*
(off Eltham High St.)
Carpenters Cl. EN5: New Bar 6E 20
Carpenters Ct. *NW1 1G 83*
(off Pratt St.)
TW2: Twick 2J 131
Carpenters M. N7 5J 65
Carpenters Pl. SW4 4H 119
Carpenter's Rd. E15 7E 68
Carpenter St. W1 3J 11 (7F 83)
Carp Ho. *E3 1B 86*
(off Old Ford Rd.)
Carradale Ho. *E14 6E 86*
(off St Leonard's Rd.)
Carrara Cl. SE24 4A 120
SW9 4B 120
Carrara M. *E8 6G 67*
(off Dalston La.)
Carrara Wharf SW6 3G 117
Carr Cl. HA7: Stan 6F 27
Carre M. *SE5 1B 120*
(off Calais St.)
Carr Gro. SE18 4C 106
Carr Ho. DA1: Cray 5K 127
Carriage Dr. E. SW11 7E 100
Carriage Dr. Nth. SW11 7H 17 (6E 100)
(Carriage Dr. E.)
SW11 7D 100
(The Parade)
Carriage Dr. Sth. SW11 1D 118
(not continuous)
Carriage Dr. W. SW11 7D 100
Carriage M. IG1: Ilf 2G 71
Carriage Pl. N16 3D 66
SW16 5G 137
Carriage St. SE18 3F 107
Carrick Cl. TW7: Isle 3A 114
Carrick Dr. IG6: Ilf 1G 53
Carrick Gdns. N17 7K 33
Carrick Ho. *N7 6K 65*
(off Caledonian Rd.)
SE11 5K 19 (5A 102)
Carrick M. SE8 6C 104
Carrill Way DA17: Belv 3D 108
Carrington Av. TW3: Houn 5F 113
Carrington Cl. CR0: C'don 7A 158
KT2: King T 5J 133
Carrington Ct. *SW11 4C 118*
(off Barnard Rd.)
Carrington Gdns. E7 4J 69
Carrington Ho. *W1 5J 11*
(off Carrington St.)
Carrington Rd. TW10: Rich 4G 115
Carrington Sq. HA3: Hrw W 6B 26
Carrington St. W1 5J 11 (1F 101)
Carrock Ct. *RM7: Rush G 6K 55*
(off Union Rd.)
Carrol Cl. NW5 4F 65
Carroll Cl. E15 5H 69

Carroll Ct. *W3* 3H 97
(off Osborne Rd.)
Carroll Ho. *W2* 2A 10
(off Craven Ter.)
Carronade Ct. N7 5K 65
Carronade Pl. SE28 3G 107
Carron Cl. E14 6D 86
Carroun Rd. SW8 7K 101
Carroway La. UB6: G'frd 3H 77
Carrow Rd. RM9: Dag 7B 72
Carr Rd. E17 2B 50
UB5: N'olt 6E 58
Carrs La. N21 5H 23
Carr St. E14 5A 86
CARSHALTON 4E 166
Carshalton Athletic FC 3C 166
CARSHALTON BEECHES 7C 166
Carshalton Gro. SM1: Sutt 4B 166
CARSHALTON ON THE HILL 7E 166
Carshalton Pk. Rd. SM5: Cars 5D 166
Carshalton Pl. SM5: Cars 5E 166
Carshalton Rd. CR4: Mitc 4E 154
SM1: Sutt 5A 166
SM5: Cars 5A 166
Carslake Rd. SW15 6E 116
Carson Rd. E16 4J 87
EN4: Cockf 4J 21
SE21 2D 138
Carson Ter. *W11* 1G 99
(off Princes Pl.)
Carstairs Rd. SE6 3E 140
Carston Cl. SE12 5H 123
Carswell Cl. IG4: Ilf 4B 52
Carswell Rd. SE6 7E 122
Carter Cl. NW9 6K 43
Carter Ct. EC4 1A 14
Carter Dr. RM5: Col R 1H 55
Carteret Ho. *W12* 7D 80
(off White City Est.)
Carteret St. SW1 7C 12 (2H 101)
Carteret Way SE8 4A 104
Carterhatch La. EN1: Enf 1A 24
Carterhatch Rd. EN3: Enf H 1D 24
Carter Ho. E1 6J 9
Carter La. EC4 1B 14 (6B 84)
Carter Pl. SE17 5C 102
Carter Rd. E13 1K 87
SW19 6B 136
Carters Cl. KT4: Wor Pk 2F 165
NW5 5H 65
(off Torriano Av.)
Carters Hill Cl. SE9 1A 142
Carters La. SE23 2A 140
Carter St. SE17 6C 102
Carter's Yd. SW18 5J 117
Carthew Rd. W6 3D 98
Carthew Vs. W6 3D 98
Carthusian St. EC1 5C 8 (5C 84)
Cartier Circ. E14 1D 104
Carting La. WC2 3F 13 (7J 83)
Cart La. E4 1B 36
Cartmel *NW1* 1A 6
(off Hampstead Rd.)
Cartmel Cl. N17 7C 34
Cartmel Ct. UB5: N'olt 6C 58
Cartmel Gdns. SM4: Mord 5A 154
Cartmel Rd. DA7: Bex 1G 127
Carton Ho. *SE16* 3G 103
(off Marine St.)
W11 7F 81
(off St Ann's Rd.)
Cartoon Mus. 6E 6
(off Lit. Russell St.)
Cartridge Pl. SE18 3F 107
Cartwright Gdns. WC1 2E 6 (3J 83)
Cartwright Ho. *SE1* 3C 102
(off County St.)
Cartwright Rd. RM9: Dag 7F 73
Cartwright St. E1 2K 15 (7F 85)
Cartwright Way SW13 7D 98
Carvel Ho. *E14* 5E 104
(off Manchester Rd.)
Carver Cl. W4 3J 97
Carver Rd. SE24 6C 120
Carville Cres. TW8: Bford 4E 96
Cary Rd. E11 4G 69
Carysfort Rd. N8 5H 47
N16 3D 66
Casby Ho. *SE16* 3G 103
(off Marine St.)
Cascade Av. N10 4G 47
Cascade Cl. IG9: Buck H 2G 37
Cascade Rd. IG9: Buck H 2G 37
Cascades Ct. SW19 7H 135
Cascades Twr. E14 1B 104
Casel Ct. *HA7: Stan* 2F 27
(off Brightwen Gro.)
Casella Rd. SE14 7K 103
Casewick Rd. SE27 5A 138
Casey Cl. NW8 2C 4 (3C 82)
Casimir Rd. E5 2J 67
Casino Av. SE24 5C 120
Caspian Ho. *E1* 5K 85
(off Shandy St.)
Caspian St. SE5 7D 102
Caspian Wlk. E16 6B 88
Caspian Wharf *E3* 5D 86
(off Violet Rd.)
Cassandra Cl. UB5: N'olt 4H 59
Casselden Rd. NW10 7K 61
Cassell Ho. *SW9* 2K 119
(off Stockwell Gdns. Est.)
Cassidy Rd. SW6 7J 99
(not continuous)
Cassilda Rd. SE2 4A 108
Cassilis Rd. E14 2C 104
TW1: Twick 5B 114
Cassini Apartments E16 6J 87
Cassiobury Av. TW14: Felt 7H 111
Cassiobury Rd. E17 5A 50
Cassland Rd. CR7: Thor H 4D 156
E9 7K 67
Casslee Rd. SE6 7B 122
Cassocks Sq. TW17: Shep 7F 147
Casson Ho. *E1* 5K 9
(off Hanbury St.)
Casson St. E1 5G 85
Castalia Sq. E14 2E 104
Castellain Mans. *W9* 4K 81
(off Castellain Rd., not continuous)
Castellain Rd. W9 4K 81
Castellane Cl. HA7: Stan 7E 26
Castell Ho. SE8 7C 104
Castello Av. SW15 5E 116
CASTELNAU 6D 98
Castelnau SW13 1C 116
Castelnau Gdns. SW13 6D 98
Castelnau Mans. *SW13* 6D 98
(off Castelnau, not continuous)
Castelnau Row SW13 6D 98
Casterbridge *NW6* 1K 81
(off Abbey Rd.)
W11 6H 81
(off Dartmouth Cl.)
Casterbridge Rd. SE3 3J 123
Casterton St. E8 6H 67
Castile Rd. SE18 4E 106
Castillon Rd. SE6 2G 141
Castlands Rd. SE6 2B 140
Castleacre *W2* 1C 10
(off Hyde Pk. Cres.)
Castle Av. E4 5A 36
KT17: Ewe 7D 164
UB7: Yiew 7A 74
Castlebar Ct. W5 5C 78
Castlebar Hill W5 5C 78
Castlebar M. W5 5C 78
Castlebar Pk. W5 5B 78
Castlebar Rd. W5 5C 78
Castle Baynard St. EC4 2B 14 (7B 84)
Castlebrook Cl. SE11 4B 102
Castle Bus. Cen. *TW12: Hamp* 1F 149
(off Castle M.)
Castle Climbing Cen., The 2C 66
Castle Cl. BR2: Brom 3G 159
E9 5A 68
SW19 3F 135
TW16: Sun 7G 129
W3 2H 97
Castlecombe Dr. SW19 7F 117
Castlecombe Rd. SE9 4C 142
Castle Ct. *EC3* 1F 15
(off Birchin La.)
SE26 4A 140
Castleden Ho. *NW3* 7B 64
(off Hilgrove Rd.)
Castledine Rd. SE20 7H 139
Castle Dr. IG4: Ilf 6C 52
Castleford Av. SE9 1F 143
Castleford Cl. N17 6A 34
Castleford Ct. *NW8* 3B 4
(off Henderson Dr.)
Castlegate TW9: Rich 3F 115
Castlehaven Rd. NW1 7F 65
Castle Hgts. RM9: Dag 1B 90
Castle Hill Av. CR0: New Ad 7D 170
Castle Hill Pde. *W13* 7B 78
(off The Avenue)
Castle Ho. *SE1* 4C 102
(off Newington Butts)
SM2: Sutt 6J 165
SW8 7J 101
(off Sth. Lambeth Rd.)
Castle Ind. Est. SE17 4C 102
Castle La. SW1 1B 18 (3G 101)
Castleleigh Ct. EN2: Enf 5J 23
Castlemaine Av. CR2: S Croy 5F 169
KT17: Ewe 7D 164
Castlemain St. E1 5H 85
Castle Mead SE5 7C 102
Castle M. N12 5F 31
NW1 6F 65
SW17 4C 136
TW12: Hamp 1F 149
(not continuous)
Castle Pde. KT17: Ewe 7C 164
Castle Pl. NW1 6F 65
W4 4A 98
Castle Point *E13* 2A 88
(off Boundary Rd.)
Castlereagh Ho. HA7: Stan 6G 27
Castlereagh St. W1 7E 4 (6D 82)
Castle Rd. EN3: Enf H 1F 25
N12 5F 31
NW1 6F 65
RM9: Dag 1B 90
TW7: Isle 2K 113
UB2: S'hall 3D 94
UB5: N'olt 6F 59
Castle Row W4 5K 97
Castle St. E6 2A 88
KT1: King T 2E 150
Castleton Av. DA7: Bex 1K 127
HA9: Wemb 4E 60
Castleton Cl. CR0: C'don 6A 158
Castleton Gdns. HA9: Wemb 3E 60
Castleton Ho. *E14* 4E 104
(off Pier St.)
Castleton Rd. CR4: Mitc 4H 155
(not continuous)
E17 2F 51
HA4: Ruis 1B 58
IG3: Ilf 1A 72
SE9 4B 142
Castletown Rd. W14 5G 99
Castleview Cl. N4 2C 66
Castleview Gdns. IG1: Ilf 6C 52
Castle Wlk. TW16: Sun 3A 148
Castle Way SW19 3F 135
TW13: Hanw 4A 130
Castle Wharf *E14* 7G 87
(off Orchard Pl.)
Castlewood Dr. SE9 2D 124
Castlewood Rd. EN4: Cockf 3G 21
N15 6G 49
N16 6G 49
Castle Yd. N6 7E 46
SE1 4B 14 (1B 102)
TW10: Rich 5D 114
Castor La. E14 7D 86
Catalina Rd. TW6: H'row A 2D 110
Catalpa Ct. SE13 6F 123
Caterham Av. IG5: Ilf 2D 52
Caterham Rd. SE13 3F 123
Catesby Ho. *E9* 7J 67
(off Frampton Pk. Rd.)
Catesby St. SE17 4D 102
CATFORD 7D 122
Catford Art Gallery 7D 122
(off Rushey Grn.)
Catford B'way. SE6 7D 122
CATFORD GYRATORY 7D 122
Catford Hill SE6 1B 140
Catford Island SE6 7D 122
Catford M. SE6 7D 122
Catford Rd. SE6 7C 122
Catford Trad. Est. SE6 2D 140
Cathall Leisure Cen. 2G 69
Cathall Rd. E11 2F 69
Cathay Ho. SE16 2H 103
Cathay St. SE16 2H 103
Cathay Wlk. *UB5: N'olt* 2E 76
(off Brabazon Rd.)
Cathcart Dr. BR6: Orp 2J 173
Cathcart Hill N19 3G 65
Cathcart Ho. *SW10* 5A 100
(off Cathcart Rd.)
Cathcart Rd. SW10 6K 99
Cathcart St. NW5 6F 65
Cathedral Lodge *EC1* 5C 8
(off Aldersgate St.)
Cathedral Mans. *SW1* 3A 18
(off Vauxhall Bri. Rd.)
Cathedral Piazza SW1 2A 18 (3G 101)
Cathedral St. SE1 4E 14 (1D 102)
Cathedral Wlk. SW1 1A 18
Catherall Rd. N5 3C 66
Catherine Cl. NW4 4D 44
Catherine Ct. IG2: Ilf 5G 53
N14 5B 22
SW3 7A 16
(off Callow St.)
SW19 5H 135
Catherine Dr. TW9: Rich 4E 114
TW16: Sun 6H 129
Catherine Gdns. TW3: Houn 4H 113
Catherine Griffiths Ct. *EC1* 3K 7
(off Northampton Rd.)
Catherine Gro. SE10 1D 122
Catherine Ho. *E3* 2C 86
(off Thomas Frye Dr.)
N1 1E 84
(off Whitmore Est.)
Catherine Howard Ct. SE9 6H 125
Catherine of Aragon Ct.
SE9 6G 125
Catherine Parr Ct. SE9 6H 125
Catherine Pl. HA1: Harr 5K 41
SW1 1A 18 (3G 101)
Catherine Rd. KT6: Surb 5D 150
Catherine St. WC2 2G 13 (7K 83)
Catherine Wheel All. E1 6H 9 (5E 84)
Catherine Wheel Rd.
TW8: Bford 7D 96
Catherine Wheel Yd. SW1 5A 12
Catherwood Ct. N1 1E 8
Cat Hill EN4: E Barn 6H 21
Cathles Rd. SW12 6F 119
Cathnor Rd. W12 2D 98
Catlin Cres. TW17: Shep 5F 147
Catling Cl. SE23 3J 139
Catlin's La. HA5: Eastc 3K 39
Catlin St. SE16 5G 103
Cator La. BR3: Beck 1B 158
Cato Rd. SW4 3H 119
Cator Pk. Sports Cen. 6A 140
Cator Rd. SE26 6K 139
SM5: Cars 5D 166

Cator St. SE15 . . . . .7F **103**
(Commercial Way)
SE15 . . . . .6F **103**
(Ebley Cl.)
Cato St. W1 . . . . .6D **4** (5C **82**)
Catsey La. WD23: Bush 1B **26**
Catsey Woods WD23: Bush 1B **26**
Catterick Cl. N11 . . . . .5K **31**
Cattistock Rd. SE9 . . . . .5C **142**
Cattley Cl. EN5: Barn 4B **20**
Catton St. WC1 . . . . .6G **7** (5K **83**)
Caudwell Ter. SW18 . . . . .6B **118**
Caughley Ho. SE11 . . . . .2J **19**
(off Baynes St.)
Caulfield Ct. NW1 . . . . .7G **65**
(off Baynes St.)
Caulfield Rd. E6 . . . . .1C **88**
SE15 .2H **121**
Causeway, The KT9: Chess 4E **162**
KT10: Clay 7A **162**
N2 . . . . .4C **46**
SM2: Sutt 7A **166**
SM5: Cars 3E **166**
SW18 .5K **117**
SW19 .5E **134**
TW4: Houn 4J **111**
TW11: Tedd 6K **131**
TW14: Felt, Houn 4J **111**
Causeyware Rd. N9 . . . . .7D **24**
Causton Cotts. E14 . . . . .6A **86**
(off Galsworthy Av.)
Causton Ho. SE5 . . . . .6C **102**
Causton Rd. N6 . . . . .7F **47**
Causton Sq. RM10: Dag 7G **73**
Causton St. SW1 . . . . . .4D **18** (4H **101**)
Cautley Av. SW4 . . . . .5G **119**
Cavalier Cl. RM6: Chad H 4D **54**
Cavalier Ct. KT5: Surb 6F **151**
Cavalier Gdns. UB3: Hayes 6F **75**
Cavalry Cres. TW4: Houn 4B **112**
Cavalry Gdns. SW15 . . . . .5H **117**
Cavalry Sq. SW3 . . . . . .5F **17** (5D **100**)
Cavan Pl. HA5: Hat E 1D **40**
Cavaye Ho. SW10 . . . . .7A **16**
(off Cavaye Pl.)
Cavaye Pl. SW10 . . . . .6A **16** (5A **100**)
Cavell Dr. EN2: Enf 2F **23**
Cavell Ho. N1 .1E **84**
(off Colville Est.)
Cavell Rd. N17 . . . . .7J **33**
Cavell St. E1 .5H **85**
Cavendish Av. DA8: Erith 6J **109**
DA15: Sidc 7A **126**
DA16: Well 3K **125**
HA1: Harr 4H **59**
HA4: Ruis 5K **57**
IG8: Wfd G 1K **51**
KT3: N Mald 5C **152**
N3 . . . . .2J **45**
NW8 . . . . .1B **4** (2B **82**)
W13 . . . . .5A **78**
Cavendish Cl. N18 . . . . .5C **34**
NW6 . . . . .6H **63**
NW8 . . . . .1B **4** (3B **82**)
TW16: Sun 6H **129**
UB4: Hayes 5G **75**
Cavendish Ct. EC3 . . . . .7H **9**
SE6 . . . . .1D **140**
(off Bromley Rd.)
SM6: Wall 6F **167**
TW16: Sun 6H **129**
HA8: Edg 6A **28**
Cavendish Dr. E11 . . . . .1F **69**
Cavendish Gdns. IG1: Ilf 1E **70**
IG11: Bark 5J **71**
RM6: Chad H 5E **54**
SW4 .6G **119**
Cavendish Ho. NW8 . . . . .1B **4**
(off Wellington Rd.)
SW1 .6H **101**
(off Monck St.)
UB7: W Dray 2B **92**
(off Park Lodge Av.)

Cavendish Ho. W1 . . . . .6A **6**
(off Mortimer St.)
W1 . . . . .5G **83**
(off Mortimer St.)
Cavendish Mans. EC1 . . . . .4J **7**
(off Rosebery Av.)
NW6 . . . . .5J **63**
Cavendish M. Nth. W1 . . . . .5K **5** (5F **83**)
Cavendish M. Sth. W1 . . . . .6K **5** (5F **83**)
Cavendish Pde. SW4 . . . . .6F **119**
(off Clapham Comn. Sth. Side)
TW4: Houn 2C **112**
Cavendish Pl. BR1: Brom 4D **160**
NW2 . . . . .6F **63**
SW4 .5H **119**
W1 . . . . .7K **5** (6F **83**)
Cavendish Rd. CR0: C'don 1B **168**
E4 . . . . .6K **35**
EN5: Barn 3A **20**
KT3: N Mald 4B **152**
N4 . . . . .6B **48**
N18 . . . . .5C **34**
NW6 . . . . .7G **63**
SM2: Sutt 7A **166**
SW12 .6F **119**
SW19 .7B **136**
TW16: Sun 6H **129**
W4 . . . . .1J **115**
Cavendish Sq. W1 . . . . .7K **5** (6F **83**)
Cavendish St. N1 . . . . .2D **84**
Cavendish Ter. E3 . . . . .3B **86**
TW13: Felt 2J **129**
Cavendish Way
BR4: W W'ck 1D **170**
Cavenham Gdns. IG1: Ilf 3H **71**
Caverleigh Way KT4: Wor Pk 1C **164**
Cave Rd. E13 . . . . .3K **87**
TW10: Ham 4C **132**
Caversham Av. N13 . . . . .3F **33**
SM3: Cheam 2G **165**
Caversham Ct. N11 . . . . .3K **31**
(off Brunswick Pk. Rd.)
Caversham Ho. KT1: King T 2E **150**
(off Lady Booth Rd.)
N15 . . . . .4C **48**
(off Caversham Rd.)
SE15 .6G **103**
(off Haymerle Rd.)
Caversham Rd. KT1: King T 2F **151**
N15 . . . . .4C **48**
NW5 . . . . .6G **65**
Caversham St. SW3 . . . . . . .7E **16** (6D **100**)
Caverswall St. W12 . . . . .6E **80**
Caveside Cl. BR7: Chst 1E **160**
Cavour Ho. SE17 . . . . .5B **102**
(off Alberta Est.)
Cawdor Cres. W7 . . . . .4A **96**
Cawnpore St. SE19 . . . . .5E **138**
Caxton Ct. SW11 . . . . .2C **118**
Caxton Gro. E3 . . . . .3C **86**
Caxton Hall SW1 . . . . .3H **101**
(off Caxton St.)
Caxton M. TW8: Bford 6D **96**
Caxton Pl. IG1: Ilf 3E **70**
Caxton Rd. N22 . . . . .2K **47**
SW19 .5A **136**
UB2: S'hall 3B **94**
W12 . . . . .2F **99**
Caxton St. SW1 . . . . .1C **18** (3G **101**)
Caxton St. Nth. E16 . . . . .6H **87**
Caxton Trad. Est.
UB3: Hayes 2G **93**
Caxton Wlk. WC2 . . . . . .1D **12** (6H **83**)
Cayenne Ct. SE1 . . . . .5K **15** (2F **103**)
Caygill Cl. BR2: Brom 4H **159**
Cayley Rd. UB2: S'hall 3F **95**
Cayton Pl. EC1 . . . . .2E **8**
Cayton Rd. UB6: G'frd 2J **77**
Cayton St. EC1 . . . . .2E **8** (3D **84**)
Cazenove Rd. E17 . . . . .1C **50**
N16 . . . . .2F **67**
Cearns Ho. E6 . . . . .1B **88**

Cecil Av. EN1: Enf 4A **24**
HA9: Wemb 5F **61**
IG11: Bark 7H **71**
Cecil Cl. KT9: Chess 4D **162**
TW15: Ashf 7E **128**
W5 . . . . .5D **78**
Cecil Ct. CR0: C'don 2F **169**
EN2: Enf 4J **23**
EN5: Barn 3A **20**
NW6 . . . . .7K **63**
SW10 .6A **100**
(off Fawcett St.)
WC2 . . . . .3E **12** (7J **83**)
Cecile Pk. N8 .6J **47**
Cecil Ho. E17 . . . . .1C **50**
Cecilia Cl. N2 . . . . .3A **46**
Cecilia Rd. E8 . . . . .5F **67**
Cecil Manning Cl.
UB6: G'frd 1A **78**
Cecil Pk. HA5: Pinn 4C **40**
Cecil Pl. CR4: Mitc 5D **154**
Cecil Rhodes Ho. NW1 . . . . .2H **83**
(off Goldington St.)
Cecil Rd. CR0: C'don 6J **155**
E11 . . . . .3H **69**
E13 . . . . .1J **87**
E17 . . . . .1C **50**
EN2: Enf 3H **23**
HA3: W'stone 3J **41**
IG1: Ilf .4F **71**
N10 . . . . .2F **47**
N14 . . . . .1B **32**
NW9 . . . . .3A **44**
NW10 .1A **80**
RM6: Chad H 7D **54**
SM1: Sutt 6H **165**
SW19 .7K **135**
TW3: Houn 2G **113**
TW15: Ashf 7E **128**
W3 . . . . .5J **79**
Cecil Rosen Ct. HA0: Wemb 3B **60**
Cecil Sharp House 1E **82**
Cecil Way BR2: Hayes 1J **171**
Cedar Av. DA15: Sidc 7A **126**
EN3: Enf H 2D **24**
EN4: E Barn 7H **21**
HA4: Ruis 5A **58**
RM6: Chad H 5E **54**
TW2: Whitt 6F **113**
UB3: Hayes 6J **75**
UB7: Yiew 7B **74**
Cedar Cl. BR2: Brom 3C **172**
E3 . . . . .1B **86**
IG1: Ilf .5H **71**
IG9: Buck H 2G **37**
KT6: E Mos 4J **149**
RM7: Rom 4J **55**
SE21 .1C **138**
SM5: Cars 6D **166**
SW15 .4K **133**
Cedar Copse BR1: Brom 2D **160**
Cedar Ct. E18 . . . . .1J **51**
N1 . . . . .7C **66**
N10 . . . . .2E **46**
N11 . . . . .5B **32**
N20 . . . . .1G **31**
SE1 . . . . .5J **15**
(off Royal Oak Yd.)
SE7 . . . . .6A **106**
SE13 .4F **123**
SM2: Sutt 6A **166**
SW19 .3F **135**
TW8: Bford 6C **96**
Cedar Cres. BR2: Brom 3C **172**
Cedarcroft Rd. KT9: Chess 4F **163**
Cedar Dr. HA5: Hat E 6A **26**
N2 . . . . .4C **46**
Cedar Gdns. SM2: Sutt 6A **166**
Cedar Grange EN1: Enf 5K **23**
Cedar Gro. DA5: Bexl 6D **126**
UB1: S'hall 5E **76**
W5 . . . . .3E **96**

Cedar Hgts. NW2 . . . . .6H **63**
TW10: Ham 1E **132**
Cedar Ho. E2 .2H **85**
(off Mowlem St.)
E14 . . . . .2E **104**
(off Manchester Rd.)
N22 . . . . .1A **48**
(off Acacia Rd.)
SE14 .1K **121**
SE16 .2K **103**
(off Woodland Cres.)
SW6 .2A **118**
TW9: Kew 1H **115**
TW16: Sun 7H **129**
(off Spelthorne Gro.)
UB4: Yead 4A **76**
W8 . . . . .3K **99**
(off Marloes Rd.)
Cedarhurst BR1: Brom 7G **141**
Cedarhurst Cotts. DA5: Bexl 7G **127**
Cedarhurst Dr. SE9 . . . . .5A **124**
Cedarland Ter. SW20 . . . . .7D **134**
Cedar Lawn Av. EN5: Barn 5B **20**
Cedar M. SW15 . . . . .5F **117**
Cedar Mt. SE9 . . . . .1B **142**
Cedarne Rd. SW6 . . . . .7K **99**
Cedar Pk. Gdns. RM6: Chad H 7D **54**
SW19 .5D **134**
Cedar Pk. Rd. EN2: Enf 1H **23**
Cedar Pl. SE7 . . . . .5A **106**
Cedar Ri. N14 . . . . .7K **21**
Cedar Rd. BR1: Brom 2A **160**
CR0: C'don 2D **168**
EN2: Enf 1G **23**
KT8: E Mos 4J **149**
N17 . . . . .1F **49**
NW2 . . . . .4E **62**
RM7: Rom 6A **166**
SM2: Sutt 6A **166**
TW4: Cran 2A **112**
TW11: Tedd 5A **132**
TW14: Bedf 1F **129**
Cedars, The E9 . . . . .7K **67**
(off Banbury Rd.)
E15 . . . . .7H **69**
IG9: Buck H 1D **36**
SM6: Wall 4G **167**
TW11: Tedd 6K **131**
W13 . . . . .6C **78**
Cedars Av. CR4: Mitc 4E **154**
E17 . . . . .5C **50**
Cedars Cl. NW4 . . . . .3F **45**
SE13 .3F **123**
Cedars Ct. N9 . . . . .2K **33**
Cedars Dr. UB10: Hil 2B **74**
Cedars Ho. E17 . . . . .3D **50**
Cedars M. SW4 . . . . .4F **119**
(not continuous)
Cedars Rd. BR3: Beck 2A **158**
CR0: Bedd 3J **167**
E15 . . . . .6G **69**
KT1: Ham W 1C **150**
N9 . . . . .2B **34**
N21 . . . . .2G **33**
SM4: Mord 4J **153**
SW4 . . . . .3F **119**
SW13 .2C **116**
W4 . . . . .5J **97**
Cedar Ter. TW9: Rich 4E **114**
Cedar Tree Gro. SE27 . . . . .5B **138**
Cedar Vw. KT1: King T 3D **150**
(off Milner Rd.)
Cedarville Gdns. SW16 . . . . .6K **137**
Cedar Way NW1 . . . . .7H **65**
TW16: Sun 7G **129**
Cedar Way Ind. Est. NW1 . . . . .7H **65**
Cedra Ct. N16 . . . . .1G **67**
Cedric Chambers NW8 . . . . .3A **4**
(off Northwick Cl.)
Cedrick Chambers NW8 . . . . .4B **82**
(off Northwick Cl.)
Cedric Rd. SE9 . . . . .3G **143**

Celadon Cl.—Chamberlain Cl.

Celadon Cl. EN3: Enf H . . . 3F 25
Celandine Cl. E14 . . . 5C 86
Celandine Ct. E4 . . . 3J 35
Celandine Dr. E8 . . . 7F 67
SE28 . . . 1B 108
Celandine Gro. N14 . . . 5B 22
Celandine Way E15 . . . 3G 87
Celbridge M. W2 . . . 5K 81
Celestial Gdns. SE13 . . . 4F 123
Celia Cres. TW15: Ashf . . . 6A 128
Celia Ho. *N1* . . . *2E 84*
(off Arden Est.)
Celia Rd. N19 . . . 4G 65
Celtic Av. BR2: Brom . . . 3G 159
Celtic St. E14 . . . 5D 86
Cemetery La. SE7 . . . 6C 106
TW17: Shep . . . 7D 146
Cemetery Rd. E7 . . . 5H 69
N17 . . . 7K 33
SE2 . . . 7B 108
Cenacle Cl. NW3 . . . 3J 63
Cenotaph . . . 6E 12 (2J 101)
Centaur Ct. TW8: Bford . . . 5E 96
Centaurs Bus. Pk. TW7: Isle . . . 6A 96
Centaur St. SE1 . . . 1H 19 (3K 101)
Centenary Rd. EN3: Brim . . . 4G 25
Centenary Trad. Est. EN3: Brim . . . 3G 25
Centennial Av. WD6: E'tree . . . 1H 27
Centennial Ct. WD6: E'tree . . . 1H 27
Centennial Pk. WD6: E'tree . . . 1H 27
Central Av. DA16: Well . . . 2K 125
E11 . . . 2F 69
E12 . . . 3B 70
EN1: Enf . . . 2C 24
HA5: Pinn . . . 6D 40
KT8: W Mole . . . 4D 148
N2 . . . 2B 46
(Oak La.)
N2 . . . 4K 45
(Rosemary Av.)
N9 . . . 3K 33
SM6: Wall . . . 5J 167
SW11 . . . 7D 100
TW3: Houn . . . 4G 113
UB3: Hayes . . . 1H 93
Central Bus. Cen. NW10 . . . 5A 62
Central Church Sports Club . . . *2K 139*
(off Normanton St.)
Central Cir. NW4 . . . 5D 44
Central Courtyard *EC2* . . . *7H 9*
(off Cutlers Gdns.)
Central Criminal Court
Old Bailey . . . 7B 8 (6B 84)
Centrale Shop. Cen. CR0: C'don . . . 2C 168
Central Gallery *IG1: Ilf* . . . *2F 71*
(in The Exchange)
Central Gdns. SM4: Mord . . . 5K 153
Central Hill SE19 . . . 5D 138
Central Ho. E15 . . . 2D 86
IG11: Bark . . . 7G 71
Central London Civil Justice Centre . . . 4J 5
Central Mall *SW18* . . . *6K 117*
(off Southside Shop. Cen.)
Central Mans. *NW4* . . . *5D 44*
(off Watford Way)
Central Markets (Smithfield) . . . 6A 8
Central Pde. DA15: Sidc . . . 3A 144
E17 . . . 4C 50
EN3: Enf H . . . 2D 24
HA1: Harr . . . 5K 41
IG2: Ilf . . . 6H 53
KT6: Surb . . . 6E 150
KT8: W Mole . . . 4D 148
SE20 . . . *7K 139*
(off High St.)
TW5: Hest . . . 7D 94
TW14: Felt . . . 7A 112
UB6: G'frd . . . 3A 78
W3 . . . 2H 97
Central Pk. Av. RM10: Dag . . . 3H 73
Central Pk. Est. TW4: Houn . . . 5B 112
Central Pk. Rd. E6 . . . 2B 88
Central Pl. SE25 . . . 5G 157
Central Rd. HA0: Wemb . . . 5B 60
KT4: Wor Pk . . . 1C 164
SM4: Mord . . . 6J 153
Central St Martins College of Art & Design . . . 6G 7
Central School Path SW14 . . . 3J 115
Central Sq. *HA9: Wemb* . . . *5E 60*
(off Sevenex Pde.)
NW11 . . . 6K 45
Central St. EC1 . . . 1C 8 (3C 84)
Central Ter. BR3: Beck . . . 3K 157
Central Walkway *N19* . . . *4H 65*
(off Pleshey Rd.)
Central Way NW10 . . . 3J 79
SE28 . . . 1A 108
SM5: Cars . . . 7C 166
TW14: Felt . . . 5J 111
Central Wharf *E14* . . . *6C 86*
(off Thomas Rd.)
Centre, The KT12: Walt T . . . 7J 147
TW3: Houn . . . 3F 113
TW13: Felt . . . 1K 129
Centre Av. N2 . . . 2C 46
NW10 . . . 3E 80
W3 . . . 1K 97
Centre Comn. Rd. BR7: Chst . . . 6G 143
Centre Ct. Shop. Cen. SW19 . . . 6H 135
Centre Dr. E7 . . . 4A 70
Centre for the Magic Arts, The . . . *3B 6*
(off Stephenson Way)
Centre for Wildlife Gardening Vis. Cen. . . . 3F 121
Centre Hgts. *NW3* . . . *7B 64*
(off Finchley Rd.)
Centre Point SE1 . . . 5G 103
Centrepoint WC2 . . . 7D 6
Centre Point Ho. *WC2* . . . *7D 6*
(off St Giles High St.)
Centre Rd. E7 . . . 2J 69
E11 . . . 2J 69
RM10: Dag . . . 2H 91
Centre Sq. *SW18* . . . *5J 117*
(off Buckhold Rd.)
Centre St. E2 . . . 2H 85
Centre Vw. Apartments *CR0: C'don* . . . *3C 168*
(off Whitgift St.)
Centre Way E17 . . . 7K 35
N9 . . . 2D 34
Centreway *IG1: Ilf* . . . *2G 71*
(off High Rd.)
Centreway Apartments *IG1: Ilf* . . . *2G 71*
(off Axon Pl.)
Centric Cl. NW1 . . . 1E 82
Centrillion Point *CR0: C'don* . . . *4C 168*
(off Mason's Av.)
Centro Ct. E6 . . . 4D 88
Centurion Bldg. SW8 . . . 7J 17 (6F 101)
Centurion Cl. N7 . . . 7K 65
Centurion Ct. SE18 . . . 4E 106
SM6: Wall . . . 2F 167
Centurion La. E3 . . . 1B 86
Centurion Sq. SE18 . . . 1C 124
Centurion Way DA18: Erith . . . 3F 109
Century Cl. NW4 . . . 5F 45
Century Ho. HA9: Wemb . . . 2F 61
SW15 . . . 4F 117
Century M. E5 . . . 4J 67
N5 . . . *3B 66*
(off Conewood St.)
Century Plaza *HA8: Edg* . . . *6B 28*
(off Station Rd.)
Century Rd. E17 . . . 3A 50
Century Yd. SE23 . . . 2J 139
(not continuous)
Cephas Av. E1 . . . 4J 85
Cephas Ho. *E1* . . . *4J 85*
(off Doveton St.)
Cephas St. E1 . . . 4J 85
Ceres Rd. SE18 . . . 4K 107
Cerise Rd. SE15 . . . 1G 121
Cerne Cl. UB4: Yead . . . 7A 76
Cerne Rd. SM4: Mord . . . 6A 154
Cerney M. W2 . . . 2A 10 (7B 82)
Cervantes Ct. W2 . . . 6K 81
Cester St. E2 . . . 1G 85
Ceylon Rd. W14 . . . 3F 99
Ceylon Wharf Apartments *SE16* . . . *2J 103*
(off St Marychurch St.)
Chabot Dr. SE15 . . . 3H 121
Chadacre Av. IG5: Ilf . . . 3D 52
Chadacre Ct. *E15* . . . *1J 87*
(off Vicars Cl.)
Chadacre Ho. *SW9* . . . *4B 120*
(off Loughborough Pk.)
Chadacre Rd. KT17: Ewe . . . 6D 164
Chadbourn St. E14 . . . 5D 86
Chadbury Ct. NW7 . . . 1C 44
Chad Cres. N9 . . . 3D 34
Chadd Dr. BR1: Brom . . . 3C 160
Chadd Grn. E13 . . . 1J 87
(not continuous)
Chadston Ho. *N1* . . . *7B 66*
(off Halton Rd.)
Chadswell *WC1* . . . *2F 7*
(off Cromer St.)
Chadview Ct. RM6: Chad H . . . 7D 54
Chadville Gdns. RM6: Chad H . . . 5D 54
Chadway RM8: Dag . . . 1C 72
Chadwell Av. RM6: Chad H . . . 7B 54
CHADWELL HEATH . . . 7D 54
Chadwell Heath Ind. Pk. RM8: Dag . . . 1E 72
Chadwell Heath La. RM6: Chad H . . . 4B 54
Chadwell Ho. *SE17* . . . *5D 102*
(off Inville Rd.)
Chadwell La. N8 . . . 3K 47
Chadwell St. EC1 . . . 1K 7 (3A 84)
Chadwick Av. E4 . . . 4A 36
N21 . . . 5E 22
SW19 . . . 6J 135
Chadwick Cl. SW15 . . . 7B 116
TW11: Tedd . . . 6A 132
W7 . . . 5K 77
Chadwick M. W4 . . . 6H 97
Chadwick Pl. KT6: Surb . . . 7C 150
Chadwick Rd. E11 . . . 6G 51
IG1: Ilf . . . 3F 71
NW10 . . . 1B 80
SE15 . . . 2F 121
Chadwick St. SW1 . . . 2C 18 (3H 101)
Chadwick Way SE28 . . . 7D 90
Chadwin Rd. E13 . . . 5K 87
Chadworth Ho. *EC1* . . . *2C 8*
(off Lever St.)
N4 . . . 1C 66
Chaffinch Av. CR0: C'don . . . 6K 157
Chaffinch Bus. Pk. BR3: Beck . . . 4K 157
Chaffinch Cl. CR0: C'don . . . 5K 157
KT6: Surb . . . 3G 163
N9 . . . 1E 34
Chaffinch Rd. BR3: Beck . . . 1A 158
Chafford Way RM6: Chad H . . . 4C 54
Chagford Ho. *E3* . . . *3D 86*
(off Talwin St.)
Chagford St. NW1 . . . 4E 4 (4D 82)
Chailey Av. EN1: Enf . . . 2A 24
Chailey Cl. TW5: Hest . . . 1B 112
Chailey Ind. Est. UB3: Hayes . . . 2J 93
Chailey St. E5 . . . 3J 67
Chalbury Wlk. N1 . . . 2K 83
Chalcombe Rd. SE2 . . . 3B 108
Chalcot Cl. SM2: Sutt . . . 7J 165
Chalcot Cres. NW1 . . . 1D 82
Chalcot Gdns. NW3 . . . 6D 64
Chalcot M. SW16 . . . 3J 137
Chalcot Rd. NW1 . . . 7E 64
Chalcot Sq. NW1 . . . 7E 64
(not continuous)
Chalcott Gdns. KT6: Surb . . . 1C 162
Chalcroft Rd. SE13 . . . 5G 123
Chaldon Ct. SE19 . . . 1D 156
Chaldon Path CR7: Thor H . . . 4B 156
Chaldon Rd. SW6 . . . 7G 99
Chale Rd. SW2 . . . 6J 119
Chalet Cl. DA5: Bexl . . . 4K 145
TW15: Ashf . . . 6F 129
Chalet Ct. CR7: Thor H . . . 5C 156
Chalet Est. NW7 . . . 4H 29
Chalfont Av. HA9: Wemb . . . 6H 61
Chalfont Ct. *HA1: Harr* . . . *6K 41*
(off Northwick Pk. Rd.)
NW1 . . . *4F 5*
(off Baker St.)
NW9 . . . 3B 44
Chalfont Grn. N9 . . . 3K 33
Chalfont Ho. *SE16* . . . *3H 103*
(off Keetons Rd.)
Chalfont M. UB10: Hil . . . 7D 56
Chalfont Rd. N9 . . . 3K 33
SE25 . . . 3F 157
UB3: Hayes . . . 2J 93
Chalfont Wlk. HA5: Pinn . . . 2A 40
Chalfont Way W13 . . . 3B 96
Chalford *NW3* . . . *6A 64*
(off Finchley Rd.)
Chalford Cl. KT8: W Mole . . . 4E 148
Chalford Rd. SE21 . . . 4D 138
Chalford Wlk. IG8: Wfd G . . . 1B 52
Chalgrove Av. SM4: Mord . . . 5J 153
Chalgrove Cres. IG5: Ilf . . . 2C 52
Chalgrove Gdns. N3 . . . 3G 45
Chalgrove Rd. N17 . . . 1H 49
SM2: Sutt . . . 7B 166
Chalice Cl. SM6: Wall . . . 6H 167
Chalice Ct. N2 . . . 4C 46
Chalkenden Cl. SE20 . . . 7H 139
CHALKER'S CORNER . . . 3H 115
CHALK FARM . . . 7E 64
Chalk Farm Pde. *NW3* . . . *7E 64*
(off Adelaide Rd.)
Chalk Farm Rd. NW1 . . . 7E 64
Chalk Hill Rd. W6 . . . 4F 99
Chalkhill Rd. HA9: Wemb . . . 3H 61
Chalklands HA9: Wemb . . . 3J 61
Chalk La. EN4: Cockf . . . 3J 21
Chalkley Cl. CR4: Mitc . . . 2D 154
Chalkmill Dr. EN1: Enf . . . 3C 24
Chalk Pit Way SM1: Sutt . . . 5A 166
Chalk Rd. E13 . . . 5K 87
Chalkstone Cl. DA16: Well . . . 1A 126
Chalkwell Ho. *E1* . . . *6K 85*
(off Pitsea St.)
Chalkwell Pk. Av. EN1: Enf . . . 4K 23
Challenge Cl. NW10 . . . 1A 80
Challenge Ct. TW2: Twick . . . 7J 113
Challenger Ho. *E14* . . . *7A 86*
(off Victory Pl.)
Challenge Rd. TW15: Ashf . . . 3F 129
Challice Way SW2 . . . 1K 137
Challin St. SE20 . . . 1J 157
Challis Rd. TW8: Bford . . . 5D 96
Challoner Cl. N2 . . . 2B 46
Challoner Ct. BR2: Brom . . . 2F 159
W14 . . . *5H 99*
(off Challoner St.)
Challoner Cres. W14 . . . 5H 99
Challoner Mans. *W14* . . . *5H 99*
(off Challoner St.)
Challoners Cl. KT8: E Mos . . . 4H 149
Challoner St. W14 . . . 5H 99
Chalmers Ho. E17 . . . 5D 50
Chalmers Rd. TW15: Ashf . . . 5D 128
Chalmers Rd. E. TW15: Ashf . . . 4D 128
Chalmers Wlk. *SE17* . . . *6B 102*
(off Hillingdon St.)
Chalmers Way TW1: Isle . . . 4B 114
TW14: Felt . . . 5K 111
Chaloner Ct. SE1 . . . 6E 14
Chalsey Rd. SE4 . . . 4B 122
Chalton Dr. N2 . . . 6B 46
Chalton Ho. *NW1* . . . *1C 6*
(off Chalton St.)
Chalton St. NW1 . . . 1C 6 (2G 83)
(not continuous)
Chamberlain Cl. IG1: Ilf . . . 3G 71
SE28 . . . 3H 107

220 A-Z London

Chamberlain Cotts. SE5 . . . . .1D 120
Chamberlain Cres.
BR4: W W'ck 1D 170
Chamberlain Gdns. TW3: Houn 1G 113
Chamberlain Ho. E1 . . . . .7J 85
(off Cable St.)
NW1 . . . . .1D 6
SE1 . . . . .7J 13
(off Westminster Bri. Rd.)
Chamberlain La. HA5: Eastc 3J 39
Chamberlain Pl. E17 . . . . .3A 50
Chamberlain Rd. N2 . . . . .2A 46
W13 . . . . .2A 96
Chamberlain St. NW1 . . . . .7D 64
Chamberlain Wlk. TW13: Hanw 4C 130
Chamberlain Way HA5: Eastc 3K 39
KT6: Surb 7E 150
Chamberlayne Av. HA9: Wemb 3E 60
Chamberlayne Mans. NW10 . . . . .3F 81
(off Chamberlayne Rd.)
Chamberlayne Rd. NW10 . . . . .1E 80
Chamberlens Garages W6 . . . . .4D 98
(off Dalling Rd.)
Chambers, The SW10 . . . . .1A 118
(off Chelsea Harbour Dr.)
Chambers Av. DA14: Sidc 6E 144
(not continuous)
Chambers Bus. Pk. UB7: Sip 6C 92
Chambers Gdns. N2 . . . . .1B 46
Chambers La. NW10 . . . . .7D 62
Chambers Pl. CR2: S Croy 7D 168
Chambers Rd. N7 . . . . .4J 65
Chambers St. SE16 . . . . .2G 103
Chamber St. E1 . . . . .2K 15 (7F 85)
Chambers Wlk. HA7: Stan 5G 27
Chambers Wharf SE16 . . . . .2G 103
Chambon Pl. W6 . . . . .4C 98
Chambord Ho. E2 . . . . .2K 9
(off Chambord St.)
Chambord St. E2 . . . . .2K 9 (3F 85)
Chamomile Ct. E17 . . . . .6C 50
(off Yunus Khan Cl.)
Champa Cl. N17 . . . . .2F 49
Champion Cres. SE26 . . . . .4A 140
Champion Gro. SE5 . . . . .3D 120
Champion Hill SE5 . . . . .3D 120
Champion Hill Est. SE5 . . . . .3E 120
Champion Ho. SE7 . . . . .6A 106
(off Charlton Rd.)
Champion Pk. SE5 . . . . .2D 120
Champion Rd. SE26 . . . . .4A 140
Champions Way NW4 . . . . .1D 44
Champlain Ho. W12 . . . . .7D 80
(off White City Est.)
Champness Cl. SE27 . . . . .4D 138
Champness Rd. IG11: Bark 6K 71
Champneys Cl. SM2: Cheam 7H 165
Chancel Ct. W1 . . . . .7H 83
(off Old Compton St.)
Chancel Ind. Est. NW10 . . . . .5B 62
Chancellor Gdns. CR2: S Croy 7B 168
Chancellor Gro. SE21 . . . . .2C 138
Chancellor Ho. E1 . . . . .1H 103
(off Green Bank)
SW7 . . . . .3A 100
(off Hyde Pk. Ga.)
Chancellor Pas. E14 . . . . .1C 104
Chancellor Pl. NW9 . . . . .2B 44
Chancellors Cl. WC1 . . . . .5G 7
Chancellor's Rd. W6 . . . . .5E 98
Chancellor's St. W6 . . . . .5E 98
Chancellors Wharf W6 . . . . .5E 98
Chancelot Rd. SE2 . . . . .4B 108
Chancel St. SE1 . . . . .5A 14 (1B 102)
Chancery Bldgs. 7H 85
(off Lowood St.)
Chancerygate UB7: Yiew 1C 92
Chancerygate Bus. Cen. HA4: Ruis . . .4C 58
UB2: S'hall 3A 94
Chancery La. BR3: Beck 2D 158
WC2 . . . . .6H 7 (6A 84)
Chancery M. SW17 . . . . .2C 136

Chance St. E1 . . . . .3J 9 (4F 85)
E2 . . . . .3J 9 (4F 85)
Chanctonbury Cl. SE9 . . . . .3F 143
Chanctonbury Gdns. SM2: Sutt 7K 165
Chanctonbury Way N12 . . . . .4C 30
Chandaria Cl. CRO: C'don 2C 168
(off Church Rd.)
Chandler Av. E16 . . . . .5J 87
Chandler Cl. TW12: Hamp 1E 148
Chandler Ct. TW14: Felt 6J 111
Chandler Ho. NW6 . . . . .1H 81
(off Willesden La.)
WC1 . . . . .4F 7
(off Colonnade)
Chandlers Cl. KT8: W Mole 5F 149
TW14: Felt 7H 111
Chandlers Ct. SE12 . . . . .1K 141
Chandlers Dr. DA8: Erith 4K 109
Chandlers M. E14 . . . . .2C 104
Chandler St. E1 . . . . .1H 103
Chandlers Way SW2 . . . . .7A 120
Chandler Way SE15 . . . . .6E 102
Chandlery, The SE1 . . . . .1K 19
(off Gerridge St.)
Chandlery Ho. E1 . . . . .6G 85
(off Gower's Wlk.)
Chandon Lodge SM2: Sutt 7A 166
Chandos Av. E17 . . . . .2C 50
N14 . . . . .3B 32
N20 . . . . .1F 31
W5 . . . . .4C 96
Chandos Cl. IG9: Buck H 2E 36
Chandos Ct. HA7: Stan 6G 27
HA8: Edg 7A 28
N14 . . . . .2C 32
Chandos Cres. HA8: Edg 7A 28
Chandos Pde. HA8: Edg 7A 28
Chandos Pl. WC2 . . . . .3E 12 (7J 83)
Chandos Rd. E15 . . . . .5F 69
HA1: Harr 5G 41
HA5: Eastc 7B 40
N2 . . . . .2B 46
N17 . . . . .2E 48
NW2 . . . . .5E 62
NW10 .4A 80
Chandos St. W1 . . . . .6K 5 (5F 83)
Chandos Way NW11 . . . . .1K 63
Change All. EC3 . . . . .1F 15 (6D 84)
Channel 4 TV 3H 101
(off Horseferry Rd.)
Channel Cl. TW5: Hest 1E 112
Channel Ga. Rd. NW10 . . . . .3A 80
Channel Ho. E14 . . . . .5A 86
(off Aston St.)
SE16 .2K 103
(off Water Gdns. Sq.)
Channel Islands Est. N1 . . . . .6C 66
(off Guernsey Rd.)
Channelsea Path E15 . . . . .1F 87
Channelsea Rd. E15 . . . . .1F 87
Channon Ct. KT6: Surb 5E 150
(off Maple Rd)
Chantress Cl. RM10: Dag 1J 91
Chantrey Ho. SW1 . . . . .3J 17
Chantrey Rd. SW9 . . . . .3K 119
Chantry, The E4 . . . . .1K 35
UB8: Hil 3B 74
Chantry Cl. DA14: Sidc 5E 144
EN2: Enf 1H 23
HA3: Kenton 5F 43
SE2 . . . . .3C 108
TW16: Sun 7J 129
UB7: Yiew 7A 74
W9 . . . . .4J 81
Chantry Ct. SM5: Cars 3C 166
Chantry Cres. NW10 . . . . .6B 62
Chantry Ho. KT1: King T 4E 150
RM13: Rain 2K 91
Chantry La. BR2: Brom 5B 160
Chantry Pl. HA3: Hrw W 1F 41
Chantry Rd. HA3: Hrw W 1F 41
KT9: Chess 5F 163

Chantry Sq. W8 . . . . .3K 99
Chantry St. N1 . . . . .1B 84
Chantry Way CR4: Mitc 3B 154
RM13: Rain 2K 91
Chant Sq. E15 . . . . .7F 69
Chant St. E15 . . . . .7F 69
Chapel, The SW15 . . . . .6G 117
Chapel Av. E12 . . . . .3B 70
Chapel Cl. DA1: Cray 5K 127
NW10 .5B 62
Chapel Ct. E10 . . . . .2D 68
(off Rosedene Ter.)
N2 . . . . .3C 46
SE1 . . . . .6E 14 (2D 102)
SE18 .6A 108
UB3: Hayes 7H 75
CHAPEL END 1D 50
Chapel Farm Rd. SE9 . . . . .3D 142
Chapel Hill DA1: Cray 5K 127
Chapel Ho. St. E14 . . . . .5D 104
Chapelier Ho. SW18 . . . . .4J 117
Chapel La. HA5: Pinn 3B 40
RM6: Chad H 7D 54
UB8: Hil 6C 74
Chapel Mkt. N1 . . . . .2A 84
Chapel M. IG8: Wfd G 6K 37
Chapel Mill Rd. KT1: King T 3F 151
Chapelmount Rd. IG8: Wfd G 6J 37
Chapel of St John the Evangelist 3J 15
(in The Tower of London)
Chapel of St Peter & St Paul 6F 105
(in Old Royal Naval College)
Chapel Path E11 . . . . .6K 51
(off Woodbine Pl.)
Chapel Pl. EC2 . . . . .2G 9 (3E 84)
N1 . . . . .2A 84
N17 . . . . .7A 34
W1 . . . . .1J 11 (6F 83)
Chapel Rd. DA7: Bex 4G 127
IG1: Ilf .3E 70
SE27 .4B 138
TW1: Twick 7B 114
TW3: Houn 3F 113
W13 . . . . .1B 96
Chapel Side W2 . . . . .7K 81
Chapel Stones N17 . . . . .1F 49
Chapel St. EN2: Enf 3H 23
NW1 . . . . .6C 4 (5C 82)
SW1 . . . . .1H 17 (3E 100)
Chapel Vw. CR2: Sels 6J 169
Chapel Wlk. CRO: C'don 2C 168
NW4 . . . . .4D 44
(not continuous)
Chapel Way N7 . . . . .3K 65
Chapel Yd. SW18 . . . . .5K 117
(off Wandsworth High St.)
Chaplin Cl. HA0: Wemb 6D 60
SE1 . . . . .6K 13 (2A 102)
Chaplin Cres. TW16: Sun 6G 129
Chaplin Ho. DA14: Sidc 4A 144
(off Sidcup High St.)
N1 . . . . .1D 84
Chaplin Rd. E15 . . . . .2H 87
HA0: Wemb 6C 60
N17 . . . . .3F 49
NW2 . . . . .6C 62
RM9: Dag 7E 72
Chaplin Sq. N12 . . . . .7G 31
Chapman Cl. UB7: W Dray 3B 92
Chapman Cres. HA3: Kenton 6E 42
Chapman Grn. N22 . . . . .1A 48
Chapman Ho. E1 . . . . .6H 85
(off Bigland St.)
Chapman Pl. N4 . . . . .2B 66
Chapman Rd. CRO: C'don 1A 168
DA17: Belv 5G 109
E9 . . . . .6B 68
Chapman's La. SE2: Belv, Lon 4C 108
Chapmans Pk. Ind. Est. NW10 . . . . . .6B 62
Chapman Sq. SW19 . . . . .2F 135
Chapman's Ter. N22 . . . . .1B 48

Chapman St. E1 . . . . .7H 85
Chapone Pl. W1 . . . . .1C 12 (6H 83)
Chapter Chambers SW1 . . . . .4C 18
(off Chapter St.)
Chapter Cl. UB10: Hil 7B 56
W4 . . . . .3J 97
Chapter House 1C 14
Chapter Rd. NW2 . . . . .5C 62
SE17 .5B 102
Chapter St. SW1 . . . . .4C 18 (4H 101)
Chapter Way SW19 . . . . .1B 154
TW12: Hamp 4E 130
Chara Pl. W4 . . . . .6K 97
Charcot Ho. SW15 . . . . .6B 116
Charcroft Ct. W14 . . . . .2F 99
(off Minford Gdns.)
Charcroft Gdns. EN3: Pond E 4E 24
Chardin Ho. SW9 . . . . .1A 120
(off Gosling Way)
Chardin Rd. W4 . . . . .4A 98
Chardmore Rd. N16 . . . . .1G 67
Chard Rd. TW6: H'row A 2D 110
Chardwell Cl. E6 . . . . .6D 88
Charecroft Way W12 . . . . .2F 99
Charfield Ct. W9 . . . . .4K 81
(off Shirland Rd.)
Charford Rd. E16 . . . . .5J 87
Chargeable La. E13 . . . . .4H 87
Chargeable St. E16 . . . . .4H 87
Chargrove Cl. SE16 . . . . .2K 103
Charing Cl. BR6: Orp 4K 173
Charing Ct. BR2: Brom 2G 159
Charing Cross SW1 . . . . .4E 12
Charing Cross Rd. WC2 . . . . . . .7D 6 (6H 83)
Charing Cross Sports Club 6F 99
Charing Cross Underground Shop. Cen.
. . . . .3E 12
Charing Ho. SE1 . . . . .6K 13
(off Windmill Wlk.)
Chariot Cl. E3 . . . . .1C 86
Charis Ho. E3 . . . . .3D 86
(off Grace St.)
Charlbert Ct. NW8 . . . . .2C 82
(off Charlbert St.)
Charlbert St. NW8 . . . . .2C 82
Charlbury Av. HA7: Stan 5J 27
Charlbury Gdns. IG3: Ilf 2K 71
Charlbury Gro. W5 . . . . .6C 78
Charlbury Rd. UB10: Ick 3B 56
Charldane Rd. SE9 . . . . .3F 143
Charlecote Gro. SE26 . . . . .3H 139
Charlecote Rd. RM8: Dag 3E 72
Charlemont Rd. E6 . . . . .4D 88
Charles II Pl. SW3 . . . . .6E 16 (5D 100)
Charles II St. SW1 . . . . .4C 12 (1H 101)
Charles Allen Ho. EC1 . . . . .1J 7
(off Amwell St.)
Charles Auffray Ho. E1 . . . . .5J 85
(off Smithy St.)
Charles Babbage Cl. KT9: Chess 7C 162
Charles Barry Cl. SW4 . . . . .3G 119
Charles Bradlaugh Ho. N17 . . . . .7C 34
(off Haynes Cl.)
Charles Chu. Wlk. IG1: Ilf 6D 52
Charles Cl. DA14: Sidc 4B 144
Charles Cobb Gdns. CRO: Wadd 5A 168
Charles Coveney Rd. SE15 . . . . .1F 121
Charles Cres. HA1: Harr 7H 41
(not continuous)
Charles Curran Ho. UB10: Ick 3D 56
Charles Darwin Ho. E2 . . . . .3H 85
(off Canrobert St.)
Charles Dickens Ho. E2 . . . . .3G 85
(off Mansford St.)
Charles Dickens Mus., The 4G 7
Charle Sevright Dr. NW7 . . . . .5A 30
Charlesfield SE9 . . . . .3A 142
Charles Flemwell M. E16 . . . . .1J 105
Charles Gardner Ct. N1 . . . . .1F 9
(off Haberdasher St.)
Charles Grinling Wlk. SE18 . . . . .4E 106
Charles Gro. N14 . . . . .1B 32

Charles Haller St.—Chatsworth Cl.

Charles Haller St. SW2 . . . 7A **120**
Charles Harrod Ct. *SW13* . . . *6E **98***
(off Somerville Av.)
Charles Hocking Ho. *W3* . . . *2J **97***
(off Bollo Bri. Rd.)
Charles House . . . *4H **99***
(off Kensington High St.)
Charles Ho. *N17* . . . *7A **34***
(off Love La.)
UB2: S'hall . . . 2E **94**
Charles Lamb Ct. *N1* . . . *2B **84***
(off Gerrard Rd.)
Charles La. NW8 . . . 2C **82**
Charles Lesser Ho. KT9: Chess . . . 5D **162**
Charles Mackenzie Ho.
SE16 . . . *4G **103***
(off Linsey St.)
Charlesmere Gdns. *SE28* . . . *2J **107***
(off Thames Reach)
Charles Nex M. SE21 . . . 2C **138**
Charles Pl. NW1 . . . 2B **6** (3G **83**)
Charles Rd. E7 . . . 7A **70**
RM6: Chad H . . . 6D **54**
RM10: Dag . . . 6K **73**
SW19 . . . 1J **153**
TW18: Staines . . . 6A **128**
W13 . . . 6A **78**
Charles Rowan Ho. *WC1* . . . *2J **7***
(off Margery St.)
Charles Simmons Ho. *WC1* . . . *2J **7***
(off Margery St.)
Charles Sq. N1 . . . 2F **9** (3D **84**)
Charles Sq. Est. N1 . . . 2F **9**
Charles St. CR0: C'don . . . 3C **168**
E16 . . . 1A **106**
EN1: Enf . . . 5A **24**
SW13 . . . 2A **116**
TW3: Houn . . . 2D **112**
UB10: Hil . . . 4D **74**
W1 . . . 4J **11** (1F **101**)
Charleston Cl. TW13: Felt . . . 3J **129**
Charleston St. SE17 . . . 4C **102**
Charles Townsend Ho.
EC1 . . . *3A **8***
(off Skinner St.)
Charles Uton Ct. E8 . . . 4G **67**
Charles Whincup Rd. E16 . . . 1K **105**
Charlesworth Ho. *E14* . . . *6B **86***
(off Dod St.)
Charlesworth Pl. SW13 . . . 3A **116**
Charleville Cir. SE26 . . . 5G **139**
Charleville Ct. *W14* . . . *5H **99***
(off Charleville Rd.)
Charleville Mans. *W14* . . . *5G **99***
(off Charleville Rd., not continuous)
Charleville M. TW7: Isle . . . 4B **114**
Charleville Rd. W14 . . . 5G **99**
CHARLIE BROWN'S RDBT. . . . 2A **52**
Charlie Chaplin Wlk. SE1 . . . 4H **13**
Charlieville Rd. DA8: Erith . . . 7J **109**
Charlmont Rd. SW17 . . . 6C **136**
Charlotte Cl. DA6: Bex . . . 5E **126**
IG6: Ilf . . . 1G **53**
Charlotte Ct. IG2: Ilf . . . 6E **52**
N8 . . . 6H **47**
SE1 . . . *4E **102***
(off Old Kent Rd.)
W6 . . . *4C **98***
(off Invermead Cl.)
Charlotte Despard Av.
SW11 . . . 1E **118**
Charlotte Ho. *E16* . . . *1K **105***
(off Fairfax M.)
W6 . . . *5E **98***
(off Queen Caroline St.)
Charlotte M. W1 . . . 5B **6** (5G **83**)
W10 . . . 6F **81**
W14 . . . 4G **99**
Charlotte Pk. Av. BR1: Brom . . . 3C **160**
Charlotte Pl. NW9 . . . 5J **43**
SW1 . . . 4A **18** (4G **101**)
W1 . . . 6B **6** (5G **83**)
Charlotte Rd. EC2 . . . 2G **9** (3E **84**)
RM10: Dag . . . 6H **73**
SM6: Wall . . . 6G **167**
SW13 . . . 1B **116**
Charlotte Row SW4 . . . 3G **119**
Charlotte Sq. TW10: Rich . . . 6F **115**
Charlotte St. W1 . . . 5B **6** (5G **83**)
Charlotte Ter. N1 . . . 1K **83**
Charlow Cl. SW6 . . . 2A **118**
CHARLTON
SE7 . . . 7B **106**
TW17 . . . 3E **146**
Charlton Athletic FC . . . 5A **106**
Charlton Chu. La. SE7 . . . 5A **106**
Charlton Cl. UB10: Ick . . . 2D **56**
Charlton Ct. E2 . . . 1F **85**
NW5 . . . 5H **65**
Charlton Cres. IG11: Bark . . . 2K **89**
Charlton Dene SE7 . . . 7A **106**
Charlton Ga. Bus. Pk. SE7 . . . 4A **106**
Charlton Ho. TW8: Bford . . . 6E **96**
Charlton King's Rd. NW5 . . . 5H **65**
Charlton La. SE7 . . . 4B **106**
TW17: Shep . . . 3E **146**
(not continuous)
Charlton Lido . . . 7B **106**
Charlton Pk. La. SE7 . . . 7B **106**
Charlton Pk. Rd. SE7 . . . 6B **106**
Charlton Pl. N1 . . . 2B **84**
Charlton Rd. HA3: Kenton . . . 4D **42**
HA9: Wemb . . . 1F **61**
N9 . . . 1E **34**
NW10 . . . 1A **80**
SE3 . . . 7J **105**
SE7 . . . 7J **105**
TW17: Shep . . . 3E **146**
Charlton Way SE3 . . . 1G **123**
Charlwood CR0: Sels . . . 7B **170**
Charlwood Cl. HA3: Hrw W . . . 6D **26**
Charlwood Ho. *SW1* . . . *4C **18***
(off Vauxhall Bri. Rd.)
TW9: Kew . . . 7H **97**
Charlwood Ho's. *WC1* . . . *2F **7***
(off Midhope St.)
Charlwood Pl. SW1 . . . 4B **18** (4G **101**)
Charlwood Rd. SW15 . . . 4F **117**
Charlwood St. SW1 . . . 6A **18** (5G **101**)
(not continuous)
Charlwood Ter. SW15 . . . 4F **117**
Charmans Ho. *SW8* . . . *7J **101***
(off Wandsworth Rd.)
Charmian Av. HA7: Stan . . . 3D **42**
Charmian Ho. *N1* . . . *1G **9***
(off Arden Est.)
Charminster Av. SW19 . . . 2J **153**
Charminster Ct. KT6: Surb . . . 7D **150**
Charminster Rd. T4: Wor Pk . . . 1F **165**
SE9 . . . 4B **142**
Charmouth Ct. TW10: Rich . . . 5F **115**
Charmouth Ho. SW8 . . . 7K **101**
Charmouth Rd. DA16: Well . . . 1C **126**
Charnock Ho. *W12* . . . *7D **80***
(off White City Est.)
Charnock Rd. E5 . . . 3H **67**
Charnwood Av. SW19 . . . 2J **153**
Charnwood Cl. KT3: N Mald . . . 4A **152**
Charnwood Dr. E18 . . . 3K **51**
Charnwood Gdns. E14 . . . 4C **104**
Charnwood Pl. N20 . . . 3F **31**
Charnwood Rd. SE25 . . . 5D **156**
UB10: Hil . . . 2C **74**
Charnwood St. E5 . . . 2H **67**
Charrington Bowl . . . 2H **163**
Charrington Rd. CR0: C'don . . . 2C **168**
Charrington St. NW1 . . . 2H **83**
Charsley Rd. SE6 . . . 2D **140**
Chart Cl. BR2: Brom . . . 1G **159**
CR0: C'don . . . 6J **157**
CR4: Mitc . . . 4D **154**
Charter Av. IG2: Ilf . . . 1H **71**
Charter Bldgs. *SE10* . . . *1D **122***
(off Catherine Gro.)
Charter Ct. KT3: N Mald . . . 3A **152**
N4 . . . 1A **66**
N22 . . . 1H **47**
UB1: S'hall . . . 1E **94**
Charter Cres. TW4: Houn . . . 4C **112**
Charter Dr. DA5: Bexl . . . 7E **126**
Charterhouse . . . 4B **8**
Charter Ho. *SM2: Sutt* . . . *6K **165***
(off Mulgrave Rd.)
WC2 . . . *1F **13***
(off Crown Ct.)
Charterhouse Apartments SW18 . . . 4A **118**
Charterhouse Av. HA0: Wemb . . . 4C **60**
Charterhouse Bldgs. EC1 . . . 4B **8** (4C **84**)
Charterhouse M. EC1 . . . 5B **8** (5B **84**)
Charterhouse Rd. BR6: Chels . . . 3K **173**
E8 . . . 4G **67**
Charterhouse Sq. EC1 . . . 5B **8** (5B **84**)
Charterhouse St. EC1 . . . 6K **7** (5A **84**)
Charteris Community Sports Cen. . . . 1J **81**
Charteris Rd. IG8: Wfd G . . . 7E **36**
N4 . . . 1A **66**
NW6 . . . 1H **81**
Charter Quay *KT1: King T* . . . *2D **150***
(off Wadbrook St.)
Charter Rd. KT1: King T . . . 3H **151**
Charter Rd., The IG8: Wfd G . . . 6B **36**
Charters Cl. SE19 . . . 5E **138**
Charter Sq. KT1: King T . . . 2H **151**
Charter Way N3 . . . 4H **45**
N14 . . . 6B **22**
Chartes Ho. *SE1* . . . *7H **15***
(off Stevens St.)
Chartfield Av. SW15 . . . 5D **116**
Chartfield Sq. SW15 . . . 5F **117**
Chartham Ct. *SW9* . . . *3A **120***
(off Canterbury Cres.)
Chartham Gro. SE27 . . . 3B **138**
Chartham Ho. *SE1* . . . *7F **15***
(off Weston St.)
Chartham Rd. SE25 . . . 3H **157**
Chart Hills Cl. SE28 . . . 6E **90**
Chart Ho. CR4: Mitc . . . 2D **154**
E14 . . . *5D **104***
(off Burrells Wharf Sq.)
Chartley Av. HA7: Stan . . . 6E **26**
NW2 . . . 3A **62**
Charton Cl. DA17: Belv . . . 6F **109**
Chartres Ct. UB6: G'frd . . . 2H **77**
Chartridge *SE17* . . . *6D **102***
(off Westmoreland Rd.)
Chart St. N1 . . . 1F **9** (3D **84**)
Chartwell Bus. Cen. BR1: Brom . . . 3B **160**
Chartwell Cl. CR0: C'don . . . 1D **168**
SE9 . . . 2H **143**
UB6: G'frd . . . 1F **77**
Chartwell Ct. EN5: Barn . . . 4B **20**
IG8: Wfd G . . . 7C **36**
UB3: Hayes . . . 7H **75**
Chartwell Dr. BR6: Farnb . . . 5H **173**
Chartwell Gdns. SM3: Cheam . . . 4G **165**
Chartwell Ho. *W11* . . . *1H **99***
(off Ladbroke Rd.)
Chartwell Lodge BR3: Beck . . . 7C **140**
Chartwell Pl. HA2: Harr . . . 2H **59**
SM3: Cheam . . . 4G **165**
Chartwell Way SE20 . . . 1H **157**
Charville Ct. HA1: Harr . . . 6K **41**
SE10 . . . *6F **105***
(off Trafalgar Gro.)
Charville La. UB4: Hayes . . . 3E **74**
Charville La. W. UB10: Hil . . . 3D **74**
(not continuous)
Charwood SW16 . . . 4A **138**
Chase, The BR1: Brom . . . 3K **159**
DA7: Bex . . . 3H **127**
E12 . . . 4B **70**
HA5: Eastc . . . 6A **40**
HA5: Pinn . . . 4D **40**
HA7: Stan . . . 6F **27**
HA8: Edg . . . 1H **43**
RM1: Rom . . . 3K **55**
Chase, The RM6: Chad H . . . 6E **54**
RM7: Rush G . . . 3K **73**
(not continuous)
SM6: Wall . . . 5J **167**
SW4 . . . 3F **119**
SW16 . . . 7K **137**
SW20 . . . 1G **153**
TW16: Sun . . . 1K **147**
UB10: Ick . . . 5C **56**
Chase Bank Ct. *N14* . . . *6B **22***
(off Avenue Rd.)
Chase Cen., The NW10 . . . 3K **79**
Chase Ct. *SW3* . . . *2E **16***
(off Beaufort Gdns.)
SW20 . . . 2G **153**
TW7: Isle . . . 2A **114**
Chase Ct. Gdns. EN2: Enf . . . 3H **23**
Chase Cross Rd. RM5: Col R . . . 1J **55**
Chasefield Rd. SW17 . . . 4D **136**
Chase Gdns. E4 . . . 4H **35**
TW2: Whitt . . . 7H **113**
Chase Grn. EN2: Enf . . . 3H **23**
Chase Grn. Av. EN2: Enf . . . 2G **23**
Chase Hill EN2: Enf . . . 3H **23**
Chase La. IG2: Ilf . . . 5H **53**
IG6: Ilf . . . 5H **53**
Chaseley Dr. W4 . . . 5H **97**
Chaseley St. E14 . . . 6A **86**
Chasemore Cl. CR4: Mitc . . . 7D **154**
Chasemore Gdns.
CR0: Wadd . . . 5A **168**
Chasemore Ho. *SW6* . . . *7G **99***
(off Williams Cl.)
Chase Ridings EN2: Enf . . . 2F **23**
Chase Rd. N14 . . . 5B **22**
NW10 . . . 4K **79**
Chase Rd. Trad. Est. NW10 . . . 4K **79**
CHASE SIDE . . . 1J **23**
Chase Side EN2: Enf . . . 3H **23**
N14 . . . 6K **21**
Chase Side Av. EN2: Enf . . . 2H **23**
SW20 . . . 1G **153**
Chase Side Cres. EN2: Enf . . . 1H **23**
Chase Side Ind. Est. N14 . . . 7C **22**
Chase Side Pl. EN2: Enf . . . 2H **23**
Chaseville Pde. N21 . . . 5E **22**
Chaseville Pk. Rd. N21 . . . 5D **22**
Chase Way N14 . . . 2A **32**
Chaseway Lodge *E16* . . . *6J **87***
(off Butchers Rd.)
Chaseways Vs. RM5: Col R . . . 1F **55**
Chasewood Av. EN2: Enf . . . 2G **23**
Chasewood Ct. NW7 . . . 5E **28**
Chasewood Pk. HA1: Harr . . . 3K **59**
Chaston Pl. *NW5* . . . *5E **64***
(off Grafton Ter.)
Chater Ho. *E2* . . . *3K **85***
(off Roman Rd.)
Chatfield Rd. CR0: C'don . . . 1B **168**
SW11 . . . 3A **118**
Chatham Av. BR2: Hayes . . . 7H **159**
Chatham Cl. NW11 . . . 5J **45**
SE18 . . . 3F **107**
SM3: Sutt . . . 7H **153**
Chatham Ho. *SM6: Wall* . . . *5F **167***
(off Melbourne Rd.)
Chatham Pl. E9 . . . 6J **67**
Chatham Rd. E17 . . . 3A **50**
E18 . . . 2H **51**
KT1: King T . . . 2G **151**
SW11 . . . 6D **118**
Chatham St. SE17 . . . 4D **102**
Chatsfield Pl. W5 . . . 6E **78**
Chats Palace Arts Cen. . . . 5K **67**
Chatsworth Av. BR1: Brom . . . 4K **141**
DA15: Sidc . . . 1A **144**
HA9: Wemb . . . 5F **61**
NW4 . . . 2E **44**
SW20 . . . 1G **153**
Chatsworth Cl. BR4: W W'ck . . . 2H **171**
NW4 . . . 2E **44**
W4 . . . 6J **97**

Chatsworth Ct. HA7: Stan 5H 27
   SW16 . . . . .3K 155
   W8 . . . . .4J 81
                  (off Pembroke Rd.)
Chatsworth Cres. TW3: Houn 4H 113
Chatsworth Dr. EN1: Enf 7B 24
Chatsworth Est. E5 . . . . .4K 67
Chatsworth Gdns. HA2: Harr 1F 59
   KT3: N Mald 5B 152
   W3 . . . . .1F 97
Chatsworth Ho. BR2: Brom 4J 159
          (off Westmoreland Rd.)
   E16 . . . . .1K 105
                    (off Wesley Av.)
Chatsworth Lodge W4 . . . . .5K 97
                    (off Bourne Rd.)
Chatsworth Pde. BR5: Pet W 5G 161
Chatsworth Pl. CR4: Mitc 3D 154
   TW11: Tedd 4A 132
Chatsworth Ri. W5 . . . . .4F 79
Chatsworth Rd. CR0: C'don 4D 168
   E5 . . . . .3J 67
   E15 . . . . .5H 69
   NW2 . . . . .6E 62
   SM3: Cheam 5F 165
   UB4: Yead 4K 75
   W4 . . . . .6J 97
   W5 . . . . .4F 79
Chatsworth Way SE27 . . . . .3B 138
CHATTERN HILL 4D 128
Chattern Hill TW15: Ashf 4D 128
Chattern Rd. TW15: Ashf 4E 128
Chatterton Ct. TW9: Kew 2F 115
Chatterton M. N4 . . . . .3B 66
              (off Chatterton Rd.)
Chatterton Rd. BR2: Brom 4B 160
   N4 . . . . .3B 66
Chatto Rd. SW11 . . . . .5D 118
Chaucer Av. TW4: Cran 2K 111
   TW9: Rich 3G 115
   UB4: Hayes 5J 75
Chaucer Cl. N11 . . . . .5B 32
Chaucer Ct. EN5: New Bar 5E 20
   N16 . . . . .4E 66
   SW17 . . . . .3B 136
           (off Lanesborough Way)
Chaucer Dr. SE1 . . . . .4F 103
Chaucer Gdns. SM1: Sutt 3J 165
Chaucer Grn. CR0: C'don 7H 157
Chaucer Ho. EN5: Barn 4A 20
   SM1: Sutt 3J 165
               (off Chaucer Gdns.)
   SW1 . . . . .6A 18
                (off Churchill Gdns.)
Chaucer Mans. W14 . . . . .6G 99
             (off Queen's Club Gdns.)
Chaucer Rd. DA15: Sidc 1C 144
   DA16: Well 1J 125
   E7 . . . . .6J 69
   E11 . . . . .6J 51
   E17 . . . . .2E 50
   SE24 . . . . .5A 120
   SM1: Sutt 4J 165
   TW15: Ashf 4A 128
   W3 . . . . .1J 97
Chaucer Way SW19 . . . . .5B 136
Chaulden Ho. EC1 . . . . .2F 9
                (off Cranwood St.)
Chauncey Cl. N9 . . . . .3B 34
Chaundrye Cl. SE9 . . . . .6D 124
Chauntler Cl. E16 . . . . .6K 87
Chaville Ct. N11 . . . . .4K 31
Chaville Way N3 .1J 45
Cheadle Ct. NW8 . . . . .4B 4
              (off Henderson Dr.)
Cheadle Ho. E14 . . . . .6B 86
             (off Copenhagen Pl.)
CHEAM 6G 165
Cheam Comn. Rd. KT4: Wor Pk 2D 164
Cheam Leisure Cen. 4F 165
Cheam Mans. SM3: Cheam 7G 165
Cheam Pk. Way SM3: Cheam 6G 165

Cheam Rd. SM1: Sutt 6H 165
   SM2: Cheam 7F 165
Cheam St. SE15 . . . . .3J 121
CHEAM VILLAGE 6G 165
Cheapside EC2 . . . . .1D 14 (6C 84)
   N13 . . . . .4J 33
   N22 . . . . .3A 48
Chearsley SE17 .4C 102
               (off Deacon Way)
Cheddar Cl. N11 . . . . .6J 31
Cheddar Waye UB4: Yead 6K 75
Cheddington Ho. E2 . . . . .1G 85
              (off Whiston Rd.)
Cheddington Rd. N18 . . . . .3K 33
Chedworth Cl. E16 . . . . .6H 87
Chedworth Ho. N15 . . . . .4D 48
              (off West Grn. Rd.)
Cheeseman Cl. TW12: Hamp 6C 130
Cheesemans Ter. W14 . . . . .5H 99
              (not continuous)
Cheethams Rd. E12 . . . . .3C 70
Cheffery Ct. TW15: Ashf 6D 128
Cheldon Av. NW7 . . . . .7A 30
Chelford Rd. BR1: Brom 5F 141
Chelmer Cres. IG11: Bark 2B 90
Chelmer Rd. E9 .5K 67
Chelmsford Cl. E6 . . . . .6D 88
   W6 . . . . .6F 99
Chelmsford Ct. N14 . . . . .7C 22
             (off Chelmsford Rd.)
Chelmsford Gdns. IG1: Ilf 7C 52
Chelmsford Ho. N7 . . . . .4K 65
              (off Holloway Rd.)
Chelmsford Rd. E11 . . . . .1F 69
   E17 . . . . .6C 50
   E18 . . . . .1H 51
   N14 . . . . .7B 22
Chelmsford Sq. NW10 . . . . .1E 80
Chelmsine Ct. HA4: Ruis 5E 38
CHELSEA 6D 16 (5C 100)
Chelsea Barracks 5E 100
Chelsea Bri. SW1 . . . . .7J 17 (6F 101)
Chelsea Bri. Rd. SW1 . . . . . . .5G 17 (5E 100)
Chelsea Bri. Wharf SW8 . . . . .6F 101
Chelsea Cinema 6D 16 (5C 100)
Chelsea Cloisters SW3 . . . . . .4D 16 (4C 100)
Chelsea Ct. HA8: Edg 2G 43
   KT4: Wor Pk 7C 152
   NW10 . . . . .1K 79
   TW12: Ham H 5G 131
Chelsea Ct. BR1: Brom 3C 160
              (off Holmdene Ct.)
   SW3 . . . . .7G 17
             (off Embankment Gdns.)
Chelsea Cres. NW2 . . . . .6H 63
   SW10 . . . . .1A 118
Chelsea Emb. SW3 . . . . .7D 16 (6C 100)
Chelsea Farm Ho. Studios SW10 . . . .6B 100
              (off Cremorne Est.)
Chelsea FC 7K 99
Chelsea Flds. SW19 . . . . .1B 154
Chelsea Gdns. SM3: Cheam 4G 165
   SW1 . . . . .6H 17 (5E 100)
   W13 . . . . .5K 77
Chelsea Ga. SW1 . . . . .6H 17
Chelsea Harbour SW10 . . . . .1A 118
Chelsea Harbour Design Cen.
   SW10 . . . . .1A 118
           (off Chelsea Harbour Dr.)
Chelsea Harbour Dr. SW10 . . . . .1A 118
Chelsea Lodge SW3 . . . . .7F 17
                (off Tite St.)
Chelsea Mnr. Ct. SW3 . . . . . . .7D 16 (6C 100)
Chelsea Mnr. Gdns. SW3 . . . . .6D 16 (5C 100)
Chelsea Mnr. St. SW3 . . . . . . .6D 16 (5C 100)
Chelsea Mnr. Studios SW3 . . . . .6D 16
                (off Flood St.)
Chelsea Pk. Gdns. SW3 . . . . . .7A 16 (6B 100)
Chelsea Physic Garden 7E 16 (6D 100)
Chelsea Reach Twr. SW10 . . . . .7B 100
             (off Worlds End Est.)
Chelsea Sports Cen. 6D 16 (5C 100)

Chelsea Sq. SW3 . . . . .5B 16 (5B 100)
Chelsea Studios SW6 . . . . .7K 99
                (off Fulham Rd.)
Chelsea Theatre, The 7A 100
Chelsea Towers SW3 . . . . .7D 16
Chelsea Village SW6 . . . . .7K 99
                (off Fulham Rd.)
Chelsea Vista SW6 . . . . .1A 118
Chelsea Wharf SW10 . . . . .7B 100
                (off Lots Rd.)
Chelsfield Av. N9 . . . . .7E 24
Chelsfield Gdns. SE26 . . . . .3J 139
Chelsfield Grn. N9 . . . . .7E 24
               (not continuous)
Chelsfield Ho. SE17 . . . . .4E 102
              (off Massinger St.)
Chelsfield Point E9 . . . . .7K 67
              (off Penshurst Rd.)
Chelsham Rd. CR2: S Croy 7D 168
   SW4 . . . . .3H 119
Chelsiter Ct. DA14: Sidc 4K 143
Chelston App. HA4: Ruis 2J 57
Chelston Rd. HA4: Ruis 1J 57
Chelsworth Dr. SE18 . . . . .6H 107
Cheltenham Av. TW1: Twick 7A 114
Cheltenham Cl. KT3: N Mald 3J 151
   UB5: N'olt 6F 59
Cheltenham Ct. HA7: Stan 5H 27
                (off Marsh La.)
Cheltenham Gdns. E6 . . . . .2C 88
Cheltenham Ho. IG8: Wfd G 6K 37
   UB3: Harl 3E 92
              (off Skipton Dr.)
Cheltenham Pl. HA3: Kenton 4E 42
   W3 . . . . .1H 97
Cheltenham Rd. BR6: Chels 3K 173
   E10 . . . . .6E 50
   SE15 . . . . .4J 121
Cheltenham Ter. SW3 . . . . . . .5F 17 (5D 100)
Chelverton Rd. SW15 . . . . .4F 117
Chelwood N20 . . . . .2G 31
Chelwood Cl. E4 .6J 25
Chelwood Ct. SW11 . . . . .1B 118
              (off Westbridge Rd.)
Chelwood Gdns. TW9: Kew 2G 115
Chelwood Gdns. Pas. TW9: Kew 2G 115
Chelwood Ho. W2 . . . . .1B 10
              (off Gloucester Sq.)
Chelwood Wlk. SE4 . . . . .4A 122
Chenappa Cl. E13 . . . . .3J 87
Chenduit Way HA7: Stan 5E 26
Cheney Ct. SE23 . . . . .1K 139
Cheney Row E17 . . . . .1B 50
Cheneys Rd. E11 . . . . .3G 69
Chenies, The BR6: Pet W 2C 161
   NW1 . . . . .2H 83
              (off Pancras Rd.)
Chenies Ho. W2 .7K 81
              (off Moscow Rd.)
   W4 . . . . .7B 98
              (off Corney Reach Way)
Chenies M. WC1 . . . . .4C 6 (4H 83)
Chenies Pl. NW1 . . . . .2H 83
Chenies St. WC1 . . . . .5C 6 (5H 83)
Cheniston Gdns. W8 . . . . .3K 99
Chenla SE13 . . . . .2D 122
Chepstow Cl. SW15 . . . . .5G 117
   KT8: W Mole 3D 148
Chepstow Cnr. W2 . . . . .6J 81
               (off Chepstow Pl.)
Chepstow Ct. W11 . . . . .7J 81
              (off Chepstow Vs.)
Chepstow Cres. IG3: Ilf 6J 53
   W11 . . . . .7J 81
Chepstow Gdns. UB1: S'hall 6D 76
Chepstow Pl. W2 . . . . .6J 81
Chepstow Ri. CR0: C'don 3E 168
Chepstow Rd. CR0: C'don 3E 168
   W2 . . . . .6J 81
   W7 . . . . .3A 96
Chepstow Vs. W11 . . . . .7H 81
Chequers IG9: Buck H 1E 36

Chequers, The HA5: Pinn 3B 40
Chequers Cl. BR5: St P 4K 161
   NW9 . . . . .3A 44
Chequers Ct. EC1 . . . . .4D 8
              (off Chequer St.)
Chequers Ho. NW8 . . . . .3C 4
              (off Jerome Cres.)
Chequers La. RM9: Dag 4F 91
              (not continuous)
Chequers Pde. N13 . . . . .5H 33
   RM9: Dag 1F 91
   SE9 . . . . .6D 124
              (off Eltham High St.)
Chequer St. EC1 . . . . .4D 8 (4C 84)
Chequers Way N13 . . . . .5G 33
Cherbury Cl. SE28 . . . . .6D 90
Cherbury Ct. N1 .2D 84
              (off St John's Est.)
Cherbury St. N1 .2D 84
Cherchefelle M. HA7: Stan 5G 27
Cherimoya Gdns. KT8: W Mole 3F 149
Cherington Rd. W7 . . . . .1J 95
Cheriton Av. BR2: Brom 5H 159
   IG5: Ilf 2D 52
Cheriton Cl. EN4: Cockf 3J 21
   W5 . . . . .5C 78
Cheriton Ct. SE12 . . . . .7J 123
Cheriton Dr. SE18 . . . . .7H 107
Cheriton Lodge HA4: Ruis 1H 57
Cheriton Sq. SW17 . . . . .2E 136
Cherry Av. UB1: S'hall 1B 94
Cherry Blossom Cl. N13 . . . . .5G 33
Cherry Cl. E17 . . . . .5D 50
   HA4: Ruis 2A 57
   NW9 . . . . .2A 44
   SM4: Mord 4G 153
   SM5: Cars 2D 166
   SW2 . . . . .7A 120
   W5 . . . . .3D 96
Cherrycot Hill BR6: Farnb 4G 173
Cherrycot Ri. BR6: Farnb 4G 173
Cherry Ct. HA5: Pinn 2B 40
   IG6: Ilf 3F 53
   W3 . . . . .1A 98
Cherry Cres. TW8: Bford 7B 96
Cherrydown Av. E4 . . . . .3G 35
Cherrydown Cl. E4 . . . . .3H 35
Cherrydown Rd. DA14: Sidc 2D 144
Cherrydown Wlk. RM7: Mawney 2H 55
Cherry Gdn. Ho. SE16 . . . . .2H 103
              (off Cherry Gdn. St.)
Cherry Gdn. St. SE16 . . . . .2H 103
Cherry Gth. TW8: Bford 5D 96
Cherry Gro. UB3: Hayes 1K 93
   UB8: Hil 5D 74
Cherry Hill EN5: New Bar 6E 20
   HA3: Hrw W 6E 26
Cherry Hill Gdns. CR0: Wadd 4K 167
Cherrylands Cl. NW9 . . . . .2J 61
Cherry La. UB7: W Dray 4B 92
Cherry Laurel Wlk. SW2 . . . . .6K 119
Cherry Orchard SE7 . . . . .6A 106
   UB7: W Dray 2A 92
Cherry Orchard Gdns. CR0: C'don . . .1D 168
   KT8: W Mole 3D 148
Cherry Orchard Rd. BR2: Brom 2C 172
   CR0: C'don 2D 168
   KT8: W Mole 3E 148
Cherry Rd. EN3: Enf W 1D 24
Cherry St. RM7: Rom 5K 55
Cherry Tree Av. UB7: Yiew 6B 74
Cherry Tree Cl. E9 . . . . .1J 85
   HA0: Wemb 4A 60
Cherry Tree Ct. NW1 . . . . .7G 65
              (off Camden Rd.)
   NW9 . . . . .4J 43
   SE7 . . . . .6A 106
Cherry Tree Dr. SW16 . . . . .3J 137
Cherry Tree Hill N2 . . . . .5C 46

Cherry Tree Ho. N22 . . . . .7D **32**
Cherry Tree Ri. IG9: Buck H 4F **37**
Cherry Tree Rd. E15 . . . . .5G **69**
   N2 . . . . .4D **46**
Cherry Tree Ter. SE1 . . . . .7H **15**
   (off Whites Grounds)
Cherry Tree Wlk. BR3: Beck 4B **158**
   BR4: W W'ck 4H **171**
   EC1 . . . . .4D 8 (4C **84**)
Cherry Tree Way E13 . . . . .4B **88**
   HA7: Stan 6G **27**
Cherry Wlk. BR2: Hayes 1J **171**
Cherry Way KT19: Ewe 6K **163**
   TW17: Shep 4F **147**
Cherrywood Cl. E3 . . . . .3A **86**
   KT2: King T 7G **133**
Cherrywood Ct. TW11: Tedd 5A **132**
Cherrywood Dr. SW15 . . . . .5F **117**
Cherrywood La. SM4: Mord 4G **153**
Cherrywood Lodge SE13 . . . . .6F **123**
   (off Birdwood Av.)
Cherry Wood Way W5 . . . . .5G **79**
Chertsey Bri. Rd. KT16: Chert 7A **146**
Chertsey Cl. SW14 . . . . .3H **115**
Chertsey Dr. SM3: Cheam 2G **165**
Chertsey Ho. E2 . . . . .2J **9**
   (off Arnold Cir.)
CHERTSEY MEADS 7A **146**
Chertsey Rd. E11 . . . . .2F **69**
   IG1: Ilf 4H **71**
   TW1: Twick 6K **113**
   TW2: Twick 1G **131**
   TW13: Felt 3G **129**
   TW15: Ashf 7F **129**
   TW16: Sun 7F **129**
   TW17: Shep 7A **146**
Chertsey St. SW17 . . . . .5E **136**
Chervil Cl. TW13: Felt 3J **129**
Chervil M. SE28 . . . . .1B **108**
Cherwell Cl. KT19: Ewe 4J **163**
Cherwell Ct. KT19: Ewe 4J **163**
Cherwell Ho. NW8 . . . . .4B **4**
Cherwell Way HA4: Ruis 6E **38**
Cheryls Cl. SW6 . . . . .1K **117**
Cheseman St. SE26 . . . . .3H **139**
Chesfield Rd. KT2: King T 7E **132**
Chesham Av. BR5: Pet W 6F **161**
Chesham Cl. RM7: Rom 4K **55**
   SW1 . . . . .2G **17**
Chesham Cres. SE20 . . . . .1J **157**
Chesham Flats W1 . . . . .2H **11**
   (off Brown Hart Gdns.)
Chesham Ho. SE8 . . . . .1C **122**
   (off Brookmill Rd.)
Chesham M. SW1 . . . . .1G **17**
Chesham Pl. SW1 . . . . .2G 17 (3E **100**)
   (not continuous)
Chesham Rd. KT1: King T 2G **151**
   SE20 . . . . .2J **157**
   SW19 . . . . .5B **136**
Chesham St. NW10 . . . . .3K **61**
   SW1 . . . . .2G 17 (3E **100**)
Chesham Ter. W13 . . . . .2B **96**
Cheshire Cl. CR4: Mitc 3J **155**
   E17 . . . . .1D **50**
   SE4 . . . . .2B **122**
Cheshire Ct. EC4 . . . . .1K **13**
   (off Fleet St.)
Cheshire Gdns. KT9: Chess 6D **162**
Cheshire Ho. N18 . . . . .4C **34**
   SM4: Mord 7K **153**
Cheshire Rd. N22 . . . . .7E **32**
Cheshire St. E2 . . . . .3K 9 (4F **85**)
Cheshir Ho. NW4 . . . . .4E **44**
Chesholm Rd. N16 . . . . .3E **66**
Cheshunt Ho. NW6 . . . . .1K **81**
   (off Mortimer Cres.)
Cheshunt Rd. DA17: Belv 5G **109**
   E7 . . . . .6K **69**
Chesil Ct. E2 .2J **85**
   SW3 . . . . .7D 16 (6C **100**)
Chesilton Rd. SW6 . . . . .1H **117**
Chesil Way UB4: Hayes 3H **75**

Chesley Gdns. E6 . . . . .2B **88**
Chesney Ct. W9 . . . . .4J **81**
   (off Shirland Rd.)
Chesney Cres. CR0: New Ad 7E **170**
Chesney Ho. SE13 . . . . .4F **123**
   (off Mercator Rd.)
Chesney St. SW11 . . . . .1E **118**
Chesnut Gro. N17 . . . . .3F **49**
Chesnut Rd. N17 . . . . .3F **49**
Chesnut Row N3 . . . . .7D **30**
   (off Nether St.)
Chessell Cl. CR7: Thor H 4B **156**
Chessholme Ct. TW16: Sun 7G **129**
   (off Scotts Av.)
Chessholme Rd. TW15: Ashf 6E **128**
Chessing Ct. N2 . . . . .3D **46**
   (off Fortis Grn.)
CHESSINGTON 5F **163**
Chessington Av. DA7: Bex 7E **108**
   N3 . . . . .3G **45**
Chessington Cl. KT19: Ewe 6J **163**
Chessington Cl. HA5: Pinn 4D **40**
   N3 . . . . .3H **45**
   (off Charter Way)
Chessington Hall Gdns.
   KT9: Chess 7D **162**
Chessington Hill Pk.
   KT9: Chess 5G **163**
Chessington Ho. SW8 . . . . .2H **119**
Chessington Lodge N3 . . . . .3H **45**
Chessington Mans. E10 . . . . .7C **50**
   E11 . . . . .7G **51**
Chessington Pde. KT9: Chess 6D **162**
Chessington Pk. KT9: Chess 4G **163**
Chessington Rd. KT17: Ewe 7B **164**
   KT19: Ewe 6G **163**
Chessington Sports Cen. 7D **162**
Chessington Trade Pk. KT9: Chess . .4G **163**
Chessington Way BR4: W W'ck 2D **170**
Chesson Rd. W14 . . . . .6H **99**
Chesswood Way HA5: Pinn 2B **40**
Chestbrook Ct. EN1: Enf 5K **23**
   (off Forsyth Pl.)
Chester Av. TW2: Whitt 1D **130**
   TW10: Rich 6F **115**
Chester Cl. SM1: Sutt 2J **165**
   SW1 . . . . .7J 11 (2F **101**)
   SW13 . . . . .3D **116**
   TW10: Rich 6F **115**
   TW15: Ashf 5F **129**
   UB8: Hil .6D **74**
Chester Cl. Nth. NW1 . . . . .1K 5 (3F **83**)
Chester Cl. Sth. NW1 . . . . .2K 5 (3F **83**)
Chester Cotts. SW1 . . . . .4G **17**
Chester Ct. BR2: Brom 4H **159**
   (off Durham Rd.)
   NW1 . . . . .1K 5 (3F **83**)
   (not continuous)
   SE5 . . . . .7D **102**
   (off Lomond Gro.)
   SE8 . . . . .5K **103**
   W6 . . . . .4F **99**
   (off Wolverton Gdns.)
Chester Cres. E8 . . . . .5F **67**
Chester Dr. HA2: Harr 6D **40**
Chesterfield Cl. SE13 . . . . .2F **123**
Chesterfield Ct. KT5: Surb 5E **150**
   (off Cranes Pk.)
Chesterfield Dr. KT10: Hin W 2A **162**
Chesterfield Flats EN5: Barn 5A **20**
   (off Bells Hill)
Chesterfield Gdns. N4 . . . . .5B **48**
   SE10 . . . . .1F **123**
   W1 . . . . .4J 11 (1F **101**)
Chesterfield Gro. SE22 . . . . .5F **121**
Chesterfield Hill W1 . . . . . .4J 11 (1F **101**)
Chesterfield Ho. W1 . . . . .4H **11**
   (off Chesterfield Gdns.)
Chesterfield Lodge N21 . . . . .7E **22**
   (off Church Hill)
Chesterfield M. N4 . . . . .5B **48**
   TW15: Ashf 4A **128**

Chesterfield Rd. E10 . . . . .6E **50**
   EN5: Barn 5A **20**
   KT19: Ewe 7K **163**
   N3 . . . . .6D **30**
   TW15: Ashf 4A **128**
   W4 . . . . .6J **97**
Chesterfield St. W1 . . . . . . .4J 11 (1F **101**)
Chesterfield Wlk. SE10 . . . . .1F **123**
Chesterfield Way SE15 . . . . .7J **103**
   UB3: Hayes 2J **93**
Chesterford Gdns. NW3 . . . . .4K **63**
Chesterford Ho. SE18 . . . . .1B **124**
   (off Tellson Av.)
Chesterford Rd. E12 . . . . .5D **70**
Chester Gdns. EN3: Pond E 6C **24**
   SM4: Mord 6A **154**
   W13 . . . . .6B **78**
Chester Ga. NW1 . . . . .2J 5 (3F **83**)
Chester Ho. N10 . . . . .2F **47**
   SE8 . . . . .6B **104**
   SW1 . . . . .3J **17**
   (off Eccleston Pl.)
   SW9 . . . . .7A **102**
   (off Cranmer Rd.)
Chesterman Ct. W4 . . . . .7A **98**
   (off Corney Reach Way)
Chester M. E17 . . . . .2C **50**
   SW1 . . . . .1J 17 (3F **101**)
Chester Pl. NW1 . . . . .1J 5 (3E **83**)
Chester Rd. DA15: Sidc 5J **125**
   (not continuous)
   E7 . . . . .7B **70**
   E11 . . . . .6K **51**
   E16 . . . . .4G **87**
   E17 . . . . .5K **49**
   HA6: Nwood 1H **39**
   IG3: Ilf 1K **71**
   IG7: Chig 3K **37**
   N9 . . . . .1C **34**
   N17 . . . . .3D **48**
   N19 . . . . .2F **65**
   NW1 . . . . .2H 5 (3E **82**)
   SW19 . . . . .6E **134**
   TW4: Houn 3K **111**
   TW6: H'row A 3C **110**
Chester Row SW1 . . . . .4G 17 (4E **100**)
Chesters, The KT3: N Mald 1A **152**
Chester Sq. SW1 . . . . .3H 17 (4E **100**)
Chester Sq. M. SW1 . . . . .2J **17**
Chester St. E2 . . . . .4G **85**
   SW1 . . . . .1H 17 (3E **100**)
Chester Ter. IG11: Bark 6H **71**
   NW1 . . . . .1J 5 (3F **83**)
   (not continuous)
Chesterton Cl. SW18 . . . . .5J **117**
   UB6: G'frd 2F **77**
Chesterton Ct. W3 . . . . .3H **97**
   (off Bollo Bri. Rd.)
   W5 . . . . .5D **78**
Chesterton Dr. TW19: Stanw 1B **128**
Chesterton Ho. CR0: C'don 4D **168**
   (off Heathfield Rd.)
   SW11 . . . . .3B **118**
   (off Ingrave St.)
   W10 . . . . .5G **81**
   (off Portobello Rd.)
Chesterton Rd. E13 . . . . .3J **87**
   W10 . . . . .5F **81**
Chesterton Sq. W8 . . . . .4J **99**
Chesterton Ter. E13 . . . . .3J **87**
   KT1: King T 2G **151**
Chester Way SE11 . . . . .4K 19 (4A **102**)
Chesthunte Rd. N17 . . . . .1C **48**
Chestlands Ct. UB10: Hil 6C **56**
Chestnut All. SW6 . . . . .6H **99**
Chestnut Av. BR4: W W'ck 5G **171**
   E7 . . . . .4K **69**
   E12 . . . . .2C **70**
   HA0: Wemb 5B **60**
   HA6: Nwood 2H **39**
   HA8: Edg 6K **27**
   IG9: Buck H 3G **37**

Chestnut Av. KT8: E Mos 3K **149**
   KT10: Esh 7H **149**
   KT19: Ewe 4A **164**
   N8 . . . . .5J **47**
   SW14 . . . . .3K **115**
   TW8: Bford 4D **96**
   TW11: Tedd 2K **149**
   TW12: Hamp 7E **130**
   UB7: View 7B **74**
Chestnut Av. Nth. E17 . . . . .4F **51**
Chestnut Av. Sth. E17 . . . . .5E **50**
Chestnut Cl. BR6: Chels 5K **173**
   DA15: Sidc 1A **144**
   IG9: Buck H 3G **37**
   N14 . . . . .5B **22**
   N16 . . . . .2D **66**
   SE6 . . . . .5E **140**
   SE14 . . . . .1B **122**
   SM5: Cars 1D **166**
   SW16 . . . . .4A **138**
   TW15: Ashf 4D **128**
   TW16: Sun 6H **129**
   UB3: Hayes 7G **75**
   UB7: Harl, Sip 7D **92**
Chestnut Ct. CR2: S Croy 4C **168**
   (off Bramley Hill)
   N8 . . . . .5J **47**
   SW6 . . . . .6H **99**
   TW13: Hanw 5B **130**
   W8 . . . . .3K **99**
   (off Abbots Wlk.)
Chestnut Dr. DA7: Bex 3D **126**
   E11 . . . . .6J **51**
   HA3: Hrw W 7E **26**
   HA5: Pinn 6B **40**
Chestnut Gro. CR2: Sels 7H **169**
   CR4: Mitc 5H **155**
   DA2: Dart 4K **145**
   EN4: E Barn 5J **21**
   HA0: Wemb 5B **60**
   KT3: N Mald 3K **151**
   SE20 . . . . .7H **139**
   SW12 . . . . .7E **118**
   TW7: Isle 4A **114**
   W5 . . . . .3D **96**
Chestnut Ho. E3 . . . . .1B **86**
   (off Sycamore Av.)
   SW15 . . . . .4B **116**
   W4 . . . . .4A **98**
   (off The Orchard)
Chestnut La. N20 . . . . .1B **30**
Chestnut Pl. SE26 . . . . .4F **139**
Chestnut Rd. SE18 . . . . .6H **107**
   WD23: Bush 1A **26**
Chestnut Rd. KT2: King T 7E **132**
   SE27 . . . . .3B **138**
   SW20 . . . . .2F **153**
   TW2: Twick 2J **131**
   TW15: Ashf 4D **128**
Chestnuts, The HA5: Hat E 1D **40**
   N5 . . . . .4C **66**
   (off Highbury Grange)
   UB10: Uxb 7A **56**
Chestnut Ter. SM1: Sutt 4K **165**
Chestnut Wlk. IG8: Wfd G 5D **36**
   TW17: Shep 4G **147**
Chestnut Way TW13: Felt 3K **129**
Cheston Av. CR0: C'don 2A **170**
Chestwood Gro. UB10: Hil 7B **56**
Chettle Cl. SE1 . . . . .3D **102**
   (off Spurgeon St.)
Chettle Ct. N8 . . . . .6A **48**
Chetwode Ho. NW8 . . . . .3C **4**
Chetwode Rd. SW17 . . . . .3D **136**
Chetwood Wlk. E6 . . . . .5C **88**
   (off Greenwich Cres.)
Chetwynd Av. EN4: E Barn 1J **31**
Chetwynd Dr. UB10: Hil 2B **74**
Chetwynd Rd. NW5 . . . . .4F **65**
Chetwynd Vs. NW5 . . . . .4F **65**
   (off Chetwynd Rd.)
Chevalier Cl. HA7: Stan 4K **27**

Cheval Pl.—Cholmeley Cl.

Cheval Pl. SW7 1D **16** (3C **100**)
Cheval St. E14 3C **104**
Cheveney Wlk. BR2: Brom 3J **159**
Chevening Rd. NW6 2F **81**
SE10 5H **105**
SE19 6D **138**
Chevenings, The DA14: Sidc 3C **144**
Cheverell Ho. *E2* *2G* ***85***
(off Pritchard's Rd.)
Cheverton Rd. N19 1H **65**
Chevet St. E9 5A **68**
Chevington NW2 6H **63**
Cheviot *N17* *7C* ***34***
(off Northumberland Gro.)
Cheviot Cl. DA7: Bex 2K **127**
EN1: Enf 2J **23**
UB3: Harl 7F **93**
Cheviot Ct. *SE14* *6J* ***103***
(off Avonley Rd.)
UB2: S'hall 4F **95**
Cheviot Gdns. NW2 2F **63**
SE27 4B **138**
Cheviot Ga. NW2 2G **63**
Cheviot Ho. *E1* *6H* ***85***
(off Commercial Rd.)
Cheviot Rd. SE27 5A **138**
Cheviot Way IG2: Ilf 4J **53**
Chevron Cl. E16 6J **87**
Chevy Rd. UB2: S'hall 2G **95**
Chewton Rd. E17 4A **50**
Cheylesmore Ho. *SW1* *5J* ***17***
(off Ebury Bri. Rd.)
Cheyne Av. E18 3H **51**
TW2: Whitt 1D **130**
Cheyne Cl. BR2: Brom 3C **172**
NW4 5E **44**
Cheyne Ct. SW3 7E **16** (6D **100**)
Cheyne Gdns. SW3 7D **16** (6C **100**)
Cheyne Hill KT5: Surb 4F **151**
Cheyne M. SW3 7D **16** (6C **100**)
Cheyne Pk. Dr. BR4: W W'ck 3E **170**
Cheyne Path W7 5K **77**
Cheyne Pl. SW3 7E **16** (6D **100**)
Cheyne Rd. TW15: Ashf 7F **129**
Cheyne Row SW3 7C **16** (6C **100**)
Cheyne Wlk. CR0: C'don 2G **169**
N21 5G **23**
NW4 6E **44**
SW3 7C **16** (6B **100**)
(not continuous)
SW10 7B **100**
Cheyneys Av. HA8: Edg 6J **27**
Chichele Gdns. CR0: C'don 4E **168**
Chichele Ho. HA8: Edg 4A **28**
Chichele Rd. NW2 5F **63**
Chicheley Gdns. HA3: Hrw W 7B **26**
(not continuous)
Chicheley Rd. HA3: Hrw W 7B **26**
Chicheley St. SE1 6H **13** (2K **101**)
Chichester Av. HA4: Ruis 2F **57**
Chichester Cl. E6 6C **88**
SE3 7A **106**
TW12: Hamp 6D **130**
Chichester Ct. HA7: Stan 3E **42**
HA8: Edg *6B* ***28***
(off Whitchurch La.)
KT17: Ewe 7B **164**
NW1 *7G* ***65***
(off Royal Coll. St.)
TW19: Stanw 1A **128**
UB5: N'olt 1D **76**
Chichester Gdns. IG1: Ilf 7C **52**
Chichester Ho. NW6 2J **81**
SW9 *7A* ***102***
(off Cranmer Rd.)
Chichester M. SE27 4A **138**
Chichester Rents WC2 7J **7**
Chichester Rd. CR0: C'don 3E **168**
E11 3G **69**
N9 1B **34**
NW6 2J **81**
W2 5K **81**
Chichester St. SW1 6B **18** (5G **101**)
Chichester Way E14 4F **105**
TW14: Felt 7A **112**
Chicken Shed Theatre 5K **21**
Chicksand Ho. *E1* *5K* ***9***
(off Chicksand St.)
Chicksand St. E1 6K **9** (5F **85**)
(not continuous)
Chiddingfold N12 3D **30**
Chiddingstone SE13 5E **122**
Chiddingstone Av. DA7: Bex 7F **109**
Chiddingstone St. SW6 2J **117**
Chieveley Pde. *DA7: Bex* *4H* ***127***
(off Chieveley Rd.)
DA7: Bex 3H **127**
(Mayplace Rd. E.)
Chieveley Rd. DA7: Bex 4H **127**
Chignell Pl. W13 1A **96**
CHIGWELL 3K **37**
Chigwell Hill E1 7H **85**
Chigwell Hurst Ct. HA5: Pinn 3B **40**
Chigwell Pk. IG7: Chig 4K **37**
Chigwell Pk. Dr. IG7: Chig 4K **37**
Chigwell Ri. IG7: Chig 2K **37**
Chigwell Rd. E18 3K **51**
IG8: Wfd G 2A **52**
Chilcombe Ho. *SW15* *7C* ***116***
(off Fontley Way)
Chilcot Cl. E14 6D **86**
Chilcott Cl. HA0: Wemb 4C **60**
Childebert Rd. SW17 2F **137**
Childeric Rd. SE14 7A **104**
Childerley *KT1: King T* *3G* ***151***
(off Burritt Rd.)
Childerley St. SW6 1G **117**
Childers, The IG8: Wfd G 5J **37**
Childers St. SE8 6A **104**
Child La. SE10 3H **105**
Children's Discovery Cen. 7F **69**
Childs Ct. UB3: Hayes 7J **75**
CHILD'S HILL 3H **63**
Childs Hill Wlk. *NW2* *3H* ***63***
(off Cricklewood La.)
Child's La. SE19 6E **138**
Child's M. *SW5* *4J* ***99***
(off Child's Pl.)
Child's Pl. SW5 4J **99**
Child's St. SW5 4J **99**
Child's Wlk. *SW5* *4J* ***99***
(off Child's St.)
Childs Way NW11 5H **45**
Chilham Cl. DA5: Bexl 7F **127**
UB6: G'frd 2A **78**
Chilham Ho. SE1 3D **102**
SE15 6J **103**
Chilham Rd. SE9 4C **142**
Chilham Way BR2: Hayes 7J **159**
Chilianwalla Memorial 7G **17** (6E **100**)
Chillerton Rd. SW17 5E **136**
Chillingford Ho. SW17 4A **136**
Chillington Dr. SW11 4B **118**
Chillingworth Gdns. TW1: Twick 3K **131**
Chillingworth Rd. N7 5A **66**
Chilmark Gdns. KT3: N Mald 6C **152**
Chilmark Rd. SW16 2H **155**
Chiltern Av. TW2: Whitt 1E **130**
Chiltern Cl. CR0: C'don 3E **168**
DA7: Bex 1K **127**
KT4: Wor Pk 1E **164**
UB10: Ick 2C **56**
Chiltern Ct. *BR2: Brom* *2C* ***172***
(off Gravel Rd.)
EN5: New Bar 5F **21**
HA1: Harr 5H **41**
N10 2E **46**
NW1 *4F* ***5***
(off Baker St.)
SE14 *7J* ***103***
(off Avonley Rd.)
UB8: Hil 4D **74**
Chiltern Dene EN2: Enf 4E **22**
Chiltern Dr. KT5: Surb 6G **151**
Chiltern Gdns. BR2: Brom 4H **159**
NW2 3F **63**
Chiltern Ho. N9 3B **34**
SE17 *6D* ***102***
(off Portland St.)
W5 5E **78**
W10 *5G* ***81***
(off Telford Rd.)
Chiltern Rd. E3 4C **86**
HA5: Eastc 5A **40**
IG2: Ilf 5J **53**
Chilterns, The *BR1: Brom* *2K* ***159***
(off Murray Av.)
Chiltern St. W1 5G **5** (5E **82**)
Chiltern Way IG8: Wfd G 3D **36**
Chilthorne Cl. SE6 7B **122**
Chilton Av. W5 4D **96**
Chilton Ct. *N22* *7D* ***32***
(off Truro Rd.)
Chilton Gro. SE8 4K **103**
Chiltonian Ind. Est. SE12 6H **123**
Chilton Rd. HA8: Edg 6B **28**
TW9: Rich 3G **115**
Chiltons, The E18 2J **51**
Chilton St. E2 3K **9** (4F **85**)
Chilvers Cl. TW2: Twick 2J **131**
Chilver St. SE10 5H **105**
Chilworth Ct. SW19 1F **135**
Chilworth Gdns. SM1: Sutt 3A **166**
Chilworth M. W2 1A **10** (6B **82**)
Chilworth St. W2 1A **10** (6A **82**)
Chimes Av. N13 5F **33**
Chimes Ho. BR3: Beck 1A **158**
Chimney Ct. *E1* *1H* ***103***
(off Brewhouse La.)
China Ct. *E1* *1H* ***103***
(off Asher Way)
China Hall M. SE16 3J **103**
China M. SW2 7K **119**
China Town *7H* ***83***
(off Gerrard St.)
China Wlk. SE11 4K **101**
China Wharf SE1 6K **15** (2G **103**)
Chinbrook Cres. SE12 3K **141**
Chinbrook Rd. SE12 3K **141**
Chinchilla Dr. TW4: Houn 2A **112**
Chine, The HA0: Wemb 5B **60**
N10 4G **47**
N21 6G **23**
Ching Ct. *WC2* *1E* ***12***
(off Monmouth St.)
Chingdale Rd. E4 3B **36**
CHINGFORD 1K **35**
Chingford Av. E4 3H **35**
CHINGFORD GREEN 7K **25**
CHINGFORD HATCH 4A **36**
Chingford Ind. Cen. E4 5F **35**
Chingford La. IG8: Wfd G 4B **36**
CHINGFORD MOUNT 4H **35**
Chingford Mt. Rd. E4 4H **35**
Chingford Rd. E4 6H **35**
E17 1D **50**
Chingley Cl. BR1: Brom 6G **141**
Ching Way E4 6G **35**
(not continuous)
Chinnery Cl. EN1: Enf 1A **24**
Chinnock's Wharf *E14* *7A* ***86***
(off Narrow St.)
Chinnor Cres. UB6: G'frd 2F **77**
Chipka St. E14 2E **104**
(not continuous)
Chipley St. SE14 6A **104**
Chipmunk Gro. UB5: N'olt 3C **76**
Chippendale All. UB8: Uxb 7A **56**
Chippendale Ho. *SW1* *6K* ***17***
(off Churchill Gdns.)
Chippendale St. E5 3K **67**
Chippendale Waye UB8: Uxb 7A **56**
Chippenham *KT1: King T* *2F* ***151***
(off Excelsior Cl.)
Chippenham Av. HA9: Wemb 5H **61**
Chippenham Cl. HA5: Eastc 4H **39**
Chippenham Gdns. NW6 3J **81**
Chippenham M. W9 4J **81**
Chippenham Rd. W9 4J **81**
Chipperfield Ho. *SW3* *5C* ***16***
(off Cale St.)
Chipperfield Rd. BR5: St P 7A **144**
(not continuous)
CHIPPING BARNET 4B **20**
Chipping Cl. EN5: Barn 3B **20**
Chipstead Av. CR7: Thor H 4B **156**
Chipstead Cl. SE19 7F **139**
SM2: Sutt 7K **165**
Chipstead Gdns. NW2 2D **62**
Chipstead St. SW6 1J **117**
Chip St. SW4 3H **119**
Chirk Cl. UB4: Yead 4C **76**
Chisenhale Rd. E3 2A **86**
Chisholm Ct. W6 5C **98**
Chisholm Rd. CR0: C'don 2E **168**
TW10: Rich 6F **115**
Chisledon Wlk. *E9* *6B* ***68***
(off Osborne Rd.)
CHISLEHURST 6F **143**
Chislehurst Av. N12 7F **31**
Chislehurst Caves 1E **160**
Chislehurst Rd. BR1: Brom 2B **160**
BR5: Pet W 4J **161**
BR6: Orp, Pet W, St M Cry 4J **161**
BR7: Chst 2B **160**
DA14: Sidc 5A **144**
TW10: Rich 5E **114**
CHISLEHURST WEST 5E **142**
Chislet Cl. BR3: Beck 7C **140**
Chisley Rd. N15 6E **48**
Chiswell Sq. SE3 2K **123**
Chiswell St. EC1 5E **8** (5C **84**)
SE5 *7D* ***102***
(off Edmund St.)
CHISWICK 5K **97**
Chiswick Bri. SW14 2J **115**
Chiswick Cl. CR0: Bedd 3K **167**
Chiswick Comn. Rd. W4 4K **97**
Chiswick Community Sports Hall 7K **97**
Chiswick Ct. HA5: Pinn 3D **40**
W4 4H **97**
Chiswick High Rd. TW8: Bford, Lon 5G **97**
(not continuous)
W4 5H **97**
Chiswick House 6A **98**
Chiswick La. W4 5A **98**
Chiswick La. Sth. W4 6B **98**
Chiswick Mall W4 6B **98**
W6 5C **98**
Chiswick Pk. W4 4H **97**
Chiswick Plaza W4 6J **97**
Chiswick Quay W4 1J **115**
Chiswick Rd. N9 2B **34**
W4 4J **97**
CHISWICK RDBT. 5G **97**
Chiswick Sq. W4 6A **98**
Chiswick Staithe W4 1J **115**
Chiswick Ter. *W4* *4J* ***97***
(off Chiswick Rd.)
Chiswick Village W4 6G **97**
Chiswick Wharf W4 6B **98**
Chitterfield Ga. UB7: Sip 7C **92**
Chitty's La. RM8: Dag 2D **72**
Chitty St. W1 5B **6** (5G **83**)
Chivalry Rd. SW11 5C **118**
Chivelston SW19 1F **135**
Chivenor Gro. KT2: King T 5D **132**
Chivers Rd. E4 3J **35**
Choats Mnr. Way RM9: Dag 2E **90**
Choats Rd. IG11: Bark 2C **90**
RM9: Bark, Dag 2C **90**
Chobham Gdns. SW19 2F **135**
Chobham Rd. E15 5F **69**
Chocolate Studios *N1* *1E* ***8***
(off Shepherdess Pl.)
Choice Vw. *IG1: Ilf* *2G* ***71***
(off Axon Pl.)
Cholmeley Cl. N6 7F **47**

Cholmeley Cres. N6 . . . 7F 47
Cholmeley Lodge N6 . . . 1F 65
Cholmeley Pk. N6 . . . 1F 65
Cholmley Gdns. NW6 . . . 5J 63
Cholmley Rd. KT7: T Ditt . . . 6B 150
Cholmley Ter. KT7: T Ditt . . . 7B 150
(off Portsmouth Rd.)
Cholmley Vs. KT7: T Ditt . . . 6B 150
(off Portsmouth Rd.)
Cholmondeley Av. NW10 . . . 2C 80
Cholmondeley Wlk. TW9: Rich . . . 5C 114
(not continuous)
Choppin's Ct. E1 . . . 1H 103
Chopwell Cl. E15 . . . 7F 69
Chorleywood Cres. BR5: St P . . . 2K 161
Choudhury Mans. N1 . . . 7J 65
(off Pembroke St.)
Choumert Gro. SE15 . . . 2G 121
Choumert M. SE15 . . . 2G 121
Choumert Rd. SE15 . . . 3F 121
Choumert Sq. SE15 . . . 2G 121
Chow Sq. E8 . . . 5F 67
Chrisp Ho. SE10 . . . 6G 105
(off Maze Hill)
Chrisp St. E14 . . . 5D 86
(not continuous)
Christabel Cl. TW7: Isle . . . 3J 113
Christchurch Av. DA8: Erith . . . 6K 109
HA0: Wemb . . . 6E 60
HA3: Kenton, W'stone . . . 4K 41
N12 . . . 6F 31
NW6 . . . 1F 81
TW11: Tedd . . . 5A 132
Christchurch Cl. EN2: Enf . . . 2H 23
N12 . . . 7G 31
SW19 . . . 7B 136
Christ Chu. Ct. NW10 . . . 1A 80
Christchurch Ct. EC4 . . . 7B 8
(off Warwick La.)
UB4: Yead . . . 4A 76
(off Dunedin Way)
Christchurch Flats TW9: Rich . . . 3E 114
Christchurch Gdns. HA3: W'stone . . . 4A 42
Christchurch Grn. HA0: Wemb . . . 6E 60
Christchurch Hill NW3 . . . 3B 64
Christchurch Ho. SW2 . . . 1K 137
(off Christchurch Rd.)
Christchurch La. EN5: Barn . . . 2B 20
Christchurch Lodge EN4: Cockf . . . 4J 21
Christchurch Pk. SM2: Sutt . . . 7A 166
Christchurch Pas. EN5: Barn . . . 2B 20
NW3 . . . 3A 64
Christchurch Path UB3: Harl . . . 3E 92
Christchurch Pl. SW8 . . . 2H 119
Christ Chu. Rd. BR3: Beck . . . 2C 158
KT5: Surb . . . 6F 151
Christchurch Rd. DA15: Sidc . . . 4K 143
IG1: Ilf . . . 1F 71
N8 . . . 6J 47
SW2 . . . 1K 137
SW14 . . . 5H 115
SW19 . . . 7B 136
TW6: H'row A . . . 3C 110
Christ Church Sports Cen. . . . 5G 31
(off Hilton Av.)
Christchurch Sq. E9 . . . 1J 85
Christchurch St. SW3 . . . 7E 16 (6D 100)
Christchurch Ter. SW3 . . . 7E 16
Christchurch Way SE10 . . . 5G 105
Christian Ct. SE16 . . . 1B 104
Christian Flds. SW16 . . . 7A 138
Christian Pl. E1 . . . 6G 85
(off Burslem St.)
Christian St. E1 . . . 6G 85
Christie Ct. N19 . . . 2J 65
Christie Dr. CR0: C'don . . . 5G 157
Christie Gdns. RM6: Chad H . . . 6B 54
Christie Ho. SE10 . . . 5H 105
(off Blackwall La.)
Christie Rd. E9 . . . 6A 68
Christina Sq. N4 . . . 1B 66
Christina St. EC2 . . . 3G 9 (4E 84)
Christine Worsley Cl. N21 . . . 1G 33
Christobel Pankhurst Ct. SE5 . . . 7D 102
(off Brisbane St.)
Christopher Av. W7 . . . 3A 96
Christopher Bell Twr. E3 . . . 2C 86
(off Pancras Way)
Christopher Cl. DA15: Sidc . . . 5K 125
SE16 . . . 2K 103
Christopher Ct. E1 . . . 6G 85
(off Leman St.)
TW15: Ashf . . . 5A 128
Christopher Gdns.
RM9: Dag . . . 5D 72
Christopher Ho. DA15: Sidc . . . 2A 144
(off Station Rd.)
Christopher Pl. N22 . . . 7D 32
(off Myddleton Rd.)
NW1 . . . 1D 6 (3H 83)
Christopher Rd. UB2: S'hall . . . 4K 93
Christophers M. W11 . . . 1G 99
Christopher St. EC2 . . . 4F 9 (4D 84)
Chryssell Rd. SW9 . . . 7A 102
Chubworthy St. SE14 . . . 6A 104
Chudleigh DA14: Sidc . . . 4B 144
Chudleigh Cres. IG3: Ilf . . . 4J 71
Chudleigh Gdns. SM1: Sutt . . . 3A 166
Chudleigh Rd. NW6 . . . 7F 63
SE4 . . . 5B 122
TW2: Twick . . . 6J 113
(not continuous)
Chudleigh St. E1 . . . 6K 85
Chudleigh Way HA4: Ruis . . . 1J 57
Chulsa Rd. SE26 . . . 5H 139
Chumleigh Gdns. SE5 . . . 6E 102
(off Chumleigh St.)
Chumleigh St. SE5 . . . 6E 102
Chumleigh Wlk. KT5: Surb . . . 4F 151
Church All. CR0: C'don . . . 1A 168
Church App. SE21 . . . 3D 138
Church Av. BR3: Beck . . . 1C 158
DA14: Sidc . . . 5A 144
E4 . . . 6A 36
(not continuous)
E12 . . . 3B 70
HA4: Ruis . . . 1F 57
HA5: Pinn . . . 6C 40
N2 . . . 2B 46
NW1 . . . 6F 65
SW14 . . . 3K 115
UB2: S'hall . . . 3C 94
UB5: N'olt . . . 7D 58
Churchbank E17 . . . 4C 50
(off Eastfield Rd.)
Churchbury Cl. EN1: Enf . . . 2K 23
Churchbury La. EN1: Enf . . . 3J 23
Churchbury Rd. EN1: Enf . . . 2K 23
SE9 . . . 7B 124
Church Cloisters EC3 . . . 3G 15
Church Cl. HA6: Nwood . . . 1H 39
HA8: Edg . . . 5D 28
N20 . . . 3H 31
TW3: Houn . . . 2C 112
UB4: Hayes . . . 5F 75
UB7: W Dray . . . 3A 92
W8 . . . 2K 99
Church Ct. EC4 . . . 6A 84
SE16 . . . 2B 104
(off Rotherhithe St.)
TW9: Rich . . . 5D 114
Church Cres. E9 . . . 7K 67
N3 . . . 1H 45
N10 . . . 4F 47
N20 . . . 3H 31
Churchcroft Cl. SW12 . . . 7E 118
Churchdown BR1: Brom . . . 4G 141
Church Dr. BR4: W W'ck . . . 3G 171
HA2: Harr . . . 6E 40
NW9 . . . 1K 61
Church Elm La. RM10: Dag . . . 6G 73
CHURCH END
N3 . . . 1H 45
NW10 . . . 7A 62
Church End E17 . . . 4D 50
NW4 . . . 3D 44
Church Entry EC4 . . . 1B 14
Church Est. Almshouses
TW9: Rich . . . 4F 115
(off Sheen Rd.)
Church Farm House Mus. . . . 3D 44
Church Farm La. SM3: Cheam . . . 6G 165
Church Farm Pool . . . 7J 21
Churchfield Av. N12 . . . 6G 31
Churchfield Cl. HA2: Harr . . . 4G 41
UB3: Hayes . . . 7H 75
Churchfield Ho. W2 . . . 4B 82
(off Hall Pl.)
Churchfield Mans. SW6 . . . 2H 117
(off New Kings Rd.)
Churchfield Pl. TW17: Shep . . . 7D 146
Churchfield Rd. DA16: Well . . . 3A 126
KT12: Walt T . . . 7J 147
W3 . . . 1J 97
W7 . . . 2J 95
W13 . . . 1B 96
Churchfields E18 . . . 1J 51
KT8: W Mole . . . 3E 148
SE10 . . . 6E 104
Churchfields Av. TW13: Hanw . . . 3D 130
Churchfields Rd. BR3: Beck . . . 2K 157
Churchfield Way N12 . . . 6F 31
Church Gdns. HA0: Wemb . . . 4A 60
W5 . . . 2D 96
Church Gth. N19 . . . 2H 65
(off St John's Gro.)
Church Ga. SW6 . . . 3G 117
Church Grn. SW9 . . . 1A 120
UB3: Hayes . . . 6H 75
Church Gro. KT1: Ham W . . . 1C 150
SE13 . . . 5D 122
Church Hill DA1: Cray . . . 4K 127
E17 . . . 4C 50
HA1: Harr . . . 1J 59
N21 . . . 7E 22
SE18 . . . 3D 106
SM5: Cars . . . 5D 166
SW19 . . . 5H 135
Church Hill Rd. E17 . . . 4D 50
EN4: E Barn . . . 6H 21
KT6: Surb . . . 5E 150
SM3: Cheam . . . 3F 165
Church Hill Wood BR5: St M Cry . . . 5K 161
Church Ho. EC1 . . . 3B 8
(off Compton St.)
SW1 . . . 1D 18
(off Gt. Smith St.)
Church Hyde SE18 . . . 6J 107
Churchill Av. HA3: Kenton . . . 6B 42
UB10: Hil . . . 3D 74
Churchill Cl. TW14: Felt . . . 1H 129
UB10: Hil . . . 3D 74
Churchill Ct. BR6: Farnb . . . 5G 173
HA2: Harr . . . 2F 59
(Eastcote Av.)
HA2: Harr . . . 5F 41
(Montrose Ct.)
HA5: Hat E . . . 1C 40
N4 . . . 7A 48
N9 . . . 1K 33
SE18 . . . 4D 106
UB5: N'olt . . . 5E 58
(off Newmarket Av.)
W5 . . . 4F 79
Churchill Gdns. SW1 . . . 6A 18
(not continuous)
W3 . . . 6G 79
Churchill Gdns. Rd. SW1 . . . 6K 17 (5F 101)
Churchill Lodge IG6: Ilf . . . 4G 53
Churchill Mus. (Cabinet War Rooms)
. . . 6D 12 (2H 101)
Churchill Pl. E14 . . . 1D 104
HA1: Harr . . . 4J 41
Churchill Rd. CR2: S Croy . . . 7C 168
E16 . . . 6A 88
HA8: Edg . . . 6A 28
Churchill Rd. NW2 . . . 6D 62
NW5 . . . 4F 65
Churchills M. IG8: Wfd G . . . 6C 36
Churchill Ter. E4 . . . 4H 35
Churchill Theatre . . . 2J 159
Churchill Wlk. E9 . . . 5J 67
Churchill Way BR1: Brom . . . 2J 159
TW16: Sun . . . 5J 129
Churchlands Way KT4: Wor Pk . . . 2F 165
Church La. BR2: Brom . . . 1C 172
BR7: Chst . . . 1G 161
E11 . . . 1G 69
E17 . . . 4D 50
EN1: Enf . . . 3J 23
HA3: W'stone . . . 1K 41
HA5: Pinn . . . 3C 40
KT7: T Ditt . . . 6K 149
KT9: Chess . . . 6F 163
N2 . . . 3B 46
N8 . . . 4K 47
N9 . . . 2B 34
N17 . . . 1E 48
NW9 . . . 6J 43
RM10: Dag . . . 7J 73
SM6: Bedd . . . 3H 167
(not continuous)
SW17 . . . 5D 136
SW19 . . . 1H 153
TW1: Twick . . . 1A 132
TW10: Ham . . . 1E 132
TW11: Tedd . . . 5K 131
UB3: Hayes . . . 6G 75
W5 . . . 2C 96
Churchley Rd. SE26 . . . 4H 139
Church Manorway DA8: Erith . . . 4K 109
SE2 . . . 5A 108
Church Mead SE5 . . . 7C 102
(off Camberwell Rd.)
Churchmead Cl. EN4: E Barn . . . 6H 21
Church Mdw. KT6: Surb . . . 2C 162
Churchmead Rd. NW10 . . . 6C 62
Churchmore Rd. SW16 . . . 1G 155
Church Mt. N2 . . . 5B 46
Church Paddock Ct.
SM6: Bedd . . . 3H 167
Church Pde. TW15: Ashf . . . 4B 128
Church Pas. EC2 . . . 7D 8
(off Gresham St.)
EN5: Barn . . . 3B 20
KT6: Surb . . . 5E 150
TW1: Twick . . . 1B 132
Church Path CR0: C'don . . . 2C 168
CR4: Mitc . . . 3C 154
(not continuous)
E11 . . . 5J 51
E17 . . . 4D 50
N5 . . . 5B 66
N8 . . . 5K 47
(off Tottenham La.)
N12 . . . 3F 31
(Woodside La.)
N12 . . . 4F 31
(Woodside Pk. Rd.)
N17 . . . 7K 33
NW10 . . . 7A 62
SW14 . . . 3K 115
(not continuous)
SW19 . . . 2H 153
(not continuous)
UB1: S'hall . . . 1E 94
UB2: S'hall . . . 3D 94
(not continuous)
W3 . . . 2J 97
(not continuous)
W4 . . . 3J 97
Church Pl. CR4: Mitc . . . 3C 154
SW1 . . . 3B 12 (7G 83)
UB10: Ick . . . 3E 56
W5 . . . 2D 96
Church Ri. KT9: Chess . . . 6F 163
SE23 . . . 2K 139
Church Road . . . 7H 75

Church Rd. BR2: Brom .2J **159**
(Glassmill La.)
BR2: Brom .3G **159**
(Shortlands Rd.)
BR2: Kes .7B **172**
BR6: Farnb .5G **173**
CR0: C'don .3C **168**
(not continuous)
CR4: Mitc .1B **154**
DA7: Bex .2F **127**
DA8: Erith .5K **109**
DA14: Sidc .4A **144**
DA16: Well .2B **126**
E10 .1C **68**
E12 .5C **70**
E17 .2A **50**
EN3: Pond E .6D **24**
HA6: Nwood .1H **39**
HA7: Stan .5G **27**
IG2: Ilf .6J **53**
IG9: Buck H .1E **36**
IG11: Bark .6G **71**
KT1: King T .2F **151**
KT4: Wor Pk .1A **164**
KT6: Surb .1C **162**
KT8: E Mos .4H **149**
KT10: Clay .7A **162**
KT19: Ewe .7K **163**
N1 .6C **66**
N6 .6E **46**
N17 .1E **48**
(not continuous)
NW4 .4D **44**
NW10 .7A **62**
SE19 .1E **156**
SM3: Cheam .6G **165**
SM6: Bedd .3H **167**
SW13 .2B **116**
SW19 .5G **135**
(High St. Wimbledon)
SW19 .1B **154**
(Western Rd.)
TW5: Cran .5K **93**
TW5: Hest .7E **94**
TW7: Isle .1H **113**
TW9: Rich .4E **114**
TW10: Ham .4D **132**
TW10: Rich .5E **114**
TW11: Tedd .4J **131**
TW13: Hanw .5B **130**
TW15: Ashf .3B **128**
TW17: Shep .7D **146**
UB2: S'hall .3D **94**
UB3: Hayes .1H **93**
UB5: N'olt .2B **76**
UB7: W Dray .3A **92**
UB8: Cowl .4A **74**
W3 .1J **97**
W7 .7H **77**
Church Rd. Almshouses *E10* .*2D* ***68***
(off Church Rd.)
Church Rd. Ind. Est. E10 .1C **68**
Church Rd. Nth. N2 .2B **46**
Church Rd. Sth. N2 .2B **46**
Church Row BR7: Chst .1G **161**
NW3 .4A **64**
SW6 .*7K* ***99***
(off Park Rd.)
Church Row M. BR7: Chst .7G **143**
Church Sq. TW17: Shep .7D **146**
Church St. CR0: C'don .3B **168**
E15 .1G **87**
E16 .1F **107**
EN2: Enf .3H **23**
KT1: King T .2D **150**
KT12: Walt T .7J **147**
KT17: Ewe .7C **164**
N9 .7J **23**
NW8 .5B **4** (5B **82**)
RM10: Dag .6H **73**
SM1: Sutt .5K **165**
TW1: Twick .1A **132**
Church St. TW7: Isle .3B **114**
TW12: Hamp .1G **149**
TW16: Sun .3K **147**
W2 .5B **4** (5B **82**)
W4 .6B **98**
Church St. Est. NW8 .4B **4** (4B **82**)
Church St. Nth. E15 .1G **87**
Church St. Pas. *E15* .*1G* ***87***
(off Church St.)
Church Stretton Rd. TW3: Houn .5G **113**
Church Ter. NW4 .3D **44**
SE13 .3G **123**
TW10: Rich .5D **114**
Church Va. N2 .3D **46**
SE23 .2K **139**
Church Vw. TW10: Rich .5E **114**
Churchview Rd. TW2: Twick .1H **131**
Church Wlk. EN2: Enf .3J **23**
KT7: T Ditt .6K **149**
KT12: Walt T .7J **147**
(not continuous)
N6 .3E **64**
N16 .3D **66**
(not continuous)
NW2 .3H **63**
NW4 .3E **44**
NW9 .2K **61**
SW13 .1C **116**
SW15 .5D **116**
SW16 .2G **155**
SW20 .3E **152**
TW8: Bford .6C **96**
(not continuous)
TW9: Rich .5D **114**
UB3: Hayes .6G **75**
Churchward Ho. *SE17* .*6B* ***102***
(off Lorrimore Sq.)
W14 .*5H* ***99***
(off Ivatt Pl.)
Church Way EN4: Cockf .4J **21**
HA8: Edg .6B **28**
N20 .3H **31**
Churchway NW1 .1D **6** (3H **83**)
(not continuous)
Churchwell Path E9 .5J **67**
Churchwood Gdns. IG8: Wfd G .4D **36**
Churchyard Pas. SE5 .2D **120**
Churchyard Row SE11 .4B **102**
Church Yd. Wlk. *W2* .*5A* ***4***
(off St Mary's Sq.)
Churnfield N4 .2A **66**
Churston Av. E13 .1K **87**
Churston Cl. SW2 .1A **138**
Churston Dr. SM4: Mord .5F **153**
Churston Gdns. N11 .6B **32**
Churston Mans. WC1 .4H **7**
Churton Pl. SW1 .4B **18** (4G **101**)
Churton St. SW1 .4B **18** (4G **101**)
Chusan Pl. E14 .6B **86**
Chute Ho. *SW9* .*2A* ***120***
(off Stockwell Pk. Rd.)
Chuter Ede Ho. *SW6* .*6H* ***99***
(off North End Rd.)
Chyngton Cl. DA15: Sidc .3K **143**
Cibber Rd. SE23 .2K **139**
Cicada Rd. SW18 .6A **118**
Cicely Ho. *NW8* .*2B* ***82***
(off Cochrane St.)
Cicely Rd. SE15 .1G **121**
Cinderella Path NW11 .1K **63**
Cinderford Way BR1: Brom .4G **141**
Cine Lumiere .**3A 16**
(off Queensberry Pl.)
Cineworld Cinema
Bexleyheath .**4H 127**
Chelsea, Fulham Rd. .**5A 100**
Chelsea, King's Rd. .**6B 100**
Ealing .***7D 78***
(off New Broadway
Enfield .**4B 24**
Feltham .**2K 129**
Hammersmith .**4D 98**
Cineworld Cinema
Haymarket .***3C 12***
(off Haymarket)
Ilford .***3F 71***
(off Clements Rd.)
Shaftesbury Av. .***3C 12***
(off Shaftesbury Av.)
Staples Corner .**1D 62**
Wandsworth .**5K 117**
West India Quay .**7C 86**
Wood Green .***2A 48***
(in Wood Green Shop. City)
Cinnabar Wharf Central *E1* .*1G* ***103***
(off Wapping High St.)
Cinnabar Wharf E. *E1* .*1G* ***103***
(off Wapping High St.)
Cinnabar Wharf W. *E1* .*1G* ***103***
(off Wapping High St.)
Cinnamon Cl. CR0: C'don .7J **155**
SE15 .7F **103**
Cinnamon Row SW11 .3A **118**
Cinnamon St. E1 .1H **103**
Cinnamon Wharf *SE1* .*6K* ***15***
(off Shad Thames)
Cintra Pk. SE19 .7F **139**
Circa Apartments NW1 .7E **64**
Circle, The NW2 .3A **62**
NW7 .6E **28**
SE1 .*6J* ***15***
(off Queen Elizabeth St.)
Circle Gdns. SW19 .2J **153**
Circuits, The HA5: Pinn .4A **40**
Circular Rd. N2 .2B **46**
N17 .3F **49**
Circular Way SE18 .6D **106**
(not continuous)
Circus Lodge NW8 .1A **4**
Circus M. W1 .5E **4**
Circus Pl. EC2 .6F **9** (5D **84**)
Circus Rd. NW8 .1A **4** (3B **82**)
Circus St. SE10 .7E **104**
Cirencester St. W2 .5K **81**
Cirrus Cl. SM6: Wall .7J **167**
Cissbury Ho. SE26 .3G **139**
Cissbury Ring Nth. N12 .5C **30**
Cissbury Ring Sth. N12 .5C **30**
Cissbury Rd. N15 .5D **48**
Citadel Pl. SE11 .5G **19** (5K **101**)
Citius Apartments *E3* .*2C* ***86***
(off Tredegar La.)
Citizen Ho. N7 .4A **66**
Citizen Rd. N7 .4A **66**
Citrus Ho. *SE8* .*5B* ***104***
(off Alverton St.)
City Apartments *E1* .*7K* ***9***
(off White Church La.)
City Bus. Cen. SE16 .3J **103**
City Central Est. *EC1* .*2C* ***8***
(off Seward St.)
City Ct. CR0: C'don .7B **156**
City Cross Bus. Pk. SE10 .4G **105**
City Forum EC1 .1C **8** (3C **84**)
City Gdn. Row N1 .1C **8** (2B **84**)
City Ga. Ho. *IG2: Ilf* .*6E* ***52***
(off Eastern Av.)
City Hall .**5H 15**
City Harbour *E14* .*3D* ***104***
(off Selsdon Way)
City Hgts. *E8* .*1F* ***85***
(off Kingsland Rd.)
City Lights Ct. *SE11* .*5A* ***102***
(off Kennington Rd.)
City Limits
Collier Row .**2F 55**
Croydon .***6A 168***
(off Purley Way)
CITY OF LONDON .1E **14** (6D **84**)
City of London Almshouses SW9 .4K **119**
City of London Crematorium
E12 .3C **70**
City of London Point *N7* .*6H* ***65***
(off York Way)
City of Westminster College
Paddington Basin Campus .**6A 4**
Paddington Green Campus .**5A 4**
City Pav. *EC1* .*5A* ***8***
(off Britton St.)
City Pl. Ho. *EC2* .*6D* ***8***
(off London Wall)
Citypoint EC2 .5E **8**
City Rd. EC1 .1A **8** (2B **84**)
City Tower *EC2* .*6E* ***8***
(off Basinghall St.)
City University London
Northampton Square Campus
. **2A 8 (3B 84)**
Whitechapel .**5H 85**
City University Saddlers Sports Cen., The
. **3B 8 (4B 84)**
City Vw. *IG1: Ilf* .*2G* ***71***
(off Axon Pl.)
Cityview SE7 .6A **106**
City Vw. Apartments *N1* .*7C* ***66***
(off Essex Rd.)
City Vw. Ct. SE22 .7G **121**
City Wlk. SE1 .7G **15** (2E **102**)
City Wlk. Apartments
EC1 .*2C* ***8***
(off Seward St.)
City Wharf Ho. KT7: T Ditt .6B **150**
Civic Way HA4: Ruis .5B **58**
IG6: Ilf .4G **53**
Clabon M. SW1 .2E **16** (3D **100**)
Clack La. HA4: Ruis .1E **56**
Clack St. SE16 .2J **103**
Clacton Rd. E6 .3B **88**
E17 .6A **50**
N17 .2F **49**
Claigmar Gdns. N3 .1K **45**
Claire Ct. HA5: Hat E .1D **40**
N12 .3F **31**
NW2 .6G **63**
WD23: B Hea .1C **26**
Claire Gdns. HA7: Stan .5H **27**
Claire Ho. IG1: Ilf .4F **71**
Claire Pl. E14 .3C **104**
Clairvale Rd. TW5: Hest .1B **112**
Clairview Rd. SW16 .5F **137**
Clairville Gdns. W7 .1J **95**
Clairville Point *SE23* .*3K* ***139***
(off Dacres Rd.)
Clamp Hill HA7: Stan .4C **26**
Clancarty Rd. SW6 .2J **117**
Clandon Cl. KT17: Ewe .6B **164**
W3 .2H **97**
Clandon Gdns. N3 .3J **45**
Clandon Ho. *SE1* .*7B* ***14***
(off Webber St.)
Clandon Rd. IG3: Ilf .2J **71**
Clandon St. SE8 .2C **122**
Clandon Ter. SW20 .2F **153**
Clanricarde Gdns. W2 .7J **81**
CLAPHAM .**4G 119**
CLAPHAM COMMON .**4H 119**
Clapham Comn. Nth. Side SW4 .4D **118**
Clapham Comn. Sth. Side SW4 .6F **119**
Clapham Comn. W. Side SW4 .4D **118**
(not continuous)
Clapham Cres. SW4 .4H **119**
Clapham High St. SW4 .4H **119**
CLAPHAM JUNCTION .**3C 118**
Clapham Junc. App. SW11 .3C **118**
Clapham Leisure Cen. .**3H 119**
Clapham Mnr. Ct. SW4 .3G **119**
Clapham Mnr. St. SW4 .3G **119**
CLAPHAM PARK .**7H 119**
Clapham Pk. Est. SW4 .6H **119**
Clapham Pk. Rd. SW4 .4G **119**
Clapham Pk. Ter. *SW2* .*5J* ***119***
(off Lyham Rd.)
Clapham Picturehouse .**4G 119**
Clapham Rd. SW9 .3J **119**
Clapham Rd. Est. SW4 .3J **119**
Clap La. RM10: Rush G, Dag .2H **73**

Claps Ga. La. E6 4E **88**
Clapton Comn. E5 7F **49**
(not continuous)
CLAPTON PARK **4K 67**
Clapton Pk. Est. E5 4K **67**
Clapton Pas. E5 5J **67**
Clapton Sq. E5 5J **67**
Clapton Ter. E5 1G **67**
Clapton Way E5 4G **67**
Clara Grant Ho. *E14* *3C* ***104***
(off Mellish St.)
Clara Nehab Ho. *NW11* *5H* ***45***
(off Leeside Cres.)
Clara Pl. SE18 4E **106**
Clare Cl. N2 3A **46**
Clare Cnr. SE9 7F **125**
Clare Ct. *W11* *7G* ***81***
(off Clarendon Rd.)
WC1 *2F* ***7***
(off Judd St.)
Claredale Ho. *E2* *2H* ***85***
(off Claredale St.)
Claredale St. E2 2G **85**
Clare Gdns. E7 4J **69**
IG11: Bark 6K **71**
W11 6G **81**
Clare Ho. E3 1B **86**
E16 *7E* ***88***
(off University Way)
HA8: Edg *2J* ***43***
(off Burnt Oak B'way.)
SE1 *5F* ***103***
(off Cooper's Rd.)
Clare La. N1 7C **66**
Clare Lawn Av. SW14 5J **115**
Clare Mkt. WC2 1H **13** (6K **83**)
Clare M. SW6 7K **99**
Claremont *TW17: Shep* *6D* ***146***
(off Laleham Rd.)
Claremont Av. HA3: Kenton 5E **42**
KT3: N Mald 5C **152**
TW16: Sun 1K **147**
Claremont Cl. BR6: Farnb 4E **172**
E16 1E **106**
N1 1K **7** (2A **84**)
SW2 1J **137**
Claremont Ct. *W2* *6K* ***81***
(off Queensway)
W9 *2H* ***81***
(off Claremont Rd.)
Claremont Dr. TW17: Shep 6D **146**
Claremont Gdns. IG3: Ilf 2J **71**
KT6: Surb 5E **150**
Claremont Gro. IG8: Wfd G 6F **37**
W4 7A **98**
Claremont Ho. SM2: Sutt 7K **165**
Claremont Pk. N3 1G **45**
Claremont Pl. KT10: Clay 6A **162**
Claremont Road 2F **63**
Claremont Rd. BR1: Brom 4C **160**
CR0: C'don 1G **169**
E7 5K **69**
E11 3F **69**
E17 2A **50**
HA3: W'stone 2J **41**
KT6: Surb 5E **150**
N6 7G **47**
NW2 7F **45**
TW1: Twick 7B **114**
TW11: Tedd 5K **131**
W9 2G **81**
W13 5A **78**
Claremont Sq. N1 1J **7** (2A **84**)
Claremont St. E16 2E **106**
N18 6B **34**
SE10 6D **104**
Claremont Ter. KT7: T Ditt 7B **150**
Claremont Vs. *SE5* *7D* ***102***
(off Southampton Way)
Claremont Way NW2 1E **62**
(not continuous)
Claremont Way Ind. Est. NW2 1E **62**
Clarence Av. BR1: Brom 4C **160**
IG2: Ilf 6E **52**
KT3: N Mald 2J **151**
SW4 7H **119**
Clarence Cl. EN4: E Barn 5G **21**
WD23: B Hea 1E **26**
Clarence Ct. NW7 5F **29**
W6 *4D* ***98***
(off Cambridge Gro.)
Clarence Cres. DA14: Sidc 3B **144**
SW4 6H **119**
Clarence Gdns. NW1 2K **5** (3F **83**)
Clarence Ga. IG8: Ilf, Wfd G 6K **37**
Clarence Ga. Gdns.
NW1 *4F* ***5***
(off Glentworth St.)
Clarence House 6B **12**
Clarence Ho. *SE17* *6C* ***102***
(off Merrow St.)
Clarence La. SW15 6A **116**
Clarence M. E5 5H **67**
SE16 1K **103**
SW12 7F **119**
Clarence Pl. E5 5H **67**
Clarence Rd. BR1: Brom 3B **160**
CR0: C'don 7D **156**
DA6: Bex 4E **126**
DA14: Sidc 3B **144**
E5 4H **67**
E12 4A **70**
E16 4G **87**
E17 2K **49**
EN3: Pond E 5C **24**
N15 5C **48**
N22 7D **32**
NW6 7H **63**
SE8 6D **104**
SE9 2C **142**
SM1: Sutt 5K **165**
SM6: Wall 5F **167**
SW19 6K **135**
TW9: Kew 1F **115**
TW11: Tedd 6K **131**
W4 5G **97**
Clarence St. KT1: King T 2D **150**
(not continuous)
TW9: Rich 4E **114**
UB2: S'hall 3B **94**
Clarence Ter. NW1 3F **5** (4D **82**)
TW3: Houn 4F **113**
Clarence Wlk. SW4 2J **119**
Clarence Way NW1 7F **65**
Clarenden Pl. DA2: Dart 5K **145**
Clarendon Cl. BR5: St P 3K **161**
E9 7J **67**
W2 2C **10** (7C **82**)
Clarendon Ct. *BR3: Beck* *1D* ***158***
(off Blair Ct.)
NW2 7E **62**
NW11 4H **45**
TW5: Cran 1J **111**
TW9: Kew 1F **115**
Clarendon Cres. TW2: Twick 3H **131**
Clarendon Cross W11 7G **81**
Clarendon Dr. SW15 4E **116**
Clarendon Flats *W1* *1H* ***11***
(off Balderton St.)
Clarendon Gdns. HA9: Wemb 3D **60**
IG1: Ilf 7D **52**
NW4 3C **44**
W9 4A **82**
Clarendon Grn. BR5: St P 4K **161**
Clarendon Gro. CR4: Mitc 3D **154**
NW1 1C **6** (3H **83**)
Clarendon Ho. *KT2: King T* *1E* ***150***
(off Cowleaze Rd.)
NW1 *1B* ***6***
(off Werrington St.)
W2 *2C* ***10***
(off Strathearn Pl.)
Clarendon Lodge *W11* *7G* ***81***
(off Clarendon Rd.)
Clarendon M. DA5: Bexl 1H **145**
W2 2C **10** (7C **82**)
Clarendon Path BR5: St P 4K **161**
(not continuous)
Clarendon Pl. W2 2C **10** (7C **82**)
Clarendon Ri. SE13 4E **122**
Clarendon Rd. CR0: C'don 2B **168**
E11 1F **69**
E17 6D **50**
E18 3J **51**
HA1: Harr 6J **41**
N8 3K **47**
N15 4C **48**
N18 6B **34**
N22 2K **47**
SM6: Wall 6G **167**
SW19 7C **136**
TW15: Ashf 4B **128**
UB3: Hayes 2H **93**
W5 3E **78**
W11 7G **81**
Clarendon St. SW1 5K **17** (5F **101**)
Clarendon Ter. W9 3A **4** (4A **82**)
Clarendon Wlk. W11 6G **81**
Clarendon Way BR5: St P 3K **161**
BR7: Chst 3K **161**
N21 6H **23**
Clarens St. SE6 2B **140**
Clare Pl. SW15 7B **116**
Clare Point *NW2* *1F* ***63***
(off Whitefield Av.)
Clare Rd. E11 6F **51**
NW10 7C **62**
SE14 1B **122**
TW4: Houn 3D **112**
TW19: Stanw 1A **128**
UB6: G'frd 6H **59**
Clare St. E2 2H **85**
Claret Gdns. SE25 3E **156**
Clareville Ct. *SW7* *4A* ***16***
(off Clareville St.)
Clareville Gro. SW7 4A **16** (4A **100**)
Clareville Gro. M. SW7 4A **16** (4A **100**)
Clareville Rd. BR5: Farnb 2G **173**
Clareville St. SW7 4A **16** (4A **100**)
Clare Way DA7: Bex 1E **126**
Clarewood Ct. *W1* *6E* ***4***
(off Seymour Pl.)
Clarewood Wlk. SW9 4A **120**
Clarges M. W1 4J **11** (1F **101**)
Clarges St. W1 4K **11** (1F **101**)
Claribel Rd. SW9 2B **120**
Clarice Way SM6: Wall 7J **167**
Claridge Ct. SW6 2H **117**
Claridge Rd. RM8: Dag 1D **72**
Clarinet Ct. HA8: Edg 7C **28**
Clarion Ho. *E3* *2A* ***86***
(off Roman Rd.)
SW1 *5B* ***18***
(off Moreton Pl.)
W1 *1C* ***12***
(off St Anne's Ct.)
Clarissa Ho. *E14* *6D* ***86***
(off Cordela St.)
Clarissa Rd. RM6: Chad H 7D **54**
Clarissa St. E8 1F **85**
Clarke Cl. CR0: C'don 6C **156**
Clarke Mans. *IG11: Bark* *7K* ***71***
(off Upney La.)
Clarke M. N9 3C **34**
Clarke Path N16 1G **67**
Clarkes Av. KT4: Wor Pk 1F **165**
Clarkes Dr. UB8: Hil 5A **74**
Clarke's M. W1 5H **5** (5E **82**)
Clark Gro. IG1: Ilf 4J **71**
Clark Ho. *SW10* *7A* ***100***
(off Coleridge Gdns.)
Clarks Mead WD23: Bush 1B **26**
Clarkson Rd. E16 6H **87**
Clarkson Row *NW1* *2G* ***83***
(off Mornington Ter.)
Clarksons, The IG11: Bark 2G **89**
Clarkson St. E2 3H **85**
Clarks Rd. IG1: Ilf 2H **71**
Clark St. E1 5H **85**
Clark Way TW5: Hest 7B **94**
Classic Mans. *E9* *7H* ***67***
(off Wells St.)
Classon Cl. UB7: W Dray 2A **92**
Claude Rd. E10 2E **68**
E13 1K **87**
SE15 2H **121**
Claude St. E14 4C **104**
Claudia Jones Ho. N17 1C **48**
Claudia Jones Way SW2 6J **119**
Claudia Pl. SW19 1G **135**
Claudius Cl. HA7: Stan 3J **27**
Claughton Rd. E13 2A **88**
Clauson Av. UB5: N'olt 5F **59**
Clavell St. SE10 6E **104**
Claverdale Rd. SW2 7K **119**
Clavering Av. SW13 6D **98**
Clavering Cl. TW1: Twick 4A **132**
Clavering Ho. *SE13* *4F* ***123***
(off Blessington Rd.)
Clavering Ind. Est. *N9* *2D* ***34***
(off Centre Way)
Clavering Pl. SW12 6E **118**
Clavering Rd. E12 1B **70**
Claverley Gro. N3 1K **45**
Claverley Vs. N3 7E **30**
Claverton St. SW1 6B **18** (5G **101**)
Clave St. E1 1J **103**
Claxton Gro. W6 5F **99**
Claxton Path *SE4* *4K* ***121***
(off Coston Wlk.)
Clay Av. CR4: Mitc 2F **155**
Claybank Gro. SE13 3D **122**
Claybourne M. SE19 7E **138**
Claybridge Rd. SE12 4A **142**
Claybrook Cl. N2 3B **46**
Claybrook Rd. W6 6F **99**
Claybury B'way. IG5: Ilf 3C **52**
Claybury Hall IG8: Wfd G 7J **37**
Claybury Rd. IG8: Wfd G 7H **37**
Clay Ct. E17 3F **51**
SE1 *7G* ***15***
(off Long La.)
Claydon *SE17* *4C* ***102***
(off Deacon Way)
Claydon Dr. CR0: Bedd 4J **167**
Claydon Ho. *NW4* *2F* ***45***
(off Holders Hill Rd.)
Claydown M. SE18 5E **106**
Clay Farm Rd. SE9 2G **143**
CLAYGATE **7A 162**
Claygate Cres. CR0: New Ad 6E **170**
Claygate La. KT7: T Ditt 1A **162**
KT10: Clay, Hin W 2A **162**
Claygate Rd. W13 3B **96**
CLAYHALL **3C 52**
Clayhall Av. IG5: Ilf 3C **52**
Clayhall Ct. *E3* *2B* ***86***
(off St Stephen's Rd.)
Clay Hill EN2: Enf 1K **23**
Clayhill KT5: Surb 5G **151**
Clayhill Cres. SE9 4B **142**
Claylands Pl. SW8 7A **102**
Claylands Rd. SW8 7H **19** (6K **101**)
Clay La. HA8: Edg 2B **28**
TW19: Stanw 7B **110**
WD23: B Hea 1D **26**
Claymill Ho. SE18 5G **107**
Claymore Cl. SM4: Mord 7J **153**
Clay Path E17 2C **50**
Claypole Ct. *E17* *5C* ***50***
(off Yunus Khan Cl.)
Claypole Dr. TW5: Hest 1C **112**
Claypole Rd. E15 2E **86**
Clayponds Av. TW8: Bford 4D **96**
Clayponds Gdns. W5 4D **96**
(not continuous)
Clayponds La. TW8: Bford 5E **96**
(not continuous)

Clay St.—Clipper Way

Clay St. W1 6F 5 (5D 82)
Clayton Av. HA0: Wemb 7E 60
Clayton Bus. Cen. UB3: Hayes 2G 93
Clayton Cl. E6 6D 88
Clayton Ct. E17 2A 50
Clayton Cres. N1 1J 83
TW8: Bford 5D 96
Clayton Dr. SE8 5A 104
Clayton Fld. NW9 7F 29
Clayton Ho. *E9* *7J 67*
(off Frampton Pk. Rd.)
KT7: T Ditt 1B 162
SW13 *7E 98*
(off Trinity Church Rd.)
Clayton M. SE10 1F 123
Clayton Rd. KT9: Chess 4C 162
RM7: Rush G 1J 73
SE15 1G 121
TW7: Isle 3J 113
UB3: Hayes 2G 93
Clayton St. SE11 7J 19 (6A 102)
Clayton Ter. UB4: Yead 5C 76
Claytonville Ter. DA17: Belv 2J 109
Clay Wood Cl. BR6: Orp 7J 161
Clayworth Cl. DA15: Sidc 6B 126
Cleanthus Cl. SE18 1F 125
Cleanthus Rd. SE18 2F 125
(not continuous)
Clearbrook Way E1 6J 85
Clearwater Pl. KT6: Surb 6C 150
Clearwater Ter. W11 2F 99
Clearwater Yd. *NW1* *1F 83*
(off Inverness St.)
Clearwell Dr. W9 4K 81
Cleave Av. BR6: Chels 6J 173
UB3: Harl 4G 93
Cleaveland Rd. KT6: Surb 5D 150
Cleaverholme Cl. SE25 6H 157
Cleaver Ho. *NW3* *7D 64*
(off Adelaide Rd.)
Cleaver Sq. SE11 6K 19 (5A 102)
Cleaver St. SE11 5K 19 (5A 102)
Cleaves Almshouses
KT2: King T *2E 150*
(off London Rd.)
Cleeve Ct. TW14: Bedf 1G 129
Cleeve Hill SE23 1H 139
Cleeve Ho. E2 2H 9
Cleeve Pk. Gdns. DA14: Sidc 2B 144
Cleeve Way SM1: Sutt 1K 165
SW15 7B 116
Cleeve Workshops *E2* *2H 9*
(off Boundary Rd.)
Clegg Ho. SE3 4K 123
SE16 *3J 103*
(off Moodkee St.)
Clegg St. E1 1H 103
E13 2J 87
Cleland Ho. *E2* *2J 85*
(off Sewardstone Rd.)
Clematis Apartments *E3* *3B 86*
(off Merchant St.)
Clematis Gdns. IG8: Wfd G 5D 36
Clematis St. W12 7C 80
Clem Attlee Ct. SW6 6H 99
Clem Attlee Pde. *SW6* *6H 99*
(off North End Rd.)
Clemence Rd. RM10: Dag 1J 91
Clemence St. E14 5B 86
Clement Av. SW4 4H 119
Clement Cl. NW6 7E 62
W4 4K 97
Clement Gdns. UB3: Harl 4G 93
Clementhorpe Rd. RM9: Dag 6C 72
Clement Ho. SE8 4A 104
W10 *5E 80*
(off Dalgarno Gdns.)
Clementina Ct. *E3* *4A 86*
(off Copperfield Rd.)
Clementina Rd. E10 1B 68
Clementine Cl. W13 2B 96
Clementine Wlk. IG8: Wfd G 7D 36
Clement Rd. BR3: Beck 2K 157
SW19 5G 135
Clement's Av. E16 7J 87
Clements Cl. N12 4E 30
Clements Ct. IG1: Ilf 3F 71
TW4: Houn 4B 112
Clement's Inn WC2 1H 13 (6K 83)
Clement's Inn Pas. WC2 1H 13
Clements La. EC4 2F 15 (7D 84)
IG1: Ilf 3F 71
Clements Pl. TW8: Bford 5D 96
Clements Rd. E6 7C 70
IG1: Ilf 3F 71
SE16 3G 103
Clemson Ho. E8 1F 85
Clendon Way SE18 4H 107
Clennam St. SE1 6D 14 (2C 102)
Clensham Ct. SM1: Sutt 2J 165
Clensham La. SM1: Sutt 2J 165
Clenston M. W1 7E 4 (6D 82)
Cleopatra Cl. HA7: Stan 3J 27
Cleopatra's Needle 4G 13 (1J 101)
Clephane Rd. N1 6C 66
Clephane Rd. Nth. N1 6C 66
Clephane Rd. Sth. N1 6D 66
Clere Pl. EC2 3F 9 (4D 84)
Clere St. EC2 3F 9 (4D 84)
Clerics Wlk. TW17: Shep 7F 147
CLERKENWELL 3J 7 (4A 84)
Clerkenwell Cl. EC1 3K 7 (4A 84)
(not continuous)
Clerkenwell Grn. EC1 4K 7 (4A 84)
Clerkenwell Rd. EC1 4J 7 (4A 84)
Clerk's Pl. EC2 7G 9 (6E 84)
Clermont Rd. E9 1J 85
Clevedon Cl. N16 3F 67
Clevedon Ct. CR2: S Croy 5E 168
SW11 *1C 118*
(off Bolingbroke Wlk.)
Clevedon Gdns. TW5: Cran 1K 111
UB3: Harl 3F 93
Clevedon Ho. SM1: Sutt 4A 166
Clevedon Mans. NW5 4E 64
Clevedon Pas. N16 2F 67
Clevedon Rd. KT1: King T 2G 151
SE20 1K 157
TW1: Twick 6D 114
(not continuous)
Cleve Ho. NW6 7K 63
Cleveland Av. SW20 2H 153
TW12: Hamp 7D 130
W4 4B 98
Cleveland Ct. W13 5B 78
Cleveland Gdns.
KT4: Wor Pk 2A 164
N4 5C 48
NW2 2F 63
SW13 2B 116
W2 6A 82
Cleveland Gro. E1 4J 85
Cleveland Ho. *N2* *2B 46*
(off The Grange)
Cleveland Mans. *NW6* *7H 63*
(off Willesden La.)
SW9 *7A 102*
(off Mowll St.)
W9 4J 81
Cleveland M. W1 5A 6 (5G 83)
Cleveland Pk. TW19: Stanw 6A 110
Cleveland Pk. Av. E17 4C 50
Cleveland Pk. Cres. E17 4C 50
Cleveland Pl. SW1 4B 12 (1G 101)
Cleveland Ri. SM4: Mord 7F 153
Cleveland Rd. DA16: Well 2K 125
E18 3J 51
IG1: Ilf 3F 71
KT3: N Mald 4A 152
KT4: Wor Pk 2A 164
N1 7D 66
N9 7C 24
SW13 2B 116
TW7: Isle 4A 114
Cleveland Rd. W4 3J 97
W13 5A 78
Cleveland Row SW1 5A 12 (1G 101)
Cleveland Sq. W2 6A 82
Cleveland St. W1 4K 5 (4F 83)
Cleveland Ter. W2 6A 82
Cleveland Way E1 4J 85
Cleveley Cl. SE7 4B 106
Cleveley Cres. W5 2E 78
Cleveleys Rd. E5 3H 67
Cleverly Est. W12 1C 98
Cleve Rd. DA14: Sidc 3D 144
NW6 7J 63
Cleves Av. KT17: Ewe 7D 164
Cleves Ho. *E16* *1J 105*
(off Southey M.)
Cleves Rd. E6 1B 88
TW10: Ham 3C 132
Cleves Wlk. IG6: Ilf 1G 53
Cleves Way HA4: Ruis 1B 58
TW12: Hamp 7D 130
TW16: Sun 6H 129
Clewer Ct. *E10* *1C 68*
(off Leyton Grange Est.)
Clewer Cres. HA3: Hrw W 1H 41
Clewer Ho. *SE2* *2D 108*
(off Wolvercote Rd.)
Cley Ho. SE4 4K 121
Clichy Est. E1 5J 85
Clichy Ho. *E1* *5J 85*
(off Stepney Way)
Clifden M. E5 4K 67
Clifden Rd. E5 5J 67
TW1: Twick 1K 131
TW8: Bford 6D 96
Cliffe Ho. *SE10* *5H 105*
(off Blackwall La.)
Cliffe Rd. CR2: S Croy 5D 168
Cliffe Wlk. *SM1: Sutt* *5A 166*
(off Greyhound Rd.)
Clifford Av. BR7: Chst 6D 142
IG5: Ilf 1F 53
SM6: Wall 4G 167
SW14 3H 115
(not continuous)
Clifford Cl. UB5: N'olt 1C 76
Clifford Ct. *W2* *5K 81*
(off Westbourne Pk. Vs.)
Clifford Dr. SW9 4B 120
Clifford Gdns. NW10 2E 80
UB3: Harl 4G 93
Clifford Gro. TW15: Ashf 4C 128
Clifford Haigh Ho. SW6 7F 99
Clifford Ho. *BR3: Beck* *6D 140*
(off Calverley Cl.)
W14 *4H 99*
(off Edith Vs.)
Clifford Rd. E16 4H 87
E17 2E 50
EN5: New Bar 3E 20
HA0: Wemb 7D 60
N1 1E 84
N9 6D 24
SE25 4G 157
TW4: Houn 3B 112
TW10: Ham 2D 132
Clifford's Inn Pas. EC4 1J 13 (6A 84)
Clifford St. W1 3A 12 (7G 83)
Clifford Way NW10 4B 62
Cliff Rd. NW1 6H 65
Cliffsend Ho. *SW9* *1A 120*
(off Cowley Rd.)
Cliff Ter. SE8 2C 122
Cliffview Rd. SE13 3C 122
Cliff Vs. NW1 6H 65
Cliff Wlk. E16 5H 87
Clifton Av. E17 3K 49
HA7: Stan 2B 42
HA9: Wemb 6F 61
N3 1H 45
TW13: Felt 3A 130
W12 1B 98
Clifton Cl. BR6: Farnb 5G 173
Clifton Ct. BR3: Beck 1D 158
IG8: Wfd G 6D 36
KT5: Surb 7F 151
N4 2A 66
NW8 3A 4
SE15 7H 103
TW19: Stanw 6A 110
Clifton Cres. SE15 7H 103
Clifton Est. SE15 1H 121
Clifton Gdns. EN2: Enf 4D 22
N15 6F 49
NW11 6H 45
UB10: Hil 2D 74
W4 4K 97
(not continuous)
W9 4A 82
Clifton Ga. SW10 6A 100
Clifton Gro. E8 6G 67
Clifton Hill NW8 2K 81
Clifton Ho. *E2* *3J 9*
(off Club Row)
E11 2G 69
Clifton M. SE25 4E 156
Clifton Pde. TW13: Felt 3A 130
Clifton Pk. Av. SW20 2E 152
Clifton Pl. SE16 2J 103
SW10 *6A 100*
(off Hollywood Rd.)
W2 1B 10 (6B 82)
Clifton Ri. SE14 7A 104
(not continuous)
Clifton Rd. DA14: Sidc 4J 143
DA16: Well 3C 126
E7 6B 70
E16 5G 87
HA3: Kenton 4F 43
IG2: Ilf 6H 53
KT2: King T 7F 133
N1 6C 66
N3 1A 46
N8 6H 47
N22 1G 47
NW10 2C 80
SE25 4E 156
SM6: Wall 5F 167
SW19 6F 135
TW7: Isle 2J 113
TW11: Tedd 4J 131
UB2: S'hall 4C 94
UB6: G'frd 4G 77
W9 3A 4 (4A 82)
Clifton St. EC2 4G 9 (4E 84)
Clifton Ter. N4 2A 66
Clifton Vs. W9 5A 82
Cliftonville Ct. SE12 1J 141
Clifton Wlk. *W6* *4D 98*
(off King St.)
Clifton Way HA0: Wemb 1E 78
SE15 7H 103
TW6: H'row A 3C 110
Climsland Ho. SE1 4K 13 (1A 102)
Cline Rd. N11 6B 32
Clinger Ct. *N1* *1E 84*
(off Hobbs Pl. Est.)
Clink Prison Mus. 4E 14
Clink St. SE1 4D 14 (1D 102)
Clink Wharf *SE1* *4E 14*
(off Clink St.)
Clinton Av. DA16: Well 4A 126
KT8: E Mos 4G 149
Clinton Ho. *KT6: Surb* *7D 150*
(off Lovelace Gdns)
Clinton Rd. E3 3A 86
E7 4J 69
N15 4D 48
Clipper Apartments *SE10* *6E 104*
(off Welland St.)
Clipper Cl. SE16 2K 103
Clipper Ho. *E14* *5E 104*
(off Manchester Rd.)
Clipper Way SE13 4E 122

A-Z London 229

Clippesby Cl. KT9: Chess 6F 163
Clipstone M. W1 5A 6 (5G 83)
Clipstone Rd. TW3: Houn 3E 112
Clipstone St. W1 5K 5 (5F 83)
Clissold Cl. N2 3D 46
Clissold Ct. N4 2C 66
Clissold Cres. N16 3D 66
Clissold Leisure Cen. 3D 66
Clissold Rd. N16 3D 66
Clitheroe Av. HA2: Harr 1E 58
Clitheroe Rd. SW9 2J 119
Clitherow Av. W7 3A 96
Clitherow Ct. TW8: Bford 5C 96
Clitherow Pas. TW8: Bford 5C 96
Clitherow Rd. TW8: Bford 5B 96
Clitterhouse Cres. NW2 1E 62
Clitterhouse Rd. NW2 1E 62
Clive Av. N18 6B 34
Clive Ct. W9 4A 82
Cliveden Cl. N12 4F 31
Cliveden Ho. *E16* *1J 105*
(off Fitzwilliam M.)
SW1 *3G 17*
(off Cliveden Pl.)
Cliveden Pl. SW1 3G 17 (4E 100)
TW17: Shep 6E 146
Cliveden Rd. SW19 1H 153
Clivedon Ct. W13 5B 78
Clivedon Rd. E4 5B 36
Clive Ho. *SE10* *6E 104*
(off Haddo St.)
Clive Lloyd Ho. *N15* *5C 48*
(off Woodlands Pk. Rd.)
Clive Lodge NW4 6F 45
Clive Pas. SE21 3D 138
Clive Rd. DA17: Belv 4G 109
EN1: Enf 4B 24
SE21 3D 138
SW19 6C 136
TW1: Twick 4K 131
TW14: Felt 6J 111
Clivesdale Dr.
UB3: Hayes 1K 93
Clive Way EN1: Enf 4B 24
Cloak La. EC4 2D 14 (7C 84)
Clochar Ct. NW10 1B 80
Clock Ct. E11 4K 51
Clock End Bri. N5 4A 66
Clock Ho. E3 3E 86
E17 *4F 51*
(off Wood St.)
Clockhouse, The SW19 3E 134
Clockhouse Av. IG11: Bark 1G 89
Clockhouse Cl. SW19 2E 134
Clockhouse Ct. BR3: Beck 2A 158
CLOCKHOUSE JUNC. 5E 32
Clockhouse La. RM5: Col R 1H 55
TW14: Bedf 4C 128
TW15: Ashf 4C 128
Clock Ho. Pde. E11 6K 51
Clockhouse Pde. N13 5F 33
Clockhouse Pl. SW15 6G 117
Clock Ho. Rd. BR3: Beck 3A 158
CLOCKHOUSE RDBT. 1D 128
Clock Mus., The 7D 8
Clock Pde. EN2: Enf 5J 23
Clock Pl. *SE1* *4B 102*
(off Newington Butts)
Clock Twr. Ind. Est. TW7: Isle 3K 113
Clock Twr. M. N1 1C 84
SE28 7B 90
W7 1J 95
Clock Twr. Pl. *N7* *6J 65*
(off Market Est.)
Clock Twr. Rd. TW7: Isle 3K 113
Clock Vw. N7 6J 65
Cloister Cl. TW11: Tedd 5B 132
Cloister Gdns. HA8: Edg 5D 28
SE25 6H 157
Cloister Rd. NW2 3H 63
W3 5J 79
Cloisters, The 1E 18
Cloisters, The E1 4J 9
SW9 1A 120
TW7: Isle *3A 114*
(off Pulteney Cl.)
Cloisters Av. BR2: Brom 5D 160
Cloisters Bus. Cen.
SW8 *7F 101*
(off Battersea Pk. Rd.)
Cloisters Ct. DA7: Bex 3H 127
Cloisters Mall KT1: King T 2E 150
Clonard Way HA5: Hat E 6A 26
Clonbrock Rd. N16 4E 66
Cloncurry St. SW6 2F 117
Clonmel Cl. HA2: Harr 2H 59
Clonmell Rd. N17 3D 48
Clonmel Rd. SW6 7H 99
TW11: Tedd 4H 131
Clonmore St. SW18 1H 135
Cloonmore Av. BR6: Chels 4K 173
Clorane Gdns. NW3 3J 63
Close, The BR3: Beck 4A 158
BR5: Pet W 6J 161
CR4: Mitc 4D 154
DA5: Bexl 6G 127
DA14: Sidc 4B 144
E4 7K 35
EN4: E Barn 6J 21
HA0: Wemb 6E 60
HA2: Harr 2G 41
HA5: Eastc 7A 40
HA5: Pinn 7D 40
HA9: Wemb 3J 61
IG2: Ilf 6J 53
KT3: N Mald 2J 151
KT6: Surb 6E 150
N10 2F 47
N14 2C 32
N20 2C 30
RM6: Chad H 6E 54
SE3 2F 123
SE25 6G 157
SM3: Sutt 7H 153
SM5: Cars 7C 166
TW7: Isle 2H 113
TW9: Rich 3H 115
UB10: Hil 1C 74
Cloth Ct. EC1 6B 8
Cloth Fair EC1 6B 8 (5B 84)
Clothier St. E1 7H 9 (6E 84)
Cloth St. EC1 5C 8 (5C 84)
Clothworkers Rd. SE18 7H 107
Cloudesdale Rd. SW17 2F 137
Cloudesley Cl. DA14: Sidc 5K 143
(not continuous)
Cloudesley Mans. *N1* *1A 84*
(off Cloudesley Pl.)
Cloudesley Pl. N1 1A 84
Cloudesley Rd. DA7: Bex 1F 127
N1 1A 84
(not continuous)
Cloudesley Sq. N1 1A 84
Cloudesley St. N1 1A 84
Clouston Cl. SM6: Wall 5J 167
Clova Rd. E7 6H 69
Clove Cres. E14 7E 86
Clove Hitch Quay
SW11 3A 118
Clovelly Av. NW9 4B 44
UB10: Ick 4E 56
Clovelly Cl. HA5: Eastc 3K 39
UB10: Ick 4E 56
Clovelly Ct. NW2 5E 62
Clovelly Gdns. EN1: Enf 7K 23
RM7: Mawney 1H 55
SE19 1F 157
Clovelly Ho. *W2* *6A 82*
(off Hallfield Est.)
Clovelly Rd. DA7: Bex 6E 108
N8 4H 47
TW3: Houn 2E 112
W4 2K 97
W5 2C 96
Clovelly Way BR6: St M Cry 6K 161
E1 6J 85
HA2: Harr 2D 58
Clover Cl. E11 2F 69
Cloverdale Ct. SM6: Wall 6F 167
Cloverdale Gdns. DA15: Sidc 6K 125
Clover M. SW3 7F 17 (6D 100)
Clover Way SM6: Wall 1E 166
Clove St. E13 4J 87
Clowders Rd. SE6 3B 140
Clowser Cl. SM1: Sutt 5A 166
Cloysters Grn. E1 1G 103
Cloyster Wood HA8: Edg 7J 27
Club Gdns. Rd. BR2: Hayes 7J 159
Club Row E1 3J 9 (4F 85)
E2 3J 9 (4F 85)
Clumps, The TW15: Ashf 4F 129
Clunbury Av. UB2: S'hall 5D 94
Clunbury St. N1 2D 84
Clunie Ho. *SW1* *1F 17*
(off Pavillion Rd.)
Cluny Est. SE1 7G 15 (3E 102)
Cluny M. SW5 4J 99
Cluny Pl. SE1 7G 15 (3E 102)
Cluse Ct. *N1* *2C 84*
(off St Peters St., not continuous)
Clutton St. E14 5D 86
Clydach Rd. EN1: Enf 4A 24
Clyde Cir. N15 4E 48
Clyde Ct. *NW1* *2H 83*
(off Hampden Cl.)
Clyde Flats *SW6* *7H 99*
(off Rhylston Rd.)
Clyde Ho. KT2: King T 1D 150
Clyde Pl. E10 7D 50
Clyde Rd. CR0: C'don 2F 169
N15 4E 48
N22 1H 47
SM1: Sutt 5J 165
SM6: Wall 6G 167
TW19: Stanw 1A 128
Clydesdale EN3: Pond E 4E 24
Clydesdale Av. HA7: Stan 3D 42
Clydesdale Cl. TW7: Isle 3K 113
Clydesdale Ct. N20 1G 31
Clydesdale Gdns. TW10: Rich 4H 115
Clydesdale Ho. *DA18: Erith* *2E 108*
(off Kale Rd.)
W11 *6H 81*
(off Clydesdale Rd.)
Clydesdale Rd. W11 6H 81
Clyde St. SE8 6B 104
Clyde Ter. SE23 2J 139
Clyde Va. SE23 2J 139
Clyde Way RM1: Rom 1K 55
Clyde Wharf E16 1J 105
Clydon Cl. DA8: Erith 6K 109
Clyfford Rd. HA4: Ruis 4H 57
Clymping Dene TW14: Felt 7K 111
Clynes Ho. *E2* *3K 85*
(off Knottisford St.)
RM10: Dag *3G 73*
(off Uvedale Rd.)
Clyston St. SW8 2G 119
Coach & Horses Yd. W1 2K 11 (7G 83)
Coach Ho. La. N5 4B 66
SW19 4F 135
Coach Ho. M. *SE1* *7G 15*
(off Long La.)
SE23 6K 121
SM2: Sutt 6K 165
Coachhouse M. SE20 7H 139
Coach Ho. Yd. *NW3* *4A 64*
(off Heath St.)
SW18 4K 117
Coachmaker M. *SW4* *3J 119*
(off Bedford Rd.)
W4 *3K 97*
(off Berrymede Rd.)
Coach Yd. M. N19 1J 65
Coaldale Wlk. SE21 7C 120
Coalecroft Rd. SW15 4E 116
Coalport Ho. SE11 2J 19
Coal Post Cl. BR6: Chels 6K 173
Coalstore Ct. E1 5A 86
Coatbridge Ho. *N1* *7K 65*
(off Carnoustie Dr.)
Coates Av. SW18 6C 118
Coates Cl. CR7: Thor H 3C 156
Coates Hill Rd. BR1: Brom 2E 160
Coate St. E2 2G 85
Coates Wlk. TW8: Bford 6E 96
Cobalt SE28 2A 108
Cobalt Bldg., The *EC2* *5C 84*
(off Bridgewater Sq.)
Cobalt Cl. BR3: Beck 4K 157
Cobalt Sq. SW8 7G 19
Cobbett Rd. SE9 3C 124
TW2: Whitt 1E 130
Cobbetts Av. IG4: Ilf 5B 52
Cobbett St. SW8 7K 101
Cobble La. N1 7B 66
Cobble M. *N6* *1E 64*
(off W. Hill)
Cobblers Wlk. KT1: Ham W 1A 150
KT8: E Mos 1A 150
TW11: Tedd 1A 150
TW12: Hamp, Tedd 1G 149
(not continuous)
Cobblestone Pl. CR0: C'don 1C 168
Cobbold Ct. *SW1* *3C 18*
(off Elverton St.)
Cobbold Ind. Est. NW10 6B 62
Cobbold M. W12 2B 98
Cobbold Rd. E11 3H 69
NW10 6B 62
W12 2A 98
Cobb's Ct. EC4 1B 14
Cobb's Hall *SW6* *6F 99*
(off Fulham Pal. Rd.)
Cobb's Rd. TW4: Houn 4D 112
Cobbsthorpe Vs. SE26 4K 139
Cobb St. E1 6J 9 (5F 85)
Cobden Bldgs. *WC1* *1G 7*
(off Weston Rd.)
Cobden Ct. BR2: Brom 4A 160
Cobden Ho. *E2* *3G 85*
(off Nelson Gdns.)
NW1 *2G 83*
(off Arlington Rd.)
Cobden M. SE26 5H 139
Cobden Rd. BR6: Farnb 4H 173
E11 3G 69
SE25 5G 157
Cobham Av. KT3: N Mald 5C 152
Cobham Cl. BR2: Brom 7C 160
DA15: Sidc 6B 126
EN1: Enf 3B 24
HA8: Edg 2H 43
SM6: Wall 6J 167
SW11 6C 118
Cobham Ct. CR4: Mitc 2B 154
Cobham Ho. IG11: Bark 1G 89
Cobham M. NW1 7H 65
Cobham Pl. DA6: Bex 5D 126
Cobham Rd. E17 1E 50
IG3: Ilf 2J 71
KT1: King T 2G 151
N22 3B 48
TW5: Hest 7A 94
Cobland Rd. SE12 4A 142
Coborn M. *E3* *3B 86*
(off Coborn St.)
Coborn Rd. E3 2B 86
Coborn St. E3 3B 86
Cobourg Rd. SE5 6F 103
Cobourg St. NW1 2B 6 (3G 83)
Coburg Cl. SW1 3B 18 (4G 101)
Coburg Cres. SW2 1K 137
Coburg Dwellings *E1* *6J 85*
(off Hardinge St.)
Coburg Gdns. IG5: Ilf 2B 52
Coburg Rd. N22 3K 47
Cochrane Cl. NW8 1B 4

Cochrane Ct. *E10* 1C *68*
(off Leyton Grange Est.)
Cochrane Ho. *E14* 2C *104*
(off Admirals Way)
Cochrane M. *NW8* 2B *82*
Cochrane Rd. *SW19* 7G *135*
Cochrane St. *NW8* 1B 4 (2B *82*)
Cochrane Theatre 6F *7*
(off Southampton Row)
Cockburn Ho. *SW1* 6D *18*
(off Aylesford St.)
COCKCROW HILL 1D *162*
Cockerell Rd. *E17* 7A *50*
COCKFOSTERS .4J *21*
Cockfosters Pde. *EN4:* Cockf 4K *21*
Cockfosters Rd. *EN4:* Cockf, Had W . .1H *21*
Cock Hill *E1* 6H 9 (5E *84*)
Cock La. *EC1* 6A 8 (5B *84*)
Cockpit Steps *SW1* 7C *12*
Cockpit Theatre 4C *4*
(off Gateforth St.)
Cockpit Yd. *WC1* 5H 7 (5K *83*)
Cocks Cres. *KT3:* N Mald 4B *152*
Cocksett Av. *BR6:* Chels 6J *173*
Cockspur Ct. *SW1* 4D *12* (1H *101*)
Cockspur St. *SW1* 4D *12* (1H *101*)
Cocksure La. *DA14:* Sidc 3G *145*
Coda Cen., The *SW6* 7G *99*
Code St. *E1* 4K *9*
Codicote Ho. *SE8* 4K *103*
(off Chilton Gro.)
Codicote Ter. *N4* 2C *66*
Codling Cl. *E1* 1G *103*
Codling Way *HA0:* Wemb 4D *60*
Codrington Ct. *E1* 4H *85*
SE16 . . . . .7A *86*
Codrington Hill *SE23* 7A *122*
Codrington M. *W11* 6G *81*
Cody Cl. *HA3:* Kenton 3D *42*
SM6: Wall 7H *167*
Cody Rd. *E16* .4F *87*
Coe Av. *SE25* 6G *157*
Coe's All. *EN5:* Barn 4B *20*
Coffey St. *SE8* 7C *104*
Cogan Av. *E17* 1A *50*
Coin St. *SE1* 4J 13 (1A *102*)
(not continuous)
Coity Rd. *NW5* 6E *64*
Cokers La. *SE21* 1D *138*
Coke St. *E1* 6G *85*
Colas M. *NW6* 1J *81*
Colbeck M. *SW7* 4K *99*
Colbeck Rd. *HA1:* Harr 7G *41*
Colberg Pl. *N16* 7F *49*
Colbert *SE5* .1E *120*
(off Sceaux Gdns.)
Colborne Ho. *E14* 7C *86*
(off E. India Dock Rd.)
Colborne Way *KT4:* Wor Pk 3E *164*
Colbrook Av. *UB3:* Harl 3F *93*
Colbrook Cl. *UB3:* Harl 3F *93*
Colburn Way *SM1:* Sutt 3B *166*
Colby M. *SE19* 5E *138*
Colby Rd. *KT12:* Walt T 7J *147*
SE19 . . . . .5E *138*
Colchester Av. *E12* 4D *70*
Colchester Dr. *HA5:* Pinn 5B *40*
Colchester Ho. *E3* 1B *86*
(off Parnell Rd.)
Colchester Rd. *E10* 7E *50*
E17 . . . . .6C *50*
HA6: Nwood .2J *39*
HA8: Edg 7D *28*
Colclough Ct. *CR0:* C'don 6C *156*
(off Simpson Cl.)
Coldbath Sq. *EC1* 3J 7 (4A *84*)
Coldbath St. *SE13* 1D *122*
COLDBLOW 1J *145*
Cold Blow Cres. *DA5:* Bexl 1K *145*
Cold Blow La. *SE14* 7K *103*
(not continuous)
Cold Blows *CR4:* Mitc 3D *154*

Coldershaw Rd. *W13* 1A *96*
Coldfall Av. *N10* 2E *46*
Coldham Ct. *N22* 1B *48*
Coldharbour *E14* 2E *104*
Coldharbour Crest *SE9* 3E *142*
Coldharbour Ind. Est. *SE5* 2C *120*
Coldharbour La. *SE5* 3C *120*
SW9 . . . . .4A *120*
UB3: Hayes .1J *93*
Coldharbour Leisure Cen. 2D *142*
Coldharbour Pl. *SE5* 2C *120*
Coldharbour Rd. *CR0:* Wadd 5A *168*
Coldharbour Way *CR0:* Wadd 5A *168*
Coldstream Gdns. *SW18* 6H *117*
Colebeck M. *N1* 6B *66*
Colebert Av. *E1* 4J *85*
Colebert Ho. *E1* 4J *85*
(off Colebert Av.)
Colebrook Cl. *NW7* 6A *30*
SW15 . . . . .7F *117*
Colebrook Ct. *SW3* 4D *16*
(off Makins St.)
Colebrooke Av. *W13* 6B *78*
Colebrooke Ct. *DA14:* Sidc 3B *144*
Colebrooke Dr. *E11* 7A *52*
Colebrooke Pl. *N1* 1B *84*
Colebrooke Ri. *BR2:* Brom 2G *159*
Colebrooke Row *N1* 2B *84*
Colebrook Ho. *E14* 6D *86*
(off Ellesmere St.)
Colebrook Rd. *SW16* 1J *155*
Colebrook Way *N11* 5A *32*
Coleby Path *SE5* 7D *102*
Colechurch Ho. *SE1* 5G *103*
(off Avondale Sq.)
Cole Cl. *SE28* 1B *108*
Cole Ct. *TW1:* Twick 7A *114*
Coledale Dr. *HA7:* Stan 1C *42*
Coleford Rd. *SW18* 5A *118*
Cole Gdns. *TW5:* Cran 7J *93*
Colegrave Rd. *E15* 5F *69*
Colegrove Rd. *SE15* 6F *103*
Coleherne Ct. *SW5* 5K *99*
Coleherne Mans. *SW5* 5K *99*
(off Old Brompton Rd.)
Coleherne M. *SW10* 5K *99*
Coleherne Rd. *SW10* 5K *99*
Colehill Gdns. *SW6* 2G *117*
Colehill La. *SW6* 1G *117*
Cole Ho. *SE1* .7K *13*
(off Baylis Rd.)
Coleman Cl. *SE25* 2G *157*
Coleman Ct. *SW18* 7J *117*
Coleman Flds. *N1* 1C *84*
Coleman Mans. *N8* 7J *47*
Coleman Rd. *DA17:* Belv 4G *109*
RM9: Dag 6E *72*
SE5 . . . . .7E *102*
Colemans Heath *SE9* 3E *142*
Coleman St. *EC2* 7E 8 (6D *84*)
Coleman St. Bldgs. *EC2* 7E *8*
Colenso Dr. *NW7* 7H *29*
Colenso Rd. *E5* 4J *67*
IG2: Ilf 1J *71*
COLE PARK 6A *114*
Cole Pk. Gdns. *TW1:* Twick 5A *114*
Cole Pk. Rd. *TW1:* Twick 6A *114*
Cole Pk. Vw. *TW1:* Twick 6A *114*
Colepits Wood Rd. *SE9* 5H *125*
Coleraine Rd. *N8* 3A *48*
SE3 . . . . .6H *105*
Coleridge Av. *E12* 6C *70*
SM1: Sutt 4C *166*
Coleridge Cl. *SW8* 2F *119*
Coleridge Ct. *EN5:* New Bar 5E *20*
(off Station Rd.)
N1 . . . . .1C *84*
(off Popham Rd.)
SW1 . . . . .3C *18*
(off Fynes St.)
W14 . . . . .3F *99*
(off Blythe Rd.)

Coleridge Cres. *SL3:* Poyle 4A *174*
Coleridge Gdns. *NW6* 7A *64*
SW10 . . . . .7K *99*
Coleridge Ho. *SE17* 5C *102*
(off Browning St.)
SW1 . . . . .6B *18*
(off Churchill Gdns.)
Coleridge La. *N8* 6J *47*
Coleridge Rd. *CR0:* C'don 7J *157*
E17 . . . . .4B *50*
N4 . . . . .2A *66*
N8 . . . . .6H *47*
N12 . . . . .5F *31*
TW15: Ashf .4A *128*
Coleridge Sq. *SW10* 7A *100*
(off Coleridge Gdns.)
W13 . . . . .6A *78*
Coleridge Wlk. *NW11* 4J *45*
Coleridge Way *UB4:* Hayes 6J *75*
UB7: W Dray 4A *92*
Cole Rd. *TW1:* Twick 6A *114*
Colesburg Rd. *BR3:* Beck 3B *158*
Coles Cres. *HA2:* Harr 2F *59*
Coles Grn. *WD23:* B Hea 1B *26*
Coles Grn. Ct. *NW2* 2C *62*
Coles Grn. Rd. *NW2* 1C *62*
Coleshill Flats *SW1* 4H *17*
Coleshill Rd. *TW11:* Tedd 6J *131*
Colestown St. *SW11* 2C *118*
Cole St. *SE1* 7D *14* (2C *102*)
Colesworth Ho. *HA8:* Edg 2J *43*
(off Burnt Oak B'way.)
Colet Cl. *N13* .6G *33*
Colet Ct. *W6* 4F *99*
(off Hammersmith Rd.)
Colet Flats *E1* .6A *86*
(off Troon St.)
Colet Gdns. *W14* 4F *99*
Colet Ho. *SE17* 5B *102*
(off Doddington Gro.)
Colette Ct. *SE16* 2K *103*
(off Eleanor Cl.)
Coley St. *WC1* 4H 7 (4K *83*)
Colfe & Hatcliffe Glebe *SE13* 5D *122*
(off Lewisham High St.)
Colfe Rd. *SE23* 1A *140*
Colfes Leisure Cen. 6J *123*
Colham Av. *UB7:* Yiew 1A *92*
COLHAM GREEN 5C *74*
Colham Grn. Rd. *UB8:* Hil 5C *74*
Colham Mill Rd. *UB7:* W Dray 2A *92*
Colham Rd. *UB8:* Hil 4B *74*
Colham Rdbt. *UB8:* Hil 6C *74*
Colina M. *N15* .4B *48*
Colina Rd. *N15* 5B *48*
Colin Cl. *BR4:* W W'ck 3H *171*
CR0: C'don .3B *170*
NW9 . . . . .4A *44*
Colin Ct. *SE6* .7B *122*
Colin Cres. *NW9* 4B *44*
COLINDALE 3K *43*
Colindale Av. *NW9* 3K *43*
Colindale Bus. Pk. *NW9* 3J *43*
Colindale Retail Pk. *NW9* 4K *43*
Colindeep Gdns. *NW4* 4C *44*
Colindeep La. *NW4* 3A *44*
NW9 . . . . .3A *44*
Colin Dr. *NW9* 5B *44*
Colinette Rd. *SW15* 4E *116*
Colin Gdns. *NW9* 4B *44*
Colin Pde. *NW9* 4A *44*
Colin Pk. Rd. *NW9* 4A *44*
Colin Pond Ct.
RM6: Chad H 4D *54*
Colin Rd. *NW10* 6C *62*
Colinsdale *N1* .2C *84*
(off Camden Wlk.)
Colinton Rd. *IG3:* Ilf 2B *72*
Colin Winter Ho. *E1* 4J *85*
(off Nicholas Rd.)
Coliseum Theatre 3E *12*
(off St Martin's La.)

Coliston Pas. *SW18* 7J *117*
(off Coliston Rd.)
Coliston Rd. *SW18* 7J *117*
Collamore Av. *SW18* 1C *136*
Collapit Cl. *HA1:* Harr 6F *41*
Collard Pl. *NW1* 7F *65*
Collards Almshouses *E17* 5E *50*
(off Maynard Rd.)
Collection Pl. *NW8* 1K *81*
(off Bolton Pl.)
College App. *SE10* 6E *104*
College Av. *HA3:* Hrw W 1J *41*
College Cl. *E9* 5J *67*
HA3: Hrw W .1J *41*
N18 . . . . .5A *34*
TW2: Twick .1H *131*
College Ct. *EN3:* Pond E 5D *24*
NW3 . . . . .6B *64*
(off College Cres.)
SW3 . . . . .6F *17*
W5 . . . . .7E *78*
W6 . . . . .5E *98*
(off Queen Caroline St.)
College Cres. *NW3* 6A *64*
College Cross *N1* 7A *66*
College Dr. *HA4:* Ruis 7J *39*
KT7: T Ditt 7J *149*
College E. *E1* 6K 9 (5F *85*)
College Flds. Bus. Cen. *SW19* 1C *154*
College Gdns. *E4* 7J *25*
EN2: Enf 1J *23*
IG4: Ilf 5C *52*
KT3: N Mald 5B *152*
N18 . . . . .5B *34*
SE21 . . . . .1E *138*
SW17 . . . . .2C *136*
(not continuous)
College Grn. *SE19* 7E *138*
College Gro. *NW1* 1G *83*
College Hill *EC4* 2D *14* (7C *84*)
College Hill Rd. *HA3:* Hrw W 7D *26*
College Ho. *TW7:* Isle 7J *95*
College La. *NW5* 4F *65*
College Mans. *NW6* 1G *81*
(off Salusbury Rd.)
College M. *N1* .7A *66*
(off College Cross, not continuous)
SW1 . . . . .1E *18*
SW18 . . . . .5K *117*
College of Arms 2C *14*
College Pde. *NW6* 1G *81*
(off Salusbury Rd.)
COLLEGE PARK 3D *80*
College Pk. Cl. *SE13* 4F *123*
College Pk. Rd. *N17* 6A *34*
College Pl. *E17* 4G *51*
NW1 . . . . .1G *83*
SW10 . . . . .7A *100*
College Point *E15* 6H *69*
College Rd. *BR1:* Brom 1J *159*
BR8: Hext 7K *145*
CR0: C'don .2D *168*
E17 . . . . .5E *50*
EN2: Enf 2J *23*
HA1: Harr 6J *41*
HA3: Hrw W .1J *41*
HA9: Wemb .1D *60*
N17 . . . . .6A *34*
N21 . . . . .2F *33*
NW10 . . . . .2E *80*
SE19 . . . . .5F *139*
SE21 . . . . .7E *120*
SW19 . . . . .6B *136*
TW7: Isle 1K *113*
W13 . . . . .6B *78*
College Rdbt. *KT1:* King T 3E *150*
College Row *E9* 5K *67*
College Slip *BR1:* Brom 1J *159*
College St. *EC4* 2D *14* (7C *84*)
College Ter. *E3* 3B *86*
N3 . . . . .2H *45*
College Vw. *SE9* 1B *142*

College Wlk. KT1: King T . . . 3E **150**
College Way TW15: Ashf . . . 4B **128**
UB3: Hayes . . . 7J **75**
College Yd. NW5 . . . 4F **65**
NW6 . . . 1G **81**
Collent St. E9 . . . 6J **67**
Collerston Ho. *SE10* . . . *5H **105***
(off Armitage Rd.)
Colless Rd. N15 . . . 5F **49**
Collett Rd. SE16 . . . 3G **103**
Collett Way UB2: S'hall . . . 2F **95**
Collier Cl. E6 . . . 7F **89**
KT19: Ewe . . . 6G **163**
Collier Dr. HA8: Edg . . . 2G **43**
COLLIER ROW . . . 1H **55**
Collier Row La. RM5: Col R . . . 1H **55**
Collier Row Rd. RM5: Col R . . . 1F **55**
Colliers Ct. *CR0: C'don* . . . *4D **168***
(off St Peter's Rd.)
Colliers Shaw BR2: Kes . . . 5B **172**
Collier St. N1 . . . 2K **83**
Colliers Water La. CR7: Thor H . . . 5A **156**
COLLIERS WOOD . . . 7B **136**
COLLIERS WOOD . . . **7B 136**
Colliers Wood SW19 . . . 6B **136**
Collindale Av. DA8: Erith . . . 7H **109**
DA15: Sidc . . . 1A **144**
Collingbourne Rd. W12 . . . 1D **98**
Collingham Gdns. SW5 . . . 4K **99**
Collingham Pl. SW5 . . . 4K **99**
Collingham Rd. SW5 . . . 4K **99**
Collings Cl. N22 . . . 6E **32**
Collington St. SE10 . . . 5F **105**
Collingtree Rd. SE26 . . . 4J **139**
Collingwood Av. KT5: Surb . . . 1J **163**
N10 . . . 3E **46**
Collingwood Cl. SE20 . . . 1H **157**
TW2: Whitt . . . 7E **112**
Collingwood Ct. EN5: New Bar . . . 5E **20**
W5 . . . 5F **79**
Collingwood Ho. *E1* . . . *4H **85***
(off Darling Row)
SE16 . . . *2H **103***
(off Cherry Gdn. St.)
SW1 . . . *6C **18***
(off Dolphin Sq.)
W1 . . . *5A **6***
(off Clipstone St.)
Collingwood Rd. CR4: Mitc . . . 3C **154**
E17 . . . 6C **50**
N15 . . . 4E **48**
SM1: Sutt . . . 3J **165**
UB8: Hil . . . 4D **74**
Collingwood St. E1 . . . 4H **85**
Collins Av. HA7: Stan . . . 2E **42**
Collins Ct. E8 . . . 6G **67**
Collins Dr. HA4: Ruis . . . 2A **58**
Collins Ho. *E14* . . . *7E **86***
(off Newby Pl.)
SE10 . . . *5H **105***
(off Armitage Rd.)
Collinson Ct. *SE1* . . . *7C **14***
(off Gt. Suffolk St.)
Collinson Ho. *SE15* . . . *7G **103***
(off Peckham Pk. Rd.)
Collinson St. SE1 . . . 7C **14** (2C **102**)
Collinson Wlk. SE1 . . . 7C **14** (2C **102**)
Collins Path TW12: Hamp . . . 6D **130**
Collins Rd. N5 . . . 4C **66**
Collins Sq. SE3 . . . 2H **123**
Collins St. SE3 . . . 2G **123**
(not continuous)
Collins Twr. *E8* . . . *6F **67***
(off Roseberry St.)
Collin's Yd. N1 . . . 1B **84**
Collinwood Av. EN3: Enf H . . . 3D **24**
Collinwood Gdns. IG5: Ilf . . . 5D **52**
Collis All. TW2: Twick . . . 1J **131**
Collison Pl. N16 . . . 1E **66**
Coll's Rd. SE15 . . . 1J **121**
Collyer Av. CR0: Bedd . . . 4J **167**
Collyer Pl. SE15 . . . 1G **121**
Collyer Rd. CR0: Bedd . . . 4J **167**
Colman Ct. HA7: Stan . . . 6G **27**
N12 . . . 6F **31**
Colman Pde. EN1: Enf . . . 3K **23**
Colman Rd. E16 . . . 5A **88**
Colmans Wharf *E14* . . . *5D **86***
(off Morris Rd.)
Colmar Cl. E1 . . . 4K **85**
Colmer Pl. HA3: Hrw W . . . 7C **26**
Colmer Rd. SW16 . . . 1J **155**
Colmore M. SE15 . . . 1H **121**
Colmore Rd. EN3: Pond E . . . 4D **24**
Colnbrook By-Pass SL3: Coln, L'ly . . . 3A **174**
UB7: Harm . . . 3A **174**
Colnbrook Ct. SL3: Poyle . . . 4A **174**
Colnbrook St. SE1 . . . 3B **102**
Colne Ct. KT19: Ewe . . . 4J **163**
W7 . . . *6H **77***
(off High La.)
Colnedale Rd. UB8: Uxb . . . 5A **56**
Colne Ho. IG11: Bark . . . 7F **71**
NW8 . . . *4B **4***
(off Penfold St.)
Colne Pk. Cvn. Site UB7: W Dray . . . 1D **174**
Colne Reach TW19: Stan M . . . 7A **174**
Colne Rd. E5 . . . 4A **68**
N21 . . . 7J **23**
TW1: Twick . . . 1J **131**
TW2: Twick . . . 1J **131**
Colne St. E13 . . . 3J **87**
COLNEY HATCH . . . **6J 31**
Colney Hatch La. N10 . . . 6J **31**
N11 . . . 6J **31**
Colnmore Ct. *E2* . . . *3K **85***
(off Meath Cres.)
Coln Trad. Est. SL3: Poyle . . . 4A **174**
Cologne Rd. SW11 . . . 4B **118**
Coloma Ct. BR4: W W'ck . . . 4G **171**
Colombo Rd. IG1: Ilf . . . 1G **71**
Colombo St. SE1 . . . 5A **14** (1B **102**)
Colombo Street Sports & Community Cen. . . . 5A **14**
Colomb St. SE10 . . . 5G **105**
Colonel's Wlk. EN2: Enf . . . 3G **23**
Colonial Av. TW2: Whitt . . . 6G **113**
Colonial Ct. N7 . . . 3K **65**
Colonial Dr. W4 . . . 4J **97**
Colonial Rd. TW14: Felt . . . 7G **111**
Colonnade WC1 . . . 4F **7** (4J **83**)
Colonnade, The SE8 . . . 4B **104**
Colonnades, The CR0: Wadd . . . 6A **168**
W2 . . . 6K **81**
Colonnade Wlk. SW1 . . . 4J **17** (4F **101**)
Colony M. *N1* . . . *5D **66***
(off Mildmay Gro. Nth.)
Colorado Apartments *N8* . . . *3K **47***
(off Gt. Amwell La.)
Colorado Bldg. *SE10* . . . *1D **122***
(off Deal's Gateway)
Colosseum Ter. NW1 . . . 2K **5**
Colour Ct. SW1 . . . 5B **12**
Colour Ho. *SE1* . . . *7H **15***
(off Bell Yd M.)
Colour House Theatre . . . 1A **154**
Colroy Ct. NW11 . . . 5G **45**
Colson Rd. CR0: C'don . . . 2E **168**
Colson Way SW16 . . . 4G **137**
Colstead Ho. *E1* . . . *6H **85***
(off Watney Mkt.)
Colsterworth Rd. N15 . . . 4F **49**
(not continuous)
Colston Av. SM5: Cars . . . 4C **166**
Colston Ct. SM5: Cars . . . 4D **166**
Colston Rd. E7 . . . 6B **70**
SW14 . . . 4J **115**
Coltash Ct. *EC1* . . . *3D **8***
(off Whitecross St.)
Colthurst Cres. N4 . . . 2B **66**
Colthurst Dr. N9 . . . 3C **34**
Coltman Ho. *SE10* . . . *6E **104***
(off Welland St.)
Coltman St. E14 . . . 5A **86**
Coltness Cres. SE2 . . . 5B **108**
Colton Gdns. N17 . . . 3C **48**
Colton Rd. HA1: Harr . . . 5J **41**
Coltsfoot Dr. UB7: Yiew . . . 6A **74**
Columbas Dr. NW3 . . . 1B **64**
Columbia Av. HA4: Ruis . . . 1K **57**
HA8: Edg . . . 1H **43**
KT4: Wor Pk . . . 7B **152**
Columbia Ho. *E3* . . . *4B **86***
(off Hamlets Way)
Columbia Point *SE16* . . . *3J **103***
(off Canada Est.)
Columbia Rd. E2 . . . 1J **9** (3F **85**)
E13 . . . 4H **87**
Columbia Road Flower Market . . . *1K 9*
(off Columbia Rd.)
Columbia Sq. SW14 . . . 4J **115**
Columbia Wharf EN3: Pond E . . . 6F **25**
Columbine Av. CR2: S Croy . . . 7B **168**
E6 . . . 5C **88**
Columbine Way SE13 . . . 2E **122**
Columbus Ct. *SE16* . . . *1J **103***
(off Rotherhithe St.)
Columbus Courtyard E14 . . . 1C **104**
Columbus Gdns. HA6: Nwood . . . 1J **39**
Colva Wlk. N19 . . . 2F **65**
Colvern Ho. RM7: Rom . . . 5J **55**
Colverson Ho. *E1* . . . *5J **85***
(off Lindley St.)
Colvestone Cres. E8 . . . 5F **67**
Colview Ct. SE9 . . . 1B **142**
Colville Est. N1 . . . 1E **84**
Colville Est. W. E2 . . . 2K **9**
Colville Gdns. W11 . . . 6H **81**
(not continuous)
Colville Ho. *E2* . . . *2J **85***
(off Waterloo Gdns.)
Colville Ho's. W11 . . . 6H **81**
Colville M. W11 . . . 6H **81**
Colville Pl. W1 . . . 6B **6** (5G **83**)
Colville Rd. E11 . . . 3E **68**
E17 . . . 2A **50**
N9 . . . 1C **34**
W3 . . . 3H **97**
W11 . . . 6H **81**
Colville Sq. W11 . . . 6H **81**
Colville Ter. W11 . . . 6H **81**
Colvin Cl. SE26 . . . 5J **139**
Colvin Gdns. E4 . . . 3K **35**
E11 . . . 4K **51**
IG6: Ilf . . . 1G **53**
Colvin Ho. *W10* . . . *6F **81***
(off Kingsdown Cl.)
Colvin Rd. CR7: Thor H . . . 5A **156**
E6 . . . 7C **70**
Colwall Gdns. IG8: Wfd G . . . 5D **36**
Colwell Rd. SE22 . . . 5F **121**
Colwick Cl. N6 . . . 7H **47**
Colwith Rd. W6 . . . 6E **98**
Colwood Gdns. SW19 . . . 7B **136**
Colworth Gro. SE17 . . . 4C **102**
Colworth Rd. CR0: C'don . . . 1G **169**
E11 . . . 6G **51**
Colwyn Av. UB6: G'frd . . . 2K **77**
Colwyn Cl. SW16 . . . 5G **137**
Colwyn Cres. TW3: Houn . . . 1G **113**
Colwyn Grn. *NW9* . . . *6A **44***
(off Snowdon Dr.)
Colwyn Ho. SE1 . . . 2J **19** (3A **102**)
Colwyn Rd. NW2 . . . 3D **62**
Colyer Cl. SE9 . . . 2F **143**
Colyers Cl. DA8: Erith . . . 1K **127**
Colyers La. DA8: Erith . . . 1J **127**
Colyers Wlk. DA8: Erith . . . 1K **127**
Colyton Cl. DA16: Well . . . 1D **126**
HA0: Wemb . . . 6C **60**
Colyton La. SW16 . . . 5A **138**
Colyton Rd. SE22 . . . 5H **121**
Colyton Way N18 . . . 5B **34**
Combe, The NW1 . . . 2K **5** (3F **83**)
Combe Av. SE3 . . . 7H **105**
Combedale Rd. SE10 . . . 5J **105**
Combe Ho. *W2* . . . *5J **81***
(off Gt. Western Rd.)
Combemartin Rd. SW18 . . . 7G **117**
Combe M. SE3 . . . 7H **105**
Comber Cl. NW2 . . . 3D **62**
Comber Gro. SE5 . . . 7C **102**
Comber Ho. SE5 . . . 7C **102**
Combermere Rd. SM4: Mord . . . 6K **153**
SW9 . . . 3K **119**
Comberton *KT1: King T* . . . *2G **151***
(off Eureka Rd.)
Comberton Rd. E5 . . . 2H **67**
Combeside SE18 . . . 7K **107**
Combwell Cres. SE2 . . . 3A **108**
Comedy Store . . . *3C 12*
(off Oxendon St.)
Comedy Theatre . . . *3C 12*
(off Panton St.)
Comely Bank Rd. E17 . . . 5E **50**
Comeragh M. W14 . . . 5G **99**
Comeragh Rd. W14 . . . 5G **99**
Comer Cres. *UB2: S'hall* . . . *1G **95***
(off Windmill Av.)
Comerell Pl. SE10 . . . 5H **105**
Comerford Rd. SE4 . . . 4A **122**
Comer Ho. EN5: New Bar . . . 4F **21**
Comet Cl. E12 . . . 4B **70**
Comet Ho. UB3: Harl . . . 7E **92**
Comet Pl. SE8 . . . 7C **104**
(not continuous)
Comet Rd. TW19: Stanw . . . 7A **110**
Comet St. SE8 . . . 7C **104**
Comfort St. SE15 . . . 6E **102**
Commerce Pk. CR0: Wadd . . . 2K **167**
Commerce Rd. N22 . . . 1K **47**
TW8: Bford . . . 6C **96**
Commerce Way CR0: Wadd . . . 2K **167**
Commercial Dock Path *SE16* . . . *3B **104***
(off Gulliver St.)
Commercial Rd. E1 . . . 7K **9** (6G **85**)
E14 . . . 6G **85**
N18 . . . 5K **33**
Commercial Rd. Ind. Est. N18 . . . 6A **34**
Commercial St. E1 . . . 4J **9** (4F **85**)
Commercial Way NW10 . . . 2H **79**
SE10 . . . 4H **105**
SE15 . . . 7F **103**
Commerell St. SE10 . . . 5G **105**
Commodity Quay E1 . . . 3K **15** (7F **85**)
Commodore Ct. *SE8* . . . *1C **122***
(off Albyn Rd.)
Commodore Ho. *E14* . . . *7E **86***
(off Poplar High St.)
SW18 . . . 3A **118**
Commodore Sq. SW10 . . . 1A **118**
Commodore St. E1 . . . 4A **86**
Common, The E15 . . . 6G **69**
HA7: Stan . . . 2D **26**
UB2: S'hall . . . 4A **94**
UB7: W Dray . . . 1D **174**
W5 . . . 7E **78**
(not continuous)
Commondale SW15 . . . 2E **116**
Commonfield La. SW17 . . . 5C **136**
Common La. KT10: Clay . . . 7A **162**
Common Mile Cl. SW4 . . . 5H **119**
Common Rd. HA7: Stan . . . 4C **26**
KT10: Clay . . . 6A **162**
SW13 . . . 3D **116**
Commonside BR2: Kes . . . 4A **172**
Commonside E. CR4: Mitc . . . 3E **154**
(not continuous)
Commonside W. CR4: Mitc . . . 3D **154**
Commonwealth Av.
UB3: Hayes . . . 6F **75**
W12 . . . 7D **80**
(not continuous)
Commonwealth Conference Cen. . . . 5B **12**
Commonwealth Rd. N17 . . . 7B **34**
Commonwealth Way SE2 . . . 5B **108**
Community Cl. TW5: Cran . . . 1K **111**
UB10: Ick . . . 3D **56**

Community La. N7 . . . . .5H 65
Community Rd. E15 . . . . .5F 69
    UB6: G'frd 1G 77
Como Rd. SE23 . . . . .2A 140
Como St. RM7: Rom 5K 55
Compass Cl. HA8: Edg 4A 28
    TW15: Ashf 7E 128
Compass Ct. SE1 . . . . .5J 15
    (off Shad Thames)
Compass Hill TW10: Rich 6D 114
Compass Ho. SW18 . . . . .4K 117
Compass La. BR1: Brom 1J 159
    (off North St.)
Compass Point E14 . . . . .7B 86
    (off Grenade St.)
Compass Theatre 3E 56
Compayne Gdns. NW6 . . . . .7K 63
Compayne Mans. NW6 . . . . .6K 63
    (off Fairhazel Gdns.)
Compter Pas. EC2 . . . . .1D 14
Compton Av. E6 . . . . .2B 88
    HA0: Wemb 4C 60
    N1 . . . . .6B 66
    N6 . . . . .7C 46
Compton Cl. E3 . . . . .5C 86
    HA8: Edg .7D 28
    NW1 . . . . .2K 5
    NW11 . . . . .3F 63
    SE15 . . . . .7G 103
    W13 . . . . .6A 78
Compton Ct. SE19 . . . . .6E 138
    SM1: Sutt 4A 166
Compton Cres. KT9: Chess 5E 162
    N17 . . . . .7H 33
    UB5: N'olt 1B 76
    W4 . . . . .6J 97
Compton Ho. SW11 . . . . .1C 118
Compton Leisure Cen., The 1C 76
Compton Pas. EC1 . . . . .3B 8 (4B 84)
Compton Pl. WC1 . . . . .3E 6 (4J 83)
Compton Ri. HA5: Pinn 5C 40
Compton Rd. CR0: C'don 1H 169
    N1 . . . . .6B 66
    N21 . . . . .1F 33
    NW10 . . . . .3F 81
    SW19 . . . . .6H 135
    UB3: Hayes 7G 75
Compton Sports Cen. 6H 31
Compton St. EC1 . . . . .3A 8 (4B 84)
Compton Ter. N1 . . . . .6B 66
    N21 . . . . .1F 33
Comreddy Cl. EN2: Enf 1G 23
Comus Ho. SE17 . . . . .4E 102
    (off Comus Pl.)
Comus Pl. SE17 . . . . .4E 102
Comyn Rd. SW11 . . . . .4C 118
Comyns, The WD23: B Hea 1B 26
Comyns Cl. E16 . . . . .5H 87
Comyns Rd. RM9: Dag 7G 73
Conant Ho. SE11 . . . . .7K 19
    (off St Agnes Pl.)
Conant Ho. E1 .7G 85
Concanon Rd. SW2 . . . . .4K 119
Concert Hall App.
    SE1 . . . . .5H 13 (1K 101)
Concord Bus. Cen. W3 . . . . .4H 79
Concord Cl. UB5: N'olt 3B 76
Concord Ct. KT1: King T 3F 151
    (off Winery La.)
Concorde Cl. TW3: Houn 2F 113
    UB10: Uxb 2A 74
Concorde Dr. E6 . . . . .5D 88
Concorde Way SE16 . . . . .4K 103
Concord Ho. KT3: N Mald 3A 152
    N17 . . . . .7A 34
    (off Park La.)
Concordia Wharf E14 . . . . .1E 104
    (off Coldharbour)
Concord Rd. EN3: Pond E 5C 24
    W3 . . . . .4H 79
Concord Ter. HA2: Harr 2F 59
    (off Coles Cres.)

Concourse, The N9 . . . . .2B 34
    (within Edmonton Grn. Shop. Cen.)
    NW9 . . . . .1A 44
Condell Rd. SW8 . . . . .1G 119
Conder St. E14 .6A 86
Condor Path UB5: N'olt 2E 76
    (off Union Rd.)
Condover Cres. SE18 . . . . .7F 107
Condray Pl. SW11 . . . . .7C 100
Conduit Av. SE10 . . . . .1F 123
Conduit Ct. WC2 . . . . .2E 12
Conduit La. CR0: C'don 5G 169
    CR2: S Croy 5G 169
    EN3: Pond E 6F 25
    N18 . . . . .5D 34
Conduit M. SE18 . . . . .5F 107
    W2 . . . . .1A 10 (6B 82)
Conduit Pas. W2 . . . . .1A 10
Conduit Pl. W2 . . . . .1A 10 (6B 82)
Conduit Rd. SE18 . . . . .5F 107
Conduit St. W1 . . . . .2K 11 (7F 83)
Conduit Way NW10 . . . . .7J 61
Conewood St. N5 . . . . .3B 66
Coney Acre SE21 . . . . .1C 138
Coney Burrows E4 . . . . .2B 36
Coney Gro. UB8: Hil 3C 74
Coneygrove Path UB5: N'olt 6C 58
    (off Arnold Rd.)
CONEY HALL .3G 171
Coney Hall Pde. BR4: W W'ck 3G 171
Coney Hill Rd. BR4: W W'ck 2G 171
Coney Way SW8 . . . . .6K 101
Conference Ct. E4 . . . . .2K 35
Conference Rd. SE2 . . . . .4C 108
Congers Ho. SE8 . . . . .7C 104
Congleton Gro. SE18 . . . . .5G 107
Congo Dr. N9 . . . . .3D 34
Congo Rd. SE18 . . . . .5H 107
Congress Rd. SE2 . . . . .4C 108
Congreve Ho. N16 . . . . .5E 66
Congreve Rd. SE9 . . . . .3D 124
Congreve St. SE17 . . . . .4E 102
Congreve Wlk. E16 . . . . .5B 88
    (off Fulmer Rd.)
Conical Cnr. EN2: Enf 2H 23
Conifer Cl. BR6: Orp 4H 173
Conifer Ct. TW15: Ashf 5B 128
    (off The Crescent)
Conifer Gdns. EN1: Enf 6K 23
    SM1: Sutt 2K 165
    SW16 . . . . .3J 137
Conifer Ho. SE4 . . . . .4B 122
    (off Brockley Rd.)
Conifers Cl. TW11: Tedd 7B 132
Conifer Way HA0: Wemb 3C 60
    UB3: Hayes 7J 75
Coniger Rd. SW6 . . . . .2J 117
Coningham M. W12 . . . . .1C 98
Coningham Rd. W12 . . . . .2D 98
Coningsby Av. NW9 . . . . .2A 44
Coningsby Cotts. W5 . . . . .2D 96
Coningsby Ct. CR4: Mitc 2E 154
Coningsby Gdns. E4 . . . . .6J 35
Coningsby Rd. CR2: S Croy 7C 168
    N4 . . . . .7B 48
    W5 . . . . .2D 96
Conington Rd. SE13 . . . . .2D 122
Conisbee Ct. N14 . . . . .5B 22
Conisborough Cres. SE6 . . . . .3E 140
Conisbrough NW1 . . . . .1G 83
    (off Bayham St.)
Coniscliffe Cl. BR7: Chst 1E 160
Coniscliffe Rd. N13 . . . . .3H 33
Coniston NW1 . . . . .1A 6
    (off Harrington St.)
Coniston Av. DA16: Well 3J 125
    IG11: Bark 7J 71
    UB6: G'frd 3B 78
Coniston Cl. DA7: Bex 1J 127
    DA8: Erith 7K 109

Coniston Cl. IG11: Bark 7J 71
    N20 . . . . .3F 31
    SW13 . . . . .7B 98
    SW20 . . . . .6F 153
    W4 . . . . .7J 97
Coniston Ct. NW7 . . . . .7B 30
    (off Langstone Way)
    SE16 . . . . .2K 103
    (off Eleanor Cl.)
    SM6: Wall 4F 167
    TW15: Ashf 3A 128
    W2 . . . . .1D 10
    (off Kendal St.)
Conistone Way N7 . . . . .7J 65
Coniston Gdns. HA5: Eastc 4J 39
    HA9: Wemb 1C 60
    IG4: Ilf 4C 52
    N9 . . . . .1D 34
    NW9 . . . . .5K 43
    SM2: Sutt 6B 166
Coniston Ho. E3 . . . . .4B 86
    (off Southern Gro.)
    SE5 . . . . .7C 102
    (off Wyndham Rd.)
Coniston Rd. BR1: Brom 6G 141
    CR0: C'don 7G 157
    DA7: Bex 1J 127
    N10 . . . . .2F 47
    N17 . . . . .6B 34
    TW2: Whitt 6F 113
Coniston Wlk. E9 . . . . .5J 67
Coniston Way KT9: Chess 3E 162
Conlan St. W10 .4G 81
Conley Rd. NW10 . . . . .6A 62
Conley St. SE10 . . . . .5G 105
Connaught Av. E4 . . . . .7K 25 & 1A 36
    EN1: Enf 2K 23
    EN4: E Barn 1J 31
    SW14 . . . . .3J 115
    TW4: Houn 4C 112
    TW15: Ashf 4A 128
Connaught Bri. E16 . . . . .1B 106
Connaught Bus. Cen. CR0: Wadd 6K 167
    CR4: Mitc 5D 154
    NW9 . . . . .5B 44
Connaught Cl. E10 . . . . .2A 68
    EN1: Enf 2K 23
    SM1: Sutt 2B 166
    UB8: Hil 4E 74
    W2 . . . . .1D 10 (6C 82)
Connaught Ct. E17 . . . . .4D 50
    (off Orford Rd.)
    W2 . . . . .1E 10
    (off Connaught Sq.)
Connaught Dr. NW11 . . . . .4J 45
Connaught Gdns. N10 . . . . .5F 47
    N13 . . . . .4G 33
    SM4: Mord 4A 154
Connaught Hgts. UB10: Hil 4E 74
    (off Uxbridge Rd.)
Connaught Ho. NW10 . . . . .3D 80
    (off Trenmar Gdns.)
    W1 . . . . .3J 11
    (off Davies St.)
Connaught La. IG1: Ilf 2G 71
Connaught Lodge N4 . . . . .7A 48
    (off Connaught Rd.)
Connaught M. NW3 . . . . .4C 64
    SE18 . . . . .5E 106
    SW6 . . . . .1G 117
Connaught Pl. W2 . . . . .2E 10 (7D 82)
Connaught Rd. E4 . . . . .1B 36
    E11 . . . . .1F 69
    E16 . . . . .1B 106
    E17 . . . . .5C 50
    EN5: Barn 6A 20
    HA3: W'stone 1K 41
    IG1: Ilf 2H 71
    KT3: N Mald 4A 152
    N4 . . . . .7A 48
    NW10 . . . . .1A 80
    SE18 . . . . .5E 106

Connaught Rd. SM1: Sutt 2B 166
    TW10: Rich 5F 115
    TW11: Tedd 5H 131
    W13 . . . . .7B 78
Connaught Rdbt. E16 . . . . .7B 88
    (off Victoria Dock Rd.)
Connaught Sq. W2 . . . . .1D 10 (6D 82)
Connaught St. W2 . . . . .1D 10 (6C 82)
Connaught Way N13 . . . . .4G 33
Connaught Works E3 . . . . .1A 86
    (off Old Ford Rd.)
Connect La. IG6: Ilf 2G 53
Connell Ct. SE14 . . . . .6K 103
    (off Myers La.)
Connell Cres. W5 . . . . .4F 79
Conniffe Ct. SE9 . . . . .6H 125
Connington Cres. E4 . . . . .3A 36
Connolly Ct. RM7: Rush G 6K 55
    (off Union Rd.)
Connor Cl. E11 .7G 51
    IG6: Ilf 1G 53
Connor Ct. SW11 . . . . .1F 119
Connor Rd. RM9: Dag 4F 73
Connor St. E9 . . . . .1K 85
Conolly Dell W7 .1J 95
    (off Conolly Rd.)
Conolly Rd. W7 .1J 95
Conrad Dr. KT4: Wor Pk 1E 164
Conrad Ho. E8 .6G 67
    E14 . . . . .7J 87
    (off Victory Pl.)
    E16 . . . . .1K 105
    (off Wesley Av.)
    N16 . . . . .5E 66
    (off Matthias Rd.)
    SW8 . . . . .7J 101
    (off Wyvil Rd.)
Conrad Twr. W3 .3H 97
Consfield Av. KT3: N Mald 4C 152
Consort Cl. W4 .3K 99
    (off Wright's La.)
Consort Ho. E14 . . . . .1E 104
    (off St Davids Sq.)
    SW6 . . . . .2A 118
    (off Lensbury Av.)
    W2 . . . . .7K 81
    (off Queensway)
Consort Lodge NW8 . . . . .1D 82
    (off Prince Albert Rd.)
Consort M. TW7: Isle 5H 113
Consort Rd. SE15 . . . . .1H 121
Cons St. SE1 . . . . .6K 13 (2A 102)
Constable Av. E16 . . . . .1K 105
Constable Cl. N11 . . . . .5J 31
    NW11 . . . . .6K 45
    UB4: Hayes 2E 74
Constable Ct. SE16 . . . . .5H 103
    (off Stubbs Dr.)
    W4 . . . . .5H 97
    (off Chaseley Dr.)
Constable Cres. N15 . . . . .5G 49
Constable Gdns. HA8: Edg 1G 43
    TW7: Isle 5H 113
Constable Ho. NW3 . . . . .7D 64
    UB5: N'olt 2B 76
    (off Gallery Gdns.)
Constable Ho's. E14 . . . . .2C 104
    (off Cassilis Rd.)
Constable Rd. BR1: Brom 2K 159
    RM8: Dag 4B 72
Constable St. E16 . . . . .1C 106
Constable Wlk. SE21 . . . . .3E 138
Constance Allen Ho. W10 . . . . .6F 81
    (off Bridge Cl.)
Constance Cl. SW15 . . . . .4K 133
Constance Cres. BR2: Hayes 7H 159
Constance Rd. CR0: C'don 7B 156
    EN1: Enf 6K 23
    SM1: Sutt 4A 166
    TW2: Whitt 7F 113
Constance St. E16 . . . . .1C 106
Constant Ho. E14 . . . . .7D 86
    (off Harrow La.)

Constantine Ct. *E1* 6G **85**
(*off Fairclough St.*)
Constantine Pl. UB10: Hil 1B **74**
Constantine Rd. NW3 4C **64**
Constitution Hill SW1 6J **11** (2F **101**)
Constitution Ri. SE18 1E **124**
Consul Av. RM9: Dag, Rain 3J **91**
RM13: Rain 3J **91**
Consul Ho. *E3* 4C **86**
(*off Wellington Way*)
Content St. SE17 4D **102**
Contessa Cl. BR6: Farnb 5J **173**
Control Twr. Rd. TW6: H'row A 3C **110**
Convair Wlk. UB5: N'olt 3B **76**
Convent Cl. BR3: Beck 7E **140**
EN5: Barn 2C **20**
Convent Gdns. W5 4C **96**
W11 6G **81**
Convent Hill SE19 6C **138**
Convent Lodge TW15: Ashf 5D **128**
Convent Rd. TW15: Ashf 5C **128**
Convent Way UB2: S'hall 4A **94**
Conway Cl. BR3: Beck 1A **158**
HA7: Stan 6F **27**
Conway Cres. RM6: Chad H 6C **54**
UB6: G'frd 2J **77**
Conway Dr. SM2: Sutt 6K **165**
TW15: Ashf 6E **128**
UB3: Harl 3E **92**
Conway Gdns. CR4: Mitc 4J **155**
EN2: Enf 1K **23**
HA9: Wemb 7C **42**
Conway Gro. W3 5K **79**
Conway Ho. *E14* 4C **104**
(*off Cahir St.*)
SW3 6F **17**
(*off Ormonde Ga.*)
Conway M. W1 4A **6**
Conway Rd. N14 3D **32**
N15 5B **48**
NW2 2E **62**
SE18 4H **107**
SW20 1E **152**
TW4: Houn 7D **112**
TW6: H'row A 3D **110**
TW13: Hanw 5B **130**
Conway St. W1 4A **6** (4G **83**)
(not continuous)
Conway Wlk. TW12: Hamp 6D **130**
Conybeare NW3 7C **64**
Conyers Cl. IG8: Wfd G 6B **36**
Conyer's Rd. SW16 5H **137**
Conyer St. E3 2A **86**
Cooden Cl. BR1: Brom 7K **141**
Cook Ct. *SE8* 5A **104**
(*off Evelyn St.*)
SE16 1J **103**
(*off Rotherhithe St.*)
Cookes Cl. E11 2H **69**
Cookes La. SM3: Cheam 6G **165**
Cooke St. IG11: Bark 1G **89**
Cookham Cl. UB2: S'hall 3F **95**
Cookham Cres. SE16 2K **103**
Cookham Dene Cl. BR7: Chst 1H **161**
Cookham Ho. *E2* 3J **9**
(*off Montclare St.*)
Cookham Rd. BR8: Swan 7G **145**
Cookhill Rd. SE2 2B **108**
Cook Rd. RM9: Dag 1E **90**
Cooks Cl. *E14* 1C **104**
(*off Cabot Sq.*)
RM5: Col R 1J **55**
Cooks Hole Rd. EN2: Enf 1H **23**
Cookson Gro. DA8: Erith 7H **109**
Cooks Rd. E15 2D **86**
SE17 6B **102**
Coolfin Rd. E16 6J **87**
Coolgardie Av. E4 5A **36**
IG7: Chig 3K **37**
Coolgardie Rd. TW15: Ashf 5E **128**
Coolhurst Lawn Tennis & Squash Raquet Club 6H **47**
Coolhurst Rd. N8 6H **47**
Cool Oak La. NW9 7A **44**
Coomassie Rd. W9 4H **81**
COOMBE 7K **133**
Coombe Av. CR0: C'don 4E **168**
Coombe Bank KT2: King T 1A **152**
Coombe Cl. HA8: Edg 2F **43**
TW3: Houn 4E **112**
Coombe Cnr. N21 1G **33**
Coombe Ct. *CR0: C'don* 4D **168**
(*off St Peter's Rd.*)
Coombe Cres. TW12: Hamp 7D **130**
Coombe Dene *BR2: Brom* 4H **159**
(*off Cumberland Rd.*)
Coombe Dr. HA4: Ruis 1K **57**
Coombe End KT2: King T 7K **133**
Coombefield Cl. KT3: N Mald 5A **152**
Coombe Gdns. KT3: N Mald 4B **152**
SW20 2C **152**
Coombe Hill Glade KT2: King T 7A **134**
Coombe Hill Rd. KT2: King T 7A **134**
Coombe Ho. E4 6G **35**
N7 5H **65**
Coombe Ho. Chase KT3: N Mald 1K **151**
Coombehurst Cl. EN4: Cockf 2J **21**
COOMBE LANE 1B **152**
Coombe La. CR0: C'don 5H **169**
SW20 1B **152**
Coombe La. Flyover SW20 1B **152**
Coombe La. W. KT2: King T 1H **151**
Coombe Lea BR1: Brom 3C **160**
Coombe Lodge SE7 6A **106**
Coombe Neville KT2: King T 7K **133**
Coombe Pk. KT2: King T 5J **133**
Coombe Pl. KT2: King T 5J **133**
Coomber Ho. *SW6* 3K **117**
(*off Wandsworth Bri. Rd.*)
Coombe Ridings KT2: King T 5J **133**
Coombe Ri. KT2: King T 1J **151**
Coombe Rd. CR0: C'don 4D **168**
KT2: King T 1G **151**
KT3: N Mald 2A **152**
N22 2A **48**
NW10 3K **61**
SE26 4H **139**
TW12: Hamp 6D **130**
W4 5A **98**
W13 3B **96**
Coomber Way CR0: Bedd 7H **155**
Coombes Rd. RM9: Dag 1F **91**
Coombe Wlk. SM1: Sutt 3K **165**
Coombewood Dr. RM6: Chad H 6F **55**
Coombe Wood Rd. KT2: King T 5J **133**
Coombrook Ct. *SE16* 2A **104**
(*off Elgar St.*)
Coombs St. N1 1B **8** (2B **84**)
Coomer M. SW6 6H **99**
Coomer Pl. SW6 6H **99**
Coomer Rd. SW6 6H **99**
Cooms Wlk. HA8: Edg 1J **43**
Coope Ct. *RM7: Rush G* 6K **55**
(*off Union Rd.*)
Cooperage, The *SE1* 6J **15**
(*off Gainsford St.*)
SW8 7K **101**
(*off Regent's Bri. Gdns.*)
Cooperage Cl. N17 6A **34**
Co-operative Ho. SE15 3G **121**
Cooper Av. E17 1A **50**
Cooper Cl. SE1 7K **13** (2A **102**)
Cooper Ct. SE18 6F **107**
Cooper Cres. SM5: Cars 3D **166**
Cooper Ho. *NW8* 4A **4**
(*off Lyons Pl.*)
SE4 5K **121**
(*off St Norbert Rd.*)
TW4: Houn 3D **112**
Cooper Rd. CR0: Wadd 4B **168**
NW4 6F **45**
NW10 5C **62**
Coopersale Cl. IG8: Wfd G 7F **37**
Coopersale Rd. E9 5K **67**
Coopers Cl. E1 4J **85**
RM10: Dag 6H **73**
Coopers Ct. *E3* 4B **86**
(*off Eric St.*)
TW7: Isle 2K **113**
(*off Woodlands Rd.*)
W3 1J **97**
(*off Church Rd.*)
Coopers La. E10 1D **68**
NW1 2H **83**
(not continuous)
SE12 2K **141**
Coopers Lodge *SE1* 6J **15**
(*off Tooley St.*)
Coopers M. BR3: Beck 2C **158**
Cooper's Rd. SE1 5F **103**
Coopers Row EC3 2J **15** (7F **85**)
Cooper St. E16 5H **87**
Coopers Wlk. E15 5G **69**
Coopers Yd. *N1* 7B **66**
(*off Upper St.*)
SE19 6E **138**
Coote Gdns. RM8: Dag 3F **73**
Coote Rd. DA7: Bex 1F **127**
RM8: Dag 3F **73**
Cope Ho. EC1 2D **8**
Copeland Dr. E14 4C **104**
Copeland Ho. SE11 2H **19**
SW17 4B **136**
Copeland Rd. E17 6D **50**
SE15 2G **121**
Copeman Cl. SE26 5J **139**
Copenhagen Gdns. W4 2K **97**
Copenhagen Ho. *N1* 1K **83**
(*off Barnsbury Est.*)
Copenhagen Pl. E14 6B **86**
(not continuous)
Copenhagen St. N1 1J **83**
Cope Pl. W8 3J **99**
Copers Cope Rd. BR3: Beck 7B **140**
Cope St. SE16 4K **103**
Copford Cl. IG8: Wfd G 6H **37**
Copford Wlk. *N1* 1C **84**
(*off Popham St.*)
Copgate Path SW16 6K **137**
Copinger Wlk. HA8: Edg 1H **43**
Copland Av. HA0: Wemb 5D **60**
Copland Cl. HA0: Wemb 5C **60**
Copland Ho. UB1: S'hall 2D **94**
Copland M. HA0: Wemb 6E **60**
Copland Rd. HA0: Wemb 6E **60**
Copleston M. SE15 2F **121**
Copleston Pas. SE5 2F **121**
Copleston Rd. SE15 3F **121**
Copley Cl. SE17 6C **102**
W7 4K **77**
Copley Dene BR1: Brom 1B **160**
Copley Pk. SW16 6K **137**
Copley Rd. HA7: Stan 5H **27**
Copley St. E1 5K **85**
Coppard Gdns. KT9: Chess 6C **162**
Coppelia Rd. SE3 4H **123**
Coppen Rd. RM8: Dag 7F **55**
Copperas St. SE8 6D **104**
Copper Beech Cl. IG5: Ilf 1E **52**
Copperbeech Cl. NW3 5B **64**
Copper Beeches Ct.
TW7: Isle 1H **113**
Copper Cl. N17 7C **34**
SE19 7F **139**
Copperdale Rd. UB3: Hayes 2J **93**
Copperfield Av. UB8: Hil 5C **74**
Copperfield Dr. N15 4F **49**
Copperfield Ho. *SE1* 7K **15**
(*off Wolseley St.*)
W1 5H **5**
(*off Marylebone High St.*)
W11 1F **99**
(*off St Ann's Rd.*)
Copperfield M. N18 4K **33**
Copperfield Rd. E3 4A **86**
SE28 6C **90**
Copperfields BR3: Beck 1E **158**
HA1: Harr 7J **41**
Copperfields Ct. W3 2G **97**
Copperfield St. SE1 6B **14** (2B **102**)
Copperfield Way BR7: Chst 6G **143**
HA5: Pinn 4D **40**
Coppergate Cl. BR1: Brom 1K **159**
Coppermead Cl. NW2 3E **62**
Copper Mill Dr. TW7: Isle 2K **113**
Copper Mill La. SW17 4A **136**
Coppermill La. E17 6J **49**
Copper Row SE1 5J **15**
Copperworks, The *N1* 2J **83**
(*off Railway St.*)
Coppetts Cen. N12 7J **31**
Coppetts Cl. N12 7H **31**
Coppetts Rd. N10 7J **31**
Coppetts Wood & Glebelands Local Nature Reserve 6J **31**
Coppice, The DA5: Bexl 3K **145**
EN2: Enf 4G **23**
EN5: New Bar 6E **20**
(*off Great Nth. Rd.*)
TW15: Ashf 6D **128**
UB7: Yiew 6A **74**
Coppice Cl. BR3: Beck 4D **158**
HA4: Ruis 6F **39**
HA7: Stan 6E **26**
SW20 3E **152**
Coppice Dr. SW15 6D **116**
Coppice Wlk. N20 3D **30**
Coppice Way E18 4H **51**
Coppies Gro. N11 4A **32**
Copping Cl. CR0: C'don 4E **168**
Coppins, The CR0: New Ad 6D **170**
HA3: Hrw W 6D **26**
Coppock Cl. SW11 2C **118**
Coppsfield KT8: W Mole 3E **148**
Copse, The E4 1C **36**
N2 3D **46**
Copse Av. BR4: W W'ck 2D **170**
Copse Cl. HA6: Nwood 2E **38**
SE7 6K **105**
Copse Glade KT6: Surb 7D **150**
COPSE HILL 7D **134**
Copse Hill SM2: Sutt 7K **165**
SW20 1C **152**
Copse Vw. CR2: Sels 7K **169**
Copsewood Cl. DA15: Sidc 6J **125**
Copse Wood Way HA6: Nwood 1D **38**
Coptain Ho. SW18 4J **117**
Coptefield Dr. DA17: Belv 3D **108**
Copthall Av. EC2 7F **9** (6D **84**)
(not continuous)
Copthall Bldgs. EC2 7F **9**
Copthall Cl. EC2 7E **8** (6D **84**)
Copthall Dr. NW7 7H **29**
Copthall Gdns. NW7 7H **29**
TW1: Twick 1K **131**
Copthall Leisure Cen. 7J **29**
Copthall Rd. E. UB10: Ick 2C **56**
Copthall Rd. W. UB10: Ick 2C **56**
Copthorne Av. BR2: Brom 2D **172**
SW12 7H **119**
Copthorne Chase TW15: Ashf 4B **128**
Copthorne Cl. TW17: Shep 6E **146**
Copthorne M. UB3: Harl 4G **93**
Coptic St. WC1 6E **6** (5J **83**)
Copwood Cl. N12 4G **31**
Coral Apartments *E16* 7J **87**
(*off Western Gateway*)
Coral Cl. RM6: Chad H 3D **54**
Coral Ho. *E1* 4A **86**
(*off Harford St.*)
NW10 3G **79**
Coraline Cl. UB1: S'hall 3D **76**
Coralline Wlk. SE2 3C **108**
Coral Mans. *NW6* 1J **81**
(*off Kilburn High Rd.*)
Coral Row SW11 3A **118**
Coral St. SE1 7K **13** (2A **102**)

Coram Ho. W4 . . . . .5A 98
(off Wood St.)
WC1 . . . . .3E 6
Coram Mans. WC1 . . . . .4G 7
(off Millman St.)
Coram St. WC1 . . . . .4E 6 (4J 83)
Coran Cl. N9 . . . . .7E 24
Corban Rd. TW3: Houn 3E 112
Corbar Cl. EN4: Had W 1G 21
Corbden Cl. SE15 . . . . .1F 121
Corbet Cl. SM6: Wall 1E 166
Corbet Ct. EC3 . . . . .1F 15 (6D 84)
Corbet Ho. N1 . . . . .2A 84
(off Barnsbury Est.)
SE5 . . . . .7C 102
(off Wyndham Rd.)
Corbet Pl. E1 . . . . .5J 9 (5F 85)
Corbett Ct. SE26 . . . . .4B 140
Corbett Gro. N22 . . . . .7D 32
Corbett Ho. SW10 . . . . .6A 100
(off Cathcart Rd.)
Corbett Rd. E11 . . . . .6A 52
E17 . . . . .3E 50
Corbetts La. SE16 . . . . .4J 103
(not continuous)
Corbetts Pas. SE16 . . . . .4J 103
(off Corbetts La.)
Corbetts Wharf SE16 . . . . .2H 103
(off Bermondsey Wall E.)
Corbicum E11 . . . . .7G 51
Corbidge Ct. SE8 . . . . .6D 104
Corbiere Ct. SW19 . . . . .6F 135
Corbiere Ho. N1 . . . . .1D 84
(off De Beauvoir Est.)
Corbin Ho. E3 . . . . .3D 86
(off Bromley High St.)
Corbins La. HA2: Harr 3F 59
Corbridge N17 . . . . .7C 34
Corbridge Cres. E2 . . . . .2H 85
Corby Cres. EN2: Enf 4D 22
Corbylands Rd.
DA15: Sidc 7J 125
Corbyn St. N4 . . . . .1J 65
Corby Rd. NW10 . . . . .2K 79
Corby Way E3 . . . . .4C 86
Cordelia Cl. SE24 . . . . .4B 120
Cordelia Gdns. TW19: Stanw 7A 110
Cordelia Ho. N1 . . . . .2E 84
(off Arden Est.)
Cordelia Rd. TW19: Stanw 7A 110
Cordelia St. E14 . . . . .6D 86
Cordell Ho. N15 . . . . .5F 49
(off Newton Rd.)
Cordingley Rd. HA4: Ruis 2F 57
Cording St. E14 . . . . .5D 86
Cordwainers Ct. E9 . . . . .7J 67
(off St Thomas's Sq.)
Cordwainers Wlk. E13 . . . . .2J 87
Cord Way E14 . . . . .3C 104
Cordwell Rd. SE13 . . . . .5G 123
Corefield Cl. N11 . . . . .2K 31
Corelli Ct. SE1 . . . . .4H 103
SW5 . . . . .4J 99
(off W. Cromwell Rd.)
Corelli Rd. SE3 . . . . .2C 124
Corfe Av. HA2: Harr 4E 58
Corfe Cl. TW4: Houn 1C 130
UB4: Yead 6A 76
Corfe Ho. SW8 . . . . .7K 101
(off Dorset Rd.)
Corfe Twr. W3 . . . . .2H 97
Corfield Rd. N21 . . . . .5E 22
Corfield St. E2 . . . . .3H 85
Corfton Lodge W5 . . . . .5E 78
Corfton Rd. W5 . . . . .6E 78
Coriander Av. E14 . . . . .6F 87
Coriander Ct. SE1 . . . . .6K 15
(off Gainsford St.)
Cories Cl. RM8: Dag 2D 72
Corinium Cl. HA9: Wemb 4F 61
Corinne Rd. N19 . . . . .4G 65
Corinthian Manorway DA8: Erith . .4K 109

Corinthian Rd. DA8: Erith 4K 109
Corinthian Way TW19: Stanw 7A 110
Corkers Path IG1: Ilf 2G 71
Corker Wlk. N7 . . . . .2K 65
Corkran Rd. KT6: Surb 7D 150
Corkscrew Hill
BR4: W W'ck 2E 170
Cork Sq. E1 . . . . .1H 103
Cork St. W1 . . . . .3A 12 (7G 83)
Cork St. M. W1 . . . . .3A 12
Cork Tree Ho. SE27 . . . . .5B 138
(off Lakeview Rd.)
Cork Tree Retail Pk. E4 . . . . .5F 35
Cork Tree Way E4 . . . . .5F 35
Corlett St. NW1 . . . . .5C 4 (5C 82)
Cormont Rd. SE5 . . . . .1B 120
Cormorant Cl. E17 . . . . .7F 35
Cormorant Ct. SE8 . . . . .6B 104
(off Pilot Cl.)
Cormorant Ho. EN3: Pond E 5E 24
Cormorant Lodge E1 . . . . .1G 103
(off Thomas More St.)
Cormorant Pl. SM1: Sutt 5H 165
Cormorant Rd. E7 . . . . .5H 69
Cornbury Ho. SE8 . . . . .6B 104
(off Evelyn St.)
Cornbury Rd. HA8: Edg 7J 27
Cornel Ho. DA15: Sidc 3A 144
Cornelia Dr. UB4: Yead 4A 76
Cornelia Ho. TW1: Twick 6D 114
(off Denton Rd.)
Cornelia St. N7 . . . . .6K 65
Cornell Bldg. E1 . . . . .6G 85
(off Coke St.)
Cornell Cl. DA14: Sidc 6E 144
Cornell Ct. EN3: Enf H 3F 25
Cornell Ho. HA2: Harr 3D 58
Corner, The W5 . . . . .1E 96
Cornercroft SM3: Cheam 5F 165
(off Wickham Av.)
Corner Fielde SW2 . . . . .1K 137
Corner Grn. SE3 . . . . .2J 123
Corner Ho. St. WC2 . . . . .4E 12
Corner Mead NW9 . . . . .7G 29
Cornerside TW15: Ashf 7E 128
Corney Reach Way
W4 . . . . .7A 98
Corney Rd. W4 . . . . .6A 98
Cornfield Cl. UB8: Uxb 2A 74
Cornflower La. CR0: C'don 1K 169
Cornflower Ter. SE22 . . . . .6H 121
Cornford Cl. BR2: Brom 5J 159
Cornford Gro. SW12 . . . . .2F 137
Cornhill EC3 . . . . .1F 15 (6D 84)
Cornick Ho. SE16 . . . . .3H 103
(off Slippers Pl.)
Cornish Ct. N9 . . . . .7C 24
Cornish Gro. SE20 . . . . .1H 157
Cornish Ho. SE17 . . . . .6B 102
(off Brandon Est.)
TW8: Bford 5F 97
Corn Mill Dr. BR6: Orp 7K 161
Cornmill La. SE13 . . . . .3E 122
Cornmow Dr. NW10 . . . . .5B 62
Cornshaw Rd. RM8: Dag 1D 72
Cornthwaite Rd. E5 . . . . .3J 67
Cornwall Av. DA16: Well 3J 125
E2 . . . . .3J 85
KT10: Clay 7A 162
N3 . . . . .7D 30
N22 .1J 47
UB1: S'hall 5D 76
Cornwall Cl. IG11: Bark 6K 71
Cornwall Cl. HA5: Hat E 1D 40
W7 . . . . .4K 77
(off Copley Cl.)
Cornwall Cres. W11 . . . . .6G 81
Cornwall Dr. BR5: St P 7C 144
Cornwall Gdns. NW10 . . . . .6D 62
SE25 .4F 157
SW7 .3K 99

Cornwall Gdns. Wlk. SW7 . . . . . . .3K 99
Cornwall Gro. W4 . . . . .5A 98
Cornwall Ho. SW7 . . . . .3K 99
(off Cornwall Gdns.)
Cornwallis Av. N9 . . . . .2C 34
SE9 .2H 143
Cornwallis Ct. SW8 . . . . .1J 119
(off Lansdowne Grn.)
Cornwallis Gro. N9 . . . . .2C 34
Cornwallis Ho. SE16 . . . . .2H 103
(off Cherry Gdn. St.)
W12 .7D 80
(off India Way)
Cornwallis Rd. E17 . . . . .4K 49
N9 . . . . .2C 34
N19 .2J 65
RM9: Dag 4D 72
SE18 . . . . .3G 107
Cornwallis Sq. N19 . . . . .2J 65
Cornwallis Wlk. SE9 . . . . .3D 124
Cornwall Mans. SW10 . . . . .7A 100
(off Cremorne Rd.)
W8 . . . . .2K 99
(off Kensington Ct.)
W14 .3F 99
(off Blythe Rd.)
Cornwall M. Sth. SW7 . . . . .3A 100
Cornwall M. W. SW7 . . . . .3K 99
Cornwall Rd. CR0: C'don 2B 168
HA1: Harr 6G 41
HA4: Ruis 3H 57
HA5: Hat E 1D 40
N4 . . . . .7A 48
N15 .5D 48
N18 .5B 34
SE1 . . . . .4J 13 (1A 102)
SM2: Sutt 7H 165
TW1: Twick 7A 114
UB8: Uxb 6A 56
Cornwall Sq. SE11 . . . . .5K 19
Cornwall St. E1 . . . . .7H 85
Cornwall Ter. NW1 . . . . . .4F 5 (4D 82)
Cornwall Ter. M. NW1 . . . . .4F 5
Corn Way E11 . . . . .3F 69
Cornwell Cres. E7 . . . . .4A 70
Cornwood Cl. N2 . . . . .5B 46
Cornwood Dr. E1 . . . . .6J 85
Cornworthy Rd. RM8: Dag 5C 72
Corona Bldg. E14 . . . . .1E 104
(off Blackwall Way)
Corona Rd. SE12 . . . . .7J 123
Coronation Av. N16 . . . . .4F 67
Coronation Cl. DA5: Bexl 6D 126
IG6: Ilf 4E 53
Coronation Ct. DA8: Erith 7K 109
E15 .6H 69
KT1: King T 4E 150
(off Surbiton Rd.)
W10 .5E 80
(off Brewster Gdns.)
Coronation Rd. E13 . . . . .3A 88
NW10 . . . . .3G 79
UB3: Harl 4H 93
Coronation Vs. NW10 . . . . .3G 79
Coronation Wlk. TW2: Whitt 1E 130
Coroners Court
City of London 2E 14 (7D 84)
Poplar 7D 86
(off Poplar High St.)
St Pancras 1H 83
Southwark 2D 102
West London 1A 118
Westminster 4H 101
Coronet Cinema 1J 99
(off Notting Hill Ga.)
Coronet Pde. HA0: Wemb 6E 60
Coronet St. N1 . . . . .2G 9 (3E 84)
Coronet Theatre 3C 102
(off New Kent Rd.)
Corporate Dr. TW13: Felt 3K 129
Corporate Ho. HA3: Hrw W 1H 41
Corporation Av. TW4: Houn 4C 112

Corporation Row EC1 . . . . . .3K 7 (4A 84)
Corporation St. E15 . . . . .2G 87
N7 . . . . .5J 65
Corrance Rd. SW2 . . . . .4J 119
Corri Av. N14 . . . . .4C 32
Corrib Cl. N13 . . . . .3E 32
Corrib Dr. SM1: Sutt 5C 166
Corrigan Cl. NW4 . . . . .3E 44
Corringham Ct. NW11 . . . . .7J 45
Corringham Ho. E1 . . . . .6K 85
(off Pitsea St.)
Corringham Rd. HA9: Wemb 2G 61
NW11 . . . . .7J 45
Corringway NW11 . . . . .7K 45
W5 . . . . .4G 79
Corris Grn. NW9 . . . . .5A 44
Corry Dr. SW9 . . . . .4B 120
Corry Ho. E14 . . . . .7D 86
(off Wade's Pl.)
Corsair Cl. TW19: Stanw 7A 110
Corsair Rd. TW19: Stanw 7A 110
Corscombe Cl. KT2: King T 5J 133
Corsehill St. SW16 . . . . .6G 137
Corsellis Sq. TW1: Isle 4B 114
(off Varley Dr.)
Corsham St. N1 . . . . .2F 9 (3D 84)
Corsica St. N5 . . . . .6B 66
Corsley Way E9 . . . . .6B 68
Cortayne Ct. TW2: Twick 2J 131
Cortayne Rd. SW6 . . . . .2H 117
Cortis Rd. SW15 . . . . .6D 116
Cortis Ter. SW15 . . . . .6D 116
Cortland Cl. IG8: Wfd G 1A 52
Corunna Rd. SW8 . . . . .1G 119
Corunna Ter. SW8 . . . . .1G 119
Corvette Sq. SE10 . . . . .6F 105
Corwell Gdns. UB8: Hil 6E 74
Corwell La. UB8: Hil 6E 74
(not continuous)
Coryton Path W9 . . . . .4H 81
(off Ashmore Rd.)
Cosbycote Av. SE24 . . . . .5C 120
Cosdach Av. SM6: Wall 7H 167
Cosedge Cres. CR0: Wadd 5A 168
Cosgrove Cl. N21 . . . . .2H 33
UB4: Yead 4C 76
Cosgrove Ho. E2 . . . . .1G 85
(off Whiston Rd.)
Cosmo Pl. WC1 . . . . .5F 7 (5J 83)
Cosmur Cl. W12 . . . . .3B 98
Cossall Wlk. SE15 . . . . .2H 121
Cossar M. SW2 . . . . .5A 120
Cosser St. SE1 . . . . .1J 19 (3A 102)
Costa St. SE15 . . . . .2G 121
Costons Av. UB6: G'frd 3H 77
Costons La. UB6: G'frd 3H 77
(not continuous)
Coston Wlk. SE4 . . . . .4K 121
Cosway Mans. NW1 . . . . .5D 4
(off Shroton St.)
Cosway St. NW1 . . . . .5D 4 (5C 82)
Cotall St. E14 . . . . .5C 86
Coteford Cl. HA5: Eastc 5J 39
Coteford St. SW17 . . . . .4D 136
Cotelands CR0: C'don 3E 168
Cotesbach Rd. E5 . . . . .3J 67
Cotes Ho. NW8 . . . . .4C 4
(off Broadley St.)
Cotesmore Gdns. RM8: Dag 4C 72
Cotford Rd. CR7: Thor H 4C 156
Cotham St. SE17 . . . . .4C 102
Cotherstone Rd. SW2 . . . . .1K 137
Cotleigh Av. DA5: Bexl 2D 144
Cotleigh Rd. NW6 . . . . .7J 63
RM7: Rom 6K 55
Cotman Cl. NW11 . . . . .6A 46
SW15 . . . . .6F 117
Cotman Gdns. HA8: Edg 2G 43
Cotman Ho. NW8 . . . . .2C 82
(off Townshend Est.)
UB5: N'olt 2B 76
(off Academy Gdns.)

Cotman M. *RM8*: Dag *5C 72*
    (off Highgrove Rd.)
Cotmans Cl. UB3: Hayes 1J 93
Coton Rd. DA16: Well 3A 126
Cotsford Av. KT3: N Mald 5J 151
Cotswold Cl. DA7: Bex 2K 127
    KT2: King T 6J 133
    KT10: Hin W 2A 162
    N11 . . . . .4K 31
Cotswold Cl. EC1 . . . . .3C 8
    UB6: G'frd 2K 77
    (off Hodder Dr.)
Cotswold Gdns. E6 . . . . .3B 88
    IG2: Ilf 7H 53
    NW2 . . . . .2F 63
Cotswold Ga. NW2 . . . . .1G 63
Cotswold Grn. EN2: Enf 4E 22
Cotswold M. SW11 . . . . .1B 118
Cotswold Ri. BR6: St M Cry 6K 161
Cotswold Rd. TW12: Hamp 5E 130
Cotswold St. SE27 . . . . .4B 138
Cotswold Way EN2: Enf 3E 22
    KT4: Wor Pk 2E 164
Cottage Av. BR2: Brom 1C 172
Cottage Cl. E1 . . . . .4J 85
    (off Mile End Rd.)
    HA2: Harr 2H 59
    HA4: Ruis 1F 57
Cottage Fld. Cl. DA14: Sidc 1C 144
Cottage Grn. SE5 . . . . .7D 102
Cottage Gro. KT6: Surb 6D 150
    SW9 . . . . .3J 119
Cottage Pl. SW3 . . . . . .1C 16 (3D 100)
Cottage Rd. KT19: Ewe 7K 163
    N7 .5K 65
    (not continuous)
Cottages, The UB10: Ick 2A 56
Cottage St. E14 . . . . .7D 86
Cottage Wlk. N16 . . . . .3F 67
Cottenham Dr. NW9 . . . . .3B 44
    SW20 . . . . .7D 134
Cottenham Pde. SW20 . . . . .2D 152
COTTENHAM PARK 1D 152
Cottenham Pk. Rd. SW20 . . . . .1C 152
    (not continuous)
Cottenham Pl. SW20 . . . . .7D 134
Cottenham Rd. E17 . . . . .4B 50
Cotterill Rd. KT6: Surb 2E 162
Cottesbrook St. SE14 . . . . .7A 104
Cottesloe Ho. NW8 . . . . .3C 4
Cottesloe M. SE1 . . . . .1K 19
    (off Emery St.)
Cottesloe Theatre 4H 13
    (in National Theatre)
Cottesmore Av. IG5: Ilf 2E 52
Cottesmore Ct. W8 . . . . .3K 99
    (off Stanford Rd.)
Cottesmore Gdns. W8 . . . . .3K 99
Cottimore Av. KT12: Walt T 7K 147
Cottimore Cres. KT12: Walt T 7K 147
Cottimore La. KT12: Walt T 7K 147
Cottimore Ter. KT12: Walt T 7K 147
Cottingham Chase HA4: Ruis 3J 57
Cottingham Rd. SE20 . . . . .7K 139
    SW8 . . . . .7K 101
Cottington Rd. TW13: Hanw 4B 130
Cottington St. SE11 . . . . . .5K 19 (5A 102)
Cottle Way SE16 . . . . .2H 103
    (off Paradise St.)
Cotton Av. W3 . . . . .6K 79
Cotton Cl. E11 . . . . .2G 69
    RM9: Dag 7C 72
Cottongrass Cl. CR0: C'don 1K 169
Cottonham Cl. N12 . . . . .5G 31
Cotton Hill BR1: Brom 4E 140
Cotton Ho. SW2 . . . . .7J 119
Cotton Row SW11 . . . . .3A 118
Cottons App. RM7: Rom 5K 55
Cottons Cen. SE1 . . . . .4G 15 (1E 102)
Cottons Ct. RM7: Rom 5K 55
Cotton's Gdns. E2 . . . . .1H 9 (3E 84)
Cottons La. SE1 . . . . .4F 15 (1D 102)

Cotton St. E14 . . . . .7E 86
Cottrell Ct. SE10 . . . . .4H 105
    (off Hop St.)
Cottrill Gdns. E8 . . . . .6H 67
Cotts Cl. W7 . . . . .5K 77
Couchmore Av. IG5: Ilf 2D 52
Coulgate St. SE4 . . . . .3A 122
Coulson Cl. RM8: Dag 1C 72
Coulson St. SW3 . . . . . .5E 16 (5D 100)
Coulter Cl. UB4: Yead 4C 76
Coulter Rd. W6 . . . . .3D 98
Coulthurst Ct. SW16 . . . . .7J 137
    (off Heybridge Av.)
Councillor St. SE5 . . . . .7C 102
Counter Cl. SE1 . . . . .5E 14
    (off Borough High St.)
Counters Ct. W14 . . . . .3G 99
    (off Holland Rd.)
Counter St. SE1 . . . . .5G 15 (1E 102)
Countess Rd. NW5 . . . . .5G 65
Countisbury Av. EN1: Enf 7A 24
Country Way TW13: Hanw 6K 129
County & Magistrates' Court
    West London 5F 99
County Court
    Bow .6H 69
    (off Romford Rd.)
    Brentford 6D 96
    Bromley 1J 159
    Central London 4K 5
    Clerkenwell and Shoreditch
    . . . . .3C 8 (4C 84)
    Edmonton 5B 34
    Ilford 2H 71
    Kingston upon Thames 2D 150
    Lambeth 5K 19 (5A 102)
    Uxbridge 5H 75
    Wandsworth 5G 117
    Willesden 2B 80
    Woolwich 3E 106
County Cl. SE11 . . . . .5A 102
    (off Cleaver St.)
County Ga. EN5: New Bar 6E 20
    SE9 . . . . .3G 143
County Gro. SE5 . . . . .1C 120
County Hall Apartments SE1 . . . . . . .6G 13
County Hall (Former) 6G 13 (2K 101)
County Ho. SW9 . . . . .1A 120
    (off Brixton Rd.)
County Pde. TW8: Bford 7D 96
County Rd. CR7: Thor H 2B 156
    E6 . . . . .5F 89
County St. SE1 . . . . .3C 102
Coupland Pl. SE18 . . . . .5G 107
Courcy Rd. N8 . . . . .3A 48
Courier Rd. RM9: Dag 4J 91
Courland Gro. SW8 . . . . .1H 119
Courland St. SW8 . . . . .1H 119
Course, The SE9 . . . . .3E 142
Court, The HA4: Ruis 4C 58
Court Annexe 2C 102
Courtauld Cl. SE28 . . . . .1A 108
Courtauld Ho. E2 . . . . .1G 85
    (off Goldsmiths Row)
Courtauld Institute of Art Gallery 2G 13
Courtauld Rd. N19 . . . . .1J 65
Court Av. DA17: Belv 5F 109
Court Cl. HA3: Kenton 3E 42
    NW8 . . . . .7B 64
    (off Boydell Ct., not continuous)
    SM6: Wall 7H 167
    TW2: Twick 3F 131
Court Cl. Av. TW2: Twick 3F 131
Court Cres. KT9: Chess 5D 162
Court Downs Rd. BR3: Beck 2D 158
Court Dr. CR0: Wadd 4K 167
    HA7: Stan 4K 27
    SM1: Sutt 4C 166
    UB10: Hil 1B 74
Courtenay Av. HA3: Hrw W 7B 26
    N6 . . . . .7C 46
    SM2: Sutt 7J 165

Courtenay Dr. BR3: Beck 2F 159
Courtenay Gdns. HA3: Hrw W 2G 41
Courtenay M. E17 . . . . .5A 50
Courtenay Pl. E17 . . . . .5A 50
Courtenay Rd. E11 . . . . .3H 69
    E17 .4K 49
    HA9: Wemb 3D 60
    KT4: Wor Pk 3E 164
    SE20 . . . . .6K 139
Courtenay Sq. SE11 . . . . . . .6J 19 (5A 102)
Courtenay St. SE11 . . . . . . .5J 19 (5A 102)
Courtens M. HA7: Stan 7H 27
Court Farm Av. KT19: Ewe 5K 163
Court Farm Ind. Est.
    TW19: Stanw 6B 110
Court Farm La. UB5: N'olt 7E 58
Court Farm Rd. SE9 . . . . .2B 142
    UB5: N'olt 7E 58
Courtfield W5 . . . . .5C 78
Courtfield Av. HA1: Harr 5K 41
Courtfield Cres. HA1: Harr 5K 41
Courtfield Gdns. HA4: Ruis 2H 57
    SW5 . . . . .4K 99
    W13 .6A 78
Courtfield Ho. EC1 . . . . .5J 7
    (off Baldwins Gdns.)
Courtfield M. SW5 . . . . .4A 100
Courtfield Ri. BR4: W W'ck 3F 171
Courtfield Rd. SW7 . . . . .4A 100
    TW15: Ashf 6D 128
Court Gdns. N1 . . . . .6A 66
    N7 . . . . .6A 66
Courtgate Cl. NW7 . . . . .6G 29
Courthill Rd. SE13 . . . . .4E 122
Courthope Ho. SE16 . . . . .3J 103
    (off Lower Rd.)
    SW8 . . . . .7J 101
    (off Hartington Rd.)
Courthope Rd. NW3 . . . . .4D 64
    SW19 . . . . .5G 135
    UB6: G'frd 2H 77
Courthope Vs. SW19 . . . . .7G 135
Courthouse Gdns. N3 . . . . .6D 30
Courthouse La. N16 . . . . .4F 67
Courthouse Rd. N12 . . . . .6E 30
Courtland Av. E4 . . . . .2C 36
    IG1: Ilf 2D 70
    NW7 .3E 28
    SW16 . . . . .7K 137
Courtland Gro. SE28 . . . . .6D 90
Courtland Rd. E6 . . . . .1C 88
Courtlands KT12: Walt T 7J 147
    TW10: Rich 5G 115
Courtlands Av. BR2: Hayes 1G 171
    SE12 . . . . .5K 123
    TW9: Kew 2G 115
    TW12: Hamp 6D 130
Courtlands Cl. HA4: Ruis 7H 39
Courtlands Dr. KT19: Ewe 6A 164
Courtlands Rd. KT5: Surb 7G 151
Court La. SE21 . . . . .6E 120
Court La. Gdns. SE21 . . . . .7E 120
Courtleet Dr. DA8: Erith 1H 127
Courtleigh NW11 . . . . .5H 45
Courtleigh Gdns. NW11 . . . . .4G 45
Court Lodge DA17: Belv 5G 109
    SW1 .4G 17
    (off Sloane Sq.)
Courtman Rd. N17 . . . . .7H 33
Court Mead UB5: N'olt 3D 76
Courtmead Cl. SE24 . . . . .6C 120
Courtnell St. W2 . . . . .6J 81
Courtney Cl. SE19 . . . . .6E 138
Courtney Ct. N7 . . . . .5A 66
Courtney Cres. SM5: Cars 7D 166
Courtney Ho. NW4 . . . . .3E 44
    (off Mulberry Cl.)
    W14 .3G 99
    (off Russell Rd.)
Courtney Pl. CR0: Wadd 3A 168
Courtney Rd. CR0: Wadd 3A 168
    N7 . . . . .5A 66

Courtney Rd. SW19 . . . . .7C 136
    TW6: H'row A 3C 110
Courtney Way TW6: H'row A 2C 110
Court Pde. HA0: Wemb 3B 60
Courtrai Rd. SE23 . . . . .6A 122
Court Rd. SE9 . . . . .6D 124
    SE25 . . . . .2F 157
    UB2: S'hall 4D 94
    UB10: Ick 5D 56
Court Royal SW15 . . . . .5G 117
Courtside N8 . . . . .6H 47
    SE26 . . . . .3H 139
Court St. BR1: Brom 2J 159
    E1 . . . . .5H 85
Courtville Ho. W10 . . . . .3G 81
    (off Third Av.)
Court Way NW9 . . . . .4A 44
    TW2: Twick 7K 113
    W3 . . . . .5J 79
Courtway IG6: Ilf 3G 53
    IG8: Wfd G 5F 37
Courtway, The CR0: Sels 7B 170
Court Yd. SE9 . . . . .6D 124
Courtyard SW3 . . . . .5E 16
    (off Smith St.)
Courtyard, The BR2: Kes 6C 172
    E2 . . . . .1K 9
    (off Erza St.)
    EC3 . . . . .1F 15
    (in Royal Exchange)
    N1 . . . . .7K 65
    NW1 .7E 64
    SE14 . . . . .1K 121
    (off Besson St.)
    SW3 .7B 16
    (off Waldron M.)
Courtyard Ho. SW6 . . . . .2A 118
Courtyard M. BR5: St P 7A 144
Courtyard Theatre 2G 9 (3E 84)
Cousin La. EC4 . . . . .3E 14 (7D 84)
Cousins Cl. UB7: Yiew 7A 74
Couthurst Rd. SE3 . . . . .6K 105
Coutts Av. KT9: Chess 5E 162
Coutt's Cres. NW5 . . . . .3E 64
Couzens Ho. E3 . . . . .5B 86
    (off Weatherley Cl.)
Coval Gdns. SW14 . . . . .4H 115
Coval La. SW14 . . . . .4H 115
Coval Pas. SW14 . . . . .4J 115
Coval Rd. SW14 . . . . .4H 115
Covelees Wall E6 . . . . .6E 88
Covell Ct. EN2: Enf 1E 22
    (off The Ridgeway)
    SE8 .7C 104
COVENT GARDEN 2F 13 (7J 83)
    Covent Garden 2F 13 (7J 83)
Covent Gdn. WC2 . . . . .2F 13 (7J 83)
Coventry Cl. E6 . . . . .6D 88
    NW6 .2J 81
Coventry Hall SW16 . . . . .5J 137
Coventry Rd. E1 . . . . .4H 85
    E2 . . . . .4H 85
    IG1: Ilf 2F 71
    SE25 . . . . .4G 157
Coventry St. W1 . . . . .3C 12 (7H 83)
Coverack Cl. CR0: C'don 7A 158
    N14 .6B 22
Coverdale Cl. HA7: Stan 5G 27
Coverdale Gdns. CR0: C'don 3F 169
Coverdale Rd. N11 . . . . .6K 31
    NW2 .7F 63
    W12 .2D 98
Coverdales, The IG11: Bark 2H 89
Coverham Ho. SE4 . . . . .4K 121
    (off Billingford Cl.)
Coverley Cl. E1 . . . . .5G 85
Coverley Point SE11 . . . . .4G 19
Covert, The BR6: Pet W 6J 161
    HA6: Nwood 1E 38
    SE19 . . . . .7F 139
    (off Fox Hill)
Coverton Rd. SW17 . . . . .5C 136

Covert Way EN4: Had W 2F **21**
Covet Wood Cl. BR5: St M Cry 6K **161**
Covey Cl. SW19 2K **153**
Covey Rd. KT4: Wor Pk 2F **165**
Covington Gdns. SW16 7B **138**
Covington Way SW16 6K **137**
(not continuous)
Cowan Cl. E6 5C **88**
Cowan Ct. NW10 7K **61**
Cowbridge La. IG11: Bark 7F **71**
Cowbridge Rd. HA3: Kenton 4F **43**
Cowcross St. EC1 5A **8** (5B **84**)
Cowdenbeath Path N1 1K **83**
Cowden Rd. BR6: Orp 7K **161**
Cowden St. SE6 4C **140**
Cowdray Rd. UB10: Hil 1E **74**
Cowdrey Cl. EN1: Enf 2K **23**
Cowdrey Rd. SW19 5K **135**
Cowen Av. HA2: Harr 2H **59**
Cowgate Rd. UB6: G'frd 3H **77**
Cowick Rd. SW17 4D **136**
Cowings Mead UB5: N'olt 6C **58**
Cowland Av. EN3: Pond E 4D **24**
Cow La. UB6: G'frd 2H **77**
Cow Leaze E6 6E **88**
Cowleaze Rd. KT2: King T 1E **150**
COWLEY 4A **74**
Cowley La. E11 3G **69**
COWLEY PEACHEY 6A **74**
Cowley Pl. NW4 5E **44**
Cowley Rd. E11 5K **51**
IG1: Ilf 7D **52**
SW9 1A **120**
(not continuous)
SW14 3A **116**
W3 1B **98**
Cowley St. SW1 1E **18** (3J **101**)
Cowling Cl. W11 1G **99**
Cowper Av. E6 7C **70**
SM1: Sutt 4B **166**
Cowper Cl. BR2: Brom 4B **160**
DA16: Well 5A **126**
Cowper Gdns. N14 6A **22**
SM6: Wall 6G **167**
Cowper Ho. *SE17* *5C* ***102***
(off Browning St.)
SW1 *6C* ***18***
(off Aylesford St.)
Cowper Rd. BR2: Brom 4B **160**
DA17: Belv 4G **109**
KT2: King T 5F **133**
N14 1A **32**
N16 5E **66**
N18 5B **34**
SW19 6A **136**
W3 1K **97**
W7 7K **77**
Cowper's Ct. *EC3* *1F* ***15***
(off Birchin La.)
Cowper St. EC2 3F **9** (4D **84**)
Cowper Ter. W10 5F **81**
Cowslip Cl. UB10: Uxb 7A **56**
Cowslip Rd. E18 2K **51**
Cowthorpe Rd. SW8 1H **119**
Cox Ct. EN4: E Barn 4H **21**
Coxe Pl. HA3: W'stone 4A **42**
Cox Ho. *W6* *6G* ***99***
(off Field Rd.)
Cox La. KT9: Chess 4F **163**
KT19: Ewe 5H **163**
(not continuous)
Coxmount Rd. SE7 5B **106**
Coxs Av. TW17: Shep 3G **147**
Coxson Way SE1 7J **15** (2F **103**)
Cox's Wlk. SE21 1G **139**
Coxwell Rd. SE18 5H **107**
SE19 7E **138**
Coxwold Path KT9: Chess 7E **162**
Crabbs Cft. Cl. BR6: Farnb 5G **173**
Crab Hill BR3: Beck 7F **141**
Crabtree Av. HA0: Wemb 2E **78**
RM6: Chad H 4D **54**
Crabtree Cl. E2 2F **85**
Crabtree Ct. EN5: New Bar 4E **20**
Crabtree Hall *SW6* *7E* ***98***
(off Crabtree La.)
Crabtree La. SW6 7E **98**
(not continuous)
Crabtree Manorway Nth.
DA17: Belv, Erith 2J **109**
Crabtree Manorway Sth.
DA17: Belv 3J **109**
Crabtree Wlk. CR0: C'don 1G **169**
SE15 *1F* ***121***
(off Peckham Rd.)
Crace St. NW1 1C **6** (3H **83**)
Craddock Rd. EN1: Enf 3A **24**
Craddock St. NW5 6E **64**
Cradley Rd. SE9 1H **143**
Crafts Council & Gallery 2A **84**
Cragie Ho. *SE1* *4F* ***103***
(off Balaclava Rd.)
Craig Dr. UB8: Hil 6D **74**
Craigen Av. CR0: C'don 1H **169**
Craigen Gdns. IG1: Ilf 4J **71**
Craigerne Rd. SE3 7K **105**
Craig Gdns. E18 2H **51**
Craigholm SE18 2E **124**
Craigmore Ct. HA6: Nwood 1G **39**
Craigmuir Pk. HA0: Wemb 1F **79**
Craignair Rd. SW2 7A **120**
Craignish Av. SW16 2K **155**
Craig Pk. Rd. N18 4C **34**
Craig Rd. TW10: Ham 4C **132**
Craig's Ct. SW1 4E **12** (1J **101**)
Craigton Rd. SE9 4D **124**
Craigweil Cl. HA7: Stan 5J **27**
Craigweil Dr. HA7: Stan 5J **27**
Craigwell Av. TW13: Felt 3J **129**
Craik Ct. *NW6* *2H* ***81***
(off Carlton Va.)
Crail Row SE17 4D **102**
Crales Ho. SE18 3C **106**
Cramer St. W1 6H **5** (5E **82**)
Crammond Cl. W6 6G **99**
Cramond Ct. TW14: Bedf 1G **129**
Cramonde Ct. DA16: Well 2A **126**
Crampton Ho. SW8 1G **119**
Crampton Rd. SE20 6J **139**
Crampton St. SE17 4C **102**
Cranberra Pl. TW9: Rich 3G **115**
Cranberry Cl. UB5: N'olt 2B **76**
Cranberry Ent. Pk. *N17* *7A* ***34***
(off White Hart La.)
Cranberry La. E16 4G **87**
Cranborne Av. KT6: Surb 3G **163**
UB2: S'hall 4E **94**
Cranborne Rd. IG11: Bark 1H **89**
Cranborne Waye UB4: Yead 6K **75**
(not continuous)
Cranbourn All. *WC2* *2D* ***12***
(off Cranbourn St.)
Cranbourne *NW1* *7H* ***65***
(off Agar Gro.)
Cranbourne Av. E11 4K **51**
Cranbourne Cl. SW16 3J **155**
Cranbourne Ct. *SW11* *7C* ***100***
(off Albert Bri. Rd.)
Cranbourne Dr. HA5: Pinn 5B **40**
Cranbourne Gdns. IG6: Ilf 3G **53**
NW11 5G **45**
Cranbourne Pas. SE16 2H **103**
Cranbourne Rd. E12 5C **70**
E15 4E **68**
HA6: Nwood 3H **39**
N10 2F **47**
Cranbourn Ho. *SE16* *2H* ***103***
(off Marigold St.)
Cranbourn St. WC2 2D **12** (7H **83**)
CRANBROOK 1D **70**
Cranbrook *NW1* *1G* ***83***
(off Camden St.)
Cranbrook Cl. BR2: Hayes 6J **159**
Cranbrook Ct. TW8: Bford 6C **96**
Cranbrook Dr. KT10: Esh 7G **149**
TW2: Whitt 1F **131**
Cranbrook Est. E2 2K **85**
Cranbrook La. N11 4A **32**
Cranbrook M. E17 5B **50**
Cranbrook Pk. N22 1A **48**
Cranbrook Ri. IG1: Ilf 6D **52**
Cranbrook Rd. CR7: Thor H 2C **156**
DA7: Bex 1F **127**
EN4: E Barn 6G **21**
IG1: Ilf 7E **52**
IG2: Ilf 5E **52**
IG6: Ilf 5E **52**
SE8 1C **122**
SW19 7G **135**
TW4: Houn 4D **112**
W4 5A **98**
Cranbrook St. E2 2K **85**
Cranbury Rd. SW6 2K **117**
Crandley Ct. SE8 4A **104**
(not continuous)
Crane Av. TW7: Isle 5A **114**
W3 7J **79**
Cranebank M. TW1: Twick 4A **114**
Cranebrook TW2: Twick 2G **131**
Crane Cl. HA2: Harr 3G **59**
RM10: Dag 6G **73**
Crane Ct. EC4 6A **84**
KT19: Ewe 4J **163**
Craneford Cl. TW2: Twick 7K **113**
Craneford Way TW2: Twick 7J **113**
Crane Gdns. UB3: Harl 4H **93**
Crane Gro. N7 6A **66**
Crane Ho. *E3* *2A* ***86***
(off Roman Rd.)
SE15 1F **121**
TW13: Hanw 3E **130**
Crane Lodge Rd. TW5: Cran 6K **93**
Crane Mead SE16 5J **103**
Crane Mead Ct. TW1: Twick 7K **113**
Crane Pk. Island Nature Reserve 2D **130**
Crane Pk. Rd. TW2: Whitt 2F **131**
Crane Rd. TW2: Twick 1J **131**
TW19: Stanw 6C **110**
Cranesbill Cl. NW9 3K **43**
SW16 2H **155**
Cranes Dr. KT5: Surb 4E **150**
Cranes Pk. KT5: Surb 4E **150**
Cranes Pk. Av. KT5: Surb 4E **150**
Cranes Pk. Cres. KT5: Surb 4F **151**
Crane St. SE10 5F **105**
SE15 1F **121**
Craneswater UB3: Harl 7H **93**
Craneswater Pk. UB2: S'hall 5D **94**
Crane Way TW2: Whitt 7G **113**
Cranfield Cl. SE27 3C **138**
Cranfield Ct. W1 6D **4**
Cranfield Dr. NW9 7F **29**
Cranfield Ho. WC1 5E **6**
Cranfield Rd. SE4 3B **122**
Cranfield Rd. E. SM5: Cars 7E **166**
Cranfield Rd. W. SM5: Cars 7D **166**
Cranfield Row SE1 1K **19**
CRANFORD 1J **111**
Cranford Av. N13 5D **32**
TW19: Stanw 7A **110**
Cranford Cl. SW20 7D **134**
TW19: Stanw 7A **110**
Cranford Community College Sports Cen.
6K **93**
Cranford Cotts. *E1* *7K* ***85***
(off Cranford St.)
Cranford Dr. UB3: Harl 4H **93**
Cranford La. TW5: Cran, Hest 7K **93**
TW6: H'row A 1H **111**
(Bath Rd., not continuous)
TW6: H'row A 3H **111**
(Elmdon Rd.)
UB3: Cran, Harl 6F **93**
Cranford M. BR2: Brom 5C **160**
Cranford Pk. Rd. UB3: Harl 4H **93**
Cranford St. E1 7K **85**
Cranford Way N8 4K **47**
Cranhurst Rd. NW2 5E **62**
Cranleigh *W11* *1H* ***99***
(off Ladbroke Rd.)
Cranleigh Cl. BR6: Chels 3K **173**
DA5: Bexl 6H **127**
SE20 2H **157**
Cranleigh Ct. CR4: Mitc 3B **154**
TW9: Rich 3G **115**
UB1: S'hall 6D **76**
Cranleigh Gdns. HA3: Kenton 5E **42**
IG11: Bark 7H **71**
KT2: King T 6F **133**
N21 5F **23**
SE25 3E **156**
SM1: Sutt 2K **165**
UB1: S'hall 6D **76**
Cranleigh Gdns. Ind. Est.
UB1: S'hall 5D **76**
Cranleigh Ho's. *NW1* *2G* ***83***
(off Cranleigh St.)
Cranleigh M. SW11 2C **118**
Cranleigh Rd. N15 5C **48**
SW19 3J **153**
TW13: Felt 4H **129**
Cranleigh St. NW1 2G **83**
Cranley Dene Ct. N10 4F **47**
Cranley Dr. HA4: Ruis 2H **57**
IG2: Ilf 7G **53**
CRANLEY GARDENS 4F **47**
Cranley Gdns. N10 4F **47**
N13 3E **32**
SM6: Wall 7G **167**
SW7 5A **16** (5A **100**)
Cranley M. SW7 5A **16** (5A **100**)
Cranley Pde. *SE9* *4C* ***142***
(off Beaconsfield Rd.)
Cranley Pl. SW7 4A **16** (4B **100**)
Cranley Rd. E13 5K **87**
IG2: Ilf 6G **53**
Cranmer Av. W13 3B **96**
Cranmer Cl. HA4: Ruis 1B **58**
HA7: Stan 7H **27**
SM4: Mord 6F **153**
Cranmer Ct. N3 2G **45**
SW3 4D **16** (4C **100**)
SW4 3H **119**
TW12: Ham H 5F **131**
Cranmere Ct. EN2: Enf 2F **23**
Cranmer Farm Cl. CR4: Mitc 4D **154**
Cranmer Gdns. RM10: Dag 4J **73**
Cranmer Ho. *SW9* *7A* ***102***
(off Cranmer Rd.)
SW11 *1C* ***118***
(off Surrey La. Est.)
Cranmer Rd. CR0: C'don 3B **168**
CR4: Mitc 4D **154**
E7 4K **69**
HA8: Edg 3C **28**
KT2: King T 5E **132**
SW9 7A **102**
TW12: Ham H 5F **131**
UB3: Hayes 6F **75**
Cranmer Ter. SW17 5B **136**
Cranmore Av. TW7: Isle 7G **95**
Cranmore Rd. BR1: Brom 3H **141**
BR7: Chst 5D **142**
Cranmore Way N10 4G **47**
Cranston Cl. TW3: Houn 2C **112**
UB10: Ick 2F **57**
Cranston Est. N1 2D **84**
Cranston Gdns. E4 6J **35**
Cranston Rd. SE23 1A **140**
Cranswick Rd. SE16 5H **103**
Crantock Rd. SE6 2D **140**
Cranwell Cl. E3 4D **86**
Cranwell Gro. TW17: Shep 4B **146**
Cranwell Rd. TW6: H'row A 2D **110**
Cranwich Av. N21 7J **23**
Cranwich Rd. N16 7D **48**
Cranwood Ct. EC1 2F **9**
Cranwood St. EC1 2E **8** (3D **84**)

Cranworth Cres. E4 . . . . .1A 36
Cranworth Gdns. SW9 . . . . .1A 120
Craster Rd. SE12 . . . . .7K 119
Crathie Rd. SE12 . . . . .6K 123
Cravan Av. TW13: Felt 2J 129
Craven Av. UB1: S'hall 5D 76
   W5 . . . . .7C 78
Craven Cl. N16 .7G 49
   UB4: Hayes 6J 75
Craven Cottage .2F 117
Craven Ct. NW10 . . . . .1A 80
   RM6: Chad H .6E 54
Craven Gdns. IG6: Ilf 2H 53
   IG11: Bark 2J 89
   SW19 . . . . .5J 135
Craven Hill W2 .7A 82
Craven Hill Gdns. W2 . . . . .7A 82
              (not continuous)
Craven Hill M. W2 . . . . .7A 82
Craven Ho. N2 . . . . .2B 46
      (off High Rd. E. Finchley)
Craven Lodge SW6 . . . . .1F 117
           (off Harbord St.)
   W2 . . . . .7A 82
          (off Craven Hill)
Craven M. SW11 . . . . .3E 118
Craven Pk. NW10 . . . . .1K 79
Craven Pk. M. NW10 . . . . .7A 62
Craven Pk. Rd. N15 . . . . .6F 49
   NW10 . . . . .1A 80
Craven Pas. WC2 . . . . .4E 12
           (off Craven St.)
Craven Rd. CR0: C'don 1H 169
   KT2: King T 1F 151
   NW10 . . . . .1K 79
   W2 .1A 10 (7A 82)
   W5 . . . . .7C 78
Craven St. WC2 . . . . .4E 12 (1J 101)
Craven Ter. W2 . . . . .2A 10 (7A 82)
Craven Wlk. N16 . . . . .7G 49
Crawford Av. HA0: Wemb 5D 60
Crawford Bldgs. W1 . . . . .6D 4
           (off Homer St.)
Crawford Cl. TW7: Isle 2J 113
Crawford Est. SE5 . . . . .2C 120
Crawford Gdns. N13 . . . . .3G 33
   UB5: N'olt 3D 76
Crawford Mans. W1 . . . . .6D 4
         (off Crawford St.)
Crawford M. W1 . . . . .6E 4 (5D 82)
Crawford Pas. EC1 . . . . .4K 7 (4A 84)
Crawford Pl. W1 . . . . .7D 4 (6C 82)
Crawford Point E16 . . . . .6H 87
        (off Wouldham Rd.)
Crawford Rd. SE5 . . . . .1C 120
Crawford St. NW10 . . . . .7K 61
   W1 .6E 4 (5C 82)
Crawley Rd. E10 . . . . .1D 68
   EN1: Enf 7K 23
   N22 . . . . .2C 48
Crawshay Cl. SW9 . . . . .1A 120
Crawthew Gro. SE22 . . . . .4F 121
Craybrooke Rd. DA14: Sidc 4B 144
Craybury End SE9 . . . . .2G 143
Crayfields Bus. Pk. BR5: St P 7C 144
CRAYFORD 5K 127
Crayford Cl. E6 . . . . .6C 88
Crayford Ho. SE1 . . . . .7F 15
          (off Long La.)
Crayford Rd. N7 .4H 65
Cray Ho. NW8 . . . . .5B 4
         (off Penfold St.)
Crayke Hill KT9: Chess 7E 162
Crayle Ho. EC1 . . . . .3B 8
          (off Malta St.)
Crayleigh Ter. DA14: Sidc 6C 144
Crayonne Cl. TW16: Sun 1G 147
Cray Rd. DA14: Sidc 6C 144
   DA17: Belv 6G 109
Cray Valley Rd. BR5: St M Cry 5K 161
Crealock Gro. IG8: Wfd G 5C 36
Crealock St. SW18 . . . . .6K 117

Creasy Est. SE1 .3E 102
Creative Ho. SW8 . . . . .7F 101
      (off Princes of Wales Dr.)
Crebor St. SE22 . . . . .6G 121
Crecy Ct. SE11 . . . . .5J 19
         (off Hotspur St.)
Credenhall Dr. BR2: Brom 1D 172
Credenhill Ho. SE15 . . . . .7H 103
Credenhill St. SW16 . . . . .6G 137
Crediton Hgts. NW10 . . . . .2F 81
      (off Okehampton Rd.)
Crediton Hill NW6 . . . . .5K 63
Crediton Rd. E16 . . . . .6J 87
   NW10 . . . . .1F 81
Crediton Way KT10: Clay 5A 162
Credon Rd. E13 .2A 88
   SE16 . . . . .5H 103
Creechurch La. EC3 . . . . .1H 15 (6B 84)
         (not continuous)
Creechurch Pl. EC3 . . . . .1H 15
Creed Ct. E1 . . . . .3A 86
   EC4 . . . . .1B 14
Creed La. EC4 . . . . .1B 14 (6B 84)
Creek, The TW16: Sun 5J 147
Creek Cotts. KT8: E Mos 4J 149
         (off Creek Rd.)
Creek Ho. W14 . . . . .3G 99
        (off Russell Rd.)
CREEKMOUTH 4K 89
Creekmouth Ind. Pk. IG11: Bark 4K 89
Creek Rd. IG11: Bark 3K 89
   KT8: E Mos 4J 149
   SE8 . . . . .6C 104
   SE10 . . . . .6C 104
Creekside SE8 . . . . .7D 104
Creekside Foyer SE8 . . . . .6D 104
         (off Stowage)
Creek Way RM13: Rain 5K 91
Creeland Gro. SE6 . . . . .1B 140
Crefeld Cl. W6 . . . . .6G 99
Creffield Rd. W3 . . . . .7F 79
   W5 . . . . .7F 79
Creighton Av. E6 . . . . .2B 88
   N2 . . . . .3C 46
   N10 . . . . .3C 46
Creighton Cl. W12 . . . . .7C 80
Creighton Rd. N17 . . . . .7K 33
   NW6 . . . . .2F 81
   W5 . . . . .3D 96
Cremer Bus. Cen. E2 . . . . .1J 9
         (off Cremer St.)
Cremer Ho. SE8 .7C 104
      (off Deptford Chu. St.)
Cremer St. E2 . . . . .1J 9 (2F 85)
         (not continuous)
Cremorne Est. SW10 . . . . .6B 100
         (not continuous)
Cremorne Riverside Cen. 7B 100
Cremorne Rd. SW10 . . . . .7A 100
Creon Ct. SW9 . . . . .7A 102
         (off Caldwell St.)
Crescent EC3 . . . . .2J 15 (7F 85)
Crescent, The BR3: Beck 1C 158
   BR4: W W'ck .6G 159
   CR0: C'don 5D 156
   DA5: Bexl 7C 126
   DA14: Sidc 4K 143
   E17 . . . . .6A 50
   EN5: New Bar 2E 20
   HA0: Wemb 2B 60
   HA2: Harr 1G 59
   IG2: Ilf 6E 52
   KT3: N Mald .3J 151
   KT6: Surb 5E 150
   KT8: W Mole .4E 148
   N9 . . . . .2C 34
   N11 . . . . .4J 31
   NW2 . . . . .3D 62
   SM1: Sutt 5B 166
   SW13 . . . . .2B 116
   SW19 . . . . .3J 135
   TW15: Ashf 5B 128
   TW17: Shep 7H 147

Crescent, The UB1: S'hall 2D 94
   UB3: Harl 7E 92
   W3 . . . . .6A 80
Crescent Arc. SE10 . . . . .6E 104
         (off Creek Rd.)
Crescent Cl. KT6: Surb 5D 150
   SW4 . . . . .5H 119
         (off Park Hill)
Crescent Ct. Bus. Cen. E16 . . . . .4F 87
Crescent Dr. BR5: Pet W 5F 161
Crescent E. EN4: Had W 1F 21
Crescent Gdns. HA4: Ruis 7K 39
   SW19 . . . . .3J 135
Crescent Gro. CR4: Mitc 4C 154
   SW4 . . . . .4G 119
Crescent Ho. EC1 . . . . .4C 8
        (off Golden La. Est.)
   SE13 . . . . .2D 122
Crescent La. SW4 . . . . .4G 119
Crescent Mans. W11 . . . . .7G 81
         (off Elgin Cres.)
Crescent M. N22 . . . . .1J 47
Crescent Pde. UB10: Hil 3C 74
Crescent Pl. SW3 . . . . .3D 16 (4C 100)
Crescent Ri. EN4: E Barn 5H 21
   N3 . . . . .1H 45
   N22 . . . . .1H 47
Crescent Rd. BR1: Brom 7J 141
   BR3: Beck 2D 158
   DA15: Sidc 3K 143
   E4 . . . . .1B 36
   E6 . . . . .1A 88
   E10 . . . . .2D 68
   E13 . . . . .1J 87
   E18 . . . . .1A 52
   EN2: Enf 4G 23
   EN4: E Barn 4G 21
   KT2: King T .7G 133
   N3 . . . . .1H 45
   N8 . . . . .6H 47
   N9 . . . . .1B 34
   N11 . . . . .4J 31
   N15 . . . . .3B 48
   N22 . . . . .1H 47
   RM10: Dag 3H 73
   SE18 . . . . .5F 107
   SW20 . . . . .1F 153
   TW17: Shep 5E 146
Crescent Row EC1 . . . . .4C 8 (4C 84)
Crescent Stables SW15 . . . . .5G 117
Crescent St. N1 .7K 65
Crescent Way BR6: Orp 5J 173
   N12 . . . . .6H 31
   SE4 . . . . .3C 122
   SW16 . . . . .6K 137
Crescent W. EN4: Had W 1F 21
Crescent Wharf E16 . . . . .2K 105
Crescent Wood Rd. SE26 . . . . .3G 139
Cresford Rd. SW6 . . . . .1K 117
Crespigny Rd. NW4 . . . . .6D 44
Cressage Cl. UB1: S'hall 4E 76
Cressage Ho. TW8: Bford 6E 96
         (off Ealing Rd.)
Cressal Ho. E14 .3C 104
         (off Tiller Rd.)
Cresset Ho. E9 . . . . .6J 67
Cresset Rd. E9 . . . . .6J 67
Cresset St. SW4 . . . . .3H 119
Cressfield Cl. NW5 . . . . .5E 64
Cressida Rd. N19 . . . . .1G 65
Cressingham Gro. SM1: Sutt 4A 166
Cressingham Rd. HA8: Edg 6C 28
   SE13 . . . . .3E 122
Cressington Cl. N16 . . . . .5E 66
Cress M. BR1: Brom 5F 141
Cresswell NW9 . . . . .2B 44
Cresswell Gdns. SW5 . . . . .5A 100
Cresswell Ho. HA9: Wemb 3E 60
   TW19: Stanw .6A 110
         (off Douglas Rd.)
Cresswell Pk. SE3 . . . . .3H 123
Cresswell Pl. SW10 . . . . .5A 100

Cresswell Rd. SE25 . . . . .4G 157
   TW1: Twick 6D 114
   TW13: Hanw .3C 130
Cresswell Way N21 . . . . .7F 23
Cressy Ct. E1 . . . . .5J 85
   W6 . . . . .3D 98
Cressy Ho. SW15 . . . . .3D 116
Cressy Ho's. E1 . . . . .5J 85
        (off Hannibal Rd.)
Cressy Pl. E1 . . . . .5J 85
Cressy Rd. NW3 .5D 64
Crest, The KT5: Surb 5G 151
   N13 . . . . .4F 33
   NW4 . . . . .5E 44
Cresta Cl. W5 . . . . .4F 79
Cresta Ho. E3 . . . . .4C 86
        (off Dimson Cres.)
   NW3 . . . . .7B 64
        (off Finchley Rd.)
Crestbrook Av. N13 . . . . .3G 33
Crestbrook Pl. N13 . . . . .3G 33
        (off Green Lanes)
Crest Ct. NW4 . . . . .5E 44
Crest Dr. EN3: Enf W 1D 24
Crestfield St. WC1 . . . . .1E 7 (3J 83)
Crest Gdns. HA4: Ruis 3A 58
Creston Way KT4: Wor Pk 1F 165
Crest Rd. BR2: Hayes 7H 159
   CR2: Sels 7H 169
   NW2 . . . . .2B 62
Crest Vw. HA5: Pinn 4B 40
Crest Vw. Dr. BR5: Pet W 5F 161
Crestway SW15 .6C 116
Crestwood Way TW4: Houn 5C 112
Creswell Dr. BR3: Beck 5D 158
Creswick Ct. W3 . . . . .7H 79
Creswick Rd. W3 . . . . .7H 79
Creswick Wlk. E3 . . . . .3C 86
   NW11 . . . . .4H 45
Creton St. SE18 .3E 106
Creukhorne Rd. NW10 . . . . .7A 62
Crewdson Rd. SW9 . . . . .7A 102
Crewe Pl. NW10 .3B 80
Crewkerne Ct. SW11 . . . . .1B 118
       (off Bolingbroke Wlk.)
Crews St. E14 . . . . .4C 104
Crewys Rd. NW2 . . . . .2H 63
   SE15 . . . . .2H 121
Crichton Av. SM6: Bedd 5H 167
Crichton Ho. DA14: Sidc 6D 144
Crichton Rd. SM5: Cars 6D 166
Crichton St. SW8 . . . . .2G 119
Crick Ct. IG11: Bark 2G 89
         (off Spring Pl.)
Cricketers Arms Rd. EN2: Enf 2H 23
Cricketers Cl. DA8: Erith 5K 109
   KT9: Chess 4D 162
   N14 . . . . .7B 22
Cricketers Ct. SE11 . . . . .4B 102
        (off Kennington La.)
Cricketers M. SW18 . . . . .5K 117
Cricketers Ter. SM5: Cars 3C 166
Cricketers Wlk. SE26 . . . . .5J 139
Cricketfield Rd. E5 . . . . .4H 67
Cricket Grn. CR4: Mitc 3D 154
Cricket Ground Rd. BR7: Chst 1F 161
Cricket La. BR3: Beck 6A 140
Cricklade Av. SW2 . . . . .2J 137
Cricklefield Stadium 2J 71
CRICKLEWOOD 4F 63
Cricklewood B'way. NW2 . . . . .3E 62
Cricklewood La. NW2 . . . . .4F 63
Cridland St. E15 .1H 87
Crieff Ct. TW11: Tedd 7C 132
Crieff Rd. SW18 .6A 118
Criffel Av. SW2 . . . . .2H 137
Crimscott St. SE1 . . . . .3E 102
Crimsworth Rd. SW8 . . . . .1H 119
Crinan St. N1 . . . . .2J 83
Cringle St. SW8 .7G 101
Cripplegate St. EC2 . . . . .5D 8 (5C 84)
Cripps Grn. UB4: Yead 4K 75

Crispe Ho. IG11: Bark .2H **89**
N1 .*1K 83*
(off Barnsbury Est.)
Crispen Rd. TW13: Hanw .4C **130**
Crispian Cl. NW10 .4A **62**
Crispin Cl. CR0: Bedd .2J **167**
Crispin Ct. *SE17* .*4E 102*
(off Freemantle St.)
Crispin Cres. CR0: Bedd .3H **167**
Crispin Ind. Cen. N18 .5D **34**
Crispin Lodge N11 .5J **31**
Crispin M. *NW11* .*4H 45*
(off Willifield Way)
Crispin Pl. E1 .5J **9** (5F **85**)
Crispin Rd. HA8: Edg .6D **28**
Crispin St. E1 .6J **9** (5F **85**)
Crispin Way UB8: Hil .4B **74**
Crisp Rd. W6 .5E **98**
Cristowe Rd. SW6 .2H **117**
Criterion Bldgs. *KT7: T Ditt* .*7B 150*
(off Portsmouth Rd.)
Criterion Ct. *E8* .*7F 67*
(off Middleton Rd.)
Criterion M. N19 .2H **65**
Criterion Theatre .*3C 12*
(off Piccadilly Cir.)
CRITTALLS CORNER .**7C 144**
Crockerton Rd. SW17 .2D **136**
Crockham Way SE9 .4E **142**
Crocus Cl. CR0: C'don .1K **169**
Crocus Fld. EN5: Barn .6C **20**
Croft, The CR0: C'don .3F **169**
E4 .2B **36**
EN5: Barn .4B **20**
HA0: Wemb .5C **60**
HA4: Ruis .4A **58**
HA5: Pinn .7D **40**
HA8: Edg .7C **28**
NW10 .2B **80**
TW5: Hest .6C **94**
W5 .5E **78**
Croft Av. BR4: W W'ck .1E **170**
Croft Cl. BR7: Chst .5D **142**
DA17: Belv .5F **109**
NW7 .3F **29**
UB3: Harl .7E **92**
UB10: Hil .7C **56**
Croft Ct. HA4: Ruis .1H **57**
SE13 .6E **122**
Croftdown Rd. NW5 .3E **64**
Croft End Cl. KT9: Chess .3F **163**
Crofters Cl. TW7: Isle .5H **113**
Crofters Ct. *SE8* .*4A 104*
(off Croft St.)
Crofters Mead CR0: Sels .7B **170**
Crofters Way NW1 .1H **83**
Croft Gdns. HA4: Ruis .1G **57**
W7 .2A **96**
Croft Ho. E17 .4D **50**
W10 .*3G 81*
(off Third Av.)
Croft Lodge Cl. IG8: Wfd G .6E **36**
Croft M. N12 .3F **31**
CROFTON .2H **173**
Crofton Av. BR6: Farnb .2G **173**
DA5: Bexl .7D **126**
W4 .7J **97**
Croftongate Way SE4 .5A **122**
Crofton Gro. E4 .4A **36**
Crofton Ho. *SW1* .*5K 17*
(off Sutherland St.)
SW3 .*7C 16*
(off Old Church St.)
Crofton La.
BR5: Farnb, Orp, Pet W .2H **173**
BR6: Pet W .7H **161**
CROFTON PARK .5B **122**
Crofton Pk. Rd. SE4 .6B **122**
Crofton Rd. BR6: Farnb, Orp .3E **172**
E13 .4K **87**
SE5 .1E **120**
Crofton Roman Villa .2J **173**
Crofton Ter. E5 .5A **68**
TW9: Rich .4F **115**
Crofton Way EN2: Enf .2F **23**
EN5: New Bar .6E **20**
Croft Rd. BR1: Brom .6J **141**
EN3: Enf H .1F **25**
SM1: Sutt .5C **166**
SW16 .1A **156**
SW19 .7A **136**
Crofts, The TW17: Shep .4G **147**
Crofts Ho. *E2* .*2G 85*
(off Teale St.)
Croftside, The SE25 .3G **157**
Crofts La. N22 .7F **33**
Crofts Rd. HA1: Harr .6A **42**
Crofts St. E1 .3K **15** (7G **85**)
Croft St. SE8 .4A **104**
Crofts Vs. HA1: Harr .6A **42**
Croft Way DA15: Sidc .3J **143**
Croftway NW3 .4J **63**
TW10: Ham .3B **132**
Crogsland Rd. NW1 .7E **64**
Croham Cl. CR2: S Croy .7E **168**
Croham Mnr. Rd. CR2: S Croy .7E **168**
Croham Mt. CR2: S Croy .7E **168**
Croham Pk. Av. CR2: S Croy .5E **168**
Croham Rd. CR2: S Croy .5D **168**
Croham Valley Rd. CR2: Sels .6G **169**
Croindene Rd. SW16 .1J **155**
Crokesley Ho. *HA8: Edg* .*2J 43*
(off Burnt Oak B'way.)
Cromartie Rd. N19 .7H **47**
Cromarty Ct. SW2 .5K **119**
Cromarty Ho. *E1* .*5A 86*
(off Ben Jonson Rd.)
Cromarty Rd. HA8: Edg .2C **28**
Cromberdale Ct. *N17* .*1G 49*
(off Spencer Rd.)
Crombie Cl. IG4: Ilf .5D **52**
Crombie M. SW11 .2C **118**
Crombie Rd. DA15: Sidc .1H **143**
Crome Ho. *UB5: N'olt* .*2C 76*
(off Parkfield Dr.)
Cromer Cl. UB8: Hil .6E **74**
Cromer Hyde SM4: Mord .5K **153**
Crome Rd. NW10 .6A **62**
Cromer Pl. BR6: Orp .1J **173**
Cromer Rd. E10 .7F **51**
EN5: New Bar .4F **21**
IG8: Wfd G .4D **36**
N17 .2G **49**
RM6: Chad H .6E **54**
RM7: Rom .6J **55**
SE25 .3H **157**
SW17 .6E **136**
TW6: H'row A .2C **110**
Cromer St. WC1 .2E **6** (3J **83**)
Cromer Ter. E8 .5G **67**
RM6: Chad H .5B **54**
Cromer Vs. Rd. SW18 .6H **117**
Cromford Cl. BR6: Orp .3J **173**
Cromford Path E5 .4K **67**
Cromford Rd. SW18 .5J **117**
Cromford Way KT3: N Mald .1K **151**
Cromlix Cl. BR7: Chst .2F **161**
Crompton Ct. SW3 .3C **16** (4C **100**)
Crompton Ho. *SE1* .*3C 102*
(off County St.)
W2 .*4A 4*
(off Hall Pl.)
Crompton Pl. EN3: Enf L .1H **25**
Crompton St. W2 .4A **4** (4B **82**)
Cromwell Av. BR2: Brom .4K **159**
KT3: N Mald .5B **152**
N6 .1F **65**
W6 .5D **98**
Cromwell Cen. IG11: Bark .3A **90**
NW10 .3K **79**
Cromwell Cen., The *RM8: Dag* .*7F 55*
(off Coppen Rd.)
Cromwell Cl. BR2: Brom .4K **159**
E1 .1G **103**
Cromwell Cl. KT12: Walt T .7K **147**
N2 .4B **46**
W3 .1J **97**
(not continuous)
W4 .*5H 97*
(off Harvard Rd.)
Cromwell Ct. EN3: Pond E .5E **24**
Cromwell Cres. SW5 .4J **99**
Cromwell Gdns. SW7 .2B **16** (3B **100**)
Cromwell Gro. W6 .3E **98**
Cromwell Highwalk EC2 .5D **8**
Cromwell Ho. CR0: C'don .3B **168**
SW11 .*1E 118*
(off Charlotte Despard Av.)
Cromwell Ind. Est. E10 .1A **68**
Cromwell Lodge DA6: Bex .5E **126**
E1 .*4J 85*
(off Cleveland Gro.)
IG11: Bark .5J **71**
Cromwell Mans. *SW5* .*4J 99*
(off Cromwell Rd.)
Cromwell M. SW7 .3B **16** (4B **100**)
Cromwell Pl. *EC2* .*5D 8*
(off Silk St.)
N6 .1F **65**
SW7 .3B **16** (4B **100**)
SW14 .3J **115**
Cromwell Rd. BR3: Beck .2A **158**
CR0: C'don .7D **156**
E7 .7A **70**
E17 .5E **50**
HA0: Wemb .2E **78**
KT2: King T .1E **150**
KT4: Wor Pk .3K **163**
N3 .1A **46**
N10 .7K **31**
(not continuous)
SW5 .4J **99**
SW7 .3A **16** (4J **99**)
SW9 .1B **120**
SW19 .5J **135**
TW3: Houn .4E **112**
TW11: Tedd .6A **132**
TW13: Felt .1K **129**
UB3: Hayes .6F **75**
Cromwell St. TW3: Houn .4E **112**
Cromwell Twr. EC2 .5D **8**
Cromwell Trad. Cen. IG11: Bark .3J **89**
Crondace Rd. SW6 .1J **117**
Crondall Ct. N1 .1F **9**
Crondall Ho. SW15 .7C **116**
Crondall St. N1 .1F **9** (2D **84**)
Crone Ct. *NW6* .*2H 81*
(off Denmark Rd.)
Cronin St. SE15 .7F **103**
CROOKED BILLET .**7H 35**
Crooked Billet SW19 .6E **134**
Crooked Billet Yd. E2 .1H **9**
Crooked Usage N3 .3G **45**
Crooke Rd. SE8 .5A **104**
Crookham Rd. SW6 .1H **117**
Crook Log DA6: Bex .3D **126**
Crook Log Sports Cen. .**3D 126**
Crookston Rd. SE9 .3E **124**
Croombs Rd. E16 .5A **88**
Croom's Hill SE10 .7E **104**
Croom's Hill Gro. SE10 .7E **104**
Cropley Ct. *N1* .*2D 84*
(off Cropley St., not continuous)
Cropley St. N1 .1E **8** (2D **84**)
Croppath Rd. RM10: Dag .4G **73**
Cropthorne Ct. W9 .3A **82**
Crosbie NW9 .2B **44**
Crosbie Ho. *E17* .*3E 50*
(off Prospect Hill)
Crosby Cl. TW13: Hanw .3C **130**
Crosby Ct. SE1 .6E **14** (2D **102**)
Crosby Ho. E7 .6J **69**
E14 .*3E 104*
(off Manchester Rd.)
Crosby Rd. E7 .6J **69**
RM10: Dag .2H **91**
Crosby Row SE1 .7E **14** (2D **102**)
Crosby Sq. EC3 .1G **15** (6E **84**)
Crosby Wlk. E8 .6F **67**
SW2 .7A **120**
Crosby Way SW2 .7A **120**
Crosier Cl. SE3 .1C **124**
Crosier Rd. UB10: Ick .4E **56**
Crosier Way HA4: Ruis .3G **57**
Crosland Pl. SW11 .3E **118**
Cross Av. SE10 .6F **105**
Crossbow Ho. *N1* .*1E 84*
(off Whitmore Est.)
W13 .*1B 96*
(off Sherwood Cl.)
Crossbrook Rd. SE3 .2C **124**
Cross Cl. SE15 .2H **121**
Cross Ct. *SE28* .*7B 90*
(off Titmuss Av.)
Cross Deep TW1: Twick .2K **131**
Cross Deep Gdns. TW1: Twick .2K **131**
Crossfield Ct. *W10* .*6F 81*
(off Cambridge Gdns.)
Crossfield Ho. *W11* .*7G 81*
(off Mary Pl.)
Crossfield Rd. N17 .3C **48**
NW3 .6B **64**
Crossfield St. SE8 .7C **104**
(not continuous)
Crossford St. SW9 .2K **119**
Cross Ga. HA8: Edg .3B **28**
Crossgate UB6: G'frd .6B **60**
Cross Keys Cl. N9 .2B **34**
W1 .6H **5** (5E **82**)
Cross Keys Sq. *EC1* .*6C 8*
(off Little Britain)
Cross Lances Rd. TW3: Houn .4F **113**
Crossland Rd. CR7: Thor H .6B **156**
Crosslands Av. UB2: S'hall .5D **94**
W5 .1F **97**
Crosslands Rd. KT19: Ewe .6K **163**
Cross La. DA5: Bexl .7F **127**
EC3 .3G **15** (7E **84**)
(not continuous)
N8 .3K **47**
(not continuous)
Crossleigh Ct. *SE14* .*7B 104*
(off New Cross Rd.)
Crosslet St. SE17 .4D **102**
Crosslet Va. SE10 .1D **122**
Crossley St. N7 .6A **66**
Crossmead SE9 .1D **142**
Crossmead Av. UB6: G'frd .3E **76**
Crossmount Ho. *SE5* .*7C 102*
(off Bowyer St.)
Crossness Engines, The .**6F 91**
Crossness Footpath DA18: Erith .1F **109**
Crossness La. SE2 .7E **90**
Crossness Nature Reserve .**1G 109**
Crossness Rd. IG11: Bark .3K **89**
Cross Rd. BR2: Brom .2C **172**
CR0: C'don .1D **168**
DA14: Sidc .4B **144**
E4 .1A **36**
EN1: Enf .4K **23**
HA1: Harr .4H **41**
HA2: Harr .3F **59**
HA3: W'stone .2A **42**
IG8: Wfd G .6J **37**
KT2: King T .7F **133**
N11 .5A **32**
N22 .7F **33**
RM6: Chad H .7C **54**
RM7: Mawney .4G **55**
SE5 .2E **120**
SM1: Sutt .5B **166**
SW19 .7J **135**
TW13: Hanw .4C **130**
Cross St. N1 .1B **84**
N18 .5B **34**
SE5 .3D **120**
SW13 .2A **116**
TW12: Ham H .5G **131**

Crossthwaite Av. SE5 ....4D 120
Crosstrees Ho. E14 ....3C 104
(off Cassilis Rd.)
Crosswall EC3 ....2J 15 (7F 85)
Cross Way NW10 ....7C 62
Cross Way. The HA3: W'stone 2J 41
Crossway BR5: Pet W 4H 161
EN1: Enf 7K 23
HA4: Ruis 4A 58
HA5: Pinn 2K 39
IG8: Wfd G 4F 37
N12 ....6G 31
N16 ....5E 66
NW9 ....4B 44
RM8: Dag 3C 72
SE28 ....6B 90
SW20 ....4E 152
UB3: Hayes 1J 93
W13 ....4A 78
Crossway, The N22 ....7G 33
SE9 ....2B 142
UB10: Hil 2B 74
Crossway Ct. SE4 ....2A 122
Crossway Pde. N22 ....7G 33
(off The Crossway)
Crossways CR2: Sels 7A 170
N21 ....6H 23
SM2: Sutt 7B 166
TW16: Sun 7H 129
Crossways, The HA9: Wemb 2G 61
KT5: Surb 1H 163
TW5: Hest 7D 94
Crossways Rd. BR3: Beck 4C 158
CR4: Mitc 3F 155
Crossways Ter. E5 ....4J 67
Crosswell Cl. TW17: Shep 2E 146
Croston St. E8 ....1G 85
Crothall Cl. N13 ....3E 32
Crouch Av. IG11: Bark 2B 90
Crouch Cl. BR3: Beck 6C 140
Crouch Cft. SE9 ....3E 142
CROUCH END 7H 47
Crouch End Hill N8 ....7H 47
Crouch Hall Cl. N19 ....1J 65
Crouch Hall Rd. N8 ....6H 47
Crouch Hill N4 ....6J 47
N8 ....6J 47
Crouchman's Cl. SE26 ....3F 139
Crouch Rd. NW10 ....7K 61
Crowborough Rd. SW17 ....6E 136
Crowden Way SE28 ....7C 90
Crowder Cl. N12 ....1A 46
Crowder St. E1 ....7H 85
Crowfield Ho. N5 ....4C 66
Crowfoot Cl. E9 ....5B 68
SE28 ....1J 107
Crowhurst Cl. SW9 ....2A 120
Crowhurst Ho. SW9 ....2K 119
(off Aytoun Rd.)
Crowland Av. UB3: Harl 4G 93
Crowland Gdns. N14 ....7D 22
Crowland Ho. NW8 ....1A 82
(off Springfield Rd.)
Crowland Rd. CR7: Thor H 4D 156
N15 ....5F 49
CROWLANDS 7H 55
Crowlands Av. RM7: Rom 6H 55
Crowland Ter. N1 ....7D 66
Crow La. RM7: Rush G 7F 55
Crowland Wlk. SM4: Mord 6K 153
Crowley Cres. CR0: Wadd 5A 168
Crowline Wlk. N1 ....6C 66
Crowmarsh Gdns. SE23 ....7J 121
Crown All. SE9 ....2K 7
(off Court Yd.)
Crown Arc. KT1: King T 2D 150
Crownbourne Ct. SM1: Sutt 4K 165
(off St Nicholas Way)
Crown Bldgs. E4 ....1K 35
Crown Cl. E3 ....1C 86
KT12: Walt T 7A 148
N22 ....1A 48

Crown Cl. NW6 ....6K 63
NW7 ....2G 29
UB3: Hayes 2H 93
Crown Cl. Bus. Cen. E3 ....1C 86
(off Crown Cl.)
Crown Cotts. RM5: Col R 1G 55
Crown Court
Blackfriars 6B 14 (2B 102)
Croydon 2D 168
Harrow 3H 41
Inner London 7C 14 (3C 102)
Isleworth 1J 113
Kingston upon Thames 3D 150
Snaresbrook 5H 51
Southwark 4G 15 (1E 102)
Wood Green 1A 48
Woolwich 2J 107
Crown Ct. EC2 ....1D 14
N10 ....7K 31
NW8 ....2D 4
(off Park Rd.)
SE12 ....6K 123
WC2 ....1F 13 (6J 83)
Crown Dale SE19 ....6B 138
Crowndale Ct. NW1 ....2H 83
(off Crowndale Rd.)
Crowndale Rd. NW1 ....2G 83
Crownfield Av. IG2: Ilf 6J 53
Crownfield Rd. E15 ....4F 69
Crowngate Ho. E3 ....2B 86
(off Hereford Rd.)
Crown Hill CR0: C'don 2C 168
Crownhill Rd. IG8: Wfd G 7H 37
NW10 ....1B 80
Crown Ho. KT3: N Mald 3J 151
NW10 ....2G 79
Crown La. BR2: Brom 5B 160
BR7: Chst 1G 161
N14 ....1B 32
SM4: Mord 4J 153
SW16 ....5A 138
Crown La. Gdns. SW16 ....5A 138
Crown La. Spur BR2: Brom 6B 160
Crown Lodge SW3 ....4D 16
Crownmead Way RM7: Mawney 4H 55
Crown M. E1 ....5K 85
(off White Horse La.)
E13 ....1A 88
W6 ....4C 98
Crown Office Row EC4 ....2J 13 (7A 84)
Crown Pde. N14 ....1B 32
SM4: Mord 3J 153
Crown Pas. KT1: King T 2D 150
(off Church St.)
SW1 ....5B 12 (1G 101)
Crown Pl. EC2 ....5G 9 (5E 84)
NW5 ....6F 65
SE16 ....5H 103
Crown Point SE19 ....6B 138
Crown Point Pde. SE19 ....6B 138
(off Crown Dale)
Crown Reach SW1 .....6D 18 (5H 101)
Crown Rd. EN1: Enf 3B 24
HA4: Ruis 5B 58
IG6: Ilf 4H 53
KT3: N Mald 1J 151
N10 ....7K 31
SM1: Sutt 4K 165
SM4: Mord 4K 153
TW1: Twick 6B 114
Crownstone Ct. SW2 ....5A 120
Crownstone Rd. SW2 ....5A 120
Crown St. HA2: Harr 1H 59
RM10: Dag 6J 73
(not continuous)
SE5 ....7C 102
W3 ....1H 97
Crown Ter. N14 ....1C 32
(off Crown La.)
TW9: Rich 4F 115
Crown Trad. Cen. UB3: Hayes 2G 93
Crowntree Cl. TW7: Isle 6K 95

Crown Wlk. HA9: Wemb 3F 61
Crown Way UB7: Yiew 1B 92
Crown Wharf E14 ....1E 104
(off Coldharbour)
SE8 ....5B 104
(off Grove St.)
Crown Woods SE18 ....2F 125
Crown Woods Way SE9 ....5H 125
Crown Yd. TW3: Houn 3G 113
Crowshott Av. HA7: Stan 2C 42
Crows Rd. E3 ....3F 87
E15 ....3F 87
IG11: Bark 6F 71
Crowther Av. TW8: Bford 4E 96
Crowther Cl. SW6 ....6H 99
(off Bucklers All.)
Crowther Rd. SE25 ....5G 157
Crowthorne Cl. SW18 ....7H 117
Crowthorne Rd. W10 ....6F 81
Croxall Ho. KT12: Walt T 6A 148
Croxden Cl. HA8: Edg 3G 43
Croxden Wlk. SM4: Mord 6A 154
Croxford Gdns. N22 ....7G 33
Croxford Way RM7: Rush G 1K 73
Croxley Grn. BR5: St P 7B 144
Croxley Rd. W9 ....3H 81
Croxted Cl. SE21 ....7C 120
Croxted M. SE24 ....6C 120
Croxted Rd. SE21 ....7C 120
SE24 ....7C 120
Croxteth Ho. SW8 ....2H 119
Croyde Av. UB3: Harl 4G 93
UB6: G'frd 3G 77
Croyde Cl. DA15: Sidc 7H 125
CROYDON 3C 168
Croydon N17 ....2D 48
(off Gloucester Rd.)
Croydon Airport Ind. Est.
CR0: Wadd 6K 167
Croydon Airport Vis. Cen. 6A 168
Croydon Clocktower 3C 168
(off Katherine St.)
Croydon Crematorium CR0: C'don ..5K 155
Croydon Flyover, The CR0: C'don ..4B 168
Croydon Gro. CR0: C'don 1B 168
Croydon Ho. SE1 ....6K 13
(off Wootton St.)
Croydon Rd. BR2: Hayes, Kes 3A 172
BR2: Kes 3A 172
BR3: Beck 4K 157
BR4: Hayes, W W'ck 3G 171
CR0: Bedd, Wadd 4F 167
CR0: C'don 4E 154
CR4: Mitc 4E 154
E13 ....4H 87
SE20 ....2H 157
SM6: Bedd, Wall 4F 167
TW6: H'row A 2D 110
Croydon Rd. Ind. Est. BR3: Beck ..4K 157
Croydon Sports Arena 5J 157
Croydon Valley Trade Pk. CR0: Bedd ..7J 155
(off Therapia La.)
Croyland Rd. N9 ....1B 34
Croylands Dr. KT6: Surb 7E 150
Croysdale Av. TW16: Sun 3J 147
Crozier Ho. SE3 ....3K 123
SW8 ....7K 101
(off Wilkinson St.)
Crozier Ter. E9 ....5A 68
E9 ....5K 67
(not continuous)
Crucible Cl. RM6: Chad H 6B 54
Crucifix La. SE1 ....6H 15 (2E 102)
Cruden Ho. E3 ....2B 86
(off Vernon Rd.)
SE17 ....6B 102
(off Brandon Est.)
Cruden St. N1 ....1B 84
Cruikshank Ho. NW8 ....2C 82
(off Townshend Rd.)
Cruikshank Rd. E15 ....4G 69
Cruikshank St. WC1 .....1J 7 (3A 84)

Crummock Gdns. NW9 ....5A 44
Crumpsall St. SE2 ....4C 108
Crundale Av. NW9 ....5G 43
Crunden Rd. CR2: S Croy 7D 168
Crusader Gdns. CR0: C'don 3E 168
Crusader Ind. Est. N4 ....6C 48
Crusoe M. N16 ....2D 66
Crusoe Rd. CR4: Mitc 7D 136
DA8: Erith 5K 109
Crutched Friars EC3 ....2H 15 (7E 84)
Crutchley Rd. SE6 ....2G 141
Crystal Ct. SE19 ....5F 139
(off College Rd.)
Crystal Ho. SE18 ....5K 107
CRYSTAL PALACE 6F 139
Crystal Palace Athletics Stadium ..6G 139
Crystal Palace Dinosaurs 6G 139
Crystal Palace FC 4E 156
Crystal Palace Indoor Bowling Club
..............................1H 157
Crystal Palace Mus. 6F 139
Crystal Palace National Sports Cen.
..............................6G 139
Crystal Pal. Pde. SE19 ....6F 139
Crystal Palace Pk. 5G 139
Crystal Palace Pk. Farm 5G 139
Crystal Pal. Pk. Rd. SE26 ....5G 139
Crystal Pal. Rd. SE22 ....6F 121
Crystal Pal. Sta. Rd. SE19 .....6G 139
Crystal Ter. SE19 ....6D 138
Crystal Vw. Ct. BR1: Brom 4F 141
Crystal Way HA1: Harr 5K 41
RM8: Dag 1C 72
Crystal Wharf N1 ....2B 84
Cuba Dr. EN3: Enf H 2D 24
Cuba St. E14 ....2C 104
Cube Ho. SE16 ....3F 103
Cubitt Bldg. SW1 ....7J 17 (5F 101)
Cubitt Ho. SW4 ....6G 119
Cubitt Sq. UB2: S'hall 1G 95
Cubitt Steps E14 ....1C 104
Cubitt St. WC1 ....2H 7 (3K 83)
Cubitt's Yd. WC2 ....2F 13
Cubitt Ter. SW4 ....3G 119
CUBITT TOWN 4E 104
Cuckoo Av. W7 ....4J 77
Cuckoo Dene W7 ....5H 77
Cuckoo Hall La. N9 ....7D 24
Cuckoo Hall Rd. N9 ....7D 24
Cuckoo Hill HA5: Eastc, Pinn 3A 40
Cuckoo Hill Dr. HA5: Pinn 3A 40
Cuckoo Hill Rd. HA5: Pinn 4A 40
Cuckoo La. W7 ....7J 77
Cuckoo Pound TW17: Shep 5G 147
Cudas Cl. KT19: Ewe 4B 164
Cuddington SE17 ....4C 102
(off Deacon Way)
Cuddington Av. KT4: Wor Pk 3B 164
Cudham La. Nth. BR6: Downe 7J 173
Cudham St. SE6 ....7E 122
Cudworth Ho. SW8 ....1G 119
Cudworth St. E1 ....4H 85
Cuff Cres. SE9 ....6B 124
Cuffley Ho. W10 ....5E 80
(off Sutton Way)
Cuff Point E2 ....1J 9
(off Columbia Rd.)
Culand Ho. SE17 ....4E 102
(off Congreve St.)
Culford Gdns. SW3 .....4F 17 (4D 100)
Culford Gro. N1 ....6E 66
Culford Mans. SW3 ....4F 17
(off Culford Gdns.)
Culford M. N1 ....6E 66
Culford Rd. N1 ....7E 66
Culford Ter. N1 ....6E 66
(off Balls Pond Rd.)
Culgaith Gdns. EN2: Enf 4D 22
Culham Ho. E2 ....2J 9
(off Palissy St.)
W2 ....5J 81
(off Gt. Western Rd.)

Cullen Way NW10 4J **79**
Culling Rd. SE16 3J **103**
Cullington Cl. HA3: W'stone 4A **42**
Cullingworth Rd. NW10 5C **62**
Culloden Cl. SE16 5G **103**
Culloden Rd. EN2: Enf 2G **23**
Cullum St. EC3 2G **15** (7E **84**)
Cullum Welch Ct. *N1* *1F 9*
(off Haberdasher St.)
Cullum Welch Ho. *EC1* *4C 8*
(off Golden La. Est.)
Culmington Pde. *W13* *1C 96*
(off Uxbridge Rd.)
Culmington Rd. CR2: S Croy 7C **168**
W13 1C **96**
Culmore Rd. SE15 7H **103**
Culmstock Rd. SW11 5E **118**
Culpepper Cl. N18 5C **34**
Culpepper Ct. SE11 3J **19**
Culross Cl. N15 4C **48**
Culross Ho. *W10* *6F 81*
(off Bridge Cl.)
Culross St. W1 3G **11** (7E **82**)
Culsac Rd. KT6: Surb 2E **162**
Culverden Rd. SW12 2G **137**
Culver Gro. HA7: Stan 2C **42**
Culverhouse *WC1* *6G 7*
(off Red Lion Sq.)
Culverhouse Gdns. SW16 3K **137**
Culverlands Cl. HA7: Stan 4G **27**
Culverley Rd. SE6 1D **140**
Culvers Av. SM5: Cars 2D **166**
Culvers Retreat SM5: Cars 1D **166**
Culverstone Cl. BR2: Brom 6H **159**
Culvers Way SM5: Cars 2D **166**
Culvert Pl. SW11 2E **118**
Culvert Rd. *N15* *5E 48*
(off Lydford Rd.)
N15 5E **48**
(Oulton Rd.)
SW11 2D **118**
Culworth Ho. *NW8* *2C 82*
(off Allitsen Rd.)
Culworth St. NW8 2C **82**
Culzean Cl. SE27 3B **138**
Cumberland Av. DA16: Well 3J **125**
NW10 3H **79**
Cumberland Bus. Pk. NW10 3H **79**
Cumberland Cl. E8 6F **67**
IG6: Ilf 1G **53**
SW20 7F **135**
TW1: Twick 6B **114**
Cumberland Ct. CR0: C'don 1D **168**
DA16: Well 2J **125**
HA1: Harr *3J 41*
(off Princes Dr.)
SW1 *5K 17*
(off Cumberland St.)
W1 *1F 11*
(off Gt. Cumberland Pl.)
Cumberland Cres. W14 4G **99**
(not continuous)
Cumberland Dr. DA7: Bex 7E **108**
KT9: Chess 3E **162**
KT10: Hin W 2A **162**
Cumberland Gdns. NW4 2G **45**
WC1 1J **7** (3A **84**)
Cumberland Ga. W1 2E **10** (7D **82**)
Cumberland Gate (Park & Ride)
2E **10** (7D **82**)
Cumberland Ho. *E16* *1J 105*
(off Wesley Av.)
KT2: King T 7H **133**
N9 *1D 34*
(off Cumberland Rd.)
SE28 2G **107**
W8 *2K 99*
(off Kensington Ct.)
Cumberland Mans. W1 7E **4**
Cumberland Mkt. NW1 1K **5** (3F **83**)
Cumberland M. SE11 6K **19** (5A **102**)
Cumberland Mills Sq. E14 5F **105**
Cumberland Pk. W3 7J **79**
Cumberland Pk. Ind. Est. NW10 3C **80**
Cumberland Pl. NW1 1J **5** (3F **83**)
SE6 1H **141**
TW16: Sun 4J **147**
Cumberland Rd. BR2: Brom 4G **159**
E12 4B **70**
E13 5K **87**
E17 2A **50**
HA1: Harr 5F **41**
HA7: Stan 3F **43**
N9 1D **34**
N22 2K **47**
SE25 6H **157**
SW13 1B **116**
TW9: Kew 7G **97**
TW15: Ashf 3A **128**
W3 7J **79**
W7 2K **95**
Cumberland St. SW1 5K **17** (5F **101**)
Cumberland Ter. NW1 1J **5** (2F **83**)
Cumberland Ter. M. NW1 1J **5**
(not continuous)
Cumberland Vs. *W3* *7J 79*
(off Cumberland Rd.)
Cumberland Wharf *SE16* *2J 103*
(off Rotherhithe St.)
Cumberlow Av. SE25 3F **157**
Cumbernauld Gdns. TW16: Sun 5H **129**
Cumberton Rd. N17 1D **48**
Cumbrae Gdns. KT6: Surb 2D **162**
Cumbrian Gdns. NW2 2F **63**
Cumbrian Way UB8: Uxb 7A **56**
Cuming Mus. *4C 102*
(off Walworth Rd.)
Cumming St. N1 1H **7** (2K **83**)
Cumnor Cl. *SW9* *2K 119*
(off Robsart St.)
Cumnor Gdns. KT17: Ewe 6C **164**
Cumnor Rd. SM2: Sutt 6A **166**
Cunard Ct. *HA7: Stan* *2F 27*
(off Brightwen Gro.)
Cunard Cres. N21 6J **23**
Cunard Pl. EC3 1H **15** (6E **84**)
Cunard Rd. NW10 3K **79**
Cunard Wlk. SE16 4K **103**
Cundy Rd. E16 6A **88**
Cundy St. SW1 4H **17** (4E **100**)
Cunliffe Pde. KT19: Ewe 4B **164**
Cunliffe Rd. KT19: Ewe 4B **164**
Cunliffe St. SW16 6G **137**
Cunningham Cl. BR4: W W'ck 2D **170**
RM6: Chad H 5C **54**
Cunningham Ct. *E10* *3D 68*
(off Oliver Rd.)
W9 *4A 4*
(off Blomfield Rd.)
Cunningham Ho. *SE5* *7D 102*
(off Elmington Est.)
Cunningham Pk. HA1: Harr 5G **41**
Cunningham Pl. NW8 3A **4** (4B **82**)
Cunningham Rd. N15 4G **49**
Cunnington St. W4 3J **97**
Cupar Rd. SW11 1E **118**
Cupola Cl. BR1: Brom 5K **141**
Cureton St. SW1 4D **18** (4H **101**)
Curfew Ho. IG11: Bark 1G **89**
Curie Ct. HA1: Harr 7B **42**
Curie Gdns. NW9 2A **44**
Curlew Cl. SE28 7D **90**
Curlew Ct. KT6: Surb 3G **163**
W13 4K **77**
Curlew Ho. EN3: Pond E 5E **24**
SE4 *4A 122*
(off St Norbert Rd.)
SE15 1F **121**
Curlew St. SE1 6K **15** (2F **103**)
Curlew Way UB4: Yead 5B **76**
Curness St. SE13 4E **122**
Curnick's La. SE27 4C **138**
Curran Av. DA15: Sidc 5K **125**
SM6: Wall 3E **166**
Curran Ho. *SW3* *4C 16*
(off Lucan Pl.)
Currey Rd. UB6: G'frd 6H **59**
Curricle St. W3 1A **98**
Currie Hill Cl. SW19 4H **135**
Currie Ho. *E14* *6F 87*
(off Abbott Rd.)
Curry Ri. NW7 6A **30**
Cursitor St. EC4 7J **7** (6A **84**)
Curtain Pl. EC2 3H **9** (3E **84**)
Curtain Rd. EC2 2H **9** (4E **84**)
Curthwaite Gdns. EN2: Enf 4C **22**
Curtis Dr. W3 6K **79**
Curtis Fld. Rd. SW16 4K **137**
Curtis Ho. *N11* *5B 32*
(off Ladderswood Way)
SE17 *5D 102*
(off Morecambe St.)
Curtis La. HA0: Wemb 6E **60**
Curtis Rd. KT19: Ewe 4J **163**
TW4: Houn 7D **112**
Curtis St. SE1 4F **103**
Curtis Way SE1 4F **103**
SE28 7B **90**
Curtlington Ho. *HA8: Edg* *2J 43*
(off Burnt Oak B'way.)
Curve, The W12 7C **80**
Curwen Av. E7 4K **69**
Curwen Rd. W12 2C **98**
Curzon Av. EN3: Pond E 5E **24**
HA7: Stan 1A **42**
Curzon Cinema
Mayfair *5J 11*
(off Curzon St.)
Richmond 5D **114**
Soho *2D 12*
(off Shaftesbury Av.)
Curzon Cl. BR6: Orp 4H **173**
Curzon Ct. *SW6* *1A 118*
(off Imperial Rd.)
Curzon Cres. IG11: Bark 2K **89**
NW10 7A **62**
Curzon Ga. W1 5H **11** (1E **100**)
Curzon Pl. HA5: Eastc 5A **40**
Curzon Rd. CR7: Thor H 6A **156**
N10 2F **47**
W5 4B **78**
Curzon Sq. W1 5H **11** (1E **100**)
Curzon St. W1 5H **11** (1E **100**)
Cusack Cl. TW1: Twick 4K **131**
Custance Ho. *N1* *1E 8*
(off Provost Est.)
Custance St. N1 1E **8** (3D **84**)
CUSTOM HOUSE 6A **88**
Custom Ho. EC3 3G **15** (7E **84**)
Custom Ho. Reach SE16 2B **104**
Custom Ho. Wlk. EC3 3G **15** (7E **84**)
Cut, The SE1 6K **13** (2A **102**)
Cutbush Ho. N7 5H **65**
Cutcombe Rd. SE5 2C **120**
Cuthberga Cl. IG11: Bark 7G **71**
Cuthbert Bell Twr. *E3* *2C 86*
(off Pancras Way)
Cuthbert Gdns. SE25 3E **156**
Cuthbert Harrowing Ho. *EC1* *4C 8*
(off Golden La. Est.)
Cuthbert Ho. *W2* *5A 4*
(off Hall Pl.)
Cuthbert Rd. CR0: C'don 2B **168**
E17 3E **50**
N18 5B **34**
Cuthbert St. W2 5A **4** (5B **82**)
Cuthill Wlk. SE5 1D **120**
Cutlers Gdns. EC2 6H **9** (6E **84**)
Cutlers Gdns. Arc. *EC2* *7H 9*
(off Devonshire Sq.)
Cutlers Sq. E14 4C **104**
Cutlers Ter. *N1* *6E 66*
(off Balls Pond Rd.)
Cutler St. E1 7H **9** (6E **84**)
Cutter Ho. DA8: Erith 4K **109**
Cutter La. SE10 1G **105**
Cutthroat All. TW10: Ham 2C **132**
Cutty Sark 6E **104**
Cutty Sark Gdns. *SE10* *6E 104*
(off King William Wlk.)
Cuxton BR5: Pet W 5G **161**
Cuxton Cl. DA6: Bex 5E **126**
Cuxton Ho. *SE17* *5E 102*
(off Mina Rd.)
Cyclamen Cl. TW12: Hamp 6E **130**
Cyclamen Way KT19: Ewe 5J **163**
Cyclops M. E14 4C **104**
Cygnet Av. TW14: Felt 7A **112**
Cygnet Cl. NW10 5K **61**
Cygnet Ho. *SW3* *6D 16*
(off King's Rd.)
Cygnet Ho. Nth. *E14* *6D 86*
(off Chrisp St.)
Cygnet Ho. Sth. *E14* *6D 86*
(off Chrisp St.)
Cygnets, The TW13: Hanw 4C **130**
Cygnet St. E1 3K **9** (4F **85**)
Cygnet Way UB4: Yead 5B **76**
Cygnus Bus. Cen. NW10 5B **62**
Cymbeline Ct. *HA1: Harr* *6K 41*
(off Gayton Rd.)
Cynthia St. N1 1H **7** (2K **83**)
Cyntra Pl. E8 7H **67**
Cypress Av. TW2: Whitt 7G **113**
Cypress Cl. E5 2G **67**
Cypress Ct. SM1: Sutt 5J **165**
Cypress Gdns. SE4 5A **122**
Cypress Ho. SE14 1K **121**
SE16 *2K 103*
(off Woodland Cres.)
Cypress Pl. W1 4B **6** (4G **83**)
Cypress Rd. HA3: Hrw W 2H **41**
SE25 2E **156**
Cypress Tree Cl. DA15: Sidc 1K **143**
CYPRUS 7E **88**
Cyprus Av. N3 2G **45**
Cyprus Cl. N4 6B **48**
Cyprus Gdns. N3 2G **45**
Cyprus Pl. E2 2J **85**
E6 7E **88**
Cyprus Rd. N3 2H **45**
N9 2A **34**
Cyprus St. E2 2J **85**
(not continuous)
Cyrena Rd. SE22 6F **121**
Cyril Lodge DA14: Sidc 4A **144**
Cyril Mans. SW11 1D **118**
Cyril Rd. BR6: Orp 7K **161**
DA7: Bex 2E **126**
Cyrus Ho. EC1 3B **8**
Cyrus St. EC1 3B **8**
Czar St. SE8 6C **104**

D

Dabbs Hill La. UB5: N'olt 6D **58**
(not continuous)
Dabbs La. *EC1* *4K 7*
(off Farringdon Rd.)
Dabin Cres. SE10 1E **122**
Dacca St. SE8 6B **104**
Dace Rd. E3 1C **86**
Dacre Av. IG5: Ilf 2E **52**
Dacre Cl. UB6: G'frd 2F **77**
Dacre Gdns. SE13 4G **123**
Dacre Ho. SW3 7B **16**
Dacre Pk. SE13 3G **123**
Dacre Pl. SE13 3G **123**
Dacre Rd. CR0: C'don 7J **155**
E11 1H **69**
E13 1K **87**
Dacres Est. SE23 3K **139**
Dacres Ho. SW4 3F **119**
Dacres Rd. SE23 2K **139**
Dacre St. SW1 1C **18** (3H **101**)
Dade Way UB2: S'hall 5D **94**
Daerwood Cl. BR2: Brom 1D **172**

Daffodil Cl. CR0: C'don . . . 1K 169
Daffodil Gdns. IG1: Ilf . . . 5F 71
Daffodil Pl. TW12: Hamp . . . 6E 130
Daffodil St. W12 . . . 7B 80
Dafforne Rd. SW17 . . . 3E 136
Da Gama Pl. E14 . . . 5C 104
DAGENHAM . . . 6G 73
Dagenham & Redbridge FC . . . 5H 73
Dagenham Av. RM9: Dag . . . 1E 90
(not continuous)
Dagenham Bowl . . . 1E 90
Dagenham Leisure Pk.
RM9: Dag . . . 1E 90
Dagenham Pk. Leisure Cen. . . . 7G 73
Dagenham Rd. E10 . . . 1B 68
RM7: Rush G . . . 7K 55
RM10: Dag, Rush G . . . 4J 73
RM13: Rain . . . 7K 73
Dagenham Swimming Pool . . . 2G 73
Dagmar Av. HA9: Wemb . . . 4F 61
Dagmar Ct. E14 . . . 3E 104
Dagmar Gdns. NW10 . . . 2F 81
Dagmar M. *UB2: S'hall* . . . *3C 94*
(off Dagmar Rd.)
Dagmar Pas. *N1* . . . *1B 84*
(off Cross St.)
Dagmar Rd. KT2: King T . . . 1F 151
N4 . . . 7A 48
N15 . . . 4D 48
N22 . . . 1H 47
RM10: Dag . . . 7J 73
SE5 . . . 1E 120
SE25 . . . 5E 156
UB2: S'hall . . . 3C 94
Dagmar Ter. N1 . . . 1B 84
Dagnall Pk. SE25 . . . 6E 156
Dagnall Rd. SE25 . . . 5E 156
Dagnall St. SW11 . . . 2D 118
Dagnan Rd. SW12 . . . 7F 119
Dagobert Ho. *E1* . . . *5J 85*
(off Smithy St.)
Dagonet Gdns. BR1: Brom . . . 3J 141
Dagonet Rd. BR1: Brom . . . 3J 141
Dahlia Gdns. CR4: Mitc . . . 4H 155
IG1: Ilf . . . 6F 71
Dahlia Rd. SE2 . . . 4B 108
Dahomey Rd. SW16 . . . 6G 137
Daimler Ho. *E3* . . . *4C 86*
(off Wellington Way)
Daimler Way SM6: Wall . . . 7J 167
Dain Ct. *W8* . . . *4J 99*
(off Lexham Gdns.)
Daines Cl. E12 . . . 3D 70
Dainford Cl. BR1: Brom . . . 5F 141
Dainton Cl. BR1: Brom . . . 1K 159
Dainton Ho. *W2* . . . *5J 81*
(off Gt. Western Rd.)
Daintry Cl. HA3: W'stone . . . 4A 42
Daintry Way E9 . . . 6B 68
Dairsie Ct. BR1: Brom . . . 1A 160
Dairsie Rd. SE9 . . . 3E 124
Dairy Cl. BR1: Brom . . . 7K 141
CR7: Thor H . . . 2C 156
NW10 . . . 1C 80
SW6 . . . 1J 117
UB6: G'frd . . . 2H 77
Dairy La. SE18 . . . 4D 106
Dairyman Cl. NW2 . . . 3F 63
Dairy M. N2 . . . 4C 46
SW9 . . . 3J 119
Dairy Wlk. SW19 . . . 4G 135
Daisy Cl. CR0: C'don . . . 1K 169
NW9 . . . 2J 61
Daisy Dobbings Wlk. *N19* . . . *7J 47*
(off Jessie Blythe La.)
Daisy La. SW6 . . . 3J 117
Daisy Rd. E16 . . . 4G 87
E18 . . . 2K 51
Dakin Pl. E1 . . . 5A 86
Dakota Bldg. *SE10* . . . *1D 122*
(off Deal's Gateway)
Dakota Cl. SM6: Wall . . . 7K 167
Dakota Gdns. E6 . . . 4C 88
UB5: N'olt . . . 3C 76
Dakota Ho. CR7: Thor H . . . 6B 156
Dalberg Rd. SW2 . . . 4A 120
(not continuous)
Dalberg Way SE2 . . . 3D 108
Dalby Rd. SW18 . . . 4A 118
Dalbys Cres. N17 . . . 6K 33
Dalby St. NW5 . . . 6F 65
Dalcross Rd. TW4: Houn . . . 2C 112
Dale, The BR2: Kes . . . 4B 172
Dale Av. HA8: Edg . . . 1F 43
TW4: Houn . . . 3C 112
Dalebury Rd. SW17 . . . 2D 136
Dale Cl. EN5: New Bar . . . 6E 20
HA5: Pinn . . . 1K 39
SE3 . . . 3J 123
Dale Ct. EN2: Enf . . . 1H 23
KT2: King T . . . *7F 133*
(off York Rd.)
Dale Dr. UB4: Hayes . . . 4H 75
Dalefield *IG9: Buck H* . . . *1F 37*
(off Roebuck La.)
Dale Gdns. IG8: Wfd G . . . 4E 36
Dale Grn. Rd. N11 . . . 3A 32
Dale Gro. N12 . . . 5F 31
Daleham Dr. UB8: Hil . . . 6D 74
Daleham Gdns. NW3 . . . 5B 64
Daleham M. NW3 . . . 6B 64
Dalehead *NW1* . . . *1A 6*
(off Hampstead Rd.)
Dale Ho. *N1* . . . *1E 84*
(off New Era Est.)
NW8 . . . *1A 82*
(off Boundary Rd.)
SE4 . . . 4A 122
Dale Lodge N6 . . . 6G 47
Dalemain M. E16 . . . 1J 105
Dale Pk. Av. SM5: Cars . . . 2D 166
Dale Pk. Rd. SE19 . . . 1C 156
Dale Rd. KT12: Walt T . . . 7H 147
NW5 . . . 5E 64
SE17 . . . 6B 102
SM1: Sutt . . . 4H 165
TW16: Sun . . . 7H 129
UB6: G'frd . . . 5F 77
Dale Row W11 . . . 6G 81
Daleside Rd. KT19: Ewe . . . 6K 163
SW16 . . . 5F 137
Dale St. W4 . . . 5A 98
Dale Vw. Av. E4 . . . 2K 35
Dale Vw. Cres. E4 . . . 2K 35
Dale Vw. Gdns. E4 . . . 3A 36
Daleview Rd. N15 . . . 6E 48
Dalewood Gdns. KT4: Wor Pk . . . 2D 164
Dale Wood Rd. BR6: Orp . . . 7J 161
Daley Ho. W12 . . . 6D 80
Daley St. E9 . . . 6K 67
Daley Thompson Way SW8 . . . 2F 119
Dalgarno Gdns. W10 . . . 5E 80
Dalgarno Way W10 . . . 4E 80
Dalgleish St. E14 . . . 6A 86
Daling Way E3 . . . 1A 86
Dali Universe, The . . . 6G 13 (2K 101)
Dalkeith Ct. *SW1* . . . *3D 18*
(off Vincent St.)
Dalkeith Gro. HA7: Stan . . . 5J 27
Dalkeith Ho. *SW9* . . . *1B 120*
(off Lothian Rd.)
Dalkeith Rd. IG1: Ilf . . . 3G 71
SE21 . . . 1C 138
Dallas Rd. NW4 . . . 7C 44
SE26 . . . 3H 139
SM3: Cheam . . . 6G 165
W5 . . . 5F 79
Dallas Ter. UB3: Harl . . . 3H 93
Dallega Cl. UB3: Hayes . . . 7F 75
Dallinger Rd. SE12 . . . 6H 123
Dalling Rd. W6 . . . 4D 98
Dallington Sq. *EC1* . . . *3B 8*
(off Dallington St.)
Dallington St. EC1 . . . 3B 8 (4B 84)
Dallin Rd. DA6: Bex . . . 4D 126
SE18 . . . 7F 107
Dalmain Rd. SE23 . . . 1K 139
Dalmally Rd. CR0: C'don . . . 7F 157
Dalmany Pas. CR0: C'don . . . 7F 157
Dalmeny Av. N7 . . . 4H 65
SW16 . . . 2A 156
Dalmeny Cl. HA0: Wemb . . . 6C 60
Dalmeny Cres. TW3: Houn . . . 4H 113
Dalmeny Rd. DA8: Erith . . . 1H 127
EN5: New Bar . . . 6F 21
KT4: Wor Pk . . . 3D 164
N7 . . . 3H 65
(not continuous)
SM5: Cars . . . 7E 166
Dalmeyer Rd. NW10 . . . 6B 62
Dalmore Rd. SE21 . . . 2C 138
Dalo Lodge *E3* . . . *5C 86*
(off Gale St.)
Dalrymple Cl. N14 . . . 7C 22
Dalrymple Rd. SE4 . . . 4A 122
DALSTON . . . 6F 67
Dalston Gdns. HA7: Stan . . . 1E 42
Dalston La. E8 . . . 6F 67
Dalton Av. CR4: Mitc . . . 2C 154
Dalton Cl. BR6: Orp . . . 3J 173
UB4: Hayes . . . 4F 75
Dalton Ho. *E3* . . . *2A 86*
(off Ford St.)
HA7: Stan . . . 5F 27
SE14 . . . *6K 103*
(off John Williams Cl.)
SW1 . . . *5J 17*
(off Ebury Bri. Rd.)
Dalton Rd. HA3: W'stone . . . 2H 41
Dalton St. SE27 . . . 2B 138
Dalwood St. SE5 . . . 1E 120
Daly Dr. BR1: Brom . . . 3E 160
Dalyell Rd. SW9 . . . 3K 119
Damascene Wlk. SE21 . . . 1C 138
Damask Ct. SM1: Sutt . . . 1K 165
Damask Cres. E16 . . . 4G 87
Damer Ter. SW10 . . . 7A 100
Dames Rd. E7 . . . 3J 69
Dame St. N1 . . . 2C 84
Damien Ct. *E1* . . . *6H 85*
(off Damien St.)
Damien St. E1 . . . 6H 85
Damon Cl. DA14: Sidc . . . 3B 144
Damory Ho. *SE16* . . . *4H 103*
(off Abbeyfield Est.)
Damson Dr. UB3: Hayes . . . 7J 75
Damsonwood Rd. UB2: S'hall . . . 3E 94
Danbrook Rd. SW16 . . . 1J 155
Danbury Cl. RM6: Chad H . . . 3D 54
Danbury Mans. *IG11: Bark* . . . *7F 71*
(off Whiting Av.)
Danbury M. SM6: Wall . . . 4F 167
Danbury St. N1 . . . 2B 84
Danbury Way IG8: Wfd G . . . 6F 37
Danby Ct. EN2: Enf . . . 3H 23
Danby Ho. *E9* . . . *7J 67*
(off Frampton Pk. Rd.)
W10 . . . *3G 81*
(off Bruckner St.)
Danby St. SE15 . . . 3F 121
Dance Ho. *SE4* . . . *5K 121*
(off St Norbert Rd.)
Dancer Rd. SW6 . . . 1H 117
TW9: Rich . . . 3G 115
Dando Cres. SE3 . . . 3K 123
Dandridge Cl. SE10 . . . 5H 105
Dandridge Ho. *E1* . . . *5J 9*
(off Lamb St.)
Danebury CR0: New Ad . . . 6E 170
Danebury Av. SW15 . . . 6A 116
(not continuous)
Daneby Rd. SE6 . . . 3D 140
Dane Cl. BR6: Farnb . . . 5H 173
DA5: Bexl . . . 7G 127
Danecourt Gdns. CR0: C'don . . . 3F 169
Danecroft Rd. SE24 . . . 5C 120
Danehill Wlk. DA14: Sidc . . . 3A 144
Danehurst TW8: Bford . . . 7C 96
Danehurst Gdns. IG4: Ilf . . . 5C 52
Danehurst St. SW6 . . . 1G 117
Daneland EN4: E Barn . . . 6J 21
Danemead Gro. UB5: N'olt . . . 5F 59
Danemere St. SW15 . . . 3E 116
Dane Pl. E3 . . . 2A 86
Dane Rd. IG1: Ilf . . . 5G 71
N18 . . . 3D 34
SW19 . . . 1A 154
TW15: Ashf . . . 6E 128
UB1: S'hall . . . 7C 76
W13 . . . 1C 96
Danesbury Rd. TW13: Felt . . . 1K 129
Danescombe SE12 . . . 1J 141
Danes Ct. HA9: Wemb . . . 3H 61
NW8 . . . *1D 82*
(off St Edmund's Ter.)
Danescourt Cres. SM1: Sutt . . . 2A 166
Danescroft NW4 . . . 5F 45
Danescroft Av. NW4 . . . 5F 45
Danescroft Gdns. NW4 . . . 5F 45
Danesdale Rd. E9 . . . 6A 68
Danesfield *SE5* . . . *6E 102*
(off Albany Rd.)
Danes Ga. HA1: Harr . . . 3J 41
Danes Ho. *W10* . . . *5E 80*
(off Sutton Way)
Danes Rd. RM7: Rush G . . . 7J 55
Dane St. WC1 . . . 6G 7 (5K 83)
Daneswood Av. SE6 . . . 3E 140
Danethorpe Rd. HA0: Wemb . . . 6D 60
Danetree Cl. KT19: Ewe . . . 7J 163
Danetree Rd. KT19: Ewe . . . 7J 163
Danette Gdns. RM10: Dag . . . 2G 73
Daneville Rd. SE5 . . . 1D 120
Dangan Rd. E11 . . . 6J 51
Daniel Bolt Cl. E14 . . . 5D 86
Daniel Cl. N18 . . . 4D 34
SW17 . . . 6C 136
TW4: Houn . . . 7D 112
Daniel Ct. NW9 . . . 1A 44
Daniel Gdns. SE15 . . . 7F 103
Daniell Ho. *N1* . . . *2D 84*
(off Cranston Est.)
Daniell Way CR0: Wadd . . . 1J 167
Daniel Pl. NW4 . . . 7D 44
Daniel Rd. W5 . . . 7F 79
Daniels Rd. SE15 . . . 3J 121
Danleigh Ct. N14 . . . 7C 22
Dan Leno Wlk. SW6 . . . 7K 99
Dan Mason Dr. W4 . . . 2J 115
Dansey Pl. W1 . . . 2C 12
Dansington Rd. DA16: Well . . . 4A 126
Danson Cres. DA16: Well . . . 3B 126
Danson House . . . 4C 126
DANSON INTERCHANGE . . . 5D 126
Danson La. DA16: Well . . . 4B 126
Danson Mead DA16: Well . . . 3C 126
Danson Pk. . . . 5C 126
Danson Pk. Watersports Cen. . . . 4C 126
Danson Rd. DA5: Bexl, Bex . . . 6C 126
DA6: Bex . . . 5D 126
SE17 . . . 5B 102
Danson Underpass DA15: Sidc . . . 6C 126
Dante Pl. SE11 . . . 4B 102
Dante Rd. SE11 . . . 4B 102
Danube Apartments *N8* . . . *3K 47*
(off Gt. Amwell La.)
Danube Cl. N9 . . . 3D 34
Danube Ct. *SE15* . . . *7F 103*
(off Daniel Gdns.)
Danube St. SW3 . . . 5D 16 (5C 100)
Danvers Ho. *E1* . . . *6G 85*
(off Christian St.)
Danvers Rd. N8 . . . 4H 47
Danvers St. SW3 . . . 7B 16 (6B 100)
Dao Ct. E13 . . . 1K 87
Da Palma Ct. *SW6* . . . *6J 99*
(off Anselm Rd.)
Daphne Ct. KT4: Wor Pk . . . 2A 164

Daphne Gdns.—Deacons Ct.

Daphne Gdns. E4 . . . . . 3K 35
Daphne Ho. N22 . . . . . 1A 48
(off Acacia Rd.)
Daphne St. SW18 . . . . . 6A 118
Daplyn St. E1 . . . . . 5K 9 (5G 85)
D'Arblay St. W1 . . . . . 1B 12 (6G 83)
Darby Cres. TW16: Sun 2A 148
Darby Gdns. TW16: Sun 2A 148
Darcy Av. SM6: Wall 4G 167
Darcy Cl. N20 . . . . . 2G 31
D'Arcy Dr. HA3: Kenton 4D 42
Darcy Gdns. HA3: Kenton 4D 42
RM9: Dag 1F 91
Darcy Ho. E8 . . . . . 1H 85
(off London Flds. E. Side)
D'Arcy Pl. BR2: Brom 4J 159
Darcy Rd. SM3: Cheam 4F 165
SW16 . . . . . 2J 155
TW7: Isle 1A 114
Dare Gdns. RM8: Dag 3E 72
Darell Rd. TW9: Rich 3G 115
Darent Ho. BR1: Brom 5F 141
NW8 . . . . . 5B 4
(off Church St. Est.)
Darenth Rd. DA16: Well 1A 126
N16 . . . . . 7F 49
Darfield NW1 . . . . . 1G 83
(off Bayham St.)
Darfield Rd. SE4 . . . . . 5B 122
Darfield Way W10 . . . . . 6F 81
Darfur St. SW15 . . . . . 3F 117
Dargate Cl. SE19 . . . . . 7F 139
Darien Ho. E1 . . . . . 5K 85
(off Shandy St.)
Darien Rd. SW11 . . . . . 3B 118
Daring Ho. E3 . . . . . 2A 86
(off Roman Rd.)
Dark Ho. Wlk. EC3 . . . . . 3F 15 (7D 84)
Darlands Dr. EN5: Barn 5A 20
Darlan Rd. SW6 . . . . . 7H 99
Darlaston Rd. SW19 . . . . . 7F 135
Darley Cl. CR0: C'don 6A 158
Darley Dr. KT3: N Mald 2K 151
Darley Gdns. SM4: Mord 6A 154
Darley Ho. SE11 . . . . . 6G 19
Darley Rd. N9 . . . . . 1A 34
SW11 . . . . . 6D 118
Darling Ho. TW1: Twick 6D 114
Darling Rd. SE4 . . . . . 3C 122
Darling Row E1 . . . . . 4H 85
Darlington Ct. SE6 . . . . . 1H 141
Darlington Ho. SW8 . . . . . 7H 101
(off Hemans St.)
Darlington Rd. SE27 . . . . . 5B 138
Darmaine Cl. CR2: S Croy 7C 168
Darnall Ho. SE10 . . . . . 1E 122
(off Royal Hill)
Darnaway Pl. E14 . . . . . 5E 86
(off Aberfeldy St.)
Darnay Apartments E15 . . . . . 6F 69
Darnay Ho. SE16 . . . . . 7K 15 (3G 103)
Darndale Cl. E17 . . . . . 2B 50
Darnley Ho. E14 . . . . . 6A 86
(off Camdenhurst St.)
Darnley Rd. E9 . . . . . 6J 67
IG8: Wfd G 1J 51
Darnley Ter. W11 . . . . . 1F 99
Darrell Charles Ct. UB8: Uxb 7A 56
Darrell Rd. SE22 . . . . . 5G 121
Darren Cl. N4 . . . . . 7K 47
Darren Ct. N7 . . . . . 4J 65
Darrick Wood Rd. BR6: Orp 2H 173
Darrick Wood Sports Cen. 3G 173
Darrick Wood Swimming Pool 3F 173
Darris Cl. UB4: Yead 4C 76
Darsley Dr. SW8 . . . . . 1H 119
Dartford Av. N9 . . . . . 6D 24
Dartford By-Pass DA5: Bexl, Dart 7K 127
Dartford Gdns. RM6: Chad H 5B 54
Dartford Ho. SE1 . . . . . 4F 103
(off Longfield Est.)
Dartford Rd. DA5: Bexl 1J 145
Dartford St. SE17 . . . . . 6C 102
Dartington NW1 . . . . . 1G 83
(off Plender St.)
Dartington Ho. SW8 . . . . . 2H 119
(off Union Gro.)
W2 . . . . . 5K 81
(off Senior St.)
Dartle Ct. SE16 . . . . . 2G 103
(off Scott Lidgett Cres.)
Dartmoor Wlk. E14 . . . . . 4C 104
(off Severnake Cl.)
Dartmouth Cl. W11 . . . . . 6H 81
Dartmouth Ct. SE10 . . . . . 1E 122
Dartmouth Gro. SE10 . . . . . 1E 122
Dartmouth Hill SE10 . . . . . 1E 122
Dartmouth Ho. KT2: King T 1E 150
(off Seven Kings Way)
SE10 . . . . . 1D 122
(off Catherine Gro.)
DARTMOUTH PARK 3F 65
Dartmouth Pk. Av. NW5 . . . . . 3F 65
Dartmouth Pk. Hill N19 . . . . . 1F 65
NW5 . . . . . 1F 65
Dartmouth Pk. Rd. NW5 . . . . . 4F 65
Dartmouth Pl. SE23 . . . . . 2J 139
W4 . . . . . 6A 98
Dartmouth Rd. BR2: Hayes 7J 159
HA4: Ruis 3J 57
NW2 . . . . . 6F 63
NW4 . . . . . 6C 44
SE23 . . . . . 3H 139
SE26 . . . . . 3H 139
Dartmouth Row SE10 . . . . . 2E 122
Dartmouth St. SW1 . . . . . 7D 12 (2H 101)
Dartmouth Ter. SE10 . . . . . 1F 123
Dartnell Rd. CR0: C'don 7F 157
Darton Ct. W3 . . . . . 1J 97
Dartrey Twr. SW10 . . . . . 7A 100
(off Worlds End Est.)
Dartrey Wlk. SW10 . . . . . 7A 100
Dart St. W10 . . . . . 3G 81
Darvell Ho. SE17 . . . . . 5D 102
(off Inville Rd.)
Darville Rd. N16 . . . . . 3F 67
Darwell Cl. E6 . . . . . 2E 88
Darwen Pl. E2 . . . . . 2H 85
Darwin Cl. BR6: Farnb 5H 173
N11 . . . . . 3A 32
Darwin Ct. E13 . . . . . 3K 87
NW1 . . . . . 1F 83
(not continuous)
SE17 . . . . . 4D 102
(off Barlow St.)
Darwin Dr. UB1: S'hall 6F 77
Darwin Ho. SW1 . . . . . 7A 18
Darwin Rd. DA16: Well 3K 125
N22 . . . . . 1B 48
W5 . . . . . 5C 96
Darwin St. SE17 . . . . . 4D 102
Darwood Ct. NW6 . . . . . 7A 64
(off Belsize Rd.)
Daryngton Dr. UB6: G'frd 2H 77
Daryngton Ho. SE1 . . . . . 7F 15
(off Manciple St.)
SW8 . . . . . 7J 101
(off Hartington Rd.)
Dashwood Cl. DA6: Bex 5G 127
Dashwood Rd. N8 . . . . . 6K 47
Dassett Rd. SE27 . . . . . 5B 138
Data Point Bus. Cen.
E16 . . . . . 4F 87
Datchelor Pl. SE5 . . . . . 1D 120
Datchet Ho. E2 . . . . . 3F 85
(off Virginia Rd.)
NW1 . . . . . 1K 5
(off Augustus St.)
Datchet Rd. SE6 . . . . . 2B 140
Datchworth Ct. EN1: Enf 5K 23
Datchworth Ho. N1 . . . . . 7B 66
(off The Sutton Est.)
Date St. SE17 . . . . . 5D 102
Daubeney Gdns. N17 . . . . . 7H 33
Daubeney Pl. TW12: Hamp 1G 149
(off High St.)
Daubeney Rd. E5 . . . . . 4A 68
N17 . . . . . 7H 33
Daubeney Twr. SE8 . . . . . 5B 104
(off Bowditch)
Dault Rd. SW18 . . . . . 6A 118
Dauncey Ho. SE1 . . . . . 7A 14
Dave Adams Ho. E3 . . . . . 2B 86
(off Norman Gro.)
Davema Cl. BR7: Chst 1E 160
Davenant Ho. E1 . . . . . 5G 85
(off Old Montague St.)
Davenant Rd. CR0: C'don 4B 168
N19 . . . . . 2H 65
Davenant St. E1 . . . . . 5G 85
Davenport Cen. IG11: Bark 1B 90
Davenport Cl. TW11: Tedd 6A 132
Davenport Ct. CR0: C'don 7B 156
Davenport Ho. SE11 . . . . . 3J 19
(off Walnut Tree Wlk.)
UB7: W Dray 2B 92
Davenport Lodge TW5: Hest 7C 94
Davenport Rd. DA14: Sidc 2E 144
SE6 . . . . . 6D 122
Daventer Dr. HA7: Stan 7E 26
Daventry Av. E17 . . . . . 6C 50
Daventry Cl. SL3: Poyle 4A 174
Daventry St. NW1 . . . . . 5C 4 (5C 82)
Daver Ct. SW3 . . . . . 5D 16 (5C 100)
W5 . . . . . 4D 78
Davern Cl. SE10 . . . . . 4H 105
Davey Cl. N7 . . . . . 6K 65
N13 . . . . . 5E 32
Davey Rd. E9 . . . . . 7C 68
Davey's Ct. WC2 . . . . . 2E 12
Davey St. SE15 . . . . . 6F 103
David Av. UB6: G'frd 3J 77
David Cl. UB3: Harl 7G 93
David Coffer Ct. DA17: Belv 4H 109
David Ct. N20 . . . . . 3F 31
Davidge Ho. SE1 . . . . . 7K 13
(off Coral St.)
Davidge St. SE1 . . . . . 7A 14 (2B 102)
David Hewitt Ho. E3 . . . . . 5D 86
(off Watts Gro.)
David Ho. DA15: Sidc 3A 144
SW8 . . . . . 7J 101
(off Wyvil Rd.)
David Lean Cinema 3C 168
(in Croydon Clocktower)
David Lee Point E15 . . . . . 1G 87
(off Leather Gdns.)
David Lloyd Leisure
Barnet 7G 31
Beckenham 5B 158
Buckhurst Hill 1J 37
Cheam 7F 165
Ealing 5H 59
Enfield 2B 24
Fulham 7J 99
(within Fulham Broadway Shopping Cen.)
Hounslow 5A 94
Kidbrooke 4K 123
Kingston upon Thames 2E 150
(in The Rotunda Cen.)
Merton 3F 153
Sidcup 5C 144
South Kensington 4K 99
(off Point W.)
David M. W1 . . . . . 5F 5 (5D 82)
David Rd. RM8: Dag 2E 72
SL3: Poyle 5A 174
David's Ct. UB1: S'hall 6G 77
(off Whitecote Rd.)
Davidson Gdns. SW8 . . . . . 7J 101
Davidson La. HA1: Harr 7K 41
Davidson Rd. CR0: C'don 1E 168
Davidson Terraces E7 . . . . . 5K 69
(off Claremont Rd.)
David's Rd. SE23 . . . . . 1J 139
David St. E15 . . . . . 6F 69
David Twigg Cl. KT2: King T 1E 150
Davies Alpine House 7F 97
Davies Cl. CR0: C'don 6G 157
Davies La. E11 . . . . . 2G 69
Davies M. W1 . . . . . 2J 11 (7F 83)
Davies St. W1 . . . . . 1J 11 (6F 83)
Davies Wlk. TW7: Isle 1H 113
Da Vinci Ct. SE16 . . . . . 5H 103
(off Rossetti Rd.)
Da Vinci Lodge SE10 . . . . . 3H 105
(off West Parkside)
Davington Gdns. RM8: Dag 5B 72
Davington Rd. RM8: Dag 6B 72
Davinia Cl. IG8: Wfd G 6J 37
Davis Ho. W12 . . . . . 7D 80
(off White City Est.)
Davis Rd. KT9: Chess 4G 163
W3 . . . . . 1B 98
Davis Road Ind. Pk. KT9: Chess 4G 163
Davis St. E13 . . . . . 2K 87
Davisville Rd. W12 . . . . . 2C 98
Davis Way DA14: Sidc 6E 144
(not continuous)
Davmor Ct. TW8: Bford 5C 96
Dawes Av. TW7: Isle 5A 114
Dawes Ho. SE17 . . . . . 4D 102
(off Orb St.)
Dawes Rd. SW6 . . . . . 7G 99
UB10: Uxb 2A 74
Dawes St. SE17 . . . . . 5D 102
Dawley Av. UB8: Hil 5E 74
Dawley Pde. UB3: Hayes 7E 74
Dawley Pk. UB3: Hayes 2F 93
Dawley Rd. UB3: Harl, Hayes 7E 74
Dawlish Av. N13 . . . . . 4D 32
SW18 . . . . . 2K 135
UB6: G'frd 2A 78
Dawlish Dr. HA4: Ruis 2J 57
HA5: Pinn 5C 40
IG3: Ilf 4J 71
Dawlish Rd. E10 . . . . . 1E 68
N17 . . . . . 3G 49
NW2 . . . . . 6F 63
Dawnay Gdns. SW18 . . . . . 2B 136
Dawnay Rd. SW18 . . . . . 2A 136
Dawn Cl. TW4: Houn 3C 112
Dawn Cres. E15 . . . . . 1F 87
Dawpool Rd. NW2 . . . . . 2B 62
Daws Hill E4 . . . . . 2K 25
Daws La. NW7 . . . . . 5G 29
Dawson Av. IG11: Bark 7J 71
Dawson Cl. SE18 . . . . . 4G 107
UB3: Hayes 5F 75
Dawson Gdns. IG11: Bark 7K 71
Dawson Ho. E2 . . . . . 3J 85
(off Sceptre Rd.)
Dawson Pl. W2 . . . . . 7J 81
Dawson Rd. KT1: King T 3F 151
NW2 . . . . . 5E 62
Dawson St. E2 . . . . . 1K 9 (2F 85)
Dawson Ter. N9 . . . . . 7D 24
Dax Ct. TW16: Sun 3A 148
Daybrook Rd. SW19 . . . . . 2K 153
Day Ho. SE5 . . . . . 7C 102
(off Bethwin Rd.)
Daylesford Av. SW15 . . . . . 4C 116
Daymer Gdns. HA5: Eastc 4K 39
Daynor Ho. NW6 . . . . . 1J 81
(off Quex Ho.)
Daysbrook Rd. SW2 . . . . . 1K 137
Days La. DA15: Sidc 7J 125
Dayton Gro. SE15 . . . . . 1J 121
Deaconess Ct. N15 . . . . . 4F 49
(off Tottenham Grn. E.)
Deacon Est., The E4 . . . . . 6G 35
Deacon Ho. SE11 . . . . . 4H 19
(off Black Prince Rd.)
Deacon M. N1 . . . . . 7D 66
Deacon Rd. KT2: King T 1F 151
NW2 . . . . . 5C 62
Deacons Cl. HA5: Pinn 2K 39
Deacons Ct. TW1: Twick 2K 131

A-Z London 243

Deacons Leas BR6: Orp 4H **173**
Deacon's Ri. N2 . . . . .5B **46**
Deacons Ter. *N1* *6C **66***
(off Harecourt Rd.)
Deacons Wlk. TW12: Hamp 4E **130**
Deacon Way IG8: Wfd G 7J **37**
SE17 . . . . .4C **102**
Deal Ct. NW9 . . . . .2B **44**
(off Hazel Cl.)
UB1: S'hall 6G **77**
(off Haldane Rd.)
Deal Ho. SE15 . . . . .6K **103**
(off Lovelinch La.)
SE17 . . . . .5E **102**
(off Mina Rd.)
Deal M. W5 . . . . .4D **96**
Deal Porters Wlk. SE16 . . . . .2K **103**
Deal Porters Way SE16 . . . . .3J **103**
Deal Rd. SW17 . . . . .6E **136**
Deal's Gateway SE10 . . . . .1C **122**
Deal St. E1 . . . . .5G **85**
Dealtry Rd. SW15 . . . . .4E **116**
Deal Wlk. SW9 . . . . .7A **102**
Dean Abbott Ho. *SW1* *3C **18***
(off Vincent St.)
Dean Bradley St. SW1 . . .2E **18** (3J **101**)
Dean Cl. E9 . . . . .5J **67**
SE16 . . . . .1K **103**
UB10: Hil 7B **56**
Dean Ct. HA0: Wemb 3B **60**
HA8: Edg 6C **28**
RM7: Rom 5K **55**
SW8 . . . .*7J **101***
(off Thorncroft St.)
W3 . . . . .6K **79**
Deancross St. E1 . . . . .6J **85**
Dean Dr. HA7: Stan 2E **42**
Deane Av. HA4: Ruis 5A **58**
Deane Ct. HA6: Nwood 1G **39**
Deane Ct. Rd. HA5: Eastc 6A **40**
Deanery Cl. N2 . . . . .4C **46**
Deanery M. W1 . . . . .4H **11**
Deanery Rd. E15 . . . . .6G **69**
Deanery St. W1 . . . . . . .4H **11** (1E **100**)
Deane Way HA4: Ruis 6K **39**
Dean Farrar St. SW1 . . .1D **18** (3H **101**)
Deanfield Gdns.
CRO: C'don 4D **168**
Dean Gdns. E17 . . . . .4F **51**
Deanhill Ct. SW14 . . . . .4H **115**
Deanhill Rd. SW14 . . . . .4H **115**
Dean Ho. E1 .6J **85**
(off Tarling St.)
SE14 . . . . .7A **104**
(off New Cross Rd.)
Dean Rd. CRO: C'don 4D **168**
NW2 . . . . .6E **62**
SE28 . . . . .1A **108**
TW3: Houn 5F **113**
TW12: Hamp 4E **130**
Dean Ryle St. SW1 . . . . . . .3E **18** (4J **101**)
Deansbrook Cl. HA8: Edg 7D **28**
Deansbrook Rd. HA8: Edg 7C **28**
Dean's Bldgs. SE17 . . . . .4D **102**
Deans Cl. CRO: C'don 3F **169**
HA8: Edg 6D **28**
W4 . . . . .6H **97**
Dean's Ct. EC4 . . . . .1B **14** (6B **84**)
Deanscroft Av. NW9 . . . . .1J **61**
Deans Dr. HA8: Edg 5E **28**
N13 . . . . .6G **33**
Deans Ga. Cl. SE23 . . . . .3K **139**
Deanshanger Ho. *SE8* *4K **103***
(off Chilton Gro.)
Deans La. HA8: Edg 6D **28**
W4 . . . . .6H **97**
(off Deans Cl.)
Dean's M. W1 . . . . .7K **5** (6F **83**)
Deans Rd. SM1: Sutt 3K **165**
W7 . . . . .1K **95**
Dean Stanley St. SW1 . . .2E **18** (3J **101**)
Deanston Wharf E16 . . . . .2K **105**

Dean St. E7 . . . . .5J **69**
W1 . . . . .7C **6** (6H **83**)
Deans Way HA8: Edg 5D **28**
Deansway N2 . . . . .4B **46**
N9 . . . . .3K **33**
Deanswood N11 . . . . .6C **32**
Dean's Yd. SW1 . . . . .1D **18** (3H **101**)
Dean Trench St. SW1 . . . .2E **18** (3J **101**)
Dean Wlk. HA8: Edg 6D **28**
Dean Way UB2: S'hall 2F **95**
Dearne Cl. HA7: Stan 5F **27**
De'Arn Gdns. CR4: Mitc 3C **154**
Dearsley Ho. RM13: Rain 2K **91**
Dearsley Rd. EN1: Enf 3B **24**
Death Trap, London's 7G **13**
Deauville Ct. *SE16* *2K **103***
(off Eleanor Cl.)
SW4 . . . . .6G **119**
De Barowe M. N5 . . . . .4B **66**
Debdale Ho. *E2* *1G **85***
(off Whiston Rd.)
Debden *N17* *2D **48***
(off Gloucester Rd.)
Debden Cl. IG8: Wfd G 7G **37**
KT2: King T 5D **132**
NW9 . . . . .1A **44**
De Beauvoir Ct. *N1* *7D **66***
(off Northchurch Rd.)
De Beauvoir Cres. N1 . . . . .1E **84**
De Beauvoir Est. N1 . . . . .1E **84**
De Beauvoir Pl. N1 . . . . .6E **66**
De Beauvoir Rd. N1 . . . . .1E **84**
De Beauvoir Sq. N1 . . . . .7E **66**
DE BEAUVOIR TOWN 1E **84**
Debenham Ct. *E8* *1G **85***
(off Pownall Rd.)
Debham Ct. NW2 . . . . .3E **62**
Debnams Rd. SE16 . . . . .4J **103**
De Bohun Av. N14 . . . . .6A **22**
Deborah Ct. TW7: Isle 1J **113**
Deborah Cl. *E18* *3K **51***
(off Victoria Rd.)
Deborah Cres. HA4: Ruis 7F **39**
Deborah Lodge HA8: Edg 1H **43**
Debrabant Cl. DA8: Erith 6K **109**
De Brome Rd. TW13: Felt 1A **130**
De Bruin Ct. *E14* *5E **104***
(off Ferry St.)
Deburgh Rd. SW19 . . . . .7A **136**
Debussy NW9 . . . . .2B **44**
Decima St. SE1 . . . . . . .7G **15** (3E **102**)
Decima Studios *SE1* *3E **102***
(off Rothsay St.)
Decimus Cl. CR7: Thor H 4D **156**
Deck Cl. SE16 . . . . .1K **103**
Decoy Av. NW11 . . . . .5G **45**
De Crespigny Pk. SE5 . . . . .2D **120**
Dee Ct. *W7* *6H **77***
(off Hobbayne Rd.)
Dee Ho. *KT2: King T* *1D **150***
(off May Bate Av.)
Deeley Rd. SW8 . . . . .1H **119**
Deena Cl. W3 . . . . .5F **79**
Deen City Farm 2A **154**
Deepdale SW19 . . . . .4F **135**
Deepdale Av. BR2: Brom 4H **159**
Deepdale Cl. N11 . . . . .6K **31**
Deepdale Ct. CRO: C'don 4D **168**
(off Birdhurst Rd.)
Deep Dene W5 . . . . .4F **79**
Deepdene Av. CRO: C'don 3F **169**
Deepdene Cl. E11 . . . . .4J **51**
Deepdene Ct. BR2: Brom 3G **159**
N21 . . . . .6G **23**
Deepdene Gdns. SW2 . . . . .7K **119**
Deepdene Mans. *SW6* *1H **117***
(off Rostrevor Rd.)
Deepdene Point SE23 . . . . .3K **139**
Deepdene Rd. DA16: Well 3A **126**
SE5 . . . . .4D **120**
Deepwell Cl. TW7: Isle 1A **114**
Deepwood La. UB6: G'frd 3H **77**

Deerbrook Rd. SE24 . . . . .1B **138**
Deerdale Rd. SE24 . . . . .4C **120**
Deerfield Cl. NW9 . . . . .5B **44**
Deerfield Cotts. NW9 . . . . .5B **44**
Deerhurst Cl. TW13: Felt 4K **129**
Deerhurst Cres. TW12: Ham H 5G **131**
Deerhurst Ho. *SE15* *6G **103***
(off Haymerle Rd.)
Deerhurst Rd. NW2 . . . . .6F **63**
SW16 . . . . .5K **137**
Deerings Dr. HA5: Eastc 5J **39**
Deerleap Gro. E4 . . . . .5J **25**
Dee Rd. TW9: Rich 4F **115**
Deer Pk. Cl. KT2: King T 7H **133**
Deer Pk. Gdns. CR4: Mitc 4B **154**
Deer Pk. Rd. SW19 . . . . .2K **153**
Deer Pk. Way BR4: W W'ck 2H **171**
Deeside Rd. SW17 . . . . .3B **136**
Dee St. E14 . . . . .6E **86**
Defence Cl. SE28 . . . . .1J **107**
Defiance Wlk. SE18 . . . . .3D **106**
Defiant *NW9* *2B **44***
(off Further Acre)
Defiant Way SM6: Wall 7J **167**
Defoe Cl. SE16 . . . . .2B **104**
SW17 . . . . .6C **136**
Defoe Ho. EC2 . . . . .5D **8**
(off Beech St.)
Defoe Pl. *EC2* *5C **8***
(off Beech St.)
SW17 . . . . .4D **136**
Defoe Rd. N16 . . . . .3E **66**
De Frene Rd. SE26 . . . . .4K **139**
Degema Rd. BR7: Chst 5F **143**
Dehar Cres. NW9 . . . . .7B **44**
Dehavilland Cl. UB5: N'olt 3B **76**
De Havilland Dr. SE18 . . . . .6F **107**
De Havilland Rd. HA8: Edg 2G **43**
TW5: Hest 7A **94**
Dehavilland Studios *E5* *2J **67***
(off Theydon Rd.)
De Havilland Way
TW19: Stanw 6A **110**
Dekker Ho. *SE5* *7D **102***
(off Elmington Est.)
Dekker Rd. SE21 . . . . .6E **120**
Delacourt Rd. SE3 . . . . .7K **105**
Delafield Ho. *E1* *6G **85***
(off Christian St.)
Delafield Rd. SE7 . . . . .5K **105**
Delaford Rd. SE16 . . . . .5H **103**
Delaford St. SW6 . . . . .7G **99**
Delamare Ct. SE6 . . . . .3D **140**
Delamare Cres. CRO: C'don 6J **157**
Delamere Ct. E17 . . . . .2E **50**
Delamere Gdns. NW7 . . . . .6E **28**
Delamere Rd. SW20 . . . . .1F **153**
UB4: Yead 7B **76**
W5 . . . . .2E **96**
Delamere St. W2 . . . . .5K **81**
Delamere Ter. W2 . . . . .5K **81**
Delancey Pas. *NW1* *1F **83***
(off Delancey St.)
Delancey St. NW1 . . . . .1F **83**
Delancey Studios NW1 . . . . .1F **83**
Delany Ho. *SE10* *6E **104***
(off Thames St.)
Delarch Ho. SE1 . . . . .7A **14**
De Laune St. SE17 . . . . . .6K **19** (5B **102**)
Delaware Mans. *W9* *4K **81***
(off Delaware Rd.)
Delaware Rd. W9 . . . . .4K **81**
Delawyk Cres. SE24 . . . . .6C **120**
Delcombe Av. KT4: Wor Pk 1E **164**
Delderfield Ho. *RM1: Rom* *2K **55***
(off Portnoi Cl.)
Delft Ho. *KT2: King T* *7F **133***
(off Acre Rd.)
Delft Way SE22 . . . . .5E **120**
Delhi Rd. EN1: Enf 7A **24**
Delhi St. N1 .1J **83**
Delia St. SW18 . . . . .7K **117**

Delisle Rd. SE28 . . . . .2J **107**
(not continuous)
Delius Gro. E15 . . . . .2F **87**
Dell, The DA5: Bexl 1K **145**
HA0: Wemb 5B **60**
HA5: Pinn 2B **40**
IG8: Wfd G 3E **36**
SE2 . . . . .5A **108**
SE19 . . . . .1F **157**
TW8: Bford 6C **96**
TW14: Felt 7K **111**
Della Path E5 . . . . .3G **67**
Dellbow Rd. TW14: Felt 5K **111**
Dell Cl. E15 . . . . .1F **87**
IG8: Wfd G 3E **36**
SM6: Wall 4G **167**
Dell Farm Rd. HA4: Ruis 5F **39**
Dellfield Cl. BR3: Beck 1E **158**
Dell La. KT17: Ewe 5C **164**
Dellors Cl. EN5: Barn 5A **20**
Dellow Cl. IG2: Ilf 7H **53**
Dellow Ho. *E1* *7H **85***
(off Dellow St.)
Dellow St. E1 . . . . .7H **85**
Dell Rd. KT17: Ewe 6C **164**
UB7: W Dray 4B **92**
Dells Cl. E4 . . . . .7J **25**
TW11: Tedd 6K **131**
Dell's M. SW1 . . . . .4B **18**
Dell Wlk. KT3: N Mald 2A **152**
Dell Way W13 . . . . .6C **78**
Dellwood Gdns. IG5: Ilf 3E **52**
Delmare Cl. SW9 . . . . .4K **119**
Delme Cres. SE3 . . . . .2K **123**
Delmerend Ho. *SW3* *5C **16***
(off Cale St.)
Delmey Cl. CRO: C'don 3F **169**
Deloraine Ho. SE8 . . . . .1C **122**
Delorme St. W6 . . . . .6F **99**
Delroy Ct. N20 . . . . .7F **21**
Delta Bldg. *E14* *6E **86***
(off Ashton St.)
Delta Cen. HA0: Wemb 1F **79**
Delta Cl. KT4: Wor Pk 3B **164**
Delta Ct. NW2 . . . . .2C **62**
SE8 . . . .*6A **104***
(off Trundleys Rd.)
Delta Gro. UB5: N'olt 3B **76**
Delta Ho. *N1* *1E **8***
(off Nile St.)
Delta Pk. SW18 . . . . .4K **117**
Delta Pk. Ind. Est.
EN3: Brim 3G **25**
Delta Point *CRO: C'don* *1C **168***
(off Wellesley Rd.)
E2 . . . .*3K **85***
(off Delta St.)
Delta Rd. KT4: Wor Pk 3A **164**
Delta St. E2 .3G **85**
De Luci Rd. DA8: Erith 5J **109**
De Lucy St. SE2 . . . . .4B **108**
Delvan Cl. SE18 . . . . .7E **106**
Delvers Mead RM10: Dag 4J **73**
Delverton Ho. *SE17* *5B **102***
(off Delverton Rd.)
Delverton Rd. SE17 . . . . .5B **102**
Delvino Rd. SW6 . . . . .1J **117**
Demesne Rd. SM6: Wall 4H **167**
Demeta Cl. HA9: Wemb 3J **61**
De Montfort Pde. SW16 . . . . .3J **137**
De Montfort Rd. SW16 . . . . .3J **137**
De Morgan Rd. SW6 . . . . .3K **117**
Dempster Cl. KT6: Surb 1C **162**
Dempster Rd. SW18 . . . . .5A **118**
Den, The 5J **103**
Denbar Pde. RM7: Rom 4J **55**
Denberry Dr. DA14: Sidc 3B **144**
Denbigh Cl. BR7: Chst 6D **142**
HA4: Ruis 2H **57**
SM1: Sutt 5H **165**
UB1: S'hall 6D **76**
W11 . . . . .7H **81**

Denbigh Ct.—Derwentwater Rd.

Denbigh Ct. E6 3B **88**
W7 *5K 77*
(*off Copley Cl.*)
Denbigh Dr. UB3: Harl 2E **92**
Denbigh Gdns. TW10: Rich 5F **115**
Denbigh Ho. *SW1* *1F 17*
(*off Hans Pl.*)
W11 *7H 81*
(*off Westbourne Gro.*)
Denbigh M. SW1 4A **18**
Denbigh Pl. SW1 5A **18** (5G **101**)
Denbigh Rd. E6 3B **88**
TW3: Houn 2F **113**
UB1: S'hall 6D **76**
W11 7H **81**
W13 7B **78**
Denbigh St. SW1 4A **18** (4G **101**)
(not continuous)
Denbigh Ter. W11 7H **81**
Denbridge Rd. BR1: Brom 2D **160**
Denbury Ho. *E3* *3D 86*
(*off Talwin St.*)
Denby Ct. SE11 3H **19**
Dence Ho. *E2* *2K 9*
(*off Turin St.*)
Denchworth Ho. SW9 2A **120**
Dencliffe TW15: Ashf 5C **128**
Den Cl. BR3: Beck 3F **159**
Dencora Cen., The EN3: Brim 3F **25**
Dene, The CR0: C'don 4K **169**
HA9: Wemb 4E **60**
KT8: W Mole 5D **148**
W13 5B **78**
Dene Av. DA15: Sidc 7B **126**
TW3: Houn 3D **112**
Dene Cl. BR2: Hayes 1H **171**
DA2: Dart 4K **145**
E10 2D **68**
KT4: Wor Pk 2B **164**
SE4 3A **122**
Dene Ct. *CR2: S Croy* *5C 168*
(*off Warham Rd.*)
W5 5C **78**
Denecroft Cres. UB10: Hil 1D **74**
Dene Gdns. HA7: Stan 5H **27**
KT7: T Ditt 2A **162**
Dene Ho. N14 7C **22**
Denehurst Gdns. IG8: Wfd G 4E **36**
NW4 6E **44**
TW2: Twick 7H **113**
TW10: Rich 4G **115**
W3 1H **97**
Dene Rd. IG9: Buck H 1G **37**
N11 1J **31**
Denesmead SE24 5C **120**
Denewood EN5: New Bar 5F **21**
Denewood Rd. N6 6D **46**
Denford St. *SE10* *5H 105*
(*off Glenforth St.*)
Dengie Wlk. *N1* *1C 84*
(*off Basire St.*)
Denham Cl. DA16: Well 3C **126**
Denham Ct. *NW6* *7A 64*
(*off Fairfax Rd.*)
SE26 *3H 139*
(*off Kirkdale*)
UB1: S'hall *7G 77*
(*off Baird Av.*)
Denham Cres. CR4: Mitc 4D **154**
Denham Dr. IG2: Ilf 6G **53**
Denham Ho. *UB7: W Dray* *2B 92*
(*off Park Lodge Av.*)
W12 *7D 80*
(*off White City Est.*)
Denham Rd. N20 3J **31**
TW14: Felt 7A **112**
Denham St. SE10 5J **105**
Denham Way IG11: Bark 1J **89**
Denholme Rd. W9 3H **81**
Denison Cl. N2 3A **46**
Denison Ho. *E14* *6C 86*
(*off Farrance St.*)
Denison Rd. SW19 6B **136**
TW13: Felt 4H **129**
W5 4C **78**
Deniston Av. DA5: Bexl 1E **144**
Denis Way SW4 3H **119**
Denland Ho. *SW8* *7K 101*
(*off Dorset Rd.*)
Denleigh Gdns. KT7: T Ditt 6J **149**
N21 1F **33**
Denman Dr. KT10: Clay 5A **162**
NW11 5J **45**
TW15: Ashf 6D **128**
Denman Dr. Nth. NW11 5J **45**
Denman Dr. Sth. NW11 5J **45**
Denman Ho. N16 2E **66**
Denman Pl. W1 2C **12**
Denman Rd. SE15 1F **121**
Denman St. W1 3C **12** (7H **83**)
Denmark Av. SW19 7G **135**
Denmark Ct. SM4: Mord 6J **153**
Denmark Gdns. SM5: Cars 3D **166**
Denmark Gro. N1 2A **84**
DENMARK HILL 3C **120**
Denmark Hill SE5 1D **120**
Denmark Hill Dr. NW9 3C **44**
Denmark Hill Est. SE5 4D **120**
Denmark Ho. SE7 4C **106**
Denmark Mans. *SE5* *2C 120*
(*off Coldharbour La.*)
Denmark Path SE25 5H **157**
Denmark Pl. E3 3C **86**
WC2 7D **6** (6H **83**)
Denmark Rd. BR1: Brom 1K **159**
KT1: King T 3E **150**
N8 4A **48**
NW6 2H **81**
(not continuous)
SE5 1C **120**
SE25 5G **157**
SM5: Cars 3D **166**
SW19 6F **135**
TW2: Twick 3H **131**
W13 7B **78**
Denmark St. E11 3G **69**
E13 5K **87**
N17 1H **49**
WC2 7D **6** (6H **83**)
Denmark Ter. N2 3D **46**
Denmark Wlk. SE27 4C **138**
Denmead Ho. *SW15* *6B 116*
(*off Highcliffe Dr.*)
Denmead Rd. CR0: C'don 1B **168**
Denmore Ct. SM6: Wall 5F **167**
Dennan Rd. KT6: Surb 1F **163**
Dennard Way BR6: Farnb 4F **173**
Denner Rd. E4 2H **35**
Denne Ter. E8 1F **85**
Dennett Rd. CR0: C'don 1A **168**
Dennett's Gro. SE14 2K **121**
Dennett's Rd. SE14 1J **121**
Denning Av. CR0: Wadd 4A **168**
Denning Cl. NW8 1A **4** (3A **82**)
TW12: Hamp 5D **130**
Denning M. SW12 6E **118**
Denning Point *E1* *7K 9*
(*off Commercial St.*)
Denning Rd. NW3 4B **64**
Dennington Cl. E5 2J **67**
Dennington Pk. Rd. NW6 6J **63**
Denningtons, The KT4: Wor Pk 2A **164**
Dennis Av. HA9: Wemb 5F **61**
Dennis Cl. TW15: Ashf 7F **129**
Dennis Gdns. HA7: Stan 5H **27**
Dennis Ho. *E3* *2B 86*
(*off Roman Rd.*)
SM1: Sutt 4K **165**
Dennis La. HA7: Stan 3G **27**
Dennison Point E15 7E **68**
Dennis Pde. N14 1C **32**
Dennis Pk. Cres. SW20 1G **153**
Dennis Reeve Cl. CR4: Mitc 1D **154**
Dennis Rd. KT8: E Mos 4G **149**
Dennis Way SW4 3H **119**
Denny Cl. E6 5C **88**
Denny Cres. SE11 5K **19** (5A **102**)
Denny Gdns. RM9: Dag 7B **72**
Denny Rd. N9 1C **34**
Denny St. SE11 5K **19** (5A **102**)
Den Rd. BR2: Brom 3F **159**
Densham Ho. *NW8* *1B 4*
(*off Cochrane St.*)
Densham Rd. E15 1G **87**
Densole Cl. BR3: Beck 1A **158**
Denstone Ho. *SE15* *6G 103*
(*off Haymerle Rd.*)
Densworth Gro. N9 2D **34**
Dent Ho. *SE17* *4E 102*
(*off Tatum St.*)
Denton NW1 6E **64**
Denton Ct. BR2: Brom 7E **160**
Denton Ho. *N1* *7B 66*
(*off Halton Rd.*)
Denton Rd. DA5: Bexl 2K **145**
DA16: Well 7C **108**
N8 5K **47**
N18 4K **33**
TW1: Twick 6D **114**
Denton St. SW18 6K **117**
Denton Ter. DA5: Bexl 2K **145**
Denton Way E5 3K **67**
Dents Rd. SW11 6D **118**
Denver Cl. BR6: Pet W 6J **161**
Denver Rd. N16 7E **48**
Denwood SE23 3K **139**
Denyer St. SW3 4D **16** (4C **100**)
Denys Ho. *EC1* *5J 7*
(*off Bourne Est.*)
Denziloe Av. UB10: Hil 3D **74**
Denzil Rd. NW10 5B **62**
Deodar Rd. SW15 4G **117**
Deodora Cl. N20 3H **31**
Department for Transport
Eland House 1A **18**
Depot App. NW2 4F **63**
Depot Rd. TW3: Houn 3H **113**
W12 7E **80**
Depot St. SE5 6D **102**
DEPTFORD 7C **104**
Deptford Bri. SE8 1C **122**
Deptford B'way. SE8 1C **122**
Deptford Bus. Pk. SE15 6J **103**
Deptford Chu. St. SE8 6C **104**
Deptford Creek Bri. *SE8* *6D 104*
(*off Creek Rd.*)
Deptford Ferry Rd. E14 4C **104**
Deptford Grn. SE8 6C **104**
Deptford High St. SE8 6C **104**
Deptford Pk. Bus. Cen. SE8 5A **104**
Deptford Strand SE8 4B **104**
Deptford Trad. Est. SE8 5A **104**
Deptford Wharf SE8 4B **104**
De Quincey Ho. *SW1* *6A 18*
(*off Lupus St.*)
De Quincey M. E16 1J **105**
De Quincey Rd. N17 1D **48**
Derby Av. HA3: Hrw W 1H **41**
N12 5F **31**
RM7: Rom 6J **55**
Derby Ga. SW1 6E **12** (2J **101**)
(not continuous)
Derby Hill SE23 2J **139**
Derby Hill Cres. SE23 2J **139**
Derby Ho. HA5: Pinn 2B **40**
SE11 3J **19**
Derby Lodge N3 2H **45**
WC1 *1G 7*
(*off Britannia St.*)
Derby Rd. CR0: C'don 1B **168**
E7 7B **70**
E9 1K **85**
E18 1H **51**
EN3: Pond E 5C **24**
KT5: Surb 1G **163**
N18 5D **34**
Derby Rd. SM1: Sutt 6H **165**
SW14 4H **115**
SW19 7J **135**
TW3: Houn 4F **113**
UB6: G'frd 1F **77**
Derby Rd. Ind. Est. TW3: Houn 4F **113**
Derbyshire St. E2 3G **85**
(not continuous)
Derby St. W1 5H **11** (1E **100**)
Dereham Ho. *SE4* *4K 121*
(*off Frendsbury Rd.*)
Dereham Pl. EC2 2H **9** (3E **84**)
Dereham Rd. IG11: Bark 5K **71**
Derek Av. HA9: Wemb 7H **61**
KT19: Ewe 6G **163**
SM6: Wall 4F **167**
Derek Cl. KT19: Ewe 5H **163**
Derek Walcott Cl.
SE24 5B **120**
Dericote St. E8 1H **85**
Deri Dene Cl. TW19: Stanw 6A **110**
Derifall Cl. E6 5D **88**
Dering Pl. CR0: C'don 4C **168**
Dering Rd. CR0: C'don 4C **168**
Dering St. W1 1K **11** (6F **83**)
Dering Yd. W1 1K **11** (6F **83**)
Derinton Rd. SW17 4D **136**
Derley Rd. UB2: S'hall 3A **94**
Dermody Gdns. SE13 5F **123**
Dermody Rd. SE13 5F **123**
Deronda Rd. SE24 1B **138**
Deroy Cl. SM5: Cars 6D **166**
Derrick Gdns. SE7 3A **106**
Derrick Rd. BR3: Beck 3B **158**
Derrycombe Ho. *W2* *5J 81*
(*off Gt. Western Rd.*)
Derry Ho. *NW8* *4B 4*
(*off Church St. Est.*)
Derry M. N19 2J **65**
Derry Rd. CR0: Bedd 3J **167**
Derry St. W8 2K **99**
Dersingham Av. E12 4D **70**
Dersingham Rd. NW2 3G **63**
Derwent *NW1* *2A 6*
(*off Robert St.*)
Derwent Av. EN4: E Barn 1J **31**
N18 5J **33**
NW7 6E **28**
NW9 5A **44**
SW15 4A **134**
UB10: Ick 2C **56**
Derwent Cl. TW14: Felt 1H **129**
Derwent Ct. *SE16* *2K 103*
(*off Eleanor Cl.*)
Derwent Cres. DA7: Bex 2G **127**
HA7: Stan 2C **42**
N20 3F **31**
Derwent Dr. BR5: Pet W 7H **161**
UB4: Hayes 5G **75**
Derwent Gdns. HA9: Wemb 7C **42**
IG4: Ilf 4C **52**
Derwent Gro. SE22 4F **121**
Derwent Ho. *E3* *4B 86*
(*off Southern Gro.*)
KT2: King T *1D 150*
(*off May Bate Av.*)
SE20 *2H 157*
(*off Derwent Rd.*)
SW7 *3A 16*
(*off Cromwell Rd.*)
Derwent Lodge KT4: Wor Pk 2D **164**
TW7: Isle 2H **113**
Derwent Ri. NW9 6A **44**
Derwent Rd. N13 4E **32**
SE20 2G **157**
SW20 6F **153**
TW2: Whitt 6F **113**
UB1: S'hall 6D **76**
W5 3C **96**
Derwent St. SE10 5G **105**
Derwent Wlk. SM6: Wall 7F **167**
Derwentwater Rd. W3 1J **97**

Derwent Yd.—Dinmont Est.

Derwent Yd. W5 . . . . 3C 96
(off Derwent Rd.)
De Salis Rd. UB10: Hil 4E 74
Desborough Cl.
TW17: Shep 7C 146
W2 . . . . 5K 81
Desborough Ho. W14 . . . . 6H 99
(off North End Rd.)
Desborough Sailing Club 7D 146
Desborough St. W2 . . . . 5K 81
(off Cirencester St.)
Desenfans Rd. SE21 . . . . 6E 120
Desford Ct. TW15: Ashf 2C 128
Desford Rd. E16 . . . . 4G 87
Desford Way TW15: Ashf 2B 128
Design Mus. 6K 15 (2F 103)
Desmond Ho. EN4: E Barn 6H 21
Desmond St. SE14 . . . . 6A 104
Desmond Tutu Dr. SE23 . . . . 1B 140
Despard Rd. N19 . . . . 1G 65
Desvignes Dr. SE13 . . . . 6F 123
Dethick Ct. E3 . . . . 1A 86
Detling Ho. SE17 . . . . 4E 102
(off Congreve St.)
Detling Rd. BR1: Brom 5J 141
DA8: Erith 7K 109
Detmold Rd. E5 . . . . 2J 67
Devalls Cl. E6 . . . . 7F 89
Devana End SM5: Cars 3D 166
Devane Way SE27 . . . . 3B 138
Devas Rd. SW20 . . . . 1E 152
Devas St. E3 . . . . 4D 86
Devenay Rd. E15 . . . . 7H 69
Devenish Rd. SE2 . . . . 2A 108
Deventer Cres. SE22 . . . . 5E 120
Deveraux Cl. BR3: Beck 5E 158
De Vere Cl. SM6: Wall 7J 167
De Vere Cotts. W8 . . . . 3A 100
(off De Vere Gdns.)
De Vere Gdns. IG1: Ilf 2D 70
W8 . . . . 2A 100
Deverell St. SE1 . . . . 3D 102
De Vere M. W8 . . . . 3A 100
(off Canning Pl.)
Devereux Ct. WC2 . . . . 1J 13
Devereux La. SW13 . . . . 7D 98
Devereux Rd. SW11 . . . . 6D 118
Deveron Way RM1: Rom 1K 55
Devey Cl. KT2: King T 7B 134
Devitt Ho. E14 . . . . 7D 86
(off Wade's Pl.)
Devizes St. N1 . . . . 1D 84
Devon Av. TW2: Twick 1G 131
Devon Cl. IG9: Buck H 2E 36
N17 . . . . 3F 49
UB6: G'frd 1C 78
Devon Ct. TW12: Hamp 7E 130
W7 . . . . 5K 77
(off Copley Cl.)
Devoncroft Gdns. TW1: Twick 7A 114
Devon Gdns. N4 . . . . 6B 48
Devon Ho. E17 . . . . 2B 50
N1 . . . . 2B 84
(off Upper St.)
Devonhurst Pl. W4 . . . . 5K 97
Devonia Gdns. N18 . . . . 6H 33
Devonia Rd. N1 . . . . 2B 84
Devon Mans. HA3: Kenton 5C 42
(off Woodcock Hill)
SE1 . . . . 6J 15
(off Tooley St.)
Devon Pde. HA3: Kenton 5C 42
HA5: Eastc 7A 40
Devonport W2 . . . . 1C 10 (6C 82)
Devonport Gdns. IG1: Ilf 6D 52
Devonport Ho. W2 . . . . 5J 81
(off Gt. Western Rd.)
Devonport M. W12 . . . . 2D 98
Devonport Rd. W12 . . . . 1D 98
(not continuous)
Devonport St. E1 . . . . 6K 85
Devon Ri. N2 . . . . 4B 46
Devon Rd. IG11: Bark 1J 89
SM2: Cheam 7G 165
Devons Est. E3 . . . . 3D 86
Devonshire Av. SM2: Sutt 7A 166
Devonshire Cl. E15 . . . . 4G 69
N13 . . . . 3F 33
W1 . . . . 5J 5 (5F 83)
Devonshire Ct. E1 . . . . 3J 85
(off Bancroft Rd.)
HA5: Hat E 1D 40
(off Devonshire Rd.)
N17 . . . . 6H 33
WC1 . . . . 5F 7
(off Boswell St.)
Devonshire Cres. NW7 . . . . 7A 30
Devonshire Dr. KT6: Surb 1D 162
SE10 . . . . 7D 104
Devonshire Gdns. N17 . . . . 6H 33
N21 . . . . 7H 23
W4 . . . . 7J 97
Devonshire Gro. SE15 . . . . 6H 103
Devonshire Hall E9 . . . . 6J 67
(off Frampton Pk. Rd.)
Devonshire Hill La. N17 . . . . 6G 33
(not continuous)
Devonshire Ho. E14 . . . . 4C 104
(off Westferry Rd.)
IG8: Wfd G 7K 37
NW6 . . . . 6H 63
(off Kilburn High Rd.)
SE1 . . . . 3C 102
(off Bath Ter.)
SM2: Sutt 7A 166
SW1 . . . . 5D 18
(off Lindsay Sq.)
Devonshire Ho. Bus. Cen.
BR2: Brom 4K 159
(off Devonshire Sq.)
Devonshire M. N13 . . . . 4F 33
SW10 . . . . 7A 16
(off Park Wlk.)
W4 . . . . 5A 98
Devonshire M. Nth. W1 . . . . 5J 5 (5F 83)
Devonshire M. Sth. W1 . . . . 5J 5 (5F 83)
Devonshire M. W. W1 . . . . 4H 5 (4E 82)
Devonshire Pas. W4 . . . . 5A 98
Devonshire Pl. NW2 . . . . 3J 63
W1 . . . . 4H 5 (4E 82)
W8 . . . . 3K 99
Devonshire Pl. M. W1 . . . . 4H 5 (5E 82)
Devonshire Point TW15: Ashf 3E 128
Devonshire Rd. BR6: Orp 7K 161
CR0: C'don 7D 156
DA6: Bex 4E 126
E16 . . . . 6K 87
E17 . . . . 6C 50
HA1: Harr 6H 41
HA5: Eastc 6A 40
HA5: Hat E 1D 40
IG2: Ilf 7H 53
N9 . . . . 1D 34
N13 . . . . 4E 32
N17 . . . . 6H 33
NW7 . . . . 7A 30
SE9 . . . . 2C 142
SE23 . . . . 1J 139
SM2: Sutt 7A 166
SM5: Cars 4E 166
SW19 . . . . 7C 136
TW13: Hanw 3C 130
UB1: S'hall 5E 76
W4 . . . . 5A 98
W5 . . . . 3C 96
Devonshire Road Nature Reserve . . . 7K 121
Devonshire Road Nature Reserve Vis. Cen.
. . . . 7K 121
Devonshire Row EC2 . . . . 6H 9 (5E 84)
Devonshire Row M. W1 . . . . 4K 5
Devonshire Sq. BR2: Brom 4K 159
EC2 . . . . 6H 9 (6E 84)
Devonshire St. W1 . . . . 5H 5 (5E 82)
W4 . . . . 5A 98
Devonshire Ter. W2 . . . . 6A 82
Devonshire Way CR0: C'don 2A 170
UB4: Yead 6K 75
Devons Rd. E3 . . . . 3D 86
Devon St. SE15 . . . . 6H 103
Devon Way KT9: Chess 5C 162
KT19: Ewe 5H 163
UB10: Hil 2B 74
Devon Waye TW5: Hest 7D 94
Devon Wharf E14 . . . . 5F 87
De Walden Ho. NW8 . . . . 2C 82
(off Allitsen Rd.)
De Walden St. W1 . . . . 6H 5 (5E 82)
Dewar St. SE15 . . . . 3G 121
Dewberry Gdns. E6 . . . . 5C 88
Dewberry St. E14 . . . . 5E 86
Dewey La. SW2 . . . . 6A 120
(off Tulse Hill)
Dewey Rd. N1 . . . . 2A 84
RM10: Dag 6H 73
Dewey St. SW17 . . . . 5D 136
Dewhurst Rd. W14 . . . . 3F 99
Dewsbury Cl. HA5: Pinn 6C 40
Dewsbury Ct. W4 . . . . 4J 97
Dewsbury Gdns.
KT4: Wor Pk 3C 164
Dewsbury Rd. NW10 . . . . 5C 62
Dewsbury Ter. NW1 . . . . 1F 83
Dews Farm Sand Pits Nature Reserve
. . . . 6A 38
Dexter Ho. DA18: Erith 3E 108
(off Kale Rd.)
Dexter Rd. EN5: Barn 6A 20
Deyncourt Rd. N17 . . . . 1C 48
Deynecourt Gdns. E11 . . . . 4A 52
D'Eynsford Rd. SE5 . . . . 1D 120
Dhonau Ho. SE1 . . . . 4F 103
(off Longfield Est.)
Diadem Ct. W1 . . . . 7C 6
Dial Wlk., The W8 . . . . 2K 99
Diameter Rd. BR5: Pet W 7F 161
Diamond Cl. RM8: Dag 1C 72
Diamond Est. SW17 . . . . 3C 136
Diamond Ho. E3 . . . . 2A 86
(off Roman Rd.)
Diamond Rd. HA4: Ruis 4B 58
Diamond St. NW10 . . . . 7K 61
SE15 . . . . 7E 102
Diamond Ter. SE10 . . . . 1E 122
Diamond Way SE8 . . . . 6C 104
Diana Cl. DA14: Sidc 2E 144
E18 . . . . 1K 51
SE8 . . . . 6B 104
Diana Gdns. KT6: Surb 2F 163
Diana Ho. SW13 . . . . 1B 116
Diana, Princess of Wales
Memorial Playground 1K 99
Diana, Princess of Wales Memorial Walk
. . . . 1A 100
(in Kensington Gdns.)
Diana Rd. E17 . . . . 3B 50
Dianne Ct. SE12 . . . . 1J 141
Dianne Way EN4: E Barn 4H 21
Dianthus Cl. SE2 . . . . 5B 108
Dibden Ho. SE5 . . . . 7E 102
Dibden St. N1 . . . . 1C 84
Dibdin Cl. SM1: Sutt 3J 165
Dibdin Ho. W9 . . . . 2K 81
Dibdin Rd. SM1: Sutt 3J 165
Dicey Av. NW2 . . . . 4E 62
Dickens Av. N3 . . . . 1A 46
UB8: Hil 6D 74
Dickens Cl. DA8: Erith 7H 109
TW10: Ham 2E 132
UB3: Harl 4G 93
Dickens Ct. E11 . . . . 4J 51
(off Makepeace Rd.)
SW17 . . . . 3B 136
(off Grosvenor Way)
Dickens Dr. BR7: Chst 6G 143
Dickens Est. SE1 . . . . 2G 103
SE16 . . . . 3G 103
Dickens Ho. NW6 . . . . 3J 81
(off Malvern Rd.)
NW8 . . . . 3B 4
SE17 . . . . 5B 102
(off Doddington Gro.)
WC1 . . . . 3E 6
Dickens La. N18 . . . . 5K 33
Dickens M. EC1 . . . . 5A 8
(off Turnmill St.)
Dickenson Cl. N9 . . . . 1B 34
Dickenson Rd. N8 . . . . 7J 47
TW13: Hanw 5A 130
Dickensons La. SE25 . . . . 5G 157
(not continuous)
Dickensons Pl. SE25 . . . . 6G 157
Dickens Pl. SL3: Poyle 4A 174
Dickens Ri. IG7: Chig 3K 37
Dickens Rd. E6 . . . . 2B 88
Dickens Sq. SE1 . . . . 7D 14 (3C 102)
Dickens St. SW8 . . . . 2F 119
Dickenswood Cl. SE19 . . . . 7B 138
Dickerage La.
KT3: N Mald 3J 151
Dickerage Rd. KT1: King T 1J 151
KT3: N Mald 1J 151
Dickinson Ct. EC1 . . . . 3B 8
(off Brewhouse Yd.)
Dicksee Ho. NW8 . . . . 4A 4
(off Lyons Pl.)
Dickson Fold HA5: Pinn 4B 40
Dickson Ho. E1 . . . . 6H 85
(off Philpot St.)
Dickson Rd. SE9 . . . . 3C 124
Dick Turpin Way TW14: Felt 4H 111
Didsbury Cl. E6 . . . . 1D 88
Dieppe Cl. W14 . . . . 5H 99
Digby Bus. Cen. E9 . . . . 6K 67
(off Digby Rd.)
Digby Cres. N4 . . . . 2C 66
Digby Gdns. RM10: Dag 1G 91
Digby Mans. W6 . . . . 5D 98
(off Hammersmith Bri. Rd.)
Digby Pl. CR0: C'don 3F 169
Digby Rd. E9 . . . . 6K 67
IG11: Bark 7K 71
Digby St. E2 . . . . 3J 85
Diggon St. E1 . . . . 5K 85
Dighton Ct. SE5 . . . . 6C 102
Dighton Rd. SW18 . . . . 5A 118
Dignum St. N1 . . . . 2A 84
Digswell St. N7 . . . . 6A 66
Dilhorne Cl. SE12 . . . . 3K 141
Dilke St. SW3 . . . . 7F 17 (6D 100)
Dilloway La. UB2: S'hall 2C 94
Dillwyn Cl. SE26 . . . . 4A 140
Dilston Cl. UB5: N'olt 3A 76
Dilston Gro. SE16 . . . . 4J 103
Dilton Gdns. SW15 . . . . 1C 134
Dilwyn Ct. E17 . . . . 2A 50
Dimes Pl. W6 . . . . 4D 98
Dimmock Dr. UB6: G'frd 5H 59
Dimond Cl. E7 . . . . 4J 69
Dimsdale Dr. EN1: Enf 7B 24
NW9 . . . . 1J 61
Dimsdale Hgts. E1 . . . . 6H 85
(off Spencer Way)
Dimsdale Wlk. E13 . . . . 2J 87
Dimson Cres. E3 . . . . 3C 86
Dinerman Ct. NW8 . . . . 1A 82
Dingle, The UB10: Hil 3D 74
Dingle Gdns. E14 . . . . 7C 86
Dingle Rd. TW15: Ashf 5D 128
Dingles Ct. HA5: Pinn 1B 40
Dingley La. SW16 . . . . 2H 137
Dingley Pl. EC1 . . . . 1D 8 (3C 84)
Dingley Rd. EC1 . . . . 2C 8 (3C 84)
Dingwall Av. CR0: C'don 2C 168
Dingwall Gdns. NW11 . . . . 6J 45
Dingwall Rd. CR0: C'don 1D 168
SM5: Cars 7D 166
SW18 . . . . 7A 118
Dinmont Est. E2 . . . . 2G 85

Dinmont Ho. E2 2G 85
(off Pritchard's Rd.)
Dinmont St. E2 2H 85
Dinmore Ho. E9 1J 85
(off Templecombe Rd.)
Dinnington Ho. E1 4H 85
(off Coventry Rd.)
Dinsdale Gdns. EN5: New Bar 5E 20
SE25 5E 156
Dinsdale Rd. SE3 6H 105
Dinsmore Rd. SW12 7F 119
Dinton Ho. NW8 3D 4
(off Lilestone St.)
Dinton Rd. KT2: King T 7F 133
SW19 6B 136
Diploma Av. N2 4C 46
Diploma Ct. N2 4C 46
Diprose Lodge SW17 4B 136
Dirleton Rd. E15 1H 87
Disbrowe Rd. W6 6G 99
Discovery Bus. Pk. SE16 3G 103
(off St James's Rd.)
Discovery Dock Apartments E14 2D 104
(off Sth. Quay Sq.)
Discovery Ho. E14 7E 86
(off Newby Pl.)
Discovery Wlk. E1 1H 103
Dishforth La. NW9 7F 29
Disley Ct. UB1: S'hall 6F 77
(off Howard Rd.)
Disney Pl. SE1 6D 14 (2C 102)
Disney St. SE1 6D 14 (2C 102)
Dison Cl. EN3: Enf H 1E 24
Disraeli Cl. SE28 1C 108
W4 3K 97
Disraeli Gdns. SW15 4H 117
Disraeli Rd. E7 6J 69
NW10 2K 79
SW15 4G 117
W5 1D 96
Diss St. E2 1J 9 (3F 85)
Distaff La. EC4 2C 14 (7C 84)
Distillery, The SE8 1C 122
Distillery La. W6 5E 98
Distillery Rd. W6 5E 98
Distillery Wlk.
TW8: Bford 6E 96
Distin St. SE11 4J 19 (4A 102)
District Rd. HA0: Wemb 5B 60
Ditch All. SE13 1D 122
Ditchburn St. E14 7E 86
Ditchfield Rd. UB4: Yead 4C 76
Ditchley Ct. W7 5K 77
(off Templeman Rd.)
Dittisham Rd. SE9 4C 142
Ditton Cl. KT7: T Ditt 7A 150
Dittoncroft Cl. CR0: C'don 4E 168
Ditton Grange Cl. KT6: Surb 1D 162
Ditton Grange Dr. KT6: Surb 1D 162
Ditton Hill KT6: Surb 1C 162
Ditton Hill Rd. KT6: Surb 1C 162
Ditton Lawn KT7: T Ditt 1A 162
Ditton Pl. SE20 1H 157
Ditton Reach KT7: T Ditt 6B 150
Ditton Rd. DA6: Bex 5D 126
KT6: Surb 2D 162
UB2: S'hall 5D 94
Divisional Rd. E12 2B 70
Divis Way SW15 6D 116
(off Dover Pk. Dr.)
Dixon Clark Ct. N1 6B 66
Dixon Cl. E6 6D 88
Dixon Ho. W10 6F 81
(off Darfield Way)
Dixon Pl. BR4: W W'ck 1D 170
Dixon Rd. SE14 1A 122
SE25 3E 156
Dixon's All. SE16 2H 103
Dixon Way NW10 7A 62
Dobbin Cl. HA3: Kenton 2A 42
Dobell Rd. SE9 5D 124
Dobree Av. NW10 7D 62
Dobson Cl. NW6 7B 64
Dobson Ho. SE14 6K 103
(off John Williams Cl.)
Doby Ct. EC4 2D 14
Dock Cotts. E1 7J 85
(off The Highway)
Dockers Tanner Rd. E14 3C 104
Dockett Eddy KT16: Chert 7A 146
Dockett Eddy La. TW17: Shep 7B 146
Dockett Moorings KT16: Chert 7A 146
Dockhead SE1 7K 15 (2F 103)
Dockhead Wharf SE1 7K 15
(off Shad Thames)
Dock Hill Av. SE16 1K 103
Docklands Ct. E14 6B 86
(off Wharf La.)
Docklands Equestrian Cen., The 4E 88
Docklands Sailing Cen. 3C 104
Dockland St. E16 1E 106
(not continuous)
Dockley Rd. SE16 3G 103
Dockley Rd. Ind. Est. SE16 3G 103
(off Dockley Rd.)
Dock Offices SE16 3J 103
(off Surrey Quays Rd.)
Dock Rd. E16 7H 87
IG11: Bark 2G 89
TW8: Bford 7D 96
Dockside Ct. E5 2J 67
Dockside Rd. E16 7B 88
Dock St. E1 7G 85
Dockwell Cl. TW14: Felt 4J 111
Dockwell's Ind. Est. TW14: Felt 5K 111
Doctor Johnson Av. SW17 3F 137
Dr Johnson's House 1K 13
(off Pemberton Row)
Doctors Cl. SE26 5J 139
Docura Ho. N7 2K 65
Docwra's Bldgs. N1 6E 66
Dodbrooke Rd. SE27 3A 138
Dodd Ho. SE16 4H 103
(off Rennie Est.)
Doddington Gro. SE17 6B 102
Doddington Pl. SE17 6B 102
Dodsley Pl. N9 3D 34
Dodson St. SE1 7K 13 (2A 102)
Dod St. E14 6B 86
Doebury Wlk. SE18 6A 108
(off Prestwood Cl.)
Doel Cl. SW19 7A 136
Dog & Duck Yd. WC1 5H 7
Doggett Rd. SE6 7C 122
Doggetts Ct. EN4: E Barn 5H 21
Doghurst Av. UB3: Harl 7D 92
Doghurst Dr. UB7: Sip 7D 92
Dog Kennel Hill SE22 3E 120
Dog Kennel Hill Est. SE22 3E 120
(off Albrighton Rd.)
Dog La. NW10 4A 62
Doherty Rd. E13 4J 87
Dokal Ind. Est. UB2: S'hall 2C 94
Dolben Ct. SW1 4D 18
(off Montaigne Cl.)
Dolben St. SE1 5A 14 (1B 102)
(not continuous)
Dolby Rd. SW6 2H 117
Dolland Ho. SE11 6H 19
Dolland St. SE11 6H 19 (5K 101)
Dollar Bay Ct. E14 2E 104
(off Lawn Ho. Cl.)
Dollary Pde. KT1: King T 3H 151
(off Kingston Rd.)
Dolliffe Cl. CR4: Mitc 2C 154
Dollis Av. N3 1H 45
Dollis Brook Wlk. EN5: Barn 6B 20
Dollis Cres. HA4: Ruis 1A 58
Dolliscroft NW7 7B 30
DOLLIS HILL 2D 62
Dollis Hill Av. NW2 3D 62
Dollis Hill La. NW2 4B 62
Dollis M. N3 1J 45
Dollis Pk. N3 1H 45
Dollis Rd. N3 7B 30
NW7 7B 30
Dollis Valley Dr. EN5: Barn 6C 20
Dollis Valley Way EN5: Barn 6C 20
Dolman Cl. N3 2A 46
Dolman Rd. W4 4K 97
Dolman St. SW4 4K 119
Dolphin Cl. KT6: Surb 5D 150
SE16 2K 103
SE28 6D 90
Dolphin Ct. NW11 6G 45
Dolphin Est. TW16: Sun 1G 147
Dolphin Ho. SW6 2A 118
(off Lensbury Av.)
SW18 4K 117
Dolphin La. E14 7D 86
Dolphin Rd. TW16: Sun 1G 147
UB5: N'olt 2D 76
Dolphin Rd. Nth. TW16: Sun 1G 147
Dolphin Rd. Sth. TW16: Sun 1F 147
Dolphin Rd. W. TW16: Sun 1G 147
Dolphin Sq. SW1 6B 18 (5G 101)
W4 7A 98
Dolphin St. KT1: King T 2E 150
Dolphin Twr. SE8 6B 104
(off Abinger Gro.)
Dombey Ho. SE1 7K 15
(off Wolseley St.)
W11 1F 99
(off St Ann's Rd.)
Dombey St. WC1 5G 7 (5K 83)
(not continuous)
Domecq Ho. EC1 3B 8
(off Dallington St.)
Dome Hill Pk. SE26 4F 139
Domelton Ho. SW18 6K 117
(off Iron Mill Rd.)
Domett Cl. SE5 4D 120
Domfe Pl. E5 4J 67
Domingo St. EC1 3C 8 (4C 84)
Dominica Cl. E13 2B 88
Dominion Bus. Pk. N9 2E 34
Dominion Cen., The UB2: S'hall 2C 94
Dominion Cl. TW3: Houn 2H 113
Dominion Ct. E8 7F 67
(off Middleton Rd.)
Dominion Ho. E14 5D 104
(off St Davids Sq.)
Dominion Ind. Est. UB2: S'hall 2C 94
(off Feather Rd.)
Dominion Pde. HA1: Harr 5K 41
Dominion Rd. CR0: C'don 7F 157
UB2: S'hall 2C 94
Dominion St. EC2 5F 9 (5D 84)
Dominion Theatre 7D 6
(off Tottenham Ct. Rd.)
Domonic Dr. SE9 4F 143
Domville Cl. N20 2G 31
Domville Ct. SE17 5E 102
(off Bagshott St.)
Donald Dr. RM6: Chad H 5C 54
Donald Hunter Ho. E7 5K 69
(off Woodgrange Rd.)
Donald Rd. CR0: C'don 7A 156
E13 1K 87
Donaldson Rd. NW6 1H 81
SE18 1E 124
Donald Woods Gdns. KT5: Surb 2H 163
Donato Dr. SE15 6E 102
Doncaster Dr. UB5: N'olt 5D 58
Doncaster Gdns. N4 6C 48
UB5: N'olt 5D 58
Doncaster Rd. N9 7C 24
Donegal Ho. E1 4H 85
(off Cambridge Heath Rd.)
Donegal St. N1 2K 83
Doneraile Ho. SW1 5J 17
(off Ebury Bri. Rd.)
Doneraile St. SW6 2F 117
Dongola Rd. E1 5A 86
E13 3K 87
N17 3E 48
Dongola Rd. W. E13 3K 87
Don Gratton Ho. E1 5G 85
(off Old Montague St.)
Donington Av. IG2: Ilf 5G 53
IG6: Ilf 5G 53
Donkey All. SE22 7G 121
Donkey La. EN1: Enf 2B 24
UB7: W Dray 1D 174
Donkin Ho. SE16 4H 103
(off Rennie Est.)
Donmar Warehouse Theatre 1E 12
(off Earlham St.)
Donnatt's Rd. SE14 1B 122
Donne Ct. SE24 6C 120
Donnefield Av. HA8: Edg 7K 27
Donne Ho. E14 6C 86
(off Dod St.)
SE14 6K 103
(off Samuel Cl.)
Donnelly Ct. SW6 7G 99
(off Dawes Rd.)
Donnelly Ho. SE1 3A 102
(off Cosser St.)
Donne Pl. CR4: Mitc 4F 155
SW3 3D 16 (4C 100)
Donne Rd. RM8: Dag 2C 72
Donnington Ct. NW1 7F 65
(off Castlehaven Rd.)
NW10 7D 62
(off Donnington Rd.)
Donnington Mans. NW10 1E 80
(off Donnington Rd.)
Donnington Rd. HA3: Kenton 5D 42
KT4: Wor Pk 2C 164
NW10 7D 62
Donnybrook Ct. E3 1B 86
(off Old Ford Rd.)
Donnybrook Rd. SW16 7G 137
Donoghue Bus. Pk. NW2 3F 63
Donoghue Cotts. E14 5A 86
(off Galsworthy Av.)
Donovan Av. N10 2F 47
Donovan Ct. SW10 6A 16
(off Drayton Gdns.)
Donovan Ho. E1 7J 85
(off Cable St.)
Donovan Pl. N21 5E 22
Don Phelan Cl. SE5 1D 120
Doone Cl. TW11: Tedd 6A 132
Doon St. SE1 5J 13 (1A 102)
Dora Ho. E14 6B 86
(off Rhodeswell Rd.)
W11 7F 81
(off St Ann's Rd.)
Doral Way SM5: Cars 5D 166
Doran Ct. E6 2D 88
Dorando Cl. W12 7D 80
Doran Gro. SE18 7J 107
Doran Mnr. N2 5D 46
(off Great Nth. Rd.)
Doran Wlk. E15 7E 68
Dora Rd. SW19 5J 135
Dora St. E14 6B 86
Dora Way SW9 2A 120
Dorchester Av. DA5: Bexl 1D 144
HA2: Harr 6G 41
N13 4H 33
Dorchester Cl. BR5: St P 7B 144
KT10: Hin W 2A 162
UB5: N'olt 5F 59
Dorchester Ct. E18 1H 51
(off Buckingham Rd.)
N1 7E 66
(off Englefield Rd.)
N10 3F 47
N14 7A 22
NW2 3F 63
SE24 5C 120
SW1 2F 17
(off Pavillion Rd.)
Dorchester Dr. SE24 5C 120
TW14: Bedf 6G 111

Dorchester Gdns. E4 ....4H 35
  NW11 ....4J 45
Dorchester Gro. W4 ....5A 98
Dorchester Ho. TW9: Kew 7H 97
Dorchester Rd. KT3: N Mald 4K 151
  TW1: Twick 6C 114
Dorchester Rd. KT4: Wor Pk 1E 164
  SM4: Mord 7K 153
  UB5: N'olt 5F 59
Dorchester Ter. NW2 ....3F 63
  (off Needham Ter.)
Dorchester Way HA3: Kenton 6F 43
Dorchester Waye UB4: Yead 6A 76
  (Quebec Rd.)
  UB4: Yead 6K 75
  (Wimborne Av.)
Dorcis Av. DA7: Bex 2E 126
Dordrecht Rd. W3 ....1A 98
Dore Av. E12 ....5E 70
Doreen Av. NW9 ....1K 61
Doreen Capstan Ho. E11 ....3G 69
  (off Apollo Pl.)
Dore Gdns. SM4: Mord 7K 153
Dorell Cl. UB1: S'hall 5D 76
Dorey Ho. TW8: Bford 7C 96
  (off High St.)
Doria Rd. SW6 ....2H 117
Doric Ho. E2 ....2K 85
  (off Mace St.)
Doric Way NW1 ....1C 6 (3H 83)
Dorie M. N12 ....4E 30
Dorien Rd. SW20 ....2F 153
Doris Ashby Cl. UB6: G'frd 1A 78
Doris Av. DA8: Erith 1J 127
Doris Emmerton Ct. SW11 ....4A 118
Doris Rd. E7 ....7J 69
  TW15: Ashf 6F 129
Dorking Cl. KT4: Wor Pk 2F 165
  SE8 ....6B 104
Dorking Ct. N17 ....1G 49
  (off Hampden La.)
Dorking Ho. SE1 ....3D 102
Dorlcote Rd. SW18 ....7C 118
Dorly Cl. TW17: Shep 5G 147
Dorman Pl. N9 ....2B 34
Dormans Cl. HA6: N'wood 1F 39
Dorman Wlk. NW10 ....5K 61
Dorman Way NW8 ....1B 82
Dorma Trad. Pk. E10 ....1K 67
Dormay St. SW18 ....5K 117
Dormer Cl. E15 ....6H 69
  EN5: Barn 5A 20
Dormer's Av. UB1: S'hall 6E 76
Dormers Ri. UB1: S'hall 6F 77
DORMER'S WELLS 6E 76
Dormer's Wells La. UB1: S'hall 6E 76
Dormers Wells Leisure Cen. 6F 77
Dormstone Ho. SE17 ....4E 102
  (off Congreve St.)
Dormywood HA4: Ruis 5H 39
Dornberg Cl. SE3 ....7J 105
Dornberg Rd. SE3 ....7K 105
Dorncliffe Rd. SW6 ....2G 117
Dorney NW3 ....7C 64
Dorney Ri. BR5: St M Cry 4K 161
Dorney Way TW4: Houn 5C 112
Dornfell St. NW6 ....5H 63
Dornoch Ho. E3 ....2B 86
  (off Anglo Rd.)
Dornton Rd. CR2: S Croy 5D 168
  SW12 ....2F 137
Dorothy Av. HA0: Wemb 7E 60
Dorothy Evans Cl. DA7: Bex 4H 127
Dorothy Gdns. RM8: Dag 4B 72
Dorothy Pettingell Ho. SM1: Sutt 3K 165
  (off Angel Hill)
Dorothy Rd. SW11 ....3D 118
Dorrell Pl. SW9 ....3A 120
Dorrien Wlk. SW16 ....2H 137
Dorrington Ct. SE25 ....2E 156
Dorrington Point E3 ....3D 86
  (off Bromley High St.)

Dorrington St. EC1 ....5J 7 (5A 84)
Dorrington Way BR3: Beck 5E 158
Dorrit Ho. W11 ....1F 99
  (off St Ann's Rd.)
Dorrit M. N18 ....5K 33
Dorrit St. SE1 ....6D 14 (2C 102)
Dorrit Way BR7: Chst 6G 143
Dorryn Ct. SE26 ....5K 139
Dors Cl. NW9 ....1K 61
Dorset Av. DA16: Well 4K 125
  RM1: Rom 4K 55
  UB2: S'hall 4E 94
  UB4: Hayes 3G 75
Dorset Bldgs. EC4 ....1A 14 (6B 84)
Dorset Cl. NW1 ....5E 4 (5D 82)
  UB4: Hayes 3G 75
Dorset Ct. HA6: N'wood 1H 39
  N1 ....7E 66
  (off Hertford Rd.)
  UB5: N'olt 3C 76
  W7 ....5K 77
  (off Copley Cl.)
Dorset Dr. HA8: Edg 6A 28
Dorset Gdns. CR4: Mitc 4K 155
  HA0: Wemb 5C 60
Dorset Ho. NW1 ....5F 5
  (off Gloucester Pl.)
Dorset Mans. SW6 ....6F 99
  (off Lille Rd.)
Dorset M. N3 ....1J 45
  SW1 ....1J 17 (3F 101)
Dorset Ri. EC4 ....1A 14 (6B 84)
Dorset Rd. BR3: Beck 3K 157
  CR4: Mitc 2C 154
  E7 ....7A 70
  HA1: Harr 6G 41
  N15 ....4D 48
  N22 ....1J 47
  SE9 ....2C 142
  SW8 ....7J 101
  SW19 ....1J 153
  TW15: Ashf 3A 128
  W5 ....3C 96
Dorset Sq. NW1 ....4E 4 (4D 82)
Dorset St. W1 ....6F 5 (5D 82)
Dorset Way TW2: Twick 1H 131
  UB10: Hil 2B 74
Dorset Waye TW5: Hest 7D 94
Dorset Wharf W6 ....7E 98
  (off Rainville Rd.)
Dorton Cl. SE15 ....7E 102
Dorton Vs. UB7: Sip 7C 92
Dorville Cres. W6 ....3D 98
Dorville Rd. SE12 ....5H 123
Dothill Rd. SE18 ....7G 107
Douai Gro. TW12: Hamp 1G 149
Doughty Cl. E1 ....1H 103
  (off Prusom St.)
Doughty Ho. SW10 ....6A 100
  (off Netherton Gro.)
Doughty M. WC1 ....4G 7 (4K 83)
Doughty St. WC1 ....3G 7 (4K 83)
Douglas Av. E17 ....1B 50
  HA0: Wemb 7E 60
  KT3: N Mald 4D 152
Douglas Bader Ho. TW7: Isle 3H 113
Douglas Cl. HA7: Stan 5F 27
  IG6: Ilf 7K 37
  SM6: Wall 6J 167
Douglas Ct. KT1: King T 4E 150
  (off Geneva Rd.)
  N3 ....2K 45
  NW6 ....7J 63
  (off Quex Rd.)
Douglas Cres. UB4: Yead 4A 76
Douglas Dr. CRO: C'don 3C 170
Douglas Est. N1 ....6C 66
  (off Oransay Rd.)
Douglas Eyre Sports Cen. 5K 49
Douglas Ho. KT6: Surb 1F 163
Douglas Johnstone Ho. SW6 ....6H 99
  (off Clem Attlee Ct.)

Douglas Mans. TW3: Houn 3F 113
Douglas M. NW2 ....3G 63
Douglas Path E14 ....5E 104
  (off Manchester Rd.)
Douglas Rd. DA16: Well 1B 126
  E4 ....1B 36
  E16 ....5J 87
  IG3: Ilf 7A 54
  KT1: King T 2H 151
  KT6: Surb 2F 163
  N1 ....7C 66
  N22 ....1A 48
  NW6 ....1H 81
  TW3: Houn 3F 113
  TW19: Stanw 6A 110
Douglas Rd. Nth. N1 ....6C 66
Douglas Rd. Sth. N1 ....6C 66
Douglas Robinson Ct. SW16 ....7J 137
  (off Streatham High Rd.)
Douglas Sq. SM4: Mord 6J 153
Douglas St. SW1 ....4C 18 (4H 101)
Douglas Ter. E17 ....1B 50
Douglas Waite Ho. NW6 ....7J 63
Douglas Way SE8 ....7B 104
  (Stanley St.)
  SE8 ....7C 104
  (Watsons St.)
Doulton Ho. SE11 ....2H 19
Doulton M. NW6 ....6K 63
Dounesforth Gdns. SW18 ....1K 135
Douro Pl. W8 ....3K 99
Douro St. E3 ....2C 86
Douthwaite Sq. E1 ....1G 103
Dove App. E6 ....5C 88
Dove Cl. NW7 ....7G 29
  SM6: Wall 7K 167
  UB5: N'olt 4B 76
Dove Commercial Cen. NW5 ....5G 65
Dovecot Cl. HA5: Eastc 5A 40
Dovecote Av. N22 ....3A 48
Dovecote Gdns. SW14 ....3K 115
Dovecote Ho. SE16 ....2K 103
  (off Water Gdns. Sq.)
Dovedale Av. HA3: Kenton 6C 42
  IG5: Ilf 2E 52
Dovedale Bus. Est. SE15 ....2G 121
  (off Blenheim Gro.)
Dovedale Cl. DA16: Well 2A 126
Dovedale Ri. CR4: Mitc 7D 136
Dovedale Rd. SE22 ....5H 121
Dovedon Cl. N14 ....2D 32
Dovehouse Mead IG11: Bark 2H 89
Dovehouse St. SW3 ....5B 16 (5B 100)
Dove M. SW5 ....4A 100
Dove Pk. HA5: Hat E 1E 40
Dover Cl. NW2 ....2F 63
  RM5: Col R 2J 55
Dover Ct. EC1 ....3A 8
  (off St John St.)
  N1 ....7D 66
  (off Southgate Rd.)
Dovercourt Av. CR7: Thor H 5A 156
Dovercourt Est. N1 ....6D 66
Dovercourt Gdns. HA7: Stan 5K 27
Dovercourt La. SM1: Sutt 3A 166
Dovercourt Rd. SE22 ....6E 120
Doverfield Rd. SW2 ....7J 119
Dover Flats SE1 ....4E 102
Dover Gdns. SM5: Cars 3D 166
Dover Ho. N18 ....5A 34
  SE15 ....6J 103
Dover Ho. Rd. SW15 ....4C 116
Doveridge Gdns. N13 ....4G 33
Dove Rd. N1 ....6C 66
Dove Row E2 ....1G 85
Dover Pk. Dr. SW15 ....6D 116
Dover Patrol SE3 ....2K 123
Dover Rd. E12 ....2A 70
  N9 ....2D 34

Dover Rd. RM6: Chad H 6E 54
  SE19 ....6D 138
Dover St. W1 ....3K 11 (7F 83)
Dover Ter. TW9: Rich 2F 115
  (off Sandycombe Rd.)
Dover Yd. W1 ....4A 12
Doves Cl. BR2: Brom 2C 172
Dove Yd. N1 ....1A 84
Dovet Ct. SW9 ....1K 119
Doveton Ho. E1 ....4J 85
  (off Doveton St.)
Doveton Rd. CR2: S Croy 5D 168
Doveton St. E1 ....4J 85
Dove Wlk. SW1 ....5G 17 (5E 100)
Dovey Lodge N1 ....7A 66
  (off Bewdley St.)
Dovill Ct. SE16 ....3G 103
  (off Marine St.)
Downahill Rd. SE6 ....1F 141
Dowd Cl. N11 ....2K 31
Dowdeswell Cl. SW15 ....4A 116
Dowding Ho. N6 ....7E 46
  (off Hillcrest)
Dowding Pl. HA7: Stan 6F 27
Dowding Rd. UB10: Uxb 7B 56
Downey Cl. NW5 ....5G 65
Dowe Ho. SE3 ....3G 123
Dower Av. SM6: Wall 7F 167
Dowes Ho. SW16 ....3J 137
Dowgate Hill EC4 ....2E 14 (7D 84)
Dowland St. W10 ....3G 81
Dowlas St. SE5 ....7E 102
Dowler Ct. KT2: King T 1E 150
Dowler Ho. E1 ....6G 85
  (off Burslem St.)
Dowlerville Rd. BR6: Chels 6K 173
Dowling Ho. DA17: Belv 3F 109
Dowman Cl. SW19 ....7K 135
Downage NW4 ....3E 44
  (not continuous)
Downalong WD23: B Hea 1C 26
Downbank Av. DA7: Bex 1K 127
Down Barns Rd. HA4: Ruis 3B 58
Downbarton Ho. SW9 ....1A 120
  (off Gosling Way)
Downbury M. SW18 ....5J 117
Down Cl. UB5: N'olt 2K 75
Downderry Rd.
  BR1: Brom 3F 141
Downe Cl. DA16: Well 7C 108
Downend SE18 ....7F 107
Downend Ct. SE15 ....6E 102
  (off Bibury Cl.)
Downe Rd. BR2: Kes 7B 172
  CR4: Mitc 2D 154
Downe's Cott. SW4 ....4G 119
Downesbury NW3 ....6D 64
  (off Steele's Rd.)
Downes Cl. TW1: Twick 6B 114
Downes Ct. N21 ....1F 33
Downes Ho. CRO: Wadd 4B 168
  (off Violet La.)
Downe Ter. TW10: Rich 6E 114
Downey Ho. E1 ....4K 85
  (off Globe Rd.)
Downfield KT4: Wor Pk 1B 164
Downfield Cl. W9 ....4K 81
Down Hall Rd. KT2: King T 1D 150
DOWNHAM 5F 141
Downham Cl. RM5: Col R 1G 55
Downham Ct. N1 ....7D 66
  (off Downham Rd.)
Downham Ent. Cen. SE6 ....2H 141
Downham La. BR1: Brom 5F 141
Downham Rd. N1 ....7D 66
Downham Way BR1: Brom 5F 141
Downhills Av. N17 ....3D 48
Downhills Pk. Rd. N17 ....3C 48
Downhills Way N17 ....3C 48
Downhurst Av. NW7 ....5E 28
Downhurst Ct. NW4 ....3E 44
Downing Cl. HA2: Harr 3G 41

Downing Ct. *WC1* *4J 83*
(off Bernard St.)
WC1 . . . . . *4F 7*
(off Grenville St.)
Downing Dr. UB6: G'frd 1H 77
Downing Ho. *W10* *6F 81*
(off Cambridge Gdns.)
Downing Rd. RM9: Dag 7F 73
Downings E6 . . . . . 6E 88
Downing St. SW1 . . . . . 6E 12 (2J 101)
Downland Cl. N20 . . . . . 1F 31
Downland Ct. E11 . . . . . 2G 69
Downleys Cl. SE9 . . . . . 2C 142
Downman Rd. SE9 . . . . . 3C 124
Down Pl. W6 . . . . . 4D 98
Down Rd. TW11: Tedd 6B 132
Downs, The SW20 . . . . . 7F 135
Downs Av. BR7: Chst 5D 142
HA5: Pinn 6C 40
Downs Bri. Rd. BR3: Beck 1F 159
Downs Ct. UB6: G'frd 3A 78
Downs Ct. Pde. *E8* *5H 67*
(off Amhurst Rd.)
Downsell Rd. E15 . . . . . 4E 68
Downsfield Rd. E17 . . . . . 6A 50
Downshall Av. IG3: Ilf 6J 53
Downs Hill BR3: Beck 7F 141
Downshire Hill NW3 . . . . . 4B 64
Downside TW1: Twick 3K 131
TW16: Sun 1J 147
Downside Cl. SW19 . . . . . 6A 136
Downside Cres. NW3 . . . . . 5C 64
W13 . . . . . 4A 78
Downside Rd. SM2: Sutt 6B 166
Downside Wlk. *TW8: Bford* *6D 96*
(off Windmill Rd.)
UB5: N'olt 3D 76
Downs La. E5 . . . . . 4H 67
Downs Pk. Rd. E5 . . . . . 5F 67
E8 . . . . . 5F 67
Downs Rd. BR3: Beck 2D 158
CR7: Thor H 1C 156
E5 . . . . . 4G 67
EN1: Enf 4K 23
Down St. KT8: W Mole 5E 148
W1 . . . . . 5J 11 (1F 101)
Down St. M. W1 . . . . . 5J 11 (1F 101)
Downs Vw. TW7: Isle 1K 113
Downsview Gdns. SE19 . . . . . 7B 138
Downsview Rd. SE19 . . . . . 7C 138
Downsway BR6: Orp 5J 173
Downsway, The SM2: Sutt 7A 166
Downton Av. SW2 . . . . . 2J 137
Downtown Rd. SE16 . . . . . 2A 104
Down Way UB5: N'olt 3K 75
Dowrey St. N1 . . . . . 1A 84
Dowsett Rd. N17 . . . . . 2F 49
Dowson Cl. SE5 . . . . . 4D 120
Dowson Ho. *E1* *6K 85*
(off Bower St.)
Doyce St. SE1 . . . . . 6C 14 (2C 102)
Doyle Gdns. NW10 . . . . . 1C 80
Doyle Ho. *SW13* *7E 98*
(off Trinity Chu. Rd.)
Doyle Rd. SE25 . . . . . 4G 157
D'Oyley St. SW1 . . . . . 3G 17 (4E 100)
Doynton St. N19 . . . . . 2F 65
Draco Ga. SW15 . . . . . 3E 116
Draco St. SE17 . . . . . 6C 102
Dragonfly Cl. E13 . . . . . 3K 87
Dragon Rd. SE15 . . . . . 6E 102
Dragons Health Club
Northolt 1E 76
Purley 7A 168
Dragon Yd. WC1 . . . . . 7F 7 (6J 83)
Dragoon Rd. SE8 . . . . . 5B 104
Dragor Rd. NW10 . . . . . 4J 79
Drake Cl. SE16 . . . . . 2K 103
Drake Ct. *KT5: Surb* *4E 150*
(off Cranes Pk. Av.)
SE1 . . . . . *7D 14*
(off Swan St.)
Drake Ct. SE19 . . . . . 5F 139
W12 . . . . . *2E 98*
(off Scott's Rd.)
Drake Cres. SE28 . . . . . 6C 90
Drakefell Rd. SE4 . . . . . 2K 121
SE14 . . . . . 2K 121
Drakefield Rd. SW17 . . . . . 3E 136
Drake Hall *E16* *1K 105*
(off Wesley Av.)
Drake Ho. *E1* *5J 85*
(off Stepney Way)
E14 . . . . . *7A 86*
(off Victory Pl.)
SW1 . . . . . *7C 18*
(off Dolphin Sq.)
Drakeland Ho. *W9* *4H 81*
(off Fernhead Rd.)
Drakeley Ct. N5 . . . . . 4B 66
Drake M. BR2: Brom 4A 160
Drake Rd. CR0: C'don 7K 155
CR4: Mitc 6E 154
HA2: Harr 2D 58
KT9: Chess 5G 163
SE4 . . . . . 3C 122
Drakes, The SE8 . . . . . 6C 104
Drakes Ct. SE23 . . . . . 1J 139
Drakes Courtyard
NW6 . . . . . 7H 63
Drakes Dr. HA6: Nwood 1D 38
Drake St. EN2: Enf 1J 23
WC1 . . . . . 6G 7 (5K 83)
Drakes Wlk. E6 . . . . . 1D 88
Drakewood Rd. SW16 . . . . . 7H 137
Draper Cl. DA17: Belv 4F 109
TW7: Isle 2H 113
Draper Ct. BR1: Brom 4C 160
Draper Ho. *SE1* *4B 102*
(off Newington Butts)
Draper Pl. *N1* *1B 84*
(off Dagmar Ter.)
Drapers Almshouses *E3* *3D 86*
(off Rainhill Way)
Drapers Cott. Homes NW7 . . . . . 4G 29
(not continuous)
Draper's Ct. *SW11* *1E 118*
(off Battersea Pk. Rd.)
Drapers Gdns. EC2 . . . . . 7F 9 (6D 84)
Drapers Rd. E15 . . . . . 4F 69
EN2: Enf 2G 23
N17 . . . . . 3F 49
Drappers Way SE16 . . . . . 4G 103
Draven Cl. BR2: Hayes 7H 159
Drawdock Rd. SE10 . . . . . 2F 105
Drawell Cl. SE18 . . . . . 5J 107
Drax Av. SW20 . . . . . 7C 134
Draxmont SW19 . . . . . 6G 135
Draycot Rd. E11 . . . . . 6K 51
KT6: Surb 1G 163
Draycott Av.
HA3: Kenton 6B 42
SW3 . . . . . 3D 16 (4C 100)
Draycott Cl. HA3: Kenton 6B 42
NW2 . . . . . 3F 63
SE5 . . . . . 7D 102
(not continuous)
Draycott Ct. *SW11* *1C 118*
(off Westbridge Rd.)
Draycott M. *SW6* *2H 117*
(off Laurel Bank Gdns.)
Draycott Pl. SW3 . . . . . 4E 16 (4D 100)
Draycott Ter. SW3 . . . . . 4F 17 (4D 100)
Dray Ct. *HA0: Wemb* *5A 60*
(off Brewery Cl.)
Drayford Cl. W9 . . . . . 4H 81
Dray Gdns. SW2 . . . . . 5K 119
Draymans M. SE15 . . . . . 2F 121
Draymans Way
TW7: Isle 3K 113
Drayside M. UB2: S'hall 2D 94
Drayson M. W8 . . . . . 2J 99
Drayton Av. BR6: Farnb 1F 173
W13 . . . . . 7A 78
Drayton Bri. Rd. W7 . . . . . 7K 77
W13 . . . . . 7K 77
Drayton Cl. IG1: Ilf 1H 71
TW4: Houn 5D 112
Drayton Ct. UB7: W Dray 4B 92
Drayton Gdns. N21 . . . . . 7G 23
SW10 . . . . . 6A 16 (5A 100)
UB7: W Dray 2A 92
W13 . . . . . 7A 78
Drayton Grn. W13 . . . . . 7A 78
Drayton Grn. Rd. W13 . . . . . 7B 78
Drayton Gro. W13 . . . . . 7A 78
Drayton Ho. E11 . . . . . 1F 69
SE5 . . . . . *7D 102*
(off Elmington Rd.)
Drayton Pk. N5 . . . . . 4A 66
Drayton Pk. M. N5 . . . . . 5A 66
Drayton Rd. CR0: C'don 2B 168
E11 . . . . . 1F 69
N17 . . . . . 2E 48
NW10 . . . . . 1B 80
W13 . . . . . 7A 78
Drayton Waye HA3: Kenton 6B 42
Dray Wlk. E1 . . . . . 4K 9
Dreadnought Cl. *SW19* *1A 154*
(off Nelson Gro. Rd.)
SW19 . . . . . 2B 154
(Brangwyn Cres.)
Dreadnought St. SE10 . . . . . 3G 105
Drenon Sq. UB3: Hayes 7H 75
Dresden Cl. NW6 . . . . . 6K 63
Dresden Ho. SE11 . . . . . 3H 19
SW11 . . . . . *2E 118*
(off Dagnall St.)
Dresden Rd. N19 . . . . . 1G 65
Dressington Av. SE4 . . . . . 6C 122
Drew Av. NW7 . . . . . 6B 30
Drewery Ct. SE3 . . . . . 3G 123
Drewett Ho. *E1* *6G 85*
(off Christian St.)
Drew Gdns. UB6: G'frd 6K 59
Drew Ho. SW16 . . . . . 3J 137
Drewitts Ct. KT12: Walt T 7H 147
Drew Rd. E16 . . . . . 1B 106
(not continuous)
Drewstead La. SW16 . . . . . 2H 137
Drewstead Rd. SW16 . . . . . 2H 137
Drey Ct. KT4: Wor Pk 1B 164
Driffield Ct. *NW9* *1A 44*
(off Pageant Av.)
Driffield Rd. E3 . . . . . 2A 86
Drift, The BR2: Brom 3B 172
Drift Ct. E16 . . . . . 7F 89
Driftway, The CR4: Mitc 1E 154
Driftway Ho. *E3* *2B 86*
(off Stafford Rd.)
Drill Hall Arts *5C 6*
(off Chenies St.)
Drinkwater Ho. *SE5* *7D 102*
(off Picton St.)
Drinkwater Rd. HA2: Harr 2F 59
Drive, The BR3: Beck 2C 158
BR4: W W'ck 7F 159
BR6: Orp 2K 173
BR7: Chst 3K 161
CR7: Thor H 4D 156
DA5: Bexl 6C 126
DA8: Erith 7H 109
DA14: Sidc 3B 144
E4 . . . . . 1A 36
E17 . . . . . 3D 50
E18 . . . . . 4J 51
EN2: Enf 1J 23
EN5: Barn 3B 20
EN5: New Bar 6F 21
HA2: Harr 7E 40
HA6: Nwood 2G 39
HA8: Edg 5B 28
HA9: Wemb 2J 61
IG1: Ilf 6C 52
IG9: Buck H 1F 37
IG11: Bark 7K 71
Drive, The KT2: King T 7J 133
KT6: Surb 7E 150
KT10: Esh 7G 149
KT19: Ewe 6B 164
N3 . . . . . 7D 30
N6 . . . . . 5D 46
N7 . . . . . 6K 65
(not continuous)
N11 . . . . . 6B 32
NW10 . . . . . 1B 80
NW11 . . . . . 7G 45
RM5: Col R 1K 55
SM4: Mord 5A 154
SW6 . . . . . 2G 117
SW20 . . . . . 7E 134
TW3: Houn 2H 113
TW7: Isle 2H 113
TW14: Felt 7A 112
TW15: Ashf 7F 129
UB10: Ick 4A 56
W3 . . . . . 6J 79
Drive Ct. HA8: Edg 5B 28
Drive Mans. *SW6* *2G 117*
(off Fulham Rd.)
Driveway, The *E17* *6D 50*
(off Hoe St.)
Droitwich Cl. SE26 . . . . . 3G 139
Dromey Gdns. HA3: Hrw W 7E 26
Dromore Rd. SW15 . . . . . 6G 117
Dronfield Gdns. RM8: Dag 5C 72
Dron Ho. *E1* *5J 85*
(off Adelina Gro.)
Droop St. W10 . . . . . 3F 81
Drovers Ct. *KT1: King T* *2E 150*
(off Fairfield E.)
Drovers Pl. SE15 . . . . . 7J 103
Drovers Rd. CR2: S Croy 5D 168
Drovers Way N7 . . . . . 6J 65
Druce Rd. SE21 . . . . . 6E 120
Druid St. SE1 . . . . . 6H 15 (2E 102)
(not continuous)
Druids Way BR2: Brom 4F 159
Drumaline Ridge
KT4: Wor Pk 2A 164
Drummond Av. RM7: Rom 4K 55
Drummond Ct. N12 . . . . . 7H 31
Drummond Cres. NW1 . . . . . 1C 6 (3H 83)
Drummond Dr. HA7: Stan 7E 26
Drummond Ga. SW1 . . . . . 5D 18 (5H 101)
Drummond Ho. *E2* *2G 85*
(off Goldsmiths Row)
N2 . . . . . *2A 46*
(off Font Hills)
Drummond Pl. TW1: Twick 7B 114
Drummond Rd. CR0: C'don 2C 168
(not continuous)
E11 . . . . . 6A 52
RM7: Rom 4K 55
SE16 . . . . . 3H 103
Drummonds, The
IG9: Buck H 2E 36
Drummonds Pl. TW9: Rich 4E 114
Drummond St. NW1 . . . . . 3A 6 (4G 83)
Druries *HA1: Harr* *1J 59*
(off High St.)
Drury Cres. CR0: Wadd 2A 168
Drury Ho. SW8 . . . . . 1G 119
Drury La. WC2 . . . . . 7F 7 (6J 83)
Drury Lane Theatre Royal *1F 13*
(off Drury La.)
Drury Rd. HA1: Harr 7G 41
Drury Way NW10 . . . . . 5K 61
Drury Way Ind. Est. NW10 . . . . . 5J 61
Dryad St. SW15 . . . . . 3F 117
Dryburgh Gdns. NW9 . . . . . 3G 43
Dryburgh Ho. *SW1* *5K 17*
(off Abbots Mnr.)
Dryburgh Rd. SW15 . . . . . 3D 116
Dryden Av. W7 . . . . . 6K 77
Dryden Bldg. *E1* *6G 85*
(off Commercial Rd.)
Dryden Cl. SW4 . . . . . 5H 119

Dryden Ct. SE11 . . . . .4K 19 (4B 102)
Dryden Mans. W14 . . . . .6G 99
(off Queen's Club Gdns.)
Dryden Rd. DA16: Well 1H 125
EN1: Enf 6K 23
HA3: W'stone 1K 41
SW19 . . . . .6A 136
Dryden St. WC2 . . . . .1F 13 (6J 83)
Dryfield Cl. NW10 . . . . .6J 61
Dryfield Rd. HA8: Edg 6D 28
Dryfield Wlk. SE8 . . . . .6C 104
Dryhill Rd. DA17: Belv 6F 109
Dryland Av. BR6: Orp 4K 173
Drylands Rd. N8 . . . . .6J 47
Drysdale Av. E4 . . . . .7J 25
Drysdale Cl. HA6: Nwood 1G 39
Drysdale Dwellings E8 . . . . .5F 67
(off Dunn St.)
Drysdale Pl. N1 . . . . .1H 9 (3E 84)
Drysdale St. N1 . . . . .1H 9 (3E 84)
Dublin Av. E8 .1G 85
Dublin Ct. HA2: Harr 2H 59
(off Northolt Rd.)
Du Burstow Ter. W7 . . . . .2J 95
Ducaine Apartments E3 . . . . .3B 86
(off Merchant St.)
Ducal St. E2 . . . . .2K 9 (3F 85)
Du Cane Cl. W12 . . . . .6E 80
Du Cane Ct. SW17 . . . . .1E 136
Du Cane Rd. W12 . . . . .6B 80
Ducavel Ho. SW2 . . . . .1K 137
Duchess Cl. N11 . . . . .5A 32
SM1: Sutt 4A 166
Duchess Gro. IG9: Buck H 2E 36
Duchess M. W1 . . . . .6K 5 (5F 83)
Duchess of Bedford Ho. W8 . . . . .2J 99
(off Duchess of Bedford's Wlk.)
Duchess of Bedford's Wlk. W8 . . . . . . .2J 99
Duchess St. W1 . . . . .6K 5 (5F 83)
Duchess Theatre 2G 13
(off Catherine St.)
Duchy Rd. EN4: Had W 1G 21
Duchy St. SE1 . . . . .4K 13 (1A 102)
(not continuous)
Ducie St. SW4 . . . . .4K 119
Duckett M. N4 . . . . .6B 48
Duckett Rd. N4 . . . . .6A 48
Duckett's Apartments E3 . . . . .7B 68
(off Wick La.)
Duckett St. E1 . . . . .4K 85
Duck La. W1 .1C 12
Duck Lees La. EN3: Pond E 4F 25
Duck's Hill Rd. HA4: Ruis 1D 38
HA6: Nwood 1D 38
DUCKS ISLAND 6A 20
Ducks Wlk. TW1: Twick 5C 114
Du Cros Dr. HA7: Stan 6J 27
Du Cros Rd. W3 . . . . .1A 98
DUDDEN HILL 5D 62
Dudden Hill La. NW10 . . . . .4B 62
Dudden Hill Pde. NW10 . . . . .4B 62
Duddington Cl. SE9 . . . . .4B 142
Dudley Av. HA3: Kenton 3C 42
Dudley Ct. NW11 . . . . .4H 45
W1 .1E 10
(off Up. Berkeley St.)
WC2 . . . . .7E 6 (6J 83)
Dudley Dr. HA4: Ruis 5K 57
SM4: Mord 1G 165
Dudley Gdns. HA2: Harr 1H 59
W13 . . . . .2B 96
Dudley Ho. W2 . . . . .6A 4
(off Nth. Wharf Rd.)
Dudley M. SW2 . . . . .6A 120
Dudley Pl. TW19: Stanw 6B 110
UB3: Harl 4F 93
Dudley Rd. E17 . . . . .2C 50
HA2: Harr 2G 59
IG1: Ilf 3F 71
KT1: King T 3F 151
KT12: Walt T 6J 147
N3 .2K 45

Dudley Rd. NW6 . . . . .2G 81
SW19 . . . . .6J 135
TW9: Rich 2F 115
TW14: Bedf 1E 128
TW15: Ashf 5B 128
UB2: S'hall 2B 94
Dudley St. W2 . . . . .6A 4 (5B 82)
Dudlington Rd. E5 . . . . .2J 67
Dudmaston M. SW3 . . . . .5B 16
Dudrich Cl. N11 . . . . .6J 31
Dudrich M. EN2: Enf 1F 23
SE22 . . . . .5F 121
Dudsbury Rd. DA14: Sidc 6B 144
Dudset La. TW5: Cran 1J 111
Duett Ct. TW5: Hest 7C 94
Duffell Ho. SE11 . . . . .6H 19
Dufferin Ct. EC1 . . . . .4E 8
Dufferin Ct. EC1 . . . . .4E 8
(off Dufferin St.)
Dufferin St. EC1 . . . . .4D 8 (4C 84)
Duffield Cl. HA1: Harr 5K 41
Duffield Dr. N15 . . . . .4F 49
Duff St. E14 . . . . .6D 86
Dufour's Pl. W1 . . . . .1B 12 (6G 83)
Dugard Way SE11 . . . . .4B 102
Dugdale Ct. NW10 . . . . .3D 80
(off Harrow Rd.)
Duggan Dr. BR7: Chst 6C 142
Dugolly Av. HA9: Wemb 3H 61
Duke Gdns. IG6: Ilf 4H 53
Duke Humphrey Rd. SE3 . . . . .1G 123
Duke of Cambridge Cl.
TW2: Whitt 6H 113
Duke of Clarence Ct. SE17 . . . . .5C 102
(off Penton Pl.)
Duke of Edinburgh Rd. SM1: Sutt 2B 166
Duke of Wellington Av. SE18 . . . . .3F 107
Duke of Wellington Pl.
SW1 . . . . .6H 11 (2E 100)
Duke of York Column (Memorial) 5C 12
Duke of York Sq. SW3 . . . . . . .4F 17 (5D 100)
Duke of York's Theatre 3E 12
(off St Martin's La.)
Duke of York St. SW1 . . . . . . .4B 12 (1G 101)
Duke Rd. IG6: Ilf 4H 53
W4 .5K 97
Dukes Av. HA1: Harr 4J 41
HA2: Harr 6D 40
HA8: Edg 6A 28
KT2: King T 4C 132
KT3: N Mald 3A 152
N3 .1K 45
N10 . . . . .3F 47
TW4: Houn 4C 112
TW10: Ham 4C 132
UB5: N'olt 7C 58
W4 .5K 97
Dukes Cl. TW12: Hamp 5D 130
TW15: Ashf 4E 128
Dukes Ct. E6 . . . . .1E 88
(not continuous)
SE13 . . . . .2E 122
SW14 . . . . .2K 115
W2 .7K 81
(off Moscow Rd.)
Dukes Ga. W4 . . . . .4J 97
Dukes Grn. Av. TW14: Felt 5J 111
Dukes Head Pas. TW12: Hamp 7G 131
Duke Shore Wharf E14 . . . . .7B 86
Duke's Ho. SW1 . . . . .3D 18
(off Vincent St.)
Dukes La. W8 .2K 99
Duke's La. Chambers W8 . . . . .2K 99
(off Dukes La.)
Duke's La. Mans. W8 . . . . .2K 99
(off Dukes La.)
Dukes Lodge W8 . . . . .1H 99
(off Holland Wlk.)
Dukes Meadows Golf & Tennis 2K 115
Dukes M. N10 .3F 47
W1 .7H 5

Dukes Orchard DA5: Bexl 1J 145
Duke's Pas. E17 . . . . .4E 50
Duke's Pl. EC3 . . . . .1H 15 (6E 84)
Dukes Point N6 . . . . .1F 65
(off Dukes Head Yd.)
Dukes Ride UB10: Ick 4A 56
Dukes Rd. E6 .1E 88
W3 .4G 79
WC1 . . . . .2D 6 (3H 83)
Dukesthorpe Rd. SE26 . . . . .4K 139
Duke St. SM1: Sutt 4B 166
TW9: Rich 4D 114
W1 . . . . .7H 5 (6E 82)
Duke St. Hill SE1 . . . . .4F 15 (1D 102)
Duke St. Mans. W1 . . . . .1H 11
(off Duke St.)
Duke St. St James's
SW1 . . . . .4B 12 (1G 101)
Dukes Way BR4: W W'ck 3G 171
HA9: Wemb 5E 60
Duke's Yd. W1 . . . . .2H 11 (7E 82)
Dulas St. N4 . . . . .1K 65
Dulford Rd. W11 . . . . .7G 81
Dulka Rd. SW11 . . . . .5D 118
Dulverton NW1 . . . . .1G 83
(off Royal College St.)
Dulverton Mans. WC1 . . . . .4H 7
Dulverton Rd. HA4: Ruis 1J 57
SE9 . . . . .2G 143
DULWICH 2E 138
Dulwich Bus. Cen. SE23 . . . . .1K 139
Dulwich Comn. SE21 . . . . .1E 138
SE22 . . . . .1E 138
Dulwich Lawn Cl. SE22 . . . . .5F 121
Dulwich Leisure Cen. 4G 121
Dulwich Oaks, The SE21 . . . . .3F 139
Dulwich Picture Gallery 7D 120
Dulwich Ri. Gdns. SE22 . . . . .5F 121
Dulwich Rd. SE24 . . . . .5A 120
Dulwich Upper Wood Nature Pk. 5F 139
DULWICH VILLAGE 7E 120
Dulwich Village SE21 . . . . .6D 120
Dulwich Wood Av. SE19 . . . . .4E 138
Dulwich Wood Pk. SE19 . . . . .4E 138
Dumain Ct. SE11 . . . . .4B 102
(off Opal St.)
Dumbarton Ct. SW2 . . . . .6J 119
Dumbarton Rd. SW2 . . . . .6J 119
Dumbleton Cl. KT1: King T 1H 151
Dumbreck Rd. SE9 . . . . .4D 124
Dumont Rd. N16 . . . . .3E 66
Dumpton Pl. NW1 . . . . .7E 64
Dumsey Eyot KT16: Chert 7A 146
Dunally Pk. TW17: Shep 7F 147
Dunbar Av. BR3: Beck 4A 158
RM10: Dag 3G 73
SW16 . . . . .2A 156
Dunbar Cl. UB4: Hayes 5K 75
Dunbar Ct. BR2: Brom 3H 159
(off Durham Rd.)
SM1: Sutt 5B 166
Dunbar Gdns. RM10: Dag 5G 73
Dunbar Rd. E7 . . . . .6J 69
KT3: N Mald 4J 151
N22 . . . . .1A 48
Dunbar St. SE27 . . . . .3C 138
Dunbar Twr. E8 . . . . .6F 67
(off Roseberry St.)
Dunbar Wharf E14 . . . . .7B 86
(off Narrow St.)
Dunblane Cl. HA8: Edg 2C 28
Dunblane Rd. SE9 . . . . .3C 124
Dunboe Pl. TW17: Shep 7E 146
Dunboyne Rd. NW3 . . . . .5D 64
Dunbridge Ho. SW15 . . . . .6B 116
(off Highcliffe Dr.)
Dunbridge St. E2 . . . . .4G 85
Duncan Cl. EN5: New Bar 4F 21
Duncan Ct. E14 . . . . .5E 86
(off Teviot St.)
N21 . . . . .1G 33
Duncan Gro. W3 . . . . .6A 80

Duncan Ho. NW3 . . . . .7D 64
(off Fellows Rd.)
SW1 . . . . .6B 18
(off Dolphin Sq.)
Duncannon Ho. SW1 . . . . .6D 18
(off Lindsay Sq.)
Duncannon St. WC2 . . . . . . .3E 12 (7J 83)
Duncan Rd. E8 . . . . .1H 85
TW9: Rich 4E 114
Duncan St. N1 . . . . .2B 84
Duncan Ter. N1 . . . . .2B 84
(not continuous)
Dunch St. E1 .6H 85
Dunchurch Ho. RM10: Dag 7G 73
Duncombe Hill SE23 . . . . .7A 122
Duncombe Rd. N19 . . . . .1H 65
Duncrievie Rd. SE13 . . . . .6F 123
Duncroft SE18 . . . . .7J 107
Dundalk Ho. E1 . . . . .6J 85
(off Clark St.)
Dundalk Rd. SE4 . . . . .3A 122
Dundas Gdns. KT8: W Mole 3F 149
Dundas Ho. E2 . . . . .2J 85
(off Bishop's Way)
Dundas Rd. SE15 . . . . .2J 121
Dundee Ct. E1 . . . . .1H 103
(off Wapping High St.)
SE1 .7G 15
(off Long La.)
Dundee Ho. W9 . . . . .3A 82
(off Maida Va.)
Dundee Rd. E13 . . . . .2K 87
SE25 . . . . .5H 157
Dundee St. E1 . . . . .1H 103
Dundee Way Brim 3F 25
Dundee Wharf E14 . . . . .7B 86
Dundela Gdns. KT4: Wor Pk 4D 164
Dundonald Cl. E6 . . . . .6C 88
Dundonald Rd. NW10 . . . . .1F 81
SW19 . . . . .7G 135
(not continuous)
Dundry Ho. SE26 . . . . .3G 139
Dunedin Ho. E16 . . . . .1D 106
(off Manwood St.)
Dunedin M. SW2 . . . . .1J 137
Dunedin Rd. E10 . . . . .3D 68
IG1: Ilf 1G 71
Dunedin Way UB4: Yead 4A 76
Dunelm Gro. SE27 . . . . .3C 138
Dunelm St. E1 .6K 85
Dunfield Gdns. SE6 . . . . .5D 140
Dunfield Rd. SE6 . . . . .5D 140
(not continuous)
Dunford Ct. HA5: Hat E 1D 40
Dunford Rd. N7 . . . . .4K 65
Dungarvan Av. SW15 . . . . .4C 116
Dunheved Cl. CR7: Thor H 6A 156
Dunheved Rd. Nth. CR7: Thor H 6A 156
Dunheved Rd. Sth. CR7: Thor H 6A 156
Dunheved Rd. W. CR7: Thor H 6A 156
Dunhill Point SW15 . . . . .1C 134
Dunholme Grn. N9 . . . . .3A 34
Dunholme La. N9 . . . . .3A 34
Dunholme Rd. N9 . . . . .3A 34
Dunkeld Ho. E14 . . . . .6F 87
(off Abbott Rd.)
Dunkeld Rd. RM8: Dag 2B 72
SE25 . . . . .4D 156
Dunkery Rd. SE9 . . . . .4B 142
Dunkirk Ho. SE1 . . . . .2D 102
(off Long La.)
Dunkirk St. SE27 . . . . .4C 138
Dunlace Rd. E5 . . . . .4J 67
Dunleary Cl. TW4: Houn 7D 112
Dunley Dr. CR0: New Ad 7D 170
Dunlin Ho. SE16 . . . . .4K 103
(off Tawny Way)
Dunloe Av. N17 . . . . .3D 48
Dunloe Ct. E2 .2F 85
Dunloe Pas. E2 . . . . .2F 85
(off Dunloe St.)
Dunloe St. E2 .2F 85

Dunlop Pl. SE16 3F 103
Dunmore Point *E2* *2J 9*
(off Gascoigne Pl.)
Dunmore Rd. NW6 1G 81
SW20 1E 152
Dunmow Cl. RM6: Chad H 5C 54
TW13: Hanw 3C 130
Dunmow Ho. RM9: Dag 1B 90
SE11 *5H 19*
(off Newburn St.)
Dunmow Rd. E15 4F 69
Dunmow Wlk. *N1* *1C 84*
(off Popham St.)
Dunnage Cres. SE16 4A 104
(not continuous)
Dunnett Ho. *E3* *2B 86*
(off Vernon Rd.)
Dunnico Ho. *SE17* *5E 102*
(off East St.)
Dunn Mead NW9 7G 29
Dunnock Cl. N9 1E 34
Dunnock Rd. E6 6C 88
Dunn's Pas. WC1 7F 7
Dunn St. E8 5F 67
Dunollie Pl. NW5 5G 65
Dunollie Rd. NW5 5G 65
Dunoon Gdns. SE23 7K 121
Dunoon Ho. *N1* *1K 83*
(off Bemerton Est.)
Dunoon Rd. SE23 7J 121
Dunoran Home BR1: Brom 1C 160
Dunraven Dr. EN2: Enf 2F 23
Dunraven Rd. W12 1C 98
Dunraven St. W1 2F 11 (7D 82)
Dunsany Rd. W14 3F 99
Dunsfold Cl. *SM2: Sutt* *7K 165*
(off Blackbush Cl.)
Dunsfold Way CR0: New Ad 7D 170
Dunsford Way SW15 6D 116
Dunsmore Cl. UB4: Yead 4C 76
Dunsmore Rd. KT12: Walt T 6K 147
Dunsmure Rd. N16 1E 66
Dunspring La. IG5: Ilf 2F 53
Dunstable M. W1 5H 5 (5E 82)
Dunstable Rd. KT8: W Mole 4D 148
TW9: Rich 4E 114
Dunstall Rd. SW20 6D 134
Dunstall Way KT8: W Mole 3F 149
Dunstall Welling Est. DA16: Well 2B 126
Dunstan Cl. N2 3A 46
Dunstan Glade BR5: Pet W 6H 161
Dunstan Ho's. *E1* *5J 85*
(off Stepney Grn.)
Dunstan Rd. NW11 1H 63
Dunstan's Gro. SE22 6H 121
Dunstan's Rd. SE22 7G 121
Dunster Av. SM4: Mord 1F 165
Dunster Cl. EN5: Barn 4A 20
RM5: Col R 2J 55
Dunster Ct. EC3 2H 15 (7E 84)
Dunster Dr. NW9 1J 61
Dunster Gdns. NW6 7H 63
Dunster Ho. SE6 3E 140
Dunsterville Way SE1 7F 15 (2D 102)
Dunster Way HA2: Harr 3C 58
SM6: Wall 1E 166
Dunston Rd. E8 1F 85
SW11 2E 118
Dunston St. E8 1E 84
Dunton Cl. KT6: Surb 1E 162
Dunton Ct. SE23 2H 139
Dunton Rd. E10 7D 50
RM1: Rom 4K 55
SE1 5F 103
Duntshill Rd. SW18 1K 135
Dunvegan Cl. KT8: W Mole 4F 149
Dunvegan Rd. SE9 4D 124
Dunwich Ct. *RM6: Chad H* *5B 54*
(off Glandford Way)
Dunwich Rd. DA7: Bex 1F 127
Dunworth M. W11 6H 81
Duplex Ride SW1 7F 11 (2D 100)
Dupont Rd. SW20 2F 153
Duppas Av. CR0: Wadd 4B 168
Duppas Cl. TW17: Shep 5F 147
Duppas Ct. *CR0: C'don* *3B 168*
(off Duppas Hill Ter.)
Duppas Hill La. CR0: C'don 4B 168
Duppas Hill Rd. CR0: Wadd 4A 168
Duppas Hill Ter. CR0: C'don 3B 168
Duppas Rd. CR0: Wadd 3A 168
Dupree Rd. SE7 5K 105
Dura Den Cl. BR3: Beck 7D 140
Durand Cl. SM5: Cars 1D 166
Durand Gdns. SW9 1K 119
Durands Wlk. SE16 2B 104
Durand Way NW10 7J 61
Durants Pk. Av. EN3: Pond E 4E 24
Durants Rd. EN3: Pond E 4D 24
Durant St. E2 2G 85
Durban Ct. E7 7B 70
Durban Gdns. RM10: Dag 7J 73
Durban Ho. *W12* *7D 80*
(off White City Est.)
Durban Rd. BR3: Beck 2B 158
E15 3G 87
E17 1B 50
IG2: Ilf 1J 71
N17 6K 33
SE27 4C 138
Durbin Rd. KT9: Chess 4E 162
Durdan Cotts. *UB1: S'hall* *6D 76*
(off Denbigh Rd.)
Durdans Ho. *NW1* *7F 65*
(off Farrier St.)
Durdans Rd. UB1: S'hall 6D 76
Durell Gdns. RM9: Dag 5D 72
Durell Ho. *SE16* *2K 103*
(off Wolfe Cres.)
Durell Rd. RM9: Dag 5D 72
Durfey Pl. SE5 7D 102
Durford Cres. SW15 1D 134
Durham Av. BR2: Brom 4H 159
IG8: Buck H, Wfd G 5G 37
TW5: Hest 5D 94
Durham Cl. SW20 2D 152
Durham Ct. *NW6* *2J 81*
(off Kilburn Pk. Rd.)
TW11: Tedd 4J 131
Durham Hill BR1: Brom 4H 141
Durham Ho. BR2: Brom 4G 159
IG11: Bark *7A 72*
(off Margaret Bondfield Av.)
NW8 *2D 4*
(off Lorne Cl.)
RM10: Dag 5J 73
Durham Ho. St. WC2 3F 13
Durham Pl. IG1: Ilf 4G 71
SW3 6E 16 (5D 100)
Durham Ri. SE18 5G 107
Durham Rd. BR2: Brom 3H 159
DA14: Sidc 5B 144
E12 4B 70
E16 4G 87
HA1: Harr 5F 41
N2 3C 46
N7 2K 65
N9 2B 34
RM10: Dag 5J 73
SW20 1D 152
TW14: Felt 7A 112
W5 3D 96
Durham Row E1 5K 85
Durham St. SE11 6G 19 (5K 101)
Durham Ter. W2 6K 81
Durham Wharf Dr. TW8: Bford 7C 96
Durham Yd. E2 3H 85
Durley Av. HA5: Pinn 7C 40
Durley Rd. N16 7E 48
Durlston Rd. E5 2G 67
KT2: King T 6E 132
Durnford Ho. SE6 3E 140
Durnford St. N15 5E 48
SE10 6E 104
Durning Rd. SE19 5D 138
Durnsford Av. SW19 2J 135
Durnsford Ct. *EN3: Enf H* *3F 25*
(off Enstone Rd.)
Durnsford Rd. N11 1H 47
SW19 2J 135
Durrant Ct. HA3: Hrw W 2J 41
Durrant Ho. *EC1* *5D 84*
(off Chiswell St.)
Durrant Way BR6: Farnb 5H 173
Durrell Rd. SW6 1H 117
Durrell Way TW17: Shep 6F 147
Durrels Ho. *W14* *4H 99*
(off Warwick Gdns.)
Durrington Av. SW20 7E 134
Durrington Pk. Rd. SW20 1E 152
Durrington Rd. E5 4A 68
Durrington Twr. SW8 2G 119
Durrisdeer Ho. *NW2* *4H 63*
(off Lyndale)
Dursley Cl. SE3 2A 124
Dursley Gdns. SE3 1B 124
Dursley Rd. SE3 2A 124
Durward Ho. *W8* *2K 99*
(off Kensington Ct.)
Durward St. E1 5H 85
Durweston M. W1 5F 5
Durweston St. W1 6F 5 (5D 82)
Dury Falls Ct. RM5: Col R 2J 55
Dury Rd. EN5: Barn 1C 20
Dutch Barn Cl. TW19: Stanw 6A 110
Dutch Gdns. KT2: King T 6H 133
Dutch Yd. SW18 5J 117
Dutton St. SE10 1E 122
Duval Ho. *N19* *2H 65*
(off Ashbrook Rd.)
Duxberry Av. TW13: Felt 3A 130
Duxberry Cl. BR2: Brom 5C 160
Duxford Ho. *SE2* *2D 108*
(off Wolvercote Rd.)
Dye Ho. La. E3 1C 86
Dyer Ho. TW12: Hamp 1F 149
Dyer's Bldgs. EC1 6J 7 (5A 84)
Dyers Hall Rd. E11 1G 69
Dyers Hill Rd. E11 2F 69
Dyers La. SW15 4D 116
Dykes Way BR2: Brom 3H 159
Dykewood Cl. DA5: Bexl 3K 145
Dylan Rd. DA17: Belv 3G 109
SE24 4B 120
Dylways SE5 4D 120
Dymchurch Cl. BR6: Orp 4J 173
IG5: Ilf 2E 52
Dymes Path SW19 2F 135
Dymock St. SW6 3K 117
Dyneley Rd. SE12 3A 142
Dyne Rd. NW6 7G 63
Dynevor Rd. N16 3E 66
TW10: Rich 5E 114
Dynham Rd. NW6 7J 63
Dyott St. WC1 7D 6 (6H 83)
Dysart Av. KT2: King T 5C 132
Dysart St. EC2 4G 9 (4D 84)
Dyson Ct. HA0: Wemb 4A 60
NW2 1E 62
Dyson Ho. *SE10* *5H 105*
(off Blackwall La.)
Dyson Rd. E11 6G 51
E15 6H 69
Dysons Rd. N18 5C 34

E

Eade Rd. N4 7C 48
Eagans Cl. N2 3B 46
Eagle Av. RM6: Chad H 6E 54
Eagle Cl. EN3: Pond E 4D 24
SE16 5J 103
SM6: Wall 6J 167
Eagle Ct. E11 4J 51
EC1 5A 8 (5B 84)
Eagle Dr. NW9 2A 44
Eagle Dwellings *EC1* *1D 8*
(off City Rd.)
Eagle Hgts. SW11 3C 118
Eagle Hill SE19 6D 138
Eagle Ho. *E1* *4H 85*
(off Headlam St.)
N1 *2D 84*
(off Eagle Wharf Rd.)
Eagle Ho. M. SW4 5G 119
Eagle La. E11 4J 51
Eagle Lodge NW11 7H 45
Eagle Mans. *N16* *5F 67*
(off Salcombe Rd.)
Eagle M. N1 6E 66
Eagle Pl. SW1 3B 12
SW7 5A 100
Eagle Rd. HA0: Wemb 7D 60
TW6: H'row A 3H 111
Eaglesfield Rd. SE18 1F 125
Eagle St. WC1 6G 7 (5K 83)
Eagle Ter. IG8: Wfd G 7E 36
Eagle Trad. Est. CR4: Mitc 6D 154
Eagle Wharf Ct. *SE1* *5J 15*
(off Lafone St.)
Eagle Wharf E. *E14* *7A 86*
(off Narrow St.)
Eagle Wharf Rd. N1 2C 84
Eagle Wharf W. *E14* *7A 86*
(off Narrow St.)
Eagle Works E. E1 4K 9
Eagle Works W. E1 4J 9
Eagling Cl. E3 3C 86
Ealdham Sq. SE9 4A 124
EALING 7D 78
Ealing B'way. Cen. W5 7D 78
EALING COMMON 7F 79
Ealing Driving Range 1E 76
Ealing Grn. W5 1D 96
Ealing Pk. Gdns. W5 4C 96
Ealing Pk. Mans. *W5* *3D 96*
(off Sth. Ealing Rd.)
Ealing Rd. HA0: Wemb 6E 60
TW8: Bford 4D 96
UB5: N'olt 1E 76
Ealing Squash & Fitness Club 6E 78
Ealing Studios 1D 96
Ealing Village W5 6E 78
Eamont Cl. HA4: Ruis 7D 38
Eamont Ct. *NW8* *2C 82*
(off Eamont St.)
Eamont St. NW8 2C 82
Eardley Cres. SW5 5J 99
Eardley Point *SE18* *4F 107*
(off Wilmount St.)
Eardley Rd. DA17: Belv 5G 109
SW16 5G 137
Earhart Way TW6: Cran, H'row A 3J 111
Earl Cl. N11 5A 32
Earldom Rd. SW15 4E 116
Earle Gdns. KT2: King T 7E 132
Earle Ho. *SW1* *4D 18*
(off Montaigne Cl.)
Earlham Ct. E11 7H 51
Earlham Gro. E7 5H 69
N22 7E 32
Earlham St. WC2 1D 12 (6J 83)
Earl Ho. *NW1* *4D 4*
(off Lisson Gro.)
Earlom Ho. *WC1* *2J 7*
(off Margery St.)
Earl Ri. SE18 5H 107
Earl Rd. SW14 4J 115
Earlsbury Gdns. HA8: Edg 4B 28
EARL'S COURT 4K 99
Earls Court Exhibition Building 5J 99
Earl's Ct. Gdns. SW5 4K 99
Earls Ct. Rd. SW5 3J 99
W8 3J 99
Earl's Ct. Sq. SW5 5K 99
Earls Cres. HA1: Harr 4J 41
Earlsdown Ho. IG11: Bark 2H 89

Earlsferry Way N1 7J **65**
(not continuous)
EARLSFIELD **1A 136**
Earlsfield Ho. *KT2: King T 1D 150*
(off Skerne Rd.)
Earlsfield Rd. SW18 1A **136**
Earlshall Rd. SE9 4D **124**
Earls Ho. TW9: Kew 7H **97**
Earlsmead HA2: Harr 4D **58**
Earlsmead Rd. N15 5F **49**
NW10 3E **80**
Earlsmead Stadium **4D 58**
Earls Ter. W8 3H **99**
Earlsthorpe M. SW12 6E **118**
Earlsthorpe Rd. SE26 4K **139**
Earlstoke St. EC1 1A **8** (3B **84**)
Earlston Gro. E9 1H **85**
Earl St. EC2 5G **9** (5D **84**)
Earls Wlk. RM8: Dag 4B **72**
W8 3J **99**
Earlswood Av. CR7: Thor H 5A **156**
Earlswood Cl. SE10 6G **105**
Earlswood Gdns. IG5: Ilf 3E **52**
Earlswood St. SE10 5G **105**
Early M. NW1 1F **83**
Earnshaw Ho. *EC1 2B 8*
(off Percival St.)
Earnshaw St. WC2 7D **6** (6H **83**)
Earsby St. W14 4G **99**
(not continuous)
Easby Cres. SM4: Mord 6K **153**
Easebourne Rd. RM8: Dag 5C **72**
Easedale Ho. TW7: Isle 5K **113**
Eashing Point *SW15 1D 134*
(off Wanborough Dr.)
Easleys M. W1 7H **5** (6E **82**)
East 10 Ent. Pk. E10 1A **68**
EAST ACTON **7B 80**
E. Acton Arc. W3 6A **80**
E. Acton Ct. W3 7A **80**
E. Acton La. W3 1A **98**
E. Arbour St. E1 6K **85**
East Av. E12 7C **70**
E17 4D **50**
N2 4K **45**
SM6: Wall 5K **167**
UB1: S'hall 7D **76**
UB3: Hayes 1H **93**
East Bank N16 7E **48**
E. Bank Cl. E17 5D **50**
Eastbank Rd. TW12: Ham H 5G **131**
EAST BARNET **6H 21**
E. Barnet Rd. EN4: E Barn 4G **21**
E. Beckton District Cen. E6 5D **88**
EAST BEDFONT **7G 111**
East Block *SE1 6H 13*
(off York Rd.)
E. Boundary Rd. E12 3D **70**
Eastbourne Av. W3 6K **79**
Eastbourne Gdns. SW14 3J **115**
Eastbourne M. W2 7A **4** (6A **82**)
Eastbourne Rd. E6 3E **88**
(not continuous)
E15 1G **87**
N15 6E **48**
SW17 6E **136**
TW8: Bford 5C **96**
TW13: Felt 2B **130**
W4 6J **97**
Eastbourne Ter. W2 7A **4** (6A **82**)
Eastbournia Av. N9 3C **34**
Eastbrook Av. N9 7D **24**
RM10: Dag 4J **73**
Eastbrook Dr. RM7: Rush G 3K **73**
Eastbrookend Country Pk. **4K 73**
Eastbrook Rd. SE3 1K **123**
Eastbury Av. EN1: Enf 1A **24**
IG11: Bark 1J **89**
Eastbury Ct. *EN5: New Bar 5F 21*
(off Lyonsdown Rd.)
IG11: Bark 1J **89**
Eastbury Gro. W4 5A **98**
Eastbury Manor House **1K 89**
Eastbury Rd. BR5: Pet W 6H **161**
E6 4E **88**
KT2: King T 7E **132**
RM7: Rom 6K **55**
Eastbury Sq. IG11: Bark 1K **89**
Eastbury Ter. E1 4K **85**
Eastcastle St. W1 7A **6** (6G **83**)
Eastcheap EC3 2G **15** (7E **84**)
E. Churchfield Rd. W3 1K **97**
Eastchurch Rd. TW6: H'row A 2G **111**
East Cl. EN4: Cockf 4K **21**
UB6: G'frd 2G **77**
W5 4G **79**
Eastcombe Av. SE7 6K **105**
EASTCOTE **7K 39**
Eastcote BR6: Orp 1K **173**
Eastcote Av. HA2: Harr 2F **59**
KT8: W Mole 5D **148**
UB6: G'frd 5A **60**
Eastcote Hockey & Badminton Club **6H 39**
Eastcote Ind. Est. HA4: Ruis 7A **40**
Eastcote La. HA2: Harr 4C **58**
UB5: N'olt 5D **58**
(not continuous)
Eastcote La. Nth. UB5: N'olt 6D **58**
Eastcote Pl. HA5: Eastc 6K **39**
Eastcote Rd. DA16: Well 2H **125**
HA2: Harr 3G **59**
HA4: Ruis 7G **39**
HA5: Pinn 5B **40**
Eastcote St. SW9 2K **119**
Eastcote Vw. HA5: Pinn 4A **40**
EASTCOTE VILLAGE **5K 39**
East Ct. HA0: Wemb 2C **60**
East Cres. EN1: Enf 5A **24**
N11 4J **31**
Eastcroft Cl. KT2: King T 5J **133**
Eastcroft Rd. KT19: Ewe 7A **164**
E. Cross Route E3 7B **68**
E9 5B **68**
(Crowfoot Cl.)
E9 7B **68**
(Wansbeck Rd.)
E10 5B **68**
Eastdown Ct. SE13 4F **123**
Eastdown Ho. E8 4G **67**
Eastdown Pk. SE13 4F **123**
East Dr. SM5: Cars 7C **166**
E. Duck Lees La. EN3: Pond E 4F **25**
EAST DULWICH **4F 121**
E. Dulwich Gro. SE22 5E **120**
E. Dulwich Rd. SE22 4F **121**
(not continuous)
East End Farm HA5: Pinn 3D **40**
East End Rd. N2 3K **45**
N3 2J **45**
East End Way HA5: Pinn 3C **40**
East Entrance RM10: Dag 2H **91**
Eastern App. IG11: Bark 1A **90**
Eastern Av. E11 6K **51**
HA5: Pinn 7B **40**
IG2: Ilf 6F **53**
IG4: Ilf 6C **52**
RM6: Chad H 4A **54**
Eastern Av. E. RM1: Rom 3K **55**
Eastern Av. Retail Pk.
RM7: Rom 4J **55**
Eastern Av. W. RM1: Rom 3K **55**
RM5: Rom 3K **55**
RM6: Chad H 4E **54**
RM7: Chad H, Mawney, Rom 4A **54**
Eastern Bus. Pk. TW6: H'row A 2G **111**
Eastern Gateway E16 7A **88**
Eastern Ho. *E2 3H 85*
(off Bethnal Grn. Rd.)
Eastern Ind. Est. DA18: Erith 2G **109**
Eastern Perimeter Rd.
TW6: H'row A 2H **111**
Eastern Quay Apartments
E16 1K 105
(off Portsmouth M.)
Eastern Rd. E13 2K **87**
E17 5E **50**
N2 3D **46**
N22 1J **47**
SE4 4C **122**
Eastern Rdbt. IG1: Ilf 2G **71**
Easternville Gdns. IG2: Ilf 6G **53**
Eastern Way DA17: Belv 2A **108**
SE2: Belv, Erith, Lon 2A **108**
SE28 2A **108**
E. Ferry Rd. E14 4D **104**
Eastfield Gdns. RM10: Dag 4G **73**
Eastfield Rd. E17 4C **50**
EN3: Enf W 1E **24**
N8 3J **47**
RM9: Dag 4F **73**
RM10: Dag 4G **73**
Eastfields HA5: Eastc 5A **40**
Eastfields Av. SW18 4J **117**
Eastfields Rd. CR4: Mitc 2E **154**
W3 5J **79**
Eastfield St. E14 5A **86**
EAST FINCHLEY **4C 46**
East Gdns. SW17 6C **136**
Eastgate Bus. Pk. E10 1A **68**
Eastgate Cl. SE28 6D **90**
Eastglade HA5: Pinn 3D **40**
EAST HAM **2D 88**
E. Ham & Barking By-Pass
IG11: Bark 2J **89**
Eastham Cl. EN5: Barn 5B **20**
E. Ham Ind. Est. E6 4C **88**
East Ham Leisure Cen. **1D 88**
E. Ham Mnr. Way E6 6E **88**
East Ham Nature Reserve **4D 88**
East Ham Nature Reserve Vis. Cen.
4D 88
E. Harding St. EC4 7K **7** (6A **84**)
E. Heath Rd. NW3 3A **64**
East Hill HA9: Wemb 2G **61**
SW18 5K **117**
Eastholm NW11 4K **45**
East Holme DA8: Erith 1K **127**
Eastholme UB3: Hayes 1J **93**
E. India Bldgs. *E14 7C 86*
(off Saltwell St.)
E. India Ct. *SE16 2J 103*
(off St Marychurch St.)
East India Dock Basin Nature Reserve
7G 87
E. India Dock Ho. E14 6E **86**
E. India Dock Rd. E14 6C **86**
E. India Way CR0: C'don 1F **169**
Eastlake Ho. NW8 4B **4**
Eastlake Rd. SE5 2C **120**
Eastlands Cres. SE21 6F **121**
East La. HA0: Wemb 3B **60**
HA9: Wemb 3B **60**
KT1: King T 3D **150**
SE16 2G **103**
(Chambers St.)
SE16 2G **103**
(Scott Lidgett Cres.)
East La. Bus. Pk. HA9: Wemb 2D **60**
Eastlea M. E16 4G **87**
Eastleigh Av. HA2: Harr 2F **59**
Eastleigh Cl. NW2 3A **62**
SM2: Sutt 7K **165**
Eastleigh Rd. DA7: Bex 3J **127**
E17 2B **50**
Eastleigh Wlk. SW15 7C **116**
Eastleigh Way TW14: Felt 1J **129**
East Lodge *E16 1J 105*
(off Wesley Av.)
E. London Crematorium E13 3H **87**
East London Gymnastic Cen. **6D 88**
Eastman Ho. SW4 6G **119**
Eastman Rd. W3 2K **97**
East Mead HA4: Ruis 3B **58**
Eastmead Av. UB6: G'frd 3F **77**
Eastmead Cl. BR1: Brom 2C **160**
Eastmearn Rd. SE21 2C **138**
EAST MOLESEY **4H 149**
Eastmoor Pl. SE7 3B **106**
Eastmoor St. SE7 3B **106**
East Mt. St. E1 5H **85**
(not continuous)
Eastney Rd. CR0: C'don 1B **168**
Eastney St. SE10 5F **105**
Eastnor Rd. SE9 1G **143**
Eastone Apartments *E1 6K 9*
(off Lolesworth Cl.)
Easton St. WC1 3J **7** (4A **84**)
East Pk. Cl. RM6: Chad H 5D **54**
East Parkside SE10 2G **105**
East Pas. EC1 5C **8**
East Pl. SE27 4C **138**
East Point SE1 5G **103**
E. Pole Cotts. N14 4C **22**
E. Poultry Av. EC1 6A **8** (5B **84**)
East Ramp TW6: H'row A 1D **110**
East Rd. DA16: Well 2B **126**
E15 1J **87**
EN3: Enf W 1D **24**
EN4: E Barn 1K **31**
HA1: Harr 7B **42**
HA8: Edg 1H **43**
KT2: King T 1E **150**
N1 2E **8** (3D **84**)
N2 1C **46**
RM6: Chad H 5E **54**
RM7: Rush G 7K **55**
SW3 6G **17** (5E **100**)
SW19 6A **136**
TW14: Bedf 7F **111**
UB7: W Dray 4B **92**
E. Rochester Way DA5: Bexl 6F **127**
DA15: Bexl, Sidc 5J **125**
East Row E11 6J **51**
W10 4G **81**
Eastry Av. BR2: Hayes 6H **159**
Eastry Ho. *SW8 7J 101*
(off Hartington Rd.)
Eastry Rd. DA8: Erith 7G **109**
EAST SHEEN **4J 115**
E. Sheen Av. SW14 5K **115**
East Side *W12 2E 98*
(off Shepherd's Bush Mkt.)
Eastside M. *E3 2C 86*
(off Morville St.)
Eastside Rd. NW11 4H **45**
East Smithfield E1 3K **15** (7F **85**)
East Sq. E10 7D **50**
East Stand N5 3B **66**
East St. BR1: Brom 2J **159**
DA7: Bex 4G **127**
IG11: Bark 1G **89**
SE17 5C **102**
(not continuous)
TW8: Bford 7C **96**
E. Surrey Gro. SE15 7F **103**
E. Tenter St. E1 1K **15** (6F **85**)
East Ter. DA15: Sidc 1J **143**
E. Thamesmead Bus. Pk.
DA18: Erith 2F **109**
East Twr. *E14 2D 104*
(off Pan Peninsula Sq.)
East Towers HA5: Pinn 5B **40**
East Va. W3 1B **98**
East Vw. E4 5K **35**
EN5: Barn 2C **20**
Eastview Av. SE18 7J **107**
Eastville Av. NW11 6H **45**
East Wlk. EN4: E Barn 7K **21**
UB3: Hayes 1J **93**
East Way BR2: Hayes 7J **159**
CR0: C'don 2A **170**
E11 5K **51**
HA4: Ruis 1J **57**
UB3: Hayes 1J **93**
Eastway E9 6B **68**
(not continuous)
SM4: Mord 5F **153**
SM6: Wall 4G **167**

Eastway Cres.—Edmonton Ct.

Eastway Cres. HA2: Harr . . . 2F 59
Eastwell Cl. BR3: Beck . . . 7A 140
Eastwell Ho. SE1 . . . 7F 15
EAST WICKHAM . . . 1C 126
East Winter Garden . . . 1D 104
(off Bank St.)
Eastwood Cl. E18 . . . 2J 51
N7 . . . 5A 66
N17 . . . 7C 34
Eastwood Rd. E18 . . . 2J 51
IG3: Ilf . . . 1A 72
N10 . . . 2E 46
UB7: W Dray . . . 2C 92
East Woodside DA5: Bexl . . . 7E 126
Eastwood St. SW16 . . . 6G 137
Eatington Rd. E10 . . . 5F 51
Eaton Cl. HA7: Stan . . . 4G 27
SW1 . . . 4G 17 (4E 100)
Eaton Ct. E18 . . . 2J 51
HA8: Edg . . . 4B 28
Eaton Dr. KT2: King T . . . 7G 133
RM5: Col R . . . 1H 55
SW9 . . . 4B 120
Eaton Gdns. RM9: Dag . . . 7E 72
Eaton Ga. SW1 . . . 3G 17 (4E 100)
Eaton Ho. E14 . . . 7B 86
(off Westferry Cir.)
SW11 . . . 1B 118
Eaton La. SW1 . . . 2K 17 (3F 101)
Eaton Mans. SW1 . . . 4G 17
(off Bourne St.)
Eaton M. Nth. SW1 . . . 3G 17 (4E 100)
Eaton M. Sth. SW1 . . . 3H 17 (4E 100)
Eaton M. W. SW1 . . . 3H 17 (4E 100)
Eaton Pk. Rd. N13 . . . 2F 33
Eaton Pl. SW1 . . . 2G 17 (4E 100)
Eaton Ri. E11 . . . 5A 52
W5 . . . 5D 78
Eaton Rd. DA14: Sidc . . . 2D 144
EN1: Enf . . . 4K 23
NW4 . . . 5E 44
SM2: Sutt . . . 6B 166
TW3: Houn . . . 4H 113
Eaton Row SW1 . . . 2J 17 (3F 101)
Eatons Mead E4 . . . 2H 35
Eaton Sq. SW1 . . . 3G 17 (4E 100)
Eaton Ter. E3 . . . 3A 86
SW1 . . . 3G 17 (4E 100)
Eaton Ter. M. SW1 . . . 3G 17
Eatonville Rd. SW17 . . . 2D 136
Eatonville Vs. SW17 . . . 2D 136
Ebb Ct. E16 . . . 7G 89
Ebbett Ct. W3 . . . 5K 79
Ebbisham Dr. SW8 . . . 7G 19 (6K 101)
Ebbisham Rd. KT4: Wor Pk . . . 2E 164
Ebbsfleet Rd. NW2 . . . 5G 63
Ebdon Way SE3 . . . 3K 123
Ebenezer Ho. SE11 . . . 4K 19 (4B 102)
Ebenezer Mussel Ho. E2 . . . 2J 85
(off Patriot Sq.)
Ebenezer St. N1 . . . 1E 8 (3D 84)
Ebenezer Wlk. SW16 . . . 1G 155
Ebley Cl. SE15 . . . 6F 103
Ebner St. SW18 . . . 5K 117
Ebony Ho. E2 . . . 3G 85
(off Buckfast St.)
Ebor Cotts. SW15 . . . 3A 134
Ebor St. E1 . . . 3J 9 (4F 85)
Ebrington Rd. HA3: Kenton . . . 6D 42
Ebsworth St. SE23 . . . 7K 121
Eburne Rd. N7 . . . 3J 65
Ebury Bri. SW1 . . . 5J 17 (5F 101)
Ebury Bri. Est. SW1 . . . 5J 17 (5F 101)
Ebury Bri. Rd. SW1 . . . 6H 17 (5E 100)
Ebury Cl. BR2: Kes . . . 3C 172
Ebury M. SE27 . . . 3B 138
SW1 . . . 3J 17 (4F 101)
Ebury M. E. SW1 . . . 2J 17 (3F 101)
Ebury Sq. SW1 . . . 4H 17 (4E 100)
Ebury St. SW1 . . . 4H 17 (4E 100)
Ecclesbourne Apartments N1 . . . 7D 66
(off Ecclesbourne Rd.)
Ecclesbourne Cl. N13 . . . 5F 33
Ecclesbourne Gdns. N13 . . . 5F 33
Ecclesbourne Rd. CR7: Thor H . . . 5C 156
N1 . . . 7C 66
Eccleshill BR2: Brom . . . 4H 159
(off Durham Rd.)
Eccles Rd. SW11 . . . 4D 118
Eccleston Bri. SW1 . . . 3K 17 (4F 101)
Eccleston Cl. BR6: Orp . . . 1H 173
EN4: Cockf . . . 4J 21
Eccleston Cres. RM6: Chad H . . . 7B 54
Ecclestone Ct. HA9: Wemb . . . 5E 60
Ecclestone M. HA9: Wemb . . . 5E 60
Ecclestone Pl. HA9: Wemb . . . 5F 61
Eccleston Ho. SW2 . . . 6A 120
Eccleston M. SW1 . . . 2H 17 (3E 100)
Eccleston Pl. SW1 . . . 3J 17 (4F 101)
Eccleston Rd. W13 . . . 7A 78
Eccleston Sq. SW1 . . . 4K 17 (4F 101)
(not continuous)
Eccleston Sq. M. SW1 . . . 4A 18 (4F 101)
Eccleston St. SW1 . . . 2J 17 (3F 101)
Echelforde Dr. TW15: Ashf . . . 4C 128
Echo Hgts. E4 . . . 1J 35
Eckford St. N1 . . . 2A 84
Eckington Ho. N15 . . . 6D 48
(off Fladbury Rd.)
Eckstein Rd. SW11 . . . 4C 118
Eclipse Bldg. N1 . . . 6A 66
(off Laycock St.)
Eclipse Ho. N22 . . . 2K 47
(off Station Rd.)
Eclipse Rd. E13 . . . 5K 87
Ecology Cen. and Arts Pavilion . . . 3A 86
Ector Rd. SE6 . . . 2G 141
Edam Ct. DA15: Sidc . . . 3A 144
Edans Ct. W12 . . . 2B 98
Edar Ho. CR0: New Ad . . . 6D 170
Edbrooke Rd. W9 . . . 4J 81
Eddinton Cl. CR0: New Ad . . . 6E 170
Eddisbury Ho. SE26 . . . 3G 139
Eddiscombe Rd. SW6 . . . 2H 117
Eddy Cl. RM7: Rom . . . 6H 55
Eddystone Rd. SE4 . . . 5A 122
Eddystone Twr. SE8 . . . 5A 104
Eddystone Wlk. TW19: Stanw . . . 7A 110
Ede Cl. TW3: Houn . . . 3D 112
Edenbridge Cl. SE16 . . . 5H 103
(off Masters Dr.)
Edenbridge Rd. E9 . . . 7K 67
EN1: Enf . . . 6K 23
Eden Cl. DA5: Bexl . . . 4K 145
HA0: Wemb . . . 1D 78
NW3 . . . 2J 63
W8 . . . 3J 99
Eden Ct. IG6: Ilf . . . 1H 53
Edencourt Rd. SW16 . . . 6F 137
Edendale W3 . . . 7H 79
Edendale Rd. DA7: Bex . . . 1K 127
Edenfield Gdns. KT4: Wor Pk . . . 3B 164
Eden Gro. E17 . . . 5D 50
N7 . . . 5K 65
NW10 . . . 6D 62
Edenham Way W10 . . . 4H 81
Eden Ho. NW8 . . . 4C 4
(off Church St.)
SE8 . . . 7C 104
(off Deptford High St.)
SE16 . . . 2K 103
(off Water Gdns. Sq.)
Edenhurst Av. SW6 . . . 3H 117
Eden Lodge NW6 . . . 7F 63
Eden M. SW17 . . . 3A 136
EDEN PARK . . . 5C 158
Eden Pk. Av. BR3: Beck . . . 4A 158
(not continuous)
Eden Rd. BR3: Beck . . . 4A 158
CR0: C'don . . . 4D 168
DA5: Bexl . . . 4J 145
E17 . . . 5D 50
SE27 . . . 4B 138
Edensor Gdns. W4 . . . 7A 98
Edensor Rd. W4 . . . 7A 98
Eden St. KT1: King T . . . 2D 150
Edenvale Cl. CR4: Mitc . . . 7E 136
Edenvale Rd. CR4: Mitc . . . 7E 136
Edenvale St. SW6 . . . 2A 118
Eden Wlk. KT1: King T . . . 2E 150
Eden Way BR3: Beck . . . 5B 158
E3 . . . 1B 86
Ederline Av. SW16 . . . 3K 155
Edgar Ct. KT3: N Mald . . . 2A 152
Edgar Ho. E9 . . . 5A 68
(off Homerton Rd.)
E11 . . . 7J 51
SW8 . . . 7J 101
(off Wyvil Rd.)
Edgar Kail Way SE22 . . . 4E 120
Edgarley Ter. SW6 . . . 1G 117
Edgar Myles Ho. E16 . . . 5H 87
(off Ordnance Rd.)
Edgar Rd. E3 . . . 3D 86
RM6: Chad H . . . 7D 54
TW4: Houn . . . 7D 112
UB7: Yiew . . . 7A 74
Edgar Wallace Cl. SE15 . . . 7E 102
Edgar Wright Ct. SW6 . . . 7H 99
(off Dawes Rd.)
Edgcott Ho. W10 . . . 5E 80
(off Sutton Way)
Edge Apartments E15 . . . 7F 69
Edgeborough Way BR1: Brom . . . 7B 142
Edgebury BR7: Chst . . . 4F 143
Edgebury Wlk. BR7: Chst . . . 4G 143
Edge Bus. Cen., The NW2 . . . 2D 62
Edgecombe Ho. SE5 . . . 2E 120
SW19 . . . 1G 135
Edgecoombe CR2: Sels . . . 7J 169
Edgecoombe Cl. KT2: King T . . . 7K 133
Edgecote Cl. W3 . . . 1J 97
Edgecot Gro. N15 . . . 5E 48
Edgefield Av. IG11: Bark . . . 7K 71
Edgefield Ct. IG11: Bark . . . 7K 71
(off Edgefield Av.)
Edge Hill SE18 . . . 6F 107
SW19 . . . 7F 135
Edge Hill Av. N3 . . . 4J 45
Edge Hill Ct. DA14: Sidc . . . 4K 143
SW19 . . . 7F 135
Edgehill Gdns. RM10: Dag . . . 4G 73
Edgehill Ho. SW9 . . . 2B 120
Edgehill Rd. BR7: Chst . . . 3G 143
CR4: Mitc . . . 1F 155
W13 . . . 5C 78
Edgeley La. SW4 . . . 3H 119
Edgeley Rd. SW4 . . . 3H 119
Edgel St. SW18 . . . 4K 117
Edge Point Cl. SE27 . . . 5B 138
Edge St. W8 . . . 1J 99
Edgewood Dr. BR6: Chels . . . 5K 173
Edgewood Grn. CR0: C'don . . . 1K 169
Edgeworth Av. NW4 . . . 5C 44
Edgeworth Cl. NW4 . . . 5C 44
Edgeworth Ct. EN4: Cockf . . . 4H 21
(off Fordham Rd.)
Edgeworth Cres. NW4 . . . 5C 44
Edgeworth Ho. NW8 . . . 1A 82
(off Boundary Rd.)
Edgeworth Rd. EN4: Cockf . . . 4H 21
SE9 . . . 4A 124
Edgington Rd. SW16 . . . 6H 137
Edgington Way DA14: Sidc . . . 7C 144
Edgson Ho. SW1 . . . 5J 17
(off Ebury Bri. Rd.)
EDGWARE . . . 6B 28
EDGWARE BURY . . . 1A 28
Edgwarebury Gdns.
HA8: Edg . . . 5B 28
Edgwarebury La. HA8: Edg . . . 1A 28
WD6: E'tree . . . 1A 28
Edgware Ct. HA8: Edg . . . 6B 28
Edgware Rd. NW2 . . . 1D 62
NW9 . . . 2J 43
W2 . . . 4A 4 (4B 82)
Edgware Way HA8: Edg . . . 4A 28
NW7 . . . 4A 28
WD6: E'tree . . . 1J 27
Edinburgh Cl. E2 . . . 2J 85
HA5: Pinn . . . 7B 40
UB10: Ick . . . 4D 56
Edinburgh Ct. DA8: Erith . . . 7K 109
KT1: King T . . . 3E 150
(off Watersplash Cl.)
SE16 . . . 1K 103
(off Rotherhithe St.)
SW20 . . . 5F 153
Edinburgh Dr. UB10: Ick . . . 4D 56
Edinburgh Ga. SW1 . . . 7E 10 (2D 100)
Edinburgh Ho. NW4 . . . 3E 44
W9 . . . 3K 81
(off Maida Va.)
Edinburgh Rd. E13 . . . 2K 87
E17 . . . 5C 50
(not continuous)
N18 . . . 5B 34
SM1: Sutt . . . 2A 166
W7 . . . 2K 95
Edington NW5 . . . 6E 64
Edington Rd. EN3: Enf H . . . 2D 24
SE2 . . . 3B 108
Edison Bldg. E14 . . . 2C 104
Edison Cl. E17 . . . 5C 50
UB7: W Dray . . . 2B 92
Edison Ct. CR0: C'don . . . 7B 156
(off Campbell Rd.)
SE10 . . . 3H 105
(off Schoolbank Rd.)
Edison Dr. HA9: Wemb . . . 3E 60
UB1: S'hall . . . 6F 77
Edison Gro. SE18 . . . 7K 107
Edison Ho. HA9: Wemb . . . 3J 61
(off Barnhill Rd.)
SE1 . . . 4D 102
(off New Kent Rd.)
Edison Rd. BR2: Brom . . . 2J 159
DA16: Well . . . 1K 125
EN3: Brim . . . 2G 25
N8 . . . 6H 47
Edis St. NW1 . . . 1E 82
Editha Mans. SW10 . . . 6A 100
(off Edith Gro.)
Edith Brinson Ho. E14 . . . 6F 87
(off Oban St.)
Edith Cavell Cl. N19 . . . 7J 47
Edith Cavell Way SE18 . . . 1C 124
Edith Gdns. KT5: Surb . . . 7H 151
Edith Gro. SW10 . . . 6A 100
Edith Ho. W6 . . . 5E 98
(off Queen Caroline St.)
Edithna St. SW9 . . . 3J 119
Edith Nesbit Wlk. SE9 . . . 5D 124
Edith Neville Cotts. NW1 . . . 1C 6
(off Drummond Cres.)
Edith Ramsay Ho. E1 . . . 5A 86
(off Duckett St.)
Edith Rd. E6 . . . 7B 70
E15 . . . 5F 69
N11 . . . 7C 32
RM6: Chad H . . . 7D 54
SE25 . . . 5D 156
SW19 . . . 6K 135
W14 . . . 4G 99
Edith Row SW6 . . . 1K 117
Edith St. E2 . . . 2G 85
Edith Summerskill Ho. SW6 . . . 7H 99
(off Clem Attlee Est.)
Edith Ter. SW10 . . . 7A 100
Edith Vs. W14 . . . 4H 99
Edith Yd. SW10 . . . 7A 100
Edmansons Cl. N17 . . . 1F 49
Edmeston Cl. E9 . . . 6A 68
Edmond Ct. SE14 . . . 1J 121
Edmonscote W13 . . . 5A 78
EDMONTON . . . 3B 34
Edmonton Ct. SE16 . . . 3J 103
(off Canada Est.)

Edmonton Grn. Shop. Cen.—Elgar Av.

Edmonton Grn. Shop. Cen. N9 2B **34**
Edmonton Leisure Cen. 3B **34**
Edmund Gro. TW13: Hanw 2D **130**
Edmund Halley Way SE10 2G **105**
Edmund Ho. SE17 6B **102**
Edmund Hurst Dr. E6 5F **89**
Edmund Rd. CR4: Mitc 3C **154**
DA16: Well 3A **126**
Edmundsbury Ct. Est. SW9 4K **119**
Edmunds Cl. UB4: Yead 5A **76**
Edmund St. SE5 7D **102**
Edmunds Wlk. N2 4C **46**
Ednam Ho. *SE15* *6G 103*
(off Haymerle Rd.)
Edna Rd. SW20 2F **153**
Edna St. SW11 1C **118**
Edred Ho. *E9* *4A 68*
(off Lindisfarne Way)
Edrich Ho. SW4 1J **119**
Edric Ho. *SW1* *3D 18*
(off Page St.)
Edrick Rd. HA8: Edg 6D **28**
Edrick Wlk. HA8: Edg 6D **28**
Edric Rd. SE14 7K **103**
Edridge Rd. CR0: C'don 3C **168**
Edward VII Mans. *NW10* *3F 81*
(off Chamberlayne Rd.)
Edward Alderton Theatre 3D **126**
Edward Av. E4 6J **35**
SM4: Mord 5B **154**
Edward Bond Ho. *WC1* *2F 7*
(off Cromer St.)
Edward Clifford Ho. *SE17* *4D 102*
(off Elsted St.)
Edward Cl. N9 7A **24**
NW2 4F **63**
TW12: Ham H 5G **131**
Edward Ct. E16 5J **87**
Edward Dodd Ct. *N1* *1F 9*
(off Chart St.)
Edward Edward's Ho. SE1 5A **14**
Edwardes Pl. W8 3H **99**
Edwardes Sq. W8 3H **99**
Edward Gro. EN4: E Barn 5G **21**
Edward Heylyn Ho. *E3* *2C 86*
(off Thomas Frye Dr.)
Edward Ho. SE11 5H **19**
W2 *4A 4*
(off Hall Pl.)
Edward Kennedy Ho. *W10* *4G 81*
(off Wornington Rd.)
Edward Mann Cl. *E1* *6K 85*
(off Pitsea St.)
Edward M. NW1 1K **5** (3F **83**)
Edward Pl. SE8 6B **104**
Edward Rd. BR1: Brom 7K **141**
BR7: Chst 5F **143**
CR0: C'don 7E **156**
E17 4K **49**
EN4: E Barn 5G **21**
HA2: Harr 3G **41**
RM6: Chad H 6E **54**
SE20 7K **139**
TW12: Ham H 5G **131**
TW14: Felt 5F **111**
UB5: N'olt 2A **76**
Edward Robinson Ho. *SE14* *7K 103*
(off Reaston St.)
Edward's Av. HA4: Ruis 6K **57**
Edwards Cl. KT4: Wor Pk 2F **165**
Edward's Cotts. N1 6B **66**
Edwards Ct. *CR0: C'don* *4E 168*
(off South Pk. Hill Rd.)
Edwards Dr. N11 7C **32**
Edward's La. N16 2E **66**
Edwards Mans. *IG11: Bark* *7K 71*
(off Upney La.)
Edwards M. N1 7A **66**
W1 1G **11** (6E **82**)
Edward Sq. N1 1K **83**
SE16 1A **104**
Edwards Rd. DA17: Belv 4G **109**
Edward St. E16 4J **87**
(not continuous)
SE8 6B **104**
SE14 7A **104**
Edwards Yd. HA0: Wemb 1E **78**
Edward Temme Av. E15 7H **69**
Edward Tyler Rd. SE12 2A **142**
Edward Way TW15: Ashf 2B **128**
Edwina Gdns. IG4: Ilf 5C **52**
Edwin Arnold Ct. DA14: Sidc 4K **143**
Edwin Av. E6 2E **88**
(not continuous)
Edwin Cl. DA7: Bex 6F **109**
Edwin Hall Pl. SE13 6F **123**
Edwin Ho. SE15 7G **103**
Edwin Pl. *CR0: C'don* *1E 168*
(off Leslie Gro.)
Edwin Rd. HA8: Edg 6E **28**
TW1: Twick 1K **131**
TW2: Twick 1J **131**
Edwin's Mead E9 4A **68**
Edwin Stray Ho. TW13: Hanw 2E **130**
Edwin St. E1 4J **85**
E16 5J **87**
Edwin Ware Ct. HA5: Pinn 2A **40**
Edwyn Cl. EN5: Barn 6A **20**
Edwyn Ho. *SW18* *6K 117*
(off Neville Gill Cl.)
Eel Brook Cl. SW6 1K **117**
Eel Pie Island TW1: Twick 1A **132**
Effie Pl. SW6 7J **99**
Effie Rd. SW6 7J **99**
Effingham Cl. SM2: Sutt 7K **165**
Effingham Lodge KT1: King T 4D **150**
Effingham Rd. CR0: C'don 7K **155**
KT6: Surb 7B **150**
N8 5A **48**
SE12 5G **123**
Effort St. SW17 5C **136**
Effra Cl. SW19 6K **135**
Effra Ct. *SW2* *5K 119*
(off Brixton Hill)
Effra Pde. SW2 5A **120**
Effra Rd. SW2 4A **120**
SW19 6K **135**
Effra Rd. Retail Pk. SW2 5A **120**
Egan Way UB3: Hayes 7G **75**
Egbert St. NW1 1E **82**
Egbury Ho. *SW15* *6B 116*
(off Tangley Gro.)
Egeremont Rd. SE13 2D **122**
Egerton Cl. HA5: Eastc 4J **39**
Egerton Ct. E11 7F **51**
Egerton Cres. SW3 3D **16** (4C **100**)
Egerton Dr. SE10 1D **122**
Egerton Gdns. IG3: Ilf 3K **71**
NW4 4D **44**
NW10 1E **80**
SW3 2C **16** (4C **100**)
W13 6B **78**
Egerton Gdns. M. SW3 2D **16** (3C **100**)
Egerton Pl. SW3 2D **16** (3C **100**)
Egerton Rd. HA0: Wemb 7F **61**
KT3: N Mald 4B **152**
N16 7F **49**
SE25 3E **156**
TW2: Twick 7J **113**
Egerton Ter. SW3 2D **16** (3C **100**)
Egerton Way UB3: Harl 7D **92**
Eggardon Ct. UB5: N'olt 6F **59**
Egham Cl. SM3: Cheam 2G **165**
SW19 2G **135**
Egham Cres. SM3: Cheam 3G **165**
Egham Rd. E13 5K **87**
Eglantine Rd. SW18 5A **118**
Egleston Rd. SM4: Mord 6K **153**
Eglington Ct. SE17 6C **102**
Eglington Rd. E4 7K **25**
Eglinton Hill SE18 6F **107**
Eglinton Rd. SE18 6E **106**
Egliston M. SW15 3E **116**
Egliston Rd. SW15 3E **116**
Eglon M. NW1 7D **64**
Egmont Av. KT6: Surb 1F **163**
Egmont Ct. *KT12: Walt T* *7K 147*
(off Egmont Rd.)
Egmont M. KT19: Ewe 4K **163**
Egmont Rd. KT3: N Mald 4B **152**
KT6: Surb 1F **163**
KT12: Walt T 7K **147**
SM2: Sutt 7A **166**
Egmont St. SE14 7K **103**
Egremont Ho. *SE13* *2D 122*
(off Russett Way)
Egremont Rd. SE27 3A **138**
Egret Ho. *SE16* *4K 103*
(off Tawny Way)
Egret Way UB4: Yead 5B **76**
Eider Cl. E7 5H **69**
UB4: Yead 5B **76**
Eider Ct. *SE8* *6B 104*
(off Pilot Cl.)
Eighteenth Rd. CR4: Mitc 4J **155**
Eighth Av. E12 4D **70**
UB3: Hayes 1J **93**
Eileen Rd. SE25 5D **156**
Eindhoven Cl. SM5: Cars 1E **166**
Einstein Ho. HA9: Wemb 3J **61**
Eisenhower Dr. E6 5C **88**
Ekarro Ho. *SW8* *1J 119*
(off Guildford Rd.)
Elaine Gro. NW5 5E **64**
Elam Cl. SE5 2B **120**
Elam St. SE5 2B **120**
Elan Ct. E1 5H **85**
Eland Ho. (Department for Transport)
SW1 1A **18**
Eland Pl. CR0: Wadd 3B **168**
Eland Rd. CR0: Wadd 3B **168**
SW11 3D **118**
Elba Pl. SE17 4C **102**
Elberon Av. CR0: Bedd 6G **155**
Elbe St. SW6 2A **118**
Elborough Rd. SE25 5G **157**
Elborough St. SW18 1J **135**
Elbourne Ct. *SE16* *3K 103*
(off Worgan St.)
Elbourne Trad. Est.
DA17: Belv 3H **109**
Elbourn Ho. *SW3* *5C 16*
(off Cale St.)
Elbow Mdw. SL3: Poyle 4A **174**
Elbury Dr. E16 6J **87**
Elcho St. SW11 7C **100**
Elcot Av. SE15 7H **103**
Elden Ho. *SW3* *3C 16*
(off Sloane Av.)
Eldenwall Ind. Est.
RM8: Dag 1E **72**
Elder Av. N8 5J **47**
Elderberry Gro. SE27 4C **138**
Elderberry Rd. W5 2E **96**
Elderberry Way E6 3D **88**
Elder Cl. DA15: Sidc 1K **143**
N20 2E **30**
UB7: Yiew 7A **74**
Elder Ct. WD23: B Hea 2D **26**
Elderfield Ho. E14 7C **86**
Elderfield Pl. SW17 4F **137**
Elderfield Rd. E5 4K **67**
Elderfield Wlk. E11 5K **51**
Elderflower Way E15 7G **69**
Elder Gdns. SE27 5C **138**
Elder Oak Cl. SE20 1H **157**
Elder Oak Ct. *SE20* *1H 157*
(off Anerley Ct.)
Elder Rd. SE27 5C **138**
Elderslie Cl. BR3: Beck 5C **158**
Elderslie Rd. SE9 5E **124**
Elder St. E1 5J **9** (4F **85**)
(not continuous)
Elderton Rd. SE26 4A **140**
Eldertree Pl. CR4: Mitc 1G **155**
Eldertree Way CR4: Mitc 1G **155**
Elder Wlk. *N1* *1B 84*
(off Popham St.)
SE13 3E **122**
Elderwood Pl. SE27 5C **138**
Eldon Av. CR0: C'don 2J **169**
TW5: Hest 7E **94**
Eldon Ct. NW6 1J **81**
Eldon Gro. NW3 5B **64**
Eldon Pk. SE25 4H **157**
Eldon Rd. E17 4B **50**
N9 1D **34**
N22 1B **48**
W8 3K **99**
Eldon St. EC2 6F **9** (5D **84**)
Eldon Way NW10 3H **79**
Eldred Rd. IG11: Bark 1J **89**
Eldrick Ct. TW14: Bedf 1F **129**
Eldridge Cl. TW14: Felt 1J **129**
Eldridge Ct. RM10: Dag 6H **73**
SE16 3G **103**
Eleanor Cl. N15 3F **49**
SE16 2K **103**
Eleanor Ct. *E2* *1G 85*
(off Whiston Rd.)
Eleanor Cres. NW7 5A **30**
Eleanor Gdns. EN5: Barn 5A **20**
RM8: Dag 2F **73**
Eleanor Gro. SW13 3A **116**
UB10: Ick 3D **56**
Eleanor Ho. *W6* *5E 98*
(off Queen Caroline St.)
Eleanor Rathbone Ho. *N6* *7H 47*
(off Avenue Rd.)
Eleanor Rd. E8 6H **67**
E15 6H **69**
N11 6D **32**
Eleanor's Station
Ruislip Lido Railway 3G **39**
Eleanor St. E3 3C **86**
Eleanor Wlk. SE18 4C **106**
Electra Av. TW6: H'row A 3H **111**
Electra Bus. Pk. E16 5F **87**
Electric Av. SW9 4A **120**
Electric Empire, The *SE14* *1K 121*
(off New Cross Rd.)
Electric Ho. *E3* *3C 86*
(off Bow Rd.)
Electric La. SW9 4A **120**
(not continuous)
Electric Pde. *E18* *2J 51*
(off George La.)
IG3: Ilf 2J **71**
KT6: Surb 6D **150**
Elektron Ho. E14 7F **87**
ELEPHANT & CASTLE 3B **102**
Elephant & Castle SE1 4B **102**
Elephant & Castle Leisure Cen. 4B **102**
Elephant & Castle Shop. Cen.
SE1 4C **102**
Elephant La. SE16 2J **103**
Elephant Rd. SE17 4C **102**
Elers Rd. UB3: Harl 4F **93**
W13 2C **96**
Eley Rd. N18 4D **34**
Eley Rd. Retail Pk. N18 5D **34**
Eleys Est. N18 3E **34**
Elfindale Rd. SE24 5C **120**
Elfin Gro. TW11: Tedd 5K **131**
Elford Cl. SE3 4K **123**
Elford M. SW4 5G **119**
Elfort Rd. N5 4A **66**
Elfrida Cres. SE6 4C **140**
Elf Row E1 7J **85**
Elfwine Rd. W7 5J **77**
Elgal Cl. BR6: Farnb 5F **173**
Elgar *N8* *3J 47*
(off Boyton Cl.)
Elgar Av. KT5: Surb 1G **163**
NW10 6K **61**
(not continuous)
SW16 3J **155**
W5 2E **96**

Elgar Cl.—Elmcroft Av.

Elgar Cl. E13 2A **88**
IG9: Buck H 2G **37**
SE8 7C **104**
UB10: Ick 2C **56**
Elgar Ct. W9 3H **81**
W14 3G 99
(off Blythe Rd.)
Elgar Ho. *NW6 7A 64*
(off Fairfax Rd.)
SW1 6K 17
(off Churchill Gdns.)
Elgar St. SE16 3A **104**
Elgin Av. HA3: Kenton 2B **42**
TW15: Ashf 6E **128**
W9 4H **81**
W12 2C **98**
Elgin Cl. W12 2D **98**
Elgin Ct. *CR2: S Croy 4C 168*
(off Bramley Hill)
W9 4K **81**
Elgin Cres. TW6: H'row A 2G **111**
W11 7G **81**
Elgin Dr. HA6: Nwood 1G **39**
Elgin Est. *W9 4J 81*
(off Elgin Av.)
Elgin Ho. *E14 6D 86*
(off Ricardo St.)
RM6: Chad H 6F 55
(off High Rd.)
Elgin Mans. W9 3K **81**
Elgin M. W11 6G **81**
Elgin M. Nth. W9 3K **81**
Elgin M. Sth. W9 3K **81**
Elgin Rd. CR0: C'don 2F **169**
IG3: Ilf 1J **71**
N22 2G **47**
SM1: Sutt 3A **166**
SM6: Wall 6G **167**
Elgood Cl. W11 7G **81**
Elgood Ho. *NW8 2B 82*
(off Wellington Rd.)
SE1 2D 102
(off Nebraska St.)
Elham Cl. BR1: Brom 7B **142**
Elham Ho. E5 5H **67**
Elia M. N1 1A **8** (2B **84**)
Elias Pl. SW8 6A **102**
Elia St. N1 1B **8** (2B **84**)
Elibank Rd. SE9 4D **124**
Elim Est. SE1 7G **15** (3E **102**)
Elim St. SE1 7G **15** (3D **102**)
(not continuous)
Elim Way E13 3H **87**
Eliot Bank SE23 2H **139**
Eliot Cotts. SE3 2G **123**
Eliot Ct. SW18 6K **117**
Eliot Dr. HA2: Harr 2F **59**
Eliot Gdns. SW15 4C **116**
Eliot Hill SE13 2E **122**
Eliot M. NW8 2A **82**
Eliot Pk. SE13 2E **122**
Eliot Pl. SE3 2G **123**
Eliot Rd. RM9: Dag 4D **72**
Eliot Va. SE3 2F **123**
Elis David Almshouses
CR0: C'don 3B **168**
Elizabethan Cl. TW19: Stanw 7A **110**
Elizabethan Way TW19: Stanw 7A **110**
Elizabeth Av. EN2: Enf 3G **23**
IG1: Ilf 2H **71**
N1 1C **84**
TW18: Staines 7A **128**
Elizabeth Barnes Ct. *SW6 2K 117*
(off Marinefield Rd.)
Elizabeth Blackwell Ho. *N22 1A 48*
(off Progress Way)
Elizabeth Blount Ct. *E14 6A 86*
(off Carr St.)
Elizabeth Bri. SW1 4J **17** (4F **101**)
Elizabeth Cl. E14 6D **86**
EN5: Barn 3A **20**
RM7: Mawney 1H **55**
Elizabeth Cl. SM1: Sutt 4H **165**
W9 4A **82**
Elizabeth Clyde Cl. N15 4E **48**
Elizabeth Cotts.
TW9: Kew 1F **115**
Elizabeth Ct. *BR1: Brom 1H 159*
(off Highland Rd.)
CR0: C'don 3E 168
(off The Avenue)
E4 5G **35**
E10 7D **50**
IG8: Wfd G 7F **37**
KT2: King T 1E **150**
NW1 3D **4**
SW1 2D **18**
SW10 6B 100
(off Milman's St.)
TW11: Tedd 5J **131**
TW16: Sun 3A 148
(off Elizabeth Gdns.)
Elizabeth Croll Ho. *WC1 1H 7*
(off Penton Ri.)
Elizabeth Fry Ho. UB3: Harl 4H **93**
Elizabeth Fry M. E8 7H **67**
Elizabeth Fry Pl. SE18 1C **124**
Elizabeth Gdns. HA7: Stan 6H **27**
TW7: Isle 4A **114**
TW16: Sun 3A **148**
W3 1B **98**
Elizabeth Garrett Anderson Ho.
DA17: Belv 3G 109
(off Ambrook Rd.)
Elizabeth Ho. *E3 3D 86*
(off St Leonard's St.)
SE11 4K 19
(off Reedworth St.)
SM3: Cheam 6G 165
(off Park La.)
W6 5E 98
(off Queen Caroline St.)
Elizabeth Ind. Est. SE14 6K **103**
Elizabeth M. *E2 2G 85*
(off Kay St.)
HA1: Harr 6J **41**
NW3 6C **64**
Elizabeth Newcomen Ho. *SE1 6E 14*
(off Newcomen St.)
Elizabeth Pl. N15 4D **48**
Elizabeth Ride N9 7C **24**
Elizabeth Rd. E6 1B **88**
N15 5E **48**
Elizabeth Sq. *SE16 7A 86*
(off Sovereign Cres.)
Elizabeth St. SW1 3H **17** (4E **100**)
Elizabeth Ter. SE9 6D **124**
Elizabeth Way SE19 7D **138**
TW13: Hanw 4A **130**
Elkanette M. N20 2F **31**
Elkington Point SE11 4J **19**
Elkington Rd. E13 4K **87**
Elkstone Rd. W10 5H **81**
Ella Cl. BR3: Beck 2C **158**
Ellacott M. SW16 2H **137**
Ellaline Rd. W6 6F **99**
Ella M. NW3 4D **64**
Ellanby Cres. N18 4C **34**
Elland Cl. EN5: New Bar 5G **21**
Elland Ho. *E14 6B 86*
(off Copenhagen Pl.)
Elland Rd. SE15 4J **121**
Ella Rd. N8 7J **47**
Ellement Cl. HA5: Pinn 5B **40**
Ellena Ct. *N14 3D 32*
(off Conway Rd.)
Ellenborough Ho. *W12 7D 80*
(off White City Est.)
Ellenborough Pl. SW15 4C **116**
Ellenborough Rd. DA14: Sidc 5D **144**
N22 1C **48**
Ellenbridge Way
CR2: Sande 7E **168**
Ellen Cl. BR1: Brom 3B **160**
Ellen Ct. *E4 1K 35*
(off The Ridgeway)
N9 2D **34**
Ellen Julia Ct. *E1 6J 85*
(off James Voller Way)
Ellen St. E1 6G **85**
Ellen Terry Ct. *NW1 7F 65*
(off Farrier St.)
Ellen Webb Dr. HA3: W'stone 3J **41**
Ellen Wilkinson Ho. *E2 3K 85*
(off Usk St.)
RM10: Dag 3G **73**
SW6 6H 99
(off Clem Attlee Ct.)
Elleray Rd. TW11: Tedd 6K **131**
Ellerby St. SW6 1F **117**
Ellerdale Cl. NW3 4A **64**
Ellerdale Rd. NW3 5A **64**
Ellerdale St. SE13 4D **122**
Ellerdine Rd. TW3: Houn 4G **113**
Ellerker Gdns. TW10: Rich 6E **114**
Ellerman Av. TW2: Whitt 1D **130**
Ellerslie Gdns. NW10 1C **80**
Ellerslie Rd. W12 1D **98**
Ellerslie Sq. Ind. Est. SW2 5J **119**
Ellerton Gdns. RM9: Dag 7C **72**
Ellerton Lodge N3 2J **45**
Ellerton Rd. KT6: Surb 2F **163**
RM9: Dag 7C **72**
SW13 1C **116**
SW18 1B **136**
SW20 7C **134**
Ellery Ho. SE17 4D **102**
Ellery Rd. SE19 7D **138**
Ellery St. SE15 2H **121**
Ellesmere Av. BR3: Beck 2D **158**
NW7 3E **28**
Ellesmere Cl. E11 5H **51**
HA4: Ruis 7E **38**
Ellesmere Ct. SE12 1J **141**
W4 5K **97**
Ellesmere Gdns. IG4: Ilf 5C **52**
Ellesmere Gro. EN5: Barn 5C **20**
Ellesmere Ho. *SW10 6A 100*
(off Fulham Rd.)
Ellesmere Mans. *NW6 6A 64*
(off Canfield Gdns.)
Ellesmere Rd. E3 2A **86**
NW10 5C **62**
TW1: Twick 6C **114**
UB6: G'frd 4G **77**
W4 6J **97**
Ellesmere St. E14 6D **86**
Ellies M. TW15: Ashf 2A **128**
Ellingfort Rd. E8 7H **67**
Ellingham Rd. E15 4F **69**
KT9: Chess 6D **162**
W12 2C **98**
Ellington Ct. N14 2C **32**
Ellington Ho. SE1 3C **102**
Ellington Rd. N10 4F **47**
TW3: Houn 2F **113**
TW13: Felt 4H **129**
Ellington St. N7 6A **66**
Elliot Cl. E15 7G **69**
HA9: Wemb 3F **61**
Elliot Ct. IG8: Wfd G 6G **37**
Elliot Ho. *SW17 3B 136*
(off Grosvenor Way)
W1 6D 4
(off Cato St.)
Elliot Rd. NW4 6D **44**
Elliott Av. HA4: Ruis 2K **57**
Elliott Gdns. TW17: Shep 4C **146**
Elliott Rd. BR2: Brom 4B **160**
CR7: Thor H 4B **156**
HA7: Stan 6F **27**
SW9 1B **120**
W4 4A **98**
Elliott's Pl. N1 1B **84**
Elliott Sq. NW3 7C **64**
Elliotts Row SE11 4B **102**
Ellis Cl. HA8: Edg 6F **29**
NW10 6D **62**
SE9 2G **143**
Elliscombe Mt. SE7 6A **106**
Elliscombe Rd. SE7 6A **106**
Ellis Ct. *E1 6J 85*
(off James Voller Way)
W7 5K **77**
Ellisfield Dr. SW15 7C **116**
Ellis Franklin Ct. *NW8 2A 82*
(off Abbey Rd.)
Ellis Ho. *SE17 5D 102*
(off Brandon St.)
Ellison Gdns. UB2: S'hall 4D **94**
Ellison Ho. *SE13 2D 122*
(off Lewisham Rd.)
Ellison Rd. DA15: Sidc 1H **143**
SW13 2B **116**
SW16 7H **137**
Ellis Rd. CR4: Mitc 6D **154**
UB2: S'hall 1G **95**
Ellis St. SW1 3F **17** (4E **100**)
Elliston Ho. *SE18 4E 106*
(off Wellington St.)
Ellora Rd. SW16 5H **137**
Ellswood Ct. KT6: Surb 7D **150**
Ellsworth St. E2 3H **85**
Ellwood Ct. *W9 4K 81*
(off Clearwell Dr.)
Elmar Rd. N15 4D **48**
Elm Av. HA4: Ruis 1J **57**
TW19: Stanw 2A **128**
W5 1E **96**
Elmbank N14 7D **22**
Elmbank Av. EN5: Barn 4A **20**
Elm Bank Dr. BR1: Brom 2B **160**
Elm Bank Gdns. SW13 2A **116**
Elmbank Way W7 5H **77**
Elmbourne Dr. DA17: Belv 4H **109**
Elmbourne Rd. SW17 3F **137**
Elmbridge Av. KT5: Surb 5H **151**
Elmbridge Cl. HA4: Ruis 6J **39**
Elmbridge Dr. HA4: Ruis 5H **39**
Elmbridge Wlk. E8 7G **67**
Elmbridge Xcel Leisure Complex 5K **147**
Elmbrook Cl. TW16: Sun 1K **147**
Elmbrook Gdns. SE9 4C **124**
Elmbrook Rd. SM1: Sutt 4H **165**
Elm Cl. CR2: S Croy 6E **168**
E11 6K **51**
HA2: Harr 6F **41**
IG9: Buck H 2G **37**
KT5: Surb 7J **151**
N19 2G **65**
NW4 5F **45**
RM7: Mawney 1H **55**
SM5: Cars 1D **166**
SW20 4E **152**
TW2: Twick 2F **131**
UB3: Hayes 6J **75**
Elmcote HA5: Pinn 2B **40**
Elm Cotts. CR4: Mitc 2D **154**
Elm Ct. CR4: Mitc 2D **154**
EC4 1J **13**
EN4: E Barn 7H **21**
KT8: W Mole 4F **149**
SE1 7G 15
(off Royal Oak Yd.)
SE13 3F **123**
SW9 1A 120
(off Cranworth Gdns.)
TW16: Sun 7H 129
(off Grangewood Dr.)
W9 5J 81
(off Admiral Wlk.)
Elmcourt Rd. SE27 2B **138**
Elm Cres. KT2: King T 1E **150**
W5 1E **96**
Elmcroft N6 7G **47**
N8 5K **47**
Elmcroft Av. DA15: Sidc 7K **125**
E11 5K **51**

Elmcroft Av.—Eltham Grn.

Elmcroft Av. N9 6C **24**
NW11 7H **45**
Elmcroft Cl. E11 4K **51**
KT9: Chess 3E **162**
TW14: Felt 6H **111**
W5 6D **78**
Elmcroft Cres. HA2: Harr 3E **40**
NW11 7G **45**
Elmcroft Dr. KT9: Chess 3E **162**
TW15: Ashf 5C **128**
Elmcroft Gdns. NW9 4G **43**
Elmcroft St. E5 4J **67**
Elmcroft Ter. UB8: Hil 6C **74**
Elmdale Rd. N13 5E **32**
Elmdene KT5: Surb 1J **163**
Elmdene Cl. BR3: Beck 6B **158**
Elmdene Rd. SE18 5F **107**
Elmdon Rd. TW4: Houn 2B **112**
TW6: H'row A 3H **111**
Elm Dr. HA2: Harr 6F **41**
TW16: Sun 2A **148**
Elmer Cl. EN2: Enf 3E **22**
Elmer Gdns. HA8: Edg 7C **28**
TW7: Isle 3H **113**
Elmer Ho. *NW8* *5C* ***4***
(off Penfold St.)
Elmer Rd. SE6 7E **122**
Elmers Dr. TW11: Tedd 6B **132**
ELMERS END 4K **157**
Elmers End Rd. BR3: Beck 2J **157**
SE20 2J **157**
Elmerside Rd. BR3: Beck 4A **158**
Elmers Lodge BR3: Beck 4K **157**
Elmers Rd. SE25 7G **157**
Elmfield HA1: Harr 7K **41**
Elmfield Av. CR4: Mitc 1E **154**
N8 5J **47**
TW11: Tedd 5K **131**
Elmfield Cl. HA1: Harr 2J **59**
Elmfield Ct. DA16: Well 1B **126**
Elmfield Ho. *N2* *2B* ***46***
(off The Grange)
NW8 *2K* ***81***
(off Carlton Hill)
W9 *4J* ***81***
(off Goldney Rd.)
Elmfield Pk. BR1: Brom 3J **159**
Elmfield Rd. BR1: Brom 2J **159**
E4 2K **35**
E17 6K **49**
N2 3B **46**
SW17 2E **136**
UB2: S'hall 3C **94**
Elmfield Way CR2: Sande 7F **169**
W9 5J **81**
Elm Friars Wlk. NW1 7H **65**
Elm Gdns. CR4: Mitc 4H **155**
KT10: Clay 6A **162**
N2 3A **46**
Elmgate Av. TW13: Felt 3K **129**
Elmgate Gdns. HA8: Edg 5D **28**
Elm Grn. W3 6A **80**
Elmgreen Cl. E15 1G **87**
Elm Gro. BR6: Orp 1K **173**
DA8: Erith 7K **109**
HA2: Harr 7E **40**
IG8: Wfd G 5C **36**
KT2: King T 1E **150**
N8 6J **47**
NW2 4F **63**
SE15 2F **121**
SM1: Sutt 4K **165**
SW19 7G **135**
UB7: Yiew 7B **74**
Elmgrove Cres. HA1: Harr 5K **41**
Elmgrove Gdns. HA1: Harr 5A **42**
Elm Gro. Pde. SM6: Wall 3E **166**
Elm Gro. Rd. SW13 1C **116**
W5 2E **96**
Elmgrove Rd. CR0: C'don 7H **157**
HA1: Harr 5K **41**
HA3: W'stone 5A **42**
Elm Hall Gdns. E11 5K **51**
(not continuous)
Elm Ho. *E3* *1B* ***86***
(off Sycamore Av.)
E14 *2E* ***104***
(off E. Ferry Rd.)
KT2: King T *7F* ***133***
(off Elm Rd.)
W10 *4G* ***81***
(off Briar Wlk.)
Elmhurst DA17: Belv 6E **108**
Elmhurst Av. CR4: Mitc 7F **137**
N2 3B **46**
Elmhurst Ct. CR0: C'don 4D **168**
Elmhurst Dr. E18 2J **51**
Elmhurst Lodge SM2: Sutt 7A **166**
Elmhurst Mans. SW4 3H **119**
Elmhurst Rd. E7 7K **69**
N17 2F **49**
SE9 2C **142**
Elmhurst St. SW4 3H **119**
Elmington Cl. DA5: Bexl 6H **127**
Elmington Est. SE5 7D **102**
Elmington Rd. SE5 7D **102**
Elmira St. SE13 3D **122**
Elm La. SE6 2B **140**
Elm Lawn Cl. UB8: Uxb 7A **56**
Elmlea Dr. UB3: Hayes 5G **75**
Elm Lea Trad. Est. N17 6C **34**
Elmlee Cl. BR7: Chst 6D **142**
Elmley Cl. E6 5C **88**
Elmley St. SE18 5H **107**
(not continuous)
Elm Lodge SW6 1E **116**
Elmore Cl. HA0: Wemb 2E **78**
Elmore Ho. SW9 2B **120**
Elmore Rd. E11 3E **68**
EN3: Enf W 1E **24**
Elmore St. N1 7C **66**
Elm Pde. DA14: Sidc 4A **144**
Elm Pk. HA7: Stan 5G **27**
SW2 6K **119**
Elm Pk. Av. N15 5F **49**
Elm Pk. Chambers
SW10 *6A* ***16***
(off Fulham Rd.)
Elm Pk. Ct. HA5: Pinn 2A **40**
Elm Pk. Gdns. NW4 5F **45**
SW10 6A **16** (5B **100**)
Elm Pk. Ho. SW10 6A **16** (5B **100**)
Elm Pk. La. SW3 6A **16** (5B **100**)
Elm Pk. Mans. SW10 7A **16**
Elm Pk. Rd. E10 1A **68**
HA5: Pinn 2A **40**
N3 7C **30**
N21 7H **23**
SE25 3F **157**
SW3 7A **16** (6B **100**)
Elm Pas. EN5: Barn 4C **20**
Elm Pl. SW7 5A **16** (5B **100**)
TW15: Ashf 5C **128**
Elm Quay Ct. SW8 7C **18** (6H **101**)
Elm Rd. BR3: Beck 2B **158**
BR6: Chels 7K **173**
CR7: Thor H 4D **156**
DA14: Sidc 4A **144**
E7 6H **69**
E11 2F **69**
E17 5E **50**
EN5: Barn 4C **20**
HA9: Wemb 5E **60**
KT2: King T 1F **151**
KT3: N Mald 2K **151**
KT9: Chess 4E **162**
KT17: Ewe 6B **164**
N22 1B **48**
RM7: Mawney 2H **55**
SM6: Wall 1E **166**
SW14 3J **115**
TW14: Bedf 1F **129**
Elm Rd. W. SM3: Sutt 7H **153**
Elm Row NW3 3A **64**
Elms, The *CR0: C'don* *1C* ***168***
(off Tavistock Rd.)
E12 6B **70**
KT10: Clay 7A **162**
SW13 3B **116**
TW15: Ashf 5C **128**
Elms Av. N10 3F **47**
NW4 5F **45**
Elmscott Gdns. N21 6H **23**
Elmscott Rd. BR1: Brom 5G **141**
Elms Ct. HA0: Wemb 4A **60**
Elms Cres. SW4 6G **119**
Elmsdale Rd. E17 4B **50**
Elms Gdns. HA0: Wemb 4A **60**
RM9: Dag 4F **73**
Elmsgrove Point SE18 4H **107**
Elmshaw Rd. SW15 5C **116**
Elmshurst Cres. N2 4B **46**
Elmside CR0: New Ad 6D **170**
Elmside Rd. HA9: Wemb 3G **61**
Elms La. HA0: Wemb 3A **60**
Elmsleigh Av. HA3: Kenton 4B **42**
Elmsleigh Ct. SM1: Sutt 3K **165**
Elmsleigh Ho. *TW2: Twick* *2H* ***131***
(off Staines Rd.)
Elmsleigh Rd. TW2: Twick 2H **131**
Elmslie Cl. IG8: Wfd G 6J **37**
Elmslie Point *E3* *5B* ***86***
(off Leopold St.)
Elms M. W2 2A **10** (7B **82**)
Elms Pk. Av. HA0: Wemb 4A **60**
Elms Rd. HA3: Hrw W 7D **26**
SW4 5G **119**
ELMSTEAD 6D **142**
Elmstead Av. BR7: Chst 5D **142**
HA9: Wemb 1E **60**
Elmstead Cl. KT19: Ewe 5A **164**
N20 2D **30**
Elmstead Gdns. KT4: Wor Pk 3C **164**
Elmstead Glade BR7: Chst 6D **142**
Elmstead La. BR7: Chst 7C **142**
Elmstead Rd. DA8: Erith 1K **127**
IG3: Ilf 2J **71**
Elmsted Cres. DA16: Well 6C **108**
Elmstone Rd. SW6 1J **117**
Elm St. WC1 4H **7** (4K **83**)
Elmsway TW15: Ashf 5C **128**
Elmsworth Av. TW3: Houn 2F **113**
Elm Ter. HA3: Hrw W 1H **41**
NW2 3J **63**
NW3 4C **64**
SE9 6E **124**
Elm Terrace Fitness Cen. 6E **124**
Elmton Ct. *NW8* *3A* ***4***
(off Cunningham Pl.)
Elm Tree Av. KT10: Esh 7H **149**
Elm Tree Cl. NW8 1A **4** (3B **82**)
TW15: Ashf 5D **128**
UB5: N'olt 2D **76**
Elm Tree Ct. NW8 1A **4**
SE7 6A **106**
Elm Tree Rd. NW8 1A **4** (3B **82**)
Elmtree Rd. TW11: Tedd 4J **131**
Elm Vw. Ct. UB2: S'hall 4E **94**
Elm Vw. Ho. UB3: Harl 4F **93**
Elm Wlk. BR6: Farnb 3D **172**
NW3 2J **63**
SW20 4E **152**
Elm Way KT4: Wor Pk 3E **164**
KT19: Ewe 5K **163**
N11 6K **31**
NW10 4A **62**
Elmwood Av. HA3: Kenton 5A **42**
N13 5D **32**
TW13: Felt 2J **129**
Elmwood Cl. KT17: Ewe 7C **164**
SM6: Wall 2F **167**
Elmwood Ct. *E10* *1C* ***68***
(off Goldsmith Rd.)
HA0: Wemb 3A **60**
SW11 1F **119**
Elmwood Cres. NW9 4J **43**
Elmwood Dr. DA5: Bexl 7E **126**
KT17: Ewe 6C **164**
Elmwood Gdns. W7 6J **77**
Elmwood Ho. *NW10* *2D* ***80***
(off All Souls Av.)
Elmwood Rd. CR0: C'don 7B **156**
CR4: Mitc 3D **154**
SE24 5D **120**
W4 6J **97**
Elmworth Gro. SE21 2D **138**
Elnathan M. W9 4K **81**
Elphinstone Ct. SW16 6J **137**
Elphinstone Rd. E17 2B **50**
Elphinstone St. N5 4B **66**
Elrington Rd. E8 6G **67**
IG8: Wfd G 5D **36**
Elsa Cotts. *E14* *5A* ***86***
(off Halley St.)
Elsa Ct. BR3: Beck 1B **158**
Elsa Rd. DA16: Well 2B **126**
Elsa St. E1 5A **86**
Elsdale St. E9 6J **67**
Elsden M. E2 2J **85**
Elsden Rd. N17 1F **49**
Elsenham Rd. E12 5E **70**
Elsenham St. SW18 1H **135**
Elsham Rd. E11 3G **69**
W14 2G **99**
Elsham Ter. *W14* *3G* ***99***
(off Elsham Rd.)
Elsiedene Rd. N21 7H **23**
Elsie La. Ct. *W2* *5J* ***81***
(off Westbourne Pk. Vs.)
Elsiemaud Rd. SE4 5B **122**
Elsie Rd. SE22 4F **121**
Elsinore Av. TW19: Stanw 7A **110**
Elsinore Gdns. NW2 3G **63**
Elsinore Ho. *N1* *1A* ***84***
(off Denmark Gro.)
SE5 *2C* ***120***
(off Denmark Rd.)
SE7 4C **106**
W6 *5F* ***99***
(off Fulham Pal. Rd.)
Elsinore Rd. SE23 1A **140**
Elsinore Way TW9: Rich 3H **115**
Elsley Ct. HA9: Wemb 6H **61**
Elsley Rd. SW11 3D **118**
Elspeth Rd. HA0: Wemb 5E **60**
SW11 4D **118**
Elsrick Av. SM4: Mord 5J **153**
Elstan Way CR0: C'don 7A **158**
Elstead Ct. SM3: Sutt 1G **165**
Elstead Ho. *SW2* *7K* ***119***
(off Redlands Way)
Elsted St. SE17 4D **102**
Elstow Cl. HA4: Ruis 7B **40**
SE9 5D **124**
(not continuous)
Elstow Gdns. RM9: Dag 1E **90**
Elstow Grange NW6 7F **63**
Elstow Rd. RM9: Dag 1E **90**
Elstree Gdns. DA17: Belv 4E **108**
IG1: Ilf 5G **71**
N9 1C **34**
Elstree Hill BR1: Brom 7G **141**
Elstree Hill Sth. WD6: E'tree 1H **27**
Elstree Rd. WD23: B Hea 1C **26**
Elswick Rd. SE13 2D **122**
Elswick St. SW6 2A **118**
Elsworth Cl. TW14: Bedf 1G **129**
Elsworthy KT7: T Ditt 6J **149**
Elsworthy Ct. *NW3* *7D* ***64***
(off Primrose Hill Rd.)
Elsworthy Ri. NW3 7C **64**
Elsworthy Rd. NW3 1C **82**
Elsworthy Ter. NW3 7C **64**
Elsynge Rd. SW18 5B **118**
ELTHAM 6D **124**
Eltham Cen. 5E **124**
Eltham Crematorium SE9 4H **125**
Eltham Grn. SE9 5B **124**

Eltham Grn. Rd.—Ennismore M.

Eltham Grn. Rd. SE9 . . . . 4A 124
Eltham High St. SE9 . . . . 6D 124
Eltham Hill SE9 . . . . 5B 124
Eltham Palace 7C 124
Eltham Pal. Rd. SE9 . . . . 6A 124
ELTHAM PARK 4E 124
Eltham Pk. Gdns. SE9 . . . . 4E 124
Eltham Rd. SE9 . . . . 5H 123
SE12 . . . . 5H 123
Elthiron Rd. SW6 . . . . 1J 117
Elthorne Av. W7 . . . . 2K 95
Elthorne Ct. TW13: Felt 1A 130
ELTHORNE HEIGHTS 5J 77
Elthorne Pk. Rd. W7 . . . . 2K 95
Elthorne Rd. N19 . . . . 2H 65
NW9 . . . . 7K 43
Elthorne Sports Cen. 3K 95
Elthorne Way NW9 . . . . 6K 43
Elthruda Rd. SE13 . . . . 6F 123
Eltisley Rd. IG1: Ilf 4F 71
Elton Av. EN5: Barn 5C 20
HA0: Wemb 5B 60
UB6: G'frd 6J 59
Elton Cl. KT1: Ham W 7C 132
Elton Ho. E3 . . . . 1B 86
(off Candy St.)
Elton Pl. N16 . . . . 5E 66
Elton Rd. KT2: King T 1F 151
Eltringham St. SW18 . . . . 4A 118
Eluna Apartments E1 . . . . 7H 85
(off Wapping La.)
Elvaston M. SW7 . . . . 2A 16 (3A 100)
Elvaston Pl. SW7 . . . . 2A 16 (3A 100)
Elveden Ho. SE24 . . . . 5B 120
Elveden Pl. NW10 . . . . 2G 79
Elveden Rd. NW10 . . . . 2G 79
Elvedon Rd. TW13: Felt 3H 129
Elvendon Rd. N13 . . . . 6D 32
Elver Gdns. E2 . . . . 3G 85
Elverson Rd. SE8 . . . . 2D 122
Elverton St. SW1 . . . . 3C 18 (4H 101)
Elvington Grn. BR2: Brom 5H 159
Elvington La. NW9 . . . . 1A 44
Elvino Rd. SE26 . . . . 5A 140
Elvis Rd. NW2 . . . . 6E 62
Elwill Way BR3: Beck 4E 158
Elwin St. E2 . . . . 1K 9 (3G 85)
Elwood Cl. EN5: New Bar 4F 21
Elwood St. N5 . . . . 3B 66
Elworth Ho. SW8 . . . . 7K 101
(off Oval Pl.)
Elwyn Gdns. SE12 . . . . 7J 123
Ely Cl. KT3: N Mald 2B 152
Ely Cotts. SW8 . . . . 7K 101
Ely Ct. EC1 . . . . 6K 7
KT1: King T 2G 151
NW6 . . . . 2J 81
(off Chichester Rd.)
Ely Gdns. IG1: Ilf 7C 52
RM10: Dag 3J 73
Ely Ho. SE15 . . . . 7G 103
(off Friary Est.)
Elyne Rd. N4 . . . . 6A 48
Ely Pl. EC1 . . . . 6K 7 (5A 84)
IG8: Wfd G 6K 37
Ely Rd. CR0: C'don 5D 156
E10 . . . . 6E 50
TW4: Houn 3A 112
Elysian Av. BR5: St M Cry 6K 161
Elysian Pl. CR2: S Croy 7C 168
Elysium Pl. SW6 . . . . 2H 117
(off Elysium St.)
Elysium St. SW6 . . . . 2H 117
Elystan Bus. Cen. UB4: Yead 7A 76
Elystan Cl. SM6: Wall 7G 167
Elystan Pl. SW3 . . . . 5D 16 (5C 100)
Elystan St. SW3 . . . . 4C 16 (4C 100)
Elystan Wlk. N1 . . . . 1A 84
Ely's Yd. E1 . . . . 5K 9
Emanuel Av. W3 . . . . 6J 79
Emanuel Dr. TW12: Hamp 5D 130
Emanuel Ho. SW1 . . . . 2C 18 (3H 101)
Embankment SW15 . . . . 2F 117
(not continuous)
Embankment, The TW1: Twick 1A 132
Embankment Galleries 3H 13
(within Somerset House)
Embankment Gdns. SW3 . . . . 7F 17 (6D 100)
Embankment Pl. WC2 . . . . 4F 13 (1J 101)
Embassy Ct. DA14: Sidc 3B 144
DA16: Well 3B 126
N11 . . . . 6C 32
(off Bounds Grn. Rd.)
NW8 . . . . 1B 4
SM6: Wall 6F 167
W5 . . . . 7F 79
Embassy Gdns. BR3: Beck 1B 158
Embassy Ho. NW6 . . . . 7K 63
Embassy Lodge N3 . . . . 2H 45
(off Cyprus Rd.)
Embassy Theatre
Central School of Speech & Drama
. . . . 7B 64
(off College Cres.)
Emba St. SE16 . . . . 2G 103
Ember Cl. BR5: Pet W 7G 161
Ember Ct. NW9 . . . . 2B 44
Embercourt Rd. KT7: T Ditt 6J 149
Ember Farm Av. KT8: E Mos 6H 149
Ember Farm Way KT8: E Mos 6H 149
Ember Gdns. KT7: T Ditt 7J 149
Ember La. KT8: E Mos 7H 149
KT10: Esh 7H 149
Emberton SE5 . . . . 6E 102
(off Albany Rd.)
Emberton Ct. EC1 . . . . 2A 8
(off Tompion St.)
Embleton Rd. SE13 . . . . 4D 122
Embleton Wlk. TW12: Hamp 5D 130
Embry Cl. HA7: Stan 4F 27
Embry Dr. HA7: Stan 6F 27
Embry Way HA7: Stan 5F 27
Emden Cl. UB7: W Dray 2C 92
Emden St. SW6 . . . . 1K 117
Emerald Cl. E16 . . . . 6B 88
Emerald Gdns. RM8: Dag 1G 73
Emerald Rd. NW10 . . . . 1K 79
(not continuous)
Emerald Sq. UB2: S'hall 3B 94
Emerald St. WC1 . . . . 5G 7 (5K 83)
Emerson Apartments
N8 . . . . 3K 47
Emerson Gdns. HA3: Kenton 6F 43
Emerson Rd. IG1: Ilf 7E 52
Emerson St. SE1 . . . . 4C 14 (1C 102)
Emerton Cl. DA6: Bex 4E 126
Emery Hill St. SW1 . . . . 2B 18 (3G 101)
Emery St. SE1 . . . . 1K 19 (3A 102)
Emery Theatre 6D 86
(off Annabel Cl.)
Emery Walker Trust 5C 98
Emes Rd. DA8: Erith 7J 109
Emilia Cl. EN3: Pond E 5C 24
Emily Ct. SE1 . . . . 7C 14
(off Sudrey St.)
Emily Duncan Pl. E7 . . . . 4K 69
Emily Ho. W10 . . . . 4G 81
(off Kensal Rd.)
Emily St. E16 . . . . 6H 87
(off Jude St.)
Emirates Stadium 4A 66
Emlyn Gdns. W12 . . . . 2A 98
Emlyn Rd. W12 . . . . 2A 98
Emma Ho. RM1: Rom 4K 55
Emmanuel Ct. E10 . . . . 7D 50
Emmanuel Ho. SE11 . . . . 4J 19 (4A 102)
Emmanuel Rd. HA6: Nwood 1H 39
SW12 . . . . 1G 137
Emma Rd. E13 . . . . 2H 87
Emma St. E2 . . . . 2H 85
Emmaus Way IG7: Chig 5K 37
Emmeline Ct. KT12: Walt T 7A 148
Emminster NW6 . . . . 1K 81
(off Abbey Rd.)
Emmott Av. IG6: Ilf 5G 53
Emmott Cl. E1 . . . . 4A 86
NW11 . . . . 6A 46
Emms Pas. KT1: King T 2D 150
Emperor's Ga. SW7 . . . . 3A 100
Empingham Ho. SE8 . . . . 4K 103
(off Chilton Gro.)
Empire Av. N18 . . . . 5H 33
Empire Cinema
Bromley 2J 159
(off High St.)
Leicester Sq. 2D 12
(off Leicester Sq.)
Sutton 5K 165
Empire Cl. SE7 . . . . 6K 105
Empire Ct. HA9: Wemb 3H 61
Empire Ho. SW7 . . . . 2C 16
Empire Pde. HA9: Wemb 3G 61
N18 . . . . 6J 33
Empire Rd. UB6: G'frd 1B 78
Empire Sq. N7 . . . . 3J 65
SE1 . . . . 7E 14
(off Long La.)
SE20 . . . . 7K 139
(off High St.)
Empire Sq. E. SE1 . . . . 7E 14
Empire Sq. Sth. SE1 . . . . 7E 14
Empire Sq. W. SE1 . . . . 7E 14
Empire Way HA9: Wemb 4F 61
Empire Wharf E3 . . . . 1A 86
(off Old Ford Rd.)
Empire Wharf Rd. E14 . . . . 4F 105
Empress App. SW6 . . . . 5J 99
Empress Av. E4 . . . . 7J 35
E12 . . . . 2A 70
IG1: Ilf 2D 70
IG8: Wfd G 7C 36
Empress Dr. BR7: Chst 6F 143
Empress M. SE5 . . . . 2C 120
Empress Pde. E4 . . . . 7H 35
Empress Pl. SW6 . . . . 5J 99
Empress State Bldg.
SW6 . . . . 5J 99
Empress St. SE17 . . . . 6C 102
Empson St. E3 . . . . 4D 86
Emsworth Cl. N9 . . . . 1D 34
Emsworth Ct. SW16 . . . . 3J 137
Emsworth Rd. IG6: Ilf 2F 53
Emsworth St. SW2 . . . . 2K 137
EMT Ho. E6 . . . . 5E 88
Emu Rd. SW8 . . . . 2F 119
Enard Ho. E3 . . . . 2B 86
(off Cardigan Rd.)
Ena Rd. SW16 . . . . 3J 155
Enbrook St. W10 . . . . 3G 81
Enclave, The SW13 . . . . 2B 116
Enclave Ct. EC1 . . . . 3B 8
(off Dallington St.)
Endale Cl. SM5: Cars 2D 166
Endeavour Ho. E14 . . . . 2C 104
(off Cuba St.)
Endeavour Way CR0: Bedd 7J 155
IG11: Bark 2A 90
SW19 . . . . 4K 135
Endell St. WC2 . . . . 7E 6 (6J 83)
Enderby St. SE10 . . . . 5F 105
Enderley Cl. HA3: Hrw W 2J 41
Enderley Rd. HA3: Hrw W 1J 41
Enders Cl. EN2: Enf 1F 23
Endersleigh Gdns. NW4 . . . . 4C 44
Endlebury Rd. E4 . . . . 2K 35
Endlesham Rd. SW12 . . . . 7E 118
Endsleigh Ct. WC1 . . . . 3D 6
Endsleigh Gdns. IG1: Ilf 2D 70
KT6: Surb 6C 150
WC1 . . . . 3C 6 (4H 83)
Endsleigh Ind. Est.
UB2: S'hall 4C 94
Endsleigh Pl. WC1 . . . . 3D 6 (4H 83)
Endsleigh Rd. UB2: S'hall 4C 94
W13 . . . . 7A 78
Endsleigh St. WC1 . . . . 3D 6 (4H 83)
Endway KT5: Surb 7H 151
Endwell Rd. SE4 . . . . 2A 122
Endymion Rd. N4 . . . . 7A 48
SW2 . . . . 6K 119
Energen Cl. NW10 . . . . 6A 62
Energize Fitness Club 5G 99
(in Hammersmith & West London College)
Energy Cen., The N1 . . . . 1G 9
(off Bowling Grn. Wlk.)
ENFIELD 3J 23
Enfield Bus. Cen. EN3: Enf H 2D 24
Enfield Cloisters N1 . . . . 1G 9
(off Fanshaw St.)
Enfield College Sports Cen. 3D 24
ENFIELD HIGHWAY 3D 24
Enfield Ho. SW9 . . . . 2J 119
(off Stockwell Rd.)
ENFIELD ISLAND VILLAGE 1H 25
ENFIELD LOCK 1H 25
Enfield Lock EN3: Enf L 1H 25
Enfield Retail Pk.
EN1: Enf 3B 24
Enfield Rd. EN2: Enf 4C 22
N1 . . . . 7E 66
TW6: H'row A 2G 111
TW8: Bford 5D 96
W3 . . . . 2H 97
Enfield Rd. Rdbt. TW6: H'row A 2G 111
ENFIELD TOWN 3J 23
Enfield Wlk. TW8: Bford 5D 96
ENFIELD WASH 1F 25
Enford St. W1 . . . . 5E 4 (5D 82)
Engadine Cl. CR0: C'don 3F 169
Engadine St. SW18 . . . . 1H 135
Engate St. SE13 . . . . 4E 122
Engel Pk. NW7 . . . . 6K 29
Engine Ct. SW1 . . . . 5B 12
(off Ambassador's Ct.)
Engineer Cl. SE18 . . . . 6E 106
Engineers Way HA9: Wemb 4G 61
England's La. NW3 . . . . 6D 64
England Way KT3: N Mald 4H 151
Englefield NW1 . . . . 2A 6
(off Clarence Gdns.)
Englefield Cl. BR5: St M Cry 5K 161
CR0: C'don 6C 156
EN2: Enf 2F 23
Englefield Cres. BR5: St M Cry 4K 161
Englefield Path BR5: St M Cry 4K 161
Englefield Rd. N1 . . . . 7D 66
Engleheart Dr. TW14: Felt 6H 111
Engleheart Rd. SE6 . . . . 7D 122
Englewood Rd. SW12 . . . . 6F 119
English Grounds SE1 . . . . 5G 15 (1E 102)
English St. E3 . . . . 4B 86
Enid St. SE16 . . . . 7K 15 (3F 103)
Enmore Av. SE25 . . . . 5G 157
Enmore Gdns. SW14 . . . . 5K 115
Enmore Rd. SE25 . . . . 5G 157
SW15 . . . . 4E 116
UB1: S'hall 4E 76
Ennerdale NW1 . . . . 1A 6
(off Varndell St.)
Ennerdale Av. HA7: Stan 3C 42
Ennerdale Cl. SM1: Sutt 4H 165
TW14: Felt 1H 129
Ennerdale Ct. E11 . . . . 7J 51
(off Cambridge Rd.)
Ennerdale Dr. NW9 . . . . 5A 44
Ennerdale Gdns. HA9: Wemb 1C 60
Ennerdale Ho. E3 . . . . 4B 86
Ennerdale Rd. DA7: Bex 1G 127
TW9: Rich 2F 115
Ennersdale Rd. SE13 . . . . 5F 123
Ennis Ho. E14 . . . . 6D 86
(off Vesey Path)
Ennismore Av. UB6: G'frd 6J 59
W4 . . . . 4B 98
Ennismore Gdns. KT7: T Ditt 6J 149
SW7 . . . . 7C 10 (2C 100)
Ennismore Gdns. M. SW7 . . . . 1C 16 (3C 100)
Ennismore M. SW7 . . . . 7C 10 (3C 100)

A-Z London 257

Ennismore St.—Eton Av.

Ennismore St. SW7 1C **16** (3C **100**)
Ennis Rd. N4 1A **66**
SE18 6G **107**
Ennor Ct. SM3: Cheam 4E **164**
Ensbury Ho. *SW8* *7K* ***101***
(off Carroun Rd.)
Ensign Cl. TW6: H'row A 3G **111**
TW19: Stanw 1A **128**
Ensign Dr. N13 3H **33**
Ensign Ho. *E14* *2C* ***104***
(off Admirals Way)
SW18 3A **118**
Ensign Ind. Cen. *E1* *7G* ***85***
(off Ensign St.)
Ensign St. E1 7G **85**
Ensign Way SM6: Wall 7J **167**
TW19: Stanw 1A **128**
Enslin Rd. SE9 6E **124**
Ensor M. SW7 5A **16** (5B **100**)
Enstone Rd. EN3: Enf H 3F **25**
UB10: Ick 3B **56**
Enterprise Bus. Pk. E14 2D **104**
Enterprise Cen., The *BR3: Beck* *5A* ***140***
(off Cricket La.)
Enterprise Cl. CR0: C'don 1A **168**
Enterprise Ho. E4 7K **25**
E9 *7J* ***67***
(off Tudor Gro.)
E14 *5D* ***104***
(off St Davids Sq.)
IG11: Bark 3K **89**
KT12: Walt T 7K **147**
Enterprise Ind. Est. SE16 5J **103**
Enterprise Row N15 5F **49**
Enterprise Trad. Est. UB2: S'hall 2F **95**
Enterprise Way NW10 3B **80**
SW18 4J **117**
TW11: Tedd 6K **131**
Enterprize Way SE8 4B **104**
Entertainment Av. SE10 1G **105**
Envoy Av. TW6: H'row A 3H **111**
Envoy Rdbt. TW6: H'row A 3H **111**
Epcot M. NW10 3F **81**
Epirus M. SW6 7J **99**
Epirus Rd. SW6 7H **99**
Epping Cl. E14 4C **104**
RM7: Mawney 3H **55**
Epping Glade E4 6K **25**
Epping New Rd. IG9: Buck H 3D **36**
Epping Pl. N1 6A **66**
Epping Way E4 6J **25**
Epple Rd. SW6 1H **117**
Epsom Cl. DA7: Bex 3H **127**
UB5: N'olt 5D **58**
Epsom Rd. CR0: Wadd 4A **168**
E10 6E **50**
IG3: Ilf 6K **53**
SM3: Sutt 7H **153**
SM4: Mord 7H **153**
Epsom Sq. TW6: H'row A 2H **111**
Epstein Rd. SE28 1A **108**
Epworth Rd. TW7: Isle 7B **96**
Epworth St. EC2 4F **9** (4D **84**)
Equana Apartments *SE8* *5A* ***104***
(off Evelyn St.)
Equinox Ct. IG2: Ilf 5F **53**
Equinox Ho. IG11: Bark 6G **71**
Equity M. W5 1D **96**
Equity Sq. *E2* *2K* ***9***
(off Shacklewell St.)
Erasmus St. SW1 4D **18** (4H **101**)
Erconwald St. W12 6B **80**
Erebus Dr. SE28 3G **107**
Eresby Dr. BR3: Beck 1C **170**
Eresby Ho. *SW7* *7D* ***10***
(off Rutland Ga.)
Eresby Pl. NW6 7J **63**
Erica Gdns. CR0: C'don 3D **170**
Erica Ho. *N22* *1A* ***48***
(off Acacia Rd.)
SE4 3B **122**
Erica St. W12 7C **80**
Eric Clarke La. IG11: Bark 4F **89**
Eric Cl. E7 4J **69**
Ericcson Cl. SW18 5J **117**
Eric Fletcher Ct. *N1* *7C* ***66***
(off Essex Rd.)
Eric Liddell Sports Cen. 2B 142
Eric Rd. E7 4J **69**
NW10 6B **62**
RM6: Chad H 7D **54**
Eric Shipman Ter. *E13* *4J* ***87***
(off Balaam St.)
Ericson Ho. *SE13* *4F* ***123***
(off Blessington Rd.)
Eric St. E3 4B **86**
(not continuous)
Eric Wilkins Ho. *SE1* *5G* ***103***
(off Old Kent Rd.)
Eridge Rd. W4 3K **97**
Erin Cl. BR1: Brom 7G **141**
IG3: Ilf 6A **54**
Erindale SE18 6H **107**
Erindale Ter. SE18 6H **107**
Erin M. N22 1B **48**
ERITH 5K **109**
Erith Cres. RM5: Col R 1J **55**
Erith Rd. DA7: Bex 4H **127**
DA8: Erith 5G **109**
DA17: Belv, Erith 5G **109**
Erith School Community Sports Cen. 7J 109
Erlanger Rd. SE14 1K **121**
Erlesmere Gdns. W13 3A **96**
Erlich Cotts. *E1* *5J* ***85***
(off Sidney St.)
Ermine Cl. TW4: Houn 2A **112**
Ermine Ho. *E3* *1B* ***86***
(off Parnell Rd.)
N17 *7A* ***34***
(off Moselle St.)
Ermine M. E2 1F **85**
Ermine Rd. N15 6F **49**
SE13 4D **122**
Ermine Side EN1: Enf 5B **24**
Ermington Rd. SE9 2G **143**
Ernald Av. E6 2C **88**
Erncroft Way TW1: Twick 6K **113**
Ernest Av. SE27 4B **138**
Ernest Cl. BR3: Beck 5C **158**
Ernest Cotts. KT17: Ewe 7B **164**
Ernest Gdns. W4 6H **97**
Ernest Gro. BR3: Beck 5B **158**
Ernest Harriss Ho. *W9* *4J* ***81***
(off Elgin Av.)
Ernest Rd. KT1: King T 2H **151**
Ernest Sq. KT1: King T 2H **151**
Ernest St. E1 4K **85**
Ernle Rd. SW20 7D **134**
Ernshaw Pl. SW15 5G **117**
Eros 3C 12 (7H 83)
Eros Ho. Shops *SE6* *7D* ***122***
(off Brownhill Rd.)
Erpingham Rd. SW15 3E **116**
Erridge Rd. SW19 2J **153**
Errington Rd. W9 4H **81**
Errol Gdns. KT3: N Mald 4C **152**
UB4: Yead 4K **75**
Errol St. EC1 4D **8** (4C **84**)
Erskine Cl. SM1: Sutt 3C **166**
Erskine Cres. N17 4H **49**
Erskine Hill NW11 4J **45**
Erskine Ho. *SW1* *6A* ***18***
(off Churchill Gdns.)
Erskine M. *NW3* *7D* ***64***
(off Erskine Rd.)
Erskine Rd. E17 4B **50**
NW3 7D **64**
SM1: Sutt 4B **166**
Erwood Rd. SE7 5C **106**
Esam Way SW16 5A **138**
Escot Rd. TW16: Sun 7G **129**
Escott Gdns. SE9 4C **142**
Escreet Gro. SE18 4E **106**
Esher Av. KT12: Walt T 7J **147**
RM7: Rom 6J **55**
SM3: Cheam 3F **165**
Esher By-Pass KT9: Chess 7B **162**
KT10: Clay 7B **162**
Esher Cl. DA5: Bexl 1E **144**
Esher Cres. TW6: H'row A 2H **111**
Esher Gdns. SW19 2F **135**
Esher M. CR4: Mitc 3E **154**
Esher Rd. IG3: Ilf 3J **71**
KT8: E Mos 6H **149**
Eskdale *NW1* *1A* ***6***
(off Stanhope St.)
Eskdale Av. UB5: N'olt 1D **76**
Eskdale Cl. HA9: Wemb 2D **60**
Eskdale Rd. DA7: Bex 2G **127**
Esk Ho. *E3* *4B* ***86***
(off British St.)
Eskmont Ridge SE19 7D **138**
Esk Rd. E13 4J **87**
Esk Way RM1: Rom 1K **55**
Esmar Cres. NW9 7C **44**
Esmeralda Rd. SE1 4G **103**
Esmond Ct. *W8* *3K* ***99***
(off Thackeray St.)
Esmond Gdns. W4 4K **97**
Esmond Rd. NW6 1H **81**
W4 4K **97**
Esmond St. SW15 4G **117**
Esparto St. SW18 7K **117**
Esporta Health & Fitness
Chislehurst 5J 143
Chiswick Pk. 4H 97
Chiswick Riverside 1A 116
Enfield 4J 23
Finchley Rd. *6A 64*
(in O2 Cen.)
Ilford *3F 71*
(off Clements Rd.)
Islington 1B 84
Kingston upon Thames 1E 150
New Southgate 5K 31
Repton Park 7K 37
Romford 5K 55
Wandsworth 4K 117
Wimbledon 6H 135
Esporta Health & Racquets Club
Purley 6K 167
Esprit Ct. *E1* *6J* ***9***
(off Brune St.)
Essan Ho. W5 5B **78**
Essence Ct. HA9: Wemb 2F **61**
Essenden Rd. CR2: S Croy 7E **168**
DA17: Belv 5G **109**
Essendine Mans. W9 3J **81**
Essendine Rd. W9 3J **81**
Essex Av. TW7: Isle 3J **113**
Essex Cl. E17 4A **50**
HA4: Ruis 1B **58**
RM7: Mawney 4H **55**
SM4: Mord 7F **153**
Essex Ct. EC4 1J **13**
SW13 2B **116**
W6 *3E* ***98***
(off Hammersmith Gro.)
Essex Gdns. N4 6B **48**
Essex Gro. SE19 6D **138**
Essex Hall E17 1K **49**
Essex Ho. *E14* *6D* ***86***
(off Girauld St.)
Essex Mans. E11 7F **51**
Essex Pk. N3 6E **30**
Essex Pk. M. W3 1A **98**
Essex Pl. W4 4J **97**
(not continuous)
Essex Pl. Sq. W4 4K **97**
Essex Rd. E4 1B **36**
E10 6E **50**
E12 5C **70**
E17 6A **50**
E18 2K **51**
EN2: Enf 4J **23**
Essex Rd. IG11: Bark 7H **71**
N1 1B **84**
NW10 7A **62**
RM6: Chad H 7C **54**
RM7: Mawney 4H **55**
RM10: Dag 5J **73**
W3 7J **79**
W4 4K **97**
(not continuous)
Essex Rd. Sth. E11 7F **51**
Essex St. E7 5J **69**
WC2 1J **13** (6A **84**)
Essex Twr. *SE20* *1H* ***157***
(off Jasmine Gro.)
Essex Vs. W8 2J **99**
Essex Wharf E5 2K **67**
Essian St. E1 5A **86**
Essoldo Way HA8: Edg 3F **43**
Estate Way E10 1B **68**
Estcourt Rd. SE25 6H **157**
SW6 7H **99**
Estella Apartments E15 6F **69**
Estella Av. KT3: N Mald 4D **152**
Estella Ho. *W11* *7F* ***81***
(off St Ann's Rd.)
Estelle Rd. NW3 4D **64**
Esterbrooke St. SW1 4C **18** (4H **101**)
Este Rd. SW11 3C **118**
Esther Cl. N21 7F **23**
Esther Randall Ct. *NW1* *3K* ***5***
(off Lit. Albany St.)
NW1 *4F* ***83***
(off Longford St.)
Esther Rd. E11 7G **51**
Estoria Cl. SW2 7A **120**
Estorick Collection of Modern Italian Art 6B 66
Estreham Rd. SW16 6H **137**
Estridge Cl. TW3: Houn 4E **112**
Estuary Cl. IG11: Bark 3B **90**
Eswyn Rd. SW17 4D **136**
Etal Ho. *N1* *7B* ***66***
(off The Sutton Est.)
Etcetera Theatre *7F 65*
(off Camden High St.)
Etchingham Ct. N3 7E **30**
Etchingham Pk. Rd. N3 7E **30**
Etchingham Rd. E15 4E **68**
Eternit Wlk. SW6 1E **116**
Etfield Gro. DA14: Sidc 5B **144**
Ethelbert Cl. BR1: Brom 2J **159**
Ethelbert Ct. *BR1: Brom* *3J* ***159***
(off Ethelbert Rd.)
Ethelbert Gdns. IG2: Ilf 5D **52**
Ethelbert Rd. BR1: Brom 3J **159**
DA8: Erith 7J **109**
SW20 1F **153**
Ethelbert St. SW12 1F **137**
Ethel Brooks Ho. SE18 6F **107**
Ethelburga St. SW11 1C **118**
Ethelburga Twr. *SW11* *1C* ***118***
(off Maskelyne Cl.)
Etheldene Av. N10 4G **47**
Ethelden Rd. W12 1D **98**
Ethel Rd. E16 6K **87**
TW15: Ashf 5A **128**
Ethel St. SE17 4C **102**
Etheridge Rd. NW4 7E **44**
(not continuous)
Etherley Rd. N15 5C **48**
Etherow St. SE22 7G **121**
Etherstone Grn. SW16 4A **138**
Etherstone Rd. SW16 4A **138**
Ethnard Rd. SE15 6H **103**
Ethos Sport Imperial 7B 10 (2B 100)
Ethronvi Rd. DA7: Bex 3E **126**
Etloe Ho. E10 1C **68**
Etloe Rd. E10 2C **68**
Eton Av. EN4: E Barn 6H **21**
HA0: Wemb 4B **60**
KT3: N Mald 5K **151**
N12 7F **31**

Eton Av. NW3 7B 64
TW5: Hest 6D 94
Eton Cl. SW18 7K 117
Eton Coll. Rd. NW3 6D 64
Eton Ct. HA0: Wemb 4C 60
NW3 7B 64
Eton Garages NW3 6C 64
Eton Gro. NW9 3G 43
SE13 3G 123
Eton Hall NW3 6D 64
Eton Ho. N5 4B 66
(off Leigh Rd.)
UB7: W Dray 2B 92
Eton Mnr. Ct. E10 2C 68
(off Leyton Grange Est.)
Eton Pl. NW3 7E 64
Eton Ri. NW3 6D 64
Eton Rd. IG1: Ilf 4G 71
NW3 7D 64
UB3: Harl 7H 93
Eton St. TW9: Rich 5E 114
Eton Vs. NW3 6D 64
Etta St. SE8 6A 104
Ettrick St. E14 6E 86
(not continuous)
Etwell Pl. KT5: Surb 6F 151
Eucalyptus M. SW16 6H 137
Euesden Cl. N9 3C 34
Eugene Cotter Ho. SE17 4D 102
(off Tatum St.)
Eugenia Rd. SE16 4J 103
Eugenie M. BR7: Chst 1F 161
Eureka Rd. KT1: King T 2G 151
Euro Cl. NW10 6C 62
Eurolink Bus. Cen. SW2 5A 120
Europa Ho. E16 6H 87
(off Shirley St.)
Europa Pl. EC1 2C 8 (3C 84)
Europa Trade Pk. E16 4G 87
Europa Trad. Est. DA8: Erith 5K 109
European Bus. Cen. NW9 3J 43
(not continuous)
European Design Cen. NW9 3K 43
Europe Rd. SE18 3D 106
Euro Trade Cen. DA17: Belv 2J 109
Eustace Bldg. SW8 6F 101
Eustace Ho. SE11 3G 19
Eustace Pl. SE18 4D 106
Eustace Rd. E6 3C 88
RM6: Chad H 7D 54
SW6 7J 99
Euston Cen. NW1 4G 83
Euston Gro. NW1 2C 6
Euston Rd. CR0: C'don 1A 168
NW1 4A 6 (4F 83)
Euston Sq. NW1 2C 6 (3H 83)
(not continuous)
Euston Sta. Colonnade NW1 2C 6 (3H 83)
Euston St. NW1 2B 6 (3G 83)
Euston Twr. NW1 3A 6 (4G 83)
EUSTON UNDERPASS 4G 83
Eva Ct. CR2: S Croy 6E 168
Evan Cook Cl. SE15 1J 121
Evandale Rd. SW9 2A 120
Evangelist Ho. EC4 1A 14
(off Black Friars La.)
Evangelist Rd. NW5 4F 65
Evans Bus. Cen. NW2 3C 62
Evans Cl. E8 6F 67
Evans Gro. TW13: Hanw 2E 130
Evans Ho. SW8 7H 101
(off Wandsworth Rd.)
TW13: Hanw 2E 130
W12 7D 80
(off White City Est.)
Evans Rd. SE6 2G 141
Evanston Av. E4 7K 35
Evanston Gdns. IG4: Ilf 6C 52
Eva Rd. RM6: Chad H 7C 54
Evedon Ho. N1 1E 84
(off New Era Est.)
Evelina Mans. SE5 7D 102
Evelina Rd. SE15 3J 121
SE20 7J 139
Eveline Lowe Est. SE16 3G 103
Eveline Rd. CR4: Mitc 1D 154
Evelyn Av. HA4: Ruis 7G 39
NW9 4K 43
Evelyn Cl. TW2: Whitt 7F 113
Evelyn Ct. E8 4G 67
N1 1E 8
(off Evelyn Wlk.)
Evelyn Cres. TW16: Sun 1H 147
Evelyn Denington Ct. N1 7B 66
(off The Sutton Est.)
Evelyn Denington Rd. E6 4C 88
Evelyn Dr. HA5: Pinn 1B 40
Evelyn Fox Ct. W10 5E 80
Evelyn Gdns. SW7 6A 16 (5A 100)
TW9: Rich 4E 114
Evelyn Gro. UB1: S'hall 6D 76
W5 1F 97
Evelyn Ho. SE14 1A 122
(off Loring Rd.)
W8 2K 99
(off Hornton Pl.)
W12 2B 98
(off Cobbold Rd.)
Evelyn Mans. SW1 2A 18
(off Carlisle Pl.)
W14 6G 99
(off Queen's Club Gdns.)
Evelyn Rd. E16 1J 105
E17 4E 50
EN4: Cockf 4J 21
SW19 5K 135
TW9: Rich 3E 114
TW10: Ham 3C 132
W4 3K 97
Evelyns Cl. UB8: Hil 6C 74
Evelyn St. SE8 4A 104
Evelyn Ter. TW9: Rich 3E 114
Evelyn Wlk. N1 1E 8 (2D 84)
Evelyn Way SM6: Bedd 4H 167
TW16: Sun 1H 147
Evelyn Yd. W1 7C 6 (6H 83)
Evening Hill BR3: Beck 7E 140
Evenlode Ho. SE2 2C 108
Evenwood Cl. SW15 5G 117
Everard Av. BR2: Hayes 1J 171
Everard Ct. N13 3E 32
Everard Ho. E1 6G 85
(off Boyd St.)
Everard Way HA9: Wemb 3E 60
Everatt Cl. SW18 6H 117
Everdon Rd. SW13 6C 98
Everest Pl. E14 5E 86
Everest Rd. SE9 5D 124
TW19: Stanw 7A 110
Everett Cl. HA5: Eastc 3H 39
WD23: B Hea 1D 26
Everett Ho. SE17 5D 102
(off East St.)
Everett Wlk. DA17: Belv 5F 109
(off Osborne Rd.)
Everglade Ho. E17 2B 50
Everglade Strand NW9 1B 44
Evergreen Apartments IG8: Wfd G 1H 51
(off High Rd. Woodford Grn.)
Evergreen Cl. SE20 7J 139
Evergreen Sq. E8 7F 67
Evergreen Way UB3: Hayes 7H 75
Everilda St. N1 1K 83
Evering Rd. E5 3F 67
N16 3F 67
Everington Rd. N10 2D 46
Everington St. W6 6F 99
(not continuous)
Everitt Rd. NW10 3K 79
Everleigh St. N4 1K 65
Eve Rd. E11 4G 69
E15 2G 87
N17 3E 48
TW7: Isle 4A 114
Eversfield Gdns. NW7 6F 29
Eversfield Rd. TW9: Kew 2F 115
Evershed Ho. E1 7K 9
(off Old Castle St.)
Evershed Wlk. W4 3J 97
Eversholt Ct. EN5: New Bar 5F 21
Eversholt St. NW1 1B 6 (2G 83)
Evershot Rd. N4 1K 65
Eversleigh Ct. N3 7C 30
Eversleigh Rd. E6 1B 88
EN5: New Bar 5F 21
N3 7C 30
SW11 3D 118
Eversley Av. DA7: Bex 2K 127
HA9: Wemb 2G 61
Eversley Cl. N21 6E 22
Eversley Cres. HA4: Ruis 2G 57
N21 6F 23
TW7: Isle 1H 113
Eversley Ho. E2 2K 9
(off Gosset St.)
Eversley Mt. N21 6E 22
Eversley Pk. SW19 6D 134
Eversley Pk. Rd. N21 6E 22
Eversley Rd. KT5: Surb 4F 151
SE7 6K 105
SE19 7D 138
Eversley Way CR0: C'don 4C 170
Everthorpe Rd. SE15 3F 121
Everton Bldgs. NW1 2A 6 (3G 83)
Everton Ct. HA7: Stan 3E 42
(off Honeypot La.)
Everton Dr. HA7: Stan 3E 42
Everton Rd. CR0: C'don 1G 169
Evesham Av. E17 2C 50
Evesham Cl. SM2: Sutt 7J 165
UB6: G'frd 2F 77
Evesham Ct. TW10: Rich 6F 115
W13 1A 96
(off Tewkesbury Rd.)
Evesham Grn. SM4: Mord 6K 153
Evesham Ho. E2 2J 85
(off Old Ford Rd.)
NW8 1A 82
(off Abbey Rd.)
SW1 5F 101
(off Sutherland Row)
Evesham Rd. E15 7H 69
N11 5B 32
SM4: Mord 6K 153
Evesham St. W11 7F 81
Evesham Ter. KT6: Surb 6D 150
Evesham Wlk. SE5 2D 120
SW9 2A 120
Evesham Way IG5: Ilf 3E 52
SW11 3E 118
Evry Rd. DA14: Sidc 6C 144
Ewald Rd. SW6 2H 117
Ewanrigg Ter. IG8: Wfd G 5F 37
Ewart Gro. N22 1K 47
Ewart Pl. E3 2B 86
Ewart Rd. SE23 7K 121
Ewe Cl. N7 6J 65
EWELL 7C 164
Ewell By-Pass KT17: Ewe 7C 164
Ewell Ct. Av. KT19: Ewe 5A 164
Ewellhurst Rd. IG5: Ilf 2C 52
Ewell Pk. Gdns. KT17: Ewe 7C 164
Ewell Pk. Way KT17: Ewe 6C 164
Ewell Rd. KT6: Surb 6E 150
(Surbiton Hill Rd.)
KT6: Surb 7B 150
(Thorkhill Rd.)
SM3: Cheam 6F 165
Ewelme Rd. SE23 1J 139
Ewen Cres. SW2 7A 120
Ewen Henderson Ct. SE14 7A 104
(off Goodwood Rd.)
Ewen Ho. N1 1K 83
(off Barnsbury Est.)
Ewer St. SE1 5C 14 (1C 102)
Ewhurst Av. CR2: Sande 7F 169
Ewhurst Cl. E1 5J 85
Ewhurst Ct. CR4: Mitc 3B 154
Ewhurst Rd. SE4 6B 122
Exbury Ho. E9 7J 67
SW1 5C 18
(off Rampayne St.)
Exbury Rd. SE6 2C 140
ExCeL 7K 87
Excel Ct. WC2 3D 12
Excel Marina E16 7J 87
Excelsior Cl. KT1: King T 2G 151
Excelsior Gdns. SE13 2E 122
Excelsior Ind. Est. SE15 6J 103
Excel Waterfront E16 7K 87
Exchange, The CR0: C'don 3C 168
(off Surrey St.)
IG1: Ilf 2F 71
Exchange Apartments BR2: Brom 4K 159
(off Sparkes Cl.)
Exchange Arc. EC2 5H 9 (5E 84)
Exchange Bldg. E1 4J 9
(off Commercial St.)
Exchange Cl. N11 2K 31
Exchange Ct. WC2 3F 13 (7J 83)
Exchange Ho. EC2 5H 9
NW10 7D 62
SW1 4C 18
(off Vauxhall Bri. Rd.)
Exchange Mans. NW11 7H 45
Exchange Pl. EC2 5G 9 (5E 84)
Exchange Sq. EC2 5G 9 (5E 84)
Exchange St. EC1 2C 8 (3C 84)
RM1: Rom 5K 55 & 6K 55
Exchange Wlk. HA5: Pinn 7C 40
Exeforde Av. TW15: Ashf 4C 128
Exeter Cl. E6 6D 88
Exeter Ct. KT6: Surb 5E 150
(off Maple Rd.)
NW6 2J 81
(off Cambridge Rd.)
Exeter Gdns. IG1: Ilf 1C 70
Exeter Ho. IG11: Bark 7A 72
(off Margaret Bondfield Av.)
N1 1E 84
(off New Era Est.)
SE15 6G 103
(off Friary Est.)
SW15 6E 116
TW13: Hanw 2D 130
(off Watermill Way)
W2 6A 82
(off Hallfield Est.)
Exeter Mans. NW2 6G 63
Exeter M. NW6 6K 63
SW6 7J 99
Exeter Rd. CR0: C'don 7E 156
DA16: Well 2K 125
E16 5J 87
E17 5C 50
EN3: Pond E 3E 24
HA2: Harr 2C 58
N9 2D 34
N14 1A 32
NW2 5G 63
RM10: Dag 6H 73
TW6: H'row A 3F 111
TW13: Hanw 3D 130
Exeter St. WC2 2F 13 (7J 83)
Exeter Way SE14 7B 104
TW6: H'row A 2G 111
Exford Ct. SW11 1B 118
(off Bolingbroke Wlk.)
Exford Gdns. SE12 1K 141
Exford Rd. SE12 2K 141
Exhibition Cl. W12 7E 80
Exhibition Grounds HA9: Wemb 4H 61
Exhibition Rd. SW7 7B 10 (2B 100)
Exit Rd. N2 2B 46
Exmoor Cl. IG6: Ilf 1G 53
Exmoor Ho. E3 2A 86
(off Gernon Rd.)
Exmoor St. W10 4F 81

Exmouth Ho. *E14* 4D 104
(off Cahir St.)
EC1 . . . . . 3J 7
(off Pine St.)
Exmouth Mkt. EC1 . . . . . 3J 7 (4A 84)
Exmouth M. NW1 . . . . . 2B 6 (3G 83)
Exmouth Pl. E8 . . . . . 7H 67
Exmouth Rd. DA16: Well 1C 126
E17 . . . . . 5B 50
HA4: Ruis 3A 58
UB4: Hayes 3G 75
Exmouth St. E1 . . . . . 6J 85
Exning Rd. E16 . . . . . 4G 87
Exonbury *NW8* 1K 81
(off Abbey Rd.)
Exon St. SE17 . . . . . 5E 102
Explorer Av. TW19: Stanw 1A 128
Explorers Ct. *E14* 7F 87
(off Newport Av.)
Export Ho. *SE1* 7H 15
(off Tower Bri. Rd.)
Express Dr. IG3: Ilf 1B 72
Express Newspapers
SE1 . . . . . 4A 14
(off Blackfriars Rd.)
Exton Gdns. RM8: Dag 5C 72
Exton Rd. NW10 . . . . . 7J 61
Exton St. SE1 . . . . . 5J 13 (1A 102)
Eyebright Cl. CR0: C'don 1K 169
Eyhurst Cl. NW2 . . . . . 2C 62
Eylewood Rd. SE27 . . . . . 5C 138
Eynella Rd. SE22 . . . . . 7F 121
Eynham Rd. W12 . . . . . 6E 80
Eynsford Cl. BR5: Pet W 7G 161
Eynsford Cres. DA5: Bexl 1C 144
Eynsford Ho. *SE1* 7E 14
(off Crosby Row)
SE15 . . . . . 6J 103
SE17 . . . . . 4E 102
(off East St.)
Eynsford Rd. IG3: Ilf 2J 71
Eynsford Ter. UB7: Yiew 6B 74
Eynsham Dr. SE2 . . . . . 4A 108
Eynswood Dr. DA14: Sidc 5B 144
Eyot Gdns. W6 . . . . . 5B 98
Eyot Grn. W4 . . . . . 5B 98
Eyot Ho. *SE16* 3G 103
(off Frean St.)
Eyre Ct. NW8 . . . . . 2B 82
Eyre St. Hill EC1 . . . . . 4J 7 (4A 84)
Eysham Ct. EN5: New Bar 5E 20
Eythorne Rd. SW9 . . . . . 1A 120
Ezra St. E2 . . . . . 1K 9 (3F 85)

F

Faber Gdns. NW4 . . . . . 5C 44
Fabian Bell Twr. *E3* 2C 86
(off Pancras Way)
Fabian Rd. SW6 . . . . . 7H 99
Fabian St. E6 . . . . . 4D 88
Facade, The SE23 . . . . . 2J 139
Factory La. CR0: C'don 1A 168
N17 . . . . . 2F 49
Factory Rd. E16 . . . . . 1B 106
Factory Yd. W7 . . . . . 1J 95
Faggs Rd. TW14: Felt 4H 111
Fairacre HA5: Eastc 4J 39
KT3: N Mald 3A 152
Fairacre Ct. HA6: Nwood 1G 39
Fair Acres BR2: Brom 5J 159
CR0: Sels 7B 170
Fairacres HA4: Ruis 7H 39
SW15 . . . . . 4B 116
Fairbairn Grn. SW9 . . . . . 1B 120
Fairbank Av. BR6: Farnb 2F 173
Fairbank Est. N1 . . . . . 1F 9 (2D 84)
Fairbanks Ct. HA0: Wemb 1E 78
Fairbanks Rd. N17 . . . . . 3F 49
Fairbourne Ho. UB3: Harl 3E 92
Fairbourne Rd. N17 . . . . . 3E 48
Fairbriar Residence *SW7* 4A 100
(off Cromwell Rd.)
Fairbridge Rd. N19 . . . . . 2H 65
Fairbrook Cl. N13 . . . . . 5F 33
Fairbrook Rd. N13 . . . . . 6F 33
Fairburn Ct. SW15 . . . . . 5G 117
Fairburn Ho. *W14* 5H 99
(off Ivatt Pl.)
Fairby Ho. *SE1* 4F 103
(off Longfield Est.)
Fairby Rd. SE12 . . . . . 5K 123
Faircharm Trad. Est.
SE8 . . . . . 7D 104
Fairchild Cl. SW11 . . . . . 2B 118
Fairchild Ho. *E2* 2H 85
(off Cambridge Cres.)
E9 . . . . . 7J 67
(off Frampton Pk. Rd.)
N1 . . . . . 1G 9
(off Fanshaw St.)
N3 . . . . . 1J 45
Fairchild Pl. EC2 . . . . . 4H 9
Fairchild St. EC2 . . . . . 3H 9 (4E 84)
Fair Cl. WD23: Bush 1A 26
Fairclough Cl. UB5: N'olt 4D 76
Fairclough St. E1 . . . . . 6G 85
Faircroft Ct. TW11: Tedd 6A 132
FAIR CROSS 5J 71
Faircross Av. IG11: Bark 6G 71
RM5: Col R 1K 55
Faircross Pde. IG11: Bark 5J 71
Fairdale Gdns. SW15 . . . . . 4D 116
UB3: Hayes 2J 93
Fairey Av. UB3: Harl 4H 93
Fairfax Av. KT17: Ewe 7D 164
Fairfax Cl. KT12: Walt T 7K 147
Fairfax Ct. *NW6* 7A 64
(off Fairfax Rd.)
Fairfax Gdns. SE3 . . . . . 1A 124
Fairfax Ho. *KT1: King T* 3F 151
(off Livesey Cl.)
Fairfax Mans. *NW3* 6A 64
(off Finchley Rd.)
Fairfax M. E16 . . . . . 1K 105
N8 . . . . . 4B 48
SW15 . . . . . 4E 116
Fairfax Pl. NW6 . . . . . 7A 64
W14 . . . . . 3G 99
Fairfax Rd. N8 . . . . . 4A 48
NW6 . . . . . 7A 64
TW11: Tedd 6A 132
W4 . . . . . 3A 98
Fairfax Way N10 . . . . . 7K 31
Fairfield *E1* 5J 85
(off Redman's Rd.)
KT1: King T 2F 151
N20 . . . . . 7G 21
NW1 . . . . . 1G 83
(off Arlington Rd.)
Fairfield Av. HA4: Ruis 7E 38
HA8: Edg 6C 28
NW4 . . . . . 6D 44
TW2: Whitt 1F 131
Fairfield Cl. CR4: Mitc 7C 136
DA15: Sidc 6K 125
EN3: Pond E 4E 24
KT19: Ewe 5A 164
N12 . . . . . 4F 31
Fairfield Ct. HA4: Ruis 1F 57
HA6: Nwood 2J 39
NW10 . . . . . 1C 80
Fairfield Cres. HA8: Edg 6C 28
Fairfield Dr. HA2: Harr 3G 41
SW18 . . . . . 5K 117
UB6: G'frd 1C 78
Fairfield E. KT1: King T 2E 150
Fairfield Gdns. N8 . . . . . 5J 47
Fairfield Gro. SE7 . . . . . 6B 106
Fairfield Halls 3D 168
Fairfield Nth. KT1: King T 2E 150
Fairfield Path CR0: C'don 3D 168
Fairfield Pl. KT1: King T 3E 150
Fairfield Rd. BR1: Brom 7J 141
BR3: Beck 2C 158
BR5: Pet W 6H 161
CR0: C'don 3D 168
DA7: Bex 2F 127
E3 . . . . . 2C 86
E17 . . . . . 2A 50
IG1: Ilf 6F 71
IG8: Wfd G 6D 36
KT1: King T 2E 150
(not continuous)
N8 . . . . . 5J 47
N18 . . . . . 4B 34
UB1: S'hall 6D 76
UB7: Yiew 7A 74
UB8: Uxb 6A 56
Fairfields Cl. NW9 . . . . . 5J 43
Fairfields Cres. NW9 . . . . . 4J 43
Fairfield Sth. KT1: King T 2E 150
Fairfields Rd. TW3: Houn 3G 113
Fairfield St. SW18 . . . . . 5K 117
Fairfield Trade Pk.
KT1: King T 3F 151
Fairfield Way EN5: Barn 5D 20
KT19: Ewe 5A 164
Fairfield W. KT1: King T 2E 150
Fairfoot Rd. E3 . . . . . 4C 86
Fairford SE6 . . . . . 1C 140
Fairford Av. CR0: C'don 5K 157
DA7: Bex 1K 127
Fairford Cl. CR0: C'don 5A 158
Fairford Ct. SM2: Sutt 7K 165
Fairford Gdns. KT4: Wor Pk 2B 164
Fairford Ho. SE11 . . . . . 4K 19 (4A 102)
Fairgreen EN4: Cockf 3J 21
Fairgreen Ct. EN4: Cockf 3J 21
Fairgreen E. EN4: Cockf 3J 21
Fairgreen Rd. CR7: Thor H 5B 156
Fairhall Ct. KT5: Surb 7F 151
Fairhaven Av. CR0: C'don 6K 157
Fairhaven Ct. *CR2: S Croy* 5C 168
(off Warham Rd.)
Fairhazel Gdns. NW6 . . . . . 6K 63
Fairhazel Mans. *NW6* 7A 64
(off Fairhazel Gdns.)
Fairholme TW14: Bedf 7F 111
Fairholme Cl. N3 . . . . . 4G 45
Fairholme Cres. UB4: Hayes 4H 75
Fairholme Gdns. N3 . . . . . 3G 45
Fairholme Rd. CR0: C'don 7A 156
HA1: Harr 5K 41
IG1: Ilf 7D 52
SM1: Sutt 6H 165
TW15: Ashf 5A 128
W14 . . . . . 5G 99
Fairholt Cl. N16 . . . . . 1E 66
Fairholt Rd. N16 . . . . . 1D 66
Fairholt St. SW7 . . . . . 1D 16 (3C 100)
Fairland Ho. BR2: Brom 4K 159
Fairland Rd. E15 . . . . . 6H 69
Fairlands Av. CR7: Thor H 4K 155
IG9: Buck H 2D 36
SM1: Sutt 2J 165
Fairlands Ct. SE9 . . . . . 6E 124
Fairlawn SE7 . . . . . 7A 106
Fairlawn Av. DA7: Bex 2D 126
N2 . . . . . 4C 46
W4 . . . . . 4J 97
Fairlawn Cl. KT2: King T 6J 133
KT10: Clay 6A 162
N14 . . . . . 6B 22
TW13: Hanw 4D 130
Fairlawn Ct. SE7 . . . . . 7A 106
(not continuous)
W4 . . . . . 4J 97
Fairlawn Dr. IG8: Wfd G 7D 36
Fairlawnes SM6: Wall 5F 167
Fairlawn Gdns. UB1: S'hall 7D 76
Fairlawn Gro. W4 . . . . . 4J 97
Fairlawn Mans. SE14 . . . . . 1K 121
Fairlawn Pk. SE26 . . . . . 5A 140
Fairlawn Rd. SW19 . . . . . 7H 135
Fairlawns HA5: Pinn 2B 40
TW1: Twick 6C 114
TW16: Sun 3J 147
Fairlead Ho. *E14* 3C 104
(off Alpha Gro.)
Fairlea Pl. W5 . . . . . 4C 78
Fairlie Ct. *E3* 3D 86
(off Stroudley Wlk.)
Fairlie Gdns. SE23 . . . . . 7J 121
Fairlight TW12: Ham H 5F 131
Fairlight Av. E4 . . . . . 2A 36
IG8: Wfd G 6D 36
NW10 . . . . . 2A 80
Fairlight Cl. E4 . . . . . 2A 36
KT4: Wor Pk 4E 164
Fairlight Ct. NW10 . . . . . 2A 80
UB6: G'frd 2G 77
Fairlight Rd. SW17 . . . . . 4B 136
Fairline Ct. BR3: Beck 2E 158
FAIRLOP 1J 53
Fairlop Ct. E11 . . . . . 1F 69
Fairlop Gdns. IG6: Ilf 1G 53
Fairlop Rd. E11 . . . . . 7F 51
IG6: Ilf 2G 53
Fairlop Sailing Cen. 1K 53
Fairlop Waters Country Pk. 2K 53
Fairmark Dr. UB10: Hil 6C 56
Fairmead BR1: Brom 4D 160
KT5: Surb 1H 163
Fairmead Cl. BR1: Brom 4D 160
KT3: N Mald 3K 151
TW5: Hest 7B 94
Fairmead Ct. TW9: Rich 2H 115
Fairmead Cres. HA8: Edg 3D 28
Fairmead Gdns. IG4: Ilf 5C 52
Fairmead Ho. E9 . . . . . 4A 68
Fairmead Rd. CR0: C'don 7K 155
N19 . . . . . 3H 65
Fairmile Av. SW16 . . . . . 5H 137
Fairmile Ho. TW11: Tedd 4A 132
Fairmont Av. E14 . . . . . 1F 105
Fairmont Cl. DA17: Belv 5F 109
Fairmont Ho. *E3* 4C 86
(off Wellington Way)
Fairmount Rd. SW2 . . . . . 6K 119
Fairoak Cl. BR5: Pet W 7F 161
Fairoak Dr. SE9 . . . . . 5H 125
Fairoak Gdns. RM1: Rom 2K 55
Fair Oak Pl. IG6: Ilf 2G 53
Fairseat Cl. WD23: B Hea 2D 26
Fairstead Lodge *IG8: Wfd G* 6D 36
(off Snakes La.)
Fairstead Wlk. *N1* 1C 84
(off Popham St.)
Fair St. SE1 . . . . . 6H 15 (2E 102)
TW3: Houn 3G 113
Fairthorne Vs. *SE7* 5J 105
(off Felltram Way)
Fairthorn Rd. SE7 . . . . . 5J 105
Fairview HA4: Ruis 4A 58
Fairview Av. HA0: Wemb 6D 60
Fairview Cl. E17 . . . . . 1A 50
SE26 . . . . . 5A 140
Fairview Ct. NW4 . . . . . 2F 45
TW15: Ashf 5C 128
Fairview Cres. HA2: Harr 1E 58
Fairview Dr. BR6: Orp 4H 173
TW17: Shep 5B 146
Fairview Est. NW10 . . . . . 3J 79
Fairview Gdns. IG8: Wfd G 1K 51
Fairview Ho. SW2 . . . . . 7K 119
Fairview Ind. Pk. RM13: Rain 5K 91
Fairview Pl. SW2 . . . . . 7K 119
Fairview Rd. EN2: Enf 1F 23
N15 . . . . . 5F 49
SM1: Sutt 5B 166
SW16 . . . . . 1K 155
Fairview Vs. E4 . . . . . 7J 35
Fairview Way HA8: Edg 4B 28
Fairwall Ho. SE5 . . . . . 1E 120
Fairwater Av. DA16: Well 4A 126
Fairwater Ho. TW11: Tedd 4A 132

Fairway—Farnham Ho.

Fairway BR5: Pet W 5H **161**
DA6: Bex 5E **126**
IG8: Wfd G 5F **37**
SW20 . . . . . 3E **152**
Fairway, The BR1: Brom 5D **160**
EN5: New Bar 6E **20**
HA0: Wemb 3B **60**
HA4: Ruis 4A **58**
KT3: N Mald 1K **151**
KT8: W Mole 3F **149**
N13 . . . . . 3H **33**
N14 . . . . . 6A **22**
NW7 . . . . . 3E **28**
UB5: N'olt 6G **59**
UB10: Hil 2B **74**
W3 . . . . . 6A **80**
Fairway Av. NW9 . . . . . 3H **43**
Fair Way Cl. KT6: Surb 3B **162**
Fairway Cl. CR0: C'don 5A **158**
KT19: Ewe 4J **163**
NW11 . . . . . 7A **46**
TW4: Houn 5A **112**
(Green La.)
TW4: Houn 5B **112**
(Staines Rd.)
Fairway Ct. EN5: New Bar 6E **20**
NW7 . . . . . 3E **28**
SE16 . . . . . *2K* ***103***
(off Christopher Cl.)
Fairway Dr. SE28 . . . . . 6D **90**
UB6: G'frd 7F **59**
Fairway Gdns. BR3: Beck 6F **159**
IG1: Ilf 5G **71**
Fairways E17 . . . . . 4E **50**
HA7: Stan 2E **42**
TW7: Isle 1H **113**
TW11: Tedd 7D **132**
TW15: Ashf 6D **128**
Fairways Bus. Pk. E10 . . . . . 2A **68**
Fairway Trad. Est. TW4: Houn 5A **112**
Fairweather Cl. N15 . . . . . 4E **48**
Fairweather Ct. N13 . . . . . 3E **32**
Fairweather Ho. N7 . . . . . 4J **65**
Fairweather Rd. N16 . . . . . 6G **49**
Fairwyn Rd. SE26 . . . . . 4A **140**
Faith Ct. *E3* *2C* ***86***
(off Lefevre Wlk.)
SE1 . . . . . *5F* ***103***
(off Cooper's Rd.)
Fakenham Cl. NW7 . . . . . 7H **29**
UB5: N'olt 6D **58**
Fakruddin St. E1 . . . . . 4G **85**
Falcon *WC1* *5F* ***7***
(off Old Gloucester St.)
Falcon Av. BR1: Brom 4C **160**
Falconberg Ct. W1 . . . . . 7D **6** (6H **83**)
Falconberg M. W1 . . . . . 7D **6** (6H **83**)
Falcon Cl. HA6: Nwood 1G **39**
W4 . . . . . 6J **97**
Falcon Ct. *E18* *3K* ***51***
(off Albert Rd.)
EC4 . . . . . 1K **13** (6A **84**)
EN5: New Bar 4F **21**
HA4: Ruis 2G **57**
N1 . . . . . *1B* ***8***
(off City Gdn. Row)
Falcon Cres. EN3: Pond E 5E **24**
Falcon Dr. TW19: Stanw 6A **110**
Falconer Ct. *N17* *7H* ***33***
(off Compton Cres.)
Falconer Wlk. N7 . . . . . 2K **65**
Falconet Ct. *E1* *1H* ***103***
(off Wapping High St.)
Falcon Gro. SW11 . . . . . 3C **118**
Falcon Highwalk EC1 . . . . . 6C **8**
Falcon Ho. *E14* *5D* ***104***
(off St Davids Sq.)
NW6 . . . . . *1K* ***81***
(off Springfield Wlk.)
SW5 . . . . . *5K* ***99***
(off Old Brompton Rd.)
Falcon La. SW11 . . . . . 3C **118**
Falcon Lodge *W9* *5J* ***81***
(off Admiral Wlk.)
Falcon Pk. Ind. Est. NW10 . . . . . 4A **62**
Falcon Point SE1 . . . . . 3B **14** (7B **84**)
Falcon Rd. EN3: Pond E 5E **24**
SW11 . . . . . 2C **118**
TW12: Hamp 7D **130**
Falconry Ct. *KT1: King T* *3E* ***150***
(off Fairfield Sth.)
Falcon St. E13 . . . . . 4H **87**
Falcon Ter. SW11 . . . . . 3C **118**
Falcon Way E11 . . . . . 4J **51**
E14 . . . . . 4D **104**
HA3: Kenton 5E **42**
NW9 . . . . . 2A **44**
TW14: Felt 5K **111**
TW16: Sun 2G **147**
Falcon Wharf SW11 . . . . . 2B **118**
FALCONWOOD 4K **125**
FALCONWOOD 4H **125**
Falconwood Av. DA16: Well 2H **125**
Falconwood Ct. *SE3* *2H* ***123***
(off Montpelier Row)
Falconwood Pde.
DA16: Well 4J **125**
Falconwood Rd. CR0: Sels 7B **170**
Falcourt Cl. SM1: Sutt 5K **165**
Falkirk Ct. *SE16* *1K* ***103***
(off Rotherhithe St.)
Falkirk Ho. *W9* *2K* ***81***
(off Maida Va.)
Falkirk St. N1 . . . . . 1H **9** (2E **84**)
Falkland Av. N3 . . . . . 7D **30**
N11 . . . . . 4A **32**
Falkland Ho. SE6 . . . . . 4E **140**
W8 . . . . . 3K **99**
W14 . . . . . *5H* ***99***
(off Edith Vs.)
Falkland Pk. Av. SE25 . . . . . 3E **156**
Falkland Pl. NW5 . . . . . 5G **65**
Falkland Rd. EN5: Barn 2B **20**
N8 . . . . . 4A **48**
NW5 . . . . . 5G **65**
Fallaize Av. IG1: Ilf 4F **71**
Falling La. UB7: Yiew 7A **74**
Falloden Way NW11 . . . . . 4J **45**
Fallodon Ho. *W11* *5H* ***81***
(off Tavistock Cres.)
FALLOW CORNER 7F **31**
Fallow Ct. *SE16* *5G* ***103***
(off Argyle Way)
Fallow Ct. Av. N12 . . . . . 7F **31**
Fallowfield HA7: Stan 4F **27**
Fallowfield Ct. HA7: Stan 3F **27**
Fallowfields Dr. N12 . . . . . 6H **31**
Fallowhurst Path N3 . . . . . 7F **31**
Fallows Cl. N2 . . . . . 2B **46**
Fallsbrook Rd. SW16 . . . . . 6F **137**
Falman Cl. N9 . . . . . 1B **34**
Falmer Rd. E17 . . . . . 3D **50**
EN1: Enf 4K **23**
N15 . . . . . 5C **48**
Falmouth Av. E4 . . . . . 5A **36**
Falmouth Cl. N22 . . . . . 7E **32**
SE12 . . . . . 5H **123**
Falmouth Gdns. IG4: Ilf 4B **52**
Falmouth Ho. HA5: Hat E 1D **40**
KT2: King T *1D* ***150***
(off Skerne Rd.)
SE11 . . . . . *5K* ***19***
(off Seaton Cl.)
W2 . . . . . *2C* ***10***
(off Clarendon Pl.)
Falmouth Rd. SE1 . . . . . 7E **14** (3C **102**)
Falmouth St. E15 . . . . . 5F **69**
Falmouth Wlk. SW15 . . . . . 6C **116**
Falmouth Way E17 . . . . . 5B **50**
Falstaff Bldg. *E1* *7H* ***85***
(off Cannon St. Rd.)
Falstaff Cl. DA1: Cray 7K **127**
Falstaff Ct. *SE11* *4B* ***102***
(off Opal St.)
Falstaff Ho. *N1* *1G* ***9***
(off Arden Est.)
Falstaff M. *TW12: Ham H* *5H* ***131***
(off High St.)
Fambridge Cl. SE26 . . . . . 4B **140**
Fambridge Ct. *RM7: Rom* *5K* ***55***
(off Marks Rd.)
Fambridge Rd. RM8: Dag 1G **73**
Fane St. W14 . . . . . 6H **99**
Fan Mus., The 7E **104**
Fann St. EC1 . . . . . 4C **8** (4C **84**)
EC2 . . . . . 4C **8** (4C **84**)
(not continuous)
Fanshawe Av. IG11: Bark 6G **71**
Fanshawe Cres. RM9: Dag 5E **72**
Fanshawe Rd. TW10: Ham 4C **132**
Fanshaw St. N1 . . . . . 1G **9** (3E **84**)
FANTAIL, THE **3D 172**
Fantail Cl. SE28 . . . . . 6C **90**
Fanthorpe St. SW15 . . . . . 3E **116**
Faraday Av. DA14: Sidc 2A **144**
Faraday Cl. N7 . . . . . 6K **65**
Faraday Ho. *E14* *7B* ***86***
(off Brightlingsea Pl.)
HA9: Wemb 3J **61**
SE1 . . . . . *7E* ***14***
(off Cole St.)
W10 . . . . . *5G* ***81***
(off Wornington Rd.)
Faraday Lodge SE10 . . . . . 3H **105**
Faraday Mans. *W14* *6G* ***99***
(off Queen's Club Gdns.)
Faraday Pl. KT8: W Mole 4E **148**
Faraday Rd. DA16: Well 3A **126**
E15 . . . . . 6H **69**
KT8: W Mole 4E **148**
SW19 . . . . . 6J **135**
UB1: S'hall 7F **77**
W3 . . . . . 7J **79**
W10 . . . . . 5G **81**
Faraday Way CR0: Wadd 1K **167**
SE18 . . . . . 3B **106**
Fareham Rd. TW14: Felt 7A **112**
Farewell Pl. CR4: Mitc 1C **154**
Fari Ct. *E17* *4C* ***50***
(off Tower M.)
Faringdon Av. BR2: Brom 7E **160**
Faringford Rd. E15 . . . . . 7G **69**
Farjeon Ho. *NW6* *7B* ***64***
(off Hilgrove Rd.)
Farjeon Rd. SE3 . . . . . 1B **124**
Farleigh Av. BR2: Hayes 7H **159**
Farleigh Ct. CR2: S Croy 5C **168**
Farleigh Ho. *N1* *7B* ***66***
(off Halton Rd.)
Farleigh Pl. N16 . . . . . 4F **67**
Farleigh Rd. N16 . . . . . 4F **67**
Farley Ct. *NW1* *4G* ***5***
(off Allsop Pl.)
W14 . . . . . 3H **99**
Farley Dr. IG3: Ilf 1J **71**
Farley Ho. SE26 . . . . . 3H **139**
Farley Pl. SE25 . . . . . 4G **157**
Farley Rd. CR2: Sels 7H **169**
SE6 . . . . . 7D **122**
Farlington Pl. SW15 . . . . . 7D **116**
Farlow Rd. SW15 . . . . . 3F **117**
Farlton Rd. SW18 . . . . . 1K **135**
Farman Gro. UB5: N'olt 3B **76**
Farman Ter. HA3: Kenton 4D **42**
Farm Av. HA0: Wemb 6C **60**
HA2: Harr 7D **40**
NW2 . . . . . 3G **63**
SW16 . . . . . 4J **137**
Farmborough Cl.
HA1: Harr 7H **41**
Farm Cl. BR4: W W'ck 3H **171**
IG9: Buck H 3F **37**
RM10: Dag 7J **73**
SM2: Sutt 7B **166**
SW6 . . . . . 7J **99**
TW17: Shep 7C **146**
Farm Cl. UB1: S'hall 7F **77**
UB10: Ick 2D **56**
Farmcote Rd. SE12 . . . . . 1J **141**
Farm Ct. NW4 . . . . . 3C **44**
Farmdale Rd. SE10 . . . . . 5J **105**
SM5: Cars 7C **166**
Farm Dr. CR0: C'don 2B **170**
Farm End HA6: Nwood 1D **38**
Farmer Rd. E10 . . . . . 1D **68**
Farmer's Rd. SE5 . . . . . 7B **102**
Farmer St. W8 . . . . . 1J **99**
Farmfield Rd. BR1: Brom 5G **141**
Farm Ho. Ct. NW7 . . . . . 7H **29**
Farmhouse Rd. SW16 . . . . . 7G **137**
Farmilo Rd. E17 . . . . . 7B **50**
Farmington Av. SM1: Sutt 3B **166**
Farmlands EN2: Enf 1F **23**
HA5: Eastc 4J **39**
Farmlands, The UB5: N'olt 6D **58**
Farmland Wlk. BR7: Chst 5F **143**
Farm La. CR0: C'don 2B **170**
N14 . . . . . 7A **22**
SW6 . . . . . 6J **99**
(not continuous)
Farm La. Trad. Est. SW6 . . . . . 6J **99**
Farmleigh N14 . . . . . 7B **22**
Farmleigh Ho. SW9 . . . . . 5B **120**
Farm M. CR4: Mitc 2F **155**
Farm Pl. W8 . . . . . 1J **99**
Farm Rd. E12 . . . . . 2C **70**
HA8: Edg 6C **28**
N21 . . . . . 1H **33**
NW10 . . . . . 1K **79**
SM2: Sutt 7B **166**
SM4: Mord 5K **153**
TW4: Houn 1C **130**
Farmstead Ct. *SM6: Wall* *5F* ***167***
(off Melbourne Rd.)
Farmstead Rd. HA3: Hrw W 1H **41**
SE6 . . . . . 4D **140**
Farm St. W1 . . . . . 3J **11** (7F **83**)
Farm Va. DA5: Bexl 6H **127**
Farm Wlk. NW11 . . . . . 5H **45**
Farm Way IG9: Buck H 4F **37**
KT4: Wor Pk 3E **164**
Farmway RM8: Dag 3C **72**
Farnaby Ho. *W10* *3H* ***81***
(off Bruckner St.)
Farnaby Rd. BR1: Brom 7F **141**
BR2: Brom 7F **141**
SE9 . . . . . 4A **124**
Farnan Av. E17 . . . . . 2C **50**
Farnan Lodge SW16 . . . . . 5J **137**
Farnan Rd. SW16 . . . . . 5J **137**
FARNBOROUGH 5G **173**
Farnborough Av. CR2: Sels 7K **169**
E17 . . . . . 3A **50**
Farnborough Cl. HA9: Wemb 2H **61**
Farnborough Comn. BR6: Farnb 3D **172**
Farnborough Cres. BR2: Hayes 1H **171**
CR2: Sels 7A **170**
Farnborough Hill BR6: Chels, Farnb . . . 5H **173**
Farnborough Ho. SW15 . . . . . 1C **134**
Farnborough Way
BR6: Chels, Farnb 5G **173**
Farncombe St. SE16 . . . . . 2G **103**
Farndale Av. N13 . . . . . 2G **33**
Farndale Ct. SE18 . . . . . 7C **106**
Farndale Cres. UB6: G'frd 3G **77**
Farndale Ho. *NW6* *1K* ***81***
(off Kilburn Va.)
Farnell M. SW5 . . . . . 5K **99**
Farnell Pl. W3 . . . . . 7H **79**
Farnell Rd. TW7: Isle 3H **113**
Farnham Cl. N20 . . . . . 7F **21**
Farnham Ct. SM3: Cheam 6G **165**
UB1: S'hall *7G* ***77***
(off Redcroft Rd.)
Farnham Gdns. SW20 . . . . . 2D **152**
Farnham Ho. NW1 . . . . . 4D **4**
SE1 . . . . . *5C* ***14***
(off Union St.)

Farnham Pl.—Fernbrook Av.

Farnham Pl. SE1	.5B 14 (1B 102)	
Farnham Rd. DA16: Well	.2C 126	
IG3: Ilf	.7F 53	
Farnham Royal SE11	.6H 19 (5K 101)	
Farningham Ct. SW16	.7H 137	
Farningham Ho. N4	.7D 48	
Farningham Rd. N17	.7B 34	
Farnley Ho. SW8	.2H 119	
Farnley Rd. E4	.1B 36	
SE25	.4D 156	
Farnsworth Ct. SE10	.3H 105	
(off West Parkside)		
Farnworth Ho. E14	.4F 105	
(off Manchester Rd.)		
Faro Cl. BR1: Brom	.2E 160	
Faroe Rd. W14	.3F 99	
Farorna Wlk. EN2: Enf	.1F 23	
Farquhar Rd. SE19	.5F 139	
SW19	.3J 135	
Farquharson Rd. CRO: C'don	.1C 168	
Farrance Rd. RM6: Chad H	.6E 54	
Farrance St. E14	.6C 86	
Farrans Ct. HA3: Kenton	.7B 42	
Farrant Av. N22	.2A 48	
Farrant Cl. BR6: Chels	.7K 173	
Farr Av. IG11: Bark	.2A 90	
Farrell Ho. E1	.6J 85	
(off Ronald St.)		
Farren Rd. SE23	.2A 140	
Farrer Ct. TW1: Twick	.7D 114	
Farrer Ho. SE8	.7C 104	
Farrer M. N8	.4G 47	
Farrer Rd. HA3: Kenton	.5E 42	
N8	.4G 47	
Farrer's Pl. CRO: C'don	.4K 169	
Farriance Rd. BR1: Brom	.3B 160	
TW16: Sun	.4J 147	
UB8: Hil	.6C 74	
Farrier Pl. SM1: Sutt	.3K 165	
Farrier Rd. UB5: N'olt	.2E 76	
Farriers Ho. EC1	.4D 8	
(off Errol St.)		
Farriers M. SE15	.3J 121	
Farrier St. NW1	.7F 65	
Fearon St. SE10	.5J 105	
Farrier Wlk. SW10	.6A 100	
Farringdon Ho. TW9: Kew	.7H 97	
UB7: W Dray	.2B 92	
Farringdon La. EC1	.4K 7 (4A 84)	
Farringdon Rd. EC1	.3J 7 (4A 84)	
Farringdon St. EC4	.6A 8 (5B 84)	
Farringdon Pl. BR7: Chst	.7H 143	
Farrins Rents SE16	.1A 104	
Farrow La. SE14	.7J 103	
Farrow Pl. SE16	.3A 104	
Farr Rd. EN2: Enf	.1J 23	
Farthingale Wlk. E15	.7F 69	
Farthing All. SE1	.7K 15 (2G 103)	
Farthing Barn La.		
BR6: Downe	.7E 172	
Farthing Ct. NW7	.7B 30	
Farthing Flds. E1	.1H 103	
Farthings, The KT2: King T	.1G 151	
Farthings Cl. E4	.3B 36	
HA5: Eastc	.6K 39	
FARTHING STREET	.7D 172	
Farthing St. BR6: Downe	.7D 172	
Farwell Rd. DA14: Sidc	.4B 144	
Farwig La. BR1: Brom	.1H 159	
Fashion & Textile Mus.	.6H 15 (2E 102)	
Fashion St. E1	.6K 9 (5F 85)	
Fashoda Rd. BR2: Brom	.4B 160	
Fassett Rd. E8	.6G 67	
KT1: King T	.4E 150	
Fassett Sq. E8	.6G 67	
Fathom Ct. E16	.7F 89	
(off Basin App.)		
Fauconberg Ct. W4	.6J 97	
(off Fauconberg Rd.)		
Fauconberg Rd. W4	.6J 97	
Faulkner Cl. RM8: Dag	.7D 54	
Faulkners All. EC1	.5A 8 (5B 84)	
Faulkner St. SE14	.1J 121	

Fauna Cl. HA7: Stan	.4J 27	
RM6: Chad H	.6C 54	
Faunce Ho. SE17	.6B 102	
(off Doddington Gro.)		
Faunce St. SE17	.5B 102	
Favart Rd. SW6	.1J 117	
Faversham Av. E4	.1B 36	
EN1: Enf	.6J 23	
Faversham Ho. NW1	.1G 83	
(off Bayham Pl.)		
SE17	.5E 102	
(off Kinglake St.)		
Faversham Rd. BR3: Beck	.2B 158	
SE6	.7B 122	
SM4: Mord	.6K 153	
Fawcett Cl. SW11	.2B 118	
SW16	.5A 138	
Fawcett Ct. SW10	.6A 100	
(off Fawcett St.)		
Fawcett Est. E5	.1G 67	
Fawcett Rd. CRO: C'don	.3C 168	
NW10	.7B 62	
Fawcett St. SW10	.6A 100	
Fawe Pk. M. SW15	.4H 117	
Fawe Pk. Rd. SW15	.4H 117	
Fawe St. E14	.5D 86	
Fawkham Ho. SE1	.4F 103	
(off Longfield Est.)		
Fawley Lodge E14	.4F 105	
(off Millennium Dr.)		
Fawley Rd. NW6	.5K 63	
Fawnbrake Av. SE24	.5B 120	
Fawn Rd. E13	.2A 88	
Fawns Mnr. Cl. TW14: Bedf	.1E 128	
Fawns Mnr. Rd. TW14: Bedf	.1F 129	
Fawood Av. NW10	.7J 61	
Faygate Cres. DA6: Bex	.5G 127	
Faygate Rd. SW2	.2K 137	
Fayland Av. SW16	.5G 137	
Fazeley Cl. W9	.5J 81	
(off Elmfield Way)		
Fearnley Cres. TW12: Hamp	.5C 130	
Fearnley Ho. SE5	.2E 120	
Fearon St. SE10	.5J 105	
Featherbed La. CRO: Sels	.7B 170	
Feathers Pl. SE10	.6F 105	
Featherstone Av. SE23	.2H 139	
Featherstone Ho. UB4: Yead	.5A 76	
Featherstone Ind. Est. UB2: S'hall	.3C 94	
(off Feather Rd.)		
Featherstone Rd. NW7	.6J 29	
UB2: S'hall	.3C 94	
Featherstone Sports Cen.	.4B 94	
Featherstone St. EC1	.3E 8 (4D 84)	
Featherstone Ter. UB2: S'hall	.3C 94	
Featley Rd. SW9	.3B 120	
Federal Rd. UB6: G'frd	.1C 78	
Federation Rd. SE2	.4B 108	
Feeny Cl. NW10	.4B 62	
Fee Farm Rd. KT10: Clay	.7A 162	
Felbridge Av. HA7: Stan	.1A 42	
Felbridge Cl. SM2: Sutt	.7K 165	
SW16	.4A 138	
Felbridge Ct. TW13: Felt	.1K 129	
(off High St.)		
UB3: Harl	.6F 93	
Felbridge Ho. SE22	.3E 120	
Felbrigge Rd. IG3: Ilf	.2K 71	
Felday Rd. SE13	.6D 122	
Felden Cl. HA5: Hat E	.1C 40	
Felden St. SW6	.1H 117	
Feldman Cl. N16	.1G 67	
Feldspar Ct. EN3: Enf H	.3F 25	
(off Enstone Rd.)		
Felgate M. W6	.4D 98	
Felhampton Rd. SE9	.2F 143	
Felhurst Cres. RM10: Dag	.4H 73	
Feline Ct. EN4: E Barn	.6H 21	
Felix Av. N8	.6J 47	
Felix Ct. E17	.5D 50	
Felix Ho. E16	.7E 88	
(off University Way)		

Felix La. TW17: Shep	.6G 147	
Felix Mnr. BR7: Chst	.6J 143	
Felix Neubergh Ho. EN1: Enf	.4K 23	
Felix Pl. SW2	.5A 120	
(off Talma Rd.)		
Felix Rd. KT12: Walt T	.6J 147	
W13	.7A 78	
Felixstowe Ct. E16	.1F 107	
Felixstowe Rd. N9	.3B 34	
N17	.3F 49	
NW10	.3D 80	
SE2	.3B 108	
Felix St. E2	.2H 85	
Fellbrigg Rd. SE22	.5F 121	
Fellbrigg St. E1	.4H 85	
Fellbrook TW10: Ham	.3B 132	
Fellmongers Path SE1	.7J 15	
Fellmongers Yd. CRO: C'don	.3C 168	
(off Surrey St.)		
Fellowes Cl. UB4: Yead	.4B 76	
Fellowes Rd. SM5: Cars	.3C 166	
Fellows Ct. E2	.1J 9 (2F 85)	
(not continuous)		
Fellows Rd. NW3	.7B 64	
Fell Rd. CRO: C'don	.3C 168	
(not continuous)		
Felltram M. SE7	.5J 105	
Felltram Way SE7	.5J 105	
Fell Wlk. HA8: Edg	.1J 43	
Felmersham Cl. SW4	.4J 119	
Felmingham Rd. SE20	.2J 157	
Felnex Trad. Est. NW10	.2K 79	
SM6: Wall	.2E 166	
Felsberg Rd. SW2	.6J 119	
Fels Cl. RM10: Dag	.3H 73	
Fels Farm Av. RM10: Dag	.3J 73	
Felsham M. SW15	.3F 117	
(off Felsham Rd.)		
Felsham Rd. SW15	.3E 116	
Felspar Cl. SE18	.5K 107	
Felstead Av. IG5: Ilf	.1E 52	
Felstead Cl. N13	.5F 33	
Felstead Gdns. E14	.5E 104	
Felstead Rd. E9	.6B 68	
E11	.7J 51	
Felstead St. E9	.6B 68	
Felstead Wharf E14	.5E 104	
Felsted Rd. E16	.6B 88	
FELTHAM	.1K 129	
Feltham Airparcs Leisure Cen.	.2B 130	
Feltham Arenas	.7J 111	
Feltham Av. KT8: E Mos	.4J 149	
Felthambrook Ind. Est. TW13: Felt	.3K 129	
Felthambrook Way TW13: Felt	.3K 129	
Feltham Bus. Complex		
TW13: Felt	.2K 129	
Feltham Corporate Cen.		
TW13: Felt	.3K 129	
FELTHAMHILL	.5H 129	
Feltham Hill Rd. TW15: Ashf	.5C 128	
Feltham Rd. CR4: Mitc	.2D 154	
TW15: Ashf	.4C 128	
Felton Cl. BR5: Pet W	.6F 161	
Felton Gdns. IG11: Bark	.1J 89	
Felton Ho. N1	.1D 84	
(off Branch Pl.)		
SE3	.4K 123	
Felton Lea DA14: Sidc	.5K 143	
Felton Rd. IG11: Bark	.2J 89	
W13	.2C 96	
Felton St. N1	.1D 84	
Fencepiece Rd. IG6: Chig, Ilf	.1G 53	
Fenchurch Av. EC3	.1G 15 (6E 84)	
Fenchurch Bldgs. EC3	.1H 15 (6E 84)	
Fenchurch Ho. EC3	.1J 15	
(off Minories)		
Fenchurch Pl. EC3	.2H 15 (6E 84)	
Fenchurch St. EC3	.2G 15 (7E 84)	
Fendall Rd. KT19: Ewe	.5J 163	
Fendall St. SE1	.3E 102	
(not continuous)		

Fendt Cl. E16	.6H 87	
Fendyke Rd. DA17: Belv	.4D 108	
Fenelon Pl. W14	.4H 99	
Fen Gro. DA15: Sidc	.5K 125	
Fenham Rd. SE15	.7G 103	
Fenland Ho. E5	.2J 67	
Fen La. SW13	.1D 116	
Fenman Ct. N17	.1H 49	
Fenman Gdns. IG3: Ilf	.1B 72	
Fenn Cl. BR1: Brom	.6J 141	
Fennel Apartments SE1	.5J 15	
(off Cayenne Ct.)		
Fennel Cl. CRO: C'don	.1K 169	
E16	.4G 87	
Fennells Mead KT17: Ewe	.7B 164	
Fennell St. SE18	.6E 106	
Fenner Cl. SE16	.4H 103	
Fenner Ho. E1	.1H 103	
(off Watts St.)		
Fenner Sq. SW11	.3B 118	
Fenn Ho. TW7: Isle	.1B 114	
Fenning St. SE1	.6G 15 (2E 102)	
Fenn St. E9	.5K 67	
Fenstanton N4	.1K 65	
(off Marquis Rd.)		
Fenstanton Av. N12	.6G 31	
Fen St. E16	.7H 87	
Fenswood Cl. DA5: Bexl	.6G 127	
Fentiman Rd. SW8	.7F 19 (6J 101)	
Fentiman Way HA2: Harr	.2F 59	
Fenton Cl. BR7: Chst	.5D 142	
E8	.6F 67	
SW9	.2K 119	
Fenton House	.4A 64	
(off Windmill Hill)		
Fenton Ho. SE14	.7A 104	
TW5: Hest	.6E 94	
Fenton Rd. N17	.7H 33	
Fentons Av. E13	.3K 87	
Fenton St. E1	.6H 85	
Fenwick Cl. SE18	.6E 106	
Fenwick Gro. SE15	.3G 121	
Fenwick Pl. CR2: S Croy	.7B 168	
SW9	.3J 119	
Fenwick Rd. SE15	.3G 121	
Ferby Ct. DA14: Sidc	.4K 143	
(off Main Rd.)		
SE9	.3H 143	
(off Main Rd.)		
Ferdinand Ho. NW1	.7E 64	
(off Ferdinand Pl.)		
Ferdinand Pl. NW1	.7E 64	
Ferdinand St. NW1	.7E 64	
Ferguson Av. KT5: Surb	.5F 151	
Ferguson Cen., The E17	.6A 50	
Ferguson Cl. BR2: Brom	.3F 159	
E14	.4C 104	
Ferguson Dr. W3	.6K 79	
Ferguson Ho. SE10	.1E 122	
(off Sparta St.)		
Fergus Rd. N5	.5B 66	
Ferial Ct. SE15	.7G 103	
(off Fenham Rd.)		
Fermain Ct. E. N1	.1E 84	
(off De Beauvoir Est.)		
Fermain Ct. Nth. N1	.1E 84	
(off De Beauvoir Est.)		
Fermain Ct. W. N1	.1E 84	
(off De Beauvoir Est.)		
Ferme Pk. Rd. N4	.5J 47	
N8	.5J 47	
Fermor Rd. SE23	.1A 140	
Fermoy Ho. W9	.4H 81	
(off Fermoy Rd.)		
Fermoy Rd. UB6: G'frd	.4F 77	
W9	.4H 81	
Fern Av. CR4: Mitc	.4H 155	
Fernbank IG9: Buck H	.1E 36	
Fernbank Av. HA0: Wemb	.4K 59	
KT12: Walt T	.7C 148	
Fernbank M. SW12	.6G 119	
Fernbrook Av. DA15: Sidc	.5J 125	

Fernbrook Cres. SE13 . . . . .6G **123**
    (off Leahurst Rd.)
Fernbrook Dr. HA2: Harr 7F **41**
Fernbrook Rd. SE13 . . . . .5G **123**
Ferncliff Rd. E8 . . . . .5G **67**
Fern Cl. N1 . . . . .2E **84**
Fern Ct. DA7: Bex 4G **127**
    RM7: Rom 5K **55**
    SE14 . . . . .2K **121**
Ferncroft Av. HA4: Ruis 2A **58**
    N12 . . . . .6J **31**
    NW3 . . . . .3J **63**
Ferndale BR1: Brom 2A **160**
Ferndale Av. E17 . . . . .5F **51**
    TW4: Houn 3C **112**
Ferndale Cl. DA7: Bex 1E **126**
Ferndale Community Sports Cen. . . .3K **119**
Ferndale Rd. E7 . . . . .7K **69**
    E11 . . . . .2G **69**
    N15 . . . . .6F **49**
    RM5: Col R 2J **55**
    SE25 . . . . .5H **157**
    SW4 . . . . .4J **119**
    SW9 . . . . .4J **119**
    TW15: Ashf 5A **128**
Ferndale St. E6 . . . . .7F **89**
Ferndale Ter. HA1: Harr 4K **41**
Ferndale Way BR6: Farnb 5H **173**
Ferndell Av. DA5: Bexl 3K **145**
Fern Dene W13 . . . . .5B **78**
Ferndene Rd. SE24 . . . . .4C **120**
Fernden Way RM7: Rom 6H **55**
Ferndown HA6: Nwood 2J **39**
    NW1 . . . . .7H **65**
    (off Camley St.)
Ferndown Av. BR6: Orp 1H **173**
Ferndown Cl. HA5: Pinn 1C **40**
    SM2: Sutt 6B **166**
Ferndown Ct. UB1: S'hall 6G **77**
    (off Haldane Rd.)
Ferndown Lodge E14 . . . . .3E **104**
    (off Manchester Rd.)
Ferndown Rd. SE9 . . . . .7B **124**
Ferney Meade Way TW7: Isle 2A **114**
Ferney Rd. EN4: E Barn 7K **21**
Fern Gro. TW14: Felt 7K **111**
Fernhall Dr. IG4: Ilf 5B **52**
Fernham Rd. CR7: Thor H 3C **156**
Fernhead Rd. W9 . . . . .3H **81**
Fernheath Way DA2: Dart 5K **145**
Fernhill Cl. E17 . . . . .1D **106**
Fernhill Gdns. KT2: King T 5D **132**
Fern Hill Pl. BR6: Farnb 5G **173**
Fernhill St. E16 . . . . .1D **106**
Fernholme Rd. SE15 . . . . .5K **121**
Fernhurst Gdns. HA8: Edg 6B **28**
Fernhurst Rd. CR0: C'don 7H **157**
    SW6 . . . . .1G **117**
    TW15: Ashf 4E **128**
Fern La. TW5: Hest 5D **94**
Fernlea Rd. CR4: Mitc 2E **154**
    SW12 . . . . .1F **137**
Fernleigh Cl. CR0: Wadd 4A **168**
    W9 . . . . .3H **81**
Fernleigh Ct. HA2: Harr 2F **41**
    HA9: Wemb 2E **60**
    RM7: Rom 5J **55**
Fernleigh Rd. N21 . . . . .2F **33**
Fernley Cl. HA5: Eastc 4A **40**
Fernsbury St. WC1 . . . . .2J **7** (3A **84**)
Fernshaw Cl. SW10 . . . . .6A **100**
Fernshaw Mans. SW10 . . . . .6A **100**
    (off Fernshaw Rd.)
Fernshaw Rd. SW10 . . . . .6A **100**
Fernside IG9: Buck H 1E **36**
    NW11 . . . . .2J **63**
Fernside Av. NW7 . . . . .3E **28**
    TW13: Felt 4K **129**
Fernside Cl. NW4 . . . . .2F **45**
    (off Holders Hill Rd.)
Fernside Rd. SW12 . . . . .1D **136**
Ferns Rd. E15 . . . . .6H **69**

Fern St. E3 . . . . .4C **86**
Fernthorpe Rd. SW16 . . . . .6G **137**
Ferntower Rd. N5 . . . . .5D **66**
Fern Wlk. SE16 . . . . .5G **103**
    TW15: Ashf 5A **128**
Fernways IG1: Ilf 4F **71**
Fenwood SW19 . . . . .1H **135**
Fenwood Av. HA0: Wemb 6C **60**
    SW16 . . . . .4H **137**
Fernwood Cl. BR1: Brom 2A **160**
Fernwood Ct. N14 . . . . .7B **22**
Fernwood Cres. N20 . . . . .3J **31**
Ferny Hill EN4: Had W 1J **21**
Ferranti Cl. SE18 . . . . .3B **106**
Ferraro Cl. TW5: Hest 6E **94**
Ferrers Av. SM6: Bedd 4H **167**
    UB7: W Dray 2A **92**
Ferrers Rd. SW16 . . . . .5H **137**
Ferrestone Rd. N8 . . . . .4K **47**
Ferrey M. SW9 . . . . .2A **120**
Ferriby Cl. N1 .7A **66**
Ferrier Ind. Est. SW18 . . . . .4K **117**
    (off Ferrier St.)
Ferrier Point E16 . . . . .5J **87**
    (off Forty Acre La.)
Ferrier St. SW18 . . . . .4K **117**
Ferring Cl. HA2: Harr 1G **59**
Ferrings SE21 . . . . .3E **138**
Ferris Av. CR0: C'don 3B **170**
Ferris Rd. SE22 . . . . .4G **121**
Ferron Rd. E5 .3H **67**
Ferry App. SE18 . . . . .3E **106**
Ferrybridge Ho. SE11 . . . . .2H **19**
Ferrydale Lodge NW4 . . . . .4E **44**
    (off Parson St.)
Ferry Ho. E5 . . . . .1H **67**
    (off Harrington Hill)
Ferry Island Retail Pk. N17 . . . . . . .3G **49**
Ferry La. N17 .4G **49**
    SW13 . . . . .6B **98**
    TW8: Bford 6E **96**
    TW9: Kew 6F **97**
    TW17: Shep 7C **146**
Ferry La. Ind. Est. E17 . . . . .4K **49**
Ferryman's Quay SW6 . . . . .2A **118**
Ferrymead Av. UB6: G'frd 3E **76**
Ferrymead Dr. UB6: G'frd 2E **76**
Ferrymead Gdns. UB6: G'frd 2G **77**
Ferrymoor TW10: Ham 3B **132**
Ferry Pl. SE18 . . . . .3E **106**
Ferry Quays TW8: Bford 7D **96**
    (off Point Wharf La.)
    TW8: Bford 7E **96**
    (Ferry La.)
Ferry Rd. KT7: T Ditt 6B **150**
    KT8: W Mole 3E **148**
    SW13 . . . . .7C **98**
    TW1: Twick 1B **132**
    TW11: Tedd 5B **132**
Ferry Sq. TW8: Bford 7E **96**
Ferry St. E14 .5E **104**
Ferry Wharf TW8: Bford 7E **96**
Festing Rd. SW15 . . . . .3F **117**
Festival Cl. DA5: Bexl 1D **144**
    UB10: Hil .1D **74**
Festival Ct. E8 . . . . .7F **67**
    (off Holly St.)
    SM1: Sutt 7K **153**
Festival Wlk. SM5: Cars 4D **166**
Festoon Way E16 . . . . .7B **88**
Fetherstone Ct. RM6: Chad H 6F **55**
    (off High Rd.)
Fetherton Ct. IG11: Bark 2G **89**
    (off Spring Pl.)
Fetter La. EC4 . . . . .1K **13** (6A **84**)
    (not continuous)
Fettes Ho. NW8 . . . . .2B **82**
    (off Wellington Rd.)
Fews Lodge RM6: Chad H 4D **54**
Ffinch St. SE8 . . . . .7C **104**
Fidelis Ho. E1 .6J **9**
    (off Gun St.)

Fidgeon Cl. BR1: Brom 3E **160**
Field Cl. BR1: Brom 2A **160**
    E4 . . . . .6J **35**
    HA4: Ruis 1E **56**
    IG9: Buck H 3F **37**
    KT8: W Mole 5F **149**
    KT9: Chess 5C **162**
    NW2 . . . . .2C **62**
    TW4: Cran 1K **111**
    UB3: Harl 7E **92**
    UB10: Ick 2D **56**
FIELDCOMMON 7D **148**
Fieldcommon La.
    KT12: Walt T 7C **148**
Field Ct. SW19 . . . . .3J **135**
    WC1 . . . . .6H **7** (5K **83**)
Field End HA4: Ruis 6A **58**
    UB5: N'olt 6B **58**
Fieldend TW1: Twick 4K **131**
Field End Rd. HA4: Ruis 1B **58**
    HA5: Eastc 5K **39**
Fieldend Rd. SW16 . . . . .1G **155**
Fielders Cl. EN1: Enf 4K **23**
    HA2: Harr 1G **59**
Fieldfare Rd. SE28 . . . . .7C **90**
Fieldgate La. CR4: Mitc 2C **154**
Fieldgate Mans. E1 . . . . .5G **85**
    (off Fieldgate St., not continuous)
Fieldgate St. E1 . . . . .5G **85**
Field Ho. NW6 . . . . .3F **81**
    (off Harvist Rd.)
Fieldhouse Cl. E18 . . . . .1J **51**
Fieldhouse Rd. SW12 . . . . .1G **137**
Fielding Av. TW2: Twick 3G **131**
Fielding Ct. WC2 . . . . .1E **12**
    (off Tower St.)
Fielding Ho. NW6 . . . . .3J **81**
    NW8 . . . . .1A **82**
    (off Ainsworth Way)
    W4 . . . . .6A **98**
    (off Devonshire Rd.)
Fielding La. BR2: Brom 4A **160**
Fielding M. SW13 . . . . .6D **98**
Fielding Rd. W4 . . . . .3K **97**
    W14 . . . . .3F **99**
Fieldings, The SE23 . . . . .1J **139**
Fielding St. SE17 . . . . .6C **102**
Fielding Ter. W5 . . . . .7F **79**
Fielding Wlk. W13 . . . . .3B **96**
Field La. TW8: Bford 7C **96**
    TW11: Tedd 5A **132**
Field Mead NW7 . . . . .7F **29**
    NW9 . . . . .7G **29**
Fieldpark Gdns. CR0: C'don 1A **170**
Field Pl. KT3: N Mald 6B **152**
Field Point E7 .4J **69**
Field Rd. E7 . . . . .4H **69**
    N17 . . . . .3D **48**
    TW14: Felt 6K **111**
    W6 . . . . .5G **99**
Fieldsend Rd. SM3: Cheam 5G **165**
Fields Est. E8 .7G **67**
Fieldside Cl. BR6: Farnb 4G **173**
Fieldside Rd. BR1: Brom 5F **141**
Fields Pk. Cres.
    RM6: Chad H 5D **54**
Field St. WC1 . . . . .1G **7** (3K **83**)
Fieldsway Ho. N5 . . . . .5A **66**
Field Vw. TW13: Felt 4F **129**
Fieldview SW18 . . . . .1B **136**
Field Vw. Cl. RM7: Mawney 3G **55**
Fieldview Cotts. N14 . . . . .2C **32**
    (off Balaams La.)
Field Way HA4: Ruis 1E **56**
    NW10 . . . . .7J **61**
    UB6: G'frd 1F **77**
Fieldway BR5: Pet W 6H **161**
    CR0: New Ad 7D **170**
    RM8: Dag 3C **72**
Fieldway Cres. N5 . . . . .5A **66**
Fiennes Cl. RM8: Dag 1C **72**
Fifehead Cl. TW15: Ashf 6A **128**

Fife Rd. E16 . . . . .5J **87**
    KT1: King T 2E **150**
    (not continuous)
    N22 . . . . .7G **33**
    SW14 . . . . .5J **115**
Fife Ter. N1 . . . . .2K **83**
Fifield Path SE23 . . . . .3K **139**
Fifth Av. E12 .4D **70**
    UB3: Hayes 1H **93**
    W10 . . . . .3G **81**
Fifth Cross Rd. TW2: Twick 2H **131**
Fifth Way HA9: Wemb 4H **61**
Figges Rd. CR4: Mitc 7E **136**
Fig Tree Cl. NW10 . . . . .1A **80**
Figure Ct. SW3 . . . . .6F **17**
Filanco Ct. W7 . . . . .1K **95**
Filby Rd. KT9: Chess 6F **163**
Filey Av. N16 .1G **67**
Filey Cl. SM2: Sutt 7A **166**
Filey Waye HA4: Ruis 2J **57**
Filigree Ct. SE16 . . . . .1B **104**
Fillebrook Av. EN1: Enf 2K **23**
Fillebrook Rd. E11 . . . . .1F **69**
Filmer Chambers SW6 . . . . .1G **117**
    (off Filmer Rd.)
Filmer Ho. SW6 . . . . .1H **117**
    (off Filmer Rd.)
Filmer M. SW6 . . . . .1H **117**
Filmer Rd. SW6 . . . . .1G **117**
Filston Rd. DA8: Erith 5J **109**
Filton Cl. NW9 . . . . .1A **44**
Filton Ct. SE14 . . . . .7J **103**
    (off Farrow La.)
Finborough Ho. SW10 . . . . .6A **100**
    (off Finborough Rd.)
Finborough Rd. SW10 . . . . .5K **99**
    SW17 . . . . .6D **136**
Finborough Theatre, The 6K **99**
    (off Finborough Rd.)
Finchale Rd. SE2 . . . . .3A **108**
Fincham Cl. UB10: Ick 3E **56**
Finch Av. SE27 . . . . .4D **138**
Finch Cl. EN5: Barn 5D **20**
    NW10 . . . . .6K **61**
Finch Ct. DA14: Sidc 3B **144**
Finchdean Ho. SW15 . . . . .7B **116**
Finch Dr. TW14: Felt 7B **112**
Finch Gdns. E4 . . . . .5H **35**
Finch Ho. E3 .1B **86**
    (off Jasmine Sq.)
    SE8 . . . . .7D **104**
    (off Bronze St.)
Finchingfield Av. IG8: Wfd G 7F **37**
Finch La. EC3 . . . . .1F **15** (6D **84**)
FINCHLEY 1J **45**
Finchley Ct. N3 . . . . .6E **30**
Finchley Ind. Est. N12 . . . . .4F **31**
Finchley La. NW4 . . . . .4E **44**
Finchley Lido .7G **31**
Finchley Manor Club 1H **45**
Finchley Pk. N12 . . . . .4F **31**
Finchley Pl. NW8 . . . . .2B **82**
Finchley Rd. NW3 . . . . .1J **63**
    NW8 . . . . .1B **82**
    NW11 . . . . .4H **45**
Finchley Way N3 . . . . .7D **30**
Finch Lodge W9 . . . . .5J **81**
    (off Admiral Wlk.)
Finch M. SE15 . . . . .1F **121**
Finch's Ct. E14 . . . . .7D **86**
Finden Rd. E7 . . . . .5K **69**
Findhorn Av. UB4: Yead 5K **75**
Findhorn St. E14 . . . . .6E **86**
Findon Cl. HA2: Harr 3F **59**
    SW18 . . . . .6J **117**
Findon Rd. N9 . . . . .1C **34**
    W12 . . . . .2C **98**
Fine Bush La. UB9: Hare 6D **38**
Fingal St. SE10 . . . . .5H **105**
Fingest Ho. NW8 . . . . .3C **4**
    (off Lilestone St.)
Finians Cl. UB10: Uxb 7B **56**

Finland Rd. SE4 . . . 3A 122
Finland St. SE16 . . . 3A 104
Finlays Cl. KT9: Chess . . . 5G 163
Finlay St. SW6 . . . 1F 117
Finmere Ho. N4 . . . 7C 48
Finnemore Ho. *N1* . . . *1C 84*
(off Britannia Row)
Finney La. TW7: Isle . . . 1A 114
Finn Ho. *N1* . . . *1F 9*
(off Bevenden St.)
Finnis St. E2 . . . 3H 85
Finnymore Rd. RM9: Dag . . . 7E 72
FINSBURY . . . 3C 8 (3A 84)
Finsbury Av. EC2 . . . 6F 9 (5D 84)
(not continuous)
Finsbury Av. Sq. EC2 . . . 5G 9 (5E 84)
Finsbury Cir. EC2 . . . 6F 9 (5D 84)
Finsbury Cotts. N22 . . . 7D 32
Finsbury Est. EC1 . . . 2K 7 (3A 84)
Finsbury Ho. N22 . . . 1J 47
Finsbury Leisure Cen. . . . 3C 8 (3C 84)
Finsbury Mkt. EC2 . . . 4G 9 (4E 84)
(not continuous)
FINSBURY PARK . . . 1A 66
Finsbury Pk. Av. N4 . . . 6C 48
Finsbury Pk. Rd. N4 . . . 2B 66
Finsbury Pavement EC2 . . . 5F 9 (5D 84)
Finsbury Rd. N22 . . . 7E 32
(not continuous)
Finsbury Sq. EC2 . . . 4F 9 (4D 84)
Finsbury St. EC2 . . . 5E 8 (5D 84)
Finsbury Way DA5: Bexl . . . 6F 127
Finsen Rd. SE5 . . . 4C 120
Finstock Rd. W10 . . . 6F 81
Finucane Ct. *TW9: Rich* . . . *3F 115*
(off Lwr. Mortlake Rd.)
Finucane Ri. WD23: B Hea . . . 2B 26
Finwhale Ho. *E14* . . . *3D 104*
(off Glengall Gro.)
Fiona Ct. EN2: Enf . . . 3G 23
NW6 . . . 2J 81
Firbank Cl. E16 . . . 5B 88
EN2: Enf . . . 4H 23
Firbank Rd. SE15 . . . 2H 121
Fir Cl. KT12: Walt T . . . 7J 147
Fircroft Gdns. HA1: Harr . . . 3J 59
Fircroft Rd. KT9: Chess . . . 4F 163
SW17 . . . 2D 136
Fir Dene BR6: Farnb . . . 3D 172
Firdene KT5: Surb . . . 1J 163
Fire Bell All. KT6: Surb . . . 6E 150
Firecrest Dr. NW3 . . . 3K 63
Firefly Gdns. E6 . . . 4C 88
Firemans Flats N22 . . . 7D 32
Firepower (The Royal Artillery Mus.)
. . . 3F 107
Fire Sta. All. EN5: Barn . . . 3B 20
Fire Sta. M. BR3: Beck . . . 1C 158
Firestone Ho. TW8: Bford . . . 5E 96
Firethorn Cl. HA8: Edg . . . 4D 28
Firewatch Ct. *E1* . . . *5A 86*
(off Candle St.)
Fir Gro. KT3: N Mald . . . 6B 152
Fir Gro. Rd. SW9 . . . 2A 120
Firhill Rd. SE6 . . . 4C 140
Fir Ho. *W10* . . . *4G 81*
(off Droop St.)
Firle Ho. *W10* . . . *5E 80*
(off Sutton Way)
Firman Cl. KT3: N Mald . . . 4A 152
Firmans Ct. E17 . . . 4F 51
Fir Rd. SM3: Sutt . . . 1H 165
TW13: Hanw . . . 5B 130
Firs, The DA5: Bexl . . . 1K 145
DA15: Sidc . . . 2K 143
E6 . . . 7C 70
HA8: Edg . . . *4E 28*
(off Stoneyfields La.)
IG8: Wfd G . . . 7F 37
N20 . . . 1G 31
SE26 . . . 5H 139
(Border Rd.)
Firs, The SE26 . . . 5J 139
(Waverley Ct.)
W5 . . . 5D 78
Firs Av. N10 . . . 3E 46
N11 . . . 6J 31
SW14 . . . 4J 115
Firsby Av. CR0: C'don . . . 1K 169
Firsby Rd. N16 . . . 1G 67
Firs Cl. CR4: Mitc . . . 2F 155
N10 . . . 4E 46
SE23 . . . 7A 122
Firscroft N13 . . . 3H 33
Firs Dr. TW5: Cran . . . 7K 93
Firs Ho. *N22* . . . *1A 48*
(off Acacia Rd.)
Firside Gro. DA15: Sidc . . . 1K 143
Firs La. N13 . . . 3H 33
N21 . . . 7H 23
Firs Pk. Av. N21 . . . 1J 33
Firs Pk. Gdns. N21 . . . 1H 33
First Av. DA7: Bex . . . 7C 108
E12 . . . 4C 70
E13 . . . 3J 87
E17 . . . 5C 50
EN1: Enf . . . 5A 24
HA9: Wemb . . . 2D 60
KT8: W Mole . . . 4D 148
KT12: Walt T . . . 6K 147
KT19: Ewe . . . 7A 164
N18 . . . 4D 34
NW4 . . . 4E 44
RM6: Chad H . . . 5C 54
RM10: Dag . . . 2H 91
SW14 . . . 3A 116
UB3: Hayes . . . 1H 93
W3 . . . 1B 98
W10 . . . 4H 81
First Cl. KT8: W Mole . . . 3G 149
First Cross Rd. TW2: Twick . . . 2J 131
First Dr. NW10 . . . 7J 61
First St. SW3 . . . 3D 16 (4C 100)
First Way HA9: Wemb . . . 4H 61
Firstway SW20 . . . 2E 152
Firs Wlk. IG8: Wfd G . . . 5D 36
Firswood Av. KT19: Ewe . . . 5A 164
Firth Gdns. SW6 . . . 1G 117
Firth Ho. *E2* . . . *3G 85*
(off Turin St.)
Fir Tree Av. UB7: W Dray . . . 3C 92
Firtree Av. CR4: Mitc . . . 2E 154
Fir Tree Cl. BR6: Chels . . . 5K 173
KT19: Ewe . . . 4B 164
RM1: Rom . . . 3K 55
SW16 . . . 5G 137
W5 . . . 6E 78
Fir Tree Gdns. CR0: C'don . . . 4C 170
Fir Tree Gro. SM5: Cars . . . 7D 166
Fir Tree Ho. *SE14* . . . *7J 103*
(off Avonley Rd.)
Firtree Ho. *SE13* . . . *7F 123*
(off Birdwood Av.)
Fir Tree Pl. TW15: Ashf . . . 5C 128
Fir Tree Rd. TW4: Houn . . . 4C 112
Fir Trees Cl. SE16 . . . 1A 104
Fir Tree Wlk. EN1: Enf . . . 3J 23
RM10: Dag . . . 3J 73
Fir Wlk. SM3: Cheam . . . 6F 165
Fisher Cl. CR0: C'don . . . 1F 169
E9 . . . 5K 67
UB6: G'frd . . . 3E 76
Fisher Ho. *E1* . . . *7J 85*
(off Cable St.)
N1 . . . *1A 84*
(off Barnsbury Est.)
Fisherman Cl. TW10: Ham . . . 4B 132
Fishermans Dr. SE16 . . . 2K 103
Fisherman's Pl. W4 . . . 6B 98
Fishermans Wlk. E14 . . . 1C 104
SE28 . . . 2J 107
Fisher Rd. HA3: W'stone . . . 2K 41
Fisher's Cl. SW16 . . . 3H 137
Fishers Ct. SE14 . . . 1K 121
Fishersdene KT10: Clay . . . 7A 162
Fisher's La. W4 . . . 4K 97
Fisher St. E16 . . . 5J 87
WC1 . . . 6G 7 (5K 83)
Fishers Way DA17: Belv . . . 1J 109
Fisherton St. NW8 . . . 4A 4 (4B 82)
Fishguard Way E16 . . . 1F 107
Fishmongers Hall Wharf EC4 . . . 3E 14
Fishponds Rd. BR2: Kes . . . 5B 172
SW17 . . . 4C 136
Fish St. Hill EC3 . . . 3F 15 (7D 84)
Fish Wharf EC3 . . . 3F 15 (7D 84)
Fisk Cl. TW16: Sun . . . 6H 129
Fiske Ct. IG11: Bark . . . 2H 89
N17 . . . 1G 49
SM2: Sutt . . . 7A 166
Fitness First Health Club
Alperton . . . 1E 78
America Square . . . 2J 15
Baker Street . . . 6F 5 (5D 82)
Beckenham . . . 5B 140
Bloomsbury . . . 4E 6
Bow Wharf . . . 2K 85
Camden . . . 1F 83
Chancery Lane . . . 6K 7
Clapham Junction . . . *3C 118*
(off Lavender Hill)
Covent Garden . . . *3F 13*
(off Bedford St.)
Crouch End . . . 6J 47
Croydon . . . 1B 168
Embankment . . . *4F 13*
(off Embankment Pl.)
Fetter Lane . . . *1K 13*
(off Fetter La.)
Gracechurch Street . . . *2G 15*
(off Gracechurch St.)
Great Marlborough Street . . . 1A 12
Hammersmith . . . 4E 98
Harrow . . . *6J 41*
(in St George's Shop. & Leisure Cen.)
High Holborn . . . *6G 7*
(off High Holborn)
Holloway . . . 3K 65
Ilford . . . 2G 71
Islington . . . 1A 8 (2B 84)
Kilburn . . . 1H 81
Kingly St. . . . 2A 12
Kingsbury . . . 5G 43
Lewisham . . . 3E 122
Leyton . . . 3E 68
London Bridge . . . *5F 15*
(off Middle Yd.)
London Victoria . . . 2K 17
Mitcham . . . 2D 154
North Finchley . . . 5F 31
Old Street . . . *3E 8*
(off Bunhill Row)
Paternoster Square . . . 7B 8
Pinner . . . 3B 40
Queen Victoria Street . . . *2C 14*
(off Queen Victoria St.)
South Kensington . . . *3A 16*
(off Harrington Rd.)
Streatham . . . 2J 137
Thomas More Square . . . *7G 85*
(off Thomas More Sq.)
Tooting Bec . . . 3E 136
Tottenham . . . 2F 49
Walworth Road . . . 5C 102
Wembley . . . 5E 60
Westminster . . . 1A 18
Fitness First (For Women)
Chalk Farm . . . *7E 64*
(off Chalk Farm Rd.)
Fitrooms . . . 6H 99
FitSpace Gym . . . 3F 107
Fitzalan Rd. N3 . . . 3G 45
Fitzalan St. SE11 . . . 3H 19 (4A 102)
Fitzgeorge Av. KT3: N Mald . . . 1K 151
W14 . . . 4G 99
Fitzgerald Av. SW14 . . . 3A 116
Fitzgerald Ct. *E10* . . . *1D 68*
(off Leyton Grange Est.)
Fitzgerald Ho. *E14* . . . *6D 86*
(off E. India Dock Rd.)
SW9 . . . 2A 120
UB3: Hayes . . . 1K 93
Fitzgerald Rd. E11 . . . 5J 51
KT7: T Ditt . . . 6A 150
SW14 . . . 3K 115
Fitzhardinge Ho. *W1* . . . *7G 5*
(off Portman Sq.)
Fitzhardinge St. W1 . . . 7G 5 (6E 82)
Fitzherbert Wlk. UB1: S'hall . . . 2H 95
Fitzhugh Gro. SW18 . . . 6B 118
Fitzjames Av. CR0: C'don . . . 2G 169
W14 . . . 4G 99
Fitzjohn Av. EN5: Barn . . . 5B 20
Fitzjohn's Av. NW3 . . . 4A 64
Fitzmaurice Ho. *SE16* . . . *4H 103*
(off Rennie Est.)
Fitzmaurice Pl. W1 . . . 4K 11 (1F 101)
Fitzneal St. W12 . . . 6B 80
FITZROVIA . . . 5K 5
Fitzrovia Apartments
W1 . . . *4K 5*
(off Bolsover St.)
W1 . . . *4F 83*
(off Bolsover St.)
Fitzroy Bri. NW1 . . . 1E 82
Fitzroy Bus. Pk. BR5: St P . . . 7D 144
Fitzroy Cl. N6 . . . 1D 64
Fitzroy Ct. CR0: C'don . . . 7D 156
N6 . . . 6G 47
W1 . . . 4B 6
Fitzroy Cres. W4 . . . 7K 97
Fitzroy Gdns. SE19 . . . 7E 138
Fitzroy Ho. *E14* . . . *5B 86*
(off Wallwood St.)
SE1 . . . *5F 103*
(off Cooper's Rd.)
Fitzroy M. W1 . . . 4A 6
Fitzroy Pk. N6 . . . 1D 64
Fitzroy Rd. NW1 . . . 1E 82
Fitzroy Sq. W1 . . . 4A 6 (4G 83)
Fitzroy St. W1 . . . 4A 6 (4G 83)
(not continuous)
Fitzroy Yd. NW1 . . . 1E 82
Fitzsimmons Ct. NW10 . . . 1K 79
Fitzstephen Rd. RM8: Dag . . . 5B 72
Fitzwarren Gdns. N19 . . . 1G 65
Fitzwilliam Av. TW9: Rich . . . 2F 115
Fitzwilliam Cl. N20 . . . 1K 31
Fitzwilliam Hgts. SE23 . . . 2J 139
Fitzwilliam Ho. TW9: Rich . . . 4D 114
Fitzwilliam M. E16 . . . 1J 105
Fitzwilliam Rd. SW4 . . . 3G 119
Fitzwygram Cl. TW12: Ham H . . . 5G 131
Five Acre NW9 . . . 1B 44
Fiveacre Cl. CR7: Thor H . . . 6A 156
Five Arches Bus. Pk. DA14: Sidc . . . 5D 144
Five Bell All. *E14* . . . *6B 86*
(off Three Colt St.)
Five Elms Rd. BR2: Hayes . . . 3K 171
RM9: Dag . . . 3F 73
Five Oaks M. BR1: Brom . . . 3J 141
Fives Ct. SE11 . . . 3B 102
FIVEWAYS . . . 2F 143
Five Ways Bus. Cen. TW13: Felt . . . 3K 129
FIVEWAYS CORNER
Croydon . . . 4A 168
Hendon . . . 1C 44
Fiveways Rd. SW9 . . . 2A 120
Flack Ct. E10 . . . 7D 50
Fladbury Rd. N15 . . . 6D 48
Fladgate Rd. E11 . . . 6G 51
Flag Cl. CR0: C'don . . . 1K 169
Flagon Ct. *CR0: C'don* . . . *4C 168*
(off St Andrew's Rd.)
Flag Wlk. HA5: Eastc . . . 6J 39
Flambard Rd. HA1: Harr . . . 6A 42
Flamborough Ho. *SE15* . . . *1G 121*
(off Clayton Rd.)

Flamborough Rd. HA4: Ruis 3J 57
Flamborough St. E14 . . . . .6A 86
Flamborough Wlk. E14 . . . . .6A 86
    (off Flamborough St.)
Flamingo Ct. SE8 . . . . .7C 104
    (off Hamilton St.)
  SE17 . . . . .5C 102
    (off Crampton St.)
Flamingo Gdns. UB5: N'olt 3C 76
Flamstead Gdns.
  RM9: Dag .7C 72
Flamstead Ho. SW3 . . . . .5C 16
    (off Cale St.)
Flamstead Rd. RM9: Dag 7C 72
Flamsted Av. HA9: Wemb 6G 61
Flamsteed Rd. SE7 . . . . .5C 106
Flanchford Rd. W12 . . . . .3B 98
Flanders Cl. E17 . . . . .7A 50
Flanders Cres. SW17 . . . . .7D 136
Flanders Mans. W4 . . . . .4B 98
Flanders Rd. E6 . . . . .2D 88
  W4 . . . . .4A 98
Flanders Way E9 . . . . .6K 67
Flandrian Cl. EN3: Enf L 1J 25
Flank St. E1 .7G 85
Flannery Ct. SE16 . . . . .3H 103
Flansham Ho. E14 . . . . .6B 86
    (off Clemence St.)
Flask Wlk. NW3 . . . . .4A 64
Flatford Ho. SE6 . . . . .4E 140
Flather Cl. SW16 . . . . .5G 137
Flat Iron Sq. SE1 . . . . .5D 14
    (off Southwark Bri. Rd.)
Flatiron Yd. SE1 . . . . .5D 14
    (off Union St.)
Flavell M. SE10 . . . . .5G 105
Flaxen Cl. E4 .3J 35
Flaxen Rd. E4 . . . . .3J 35
Flaxley Ho. SW1 . . . . .5F 101
    (off Abbots Mnr.)
Flaxley Rd. SM4: Mord 7K 153
Flaxman Ct. DA17: Belv 5G 109
    (off Hoddesdon Rd.)
  W1 . . . . .1C 12
  WC1 . . . . .2D 6
    (off Flaxman Ter.)
Flaxman Ho. SE1 . . . . .3B 102
    (off London Rd.)
  W4 . . . . .5A 98
    (off Devonshire St.)
Flaxman Rd. SE5 . . . . .3B 120
Flaxman Sports Cen. 2C 120
Flaxman Ter. WC1 . . . . .2D 6 (3H 83)
Flaxton Rd. SE18 . . . . .1H 125
Flecker Cl. HA7: Stan 5E 26
Flecker Ho. SE5 . . . . .7D 102
    (off Lomond Gro.)
Fleece Dr. N9 . . . . .4B 34
Fleece Rd. KT6: Surb 1C 162
Fleece Wlk. N7 . . . . .6J 65
Fleeming Cl. E17 . . . . .2B 50
Fleeming Rd. E17 . . . . .2B 50
Fleetbank Ho. EC4 . . . . .1K 13
    (off Salisbury Sq.)
Fleet Bldg. EC4 . . . . .7A 8
Fleet Cl. HA4: Ruis 6E 38
  KT8: W Mole 5D 148
Fleetfield WC1 . . . . .1F 7
    (off Birkenhead St.)
Fleet Ho. E14 .7A 86
    (off Victory Pl.)
Fleet La. KT8: W Mole 6D 148
Fleet Pl. EC4 . . . . .7A 8 (6B 84)
    (not continuous)
Fleet Rd. NW3 . . . . .5C 64
Fleetside KT8: W Mole 6F 148
Fleet Sq. WC1 . . . . .2H 7 (3K 83)
Fleet St. EC4 . . . . .1J 13 (6A 84)
Fleet St. Hill E1 . . . . .4G 85
Fleetway WC1 . . . . .1F 7
    (off Birkenhead St.)
Fleetway W. Bus. Pk. UB6: G'frd 2B 78

Fleetwood Cl. CR0: C'don 3F 169
  E16 . . . . .5B 88
  KT9: Chess 7D 162
Fleetwood Ct. E6 . . . . .5D 88
    (off Evelyn Dennington Rd.)
  TW19: Stanw 6A 110
    (off Douglas Rd.)
Fleetwood Rd. KT1: King T 3H 151
  NW10 . . . . .5C 62
Fleetwood Sq. KT1: King T 3H 151
Fleetwood St. N16 . . . . .2E 66
Fleming N8 . . . . .3J 47
    (off Boyton Cl.)
Fleming Cl. SW10 . . . . .7A 16
    (off Park Wlk.)
  W9 . . . . .4J 81
Fleming Ct. CR0: Wadd 5A 168
  W2 . . . . .5A 4
Fleming Dr. N21 . . . . .5E 22
Fleming Ho. HA9: Wemb 3J 61
    (off Barnhill Rd.)
  N4 . . . . .1C 66
  SE16 . . . . .2G 103
    (off George Row)
  SW17 . . . . .3B 136
Fleming Lodge W9 . . . . .5J 81
    (off Admiral Wlk.)
Fleming Mead CR4: Mitc 7C 136
Fleming Rd. SE17 . . . . .6B 102
  UB1: S'hall 6F 77
Fleming Wlk. NW9 . . . . .3A 44
Fleming Way SE28 . . . . .7D 90
  TW7: Isle 4K 113
Flemming Av. HA4: Ruis 1K 57
Flempton Rd. E10 . . . . .1A 68
Fletcher Bldgs. WC2 . . . . .1F 13
    (off Martlett Ct.)
Fletcher Cl. E6 . . . . .6F 89
Fletcher Ho. N1 . . . . .1E 84
    (off Nuttall St.)
  SE15 . . . . .7J 103
    (off Clifton Way)
Fletcher La. E10 . . . . .7E 50
Fletcher Path SE8 . . . . .7C 104
Fletcher Rd. W4 . . . . .3J 97
Fletchers Cl.
  BR2: Brom 4K 159
Fletcher St. E1 . . . . .7G 85
Fletching Rd. E5 . . . . .3J 67
  SE7 . . . . .6A 106
Fletton Rd. N11 . . . . .7D 32
Fleur-de-Lis St. E1 . . . . .4H 9 (4F 85)
Fleur Gates SW19 . . . . .7F 117
Flexmere Gdns. N17 . . . . .1D 48
Flexmere Rd. N17 . . . . .1D 48
Flight App. NW9 . . . . .2B 44
Flight Ho. N1 .1E 84
    (off Whitmore Est.)
Flimwell Cl. BR1: Brom 5G 141
Flinders Ho. E1 . . . . .1H 103
    (off Green Bank)
Flint Cl. BR6: Chels 6K 173
  CR0: C'don 6K 155
  E15 . . . . .7H 69
Flintlock Cl.
  TW19: Stan M 7B 174
Flintmill Cres. SE3 . . . . .2C 124
Flinton St. SE17 . . . . .5E 102
Flint St. SE17 . . . . .4D 102
Flitcroft St. WC2 . . . . .1D 12 (6H 83)
Flitton Ho. N1 .7B 66
    (off The Sutton Est.)
Floathaven Cl. SE28 . . . . .1A 108
Flock Mill Pl. SW18 . . . . .1K 135
Flockton St. SE16 . . . . .2G 103
Flodden Rd. SE5 . . . . .1C 120
Flood La. TW1: Twick 1A 132
Flood Pas. SE18 . . . . .3C 106
Flood St. SW3 . . . . .6D 16 (5C 100)
Flood Wlk. SW3 . . . . .7D 16 (6C 100)
Flora Cl. E14 .6D 86
  HA7: Stan 3K 27

Flora Gdns. RM6: Chad H 6C 54
  W6 . . . . .4D 98
    (off Albion Gdns.)
Flora Ho. E3 .1C 86
    (off Garrison Rd.)
Floral Pl. N1 .5D 66
Floral St. WC2 . . . . .2E 12 (7J 83)
Flora St. DA17: Belv 5F 109
Florence Av. EN2: Enf 3H 23
  SM4: Mord 5A 154
Florence Cantwell Wlk. N19 . . . . .7J 47
    (off Jessie Blythe La.)
Florence Cl. KT12: Walt T 7K 147
Florence Ct. E11 . . . . .4K 51
  N1 . . . . .7B 66
    (off Florence St.)
  SW19 . . . . .6G 135
  W9 . . . . .3A 82
    (off Maida Va.)
Florence Dr. EN2: Enf 3H 23
Florence Elson Cl. E12 . . . . .4E 70
Florence Gdns. RM6: Chad H 7C 54
  W4 . . . . .6J 97
Florence Ho. KT2: King T 7F 133
    (off Florence Rd)
  SE16 . . . . .5H 103
    (off Rotherhithe New Rd.)
  W11 . . . . .7F 81
    (off St Ann's Rd.)
Florence Mans. NW4 . . . . .5D 44
    (off Vivian Av.)
  SW6 . . . . .1H 117
    (off Rostrevor Rd.)
Florence Nightingale Mus.
  . . . . .7G 13 (2K 101)
Florence Rd. BR1: Brom 1J 159
  BR3: Beck 2A 158
  CR2: Sande 7D 168
  E6 . . . . .1A 88
  E13 . . . . .2J 87
  KT2: King T 7F 133
  KT12: Walt T 7K 147
  N4 . . . . .7K 47
    (not continuous)
  SE2 . . . . .4C 108
  SE14 . . . . .1B 122
  SW19 . . . . .6K 135
  TW13: Felt 1K 129
  UB2: S'hall 4B 94
  W4 . . . . .3K 97
  W5 . . . . .7E 78
Florence Root Ho. IG4: Ilf 5C 52
Florence Sq. E3 . . . . .4D 86
Florence St. E16 . . . . .4H 87
  N1 . . . . .7B 66
  NW4 . . . . .4E 44
Florence Ter. SE14 . . . . .1B 122
  SW15 . . . . .3A 134
Florence Way SW12 . . . . .1D 136
Flores Ho. E1 . . . . .5K 85
    (off Shandy St.)
Florey Lodge W9 . . . . .5J 81
    (off Admiral Wlk.)
Florey Sq. N21 . . . . .5E 22
Florfield Pas. E8 . . . . .6H 67
    (off Reading La.)
Florfield Rd. E8 . . . . .6H 67
Florian SE5 . . . . .1E 120
Florian Av. SM1: Sutt 4B 166
Florian Rd. SW15 . . . . .4G 117
Florida Cl. WD23: B Hea 2C 26
Florida Ct. BR2: Brom 4H 159
    (off Westmoreland Rd.)
Florida Rd. CR7: Thor H 1B 156
Florida St. E2 . . . . .3G 85
Florin Ct. EC1 . . . . .5C 8
  N18 . . . . .4K 33
  SE1 . . . . .7J 15
    (off Tanner St.)
Floris Pl. SW4 . . . . .3G 119
Floriston Av. UB10: Hil 7E 56
Floriston Cl. HA7: Stan 1B 42

Floriston Ct. UB5: N'olt 5F 59
Floriston Gdns. HA7: Stan 1B 42
Florys Ct. SW19 . . . . .1G 135
Floss St. SW15 . . . . .2E 116
Flower & Dean Wlk. E1 . . . . . .6K 9 (5F 85)
Flower La. NW7 . . . . .5G 29
Flower M. NW11 . . . . .6G 45
Flower Pot Cl. N15 . . . . .6F 49
Flowers Cl. NW2 . . . . .3C 62
Flowersmead SW17 . . . . .2E 136
Flowers M. N19 . . . . .2G 65
Flower Wlk., The SW7 . . . . . .6A 10 (2A 100)
Floyd Rd. SE7 . . . . .5A 106
Floyer Cl. TW10: Rich 5F 115
Fludyer St. SE13 . . . . .4G 123
Flying Angel Ho. E16 . . . . .7K 87
    (off Victoria Dock Rd.)
Flynn Ct. E14 .7C 86
    (off Garford St.)
Foley Ho. E1 .6J 85
    (off Tarling St.)
Foley St. W1 . . . . .6A 6 (5G 83)
Folgate St. E1 . . . . .5H 9 (5E 84)
    (not continuous)
Foliot Ho. N1 .2K 83
    (off Priory Grn. Est.)
Foliot St. W12 . . . . .6B 80
Folkestone Ct. UB5: N'olt 5F 59
    (off Newmarket Av.)
Folkestone Ho. SE17 . . . . .5E 102
    (off Upnor Way)
Folkestone Rd. E6 . . . . .2E 88
  E17 . . . . .4D 50
  N18 . . . . .4B 34
Folkingham La. NW9 . . . . .1K 43
Folkington Cnr. N12 . . . . .5C 30
Folland NW9 .2B 44
    (off Hundred Acre)
Follett Ho. SW10 . . . . .7B 100
    (off Worlds End Est.)
Follett St. E14 . . . . .6E 86
Follingham Ct. N1 . . . . .1H 9
    (off Drysdale Pl.)
Folly Brook & Darland's Lake Nature Reserve
  . . . . .3B 30
Folly La. E4 .6G 35
  E17 . . . . .1A 50
Folly M. W11 .6H 81
Folly Wall E14 . . . . .2E 104
Fonda Ct. E14 .7C 86
    (off Premiere Pl.)
Fontaine Rd. SW16 . . . . .7K 137
Fontarabia Rd. SW11 . . . . .4E 118
Fontayne Av. RM1: Rom 2K 55
Fontenelle SE5 . . . . .1E 120
Fontenoy Ho. SE11 . . . . .4B 102
    (off Kennington La.)
Fontenoy Rd. SW12 . . . . .2F 137
Fonteyne Gdns. IG8: Wfd G 2B 52
Fonthill Cl. SE20 . . . . .2G 157
Fonthill Ho. SW1 . . . . .5F 101
    (off Sutherland St.)
  W14 . . . . .3G 99
    (off Russell Rd.)
Fonthill M. N4 . . . . .2K 65
Fonthill Rd. N4 . . . . .1K 65
Font Hills N2 .2A 46
Fontley Way SW15 . . . . .7C 116
Fontmell Cl. TW15: Ashf 5C 128
Fontmell Pk. TW15: Ashf 5B 128
    (not continuous)
Fontwell Cl. HA3: Hrw W 7D 26
  UB5: N'olt 6E 58
Fontwell Dr. BR2: Brom 5E 160
Football La. HA1: Harr 1K 59
Footpath, The SW15 . . . . .6C 116
FOOTS CRAY 6C 144
Foots Cray High St. DA14: Sidc 6C 144
Foots Cray La. DA14: Sidc 1C 144
Foots Cray Meadows (Nature Reserve)
  . . . . .4D 144
Footscray Rd. SE9 . . . . .6E 124

Forber Ho. *E2* .3J *85*
(off Cornwall Av.)
Forbes Cl. NW2 .3C *62*
Forbes Ho. *E7* .5A *70*
(off Romford Rd.)
W4 . . . . .5G *97*
(off Stonehall Rd.)
Forbes St. E1 . . . . .6G *85*
Forbes Way HA4: Ruis 2K *57*
Forburg Rd. N16 . . . . .1G *67*
Fordbridge Ct. TW15: Ashf 6A *128*
Fordbridge Pk. TW16: Sun 6H *147*
Fordbridge Rd. TW15: Ashf 6A *128*
TW16: Sun 6G *147*
TW17: Shep 6G *147*
FORDBRIDGE RDBT. 6A *128*
Ford Cl. CR7: Thor H 5B *156*
E3 . . . . .2A *86*
HA1: Harr .7H *41*
TW15: Ashf 6A *128*
TW17: Shep 4C *146*
Forde Av. BR1: Brom 3A *160*
Fordel Rd. SE6 .1E *140*
Ford End IG8: Wfd G 6E *36*
Fordgate Bus. Pk. DA17: Belv 2J *109*
Fordham *KT1: King T* 2G *151*
(off Excelsior Cl.)
Fordham Cl. EN4: Cockf 3H *21*
KT4: Wor Pk 1D *164*
Fordham Ho. *SE14* 7A *104*
(off Angus St.)
Fordham Rd. EN4: Cockf 3G *21*
Fordham St. E1 .6G *85*
Fordhook Av. W5 . . . . .1F *97*
Ford Ho. EN5: New Bar 5E *20*
Fordie Ho. *SW1* 2F *17*
(off Sloane St.)
Ford Ind. Pk. RM9: Dag 4H *91*
Fordingley Rd. W9 . . . . .3H *81*
Fordington Ho. SE26 . . . . .3G *139*
Fordington Rd. N6 . . . . .5D *46*
Ford Lodge RM7: Rom 4K *55*
Fordmill Rd. SE6 . . . . .2C *140*
Ford Rd. E3 . . . . .2B *86*
RM9: Dag 7F *73*
RM10: Dag 7G *73*
TW15: Ashf 4B *128*
Fords Gro. N21 .1H *33*
Fords Pk. Rd. E16 . . . . .5J *87*
Ford Sq. E1 . . . . .5H *85*
Ford St. E3 . . . . .1A *86*
E16 . . . . .6H *87*
Fordview Ind. Est. RM13: Rain 3K *91*
Fordwich Cl. BR6: Orp 7K *161*
Fordwych Rd. NW2 . . . . .4G *63*
Fordyce Rd. SE13 . . . . .6E *122*
Fordyke Rd. RM8: Dag 2F *73*
Foreign St. SE5 .2B *120*
Foreland Ct. NW4 . . . . .1F *45*
Foreland Ho. *W11* 7G *81*
(off Walmer Rd.)
Foreland St. SE18 . . . . .4H *107*
Foreman Ct. TW1: Twick 1K *131*
Foreman Ho. *SE4* 4K *121*
(off Billingford Cl.)
Foreshore SE8 .4B *104*
Forest, The E11 .4G *51*
Forest App. E4 .1B *36*
IG8: Wfd G 7D *36*
Forest Av. E4 . . . . .1B *36*
IG7: Chig .5K *37*
Forest Bus. Pk. E10 . . . . .7K *49*
Forest Cl. BR7: Chst 1E *160*
E11 . . . . .5J *51*
IG8: Wfd G 3E *36*
N10 . . . . .1F *47*
NW6 . . . . .7G *63*
Forest Ct. E4 . . . . .1C *36*
E11 . . . . .4G *51*
N12 . . . . .5E *30*
Forest Cft. SE23 . . . . .2H *139*
FORESTDALE 7B *170*

Forestdale N14 .4C *32*
Forestdale Cen., The CR0: Sels 7B *170*
Forest Dene Ct. SM2: Sutt 6A *166*
Forest Dr. BR2: Kes 4C *172*
E12 . . . . .3B *70*
IG8: Wfd G 7A *36*
TW16: Sun 7H *129*
Forest Dr. E. E11 . . . . .7F *51*
Forest Dr. W. E11 . . . . .7E *50*
Forest Edge IG9: Buck H 4F *37*
Forester Ho. *E14* 7A *86*
(off Victory Pl.)
Forester Rd. SE15 . . . . .3H *121*
Foresters Cl. SM6: Wall 7H *167*
Foresters Cres. DA7: Bex 4H *127*
Foresters Dr. E17 . . . . .4F *51*
SM6: Wall 7H *167*
Forest Gdns. N17 . . . . .2F *49*
FOREST GATE .5J *69*
Forest Ga. NW9 .4A *44*
Forest Ga. Retreat *E7* 5J *69*
(off Odessa Rd.)
Forest Glade E4 .4B *36*
E11 . . . . .6G *51*
Forest Gro. E8 . . . . .6F *67*
Forest Hgts. IG9: Buck H 2D *36*
FOREST HILL 2J *139*
Forest Hill Bus. Cen. *SE23* 2J *139*
(off Clyde Va.)
Forest Hill Ind. Est. SE23 . . . . .2J *139*
Forest Hill Pool .2J *139*
Forest Hill Rd. SE22 . . . . .5H *121*
SE23 . . . . .5H *121*
Forestholme Cl. SE23 . . . . .2J *139*
Forest Ind. Pk. IG6: Ilf 1J *53*
Forest La. E7 . . . . .5G *69*
E15 . . . . .5G *69*
IG7: Chig .5K *37*
Forest Lodge *SE23* 3J *139*
(off Dartmouth Rd.)
Forest Mt. Rd. IG8: Wfd G 7A *36*
Forest Point *E7* 5K *69*
(off Windsor Rd.)
Fore St. EC2 . . . . .6D *8* (5C *84*)
HA5: Eastc 4H *39*
N9 . . . . .4B *34*
N18 . . . . .6A *34*
Fore St. Av. EC2 . . . . .6E *8* (5D *84*)
Forest Ridge BR2: Kes 4C *172*
BR3: Beck 3C *158*
Forest Ri. E17 . . . . .3F *51*
(not continuous)
Forest Rd. E7 . . . . .4J *69*
E8 . . . . .6F *67*
E11 . . . . .7F *51*
E17 . . . . .3D *50*
IG6: Chig, Ilf 2H *53*
IG8: Wfd G 3D *36*
N9 . . . . .1C *34*
N17 . . . . .4J *49*
RM7: Mawney 3H *55*
SM3: Sutt 1J *165*
TW9: Kew 7G *97*
TW13: Felt 2A *130*
Forest Side E4 . . . . .1C *36*
E7 . . . . .4K *69*
IG9: Buck H 1F *37*
KT4: Wor Pk 1B *164*
Forest St. E7 . . . . .5J *69*
Forest Ter. IG7: Chig 5K *37*
Forest Trad. Est. E17 . . . . .3K *49*
Forest Vw. E4 . . . . .7K *25* & *1B 36*
E11 . . . . .7H *51*
Forest Vw. Av. E10 . . . . .5F *51*
Forest Vw. Rd. E12 . . . . .4C *70*
E17 . . . . .1E *50*
Forest Wlk. N10 .1F *47*
Forest Way BR5: St M Cry 5K *161*
DA15: Sidc 7H *125*
IG8: Wfd G 4E *36*
N19 . . . . .2G *65*
Forest Works Ind. Est. E17 . . . . .3K *49*

Forfar Rd. N22 . . . . .1B *48*
SW11 . . . . .1E *118*
Forge, The UB3: Harl 6F *93*
Forge Cl. BR2: Hayes 1J *171*
Forge Cotts. W5 .1D *96*
Forge Dr. KT10: Clay 7A *162*
Forge La. HA6: Nwood 1G *39*
SM3: Cheam 7G *165*
TW10: Ham 1E *132*
TW13: Hanw 5C *130*
TW16: Sun 3J *147*
Forge Pl. NW1 . . . . .6E *64*
Forge Sq. E14 . . . . .4D *104*
Forges Rd. E12 .2B *70*
Forman Pl. N16 .4F *67*
Formation, The *E16* 2F *107*
(off Woolwich Mnr. Way)
Formby Av. HA7: Stan 3C *42*
Formby Ho. *E7* .5A *66*
(off Morgan Rd.)
Formosa Ho. *E1* 4A *86*
(off Ernest St.)
Formosa St. W9 .4K *81*
Formunt Cl. E16 .5H *87*
Forres Gdns. NW11 . . . . .6J *45*
Forrester Path SE26 . . . . .4J *139*
Forrest Gdns. SW16 . . . . .3K *155*
Forris Av. UB3: Hayes 1H *93*
Forset Cl. W2 . . . . .7D *4*
(off Edgware Rd.)
Forset St. W1 . . . . .7D *4* (6C *82*)
(not continuous)
Forstal Cl. BR2: Brom 3J *159*
Forster Cl. IG8: Wfd G 7A *36*
Forster Ho. BR1: Brom 4F *141*
SW17 . . . . .3B *136*
(off Grosvenor Way)
Forster Rd. BR3: Beck 3A *158*
E17 . . . . .6A *50*
N17 . . . . .3F *49*
SW2 . . . . .7J *119*
Forsters Cl. RM6: Chad H 6F *55*
Forsters Way UB4: Yead 6K *75*
Forston St. N1 . . . . .2C *84*
Forsyte Cres. SE19 . . . . .1E *156*
Forsyte Ho. SW3 . . . . .6D *16*
Forsythe Shades Ct. BR3: Beck 1E *158*
Forsyth Gdns. SE17 . . . . .6B *102*
Forsyth Ho. *E9* .7J *67*
(off Frampton Pk. Rd.)
SW1 . . . . .5B *18*
(off Tachbrook St.)
Forsythia Cl. IG1: Ilf 5F *71*
Forsyth Pl. EN1: Enf 5K *23*
Forterie Gdns. IG3: Bark, Ilf 3A *72*
Fortescue Av. E8 . . . . .7H *67*
TW2: Twick 3G *131*
Fortescue Rd. HA8: Edg 1K *43*
SW19 . . . . .7B *136*
Fortess Gro. NW5 . . . . .5G *65*
Fortess Rd. NW5 . . . . .5F *65*
Fortess Wlk. NW5 . . . . .5F *65*
Fortess Yd. NW5 . . . . .4F *65*
Forthbridge Rd. SW11 . . . . .4E *118*
Forth Ho. *E3* 2B *86*
(off Tredegar Rd.)
Fortis Cl. E16 . . . . .6A *88*
Fortis Ct. N10 . . . . .3E *46*
FORTIS GREEN 4D *46*
Fortis Grn. N2 . . . . .4C *46*
N10 . . . . .4C *46*
Fortis Grn. Av. N2 . . . . .3D *46*
Fortis Grn. Rd. N10 . . . . .3E *46*
Fortismere Av. N10 . . . . .3E *46*
Fortius Apartments *E3* 2C *86*
(off Tredegar La.)
Fortnam Rd. N19 . . . . .2H *65*
Fortnum's Acre HA7: Stan 6E *26*
Fort Rd. SE1 . . . . .4F *103*
UB5: N'olt 7E *58*
Fortrose Cl. E14 .6F *87*

Fortrose Gdns. SW2 . . . . .1J *137*
Fort St. E1 . . . . .6H *9* (5E *84*)
E16 . . . . .1K *105*
Fortuna Cl. N7 . . . . .6K *65*
Fortune Av. HA8: Edg 1H *43*
Fortune Ct. E8 . . . . .7F *67*
(off Queensbridge Rd.)
IG11: Bark 2C *90*
Fortunegate Rd. NW10 . . . . .1A *80*
FORTUNE GREEN 5J *63*
Fortune Grn. Rd. NW6 . . . . .4J *63*
Fortune Ho. *EC1* 4D *8*
(off Fortune St.)
SE11 . . . . .4J *19*
Fortune Pl. SE1 .5F *103*
Fortunes Mead UB5: N'olt 6C *58*
Fortune St. EC1 . . . . .4D *8* (4C *84*)
Fortune Theatre 1F *13*
(off Russell St.)
Fortune Wlk. *SE28* 3H *107*
(off Broadwater Rd.)
Fortune Way NW10 . . . . .3C *80*
Forty Acre La. E16 . . . . .5J *87*
Forty Av. HA9: Wemb 3F *61*
Forty Cl. HA9: Wemb 3F *61*
Forty Footpath SW14 . . . . .3J *115*
Forty Foot Way SE9 . . . . .7G *125*
FORTY HILL 1K *23*
Forty Hill EN2: Enf 1K *23*
Forty La. HA9: Wemb 2H *61*
Forum, The KT8: W Mole 4F *149*
Forum Cl. E3 . . . . .1C *86*
Forum Ho. HA9: Wemb 4G *61*
(not continuous)
Forum Magnum Sq. *SE1* 6H *13*
(off York Rd.)
Forumside HA8: Edg 6B *28*
Forum Way HA8: Edg 6B *28*
Forval Cl. CR4: Mitc 5D *154*
Forward Bus. Cen., The E16 . . . . .4F *87*
Forward Dr. HA3: W'stone 4K *41*
Fosbrooke Ho. *SW8* 7J *101*
(off Davidson Gdns.)
Foskett M. E8 . . . . .5F *67*
Foskett Rd. SW6 . . . . .2H *117*
Foss Av. CR0: Wadd 5A *168*
Fossdene Rd. SE7 . . . . .5K *105*
Fossdyke Cl. UB4: Yead 5C *76*
Fosset Lodge DA7: Bex 1J *127*
Fosse Way W13 .5A *78*
Foss Ho. *NW8* 2K *81*
(off Carlton Hill)
Fossil Ct. *SE1* 7G *15*
(off Long La.)
Fossil Rd. SE13 .3C *122*
Fossington Rd. DA17: Belv 4D *108*
Foss Rd. SW17 .4B *136*
Fossway RM8: Dag 2C *72*
Foster Ct. E16 . . . . .7H *87*
(off Tarling Rd.)
NW1 . . . . .7G *65*
(off Royal College St.)
NW4 . . . . .4E *44*
Foster Ho. SE14 . . . . .1B *122*
Foster La. EC2 . . . . .7C *8* (6C *84*)
Foster Rd. E13 . . . . .4J *87*
W3 . . . . .7A *80*
W4 . . . . .5K *97*
Fosters Cl. BR7: Chst 5D *142*
E18 . . . . .1K *51*
Foster St. NW4 . . . . .4E *44*
Foster's Way SW18 . . . . .1K *135*
Foster Wlk. NW4 . . . . .4E *44*
Fothergill Cl. E13 . . . . .2J *87*
Fothergill Dr. N21 . . . . .5D *22*

Fotheringham Rd.—Fraserburgh Ho.

Fotheringham Rd. EN1: Enf 4A **24**
(not continuous)
Foubert's Pl. W1 . . . . 1A **12** (6G **83**)
Foulden Rd. N16 . . . . 4F **67**
Foulden Ter. N16 . . . . 4F **67**
Foulis Ter. SW7 . . . . 5B **16** (5B **100**)
Foulser Rd. SW17 . . . . 3D **136**
Foulsham Rd.
CR7: Thor H 3C **156**
Foundation Pl. *SE9* *6E* ***124***
(off Archery Rd.)
Founder Cl. E6 . . . . 6F **89**
Founders Cl. UB5: N'olt 3D **76**
Founders Ct. EC2 . . . . 7E **8**
Founders Gdns. SE19 . . . . 7C **138**
Founders Ho. *SW1* *6C* ***18***
(off Aylesford St.)
Foundling Ct. *WC1* *3E* ***6***
(off Brunswick Cen.)
Foundling Mus., The 3F 7 (4J 83)
Foundry, The *EC2* *2H* ***9***
(off Dereham Pl.)
EC2 . . . . *3E* ***84***
(off Dereham Pl.)
Foundry Cl. SE16 . . . . 1A **104**
Foundry Ho. *E14* *5D* ***86***
(off Morris Rd.)
Foundry M. NW1 . . . . 3B **6**
TW3: Houn 4F **113**
Foundry Pl. *E1* *5J* ***85***
(off Jubilee St.)
SW18 . . . . 7K **117**
Fountain Cl. SE18 . . . . 5F **107**
UB8: Hil 5E **74**
Fountain Ct. DA15: Sidc 6B **126**
EC4 . . . . 2J **13** (7A **84**)
SE23 . . . . 2K **139**
SW1 . . . . *4J* ***17***
(off Buckingham Pal. Rd.)
W11 . . . . *2F* ***99***
(off Clearwater Ter.)
Fountain Dr. SE19 . . . . 4F **139**
SM5: Cars 7D **166**
Fountain Grn. Sq. SE16 . . . . 2G **103**
Fountain Ho. CR4: Mitc 2D **154**
E2 . . . . *3J* ***9***
(off Redchurch St.)
NW6 . . . . 7G **63**
SE16 . . . . *2G* ***103***
(off Bermondsey Wall E.)
SW6 . . . . 2A **118**
W1 . . . . *4G* ***11***
(off Park St.)
Fountain M. *N5* *4C* ***66***
(off Highbury Grange)
NW3 . . . . 6D **64**
Fountain Pl. SW9 . . . . 1A **120**
Fountain Rd. CR7: Thor H 3C **156**
SW17 . . . . 5B **136**
Fountain Rdbt. KT3: N Mald 4A **152**
Fountains, The *N3* *7E* ***30***
(off Ballards La.)
Fountains Av. TW13: Hanw 3D **130**
Fountains Cl. TW13: Hanw 2D **130**
(not continuous)
Fountains Cres. N14 . . . . 7D **22**
Fountain Sq. SW1 . . . . 3K **17** (4F **101**)
Fountayne Bus. Cen. N15 . . . . 4G **49**
Fountayne Rd. N15 . . . . 4G **49**
N16 . . . . 2G **67**
Fount St. SW8 . . . . 7H **101**
Fouracre Path SE25 . . . . 6E **156**
Four Acres N12 . . . . 3E **30**
Fouracres EN3: Enf H 1F **25**
Fourland Wlk. HA8: Edg 6D **28**
Fournier St. E1 . . . . 5J **9** (5F **85**)
Fourscore Mans. *E8* *7G* ***67***
(off Shrubland Rd.)
Four Seasons Cl. E3 . . . . 2C **86**
Four Seasons Cres.
SM3: Sutt 2H **165**
Four Sq. Ct. TW3: Houn 6E **112**
Fourth Av. E12 . . . . 4D **70**
RM7: Rush G 1K **73**
UB3: Hayes 1H **93**
W10 . . . . 4G **81**
Fourth Cross Rd. TW2: Twick 2H **131**
Fourth Way HA9: Wemb 4H **61**
Four Wents, The E4 . . . . 1A **36**
Fovant Ct. SW8 . . . . 2G **119**
Fowey Av. IG4: Ilf 5B **52**
Fowey Cl. E1 . . . . 1H **103**
Fowey Ho. SE11 . . . . 5K **19**
Fowler Cl. SW11 . . . . 3B **118**
Fowler Ho. *N15* *5D* ***48***
(off South Gro.)
Fowler Rd. CR4: Mitc 2E **154**
E7 . . . . 4J **69**
N1 . . . . 1B **84**
Fowlers Cl. DA14: Sidc 5E **144**
Fowlers M. *N19* *2G* ***65***
(off Holloway Rd.)
Fowler's Wlk. W5 . . . . 4D **78**
Fownes St. SW11 . . . . 3C **118**
Fox & Knot St. EC1 . . . . 5B **8**
Foxberry Rd. SE4 . . . . 3A **122**
Foxborough Gdns. SE4 . . . . 5C **122**
Foxbourne Rd. SW17 . . . . 2E **136**
Foxbury Av. BR7: Chst 6H **143**
Foxbury Cl. BR1: Brom 6K **141**
Foxbury Rd. BR1: Brom 6J **141**
Fox Cl. BR6: Chels 5K **173**
E1 . . . . 4J **85**
E16 . . . . 5J **87**
Foxcombe CR0: New Ad 6D **170**
(not continuous)
Foxcombe Cl. E6 . . . . 2B **88**
Foxcombe Rd. SW15 . . . . 1C **134**
Foxcote SE5 . . . . 5E **102**
Foxcroft *WC1* *1H* ***7***
(off Penton Ri.)
Foxcroft Rd. SE18 . . . . 1F **125**
Foxearth Spur CR2: Sels 7J **169**
Foxes Dale BR2: Brom 3F **159**
SE3 . . . . 3J **123**
Foxfield *NW1* *1F* ***83***
(off Arlington Rd.)
Foxfield Rd. BR6: Orp 2H **173**
Foxglove Cl. DA15: Sidc 6A **126**
N9 . . . . 1D **34**
UB1: S'hall 7C **76**
Foxglove Ct. *E3* *2C* ***86***
(off Four Seasons Cl.)
HA0: Wemb 2E **78**
Foxglove Gdns. E11 . . . . 4A **52**
Foxglove La. KT9: Chess 4G **163**
Foxglove Path *SE28* *1J* ***107***
(off Martins Pl.)
Foxglove Rd. RM7: Rush G 2K **73**
Foxglove St. W12 . . . . 7B **80**
Foxglove Way SM6: Wall 1F **167**
Fox Gro. KT12: Walt T 7K **147**
Foxgrove N14 . . . . 3D **32**
Foxgrove Av. BR3: Beck 7D **140**
Foxgrove Rd. BR3: Beck 7D **140**
Foxham Rd. N19 . . . . 3H **65**
Fox Hill BR2: Kes 5A **172**
SE19 . . . . 7F **139**
Fox Hill Gdns. SE19 . . . . 7F **139**
Foxhole Rd. SE9 . . . . 5C **124**
Fox Hollow Cl. SE18 . . . . 5J **107**
Fox Hollow Dr. DA7: Bex 3D **126**
Foxholt Gdns. NW10 . . . . 7J **61**
Foxhome Cl. BR7: Chst 6E **142**
Fox Ho. Rd. DA17: Belv 5H **109**
(not continuous)
Foxlands Cres. RM10: Dag 5J **73**
Foxlands La. RM10: Dag 5K **73**
Foxlands Rd. RM10: Dag 5J **73**
Fox La. BR2: Kes 5K **171**
N13 . . . . 2E **32**
W5 . . . . 4E **78**
Foxleas Ct. BR1: Brom 7G **141**
Foxlees HA0: Wemb 4A **60**
Foxley Cl. E8 . . . . 5G **67**
Foxley Ct. SM2: Sutt 7A **166**
Foxley Ho. *E3* *3D* ***86***
(off Bow Rd.)
Foxley Rd. CR7: Thor H 4B **156**
SW9 . . . . 7A **102**
Foxley Sq. SW9 . . . . 1B **120**
Foxmead Cl. EN2: Enf 3E **22**
Foxmore St. SW11 . . . . 1D **118**
Fox Rd. E16 . . . . 5H **87**
Fox's Path CR4: Mitc 2C **154**
Fox's Yd. E2 . . . . 3K **9**
E2 . . . . *4F* ***85***
(off Rhoda St.)
Foxton Gro. CR4: Mitc 2B **154**
Foxton Ho. *E16* *2E* ***106***
(off Albert Rd.)
Foxwarren KT10: Clay 7A **162**
Foxwell M. SE4 . . . . 3A **122**
Foxwell St. SE4 . . . . 3A **122**
Foxwood Cl. NW7 . . . . 4F **29**
TW13: Felt 3K **129**
Foxwood Grn. Cl. EN1: Enf 6K **23**
Fox Wood Nature Reserve 4E 78
Foxwood Rd. SE3 . . . . 4H **123**
Foyle Rd. N17 . . . . 1G **49**
SE3 . . . . 6H **105**
Framfield Cl. N12 . . . . 3D **30**
Framfield Ct. *EN1: Enf* *6K* ***23***
(off Queen Anne's Gdns.)
Framfield Rd. CR4: Mitc 7E **136**
N5 . . . . 5B **66**
W7 . . . . 6J **77**
Framlingham Cl. E5 . . . . 2J **67**
Framlingham Ct. *RM6: Chad H* *5B* ***54***
(off Norwich Cres.)
Framlingham Cres. SE9 . . . . 4C **142**
Frampton *NW1* *7H* ***65***
(off Wrotham Rd.)
Frampton Cl. SM2: Sutt 7J **165**
Frampton Ct. *W3* *2J* ***97***
(off Avenue Rd.)
Frampton Ho. *NW8* *4B* ***4***
(off Frampton St.)
Frampton Pk. Est. E9 . . . . 7J **67**
Frampton Pk. Rd. E9 . . . . 6J **67**
Frampton Rd. TW4: Houn 5C **112**
Frampton St. NW8 . . . . 4B **4** (4B **82**)
Francemary Rd. SE4 . . . . 5C **122**
Frances Ct. E17 . . . . 6C **50**
SE25 . . . . 3G **157**
Frances Rd. E4 . . . . 6H **35**
Frances St. SE18 . . . . 3D **106**
Frances Wharf E14 . . . . 6B **86**
Franche Ct. Rd. SW17 . . . . 3A **136**
Francis & Dick James Ct. NW7 . . . . 7B **30**
Francis Av. DA7: Bex 2G **127**
IG1: Ilf 2H **71**
TW13: Felt 3J **129**
Francis Barber Cl. SW16 . . . . 5K **137**
Francis Bentley M. SW4 . . . . 3G **119**
Franciscan Rd. SW17 . . . . 5D **136**
Francis Chichester Way SW11 . . . . 1E **118**
Francis Cl. E14 . . . . 4F **105**
KT19: Ewe 4K **163**
TW17: Shep 4C **146**
Francis Ct. DA8: Erith 5K **109**
EC1 . . . . 5A **8**
KT5: Surb *4E* ***150***
(off Cranes Pk. Av.)
NW7 . . . . *5G* ***29***
(off Watford Way)
SE14 . . . . *6K* ***103***
(off Myers La.)
Francis Gro. SW19 . . . . 6H **135**
(not continuous)
Francis Ho. E17 . . . . 6B **50**
N1 . . . . *1E* ***84***
(off Colville Est.)
SW10 . . . . *7K* ***99***
(off Coleridge Gdns.)
Francis M. SE12 . . . . 7J **123**
Francis Pl. *N6* *7F* ***47***
(off Shepherd's Cl.)
Francis Rd. CR0: C'don 7B **156**
E10 . . . . 1E **68**
HA1: Harr 5A **42**
HA5: Eastc 5A **40**
IG1: Ilf 2H **71**
N2 . . . . 4D **46**
SM6: Wall 6G **167**
TW4: Houn 2B **112**
UB6: G'frd 2B **78**
Francis St. E15 . . . . 5G **69**
IG1: Ilf 2H **71**
SW1 . . . . 3A **18** (4G **101**)
Francis Ter. N19 . . . . 3G **65**
Francis Wlk. N1 . . . . 1K **83**
Francklyn Gdns. HA8: Edg 3B **28**
Franconia Rd. SW4 . . . . 5H **119**
Frank Bailey Wlk. E12 . . . . 5E **70**
Frank Beswick Ho. *SW6* *6H* ***99***
(off Clem Attlee Ct.)
Frank Burton Cl. SE7 . . . . 5K **105**
Frank Dixon Cl. SE21 . . . . 7E **120**
Frank Dixon Way SE21 . . . . 1E **138**
Frankfurt Rd. SE24 . . . . 5C **120**
Frank Godley Ct. DA14: Sidc 5B **144**
Frankham Ho. *SE8* *7C* ***104***
(off Frankham St.)
Frankham St. SE8 . . . . 7C **104**
Frank Ho. *SW8* *7J* ***101***
(off Wyvil Rd.)
Frankland Cl. IG8: Wfd G 5F **37**
SE16 . . . . 3H **103**
Frankland Rd. E4 . . . . 5H **35**
SW7 . . . . 2A **16** (3B **100**)
Franklin Bldg. E14 . . . . 2C **104**
Franklin Cl. KT1: King T 3G **151**
N20 . . . . 7F **21**
SE13 . . . . 1D **122**
SE27 . . . . 3B **138**
Franklin Cotts. HA7: Stan 4G **27**
Franklin Cres. CR4: Mitc 4G **155**
Franklin Ho. BR2: Brom 3G **159**
E1 . . . . *1H* ***103***
(off Watts St.)
E14 . . . . *6F* ***87***
(off E. India Dock Rd.)
NW9 . . . . 6B **44**
Franklin Ind. Est. *SE20* *1J* ***157***
(off Franklin Rd.)
Franklin Pas. SE9 . . . . 3C **124**
Franklin Pl. SE13 . . . . 1D **122**
Franklin Rd. DA7: Bex 1E **126**
SE20 . . . . 7J **139**
Franklins M. HA2: Harr 2G **59**
Franklin Sq. W14 . . . . 5H **99**
Franklin's Row SW3 . . . . 5F **17** (5D **100**)
Franklin St. E3 . . . . 3D **86**
N15 . . . . 6E **48**
Franklin Way CR0: Wadd 7J **155**
Franklyn Rd. KT12: Walt T 6J **147**
NW10 . . . . 6B **62**
Frank M. SE1 . . . . 4H **103**
Franks Av. KT3: N Mald 4J **151**
Frank Soskice Ho. *SW6* *6H* ***99***
(off Clem Attlee Ct.)
Frank St. E13 . . . . 4J **87**
Franks Wood Av. BR5: Pet W 5F **161**
Frankswood Av. UB7: Yiew 6B **74**
Frank Towell Ct. TW14: Felt 7J **111**
Frank Whymark Ho. *SE16* *2J* ***103***
(off Rupack St.)
Franlaw Cres. N13 . . . . 4H **33**
Fransfield Gro. SE26 . . . . 3H **139**
Frans Hals Ct. E14 . . . . 3F **105**
Franshams *WD23: B Hea* *2D* ***26***
(off Hartsbourne Rd.)
Frant Cl. SE20 . . . . 7J **139**
Franthorne Way SE6 . . . . 2D **140**
Frant Rd. CR7: Thor H 5B **156**
Fraserburgh Ho. *E3* *2B* ***86***
(off Vernon Rd.)

Fraser Cl. DA5: Bexl 1J 145
E6 6C 88
Fraser Ct. *E14* *5E 104*
(off Ferry St.)
SE1 7D 14
SW11 *1C 118*
(off Surrey La. Est.)
Fraser Ho. TW8: Bford 5F 97
Fraser Rd. DA8: Erith 5K 109
E17 5D 50
N9 3C 34
UB6: G'frd 1B 78
Fraser St. W4 5A 98
Frating Cres. IG8: Wfd G 6E 36
Frazer Av. HA4: Ruis 5A 58
Frazier St. SE1 7J 13 (2A 102)
Frean St. SE16 3G 103
Frearson Ho. *WC1* *1H 7*
(off Penton Ri.)
Freda Corbet Cl. SE15 7G 103
Frederica Ct. SW2 1B 138
Frederica Rd. E4 1A 36
Frederica St. N7 7K 65
Frederick Charrington Ho.
E1 *4J 85*
(off Wickford St.)
Frederick Cl. SM1: Sutt 4H 165
W2 2D 10 (7D 82)
Frederick Ct. *SW3* *4F 17*
(off Duke of York Sq.)
Frederick Cres. EN3: Enf H 2D 24
SW9 7B 102
Frederick Dobson Ho. *W11* *7G 81*
(off Cowling Cl.)
Frederick Gdns. CR0: C'don 6B 156
SM1: Sutt 5H 165
Frederick Ho. *SE18* *4C 106*
(off Pett St.)
Frederick Pl. *N8* *6J 47*
(off Crouch Hall Rd.)
SE18 5F 107
Frederick Rd. RM13: Rain 2K 91
SE17 6B 102
SM1: Sutt 5H 165
Fredericks Pl. EC2 1E 14 (6D 84)
N12 4F 31
Frederick Sq. *SE16* *7A 86*
(off Sovereign Cres.)
Frederick's Row EC1 1A 8 (3B 84)
Frederick St. WC1 2G 7 (3K 83)
Frederick Ter. E8 7F 67
Frederick Vs. *W7* *1J 95*
(off Lwr. Boston Rd.)
Frederic M. SW1 7F 11
Frederic St. E17 5A 50
Fredora Av. UB4: Hayes 4H 75
Fred Styles Ho. SE7 6A 106
Fred Tibble Ct. RM9: Dag 4E 72
Fred White Wlk. N7 6J 65
Freedom Cl. E17 4A 50
Freedom Rd. N17 2D 48
Freedom St. SW11 2D 118
Freegrove Rd. N7 5J 65
(not continuous)
Freeland Ct. DA15: Sidc 3A 144
Freeland Pk. NW4 2G 45
Freeland Rd. W5 7F 79
Freelands Av. CR2: Sels 7K 169
Freelands Gro. BR1: Brom 1K 159
Freelands Rd. BR1: Brom 1K 159
Freeling Ho. *NW8* *1B 82*
(off Dorman Way)
Freeling St. N1 7K 65
(Carnoustie Dr.)
N1 7J 65
(Pembroke St.)
Freeman Cl. TW17: Shep 4G 147
UB5: N'olt 7C 58
Freeman Ct. SW16 2J 155
Freeman Dr. KT8: W Mole 3D 148
Freeman Rd. SM4: Mord 5B 154
Freemans La. UB3: Hayes 7G 75
Freemantle Av. EN3: Pond E 5E 24
Freemantle St. SE17 5E 102
Freemasons' Hall *7F 7*
(off Gt. Queen St.)
Freemasons Pl. *CR0: C'don* *1E 168*
(off Freemasons Rd.)
Freemasons Rd. CR0: C'don 1E 168
E16 5K 87
Freesia Cl. BR6: Chels 5K 173
Freethorpe Cl. SE19 7D 138
Free Trade Wharf E1 7K 85
Freezeland Way UB10: Hil 6D 56
Freke Rd. SW11 3E 118
Fremantle Ho. *E1* *4H 85*
(off Somerford St.)
Fremantle Rd. DA17: Belv 4G 109
IG6: Ilf 2F 53
Fremont St. E9 1H 85
(not continuous)
French Horn Yd. WC1 6G 7
French Ordinary Ct.
EC3 2H 15
French Pl. E1 2H 9 (3E 84)
French St. TW16: Sun 2A 148
Frendsbury Rd. SE4 4A 122
Frensham Cl. UB1: S'hall 4D 76
Frensham Ct. SW19 3A 154
Frensham Dr. CR0: New Ad 7E 170
SW15 3B 134
(not continuous)
Frensham Rd. SE9 2H 143
Frensham St. SE15 6G 103
Frere St. SW11 2C 118
Fresham Ho. *BR2: Brom* *3H 159*
(off Durham Rd.)
Freshfield Av. E8 7F 67
Freshfield Cl. SE13 4F 123
Freshfield Dr. N14 7A 22
Freshfields CR0: C'don 1B 170
Freshford St. SW18 3A 136
Freshill La. UB1: S'hall 4E 76
Freshwater Cl. SW17 6E 136
Freshwater Ct. UB1: S'hall 3E 76
W1 *6D 4*
(off Crawford St.)
Freshwater Rd. RM8: Dag 1D 72
SW17 6E 136
Freshwell Av. RM6: Chad H 4C 54
Fresh Wharf Est.
IG11: Bark 2F 89
Fresh Wharf Rd. IG11: Bark 1F 89
Freshwood Cl. BR3: Beck 1D 158
Freshwood Way SM6: Wall 7F 167
Freston Gdns. EN4: Cockf 5K 21
Freston Pk. N3 2H 45
Freston Rd. W10 7F 81
W11 7F 81
Freswick Ho. *SE8* *4A 104*
(off Chilton Gro.)
Freta Rd. DA6: Bex 5F 127
Freud Mus. 6A 64
Frewell Ho. *EC1* *5J 7*
(off Bourne Est.)
Frewing Cl. BR7: Chst 6D 142
Frewin Rd. SW18 1B 136
Friar M. SE27 3B 138
Friar Rd. BR5: St M Cry 5K 161
UB4: Yead 4B 76
Friars Av. N20 3H 31
SW15 3B 134
Friars Cl. E4 3K 35
IG1: Ilf 1H 71
SE1 5B 14
UB5: N'olt 3B 76
Friars Ct. E17 1B 50
SM6: Wall 4F 167
Friars Gdns. W3 6K 79
Friarsgate NW10 2H 79
Friars Ga. Cl. IG8: Wfd G 4D 36
Friars La. TW9: Rich 5D 114
Friars Mead E14 3E 104
Friars M. SE9 5E 124
Friars Pl. La. W3 7K 79
Friars Rd. E6 1B 88
Friars Stile Pl. TW10: Rich 6E 114
Friars Stile Rd. TW10: Rich 6E 114
Friar St. EC4 1B 14 (6B 84)
Friars Wlk. N14 7A 22
SE2 5D 108
Friars Way W3 6K 79
Friars Wood CR0: Sels 7A 170
Friary Cl. N12 5H 31
Friary Ct. SW1 5B 12
Friary Est. SE15 6G 103
(not continuous)
Friary La. IG8: Wfd G 4D 36
Friary Pk. Ct. W3 6J 79
Friary Rd. N12 4G 31
SE15 7G 103
W3 6J 79
Friary Way N12 4H 31
FRIDAY HILL 2B 36
Friday Hill E4 2B 36
Friday Hill E. E4 3B 36
(not continuous)
Friday Hill W. E4 2B 36
Friday Rd. CR4: Mitc 7D 136
DA8: Erith 5K 109
Friday St. EC4 2C 14 (7C 84)
Frideswide Pl. NW5 5G 65
Freightliners City Farm 6A 66
Friendly Pl. SE13 1D 122
Friendly St. SE8 2C 122
Friendly St. M. SE8 2C 122
Friendship Ho. *SE1* *7B 14*
(off Belvedere Pl.)
Friendship Wlk. UB5: N'olt 3B 76
Friendship Way E15 1E 86
Friends Rd. CR0: C'don 3D 168
Friend St. EC1 1A 8 (3B 84)
FRIERN BARNET 5J 31
Friern Barnet La. N11 2G 31
N20 2G 31
Friern Barnet Rd. N11 5J 31
Friern Barnet School Sports Cen. *5J 31*
(off Hemington Av.)
Friern Bri. Retail Pk. N11 6A 32
Friern Ct. N20 3G 31
Friern Mt. Dr. N20 7F 21
Friern Pk. N12 5F 31
Friern Rd. SE22 7G 121
Friern Watch Av. N12 4F 31
Frigate Ho. *E14* *4E 104*
(off Stebondale St.)
Frigate M. SE8 6C 104
Frimley Av. SM6: Wall 5J 167
Frimley Cl. CR0: New Ad 7E 170
SW19 2G 135
Frimley Ct. DA14: Sidc 5C 144
Frimley Cres. CR0: New Ad 7E 170
Frimley Gdns. CR4: Mitc 3C 154
Frimley Rd. IG3: Ilf 3J 71
KT9: Chess 5D 162
Frimley St. *E1* *4K 85*
(off Frimley Way)
Frimley Way E1 4K 85
Fringewood Cl. HA6: Nwood 1D 38
Frinstead Ho. *W10* *7F 81*
(off Freston Rd.)
Frinsted Rd. DA8: Erith 7K 109
Frinton Ct. *W13* *5B 78*
(off Hardwick Grn.)
Frinton Dr. IG8: Wfd G 7A 36
Frinton M. IG2: Ilf 6E 52
Frinton Rd. DA14: Sidc 2E 144
E6 3B 88
N15 6E 48
SW17 6E 136
Friston St. SW6 2K 117
Friswell Pl. DA6: Bex 4G 127
Fritham Cl. KT3: N Mald 6A 152
Frith Ct. NW7 7B 30
Frith Ho. *NW8* *4B 4*
(off Frampton St.)
Frith La. NW7 7B 30
Frith Rd. CR0: C'don 2C 168
E11 4E 68
Frith St. W1 1C 12 (6H 83)
Frithville Ct. *W12* *1E 98*
(off Frithville Gdns.)
Frithville Gdns. W12 1E 98
Frizlands La. RM10: Dag 2H 73
Frobisher Cl. HA5: Pinn 7B 40
Frobisher Ct. NW9 2A 44
SE8 *5A 104*
(off Evelyn St.)
SE10 *6F 105*
(off Old Woolwich Rd.)
SE23 2H 139
SM3: Cheam 7G 165
W12 *2E 98*
(off Lime Gro.)
Frobisher Cres. *EC2* *5D 8*
(off Silk St.)
TW19: Stanw 7A 110
Frobisher Gdns. E10 7D 50
TW19: Stanw 7A 110
Frobisher Ho. *E1* *1H 103*
(off Watts St.)
SW1 *7C 18*
(off Dolphin Sq.)
Frobisher M. EN2: Enf 4J 23
Frobisher Pas. E14 1C 104
Frobisher Pl. SE15 1J 121
Frobisher Rd. E6 6D 88
N8 4A 48
Frobisher St. SE10 6G 105
Frog La. RM13: Rain 6K 91
Frogley Rd. SE22 4F 121
Frogmore SW18 5J 117
Frogmore Av. UB4: Hayes 4G 75
Frogmore Cl. SM3: Cheam 3F 165
Frogmore Ct. UB2: S'hall 4D 94
Frogmore Gdns. SM3: Cheam 4G 165
UB4: Hayes 4G 75
Frogmore Ind. Est. N5 5C 66
NW10 3J 79
UB3: Hayes 2G 93
Frognal NW3 4A 64
Frognal Av. DA14: Sidc 5A 144
HA1: Harr 4K 41
Frognal Cl. NW3 5A 64
FROGNAL CORNER 6K 143
Frognal Ct. NW3 6A 64
Frognal Gdns. NW3 4A 64
Frognal La. NW3 5K 63
Frognal Pde. NW3 6A 64
Frognal Pl. DA14: Sidc 6A 144
Frognal Ri. NW3 3A 64
Frognal Way NW3 4A 64
Frogwell Cl. N4 6D 48
Froissart Rd. SE9 5B 124
Frome Ho. SE15 4H 121
Frome Rd. N22 3B 48
Frome St. N1 2C 84
Fromondes Rd. SM3: Cheam 5G 165
Frontenac NW10 7D 62
Frontier Works N17 6K 33
Frostic Wlk. E1 6K 9 (5G 85)
Froude St. SW8 2F 119
Fruen Rd. TW14: Felt 7H 111
Fruiterers Pas. *EC4* *3D 14*
(off Queen St. Pl.)
Fryatt Rd. N17 7J 33
(not continuous)
Fryday Gro. M. *SW12* *7G 119*
(off Weir Rd.)
Frye Ct. *E3* *3B 86*
(off Benworth St.)
Fryent Cl. NW9 6G 43
Fryent Country Pk. 7G 43
Fryent Country Pk. Local Nature Reserve
7G 43
Fryent Cres. NW9 6A 44
Fryent Flds. NW9 6A 44
Fryent Gro. NW9 6A 44

Fryent Way NW9 5G **43**
Fry Ho. E6 7A **70**
Frying Pan All. E1 6J **9**
Fry Rd. E6 7B **70**
NW10 1B **80**
Fryston Av. CR0: C'don 2G **169**
Fuchsia Cl. RM7: Rush G 2K **73**
Fuchsia St. SE2 5B **108**
Fulbeck Dr. NW9 1A **44**
Fulbeck Ho. *N7* *6K* ***65***
(off Sutterton St.)
Fulbeck Rd. N19 4G **65**
Fulbeck Wlk. HA8: Edg 2C **28**
Fulbeck Way HA2: Harr 2G **41**
Fulbourn *KT1: King T* *2G* ***151***
(off Eureka Rd.)
Fulbourne Rd. E17 1E **50**
Fulbourne St. E1 5H **85**
Fulbrook M. N19 4G **65**
Fulcher Ho. *N1* *1E* ***84***
(off Colville Est.)
SE8 5B **104**
Fulford Ho. KT19: Ewe 7K **163**
Fulford Rd. KT19: Ewe 7K **163**
Fulford St. SE16 2H **103**
FULHAM 2G 117
FULHAM BROADWAY 7J **99**
Fulham B'way. SW6 7J **99**
Fulham Broadway Shop. Cen.
SW6 7J **99**
Fulham Bus. Exchange
SW6 *1A* ***118***
(off The Boulevard)
Fulham Cl. UB10: Hil 4E **74**
Fulham Ct. SW6 1J **117**
(not continuous)
Fulham FC 1F 117
Fulham High St. SW6 2G **117**
Fulham Palace 2G 117
Fulham Pal. Rd. SW6 5E **98**
W6 5E **98**
Fulham Pk. Gdns. SW6 2H **117**
Fulham Pk. Rd. SW6 2H **117**
Fulham Pools
Virgin Active 6G 99
Fulham Rd. SW3 7A **16** (7K **99**)
SW6 2G **117**
(Fulham High St.)
SW6 7K **99**
(King's Rd.)
SW10 7A **16** (7K **99**)
Fullbrooks Av. KT4: Wor Pk 1B **164**
Fuller Cl. BR6: Chels 5K **173**
E2 *4G* ***85***
(off Cheshire St.)
WD23: Bush 1C **26**
Fuller Rd. RM8: Dag 3B **72**
Fullers Av. IG8: Wfd G 7C **36**
KT6: Surb 2F **163**
Fullers Cl. RM5: Col R 1J **55**
Fuller's Griffin Brewery & Vis. Cen. 6B 98
Fullers La. RM5: Col R 1J **55**
Fullers Rd. E18 7C **36**
Fuller St. NW4 4E **44**
Fullers Way Nth.
KT6: Surb 3F **163**
Fullers Way Sth.
KT9: Chess 4E **162**
Fuller's Wood CR0: C'don 5C **170**
Fullerton Ct. TW11: Tedd 6A **132**
Fullerton Rd. CR0: C'don 7F **157**
SM5: Cars 7C **166**
SW18 5K **117**
Fuller Way UB3: Harl 5H **93**
Fullwell Av. IG5: Ilf 1D **52**
IG6: Ilf 1F **53**
FULLWELL CROSS 2G **53**
Fullwell Cross IG6: Ilf 2H **53**
Fullwell Cross Swimming Pool &
Recreation Cen. 2G 53
Fullwell Pde. IG5: Ilf 1E **52**
Fullwood's M. N1 1F **9** (3D **84**)
Fulmar Cl. KT5: Surb 6F **151**
Fulmar Ho. *SE16* *4K* ***103***
(off Tawny Way)
Fulmead St. SW6 1K **117**
Fulmer Cl. TW12: Hamp 5C **130**
Fulmer Ho. *NW8* *4D* ***4***
(off Mallory St.)
UB8: Uxb 6A **56**
Fulmer Rd. E16 5B **88**
Fulmer Way W13 3B **96**
Fulneck *E1* *5J* ***85***
(off Mile End Rd.)
Fulready Rd. E10 5F **51**
Fulstone Cl. TW4: Houn 4D **112**
Fulthorp Rd. SE3 2H **123**
Fulton M. W2 7A **82**
Fulton Rd. HA9: Wemb 3G **61**
FULWELL 4H 131
Fulwell Ct. IG5: Ilf 1E **52**
UB1: S'hall *7G* ***77***
(off Baird Av.)
Fulwell Pk. Av. TW2: Twick 2F **131**
Fulwell Rd. TW11: Tedd 4H **131**
Fulwood Av. HA0: Wemb 2F **79**
Fulwood Cl. UB3: Hayes 6H **75**
Fulwood Ct. HA3: Kenton 6A **42**
Fulwood Gdns. TW1: Twick 6K **113**
Fulwood Pl. WC1 6H **7** (5K **83**)
Fulwood Wlk. SW19 1G **135**
Funland *2C 12*
(in Trocadero Cen.)
Furber St. W6 3D **98**
Furham Fld. HA5: Hat E 7A **26**
Furley Ho. *SE15* *7G* ***103***
(off Peckham Pk. Rd.)
Furley Rd. SE15 7G **103**
Furlong Cl. SM6: Wall 1F **167**
Furlong Path *UB5: N'olt* *6C* ***58***
(off Cowings Mead)
Furlong Rd. N7 6A **66**
Furmage St. SW18 7K **117**
Furneaux Av. SE27 5B **138**
Furness Ho. *SW1* *5J* ***17***
(off Abbots Mnr.)
Furness Rd. HA2: Harr 7F **41**
NW10 2C **80**
SM4: Mord 6K **153**
SW6 2K **117**
Furnival Ct. *E3* *2C* ***86***
(off Four Seasons Cl.)
Furnival Mans. *W1* *6A* ***6***
(off Wells St.)
Furnival St. EC4 7J **7** (6A **84**)
Furrow La. E9 5J **67**
Fursby Av. N3 6D **30**
Fursecroft W1 7E **4**
Further Acre NW9 2B **44**
Furtherfield Cl. CR0: C'don 6A **156**
Further Grn. Rd. SE6 7G **123**
FURZEDOWN 5F 137
Furzedown Dr. SW17 5F **137**
Furzedown Rd. SW17 5F **137**
Furze Farm Cl. RM6: Chad H 2E **54**
Furzefield Cl. BR7: Chst 6F **143**
Furzefield Rd. SE3 6K **105**
Furzeground Way UB11: Stock P 1E **92**
Furzeham Rd. UB7: W Dray 2A **92**
Furze Rd. CR7: Thor H 3C **156**
Furze St. E3 5C **86**
Furzewood TW16: Sun 1J **147**
Fye Foot La. *EC4* *2C* ***14***
(off Queen Victoria St.)
Fyfe Apartments N8 3K **47**
Fyfe Way BR1: Brom 2J **159**
Fyfield *N4* *2A* ***66***
(off Six Acres Est.)
Fyfield Cl. BR2: Brom 4F **159**
Fyfield Ct. E7 6J **69**
Fyfield Ho. *E6* *1C* ***88***
(off Ron Leighton Way)
Fyfield Rd. E17 3F **51**
EN1: Enf 3K **23**
Fyfield Rd. IG8: Wfd G 7F **37**
SW9 3A **120**
Fynes St. SW1 3C **18** (4H **101**)

G

Gable Cl. HA5: Hat E 1E **40**
Gable Ct. SE26 4H **139**
Gables, The BR1: Brom 7K **141**
HA9: Wemb 3G **61**
IG11: Bark 6G **71**
N10 *3E* ***46***
(off Fortis Grn.)
Gables Av. TW15: Ashf 5B **128**
Gables Cl. SE5 1E **120**
SE12 1J **141**
Gables Lodge EN4: Had W 1F **21**
Gabriel Cl. TW13: Hanw 4C **130**
Gabriel Ho. *N1* *1B* ***84***
(off Islington Grn.)
SE11 3G **19** (4K **101**)
SE16 *3B* ***104***
(off Odessa St.)
Gabrielle Cl. HA9: Wemb 3F **61**
Gabrielle Ct. NW3 6B **64**
Gabriel M. BR3: Beck 1K **157**
NW2 2H **63**
Gabriel St. SE23 7K **121**
Gabriels Wharf SE1 4J **13** (1A **102**)
Gad Cl. E13 3K **87**
Gaddesden Av. HA9: Wemb 6F **61**
Gaddesden Ho. *EC1* *2F* ***9***
(off Cranwood St.)
Gadebridge Ho. *SW3* *5C* ***16***
(off Cale St.)
Gade Cl. UB3: Hayes 1K **93**
Gadesden Rd. KT19: Ewe 6J **163**
(not continuous)
Gadsbury Cl. NW9 6B **44**
Gadsden Ho. *W10* *4G* ***81***
(off Hazlewood Cres.)
Gadwall Cl. E16 6K **87**
Gadwall Way SE28 2H **107**
Gage Brown Ho. *W10* *6F* ***81***
(off Bridge Cl.)
Gage Rd. E16 5G **87**
Gage St. WC1 5F **7** (5J **83**)
Gainford Ho. *E2* *3H* ***85***
(off Ellsworth St.)
Gainford St. N1 1A **84**
Gainsboro Gdns. UB6: G'frd 5J **59**
Gainsborough Av.
E12 *6E* ***70***
(off Barrington Rd.)
E12 5E **70**
(Landseer Av.)
Gainsborough Cl. BR3: Beck 7C **140**
KT10: Esh 7J **149**
Gainsborough Ct. BR2: Brom 4A **160**
KT19: Ewe 6B **164**
N12 5E **30**
SE16 *5H* ***103***
(off Stubbs Dr.)
SE21 2E **138**
W4 *5H* ***97***
(off Chaseley Dr.)
W12 2E **98**
Gainsborough Gdns.
HA8: Edg 2F **43**
NW3 3B **64**
NW11 7H **45**
TW7: Isle 5H **113**
Gainsborough Ho. *E14* *2C* ***104***
(off Cassilis Rd.)
E14 *7A* ***86***
(off Victory Pl.)
EN1: Enf 5B **24**
RM8: Dag *4B* ***72***
(off Longbridge Rd.)
SW1 *4D* ***18***
(off Erasmus St.)
Gainsborough Lodge *HA1: Harr* *5K* ***41***
(off Hindes Rd.)
Gainsborough Mans. *W14* *6G* ***99***
(off Queen's Club Gdns.)
Gainsborough M. SE26 3H **139**
Gainsborough Rd. E11 7G **51**
E15 3G **87**
IG8: Wfd G 6H **37**
KT3: N Mald 6K **151**
N12 5E **30**
RM8: Dag 4B **72**
TW9: Rich 2F **115**
UB4: Hayes 2E **74**
W4 4B **98**
Gainsborough Sq. DA6: Bex 3D **126**
Gainsborough St. E9 6B **68**
Gainsborough Studios E. *N1* *1D* ***84***
(off Poole St.)
Gainsborough Studios Nth. *N1* *1D* ***84***
(off Poole St.)
Gainsborough Studios Sth. *N1* *1D* ***84***
(off Poole St.)
Gainsborough Studios W. *N1* *1D* ***84***
(off Poole St.)
Gainsborough Ter. *SM2: Sutt* *7H* ***165***
(off Belmont Ri.)
Gainsborough Twr. *UB5: N'olt* *2B* ***76***
(off Academy Gdns.)
Gainsfield Ct. E11 3G **69**
Gainsford Rd. E17 4B **50**
Gainsford St. SE1 6J **15** (2F **103**)
Gairloch Ho. *NW1* *7H* ***65***
(off Stratford Vs.)
Gairloch Rd. SE5 2E **120**
Gaisford St. NW5 6G **65**
Gaitskell Ct. SW11 2C **118**
Gaitskell Ho. E6 1B **88**
E17 3D **50**
SE17 *6E* ***102***
(off Villa St.)
Gaitskell Rd. SE9 1G **143**
Gaitskell Way *SE1* *6C* ***14***
(off Weller St.)
Gala Bingo
Acton 1K 97
(off High St.)
Bexleyheath 4H 127
Camberwell 7C 102
Crystal Palace 6F 139
Enfield 4B 24
Feltham 2K 129
Harrow 5K 41
Hounslow 4E 112
Ilford 2G 53
Kingston upon Thames 1E 150
Leyton 1B 68
Stratford 1F 87
Surrey Quays 3K 103
Tooting 5C 136
Upton Pk. 1C 88
Woolwich 3E 106
Gala Ct. CR7: Thor H 5A **156**
Galahad Rd. BR1: Brom 4J **141**
N9 3B **34**
Galata Rd. SW13 7C **98**
Galatea Sq. SE15 3H **121**
Galaxy Bldg. *E14* *4C* ***104***
(off Crews St.)
Galaxy Ho. *EC2* *3F* ***9***
(off Leonard St.)
Galba Ct. TW8: Bford 7D **96**
Galbraith St. E14 3E **104**
Galdana Av. EN5: New Bar 3F **21**
Galeborough Av. IG8: Wfd G 7A **36**
Gale Cl. CR4: Mitc 3B **154**
TW12: Hamp 6C **130**
Gale Ct. BR2: Brom 2G **159**
Galena Arches *W6* *4D* ***98***
(off Galena Rd.)
Galena Ho. *SE18* *5K* ***107***
(off Grosmont Rd.)
Galena Rd. W6 4D **98**

Galen Pl.—Garth Cl.

Galen Pl. WC1 . . . . .6F 7 (5J 83)
Galesbury Rd. SW18 . . . . .6A 118
Gales Gdns. E2 . . . . .3H 85
Gale St. E3 . . . . .5C 86
RM9: Dag 5C 72
Gales Way IG8: Wfd G 7H 37
Galgate Cl. SW19 . . . . .1F 135
Gallants Farm Rd. EN4: E Barn 7H 21
Galleon Cl. DA8: Erith 4K 109
SE16 .2K 103
Galleon Ho. E14 . . . . .4E 104
(off Glengarnock Av.)
Galleons Dr. IG11: Bark 3A 90
Galleria Ct. SE15 . . . . .6F 103
Galleria Shop. Mall, The E18 . . . . .2J 51
Gallery Ct. SE1 . . . . .7E 14
(off Pilgrimage St.)
SW10 . . . . .6A 100
(off Gunter Gro.)
Gallery Gdns. UB5: N'olt 2B 76
Gallery Rd. SE21 . . . . .1D 138
Galley, The E16 . . . . .7F 89
Galleymead Rd. SL3: Poyle 4A 174
Galleywall Rd. SE16 . . . . .4H 103
Galleywall Rd. Trad. Est. SE16 . . . . . .4H 103
Galleywood Ho. W10 . . . . .5E 80
(off Sutton Way)
Galliard Cl. N9 . . . . .6D 24
Galliard Ct. N9 . . . . .6B 24
Galliard Rd. N9 . . . . .1B 34
Gallia Rd. N5 . . . . .5B 66
Gallica Ct. SM1: Sutt 1K 165
Gallions Cl. IG11: Bark 3A 90
Gallions Entrance E16 . . . . .1G 107
Gallions Reach Shop. Pk. E6 . . . . .5G 89
Gallions Rd. E16 . . . . .7F 89
SE7 . . . . .4K 105
(not continuous)
Gallions Rdbt. E16 . . . . .7F 89
Gallions Vw. Rd. SE28 . . . . .2J 107
Gallon Cl. SE7 . . . . .4A 106
Gallop, The CR2: Sels 7H 169
SM2: Sutt 7B 166
Gallosson Rd. SE18 . . . . .4J 107
Galloway Path CR0: C'don 4D 168
Galloway Rd. W12 . . . . .1C 98
Gallus Cl. N21 . . . . .6E 22
Gallus Sq. SE3 . . . . .3K 123
Galpins Rd. CR7: Thor H 5J 155
Galsworthy Av. E14 . . . . .6A 86
RM6: Chad H 7B 54
Galsworthy Cl. NW2 . . . . .4G 63
SE28 .1B 108
Galsworthy Ct. W3 . . . . .3H 97
(off Bollo Bri. Rd.)
Galsworthy Cres. SE3 . . . . .7A 106
Galsworthy Ho. W11 . . . . .6G 81
(off Elgin Cres.)
Galsworthy Rd. KT2: King T 7H 133
NW2 . . . . .4G 63
Galsworthy Ter. N16 . . . . .3E 66
Galton St. W10 . . . . .3G 81
Galva Cl. EN4: Cockf 4K 21
Galvani Way CR0: Wadd 1K 167
Galveston Ho. E1 . . . . .4A 86
(off Harford St.)
Galveston Rd. SW15 . . . . .5H 117
Galway Cl. SE16 . . . . .5H 103
(off Masters Dr.)
Galway Ho. E1 .5K 85
(off White Horse La.)
EC1 . . . . .2D 8
Galway St. EC1 . . . . .2D 8 (3C 84)
Galy NW9 . . . . .2B 44
Gambado
Beckenham 6C 140
Chelsea 1A 118
(off Station Ct.)
Gambetta St. SW8 . . . . .2F 119
Gambia St. SE1 . . . . .5B 14 (1B 102)
Gambier Ho. EC1 . . . . .2D 8
(off Mora St.)
Gambole Rd. SW17 . . . . .4C 136
Games Rd. EN4: Cockf 3H 21
Gamlen Rd. SW15 . . . . .4F 117
Gamma Ct. CR0: C'don 1D 168
(off Sydenham Rd.)
Gamuel Cl. E17 . . . . .6C 50
Gander Grn. Cres. TW12: Hamp 1E 148
Gander Grn. La. SM1: Sutt 3H 165
SM3: Cheam 2G 165
Gandhi Cl. E17 . . . . .6C 50
Gandolfi St. SE15 . . . . .6E 102
Ganley Ct. SW11 . . . . .3B 118
(off Winstanley Est.)
Ganton St. W1 . . . . .2A 12 (7G 83)
GANTS HILL 6E 52
GANTS HILL 6E 52
Gants Hill IG2: Ilf 6E 52
Gantshill Cres. IG2: Ilf 5E 52
Gap Rd. SW19 . . . . .5J 135
Garage Rd. W3 .6G 79
Garand Ct. N7 .5K 65
Garbett Ho. SE17 . . . . .6B 102
(off Doddington Gro.)
Garbutt Pl. W1 . . . . .5H 5 (5E 82)
Garden Av. CR4: Mitc 7F 137
DA7: Bex 3F 127
Garden City HA8: Edg 6B 28
Garden Cl. E4 .5H 35
HA4: Ruis 2G 57
KT3: N Mald 4A 152
SE12 .3K 141
SM6: Wall 5J 167
SW15 .7E 116
TW12: Hamp 5D 130
TW15: Ashf 6E 128
UB5: N'olt 1C 76
Garden Ct. CR0: C'don 2F 169
EC4 . . . . .2J 13
HA7: Stan 5H 27
N12 . . . . .5E 30
NW8 . . . . .1A 4
(off Garden Rd.)
TW9: Kew 1F 115
TW12: Hamp 5D 130
W4 . . . . .3J 97
W11 . . . . .7G 81
(off Clarendon Rd.)
Gardener Gro. TW13: Hanw 2D 130
Gardeners Cl. N11 . . . . .2K 31
SE9 . . . . .3C 142
Gardeners Rd. CR0: C'don 1B 168
Garden Ho. N2 .2B 46
(off The Grange)
SW7 . . . . .3K 99
(off Cornwall Gdns.)
Garden Ho., The W6 . . . . .6F 99
(off Bothwell St.)
Gardenia Rd. BR1: Brom 3E 160
EN1: Enf 6K 23
Gardenia Way IG8: Wfd G 6D 36
Garden La. BR1: Brom 6K 141
SW2 . . . . .1K 137
Garden M. W2 .7J 81
Garden Mus., The 2G 19 (3K 101)
Garden Pl. E8 .1F 85
Garden Rd. BR1: Brom 7K 141
KT12: Walt T 6K 147
NW8 . . . . .1A 4 (3A 82)
SE20 .1J 157
TW9: Rich 3G 115
Garden Row SE1 . . . . .3B 102
Garden Royal SW15 . . . . .6F 117
Gardens, The BR3: Beck 1E 158
E5 . . . . .7F 49
HA1: Harr 6G 41
HA5: Pinn 6D 40
N8 . . . . .4J 47
(not continuous)
SE22 .4G 121
TW14: Felt 5F 111
Garden St. E1 .5K 85
Gardens Way E12 . . . . .3C 70
Garden Ter. SW1 . . . . .5C 18 (5H 101)
SW7 . . . . .7D 10
Garden Vw. E7 .4A 70
Garden Wlk. BR3: Beck 1B 158
EC2 . . . . .2G 9 (3E 84)
Garden Way NW10 . . . . .6J 61
Gardiner Av. NW2 . . . . .5E 62
Gardiner Cl. EN3: Pond E 6E 24
RM8: Dag 4D 72
Gardiner Ct. CR2: S Croy 6D 168
NW10 . . . . .1K 79
Gardiner Ho. SW11 . . . . .1C 118
Gardner Cl. E11 . . . . .6K 51
Gardner Ct. EC1 . . . . .3A 8
(off Brewery Sq.)
N5 . . . . .4C 66
Gardner Ho. TW13: Hanw 2D 130
UB1: S'hall 7B 76
(off The Broadway)
Gardner Ind. Est. SE26 . . . . .5B 140
Gardner Pl. TW14: Felt 6K 111
Gardner Rd. E13 . . . . .4K 87
Gardners La. EC4 . . . . .2C 14 (7C 84)
Gardnor Rd. NW3 . . . . .4B 64
Gard St. EC1 . . . . .1B 8 (3B 84)
Garendon Gdns.
SM4: Mord 7K 153
Garendon Rd. SM4: Mord 7K 153
Garenne Ct. E4 . . . . .1K 35
Gareth Cl. KT4: Wor Pk 2F 165
Gareth Ct. SW16 . . . . .3H 137
Gareth Dr. N9 .2B 34
Gareth Gro. BR1: Brom 4J 141
Garfield EN2: Enf 5J 23
(off London Rd.)
Garfield Ct. NW6 . . . . .7G 63
(off Willesden La.)
Garfield M. SW11 . . . . .3E 118
Garfield Rd. E4 . . . . .1A 36
E13 . . . . .4H 87
EN3: Pond E 4D 24
SW11 .3E 118
SW19 .5A 136
TW1: Twick 1A 132
Garford St. E14 . . . . .7C 86
Garganey Ct. NW10 . . . . .6K 61
(off Elgar Av.)
Garganey Wlk. SE28 . . . . .7C 90
Garibaldi St. SE18 . . . . .4J 107
Garland Ct. E14 . . . . .7C 86
(off Premiere Pl.)
SE17 .4C 102
(off Wansey St.)
Garland Dr. TW3: Houn 2G 113
Garland Ho. KT2: King T 1E 150
(off Seven Kings Way)
UB7: W Dray 2B 92
Garland Rd. HA7: Stan 1E 42
SE18 .7H 107
Garlands Ct. CR0: C'don 4D 168
(off Chatsworth Rd.)
Garlands Ho. NW8 . . . . .2A 82
(off Carlton Hill)
Garlands La. HA1: Harr 1K 59
Garlick Hill EC4 . . . . .2D 14 (7C 84)
Garlies Rd. SE23 . . . . .3A 140
Garlinge Ho. SW9 . . . . .1A 120
(off Gosling Way)
Garlinge Rd. NW2 . . . . .6H 63
Garman Cl. N18 . . . . .5J 33
Garman Rd. N17 . . . . .7C 34
(not continuous)
Garnault M. EC1 . . . . .2K 7
Garnault Pl. EC1 . . . . .2K 7 (3A 84)
Garnault Rd. EN1: Enf 1A 24
Garner Cl. RM8: Dag 1D 72
Garner Ct. TW19: Stanw 6A 110
(off Douglas Rd.)
Garner Rd. E17 . . . . .1E 50
Garner St. E2 .2G 85
Garnet Ho. E1 . . . . .1J 103
(off Garnet St.)
Garnet Rd. CR7: Thor H 4C 156
NW10 . . . . .6A 62
Garnet St. E1 . . . . .7J 85
Garnett Cl. SE9 . . . . .3D 124
Garnett Rd. NW3 . . . . .5D 64
Garnett Way E17 . . . . .1A 50
(off McEntee Av.)
Garnet Wlk. E6 . . . . .5C 88
Garnham Cl. N16 . . . . .2F 67
Garnham St. N16 . . . . .2F 67
Garnies Cl. SE15 . . . . .7F 103
Garrad's Rd. SW16 . . . . .3H 137
Garrard Cl. BR7: Chst 5F 143
DA7: Bex 3G 127
Garrard Wlk. NW10 . . . . .6A 62
Garratt Cl. CR0: Bedd 4J 167
Garratt Ct. SW18 . . . . .7K 117
Garratt La. SW17 . . . . .6K 117
SW18 .6K 117
Garratt Rd. HA8: Edg 7B 28
Garratts Rd. WD23: Bush 1B 26
Garratt Ter. SW17 . . . . .4C 136
Garraway Ct. SW13 . . . . .7E 98
(off Wyatt Dr.)
Garrett Cl. W3 .5K 79
Garrett Ho. SE1 . . . . .6A 14
(off Burrows M.)
W12 . . . . .6D 80
(off Du Cane Rd.)
Garrett St. EC1 . . . . .3D 8 (4C 84)
Garrick Av. NW11 . . . . .6G 45
Garrick Cl. SW18 . . . . .4A 118
TW9: Rich 5D 114
W5 . . . . .4E 78
Garrick Ct. E8 .7F 67
(off Jacaranda Gro.)
HA8: Edg 4A 28
Garrick Cres. CR0: C'don 2E 168
Garrick Dr. NW4 . . . . .2E 44
SE28 .3H 107
Garrick Gdns.
KT8: W Mole 3E 148
Garrick Ho. KT1: King T 4E 150
(off Surbiton Rd.)
W1 . . . . .5J 11
W4 . . . . .6A 98
Garrick Ind. Est.
NW9 . . . . .5B 44
Garrick Pk. NW4 . . . . .2F 45
Garrick Rd. NW9 . . . . .6B 44
TW9: Rich 2G 115
UB6: G'frd 4F 77
Garricks Ho. KT1: King T 2D 150
(off Wadbrook St.)
Garrick St. WC2 . . . . .2E 12 (7J 83)
Garrick Theatre 3E 12
(off Charing Cross Rd.)
Garrick Way NW4 . . . . .4F 45
Garrick Yd. WC2 . . . . .2E 12
Garrison Cl. SE18 . . . . .7E 106
TW4: Houn 5D 112
Garrison La. KT9: Chess 7D 162
Garrison Rd. E3 . . . . .1C 86
Garrowsfield EN5: Barn 6C 20
Garry Way RM1: Rom 1K 55
Garsdale Cl. N11 . . . . .6K 31
Garsdale Ter. W14 . . . . .5H 99
(off Aisgill Av.)
Garside Cl. SE28 . . . . .3H 107
TW12: Hamp 6F 131
Garside Ct. TW11: Ham W 1C 150
Garsington M. SE4 . . . . .3B 122
Garson Ho. W2 .2A 10
(off Gloucester Ter.)
Garston Ho. N1 . . . . .7B 66
(off The Sutton Est.)
Garter Way SE16 . . . . .2K 103
Garth, The HA3: Kenton 6F 43
TW12: Ham H 6F 131
Garth Cl. HA4: Ruis 1B 58
KT2: King T 5F 133
SM4: Mord 7F 153

270 A-Z London

Garth Ct. *HA1: Harr* 6K *41*
    (off Northwick Pk. Rd.)
  W4 . . . . .5K *97*
Garth Ho. NW2 . . . . .2H *63*
Garth M. W5 . . . . .4E *78*
Garthorne Rd. SE23 . . . . .7K *121*
Garthorne Road Nature Reserve . . .7K *121*
Garth Rd. KT2: King T 5F *133*
  NW2 . . . . .2H *63*
  SM4: Mord 6E *152*
  W4 . . . . .5K *97*
Garth Rd. Ind. Cen., The
  SM4: Mord 1F *165*
Garthside TW10: Ham 5E *132*
Garthway N12 . . . . .6H *31*
Gartmoor Gdns. SW19 . . . . .1H *135*
Gartmore Rd. IG3: Ilf 2K *71*
Garton Pl. SW18 . . . . .6A *118*
Gartons Cl. EN3: Pond E 4D *24*
Gartons Way SW11 . . . . .3A *118*
Garvary Rd. E16 . . . . .6K *87*
Garway Ct. *E3* 2C *86*
  (off Matilda Gdns.)
Garway Rd. W2 . . . . .6K *81*
Garwood Cl. N17 . . . . .1H *49*
Gascoigne Cl. N17 . . . . .1F *49*
  (off King's Rd.)
Gascoigne Gdns. IG8: Wfd G 7B *36*
Gascoigne Pl. E2 . . . . .1J *9* (3F *85*)
  (not continuous)
Gascoigne Rd. CR0: New Ad 7F *171*
  IG11: Bark 1G *89*
Gascony Av. NW6 . . . . .7J *63*
Gascony Pl. W12 . . . . .1F *99*
Gascoyne Ho. E9 . . . . .7A *68*
Gascoyne Rd. E9 . . . . .7K *67*
Gaselee St. *E14* 1E *104*
  (off Baffin Way)
Gaskarth Rd. HA8: Edg 1J *43*
  SW12 . . . . .6F *119*
Gaskell Ct. SE20 . . . . .7K *139*
Gaskell Rd. N6 . . . . .6D *46*
Gaskell St. SW4 . . . . .2J *119*
Gaskin St. N1 . . . . .1B *84*
Gaspar Cl. SW5 . . . . .4K *99*
Gaspar M. SW5 . . . . .4K *99*
Gassiot Rd. SW17 . . . . .4D *136*
Gassiot Way SM1: Sutt 3B *166*
Gasson Ho. *SE14* 6K *103*
  (off John Williams Cl.)
Gastein Rd. W6 . . . . .6F *99*
Gastigny Ho. EC1 . . . . .2D *8*
Gaston Bell Cl. TW9: Rich 3F *115*
Gaston Bri. Rd. TW17: Shep 6F *147*
Gaston Rd. CR4: Mitc 3E *154*
Gaston Way TW17: Shep 5F *147*
Gataker Ho. *SE16* 3H *103*
  (off Slippers Pl.)
Gataker St. SE16 . . . . .3H *103*
Gatcombe Ct. BR3: Beck 7C *140*
Gatcombe Ho. SE22 . . . . .3E *120*
Gatcombe M. W5 . . . . .7F *79*
Gatcombe Rd. E16 . . . . .1J *105*
  N19 . . . . .3H *65*
Gatcombe Way EN4: Cockf 3J *21*
Gateacre Ct. DA14: Sidc 4B *144*
Gate Cen., The TW8: Bford 7A *96*
Gate Cinema 1J *99*
  (off Notting Hill Ga.)
Gateforth St. NW8 . . . . .4C *4* (4C *82*)
Gate Hill Ct. W11 . . . . .1H *99*
  (off Ladbroke Ter.)
Gate Ho. *E3* 1A *86*
  (off Gunmakers La.)
  N1 . . . . .7D *66*
  (off Ufton Rd.)
Gatehouse Cl. KT2: King T 7J *133*
Gatehouse Sq. SE1 . . . . .4D *14*
Gatehouse Theatre 1E *64*
Gateley Ho. *SE4* 4A *122*
  (off Coston Wlk.)
Gateley Rd. SW9 . . . . .3K *119*

Gate Lodge W9 . . . . .5J *81*
  (off Admiral Wlk.)
Gately Ct. SE15 . . . . .7F *103*
Gate M. SW7 . . . . .7D *10*
Gater Dr. EN2: Enf 1J *23*
Gates NW9 .2B *44*
Gatesborough St. EC2 . . . . . .3G *9* (4E *84*)
Gates Cl. SE17 . . . . .5C *102*
Gatesden WC1 . . . . .2G *7* (3J *83*)
Gates Grn. Rd.
  BR2: Kes 3H *171*
  BR4: W W'ck 3H *171*
Gateside Rd. SW17 . . . . .3D *136*
Gatestone Ct. SE19 . . . . .6E *138*
Gatestone Rd. SE19 . . . . .6E *138*
Gate St. WC2 . . . . .7G *7* (6K *83*)
Gate Theatre, The 1J *99*
  (off Pembridge Rd.)
Gateway SE17 . . . . .6C *102*
Gateway Arc. *N1* 2B *84*
  (off Upper St.)
Gateway Bus. Cen.
  BR3: Beck 6A *140*
  SE28 . . . . .3H *107*
Gateway Cl. *IG2: Ilf* 6E *52*
  (off Parham Dr.)
Gateway Ho. IG11: Bark 1G *89*
Gateway Ind. Est. NW10 . . . . .3B *80*
Gateway M. E8 . . . . .5F *67*
  N11 . . . . .6B *32*
Gateway Rd. E10 . . . . .3D *68*
Gateways KT6: Surb 5E *150*
  (off Surbiton Hill Rd.)
Gateways, The SW3 . . . . .4D *16*
  TW9: Rich 4D *114*
  (off Park La.)
Gateways Ct. SM6: Wall 5F *167*
Gatfield Gro. TW13: Hanw 2E *130*
Gatfield Ho. TW13: Hanw 2D *130*
Gathorne Rd. N22 . . . . .2A *48*
Gathorne St. E2 . . . . .2K *85*
Gatley Av. KT19: Ewe 5H *163*
Gatliff Cl. SW1 . . . . .6H *17*
Gatliff Rd. SW1 . . . . .6J *17* (5F *101*)
  (not continuous)
Gatling Rd. SE2 . . . . .5A *108*
Gatonby St. SE15 . . . . .1F *121*
Gatton Cl. HA8: Edg 7D *28*
Gatting Way UB8: Uxb 6A *56*
Gattis Wharf *N1* 2J *83*
  (off New Wharf Rd.)
Gatton Cl. SM2: Sutt 7K *165*
Gatton Rd. SW17 . . . . .4C *136*
Gattons Way DA14: Sidc 4F *145*
Gatward Cl. N21 . . . . .6G *23*
Gatward Grn. N9 . . . . .2A *34*
Gatwick Ho. *E14* 6B *86*
  (off Clemence St.)
Gatwick Rd. SW18 . . . . .7H *117*
Gauden Cl. SW4 . . . . .3H *119*
Gauden Rd. SW4 . . . . .2H *119*
Gaudi Apartments *N8* 3K *47*
  (off Gt. Amwell La.)
Gaugin Ct. *SE16* 5H *103*
  (off Stubbs Dr.)
Gaumont Ter. W12 . . . . .2E *98*
  (off Lime Gro.)
Gaumont Twr. *E8* 6F *67*
  (off Roseberry St.)
Gauntlet NW9 . . . . .2B *44*
  (off Five Acre)
Gauntlet Cl. UB5: N'olt 7C *58*
Gauntlett Ct. HA0: Wemb 5B *60*
Gauntlett Rd. SM1: Sutt 5B *166*
Gaunt St. SE1 . . . . .3C *102*
Gautrey Rd. SE15 . . . . .2J *121*
Gautrey Sq. E6 . . . . .6D *88*
Gavel St. SE17 . . . . .4D *102*
Gaverick M. E14 . . . . .4C *104*
Gavestone Cres. SE12 . . . . .7K *123*
Gavestone Rd. SE12 . . . . .7K *123*

Gaviller Pl. E5 . . . . .4H *67*
Gavina Cl. SM4: Mord 5C *154*
Gavin Ho. SE18 . . . . .4J *107*
Gawain Wlk. N9 . . . . .3B *34*
Gawber St. E2 . . . . .3J *85*
Gawsworth Cl. E15 . . . . .5H *69*
Gawthorne Ct. E3 . . . . .2C *86*
Gay Cl. NW2 . . . . .5D *62*
Gaydon Ho. *W2* 5K *81*
  (off Bourne Ter.)
Gaydon La. NW9 . . . . .1A *44*
Gayfere Rd. IG5: Ilf 3D *52*
  KT17: Ewe 5C *164*
Gayfere St. SW1 . . . . .2E *18* (3J *101*)
Gayford Rd. W12 . . . . .2B *98*
Gay Gdns. RM10: Dag 4J *73*
Gay Ho. N16 . . . . .5E *66*
Gayhurst *SE17* 6D *102*
  (off Hopwood Rd.)
Gayhurst Ct. UB5: N'olt 3A *76*
Gayhurst Ho. *NW8* 3C *4*
  (off Mallory St.)
Gayhurst Rd. E8 . . . . .7G *67*
Gaylor Rd. UB5: N'olt 5D *58*
Gaymead NW8 . . . . .1K *81*
  (off Abbey Rd.)
Gaynesford Rd. SE23 . . . . .2K *139*
  SM5: Cars 7D *166*
Gaynes Hill Rd. IG8: Wfd G 6H *37*
Gay Rd. E15 . . . . .2F *87*
Gaysham Av. IG2: Ilf 5E *52*
Gaysham Hall IG5: Ilf 3F *53*
Gaysley Ho. SE11 . . . . .4J *19*
Gayton *HA1: Harr* 7J *41*
  (off Grove Hill)
Gayton Cl. HA1: Harr 6K *41*
Gayton Cres. NW3 . . . . .4B *64*
Gayton Ho. *E3* 4C *86*
  (off Chiltern Rd.)
Gayton Rd. HA1: Harr 6K *41*
  NW3 . . . . .4B *64*
  SE2 .3C *108*
Gayville Rd. SW11 . . . . .6D *118*
Gaywood Cl. SW2 . . . . .1K *137*
Gaywood Ho. E17 . . . . .3C *50*
Gaywood St. SE1 . . . . .3B *102*
Gaza St. SE17 . . . . .5B *102*
Gaze Ho. *E14* 6F *87*
  (off Blair St.)
Gazelle Ho. E15 . . . . .6G *69*
Gean Ct. E11 . . . . .4F *69*
  N11 . . . . .6B *32*
  (off Cline Rd.)
Geariesville Gdns. IG6: Ilf 4F *53*
Gearing Cl. SW17 . . . . .4E *136*
Gearing Rd. NW10 . . . . .5C *62*
Geary St. N7 . . . . .5K *65*
Geddes Pl. *DA7: Bex* 4G *127*
  (off Arnsberg Way)
Gedeney Rd. N17 . . . . .1C *48*
Gedling Ct. *SE1* 7K *15*
  (off Jamaica Rd.)
Gedling Pl. SE1 . . . . .7K *15* (3F *103*)
Geere Rd. E15 . . . . .1H *87*
Gees Ct. W1 . . . . .1H *11* (6E *82*)
Gee St. EC1 . . . . .3C *8* (4C *84*)
Geffery's Ct. SE9 . . . . .3C *142*
Geffrye Cl. N1 . . . . .2E *84*
Geffrye Est. N1 . . . . .2E *84*
Geffrye Mus. 1J *9*
Geffrye St. E2 . . . . .1J *9* (2F *85*)
Geldart Rd. SE15 . . . . .7H *103*
Geldeston Rd. E5 . . . . .2G *67*
Gellatly Rd. SE14 . . . . .2J *121*
Gell Cl. UB10: Ick 3B *56*
Gelsthorpe Rd. RM5: Col R 1H *55*
Gemini Bus. Cen. E16 . . . . .4F *87*
Gemini Bus. Est. SE14 . . . . .5K *103*
Gemini Bus. Pk. E6 . . . . .5H *89*
Gemini Ct. *E1* 7G *85*
  (off Vaughan Way)

Gemini Gro. UB5: N'olt 3C *76*
Gemini Ho. *E3* 1C *86*
  (off Garrison Rd.)
Gemini Pl. TW15: Ashf 6G *129*
Gemma Knowles Cl. *SW2* 1A *138*
  (off Tulse Hill)
Genas Cl. IG6: Ilf 1F *53*
General Gordon Pl. SE18 . . . . .4F *107*
General Wolfe Rd. SE10 . . . . .1F *123*
Genesis Bus. Pk. NW10 . . . . .2H *79*
Genesis Cl. TW19: Stanw 1B *128*
Genesta Rd. SE18 . . . . .6F *107*
Geneva Cl. TW17: Shep 2G *147*
Geneva Ct. NW9 . . . . .5B *44*
Geneva Dr. SW9 . . . . .4A *120*
Geneva Gdns. RM6: Chad H 5E *54*
Geneva Rd. CR7: Thor H 5C *156*
  KT1: King T 4E *150*
Genever Cl. E4 . . . . .5H *35*
Genista Rd. N18 . . . . .5C *34*
Genoa Av. SW15 . . . . .5E *116*
Genoa Ho. *E1* 4K *85*
  (off Ernest St.)
Genoa Rd. SE20 . . . . .1J *157*
Genotin Rd. EN1: Enf 3J *23*
Genotin Ter. EN1: Enf 3J *23*
Gentlemans Row EN2: Enf 3H *23*
Gentry Gdns. E13 . . . . .4J *87*
Geoffrey Bower Sports Cen. 2D *52*
Geoffrey Cl. SE5 . . . . .2C *120*
Geoffrey Ct. SE4 . . . . .2B *122*
Geoffrey Gdns. E6 . . . . .2C *88*
Geoffrey Ho. *SE1* 7F *15*
  (off Pardoner St.)
Geoffrey Jones Ct. NW10 . . . . .1C *80*
Geoffrey Rd. SE4 . . . . .3B *122*
George V Av. HA5: Pinn 2D *40*
George V Cl. HA5: Pinn 3E *40*
George V Way UB6: G'frd 1B *78*
George Beard Rd. SE8 . . . . .4B *104*
George Belt Ho. *E2* 3K *85*
  (off Smart St.)
George Comberton Wlk. E12 . . . . . .5E *70*
George Ct. *TW15: Ashf* 4B *128*
  (off Church Rd.)
  WC2 . . . . .3F *13*
George Cres. N10 . . . . .7K *31*
George Davies Lodge *IG6: Ilf* 5G *53*
  (off Veronique Gdns.)
George Downing Est. N16 . . . . .2F *67*
George Eliot Ho. SW1 . . . . .4B *18*
  (off Vauxhall Bri. Rd.)
George Elliot Ho. *SE17* 5C *102*
  (off Crampton St.)
George Elliston Ho. *SE1* 5G *103*
  (off Old Kent Rd.)
George Eyre Ho. *NW8* 2B *82*
  (off Cochrane St.)
George Furness Ho. NW10 . . . . .6D *62*
  (off Grange Rd.)
George Gange Way HA3: W'stone . . .3J *41*
George Gillett Ct. EC1 . . . . .3D *8*
George Groves Rd. SE20 . . . . .1G *157*
George Hudson Twr. E15 . . . . .2D *86*
  (off High St.)
George Inn Yd. SE1 . . . . . . .5E *14* (1D *102*)
George La. BR2: Hayes 1K *171*
  E18 . . . . .2J *51*
  (not continuous)
  SE13 . . . . .6D *122*
George Lansbury Ho. *E3* 3B *86*
  (off Bow Rd.)
  N22 . . . . .1A *48*
  (off Progress Way)
  NW10 .7A *62*
George Lindgren Ho. *SW6* 7H *99*
  (off Clem Attlee Ct.)
George Loveless Ho. *E2* 1K *9*
  (off Diss St.)
George Lowe Ct. W2 . . . . .5K *81*
  (off Bourne Ter.)
George Mathers Rd. SE11 . . . . . . .4B *102*

George M.—Given Wilson Wlk.

George M. EN2: Enf 3J **23**
NW1 2B **6**
SW9 2A **120**
George Padmore Ho. *E8* *1G 85*
(off Brougham Rd.)
George Peabody Ct. *NW1* *5C 4*
(off Burne St.)
George Pl. N17 3E **48**
George Potter Ho. *SW11* *2B 118*
(off George Potter Way)
George Potter Way SW11 2B **118**
George Rd. E4 6H **35**
KT2: King T 7H **133**
(not continuous)
KT3: N Mald 4B **152**
George Row SE16 2G **103**
George Sq. SW19 3J **153**
George's Rd. N7 5K **65**
George's Sq. *SW6* *6H 99*
(off North End Rd.)
George St. CR0: C'don 2C **168**
E16 6H **87**
IG11: Bark 7G **71**
TW3: Houn 2D **112**
TW9: Rich 5D **114**
UB2: S'hall 4C **94**
W1 7E **4** (6D **82**)
W7 1J **95**
George Tingle Ho. *SE1* *3F 103*
(off Grange Wlk.)
Georgetown Cl. SE19 5E **138**
Georgette Pl. SE10 7E **104**
George Vale Ho. *E2* *2G 85*
(off Mansford St.)
Georgeville Gdns. IG6: Ilf 4F **53**
George Walter Ct. *SE16* *4J 103*
(off Millender Wlk.)
George Wyver Cl. SW19 7G **117**
George Yd. EC3 1F **15** (6D **84**)
W1 2H **11** (7E **82**)
Georgia Ct. *SE16* *3G 103*
(off Priter Rd.)
Georgiana St. NW1 1G **83**
Georgian Cl. BR2: Hayes 1K **171**
HA7: Stan 7F **27**
UB10: Ick 4A **56**
Georgian Ct. *CR0: C'don* *1D 168*
(off Cross Rd.)
E9 1J **85**
EN5: New Bar 4F **21**
HA9: Wemb 6G **61**
N3 1H **45**
NW4 5D **44**
SW16 4J **137**
Georgian Ho. *E16* *1J 105*
(off Capulet M.)
Georgian Way HA1: Harr 2H **59**
Georgia Rd. CR7: Thor H 1B **156**
KT3: N Mald 4J **151**
Georgina Gdns. E2 1K **9** (3F **85**)
Geraint Rd. BR1: Brom 4J **141**
Geraldine Rd. SW18 5A **118**
W4 6G **97**
Geraldine St. SE11 2K **19** (3B **102**)
Gerald M. SW1 3H **17**
Gerald Rd. E16 4H **87**
RM8: Dag 2F **73**
SW1 3H **17** (4E **100**)
Gerard Av. TW4: Houn 7E **112**
Gerard Gdns. RM13: Rain 2K **91**
Gerard Pl. E9 7K **67**
Gerard Rd. HA1: Harr 6A **42**
SW13 1B **116**
Gerards Cl. SE16 5J **103**
Gerda Rd. SE9 2G **143**
Germander Way E15 3G **87**
Gernigan Ho. SW18 6B **118**
Gernon Rd. E3 2A **86**
Geron Way NW2 1D **62**
Gerrard Gdns. HA5: Eastc 5J **39**
Gerrard Ho. *SE14* *7J 103*
(off Briant St.)
Gerrard Pl. W1 2D **12** (7H **83**)
Gerrard Rd. N1 2B **84**
Gerrards Cl. N14 5B **22**
Gerrards Ct. W5 3D **96**
Gerrards Pl. SW4 4H **119**
Gerrard St. W1 2D **12** (7H **83**)
Gerridge Ct. *SE1* *1K 19*
(off Gerridge St.)
Gerridge St. SE1 1K **19** (3A **102**)
Gerry Raffles Sq. E15 7F **69**
Gertrude Rd. DA17: Belv 4G **109**
Gertrude St. SW10 7A **16** (6A **100**)
Gervase Cl. HA9: Wemb 3J **61**
Gervase Rd. HA8: Edg 1J **43**
Gervase St. SE15 7H **103**
Gervis Ct. TW7: Isle 7G **95**
Ghent St. SE6 2C **140**
Ghent Way E8 6F **67**
Gherkin, The 1H **15**
Giant Arches Rd. SE24 7C **120**
Giant Tree Hill WD23: B Hea 1C **26**
Gibbfield Cl. RM6: Chad H 3E **54**
Gibbings Ho. *SE1* *7B 14*
(off King James St.)
Gibbins Rd. E15 7E **68**
Gibbon Ho. *NW8* *4B 4*
(off Fisherton St.)
Gibbon Rd. KT2: King T 1E **150**
SE15 2J **121**
W3 7A **80**
Gibbons M. NW11 5H **45**
Gibbon's Rents SE1 5G **15**
Gibbons Rd. NW10 6A **62**
Gibbon Wlk. SW15 4C **116**
Gibbs Av. SE19 5D **138**
Gibbs Cl. SE19 6D **138**
Gibbs Grn. HA8: Edg 4D **28**
W14 5H **99**
(not continuous)
Gibbs Ho. *BR1: Brom* *1H 159*
(off Longfield)
Gibb's Rd. N18 4D **34**
Gibbs Sq. SE19 5D **138**
Gibney Ter. BR1: Brom 4H **141**
Gibraltar Wlk. E2 2K **9**
Gibson Bus. Cen., The N17 7A **34**
Gibson Cl. E1 4J **85**
KT9: Chess 5C **162**
N21 6F **23**
TW7: Isle 3J **113**
Gibson Gdns. N16 2F **67**
Gibson Ho. SM1: Sutt 4J **165**
Gibson M. TW1: Twick 6C **114**
Gibson Rd. RM8: Dag 1C **72**
SE11 4H **19** (4K **101**)
SM1: Sutt 5K **165**
UB10: Ick 4B **56**
Gibsons Hill SW16 7A **138**
(not continuous)
Gibson Sq. N1 1A **84**
Gibson Sq. Gdns. *N1* *1A 84*
(off Gibson Sq.)
Gibson St. SE10 5G **105**
Gideon Cl. DA17: Belv 4H **109**
Gideon M. W5 2D **96**
Gideon Rd. SW11 3E **118**
Gielgud Theatre *2C 12*
(off Shaftesbury Av.)
Giesbach Rd. N19 2H **65**
Giffard Rd. N18 6K **33**
Giffen Sq. Mkt. *SE8* *7C 104*
(off Giffen St.)
Giffin St. SE8 7C **104**
Gifford Gdns. W7 5H **77**
Gifford Ho. *SE10* *5F 105*
(off Eastney St.)
SW1 *6A 18*
(off Churchill Gdns.)
Gifford Rd. NW10 7A **62**
Gifford St. N1 7J **65**
Gift La. E15 1G **87**
GIGGSHILL 7A **150**
Giggs Hill BR5: St P 2K **161**
Giggs Hill Gdns. KT7: T Ditt 1A **162**
Giggs Hill Rd. KT7: T Ditt 7A **150**
Gilbert Bri. *EC2* *5D 8*
(off Wood St.)
Gilbert Cl. SE18 1D **124**
SW19 *1K 153*
(off High Path)
Gilbert Ct. *W5* *6F 79*
(off Green Va.)
Gilbert Gro. HA8: Edg 1K **43**
Gilbert Ho. *E2* *3K 85*
(off Usk St.)
E17 3D **50**
EC2 5D **8**
SE8 6C **104**
SW1 *6K 17*
(off Churchill Gdns.)
SW8 *7J 101*
(off Wyvil Rd.)
SW13 *7D 98*
(off Trinity Chu. Rd.)
Gilbert Pl. WC1 6E **6** (5J **83**)
Gilbert Rd. BR1: Brom 7J **141**
DA17: Belv 3G **109**
HA5: Pinn 4B **40**
SE11 4K **19** (4A **102**)
SW19 7A **136**
UB9: Hare 2A **38**
Gilbert Scott Bldg. SW15 6G **117**
Gilbert Sheldon Ho. *W2* *5B 4*
(off Edgware Rd.)
Gilbertson Ho. *E14* *3C 104*
(off Mellish St.)
Gilbert St. E15 4G **69**
TW3: Houn 3G **113**
W1 1H **11** (6E **82**)
Gilbert Way CR0: Wadd 2K **167**
Gilbert White Cl. UB6: G'frd 1A **78**
Gilbey Cl. UB10: Ick 4D **56**
Gilbey Ho. NW1 7F **65**
Gilbey Rd. SW17 4C **136**
Gilbeys Yd. NW1 7E **64**
Gilbourne Rd. SE18 6K **107**
Gilby Ho. E9 6K **67**
Gilda Av. EN3: Pond E 5F **25**
Gilda Ct. NW7 1C **44**
Gilda Cres. N16 1G **67**
Gildea Cl. HA5: Hat E 1E **40**
Gildea St. W1 6K **5** (5F **83**)
Gilden Cres. NW5 5E **64**
Gildersome St. SE18 6E **106**
Gilders Rd. KT9: Chess 7F **163**
Giles Coppice SE19 4F **139**
Giles Ho. SE16 7K **15**
W11 *6J 81*
(off Westbourne Gro.)
Gilesmead SE5 1D **120**
Gilford Ho. *IG1: Ilf* *2F 71*
(off Clements Rd.)
Gilfrid Cl. UB8: Hil 6D **74**
Gilkes Cres. SE21 6E **120**
Gilkes Pl. SE21 6E **120**
Gillam Ho. *SE16* *4J 103*
(off Silwood St.)
Gillan Ct. SE12 3K **141**
Gillan Grn. WD23: B Hea 2B **26**
Gillards M. E17 4C **50**
Gillards Way E17 4C **50**
Gill Av. E16 6J **87**
Gillender St. E14 4E **86**
Gillespie Pk. Nature Reserve 3A **66**
Gillespie Rd. N5 3A **66**
Gillett Av. E6 2C **88**
GILLETTE CORNER 7A **96**
Gillett Ho. *N8* *3J 47*
(off Campsfield Rd.)
Gillett Pl. N16 5E **66**
Gillett Rd. CR7: Thor H 4D **156**
Gillett Sq. N16 5E **66**
Gillfoot *NW1* *1A 6*
(off Hampstead Rd.)
Gillham Ter. N17 6B **34**
Gillian Ho. HA3: Hrw W 6D **26**
Gillian Pk. Rd. SM3: Sutt 1H **165**
Gillian St. SE13 5D **122**
Gillies Ho. *NW6* *7B 64*
(off Hilgrove Rd.)
Gillies St. NW5 5E **64**
Gilling Ct. NW3 6C **64**
Gillingham M. SW1 3A **18** (4G **101**)
Gillingham Rd. NW2 3G **63**
Gillingham Row SW1 3A **18** (4G **101**)
Gillingham St. SW1 3A **18** (4G **101**)
Gillings Ct. *EN5: Barn* *4B 20*
(off Wood St.)
Gillison Wlk. SE16 3H **103**
Gillman Dr. E15 1H **87**
Gillman Ho. *E2* *2G 85*
(off Pritchard's Rd.)
Gillray Ho. *SW10* *6B 100*
(off Ann La.)
Gill St. E14 6B **86**
Gillum Cl. EN4: E Barn 1J **31**
Gilmore Cl. UB10: Ick 3C **56**
Gilmore Ct. N11 5J **31**
Gilmore Cres.
TW15: Ashf 5C **128**
Gilmore Rd. SE13 4F **123**
Gilpin Av. SW14 4K **115**
Gilpin Cl. CR4: Mitc 2C **154**
W2 *5A 4*
(off Porteus Rd.)
Gilpin Cres. N18 5A **34**
TW2: Whitt 7F **113**
Gilpin Rd. E5 4A **68**
Gilpin Way UB3: Harl 7F **93**
Gilray Ho. *W2* *2A 10*
(off Gloucester Ter.)
Gilsland Rd. CR7: Thor H 4D **156**
Gilson Pl. N10 7J **31**
Gilstead Ho. IG11: Bark 2B **90**
Gilstead Rd. SW6 2K **117**
Gilston Rd. SW10 7A **16** (5A **100**)
Gilton Rd. SE6 3G **141**
Giltspur St. EC1 7B **8** (6B **84**)
Gilwell Cl. E4 4J **25**
Gilwell La. E4 4J **25**
(not continuous)
GILWELL PARK 4K **25**
Gilwell Pk. E4 3K **25**
Ginger Apartments *SE1* *6K 15*
(off Cayenne Ct.)
Ginsburg Yd. NW3 4A **64**
Gippeswyck Cl. HA5: Pinn 1B **40**
Gipsy Hill SE19 4E **138**
Gipsy La. SW15 3D **116**
Gipsy Rd. DA16: Well 7D **108**
SE27 4C **138**
Gipsy Rd. Gdns. SE27 4C **138**
Giralda Cl. E16 5B **88**
Giraud St. E14 6D **86**
Girdler's Rd. W14 4F **99**
Girdlestone Wlk. N19 2G **65**
Girdwood Rd. SW18 7G **117**
Girling Ho. *N1* *1E 84*
(off Colville Est.)
Girling Way TW14: Felt 3J **111**
Gironde Rd. SW6 7H **99**
Girtin Ho. *UB5: N'olt* *2B 76*
(off Academy Gdns.)
Girton Av. NW9 3G **43**
Girton Cl. UB5: N'olt 6G **59**
Girton Gdns. CR0: C'don 3C **170**
Girton Rd. SE26 5K **139**
UB5: N'olt 6G **59**
Girton Vs. W10 6F **81**
Gisbourne Cl. SM6: Bedd 3H **167**
Gisburn Ho. *SE15* *6G 103*
(off Friary Est.)
Gisburn Rd. N8 4K **47**
Gissing Wlk. N1 7A **66**
Gittens Cl. BR1: Brom 4H **141**
Given Wilson Wlk. E13 2H **87**

Giverny Ho. *SE16* 2K 103
(off Water Gdns. Sq.)
Glacier Way HA0: Wemb 2D 78
Gladbeck Way EN2: Enf 4G 23
Gladding Rd. E12 4B 70
Glade, The BR1: Brom 2B 160
BR4: W W'ck 3D 170
CR0: C'don 5K 157
E8 6G 67
EN2: Enf 3F 23
IG5: Ilf 1D 52
IG8: Wfd G 3E 36
KT17: Ewe 6C 164
N12 3G 31
N21 6E 22
SE7 7A 106
SM2: Cheam 7G 165
W12 2D 98
(off Coningham Rd.)
Glade Cl. KT6: Surb 2D 162
Glade Ct. IG5: Ilf 1D 52
Glade Gdns. CR0: C'don 7A 158
Glade La. UB2: S'hall 2F 95
Glade Rd. E12 3D 70
Glades, The KT6: Surb 7E 150
Gladeside CR0: C'don 6K 157
N21 6E 22
Gladeside Cl. KT9: Chess 7D 162
Gladesmore Community School & Sports Cen. 5G 49
Gladesmore Rd. N15 6F 49
Glades Pl. BR1: Brom 2J 159
Glades Shop. Cen., The BR1: Brom 2J 159
Gladeswood Rd. DA17: Belv 4H 109
Gladiator St. SE23 7A 122
Glading Ter. N16 3F 67
Gladioli Cl. TW12: Hamp 6E 130
Gladsdale Dr. HA5: Eastc 4J 39
Gladsmuir Rd. EN5: Barn 2B 20
N19 1G 65
Gladstone Av. E12 7C 70
N22 2A 48
TW2: Twick 1H 131
TW14: Felt 6J 111
Gladstone Ct. *NW6* 7A 64
(off Fairfax Rd.)
SW1 4D 18
(off Regency St.)
Gladstone Ct. Bus. Cen. *SW8* 1F 119
(off Pagden St.)
Gladstone Gdns. TW3: Houn 1G 113
Gladstone Ho. CR4: Mitc 2D 154
E14 6C 86
(off E. India Dock Rd.)
Gladstone M. N22 2A 48
NW6 7H 63
SE20 7J 139
Gladstone Pde. NW2 2E 62
Gladstone Pk. Gdns. NW2 3D 62
Gladstone Pl. E3 2B 86
EN5: Barn 4A 20
KT8: E Mos 5J 149
Gladstone Rd. BR6: Farnb 5G 173
CR0: C'don 7D 156
IG9: Buck H 1F 37
KT1: King T 3G 151
KT6: Surb 2D 162
SW19 7J 135
UB2: S'hall 2C 94
W4 3K 97
Gladstone St. SE1 3B 102
Gladstone Ter. *SE27* 5C 138
(off Bentons La.)
SW8 1F 119
Gladstone Way HA3: W'stone 3J 41
Gladwell Rd. BR1: Brom 6J 141
N8 6K 47
Gladwin Ho. *NW1* 1B 6
(off Werrington St.)
Gladwyn Rd. SW15 3F 117
Gladys Dimson Ho. E7 5H 69
Gladys Rd. NW6 7J 63
Glaisher St. SE8 6C 104
Glamis Ct. W3 2H 97
Glamis Cres. UB3: Harl 3E 92
Glamis Pl. E1 7J 85
Glamis Rd. E1 7J 85
Glamis Way UB5: N'olt 6G 59
Glamorgan Cl. CR4: Mitc 3J 155
Glamorgan Ct. *W7* 5K 77
(off Copley Cl.)
Glamorgan Rd. KT1: Ham W 7C 132
Glandford Way RM6: Chad H 5B 54
Glanfield Rd. BR3: Beck 4B 158
Glanleam Rd. HA7: Stan 4J 27
Glanville M. HA7: Stan 5F 27
Glanville Rd. BR2: Brom 3K 159
SW2 5J 119
Glasbrook Av. TW2: Whitt 1D 130
Glasbrook Rd. SE9 7B 124
Glaserton Rd. N16 7E 48
Glasford St. SW17 6D 136
Glasfryn Ct. *HA2: Harr* 2H 59
(off Roxeth Hill)
Glasfryn Ho. *HA2: Harr* 2H 59
(off Roxeth Hill)
Glasgow Ho. *W9* 2K 81
(off Maida Va.)
Glasgow Rd. E13 2K 87
N18 5C 34
Glasgow Ter. SW1 6A 18 (5G 101)
Glasier Ct. E15 7G 69
Glaskin M. E9 6A 68
Glass Art Gallery, The 6G 15
Glass Building, The *NW1* 1F 83
(off Jamestown Rd.)
Glasse Cl. W13 7A 78
Glass Foundry Yd. *E13* 5K 87
(off Denmark St.)
Glasshill St. SE1 6B 14 (2B 102)
Glass Ho. *WC2* 1E 12
(off Shaftesbury Av.)
Glass Ho., The *SE1* 7G 15
(off Royal Oak Yd.)
Glasshouse Cl. UB8: Hil 5D 74
Glasshouse Flds. E1 7K 85
(not continuous)
Glasshouse St. W1 3B 12 (7G 83)
Glasshouse Wlk. SE11 5F 19 (5J 101)
Glasshouse Yd. EC1 4C 8 (4C 84)
Glasslyn Rd. N8 5H 47
Glassmill La. BR2: Brom 2H 159
(not continuous)
Glass St. E2 4H 85
Glassworks Studios *E2* 1H 9
(off Basing Pl.)
Glass Yd. SE18 3E 106
Glastonbury Av. IG8: Wfd G 7G 37
Glastonbury Ct. *SE14* 7J 103
(off Farrow La.)
W13 1A 96
(off Talbot Rd.)
Glastonbury Ho. *SE12* 5H 123
(off Wantage Rd.)
SW1 5J 17
(off Abbots Mnr.)
Glastonbury Pl. E1 6J 85
Glastonbury Rd. N9 1B 34
SM4: Mord 7J 153
Glastonbury St. NW6 5H 63
Glaston Ct. *W5* 1D 96
(off Grange Rd.)
Glaucus St. E3 5D 86
Glazbury Rd. W14 4G 99
Glazebrook Cl. SE21 2D 138
Glazebrook Rd. TW11: Tedd 7K 131
Glebe, The BR7: Chst 1G 161
KT4: Wor Pk 1B 164
SE3 3G 123
SW16 4H 137
UB7: W Dray 4B 92
Glebe Av. CR4: Mitc 2C 154
EN2: Enf 3G 23
HA3: Kenton 4E 42
Glebe Av. HA4: Ruis 6K 57
IG8: Wfd G 6D 36
UB10: Ick 3E 56
Glebe Cl. UB10: Ick 4E 56
W4 5A 98
Glebe Cotts. *TW13: Hanw* 3E 130
(off Twickenham Rd.)
Glebe Ct. CR4: Mitc 3D 154
E3 3D 86
(off Rainhill Way)
HA7: Stan 5H 27
N13 3F 33
SE3 3G 123
W5 1D 96
W7 7H 77
Glebe Cres. HA3: Kenton 3E 42
NW4 4E 44
Glebe Farm Bus. Pk. BR2: Kes 7B 172
Glebe Gdns. KT3: N Mald 7A 152
Glebe Ho. *SE16* 3H 103
(off Slippers Pl.)
Glebe Ho. Dr. BR2: Hayes 1K 171
Glebe Hyrst SE19 4E 138
Glebe Knoll BR2: Brom 2H 159
Glebeland Gdns. TW17: Shep 6E 146
Glebelands E10 2D 68
KT8: W Mole 5F 149
Glebelands Av. E18 2J 51
IG2: Ilf 7H 53
Glebelands Cl. N12 1B 46
SE5 3E 120
Glebelands Rd. TW14: Felt 1J 129
Glebe La. HA3: Kenton 4E 42
Glebe M. DA15: Sidc 6K 125
(not continuous)
Glebe Path CR4: Mitc 3D 154
Glebe Pl. SW3 7C 16 (6C 100)
Glebe Rd. BR1: Brom 1J 159
E8 7F 67
HA7: Stan 5H 27
N3 1A 46
N8 4K 47
NW10 6C 62
RM10: Dag 6H 73
SM2: Cheam 7G 165
SM5: Cars 6D 166
SW13 2C 116
UB3: Hayes 1H 93
Glebe Side TW1: Twick 6K 113
Glebe Sq. CR4: Mitc 3D 154
Glebe St. W4 5A 98
Glebe Ter. W4 5A 98
Glebe Way BR4: W W'ck 2E 170
IG8: Wfd G 5F 37
TW13: Hanw 3E 130
Gledhow Gdns. SW5 4A 100
Gledstanes Rd. W14 5G 99
Gledwood Av. UB4: Hayes 5H 75
Gledwood Cres. UB4: Hayes 5H 75
Gledwood Dr. UB4: Hayes 5H 75
Gledwood Gdns. UB4: Hayes 5H 75
Gleed Av. WD23: B Hea 2C 26
Gleeson Dr. BR6: Chels 5K 173
Glegg Pl. SW15 4F 117
Glen, The BR2: Brom 2G 159
BR6: Farnb 3D 172
CR0: C'don 3K 169
EN2: Enf 4G 23
HA5: Eastc 5K 39
HA5: Pinn 7C 40
HA9: Wemb 4E 60
UB2: S'hall 5D 94
Glenaffric Av. E14 4E 104
Glen Albyn Rd. SW19 2F 135
Glenallan Ho. *W14* 4H 99
(off North End Cres.)
Glenalla Rd. HA4: Ruis 7H 39
Glenalmond Ho. TW15: Ashf 3A 128
Glenalmond Rd. HA3: Kenton 4E 42
Glenalvon Way SE18 4C 106
Glena Mt. SM1: Sutt 4A 166
Glenarm Rd. E5 4J 67
Glen Av. TW15: Ashf 4C 128
Glenavon Cl. KT10: Clay 6A 162
Glenavon Ct. KT4: Wor Pk 2D 164
Glenavon Lodge BR3: Beck 7C 140
Glenavon Rd. E15 7G 69
Glenbarr Cl. SE9 3F 125
Glenbow Rd. BR1: Brom 6G 141
Glenbrook Nth. EN2: Enf 4E 22
Glenbrook Rd. NW6 5J 63
Glenbrook Sth. EN2: Enf 4E 22
Glenbuck Ct. KT6: Surb 6E 150
Glenbuck Rd. KT6: Surb 6D 150
Glenburnie Rd. SW17 3D 136
Glencairn Dr. W5 4C 78
Glencairne Cl. E16 5B 88
Glencairn Rd. SW16 1J 155
Glencar Ct. SE19 6B 138
Glen Cl. TW17: Shep 4C 146
Glencoe Av. IG2: Ilf 7H 53
Glencoe Dr. RM10: Dag 4G 73
Glencoe Mans. *SW9* 7A 102
(off Mowll St.)
Glencoe Rd. UB4: Yead 5B 76
Glen Ct. DA15: Sidc 4A 144
Glen Cres. IG8: Wfd G 6E 36
Glendale Av. HA8: Edg 4A 28
N22 7F 33
RM6: Chad H 7C 54
Glendale Cl. SE9 3E 124
Glendale Dr. SW19 5H 135
Glendale Gdns. HA9: Wemb 1D 60
Glendale M. BR3: Beck 1D 158
Glendale Rd. DA8: Erith 4J 109
Glendale Way SE28 7C 90
Glendall St. SW9 4K 119
Glendarvon St. SW15 3F 117
Glendevon Cl. HA8: Edg 3C 28
Glendish Rd. N17 1H 49
Glendor Gdns. NW7 4E 28
Glendower Gdns. SW14 3K 115
Glendower Pl. SW7 3A 16 (4B 100)
Glendower Rd. E4 1A 36
SW14 3K 115
Glendown Ho. E8 5G 67
Glendown Rd. SE2 5A 108
Glendun Ct. W3 7A 80
Glendun Rd. W3 7A 80
Gleneagle M. SW16 5H 137
Gleneagle Rd. SW16 5H 137
Gleneagles HA7: Stan 7G 27
W13 5B 78
(off Malvern Way)
Gleneagles Cl. BR6: Orp 1H 173
SE16 5H 103
Gleneagles Grn. BR6: Orp 1H 173
Gleneagles Twr. *UB1: S'hall* 6G 77
(off Fleming Rd.)
Gleneldon M. SW16 4J 137
Gleneldon Rd. SW16 4J 137
Glenelg Rd. SW2 5J 119
Glenesk Rd. SE9 3E 124
Glenfarg Rd. SE6 1E 140
Glenfield Cres. HA4: Ruis 7F 39
Glenfield Rd. SW12 1G 137
TW15: Ashf 6D 128
W13 2B 96
Glenfield Ter. W13 2B 96
Glenfinlas Way SE5 7B 102
Glenforth St. SE10 5H 105
Glengall Bus. Cen. SE15 6F 103
Glengall Gro. E14 3D 104
Glengall Pas. *NW6* 1J 81
(off Priory Pk. Rd.)
Glengall Rd. DA7: Bex 3E 126
HA8: Edg 3C 28
IG8: Wfd G 6D 36
NW6 1H 81
SE15 5F 103
Glengall Ter. SE15 6F 103
Glen Gdns. CR0: Wadd 3A 168
Glengariff Mans. *SW9* 7A 102
(off Sth. Island Pl.)

Glengarnock Av.—Golda Cl.

Glengarnock Av. E14 4E 104
Glengarry Rd. SE22 5E 120
Glenham Dr. IG2: Ilf 5F 53
Glenhead Cl. SE9 3F 125
Glenhill Cl. N3 2J 45
Glen Ho. *E16* 1E 106
(off Storey St.)
Glenhouse Rd. SE9 5E 124
Glenhurst BR3: Beck 1E 158
Glenhurst Av. DA5: Bexl 1F 145
HA4: Ruis 7E 38
NW5 4E 64
Glenhurst Ct. SE19 5F 139
Glenhurst Ri. SE19 7C 138
Glenhurst Rd. N12 5G 31
TW8: Bford 6C 96
Glenilla Rd. NW3 6C 64
Glenister Ho. *UB3: Hayes* 1K 93
(off Avondale Dr.)
Glenister Pk. Rd. SW16 7H 137
Glenister Rd. SE10 5H 105
Glenister St. E16 1E 106
Glenkerry Ho. *E14* 6E 86
(off Burcham St.)
Glenlea Rd. SE9 5D 124
Glenloch Rd. EN3: Enf H 2D 24
NW3 6C 64
Glenluce Rd. SE3 6J 105
Glenlyon Rd. SE9 5E 124
Glenmead IG9: Buck H 1F 37
Glenmere Av. NW7 7H 29
Glenmere Row SE12 6J 123
Glen M. E17 5B 50
Glenmill TW12: Hamp 5D 130
Glenmore Lawns W13 6A 78
Glenmore Lodge BR3: Beck 1D 158
Glenmore Pde. HA0: Wemb 1E 78
Glenmore Rd. DA16: Well 7K 107
NW3 6C 64
Glenmore Way IG11: Bark 2A 90
Glenmount Path SE18 5G 107
Glennie Ct. SE22 1G 139
Glennie Ho. *SE10* 1E 122
(off Blackheath Hill)
Glennie Rd. SE27 3A 138
Glenny Rd. IG11: Bark 6G 71
Glenorchy Cl. UB4: Yead 5C 76
Glenpark Ct. W13 7A 78
Glenparke Rd. E7 6K 69
Glenridding *NW1* 1B 6
(off Ampthill Est.)
Glen Ri. IG8: Wfd G 6E 36
Glen Rd. E13 4A 88
E17 5B 50
KT9: Chess 4F 163
Glen Rd. End SM6: Wall 7F 167
Glenrosa St. SW6 2A 118
Glenrose Ct. DA14: Sidc 5B 144
SE1 7G 15
(off Long La.)
Glenroy St. W12 6E 80
Glensdale Rd. SE4 3B 122
Glenshaw Mans. *SW9* 7A 102
(off Brixton Rd.)
Glenshiel Rd. SE9 5E 124
Glentanner Way SW17 3B 136
Glen Ter. *E14* 2E 104
(off Manchester Rd.)
Glentham Gdns. SW13 6D 98
Glentham Rd. SW13 6C 98
Glenthorne Av. CR0: C'don 1H 169
Glenthorne Cl. SM3: Sutt 1J 165
UB10: Hil 3C 74
Glenthorne Gdns. IG6: Ilf 3E 52
SM3: Sutt 1J 165
Glenthorne M. W6 4D 98
Glenthorne Rd. E17 5A 50
KT1: King T 4F 151
N11 5J 31
W6 4D 98
Glenthorpe Av. SW15 4C 116
Glenthorpe Rd. SM4: Mord 5F 153
Glenton Rd. SE13 4G 123
Glentrammon Av. BR6: Chels 6K 173
Glentrammon Cl. BR6: Chels 5K 173
Glentrammon Gdns. BR6: Chels 6K 173
Glentrammon Rd. BR6: Chels 6K 173
Glentworth St. NW1 4F 5 (4D 82)
Glenure Rd. SE9 5E 124
Glenvern Ct. *TW7: Isle* 2A 114
(off White Lodge Cl.)
Glenview SE2 6D 108
Glenview Rd. BR1: Brom 2B 160
Glenville Av. EN2: Enf 1H 23
Glenville Gro. SE8 7B 104
Glenville M. SW18 7K 117
Glenville M. Ind. Est. SW18 7J 117
Glenville Rd. KT2: King T 1G 151
Glen Wlk. TW7: Isle 5H 113
(not continuous)
Glenwood Av. NW9 1A 62
Glenwood Cl. HA1: Harr 5K 41
Glenwood Ct. DA14: Sidc 4A 144
E18 3J 51
Glenwood Gdns. IG2: Ilf 5E 52
Glenwood Gro. NW9 1J 61
Glenwood Rd. KT17: Ewe 6C 164
N15 5B 48
NW7 3F 29
SE6 1B 140
TW3: Houn 3H 113
Glenwood Way CR0: C'don 6K 157
Glenworth Av. E14 4F 105
Gliddon Dr. E5 4H 67
Gliddon Rd. W14 4G 99
Glimpsing Grn. DA18: Erith 3E 108
Glisson Rd. UB10: Hil 2C 74
Global App. E3 2E 86
Globe Pond Rd. SE16 1A 104
Globe Rd. E1 3J 85
E2 3J 85
E15 5H 69
IG8: Wfd G 6F 37
Globe Rope Wlk. *E14* 4D 104
(off E. Ferry Rd.)
Globe St. SE1 7E 14 (3D 102)
Globe Ter. E2 3J 85
GLOBE TOWN 3K 85
Globe Town Mkt. E2 3K 85
Globe Vw. *EC4* 2C 14
(off High Timber St.)
Globe Wharf SE16 7K 85
Globe Yd. W1 1J 11
Glossop Rd. CR2: Sande 7D 168
Gloster Rd. KT3: N Mald 4A 152
Gloucester *W14* 4H 99
(off Mornington Av.)
Gloucester Arc. SW7 4A 100
Gloucester Av. DA15: Sidc 2J 143
DA16: Well 4K 125
NW1 7E 64
Gloucester Cir. SE10 7E 104
Gloucester Cl. KT7: T Ditt 1A 162
NW10 7K 61
Gloucester Ct. CR4: Mitc 5J 155
EC3 3H 15 (7E 84)
HA1: Harr 3J 41
NW11 7H 45
(off Golders Grn. Rd.)
SE1 5F 103
(off Rolls Rd.)
SE1 7D 14
(off Swan St.)
SE22 1G 139
TW9: Kew 7G 97
W7 5K 77
(off Copley Cl.)
Gloucester Cres. NW1 1F 83
TW18: Staines 6A 128
Gloucester Dr. N4 2B 66
NW11 4J 45
Gloucester Gdns. EN4: Cockf 4K 21
IG1: Ilf 7C 52
NW11 7H 45
Gloucester Gdns. SM1: Sutt 2K 165
W2 6A 82
Gloucester Ga. NW1 2F 83
(not continuous)
Gloucester Ga. Bri. *NW1* 1F 83
(off Gloucester Ga.)
Gloucester Ga. M. NW1 2F 83
Gloucester Gro. HA8: Edg 1K 43
Gloucester Ho. *E16* 1J 105
(off Gatcombe Rd.)
NW6 2J 81
(off Cambridge Rd.)
SW9 7A 102
TW10: Rich 5G 115
Gloucester M. E10 7C 50
W2 1A 10 (6A 82)
Gloucester M. W.
W2 6A 82
Gloucester Pde. DA15: Sidc 5A 126
UB3: Harl 3E 92
Gloucester Pk. Apartments
SW7 4A 100
Gloucester Pl. NW1 4E 4 (4D 82)
W1 4E 4 (4D 82)
Gloucester Pl. M. W1 6F 5 (5D 82)
Gloucester Rd. CR0: C'don 1D 168
DA17: Belv 5F 109
E10 7C 50
E11 5K 51
E12 3D 70
E17 2K 49
EN2: Enf 1H 23
EN5: New Bar 5E 20
HA1: Harr 5F 41
KT1: King T 2G 151
N17 2D 48
N18 5A 34
SW7 4A 16 (3A 100)
TW2: Twick 1G 131
TW4: Houn 4C 112
TW9: Kew 7G 97
TW11: Tedd 5J 131
TW12: Hamp 7F 131
TW13: Felt 1A 130
W3 2J 97
W5 2C 96
Gloucester Sq. E2 1G 85
W2 1B 10 (6B 82)
Gloucester St. SW1 6A 18 (5G 101)
Gloucester Ter. *N14* 1C 32
(off Crown La.)
W2 1A 10 (6K 81)
Gloucester Wlk. W8 2J 99
Gloucester Way EC1 2K 7 (3A 84)
Glover Cl. SE2 4C 108
Glover Dr. N18 6D 34
Glover Ho. *NW6* 7A 64
(off Harben Rd.)
SE15 4H 121
Glover Rd. HA5: Pinn 6B 40
Glovers Gro. HA4: Ruis 7D 38
Gloxinia Wlk. TW12: Hamp 6E 130
Glycena Rd. SW11 3D 118
Glyn Av. EN4: E Barn 4G 21
Glyn Cl. SE25 2E 156
Glyn Ct. HA7: Stan 6G 27
SW16 3A 138
Glyndale Grange SM2: Sutt 6K 165
Glyndebourne Ct. *UB5: N'olt* 3A 76
(off Canberra Dr.)
Glyndebourne Pk. BR6: Farnb 2F 173
Glynde M. SW3 2D 16
Glynde Reach WC1 2F 7
Glynde Rd. DA7: Bex 3D 126
Glynde St. SE4 6B 122
Glyndon Rd. SE18 4G 107
(not continuous)
Glyn Dr. DA14: Sidc 4B 144
Glynfield Rd. NW10 7A 62
Glyn Mans. *W14* 4G 99
(off Hammersmith Rd.)
Glynne Rd. N22 2A 48
Glyn Rd. E5 3K 67
EN3: Pond E 4D 24
KT4: Wor Pk 2F 165
Glyn St. SE11 6G 19 (5K 101)
Glynswood Pl. HA6: Nwood 1D 38
Glynwood Ct. SE23 2J 139
Goals Soccer Cen.
Bexleyheath 3F 127
Hayes 1A 94
Heathrow 4E 92
Ruislip 5B 58
Walthamstow 7H 35
Goater's All. *SW6* 7H 99
(off Dawes Rd.)
Goat Ho. Bri. SE25 3G 157
Goat La. EN1: Enf 1A 24
Goat Rd. CR4: Cars, Mitc 7D 154
Goat Wharf TW8: Bford 6E 96
Gobions Av. RM5: Col R 1K 55
Godalming Av. SM6: Wall 5J 167
Godalming Rd. E14 5D 86
Godbold Rd. E15 4G 87
Goddard Cl. TW17: Shep 3B 146
Goddard Ct. HA3: Kenton 2A 42
Goddard Pl. N19 3G 65
Goddard Rd. BR3: Beck 4K 157
Goddards Way IG1: Ilf 1H 71
Goddarts Ho. E17 3C 50
Goddington La. BR6: Chels 3K 173
Godfree Ct. *SE1* 6E 14
(off Long La.)
Godfrey Av. TW2: Whitt 7H 113
UB5: N'olt 1C 76
Godfrey Hill SE18 4C 106
Godfrey Ho. EC1 2E 8
Godfrey Pl. *E2* 2J 9
(off Austin St.)
Godfrey Rd. SE18 4D 106
Godfrey St. E15 2E 86
SW3 5D 16 (5C 100)
Godfrey Way TW4: Houn 7C 112
Goding St. SE11 5F 19 (5J 101)
Godley Cl. SE14 1J 121
Godley Rd. SW18 1B 136
Godliman St. EC4 1B 14 (6B 84)
Godman Rd. SE15 2H 121
Godolphin Cl. N13 6G 33
Godolphin Ho. *NW3* 7C 64
(off Fellows Rd.)
Godolphin Pl. W3 7K 79
Godolphin Rd. W12 1D 98
(not continuous)
Godric Cres. CR0: New Ad 7F 171
Godson Rd. CR0: Wadd 3A 168
Godson St. N1 2A 84
Godson Yd. *W9* 3J 81
(off Kilburn Pk. Rd.)
Godstone Ho. *SE1* 7F 15
(off Pardoner St.)
Godstone Rd. SM1: Sutt 4A 166
TW1: Twick 6B 114
Godstow Rd. SE2 2B 108
Godwin Cl. E4 1K 25
KT19: Ewe 6J 163
N1 2C 84
Godwin Ct. *NW1* 2G 83
(off Chalton St.)
Godwin Ho. *E2* 2F 85
(off Thurtle Rd.)
NW6 2K 81
(off Tollgate Gdns., not continuous)
Godwin Rd. BR2: Brom 3A 160
E7 4K 69
Goffers Rd. SE3 1G 123
Goffs Rd. TW15: Ashf 6F 129
Goidel Cl. SM6: Bedd 4H 167
Golborne Gdns. W10 4G 81
Golborne Ho. *W10* 4G 81
(off Adair Rd.)
Golborne M. W10 5G 81
Golborne Rd. W10 5G 81
Golda Cl. EN5: Barn 6A 20

Golda Ct. N3 2H 45
Goldbeaters Gro. HA8: Edg 6F 29
Goldbeaters Ho. W1 1D 12
(off Manette St.)
Goldcliff Cl. SM4: Mord 7J 153
Goldcrest Cl. E16 5B 88
SE28 7C 90
Goldcrest M. W5 5D 78
Goldcrest Way CR0: New Ad 7F 171
WD23: Bush 1B 26
Golden Bus. Pk. E10 1A 68
Golden Ct. EN4: E Barn 4H 21
TW7: Isle 2H 113
TW9: Rich 5D 114
Golden Cres. UB3: Hayes 1H 93
Golden Cross M. W11 6H 81
(off Portobello Rd.)
Golden Hinde 4E 14 (1D 102)
Golden Hind Pl. SE8 4B 104
(off Grove St.)
Golden Jubilee Bridges 5G 13
Golden La. EC1 3C 8 (4C 84)
Golden La. Campus EC1 4D 8
Golden La. Est. EC1 4C 8 (4C 84)
Golden Lane Leisure Cen. 4C 8
Golden Mnr. W7 7J 77
Golden M. SE20 1J 157
Golden Pde. E17 3E 50
(off Wood St.)
Golden Plover Cl. E16 6J 87
Golden Sq. W1 2B 12 (7G 83)
Golden Yd. NW3 4A 64
(off Holly Mt.)
Golders Cl. HA8: Edg 5C 28
Golders Ct. NW11 7H 45
Golders Gdns. NW11 7G 45
GOLDERS GREEN 6G 45
Golders Grn. Crematorium NW11 7J 45
Golders Grn. Cres. NW11 7H 45
Golders Grn. Rd. NW11 6G 45
Golderslea NW11 1J 63
Golders Mnr. Dr. NW11 6F 45
Golders Pk. Cl. NW11 1J 63
Golders Ri. NW4 5F 45
Golders Way NW11 7H 45
Golderton NW4 4D 44
(off Prince of Wales Cl.)
Goldfinch Ct. E3 2C 86
(off Four Seasons Cl.)
Goldfinch Rd. SE28 3H 107
Goldhawk Ind. Est. W6 3D 98
Goldhawk M. W12 2D 98
Goldhawk Rd. W6 4B 98
W12 3C 98
Goldhaze Cl. IG8: Wfd G 7F 37
Gold Hill HA8: Edg 6E 28
Goldhurst Mans. NW6 6A 64
(off Goldhurst Ter.)
Goldhurst Ter. NW6 7K 63
Goldie Ho. N19 7H 47
Goldie Leigh Hospital SE2 7B 108
Golding Cl. KT9: Chess 6C 162
Golding Ct. IG1: Ilf 3E 70
Golding St. E1 6G 85
Golding Ter. E1 6G 85
SW11 2E 118
Goldington Bldgs. NW1 1H 83
(off Royal College St.)
Goldington Cres. NW1 2H 83
Goldington St. NW1 2H 83
Gold La. HA8: Edg 6E 28
Goldman Cl. E2 3K 9 (4G 85)
Goldmark Ho. SE3 3K 123
Goldney Rd. W9 4J 81
Goldrill Dr. N11 2K 31
Goldsboro' Rd. SW8 1H 119
Goldsborough Cres. E4 2J 35
Goldsborough Ho. E14 5D 104
(off St Davids Sq.)
Goldsdown Cl. EN3: Enf H 2F 25
Goldsdown Rd. EN3: Enf H 2E 24
Goldsmid St. SE18 5J 107
Goldsmith Av. E12 6C 70
NW9 5A 44
RM7: Rush G 7G 55
W3 7K 79
Goldsmith Cl. HA2: Harr 1E 58
Goldsmith Ct. HA8: Edg 4A 28
WC2 7F 7
(off Stukeley St.)
Goldsmith Est. SE15 1G 121
Goldsmith La. NW9 4H 43
Goldsmith Rd. E10 1C 68
E17 2K 49
N11 5J 31
SE15 1G 121
W3 1K 97
Goldsmith's Bldgs. W3 1K 97
Goldsmiths Cl. W3 1K 97
Goldsmiths College 1A 122
Goldsmith's Pl. NW6 1K 81
(off Springfield La.)
Goldsmith's Row E2 2G 85
Goldsmith's Sq. E2 2G 85
Goldsmith St. EC2 7D 8 (6C 84)
Goldsworthy Gdns. SE16 5J 103
Goldthorpe NW1 1G 83
(off Camden St.)
Goldwell Ho. SE22 3E 120
(off Dog Kennel Hill Est.)
Goldwell Rd. CR7: Thor H 4K 155
Goldwin Cl. SE14 1J 121
Goldwing Cl. E16 6J 87
Golf Cl. CR7: Thor H 1A 156
HA7: Stan 7H 27
Golf Club Dr. KT2: King T 7K 133
Golfe Rd. IG1: Ilf 3H 71
Golf Rd. BR1: Brom 3E 160
W5 6F 79
Golf Side TW2: Twick 3H 131
Golfside Cl. KT3: N Mald 2A 152
N20 3H 31
Gollogly Ter. SE7 5A 106
Gomer Gdns. TW11: Tedd 6A 132
Gomer Pl. TW11: Tedd 6A 132
Gomm Rd. SE16 3J 103
Gomshall Av. SM6: Wall 5J 167
Gondar Gdns. NW6 5H 63
Gonson St. SE8 6D 104
Gonston Cl. SW19 2G 135
Gonville Cres. UB5: N'olt 6F 59
Gonville Rd. CR7: Thor H 5K 155
Gonville St. SW6 3G 117
Gooch Ho. E5 3H 67
EC1 5J 7
(off Portpool La.)
Goodall Ho. SE4 4K 121
Goodall Rd. E11 3E 68
Gooden Ct. HA1: Harr 3J 59
Goodenough Rd. SW19 7H 135
Goodey Rd. IG11: Bark 7K 71
Goodfaith Ho. E14 7D 86
(off Simpson's Rd.)
Goodge Pl. W1 6B 6 (5G 83)
Goodge St. W1 6B 6 (5G 83)
Goodhall Cl. HA7: Stan 6F 27
Goodhall St. NW10 3B 80
(not continuous)
Goodhart Pl. E14 7A 86
Goodhart Way BR4: W W'ck 7G 159
Goodhew Rd. CR0: C'don 6G 157
Goodhope Ho. E14 7D 86
(off Poplar High St.)
Gooding Cl. KT3: N Mald 4J 151
Goodinge Cl. N7 6J 65
Gooding Ho. SE7 5A 106
Goodman Cres. CR0: C'don 6B 156
SW2 2J 137
Goodman Rd. E10 7E 50
Goodmans Ct. E1 2J 15 (7F 85)
HA0: Wemb 4D 60
Goodman's Stile E1 6G 85
Goodmans Yd. E1 2J 15 (7F 85)
GOODMAYES 2A 72
Goodmayes Av. IG3: Ilf 1A 72
Goodmayes La. IG3: Ilf 4A 72
Goodmayes Lodge RM8: Dag 4A 72
Goodmayes Retail Pk.
RM6: Chad H 1B 72
Goodmayes Rd. IG3: Ilf 1A 72
Goodrich Ct. W10 6F 81
Goodrich Ho. E2 2J 85
(off Sewardstone Rd.)
Goodrich Rd. SE22 6F 121
Goodson Ho. SM4: Mord 7A 154
(off Green La.)
Goodson Rd. NW10 7A 62
Goodspeed Ho. E14 7D 86
(off Simpson's Rd.)
Goods Way NW1 2J 83
Goodway Gdns. E14 6F 87
Goodwill Dr. HA2: Harr 1E 58
Goodwill Ho. E14 7D 86
(off Simpson's Rd.)
Goodwin Cl. CR4: Mitc 3B 154
SE16 3F 103
Goodwin Ct. EN4: E Barn 6H 21
N8 3J 47
(off Campsbourne Rd.)
SW19 7C 136
Goodwin Dr. DA14: Sidc 3D 144
Goodwin Gdns. CR0: Wadd 6B 168
Goodwin Ho. N9 1D 34
Goodwin Rd. CR0: Wadd 5B 168
N9 1E 34
W12 2C 98
Goodwins Ct. WC2 2E 12 (7J 83)
Goodwin St. N4 2A 66
Goodwood Cl. HA7: Stan 5H 27
SM4: Mord 4J 153
Goodwood Ct. W1 5K 5
(off Devonshire St.)
Goodwood Dr. UB5: N'olt 6E 58
Goodwood Ho. SE14 7A 104
(off Goodwood Rd.)
Goodwood Pde. BR3: Beck 4A 158
Goodwood Rd. SE14 7A 104
Goodwyn Av. NW7 5F 29
Goodwyns Va. N10 1E 46
Goodyear Ho. N2 2B 46
(off The Grange)
Goodyear Pl. SE5 6C 102
Goodyer Ho. SW1 5C 18
(off Tachbrook St.)
Goodyers Gdns. NW4 5F 45
Goosander Way SE28 3H 107
Gooseacre La. HA3: Kenton 5D 42
Goose Grn. Trad. Est.
SE22 4F 121
Gooseley La. E6 3E 88
(Brighton Rd.)
E6 4F 89
(Claps Ga. La.)
Goosens Cl. SM1: Sutt 5A 166
Goose Sq. E6 6D 88
Gophir La. EC4 2E 14 (7D 84)
Gopsall St. N1 1D 84
Gordon Av. E4 6B 36
HA7: Stan 7E 26
SW14 4A 116
TW1: Twick 5A 114
Gordonbrock Rd. SE4 5C 122
Gordon Cl. E17 6C 50
N19 1G 65
Gordon Cotts. W8 2K 99
(off Dukes La.)
Gordon Ct. HA8: Edg 5A 28
Gordon Cres. CR0: C'don 1E 168
UB3: Hayes 4J 93
Gordondale Rd. SW19 2J 135
Gordon Dr. TW17: Shep 7F 147
Gordon Gdns. HA8: Edg 2H 43
Gordon Gro. SE5 2B 120
Gordon Hill EN2: Enf 1H 23
Gordon Ho. E1 7J 85
(off Glamis Rd.)
Gordon Ho. SW1 2B 18
(off Greencoat Pl.)
W5 3E 78
Gordon Ho. Rd. NW5 4E 64
Gordon Mans. W14 3F 99
(off Addison Gdns.)
WC1 4C 6
(off Torrington Pl.)
Gordon Pl. W8 2J 99
Gordon Rd. BR3: Beck 3B 158
DA15: Sidc 5J 125
DA17: Belv 4J 109
E4 1B 36
E11 6J 51
E15 4E 68
E18 1K 51
EN2: Enf 1H 23
HA3: W'stone 3J 41
IG1: Ilf 3H 71
IG11: Bark 1J 89
KT2: King T 1F 151
KT5: Surb 7F 151
N3 7C 30
N9 2C 34
N11 7C 32
RM6: Chad H 6F 55
SE15 2H 121
SM5: Cars 6D 166
TW3: Houn 4G 113
TW9: Rich 2F 115
TW15: Ashf 3A 128
TW17: Shep 6F 147
UB2: S'hall 4C 94
UB7: Yiew 7A 74
W4 6H 97
W5 7B 78
W13 7B 78
Gordon Sq. WC1 3C 6 (4H 83)
Gordon St. E13 3J 87
WC1 3C 6 (4H 83)
Gordon Way BR1: Brom 1J 159
EN5: Barn 4C 20
Gore Ct. NW9 5G 43
Gorefield Ho. NW6 2J 81
(off Gorefield Pl.)
Gorefield Pl. NW6 2J 81
Gore Rd. E9 1J 85
SW20 2E 152
GORESBROOK INTERCHANGE 2F 91
Goresbrook Leisure Cen. 1D 90
Goresbrook Rd. RM9: Dag 1B 90
Gore St. SW7 3A 100
Gorham Ho. SE16 2K 103
(off Wolfe Cres.)
Gorham Pl. W11 7G 81
Goring Cl. RM5: Col R 1J 55
Goring Gdns. RM8: Dag 4C 72
Goring Rd. N11 6D 32
RM10: Dag 6K 73
Goring St. EC3 7H 9
Goring Way UB6: G'frd 2G 77
Gorleston Rd. N15 5D 48
Gorleston St. W14 4G 99
(not continuous)
Gorman Rd. SE18 4D 106
Gorringe Pk. Av. CR4: Mitc 7D 136
Gorse Cl. E16 6J 87
Gorsefield Ho. E14 7C 86
(off E. India Dock Rd.)
Gorse Ri. SW17 5E 136
Gorse Rd. CR0: C'don 4C 170
Gorse Wlk. UB7: Yiew 6A 74
Gorseway RM7: Rush G 1K 73 & 2K 73
Gorst Rd. NW10 4J 79
SW11 6D 118
Gorsuch Pl. E2 1J 9 (3F 85)
Gorsuch St. E2 1J 9 (2F 85)
Gosberton Rd. SW12 1D 136
Gosbury Hill KT9: Chess 4E 162
Gosfield Rd. RM8: Dag 2G 73
Gosfield St. W1 6A 6 (5G 83)
Gosford Gdns. IG4: Ilf 5D 52

Gosford Ho. *E3* *2B* ***86***
(off Tredegar Rd.)
Goshawk Gdns. UB4: Hayes 3G **75**
Goslett Yd. WC2 1D **12** (6H **83**)
Gosling Cl. UB6: G'frd 3E **76**
Gosling Ho. *E1* *7J* ***85***
(off Sutton St.)
Gosling Way SW9 1A **120**
Gospatrick Rd. N17 7H **33**
GOSPEL OAK 4E **64**
Gosport Rd. E17 5B **50**
Gosport Wlk. N17 4H **49**
Gossage Rd. SE18 5H **107**
UB10: Uxb 7B **56**
Gosset St. E2 1K **9** (3F **85**)
Gosshill Rd. BR7: Chst 2E **160**
Gossington Cl. BR7: Chst 4F **143**
Gosterwood St. SE8 6A **104**
Gostling Rd. TW2: Whitt 1E **130**
Goston Gdns.
CR7: Thor H 3A **156**
Goston Ga. *SW8* *1K* ***119***
(off Hampson Way)
Goswell Pl. EC1 2B **8**
Goswell Rd. EC1 1A **8** (2B **84**)
Gothic Cotts. *EN2: Enf* *2H* ***23***
(off Chase Grn. Av.)
Gothic Ct. *SE5* *7C* ***102***
(off Wyndham Rd.)
UB3: Harl 6F **93**
Gothic Rd. TW2: Twick 2H **131**
Gottfried M. NW5 4G **65**
Goudhurst Rd. BR1: Brom 5G **141**
Gough Ho. *KT1: King T* *2E* ***150***
(off Eden St.)
N1 *1B* ***84***
(off Windsor St.)
Gough Rd. E15 4H **69**
EN1: Enf 2C **24**
Gough Sq. EC4 1K **13** (6A **84**)
Gough St. WC1 3H **7** (4K **83**)
Gough Wlk. E14 6C **86**
Goulden Ho. SW11 2C **118**
Goulden Ho. App. SW11 2C **118**
Goulding Gdns. CR7: Thor H 2C **156**
Gouldman Ho. *E1* *4J* ***85***
(off Wyllen Cl.)
Gould Rd. TW2: Twick 1J **131**
TW14: Felt 7G **111**
GOULDS GREEN 5D **74**
Gould's Grn. UB8: Hil 7D **74**
Gould Ter. E8 5H **67**
Goulston St. E1 7J **9** (6F **85**)
Goulton Rd. E5 4H **67**
Gourley Pl. N15 5E **48**
Gourley St. N15 5E **48**
Gourock Rd. SE9 5E **124**
Govan St. E2 1G **85**
Gover Ct. SW4 2J **119**
Govett Av. TW17: Shep 5E **146**
Govier Cl. E15 7G **69**
Gowan Av. SW6 1G **117**
Gowan Ho. *E2* *2K* ***9***
(off Chambord St.)
Gowan Rd. NW10 6D **62**
Gower Cl. SW4 6G **119**
Gower Ct. WC1 3C **6** (4H **83**)
Gower Ho. E17 3D **50**
SE17 *5C* ***102***
(off Morecambe St.)
Gower M. WC1 6D **6** (5H **83**)
Gower M. Mans. *WC1* *5D* ***6***
(off Gower M.)
Gower Pl. WC1 3B **6** (4H **83**)
Gower Rd. E7 6J **69**
TW7: Isle 6K **95**
Gower St. WC1 3B **6** (4G **83**)
Gower's Wlk. E1 6G **85**
Gowland Pl. BR3: Beck 2B **158**
Gowlett Rd. SE15 3G **121**
Gowlland Cl. CR0: C'don 7G **157**
Gowrie Rd. SW11 3E **118**
Graburn Way KT8: E Mos 3H **149**
Grace Av. DA7: Bex 2F **127**
Grace Bus. Cen. CR4: Mitc 6D **154**
Gracechurch St. EC3 2F **15** (7D **84**)
Grace Cl. HA8: Edg 7D **28**
SE9 3B **142**
Grace Ct. *CR0: C'don* *3B* ***168***
(off Waddon Rd.)
SM2: Sutt 7K **165**
Gracedale Rd. SW16 5F **137**
Gracefield Gdns. SW16 3J **137**
Gracehill *E1* *5J* ***85***
(off Hannibal Rd.)
Grace Ho. SE11 7H **19**
Grace Jones Cl. E8 6G **67**
Grace M. BR3: Beck 6C **140**
SE20 *2J* ***157***
(off Marlow Rd.)
Grace Path SE26 4J **139**
Grace Pl. E3 3D **86**
Grace Rd. CR0: C'don 6C **156**
Graces All. E1 7G **85**
Graces M. NW8 2A **82**
SE5 2D **120**
Grace's Rd. SE5 2E **120**
Grace St. E3 3D **86**
Gradient, The SE26 4G **139**
Graduate Pl. SE1 7F **15**
Graeme Rd. EN1: Enf 2J **23**
Graemesdyke Av. SW14 3H **115**
Grafton Chambers *NW1* *2D* ***6***
(off Churchway)
Grafton Cl. KT4: Wor Pk 3A **164**
TW4: Houn 1C **130**
W13 6A **78**
Grafton Ct. TW14: Bedf 1F **129**
Grafton Cres. NW1 6F **65**
Grafton Gdns. N4 6C **48**
RM8: Dag 2E **72**
Grafton Ho. *E3* *3C* ***86***
(off Wellington Way)
SE8 5B **104**
Grafton M. W1 4A **6** (4G **83**)
Grafton Pk. Rd. KT4: Wor Pk 2A **164**
Grafton Pl. NW1 2D **6** (3H **83**)
Grafton Rd. CR0: C'don 1A **168**
EN2: Enf 3E **22**
HA1: Harr 5G **41**
KT3: N Mald 3A **152**
KT4: Wor Pk 3K **163**
NW5 5E **64**
RM8: Dag 2E **72**
W3 7J **79**
Graftons, The NW2 3J **63**
Grafton Sq. SW4 3G **119**
Grafton St. W1 3K **11** (7F **83**)
Grafton Ter. NW5 5D **64**
Grafton Way KT8: W Mole 4D **148**
W1 4A **6** (4G **83**)
WC1 4A **6** (4G **83**)
Grafton Yd. NW5 6F **65**
Graham Av. CR4: Mitc 1E **154**
W13 2B **96**
Graham Cl. CR0: C'don 2C **170**
Graham Ct. *SE14* *6K* ***103***
(off Myers La.)
UB5: N'olt 5D **58**
GRAHAME PARK 1A **44**
Grahame Pk. Est. NW9 1A **44**
Grahame Pk. Way NW7 7G **29**
NW9 2B **44**
Grahame Twr. *W3* *3H* ***97***
(off Hanbury Rd.)
Grahame White Ho. HA3: Kenton 3D **42**
Graham Gdns. KT6: Surb 1E **162**
Graham Ho. *N9* *1D* ***34***
(off Cumberland Rd.)
Graham Lodge NW4 6D **44**
Graham Mans. *IG11: Bark* *7A* ***72***
(off Lansbury Av.)
Graham Rd. CR4: Mitc 1E **154**
DA6: Bex 4F **127**
Graham Rd. E8 6G **67**
E13 4J **87**
HA3: W'stone 3J **41**
N15 3B **48**
NW4 6D **44**
SW19 7H **135**
TW12: Ham H 4E **130**
W4 3K **97**
Graham St. N1 1B **8** (2B **84**)
Graham Ter. *DA15: Sidc* *6B* ***126***
(off Westerham Dr.)
SW1 4G **17** (4E **100**)
Grainger Cl. UB5: N'olt 5F **59**
Grainger Ct. SE5 7C **102**
Grainger Rd. N22 1C **48**
TW7: Isle 2K **113**
Grainstore, The E16 7J **87**
Gramer Cl. E11 2F **69**
Gramophone La. UB3: Hayes 2G **93**
Grampian Cl. BR6: St M Cry 6K **161**
SM2: Sutt 7A **166**
UB3: Harl 7F **93**
Grampian Gdns. NW2 1G **63**
Grampians, The *W6* *2F* ***99***
(off Shepherd's Bush Rd.)
Gramsci Way SE6 3D **140**
Granada St. SW17 5D **136**
Granard Av. SW15 5D **116**
Granard Bus. Cen. NW7 6F **29**
Granard Ho. E9 6K **67**
Granard Rd. SW12 7D **118**
Granary Cl. N9 7D **24**
Granary Complex, The & Goods Yard
1J **83**
Granary Mans. SE28 2G **107**
Granary Rd. E1 4H **85**
Granary Sq. N1 6A **66**
Granary St. NW1 1H **83**
Granby Pl. *SE1* *7J* ***13***
(off Lower Marsh)
Granby Rd. SE9 2D **124**
Granby St. E2 3K **9** (4G **85**)
(not continuous)
Granby Ter. NW1 1A **6** (2G **83**)
Grand Arc. N12 5F **31**
Grand Av. EC1 5B **8** (5B **84**)
(not continuous)
HA9: Wemb 5G **61**
KT5: Surb 5H **151**
N10 4E **46**
Grand Av. E. HA9: Wemb 5H **61**
Grand Courts RM8: Dag 3E **72**
Grand Dpt. Rd. SE18 5E **106**
Grand Dr. SW20 2E **152**
UB2: S'hall 2G **95**
Granden Rd. SW16 2J **155**
Grandfield Ct. W4 6K **97**
Grandison Rd. KT4: Wor Pk 2E **164**
SW11 5D **118**
Grand Junc. Wharf N1 2C **84**
Grand Pde. HA9: Wemb 2G **61**
KT6: Surb 1G **163**
N4 5B **48**
SW14 *4J* ***115***
(off Up. Richmond Rd. W.)
Grand Pde. M. SW15 5G **117**
Grand Union Canal Wlk. *W10* *4E* ***80***
(off Canal Way)
Grand Union Cen. *W10* *4F* ***81***
(off West Row)
Grand Union Cl. W9 5J **81**
Grand Union Cres. E8 1G **85**
Grand Union Ent. Pk. UB2: S'hall 3E **94**
Grand Union Hgts. HA0: Wemb 1D **78**
Grand Union Ind. Est. NW10 2H **79**
Grand Union Village UB5: N'olt 3D **76**
Grand Union Wlk. *NW1* *7F* ***65***
(off Kentish Town Rd.)
Grand Union Way UB2: S'hall 2E **94**
Grand Vitesse Ind. Cen. *SE1* *5B* ***14***
(off Gt. Suffolk St.)
Grand Wlk. E1 4A **86**
Granfield St. SW11 1B **118**
Grange, The CR0: C'don 2B **170**
E17 *5A* ***50***
(off Lynmouth Rd.)
HA0: Wemb 7G **61**
KT3: N Mald 5B **152**
KT4: Wor Pk 4K **163**
N2 2B **46**
N20 1F **31**
(Grangeview Rd.)
N20 1G **31**
(Oxford Gdns.)
SE1 3F **103**
SW19 6F **135**
W3 2H **97**
W4 5H **97**
W13 5C **78**
W14 4H **99**
Grange Av. EN4: E Barn 1H **31**
HA7: Stan 2B **42**
IG8: Wfd G 6D **36**
N12 5F **31**
N20 7B **20**
SE25 2E **156**
TW2: Twick 2J **131**
Grangecliffe Gdns. SE25 2E **156**
Grange Cl. DA15: Sidc 3A **144**
HA8: Edg 5D **28**
IG8: Wfd G 7D **36**
KT8: W Mole 4F **149**
TW5: Hest 6D **94**
UB3: Hayes 5G **75**
Grange Ct. HA1: Harr 4K **59**
HA5: Pinn 3C **40**
NW10 *3A* ***62***
(off Neasden La.)
SM2: Sutt 7K **165**
SM6: Wall 3F **167**
TW17: Shep 4C **146**
UB5: N'olt 2A **76**
WC2 1H **13** (6K **83**)
Grangecourt Rd. N16 1E **66**
Grange Cres. SE28 6C **90**
Grangedale Cl. HA6: Nwood 1G **39**
Grange Dr. BR7: Chst 6C **142**
Grange Farm Cl. HA2: Harr 2G **59**
Grangefield *NW1* *7H* ***65***
(off Marquis Rd.)
Grange Gdns. HA5: Pinn 3C **40**
N14 1C **32**
NW3 3K **63**
SE25 2E **156**
Grange Gro. N1 6C **66**
Grange Hill HA8: Edg 5D **28**
SE25 2E **156**
Grangehill Pl. SE9 3D **124**
Grangehill Rd. SE9 4D **124**
Grange Ho. IG11: Bark 1H **89**
NW10 7D **62**
SE1 3F **103**
Grange La. SE21 2F **139**
Grange Lodge SW19 6F **135**
Grange Mans. KT17: Ewe 7B **164**
Grange M. N21 6G **23**
TW13: Felt 4J **129**
Grangemill Rd. SE6 3C **140**
Grangemill Way SE6 2C **140**
GRANGE PARK 6G **23**
Grange Pk. W5 1E **96**
Grange Pk. Av. N21 6H **23**
Grange Pk. Pl. SW20 7D **134**
Grange Pk. Rd. CR7: Thor H 4D **156**
E10 1D **68**
Grange Pl. NW6 7J **63**
Grange Rd. BR6: Orp 2H **173**
CR2: S Croy 7C **168**
CR7: Thor H 4D **156**
E10 1C **68**
E13 3H **87**
E17 5A **50**
(not continuous)
HA1: Harr 5A **42**

Grange Rd. HA2: Harr 2H 59
HA8: Edg 6E 28
IG1: Ilf 4F 71
KT1: King T 3E 150
KT8: W Mole 4F 149
KT9: Chess 4E 162
N6 .6E 46
N17 . . . . .6B 34
N18 . . . . .6B 34
NW10 . . . . .6D 62
SE1 . . . . .3E 102
SE19 . . . . .4D 156
SE25 . . . . .4D 156
SM2: Sutt 7J 165
SW13 . . . . .1C 116
UB1: S'hall 2C 94
UB3: Hayes 6G 75
W4 .5H 97
W5 .1D 96
Grange St. N1 . . . . .1D 84
Grange Va. SM2: Sutt 7K 165
Grangeview Rd. N20 . . . . .1F 31
Grange Wlk. SE1 . . . . .3E 102
Grange Wlk. M. SE1 . . . . .3E 102
(off Grange Wlk.)
Grange Way N12 . . . . .4E 30
NW6 . . . . .7J 63
Grangeway IG8: Wfd G 4F 37
Grangeway, The N12 . . . . .6G 23
Grangeway Gdns. IG4: Ilf 5C 52
Grangewood DA5: Bexl 1F 145
Grangewood Cl. HA5: Eastc 5J 39
Grangewood Dr. TW16: Sun 7H 129
Grangewood La. BR3: Beck 6B 140
Grangewood St. E6 . . . . .1B 88
Grangewood Ter. SE25 . . . . .2D 156
Grange Yd. SE1 . . . . .3F 103
Granham Gdns. N9 . . . . .2A 34
Granite Apartments E15 . . . . .6G 69
Granite St. SE18 . . . . .5K 107
Granleigh Rd. E11 . . . . .2G 69
Gransden Av. E8 . . . . .7H 67
Gransden Ho. SE8 . . . . .5B 104
Gransden Rd. W12 . . . . .2B 98
Grantbridge St. N1 . . . . .2B 84
Grantchester KT1: King T 2G 151
(off St Peters Rd.)
Grantchester Cl. HA1: Harr 3K 59
Grant Cl. N14 . . . . .7B 22
N17 . . . . .2E 48
TW17: Shep 6D 146
Grant Ct. E4 . . . . .1K 35
(off The Ridgeway)
NW9 . . . . .2B 44
(off Hazel Cl.)
Grantham Cl. HA8: Edg 3K 27
Grantham Ct. KT2: King T 5D 132
RM6: Chad H 7F 55
SE16 . . . . .2K 103
(off Eleanor Cl.)
Grantham Gdns. RM6: Chad H 6F 55
Grantham Ho. SE15 . . . . .6G 103
(off Friary Est.)
TW16: Sun 7G 129
Grantham Pl. W1 . . . . .5J 11 (1F 101)
Grantham Rd. E12 . . . . .4E 70
SW9 . . . . .2J 119
W4 .7A 98
Grantley Ho. SE14 . . . . .6K 103
(off Myers La.)
Grantley Rd. TW4: Cran 2A 112
Grantley St. E1 . . . . .3K 85
Grant Mus. of Zoology 4C 6
Grantock Rd. E17 . . . . .1F 51
Granton Rd. DA14: Sidc 6C 144
IG3: Ilf 1A 72
SW16 . . . . .1G 155
Grant Pl. CR0: C'don 1F 169
Grant Rd. CR0: C'don 1F 169
HA3: W'stone 3K 41
SW11 . . . . .4B 118
Grants Cl. NW7 . . . . .7K 29

Grants Quay Wharf EC3 . . . . . .3F 15 (7D 84)
Grant St. E13 . . . . .3J 87
N1 .2A 84
Grant Ter. N16 . . . . .7G 49
(off Castlewood Rd.)
Grantully Rd. W9 . . . . .3K 81
Grant Way TW7: Isle 6A 96
Granville Arc. SW9 . . . . .4A 120
Granville Av. N9 . . . . .3D 34
TW3: Houn 5E 112
TW13: Felt 2J 129
Granville Cl. CR0: C'don 2E 168
Granville Ct. N1 . . . . .1E 84
N4 .6K 47
SE14 . . . . .7A 104
(off Nynehead St.)
Granville Gdns. SW16 . . . . .1K 155
W5 .1F 97
Granville Gro. SE13 . . . . .3E 122
Granville Ho. E14 . . . . .6C 86
(off E. India Dock Rd.)
Granville Mans. W12 . . . . .2E 98
(off Shepherd's Bush Grn.)
Granville M. DA14: Sidc 4A 144
Granville Pk. SE13 . . . . .3E 122
Granville Pl. HA5: Pinn 3B 40
N12 . . . . .7F 31
SW6 . . . . .7K 99
W1 . . . . .1G 11 (6E 82)
Granville Point NW2 . . . . .2H 63
Granville Rd. DA14: Sidc 4A 144
DA16: Well 3C 126
E17 . . . . .6D 50
E18 . . . . .2K 51
EN5: Barn 4A 20
IG1: Ilf 1F 71
N4 .6K 47
N12 . . . . .7F 31
N13 . . . . .6E 32
N22 . . . . .1B 48
NW2 . . . . .2H 63
NW6 . . . . .2J 81
(not continuous)
SW18 . . . . .7H 117
SW19 . . . . .7J 135
UB3: Harl 4H 93
UB10: Hil 6D 56
Granville Sq. SE15 . . . . .7E 102
WC1 . . . . .2H 7 (3K 83)
Granville St. WC1 . . . . . .2H 7 (3K 83)
Granwood Ct. TW7: Isle 1J 113
Grape St. WC2 . . . . .7E 6 (6J 83)
Graphite Apartments, The N1 . . . . .1E 8
(off Murray Gro.)
Graphite Sq. SE11 . . . . .5G 19 (5K 101)
Grapsome Cl. KT9: Chess 7C 162
Grasdene Rd. SE18 . . . . .7A 108
Grasgarth Cl. W3 . . . . .7J 79
Grasmere NW1 . . . . .2K 5
(off Osnaburgh St.)
Grasmere Av. BR6: Farnb 3F 173
HA4: Ruis 7E 38
HA9: Wemb 7C 42
SW15 . . . . .4K 133
SW19 . . . . .3J 153
TW3: Houn 6F 113
W3 .7K 79
Grasmere Cl. TW14: Felt 1H 129
Grasmere Ct. N22 . . . . .6E 32
SE26 . . . . .5G 139
SM2: Sutt 6A 166
SW13 . . . . .6C 98
(off Verdun Rd.)
Grasmere Gdns. BR6: Farnb 3F 173
HA3: W'stone 2A 42
IG4: Ilf 5D 52
Grasmere Point SE15 . . . . .7J 103
(off Old Kent Rd.)
Grasmere Rd. BR1: Brom 1H 159
BR6: Farnb 3F 173
DA7: Bex 2J 127
E13 . . . . .2J 87

Grasmere Rd. N10 . . . . .1F 47
N17 . . . . .6B 34
SE25 . . . . .6H 157
SW16 . . . . .5K 137
Grasshaven Way SE28 . . . . .1K 107
(not continuous)
Grassington Cl. N11 . . . . .6K 31
Grassington Rd. DA14: Sidc 4A 144
Grassmount SE23 . . . . .2H 139
Grass Pk. N3 . . . . .1H 45
Grassway SM6: Wall 4G 167
Grasvenor Av. EN5: Barn 5D 20
Gratton Rd. W14 . . . . .3G 99
Gratton Ter. NW2 . . . . .3F 63
Gravel Hill CR0: Addtn 6K 169
DA6: Bex 4H 127
N3 .2H 45
UB8: Uxb 5A 56
Gravel Hill Cl. DA6: Bex 5H 127
Gravel La. E1 . . . . .7J 9 (6F 85)
Gravel Pit La. SE9 . . . . .5F 125
Gravel Pit Way BR6: Orp 2K 173
Gravel Rd. BR2: Brom 3C 172
TW2: Twick 1J 131
Gravelwood Cl. BR7: Chst 3G 143
Gravely Ho. SE8 . . . . .4A 104
(off Chilton Gro.)
Gravenel Gdns. SW17 . . . . .5C 136
(off Nutwell St.)
Graveney Gro. SE20 . . . . .7J 139
Graveney Rd. SW17 . . . . .4C 136
Gravesend Rd. W12 . . . . .7C 80
Gray Av. RM8: Dag 1F 73
Gray Cl. E1 . . . . .5A 86
HA5: Pinn 4C 40
Grayham Cres. KT3: N Mald 4K 151
Grayham Rd. KT3: N Mald 4K 151
Gray Ho. SE17 . . . . .5C 102
(off King & Queen St.)
Grayland Cl. BR1: Brom 1B 160
Grayling Cl. E16 . . . . .4G 87
Grayling Ct. W5 . . . . .1D 96
(off Grange Rd.)
Grayling Rd. N16 . . . . .2D 66
Grayling Sq. E2 . . . . .3G 85
(off Nelson Gdns.)
Grays Ct. RM10: Dag 7H 73
Grayscroft Rd. SW16 . . . . .7H 137
Grays Farm Production Village
BR5: St P 7B 144
Grays Farm Rd.
BR5: St P 7B 144
Grayshott Rd. SW11 . . . . .2E 118
Gray's Inn 5H 7 (5K 83)
Gray's Inn Bldgs. EC1 . . . . .4J 7
(off Rosebery Av.)
Gray's Inn Pl. WC1 . . . . .6H 7 (5K 83)
Gray's Inn Rd. WC1 . . . . .1F 7 (3J 83)
Gray's Inn Sq. WC1 . . . . .5J 7 (5K 83)
Grays La. TW15: Ashf 4D 128
Grayson Ho. EC1 . . . . .2D 8
Grays Rd. UB10: Uxb 2A 74
Grays Ter. E7 . . . . .6A 70
Gray St. SE1 . . . . .7K 13 (2A 102)
Grayswood Gdns. SW20 . . . . .2D 152
Grayswood Point SW15 . . . . .1C 134
Gray's Yd. W1 . . . . .1H 11
Graywood Ct. N12 . . . . .7F 31
Grazebrook Rd. N16 . . . . .2D 66
Grazeley Cl. DA6: Bex 5J 127
Grazeley Ct. SE19 . . . . .5E 138
Gt. Acre Ct. SW4 . . . . .4H 119
Gt. Amwell La. N8 . . . . .3K 47
Gt. Arthur Ho. EC1 . . . . .4C 8
(off Golden La. Est.)
Gt. Bell All. EC2 . . . . .7E 8 (6D 84)
Gt. Benty UB7: W Dray 4A 92
Great Brownings SE21 . . . . .4F 139
Gt. Bushey Dr. N20 . . . . .1E 30
Gt. Cambridge Ind. Est.
EN1: Enf 5C 24
GREAT CAMBRIDGE JUNC. 4J 33

Gt. Cambridge Rd. EN1: Enf 4J 33
N9 .4J 33
N17 . . . . .5J 33
N18 . . . . .4J 33
Gt. Castle St. W1 . . . . .7K 5 (6F 83)
Gt. Central Av. HA4: Ruis 5A 58
Gt. Central St. NW1 . . . . .5E 4 (5D 82)
Gt. Central Way HA9: Wemb 4J 61
NW10 . . . . .4J 61
Gt. Chapel St. W1 . . . . .7C 6 (6H 83)
Gt. Chart St. SW11 . . . . .4B 118
Gt. Chertsey Rd. TW2: Twick 2F 131
TW13: Hanw, Twick 3D 130
W4 .1J 115
Gt. Church La. W6 . . . . .4F 99
Gt. College St. SW1 . . . . . . .1E 18 (3J 101)
Great Cft. WC1 . . . . .2F 7
(off Cromer St.)
Gt. Cross Av. SE10 . . . . .7F 105
(not continuous)
Gt. Cumberland M. W1 . . . . . .1E 10 (6D 82)
Gt. Cumberland Pl. W1 . . . . . .7E 4 (6D 82)
Gt. Dover St. SE1 . . . . .7D 14 (2C 102)
Greatdown Rd. W7 . . . . .4K 77
Gt. Eastern Ent. Cen. E14 . . . . .2D 104
Gt. Eastern Rd. E15 . . . . .7F 69
Gt. Eastern St. EC2 . . . . .2G 9 (3E 84)
Gt. Eastern Wlk. EC2 . . . . .6H 9
Gt. Eastern Wharf SW11 . . . . .7C 100
Gt. Elms Rd. BR2: Brom 4A 160
Great Fld. NW9 . . . . .1A 44
Greatfield NW5 . . . . .5G 65
Greatfield Av. E6 . . . . .4D 88
Greatfield Cl. N19 . . . . .4G 65
SE4 . . . . .4C 122
Greatfields Dr. UB8: Hil 5C 74
Greatfields Rd. IG11: Bark 1H 89
Gt. Fleete Way IG11: Bark 2C 90
Gt. Galley Cl. IG11: Bark 3B 90
Gt. Gatton Cl. CR0: C'don 7A 158
Gt. George St. SW1 . . . . .7D 12 (2H 101)
Gt. Guildford Bus. Sq. SE1 . . .5C 14 (1C 102)
Gt. Guildford St. SE1 . . . . .4C 14 (1C 102)
Great Hall 6F 17 (5D 100)
Great Hall SW11 . . . . .1E 118
(off Battersea Pk. Rd.)
Greatham Wlk. SW15 . . . . .1C 134
Gt. Harry Dr. SE9 . . . . .3E 142
Gt. James St. WC1 . . . . .5G 7 (5K 83)
Gt. Marlborough St. W1 . . . . .1A 12 (6G 83)
Gt. Maze Pond SE1 . . . . .6F 15 (2D 102)
Gt. Newport St. WC2 . . . . . . .2E 12 (7J 83)
Gt. New St. EC4 . . . . .7K 7
(off New Fetter La.)
Great Nth. Leisure Pk. N12 . . . . .7G 31
Great Nth. Rd. EN5: Barn 2C 20
EN5: New Bar 5D 20
N2 .5C 46
N6 .5C 46
Gt. Nth. Way NW4 . . . . .2D 44
Greatorex Ho. E1 . . . . .5G 85
(off Greatorex St.)
Greatorex St. E1 . . . . .5G 85
Gt. Ormond St. WC1 . . . . .5F 7 (5J 83)
Gt. Owl Rd. IG7: Chig 3K 37
Great Pk. Cl. UB10: Hil 7C 56
Gt. Percy St. WC1 . . . . .1H 7 (3K 83)
Gt. Peter St. SW1 . . . . .2C 18 (3H 101)
Gt. Portland St. W1 . . . . .4K 5 (4F 83)
Gt. Pulteney St. W1 . . . . .2B 12 (7G 83)
Gt. Queen St. WC2 . . . . .1F 13 (6J 83)
Gt. Russell Mans. WC1 . . . . .6E 6
(off Gt. Russell St.)
Gt. Russell St. WC1 . . . . .7D 6 (6H 83)
Gt. St Helen's EC3 . . . . .7G 9 (6E 84)
Gt. St Thomas Apostle EC4 . . .2D 14 (7C 84)
Gt. Scotland Yd. SW1 . . . . . . .5E 12 (1J 101)
Gt. Smith St. SW1 . . . . .1D 18 (3H 101)
Great Sth. W. Rd. TW4: Houn 4H 111
TW14: Bedf, Felt 7E 110
Great Spilmans SE22 . . . . .5E 120
Great Strand NW9 . . . . .1B 44

Gt. Suffolk St.—Greenoak Way

Gt. Suffolk St. SE1 .....5B **14** (1B **102**)
Gt. Sutton St. EC1 .....4B **8** (4B **84**)
Gt. Swan All. EC2 .....7E **8** (6D **84**)
Great Thrift BR5: Pet W 4G **161**
Gt. Titchfield St. W1 .....4K **5** (4F **83**)
Gt. Tower St. EC3 .....2G **15** (7E **84**)
Gt. Trinity La. EC4 .....2D **14** (7C **84**)
Great Turnstile WC1 .....6H **7** (5K **83**)
Gt. Turnstile Ho. *WC1* *6H 7*
(off Great Turnstile)
Gt. Western Ind. Pk. UB2: S'hall 2F **95**
Gt. Western Rd. W9 .....5H **81**
W11 .....5H **81**
Gt. West Rd. TW5: Hest 2B **112**
TW7: Bford, Isle 2B **112**
TW8: Bford 2B **112**
W4 .....5B **98**
(Cedars Rd.)
W4 .....5H **97**
(Harvard Rd.)
W6 .....5B **98**
Gt. West Trad. Est. TW8: Bford 6B **96**
Gt. Winchester St. EC2 .....7F **9** (6D **84**)
Gt. Windmill St. W1 .....2C **12** (7H **83**)
Greatwood BR7: Chst 7E **142**
Great Yd. SE1 .....6H **15**
Greaves Cl. IG11: Bark 7H **71**
Greaves Cotts. *E14* *5A 86*
(off Maroon St.)
Greaves Pl. SW17 .....4C **136**
Greaves Twr. *SW10* *7A 100*
(off Worlds End Est.)
Grebe Av. UB4: Yead 6B **76**
Grebe Cl. E7 .....5H **69**
E17 .....7F **35**
IG11: Bark 4A **90**
Grebe Ct. *E14* *2E 104*
(off River Barge Cl.)
SE8 .....*6B 104*
(off Dorking Cl.)
SM1: Sutt 5H **165**
Grebe Ter. KT1: King T 3E **150**
Grecian Cres. SE19 .....6B **138**
Greek Ct. W1 .....1D **12** (6H **83**)
Greek St. W1 .....1D **12** (6H **83**)
Green, The BR1: Brom 3J **141**
(not continuous)
BR2: Hayes 7J **159**
BR5: St P 7B **144**
CR0: Sels 7B **170**
DA7: Bex 1G **127**
DA14: Sidc 4A **144**
DA16: Well 4J **125**
E4 .....1K **35**
E11 .....6K **51**
E15 .....6G **69**
HA0: Wemb 2A **60**
IG8: Wfd G 5D **36**
IG9: Buck H 1E **36**
KT3: N Mald 3K **151**
N9 .....2B **34**
N14 .....2C **32**
N17 .....6H **33**
N21 .....7F **23**
SM1: Sutt 3K **165**
SM4: Mord 4G **153**
SM5: Cars 4E **166**
SM6: Wall 2E **166**
SW19 .....5F **135**
TW2: Twick 1J **131**
TW5: Hest 6E **94**
TW9: Rich 5D **114**
TW13: Felt 2K **129**
TW17: Shep 4G **147**
UB2: S'hall 3C **94**
UB7: W Dray 3A **92**
UB10: Ick 2E **56**
W3 .....6A **80**
W5 .....7D **78**
Greenacre Cl. EN5: Barn 1C **20**
UB5: N'olt 5D **58**
Greenacre Gdns. E17 .....4E **50**
Greenacre Pl. SM6: Wall 2F **167**
Green Acres CR0: C'don 3F **169**
Greenacres DA14: Sidc 4A **144**
N3 .....2H **45**
SE9 .....6E **124**
WD23: B Hea 2C **26**
Greenacres Av. UB10: Ick 3B **56**
Greenacres Cl. BR6: Farnb 4G **173**
Greenacres Dr. HA7: Stan 6G **27**
Greenacre Sq. SE16 .....2K **103**
Greenacre Wlk. N14 .....3C **32**
Greenan Ct. *E2* *3K 85*
(off Meath Cres.)
Green Arbour Ct. EC1 .....7A **8**
Green Av. NW7 .....4E **28**
W13 .....3B **96**
Greenaway Av. N18 .....6E **34**
Greenaway Gdns. NW3 .....4K **63**
Greenaway Ho. *NW8* *1A 82*
(off Boundary Rd.)
WC1 .....*2J 7*
(off Fernsbury St.)
Greenaway Ter. *TW19: Stanw* *1A 128*
(off Victory Cl.)
Green Bank E1 .....1H **103**
N12 .....4E **30**
Greenbank Av. HA0: Wemb 5A **60**
Greenbank Cl. E4 .....2K **35**
Greenbank Ct. *TW7: Isle* *2K 113*
(off Lanadron Cl.)
Greenbank Cres. NW4 .....4G **45**
Greenbank Lodge *BR7: Chst* *2E 160*
(off Forest Cl.)
Greenbanks HA1: Harr 4J **59**
Greenbay Rd. SE7 .....7B **106**
Greenberry St. NW8 .....1C **4** (2C **82**)
Greenbrook Av. EN4: Had W 1F **21**
Green Cl. BR2: Brom 3G **159**
NW9 .....6J **43**
NW11 .....7A **46**
SM5: Cars 2D **166**
TW13: Hanw 5C **130**
Greencoat Mans. *SW1* *2B 18*
(off Greencoat Row)
Greencoat Pl. SW1 .....3B **18** (4G **101**)
Greencoat Row SW1 .....2B **18** (3G **101**)
Green Ct. TW16: Sun 6H **129**
Greencourt Av. CR0: C'don 2H **169**
HA8: Edg 1H **43**
Greencourt Gdns. CR0: C'don 1H **169**
Greencourt Ho. *E1* *4K 85*
(off Mile End Rd.)
Greencourt Rd. BR5: Pet W 5H **161**
Greencrest Pl. NW2 .....3C **62**
Greencroft HA8: Edg 5D **28**
Greencroft Av. HA4: Ruis 2A **58**
Greencroft Cl. E6 .....5B **88**
Greencroft Gdns. EN1: Enf 3K **23**
NW6 .....7K **63**
Greencroft Rd. TW5: Hest 1D **112**
Green Dale SE5 .....4D **120**
SE22 .....5E **120**
Greendale NW7 .....4F **29**
Green Dale Cl. SE22 .....5E **120**
Green Dragon Ct. SE1 .....4E **14**
Green Dragon Ho. *WC2* *7F 7*
(off Dragon Yd.)
Green Dragon La. N21 .....6F **23**
TW8: Bford 5E **96**
Green Dragon Yd. E1 .....6K **9** (5G **85**)
Green Dr. UB1: S'hall 1E **94**
Greene Ct. *SE14* *6K 103*
(off Samuel Cl.)
Greene Ho. *SE1* *3D 102*
(off Burbage Cl.)
Green End KT9: Chess 4E **162**
N21 .....2G **33**
Greenend Rd. W4 .....2A **98**
Greener Ct. *CR0: C'don* *6C 156*
(off Goodman Ct.)
Greener Ho. SW4 .....3H **119**
Green Farm Cl. BR6: Chels 6K **173**
Greenfell Mans. SE8 .....6D **104**
Green Ferry Way E17 .....3K **49**
Greenfield Av. KT5: Surb 7H **151**
Greenfield Dr. BR1: Brom 2A **160**
N2 .....4D **46**
Greenfield Gdns.
BR5: Pet W 7H **161**
NW2 .....2G **63**
RM9: Dag 1D **90**
Greenfield Ho. SW19 .....1F **135**
Greenfield Rd. DA2: Dart 5K **145**
E1 .....5G **85**
N15 .....5E **48**
RM9: Dag 7C **72**
Greenfields UB1: S'hall 6E **76**
Greenfield Way HA2: Harr 3F **41**
GREENFORD **3E 76**
Greenford Av. UB1: S'hall 7D **76**
W7 .....4J **77**
Greenford Bus. Cen.
UB6: G'frd 7H **59**
Greenford Gdns. UB6: G'frd 3F **77**
GREENFORD GREEN **6J 59**
Greenford Ind. Est. UB6: G'frd 7F **59**
Greenford Pk. UB6: G'frd 7H **59**
Greenford Rd. HA1: Harr 7J **59**
SM1: Sutt 4K **165**
(not continuous)
UB1: S'hall 1G **95**
UB6: G'frd 7G **77**
GREENFORD RDBT. **2H 77**
Greenford Sports Cen. 3E 76
Green Gdns. BR6: Farnb 5G **173**
Greengate UB6: G'frd 6B **60**
Greengate Lodge *E13* *2K 87*
(off Hollybush St.)
Greengate Pde. IG2: Ilf 6H **53**
Greengate St. E13 .....2K **87**
Greenhalgh Wlk. N2 .....4A **46**
Greenham Cl. SE1 .....7J **13** (2A **102**)
Greenham Cres. E4 .....6G **35**
Greenham Ho. *E9* *1J 85*
(off Templecombe Rd.)
TW7: Isle 3H **113**
Greenham Rd. N10 .....2E **46**
Greenhaven Dr. SE28 .....6B **90**
Greenheath Bus. Cen. *E2* *4H 85*
(off Three Colts La.)
Green Hedges TW1: Twick 5C **114**
Greenheys Cl. HA6: Nwood 1G **39**
Greenheys Dr. E18 .....3H **51**
GREENHILL **5J 41**
Green Hill SE18 .....5D **106**
Greenhill HA9: Wemb 2H **61**
IG9: Buck H 1F **37**
NW3 .....4B **64**
SM1: Sutt 2A **166**
Greenhill Ct. EN5: New Bar 5E **20**
SE18 .....5D **106**
Greenhill Gdns. UB5: N'olt 2D **76**
Greenhill Gro. E12 .....4C **70**
Greenhill Pde. EN5: New Bar 5E **20**
Greenhill Pk. EN5: New Bar 5E **20**
NW10 .....1A **80**
Greenhill Rd. HA1: Harr 6J **41**
NW10 .....1A **80**
Greenhill's Rents EC1 .....5A **8** (5B **84**)
Greenhills Ter. N1 .....6D **66**
Greenhill Ter. SE18 .....5D **106**
UB5: N'olt 2D **76**
Greenhill Way HA1: Harr 6J **41**
HA9: Wemb 2H **61**
Greenhithe Cl. DA15: Sidc 7J **125**
Greenholm Rd. SE9 .....5F **125**
Green Hundred Rd. SE15 .....6G **103**
Greenhurst Rd. SE27 .....5A **138**
Greening St. SE2 .....4C **108**
Greenland Cres. UB2: S'hall 3A **94**
Greenland Ho. *E1* *4A 86*
(off Ernest St.)
Greenland M. SE8 .....5K **103**
Greenland Pl. NW1 .....1F **83**
Greenland Quay SE16 .....4K **103**
Greenland Rd. EN5: Barn 6A **20**
NW1 .....1G **83**
Greenlands KT19: Ewe 5H **163**
Greenlands La. NW4 .....1D **44**
Greenland St. NW1 .....1F **83**
Greenland Way CR0: Bedd 7H **155**
Green La. BR7: Chst 4F **143**
CR7: Thor H 7K **137**
HA1: Harr 3J **59**
HA7: Stan 4G **27**
HA8: Edg 4A **28**
(not continuous)
IG1: Ilf 2H **71**
IG3: Ilf 2H **71**
KT3: N Mald 5J **151**
KT4: Wor Pk 1C **164**
KT8: W Mole 5F **149**
KT9: Chess 7D **162**
NW4 .....4F **45**
RM8: Dag 2H **71**
SE9 .....1F **143**
SE20 .....7K **139**
SM4: Mord 6J **153**
(Central Rd.)
SM4: Mord 7E **152**
(Lwr. Morden La.)
SW16 .....7K **137**
TW4: Houn 3K **111**
TW13: Hanw 5C **130**
TW16: Sun 7H **129**
TW17: Shep 6E **146**
UB8: Hil 5E **74**
W7 .....2J **95**
Green La. Bus. Pk. SE9 .....2E **142**
Green La. Cotts. HA7: Stan 4G **27**
Green La. Gdns. CR7: Thor H 2C **156**
Green Lanes KT19: Ewe 7A **164**
(not continuous)
N4 .....1C **66**
N8 .....3B **48**
N13 .....6E **32**
N15 .....3B **48**
N16 .....1C **66**
N21 .....3F **33**
Greenlaw Ct. *W5* *6D 78*
(off Mount Pk. Rd.)
Greenlaw Gdns. KT3: N Mald 7B **152**
Greenlawn La. TW8: Bford 4D **96**
Green Lawns HA4: Ruis 1A **58**
Greenlawns N12 .....6E **30**
Greenlawns, The *SE18* *4F 107*
(off Vincent Rd.)
Greenlaw St. SE18 .....3E **106**
Green Leaf Av. SM6: Bedd 4H **167**
Greenleaf Cl. SW2 .....7A **120**
Greenleafe Dr. IG6: Ilf 3F **53**
Greenleaf Rd. E6 .....1A **88**
E17 .....3B **50**
Greenleaf Way HA3: W'stone 3K **41**
Greenlea Pk. SW19 .....7B **136**
Green Leas *KT1: King T* *3E 150*
(off Mill St.)
TW16: Sun 6H **129**
Green Leas Cl. TW16: Sun 6H **129**
Greenleaves Ct. TW15: Ashf 6D **128**
Greenlink Wlk. TW9: Kew 1H **115**
Green Man Gdns. W13 .....7A **78**
Green Man La. TW14: Felt 4J **111**
(not continuous)
W13 .....7A **78**
Green Man Pas. W13 .....7B **78**
(not continuous)
GREEN MAN RDBT. **7H 51**
Greenman St. N1 .....7C **66**
Greenmead DA18: Erith 3E **108**
Greenmead Cl. SE25 .....5G **157**
Green Moor Link N21 .....7G **23**
Greenmoor Rd. EN3: Enf H 2D **24**
Greenoak Pl. EN4: Cockf 2J **21**
Green Oaks UB2: S'hall 4B **94**
Greenoak Way SW19 .....4F **135**

Greenock Rd. SW16 1H 155
W3 3H 97
Greeno Cres. TW17: Shep 5C 146
Green Pde. TW3: Houn 5F 113
Green Pk. 5K 11 (2F 101)
Greenpark Ct. HA0: Wemb 7C 60
Green Pk. Way UB6: G'frd 7J 59
(not continuous)
Green Pl. SE10 2G 105
Green Point E15 6G 69
Green Pond Cl. E17 3B 50
Green Pond Rd. E17 3A 50
Green Rd. N14 6A 22
N20 3F 31
Green Rd. Nth. EN3: Pond E 4F 25
Greenrod Pl. *TW8: Bford* 5E 96
(off Clayponds La.)
Greenroof Way SE10 3H 105
Green's Ct. W1 2C 12
W11 1H 99
(off Lansdowne M.)
Green's End SE18 4F 107
Greenshank Cl. E17 7F 35
Greens Health & Fitness
Chingford 4K 35
Purley 6A 168
Greenshields Ind. Est. E16 2J 105
Greenside DA5: Bexl 1E 144
RM8: Dag 1C 72
Greenside Cl. N20 2G 31
SE6 2F 141
Greenside Rd. CR0: C'don 7A 156
W12 3C 98
Greenslade Rd. IG11: Bark 7H 71
Greenstead Av. IG8: Wfd G 7F 37
Greenstead Cl. IG8: Wfd G 6F 37
Greenstead Gdns. IG8: Wfd G 6F 37
SW15 5D 116
Greensted Rd. IG10: Lough 1H 37
Greenstone M. E11 6J 51
Green St. E7 6K 69
E13 6K 69
EN3: Brim, Enf H 2D 24
TW16: Sun 1J 147
W1 2G 11 (7E 82)
GREEN STREET GREEN 6K 173
Greenstreet Hill SE14 2K 121
Green Ter. EC1 2K 7 (3A 84)
Green Va. DA6: Bex 5D 126
W5 6F 79
Greenvale Rd. SE9 4D 124
Green Verges HA7: Stan 7J 27
Green Vw. KT9: Chess 7F 163
Greenview Av. BR3: Beck 6A 158
CR0: C'don 6A 158
Greenview Cl. W3 1A 98
Greenview Ct. TW15: Ashf 4B 128
Green Wlk. HA4: Ruis 1H 57
IG8: Wfd G 6H 37
IG10: Lough 1H 37
NW4 5F 45
SE1 3E 102
TW12: Hamp 6D 130
UB2: S'hall 5E 94
Green Wlk., The E4 1A 36
Green Way BR2: Brom 6C 160
SE9 5B 124
TW16: Sun 4J 147
Greenway BR7: Chst 5E 142
E15 1C 86
(not continuous)
HA3: Kenton 5E 42
HA5: Pinn 2K 39
IG8: Wfd G 5F 37
N14 2D 32
N20 2D 30
RM8: Dag 2C 72
SM6: Wall 4G 167
SW20 4E 152
UB4: Yead 3J 75
Greenway, The HA3: W'stone 1J 41
HA5: Pinn 6D 40
Greenway, The NW9 2K 43
TW4: Houn 4D 112
UB8: Uxb 2A 74
UB10: Ick 2D 56
Greenway Av. E17 4F 51
Greenway Cl. N4 2C 66
N11 6K 31
N15 4F 49
N20 2D 30
NW9 2K 43
Greenway Ct. IG1: Ilf 1E 70
Greenway Gdns. CR0: C'don 3B 170
HA3: W'stone 2J 41
NW9 2K 43
UB6: G'frd 3E 76
Greenways BR3: Beck 3C 158
Greenways, The TW1: Twick 6A 114
Greenwell St. W1 4K 5 (4F 83)
GREENWICH 7E 104
Greenwich Bus. Pk. SE10 7D 104
Greenwich Chu. St. SE10 6E 104
Greenwich Commercial Cen. SE10 7D 104
Greenwich Ct. *E1* 6H 85
(off Cavell St.)
Greenwich Cres. E6 5C 88
Greenwich Foot Tunnel SE10 5E 104
Greenwich Gateway Vis. Cen. 6E 104
Greenwich Hgts. SE18 7C 106
Greenwich Heritage Cen. 3F 107
Greenwich High Rd. SE10 1D 122
Greenwich Ho. SE13 6F 123
Greenwich Mkt. SE10 6E 104
GREENWICH MILLENNIUM VILLAGE 3H 105
Greenwich Pk. 7F 105
Greenwich Pk. St. SE10 6F 105
Greenwich Peninsula Ecology Pk. 3J 105
Greenwich Picturehouse 7E 104
Greenwich Quay SE8 6D 104
Greenwich Shop. Pk. SE7 4K 105
Greenwich Sth. St. SE10 1D 122
Greenwich Theatre 7E 104
Greenwich Vw. Pl. E14 3D 104
Greenwich Yacht Club 3J 105
Greenwood Av. EN3: Enf H 2F 25
RM10: Dag 4H 73
Greenwood Bus. Cen. CR0: C'don 7F 157
Greenwood Cl. BR5: Pet W 6J 161
DA15: Sidc 2A 144
KT7: T Ditt 1A 162
SM4: Mord 4G 153
UB3: Hayes 1J 93
WD23: B Hea 1D 26
Greenwood Dr. E4 5A 36
Greenwood Gdns. IG6: Ilf 1G 53
N13 3G 33
Greenwood Ho. *EC1* 2J 7
(off Rosebery Av.)
N22 1A 48
SE4 4K 121
Greenwood La. TW12: Ham H 5F 131
Greenwood Mans. *IG11: Bark* 7A 72
(off Lansbury Av.)
Greenwood Pk. KT2: King T 7A 134
Greenwood Pl. NW5 5F 65
Greenwood Rd. CR0: C'don 7B 156
CR4: Mitc 3H 155
DA5: Bexl 4K 145
E8 6G 67
E13 2H 87
KT7: T Ditt 1A 162
TW7: Isle 3K 113
Greenwoods, The HA2: Harr 3G 59
Greenwood Ter. NW10 1K 79
Greenwood Theatre 2D 102
Green Wrythe Cres. SM5: Cars 1C 166
Green Wrythe La. SM5: Cars 6B 154
Green Yd. WC1 3H 7 (4K 83)
Green Yd., The EC3 1G 15
Greer Rd. HA3: Hrw W 1G 41
Greet Ho. SE1 7K 13
Greet St. SE1 5K 13 (1A 102)
Greg Cl. E10 6E 50
Gregor M. SE3 7J 105
Gregory Cl. BR2: Brom 4G 159
Gregory Cres. SE9 7B 124
Gregory Pl. W8 2K 99
Gregory Rd. RM6: Chad H 4D 54
UB2: S'hall 3E 94
Greig Cl. N8 5J 47
Greig Ter. SE17 6B 102
Grenaby Av. CR0: C'don 7D 156
Grenaby Rd. CR0: C'don 7D 156
Grenada Ho. *E14* 7B 86
(off Limehouse C'way.)
Grenada Rd. SE7 7A 106
Grenade St. E14 7B 86
Grenadier St. E16 1E 106
Grena Gdns. TW9: Rich 4F 115
Grenard Cl. SE15 7G 103
Grena Rd. TW9: Rich 4F 115
Grendon Gdns.
HA9: Wemb 2G 61
Grendon Ho. *E9* 7J 67
(off Shore Pl.)
N1 2K 83
(off Calshot St.)
Grendon Lodge HA8: Edg 2D 28
Grendon St. NW8 3C 4 (4C 82)
Grenfell Ct. NW7 6J 29
Grenfell Gdns. HA3: Kenton 7E 42
IG3: Ilf 5K 53
Grenfell Ho. SE5 7C 102
Grenfell Rd. CR4: Mitc 6D 136
W11 7F 81
Grenfell Twr. W11 7F 81
Grenfell Wlk. W11 7F 81
Grenier Apartments SE15 7H 103
Grennell Cl. SM1: Sutt 2B 166
Grennell Rd. SM1: Sutt 2A 166
Grenoble Gdns. N13 6F 33
Grenville Cl. KT5: Surb 1J 163
N3 1G 45
Grenville Ct. W13 5B 78
Grenville Gdns. IG8: Wfd G 1A 52
Grenville Ho. *E3* 2A 86
(off Arbery Rd.)
SE8 6C 104
(off New King St.)
SW1 7C 18
(off Dolphin Sq.)
Grenville M. N19 1J 65
SW7 4A 100
TW12: Ham H 5F 131
Grenville Pl. NW7 5E 28
SW7 3A 100
Grenville Rd. N19 1J 65
Grenville St. WC1 4F 7 (4J 83)
Gresham Av. N20 4J 31
Gresham Cl. DA5: Bexl 6E 126
EN2: Enf 3H 23
Gresham Dr. RM6: Chad H 5B 54
Gresham Gdns. NW11 1G 63
Gresham Lodge E17 5D 50
Gresham Pl. N19 2H 65
Gresham Rd. BR3: Beck 2A 158
E6 2D 88
E16 6K 87
HA8: Edg 6A 28
NW10 5K 61
SE25 4G 157
SW9 3A 120
TW3: Houn 1G 113
TW12: Hamp 6E 130
UB10: Hil 2C 74
Gresham St. EC2 7C 8 (6C 84)
Gresham Way SW19 3K 135
Gresham Way Ind. Est. *SW19* 3K 135
(off Gresham Way)
Gresley Cl. E17 6A 50
N15 4D 48
Gresley Rd. N19 1G 65
Gressenhall Rd. SW18 6H 117
Gresse St. W1 6C 6 (6H 83)
Gresswell Cl. DA14: Sidc 3A 144
Greswell St. SW6 1F 117
Gretton Ho. *E2* 3J 85
(off Globe Rd.)
Gretton Rd. N17 7A 34
Greville Cl. TW1: Twick 7B 114
Greville Ct. *E5* 3H 67
(off Napoleon Rd.)
HA1: Harr 4J 59
Greville Hall NW6 2K 81
Greville Ho. *SW1* 1G 17
(off Halkin Arc.)
Greville Lodge E13 1K 87
HA8: Edg 4C 28
(off Broadhurst Av.)
N12 5E 30
Greville M. *NW6* 1K 81
(off Greville Rd.)
Greville Pl. NW6 2K 81
Greville Rd. E17 4E 50
NW6 2K 81
TW10: Rich 6F 115
Greville St. EC1 6J 7 (5A 84)
(not continuous)
Grey Cl. NW11 6A 46
Greycoat Gdns. *SW1* 2C 18
(off Greycoat St.)
Greycoat Pl. SW1 2C 18 (3H 101)
Greycoat St. SW1 2C 18 (3H 101)
Greycot Rd. BR3: Beck 5C 140
Grey Eagle St. E1 4K 9 (4F 85)
Greyfell Cl. HA7: Stan 5G 27
Greyfriars *SE26* 3G 139
(off Wells Pk. Rd.)
Greyfriars Pas. EC1 7B 8 (6B 84)
Greyhound Ct. WC2 2H 13 (7K 83)
Greyhound Hill NW4 3C 44
Greyhound La. SW16 6H 137
Greyhound Mans. *W6* 6G 99
(off Greyhound Rd.)
Greyhound Rd. N17 3E 48
NW10 3D 80
SM1: Sutt 5A 166
W6 6F 99
W14 6F 99
Greyhound Ter. SW16 1G 155
Grey Ho. *W12* 7D 80
(off White City Est.)
Greyladies Gdns. SE10 2E 122
Greys Pk. Cl. BR2: Kes 5B 172
Greystead Rd. SE23 7J 121
Greystoke Av. HA5: Pinn 3E 40
Greystoke Ct. W5 4E 78
Greystoke Dr. HA4: Ruis 6D 38
Greystoke Gdns. EN2: Enf 4C 22
W5 4E 78
Greystoke Ho. *SE15* 6G 103
(off Peckham Pk. Rd.)
W5 4E 78
Greystoke Lodge *W5* 4F 79
(off Hanger La.)
Greystoke Pk. Ter. W5 3D 78
Greystoke Pl. EC4 7J 7 (6A 84)
Greystone Gdns. HA3: Kenton 6C 42
IG6: Ilf 2G 53
Greyswood Av. N18 6E 34
Greyswood St. SW16 6F 137
Grey Turner Ho. W12 6C 80
Grierson Ho. SW16 4G 137
Grierson Rd. SE23 7K 121
Griffen Ct. BR3: Beck 1D 158
Griffin Cen. TW14: Felt 5K 111
Griffin Cen., The *KT1: King T* 2D 150
(off Market Pl.)
Griffin Cl. NW10 5D 62
Griffin Ct. TW8: Bford 6E 96
W4 5B 98
Griffin Ho. CR0: C'don 7B 156
E14 6D 86
(off Ricardo St.)
N1 1E 84
(off New Era Est.)

Griffin Ho.—Grove Rd.

Griffin Ho. *W6* 4F 99
(off Hammersmith Rd.)
Griffin Mnr. Way SE28 .... 3H 107
Griffin Pk. 6D 96
Griffin Rd. N17 .... 2E 48
SE18 .... 5H 107
Griffins Cl. N21 .... 7J 23
Griffin Way TW16: Sun 2J 147
Griffith Cl. RM8: Dag 7C 54
Griffiths Cl. KT4: Wor Pk 2D 164
Griffiths Rd. SW19 .... 7J 135
Griggs App. IG1: Ilf 2G 71
Griggs Cl. IG1: Ilf 4J 71
Griggs Ct. *SE1* 3E 102
(off Grigg's Pl.)
Grigg's Pl. SE1 .... 3E 102
Griggs Rd. E10 .... 6E 50
Grilse Cl. N9 .... 4C 34
Grimaldi Ho. *N1* 2K 83
(off Calshot St.)
Grimsby Gro. E16 .... 2F 107
Grimsby St. E2 .... 4K 9 (4F 85)
Grimsdyke Rd. HA5: Hat E 1D 40
Grimsel Path SE5 .... 7B 102
Grimshaw Cl. N6 .... 7E 46
Grimston Rd. SW6 .... 2H 117
Grimthorpe Ho. EC1 .... 3A 8
Grimwade Av. CR0: C'don 3G 169
Grimwade Cl. SE15 .... 3J 121
Grimwood Rd. TW1: Twick 7K 113
Grindall Cl. CR0: Wadd 4B 168
Grindall Ho. *E1* 4H 85
(off Darling Row)
Grindal St. SE1 .... 7J 13 (2A 102)
Grindleford Av. N11 .... 2K 31
Grindley Gdns. CR0: C'don 6F 157
Grindley Ho. *E3* 5B 86
(off Leopold St.)
Grinling Pl. SE8 .... 6C 104
Grinstead Rd. SE8 .... 5A 104
Grisedale *NW1* 1A 6
(off Cumberland Mkt.)
Grittleton Av. HA9: Wemb 6H 61
Grittleton Rd. W9 .... 4J 81
Grizedale Ter. SE23 .... 2H 139
Grocer's Hall Ct. EC2 .... 1E 14 (6D 84)
Grocer's Hall Gdns.
EC2 .... 1E 14
Grogan Cl. TW12: Hamp 6D 130
Groombridge Cl. DA16: Well 5A 126
Groombridge Ho. *SE17* 5E 102
(off Upnor Way)
Groombridge Rd. E9 .... 7K 67
Groom Cl. BR2: Brom 4K 159
Groom Cres. SW18 .... 7B 118
Groome Ho. SE11 .... 4H 19 (4K 101)
Groomfield Cl. SW17 .... 4E 136
Groom Pl. SW1 .... 1H 17 (3E 100)
Grooms Dr. HA5: Eastc 5J 39
Grosmont Rd. SE18 .... 5K 107
Grosse Way SW15 .... 6D 116
Grosvenor Av. HA2: Harr 6F 41
N5 .... 5C 66
SM5: Cars 6D 166
SW14 .... 3A 116
TW10: Rich 5E 114
UB4: Hayes 2H 75
Grosvenor Cotts. SW1 .... 3G 17 (4E 100)
Grosvenor Ct. E10 .... 1D 68
E14 .... 6B 86
(off Wharf La.)
N14 .... 7B 22
NW6 .... 1F 81
NW7 .... 5E 28
(off Hale La.)
SE5 .... 6C 102
SM2: Sutt 6K 165
SM4: Mord 4J 153
TW11: Tedd 6A 132
W3 .... 1G 97
W5 .... 7E 78
(off The Grove)
Grosvenor Ct. *W14* 3F 99
(off Irving Rd.)
Grosvenor Ct. Mans. *W2* 1E 10
(off Edgware Rd.)
Grosvenor Cres. NW9 .... 4G 43
SW1 .... 7H 11 (2E 100)
UB10: Hil 7D 56
Grosvenor Cres. M. SW1 .... 7G 11 (2E 100)
Grosvenor Est. SW1 .... 3D 18 (4H 101)
Grosvenor Gdns. E6 .... 3B 88
IG8: Wfd G 6D 36
KT2: King T 6D 132
N10 .... 3G 47
N14 .... 4C 22
NW2 .... 6E 62
NW11 .... 6H 45
SM6: Wall 7G 167
SW1 .... 1J 17 (3F 101)
SW14 .... 3A 116
Grosvenor Gdns. M. E. SW1 .... 1K 17
Grosvenor Gdns. M. Nth. SW1 .... 2J 17
Grosvenor Gdns. M. Sth. SW1 .... 2K 17
Grosvenor Ga. W1 .... 3G 11 (7E 82)
Grosvenor Hill SW19 .... 6G 135
W1 .... 2J 11 (7F 83)
Grosvenor Hill Ct. *W1* 2J 11
(off Bourdon St.)
Grosvenor Ho. *SM1: Sutt* 5K 165
(off West St.)
Grosvenor Pde. *W5* 1G 97
(off Uxbridge Rd.)
Grosvenor Pk. SE5 .... 7C 102
Grosvenor Pk. Rd. E17 .... 5C 50
Grosvenor Pl. SW1 .... 7H 11 (2E 100)
Grosvenor Ri. E. E17 .... 5D 50
Grosvenor Rd. BR4: W W'ck 1D 170
BR5: St M Cry 6J 161
DA6: Bex 5D 126
DA17: Belv 6G 109
E6 .... 1B 88
E7 .... 6K 69
E10 .... 1E 68
E11 .... 5K 51
IG1: Ilf 3G 71
N3 .... 7C 30
N9 .... 1C 34
N10 .... 1F 47
RM7: Rush G 7K 55
RM8: Dag 1F 73
SE25 .... 4F 157
SM6: Wall 6F 167
SW1 .... 7J 17 (6F 101)
TW1: Twick 1A 132
TW3: Houn 3D 112
TW8: Bford 6D 96
TW10: Rich 5E 114
UB2: S'hall 3D 94
W4 .... 5H 97
W7 .... 1A 96
Grosvenor Sq. W1 .... 2H 11 (7E 82)
Grosvenor St. W1 .... 2J 11 (7F 83)
Grosvenor Studios *SW1* 3G 17
(off Eaton Ter.)
Grosvenor Ter. SE5 .... 7C 102
Grosvenor Va. HA4: Ruis 2H 57
Grosvenor Way E5 .... 2J 67
SW17 .... 3B 136
Grosvenor Wharf Rd. E14 .... 4F 105
Grotes Bldgs. SE3 .... 2G 123
Grote's Pl. SE3 .... 2G 123
Groton Rd. SW18 .... 2K 135
Grotto Ct. SE1 .... 6B 14 (2B 102)
Grotto Pas. W1 .... 5H 5 (5E 82)
Grotto Rd. TW1: Twick 2K 131
GROVE, THE 1G 139
Grove, The BR4: W W'ck 3D 170
DA6: Bex 4D 126
DA14: Sidc 5E 144
E15 .... 6G 69
EN2: Enf 2F 23
HA1: Harr 7J 41
HA8: Edg 4C 28
Grove, The KT12: Walt T 7K 147
N3 .... 1J 45
N4 .... 7K 47
N6 .... 1E 64
N8 .... 5H 47
N13 .... 4F 33
(not continuous)
N14 .... 5B 22
NW9 .... 5K 43
NW11 .... 7G 45
TW1: Twick 6B 114
TW7: Isle 1J 113
TW11: Tedd 4A 132
UB6: G'frd 6G 77
UB10: Ick 5C 56
W5 .... 1D 96
Grove Av. HA5: Pinn 4C 40
N3 .... 7D 30
N10 .... 2G 47
SM1: Sutt 6J 165
TW1: Twick 1K 131
W7 .... 7J 77
Grovebury Cl. DA8: Erith 6K 109
Grovebury Ct. DA6: Bex 5H 127
N14 .... 7C 22
Grovebury Rd. SE2 .... 2B 108
Grove Cl. BR2: Hayes 2J 171
KT1: King T 4F 151
N14 .... 7B 22
SE23 .... 1A 140
TW13: Hanw 4C 130
UB10: Ick 5C 56
Grove Cotts. SW3 .... 7D 16
W4 .... 6A 98
Grove Ct. *EN5: Barn* 3C 20
(off Hadley Ridge)
KT1: King T 3E 150
(off Grove Cres.)
KT8: E Mos 4H 149
NW8 .... 1A 4
SE15 .... 7E 102
(off Blake's Rd.)
SW10 .... 6A 16
(off Drayton Gdns.)
TW3: Houn 4E 112
W5 .... 1E 96
Grove Cres. E18 .... 2H 51
KT1: King T 3E 150
KT12: Walt T 7K 147
NW9 .... 4J 43
TW13: Hanw 4C 130
Grove Cres. Rd. E15 .... 6F 69
Grovedale Rd. N19 .... 2H 65
Grove Dwellings E1 .... 5J 85
Grove End E18 .... 2H 51
NW5 .... 4F 65
Grove End Gdns. NW8 .... 2B 82
Grove End Ho. NW8 .... 2A 4
Grove End La. KT10: Esh 7H 149
Grove End Rd. NW8 .... 1A 4 (2B 82)
Grove Farm Retail Pk. RM6: Chad H 7C 54
Grovefield *N11* 4A 32
(off Coppies Gro.)
Grove Footpath KT5: Surb 4E 150
Grove Gdns. EN3: Enf W 1E 24
NW4 .... 5C 44
NW8 .... 2D 4 (3C 82)
RM10: Dag 3J 73
TW10: Rich 6F 115
TW11: Tedd 4A 132
Grove Grn. Rd. E11 .... 3E 68
Grove Hall Ct. *E3* 2C 86
(off Jebb St.)
NW8 .... 1A 4 (3A 82)
Grove Hill E18 .... 2H 51
HA1: Harr 7J 41
Grovehill Ct. BR1: Brom 6H 141
Grove Hill Rd. HA1: Harr 7K 41
SE5 .... 3E 120
Grove Ho. N3 .... 3F 45
SW3 .... 7D 16
(off Chelsea Mnr. St.)
Grove Ho. Rd. N8 .... 4J 47
Groveland Av. SW16 .... 7K 137
Groveland Ct. EC4 .... 1D 14
Groveland Rd. BR3: Beck 3B 158
Grovelands *KT1: King T* 4D 150
(off Palace Rd.)
KT8: W Mole 4E 148
Grovelands Cl. HA2: Harr 3F 59
SE5 .... 2E 120
Grovelands Ct. N14 .... 7C 22
Grovelands Rd. BR5: St P 7A 144
N13 .... 4E 32
N15 .... 6G 49
Groveland Way KT3: N Mald 5J 151
Grove La. KT1: King T 4E 150
SE5 .... 1D 120
UB8: Hil 4B 74
Grove La. Ter. SE5 .... 2D 120
Groveley Rd. TW13: Felt 5H 129
TW16: Sun 5H 129
Grove Mans. *W6* 2E 98
(off Hammersmith Gro.)
Grove Mkt. Pl. SE9 .... 6D 124
Grove M. W6 .... 3E 98
Grove Mill Pl. SM5: Cars 3E 166
Grove Nature Reserve, The 4B 74
GROVE PARK
BR1 .... 3K 141
W4 .... 1J 115
Grove Pk. E11 .... 6K 51
NW9 .... 4J 43
SE5 .... 2E 120
Grove Pk. Av. E4 .... 7J 35
Grove Pk. Bri. W4 .... 7J 97
Grove Pk. Gdns. W4 .... 7H 97
Grove Pk. Ind. Est. NW9 .... 3K 43
Grove Pk. M. W4 .... 7J 97
Grove Pk. Nature Reserve 2J 141
Grove Pk. Rd. N15 .... 4E 48
SE9 .... 3A 142
W4 .... 7H 97
Grove Pk. Ter. W4 .... 7H 97
(not continuous)
Grove Pas. E2 .... 2H 85
Grove Pl. IG11: Bark 7G 71
NW3 .... 3B 64
SW12 .... 7F 119
W3 .... 1J 97
Grover Ct. SE13 .... 2D 122
Grover Ho. SE11 .... 6H 19 (5K 101)
Grove Rd. CR4: Mitc 3E 154
(not continuous)
CR7: Thor H 4A 156
DA7: Bex 4J 127
DA17: Belv 6F 109
E3 .... 1K 85
E4 .... 4K 35
E11 .... 7H 51
E17 .... 6D 50
E18 .... 2H 51
EN4: Cockf 3H 21
HA5: Pinn 5D 40
HA8: Edg 6B 28
KT6: Surb 5D 150
KT8: E Mos 4H 149
N11 .... 5A 32
N12 .... 5G 31
N15 .... 5E 48
NW2 .... 6E 62
RM6: Chad H 7B 54
SM1: Sutt 6J 165
SW13 .... 2B 116
SW19 .... 7A 136
TW2: Twick 3H 131
TW3: Houn 4E 112
TW7: Isle 1J 113
TW8: Bford 5C 96
TW10: Rich 6F 115
TW17: Shep 6E 146
UB8: Uxb 7A 56
W3 .... 1J 97
W5 .... 7D 78

Groveside Cl. SM5: Cars 2C 166
  W3 . . . . .5G 79
Groveside Cl. SW11 . . . . .2B 118
Groveside Rd. E4 . . . . .2B 36
Grovestile Waye TW14: Bedf 7F 111
Grove St. N18 . . . . .5A 34
  SE8 . . . . .4B 104
Grove Ter. NW5 . . . . .3F 65
  TW11: Tedd 4A 132
  UB1: S'hall .7E 76
Grove Ter. M. NW5 . . . . .3F 65
Grove Va. BR7: Chst 6E 142
  SE22 . . . . .4F 121
Grove Vs. E14 . . . . .7D 86
Grove Way HA9: Wemb 5H 61
  KT10: Esh .7G 149
  UB8: Uxb 7A 56
Groveway RM8: Dag 4D 72
  SW9 . . . . .1K 119
Grovewood TW9: Kew 1G 115
Grove Wood Cl. BR1: Brom 3E 160
Grovewood Pl. IG8: Wfd G 6J 37
Grummant Rd. SE15 . . . . .1F 121
Grundy St. E14 . . . . .6D 86
Gruneisen Rd. N3 . . . . .7E 30
Guardian Ct. SE12 . . . . .5G 123
Guards Memorial 5D 12 (1H 101)
Guards' Mus. 7B 12 (2G 101)
Gubyon Av. SE24 . . . . .5B 120
Guerin Sq. E3 . . . . .3B 86
Guernsey Cl. TW5: Hest 7E 94
Guernsey Gro. SE24 . . . . .7C 120
Guernsey Ho. EN3: Enf W 1E 24
                 (off Eastfield Rd.)
  N1 . . . . .6C 66
           (off Douglas Rd. Nth.)
Guernsey Rd. E11 . . . . .1F 69
Guibal Rd. SE12 . . . . .7K 123
Guildersfield Rd. SW16 . . . . .7J 137
Guildford Av. TW13: Felt 2H 129
Guildford Ct. SW8 . . . . .7J 101
              (off Guildford Rd.)
Guildford Gro. SE10 . . . . .1D 122
Guildford Rd. CRO: C'don 6D 156
  E6 . . . . .6D 88
  E17 . . . . .1E 50
  IG3: Ilf 2J 71
  SW8 . . . . .1J 119
Guildford Way SM6: Wall 5J 167
Guildhall
  City 7E 8
  Westminster 7E 12
Guildhall Art Gallery 7E 8
           (off Aldermanbury)
Guildhall Bldgs. EC2 . . . . .7E 8
Guildhall Library 7D 8
Guildhall Offices EC2 . . . . .7D 8
Guildhall Yd. EC2 . . . . . . .7D 8 (6C 84)
Guildhouse St. SW1 . . . . .3A 18 (4G 101)
Guildown Av. N12 . . . . .4E 30
Guild Rd. SE7 . . . . .6B 106
Guildsway E17 . . . . .1B 50
Guilford Av. KT5: Surb 5F 151
Guilford Pl. WC1 . . . . .4G 7 (4K 83)
Guilford St. WC1 . . . . .4E 6 (4J 83)
Guilfoyle NW9 . . . . .2B 44
Guillemot Ct. SE8 . . . . .6B 104
           (off Alexandra Cl.)
Guillemot Pl. N22 . . . . .2K 47
Guinea Ct. E1 . . . . .7G 85
           (off Royal Mint St.)
Guinness Cl. E9 . . . . .7A 68
  UB3: Harl 3F 93
Guinness Cl. CRO: C'don 2F 169
  E1 . . . . .1J 15
  EC1 . . . . .2D 8
  NW8 . . . . .1C 82
  SE1 . . . . .6G 15
  SW3 . . . . .4E 16 (4D 100)
Guinness Sq. SE1 . . . . .4E 102
Guinness Trust SW3 . . . . .4E 16
           (off Cadogan St.)

Guinness Trust Bldgs. SE11 . . . . . .5B 102
  W6 . . . . .5F 99
           (off Fulham Pal. Rd.)
Guinness Trust Est., The N16 . . . . .1F 66
Guion Rd. SW6 . . . . .2H 117
Gulland Wlk. N1 . . . . .6C 66
           (off Church Rd.)
Gullane Ho. E3 . . . . .2B 86
           (off Shetland Rd.)
Gulliver Cl. UB5: N'olt 1D 76
Gulliver Rd. DA15: Sidc 2H 143
Gulliver's Ho. EC1 . . . . .4C 8
Gulliver St. SE16 . . . . .3A 104
Gulston Wlk. SW3 . . . . .4F 17
Gumleigh Rd. W5 . . . . .4C 96
Gumley Gdns. TW7: Isle 3A 114
Gumping Rd. BR5: Farnb 2G 173
Gundulph Rd. BR2: Brom 3A 160
Gun Ho. E1 .1H 103
        (off Wapping High St.)
Gunmakers La. E3 . . . . .1A 86
Gunnell Cl. CRO: C'don 6F 157
  SE25 . . . . .6G 157
           (off Backley Gdns.)
  SE26 . . . . .4G 139
Gunner La. SE18 . . . . .5E 106
GUNNERSBURY 5H 97
Gunnersbury Av. W3 . . . . .3G 97
  W4 . . . . .1F 97
  W5 . . . . .1F 97
Gunnersbury Cl. W4 . . . . .5H 97
Gunnersbury Cl. W3 . . . . .3H 97
Gunnersbury Cres. W3 . . . . .2G 97
Gunnersbury Dr. W5 . . . . .2F 97
Gunnersbury Gdns. W3 . . . . .2G 97
Gunnersbury La. W3 . . . . .3G 97
Gunnersbury Mnr. W5 . . . . .1F 97
Gunnersbury M. W4 . . . . .5H 97
GUNNERSBURY PARK 3G 97
Gunnersbury Pk. Mus. 3G 97
Gunnersbury Triangle Nature Reserve
  . . . . .4J 97
Gunnersbury Triangle Nature Reserve
  Vis. Cen. 4J 97
Gunners Gro. E4 . . . . .3K 35
Gunners Rd. SW18 . . . . .2B 136
Gunnery Ter. SE18 . . . . .3G 107
Gunning St. SE18 . . . . .4J 107
Gunpowder Sq. EC4 . . . . .7K 7
    (off E. Harding St., not continuous)
Gunstor Rd. N16 . . . . .4E 66
Gun St. E1 . . . . .6J 9 (5F 85)
Gunter Gro. HA8: Edg 1K 43
  SW10 . . . . .6A 100
Gunter Hall Studios SW10 . . . . . . .6A 100
           (off Gunter Gro.)
Gunterstone Rd. W14 . . . . .4G 99
Gunthorpe St. E1 . . . . .6K 9 (5F 85)
Gunton Rd. E5 . . . . .3H 67
  SW17 . . . . .6E 136
Gunwhale Cl. SE16 . . . . .1K 103
Gun Wharf E1 . . . . .1J 103
        (off Wapping High St.)
Gun Wharf Bus. Cen. E3 . . . . .1A 86
         (off Old Ford Rd.)
Gunyard M. SE18 . . . . .7C 106
Gurdon Ho. E14 . . . . .6C 86
           (off Dod St.)
Gurdon Rd. SE7 . . . . .5J 105
Gurnard Cl. UB7: Yiew 7A 74
Gurnell Gro. W13 . . . . .4K 77
Gurnell Leisure Cen. 3K 77
Gurney Cl. E15 . . . . .5G 69
  E17 . . . . .1K 49
  IG11: Bark 6F 71
Gurney Cres. CRO: C'don 1K 167
Gurney Dr. N2 . . . . .4A 46
Gurney Ho. E2 . . . . .2G 85
         (off Goldsmiths Row)
  UB3: Harl 5G 93
Gurney Rd. E15 . . . . .5G 69
  SM5: Cars 4E 166

Gurney Rd. SW6 . . . . .3A 118
  UB5: N'olt 3K 75
Guthrie Cl. SE1 . . . . .7K 13
Guthrie St. SW3 . . . . .5C 16 (5B 100)
Gutter La. EC2 . . . . .7C 8 (6C 84)
Guyatt Gdns. CR4: Mitc 2E 154
Guy Barnett Gro. SE3 . . . . .3J 123
Guy Rd. SM6: Bedd 3H 167
Guyscliff Rd. SE13 . . . . .5E 122
Guys Retreat IG9: Buck H 1F 37
Guy St. SE1 . . . . .6F 15 (2D 102)
Gwalior Ho. N14 . . . . .6B 22
Gwalior Rd. SW15 . . . . .4F 117
Gwendolen Av. SW15 . . . . .4F 117
Gwendolen Cl. SW15 . . . . .5F 117
Gwendolen Ho. TW19: Stanw 1A 128
           (off Yeoman Dr.)
Gwendoline Av. E13 . . . . .1K 87
Gwendwr Rd. W14 . . . . .5G 99
Gweneth Cotts. HA8: Edg 6B 28
Gwen Morris Ho. SE5 . . . . .7C 102
Gwent Cl. SE16 . . . . .1K 103
         (off Rotherhithe St.)
Gwillim Cl. DA15: Sidc 5A 126
Gwilym Maries Ho. E2 . . . . .3H 85
           (off Blythe St.)
Gwydor Rd. BR3: Beck 3K 157
Gwydyr Rd. BR2: Brom 3H 159
Gwyn Cl. SW6 . . . . .7A 100
Gwynne Av. CRO: C'don 7K 157
Gwynne Cl. W4 . . . . .6B 98
Gwynne Ho. E1 . . . . .5H 85
           (off Turner St.)
  SW1 . . . . .5G 17
         (off Lwr. Sloane St.)
  WC1 . . . . .2J 7
          (off Lloyd Baker St.)
Gwynne Pk. Av. IG8: Wfd G 6J 37
Gwynne Rd. SW11 . . . . .2B 118
Gylcote Cl. SE5 . . . . .4D 120
Gyles Pk. HA7: Stan 1C 42
Gyllyngdune Gdns. IG3: Ilf 2K 71
Gym, The 3F 113
GYPSY CORNER 5K 79

H

Haarlem Rd. W14 . . . . .3F 99
Haberdasher Est. N1 . . . . . .1F 9 (3D 84)
Haberdasher Pl. N1 . . . . . . .1F 9 (3D 84)
Haberdashers Ct. SE14 . . . . .3K 121
Haberdasher St. N1 . . . . . . .1F 9 (3D 84)
Habitat Cl. SE15 . . . . .2H 121
Habitat Sq. SE10 . . . . .3H 105
           (off Teal St.)
Haccombe Rd. SW19 . . . . .6A 136
HACKBRIDGE 1E 166
Hackbridge Pk. Gdns.
    SM5: Cars 2D 166
Hackbridge Rd. SM6: Wall 2E 166
Hackford Rd. SW9 . . . . .1K 119
Hackford Wlk. SW9 . . . . .1K 119
Hackington Cres.
    BR3: Beck 6C 140
HACKNEY 6H 67
Hackney City Farm 2G 85
Hackney Empire Theatre 6H 67
Hackney Gro. E8 . . . . .6H 67
Hackney Mus. 6H 67
Hackney Rd. E2 . . . . .2J 9 (3F 85)
HACKNEY WICK 6B 68
HACKNEY WICK 6A 68
Hackworth Point E3 . . . . .3D 86
           (off Rainhill Way)
Hacon Sq. E8 . . . . .7H 67
           (off Mare St.)
Hadar Cl. N20 . . . . .1D 30
Hadden Rd. SE28 . . . . .3J 107
Hadden Way UB6: G'frd 6H 59
Haddington Rd. BR1: Brom 3F 141

Haddo Ho. SE10 . . . . .6D 104
           (off Haddo St.)
Haddon Cl. EN1: Enf 6B 24
  KT3: N Mald 5B 152
Haddon Cl. NW4 . . . . .3E 44
  W3 . . . . .7B 80
Haddonfield SE8 . . . . .4K 103
Haddon Gro. DA15: Sidc 7K 125
Haddon Hall St. SE1 . . . . .3D 102
           (off Rephidim St.)
Haddon Rd. SM1: Sutt 4K 165
           (not continuous)
Haddo St. SE10 . . . . .6D 104
Haden Ct. N4 . . . . .2A 66
Haden La. N11 . . . . .4B 32
Hadfield Cl. UB1: S'hall 3D 76
Hadfield Ho. E1 . . . . .6G 85
           (off Ellen St.)
Hadleigh Cl. E1 . . . . .4J 85
  SW20 . . . . .2H 153
Hadleigh Cl. E4 . . . . .1B 36
  NW2 . . . . .6E 62
Hadleigh Ho. E1 . . . . .4J 85
           (off Hadleigh Cl.)
Hadleigh Lodge IG8: Wfd G 6D 36
           (off Snakes La.)
Hadleigh Rd. N9 . . . . .7C 24
Hadleigh St. E2 . . . . .3J 85
Hadleigh Wlk. E6 . . . . .6C 88
HADLEY 3C 20
Hadley Cl. N21 . . . . .6F 23
Hadley Comn. EN5: Barn, New Bar . . .2D 20
Hadley Ct. EN5: New Bar 3E 20
  N16 . . . . .1G 67
  SL3: Poyle 4A 174
          (off Coleridge Cres.)
Hadley Gdns. UB2: S'hall 5D 94
  W4 . . . . .5K 97
Hadley Grn. EN5: Barn 2C 20
Hadley Grn. Rd. EN5: Barn 2C 20
Hadley Grn. W. EN5: Barn 2C 20
Hadley Gro. EN5: Barn 2B 20
Hadley Highstone EN5: Barn 1C 20
Hadley M. EN5: Barn 3C 20
Hadley Pde. EN5: Barn 3B 20
           (off High St.)
Hadley Ridge EN5: Barn 3C 20
Hadley Rd. CR4: Mitc 4H 155
  DA17: Belv 4F 109
  EN2: Enf 1A 22
  EN4: Had W 1K 21
  EN5: New Bar 2E 20
Hadley St. NW1 . . . . .6F 65
           (not continuous)
Hadley Way N21 . . . . .6F 23
HADLEY WOOD 1F 21
Hadley Wood Nature Reserve 2F 21
Hadley Wood Rd. EN4: Cock'f 2F 21
  EN5: Cock'f, New Bar 2F 21
Hadlow Ho. SE17 . . . . .5E 102
           (off Kinglake Est.)
Hadlow Pl. SE19 . . . . .7G 139
Hadlow Rd. DA14: Sidc 4A 144
  DA16: Well 7C 108
Hadrian Cl. E3 . . . . .1C 86
           (off Garrison Rd.)
  TW19: Stanw 7A 110
Hadrian Ct. SM2: Sutt 7K 165
Hadrian Est. E2 . . . . .2G 85
Hadrian M. N7 . . . . .7K 65
Hadrians Ride EN1: Enf 5A 24
Hadrian St. SE10 . . . . .5G 105
Hadrian Way TW19: Stanw 7A 110
           (not continuous)
Hadstock Ho. NW1 . . . . .1D 6
           (off Ossulston St.)
Hadyn Pk. Ct. W12 . . . . .2C 98
           (off Curwen Rd.)
Hadyn Pk. Rd. W12 . . . . .2C 98
Hafer Rd. SW11 . . . . .4D 118
Hafton Rd. SE6 . . . . .1G 141
Haggard Rd. TW1: Twick 7B 114

Hagger Ct. E17 3F **51**
HAGGERSTON 7F **67**
Haggerston Rd. E8 7F **67**
Haggerston Studios *E8* *1F 85*
(off Kingsland Rd.)
Hague St. E2 3G **85**
Ha Ha Rd. SE18 6D **106**
Haig Ho. *E2* *1K 9*
(off Shipton St.)
Haig Pl. SM4: Mord 6J **153**
Haig Rd. HA7: Stan 5H **27**
UB8: Hil 5D **74**
Haig Rd. E. E13 3A **88**
Haig Rd. W. E13 3A **88**
Haigville Gdns. IG6: Ilf 4F **53**
Hailes Cl. CR0: Bedd 2H **167**
SW19 6A **136**
Haileybury Av. EN1: Enf 6A **24**
Hailey Rd. DA18: Erith 2G **109**
Hailey Rd. Bus. Pk.
DA18: Erith 2G **109**
Hailing M. *BR2: Brom* *3K 159*
(off Wendover Rd.)
Hailsham Av. SW2 2K **137**
Hailsham Cl. KT6: Surb 7D **150**
Hailsham Dr. HA1: Harr 3H **41**
Hailsham Ho. *NW8* *4C 4*
(off Salisbury St.)
Hailsham Rd. SW17 6E **136**
Hailsham Ter. N18 5J **33**
Haimo Rd. SE9 5B **124**
Hainault Ct. *E17* *4F 51*
(off Forest Ri.)
Hainault Gore RM6: Chad H 5E **54**
Hainault Rd. E11 1E **68**
RM5: Col R, Rom 2J **55**
RM6: Chad H 1B **54**
(Forest Rd.)
RM6: Chad H 6F **55**
(Sylvan Av.)
Hainault St. IG1: Ilf 2G **71**
SE9 1F **143**
Haines Cl. N1 7E **66**
Haines St. SW8 7G **101**
Haines Wlk. SM4: Mord 7K **153**
Hainford Cl. SE4 4K **121**
Haining Cl. W4 5G **97**
Hainthorpe Rd. SE27 3B **138**
Hainton Cl. E1 6H **85**
Halberd M. E5 2H **67**
Halbutt Gdns. RM9: Dag 3F **73**
Halbutt St. RM9: Dag 4F **73**
Halcomb St. N1 1E **84**
Halcot Av. DA6: Bex 5H **127**
Halcrow St. E1 5H **85**
Halcyon *EN1: Enf* *5K 23*
(off Private Rd.)
Halcyon Wharf *E1* *1G 103*
(off Hermitage Wall)
Haldane Cl. N10 7A **32**
Haldane Pl. SW18 1K **135**
Haldane Rd. E6 3B **88**
SE28 7D **90**
SW6 7H **99**
UB1: S'hall 7G **77**
Haldan Rd. E4 6K **35**
Haldon Rd. SW18 6H **117**
HALE, THE 5E **28**
Hale, The E4 7A **36**
N17 3G **49**
(not continuous)
Hale Cl. BR6: Farnb 4G **173**
E4 3K **35**
HA8: Edg 5D **28**
Hale Ct. HA8: Edg 5D **28**
Hale Dr. NW7 6D **28**
HALE END 6B **36**
Hale End Cl. HA4: Ruis 6J **39**
Hale End Rd. E4 6A **36**
E17 1E **50**
IG8: Wfd G 7A **36**
Halefield Rd. N17 1H **49**
Hale Gdns. N17 4G **49**
W3 1G **97**
Hale Gro. Gdns. NW7 5F **29**
Hale Ho. *SW1* *5D 18*
(off Lindsay Sq.)
Hale La. HA8: Edg 5C **28**
NW7 5E **28**
Hale Path SE27 4B **138**
Hale Rd. E6 4C **88**
N17 3G **49**
Halesowen Rd.
SM4: Mord 7K **153**
Hales Prior *N1* *1G 7*
(off Calshot St.)
Hales St. SE8 7C **104**
Hale St. E14 7D **86**
Halesworth Cl. E5 2J **67**
Halesworth Rd. SE13 3D **122**
Hale Wlk. W7 5J **77**
Haley Rd. NW4 6E **44**
Half Acre HA7: Stan 5H **27**
TW8: Bford 6D **96**
Half Acre Rd. W7 1J **95**
Half Moon Ct. EC1 6C **8**
Half Moon Cres. N1 2K **83**
(not continuous)
Half Moon La. SE24 6C **120**
Half Moon Pas. E1 1K **15** (6F **85**)
(not continuous)
Half Moon St. W1 4K **11** (1F **101**)
Halford Cl. HA8: Edg 2H **43**
Halford Rd. E10 5F **51**
SW6 6J **99**
TW10: Rich 5E **114**
UB10: Ick 4C **56**
Halfway St. DA15: Sidc 7H **125**
Haliburton Rd. TW1: Twick 5A **114**
Haliday Ho. *N1* *6D 66*
(off Mildmay St.)
Haliday Wlk. N1 6D **66**
Halidon Cl. E9 5J **67**
Halifax NW9 2B **44**
Halifax Cl. TW11: Tedd 6J **131**
Halifax Rd. EN2: Enf 2H **23**
UB6: G'frd 1F **77**
Halifax St. SE26 3H **139**
Halifield Dr. DA17: Belv 3E **108**
Haling Down Pas. CR8: Purl 7C **168**
(not continuous)
Haling Gro. CR2: S Croy 7C **168**
Haling Pk. Gdns. CR2: S Croy 6B **168**
Haling Pk. Rd. CR2: S Croy 5B **168**
Haling Rd. CR2: S Croy 6D **168**
Haliwell Ho. *NW6* *1K 81*
(off Mortimer Cres.)
Halkett Ho. *E2* *1J 85*
(off Waterloo Gdns.)
Halkin Arc. SW1 1F **17** (3D **100**)
Halkin M. SW1 1G **17** (3E **100**)
Halkin Pl. SW1 1G **17** (3E **100**)
Halkin St. SW1 7H **11** (2E **100**)
Hall, The SE3 3J **123**
Hallam Cl. BR7: Chst 5D **142**
Hallam Ct. *W1* *5K 5*
(off Hallam St.)
Hallam Gdns. HA5: Hat E 1C **40**
Hallam Ho. *SW1* *6B 18*
(off Churchill Gdns.)
Hallam M. W1 5K **5** (5F **83**)
Hallam Rd. N15 4B **48**
SW13 3D **116**
Hallam St. W1 4K **5** (4F **83**)
Hallane Ho. SE27 5C **138**
Hall Cl. W5 5E **78**
Hall Ct. TW11: Tedd 5K **131**
Hall Dr. SE26 5J **139**
W7 6J **77**
Halley Gdns. SE13 4F **123**
Halley Ho. *E2* *2G 85*
(off Pritchards Rd.)
SE10 *5H 105*
(off Armitage Rd.)
Halley Rd. E7 6A **70**
E12 6A **70**
Halley St. E14 5A **86**
Hall Farm Cl. HA7: Stan 4G **27**
Hall Farm Dr. TW2: Whitt 7H **113**
Hallfield Est. W2 6A **82**
(not continuous)
Hall Gdns. E4 4G **35**
Hall Ga. NW8 1A **4** (3B **82**)
Halliards, The KT12: Walt T 6J **147**
Halliday Ho. *E1* *6G 85*
(off Christian St.)
Halliday Sq. UB2: S'hall 1H **95**
Halliford Cl. TW17: Shep 4F **147**
Halliford Rd. TW16: Sun 5G **147**
TW17: Shep 5G **147**
Halliford St. N1 7C **66**
Hallingbury Ct. E17 3D **50**
Halling Ho. *SE1* *7F 15*
(off Long La.)
Hallings Wharf Studios E15 1F **87**
Halliwell Ct. SE22 5G **121**
Halliwell Rd. SW2 6K **119**
Halliwick Ct. Pde. *N12* *6J 31*
(off Woodhouse Rd.)
Halliwick Rd. N10 1E **46**
Hall La. E4 5F **35**
NW4 1C **44**
UB3: Harl 7F **93**
HALL LANE JUNC. 5E **34**
Hallmark Trad. Est.
HA9: Wemb 4J **61**
Hallmead Rd. SM1: Sutt 3K **165**
Hall Oak Wlk. NW6 6H **63**
Hallowell Av. CR0: Bedd 4J **167**
Hallowell Cl. CR4: Mitc 3E **154**
Hallowell Gdns. CR7: Thor H 2C **156**
Hallowell Rd. HA6: Nwood 1G **39**
Hallowfield Way CR4: Mitc 3B **154**
Hallows Gro. TW16: Sun 5H **129**
Hall Pl. W2 4A **4** (4B **82**)
(not continuous)
Hall Pl. Cres. DA5: Bexl 5J **127**
Hall Place House & Gardens 6J 127
Hall Rd. E6 1D **88**
E15 4F **69**
NW8 1A **4** (3A **82**)
RM6: Chad H 6C **54**
SM6: Wall 7F **167**
TW7: Isle 5H **113**
Hallside Rd. EN1: Enf 1A **24**
Hall St. EC1 1B **8** (3B **84**)
N12 5F **31**
Hallsville Rd. E16 6H **87**
Hallswelle Pde. NW11 5H **45**
Hallswelle Rd. NW11 5H **45**
Hall Twr. W2 5B **4**
Hall Vw. SE9 2B **142**
Hallywell Cres. E6 5D **88**
Halons Rd. SE9 7E **124**
Halpin Pl. SE17 4D **102**
Halsbrook Rd. SE3 3A **124**
Halsbury Cl. HA7: Stan 4G **27**
Halsbury Ct. HA7: Stan 5G **27**
Halsbury Ho. *N7* *4K 65*
(off Biddestone Rd.)
Halsbury Rd. W12 1D **98**
Halsbury Rd. E. UB5: N'olt 4G **59**
Halsbury Rd. W. UB5: N'olt 5F **59**
Halsend UB3: Hayes 1K **93**
Halsey Ho. *WC1* *6G 7*
(off Dane St.)
Halsey M. SW3 3E **16** (4D **100**)
Halsey St. SW3 3E **16** (4D **100**)
Halsham Cres.
IG11: Bark 5K **71**
Halsmere Rd. SE5 1B **120**
Halstead Cl. CR0: C'don 3C **168**
Halstead Ct. E17 7B **50**
N1 *1F 9*
(off Murray Gro.)
Halstead Gdns. N21 1J **33**
Halstead Rd. E11 5J **51**
EN1: Enf 4K **23**
N21 1H **33**
Halston Cl. SW11 6D **118**
Halstow Rd. NW10 3F **81**
SE10 5J **105**
Halsway UB3: Hayes 1J **93**
Halton Cl. N11 6J **31**
Halton Cross St. N1 1B **84**
Halton Ho. *N1* *7B 66*
(off Halton Rd.)
Halton Mans. N1 7B **66**
Halton Pl. N1 1C **84**
Halton Rd. N1 7B **66**
Halt Robin La. DA17: Belv 4H **109**
Halt Robin Rd. DA17: Belv 4G **109**
(not continuous)
Halyard Ho. E14 3E **104**
HAM 3C **132**
Ham, The TW8: Bford 7C **96**
Hamara Ghar E13 1A **88**
Hambalt Rd. SW4 5G **119**
Hamble Cl. HA4: Ruis 2G **57**
Hambledon *SE17* *6D 102*
(off Villa St.)
Hambledon Cl. UB8: Hil 4D **74**
Hambledon Ct. SE22 4E **120**
W5 7E **78**
Hambledon Gdns. SE25 3F **157**
Hambledon Pl. SE21 1E **138**
Hambledon Rd. SW18 7H **117**
Hambledown Rd.
DA15: Sidc 7H **125**
Hamblehyrst BR3: Beck 2D **158**
Hamble St. SW6 3K **117**
Hambleton Cl.
KT4: Wor Pk 2E **164**
Hamble Wlk. *UB5: N'olt* *2E 76*
(off Brabazon Rd.)
Hambley Ho. *SE16* *4H 103*
(off Camilla Rd.)
Hamblin Ho. *UB1: S'hall* *7C 76*
(off The Broadway)
Hambridge Way SW2 7A **120**
Hambro Av. BR2: Hayes 1J **171**
Hambrook Rd. SE25 3H **157**
Hambro Rd. SW16 6H **137**
Hambrough Ho. UB4: Yead 5A **76**
Hambrough Rd. UB1: S'hall 1C **94**
Ham Cl. TW10: Ham 3C **132**
(not continuous)
Ham Comn. TW10: Ham 3D **132**
Ham Ct. NW9 2A **44**
Ham Cft. Cl. TW13: Felt 3J **129**
Hamden Cres. RM10: Dag 3H **73**
Hamel Cl. HA3: Kenton 4D **42**
Hameway E6 4E **88**
Ham Farm Rd. TW10: Ham 4D **132**
Ham Flds. TW10: Ham 3B **132**
Hamfrith Rd. E15 6H **69**
Ham Ga. Av. TW10: Ham 3D **132**
Ham House 1C 132
Hamilton Av. IG6: Ilf 4F **53**
KT6: Surb 2G **163**
N9 7B **24**
RM1: Rom 2K **55**
SM3: Cheam 2G **165**
Hamilton Cl. EN4: Cockf 4H **21**
HA7: Stan 2D **26**
N17 3F **49**
NW8 2A **4** (3B **82**)
SE16 2A **104**
TW11: Tedd 6B **132**
TW13: Felt 5H **129**
Hamilton Ct. CR0: C'don 1G **169**
SE6 1H **141**
SW15 3G **117**
TW3: Houn *4F 113*
(off Hanworth Rd.)
W5 7E **78**
W9 *3A 82*
(off Maida Va.)

Hamilton Cres. HA2: Harr 3D 58
N13 4F 33
TW3: Houn 5F 113
Hamilton Gdns. NW8 1A 4 (3A 82)
Hamilton Hall NW8 2A 82
(off Hamilton Ter.)
Hamilton Ho. E3 3B 86
(off British St.)
E14 5D 104
(off St Davids Sq.)
E14 7B 86
(off Victory Pl.)
NW8 1A 4
W4 6A 98
W8 2K 99
(off Vicarage Ga.)
Hamilton La. N5 4B 66
Hamilton Lodge E1 4J 85
(off Cleveland Gro.)
Hamilton M. SW18 1J 135
SW19 7J 135
W1 6J 11 (2F 101)
Hamilton Pde. TW13: Felt 4H 129
Hamilton Pk. N5 4B 66
Hamilton Pk. W. N5 4B 66
Hamilton Pl. N19 3H 65
TW16: Sun 7K 129
W1 5H 11 (1E 100)
Hamilton Rd. CR7: Thor H 3D 156
DA7: Bex 2E 126
DA15: Sidc 4A 144
E15 3G 87
E17 2A 50
EN4: Cockf 4H 21
HA1: Harr 5J 41
IG1: Ilf 4F 71
N2 3A 46
N9 7B 24
NW10 5C 62
NW11 7F 45
SE27 4D 138
SW19 7K 135
TW2: Twick 1J 131
TW8: Bford 6D 96
TW13: Felt 4H 129
UB1: S'hall 1D 94
UB3: Hayes 7K 75
W4 2A 98
W5 7E 78
Hamilton Rd. Ind. Est. SE27 4D 138
Hamilton Rd. M. SW19 7K 135
Hamilton Sq. N12 6G 31
SE1 6F 15 (2D 102)
Hamilton St. SE8 6C 104
Hamilton Ter. NW8 2A 4 (2K 81)
Hamilton Way N3 6D 30
N13 4G 33
SM6: Wall 7H 167
Ham Lands Nature Reserve 2A 132
Hamlea Cl. SE12 5J 123
Hamlet, The SE5 3D 120
Hamlet Cl. RM5: Col R 1G 55
SE13 4G 123
Hamlet Ct. E3 3C 86
(off Tomlin's Gro.)
EN1: Enf 5K 23
SE11 5B 102
(off Opal St.)
W6 4C 98
Hamlet Gdns. W6 4C 98
Hamlet Ind. Est. E9 7C 68
Hamlet Intl. Ind. Est. DA8: Erith 5K 109
Hamlet Lodge UB10: Hil 6D 56
Hamlet M. SE21 1D 138
Hamleton Ter. RM9: Dag 7C 72
(off Flamstead Rd.)
Hamlet Rd. RM5: Col R 1G 55
SE19 7F 139
Hamlet Sq. NW2 3G 63
Hamlets Way E3 4B 86
Hamlet Way SE1 6F 15 (2D 102)
Hamlin Cres. HA5: Eastc 5A 40
Hamlyn Cl. HA8: Edg 3K 27
Hamlyn Gdns. SE19 7E 138
Hamlyn Ho. TW13: Felt 1K 129
Hammelton Ct. BR1: Brom 1H 159
(off London Rd.)
Hammelton Grn. SW9 1B 120
Hammelton Rd.
BR1: Brom 1H 159
Hammerfield Ho. SW3 5D 16
(off Cale St.)
Hammers La. NW7 5H 29
Hammersley Ho. SE14 7J 103
(off Pomeroy St.)
HAMMERSMITH 4E 98
Hammersmith Apollo 5E 98
Hammersmith Bri. SW13 6D 98
Hammersmith Bri. Rd. W6 5E 98
HAMMERSMITH BROADWAY 4E 98
Hammersmith B'way. W6 4E 98
Hammersmith Emb. W6 6E 98
Hammersmith Fitness & Squash Cen.
4F 99
(off Chalk Hill Rd.)
HAMMERSMITH FLYOVER 5E 98
Hammersmith Flyover W6 5E 98
Hammersmith Gro. W6 2E 98
Hammersmith Rd. W6 4F 99
W14 4F 99
Hammersmith Ter. W6 5C 98
Hammet Cl. UB4: Yead 5B 76
Hammett St. EC3 2J 15 (7F 85)
Hammond Av. CR4: Mitc 2F 155
Hammond Cl. EN5: Barn 5B 20
TW12: Hamp 1E 148
UB6: G'frd 5H 59
Hammond Ct. E10 2D 68
(off Leyton Grange Est.)
E17 5A 50
(off Maude Rd.)
SE11 5J 19
(off Hotspur St.)
Hammond Ho. E14 3C 104
(off Tiller Rd.)
SE14 7J 103
(off Lubbock St.)
Hammond Lodge W9 5J 81
(off Admiral Wlk.)
Hammond Rd. EN1: Enf 2C 24
UB2: S'hall 3C 94
Hammonds Cl. RM8: Dag 3C 72
Hammond St. NW5 6G 65
Hammond Way SE28 7B 90
Hamond Cl. CR2: S Croy 7B 168
Hamonde Cl. HA8: Edg 2C 28
Hamond Sq. N1 2E 84
Ham Pk. Rd. E7 7H 69
E15 7H 69
Hampden Av. BR3: Beck 2A 158
Hampden Cl. NW1 2H 83
Hampden Ct. N10 7K 31
Hampden Gurney St. W1 1E 10 (6D 82)
Hampden Ho. SW9 2A 120
(off Overton Rd.)
Hampden La. N17 1F 49
Hampden Rd. BR3: Beck 2A 158
HA3: Hrw W 1G 41
KT1: King T 3G 151
N8 4A 48
N10 7K 31
N17 1G 49
N19 2H 65
RM5: Col R 1H 55
Hampden Sq. N14 1A 32
Hampden Way N14 1A 32
Hampshire Cl. N18 5C 34
Hampshire Hog La. W6 5D 98
Hampshire Rd. N22 7E 32
Hampshire St. NW5 6H 65
Hampson Way SW8 1K 119
HAMPSTEAD 4B 64
Hampstead Av. IG8: Wfd G 7K 37
Hampstead Cl. SE28 1B 108
Hampstead Gdns. NW11 6J 45
RM6: Chad H 5B 54
HAMPSTEAD GARDEN SUBURB 5A 46
Hampstead Ga. NW3 5A 64
Hampstead Grn. NW3 5C 64
Hampstead Gro. NW3 3A 64
Hampstead Heath 2B 64
Hampstead Heath Info. Cen. 4E 64
(off Lissenden Gdns.)
Hampstead Hgts. N2 3A 46
Hampstead High St. NW3 4B 64
Hampstead Hill Gdns. NW3 4B 64
Hampstead Ho. NW1 2A 6
(off William Rd.)
Hampstead La. N6 1B 64
NW3 1B 64
Hampstead Lodge NW1 5C 4
(off Bell St.)
Hampstead Mus. 4B 64
(off New End Sq.)
Hampstead Rd. NW1 1A 6 (2G 83)
Hampstead Sq. NW3 3A 64
Hampstead Theatre 7B 64
Hampstead Wlk. E3 1B 86
Hampstead Way NW11 5H 45
Hampstead W. NW6 6J 63
HAMPTON 1F 149
Hampton & Richmond Borough FC 1F 149
Hampton Cl. N11 5A 32
NW6 3J 81
SW20 7E 134
HAMPTON COURT 4J 149
HAMPTON COURT 3J 149
Hampton Ct. N1 6B 66
N22 1G 47
SE16 7K 85
(off King & Queen Wharf)
Hampton Ct. Av. KT8: E Mos 6H 149
Hampton Ct. Bri. KT8: E Mos 4J 149
Hampton Ct. Cres. KT8: E Mos 3H 149
Hampton Ct. Est. KT7: T Ditt 4J 149
Hampton Ct. M. KT8: E Mos 4J 149
(off Feltham Av.)
Hampton Court Palace 4K 149
Hampton Ct. Pde. KT8: E Mos 4J 149
Hampton Ct. Rd. KT1: Ham W 3K 149
KT8: E Mos 3K 149
TW12: E Mos, Hamp 2G 149
Hampton Ct. Way KT7: T Ditt 7J 149
KT8: E Mos 7J 149
Hampton Farm Ind. Est.
TW13: Hanw 3C 130
HAMPTON HILL 5G 131
Hampton Hill Bus. Pk.
TW12: Ham H 5G 131
(off High St.)
Hampton Hill Playhouse Theatre 5G 131
Hampton Ho. DA7: Bex 2H 127
(off Erith Rd.)
SW8 7G 101
(off Ascalon St.)
Hampton La. TW13: Hanw 4C 130
Hampton M. NW10 3K 79
Hampton Open Air Pool 7G 131
Hampton Ri. HA3: Kenton 6E 42
Hampton Rd. CR0: C'don 6C 156
E4 5G 35
E7 5K 69
E11 1F 69
IG1: Ilf 4G 71
KT4: Wor Pk 2C 164
TW2: Twick 3H 131
TW11: Tedd 5H 131
TW12: Ham H 5H 131
Hampton Rd. E. TW13: Hanw 4D 130
Hampton Rd. Ind. Pk. CR0: C'don 6C 156
Hampton Rd. W. TW13: Hanw 3C 130
Hampton Sports & Fitness Cen. 5E 130
Hampton St. SE17 4B 102
HAMPTON WICK 1C 150
Hampton Youth Project (Sports Hall)
6D 130
Ham Ridings TW10: Ham 5F 133
Hamshades Cl. DA15: Sidc 3K 143
Hamston Ho. W8 3K 99
(off Kensington Ct. Pl.)
Ham St. TW10: Ham 1B 132
Ham Vw. CR0: C'don 6A 158
Ham Yd. W1 2C 12 (7H 83)
Hanah Ct. SW19 7F 135
Hanameel St. E16 1J 105
Hana M. E5 4H 67
Hanbury Cl. NW4 3E 44
Hanbury Ct. HA1: Harr 6K 41
Hanbury Dr. E11 7H 51
N21 5E 22
Hanbury Ho. E1 5G 85
(off Hanbury St.)
SW8 7J 101
(off Regent's Bri. Gdns.)
Hanbury M. N1 1C 84
Hanbury Rd. N17 2H 49
W3 2H 97
Hanbury St. E1 5K 9 (5F 85)
Hanbury Wlk. DA5: Bexl 3K 145
Hancock Nunn Ho. NW3 6D 64
(off Fellows Rd.)
Hancock Rd. E3 3E 86
SE19 6D 138
Handa Wlk. N1 6D 66
Hand Ct. WC1 6H 7 (5K 83)
Handcroft Rd. CR0: C'don 7B 156
Handel Bus. Cen. SW8 7E 18 (6J 101)
Handel Cl. HA8: Edg 6A 28
Handel House Mus. 2J 11
(off Brook St.)
Handel Mans. SW13 7E 98
WC1 3F 7
(off Handel St.)
Handel Pde. HA8: Edg 7B 28
(off Whitchurch La.)
Handel Pl. NW10 6K 61
Handel St. WC1 3E 6 (4J 83)
Handel Way HA8: Edg 7B 28
Handen Rd. SE12 5G 123
Handforth Rd. IG1: Ilf 3F 71
SW9 7A 102
Handley Gro. NW2 3F 63
Handley Page Rd. SM6: Wall 7K 167
Handley Rd. E9 7J 67
Handowe Cl. NW4 4C 44
Handside Cl. KT4: Wor Pk 1F 165
Hands Wlk. E16 6J 87
Handsworth Av. E4 6A 36
Handsworth Rd. N17 3D 48
Handtrough Way IG11: Bark 2F 89
Hanford Cl. SW18 1J 135
Hanford Row SW19 6E 134
Hanger Ct. W5 4F 79
Hanger Grn. W5 4G 79
HANGER HILL 4F 79
HANGER LANE 3E 78
Hanger La. W5 2E 78
Hanger Va. La. W5 6F 79
(not continuous)
Hanger Vw. Way W3 6G 79
Hanging Sword All. EC4 1K 13
Hankey Ho. SE1 7F 15
(off Manciple St.)
Hankey Pl. SE1 7F 15 (2D 102)
Hankins La. NW7 2F 29
Hanley Gdns. N4 1K 65
Hanley Pl. BR3: Beck 7C 140
Hanley Rd. N4 1J 65
Hanmer Wlk. N7 2K 65
Hannaford Wlk. E3 4D 86
Hannah Barlow Ho. SW8 1K 119
Hannah Bldg. E1 6H 85
(off Watney St.)
Hannah Cl. BR3: Beck 3E 158
NW10 4J 61
Hannah Mary Way SE1 4G 103
Hannah M. SM6: Wall 7G 167
Hannay Ho. SW15 6G 117

Hannay La.—Harleyford

Hannay La. N8 7H **47**
Hannay Wlk. SW16 2H **137**
Hannell Rd. SW6 7G **99**
Hannen Rd. SE27 3B **138**
Hannibal Rd. E1 5J **85**
TW19: Stanw 7A **110**
Hannibal Way CR0: Wadd 5K **167**
Hannington Rd. SW4 3F **119**
Hanno Cl. SM6: Wall 7H **167**
Hanover Av. E16 1J **105**
TW13: Felt 1J **129**
Hanover Circ. UB3: Hayes 6E **74**
Hanover Cl. SM3: Cheam 4G **165**
TW9: Kew 7G **97**
Hanover Ct. HA4: Ruis 3J **57**
NW9 3A **44**
SE19 7G ***139***
(off Anerley Rd.)
SW15 4B **116**
W12 1C ***98***
(off Uxbridge Rd.)
Hanover Dr. BR7: Chst 4G **143**
Hanover Flats *W1 2H* ***11***
(off Binney St.)
Hanover Gdns. IG6: Ilf 1G **53**
SE11 6A **102**
Hanover Ga. NW1 2D **4** (3C **82**)
Hanover Ga. Mans. NW1 3D **4** (4C **82**)
Hanover Ho. *E14 1B* ***104***
(off Westferry Cir.)
NW8 1C **4**
SW9 3A **120**
Hanover Mans. *SW2 5A* ***120***
(off Barnwell Rd.)
Hanover Mead NW11 5G **45**
Hanover Pk. SE15 1G **121**
Hanover Pl. E3 3B **86**
WC2 1F **13** (6J **83**)
Hanover Rd. N15 4F **49**
NW10 7E **62**
SW19 7A **136**
Hanover Sq. W1 1K **11** (6F **83**)
Hanover Steps W2 1D **10**
Hanover St. CR0: C'don 3B **168**
W1 1K **11** (6F **83**)
Hanover Ter. NW1 2E **4** (3C **82**)
TW7: Isle 1A **114**
Hanover Ter. M. NW1 2D **4** (3C **82**)
Hanover Trad. Est. N7 5J **65**
Hanover Way DA6: Bex 3D **126**
Hanover W. Ind. Est. NW10 3K **79**
Hanover Yd. *N1 2C* ***84***
(off Noel Rd.)
Hansa Cl. UB2: S'hall 3A **94**
Hansard M. W14 2F **99**
Hansart Way EN2: Enf 1F **23**
Hanscomb M. SW4 4G **119**
Hans Ct. SW3 1E **16**
Hans Cres. SW1 1E **16** (3D **100**)
Hanseatic Wlk. EC4 3E **14**
Hanselin Cl. HA7: Stan 5E **26**
Hansen Dr. N21 5E **22**
Hanshaw Dr. HA8: Edg 1K **43**
Hansler Ct. *SW19 1G* ***135***
(off Princes Way)
Hansler Gro. KT8: E Mos 4H **149**
Hansler Rd. SE22 5F **121**
Hansol Rd. DA6: Bex 5E **126**
Hansom Ter. *BR1: Brom 1K* ***159***
(off Freelands Gro.)
Hanson Cl. BR3: Beck 6D **140**
SW12 7F **119**
SW14 3J **115**
UB7: W Dray 3B **92**
Hanson Ct. E17 6D **50**
Hanson Gdns. UB1: S'hall 2C **94**
Hanson Ho. *E1 7G* ***85***
(off Pinchin St.)
Hanson St. W1 5A **6** (5G **83**)
Hans Pl. SW1 1F **17** (3D **100**)
Hans Rd. SW3 1E **16** (3D **100**)
Hans St. SW1 2F **17** (3D **100**)
Hanway Pl. W1 7C **6** (6H **83**)
Hanway Rd. W7 6H **77**
Hanway St. W1 7C **6** (6H **83**)
HANWELL 1K **95**
Hanwell Fitness Cen. 1K **95**
Hanwell Ho. *W2 5J* ***81***
(off Gt. Western Rd.)
HANWORTH 4B **130**
Hanworth Ho. SE5 7B **102**
Hanworth Rd. TW3: Houn 1C **130**
TW4: Houn 1C **130**
TW12: Hamp 4D **130**
TW13: Felt 1K **129**
TW16: Sun 7J **129**
(not continuous)
Hanworth Ter. TW3: Houn 4F **113**
Hanworth Trad. Est. TW13: Hanw 3C **130**
Hapgood Cl. UB6: G'frd 5H **59**
Harad's Pl. E1 7G **85**
Harbans Ct. SL3: Poyle 4A **174**
Harben Pde. *NW3 7A* ***64***
(off Finchley Rd.)
Harben Rd. NW6 7A **64**
Harberson Rd. E15 1H **87**
SW12 1F **137**
Harberton Rd. N19 1G **65**
Harbet Rd. E4 5F **35**
N18 5F **35**
W2 6B **4** (5B **82**)
Harbex Cl. DA5: Bexl 7H **127**
Harbinger Rd. E14 4D **104**
Harbledown Ho. *SE1 7E* ***14***
(off Manciple St.)
Harbledown Rd. SW6 1J **117**
Harbord Cl. SE5 2D **120**
Harbord Ho. *SE16 4K* ***103***
(off Cope St.)
Harbord St. SW6 1F **117**
Harborough Av. DA15: Sidc 7J **125**
Harborough Rd. SW16 4K **137**
Harbour Av. SW10 1A **118**
Harbour Cl. CR4: Mitc 1E **154**
Harbour Club Leisure Cen., The 2A **118**
Harbour Club Notting Hill 5J **81**
Harbour Exchange Sq. E14 2D **104**
Harbour Quay E14 1E **104**
Harbour Reach SW6 1A **118**
Harbour Rd. SE5 3C **120**
Harbour Yd. SW10 1A **118**
Harbridge Av. SW15 7B **116**
Harbury Rd. SM5: Cars 7C **166**
Harbut Rd. SW11 4B **118**
(not continuous)
Harcombe Rd. N16 3E **66**
Harcourt Av. DA15: Sidc 6C **126**
E12 4D **70**
HA8: Edg 3D **28**
SM6: Wall 4F **167**
Harcourt Bldgs. EC4 2J **13**
Harcourt Cl. TW7: Isle 3A **114**
Harcourt Fld. SM6: Wall 4F **167**
Harcourt Ho. W1 7J **5**
Harcourt Lodge SM6: Wall 4F **167**
Harcourt Rd. CR7: Thor H 6K **155**
DA6: Bex 4E **126**
E15 2H **87**
N22 1H **47**
SE4 3B **122**
SM6: Wall 4F **167**
SW19 7J **135**
Harcourt St. W1 6D **4** (5C **82**)
Harcourt Ter. SW10 5K **99**
Hardcastle Cl. CR0: C'don 6G **157**
Hardcastle Ho. *SE14 1A* ***122***
(off Loring Rd.)
Hardcourts Cl. BR4: W W'ck 3D **170**
Hardel Ri. SW2 1B **138**
Hardel Wlk. SW2 7A **120**
Harden Ct. SE7 4C **106**
Harden Ho. SE5 2E **120**
Harden's Manorway SE7 3B **106**
(not continuous)
Harders Rd. SE15 2H **121**
Hardess St. SE24 3C **120**
Hardie Cl. NW10 5K **61**
Hardie Rd. RM10: Dag 3J **73**
Harding Cl. CR0: C'don 3F **169**
SE17 6C **102**
Hardinge Cl. UB8: Hil 5D **74**
Hardinge Cres. SE18 3G **107**
Hardinge La. E1 6J **85**
(not continuous)
Hardinge Rd. N18 6K **33**
NW10 1D **80**
Hardinge St. E1 7J **85**
(not continuous)
Harding Ho. *SW13 6D* ***98***
(off Wyatt Dr.)
UB3: Hayes 6K **75**
Harding Rd. DA7: Bex 2F **127**
Harding's Cl. KT2: King T 1F **151**
Hardings La. SE20 6K **139**
Hardington *NW1 7E* ***64***
(off Belmont St.)
Hardman Rd. KT2: King T 2E **150**
SE7 5K **105**
Hardwick Cl. HA7: Stan 5H **27**
Hardwick Ct. DA8: Erith 6K **109**
Hardwicke Av. TW5: Hest 1E **112**
Hardwicke M. WC1 2H **7**
Hardwicke Rd. N13 6D **32**
TW10: Ham 4C **132**
W4 4K **97**
Hardwicke St. IG11: Bark 1G **89**
Hardwick Grn. W13 5B **78**
Hardwick Ho. *NW8 3D* ***4***
(off Lilestone St.)
Hardwick Pl. SW16 7G **137**
Hardwick St. EC1 2K **7** (3A **84**)
Hardwick's Way SW18 5J **117**
Hardwidge St. SE1 6G **15** (2E **102**)
Hardy Av. E16 1J **105**
HA4: Ruis 5K **57**
Hardy Cl. EN5: Barn 6B **20**
HA5: Pinn 7B **40**
SE16 2K **103**
Hardy Cotts. SE10 6F **105**
Hardy Ct. *SW17 3B* ***136***
(off Grosvenor Way)
Hardy Ho. SW4 7G **119**
SW18 7K **117**
Hardying Ho. E17 4A **50**
Hardy Pas. N22 1K **47**
Hardy Rd. E4 6G **35**
SE3 7H **105**
SW19 7K **135**
Hardy's M. KT8: E Mos 4J **149**
Hardy Way EN2: Enf 1F **23**
Hare & Billet Rd. SE3 1F **123**
Harebell Dr. E6 5E **88**
Harecastle Cl. UB4: Yead 4C **76**
Hare Ct. EC4 1J **13**
Harecourt Rd. N1 6C **66**
Haredale Ho. *SE16 2G* ***103***
(off East La.)
Haredale Rd. SE24 4C **120**
Haredon Cl. SE23 7K **121**
HAREFIELD 1A **38**
Harefield Cl. EN2: Enf 1F **23**
Harefield Grn. NW7 6K **29**
Harefield M. SE4 3B **122**
Harefield Rd. DA14: Sidc 2D **144**
N8 5H **47**
SE4 3B **122**
SW16 7K **137**
UB8: Uxb 5A **56**
Hare Marsh E2 4G **85**
Harepit Cl. CR2: S Croy 7B **168**
Hare Pl. *EC4 1K* ***13***
(off Fleet St.)
Hare Row E2 2H **85**
Haresfield Rd.
RM10: Dag 6G **73**
Hare St. SE18 3E **106**
Hare Wlk. N1 2E **84**
(not continuous)
Harewood Av. NW1 4D **4** (4C **82**)
UB5: N'olt 7D **58**
Harewood Cl. UB5: N'olt 7D **58**
Harewood Dr. IG5: Ilf 2D **52**
Harewood Pl. W1 1K **11** (6F **83**)
Harewood Rd. CR2: S Croy 6E **168**
SW19 6C **136**
TW7: Isle 7K **95**
Harewood Row NW1 5D **4** (5C **82**)
Harewood Ter. UB2: S'hall 4D **94**
Harfield Gdns. SE5 3E **120**
Harfield Rd. TW16: Sun 2B **148**
Harfleur Ct. *SE11 4B* ***102***
(off Opal St.)
Harford Cl. E4 7J **25**
Harford Ho. *SE5 6C* ***102***
(off Bethwin Rd.)
W11 5H **81**
Harford M. N19 3H **65**
Harford Rd. E4 7J **25**
Harford St. E1 4A **86**
Harford Wlk. N2 4B **46**
Harfst Way BR8: Swan 7J **145**
Hargood Cl. HA3: Kenton 6E **42**
Hargood Rd. SE3 1A **124**
Hargrave Mans. N19 2H **65**
Hargrave Pk. N19 2G **65**
Hargrave Pl. N7 5H **65**
Hargrave Rd. N19 2G **65**
Hargraves Ho. *W12 7D* ***80***
(off White City Est.)
Hargwyne St. SW9 3K **119**
Hari Cl. UB5: N'olt 5F **59**
Haringey Mus. 1E **48**
Haringey Pk. N8 6J **47**
Haringey Pas. N8 4A **48**
Haringey Rd. N8 4J **47**
Harington Ter. N9 3J **33**
N18 3J **33**
Harkett Cl. HA3: W'stone 2K **41**
Harkett Ct. HA3: W'stone 2K **41**
Harkness Ct. *SM1: Sutt 1K* ***165***
(off Cleeve Way)
Harkness Ho. *E1 6G* ***85***
(off Christian St.)
Harland Av. CR0: C'don 3F **169**
DA15: Sidc 3H **143**
Harland Cl. SW19 3K **153**
Harland Rd. SE12 1J **141**
Harlands Gro. BR6: Farnb 4F **173**
Harlech Gdns. HA5: Pinn 7B **40**
TW5: Hest 6A **94**
Harlech Rd. N14 3D **32**
Harlech Twr. W3 2J **97**
Harlequin Av. TW8: Bford 6A **96**
Harlequin Cl. TW7: Isle 5J **113**
UB4: Yead 5B **76**
Harlequin Ct. *E1 7G* ***85***
(off Thomas More St.)
NW10 6K ***61***
(off Mitchellbrook Way)
W5 7C **78**
Harlequin Ho. *DA18: Erith 3E* ***108***
(off Kale Rd.)
Harlequin Rd. TW11: Tedd 7B **132**
Harlequins RLFC 7J **113**
Harlequins RUFC 7J **113**
Harlescott Rd. SE15 4K **121**
HARLESDEN 2B **80**
Harlesden Gdns. NW10 1B **80**
Harlesden La. NW10 1C **80**
Harlesden Plaza NW10 2B **80**
Harlesden Rd. NW10 1C **80**
Harleston Cl. E5 2J **67**
Harley Cl. HA0: Wemb 6D **60**
Harley Ct. E11 7J **51**
HA1: Harr 4H **41**
N20 3F **31**
Harley Cres. HA1: Harr 4H **41**
Harleyford BR1: Brom 1K **159**

Harleyford Ct. SE11 . . . . .7G 19
Harleyford Mnr. W3 . . . . .1J 97
(off Edgecote Cl.)
Harleyford Rd. SE11 . . . . . . .7G 19 (6K 101)
Harleyford St. SE11 . . . . . . .7J 19 (6A 102)
Harley Gdns. BR6: Orp 4J 173
SW10 . . . . .5A 100
Harley Gro. E3 . . . . .3B 86
Harley Ho. E11 . . . . .7F 51
E14 . . . . .6B 86
(off Frances Wharf)
NW1 . . . . .4H 5
Harley Pl. W1 . . . . .6J 5 (5F 83)
Harley Rd. HA1: Harr 4H 41
NW3 .7B 64
NW10 . . . . .2A 80
Harley St. W1 . . . . .4J 5 (4F 83)
Harley Vs. NW10 . . . . .2A 80
Harling Cl. SW11 . . . . .2D 118
Harlinger St. SE18 . . . . .3C 106
HARLINGTON 6F 93
Harlington Cl. UB3: Harl 7E 92
HARLINGTON CORNER 1F 111
Harlington Rd. DA7: Bex 3E 126
UB8: Hil 3C 74
Harlington Rd. E. TW13: Felt 7K 111
TW14: Felt 7K 111
Harlington Rd. W. TW14: Felt 6K 111
Harlington Sports Cen., The 4F 93
(off Pinkwell La.)
Harlowe Ho. E8 . . . . .1F 85
(off Clarissa St.)
Harlow Mans. IG11: Bark 7F 71
(off Whiting Av.)
Harlow Rd. N13 . . . . .3J 33
Harlyn Dr. HA5: Eastc 3K 39
Harlynwood SE5 . . . . .7C 102
(off Wyndham Rd.)
Harman Av. IG8: Wfd G 6C 36
Harman Cl. E4 . . . . .4A 36
NW2 .3G 63
SE1 .5G 103
Harman Dr. DA15: Sidc 6K 125
NW2 .3G 63
Harman Ri. IG1: Ilf 4J 71
Harman Rd. EN1: Enf 5A 24
HARMONDSWORTH 2E 174
Harmondsworth La. UB7: Harm, Sip . .6A 92
Harmondsworth Moor Waterside 2C 174
Harmondsworth Moor Waterside Vis. Cen.
. . . . .2C 174
Harmondsworth Rd. UB7: W Dray . . .5A 92
Harmon Ho. SE8 . . . . .4B 104
Harmont Ho. W1 . . . . .6J 5
(off Harley St.)
Harmony Cl. NW11 . . . . .5G 45
SM6: Wall 7J 167
Harmony Pl. SE1 . . . . .5F 103
Harmony Ter. HA2: Harr 1F 59
Harmony Way BR1: Brom 2J 159
NW4 .4E 44
Harmood Gro. NW1 . . . . .7F 65
Harmood Ho. NW1 . . . . .7F 65
(off Harmood St.)
Harmood Pl. NW1 . . . . .7F 65
Harmood St. NW1 . . . . .7F 65
Harmsworth M. SE11 . . . . . .2K 19 (3A 102)
Harmsworth St. SE17 . . . . . .6K 19 (5B 102)
Harmsworth Way N20 . . . . .1C 30
Harold Av. DA17: Belv 5F 109
UB3: Hayes 3H 93
Harold Ct. SE16 . . . . .2K 103
(off Christopher Cl.)
Harold Est. SE1 . . . . .3E 102
Harold Gibbons Ct. SE7 . . . . .6A 106
Harold Ho. E2 . . . . .2K 85
(off Mace St.)
Harold Laski Ho. EC1 . . . . .2B 8
(off Percival St.)
Harold Maddison Ho. SE17 . . . . .5B 102
(off Penton Pl.)
Harold Pl. SE11 . . . . .6J 19 (5A 102)

Harold Rd. E4 . . . . .4K 35
E11 . . . . .1G 69
E13 . . . . .1K 87
IG8: Wfd G 1J 51
N8 . . . . .5K 47
N15 . . . . .5F 49
NW10 . . . . .3K 79
SE19 . . . . .7D 138
SM1: Sutt 4B 166
Haroldstone Rd. E17 . . . . .5K 49
Harold Wilson Ho. SE28 . . . . .1B 108
SW6 .6H 99
(off Clem Attlee Ct.)
Harp All. EC4 . . . . .7A 8 (6B 84)
Harp Bus. Cen., The NW2 . . . . .2C 62
Harpenden Rd. E12 . . . . .2A 70
SE27 . . . . .3B 138
Harpenmead Point NW2 . . . . .2H 63
Harper Cl. N14 . . . . .5B 22
Harper Ho. SW9 . . . . .3B 120
Harper M. SW17 . . . . .3A 136
Harper Rd. E6 . . . . .6D 88
SE1 . . . . .7C 14 (3C 102)
Harpers Ter. N17 . . . . .1F 49
(off Rennels Way)
Harp Island Cl. NW10 . . . . .2K 61
Harp La. EC3 . . . . .3G 15 (7E 84)
Harpley Sq. E1 . . . . .4K 85
Harpour Rd. IG11: Bark 6G 71
Harp Rd. W7 .4K 77
Harpsden St. SW11 . . . . .1E 118
Harpur M. WC1 . . . . .5G 7 (5K 83)
Harpur St. WC1 . . . . .5G 7 (5K 83)
Harraden Rd. SE3 . . . . .1A 124
Harrier Av. E11 . . . . .6K 51
Harrier Cen., The 6K 163
Harrier Ct. TW4: Houn 3C 112
Harrier M. SE28 . . . . .2H 107
Harrier Rd. NW9 . . . . .2A 44
Harriers Cl. W5 . . . . .7E 78
Harrier Way E6 . . . . .5D 88
Harries Rd. UB4: Yead 4A 76
Harriet Cl. E8 . . . . .1G 85
Harriet Gdns. CR0: C'don 2G 169
Harriet Ho. SW6 . . . . .7K 99
(off Wandon Rd.)
Harriet M. DA16: Well 2B 126
(not continuous)
Harriet St. SW1 . . . . .7F 11 (2D 100)
Harriet Tubman Cl. SW2 . . . . .7K 119
Harriet Wlk. SW1 . . . . .7F 11 (2D 100)
Harriet Way WD23: Bush 1C 26
HARRINGAY .5B 48
Harringay Gdns. N8 . . . . .4B 48
Harringay Rd. N15 . . . . .5B 48
(not continuous)
Harrington Cl. CR0: Bedd 2J 167
NW10 . . . . .3K 61
Harrington Ct. CR0: C'don 2D 168
SW7 . . . . .3B 16
(off Harrington Rd.)
W10 . . . . .3H 81
Harrington Gdns. SW7 . . . . .4K 99
Harrington Hill E5 . . . . .1H 67
Harrington Ho. NW1 . . . . .1A 6
(off Harrington St.)
UB10: Ick 4D 56
Harrington Rd. E11 . . . . .1G 69
SE25 .4G 157
SW7 . . . . .3A 16 (4B 100)
Harrington Sq. NW1 . . . . .2G 83
Harrington St. NW1 . . . . . . .1A 6 (2G 83)
(not continuous)
Harrington Way SE18 . . . . .3B 106
Harriott Cl. SE10 . . . . .4H 105
Harriott Ho. E1 . . . . .5J 85
(off Jamaica St.)
Harris Bldgs. E1 . . . . .6G 85
(off Burslem St.)
Harris Cl. EN2: Enf 1G 23
TW3: Houn 1E 112

Harris Ct. HA9: Wemb 3F 61
KT19: Ewe 4K 163
Harris Ho. E3 . . . . .3C 86
(off Alfred St.)
SW9 .3A 120
(off St James's Cres.)
Harris Lodge SE6 . . . . .1E 140
Harrison Cl. N20 . . . . .1H 31
Harrison Ct. E18 . . . . .1J 51
(off Queen Mary Av.)
Harrison Dr. BR1: Brom 4E 160
Harrison Ho. SE17 . . . . .5D 102
(off Brandon St.)
Harrison Rd. NW10 . . . . .1K 79
RM10: Dag 6H 73
Harrisons Ct. SE14 . . . . .6K 103
(off Myers La.)
Harrison's Ri. CR0: Wadd 3B 168
Harrison St. WC1 . . . . .2F 7 (3J 83)
Harrison Way TW17: Shep 5D 146
Harris Rd. DA7: Bex 1E 126
RM9: Dag 5F 73
Harris Sports Cen. 5J 121
Harris St. E17 . . . . .7B 50
SE5 .7D 102
Harris Way TW16: Sun 1G 147
Harrod Cl. NW9 . . . . .4J 43
Harrods 1E 16 (3D 100)
Harrogate Ct. N11 . . . . .6K 31
SE12 . . . . .7J 123
SE26 . . . . .3G 139
(off Droitwich Cl.)
Harrold Ho. NW3 . . . . .7B 64
Harrold Rd. RM8: Dag 5B 72
Harrovian Bus. Village HA1: Harr 7J 41
HARROW 6J 41
Harrow Arts Cen. 7A 26
Harrow Av. EN1: Enf 6A 24
Harroway Rd. SW11 . . . . .2B 118
Harrow Borough FC 4D 58
Harrowby Ho. W1 . . . . .6D 82
(off Harrowby St.)
Harrowby St. W1 . . . . .7D 4 (6C 82)
Harrow Cl. KT9: Chess 7D 162
Harrow Club Sports Cen. 7F 81
Harrowdene Cl. HA0: Wemb 4D 60
Harrowdene Gdns. TW11: Tedd 6A 132
Harrowdene Rd. HA0: Wemb 3D 60
Harrow Dr. N9 . . . . .1A 34
Harrowes Meade HA8: Edg 3B 28
Harrow Flds. Gdns. HA1: Harr 3J 59
Harrowgate Ho. E9 . . . . .6K 67
Harrowgate Rd. E9 . . . . .6A 68
Harrow Grn. E11 . . . . .3G 69
Harrow La. E14 . . . . .7D 86
Harrow Leisure Cen. 3K 41
Harrow Lodge NW8 . . . . .3A 4
(off Northwick Ter.)
Harrow Mnr. Way SE2 . . . . .1C 108
SE28 .7C 90
Harrow Mus. & Heritage Cen. 3G 41
HARROW ON THE HILL 1J 59
Harrow Pk. HA1: Harr 2J 59
Harrow Pl. E1 . . . . .7H 9 (6E 84)
HARROW ROAD 7H 61
Harrow Rd. E6 . . . . .1C 88
E11 . . . . .3G 69
HA0: Wemb 4K 59
HA9: Wemb 5G 61
IG1: Ilf 4G 71
IG11: Bark 1J 89
NW10 . . . . .3D 80
SM5: Cars 6C 166
TW14: Bedf 2C 128
W2 . . . . .6A 4 (5A 82)
(not continuous)
W9 . . . . .4F 81
W10 . . . . .4G 81
Harrow Rd. Bri. W2 . . . . .5A 82
HARROW ROAD JUNC. 6H 61
Harrow Safari Cinema 5K 41
Harrow St. NW1 . . . . .5D 4

Harrow Vw. HA1: Harr 2G 41
HA2: Harr 2G 41
UB3: Hayes 6J 75
UB10: Hil 3E 74
Harrow Vw. Rd. W5 . . . . .4B 78
Harrow Way TW17: Shep 2E 146
HARROW WEALD 1J 41
Harrow Weald Pk. HA3: Hrw W 6C 26
Harry Cl. CR0: C'don 6C 156
Harry Day M. SE27 . . . . .3C 138
Harry Hinkins Ho. SE17 . . . . .5C 102
(off Bronti Cl.)
Harry Lambourn Ho. SE15 . . . . .7H 103
(off Gervase St.)
Harry Zeital Way E5 . . . . .2J 67
Hartcliff Ct. W7 . . . . .2K 95
Hart Cl. CR0: C'don 3B 168
Hart Ct. E6 . . . . .7E 70
Harte Rd. TW3: Houn 2D 112
Hartfield Av. UB5: N'olt 2K 75
Hartfield Cres. BR4: W W'ck 3J 171
SW19 . . . . .7H 135
Hartfield Gro. SE20 . . . . .1J 157
Hartfield Ho. UB5: N'olt 2K 75
(off Hartfield Av.)
Hartfield Rd. BR4: W W'ck 4J 171
KT9: Chess 5D 162
SW19 . . . . .7H 135
Hartfield Ter. E3 . . . . .2C 86
Hartford Av. HA3: Kenton 3A 42
Hartford Rd. DA5: Bexl 6G 127
KT19: Ewe 6H 163
Hart Gro. UB1: S'hall 5E 76
W5 . . . . .1G 97
Hart Gro. Ct. W5 . . . . .1G 97
Hartham Cl. N7 . . . . .5J 65
TW7: Isle 1A 114
Hartham Rd. N7 . . . . .5J 65
N17 . . . . .2F 49
TW7: Isle 7K 95
Harting Rd. SE9 . . . . .3C 142
Hartington Cl. BR6: Farnb 5G 173
HA1: Harr 4J 59
Hartington Ct. SW8 . . . . .1J 119
W4 . . . . .7H 97
Hartington Ho. SW1 . . . . .5D 18
(off Drummond Ga.)
Hartington Rd. E16 . . . . .6K 87
E17 . . . . .6A 50
SW8 .1J 119
TW1: Twick 7B 114
UB2: S'hall 3C 94
W4 . . . . .7H 97
W13 .7B 78
Hartismere Rd. SW6 . . . . .7H 99
Hartlake Rd. E9 . . . . .6K 67
Hartland NW1 . . . . .1G 83
(off Royal College St.)
Hartland Cl. HA8: Edg 2B 28
N21 . . . . .6H 23
Hartland Ct. N11 . . . . .5J 31
(off Hartland Rd.)
Hartland Dr. HA4: Ruis 3K 57
HA8: Edg 2B 28
Hartland Rd. E15 . . . . .7H 69
N11 . . . . .5J 31
NW1 . . . . .7F 65
NW6 .2H 81
SM4: Mord 7J 153
TW7: Isle 3A 114
TW12: Ham H 4F 131
Hartlands, The TW5: Cran 6K 93
Hartlands Cl. DA5: Bexl 6F 127
Hartland Way CR0: C'don 3A 170
SM4: Mord 7H 153
Hartlepool Ct. E16 . . . . .1F 107
Hartley Av. E6 . . . . .1C 88
NW7 .5G 29
Hartley Cl. BR1: Brom 2D 160
NW7 .5G 29
Hartley Ho. SE1 . . . . .4F 103
(off Longfield Est.)

Hartley Rd.—Haven Pl.

Hartley Rd. CR0: C'don 7C 156
DA16: Well 7C 108
E11 1H 69
Hartley St. E2 3J 85
(not continuous)
Hart Lodge EN5: Barn 3B 20
Hartmann Rd. E16 1B 106
Hartnoll St. N7 5K 65
Harton Cl. BR1: Brom 1B 160
Harton Lodge *SE8* *1C 122*
(off Harton St.)
Harton Rd. N9 2C 34
Harton St. SE8 1C 122
Hartop Point *SW6* *7G 99*
(off Pellant Rd.)
Hartsbourne Av. WD23: B Hea 2B 26
Hartsbourne Cl. WD23: B Hea 2C 26
Hartsbourne Ct. *UB1: S'hall* *6G 77*
(off Fleming Rd.)
Hartsbourne Pk. WD23: B Hea 2D 26
Hartsbourne Rd. WD23: B Hea 2C 26
Harts Gro. IG8: Wfd G 5D 36
Hartshill Cl. UB10: Hil 7D 56
Hartshorn All. EC3 1H 15
Hartshorn Gdns. E6 4E 88
Harts La. IG11: Bark 6F 71
SE14 1A 122
Hartslock Dr. SE2 2D 108
Hartsmead Rd. SE9 2D 142
Hart St. EC3 2H 15 (7E 84)
Hartsway EN3: Pond E 4D 24
Hartswood Gdns. W12 3B 98
Hartswood Grn. WD23: B Hea 2C 26
Hartswood Rd. W12 2B 98
Hartsworth Cl. E13 2H 87
Hartville Rd. SE18 4J 107
Hartwell Cl. SW2 1K 137
Hartwell Dr. E4 6K 35
Hartwell Ho. *SE7* *5K 105*
(off Troughton Rd.)
Hartwell St. E8 6F 67
Harvard Ct. NW6 5K 63
Harvard Hill W4 6H 97
Harvard Ho. *SE17* *6B 102*
(off Doddington Gro.)
Harvard La. W4 5J 97
Harvard Rd. SE13 5E 122
TW7: Isle 1J 113
W4 5H 97
Harvel Cl. BR5: St P 3K 161
Harvel Cres. SE2 5D 108
Harvest Bank Rd. BR4: W W'ck 3H 171
Harvest Ct. TW17: Shep 4C 146
Harvesters Cl. TW7: Isle 5H 113
Harvest La. KT7: T Ditt 6A 150
Harvest Rd. TW13: Felt 4J 129
Harvey Ct. E17 5C 50
Harvey Dr. TW12: Hamp 1F 149
Harvey Gdns. E11 1H 69
SE7 5A 106
Harvey Ho. *E1* *4H 85*
(off Brady St.)
N1 *1D 84*
(off Colville Est.)
RM6: Chad H 4D 54
SW1 *6D 18*
(off Aylesford St.)
TW8: Bford 5E 96
Harvey Lodge *W9* *5J 81*
(off Admiral Wlk.)
Harvey M. *N8* *5K 47*
(off Harvey Rd.)
Harvey Rd. E11 1G 69
IG1: Ilf 5F 71
KT12: Walt T 7H 147
N8 5K 47
SE5 1D 120
(not continuous)
TW4: Houn 7D 112
UB5: N'olt 7A 58
UB10: Hil 2C 74
Harvey's Bldgs. WC2 3F 13 (7J 83)
Harveys La. RM7: Rush G 2K 73
Harvey St. N1 1D 84
Harvill Rd. DA14: Sidc 5E 144
Harvil Rd. UB9: Hare 6A 38
UB10: Ick 6A 38
Harvington Wlk. E8 7G 67
Harvist Est. N7 4A 66
Harvist Rd. NW6 2F 81
Harwell Cl. HA4: Ruis 1F 57
Harwell Pas. N2 4D 46
Harwicke Ho. *E3* *3D 86*
(off Bromley High St.)
Harwood Av. BR1: Brom 2K 159
CR4: Mitc 3C 154
Harwood Cl. HA0: Wemb 4D 60
N12 6H 31
Harwood Ct. *N1* *1D 84*
(off Colville Est.)
SW15 4E 116
Harwood Dr. UB10: Hil 1B 74
Harwood M. SW6 7J 99
Harwood Point SE16 2B 104
Harwood Rd. SW6 7J 99
Harwoods Yd. N21 7F 23
Harwood Ter. SW6 1K 117
Haselbury Rd. N9 4K 33
N18 4K 33
Haseley End SE23 7J 121
Haselrigge Rd. SW4 4H 119
Haseltine Rd. SE26 4B 140
Haselwood Dr. EN2: Enf 4G 23
Haskard Rd. RM9: Dag 4D 72
Hasker St. SW3 3D 16 (4C 100)
Haslam Av. SM3: Sutt 1G 165
Haslam Cl. N1 7A 66
UB10: Ick 2E 56
Haslam Ct. N11 4A 32
Haslam Ho. *N1* *7C 66*
(off Canonbury Rd.)
Haslam St. SE15 7F 103
Haslemere Av.
CR4: Mitc 2B 154
EN4: E Barn 1J 31
NW4 6F 45
SW18 2K 135
TW5: Cran 2A 112
W7 3A 96
W13 3A 96
Haslemere Bus. Cen.
EN1: Enf 4C 24
Haslemere Cl. SM6: Wall 5J 167
TW12: Hamp 5D 130
Haslemere Gdns. N3 3H 45
Haslemere Ind. Est. SW18 2K 135
Haslemere Rd. CR7: Thor H 5B 156
DA7: Bex 2F 127
IG3: Ilf 2K 71
N8 7H 47
N21 2G 33
Hasler Cl. SE28 7B 90
Haslers Wharf *E3* *1A 86*
(off Old Ford Rd.)
Haslett Rd. TW17: Shep 2G 147
Hasluck Gdns.
EN5: New Bar 6E 20
Hassard St. E2 1K 9 (2F 85)
Hassendean Rd. SE3 7K 105
Hassett Rd. E9 6K 67
Hassocks Cl. SE26 3H 139
Hassocks Rd. SW16 1H 155
Hassock Wood BR2: Kes 4B 172
Hassop Rd. NW2 4F 63
Hassop Wlk. SE9 4C 142
Hasted Rd. SE7 5B 106
Haste Hill Station
Ruislip Lido Railway 3G 39
Hastings Av. IG6: Ilf 4G 53
Hastings Cl. EN5: New Bar 4F 21
HA0: Wemb 4C 60
SE15 7G 103
Hastings Ct. TW11: Tedd 5H 131
Hastings Dr. KT6: Surb 6C 150
Hastings Ho. EN3: Enf H 2D 24
SE18 *4D 106*
(off Mulgrave Rd.)
W12 *7D 80*
(off White City Est.)
W13 7B 78
WC1 *2E 6*
(off Hastings St.)
Hastings Pl. *CR0: C'don* *1F 169*
(off Hastings Rd.)
Hastings Rd. BR2: Brom 1C 172
CR0: C'don 1F 169
N11 5B 32
N17 3D 48
W13 7B 78
Hastings St. SE18 3G 107
WC1 2E 6 (3J 83)
Hastingwood Ct. E17 5D 50
Hastingwood Trad. Est. N18 6E 34
Hastoe Cl. UB4: Yead 4C 76
Hasty Cl. CR4: Mitc 1F 155
Hat & Mitre Ct. EC1 4B 8
Hatch, The EN3: Enf H 1E 24
Hatcham M. Bus. Cen. *SE14* *1K 121*
(off Hatcham Pk. Rd.)
Hatcham Pk. M. SE14 1K 121
Hatcham Pk. Rd. SE14 1K 121
Hatcham Rd. SE15 6J 103
Hatchard Rd. N19 2H 65
Hatchcroft NW4 3D 44
HATCH END 7A 26
Hatch End Swimming Pool 7A 26
Hatchers M. SE1 7H 15
Hatchett Rd. TW14: Bedf 1E 128
Hatchfield Ho. *N15* *6E 48*
(off Albert Rd.)
Hatch Gro. RM6: Chad H 4E 54
Hatch La. E4 4A 36
(not continuous)
UB7: Harm 3E 174
Hatch Pl. KT2: King T 5F 133
Hatch Rd. SW16 2J 155
Hatch Side IG7: Chig 5K 37
Hatchwood Cl. IG8: Wfd G 4C 36
Hatcliffe Almshouses *SE10* *5G 105*
(off Tuskar St.)
Hatcliffe Cl. SE3 3H 123
Hatcliffe St. SE10 5H 105
Hatfeild Mead SM4: Mord 5J 153
Hatfield Cl. CR4: Mitc 4B 154
IG6: Ilf 3F 53
SE14 7K 103
Hatfield Ct. SE3 7J 105
UB5: N'olt *3A 76*
(off Canberra Dr.)
Hatfield Ho. EC1 4C 8
Hatfield M. RM9: Dag 7E 72
Hatfield Rd. E15 5G 69
RM9: Dag 6E 72
W4 2K 97
W13 1A 96
Hatfields SE1 4K 13 (1A 102)
Hathaway Cl. BR2: Brom 1D 172
HA4: Ruis 4H 57
HA7: Stan 5F 27
Hathaway Cres. E12 6D 70
Hathaway Gdns. RM6: Chad H 5D 54
W13 5A 78
Hathaway Ho. N1 1G 9 (2E 84)
Hathaway Rd. CR0: C'don 7B 156
Hatherleigh Cl. KT9: Chess 5D 162
NW7 6A 30
SM4: Mord 4J 153
Hatherleigh Rd. HA4: Ruis 2J 57
Hatherley Ct. *W2* *6K 81*
(off Hatherley Gro.)
Hatherley Cres. DA14: Sidc 2A 144
Hatherley Gdns. E6 3B 88
N8 6J 47
Hatherley Gro. W2 6K 81
Hatherley Ho. E17 4C 50
Hatherley M. E17 4C 50
Hatherley Rd. DA14: Sidc 4A 144
E17 4B 50
TW9: Kew 1F 115
Hatherley St. SW1 4B 18 (4G 101)
Hathern Gdns. SE9 4E 142
Hatherop Rd. TW12: Hamp 7D 130
Hathersage Ct. N1 5D 66
Hathorne Cl. SE15 2H 121
Hathway St. SE14 2K 121
Hathway Ter. *SE14* *2K 121*
(off Hathway St.)
Hatley Av. IG6: Ilf 4G 53
Hatley Cl. N11 5J 31
Hatley Rd. N4 2K 65
Hatteraick St. SE16 2J 103
Hattersfield Cl. DA17: Belv 4F 109
HATTON 4H 111
Hatton Cl. SE18 7H 107
HATTON CROSS 4H 111
Hatton Cross Cen.
TW6: H'row A 3H 111
Hatton Gdn. EC1 5K 7 (5A 84)
Hatton Gdns. CR4: Mitc 5D 154
Hatton Grn. TW14: Felt 4J 111
Hatton Gro. UB7: W Dray 2A 92
Hatton Ho. *KT1: King T* *2F 151*
(off Victoria Rd.)
Hatton Pl. EC1 5K 7 (5A 84)
Hatton Rd. CR0: C'don 1A 168
TW14: Bedf, Felt 7E 110
Hatton Rd. Sth. TW14: Felt 4H 111
Hatton Row NW8 4B 4
Hatton St. NW8 4B 4 (4B 82)
Hatton Wlk. *EN2: Enf* *4J 23*
(off London Rd.)
Hatton Wall EC1 5K 7 (5A 84)
Haughmond N12 4E 30
Haunch of Venison Yd. W1 1J 11 (6F 83)
Hauteville Ct. Gdns. *W6* *3B 98*
(off South Side)
Havana Rd. SW19 2J 135
Havannah St. E14 2C 104
Havant Rd. E17 3E 50
Havelock Cl. W12 7D 80
Havelock Ct. *UB2: S'hall* *3D 94*
(off Havelock Rd.)
Havelock Ho. *SE1* *4F 103*
(off Fort Rd.)
SE23 1J 139
Havelock Pl. HA1: Harr 6J 41
Havelock Rd. BR2: Brom 4A 160
CR0: C'don 2F 169
DA17: Belv 4F 109
HA3: W'stone 3J 41
N17 2G 49
SW19 5A 136
UB2: S'hall 3C 94
Havelock St. IG1: Ilf 2F 71
N1 1J 83
Havelock Ter. SW8 1F 119
Havelock Ter. Arches *SW8* *1F 119*
(off Havelock Ter.)
Havelock Wlk. SE23 1J 139
Haven, The TW9: Rich 3G 115
TW16: Sun 7J 129
Haven Cl. DA14: Sidc 6C 144
SE9 3D 142
SW19 3F 135
UB4: Hayes 4G 75
Haven Ct. BR3: Beck 2E 158
KT5: Surb 6F 151
Haven Grn. W5 6D 78
Haven Grn. Ct. W5 6D 78
Havenhurst Ri. EN2: Enf 2F 23
Haven La. W5 6E 78
Haven Lodge *EN1: Enf* *6K 23*
(off Village Rd.)
SE18 *4F 107*
(off Vincent Rd.)
Haven M. E3 5B 86
N1 7A 66
Haven Pl. W5 7D 78

286 A-Z London

Havenpool—Hayward's Pl.

Havenpool *NW8* 1K **81**
(off Abbey Rd.)
Haven Rd. TW15: Ashf 4D **128**
Haven St. NW1 7F **65**
Havenwood HA9: Wemb 3H **61**
Haverfield Gdns. TW9: Kew 7G **97**
Haverfield Rd. E3 3A **86**
Haverford Way HA8: Edg 1F **43**
Haverhill Rd. E4 1K **35**
SW12 1G **137**
Havering *NW1* 7F **65**
(off Castlehaven Rd.)
Havering Dr. RM1: Rom 4K **55**
Havering Gdns. RM6: Chad H 5C **54**
Havering Mus. 5K **55**
Havering Rd.
RM1: Have B, Rom 3K **55**
Havering St. E1 6K **85**
Havering Way IG11: Bark 3B **90**
Haversham Cl. TW1: Twick 6D **114**
Haversham Ct. UB6: G'frd 6K **59**
Haversham Pl. N6 2D **64**
Haverstock Hill NW3 5C **64**
Haverstock Pl. *N1* 1B **8**
(off Haverstock St.)
Haverstock Rd. NW5 5E **64**
Haverstock St. N1 1B **8** (2B **84**)
Haverthwaite Rd. BR6: Orp 2H **173**
Havilland Ct. HA8: Edg 4A **28**
Havil St. SE5 7E **102**
Havisham Apartments *E15* 6F **69**
(off Grove Cres. Rd.)
Havisham Ho. SE16 2G **103**
Havisham Pl. SE19 7B **138**
Hawarden Gro. SE24 7C **120**
Hawarden Hill NW2 3C **62**
Hawarden Rd. E17 4K **49**
Hawbridge Rd. E11 1F **69**
Hawes Ho. E17 4K **49**
Hawes La. BR4: W W'ck 1E **170**
Hawes Rd. BR1: Brom 1K **159**
(not continuous)
N18 6C **34**
Hawes St. N1 7B **66**
Haweswater Ho. TW7: Isle 5K **113**
Hawgood St. E3 5C **86**
Hawkdene E4 6J **25**
Hawke Ct. *UB4: Yead* 4A **76**
(off Perth Av.)
Hawke Ho. *E1* 4K **85**
(off Ernest St.)
Hawke Pk. Rd. N22 3B **48**
Hawke Pl. SE16 2K **103**
Hawker *NW9* 1B **44**
(off Everglade Strand)
Hawker Ct. *KT1: King T* 2F **151**
(off Church Rd.)
Hawke Rd. SE19 6D **138**
Hawker Pl. E17 2E **50**
Hawker Rd. CR0: Wadd 6A **168**
Hawkesbury Rd. SW15 5D **116**
Hawkesfield Rd. SE23 2A **140**
Hawkesley Cl. TW1: Twick 4A **132**
Hawkes Rd. CR4: Mitc 1D **154**
TW14: Felt 7J **111**
Hawkesworth Cl. HA6: Nwood 1G **39**
Hawke Twr. SE14 6A **104**
Hawkewood Rd. TW16: Sun 3J **147**
Hawkfield Ct. TW7: Isle 2J **113**
Hawkhurst Gdns. KT9: Chess 4E **162**
Hawkhurst Rd. SW16 1H **155**
Hawkhurst Way BR4: W W'ck 2D **170**
KT3: N Mald 5K **151**
Hawkinge *N17* 2D **48**
(off Gloucester Rd.)
Hawkins Cl. HA1: Harr 7H **41**
NW7 5E **28**
Hawkins Ct. SE18 4C **106**
Hawkins Ho. *SE8* 6C **104**
(off New King St.)
SW1 7B **18**
(off Dolphin Sq.)
Hawkins Rd. NW10 7A **62**
TW11: Tedd 6B **132**
Hawkins Ter. SE7 5C **106**
Hawkins Way SE6 5C **140**
Hawkley Gdns. SE27 2B **138**
Hawkridge Cl.
RM6: Chad H 6C **54**
Hawksbrook La. BR3: Beck 6D **158**
(not continuous)
Hawkshaw Cl. SW2 7J **119**
Hawkshead NW1 1A **6**
Hawkshead Cl. BR1: Brom 7G **141**
Hawkshead Rd. NW10 7B **62**
W4 2A **98**
Hawkslade Rd. SE15 5K **121**
Hawksley Rd. N16 3E **66**
Hawks M. SE10 7E **104**
Hawksmoor Cl. E6 6C **88**
SE18 5J **107**
Hawksmoor M. E1 7H **85**
Hawksmoor Pl. *E2* 3K **9**
(off Cheshire St.)
Hawksmoor St. W6 6F **99**
Hawksmouth E4 7K **25**
Hawks Pas. *KT1: King T* 2F **151**
(off Minerva Rd.)
Hawks Rd. KT1: King T 2F **151**
Hawkstone Rd. SE16 4J **103**
Hawksworth Ho. BR1: Brom 2J **159**
Hawkwell Ct. E4 3K **35**
Hawkwell Ho. RM8: Dag 1G **73**
Hawkwell Wlk. *N1* 1C **84**
(off Maldon Cl.)
Hawkwood Cres. E4 6J **25**
Hawkwood La. BR7: Chst 1G **161**
Hawkwood Mt. E5 1H **67**
Hawlands Dr. HA5: Pinn 7C **40**
Hawley Cl. TW12: Hamp 6D **130**
Hawley Cres. NW1 7F **65**
Hawley M. NW1 7F **65**
Hawley Rd. N18 5E **34**
NW1 7F **65**
Hawley St. NW1 7F **65**
Hawley Way TW15: Ashf 5C **128**
Hawstead Rd. SE6 6D **122**
Hawsted IG9: Buck H 1E **36**
Hawthorn Av. CR7: Thor H 1B **156**
E3 1B **86**
N13 5D **32**
Hawthorn Cen., The HA1: Harr 5K **41**
Hawthorn Cl. BR5: Pet W 6H **161**
TW5: Cran 7K **93**
TW12: Hamp 5E **130**
Hawthorn Cotts. *DA16: Well* 3A **126**
(off Hook La.)
Hawthorn Ct. *HA5: Pinn* 2A **40**
(off Rickmansworth Rd.)
TW9: Kew 1H **115**
TW15: Ashf 7E **128**
Hawthorn Cres. SW17 5E **136**
Hawthornden Cl. N12 6H **31**
Hawthorndene Cl. BR2: Hayes 2H **171**
Hawthorndene Rd. BR2: Hayes 2H **171**
Hawthorn Dr. BR4: W W'ck 4G **171**
HA2: Harr 6E **40**
Hawthorne Av. CR4: Mitc 2B **154**
HA3: Kenton 6A **42**
HA4: Ruis 6K **39**
SM5: Cars 7E **166**
Hawthorne Cl. BR1: Brom 3D **160**
N1 6E **66**
SM1: Sutt 2A **166**
Hawthorne Ct. HA6: Nwood 2J **39**
W5 1E **96**
Hawthorne Cres. UB7: W Dray 2B **92**
Hawthorne Farm Av. UB5: N'olt 1C **76**
Hawthorne Gro. NW9 7J **43**
Hawthorne Ho. N15 5G **49**
SW1 6B **18**
(off Churchill Gdns.)
Hawthorne M. UB6: G'frd 6G **77**
Hawthorne Pl. UB3: Hayes 7H **75**
Hawthorne Rd. BR1: Brom 3C **160**
E17 3C **50**
Hawthorne Way N9 2A **34**
Hawthorn Gdns. W5 3D **96**
Hawthorn Gro. EN2: Enf 1J **23**
SE20 7H **139**
Hawthorn Hatch TW8: Bford 7B **96**
Hawthorn M. NW7 1G **45**
Hawthorn Pl. DA8: Erith 5J **109**
Hawthorn Rd. DA6: Bex 4F **127**
IG9: Buck H 4G **37**
N8 3H **47**
N18 6A **34**
NW10 7C **62**
SM1: Sutt 6C **166**
SM6: Wall 7F **167**
TW8: Bford 7B **96**
TW13: Felt 1J **129**
Hawthorns *CR2: S Croy* 4B **168**
(off Bramley Hill)
IG8: Wfd G 3D **36**
Hawthorns, The KT17: Ewe 7B **164**
SL3: Poyle 4A **174**
Hawthorn Ter. DA15: Sidc 5K **125**
N19 1H **65**
(off Calverley Gro.)
Hawthorn Wlk. W10 4G **81**
Hawthorn Way TW17: Shep 4F **147**
Hawtrey Av. UB5: N'olt 2B **76**
Hawtrey Dr. HA4: Ruis 7J **39**
Hawtrey Rd. NW3 7C **64**
Haxted Rd. BR1: Brom 1K **159**
Hay Cl. E15 7G **69**
Haycroft Gdns. NW10 1C **80**
Haycroft Rd. KT6: Surb 2D **162**
SW2 5J **119**
Hay Currie St. E14 6D **86**
Hayday Rd. E16 5J **87**
(not continuous)
Hayden Ct. TW13: Felt 4G **129**
Hayden Piper Ho. *SW3* 7E **16**
(off Caversham St.)
Haydens M. W3 6J **79**
Hayden's Pl. W11 6H **81**
Hayden Way RM5: Col R 2J **55**
Haydock Av. UB5: N'olt 6E **58**
Haydock Grn. UB5: N'olt 6E **58**
Haydock Grn. Flats *UB5: N'olt* 6E **58**
(off Haydock Grn.)
Haydon Cl. EN1: Enf 6K **23**
NW9 4J **43**
Haydon Ct. NW9 4J **43**
Haydon Dr. HA5: Eastc 4J **39**
Haydon Pk. Rd. SW19 5J **135**
Haydon Rd. RM8: Dag 2C **72**
Haydons Rd. SW19 5K **135**
Haydon St. EC3 2J **15** (7F **85**)
Haydon Wlk. E1 1K **15** (6F **85**)
Haydon Way SW11 4B **118**
HAYES
BR2 1J **171**
UB3 6G **75**
Hayes & Yeading United FC 7H **75**
Hayes Botanical Gdns. 6H **75**
Hayes Bri. Retail Pk. UB4: Yead 7A **76**
Hayes Chase BR4: W W'ck 6F **159**
Hayes Cl. BR2: Hayes 2J **171**
Hayes Ct. HA0: Wemb 1E **78**
SE5 7C **102**
(off Camberwell New Rd.)
SW2 1J **137**
Hayes Cres. NW11 5H **45**
SM3: Cheam 4F **165**
HAYES END 4F **75**
Hayes End Cl. UB4: Hayes 4F **75**
Hayes End Dr. UB4: Hayes 4F **75**
Hayes End Rd. UB4: Hayes 4F **75**
Hayesens Ho. SW17 4A **136**
Hayesford Pk. Dr. BR2: Brom 5H **159**
Hayes Gdn. BR2: Hayes 1J **171**
Hayes Gro. SE22 3F **121**
Hayes Hill BR2: Hayes 1G **171**
Hayes Hill Rd. BR2: Hayes 1H **171**
Hayes La. BR2: Brom, Hayes 5K **159**
BR3: Beck 3E **158**
Hayes Mead Rd. BR2: Hayes 1G **171**
Hayes Metro Cen.
UB4: Yead 7A **76**
Hayes Pl. NW1 4D **4** (4C **82**)
Hayes Rd. BR2: Brom 4J **159**
UB2: S'hall 4K **93**
Hayes Stadium & Sports Cen. 6F **75**
Hayes St. BR2: Hayes 1K **171**
Hayes Swimming Pool 1H **93**
HAYES TOWN 2H **93**
Hayes Way BR3: Beck 4E **158**
Hayes Wood Av. BR2: Hayes 1K **171**
Hayfield Pas. E1 4J **85**
Hayfield Yd. E1 4J **85**
Haygarth Pl. SW19 5F **135**
Haygreen Cl. KT2: King T 6H **133**
Hay Hill W1 3K **11** (7F **83**)
Hayhurst Ct. *N1* 1B **84**
(off Dibden St.)
Hayland Cl. NW9 4K **43**
Hay La. NW9 4J **43**
Hayles Bldgs. *SE11* 4B **102**
(off Elliotts Row)
Hayles St. SE11 4B **102**
Haylett Gdns. KT1: King T 4D **150**
Hayling Av. TW13: Felt 3J **129**
Hayling Cl. N16 5E **66**
Hayling Ct. SM3: Cheam 4E **164**
Haymaker Cl. UB10: Uxb 7B **56**
Hayman Cres. UB4: Hayes 2F **75**
Haymans Point SE11 5G **19** (4K **101**)
Hayman St. N1 7B **66**
Haymarket SW1 3C **12** (7H **83**)
Haymarket Arc. SW1 3C **12**
Haymarket Ct. *E8* 7F **67**
(off Jacaranda Gro.)
Haymarket Theatre Royal 3D **12**
(off Haymarket)
Haymer Gdns. KT4: Wor Pk 3C **164**
Haymerle Ho. *SE15* 6G **103**
(off Haymerle Rd.)
Haymerle Rd. SE15 6G **103**
Hay M. NW3 6D **64**
Haymill Cl. UB6: G'frd 3K **77**
Hayne Ho. *W11* 1G **99**
(off Penzance Pl.)
Hayne Rd. BR3: Beck 2B **158**
Haynes Cl. N11 3K **31**
N17 7C **34**
SE3 3G **123**
Haynes Dr. N9 3C **34**
Haynes La. SE19 6E **138**
Haynes Rd. HA0: Wemb 7E **60**
Hayne St. EC1 5B **8** (5B **84**)
Haynt Wlk. SW20 3G **153**
Hay's Ct. *SE16* 2J **103**
(off Rotherhithe St.)
Hay's Galleria SE1 4G **15** (1E **102**)
Hays La. SE1 4G **15** (1E **102**)
Haysleigh Gdns. SE20 2G **157**
Hay's M. W1 4J **11** (1F **101**)
Haysoms Cl. RM1: Rom 4K **55**
Haystall Cl. UB4: Hayes 2G **75**
Hay St. E2 1G **85**
Hayter Ct. E11 2K **69**
Hayter Rd. SW2 5J **119**
Hayton Cl. E8 6F **67**
Hayward Cl. DA1: Cray 5K **127**
SW19 7K **135**
Hayward Ct. *SW9* 2J **119**
(off Studley Rd.)
Hayward Gallery 5H **13**
Hayward Gdns. SW15 6E **116**
Hayward Ho. *N1* 2A **84**
(off Penton St.)
Hayward Rd. KT7: T Ditt 7K **149**
N20 2F **31**
Haywards Cl. RM6: Chad H 5B **54**
Hayward's Pl. EC1 3A **8** (4B **84**)

Haywards Yd. *SE4* 5B 122
(off Lindal Rd.)
Haywood Cl. HA5: Pinn 2B 40
Haywood Lodge *N11* 6D 32
(off York Rd.)
Haywood Ri. BR6: Orp 5J 173
Haywood Rd. BR2: Brom 4B 160
Hazel Av. UB7: W Dray 3C 92
Hazel Bank SE25 2E 156
Hazelbank KT5: Surb 1J 163
Hazelbank Rd. SE6 2F 141
Hazelbourne Rd. SW12 6F 119
Hazelbury Cl. SW19 2J 153
Hazelbury Grn. N9 3K 33
Hazelbury La. N9 3K 33
Hazel Cl. CR0: C'don 7K 157
CR4: Mitc 4H 155
N13 3J 33
N19 2G 65
NW9 2A 44
SE15 2G 121
(off Bournemouth Cl.)
TW2: Whitt 7G 113
TW8: Bford 7B 96
Hazel Ct. W5 7E 78
Hazel Cres. RM5: Col R 1H 55
Hazelcroft HA5: Hat E 6A 26
Hazelcroft Cl. UB10: Hil 7B 56
Hazeldean Rd. NW10 7K 61
Hazeldene Dr. HA5: Pinn 3A 40
Hazeldene Gdns. UB10: Hil 1E 74
Hazeldene Rd. DA16: Well 2C 126
IG3: Ilf 2B 72
Hazeldon Rd. SE4 5A 122
Hazeleigh Gdns. IG8: Wfd G 5H 37
Hazel Gdns. HA8: Edg 4C 28
Hazelgreen Cl. N21 1G 33
Hazel Gro. BR6: Farnb 2F 173
EN1: Enf 6B 24
HA0: Wemb 1E 78
RM6: Chad H 3E 54
SE26 4K 139
TW13: Felt 1J 129
Hazel Ho. *E3* 1B 86
(off Barge La.)
Hazelhurst BR3: Beck 1F 159
Hazelhurst Ct. *SE6* 5E 140
(off Beckenham Hill Rd.)
Hazelhurst Rd. SW17 4A 136
Hazel La. IG6: Ilf 6K 37
TW10: Ham 2E 132
Hazellville Rd. N19 7H 47
Hazelmere Cl. TW14: Felt 6G 111
UB5: N'olt 2D 76
Hazelmere Ct. SW2 1K 137
Hazelmere Dr. UB5: N'olt 2D 76
Hazelmere Rd. BR5: Pet W 4G 161
NW6 1H 81
UB5: N'olt 2D 76
Hazelmere Wlk. UB5: N'olt 2D 76
(not continuous)
Hazelmere Way BR2: Hayes 6J 159
Hazel M. *N22* 3A 48
(off High Rd.)
Hazel Rd. E15 5G 69
NW10 3D 80
(not continuous)
Hazeltree La. UB5: N'olt 3C 76
Hazel Wlk. BR2: Brom 6E 160
Hazel Way E4 6G 35
SE1 4F 103
Hazelwood Av. SM4: Mord 4K 153
Hazelwood Cl. HA2: Harr 4F 41
W5 2E 96
Hazelwood Ct. KT6: Surb 6E 150
N13 4F 33
(off Hazelwood La.)
NW10 3A 62
Hazelwood Cres. N13 4F 33
Hazelwood Dr. HA5: Pinn 2K 39
Hazelwood Ho. SE8 4A 104
Hazelwood Ho's. BR2: Brom 3G 159
Hazelwood La. N13 4F 33
Hazelwood Rd. E17 5A 50
EN1: Enf 6A 24
Hazlebury Rd. SW6 2K 117
Hazledean Rd. CR0: C'don 2D 168
Hazledene Rd. W4 6J 97
Hazlemere Gdns.
KT4: Wor Pk 1C 164
Hazlewell Rd. SW15 5E 116
Hazlewood Cl. E5 3A 68
Hazlewood Cres. W10 4G 81
Hazlewood M. SW9 3J 119
Hazlewood Twr. *W10* 4G 81
(off Golborne Gdns.)
Hazlitt Cl. TW13: Hanw 4C 130
Hazlitt M. W14 3G 99
Hazlitt Rd. W14 3G 99
Heacham Av. UB10: Ick 3E 56
Headbourne Ho. SE1 7F 15 (3D 102)
Headcorn Pl. CR7: Thor H 4K 155
Headcorn Rd. BR1: Brom 5H 141
CR7: Thor H 4K 155
N17 7A 34
Headfort Pl. SW1 7H 11 (2E 100)
Headingley Dr. BR3: Beck 6C 140
Headington Ct. *CR0: C'don* 4C 168
(off Tanfield Rd.)
Headington Rd. SW18 2A 136
Headlam Rd. SW4 6H 119
(not continuous)
Headlam St. E1 4H 85
Headley App. IG2: Ilf 5F 53
Headley Av. SM6: Wall 5K 167
Headley Cl. KT19: Ewe 6G 163
Headley Ct. SE26 5J 139
Headley Dr. CR0: New Ad 7D 170
IG2: Ilf 6F 53
Head's M. W11 6J 81
HEADSTONE 3H 41
Headstone Dr. HA1: Harr 3H 41
HA3: W'stone 3H 41
Headstone Gdns. HA2: Harr 4G 41
Headstone La. HA2: Harr 4E 40
HA3: Hrw W 7A 26
Headstone Manor 3G 41
Headstone Pde. HA1: Harr 4H 41
Headstone Rd. HA1: Harr 5J 41
Head St. E1 6K 85
(not continuous)
Headway Cl. TW10: Ham 4C 132
Heald St. SE14 1C 122
Healey Ho. *E3* 4C 86
(off Wellington Way)
SW9 7A 102
Healey St. NW1 6F 65
Healy Dr. BR6: Orp 4K 173
Hearne Rd. W4 6G 97
Hearn Ri. UB5: N'olt 1B 76
Hearn's Bldgs. SE17 4D 102
Hearnshaw St. E14 6A 86
Hearn St. EC2 4H 9 (4E 84)
Hearnville Rd. SW12 1E 136
Heart, The KT12: Walt T 7J 147
Heath, The W7 1J 95
Heatham Pk. TW2: Twick 7K 113
Heath Av. DA7: Bex 6D 108
Heathbourne Rd. HA7: Stan 2D 26
WD23: B Hea 1D 26
Heath Brow NW3 3A 64
Heath Bus. Cen. TW3: Houn 4G 113
Heath Cl. CR2: S Croy 6B 168
NW11 7K 45
UB3: Harl 7F 93
W5 4F 79
Heathcock Ct. *WC2* 3F 13
(off Exchange Ct.)
Heathcote Av. IG5: Ilf 2D 52
Heathcote Ct. IG5: Ilf 1D 52
(not continuous)
Heathcote Gro. E4 3K 35
Heathcote Rd. TW1: Twick 6B 114
Heathcote St. WC1 3G 7 (4K 83)
Heath Ct. *CR0: C'don* 4D 168
(off Heathfield Rd.)
SE9 1G 143
TW4: Houn 4D 112
UB8: Uxb 7A 56
Heath Cft. NW11 1K 63
Heathcroft W5 4F 79
Heathcroft Av. TW16: Sun 7H 129
Heathcroft Gdns. E17 1F 51
Heathdale Av. TW4: Houn 3C 112
Heathdene Dr. DA17: Belv 4H 109
Heathdene Rd. SM6: Wall 7F 167
SW16 7K 137
Heath Dr. NW3 4K 63
SM2: Sutt 7A 166
SW20 4E 152
Heathedge SE26 2H 139
Heath End Rd. DA5: Bexl 1K 145
Heather Av. RM1: Rom 2K 55
Heatherbank BR7: Chst 2E 160
SE9 2D 124
Heather Cl. E6 6E 88
N7 3K 65
RM1: Rom 1K 55
SE13 7F 123
SW8 3F 119
TW7: Isle 5H 113
TW12: Hamp 1D 148
UB8: Hil 5B 74
Heather Ct. DA14: Sidc 6D 144
Heatherdale Cl. KT2: King T 6G 133
Heatherdene Cl. CR4: Mitc 4B 154
N12 7F 31
Heather Dr. EN2: Enf 2G 23
RM1: Rom 2K 55
Heatherfold Way HA5: Eastc 3H 39
Heather Gdns. NW11 6G 45
RM1: Rom 2K 55
SM2: Sutt 6J 165
Heather Glen RM1: Rom 2K 55
Heather Ho. *E14* 6E 86
(off Dee St.)
Heatherlands TW16: Sun 6J 129
Heather La. UB7: Yiew 6A 74
Heatherlea Gro. KT4: Wor Pk 1D 164
Heatherley Ct. E5 3G 67
Heatherley Dr. IG5: Ilf 3C 52
Heather Pk. Dr. HA0: Wemb 7G 61
Heather Pk. Pde. *HA0: Wemb* 7F 61
(off Heather Pk. Dr.)
Heather Rd. E4 6G 35
NW2 2B 62
SE12 2J 141
Heathers, The TW19: Stanw 7B 110
Heatherset Gdns. SW16 7K 137
Heatherside Rd. DA14: Sidc 3C 144
KT19: Ewe 7K 163
Heatherton Ter. N3 2K 45
Heather Wlk. HA8: Edg 5C 28
TW2: Whitt 7E 112
(off Stephenson Rd.)
W10 4G 81
Heather Way CR2: Sels 7K 169
HA7: Stan 6E 26
RM1: Rom 2K 55
Heatherwood Cl. E12 2A 70
Heatherwood Dr. UB4: Hayes 2F 75
Heathfield BR7: Chst 6G 143
E4 3K 35
HA1: Harr 7K 41
Heathfield Av. SW18 7B 118
Heathfield Cl. BR2: Kes 5A 172
E16 5B 88
Heathfield Ct. *E3* 2C 86
(off Tredegar Rd.)
SE20 7J 139
W4 5K 97
Heathfield Dr. CR4: Mitc 1C 154
Heathfield Gdns. CR0: C'don 4D 168
NW11 6F 45
SE3 2G 123
(off Baizdon Rd.)
Heathfield Gdns. SW18 6B 118
W4 5J 97
Heathfield Ho. SE3 2G 123
Heathfield La. BR7: Chst 6G 143
Heathfield Nth. TW2: Twick 7J 113
Heathfield Pk. NW2 6E 62
Heathfield Pk. Dr. RM6: Chad H 5B 54
Heathfield Ri. HA4: Ruis 7E 38
Heathfield Rd. BR1: Brom 7H 141
BR2: Kes 5A 172
CR0: C'don 4D 168
DA6: Bex 4F 127
SW18 6A 118
W3 2H 97
Heathfields Ct. TW4: Houn 5C 112
Heathfield Sth. TW2: Twick 7K 113
Heathfield Sq. SW18 7B 118
Heathfield Ter. SE18 6J 107
W4 5J 97
Heathfield Va. CR2: Sels 7K 169
Heath Gdns. TW1: Twick 1K 131
Heathgate NW11 6K 45
Heathgate Pl. NW3 5D 64
Heath Gro. SE20 7J 139
TW16: Sun 7H 129
Heath Ho. DA15: Sidc 4K 143
Heath Hurst Rd. NW3 4C 64
Heathhurst Rd. CR2: Sande 7E 168
Heathland Rd. N16 1E 66
Heathlands Cl. TW1: Twick 2K 131
TW16: Sun 2J 147
Heathlands Way TW4: Houn 5C 112
Heath La. SE3 2F 123
(not continuous)
Heathlee Rd. SE3 4H 123
Heathley End BR7: Chst 6G 143
Heath Lodge WD23: B Hea 1D 26
Heathmans Rd. SW6 1H 117
Heath Mead SW19 3F 135
Heath Pk. Dr. BR1: Brom 3C 160
Heath Pas. NW3 2K 63
Heathpool Ct. E1 4H 85
Heath Ri. BR2: Hayes 6H 159
SW15 6F 117
Heath Rd. CR7: Thor H 3C 156
DA5: Bexl 1J 145
HA1: Harr 7G 41
RM6: Chad H 7D 54
SW8 2F 119
TW1: Twick 1K 131
TW2: Twick 1K 131
TW3: Houn, Isle 4F 113
UB10: Hil 4E 74
Heathrow Academy 1E 110
HEATHROW AIRPORT
Terminals 1 & 3 3C 110
Terminal 4 5D 110
Terminal 5 6D 174
Heathrow Blvd. UB7: Sip 7B 92
(not continuous)
Heathrow C'way. Cen. TW4: Houn 3K 111
Heathrow Cl. UB7: Lford 4C 174
Heathrow Est., The TW4: Cran 2K 111
Heathrow Gateway TW4: Houn 7C 112
Heathrow Interchange UB4: Yead 1A 94
Heathrow Intl. Trad. Est.
TW4: Houn 3K 111
Heathrow Prologis Pk. UB3: Harl 3D 92
Heath Royal SW15 6F 117
Heaths Cl. EN1: Enf 2K 23
Heath Side BR5: Pet W 1G 173
NW3 4B 64
Heathside NW11 1J 63
SE13 2E 122
TW4: Houn 7D 112
Heathside Av. DA7: Bex 1E 126
Heathside Cl. IG2: Ilf 5H 53
Heathstan Rd. W12 6C 80
Heath St. NW3 3A 64
Heath Vw. N2 4A 46
Heathview NW5 4E 64
Heath Vw. Cl. N2 4A 46

Heathview Dr. SE2 6D **108**
Heathview Gdns. SW15 7E **116**
Heathview Rd. CR7: Thor H 4A **156**
Heath Vs. NW3 3B **64**
SE18 5K **107**
Heathville Rd. N19 7J **47**
Heathwall St. SW11 3D **118**
HEATHWAY **1G 91**
Heath Way DA8: Erith 1J **127**
Heathway CR0: C'don 3B **170**
IG8: Wfd G 5F **37**
RM9: Dag 3F **73**
RM10: Dag 3F **73**
SE3 7J **105**
UB2: S'hall 4B **94**
Heathway Ct. NW3 2J **63**
Heathway Ind. Est. RM10: Dag 4H **73**
Heathwood Gdns. SE7 4C **106**
Heathwood Point SE23 3K **139**
Heathwood Wlk. DA5: Bexl 1K **145**
Heaton Cl. E4 3K **35**
Heaton Ho. *SW10* *6A* ***100***
(off Seymour Wlk.)
Heaton Rd. CR4: Mitc 7E **136**
SE15 2H **121**
Heaven Tree Cl. N1 6C **66**
Heaver Rd. SW11 3B **118**
Heavitree Cl. SE18 5H **107**
Heavitree Rd. SE18 5H **107**
(not continuous)
Hebden Ct. E2 1F **85**
Hebden Ter. N17 6K **33**
Hebdon Rd. SW17 3C **136**
Heber Mans. *W14* *6G* ***99***
(off Queen's Club Gdns.)
Heber Rd. NW2 5F **63**
SE22 6F **121**
Hebert Pl. TW7: Isle 2H **113**
Hebron Rd. W6 3E **98**
Hecham Cl. E17 2A **50**
Heckfield Pl. SW6 7J **99**
Heckford Ho. *E14* *6D* ***86***
(off Grundy St.)
Heckford St. E1 7K **85**
Hector *NW9* *1B* ***44***
(off Five Acre)
Hector Cl. N9 2B **34**
Hector Ct. *SW9* *7A* ***102***
(off Caldwell St.)
Hector Ho. *E2* *2H* ***85***
(off Old Bethnal Grn. Rd.)
Hector St. SE18 4J **107**
Heddington Gro. N7 5K **65**
Heddon Cl. TW7: Isle 4A **114**
Heddon Ct. Av. EN4: Cockf 5J **21**
Heddon Ct. Pde. EN4: Cockf 5K **21**
Heddon Rd. EN4: Cockf 5J **21**
Heddon St. W1 2A **12** (7G **83**)
Hedgegate Ct. *W11* *6H* ***81***
(off Powis Ter.)
Hedge Hill EN2: Enf 1G **23**
Hedge La. N13 3G **33**
Hedgeley IG4: Ilf 4D **52**
Hedgemans Rd. RM9: Dag 7D **72**
Hedgemans Way RM9: Dag 6E **72**
Hedgerley Gdns. UB6: G'frd 2G **77**
Hedgerow Ct. *E6* *1D* ***88***
(off Nelson St.)
Hedgers Gro. E9 6A **68**
Hedger St. SE11 4B **102**
Hedge Wlk. SE6 5D **140**
Hedgewood Gdns. IG5: Ilf 5E **52**
Hedgley M. SE12 5H **123**
Hedgley St. SE12 5H **123**
Hedingham Cl. N1 7C **66**
Hedingham Ho. *KT2: King T* *1E* ***150***
(off Royal Quarter)
Hedingham Rd. RM8: Dag 5B **72**
Hedley Cl. RM1: Rom 5K **55**
Hedley Ho. *E14* *3E* ***104***
(off Stewart St.)
Hedley Rd. TW2: Whitt 7E **112**
Hedley Row N5 5D **66**
Hedsor Ho. *E2* *3J* ***9***
(off Ligonier St.)
Heenan Cl. IG11: Bark 6G **71**
Heene Rd. EN2: Enf 1J **23**
Hega Ho. *E14* *5E* ***86***
(off Ullin St.)
Heidegger Cres. SW13 7D **98**
Heigham Rd. E6 7C **70**
Heighton Gdns. CR0: Wadd 5B **168**
Heights, The BR3: Beck 7E **140**
(not continuous)
SE7 5A **106**
UB5: N'olt 5D **58**
Heights Cl. SW20 7D **134**
Heiron St. SE17 6B **102**
Helby Rd. SW4 6H **119**
Heldar Ct. SE1 7F **15** (2D **102**)
Helder Gro. SE12 7H **123**
Helder St. CR2: S Croy 6D **168**
Heldmann Cl. TW3: Houn 4H **113**
Helegan Cl. BR6: Chels 4K **173**
Helena Ct. W5 5D **78**
Helena Pl. E9 1H **85**
Helena Rd. E13 2H **87**
E17 5C **50**
NW10 5D **62**
W5 5D **78**
Helena Sq. *SE16* *7A* ***86***
(off Sovereign Cres.)
Helen Av. TW14: Felt 7K **111**
Helen Cl. KT8: W Mole 4F **149**
N2 3A **46**
Helen Gladstone Ho. *SE1* *6A* ***14***
(off Surrey Row)
Helen Ho. *E2* *2H* ***85***
(off Old Bethnal Grn. Rd.)
Helen Mackay Ho. *E14* *6F* ***87***
(off Blair St.)
Helen Peele Cotts. *SE16* *3J* ***103***
(off Lower Rd.)
Helenslea Av. NW11 1J **63**
Helen's Pl. E2 3J **85**
Helen St. SE18 4F **107**
Helen Taylor Ho. *SE16* *3G* ***103***
(off Evelyn Lowe Est.)
Helford Cl. HA4: Ruis 2G **57**
Helgiford Gdns. TW16: Sun 7G **129**
Heligan Ho. *SE16* *2K* ***103***
(off Water Gdns. Sq.)
Helios Rd. SM6: Wall 1E **166**
Heliport Ind. Est. SW11 2B **118**
Helix Ct. *W11* *1F* ***99***
(off Swanscombe Rd.)
Helix Gdns. SW2 6K **119**
Helix Rd. SW2 6K **119**
Helix Ter. SW19 2F **135**
Hellings St. E1 1G **103**
Helm, The E16 7F **89**
Helme Cl. SW19 5H **135**
Helmet Row EC1 2D **8** (4C **84**)
Helmore Rd. IG11: Bark 7K **71**
Helmsdale Cl. UB4: Yead 4C **76**
Helmsdale Ho. *NW6* *2K* ***81***
(off Carlton Va.)
Helmsdale Rd. SW16 1H **155**
Helmsley Pl. E8 7H **67**
Helmsley St. E8 7H **67**
Helperby Rd. NW10 7A **62**
Helsby Ct. *NW8* *3A* ***4***
(off Pollitt Dr.)
Helsinki Sq. SE16 3A **104**
Helston *NW1* *1G* ***83***
(off Camden St.)
Helston Cl. HA5: Hat E 1D **40**
Helston Ct. *N15* *5E* ***48***
(off Culvert Rd.)
Helston Ho. *SE11* *5K* ***19***
(off Kennings Way)
Helvetia St. SE6 2B **140**
Helwys Ct. E4 6J **35**
Hemans St. SW8 7H **101**
Hemans St. Est. SW8 7H **101**
Hemberton Rd. SW9 3J **119**
Hemery Rd. UB6: G'frd 5H **59**
Hemingford Cl. N12 5G **31**
Hemingford Rd. N1 1K **83**
SM3: Cheam 4E **164**
Heming Rd. HA8: Edg 7C **28**
Hemington Av. N11 5J **31**
Hemingway Cl. NW5 4E **64**
Hemlock Cl. SW16 2G **155**
Hemlock Rd. W12 7B **80**
(not continuous)
Hemmen La. UB3: Hayes 6H **75**
Hemming Cl. TW12: Hamp 1E **148**
Hemmings Cl. DA14: Sidc 2B **144**
Hemmings Mead KT19: Ewe 6J **163**
Hemming St. E1 4G **85**
Hempstead Cl. IG9: Buck H 2D **36**
Hempstead Rd. E17 3F **51**
Hemp Wlk. SE17 4D **102**
Hemsby Rd. KT9: Chess 6F **163**
Hemstal Rd. NW6 7J **63**
Hemsted Rd. DA8: Erith 7K **109**
Hemswell Dr. NW9 1A **44**
Hemsworth Ct. N1 2E **84**
Hemsworth St. N1 2E **84**
Hemus Pl. SW3 6D **16** (5C **100**)
Hen & Chicken Ct. *EC4* *1J* ***13***
(off Fleet St.)
Hen & Chickens Theatre *6B* ***66***
(off St Paul's Rd.)
Henchman St. W12 6B **80**
Hendale Av. NW4 3D **44**
Henderson Cl. NW10 6J **61**
Henderson Ct. N12 4E **30**
NW3 *5B* ***64***
(off Fitzjohn's Av.)
SE14 *6K* ***103***
(off Myers La.)
Henderson Dr. NW8 3A **4** (4B **82**)
Henderson Ho. *RM10: Dag* *3G* ***73***
(off Kershaw Rd.)
Henderson Rd. CR0: C'don 6D **156**
E7 6A **70**
N9 1C **34**
SW18 7C **118**
UB4: Yead 3J **75**
Hendfield Ct. SM6: Wall 6F **167**
Hendham Rd. SW17 2C **136**
HENDON 4E **44**
Hendon Av. N3 1G **45**
Hendon Crematorium NW7 1F **45**
Hendon FC 1F **63**
Hendon Hall Ct. NW4 3F **45**
Hendon Ho. NW4 5F **45**
Hendon La. N3 3G **45**
Hendon Leisure Cen. 7F **45**
Hendon Lodge NW4 3D **44**
Hendon Pk. Mans. NW4 5E **44**
Hendon Pk. Row NW11 6H **45**
Hendon Rd. N9 2B **34**
Hendon Way NW2 7F **45**
NW4 6D **44**
Hendon Wood La. NW7 1G **29**
Hendre Ho. *SE1* *4E* ***102***
(off Old Kent Rd.)
Hendren Cl. UB6: G'frd 5H **59**
Hendre Rd. SE1 4E **102**
Hendrick Av. SW12 7D **118**
Heneage La. EC3 1H **15** (6E **84**)
Heneage Pl. EC3 1H **15** (6E **84**)
Heneage St. E1 5K **9** (5F **85**)
Henera's Ct. *BR1: Brom* *3E* ***160***
(off Brady Dr.)
Henfield Cl. DA5: Bexl 6G **127**
N19 1G **65**
Henfield Rd. SW19 1H **153**
Hengelo Gdns.
CR4: Mitc 4B **154**
Hengest Av. KT6: Surb 3A **162**
Hengist Rd. DA8: Erith 7H **109**
SE12 7K **123**
Hengist Way BR2: Brom 4G **159**
SM6: Wall 7H **167**
Hengrave Rd. SE23 6J **121**
Hengrove Ct. DA5: Bexl 1E **144**
Hengrove Cres. TW15: Ashf 3A **128**
Henham Ct. RM5: Col R 1J **55**
Henley Av. SM3: Cheam 3G **165**
Henley Cl. *SE16* *2J* ***103***
(off St Marychurch St.)
TW7: Isle 1K **113**
UB6: G'frd 2G **77**
Henley Ct. N14 7B **22**
NW2 6F **63**
Henley Dr. KT2: King T 7B **134**
SE1 4F **103**
Henley Gdns. HA5: Eastc 3K **39**
RM6: Chad H 5E **54**
Henley Ho. *E2* *3K* ***9***
(off Swanfield St.)
Henley Prior *N1* *1G* ***7***
(off Affleck St.)
Henley Rd. E16 2D **106**
IG1: Ilf 4G **71**
N18 4K **33**
NW10 1E **80**
Henley St. SW11 2E **118**
Henley Way TW13: Hanw 5B **130**
Henlow Pl. TW10: Ham 2D **132**
HENLYS CORNER **4H 45**
HENLYS RDBT. **2A 112**
Hennel Cl. SE23 3J **139**
Hennessy Ct. E10 6E **50**
Hennessy Rd. N9 2D **34**
Henniker Gdns. E6 3B **88**
Henniker M. SW3 7A **16** (6B **100**)
Henniker Point *E15* *5G* ***69***
(off Leytonstone Rd.)
Henniker Rd. E15 5F **69**
Henningham Rd. N17 1D **48**
Henning St. SW11 1C **118**
Henrietta Barnet Wlk. NW11 6J **45**
Henrietta Cl. SE8 6C **104**
Henrietta Ct. *TW1: Twick* *7C* ***114***
(off Richmond Rd.)
Henrietta Ho. *N15* *6E* ***48***
(off St Ann's Rd.)
W6 *5E* ***98***
(off Queen Caroline St.)
Henrietta M. WC1 3F **7** (4J **83**)
Henrietta Pl. W1 1J **11** (6F **83**)
Henrietta St. WC2 2F **13** (7J **83**)
Henriques St. E1 6G **85**
Henry Addlington Cl. E6 5F **89**
Henry Cl. EN2: Enf 1K **23**
Henry Cooper Way SE9 3B **142**
Henry Darlot Dr. NW7 5A **30**
Henry Dent Cl. SE5 3D **120**
Henry Dickens Ct. W11 7F **81**
Henry Doulton Dr. SW17 4E **136**
Henry Hatch Ct. SM2: Sutt 7A **166**
Henry Ho. SE1 5J **13** (1A **102**)
SW8 *7J* ***101***
(off Wyvil Rd.)
Henry Jackson Rd. SW15 3F **117**
Henry Macaulay Av. KT2: King T 1D **150**
Henry Moore Ct. SW3 5C **100**
Henry Peters Dr. *TW11: Tedd* *5J* ***131***
(off Somerset Gdns.)
Henry Purcell Ho. *E16* *1K* ***105***
(off Evelyn Rd.)
Henry Rd. E6 2C **88**
EN4: E Barn 5G **21**
N4 1C **66**
Henrys Av. IG8: Wfd G 5C **36**
Henryson Rd. SE4 5C **122**
Henry St. BR1: Brom 1K **159**
Henry's Wlk. IG6: Ilf 1H **53**
Henry Tate M. SW16 5K **137**
Henry Tudor Ct. SE9 7G **125**
Henry Wise Ho. *SW1* *4B* ***18***
(off Vauxhall Bri. Rd.)
Hensford Gdns. SE26 4H **139**

Henshall Point *E3* *3D 86*
(off Bromley High St.)
Henshall St. N1 . . . . .6D **66**
Henshawe Rd. RM8: Dag 3D **72**
Henshaw St. SE17 . . . . .4D **102**
Henslowe Rd. SE22 . . . . .5G **121**
Henslow Ho. *SE15* *7G 103*
(off Peckham Pk. Rd.)
Henson Av. NW2 . . . . .5E **62**
Henson Cl. BR6: Farnb 2F **173**
Henson Path HA3: Kenton 3D **42**
Henson Pl. UB5: N'olt 1A **76**
Henstridge Pl. NW8 . . . . .1C **82**
Henty Cl. SW11 . . . . .7C **100**
Henty Wlk. SW15 . . . . .5D **116**
Henville Rd. BR1: Brom 1K **159**
Henwick Rd. SE9 . . . . .3B **124**
Henwood Side IG8: Wfd G 6J **37**
Hepburn Gdns. BR2: Hayes 1G **171**
Hepburn M. SW11 . . . . .5D **118**
Hepple Cl. TW7: Isle 2B **114**
Hepplestone Cl. SW15 . . . . .6D **116**
Hepscott Rd. E9 . . . . .6C **68**
Hepworth Ct. *N1* *1B 84*
(off Gaskin St.)
NW3 . . . . .5C **64**
SM3: Sutt 1J **165**
SW1 . . . . .6J **17**
Hepworth Gdns. IG11: Bark 5A **72**
Hepworth Rd. SW16 . . . . .7J **137**
Hepworth Way KT12: Walt T 7H **147**
Heracles *NW9* *1B 44*
(off Five Acre)
Hera Ct. *E14* *4C 104*
(off Homer Dr.)
Herald Gdns. SM6: Wall 2F **167**
Herald's Pl. SE11 . . . . .3K **19** (4B **102**)
Herald St. E2 . . . . .4H **85**
Herbal Hill EC1 . . . . .4K **7** (4A **84**)
Herbal Hill Gdns. *EC1* *4K 7*
(off Herbal Hill)
Herbal Pl. EC1 . . . . .4K **7**
Herbert Cres. SW1 . . . . .1F **17** (3D **100**)
Herbert Gdns. NW10 . . . . .2D **80**
RM6: Chad H 7D **54**
W4 . . . . .6H **97**
Herbert Ho. *E1* *7J 9*
(off Old Castle St.)
Herbert M. SW2 . . . . .6A **120**
Herbert Morrison Ho. *SW6* *6H 99*
(off Clem Attlee Ct.)
Herbert Pl. SE18 . . . . .6F **107**
Herbert Rd. BR2: Brom 5B **160**
DA7: Bex 2E **126**
E12 . . . . .4C **70**
E17 . . . . .7B **50**
IG3: Ilf 2J **71**
KT1: King T 3F **151**
N11 . . . . .7D **32**
N15 . . . . .5F **49**
NW9 . . . . .6C **44**
SE18 . . . . .7E **106**
(not continuous)
SW19 . . . . .7H **135**
(not continuous)
UB1: S'hall 1D **94**
Herbert St. E13 . . . . .2J **87**
NW5 . . . . .6E **64**
Herbrand Est. WC1 . . . . .3E **6** (4J **83**)
Herbrand St. WC1 . . . . .3E **6** (4J **83**)
Hercies Rd. UB10: Hil 7B **56**
Hercules Ct. SE14 . . . . .6A **104**
Hercules Pl. N7 . . . . .3J **65**
(not continuous)
Hercules Rd. SE1 . . . . .2H **19** (3K **101**)
Hercules St. N7 . . . . .3J **65**
Hercules Wharf *E14* *7G 87*
(off Orchard Pl.)
Hercules Yd. N7 . . . . .3J **65**
Hereford Av. EN4: E Barn 1J **31**
Hereford Bldgs. *SW3* *7B 16*
(off Old Church St.)
Hereford Ct. HA1: Harr 4J **41**
SM2: Sutt 7J **165**
W7 . . . .*5K 77*
(off Copley Cl.)
Hereford Gdns. HA5: Pinn 5C **40**
IG1: Ilf 7C **52**
SE13 . . . . .5G **123**
TW2: Twick 1G **131**
Hereford Ho. *N18* *5C 34*
(off Cavendish Cl.)
NW6 . . . .*2J 81*
(off Carlton Va.)
SW3 . . . .*1D 16*
(off Ovington Gdns.)
SW10 . . . .*7K 99*
(off Fulham Rd.)
Hereford M. W2 . . . . .6J **81**
Hereford Pl. SE14 . . . . .7B **104**
Hereford Retreat SE15 . . . . .7G **103**
Hereford Rd. E3 . . . . .2B **86**
E11 . . . . .5K **51**
TW13: Felt 1A **130**
W2 . . . . .6J **81**
W3 . . . . .7H **79**
W5 . . . . .3C **96**
Hereford Sq. SW7 . . . . .4A **100**
Hereford St. E2 . . . . .4G **85**
Hereford Way KT9: Chess 5C **162**
Herent Dr. IG5: Ilf 4C **52**
Hereward Gdns. N13 . . . . .5F **33**
Hereward Rd. SW17 . . . . .4D **136**
Herga Ct. HA1: Harr 3J **59**
Herga Rd. HA3: W'stone 4K **41**
Heriot Av. E4 . . . . .2H **35**
Heriot Rd. NW4 . . . . .5E **44**
Heriots Cl. HA7: Stan 4F **27**
Heritage Av. NW9 . . . . .3B **44**
Heritage Cl. SW9 . . . . .3B **120**
TW16: Sun 1J **147**
Heritage Ct. *SE8* *5K 103*
(off Trundley's Rd.)
Heritage Hill BR2: Kes 5A **172**
Heritage Pl. E4 . . . . .7K **25**
SW18 . . . . .1A **136**
Heritage Vw. HA1: Harr 3K **59**
Herlwyn Av. HA4: Ruis 2G **57**
Herlwyn Gdns. SW17 . . . . .4D **136**
Her Majesty's Theatre *4C 12*
(off Haymarket)
Herm Cl. TW7: Isle 7G **95**
Hermes Cl. W9 . . . . .4J **81**
Hermes Ct. SW2 . . . . .6K **119**
SW9 . . . .*1A 120*
(off Southey Rd.)
Hermes St. N1 . . . . .1J **7** (2A **84**)
Hermes Wlk. UB5: N'olt 2E **76**
Herm Ho. EN3: Enf W 1E **24**
N1 . . . .*6C 66*
(off Clifton Rd.)
Hermiston Av. N8 . . . . .5J **47**
Hermitage, The
KT1: King T 4D **150**
SE13 . . . . .2E **122**
SE23 . . . . .1J **139**
SW13 . . . . .1B **116**
TW10: Rich 5E **114**
TW13: Felt 3H **129**
UB8: Uxb 6A **56**
Hermitage Cl. E18 . . . . .4H **51**
EN2: Enf 2G **23**
KT10: Clay 6A **162**
SE2 . . . . .3C **108**
TW17: Shep 4C **146**
Hermitage Ct. *E1* *1G 103*
(off Knighten St.)
E18 . . . . .4J **51**
NW2 . . . . .3J **63**
Hermitage Gdns. NW2 . . . . .3J **63**
SE19 . . . . .7C **138**
Hermitage Grn. SW16 . . . . .1J **155**
Hermitage Ho. *N1* *2B 84*
(off Gerrard Rd.)
Hermitage La. CR0: C'don 7G **157**
N18 . . . . .5J **33**
NW2 . . . . .3J **63**
SE25 . . . . .6G **157**
(not continuous)
SW16 . . . . .7K **137**
Hermitage Path SW16 . . . . .1J **155**
Hermitage Rd. N4 . . . . .7B **48**
N15 . . . . .7B **48**
SE19 . . . . .7C **138**
Hermitage Row E8 . . . . .5G **67**
Hermitage St. W2 . . . . .6A **4** (5B **82**)
Hermitage Vs. *SW6* *6J 99*
(off Lillie Rd.)
Hermitage Wlk. E18 . . . . .4H **51**
Hermitage Wall E1 . . . . .1G **103**
Hermitage Waterside *E1* *1G 103*
(off Thomas More St.)
Hermitage Way HA7: Stan 1A **42**
Hermit Pl. NW6 . . . . .1K **81**
Hermit Rd. E16 . . . . .5H **87**
Hermit St. EC1 . . . . .1A **8** (3B **84**)
Hermon Gro. UB3: Hayes 1J **93**
Hermon Hill E11 . . . . .5J **51**
E18 . . . . .5J **51**
Herndon Rd. SW18 . . . . .5A **118**
Herne Cl. NW10 . . . . .5K **61**
UB3: Hayes 6H **75**
Herne Ct. WD23: Bush 1B **26**
HERNE HILL 5C **120**
Herne Hill SE24 . . . . .6C **120**
Herne Hill Ho. *SE24* *6B 120*
(off Railton Rd.)
Herne Hill Rd. SE24 . . . . .3C **120**
Herne Hill Stadium 6D **120**
Herne M. N18 . . . . .4B **34**
Herne Pl. SE24 . . . . .5B **120**
Herne Rd. KT6: Surb 2D **162**
Heron Cl. E17 . . . . .2B **50**
IG9: Buck H 1D **36**
NW10 . . . . .6A **62**
SM1: Sutt 5H **165**
Heron Ct. BR2: Brom 4A **160**
E14 . . . .*3E 104*
(off New Union Cl.)
HA4: Ruis 2F **57**
KT1: King T 3E **150**
NW9 . . . . .2A **44**
TW19: Stanw 1A **128**
Heron Cres. DA14: Sidc 3J **143**
Herondale Av. SW18 . . . . .1B **136**
Heron Dr. N4 . . . . .2C **66**
Herongate *N1* *1C 84*
(off Ridgewell Cl.)
Herongate Cl. EN1: Enf 2A **24**
Herongate Rd. E12 . . . . .2A **70**
Heron Hill DA17: Belv 5F **109**
Heron Ho. DA14: Sidc 3B **144**
E3 . . . .*1B 86*
(off Sycamore Av.)
E6 . . . . .7C **70**
NW8 . . . .*1C 4*
(off Newcourt St.)
SW11 . . . .*7C 100*
(off Searles Cl.)
W13 . . . . .4A **78**
Heron Mead EN3: Enf L 1H **25**
Heron M. IG1: Ilf 2F **71**
Heron Pl. SE16 . . . . .1A **104**
W1 . . . .*7H 5*
(off Thayer St.)
Heron Quay E14 . . . . .1C **104**
Heron Rd. CR0: C'don 2E **168**
SE24 . . . . .4C **120**
TW1: Twick 4A **114**
Herons, The E11 . . . . .6H **51**
Heronsforde W13 . . . . .6C **78**
Heronsgate HA8: Edg 5B **28**
Heron's Lea N6 . . . . .6D **46**
Heronslea Dr. HA7: Stan 5K **27**
Heron's Pl. TW7: Isle 3B **114**
Heron Sq. TW9: Rich 5D **114**
Herons Ri. EN4: E Barn 4H **21**
Heron Trad. Est. W3 . . . . .5H **79**
Heron Vw. *TW8: Bford* *7C 96*
(off Commerce Rd.)
Heron Way SM6: Wall 7H **167**
TW14: Felt 4J **111**
Heronway IG8: Wfd G 4F **37**
Herrick Ho. *N16* *4D 66*
(off Howard Rd.)
SE5 . . . .*7D 102*
(off Elmington Est.)
Herrick Rd. N5 . . . . .3C **66**
Herrick St. SW1 . . . . .4D **18** (4H **101**)
Herries St. W10 . . . . .2G **81**
Herringham Rd. SE7 . . . . .3A **106**
Herron Ct. BR2: Brom 4H **159**
Hersant Cl. NW10 . . . . .1C **80**
Herschell M. SE5 . . . . .3C **120**
Herschell Rd. SE23 . . . . .7A **122**
Hersham Cl. SW15 . . . . .7C **116**
Hershell Ct. SW14 . . . . .4H **115**
Hertford Av. SW14 . . . . .5K **115**
Hertford Cl. EN4: Cockf 3G **21**
Hertford Ct. E6 . . . . .3D **88**
N13 . . . . .3F **33**
Hertford Ho. UB5: N'olt 4D **76**
Hertford Lock Ho. *E3* *1B 86*
(off Parnell Rd.)
Hertford Pl. W1 . . . . .4B **6** (4G **83**)
Hertford Rd. EN3: Enf H, Enf W 3D **24**
EN4: Cockf 3F **21**
IG2: Ilf 6J **53**
IG11: Bark 7E **70**
N1 . . . . .1E **84**
(not continuous)
N2 . . . . .3C **46**
N9 . . . . .2C **34**
Hertford St. W1 . . . . .5J **11** (1F **101**)
Hertford Wlk. DA17: Belv 5G **109**
Hertford Way CR4: Mitc 4J **155**
Hertslet Rd. N7 . . . . .3K **65**
Hertsmere Ho. *E14* *7C 86*
(off Hertsmere Rd.)
Hertsmere Rd. E14 . . . . .1C **104**
Hertswood Ct. EN5: Barn 4B **20**
Hervey Cl. N3 . . . . .1J **45**
Hervey Pk. Rd. E17 . . . . .4A **50**
Hervey Rd. SE3 . . . . .1K **123**
Hervey Way N3 . . . . .1J **45**
Hesa Rd. UB3: Hayes 6J **75**
Hesewall Cl. SW4 . . . . .2G **119**
Hesketh Pl. W11 . . . . .7G **81**
Hesketh Rd. E7 . . . . .3J **69**
Heslop Rd. SW12 . . . . .1D **136**
Hesper M. SW5 . . . . .4K **99**
Hesperus Cres. E14 . . . . .4D **104**
Hessel Rd. W13 . . . . .2A **96**
Hessel St. E1 . . . . .6H **85**
Hestercombe Av. SW6 . . . . .2G **117**
Hesterman Way CR0: Wadd 1K **167**
Hester Rd. N18 . . . . .5B **34**
SW11 . . . . .7C **100**
Hester Ter. TW9: Rich 3G **115**
Hestia Ho. SE1 . . . . .7G **15**
HESTON 7E **94**
Heston Av. TW5: Hest 6C **94**
Heston Cen., The TW5: Cran 5A **94**
Heston Community Sports Hall 7E **94**
Heston Grange TW5: Hest 6D **94**
Heston Grange La. TW5: Hest 6D **94**
Heston Ho. SE8 . . . . .1C **122**
Heston Ind. Mall TW5: Hest 7D **94**
Heston Phoenix Distribution Pk.
TW5: Hest 6A **94**
Heston Pool 6D **94**
Heston Rd. TW5: Hest 6E **94**
HESTON SERVICE AREA **6B 94**
Heston St. SE14 . . . . .1C **122**
Hetherington Rd. SW4 . . . . .4J **119**
TW17: Shep 2E **146**
Hetherington Way UB10: Ick 4A **56**
Hethpool Ho. W2 . . . . .4A **4**

Hetley Gdns. SE19 .....7F 139
Hetley Rd. W12 .....1D 98
Heton Gdns. NW4 .....4D 44
Hevelius Cl. SE10 .....5H 105
Hever Cft. SE9 .....4E 142
Hever Gdns. BR1: Brom 2E 160
Heverham Rd. SE18 .....4J 107
Hever Ho. SE15 .....6K 103
(off Lovelinch Cl.)
Heversham Ho. SE15 .....6J 103
Heversham Rd. DA7: Bex 2G 127
Hevingham Dr. RM6: Chad H 5C 54
Hewens Rd. UB4: Hil 4E 74
UB10: Hil 4E 74
Hewer St. W10 .....5F 81
Hewett Cl. HA7: Stan 4G 27
Hewett Rd. RM8: Dag 5D 72
Hewetts Quay IG11: Bark 1F 89
Hewett St. EC2 .....4H 9 (4E 84)
Hewish Rd. N18 .....4K 33
Hewison St. E3 .....2B 86
Hewitt Av. N22 .....2B 48
Hewitt Cl. CR0: C'don 3C 170
Hewitt Rd. N8 .....5A 48
Hewlett Ho. SW8 .....7F 101
(off Havelock La.)
Hewlett Rd. E3 .....2A 86
Hexagon, The N6 .....1D 64
Hexagon Bus. Pk.
UB4: Yead 7A 76
Hexal Rd. SE6 .....3G 141
Hexham Gdns. TW7: Isle 7A 96
Hexham Rd. EN5: New Bar 4E 20
SE27 .....2C 138
SM4: Mord 1K 165
Heybourne Rd. N17 .....7C 34
Heybridge NW1 .....6F 65
(off Lewis St.)
Heybridge Av. SW16 .....7J 137
Heybridge Dr. IG6: Ilf 2H 53
Heybridge Way E10 .....7A 50
Heydon Ho. SE14 .....1J 121
(off Kender St.)
Heyford Av. SW8 .....7J 101
SW20 .....3H 153
Heyford Rd. CR4: Mitc 2C 154
Heyford Ter. SW8 .....7J 101
Heygate St. SE17 .....4C 102
Heylyn Sq. E3 .....3B 86
Heynes Rd. RM8: Dag 4C 72
Heysham La. NW3 .....3K 63
Heysham Rd. N15 .....6D 48
Heythorp St. SW18 .....1H 135
Heythrop Dr. UB10: Ick 4B 56
Heywood Av. NW9 .....1A 44
Heywood Ct. HA7: Stan 5H 27
Heywood Ho. SE14 .....6K 103
(off Myers La.)
Heyworth Rd. E5 .....4H 67
E15 .....5H 69
Hibbert Ho. E14 .....3C 104
(off Tiller Rd.)
Hibbert Rd. E17 .....7B 50
HA3: W'stone 2K 41
Hibbert St. SW11 .....3B 118
Hibernia Gdns. TW3: Houn 4E 112
Hibernia Point SE2 .....2D 108
(off Wolvercote Rd.)
Hibernia Rd. TW3: Houn 4E 112
Hibiscus Cl. HA8: Edg 4D 28
Hibiscus Ho. TW13: Felt 1J 129
Hichisson Rd. SE15 .....5J 121
Hicken Rd. SW2 .....5K 119
Hickes Ho. NW6 .....7J 63
Hickey's Almshouses TW9: Rich 4F 115
Hickin Cl. SE7 .....4B 106
Hickin St. E14 .....3E 104
Hickleton NW1 .....1G 83
(off Camden St.)
Hickling Ho. SE16 .....3H 103
(off Slippers Pl.)
Hickling Rd. IG1: Ilf 5F 71

Hickman Av. E4 .....6K 35
Hickman Cl. E16 .....5B 88
Hickman Rd. RM6: Chad H 7C 54
Hickmore Wlk. SW4 .....3H 119
Hickory Cl. N9 .....7B 24
Hicks Av. UB6: G'frd 3H 77
Hicks Bolton Ho. NW6 .....2H 81
(off Denmark Ho.)
Hicks Cl. SW11 .....3C 118
Hicks Ho. RM10: Dag 3H 73
Hicks Gallery 5J 135
Hicks Ho. SE16 .....3G 103
(off Spa Rd.)
Hicks St. SE8 .....5A 104
Hidcote Gdns. SW20 .....3D 152
Hidden Cl. KT8: W Mole 4G 149
Hide E6 .....6E 88
Hide Pl. SW1 .....4C 18 (4H 101)
Hider Cl. SE3 .....7A 106
Hide Rd. HA1: Harr 4G 41
Hides St. N7 .....6K 65
Hide Twr. SW1 .....4C 18
(off Regency St.)
Higgins Ho. N1 .....1E 84
(off Colville Est.)
Higginson Ho. NW3 .....7D 64
(off Fellows Rd.)
Higgins Wlk. TW12: Hamp 6C 130
(off Abbott Cl.)
Higgs Ind. Est. SE24 .....3B 120
High Acres EN2: Enf 3G 23
HIGHAM HILL 2A 50
Higham Hill Rd. E17 .....1A 50
Higham M. UB5: N'olt 4D 76
Higham Path E17 .....3A 50
Higham Pl. E17 .....3A 50
Higham Rd. IG8: Wfd G 6D 36
N17 .....3D 48
Highams, The E17 .....1E 50
Highams Ct. E4 .....3A 36
Highams Lodge Bus. Cen. E17 .....3K 49
HIGHAMS PARK 6A 36
Highams Pk. Ind. Est. E4 .....6K 35
Higham Sta. Av. E4 .....6H 35
Higham St. E17 .....3A 50
High Ashton KT2: King T 7H 133
Highbanks Cl. DA16: Well 7B 108
Highbanks Rd. HA5: Hat E 6A 26
Highbank Way N8 .....6A 48
HIGH BARNET 2A 20
Highbarrow Rd. CR0: C'don 1G 169
High Beech CR2: S Croy 7E 168
N21 .....6E 22
High Beeches DA14: Sidc 5E 144
High Birch Ct. EN4: E Barn 4H 21
(off Park Rd.)
High Bri. SE10 .....5F 105
Highbridge Ct. SE14 .....7J 103
(off Farrow La.)
Highbridge Rd. IG11: Bark 1F 89
High Bri. Wharf SE10 .....5F 105
(off High Bri.)
Highbrook Rd. SE3 .....3B 124
High Broom Cres. BR4: W W'ck 7D 158
HIGHBURY 4B 66
Highbury Av. CR7: Thor H 2A 156
Highbury Cl. BR4: W W'ck 2D 170
KT3: N Mald 4J 151
HIGHBURY CORNER 6B 66
Highbury Cres. N5 .....5B 66
Highbury Est. N5 .....5C 66
Highbury Gdns. IG3: Ilf 2J 71
Highbury Grange N5 .....4C 66
Highbury Gro. N5 .....5B 66
Highbury Gro. Ct. N5 .....6C 66
Highbury Hill N5 .....3A 66
Highbury Mans. N1 .....7B 66
(off Upper St.)
Highbury New Pk. N5 .....5C 66
Highbury Pk. N5 .....3B 66
Highbury Pk. M. N5 .....4C 66
Highbury Pl. N5 .....6B 66

Highbury Pool 6B 66
Highbury Quad. N5 .....3C 66
Highbury Rd. SW19 .....5G 135
Highbury Sq. N14 .....1B 32
Highbury Sta. Rd. N1 .....6A 66
Highbury Ter. N5 .....5B 66
Highbury Ter. M. N5 .....5B 66
High Cedar Dr. SW20 .....7E 134
Highclere Rd. KT3: N Mald 3K 151
Highclere St. SE26 .....4A 140
Highcliffe W13 .....5B 78
(off Clivedon Ct.)
Highcliffe Dr. SW15 .....6B 116
Highcliffe Gdns. IG4: Ilf 5C 52
Highcombe SE7 .....6K 105
Highcombe Cl. SE9 .....1B 142
High Coombe Pl. KT2: King T 6H 133
Highcroft NW9 .....5A 44
Highcroft Av. HA0: Wemb 7G 61
Highcroft Est. N19 .....7J 47
Highcroft Gdns. NW11 .....6H 45
Highcroft Rd. N19 .....7J 47
High Cross Cen., The N15 .....4G 49
High Cross Rd. N17 .....3G 49
Highcross Way SW15 .....1C 134
Highdaun Dr. SW16 .....4K 155
Highdown KT4: Wor Pk 2A 164
Highdown Rd. SW15 .....6D 116
High Dr. KT3: N Mald 1J 151
High Elms IG8: Wfd G 5D 36
High Elms Country Pk.
(Local Nature Reserve) 7H 173
High Elms Rd. BR6: Downe 7G 173
Highfield WD23: B Hea 2D 26
Highfield Av. BR6: Chels 5K 173
DA8: Erith 6H 109
HA5: Pinn 5D 40
HA9: Wemb 3F 61
NW9 .....5J 43
NW11 .....7F 45
UB6: G'frd 5J 59
Highfield Cl. HA6: Nwood 1G 39
KT6: Surb 1C 162
N22 .....1A 48
NW9 .....5J 43
SE13 .....6E 123
Highfield Ct. N14 .....6B 22
NW11 .....6G 45
Highfield Cres. HA6: Nwood 1G 39
Highfield Dr. BR2: Brom 4G 159
BR4: W W'ck 2D 170
KT19: Ewe 6B 164
UB10: Ick 4A 56
Highfield Gdns. NW11 .....6G 45
Highfield Hill SE19 .....7D 138
Highfield M. NW6 .....7K 63
(off Compayne Gdns.)
Highfield Rd. BR1: Brom 4D 160
BR7: Chst 3K 161
DA6: Bex 5F 127
HA6: Nwood 1G 39
IG8: Wfd G 7H 37
KT5: Surb 7J 151
KT12: Walt T 7J 147
N21 .....2G 33
NW11 .....6G 45
SM1: Sutt 5C 166
TW7: Isle 1K 113
TW13: Felt 2J 129
TW16: Sun 5H 147
W3 .....5H 79
Highfields SM1: Sutt 2J 165
Highfields Gro. N6 .....1D 64
High Foleys KT10: Clay 7B 162
High Gables BR2: Brom 2G 159
HIGHGATE 6E 46
Highgate Av. N6 .....7F 47
Highgate Cemetery N6 .....1E 64
Highgate Cl. N6 .....7E 46
Highgate Edge N2 .....5C 46
Highgate Hgts. N6 .....6G 47
Highgate High St. N6 .....1E 64

Highgate Hill N6 .....1F 65
N19 .....1F 65
Highgate Ho. SE26 .....3G 139
Highgate Rd. NW5 .....3E 64
Highgate Spinney N8 .....6H 47
Highgate Wlk. SE23 .....2J 139
Highgate W. Hill N6 .....1E 64
Highgate Wood School Sports Cen. 5G 47
High Gro. BR1: Brom 1B 160
SE18 .....7H 107
Highgrove Cl. BR7: Chst 1C 160
N11 .....5K 31
Highgrove Ct. BR3: Beck 7C 140
SM1: Sutt 6J 165
Highgrove M. SM5: Cars 3D 166
Highgrove Rd. RM8: Dag 5C 72
Highgrove Swimming Pool 6J 39
Highgrove Ter. E4 .....2A 36
Highgrove Way HA4: Ruis 6J 39
High Hill Est. E5 .....1H 67
High Hill Ferry E5 .....1H 67
High Holborn WC1 .....7E 6 (6J 83)
(not continuous)
Highland Av. RM10: Dag 3J 73
W7 .....6J 77
Highland Cotts. SM6: Wall 4G 167
Highland Ct. E18 .....1K 51
Highland Cft. BR3: Beck 5D 140
Highland Dr. WD23: Bush 1A 26
Highland Pk. TW13: Felt 4H 129
Highland Rd. BR1: Brom 1H 159
BR2: Brom 1H 159
DA6: Bex 5G 127
HA6: Nwood 2H 39
SE19 .....6E 138
Highlands N20 .....2G 31
Highlands, The EN5: New Bar 4D 20
HA8: Edg 2H 43
Highlands Av. N21 .....5E 22
W3 .....7J 79
Highlands Cl. N4 .....7J 47
TW3: Houn 1F 113
Highlands Ct. SE19 .....6E 138
Highlands Gdns. IG1: Ilf 1D 70
Highlands Heath SW15 .....7E 116
Highlands Rd. EN5: New Bar 5D 20
HIGHLANDS VILLAGE 5E 22
Highland Ter. SE13 .....3D 122
(off Algernon Rd.)
Highland Vw. Pk. Homes
UB7: W Dray 1D 174
High La. W7 .....5H 77
Highlawn Hall HA1: Harr 3J 59
Highlea Cl. NW9 .....7F 29
High Level Dr. SE26 .....4G 139
Highlever Rd. W10 .....5E 80
HA1: Harr 5J 41
Highmead N18 .....5B 34
(off Fore St.)
SE18 .....7K 107
Highmead Cres. HA0: Wemb 7F 61
High Mdw. Cl. HA5: Eastc 4A 40
Highmeadow Cres. NW9 .....5K 43
High Meads Rd. E16 .....6B 88
Highmore Rd. SE3 .....7G 105
High Mt. NW4 .....6C 44
High Oaks EN2: Enf 1E 22
High Pde., The SW16 .....3J 137
High Pk. Av. TW9: Kew 1G 115
High Pk. Rd. TW9: Kew 1G 115
High Path SW19 .....1K 153
High Point N6 .....7E 46
SE9 .....3F 143
High Ridge N10 .....1F 47
Highridge Pl. EN2: Enf 1E 22
(off Oak Av.)
High Rd. E18 .....1J 51
HA0: Wemb 5D 60
HA3: Hrw W 7D 26
HA5: Eastc 6J 39
HA9: Wemb 5D 60

High Rd. IG1: Ilf 3F **71**
(not continuous)
IG3: Chad H, Ilf 2G **71**
IG7: Chig 5K **37**
IG8: Wfd G 7C **36**
IG9: Buck H 2E **36**
N11 5A **32**
N15 4F **49**
N17 2F **49**
N22 1K **47**
NW10 6A **62**
RM6: Chad H 7D **54**
UB4: Hayes 5G **75**
UB10: Ick 3E **56**
WD23: B Hea 1C **26**
High Rd. E. Finchley N2 1B **46**
High Rd. Leyton E10 6D **50**
E15 2D **68**
High Rd. Leytonstone E11 4G **69**
E15 4G **69**
High Rd. Nth. Finchley N12 3F **31**
High Rd. Whetstone N20 7F **21**
High Rd. Woodford Grn. IG8: Wfd G 6C **36**
High Sheldon N6 6D **46**
Highshore Rd. SE15 2F **121**
(not continuous)
Highstead Cres. DA8: Erith 1K **127**
Highstone Av. E11 6J **51**
Highstone Ct. *E11 6H **51***
(off New Wanstead)
Highstone Mans. *NW1 7G **65***
(off Camden Rd.)
High St. BR1: Brom 2J **159**
BR3: Beck 2C **158**
BR4: W W'ck 1D **170**
BR6: Chels 7K **173**
BR6: Farnb 5F **173**
BR6: Orp 2K **173**
BR7: Chst 6F **143**
CR0: C'don 3C **168**
(not continuous)
CR7: Thor H 4C **156**
E11 5J **51**
E13 2J **87**
E15 2E **86**
E17 5A **50**
EN3: Pond E 6D **24**
EN5: Barn 3B **20**
HA1: Harr 1J **59**
HA3: W'stone 2J **41**
(not continuous)
HA4: Ruis 7G **39**
HA5: Pinn 3C **40**
HA6: Nwood 1H **39**
HA8: Edg 6B **28**
HA9: Wemb 4F **61**
IG6: Ilf 3G **53**
KT1: Ham W 1C **150**
KT1: King T 3D **150**
KT3: N Mald 4A **152**
KT7: T Ditt 6A **150**
KT8: W Mole 4E **148**
KT12: Walt T 7J **147**
KT17: Ewe 7B **164**
N8 4J **47**
N14 1C **32**
NW7 5J **29**
NW10 2B **80**
RM1: Rom 5K **55**
SE20 6J **139**
SE25 4F **157**
SM1: Sutt 4K **165**
SM3: Cheam 6G **165**
SM5: Cars 5E **166**
SW19 5F **135**
TW2: Whitt 7G **113**
TW3: Houn 3F **113**
(not continuous)
TW5: Cran 1J **111**
TW8: Bford 7C **96**
TW11: Tedd 5K **131**
TW12: Hamp, Ham H 1G **149**
High St. TW13: Felt 3H **129**
TW17: Shep 6D **146**
TW19: Stanw 6A **110**
UB1: S'hall 1D **94**
UB3: Harl 6F **93**
UB7: Harm 2E **174**
UB7: Yiew 7A **74**
UB8: Uxb 1A **74**
W3 1H **97**
W5 1D **96**
High St. Colliers Wood SW19 7B **136**
High St. Harlesden NW10 2B **80**
High St. M. SW19 5G **135**
High St. Nth. E6 5C **70**
E12 5C **70**
High St. Sth. E6 2D **88**
High Timber St. EC4 2C **14** (7C **84**)
High Tor Cl. BR1: Brom 7K **141**
High Tor Vw. SE28 1J **107**
High Trees CR0: C'don 1A **170**
EN4: E Barn 5H **21**
N20 3F **31**
SW2 1A **138**
Hightrees Ct. W7 7J **77**
Hightrees Ho. SW12 6E **118**
High Vw. HA5: Pinn 4A **40**
Highview N6 6G **47**
NW7 3E **28**
UB5: N'olt 3C **76**
Highview Av. HA8: Edg 4D **28**
SM6: Wall 5K **167**
High Vw. Cl. SE19 2F **157**
High Vw. Ct. HA3: Hrw W 7D **26**
Highview Gdns. HA8: Edg 4D **28**
N3 3G **45**
N11 5B **32**
Highview Ho. RM6: Chad H 4E **54**
Highview Lodge *EN2: Enf 3G **23***
(off The Ridgeway)
High Vw. Pde. IG4: Ilf 5D **52**
High Vw. Rd. E18 2H **51**
N2 1D **46**
SE19 6D **138**
Highview Rd. DA14: Sidc 4B **144**
W13 5A **78**
Highway, The E1 7G **85**
HA7: Stan 1K **41**
SM2: Sutt 7A **166**
Highway Bus. Pk., The *E1 7K **85***
(off Heckford St.)
Highway Trad. Cen., The *E1 7K **85***
(off Heckford St.)
Highwood BR2: Brom 3F **159**
Highwood Av. N12 4F **31**
Highwood Cl. BR6: Farnb 2G **173**
SE22 1G **139**
Highwood Ct. EN5: New Bar 5D **20**
N12 3F **31**
Highwood Dr. BR6: Farnb 2G **173**
Highwood Gdns. IG5: Ilf 5D **52**
Highwood Gro. NW7 5E **28**
HIGHWOOD HILL 3G **29**
Highwood Hill NW7 2G **29**
Highwood Rd. N19 3J **65**
High Worple HA2: Harr 7D **40**
Highworth Rd. N11 6C **32**
Highworth St. NW1 5D **4**
Hi-Gloss Cen. SE8 5A **104**
Hilary Av. CR4: Mitc 3E **154**
Hilary Cl. DA8: Erith 1H **127**
SW6 7K **99**
Hilary Dennis Ct. E11 4J **51**
Hilary Rd. W12 6B **80**
(not continuous)
Hilberry Ct. WD23: Bush 1A **26**
Hilbert Rd. SM3: Cheam 3F **165**
Hilborough Cl. SW19 7A **136**
Hilborough Ct. E8 7F **67**
Hilborough Way BR6: Farnb 5H **173**
Hilda Ct. KT6: Surb 7D **150**
Hilda Lockert Wlk. *SW9 2B **120***
(off Loughborough Rd.)
Hilda Rd. E6 7B **70**
E16 4G **87**
(not continuous)
Hilda Ter. SW9 2A **120**
Hilda Va. Cl. BR6: Farnb 4F **173**
Hilda Va. Rd. BR6: Farnb 4E **172**
Hildenborough Gdns. BR1: Brom 6G **141**
Hildenborough Ho. *BR3: Beck 7B **140***
(off Bethersden Cl.)
Hildenlea Pl. BR2: Brom 2F **159**
Hilderley Ho. *KT1: King T 3F **151***
(off Winery La.)
Hildreth St. SW12 1F **137**
Hildreth St. M. SW12 1F **137**
Hildyard Rd. SW6 6J **99**
Hiley Rd. NW10 3E **80**
Hilgrove Rd. NW6 7A **64**
Hiliary Gdns. HA7: Stan 2C **42**
Hillary *N8 3J **47***
(off Boyton Cl.)
Hillary Ct. *TW19: Stanw 1A **128***
(off Explorer Av.)
*W12 2E **98***
(off Titmuss St.)
Hillary Cres. KT12: Walt T 7A **148**
Hillary Dr. TW7: Isle 5K **113**
Hillary Ri. EN5: New Bar 4D **20**
Hillary Rd. UB2: S'hall 3E **94**
Hillbeck Cl. SE15 7J **103**
(not continuous)
Hillbeck Way UB6: G'frd 1H **77**
Hillborne Cl. UB3: Harl 5J **93**
Hillboro Ct. E11 7F **51**
Hillbrook Rd. SW17 3D **136**
Hill Brow BR1: Brom 1B **160**
Hillbrow KT3: N Mald 3B **152**
Hillbrow Cl. DA5: Bexl 4K **145**
Hillbrow Rd. BR1: Brom 7G **141**
Hillbury Av. HA3: Kenton 5B **42**
Hillbury Rd. SW17 3F **137**
Hill Cl. BR7: Chst 5F **143**
HA1: Harr 3J **59**
HA7: Stan 4G **27**
NW2 3D **62**
NW11 6J **45**
Hillcote Av. SW16 7A **138**
Hill Ct. EN4: E Barn 4H **21**
UB5: N'olt 5E **58**
W5 4F **79**
Hillcourt Av. N12 6E **30**
Hillcourt Est. N16 1D **66**
Hillcourt Rd. SE22 6H **121**
Hill Cres. DA5: Bexl 1J **145**
HA1: Harr 5A **42**
KT4: Wor Pk 2E **164**
KT5: Surb 5F **151**
N20 2E **30**
Hill Crest DA15: Sidc 7A **126**
KT6: Surb 7E **150**
Hillcrest N6 7E **46**
N21 7F **23**
SE24 4D **120**
*W11 7H **81***
(off St John's Gdns.)
Hillcrest Av. HA5: Pinn 4B **40**
HA8: Edg 4C **28**
NW11 5H **45**
Hillcrest Cl. BR3: Beck 6B **158**
SE26 4G **139**
Hillcrest Ct. RM5: Col R 1K **55**
*SM2: Sutt 6B **166***
(off Eaton Rd.)
Hillcrest Gdns. KT10: Hin W 3A **162**
N3 4G **45**
NW2 3C **62**
Hillcrest Rd. BR1: Brom 5J **141**
BR6: Chels 2K **173**
E17 2F **51**
E18 2H **51**
W3 1H **97**
W5 5E **78**
Hillcrest Vw. BR3: Beck 6B **158**
Hillcroft Av. HA5: Pinn 6D **40**
Hillcroft Cres. HA4: Ruis 3B **58**
HA9: Wemb 4F **61**
W5 6D **78**
Hillcroft Rd. E6 5F **89**
Hillcroome Rd. SM2: Sutt 6B **166**
Hillcross Av. SM4: Mord 6F **153**
Hilldale Rd. SM1: Sutt 4H **165**
Hilldown Ct. SW16 7J **137**
Hilldown Rd. BR2: Hayes 1G **171**
SW16 7J **137**
Hill Dr. NW9 1J **61**
SW16 3K **155**
Hilldrop Cres. N7 5H **65**
Hilldrop Est. N7 5H **65**
(not continuous)
Hilldrop La. N7 5H **65**
Hilldrop Rd. BR1: Brom 6K **141**
N7 5H **65**
Hill End BR6: Orp 2K **173**
Hillend SE18 1E **124**
Hillersden Ho. *SW1 5J **17***
(off Ebury Bri. Rd.)
Hillersdon Av. HA8: Edg 5A **28**
SW13 2C **116**
Hillery Cl. SE17 4D **102**
Hill Farm Cotts. HA4: Ruis 7E **38**
Hill Farm Rd. UB10: Ick 4F **57**
W10 5E **80**
Hillfield Av. HA0: Wemb 7E **60**
N8 5J **47**
NW9 5A **44**
SM4: Mord 6C **154**
Hillfield Cl. HA2: Harr 4G **41**
Hillfield Ct. NW3 5C **64**
Hillfield Ho. N5 5C **66**
Hillfield M. N8 4K **47**
Hillfield Pk. N10 4F **47**
N21 2F **33**
Hillfield Pk. M. N10 4F **47**
Hill Fld. Rd. TW12: Hamp 7D **130**
Hillfield Rd. NW6 5H **63**
Hillfoot Av. RM5: Col R 1J **55**
Hillfoot Rd. RM5: Col R 1J **55**
Hillgate Pl. SW12 7F **119**
W8 1J **99**
Hillgate St. W8 1J **99**
Hill Ga. Wlk. N6 6G **47**
Hill Gro. RM1: Rom 3K **55**
TW13: Hanw 2D **130**
Hill Ho. BR2: Brom 2H **159**
*E5 1H **67***
(off Harrington Hill)
SE28 1H **107**
Hill Ho. Apartments *N1 1H **7***
(off Pentonville Rd.)
Hill Ho. Av. HA7: Stan 7E **26**
Hill Ho. Cl. N21 7F **23**
Hill Ho. Dr. TW12: Hamp 1E **148**
Hill Ho. M. BR2: Brom 2H **159**
Hill Ho. Rd. SW16 5K **137**
Hilliard Ho. *E1 1H **103***
(off Prusom St.)
Hilliard Rd. HA6: Nwood 1H **39**
Hilliards Ct. E1 1J **103**
Hillier Cl. EN5: New Bar 6E **20**
Hillier Gdns. CR0: Wadd 5A **168**
Hillier Ho. *NW1 7H **65***
(off Camden Sq.)
Hillier Lodge TW11: Tedd 5H **131**
Hillier Pl. KT9: Chess 6D **162**
Hillier Rd. SW11 6D **118**
Hilliers Av. UB8: Hil 3C **74**
Hilliers La. CR0: Bedd 3J **167**
HILLINGDON 3C **74**
Hillingdon Athletic Club 5F **39**
Hillingdon Athletics Stadium 6A **56**
Hillingdon Av. TW19: Stanw 1A **128**
HILLINGDON CIRCUS 6D **56**
Hillingdon Ct. HA3: Kenton 4D **42**
Hillingdon Cycling Circuit 1A **94**
HILLINGDON HEATH 4D **74**

Hillingdon Hill UB10: Hil 2A 74
Hillingdon Rd. DA7: Bex 2J 127
   UB8: Uxb 1A 74
   UB10: Uxb 1A 74
Hillingdon Sports & Leisure Complex
   ....6A 56
Hillingdon St. SE17 ....6B 102
Hillington Gdns.
   IG8: Wfd G 2B 52
Hill La. HA4: Ruis 1E 56
Hillman Cl. UB8: Uxb 5A 56
Hillman Dr. W10 ....4E 80
Hillman St. E8 ....6H 67
Hillmarton Rd. N7 ....5J 65
Hillmarton Ter. N7 ....5J 65
   (off Hillmarton Rd.)
Hillmead Dr. SW9 ....4B 120
Hillmore Ct. SE13 ....3F 123
   (off Belmont Hill)
Hillmore Gro. SE26 ....5A 140
Hill Path SW16 ....5K 137
Hillreach SE18 ....5D 106
Hill Ri. HA4: Ruis 1E 56
   KT10: Hin W 2B 162
   N9 ....6C 24
   NW11 ....4K 45
   SE23 ....1H 139
   TW10: Rich 5D 114
   UB6: G'frd 7G 59
Hillrise KT12: Walt T 7H 147
Hillrise Mans. N19 ....7J 47
   (off Warltersville Rd.)
Hillrise Rd. N19 ....7J 47
Hill Rd. CR4: Mitc 1F 155
   HA0: Wemb 3B 60
   HA1: Harr 5A 42
   HA5: Pinn 5C 40
   N10 ....1D 46
   NW8 ....2A 82
   SM1: Sutt 5K 165
   SM5: Cars 6C 166
Hillsboro' Rd. SE22 ....5E 120
Hillsborough Ct. NW6 ....1K 81
   (off Mortimer Cres.)
Hillsgrove Cl. DA16: Well 7C 108
HILLSIDE 4J 109
Hillside DA8: Erith 4J 109
   EN5: New Bar 5F 21
   N8 ....6H 47
   NW5 ....3E 64
   NW9 ....4K 43
   NW10 ....7J 61
   SE10 ....7F 105
   (off Crooms Hill)
   SW19 ....6F 135
Hillside Av. HA9: Wemb 4F 61
   IG8: Wfd G 6F 37
   N11 ....6J 31
Hillside Cl. IG8: Wfd G 5F 37
   NW8 ....2K 81
   SM4: Mord 4G 153
Hillside Cres. HA2: Harr 1G 59
   HA6: Nwood 1J 39
Hillside Dr. HA8: Edg 6B 28
Hillside Gdns. E17 ....3F 51
   EN5: Barn 4B 20
   HA3: Kenton 7E 42
   HA6: Nwood 1J 39
   HA8: Edg 4A 28
   N6 ....6F 47
   N11 ....6B 32
   SM6: Wall 7G 167
   SW2 ....2A 138
Hillside Gro. N14 ....7C 22
   NW7 ....7H 29
Hillside Ho. CR0: Wadd 4B 168
   (off Violet La.)
Hillside La. BR2: Hayes 7H 159
   (not continuous)
Hillside Mans. EN5: Barn 4C 20
Hillside Pas. SW16 ....2K 137
Hillside Ri. HA6: Nwood 1J 39

Hillside Rd. BR2: Brom 3H 159
   CR0: Wadd 5B 168
   HA5: Pinn 1K 39
   HA6: Nwood 1J 39
   KT5: Surb 4F 151
   N15 ....7E 48
   SM2: Sutt 7H 165
   SW2 ....2K 137
   UB1: S'hall 4E 76
   W5 ....5E 78
Hills La. HA6: Nwood 1G 39
Hillsleigh Rd. W8 ....1H 99
Hills M. W5 ....7E 78
Hills Pl. W1 ....1A 12 (6G 83)
Hills Rd. IG9: Buck H 1E 36
Hillstone Ct. E3 ....4D 86
   (off Empson St.)
Hillstowe St. E5 ....3J 67
Hill St. TW9: Rich 5D 114
   W1 ....4H 11 (1E 100)
Hill Top NW11 ....4K 45
   SM3: Sutt 7H 153
   SM4: Mord 6J 153
Hilltop E17 ....3D 50
Hilltop Av. NW10 ....7J 61
Hill Top Ct. IG8: Wfd G 6J 37
Hilltop Ct. NW8 ....7A 64
   (off Alexandra Rd.)
Hilltop Gdns. BR6: Orp 2J 173
   NW4 ....2D 44
Hilltop Ho. N6 ....7H 47
Hilltop Rd. NW6 ....7J 63
Hill Top Vw. IG8: Wfd G 6J 37
Hilltop Way HA7: Stan 3F 27
Hill Vw. NW3 ....1D 82
   (off Ainger Rd.)
Hillview SW20 ....7D 134
Hillview Av. HA3: Kenton 5E 42
Hillview Cl. HA9: Wemb 2F 61
Hill Vw. Cres. IG1: Ilf 6D 52
Hillview Cres. BR6: Orp 1J 173
Hill Vw. Dr. DA16: Well 2J 125
   SE28 ....1J 107
Hill Vw. Gdns. NW9 ....5K 43
Hillview Gdns. HA2: Harr 3E 40
   NW4 ....4F 45
Hill Vw. Rd. KT10: Clay 7A 162
   TW1: Twick 6A 114
Hillview Rd. BR6: Orp 1K 173
   BR7: Chst 5E 142
   HA5: Hat E 1D 40
   NW7 ....4A 30
   SM1: Sutt 3A 166
Hillway N6 ....2E 64
   NW9 ....1A 62
Hill-Wood Ho. NW1 ....1B 6
   (off Polygon Rd.)
Hillworth BR3: Beck 2D 158
Hillworth Rd. SW2 ....7A 120
Hillyard Ho. SW9 ....1A 120
Hillyard Rd. W7 ....5J 77
Hillyard St. SW9 ....1A 120
Hillyfield E17 ....2A 50
Hillyfield Cl. E9 ....5A 68
Hilly Flds. Cres. SE4 ....3C 122
   SE13 ....3C 122
Hilsea Point SW15 ....1D 134
Hilsea St. E5 ....4J 67
Hilton Av. N12 ....5G 31
Hilton Ho. SE4 ....4K 121
Hilton's Wharf SE10 ....6D 104
   (off Norman Rd.)
Hilversum Cres. SE22 ....5E 120
Himalaya Palace Cinema 1D 94
Himley Rd. SW17 ....5C 136
Hinchinbrook Ho. NW6 ....1K 81
   (off Mortimer Cres.)
Hinchley Cl. KT10: Hin W 4A 162
Hinchley Dr. KT10: Hin W 3A 162
Hinchley Mnr. KT10: Hin W 3A 162
Hinchley Way KT10: Hin W 3A 162
HINCHLEY WOOD 3A 162

Hinckley Rd. SE15 ....4G 121
Hind Cl. EC4 ....1K 13 (6A 84)
Hind Cres. DA8: Erith 6K 109
Hinde Ho. W1 ....7H 5
   (off Hinde St.)
Hinde M. W1 ....7H 5
Hindes Rd. HA1: Harr 5H 41
Hinde St. W1 ....7H 5 (6E 82)
Hind Gro. E14 ....6C 86
Hindhead Cl. N16 ....1E 66
   UB8: Hil 5D 74
Hindhead Gdns. UB5: N'olt 1C 76
Hindhead Point SW15 ....1D 134
Hindhead Way SM6: Wall 5J 167
Hind Ho. N7 ....4A 66
   SE14 ....6K 103
   (off Myers La.)
Hindle Ho. E8 ....5F 67
Hindlip Ho. SW8 ....1H 119
Hindmans Rd. SE22 ....5G 121
Hindmans Way RM9: Dag 4F 91
Hindmarsh Cl. E1 ....7G 85
Hindon Cl. SW1 ....3A 18
Hindrey Rd. E5 ....5H 67
Hindsley's Pl. SE23 ....2J 139
Hinkler Rd. HA3: Kenton 3D 42
Hinksey Path SE2 ....2D 108
Hinstock NW6 ....1K 81
   (off Belsize Rd.)
Hinstock Rd. SE18 ....6G 107
Hinton Av. TW4: Houn 4B 112
Hinton Cl. SE9 ....1C 142
Hinton Cl. E10 ....2D 68
   (off Leyton Grange Est.)
Hinton Ho. W5 ....6C 78
Hinton Rd. N18 ....4K 33
   SE24 ....3B 120
   SM6: Wall 6G 167
Hippisley Ct. TW7: Isle 3K 113
Hippodrome M. W11 ....7G 81
Hippodrome Pl. W11 ....7G 81
Hiroshima Prom. SE7 ....3A 106
Hirst Cl. SW1 ....7J 17 (6F 101)
Hirst Cres. HA9: Wemb 3E 60
Hitcham Rd. E17 ....7B 50
Hitchcock Cl. TW17: Shep 3B 146
Hitchin Sq. E3 ....2A 86
Hithe Gro. SE16 ....3J 103
Hitherbroom Rd. UB3: Hayes 1J 93
Hither Farm Rd. SE3 ....3A 124
Hitherfield Rd. RM8: Dag 2E 72
   SW16 ....2K 137
HITHER GREEN 6G 123
Hither Grn. La. SE13 ....5E 122
Hithermoor Rd. TW19: Stan M 7B 174
Hitherwell Dr. HA3: Hrw W 1H 41
Hitherwood Dr. SE19 ....4F 139
Hive Cl. WD23: B Hea 2C 26
Hive Rd. WD23: B Hea 2C 26
   (not continuous)
HMP Belmarsh SE28 ....2J 107
HMP Brixton SW2 ....6J 119
HMP Holloway N7 ....4J 65
HMP Latchmere House
   TW10: Ham 5F 133
HMP Pentonville N7 ....6K 65
HMP Wandsworth SW18 ....7B 118
HMP Wormwood Scrubs W12 ....6C 80
HMS Belfast 4H 15 (1E 102)
HMYOI Feltham TW13: Felt 3F 129
Hoadly Ho. SE1 ....5C 14
   (off Union St.)
Hoadly Rd. SW16 ....3H 137
Hobart Cl. N20 ....2H 31
   UB4: Yead 4B 76
Hobart Ct. CR2: S Croy 5D 168
   (off South Pk. Hill Rd.)
Hobart Dr. UB4: Yead 4B 76
Hobart Gdns. CR7: Thor H 3D 156
Hobart La. UB4: Yead 4B 76
Hobart Pl. SW1 ....1J 17 (3F 101)
   TW10: Rich 7F 115

Hobart Rd. IG6: Ilf 2G 53
   KT4: Wor Pk 3D 164
   RM9: Dag 4D 72
   UB4: Yead 4B 76
Hobbayne Rd. W7 ....6H 77
Hobbes Wlk. SW15 ....5D 116
Hobbs Ct. SE1 ....6K 15
   (off Mill St.)
Hobbs Grn. N2 ....3A 46
Hobbs M. IG3: Ilf 2K 71
Hobbs Pl. N1 ....1E 84
Hobbs Pl. Est. N1 ....2E 84
   (off Hobbs Pl.)
Hobbs Rd. SE27 ....4C 138
Hobby St. EN3: Enf W 4F 25
Hobday St. E14 ....6D 86
Hobill Wlk. KT5: Surb 6F 151
Hoblands End BR7: Chst 6J 143
Hobson's Pl. E1 ....5G 85
Hobury St. SW10 ....7A 16 (6A 100)
Hocker St. E2 ....2J 9 (3F 85)
Hockett Cl. SE8 ....4A 104
Hockington Cl. EN5: New Bar 4E 20
Hockley Av. E6 ....2C 88
Hockley Cl. E18 ....1J 51
Hockley M. IG11: Bark 3J 89
Hockliffe Ho. W10 ....5E 80
   (off Sutton Way)
Hockney Ct. SE16 ....5H 103
   (off Rossetti Rd.)
Hocroft Av. NW2 ....3H 63
Hocroft Ct. NW2 ....3H 63
Hocroft Rd. NW2 ....3H 63
Hocroft Wlk. NW2 ....3H 63
Hodder Dr. UB6: G'frd 2K 77
Hoddesdon Rd. DA17: Belv 5G 109
Hodes Row NW3 ....4E 64
Hodford Rd. NW11 ....1H 63
Hodgkin Cl. SE28 ....7D 90
Hodgkins M. HA7: Stan 5G 27
Hodister Cl. SE5 ....7C 102
Hodnet Gro. SE16 ....4K 103
Hodson Cl. HA2: Harr 3D 58
Hoecroft Ct. EN3: Enf W 1D 24
   (off Hoe La.)
Hoe La. EN1: Enf 1B 24
   EN3: Enf W 1C 24
Hoe St. E17 ....4C 50
Hoever Ho. SE6 ....4E 140
Hoffmann Gdns. CR2: Sels 7H 169
Hoffman Sq. N1 ....1F 9
Hofland Rd. W14 ....3G 99
Hogan M. W2 ....5A 4 (5A 82)
Hogan Way E5 ....2G 67
Hogarth Av. TW15: Ashf 6E 128
Hogarth Bus. Pk. W4 ....6A 98
Hogarth Cl. E16 ....5B 88
   W5 ....5E 78
Hogarth Ct. E1 ....6G 85
   (off Batty St.)
   EC3 ....2H 15 (6E 84)
   NW1 ....7G 65
   (off St Pancras Way)
   SE19 ....4F 139
   TW5: Hest 7C 94
Hogarth Cres. CR0: C'don 7C 156
   SW19 ....1B 154
Hogarth Gdns. TW5: Hest 7E 94
Hogarth Health Club, The 4B 98
Hogarth Hill NW11 ....4H 45
Hogarth Ho. SW1 ....4D 18
   (off Erasmus St.)
   UB5: N'olt 2B 76
   (off Gallery Gdns.)
Hogarth Ind. Est. NW10 ....4C 80
Hogarth La. W4 ....6A 98
Hogarth Pl. SW5 ....4K 99
   (off Hogarth Rd.)
Hogarth Rd. HA8: Edg 2G 43
   RM8: Dag 5B 72
   SW5 ....4K 99

HOGARTH RDBT. 6A 98
Hogarth's House 6A 98
   (off Hogarth La.)
Hogarth Ter. W4 . . . . .6A 98
Hogarth Way TW12: Hamp 1G 149
Hog Hill Rd. RM5: Col R 1F 55
Hogshead Pas. E1 . . . . .7H 85
   (off Tobacco Dock)
Hogsmill Ho. KT1: King T 3F 151
   (off Vineyard Cl.)
Hogsmill La. KT1: King T 3F 151
Hogsmill Local Nature Reserve 5H 163
Hogsmill Wlk. KT1: King T 3E 150
   (off Penrhyn Rd.)
Hogsmill Way KT19: Ewe 5J 163
Holbeach Cl. NW9 . . . . .1A 44
Holbeach Gdns. DA15: Sidc 6J 125
Holbeach M. SW12 . . . . .1F 137
Holbeach Rd. SE6 . . . . .7C 122
Holbeck Row SE15 . . . . .7G 103
Holbein Ho. SW1 . . . . .5G 17
   (off Holbein M.)
Holbein M. SW1 . . . . .5G 17 (5E 100)
Holbein Pl. SW1 . . . . .4G 17 (4E 100)
Holbein Ter. RM8: Dag 4C 72
   (off Marlborough Rd.)
Holberton Gdns. NW10 . . . . .3D 80
HOLBORN 6G 7 (5K 83)
Holborn EC1 . . . . .5A 84
Holborn Cir. EC1 . . . . .6K 7 (5A 84)
Holborn Pl. WC1 . . . . .6G 7
Holborn Rd. E13 . . . . .4K 87
Holborn Viaduct EC1 . . . . . . .6K 7 (5B 84)
Holborn Way CR4: Mitc 2D 154
Holbrook Cl. EN1: Enf 1A 24
   N19 . . . . .1F 65
Holbrooke Ct. N7 . . . . .4J 65
Holbrooke Pl. TW10: Rich 5D 114
Holbrook La. BR7: Chst 1H 161
Holbrook Rd. E15 . . . . .2H 87
Holbrook Way BR2: Brom 6D 160
Holburne Cl. SE3 . . . . .1A 124
Holburne Gdns. SE3 . . . . .1B 124
Holburne Rd. SE3 . . . . .1A 124
Holcombe Hill NW7 . . . . .3H 29
Holcombe Ho. SW9 . . . . .3J 119
   (off Landor Rd.)
Holcombe Pl. SE4 . . . . .3A 122
   (off St Asaph Rd.)
Holcombe Rd. IG1: Ilf 7E 52
   N17 . . . . .3F 49
   (not continuous)
Holcombe St. W6 . . . . .4D 98
Holcote Cl. DA17: Belv 3E 108
Holcroft Ct. W1 . . . . .5A 6
Holcroft Ho. SW11 . . . . .3B 118
Holcroft Rd. E9 . . . . .7J 67
Holden Av. N12 . . . . .5E 30
   NW9 . . . . .1J 61
Holdenby Rd. SE4 . . . . .5A 122
Holden Cl. RM8: Dag 3B 72
Holden Ho. N1 . . . . .1C 84
   (off Prebend St.)
   SE8 . . . . .7C 104
Holdenhurst Av. N12 . . . . .7F 31
Holden Rd. N12 . . . . .5E 30
Holden St. SW11 . . . . .2E 118
Holder Cl. N3 . . . . .7E 30
Holdernesse Cl. TW7: Isle 1A 114
Holdernesse Rd. SW17 . . . . .3D 136
Holderness Ho. SE5 . . . . .3E 120
Holderness Way SE27 . . . . .5B 138
HOLDERS HILL 2F 45
Holder's Hill Av. NW4 . . . . .2F 45
Holders Hill Cir. NW7 . . . . .7B 30
Holders Hill Cres. NW4 . . . . .2F 45
Holders Hill Dr. NW4 . . . . .3F 45
Holder's Hill Gdns. NW4 . . . . .2G 45
Holders Hill Pde. NW7 . . . . .1G 45
Holders Hill Rd. NW4 . . . . .2F 45
   NW7 . . . . .2F 45

Holford Ho. SE16 . . . . .4H 103
   (off Camilla Rd.)
   WC1 . . . . .1H 7
   (off St. Percy St.)
Holford M. WC1 . . . . .1J 7
Holford Pl. WC1 . . . . .1H 7 (3K 83)
Holford Rd. NW3 . . . . .3A 64
Holford St. WC1 . . . . .1J 7 (3K 83)
Holford Way SW15 . . . . .6C 116
Holford Yd. WC1 . . . . .1J 7
   (off Cruikshank St.)
Holgate Av. SW11 . . . . .3B 118
Holgate Gdns. RM10: Dag 6G 73
Holgate Rd. RM10: Dag 5G 73
Holgate St. SE7 . . . . .3B 106
Hollam Ho. N8 . . . . .4K 47
Holland Av. SM2: Sutt 7J 165
   SW20 . . . . .1B 152
Holland Cl. BR2: Hayes 2H 171
   EN5: New Bar 7G 21
   HA7: Stan 5G 27
   RM7: Rom 5J 55
Holland Ct. E17 . . . . .4E 50
   (off Evelyn Rd.)
   KT6: Surb 7D 150
   NW7 . . . . .6H 29
Holland Dr. SE23 . . . . .3A 140
Holland Dwellings WC2 . . . . .7F 7
   (off Newton St.)
Holland Gdns. TW8: Bford 6F 97
   W14 . . . . .3G 99
Holland Gro. SW9 . . . . .7A 102
Holland Ho. E4 . . . . .4K 35
   NW10 . . . . .2D 80
   (off Holland Rd.)
HOLLAND PARK 1H 99
Holland Pk. .2H 99
Holland Pk. W11 . . . . .1G 99
Holland Pk. Av. IG3: Ilf 6J 53
   W11 . . . . .2G 99
Holland Pk. Ct. W14 . . . . .2G 99
   (off Holland Pk. Gdns.)
Holland Pk. Gdns. W14 . . . . .2G 99
Holland Pk. Mans. W14 . . . . .1G 99
   (off Holland Pk. Gdns.)
Holland Pk. M. W11 . . . . .1G 99
Holland Pk. Rd. W14 . . . . .3H 99
HOLLAND PARK RDBT. 2F 99
Holland Pk. Ter. W11 . . . . .1G 99
   (off Portland Rd.)
Holland Park Theatre (Open Air) 2H 99
Holland Pas. N1 . . . . .1C 84
   (off Basire St.)
Holland Pl. W8 . . . . .2K 99
   (off Kensington Chu. St.)
Holland Pl. Chambers W8 . . . . .2K 99
   (off Holland Pl.)
Holland Ri. Ho. SW9 . . . . .7K 101
   (off Clapham Rd.)
Holland Rd. E6 . . . . .1D 88
   E15 . . . . .3G 87
   HA0: Wemb 6D 60
   NW10 . . . . .1C 80
   SE25 . . . . .5G 157
   W14 . . . . .2F 99
Hollands, The
   KT4: Wor Pk 1B 164
   TW13: Hanw 4B 130
Holland St. SE1 . . . . .4B 14 (1B 102)
   W8 . . . . .2J 99
Holland Vs. Rd. W14 . . . . .2G 99
Holland Wlk. HA7: Stan 5F 27
   N19 . . . . .1H 65
   W8 . . . . .1H 99
Holland Way BR2: Hayes 2H 171
Hollar Rd. N16 . . . . .3F 67
Hollen St. W1 . . . . .7C 6 (6H 83)
Holles Cl. TW12: Hamp 6E 130
Holles Ho. SW9 . . . . .2A 120
Holles St. W1 . . . . .7K 5 (6F 83)
Holley Rd. W3 . . . . .2A 98
Hollickwood Av. N12 . . . . .6J 31

Holliday Sq. SW11 . . . . .3B 118
   (off Fowler Cl.)
Hollidge Way RM10: Dag 7H 73
Hollies, The E11 . . . . .5J 51
   (off New Wanstead)
   HA3: W'stone 4A 42
   N20 . . . . .1G 31
Hollies Av. DA15: Sidc 2K 143
Hollies Cl. SW16 . . . . .6A 138
   TW1: Twick 2K 131
Hollies End NW7 . . . . .5J 29
Hollies Rd. W5 . . . . .4C 96
Hollies Way SW12 . . . . .7E 118
Holligrave Rd. BR1: Brom 1J 159
Hollingbourne Av. DA7: Bex 1F 127
Hollingbourne Gdns. W13 . . . . .5B 78
Hollingbourne Rd. SE24 . . . . .5C 120
Hollingsworth Ct. KT6: Surb 7D 150
Hollingsworth Rd. CR0: C'don 6H 169
Hollington Ct. BR7: Chst 6F 143
Hollington Cres. KT3: N Mald 6B 152
Hollington Rd. E6 . . . . .3D 88
   N17 . . . . .2G 49
Hollingworth Cl. KT8: W Mole 4D 148
Hollingworth Rd. BR5: Pet W 6F 161
Hollins Ho. N7 . . . . .4J 65
Hollisfield WC1 . . . . .2F 7
   (off Cromer St.)
Hollman Gdns. SW16 . . . . .6B 138
Hollow, The IG8: Wfd G 4C 36
HOLLOWAY .3J 65
Holloway Cl. UB7: Harm 5A 92
Holloway Ho. NW2 . . . . .3E 62
   (off Stoll Cl.)
Holloway La. UB7: Harm, W Dray . . .2E 174
Holloway Rd. E6 . . . . .3D 88
   E11 . . . . .3F 69
   N7 . . . . .4K 65
   N19 . . . . .2H 65
Holloway St. TW3: Houn 3F 113
Hollowfield Wlk. UB5: N'olt 6C 58
Hollows, The TW8: Bford 6F 97
Holly Av. HA7: Stan 2E 42
   KT12: Walt T 7B 148
Hollybank Cl. TW12: Hamp 5E 130
Hollyberry La. NW3 . . . . .4A 64
Hollybrake Cl. BR7: Chst 7H 143
Hollybush Cl. E11 . . . . .5J 51
   HA3: Hrw W 1J 41
Hollybush Gdns. E2 . . . . .3H 85
Holly Bush Hill NW3 . . . . .4A 64
Hollybush Hill E11 . . . . .6H 51
Hollybush Ho. E2 . . . . .3H 85
Holly Bush La. TW12: Hamp 7D 130
Hollybush Pl. E2 . . . . .3H 85
Hollybush Rd. KT2: King T 5E 132
Holly Bush Steps NW3 . . . . .4A 64
   (off Holly Mt.)
Hollybush St. E13 . . . . .3K 87
Holly Bush Va. NW3 . . . . .4A 64
Hollybush Wlk. SW9 . . . . .4B 120
Holly Cl. BR3: Beck 4E 158
   IG9: Buck H 3G 37
   SM6: Wall 7F 167
   TW13: Hanw 5C 130
   TW16: Sun 3K 147
Holly Cott. M. UB8: Hil 5C 74
Holly Ct. DA14: Sidc 4B 144
   (off Sidcup Hill)
   N15 . . . . .4E 48
   SE10 . . . . .3H 105
   SM2: Sutt 7J 165
Holly Cres. BR3: Beck 5B 158
   IG8: Wfd G 7A 36
Hollycroft Av. HA9: Wemb 2F 61
   NW3 . . . . .3J 63
Hollycroft Cl. CR2: S Croy 5E 168
   SE7: Sip 6C 92
Hollycroft Gdns. UB7: Sip 6C 92
Hollydale Cl. UB5: N'olt 4F 59
Hollydale Dr. BR2: Brom 3D 172
Hollydale Rd. SE15 . . . . .1J 121

Hollydene BR2: Brom 1H 159
   (off Beckenham La.)
   SE13 . . . . .6F 123
   SE15 . . . . .1H 121
Hollydown Way E11 . . . . .3F 69
Holly Dr. E4 .7J 25
Holly Farm Rd. UB2: S'hall 5C 94
Hollyfield Av. N11 . . . . .5J 31
Hollyfield Rd. KT5: Surb 7F 151
Holly Gdns. DA7: Bex 4J 127
   UB7: W Dray 2B 92
Holly Gro. HA5: Pinn 1C 40
   NW9 . . . . .7J 43
   SE15 . . . . .2F 121
Hollygrove WD23: Bush 1C 26
Hollygrove Cl. TW3: Houn 4D 112
Holly Hedge Ter. SE13 . . . . .5F 123
Holly Hill N21 . . . . .6E 22
   NW3 . . . . .4A 64
Holly Hill Rd. DA8: Erith 5H 109
   DA17: Belv, Erith 5H 109
Holly Ho. TW8: Bford 6C 96
   W10 . . . . .4G 81
   (off Hawthorn Wlk.)
Holly Lodge HA1: Harr 5H 41
   W8 . . . . .2J 99
   (off Thornwood Gdns.)
Holly Lodge Gdns. N6 . . . . .2E 64
Holly Lodge Mans. N6 . . . . .2E 64
Hollymead SM5: Cars 3D 166
Holly M. SW10 . . . . .6A 16 (5A 100)
Holly Mt. NW3 . . . . .4A 64
Hollymount Cl. SE10 . . . . .1E 122
Holly Pk. N3 .3H 45
   N4 . . . . .7J 47
   (not continuous)
Holly Pk. Est. N4 . . . . .7K 47
Holly Pk. Gdns. N3 . . . . .3J 45
Holly Pk. Rd. N11 . . . . .5K 31
   W7 . . . . .1K 95
Holly Pl. NW3 . . . . .4A 64
   (off Holly Berry La.)
Holly Rd. E11 . . . . .7H 51
   TW1: Twick 1K 131
   TW3: Houn 4F 113
   TW12: Ham H 6G 131
   W4 . . . . .4K 97
Holly St. E8 . . . . .7F 67
Holly Ter. N6 . . . . .1E 64
   N20 . . . . .2F 31
Holly Tree Cl. SW19 . . . . .1F 135
Holly Tree Ho. SE4 . . . . .3B 122
   (off Brockley Rd.)
Hollytree Pde. DA14: Sidc 6C 144
   (off Sidcup Hill)
Hollyview Cl. NW4 . . . . .6C 44
Holly Village N6 . . . . .2F 65
Holly Vs. W6 .3D 98
   (off Wellesley Av.)
Holly Wlk. EN2: Enf 3H 23
   NW3 . . . . .4A 64
Holly Way CR4: Mitc 4H 155
Hollywood Bowl
   Barking .3G 89
   Finchley .7G 31
   Surrey Quays 3K 103
Hollywood Ct. SW10 . . . . .6A 100
   (off Hollywood Rd.)
   W5 . . . . .7F 79
Hollywood Gdns. UB4: Yead 6K 75
Hollywood M. SW10 . . . . .6A 100
Hollywood Rd. E4 . . . . .5F 35
   SW10 . . . . .6A 100
Hollywood Way IG8: Wfd G 7A 36
Holman Cl. KT17: Ewe 7C 164
Holman Ho. E2 . . . . .3K 85
   (off Roman Rd.)
Holman Hunt Ho. W6 . . . . .5G 99
   (off Field Rd.)
Holman Rd. KT19: Ewe 5J 163
   SW11 . . . . .2B 118
Holmbank Dr. TW17: Shep 4G 147

Holmbridge Gdns. EN3: Pond E 4E 24
Holmbrook *NW1* *2G 83*
(off Eversholt St.)
Holmbrook Dr. NW4 5F 45
Holmbury Ct. CR2: S Croy 5E 168
SW17 3D 136
SW19 7C 136
Holmbury Gdns. UB3: Hayes 1H 93
Holmbury Gro. CR0: Sels 7B 170
Holmbury Ho. SE24 5B 120
Holmbury Mnr. DA14: Sidc 4A 144
Holmbury Pk. BR1: Brom 7C 142
Holmbury Vw. E5 1H 67
Holmbush Rd. SW15 6G 117
Holmcote Gdns. N5 5C 66
Holm Ct. SE12 3K 141
Holmcroft Ho. E17 4D 50
Holmcroft Way BR2: Brom 5D 160
Holmdale Gdns. NW4 5F 45
Holmdale Rd. BR7: Chst 5G 143
NW6 5J 63
Holmdale Ter. N15 7E 48
Holmdene N12 5E 30
Holmdene Av. HA2: Harr 3F 41
NW7 6H 29
SE24 5C 120
Holmdene Cl. BR3: Beck 2E 158
Holmdene Ct. BR1: Brom 3C 160
Holmead Rd. SW6 7K 99
Holmebury Cl. WD23: B Hea 2D 26
Holme Ct. TW7: Isle 3A 114
Holmefield Ho. *W10* *4G 81*
(off Hazlewood Cres.)
Holme Ho. *SE15* *7H 103*
(off Studholme St.)
Holme Lacey Rd. SE12 6H 123
Holme Rd. E6 1C 88
Holmes Av. E17 3B 50
NW7 5B 30
Holmes Cl. SE22 4G 121
Holmesdale Av. SW14 3H 115
Holmesdale Cl. SE25 3F 157
Holmesdale Ho. *NW6* *1J 81*
(off Kilburn Va.)
Holmesdale Rd. CR0: C'don 5D 156
DA7: Bex 2D 126
N6 7F 47
SE25 5D 156
TW9: Kew 1F 115
TW11: Tedd 7C 132
Holmesley Rd. SE23 6A 122
Holmes Pl. SW10 6A 100
Holmes Rd. NW5 5F 65
SW19 7A 136
TW1: Twick 2K 131
Holmes Ter. SE1 6J 13
Holmeswood SM2: Sutt 6K 165
Holmeswood Ct. N22 2A 48
Holme Way HA7: Stan 6E 26
Holmewood Gdns. SW2 7K 119
Holmewood Rd. SE25 3E 156
SW2 7J 119
Holmfield Av. NW4 5F 45
Holmfield Ct. NW3 5C 64
Holm Gro. UB10: Hil 7C 56
Holmhurst SE13 6F 123
Holmhurst Rd. DA17: Belv 5H 109
Holmlea Ct. *CR0: C'don* *4D 168*
(off Chatsworth Rd.)
Holmleigh Ct. EN3: Pond E 4D 24
Holmleigh Rd. N16 1E 66
Holmleigh Rd. Est. N16 1E 66
Holm Oak Cl. SW15 6H 117
Holm Oak M. SW4 5J 119
Holmoaks Ho. BR3: Beck 2E 158
Holmsdale Ho. *E14* *7D 86*
(off Poplar High St.)
N11 *4A 32*
(off Coppies Gro.)
Holmshaw Cl. SE26 4A 140
Holmside Rd. SW12 6E 118
Holmsley Cl. KT3: N Mald 6B 152
Holmsley Ho. *SW15* *7B 116*
(off Tangley Gro.)
Holmstall Av. HA8: Edg 3J 43
Holmstall Pde. HA8: Edg 2J 43
Holmstead Ct. CR2: S Croy 5D 168
Holm Wlk. SE3 2J 123
Holmwood Cl. HA2: Harr 3G 41
SM2: Cheam 7F 165
UB5: N'olt 6F 59
Holmwood Gdns. N3 2J 45
SM6: Wall 6F 167
Holmwood Gro. NW7 5E 28
Holmwood Rd. IG3: Ilf 2J 71
KT9: Chess 5D 162
SM2: Cheam 7E 164
Holmwood Vs. SE7 5J 105
Holne Chase N2 6A 46
SM4: Mord 6H 153
Holness Rd. E15 6H 69
Holocaust Memorial Garden, The 6F 11
Holroyd Rd. KT10: Clay 7A 162
SW15 4E 116
Holst Ct. *SE1* *1J 19*
(off Westminster Bri. Rd.)
Holstein Way DA18: Erith 3D 108
Holst Mans. SW13 6E 98
Holstock Rd. IG1: Ilf 2G 71
Holsworth Cl. HA2: Harr 5G 41
Holsworthy Ho. *E3* *3D 86*
(off Talwin St.)
Holsworthy Sq. WC1 4H 7
Holsworthy Way KT9: Chess 5C 162
Holt, The SM4: Mord 4J 153
SM6: Wall 4G 167
Holt Cl. DA14: Sidc 4E 144
(not continuous)
N10 4E 46
SE28 7B 90
Holt Ct. *SE10* *6E 104*
(off Horseferry Pl.)
Holt Ho. SW2 6A 120
Holton St. E1 4K 85
Holt Rd. E16 1C 106
HA0: Wemb 3B 60
Holtwhite Av. EN2: Enf 2H 23
Holtwhite's Hill EN2: Enf 1G 23
Holwell Pl. HA5: Pinn 4C 40
Holwood Pk. Av. BR6: Farnb 4D 172
Holwood Pl. SW4 4H 119
Holybourne Av. SW15 7C 116
Holyhead Cl. E3 3C 86
E6 5D 88
Holyhead Ct. *KT1: King T* *4D 150*
(off Anglesea Rd.)
Holyoake Ct. SE16 2B 104
Holyoake Ho. W5 4C 78
Holyoake Wlk. N2 3A 46
W5 4C 78
Holyoak Rd. SE11 4B 102
Holyport Rd. SW6 7F 99
Holyrood Av. HA2: Harr 4C 58
Holyrood Ct. *NW1* *1F 83*
(off Gloucester Av.)
Holyrood Gdns. HA8: Edg 3H 43
Holyrood M. E16 1J 105
Holyrood Rd. EN5: New Bar 6F 21
Holyrood St. SE1 5G 15 (1E 102)
Holywell Cen. *EC2* *3G 9*
(off Phipp St.)
Holywell Cl. BR6: Chels 4K 173
SE3 6J 105
SE16 5H 103
TW19: Stanw 1A 128
Holywell La. EC2 3H 9 (4E 84)
Holywell Row EC2 4G 9 (4E 84)
Holywell Way TW19: Stanw 1A 128
Homan Ct. N12 4G 31
Homebush Ho. E4 7J 25
Homecedars Ho. WD23: B Hea 1C 26
Home Cl. SM5: Cars 2D 166
UB5: N'olt 3D 76
Home Ct. KT6: Surb 5D 150
Homecroft Rd. N22 1C 48
SE26 5J 139
Home Farm Cl. KT7: T Ditt 7K 149
TW17: Shep 4G 147
Homefarm Rd. W7 6J 77
Home Fld. EN5: Barn 5C 20
Homefield SM4: Mord 4J 153
Homefield Av. IG2: Ilf 5J 53
Homefield Cl. NW10 6J 61
UB4: Yead 4B 76
Homefield Gdns. CR4: Mitc 2A 154
N2 3B 46
Homefield Ho. SE23 3K 139
Homefield M. BR3: Beck 1C 158
Homefield Pk. SM1: Sutt 6K 165
Homefield Rd. BR1: Brom 1A 160
HA0: Wemb 4A 60
HA8: Edg 6E 28
KT12: Walt T 7C 148
SW19 6F 135
W4 5B 98
Homefield St. N1 1G 9 (2E 84)
Homefirs Ho. HA9: Wemb 3F 61
Home Gdns. RM10: Dag 3J 73
Homeheather Ho. IG4: Ilf 5D 52
Homeland Dr. SM2: Sutt 7K 165
Homelands Dr. SE19 7E 138
Home Lea BR6: Chels 5K 173
Homeleigh Ct. SW16 3J 137
Homeleigh Rd. SE15 5K 121
Home Mead HA7: Stan 1C 42
Home Mdw. M. SE22 5G 121
Homemead Rd. BR2: Brom 5D 160
CR0: C'don 6G 155
Home Pk. KT8: E Mos 5C 150
Home Pk. Ct. *KT1: King T* *4D 150*
(off Palace Rd.)
Home Pk. Pde. *KT1: Ham W* *2D 150*
(off High St.)
Home Pk. Rd. SW19 4H 135
Home Pk. Ter. *KT1: Ham W* *2D 150*
(off Hampton Ct. Rd.)
Home Pk. Wlk. KT1: King T 4D 150
Homer Cl. DA7: Bex 1J 127
Homer Dr. E14 4C 104
Home Rd. SW11 2C 118
Homer Rd. CR0: C'don 6K 157
E9 6A 68
Homer Row W1 6D 4 (5C 82)
Homersham Rd. KT1: King T 2G 151
Homer St. W1 6D 4 (5C 82)
HOMERTON 5K 67
Homerton Gro. E9 5K 67
Homerton High St. E9 5K 67
Homerton Rd. E9 5A 68
Homerton Row E9 5J 67
Homerton Ter. E9 6J 67
(not continuous)
Homesdale Cl. E11 5J 51
Homesdale Rd. BR1: Brom 4A 160
BR2: Brom 4A 160
BR5: Pet W 7J 161
Homesfield NW11 5J 45
Homestall Rd. SE22 5J 121
Homestead Ct. EN5: New Bar 5D 20
Homestead Paddock N14 5A 22
Homestead Pk. NW2 3B 62
Homestead Rd. RM8: Dag 2F 73
SW6 7H 99
Homesteads, The N11 4A 32
Homewalk Ho. SE26 4H 139
Homewaters Av. TW16: Sun 1H 147
Homewillow Cl. N21 6G 23
Homewood Cl. TW12: Hamp 6D 130
Homewood Cres. BR7: Chst 6J 143
Homewoods SW12 7G 119
Homildon Ho. SE26 3G 139
Honduras St. EC1 3C 8 (4C 84)
Honeybourne Rd. NW6 5K 63
Honeybourne Way BR5: Pet W 1H 173
Honeybrook Rd. SW12 7G 119
Honey Cl. RM10: Dag 6H 73
Honeycroft Hill UB10: Uxb 7A 56
Honeyden Rd. DA14: Sidc 6E 144
Honey Hill UB10: Uxb 7B 56
Honey La. EC2 1D 14
Honey La. Ho. *SW10* *6K 99*
(off Finborough Rd.)
Honeyman Cl. NW6 7F 63
Honeymead *N8* *3J 47*
(off Campsfield Rd.)
Honey M. *SE27* *4C 138*
(off Norwood High St.)
Honeypot Bus. Cen. HA7: Stan 1E 42
Honeypot Cl. NW9 4F 43
Honeypot La. HA7: Stan 7J 27
NW9 1D 42
Honeysett Rd. N17 2F 49
Honeysuckle Cl. UB1: S'hall 7C 76
Honeysuckle Ct. IG1: Ilf 6F 71
IG9: Buck H 3G 37
Honeysuckle Gdns. CR0: C'don 7K 157
Honeysuckle La. N22 2C 48
Honeywell Rd. SW11 6D 118
Honeywood Heritage Cen. 5D 166
Honeywood Ho. *SE15* *1G 121*
(off Goldsmith Rd.)
Honeywood Rd. NW10 2B 80
TW7: Isle 4A 114
Honeywood Wlk. SM5: Cars 4D 166
Honister Cl. HA7: Stan 1B 42
Honister Gdns. HA7: Stan 7G 27
Honister Pl. HA7: Stan 1B 42
Honiton Gdns. NW7 7A 30
SE15 *2J 121*
(off Gibbon Rd.)
Honiton Ho. EN3: Pond E 3E 24
Honiton Rd. DA16: Well 2K 125
NW6 2H 81
RM7: Rom 6K 55
Honley Rd. SE6 7D 122
Honnor Gdns. TW7: Isle 2H 113
HONOR OAK 6J 121
Honor Oak Crematorium SE23 5K 121
HONOR OAK PARK 7A 122
Honor Oak Pk. SE23 6J 121
Honor Oak Ri. SE23 6J 121
Honor Oak Rd. SE23 1J 139
Hood Av. N14 6A 22
SW14 5J 115
Hood Cl. CR0: C'don 1B 168
Hoodcote Gdns. N21 7G 23
Hood Ct. EC4 1K 13
Hood Ho. *SE5* *7D 102*
(off Elmington Est.)
SW1 *6C 18*
(off Dolphin Sq.)
Hood Point *SE16* *2B 104*
(off Rotherhithe St.)
Hood Rd. SW20 7B 134
Hood Wlk. RM7: Mawney 1H 55
HOOK 5E 162
Hook, The EN5: New Bar 6G 21
Hooke Ct. *SE10* *1E 122*
(off Winforton St.)
Hooke Ho. *E3* *2A 86*
(off Gernon Rd.)
Hookers Rd. E17 3K 49
Hook Farm Rd. BR2: Brom 5B 160
Hookham Ct. SW8 1H 119
Hooking Grn. HA2: Harr 5F 41
HOOK JUNC. 3E 162
Hook La. DA16: Well 4K 125
Hook Ri. Nth. KT6: Surb 3E 162
Hook Ri. Sth. KT6: Surb 3E 162
Hook Ri. Sth. Ind. Pk. KT6: Surb 3F 163
Hook Rd. KT6: Surb 2E 162
KT9: Chess 5D 162
KT19: Eps, Ewe 7J 163
Hooks Cl. SE15 1H 121
Hooks Hall Dr. RM10: Dag 3J 73
Hookstone Way IG8: Wfd G 7G 37
Hook Wlk. HA8: Edg 6D 28
Hool Cl. NW9 5J 43

Hooper Dr. UB8: Hil 5D 74
Hooper Ho. TW15: Ashf 3A 128
Hooper Rd. E16 . . . . .6J 87
Hooper's Ct. SW3 . . . . .7E 10 (2D 100)
Hoopers M. W3 . . . . .1J 97
    WD23: Bush 1A 26
Hooper Sq. E1 . . . . .6G 85
                            (off Hooper St.)
Hooper St. E1 . . . . .6G 85
Hoopers Yd. E1 . . . . .6G 85
                            (off Hooper St.)
    NW6 . . . . .1H 81
                         (off Kimberley Rd.)
Hoop La. NW11 . . . . .7H 45
Hop Cl. HA0: Wemb 5A 60
                           (off Brewery Cl.)
Hope Cl. IG8: Wfd G 6F 37
    N1 . . . . .6C 66
    RM6: Chad H 4D 54
    SE12 . . . . .3A 141
    SM1: Sutt 5A 166
    TW8: Bford 5E 96
Hope Ct. NW10 . . . . .3F 81
                     (off Chamberlayne Rd.)
    SE1 . . . . .5G 103
                             (off Avocet Cl.)
Hopedale Rd. SE7 . . . . .6K 105
Hopefield Av. NW6 . . . . .2G 81
Hope Gdns. W3 . . . . .2H 97
Hope Ho. CRO: C'don 4E 168
                          (off Steep Hill)
Hope La. SE9 . . . . .2F 143
Hope Pk. BR1: Brom 7H 141
Hopes Cl. TW5: Hest 6E 94
Hope Sq. EC2 . . . . .6G 9
Hope St. SW11 . . . . .3B 118
Hopetown St. E1 . . . . .6K 9 (5F 85)
Hopewell St. SE5 . . . . .7D 102
Hopewell Yd. SE5 . . . . .7D 102
                          (off Hopewell St.)
Hope Wharf SE16 . . . . .2J 103
Hop Gdns. WC2 . . . . .3E 12 (7J 83)
Hopgood St. W12 . . . . .1E 98
Hopkins Cl. N10 . . . . .7K 31
Hopkins Ho. E14 . . . . .6C 86
                             (off Canton St.)
Hopkins M. E15 . . . . .1H 87
Hopkinsons Pl. NW1 . . . . .1E 82
Hopkins Rd. E10 . . . . .7D 50
Hopkins St. W1 . . . . .1B 12 (6G 83)
Hoppers Rd. N13 . . . . .2F 33
    N21 . . . . .2F 33
Hoppett Rd. E4 . . . . .2B 36
Hopping La. N1 . . . . .6B 66
Hoppingwood Av. KT3: N Mald 3A 152
Hoppner Rd. UB4: Hayes 2F 75
Hop St. SE10 . . . . .4H 105
Hopton Cl. BR2: Hayes 1K 171
Hopton Gdns. KT3: N Mald 6C 152
Hopton Rd. SE18 . . . . .3F 107
    SW16 .5J 137
Hopton's Gdns. SE1 . . . . .4B 14
Hopton St. SE1 . . . . .3A 14 (7B 84)
Hoptree Cl. N12 . . . . .5E 30
Hopwood Cl. SW17 . . . . .3A 136
Hopwood Rd. SE17 . . . . .6D 102
Hopwood Wlk. E8 . . . . .7G 67
Horace Av. RM7: Rush G 1J 73
Horace Bldg. SW8 . . . . .7F 101
Horace Rd. E7 . . . . .4K 69
    IG6: Ilf .3G 53
    KT1: King T 3F 151
Horatio Ct. SE16 . . . . .1J 103
                         (off Rotherhithe St.)
Horatio Ho. E2 . . . . .2F 85
                           (off Horatio St.)
    W6 . . . . .5F 99
                          (off Fulham Pal. Rd.)
Horatio Pl. E14 . . . . .1E 104
                          (off Managers St.)
    SW19 .1J 153
Horatio St. E2 . . . . .2F 85

Horatius Way CRO: Wadd 5K 167
Horbury Cres. W11 . . . . .7J 81
Horbury M. W11 . . . . .7H 81
Horder Rd. SW6 . . . . .1G 117
Hordle Prom. E. SE15 . . . . .7F 103
Hordle Prom. Sth. SE15 . . . . .7F 103
                           (off Quarley Way)
Horizon Bldg. E14 . . . . .7C 86
                          (off Hertsmere Rd.)
Horizon Bus. Cen. N9 . . . . .2E 34
                            (off Goodwin Rd.)
Horizon Ct. SM2: Cheam 7G 165
                          (off Up. Mulgrave Rd.)
Horizon Ind. Est. SE15 . . . . .6G 103
Horizon Way SE7 . . . . .4K 105
Horle Wlk. SE5 . . . . .2B 120
Horley Cl. DA6: Bex 5G 127
Horley Rd. SE9 . . . . .4C 142
Hormead Rd. W9 . . . . .4H 81
Hornbeam Cl. IG1: Ilf 5H 71
    IG9: Buck H 3G 37
    IG11: Bark 3A 90
    NW7 . . . . .3G 29
    SE11 . . . . .3J 19 (4A 102)
    UB5: N'olt 5D 58
Hornbeam Cres. TW8: Bford 7B 96
Hornbeam Gdns. KT3: N Mald 6C 152
Hornbeam Gro. E4 . . . . .3B 36
Hornbeam Ho. IG9: Buck H 3H 37
    UB4: Yead 5A 76
Hornbeam Sq. E3 . . . . .1B 86
Hornbeams Ri. N11 . . . . .6K 31
Hornbeam Ter. SM5: Cars 1C 166
Hornbeam Wlk. TW10: Rich 2F 133
Hornbeam Way BR2: Brom 6E 160
Hornblower Cl. SE16 . . . . .3A 104
Hornbuckle Cl. HA2: Harr 2H 59
Hornby Cl. NW3 . . . . .7B 64
Hornby Ho. SE11 . . . . .7J 19
Horncastle Cl. SE12 . . . . .7J 123
Horncastle Rd. SE12 . . . . .7J 123
Hornchurch N17 . . . . .2D 48
                          (off Gloucester Rd.)
Hornchurch Cl. KT2: King T 4D 132
Horndean Cl. SW15 . . . . .1C 134
Horndon Cl. RM5: Col R 1J 55
Horndon Grn. RM5: Col R 1J 55
Horndon Rd. RM5: Col R 1J 55
Horner Ho. N1 . . . . .1E 84
                          (off Whitmore Est.)
Horner La. CR4: Mitc 2B 154
Horne Rd. TW17: Shep 4C 146
Horner Sq. E1 . . . . .5J 9
                       (off Old Spitalfields Market)
Hornet Way E6 . . . . .5H 89
Horne Way SW15 . . . . .2E 116
Hornfair Rd. SE7 . . . . .6A 106
Horniman Dr. SE23 . . . . .1H 139
Horniman Mus. 1H 139
Horning Cl. SE9 . . . . .4C 142
Horn La. IG8: Wfd G 6D 36
    SE10 . . . . .5J 105
                         (not continuous)
    W3 . . . . .7J 79
                         (not continuous)
Horn Link Way SE10 . . . . .4J 105
HORN PARK 5K 123
Horn Pk. Cl. SE12 . . . . .5K 123
Hornpark La. SE12 . . . . .5K 123
Hornscroft Cl. IG11: Bark 7J 71
Horns End Pl. HA5: Eastc 4A 40
HORNSEY 4J 47
Hornsey N8 .4J 47
Hornsey Club, The 5H 47
Hornsey La. N6 . . . . .1F 65
Hornsey La. Est. N19 . . . . .7H 47
Hornsey La. Gdns. N6 . . . . .7G 47
Hornsey Pk. Rd. N8 . . . . .3K 47
Hornsey Ri. N19 . . . . .7H 47
Hornsey Ri. Gdns. N19 . . . . .7H 47

Hornsey Rd. N7 . . . . .1J 65
    N19 . . . . .1J 65
Hornsey St. N7 . . . . .5K 65
HORNSEY VALE 5K 47
Hornshay St. SE15 . . . . .6J 103
Horns Rd. IG2: Ilf 5G 53
    IG6: Ilf .4H 53
Hornton Ct. W8 . . . . .2J 99
                    (off Kensington High St.)
Hornton Pl. W8 . . . . .2K 99
Hornton St. W8 . . . . .2J 99
Horsa Rd. DA8: Erith 7H 109
    SE12 .7A 124
Horse & Dolphin Yd. W1 . . . . .2D 12
Horsebridge Cl. RM9: Dag 1E 90
Horsecroft Rd. HA8: Edg 7E 28
Horse Fair KT1: King T 2D 150
Horseferry Pl. SE10 . . . . .6E 104
Horseferry Rd. E14 . . . . .7A 86
    SW1 . . . . .2C 18 (3H 101)
Horseferry Rd. Est. SW1 . . . . .2C 18
Horse Guards Av. SW1 . . . .5E 12 (1J 101)
Horse Guards Parade 5E 12 (1H 101)
Horse Guards Rd. SW1 . . . .5D 12 (1H 101)
Horse Leaze E6 . . . . .6E 88
Horseley Ct. E1 . . . . .5A 86
Horsell Rd. BR5: St P 7B 144
    N5 . . . . .5A 66
                         (not continuous)
Horselydown La. SE1 . . . . .6J 15 (2F 103)
Horselydown Mans. SE1 . . . . .6J 15
                            (off Lafone St.)
Horsemongers M. SE1 . . . . .7D 14
Horsenden Av. UB6: G'frd 5K 59
Horsenden Cres. UB6: G'frd 5K 59
Horsenden La. Nth. UB6: G'frd 6J 59
Horsenden La. Sth.
    UB6: G'frd 1A 78
Horse Ride SW1 . . . . .5C 12 (1G 101)
Horseshoe Cl. E14 . . . . .5E 104
    NW2 . . . . .2D 62
Horseshoe Ct. EC1 . . . . .3B 8
                          (off Brewhouse Yd.)
Horse Shoe Cres. UB5: N'olt 2E 76
Horseshoe Dr. UB8: Hil 6C 74
Horse Shoe Grn. SM1: Sutt 2K 165
Horseshoe La. EN2: Enf 3H 23
    N20 . . . . .1A 30
Horseshoe M. SW2 . . . . .4J 119
Horseshoe Wharf SE1 . . . . .4E 14
                            (off Clink St.)
Horse Yd. N1 . . . . .1B 84
                            (off Essex Rd.)
Horsfeld Gdns. SE9 . . . . .5C 124
Horsfeld Rd. SE9 . . . . .5B 124
Horsfield Ho. N1 . . . . .7C 66
                          (off Northampton St.)
Horsford Rd. SW2 . . . . .5K 119
Horsham Av. N12 . . . . .5H 31
Horsham Ct. N17 . . . . .1G 49
                          (off Lansdowne Rd.)
Horsham Rd. DA6: Bex 5G 127
    TW14: Bedf 6E 110
Horsley Ct. SW1 . . . . .4H 101
                           (off Vincent St.)
Horsley Dr. CRO: New Ad 7E 170
    KT2: King T 5D 132
Horsley Rd. BR1: Brom 1K 159
    E4 . . . . .2K 35
Horsley St. SE17 . . . . .6D 102
Horsman Ho. SE5 . . . . .6C 102
                            (off Bethwin Rd.)
Horsman St. SE5 . . . . .6C 102
Horsmonden Cl. BR6: Orp 7K 161
Horsmonden Rd. SE4 . . . . .5B 122
Hortensia Ho. SW10 . . . . .7A 100
                           (off Gunter Gro.)
Hortensia Rd. SW10 . . . . .7A 100
Horticultural Pl. W4 . . . . .5K 97
Horton Av. NW2 . . . . .4G 63
Horton Bri. Rd. UB7: Yiew 1B 92
Horton Cl. UB7: Yiew 1C 92

Horton Country Pk. Local Nature Reserve
    . . . . .7F 163
Horton Halls SW17 . . . . .3B 136
Horton Ho. SE15 . . . . .6J 103
    SW8 . . . . .7K 101
    W6 . . . . .5G 99
                            (off Field Rd.)
Horton Ind. Pk. UB7: Yiew 1B 92
Horton La. KT19: Eps 7H 163
Horton Pde. UB7: Yiew 1A 92
Horton Rd. E8 . . . . .6H 67
    SL3: Poyle 6A 174
    TW19: Stan M 7A 174
    UB7: Yiew 1A 92
    UB11: Stock P 1A 92
Horton Rd. Ind. Est. UB7: Yiew 1B 92
Horton St. SE13 . . . . .3D 122
Horton Way CRO: C'don 5K 157
Hortus Rd. E4 . . . . .2K 35
    UB2: S'hall 2D 94
Horwood Ho. E2 . . . . .3H 85
                            (off Pott St.)
    NW8 . . . . .3D 4
                           (off Paveley St.)
Hosack Rd. SW17 . . . . .2E 136
Hoser Av. SE12 . . . . .2J 141
Hosier La. EC1 . . . . .6A 8 (5B 84)
Hoskins Cl. E16 . . . . .6A 88
    UB3: Harl 5H 93
Hoskins St. SE10 . . . . .5F 105
Hospital Bri. Rd. TW2: Twick, Whitt . . .7F 113
HOSPITAL BRIDGE RDBT. 2F 131
Hospital Rd. E9 . . . . .5K 67
    TW3: Houn 3E 112
Hospital Way SE13 . . . . .7F 123
Hotel 5G 85
                         (off Greenfield Rd.)
Hotham Cl. KT8: W Mole 3E 148
Hotham Rd. SW15 . . . . .3E 116
    SW19 .7A 136
Hotham Rd. M. SW19 . . . . .7A 136
Hotham St. E15 . . . . .1G 87
Hothfield Pl. SE16 . . . . .3J 103
Hotspur Ind. Est. N17 . . . . .6C 34
Hotspur Rd. UB5: N'olt 2E 76
Hotspur St. SE11 . . . . .5J 19 (4A 102)
Houblon Rd. TW10: Rich 5E 114
Houghton Cl. E8 . . . . .6F 67
    TW12: Hamp 6C 130
Houghton Ct. EC1 . . . . .4C 8
                         (off Glasshouse Yd.)
Houghton Rd. N15 . . . . .4F 49
Houghton Sq. SW9 . . . . .2J 119
                          (off Clapham Rd.)
Houghton St. WC2 . . . . . . .1H 13 (6K 83)
                         (not continuous)
Houlder Cres. CRO: Wadd 6B 168
Houndsden Rd. N21 . . . . .6E 22
Houndsditch EC3 . . . . .7H 9 (6E 84)
Houndsfield Rd. N9 . . . . .7C 24
HOUNSLOW .3F 113
Hounslow and District Indoor Bowls Club
    . . . . .2D 112
                            (off Sutton La.)
Hounslow Av. TW3: Houn 5F 113
Hounslow Bus. Pk. TW3: Houn 4E 112
Hounslow Cen. TW3: Houn 3F 113
Hounslow Gdns. TW3: Houn 5F 113
Hounslow Heath Nature Reserve 6C 112
Hounslow Heath Nature Reserve Vis. Cen.
    . . . . .5C 112
Hounslow Rd. TW2: Whitt 6J 113
    TW13: Hanw 4B 130
    TW14: Felt 1K 129
Hounslow Urban Farm 5J 111
HOUNSLOW WEST 2C 112
Household Cavalry Mus., The
    Whitehall 5D 12 (1H 101)
Houseman Way SE5 . . . . .7D 102
House Mill 3E 86
Houses of Parliament 1F 19 (3J 101)
Houston Bus. Pk. UB4: Yead 1A 94

Houston Pl.—Huntsworth M.

Houston Pl. KT10: Esh 7H **149**
Houston Rd. KT6: Surb 6B **150**
SE23 . . . . . 2A **140**
Houstoun Ct. TW5: Hest 7D **94**
Hove Av. E17 . . . . . 5B **50**
Hoveden Rd. NW2 . . . . . 5G **63**
Hove Gdns. SM1: Sutt 1K **165**
Hove St. *SE15* *7J* ***103***
(off Culmore Rd.)
Hoveton Rd. SE28 . . . . . 6C **90**
Hoveton Way IG6: Ilf 1F **53**
Howard Av. DA5: Bexl 1C **144**
Howard Bldg. SW8 . . . . . 7J **17** (6F **101**)
Howard Cl. N11 . . . . . 2K **31**
NW2 . . . . . 4G **63**
TW12: Hamp 7G **131**
TW16: Sun 6H **129**
W3 . . . . . 6H **79**
WD23: B Hea 1D **26**
Howard Ct. IG11: Bark 1H **89**
Howard Ho. *E16* *1K* ***105***
(off Wesley Av.)
SE8 . . . . . *6B* ***104***
(off Evelyn St.)
SW1 . . . . . *6B* ***18***
(off Dolphin Sq.)
SW9 . . . . . *3B* ***120***
(off Barrington Rd.)
W1 . . . . . *4K* ***5***
(off Cleveland St.)
Howard M. N5 . . . . . 4B **66**
Howard Rd. BR1: Brom 7J **141**
E6 . . . . . 2D **88**
E11 . . . . . 3G **69**
E17 . . . . . 3C **50**
IG1: Ilf 4F **71**
IG11: Bark 1H **89**
KT3: N Mald 3A **152**
KT5: Surb 6F **151**
N15 . . . . . 6E **48**
N16 . . . . . 4D **66**
NW2 . . . . . 4F **63**
SE20 . . . . . 1J **157**
SE25 . . . . . 5G **157**
TW7: Isle 3K **113**
UB1: S'hall 6F **77**
Howards Cl. HA5: Pinn 2K **39**
Howards Crest Cl. BR3: Beck 2E **158**
Howard's La. SW15 . . . . . 4D **116**
Howards Rd. E13 . . . . . 3J **87**
Howard St. KT7: T Ditt 7B **150**
Howard Wlk. N2 . . . . . 4A **46**
Howard Way EN5: Barn 5A **20**
Howarth Rd. SE2 . . . . . 5A **108**
Howberry Cl. HA8: Edg 6J **27**
Howberry Rd. CR7: Thor H 1D **156**
HA7: Stan 6J **27**
HA8: Edg 6J **27**
Howbury Rd. SE15 . . . . . 3J **121**
Howcroft Cres. N3 . . . . . 7D **30**
Howcroft Ho. *E3* *3B* ***86***
(off Benworth St.)
Howcroft La. UB6: G'frd 3H **77**
Howden Cl. SE28 . . . . . 7D **90**
Howden Rd. SE25 . . . . . 2F **157**
Howden St. SE15 . . . . . 3G **121**
Howe Cl. RM7: Mawney 1G **55**
Howell Cl. RM6: Chad H 5D **54**
Howell Ct. E10 . . . . . 7D **50**
Howell Wlk. SE1 . . . . . 4B **102**
Howerd Way SE18 . . . . . 1C **124**
(not continuous)
Howes Cl. N3 . . . . . 3J **45**
Howeth Ct. *N11* *6J* ***31***
(off Ribblesdale Av.)
Howfield Pl. N17 . . . . . 3F **49**
Howgate Rd. SW14 . . . . . 3K **115**
Howick Pl. SW1 . . . . . 2B **18** (3G **101**)
Howie St. SW11 . . . . . 7C **100**
Howitt Cl. N16 . . . . . 4E **66**
NW3 . . . . . 6C **64**
Howitt Rd. NW3 . . . . . 6C **64**
Howland Est. SE16 . . . . . 3J **103**
Howland Ho. SW16 . . . . . 3J **137**
Howland M. E. W1 . . . . . 5B **6** (5G **83**)
Howland St. W1 . . . . . 5A **6** (5G **83**)
Howland Way SE16 . . . . . 2A **104**
Howletts La. HA4: Ruis 5E **38**
Howlett's Rd. SE24 . . . . . 6C **120**
Howley Pl. W2 . . . . . 5A **4** (5A **82**)
Howley Rd. CR0: C'don 3B **168**
Howsman Rd. SW13 . . . . . 6C **98**
Howson Rd. SE4 . . . . . 4A **122**
Howson Ter. TW10: Rich 6E **114**
How's St. E2 . . . . . 2F **85**
Howton Pl. WD23: B Hea 1C **26**
HOXTON 2E **84**
Hoxton Hall Theatre *2E* ***84***
(off Hoxton St.)
Hoxton Mkt. N1 . . . . . 2G **9**
Hoxton Sq. N1 . . . . . 2G **9** (3E **84**)
Hoxton St. N1 . . . . . 2H **9** (1E **84**)
Hoylake Cres. UB10: Ick 2C **56**
Hoylake Gdns. CR4: Mitc 3G **155**
HA4: Ruis 1K **57**
Hoylake Rd. W3 . . . . . 6A **80**
Hoyland Cl. SE15 . . . . . 7H **103**
Hoyle Rd. SW17 . . . . . 5C **136**
Hoy St. E16 . . . . . 6H **87**
HQS Wellington 3J **13**
Hub, The
Westminster 1F **5** (2D **82**)
Hubbard Ct. IG10: Lough 1H **37**
Hubbard Dr. KT9: Chess 6D **162**
Hubbard Ho. *SW10* *7B* ***100***
(off Worlds End Pas.)
Hubbard Rd. SE27 . . . . . 4C **138**
Hubbards Cl. UB8: Hil 6D **74**
Hubbard St. E15 . . . . . 1G **87**
Hubbinet Ind. Est. RM7: Mawney 3J **55**
Huberd Ho. *SE1* *7F* ***15***
(off Manciple St.)
Hubert Cl. *SW19* *1A* ***154***
(off Nelson Gro. Rd.)
Hubert Gro. SW9 . . . . . 3J **119**
Hubert Ho. *NW8* *4C* ***4***
(off Ashbridge St.)
Hubert Rd. E6 . . . . . 3B **88**
Hucknall Ct. *NW8* *3A* ***4***
(off Cunningham Pl.)
Huddart St. E3 . . . . . 5B **86**
(not continuous)
Huddleston Cl. E2 . . . . . 2J **85**
Huddlestone Rd. E7 . . . . . 4H **69**
NW2 . . . . . 6D **62**
Huddleston Rd. N7 . . . . . 3G **65**
Hudson *NW9* *1B* ***44***
(off Five Acre)
Hudson Apartments N8 . . . . . 3K **47**
Hudson Bldg. *E1* *6K* ***9***
(off Chicksand St.)
Hudson Cl. E15 . . . . . 1J **87**
W12 . . . . . 7D **80**
Hudson Ct. *E14* *5C* ***104***
(off Maritime Quay)
Hudson Gdns. BR6: Chels 6K **173**
Hudson Ho. *SW10* *7A* ***100***
(off Hortensia Rd.)
W11 . . . . . *6G* ***81***
(off Ladbroke Gro.)
Hudson Pl. SE18 . . . . . 5G **107**
Hudson Rd. DA7: Bex 2F **127**
UB3: Harl 6F **93**
Hudson's Pl. SW1 . . . . . 3A **18** (4F **101**)
Hudson Way N9 . . . . . 3D **34**
NW2 . . . . . 3F **63**
Huggin Ct. EC4 . . . . . 2D **14**
Huggin Hill EC4 . . . . . 2C **14** (7C **84**)
Huggins Ho. *E3* *3C* ***86***
(off Alfred St.)
Huggins Pl. SW2 . . . . . 1K **137**
Hughan Rd. E15 . . . . . 5F **69**
Hugh Astor Ct. *SE1* *7B* ***14***
(off Keyworth St.)
Hugh Clark Ho. *W13* *1A* ***96***
(off Singapore Rd.)
Hugh Cubitt Ho. *N1* *2K* ***83***
(off Collier St.)
Hugh Dalton Av. SW6 . . . . . 6H **99**
Hughenden Av. HA3: Kenton 5B **42**
Hughenden Gdns. UB5: N'olt 3A **76**
(not continuous)
Hughenden Ho. NW8 . . . . . 3C **4**
Hughenden Rd. KT4: Wor Pk 7C **152**
Hughendon EN5: New Bar 4E **20**
Hughendon Ter. E15 . . . . . 4E **68**
Hughes Cl. N12 . . . . . 5F **31**
Hughes Ct. N7 . . . . . 5H **65**
Hughes Ho. *E2* *3J* ***85***
(off Sceptre Ho.)
SE5 . . . . . *1C* ***120***
(off Flodden Rd.)
SE8 . . . . . *6C* ***104***
(off Benbow St.)
SE17 . . . . . *4B* ***102***
(off Peacock St.)
Hughes Mans. E1 . . . . . 4G **85**
Hughes Rd. TW15: Ashf 6E **128**
UB3: Hayes 7K **75**
Hughes Ter. *E16* *5H* ***87***
(off Clarkson Rd.)
SW9 . . . . . *3B* ***120***
(off Styles Gdns.)
Hughes Wlk. CR0: C'don 7C **156**
Hugh Gaitskell Cl. SW6 . . . . . 6H **99**
Hugh Gaitskell Ho. N16 . . . . . 2F **67**
Hugh Herland Ho. KT1: King T 3E **150**
Hugh M. SW1 . . . . . 4K **17** (4F **101**)
Hugh Platt Ho. *E2* *2H* ***85***
(off Patriot Sq.)
Hugh St. SW1 . . . . . 4K **17** (4F **101**)
Hugo Ho. *SW1* *1F* ***17***
(off Sloane St.)
Hugon Rd. SW6 . . . . . 3K **117**
Hugo Rd. N19 . . . . . 4G **65**
Huguenot Pl. E1 . . . . . 5K **9** (5F **85**)
SW18 . . . . . 5A **118**
Huguenot Sq. SE15 . . . . . 3H **121**
Hullbridge M. N1 . . . . . 1D **84**
Hull Cl. SE16 . . . . . 2K **103**
Hull Pl. E16 . . . . . 1G **107**
Hull St. EC1 . . . . . 2C **8** (3C **84**)
Hulme Pl. SE1 . . . . . 7D **14** (2C **102**)
Hulse Av. IG11: Bark 6H **71**
RM7: Mawney 1H **55**
Hulverston Cl. SM2: Sutt 7K **165**
Humber Cl. UB7: W Dray 1A **92**
Humber Ct. *W7* *6H* ***77***
(off Hobbayne Rd.)
Humber Dr. W10 . . . . . 4F **81**
Humber Rd. NW2 . . . . . 2D **62**
SE3 . . . . . 6H **105**
Humberstone Rd. E13 . . . . . 3A **88**
Humberton Cl. E9 . . . . . 5A **68**
Humber Trad. Est. NW2 . . . . . 2D **62**
Humbolt Rd. W6 . . . . . 6G **99**
Hume Ct. *N1* *7B* ***66***
(off Hawes St.)
Hume Ho. *W11* *1F* ***99***
(off Queensdale Cres.)
Humes Av. W7 . . . . . 3J **95**
Hume Ter. E16 . . . . . 5K **87**
Hume Way HA4: Ruis 6J **39**
Humphrey Cl. IG5: Ilf 1D **52**
Humphrey St. SE1 . . . . . 5F **103**
Humphries Cl. RM9: Dag 4F **73**
Hundred Acre NW9 . . . . . 2B **44**
Hungerdown E4 . . . . . 1K **35**
Hungerford Ho. *SW1* *7B* ***18***
(off Churchill Gdns.)
Hungerford La. WC2 . . . . . 4F **13**
(not continuous)
Hungerford Rd. N7 . . . . . 6H **65**
Hungerford St. E1 . . . . . 6H **85**
Hunsdon Cl. RM9: Dag 6E **72**
Hunsdon Rd. SE14 . . . . . 7K **103**
Hunslett St. E2 . . . . . 3J **85**
Hunstanton Ho. *NW1* *5D* ***4***
(off Cosway St.)
Hunston Rd. SM4: Mord 1K **165**
Hunt Cl. W11 . . . . . 1F **99**
Hunt Ct. N14 . . . . . 7A **22**
RM7: Rush G *6K* ***55***
(off Union Rd.)
UB5: N'olt *2B* ***76***
(off Gallery Gdns.)
Hunter Cl. SE1 . . . . . 3D **102**
SM6: Wall 7J **167**
Hunter Ho. *SE1* *7B* ***14***
(off King James St.)
SW5 . . . . . *5J* ***99***
(off Old Brompton Rd.)
SW8 . . . . . *7H* ***101***
(off Fount St.)
TW13: Felt *1J* ***129***
(off Lemon Gro.)
WC1 . . . . . *3F* ***7***
(off Hunter St.)
Hunterian Mus., The *7H* ***7***
(off Portugal St.)
Hunter Lodge *W9* *5J* ***81***
(off Admiral Wlk.)
Hunter Rd. CR7: Thor H 3D **156**
IG1: Ilf 5F **71**
SW20 . . . . . 1E **152**
Hunters Cl. DA5: Bexl 3K **145**
SW12 . . . . . 1E **136**
Hunters Ct. TW9: Rich 5D **114**
Hunters Gro. BR6: Farnb 4G **173**
HA3: Kenton 4C **42**
UB3: Hayes 1J **93**
Hunters Hall Rd. RM10: Dag 4G **73**
Hunters Hill HA4: Ruis 3A **58**
Hunters Mdw. SE19 . . . . . 4E **138**
Hunter's Rd. KT9: Chess 3E **162**
Hunters Sq. RM10: Dag 4G **73**
Hunter St. WC1 . . . . . 3F **7** (4J **83**)
Hunters Way CR0: C'don 4E **168**
EN2: Enf 1F **23**
Hunter Wlk. E13 . . . . . 2J **87**
Huntingdon Cl. CR4: Mitc 3J **155**
UB5: N'olt 6E **58**
Huntingdon Gdns. KT4: Wor Pk 3E **164**
W4 . . . . . 7J **97**
Huntingdon Rd. N2 . . . . . 3C **46**
N9 . . . . . 2D **34**
Huntingdon St. E16 . . . . . 6H **87**
N1 . . . . . 7K **65**
Huntingfield CR0: Sels 7B **170**
Huntingfield Rd. SW15 . . . . . 4C **116**
Hunting Ga. Cl. EN2: Enf 3F **23**
Hunting Ga. Dr. KT9: Chess 7E **162**
Hunting Ga. M. SM1: Sutt 3K **165**
TW2: Twick 1J **131**
Huntings Farm IG1: Ilf 2J **71**
Huntings Rd. RM10: Dag 6G **73**
Huntley Cl. TW19: Stanw 7A **110**
Huntley St. WC1 . . . . . 4B **6** (4G **83**)
Huntley Way SW20 . . . . . 2C **152**
Huntloe Ho. *SE14* *1J* ***121***
(off Kender St.)
Huntly Dr. N3 . . . . . 6D **30**
Huntly Rd. SE25 . . . . . 4E **156**
Hunton St. E1 . . . . . 4K **9** (5G **85**)
Hunt Rd. UB2: S'hall 3E **94**
Hunt's Cl. SE3 . . . . . 2J **123**
Hunt's Ct. WC2 . . . . . 3D **12** (7H **83**)
Huntshaw Ho. *E3* *3D* ***86***
(off Devons Rd.)
Hunts La. E15 . . . . . 2E **86**
Huntsmans Cl. TW13: Felt 4K **129**
Huntsman St. SE17 . . . . . 4E **102**
Hunts Mead EN3: Enf H 3E **24**
Huntsmead Cl. BR7: Chst 7D **142**
Huntsmoor Rd. KT19: Ewe 5K **163**
Huntspill St. SW17 . . . . . 3A **136**
Hunts Slip Rd. SE21 . . . . . 3E **138**
Huntsworth M. NW1 . . . . . 3E **4** (4D **82**)

Hurdwick Ho. NW1 2G 83
(off Harrington Sq.)
Hurdwick Pl. NW1 2G 83
(off Hampstead Rd.)
Hurleston Ho. SE8 5B 104
Hurley Ct. SW17 6E 136
(off Mitcham Rd.)
W5 6C 78
Hurley Cres. SE16 2K 103
Hurley Ho. SE11 4K 19 (4B 102)
UB7: W Dray 2B 92
Hurley Rd. UB6: G'frd 6F 77
HURLINGHAM 3K 117
Hurlingham Bus. Pk. SW6 3J 117
Hurlingham Club, The 3J 117
Hurlingham Ct. SW6 3H 117
Hurlingham Gdns. SW6 3H 117
Hurlingham Pk. 2H 117
Hurlingham Retail Pk. SW6 3K 117
Hurlingham Rd. DA7: Bex 7F 109
SW6 2H 117
Hurlingham Sq. SW6 3J 117
Hurlock St. N5 3B 66
Hurlstone Rd. SE25 5E 156
Hurn Ct. TW4: Houn 2B 112
Hurn Ct. Rd. TW4: Houn 2B 112
Huron Cl. BR6: Chels 6J 173
Huron Rd. SW17 2E 136
Hurren Cl. SE3 3G 123
Hurricane Rd. SM6: Wall 7J 167
Hurricane Trad. Cen. NW9 1C 44
Hurry Cl. E15 7G 69
Hurst Av. E4 4H 35
N6 6G 47
Hurstbourne KT10: Clay 6A 162
Hurstbourne Gdns. IG11: Bark 6J 71
Hurstbourne Ho. SW15 6B 116
(off Tangley Gro.)
Hurstbourne Rd. SE23 1A 140
Hurst Cl. BR2: Hayes 1H 171
E4 3H 35
KT9: Chess 5G 163
NW11 6K 45
UB5: N'olt 6D 58
Hurstcombe IG9: Buck H 2D 36
Hurst Ct. DA15: Sidc 2A 144
E6 5B 88
(off Tollgate Rd.)
IG8: Wfd G 6E 36
(off Snakes La.)
Hurstcourt Rd. SM1: Sutt 2K 165
Hurstdene Av. BR2: Hayes 1H 171
Hurstdene Gdns. N15 7E 48
Hurstfield BR2: Brom 5J 159
Hurstfield Cres. UB4: Hayes 4G 75
Hurstfield Rd. KT8: W Mole 3E 148
Hurst Gro. KT12: Walt T 7H 147
Hurst Ho. WC1 1H 7
(off Penton Ri.)
Hurst La. KT8: E Mos 4G 149
SE2 5D 108
Hurst La. Est. SE2 5D 108
Hurstleigh Gdns. IG5: Ilf 1D 52
Hurstmead Ct. HA8: Edg 4C 28
HURST PARK 2G 149
Hurst Pl. HA6: Nwood 1D 38
Hurst Pool 3F 149
Hurst Ri. EN5: New Bar 3D 20
Hurst Rd. CR0: C'don 5D 168
DA5: Bexl 1D 144
DA8: Erith 1J 127
DA15: Bexl, Sidc 2A 144
E17 3D 50
IG9: Buck H 1G 37
KT8: W Mole, E Mos 3F 149
KT12: Walt T 5A 148
N21 1F 33
Hurst Springs DA5: Bexl 1E 144
Hurst St. SE24 6B 120
Hurstview Grange CR2: S Croy 7B 168
Hurst Vw. Rd. CR2: S Croy 7E 168
Hurst Way CR2: S Croy 6E 168
Hurstway Rd. W11 7F 81
Hurstway Wlk. W11 7F 81
Hurstwood Av. DA5: Bexl 1E 144
E18 4K 51
Hurstwood Ct. N12 6H 31
NW11 4H 45
(off Finchley Rd.)
Hurstwood Dr. BR1: Brom 3D 160
Hurstwood Rd. NW11 4G 45
Hurtwood Rd. KT12: Walt T 7D 148
Husborne Ho. SE8 4A 104
(off Chilton Gro.)
Huson Cl. NW3 7C 64
Hussain Cl. HA1: Harr 4K 59
Hussars Cl. TW4: Houn 3C 112
Husseywell Cres. BR2: Hayes 1J 171
Hutchings St. E14 2C 104
Hutchings Wlk. NW11 4K 45
Hutchings Wharf E14 2C 104
(off Hutchings St.)
Hutchins Cl. E15 7E 68
Hutchinson Ct. RM6: Chad H 4D 54
Hutchinson Ho. NW3 7D 64
SE14 7J 103
Hutchinson Ter. HA9: Wemb 3D 60
Hutchins Rd. SE28 7A 90
Hutton Cl. IG8: Wfd G 6E 36
UB6: G'frd 5H 59
Hutton Ct. N4 1K 65
(off Victoria Rd.)
N9 7D 24
(off Tramway Av.)
W5 5B 78
Hutton Gdns. HA3: Hrw W 7B 26
Hutton Gro. N12 5E 30
Hutton La. HA3: Hrw W 7B 26
Hutton M. SW15 5D 116
Hutton Row HA8: Edg 7D 28
Hutton St. EC4 2K 13 (6B 84)
Hutton Wlk. HA3: Hrw W 7B 26
Huxbear St. SE4 5B 122
Huxley Cl. UB5: N'olt 2C 76
UB8: Cowl 4A 74
Huxley Dr. RM6: Chad H 7B 54
Huxley Gdns. NW10 3F 79
Huxley Ho. NW8 4B 4
(off Fisherton St.)
Huxley Pde. N18 5J 33
Huxley Pl. N13 3G 33
Huxley Rd. DA16: Well 3K 125
E10 2E 68
N18 4J 33
Huxley Sayze N18 5J 33
Huxley Sth. N18 5J 33
Huxley St. W10 3G 81
Hyacinth Cl. IG1: Ilf 6F 71
TW12: Hamp 6E 130
Hyacinth Dr. UB10: Uxb 7A 56
Hyacinth Rd. SW15 1C 134
HYDE, THE 5B 44
Hyde, The NW9 4A 44
(not continuous)
Hyde Cl. E13 2J 87
EN5: Barn 3C 20
TW15: Ashf 6G 129
Hyde Ct. N20 3G 31
Hyde Cres. NW9 5A 44
Hyde Est. Rd. NW9 5B 44
Hyde Farm M. SW12 1H 137
Hydefield Cl. N21 1J 33
Hydefield Ct. N9 2K 33
Hyde Ho. TW3: Houn 3G 113
UB8: Uxb 6A 56
W13 1A 96
(off Singapore Rd.)
Hyde Ind. Est., The NW9 5B 44
Hyde La. SW11 1C 118
Hyde Pk. 4D 10 (1C 100)
Hyde Pk. Av. N21 2H 33
Hyde Pk. Barracks 7D 10
HYDE PARK CORNER 2F 101
Hyde Pk. Cnr. W1 6H 11 (2E 100)
Hyde Pk. Cres. W2 1C 10 (6C 82)
Hyde Pk. Gdns. N21 1H 33
W2 2B 10 (7B 82)
Hyde Pk. Gdns. M.
W2 2B 10 (7B 82)
Hyde Pk. Ga. SW7 2A 100
(not continuous)
Hyde Pk. Ga. M. SW7 2A 100
Hyde Pk. Mans. NW1 6C 4
(off Cabbell St., not continuous)
Hyde Pk. Pl. W2 2D 10 (7C 82)
Hyde Pk. Sq. W2 1C 10 (6C 82)
Hyde Pk. Sq. M. W2 1C 10
Hyde Pk. St. W2 1C 10 (6C 82)
Hyde Pk. Towers W2 7A 82
Hyderabad Way E15 7G 69
Hyde Rd. DA7: Bex 2F 127
N1 1E 84
TW10: Rich 5F 115
Hydeside Gdns. N9 2A 34
Hyde's Pl. N1 7B 66
Hyde St. SE8 6C 104
Hyde Ter. TW15: Ashf 6G 129
Hydethorpe Av. N9 2A 34
Hydethorpe Rd. SW12 1G 137
Hyde Va. SE10 7E 104
Hyde Wlk. SM4: Mord 7J 153
Hyde Way N9 2A 34
UB3: Harl 4H 93
Hydon Ct. N11 5J 31
Hydra Bldg., The EC1 2K 7
Hylands Rd. E17 2F 51
Hylton St. SE18 4K 107
Hyndewood SE23 3K 139
Hyndman Ho. RM10: Dag 3G 73
(off Kershaw Rd.)
Hyndman St. SE15 6H 103
Hynton Rd. RM8: Dag 2C 72
Hyperion Ho. E3 2A 86
(off Arbery Rd.)
SW2 6K 119
Hyrstdene CR2: S Croy 4B 168
Hyson Rd. SE16 5H 103
Hythe Av. DA7: Bex 7E 108
Hythe Cl. N18 4B 34
Hythe Ho. SE16 2J 103
(off Swan Rd.)
W6 4E 98
(off Shepherd's Bush Rd.)
Hythe Rd. CR7: Thor H 2D 156
NW10 3B 80
Hythe Rd. Ind. Est. NW10 3C 80

I

Ian Bowater Ct. N1 1F 9
(off East Rd.)
Ian Ct. SE23 2J 139
Ian Sq. EN3: Enf H 1E 24
Ibberton Ho. SW8 7K 101
(off Meadow Rd.)
W14 3G 99
(off Russell Rd.)
Ibbotson Av. E16 6H 87
Ibbott St. E1 4J 85
Iberia Ho. N19 7H 47
Iberian Av. SM6: Bedd 4H 167
Ibex Ho. E15 5G 69
(off Forest La.)
Ibis Ct. SE8 6B 104
(off Edward Pl.)
Ibis La. W4 1J 115
Ibis Way UB4: Yead 6B 76
Ibrox Ct. IG9: Buck H 2F 37
Ibscott Cl. RM10: Dag 6J 73
Ibsley Gdns. SW15 1C 134
Ibsley Way EN4: Cockf 5H 21
ICA Cinema 4D 12
(off Carlton Ho. Ter.)
Icarus Ho. E3 3B 86
(off British St.)
ICA Theatre 4D 12
(off Carlton Ho. Ter.)
Iceland Rd. E3 1C 86
Iceland Wharf SE8 4A 104
Iceni Ct. E3 1B 86
(off Parnell Rd.)
IG9: Buck H 1E 36
Ice Wharf N1 2J 83
Ice Wharf Marina N1 2J 83
(off New Wharf Rd.)
Ice Works, The NW1 7F 65
(off Jamestown Rd.)
Ickburgh Est. E5 2H 67
Ickburgh Rd. E5 3H 67
ICKENHAM 3D 56
Ickenham Cl. HA4: Ruis 2F 57
Ickenham Grn. UB10: Ick 1D 56
Ickenham Rd. HA4: Ruis 2E 56
Ickleton Rd. SE9 4C 142
Icknield Dr. IG2: Ilf 5F 53
Icknield Ho. SW3 5D 16
(off Cale St.)
Ickworth Pk. Rd. E17 4A 50
Icon Apartments SE1 7G 15
(off Cluny Pl.)
Icona Point E15 1E 86
(off Warton Rd.)
Idaho Bldg. SE10 1D 122
(off Deal's Gateway)
Ida Rd. N15 4D 48
Ida St. E14 6E 86
(not continuous)
Ide Mans. E1 7K 85
(off Cable St.)
Iden Cl. BR2: Brom 3G 159
Idlecombe Rd. SW17 6E 136
Idmiston Rd. E15 4H 69
KT4: Wor Pk 7B 152
SE27 3C 138
Idmiston Sq. KT4: Wor Pk 7B 152
Idol La. EC3 3G 15 (7E 84)
Idonia St. SE8 7C 104
Iffley Cl. UB8: Uxb 7A 56
Iffley Rd. W6 3D 98
Ifield Ho. SE17 5E 102
(off Madron St.)
Ifield Rd. SW10 6K 99
Ifor Evans Pl. E1 4K 85
Ightham Ho. BR3: Beck 7B 140
(off Bethersden Cl.)
SE17 4E 102
(off Beckway St.)
Ightham Rd. DA8: Erith 7G 109
Ikon Ho. E1 7J 85
(off Devonport St.)
Ilbert St. W10 3F 81
Ilchester Gdns. W2 7K 81
Ilchester Mans. W8 3J 99
(off Abingdon Rd.)
Ilchester Pl. W14 3H 99
Ilchester Rd. RM8: Dag 5B 72
Ildersly Gro. SE21 2D 138
Ilderton Rd. SE15 5J 103
SE16 5J 103
Ilderton Wharf SE15 6J 103
(off Rollins St.)
Ilex Cl. TW16: Sun 2A 148
Ilex Rd. NW10 6B 62
Ilex Way SW16 5A 138
ILFORD 3F 71
Ilford FC 2J 71
Ilford Hill IG1: Ilf 3E 70
Ilford Ho. N1 6D 66
(off Dove Rd.)
Ilford La. IG1: Bark, Ilf 3F 71
Ilfracombe Flats SE1 6D 14
(off Marshalsea Rd.)
Ilfracombe Gdns. RM6: Chad H 7B 54
Ilfracombe Rd. BR1: Brom 3H 141
Iliffe St. SE17 5B 102
Iliffe Yd. SE17 5B 102
(off Crampton St.)

Ilkeston Ct. E5 . . . 4K 67
(off Overbury St.)
Ilkley Cl. SE19 . . . 6D 138
Ilkley Rd. E16 . . . 5A 88
Illingworth Cl. CR4: Mitc . . . 3B 154
Illingworth Way EN1: Enf . . . 5K 23
Ilmington Rd. HA3: Kenton . . . 6D 42
Ilminster Gdns. SW11 . . . 4C 118
Ilsley Ct. SW8 . . . 2G 119
Images IG2: Ilf . . . 6E 52
Imani Mans. SW11 . . . 2B 118
IMAX National Film Theatre
. . . 5J 13 (1A 102)
Imber Cl. N14 . . . 7B 22
Imber Ct. Trad. Est. KT8: E Mos . . . 6H 149
Imber Cross KT7: T Ditt . . . 6K 149
Imber Gro. KT10: Esh . . . 7H 149
Imber Pk. Rd. KT10: Esh . . . 7H 149
Imber St. N1 . . . 1D 84
Impact Bus. Pk. UB6: G'frd . . . 2B 78
Impact Ct. SE20 . . . 2H 157
Imperial Av. N16 . . . 4E 66
Imperial Cl. HA2: Harr . . . 6E 40
NW2 . . . 5D 62
Imperial College London
Chelsea & Westminster Campus
. . . 6A 100
(within Chelsea & Westminster Hospital)
Royal Brompton Campus . . . 6C 16
St Mary's . . . 7B 4
Sth. Kensington Campus
. . . 1A 16 (3B 100)
Imperial Coll. Rd. SW7 . . . 2A 16 (3B 100)
Imperial Ct. HA2: Harr . . . 7E 40
N6 . . . 6G 47
N20 . . . 3F 31
NW8 . . . 2C 82
(off Prince Albert Rd.)
SE11 . . . 6J 19 (5A 102)
Imperial Cres. SW6 . . . 2A 118
Imperial Dr. HA2: Harr . . . 7E 40
Imperial Fields . . . 5C 154
Imperial Gdns. CR4: Mitc . . . 3F 155
Imperial Hgts. E18 . . . 1J 51
(off Queen Mary Av.)
Imperial Ho. E3 . . . 3A 86
(off Grove Rd.)
E14 . . . 7B 86
(off Victory Pl.)
Imperial M. E6 . . . 2B 88
Imperial Pl. BR7: Chst . . . 1E 160
Imperial Rd. N22 . . . 7D 32
SW6 . . . 1K 117
TW14: Felt . . . 7G 111
Imperial Sq. SW6 . . . 1K 117
Imperial St. E3 . . . 3E 86
Imperial War Mus.
All Saints Annexe . . . 3K 19
(off Austral St.)
Lambeth Rd. . . . 2K 19 (3A 102)
Imperial Way BR7: Chst . . . 3G 143
CR0: Wadd . . . 6K 167
HA3: Kenton . . . 6E 42
Imperial Wharf E2 . . . 2H 85
(off Darwen Pl.)
SW6 . . . 2A 118
Imre Cl. W12 . . . 1D 98
Inca Dr. SE9 . . . 7F 125
Inca Ter. N15 . . . 3B 48
Inchmery Rd. SE6 . . . 2D 140
Inchwood CR0: Addtn . . . 4D 170
Independence Ho. SW19 . . . 1B 154
(off Chapter Way)
Independent Ind. Est. UB7: Yiew . . . 1A 92
Independent Pl. E8 . . . 5F 67
Independents Rd. SE3 . . . 3H 123
Inderwick Rd. N8 . . . 5K 47
Indescon Ct. E14 . . . 2D 104
Indescon Sq. E14 . . . 2C 104
India Gdns. UB5: N'olt . . . 7A 58
India Ho. WC2 . . . 7K 83
(off Aldwych)
Indiana Bldg. SE10 . . . 1C 122
(off Deal's Gateway)
India Pl. WC2 . . . 2G 13
India St. EC3 . . . 1J 15 (6F 85)
India Way W12 . . . 7D 80
Indigo M. E14 . . . 7E 86
N16 . . . 3D 66
Indigo Wlk. N2 . . . 4D 46
Indus Ct. SE15 . . . 7F 103
(off Amstel Ct.)
Indus Rd. SE7 . . . 7A 106
Infirmary Ct. SW3 . . . 7F 17
Inforum M. SE15 . . . 7G 103
Ingal Rd. E13 . . . 4J 87
Ingate Pl. SW8 . . . 1F 119
Ingatestone Rd. E12 . . . 1A 70
IG8: Wfd G . . . 7E 36
SE25 . . . 4H 157
Ingelow Ho. W8 . . . 2K 99
(off Holland St.)
Ingelow Rd. SW8 . . . 2F 119
Ingersoll Rd. EN3: Enf W . . . 1D 24
W12 . . . 1D 98
Ingestre Pl. W1 . . . 1B 12 (6G 83)
Ingestre Rd. E7 . . . 4J 69
NW5 . . . 4F 65
Ingham Cl. CR2: Sels . . . 7K 169
Ingham Rd. CR2: Sels . . . 7J 169
NW6 . . . 4J 63
Inglebert St. EC1 . . . 1J 7 (3A 84)
Ingleborough St. SW9 . . . 2A 120
Ingleby Dr. HA1: Harr . . . 3H 59
Ingleby Rd. IG1: Ilf . . . 1F 71
N7 . . . 3J 65
RM10: Dag . . . 6H 73
Ingleby Way BR7: Chst . . . 5E 142
SM6: Wall . . . 7H 167
Ingle Cl. HA5: Pinn . . . 3C 40
Ingledew Rd. SE18 . . . 5H 107
Inglefield Sq. E1 . . . 1H 103
(off Prusom St.)
Inglehurst Gdns. IG4: Ilf . . . 5D 52
Inglemere Rd. CR4: Mitc . . . 7D 136
SE23 . . . 3K 139
Ingle M. EC1 . . . 1J 7 (3A 84)
Inglesham Wlk. E9 . . . 6B 68
Ingleside SL3: Poyle . . . 4A 174
Ingleside Cl. BR3: Beck . . . 7C 140
Ingleside Gro. SE3 . . . 6H 105
Inglethorpe St. SW6 . . . 1F 117
Ingleton Av. DA16: Well . . . 5A 126
Ingleton Rd. N18 . . . 6B 34
SM5: Cars . . . 7C 166
Ingleton St. SW9 . . . 2A 120
Ingleway N12 . . . 6G 31
Inglewood BR7: Chst . . . 6H 143
CR0: Sels . . . 7A 170
Inglewood Cl. E14 . . . 4C 104
Inglewood Copse BR1: Brom . . . 2C 160
Inglewood Ct. BR1: Brom . . . 7G 141
Inglewood M. KT6: Surb . . . 1G 163
Inglewood Rd. DA7: Bex . . . 4K 127
NW6 . . . 5J 63
Inglis Rd. CR0: C'don . . . 1F 169
W5 . . . 7F 79
Inglis St. SE5 . . . 1B 120
Ingoldisthorpe Gro. SE15 . . . 6F 103
Ingram Av. NW11 . . . 7A 46
Ingram Cl. HA7: Stan . . . 5H 27
SE11 . . . 3H 19 (4K 101)
Ingram Ho. E3 . . . 1A 86
Ingram Rd. CR7: Thor H . . . 1C 156
N2 . . . 4C 46
Ingram Way UB6: G'frd . . . 1H 77
Ingrave Ho. RM9: Dag . . . 1B 90
Ingrave Rd. RM1: Rom . . . 4K 55
Ingrave St. SW11 . . . 3B 118
Ingrebourne Ct. E4 . . . 3J 35
Ingrebourne Ho. BR1: Brom . . . 5F 141
(off Brangbourne Rd.)
NW8 . . . 5B 4
(off Broadley St.)
Ingress St. W4 . . . 5A 98
Inigo Jones Rd. SE7 . . . 7C 106
Inigo Pl. WC2 . . . 2E 12
Ink Bldg. W10 . . . 5F 81
Inkerman Rd. NW5 . . . 6F 65
Inkerman Ter. W8 . . . 3J 99
(off Allen St.)
Inks Grn. E4 . . . 5K 35
Inkster Ho. SW11 . . . 3C 118
Inkwell Cl. N12 . . . 3F 31
Ink Works Ct. SE1 . . . 2E 102
(off Bell Yd. M.)
Inman Rd. NW10 . . . 1A 80
SW18 . . . 7A 118
Inmans Row IG8: Wfd G . . . 4D 36
Inner Circ. NW1 . . . 2G 5 (3E 82)
Inner Ct. SW3 . . . 7C 16 (6C 100)
Innerd Ct. CR0: C'don . . . 6C 156
(off Harry Cl.)
Inner London Family Proceedings Court
(Magistrates') . . . 7A 6 (5G 83)
Inner Pk. Rd. SW19 . . . 1F 135
Inner Ring E. TW6: H'row A . . . 3D 110
Inner Ring W. TW6: H'row A . . . 3C 110
Inner Temple La. EC4 . . . 1J 13
Innes Cl. SW20 . . . 2G 153
Innes Gdns. SW15 . . . 6D 116
Innes St. SE15 . . . 7E 102
Innes Yd. CR0: C'don . . . 3C 168
Innis Ho. SE17 . . . 5E 102
(off East St.)
Inniskilling Rd. E13 . . . 2A 88
Innova Ct. CR0: C'don . . . 1E 168
Innovation Cen., The E14 . . . 2E 104
(off Marsh Wall)
Innovation Cl. HA0: Wemb . . . 1E 78
Inns of Court & City Yeomanry Mus.
. . . 6H 7 (5K 83)
Inskip Cl. E10 . . . 2D 68
Inskip Rd. RM8: Dag . . . 1D 72
Insley Ho. E3 . . . 3D 86
(off Bow Rd.)
Institute of Archaeology Collections
. . . 4H 83
Institute of Contemporary Arts . . . 4D 12
Institute Pl. E8 . . . 5H 67
Integer Gdns. E11 . . . 7F 51
Interface Ho. TW3: Houn . . . 3E 112
(off Staines Rd.)
International Av. TW5: Cran . . . 5A 94
International Bus. Pk. E15 . . . 1F 87
International Ho. E1 . . . 3K 15
(off St Katharine's Way)
International Trad. Est. UB2: S'hall . . . 3K 93
International Way TW16: Sun . . . 1G 147
Inverary Pl. SE18 . . . 6H 107
Inver Cl. E5 . . . 2J 67
Inverclyde Gdns. RM6: Chad H . . . 4C 54
(not continuous)
Inver Ct. W2 . . . 6K 81
W6 . . . 3C 98
Inveresk Gdns. KT4: Wor Pk . . . 3C 164
Inverforth Cl. NW3 . . . 2A 64
Inverforth Rd. N11 . . . 5A 32
Invergarry Ho. NW6 . . . 2K 81
(off Carlton Va.)
Inverine Rd. SE7 . . . 5K 105
Invermead Cl. W6 . . . 3C 98
Invermore Pl. SE18 . . . 4G 107
Inverness Av. EN1: Enf . . . 1K 23
Inverness Ct. SE6 . . . 1H 141
Inverness Gdns. W8 . . . 1K 99
Inverness M. E16 . . . 1G 107
W2 . . . 7K 81
Inverness Pl. W2 . . . 7K 81
Inverness Rd. KT4: Wor Pk . . . 1F 165
N18 . . . 5C 34
TW3: Houn . . . 4D 112
UB2: S'hall . . . 4C 94
Inverness St. NW1 . . . 1F 83
Inverness Ter. W2 . . . 6K 81
Inverton Rd. SE15 . . . 4K 121
Invicta Cen., The IG11: Bark . . . 1A 90
Invicta Cl. BR7: Chst . . . 5E 142
E3 . . . 5C 86
TW14: Felt . . . 1H 129
Invicta Gro. UB5: N'olt . . . 3D 76
Invicta Pde. DA14: Sidc . . . 4B 144
Invicta Plaza SE1 . . . 4A 14 (1B 102)
Invicta Rd. SE3 . . . 7J 105
Inville Rd. SE17 . . . 5D 102
(not continuous)
Inville Wlk. SE17 . . . 5D 102
Invito IG2: Ilf . . . 6E 52
Inwen Ct. SE8 . . . 5A 104
Inwood Av. TW3: Houn . . . 3G 113
Inwood Bus. Pk. TW3: Houn . . . 4F 113
Inwood Cl. CR0: C'don . . . 2A 170
Inwood Ct. NW1 . . . 7G 65
(off Rochester Sq.)
Inwood Rd. TW3: Houn . . . 4F 113
Inworth St. SW11 . . . 2C 118
Inworth Wlk. N1 . . . 1C 84
(off Popham St.)
IO Centre SE18 . . . 3G 107
(not continuous)
Iona Cl. SE6 . . . 7C 122
SM4: Mord . . . 7K 153
Ion Ct. E2 . . . 2G 85
Ionian Bldg. E14 . . . 7A 86
Ionian Ho. E1 . . . 4K 85
(off Duckett St.)
Ion Sq. E2 . . . 2G 85
Ipsden Bldgs. SE1 . . . 5K 13
Ipswich Rd. SW17 . . . 6E 136
Ira Ct. SE27 . . . 2B 138
Ireland Cl. E6 . . . 5D 88
Ireland Pl. N22 . . . 7D 32
Ireland Yd. EC4 . . . 1B 14 (6B 84)
Irene M. W7 . . . 1K 95
(off Uxbridge Rd.)
Irene Rd. BR6: Orp . . . 7K 161
SW6 . . . 1J 117
Ireton Cl. N10 . . . 7K 31
Ireton St. E3 . . . 4C 86
Iris Av. DA5: Bexl . . . 5E 126
Iris Cl. CR0: C'don . . . 1K 169
E6 . . . 5C 88
KT6: Surb . . . 7F 151
Iris Ct. SE14 . . . 1J 121
(off Briant St.)
Iris Cres. DA7: Bex . . . 6F 109
Iris Rd. KT19: Ewe . . . 5H 163
Iris Wlk. HA8: Edg . . . 4D 28
Iris Way E4 . . . 6G 35
Irkdale Av. EN1: Enf . . . 1A 24
Iron Bri. Cl. NW10 . . . 5A 62
Ironbridge Cl. UB2: S'hall . . . 1G 95
Iron Bri. Ho. NW1 . . . 7D 64
Iron Bri. Rd. Nth. UB11: Stock P . . . 2C 92
Iron Bri. Rd. Sth. UB7: W Dray . . . 2C 92
Iron Mill Pl. SW18 . . . 6K 117
Iron Mill Rd. SW18 . . . 6K 117
Ironmonger La. EC2 . . . 1D 14 (6C 84)
Ironmonger Pas. EC1 . . . 2D 8
(off Ironmonger Row)
Ironmonger Row EC1 . . . 2D 8 (3C 84)
Ironmonger Row Baths . . . 2D 8
Ironmongers Pl. E14 . . . 4C 104
Ironside Cl. SE16 . . . 2K 103
Ironside Ct. TW11: Ham W . . . 1C 150
Ironside Ho. E9 . . . 4A 68
Irons Way RM5: Col R . . . 1J 55
Iron Works E3 . . . 1C 86
Ironworks, The N1 . . . 2J 83
(off Albion Wlk.)
Irvine Av. HA3: Kenton . . . 3A 42
Irvine Cl. E14 . . . 5D 86
N20 . . . 2H 31
Irvine Ct. W1 . . . 4B 6
(off Whitfield St.)
Irvine Ho. N7 . . . 6K 65
(off Caledonian Rd.)
Irvine Way BR6: Orp . . . 7K 161

Irving Av. UB5: N'olt 1B 76
Irving Gro. SW9 . . . . .2K 119
Irving Ho. SE17 . . . . .5B 102
   (off Doddington Gro.)
Irving Mans. W14 . . . . .6G 99
   (off Queen's Club Gdns.)
Irving M. N1 . . . . .6C 66
Irving Rd. W14 . . . . .3F 99
Irving St. WC2 . . . . .3D 12 (7H 83)
Irving Way NW9 . . . . .5C 44
Irwell Ct. W7 . . . . .6H 77
   (off Hobbayne Rd.)
Irwell Est. SE16 . . . . .3J 103
Irwin Av. SE18 . . . . .7J 107
Irwin Cl. UB10: Ick 3C 56
Irwin Gdns. NW10 . . . . .1D 80
Isaac Way SE1 . . . . .6D 14
   (off Sanctuary St.)
Isabel Hill Cl. TW12: Hamp 2F 149
Isabella Cl. N14 . . . . .7B 22
Isabella Dr. BR6: Farnb 4G 173
Isabella Ho. SE11 . . . . .5K 19
   W6 . . . . .5E 98
   (off Queen Caroline St.)
Isabella Pl. KT2: King T 5F 133
Isabella Rd. E9 . . . . .5J 67
Isabella St. SE1 . . . . . . .5A 14 (1B 102)
Isabel St. SW9 . . . . .1K 119
Isambard M. E14 . . . . .3E 104
Isambard Pl. SE16 . . . . .1J 103
Isard Ho. BR2: Hayes 1K 171
Isel Way SE22 . . . . .5E 120
Isham Rd. SW16 . . . . .2J 155
Isis Cl. HA4: Ruis 6E 38
   SW15 . . . . .4E 116
Isis Ct. W4 . . . . .7H 97
Isis Ho. N18 .6A 34
   NW8 . . . . .4B 4
   (off Church St. Est.)
Isis St. SW18 . . . . .2A 136
Island, The KT7: T Ditt 6A 150
   UB7: Lford 3D 174
Island Apartments N1 . . . . .1C 84
Island Barn Reservoir Sailing Club
   . . . . .6F 149
Island Farm Av. KT8: W Mole 5D 148
Island Farm Rd. KT8: W Mole 5D 148
Island Ho. E3 .3E 86
Island Rd. CR4: Mitc 7D 136
   SE16 . . . . .4K 103
Island Row E14 . . . . .6B 86
Isla Rd. SE18 . . . . .6G 107
Islay Gdns. TW4: Houn 5B 112
Islay Wlk. N1 .6C 66
   (off Douglas Rd. Sth.)
Isleden Ho. N1 . . . . .1C 84
   (off Prebend St.)
Isledon Rd. N7 . . . . .3A 66
ISLEDON VILLAGE 3A 66
Islehurst Cl. BR7: Chst 1E 160
ISLEWORTH .3A 114
Isleworth Ait Nature Reserve 3B 114
Isleworth Bus. Complex TW7: Isle . .2K 113
Isleworth Prom. TW1: Twick 4B 114
Isleworth Recreation Cen. 4K 113
Isley Ct. SW8 . . . . .2G 119
ISLINGTON 7B 66
Islington Bus. Cen. N1 . . . . .1C 84
   (off Coleman Flds.)
Islington Crematorium N2 . . . . . . .1D 46
Islington Ecology Cen., The 3A 66
Islington Grn. N1 . . . . .1B 84
Islington High St. N1 . . . . .2A 84
   (not continuous)
Islington Mus. 4B (3B 84)
Islington Pk. M. N1 . . . . .7B 66
Islington Pk. St. N1 . . . . .7A 66
Islington Pl. N1 . . . . .1A 84
Islington Tennis Cen. 6J 65
Islip Gdns. HA8: Edg 7E 28
   UB5: N'olt 7C 58
Islip Mnr. Rd. UB5: N'olt 7C 58

Islip St. NW5 .5G 65
Ismailia Rd. E7 . . . . .7K 69
Isobel Ho. HA1: Harr 5K 41
Isola Ct. N1 . . . . .1C 84
   (off Popham Rd.)
Isom Cl. E13 .3K 87
Issa Rd. TW3: Houn 4D 112
Issigonis Ho. W3 . . . . .1B 98
   (off Cowley Rd.)
Italia Conti Academy of Theatre Arts
   Avondale 3J 119
   (off Landor Rd.)
Itaska Cotts. WD23: B Hea 1D 26
Ivanhoe Cl. UB8: Cowl 5A 74
Ivanhoe Dr. HA3: Kenton 3A 42
Ivanhoe Ho. E3 . . . . .2A 86
   (off Grove Rd.)
Ivanhoe Rd. SE5 . . . . .3F 121
   TW4: Houn 3B 112
Ivatt Pl. W14 .5H 99
Ivatt Way N17 . . . . .3B 48
Iveagh Av. NW10 . . . . .2G 79
Iveagh Cl. E9 .1K 85
   HA6: Nwood 1D 38
   NW10 . . . . .2G 79
Iveagh Ct. BR3: Beck 3E 158
   E1 . . . . .1J 15
Iveagh Ho. SW9 . . . . .2B 120
   SW10 . . . . .7A 100
   (off King's Rd.)
Iveagh Ter. NW10 . . . . .2G 79
   (off Iveagh Av.)
Ivedon Rd. DA16: Well 2C 126
Ive Farm Cl. E10 . . . . .2C 68
Ive Farm La. E10 . . . . .2C 68
Iveley Rd. SW4 . . . . .2G 119
Ivere Dr. EN5: New Bar 6E 20
Iver Ho. N1 . . . . .1E 84
   (off New Era Est.)
Iverhurst Cl. DA6: Bex 5D 126
Iverna Ct. W8 . . . . .3J 99
Iverna Gdns. TW14: Felt 5F 111
   W8 . . . . .3J 99
Iverson Rd. NW6 . . . . .6H 63
Ivers Way CR0: New Ad 7D 170
Ives Rd. E16 .5G 87
Ives St. SW3 . . . . .3D 16 (4C 100)
Ivestor Ter. SE23 . . . . .7J 121
Ivimey St. E2 .3G 85
Ivinghoe Cl. EN1: Enf 1K 23
Ivinghoe Ho. N7 . . . . .5H 65
Ivinghoe Rd. RM8: Dag 5B 72
Ivor Ct. N8 . . . . .6J 47
   NW1 . . . . .3E 4
   (off Gloucester Pl.)
Ivor Gro. SE9 . . . . .1F 143
Ivories, The N1 . . . . .7C 66
   (off Northampton St.)
Ivor Pl. NW1 . . . . .4E 4 (4D 82)
Ivor St. NW1 .7G 65
Ivory Ct. E18 .1J 51
   TW13: Felt 1J 129
Ivorydown BR1: Brom 4J 141
Ivory Ho. E1 . . . . .3K 15 (1F 103)
Ivory Pl. W11 .7G 81
   (off Treadgold St.)
Ivory Sq. SW11 . . . . .3A 118
Ivybridge Cl. TW1: Twick 7A 114
   UB8: Uxb 3A 74
Ivybridge Ct. BR7: Chst 1E 160
   (off Old Hill)
   NW1 . . . . .7F 65
   (off Lewis St.)
Ivybridge La. WC2 . . . . . . .3F 13 (7J 83)
Ivy Bri. Retail Pk. TW7: Isle 5K 113
Ivychurch Cl. SE20 . . . . .7J 139
Ivychurch La. SE17 . . . . .5F 103
Ivy Cl. HA2: Harr 4D 58
   HA5: Eastc 7A 40
   TW16: Sun 2A 148
Ivy Cotts. E14 . . . . .7E 86
   UB10: Hil .3C 74

Ivy Ct. SE16 .5G 103
   (off Argyle Way)
Ivy Cres. W4 .4J 97
Ivydale Rd. SE15 . . . . .3K 121
   SM5: Cars 2D 166
Ivyday Gro. SW16 . . . . .3K 137
Ivydene KT8: W Mole 5D 148
Ivydene Cl. SM1: Sutt 4A 166
Ivy Gdns. CR4: Mitc 3H 155
   N8 . . . . .6J 47
Ivy Ho. Rd. UB10: Ick 3D 56
Ivyhouse Rd. RM9: Dag 6D 72
Ivy La. TW4: Houn 4D 112
Ivy Lodge W11 . . . . .1J 99
   (off Notting Hill Ga.)
Ivymount Rd. SE27 . . . . .3A 138
Ivy Rd. E16 . . . . .6J 87
   E17 . . . . .6C 50
   KT6: Surb 1G 163
   N14 . . . . .7B 22
   NW2 . . . . .4E 62
   SE4 . . . . .4B 122
   SW17 . . . . .5C 136
   TW3: Houn 4F 113
Ivy St. N1 . . . . .2E 84
Ivy Wlk. HA6: Nwood 1G 39
   RM9: Dag .6E 72
Ixworth Pl. SW3 . . . . . .5C 16 (5C 100)
Izane Rd. DA6: Bex 4F 127

J

Jacana Ct. E1 .3K 15
   (off Star Pl.)
Jacaranda Cl. KT3: N Mald 3A 152
Jacaranda Gro. E8 . . . . .7F 67
Jackass La. BR2: Kes 5K 171
Jack Barnett Way N22 . . . . .2K 47
Jack Clow Rd. E15 . . . . .2G 87
Jack Cook Ho. IG11: Bark 7F 71
Jack Cornwell St. E12 . . . . .4E 70
Jack Dash Way E6 . . . . .4C 88
Jackets La. HA6: Nwood 1D 38
Jack Goodchild Way
   KT1: King T 3H 151
Jack Jones Way RM9: Dag 1F 91
Jacklin Grn. IG8: Wfd G 4D 36
Jackman Ho. E1 . . . . .1H 103
   (off Watts St.)
Jackman M. NW2 . . . . .3A 62
Jackman St. E8 . . . . .1H 85
Jackson Cl. E9 . . . . .7J 67
   UB10: Uxb 7A 56
Jackson Ct. E7 . . . . .6K 69
Jackson Ho. N11 . . . . .5B 32
Jackson Rd. BR2: Brom 2D 172
   EN4: E Barn 6H 21
   IG11: Bark 1H 89
   N7 . . . . .4K 65
   UB10: Uxb 7A 56
Jacksons La. N6 . . . . .7E 46
Jacksons Lane Theatre 6F 47
   (off Archway Rd.)
Jacksons Pl. CR0: C'don 1D 168
Jackson St. SE18 . . . . .6E 106
Jackson's Way CR0: C'don 3C 170
Jackson Way UB2: S'hall 2F 95
Jacks Pl. E1 . . . . .5J 9
   (off Corbet Pl.)
Jack Walker Ct. N5 . . . . .4B 66
Jacob Ho. DA18: Erith 2D 108
   (off Kale Rd.)
Jacobin Lodge N7 . . . . .5J 65
   (off Commercial Rd.)
Jacob M. HA7: Stan 2F 27
Jacob Rd. CR10: Dag 4H 73
Jacobs Ho. E13 . . . . .3A 88
   (off New City Rd.)
Jacobs Island Ho. SE16 . . . . .3F 103
   (off Dunlop Pl.)

Jacobs Island Pier SE16 . . . . .2G 103
   (off Bermondsey Wall W.)
Jacob St. SE1 . . . . .6K 15 (2G 103)
Jacob's Well M. W1 . . . . . . .6H 5 (5E 82)
Jacotts Ho. W10 . . . . .4E 80
   (off Sutton Way)
Jacqueline Cl. UB5: N'olt 1C 76
Jacqueline Creft Ter. N6 . . . . .6E 46
   (off Grange Rd.)
Jacqueline Ho. NW1 . . . . .1D 82
   (off Regent's Pk. Rd.)
Jacqueline Vs. E17 . . . . .5E 50
   (off Shernhall St.)
Jade Cl. E16 .6B 88
   NW2 . . . . .7F 45
   RM8: Dag .1C 72
Jade Ter. NW6 . . . . .7A 64
Jaffe Rd. IG1: Ilf 1H 71
Jaffray Pl. SE27 . . . . .4B 138
Jaffray Rd. BR2: Brom 4B 160
Jaggard Way SW12 . . . . .7D 118
Jagger Ho. SW11 . . . . .1D 118
   (off Rosenau Rd.)
Jago Cl. SE18 . . . . .6G 107
Jago Wlk. SE5 . . . . .7D 102
Jake Russell Wlk. E16 . . . . .7A 88
Jamaica Rd. CR7: Thor H 6B 156
   SE1 . . . . .7K 15 (2F 103)
   SE16 . . . . .7K 15 (2F 103)
Jamaica St. E1 . . . . .6J 85
James Allens School Swimming Pool
   . . . . .5E 120
James Anderson Ct. E2 . . . . .2E 84
   (off Kingsland Rd.)
James Av. NW2 . . . . .5E 62
   RM8: Dag .1F 73
James Bedford Cl.
   HA5: Pinn .2A 40
James Boswell Cl. SW16 . . . . .4K 137
James Brine Ho. E2 . . . . .1K 9
   (off Ravenscroft St.)
James Campbell Ho. E2 . . . . .2J 85
   (off Old Ford Rd.)
James Clavell Sq. SE18 . . . . .3F 107
   (off No. 1 St.)
James Cl. E13 . . . . .2J 87
   NW11 . . . . .6G 45
James Collins Cl. W9 . . . . .4H 81
James Ct. HA6: Nwood 1H 39
   N1 . . . . .1C 84
   (off Raynor Pl.)
   NW9 . . . . .2A 44
   UB5: N'olt .2C 76
   (off Church Rd.)
James Docherty Ho. E2 . . . . .2H 85
   (off Patriot Sq.)
James Dudson Ct. NW10 . . . . .7J 61
James Est. CR4: Mitc 2D 154
James Gdns. N22 . . . . .7G 33
James Hammett Ho. E2 . . . . .1K 9
   (off Ravenscroft St.)
James Hill Ho. W10 . . . . .4G 81
   (off Kensal Rd.)
James Ho. E1 . . . . .4A 86
   (off Solebay St.)
   SE16 . . . . .2K 103
   (off Wolfe Cres.)
   SW8 . . . . .7J 101
   (off Wheatsheaf La.)
   W10 . . . . .4G 81
James Joyce Wlk. SE24 . . . . .4B 120
James La. E10 . . . . .7E 50
   E11 . . . . .7F 51
James Leal Cen. 5G 37
James Lighthill Ho. WC1 . . . . .1H 7
   (off Penton Ri.)
James Lind Ho. SE8 . . . . .4B 104
   (off Grove St.)
James Middleton Ho. E2 . . . . .3H 85
   (off Middleton St.)
James Newman Ct. SE9 . . . . .3E 142
Jameson Cl. W3 . . . . .2J 97

Jameson Ct. E2 . . . . .2J 85
(off Russia La.)
Jameson Ho. SE11 . . . . .5G 19
(off Glasshouse Wlk.)
Jameson Lodge N6 . . . . .6G 47
Jameson St. W8 . . . . .1J 99
James Pl. N17 . . . . .1F 49
James's Cotts. TW9: Kew 7G 97
James Stewart Ho. NW6 . . . . .7H 63
James St. EN1: Enf 5A 24
IG11: Bark 7G 71
TW3: Houn 3H 113
W1 . . . . .1H 11 (6E 82)
WC2 . . . . .1F 13 (7J 83)
James Stroud Ho. SE17 . . . . .5C 102
(off Walworth Pl.)
James Ter. SW14 . . . . .3K 115
(off Church Path)
TW12: Ham H 6G 131
(off Church Path)
James Terry Ct. CR2: S Croy 5C 168
(off Warham Rd.)
Jameston Lodge HA4: Ruis 1H 57
Jamestown Rd. NW1 . . . . .1F 83
Jamestown Way E14 . . . . .7F 87
James Voller Way E1 . . . . .6J 85
James Yd. E4 . . . . .6A 36
Jam Factory, The SE1 . . . . .3E 102
(off Green Wlk.)
Jamieson Ho. TW4: Houn 6D 112
Jamilah Ho. E16 . . . . .7E 88
(off University Way)
Jamuna Cl. E14 . . . . .5A 86
Jane Austen Hall E16 . . . . .1K 105
(off Wesley Av.)
Jane Austen Ho. SW1 . . . . .6A 18
(off Churchill Gdns.)
Jane Seymour Ct. SE9 . . . . .7H 125
Jane St. E1 . . . . .6H 85
Janet Adegoke Swimming Pool 7C 80
Janet St. E14 . . . . .3C 104
Janeway Pl. SE16 . . . . .2H 103
Janeway St. SE16 . . . . .2G 103
Janice M. IG1: Ilf 2F 71
Jansen Wlk. SW11 . . . . .3B 118
Janson Cl. E15 . . . . .5G 69
NW10 . . . . .3A 62
Janson Rd. E15 . . . . .5G 69
Jansons Rd. N15 . . . . .3E 48
Japan Cres. N4 . . . . .1K 65
Japan Rd. RM6: Chad H 6D 54
Jardine Rd. E1 . . . . .7K 85
Jarman Ho. E1 . . . . .5J 85
(off Jubilee La.)
SE16 . . . . .4K 103
(off Hawkstone Rd.)
Jarret Ho. E3 . . . . .3C 86
(off Bow Rd.)
Jarrett Cl. SW2 . . . . .1B 138
Jarrow Cl. SM4: Mord 5K 153
Jarrow Rd. N17 . . . . .4H 49
RM6: Chad H 6C 54
SE16 . . . . .4J 103
Jarrow Way E9 . . . . .4B 68
Jarvis Cl. EN5: Barn 5A 20
IG11: Bark 1H 89
Jarvis Ho. SE15 . . . . .1G 121
(off Goldsmith Rd.)
Jarvis Rd. CR2: S Croy 6D 168
SE22 . . . . .4E 120
Jashoda Ho. SE18 . . . . .5E 106
(off Connaught M.)
Jasmin Cl. HA6: Nwood 1H 39
Jasmin Cl. SE12 . . . . .6J 123
Jasmine Cl. BR6: Farnb 2F 173
IG1: Ilf 5F 71
UB1: S'hall 7C 76
Jasmine Cl. SW19 . . . . .5J 135
Jasmine Gdns. CR0: C'don 3D 170
HA2: Harr 2E 58
Jasmine Gro. SE20 . . . . .1H 157
Jasmine Rd. RM7: Rush G 2K 73

Jasmine Sq. E3 . . . . .1B 86
(off Hawthorn Av.)
Jasmine Ter. UB7: W Dray 2C 92
Jasmine Way KT8: E Mos 4J 149
Jasmin Lodge SE16 . . . . .5H 103
(off Sherwood Gdns.)
Jasmin Rd. KT19: Ewe 5H 163
Jason Cl. SW9 . . . . .1A 120
(off Southey Rd.)
W1 . . . . .7H 5
Jason Wlk. SE9 . . . . .4E 142
Jasper Cl. EN3: Enf W 1D 24
Jasper Pas. SE19 . . . . .6F 139
Jasper Rd. E16 . . . . .6B 88
SE19 . . . . .5F 139
Jasper Wlk. N1 . . . . .3D 84
Java Wharf SE1 . . . . .6K 15
(off Shad Thames)
Javelin Cl. HA7: Stan 5G 27
(off William Dr.)
Javelin Way UB5: N'olt 3B 76
Jaycroft EN2: Enf 1F 23
Jay Gdns. BR7: Chst 4D 142
Jay Ho. E3 . . . . .1B 86
(off Hawthorn Av.)
Jay M. SW7 . . . . .7A 10 (2A 100)
Jazzfern Ter. HA0: Wemb 5A 60
Jean Batten Cl. SM6: Wall 7K 167
Jean Darling Ho. SW10 . . . . .6B 100
(off Milman's St.)
Jean Ho. SW17 . . . . .5C 136
Jean Pardies Ho. E1 . . . . .5J 85
(off Jubilee St.)
Jebb Av. SW2 . . . . .6J 119
(not continuous)
Jebb St. E3 . . . . .2C 86
Jedburgh Rd. E13 . . . . .3A 88
Jedburgh St. SW11 . . . . .4E 118
Jeddo M. W12 . . . . .2B 98
Jeddo Rd. W12 . . . . .2B 98
Jefferson Bldg. E14 . . . . .2C 104
Jefferson Cl. IG2: Ilf 5F 53
W13 . . . . .3B 96
Jefferson Ho. UB7: W Dray 2B 92
Jefferson Wlk. SE18 . . . . .6E 106
Jeffrey Row SE12 . . . . .5K 123
Jeffrey's Pl. NW1 . . . . .7G 65
Jeffreys Rd. EN3: Brim 4F 25
SW4 . . . . .2J 119
Jeffrey's St. NW1 . . . . .7G 65
Jeffreys Walk SW4 . . . . .2J 119
Jeffries Ho. NW10 . . . . .7K 61
Jeffs Cl. TW12: Hamp 6F 131
Jeffs Rd. SM1: Sutt 4H 165
Jeger Av. E2 . . . . .1F 85
Jeken Rd. SE9 . . . . .4A 124
Jelf Rd. SW2 . . . . .5A 120
Jelico Point SE16 . . . . .2B 104
(off Rotherhithe St.)
Jellicoe Gdns. HA7: Stan 6E 26
Jellicoe Ho. E2 . . . . .2G 85
(off Ropley St.)
Jellicoe Rd. E13 . . . . .4J 87
N17 . . . . .7J 33
Jemmett Cl. KT2: King T 1H 151
Jemotts Ct. SE14 . . . . .6K 103
(off Myers La.)
Jem Paterson Ct. HA1: Harr 4J 59
Jengar Cl. SM1: Sutt 4K 165
Jenkins La. IG11: Bark 2G 89
Jenkinson Ho. E2 . . . . .3K 85
(off Usk St.)
Jenkins Rd. E13 . . . . .4K 87
Jenner Av. W3 . . . . .5K 79
Jenner Cl. DA14: Sidc 4A 144
Jenner Ct. N21 . . . . .5D 22
(off Pennington Dr.)
Jenner Ho. WC1 . . . . .3F 7
(off Hunter St.)
Jenner Pl. SW13 . . . . .6D 98
Jenner Rd. N16 . . . . .3F 67
Jennett Rd. CR0: Wadd 3A 168

Jennifer Ho. SE11 . . . . .4K 19
(off Reedworth St.)
Jennifer Rd. BR1: Brom 3H 141
Jenningsbury Ho. SW3 . . . . .5D 16
(off Cale St.)
Jennings Cl. KT6: Surb 7C 150
Jennings Ho. SE10 . . . . .5F 105
(off Old Woolwich Rd.)
Jennings Rd. SE22 . . . . .6F 121
Jennings Way EN5: Barn 3A 20
Jenningtree Way DA17: Belv 2J 109
Jenny Hammond Cl. E11 . . . . .3H 69
Jensen Ho. E3 . . . . .4C 86
(off Wellington Way)
Jenson Way SE19 . . . . .7F 139
Jenton Av. DA7: Bex 1E 126
Jephson Cl. SW4 . . . . .2J 119
Jephson Ho. SE17 . . . . .6B 102
(off Doddington Gro.)
Jephson Rd. E7 . . . . .7A 70
Jephson St. SE5 . . . . .1D 120
Jephtha Rd. SW18 . . . . .6J 117
Jeppos La. CR4: Mitc 4D 154
Jepson Ho. SW6 . . . . .1K 117
(off Pearscroft Rd.)
Jerdan Ho. SW6 . . . . .7J 99
(off North End Rd.)
Jerdan Pl. SW6 . . . . .7J 99
Jeremiah St. E14 . . . . .6D 86
Jeremy Bentham Ho. E2 . . . . .3G 85
(off Mansford St.)
Jeremy's Grn. N18 . . . . .4C 34
Jermyn St. SW1 . . . . .4A 12 (1G 101)
Jermyn Street Theatre 3C 12
(off Jermyn St.)
Jerningham Av. IG5: Ilf 2F 53
Jerningham Ct. SE14 . . . . .1A 122
Jerningham Rd. SE14 . . . . .2A 122
Jerome Cres. NW8 . . . . .3C 4 (4C 82)
Jerome Ho. KT1: Ham W 2D 150
(off Old Bridge St.)
NW1 . . . . .5D 4
(off Lisson Gro.)
SW7 . . . . .3A 16
(off Glendower Pl.)
Jerome Pl. KT1: King T 2D 150
(off Wadbrook St.)
Jerome St. E1 . . . . .5J 9 (4F 85)
Jerome Twr. W3 . . . . .2H 97
Jerrard St. SE13 . . . . .3D 122
Jerrold St. N1 . . . . .1H 9 (2E 84)
Jersey Av. HA7: Stan 2B 42
Jersey Dr. BR5: Pet W 6H 161
Jersey Ho. EN3: Enf W 1E 24
(off Eastfield Rd.)
N1 .6C 66
(off Jersey Rd.)
Jersey Rd. E11 . . . . .1F 69
E16 . . . . .6A 88
IG1: Ilf 4F 71
N1 .6C 66
SW17 . . . . .6F 137
TW3: Houn 1F 113
TW5: Hest, Isle 1F 113
TW7: Isle 7H 95
W7 .2A 96
Jersey St. E2 . . . . .3H 85
Jerusalem Pas. EC1 . . . . . . .4A 8 (4B 84)
Jervis Bay Ho. E14 . . . . .6F 87
(off Blair St.)
Jervis Ct. RM10: Dag 6H 73
SE10 . . . . .1E 122
(off Blissett St.)
W1 . . . . .1K 11
Jervis Rd. SW6 . . . . .6H 99
Jerviston Gdns. SW16 . . . . .6A 138
Jerwood Space Art Gallery 6C 14
Jesmond Av. HA9: Wemb 6F 61
Jesmond Cl. CR4: Mitc 3F 155
Jesmond Rd. CR0: C'don 7F 157
Jesmond Way HA7: Stan 5K 27
Jessam Av. E5 . . . . .1H 67

Jessamine Rd. W7 . . . . .1K 95
Jessel Ho. SW1 . . . . .3D 18
(off Page St.)
WC1 . . . . .2E 6
(off Judd St.)
Jessel Mans. W14 . . . . .6G 99
(off Queen's Club Gdns.)
Jesse Rd. E10 . . . . .1E 68
Jessett Cl. DA8: Erith 4K 109
Jessica Rd. SW18 . . . . .6A 118
Jessie Blythe La. N19 . . . . .7J 47
Jessie Duffett Ho. SE5 . . . . .7C 102
(off Pitman St.)
Jessie Wood Ct. SW9 . . . . .7A 102
(off Caldwell St.)
Jessiman Ter. TW17: Shep 5C 146
Jesson Ho. SE17 . . . . .4D 102
(off Orb St.)
Jessop Av. UB2: S'hall 4D 94
Jessop Ct. N1 . . . . .2B 84
Jessop Ho. W4 . . . . .4K 97
(off Kirton Cl.)
Jessop Rd. SE24 . . . . .4B 120
Jessop Sq. E14 . . . . .1C 104
Jessops Way CR0: Bedd, Mitc 6G 155
Jessup Cl. SE18 . . . . .4G 107
Jetstar Way UB5: N'olt 3C 76
Jevington Way SE12 . . . . .1K 141
Jevons Ho. NW8 . . . . .7B 64
(off Hilgrove Rd.)
Jewel Rd. E17 . . . . .3C 50
Jewel Tower 1E 18
(off College M.)
Jewish Mus.
Camden Town 1F 83
Jewry St. EC3 . . . . .1J 15 (6F 85)
Jew's Row SW18 . . . . .4K 117
Jews' Wlk. SE26 . . . . .4H 139
Jeymer Av. NW2 . . . . .5D 62
Jeymer Dr. UB6: G'frd 1F 77
(not continuous)
Jeypore Pas. SW18 . . . . .6A 118
Jeypore Rd. SW18 . . . . .7A 118
Jigger Mast Ho. SE18 . . . . .3E 106
Jillian Cl. TW12: Hamp 7E 130
Jim Bradley Cl. SE18 . . . . .4E 106
Jim Griffiths Ho. SW6 . . . . .6H 99
(off Clem Attlee Ct.)
Jim Veal Dr. N7 . . . . .6J 65
Joan Cres. SE9 . . . . .7B 124
Joan Gdns. RM8: Dag 2E 72
Joanna Ho. W6 . . . . .5E 98
(off Queen Caroline St.)
Joan Rd. RM8: Dag 2E 72
Joan St. SE1 . . . . .5A 14 (1B 102)
Jocelin Ho. N1 . . . . .1K 83
(off Barnsbury Est.)
Jocelyn Rd. TW9: Rich 3E 114
Jocelyn St. SE15 . . . . .1G 121
Jockey's Flds. WC1 . . . . .5H 7 (5K 83)
Jodane St. SE8 . . . . .4B 104
Jodrell Cl. TW7: Isle 1A 114
Jodrell Rd. E3 . . . . .1B 86
Joe Hunte Ct. SE27 . . . . .5B 138
Joel St. HA5: Eastc 3J 39
HA6: Nwood 2J 39
Johanna St. SE1 . . . . .7J 13 (2A 102)
John Adams Ct. N9 . . . . .2A 34
John Adam St. WC2 . . . . . . .3F 13 (7J 83)
John Aird Ct. W2 . . . . .5A 4
(not continuous)
John Archer Way SW18 . . . . .6B 118
John Ashby Cl. SW2 . . . . .6J 119
John Austin Cl. KT2: King T 1F 151
John Baird Cl. SE26 . . . . .4J 139
John Barker Cl. NW6 . . . . .7G 63
John Barnes Wlk. E15 . . . . .6H 69
John Bell Twr. E. E3 . . . . .2C 86
(off Pancras Way)
John Bell Twr. W. E3 . . . . .2C 86
(off Pancras Way)
John Betts' Ho. W12 . . . . .3B 98

John Bond Ho. *E3* 2B *86*
(off Wright's Rd.)
John Bowles Ct. *E1* 7K *85*
(off Schoolhouse La.)
John Bradshaw Rd. N14 . . . . .1C *32*
John Brent Ho. *SE8* 4K *103*
(off Haddonfield)
John Buck Ho. NW10 . . . . .1B *80*
John Burns Dr. IG11: Bark 7J *71*
John Campbell Rd. N16 . . . . .5E *66*
John Carpenter St. EC4 . . . . .2A *14* (7B *84*)
John Cartwright Ho. *E2* 3H *85*
(off Old Bethnal Grn. Rd.)
John Drinkwater Cl. E11 . . . . .7H *51*
John Fearon Wlk. *W10* 3G *81*
(off Dart St.)
John Felton Rd. SE16 . . . . .2G *103*
John Fielden Ho. *E2* 3H *85*
(off Canrobert St.)
John Fisher St. E1 . . . . .2K *15* (7G *85*)
John Goddard Way TW13: Felt 2K *129*
John Gooch Dr. EN2: Enf 1G *23*
John Harrison Way SE10 . . . . .3H *105*
John Horner M. N1 . . . . .2C *84*
John Islip St. SW1 . . . . . . .5D *18* (4H *101*)
John Kaye Ct. TW17: Shep 5C *146*
John Keats Ho. N22 . . . . .7E *32*
John Keats Lodge EN2: Enf 1J *23*
John Kennedy Ct. *N1* 6D *66*
(off Newington Grn. Rd.)
John Kennedy Ho. *SE16* 4K *103*
(off Rotherhithe Old Rd.)
John Kirk Ho. *E6* 6E *88*
(off Pearl Cl.)
John Knight Lodge SW6 . . . . .7J *99*
John Lamb Cl. HA3: W'stone 1J *41*
John McDonald Ho. *E14* 3E *104*
(off Glengall Gro.)
John McKenna Wlk. SE16 . . . . .3G *103*
John Masefield Ho. *N15* 6D *48*
(off Fladbury Rd.)
John Maurice Cl. SE17 . . . . .4D *102*
John Milton Pas. EC4 . . . . .6C *84*
John Newton Ct. DA16: Well 3B *126*
John Orwell Sports Cen. 1H *103*
John Parker Cl. RM10: Dag 7H *73*
John Parker Sq. SW11 . . . . .3B *118*
John Parry Ct. *N1* 2E *84*
(off Hare Wlk.)
John Penn Ho. *SE14* 7B *104*
(off Amersham Va.)
John Penn St. SE13 . . . . .1D *122*
John Penry Ho. *SE1* 5G *103*
(off Marlborough Gro.)
John Perrin Pl.
HA3: Kenton 7E *42*
John Prince's St. W1 . . . . .7K 5 (6F *83*)
John Pritchard Ho. *E1* 4G *85*
(off Buxton St.)
John Ratcliffe Ho. NW6 . . . . .3J *81*
(off Chippenham Gdns.)
John Rennie Wlk. E1 . . . . .7H *85*
John Roll Way SE16 . . . . .3G *103*
John Ruskin St. SE5 . . . . .7B *102*
John's Av. NW4 . . . . .4E *44*
John's Cl. TW15: Ashf 4E *128*
John Scurr Ho. *E14* 6A *86*
(off Ratcliffe La.)
John Silkin La. SE8 . . . . .5K *103*
John's La. SM4: Mord 5A *154*
John's M. WC1 . . . . .4H 7 (4K *83*)
John Smith Av. SW6 . . . . .7H *99*
John Smith M. E14 . . . . .7F *87*
Johnson Cl. E8 . . . . .1G *85*
Johnson Ho. *E2* 3G *85*
(off Roberta St.)
NW1 .2G *83*
(off Cranleigh St.)
NW3 .7D *64*
(off Adelaide Rd.)
SW1 .4H *17*
(off Cundy St.)

Johnson Ho. SW8 . . . . .7H *101*
(off Wandsworth Rd.)
W8 . . . . .2J *99*
(off Campden Hill)
Johnson Lock Cl. E1 . . . . .5A *86*
Johnson Lodge W9 . . . . .5J *81*
(off Admiral Wlk.)
Johnson Mans. W14 . . . . .6G *99*
(off Queen's Club Gdns.)
Johnson Rd. BR2: Brom 5B *160*
CR0: C'don 7D *156*
NW10 . . . . .1K *79*
TW5: Hest 7A *94*
Johnsons Cl. SM5: Cars 2D *166*
Johnson's Ct. EC4 . . . . .6A *84*
Johnsons Dr. TW12: Hamp 1G *149*
Johnsons Ind. Est.
UB3: Hayes 2H *93*
Johnson's Pl. SW1 . . . . . .6A *18* (5G *101*)
Johnson St. E1 . . . . .7J *85*
UB2: S'hall 3A *94*
Johnsons Way NW10 . . . . .4H *79*
John Spencer Sq. N1 . . . . .6B *66*
John's Pl. E1 . . . . .6H *85*
John's Ter. CR0: C'don 1E *168*
Johnston Cl. SW9 . . . . .1K *119*
Johnston Cl. E10 . . . . .3D *68*
Johnstone Ho. *SE13* 3F *123*
(off Belmont Hill)
Johnstone Rd. E6 . . . . .3D *88*
Johnston Rd. IG8: Wfd G 6D *36*
Johnston Ter. NW2 . . . . .3F *63*
John Strachey Ho. SW6 . . . . .6H *99*
(off Clem Attlee Ct.)
John St. E15 . . . . .1H *87*
EN1: Enf 5A *24*
SE25 . . . . .4G *157*
TW3: Houn 2C *112*
WC1 . . . . .4H 7 (4K *83*)
John Strype St. E10 . . . . .1D *68*
John Trundle Ct. EC2 . . . . .5C 8
John Trundle Highwalk *EC2* 5C 8
(off Aldersgate St.)
John Tucker Ho. *E14* 3C *104*
(off Mellish St.)
John Watkin Cl. KT19: Eps 7H *163*
John Wesley Cl. E6 . . . . .3D *88*
John Wesley Ct. TW1: Twick 1A *132*
John Wesley Highwalk *EC2* 6C 8
(off Aldersgate St.)
John Wheatley Ho. SW6 . . . . .6H *99*
(off Clem Attlee Ct.)
John Williams Cl. KT2: King T 1D *150*
SE14 . . . . .6K *103*
John Wilson St. SE18 . . . . .3E *106*
John Woolley Cl. SE13 . . . . .4G *123*
Joiners Arms Yd. SE5 . . . . .1D *120*
Joiners Pl. N5 . . . . .4D *66*
Joiner St. SE1 . . . . .5F *15* (1D *102*)
Joiners Yd. *N1* 1F 7
(off Caledonia St.)
Joint Rd. N2 . . . . .1C *46*
Jolles Ho. *E3* 3D *86*
(off Bromley High St.)
Jollys La. HA2: Harr 1H *59*
UB4: Yead 5B *76*
Jonathan St. SE11 . . . . . .5G *19* (5K *101*)
Jones Ho. *E14* 6F *87*
(off Blair St.)
Jones M. SW15 . . . . .4G *117*
Jones Rd. E13 . . . . .4K *87*
Jones St. W1 . . . . .3J *11* (7F *83*)
Jones Wlk. TW10: Rich 6F *115*
Jonquil Gdns. TW12: Hamp 6E *130*
Jonson Cl. CR4: Mitc 4F *155*
UB4: Hayes 5J *75*
Jonson Ho. *SE1* 3D *102*
(off Burbage Cl.)
Jordan Cl. HA2: Harr 3D *58*
Jordan Cl. SW15 . . . . .4F *117*
Jordan Ho. *N1* 1D *84*
(off Colville Est.)

Jordan Ho. SE4 . . . . .4K *121*
(off St Norbert Rd.)
Jordan Rd. UB6: G'frd 1B *78*
Jordans Cl. RM10: Dag 4H *73*
TW7: Isle 1J *113*
Jordans Ho. *NW8* 3C *4*
(off Capland St.)
Jordans M. TW2: Twick 2J *131*
Joscoyne Ho. *E1* 6H *85*
(off Philpot St.)
Joseph Av. W3 . . . . .6K *79*
Joseph Conrad Ho. SW1 . . . . .4B *18*
(off Tachbrook St.)
Joseph Ct. *N16* 6E *48*
(off Amhurst Pk.)
Joseph Hardcastle Cl. SE14 . . . . . . .7K *103*
Josephine Av. SW2 . . . . .5K *119*
Joseph Irwin Ho. *E14* 7B *86*
(off Gill St.)
Joseph Lister Ct. E7 . . . . .7J *69*
Joseph Powell Cl. SW12 . . . . .6G *119*
Joseph Priestley Ho. *E2* 3H *85*
(off Canrobert St.)
Joseph Ray Rd. E11 . . . . .2G *69*
Joseph St. E3 . . . . .4B *86*
Joseph Trotter Cl. EC1 . . . . .2K 7
Joshua Cl. CR2: S Croy 7B *168*
N10 . . . . .7A *32*
Joshua St. E14 . . . . .6E *86*
Joslings Cl. W12 . . . . .7C *80*
Joslyn Cl. EN3: Enf L 1H *25*
Jossiline Ct. *E3* 2A *86*
(off Ford St.)
Joubert Mans. SW3 . . . . .5D *16*
(off Jubilee Pl.)
Joubert St. SW11 . . . . .2D *118*
Jowett St. SE15 . . . . .7F *103*
Jowitt Ho. *E2* 3K *85*
(off Morpeth St.)
Joyce Av. N18 . . . . .5A *34*
Joyce Butler Ho. N22 . . . . .1K *47*
Joyce Dawson Way SE28 . . . . .7A *90*
Joyce Latimore Ct. N9 . . . . .3C *34*
(off Colthurst Dr.)
Joyce Page Cl. SE7 . . . . .6B *106*
Joyce Wlk. SW2 . . . . .6A *120*
JOYDENS WOOD 4K *145*
Joydens Wood Rd.
DA5: Bexl 4K *145*
Joydon Dr. RM6: Chad H 6B *54*
Joyners Cl. RM9: Dag 4F *73*
Joystone Ct. EN4: E Barn 4H *21*
(off Park Rd.)
Jubb Powell Ho. N15 . . . . .6E *48*
Jubilee, The SE10 . . . . .7D *104*
Jubilee Av. E4 . . . . .6K *35*
RM7: Rom 5H *55*
TW2: Whitt 1G *131*
Jubilee Bldgs. NW8 . . . . .1B *82*
Jubilee Cl. HA5: Pinn 2A *40*
KT1: Ham W 1C *150*
NW9 . . . . .6K *43*
NW10 . . . . .2A *80*
RM7: Rom 5H *55*
Jubilee Country Pk. 4K *161*
Jubilee Cl. BR4: W W'ck 1E *170*
E18 .1J *51*
HA3: Kenton 7E *42*
N10 . . . . .3E *46*
TW3: Houn 3F *113*
(off Bristow Rd.)
Jubilee Cres. E14 . . . . .3E *104*
N9 . . . . .1B *34*
Jubilee Dr. HA4: Ruis 4B *58*
Jubilee Gdns. UB1: S'hall 5E *76*
Jubilee Hall Sports Cen. 2F *13*
(off The Piazza)
Jubilee Ho. HA7: Stan 5J *27*
SE11 . . . . .4K *19*
(off Reedworth St.)
WC1 .3G 7
Jubilee La. W5 . . . . .6E *78*

Jubilee Mans. *E1* 6J *85*
(off Jubilee St.)
Jubilee Mkt. IG8: Wfd G 6F *37*
WC2 .2F *13*
Jubilee Pde. IG8: Wfd G 6F *37*
Jubilee Pk. Local Nature Reserve . . .5F *161*
Jubilee Pl. SW3 . . . . .5D *16* (5C *100*)
Jubilee Pl. Shop. Mall *E14* 1D *104*
(off Bank St.)
Jubilee Rd. SM3: Cheam 7F *165*
UB6: G'frd 1B *78*
Jubilee Sports Cen. & Baths 3H *81*
Jubilee St. E1 . . . . .6J *85*
Jubilee Vs. KT10: Esh 7H *149*
Jubilee Walkway SE1 . . . . . .3B *14* (7B *84*)
Jubilee Way DA14: Sidc 2A *144*
KT9: Chess 4G *163*
SW19 . . . . .1K *153*
TW14: Felt 1J *129*
Jubilee Yd. SE1 . . . . .6J *15*
Judd Apartments *N8* 3K *47*
(off Gt. Amwell La.)
Judd St. WC1 . . . . .2E 6 (3J *83*)
Jude St. E16 . . . . .6H *87*
Judge Heath La. UB3: Hayes 6E *74*
Judges Wlk. NW3 . . . . .3A *64*
Juer St. SW11 . . . . .7C *100*
Jules Thorn Av. EN1: Enf 4B *24*
Julia Cl. E17 . . . . .5D *50*
Julia Gdns. IG11: Bark 2D *90*
Julia Garfield M. E16 . . . . .1K *105*
(not continuous)
Juliana Cl. N2 . . . . .2A *46*
Julian Av. W3 . . . . .7H *79*
Julian Cl. EN5: New Bar 3E *20*
Julian Ct. *NW1* 7G *65*
(off Rochester Sq.)
Julian Hill HA1: Harr 2J *59*
Julian Ho. SE21 . . . . .4E *138*
Julian Pl. E14 . . . . .5D *104*
Julian Taylor Path SE23 . . . . .2H *139*
Julia St. NW5 . . . . .4E *64*
Julia Rd. W5 . . . . .3C *96*
Juliet Ho. *N1* 2E *84*
(off Arden Est.)
Juliette Rd. E13 . . . . .2J *87*
Julius Caesar Way HA7: Stan 3J *27*
Julius Ho. *E14* 6F *87*
(off E. India Dock Rd.)
Julius Nyerere Cl. *N1* 1K *83*
(off Copenhagen St.)
Junction Av. NW10 . . . . .4E *80*
Junction M. W2 . . . . .7C 4 (6C *82*)
Junction Pl. W2 . . . . .7B 4
Junction Rd. CR2: S Croy 5D *168*
E13 .2K *87*
HA1: Harr 6J *41*
N9 . . . . .1B *34*
N17 .3G *49*
N19 .4G *65*
TW8: Bford 5D *96*
TW15: Ashf 5C *128*
W5 .4C *96*
Junction Rd. E. RM6: Chad H 7E *54*
Junction Rd. W. RM6: Chad H 7E *54*
Juniper Cl. EN5: Barn 5A *20*
HA9: Wemb 5G *61*
KT9: Chess 5F *163*
Juniper Ct. HA3: Hrw W 1K *41*
HA6: Nwood 1J *39*
KT8: W Mole 4F *149*
RM6: Chad H 6B *54*
TW3: Houn 4F *113*
(off Grove Rd.)
W8 . . . . .3K *99*
(off St Mary's Pl.)
Juniper Cres. NW1 . . . . .7E *64*
Juniper Dr. SW18 . . . . .4A *118*
Juniper Gdns. SW16 . . . . .1G *155*
TW16: Sun 6H *129*

Juniper Ho. *E16* .6H **87**
(off Turner St.)
SE14 . . . . .7J **103**
TW9: Kew 1H **115**
W10 . . . . .3B **81**
(off Fourth Av.)
Juniper La. *E6* .5C **88**
Juniper Rd. IG1: Ilf 3E **70**
Juniper St. *E1* .7J **85**
Juniper Way UB3: Hayes 7F **75**
Juno Ct. *SW9* .7A **102**
(off Caldwell St.)
Juno Ho. *E3* 1C **86**
(off Garrison Rd.)
Juno Way SE14 .6K **103**
Juno Way Ind. Est. SE14 . . . . .6K **103**
Jupiter Ct. *E3* 2C **86**
(off Four Seasons Cl.)
SW9 . . . . .7A **102**
(off Caldwell St.)
UB5: N'olt 3B **76**
(off Seasprite Cl.)
Jupiter Hgts. UB10: Uxb 1B **74**
Jupiter Ho. *E14* 5D **104**
(off St Davids Sq.)
Jupiter Way N7 .6K **65**
Jupp Rd. E15 . . . . .7F **69**
Jupp Rd. W. E15 . . . . .1F **87**
Jura Ho. *SE16* .4K **103**
(off Plough Way)
Jurassic Encounter 3C **152**
Jurston Ct. SE1 . . . . .7K **13**
Justice Wlk. SW3 . . . . .7C **16** (6C **100**)
Justin Cl. TW8: Bford 7D **96**
Justines Pl. E2 .3K **85**
Justin Pl. N22 .7E **32**
Justin Plaza CR4: Mitc 4C **154**
Justin Rd. E4 . . . . .6G **35**
Jute La. EN3: Brim 2F **25**
Jutland Cl. N19 . . . . .1J **65**
Jutland Ho. SE5 . . . . .2C **120**
SE18 . . . . .4C **106**
(off Prospect Vale)
Jutland Rd. E13 . . . . .4J **87**
SE6 . . . . .7E **122**
Jutsums Av. RM7: Rom 6H **55**
Jutsums Ct. RM7: Rom 6H **55**
Jutsums La. RM7: Rom, Rush G 6H **55**
Juxon Cl. HA3: Hrw W 1F **41**
Juxon Ho. *EC4* 1B **14**
(off St Paul's Churchyd.)
Juxon St. SE11 . . . . .3H **19** (4K **101**)
JVC Bus. Pk. NW2 . . . . .1C **62**

K

Kaduna Cl. HA5: Eastc 5J **39**
Kaine Pl. CRO: C'don 7A **158**
Kale Rd. DA18: Erith 2D **108**
Kambala Rd. SW11 . . . . .3B **118**
Kamen Ho. *SE1* 5G **15**
(off Magdalen St.)
Kangley Bri. Rd. SE26 . . . . .6B **140**
Kangley Bus. Cen. SE26 . . . . .5B **140**
Kaplan Dr. N21 .5E **22**
Kapuvar Cl. SE15 . . . . .2G **121**
Karanjia Cl. NW2 . . . . .6E **62**
Kara Way NW2 .4F **63**
Karen Ct. BR1: Brom 1H **159**
Karen Ter. E11 .2H **69**
Karenza Ct. HA9: Wemb 7C **42**
Kariba Cl. N9 . . . . .3D **34**
Karma Way HA2: Harr 1E **58**
Karoline Gdns. UB6: G'frd 2H **77**
Kashgar Rd. SE18 . . . . .4K **107**
Kashmir Rd. SE7 . . . . .7B **106**
Kassala Rd. SW11 . . . . .1D **118**
Katella Trad. Est. IG11: Bark 3J **89**
Katharine Ho. *CRO: C'don* 3C **168**
(off Katharine St.)
Katharine St. CRO: C'don 3C **168**

Katherine Bell Twr. *E3* 2C **86**
(off Pancras Way)
Katherine Cl. SE16 . . . . .1K **103**
Katherine Ct. SE23 . . . . .1H **139**
Katherine Gdns. SE9 . . . . .4B **124**
Katherine Ho. *W10* 4G **81**
(off Portobello Rd.)
Katherine Rd. E6 . . . . .5A **70**
E7 . . . . .5A **70**
TW1: Twick 1A **132**
Katherine Sq. W11 . . . . .1G **99**
Kathleen Av. HA0: Wemb 7E **60**
W3 . . . . .5J **79**
Kathleen Godfree Ct. SW19 . . . . .6J **135**
Kathleen Rd. SW11 . . . . .3D **118**
Kayani Ho. *E16* 6K **87**
(off Burrard Rd.)
Kayemoor Rd. SM2: Sutt 6B **166**
Kay Rd. SW9 . . . . .2J **119**
Kays Ter. E18 . . . . .1H **51**
Kay St. DA16: Well 1B **126**
E2 . . . . .2G **85**
E15 . . . . .7F **69**
Kean Ho. SE17 . . . . .6B **102**
TW1: Twick 6D **114**
(off Arosa Rd.)
Kean St. WC2 . . . . .1G **13** (6K **83**)
Keatley Grn. E4 . . . . .6G **35**
Keats Av. E16 .1K **105**
Keats Cl. E11 . . . . .5K **51**
EN3: Pond E 5E **24**
NW3 . . . . .4C **64**
SE1 . . . . .4F **103**
SW19 . . . . .6B **136**
UB4: Hayes .5J **75**
Keats Est. *N16* 2F **67**
(off Kyverdale Rd.)
Keats Gro. NW3 . . . . .4C **64**
Keats House 4C **64**
Keats Ho. *E2* 3J **85**
(off Roman Rd.)
HA2: Harr 2J **59**
SE5 . . . . .7C **102**
(off Elmington Est.)
SW1 . . . . .7B **18**
(off Churchill Gdns.)
Keats Pde. N9 .2B **34**
(off Church St.)
Keats Pl. *EC2* .6E **8**
(off Moorfields)
Keats Rd. DA16: Well 1J **125**
DA17: Belv .3J **109**
E10 . . . . .7D **50**
Keats Way CRO: C'don 6J **157**
UB6: G'frd .5F **77**
UB7: W Dray 4B **92**
Kebbell Ter. *E7* 5K **69**
(off Claremont Rd.)
Keble Cl. KT4: Wor Pk 1B **164**
UB5: N'olt 5G **59**
Keble Pl. SW13 . . . . .6D **98**
Keble St. SW17 . . . . .4A **136**
Kechill Gdns. BR2: Hayes 7J **159**
Kedeston Ct. SM1: Sutt 1K **165**
Kedge Ho. *E14* 3C **104**
(off Tiller Rd.)
Kedleston Dr. BR5: St M Cry 6K **161**
Kedleston Wlk. E2 . . . . .3H **85**
Kedyngton Ho. *HA8: Edg* 2J **43**
(off Burnt Oak B'way.)
Keeble Cl. SE18 . . . . .6F **107**
Keedonwood Rd. BR1: Brom 5G **141**
Keel Cl. IG11: Bark 2C **90**
N18 . . . . .6K **33**
SE16 . . . . .1K **103**
Keel Ct. *E14* 7F **87**
(off Newport Av.)
Keeley Rd. CRO: C'don 2C **168**
Keeley St. WC2 . . . . .1G **13** (6K **83**)
Keeling Ho. *E2* 2H **85**
(off Claredale St.)
Keeling Rd. SE9 . . . . .5B **124**

Keelson Ho. *E14* 3C **104**
(off Mellish St.)
Keely Cl. EN4: E Barn 5H **21**
Keemor Cl. SE18 . . . . .7E **106**
Keens Cl. SW16 . . . . .5H **137**
Keens Rd. CRO: C'don 4C **168**
Keen's Yd. N1 .6B **66**
Keep, The KT2: King T 6F **133**
SE3 . . . . .2J **123**
Keepers Ct. *CR2: S Croy* 5C **168**
(off Warham Rd.)
Keepers M. TW11: Tedd 6C **132**
Keepier Wharf *E14* 7K **85**
(off Narrow St.)
Keeton's Rd. SE16 . . . . .3H **103**
(not continuous)
Keevil Dr. SW19 . . . . .7F **117**
Keighley Cl. N7 . . . . .5J **65**
Keightley Dr. SE9 . . . . .1G **143**
Keilder Cl. UB10: Hil 2C **74**
Keildon Rd. SW11 . . . . .4D **118**
Keiller Ho. *E16* 1D **106**
(off Kennard St.)
Keir, The SW19 . . . . .5E **134**
Keir Hardie Est. E5 . . . . .1H **67**
Keir Hardie Ho. N19 . . . . .7H **47**
NW10 . . . . .7B **62**
W6 . . . . .6F **99**
(off Fulham Pal. Rd.)
Keir Hardie Way IG11: Bark 7A **72**
UB4: Yead .3J **75**
Keith Connor Cl. SW8 . . . . .3F **119**
Keith Gro. W12 . . . . .2C **98**
Keith Ho. NW6 .2K **81**
(off Carlton Va.)
SW8 . . . . .7J **101**
(off Wheatsheaf La.)
Keith Pk. Rd. UB10: Uxb 7B **56**
Keith Rd. E17 .1B **50**
IG11: Bark .2H **89**
UB3: Hayes 3G **93**
Kelbrook Rd. SE3 . . . . .2C **124**
Kelby Ho. N7 . . . . .6K **65**
(off Sutterton St.)
Kelby Path SE9 . . . . .3F **143**
Kelceda Cl. NW2 . . . . .2C **62**
Kelday Hgts. *E1* 6H **85**
(off Spencer Way)
Kelf Gro. UB3: Hayes 6H **75**
Kelfield Ct. W10 . . . . .6F **81**
Kelfield Gdns. W10 . . . . .6E **80**
Kelfield M. W10 . . . . .6F **81**
Kelland Cl. N8 .5H **47**
Kelland Rd. E13 . . . . .4J **87**
Kellaway Rd. SE3 . . . . .2B **124**
Keller Cres. E12 . . . . .4B **70**
Kellerton Rd. SE13 . . . . .5G **123**
Kellet Ho's. *WC1* 2F **7**
(off Tankerton St.)
Kellett Ho. *N1* 1E **84**
(off Colville St.)
Kellett Rd. SW2 . . . . .4A **120**
Kelling Gdns. CRO: C'don 7B **156**
Kellino St. SW17 . . . . .4D **136**
Kellner Rd. SE28 . . . . .3K **107**
Kellogg Twr. UB6: G'frd 5J **59**
Kellow Ho. *SE1* 6E **14**
(off Tennis St.)
Kell St. SE1 . . . . .7B **14** (3B **102**)
Kelly Av. SE15 .7F **103**
Kelly Cl. NW10 . . . . .3K **61**
TW17: Shep 2G **147**
Kelly Ct. *E14* 7C **86**
(off Garford St.)
Kelly M. W9 . . . . .4H **81**
Kelly Rd. NW7 .6B **30**
Kelly St. NW1 .6F **65**
Kelly Way RM6: Chad H 5E **54**
Kelman Cl. SW4 . . . . .2H **119**
Kelmore Gro. SE22 . . . . .4G **121**
Kelmscott Cl. E17 . . . . .1B **50**
Kelmscott Gdns. W12 . . . . .3C **98**

Kelmscott House 5C **98**
(off Upper Mall)
Kelmscott Leisure Cen. 6B **50**
Kelmscott Rd. SW11 . . . . .5C **118**
Kelross Pas. N5 . . . . .4C **66**
Kelross Rd. N5 . . . . .4C **66**
Kelsall Cl. SE3 . . . . .2K **123**
Kelsall M. TW9: Kew 1H **115**
Kelsey Ga. BR3: Beck 2D **158**
Kelsey La. BR3: Beck 2C **158**
Kelsey Pk. Av. BR3: Beck 2D **158**
Kelsey Pk. Rd. BR3: Beck 2C **158**
Kelsey Sq. BR3: Beck 2C **158**
Kelsey St. E2 .4G **85**
Kelsey Way BR3: Beck 3C **158**
Kelson Ho. E14 . . . . .3E **104**
Kelso Pl. W8 . . . . .3K **99**
Kelso Rd. SM5: Cars 7A **154**
Kelston Rd. IG6: Ilf 2F **53**
Kelvedon Cl. KT2: King T 6G **133**
Kelvedon Ho. SW8 . . . . .1J **119**
Kelvedon Rd. SW6 . . . . .7H **99**
Kelvedon Way IG8: Wfd G 6J **37**
Kelvin Av. N13 .6E **32**
TW11: Tedd 6J **131**
Kelvinbrook KT8: W Mole 3F **149**
Kelvin Cl. KT19: Ewe 6G **163**
Kelvin Ct. SE20 . . . . .1H **157**
TW7: Isle 2J **113**
W11 . . . . .7J **81**
(off Kensington Pk. Rd.)
Kelvin Cres. HA3: Hrw W 7D **26**
Kelvin Dr. TW1: Twick 6B **114**
Kelvin Gdns. CRO: Wadd 7J **155**
UB1: S'hall .6E **76**
Kelvin Gro. KT9: Chess 3D **162**
SE26 . . . . .3H **139**
Kelvington Cl. CRO: C'don 7A **158**
Kelvington Rd. SE15 . . . . .5K **121**
Kelvin Ind. Est. UB6: G'frd 7F **59**
Kelvin Pde. BR6: Orp 1J **173**
Kelvin Rd. DA16: Well 3A **126**
N5 . . . . .4C **66**
Kember St. N1 .7K **65**
Kemble Dr. BR2: Brom 3C **172**
Kemble Ho. SW9 . . . . .3B **120**
(off Barrington Rd.)
Kemble Rd. CRO: Wadd 3B **168**
N17 . . . . .1G **49**
SE23 . . . . .1K **139**
Kemble St. WC2 . . . . .1G **13** (6K **83**)
Kemerton Rd. BR3: Beck 2D **158**
CRO: C'don .7F **157**
SE5 . . . . .3C **120**
Kemeys St. E9 .5A **68**
Kemnal Rd. BR7: Chst 4H **143**
Kemp NW9 . . . . .1B **44**
(off The Concourse)
Kemp Ct. SW8 . . . . .7J **101**
(off Hartington Rd.)
Kempe Ho. SE1 . . . . .3D **102**
(off Burbage Cl.)
Kempe Rd. NW6 . . . . .2F **81**
Kemp Gdns. CRO: C'don 6C **156**
Kemp Ho. *E2* 2K **85**
(off Sewardstone Rd.)
E6 . . . . .6E **70**
W1 . . . . .2C **12**
(off Berwick St.)
Kempis Way SE22 . . . . .5E **120**
Kemplay Rd. NW3 . . . . .4B **64**
Kemp Rd. RM8: Dag 1D **72**
Kemps Ct. *W1* 1B **12**
(off Hopkins St.)
Kemps Dr. E14 . . . . .7C **86**
HA6: Nwood 1H **39**
Kempsford Gdns. SW5 . . . . .5J **99**
Kempsford Rd. SE11 . . . . . .4K **19** (4A **102**)
(not continuous)
Kemps Gdns. SE13 . . . . .5E **122**
Kempshott Rd. SW16 . . . . .7H **137**
Kempson Rd. SW6 . . . . .1J **117**

Kempthorne Rd. SE8 . . . . .4B **104**
Kempton Av. TW16: Sun 1K **147**
   UB5: N'olt 6E **58**
Kempton Cl. DA8: Erith 6J **109**
   UB10: Ick 4E **56**
Kempton Ct. E1 . . . . .5H **85**
   TW16: Sun 1K **147**
Kempton Ga. TW12: Hamp 1D **148**
Kempton Ho. N1 . . . . .1E **84**
               (off Hoxton St.)
Kempton Pk. Racecourse 7A **130**
Kempton Rd. E6 . . . . .1D **88**
   TW12: Hamp 2D **148**
             (not continuous)
Kempton Wlk. CR0: C'don 6A **158**
Kempt St. SE18 . . . . .6E **106**
Kemsing Cl. BR2: Hayes 2H **171**
   CR7: Thor H 4C **156**
   DA5: Bexl 7E **126**
Kemsing Ho. SE1 . . . . .7F **15**
                (off Long La.)
Kemsing Rd. SE10 . . . . .5J **105**
Kemsley SE13 . . . . .5D **122**
Kemsley Ct. W13 . . . . .1C **96**
Kenbrook Ho. NW5 . . . . .5G **65**
   W14 . . . . .3H **99**
Kenbury Cl. UB10: Ick 3C **56**
Kenbury Gdns. SE5 . . . . .2C **120**
Kenbury Mans. SE5 . . . . .2C **120**
              (off Kenbury St.)
Kenbury St. SE5 . . . . .2C **120**
Kenchester Cl. SW8 . . . . .7J **101**
Kencot Way DA18: Erith 2F **109**
Kendal NW1 . . . . .1K **5**
             (off Augustus St.)
Kendal Av. IG11: Bark 1J **89**
   N18 . . . . .4J **33**
   W3 . . . . .4G **79**
             (not continuous)
Kendal Cl. IG8: Wfd G 2C **36**
   N20 . . . . .2H **31**
   SW9 . . . . .7B **102**
   TW14: Felt 1H **129**
   UB4: Hayes 2G **75**
Kendal Ct. W3 . . . . .5G **79**
Kendale Rd. BR1: Brom 5G **141**
Kendal Gdns. N18 . . . . .4J **33**
   SM1: Sutt 2A **166**
Kendal Ho. E9 . . . . .1J **85**
   N1 . . . . .2K **83**
          (off Priory Grn. Est.)
   SE20 .2G **157**
             (off Derwent Rd.)
Kendall Av. BR3: Beck 2A **158**
   CR2: Sande 7D **168**
Kendall Ct. DA15: Sidc 3A **144**
   SW19 . . . . .6B **136**
Kendall Lodge BR1: Brom 1K **159**
          (off Willow Tree Wlk.)
Kendall Pl. W1 . . . . .6G **5** (5E **82**)
Kendall Rd. BR3: Beck 2A **158**
   SE18 .1C **124**
   TW7: Isle 2A **114**
Kendalmere Cl. N10 . . . . .1F **47**
Kendal Pde. N18 . . . . .4J **33**
Kendal Pl. SW15 . . . . .5H **117**
Kendal Rd. NW10 . . . . .4C **62**
Kendal Steps W2 . . . . .1D **10**
Kendal St. W2 . . . . .1D **10** (6C **82**)
Kender Est. SE14 . . . . .1J **121**
             (off Queen's Rd.)
Kender St. SE14 . . . . .7J **103**
Kendoa Rd. SW4 . . . . .4H **119**
Kendon Cl. E11 . . . . .5K **51**
Kendra Hall Rd. CR2: S Croy 7D **168**
Kendrey Gdns. TW2: Whitt 7J **113**
Kendrick Ct. SE15 . . . . .1H **121**
             (off Woods Rd.)
Kendrick M. SW7 . . . . .3A **16** (4B **100**)
Kendrick Pl. SW7 . . . . .4A **16** (4B **100**)
Kenelm Cl. HA1: Harr 3A **60**
Kenerne Dr. EN5: Barn 5B **20**

Kenilford Rd. SW12 . . . . .7F **119**
Kenilworth Av. E17 . . . . .2C **50**
   HA2: Harr 4D **58**
   SW19 . . . . .5J **135**
Kenilworth Ct. SW15 . . . . .3G **117**
      (off Lwr. Richmond Rd.)
Kenilworth Cres. EN1: Enf 1K **23**
Kenilworth Gdns. IG3: Ilf 2K **71**
   SE18 .2F **125**
   UB1: S'hall 3D **76**
   UB4: Hayes 5H **75**
Kenilworth Rd. BR5: Pet W 6G **161**
   E3 . . . . .2A **86**
   HA8: Edg 3D **28**
   KT17: Ewe 5C **164**
   NW6 . . . . .1H **81**
   SE20 .1K **157**
   TW15: Ashf 3A **128**
   W5 . . . . .1E **96**
Kenley N17 . . . . .2D **48**
           (off Gloucester Rd.)
Kenley Av. NW9 . . . . .1A **44**
Kenley Cl. BR7: Chst 3J **161**
   DA5: Bexl 7G **127**
   EN4: E Barn 4H **21**
Kenley Gdns. CR7: Thor H 4B **156**
Kenley Rd. KT1: King T 2H **151**
   SW19 . . . . .2J **153**
   TW1: Twick 6B **114**
Kenley Wlk. SM3: Cheam 4F **165**
   W11 . . . . .1G **99**
Kenlor Rd. SW17 . . . . .5B **136**
Kenmare Dr. CR4: Mitc 7D **136**
   N17 . . . . .2F **49**
Kenmare Gdns. N13 . . . . .4H **33**
Kenmare Rd. CR7: Thor H 6A **156**
Kenmere Gdns. HA0: Wemb 1G **79**
Kenmere Rd. DA16: Well 2C **126**
Kenmont Gdns. NW10 . . . . .3D **80**
Kenmore Av.
   HA3: Kenton, W'stone 4A **42**
Kenmore Cl. TW9: Kew 7G **97**
Kenmore Ct. NW6 . . . . .7K **63**
             (off Acol Rd.)
Kenmore Cres. UB4: Hayes 3H **75**
Kenmore Gdns. HA8: Edg 2H **43**
Kenmore Rd. HA3: Kenton 3D **42**
   UB4: Hayes 5H **67**
Kenmure Rd. E8 . . . . .5H **67**
Kenmure Yd. E8 . . . . .5H **67**
Kennacraig Cl. E16 . . . . .1J **105**
Kennard Ho. SW11 . . . . .2E **118**
Kennard Rd. E15 . . . . .7F **69**
   N11 . . . . .5J **31**
Kennard St. E16 . . . . .1D **106**
   SW11 . . . . .1E **118**
Kennedy Av. EN3: Pond E 6D **24**
Kennedy Cl. BR5: Pet W 1H **173**
   CR4: Mitc 1E **154**
   E13 . . . . .2J **87**
Kennedy Ct. TW15: Ashf 5E **128**
   WD23: B Hea 2C **26**
Kennedy Cox Ho. E16 . . . . .5H **87**
              (off Burke St.)
Kennedy Ho. SE11 . . . . .5G **19**
            (off Vauxhall Wlk.)
Kennedy Path W7 . . . . .4K **77**
Kennedy Rd. IG11: Bark 1J **89**
   W7 . . . . .5J **77**
Kennedy Wlk. SE17 . . . . .4D **102**
             (off Elsted St.)
Kennet Cl. SW11 . . . . .4B **118**
Kennet Ct. W9 . . . . .5J **81**
           (off Elmfield Way)
Kenneth Av. IG1: Ilf 4F **71**
Kenneth Campbell Ho. NW8 . . . . . . .3B **4**
          (off Orchardson St.)
Kenneth Chambers Ct. IG8: Wfd G . .1H **37**
Kenneth Ct. SE11 . . . . .3K **19** (4A **102**)
Kenneth Cres. NW2 . . . . .5D **62**
Kenneth Gdns. HA7: Stan 6F **27**
Kenneth Moore Rd. IG1: Ilf 3F **71**
Kenneth More Theatre 3F **71**

Kennet Ho. NW8 . . . . .4B **4**
          (off Church St. Est.)
Kenneth Rd. RM6: Chad H 7D **54**
Kenneth Robbins Ho. N17 . . . . .7C **34**
Kenneth Younger Ho. SW6 . . . . . . .6H **99**
          (off Clem Attlee Ct.)
Kennet Rd. TW7: Isle 3K **113**
   W9 . . . . .4H **81**
Kennet Sq. CR4: Mitc 1C **154**
Kennet St. E1 . . . . .1G **103**
Kennett Ct. W4 . . . . .7H **97**
Kennett Dr. UB4: Yead 5C **76**
Kennett Wharf La. EC4 . . . .3D **14** (7C **84**)
KENNINGHALL JUNC. 5D **34**
Kenninghall Rd. E5 . . . . .3G **67**
   N18 . . . . .5D **34**
Kenning Ho. N1 . . . . .1E **84**
             (off Colville Est.)
Kenning St. SE16 . . . . .2J **103**
Kennings Way SE11 . . . . . . .5K **19** (5A **102**)
KENNINGTON 7K **19** (6A **102**)
Kennington Grn. SE11 . . . . . .6J **19** (5A **102**)
Kennington La. SE11 . . . . . . .6G **19** (5K **101**)
KENNINGTON OVAL 6A **102**
Kennington Oval SE11 . . . . .7H **19** (6K **101**)
Kennington Pal. Ct. SE11 . . . . .5J **19**
Kennington Pk. Gdns.
   SE11 . . . . .7K **19** (6B **102**)
Kennington Pk. Ho. SE11 . . . . .6K **19**
Kennington Pk. Pl. SE11 . . . .7K **19** (6A **102**)
Kennington Pk. Rd. SE11 . . . .7K **19** (6A **102**)
Kennington Rd. SE1 . . . . . . .1J **19** (3A **102**)
   SE11 . . . . .1J **19** (3A **102**)
Kennistoun Ho. NW5 . . . . .5G **65**
Kennoldes SE21 . . . . .2D **138**
           (off Croxted Rd.)
Kenny Dr. SM5: Cars 7E **166**
Kennyland Ct. NW4 . . . . .6D **44**
            (off Hendon Way)
Kenrick Pl. W1 . . . . .6G **5** (5E **82**)
KENSAL GREEN 3E **80**
Kensal Ho. W10 . . . . .4G **81**
          (off Ladbroke Gro.)
KENSAL RISE 2F **81**
Kensal Rd. W10 . . . . .4G **81**
KENSAL TOWN 4G **81**
Kensal Wharf W10 . . . . .4F **81**
KENSINGTON 3J **99**
Kensington Arc. W8 . . . . .2K **99**
        (off Kensington High St.)
Kensington Av. CR7: Thor H 1A **156**
   E12 . . . . .6C **70**
Kensington Cen. W14 . . . . .4G **99**
Kensington Chu. Ct. W8 . . . . .2K **99**
Kensington Chu. St. W8 . . . . .1J **99**
Kensington Chu. Wlk. W8 . . . . .2K **99**
            (not continuous)
Kensington Cl. N11 . . . . .6K **31**
Kensington Ct. SE16 . . . . .1K **103**
        (off King & Queen Wharf)
   W8 . . . . .2K **99**
Kensington Ct. Gdns. W8 . . . . .3K **99**
         (off Kensington Ct. Pl.)
Kensington Ct. Mans. W8 . . . . .2K **99**
          (off Kensington Ct.)
Kensington Ct. M. W8 . . . . .3K **99**
         (off Kensington Ct. Pl.)
Kensington Ct. Pl. W8 . . . . .3K **99**
Kensington Dr. IG8: Wfd G 2B **52**
Kensington Gdns. 5A **10** (1A **100**)
Kensington Gdns. IG1: Ilf 1D **70**
   KT1: King T 2D **150**
             (not continuous)
Kensington Gdns. Sq. W2 . . . . .6K **81**
Kensington Ga. W8 . . . . .3A **100**
Kensington Gore SW7 . . . . . .7A **10** (2A **100**)
Kensington Hall Gdns. W14 . . . . . . .5H **99**
Kensington Hgts. HA1: Harr 6K **41**
           (off Sheepcote Rd.)
   W8 . . . . .1J **99**
Kensington High St. W8 . . . . .3H **99**
   W14 . . . . .3H **99**

Kensington Ho. IG8: Wfd G 7K **37**
   UB7: W Dray 2B **92**
   W8 . . . . .2K **99**
           (off Kensington Ct.)
   W14 . . . . .2F **99**
Kensington Mall W8 . . . . .1J **99**
Kensington Mans. SW5 . . . . .5J **99**
       (off Trebovir Rd., not continuous)
Kensington Palace 1K **99**
Kensington Pal. Gdns. W8 . . . . . . .1K **99**
Kensington Pk. Gdns. W11 . . . . . . .7H **81**
Kensington Pk. M. W11 . . . . .6H **81**
Kensington Pk. Rd. W11 . . . . .6H **81**
Kensington Path E10 . . . . .2D **68**
            (off Osborne Rd.)
Kensington Pl. W8 . . . . .1J **99**
Kensington Rd. RM7: Rom 6J **55**
   SW7 . . . . .7B **10** (2A **100**)
   UB5: N'olt 3E **76**
   W8 . . . . .2A **100**
Kensington Sports Cen. 7G **81**
Kensington Sq. W8 . . . . .3K **99**
Kensington Ter. CR2: S Croy 7D **168**
Kensington Village W14 . . . . .4H **99**
Kensington W. W14 . . . . .4G **99**
Kensworth Ho. EC1 . . . . .2F **9**
           (off Cranwood St.)
Kent Av. DA16: Well 5K **125**
   RM9: Dag 4G **91**
   W13 . . . . .5B **78**
Kent Cl. BR6: Chels 6J **173**
   CR4: Mitc 4J **155**
Kent Ct. E2 . . . . .2F **85**
   NW9 . . . . .2A **44**
Kent Dr. EN4: Cockf 4K **21**
   TW11: Tedd 5J **131**
Kentford Way UB5: N'olt 1C **76**
Kent Gdns. HA4: Ruis 6J **39**
   W13 . . . . .5B **78**
Kent Ga. Way CR0: Addtn 6B **170**
Kent Ho. SE1 . . . . .5F **103**
   SW1 . . . . .5C **18**
            (off Aylesford St.)
   W4 . . . . .5A **98**
           (off Devonshire St.)
   W8 . . . . .2K **99**
           (off Kensington Ct.)
   W11 . . . . .1H **99**
          (off Boyne Ter. M.)
Kent Ho. App. Rd. BR3: Beck 1A **158**
Kent Ho. La. BR3: Beck 6A **140**
Kent Ho. Rd. BR3: Beck 1K **157**
   SE26 .5A **140**
Kentish Bldgs. SE1 . . . . . . .5E **14** (2D **102**)
Kentish Rd. DA17: Belv 4G **109**
KENTISH TOWN 5F **65**
Kentish Town Forum 5F **65**
Kentish Town Ind. Est. NW5 . . . . . . .5F **65**
Kentish Town Rd. NW1 . . . . .7F **65**
   NW5 . . . . .7F **65**
Kentish Town Sports Cen. 6F **65**
Kentish Way BR1: Brom 2K **159**
   BR2: Brom 2K **159**
Kentlea Rd. SE28 . . . . .2J **107**
Kentmere Ho. SE15 . . . . .6J **103**
Kentmere Mans. W5 . . . . .4B **78**
Kentmere Rd. SE18 . . . . .4J **107**
KENTON 5C **42**
Kenton Av. HA1: Harr 7K **41**
   TW16: Sun 2B **148**
   UB1: S'hall 7E **76**
Kenton Ct. HA3: Kenton 6B **42**
   SE26 .4A **140**
           (off Adamsrill Rd.)
   TW1: Twick 6D **114**
   W14 . . . . .3H **99**
Kentone Ct. SE25 . . . . .4H **157**
Kenton Gdns. HA3: Kenton 5C **42**
Kenton Ho. E1 . . . . .4J **85**
             (off Mantus Cl.)
Kenton La.
   HA3: Hrw W, Kenton, W'stone . . .6E **26**

Kenton Pk. Av. HA3: Kenton 5D **42**
Kenton Pk. Cl. HA3: Kenton 4C **42**
Kenton Pk. Cres. HA3: Kenton 4D **42**
Kenton Pk. Mans. HA3: Kenton 5C **42**
                   (off Kenton Rd.)
Kenton Pk. Pde. HA3: Kenton 5C **42**
Kenton Pk. Rd. HA3: Kenton 4C **42**
Kenton Rd. E9 . . . . .6K **67**
  HA1: Harr 7K **41**
  HA3: Kenton 6A **42**
Kenton St. WC1 . . . . .3E 6 (4J **83**)
Kenton Way UB4: Hayes 3G **75**
Kent Pk. Ind. Est.
  SE15 . . . . .6H **103**
Kent Pas. NW1 . . . . .3E 4 (4D **82**)
Kent Rd. BR4: W W'ck 1D **170**
  KT1: King T 3D **150**
  KT8: E Mos 4G **149**
  N21 . . . . .1J **33**
  RM10: Dag 5H **73**
  TW9: Kew 7G **97**
  W4 . . . . .3J **97**
Kent's Pas. TW12: Hamp 1D **148**
Kent St. E2 .2F **85**
  E13 . . . . .3A **88**
Kent Ter. NW1 . . . . .2D 4 (3C **82**)
Kent Vw. Gdns. IG3: Ilf 2J **71**
Kent Wlk. SW9 . . . . .4B **120**
Kent Way KT6: Surb 3E **162**
Kentwell Cl. SE4 . . . . .4A **122**
Kent Wharf SE8 . . . . .7D **104**
                  (off Creekside)
Kentwode Grn. SW13 . . . . .7C **98**
Kent Yd. SW7 . . . . .7D **10** (2C **100**)
Kenver Av. N12 . . . . .6G **31**
Kenward Rd. SE9 . . . . .5A **124**
Kenward Way SW11 . . . . .2E **118**
Ken Way HA9: Wemb 3J **61**
Kenway RM5: Col R 2J **55**
Kenway Rd. SW5 . . . . .4K **99**
Ken Wilson Ho. E2 . . . . .2G **85**
           (off Pritchards Rd.)
Kenwood Av. N14 . . . . .5C **22**
Kenwood Cl. NW3 . . . . .1B **64**
  UB7: Sip 6C **92**
Kenwood Ct. NW9 . . . . .4J **43**
           (off Elmwood Cres.)
Kenwood Dr. BR3: Beck 3E **158**
Kenwood Gdns. E18 . . . . .3K **51**
  IG2: Ilf 5E **52**
  IG5: Ilf 4E **52**
Kenwood House 1C **64**
Kenwood Ho. SW9 . . . . .4B **120**
Kenwood Pl. N6 . . . . .1D **64**
Kenwood Rd. N6 . . . . .6D **46**
  N9 . . . . .1B **34**
Kenworthy Rd. E9 . . . . .5A **68**
Kenwrick Ho. N1 . . . . .1K **83**
           (off Barnsbury Est.)
Kenwyn Dr. NW2 . . . . .2A **62**
Kenwyn Lodge N2 . . . . .4D **46**
Kenwyn Rd. SW4 . . . . .4H **119**
  SW20 .1E **152**
Kenya Rd. SE7 . . . . .7B **106**
Kenyngton Ct. TW16: Sun 5J **129**
Kenyngton Dr. TW16: Sun 5J **129**
Kenyngton Pl. HA3: Kenton 5C **42**
Kenyon Ho. SE5 . . . . .7C **102**
          (off Camberwell Rd.)
Kenyon Mans. W14 . . . . .6G **99**
         (off Queen's Club Gdns.)
Kenyon St. SW6 . . . . .1F **117**
Keogh Rd. E15 . . . . .6G **69**
Kepler Ho. SE10 . . . . .5H **105**
            (off Armitage Rd.)
Kepler Rd. SW4 . . . . .4J **119**
Keppel Ho. SE8 . . . . .5B **104**
  SW3 . . . . .4C **16**
            (off Elystan St.)
Keppel Rd. E6 . . . . .7D **70**
  RM9: Dag 4E **72**
Keppel Row SE1 . . . . .5C **14** (1C **102**)

Keppel St. WC1 . . . . .5D 6 (5H **83**)
Kepplestone M. BR3: Beck 2E **158**
Kerbela St. E2 . . . . .3K 9 (4G **85**)
Kerbey St. E14 . . . . .6D **86**
Kerfield Cres. SE5 . . . . .1D **120**
Kerfield Pl. SE5 . . . . .1D **120**
Kerridge Ct. N1 . . . . .6E **66**
            (off Balls Pond Rd.)
Kerrier Ho. SW10 . . . . .7A **100**
             (off Stadium St.)
Kerrington Ct. W10 . . . . .4G **81**
          (off Wornington Rd.)
  W12 . . . . .2E **98**
             (off Uxbridge Rd.)
Kerris Ho. SE11 . . . . .5K **19**
              (off Tavy Cl.)
Kerrison Pl. W5 . . . . .1D **96**
Kerrison Rd. E15 . . . . .1F **87**
  SW11 .3C **118**
  W5 . . . . .1D **96**
Kerrison Vs. W5 . . . . .1D **96**
Kerry Av. HA7: Stan 4H **27**
Kerry Cl. E16 . . . . .6K **87**
  N13 . . . . .2E **32**
Kerry Ct. HA7: Stan 4J **27**
Kerry Ho. E1 .6J **85**
             (off Sidney St.)
Kerry Path SE14 . . . . .6B **104**
Kerry Rd. SE14 . . . . .6B **104**
Kerscott Ho. E3 . . . . .3D **86**
            (off Rainhill Way)
Kersey Gdns. SE9 . . . . .4C **142**
Kersfield Ho. SW15 . . . . .6F **117**
Kersfield Rd. SW15 . . . . .6F **117**
Kershaw Cl. SW18 . . . . .6B **118**
Kershaw Rd. RM10: Dag 3G **73**
Kersley M. SW11 . . . . .1D **118**
Kersley Rd. N16 . . . . .2E **66**
Kersley St. SW11 . . . . .2D **118**
Kerstin Cl. UB3: Hayes 7H **75**
Kerswell Cl. N15 . . . . .5E **48**
Kerwick Cl. N7 . . . . .7J **65**
Keslake Mans. NW10 . . . . .2F **81**
            (off Station Ter.)
Keslake Rd. NW6 . . . . .2F **81**
Kessock Cl. N17 . . . . .5H **49**
Kestlake Rd. DA5: Bexl 6C **126**
KESTON 5A **172**
Keston Av. BR2: Kes 5A **172**
Keston Cl. DA16: Well 7C **108**
  N18 . . . . .3J **33**
Keston Ct. DA5: Bexl 7F **127**
  KT5: Surb 5F **151**
             (off Cranes Pk.)
Keston Gdns. BR2: Kes 4A **172**
Keston Ho. SE17 . . . . .5E **102**
           (off Kinglake Est.)
KESTON MARK 4C **172**
KESTON MARK 3C **172**
Keston Pk. Cl. BR2: Kes 3D **172**
Keston Rd. CR7: Thor H 6A **156**
  N17 . . . . .3D **48**
  SE15 . . . . .3G **121**
Keston Windmill 5A **172**
Kestrel Av. E6 . . . . .5C **88**
  SE24 . . . . .5B **120**
Kestrel Cl. KT2: King T 4D **132**
  NW9 . . . . .2A **44**
  NW10 . . . . .5K **61**
Kestrel Ct. CR2: S Croy 6C **168**
  E3 . . . . .2C **86**
          (off Four Seasons Cl.)
  E17 . . . . .2K **49**
  HA4: Ruis 2G **57**
  SM6: Wall 5G **167**
Kestrel Ho. EC1 . . . . .1C **8**
             (off Pickard St.)
  EN3: Pond E 5F **25**
Kestrel Pl. SE14 . . . . .6A **104**
Kestrel Way
  CR0: New Ad 7F **171**
  UB3: Hayes 2F **93**

Keswick Av. SW15 . . . . .5A **134**
  SW19 .2J **153**
  TW17: Shep 3G **147**
Keswick B'way. SW15 . . . . .5H **117**
         (off Up. Richmond Rd.)
Keswick Cl. SM1: Sutt 4A **166**
Keswick Ct. BR2: Brom 4H **159**
  SE6 . . . . .1H **141**
  SE13 . . . . .5D **122**
Keswick Gdns. HA4: Ruis 6F **39**
  HA9: Wemb 4E **60**
  IG4: Ilf 4C **52**
Keswick Ho. SE5 . . . . .2C **120**
Keswick M. W5 . . . . .1E **96**
Keswick Rd. BR4: W W'ck 2G **171**
  BR6: Orp 1K **173**
  DA7: Bex 1G **127**
  SW15 .5G **117**
  TW2: Whitt 6G **113**
Kettering Ct. CR7: Thor H 4C **156**
Kettering St. SW16 . . . . .6G **137**
Kett Gdns. SW2 . . . . .5K **119**
Kettlebaston Rd. E10 . . . . .1B **68**
Kettleby Ho. SW9 . . . . .3B **120**
           (off Barrington Rd.)
Kettlewell Cl. N11 . . . . .6K **31**
Ketton Ho. W10 . . . . .4E **80**
            (off Sutton Way)
Kevan Ct. E17 . . . . .4C **50**
Kevan Ho. SE5 . . . . .7C **102**
Kevelioc Rd. N17 . . . . .1C **48**
Kevin Cl. TW4: Houn 2B **112**
Kevington Cl. BR5: St P 4K **161**
Kevington Dr. BR5: St P 4K **161**
  BR7: Chst 4K **161**
KEW 7G **97**
KEW BRIDGE 5F **97**
Kew Bri. TW8: Bford 6G **97**
Kew Bri. Arches TW9: Kew 6G **97**
Kew Bri. Ct. W4 . . . . .5G **97**
Kew Bri. Distribution Cen.
  TW8: Bford 5F **97**
Kew Bri. Rd. TW8: Bford 6F **97**
Kew Bridge Steam Mus. 5F **97**
Kew Ct. KT2: King T 1E **150**
Kew Cres. SM3: Cheam 3G **165**
Kew Foot Rd. TW9: Rich 4E **114**
Kew Gdns. .7E **96**
Kew Gdns. Rd. TW9: Kew 7F **97**
Kew Gdns. Vis. Cen. 1F **115**
KEW GREEN 7G **97**
Kew Grn. TW9: Kew 6F **97**
Kew Mdw. Path TW9: Kew 2J **115**
               (Clifford Av.)
  TW9: Kew 1H **115**
             (Mortlake Rd.)
Kew Palace .7E **96**
Kew Retail Pk. TW9: Kew 1H **115**
Kew Rd. TW9: Kew 6G **97**
  TW9: Rich, Kew 4E **114**
Keybridge Ho. SW8 . . . . .7J **19**
               (off Miles St.)
Key Cl. E1 . . . . .4J **85**
Keyes Ho. SW1 . . . . .6C **18**
             (off Dolphin Sq.)
Keyes Rd. NW2 . . . . .5F **63**
Keyham Ho. W2 . . . . .5J **81**
        (off Westbourne Pk. Rd.)
Key Ho. SE11 . . . . .7K **19** (6A **102**)
Keymer Rd. SW2 . . . . .2K **137**
Keynes Cl. N2 . . . . .4D **46**
Keynes Ct. SE28 . . . . .7B **90**
              (off Attlee Rd.)
Keynsham Av. IG8: Wfd G 4B **36**
Keynsham Gdns. SE9 . . . . .5C **124**
Keynsham Rd. SE9 . . . . .5B **124**
  SM4: Mord 1K **165**
Keynsham Wlk. SM4: Mord 1K **165**
Keys Ct. CR0: C'don 3D **168**
           (off Beech Ho. Rd.)
Keyse Rd. SE1 . . . . .3F **103**

Keysham Av. TW5: Cran 1J **111**
Keystone Cres. N1 . . . . .1F 7 (2J **83**)
Keywood Dr. TW16: Sun 6J **129**
Keyworth Cl. E5 . . . . .4A **68**
Keyworth Pl. SE1 . . . . .7B **14**
Keyworth St. SE1 . . . . .7B **14** (3B **102**)
Kezia M. SE8 . . . . .5A **104**
Kezia St. SE8 . . . . .5A **104**
Khalsa Ct. N22 . . . . .1B **48**
Khama Rd. SW17 . . . . .4C **136**
Khartoum Rd. E13 . . . . .3K **87**
  IG1: Ilf 5F **71**
  SW17 .4B **136**
Khyber Rd. SW11 . . . . .2C **118**
Kibworth St. SW8 . . . . .7K **101**
KIDBROOKE 2K **123**
Kidbrooke Est. SE3 . . . . .3A **124**
Kidbrooke Gdns. SE3 . . . . .2J **123**
Kidbrooke Green Nature Reserve . . .3A **124**
Kidbrooke Gro. SE3 . . . . .1J **123**
Kidbrooke La. SE9 . . . . .4C **124**
Kidbrooke Pk. Cl. SE3 . . . . .1K **123**
Kidbrooke Pk. Rd. SE3 . . . . .1K **123**
Kidbrooke Way SE3 . . . . .2K **123**
Kidderminster Pl. CR0: C'don 1B **168**
Kidderminster Rd. CR0: C'don 1B **168**
Kidderpore Av. NW3 . . . . .4J **63**
Kidderpore Gdns. NW3 . . . . .4J **63**
Kidd Pl. SE7 . . . . .5C **106**
Kierbeck Bus. Complex E16 . . . . . .2K **105**
Kiffen St. EC2 . . . . .3F 9 (4D **84**)
Kilberry Cl. TW7: Isle 1H **113**
Kilbrennan Ho. E14 . . . . .6E **86**
           (off Findhorn St.)
KILBURN 2H **81**
Kilburn Bri. NW6 . . . . .1J **81**
Kilburn Ga. NW6 . . . . .2K **81**
Kilburn High Rd. NW6 . . . . .7H **63**
Kilburn Ho. NW6 . . . . .2H **81**
           (off Malvern Pl.)
Kilburn La. W9 . . . . .3F **81**
  W10 . . . . .3F **81**
Kilburn Pk. Rd. NW6 . . . . .3J **81**
Kilburn Pl. NW6 . . . . .1J **81**
Kilburn Priory NW6 . . . . .1K **81**
Kilburn Sq. NW6 . . . . .1J **81**
Kilburn Va. NW6 . . . . .1K **81**
Kilburn Va. Est. NW6 . . . . .1K **81**
           (off Kilburn Va.)
Kilby Ct. SE10 . . . . .3H **105**
          (off Greenroof Way)
Kildare Cl. HA4: Ruis 1A **58**
Kildare Ct. W2 . . . . .6J **81**
             (off Kildare Ter.)
Kildare Gdns. W2 . . . . .6J **81**
Kildare Rd. E16 . . . . .5J **87**
Kildare Ter. W2 . . . . .6J **81**
Kildare Wlk. E14 . . . . .6C **86**
Kildoran Rd. SW2 . . . . .5J **119**
Kildowan Rd. IG3: Ilf 1A **72**
Kilgour Rd. SE23 . . . . .6A **122**
Kilkie St. SW6 . . . . .2A **118**
Killarney Rd. SW18 . . . . .6A **118**
Killburns Mill Cl. SM6: Wall 2F **167**
Killearn Rd. SE6 . . . . .1F **141**
Killester Gdns. KT4: Wor Pk 4D **164**
Killick Ho. SM1: Sutt 4K **165**
Killick St. N1 . . . . .1G 7 (2K **83**)
Killieser Av. SW2 . . . . .2J **137**
Killigarth Ct. DA14: Sidc 4A **144**
Killigrew Ho. TW16: Sun 7G **129**
Killip Cl. E16 . . . . .6H **87**
Killoran Ho. E14 . . . . .3E **104**
           (off Galbraith St.)
Killowen Av. UB5: N'olt 5G **59**
Killowen Rd. E9 . . . . .6K **67**
Killowen St. SW8 . . . . .2G **119**
Killyon Rd. SW8 . . . . .2G **119**
Killyon Ter. SW8 . . . . .2G **119**
Kilmaine Rd. SW6 . . . . .7G **99**
Kilmarnock Gdns. RM8: Dag 3C **72**
Kilmarsh Rd. W6 . . . . .4E **98**

Kilmartin Av. SW16	.3A 156
Kilmartin Rd. IG3: Ilf	.2A 72
Kilmington Rd. SW13	.6C 98
Kilmiston Ho. TW17: Shep	.6E 146
Kilmore Ho. E14	.6D 86
	(off Vesey Path)
Kilmorey Gdns. TW1: Twick	.5B 114
Kilmorey Rd. TW1: Twick	.4B 114
Kilmorie Rd. SE23	.1A 140
Kilmuir Ho. SW1	.4H 17
	(off Bury St.)
Kiln Cl. UB3: Harl	.6F 93
Kiln Ct. E14	.7B 86
	(off Newell St.)
Kilner Ho. E16	.5K 87
	(off Freemasons Rd.)
SE11	.7J 19
Kilner St. E14	.5C 86
Kiln M. SW17	.5B 136
Kiln Pl. NW5	.5E 64
Kilnside KT10: Clay	.7A 162
Kilpatrick Way UB4: Yead	.5C 76
Kilravock St. W10	.3G 81
Kilronan W3	.6K 79
Kilross Rd. TW14: Bedf	.1F 129
Kilsby Wlk. RM9: Dag	.6B 72
Kilsha Rd. KT12: Walt T	.6A 148
Kimbell Gdns. SW6	.1G 117
Kimbell Pl. SE3	.4A 124
Kimber Ct. SE1	.7G 15
	(off Long La.)
Kimberley Av. E6	.2C 88
IG2: Ilf	.7H 53
RM7: Rom	.6J 55
SE15	.2H 121
Kimberley Ct. NW6	.1G 81
	(off Kimberley Rd.)
Kimberley Dr. DA14: Sidc	.2D 144
Kimberley Gdns. EN1: Enf	.3A 24
N4	.5B 48
Kimberley Ga. BR1: Brom	.7G 141
Kimberley Ho. E14	.3E 104
	(off Galbraith St.)
Kimberley Ind. Est. E17	.1B 50
Kimberley Rd. BR3: Beck	.2K 157
CRO: C'don	.6B 156
E4	.1B 36
E11	.2F 69
E16	.4H 87
E17	.1A 50
N17	.2G 49
N18	.6C 34
NW6	.1G 81
SW9	.2J 119
Kimberley Wlk. KT12: Walt T	.7K 147
Kimberley Way E4	.1B 36
Kimber Pl. TW4: Houn	.7D 112
Kimber Rd. SW18	.7J 117
Kimble Cres. WD23: Bush	.1B 26
Kimble Ho. NW8	.3D 4
Kimble Rd. SW19	.6B 136
Kimbolton Cl. SE12	.6H 123
Kimbolton Ct. SW3	.4C 16
	(off Fulham Rd.)
Kimbolton Row SW3	.4C 16
	(off Fulham Rd.)
Kimiston Av. TW17: Shep	.6E 146
Kimmeridge Gdns. SE9	.4C 142
Kimmeridge Rd. SE9	.4C 142
Kimpton Ho. SW15	.7C 116
Kimpton Ind. Est. SM3: Sutt	.2H 165
Kimpton Link Bus. Cen.	
SM3: Sutt	.2H 165
Kimpton Pk. Way SM1: Sutt	.2G 165
SM3: Sutt	.2G 165
Kimpton Rd. SE5	.1D 120
SM3: Sutt	.2H 165
Kimpton Trade & Bus. Cen.	
SM3: Sutt	.2H 165
Kinber Pl. TW4: Houn	.4D 112
Kinburn St. SE16	.2K 103
Kincaid Rd. SE15	.7H 103

Kincardine Gdns. W9	.4J 81
	(off Harrow Rd.)
Kincha Lodge KT2: King T	.1F 151
	(off Elm Rd.)
Kinch Gro. HA9: Wemb	.7F 43
Kinder Cl. SE28	.7D 90
Kinder Ho. N1	.2D 84
	(off Cranston Est.)
Kindersley Ho. E1	.6G 85
	(off Pinchin St.)
Kinder St. E1	.6H 85
Kinderton Ct. N14	.1B 32
Kinefold Ho. N7	.6J 65
	(off York Way Est.)
Kinfauns Rd. IG3: Ilf	.1A 72
SW2	.2A 138
King Alfred Av. SE6	.4C 140
	(not continuous)
King & Queen Cl. SE9	.4C 142
King & Queen St. SE17	.5C 102
King & Queen Wharf SE16	.7K 85
King Arthur Cl. SE15	.7J 103
King Charles I Island SW1	.4E 12
King Charles Ct. SE17	.6B 102
	(off Royal Rd.)
King Charles Cres. KT5: Surb	.7F 151
King Charles Ho. SW6	.7K 99
	(off Wandon Rd.)
King Charles Rd. KT5: Surb	.5F 151
King Charles's Ct. SE10	.6E 104
	(off Park Row)
King Charles St. SW1	.6D 12 (2H 101)
King Charles Ter. E1	.7H 85
	(off Sovereign Cl.)
King Charles Wlk. SW19	.1G 135
King Cl. E10	.7D 50
Kingcup Cl. CRO: C'don	.7K 157
King David La. E1	.7J 85
Kingdom St. W2	.5A 82
Kingdon Ho. E14	.3E 104
	(off Galbraith St.)
Kingdon Rd. NW6	.6J 63
King Edward III M. SE16	.2H 103
King Edward Bldg. EC1	.7B 8
	(off Newgate St.)
King Edward Ct. HA9: Wemb	.5E 60
	(off Elm Rd.)
King Edward Dr. KT9: Chess	.3E 162
King Edward Mans. E8	.1H 85
	(off Mare St.)
King Edward M. SW13	.1C 116
King Edward Rd. E10	.1E 68
E17	.3C 50
EN5: New Bar	.4D 20
King Edward's Gdns. W3	.1G 97
King Edwards Gro. TW11: Tedd	.6B 132
King Edwards Mans. SW6	.7J 99
	(off Fulham Rd.)
King Edward's Pl. W3	.1G 97
King Edwards Rd. E9	.1H 85
EN3: Pond E	.4E 24
HA4: Ruis	.1F 57
IG11: Bark	.1H 89
N9	.7C 24
King Edward St. EC1	.7C 8 (6C 84)
King Edward Wlk. SE1	.1K 19 (3A 102)
Kingfield Rd. W5	.4D 78
Kingfield St. E14	.4E 104
Kingfisher Av. E11	.6K 51
Kingfisher Cl. HA3: Hrw W	.7E 26
HA6: Nwood	.1D 38
SE28	.7C 90
Kingfisher Ct. E14	.2E 104
	(off River Barge Cl.)
EN2: Enf	.1E 22
KT8: E Mos	.4J 149
SE1	.7D 14
	(off Swan St.)
SM1: Sutt	.5H 165
SW19	.2F 135
TW3: Houn	.5F 113
TW7: Isle	.2H 113

Kingfisher Dr. TW10: Ham	.4B 132
Kingfisher Ho. SW18	.3A 118
W14	.3H 99
	(off Melbury Rd.)
Kingfisher Leisure Cen.	.2E 150
Kingfisher M. SE13	.4C 122
Kingfisher Pl. N22	.2K 47
Kingfisher Sq. SE8	.6B 104
	(off Clyde St.)
Kingfisher St. E6	.5C 88
Kingfisher Wlk. NW9	.2A 44
Kingfisher Way BR3: Beck	.5K 157
NW10	.6K 61
King Frederick IX Twr. SE16	.3B 104
King Gdns. CRO: Wadd	.5B 168
King George IV Ct. SE17	.5D 102
	(off Dawes St.)
King George VI Av. CR4: Mitc	.4D 154
King George VI Memorial	.5C 12
King George Av. E16	.6A 88
IG2: Ilf	.6G 53
King George Cl. RM7: Mawney	.3J 55
TW16: Sun	.5G 129
King George Cres. HA0: Wemb	.5D 60
King George's Dr. UB1: S'hall	.5D 76
King George Sq. TW10: Rich	.6F 115
King George's Sailing Club	.6H 25
King George's Trad. Est.	
KT9: Chess	.4G 163
King George St. SE10	.7E 104
Kingham Cl. SW18	.7A 118
W11	.2G 99
King Harolds Way DA7: Belv, Bex	.7D 108
DA17: Belv	.7D 108
King Henry M. BR6: Chels	.5K 173
HA2: Harr	.1J 59
King Henry's Dr. CRO: New Ad	.7D 170
King Henry's Reach W6	.6E 98
King Henry's Rd. KT1: King T	.3H 151
NW3	.7C 64
King Henry's Stairs E1	.1H 103
King Henry St. N16	.5E 66
King Henry's Wlk. N1	.6E 66
King Henry Ter. E1	.7H 85
	(off Sovereign Cl.)
Kinghorn St. EC1	.6C 8 (5C 84)
King Ho. W12	.6D 80
Kingisholt Ct. NW10	.3F 81
	(off Wellington Rd.)
King James Ct. SE1	.7B 14
King James St. SE1	.7B 14 (2B 102)
King John Ct. EC2	.3H 9 (4E 84)
King John St. E1	.5K 85
King John's Wlk. SE9	.7C 124
	(not continuous)
Kinglake Est. SE17	.5E 102
Kinglake St. SE17	.5E 102
	(not continuous)
Kinglet Cl. E7	.6J 69
Kingly Ct. W1	.2B 12
Kingly St. W1	.1A 12 (6G 83)
Kingsand Rd. SE12	.2J 141
Kings Arbour UB2: S'hall	.5C 94
King's Arms All. TW8: Bford	.6D 96
Kings Arms Ct. E1	.5G 85
Kings Arms Yd. EC2	.7E 8 (6D 84)
Kingsash Dr. UB4: Yead	.4C 76
Kings Av. BR1: Brom	.6H 141
IG8: Wfd G	.6E 36
IG9: Buck H	.2G 37
	(Langfords)
IG9: Buck H	.6E 36
	(The Broadway)
KT3: N Mald	.4A 152
N10	.3E 46
N21	.1G 33
RM6: Chad H	.6F 55
SM5: Cars	.7C 166
SW4	.1H 137
SW12	.1H 137
TW3: Houn	.1F 113
TW16: Sun	.5H 129

Kings Av. UB6: G'frd	.5F 77
W5	.6D 78
King's Bench St. SE1	.6B 14 (2B 102)
King's Bench Wlk. EC4	.1K 13 (6A 84)
Kingsbridge Av. W3	.2F 97
Kingsbridge Ct. E14	.3C 104
	(off Dockers Tanner Rd.)
	1F 65
NW1	(off Castlehaven Rd.)
Kingsbridge Cres. UB1: S'hall	.5D 76
Kingsbridge Dr. NW7	.7A 30
Kingsbridge Rd. IG11: Bark	.2H 89
KT12: Walt T	.7K 147
SM4: Mord	.6F 153
UB2: S'hall	.4D 94
W10	.6E 80
Kingsbridge Way UB4: Hayes	.3G 75
Kingsbridge Wharf	
IG11: Bark	.3J 89
KINGSBURY	.5H 43
Kingsbury Circ. NW9	.5G 43
KINGSBURY GREEN	.5K 43
Kingsbury Rd. N1	.6E 66
NW9	.5G 43
Kingsbury Ter. N1	.6E 66
Kingsbury Trad. Est. NW9	.6K 43
Kings Chase KT8: E Mos	.3G 149
Kings Chase Vw. EN2: Enf	.2F 23
Kingsclere Cl. SW15	.7C 116
Kingsclere Ct. N12	.5H 31
Kingsclere Pl. EN2: Enf	.2H 23
Kingscliffe Gdns. SW19	.1H 135
Kings Cl. DA1: Cray	.4K 127
E10	.7D 50
KT7: T Ditt	.6A 150
KT12: Walt T	.7K 147
NW4	.4F 45
TW18: Staines	.7A 128
King's Club, The (Sports Cen.)	.6E 134
Kings Coll. Cl. NW3	.7C 64
King's College London	
Guy's Campus	.5E 14
	(within Guy's Hospital)
Denmark Hill Campus -	
Dental Institute	.2D 120
St Thomas' Campus -	
Lambeth Pal. Rd.	.2F 19
St Thomas' House	.1G 19
Strand Campus	.2H 13 (7K 83)
Waterloo Campus	.5J 13 (1A 102)
Kings Coll. Rd. HA4: Ruis	.6H 39
NW3	.7C 64
King's College School of Medicine & Dentistry	
	.2C 120
Kingscote Rd. CRO: C'don	.7H 157
KT3: N Mald	.3K 151
W4	.3J 97
Kingscote St. EC4	.2A 14 (7B 84)
Kings Ct. E13	.1K 87
HA9: Wemb	.2H 61
IG9: Buck H	.2G 37
N7	.7K 65
	(off Caledonian Rd.)
NW8	.1B 82
	(off Prince Albert Rd.)
SE1	.6B 14 (2B 102)
W6	.4C 98
Kings Ct. Mans. SW6	.1H 117
	(off Fulham Rd.)
Kings Ct. M. KT8: E Mos	.5H 149
Kings Ct. Nth. SW3	.6C 16 (5C 100)
Kingscourt Rd. SW16	.3H 137
Kings Ct. Sth. SW3	.6C 16
King's Cres. N4	.3C 66
Kings Cres. Est. N4	.2C 66
Kingscroft SW4	.6J 119
Kingscroft Rd. NW2	.6H 63
King's Cross Bri. N1	.1F 7
King's Cross Rd. WC1	.1G 7 (3K 83)
Kingsdale Gdns. W11	.1F 99
Kingsdale Rd. SE18	.7K 107
SE20	.7K 139

Kingsdown Av. CR2: S Croy 7C **168**
W3 . . . . .7A **80**
W13 . . . . .2B **96**
Kingsdown Cl. *SE16* *5H 103*
(off Masters Dr.)
W10 . . . . .6F **81**
Kingsdowne Rd. KT6: Surb 7E **150**
Kingsdown Ho. E8 . . . . .5G **67**
Kingsdown Point SW2 . . . . .2A **138**
Kingsdown Rd. E11 . . . . .3G **69**
N19 . . . . .2J **65**
SM3: Cheam 5G **165**
Kingsdown Way BR2: Hayes 7J **159**
Kings Dr. HA8: Edg 4A **28**
HA9: Wemb 2H **61**
KT5: Surb 7G **151**
KT7: T Ditt 7B **150**
TW11: Tedd 5H **131**
Kingsend HA4: Ruis 1F **57**
Kingsend Ct. HA4: Ruis 1G **57**
Kings Farm E17 . . . . .1D **50**
Kings Farm Av. TW10: Rich 4G **115**
Kingsfield Av. HA2: Harr 4F **41**
Kingsfield Ho. SE9 . . . . .3B **142**
Kingsfield Rd. HA1: Harr 7H **41**
Kingsfield Ter. HA1: Harr 1H **59**
Kingsford St. NW5 . . . . .5D **64**
Kingsford Way E6 . . . . .5D **88**
Kings Gdns. IG1: Ilf 1H **71**
NW6 . . . . .7J **63**
Kings Gth. M. SE23 . . . . .2J **139**
Kingsgate HA9: Wemb 3J **61**
Kingsgate Av. N3 . . . . .3J **45**
Kingsgate Bus. Cen. *KT2: King T* *1E 150*
(off Kingsgate Rd.)
Kingsgate Cl. DA7: Bex 1E **126**
Kingsgate Est. N1 . . . . .6E **66**
Kingsgate Ho. SW9 . . . . .1A **120**
Kingsgate Mans. *WC1* *6G 7*
(off Red Lion Sq.)
Kingsgate Pde. SW1 . . . . .2B **18**
Kingsgate Pl. NW6 . . . . .7J **63**
Kingsgate Rd. KT1: King T 1E **150**
KT2: King T 1E **150**
NW6 . . . . .7J **63**
Kings Grange HA4: Ruis 1H **57**
Kingsground SE9 . . . . .7B **124**
King's Gro. SE15 . . . . .7H **103**
(not continuous)
Kings Hall Leisure Cen. 5J **67**
Kingshall M. SE13 . . . . .3E **122**
Kings Hall Rd. BR3: Beck 7A **140**
Kings Head Hill E4 . . . . .7J **25**
Kingshead Ho. NW7 . . . . .4J **29**
Kings Head Pas. *SW4* *4H 119*
(off Clapham Pk. Rd.)
Kings Head Theatre *1B 84*
(off Upper St.)
King's Head Yd. SE1 . . . . .5E **14** (1D **102**)
King's Highway SE18 . . . . .6J **107**
Kingshill *SE17* *4C 102*
(off Brandon St.)
Kingshill Av. HA3: Kenton 4B **42**
KT4: Wor Pk 7C **152**
UB4: Hayes 3G **75**
UB5: N'olt 3G **75**
Kingshill Cl. UB4: Hayes 3J **75**
Kingshill Ct. EN5: Barn 4B **20**
Kingshill Dr. HA3: Kenton 2B **42**
Kingshold Rd. E9 . . . . .7J **67**
Kingsholm Gdns. SE9 . . . . .4B **124**
Kings Ho. *SW8* *7J 101*
(off Sth. Lambeth Rd.)
SW10 . . . .*7A 16*
(off King's Rd.)
King's Ho. Studios *SW10* *7A 16*
(off Lamont Rd. Pas.)
Kingshurst Rd. SE12 . . . . .7J **123**
Kingside SE18 . . . . .3C **106**
Kings Keep BR2: Brom 2G **159**
KT1: King T 4E **150**
SW15 . . . . .5F **117**
KINGSLAND .6E **66**
Kingsland NW8 . . . . .1C **82**
Kingsland Grn. E8 . . . . .6E **66**
Kingsland High St. E8 . . . . .6F **67**
Kingsland Pas. E8 . . . . .6E **66**
Kingsland Rd. E2 . . . . .2H **9** (3E **84**)
E8 . . . . .3E **84**
E13 . . . . .3A **88**
Kingsland Shop. Cen. E8 . . . . .6F **67**
Kings La. SM1: Sutt 6B **166**
Kingslawn Cl. SW15 . . . . .5D **116**
Kingslee Ct. SM2: Sutt 7K **165**
Kingsleigh Cl. TW8: Bford 6D **96**
Kingsleigh Pl. CR4: Mitc 3D **154**
Kingsleigh Wlk. *BR2: Brom* *4H 159*
(off Stamford Dr.)
Kingsley Av. SM1: Sutt 4B **166**
TW3: Houn 2G **113**
UB1: S'hall 7E **76**
W13 . . . . .5A **78**
Kingsley Cl. N2 . . . . .5A **46**
RM10: Dag 4H **73**
Kingsley Ct. DA6: Bex 4G **127**
HA8: Edg 3C **28**
KT4: Wor Pk *2B 164*
(off The Avenue)
NW2 . . . . .6D **62**
Kingsley Dr. KT4: Wor Pk 2B **164**
Kingsley Flats *SE1* *4E 102*
(off Old Kent Rd.)
Kingsley Gdns. E4 . . . . .5H **35**
Kingsley Ho. *SW3* *6B 100*
(off Beaufort St.)
W14 . . . .*4G 99*
(off Avonmore Pl.)
Kingsley Mans. *W14* *6G 99*
(off Greyhound Rd.)
Kingsley M. BR7: Chst 6F **143**
E1 . . . . .7H **85**
W8 . . . . .3K **99**
Kingsley Pl. N6 . . . . .7E **46**
Kingsley Rd. BR6: Chels 7K **173**
CR0: C'don 1A **168**
E7 . . . . .7J **69**
E17 . . . . .2E **50**
HA2: Harr 4G **59**
HA5: Pinn 4D **40**
IG6: Ilf 1G **53**
N13 . . . . .4F **33**
NW6 . . . . .1H **81**
SW19 . . . . .5K **135**
TW3: Houn 1F **113**
Kingsley St. SW11 . . . . .3D **118**
Kingsley Way N2 . . . . .5A **46**
Kingsley Wood Dr. SE9 . . . . .3D **142**
Kings Lodge *HA4: Ruis* *1G 57*
(off Pembroke Rd.)
N12 . . . . .6F **31**
Kingslyn Cres. SE19 . . . . .1E **156**
Kings Mall W6 . . . . .4E **98**
Kingsman Pde. SE18 . . . . .3D **106**
Kings Mans. *SW3* *7C 16*
(off Lawrence St.)
Kingsman St. SE18 . . . . .3D **106**
Kingsmead EN5: New Bar 4D **20**
TW10: Rich 6F **115**
Kingsmead Av. CR4: Mitc 3G **155**
KT4: Wor Pk 2D **164**
KT6: Surb 2G **163**
N9 . . . . .1C **34**
NW9 . . . . .7K **43**
TW16: Sun 2A **148**
Kingsmead Cl. DA15: Sidc 2A **144**
KT19: Ewe 7K **163**
TW11: Tedd 6B **132**
Kingsmead Cotts. BR2: Brom 1C **172**
Kingsmead Ct. N6 . . . . .7H **47**
Kingsmead Dr. UB5: N'olt 7D **58**
Kingsmead Ho. E9 . . . . .4A **68**
Kingsmead Lodge SM2: Sutt 6B **166**
Kingsmeadow 3H **151**
Kingsmeadow Athletics Cen. 3G **151**
Kingsmead Rd. SW2 . . . . .2A **138**
Kingsmead Way E9 . . . . .4A **68**
Kingsmere Cl. SW15 . . . . .3F **117**
Kingsmere Pk. NW9 . . . . .1H **61**
Kingsmere Pl. N16 . . . . .1D **66**
Kingsmere Rd. SW19 . . . . .2F **135**
King's M. SW4 . . . . .5J **119**
WC1 . . . . .4H **7** (4K **83**)
Kingsmill *NW8* *2B 82*
(off Kingsmill Ter.)
Kingsmill Bus. Pk.
KT1: King T 3F **151**
Kingsmill Gdns. RM9: Dag 5F **73**
Kingsmill Ho. *SW3* *5D 16*
(off Cale St.)
Kingsmill Rd. RM9: Dag 5F **73**
Kingsmill Ter. NW8 . . . . .2B **82**
Kingsnorth Ho. W10 . . . . .6F **81**
Kingsnympton Pk. KT2: King T 7H **133**
Kings Oak RM7: Mawney 3G **55**
King's Orchard SE9 . . . . .6C **124**
King's Paddock TW12: Hamp 1G **149**
Kings Pde. *HA8: Edg* *5B 28*
(off Edgwarebury La.)
N17 . . . . .3F **49**
NW10 . . . . .1E **80**
SM5: Cars *3D 166*
(off Wrythe La.)
W12 . . . . .3C **98**
Kingspark Bus. Cen.
KT3: N Mald 4J **151**
Kingspark Ct. E18 . . . . .3J **51**
Kings Pas. E11 . . . . .7G **51**
KT1: King T 2D **150**
KT2: King T 1D **150**
Kings Place 2J **83**
Kings Pl. IG9: Buck H 2F **37**
SE1 . . . . .7C **14**
W4 . . . . .5J **97**
King Sq. EC1 . . . . .2C **8** (3C **84**)
Kings Quarter Apartments
N1 . . . .*1K 83*
(off Copenhagen St.)
King's Quay *SW10* *1A 118*
(off Chelsea Harbour Dr.)
Kings Reach Twr. SE1 . . . . .4A **14**
Kings Ride Ga. TW10: Rich 4G **115**
Kingsridge SW19 . . . . .2G **135**
Kings Rd. BR6: Orp 4K **173**
CR4: Mitc 3E **154**
E4 . . . . .1A **36**
E6 . . . . .1A **88**
E11 . . . . .7G **51**
EN5: Barn 3A **20**
HA2: Harr 2D **58**
IG11: Bark 7G **71**
KT2: King T 7E **132**
KT6: Surb 1C **162**
KT12: Walt T 7K **147**
N17 . . . . .1F **49**
N18 . . . . .5B **34**
N22 . . . . .1K **47**
NW10 . . . . .7D **62**
SE25 . . . . .3G **157**
SW3 . . . . .6D **16** (2J **117**)
SW6 . . . . .7K **99**
SW10 . . . . .7A **16** (7K **99**)
SW14 . . . . .3K **115**
SW19 . . . . .6J **135**
TW1: Twick 6B **114**
TW10: Rich 6F **115**
TW11: Tedd 5H **131**
TW13: Felt 1A **130**
UB7: W Dray 2B **92**
W5 . . . . .5D **78**
King's Scholars' Pas. SW1 . . . . .2A **18**
King Stairs Cl. SE16 . . . . .2H **103**
King's Ter. NW1 . . . . .1G **83**
TW7: Isle 4A **114**
Kingsthorpe Rd. SE26 . . . . .4K **139**
Kingston Av. SM3: Cheam 3G **165**
TW14: Felt 6G **111**
Kingston Av. UB7: Yiew 7B **74**
(Ash Gro.)
UB7: Yiew 1B **92**
(Whitethorn Av.)
Kingston Bri. KT1: King T 2D **150**
Kingston Bus. Cen. KT9: Chess 3E **162**
Kingston By-Pass KT3: N Mald 5A **152**
KT6: Surb 3D **162**
SW15 . . . . .4A **134**
SW20 . . . . .2C **152**
Kingston By-Pass Rd. KT6: Surb 3A **162**
KT10: Esh, Hin W 3A **162**
Kingston Cl. RM6: Chad H 3E **54**
(not continuous)
TW11: Tedd 6B **132**
UB5: N'olt 1D **76**
Kingston Crematorium KT1: King T . . .3G **151**
Kingston Cres. BR3: Beck 1B **158**
Kingston Gdns. CR0: Bedd 3J **167**
Kingston Hall Rd. KT1: King T 3D **150**
Kingston Hill KT2: King T 1G **151**
Kingston Hill Av. RM6: Chad H 3E **54**
Kingston Hill Pl. KT2: King T 4J **133**
Kingston Ho. *KT1: King T* *4D 150*
(off Surbiton Rd.)
NW1 . . . .*1G 83*
(off Camden St.)
NW6 . . . . .7G **63**
Kingston Ho. E. *SW7* *7C 10*
(off Prince's Ga.)
Kingston Ho. Est. KT6: Surb 6B **150**
Kingston Ho. Nth. *SW7* *7C 10*
(off Prince's Ga.)
Kingston Ho. Sth. *SW7* *7C 10*
(off Ennismore Gdns.)
Kingstonian FC 3G **151**
Kingston La. TW11: Tedd 5A **132**
UB7: W Dray 2B **92**
UB8: Hil .3A **74**
Kingston Lodge KT3: N Mald 4A **152**
Kingston Pl. HA3: Hrw W 7E **26**
Kingston Rd. EN4: E Barn 5G **21**
IG1: Ilf 4F **71**
KT1: King T 3H **151**
KT3: N Mald 3H **151**
KT4: Wor Pk 2H **163**
KT5: Surb 2H **163**
KT17: Ewe 7B **164**
KT19: Ewe 2H **163**
N9 . . . . .2B **34**
SW15 . . . . .2C **134**
SW19 . . . . .2C **134**
(Norstead Pl.)
SW19 . . . . .2H **153**
(Watery La.)
SW20 . . . . .2F **153**
TW11: Tedd 5B **132**
TW15: Ashf 6A **128**
UB2: S'hall 2D **94**
Kingston Sq. SE19 . . . . .5D **138**
Kingston University
Kingston Hill Campus 5K **133**
Knights Pk. Campus 3E **150**
Penrhyn Road Campus 4E **150**
Reg Bailey Building 3D **150**
Roehampton Vale Cen. 3B **134**
Kingston upon Thames Art Gallery & Mus.
. . . . .2E **150**
Kingston Upon Thames (Park & Ride)
. . . . .7C **162**
KINGSTON VALE 4A **134**
Kingston Va. SW15 . . . . .4K **133**
Kingstown St. NW1 . . . . .1E **82**
(not continuous)
King St. E13 . . . . .4J **87**
EC2 . . . . .1D **14** (6C **84**)
N2 . . . . .3B **46**
N17 . . . . .1F **49**
SW1 . . . . .5B **12** (1G **101**)
TW1: Twick 1A **132**
TW9: Rich 5D **114**
UB2: S'hall 3C **94**

King St. W3 . . . 1J **97**
W6 . . . 4C **98**
WC2 . . . 2E **12** (7J **83**)
King St. Cloisters *W6* . . . *4D 98*
(off Clifton Wlk.)
King St. Pde. *TW1: Twick* . . . *1A 132*
(off King St.)
Kings Wlk. Shop. Cen. SW3 . . . 5E **16** (5D **100**)
Kingswater Pl. SW11 . . . 7C **100**
Kings Way CR0: Wadd . . . 5K **167**
HA1: Harr . . . 4J **41**
Kingsway BR4: W W'ck . . . 3G **171**
BR5: Pet W . . . 5H **161**
EN3: Pond E . . . 5C **24**
HA9: Wemb . . . 4E **60**
IG8: Wfd G . . . 5F **37**
KT3: N Mald . . . 4E **152**
N12 . . . 6F **31**
SW14 . . . 3H **115**
TW19: Stanw . . . 1A **128**
UB3: Hayes . . . 5E **74**
WC2 . . . 7G **7** (6K **83**)
Kingsway Bus. Pk. TW12: Hamp . . . 1D **148**
Kingsway Cres. HA2: Harr . . . 4G **41**
Kingsway Est. N18 . . . 6E **34**
Kingsway Mans. *WC1* . . . *5G 7*
(off Red Lion Sq.)
Kingsway Pde. *N16* . . . *3D 66*
(off Albion Rd.)
Kingsway Pl. *EC1* . . . *3K 7*
(off Sans Wlk.)
Kingsway Rd. SM3: Cheam . . . 7G **165**
Kingswear Rd. HA4: Ruis . . . 2J **57**
NW5 . . . 3F **65**
Kings Wharf *E8* . . . *1E 84*
(off Kingsland Rd.)
Kingswood *E2* . . . *2J 85*
(off Cyprus St.)
Kingswood Av. BR2: Brom . . . 3G **159**
CR7: Thor H . . . 5A **156**
DA17: Belv . . . 4F **109**
NW6 . . . 1G **81**
TW3: Houn . . . 1D **112**
TW12: Hamp . . . 6F **131**
Kingswood Cl. BR6: Orp . . . 7J **161**
EN1: Enf . . . 5K **23**
KT3: N Mald . . . 6B **152**
KT6: Surb . . . 7E **150**
N20 . . . 7F **21**
SW8 . . . 7J **101**
TW15: Ashf . . . 5E **128**
Kingswood Ct. E4 . . . 5H **35**
NW6 . . . *7J 63*
(off West End La.)
SE13 . . . 6F **123**
Kingswood Dr. SE19 . . . 4E **138**
SM2: Sutt . . . 7K **165**
SM5: Cars . . . 1D **166**
Kingswood Est. SE21 . . . 4E **138**
Kingswood Hgts. *E18* . . . *1J 51*
(off Queen Mary Av.)
Kingswood M. N15 . . . 4B **48**
Kingswood Pk. N3 . . . 2H **45**
Kingswood Pl. SE13 . . . 4G **123**
Kingswood Rd. BR2: Brom . . . 4F **159**
E11 . . . 7G **51**
HA9: Wemb . . . 3G **61**
IG3: Ilf . . . 1A **72**
SE20 . . . 6J **139**
SW2 . . . 6J **119**
SW19 . . . 7H **135**
W4 . . . 3J **97**
Kingswood Ter. W4 . . . 3J **97**
Kingswood Way SM6: Wall . . . 5J **167**
Kingsworth Cl. BR3: Beck . . . 5A **158**
Kingsworthy Cl. KT1: King T . . . 3F **151**
Kings Yd. *SW15* . . . *3E 116*
(off Lwr. Richmond Rd.)
Kingthorpe Rd. NW10 . . . 7K **61**
Kingthorpe Ter. NW10 . . . 6K **61**
Kington Ho. *NW6* . . . *1K 81*
(off Mortimer Cres.)
Kingward Ho. *E1* . . . *5G 85*
(off Hanbury St.)
Kingweston Cl. NW2 . . . 3G **63**
King William IV Gdns. SE20 . . . 6J **139**
King William La. SE10 . . . 5G **105**
King William's Ct. *SE10* . . . *6F 105*
(off Park Row)
King William St. EC4 . . . 1F **15** (6D **84**)
King William Wlk. SE10 . . . 6E **104**
(not continuous)
Kingwood Rd. SW6 . . . 1G **117**
Kinlet Rd. SE18 . . . 1G **125**
Kinloch Dr. NW9 . . . 7K **43**
Kinloch St. N7 . . . 3K **65**
Kinloss Ct. N3 . . . 4H **45**
Kinloss Gdns. N3 . . . 3H **45**
Kinloss Rd. SM5: Cars . . . 7A **154**
Kinnaird Av. BR1: Brom . . . 6H **141**
W4 . . . 7J **97**
Kinnaird Cl. BR1: Brom . . . 6H **141**
Kinnaird Way IG8: Wfd G . . . 6J **37**
Kinnear Apartments N8 . . . 3K **47**
Kinnear Rd. W12 . . . 2B **98**
Kinnerton Pl. Nth. SW1 . . . 7F **11**
Kinnerton Pl. Sth. SW1 . . . 7F **11**
Kinnerton St. SW1 . . . 7G **11** (2E **100**)
Kinnerton Yd. SW1 . . . 7G **11**
Kinnoul Rd. W6 . . . 6G **99**
Kinross Av. KT4: Wor Pk . . . 2C **164**
Kinross Cl. HA3: Kenton . . . 5F **43**
HA8: Edg . . . 2C **28**
TW16: Sun . . . 5H **129**
Kinross Ct. *BR1: Brom* . . . *1H 159*
(off Highland Rd.)
SE6 . . . 1H **141**
Kinross Dr. TW16: Sun . . . 5H **129**
Kinross Ho. *N1* . . . *1K 83*
(off Bemerton Est.)
Kinross Ter. E17 . . . 2B **50**
Kinsale Rd. SE15 . . . 3G **121**
Kinsella Gdns. SW19 . . . 5D **134**
Kinsham Ho. *E2* . . . *4G 85*
(off Ramsey St.)
Kintore Way SE1 . . . 4F **103**
Kintyre Cl. SW16 . . . 2K **155**
Kintyre Ct. SW2 . . . 7J **119**
Kintyre Ho. *E14* . . . *1E 104*
(off Coldharbour)
Kinveachy Gdns. SE7 . . . 5C **106**
Kinver Ho. N19 . . . 2H **65**
Kinver Rd. SE26 . . . 4J **139**
Kipling Ct. W7 . . . 7K **77**
Kipling Dr. SW19 . . . 6B **136**
Kipling Est. SE1 . . . 7F **15** (2D **102**)
Kipling Ho. *E16* . . . *1K 105*
(off Southampton M.)
SE5 . . . *7D 102*
(off Elmington Est.)
Kipling Pl. HA7: Stan . . . 6E **26**
Kipling Rd. DA7: Bex . . . 1E **126**
Kipling St. SE1 . . . 7F **15** (2D **102**)
Kipling Ter. N9 . . . 3J **33**
Kipling Twr. *W3* . . . *3J 97*
(off Palmerston Rd.)
Kippington Dr. SE9 . . . 1B **142**
Kira Bldg. E3 . . . 3B **86**
Kiran Apartments *E1* . . . *6K 9*
(off Chicksand St.)
Kirby Cl. KT19: Ewe . . . 5B **164**
Kirby Est. SE16 . . . 3H **103**
Kirby Gro. SE1 . . . 6G **15** (2E **102**)
Kirby Ind. Est. UB7: Yiew . . . 7A **74**
Kirby St. EC1 . . . 5K **7** (5A **84**)
Kirby Way KT12: Walt T . . . 6A **148**
UB8: Hil . . . 4B **74**
Kirchen Rd. W13 . . . 7B **78**
Kirkby Cl. N11 . . . 6K **31**
Kirkdale SE26 . . . 2H **139**
Kirkdale Cnr. SE26 . . . 4J **139**
Kirkdale Rd. E11 . . . 1G **69**
Kirkeby Ho. *EC1* . . . *5J 7*
(off Leather La.)
Kirkfield Cl. W13 . . . 1B **96**
Kirkham Rd. E6 . . . 6C **88**
Kirkham St. SE18 . . . 6J **107**
Kirk Ho. HA9: Wemb . . . 3E **60**
Kirkland Av. IG5: Ilf . . . 2E **52**
Kirkland Cl. DA15: Sidc . . . 6J **125**
Kirkland Dr. EN2: Enf . . . 1H **23**
Kirkland Ho. *E14* . . . *5D 104*
(off St Davids Sq.)
E14 . . . *5D 104*
(off Westferry Rd.)
Kirkland Ter. BR3: Beck . . . 6C **140**
Kirkland Wlk. E8 . . . 6F **67**
Kirk La. SE18 . . . 6G **107**
Kirkleas Rd. KT6: Surb . . . 1E **162**
Kirklees Rd. CR7: Thor H . . . 5A **156**
RM8: Dag . . . 5C **72**
Kirkley Rd. SW19 . . . 1J **153**
Kirkman Pl. W1 . . . 6C **6**
Kirkmichael Rd. E14 . . . 6E **86**
Kirk Ri. SM1: Sutt . . . 3K **165**
Kirk Rd. E17 . . . 6B **50**
Kirkside Rd. SE3 . . . 6J **105**
Kirk's Place . . . 5B **86**
Kirkstall Av. N17 . . . 4D **48**
Kirkstall Gdns. SW2 . . . 1J **137**
Kirkstall Ho. *SW1* . . . *5F 101*
(off Sutherland St.)
Kirkstall Rd. SW2 . . . 1H **137**
Kirkstead Ct. E5 . . . 4K **67**
Kirksted Rd. SM4: Mord . . . 1K **165**
Kirkstone *NW1* . . . *1A 6*
(off Harrington St.)
Kirkstone Way BR1: Brom . . . 7G **141**
Kirk St. WC1 . . . 4G **7**
Kirkton Rd. N15 . . . 4E **48**
Kirkwall Pl. E2 . . . 3J **85**
Kirkwood Pl. NW1 . . . 7E **64**
Kirkwood Rd. SE15 . . . 2H **121**
Kirn Rd. W13 . . . 7B **78**
Kirrane Cl. KT3: N Mald . . . 5B **152**
Kirtley Ho. SW8 . . . 1G **119**
Kirtley Rd. SE26 . . . 4A **140**
Kirtling St. SW8 . . . 7G **101**
Kirton Cl. W4 . . . 4K **97**
Kirton Gdns. E2 . . . 2K **9** (3F **85**)
(not continuous)
Kirton Lodge SW18 . . . 6K **117**
Kirton Rd. E13 . . . 2A **88**
Kirton Wlk. HA8: Edg . . . 7D **28**
Kirwyn Way SE5 . . . 7B **102**
Kitcat Ter. E3 . . . 3C **86**
Kitchen Ct. E10 . . . 2D **68**
Kitchener Rd. CR7: Thor H . . . 3D **156**
E7 . . . 6K **69**
E17 . . . 1D **50**
N2 . . . 3C **46**
N17 . . . 3E **48**
RM10: Dag . . . 6H **73**
Kite Ho. SE1 . . . 4H **103**
Kite Pl. *E2* . . . *3G 85*
(off Warner Pl.)
Kite Yd. *SW11* . . . *1D 118*
(off Cambridge Rd.)
Kitley Gdns. SE19 . . . 1F **157**
Kitson Rd. SE5 . . . 7D **102**
SW13 . . . 1C **116**
Kittiwake Ct. *SE1* . . . *7D 14*
(off Gt. Dover St.)
SE8 . . . *6B 104*
(off Abinger Gro.)
Kittiwake Pl. SM1: Sutt . . . 5H **165**
Kittiwake Rd. UB5: N'olt . . . 3B **76**
Kittiwake Way UB4: Yead . . . 5B **76**
Kitto Rd. SE14 . . . 2K **121**
Kitts End Rd. EN5: Barn . . . 1C **20**
Kiver Rd. N19 . . . 2H **65**
Klea Av. SW4 . . . 6G **119**
Kleine Wharf N1 . . . 1E **84**
Klein's Wharf *E14* . . . *3C 104*
(off Westferry Rd.)
Knapdale Cl. SE23 . . . 2H **139**
Knapmill Rd. SE6 . . . 2C **140**
Knapmill Way SE6 . . . 2D **140**
Knapp Cl. NW10 . . . 6A **62**
Knapp Rd. E3 . . . 4C **86**
TW15: Ashf . . . 4B **128**
Knapton M. SW17 . . . 6E **136**
Knaresborough Dr. SW18 . . . 1K **135**
Knaresborough Pl. SW5 . . . 4K **99**
Knatchbull Rd. NW10 . . . 1K **79**
SE5 . . . 2B **120**
Knebworth Av. E17 . . . 1C **50**
Knebworth Cl. EN5: New Bar . . . 4E **20**
Knebworth Ho. SW8 . . . 2H **119**
Knebworth Rd. N16 . . . 4E **66**
Knee Hill SE2 . . . 4C **108**
Knee Hill Cres. SE2 . . . 4C **108**
Kneller Gdns. TW7: Isle . . . 6H **113**
Kneller Ho. *UB5: N'olt* . . . *2B 76*
(off Academy Gdns.)
Kneller Rd. KT3: N Mald . . . 7A **152**
SE4 . . . 4A **122**
TW2: Whitt . . . 6G **113**
Knevett Ter. TW3: Houn . . . 4E **112**
Knight Cl. RM8: Dag . . . 2C **72**
Knight Ct. *E4* . . . *1K 35*
(off The Ridgeway)
N15 . . . 5E **48**
Knighten St. E1 . . . 1H **103**
Knighthead Point E14 . . . 2C **104**
Knight Ho. *SE17* . . . *4E 102*
(off Tatum St.)
Knightland Rd. E5 . . . 2H **67**
Knightleas Ct. NW2 . . . 6E **62**
Knightleys Ct. *E10* . . . *1A 68*
(off Wellington Rd.)
Knighton Cl. CR2: S Croy . . . 7B **168**
IG8: Wfd G . . . 4E **36**
RM7: Rom . . . 6K **55**
Knighton Dr. IG8: Wfd G . . . 4E **36**
Knighton Grn. IG9: Buck H . . . 2E **36**
Knighton La. IG9: Buck H . . . 2E **36**
Knighton Pk. Rd. SE26 . . . 5K **139**
Knighton Rd. E7 . . . 3J **69**
RM7: Rom . . . 6J **55**
Knightrider Ct. EC4 . . . 2B **14**
Knightrider St. EC4 . . . 2B **14** (6B **84**)
Knights Arc. SW1 . . . 7E **10**
Knights Av. W5 . . . 2E **96**
KNIGHTSBRIDGE . . . 7E **10** (2C **100**)
Knightsbridge SW1 . . . 7D **10** (2D **100**)
SW7 . . . 7D **10** (2D **100**)
Knightsbridge Apartments, The
SW7 . . . *7E 10*
(off Knightsbridge)
Knightsbridge Ct. SW1 . . . 7F **11**
Knightsbridge Gdns. RM7: Rom . . . 5K **55**
Knightsbridge Grn. SW1 . . . 7E **10** (2D **100**)
(not continuous)
Knights Cl. E9 . . . 5J **67**
KT8: W Mole . . . 5D **148**
Knightscote Cl. UB9: Hare . . . 2A **38**
Knights Ct. BR1: Brom . . . 3H **141**
KT1: King T . . . 3E **150**
RM6: Chad H . . . *6E 54*
(off High Rd.)
WD23: B Hea . . . 1C **26**
Knights Hill SE27 . . . 5B **138**
Knight's Hill Sq. SE27 . . . 4B **138**
Knights Ho. *SW8* . . . *7J 101*
(off Sth. Lambeth Rd.)
SW10 . . . *7A 100*
(off Hortensia Rd.)
W14 . . . *5H 99*
(off Baron's Ct. Rd.)
Knight's Pk. KT1: King T . . . 3E **150**
Knight's Pl. TW2: Twick . . . 1J **131**
Knights Rd. E16 . . . 2J **105**
HA7: Stan . . . 4H **27**
Knight's Wlk. SE11 . . . 4K **19** (4B **102**)
(not continuous)
Knightswood Cl. HA8: Edg . . . 2D **28**
Knightswood Ct. N6 . . . 7H **47**

Knightswood Ho. N12 . . . . .6F 31
Knightwood Cres.
　KT3: N Mald 6A 152
Knivet Rd. SW6 . . . . .6J 99
Knockholt Rd. SE9 . . . . .5B 124
Knole, The SE9 . . . . .4E 142
Knole Cl. CR0: C'don 6J 157
Knole Cl. UB5: N'olt 3A 76
　　　　　　　　(off Broomcroft Av.)
Knole Ga. DA15: Sidc 3J 143
Knoll, The BR2: Hayes 2J 171
　BR3: Beck 1D 158
　HA1: Harr 1K 59
　W13 . . . . .5C 78
Knoll Cl. SE19 . . . . .5F 139
　　　　　　　　　(off Farquhar Rd.)
Knoll Cres. HA6: Nwood 2G 39
　　　　　　　　　(not continuous)
Knoll Dr. N14 . . . . .7K 21
Knoll Ho. NW8 . . . . .2A 82
　　　　　　　　　(off Carlton Hill)
Knollmead KT5: Surb 1J 163
Knoll Ri. BR6: Orp 1K 173
Knoll Rd. DA5: Bexl 7G 127
　DA14: Sidc 5B 144
　SW18 .5A 118
Knolls Cl. KT4: Wor Pk 3D 164
Knollys Cl. SW16 . . . . .3A 138
Knolly's Ho. WC1 . . . . .3E 6
　　　　　　　　　(off Tavistock Pl.)
Knollys Rd. SW16 . . . . .3K 137
Knot Ho. SE1 . . . . .5J 15
　　　　　　　　　(off Brewery Sq.)
Knotley Way BR4: W W'ck 2D 170
Knottisford St. E2 . . . . .3J 85
Knotts Grn. M. E10 . . . . .6D 50
Knotts Grn. Rd. E10 . . . . .6D 50
Knowlden Ho. E1 . . . . .7J 85
　　　　　　　　　　(off Cable St.)
Knowle Av. DA7: Bex 7E 108
Knowle Cl. SW9 . . . . .3A 120
Knowledge Ct. SW16 . . . . .3K 155
Knowle Rd. BR2: Brom 2D 172
　TW2: Twick 1J 131
Knowles Cl. UB7: Yiew 1A 92
Knowles Ct. HA1: Harr 6K 41
　　　　　　　　　(off Gayton Rd.)
Knowles Hill Cres. SE13 . . . . .5F 123
Knowles Ho. SW18 . . . . .6K 117
　　　　　　　　　(off Neville Gill Cl.)
Knowles Wlk. SW4 . . . . .3G 119
Knowles Wharf NW1 . . . . .1G 83
　　　　　　　　　(off St Pancras Way)
Knowlton Grn. BR2: Brom 5H 159
Knowlton Ho. SW9 . . . . .1A 120
　　　　　　　　　(off Cowley Rd.)
Knowsley Av. UB1: S'hall 1F 95
Knowsley Rd. SW11 . . . . .2D 118
Knox Cl. SW4 . . . . .2J 119
Knox Rd. E7 . . . . .6H 69
Knox St. W1 . . . . .5E 4 (5D 82)
Knoyle Ho. W14 . . . . .3G 99
　　　　　　　　　(off Russell Rd.)
Knoyle St. SE14 . . . . .6A 104
Koblenz Ho. N8 . . . . .3J 47
　　　　　　　　　(off Newland Rd.)
Kohat Rd. SW19 . . . . .5K 135
Korda Cl. TW17: Shep 3B 146
Kossuth St. SE10 . . . . .5G 105
Kotree Way SE1 . . . . .4G 103
Kramer M. SW5 . . . . .5J 99
Kreedman Wlk. E8 . . . . .5G 67
Kreisel Wlk. TW9: Kew 6F 97
Kristina Ct. SM2: Sutt 6J 165
　　　　　　　　　(off Overton Rd.)
Krupnik Pl. EC2 . . . . .3H 9
　　　　　　　　(shown as Curtail Pl.)
Kuala Gdns. SW16 . . . . .1K 155
Kubrick Bus. Est. E7 . . . . .4H 69
　　　　　　　　　(off Station App.)
Kuhn Way E7 . . . . .5J 69
Kurdish Mus. 4C 98

Kwame Ho. E16 . . . . .7F 89
　　　　　　　　(off University Way)
Kydbrook Cl. BR5: Pet W 7G 161
Kyle Ho. NW6 . . . . .1J 81
Kylemore Cl. E6 . . . . .2B 88
Kylemore Rd. NW6 . . . . .7J 63
Kylestrome Ho. SW1 . . . . .4H 17
　　　　　　　　　(off Cundy St.)
Kymberley Rd. HA1: Harr 6J 41
Kymberley Ct. HA2: Harr 2H 59
Kynance Gdns. HA7: Stan 1C 42
Kynance M. SW7 . . . . .3K 99
Kynance Pl. SW7 . . . . .3A 100
Kynaston Av. CR7: Thor H 5C 156
　N16 . . . . .3F 67
Kynaston Cl. HA3: Hrw W 7C 26
Kynaston Cres. CR7: Thor H 5C 156
Kynaston Rd. BR1: Brom 5J 141
　CR7: Thor H 5C 156
　EN2: Enf 1J 23
　N16 . . . . .3E 66
Kynaston Wood
　HA3: Hrw W 7C 26
Kynersley Cl. SM5: Cars 3D 166
Kynoch Rd. N18 . . . . .4D 34
Kyrle Rd. SW11 . . . . .6E 118
Kyverdale Rd. N16 . . . . .7F 49

L

Laban Cen. 6D 104
　　　　　　　　　(off Creekside)
Laboratory Spa and Health Club, The
　. . . . . .3G 47
Laburnam Av. N9 . . . . .2A 34
　N17 . . . . .7J 33
　SM1: Sutt 3C 166
　UB7: Yiew 7B 74
Laburnum Cl. E4 . . . . .6G 35
　HA0: Wemb 1G 79
　N11 . . . . .6K 31
　SE15 . . . . .7J 103
Laburnum Ct. E2 . . . . .1F 85
　HA1: Harr 6F 41
　HA7: Stan 4H 27
　SE16 . . . . .2J 103
　　　　　　　　　(off Albion St.)
Laburnum Cres. TW16: Sun 1K 147
Laburnum Gdns. CR0: C'don 7K 157
　N21 . . . . .2H 33
Laburnum Gro. HA4: Ruis 6F 39
　KT3: N Mald 2K 151
　N21 . . . . .2H 33
　NW9 . . . . .7J 43
　TW3: Houn 4D 112
　UB1: S'hall 4D 76
Laburnum Ho. BR2: Brom 1F 159
　RM10: Dag 2G 73
Laburnum Lodge N3 . . . . .2H 45
Laburnum Pl. SE9 . . . . .5E 124
Laburnum Rd. CR4: Mitc 2E 154
　SW19 .7A 136
　UB3: Harl 4H 93
Laburnums, The E6 . . . . .4C 88
Laburnum St. E2 . . . . .1F 85
Laburnum Way BR2: Brom 7E 160
　TW19: Stanw 1B 128
Labyrinth Twr. E8 . . . . .6F 67
　　　　　　　　(off Roseberry St.)
La Caye Apartments E14 . . . . .4F 105
　　　　　　　　　(off Glenaffric Av.)
Lacebark Cl. DA15: Sidc 7K 125
Lacewing Cl. E13 . . . . .3J 87
Lacey Cl. N9 . . . . .2B 34
Lacey Dr. HA8: Edg 4A 28
　RM8: Dag 3C 72
　TW12: Hamp 1D 148
Lacey M. E3 .2C 86
Lacine Ct. SE16 . . . . .2K 103
　　　　　　　　(off Christopher Cl.)
Lackington St. EC2 . . . . .5F 9 (5D 84)

Lackland Ho. SE1 . . . . .5F 103
　　　　　　　　　(off Rowcross St.)
Lacland Ho. SW10 . . . . .7B 100
　　　　　　　　(off Worlds End Est.)
Lacock Cl. SW19 . . . . .6A 136
Lacock Ct. W13 . . . . .1A 96
Lacon Ho. WC1 . . . . .5G 7
　　　　　　　　(off Theobald's Rd.)
Lacon Rd. SE22 . . . . .4G 121
Lacrosse Way SW16 . . . . .1H 155
Lacy Rd. SW15 . . . . .4F 117
　　　　　　　　　(not continuous)
Ladas Rd. SE27 . . . . .4C 138
Ladbroke Cres. W11 . . . . .6G 81
Ladbroke Gdns. W11 . . . . .7H 81
Ladbroke Gro. W10 . . . . .4F 81
　W11 . . . . .4F 81
Ladbroke Gro. Ho. W11 . . . . .7H 81
　　　　　　　　　(off Ladbroke Gro.)
Ladbroke Grove Memorial 4F 81
　　　　　　　　　(off Canal Way)
Ladbroke M. W11 . . . . .1G 99
Ladbroke Rd. EN1: Enf 6A 24
　W11 . . . . .1H 99
Ladbroke Sq. W11 . . . . .7H 81
Ladbroke Ter. W11 . . . . .7H 81
Ladbroke Wlk. W11 . . . . .1H 99
Ladbrook Cl. BR1: Brom 6G 141
　HA5: Pinn 5D 40
Ladbrooke Cres. DA14: Sidc 3D 144
Ladbrook Rd. SE25 . . . . .4D 156
Ladderstile Ride KT2: King T 5H 133
Ladderswood Way N11 . . . . .5B 32
Ladlands SE22 . . . . .7G 121
Lady Anne Ct. E18 . . . . .1J 51
　　　　　　　　(off Queen Mary Av.)
Lady Aylesford Av. HA7: Stan 5F 27
Lady Booth Rd. KT1: King T 2E 150
Ladycroft Gdns. BR6: Farnb 5G 173
Ladycroft Rd. SE13 . . . . .3D 122
Ladycroft Wlk. HA7: Stan 1D 42
Ladycroft Way BR6: Farnb 5G 173
Lady Dock Path SE16 . . . . .2A 104
Lady Elizabeth Ho. SW14 . . . . .3J 115
Ladyfern Ho. E3 . . . . .5C 86
　　　　　　　　　　(off Gail St.)
Lady Florence Courtyard SE8 . . . . . . .7C 104
　　　　　　　　　(off Reginald Sq.)
Lady Forsdyke Way KT19: Eps 7G 163
Ladygate Bowls Club 6E 38
　　　　　　　　　(off Ladygate La.)
Ladygate La. HA4: Ruis 6D 38
Lady Harewood Way KT19: Eps 7G 163
Lady Hay KT4: Wor Pk 2B 164
Lady Jane Ct. KT2: King T 2F 151
　　　　　　　　　(off London Rd.)
Lady Margaret Ho. SE17 . . . . .6D 102
　　　　　　　　　(off Queen's Row)
Lady Margaret Rd. N19 . . . . .5G 65
　NW5 . . . . .5G 65
　UB1: S'hall 7D 76
Lady May Ho. SE5 . . . . .7C 102
　　　　　　　　　(off Pitman St.)
Lady Micos Almshouses E1 . . . . .6J 85
　　　　　　　　　(off Aylward St.)
Lady Sarah Cohen Ho. N11 . . . . .6J 31
　　　　　　　　(off Asher Loftus Way)
Lady Shaw Ct. N13 . . . . .2E 32
Ladyship Ter. SE22 . . . . .7G 121
Ladysmith Av. E6 . . . . .2C 88
　IG2: Ilf .7H 53
Ladysmith Cl. NW7 . . . . .7H 29
Ladysmith Rd. E16 . . . . .3H 87
　EN1: Enf 3K 23
　　　　　　　　　(not continuous)
　HA3: W'stone 2J 41
　N17 . . . . .2G 49
　N18 . . . . .5C 34
　SE9 . . . . .6E 124
Lady Somerset Rd. NW5 . . . . .4F 65
LADYWELL .5D 122
Ladywell Arena (Running Track) 6C 122

Ladywell Cl. SE4 . . . . .5C 122
Ladywell Hgts. SE4 . . . . .6B 122
Ladywell Leisure Cen. 5E 122
Ladywell Rd. SE13 . . . . .5C 122
Ladywell St. E15 . . . . .1H 87
Ladywood Av. BR5: Pet W 5J 161
Ladywood Rd. KT6: Surb 2G 163
LA Fitness
　Aldgate .2K 15
　　　　　　　　(off Portsoken St.)
　Bayswater 7K 81
　　　　　　　　　(off Moscow Rd.)
　Bloomsbury 5G 7
　　　　　　　　(off Theobald's Rd.)
　Bromley 7D 144
　Edgware 6B 28
　Epsom .4K 163
　Finchley 3K 45
　Golders Green 7H 45
　Gospel Oak 4F 65
　Isleworth 3B 114
　　　　　　　　　(off Swan St.)
　Leadenhall 1H 15
　　　　　　　　(off Leadenhall St.)
　London Wall 6E 8
　Marylebone 5E 4 (5D 82)
　Muswell Hill 4F 47
　　　　　　　　　(off Hillfield Pk.)
　New Barnet 4G 21
　Northwood 2H 39
　Novello .2G 13
　Piccadilly 3C 12
　　　　　　　　　(off Regent St.)
　St Pauls .6C 8
　　　　　　　　　(off Little Britain)
　South Kensington 3C 16 (4C 100)
　Southgate 1C 32
　Sydenham 4J 139
　Victoria .2A 18
　　　　　　　　(off Bressenden Pl.)
　West India Quay 7C 86
Lafone Av. TW13: Felt 2A 130
Lafone St. SE1 . . . . .6J 15 (2F 103)
Lagado M. SE16 . . . . .1K 103
Lagare Apartments SE1 . . . . .6B 14
　　　　　　　　　(off Surrey Row)
Lagonda Ho. E3 . . . . .4C 86
　　　　　　　　　(off Tidworth Rd.)
Lagonier Ho. EC1 . . . . .2D 8
　　　　　　　　　(off Dingley Rd.)
Laidlaw Dr. N21 . . . . .5E 22
Laing Dean UB5: N'olt 1A 76
Laing Ho. SE5 . . . . .7C 102
Laings Av. CR4: Mitc 2D 154
Lainlock Pl. TW3: Houn 1F 113
Lainson St. SW18 . . . . .7J 117
Lairdale Cl. SE21 . . . . .1C 138
Laird Ho. SE5 . . . . .7C 102
　　　　　　　　　(off Redcar St.)
Lairs Cl. N7 .5J 65
Lait Ho. BR3: Beck 1D 158
Laitwood Rd. SW12 . . . . .1F 137
Lakanal SE5 . . . . .1E 120
　　　　　　　　(off Sceaux Gdns.)
Lake, The WD23: B Hea 1C 26
Lake Av. BR1: Brom 6J 141
Lake Bus. Cen. N17 . . . . .7B 34
Lake Cl. RM8: Dag 3D 72
　SW19 .5H 135
Lakedale Ct. IG11: Bark 4B 90
Lakedale Rd. SE18 . . . . .6J 107
Lake Dr. WD23: B Hea 2C 26
Lake Farm Country Pk. 1G 93
Lakefield Cl. SE20 . . . . .7H 139
Lakefield Rd. N22 . . . . .2B 48
Lake Footpath SE2 . . . . .2D 108
Lake Gdns. RM10: Dag 5G 73
　SM6: Wall 3F 167
　TW10: Ham 2B 132
Lakehall Gdns.
　CR7: Thor H 5B 156
Lakehall Rd. CR7: Thor H 5B 156

Lake Ho. *SE1* . . . *7C 14*
(off Southwark Bri. Rd.)
Lake Ho. Rd. E11 . . . 3J 69
Lakehurst Rd. KT19: Ewe . . . 5A 164
Lakeland Cl. HA3: Hrw W . . . 6C 26
Lakenheath N14 . . . 5B 22
Laker Ct. SW4 . . . 1J 119
Laker Ind. Est. *BR3: Beck* . . . *5A 140*
(off Kent Ho. La.)
Lake Rd. CR0: C'don . . . 2B 170
E10 . . . 7D 50
RM6: Chad H . . . 4D 54
RM9: Dag . . . 3H 91
SW19 . . . 5H 135
Laker Pl. SW15 . . . 6G 117
Lakeside BR3: Beck . . . 3D 158
EN2: Enf . . . 4C 22
KT2: King T . . . 7H 133
KT19: Ewe . . . 6A 164
N3 . . . 2K 45
SM6: Wall . . . 4F 167
W13 . . . 6C 78
Lakeside Av. IG4: Ilf . . . 4B 52
SE28 . . . 1A 108
Lakeside Cl. DA15: Sidc . . . 5C 126
HA4: Ruis . . . 4F 39
SE25 . . . 2G 157
Lakeside Ct. N4 . . . 2C 66
Lakeside Cres. EN4: E Barn . . . 5J 21
Lakeside Dr. BR2: Brom . . . 3C 172
NW10 . . . 3F 79
Lakeside Ind. Est. SL3: Coln . . . 2A 174
Lakeside Rd. N13 . . . 4E 32
SL0: Rich P . . . 3A 174
SL3: Coln, Rich P . . . 3A 174
W14 . . . 3F 99
Lakeside Station
Ruislip Lido Railway . . . 4F 39
Lakeside Ter. EC2 . . . 5D 8
Lakeside Way HA9: Wemb . . . 4G 61
Lakes Rd. BR2: Kes . . . 5A 172
Lakeswood Rd. BR5: Pet W . . . 6F 161
Lake Vw. HA8: Edg . . . 5A 28
Lake Vw. Ct. *SW1* . . . *1K 17*
(off Bressenden Pl.)
Lake Vw. Est. E3 . . . 2A 86
Lakeview Rd. DA16: Well . . . 4B 126
SE27 . . . 5A 138
Lake Vw. Ter. *N18* . . . *4A 34*
(off Sweet Briar Wlk.)
Lakis Cl. NW3 . . . 4A 64
Laleham Av. NW7 . . . 3E 28
Laleham Ct. SM1: Sutt . . . 5A 166
Laleham Ho. *E2* . . . *3J 9*
(off Camlet St.)
Laleham Rd. SE6 . . . 7E 122
TW17: Shep . . . 4B 146
Lalor St. SW6 . . . 2G 117
Lambarde Av. SE9 . . . 4E 142
Lambard Ho. *SE10* . . . *7E 104*
(off Langdale Rd.)
Lamb Cl. UB5: N'olt . . . 3C 76
Lamb Ct. *E14* . . . *7A 86*
(off Narrow St.)
Lamberhurst Ho. SE15 . . . 6J 103
Lamberhurst Rd. RM8: Dag . . . 1F 73
SE27 . . . 4A 138
Lambert Av. TW9: Rich . . . 3G 115
Lambert Ct. *DA8: Erith* . . . *6J 109*
(off Park Cres.)
Lambert Jones M. EC2 . . . 5C 8
Lambert Lodge *TW8: Bford* . . . *5D 96*
(off Layton Rd.)
Lambert Rd. E16 . . . 6K 87
N12 . . . 5G 31
SW2 . . . 5J 119
Lambert's Pl. CR0: C'don . . . 1D 168
Lamberts Rd. KT5: Surb . . . 5E 150
Lambert St. N1 . . . 7A 66
Lambert Wlk. HA9: Wemb . . . 3E 60
Lambert Way N12 . . . 5F 31
LAMBETH . . . 3G 19 (3K 101)
Lambeth Bri. SW1 . . . 3F 19 (4J 101)
Lambeth Crematorium
SW17 . . . 4A 136
Lambeth High St. SE1 . . . 4G 19 (4K 101)
Lambeth Hill EC4 . . . 2C 14 (7C 84)
Lambeth Palace . . . 2G 19 (3K 101)
Lambeth Pal. Rd. SE1 . . . 2G 19 (3K 101)
Lambeth Rd. CR0: C'don . . . 7A 156
SE1 . . . 3G 19 (4K 101)
Lambeth Towers SE11 . . . 2J 19
Lambeth Wlk. SE11 . . . 4H 19 (4K 101)
(not continuous)
Lambfold Ho. *N7* . . . *6J 65*
(off North Rd.)
Lamb Ho. *SE5* . . . *7C 102*
(off Elmington Est.)
SE10 . . . *6E 104*
(off Haddo St.)
Lambkins M. E17 . . . 4E 50
Lamb La. E8 . . . 7H 67
Lamble St. NW5 . . . 5E 64
Lambley Rd. RM9: Dag . . . 6B 72
Lambolle Pl. NW3 . . . 6C 64
Lambolle Rd. NW3 . . . 6C 64
Lambourn Cl. CR2: S Croy . . . 7B 168
NW5 . . . 4G 65
W7 . . . 2K 95
Lambourne Av. SW19 . . . 4H 135
Lambourne Ct. IG8: Wfd G . . . 7F 37
Lambourne Gdns. E4 . . . 2H 35
EN1: Enf . . . 2A 24
IG11: Bark . . . 7K 71
Lambourne Gro. SE16 . . . 5K 103
Lambourne Ho. *NW8* . . . *5B 4*
(off Broadley St.)
Lambourne Pl. SE3 . . . 1K 123
Lambourne Rd. E11 . . . 7E 50
IG3: Ilf . . . 2J 71
IG11: Bark . . . 7J 71
Lambourn Gro. KT1: King T . . . 2H 151
Lambourn Rd. SW4 . . . 3F 119
Lambrook Ho. SE15 . . . 1G 121
Lambrook Ter. SW6 . . . 1G 117
Lamb's Bldgs. EC1 . . . 4E 8 (4D 84)
Lamb's Cl. N9 . . . 2B 34
Lamb's Conduit Pas.
WC1 . . . 5G 7 (5K 83)
Lamb's Conduit St. WC1 . . . 4G 7 (4K 83)
(not continuous)
Lambscroft Av. SE9 . . . 3A 142
Lambs Mdw. IG8: Wfd G . . . 2B 52
Lamb's M. N1 . . . 1B 84
Lamb's Pas. EC1 . . . 5E 8 (4D 84)
Lambs Ter. N9 . . . 2J 33
Lamb St. E1 . . . 5J 9 (5F 85)
Lamb's Wlk. EN2: Enf . . . 2H 23
Lambton M. *N19* . . . *1J 65*
(off Lambton Rd.)
Lambton Pl. W11 . . . 7H 81
Lambton Rd. N19 . . . 1J 65
SW20 . . . 1E 152
Lamb Wlk. SE1 . . . 7G 15 (2E 102)
LAMDA . . . *5F 99*
(off Talgarth Rd.)
LAMDA Theatre . . . *4J 99*
(off Logan Pl.)
Lamerock Rd. BR1: Brom . . . 4H 141
Lamerton Rd. IG6: Ilf . . . 2F 53
Lamerton St. SE8 . . . 6C 104
Lamford Cl. N17 . . . 7J 33
Lamington St. W6 . . . 4D 98
Lamlash St. SE11 . . . 4B 102
Lamley Ho. *SE10* . . . *7D 104*
(off Ashburnham Pl.)
Lammas Av. CR4: Mitc . . . 2E 154
Lammas Grn. SE26 . . . 3H 139
Lammas Pk. Gdns. W5 . . . 1C 96
Lammas Pk. Rd. W5 . . . 2D 96
Lammas Rd. E9 . . . 7K 67
E10 . . . 2A 68
TW10: Ham . . . 4C 132
Lammermoor Rd. SW12 . . . 7F 119
Lamont Rd. SW10 . . . 7A 16 (6B 100)
Lamont Rd. Pas. SW10 . . . 7A 16
LAMORBEY . . . 1K 143
Lamorbey Cl. DA15: Sidc . . . 1K 143
Lamorna Cl. BR6: Orp . . . 7K 161
E17 . . . 2E 50
Lamorna Gro. HA7: Stan . . . 1D 42
Lampard Gro. N16 . . . 1F 67
Lampern Sq. E2 . . . 3G 85
Lampeter Cl. NW9 . . . 6A 44
Lampeter Sq. W6 . . . 6G 99
Lamplighter Cl. E1 . . . 4J 85
Lampmead Rd. SE12 . . . 5H 123
Lamp Office Ct. WC1 . . . 4G 7
Lamport Cl. SE18 . . . 4D 106
LAMPTON . . . 1F 113
Lampton Av. TW3: Houn . . . 1F 113
Lampton Ct. TW3: Houn . . . 1F 113
Lampton Ho. Cl. SW19 . . . 4F 135
Lampton Pk. Rd. TW3: Houn . . . 2F 113
Lampton Rd. TW3: Houn . . . 2F 113
Lampton Sports Cen. . . . 2E 112
Lanacre Av. NW9 . . . 1K 43
Lanadron Cl. TW7: Isle . . . 2K 113
Lanain Ct. SE12 . . . 7H 123
Lanark Cl. W5 . . . 5C 78
Lanark Ct. *UB5: N'olt* . . . *5E 58*
(off Newmarket Av.)
Lanark Ho. *SE1* . . . *5G 103*
(off Old Kent Rd.)
Lanark Mans. *W9* . . . *4A 82*
(off Lanark Rd.)
W12 . . . *2E 98*
(off Pennard Rd.)
Lanark M. W9 . . . 3A 82
Lanark Pl. W9 . . . 3A 4 (4A 82)
Lanark Rd. W9 . . . 2K 81
Lanark Sq. E14 . . . 3D 104
Lanata Wlk. *UB4: Yead* . . . *4B 76*
(off Alba Cl.)
Lanbury Rd. SE15 . . . 4K 121
Lancashire Ct. W1 . . . 2K 11
Lancaster Av. CR4: Mitc . . . 5J 155
E18 . . . 4K 51
EN4: Had W . . . 1F 21
IG11: Bark . . . 7J 71
SE27 . . . 2B 138
SW19 . . . 5F 135
Lancaster Cl. BR2: Brom . . . 4H 159
KT2: King T . . . 5D 132
N1 . . . 7E 66
N17 . . . 7B 34
NW9 . . . 7G 29
TW15: Ashf . . . 4A 128
TW19: Stanw . . . 6A 110
W2 . . . *7K 81*
(off St Petersburgh Pl.)
Lancaster Cotts. TW10: Rich . . . 6E 114
Lancaster Ct. KT12: Walt T . . . 7J 147
SE27 . . . 2B 138
SM2: Sutt . . . *7J 165*
(off Mulgrave Rd.)
SW6 . . . 7H 99
TW19: Stanw . . . 1A 128
W2 . . . *2A 10*
(off Lancaster Ga.)
Lancaster Dr. E14 . . . 1E 104
NW3 . . . 6C 64
Lancaster Gdns. BR1: Brom . . . 5C 160
KT2: King T . . . 5D 132
SW19 . . . 5G 135
W13 . . . 2B 96
Lancaster Ga. W2 . . . 2A 10 (7A 82)
Lancaster Gro. NW3 . . . 6B 64
Lancaster Hall *E16* . . . *1J 105*
(off Wesley Av.)
Lancaster House . . . 6A 12
Lancaster Ho. E11 . . . 2H 69
EN2: Enf . . . 1J 23
TW7: Isle . . . 7K 95
Lancaster Lodge *W11* . . . *6G 81*
(off Lancaster Rd.)
Lancaster M. SW18 . . . 5K 117
TW10: Rich . . . 6E 114
W2 . . . 2A 10 (7A 82)
Lancaster Pk. TW10: Rich . . . 5E 114
Lancaster Pl. IG1: Ilf . . . 5G 71
SW19 . . . 5F 135
TW1: Twick . . . 6A 114
TW4: Houn . . . 2A 112
WC2 . . . 2G 13 (7K 83)
Lancaster Rd. E7 . . . 7J 69
E11 . . . 2G 69
E17 . . . 2K 49
EN2: Enf . . . 1J 23
EN4: E Barn . . . 5G 21
HA2: Harr . . . 5E 40
N4 . . . 7K 47
N11 . . . 6C 32
N18 . . . 5A 34
NW10 . . . 5C 62
SE25 . . . 2F 157
SW19 . . . 5F 135
UB1: S'hall . . . 7C 76
UB5: N'olt . . . 6G 59
W11 . . . 6G 81
Lancaster Rd. Ind. Est. EN4: E Barn . . . 5G 21
Lancaster Stables NW3 . . . 6C 64
Lancaster St. SE1 . . . 7A 14 (2B 102)
Lancaster Ter. W2 . . . 2A 10 (7B 82)
Lancaster Wlk. UB3: Hayes . . . 6E 74
W2 . . . 3A 10 (1A 100)
Lancaster Way KT4: Wor Pk . . . 7D 152
Lancastrian Rd. SM6: Wall . . . 7J 167
Lancefield Ho. SE15 . . . 4H 121
Lancefield St. W10 . . . 3H 81
Lancell St. N16 . . . 2F 67
Lancelot Av. HA0: Wemb . . . 4D 60
Lancelot Cres. HA0: Wemb . . . 4D 60
Lancelot Gdns. EN4: E Barn . . . 7K 21
Lancelot Pl. SW7 . . . 7E 10 (2D 100)
Lancelot Rd. DA16: Well . . . 4A 126
HA0: Wemb . . . 4D 60
Lance Rd. HA1: Harr . . . 7G 41
Lancer Sq. *W8* . . . *2K 99*
(off Kensington Chu. St.)
Lancey Cl. SE7 . . . 4C 106
Lanchester Ct. *W2* . . . *1E 10*
(off Seymour St.)
Lanchester Rd. N6 . . . 5D 46
Lanchester Way SE14 . . . 1J 121
Lancing Gdns. N9 . . . 1A 34
Lancing Ho. *CR0: C'don* . . . *4D 168*
(off Coombe Rd.)
Lancing Rd. CR0: C'don . . . 7K 155
IG2: Ilf . . . 6H 53
TW13: Felt . . . 2H 129
W13 . . . 7B 78
Lancing St. NW1 . . . 2C 6 (3H 83)
Lancresse Ct. *N1* . . . *1E 84*
(off De Beauvoir Est.)
Landale Ho. *SE16* . . . *3J 103*
(off Lower Rd.)
Landau Ct. *CR2: S Croy* . . . *5C 168*
(off Warham Rd.)
Landcroft Rd. SE22 . . . 5F 121
Landells Rd. SE22 . . . 6F 121
Landford Rd. SW15 . . . 3E 116
Landgrove Rd. SW19 . . . 5J 135
Landin Ho. *E14* . . . *6C 86*
(off Thomas Rd.)
Landleys Fld. *N7* . . . *5H 65*
(off Long Mdw.)
Landmann Ho. *SE16* . . . *4H 103*
(off Rennie Est.)
Landmann Way SE14 . . . 5K 103
Landmark Arts Cen. . . . 5B 132
Landmark Commercial Cen. N18 . . . 6K 33
Landmark E. Twr. *E14* . . . *2C 104*
(off Marsh Wall)
Landmark Hgts. E5 . . . 4A 68
Landmark Ho. *W6* . . . *5E 98*
(off Hammersmith Bri. Rd.)
Landmark Sq. E14 . . . 2C 104

Landmark W. Twr. *E14* 2C **104**
(*off Marsh Wall*)
Landon Pl. SW1 .....1E **16** (3D **100**)
Landon's Cl. E14 .....1E **104**
Landon Wlk. E14 .....7D **86**
Landon Way TW15: Ashf 6D **128**
Landor Ho. *SE5* *7D* **102**
(*off Elmington Est.*)
W2 .....*5J* **81**
(*off Westbourne Pk. Rd.*)
Landor Rd. SW9 .....3J **119**
Landor Theatre 3J **119**
Landor Wlk. W12 .....2C **98**
Landra Gdns. N21 .....6G **23**
Landrake *NW1* *1G* **83**
(*off Plender St.*)
Landridge Dr. EN1: Enf 1C **24**
Landridge Rd. SW6 .....2H **117**
Landrock Rd. N8 .....6J **47**
Landscape Rd. IG8: Wfd G 7E **36**
Landsdown Cl.
EN5: New Bar 4F **21**
Landseer Av. E12 .....5E **70**
Landseer Cl. HA8: Edg 2G **43**
SW19 .....1A **154**
Landseer Ct. UB4: Hayes 2F **75**
Landseer Ho. *NW8* *3B* **4**
(*off Frampton St.*)
SW1 .....*4D* **18**
(*off Herrick St.*)
SW11 .....1E **118**
UB5: N'olt *2B* **76**
(*off Parkfield Dr.*)
Landseer Rd. EN1: Enf 5B **24**
KT3: N Mald 7K **151**
N19 .....3J **65**
(not continuous)
SM1: Sutt 6J **165**
Landstead Rd. SE18 .....7H **107**
Landulph Ho. *SE11* *5K* **19**
(*off Kennings Way*)
Landward Ct. *W1* *7D* **4**
(*off Harrowby St.*)
Lane, The NW8 .....2A **82**
SE3 .....3J **123**
Lane Cl. NW2 .....3D **62**
Lane End DA7: Bex 3H **127**
SW15 .....6F **117**
Lane Gdns. WD23: B Hea 1D **26**
Lane M. E12 .....3D **70**
Lanercost Cl. SW2 .....2A **138**
Lanercost Gdns. N14 .....7D **22**
Lanercost Rd. SW2 .....2A **138**
Lanesborough Ct. *N1* *1G* **9**
(*off Fanshaw St.*)
Lanesborough Pl. SW1 .....6H **11**
Laneside BR7: Chst 5F **143**
HA8: Edg 5D **28**
Laneside Av. RM8: Dag 7F **55**
Laneway SW15 .....5D **116**
Laney Ho. *EC1* *5J* **7**
(*off Leather La.*)
Lanfranc Ct. HA1: Harr 3K **59**
Lanfranc Rd. E3 .....2A **86**
Lanfrey Pl. W14 .....5H **99**
Langbourne Av. N6 .....2E **64**
Langbourne Ct. E17 .....6A **50**
Langbourne Mans. N6 .....2E **64**
Langbourne Pl. E14 .....5D **104**
Langbourne Way KT10: Clay 6A **162**
Langbrook Rd. SE3 .....3B **124**
Langcroft Cl. SM5: Cars 3D **166**
Langdale *NW1* *1A* **6**
(*off Stanhope St.*)
Langdale Av. CR4: Mitc 3D **154**
Langdale Cl. BR6: Farnb 3F **173**
RM8: Dag 1C **72**
SE17 .....6C **102**
SW14 .....4H **115**
Langdale Cres. DA7: Bex 7G **109**
Langdale Dr. UB4: Hayes 2G **75**
Langdale Gdns. UB6: G'frd 3B **78**
Langdale Ho. *SW1* *6A* **18**
(*off Churchill Gdns.*)
Langdale Pde. CR4: Mitc 3D **154**
Langdale Rd. CR7: Thor H 4A **156**
SE10 .....7E **104**
Langdale St. E1 .....6H **85**
Langdon Ct. *EC1* *1B* **8**
(*off City Rd.*)
NW10 .....1A **80**
Langdon Cres. E6 .....2E **88**
Langdon Dr. NW9 .....1J **61**
Langdon Ho. *E14* *6E* **86**
(*off Ida St.*)
Langdon Pk. TW11: Tedd 7C **132**
Langdon Park Leisure Cen. 6E **86**
Langdon Pk. Rd. N6 .....7G **47**
Langdon Pl. SW14 .....3J **115**
Langdon Rd. BR2: Brom 3K **159**
E6 .....1E **88**
SM4: Mord 5A **154**
Langdons Ct. UB2: S'hall 3E **94**
Langdon Shaw DA14: Sidc 5K **143**
Langdon Wlk. SM4: Mord 5A **154**
Langdon Way SE1 .....4G **103**
Langford Cl. E8 .....5G **67**
NW8 .....2A **82**
W3 .....2H **97**
Langford Ct. *NW8* *2A* **82**
(*off Abbey Rd.*)
Langford Cres. EN4: Cockf 4J **21**
Langford Grn. SE5 .....3E **120**
Langford Ho. SE8 .....6C **104**
Langford M. N1 .....7A **66**
SW11 .....*4B* **118**
(*off St John's Hill*)
Langford Pl. DA14: Sidc 3A **144**
NW8 .....2A **82**
Langford Rd. EN4: Cockf 4J **21**
IG8: Wfd G 6F **37**
SW6 .....2K **117**
Langfords IG9: Buck H 2G **37**
Langham Cl. BR2: Brom 2C **172**
N15 .....*3B* **48**
(*off Langham Rd.*)
Langham Ct. HA4: Ruis 5K **57**
NW4 .....5F **45**
SW20 .....2E **152**
Langham Dr. RM6: Chad H 6B **54**
Langham Gdns. HA0: Wemb 2C **60**
HA8: Edg 7D **28**
N21 .....5F **23**
TW10: Ham 4C **132**
W13 .....7B **78**
Langham Ho. Cl. TW10: Ham 4D **132**
Langham Mans. *SW5* *5K* **99**
(*off Earl's Ct. Sq.*)
Langham Pk. Pl. BR2: Brom 4H **159**
Langham Pl. N15 .....3B **48**
W1 .....6K **5** (5F **83**)
W4 .....6A **98**
Langham Rd. HA8: Edg 6D **28**
N15 .....3B **48**
SW20 .....1E **152**
TW11: Tedd 5B **132**
Langham St. W1 .....6K **5** (5F **83**)
Langhedge Cl. N18 .....6A **34**
Langhedge La. N18 .....6A **34**
Langhedge La. Ind. Est.
N18 .....6A **34**
Langholm Cl. SW12 .....7H **119**
Langholme WD23: Bush 1B **26**
Langhorn Dr. TW2: Twick 7J **113**
Langhorne Ct. *NW8* *7B* **64**
(*off Dorman Way*)
Langhorne Rd. RM10: Dag 7G **73**
Lang Ho. *SW8* *7J* **101**
(*off Hartington Rd.*)
TW19: Stanw 1A **128**
Langland Cres. HA7: Stan 2D **42**
Langland Dr. HA5: Pinn 1C **40**
Langland Gdns. CR0: C'don 2B **170**
NW3 .....5K **63**
Langland Ho. *SE5* *7D* **102**
(*off Edmund St.*)
Langler Rd. NW10 .....2E **80**
Langley Av. HA4: Ruis 2K **57**
KT4: Wor Pk 1F **165**
KT6: Surb 1D **162**
Langley Ct. WC2 .....2E **12** (7J **83**)
Langley Cres. E11 .....7A **52**
HA8: Edg 3D **28**
RM9: Dag 7C **72**
UB3: Harl 7H **93**
Langley Dr. E11 .....7K **51**
W3 .....2H **97**
Langley Gdns. BR2: Brom 4A **160**
BR5: Pet W 6F **161**
RM9: Dag 7D **72**
Langley Gro. KT3: N Mald 2A **152**
Langley Ho. *W2* *5J* **81**
(*off Alfred Rd.*)
Langley La. SW8 .....7F **19** (6K **101**)
Langley Mans. SW8 .....7F **19**
Langley M. RM9: Dag 7D **72**
Langley Pk. NW7 .....6F **29**
Langley Pk. Rd. SM1: Sutt 5A **166**
SM2: Sutt 6A **166**
Langley Pk. Sports Cen. 6E **158**
Langley Rd. BR3: Beck 4A **158**
DA16: Well 6C **108**
KT6: Surb 7E **150**
SW19 .....1H **153**
TW7: Isle 2K **113**
Langley Row EN5: Barn 1C **20**
Langley St. WC2 .....1E **12** (6J **83**)
Langley Way BR4: W W'ck 1F **171**
Langmead Dr. WD23: B Hea 1D **26**
Langmead Ho. *E3* *3D* **86**
(*off Bruce Rd.*)
Langmead St. SE27 .....4B **138**
Langmore Ct. DA6: Bex 3D **126**
Langmore Ho. *E1* *6G* **85**
(*off Stutfield St.*)
Langport Ct. KT12: Walt T 7A **148**
Langport Ho. SW9 .....2B **120**
Langridge M. TW12: Hamp 6D **130**
Langroyd Rd. SW17 .....2D **136**
Langside Av. SW15 .....4C **116**
Langside Cres. N14 .....3C **32**
Langstone Way NW7 .....7A **30**
Langston Hughes Cl. SE24 .....4B **120**
Lang St. E1 .....4J **85**
Langthorn Ct. EC2 .....7E **8** (6D **84**)
Langthorne Ct. BR1: Brom 4E **140**
Langthorne Ho. *E3* *3B* **86**
(*off Merchant St.*)
UB3: Harl 4G **93**
Langthorne Rd. E11 .....3E **68**
Langthorne St. SW6 .....7F **99**
Langton Av. E6 .....3E **88**
N20 .....7F **21**
Langton Cl. WC1 .....3H **7** (4K **83**)
Langton Ho. SE11 .....3H **19**
Langton Pl. SW18 .....1J **135**
Langton Ri. SE23 .....7H **121**
Langton Rd. HA3: Hrw W 7B **26**
KT8: W Mole 4G **149**
NW2 .....3E **62**
SW9 .....7B **102**
Langton St. SW10 .....6A **100**
Langton Way CR0: C'don 3E **168**
SE3 .....1H **123**
Langtry Ct. TW7: Isle 2K **113**
Langtry Ho. *KT2: King T* *1G* **151**
(*off London Rd.*)
Langtry Pl. SW6 .....6J **99**
Langtry Rd. NW8 .....1K **81**
UB5: N'olt 2B **76**
Langtry Wlk. NW8 .....1K **81**
Langwood Chase TW11: Tedd 6C **132**
Langworth Dr. UB4: Yead 6K **75**
Lanhill Rd. W9 .....4J **81**
Lanier Rd. SE13 .....6F **123**
Lanigan Dr. TW3: Houn 5F **113**
Lankaster Gdns. N2 .....1B **46**
Lankers Dr. HA2: Harr 6D **40**
Lankton Cl. BR3: Beck 1E **158**
Lannock Rd. UB3: Hayes 1H **93**
Lannoy Point *SW6* *7G* **99**
(*off Pellant Rd.*)
Lannoy Rd. SE9 .....1G **143**
Lanrick Ho. *E14* *6F* **87**
(*off Lanrick Rd.*)
Lanrick Rd. E14 .....6F **87**
Lanridge Rd. SE2 .....3D **108**
Lansbury Av. IG11: Bark 7A **72**
N18 .....5J **33**
RM6: Chad H 5E **54**
TW14: Felt 6K **111**
Lansbury Cl. NW10 .....5J **61**
Lansbury Ct. *SE28* *7B* **90**
(*off Saunders Way*)
Lansbury Dr. UB4: Hayes 2G **75**
Lansbury Est. E14 .....6D **86**
Lansbury Gdns. E14 .....6F **87**
Lansbury Rd. EN3: Enf H 1E **24**
Lansbury Way N18 .....5K **33**
Lanscombe Wlk. SW8 .....1J **119**
Lansdell Ho. *SW2* *6A* **120**
(*off Tulse Hill*)
Lansdell Rd. CR4: Mitc 2E **154**
Lansdowne Av. BR6: Farnb 1F **173**
DA7: Bex 7D **108**
Lansdowne Cl. KT6: Surb 2H **163**
SW20 .....7F **135**
TW1: Twick 1K **131**
Lansdowne Ct. IG5: Ilf 3C **52**
KT4: Wor Pk 2C **164**
W11 .....*7G* **81**
(*off Lansdowne Ri.*)
Lansdowne Cres. W11 .....7G **81**
Lansdowne Dr. E8 .....6G **67**
Lansdowne Gdns. SW8 .....1J **119**
Lansdowne Grn. SW8 .....1J **119**
Lansdowne Gro. NW10 .....4A **62**
Lansdowne Hill SE27 .....3B **138**
Lansdowne Ho. *W11* *1H* **99**
(*off Ladbroke Rd.*)
Lansdowne La. SE7 .....6B **106**
Lansdowne M. SE7 .....5B **106**
W11 .....1H **99**
Lansdowne Pl. SE1 .....3D **102**
SE19 .....7F **139**
Lansdowne Ri. W11 .....7G **81**
Lansdowne Rd. BR1: Brom 7J **141**
CR0: C'don 2D **168**
E4 .....2H **35**
E11 .....2H **69**
E17 .....6C **50**
E18 .....3J **51**
HA1: Harr 7J **41**
HA7: Stan 6H **27**
IG3: Ilf 1K **71**
KT19: Ewe 7J **163**
N3 .....7D **30**
N10 .....2G **47**
N17 .....1F **49**
SW20 .....7E **134**
TW3: Houn 3F **113**
UB8: Hil 6E **74**
W11 .....7G **81**
Lansdowne Row W1 .....4K **11** (1F **101**)
Lansdowne Ter. WC1 .....4F **7** (4J **83**)
Lansdowne Wlk. W11 .....1H **99**
Lansdowne Way SW8 .....1H **119**
Lansdowne Wood Cl. SE27 .....3B **138**
Lansdowne Workshops SE7 .....5A **106**
Lansdown Rd. DA14: Sidc 3B **144**
E7 .....7A **70**
Lansfield Av. N18 .....4B **34**
Lanson Apartments SW8 .....7F **101**
Lantern *SE1* *6C* **14**
(*off Lant St.*)
Lantern Cl. BR6: Farnb 4F **173**
HA0: Wemb 5D **60**
SW15 .....4C **116**

Lantern Ho. *UB3: Harl* 3E *92*
            (off Nine Acres Cl.)
Lanterns Ct. E14 . . . . .2D 104
Lantern Way UB7: W Dray 2A 92
Lant Ho. *SE1* 7C 14
            (off Toulmin St.)
Lantry Ct. W3 .1H 97
Lant St. SE1 . . . . .6C 14 (2C 102)
Lanvanor Rd. SE15 . . . . .2J 121
Lanyard Ho. SE8 . . . . .4B 104
Lapford Cl. W9 . . . . .4H 81
Lapis Cl. NW10 . . . . .3G 79
Lapponum Wlk. UB4: Yead 4B 76
Lapse Wood Wlk. SE23 . . . . .1H 139
Lapstone Gdns. HA3: Kenton 6C 42
Lapwing Ct. KT6: Surb 3G 163
  SE1 . . . . .7D 14
            (off Swan St.)
Lapwing Ter. E7 . . . . .5B 70
Lapwing Twr. *SE8* 6B *104*
            (off Taylor Cl.)
Lapwing Way UB4: Yead 6B 76
Lapworth *N11* 4A *32*
            (off Coppies Gro.)
Lapworth Ct. *W2* 5K *81*
            (off Delamere Ter.)
Lara Cl. KT9: Chess 7E *162*
  SE13 . . . . .6E 122
Larbert Rd. SW16 . . . . .7G 137
Larch Av. W3 .1A 98
Larch Cl. E13 .4K 87
  N11 . . . . .7K 31
  N19 . . . . .2G 65
  SE8 . . . . .6B 104
  SW12 . . . . .2F 137
Larch Ct. *SE1* .7G *15*
            (off Royal Oak Yd.)
  W9 . . . . .5J *81*
            (off Admiral Wlk.)
Larch Cres. KT19: Ewe 6H 163
  UB4: Yead 4A 76
Larch Dene BR6: Farnb 2E 172
Larch Dr. W4 .5G 97
Larches, The N13 . . . . .3H 33
  UB10: Hil .3D 74
Larches Av. SW14 . . . . .4K 115
Larch Grn. NW9 . . . . .1A 44
Larch Gro. DA15: Sidc 1K 143
Larch Ho. BR2: Brom 1G 159
  SE16 . . . . .2J *103*
            (off Ainsty Est.)
  UB4: Yead 5A 76
  W10 . . . . .4G *81*
            (off Rowan Wlk.)
Larch Rd. E10 . . . . .2C 68
  NW2 . . . . .4E 62
Larch Tree Way CRO: C'don 3C 170
Larchvale Ct. SM2: Sutt 7K 165
Larch Way BR2: Brom 7E 160
Larchwood Ho. *UB7: W Dray* 2B *92*
            (off Park Lodge Av.)
Larchwood Rd. SE9 . . . . .2F 143
Larcombe Cl. CRO: C'don 4F 169
Larcombe Ct. *SM2: Sutt* 7K *165*
            (off Worcester Rd.)
Larcom St. SE17 . . . . .4C *102*
Larden Rd. W3 . . . . .1A 98
Largewood Av. KT6: Surb 2G 163
Larissa St. SE17 . . . . .5D *102*
Larkbere Rd. SE26 . . . . .4A 140
Larken Cl. WD23: Bush 1B 26
Larken Dr. WD23: Bush 1B 26
Larkfield Av. HA3: Kenton 3B 42
Larkfield Cl. BR2: Hayes 2H 171
Larkfield Rd. DA14: Sidc 3K 143
  TW9: Rich 4E 114
Larkhall La. SW4 . . . . .2H 119
Larkhall Ri. SW4 . . . . .3G 119
            (not continuous)
Larkham Cl. TW13: Felt 3G 129
Larkhill Ter. SE18 . . . . .7E 106
Lark Row E2 . . . . .1J 85

Larksfield Gro. EN1: Enf 1C 24
Larks Gro. IG11: Bark 7J 71
Larkshall Ct. RM7: Mawney 2J 55
Larkshall Cres. E4 . . . . .4K 35
Larkshall Rd. E4 . . . . .5K 35
Larkspur Cl. E6 . . . . .5C 88
  HA4: Ruis .7E 38
  N17 . . . . .7J 33
  NW9 . . . . .5H 43
Larkspur Gro. HA8: Edg 4D 28
Larkspur Lodge DA14: Sidc 3B 144
Larkspur Way KT19: Ewe 5J 163
Larkswood Cl. E4 . . . . .5A 36
Larkswood Leisure Cen. 4K 35
Larkswood Ri. HA5: Eastc 4A 40
Larkswood Rd. E4 . . . . .4H 35
Lark Way SM5: Cars 7C 154
Larkway Cl. NW9 . . . . .4K 43
Larnaca Ho. *SE1* 3F *103*
            (off Grange Wlk.)
Larnach Rd. W6 . . . . .6F 99
Larne Rd. HA4: Ruis 7H 39
Larpent Av. SW15 . . . . .5E 116
Larwood Cl. UB6: G'frd 5H 59
Lascelles Av. HA1: Harr 7H 41
Lascelles Cl. E11 . . . . .2F 69
Lascelles Ho. NW1 . . . . .4D 4
Lascotts Rd. N22 . . . . .6E 32
Laseron Ho. *N15* 4F *49*
          (off Tottenham Grn. E.)
Las Palmas Est. TW17: Shep 7E 146
Lassa Rd. SE9 . . . . .5C 124
Lassell St. SE10 . . . . .5F 105
Lasseter Pl. SE3 . . . . .6H 105
Latchett Rd. E18 . . . . .1K 51
Latchingdon Ct. E17 . . . . .4K 49
Latchingdon Gdns. IG8: Wfd G 6H 37
Latchmere Cl. TW10: Ham 5E 132
Latchmere La. KT2: King T 6F 133
  TW10: Ham 6F 133
Latchmere Leisure Cen. 2D 118
Latchmere Pas. SW11 . . . . .2C 118
Latchmere Rd. KT2: King T 7E 132
  SW11 . . . . .2D 118
Latchmere St. SW11 . . . . .2D 118
Lateward Rd. TW8: Bford 6D 96
Latham Cl. E6 .5C 88
  TW1: Twick 7A 114
Latham Ct. *N11* 6D *32*
            (off Brownlow Rd.)
  SW5 . . . . .4J *99*
          (off W. Cromwell Rd.)
  UB5: N'olt .3B 76
            (off Delta Gro.)
Latham Ho. *E1* 6K *85*
            (off Chudleigh St.)
Latham Rd. DA6: Bex 5G 127
  TW1: Twick 7K 113
Latham's Way CRO: Wadd 1K 167
Lathkill Cl. EN1: Enf 7B 24
Lathkill Ct. BR3: Beck 1B 158
Lathom Rd. E6 . . . . .7C 70
Latimer Av. E6 . . . . .1D 88
Latimer Cl. HA5: Pinn 1A 40
  KT4: Wor Pk 4D 164
Latimer Ct. *BR2: Brom* 4H *159*
            (off Durham Rd.)
Latimer Gdns. HA5: Pinn 1A 40
Latimer Ho. E9 . . . . .6K 67
  W11 . . . . .7H *81*
          (off Kensington Pk. Rd.)
Latimer Ind. Est. W10 . . . . .6E 80
Latimer Pl. W10 . . . . .6E 80
Latimer Rd. CRO: C'don 3B 168
  E7 . . . . .4K 69
  EN5: New Bar 3E 20
  N15 . . . . .6E 48
  SW19 . . . . .6K 135
  TW11: Tedd 5K 131
  W10 . . . . .5E 80
            (not continuous)
Latitude Ct. E16 . . . . .7G 89

Latitude Ho. *NW1* 1F *83*
            (off Oval Rd.)
Latona Ct. *SW9* 7A *102*
            (off Caldwell St.)
Latona Rd. SE15 . . . . .6G 103
La Tourne Gdns. BR6: Farnb 3G 173
Lattimer Pl. W4 . . . . .7A 98
Latton Cl. KT12: Walt T 7C 148
Latvia Ct. *SE17* 5C *102*
            (off Sutherland Sq.)
Latymer Ct. W6 . . . . .4F 99
Latymer Gdns. N3 . . . . .2G 45
Latymer Rd. N9 . . . . .1A 34
Latymer Way N9 . . . . .2K 33
Laubin Cl. TW1: Twick 4B 114
Lauder Cl. UB5: N'olt 2B 76
Lauder Ct. N14 . . . . .7D 22
Lauderdale Community Arts Cen. 1F *65*
        (within Lauderdale House)
Lauderdale Dr. TW10: Ham 3D 132
Lauderdale House 1F 65
Lauderdale Ho. *SW9* 1A *120*
            (off Gosling Way)
Lauderdale Pde. W9 . . . . .4K 81
            (off Lauderdale Rd.)
Lauderdale Pl. *EC2* 5C *8*
            (off Beech St.)
Lauderdale Rd. W9 . . . . .3K 81
Lauderdale Twr. EC2 . . . . .5C *8*
Laud St. CRO: C'don 3D 168
  SE11 . . . . .5G 19 (5K 101)
Laugan Wlk. SE17 . . . . .5C 102
Laughton Rd. UB5: N'olt 1B 76
Launcelot Rd. BR1: Brom 4J 141
Launcelot St. SE1 . . . . .7J 13 (2A 102)
Launceston Gdns. UB6: G'frd 1C 78
Launceston Pl. W8 . . . . .3A 100
Launceston Rd. UB6: G'frd 1C 78
Launch St. E14 . . . . .3E 104
Launders Ga. W3 . . . . .2H 97
Laundress La. N16 . . . . .3G 67
Laundry La. N1 . . . . .1C 84
Laundry M. SE23 . . . . .7A 122
Laundry Rd. W6 . . . . .6G 99
Launton Dr. DA6: Bex 4D 126
Laura Cl. E11 .5A 52
  EN1: Enf 5K 23
Lauradale Rd. N2 . . . . .4D 46
Laura Pl. E5 . . . . .4J 67
Laura Ter. N4 .2B 66
Laurel Apartments *SE17* 4E *102*
            (off Townsend St.)
Laurel Av. TW1: Twick 1K 131
Laurel Bank N12 . . . . .4F 31
Laurel Bank Gdns. SW6 . . . . .2H 117
Laurel Bank Rd. EN2: Enf 1H 23
Laurel Bank Vs. W7 . . . . .2J *95*
           (off Lwr. Boston Rd.)
Laurelbrook SE6 . . . . .3G 141
Laurel Cl. DA14: Sidc 3A 144
  N19 . . . . .2G 65
  SW17 . . . . .5C 136
Laurel Ct. *CR2: S Croy* 4E *168*
           (off South Pk. Hill Rd.)
  HA0: Wemb 2E 78
Laurel Cres. CRO: C'don 3C 170
  RM7: Rush G 1K 73
Laurel Dr. N21 . . . . .7F 23
Laurel Gdns. BR1: Brom 4C 160
  E4 . . . . .7J 25
  NW7 . . . . .3E 28
  TW4: Houn 4C 112
  W7 . . . . .1J 95
Laurel Gro. SE20 . . . . .7H 139
  SE26 . . . . .4K 139
Laurel Ho. BR2: Brom 1G 159
  E3 . . . . .1B *86*
            (off Hornbeam Sq.)
  SE8 . . . . .6B 104
Laurel La. UB7: W Dray 4A 92
Laurel Mnr. SM2: Sutt 7A 166

Laurel Pk. HA3: Hrw W 7E 26
Laurel Rd. SW13 . . . . .2C 116
  SW20 . . . . .1D 152
  TW12: Ham H 5H 131
Laurels, The BR1: Brom 1K 159
  BR2: Brom 4J 159
  IG9: Buck H 1F 37
  NW10 . . . . .1D 80
  WD23: B Hea 2D 26
Laurel St. E8 . . . . .6F 67
Laurel Vw. N12 . . . . .3E 30
Laurel Way E18 . . . . .4H 51
  N20 . . . . .3D 30
Laurence Ct. E10 . . . . .7D 50
  W11 . . . . .7G *81*
           (off Lansdowne Rd.)
Laurence M. W12 . . . . .2C 98
Laurence Pountney Hill EC4 . .2E 14 (7D 84)
Laurence Pountney La. EC4 . .2E 14 (7D 84)
Laurence Rd. TW3: Houn 3G 113
Laurie Gro. SE14 . . . . .1A 122
Laurie Ho. *SE1* 3B *102*
           (off St George's Rd.)
  W8 . . . . .1J *99*
            (off Airlie Gdns.)
Laurie Rd. W7 .5J 77
Laurier Rd. CRO: C'don 7F 157
  NW5 . . . . .3F 65
Laurimel Cl. HA7: Stan 6G 27
Laurino Pl. WD23: B Hea 2B 26
Lauriston Ho. *E9* 7J *67*
            (off Lauriston Rd.)
Lauriston Rd. E9 . . . . .7J 67
  SW19 . . . . .6F 135
Lausanne Rd. N8 . . . . .4A 48
  SE15 . . . . .1J 121
Lavell Ho. N16 . . . . .4D 66
Lavender Av. CR4: Mitc 1C 154
  KT4: Wor Pk 3E 164
  NW9 . . . . .1J 61
Lavender Cl. BR2: Brom 6C 160
  E4 . . . . .6A 35
  SM5: Cars 4F 167
  SW3 . . . . .7B 16 (6B 100)
Lavender Ct. KT8: W Mole 3F 149
  SM2: Sutt 7A 166
  TW14: Felt 6K 111
Lavender Gdns. EN2: Enf 1G 23
  HA3: Hrw W 6D 26
  SW11 . . . . .4D 118
Lavender Gro. CR4: Mitc 1C 154
  E8 . . . . .7G 67
Lavender Hill EN2: Enf 1F 23
  SW11 . . . . .4C 118
Lavender Ho. *SE16* 1K *103*
            (off Rotherhithe St.)
  TW9: Kew 1H 115
Lavender Pl. IG1: Ilf 5F 71
Lavender Pond Nature Pk. 1A 104
Lavender Ri. UB7: W Dray 2C 92
Lavender Rd. CRO: C'don 6K 155
  EN2: Enf 1J 23
  KT19: Ewe 5H 163
  SE16 . . . . .1A 104
  SM1: Sutt .4B 166
  SM5: Cars 4E 166
  SW11 . . . . .3B 118
  UB8: Hil 5B 74
Lavender St. E15 . . . . .6G 69
Lavender Sweep SW11 . . . . .4D 118
Lavender Ter. SW11 . . . . .3C 118
Lavender Va. SM6: Wall 6H 167
Lavender Wlk. CR4: Mitc 3E 154
  SW11 . . . . .4D 118
Lavender Way CRO: C'don 6K 157
Lavendon Ho. *NW8* 3D *4*
            (off Paveley St.)
Lavengro Rd. SE27 . . . . .2C 138
Lavenham Rd. SW18 . . . . .2H 135
Lavernock Rd. DA7: Bex 2G 127
Lavers Rd. N16 . . . . .3E 66
Laverstoke Gdns. SW15 . . . . .7B 116

Laverton M.—Lebus Ho.

Laverton M. SW5 4K 99
Laverton Pl. SW5 4K 99
Lavette Ho. *E3* *3C 86*
(off Rainhill Way)
Lavidge Rd. SE9 2C 142
Lavina Gro. N1 2K 83
Lavington Cl. E9 6B 68
Lavington Rd. CR0: Bedd 3K 167
W13 1B 96
Lavington St. SE1 5B 14 (1B 102)
Lavisham Ho. BR1: Brom 5K 141
Lawdons Gdns. CR0: Wadd 4B 168
Lawes Ho. *W10* *3H 81*
(off Lancefield St.)
Lawford Rd. N1 7E 66
NW5 6G 65
W4 7J 97
Lawfords Wharf *NW1* *7G 65*
(off Lyme St.)
Law Ho. IG11: Bark 2A 90
Lawless Ho. *E14* *7E 86*
(off Bazely St.)
Lawless St. E14 7D 86
Lawley Ho. TW1: Twick 6D 114
Lawley Rd. N14 7A 22
Lawley St. E5 4J 67
Lawn, The UB2: S'hall 5E 94
Lawn Cl. BR1: Brom 6K 141
HA4: Ruis 3H 57
KT3: N Mald 2A 152
N9 7A 24
Lawn Cres. TW9: Kew 2G 115
Lawn Dr. E7 4B 70
Lawn Farm Gro. RM6: Chad H 4E 54
Lawnfield Ct. *NW6* *7F 63*
(off Coverdale Rd.)
Lawn Gdns. W7 1J 95
Lawn Ho. Cl. E14 2E 104
Lawn La. SW8 7F 19 (6K 101)
Lawn Rd. BR3: Beck 7B 140
NW3 5D 64
Lawns, The DA14: Sidc 4B 144
E4 5H 35
HA5: Hat E 7A 26
SE3 3H 123
SE19 1D 156
SL3: Poyle 4A 174
SM2: Cheam 7G 165
SW19 5H 135
Lawns Ct. HA9: Wemb 2F 61
Lawnside SE3 4H 123
Lawns Way RM5: Col R 1J 55
Lawnswood EN5: Barn 5B 20
Lawn Ter. SE3 3G 123
Lawn Va. HA5: Pinn 2C 40
Lawrence Av. E12 4E 70
E17 1K 49
KT3: N Mald 6K 151
N13 4G 33
NW7 4F 29
NW10 1K 79
Lawrence Bldgs. N16 3F 67
Lawrence Campe Cl. N20 3G 31
Lawrence Cl. E3 3C 86
N15 4E 48
W12 7D 80
Lawrence Ct. N10 3G 47
N16 *3F 67*
(off Smalley Rd. Est.)
NW7 5F 29
W3 *3J 97*
(off Stanley Rd.)
Lawrence Cres. HA8: Edg 2G 43
RM10: Dag 3H 73
Lawrence Dr. UB10: Ick 4E 56
Lawrence Est. TW4: Houn 4A 112
Lawrence Gdns. NW7 3G 29
Lawrence Hill E4 2H 35
Lawrence Ho. *NW1* *7F 65*
(off Hawley Cres.)
SW1 *4D 18*
(off Cureton St.)
Lawrence La. EC2 7D 8 (6C 84)
Lawrence Mans. *SW1* *5J 17*
(off Sutherland St.)
SW3 *7C 16*
(off Lordship Pl.)
Lawrence Pde. *TW7: Isle* *3B 114*
(off Lower Sq.)
Lawrence Pl. *N1* *1J 83*
(off Brydon Wlk.)
Lawrence Rd. BR4: W W'ck 4J 171
DA8: Erith 7H 109
E6 1C 88
E13 1K 87
HA5: Pinn 6B 40
N15 4E 48
N18 4C 34
(not continuous)
SE25 4F 157
TW4: Houn 4A 112
TW10: Ham 4C 132
TW12: Hamp 7D 130
UB4: Hayes 2E 74
W5 4D 96
Lawrence St. E16 5H 87
NW7 5G 29
SW3 7C 16 (6C 100)
Lawrence Trad. Est. SE10 4G 105
Lawrence Way NW10 3J 61
Lawrence Weaver Cl. SM4: Mord 6J 153
Lawrence Yd. N15 4E 48
Lawrie Ho. *SW19* *5K 135*
(off Dunsford Av.)
Lawrie Pk. Av. SE26 5H 139
Lawrie Pk. Cres. SE26 5H 139
Lawrie Pk. Gdns. SE26 4H 139
Lawrie Pk. Rd. SE26 6H 139
Laws Cl. SE25 4D 156
Lawson Cl. E16 5A 88
IG1: Ilf 5H 71
SW19 3F 135
Lawson Ct. KT6: Surb 7D 150
N4 *1K 65*
(off Lorne Rd.)
N11 *6B 32*
(off Ring Way)
Lawson Gdns. HA5: Eastc 3K 39
Lawson Ho. *SE18* *6E 106*
(off Nightingale Pl.)
W12 *7D 80*
(off White City Est.)
Lawson Rd. EN3: Enf H 1D 24
UB1: S'hall 4E 76
Law St. SE1 3D 102
Lawton Rd. E3 3A 86
(not continuous)
E10 1E 68
EN4: Cockf 3G 21
Laxcon Cl. NW10 5K 61
Laxey Rd. BR6: Chels 6K 173
Laxfield Ct. *E8* *1G 85*
(off Pownall Rd.)
Laxford Ho. *SW1* *4H 17*
(off Cundy St.)
Laxley Cl. SE5 7B 102
Laxton Ct. CR7: Thor H 4C 156
Laxton Pl. NW1 3K 5 (4F 83)
Layard Rd. CR7: Thor H 2D 156
EN1: Enf 1A 24
SE16 4H 103
Layard Sq. SE16 4H 103
Laybourne Ho. *E14* *2C 104*
(off Admirals Way)
Laybrook Lodge E18 4H 51
Laycock St. N1 6A 66
Layer Gdns. W3 7G 79
Layfield Cl. NW4 7D 44
Layfield Cres. NW4 7D 44
Layfield Ho. *SE10* *5J 105*
(off Kemsing Rd.)
Layfield Rd. NW4 7D 44
Layhams Rd. BR2: Kes 4G 171
BR4: W W'ck 4G 171
Laymarsh Cl. DA17: Belv 3F 109
Laymead Cl. UB5: N'olt 6C 58
Laystall Ct. *WC1* *4J 7*
(off Mt. Pleasant)
Laystall St. EC1 4J 7 (4A 84)
Layton Ct. TW8: Bford 5D 96
Layton Cres. CR0: Wadd 5A 168
Layton Pl. TW9: Kew 1G 115
Layton Rd. TW3: Houn 4F 113
TW8: Bford 5D 96
Layton's La. TW16: Sun 2H 147
Layzell Wlk. SE9 1B 142
Lazar Wlk. N7 2K 65
Lazenby Ct. WC2 2E 12
Leabank Cl. HA1: Harr 3J 59
Leabank Sq. E9 6C 68
Leabank Vw. N15 6G 49
Lea Bon Ct. *E15* *1H 87*
(off Plaistow Gro.)
Leabourne Rd. N16 7G 49
LEA BRIDGE 3K 67
Lea Bri. Ind. Cen.
E10 1A 68
Lea Bri. Rd. E5 3J 67
E10 3J 67
E17 5F 51
Lea Cl. TW2: Whitt 7D 112
Lea Ct. E4 2K 35
E13 3J 87
N15 4G 49
Lea Cres. HA4: Ruis 4H 57
Leacroft Av. SW12 7D 118
Leacroft Cl. N21 2G 33
UB7: Yiew 6A 74
Leadale Av. E4 2H 35
Leadale Rd. N15 6G 49
N16 6G 49
Leadbeaters Cl. N11 5J 31
Leadbetter Ct. *NW10* *7K 61*
(off Melville Rd.)
Leadenhall Mkt. EC3 1G 15 (6E 84)
Leadenhall Pl. EC3 1G 15 (6E 84)
Leadenhall St. EC3 1G 15 (6E 84)
Leadenham Ct. E3 4C 86
Leader Av. E12 5E 70
Leadings, The HA9: Wemb 3J 61
Leaf Cl. HA6: Nwood 1F 39
KT7: T Ditt 5J 149
Leaf Gro. SE27 5A 138
Leaf Ho. *HA1: Harr* *5K 41*
(off Catherine Pl.)
Leafield Cl. SW16 6B 138
Leafield La. DA14: Sidc 3F 145
Leafield Rd. SM1: Sutt 2J 165
SW20 3H 153
Leafy Gro. BR2: Kes 5A 172
Leafy Oak Rd. SE12 4A 142
Leafy Way CR0: C'don 2F 169
Lea Gdns. HA9: Wemb 4F 61
Leagrave St. E5 3J 67
Lea Hall Gdns. E10 1C 68
Lea Hall Rd. E10 1C 68
Leaholme Way HA4: Ruis 6E 38
Lea Ho. *NW8* *4C 4*
(off Salisbury St.)
Leahurst Rd. SE13 5F 123
(not continuous)
LEA INTERCHANGE 5C 68
Leake Ct. SE1 7H 13 (2K 101)
Leake St. SE1 6H 13 (2K 101)
(not continuous)
Lealand Rd. N15 6F 49
Leamington Av. BR1: Brom 5A 142
BR6: Orp 4J 173
E17 5C 50
SM4: Mord 4G 153
Leamington Cl. BR1: Brom 4A 142
E12 5C 70
TW3: Houn 5G 113
Leamington Ct. SE3 6G 105
Leamington Cres. HA2: Harr 3C 58
Leamington Gdns. IG3: Ilf 2K 71
Leamington Ho. HA8: Edg 5A 28
W11 *5H 81*
(off Leamington Rd. Vs.)
Leamington Pk. W3 5K 79
Leamington Pl. UB4: Hayes 4H 75
Leamington Rd. UB2: S'hall 4B 94
Leamington Rd. Vs. W11 5H 81
Leamore Ct. E2 3K 85
Leamore St. W6 4E 98
LEAMOUTH 7G 87
Leamouth Rd. E6 5C 88
E14 6F 87
Leander Ct. *E9* *7K 67*
(off Lauriston Rd.)
KT6: Surb 7D 150
NW9 1A 44
SE8 1C 122
Leander Rd. CR7: Thor H 4K 155
SW2 6K 119
UB5: N'olt 2E 76
Lea Pk. Trad. Est. E10 7B 50
Learner Dr. HA2: Harr 2E 58
Lea Rd. BR3: Beck 2C 158
EN2: Enf 1J 23
UB2: S'hall 4C 94
Learoyd Gdns. E6 7E 88
Leary Ho. SE11 5K 101
Leas Cl. KT9: Chess 7F 163
Leas Dale SE9 3E 142
Leas Grn. BR7: Chst 6K 143
Leaside Av. N10 3E 46
Leaside Bus. Cen. EN3: Brim 2G 25
Leaside Ct. UB10: Hil 3D 74
Leaside Mans. *N10* *3E 46*
(off Fortis Grn.)
Leaside Rd. E5 1J 67
Leasowes Rd. E10 1C 68
Lea Sq. E3 1B 86
Leatherbottle Grn. DA18: Erith 3F 109
Leather Bottle La. DA17: Belv 4E 108
Leather Cl. CR4: Mitc 2E 154
Leatherdale St. E1 4J 85
(Harpley Sq.)
E1 3K 85
(Portelet Rd.)
Leather Gdns. E15 1G 87
Leatherhead Cl. N16 1F 67
Leatherhead Rd. KT9: Chess 7D 162
Leather La. EC1 5J 7 (5A 84)
(not continuous)
Leathermarket, The SE1 7G 15
Leathermarket Ct. SE1 7G 15 (2E 102)
Leathermarket St. SE1 7G 15 (2E 102)
Leather Rd. SE16 4K 103
Leathersellers Cl. *EN5: Barn* *3B 20*
(off The Avenue)
Leather St. E1 7K 85
Leathsail Rd. HA2: Harr 3F 59
Leathwaite Rd. SW11 4D 118
Leathwell Rd. SE8 2D 122
Lea Va. DA1: Cray 4K 127
Lea Valley Bus. Pk. E10 2A 68
Lea Valley Rd. E4 5F 25
EN3: Pond E 5F 25
Lea Valley Trad. Est. N18 6E 34
Lea Valley Viaduct E4 5E 34
N18 5E 34
Leaveland Cl. BR3: Beck 4C 158
Leaver Gdns. UB6: G'frd 2H 77
Leavesden Rd. HA7: Stan 6F 27
Leaves Grn. Rd. BR2: Kes 7B 172
Lea Vw. Ho. E5 1H 67
Leaway E10 1K 67
Lebanon Av. TW13: Hanw 5B 130
Lebanon Ct. TW1: Twick 7B 114
Lebanon Gdns. SW18 6J 117
Lebanon Pk. TW1: Twick 7B 114
Lebanon Rd. CR0: C'don 1E 168
SW18 5J 117
Lebrun Sq. SE3 4K 123
Lebus Ho. *NW8* *1C 4*
(off Cochrane St.)

Le Chateau *CR0: C'don* 3D 168
(off Chatsworth Rd.)
Lechmere App. IG8: Wfd G 2A 52
Lechmere Av. IG8: Wfd G 2B 52
Lechmere Rd. NW2 6D 62
Leckford Rd. SW18 2A 136
Leckhampton Pl. SW2 7A 120
Leckwith Av. DA7: Bex 6E 108
Lecky St. SW7 5A 16 (5B 100)
Leclair Ho. SE3 3K 123
Leconfield Av. SW13 3B 116
Leconfield Ho. SE5 4E 120
Leconfield Rd. N5 4D 66
Le Cordon Bleu London Culinary Arts Institute 6H 5
(off Marylebone La.)
Leda Av. EN3: Enf W 1E 24
Leda Ct. *SW9* 7A 102
(off Caldwell St.)
Ledam Ho. *EC1* 5J 7
(off Bourne Est.)
Leda Rd. SE18 3D 106
Ledbury Ho. SE22 3E 120
W11 6H 81
(off Colville Rd.)
Ledbury M. Nth. W11 7J 81
Ledbury M. W. W11 7J 81
Ledbury Pl. CR0: C'don 4C 168
Ledbury Rd. CR0: C'don 4D 168
W11 6H 81
Ledbury St. SE15 7G 103
Ledrington Rd. SE19 6G 139
Ledway Dr. HA9: Wemb 7F 43
LEE 6J 123
Lee Av. RM6: Chad H 6E 54
Lee Bri. SE13 3E 122
Leechcroft Av. DA15: Sidc 5K 125
Leechcroft Rd. SM6: Wall 3E 166
Lee Chu. St. SE13 4G 123
Lee Cl. E17 1K 49
EN5: New Bar 4F 21
Lee Conservancy Rd. E9 5B 68
Lee Ct. *SE13* 4F 123
(off Lee High Rd.)
Leecroft Rd. EN5: Barn 5B 20
Leeds Ct. *EC1* 3A 8
(off St John St.)
Leeds Pl. N4 1K 65
Leeds Rd. IG1: Ilf 1H 71
Leeds St. N18 5B 34
Leefern Rd. W12 2C 98
Leegate SE12 5H 123
LEE GREEN 5H 123
Lee Gro. IG7: Chig 2K 37
Lee High Rd. SE12 3E 122
SE13 3E 122
Leeke St. WC1 1G 7 (3K 83)
Leeland Rd. W13 1A 96
Leeland Ter. W13 1A 96
Leeland Way NW10 4B 62
Lee M. BR3: Beck 3A 158
Leemount Ho. NW4 4F 45
Lee Pk. SE3 4H 123
Lee Pk. Way N9 4E 34
N18 4E 34
Leerdam Dr. E14 3E 104
Lee Rd. EN1: Enf 6B 24
NW7 7A 30
SE3 3H 123
SW19 1K 153
UB6: G'frd 1C 78
Lees, The CR0: C'don 2B 170
Lees Av. HA6: Nwood 1H 39
Lees Ct. *W1* 2G 11
(off Lees Pl.)
Lees Ho. *SE17* 5D 102
(off Inville Rd.)
Leeside EN5: Barn 5B 20
Leeside Ct. *SE16* 1K 103
(off Rotherhithe St.)
Leeside Cres. NW11 6G 45
Leeside Ind. Est. N17 7D 34
Leeside Rd. N17 6C 34
Leeside Works N17 7D 34
Leeson Ho. TW1: Twick 7B 114
Leeson Rd. SE24 4A 120
Leesons Hill BR5: St P 3J 161
BR7: Chst 3J 161
Leeson's Way BR5: St P 2K 161
Lees Pde. UB10: Hil 4D 74
Lees Pl. W1 2G 11 (7E 82)
Lees Rd. UB8: Hil 4D 74
Lee St. E8 1F 85
Lee Ter. SE3 3G 123
SE13 3G 123
Lee Valley Athletics Cen. 1E 34
Lee Valley Ice Cen. 2K 67
Lee Valley Pk.
Haringey 7E 34
Lee Valley Technopark N17 3G 49
Leeve Ho. *W10* 3H 81
(off Lancefield St.)
Lee Vw. EN2: Enf 1G 23
Leeward Ct. E1 7G 85
Leeward Gdns. SW19 5G 135
Leeward Ho. *N1* 1E 84
(off New Era Est.)
Leeway SE8 5B 104
Leeway Cl. HA5: Hat E 1D 40
Leeways, The SM3: Cheam 6G 165
Leewood Cl. SE12 6J 123
Lefa Bus. & Ind. Pk.
DA14: Sidc 6D 144
Lefevre Wlk. E3 2C 86
Leff Ho. NW6 1G 81
Lefroy Ho. *SE1* 7C 14
(off Southwark Bri. Rd.)
Lefroy Rd. W12 2B 98
Left Side *N14* 1C 32
(off Statione Pde.)
Legard Rd. N5 3B 66
Legatt Rd. SE9 5B 124
Leggatt Rd. E15 2E 86
Legge St. SE13 5E 122
Leghorn Rd. NW10 2B 80
SE18 5H 107
Legion Cl. N1 7A 66
Legion Ct. SM4: Mord 6J 153
Legion Rd. UB6: G'frd 1G 77
Legion Ter. E3 1B 86
Legion Way N12 7H 31
Legon Av. RM7: Rush G 1J 73
Legrace Av. TW4: Houn 2B 112
Leicester Av. CR4: Mitc 4J 155
Leicester Cl. KT4: Wor Pk 4E 164
Leicester Ct. *TW1: Twick* 6D 114
(off Clevedon Rd.)
W9 5J 81
(off Elmfield Way)
WC2 2D 12
Leicester Flds. WC2 3D 12
Leicester Gdns. IG3: Ilf 7J 53
Leicester Ho. *N18* 5C 34
(off Cavendish Cl.)
SW9 3B 120
(off Loughborough Rd.)
Leicester M. N2 3C 46
Leicester Pl. WC2 2D 12 (7H 83)
Leicester Rd. CR0: C'don 7E 156
E11 5K 51
EN5: New Bar 5E 20
N2 3C 46
NW10 7K 61
Leicester Sq. WC2 3D 12 (7H 83)
Leicester Square Theatre 7H 83
(off Leicester Pl.)
Leicester St. WC2 2D 12 (7H 83)
Leigh, The KT2: King T 7A 134
Leigham Av. SW16 3J 137
Leigham Cl. SW16 3K 137
Leigham Ct. Rd. SW16 2J 137
Leigham Dr. TW7: Isle 7J 95
Leigham Hall Pde. *SW16* 3J 137
(off Streatham High Rd.)
Leigham Va. SW2 3K 137
SW16 3K 137
Leigh Av. IG4: Ilf 4B 52
Leigh Cl. KT3: N Mald 4J 151
Leigh Cl. Ind. Est. KT3: N Mald 4K 151
Leigh Ct. HA2: Harr 1J 59
W14 4H 99
(off Avonmore Pl.)
Leigh Cres. CR0: New Ad 7D 170
Leigh Gdns. NW10 2E 80
Leigh Hunt Dr. N14 1C 32
Leigh Orchard Cl. SW16 3K 137
Leigh Pl. DA16: Well 2A 126
EC1 5J 7 (5A 84)
TW13: Felt 1A 130
Leigh Rd. E6 6E 70
E10 7E 50
N5 4B 66
TW3: Houn 4H 113
Leigh St. WC1 2E 6 (3J 83)
Leighton Av. E12 5E 70
HA5: Pinn 3C 40
Leighton Cl. HA8: Edg 2G 43
Leighton Cres. NW5 5G 65
Leighton Gdns. CR0: C'don 1B 168
NW10 2D 80
Leighton Gro. NW5 5G 65
Leighton Ho. *SW1* 4D 18
(off Herrick St.)
Leighton House Mus. 3H 99
Leighton Mans. *W14* 6G 99
(off Greyhound Rd.)
Leighton Pl. NW5 5G 65
Leighton Rd. EN1: Enf 5A 24
HA3: Hrw W 2H 41
NW5 5G 65
W13 2A 96
Leighton St. CR0: C'don 1B 168
Leila Parnell Pl. SE7 6A 106
Leinster Av. SW14 3J 115
Leinster Gdns. W2 6A 82
Leinster M. EN5: Barn 3B 20
W2 7A 82
Leinster Pl. W2 6A 82
Leinster Rd. N10 4F 47
Leinster Sq. W2 6J 81
(not continuous)
Leinster Ter. W2 7A 82
Leisure Way N12 7G 31
Leisure W. TW13: Felt 2K 129
Leitch Ho. *NW8* 7B 64
(off Hilgrove Rd.)
Leith Cl. NW9 1K 61
Leithcote Gdns. SW16 4K 137
Leithcote Path SW16 3K 137
Leith Hill BR5: St P 1K 161
Leith Hill Grn. BR5: St P 1K 161
Leith Mans. *W9* 3K 81
(off Grantully Rd.)
Leith Rd. N22 1B 48
Leith Towers SM2: Sutt 7K 165
Leith Yd. *NW6* 1J 81
(off Quex Rd.)
Lela Av. TW4: Houn 2A 112
Lelitia Cl. E8 1G 85
Lely Ho. *UB5: N'olt* 2B 76
(off Academy Gdns.)
Leman Pas. E1 1K 15
Leman St. E1 7K 9 (6F 85)
Lemark Cl. HA7: Stan 6H 27
Le May Av. SE12 3K 141
Lemmon Rd. SE10 6G 105
Lemna Rd. E11 7H 51
Le Moal Ho. *E1* 5J 85
(off Stepney Way)
Lemonade Bldg. *IG11: Bark* 7G 71
(off Ripple Rd.)
Lemon Gro. TW13: Felt 1J 129
Lemon Tree Ho. *E3* 3B 86
(off Bow Rd.)
Lemonwell Dr. SE9 5G 125
Lemsford Cl. N15 6G 49
Lemsford Ct. N4 2C 66
Lemuel St. SW18 6A 118
Lena Cres. N9 2D 34
Lena Gdns. W6 3E 98
Lena Kennedy Cl. E4 6K 35
Lenanton Steps *E14* 2C 104
(off Manilla St.)
Len Bishop Ct. *E1* 7K 85
(off Schoolhouse La.)
Len Clifton Ho. *SE18* 4D 106
(off Cambridge Barracks Rd.)
Lendal Ter. SW4 3H 119
Lenelby Rd. KT6: Surb 1G 163
Len Freeman Pl. SW6 6H 99
W6 4B 98
(off Goldhawk Rd.)
Lenham Ho. *SE1* 7F 15
(off Staple St.)
Lenham Rd. CR7: Thor H 2D 156
DA7: Bex 6F 109
SE12 4H 123
SM1: Sutt 4K 165
Lennard Av. BR4: W W'ck 2G 171
Lennard Cl. BR4: W W'ck 2G 171
Lennard Rd. BR2: Brom 1D 172
BR3: Beck 6K 139
CR0: C'don 1C 168
SE20 6K 139
Lennon Rd. NW2 5E 62
Lennox Gdns. CR0: Wadd 4B 168
IG1: Ilf 1D 70
NW10 4B 62
SW1 2E 16 (3D 100)
Lennox Gdns. M. SW1 2E 16 (3D 100)
Lennox Ho. *DA17: Belv* 3G 109
(off Picardy St.)
TW1: Twick 6D 114
(off Clevedon Rd.)
Lennox Rd. E17 6B 50
N4 2K 65
Lenor Cl. DA6: Bex 4E 126
Lensbury Av. SW6 2A 118
Lensbury Way SE2 3C 108
Lens Rd. E7 7A 70
Len Taylor Cl. UB4: Hayes 4G 75
Lenthall Ho. *SW1* 6B 18
(off Churchill Gdns.)
Lenthall Rd. E8 7G 67
Lenthorp Rd. SE10 4H 105
Lentmead Rd. BR1: Brom 3H 141
Lenton Path SE18 6H 107
Lenton Ri. TW9: Rich 3E 114
Lenton St. SE18 4H 107
Lenton Ter. N4 2A 66
Len Williams Ct. NW6 2J 81
Leo Ct. TW8: Bford 7D 96
Leof Cres. SE6 5D 140
Leominster Rd. SM4: Mord 6A 154
Leominster Wlk. SM4: Mord 6A 154
Leonard Av. RM7: Rush G 1K 73
SM4: Mord 5A 154
Leonard Ct. HA3: Hrw W 1J 41
W8 3J 99
WC1 3D 6 (4H 83)
Leonard Pl. N16 4E 66
Leonard Rd. E4 6H 35
E7 4J 69
N9 3A 34
SW16 1G 155
UB2: S'hall 3B 94
Leonard Robbins Path *SE28* 7B 90
(off Tawney Rd.)
Leonard St. E16 1C 106
EC2 3F 9 (4D 84)
Leonora Ho. *W9* 4A 82
(off Lanark Rd.)
Leonora Tyson M. SE21 2D 138
Leontine Cl. SE15 7G 103
Leopards Ct. EC1 5J 7
Leopold Av. SW19 5H 135
Leopold Bldgs. *E2* 1J 9
(off Columbia Rd.)

Leopold M. E9 . . . . 1J 85
Leopold Rd. E17 . . . . 5C 50
N2 . . . . 3B 46
N18 . . . . 5C 34
NW10 . . . . 7A 62
SW19 . . . . 4H 135
W5 . . . . 1F 97
Leopold St. E3 . . . . 5B 86
Leopold Ter. SW19 . . . . 5H 135
Leopold Wlk. SE11 . . . . 6G 19
(off Tyers St.)
Leo St. SE15 . . . . 7H 103
Leo Yd. EC1 . . . . 4B 8
Leppoc Rd. SW4 . . . . 5H 119
Leroy St. SE1 . . . . 4E 102
Lerry Cl. W14 . . . . 6H 99
Lerwick Ct. EN1: Enf 5K 23
Lescombe Cl. SE23 . . . . 3A 140
Lescombe Rd. SE23 . . . . 3A 140
Lesley Cl. DA5: Bexl 7H 127
Lesley Ct. SW1 . . . . 2C 18
(off Strutton Ground)
Leslie Gdns. SM2: Sutt 6J 165
Leslie Gro. CR0: C'don 1E 168
Leslie Gro. Pl. CR0: C'don 1E 168
Leslie Ho. SW8 . . . . 7J 101
(off Wheatsheaf La.)
Leslie Pk. Rd. CR0: C'don 1E 168
Leslie Prince Ct. SE5 . . . . 7D 102
Leslie Rd. E11 . . . . 4E 68
E16 . . . . 6K 87
N2 . . . . 3B 46
Leslie Smith Sq. SE18 . . . . 6E 106
Lesnes Abbey 4D 108
Lesney Farm Est. DA8: Erith 7K 109
Lesney Pk. DA8: Erith 6K 109
Lesney Pk. Rd. DA8: Erith 6K 109
Lessar Av. SW4 . . . . 6G 119
Lessingham Av. IG5: Ilf 3E 52
SW17 . . . . 4D 136
Lessing St. SE23 . . . . 7A 122
Lessington Av. RM7: Rom 6J 55
Lessness Av. DA7: Bex 7D 108
LESSNESS HEATH 5H 109
Lessness Pk. DA17: Belv 5F 109
Lessness Rd. DA17: Belv 6G 109
SM4: Mord 6A 154
Lester Av. E15 . . . . 4G 87
Lester Ct. E3 . . . . 3D 86
(off Bruce Rd.)
Lestock Cl. SE25 . . . . 3G 157
(off Manor Rd.)
Leswin Pl. N16 . . . . 3F 67
Leswin Rd. N16 . . . . 3F 67
Letchford Gdns. NW10 . . . . 3C 80
Letchford Ho. E3 . . . . 2C 86
(off Thomas Frye Dr.)
Letchford M. NW10 . . . . 3C 80
Letchford Ter. HA3: Hrw W 1F 41
Letchmore Ho. W10 . . . . 4E 80
(off Sutton Way)
Letchworth Av. TW14: Felt 7H 111
Letchworth Cl. BR2: Brom 5J 159
Letchworth Dr. BR2: Brom 5J 159
Letchworth St. SW17 . . . . 4D 136
Lethbridge Cl. SE13 . . . . 1E 122
Letterstone Rd. SW6 . . . . 7H 99
Lettice St. SW6 . . . . 1H 117
Lett Rd. E15 . . . . 7F 69
Lettsom St. SE5 . . . . 2E 120
Lettsom Wlk. E13 . . . . 2J 87
Leucha Rd. E17 . . . . 5A 50
Levana Cl. SW19 . . . . 1G 135
Levant Ho. E1 . . . . 4K 85
(off Ernest St.)
Levehurst Ho. SE27 . . . . 5C 138
Levendale Rd. SE23 . . . . 2A 140
Levenhurst Way SW4 . . . . 2J 119
Leven Rd. E14 . . . . 5E 86
Leven Way UB3: Hayes 6G 75
Leverett St. SW3 . . . . 3D 16 (4C 100)
Leverholme Gdns. SE9 . . . . 3E 142
Leverington Pl. N1 . . . . 2F 9 (3D 84)
Leverson St. SW16 . . . . 6G 137
Leverstock Ho. SW3 . . . . 5D 16
(off Cale St.)
Lever St. EC1 . . . . 2B 8 (3B 84)
Leverton Pl. NW5 . . . . 5G 65
Leverton St. NW5 . . . . 5G 65
Levett Gdns. IG3: Ilf 4K 71
Levett Rd. IG11: Bark 6J 71
Levine Gdns. IG11: Bark 2D 90
Levison Way N19 . . . . 1H 65
Levita Ho. NW1 . . . . 1D 6
(not continuous)
Levyne Ct. EC1 . . . . 3J 7
(off Pine St.)
Lewes Cl. UB5: N'olt 6E 58
Lewes Ct. CR4: Mitc 3D 154
(off Chatsworth Pl.)
Lewesdon Cl. SW19 . . . . 1F 135
Lewes Ho. SE1 . . . . 6H 15
(off Druid St.)
SE15 . . . . 6G 103
(off Friary Est.)
Lewes Rd. BR1: Brom 2B 160
N12 . . . . 5H 31
Leweston Pl. N16 . . . . 7F 49
Lew Evans Ho. SE22 . . . . 5G 121
Lewey Ho. E3 . . . . 4B 86
(off Joseph St.)
Lewgars Av. NW9 . . . . 6J 43
Lewing Cl. BR6: Orp 1J 173
Lewington Apartments
SE16 . . . . 4J 103
(off Alpine Rd.)
Lewington Cen. SE16 . . . . 4J 103
(off Alpine Rd.)
Lewin Rd. DA6: Bex 5E 126
SW14 . . . . 3K 115
SW16 . . . . 6H 137
Lewin Ter. TW14: Bedf 7F 111
Lewis Av. E17 . . . . 1C 50
Lewis Cl. N14 . . . . 7B 22
Lewis Ct. SE16 . . . . 5H 103
(off Stubbs Dr.)
Lewis Cres. NW10 . . . . 5K 61
Lewis Gdns. N2 . . . . 2B 46
N16 . . . . 6F 49
Lewis Gro. SE13 . . . . 4E 122
LEWISHAM 3E 122
Lewisham Bus. Cen. SE14 . . . . 6K 103
Lewisham Cen. SE13 . . . . 4E 122
Lewisham Crematorium SE6 . . . . 2H 141
Lewisham Hgts. SE23 . . . . 1J 139
Lewisham High St. SE13 . . . . 3E 122
(not continuous)
Lewisham Hill SE13 . . . . 2E 122
Lewisham Lions Cen. 5J 103
Lewisham Model Mkt. SE13 . . . . 4E 122
(off Lewisham High St.)
Lewisham Pk. SE13 . . . . 5E 122
Lewisham Rd. SE13 . . . . 1D 122
Lewisham St. SW1 . . . . 7D 12 (2H 101)
Lewisham Way SE4 . . . . 1B 122
SE14 . . . . 1B 122
Lewis Ho. E14 . . . . 1E 104
(off Coldharbour)
Lewis Pl. E8 . . . . 5G 67
Lewis Rd. CR4: Mitc 2B 154
(not continuous)
DA14: Sidc 3C 144
DA16: Well 3C 126
SM1: Sutt 4K 165
TW10: Rich 5D 114
UB1: S'hall 2C 94
Lewis Silkin Ho. SE15 . . . . 6J 103
(off Lovelinch Cl.)
Lewis Sports and Leisure Cen. 1F 157
Lewis St. NW1 . . . . 6F 65
(not continuous)
Lewiston Cl. KT4: Wor Pk 7D 152
Lewis Way RM10: Dag 6H 73
Lexden Dr. RM6: Chad H 6B 54
Lexden Rd. CR4: Mitc 4H 155
W3 . . . . 7H 79
Lexham Gdns. W8 . . . . 4J 99
Lexham Gdns. M. W8 . . . . 3K 99
Lexham Ho. IG11: Bark 1H 89
(off St Margarets)
W8 . . . . 4K 99
(off Lexham Gdns.)
Lexham M. W8 . . . . 4J 99
Lexham Wlk. W8 . . . . 3K 99
Lexington Apartments EC1 . . . . 3F 9 (4D 84)
Lexington Bldg. E3 . . . . 2C 86
Lexington Ho. UB7: W Dray 2B 92
Lexington Pl. KT1: Ham W 7D 132
Lexington St. W1 . . . . 2B 12 (7G 83)
Lexington Way EN5: Barn 4A 20
Lexton Gdns. SW12 . . . . 1H 137
Leyborne Av. W13 . . . . 2B 96
Leyborne Pk. TW9: Kew 1G 115
Leybourne Cl. BR2: Brom 6J 159
Leybourne Ho. E14 . . . . 6B 86
(off Dod St.)
SE15 . . . . 6J 103
Leybourne Rd. E11 . . . . 1H 69
NW1 . . . . 7F 65
NW9 . . . . 5G 43
UB10: Hil 1E 74
Leybourne St. NW1 . . . . 7F 65
Leybridge Ct. SE12 . . . . 5J 123
Leyburn Cl. E17 . . . . 4D 50
Leyburn Gdns. CR0: C'don 2E 168
Leyburn Gro. N18 . . . . 6B 34
Leyburn Rd. N18 . . . . 6B 34
Leydenhatch La. BR8: Dart, Swan 7J 145
Leyden Mans. N19 . . . . 7J 47
Leyden St. E1 . . . . 6J 9 (5F 85)
Leydon Cl. SE16 . . . . 1K 103
Leyes Rd. E16 . . . . 6B 88
Leyfield KT4: Wor Pk 1A 164
Ley Ho. SE1 . . . . 2C 102
(off Southwark Bri. Rd.)
Leyland Av. EN3: Enf H 2F 25
Leyland Gdns. IG8: Wfd G 5F 37
Leyland Ho. E14 . . . . 7D 86
(off Hale St.)
Leyland Rd. SE12 . . . . 5J 123
Leylands SW18 . . . . 6H 117
Leylands La. TW19: Stan M 7A 174
(not continuous)
Leylang Rd. SE14 . . . . 7K 103
Leys, The HA3: Kenton 6F 43
N2 . . . . 4A 46
Leys Av. RM10: Dag 1J 91
Leys Cl. HA1: Harr 5H 41
RM10: Dag 7J 73
Leys Ct. SW9 . . . . 2A 120
Leysdown Av. DA7: Bex 4J 127
Leysdown Ho. SE17 . . . . 5E 102
(off Madron St.)
Leysdown Rd. SE9 . . . . 2C 142
Leysfield Rd. W12 . . . . 3C 98
Leys Gdns. EN4: Cockf 5K 21
Leyspring Rd. E11 . . . . 1H 69
Leys Rd. E. EN3: Enf H 1F 25
Leys Rd. W. EN3: Enf H 1F 25
Leys Sq. N3 . . . . 1K 45
Ley St. IG1: Ilf 2F 71
IG2: Ilf 2F 71
Leyswood Dr. IG2: Ilf 5J 53
Leythe Rd. W3 . . . . 2J 97
LEYTON 2E 68
Leyton Bus. Cen. E10 . . . . 2C 68
Leyton Ct. SE23 . . . . 1J 139
Leyton Grange Est. E10 . . . . 1C 68
Leyton Grn. Rd. E10 . . . . 6E 50
Leyton Grn. Twr. E10 . . . . 6E 50
(off Leyton Grn. Rd.)
Leyton Ind. Village E10 . . . . 7K 49
Leyton Leisure Lagoon 7D 50
Leyton Link Est. E10 . . . . 7A 50
Leyton Mills E10 . . . . 4E 68
Leyton Orient FC 3D 68
Leyton Pk. Rd. E10 . . . . 3E 68
Leyton Rd. E15 . . . . 5E 68
SW19 . . . . 7A 136
LEYTONSTONE 1G 69
Leytonstone Ho. E11 . . . . 7H 51
(off Hanbury Dr.)
Leytonstone Rd. E15 . . . . 6G 69
Leyton Way E11 . . . . 7G 51
Leywick St. E15 . . . . 2G 87
Lezayre Rd. BR6: Chels 6K 173
Liardet St. SE14 . . . . 6A 104
Liberia Rd. N5 . . . . 6B 66
Liberty Av. SW19 . . . . 1B 154
Liberty Cen. HA0: Wemb 1F 79
Liberty Cl. KT4: Wor Pk 1E 164
N18 . . . . 4A 34
Liberty Ct. IG11: Bark 2B 90
Liberty Ho. E1 . . . . 7G 85
(off Ensign St.)
E13 . . . . 2J 87
Liberty M. N22 . . . . 1B 48
SW12 . . . . 6F 119
Liberty Point CR0: C'don 7G 157
(off Blackhorse La.)
Liberty St. SW9 . . . . 1K 119
Libra Mans. E3 . . . . 2B 86
(off Libra Rd.)
Libra Rd. E3 . . . . 2B 86
E13 . . . . 2J 87
Library Ct. N17 . . . . 3F 49
Library Mans. W12 . . . . 2E 98
(off Pennard Rd.)
Library Pde. NW10 . . . . 1A 80
(off Craven Pk. Rd.)
Library Pl. E1 . . . . 7H 85
Library St. SE1 . . . . 7A 14 (2B 102)
Library Way TW2: Whitt 7G 113
Libro Ct. E4 . . . . 4H 35
Lichfield Cl. EN4: Cockf 3J 21
Lichfield Ct. KT6: Surb 5E 150
(off Claremont Rd.)
TW9: Rich 5E 114
Lichfield Gdns. TW9: Rich 4E 114
Lichfield Gro. N3 . . . . 1J 45
Lichfield Rd. E3 . . . . 3A 86
E6 . . . . 3B 88
HA6: Nwood 3J 39
IG8: Wfd G 4B 36
N9 . . . . 2B 34
NW2 . . . . 4G 63
RM8: Dag 4B 72
TW4: Houn 3A 112
TW9: Kew 1F 115
Lichfield Ter. TW9: Rich 5E 114
(off Sheen Rd.)
Lichlade Cl. BR6: Orp 4K 173
Lickey Ho. W14 . . . . 6H 99
(off North End Rd.)
Lidbury Rd. NW7 . . . . 6B 30
Lidcote Gdns. SW9 . . . . 2K 119
Liddall Way UB7: Yiew 1B 92
Liddell Cl. HA3: Kenton 3D 42
Liddell Gdns. NW10 . . . . 2E 80
Liddell Rd. NW6 . . . . 6J 63
Liddiard Ho. W11 . . . . 7G 81
(off Lansdowne Rd.)
Lidding Rd. HA3: Kenton 5D 42
Liddington Rd. E15 . . . . 1H 87
Liddon Rd. BR1: Brom 3A 160
E13 . . . . 3K 87
Liden Cl. E17 . . . . 7B 50
Lidfield Rd. N16 . . . . 4D 66
Lidgate Rd. SE15 . . . . 7F 103
Lidgould Gro. HA4: Ruis 6J 39
Lidiard Rd. SW18 . . . . 2A 136
Lidlington Pl. NW1 . . . . 2G 83
Lido Sq. N17 . . . . 2D 48
Lidyard Rd. N19 . . . . 1G 65
Liffler Rd. SE18 . . . . 5J 107
Liffords Pl. SW13 . . . . 2B 116
Lifford St. SW15 . . . . 4F 117
Lightcliffe Rd. N13 . . . . 4F 33

Lighter Cl. SE16 .4A 104
Lighterman Ho. E14 .7E 86
Lighterman M. E1 .6K 85
Lightermans Rd. E14 .2C 104
Lightermans Wlk. SW18 .4J 117
Lightfoot Rd. N8 .5J 47
Light Horse Ct. SW3 .6G 17
Lightley Cl. HA0: Wemb .1E 78
Ligonier St. E2 .3J 9 (4F 85)
Lilac Cl. E4 .6G 35
Lilac Ct. E13 .1A 88
TW11: Tedd .4K 131
Lilac Gdns. CR0: C'don .3C 170
RM7: Rush G .1K 73
UB3: Hayes .6G 75
W5 .3D 96
Lilac Ho. SE4 .3C 122
Lilac M. *N22* .*3A 48*
(off High Rd.)
Lilac Pl. SE11 .4G 19 (4K 101)
UB7: Yiew .7B 74
Lilac St. W12 .7C 80
Lilah M. BR2: Brom .2H 159
Lilburne Gdns. SE9 .5C 124
Lilburne Rd. SE9 .5C 124
Lilburne Wlk. NW10 .6J 61
Lile Cres. W7 .5J 77
Lilestone Ho. *NW8* .*3B 4*
(off Frampton St.)
Lilestone St. NW8 .3C 4 (4C 82)
Lilford Ho. SE5 .2C 120
Lilford Rd. SE5 .2B 120
Lilian Barker Cl. SE12 .5J 123
Lilian Board Way
UB6: G'frd .5H 59
Lilian Cl. N16 .3E 66
Lilian Gdns. IG8: Wfd G .1K 51
Lilian Rd. SW16 .1G 155
Lillechurch Rd. RM8: Dag .6B 72
Lilleshall Rd. SM4: Mord .6B 154
Lilley Cl. E1 .1G 103
Lilley La. NW7 .5E 28
Lillian Av. W3 .2G 97
Lillian Rd. SW13 .6C 98
Lillie Bri. Dpt. W14 .5H 99
Lillie Mans. *SW6* .*6G 99*
(off Lillie Rd.)
Lillie Rd. SW6 .6G 99
Lillie Road Fitness Cen. .7F 99
Lillieshall Rd. SW4 .3F 119
Lillie Yd. SW6 .6J 99
Lillingston Ho. N7 .4A 66
Lillington Gdns. Est. SW1 .4B 18
Lilliput Av. UB5: N'olt .1C 76
Lilliput Ct. SE12 .5K 123
Lilliput Rd. RM7: Rush G .7K 55
Lily Cl. W14 .4F 99
(not continuous)
Lily Gdns. HA0: Wemb .2C 78
Lily Nichols Ho. *E16* .*1B 106*
(off Connaught Rd.)
Lily Pl. EC1 .5K 7 (5A 84)
Lily Rd. E17 .6C 50
Lilyville Rd. SW6 .1H 117
Limborough Ho. *E14* .*5C 86*
(off Thomas Rd.)
Limbourne Av. RM8: Dag .7F 55
Limburg Rd. SW11 .4C 118
Lime Av. UB7: Yiew .7B 74
Limeburner La. EC4 .1A 14 (6B 84)
Lime Cl. BR1: Brom .4C 160
E1 .1G 103
HA3: W'stone .2A 42
HA5: Eastc .3H 39
IG9: Buck H .2G 37
RM7: Rom .4J 55
SM5: Cars .2D 166
Lime Ct. CR4: Mitc .2B 154
E11 .*2G 69*
(off Trinity Cl.)
E17 .5E 50
HA1: Harr .6K 41
Lime Ct. HA4: Ruis .7K 39
SE9 .2F 143
Lime Cres. TW16: Sun .2A 148
Limecroft Cl. KT19: Ewe .7K 163
Limedene Cl.
HA5: Pinn .1B 40
Lime Gro. BR6: Farnb .2F 173
DA15: Sidc .6K 125
E4 .6G 35
HA4: Ruis .6K 39
KT3: N Mald .3K 151
N20 .1C 30
TW1: Twick .6K 113
UB3: Hayes .7F 75
W12 .2E 98
Limeharbour E14 .3D 104
LIMEHOUSE .6B 86
Lime Ho. TW9: Kew .1H 115
Limehouse C'way. E14 .7B 86
Lime Ho. Ct. *E14* .*6B 86*
(off Wharf La.)
Limehouse Ct. E14 .6C 86
Limehouse Cut *E14* .*5D 86*
(off Morris Rd.)
Limehouse Flds. Est. E14 .5A 86
Limehouse Link E14 .6A 86
Lime Kiln Dr. SE7 .6K 105
Limekiln Pl. SE19 .7F 139
Limelight Ho. *SE11* .*4B 102*
(off Dugard Way)
Lime Lodge *TW16: Sun* .*7H 129*
(off Forest Dr.)
Limerick Cl. SW12 .7G 119
Lime Rd. TW9: Rich .4F 115
Lime Row DA18: Erith .3F 109
Limerston St. SW10 .7A 16 (6A 100)
Limes, The BR2: Brom .2C 172
KT8: W Mole .4F 149
SW18 .6J 117
W2 .7J 81
Limes Av. CR0: Wadd .3A 168
E11 .4K 51
E12 .3C 70
N12 .4F 31
NW7 .6F 29
NW11 .7G 45
SE20 .7H 139
SM5: Cars .1D 166
SW13 .2B 116
Limes Av., The N11 .5A 32
Limes Cl. N11 .5B 32
TW15: Ashf .5C 128
Limes Ct. *NW6* .*7G 63*
(off Brondesbury Pk.)
Limesdale Gdns. HA8: Edg .2J 43
Limes Fld. Rd. SW14 .3A 116
Limesford Rd. SE15 .4K 121
Limes Gdns. SW18 .6J 117
Limes Gro. SE13 .4E 122
Limes Pl. CR0: C'don .7D 156
Limes Rd. BR3: Beck .2D 158
CR0: C'don .7D 156
Limes Row BR6: Farnb .5F 173
Limestone Wlk.
DA18: Erith .2D 108
Lime St. E17 .4A 50
EC3 .2G 15 (7E 84)
Lime St. Pas. EC3 .1G 15 (6E 84)
Limes Wlk. SE15 .4J 121
W5 .2D 96
Lime Ter. W7 .7J 77
Lime Tree Av. KT7: T Ditt .7J 149
KT10: Esh .7H 149
Lime Tree Cl. E18 .4A 52
Limetree Cl. SW2 .1K 137
Lime Tree Ct. CR2: S Croy .6C 168
E3 .5C 86
Lime Tree Gro. CR0: C'don .3B 170
Lime Tree Pl. CR4: Mitc .1F 155
Lime Tree Rd. TW5: Hest .1F 113
Limetree Ter. DA16: Well .3A 126
SE6 .1B 140
Lime Tree Wlk. BR4: W W'ck .4H 171
EN2: Enf .1H 23
WD23: B Hea .1D 26
Limetree Wlk. SW17 .5E 136
Lime Wlk. E15 .1G 87
KT8: E Mos .4K 149
Limewood Cl. BR3: Beck .5E 158
E17 .4B 50
W13 .6B 78
Limewood Ct. IG4: Ilf .5D 52
Limewood Rd. DA8: Erith .7J 109
Limpsfield Av.
CR7: Thor H .5K 155
SW19 .2F 135
Limscott Ho. *E3* .*3D 86*
(off Bruce Rd.)
Linacre Cl. SE15 .3H 121
Linacre Ct. W6 .5F 99
Linacre Rd. NW2 .6D 62
Linale Ho. N1 .1E 8
Linberry Wlk. SE8 .4B 104
Linchmere Rd. SE12 .7H 123
Lincoln Av. N14 .3B 32
RM7: Rush G .2K 73
SW19 .3F 135
TW2: Twick .2G 131
Lincoln Cl. HA2: Harr .5D 40
SE25 .6G 157
UB6: G'frd .1G 77
Lincoln Ct. *CR2: S Croy* .*5C 168*
(off Warham Rd.)
IG2: Ilf .6G 53
N16 .7D 48
SE12 .3A 142
Lincoln Cres. EN1: Enf .5K 23
Lincoln Gdns. IG1: Ilf .7C 52
Lincoln Grn. Rd. BR5: St M Cry .5K 161
Lincoln Ho. SE5 .7A 102
SW3 .2D 100
Lincoln M. N15 .4C 48
NW6 .1H 81
SE21 .2D 138
Lincoln Pde. HA9: Wemb .1E 60
N2 .*3C 46*
(off Lincoln Rd.)
Lincoln Rd. CR4: Mitc .5J 155
DA14: Sidc .5B 144
E7 .6B 70
E13 .4K 87
E18 .1J 51
EN1: Enf .4K 23
EN3: Pond E .5B 24
HA0: Wemb .6D 60
HA2: Harr .5D 40
HA6: Nwood .3H 39
KT3: N Mald .3J 151
KT4: Wor Pk .1D 164
N2 .3C 46
SE25 .3H 157
TW13: Hanw .3D 130
Lincolns, The NW7 .3G 29
Lincolns Inn Flds. WC2 .7G 7 (6K 83)
Lincoln's Inn Hall .7H 7 (6K 83)
Lincoln St. E11 .2G 69
SW3 .4E 16 (4D 100)
Lincoln Way EN1: Enf .5C 24
TW16: Sun .1G 147
Lincombe Rd. BR1: Brom .3H 141
Lindal Ct. E18 .1H 51
Lindal Cres. EN2: Enf .4D 22
Lindales, The *N17* .*6B 34*
(off Grasmere Rd.)
Lindal Rd. SE4 .5B 122
Lindbergh Rd. SM6: Wall .7J 167
Linden Av. CR7: Thor H .4B 156
EN1: Enf .1B 24
HA4: Ruis .1J 57
HA9: Wemb .5F 61
NW10 .2F 81
TW3: Houn .5F 113
Linden Cl. HA4: Ruis .1J 57
HA7: Stan .5G 27
Linden Cl. KT7: T Ditt .7K 149
N14 .6B 22
Linden Ct. DA14: Sidc .4J 143
SE20 .*7H 139*
(off Anerley Pk.)
W12 .1E 98
Linden Cres. IG8: Wfd G .6E 36
KT1: King T .2F 151
UB6: G'frd .6K 59
Lindenfield BR7: Chst .2F 161
Linden Gdns. EN1: Enf .1B 24
W2 .7J 81
W4 .5A 98
Linden Gro. KT3: N Mald .3A 152
SE15 .3H 121
SE26 .6J 139
TW11: Tedd .5K 131
Linden Ho. *SE8* .*6B 104*
(off Abinger Gro.)
TW12: Hamp .6E 130
Linden Lawns HA9: Wemb .4F 61
Linden Lea N2 .5A 46
Linden Leas BR4: W W'ck .2F 171
Linden Mans. *N6* .*1F 65*
(off Hornsey La.)
Linden M. N1 .5D 66
W2 .7J 81
Linden Pl. CR4: Mitc .4C 154
Linden Rd. N10 .4F 47
N11 .2J 31
N15 .4C 48
TW12: Hamp .7E 130
Lindens, The CR0: New Ad .6E 170
E17 .*4D 50*
(off Prospect Hill)
N12 .5G 31
W4 .1J 115
Linden St. RM7: Rom .4K 55
Linden Wlk. N19 .2G 65
Linden Way N14 .6B 22
TW17: Shep .5E 146
Lindeth Cl. HA7: Stan .6G 27
Lindfield Gdns. NW3 .5K 63
Lindfield Rd. CR0: C'don .6F 157
W5 .4C 78
Lindfield St. E14 .6C 86
Lindhill Cl. EN3: Enf H .2E 24
Lindholme Ct. *NW9* .*1A 44*
(off Pageant Av.)
Lindisfarne Rd. RM8: Dag .3C 72
SW20 .7C 134
Lindisfarne Way E9 .4A 68
Lindley Ct. KT1: Ham W .1C 150
Lindley Est. SE15 .7G 103
Lindley Ho. *E1* .*5J 85*
(off Lindley St.)
SE15 .*7G 103*
(off Peckham Pk. Rd.)
Lindley Pl. TW9: Kew .1G 115
Lindley Rd. E10 .2E 68
Lindley St. E1 .5J 85
Lindop Ho. *E1* .*4A 86*
(off Mile End Rd.)
Lindore Rd. SW11 .4D 118
Lindores Rd. SM5: Cars .7A 154
Lindo St. SE15 .2J 121
Lind Rd. SM1: Sutt .5A 166
Lindrop St. SW6 .2A 118
Lindsay Cl. KT9: Chess .7E 162
TW19: Stanw .5A 110
Lindsay Ct. *CR0: C'don* .*4D 168*
(off Eden Rd.)
SW11 .*1B 118*
(off Battersea High St.)
Lindsay Dr. HA3: Kenton .6E 42
TW17: Shep .6F 147
Lindsay Ho. *SW7* .*3A 100*
(off Gloucester Rd.)
Lindsay Rd. KT4: Wor Pk .2D 164
TW12: Ham H .4F 131
Lindsay Sq. SW1 .5D 18 (5H 101)
Lindsell St. SE10 .1E 122

Lindsey Cl. BR1: Brom ... 3B 160
CR4: Mitc ... 4J 155
Lindsey Ct. N13 ... 3F 33
(off Green Lanes)
Lindsey Gdns. TW14: Bedf ... 7F 111
Lindsey Ho. W5 ... 4D 96
Lindsey M. N1 ... 7C 66
Lindsey Rd. RM8: Dag ... 4C 72
Lindsey St. EC1 ... 5B 8 (5B 84)
Lind St. SE8 ... 2C 122
Lindum Rd. TW11: Tedd ... 7C 132
Lindway SE27 ... 5B 138
Lindwood Cl. E6 ... 6D 88
Linen Ho., The W10 ... 2G 81
Linfield WC1 ... 2G 7
(off Sidmouth St.)
Linfield Cl. NW4 ... 3E 44
Linford Christie Stadium ... 5C 80
Linford Ho. E2 ... 1G 85
(off Whiston Rd.)
Linford Rd. E17 ... 3E 50
Linford St. SW8 ... 1G 119
Linford St. Bus. Est. SW8 ... 1G 119
(off Linford St.)
Lingard Ho. E14 ... 3E 104
(off Marshfield St.)
Lingards Rd. SE13 ... 4E 122
Lingey Cl. DA15: Sidc ... 2K 143
Lingfield Av. KT1: King T ... 4E 150
Lingfield Cl. EN1: Enf ... 6K 23
HA6: Nwood ... 1G 39
Lingfield Ct. UB5: N'olt ... 2E 76
Lingfield Cres. SE9 ... 4H 125
Lingfield Gdns. N9 ... 7C 24
Lingfield Ho. SE1 ... 7B 14
Lingfield Rd. KT4: Wor Pk ... 3E 164
SW19 ... 5F 135
Lingham Ct. SW9 ... 2J 119
Lingham St. SW9 ... 2J 119
Lingholm Way EN5: Barn ... 5A 20
Ling Rd. DA8: Erith ... 6J 109
E16 ... 5J 87
Lingrove Gdns. IG9: Buck H ... 2E 36
Lings Coppice SE21 ... 2D 138
Lingwell Rd. SW17 ... 3C 136
Lingwood DA7: Bex ... 2H 127
Lingwood Ct. N2 ... 3C 46
(off Norfolk Cl.)
Lingwood Gdns. TW7: Isle ... 7J 95
Lingwood Rd. E5 ... 7G 49
Linhope St. NW1 ... 3E 4 (4D 82)
Link, The EN3: Enf H ... 1F 25
HA0: Wemb ... 1C 60
HA5: Eastc ... 7A 40
NW2 ... 1C 62
SE9 ... 3E 142
(off William Barefoot Dr.)
TW11: Tedd ... 6K 131
UB5: N'olt ... 5D 58
W3 ... 6H 79
Linkenholt Mans. W6 ... 4B 98
(off Stamford Brook Av.)
Linkfield BR2: Hayes ... 6J 159
KT8: W Mole ... 3F 149
Linkfield Rd. TW7: Isle ... 2K 113
Link Ho. E3 ... 2D 86
W10 ... 6F 81
(off Kingsdown Cl.)
Link La. SM6: Wall ... 6H 167
Linklea Cl. NW9 ... 7F 29
Link Rd. E1 ... 2K 15 (7G 85)
E12 ... 2C 70
N11 ... 4K 31
RM9: Dag ... 2H 91
SM6: Wall ... 1E 166
TW14: Felt ... 7H 111
Links, The E17 ... 4A 50
Links Av. SM4: Mord ... 4J 153
(not continuous)
Linkscroft Av. TW15: Ashf ... 6D 128
Links Dr. N20 ... 1D 30
Links Gdns. SW16 ... 7A 138
Linkside KT3: N Mald ... 2A 152
N12 ... 6D 30
Linkside Cl. EN2: Enf ... 3E 22
Linkside Gdns. EN2: Enf ... 3E 22
Links Rd. BR4: W W'ck ... 1E 170
IG8: Wfd G ... 5D 36
NW2 ... 2B 62
SW17 ... 6E 136
TW15: Ashf ... 5A 128
W3 ... 6G 79
Links Side EN2: Enf ... 3E 22
Link St. E9 ... 6J 67
Links Vw. N3 ... 7C 30
Linksview N2 ... 5D 46
(off Great Nth. Rd.)
Links Vw. Cl. HA7: Stan ... 7F 27
Links Vw. Ct. TW12: Ham H ... 4H 131
Links Vw. Rd. CR0: C'don ... 3C 170
TW12: Ham H ... 5G 131
Links Way BR3: Beck ... 6C 158
Linksway HA6: Nwood ... 1E 38
NW4 ... 2F 45
Links Yd. E1 ... 5K 9
Link Way BR2: Brom ... 7C 160
HA5: Pinn ... 1B 40
Linkway N4 ... 7C 48
RM8: Dag ... 4C 72
SW20 ... 3D 152
TW10: Ham ... 2B 132
Linkway, The EN5: Barn ... 6E 20
Linkwood Wlk. NW1 ... 7H 65
Linley Ct. SM1: Sutt ... 4A 166
Linley Cres. RM7: Mawney ... 3H 55
Linley Rd. N17 ... 2E 48
Linley Sambourne House ... 3J 99
(off Stafford Ter.)
Linnell Cl. NW11 ... 6K 45
Linnell Dr. NW11 ... 6K 45
Linnell Ho. E1 ... 5J 9
(off Folgate St.)
NW8 ... 1A 82
(off Ainsworth Way)
Linnell Rd. N18 ... 5B 34
SE5 ... 2E 120
Linnet Cl. N9 ... 1E 34
SE28 ... 7C 90
WD23: Bush ... 1B 26
Linnet M. SW12 ... 7E 118
Linnett Cl. E4 ... 4K 35
Linom Rd. SW4 ... 4J 119
Linscott Rd. E5 ... 4J 67
Linsdell Rd. IG11: Bark ... 1G 89
Linsey Ct. E10 ... 1C 68
(off Grange Rd.)
Linsey St. SE16 ... 4G 103
(not continuous)
Linslade Cl. HA5: Eastc ... 3K 39
TW4: Houn ... 5C 112
Linslade Ho. E2 ... 1G 85
NW8 ... 3D 4
(off Paveley St.)
Linslade Rd. BR6: Chels ... 6K 173
Linstead Hall SW7 ... 1B 16
(off Princes Gdns.)
Linstead St. NW6 ... 7J 63
Linstead Way SW18 ... 7G 117
Linsted Ct. SE9 ... 6J 125
Lintaine Cl. W6 ... 6G 99
Linthorpe Av. HA0: Wemb ... 6C 60
Linthorpe Rd. EN4: Cockf ... 3H 21
N16 ... 7E 48
Linton Cl. CR4: Mitc ... 7D 154
DA16: Well ... 1B 126
SE7 ... 5A 106
Linton Ct. NW1 ... 7G 65
(off Agar Gro.)
RM1: Rom ... 2K 55
Linton Gdns. E6 ... 6C 88
Linton Gro. SE27 ... 5B 138
Linton Ho. E3 ... 5C 86
(off St Paul's Way)
Linton Rd. IG11: Bark ... 7G 71
Lintons, The IG11: Bark ... 7G 71
Linton St. N1 ... 1C 84
(not continuous)
Lintott Ct. TW19: Stanw ... 6A 110
Linver Rd. SW6 ... 2J 117
Linwood Cl. SE5 ... 2F 121
Linwood Cres. EN1: Enf ... 1B 24
Linzee Rd. N8 ... 4J 47
Lion Av. TW1: Twick ... 1K 131
Lion Cl. SE4 ... 6C 122
TW17: Shep ... 3A 146
Lion Ct. E1 ... 7K 85
(off The Highway)
N1 ... 1K 83
(off Copenhagen St.)
SE1 ... 5G 15
(off Magdalen St.)
Lionel Gdns. SE9 ... 5B 124
Lionel Ho. W10 ... 5G 81
(off Portobello Rd.)
Lionel Mans. W14 ... 3F 99
(off Haarlem Rd.)
Lionel M. W10 ... 5G 81
Lionel Rd. SE9 ... 5B 124
Lionel Rd. Nth. TW8: Bford ... 3E 96
Lionel Rd. Sth. TW8: Bford ... 5F 97
Liongate Ent. Pk. CR4: Mitc ... 4B 154
Lion Ga. Gdns. TW9: Rich ... 3F 115
Lion Ga. M. SW18 ... 7J 117
Liongate M. KT8: E Mos ... 3K 149
Lion Head Ct. CR0: C'don ... 4C 168
(off Southbridge Rd.)
Lion Mills E2 ... 2G 85
Lion Pk. Av. KT9: Chess ... 4G 163
Lion Rd. CR0: C'don ... 5C 156
DA6: Bex ... 4E 126
E6 ... 5D 88
N9 ... 2B 34
TW1: Twick ... 1K 131
Lions Cl. SE9 ... 3A 142
Lion Way TW8: Bford ... 7D 96
Lion Wharf Rd. TW7: Isle ... 3B 114
Lion Yd. SW4 ... 4H 119
Liphook Cres. SE23 ... 7J 121
Lipton Cl. SE28 ... 7C 90
Lipton Rd. E1 ... 6K 85
Lisbon Av. TW2: Twick ... 2G 131
Lisbon Cl. E17 ... 2B 50
Lisburne Rd. NW3 ... 4D 64
Lisford St. SE15 ... 1F 121
Lisgar Ter. W14 ... 4H 99
Liskeard Cl. BR7: Chst ... 6G 143
Liskeard Gdns. SE3 ... 1J 123
Liskeard Ho. SE11 ... 5K 19
(off Kennings Way)
Lisle Cl. SW17 ... 4F 137
Lisle Ct. NW2 ... 3G 63
Lisle St. WC2 ... 2D 12 (7H 83)
Lismore SW19 ... 5H 135
(off Woodside)
Lismore Cir. NW5 ... 5E 64
Lismore Cl. TW7: Isle ... 2A 114
Lismore Rd. CR2: S Croy ... 6E 168
N17 ... 3D 48
Lismore Wlk. N1 ... 6C 66
(off Clephane Rd. Nth.)
Lissant Cl. KT6: Surb ... 7D 150
Lisselton Ho. NW4 ... 4F 45
(off Belle Vue Est.)
Lissenden Gdns. NW5 ... 4E 64
(not continuous)
Lissenden Mans. NW5 ... 4E 64
Lisson Grn. Est. NW8 ... 3C 4
(off Tresham Cres.)
LISSON GROVE ... 5B 4 (5C 82)
Lisson Gro. NW1 ... 3B 4 (4B 82)
NW8 ... 3B 4 (4B 82)
Lisson Ho. NW1 ... 5C 4
(off Lisson St.)
Lisson St. NW1 ... 5C 4 (5C 82)
Lister Cl. CR4: Mitc ... 1C 154
W3 ... 5K 79
Lister Ct. HA1: Harr ... 7B 42
N16 ... 2E 66
NW9 ... 2A 44
Lister Gdns. N18 ... 5H 33
Listergate Ct. SW15 ... 4E 116
Lister Ho. E1 ... 5G 85
HA9: Wemb ... 3J 61
(off Barnhill Rd.)
UB3: Harl ... 4G 93
Lister Lodge W9 ... 5J 81
(off Admiral Wlk.)
Lister Rd. E11 ... 1G 69
Lister Wlk. SE28 ... 7D 90
Liston Rd. N17 ... 1G 49
SW4 ... 3G 119
Liston Way IG8: Wfd G ... 7F 37
Listowel Cl. SW9 ... 7A 102
Listowel Rd. RM10: Dag ... 3G 73
Listria Pk. N16 ... 2E 66
Litcham Ho. E1 ... 3K 85
(off Longnor Rd.)
Litchfield Av. E15 ... 6G 69
SM4: Mord ... 7H 153
Litchfield Ct. E17 ... 6C 50
Litchfield Gdns. NW10 ... 6C 62
Litchfield Rd. SM1: Sutt ... 4A 166
Litchfield St. WC2 ... 2D 12 (7H 83)
Litchfield Way NW11 ... 5K 45
Lithgow's Rd. TW6: H'row A ... 4G 111
Lithos Rd. NW3 ... 6K 63
Litten Nature Reserve ... 3G 77
Little Acre BR3: Beck ... 3C 158
Lit. Albany St. NW1 ... 3K 5
Little Angel Theatre ... 1B 84
(off Dagmar Pl.)
Lit. Argyll St. W1 ... 1A 12 (6G 83)
Little Benty UB7: W Dray ... 1E 174
Little Birches DA15: Sidc ... 2J 143
Lit. Boltons, The SW5 ... 5K 99
SW10 ... 5K 99
Little Bornes SE21 ... 4E 138
Littlebourne SE13 ... 7G 123
Littlebourne Ho. SE17 ... 5E 102
(off Kinglake St.)
Little Britain EC1 ... 6B 8 (5B 84)
Littlebrook Cl. CR0: C'don ... 6K 157
Little Brownings SE23 ... 2H 139
Littlebury Rd. SW4 ... 3H 119
Lit. Bury St. N9 ... 1J 33
Lit. Bushey La. WD23: Bush ... 1C 26
Little Cedars N12 ... 4F 31
Lit. Chelsea Ho. SW10 ... 6A 100
(off Netherton Gro.)
Lit. Chester St. SW1 ... 1J 17 (3F 101)
Little Cloisters SW1 ... 1E 18 (3J 101)
Lit. College La. EC4 ... 2E 14
(off College St.)
Lit. College St. SW1 ... 1E 18 (3J 101)
Littlecombe SE7 ... 6K 105
Littlecombe Cl. SW15 ... 6F 117
Little Comn. HA7: Stan ... 3F 27
Littlecote Cl. SW19 ... 7G 117
Littlecote Pl. HA5: Hat E ... 1C 40
Lit. Cottage Pl. SE10 ... 7D 104
Little Ct. BR4: W W'ck ... 2G 171
Littlecroft SE9 ... 3E 124
Littledale SE2 ... 6A 108
Lit. Dean's Yd. SW1 ... 1E 18
Little Dimocks SW12 ... 2F 137
Lit. Dorrit Ct. SE1 ... 6D 14 (2C 102)
LITTLE EALING ... 3D 96
Lit. Ealing La. W5 ... 4C 96
Lit. Edward St. NW1 ... 1K 5 (3F 83)
Little Elms UB3: Harl ... 7F 93
Lit. Essex St. WC2 ... 2J 13
Lit. Ferry Rd. TW1: Twick ... 1B 132
Littlefield Cl. KT1: King T ... 2E 150
N19 ... 4G 65
Littlefield Ho. KT1: King T ... 2E 150
(off Littlefield Cl)
Littlefield Rd. HA8: Edg ... 7D 28
Lit. Friday Rd. E4 ... 2B 36

Little Gearies IG6: Ilf . . . 4F 53
Lit. George St. SW1 . . . 7E 12 (2J 101)
Little Grange UB6: G'frd . . . 3A 78
Little Green TW9: Rich . . . 4D 114
Lit. Green St. NW5 . . . 4F 65
Littlegrove EN4: E Barn . . . 6H 21
Little Halliards
KT12: Walt T . . . 6J 147
LITTLE HEATH . . . 4B 54
Little Heath RM6: Chad H . . . 4B 54
SE7 . . . 6C 106
Lit. Heath Rd. DA7: Bex . . . 1F 127
Littleheath Rd. CR2: Sels . . . 7H 169
Little Holt E11 . . . 5J 51
LITTLE ILFORD . . . 5D 70
Lit. Ilford La. E12 . . . 4D 70
Littlejohn Rd. W7 . . . 6K 77
Little Larkins EN5: Barn . . . 6B 20
Lit. London Cl. UB8: Hil . . . 5D 74
Lit. London Ct. *SE1* . . . *7K 15*
(off Wolseley St.)
Lit. Marlborough St. W1 . . . 1A 12
Littlemede SE9 . . . 3D 142
Littlemoor Rd. IG1: Ilf . . . 3H 71
Littlemore Rd. SE2 . . . 2A 108
Lit. Moss La. HA5: Pinn . . . 2C 40
Lit. Newport St. WC2 . . . 2D 12 (7H 83)
Lit. New St. EC4 . . . 7K 7 (6A 84)
Lit. Oaks Cl. TW17: Shep . . . 4B 146
Lit. Orchard Cl. HA5: Pinn . . . 2C 40
Lit. Park Dr. TW13: Felt . . . 2C 130
Lit. Park Gdns. EN2: Enf . . . 3H 23
Lit. Pluckett's Way
IG9: Buck H . . . 1G 37
Lit. Portland St. W1 . . . 7K 5 (6G 83)
Little Potters WD23: Bush . . . 1C 26
Lit. Queen's Rd. TW11: Tedd . . . 6K 131
Little Redlands BR1: Brom . . . 2C 160
Little Rd. UB3: Hayes . . . 2H 93
Littlers Cl. SW19 . . . 1B 154
Lit. Russell St. WC1 . . . 6E 6 (5J 83)
Lit. St James's St. SW1 . . . 5A 12 (1G 101)
Lit. St Leonard's SW14 . . . 3J 115
Little Sanctuary SW1 . . . 7D 12 (2H 101)
Lit. Smith St. SW1 . . . 1D 18 (3H 101)
Lit. Somerset St. E1 . . . 1J 15 (6F 85)
LITTLE STANMORE . . . 7A 28
Littlestone Cl. BR3: Beck . . . 6C 140
Little Strand NW9 . . . 2B 44
Little Thrift BR5: Pet W . . . 4G 161
Lit. Titchfield St. W1 . . . 6A 6 (5G 83)
LITTLETON . . . 3C 146
Littleton Av. E4 . . . 1C 36
LITTLETON COMMON . . . 7E 128
Littleton Cres. HA1: Harr . . . 2K 59
Littleton Ho. *SW1* . . . *6A 18*
(off Lupus St.)
Littleton La. TW17: Shep . . . 7A 146
Littleton Rd. HA1: Harr . . . 2K 59
TW15: Ashf . . . 7E 128
Littleton St. SW18 . . . 2A 136
Lit. Trinity La. EC4 . . . 2D 14 (7C 84)
Little Turnstile WC1 . . . 6G 7 (5K 83)
Little Venice Sports Cen. . . . 5A 4 (5A 82)
Littlewood SE13 . . . 6E 122
Littlewood Cl. W13 . . . 3B 96
Lit. Wood St. KT1: King T . . . 2D 150
Livermere Ct. *E8* . . . *1F 85*
(off Queensbridge Rd.)
Livermere Rd. E8 . . . 1F 85
Liverpool Gro. SE17 . . . 5C 102
Liverpool Rd. CR7: Thor H . . . 3C 156
E10 . . . 6E 50
E16 . . . 5G 87
KT2: King T . . . 7G 133
N1 . . . 5A 66
N7 . . . 5A 66
W5 . . . 2D 96
Liverpool St. EC2 . . . 6G 9 (5E 84)
Livesey Cl. KT1: King T . . . 3F 151
SE28 . . . 3G 107
Livesey Pl. SE15 . . . 6G 103
Livingstone Ct. E10 . . . 6E 50
EN5: Barn . . . *2B 20*
(off Church La.)
HA3: W'stone . . . 3K 41
TW19: Stanw . . . *1A 128*
(off Explorer Av.)
Livingstone Ho. NW10 . . . 7K 61
SE5 . . . *7C 102*
(off Wyndham Rd.)
Livingstone Lodge *W9* . . . *5J 81*
(off Admiral Wlk.)
Livingstone Mans. *W14* . . . *6G 99*
(off Queen's Club Gdns.)
Livingstone Pl. E14 . . . 5E 104
Livingstone Rd. CR7: Thor H . . . 2C 156
E17 . . . 6D 50
N13 . . . 6D 32
SW11 . . . 3B 118
TW3: Houn . . . 4G 113
UB1: S'hall . . . 7B 76
LivingWell Health Club
Wembley . . . 5F 61
LivingWell Sports Club
Regents Plaza . . . 2K 81
(off Greville Rd.)
Livonia St. W1 . . . 1B 12 (6G 83)
Lizard St. EC1 . . . 2D 8 (3C 84)
Lizban St. SE3 . . . 7K 105
Lizmans Ter. *W8* . . . *3J 99*
(off Earl's Ct. Rd.)
Llandovery Ho. *E14* . . . *2E 104*
(off Chipka St.)
Llanelly Rd. NW2 . . . 2H 63
Llanover Rd. HA9: Wemb . . . 3D 60
SE18 . . . 6E 106
Llanthony Rd.
SM4: Mord . . . 5B 154
Llanvanor Rd. NW2 . . . 2H 63
Llewellyn Ct. SE20 . . . 1J 157
Llewellyn Mans. *W14* . . . *4G 99*
(off Hammersmith Rd.)
Llewellyn St. SE16 . . . 2G 103
Lloyd Av. SW16 . . . 1J 155
Lloyd Baker St. WC1 . . . 2H 7 (3K 83)
(not continuous)
Lloyd Ct. HA5: Pinn . . . 5B 40
Lloyd Ho. BR3: Beck . . . 6D 140
Lloyd M. EN3: Enf L . . . 1H 25
Lloyd Pk. Av. CR0: C'don . . . 4F 169
Lloyd Pk. Ho. E17 . . . 3C 50
Lloyd Rd. E6 . . . 1D 88
E17 . . . 4K 49
KT4: Wor Pk . . . 3E 164
RM9: Dag . . . 6F 73
Lloyd's Av. EC3 . . . 1H 15 (6E 84)
Lloyd's Building . . . 1G 15 (6E 84)
Lloyds Lanes Raynes Pk. . . . 3F 153
Lloyd's Pl. SE3 . . . 2G 123
Lloyd Sq. WC1 . . . 1J 7 (3A 84)
Lloyd's Row EC1 . . . 2K 7 (3A 84)
Lloyd St. WC1 . . . 1J 7 (3A 84)
Lloyds Way BR3: Beck . . . 5A 158
Lloyds Wharf SE1 . . . 6K 15
Lloyd Thomas Ct. N22 . . . 7E 32
Lloyd Vs. E6 . . . 4C 88
SE4 . . . 2C 122
Loampit Hill SE13 . . . 2C 122
LOAMPIT VALE . . . 3E 122
Loampit Va. SE13 . . . 3D 122
Loanda Cl. E8 . . . 1F 85
Loats Rd. SW2 . . . 6J 119
Lobelia Cl. E6 . . . 5C 88
Locarno Ct. SW16 . . . 5G 137
Locarno Rd. UB6: G'frd . . . 4H 77
W3 . . . 1J 97
Lochaber Rd. SE13 . . . 4G 123
Lochaline St. W6 . . . 6E 98
Lochan Cl. UB4: Yead . . . 4C 76
Lochinvar St. SW12 . . . 7F 119
Lochleven Ho. *N2* . . . *2B 46*
(off The Grange)
Lochmere Cl. DA8: Erith . . . 6H 109
Lochmore Ho. *SW1* . . . *4H 17*
(off Cundy St.)
Lochnagar St. E14 . . . 5E 86
Lockbridge Ct. *W9* . . . *5J 81*
(off Woodfield Rd.)
Lock Bldg., The E15 . . . 2E 86
Lock Chase SE3 . . . 3G 123
Lock Cl. UB2: S'hall . . . 2G 95
Locke Ho. *SW8* . . . *1G 119*
(off Wadhurst Rd.)
Lockesfield Pl. E14 . . . 5D 104
Lockesley Dr.
BR5: St M Cry . . . 6K 161
Lockesley Sq. KT6: Surb . . . 6D 150
Locket Rd. HA3: W'stone . . . 3J 41
Locket Rd. M. HA3: W'stone . . . 2J 41
Lockfield Av. EN3: Brim . . . 2F 25
Lockgate Cl. E9 . . . 5B 68
Lockhart Cl. EN3: Pond E . . . 5C 24
N7 . . . 6K 65
Lockhart St. E3 . . . 4B 86
Lockhouse, The NW1 . . . 1E 82
Lockhurst St. E5 . . . 4K 67
Lockie Pl. SE25 . . . 3G 157
Lockier Wlk. HA9: Wemb . . . 3D 60
Lockington Rd. SW8 . . . 1F 119
Lock Keepers Quay *SE16* . . . *3K 103*
(off Brunswick Quay)
Lockmead Rd. N15 . . . 6G 49
SE13 . . . 3E 122
Lock M. *NW1* . . . *6H 65*
(off Northpoint Sq.)
Lock Rd. TW10: Ham . . . 4C 132
LOCKSBOTTOM . . . 3E 172
Locksfields *SE17* . . . *4D 102*
(off Catesby St.)
Lockside *E14* . . . *7A 86*
(off Narrow St.)
Locks La. CR4: Mitc . . . 1E 154
Locksley Est. E14 . . . 6B 86
Locksley St. E14 . . . 5B 86
Locksmeade Rd. TW10: Ham . . . 4C 132
Locksons Cl. E14 . . . 5D 86
Lockswood Cl. EN4: Cockf . . . 4J 21
Lockton St. *W10* . . . *7F 81*
(off Bramley Rd.)
Lock Vw. Ct. *E14* . . . *7A 86*
(off Narrow St.)
Lockwell Rd. RM10: Dag . . . 3G 73
Lockwood Cl. SE26 . . . 4K 139
Lockwood Ho. E5 . . . 2J 67
SE11 . . . 7J 19 (6A 102)
Lockwood Ind. Pk. N17 . . . 3H 49
Lockwood Pl. E4 . . . 6H 35
Lockwood Sq. SE16 . . . 3H 103
Lockwood Way E17 . . . 2K 49
KT9: Chess . . . 5G 163
Lockyer Est. SE1 . . . 7F 15
(not continuous)
Lockyer Ho. *SE10* . . . *5H 105*
(off Armitage Rd.)
SW8 . . . *7H 101*
(off Wandsworth Rd.)
SW15 . . . 3F 117
Lockyer M. EN3: Enf L . . . 1J 25
Lockyer St. SE1 . . . 7F 15 (2D 102)
Locomotive Dr.
TW14: Felt . . . 1J 129
Locton Grn. E3 . . . 1B 86
Loddiges Ho. E9 . . . 7J 67
Loddiges Rd. E9 . . . 7J 67
Loddon Ho. *NW8* . . . *4B 4*
(off Church St. Est.)
Loder St. SE15 . . . 7J 103
Lodge, The *W12* . . . *2F 99*
(off Richmond Way)
Lodge Av. CR0: Wadd . . . 3A 168
HA3: Kenton . . . 4E 42
RM8: Dag . . . 6B 72
RM9: Dag . . . 1A 90
SW14 . . . 3A 116
LODGE AVENUE FLYOVER JUNC. . . . 1A 90
Lodge Cl. HA8: Edg . . . 6A 28
N18 . . . 5H 33
SM6: Wall . . . 1E 166
TW7: Isle . . . 1B 114
Lodge Dr. N13 . . . 4F 33
Lodge Gdns. BR3: Beck . . . 5B 158
Lodge Hill IG4: Ilf . . . 4C 52
SE2 . . . 7B 108
Lodgehill Pk. Cl. HA2: Harr . . . 2F 59
Lodge La. CR0: New Ad . . . 6C 170
DA5: Bexl . . . 6D 126
N12 . . . 5F 31
RM5: Col R . . . 1G 55
Lodge Pl. SM1: Sutt . . . 5K 165
Lodge Rd. BR1: Brom . . . 7A 142
CR0: C'don . . . 6B 156
NW4 . . . 4E 44
NW8 . . . 2B 4 (3B 82)
SM6: Wall . . . 5F 167
Lodge Vs. IG8: Wfd G . . . 6C 36
Lodge Way TW15: Ashf . . . 2A 128
TW17: Shep . . . 2E 146
Lodore Gdns. NW9 . . . 5A 44
Lodore Grn. UB10: Ick . . . 3A 56
Lodore St. E14 . . . 6E 86
Lofthouse Pl. KT9: Chess . . . 6C 162
Loftie St. SE16 . . . 2G 103
Lofting Ho. *N1* . . . *7A 66*
(off Liverpool Rd.)
Lofting Rd. N1 . . . 7K 65
Loftus Road . . . 1D 98
Loftus Rd. IG11: Bark . . . 6G 71
W12 . . . 1D 98
Loftus Vs. *W12* . . . *1D 98*
(off Loftus Rd.)
Logan Cl. EN3: Enf H . . . 1E 24
TW4: Houn . . . 3D 112
Logan M. RM1: Rom . . . 5K 55
W8 . . . 4J 99
Logan Pl. W8 . . . 4J 99
Logan Rd. HA9: Wemb . . . 2D 60
N9 . . . 2C 34
Loggetts SE21 . . . 2E 138
Logs Hill BR1: Brom . . . 7C 142
BR7: Chst . . . 7C 142
Logs Hill Cl. BR7: Chst . . . 1C 160
Lohmann Ho. SE11 . . . 7J 19
Lois Dr. TW17: Shep . . . 5D 146
Lolesworth Cl. E1 . . . 6J 9 (5F 85)
Lolland Ho. SE7 . . . 4C 106
Lollard St. SE11 . . . 3H 19 (4K 101)
(not continuous)
Loman St. SE1 . . . 6B 14 (2B 102)
Lomas Cl. CR0: New Ad . . . 7E 170
Lomas Dr. E8 . . . 7F 67
Lomas St. E1 . . . 5G 85
Lombard Av. EN3: Enf H . . . 1D 24
IG3: Ilf . . . 1J 71
Lombard Bus. Pk. CR0: C'don . . . 7K 155
SW19 . . . 2K 153
Lombard Ct. EC3 . . . 2F 15 (7D 84)
RM7: Rom . . . 4J 55
W3 . . . 1H 97
Lombard La. EC4 . . . 1K 13 (6A 84)
Lombard Rd. N11 . . . 5A 32
SW11 . . . 2B 118
SW19 . . . 2K 153
LOMBARD RDBT. . . . 7K 155
Lombard St. EC3 . . . 1F 15 (6D 84)
Lombard Trad. Est. SE7 . . . 4K 105
Lombard Wall SE7 . . . 3K 105
(not continuous)
Lombardy Cl. IG6: Ilf . . . 7K 37
Lombardy Pl. W2 . . . 7K 81
Lombardy Retail Pk. UB3: Hayes . . . 7K 75
Lomond Cl. HA0: Wemb . . . 7F 61
N15 . . . 5E 48
Lomond Gdns. CR2: Sels . . . 7A 170
Lomond Gro. SE5 . . . 7D 102
Lomond Ho. SE5 . . . 7D 102
Loncroft Rd. SE5 . . . 6E 102
Londesborough Rd. N16 . . . 4E 66

Londinium Twr. *E1* 2K **15**
                (off W. Tenter St.)
London 2012 Olympic Pk. . . .7D 68 & 1D **86**
London Ambulance Service Hq. . . .5K **53**
London Bombing Memorial . . .5H 11 (1E 100)
London Bri. SE1 . . . . .4F **15** (1D **102**)
London Bridge Experience 4F **15**
                (off Tooley St.)
London Bri. St. SE1 . . . . . .5F **15** (1D **102**)
London Bri. Twr. *SE1* 5F **15**
                (off St Thomas St.)
London Bri. Wlk. *SE1* 4F **15**
                (off Duke St. Hill)
London Business School . . .3E 4 (4D **82**)
London Canal Mus. 2J **83**
LONDON CITY AIRPORT 1C **106**
London City College 5J **13**
                (off Waterloo Rd.)
London Coliseum 3E **12**
             (off St Martin's La.)
London College of Fashion, The
  Hackney .7H **67**
Londonderry Pde. DA8: Erith 7K **109**
London Dungeon 5F **15**
London Eye 6G **13** (2K **101**)
London Flds. E. Side E8 . . . . .7H **67**
London Fields Lido 7H **67**
London Flds. W. Side E8 . . . . .7G **67**
London Film Mus. 6G **13** (2K **101**)
London Fire Brigade Mus. 2C **102**
London Fruit Exchange *E1* 6J **9**
               (off Brushfield St.)
London Ga. UB3: Hayes 2G **93**
LONDON GATEWAY SERVICE AREA . . .2D **28**
London Group Bus. Pk. NW2 . . . . . . .1B **62**
LONDON - HEATHROW AIRPORT
  Terminals 1 & 3 . . . . .3C **110**
  Terminal 4 . . . . .5D **110**
  Terminal 5 . . . . .6D **174**
London Ho. *NW8* 2C **82**
                (off Avenue Rd.)
  WC1 . . . . .3G **7** (4K **83**)
London Ind. Pk., The E6 . . . . .5F **89**
London International Gallery of Children's Art
                     .1F **65**
           (off Dartmouth Pk. Hill)
London La. BR1: Brom 7H **141**
  E8 . . . . .7H **67**
London Master Bakers Almshouses
  E10 . . . . .6D **50**
London Metropolitan Archives
                   .3K **7** (4A **84**)
London Metropolitan University
  London City Campus -
    Central House 7K **9** (6G **85**)
    Commercial Rd. 6G **85**
    Jewry St. 1J **15**
               (off Jewry St.)
    Moorgate 6E **8**
    Tower Hill 2J **15**
  North London Campus -
    Eden Grove 5K **65**
    Stapleton House 5K **65**
    Tower Bldg. & Graduate Cen.
                     .5A **66**
    Old Castle St. 7K **9** (6F **85**)
London M. W2 . . . . .7B **4** (6B **82**)
London Motorcycle Mus. 3G **77**
London Motor Mus. 3H **93**
London Palladium 1A **12**
                (off Argyll St.)
London Pavilion 3C **12**
             (off Shaftesbury Av.)
London Regatta Cen. 7B **88**
London Rd. BR1: Brom 7H **141**
  CR0: C'don 7B **156**
  CR4: Mitc 5C **154**
               (Bishopsford Rd.)
  CR4: Mitc 1E **154**
              (Carshalton Rd.)
  CR4: Mitc 2D **154**
              (Holborn Way)

London Rd. CR7: C'don, Thor H 1K **155**
  DA1: Bexl, Cray 5K **127**
  E13 . . . . .2J **87**
  EN2: Enf 3J **23**
  HA1: Harr 2J **59**
  HA7: Stan 5H **27**
  HA9: Wemb 5E **60**
  IG11: Bark 7F **71**
  KT2: King T 2F **151**
             (not continuous)
  KT17: Ewe 7B **164**
  RM7: Chad H, Rom 6G **55**
  SE1 . . . . .7A **14** (3B **102**)
  SE23 . . . . .1H **139**
  SM3: Cheam 3F **165**
  SM4: Mord 5J **153**
  SM6: Wall 4F **167**
  SW16 . . . . .1K **155**
  SW17 . . . . .7D **136**
  TW1: Twick 7A **114**
  TW3: Houn, Isle 3G **113**
  TW7: Bford, Isle 2K **113**
  TW7: Isle, Twick 5A **114**
  TW8: Bford 2K **113**
  TW14: Bedf 2A **128**
  TW15: Ashf 2A **128**
LONDON ROAD RDBT. 6A **114**
London School of Economics &
  Political Science, The
                 .1G **13** (6K **83**)
London Scottish RUFC 3D **114**
               (off Kew Foot Rd.)
London's Death Trap 7G **13**
London South Bank University
  Keyworth St. 7B **14** (3B **102**)
  London Rd. 7F **77**
  Southwark Campus . . .7B **14** (3B **102**)
London South Bank University Sports Cen.
                     .7B **14**
    (in London South Bank University)
London South Bank University Technopark
                     .3B **102**
                (off London Rd.)
London Stile W4 . . . . .5G **97**
London Stock Exchange 7B **8**
London St. EC3 . . . . .2H **15** (7E **84**)
  W2 . . . . .7A **4** (6B **82**)
London Telecom Tower, The 5A **6**
London Television Cen., The
               .4J **13** (7A **84**)
London Ter. E2 . . . . .2G **85**
London Transport Mus. 2F **13** (7J **83**)
London Transport Mus. Depot 2G **97**
London Trocadero 3C **12** (7H **83**)
London Underwriting Cen. 2H **15**
London Wall EC2 . . . . .6D **8** (5C **84**)
London Wall Bldgs. EC2 . . . . .6F **9**
London Welsh RUFC 3E **114**
London Wetland Cen. 1D **116**
London Wharf E2 . . . . .1H **85**
                (off Wharf Pl.)
London Zoo .2E **82**
LONESOME 1G **155**
Lonesome Cvn. Pk.
  CR4: Mitc 1F **155**
Lonesome Way SW16 . . . . .1F **155**
Long Acre WC2 . . . . .2E **12** (7J **83**)
Long Acre St. W13 . . . . .5A **78**
Longacre Pl. SM5: Cars 6E **166**
Longacre Rd. E17 . . . . .1F **51**
Longbeach Rd. SW11 . . . . .3D **118**
Longberrys NW2 . . . . .3H **63**
Longboat Row UB1: S'hall 6D **76**
Longbow Ho. EC1 . . . . .5D **84**
               (off Chiswell St.)
Longbridge Ho. E16 . . . . .7F **89**
              (off University Way)
  RM8: Dag 4B **72**
             (off Longbridge Rd.)
Longbridge Rd. IG11: Bark 6H **71**
  RM8: Dag 4A **72**
Longbridge Way SE13 . . . . .5E **122**

Longcourt M. E11 . . . . .4A **52**
               (off Elmcroft Av.)
Longcroft SE9 . . . . .3D **142**
Longcrofte Rd. HA8: Edg 7J **27**
Long Deacon Rd. E4 . . . . .1B **36**
LONG DITTON 1C **162**
Longdon Wood BR2: Kes 3C **172**
Longdown Rd. SE6 . . . . .4C **140**
Long Dr. HA4: Ruis 5A **58**
  UB6: G'frd 1F **77**
  UB7: W Dray 2A **92**
  W3 . . . . .6A **80**
Long Elmes HA3: Hrw W 1F **41**
Longfellow Rd. E17 . . . . .6B **50**
  KT4: Wor Pk 2C **164**
Longfellow Way SE1 . . . . .4F **103**
Long Fld. NW9 . . . . .7F **29**
Longfield BR1: Brom 1H **159**
Longfield Av. E17 . . . . .4A **50**
  HA9: Wemb 1E **60**
  NW7 .7H **29**
  SM6: Wall 1E **166**
  W5 . . . . .7C **78**
Longfield Cres. SE26 . . . . .3J **139**
Longfield Dr. CR4: Mitc 1C **154**
  SW14 . . . . .5H **115**
Longfield Est. SE1 . . . . .4F **103**
Longfield Ho. W5 . . . . .7C **78**
Longfield Rd. W5 . . . . .6C **78**
Longfield St. SW18 . . . . .7J **117**
Longfield Wlk. W5 . . . . .6C **78**
LONGFORD .4C **174**
Longford Av. TW14: Felt 6G **111**
  TW19: Stanw 1A **128**
  UB1: S'hall 7F **77**
Longford Cir. CR0: C'don 4C **174**
Longford Cl. TW12: Ham H 4E **130**
  TW13: Hanw 3C **130**
  UB4: Yead 7B **76**
Longford Ct. E5 . . . . .4K **67**
                (off Pedro St.)
  KT19: Ewe 4J **163**
  NW4 .4F **45**
  TW12: Ham H 6F **131**
  UB1: S'hall 1E **94**
              (off Uxbridge Rd.)
Longford Gdns. SM1: Sutt 3A **166**
  UB4: Yead 7B **76**
Longford Ho. BR1: Brom 5F **141**
           (off Brangbourne Rd.)
  E1 . . . . .6J **85**
               (off Jubilee St.)
  TW12: Ham H 4E **130**
Longford Ind. Est. TW12: Hamp 6F **131**
LONGFORDMOOR 4B **174**
Longford Rd. TW2: Whitt 1E **130**
Longford St. NW1 . . . . . .3K **5** (4F **83**)
Longford Wlk. SW2 . . . . .7A **120**
Longford Way TW19: Stanw 1A **128**
Longhayes Av. RM6: Chad H 4D **54**
Longhayes Ct. RM6: Chad H 4D **54**
Longheath Gdns. CR0: C'don 5J **157**
Longhedge Ho. SE26 . . . . .4G **139**
              (off High Level Dr.)
Long Hedges TW3: Houn 2E **112**
Longhedge St. SW11 . . . . .2E **118**
Longhill Rd. SE6 . . . . .2F **141**
Longhook Gdns. UB5: N'olt 2J **75**
Longhope Cl. SE15 . . . . .6E **102**
Longhurst Ho. W10 . . . . .3H **81**
              (off Lancefield St.)
Longhurst Rd. CR0: C'don 6H **157**
  SE13 .5F **123**
Longland Ct. SE1 . . . . .5G **103**
  Longland Dr. N20 . . . . .3E **30**
LONGLANDS 3G **143**
Longlands Cl. CR4: Mitc 1E **154**
  DA15: Sidc 2K **143**
  W11 . . . . .7H **81**
Longlands Pk. Cres.
  DA15: Sidc 3J **143**
Longlands Rd. DA15: Sidc 3J **143**

Long La. CR0: C'don 6J **157**
  DA7: Bex 7D **108**
  EC1 . . . . .6B **8** (5B **84**)
  N2 . . . . .1K **45**
  N3 . . . . .1K **45**
             (not continuous)
  SE1 . . . . .7E **14** (2D **102**)
  TW19: Stanw 2B **128**
  UB10: Hil, Ick 3C **74**
Longleat Ho. SW1 . . . . .5C **18**
             (off Rampayne St.)
Longleat Rd. EN1: Enf 5K **23**
Longleat Way TW14: Bedf 7F **111**
Longleigh Ho. SE5 . . . . .1E **120**
              (off Peckham Rd.)
Longleigh La. DA7: Bex 6C **108**
  SE2 . . . . .6C **108**
Long Lents Ho. NW10 . . . . .1K **79**
             (off Shrewsbury Cres.)
Longley Av. HA0: Wemb 1F **79**
Longley Ct. SW8 . . . . .1J **119**
Longley Rd. CR0: C'don 7B **156**
  HA1: Harr 5G **41**
  SW17 . . . . .6C **136**
Long Leys E4 . . . . .6J **35**
Longley St. SE1 . . . . .4G **103**
Longley Way NW2 . . . . .3E **62**
Longman Ho. E2 . . . . .2K **85**
                (off Mace St.)
  E8 . . . . .1F **85**
             (off Haggerston Rd.)
Long Mark Rd. E16 . . . . .5B **88**
Longmarsh La. SE28 . . . . .1J **107**
Long Mead NW9 . . . . .1B **44**
Longmead BR7: Chst 2E **160**
Longmead Dr. DA14: Sidc 2D **144**
Longmead Ho. SE27 . . . . .5C **138**
Long Meadow NW5 . . . . .5H **65**
Long Mdw. Cl. BR4: W W'ck 7E **158**
Longmeadow Rd. DA15: Sidc 1J **143**
Longmead Rd. KT7: T Ditt 7J **149**
  SW17 . . . . .5D **136**
  UB3: Hayes 7H **75**
Long Mill SE10 . . . . .1D **122**
             (off Greenwich High Rd.)
Longmoore St. SW1 . . . . . .4A **18** (4G **101**)
Longmoor Point SW15 . . . . .1D **134**
                (off Norley Va.)
Longmore Av. EN4: E Barn 6F **21**
  EN5: New Bar 6F **21**
Longmore Gdns. Est. SW1 . . . . .4B **18**
Longnor Est. E1 . . . . .3K **85**
Longnor Rd. E1 . . . . .3K **85**
Long Pond Rd. SE3 . . . . .1G **123**
Longreach Ct. IG11: Bark 2H **89**
Long Reach Rd. IG11: Bark 4K **89**
Longridge Ho. SE1 . . . . .3C **102**
Longridge La. UB1: S'hall 6F **77**
Longridge Rd. IG11: Bark 7G **71**
  SW5 . . . . .4J **99**
Long Ridges N2 . . . . .3K **45**
                (off Fortis Grn.)
Long Rd. SW4 . . . . .4F **119**
Longs Ct. TW9: Rich 4F **115**
  WC2 . . . . .3D **12**
Longshaw Rd. E4 . . . . .3A **36**
Longshore SE8 . . . . .4B **104**
Longshott Ct. SW5 . . . . .4J **99**
             (off W. Cromwell Rd.)
Longstaff Cres. SW18 . . . . .6J **117**
Longstaff Rd. SW18 . . . . .6J **117**
Longstone Av. NW10 . . . . .7B **62**
Longstone Ct. SE1 . . . . .7E **14**
               (off Gt. Dover St.)
Longstone Rd. SW17 . . . . .5F **137**
Long St. E2 . . . . .1J **9** (3F **85**)
Longthornton Rd. SW16 . . . . .2G **155**
Longthorpe Ct. W6 . . . . .4C **98**
Longton Av. SE26 . . . . .4G **139**
Longton Gro. SE26 . . . . .4H **139**
Longview Vs. RM5: Col R 1F **55**
Longview Way RM5: Col R 1K **55**

Longville Rd. SE11 . . . . .4B 102
Long Wlk. KT3: N Mald 3J 151
  SE1 . . . . .3E 102
  SE18 . . . . .6F 107
  SW13 . . . . .2A 116
Longwalk Rd. UB11: Stock P 1D 92
Long Wall E15 . . . . .3F 87
Longwater Ho. KT1: King T 3D 150
  (off Portsmouth Rd.)
Longwood Bus. Pk. TW16: Sun . . .5H 147
Longwood Dr. SW15 . . . . .6C 116
Longwood Gdns. IG5: Ilf 4D 52
  IG6: Ilf 4D 52
Longworth Cl. SE28 . . . . .6D 90
Long Yd. WC1 . . . . .4G 7 (4K 83)
Loning, The NW9 . . . . .4A 44
Lonsdale Av. E6 . . . . .4B 88
  HA9: Wemb 5E 60
  RM7: Rom 6J 55
Lonsdale Cl. E6 . . . . .4C 88
  HA5: Hat E 1C 40
  HA8: Edg 5A 28
  SE9 .3B 142
  UB8: Hil 5E 74
Lonsdale Cl. KT6: Surb 7D 150
Lonsdale Cres. IG2: Ilf 6F 53
Lonsdale Dr. EN2: Enf 4C 22
Lonsdale Dr. Nth. EN2: Enf 5D 22
Lonsdale Gdns. CR7: Thor H 4K 155
Lonsdale Ho. W11 . . . . .6H 81
  (off Lonsdale Rd.)
Lonsdale M. TW9: Kew 1G 115
  W11 .6H 81
  (off Colville M.)
Lonsdale Pl. N1 . . . . .7A 66
Lonsdale Rd. DA7: Bex 2F 127
  E11 . . . . .6H 51
  NW6 .2H 81
  SE25 . . . . .4H 157
  SW13 . . . . .1B 116
  UB2: S'hall 3B 94
  W4 . . . . .4B 98
  W11 .6H 81
Lonsdale Road Reservoir
  Local Nature Reserve 7B 98
Lonsdale Sq. N1 . . . . .7A 66
Lonsdale Yd. W11 . . . . .7J 81
Loobert Rd. N15 . . . . .3E 48
Looe Gdns. IG6: Ilf 3F 53
Lookout Education Cen., The
  . . . . .4E 10 (1D 100)
Loop Rd. BR7: Chst 6G 143
Lopen Rd. N18 . . . . .4K 33
Lopez Ho. SW9 . . . . .3J 119
Lorac Ct. SM2: Sutt 7J 165
Loraine Cl. EN3: Pond E 5D 24
Loraine Cotts. N7 . . . . .4K 65
Loraine Ct. BR7: Chst 5F 143
Loraine Ho. SM6: Wall 4F 167
Loraine Rd. N7 . . . . .4K 65
  W4 . . . . .6H 97
Lord Admiral's Vw. SE18 . . . . . . .4D 106
  (off Frances St.)
Lord Amory Way E14 . . . . .2E 104
Lord Av. IG5: Ilf 4D 52
Lord Chancellor Wlk. KT2: King T . .1J 151
Lord Ct. IG5: Ilf 4D 52
Lordell Pl. SW19 . . . . .6E 134
Lorden Wlk. E2 . . . . .2K 9 (3G 85)
Lord Gdns. IG5: Ilf 4D 52
Lord Hills Bri. W2 . . . . .5K 81
Lord Hills Rd. W2 . . . . .5K 81
Lord Holland La. SW9 . . . . .2A 120
Lord Knyvetts Ct. TW19: Stanw . . .6A 110
Lord Napier Pl. W6 . . . . .5C 98
Lord Nth. St. SW1 . . . . . . .2E 18 (3J 101)
Lord Roberts M. SW6 . . . . .7K 99
Lord Robert's Ter. SE18 . . . . .5E 106
Lords Cl. SE21 . . . . .2C 138
  TW13: Hanw 2C 130
Lord's Cricket Ground 29 4 (3B 82)
Lordship Gro. N16 . . . . .2D 66

Lordship La. N17 . . . . .1D 48
  N22 . . . . .2A 48
  SE22 . . . . .4F 121
Lordship La. Est. SE21 . . . . .7G 121
Lordship Pk. N16 . . . . .2C 66
Lordship Pk. M. N16 . . . . .2C 66
Lordship Pl. SW3 . . . . . . .7C 16 (6C 100)
Lordship Rd. N16 . . . . .1D 66
  UB5: N'olt 7C 58
Lordship Ter. N16 . . . . .2D 66
Lordsmead Rd. N17 . . . . .1E 48
Lord St. E16 . . . . .1C 106
Lords Vw. NW8 . . . . .2A (3B 82)
  (not continuous)
Lord Warwick St. SE18 . . . . .3D 106
Lordwood Cl. DA6: Bex 5E 126
Loreburn Ho. N7 . . . . .4K 65
Lorenzo Ho. IG3: Ilf 6A 54
Lorenzo St. WC1 . . . . .1G 7 (3K 83)
Loretto Gdns. HA3: Kenton 4E 42
Lorian Cl. N12 . . . . .4E 30
Loring Rd. N20 . . . . .2H 31
  SE14 . . . . .1A 122
  TW7: Isle 2K 113
Loris Rd. W6 . . . . .3E 98
Lorn Cl. SW9 . . . . .2A 120
Lorne Av. CR0: C'don 7K 157
Lorne Cl. NW8 . . . . .2D 4 (3C 82)
Lorne Gdns. CR0: C'don 7K 157
  E11 . . . . .4A 52
  W11 . . . . .2F 99
Lorne Ho. E1 . . . . .5A 86
  (off Ben Jonson Rd.)
Lorne Rd. E7 . . . . .4K 69
  E17 . . . . .5C 50
  HA3: W'stone 2K 41
  N4 . . . . .1K 65
  TW10: Rich 5F 115
Lorne Ter. N3 . . . . .2H 45
Lorn Rd. SW9 . . . . .2K 119
Lorraine Ct. NW1 . . . . .7F 65
Lorraine Pk. HA3: Hrw W 7D 26
Lorrimore Rd. SE17 . . . . .6B 102
Lorrimore Sq. SE17 . . . . .6B 102
Lorton Ho. NW6 . . . . .1J 81
  (off Kilburn Va.)
Lothair Rd. W5 . . . . .2D 96
Lothair Rd. Nth. N4 . . . . .6B 48
Lothair Rd. Sth. N4 . . . . .7A 48
Lothbury EC2 . . . . .7E 8 (6D 84)
Lothian Av. UB4: Yead 5K 75
Lothian Cl. HA0: Wemb 3A 60
Lothian Rd. SW9 . . . . .1B 120
Lothrop St. W10 . . . . .3G 81
Lots Rd. SW10 . . . . .7A 100
Lotus Cl. SE21 . . . . .3D 138
Loubet St. SW17 . . . . .6D 136
Loudoun Av. IG6: Ilf 5F 53
Loudoun Rd. NW8 . . . . .1A 82
Loudwater Cl. TW16: Sun 4J 147
Loudwater Rd. TW16: Sun 4J 147
Loughborough Est. SW9 . . . . .3B 120
Loughborough Pk. SW9 . . . . .4B 120
Loughborough Rd. SW9 . . . . .2A 120
Loughborough St. SE11 . . . .5H 19 (5K 101)
Lough Rd. N7 . . . . .5K 65
Loughton Way IG9: Buck H 1G 37
Louisa Cl. E9 . . . . .1K 85
Louisa Cl. TW2: Twick 2J 131
Louisa Gdns. E1 . . . . .4K 85
Louisa Ho. IG3: Ilf 6A 54
Louisa St. E1 . . . . .4K 85
Louise Aumonier Wlk. N19 . . . . . . .7J 47
  (off Jessie Blythe La.)
Louise Bennett Cl. SE24 . . . . .4B 120
Louise Cl. N22 . . . . .1A 48
Louise De Marillac Ho. E1 . . . . . . .5J 85
  (off Smithy St.)
Louise Rd. E15 . . . . .6G 69
Louise White Ho. N19 . . . . .1H 65
Louis Gdns. BR7: Chst 4D 142
Louis M. N10 . . . . .1F 47

Louisville Rd. SW17 . . . . .3E 136
Lousada Lodge N14 . . . . .6B 22
  (off Avenue Rd.)
Louvaine Rd. SW11 . . . . .4B 118
Louvage App. E6 . . . . .5C 88
Lovat Cl. NW2 . . . . .3B 62
Lovat La. EC3 . . . . .2G 15 (7E 84)
  (not continuous)
Lovatt Cl. HA8: Edg 6C 28
Lovatt Ct. SW12 . . . . .1F 137
Lovatt Dr. HA4: Ruis 5J 39
Lovat Wlk. TW5: Hest 7C 94
Loveday Rd. W13 . . . . .2B 96
Lovegrove St. SE1 . . . . .5G 103
Lovegrove Wlk. E14 . . . . .1E 104
Lovekyn Cl. KT2: King T 2E 150
Lovelace Av. BR2: Brom 6E 160
Lovelace Gdns. IG11: Bark 4A 72
  KT6: Surb 7D 150
Lovelace Grn. SE9 . . . . .3D 124
Lovelace Ho. E8 . . . . .1F 85
  (off Haggerston Rd.)
  W13 . . . . .7B 78
Lovelace Rd. EN4: E Barn 7H 21
  KT6: Surb 7C 150
  SE21 . . . . .2C 138
Lovelace Vs. KT7: T Ditt 7B 150
  (off Portsmouth Rd.)
Loveland Mans. IG11: Bark 7H 71
  (off Upney La.)
Love La. BR1: Brom 3K 159
  (off Elmfield Rd.)
  BR1: Brom 3K 159
  (Rafford Way)
  CR4: Mitc 3C 154
  (not continuous)
  DA5: Bexl 6F 127
  (not continuous)
  EC2 . . . . .7D 8 (6C 84)
  HA5: Pinn 2B 40
  IG8: Wfd G 6J 37
  KT6: Surb 2C 162
  N17 . . . . .7A 34
  SE25 . . . . .3H 157
  (not continuous)
  SM1: Sutt 6H 165
  SM3: Cheam, Sutt 6G 165
  SM4: Mord 7J 153
Lovel Av. DA16: Well 2A 126
Lovelinch Cl. SE15 . . . . .6J 103
Lovell Ho. E8 . . . . .1G 85
  (off Shrubland Rd.)
Lovell Pl. SE16 . . . . .3A 104
Lovell Rd. TW10: Ham 3C 132
  UB1: S'hall 6F 77
Loveridge M. NW6 . . . . .6H 63
Loveridge Rd. NW6 . . . . .6H 63
Lovers Wlk. N3 . . . . .7D 30
  (not continuous)
  NW7 .6C 30
  SE10 . . . . .6F 105
  W1 . . . . .4G 11 (1E 100)
Lovett Dr. SM5: Cars 7A 154
Lovett's Cl. SW18 . . . . .4K 117
Lovett Way NW10 . . . . .5J 61
Love Wlk. SE5 . . . . .2D 120
Lovibonds Av. BR6: Farnb 4F 173
  UB7: Yiew 6B 74
Lowbrook Rd. IG1: Ilf 4F 71
Low Cross Wood La. SE21 . . . . . . .3F 139
Lowdell Cl. UB7: Yiew 6A 74
Lowden Rd. N9 . . . . .1C 34
  SE24 . . . . .4B 120
  UB1: S'hall 7C 76
Lowder Ho. E1 . . . . .1H 103
  (off Wapping La.)
Lowe Av. E16 . . . . .5J 87
Lowell Ho. SE5 . . . . .7C 102
  (off Wyndham Est.)
Lowell St. E14 . . . . .6A 86
Lowen Rd. RM13: Rain 2K 91
Lwr. Addiscombe Rd. CR0: C'don . .1E 168

Lwr. Addison Gdns. W14 . . . . .2G 99
Lwr. Ash Est. TW17: Shep 6H 147
Lwr. Belgrave St. SW1 . . . .2J 17 (3F 101)
Lwr. Boston Rd. W7 . . . . .1J 95
Lwr. Broad St. RM10: Dag 1G 91
Lower Camden BR7: Chst 7D 142
Lwr. Church St. CR0: C'don 2B 168
LOWER CLAPTON 4H 67
Lwr. Clapton Rd. E5 . . . . .3H 67
Lwr. Clarendon Wlk. W11 . . . . .6G 81
  (off Clarendon Rd.)
Lwr. Common Sth. SW15 . . . . . . .3D 116
Lwr. Coombe St. CR0: C'don 4C 168
Lwr. Downs Rd. SW20 . . . . .1F 153
Lwr. Drayton Pl. CR0: C'don 2B 168
LOWER EDMONTON 2B 34
LOWER FELTHAM 3J 129
Lower Fosters NW4 . . . . .5E 44
  (off New Brent St.)
Lwr. George St. TW9: Rich 5D 114
Lwr. Gravel Rd. BR2: Brom 1C 172
Lower Grn. Gdns. KT4: Wor Pk . . .1C 164
Lwr. Grn. W. CR4: Mitc 3C 154
Lwr. Grosvenor Pl. SW1 . . . .1K 17 (3F 101)
Lower Gro. Rd. TW10: Rich 6F 115
LOWER HALLIFORD 6F 147
Lwr. Hall La. E4 . . . . .5F 35
  (not continuous)
Lwr. Hampton Rd. TW16: Sun 3A 148
Lwr. Ham Rd. KT2: King T 5D 132
LOWER HOLLOWAY 5K 65
Lwr. Hook Bus. Pk. BR6: Downe . . .7D 172
Lwr. James St. W1 . . . . . .2B 12 (7G 83)
Lwr. John St. W1 . . . . .2B 12 (7G 83)
Lwr. Kenwood Av. EN2: Enf 5D 22
Lwr. King's Rd. KT2: King T 1E 150
Lwr. Lea Crossing E14 . . . . .7G 87
  E16 . . . . .7G 87
Lwr. Maidstone Rd. N11 . . . . .6B 32
Lower Mall W6 . . . . .5D 98
Lwr. Mardyke Av. RM13: Rain 2J 91
Lower Marsh SE1 . . . . . . .7J 13 (2A 102)
Lwr. Marsh La. KT1: King T 4F 151
  (not continuous)
Lwr. Merton Ri. NW3 . . . . .7C 64
Lower Mill KT17: Ewe 7B 164
Lwr. Morden La. SM4: Mord 6E 152
Lwr. Mortlake Rd. TW9: Rich 4E 114
Lwr. Park Rd. DA17: Belv 4G 109
  N11 . . . . .5B 32
Lwr. Park Trad. Est. NW10 . . . . . . .4J 79
LOWER PLACE 2J 79
Lower Pl. Bus. Cen. NW10 . . . . . . .2K 79
  (off Steele Rd.)
Lwr. Queen's Rd. IG9: Buck H 2G 37
Lwr. Richmond Rd. SW14 . . . . . . .3G 115
  SW15 . . . . .3D 116
  TW9: Rich 3G 115
Lower Rd. DA8: Erith 3H 109
  DA17: Belv 3H 109
  HA2: Harr 1H 59
  SE1 . . . . .6J 13 (2A 102)
  SE8 . . . . .4K 103
  SE16 .2J 103
  (not continuous)
  SM1: Sutt 4A 166
Lwr. Robert St. WC2 . . . . .3F 13
  (off Robert St.)
Lwr. Sand Hills KT6: Surb 7C 150
Lwr. Sloane St. SW1 . . . .4G 17 (4E 100)
Lower Sq. TW7: Isle 3B 114
Lower Sq., The SM1: Sutt 5K 165
  (off St Nicholas Way)
Lower Strand NW9 . . . . .2B 44
Lwr. Sunbury Rd. TW12: Hamp . . .2D 148
LOWER SYDENHAM 4K 139
Lwr. Sydenham Ind. Est. SE26 . . . .5B 140
Lwr. Teddington Rd. KT1: Ham W . .1D 150
Lower Ter. NW3 . . . . .3A 64
  SE27 . . . . .5B 138
  (off Woodcote Pl.)
Lwr. Thames St. EC3 . . . . . .3F 15 (7D 84)

Lowerwood Ct. *W11* 6G 81
(off Westbourne Pk. Rd.)
Lwr. Wood Rd. KT10: Clay 6B 162
Lowestoft Cl. *E5* 2J 67
(off Theydon Rd.)
Lowestoft M. E16 2F 107
Loweswater Cl. HA9: Wemb 2D 60
Loweswater Ho. E3 4B 86
Lowfield Rd. NW6 7J 63
W3 6H 79
Low Hall Cl. E4 7J 25
Low Hall La. E17 6A 50
Low Hall Mnr. Bus. Cen. E17 6A 50
Lowick Rd. HA1: Harr 4J 41
Lowlands Gdns. RM7: Rom 6H 55
Lowlands Rd. HA1: Harr 6J 41
HA5: Eastc 7A 40
Lowman Rd. N7 4K 65
Lownde M. SW16 2J 137
Lowndes Cl. SW1 2H 17 (3E 100)
Lowndes Ct. SW1 1F 17 (3D 100)
W1 1A 12
(off Carnaby St.)
Lowndes Lodge *SW1* 1F 17
(off Lowndes St.)
Lowndes M. SW16 2J 137
Lowndes Pl. SW1 2G 17 (3E 100)
Lowndes Sq. SW1 7F 11 (2D 100)
Lowndes St. SW1 1F 17 (3E 100)
Lownds Ct. BR1: Brom 2J 159
Lowood Ct. *SE19* 5F 139
(off Farquhar Rd.)
Lowood Ho. *E1* 7J 85
(off Bewley St.)
Lowood St. E1 7H 85
Lowry Cl. DA8: Erith 4K 109
Lowry Ct. *SE16* 5H 103
(off Stubbs Dr.)
Lowry Cres. CR4: Mitc 2C 154
Lowry Ho. *E14* 2C 104
(off Cassilis Rd.)
N17 1F 49
(off Pembury Rd.)
Lowry Rd. RM8: Dag 5B 72
Lowshoe La. RM5: Col R 1G 55
Lowswood Cl. HA6: Nwood 1E 38
Lowther Dr. EN2: Enf 4D 22
Lowther Hill SE23 7A 122
Lowther Ho. *E8* 1F 85
(off Clarissa St.)
SW1 6B 18
(off Churchill Gdns.)
Lowther Rd. E17 2A 50
HA7: Stan 3F 43
KT2: King T 1F 151
N7 5A 66
SW13 1B 116
Lowth Rd. SE5 1C 120
LOXFORD 5G 71
Loxford Av. E6 2B 88
Loxford La. IG1: Ilf 5G 71
IG3: Ilf 5G 71
Loxford Rd. IG11: Bark 6F 71
Loxford Ter. IG11: Bark 6G 71
Loxham Rd. E4 7J 35
Loxham St. WC1 2F 7 (3J 83)
Loxley Cl. SE26 5K 139
Loxley Ho. HA9: Wemb 3E 60
Loxley Rd. SW18 1B 136
TW12: Hamp 4D 130
Loxton Rd. SE23 1K 139
Loxwood Cl. TW14: Bedf 1F 129
Loxwood Rd. N17 3E 48
LSO St Lukes 3D 8
(off St Lukes Cl.)
Lubbock Ho. *E14* 7D 86
(off Poplar High St.)
Lubbock Rd. BR7: Chst 7D 142
Lubbock St. SE14 7J 103
Lucan Ho. *N1* 1D 84
(off Colville Est.)
Lucan Pl. SW3 4C 16 (4C 100)
Lucan Rd. EN5: Barn 3B 20
Lucas Av. E13 1K 87
HA2: Harr 2E 58
Lucas Cl. NW10 7C 62
Lucas Ct. SE26 5A 140
SW11 1E 118
Lucas Gdns. N2 2A 46
Lucas Ho. *SW10* 7K 99
(off Coleridge Gdns.)
WC1 3J 83
(off Argyle Wlk.)
Lucas Rd. SE20 6J 139
Lucas Sq. NW11 6J 45
Lucas St. SE8 1C 122
Lucerne Cl. N13 3D 32
Lucerne Ct. DA18: Erith 3E 108
Lucerne Gro. E17 4F 51
Lucerne M. W8 1J 99
Lucerne Rd. BR6: Orp 1K 173
CR7: Thor H 5B 156
N5 4B 66
Lucey Rd. SE16 3G 103
Lucey Way SE16 3G 103
Lucie Av. TW15: Ashf 6D 128
Lucien Rd. SW17 4E 136
SW19 2K 135
Lucinda Ct. E17 2A 50
EN1: Enf 4K 23
Lucknow St. SE18 7J 107
Lucorn Cl. SE12 6H 123
Luctons Av. IG9: Buck H 1F 37
Lucy Brown Ho. SE1 5D 14
Lucy Cres. W3 5J 79
Lucy Gdns. RM8: Dag 3F 73
Luddesdon Rd. DA8: Erith 7G 109
Ludford Cl. CR0: Wadd 3B 168
Ludgate B'way. EC4 1A 14 (6B 84)
Ludgate Cir. EC4 1A 14 (6B 84)
Ludgate Hill EC4 1A 14 (6B 84)
Ludgate Sq. EC4 1B 14 (6B 84)
Ludham NW5 5D 64
Ludham Cl. IG6: Ilf 1G 53
SE28 6C 90
Ludlow Cl. BR2: Brom 3J 159
HA2: Harr 4D 58
Ludlow Ct. W3 2J 97
Ludlow Rd. TW13: Felt 4J 129
W5 4C 78
Ludlow St. EC1 3C 8 (4C 84)
Ludlow Way N2 4A 46
Ludovick Wlk. SW15 4A 116
Ludwell Ho. *W14* 3G 99
(off Russell Rd.)
Ludwick M. SE14 7A 104
Luffield Rd. SE2 3B 108
Luffman Rd. SE12 3K 141
Lugard Ho. *W12* 1D 98
(off Bloemfontein Rd.)
Lugard Rd. SE15 2H 121
Lugg App. E12 3E 70
Luke Ho. *E1* 6H 85
(off Tillman St.)
Luke St. EC2 3G 9 (4E 84)
Lukin Cres. E4 3A 36
Lukin St. E1 6J 85
Luli Ct. SE14 6B 104
Lullingstone Cl. BR5: St P 7B 144
Lullingstone Cres.
BR5: St P 7A 144
Lullingstone Ho. *SE15* 6J 103
(off Lovelinch Cl.)
Lullingstone La. SE13 6F 123
Lullingstone Rd. DA17: Belv 6F 109
Lullington Gth. BR1: Brom 7G 141
N12 5C 30
Lullington Rd. RM9: Dag 7E 72
SE20 7G 139
Lulot Gdns. N19 2F 65
Lulworth *NW1* 7H 65
(off Wrotham Rd.)
SE17 5D 102
(off Portland St.)
Lulworth Av. HA9: Wemb 7C 42
TW5: Hest 1F 113
Lulworth Cl. HA2: Harr 3D 58
Lulworth Ct. *N1* 7E 66
(off St Peter's Way)
Lulworth Cres. CR4: Mitc 2C 154
Lulworth Dr. HA5: Pinn 6B 40
Lulworth Gdns. HA2: Harr 2C 58
Lulworth Ho. SW8 7K 101
Lulworth Rd. DA16: Well 2K 125
SE9 2C 142
SE15 2H 121
Lulworth Waye UB4: Yead 6K 75
Lumen Rd. HA9: Wemb 2D 60
Lumiere Apartments SW11 4B 118
Lumiere Bldg., The *E7* 5B 70
(off Romford Rd.)
Lumiere Ct. SW17 2E 136
Lumina Bldgs. *E14* 1E 104
(off Prestons Rd.)
Lumina Loft Apartments *SE1* 7H 15
(off Tower Bri. Rd.)
Luminosity Ct. W13 7B 78
Lumley Cl. DA17: Belv 5G 109
Lumley Ct. WC2 3F 13 (7J 83)
Lumley Flats *SW1* 5G 17
(off Holbein Pl.)
Lumley Gdns. SM3: Cheam 5G 165
Lumley Rd. SM3: Cheam 5G 165
Lumley St. W1 1H 11 (6E 82)
Lumsdon *NW8* 1K 81
(off Abbey Rd.)
Luna Ho. SE16 2G 103
Lunan Ho. *E3* 2B 86
(off Shetland Rd.)
Luna Rd. CR7: Thor H 3C 156
Lund Point E15 1E 86
Lundy Dr. UB3: Harl 4G 93
Lundy Wlk. N1 6C 66
Lunham Rd. SE19 6E 138
Luntley Pl. E1 6K 9
Lupin Cl. CR0: C'don 1K 169
RM7: Rush G 2K 73
SW2 2B 138
UB7: W Dray 1E 174
Lupin Cres. IG1: Ilf 6F 71
Lupino Ct. SE11 3H 19 (4K 101)
Lupin Point SE1 7K 15
Lupton Cl. SE12 3K 141
Lupton St. NW5 4G 65
(not continuous)
Lupus St. SW1 6K 17 (5F 101)
Luralda Wharf E14 5F 105
Lurgan Av. W6 6F 99
Lurline Gdns. SW11 1E 118
Luscombe Ct. BR2: Brom 2G 159
Luscombe Way SW8 7J 101
Lushington Ho. KT12: Walt T 6A 148
Lushington Rd. NW10 2D 80
SE6 4D 140
Lushington Ter. E8 5G 67
Lutea Ho. *SM2: Sutt* 7A 166
(off Walnut M.)
Luther Cl. HA8: Edg 2D 28
Luther King Cl. E17 6B 50
Luther M. TW11: Tedd 5K 131
Luther Rd. TW11: Tedd 5K 131
Luton Ho. *E13* 4J 87
(off Luton Rd.)
Luton Pl. SE10 7E 104
Luton Rd. DA14: Sidc 3C 144
E13 4J 87
E17 3B 50
Luton St. NW8 4B 4 (4B 82)
Lutton Ter. *NW3* 4A 64
(off Lakis Cl.)
Luttrell Av. SW15 5D 116
Lutwyche Rd. SE6 2B 140
Lutyens Ho. *SW1* 6A 18
(off Churchill Gdns.)
Luxborough Ho. *W1* 5G 5
(off Luxborough St.)
Luxborough La. IG7: Chig 3H 37
Luxborough St. W1 5G 5 (5E 82)
Luxborough Twr. W1 5G 5
Luxembourg M. E15 5G 69
Luxemburg Gdns. W6 4F 99
Luxfield Rd. SE9 1C 142
Luxford St. SE16 4K 103
Luxmore St. SE4 1B 122
Luxor St. SE5 3C 120
Lyall Av. SE21 4E 138
Lyall M. SW1 2G 17 (3E 100)
Lyall M. W. SW1 2G 17 (3E 100)
Lyall St. SW1 2G 17 (3E 100)
Lyal Rd. E3 2A 86
Lycett Pl. W12 2C 98
Lyceum Theatre
Covent Garden 2G 13
Lychgate Mnr. HA1: Harr 7J 41
Lych Ga. Wlk. UB3: Hayes 7H 75
(not continuous)
Lyconby Gdns. CR0: C'don 7A 158
Lydd Cl. DA14: Sidc 3J 143
Lydden Ct. SE9 6J 125
Lydden Gro. SW18 7K 117
Lydden Rd. SW18 7K 117
Lydd Rd. DA7: Bex 7F 109
Lydeard Rd. E6 7D 70
Lydford *NW1* 1G 83
(off Royal College St.)
Lydford Cl. *N16* 5E 66
(off Pellerin Rd.)
Lydford Rd. N15 5D 48
NW2 6E 62
W9 4H 81
Lydhurst Av. SW2 2K 137
Lydia Ct. *KT1: King T* 3E 150
(off Grove Cres.)
N12 6F 31
Lydney Cl. SW19 2G 135
Lydon Rd. SW4 3G 119
Lydstep Rd. BR7: Chst 4E 142
Lyford Rd. SW18 7B 118
Lyford St. SE7 4C 106
Lygon Ho. *E2* 1K 9
(off Gosset St.)
SW6 1G 117
(off Fulham Pal. Rd.)
Lygon Pl. SW1 2J 17 (3F 101)
Lyham Cl. SW2 6J 119
Lyham Rd. SW2 5J 119
Lyle Cl. CR4: Mitc 7E 154
Lyle Ct. SM4: Mord 6B 154
Lyly Ho. *SE1* 3D 102
(off Burbage Cl.)
Lyme Farm Rd. SE12 4J 123
Lyme Gro. E9 7J 67
Lyme Gro. Ho. *E9* 7J 67
(off Lyme Gro.)
Lymer Av. SE19 5F 139
Lyme Rd. DA16: Well 1B 126
Lymescote Gdns. SM1: Sutt 2J 165
Lyme St. NW1 7G 65
Lyme Ter. NW1 7G 65
Lyminge Cl. DA14: Sidc 4K 143
Lyminge Gdns. SW18 1C 136
Lymington Av. N22 2A 48
Lymington Cl. E6 5D 88
SW16 2H 155
Lymington Ct. SM1: Sutt 3K 165
Lymington Dr. HA4: Ruis 2F 57
Lymington Gdns. KT19: Ewe 5B 164
Lymington Lodge *E14* 3F 105
(off Schooner Cl.)
Lymington Rd. NW6 6K 63
RM8: Dag 1D 72
Lyminster Cl. UB4: Yead 5C 76
Lympne *N17* 2D 48
(off Gloucester Rd.)
Lympstone Gdns. SE15 7G 103
Lynbridge Gdns. N13 4G 33
Lynbrook Cl. RM13: Rain 2K 91
Lynbrook Gro. SE15 7E 102

Lynch Cl. SE3 ....2H 123
Lynchen Cl. TW5: Cran 1K 111
Lynch Wlk. SE8 ....6B 104
  (off Prince St.)
Lyncott Cres. SW4 ....4F 119
Lyncourt SE3 ....2F 123
Lyncroft Av. HA5: Pinn 5C 40
Lyncroft Gdns. NW6 ....5J 63
  TW3: Houn 5G 113
  W13 ....2C 96
Lyncroft Mans. NW6 ....5J 63
Lyndale KT7: T Ditt 7J 149
  NW2 ....4H 63
Lyndale Av. NW2 ....3H 63
Lyndale Cl. SE3 ....6H 105
Lyndean Ind. Est. SE2 ....3C 108
Lynde Ho. KT12: Walt T 6A 148
  SW4 ....3H 119
Lynden Ho. E1 ....3K 85
  (off Westfield Way)
Lynden Hyrst CR0: C'don 2F 169
Lyndhurst Av. HA5: Pinn 1K 39
  KT5: Surb 1H 163
  N12 ....6J 31
  NW7 ....6F 29
  SW16 ....2H 155
  TW2: Whitt 1D 130
  TW16: Sun 3J 147
  UB1: S'hall 1F 95
Lyndhurst Cl. BR6: Farnb 4F 173
  CR0: C'don 3F 169
  DA7: Bex 3H 127
  NW10 ....3K 61
Lyndhurst Ct. E18 ....1J 51
  NW8 ....1B 82
  (off Finchley Rd.)
  SM2: Sutt 7J 165
  (off Grange Rd.)
Lyndhurst Dr. E10 ....7E 50
  KT3: N Mald 7A 152
Lyndhurst Gdns. EN1: Enf 4K 23
  HA5: Pinn 1K 39
  IG2: Ilf 6H 53
  IG11: Bark 6J 71
  N3 ....1G 45
  NW3 ....5B 64
Lyndhurst Gro. SE15 ....2E 120
Lyndhurst Lodge E14 ....4F 105
  (off Millennium Dr.)
Lyndhurst Ri. IG7: Chig 4K 37
Lyndhurst Rd. CR7: Thor H 4A 156
  DA7: Bex 3H 127
  E4 ....7K 35
  N18 ....4B 34
  N22 ....6F 33
  NW3 ....5B 64
  UB6: G'frd 4F 77
Lyndhurst Sq. SE15 ....1F 121
Lyndhurst Ter. NW3 ....5B 64
Lyndhurst Way SE15 ....1F 121
  SM2: Sutt 7J 165
  SM6: Wall 3E 166
Lyndon Ho. E18 ....1J 51
  (off Queen Mary Av.)
Lyndon Rd. DA17: Belv 4G 109
Lyndon Yd. SW17 ....4A 136
Lyne Cres. E17 ....1B 50
Lynegrove Av. TW15: Ashf 5E 128
Lyneham Dr. NW9 ....1A 44
Lyneham Wlk. E5 ....5A 68
  HA5: Eastc 3H 39
Lynette Av. SW4 ....6F 119
Lynford Cl. HA8: Edg 1J 43
Lynford Ct. CR0: C'don 4E 168
  (off Coombe Rd.)
Lynford French Ho. SE17 ....5C 102
  (off Penton Pl.)
Lynford Gdns. HA8: Edg 3C 28
  IG3: Ilf 2K 71
Lynford Ter. N9 ....1A 34
Lynhurst Cres. UB10: Hil 7E 56

Lynhurst Rd. UB10: Hil 7E 56
Lynmere Rd. DA16: Well 2B 126
Lyn M. E3 ....3B 86
  N16 ....4E 66
Lynmouth Av. EN1: Enf 6A 24
  SM4: Mord 6F 153
Lynmouth Dr. HA4: Ruis 2K 57
Lynmouth Gdns. TW5: Hest 7B 94
  UB6: G'frd 1B 78
Lynmouth Rd. E17 ....6A 50
  N2 ....3D 46
  N16 ....1F 67
  UB6: G'frd 1B 78
Lynn Cl. HA3: Hrw W 2H 41
  TW15: Ashf 5F 129
Lynne Cl. BR6: Chels 6K 173
  SE23 ....7B 122
Lynne Ct. CR2: S Croy 4E 168
  (off Birdhurst Rd.)
  NW6 ....7K 63
  (off Priory Rd.)
Lynnett Rd. RM8: Dag 2D 72
Lynne Way UB5: N'olt 2B 76
Lynn Ho. SE15 ....6H 103
  (off Friary Est.)
Lynn M. E11 ....2G 69
Lynn Rd. E11 ....2G 69
  IG2: Ilf 7H 53
  SW12 ....7F 119
Lynn St. EN2: Enf 1J 23
Lynscott Way CR2: S Croy 7B 168
Lynstead Cl. BR3: Beck 2A 158
Lynsted Cl. BR1: Brom 2A 160
  DA6: Bex 5H 127
Lynsted Gdns. SE9 ....4B 124
Lynton Av. N12 ....4G 31
  NW9 ....4B 44
  RM7: Mawney 1G 55
  W13 ....6A 78
Lynton Cl. KT9: Chess 4E 162
  NW10 ....5A 62
  TW7: Isle 4K 113
Lynton Cres. IG2: Ilf 6F 53
Lynton Est. SE1 ....4G 103
Lynton Gdns. EN1: Enf 7K 23
  N11 ....6C 32
Lynton Grange N2 ....3D 46
Lynton Ho. IG1: Ilf 2G 71
  (off High Rd.)
  W2 ....6A 82
  (off Hallfield Est.)
Lynton Mans. SE1 ....1J 19
  (off Kennington Rd.)
Lynton Mead N20 ....3D 30
Lynton Rd. CR0: C'don 6A 156
  E4 ....5J 35
  HA2: Harr 2C 58
  KT3: N Mald 5K 151
  N8 ....5H 47
  (not continuous)
  NW6 ....2H 81
  SE1 ....4F 103
  W3 ....7G 79
Lynton Ter. W3 ....6J 79
Lynton Wlk. UB4: Hayes 3G 75
Lynwood Cl. E18 ....1A 52
  HA2: Harr 3C 58
Lynwood Ct. KT1: King T 2H 151
Lynwood Dr. HA6: Nwood 1H 39
  KT4: Wor Pk 2C 164
Lynwood Gdns. CR0: Wadd 4K 167
  UB1: S'hall 6D 76
Lynwood Gro. BR6: Orp 7J 161
  N21 ....1F 33
Lynwood Rd. KT7: T Ditt 2A 162
  SW17 ....3D 136
  W5 ....3D 78
Lynx E16 ....7B 88
Lyon Bus. Pk. IG11: Bark 2J 89
Lyon Cl. HA4: Ruis 1H 57
Lyon Ho. NW8 ....4C 4
  (off Broadley St.)

Lyon Ind. Est. NW2 ....2D 62
Lyon Meade HA7: Stan 1C 42
Lyon Pk. Av. HA0: Wemb 6C 60
  (not continuous)
Lyon Rd. HA1: Harr 6K 41
  SW19 ....1A 154
LYONSDOWN 5F 21
Lyonsdown Av. EN5: New Bar ..6F 21
Lyonsdown Rd. EN5: New Bar ..6F 21
Lyons Pl. NW8 ....4A 4 (4B 82)
Lyon St. N1 ....7K 65
Lyons Wlk. W14 ....4G 99
Lyon Way HA0: G'frd 1J 77
Lyoth Rd. BR5: Farnb 2G 173
Lyric Cl. E8 ....7F 67
  (off Holly St.)
Lyric Dr. UB6: G'frd 4F 77
Lyric M. SE26 ....4J 139
Lyric Rd. SW13 ....1B 116
Lyric Sq. W6 ....4E 98
  (off King St.)
Lyric Theatre
  Hammersmith 4E 98
  Westminster 2C 12
  (off Shaftesbury Av.)
Lysander NW9 ....1B 44
Lysander Gdns. KT6: Surb 6F 151
Lysander Gro. N19 ....1H 65
Lysander Ho. E2 ....2H 85
  (off Temple St.)
Lysander M. N19 ....1G 65
Lysander Rd. CR0: Wadd 6K 167
  HA4: Ruis 2F 57
Lysander Way BR6: Farnb 3G 173
Lysia Ct. SW6 ....7F 99
  (off Lysia St.)
Lysias Rd. SW12 ....6F 119
Lysia St. SW6 ....7F 99
Lysons Wlk. SW15 ....4C 116
Lytchet Rd. BR1: Brom 7J 141
Lytchet Way EN3: Enf H 1D 24
Lytchgate Cl. CR2: S Croy 7E 168
Lytcott Dr. KT8: W Mole 3D 148
Lytcott Gro. SE22 ....5E 120
Lytham Cl. SE28 ....6E 90
Lytham Ct. UB1: S'hall 6F 77
  (off Whitecote Rd.)
Lytham Gro. W5 ....3F 79
Lytham St. SE17 ....5D 102
Lyttelton Cl. NW3 ....7C 64
Lyttelton Ct. N2 ....5A 46
Lyttelton Ho. E9 ....7J 67
  (off Well St.)
Lyttelton Rd. E10 ....3D 68
  N2 ....5A 46
Lyttelton Theatre 4H 13
  (in National Theatre)
Lyttleton Ct. UB4: Yead 4A 76
  (off Dunedin Way)
Lyttleton Rd. N8 ....3A 48
Lytton Av. EN3: Enf L 1F 25
  N13 ....2F 33
Lytton Cl. N2 ....6B 46
  UB5: N'olt 7D 58
Lytton Ct. WC1 ....5J 83
  (off Barter St.)
Lytton Gdns. SM6: Bedd 4H 167
Lytton Gro. SW15 ....5F 117
Lytton Rd. E11 ....7G 51
  EN5: New Bar 4F 21
  HA5: Pinn 1C 40
Lytton Strachey Path SE28 .....7B 90
Lytton Ter. E12 ....6D 70
Lyveden Rd. SE3 ....7K 105
  SW17 ....6D 136

M

Mabbott Ho. SE18 ....6E 106
  (off Nightingale Pl.)
Mabel Evetts Cl. UB3: Hayes ...7K 75

Maberley Cres. SE19 ....7G 139
Maberley Rd. BR3: Beck 3K 157
  SE19 ....7F 157
Mabledon Pl. WC1 ....2D 6 (3H 83)
Mablethorpe Rd.
  SW6 ....7G 99
Mabley St. E9 ....5A 68
Mablin Lodge IG9: Buck H 1F 37
McAdam Dr. EN2: Enf 2G 23
Macaret Cl. N20 ....7E 20
Macarthur Cl. DA8: Erith 5K 109
  E7 ....6J 69
  HA9: Wemb 6H 61
Macarthur Ter. SE7 ....6B 106
Macartney Ho. SE10 ....7F 105
  (off Chesterfield Wlk.)
  SW9 ....1A 120
  (off Gosling Way)
Macaulay Ct. SW4 ....3F 119
Macaulay Rd. E6 ....2B 88
  SW4 ....3F 119
Macaulay Sq. SW4 ....4F 119
Macaulay Way SE28 ....1B 108
McAuley Cl. SE1 ....1J 19 (3A 102)
  SE9 ....5F 125
Macauley Ho. W10 ....5G 81
  (off Portobello Rd.)
Macauley M. SE13 ....2E 122
McAusland Ho. E3 ....2B 86
  (off Wright's Rd.)
Macbean St. SE18 ....3F 107
Macbeth Ho. N1 ....2E 84
Macbeth St. W6 ....5D 98
McBride Ho. E3 ....2B 86
  (off Libra Rd.)
McCabe Ct. E16 ....5H 87
  (off Barking Rd.)
McCall Cl. SW4 ....2J 119
McCall Cres. SE7 ....5C 106
McCall Ho. N7 ....4J 65
McCarthy Rd. TW13: Hanw 5B 130
Macclesfield Rd. EC1 ....2C 8
  (off Central St.)
Macclesfield Rd. EC1 ....1C 8 (3C 84)
  SE25 ....5J 157
Macclesfield St. W1 ....2D 12 (7H 83)
McCoid Way SE1 ....7C 14 (2C 102)
McCrone M. NW3 ....6B 64
McCullum Rd. E3 ....1B 86
McDermott Cl. SW11 ....3C 118
McDermott Rd. SE15 ....3G 121
Macdonald Av. RM10: Dag 3H 73
Macdonald Ho. SW11 ....2E 118
  (off Dagnall St.)
Macdonald Rd. E7 ....4J 69
  E17 ....1E 50
  (not continuous)
  N11 ....5J 31
  N19 ....2G 65
McDonough Cl. KT9: Chess 4E 162
McDougall Ct. TW9: Rich 2G 115
McDowall Cl. E16 ....5H 87
McDowall Rd. SE5 ....1C 120
Macduff Rd. SW11 ....1E 118
Mace Cl. E1 ....1H 103
McEntee Av. E17 ....1A 50
Mace St. E2 ....2K 85
McEwan Ho. E3 ....2B 86
  (off Roman Rd.)
McEwen Way E15 ....1F 87
  (off Rokeby St.)
Macey Ho. SW11 ....1C 118
Macey St. SE10 ....6E 104
  (off Thames St.)
McFadden Cl. E10 ....3D 68
  (off Buckingham Rd.)
Macfarland Gro. SE15 ....7E 102
Macfarlane La. TW7: Isle 6K 95
Macfarlane Rd. W12 ....1E 98
Macfarren Pl. NW1 ....4H 5 (4E 82)
Macfarron Ho. W10 ....3G 81
  (off Parry Rd.)

McGlashon Ho. E1 . . . . .4K 9
(off Hunton St.)
McGrath Rd. E15 . . . . .5H 69
McGregor Ct. N1 . . . . .1H 9
Macgregor Rd. E16 . . . . .5A 88
McGregor Rd. W11 . . . . .6H 81
McIndoe Ct. N1 . . . . .1D 84
(off Sherborne St.)
McIntosh Cl. RM1: Rom 3K 55
SM6: Wall 7J 167
Macintosh Ho. W1 . . . . .5H 5
(off Beaumont St.)
McIntosh Ho. SE16 . . . . .4J 103
(off Millender Wlk.)
McIntosh Rd. RM1: Rom 3K 55
McIntyre Ct. SE18 . . . . .4C 106
(off Prospect Va.)
Mackay Ho. W12 . . . . .7D 80
(off White City Est.)
Mackay Rd. SW4 . . . . .3F 119
McKay Rd. SW20 . . . . .7D 134
McKellar Cl. WD23: B Hea 2B 26
McKenna Ho. E3 . . . . .2B 86
(off Wright's Rd.)
Mackennal St. NW8 . . . . .2C 82
Mackenzie Cl. W12 . . . . .7D 80
Mackenzie Ho. N8 . . . . .4J 47
(off Pembroke Rd.)
NW2 . . . . .3C 62
Mackenzie Ho. BR3: Beck 2J 157
N7 . . . . .6K 65
Mackenzie Wlk. E14 . . . . .1C 104
McKerrell Rd. SE15 . . . . .1G 121
Mackeson Rd. NW3 . . . . .4D 64
Mackie Rd. SW2 . . . . .7A 120
McKillop Way DA14: Sidc 7C 144
Mackintosh La. E9 . . . . .5K 67
Macklin St. WC2 . . . . .7F 7 (6J 83)
Mackonochie Ho. EC1 . . . . .5J 7
(off Baldwins Gdns.)
Mackrow Wlk. E14 . . . . .7E 86
Mack's Rd. SE16 . . . . .4G 103
Mackworth Ho. NW1 . . . . .1A 6
(off Augustus St.)
Mackworth St. NW1 . . . . .1A 6 (3G 83)
McLaren Ho. SE1 . . . . .7A 14
(off St Georges Cir.)
Maclaren M. SW15 . . . . .4E 116
Maclean Rd. SE23 . . . . .6A 122
McLeod Cl. SE22 . . . . .1G 139
Macleod Rd. N21 . . . . .5D 22
McLeod Rd. SE2 . . . . .4B 108
McLeod's M. SW7 . . . . .4K 99
Macleod St. SE17 . . . . .5C 102
Maclise Ho. SW1 . . . . .4E 18
(off Marsham St.)
Maclise Rd. W14 . . . . .3G 99
Macmillan Ct. HA2: Harr 1E 58
UB6: G'frd 4H 77
Macmillan Ho. NW8 . . . . .2D 4
(off Lorne Cl.)
McMillan Ho. SE4 . . . . .3A 122
(off Arica Rd.)
SE14 . . . . .1A 122
McMillan St. SE8 . . . . .6C 104
McMillan Student Village SE8 . . . . .6C 104
Macmillan Way SW17 . . . . .4F 137
McNair Rd. UB2: S'hall 3F 95
Macnamara Ho. SW10 . . . . .7B 100
(off Worlds End Est.)
McNeil Rd. SE5 . . . . .2E 120
McNicol Dr. NW10 . . . . .2J 79
Macoma Rd. SE18 . . . . .6H 107
Macoma Ter. SE18 . . . . .6H 107
Maconochies Rd. E14 . . . . .5D 104
Macquarie Way E14 . . . . .4D 104
McRae La. CR4: Mitc 7D 154
Macready Ho. W1 . . . . .6E 4
(off Crawford St.)
Macready Pl. N7 . . . . .4J 65
(not continuous)

Macrea Ho. E3 . . . . .3B 86
(off Bow Rd.)
Macroom Ho. W9 . . . . .3H 81
(off Macroom Rd.)
Macroom Rd. W9 . . . . .3H 81
Macs Ho. E17 . . . . .3D 50
Mac's Pl. EC4 . . . . .7J 7
Madame Tussaud's 4G 5 (4E 82)
Mada Rd. BR6: Farnb 3F 173
Maddams St. E3 . . . . .4D 86
Maddfields Ct. N11 . . . . .1H 47
Maddison Cl. N2 . . . . .2A 46
TW11: Tedd 6K 131
Maddocks Cl. DA14: Sidc 5E 144
Maddocks Ho. E1 . . . . .7H 85
(off Cornwall St.)
Maddock Way SE17 . . . . .6B 102
Madeira Av. BR1: Brom 7G 141
Madeira Gro. IG8: Wfd G 6F 37
Madeira Rd. CR4: Mitc 4D 154
E11 .1F 69
N13 . . . . .4G 33
SW16 . . . . .5J 137
Madeleine Cl. RM6: Chad H 6C 54
Madeley Rd. W5 . . . . .6D 78
Madeline Gro. IG1: Ilf 5H 71
Madeline Rd. SE20 . . . . .7G 139
Madge Gill Way E6 . . . . .1C 88
(off High St. Nth.)
Madge Hill W7 . . . . .7J 77
Madinah Rd. E8 . . . . .6G 67
Madison, The SE1 . . . . .6E 14
(off Long La.)
Madison Bldg. SE10 . . . . .1D 122
(off Blackheath Rd.)
Madison Cl. SM2: Sutt 7B 166
Madison Ct. RM10: Dag 6H 73
Madison Cres. DA7: Bex 7C 108
Madison Gdns. BR2: Brom 3H 159
DA7: Bex 7C 108
Madison Ho. E14 . . . . .7B 86
(off Victory Pl.)
Madison Cl. NW2 . . . . .2J 63
Madras Pl. N7 . . . . .6A 66
Madras Rd. IG1: Ilf 4F 71
Madrid Rd. SW13 . . . . .1C 116
Madrigal La. SE5 . . . . .7B 102
Madron St. SE17 . . . . .5E 102
Mafeking Av. E6 . . . . .2C 88
IG2: Ilf 7H 53
TW8: Bford 6E 96
Mafeking Rd. E16 . . . . .4H 87
EN1: Enf 3A 24
N17 . . . . .2G 49
Magazine Ga. W2 . . . . .4D 10 (1C 100)
Magdala Av. N19 . . . . .2G 65
Magdala Rd. CR2: S Croy 7D 168
TW7: Isle 3A 114
Magdalene Cl. SE15 . . . . .2H 121
Magdalene Gdns. E6 . . . . .4E 88
N20 .1J 31
Magdalen Ho. E16 . . . . .1K 105
(off Keats Av.)
Magdalen M. NW3 . . . . .6A 64
(off Frognal)
Magdalen Pas. E1 . . . . .2K 15 (7F 85)
Magdalen Rd. SW18 . . . . .1A 136
Magee St. SE11 . . . . .7J 19 (6A 102)
Magellan Blvd. E16 . . . . .7G 89
Magellan Ct. NW10 . . . . .7K 61
(off Brentfield Rd.)
Magellan Ho. E1 . . . . .4K 85
(off Ernest St.)
Magellan Pl. E14 . . . . .4C 104
Magistrates' Court
Acton 2J 97
Belmarsh 2J 107
Bexley 4G 127
Brentford 7D 96

Magistrates' Court
Bromley 1H 159
Camberwell Green 1D 120
City of Westminster
. . . . .2E 18 (4J 101)
Clerkenwell 1H 7 (3K 83)
Croydon 3D 168
Enfield 1F 49
Feltham 1K 129
Greenwich 1D 122
Haringey 6E 46
Hendon 6B 44
Highbury Corner 6A 66
Inner London Family Proceedings
. . . . .7A 6 (5G 83)
Kingston upon Thames 2D 150
Redbridge 3G 53
Richmond-upon-Thames 4D 114
South Western 3D 118
Stratford 7F 69
Sutton 6F 167
Thames 3C 86
Tower Bridge 6J 15
Waltham Forest 3D 50
Wimbledon 6J 135
Woolwich 4E 106
Magnaville Rd. WD23: B Hea 1D 26
Magnet Rd. HA9: Wemb 2C 60
Magnin Cl. E8 . . . . .1G 85
Magnolia Cl. E10 . . . . .2C 68
KT2: King T 6H 133
Magnolia Cl. HA3: Kenton 7F 43
SM2: Sutt 7J 165
(off Grange Rd.)
SM6: Wall 5F 167
TW9: Kew 1H 115
TW13: Felt 1J 129
(off Plum Cl.)
UB5: N'olt 4C 76
UB10: Hil 6D 56
Magnolia Gdns. E10 . . . . .2C 68
HA8: Edg 4D 28
Magnolia Ho. SE8 . . . . .6B 104
(off Evelyn St.)
Magnolia Lodge E4 . . . . .3J 35
W8 .3K 99
(off St Mary's Ga.)
Magnolia Pl. SW4 . . . . .5J 119
W5 .5D 78
Magnolia Rd. W4 . . . . .6H 97
Magnolia St. UB7: W Dray . . . .4A 92 & 1E 174
Magnolia Way KT19: Ewe 5J 163
Magnolia Wharf W4 . . . . .6G 97
Magpie All. EC4 . . . . .1K 13 (6A 84)
Magpie Cl. E7 . . . . .5H 69
EN1: Enf 1B 24
NW9 . . . . .2A 44
Magpie Hall Cl. BR2: Brom 6C 160
Magpie Hall La. BR2: Brom 5D 160
Magpie Hall Rd. WD23: B Hea 2D 26
Magpie Ho. E3 . . . . .1B 86
(off Sycamore Av.)
Magpie Pl. SE14 . . . . .6A 104
Magri Wlk. E1 . . . . .5J 85
Maguire Dr. TW10: Ham 4C 132
Maguire St. SE1 . . . . .6K 15 (2F 103)
Mahatma Gandhi Ind. Est.
SE24 . . . . .4B 120
Mahlon Av. HA4: Ruis 5K 57
(not continuous)
Mahogany Cl. SE16 . . . . .1A 104
Mahon Cl. EN1: Enf 1A 24
Mahoney Ho. SE14 . . . . .1B 122
(off Heald St.)
Maibeth Gdns. BR3: Beck 4A 158
Maida Av. E4 . . . . .7J 25
W2 . . . . .4A 4 (5A 82)
MAIDA HILL 4H 81
Maida Va. DA7: Belv 3G 109
MAIDA VALE 4K 81
Maida Va. W9 . . . . .3A 4 (2K 81)
Maida Way E4 . . . . .7J 25

Maiden Erlegh Av. DA5: Bexl 1E 144
Maiden La. NW1 . . . . .7H 65
SE1 . . . . .5D 14 (1C 102)
WC2 . . . . .3F 13 (7J 83)
Maiden Pl. NW5 . . . . .3G 65
Maiden Rd. E15 . . . . .7G 69
Maidenstone Hill SE10 . . . . .1E 122
Maids of Honour Row TW9: Rich 5D 114
Maidstone Av. RM5: Col R 2J 55
Maidstone Bldgs. M. SE1 . . .5D 14 (1C 102)
Maidstone Ho. E14 . . . . .6D 86
(off Carmen St.)
Maidstone Rd. DA14: Sidc, Swan . . .6D 144
N11 . . . . .6B 32
Mail Coach Yd. E2 . . . . .1H 9 (3E 84)
Main Av. EN1: Enf 5A 24
Main Dr. HA9: Wemb 3D 60
Main Mill SE10 . . . . .7D 104
(off Greenwich High St.)
Mainridge Rd. BR7: Chst 4E 142
Main Rd. DA14: Sidc 3H 143
Main St. TW13: Hanw 5B 130
Mainwaring Ct. CR4: Mitc 2E 154
Mais Ho. SE26 . . . . .2H 139
Maismore St. SE15 . . . . .6G 103
Maisonettes, The SM1: Sutt 5H 165
Maitland Cl. E10 . . . . .7D 104
TW4: Houn 3D 112
Maitland Cl. W2 . . . . .2A 10
(off Lancaster Ter.)
Maitland Ho. E2 . . . . .2J 85
(off Waterloo Gdns.)
SW1 . . . . .7A 18
(off Churchill Gdns.)
Maitland Pk. Est. NW3 . . . . .6D 64
Maitland Pk. Rd. NW3 . . . . .6D 64
Maitland Pk. Vs. NW3 . . . . .6D 64
Maitland Pl. E5 . . . . .4H 67
Maitland Rd. E15 . . . . .6H 69
SE26 . . . . .6K 139
Maitland Yd. W13 . . . . .1A 96
Maize Row E14 . . . . .7B 86
Majendie Rd. SE18 . . . . .5H 107
Majestic Way CR4: Mitc 2D 154
Major Cl. SW9 . . . . .3B 120
Major Draper St. SE18 . . . . .3F 107
Major Rd. E15 . . . . .5F 69
SE16 . . . . .3G 103
Makepeace Av. N6 . . . . .2E 64
Makepeace Mans. N6 . . . . .2E 64
Makepeace Rd. E11 . . . . .4J 51
UB5: N'olt 2C 76
Makinen Ho. IG9: Buck H 1F 37
Makins St. SW3 . . . . .4D 16 (4C 100)
Malabar Ct. W12 . . . . .7D 80
(off India Way)
Malabar St. E14 . . . . .1C 104
Malam Ct. SE11 . . . . .4J 19 (4A 102)
Malam Gdns. E14 . . . . .7D 86
Malbrook Rd. SW15 . . . . .4D 116
Malcolm Cl. SE20 . . . . .7J 139
Malcolm Ct. E7 . . . . .6H 69
HA7: Stan 5H 27
NW4 . . . . .6C 44
Malcolm Cres. NW4 . . . . .6C 44
Malcolm Dr. KT6: Surb 1E 162
Malcolm Ho. N1 . . . . .2E 84
(off Arden Est.)
Malcolm Pl. E2 . . . . .4J 85
Malcolm Rd. E1 . . . . .4J 85
SE20 . . . . .7J 139
SE25 . . . . .6G 157
SW19 . . . . .6G 135
UB10: Ick 4B 56
Malcolm Sargent Ho. E16 . . . . .1K 105
(off Evelyn Rd.)
Malcolmson Ho. SW1 . . . . .6C 18
(off Aylesford St.)
Malcolm Way E11 . . . . .5J 51
Malcoms Way N14 . . . . .5B 22
Malden Av. SE25 . . . . .4H 157
UB6: G'frd 5J 59

Malden Cen., The 4B **152**
Malden Ct. KT3: N Mald 3D **152**
N4 6C **48**
Malden Cres. NW1 6E **64**
MALDEN GREEN 1C **164**
Malden Grn. Av. KT4: Wor Pk 1B **164**
Malden Grn. M. KT4: Wor Pk 1C **164**
Malden Hill KT3: N Mald 3B **152**
Malden Hill Gdns. KT3: N Mald 3B **152**
MALDEN JUNC. 5B **152**
Malden Pk. KT3: N Mald 6B **152**
Malden Pl. NW5 5E **64**
Malden Rd. KT3: N Mald 5A **152**
KT4: Wor Pk 5A **152**
NW5 5D **64**
SM3: Cheam 4F **165**
Malden Way KT3: N Mald 6K **151**
Maldon Cl. E15 5G **69**
N1 1C **84**
SE5 3E **120**
Maldon Ct. E6 1E **88**
SM6: Wall 5G **167**
Maldon Rd. N9 3A **34**
RM7: Rush G 7J **55**
SM6: Wall 5F **167**
W3 7J **79**
Maldon Wlk. IG8: Wfd G 6F **37**
Malet Pl. WC1 4C **6** (4H **83**)
Malet St. WC1 4C **6** (4H **83**)
Maley Av. SE27 2B **138**
Malford Ct. E18 2J **51**
Malford Gro. E18 4H **51**
Malfort Rd. SE5 3E **120**
Malham Cl. N11 6K **31**
Malham Rd. SE23 1K **139**
Malham Rd. Ind. Est. SE23 1K **139**
Malham Ter. N18 5C **34**
Malibu Ct. SE26 3H **139**
Mall, The BR1: Brom 3J **159**
CR0: C'don 2C **168**
DA6: Bex 4G **127**
E15 7F **69**
HA3: Kenton 6F **43**
KT6: Surb 5D **150**
N14 3D **32**
RM10: Dag 6G **73**
SW1 6B **12** (2G **101**)
SW14 5J **115**
TW8: Bford 6D **96**
W5 7E **78**
Mallams M. SW9 3B **120**
Mallard Cl. E9 6B **68**
EN5: New Bar 6G **21**
NW6 2J **81**
TW2: Whitt 7E **112**
W7 2J **95**
Mallard Ct. E17 3F **51**
Mallard Ho. *NW8* *2C **82***
(off Bridgeman St.)
SW6 *1A **118***
(off Station Ct.)
Mallard Path SE28 3H **107**
Mallard Pl. N22 2K **47**
TW1: Twick 3A **132**
Mallard Point *E3* *3D **86***
(off Rainhill Way)
Mallards *E11* *7J **51***
(off Blake Hall Rd.)
Mallards Rd. IG8: Wfd G 7E **36**
IG11: Bark 3A **90**
Mallard Wlk. BR3: Beck 5K **157**
DA14: Sidc 6C **144**
Mallard Way NW9 7J **43**
SM6: Wall 7G **167**
Mall Chambers *W8* *1J **99***
(off Kensington Mall)
Mallet Dr. UB5: N'olt 5D **58**
Mallet Rd. SE13 6F **123**
Mall Galleries 4D **12**
Malling SE13 5D **122**
Malling Cl. CR0: C'don 6J **157**
Malling Gdns. SM4: Mord 6A **154**
Malling Way BR2: Hayes 7H **159**
Mallinson Rd. CR0: Bedd 3H **167**
SW11 5C **118**
Mallinson Sports Cen. 7D **46**
Mallon Gdns. *E1* *7K **9***
(off Commercial St.)
Mallord St. SW3 7B **16** (6B **100**)
Mallory Bldgs. *EC1* *4A **8***
(off St John St.)
Mallory Cl. E14 5D **86**
SE4 4A **122**
Mallory Ct. SE12 7K **123**
Mallory Gdns. EN4: E Barn 7K **21**
Mallory St. NW8 3D **4** (4C **82**)
Mallow Cl. CR0: C'don 1K **169**
Mallow Mead NW7 7B **30**
Mallows, The UB10: Ick 3D **56**
Mallow St. EC1 3E **8** (4D **84**)
Mall Rd. W6 5D **98**
Mall Vs. *W6* *5D **98***
(off Mall Rd.)
Malmains Cl. BR3: Beck 4F **159**
Malmains Way BR3: Beck 4E **158**
Malmesbury *E2* *2J **85***
(off Cyprus St.)
Malmesbury Cl. HA5: Eastc 4H **39**
Malmesbury Rd. E3 3B **86**
E16 5G **87**
E18 1H **51**
SM4: Mord 7A **154**
Malmesbury Ter. E16 5H **87**
Malmsey Ho. SE11 5H **19** (5K **101**)
Malmsmead Ho. *E9* *5B **68***
(off King's Mead Way)
Malory Cl. BR3: Beck 2A **158**
Malpas Dr. HA5: Pinn 5B **40**
Malpas Rd. E8 5H **67**
RM9: Dag 6D **72**
SE4 2B **122**
Malswick Ct. *SE15* *7E **102***
(off Tower Mill Rd.)
Malta Rd. E10 1C **68**
Malta St. EC1 3A **8** (4B **84**)
Maltby Cl. BR6: Orp 1K **173**
Maltby Dr. EN1: Enf 1C **24**
Maltby Ho. *SE1* *3F **103***
(off Maltby St.)
Maltby Rd. KT9: Chess 6G **163**
Maltby St. SE1 7J **15** (2F **103**)
Malthouse Dr. TW13: Hanw 5B **130**
W4 6B **98**
Malthouse Pas. *SW13* *2B **116***
(off Clevelands Gdns.)
Malthus Path SE28 1C **108**
Malting Ho. *E14* *7B **86***
(off Oak La.)
Maltings *W4* *5G **97***
(off Spring Gro.)
Maltings, The BR6: Orp 1K **173**
Maltings Cl. E3 3E **86**
SW13 2B **116**
Maltings Lodge *W4* *6A **98***
(off Corney Reach Way)
Maltings M. DA15: Sidc 3A **144**
Maltings Pl. SE1 7H **15**
SW6 1K **117**
Malting Way TW7: Isle 3K **113**
Malton M. SE18 6J **107**
W10 6G **81**
Malton Rd. W10 6G **81**
Malton St. SE18 6J **107**
Maltravers St. WC2 2H **13** (7K **83**)
Malt St. SE1 6G **103**
Malva Cl. SW18 5K **117**
Malvern Av. DA7: Bex 7E **108**
E4 7A **36**
HA2: Harr 3C **58**
Malvern Cl. CR4: Mitc 3G **155**
KT6: Surb 1E **162**
SE20 2G **157**
UB10: Ick 2C **56**
W10 5H **81**
Malvern Ct. SM2: Sutt 7J **165**
SW7 3B **16**
Malvern Ct. *W12* *2C **98***
(off Hadyn Pk. Rd.)
Malvern Dr. IG3: Bark, Ilf 4K **71**
IG8: Wfd G 5F **37**
TW13: Hanw 5B **130**
Malvern Gdns. HA3: Kenton 4E **42**
NW2 2G **63**
Malvern Ho. N16 1F **67**
SE17 *5C **102***
(off Liverpool Gro.)
Malvern M. NW6 3J **81**
Malvern Pl. NW6 3H **81**
Malvern Rd. CR7: Thor H 4A **156**
E6 1C **88**
E8 7G **67**
E11 2G **69**
KT6: Surb 2E **162**
N8 3A **48**
N17 3G **49**
NW6 2H **81**
(not continuous)
TW12: Hamp 7E **130**
UB3: Harl 7G **93**
Malvern Ter. N1 1A **84**
N9 1A **34**
Malvern Way W13 5B **78**
Malwood Rd. SW12 6F **119**
Malyons, The TW17: Shep 6F **147**
Malyons Rd. SE13 6D **122**
Malyons Ter. SE13 5D **122**
Managers St. E14 1E **104**
Manatee Pl. SM6: Bedd 3H **167**
Manaton Cl. SE15 3H **121**
Manaton Cres. UB1: S'hall 6E **76**
Manbey Gro. E15 6G **69**
Manbey Pk. Rd. E15 6G **69**
Manbey Rd. E15 6G **69**
Manbey St. E15 6G **69**
Manbre Rd. W6 6E **98**
Manbrough Av. E6 3D **88**
Manchester Ct. *E16* *6K **87***
(off Garvary Rd.)
Manchester Dr. W10 4G **81**
Manchester Gro. E14 5E **104**
Manchester Ho. *SE17* *5C **102***
(off East St.)
Manchester M. W1 6G **5**
Manchester Rd. CR7: Thor H 3C **156**
E14 5E **104**
N15 6D **48**
Manchester Sq. W1 7G **5** (6E **82**)
Manchester St. W1 6G **5** (5E **82**)
Manchester Way RM10: Dag 4H **73**
Manchuria Rd. SW11 6E **118**
Manciple St. SE1 7E **14** (2D **102**)
Mancroft Ct. *NW8* *1B **82***
(off St John's Wood Pk.)
Mandalay Rd. SW4 5G **119**
Mandarin Ct. *NW10* *6K **61***
(off Mitchellbrook Way)
SE8 6B **104**
Mandarin St. E14 7C **86**
Mandarin Way UB4: Yead 6C **76**
Mandarin Wharf N1 1E **84**
Mandela Cl. NW10 7J **61**
W12 7D **80**
Mandela Ho. *E2* *2J **9***
(off Virginia Rd.)
SE5 2B **120**
Mandela Rd. E16 6J **87**
Mandela St. NW1 1G **83**
SW9 7A **102**
(not continuous)
Mandela Way SE1 4E **102**
Mandel Ho. SW18 4J **117**
Manderley *W14* *3H **99***
(off Oakwood La.)
Mandeville Cl. SE3 7H **105**
SW20 7G **135**
Mandeville Ct. E4 5F **35**
Mandeville Dr. KT6: Surb 1D **162**
Mandeville Ho. *SE1* *5F **103***
(off Rolls Rd.
SW4 5G **119**
Mandeville M. SW4 4J **119**
Mandeville Pl. W1 7H **5** (6E **82**
Mandeville Rd. N14 2A **32**
TW7: Isle 2A **114**
TW17: Shep 5C **146**
UB5: N'olt 7E **58**
Mandeville St. E5 3A **68**
Mandrake Rd. SW17 3D **136**
Mandrake Way E15 7G **69**
Mandrell Rd. SW2 5J **119**
Manesty Ct. *N14* *7C **2***
(off Ivy Rd.
Manette St. W1 1D **12** (6H **83**
Manfred Rd. SW15 5H **11**
Manger Rd. N7 6J **65**
Mangold Way DA18: Erith 3D **108**
Manhattan Bldg. E3 2C **86**
Manhattan Bus. Pk. W5 3E **78**
Manilla Ct. *RM6: Chad H* *6B **5***
(off Quarles Pk. Rd.
Manilla St. E14 2C **10**
Manister Rd. SE2 3A **108**
Manitoba Ct. *SE16* *2J **10***
(off Canada Est
Manitoba Gdns. BR6: Chels 6K **17**
Manley Ct. N16 3F **6**
Manley Ho. SE11 5J **19** (4A **102**
Manley St. NW1 1E **8**
Mannan Ho. *E3* *2B **8***
(off Roman Rd
Mann Cl. CR0: C'don 3C **16**
Manneby Prior *N1* *1H*
(off Cumming St.
Manning Ct. *SE28* *1B **10***
(off Titmuss Av.
Manningford Cl. EC1 1A **8** (3B **84**
Manning Gdns. CR0: C'don 7H **15**
HA3: Kenton 7D **4**
Manning Ho. *W11* *6G **8***
(off Westbourne Pk. Rd.
Manning Pl. TW10: Rich 6F **11**
Manning Rd. E17 5A **5**
RM10: Dag 6G **7**
Manningtree Cl. SW19 1G **13**
Manningtree Rd. HA4: Ruis 4K **5**
Manningtree St. E1 6G **8**
Mannin Rd. RM6: Chad H 7B **5**
Mannock Cl. NW9 3K **4**
Mannock M. E18 1A **5**
Mannock Rd. N22 3B **4**
Mann's Cl. TW7: Isle 5K **11**
Manns Rd. HA8: Edg 6B **2**
Manny Shinwell Ho. *SW6* *6H **9***
(off Clem Attlee Ct
Manoel Rd. TW2: Twick 3G **13**
Manor, The IG8: Wfd G 7K **3**
SE23 7J **12**
Manor Av. E7 4A **7**
SE4 2B **12**
TW4: Houn 3B **11**
UB5: N'olt 7D **5**
Manorbrook SE3 4J **12**
MANOR CIRCUS **3G 11**
Manor Cl. DA1: Cray 4K **12**
E17 1A **5**
EN5: Barn 4B **2**
HA4: Ruis 1H **5**
KT4: Wor Pk 1A **16**
NW7 5E **2**
NW9 5H **4**
RM10: Dag 6K **7**
SE28 7C **9**
Manor Cotts. HA6: Nwood 1H **3**
N2 *2A **4***
(off Manor Cotts. App
Manor Cotts. App. N2 2A **4**
Manor Ct. BR4: W W'ck 1D **17**
DA7: Bex 4H **12**

Manor Ct. E4 . . . . .1B **36**
E10 . . . . .1D **68**
HA1: Harr 6K **41**
HA9: Wemb 5E **60**
IG11: Bark 7K **71**
KT2: King T .1G **151**
KT8: W Mole 4E **148**
N2 . . . . .5D **46**
N14 . . . . .2C **32**
N20 . . . . .3J **31**
(off York Way)
SM5: Cars 3E **166**
SW2 . . . . .5K **119**
SW3 . . . . .6D **16**
(off Hemus Pl.)
SW6 . . . . .1K **117**
SW16 . . . . .3J **137**
TW2: Twick .2G **131**
W3 . . . . .4G **97**
Manor Ct. Rd. W7 . . . . .7J **77**
Manor Cres. KT5: Surb 6G **151**
Manor Dene SE28 . . . . .6C **90**
Manordene Cl. KT7: T Ditt 1A **162**
Manordene Rd. SE28 . . . . .6C **90**
Manor Dr. HA9: Wemb 4F **61**
KT5: Surb 6F **151**
KT10: Hin W 2A **162**
KT19: Ewe 6A **164**
N14 . . . . .1A **32**
N20 . . . . .4J **31**
NW7 . . . . .5E **28**
TW13: Hanw 5B **130**
TW16: Sun 2J **147**
Manor Dr., The KT4: Wor Pk 1A **164**
Manor Dr. Nth. KT3: N Mald 7K **151**
KT4: Wor Pk 1A **164**
Manor Est. SE16 . . . . .4H **103**
Mnr. Farm Av. TW17: Shep 6D **146**
Mnr. Farm Cl. KT4: Wor Pk 1A **164**
Mnr. Farm Ct. E6 . . . . .3D **88**
Mnr. Farm Dr. E4 . . . . .3B **36**
Mnr. Farm Rd. HA0: Wemb 2D **78**
SW16 . . . . .2A **156**
Manorfield Cl. N19 . . . . .4G **65**
(off Fulbrook M.)
Manor Flds. SW15 . . . . .6F **117**
Manorfields Cl. BR7: Chst 3K **161**
Manor Gdns. CR2: S Croy 6F **169**
HA4: Ruis 5A **58**
N7 . . . . .3J **65**
SW4 . . . . .2G **119**
(off Larkhall Ri.)
SW20 . . . . .2H **153**
TW9: Rich 4F **115**
TW12: Hamp 7F **131**
TW16: Sun 1J **147**
W3 . . . . .4G **97**
W4 . . . . .5A **98**
Manor Ga. UB5: N'olt 7C **58**
Manorgate Rd. KT2: King T 1G **151**
Manor Gro. BR3: Beck 2D **158**
SE15 . . . . .6J **103**
TW9: Rich 4G **115**
Mnr. Hall Av. NW4 . . . . .2F **45**
Mnr. Hall Dr. NW4 . . . . .2F **45**
Manorhall Gdns. E10 . . . . .1C **68**
MANOR HOUSE .7D **48**
MANOR HOUSE 7C **48**
Manor Ho. NW1 . . . . .5D **4**
(off Lisson Gro.)
UB2: S'hall 3C **94**
Manor Ho. Ct. TW17: Shep 7D **146**
W9 . . . . .4A **82**
(off Warrington Gdns.)
Manor Ho. Dr. HA6: Nwood 1D **38**
NW6 . . . . .7F **63**
Manor Ho. Est. HA7: Stan 6G **27**
Manor Ho. Gdn. E11 . . . . .6K **51**
Manor Ho. Way TW7: Isle 3B **114**
Manor La. SE12 . . . . .5G **123**
SE13 . . . . .5G **123**
SM1: Sutt 5A **166**

Manor La. TW13: Felt 2J **129**
TW16: Sun 2J **147**
UB3: Harl 6F **93**
Manor La. Ter. SE13 . . . . .4G **123**
Manor Lodge NW2 . . . . .6F **63**
(off Willesden La.)
Manor M. NW6 . . . . .2J **81**
(off Cambridge Av.)
SE4 . . . . .2B **122**
Manor Mt. SE23 . . . . .1J **139**
Manor Pde. HA1: Harr 6K **41**
N16 . . . . .2F **67**
NW10 . . . . .2B **80**
(off High St. Harlesden)
MANOR PARK 4B **70**
Manor Pk. BR7: Chst 2H **161**
SE13 . . . . .4F **123**
TW9: Rich 4F **115**
TW13: Felt 2J **129**
Manor Pk. Cl. BR4: W W'ck 1D **170**
Manor Pk. Crematorium E7 . . . . .4A **70**
Manor Pk. Cres. HA8: Edg 6B **28**
Manor Pk. Dr. HA2: Harr 3F **41**
Manor Pk. Gdns. HA8: Edg 5B **28**
Manor Pk. Pde. SE13 . . . . .4F **123**
(off Lee High Rd.)
Manor Pk. Rd. BR4: W W'ck 1D **170**
BR7: Chst 1G **161**
E12 . . . . .4B **70**
(not continuous)
N2 . . . . .3A **46**
NW10 . . . . .1B **80**
SM1: Sutt 5A **166**
Manor Pl. BR7: Chst 2H **161**
CR4: Mitc 3G **155**
KT12: Walt T 7H **147**
(not continuous)
SE17 . . . . .5B **102**
SM1: Sutt 4K **165**
TW14: Felt 1J **129**
Manor Rd. BR3: Beck 2D **158**
BR4: W W'ck 2D **170**
CR4: Mitc 4G **155**
DA1: Cray 4K **127**
DA5: Bexl 1H **145**
DA15: Sidc 3K **143**
E10 . . . . .7C **50**
E15 . . . . .2G **87**
E16 . . . . .2G **87**
E17 . . . . .2A **50**
EN2: Enf 2H **23**
EN5: Barn 4B **20**
HA1: Harr 6A **42**
HA4: Ruis 1F **57**
IG7: Chig 6J **37**
IG8: Wfd G 6J **37**
IG11: Bark 6K **71**
KT8: E Mos .4H **149**
KT12: Walt T 7H **147**
N16 . . . . .2D **66**
N17 . . . . .1G **49**
N22 . . . . .6D **32**
RM6: Chad H 6D **54**
RM10: Dag .6J **73**
SE25 . . . . .4G **157**
SM2: Cheam 7H **165**
SM6: Wall 4F **167**
SW20 . . . . .2H **153**
TW2: Twick .2G **131**
TW9: Rich 4G **115**
TW11: Tedd .5A **132**
(not continuous)
TW15: Ashf 5B **128**
UB3: Hayes 6J **75**
W13 . . . . .7A **78**
Manor Rd. Ho. HA1: Harr 6A **42**
Manor Rd. Nth. KT7: T Ditt 3A **162**
KT10: Hin W, T Ditt 3A **162**
SM6: Wall 4F **167**
Manorside EN5: Barn 4B **20**
Manorside Cl. SE2 . . . . .4C **108**
Manor Sq. RM8: Dag 2C **72**

Manor Va. TW8: Bford 5C **96**
Manor Vw. N3 .2K **45**
Manor Way BR2: Brom 6C **160**
BR3: Beck 2C **158**
BR5: Pet W 4G **161**
CR2: S Croy .6E **168**
CR4: Mitc 3G **155**
DA5: Bexl 1G **145**
DA7: Bex 3K **127**
E4 . . . . .4A **36**
HA2: Harr 4F **41**
HA4: Ruis 7G **39**
KT4: Wor Pk 1A **164**
NW9 . . . . .4A **44**
RM13: Rain .4K **91**
SE3 . . . . .4H **123**
SW3 . . . . .4B **94**
Manor Way, The SM6: Wall 4F **167**
Manorway EN1: Enf 7K **23**
IG8: Wfd G 5F **37**
SE7 . . . . .4B **106**
Mnr. Way Bus. Cen. RM13: Rain 5K **91**
Manor Waye UB8: Uxb 1A **74**
Manpreet Ct. E12 . . . . .5D **70**
Manresa Rd. SW3 . . . . . . .6C **16** (5C **100**)
Mansard Beeches SW17 . . . . .5E **136**
Mansard Cl. HA5: Pinn 3B **40**
Manse Cl. UB3: Harl 6F **93**
Mansel Gro. E17 . . . . .1C **50**
Mansell Rd. UB6: G'frd 5F **77**
W3 . . . . .2K **97**
Mansell St. E1 . . . . .1K **15** (6F **85**)
Mansel Rd. SW19 . . . . .6G **135**
Manser Cl. RM13: Rain 3K **91**
Mansergh Cl. SE18 . . . . .7C **106**
Manser Rd. N16 . . . . .3F **67**
Manser Rd. RM13: Rain 3K **91**
Mansfield Av. EN4: E Barn 6J **21**
HA4: Ruis 1K **57**
N15 . . . . .4D **48**
Mansfield Cl. N9 . . . . .6B **24**
Mansfield Ct. E2 . . . . .1F **85**
(off Whiston Rd.)
Mansfield Dr. UB4: Hayes 4G **75**
Mansfield Hgts. N2 . . . . .5C **46**
Mansfield Hill E4 . . . . .7J **25**
Mansfield Ho. N1 . . . . .1E **84**
(off New Era Est.)
Mansfield M. W1 . . . . .6J **5** (5F **83**)
Mansfield Pl. CR2: S Croy 6D **168**
NW3 . . . . .4A **64**
Mansfield Rd. CR2: S Croy 6D **168**
E11 . . . . .6K **51**
E17 . . . . .4B **50**
IG1: Ilf 2E **70**
KT9: Chess 5C **162**
NW3 . . . . .5D **64**
W3 . . . . .4H **79**
Mansfield St. W1 . . . . .6J **5** (5F **83**)
Mansford St. E2 . . . . .2G **85**
Manship Rd. CR4: Mitc 7E **136**
Mansion Cl. SW9 . . . . .1A **120**
(not continuous)
Mansion Gdns. NW3 . . . . .3K **63**
Mansion House 1E **14** (6D **84**)
Mansion Ho. Pl. EC4 . . . . . .1E **14** (6D **84**)
Mansion Ho. St. EC4 . . . . .1E **14**
Mansions, The SW5 . . . . .5K **99**
Manson M. SW7 . . . . .4A **16** (4B **100**)
Manson Pl. SW7 . . . . .4A **16** (4B **100**)
Mansted Gdns. RM6: Chad H 7C **54**
Manston N17 .2D **48**
(off Adams Rd.)
NW1 . . . . .7G **65**
(off Agar Gro.)
Manston Av. UB2: S'hall 4E **94**
Manston Cl. SE20 . . . . .1J **157**
Manstone Rd. NW2 . . . . .5G **63**
Manston Gro. KT2: King T 5D **132**
Manston Ho. W14 . . . . .3G **99**
(off Russell Rd.)
Manthorp Rd. SE18 . . . . .5G **107**

Mantilla Rd. SW17 . . . . .4E **136**
Mantle Cl. SW18 . . . . .6K **117**
(off Mapleton Rd.)
Mantle Rd. SE4 . . . . .3A **122**
Mantlet Cl. SW16 . . . . .7G **137**
Mantle Way DA8: Erith 7K **109**
E15 . . . . .7G **69**
Manton Av. W7 . . . . .2K **95**
Manton Cl. UB3: Hayes 7G **75**
Manton Rd. EN3: Enf L 1H **25**
SE2 . . . . .4A **108**
Manton Way EN3: Enf L 1J **25**
Mantua St. SW11 . . . . .3B **118**
Mantus Cl. E1 . . . . .4J **85**
Mantus Rd. E1 . . . . .4J **85**
Manuka Cl. W7 . . . . .1A **96**
Manus Way N20 . . . . .2F **31**
Manville Gdns. SW17 . . . . .3F **137**
Manville Rd. SW17 . . . . .2E **136**
Manwood Rd. SE4 . . . . .5B **122**
Manwood St. E16 . . . . .1D **106**
Manygate La. TW17: Shep 7E **146**
Manygate Pk. Cvn. Site
TW17: Shep 6F **147**
(off Mitre Cl.)
Manygates SW12 . . . . .2F **137**
Mapesbury Ct. NW2 . . . . .5G **63**
Mapesbury M. NW4 . . . . .6C **44**
Mapesbury Rd. NW2 . . . . .7G **63**
Mapeshill Pl. NW2 . . . . .6E **62**
Mapes Ho. NW6 . . . . .7G **63**
Mape St. E2 . . . . .4H **85**
(not continuous)
Maple Av. E4 .5G **35**
HA2: Harr 2F **59**
UB7: View 7A **74**
W3 . . . . .1A **98**
Maple Cl. BR5: Pet W 5H **161**
CR4: Mitc 1F **155**
HA4: Ruis 6K **39**
IG9: Buck H .3G **37**
N3 . . . . .6D **30**
N16 . . . . .6D **49**
SW4 . . . . .6H **119**
TW12: Hamp 6D **130**
UB4: Yead 3B **76**
Maple Ct. CR0: C'don 4C **168**
(Lwr. Coombe St.)
CR0: C'don 4C **168**
(off The Waldrons)
E3 . . . . .2C **86**
(off Four Seasons Cl.)
E6 . . . . .5E **88**
KT3: N Mald 3K **151**
SE6 . . . . .1D **140**
TW15: Ashf 7F **129**
Maple Cres. DA15: Sidc 6A **126**
Maplecroft Cl. E6 . . . . .6B **88**
Mapledale Av. CR0: C'don 2G **169**
Mapledene BR7: Chst 6G **143**
Mapledene Est. E8 . . . . .7G **67**
Mapledene Rd. E8 . . . . .7F **67**
Maple Gdns. HA8: Edg 7F **29**
TW19: Stanw 2A **128**
Maple Gro. NW9 . . . . .7J **43**
TW8: Bford 7B **96**
UB1: S'hall 5D **76**
W5 . . . . .3D **96**
Maple Gro. Bus. Cen. TW4: Houn 4A **112**
Maple Ho. E17 . . . . .3D **50**
KT1: King T .5E **150**
(off Maple Rd.)
N19 . . . . .3G **65**
SE8 . . . . .7B **104**
(off Idonia St.)
TW9: Kew 1H **115**
Maplehurst BR2: Brom 2G **159**
Maplehurst Cl. KT1: King T 4E **150**
Maple Ind. Est. TW13: Felt 3J **129**
Maple Leaf Dr. DA15: Sidc 1K **143**
Mapleleafe Gdns. IG6: Ilf 3F **53**
Maple Leaf Sq. SE16 . . . . .2K **103**

Maple Lodge *W8* . . . *3K 99*
(off Abbots Wlk.)
Maple M. NW6 . . . 2K 81
SE16 . . . 2K 103
SW16 . . . 5K 137
Maple Pl. N17 . . . 7B 34
UB7: Yiew . . . 1A 92
W1 . . . 5B 6 (4G 83)
Maple Rd. E11 . . . 6G 51
KT6: Surb . . . 6D 150
SE20 . . . 1H 157
UB4: Yead . . . 3A 76
Maples, The KT10: Clay . . . 7A 162
Maples Pl. E1 . . . 5H 85
Maplestead Rd. RM9: Dag . . . 1B 90
SW2 . . . 7K 119
Maple St. E2 . . . 2H 85
RM7: Rom . . . 4J 55
W1 . . . 5A 6 (5G 83)
Maplethorpe Rd. CR7: Thor H . . . 4A 156
Mapleton Cl. BR2: Brom . . . 6J 159
Mapleton Cres. EN3: Enf W . . . 1D 24
SW18 . . . 6K 117
Mapleton Rd. E4 . . . 3K 35
EN1: Enf . . . 2C 24
SW18 . . . 6J 117
(not continuous)
Maple Tree Pl. SE3 . . . 1C 124
Maple Wlk. W10 . . . 3F 81
Maple Way TW13: Felt . . . 3J 129
Maplin Cl. N21 . . . 6E 22
Maplin Ho. *SE2* . . . *2D 108*
(off Wolvercote Rd.)
Maplin Rd. E16 . . . 6J 87
Maplin St. E3 . . . 3B 86
Mapperley Cl. E11 . . . 6H 51
Mapperley Dr. IG8: Wfd G . . . 7B 36
Marabou Cl. E12 . . . 5C 70
Maran Way DA18: Erith . . . 2D 108
Marathon Ho. *NW1* . . . *5E 4*
(off Marylebone Rd.)
Marathon Way SE28 . . . 2K 107
Marban Rd. W9 . . . 3H 81
Marble Arch . . . 2F 11
MARBLE ARCH . . . 7D 82
Marble Arch W1 . . . 2E 10 (7D 82)
Marble Arch Apartments *W1* . . . *7E 4*
(off Harrowby St.)
Marble Cl. W3 . . . 1H 97
Marble Dr. NW2 . . . 1F 63
Marble Hill Cl. TW1: Twick . . . 7B 114
Marble Hill Gdns. TW1: Twick . . . 7B 114
Marble Hill House . . . 7C 114
Marble Ho. SE18 . . . 5K 107
W9 . . . 4H 81
Marble Quay E1 . . . 4K 15 (1G 103)
Marbles Ho. *SE5* . . . *6C 102*
(off Grosvenor Ter.)
Marbrook Ct. SE12 . . . 3A 142
Marcella Rd. SW9 . . . 2A 120
Marcellina Way BR6: Orp . . . 3J 173
March *NW9* . . . *1B 44*
(off The Concourse)
Marchant Cl. NW7 . . . 6F 29
Marchant Ho. *N1* . . . *1E 84*
(off New Era Est.)
Marchant Rd. E11 . . . 2F 69
Marchant St. SE14 . . . 6A 104
Marchbank Rd. W14 . . . 6H 99
March Ct. SW15 . . . 4D 116
Marchmont Gdns. TW10: Rich . . . 5F 115
Marchmont Rd. SM6: Wall . . . 7G 167
TW10: Rich . . . 5F 115
Marchmont St. WC1 . . . 3E 6 (4J 83)
March Rd. TW1: Twick . . . 7A 114
Marchside Cl. TW5: Hest . . . 1B 112
Marchwood Cl. SE5 . . . 7E 102
Marchwood Cres. W5 . . . 6C 78
Marcia Ct. *SE1* . . . *4E 102*
(off Marcia Rd.)
Marcia Rd. SE1 . . . 4E 102
Marcilly Rd. SW18 . . . 5B 118
Marco Dr. HA5: Hat E . . . 1D 40
Marcon Ct. *E8* . . . *5H 67*
(off Amhurst Rd.)
Marconi Pl. N11 . . . 4A 32
Marconi Rd. E10 . . . 1C 68
Marconi Way UB1: S'hall . . . 6F 77
Marcon Pl. E8 . . . 6H 67
Marco Polo Ho. SW8 . . . 7F 101
Marco Rd. W6 . . . 3E 98
Marcourt Lawns W5 . . . 4E 78
Marcus Ct. E15 . . . 1G 87
Marcus Garvey M. SE22 . . . 6H 121
Marcus Garvey Way SE24 . . . 4A 120
Marcus St. E15 . . . 1H 87
SW18 . . . 6K 117
Marcus Ter. SW18 . . . 6K 117
Mardale Ct. NW7 . . . 7H 29
Mardale Dr. NW9 . . . 5K 43
Mardell Rd. CR0: C'don . . . 5K 157
Marden Av. BR2: Hayes . . . 6J 159
Marden Cres. CR0: C'don . . . 6K 155
DA5: Bexl . . . 5J 127
Marden Ho. E8 . . . 5H 67
Marden Rd. CR0: C'don . . . 6K 155
N17 . . . 2E 48
Marden Sq. SE16 . . . 3H 103
Marder Rd. W13 . . . 2A 96
Mardyke Cl. RM13: Rain . . . 2J 91
Mardyke Ho. RM13: Rain . . . 2K 91
SE17 . . . *4D 102*
(off Mason St.)
Marechal Niel Av. DA15: Sidc . . . 3H 143
Marechal Niel Pde.
DA14: Sidc . . . *3H 143*
(off Main Rd.)
Maresby Ho. E4 . . . 2J 35
Maresfield CR0: C'don . . . 3E 168
Maresfield Gdns. NW3 . . . 5A 64
Mare St. E8 . . . 1H 85
Marfleet Cl. SM5: Cars . . . 2C 166
Margaret Av. E4 . . . 6J 25
Margaret Bondfield Av. IG11: Bark . . . 7A 72
Margaret Bondfield Ho. *E3* . . . *2A 86*
(off Driffield Rd.)
Margaret Bldgs. N16 . . . 1F 67
Margaret Ct. EN4: E Barn . . . 4G 21
W1 . . . 7A 6
Margaret Gardner Dr. SE9 . . . 2D 142
Margaret Herbison Ho. *SW6* . . . *6H 99*
(off Clem Attlee Ct.)
Margaret Ho. *W6* . . . *5E 98*
(off Queen Caroline St.)
Margaret Ingram Cl. SW6 . . . 6H 99
Margaret Lockwood Cl.
KT1: King T . . . 4F 151
Margaret McMillan Ho. E16 . . . 6A 88
Margaret Rd. DA5: Bexl . . . 6D 126
EN4: E Barn . . . 4G 21
N16 . . . 1F 67
Margaret Rutherford Pl. SW12 . . . 1G 137
Margaret St. W1 . . . 7K 5 (6F 83)
Margaretta Ter. SW3 . . . 7C 16 (6C 100)
Margaretting Rd. E12 . . . 1A 70
Margaret Way IG4: Ilf . . . 6C 52
Margaret White Ho. *NW1* . . . *1D 6*
(off Chalton St.)
Margate Rd. SW2 . . . 5J 119
Margery Fry Ct. N7 . . . 3J 65
Margery Pk. Rd. E7 . . . 6J 69
Margery Rd. RM8: Dag . . . 3D 72
Margery St. WC1 . . . 2J 7 (3A 84)
Margery Ter. *E7* . . . *6J 69*
(off Margery Pk. Rd.)
Margin Dr. SW19 . . . 5F 135
Margravine Gdns. W6 . . . 5F 99
Margravine Rd. W6 . . . 5F 99
Marham Dr. NW9 . . . 1A 44
Marham Gdns. SM4: Mord . . . 6A 154
SW18 . . . 1C 136
Maria Cl. SE1 . . . 4H 103
Maria Ct. SE25 . . . 2E 156
Marian Cl. UB4: Yead . . . 4B 76
Marian Ct. E9 . . . 5J 67
SM1: Sutt . . . 5K 165
Marianne North Gallery . . . 2F 115
Marian Pl. E2 . . . 2H 85
Marian Rd. SW16 . . . 1G 155
Marian St. E2 . . . 2H 85
Marian Way NW10 . . . 7B 62
Maria Ter. E1 . . . 5K 85
Maria Theresa Cl. KT3: N Mald . . . 5K 151
Maribor *SE10* . . . *7E 104*
(off Burney St.)
Maricas Av. HA3: Hrw W . . . 1H 41
Marie Curie SE5 . . . 1E 120
Marie Lloyd Gdns. N19 . . . 7J 47
Marie Lloyd Ho. *N1* . . . *1E 8*
(off Murray Gro.)
Marie Lloyd Wlk. E8 . . . 6F 67
Mariette Way SM6: Wall . . . 7J 167
Marigold All. SE1 . . . 3A 14 (7B 84)
Marigold Cl. UB1: S'hall . . . 7C 76
Marigold Rd. N17 . . . 7D 34
Marigold St. SE16 . . . 2H 103
Marigold Way CR0: C'don . . . 1K 169
Marina App. UB4: Yead . . . 5C 76
Marina Av. KT3: N Mald . . . 5D 152
Marina Cl. BR2: Brom . . . 3J 159
Marina Ct. *E3* . . . *3B 86*
(off Alfred St.)
SW6 . . . 2A 118
Marina Dr. DA16: Well . . . 2J 125
Marina Gdns. RM7: Rom . . . 5J 55
Marina One *N1* . . . *2J 83*
(off New Wharf Rd.)
Marina Pl. KT1: Ham W . . . 1D 150
Marina Point *E14* . . . *3D 104*
(off Goulston St.)
Marina Way TW11: Tedd . . . 7D 132
Marine Ct. E11 . . . 2G 69
Marine Dr. IG11: Bark . . . 4A 90
SE18 . . . 4D 106
Marinefield Rd. SW6 . . . 2K 117
Marinel Ho. SE5 . . . 7C 102
Mariner Bus. Cen. CR0: Wadd . . . 5A 168
Mariner Gdns. TW10: Ham . . . 3C 132
Mariner Rd. E12 . . . 4E 70
Mariners Cl. EN4: E Barn . . . 5G 21
Mariners M. E14 . . . 4F 105
Marine St. SE16 . . . 3G 103
Marine Twr. *SE8* . . . *6B 104*
(off Abinger Gro.)
Marion Av. TW17: Shep . . . 5D 146
Marion Gro. IG8: Wfd G . . . 5B 36
Marion Ho. *NW1* . . . *1D 82*
(off Regent's Pk. Rd.)
Marion M. SE21 . . . 3D 138
Marion Rd. CR7: Thor H . . . 5C 156
NW7 . . . 5H 29
Marischal Rd. SE13 . . . 3F 123
Maritime Ho. SE18 . . . 4F 107
Maritime Ind. Est. SE7 . . . 4K 105
Maritime Quay E14 . . . 5C 104
Maritime St. E3 . . . 4B 86
Marius Mans. SW17 . . . 2E 136
Marius Rd. SW17 . . . 2E 136
Marjorie Gro. SW11 . . . 4D 118
Marjorie M. E1 . . . 6K 85
Mark Av. E4 . . . 6J 25
Mark Cl. DA7: Bex . . . 1E 126
UB1: S'hall . . . 7F 77
Marke Cl. BR2: Kes . . . 4C 172
Market, The SM1: Sutt . . . 1A 166
Market Cen., The UB2: S'hall . . . 4K 93
Market Chambers *EN2: Enf* . . . *3J 23*
(off Church St.)
Market Ct. W1 . . . 7A 6
Market Dr. W4 . . . 7A 98
Market Entrance SW8 . . . 7G 101
Market Est. N7 . . . 6J 65
Market Hall N22 . . . 2A 48
Market Hill SE18 . . . 3E 106
Market La. HA8: Edg . . . 1J 43
W12 . . . 2E 98
Market Link RM1: Rom . . . 4K 55
Market M. W1 . . . 5J 11 (1F 101)
Market Pde. *BR1: Brom* . . . *1J 159*
(off East St.)
DA14: Sidc . . . 4B 144
E10 . . . *6E 50*
(off High Rd. Leyton)
E17 . . . *3B 50*
(off Higham Hill Rd.)
N9 . . . *2B 34*
(off Winchester Rd.)
N16 . . . *1G 67*
(off Oldhill St.)
SE25 . . . 4G 157
TW13: Hanw . . . 3C 130
Market Pav. E10 . . . 3C 68
Market Pl. DA6: Bex . . . 4G 127
EN2: Enf . . . 3J 23
KT1: King T . . . 2D 150
N2 . . . 3C 46
SE16 . . . 4G 103
(not continuous)
TW8: Bford . . . 7C 96
UB1: S'hall . . . 1D 94
W1 . . . 7A 6 (6G 83)
W3 . . . 1J 97
Market Pl., The NW11 . . . 4A 46
Market Rd. N7 . . . 6J 65
TW9: Rich . . . 3G 115
Market Row SW9 . . . 4A 120
Market Sq. BR1: Brom . . . 2J 159
(not continuous)
E14 . . . 6D 86
KT1: King T . . . *2D 150*
(off Market Pl.)
Market Sq., The *N9* . . . *2C 34*
(within Edmonton Grn. Shop. Cen.)
Market St. E1 . . . 5J 9 (5F 85)
E6 . . . 2D 88
SE18 . . . 4E 106
Market Ter. *TW8: Bford* . . . *6E 96*
(off Albany Rd.)
Market Trad. Est. UB2: S'hall . . . 4K 93
Market Way E14 . . . 6D 86
HA0: Wemb . . . 5E 60
Market Yd. M. SE1 . . . 7G 15 (2E 102)
Markfield Beam Engine and Mus. . . . 5G 49
Markfield Gdns. E4 . . . 7J 25
Markfield Rd. N15 . . . 4G 49
Markham Ho. *RM10: Dag* . . . *3G 73*
(off Uvedale Rd.)
Markham Pl. SW3 . . . 5E 16 (5D 100)
Markham Sq. SW3 . . . 5E 16 (5D 100)
Markham St. SW3 . . . 5D 16 (5C 100)
Markhole Cl. TW12: Hamp . . . 7D 130
Mark Ho. *E2* . . . *2K 85*
(off Sewardstone Rd.)
Markhouse Av. E17 . . . 6A 50
Markhouse Pas. *E17* . . . *6B 50*
(off Downsfield Rd.)
Markhouse Rd. E17 . . . 6B 50
Markland Ho. *W10* . . . *7F 81*
(off Darfield Way)
Mark La. EC3 . . . 2H 15 (7E 84)
Mark Lodge *EN4: Cockf* . . . *4H 21*
(off Edgeworth Rd.)
Markmanor Av. E17 . . . 7A 50
Mark Rd. N22 . . . 2B 48
Marksbury Av. TW9: Rich . . . 3G 115
MARKS GATE . . . 1E 54
Mark Sq. EC2 . . . 3G 9 (4E 84)
Marks Rd. RM7: Rom . . . 5J 55
(not continuous)
Markstone Ho. *SE1* . . . *7A 14*
(off Lancaster St.)
Mark St. E15 . . . 7G 69
EC2 . . . 3G 9 (4E 84)
Mark Wade Cl. E12 . . . 1B 70
Markway TW16: Sun . . . 2A 148
Markwell Cl. SE26 . . . 4H 139
Markyate Ho. *W10* . . . *4E 80*
(off Sutton Way)

Markyate Rd.—Martindale

Markyate Rd. RM8: Dag 5B **72**
Marland Ho. *SW1* *1F 17*
(off Sloane St.)
Marlands Rd. IG5: Ilf 3C **52**
Marlborough *SW19* *1F 135*
(off Inner Pk. Rd.)
W9 . . . .*3A 82*
(off Maida Va.)
Marlborough Av. E8 . . . . .1G **85**
(not continuous)
HA4: Ruis 6E **38**
HA8: Edg 3C **28**
N14 . . . . .3B **32**
Marlborough Cl. BR6: Orp 6K **161**
N20 . . . . .3J **31**
SE17 .4C **102**
SW19 . . . . .6C **136**
Marlborough Ct. *CR2: S Croy* *4E 168*
(off Birdhurst Rd.)
EN1: Enf 5K **23**
HA1: Harr 4H **41**
HA6: Nwood 1H **39**
IG9: Buck H 2F **37**
N17 . . . .*1G 49*
(off Kemble Rd.)
SM6: Wall 7G **167**
W1 . . . .*1B 12*
(off Carnaby St.)
W8 . . . .*4J 99*
(off Pembroke Rd.)
Marlborough Cres. UB3: Harl 7F **93**
W4 . . . . .3K **97**
Marlborough Dr. IG5: Ilf 3C **52**
Marlborough Flats SW3 . . . . .3D **16**
Marlborough Gdns. KT6: Surb 7D **150**
N20 . . . . .3J **31**
Marlborough Ga. Ho. *W2* *2A 10*
(off Elms M.)
Marlborough Gro. SE1 . . . . .5G **103**
Marlborough Hill HA1: Harr 4H **41**
NW8 . . . . .2A **82**
Marlborough House 5B **12** (1G **101**)
Marlborough Ho. *E16* *1J 105*
(off Hardy Av.)
UB7: W Dray 2B **92**
Marlborough La. SE7 . . . . .6A **106**
Marlborough Lodge *NW8* *2A 82*
(off Marlborough Pl.)
Marlborough Mans. *NW6* *5K 63*
(off Canon Hill)
Marlborough M. SW2 . . . . .4K **119**
Marlborough Pde. *HA8: Edg* *3C 28*
(off Marlborough Av.)
UB10: Hil 4D **74**
Marlborough Pk. Av.
DA15: Sidc 7A **126**
Marlborough Pl. NW8 . . . . .2A **82**
Marlborough Rd. BR2: Brom 4A **160**
CR2: S Croy 7C **168**
DA7: Bex 3D **126**
E4 . . . . .6J **35**
E7 . . . . .7A **70**
E15 . . . . .4G **69**
E18 . . . . .2J **51**
N9 . . . . .1B **34**
N19 . . . . .2H **65**
N22 . . . . .7D **32**
RM7: Mawney 4G **55**
RM8: Dag 4B **72**
SE18 . . . . .3F **107**
SM1: Sutt 3J **165**
SW1 . . . . .5B **12** (1G **101**)
SW19 .6C **136**
TW7: Isle 1B **114**
TW10: Rich 6F **115**
TW12: Hamp 6E **130**
TW13: Felt 2B **130**
TW15: Ashf 5A **128**
UB2: S'hall 3A **94**
UB10: Hil 4D **74**
W4 . . . . .5J **97**
W5 . . . . .2D **96**
Marlborough St. SW3 . . . . . . .4C **16** (4C **100**)
Marlborough Yd. N19 . . . . .2H **65**
Marlbury *NW8* *1K 81*
(off Abbey Rd.)
Marler Rd. SE23 . . . . .1A **140**
Marley Av. DA7: Bex 6D **108**
Marley Cl. N15 . . . . .4B **48**
UB6: G'frd 3E **76**
Marley Ho. *E16* *7F 89*
(off University Way)
W11 . . . .*7F 81*
(off St Ann's Rd.)
Marley St. SE16 . . . . .4K **103**
Marley Wlk. NW2 . . . . .5E **62**
Marlfield Cl. KT4: Wor Pk 1C **164**
Marlin Cl. TW16: Sun 6G **129**
Marling Ct. TW12: Hamp 6D **130**
Marlingdene Cl. TW12: Hamp 6E **130**
MARLING PARK 7D **130**
Marlings Cl. BR7: Chst 4J **161**
Marlings Pk. Av. BR7: Chst 4J **161**
Marlins Cl. SM1: Sutt 5A **166**
Marloes Cl. HA0: Wemb 4D **60**
Marloes Rd. W8 . . . . .3K **99**
Marlow Cl. SE20 . . . . .3H **157**
Marlow Ct. N14 . . . . .7B **22**
NW6 . . . . .7F **63**
NW9 . . . . .3B **44**
Marlow Cres. TW1: Twick 6K **113**
Marlow Dr. SM3: Cheam 2F **165**
Marlowe Bus. Cen. *SE14* *7A 104*
(off Batavia Rd.)
Marlowe Cl. BR7: Chst 6H **143**
IG6: Ilf .1G **53**
Marlowe Ct. SE19 . . . . .5F **139**
SW3 . . . .*4D 16*
(off Petyward)
Marlowe Gdns. SE9 . . . . .6E **124**
Marlowe Ho. IG8: Wfd G 7K **37**
KT1: King T *4D 150*
(off Portsmouth Rd.)
Marlowe Path SE8 . . . . .6C **104**
Marlowe Rd. E17 . . . . .4E **50**
Marlowes, The DA1: Cray 4K **127**
NW8 . . . . .1B **82**
Marlowe Sq. CR4: Mitc 4G **155**
Marlowe Way CR0: Bedd 2J **167**
Marlow Gdns. UB3: Harl 3F **93**
Marlow Ho. *E2* *2J 9*
(off Calvert Av.)
KT5: Surb *5E 150*
(off Cranes Pk.)
SE1 . . . .*7J 15*
(off Abbey St.)
TW11: Tedd 4A **132**
W2 . . . .*6K 81*
(off Hallfield Est.)
Marlow Rd. E6 . . . . .3D **88**
SE20 . . . . .3H **157**
UB2: S'hall 3D **94**
Marlow Way SE16 . . . . .2K **103**
Marlow Workshops *E2* *2J 9*
(off Virginia Rd.)
Marl Rd. SW18 . . . . .4A **118**
Marlton St. SE10 . . . . .5H **105**
Marlwood Cl. DA15: Sidc 2J **143**
Marmadon Rd. SE18 . . . . .4K **107**
Marmara Apartments *E16* *7J 87*
(off Western Gateway)
Marmion App. E4 . . . . .4H **35**
Marmion Av. E4 . . . . .4G **35**
Marmion Cl. E4 . . . . .4G **35**
Marmion M. SW11 . . . . .3E **118**
Marmion Rd. SW11 . . . . .4E **118**
Marmont Rd. SE15 . . . . .1G **121**
Marmora Ho. *E1* *5A 86*
(off Ben Jonson Rd.)
Marmora Rd. SE22 . . . . .6J **121**
Marmot Rd. TW4: Houn 3B **112**
Marne Av. DA16: Well 3A **126**
N11 . . . . .4A **32**
Marnell Way TW4: Houn 3B **112**
Marne St. W10 . . . . .3G **81**
Marney Rd. SW11 . . . . .4E **118**
Marnfield Cres. SW2 . . . . .1A **138**
Marnham Av. NW2 . . . . .4G **63**
Marnham Ct. HA0: Wemb 5C **60**
Marnham Cres. UB6: G'frd 3F **77**
Marnock Ho. *SE17* *5D 102*
(off Brandon St.)
Marnock Rd. SE4 . . . . .5B **122**
Maroon St. E14 . . . . .5A **86**
Maroons Way SE6 . . . . .5C **140**
Marqueen Ct. *W8* *2K 99*
(off Kensington Chu. St.)
Marqueen Towers SW16 . . . . .7K **137**
Marquess Hgts. E18 . . . . .1K **51**
Marquess Rd. N1 . . . . .6D **66**
Marquis Cl. HA0: Wemb 7F **61**
Marquis Ct. IG11: Bark 5J **71**
KT1: King T *4D 150*
(off Anglesea Rd.)
N4 . . . .*1K 65*
(off Marquis Rd.)
TW19: Stanw 1A **128**
Marquis Rd. N4 . . . . .1K **65**
N22 . . . . .6E **32**
NW1 . . . . .6H **65**
Marrabon Cl. DA15: Sidc 1A **144**
Marrick Cl. SW15 . . . . .4C **116**
Marrick Ho. *NW6* *1K 81*
(off Mortimer Cres.)
Marriett Ho. SE6 . . . . .4E **140**
Marrilyne Av. EN3: Enf L 1G **25**
Marriner Ct. *UB3: Hayes* *7G 75*
(off Barra Hall Rd.)
Marriott Cl. TW14: Felt 6F **111**
Marriott Rd. E15 . . . . .1G **87**
EN5: Barn 3A **20**
N4 . . . . .1K **65**
N10 . . . . .1D **46**
Marriotts Cl. NW9 . . . . .6B **44**
Marryat Cl. TW4: Houn 4D **112**
Marryat Ho. *SW1* *6A 18*
(off Churchill Gdns.)
Marryat Pl. SW19 . . . . .4G **135**
Marryat Rd. SW19 . . . . .5F **135**
Marryat Sq. SW6 . . . . .1G **117**
Marsala Rd. SE13 . . . . .4D **122**
Marsalis Ho. *E3* *3C 86*
(off Rainhill Way)
Marsden Rd. N9 . . . . .2C **34**
SE15 . . . . .3F **121**
Marsden St. NW5 . . . . .6E **64**
Marsden Way BR6: Orp 4K **173**
Marshall Bldg. *W2* *6A 4*
(off Hermitage St.)
Marshall Cl. HA1: Harr 7H **41**
SW18 .6A **118**
TW4: Houn 5D **112**
Marshall Ct. *NW6* *7F 63*
(off Coverdale Rd.)
SE20 . . . .*7H 139*
(off Anerley Pk.)
Marshall Dr. UB4: Hayes 5H **75**
Marshall Est. NW7 . . . . .4H **29**
Marshall Ho. *N1* *2D 84*
(off Cranston Est.)
NW6 . . . .*2H 81*
(off Albert Rd.)
SE1 . . . .*3E 102*
(off Page's Wlk.)
SE17 . . . .*5D 102*
(off East St.)
Marshall Path SE28 . . . . .7B **90**
Marshall Rd. E10 . . . . .3D **68**
(not continuous)
N17 . . . . .1D **48**
Marshalls Cl. N11 . . . . .4A **32**
Marshalls Dr. RM1: Rom 3K **55**
Marshalls Gro. SE18 . . . . .4C **106**
Marshall's Pl. SE16 . . . . .3F **103**
Marshalls Rd. RM7: Rom 4K **55**
SM1: Sutt 4K **165**
Marshall St. NW10 . . . . .7K **61**
W1 . . . . .1B **12** (6G **83**)
Marshall Street Leisure Cen.
. . . . .1B **12** (6G **83**)
Marshalsea Rd. SE1 . . . . .6D **14** (2C **102**)
Marsham Cl. BR7: Chst 5F **143**
Marsham Ct. SW1 . . . . .3D **18** (4H **101**)
Marsham St. SW1 . . . . .2D **18** (3H **101**)
Marsh Av. CR4: Mitc 2D **154**
Marshbrook Cl. SE3 . . . . .3B **124**
Marsh Cen., The *E1* *7K 9*
(off Whitechapel High St.)
Marsh Cl. NW7 . . . . .3G **29**
Marsh Ct. E8 .6G **67**
SW19 .1A **154**
Marsh Dr. NW9 . . . . .6B **44**
Marsh Farm Rd. TW2: Twick 1K **131**
Marshfield St. E14 . . . . .3E **104**
Marshgate La. E15 . . . . .2E **86**
Marshgate Path SE28 . . . . .3G **107**
Marsh Grn. Rd. RM10: Dag 1G **91**
Marsh Hall HA9: Wemb 3F **61**
Marsh Hill E9 .5A **68**
Marsh Ho. *SW1* *6D 18*
(off Aylesford St.)
SW8 . . . . .1G **119**
Marsh La. E10 . . . . .2B **68**
HA7: Stan 5H **27**
N17 . . . . .7C **34**
NW7 . . . . .3F **29**
Marsh Rd. HA0: Wemb 3D **78**
HA5: Pinn 4C **40**
Marshside Cl. N9 . . . . .1D **34**
Marsh St. E14 . . . . .4D **104**
Marsh Wall E14 . . . . .1C **104**
Marsh Way RM13: Dag, Rain 3K **91**
Marshwood Ho. *NW6* *1J 81*
(off Kilburn Va.)
Marsland Cl. SE17 . . . . .5B **102**
Marsom Ho. *N1* *1E 8*
(off Provost Est.)
Marston Av. KT9: Chess 6E **162**
RM10: Dag 2G **73**
Marston Cl. NW6 . . . . .7A **64**
RM10: Dag 3G **73**
Marston Ho. SW9 . . . . .2A **120**
Marston Rd. IG5: Ilf 1C **52**
TW11: Tedd 5B **132**
Marston Way SE19 . . . . .7B **138**
Marsworth Av. HA5: Pinn 1B **40**
Marsworth Cl. UB4: Yead 5C **76**
Marsworth Ho. *E2* *1G 85*
(off Whiston Rd.)
Martaban Rd. N16 . . . . .2F **67**
Martara M. SE17 . . . . .5C **102**
Marta Rose Ct. *SE20* *2H 157*
(off Wadhurst Cl.)
Martello St. E8 . . . . .7H **67**
Martello Ter. E8 . . . . .7H **67**
Martell Rd. SE21 . . . . .3D **138**
Martel Pl. E8 .6F **67**
Marten Rd. E17 . . . . .2C **50**
Martens Av. DA7: Bex 4H **127**
Martens Cl. DA7: Bex 4J **127**
Martha Ct. E2 . . . . .2H **85**
Martham Cl. IG6: Ilf 1F **53**
SE28 . . . . .7D **90**
Martha Rd. E15 . . . . .6G **69**
Martha's Bldgs. EC1 . . . . .3E **8** (4D **84**)
Martha St. E1 . . . . .6J **85**
Marthorne Cres. HA3: Hrw W 2H **41**
Martin Bowes Rd. SE9 . . . . .3D **124**
Martinbridge Trad. Est.
EN1: Enf 5B **24**
Martin Cl. N9 .1E **34**
UB10: Uxb 2A **74**
Martin Ct. *CR2: S Croy* *5D 168*
(off Birdhurst Rd.)
E14 . . . .*2E 104*
(off River Barge Cl.)
Martin Cres. CR0: C'don 1A **168**
Martindale SW14 . . . . .5J **115**

Martindale Av. BR6: Chels 5K 173
E16 7J 87
Martindale Ho. *E14* *7D 86*
(off Poplar High St.)
Martin Dale Ind. Est. EN1: Enf 3C 24
Martindale Rd. SW12 7F 119
TW4: Houn 3C 112
Martin Dene DA6: Bex 5F 127
Martin Dr. UB5: N'olt 5D 58
Martineau Dr. TW1: Twick 4B 114
Martineau Est. E1 7J 85
Martineau Ho. *SW1* *6A 18*
(off Churchill Gdns.)
Martineau M. N5 4B 66
Martineau Rd. N5 4B 66
Martingale Cl. TW16: Sun 4J 147
Martingales Cl. TW10: Ham 3D 132
Martin Gdns. RM8: Dag 4C 72
Martin Gro. SM4: Mord 3J 153
Martin Ho. *E3* *1B 86*
(off Old Ford Rd.)
SE1 3C 102
SW8 *7J 101*
(off Wyvil Rd.)
Martin La. EC4 2F 15 (7D 84)
(not continuous)
Martin Pl. *SE28* *1J 107*
(off Martin St.)
Martin Ri. DA6: Bex 5F 127
Martin Rd. RM8: Dag 4C 72
Martins, The HA9: Wemb 3F 61
SE26 5H 139
Martins Cl. BR4: W W'ck 1F 171
Martin's Mt. EN5: New Bar 4D 20
Martins Pl. SE28 1J 107
Martin's Rd. BR2: Brom 2G 159
Martin St. SE28 1J 107
Martins Wlk. N10 1E 46
N22 3A 48
SE28 *1J 107*
(off Martin St.)
Martin Way SM4: Mord 2F 153
SW20 2F 153
Martlesham *N17* *2E 48*
(off Adams Rd.)
Martlesham Wlk. NW9 2A 44
(not continuous)
Martlet Gro. UB5: N'olt 3B 76
Martlett Ct. WC2 1F 13 (6J 83)
Martley Dr. IG2: Ilf 5F 53
Martock Cl. HA3: W'stone 4A 42
Martock Gdns. N11 5J 31
Marton Cl. SE6 3C 140
Marton Rd. N16 2E 66
Martynside NW9 1B 44
Martys Yd. NW3 4B 64
Marvell Av. UB4: Hayes 5J 75
Marvell Ct. *RM6: Chad H* *6B 54*
(off Quarles Pk. Rd.)
Marvell Ho. *SE5* *7D 102*
(off Camberwell Rd.)
Marvels Cl. SE12 2K 141
Marvels La. SE12 2K 141
(not continuous)
Marville Rd. SW6 7H 99
Marvin St. E8 6H 67
Marwell Cl. BR4: W W'ck 2H 171
Marwood Cl. DA16: Well 3B 126
Marwood Dr. NW7 7A 30
Mary Adelaide Cl. SW15 4A 134
Mary Ann Gdns. SE8 6C 104
Maryatt Av. HA2: Harr 2F 59
Marybank SE18 4D 106
Mary Bayly Ho. *W11* *1G 99*
(off Wilsham St.)
Mary Cl. HA7: Stan 4F 43
Mary Datchelor Cl. SE5 1D 120
Mary Datchelor Ho. *SE5* *1D 120*
(off Grove La.)
Maryfield Cl. DA5: Bexl 3K 145
Mary Flux Ct. *SW5* *5K 99*
(off Bramham Gdns.)
Mary Grn. NW8 1K 81
Mary Holben Ho. SW16 5G 137
Mary Ho. *W6* *5E 98*
(off Queen Caroline St.)
Mary Jones Ct. *E14* *7C 86*
(off Garford St.)
Maryland Ind. Est. E15 5G 69
Maryland Pk. E15 5G 69
(not continuous)
Maryland Point *E15* *6G 69*
(off The Grove)
Maryland Rd. CR7: Thor H 1B 156
E15 5F 69
N22 6E 32
Maryland Sq. E15 5G 69
Marylands Rd. W9 4J 81
Maryland St. E15 5F 69
Maryland Wlk. *N1* *1C 84*
(off Popham St.)
Maryland Way TW16: Sun 2J 147
Mary Lawrenson Pl. SE3 7J 105
MARYLEBONE 5H 5 (5E 82)
Marylebone Cricket Club 2B 4
MARYLEBONE FLYOVER 5C 82
Marylebone Fly-Over W2 6B 4 (5B 82)
Marylebone Gdns. TW9: Rich 4G 115
Marylebone High St. W1 5H 5 (5E 82)
Marylebone La. W1 6H 5 (6E 82)
Marylebone M. W1 6J 5 (5F 83)
Marylebone Pas. W1 7B 6 (6G 83)
Marylebone Rd. NW1 5D 4 (5C 82)
Marylebone St. W1 6H 5 (5E 82)
Marylee Way SE11 4H 19 (4K 101)
Mary Macarthur Ho. *E2* *3K 85*
(off Warley St.)
RM10: Dag *3G 73*
(off Wythenshawe Rd.)
W6 6G 99
Mary Neuner Rd. N8 3K 47
N22 3K 47
Maryon Gro. SE7 4C 106
Maryon Ho. *NW6* *7A 64*
(off Goldhurst Ter.)
Maryon M. NW3 4C 64
Maryon Rd. SE7 4C 106
SE18 4C 106
Mary Peters Dr. UB6: G'frd 5H 59
Mary Pl. W11 7G 81
Mary Rose Cl. TW12: Hamp 1E 148
Mary Rose Mall E6 5D 88
Maryrose Way N20 1G 31
Marys Ct. NW1 3D 4
Mary Seacole Cl. E8 1F 85
Mary Seacole Ho. *W6* *3C 98*
(off Invermead Cl.)
Mary Smith Ct. *SW5* *4J 99*
(off Trebovir Rd.)
Marysmith Ho. *SW1* *5D 18*
(off Cureton St.)
Mary's Ter. TW1: Twick 7A 114
(not continuous)
Mary St. E16 5H 87
N1 1C 84
Mary Ter. NW1 1F 83
Maryville DA16: Well 2K 125
Mary Wallace Theatre 1A 132
Mary Wharrie Ho. *NW3* *7D 64*
(off Fellows Rd.)
Marzell Ho. *W14* *5H 99*
(off North End Rd.)
Marzena Ct. TW3: Houn 6G 113
Masault Ct. *TW9: Rich* *4E 114*
(off Kew Foot Rd.)
Masbro' Rd. W14 3F 99
Mascalls Ct. SE7 6A 106
Mascalls Rd. SE7 6A 106
Mascotte Rd. SW15 4F 117
Mascotts Cl. NW2 3D 62
Masefield Av. HA7: Stan 5E 26
UB1: S'hall 7E 76
Masefield Ct. EN5: New Bar 4F 21
KT6: Surb 7D 150
Masefield Cres. N14 5B 22
Masefield Gdns. E6 4E 88
Masefield Ho. *NW6* *3J 81*
(off Stafford Rd.)
Masefield La. UB4: Yead 4K 75
Masefield Rd. TW12: Hamp 4D 130
Masefield Vw. BR6: Farnb 3G 173
Masefield Way TW19: Stanw 1B 128
Masham Ho. *DA18: Erith* *2D 108*
(off Kale Rd.)
Mashie Rd. W3 6A 80
Mashiters Hill RM1: Rom 1K 55
Maskall Cl. SW2 1A 138
Maskani Wlk. SW16 7G 137
Maskell Rd. SW17 3A 136
Maskelyne Cl. SW11 1C 118
Mason Cl. DA7: Bex 3H 127
E16 7J 87
SE16 5G 103
SW20 1F 153
TW12: Hamp 1D 148
Mason Ho. *E9* *7J 67*
(off Frampton Pk. Rd.)
SE1 *4G 103*
(off Simms Rd.)
Mason Rd. IG8: Wfd G 4B 36
SM1: Sutt 5K 165
Mason's Arms M. W1 1K 11 (6F 83)
Masons Av. CR0: C'don 3C 168
EC2 7E 8 (6D 84)
HA3: W'stone 4K 41
Masons Grn. La. W3 4G 79
W5 4G 79
Masons Hill BR2: Brom 3J 159
SE18 4F 107
Masons Pl. CR4: Mitc 1D 154
EC1 1B 8 (3C 84)
Mason St. SE17 4D 102
Masons Yd. EC1 1B 8 (3B 84)
SW1 4B 12 (1G 101)
SW19 5F 135
Massey Cl. N11 5A 32
Massey Ct. *E6* *1A 88*
(off Florence Rd.)
Massie Rd. E8 6G 67
Massingberd Way SW17 4F 137
Massinger St. SE17 4E 102
Massingham St. E1 4K 85
Masson Av. HA4: Ruis 6A 58
Mast, The E16 7G 89
Mast Ct. *SE16* *4A 104*
(off Boat Lifter Way)
Master Gunner Pl. SE18 7C 106
Masterman Ho. *SE5* *7D 102*
(off Elmington Est.)
Masterman Rd. E6 3C 88
Masters Cl. SW16 6G 137
Masters Dr. SE16 5H 103
Masters Lodge *E1* *6J 85*
(off Johnson St.)
Masters St. E1 5K 85
Mast Ho. Ter. E14 4C 104
(not continuous)
Mastmaker Ct. E14 2C 104
Mastmaker Rd. E14 2C 104
Mast Quay SE18 3D 106
MASWELL PARK 5G 113
Maswell Pk. Cres. TW3: Houn 5G 113
Maswell Pk. Rd. TW3: Houn 5F 113
Matcham Ct. *TW1: Twick* *6D 114*
(off Clevedon Rd.)
Matcham Rd. E11 3G 69
Matching Ct. *E3* *3B 86*
(off Merchant St.)
Matchless Dr. SE18 7E 106
Matfield Cl. BR2: Brom 5J 159
Matfield Rd. DA17: Belv 6G 109
Matham Gro. SE22 4F 121
Matham Rd. KT8: E Mos 5H 149
Matheson Lang Ho. SE1 7J 13
Matheson Rd. W14 4H 99
Mathews Av. E6 2E 88
Mathews Pk. Av. E15 6H 69
Mathews Yd. WC2 1E 12 (6J 83)
Mathieson Ct. *SE1* *7B 14*
(off King James St.)
Mathison Ho. *SW10* *7A 100*
(off Coleridge Gdns.)
Matilda Cl. SE19 7D 138
Matilda Gdns. E3 2C 86
Matilda Ho. *E1* *1G 103*
(off St Katherine's Way)
Matilda St. N1 1K 83
Matisse Ct. EC1 3E 8 (4D 84)
Matisse Rd. TW3: Houn 3F 113
Matlock Cl. EN5: Barn 5A 20
SE24 4C 120
Matlock Ct. *NW8* *2A 82*
(off Abbey Rd.)
SE5 4D 120
W11 *7J 81*
(off Kensington Pk. Rd.)
Matlock Cres. SM3: Cheam 4G 165
Matlock Gdns. SM3: Cheam 4G 165
Matlock Pl. SM3: Cheam 4G 165
Matlock Rd. E10 6E 50
Matlock St. E14 6A 86
Matlock Way KT3: N Mald 1K 151
Maton Ho. *SW6* *7H 99*
(off Estcourt Rd.)
Matrimony Pl. SW4 2G 119
Matson Ct. IG8: Wfd G 7B 36
Matson Ho. SE16 3H 103
Matthew Cl. W10 4F 81
Matthew Ct. CR4: Mitc 5H 155
E17 3E 50
Matthew Parker St. SW1 7D 12 (2H 101)
Matthews Ct. *E17* *1C 50*
(off Chingford Rd.)
Matthews Ho. *E14* *5C 86*
(off Burgess St.)
Matthews Rd. UB6: G'frd 5H 59
Matthews St. SW11 2D 118
Matthews Yd. *CR0: C'don* *3C 168*
(off Surrey St.)
Matthias Apartments *N1* *7D 66*
(off Northchurch Rd.)
Matthias Ct. TW10: Rich 5E 114
Matthias Rd. N16 5E 66
Mattison Rd. N4 6A 48
Mattock La. W5 1B 96
W13 1B 96
Maud Cashmore Way
SE18 3D 106
Maud Chadburn Pl. SW12 6F 119
Maude Ho. *E2* *2G 85*
(off Ropley St.)
Maude Rd. E17 5A 50
SE5 1E 120
Maude Ter. E17 5A 50
Maud Gdns. E13 1H 87
IG11: Bark 2K 89
Maudlins Grn. E1 4K 15 (1G 103)
Maud Rd. E10 3E 68
E13 2H 87
Maudslay Rd. SE9 3D 124
Maudsley Ho. TW8: Bford 5E 96
Maud St. E16 5H 87
Maudsville Cotts. W7 1J 95
Maud Wilkes Cl. NW5 5G 65
Maugham Ct. *W3* *3J 97*
(off Palmerston Rd.)
Mauleverer Rd. SW2 5J 119
Maundeby Wlk. NW10 6A 62
Maunder Rd. W7 1K 95
Maunsel St. SW1 3C 18 (4H 101)
Maureen Campbell Ct.
TW17: Shep *5D 146*
(off Harrison Way)
Maureen Ct. BR3: Beck 2J 157
Maurer Ct. SE10 3H 105
Mauretania Bldg. *E1* *7K 85*
(off Jardine Rd.)
Maurice Av. N22 2B 48

Maurice Bishop Ter.—Meadow Cl.

Maurice Bishop Ter. N6 . . . 6E 46
(off View Rd.)
Maurice Brown Cl. NW7 . . . 5A 30
Maurice Ct. E1 . . . 3K 85
N22 . . . 1K 47
TW8: Bford . . . 7D 96
Maurice Drummond Ho.
SE10 . . . 1D 122
(off Catherine Gro.)
Maurice St. W12 . . . 6D 80
Maurice Wlk. NW11 . . . 4A 46
Maurier Cl. UB5: N'olt . . . 1A 76
Mauritius Rd. SE10 . . . 4G 105
Maury Rd. N16 . . . 2G 67
Mauveine Gdns. TW3: Houn . . . 4E 112
Mavelstone Cl. BR1: Brom . . . 1C 160
Mavelstone Rd. BR1: Brom . . . 1B 160
Maverton Rd. E3 . . . 1C 86
Mavis Av. KT19: Ewe . . . 5A 164
Mavis Cl. KT19: Ewe . . . 5A 164
Mavis Wlk. E6 . . . 5C 88
(off Greenwich Cres.)
Mavor Ho. N1 . . . 1K 83
(off Barnsbury Est.)
Mawbey Ho. SE1 . . . 5G 103
Mawbey Pl. SE1 . . . 5F 103
Mawbey Rd. SE1 . . . 5F 103
Mawbey St. SW8 . . . 7J 101
Mawdley Ho. SE1 . . . 7A 14
MAWNEY . . . 4J 55
Mawney Cl. RM7: Mawney . . . 2H 55
Mawney Rd. RM7: Mawney, Rom . . . 2H 55
Mawson Cl. SW20 . . . 2G 153
Mawson Ct. N1 . . . 1D 84
(off Gopsall St.)
Mawson Ho. EC1 . . . 5J 7
(off Baldwins Gdns.)
Mawson La. W4 . . . 6B 98
Maxden Ct. SE15 . . . 3F 121
Maxey Gdns. RM9: Dag . . . 4E 72
Maxey Rd. RM9: Dag . . . 4E 72
SE18 . . . 4G 107
Maxfield Cl. N20 . . . 7F 21
Maxilla Wlk. W10 . . . 6F 81
Maxim Apartments BR2: Brom . . . 4K 159
(off Tiger La.)
Maximfeldt Rd. DA8: Erith . . . 5K 109
Maxim Rd. DA8: Erith . . . 4K 109
N21 . . . 6F 23
Maxted Pk. HA1: Harr . . . 7J 41
Maxted Rd. SE15 . . . 3F 121
Maxwell Cl. CR0: Wadd . . . 1J 167
UB3: Hayes . . . 7J 75
Maxwell Ct. SE22 . . . 1G 139
SW4 . . . 5H 119
Maxwell Gdns. BR6: Orp . . . 3K 173
Maxwell Rd. DA16: Well . . . 3K 125
HA6: Nwood . . . 1F 39
SW6 . . . 7K 99
TW15: Ashf . . . 6E 128
UB7: W Dray . . . 4B 92
Maxwelton Av. NW7 . . . 5E 28
Maxwelton Cl. NW7 . . . 5E 28
Maya Angelou Ct. E4 . . . 4K 35
Maya Cl. SE15 . . . 2H 121
Mayall Cl. EN3: Enf L . . . 1H 25
Mayall Rd. SE24 . . . 5B 120
Maya Pl. N11 . . . 7C 32
Maya Rd. N2 . . . 4A 46
Maybank Av. E18 . . . 2K 51
HA0: Wemb . . . 5K 59
Maybank Gdns. HA5: Eastc . . . 5J 39
Maybank Rd. E18 . . . 1K 51
May Bate Av. KT2: King T . . . 1D 150
Maybells Commercial Est.
IG11: Bark . . . 2D 90
Mayberry Ct. BR3: Beck . . . 7B 140
(off Copers Cope Rd.)
Mayberry Pl. KT5: Surb . . . 7F 151
Maybourne Cl. SE26 . . . 6H 139
Maybury Cl. BR5: Pet W . . . 5F 161
EN1: Enf . . . 1C 24
Maybury Ct. CR2: S Croy . . . 5B 168
(off Haling Pk. Rd.)
HA1: Harr . . . 6H 41
W1 . . . 6H 5
(off Marylebone St.)
Maybury Gdns. NW10 . . . 6D 62
Maybury M. N6 . . . 7G 47
Maybury Rd. E13 . . . 4A 88
IG11: Bark . . . 2K 89
Maybury St. SW17 . . . 5C 136
Maychurch Cl. HA7: Stan . . . 7J 27
May Cl. KT9: Chess . . . 6F 163
May Ct. SW19 . . . 1A 154
(off Pincott Rd.)
Maycroft HA5: Pinn . . . 2K 39
Maycross Av. SM4: Mord . . . 4H 153
Mayday Gdns. SE3 . . . 2C 124
Mayday Rd. CR7: Thor H . . . 6B 156
Maydeb Ct. RM6: Chad H . . . 6F 55
Maydew Ho. SE16 . . . 4J 103
(off Abbeyfield Est.)
Maydwell Ho. E14 . . . 5C 86
(off Thomas Rd.)
Mayerne Rd. SE9 . . . 5B 124
Mayesbrook Pk. Arena . . . 5A 72
Mayesbrook Rd. IG3: Ilf . . . 3A 72
IG11: Bark . . . 1K 89
RM8: Dag . . . 3A 72
Mayes Cl. CR0: New Ad . . . 7F 171
Mayesford Rd. RM6: Chad H . . . 7C 54
Mayes Rd. N22 . . . 2K 47
Mayeswood Rd. SE12 . . . 4A 142
MAYFAIR . . . 3J 11 (7F 83)
Mayfair Av. DA7: Bex . . . 1D 126
IG1: Ilf . . . 2D 70
KT4: Wor Pk . . . 1C 164
RM6: Chad H . . . 6D 54
TW2: Whitt . . . 7G 113
Mayfair Cl. BR3: Beck . . . 1D 158
KT6: Surb . . . 1E 162
Mayfair Ct. HA8: Edg . . . 5A 28
Mayfair Gdns. IG8: Wfd G . . . 7D 36
N17 . . . 6H 33
Mayfair M. NW1 . . . 7D 64
(off Regents Pk. Rd.)
Mayfair Pl. W1 . . . 4K 11 (1F 101)
Mayfair Ter. N14 . . . 7C 22
Mayfield DA7: Bex . . . 3F 127
Mayfield Av. BR6: Orp . . . 1K 173
HA3: Kenton . . . 5B 42
IG8: Wfd G . . . 6D 36
N12 . . . 4F 31
N14 . . . 2C 32
W4 . . . 4A 98
W13 . . . 3B 96
Mayfield Cl. E8 . . . 6F 67
KT7: T Ditt . . . 1B 162
SE20 . . . 1H 157
SW4 . . . 5H 119
TW15: Ashf . . . 6D 128
UB10: Hil . . . 3D 74
Mayfield Cres. CR7: Thor H . . . 4K 155
N9 . . . 6C 24
Mayfield Dr. HA5: Pinn . . . 4D 40
Mayfield Gdns. NW4 . . . 6F 45
W7 . . . 6H 77
Mayfield Ho. E2 . . . 2H 85
(off Cambridge Heath Rd.)
Mayfield Mans. SW15 . . . 5H 117
Mayfield Rd. BR1: Brom . . . 5C 160
CR2: Sande . . . 7D 168
CR7: Thor H . . . 4K 155
DA17: Belv . . . 4J 109
E4 . . . 2K 35
E8 . . . 7F 67
E13 . . . 4H 87
E17 . . . 2A 50
EN3: Enf H . . . 2E 24
N8 . . . 5K 47
RM8: Dag . . . 1C 72
SM2: Sutt . . . 6B 166
SW19 . . . 1H 153
Mayfield Rd. W3 . . . 7H 79
W12 . . . 2A 98
Mayfield Rd. Flats N8 . . . 6K 47
Mayfields HA9: Wemb . . . 2G 61
Mayfields Cl. HA9: Wemb . . . 2G 61
Mayfield Vs. DA14: Sidc . . . 6C 144
Mayflower Cl. HA4: Ruis . . . 6E 38
SE16 . . . 4K 103
Mayflower Ho. E14 . . . 2C 104
(off Westferry Rd.)
IG11: Bark . . . 1H 89
(off Westbury Rd.)
Mayflower Rd. SW9 . . . 3J 119
Mayflower St. SE16 . . . 2J 103
Mayfly Cl. HA5: Eastc . . . 7A 40
Mayfly Gdns. UB5: N'olt . . . 3B 76
Mayford NW1 . . . 2G 83
(not continuous)
Mayford Cl. BR3: Beck . . . 3K 157
SW12 . . . 7D 118
Mayford Rd. SW12 . . . 7D 118
May Gdns. HA0: Wemb . . . 3C 78
Maygood Ho. N1 . . . 2K 83
(off Maygood St.)
Maygood St. N1 . . . 2A 84
Maygrove Rd. NW6 . . . 6H 63
Mayhew Cl. E4 . . . 3H 35
Mayhew Ct. SE5 . . . 4D 120
Mayhill Ct. SE15 . . . 7E 102
(off Newent Cl.)
Mayhill Rd. EN5: Barn . . . 6B 20
SE7 . . . 6K 105
May Ho. E3 . . . 2C 86
(off Thomas Frye Dr.)
Mayland Mans. IG11: Bark . . . 7F 71
(off Whiting Av.)
Maylands Dr. DA14: Sidc . . . 3D 144
UB8: Uxb . . . 6A 56
Maylands Ho. SW3 . . . 4D 16
(off Cale St.)
Maylie Ho. SE16 . . . 2H 103
(off Marigold St.)
Maynard Cl. N15 . . . 5E 48
SW6 . . . 7K 99
Maynard Path E17 . . . 5E 50
Maynard Rd. E17 . . . 5E 50
Maynards Quay E1 . . . 7J 85
Mayne Ct. SE26 . . . 5H 139
Maynooth Gdns. SM5: Cars . . . 7D 154
Mayo Ct. W13 . . . 3B 96
Mayo Ho. E1 . . . 5J 85
(off Lindley St.)
Mayola Rd. E5 . . . 4J 67
Mayo Rd. CR0: C'don . . . 5D 156
KT12: Walt T . . . 7J 147
NW10 . . . 6A 62
Mayor's and City of London Court, The
. . . 7E 8
Mayow Rd. SE23 . . . 4K 139
SE26 . . . 4K 139
Mayplace Cl. DA7: Bex . . . 3H 127
Mayplace La. SE18 . . . 6F 107
(not continuous)
Mayplace Rd. E. DA1: Cray . . . 3J 127
DA7: Bex . . . 3H 127
Mayplace Rd. W. DA7: Bex . . . 4G 127
MAYPOLE . . . 1K 145
Maypole Ct. UB2: S'hall . . . 2D 94
(off Merrick Rd.)
May Rd. E4 . . . 6H 35
E13 . . . 2J 87
TW2: Twick . . . 1J 131
Mayroyd Av. KT6: Surb . . . 2G 163
May's Bldgs. M. SE10 . . . 7E 104
Mays Ct. SE10 . . . 7F 105
WC2 . . . 3E 12 (7J 83)
Mays Hill Rd. BR2: Brom . . . 2G 159
Mays La. EN5: Ark, Barn . . . 1H 29 & 6A 20
Maysoule Rd. SW11 . . . 4B 118
Mays Rd. TW11: Tedd . . . 5H 131
Mayston M. SE10 . . . 5J 105
(off Ormiston Rd.)
May St. W14 . . . 5H 99
(North End Rd.)
W14 . . . 5H 99
(Vereker Rd.)
Mayswood Gdns. RM10: Dag . . . 6J 73
Maythorne Cotts. SE13 . . . 5F 123
Mayton St. N7 . . . 3K 65
Maytree Cl. HA8: Edg . . . 3D 28
Maytree Ct. CR4: Mitc . . . 3E 154
UB5: N'olt . . . 3C 76
Maytree Gdns. W5 . . . 2D 96
May Tree Ho. SE4 . . . 3B 122
(off Wickham Rd.)
Maytree La. HA7: Stan . . . 7F 27
Maytree Wlk. SW2 . . . 2A 138
Mayville Est. N16 . . . 5E 66
Mayville Rd. E11 . . . 2G 69
(not continuous)
IG1: Ilf . . . 5F 71
May Wlk. E13 . . . 2K 87
Mayward Ho. SE5 . . . 1E 120
(off Peckham Rd.)
Maywood Cl. BR3: Beck . . . 7D 140
May Wynne Ho. E16 . . . 7K 87
(off Murray Sq.)
Maze Hill SE3 . . . 7H 105
SE10 . . . 6G 105
Maze Hill Lodge SE10 . . . 6F 105
(off Park Vista)
Mazenod Av. NW6 . . . 7J 63
Maze Rd. TW9: Kew . . . 7G 97
MCC Cricket Mus. & Tours . . . 1A 4 (3B 82)
Mead, The BR3: Beck . . . 1E 158
BR4: W W'ck . . . 1F 171
N2 . . . 2A 46
SM6: Wall . . . 6H 167
UB10: Ick . . . 2C 56
W13 . . . 5B 78
Meadbank Studios SW11 . . . 7C 100
(off Parkgate Rd.)
Mead Cl. HA3: Hrw W . . . 1H 41
NW1 . . . 6E 64
Mead Ct. NW9 . . . 5J 43
Mead Cres. E4 . . . 4K 35
SM1: Sutt . . . 3C 166
Meadcroft Rd. SE11 . . . 7K 19 (6B 102)
(not continuous)
SE17 . . . 6B 102
Meade Cl. W4 . . . 6G 97
Meader Ct. SE14 . . . 7K 103
Mead Fld. HA2: Harr . . . 3D 58
Meadfield HA8: Edg . . . 2C 28
(not continuous)
Meadfield Grn. HA8: Edg . . . 2C 28
Meadfoot Rd. SW16 . . . 7G 137
Meadgate Av. IG8: Wfd G . . . 5H 37
Mead Gro. RM6: Chad H . . . 3D 54
Mead Ho. W11 . . . 1H 99
(off Ladbroke Rd.)
Mead Ho. La. UB4: Hayes . . . 4F 75
Meadhurst Club . . . 5H 129
Meadhurst Pk. TW16: Sun . . . 6G 129
Meadlands Dr. TW10: Ham . . . 2D 132
Mead Lodge W4 . . . 2K 97
Meadow, The BR7: Chst . . . 6G 143
N10 . . . 3E 46
Meadow Av. CR0: C'don . . . 6K 157
Meadow Bank N21 . . . 6E 22
Meadowbank KT5: Surb . . . 6F 151
NW3 . . . 7D 64
SE3 . . . 3H 123
Meadowbank Cl. SW6 . . . 7E 98
TW7: Isle . . . 1J 113
Meadowbank Gdns. TW5: Cran . . . 1J 111
Meadowbank Rd. NW9 . . . 7K 43
Meadowbridge Ct. CR0: C'don . . . 5D 156
(off Princess Rd.)
Meadowbrook Cl. SL3: Poyle . . . 4A 174
Meadowbrook Ct. TW7: Isle . . . 3J 113
Meadow Cl. BR7: Chst . . . 5F 143
DA6: Bex . . . 5F 127
E4 . . . 1J 35

A-Z London 329

Meadow Cl. E9 6B 68
EN3: Enf W 1F 25
EN5: Barn 6C 20
HA4: Ruis 6H 39
IG11: Bark 7A 72
KT10: Hin W 3A 162
SE6 5C 140
SM1: Sutt 2A 166
SW20 4E 152
TW4: Houn 6E 112
TW10: Ham 1E 132
UB5: N'olt 2E 76
Meadow Ct. N1 2E 84
TW3: Houn 6F 113
Meadowcourt Rd. SE3 4H 123
Meadowcroft BR1: Brom 3D 160
W4 *5G 97*
(off Brooks Rd.)
Meadowcroft Cl. N13 2F 33
Meadowcroft Rd. N13 2F 33
Meadow Dr. N10 3F 47
NW4 2E 44
Meadowford Cl. SE28 7A 90
Meadow Gdns. HA8: Edg 6C 28
Meadow Gth. NW10 6J 61
(not continuous)
Meadowgate Cl. NW7 5G 29
Meadow Hill KT3: N Mald 6A 152
Meadow La. SE12 3K 141
Meadowlea Cl. UB7: Harm 2E 174
Meadow M. SW8 6K 101
Meadow Pl. SW8 7J 101
W4 7A 98
Meadow Rd. BR2: Brom 2G 159
HA5: Pinn 4B 40
IG11: Bark 7K 71
RM7: Rush G 1J 73
RM9: Dag 6F 73
SM1: Sutt 4C 166
SW8 7H 19 (7K 101)
SW19 7A 136
TW13: Felt 2C 130
TW15: Ashf 5F 129
UB1: S'hall 7D 76
Meadow Row SE1 3C 102
Meadows, The E4 4A 36
Meadows Cl. E10 2C 68
Meadows Ct. DA14: Sidc 6B 144
Meadows End TW16: Sun 1J 147
Meadowside SE9 4A 124
TW1: Twick 7D 114
Meadowside Leisure Cen. 4A 124
Meadow Stile CR0: C'don 3C 168
Meadowsweet Cl. E16 5B 88
SW20 4E 152
Meadow Vw. DA15: Sidc 7B 126
HA1: Harr 1J 59
Meadowview TW19: Stan M 7A 174
Meadow Vw. Rd. CR7: Thor H 5B 156
UB4: Hayes 4F 75
Meadowview Rd. DA5: Bexl 6E 126
KT19: Ewe 7A 164
SE6 5B 140
Meadow Wlk. E18 4J 51
KT17: Ewe 6A 164
KT19: Ewe 6A 164
(not continuous)
RM9: Dag 6F 73
SM6: Wall 3F 167
Meadow Walks EN5: New Bar 6E 20
Meadow Way BR6: Farnb 3E 172
HA4: Ruis 6K 39
HA9: Wemb 4D 60
KT9: Chess 5E 162
NW9 5K 43
Meadow Way, The
HA3: Hrw W 1J 41
Meadow Waye TW5: Hest 6C 94
Mead Path SW17 4A 136
Mead Pl. CR0: C'don 1C 168
E9 6J 67
Mead Plat NW10 6J 61
Mead Rd. BR7: Chst 6G 143
HA8: Edg 6B 28
TW10: Ham 3C 132
Mead Row SE1 1J 19 (3A 102)
Meads, The HA8: Edg 6E 28
SM3: Cheam 3G 165
SM4: Mord 5C 154
UB8: Cowl 4A 74
Meads Ct. E15 6H 69
Meadside Cl. BR3: Beck 1A 158
Meads La. IG3: Ilf 7J 53
Meads Rd. EN3: Enf H 1F 25
N22 2B 48
Mead Ter. HA9: Wemb 4D 60
Meadvale Rd. CR0: C'don 7F 157
W5 4B 78
Mead Way BR2: Hayes 6H 159
CR0: C'don 2A 170
HA4: Ruis 6F 39
Meadway BR3: Beck 1E 158
EN5: Barn, New Bar 4D 20
IG3: Bark, Ilf 4J 71
IG8: Wfd G 5F 37
KT5: Surb 1J 163
N14 2C 32
NW11 6J 45
SW20 4E 152
TW2: Twick 1H 131
TW15: Ashf 4C 128
Meadway, The IG9: Buck H 1G 37
SE3 2F 123
Meadway Cl. EN5: Barn 4D 20
HA5: Hat E 6A 26
NW11 6K 45
Meadway Ct. RM8: Dag 2F 73
TW11: Tedd 5C 132
W5 4F 79
Meadway Gdns. HA4: Ruis 6F 39
Meadway Ga. NW11 6J 45
Meaford Way SE20 7H 139
Meakin Est. SE1 3E 102
Meanley Rd. E12 4C 70
Meard St. W1 1C 12 (6H 83)
(not continuous)
Meath Cres. E2 3K 85
Meath Ho. *SE24* *6B 120*
(off Dulwich Rd.)
Meath Rd. E15 2H 87
IG1: Ilf 3G 71
Meath St. SW11 1F 119
Mecca Bingo
Burnt Oak 2J 43
Camden *1F 83*
(off Arlington Rd.)
Catford 7D 122
Chadwell Heath 7D 54
Croydon *2C 168*
(off Tamworth Rd.)
Dagenham 1E 90
Hackney 1K 9
Hayes 6K 75
Rosehill 7A 154
Wandsworth 1K 135
Wood Green *2A 48*
(off Lordship La.)
Mecklenburgh Pl. WC1 3G 7 (4K 83)
Mecklenburgh Sq. WC1 3G 7 (4K 83)
Mecklenburgh St. WC1 3G 7 (4K 83)
Medburn St. NW1 2H 83
Medcroft Gdns. SW14 4J 115
Medebourne Cl. SE3 3J 123
Mede Ho. *BR1: Brom* *5K 141*
(off Pike Cl.)
Medesenge Way N13 6G 33
Medfield St. SW15 7C 116
Medhurst Cl. E3 2A 86
(not continuous)
Medhurst Dr. BR1: Brom 5G 141
Median Rd. E5 5J 67
Medici Cl. IG3: Ilf 6A 54
(not continuous)
Medina Gro. N7 3A 66
Medina Rd. N7 3A 66
Medland Cl. SM6: Wall 1E 166
Medland Ho. E14 7A 86
Medlar Cl. UB5: N'olt 2B 76
Medlar Ho. DA15: Sidc 3A 144
Medlar St. SE5 1C 120
Medley Rd. NW6 6J 63
Medora Rd. RM7: Rom 4K 55
SW2 7K 119
Medusa Rd. SE6 6D 122
Medway Bldgs. *E3* *2A 86*
(off Medway Rd.)
Medway Cl. CR0: C'don 6J 157
IG1: Ilf 5G 71
Medway Ct. NW11 6K 45
WC1 *2E 6*
(off Judd St.)
Medway Dr. UB6: G'frd 2K 77
Medway Gdns. HA0: Wemb 4A 60
Medway Ho. KT2: King T 1D 150
NW8 *4C 4*
(off Penfold St.)
SE1 *7F 15*
(off Hankey Pl.)
Medway M. E3 2A 86
Medway Pde. UB6: G'frd 2K 77
Medway Rd. E3 2A 86
Medway St. SW1 2D 18 (3H 101)
Medwin St. SW4 4K 119
Meerbrook Rd. SE3 3A 124
Meeson Rd. E15 7H 69
Meeson St. E5 4A 68
Meeson's Wharf E15 2E 86
Meeting Fld. Path E9 6J 67
Meeting Ho. All. E1 1H 103
Meeting Ho. La. SE15 1H 121
Megelish M. UB1: S'hall 3E 76
Mehetabel Rd. E9 5J 67
Meister Cl. IG1: Ilf 1H 71
Melancholy Wlk. TW10: Ham 2C 132
Melanda Cl. BR7: Chst 5D 142
Melanie Cl. DA7: Bex 1E 126
Melba Way SE13 1D 122
Melbourne Av. HA5: Pinn 3F 41
N13 6E 32
W13 1A 96
Melbourne Cl. BR6: Orp 7J 161
SE20 7G 139
SM6: Wall 5G 167
UB10: Ick 4C 56
Melbourne Ct. N10 7A 32
W9 *4A 82*
(off Randolph Av.)
Melbourne Gdns. RM6: Chad H 5E 54
Melbourne Gro. SE22 4E 120
Melbourne Ho. UB4: Yead 4A 76
W8 *1J 99*
(off Kensington Pl.)
Melbourne Mans. *W14* *6G 99*
(off Musard Rd.)
Melbourne M. SE6 7E 122
SW9 1A 120
Melbourne Pl. WC2 1H 13 (6K 83)
Melbourne Rd. E6 2D 88
E10 7D 50
E17 4A 50
IG1: Ilf 1F 71
SM6: Wall 5F 167
SW19 1J 153
TW11: Tedd 6C 132
Melbourne Sq. SW9 1A 120
Melbourne Ter. *SW6* *7K 99*
(off Moore Pk. Rd.)
Melbourne Way EN1: Enf 6A 24
Melbray M. SW6 2H 117
Melbreak Ho. SE22 3E 120
Melbury Av. UB2: S'hall 3F 95
Melbury Cl. BR7: Chst 6C 142
KT10: Clay 6B 162
Melbury Ct. W8 3H 99
Melbury Dr. SE5 7E 102
Melbury Gdns. SW20 1D 152
Melbury Ho. *SW8* *7K 10*
(off Richborne Ter
Melbury Rd. HA3: Kenton 5F 4
W14 3H 9
Melchester *W11* *6H 8*
(off Ledbury Rd
Melchester Ho. *N19* *3H 6*
(off Wedmore St
Melcombe Ct. *NW1* *5E*
(off Melcombe Pl
Melcombe Gdns. HA3: Kenton 6F 4
Melcombe Ho. *SW8* *7K 10*
(off Dorset Rd
Melcombe Pl. NW1 5E 4 (5D 82
Melcombe Regis Ct. *W1* *6H*
(off Weymouth St
Melcombe St. NW1 4F 5 (4D 82
Meldex Cl. NW7 6K 2
Meldon Cl. SW6 1K 11
Meldone Cl. KT5: Surb 7H 15
Meldrum Rd. IG3: Ilf 2A 7
Melfield Gdns. SE6 4E 14
Melford Av. IG11: Bark 6J 7
Melford Cl. KT9: Chess 5F 16
Melford Ct. *SE1* *3E 10*
(off Fendall St
SE22 1G 13
(not continuous
Melford Pas. SE22 7G 12
Melford Rd. E6 4D 8
E11 2G 6
E17 4A 5
IG1: Ilf 2H 7
SE22 7G 12
Melfort Av. CR7: Thor H 3B 15
Melfort Rd. CR7: Thor H 3B 15
Melgund Rd. N5 5A 6
Melina Cl. UB3: Hayes 5F 7
Melina Ct. SW15 3C 11
Melina Pl. NW8 2A 4 (3B 82
Melina Rd. W12 2D 9
Melior Ct. N6 6G 4
Melior Pl. SE1 6G 15 (2E 102
Melior St. SE1 6G 15 (2E 102
Meliot Rd. SE6 2F 14
Meller Cl. CR0: Bedd 3J 16
Mellifont Cl. SM5: Cars 7B 15
Melling Dr. EN1: Enf 1B 2
Melling St. SE18 6J 10
Mellish Cl. IG11: Bark 1K 8
Mellish Flats E10 7C 5
Mellish Gdns. IG8: Wfd G 5D 3
Mellish Ho. *E1* *6H 8*
(off Varden St
Mellish Ind. Est. SE18 3B 10
Mellish St. E14 3C 10
Mellison Rd. SW17 5C 13
Melliss Av. TW9: Kew 1H 11
Mellitus St. W12 5B 8
Mellor Cl. KT12: Walt T 7D 14
Mellow La. E. UB4: Hayes 3E 7
Mellow La. W. UB10: Hil 3E 7
Mellows Rd. IG5: Ilf 3D 5
SM6: Wall 5H 16
Mells Cres. SE9 4D 14
Mell St. SE10 5G 10
Melody La. N5 5C 6
Melody Rd. SW18 5A 11
Melon Pl. W8 2J 9
Melon Rd. E11 3G 6
SE15 1G 12
Melrose Av. CR4: Mitc 7F 13
DA1: Cray 7K 12
N22 1B 4
NW2 5D 6
SW16 3K 15
SW19 2H 13
TW2: Whitt 7F 11
UB6: G'frd 2F 7
Melrose Cl. SE12 1J 14
UB4: Hayes 5J 7
UB6: G'frd 2F 7

Melrose Ct. W13 1A 96
(off Williams Rd.)
Melrose Cres. BR6: Orp 4H 173
Melrose Dr. UB1: S'hall 1E 94
Melrose Gdns. HA8: Edg 3H 43
KT3: N Mald 3K 151
W6 3E 98
Melrose Ho. NW6 3J 81
(off Carlton Va.)
SW1 5F 101
(off Sutherland St.)
Melrose Rd. HA5: Pinn 4D 40
SW13 2B 116
SW18 6H 117
SW19 2J 153
W3 3J 97
Melrose Ter. W6 3E 98
Melrose Tudor SM6: Wall 5J 167
(off Plough La.)
Melsa Rd. SM4: Mord 6A 154
Melthorne Dr. HA4: Ruis 3A 58
Melthorpe Gdns. SE3 1C 124
Melton Cl. HA4: Ruis 1A 58
Melton Ct. SM2: Sutt 7A 166
SW7 3B 16 (4B 100)
Melton St. NW1 2B 6 (3G 83)
Melville Av. CR2: S Croy 5F 169
SW20 7C 134
UB6: G'frd 5K 59
Melville Cl. UB10: Ick 2F 57
Melville Ct. SE8 4A 104
W4 5G 97
(off Haining Cl.)
W12 3D 98
(off Goldhawk Rd.)
Melville Gdns. N13 5G 33
Melville Ho. EN5: New Bar 5G 21
SE10 1E 122
(off Sparta St.)
Melville Pl. N1 7C 66
Melville Rd. DA14: Sidc 2C 144
E17 3B 50
NW10 7K 61
RM5: Col R 1H 55
SW13 1C 116
Melville Vs. Rd. W3 1J 97
Melvin Rd. SE20 1J 157
Melwood Ho. E1 6H 85
(off Watney Mkt.)
Melyn Cl. N7 4G 65
Memel Ct. EC1 4C 8
Memel St. EC1 4C 8 (4C 84)
Memess Path SE18 6E 106
Memorial Av. E12 2C 70
E15 3G 87
Memorial Cl. TW5: Hest 6D 94
Menai Pl. E3 2C 86
(off Blondin St.)
Menard Ct. EC1 2D 8
(off Galway St.)
Mendez Way SW15 6C 116
Mendham Ho. SE1 7G 15
(off Cluny Pl.)
Mendip Cl. KT4: Wor Pk 1E 164
SE26 4J 139
UB3: Harl 7F 93
Mendip Ct. SE14 6J 103
(off Avonley Rd.)
SW11 3A 118
Mendip Dr. NW2 2G 63
Mendip Ho. N9 2B 34
(within Edmonton Grn. Shop. Cen.)
Mendip Ho's. E2 3J 85
(off Welwyn St.)
Mendip Rd. DA7: Bex 1K 127
IG2: Ilf 5J 53
SW11 3A 118
Mendora Rd. SW6 7G 99
Menelik Rd. NW2 4G 63
Menier Chocolate Factory
(Theatre and Art Gallery) 5D 14
(off Southwark St.)
Menlo Gdns. SE19 7D 138
Menlo Lodge N13 3E 32
(off Crothall Cl.)
Menon Dr. N9 3C 34
Menotti St. E2 4G 85
Menteath Ho. E14 6C 86
(off Dod St.)
Mentmore Cl. HA3: Kenton 6C 42
Mentmore Ter. E8 7H 67
Mentone Mans. SW10 7K 99
(off Fulham Rd.)
Meon Ct. TW7: Isle 2J 113
Meon Rd. W3 2J 97
Meopham Rd. CR4: Mitc 1G 155
Mepham Cres. HA3: Hrw W 7B 26
Mepham Gdns. HA3: Hrw W 7B 26
Mepham St. SE1 5H 13 (1A 102)
Mera Dr. DA7: Bex 4G 127
Merantun Way SW19 1K 153
Merbury Cl. SE13 5E 122
SE28 1H 107
Merbury Rd. SE28 1H 107
Mercator Pl. E14 5C 104
Mercator Rd. SE13 4F 123
Mercer Bldg. EC2 3H 9
(off Bateman's Row)
Mercer Cl. KT7: T Ditt 7K 149
Mercer Ct. E1 5A 86
Mercer Ho. SW1 5J 17
(off Ebury Bri. Rd.)
Merceron Ho's. E2 3J 85
(off Globe Rd.)
Merceron St. E1 4H 85
Mercer Pl. HA5: Pinn 2A 40
Mercers Cl. SE10 4H 105
Mercer's Cotts. E1 6A 86
(off White Horse Rd.)
Mercers M. N19 3H 65
Mercers Pl. W6 4F 99
Mercers Rd. N19 3H 65
(not continuous)
Mercer St. WC2 1E 12 (6J 83)
Merchant Ct. E1 1J 103
(off Wapping Wall)
Merchant Ho. E14 3D 104
(off Goulston St.)
Merchant Ind. Ter. NW10 4J 79
Merchants Cl. SE25 4G 157
Merchants Ho. SE10 5F 105
(off Collington St.)
Merchants Lodge E17 4C 50
(off Westbury Rd.)
Merchant Sq. W2 5B 82
(off Nth. Wharf Rd.)
Merchants Row SE10 5F 105
(off Hoskins St.)
Merchant St. E3 3B 86
Merchiston Rd. SE6 2F 141
Merchland Rd. SE9 1G 143
Mercia Gro. SE13 4E 122
Mercia Ho. SE5 2C 120
(off Denmark Rd.)
TW15: Ashf 1E 146
Mercier Rd. SW15 5G 117
Mercury NW9 1B 44
(off The Concourse)
Mercury Cen. TW14: Felt 5J 111
Mercury Ct. E14 4C 104
(off Homer Dr.)
SW9 1A 120
(off Southey Rd.)
Mercury Hgts. IG2: Ilf 6H 53
Mercury Ho. E3 1C 86
(off Garrison Rd.)
E16 6H 87
(off Jude St.)
TW8: Bford 6C 96
(off Glenhurst Rd.)
W5 4F 79
Mercury Rd. TW8: Bford 6C 96
Mercury Way SE14 6K 103
Mercy Ter. SE13 5D 122
Merebank La. CR0: Wadd 5K 167
Mere Cl. BR6: Farnb 2E 172
SW15 7F 117
Meredith Av. NW2 5E 62
Meredith Cl. HA5: Pinn 1B 40
Meredith Ho. N16 5E 66
Meredith M. SE4 4B 122
Meredith St. E13 3J 87
EC1 2A 8 (3B 84)
Meredith Twr. W3 3H 97
(off Hanbury Rd.)
Meredyth Rd. SW13 2C 116
Mere End CR0: C'don 7K 157
Mere Rd. TW17: Shep 6D 146
Mereside BR6: Farnb 2E 172
Mereside Pk.
TW15: Ashf 4E 128
Meretone Cl. SE4 4A 122
Mereton Mans. SE8 1C 122
(off Brookmill Rd.)
Merevale Cres. SM4: Mord 6A 154
Mereway Rd. TW2: Twick 1H 131
Merewood Cl. BR1: Brom 2E 160
Merewood Gdns.
CR0: C'don 7K 157
Merewood Rd. DA7: Bex 2J 127
Mereworth Cl. BR2: Brom 5H 159
Mereworth Dr. SE18 7F 107
Mereworth Ho. SE15 6J 103
Merganser Ct. E1 3K 15
(off Star Pl.)
SE8 6B 104
(off Edward St.)
Merganser Gdns. SE28 3H 107
Meriden Cl. BR1: Brom 7B 142
IG6: Ilf 1G 53
Meriden Ct. SW3 6C 16
Meriden Ho. N1 1E 84
(off Wilmer Gdns.)
Merideth Ct. KT1: King T 2F 151
Meridia Ct. E15 1E 86
(off Biggerstaff Rd.)
Meridiam Ct. UB4: Yead 4A 76
Meridian Cl. NW7 4E 28
Meridian Ct. SE15 7H 103
(off Gervase St.)
SE16 2G 103
(off East La.)
Meridian Ga. E14 2D 104
Meridian Ho. NW1 7G 65
(off Baynes St.)
SE10 4G 105
(off Azof St.)
SE10 7E 104
(off Royal Hill)
Meridian Pl. E14 2D 104
Meridian Point SE8 6D 104
Meridian Rd. SE7 7B 106
Meridian Sq. E15 7F 69
Meridian Trad. Est.
SE7 4K 105
Meridian Wlk. N17 6K 33
Meridian Way EN3: Pond E 7E 24
N9 4D 34
N18 5D 34
Merifield Rd. SE9 4A 124
Merino Cl. E11 4A 52
Merino Ct. EC1 2D 8
(off Lever St.)
Merino Pl. DA15: Sidc 6A 126
Merioneth Ct. W7 5K 77
(off Copley Cl.)
Merivale Rd. HA1: Harr 7G 41
SW15 4G 117
Merlewood Dr. BR7: Chst 1D 160
Merley Ct. NW9 1J 61
Merlin NW9 1B 44
(off The Concourse)
Merlin Cl. CR0: C'don 4E 168
CR4: Mitc 3C 154
SM6: Wall 6K 167
UB5: N'olt 3A 76
Merlin Ct. BR2: Brom 3H 159
HA4: Ruis 2F 57
HA7: Stan 5G 27
(off William Dr.)
Merlin Cres. HA8: Edg 1F 43
Merlin Gdns. BR1: Brom 3J 141
Merling Cl. KT9: Chess 5C 162
Merlin Gro. BR3: Beck 4B 158
Merlin Ho. EN3: Pond E 5E 24
Merlin Rd. DA16: Well 4A 126
E12 2B 70
Merlin Rd. Nth. DA16: Well 4A 126
Merlins Av. HA2: Harr 3D 58
Merlins Ct. WC1 2J 7
(off Margery St.)
Merlin St. WC1 2J 7 (3A 84)
Mermaid Ct. E8 7F 67
(off Celandine Dr.)
SE1 6E 14 (2D 102)
SE16 1B 104
Mermaid Ho. E14 7E 86
(off Bazely St.)
Mermaid Twr. SE8 6B 104
(off Abinger Gro.)
Meroe Ct. N16 2E 66
Merredene St. SW2 6K 119
Merriam Av. E9 6B 68
Merriam Cl. E4 5K 35
Merrick Rd. UB2: S'hall 2D 94
Merrick Sq. SE1 7E 14 (3D 102)
Merridene N21 6G 23
Merrielands Cres. RM9: Dag 2F 91
Merrielands Retail Pk. RM9: Dag 1F 91
Merrilands Rd. KT4: Wor Pk 1E 164
Merrilees Rd. DA15: Sidc 7J 125
Merrilyn Cl. KT10: Clay 6A 162
Merriman Rd. SE3 1A 124
Merrington Rd. SW6 6J 99
Merrion Av. HA7: Stan 5J 27
Merrion Ct. HA4: Ruis 1H 57
(off Pembroke Rd.)
Merritt Gdns. KT9: Chess 6C 162
(not continuous)
Merritt Rd. SE4 5B 122
Merrivale N14 6C 22
NW1 1G 83
(off Camden St.)
Merrivale Av. IG4: Ilf 4B 52
Merrow Bldgs. SE1 6B 14
(off Rushworth St.)
Merrow Ct. CR4: Mitc 2B 154
Merrow Rd. SM2: Cheam 7F 165
Merrow St. SE17 5D 102
Merrow Wlk. SE17 5D 102
Merrow Way CR0: New Ad 6E 170
Merrydown Way BR7: Chst 1C 160
Merryfield SE3 2H 123
Merryfield Gdns. HA7: Stan 5H 27
Merryfield Ho. SE9 3A 142
(off Grove Pk. Rd.)
Merryfields UB8: Uxb 2A 74
UB10: Uxb 2A 74
Merryfields Way SE6 7D 122
MERRY HILL 1A 26
Merryhill Cl. E4 7J 25
Merry Hill Mt. WD23: Bush 1A 26
Merry Hill Rd. WD23: Bush 1A 26
Merryhills Ct. N14 5B 22
Merryhills Dr. EN2: Enf 4C 22
Merryweather Ct. KT3: N Mald 5A 152
N19 3G 65
Mersea Ho. IG11: Bark 6F 71
Mersey Ct. KT2: King T 1D 150
(off Samuel Gray Gdns.)
Mersey Rd. E17 3B 50
Mersey Wlk. UB5: N'olt 2E 76
Mersham Dr. NW9 5G 43
Mersham Pl. CR7: Thor H 2D 156
(off Livingstone Rd.)
SE20 1H 157
Mersham Rd. CR7: Thor H 3D 156
Merten Rd. RM6: Chad H 7E 54

Merthyr Ter. SW13 6D **98**
MERTON 7A **136**
Merton Abbey Mills SW19 1A **154**
Merton Av. UB5: N'olt 5G **59**
UB10: Hil 7D **56**
W4 4B **98**
Merton Ct. DA16: Well 2B **126**
IG1: Ilf 6C **52**
Merton Gdns. BR5: Pet W 5F **161**
Merton Hall Gdns. SW20 1G **153**
Merton Hall Rd. SW19 7G **135**
Merton High St. SW19 7K **135**
Merton Ind. Est. SW19 1A **154**
Merton La. N6 2D **64**
Merton Lodge EN5: New Bar 5F **21**
Merton Mans. SW20 2F **153**
MERTON PARK 2J **153**
Merton Pk. Pde. SW19 1H **153**
Merton Pl. *SW19* *1A **154***
(off Nelson Gro. Rd.)
Merton Ri. NW3 7C **64**
Merton Rd. E17 5E **50**
EN2: Enf 1J **23**
HA2: Harr 1G **59**
IG3: Ilf 7K **53**
IG11: Bark 7K **71**
SE25 5F **157**
SW18 6J **117**
SW19 7K **135**
Merton's Intergenerational Cen. 2F **155**
Merton Way KT8: W Mole 4F **149**
UB10: Hil 7D **56**
Mertoun Ter. *W1* *7E **4***
(off Seymour Pl.)
Merttins Rd. SE15 5K **121**
Meru Cl. NW5 4E **64**
Mervan Rd. SW2 4A **120**
Mervyn Av. SE9 3G **143**
Mervyn Rd. TW17: Shep 7E **146**
W13 3A **96**
Messaline Av. W3 6J **79**
Messent Rd. SE9 5A **124**
Messeter Pl. SE9 6E **124**
Messina Av. NW6 7J **63**
Messiter Ho. *N1* *1K **83***
(off Barnsbury Est.)
Metcalfe Ct. SE10 3H **105**
Metcalf Rd. TW15: Ashf 5D **128**
Metcalf Wlk. TW13: Hanw 4C **130**
Meteor St. SW11 4E **118**
Meteor Way SM6: Wall 7J **167**
Methley St. SE11 6K **19** (5A **102**)
Methuen Cl. HA8: Edg 7B **28**
Methuen Pk. N10 3F **47**
Methuen Rd. DA6: Bex 4F **127**
DA17: Belv 4H **109**
HA8: Edg 7B **28**
Methven Ct. *N9* *3B **34***
(off The Broadway)
Methwold Rd. W10 5F **81**
Metro Bus. Cen. SE26 6B **140**
Metro Central Hgts. *SE1* *3C **102***
(off Newington C'way.)
Metro Ind. Cen. TW7: Isle 2J **113**
Metro Playgolf Driving Range 7K **29**
Metropolis *SE11* *3B **102***
(off Oswin St.)
Metropolitan Bus. Cen. *N1* *7E **66***
(off Enfield Rd.)
Metropolitan Cen., The UB6: G'frd 1F **77**
Metropolitan Cl. E14 5C **86**
Metropolitan Police Norwood Cadet Training Cen. *1E **156***
(off Sylvan Hill)
Metropolitan Sta. Bldgs. *W6* *4E **98***
(off Beadon Rd.)
Metropolitan Wharf E1 1J **103**
Metro Trad. Est. HA9: Wemb 4H **61**
Mews, The DA14: Sidc 4A **144**
IG4: Ilf 5B **52**
N1 1C **84**
N8 3A **48**
Mews, The RM1: Rom 4K **55**
TW1: Twick 6B **114**
Mews Pl. IG8: Wfd G 4D **36**
Mews St. E1 4K **15** (1G **103**)
Mexborough NW1 1G **83**
Mexfield Rd. SW15 5H **117**
Meyer Grn. EN1: Enf 1B **24**
Meyer Rd. DA8: Erith 6K **109**
Meymott St. SE1 5A **14** (1B **102**)
Meynell Cres. E9 7K **67**
Meynell Gdns. E9 7K **67**
Meynell Rd. E9 7K **67**
Meyrick Ho. *E14* *5C **86***
(off Burgess St.)
Meyrick Rd. NW10 6C **62**
SW11 3B **118**
Miah Ter. E1 1G **103**
Miall Wlk. SE26 4A **140**
Micawber Av. UB8: Hil 4C **74**
Micawber Ct. *N1* *1D **8***
(off Windsor Ter.)
Micawber Ho. *SE16* *2G **103***
(off Llewellyn St.)
Micawber St. N1 1D **8** (3C **84**)
Michael Cliffe Ho. EC1 2A **8**
Michael Faraday Ho. *SE17* *5E **102***
(off Beaconsfield Rd.)
Michael Gaynor Cl. W7 1K **95**
Michael Haines Ho. *SW9* *7A **102***
(off Sth. Island Pl.)
Michael Manley Ind. Est.
SW8 2G **119**
Michaelmas Cl. SW20 3E **152**
Michael Rd. E11 1G **69**
SE25 3E **156**
SW6 1K **117**
Michaels Cl. SE13 4G **123**
Michael Stewart Ho. *SW6* *6H **99***
(off Clem Attlee Ct.)
Michelangelo Ct. *SE16* *5H **103***
(off Stubbs Dr.)
Micheldever Rd. SE12 6G **123**
Michelham Gdns. TW1: Twick 3K **131**
Michelle Ct. *BR1: Brom* *1H **159***
(off Blyth Rd.)
N12 5F **31**
W3 7K **79**
Michelsdale Dr. TW9: Rich 4E **114**
Michelson Ho. SE11 4H **19**
Michel's Row *TW9: Rich* *4E **114***
(off Michelsdale Dr.)
Michel Wlk. SE18 5F **107**
Michigan Av. E12 4D **70**
Michigan Bldg. *E14* *1F **105***
(off Biscayne Av.)
Michigan Ho. E14 3C **104**
Michleham Down N12 4C **30**
Mickledore *NW1* *1B **6***
(off Ampthill Est.)
Mickleham Cl. BR5: St P 2K **161**
Mickleham Gdns. SM3: Cheam 6G **165**
Mickleham Rd. BR5: St P 1K **161**
Mickleham Way CR0: New Ad 7F **171**
Micklethwaite Rd. SW6 6J **99**
Mickleton Ho. *W2* *5J **81***
(off Westbourne Pk. Rd.)
Midas Bus. Cen. RM10: Dag 4H **73**
Midas Metropolitan Ind. Est.
SM4: Mord 7E **152**
MID BECKTON 6D **88**
Mid City Lanes
Croydon 6A **168**
Midcroft HA4: Ruis 1G **57**
Middle Dartrey Wlk. *SW10* *7A **100***
(off Dartrey Wlk.)
Middle Dene NW7 3E **28**
Middlefield NW8 1B **82**
Middlefielde W13 5B **78**
Middlefield Gdns. IG2: Ilf 6F **53**
Middle Grn. Cl. KT5: Surb 6F **151**
Middleham Gdns. N18 6B **34**
Middleham Rd. N18 6B **34**
Middle La. N8 5J **47**
TW11: Tedd 6K **131**
Middle La. M. N8 5J **47**
Middle Mill Halls of Residence
KT1: King T 3F **151**
Middle New St. *EC4* *7K **7***
(off Pemberton Row)
Middle Pk. Av. SE9 6B **124**
Middle Path HA2: Harr 1H **59**
Middle Rd. E13 2J **87**
EN4: E Barn 6H **21**
HA2: Harr 2H **59**
SW16 2H **155**
Middle Row W10 4G **81**
Middlesborough Rd. N18 6B **34**
Middlesex Bldg., The *E1* *6H **9***
(off Artillery La.)
Middlesex Bus. Cen. UB2: S'hall 2E **94**
Middlesex Cl. UB1: S'hall 4F **77**
Middlesex County Cricket Club 1B **4** (3B **82**)
Middlesex County Cricket School 2K **45**
Middlesex Ct. HA1: Harr 5K **41**
W4 4B **98**
Middlesex Filter Beds Nature Reserve 3K **67**
Middlesex Ho. HA0: Wemb 1D **78**
Middlesex Pas. EC1 6B **8**
Middlesex Pl. *E9* *6J **67***
(off Elsdale St.)
Middlesex Rd. CR4: Mitc 5J **155**
Middlesex St. E1 6H **9** (5E **84**)
Middlesex University
Cat Hill Campus 5K **21**
Hendon Campus 4D **44**
The Archway Campus 1G **65**
Trent Pk. Campus 2B **22**
Middlesex Wharf E5 2J **67**
Middle St. CR0: C'don 2C **168**
(not continuous)
EC1 5C **8** (5C **84**)
Middle Temple La. EC4 1J **13** (6A **84**)
Middleton Av. DA14: Sidc 6B **144**
E4 4G **35**
UB6: G'frd 2H **77**
Middleton Cl. E4 3G **35**
Middleton Dr. HA5: Eastc 3J **39**
SE16 2K **103**
Middleton Gdns. IG2: Ilf 6F **53**
Middleton Gro. N7 5J **65**
Middleton Ho. E8 7G **67**
SE1 *3D **102***
(off Burbage Cl.)
SW1 *4D **18***
(off Causton St.)
Middleton M. N7 5J **65**
Middleton Pl. W1 6A **6**
Middleton Rd. E8 7F **67**
NW11 7J **45**
SM4: Mord 6K **153**
SM5: Cars 6K **153**
UB3: Hayes 5F **75**
Middleton St. E2 3H **85**
Middleton Way SE13 4F **123**
Middle Way DA18: Erith 3E **108**
SW16 2H **155**
UB4: Yead 4A **76**
Middle Way, The HA3: W'stone 2K **41**
Middleway NW11 5K **45**
Middle Yd. SE1 4G **15** (1E **102**)
Midfield Av. DA7: Bex 3J **127**
Midfield Pde. DA7: Bex 3J **127**
Midfield Way BR5: St P 7A **144**
Midford Ho. *NW4* *4E **44***
(off Stratford Rd.)
Midford Pl. W1 4B **6** (4G **83**)
Midholm HA9: Wemb 1G **61**
NW11 4K **45**
Midholm Cl. NW11 4K **45**
Midholm Rd. CR0: C'don 2A **170**
Midhope Ho. *WC1* *2F **7***
(off Midhope St.)
Midhope St. WC1 2F **7** (3J **83**)
Midhurst SE26 6J **139**
Midhurst Av. CR0: C'don 7A **156**
N10 3E **46**
Midhurst Gdns. UB10: Hil 1E **74**
Midhurst Hill DA6: Bex 6G **127**
Midhurst Ho. *E14* *6B **86***
(off Salmon La.)
Midhurst Pde. *N10* *3E **46***
(off Fortis Grn.)
Midhurst Rd. W13 2A **96**
Midhurst Way E5 4G **67**
Midland Pde. NW6 6K **63**
Midland Pl. E14 5E **104**
Midland Rd. E10 7E **50**
NW1 1D **6** (2H **83**)
Midland Ter. NW2 3F **63**
NW10 4A **80**
Midleton Rd. KT3: N Mald 3J **151**
Midlothian Rd. *E3* *4B **86***
(off Burdett Rd.)
Midmoor Rd. SW12 1G **137**
SW19 1F **153**
Midship Cl. SE16 1K **103**
Midship Point *E14* *2C **104***
(off The Quarterdeck)
Midstrath Rd. NW10 4A **62**
Midsummer Av. TW4: Houn 4D **112**
Midway SM3: Sutt 7H **153**
Midway Ho. EC1 1A **8**
Midwinter Cl. DA16: Well 3A **126**
Midwood Cl. NW2 3D **62**
Miers Cl. E6 1E **88**
Mighell Av. IG4: Ilf 5B **52**
Mikardo Ct. *E14* *7E **86***
(off Poplar High St.)
Milan Ct. N11 1H **47**
Milan Rd. UB1: S'hall 2D **94**
Milborne Gro. SW10 6A **16** (5A **100**)
Milborne St. E9 6J **67**
Milborough Cres. SE12 6G **123**
Milburn Dr. UB7: Yiew 7A **74**
Milcote St. SE1 7A **14** (2B **102**)
Mildenhall Rd. E5 4J **67**
Mildmay Av. N1 6D **66**
Mildmay Gro. Nth. N1 5D **66**
Mildmay Gro. Sth. N1 5D **66**
Mildmay Pk. N1 5D **66**
Mildmay Pl. N16 5E **66**
Mildmay Rd. IG1: Ilf 3F **71**
N1 5D **66**
RM7: Rom 5J **55**
Mildmay St. N1 6D **66**
Mildred Av. UB3: Harl 4F **93**
UB5: N'olt 5F **59**
Mildred Ct. CR0: C'don 1G **169**
Mildred Rd. DA8: Erith 5K **109**
Mildrose Ct. *NW6* *3J **81***
(off Malvern M.)
Mildura Ct. N8 4K **47**
MILE END 4B **86**
Mile End, The E17 1K **49**
Mile End Climbing Wall 3A **86**
Mile End Pk. 2A **86**
Mile End Pk. Leisure Cen. 5A **86**
Mile End Pl. E1 4K **85**
Mile End Rd. E1 5J **85**
E3 5J **85**
Mile End Stadium 5B **86**
Mile Rd. SM6: Bedd, Wall 1F **167**
(not continuous)
Miles Bldgs. *NW1* *5C **4***
(off Penfold Pl.)
Miles Cl. SE28 1H **107**
Miles Ct. *CR0: C'don* *2B **168***
(off Cuthbert Rd.)
E1 *6H **85***
(off Tillman St.)
Miles Dr. SE28 1J **107**
Miles Ho. *SE10* *5G **105***
(off Tuskar St.)
Miles Lodge HA1: Harr 5H **41**

Milespit Hill NW7 . . . 5J **29**
Miles Pl. KT5: Surb . . . 4F **151**
NW8 . . . 5B **4**
Miles Rd. CR4: Mitc . . . 3C **154**
N8 . . . 3J **47**
Miles St. SW8 . . . 7E **18** (6J **101**)
(not continuous)
Milestone Cl. N9 . . . 2B **34**
SM2: Sutt . . . 6B **166**
Milestone Ct. E10 . . . 7D **50**
MILESTONE GREEN . . . 4J **115**
Milestone Ho. *KT1: King T* . . . *3D* ***150***
(off Surbiton Rd.)
Milestone Rd. SE19 . . . 6F **139**
Miles Way N20 . . . 2H **31**
Milfoil St. W12 . . . 7C **80**
Milford Cl. SE2 . . . 6E **108**
Milford Ct. UB1: S'hall . . . 1E **94**
Milford Gdns. CR0: C'don . . . 5J **157**
HA0: Wemb . . . 4D **60**
HA8: Edg . . . 7B **28**
Milford Gro. SM1: Sutt . . . 4A **166**
Milford La. WC2 . . . 2H **13** (7A **84**)
Milford M. SW16 . . . 3K **137**
Milford Rd. UB1: S'hall . . . 7E **76**
W13 . . . 1B **96**
Milford Towers SE6 . . . 7D **122**
Milk St. BR1: Brom . . . 6K **141**
E16 . . . 1F **107**
EC2 . . . 7D **8** (6C **84**)
Milkwell Gdns. IG8: Wfd G . . . 7E **36**
Milkwell Yd. SE5 . . . 1C **120**
Milkwood Rd. SE24 . . . 5B **120**
Milk Yd. E1 . . . 7J **85**
Millais Av. E12 . . . 5E **70**
Millais Ct. *UB5: N'olt* . . . *2B* ***76***
(off Academy Gdns.)
Millais Cres. KT19: Ewe . . . 5A **164**
Millais Gdns. HA8: Edg . . . 2G **43**
Millais Ho. *SW1* . . . *4E* ***18***
(off Marsham St.)
Millais Rd. E11 . . . 4E **68**
EN1: Enf . . . 5A **24**
KT3: N Mald . . . 7A **152**
Millais Way KT19: Ewe . . . 4J **163**
Millard Cl. N16 . . . 5E **66**
Millard Rd. SE8 . . . 5B **104**
Millard Ter. RM10: Dag . . . 6G **73**
Millbank SM6: Wall . . . 5H **167**
SW1 . . . 2E **18** (3J **101**)
Millbank Ct. SW1 . . . 3E **18**
Millbank Twr. SW1 . . . 4E **18** (4J **101**)
Millbank Way SE12 . . . 5J **123**
Millbourne Rd. TW13: Hanw . . . 4C **130**
Mill Bri. EN5: Barn . . . 6C **20**
Millbrook Av. DA16: Well . . . 4H **125**
Millbrook Gdns. RM6: Chad H . . . 6F **55**
Millbrook Ho. *SE15* . . . *6G* ***103***
(off Peckham Pk. Rd.)
Millbrook Pas. SW9 . . . 3B **120**
Millbrook Pl. *NW1* . . . *2G* ***83***
(off Hampstead Rd.)
Millbrook Rd. N9 . . . 1C **34**
SW9 . . . 3B **120**
Mill Cl. SM5: Cars . . . 2E **166**
Mill Cnr. EN5: Barn . . . 1C **20**
Mill Ct. E10 . . . 3E **68**
SE28 . . . *7B* ***90***
(off Titmuss Av.)
Millcroft Ho. *SE6* . . . *4E* ***140***
(off Melfield Gdns.)
Millender Wlk. *SE16* . . . *4J* ***103***
(off New Rotherhithe Rd.)
Millennium Arena . . . 7E **100**
Millennium Bridge . . . 3B **14** (7B **84**)
Millennium Bri. Ho. *EC4* . . . *2C* ***14***
(off Up. Thames St.)
Millennium Bus. Cen. NW2 . . . 2D **62**
Millennium Cen., The . . . 4K **73**
Millennium Cl. E16 . . . 6K **87**
Millennium Dome
(The O2) . . . 1G **105**
Millennium Dr. E14 . . . 4F **105**
Millennium Ho. E17 . . . 5K **49**
Millennium Pl. E2 . . . 2H **85**
Millennium Sq. SE1 . . . 6K **15** (2F **103**)
Millennium Way SE10 . . . 2G **105**
Miller Av. EN3: Enf L . . . 1H **25**
Miller Cl. BR1: Brom . . . 5K **141**
CR4: Mitc . . . 7D **154**
HA5: Pinn . . . 2A **40**
RM5: Col R . . . 1G **55**
Miller Ct. DA7: Bex . . . 3J **127**
Miller Rd. CR0: C'don . . . 1K **167**
SW19 . . . 6B **136**
Miller's Av. E8 . . . 5F **67**
Millers Cl. NW7 . . . 4H **29**
Millers Ct. *HA0: Wemb* . . . *2E* ***78***
(off Vicars Bri. Cl.)
Millers Grn. Cl. EN2: Enf . . . 3G **23**
Miller's House Vis. Cen. . . . 3E **86**
Millers Mdw. Cl. SE3 . . . 4H **123**
Miller's Ter. E8 . . . 5F **67**
Miller St. NW1 . . . 2G **83**
(not continuous)
Millers Way W6 . . . 2E **98**
Millers Wharf Ho. *E1* . . . *5K* ***15***
(off St Katherine's Way)
Millers Yd. N3 . . . 1K **45**
Miller Wlk. SE1 . . . 5K **13** (1A **102**)
Millet Rd. UB6: G'frd . . . 2F **77**
Mill Farm Av. TW16: Sun . . . 7G **129**
Mill Farm Bus. Pk. TW4: Houn . . . 7C **112**
Mill Farm Cl. HA5: Pinn . . . 2A **40**
Mill Farm Cres. TW4: Houn . . . 1C **130**
Millfield KT1: King T . . . 3F **151**
N4 . . . 2A **66**
TW16: Sun . . . 1F **147**
Millfield Av. E17 . . . 1A **50**
Millfield La. N6 . . . 1C **64**
Millfield Pl. N6 . . . 2E **64**
Millfield Rd. HA8: Edg . . . 2J **43**
TW4: Houn . . . 1C **130**
Millfields Rd. E5 . . . 4J **67**
Millfield Theatre . . . 4J **33**
Mill Gdns. SE26 . . . 3H **139**
Mill Grn. CR4: Mitc . . . 7E **154**
Mill Grn. Bus. Pk. CR4: Mitc . . . 7E **154**
Mill Grn. Rd. CR4: Mitc . . . 7D **154**
Millgrove St. SW11 . . . 1E **118**
Millharbour E14 . . . 2D **104**
Millhaven Cl. RM6: Chad H . . . 6B **54**
MILL HILL . . . 5F **29**
Mill Hill SW13 . . . 2C **116**
MILL HILL CIRCUS . . . 5G **29**
Mill Hill Cir. NW7 . . . 5G **29**
Mill Hill Gro. W3 . . . 1J **97**
Mill Hill Ind. Est. NW7 . . . 6G **29**
Mill Hill Rd. SW13 . . . 2C **116**
W3 . . . 2H **97**
Mill Hill School Leisure Cen. . . . 4H **29**
Mill Hill Ter. W3 . . . 1H **97**
Mill Ho. IG8: Wfd G . . . 5C **36**
Millhouse Pl. SE27 . . . 4B **138**
Millicent Fawcett Ct. N17 . . . 1F **49**
Millicent Gro. N13 . . . 5G **33**
Millicent Preston Ho. *IG11: Bark* . . . *1H* ***89***
(off Ripple Rd.)
Millicent Rd. E10 . . . 1B **68**
Milligan St. E14 . . . 7B **86**
Milliners Ho. *SE1* . . . *7H* ***15***
(off Bermondsey St.)
SW18 . . . 4J **117**
Milling Rd. HA8: Edg . . . 7E **28**
Millington Ho. N16 . . . 3D **66**
Millington Rd. UB3: Harl . . . 3G **93**
Mill La. CR0: Wadd . . . 3K **167**
E4 . . . 3J **25**
IG8: Wfd G . . . 5C **36**
KT17: Ewe . . . 7B **164**
NW6 . . . 5H **63**
RM6: Chad H . . . 6E **54**
SE18 . . . 5E **106**
SM5: Cars . . . 4D **166**
Mill La. Trad. Est. CR0: Wadd . . . 3K **167**
Millman Ct. *WC1* . . . *4G* ***7***
(off Millman Ct.)
Millman M. WC1 . . . 4G **7** (4K **83**)
Millman Pl. *WC1* . . . *4G* ***7***
(off Millman St.)
Millman Rd. E16 . . . 7D **88**
Millman St. WC1 . . . 4G **7** (4K **83**)
Millmark Gro. SE14 . . . 2A **122**
Millmarsh La. EN3: Brim . . . 2F **25**
Millmead Ind. Cen. N17 . . . 2H **49**
Mill Mead Rd. N17 . . . 3H **49**
MILL MEADS . . . 2F **87**
Mill Pl. BR7: Chst . . . 1E **160**
E14 . . . 6A **86**
KT1: King T . . . 3F **151**
Mill Plat TW7: Isle . . . 2A **114**
(not continuous)
Mill Plat Av. TW7: Isle . . . 2A **114**
Mill Pond Cl. SW8 . . . 7H **101**
Millpond Est. SE16 . . . 2H **103**
Millpond Pl. SM5: Cars . . . 3E **166**
Mill Ridge HA8: Edg . . . 5A **28**
Mill River Trad. Est.
EN3: Pond E . . . 3F **25**
Mill Rd. DA8: Erith . . . 7J **109**
E16 . . . 1K **105**
IG1: Ilf . . . 3E **70**
SW19 . . . 7A **136**
TW2: Twick . . . 2G **131**
Mill Row DA5: Bexl . . . 1H **145**
N1 . . . 1E **84**
Mills Cl. UB10: Hil . . . 2C **74**
Mills Ct. EC2 . . . 3G **9**
Mills Gro. E14 . . . 6E **86**
NW4 . . . 3F **45**
Millshot Cl. SW6 . . . 1E **116**
Mills Ho. E17 . . . 3F **51**
SW8 . . . *1G* ***119***
(off Thessaly Rd.)
Millside SM5: Cars . . . 2D **166**
Millside Pl. TW7: Isle . . . 2B **114**
Millson Cl. N20 . . . 2G **31**
Mills Row W4 . . . 4K **97**
Millstone Cl. E15 . . . 6F **69**
Millstream Cl. N13 . . . 5F **33**
Millstream Ho. *SE16* . . . *2H* ***103***
(off Jamaica Rd.)
Millstream Rd. SE1 . . . 7J **15** (2F **103**)
Mill St. KT1: King T . . . 3E **150**
SE1 . . . 7K **15** (2F **103**)
W1 . . . 2A **12** (7F **83**)
Mills Yd. SW6 . . . 3K **117**
Mill Trad. Est., The NW10 . . . 3J **79**
Mill Va. BR2: Brom . . . 2H **159**
Mill Vw. Cl. KT17: Ewe . . . 7B **164**
Mill Vw. Gdns. CR0: C'don . . . 3K **169**
MILLWALL . . . 4D **104**
Millwall Dock Rd. E14 . . . 3C **104**
Millwall FC . . . 5J **103**
Millwall Pk. . . . 4E **104**
Mill Way TW14: Felt . . . 5K **111**
Millway NW7 . . . 4F **29**
Millway Gdns. UB5: N'olt . . . 6D **58**
Millwood Rd. TW3: Houn . . . 5G **113**
Millwood St. W10 . . . 5G **81**
Mill Yd. E1 . . . 7G **85**
Mill Yd. Ind. Est. HA8: Edg . . . 1H **43**
Milman Cl. HA5: Pinn . . . 3B **40**
Milman Rd. NW6 . . . 2F **81**
Milman's Ho. *SW1* . . . *5J* ***17***
(off Warwick Way)
SW10 . . . *6B* ***100***
(off Milman's St.)
Milman's St. SW10 . . . 6B **100**
Milne Ct. E18 . . . 1J **51**
Milne Gdns. SE9 . . . 5C **124**
Milne Ho. *SE18* . . . *4D* ***106***
(off Ogilby St.)
Milner Ct. *SE15* . . . *7F* ***103***
(off Colegrove Rd.)
Milner Dr. TW2: Whitt . . . 7H **113**
Milner Pl. N1 . . . 1A **84**
SM5: Cars . . . 4E **166**
Milner Rd. CR7: Thor H . . . 3D **156**
E15 . . . 3G **87**
KT1: King T . . . 3D **150**
RM8: Dag . . . 2C **72**
SM4: Mord . . . 5B **154**
SW19 . . . 1K **153**
Milner Sq. N1 . . . 7B **66**
Milner St. SW3 . . . 3E **16** (4D **100**)
Milner Wlk. SE9 . . . 2H **143**
Milnthorpe Rd. W4 . . . 6K **97**
Milo Gdns. SE22 . . . 6F **121**
Milo Rd. SE22 . . . 6F **121**
Milrood Ho. *E1* . . . *5K* ***85***
(off Stepney Grn.)
Milroy Wlk. SE1 . . . 4A **14** (1B **102**)
Milson Rd. W14 . . . 3F **99**
Milstead Ho. E5 . . . 5H **67**
Milton Av. CR0: C'don . . . 7D **156**
E6 . . . 7B **70**
EN5: Barn . . . 5C **20**
N6 . . . 7G **47**
NW9 . . . 3J **43**
NW10 . . . 1J **79**
SM1: Sutt . . . 3B **166**
Milton Cl. N2 . . . 5A **46**
SE1 . . . 4F **103**
SM1: Sutt . . . 3B **166**
UB4: Hayes . . . 6J **75**
Milton Ct. E17 . . . 4C **50**
EC2 . . . 5E **8** (5D **84**)
RM6: Chad H . . . 7C **54**
SE14 . . . 6B **104**
(not continuous)
SW18 . . . 5J **117**
TW2: Twick . . . 3J **131**
UB10: Ick . . . 3D **56**
Milton Ct. Rd. SE14 . . . 6A **104**
Milton Ct. Wlk. *EC2* . . . *5E* ***8***
(off Silk St.)
Milton Cres. IG2: Ilf . . . 7F **53**
Milton Dr. TW17: Shep . . . 4A **146**
Milton Gdn. Est. N16 . . . 4D **66**
Milton Gdns. TW19: Stanw . . . 1B **128**
Milton Gro. N11 . . . 5B **32**
N16 . . . 4D **66**
Milton Ho. *E2* . . . *3J* ***85***
(off Roman Rd.)
E17 . . . 4C **50**
SE5 . . . *7D* ***102***
(off Elmington Est.)
SM1: Sutt . . . 3J **165**
Milton Lodge DA14: Sidc . . . 4A **144**
TW2: Twick . . . 7K **113**
Milton Mans. *W14* . . . *6G* ***99***
(off Queen's Club Gdns.)
Milton Pk. N6 . . . 7G **47**
Milton Pl. *N7* . . . *5A* ***66***
(off Eastwood Cl.)
Milton Rd. CR0: C'don . . . 7D **156**
CR4: Mitc . . . 7E **136**
DA16: Well . . . 1K **125**
DA17: Belv . . . 4G **109**
E17 . . . 4C **50**
HA1: Harr . . . 4J **41**
N6 . . . 7G **47**
N15 . . . 4B **48**
NW7 . . . 5H **29**
NW9 . . . 7C **44**
SE24 . . . 5B **120**
SM1: Sutt . . . 3J **165**
SM6: Wall . . . 6G **167**
SW14 . . . 3K **115**
SW19 . . . 6A **136**
TW12: Hamp . . . 7E **130**
UB10: Ick . . . 4D **56**
W3 . . . 1K **97**
W7 . . . 7K **77**
Milton St. EC2 . . . 5E **8** (5D **84**)
Milton Way UB7: W Dray . . . 4B **92**
Milverton Dr. UB10: Ick . . . 4E **56**

Milverton Gdns. IG3: Ilf 2K **71**
Milverton Ho. SE6 . . . . . 3A **140**
Milverton Rd. NW6 . . . . . 7E **62**
Milverton St. SE11 . . . . . 6K **19** (5A **102**)
Milverton Way SE9 . . . . . 4E **142**
Milward St. E1 . . . . . 5H **85**
Milward Wlk. SE18 . . . . . 6E **106**
Mimosa Ho. UB4: Yead 5A **76**
Mimosa Lodge NW10 . . . . . 5B **62**
Mimosa Rd. UB4: Yead 5A **76**
Mimosa St. SW6 . . . . . 1H **117**
Minard Rd. SE6 . . . . . 7G **123**
Mina Rd. SE17 . . . . . 5E **102**
SW19 . . . . . 1J **153**
Minchenden Ct. N14 . . . . . 2C **32**
Minchenden Cres. N14 . . . . . 3B **32**
Minchin Ho. *E14* *6C* ***86***
(off Dod St.)
Mincing La. EC3 . . . . . 2G **15** (7E **84**)
Minden Rd. SE20 . . . . . 1H **157**
SM3: Sutt 2G **165**
Minehead Rd. HA2: Harr 3E **58**
SW16 . . . . . 5K **137**
Mineral Cl. EN5: Barn 6A **20**
Mineral St. SE18 . . . . . 4J **107**
Minera M. SW1 . . . . . 3G **17** (4E **100**)
Minerva Cl. DA14: Sidc 3J **143**
SW9 . . . . . 7A **102**
TW19: Stan M 7B **174**
Minerva Ct. *EC1* *4K* ***7***
(off Bowling Grn. La.)
Minerva Lodge N7 . . . . . 6K **65**
Minerva Rd. E4 . . . . . 7J **35**
KT1: King T 2F **151**
NW10 . . . . . 4J **79**
Minerva St. E2 . . . . . 2H **85**
Minerva Wlk. EC1 . . . . . 7B **8** (6B **84**)
Minet Av. NW10 . . . . . 2A **80**
Minet Country Pk. 2A **94**
Minet Dr. UB3: Hayes 1J **93**
Minet Gdns. NW10 . . . . . 2A **80**
UB3: Hayes 1K **93**
Minet Rd. SW9 . . . . . 2B **120**
Minford Gdns. W14 . . . . . 2F **99**
Minford Ho. *W14* *2F* ***99***
(off Minford Gdns.)
Mingard Wlk. N7 . . . . . 2K **65**
Ming St. E14 . . . . . 7C **86**
Minimax Cl. TW14: Felt 6J **111**
Ministry Way SE9 . . . . . 2D **142**
Miniver Pl. EC4 . . . . . 2D **14**
Mink Ct. TW4: Houn 2A **112**
Minniedale KT5: Surb 5F **151**
Minnow St. SE17 . . . . . 4E **102**
Minnow Wlk. SE17 . . . . . 4E **102**
Minories EC3 . . . . . 1J **15** (6F **85**)
Minshaw Ct. DA14: Sidc 4K **143**
Minshill St. SW8 . . . . . 1H **119**
Minshull Pl. BR3: Beck 7C **140**
Minson Rd. E9 . . . . . 1K **85**
Minstead Gdns. SW15 . . . . . 7B **116**
Minstead Way KT3: N Mald 6A **152**
Minster Av. SM1: Sutt 2J **165**
Minster Ct. EC3 . . . . . 2H **15**
W5 . . . . . 4E **78**
Minster Dr. CR0: C'don 4E **168**
Minster Gdns. KT8: W Mole 4D **148**
Minsterley Av. TW17: Shep 4G **147**
Minster Pavement *EC3* *2H* ***15***
(off Mincing La.)
Minster Rd. BR1: Brom 7K **141**
NW2 . . . . . 5G **63**
Minster Wlk. N8 . . . . . 4J **47**
Minstrel Gdns. KT5: Surb 4F **151**
Mint Bus. Pk. E16 . . . . . 5K **87**
Mint Cl. UB10: Hil 3D **74**
Mintern Cl. N13 . . . . . 3G **33**
Minterne Av. UB2: S'hall 4E **94**
Minterne Rd. HA3: Kenton 5F **43**
Minterne Waye UB4: Yead 6A **76**
Mintern St. N1 . . . . . 2D **84**
Minton Ho. SE11 . . . . . 3J **19**
Minton M. NW6 . . . . . 6K **63**
Mint Rd. SM6: Wall 4F **167**
Mint St. SE1 . . . . . 6C **14** (2C **102**)
Mint Wlk. CR0: C'don 3C **168**
Mirabel Rd. SW6 . . . . . 7H **99**
Miranda Cl. E1 . . . . . 5J **85**
Miranda Ct. W3 . . . . . 6F **79**
Miranda Ho. *N1* *1G* ***9***
(off Arden Est.)
Miranda Rd. N19 . . . . . 1G **65**
Mirfield St. SE7 . . . . . 4B **106**
Miriam Rd. SE18 . . . . . 5J **107**
Mirravale Trad. Est. RM8: Dag 7E **54**
Mirren Cl. HA2: Harr 4D **58**
Mirror Path SE9 . . . . . 3A **142**
Misbourne Rd. UB10: Hil 1C **74**
Missenden *SE17* *5D* ***102***
(off Roland Way)
Missenden Cl. TW14: Felt 1H **129**
Missenden Gdns. SM4: Mord 6A **154**
Missenden Ho. NW8 . . . . . 3C **4**
Mission, The *E14* *6B* ***86***
(off Commercial Rd.)
Mission Gro. E17 . . . . . 5A **50**
Mission Pl. SE15 . . . . . 1G **121**
Mission Sq. TW8: Bford 6E **96**
Missouri Ct. HA5: Eastc 6A **40**
Mistletoe Cl. CR0: C'don 1K **169**
Mistral SE5 . . . . . 1E **120**
Misty's Fld. KT12: Walt T 7A **148**
Mitali Pas. E1 . . . . . 6G **85**
MITCHAM 3D **154**
Mitcham Gdn. Village CR4: Mitc 5E **154**
Mitcham Ho. SE5 . . . . . 1C **120**
Mitcham Ind. Est. CR4: Mitc 1E **154**
Mitcham La. SW16 . . . . . 6G **137**
Mitcham Pk. CR4: Mitc 4C **154**
Mitcham Rd. CR0: C'don 6J **155**
E6 . . . . . 3C **88**
IG3: Ilf 7K **53**
SW17 . . . . . 5D **136**
Mitchell *NW9* *1B* ***44***
(off The Concourse)
Mitchellbrook Way NW10 . . . . . 6K **61**
Mitchell Cl. DA17: Belv 3J **109**
SE2 . . . . . 4C **108**
Mitchell Ho. *N1* *7B* ***66***
(off College Cross)
W12 . . . . . *7D* ***80***
(off White City Est.)
Mitchell Rd. BR6: Orp 4K **173**
N13 . . . . . 5H **33**
Mitchell's Pl. *SE21* *6E* ***120***
(off Aysgarth Rd.)
Mitchell St. EC1 . . . . . 3C **8** (4C **84**)
(not continuous)
Mitchell Wlk. *E6* *5C* ***88***
(off Allhallows Rd.)
E6 . . . . . 5D **88**
(Elmley Cl.)
Mitchell Way BR1: Brom 1J **159**
NW10 . . . . . 6J **61**
Mitchison Ct. *TW16: Sun* *1J* ***147***
(off Downside)
Mitchison Rd. N1 . . . . . 6D **66**
Mitchley Rd. N17 . . . . . 3G **49**
Mitford Bldgs. *SW6* *7J* ***99***
(off Dawes Rd.)
Mitford Cl. KT9: Chess 6C **162**
Mitford Rd. N19 . . . . . 2J **65**
Mitre, The E14 . . . . . 7B **86**
Mitre Av. E17 . . . . . 3C **50**
Mitre Bri. Ind. Pk. W10 . . . . . 4D **80**
(not continuous)
Mitre Cl. BR2: Brom 2H **159**
SM2: Sutt 7A **166**
TW17: Shep 6F **147**
Mitre Ho. *SW3* *5E* ***16***
(off King's Rd.)
Mitre Pas. SE10 . . . . . 2G **105**
Mitre Rd. E15 . . . . . 2G **87**
SE1 . . . . . 6K **13** (2A **102**)
Mitre Sq. EC3 . . . . . 1H **15** (6E **84**)
Mitre St. EC3 . . . . . 1H **15** (6E **84**)
Mitre Way W10 . . . . . 4D **80**
Mitre Yd. SW3 . . . . . 3D **16** (4C **100**)
Mizen Ct. *E14* *2C* ***104***
(off Alpha Gro.)
Mizzen Mast Ho. SE18 . . . . . 3D **106**
Moat, The KT3: N Mald 1A **152**
Moat Cl. BR6: Chels 6K **173**
Moat Ct. DA15: Sidc 3K **143**
SE9 . . . . . 6D **124**
Moat Cres. N3 . . . . . 3K **45**
Moat Cft. DA16: Well 3C **126**
Moat Dr. E13 . . . . . 2A **88**
HA1: Harr 4G **41**
HA4: Ruis 7G **39**
Moat Farm Rd. UB5: N'olt 6D **58**
Moatfield NW6 . . . . . 7G **63**
Moatlands Ho. *WC1* *2F* ***7***
(off Cromer St.)
Moat La. KT8: E Mos 3K **149**
Moat Lodge, The HA2: Harr 2J **59**
Moat Pl. SW9 . . . . . 3K **119**
W3 . . . . . 6H **79**
Moat Side EN3: Pond E 4E **24**
TW13: Hanw 4A **130**
Moberly Rd. SW4 . . . . . 7H **119**
Moberly Sports & Education Cen. *3F* ***81***
(off Chamberlayne Rd.)
Mobil Ct. *WC2* *1H* ***13***
(off Clement's Inn)
MOBY DICK 4E **54**
Mocatta Ho. *E1* *4H* ***85***
(off Brady St.)
Modbury Gdns. NW5 . . . . . 6E **64**
Modder Pl. SW15 . . . . . 4F **117**
Model Cotts. SW14 . . . . . 4J **115**
W13 . . . . . 2B **96**
Model Farm Cl. SE9 . . . . . 3C **142**
Modern Ct. EC4 . . . . . 7A **8**
Modling Ho. *E2* *2K* ***85***
(off Mace St.)
Moelwyn N7 . . . . . 5H **65**
Moelyn M. HA1: Harr 5A **42**
Moffat Ct. SW19 . . . . . 5J **135**
Moffat Ho. SE5 . . . . . 7C **102**
Moffat Rd. CR7: Thor H 2C **156**
N13 . . . . . 6D **32**
SW17 . . . . . 4D **136**
Mogden La. TW7: Isle 5K **113**
Mohammedi Pk. UB5: N'olt 1E **76**
Mohawk Ho. *E3* *2A* ***86***
(off Gernon Rd.)
Mohmmad Khan Rd. E11 . . . . . 1H **69**
Moineau *NW9* *1B* ***44***
(off The Concourse)
Moira Cl. N17 . . . . . 2E **48**
Moira Ho. *SW9* *1A* ***120***
(off Gosling Way)
Moira Rd. SE9 . . . . . 4D **124**
Mokswell Ct. N10 . . . . . 1E **46**
Molasses Ho. *SW11* *3A* ***118***
(off Clove Hitch Quay)
Molasses Row SW11 . . . . . 3A **118**
Mole Abbey Gdns. KT8: W Mole 3F **149**
Mole Ct. KT19: Ewe 4J **163**
Mole Ho. *NW8* *4B* ***4***
(off Church St. Est.)
Molember Ct. KT8: E Mos 4J **149**
Molember Rd. KT8: E Mos 5J **149**
Molescroft SE9 . . . . . 3G **143**
Molesey Av. KT8: W Mole 5D **148**
Molesey Dr. SM3: Cheam 2G **165**
Molesey Pk. Av. KT8: W Mole 5F **149**
Molesey Pk. Cl. KT8: E Mos 5G **149**
Molesey Pk. Rd.
KT8: W Mole, E Mos 5F **149**
Molesey Rd. KT8: W Mole 7C **148**
KT12: Hers, Walt T, W Mole . . . 7C **148**
Molesford Rd. SW6 . . . . . 1J **117**
Molesham Cl. KT8: W Mole 3F **149**
Molesham Way KT8: W Mole 3F **149**
Molesworth Ho. *SE17* *6B* ***102***
(off Brandon Est.)
Molesworth St. SE13 . . . . . 4E **122**
Moliner Ct. BR3: Beck 7C **140**
Mollis Ho. *E3* *5C* ***86***
(off Gale St.)
Mollison Av.
EN3: Brim, Enf L, Enf W, Pond E, Walt C 4F **25**
EN3: Brim, Pond E 4F **25**
Mollison Dr. SM6: Wall 7H **167**
Mollison Sq. *SM6: Wall* *7H* ***167***
(off Mollison Dr.)
Mollison Way HA8: Edg 2F **43**
Molly Huggins Cl. SW12 . . . . . 7G **119**
Molton Ho. *N1* *1K* ***83***
(off Barnsbury Est.)
Molyneux Dr. SW17 . . . . . 4F **137**
Molyneux St. W1 . . . . . 6D **4** (5C **82**)
Monarch Cl. BR4: W W'ck 4H **171**
TW14: Felt 7G **111**
Monarch Ct. N2 . . . . . 5B **46**
Monarch Dr. E16 . . . . . 5B **88**
Monarch Ho. *W8* *3J* ***99***
(off Earl's Ct. Rd.)
W8 . . . . . *3J* ***99***
(off Kensington High St.)
Monarch M. E17 . . . . . 6D **50**
SW16 . . . . . 5A **138**
Monarch Pde. CR4: Mitc 2D **154**
Monarch Pl. IG9: Buck H 2F **37**
Monarch Point SW6 . . . . . 2A **118**
Monarch Rd. DA17: Belv 3G **109**
Monarchs Way HA4: Ruis 1F **57**
Monarch Way IG2: Ilf 6H **53**
Mona Rd. SE15 . . . . . 2J **121**
Monastery Gdns. EN2: Enf 2J **23**
Mona St. E16 . . . . . 5H **87**
Monaveen Gdns. KT8: W Mole 3F **149**
Moncks Row SW18 . . . . . 6H **117**
Monck St. SW1 . . . . . 2D **18** (3H **101**)
Monckton Ct. *W14* *3H* ***99***
(off Strangways Ter.)
Monclar Rd. SE5 . . . . . 4D **120**
Moncorvo Cl. SW7 . . . . . 7C **10** (2C **100**)
Moncrieff Cl. E6 . . . . . 6C **88**
Moncrieff Pl. SE15 . . . . . 2G **121**
Moncrieff St. SE15 . . . . . 2G **121**
Monday All. *N16* *2F* ***67***
(off High St.)
Mondial Way UB3: Harl 7E **92**
Mondragon Ho. *SW8* *1J* ***119***
(off Guildford Rd.)
Monega Rd. E7 . . . . . 6A **70**
E12 . . . . . 6A **70**
Monet Ct. *SE16* *5H* ***103***
(off Stubbs Dr.)
Moneyer Ho. *N1* *1E* ***8***
(off Provost Est.)
Money La. UB7: W Dray 3A **92**
Mongers Almshouses *E9* *7K* ***67***
(off Church Cres.)
Monica Ct. EN1: Enf 5K **23**
Monica James Ho.
DA14: Sidc 3A **144**
Monica Shaw Ct. *NW1* *1D* ***6***
(off Purchese St., not continuous)
Monier Rd. E3 . . . . . 7C **68**
Monivea Rd. BR3: Beck 7B **140**
Monk Ct. W12 . . . . . 1C **98**
Monk Dr. E16 . . . . . 7J **87**
MONKEN HADLEY 2C **20**
Monkfrith Av. N14 . . . . . 6A **22**
Monkfrith Cl. N14 . . . . . 7A **22**
Monkfrith Way N14 . . . . . 7K **21**
Monkham's Av. IG8: Wfd G 5E **36**
Monkham's Dr. IG8: Wfd G 5E **36**
Monkham's La. IG8: Wfd G 5D **36**
IG9: Buck H 3E **36**
Monkleigh Rd. SM4: Mord 3G **153**
Monk Pas. *E16* *7J* ***87***
(off Monk Dr.)

Monks Av.—Morat St.

Monks Av. EN5: New Bar 6F 21
KT8: W Mole 5D 148
Monks Cl. EN2: Enf 2H 23
HA2: Harr 2E 58
HA4: Ruis 4B 58
SE2 4D 108
Monks Cres. KT12: Walt T 7K 147
Monksdene Gdns. SM1: Sutt 3K 165
Monks Dr. W3 5G 79
Monks Hill Sports Cen. 7K 169
MONKS ORCHARD 7A 158
Monks Orchard Rd. BR3: Beck 1C 170
Monks Pk. HA9: Wemb 6H 61
Monks Pk. Gdns. HA9: Wemb 7H 61
Monks Rd. EN2: Enf 2G 23
Monk St. SE18 4E 106
Monks Way BR3: Beck 6C 158
BR5: Farnb 1G 173
NW11 4H 45
UB7: Harm 6A 92
Monkswood Gdns. IG5: Ilf 3E 52
Monkton Ho. E5 5H 67
SE16 *2K 103*
(off Wolfe Cres.)
Monkton Rd. DA16: Well 2K 125
Monkton St. SE11 3K 19 (4A 102)
Monkville Av. NW11 4H 45
Monkville Pde. NW11 4H 45
Monkwell Sq. EC2 6D 8 (5C 84)
Monmouth Av. E18 3K 51
KT1: Ham W 7C 132
Monmouth Cl. CR4: Mitc 4J 155
DA16: Well 4A 126
W4 3J 97
Monmouth Ct. *W7* *5K 77*
(off Copley Cl.)
Monmouth Gro. TW8: Bford 4E 96
Monmouth Pl. *W2* *6K 81*
(off Monmouth Rd.)
Monmouth Rd. E6 3D 88
N9 2C 34
RM9: Dag 5F 73
UB3: Harl 4G 93
W2 6J 81
Monmouth St. WC2 1E 12 (6J 83)
Monnery Rd. N19 3G 65
Monnow Rd. SE1 5G 103
Mono La. TW13: Felt 2K 129
Monoux Almshouses E17 4D 50
Monoux Gro. E17 1C 50
Monroe Cres. EN1: Enf 1C 24
Monroe Dr. SW14 5H 115
Monroe Ho. *NW8* *2D 4*
(off Lorne Cl.)
Monro Gdns. HA3: Hrw W 7D 26
Monro Way E5 4G 67
Monsell Ct. N4 3B 66
Monsell Rd. N4 3A 66
Monson Rd. NW10 2C 80
SE14 7K 103
Mons Way BR2: Brom 6C 160
Montacute Rd. CR0: New Ad 7E 170
SE6 7B 122
SM4: Mord 6B 154
WD23: B Hea 1E 26
Montagu Ct. *W1* *6F 5*
(off Montagu Sq.)
Montagu Cres. N18 4C 34
Montague Av. SE4 4B 122
W7 1K 95
Montague Cl. EN5: Barn 4C 20
KT12: Walt T 7K 147
SE1 4E 14 (1D 102)
Montague Ct. DA15: Sidc 3A 144
N7 *7A 66*
(off St Clements St.)
Montague Gdns. W3 7G 79
Montague Ho. *E16* *1K 105*
(off Wesley Av.)
IG3: Ilf 1A 72
N1 *1E 84*
(off New Era Est.)
Montague M. *E3* *3B 86*
(off Tredegar Ter.)
Montague Pas. UB8: Uxb 7A 56
Montague Pl. WC1 5D 6 (5H 83)
Montague Rd. CR0: C'don 1B 168
E8 5G 67
E11 2H 69
N8 5K 47
N15 4G 49
SW19 7K 135
TW3: Houn 3F 113
TW10: Rich 6E 114
UB2: S'hall 4C 94
UB8: Uxb 7A 56
W7 1K 95
W13 6B 78
Montague Sq. SE15 7J 103
Montague St. EC1 6C 8 (5C 84)
WC1 5E 6 (5J 83)
Montague Ter. BR2: Brom 4H 159
Montague Walks HA0: Wemb 1F 79
Montague Waye UB2: S'hall 3C 94
Montagu Gdns. N18 4C 34
SM6: Wall 4G 167
Montagu Ind. Est. N18 4D 34
Montagu Mans. W1 5F 5 (5D 82)
Montagu M. Nth. W1 6F 5 (5D 82)
Montagu M. Sth. W1 7F 5 (6D 82)
Montagu M. W. W1 7F 5 (6D 82)
Montagu Pl. W1 6E 4 (5D 82)
Montagu Rd. N9 4C 34
N18 5C 34
NW4 6C 44
Montagu Row W1 6F 5 (5D 82)
Montagu Sq. W1 6F 5 (5D 82)
Montagu St. W1 7F 5 (6D 82)
Montaigne Cl. SW1 4D 18 (4H 101)
Montalt Rd. IG8: Wfd G 4C 36
Montana Bldg. *SE10* *1D 122*
(off Deal's Gateway)
Montana Gdns. SE26 5B 140
SM1: Sutt 5A 166
Montana Rd. SW17 3E 136
SW20 1E 152
Montbelle Rd. SE9 3F 143
Montcalm Cl. BR2: Hayes 6J 159
UB4: Yead 3K 75
Montcalm Ho. E14 4B 104
Montcalm Rd. SE7 7B 106
Montclare St. E2 3J 9 (4F 85)
Monteagle Av. IG11: Bark 6G 71
Monteagle Ct. N1 2E 84
Monteagle Way E5 3G 67
SE15 3H 121
Montefiore Ct. N16 1F 67
Montefiore St. SW8 2F 119
Montego Cl. SE24 4A 120
Montem Rd. KT3: N Mald 4A 152
SE23 7B 122
Montem St. N4 1K 65
Montenotte Rd. N8 5G 47
Monterey Apartments N15 5D 48
Monterey Cl. DA5: Bexl 2J 145
NW7 5F 29
UB10: Hil 7C 56
Monterey Studios W10 2G 81
Montesole Ct. HA5: Pinn 2A 40
Montesquieu Ter. *E16* *6H 87*
(off Clarkson Rd.)
Montevetro SW11 1B 118
Montford Pl. SE11 6J 19 (5A 102)
Montford Rd. TW16: Sun 4J 147
Montfort Ho. *E2* *3J 85*
(off Victoria Pk. Sq.)
E14 *3E 104*
(off Galbraith St.)
Montfort Pl. SW19 1F 135
Montgolfier Wlk.
UB5: N'olt 3C 76
Montgomerie M. SE23 7J 121
Montgomery Cl. CR4: Mitc 4J 155
DA15: Sidc 6K 125
Montgomery Ct. *CR2: S Croy* *5E 168*
(off Birdhurst Rd.)
W4 7J 97
Montgomery Gdns. SM2: Sutt 7B 166
Montgomery Ho. *W2* *6A 4*
(off Harrow Rd.)
Montgomery Lodge *E1* *4J 85*
(off Cleveland Gro.)
Montgomery Rd. HA8: Edg 6A 28
W4 4J 97
Montgomery St. E14 1D 104
Montholme Rd. SW11 6D 118
Monthope Rd. E1 6K 9 (5G 85)
Montolieu Gdns. SW15 5D 116
Montpelier Av. DA5: Bexl 7D 126
W5 5C 78
Montpelier Cl. UB10: Hil 1C 74
Montpelier Ct. *BR2: Brom* *4H 159*
(off Westmoreland Rd.)
W5 5D 78
Montpelier Gdns. E6 3B 88
RM6: Chad H 7C 54
Montpelier Gro. NW5 5G 65
Montpelier M. SW7 1D 16 (3C 100)
Montpelier Pl. E1 6J 85
SW7 1D 16 (3C 100)
Montpelier Ri. HA9: Wemb 1D 60
NW11 7G 45
Montpelier Rd. N3 1A 46
SE15 1H 121
SM1: Sutt 4A 166
W5 5D 78
Montpelier Row SE3 2H 123
TW1: Twick 7C 114
Montpelier Sq. SW7 7D 10 (2C 100)
Montpelier St. SW7 1D 16 (3C 100)
Montpelier Ter. SW7 7D 10 (2C 100)
Montpelier Va. SE3 2H 123
Montpelier Wlk. SW7 1D 16 (3C 100)
Montpelier Way NW11 7G 45
Montpellier Ct. KT12: Walt T 6J 147
Montrave Rd. SE20 6J 139
Montreal Ho. SE16 2J 103
Montreal Pl. WC2 2G 13 (7K 83)
Montreal Rd. IG1: Ilf 7G 53
Montrell Rd. SW2 1J 137
Montrose Av. DA15: Sidc 7A 126
DA16: Well 3H 125
HA8: Edg 2J 43
NW6 2G 81
TW2: Whitt 7F 113
Montrose Cl. DA16: Well 3K 125
IG8: Wfd G 4D 36
TW15: Ashf 6E 128
Montrose Ct. HA1: Harr 5F 41
NW9 2J 43
NW11 4H 45
SE6 2H 141
SW7 7B 10 (2B 100)
Montrose Cres. HA0: Wemb 6E 60
N12 6F 31
Montrose Gdns. CR4: Mitc 2D 154
SM1: Sutt 2K 165
Montrose Ho. E14 3C 104
SW1 *7H 11*
(off Montrose Pl.)
Montrose Pl. SW1 7H 11 (2E 100)
Montrose Rd. HA3: W'stone 2J 41
TW14: Bedf 6F 111
Montrose Wlk. HA7: Stan 6G 27
Montrose Way SE23 1K 139
Montserrat Av. IG8: Wfd G 7A 36
Montserrat Cl. SE19 5D 138
Montserrat Rd. SW15 4G 117
Monument, The 3F 15 (7D 84)
Monument Gdns. SE13 5E 122
Monument St. EC3 2F 15 (7D 84)
Monument Way N17 3F 49
Monza St. E1 7J 85
Moodkee St. SE16 3J 103
Moody Rd. SE15 1F 121
Moody St. E1 3K 85
Moon Ct. SE12 4J 123
Moon Ho. HA1: Harr 4J 41
Moon La. EN5: Barn 3C 20
Moon St. N1 1B 84
Moorcroft HA8: Edg 1H 43
Moorcroft Gdns. BR2: Brom 5C 160
Moorcroft La. UB8: Hil 5C 74
Moorcroft Rd. SW16 3J 137
Moorcroft Way HA5: Pinn 5C 40
Moordown SE18 7F 107
Moore Cl. CR4: Mitc 2F 155
SW14 3J 115
Moore Ct. HA0: Wemb 6E 60
N1 *1B 84*
(off Gaskin St.)
Moore Cres. RM9: Dag 1B 90
Moorefield Rd. N17 2F 49
Moorehead Way SE3 3J 123
Moore Ho. *E1* *7J 85*
(off Cable St.)
E2 *3J 85*
(off Roman Rd.)
E14 2C 104
N8 *4J 47*
(off Pembroke Rd.)
SE10 *5H 105*
(off Armitage Rd.)
SW1 6J 17
SW1 *5F 101*
(off Gatliff Rd.)
Mooreland Rd. BR1: Brom 7H 141
Moore Pk. Ct. *SW6* *7K 99*
(off Fulham Rd.)
Moore Pk. Rd. SW6 7J 99
Moore Rd. SE19 6C 138
Moore St. SW3 3E 16 (4D 100)
Moore Wlk. E7 4J 69
Moore Way SM2: Sutt 7J 165
Moorey Cl. E15 1H 87
Moorfield Av. W5 4D 78
Moorfield Rd. EN3: Enf H 1D 24
KT9: Chess 5E 162
UB8: Cowl 6A 74
Moorfields EC2 6E 8 (5D 84)
Moorfields Highwalk *EC2* *6E 8*
(off New Union St., not continuous)
Moorgate EC2 7E 8 (6D 84)
Moorgate Pl. EC2 7E 8
Moorgreen Ho. EC1 1A 8
Moorhen Ho. *E3* *1B 86*
(off Old Ford Rd.)
Moorhouse NW9 1B 44
Moorhouse Rd. HA3: Kenton 3D 42
W2 6J 81
Moorings, The *E16* *5A 88*
(off Prince Regent La.)
Moorings Ho. TW8: Bford 7C 96
MOOR JUNC. 3C 174
Moorland Cl. RM5: Col R 1H 55
TW2: Whitt 7E 112
Moorland Rd. SW9 4B 120
UB7: Harm 2D 174
Moorlands UB5: N'olt 1C 76
Moorlands Av. NW7 6J 29
Moor La. EC2 6E 8 (5D 84)
(not continuous)
KT9: Chess 4E 162
UB7: Harm 2D 174
Moormead Dr. KT19: Ewe 5A 164
Moor Mead Rd. TW1: Twick 6A 114
Moor Pk. Gdns. KT2: King T 7A 134
Moor Pl. EC2 6E 8 (5D 84)
Moorside Rd. BR1: Brom 3G 141
Moor St. W1 1D 12 (6H 83)
Moot Ct. NW9 5G 43
Moran Ho. *E1* *1H 103*
(off Wapping La.)
Morant Pl. N22 1K 47
Morant St. E14 7C 86
Mora Rd. NW2 4E 62
Mora St. EC1 2D 8 (3C 84)
Morat St. SW9 1K 119

Moravian Cl. —Moscow Rd.

Moravian Cl. SW10 ....7A **16** (6B **100**)
Moravian Pl. SW10 ....6B **100**
Moravian St. E2 ....2J **85**
Moray Av. UB3: Hayes 1H **93**
Moray Cl. HA8: Edg 2C **28**
RM1: Rom 1K **55**
Moray Ct. *CR2: S Croy* *5C* ***168***
(off Warham Rd.)
Moray Ho. *E1* *4A* ***86***
(off Harford St.)
Moray M. N7 ....2K **65**
Moray Rd. N4 ....2K **65**
Moray Way RM1: Rom 1K **55**
Mordaunt Gdns. RM9: Dag 7E **72**
Mordaunt Ho. *NW10* *1K* ***79***
(off Stracey Rd.)
Mordaunt Rd. NW10 ....1K **79**
Mordaunt St. SW9 ....3K **119**
MORDEN 3K **153**
Morden Ct. SM4: Mord 4K **153**
Morden Ct. Pde. SM4: Mord 4K **153**
Morden Gdns. CR4: Mitc 4B **154**
UB6: G'frd 5K **59**
Morden Hall Pk. 3A **154**
Morden Hall Rd. SM4: Mord 3K **153**
Morden Hill SE13 ....2E **122**
(not continuous)
Morden Ho. SM4: Mord 4J **153**
Morden La. SE13 ....2E **122**
MORDEN PARK 6G **153**
Morden Pk. Pool 6H **153**
Morden Rd. CR4: Mitc 4A **154**
RM6: Chad H 7E **54**
SE3 ....2J **123**
SM4: Mord 4A **154**
SW19 ....1K **153**
Morden Rd. M. SE3 ....2J **123**
Morden St. SE13 ....1D **122**
Morden Way SM3: Sutt 7J **153**
Morden Wharf *SE10* *3G* ***105***
(off Morden Wharf Rd.)
Morden Wharf Rd. SE10 ....3G **105**
Mordern Ho. NW1 ....3D **4**
Mordon Rd. IG3: Ilf 7K **53**
Mordred Rd. SE6 ....2G **141**
Morecambe Cl. E1 ....5K **85**
Morecambe Gdns. HA7: Stan 4J **27**
Morecambe St. SE17 ....4C **102**
Morecambe Ter. *N18* *4J* ***33***
(off Gt. Cambridge Rd.)
More Cl. E16 ....6H **87**
W14 ....4F **99**
Morecoombe Cl. KT2: King T 7H **133**
More Copper Ho. *SE1* *5G* ***15***
(off Magdalen St.)
Moree Way N18 ....4B **34**
Moreland Cotts. *E3* *2C* ***86***
(off Fairfield Rd.)
Moreland Ct. NW2 ....3J **63**
Moreland St. EC1 ....1B **8** (3B **84**)
Moreland Way E4 ....3J **35**
Morella Rd. SW12 ....7D **118**
Morell Cl. EN5: New Bar 3F **21**
Morello Av. UB8: Hil 5D **74**
More London Pl. SE1 ....5G **15** (1E **102**)
More London Riverside
SE1 ....5H **15** (1E **102**)
(not continuous)
Moremead Rd. SE6 ....4B **140**
Morena St. SE6 ....7D **122**
Moresby Av. KT5: Surb 7H **151**
Moresby Rd. E5 ....1H **67**
Moresby Wlk. SW8 ....2G **119**
More's Gdn. *SW3* *6B* ***100***
(off Cheyne Wlk.)
Moreton Av. TW7: Isle 1J **113**
Moreton Cl. E5 ....2H **67**
N15 ....6D **48**
NW7 ....6K **29**
SW1 ....5B **18**
Moreton Gdns. IG8: Wfd G 5H **37**
Moreton Ho. SE16 ....3H **103**
Moreton Pl. SW1 ....5B **18** (5G **101**)
Moreton Rd. CR2: S Croy 5D **168**
KT4: Wor Pk 2C **164**
N15 ....6D **48**
Moretons HA1: Harr 1J **59**
Moreton St. SW1 ....5B **18** (5G **101**)
Moreton Ter. SW1 ....5B **18** (5G **101**)
Moreton Ter. M. Nth. SW1 ....5B **18** (5G **101**)
Moreton Ter. M. Sth. SW1 ....5B **18** (5G **101**)
Moreton Twr. W3 ....1H **97**
Morford Cl. HA4: Ruis 7K **39**
Morford Way HA4: Ruis 7K **39**
Morgan Av. E17 ....4F **51**
Morgan Cl. RM10: Dag 7G **73**
Morgan Ct. SM5: Cars 4D **166**
TW15: Ashf 5D **128**
Morgan Ho. *SW1* *4B* ***18***
(off Vauxhall Bri. Rd.)
SW8 ....*1G* ***119***
(off Wadhurst Rd.)
Morgan Mans. *N7* *5A* ***66***
(off Morgan Rd.)
Morgan Rd. BR1: Brom 7J **141**
N7 ....5A **66**
W10 ....5H **81**
Morgans La. *SE1* *5G* ***15***
(off Tooley St.)
UB3: Hayes 5F **75**
Morgan St. E3 ....3A **86**
(not continuous)
E16 ....5H **87**
Morgan Wlk. BR3: Beck 4D **158**
Morgan Way IG8: Wfd G 6H **37**
Moriarty Cl. BR1: Brom 4E **160**
Moriatry Cl. N7 ....4J **65**
Morie St. SW18 ....5K **117**
Morieux Rd. E10 ....1B **68**
Moring Rd. SW17 ....4E **136**
Morkyns Wlk. SE21 ....3E **138**
Morland Av. CR0: C'don 1E **168**
Morland Cl. CR4: Mitc 3C **154**
NW11 ....1K **63**
TW12: Hamp 5D **130**
Morland Ct. *W12* *2D* ***98***
(off Coningham Rd.)
Morland Est. E8 ....7G **67**
Morland Gdns. NW10 ....7K **61**
UB1: S'hall 1F **95**
Morland Ho. *NW1* *1B* ***6***
(off Werrington St.)
NW6 ....1J **81**
SW1 ....*3E* ***18***
(off Marsham St.)
W11 ....*6G* ***81***
(off Lancaster Rd.)
Morland M. N1 ....7A **66**
Morland Pl. N15 ....4E **48**
Morland Rd. CR0: C'don 1E **168**
E17 ....5K **49**
HA3: Kenton 5E **42**
IG1: Ilf 2F **71**
RM10: Dag 7G **73**
SE20 ....6K **139**
SM1: Sutt 5A **166**
Morley Av. E4 ....7A **36**
N18 ....4B **34**
N22 ....2A **48**
Morley Cl. BR6: Farnb 2F **173**
Morley Ct. BR2: Brom 4H **159**
E4 ....5G **35**
Morley Cres. HA4: Ruis 2A **58**
HA8: Edg 2D **28**
Morley Cres. E. HA7: Stan 2C **42**
Morley Cres. W. HA7: Stan 3C **42**
Morley Hill EN2: Enf 1J **23**
Morley Ho. *SE15* *7F* ***103***
(off Commercial Way)
Morley Rd. BR7: Chst 1G **161**
E10 ....1E **68**
E15 ....2H **87**
IG11: Bark 1H **89**
RM6: Chad H 5E **54**
Morley Rd. SE13 ....4E **122**
SM3: Sutt 1H **165**
TW1: Twick 6D **114**
Morley St. SE1 ....1K **19** (3A **102**)
Morna Rd. SE5 ....2C **120**
Morning La. E9 ....6J **67**
Morningside Rd.
KT4: Wor Pk 2E **164**
Mornington Av. BR1: Brom 3A **160**
IG1: Ilf 7E **52**
W14 ....4H **99**
Mornington Av. Mans. *W14* *4H* ***99***
(off Mornington Av.)
Mornington Cl. IG8: Wfd G 4D **36**
Mornington Ct. DA5: Bexl 1K **145**
NW1 ....*2G* ***83***
(off Mornington Cres.)
Mornington Cres. NW1 ....2G **83**
TW5: Cran 1K **111**
Mornington Gro. E3 ....3C **86**
Mornington M. SE5 ....1C **120**
Mornington Pl. NW1 ....2G **83**
SE8 ....*7B* ***104***
(off Mornington Rd.)
Mornington Rd. E4 ....7K **25**
E11 ....7H **51**
(not continuous)
IG8: Wfd G 4C **36**
SE8 ....7B **104**
TW15: Ashf 5E **128**
UB6: G'frd 5F **77**
Mornington Sports & Leisure Cen. *1F* ***83***
(off Arlington Rd.)
Mornington St. NW1 ....2F **83**
Mornington Ter. NW1 ....1F **83**
Mornington Wlk.
TW10: Ham 4C **132**
Morocco St. SE1 ....7G **15** (2E **102**)
Morocco Wharf *E1* *1H* ***103***
(off Wapping High St.)
Morpeth Gro. E9 ....1K **85**
Morpeth Mans. *SW1* *2A* ***18***
(off Morpeth Ter.)
Morpeth Rd. E9 ....1K **85**
Morpeth St. E2 ....3J **85**
Morpeth Ter. SW1 ....2A **18** (3G **101**)
Morpeth Wlk. N17 ....7C **34**
Morphou Rd. NW7 ....6B **30**
Morrab Gdns. IG3: Ilf 3K **71**
Morrel Ct. *E2* *2G* ***85***
(off Goldsmiths Row)
Morrells Yd. *SE11* *5K* ***19***
(off Cleaver St.)
Morris Av. E12 ....5D **70**
Morris Blitz Ct. N16 ....4F **67**
Morris Cl. BR6: Orp 3J **173**
CR0: C'don 5A **158**
Morris Ct. E4 ....3J **35**
Morris Gdns. SW18 ....7J **117**
Morris Ho. *E2* *3J* ***85***
(off Roman Rd.)
NW8 ....*4C* ***4***
(off Salisbury St.)
W3 ....2B **98**
Morrish Rd. SW2 ....7J **119**
Morrison Av. E4 ....6H **35**
N17 ....3E **48**
Morrison Bldgs. Nth. *E1* *6G* ***85***
(off Commercial Rd.)
Morrison Ct. *EN5: Barn* *4B* ***20***
(off Manor Way)
N12 ....7H **31**
SW1 ....*3H* ***101***
(off Gt. Smith St.)
Morrison Ho. *SW2* *1A* ***138***
(off High Trees)
Morrison Rd. IG11: Bark 2E **90**
RM9: Bark, Dag 2E **90**
SW9 ....2A **120**
UB4: Yead 3K **75**
Morrison St. SW11 ....3E **118**
Morris Pl. N4 ....2A **66**
Morris Rd. E14 ....5D **86**
E15 ....4G **69**
RM8: Dag 2F **73**
TW7: Isle 3K **113**
Morriss Ho. *SE16* *2H* ***103***
(off Cherry Gdn. St.)
Morris St. E1 ....6H **85**
Morritt Ho. *HA0: Wemb* *5D* ***60***
(off Talbot Rd.)
Morse Cl. E13 ....3J **87**
Morshead Mans. *W9* *3J* ***81***
(off Morshead Rd.)
Morshead Rd. W9 ....3J **81**
Morson Rd. EN3: Pond E 6F **25**
Morston Gdns. SE9 ....4D **142**
Mortain Ho. *SE16* *4H* ***103***
(off Roseberry St.)
Morten Cl. SW4 ....6H **119**
Morteyne Rd. N17 ....1D **48**
Mortgramit Sq. SE18 ....3E **106**
Mortham St. E15 ....1G **87**
Mortimer Cl. NW2 ....2H **63**
SW16 ....2H **137**
Mortimer Ct. *NW8* *1A* ***4***
(off Abbey Rd.)
Mortimer Cres. KT4: Wor Pk 3K **163**
NW6 ....1K **81**
Mortimer Dr. EN1: Enf 5K **23**
Mortimer Est. *NW6* *1K* ***81***
(off Mortimer Pl.)
Mortimer Ho. W11 ....1F **99**
W14 ....*4G* ***99***
(off North End Rd.)
Mortimer Mkt. WC1 ....4B **6** (4G **83**)
Mortimer Pl. NW6 ....1K **81**
Mortimer Rd. CR4: Mitc 1D **154**
DA8: Erith 6K **109**
E6 ....3D **88**
N1 ....7E **66**
(not continuous)
NW10 ....3E **80**
W13 ....6C **78**
Mortimer Sq. W11 ....7F **81**
Mortimer St. W1 ....7K **5** (6G **83**)
Mortimer Ter. NW5 ....4F **65**
MORTLAKE 3K **115**
Mortlake Cl. CR0: Bedd 3J **167**
Mortlake Crematorium
TW9: Kew 2H **115**
Mortlake Dr. CR4: Mitc 1C **154**
Mortlake High St. SW14 ....3K **115**
Mortlake Rd. E16 ....6K **87**
IG1: Ilf 4G **71**
TW9: Kew, Rich 7G **97**
Mortlake Ter. *TW9: Kew* *7G* ***97***
(off Mortlake Rd.)
Mortlock Cl. SE15 ....1H **121**
Mortlock Ct. E7 ....4B **70**
Morton Cl. E1 ....6J **85**
SM6: Wall 7K **167**
UB8: Hil 4B **74**
Morton Ct. UB5: N'olt 5G **59**
Morton Cres. N14 ....4C **32**
Morton Gdns. SM6: Wall 5G **167**
Morton Ho. SE17 ....6B **102**
Morton M. SW5 ....4K **99**
Morton Pl. SE1 ....2J **19** (3A **102**)
Morton Rd. E15 ....7H **69**
N1 ....7C **66**
SM4: Mord 5B **154**
Morton Way N14 ....3B **32**
Morvale Cl. DA17: Belv 4F **109**
Morval Rd. SW2 ....5A **120**
Morven Rd. SW17 ....3D **136**
Morville Ho. *SW18* *6B* ***118***
(off Fitzhugh Gro.)
Morville St. E3 ....2C **86**
Morwell St. WC1 ....6C **6** (5H **83**)
Moscow Mans. *SW5* *4J* ***99***
(off Cromwell Rd.)
Moscow Pl. W2 ....7K **81**
Moscow Rd. W2 ....7J **81**

336 A-Z London

Mosedale—Mulberry Way

Mosedale *NW1* *2K* ***5***
(off Cumberland Mkt.)
Moseley Row SE10 . . . . . 4H **105**
Moselle Av. N22 . . . . . 2A **48**
Moselle Cl. N8 . . . . . 3K **47**
Moselle Ho. *N17* *7A* ***34***
(off William St.)
Moselle Pl. N17 . . . . . 7A **34**
Moselle St. N17 . . . . . 7A **34**
Mosque Ter. *E1* *5G* ***85***
(off Whitechapel Rd.)
Mosque Twr. *E1* *5G* ***85***
(off Fieldgate St.)
E3 . . . . . *2A* ***86***
(off Ford St.)
Mosquite Cl. SM6: Wall 7J **167**
Mossborough Cl. N12 . . . . . 6E **30**
Mossbury Rd. SW11 . . . . . 3C **118**
Moss Cl. E1 . . . . . 5G **85**
HA5: Pinn 2D **40**
N9 . . . . . 1B **34**
Mossdown Cl. DA17: Belv 4G **109**
Mossford Ct. IG6: Ilf 3F **53**
Mossford Grn. IG6: Ilf 3F **53**
Mossford La. IG6: Ilf 2F **53**
Mossford St. E3 . . . . . 4B **86**
Moss Gdns. CR2: Sels 7K **169**
TW13: Felt 2J **129**
Moss Hall Ct. N12 . . . . . 6E **30**
Moss Hall Cres. N12 . . . . . 6E **30**
Moss Hall Gro. N12 . . . . . 6E **30**
Mossington Gdns. SE16 . . . . . 4J **103**
Moss La. HA5: Pinn 1C **40**
Mosslea Rd. BR2: Brom 5B **160**
BR6: Farnb 3G **173**
SE20 . . . . . 6J **139**
(not continuous)
Mossop St. SW3 . . . . . 3D **16** (4C **100**)
Moss Rd. RM10: Dag 7G **73**
Mossville Gdns. SM4: Mord 3H **153**
Mosswell Ho. N10 . . . . . 1E **46**
Moston Cl. UB3: Harl 5H **93**
Mostyn Av. HA9: Wemb 5F **61**
Mostyn Gdns. NW10 . . . . . 3F **81**
Mostyn Gro. E3 . . . . . 2C **86**
Mostyn Rd. HA8: Edg 7F **29**
SW9 . . . . . 1A **120**
SW19 . . . . . 1H **153**
Mosul Way BR2: Brom 6C **160**
Motcomb St. SW1 . . . . . 1G **17** (3E **100**)
Moth Cl. SM6: Wall 7J **167**
Mothers Sq. E5 . . . . . 4H **67**
Motley Av. EC2 . . . . . 4G **9**
Motley St. SW8 . . . . . 2G **119**
MOTSPUR PARK 6C **152**
Motspur Pk. KT3: N Mald 6B **152**
MOTTINGHAM 2C **142**
Mottingham Gdns. SE9 . . . . . 1B **142**
Mottingham La. SE9 . . . . . 1A **142**
SE12 . . . . . 1A **142**
Mottingham Rd. N9 . . . . . 6E **24**
SE9 . . . . . 2C **142**
Mottisfont Rd. SE2 . . . . . 3A **108**
Motts La. RM8: Dag 2F **73**
Mott St. E4: Lough 1K **25**
Moules Ct. SE5 . . . . . 7C **102**
Moulins Rd. E9 . . . . . 7J **67**
Moulsford Ho. N7 . . . . . 5H **65**
W2 . . . . . *5J* ***81***
(off Westbourne Pk. Rd.)
Moulton Av. TW3: Houn 2C **112**
Mound, The SE9 . . . . . 3E **142**
Moundfield Rd. N16 . . . . . 6G **49**
Mounsey Ho. *W10* *3G* ***81***
(off Third Av.)
Mount, The *CR2: S Croy* *5C* ***168***
(off Warham Rd.)
DA6: Bex 5H **127**
E5 . . . . . 2H **67**
(not continuous)
HA9: Wemb 2H **61**
KT3: N Mald 3B **152**
Mount, The KT4: Wor Pk 4D **164**
N20 . . . . . 2F **31**
NW3 . . . . . 3A **64**
UB5: N'olt 5F **59**
W3 . . . . . 1J **97**
W8 . . . . . *1J* ***99***
(off Bedford Gdns.)
Mountacre Cl. SE26 . . . . . 4F **139**
Mt. Adon Pk. SE22 . . . . . 7G **121**
Mountague Pl. E14 . . . . . 7E **86**
Mountain Ho. SE11 . . . . . 4H **19** (4K **101**)
Mt. Angelus Rd.
SW15 . . . . . 7B **116**
Mt. Ararat Rd. TW10: Rich 5E **114**
Mt. Arlington *BR2: Brom* *2G* ***159***
(off Park Hill Rd.)
Mt. Ash Rd. SE26 . . . . . 3H **139**
Mount Av. E4 . . . . . 3H **35**
UB1: S'hall 6E **76**
W5 . . . . . 5C **78**
Mountbatten Cl. SE18 . . . . . 6J **107**
SE19 . . . . . 5E **138**
Mountbatten Ct. IG9: Buck H 2G **37**
SE16 . . . . . *1J* ***103***
(off Rotherhithe St.)
Mountbatten Gdns. BR3: Beck 4A **158**
Mountbatten Ho. *N6* *7E* ***46***
(off Hillcrest)
Mountbatten M. SW18 . . . . . 7A **118**
Mountbel Rd. HA7: Stan 1A **42**
Mt. Carmel Chambers *W8* *2J* ***99***
(off Dukes La.)
Mount Cl. BR1: Brom 1C **160**
EN4: Cockf 4K **21**
SM5: Cars 7E **166**
W5 . . . . . 5C **78**
Mountcombe Cl. KT6: Surb 7E **150**
Mount Ct. BR4: W W'ck 2G **171**
SW15 . . . . . 3G **117**
Mt. Culver Av. DA14: Sidc 6D **144**
Mount Dr. DA6: Bex 5E **126**
HA2: Harr 5D **40**
HA9: Wemb 2J **61**
Mountearl Gdns. SW16 . . . . . 3K **137**
Mt. Eaton Ct. *W5* *5C* ***78***
(off Mount Av.)
Mt. Echo Av. E4 . . . . . 2J **35**
Mt. Echo Dr. E4 . . . . . 1J **35**
Mt. Ephraim La. SW16 . . . . . 3H **137**
Mt. Ephraim Rd. SW16 . . . . . 3H **137**
Mount Felix KT12: Walt T 7H **147**
Mountfield Cl. SE6 . . . . . 7F **123**
Mountfield Rd. E6 . . . . . 2E **88**
N3 . . . . . 3H **45**
W5 . . . . . 6D **78**
Mountfield Ter. SE6 . . . . . 7F **123**
Mountford Mans. *SW11* *1E* ***118***
(off Battersea Pk. Rd.)
Mountford Rd. E8 . . . . . 5G **67**
Mountfort Cres. N1 . . . . . 7A **66**
Mountfort Ter. N1 . . . . . 7A **66**
Mount Gdns. SE26 . . . . . 3H **139**
Mount Gro. HA8: Edg 3D **28**
Mountgrove Rd. N5 . . . . . 3B **66**
Mount Holme KT7: T Ditt 7B **150**
Mounthurst Rd. BR2: Hayes 7H **159**
Mountington Pk. Cl.
HA3: Kenton 6D **42**
Mountjoy Cl. *EC2* *6D* ***8***
(off Monkwell Sq.)
SE2 . . . . . 2B **108**
Mountjoy Ho. EC2 . . . . . 6C **8**
Mount Lodge N6 . . . . . 6G **47**
Mount M. TW12: Hamp 1F **149**
Mount Mills EC1 . . . . . 2B **8** (3B **84**)
Mt. Nod Rd. SW16 . . . . . 3K **137**
Mt. Olive Ct. W7 . . . . . 2J **95**
Mount Pde. EN4: Cockf 4H **21**
Mount Pk. SM5: Cars 7E **166**
Mount Pk. Av. CR2: S Croy 7B **168**
HA1: Harr 2H **59**
Mount Pk. Cres. W5 . . . . . 6D **78**
Mount Pk. Rd. HA1: Harr 3H **59**
HA5: Eastc 5J **39**
W5 . . . . . 5D **78**
Mount Pl. W3 . . . . . 1H **97**
Mt. Pleasant EN4: Cockf 4H **21**
HA0: Wemb 1E **78**
HA4: Ruis 2A **58**
IG1: Ilf 5G **71**
SE27 . . . . . 4C **138**
WC1 . . . . . 4J **7** (4A **84**)
Mt. Pleasant Cotts. *N14* *7C* ***22***
(off The Wells)
Mt. Pleasant Cres. N4 . . . . . 1K **65**
Mt. Pleasant Hill E5 . . . . . 2H **67**
Mt. Pleasant La. E5 . . . . . 1H **67**
Mt. Pleasant Pl. SE18 . . . . . 4H **107**
Mt. Pleasant Rd. E17 . . . . . 2A **50**
KT3: N Mald 3J **151**
N17 . . . . . 2E **48**
NW10 . . . . . 7E **62**
SE13 . . . . . 6D **122**
W5 . . . . . 4C **78**
Mt. Pleasant Vs. N4 . . . . . 7K **47**
Mt. Pleasant Wlk. DA5: Bexl 5J **127**
Mount Rd. CR4: Mitc 2B **154**
DA6: Bex 5D **126**
EN4: E Barn 5H **21**
KT3: N Mald 3K **151**
KT9: Chess 5F **163**
NW2 . . . . . 3D **62**
NW4 . . . . . 6C **44**
RM8: Dag 1F **73**
SE19 . . . . . 6D **138**
SW19 . . . . . 2J **135**
TW13: Hanw 3C **130**
UB3: Hayes 2J **93**
Mount Row W1 . . . . . 3J **11** (7F **83**)
Mountsfield Ct. SE13 . . . . . 6F **123**
Mountside HA7: Stan 1A **42**
Mounts Pond Rd. SE3 . . . . . 2F **123**
(not continuous)
Mount Sq., The NW3 . . . . . 3A **64**
Mt. Stewart Av. HA3: Kenton 7D **42**
Mount St. W1 . . . . . 3G **11** (7E **82**)
Mount St. M. W1 . . . . . 3J **11** (7F **83**)
Mountstuart Ct. TW11: Ham W 1B **150**
Mount Ter. E1 . . . . . 5H **85**
Mount Vernon NW3 . . . . . 4A **64**
Mount Vw. EN2: Enf 1E **22**
NW7 . . . . . 3E **28**
UB2: S'hall 4B **94**
W5 . . . . . 4D **78**
Mountview Cl. NW11 . . . . . 1K **63**
Mountview Ct. N8 . . . . . 4B **48**
Mount Vw. Rd. E4 . . . . . 7K **25**
KT10: Clay 7B **162**
N4 . . . . . 7J **47**
NW9 . . . . . 5K **43**
Mountview Rd. BR6: St M Cry 7K **161**
(not continuous)
Mount Vs. SE27 . . . . . 3B **138**
Mount Way SM5: Cars 7E **166**
Mountwood KT8: W Mole 3F **149**
MOVERS LANE 2J **89**
Movers La. IG11: Bark 1H **89**
Mowat Ct. *KT4: Wor Pk* *2B* ***164***
(off The Avenue)
Mowatt Cl. N19 . . . . . 1H **65**
Mowbray Ct. N22 . . . . . 1A **48**
SE19 . . . . . 7F **139**
Mowbray Gdns. UB5: N'olt 1E **76**
Mowbray Ho. *N2* *2B* ***46***
(off The Grange)
Mowbray Pde. HA8: Edg 4B **28**
Mowbray Rd. EN5: New Bar 5F **21**
HA8: Edg 4B **28**
NW6 . . . . . 7G **63**
SE19 . . . . . 1F **157**
TW10: Ham 3C **132**
Mowbrays Cl. RM5: Col R 1J **55**
Mowbrays Rd. RM5: Col R 2J **55**
Mowlem St. E2 . . . . . 2H **85**
Mowlem Trad. Est. N17 . . . . . 7D **34**
Mowll St. SW9 . . . . . 7A **102**
Moxon Cl. E13 . . . . . 2H **87**
Moxon St. EN5: Barn 3C **20**
W1 . . . . . 6G **5** (5E **82**)
Moye Cl. E2 . . . . . 2G **85**
Moyers Rd. E10 . . . . . 7E **50**
Moylan Rd. W6 . . . . . 6G **99**
Moyle Ho. *SW1* *6B* ***18***
(off Churchill Gdns.)
Moyne Ho. SW9 . . . . . 5B **120**
Moyne Pl. NW10 . . . . . 2G **79**
Moynihan Dr. N21 . . . . . 5D **22**
Moys Cl. CR0: C'don 6J **155**
Moyser Rd. SW16 . . . . . 5F **137**
Mozart St. W10 . . . . . 3H **81**
Mozart Ter. SW1 . . . . . 4H **17** (4E **100**)
Muchelney Rd. SM4: Mord 6A **154**
Mudchute Park & Farm 4E **104**
Mudlarks Blvd. SE10 . . . . . 3H **105**
Mudlarks Way SE7 . . . . . 3J **105**
SE10 . . . . . 3H **105**
(not continuous)
Muggeridge Cl. CR2: S Croy 5D **168**
Muggeridge Rd. RM10: Dag 4H **73**
Muirdown Av. SW14 . . . . . 4K **115**
Muir Dr. SW18 . . . . . 6C **118**
Muirfield W3 . . . . . 6A **80**
Muirfield Cl. SE16 . . . . . 5H **103**
Muirfield Cres. E14 . . . . . 3D **104**
Muirhead Quay IG11: Bark 2G **89**
Muirkirk Rd. SE6 . . . . . 1E **140**
Muir Rd. E5 . . . . . 3G **67**
Muir St. E16 . . . . . 1C **106**
(not continuous)
Mulberry Av. TW19: Stanw 1A **128**
Mulberry Bus. Cen. SE16 . . . . . 2K **103**
Mulberry Cl. E4 . . . . . 2H **35**
EN4: E Barn 4G **21**
N8 . . . . . 5J **47**
NW3 . . . . . 4B **64**
NW4 . . . . . 3E **44**
SE7 . . . . . 6B **106**
SE22 . . . . . 5G **121**
SW16 . . . . . 4G **137**
UB5: N'olt 2C **76**
Mulberry Ct. *E11* *4F* ***69***
(off Langthorne Rd.)
EC1 . . . . . *2B* ***8***
(off Tompion St.)
IG11: Bark 6K **71**
KT6: Surb 7D **150**
N2 . . . . . *3C* ***46***
(off Bedford Rd.)
SW3 . . . . . 7B **16** (6B **100**)
TW1: Twick 3K **131**
W9 . . . . . *3H* ***81***
(off Ashmore Rd.)
Mulberry Cres. TW8: Bford 7B **96**
UB7: W Dray 2C **92**
Mulberry Ho. BR2: Brom 1G **159**
E2 . . . . . *3J* ***85***
(off Victoria Pk. Sq.)
SE8 . . . . . 6B **104**
Mulberry Housing Co-operative
SE1 . . . . . 4K **13**
Mulberry La. CR0: C'don 1F **169**
Mulberry M. SE14 . . . . . 1B **122**
SM6: Wall 6G **167**
Mulberry Pde. UB7: W Dray 3C **92**
Mulberry Pl. *E14* *7E* ***86***
(off Clove Cres.)
SE9 . . . . . 4B **124**
W6 . . . . . 5C **98**
Mulberry Rd. E8 . . . . . 7F **67**
Mulberry St. E1 . . . . . 6G **85**
Mulberry Tree M. W4 . . . . . 2J **97**
Mulberry Trees TW17: Shep 7F **147**
Mulberry Wlk. SW3 . . . . . 7B **16** (6B **100**)
Mulberry Way DA17: Belv 2J **109**
E18 . . . . . 2K **51**
IG6: Ilf 4G **53**

Mulgrave Ct.—Narrow Way

Mulgrave Ct. *SM2: Sutt* 6K 165
(off Mulgrave Rd.)
Mulgrave Rd. CR0: C'don 3D 168
HA1: Harr 2A 60
NW10 4B 62
SE18 4D 106
SM2: Sutt 7H 165
SW6 6H 99
W5 3D 78
Mulholland Cl. CR4: Mitc 2F 155
Mulkern Rd. N19 1H 65
(not continuous)
Mullards Cl. CR4: Mitc 1D 166
Mullen Twr. *WC1* 4J 7
(off Mt. Pleasant)
Muller Ho. SE18 5E 106
Muller Rd. SW4 6H 119
Mullet Gdns. E2 3G 85
Mulletsfield *WC1* 2F 7
(off Cromer St.)
Mull Ho. *E3* 2B 86
(off Stafford Rd.)
Mulligans Apartments *NW6* 7J 63
(off Kilburn High Rd.)
Mullins Path SW14 3K 115
Mullion Cl. HA3: Hrw W 1F 41
Mull Wlk. *N1* 6C 66
(off Clephane Rd.)
Mulready Ho. *SW1* 4E 18
(off Marsham St.)
Mulready St. NW8 4C 4 (4C 82)
Multimedia Ho. NW10 4J 79
Multi Way W3 2A 98
Multon Ho. E9 7J 67
Multon Rd. SW18 7B 118
Mulvaney Way SE1 7F 15 (2D 102)
(not continuous)
Mumford Mills *SE10* 1D 122
(off Greenwich High Rd.)
Mumford Rd. SE24 5B 120
Muncaster Cl. TW15: Ashf 4C 128
Muncaster Rd. SW11 5D 118
TW15: Ashf 5D 128
Muncies M. SE6 2E 140
Mundania Ct. SE22 6H 121
Mundania Rd. SE22 6H 121
Munday Ho. *SE1* 3D 102
(off Burbage Cl.)
Munday Rd. E16 7J 87
Munden Ho. *E3* 3D 86
(off Bromley High St.)
Munden St. W14 4G 99
Mundford Rd. E5 2J 67
Mundon Gdns. IG1: Ilf 1H 71
Mund St. W14 5H 99
Mundy Ho. *W10* 3G 81
(off Dart St.)
Mundy St. N1 1G 9 (3E 84)
Mungo Pk. Cl. WD23: B Hea 2B 26
Munkenbeck Bldg.
W2 6A 4
(off Hermitage St.)
Munnery Way BR6: Farnb 3E 172
Munnings Gdns. TW7: Isle 5H 113
Munnings Ho. *E16* 1K 105
(off Portsmouth M.)
Munro Dr. N11 6B 32
Munro Ho. SE1 7J 13 (2A 102)
Munro M. W10 5G 81
(not continuous)
Munro Ter. SW10 7B 100
Munslow Gdns. SM1: Sutt 4B 166
Munster Av. TW4: Houn 5C 112
Munster Ct. SW6 2H 117
TW11: Tedd 6C 132
Munster Gdns. N13 4G 33
Munster M. SW6 7G 99
Munster Rd. SW6 7G 99
TW11: Tedd 6B 132
Munster Sq. NW1 2K 5 (3F 83)
Munton Rd. SE17 4C 102
Murchison Av. DA5: Bexl 1D 144
Murchison Ho. *W10* 5G 81
(off Ladbroke Gro.)
Murchison Rd. E10 2E 68
Murdoch Ho. *SE16* 3J 103
(off Moodkee St.)
Murdock Cl. E16 6H 87
Murdock St. SE15 6H 103
Murfett Cl. SW19 2G 135
Muriel St. N1 2K 83
(not continuous)
Murillo Rd. SE13 4F 123
Murphy Ho. *SE1* 7B 14
(off Borough Rd.)
Murphy St. SE1 7J 13 (2A 102)
Murray Av. BR1: Brom 3K 159
TW3: Houn 5F 113
Murray Cl. SE28 1J 107
Murray Ct. HA1: Harr 6K 41
TW2: Twick 2H 131
W7 2J 95
Murray Cres. HA5: Pinn 1B 40
Murray Gro. N1 1D 8 (2C 84)
Murray Ho. *SE18* 4D 106
(off Rideout St.)
Murray M. NW1 7H 65
Murray Rd. HA6: Nwood 1G 39
SW19 6F 135
TW10: Ham 2B 132
W5 4C 96
Murray Sq. E16 6J 87
Murray St. NW1 7G 65
Murrays Yd. SE18 4F 107
Murray Ter. NW3 4A 64
W5 4D 96
Mursell Est. SW8 1K 119
Musard Rd. W6 6G 99
Musbury St. E1 6J 85
Muscal *W6* 6G 99
(off Field Rd.)
Muscatel Pl. SE5 1E 120
Muschamp Rd. SE15 3F 121
SM5: Cars 2C 166
Muscott Ho. *E2* 1G 85
(off Whiston Rd.)
Muscovy Ho. *DA18: Erith* 2E 108
(off Kale Rd.)
Muscovy St. EC3 2H 15 (7E 84)
Museum Chambers *WC1* 6E 6
(off Bury Pl.)
Museum Ho. *E2* 3J 85
(off Burnham St.)
Museum La. SW7 2B 16 (3B 100)
Museum Mans. *WC1* 6E 6
(off Gt. Russell St.)
Mus. of Brands, Packaging & Advertising
6H 81
(off Colville M.)
Mus. of Classical Archaeology 3C 6
(off Gower Pl.)
Mus. of Croydon 3C 168
(off High St.)
Mus. of Domestic Design & Architecture
5K 21
Mus. of Freemasonry 7F 7
(off Gt. Queen St.)
Mus. of London 6C 8 (5C 84)
Mus. of London Docklands 7C 86
Mus. of Richmond 5D 114
Mus. of The Order of St John 4A 8
(off St John's La.)
Museum Pas. E2 3J 85
Museum St. WC1 6E 6 (5J 83)
Museum Way W3 2G 97
Musgrave Cl. EN4: Had W 1F 21
Musgrave Ct. SW11 1C 118
Musgrave Cres. SW6 7J 99
Musgrave Rd. TW7: Isle 1K 113
Musgrove Rd. SE14 1K 121
Musjid Rd. SW11 2B 118
Musket Cl. EN4: E Barn 6G 21
Musquash Way TW4: Houn 2A 112
Muston Rd. E5 2H 67
Mustow Pl. SW6 2H 117
Muswell Av. N10 1F 47
MUSWELL HILL 3F 47
Muswell Hill N10 3F 47
Muswell Hill B'way. N10 3F 47
Muswell Hill Pl. N10 4F 47
Muswell Hill Rd. N6 6E 46
N10 6E 46
Muswell M. N10 3F 47
Muswell Rd. N10 3F 47
Mutrix Rd. NW6 1J 81
Mutton Pl. NW1 6E 64
Muybridge Rd. KT3: N Mald 2J 151
Muybridge Yd. KT5: Surb 7F 151
Myatt Rd. SW9 1B 120
Myatts Flds. Sth. SW9 2A 120
Myatts Flds. St. SW9 2A 120
Mycenae Rd. SE3 7J 105
Myddelton Av. EN1: Enf 1K 23
Myddelton Cl. EN1: Enf 1A 24
Myddelton Gdns. N21 7H 23
Myddelton Pk. N20 3G 31
Myddelton Pas. EC1 1K 7 (3A 84)
Myddelton Rd. N8 4J 47
(not continuous)
Myddelton Sq. EC1 1K 7 (3A 84)
Myddelton St. EC1 2K 7 (3A 84)
Myddleton Av. N4 2C 66
Myddleton Cl. HA7: Stan 2F 27
Myddleton Ho. N1 1J 7
Myddleton M. N22 7D 32
Myddleton Rd. N22 7D 32
Myers Ho. *SE5* 7C 102
(off Bethwin Rd.)
Myers La. SE14 6K 103
Myles Ct. *SE16* 3J 103
(off Neptune St.)
Mylis Cl. SE26 4H 139
Mylius Cl. SE14 7J 103
Mylne Cl. W6 5C 98
Mylne St. EC1 1J 7 (3A 84)
Myra St. SE2 4A 108
Myrdle Ct. *E1* 6G 85
(off Myrdle St.)
Myrdle St. E1 5G 85
Myrna Cl. SW19 7C 136
Myron Pl. SE13 3E 122
Myrtle Av. HA4: Ruis 7J 39
TW14: Felt 5G 111
Myrtleberry Cl. *E8* 6F 67
(off Beechwood Rd.)
Myrtle Cl. EN4: E Barn 1J 31
UB7: W Dray 3B 92
UB8: Hil 5B 74
Myrtledene Rd. SE2 5A 108
Myrtle Gdns. W7 1J 95
Myrtle Gro. EN2: Enf 1J 23
KT3: N Mald 2J 151
Myrtle Rd. CR0: C'don 3C 170
E6 1D 88
E17 6A 50
IG1: Ilf 2F 71
N13 3H 33
SM1: Sutt 5A 166
TW3: Houn 2G 113
TW12: Ham H 6G 131
W3 1J 97
Myrtle Wlk. N1 1G 9 (2E 84)
Mysore Rd. SW11 3D 118
Myton Rd. SE21 3D 138
Mytton Ho. *SW8* 7K 101
(off St Stephens Ter.)

N

N1 Shop. Cen. N1 2A 84
N16 Fitness Cen. 4D 66
Nacton Ct. *RM6: Chad H* 5C 54
(off Hevingham Dr.)
Nadine Ct. SM6: Wall 7G 167
Nadine St. SE7 5A 106
Nagasaki Wlk. SE7 3K 105
Nagle Cl. E17 2F 51
NAG'S HEAD 3J 65
Nags Head Ct. EC1 4D 8
Nags Head La. DA16: Well 3B 126
Nags Head Rd. EN3: Pond E 4D 24
Nags Head Shop. Cen. N7 4K 65
Nainby Ho. SE11 4J 19
Nairne Gro. SE24 5D 120
Nairn Rd. HA4: Ruis 6A 58
Nairn St. E14 5E 86
Naldera Gdns. SE3 6J 105
Nallhead Rd. TW13: Hanw 5A 130
Nalton Ho. *NW6* 7A 64
(off Belsize Rd.)
Namba Roy Cl. SW16 4K 137
Namton Dr. CR7: Thor H 4K 155
Nan Clark's La. NW7 2F 29
Nankin St. E14 6C 86
Nansen Ho. *NW10* 7K 61
(off Stonebridge Pk.)
Nansen Rd. SW11 3E 118
Nansen Village N12 4E 30
Nant Ct. NW2 2H 63
Nantes Cl. SW18 4A 118
Nantes Pas. E1 5J 9 (5F 85)
Nant Rd. NW2 2H 63
Nant St. E2 3H 85
Naoroji St. WC1 2J 7 (3A 84)
Napier NW9 1B 44
Napier Av. E14 5C 104
SW6 3H 117
Napier Cl. SE8 7B 104
UB7: W Dray 3B 92
W14 3G 99
Napier Ct. *N1* 2D 84
(off Cropley St.)
SE12 3K 141
SW6 3H 117
(off Ranelagh Gdns.)
UB4: Yead 4A 76
(off Dunedin Way)
Napier Gro. N1 2C 84
Napier Ho. *SE17* 6B 102
(off Cooks Rd.)
Napier Lodge TW15: Ashf 6F 129
Napier Pl. W14 3H 99
Napier Rd. BR2: Brom 4K 159
CR2: S Croy 7D 168
DA17: Belv 4F 109
E6 1E 88
E11 4G 69
E15 2G 87
(not continuous)
EN3: Pond E 5E 24
HA0: Wemb 6D 60
N17 3E 48
NW10 3D 80
SE25 4H 157
TW7: Isle 4A 114
TW15: Ashf 7F 129
W14 3H 99
Napier St. *SE8* 7B 104
(off Napier Cl.)
Napier Ter. N1 7B 66
Napier Wlk. TW15: Ashf 7F 129
Napoleon Rd. E5 3H 67
TW1: Twick 7B 114
Napton Cl. UB4: Yead 4C 76
Nara SE13 2D 122
Narbonne Av. SW4 5G 119
Narborough Cl. UB10: Ick 2E 56
Narborough St. SW6 2K 117
Narcissus Rd. NW6 5J 63
Nardini *NW9* 1B 44
(off The Concourse)
Naresby Fold HA7: Stan 6H 27
Narford Rd. E5 3G 67
Narrow Boat Cl. SE28 2H 107
Narrow St. E14 7A 86
W3 1H 97
Narrow Way BR2: Brom 6C 160

338 A-Z London

Narvic Ho.—Neville Pl.

Narvic Ho. SE5 2C 120
Narwhal Inuit Art Gallery 4K 97
Nascot St. W12 6E 80
Naseby Cl. NW6 7A 64
TW7: Isle 1J 113
Naseby Ct. DA14: Sidc 4K 143
Naseby Rd. IG5: Ilf 1D 52
RM10: Dag 3G 73
SE19 6D 138
NASH 6J 171
Nash Cl. SM1: Sutt 3B 166
Nash Ct. HA3: Kenton 6B 42
Nashe Ho. SE1 3D 102
(off Burbage Cl.)
Nash Grn. BR1: Brom 6J 141
Nash Ho. E14 2C 104
(off Alpha Gro.)
E17 3D 50
NW1 2F 83
(off Park Village E.)
SW1 6K 17
(off Lupus St.)
Nash La. BR2: Kes 7J 171
Nash Pl. E14 1D 104
Nash Rd. N9 2D 34
RM6: Chad H 4D 54
SE4 4A 122
Nash St. NW1 1K 5 (3F 83)
Nash Way HA3: Kenton 6B 42
Nasmyth St. W6 3D 98
Nassau Path SE28 1C 108
Nassau Rd. SW13 1B 116
Nassau St. W1 6A 6 (5G 83)
Nassington Rd. NW3 4D 64
Natalie Cl. TW14: Bedf 7F 111
Natalie M. TW2: Twick 3H 131
Natal Rd. CR7: Thor H 3D 156
IG1: Ilf 4F 71
N11 6D 32
SW16 6H 137
Nathan Ct. N9 7D 24
(off Causeyware Rd.)
Nathan Ho. SE11 4K 19
(off Reedworth St.)
Nathaniel Cl. E1 6K 9 (5F 85)
Nathaniel Ct. E17 7A 50
Nathans Rd. HA0: Wemb 1C 60
Nathan Way SE28 4J 107
National Archives, The 7G 97
National Army Mus. 7F 17 (6D 100)
National Gallery 3D 12 (7H 83)
National Maritime Mus. 6F 105
National Portrait Gallery 3D 12
National Tennis Cen. 5A 116
National Ter. SE16 2H 103
(off Bermondsey Wall E.)
National Theatre 4H 13 (1K 101)
National Walks TW4: Houn 3D 112
Nation Way E4 1K 35
Natural History Mus.
Knightsbridge 2A 16 (3B 100)
Nautilus Bldg., The EC1 1K 7
(off Myddelton Pas.)
Naval Ho. E14 7F 87
(off Quixley St.)
Naval Row E14 7E 86
Naval Wlk. BR1: Brom 2J 159
(off Mitre Cl.)
Navarino Gro. E8 6G 67
Navarino Mans. E8 6G 67
Navarino Rd. E8 6G 67
Navarre Rd. E6 2C 88
Navarre St. E2 3J 9 (4F 85)
Navenby Wlk. E3 4C 86
Navestock Cl. E4 3K 35
Navestock Cres. IG8: Wfd G 7F 37
Navestock Ho. IG11: Bark 2B 90
Navigation Ct. E16 7G 89
Navigation Dr. EN3: Enf L 1H 25
Navigator Dr. UB2: S'hall 2G 95
Navigator Pk. UB2: S'hall 4A 94
Navy St. SW4 3H 119
Naxos Bldg. E14 2B 104
Nayim Pl. E8 5H 67
Nayland Ho. SE6 4E 140
Naylor Bldg. E. E1 6G 85
(off Assam St.)
Naylor Bldg. W. E1 6G 85
(off Adler St.)
Naylor Gro. EN3: Pond E 5E 24
Naylor Ho. SE17 4D 102
(off Flint St.)
W10 3G 81
(off Dart St.)
Naylor Rd. N20 2F 31
SE15 7H 103
Nazareth Gdns. SE15 2H 121
Nazrul St. E2 1J 9 (3F 85)
NCR Bus. Cen. NW10 5A 62
Neagle Ho. NW2 3E 62
(off Stoll Cl.)
Neal Av. UB1: S'hall 4D 76
Neal Cl. HA6: Nwood 1J 39
Nealden St. SW9 3K 119
Neale Cl. N2 3A 46
Neale Ct. RM9: Dag 6B 72
Neal St. WC2 1E 12 (6J 83)
Neal's Yd. WC2 1E 12 (6J 83)
Near Acre NW9 1B 44
NEASDEN 3A 62
Neasden Cl. NW10 5A 62
NEASDEN JUNC. 4A 62
Neasden La. NW10 3A 62
Neasden La. Nth. NW10 3K 61
Neasham Rd. RM8: Dag 5B 72
Neate Ho. SW1 6B 18
(off Lupus St.)
Neate St. SE5 6E 102
Neath Gdns. SM4: Mord 6A 154
Neathouse Pl. SW1 3A 18 (4G 101)
Neats Acre HA4: Ruis 7F 39
Neatscourt Rd. E6 5B 88
Nebraska Bldg. SE10 1D 122
(off Deal's Gateway)
Nebraska St. SE1 7E 14 (2D 102)
Nebula SW11 2D 118
Nebula Ct. E13 2J 87
(off Umbriel Pl.)
Neckinger SE16 7K 15 (3F 103)
Neckinger Est. SE16 3F 103
Neckinger St. SE1 7K 15 (2F 103)
Nectarine Way SE13 2D 122
Needham Ho. SE11 4J 19
Needham Rd. W11 6J 81
Needham Ter. NW2 3F 63
Needleman St. SE16 2K 103
Needwood Ho. N4 1C 66
Neela Cl. UB10: Ick 4D 56
Neeld Cres. HA9: Wemb 5G 61
NW4 5D 44
Neeld Pde. HA9: Wemb 5F 61
Neil Cl. TW15: Ashf 5E 128
Neil Wates Cres. SW2 1A 138
Nelgarde Rd. SE6 7C 122
Nella Rd. W6 6F 99
Nelldale Rd. SE16 4J 103
Nellgrove Rd. UB10: Hil 4D 74
Nell Gwynne Av.
TW17: Shep 6F 147
Nell Gwynn Ho. SW3 4D 16 (4C 100)
Nello James Gdns. SE27 4D 138
Nelson Cl. CR0: C'don 1B 168
KT12: Walt T 7K 147
NW6 3J 81
RM7: Mawney 1H 55
TW14: Felt 1H 129
UB10: Hil 3D 74
Nelson Ct. SE16 1J 103
(off Brunel Rd.)
Nelson Gdns. E2 3G 85
TW3: Houn 6E 112
Nelson Gro. Rd. SW19 1K 153
Nelson Ho. SW1 7B 18
(off Dolphin Sq.)
Nelson La. UB10: Hil 3D 74
Nelson Mandela Cl. N10 2E 46
Nelson Mandela Ho. N16 2G 67
Nelson Mandela Rd. SE3 3A 124
Nelson Pas. EC1 1D 8 (3C 84)
Nelson Pl. DA14: Sidc 4A 144
N1 1B 8 (2B 84)
Nelson Rd. BR2: Brom 4A 160
DA14: Sidc 4A 144
DA17: Belv 5F 109
E4 6J 35
E11 4J 51
EN3: Pond E 6E 24
HA1: Harr 1H 59
HA7: Stan 6H 27
KT3: N Mald 5K 151
N8 5K 47
N9 2C 34
N15 4E 48
SE10 6E 104
SW19 7K 135
TW2: Whitt 7F 113
TW3: Houn 6E 112
TW6: H'row A 1B 110
TW15: Ashf 5A 128
UB10: Hil 3D 74
Nelson Rd. M. SW19 7K 135
(off Nelson Rd.)
Nelson's Column 4D 12 (1H 101)
Nelson Sq. SE1 6A 14 (2B 102)
Nelson's Row SW4 4H 119
Nelson St. E1 6H 85
E6 2D 88
(not continuous)
E16 7H 87
(not continuous)
Nelsons Yd. NW1 2G 83
(off Mornington Cres.)
Nelson Ter. N1 1B 8 (2B 84)
Nelson Trad. Est. SW19 1K 153
Nelson Wlk. E3 4D 86
KT19: Eps 7G 163
SE16 1A 104
Nemoure Rd. W3 7J 79
Nene Gdns. TW13: Hanw 3D 130
Nene Rd. TW6: H'row A 1D 110
Nene Rd. Rdbt. TW6: H'row A 1D 110
Nepaul Rd. SW11 2C 118
Nepean St. SW15 6C 116
Neptune Ct. E14 4C 104
(off Homer Dr.)
Neptune Ho. E3 1C 86
(off Garrison Rd.)
SE16 3J 103
(off Moodkee St.)
Neptune Rd. HA1: Harr 6H 41
TW6: H'row A 1F 111
Neptune St. SE16 3J 103
Neptune Wlk. DA8: Erith 4K 109
Nero Ct. TW8: Bford 7D 96
Nesbit Rd. SE9 4B 124
Nesbitt Cl. SE3 3G 123
Nesbitts All. EN5: Barn 3C 20
Nesbitt Sq. SE19 7E 138
Nesham Ho. N1 1E 84
(off Hoxton St.)
Nesham St. E1 7G 85
Ness St. SE16 3G 103
Nesta Rd. IG8: Wfd G 6B 36
Nestles Av. UB3: Hayes 3H 93
Nestor Av. N21 6G 23
Nestor Ho. E2 2H 85
(off Old Bethnal Grn. Rd.)
Netheravon Rd. W4 4B 98
W7 1K 95
Netheravon Rd. Sth. W4 5B 98
Netherbury Rd. W5 3D 96
Netherby Gdns. EN2: Enf 4D 22
Netherby Rd. SE23 7J 121
Nether Cl. N3 7D 30
Nethercott Ho. E3 3D 86
(off Bruce Rd.)
Nethercourt Av. N3 6D 30
Netherfield Gdns. IG11: Bark 6H 71
Netherfield Rd. N12 5E 30
SW17 3E 136
Netherford Rd. SW4 2G 119
Netherhall Gdns. NW3 6A 64
Netherhall Way NW3 5A 64
Netherheys Dr. CR2: S Croy 7B 168
Netherlands Rd. EN5: New Bar 6G 21
Netherleigh Cl. N6 1F 65
Nether St. N3 7D 30
N12 7D 30
(not continuous)
Netherton Gro. SW10 6A 100
Netherton Rd. N15 6D 48
TW1: Twick 5A 114
Netherwood N2 2B 46
Netherwood Pl. W14 3F 99
(off Netherwood Rd.)
Netherwood Rd. W14 3F 99
Netherwood St. NW6 7H 63
Nethewode Ct. DA17: Belv 3H 109
(off Lower Pk. Rd.)
Netley SE5 1E 120
(off Redbridge Gdns.)
Netley Cl. CR0: New Ad 7E 170
SM3: Cheam 5F 165
Netley Dr. KT12: Walt T 7D 148
Netley Gdns. SM4: Mord 7A 154
Netley Rd. E17 5B 50
IG2: Ilf 5H 53
SM4: Mord 7A 154
TW8: Bford 6E 96
Netley St. NW1 2A 6 (3G 83)
Nettlecombe NW1 7H 65
(off Agar Gro.)
Nettleden Av. HA9: Wemb 6G 61
Nettleden Ho. SW3 4D 16
(off Cale St.)
Nettlefold Pl. SE27 3B 138
Nettlefold Wlk.
KT12: Walt T 7H 147
Nettlestead Cl. BR3: Beck 7B 140
Nettleton Ct. EC2 6C 8
(off London Wall)
Nettleton Rd. SE14 1K 121
TW6: H'row A 1D 110
UB10: Ick 4B 56
Nettlewood Rd. SW16 7H 137
Neuchatel Rd. SE6 2B 140
Nevada Bldg. SE10 1D 122
(off Blackheath Rd.)
Nevada Cl. KT3: N Mald 4J 151
Nevada St. SE10 6E 104
Nevern Mans. SW5 5J 99
(off Warwick Rd.)
Nevern Pl. SW5 4J 99
Nevern Rd. SW5 4J 99
Nevern Sq. SW5 4J 99
Nevil Ho. SW9 2B 120
(off Loughborough Est.)
Nevill Ct. SW10 7A 100
(off Edith Ter.)
Neville Av. KT3: N Mald 1K 151
Neville Cl. DA15: Sidc 4K 143
E11 3H 69
NW1 2H 83
NW6 2H 81
SE15 1G 121
TW3: Houn 2F 113
W3 2J 97
Neville Ct. NW8 1A 4
Neville Dr. N2 6A 46
Neville Gdns. RM8: Dag 3D 72
Neville Gill Cl. SW18 6J 117
Neville Ho. N11 4K 31
N22 1K 47
(off Neville Pl.)
NW6 2H 81
(off Denmark Rd.)
Neville Ho. Yd. KT1: King T 2E 150
Neville Pl. N22 1K 47

A-Z London 339

Neville Rd. CR0: C'don 7D 156
  E7 . . . . .7J 69
  IG6: Ilf 1G 53
  KT1: King T 2G 151
  NW6 .2H 81
  RM8: Dag 2D 72
  TW10: Ham 3C 132
  W5 . . . . .4D 78
Nevilles Ct. NW2 . . . . .3C 62
Neville St. SW7 . . . . . .5A 16 (5B 100)
Neville Ter. SW7 . . . . . .5A 16 (5B 100)
Neville Wlk. SM5: Cars 7C 154
Nevill La. EC4 . . . . .7K 7
Nevill Rd. N16 . . . . .4E 66
Nevin Dr. E4 . . . . .1J 35
Nevin Ho. UB3: Harl 3E 92
Nevinson Cl. SW18 . . . . .6B 118
Nevis Cl. E13 . . . . .2K 87
Nevis Rd. SW17 . . . . .2E 136
Nevitt Ho. N1 . . . . .2F 9
            (off Cranston Est.)
New Acres Rd. SE28 . . . . .2J 107
            (not continuous)
NEW ADDINGTON 7F 171
Newall Ho. SE1 . . . . .3C 102
            (off Bath Ter.)
Newall Rd. TW6: H'row A 1E 110
Newark Cres. NW10 . . . . .3K 79
Newark Ho. SW9 . . . . .2B 120
Newark Knok E6 . . . . .6E 88
Newark Rd. CR2: S Croy 6D 168
Newark St. E1 . . . . .5H 85
           (not continuous)
Newark Way NW4 . . . . .4C 44
New Ash Cl. N2 . . . . .3B 46
New Atlas Wharf E14 . . . . .3C 104
           (off Arnhem Pl.)
New Baltic Wharf SE8 . . . . .5A 104
           (off Evelyn St.)
New Barn Cl. SM6: Wall 6K 167
NEW BARNET 4G 21
New Barn Rd. BR8: Swan 7K 145
New Barns Av. CR4: Mitc 4H 155
           (not continuous)
New Barn St. E13 . . . . .4J 87
New Barns Way IG7: Chig 3K 37
NEW BECKENHAM 6B 140
New Bell Yd. EC4 . . . . .1B 14
        (off Knightridge St.)
New Bentham Ct. N1 . . . . .7C 66
       (off Ecclesbourne Rd.)
Newbery Ho. N1 . . . . .7C 66
       (off Northampton St.)
Newbold Cotts. E1 . . . . .6J 85
Newbolt Av. SM3: Cheam 5E 164
Newbolt Ho. SE17 . . . . .5D 102
          (off Brandon St.)
Newbolt Rd. HA7: Stan 5E 26
New Bond St. W1 . . . . . . .1J 11 (6F 83)
Newborough Grn.
  KT3: N Mald 4K 151
New Brent St. NW4 . . . . .5E 44
Newbridge Point SE23 . . . . .3K 139
         (off Windrush La.)
New Bri. St. EC4 . . . . . .1A 14 (6B 84)
New Broad St. EC2 . . . . . .6G 9 (5E 84)
New Broadway TW12: Ham H 5H 131
  UB10: Hil 3D 74
  W5 . . . . .7D 78
New Broadway Bldgs.
  W5 . . . . .7D 78
Newburgh Rd. W3 . . . . .1J 97
Newburgh St. W1 . . . . . .1B 12 (6G 83)
New Burlington M. W1 . . . .2A 12 (7G 83)
New Burlington Pl. W1 . . . .2A 12 (7G 83)
New Burlington St. W1 . . . .2A 12 (7G 83)
Newburn Ho. SE11 . . . . .5H 19
         (off Newburn St.)
Newburn St. SE11 . . . . . .5H 19 (5K 101)
Newbury Cl. UB5: N'olt 6D 58
Newbury Ct. DA14: Sidc 4K 143
Newbury Gdns. KT19: Ewe 4B 164

Newbury Ho. N22 . . . . .1J 47
  SW9 . . . . .2B 120
  W2 . . . . .6K 81
         (off Hallfield Est.)
Newbury M. NW5 . . . . .6E 64
NEWBURY PARK 5H 53
Newbury Rd. BR2: Brom 3J 159
  E4 . . . . .6K 35
  IG2: Ilf 6J 53
  TW6: H'row A 1B 110
Newbury St. EC1 . . . . . . .6C 8 (5C 84)
Newbury Way UB5: N'olt 6C 58
New Bus. Cen., The NW10 . . . . . .3B 80
New Butt La. SE8 . . . . .7C 104
New Butt La. Nth. SE8 . . . . .7C 104
          (off Hales St.)
Newby NW1 . . . . .2A 6
          (off Robert St.)
Newby Cl. EN1: Enf 2K 23
Newby Ho. E14 . . . . .7E 86
          (off Newby Pl.)
Newby Pl. E14 . . . . .7E 86
Newby St. SW8 . . . . .3F 119
New Caledonian Mkt. SE1 . . . . . .7H 15
       (off Bermondsey Sq.)
New Caledonian Wharf SE16 . . . .3B 104
Newcastle Cl. EC4 . . . . .7A 8 (6B 84)
Newcastle Ct. EC4 . . . . .2D 14
          (off College Hill)
Newcastle Ho. W1 . . . . .5G 5
        (off Luxborough St.)
Newcastle Pl. W2 . . . . . . .5B 4 (5B 82)
Newcastle Row EC1 . . . . .4K 7 (4A 84)
New Cavendish St. W1 . . .6H 5 (5E 82)
          (6H 87)
New Century Ho. E16 . . . . .6H 87
          (off Jude St.)
New Change EC4 . . . . .1C 14 (6C 84)
New Change Pas. EC4 . . . . .1C 14
        (off New Change)
New Chapel Sq. TW13: Felt 1K 129
New Charles St. EC1 . . . . .1B 8 (3B 84)
NEW CHARLTON 4A 106
New Chiswick Pool 7A 98
New Church Rd. SE5 . . . . .7C 102
          (not continuous)
New City Rd. E13 . . . . .3A 88
New Clock Twr. Pl. N7 . . . . .6J 65
New Cl. SW19 . . . . .3A 154
  TW13: Hanw 5C 130
New Colebrooke Ct. SM5: Cars . . .7D 166
         (off Stanley Rd.)
New College Ct. NW3 . . . . .6A 64
        (off College Cres.)
New College M. N1 . . . . .7A 66
New College Pde. NW3 . . . . .6B 64
         (off Finchley Rd.)
Newcombe Gdns. SW16 . . . . . . .4J 137
  TW4: Houn 4D 112
Newcombe Ho. E5 . . . . .3H 67
Newcombe Pk. HA0: Wemb 1F 79
  NW7 .5F 29
Newcombe Ri. UB7: Yiew 6A 74
Newcombe St. W8 . . . . .1J 99
Newcomen Rd. E11 . . . . .3H 69
  SW11 . . . . .3B 118
Newcomen St. SE1 . . . . .6E 14 (2D 102)
New Compton St. WC2 . . .1D 12 (6H 83)
New Concordia Wharf SE1 . . .6K 15 (2G 103)
New Ct. EC4 . . . . .2J 13
  UB5: N'olt 5E 59
Newcourt Ho. E2 . . . . .3H 85
          (off Pott St.)
Newcourt St. NW8 . . . . . . .1C 4 (2C 82)
New Covent Garden Market
          . . . . . .7D 18 (7H 101)
New Crane Pl. E1 . . . . .1J 103
New Crane Wharf E1 . . . . .1J 103
         (off New Crane Pl.)
New Cres. Yd. NW10 . . . . .2B 80
Newcroft Cl. UB8: Hil 5B 74
NEW CROSS 7B 104
NEW CROSS 1B 122

NEW CROSS GATE 1K 121
NEW CROSS GATE 1K 121
New Cross Rd. SE14 . . . . .7J 103
New Curzon Cinema 4B 48
Newdales Cl. N9 . . . . .2B 34
Newdene Av. UB5: N'olt 2B 76
Newdigate Ho. E14 . . . . .6B 86
         (off Norbiton Rd.)
Newell St. E14 . . . . .6B 86
NEW ELTHAM 2G 143
New End NW3 . . . . .4A 64
New End Sq. NW3 . . . . .4B 64
New End Theatre
  Hampstead 3A 64
          (off New End)
New England Ind. Est. IG11: Bark . . .2G 89
Newent Cl. SE15 . . . . .7E 102
  SM5: Cars 1D 166
New Era Est. N1 . . . . .1E 84
         (off Halcombe St.)
  N1 . . . . .1E 84
         (off Phillipp St.)
New Era Ho. N1 . . . . .1E 84
         (off New Era Est.)
New Farm Av. BR2: Brom 4J 159
New Farm La. HA6: Nwood 1G 39
New Fetter La. EC4 . . . . .7K 7 (6A 84)
Newfield Cl. TW12: Hamp 1E 148
Newfield Ri. NW2 . . . . .3C 62
New Forest La. IG7: Chig 6K 37
Newgale Gdns. HA8: Edg 1F 43
New Garden Dr. UB7: W Dray 2A 92
Newgate CR0: C'don 1C 168
Newgate Cl. TW13: Hanw 2C 130
Newgate St. E4 . . . . .3B 36
         (not continuous)
  EC1 . . . . .7B 8 (6B 84)
New Globe Wlk. SE1 . . . .4C 14 (1C 102)
New Goulston St. E1 . . . . . . .7J 9 (6F 85)
New Grn. Pl. SE19 . . . . .6E 138
Newhall Cl. N1 . . . . .1C 84
         (off Popham Rd.)
Newham City Farm 6B 88
Newham Leisure Cen. 4A 88
Newham's Row SE1 . . . . .7H 15 (3E 102)
Newham Way E6 . . . . .5A 88
  E16 . . . . .5H 87
Newhaven Cl. UB3: Harl 4H 93
Newhaven Cres. TW15: Ashf 5F 129
Newhaven Gdns. SE9 . . . . .4B 124
Newhaven La. E16 . . . . .4H 87
Newhaven Rd. SE25 . . . . .5D 156
New Heston Rd. TW5: Hest 7D 94
New Horizons Ct. TW8: Bford 6A 96
Newhouse Av. RM6: Chad H 3D 54
Newhouse Cl. KT3: N Mald 7A 152
Newhouse Wlk. SM4: Mord 7A 154
Newick Cl. DA5: Bexl 6H 127
Newick Rd. E5 . . . . .4H 67
Newing Grn. BR1: Brom 7B 142
NEWINGTON 7C 14 (3C 102)
Newington Barrow Way N7 . . . . . .3K 65
Newington Butts SE1 . . . . .4B 102
  SE11 . . . . .4B 102
Newington C'way. SE1 . . . .7C 14 (3B 102)
Newington Ct. Bus. Cen. SE1 . . . .7C 14
Newington Grn. N1 . . . . .5D 66
  N16 .5D 66
Newington Grn. Community Gdns.
  N16 .5D 66
Newington Grn. Mans. N16 . . . . .5D 66
Newington Grn. Rd. N1 . . . . .6D 66
Newington Ind. Est. SE17 . . . . . .4B 102
New Inn B'way. EC2 . . . . . .3H 9 (4E 84)
New Inn Pas. WC2 . . . . .1H 13
New Inn Sq. EC2 . . . . .3H 9
New Inn St. EC2 . . . . .3H 9 (4E 84)
New Inn Yd. EC2 . . . . .3H 9 (4E 84)
New Jubilee Ct. IG8: Wfd G 7D 36
New Jubilee Wharf E1 . . . . .1J 103
        (off Wapping Wall)
New Kelvin Av. TW11: Tedd 6J 131

New Kent Rd. SE1 . . . . .3C 102
New Kings Rd. SW6 . . . . .2H 117
New King St. SE8 . . . . .6C 104
Newland Cl. EC1 . . . . .2E 8
  HA9: Wemb 2G 61
Newland Dr. EN1: Enf 1C 24
Newland Gdns. W13 . . . . .2A 96
Newland Ho. N8 . . . . .3J 47
         (off Newland Rd.)
  SE14 . . . . .6K 103
       (off John Williams Cl.)
Newland Rd. N8 . . . . .3J 47
NEWLANDS
  HA8 .3K 27
  SE23 . . . . .5K 121
Newlands HA1: Harr 1J 59
  NW1 . . . . .1A 6
        (off Harrington St.)
Newlands, The KT7: T Ditt 7J 149
  SM6: Wall 7G 167
Newlands Av. KT7: T Ditt 7J 149
Newlands Cl. HA0: Wemb 6C 60
  HA8: Edg 3K 27
  UB2: S'hall 5C 94
Newlands Cl. SE9 . . . . .6E 124
Newlands Dr. SL3: Poyle 6A 174
Newlands Pk. SE26 . . . . .6J 139
Newlands Pl. EN5: Barn 5A 20
Newlands Quay E1 . . . . .7J 85
Newlands Rd. IG8: Wfd G 2C 36
  SW16 . . . . .2J 155
Newland St. E16 . . . . .1C 106
Newlands Way KT9: Chess 5C 162
Newlands Woods CR0: Sels 7B 170
Newling Cl. E6 . . . . .6D 88
New London St. EC3 . . . . .2H 15
New London Theatre 7F 7
          (off Parker St.)
New Lydenburg Commercial Est.
  SE7 .3A 106
New Lydenburg St. SE7 . . . . .3A 106
Newlyn NW1 . . . . .1G 83
          (off Plender St.)
Newlyn Cl. BR6: Chels 4K 173
  UB8: Hil 5C 74
Newlyn Gdns. HA2: Harr 7D 40
Newlyn Ho. HA5: Hat E 1D 40
Newlyn Rd. DA16: Well 2K 125
  EN5: Barn 4C 20
  N17 . . . . .1F 49
NEW MALDEN 4A 152
Newman Ct. BR1: Brom 1J 159
          (off North St.)
  TW15: Ashf 6D 128
         (off Staines Rd.)
Newman Ho. SE1 . . . . .3B 102
Newman Pas. W1 . . . . . . .6B 6 (5G 83)
Newman Rd. BR1: Brom 1J 159
  CR0: C'don 1K 167
  E13 . . . . .3K 87
  E17 . . . . .5K 49
  UB3: Hayes 7K 75
Newman Rd. Ind. Est. CR0: C'don . . .7K 155
Newman's Ct. EC3 . . . . .1F 15
Newmans La. KT6: Surb 6D 150
Newman's Row WC2 . . . . .6H 7 (5K 83)
Newman St. W1 . . . . .6B 6 (5G 83)
Newman's Way EN4: Had W 1F 21
Newman Yd. W1 . . . . .7C 6 (6G 83)
Newmarket Av. UB5: N'olt 5E 58
Newmarket Grn. SE9 . . . . .7B 124
Newmarsh Rd. SE28 . . . . .1K 107
Newmill Ho. E3 . . . . .4E 86
Newminster Rd. SM4: Mord 6A 154
New Mount St. E15 . . . . .7F 69
Newnes Path SW15 . . . . .4D 116
Newnham Av. HA4: Ruis 1A 58
Newnham Cl. CR7: Thor H 2C 156
  UB5: N'olt 6G 59
Newnham Gdns. UB5: N'olt 6G 59
Newnham Grn. N22 . . . . .1A 48
         (off Highfield Cl.)

Newnham Lodge—Nimmo Dr.

Newnham Lodge *DA17: Belv* *5G 109*
(off Erith Rd.)
Newnham M. N22 .... 7F 33
Newnham Rd. N22 .... 1K 47
Newnhams Cl. BR1: Brom 3D 160
Newnham Ter. SE1 ....1J 19 (3A 102)
Newnham Way HA3: Kenton 5E 42
New North Pl. EC2 ....3G 9 (4E 84)
New North Rd. IG6: Ilf 1G 53
N1 ....1F 9 (7C 66)
New North St. WC1 ....5G 7 (5K 83)
Newnton Cl. N4 .... 7D 48
(not continuous)
New Oak Rd. N2 .... 2A 46
New Orleans Wlk. N19 .... 7H 47
New Oxford St. WC1 ....7D 6 (6H 83)
New Pde. TW15: Ashf 4B 128
UB7: Yiew 1A 92
New Pk. Av. N13 .... 3H 33
New Pk. Cl. UB5: N'olt 6C 58
New Pk. Est. N18 .... 5D 34
New Pk. Ho. N13 .... 4E 32
New Pk. Pde. *SW2* *7J 119*
(off New Pk. Rd.)
New Pk. Rd. SW2 .... 1H 137
TW15: Ashf 5E 128
New Pl. CR0: Addtn 6C 170
New Pl. Sq. SE16 .... 3H 103
New Plaistow Rd. E15 .... 1G 87
New Players Theatre *1J 101*
(off Villiers St.)
New Pond Pde. HA4: Ruis 3J 57
Newport Av. E13 .... 4K 87
E14 .... 7F 87
Newport Ct. WC2 ....2D 12 (7H 83)
Newport Ho. *E3* *3A 86*
(off Strahan Rd.)
Newport Lodge *EN1: Enf* *5K 23*
(off Village Rd.)
Newport Pl. WC2 ....2D 12 (7H 83)
Newport Rd. E10 .... 2E 68
E17 .... 4A 50
SW13 .... 1C 116
TW6: H'row A 1C 110
UB4: Hayes 5F 75
W3 .... 2J 97
Newport St. SE11 ....4G 19 (4K 101)
New Priory Ct. *NW6* *7J 63*
(off Mazenod Av.)
New Providence Wharf E14 .... 1F 105
Newquay Cres. HA2: Harr 2C 58
Newquay Ho. SE11 ....5J 19 (5A 102)
Newquay Rd. SE6 .... 2D 140
New Quebec St. W1 ....1F 11 (6D 82)
New Ride SW1 .... 2C 100
SW7 ....6C 10 (2C 100)
New River Av. N8 .... 3K 47
New River Ct. N5 .... 4C 66
New River Cres. N13 .... 4G 33
New River Head EC1 ....1K 7 (3A 84)
New River Stadium 7G 33
New River Wlk. N1 .... 6C 66
New River Way N4 .... 7D 48
New Rd. CR4: Mitc 1D 166
DA16: Well 2B 126
E1 .... 5H 85
E4 .... 4J 35
E12 .... 2C 70
HA1: Harr 4K 59
IG3: Ilf 2J 71
KT2: King T 7G 133
KT8: W Mole 4E 148
N8 .... 5J 47
N9 .... 2C 34
N17 .... 1F 49
N22 .... 1C 48
NW7 .... 7B 30
RM9: Dag 2G 91
RM10: Dag 2G 91
RM13: Avel, Rain, Wenn 2G 91
SE2 .... 4D 108
SE18 .... 4F 107
New Rd. TW3: Houn 4F 113
TW8: Bford 6D 96
TW10: Ham 4C 132
TW13: Hanw 5C 130
TW14: Bedf 6F 111
TW14: Felt 1K 129
TW17: Shep 3C 146
UB3: Harl 7E 92
UB8: Hil 4E 74
New Rd. Hill BR2: Kes 7C 172
BR6: Downe 7C 172
New Rochford St. NW5 .... 5D 64
New Row NW2 .... 3E 62
WC2 ....2E 12 (7J 83)
Newry Rd. TW1: Twick 5A 114
Newsam Av. N15 .... 5D 48
Newsholme Dr. N21 .... 5E 22
NEW SOUTHGATE 5A 32
New Southgate Crematorium N11 ..... 3A 32
New Southgate Ind. Est. N11 .... 5B 32
New Spitalfields Mkt. E10 .... 3C 68
New Spring Gdns. Wlk.
SE11 ....6F 19 (5J 101)
New Sq. TW14: Bedf 1E 128
WC2 ....7J 7 (6A 84)
New Sq. Pk. TW14: Bedf 1E 128
New Sq. Pas. WC2 .... 7J 7
Newstead Av. BR6: Orp 3H 173
Newstead Cl. N12 .... 6H 31
Newstead Ct. UB5: N'olt 3C 76
Newstead Ho. *N1* *2A 84*
(off Tolpuddle St.)
Newstead Rd. SE12 .... 7H 123
Newstead Wlk. SM5: Cars 7A 154
Newstead Way SW19 .... 4F 135
New St. EC2 ....6H 9 (5E 84)
New St. Hill BR1: Brom 5K 141
New St. Sq. EC4 ....7K 7 (6A 84)
(not continuous)
Newton Av. N10 .... 1E 46
W3 .... 2J 97
Newton Cl. E17 .... 6A 50
HA2: Harr 2E 58
Newton Ct. *NW6* *7A 64*
(off Fairfax Rd.)
SW17 .... *3B 136*
(off Grosvenor Way)
W8 .... *2J 99*
(off Kensington Chu. St.)
Newton Gro. W4 .... 4A 98
Newton Ho. *E1* *7H 85*
(off Cornwall St.)
E17 .... *3D 50*
(off Prospect Hill)
EN3: Enf H 3E 24
NW8 .... *1K 81*
(off Abbey Rd.)
SE20 .... 7K 139
Newton Ind. Est. RM6: Chad H 4D 54
Newton Lodge *SE10* *3H 105*
(off Teal St.)
Newton Mans. *W14* *6G 99*
(off Queen's Club Gdns.)
Newton Pk. Pl. BR7: Chst 7D 142
Newton Pl. E14 .... 4C 104
Newton Point *E16* *6H 87*
(off Clarkson Rd.)
Newton Rd. DA16: Well 3A 126
E15 .... 5F 69
HA0: Wemb 7F 61
HA3: Hrw W 2J 41
N15 .... 5G 49
NW2 .... 4E 62
SW19 .... 7G 135
TW7: Isle 2K 113
W2 .... 6K 81
Newton St. WC2 ....7F 7 (6J 83)
Newton's Yd. SW18 .... 5J 117
Newton Ter. BR2: Brom 6B 160
Newton Wlk. HA8: Edg 1H 43
Newton Way N18 .... 5H 33
New Twr. Bldgs. E1 .... 1H 103
Newtown St. SW11 .... 1F 119
New Trinity Rd. N2 .... 3B 46
New Turnstile WC1 .... 6G 7
New Union Cl. E14 .... 3E 104
New Union St. EC2 ....6E 8 (5D 84)
New Wanstead E11 .... 6H 51
New Way Rd. NW9 .... 4A 44
New Wharf Rd. N1 .... 2J 83
NEWYEARS GREEN 7B 38
New Years Grn. La. UB9: Hare 6A 38
New Zealand Av. KT12: Walt T 7H 147
New Zealand Way W12 .... 7D 80
Nexus Ct. E11 .... 1G 69
W9 .... 3J 81
Niagara Av. W5 .... 4C 96
Niagara Cl. N1 .... 2C 84
Niagra Ct. *SE16* *3J 103*
(off Canada Est.)
Nibthwaite Rd. HA1: Harr 5J 41
Nice Bus. Pk. SE15 .... 6H 103
Nicholas Cl. UB6: G'frd 2F 77
Nicholas Ct. E13 .... 3K 87
SE12 .... 1J 141
W4 .... *6A 98*
(off Corney Reach Way)
Nicholas Gdns. W5 .... 2D 96
Nicholas La. EC4 ....2F 15 (7D 84)
(not continuous)
Nicholas M. W4 .... 6A 98
Nicholas Pas. EC4 .... 2F 15
Nicholas Rd. CR0: Bedd 4J 167
E1 .... 4J 85
RM8: Dag 2F 73
W11 .... 7F 81
Nicholas Stacey Ho. *SE7* *5K 105*
(off Frank Burton Cl.)
Nicholas Way HA6: Nwood 1E 38
Nicholay Rd. N19 .... 1H 65
(not continuous)
Nichol Cl. N14 .... 1C 32
Nicholes Rd. TW3: Houn 4E 112
Nichol La. BR1: Brom 7J 141
Nicholl Ho. N4 .... 1C 66
Nicholls Av. UB8: Hil 4C 74
Nichollsfield Wlk. N7 .... 5K 65
Nicholls M. SW16 .... 4J 137
Nicholls Point *E15* *1J 87*
(off Park Gro.)
Nicholl St. E2 .... 1G 85
Nichols Cl. KT9: Chess 6C 162
N4 .... *1A 66*
(off Osborne Rd.)
Nichols Ct. E2 .... 2F 85
Nichols Grn. W5 .... 5E 78
Nicholson Ct. E17 .... 4A 50
N17 .... 3F 49
Nicholson Ho. SE17 .... 5D 102
Nicholson M. KT1: King T 4E 150
Nicholson Rd. CR0: C'don 1F 169
Nicholson St. SE1 ....5A 14 (1B 102)
Nickelby Apartments *E15* *6F 69*
(off Grove Cres. Rd.)
Nickelby Cl. SE28 .... 6C 90
Nickleby Cl. UB8: Hil 6D 74
Nickleby Ho. *SE16* *7K 15*
(off Parkers Row)
W11 .... *1F 99*
(off St Ann's Rd.)
Nickols Wlk. SW18 .... 4K 117
Nicola Cl. CR2: S Croy 6C 168
HA3: Hrw W 2H 41
Nicola Ter. DA7: Bex 1E 126
Nicol Cl. TW1: Twick 6B 114
Nicoll Ct. N10 .... 7A 32
NW10 .... 1A 80
Nicoll Pl. NW4 .... 6D 44
Nicoll Rd. NW10 .... 1A 80
Nicolson NW9 .... 1A 44
Nicolson Dr. WD23: B Hea 1B 26
Nicosia Rd. SW18 .... 7C 118
Niederwald Rd. SE26 .... 4A 140
Nield Rd. UB3: Hayes 2H 93
Nigel Cl. UB5: N'olt 1C 76
Nigel Ct. N3 .... 7E 30
Nigel Fisher Way KT9: Chess 7C 162
Nigel Ho. *EC1* *5J 7*
(off Portpool La.)
Nigel M. IG1: Ilf 4F 71
Nigel Playfair Av. W6 .... 4D 98
Nigel Rd. E7 .... 5A 70
SE15 .... 3G 121
Nigeria Rd. SE7 .... 7A 106
Nighthawk NW9 .... 1B 44
Nightingale Av. E4 .... 5B 36
HA1: Harr 7B 42
Nightingale Cl. E4 .... 4A 36
HA5: Eastc 5A 40
SM5: Cars 2E 166
W4 .... 6J 97
Nightingale Ct. BR2: Brom 2G 159
E14 .... *2E 104*
(off Ovex Cl.)
HA1: Harr 6K 41
N4 .... *2K 65*
(off Tollington Pk.)
SM1: Sutt 5A 166
SW6 .... *1K 117*
(off Maltings Pl.)
Nightingale Dr. KT19: Ewe 6H 163
Nightingale Gro. SE13 .... 5F 123
Nightingale Hgts. SE18 .... 6F 107
Nightingale Ho. *E1* *1G 103*
(off Thomas More St.)
E2 .... *1E 84*
(off Kingsland Rd.)
NW8 .... *4C 4*
(off Samford St.)
SE18 .... *5E 106*
(off Connaught M.)
UB7: W Dray 2B 92
W12 .... *6E 80*
(off Du Cane Rd.)
Nightingale La. BR1: Brom 2A 160
E11 .... 4K 51
N8 .... 4J 47
SW4 .... 7D 118
SW12 .... 7D 118
TW10: Rich 7E 114
Nightingale Lodge *W9* *5J 81*
(off Admiral Wlk.)
Nightingale M. E3 .... 2K 85
E11 .... 5J 51
KT1: King T *3D 150*
(off South La.)
SE11 ....3K 19 (4B 102)
Nightingale Pl. SE18 .... 6E 106
SW10 ....7A 16 (6A 100)
Nightingale Rd. BR5: Pet W 6G 161
E5 .... 3H 67
KT8: W Mole 5F 149
KT12: Walt T 7A 148
N1 .... 6C 66
N9 .... 6D 24
N22 .... 1J 47
NW10 .... 2B 80
SM5: Cars 3D 166
TW12: Hamp 5E 130
W7 .... 1K 95
Nightingales, The TW19: Stanw 1B 128
Nightingale Sq. SW12 .... 7E 118
Nightingale Va. SE18 .... 6E 106
Nightingale Wlk. N1 .... 6C 66
SW4 .... 6F 119
Nightingale Way E6 .... 5C 88
Nile Cl. N16 .... 3F 67
Nile Dr. N9 .... 2D 34
Nile Ho. *N1* *1E 8*
(off Provost St.)
Nile Path SE18 .... 6E 106
Nile Rd. E13 .... 2A 88
Nile St. N1 ....1D 8 (3C 84)
Nile Ter. SE15 .... 5F 103
Nimegen Way SE22 .... 5E 120
Nimmo Dr. WD23: B Hea 1C 26

Nimrod NW9 ....1A 44
Nimrod Cl. UB5: N'olt 3B 76
Nimrod Ho. E16 ....5K 87
(off Vanguard Cl.)
Nimrod Pas. N1 ....6E 66
Nimrod Rd. SW16 ....6F 137
Nina Mackay Cl. E15 ....1G 87
Nine Acres Cl. E12 ....5C 70
UB3: Harl 3E 92
NINE ELMS 7G 101
Nine Elms Cl. TW14: Felt 1H 129
Nine Elms La. SW8 ....7C 18 (7G 101)
Nineteenth Rd. CR4: Mitc 4J 155
Ninhams Wood BR6: Farnb 4E 172
Ninth Av. UB3: Hayes 7J 75
Nipponzan Myohoji Peace Pagoda 6D 100
Nisbet Ho. E9 ....5K 67
Nisbett Wlk. DA14: Sidc 4A 144
(off Sidcup High St.)
Nita Ct. SE12 ....1J 141
Nithdale Rd. SE18 ....7F 107
Nithsdale Gro. UB10: Ick 3E 56
Niton Cl. EN5: Barn 6A 20
Niton Rd. TW9: Rich 3G 115
Niton St. SW6 ....7F 99
No 1 St. SE18 ....3F 107
Nobel Dr. UB3: Harl 1F 111
Nobel Ho. SE5 ....2C 120
Nobel Rd. N18 ....4D 34
Noble Cnr. TW5: Hest 1E 112
Noble Ct. CR4: Mitc 2B 154
E1 ....7H 85
(not continuous)
Noblefield Hgts. N2 ....5C 46
Noble M. N16 ....3D 66
(off Albion Rd.)
Noble St. EC2 ....7C 8 (6C 84)
Noble Yd. N1 ....1B 84
(off Camden Pas.)
Nocavia Ho. SW6 ....1A 44
(off Townmead Rd.)
Noel NW9 ....1A 44
Noel Ct. TW4: Houn 3D 112
Noel Coward Ho. SW1 ....4B 18
(off Vauxhall Bri. Rd.)
Noel Coward Theatre 2E 12
(off St Martin's La.)
Noel Ho. NW6 ....7B 64
(off Harben Rd.)
NOEL PARK 2B 48
Noel Pk. Rd. N22 ....2A 48
Noel Rd. E6 ....4C 88
N1 ....2B 84
W3 ....7G 79
Noel Sq. RM8: Dag 4C 72
Noel St. W1 ....1B 12 (6G 83)
Noel Ter. DA14: Sidc 4B 144
SE23 ....2J 139
Noko W10 ....3F 81
Nolan Way E5 ....4G 67
Noll Ho. N7 ....2K 65
(off Tomlins Wlk.)
Nolton Pl. HA8: Edg 1F 43
Nonsuch Ho. SW19 ....1B 154
Nonsuch Pl. SM3: Cheam 7F 165
(off Ewell Rd.)
Nonsuch Wlk. SM2: Cheam 7F 165
Nora Gdns. NW4 ....4F 45
Nora Leverton Ct. NW1 ....7G 65
(off Randolph St.)
NORBITON 2G 151
Norbiton Av. KT1: King T 1G 151
Norbiton Comn. Rd.
KT1: King T 3H 151
Norbiton Hall KT2: King T 2F 151
Norbiton Ho. NW1 ....1G 83
(off Camden St.)
Norbiton Rd. E14 ....6B 86
Norbreck Gdns. NW10 ....3F 79
Norbreck Pde. NW10 ....3E 78
Norbroke St. W12 ....7B 80
Norburn St. W10 ....5G 81

NORBURY 2K 155
Norbury Av. CR7: Thor H 1K 155
SW16 ....1K 155
TW3: Houn 4H 113
Norbury Cl. SW16 ....1A 156
Norbury Ct. Rd. SW16 ....3J 155
Norbury Cres. SW16 ....1K 155
Norbury Cross SW16 ....3J 155
Norbury Gdns. RM6: Chad H 5D 54
Norbury Gro. NW7 ....3F 29
Norbury Hill SW16 ....7A 138
Norbury Ri. SW16 ....3J 155
Norbury Rd. CR7: Thor H 2C 156
E4 ....5H 35
TW13: Felt 3H 129
Norbury Trad. Est. SW16 ....2K 155
Norcombe Gdns. HA3: Kenton 6C 42
Norcombe Ho. N19 ....3H 65
(off Wedmore St.)
Norcott Cl. UB4: Yead 4A 76
Norcott Rd. N16 ....2G 67
Norcroft Gdns. SE22 ....7G 121
Norcutt Rd. TW2: Twick 1J 131
Nordenfeldt Rd. DA8: Erith 5K 109
Norden Ho. E2 ....3H 85
(off Pott St.)
Norfield Rd. DA2: Dart 4J 145
Norfolk Av. N13 ....6G 33
N15 ....6F 49
Norfolk Cl. EN4: Cockf 4K 21
N2 ....3C 46
N13 ....6G 33
TW1: Twick 6B 114
Norfolk Ct. EN5: Barn 4B 20
RM6: Chad H 5B 54
(off Norwich Cres.)
Norfolk Cres. DA15: Sidc 7J 125
W2 ....7C 4 (6C 82)
Norfolk Gdns. DA7: Bex 1F 127
Norfolk Ho. BR2: Brom 4H 159
(off Westmoreland Rd.)
EC4 ....2C 14
SE20 ....1J 157
SW1 ....3D 18
(off Page St.)
Norfolk Ho. Rd. SW16 ....3H 137
Norfolk Mans. SW11 ....1D 118
(off Prince of Wales Dr.)
Norfolk M. W10 ....5G 81
(off Blagrove Rd.)
Norfolk Pl. DA16: Well 2A 126
W2 ....7B 4 (6B 82)
(not continuous)
Norfolk Rd. CR7: Thor H 3C 156
E6 ....1D 88
E17 ....2K 49
EN3: Pond E 6C 24
EN5: New Bar 3D 20
HA1: Harr 5F 41
IG3: Ilf 1J 71
IG11: Bark 7J 71
NW8 ....1B 82
NW10 ....7A 62
RM7: Rom 6J 55
RM10: Dag 5H 73
SW19 ....7C 136
TW13: Felt 1A 130
Norfolk Row SE1 ....3G 19 (4K 101)
(not continuous)
Norfolk Sq. W2 ....1B 10 (6B 82)
Norfolk Sq. M. W2 ....1B 10
Norfolk St. E7 ....5J 69
Norfolk Ter. W6 ....5G 99
Norgrove St. SW12 ....7E 118
Norhyrst Av. SE25 ....3F 157
Norland Ho. W11 ....1F 99
(off Queensdale Cres.)
Norland Pl. W11 ....1G 99
Norland Rd. W11 ....1F 99
Norlands Cres. BR7: Chst 1F 161
Norland Sq. W11 ....1G 99

Norland Sq. Mans. W11 ....1G 99
(off Norland Sq.)
Norley Va. SW15 ....1C 134
Norlington Rd. E10 ....1E 68
E11 ....1E 68
Norman Av. N22 ....1B 48
TW1: Twick 7C 114
TW13: Hanw 2C 130
UB1: S'hall 7C 76
Norman Butler Ho. W10 ....4G 81
(off Ladbroke Gro.)
Normanby Cl. SW15 ....5H 117
Normanby Rd. NW10 ....4B 62
Norman Cl. BR6: Farnb 3G 173
N22 ....1C 48
RM5: Col R 1H 55
Norman Ct. IG2: Ilf 7H 53
N3 ....1J 45
(off Nether St.)
N4 ....7A 48
NW10 ....7C 62
W13 ....4G 77
(off Kirkfield Cl.)
Norman Cres. HA5: Pinn 1A 40
TW5: Hest 7B 94
Normand Gdns. W14 ....6G 99
(off Greyhound Rd.)
Normand Mans. W14 ....6G 99
(off Normand M.)
Normand M. W14 ....6G 99
Normand Rd. W14 ....6H 99
Normandy Av. EN5: Barn 5C 20
Normandy Cl. SE26 ....3A 140
Normandy Dr. UB3: Hayes 6E 74
Normandy Ho. E14 ....2E 104
(off Plevna St.)
EN2: Enf 1H 23
Normandy Pl. W12 ....1F 99
Normandy Rd. SW9 ....1A 120
Normandy Ter. E16 ....6K 87
Normandy Way DA8: Erith 1K 127
Norman Gro. E3 ....2A 86
Norman Hay Trad. Est., The UB7: Sip 7B 92
Norman Ho. SE1 ....3E 102
(off Riley Rd.)
SW8 ....7J 101
(off Wyvil Rd.)
TW13: Hanw 2D 130
(off Watermill Way)
Normanhurst TW15: Ashf 5C 128
Normanhurst Av. DA7: Bex 1D 126
DA16: Well 1D 126
Normanhurst Dr. TW1: Twick 5A 114
Normanhurst Rd. SW2 ....2K 137
Norman Pde. DA14: Sidc 2D 144
Norman Pk. Athletics Track 6K 159
Norman Rd. CR7: Thor H 5B 156
DA17: Belv 3H 109
(not continuous)
E6 ....4D 88
E11 ....2F 69
IG1: Ilf 5F 71
N15 ....5F 49
SE10 ....7D 104
SM1: Sutt 5J 165
SW19 ....7A 136
TW15: Ashf 6F 129
Normans Cl. NW10 ....6K 61
UB8: Hil 5B 74
Normansfield Av. TW11: Tedd 7C 132
Normanshire Dr. E4 ....4H 35
Norman's Mead NW10 ....6K 61
Norman St. EC1 ....2D 8 (3C 84)
Norman Ter. NW6 ....5H 63
Normanton Av. SW19 ....2J 135
Normanton Pk. E4 ....2B 36
Normanton Rd. CR2: S Croy 5E 168
Normanton St. SE23 ....2K 139
Norman Way N14 ....2D 32
W3 ....5H 79
Normington Cl. SW16 ....5A 138
Norrice Lea N2 ....5B 46

Norris NW9 ....1B 44
(off The Concourse)
Norris Ho. E9 ....1J 85
(off Handley Rd.)
N1 ....1E 84
(off Colville St.)
SE8 ....5B 104
(off Grove St.)
Norris St. SW1 ....3C 12 (7H 83)
Norroy Rd. SW15 ....4F 117
Norry's Cl. EN4: Cockf 4J 21
Norry's Rd. EN4: Cockf 4J 21
Norseman Cl. IG3: Ilf 1B 72
Norseman Way UB6: G'frd 1F 77
Norstead Pl. SW15 ....2C 134
Nth. Access Rd. E17 ....6K 49
North Acre NW9 ....1A 44
NORTH ACTON 4K 79
Nth. Acton Bus. Pk. W3 ....5K 79
Nth. Acton Rd. NW10 ....2K 79
Northall Rd. DA7: Bex 2J 127
Northampton Gro. N1 ....5D 66
Northampton Pk. N1 ....6C 66
Northampton Rd. CR0: C'don 2G 169
EC1 ....3K 7 (4A 84)
EN3: Pond E 4F 25
Northampton Row EC1 ....3K 7
Northampton Sq. EC1 ....2A 8 (3B 84)
Northampton St. N1 ....7C 66
Northanger Rd. SW16 ....6J 137
Nth. Audley St. W1 ....1G 11 (7E 82)
Nth. Av. HA2: Harr 6F 41
N18 ....3E 80
NW10 ....3E 80
SM5: Cars 7E 166
TW9: Kew 1G 115
UB1: S'hall 7D 76
UB3: Hayes 7J 75
W13 ....5B 78
Northaw Ho. W10 ....4E 80
(off Sutton Way)
North Bank NW8 ....2C 4 (3C 82)
Nth. Bank Bri. N7 ....4A 66
Northbank Rd. E17 ....2E 50
NORTH BECKTON 5C 88
Nth. Birkbeck Rd. E11 ....3F 69
North Block SE1 ....6H 13
(off Chicheley St.)
Northborough Rd. SW16 ....3H 155
Nth. Boundary Rd. E12 ....3B 70
Northbourne BR2: Hayes 7J 159
Northbourne Rd. SW4 ....5H 119
Nth. Branch Av. NW10 ....3E 80
Northbrook Dr. HA6: Nwood 1G 39
Northbrook Rd. CR0: C'don 5D 156
EN5: Barn 6B 20
IG1: Ilf 2E 70
N22 ....7D 32
SE13 ....5G 123
Northburgh St. EC1 ....4B 8 (4B 84)
Nth. Carriage Dr. W2 ....2C 10
NORTH CHEAM 3E 164
Nth. Cheam Sports Club 3F 165
Northchurch SE17 ....5D 102
(not continuous)
Northchurch Ho. E2 ....1G 85
(off Whiston Rd.)
Northchurch Rd. HA9: Wemb 6G 61
N1 ....7D 66
(not continuous)
Northchurch Ter. N1 ....7E 66
Nth. Circular Rd. E4 ....6G 35
E18 ....2A 52
IG1: Ilf 4E 70
IG11: Bark 1F 89
N3 ....4H 45
N12 ....3H 31
N13 ....5F 33
NW2 ....3A 62
NW4 ....7E 44
NW10 ....2F 79
NW11 ....7E 44

Northcliffe Cl. KT4: Wor Pk 3A 164
Northcliffe Dr. N20 . . . . 1C 30
North Cl. DA6: Bex 4D 126
RM10: Dag 1G 91
SM4: Mord 4G 153
TW14: Bedf 6F 111
Nth. Colonnade, The E14 . . . . 1C 104
(not continuous)
North Comn. Rd. UB8: Uxb 5A 56
W5 . . . . 7E 78
Northcote HA5: Pinn 2A 40
Northcote Av. KT5: Surb 7H 151
TW7: Isle 5A 114
UB1: S'hall 7C 76
W5 . . . . 7E 78
Northcote M. SW11 . . . . 4C 118
Northcote Rd. CR0: C'don 6D 156
DA14: Sidc 4J 143
E17 . . . . 4A 50
KT3: N Mald 3J 151
NW10 . . . . 7A 62
SW11 . . . . 5C 118
TW1: Twick 5A 114
Northcott Av. N22 . . . . 1J 47
Nth. Countess Rd. E17 . . . . 2B 50
North Ct. *BR1: Brom* *1K 159*
(off Palace Gro.)
SE24 . . . . 3B 120
SW1 . . . . *2E 18*
(off Gt. Peter St.)
W1 . . . . 5B 6 (5G 83)
NORTH CRAY 5E 144
Nth. Cray Rd. DA5: Bexl 1H 145
DA14: Sidc 6E 144
North Cray Woods 4D 144
North Cres. E16 . . . . 4F 87
N3 . . . . 2H 45
WC1 . . . . 5C 6 (5H 83)
Northcroft Ct. W12 . . . . 2C 98
Northcroft Rd. KT19: Ewe 7A 164
W13 . . . . 2B 96
North Crofts SE23 . . . . 1H 139
Northcroft Ter. W13 . . . . 2B 96
Nth. Cross Rd. IG6: Ilf 4G 53
SE22 . . . . 5F 121
Northdale Ct. SE25 . . . . 3F 157
North Dene NW7 . . . . 3E 28
TW3: Houn 1F 113
Northdene Gdns. N15 . . . . 6F 49
Northdown Cl. HA4: Ruis 3H 57
Northdown Gdns.
IG2: Ilf 5J 53
Northdown Rd. DA16: Well 2B 126
Northdown St. N1 . . . . 1G 7 (2J 83)
North Dr. BR3: Beck 4D 158
BR6: Orp 4J 173
HA4: Ruis 7G 39
SW16 . . . . 4G 137
TW3: Houn 2G 113
North E. Surrey Crematorium
SM4: Mord 6E 152
NORTH END 2A 64
North End CR0: C'don 2C 168
IG9: Buck H 1F 37
NW3 . . . . 2A 64
North End Av. NW3 . . . . 2A 64
North End Cres. W14 . . . . 4H 99
North End Ho. W14 . . . . 4G 99
North End La. BR6: Downe 7F 173
North End Pde. *W14* *4G 99*
(off North End Rd.)
North End Rd. HA9: Wemb 3G 61
NW11 . . . . 1J 63
SW6 . . . . 4G 99
W14 . . . . 4G 99
North End Way NW3 . . . . 2A 64
Northern Av. N9 . . . . 2K 33
Northernhay Wlk. SM4: Mord 4G 153
Northern Hgts. *N8* *7H 47*
(off Crescent Rd.)
Northern Perimeter Rd.
TW6: H'row A 1D 110
Northern Perimeter Rd. (West)
TW6: H'row A 4E 174
Northern Rd. E13 . . . . 2K 87
Northesk Ho. *E1* *4H 85*
(off Tent St.)
Nth. Eyot Gdns. W6 . . . . 5B 98
Northey St. E14 . . . . 7A 86
NORTH FELTHAM 6K 111
Nth. Feltham Trad. Est. TW14: Felt . . . 5K 111
Northfield Av. HA5: Pinn 4B 40
W5 . . . . 1B 96
W13 . . . . 1B 96
Northfield Cl. BR1: Brom 1C 160
UB3: Harl 3H 93
Northfield Cres. SM3: Cheam 4G 165
Northfield Gdns. RM9: Dag 4F 73
Northfield Ho. SE15 . . . . 6G 103
Northfield Pde. UB3: Harl 3G 93
Northfield Pk. UB3: Harl 3H 93
Northfield Path RM9: Dag 4F 73
Northfield Rd. E6 . . . . 7D 70
EN3: Pond E 5C 24
EN4: Cockf 3H 21
N16 . . . . 7E 48
RM9: Dag 4F 73
TW5: Hest 6B 94
W13 . . . . 2B 96
NORTHFIELDS 3B 96
Northfields SW18 . . . . 4J 117
Northfields Ind. Est. HA0: Wemb 1G 79
Northfields Prospect Bus. Cen.
SW18 . . . . 4J 117
Northfields Rd. W3 . . . . 5H 79
NORTH FINCHLEY 5F 31
Northfleet Ho. *SE1* *6E 14*
(off Tennis St.)
Northflock St. SE16 . . . . 2G 103
Nth. Flower Wlk. W2 . . . . 3A 10
North Gdn. E14 . . . . 1B 104
North Gdns. SW19 . . . . 7B 136
North Gate NW8 . . . . 1C 4
Northgate HA6: Nwood 1E 38
Northgate Bus. Cen. EN1: Enf 3C 24
Northgate Ct. SW9 . . . . 3A 120
Northgate Dr. NW9 . . . . 6A 44
Northgate Ho. *E14* *7C 86*
(off E. India Dock Rd.)
Northgate Ind. Pk. RM5: Col R 1F 55
North Gates *N12* *1A 46*
(off Bow La.)
Nth. Glade, The DA5: Bexl 7F 127
Nth. Gower St. NW1 . . . . 2B 6 (3G 83)
North Grn. NW9 . . . . 7F 29
North Gro. N6 . . . . 7E 46
N15 . . . . 5D 48
NORTH HARROW 5F 41
Nth. Hatton Rd. TW6: H'row A 1F 111
North Hill N6 . . . . 6D 46
Nth. Hill Av. N6 . . . . 6E 46
NORTH HILLINGDON 7E 56
North Ho. SE8 . . . . 5B 104
Nth. Hyde Gdns. UB3: Harl, Hayes 3J 93
Nth. Hyde La. TW5: Hest 5C 94
UB2: S'hall 5B 94
Nth. Hyde Rd. UB3: Harl 3G 93
Northiam N12 . . . . 4D 30
(not continuous)
WC1 . . . . *2F 7*
(off Cromer St.)
Northiam St. E9 . . . . 1H 85
Northington St. WC1 . . . . 4H 7 (4K 83)
NORTH KENSINGTON 5F 81
North Kent Indoor Bowls Club 3H 109
Northlands Av. BR6: Orp 4J 173
Northlands St. SE5 . . . . 2C 120
North La. TW11: Tedd 6K 131
Northleigh Ho. *E3* *3D 86*
(off Powis Rd.)
North Lodge *E16* *1K 105*
(off Wesley Av.)
EN5: New Bar 5F 21
Nth. Lodge Cl. SW15 . . . . 5F 117
Nth. London Bus. Pk. N11 . . . . 2K 31
North Mall *N9* *2C 34*
(within Edmonton Grn. Shop. Cen.)
SW18 . . . . *5K 117*
(off Southside Shop. Cen.)
North M. WC1 . . . . 4H 7 (4K 83)
North Mt. *N20* *2F 31*
(off High Rd.)
Northolm HA8: Edg 4E 28
Northolme Gdns. HA8: Edg 1G 43
Northolme Ri. BR6: Orp 2J 173
Northolme Rd. N5 . . . . 4C 66
NORTHOLT 7E 58
Northolt *N17* *2E 48*
(off Griffin Rd.)
Northolt Av. HA4: Ruis 5K 57
Northolt Gdns. UB6: G'frd 5K 59
Northolt Leisure Cen. 6E 58
Northolt Rd. HA2: Harr 4F 59
TW6: H'row A 1A 110
(not continuous)
Northolt Trad. Est. UB5: N'olt 7F 59
Northover BR1: Brom 3H 141
North Pde. HA8: Edg 2G 43
KT9: Chess 5F 163
UB1: S'hall *6E 76*
(off North Rd.)
North Pk. SE9 . . . . 6D 124
North Pas. SW18 . . . . 5J 117
North Pl. CR4: Mitc 7D 136
TW11: Tedd 6K 131
North Point N8 . . . . 5K 47
Northpoint Cl. SM1: Sutt 3A 166
Northpoint Ho. *N1* *6D 66*
(off Essex Rd.)
Northpoint Sq. NW1 . . . . 6H 65
Nth. Pole La. BR2: Kes 6H 171
Nth. Pole Rd. W10 . . . . 5E 80
Northport St. N1 . . . . 1D 84
Nth. Quay Pl. E14 . . . . 7D 86
North Ride W2 . . . . 3C 10 (7C 82)
North Ri. W2 . . . . 1D 10 (6C 82)
North Rd. BR1: Brom 1K 159
BR4: W W'ck 1D 170
DA17: Belv 3H 109
HA1: Harr 7A 42
HA8: Edg 1H 43
IG3: Ilf 2J 71
KT6: Surb 6D 150
N2 . . . . 2C 46
N6 . . . . 7E 46
N7 . . . . 6J 65
N9 . . . . 1C 34
RM6: Chad H 5E 54
SE18 . . . . 4J 107
SW19 . . . . 6A 136
TW5: Hest 6A 94
TW8: Bford 6E 96
TW9: Kew 1G 115
TW9: Rich 3G 115
TW14: Bedf 6F 111
UB1: S'hall 6E 76
UB3: Hayes 5F 75
UB7: W Dray 3B 92
W5 . . . . 3D 96
Northrop Rd. TW6: H'row A 1G 111
North Row W1 . . . . 2F 11 (7D 82)
Nth. Row Bldgs. *W1* *2G 11*
(off North Row)
North Several SE3 . . . . 2F 123
NORTH SHEEN 3G 115
Northside Rd. BR1: Brom 1J 159
Northside Studios *E8* *1H 85*
(off Andrew's Rd.)
Nth. Side Wandsworth Comn.
SW18 . . . . 5B 118
Northspur Rd. SM1: Sutt 3J 165
North Sq. *N9* *2C 34*
(off New Rd.)
NW11 . . . . 5J 45
North Stand N5 . . . . 3B 66
Northstead Rd. SW2 . . . . 2A 138
North St. BR1: Brom 1J 159
DA7: Bex 4G 127
E13 . . . . 2K 87
IG11: Bark 6F 71
NW4 . . . . 5E 44
RM1: Rom 3K 55
(not continuous)
SM5: Cars 3D 166
SW4 . . . . 3G 119
TW7: Isle 3A 114
North St. Pas. E13 . . . . 2K 87
Nth. Tenter St. E1 . . . . 1K 15 (6F 85)
North Ter. SW3 . . . . 2C 16 (3C 100)
WC2 . . . . 4E 12
Northumberland All. EC3 . . . . . 1H 15 (6E 84)
(not continuous)
Northumberland Av. DA16: Well 4H 125
E12 . . . . 1A 70
EN1: Enf 1C 24
TW7: Isle 1K 113
WC2 . . . . 4E 12 (1J 101)
Northumberland Cl. DA8: Erith 7J 109
TW19: Stanw 6A 110
Northumberland Cres. TW14: Felt 6G 111
Northumberland Gdns. BR1: Brom . . . 4E 160
CR4: Mitc 5H 155
N9 . . . . 3A 34
TW7: Isle 7A 96
Northumberland Gro. N17 . . . . 7C 34
NORTHUMBERLAND HEATH 7J 109
Northumberland Ho. IG8: Wfd G 7K 37
SW1 . . . . *4E 12*
(off Northumberland Av.)
Northumberland Pk. DA8: Erith 7J 109
N17 . . . . 7A 34
Northumberland Pk. Ind. Est. N17 . . . . 7C 34
Northumberland Pk. Sports Cen. 7B 34
Northumberland Pl. TW10: Rich 5D 114
W2 . . . . 6J 81
Northumberland Rd. E6 . . . . 6C 88
E17 . . . . 7C 50
EN5: New Bar 6F 21
HA2: Harr 5D 40
Northumberland St. WC2 . . . . 4E 12 (1J 101)
Northumberland Way DA8: Erith 1J 127
Northumbria St. E14 . . . . 6C 86
Nth. Verbena Gdns. W6 . . . . 5C 98
North Vw. HA5: Eastc 7A 40
SW19 . . . . 5E 134
W5 . . . . 4C 78
Northview N7 . . . . 3J 65
North Vw. Cvn. Site IG6: Ilf 1A 54
Northview Cres. NW10 . . . . 4B 62
North Vw. Dr. IG8: Wfd G 2B 52
North Vw. Rd. N8 . . . . 4H 47
North Vs. NW1 . . . . 6H 65
North Wlk. CR0: New Ad 6D 170
(not continuous)
W2 . . . . 7K 81
W8 . . . . *7K 81*
(off The Broad Wlk.)
North Way HA5: Pinn 4B 40
N9 . . . . 2E 34
N11 . . . . 6B 32
NW9 . . . . 3H 43
UB10: Uxb 7A 56
Northway NW11 . . . . 5K 45
SM4: Mord 3G 153
SM6: Wall 4G 167
Northway Cir. NW7 . . . . 4E 28
Northway Ct. NW7 . . . . 4F 29
Northway Cres. NW7 . . . . 4E 28
Northway Gdns. NW11 . . . . 5K 45
Northway Rd. CR0: C'don 6F 157
SE5 . . . . 3C 120
Northways Pde. *NW3* *7B 64*
(off College Cres., not continuous)
Northweald La. KT2: King T 5D 132
NORTH WEMBLEY 3D 60
Nth. Western Commercial Cen.
NW1 . . . . 7J 65
Northwest Pl. N1 . . . . 2A 84

North Wharf *E14* *1E 104*
(off Coldharbour)
Nth. Wharf Rd. W2 6A 4 (5B 82)
Northwick Av. HA3: Kenton 6A 42
Northwick Circ. HA3: Kenton 6C 42
Northwick Cl. HA1: Harr 1B 60
NW8 3A 4 (4B 82)
Northwick Ho. NW8 3A 4
Northwick Pk. Rd. HA1: Harr 6K 41
Northwick Pk. Rdbt. HA1: Harr 7A 42
Northwick Rd. HA0: Wemb 1D 78
Northwick Ter. NW8 3A 4 (4B 82)
Northwick Wlk. HA1: Harr 7K 41
Northwold Dr. HA5: Pinn 2A 40
Northwold Rd. E5 2F 67
N16 2F 67
NORTHWOOD 1H 39
Nth. Wood Ct. SE25 3G 157
Northwood Est. E5 2G 67
Northwood FC 2H 39
Northwood Gdns. IG5: Ilf 4E 52
N12 5G 31
UB6: G'frd 5K 59
Northwood Hall N6 7G 47
NORTHWOOD HILLS 2J 39
Northwood Hills Cir.
HA6: Nwood 1J 39
Northwood Ho. *KT2: King T* *2G 151*
(off Coombe Rd.)
SE27 4D 138
Northwood Pk. 2H 39
Northwood Pl. DA18: Erith 3F 109
Northwood Rd. CR7: Thor H 2B 156
N6 7F 47
SE23 1B 140
SM5: Cars 6E 166
TW6: H'row A 4E 174
UB9: Hare 1A 38
Northwood Sports Cen. 1K 39
Northwood Way HA6: Nwood 1J 39
SE19 6D 138
UB9: Hare 1A 38
NORTH WOOLWICH 2E 106
Nth. Woolwich Rd. E16 1H 105
Nth. Worple Way SW14 3K 115
Norton Av. KT5: Surb 7H 151
Norton Cl. E4 5H 35
EN1: Enf 2C 24
Norton Ct. BR3: Beck 1B 158
Norton Folgate E1 5H 9 (5E 84)
Norton Folgate Ho. *E1* *5J 9*
(off Puma Ct.)
Norton Gdns. SW16 2J 155
Norton Ho. *E1* *6H 85*
(off Bigland St.)
E2 *2K 85*
(off Mace St.)
SW1 *2D 18*
(off Arneway St.)
SW9 *2K 119*
(off Aytoun Rd.)
Norton Rd. E10 1B 68
HA0: Wemb 6D 60
RM10: Dag 6K 73
Norval Rd. HA0: Wemb 2B 60
Norway Ga. SE16 3A 104
Norway Pl. E14 6B 86
Norway St. SE10 6D 104
Norway Wharf E14 6B 86
Norwich Cres. RM6: Chad H 5B 54
Norwich Ho. *E14* *6D 86*
(off Cordelia St.)
Norwich M. IG3: Ilf 1A 72
Norwich Pl. DA6: Bex 4G 127
Norwich Rd. CR7: Thor H 3C 156
E7 5J 69
HA6: Nwood 3H 39
RM9: Dag 2G 91
UB6: G'frd 1F 77
Norwich St. EC4 7J 7 (6A 84)
Norwich Wlk. HA8: Edg 7D 28
NORWOOD 6E 138
Norwood Av. HA0: Wemb 1F 79
RM7: Rush G 7K 55
Norwood Cl. NW2 3G 63
TW2: Twick 2H 131
UB2: S'hall 4E 94
Norwood Dr. HA2: Harr 6D 40
Norwood Gdns. UB2: S'hall 4D 94
UB4: Yead 4A 76
NORWOOD GREEN 4D 94
Norwood Grn. Rd. UB2: S'hall 4E 94
Norwood High St. SE27 3B 138
Norwood Ho. *E14* *7D 86*
(off Poplar High St.)
NORWOOD NEW TOWN 6C 138
Norwood Pk. Rd. SE27 5C 138
Norwood Rd. SE24 1B 138
SE27 2B 138
UB2: S'hall 3C 94
Norwood Ter. UB2: S'hall 4F 95
Nota M. N3 1J 45
Notley St. SE5 7D 102
Notson Rd. SE25 4H 157
Notting Barn Rd. W10 4F 81
Nottingdale Sq. W11 1G 99
Nottingham Av. E16 5A 88
Nottingham Ct. WC2 1E 12 (6J 83)
Nottingham Ho. *WC2* *1E 12*
(off Shorts Gdns.)
Nottingham Pl. W1 4G 5 (5E 82)
Nottingham Rd. CR2: S Croy 4C 168
E10 6E 50
SW17 1D 136
TW7: Isle 2K 113
Nottingham St. W1 5G 5 (5E 82)
Nottingham Ter. NW1 4G 5
NOTTING HILL 7H 81
Notting Hill Ga. W11 1J 99
Nottingwood Ho. *W11* *7G 81*
(off Clarendon Rd.)
Nova Bldg. E14 4C 104
Nova Ct. E. *E14* *1E 104*
(off Yabsley St.)
Nova Ct. W. *E14* *1E 104*
(off Yabsley St.)
Nova M. SM3: Sutt 1G 165
Novar Cl. BR6: Orp 7K 161
Nova Rd. CR0: C'don 1B 168
Novar Rd. SE9 1G 143
Novello Ct. *N1* *1C 84*
(off Popham Rd.)
Novello St. SW6 1J 117
Novello Theatre *7K 83*
(off Aldwych)
Novem Ho. *E1* *6K 9*
(off Chicksand St.)
Nowell Rd. SW13 6C 98
Nower Ct. HA5: Pinn 4D 40
Nower Hill HA5: Pinn 4D 40
Noyna Rd. SW17 3D 136
Nubia Way BR1: Brom 3G 141
Nuding Cl. SE13 3C 122
Nuffield Ct. TW5: Hest 7D 94
Nuffield Health Club
Battersea *2D 118*
(within Latchmere Leisure Cen.)
Bloomsbury *3G 7*
(off Mecklenburgh Pl.)
Bromley 5K 159
Cannon Street 3E 14
Cheam 7F 165
Fulham 1F 117
Norbury 2K 155
Southfields 7J 117
Sutton 6J 165
Twickenham 7J 113
Westminster 5A 82
Willesden Green 7E 62
Nuffield Lodge N6 6G 47
W9 *5J 81*
(off Admiral Wlk.)
Nugent Rd. N19 1J 65
SE25 3F 157
Nugents Ct. HA5: Pinn 1C 40
Nugent's Pk. HA5: Hat E 1C 40
Nugent Ter. NW8 2A 82
Numa Ct. TW8: Bford 7D 96
No. 10 Bowling Alley 6K 55
Number One EC1 4D 8 (4C 84)
Nun Ct. EC2 7E 8
Nuneaton Rd. RM9: Dag 7E 72
NUNHEAD 3H 121
Nunhead Cemetery Nature Reserve
4J 121
Nunhead Cres. SE15 3H 121
Nunhead Est. SE15 4H 121
Nunhead Grn. SE15 3H 121
Nunhead Gro. SE15 3H 121
Nunhead La. SE15 3H 121
Nunhead Pas. SE15 3G 121
Nunnington Cl. SE9 3C 142
Nunns Rd. EN2: Enf 2H 23
Nupton Dr. EN5: Barn 6A 20
Nurse Cl. HA8: Edg 1J 43
Nursery App. N12 6H 31
Nursery Av. CR0: C'don 2K 169
DA7: Bex 3F 127
N3 2A 46
Nursery Cl. BR6: Orp 7K 161
CR0: C'don 2K 169
EN3: Enf H 1E 24
IG8: Wfd G 5E 36
RM6: Chad H 6D 54
SE4 2B 122
SW15 4F 117
TW14: Felt 7K 111
(not continuous)
Nursery Ct. N17 7A 34
W13 5A 78
Nursery Gdns. BR7: Chst 6F 143
EN3: Enf H 1E 24
TW4: Houn 5D 112
TW12: Hamp 4D 130
TW16: Sun 2H 147
Nursery La. E2 1F 85
E7 6J 69
UB8: Cowl 4A 74
W10 5E 80
Nurserymans Rd. N11 2K 31
Nursery Rd. CR4: Mitc 3C 154
CR7: Thor H 4D 156
E9 6J 67
E12 2C 70
HA5: Pinn 3A 40
N2 1B 46
N14 7B 22
SM1: Sutt 4A 166
SW9 4K 119
SW19 7G 135
(Elm Gro.)
SW19 2K 153
(Parkleigh Rd.)
TW16: Sun 2G 147
Nursery Row EN5: Barn 3B 20
SE17 4D 102
Nursery St. N17 7A 34
Nursery Wlk. NW4 3E 44
RM7: Rush G 7K 55
Nursery Waye UB8: Uxb 1A 74
Nurstead Rd. DA8: Erith 7G 109
Nutbourne St. W10 3G 81
Nutbrook St. SE15 3G 121
Nutbrowne Rd. RM9: Dag 1F 91
Nutcroft Rd. SE15 7H 103
Nutfield Cl. N18 6B 34
SM5: Cars 3C 166
Nutfield Ct. BR1: Brom 3J 159
Nutfield Gdns. IG3: Ilf 2K 71
UB5: N'olt 2A 76
Nutfield Pas. *CR7: Thor H* *4B 156*
(off Nutfield Rd.)
Nutfield Rd. CR7: Thor H 4B 156
E15 4E 68
NW2 3C 62
SE22 4F 121
Nutfield Way BR6: Farnb 2F 173
Nutford Pl. W1 7D 4 (6D 82)
Nuthatch Cl. TW19: Stanw 1B 128
Nuthatch Gdns. SE28 2H 107
(not continuous)
Nuthurst Av. SW2 2K 137
Nutkin Wlk. UB8: Uxb 7A 56
Nutley Ter. NW3 6A 64
Nutmead Cl. DA5: Bexl 1J 145
Nutmeg Cl. E16 4G 87
Nutmeg La. E14 6F 87
Nuttall St. N1 2E 84
Nutter La. E11 6A 52
Nutt Gro. HA8: Edg 2J 27
Nutt St. SE15 7F 103
Nutty La. TW17: Shep 3E 146
Nutwell St. SW17 5C 136
Nuxley Rd. DA17: Belv 6F 109
Nyanza St. SE18 6H 107
Nye Bevan Est. E5 3K 67
Nye Bevan Ho. *SW6* *7H 99*
(off St Thomas's Way)
Nylands Av. TW9: Kew 1G 115
Nymans Gdns. SW20 3D 152
Nynehead St. SE14 7A 104
Nyon Gro. SE6 2B 140
Nyssa Cl. IG8: Wfd G 6J 37
Nyssa Ct. *E15* *3G 87*
(off Teasel Way)
Nyton Cl. N19 1J 65

O

O2, The
(Millennium Dome) 1G 105
O2 Academy
Brixton 3A 120
O2 Cen. NW3 6A 64
Oak Apple Ct. SE12 1J 141
Oak Av. CR0: C'don 1C 170
EN2: Enf 1E 22
N8 4J 47
N10 7A 32
N17 7J 33
TW5: Hest 7B 94
TW12: Hamp 5C 130
UB7: W Dray 3C 92
UB10: Ick 2D 56
Oak Bank CR0: New Ad 6E 170
Oakbank Av. KT12: Walt T 7D 148
Oakbank Gro. SE24 4C 120
Oakbark Ho. *TW8: Bford* *7C 96*
(off High St.)
Oakbrook Cl. BR1: Brom 4K 141
Oakbury Rd. SW6 2K 117
Oak Cl. N14 7A 22
SM1: Sutt 2A 166
Oakcombe Cl. KT3: N Mald 1A 152
Oak Cott. Cl. SE6 1H 141
Oak Cotts. W7 2J 95
Oak Ct. *SE15* *7F 103*
(off Sumner Rd.)
Oak Cres. E16 5G 87
Oakcroft Bus. Cen. KT9: Chess 4F 163
Oakcroft Cl. HA5: Pinn 2K 39
Oakcroft Rd. KT9: Chess 4F 163
SE13 2F 123
Oakcroft Vs. KT9: Chess 4F 163
Oakdale N14 1A 32
Oakdale Av. HA3: Kenton 5E 42
HA6: Nwood 2J 39
Oakdale Ct. E4 5K 35
Oakdale Gdns. E4 5K 35
Oakdale Rd. E7 7K 69
E11 2F 69
E18 2K 51
KT19: Ewe 7K 163
N4 6C 48
SE15 3J 121
SW16 5J 137
Oakdale Way CR4: Mitc 7E 154

Oak Dene W13 5B **78**
Oakdene SE15 1H **121**
Oakdene Av. BR7: Chst 5E **142**
DA8: Erith 6J **109**
KT7: T Ditt 1A **162**
Oakdene Cl. HA5: Hat E 1D **40**
Oakdene Dr. KT5: Surb 7J **151**
Oakdene M. SM3: Sutt 1H **165**
Oakdene Pk. N3 7C **30**
Oakdene Rd. BR5: St M Cry 5K **161**
UB10: Hil 2D **74**
Oakden St. SE11 3K **19** (4A **102**)
Oake Ct. SW15 5G **117**
Oakeford Ho. *W14* *3G **99***
(off Russell Rd.)
Oakend Ho. N4 7D **48**
Oakenholt Ho. SE2 1D **108**
Oakenshaw Cl. KT6: Surb 7E **150**
Oakes Cl. E6 6D **88**
Oakeshott Av. N6 2E **64**
Oakey La. SE1 1J **19** (3A **102**)
Oakfield E4 5J **35**
Oakfield Av. HA3: Kenton 3B **42**
Oakfield Cen. SE20 7H **139**
Oakfield Cl. HA4: Ruis 6H **39**
KT3: N Mald 5B **152**
Oakfield Ct. N8 7J **47**
NW2 7F **45**
Oakfield Gdns. BR3: Beck 5D **158**
N18 4K **33**
SE19 5E **138**
(not continuous)
SM5: Cars 1C **166**
UB6: G'frd 4H **77**
Oakfield Ho. *E3* *5C **86***
(off Gale St.)
Oakfield La. BR2: Kes 4A **172**
Oakfield Lodge *IG1: Ilf* *3F **71***
(off Albert Rd.)
Oakfield Rd. CR0: C'don 1C **168**
E6 1C **88**
E17 2A **50**
IG1: Ilf 3F **71**
N3 1K **45**
N4 6A **48**
N14 2D **32**
SE20 7H **139**
Oakfield Rd. SW19 3F **135**
TW15: Ashf 5D **128**
Oakfield Rd. Ind. Est. SE20 7H **139**
Oakfields Rd. NW11 6G **45**
Oakfield St. SW10 6A **100**
Oakford Rd. NW5 4G **65**
Oak Gdns. CR0: C'don 2C **170**
HA8: Edg 2J **43**
Oak Glade HA6: Nwood 1D **38**
Oak Gro. BR4: W W'ck 1E **170**
HA4: Ruis 7K **39**
NW2 4G **63**
TW16: Sun 7K **129**
Oak Gro. Rd. SE20 1J **157**
Oakhall Ct. E11 6K **51**
Oakhall Dr. TW16: Sun 5H **129**
Oak Hall Rd. E11 6K **51**
Oakham Cl. EN4: Cockf 3J **21**
SE6 2B **140**
Oakham Dr. BR2: Brom 4H **159**
Oakham Ho. *W10* *4E **80***
(off Sutton Way)
Oakhampton Rd. NW7 7A **30**
Oak Hill IG8: Wfd G 7A **36**
KT6: Surb 7E **150**
Oakhill KT10: Clay 6A **162**
Oakhill Av. HA5: Pinn 2C **40**
NW3 4K **63**
Oak Hill Cl. IG8: Wfd G 7A **36**
Oak Hill Ct. IG8: Wfd G 7A **36**
Oakhill Ct. SE23 6J **121**
SW19 7F **135**
Oak Hill Cres. IG8: Wfd G 7A **36**
KT6: Surb 7E **150**
Oakhill Dr. KT6: Surb 7E **150**
Oak Hill Gdns. IG8: Wfd G 1G **51**
Oak Hill Gro. KT6: Surb 6E **150**
Oak Hill Pk. NW3 4K **63**
Oak Hill Pk. M. NW3 4A **64**
Oak Hill Path KT6: Surb 6E **150**
Oakhill Pl. SW15 5J **117**
Oak Hill Rd. KT6: Surb 6E **150**
Oakhill Rd. BR3: Beck 2E **158**
BR6: Orp 1K **173**
SM1: Sutt 3K **165**
SW15 5H **117**
SW16 1K **155**
Oak Hill Way NW3 4K **63**
(not continuous)
Oak Hill Woods Nature Reserve 6J **21**
Oak Ho. N2 2B **46**
RM7: Rom 5K **55**
TW9: Kew 1H **115**
W10 *4G **81***
(off Sycamore Wlk.)
Oakhouse Rd. DA6: Bex 5G **127**
Oakhurst Av. DA7: Bex 7E **108**
EN4: E Barn 7H **21**
Oakhurst Cl. BR7: Chst 1D **160**
E17 4G **51**
IG6: Ilf 1G **53**
KT2: King T 6F **133**
TW11: Tedd 5J **131**
Oakhurst Ct. *E17* *4G **51***
(off Woodford New Rd.)
Oakhurst Gdns. DA7: Bex 7E **108**
E4 1C **36**
E17 4G **51**
Oakhurst Gro. SE22 4G **121**
Oakhurst Rd. KT19: Ewe 6J **163**
Oakington Av. HA2: Harr 7E **40**
HA9: Wemb 3F **61**
UB3: Harl 4F **93**
Oakington Cl. TW16: Sun 2A **148**
Oakington Ct. EN2: Enf 2G **23**
Oakington Dr. TW16: Sun 2A **148**
Oakington Mnr. Dr. HA9: Wemb 5G **61**
Oakington Rd. W9 4J **81**
Oakington Way N8 7J **47**
Oakland Pl. IG9: Buck H 2D **36**
Oakland Quay E14 3D **104**
Oakland Rd. E15 4F **69**
Oaklands BR3: Beck 1D **158**
N21 2E **32**
W13 5A **78**
Oaklands Av. BR4: W W'ck 3D **170**
CR7: Thor H 4A **156**
DA15: Sidc 7K **125**
KT10: Esh 7H **149**
N9 6C **24**
TW7: Isle 6K **95**
Oaklands Cl. BR5: Pet W 6J **161**
DA6: Bex 5F **127**
HA0: Wemb 5D **60**
KT9: Chess 4C **162**
Oaklands Ct. HA0: Wemb 5D **60**
NW10 *1A **80***
(off Nicoll Rd.)
SE20 *7J **139***
(off Chestnut Gro.)
Oaklands Dr. TW2: Whitt 7G **113**
Oaklands Est. SW4 6G **119**
Oaklands Gro. W12 1C **98**
Oaklands M. *NW2* *4F **63***
(off Oaklands Rd.)
Oaklands Pk. Av. IG1: Ilf 2G **71**
Oaklands Pas. *NW2* *4F **63***
(off Oaklands Rd.)
Oaklands Pl. SW4 4G **119**
Oaklands Rd. BR1: Brom 7G **141**
DA6: Bex 4F **127**
N20 7C **20**
NW2 4F **63**
SW14 3K **115**
W7 2K **95**
(not continuous)
Oaklands Way SM6: Wall 7H **167**
Oakland Way KT19: Ewe 6A **164**
Oak La. E14 7B **86**
IG8: Wfd G 4C **36**
N2 2B **46**
N11 6C **32**
TW1: Twick 7A **114**
TW7: Isle 4J **113**
Oakleafe Gdns. IG6: Ilf 3F **53**
Oaklea Lodge IG3: Ilf 3A **72**
Oaklea Pas. KT1: King T 3D **150**
Oakleigh Av. HA8: Edg 2H **43**
KT6: Surb 1G **163**
N20 2G **31**
Oakleigh Cl. N20 3J **31**
Oakleigh Ct. EN4: E Barn 6H **21**
HA8: Edg 2J **43**
N1 1E **8**
UB1: S'hall 1D **94**
Oakleigh Cres. N20 2H **31**
Oakleigh Gdns. BR6: Orp 4J **173**
HA8: Edg 5A **28**
N20 1F **31**
Oakleigh M. N20 1F **31**
OAKLEIGH PARK 1F **31**
Oakleigh Pk. Av. BR7: Chst 1E **160**
Oakleigh Pk. Nth. N20 1G **31**
Oakleigh Pk. Sth. N20 7H **21**
Oakleigh Rd. UB10: Hil 7E **56**
Oakleigh Rd. Nth. N20 2G **31**
Oakleigh Rd. Sth. N11 3K **31**
Oakleigh Way CR4: Mitc 1F **155**
KT6: Surb 1G **163**
Oakley Av. CR0: Bedd 4K **167**
IG11: Bark 7K **71**
W5 7G **79**
Oakley Cl. E4 3K **35**
E6 6C **88**
TW7: Isle 1H **113**
W7 7J **77**
Oakley Ct. CR4: Mitc 7E **154**
Oakley Cres. EC1 2B **84**
Oakley Dr. BR2: Brom 3C **172**
SE9 1H **143**
SE13 6F **123**
Oakley Gdns. N8 5K **47**
SW3 7D **16** (6C **100**)
Oakley Grange HA1: Harr 2H **59**
Oakley Ho. *SE11* *4J **19***
(off Hotspur St.)
SW1 2F **17** (4D **100**)
W5 7G **79**
Oakley Pk. DA5: Bexl 7C **126**
Oakley Pl. SE1 5F **103**
Oakley Rd. BR2: Brom 3C **172**
HA1: Harr 6J **41**
N1 7D **66**
SE25 5H **157**
Oakley Sq. NW1 2G **83**
Oakley St. SW3 7C **16** (6C **100**)
Oakley Studios *SW3* *7C **16***
(off Up. Cheyne Row)
Oakley Wlk. W6 6F **99**
Oakley Yd. E2 3K **9** (4F **85**)
Oak Lodge E11 6J **51**
SM1: Sutt 4A **166**
TW16: Sun *7H **129***
(off Forest Dr.)
W8 *3K **99***
(off Chantry Sq.)
Oak Lodge Cl. HA7: Stan 5H **27**
Oak Lodge Dr. BR4: W W'ck 7D **158**
Oaklodge Way NW7 5G **29**
Oakman Ho. SW19 1F **135**
Oakmead Av. BR2: Hayes 6J **159**
Oakmead Ct. HA7: Stan 4H **27**
Oakmeade HA5: Hat E 6A **26**
Oakmead Gdns. HA8: Edg 4E **28**
Oakmead Pl. CR4: Mitc 1C **154**
Oakmead Rd. CR0: C'don 6H **155**
SW12 1E **136**
Oakmede EN5: Barn 4A **20**
Oakmere Rd. SE2 6A **108**
Oakmont Pl. BR6: Orp 1H **173**
Oak Pk. Gdns. SW19 1F **135**
Oak Pk. M. N16 3F **67**
Oak Pl. SW18 5K **117**
Oakridge Dr. N2 3B **46**
Oakridge La. BR1: Brom 5F **141**
Oakridge Rd. BR1: Brom 4F **141**
Oak Ri. IG9: Buck H 3G **37**
Oak Rd. BR6: Chels 7K **173**
DA8: Erith 7J **109**
KT3: N Mald 2K **151**
W5 7D **78**
Oak Row SW16 2G **155**
Oaks, The BR2: Brom 6E **160**
EN2: Enf 3G **23**
HA4: Ruis 7F **39**
IG8: Wfd G 7B **36**
N12 4E **30**
NW6 *7F **63***
(off Brondesbury Pk.)
NW10 7D **62**
SE18 5G **107**
SM4: Mord 4G **153**
UB4: Hayes 2E **74**
Oaks Av. KT4: Wor Pk 3D **164**
RM5: Col R 2J **55**
SE19 5E **138**
TW13: Felt 2C **130**
Oaks Cvn. Pk., The KT9: Chess 3C **162**
Oaksford Av. SE26 3H **139**
Oaks Gro. E4 2B **36**
Oakshade Rd. BR1: Brom 4F **141**
Oakshaw Rd. SW18 7K **117**
Oakshott Ct. NW1 1C **6** (2H **83**)
(not continuous)
Oakside Ct. IG6: Ilf 2H **53**
Oakside Stadium 4H **53**
Oaks La. CR0: C'don 3H **169**
IG2: Ilf 5J **53**
Oak Sq. SW9 2K **119**
Oaks Rd. CR0: C'don 5H **169**
TW19: Stanw 5A **110**
Oaks Shop. Cen., The W3 1J **97**
Oak St. *E14* *2E **104***
(off Stewart St.)
RM7: Rom 5J **55**
Oaks Way KT6: Surb 1D **162**
SM5: Cars 7D **166**
Oakthorpe Ct. N13 5H **33**
Oakthorpe Est. N13 5H **33**
Oakthorpe Rd. N13 5F **33**
Oaktree Av. N13 3G **33**
Oak Tree Cl. HA7: Stan 7H **27**
W5 6C **78**
UB5: N'olt 2A **76**
W3 7H **79**
Oak Tree Dell NW9 5J **43**
Oak Tree Dr. N20 1E **30**
Oak Tree Gdns. BR1: Brom 5K **141**
Oaktree Gro. IG1: Ilf 5H **71**
Oak Tree Ho. *W9* *4J **81***
(off Shirland Rd.)
Oak Tree Rd. NW8 2B **4** (3C **82**)
Oakview Apartments SM1: Sutt 4B **166**
Oakview Gdns. N2 4B **46**
Oakview Gro. CR0: C'don 1A **170**
Oakview Lodge *NW11* *7H **45***
(off Beechcroft Av.)
Oakview Rd. SE6 5D **140**
Oak Village NW5 4E **64**
Oak Vs. *NW11* *6H **45***
(off Hendon Pk. Row)
Oak Wlk. *SM6: Wall* *1E **166***
(off Helios Rd.)
Oak Way CR0: C'don 6K **157**
N14 7A **22**
TW14: Felt 1G **129**
W3 1A **98**
Oakway BR2: Brom 2F **159**
SW20 4E **152**
Oakway Cl. DA5: Bexl 6E **126**
Oakways SE9 6F **125**

Oakwood—Oldfield Rd.

OAKWOOD 4C 22
Oakwood SM6: Wall 7F 167
Oakwood Av. BR2: Brom 3K 159
BR3: Beck 2E 158
CR4: Mitc 2B 154
N14 7C 22
UB1: S'hall 7E 76
Oakwood Bus. Pk.
NW10 4K 79
Oakwood Cl. BR7: Chst 6D 142
IG8: Wfd G 6H 37
N14 6B 22
SE13 6F 123
Oakwood Ct. E6 1C 88
HA1: Harr 6H 41
W14 3H 99
Oakwood Cres. N21 6D 22
UB6: G'frd 6A 60
Oakwood Dr. DA7: Bex 4J 127
HA8: Edg 6D 28
SE19 6D 138
Oakwood Gdns. BR6: Farnb 2G 173
IG3: Ilf 2K 71
SM1: Sutt 2J 165
Oakwood Ho. E9 6J 67
(off Frampton Pk. Rd.)
Oakwood La. W14 3H 99
Oakwood Lodge N14 6B 22
(off Avenue Rd.)
Oakwood Mans. W14 3H 99
(off Oakwood Ct.)
Oakwood Pde. EN4: Cockf 5B 22
Oakwood Pk. Rd. N14 7C 22
Oakwood Pl. CR0: C'don 6A 156
Oakwood Rd. BR6: Farnb 2G 173
CR0: C'don 6A 156
HA5: Pinn 2K 39
NW11 4J 45
SW20 1C 152
Oakwood Vw. N14 6C 22
Oakworth Rd. W10 5E 80
Oarsman Pl. KT8: E Mos 4J 149
Oasis, The BR1: Brom 2A 160
Oasis Sports Cen. 7E 6 (6J 83)
Oast Ct. E14 7B 86
(off Newell St.)
Oast Lodge W4 7A 98
(off Corney Reach Way)
Oates Cl. BR2: Brom 3F 159
Oatfield Ho. N15 6E 48
(off Perry Ct.)
Oatfield Rd. BR6: Orp 1K 173
Oatland Ri. E17 2A 50
Oatlands Dr. KT13: Weyb 7G 147
Oatlands Rd. EN3: Enf H 1D 24
Oat La. EC2 7C 8 (6C 84)
Oatwell Ho. SW3 4D 16
(off Cale St.)
Oban Cl. E13 4A 88
Oban Ho. E14 6F 87
(off Oban St.)
IG11: Bark 2H 89
Oban Rd. E13 3A 88
SE25 4D 156
Oban St. E14 6F 87
Oberon Ho. N1 2E 84
(off Arden Est.)
Oberon Way TW17: Shep 3A 146
Oberstein Rd. SW11 4B 118
Oborne Cl. SE24 5B 120
O'Brien Ho. E2 3K 85
(off Roman Rd.)
Observatory Gdns. W8 2J 99
Observatory M. E14 4F 105
Observatory Rd. SW7 2A 16 (3B 100)
SW14 4J 115
Occupation La. SE18 1F 125
W5 4D 96
Occupation Rd.
KT19: Ewe 7K 163
SE17 5C 102
W13 2B 96
Ocean Est. E1 5A 86
(Ben Jonson Rd.)
E1 4K 85
(Ernest St.)
Oceanis Apartments E16 7J 87
(off Seagull La.)
Ocean Music Venue 6H 67
(off Mare St.)
Ocean St. E1 5K 85
Ocean Wharf E14 2B 104
Ockbrook E1 5J 85
(off Hannibal Rd.)
Ockendon M. N1 6D 66
Ockendon Rd. N1 6D 66
Ockham Dr. BR5: St P 7A 144
UB6: G'frd 7G 59
Ockley Ct. DA14: Sidc 3J 143
SM1: Sutt 4A 166
Ockley Rd. CR0: C'don 7K 155
SW16 4J 137
Octagon, The SW10 7K 99
(off Coleridge Gdns.)
Octagon Arc. EC2 6G 9 (5E 84)
Octagon Ct. SE16 1K 103
(off Rotherhithe St.)
Octavia Cl. CR4: Mitc 5C 154
Octavia Ho. SW1 2C 18
(off Medway St.)
W10 4G 81
Octavia M. W9 4H 81
Octavia Rd. TW7: Isle 3J 113
Octavia St. SW11 1C 118
Octavia Way SE28 7B 90
Octavius St. SE8 7C 104
October Pl. NW4 3F 45
Odard Rd. KT8: W Mole 4E 148
Oddmark Ho.
IG11: Bark 2H 89
Odelia Ct. E15 1E 86
(off Biggerstaff Rd.)
Odell Cl. IG11: Bark 7K 71
Odell Wlk. SE13 3E 122
Odeon, The IG11: Bark 7H 71
Odeon Cinema
Barnet 5D 20
Beckenham 2B 158
Camden Town 1F 83
(off Parkway)
Covent Garden 6H 83
(off Shaftesbury Av.)
Edmonton 7E 24
Eltham Pk. 4C 124
(off Well Hall Rd.)
Greenwich 4H 105
Holloway 3J 65
Kensington 3J 99
Kingston upon Thames 2E 150
(in The Rotunda Cen.)
Leicester Square 3D 12
(off Leicester Sq.)
Marble Arch 6D 82
(off Marble Arch)
Muswell Hill 4F 47
Panton Street 3D 12
(off Panton St.)
Putney 3G 117
Richmond, Hill Street 5D 114
Richmond, Red Lion Street
5D 114
South Woodford 2J 51
Streatham 3J 137
Surrey Quays 3K 103
Swiss Cottage 7B 64
Tottenham Court Road 5H 83
(off Tottenham Ct. Rd.)
West End 3D 12
(off Leicester Sq.)
Whiteleys 6K 81
Wimbledon 6H 135
Odeon Ct. E16 5J 87
NW10 1A 80
(off St Albans Rd.)
Odeon Pde. SE9 4C 124
(off Well Hall Rd.)
UB6: G'frd 6B 60
(off Allendale Rd.)
W3 2G 97
(off Allendale Rd.)
Odessa Rd. E7 3H 69
NW10 2C 80
Odessa St. SE16 2B 104
Odessa Wharf SE16 3B 104
(off Odessa St.)
Odette Duval Ho. E1 5J 85
(off Stepney Way)
Odger St. SW11 2D 118
Odhams Wlk. WC2 1F 13 (6J 83)
Odin Ho. SE5 2C 120
O'Donnell Ct. WC1 3F 7 (4J 83)
Odontological Mus., The 7H 7
(within Royal College of Surgeons)
O'Driscoll Ho. W12 6D 80
Odyssey Bus. Pk. HA4: Ruis 5K 57
Offa's Mead E9 4B 68
Offenbach Ho. E2 2K 85
(off Mace St.)
Offenham Rd. SE9 4D 142
Offers Ct. KT1: King T 3F 151
Offerton Rd. SW4 3G 119
Offham Ho. SE17 4E 102
(off Beckway St.)
Offham Slope N12 5C 30
Offley Pl. TW7: Isle 2H 113
Offley Rd. SW9 7A 102
Offord Cl. N17 6B 34
Offord Rd. N1 7K 65
Offord St. N1 7K 65
Ogden Ho. TW13: Hanw 3C 130
Ogilby St. SE18 4D 106
Ogilvie Ho. E1 6K 85
(off Stepney C'way.)
Oglander Rd. SE15 4F 121
Ogle St. W1 5A 6 (5G 83)
Oglethorpe Rd. RM10: Dag 3F 73
O'Gorman Ho. SW10 7A 100
(off King's Rd.)
O'Grady Ho. E17 3D 50
Ohio Bldg. SE10 1D 122
(off Deal's Gateway)
Ohio Cotts. HA5: Pinn 2A 40
Ohio Rd. E13 4H 87
Oil Mill La. W6 5C 98
Okeburn Rd. SW17 5E 136
Okehampton Cl. N12 5G 31
Okehampton Cres. DA16: Well 1B 126
Okehampton Rd. NW10 1E 80
Olaf Ct. W8 2J 99
(off Kensington Chu. St.)
Olaf St. W11 7F 81
Oldacre M. SW12 7E 118
Old Bailey
Central Criminal Court
7B 8 (6B 84)
Old Bailey EC4 1B 14 (6B 84)
Old Barge Ho. All. SE1 3K 13
Old Barn Cl. SM2: Cheam 7G 165
Old Barn Way DA7: Bex 3K 127
Old Barracks W8 2K 99
Old Barrack Yd. SW1 7G 11 (2E 100)
(not continuous)
Old Barrowfield E15 1G 87
Old Bellgate Pl. E14 3C 104
Oldberry Rd. HA8: Edg 6E 28
Old Bethnal Grn. Rd. E2 3G 85
OLD BEXLEY 7H 127
Old Bexley Bus. Pk. DA5: Bexl 7H 127
Old Bexley La. DA5: Bexl, Dart 2K 145
Old Billingsgate Mkt. EC3 3F 15
Old Billingsgate Wlk. EC3 3G 15 (7E 84)
Old Bond St. W1 3A 12 (7G 83)
Oldborough Rd. HA0: Wemb 3C 60
OLD BRENTFORD 7D 96
Old Brewer's Yd. WC2 1E 12 (6J 83)
Old Brewery M. NW3 4B 64
Old Bridge Cl. UB5: N'olt 2E 76
Old Bridge St. KT1: Ham W 2D 150
Old Broad St. EC2 7F 9 (6D 84)
Old Bromley Rd. BR1: Brom 5F 141
Old Brompton Rd. SW5 5J 99
SW7 4A 16 (5J 99)
Old Bldgs. WC2 7J 7
Old Burlington St. W1 2A 12 (7G 83)
Oldbury Ho. W2 5K 81
(off Harrow Rd.)
Oldbury Pl. W1 5H 5 (5E 82)
Oldbury Rd. EN1: Enf 2B 24
Old Canal M. SE15 5F 103
(off Trafalgar Av.)
Old Castle St. E1 7J 9 (6F 85)
Old Cavendish St. W1 7J 5 (6F 83)
Old Change Ct. EC4 1C 14
Old Chapel Pl. SW9 2A 120
Old Charlton Rd.
TW17: Shep 5E 146
Old Chelsea M. SW3 7C 16 (6C 100)
Old Chiswick Yd. W4 6A 98
(off Pumping Sta. Rd.)
Old Church Ct. N11 5A 32
Oldchurch Gdns. RM7: Rush G 7K 55
Old Church La. HA7: Stan 5G 27
NW9 2K 61
UB6: G'frd 3A 78
Oldchurch Ri. RM7: Rush G 7K 55
Old Church Rd. E1 6K 85
E4 4H 35
Oldchurch Rd. RM7: Rush G 7K 55
Old Church St. SW3 6B 16 (5B 100)
Old Claygate La. KT10: Clay 6A 162
Old Clem Sq. SE18 6E 106
(off Woolwich Comn.)
Old Coal Yd. SE28 4H 107
Old College Ct. DA17: Belv 5H 109
Old Compton St. W1 2C 12 (7H 83)
Old Cote Dr. TW5: Hest 6E 94
Old Court Ho. W8 2K 99
(off Old Court Pl.)
Old Court Pl. W8 2K 99
Old Courtyard, The BR1: Brom 1K 159
Old Curiosity Shop 7G 7
(off Portsmouth St.)
Old Dairy M. NW5 6F 65
SW12 1E 136
Old Dairy Sq. N21 7F 23
(off Wade Hill)
Old Deer Pk. 2C 114
Old Deer Pk. Gdns. TW9: Rich 3E 114
Old Devonshire Rd. SW12 7F 119
Old Dock Cl. TW9: Kew 6G 97
Old Dover Rd. SE3 7J 105
Oldegate Ho. E6 7B 70
Old Farm Av. DA15: Sidc 1H 143
N14 7B 22
Old Farm Cl. SW17 2C 136
TW4: Houn 4D 112
Old Farm Pas. TW12: Hamp 1G 149
Old Farm Rd. N2 1B 46
TW12: Hamp 6D 130
(not continuous)
UB7: W Dray 2A 92
Old Farm Rd. E. DA15: Sidc 2A 144
Old Farm Rd. W. DA15: Sidc 2K 143
Oldfield Cl. BR1: Brom 4D 160
HA7: Stan 5F 27
UB6: G'frd 5J 59
Oldfield Ct. KT5: Surb 4F 151
(off Cranes Pk. Cres.)
Oldfield Farm Gdns. UB6: G'frd 1H 77
Oldfield Gro. SE16 4K 103
Oldfield Ho. W4 5A 98
(off Devonshire Rd.)
Oldfield La. Nth. UB6: G'frd 2H 77
Oldfield La. Sth. UB6: G'frd 4G 77
Oldfield M. N6 7G 47
Oldfield Rd. BR1: Brom 4D 160
DA7: Bex 2E 126
N16 3E 66

Oldfield Rd. NW10 7B 62
SW19 6G 135
TW12: Hamp 1D 148
W3 2B 98
Oldfields Cir. UB5: N'olt 6G 59
Oldfields Rd. SM1: Sutt 3H 165
Oldfields Trad. Est. SM1: Sutt 3J 165
Old Fire Station, The SE18 7F 107
Old Fish St. Hill *EC4* *2C 14*
(off Queen Victoria St.)
Old Fleet La. EC4 7A 8 (6B 84)
Old Fold Cl. EN5: Barn 1C 20
Old Fold La. EN5: Barn 1C 20
Old Fold Vw. EN5: Barn 3A 20
OLD FORD 1B 86
OLD FORD 1C 86
Old Ford Rd. E2 2J 85
E3 2A 86
Old Ford Trading Cen. *E3* *1C 86*
(off Maverton Rd.)
Old Forge Cl. HA7: Stan 4F 27
Old Forge Cres. TW17: Shep 6D 146
Old Forge M. W12 2D 98
Old Forge Rd. EN1: Enf 1A 24
N19 2H 65
Old Forge Way DA14: Sidc 4B 144
Old Gloucester St. WC1 5F 7 (5J 83)
Old Goods Yd., The W2 5A 82
Old Hall Cl. HA5: Pinn 1C 40
Old Hall Dr. HA5: Pinn 1C 40
Oldham Ter. W3 1J 97
(not continuous)
Old Hatch Mnr. HA4: Ruis 7H 39
Old Hill BR6: Downe 6H 173
BR7: Chst 1E 160
Oldhill St. N16 1G 67
Old Homesdale Rd. BR2: Brom 4A 160
Old Hospital Cl. SW12 1D 136
Old House Cl. SW19 5G 135
Old House Gdns. TW1: Twick 6C 114
Old Howlett's La. HA4: Ruis 6F 39
OLD ISLEWORTH 3B 114
Old Jamaica Rd. SE16 7K 15 (3G 103)
Old James St. SE15 3H 121
Old Jewry EC2 1E 14 (6D 84)
Old Kenton La. NW9 5H 43
Old Kent Rd. SE1 4E 102
SE15 4E 102
Old Kingston Rd. KT4: Wor Pk 2J 163
Old Laundry, The BR7: Chst 1G 161
Old Lodge Pl. TW1: Twick 6B 114
Old Lodge Way HA7: Stan 5F 27
Old London Rd. DA14: Sidc, Swan 7G 145
KT2: King T 2E 150
Old Lyonian Sports Club *5G 41*
(off Pinner Vw.)
Old Maidstone Rd. DA14: Sidc 7F 145
OLD MALDEN 1A 164
Old Malden La. KT4: Wor Pk 2K 163
Old Manor Ct. NW8 2A 82
Old Manor Dr. TW7: Isle 6G 113
Old Manor Ho. M. TW17: Shep 3C 146
Old Manor Rd. UB2: S'hall 4B 94
Old Manor Way BR7: Chst 5D 142
DA7: Bex 2K 127
Old Manor Yd. SW5 4K 99
Old Market Ct. SM1: Sutt 4K 165
Old Market Sq. E2 1J 9 (3F 85)
Old Marylebone Rd. NW1 6D 4 (5C 82)
Oldmead Ho. RM10: Dag 6H 73
Old Mews HA1: Harr 5J 41
Old Mill Ct. E18 3A 52
Old Mill Pl. RM7: Rom 6K 55
Old Mill Rd. SE18 6H 107
Old Mitre Ct. EC4 1K 13 (6A 84)
Old Montague St. E1 6K 9 (5G 85)
Old Nichol St. E2 3J 9 (4F 85)
Old North St. WC1 5G 7
Old Nursery Ct. *E2* *2F 85*
(off Dunloe St.)
Old Nursery Pl. TW15: Ashf 5D 128
Old Oak Cl. KT9: Chess 4F 163
OLD OAK COMMON 5A 80
Old Oak Comn. La. NW10 5A 80
W3 5A 80
Old Oak La. NW10 3A 80
Old Oak Rd. W3 7B 80
Old Operating Theatre Mus. & Herb Garret 5F 15
Old Orchard TW16: Sun 2A 148
Old Orchard, The NW3 4D 64
Old Orchard Cl. EN4: Had W 1G 21
UB8: Hil 6C 74
Old Palace La. TW9: Rich 5C 114
Old Palace Rd. CR0: C'don 3B 168
Old Palace Ter. TW9: Rich 5D 114
Old Palace Yd. SW1 1E 18 (3J 101)
TW9: Rich 5C 114
Old Paradise St. SE11 3G 19 (4K 101)
Old Park Av. EN2: Enf 5H 23
SW12 6E 118
Old Park Gro. EN2: Enf 4H 23
Old Park La. W1 5J 11 (1F 101)
Old Park M. TW5: Hest 7D 94
Old Park Ridings N21 6G 23
Old Park Rd. EN2: Enf 3G 23
N13 4E 32
SE2 5A 108
Old Park Rd. Sth. EN2: Enf 4G 23
Old Park Vw. EN2: Enf 3F 23
Old Pearson St. SE10 7D 104
Old Perry St. BR7: Chst 6J 143
Old Police House, The 1D 100
Old Post Office La. SE3 3K 123
Old Post Office Wlk. *KT6: Surb* *6D 150*
(off Victoria Rd.)
Old Pound Cl. TW7: Isle 1A 114
Old Priory UB9: Hare 7D 38
Old Pye St. SW1 1C 18 (3H 101)
Old Pye St. Est. *SW1* *2C 18*
(off Old Pye St.)
Old Quebec St. W1 1F 11 (6D 82)
Old Queen St. SW1 7D 12 (2H 101)
Old Rectory Gdns. HA8: Edg 6B 28
Old Redding HA3: Hrw W 5A 26
Old Red Lion Theatre *1K 7*
(off St John St.)
Oldridge Rd. SW12 7E 118
Old Rd. DA1: Cray 5K 127
EN3: Enf H 1D 24
SE13 4G 123
Old Rope Wlk. TW16: Sun 3K 147
Old Royal Free Pl. N1 1A 84
Old Royal Free Sq. N1 1A 84
Old Royal Naval College 5F 105
Old Ruislip Rd. UB5: N'olt 2A 76
Old School, The *WC1* *5K 83*
(off Princeton St.)
Old School Cl. BR3: Beck 2K 157
SE10 3G 105
SW19 2J 153
Old School Ct. N17 3F 49
Old School Cres. E7 6J 69
Old School Pl. CR0: Wadd 4A 168
Old School Rd. UB8: Hil 4B 74
Old Schools La. KT17: Ewe 7B 164
Old School Sq. *E14* *6C 86*
(off Pelling St.)
KT7: T Ditt 6K 149
Old School Ter. SM3: Cheam 7F 165
Old Seacoal La. EC4 7A 8 (6B 84)
Old Slade La. SL0: Rich P 1A 174
SL3: Coln 1A 174
Old South Cl. HA5: Pinn 1B 40
Old Sth. Lambeth Rd. SW8 7J 101
Old Speech Room Gallery 1J 59
Old Spitalfields Market 5J 9 (5F 85)
Old Sq. WC2 7J 7 (6K 83)
Old Stable M. N5 3C 66
Old Stables Ct. *SE5* *1C 120*
(off Camberwell New Rd.)
Old Station Gdns. *TW11: Tedd* *6A 132*
(off Victoria Rd.)
Old Station Ho. SE17 5C 102
Old Station Pas. *TW9: Rich* *4D 114*
(off Little Green)
Old Station Rd. UB3: Harl 3H 93
Old Station Way *SW4* *3H 119*
(off Voltaire Rd.)
Old Station Yd., The E17 4E 50
Oldstead Rd. BR1: Brom 4E 140
Old Stockley Rd. UB7: W Dray 2D 92
OLD STREET 4D 84
Old St. E13 2K 87
EC1 3C 8 (4C 84)
Old Studio Cl. CR0: C'don 7D 156
Old Sungate Cotts.
RM5: Col R 1F 55
Old Sun Wharf *E14* *7A 86*
(off Narrow St.)
Old Swan Wharf SW11 1B 118
Old Swan Yd. SM5: Cars 4D 166
Old Theatre Ct. SE1 4D 14
Old Town CR0: C'don 3B 168
SW4 3G 119
Old Tramyard SE18 4J 107
Old Twelve Cl. W7 4J 77
Old Vic Theatre, The 6K 13
Old Woolwich Rd. SE10 6F 105
Old York Rd. SW18 5K 117
Oleander Cl. BR6: Farnb 5H 173
O'Leary Sq. E1 5J 85
Olga St. E3 2A 86
Olinda Rd. N16 6F 49
Oliphant St. W10 3F 81
Olive Blythe Ho. *W10* *4G 81*
(off Ladbroke Gro.)
Olive Ct. *E5* *2J 67*
(off Woodmill Rd.)
N1 *1A 84*
(off Liverpool Rd.)
Olive Gro. N15 4C 48
Olive Ho. *EC1* *3K 7*
(off Bowling Grn. La.)
Oliver Av. SE25 3F 157
Oliver Bus. Pk. NW10 2J 79
Oliver Cl. W4 6H 97
Oliver Ct. SE18 4G 107
Oliver Gdns. E6 5C 88
Oliver Goldsmith Est. SE15 1G 121
Oliver Gro. SE25 4F 157
Oliver Ho. *SE14* *7B 104*
(off New Cross Rd.)
SE16 *2G 103*
(off George Row)
SW8 *7J 101*
(off Wyvil Rd.)
Oliver M. SE15 2G 121
Olive Rd. E13 3A 88
NW2 4E 62
SW19 7A 136
W5 3D 96
Oliver Rd. E10 2D 68
E17 5E 50
KT3: N Mald 2J 151
NW10 2J 79
SM1: Sutt 4B 166
Olivers Wharf *E1* *1H 103*
(off Wapping High St.)
Olivers Yd. EC1 3F 9 (4D 84)
Olive St. RM7: Rom 5K 55
Olive Tree Ho. *SE15* *6J 103*
(off Sharratt St.)
Olivette St. SW15 3F 117
Olive Waite Ho. NW6 7J 63
Olivia Ct. *EN2: Enf* *1H 23*
(off Chase Side)
Olivia M. HA3: Hrw W 7D 26
Olivier Theatre *4H 13*
(in National Theatre)
Ollerton Grn. E3 1B 86
Ollerton Rd. N11 5C 32
Olley Cl. SM6: Wall 7J 167
Ollgar Cl. W12 1B 98
Olliffe St. E14 3E 104
Olmar St. SE1 6G 103
Olney Ho. *NW8* *3D 4*
(off Tresham Cres.)
Olney Rd. SE17 6B 102
(not continuous)
Olron Cres. DA6: Bex 5D 126
Olven Rd. SE18 6G 107
Olveston Wlk. SM5: Cars 6B 154
Olwen M. HA5: Pinn 2B 40
Olyffe Av. DA16: Well 1A 126
Olyffe Dr. BR3: Beck 1E 158
Olympia 3G 99
Olympia Ind. Est. N22 3K 47
Olympia M. W2 7K 81
Olympian Ct. *E3* *2C 86*
(off Wick La.)
E14 *4C 104*
(off Homer Dr.)
Olympia Way W14 3G 99
Olympic Ho. N16 4F 67
Olympic Sq. HA9: Wemb 3G 61
Olympic Way HA9: Wemb 3G 61
UB6: G'frd 1G 77
Olympus Gro. N22 1A 48
Olympus Sq. E5 3G 67
O'Mahoney Ct. SW17 3A 136
Oman Av. NW2 4E 62
O'Meara St. SE1 5D 14 (1C 102)
Omega Cl. E14 3D 104
Omega Ct. RM7: Rom 5K 55
Omega Ho. *SW10* *7A 100*
(off King's Rd.)
Omega Pl. N1 1F 7
Omega St. SE14 1C 122
Omega Works E3 7C 68
Ommaney Rd. SE14 1K 121
Omnibus Ho. *N22* *2A 48*
(off Lordship La.)
Omnibus Way E17 2C 50
Omnium Ct. *WC1* *5G 7*
(off Princeton St.)
Ondine Rd. SE15 4F 121
Onega Ga. SE16 3A 104
One Hyde Pk. SW1 7E 10 (2D 100)
O'Neill Ho. *NW8* *1B 4*
(off Cochrane St.)
O'Neill Path SE18 6E 106
One New Change EC4 1C 14 (6C 84)
One Owen St. *EC1* *1A 8*
(off Goswell St.)
One Tree Cl. SE23 6J 121
One Tree Hill Local Nature Reserve 6J 121
Ongar Cl. RM6: Chad H 5C 54
Ongar Rd. SW6 6J 99
Onra Rd. E17 7C 50
Onslow Av. TW10: Rich 5E 114
Onslow Cl. E4 2K 35
KT7: T Ditt 7J 149
W10 3H 81
Onslow Ct. SW10 6A 16
Onslow Cres. BR7: Chst 1F 161
SW7 4B 16 (4B 100)
Onslow Dr. DA14: Sidc 2D 144
Onslow Gdns. E18 3K 51
KT7: T Ditt 7J 149
N10 5F 47
N21 5F 23
SM6: Wall 6G 167
SW7 4A 16 (4B 100)
Onslow Ho. *KT2: King T* *1F 151*
(off Acre Rd.)
Onslow M. E. SW7 4A 16 (4B 100)
Onslow M. W. SW7 4A 16 (4B 100)
Onslow Pde. N14 1A 32
Onslow Rd. CR0: C'don 7K 155
KT3: N Mald 4C 152
TW10: Rich 5E 114
Onslow Sq. SW7 3B 16 (4B 100)
Onslow St. EC1 4K 7 (4A 84)
Onslow Way KT7: T Ditt 7J 149
Ontario St. SE1 3B 102
Ontario Twr. E14 7F 87

Ontario Way E14 . . . . .7C 86
(not continuous)
Onyx M. E15 . . . . .6H 69
Opal Cl. E16 . . . . .6B 88
Opal M. IG1: Ilf 2F 71
NW6 . . . . .1H 81
Opal St. SE11 . . . . .5K 19 (5B 102)
Open Air Stage 1C 64
Openshaw Rd. SE2 . . . . .4B 108
Openview SW18 . . . . .1A 136
Opera Ct. N19 .3H 65
(off Wedmore St.)
Ophelia Gdns. NW2 . . . . .3G 63
Ophelia Ho. W6 . . . . .5F 99
(off Fulham Pal. Rd.)
Ophir Ter. SE15 . . . . .1G 121
Opie Ho. NW8 .2C 82
(off Townshend Est.)
Opossum Way TW4: Houn 3A 112
Oppenheim Rd. SE13 . . . . .2E 122
Oppidan Apartments
NW6 . . . . .7J 63
(off Netherwood St.)
Oppidans Rd. NW3 . . . . .7D 64
Opulens Pl. HA6: Nwood 1D 38
Orange Ct. La. BR6: Downe 7E 172
Orange Gro. E11 . . . . .3G 69
Orange Hill Rd. HA8: Edg 7D 28
Orange Pl. SE16 . . . . .3J 103
Orangery, The TW10: Ham 2C 132
Orangery Gallery, The 2H 99
Orangery La. SE9 . . . . .5D 124
Orange St. WC2 . . . . .3D 12 (7H 83)
Orange Tree Ct. SE5 . . . . .7E 102
(off Havil St.)
Orange Tree Theatre 4E 114
Orange Yd. W1 . . . . .1D 12
Oransay Rd. N1 . . . . .6C 66
Oratory La. SW3 . . . . . . .5B 16 (5B 100)
Orbain Rd. SW6 . . . . .7G 99
Orbel St. SW11 . . . . .1C 118
Orbis Sq. SW11 . . . . .3B 118
Orbital Cen., The IG8: Wfd G 2B 52
Orb St. SE17 . . . . .4D 102
Orchard, The KT17: Ewe 7B 164
N14 . . . . .5A 22
N20 . . . . .1E 30
N21 . . . . .6J 23
NW11 . . . . .5J 45
SE3 . . . . .2F 123
TW3: Houn 2G 113
W4 . . . . .4K 97
W5 . . . . .5D 78
(off Montpelier Rd.)
Orchard Av. CRO: C'don 2A 170
CR4: Mitc 1E 166
DA17: Belv 6E 108
KT3: N Mald 2A 152
KT7: T Ditt 1A 162
N3 . . . . .3J 45
N14 . . . . .6B 22
N20 . . . . .2G 31
TW5: Hest 7C 94
TW14: Felt 5F 111
TW15: Ashf 6E 128
UB1: S'hall 1D 94
Orchard Bus. Cen. SE26 . . . . .5B 140
Orchard Cl. DA7: Bex 1E 126
E4 . . . . .4H 35
E11 . . . . .4K 51
HA0: Wemb 1E 78
HA4: Ruis 7E 38
HA8: Edg 6K 27
KT6: Surb 1B 162
KT12: Walt T 7K 147
KT19: Ewe 6H 163
N1 . . . . .7C 66
NW2 . . . . .3C 62
SE23 . . . . .6J 121
SW20 . . . . .4E 152
TW15: Ashf 6E 128
UB5: N'olt 6G 59

Orchard Cl. W10 . . . . .5H 81
WD23: B Hea 1C 26
Orchard Cotts. KT2: King T 1F 151
UB3: Hayes 2G 93
Orchard Ct. E10 . . . . .1D 68
EN5: New Bar 3E 20
HA8: Edg 5A 28
KT4: Wor Pk 1C 164
KT12: Walt T 7H 147
(off Bridge St.)
N14 . . . . .6B 22
SM6: Wall 5F 167
TW2: Twick 2H 131
TW7: Isle 1H 113
UB7: Lford 3D 174
UB8: Uxb 2A 74
(off The Greenway)
Orchard Cres. EN1: Enf 1A 24
HA8: Edg 5D 28
Orchard Dr. HA8: Edg 5A 28
SE3 . . . . .2F 123
TW17: Shep 3G 147
Orchard Gdns. KT9: Chess 4E 162
SM1: Sutt 5J 165
Orchard Ga. KT10: Esh 7H 149
NW9 . . . . .4A 44
UB6: G'frd 6B 60
Orchard Grn. BR6: Orp 2J 173
Orchard Gro. BR6: Orp 2K 173
CRO: C'don 7A 158
HA3: Kenton 5F 43
HA8: Edg 1G 43
SE20 . . . . .7G 139
Orchard Hill DA1: Cray 5K 127
SE13 . . . . .2D 122
SM5: Cars 5D 166
Orchard Ho. SE5 . . . . .1C 120
(off County Gro.)
SE16 . . . . .3J 103
SW6 . . . . .7H 99
(off Varna Rd.)
W1 . . . . .7G 5
(off Fitzhardinge St.)
W12 . . . . .1C 98
Orchard La. IG8: Wfd G 4F 37
KT8: E Mos 6H 149
SW20 . . . . .1D 152
Orchardleigh Av. EN3: Enf H 2D 24
Orchard Mead Ho. NW2 . . . . .2J 63
Orchardmede N21 . . . . .6J 23
Orchard M. N1 . . . . .7D 66
N6 . . . . .7F 47
SW17 . . . . .3A 136
Orchard Pl. BR2: Kes 7A 172
E5 . . . . .5H 67
E14 . . . . .7G 87
(not continuous)
N17 . . . . .7A 34
Orchard Ri. CRO: C'don 1A 170
HA5: Eastc 3H 39
KT2: King T 1J 151
TW10: Rich 4H 115
Orchard Ri. E. DA15: Sidc 5K 125
Orchard Ri. W. DA15: Sidc 5J 125
Orchard Rd. BR1: Brom 1A 160
BR6: Farnb 5F 173
CR4: Mitc 1E 166
DA14: Sidc 4J 143
DA16: Well 3B 126
DA17: Belv 4G 109
EN3: Pond E 5D 24
EN5: Barn 4C 20
KT1: King T 2E 150
KT9: Chess 4E 162
N6 . . . . .7F 47
RM7: Mawney 1H 55
RM10: Dag 1G 91
SE3 . . . . .2G 123
SE18 . . . . .4H 107
SM1: Sutt 5J 165
TW1: Twick 5A 114
TW4: Houn 5D 112

Orchard Rd. TW8: Bford 6C 96
TW9: Rich 3G 115
TW12: Hamp 7D 130
TW14: Felt 1J 129
TW16: Sun 7K 129
UB3: Hayes 7J 75
Orchardson Ho. NW8 . . . . .4A 4
Orchardson St. NW8 . . . . . . .4A 4 (4B 82)
Orchard Sq. W14 . . . . .5H 99
Orchard St. E17 . . . . .4A 50
W1 . . . . .1G 11 (6E 82)
Orchard Studios W6 . . . . .4F 99
(off Brook Grn.)
Orchard Ter. EN1: Enf 6B 24
NW10 . . . . .4B 62
Orchard Vs. DA14: Sidc 6C 144
Orchard Wlk. KT2: King T 1G 151
(off Gordon Rd.)
Orchard Way BR3: Beck 1A 170
CRO: C'don 1A 170
EN1: Enf 3K 23
SM1: Sutt 4B 166
TW15: Ashf 2B 128
Orchard Waye UB8: Uxb 2A 74
Orchard Wharf E14 . . . . .7G 87
(off Orchard Pl.)
Orchestra Ct. HA8: Edg 7C 28
Orchid Cl. E6 .5C 88
KT9: Chess 7C 162
SE13 . . . . .5F 123
UB1: S'hall 7C 76
Orchid Ct. HA9: Wemb 2E 60
Orchid Gdns. TW3: Houn 4D 112
Orchid Grange N14 . . . . .7B 22
Orchid Rd. N14 . . . . .7B 22
Orchid St. W12 . . . . .7C 80
Orde NW9 . . . . .1B 44
Orde Hall St. WC1 . . . . .4G 7 (4K 83)
Ordell Ct. E3 .2B 86
(off Ordell Rd.)
Ordell Rd. E3 .2B 86
Ordnance Cl. TW13: Felt 2J 129
Ordnance Cres. SE10 . . . . .2G 105
Ordnance Hill NW8 . . . . .1B 82
Ordnance M. NW8 . . . . .2B 82
Ordnance Rd. E16 . . . . .5H 87
SE18 . . . . .6E 106
SW20 . . . . .1K 153
Oregano Cl. UB7: Yiew 6A 74
Oregano Dr. E14 . . . . .6F 87
Oregon Av. E12 . . . . .4D 70
Oregon Bldg. SE10 . . . . .1D 122
(off Deal's Gateway)
Oregon Cl. KT3: N Mald 4J 151
Oregon Sq. BR6: Orp 1H 173
Orestes M. NW6 . . . . .5J 63
Orford Ct. HA7: Stan 6H 27
SE27 . . . . .2B 138
Orford Gdns. TW1: Twick 2K 131
Orford Rd. E17 . . . . .5C 50
E18 . . . . .3K 51
SE6 . . . . .3D 140
ORGAN CROSSROADS 7C 164
Organ La. E4 .2K 35
Oriana Ho. E14 . . . . .7B 86
(off Victory Pl.)
Oriel Cl. CR4: Mitc 4H 155
Oriel Ct. CRO: C'don 1D 168
NW3 . . . . .4A 64
Oriel Dr. SW13 . . . . .6E 98
Oriel Gdns. IG5: Ilf 3D 52
Oriel Ho. NW6 . . . . .1J 81
(off Priory Pk. Rd.)
RM7: Rom 6K 55
Oriel M. E18 .2J 51
Oriel Pl. NW3 . . . . .4A 64
(off Heath St.)
Oriel Rd. E9 . . . . .6K 67
Oriel Way UB5: N'olt 7F 59
Oriental City NW9 . . . . .3K 43
Oriental Rd. E16 . . . . .1B 106
Oriental St. E14 . . . . .7C 86
(off Pennyfields)

Orient Ho. SW6 . . . . .1A 118
(off Station Ct.)
Orient Ind. Pk. E10 . . . . .2C 68
Orient St. SE11 . . . . .4B 102
Orient Way E5 . . . . .3K 67
E10 . . . . .1A 68
Orient Wharf E1 . . . . .1J 103
(off Wapping High St.)
Oriole Way SE28 . . . . .7B 90
Orion E14 . . . . .4C 104
(off Crews St.)
Orion Bus. Cen. SE14 . . . . .5K 103
Orion Cen., The CRO: Bedd 2J 167
Orion Ho. E1 .4H 85
(off Coventry Rd.)
Orion Rd. N11 . . . . .7K 31
Orissa Rd. SE18 . . . . .5J 107
Orkney Ho. N1 . . . . .1K 83
(off Bemerton Est.)
Orkney St. SW11 . . . . .2E 118
Orlando Rd. SW4 . . . . .3G 119
Orleans Ct. TW1: Twick 7B 114
Orleans House Gallery 1B 132
Orleans Pk. School Sports Cen. 7B 114
(off Richmond Rd.)
Orleans Rd. SE19 . . . . .6D 138
TW1: Twick 7B 114
Orleston M. N7 . . . . .6A 66
Orleston Rd. N7 . . . . .6A 66
Orley Cl. HA1: Harr 4K 59
Orley Farm Rd. HA1: Harr 3J 59
Orlop St. SE10 . . . . .5G 105
Ormanton Rd. SE26 . . . . .4G 139
Orme Ct. W2 .7K 81
Orme Ct. M. W2 . . . . .7K 81
(off Orme La.)
Orme Ho. E8 .1F 85
Orme La. W2 .7K 81
Ormeley Rd. SW12 . . . . .1F 137
Orme Rd. KT1: King T 2H 151
SM1: Sutt 6K 165
Ormerod Gdns. CR4: Mitc 2E 154
Ormesby Cl. SE28 . . . . .7D 90
Ormesby Way HA3: Kenton 6F 43
Orme Sq. W2 .7K 81
Ormiston Gro. W12 . . . . .1D 98
Ormiston Rd. SE10 . . . . .5J 105
Ormond Av. TW10: Rich 5D 114
TW12: Hamp 1F 149
Ormond Cl. WC1 . . . . .5F 7 (5J 83)
Ormond Cres. TW12: Hamp 1F 149
Ormond Dr. TW12: Hamp 7F 131
Ormonde Av. BR6: Farnb 2G 173
Ormonde Ct. NW8 . . . . .1D 82
(off St Edmund's Cl.)
SW15 . . . . .4E 116
Ormonde Ga. SW3 . . . . . . .6F 17 (5D 100)
(not continuous)
Ormonde Mans. WC1 . . . . .5F 7
(off Southampton Row)
Ormonde Pl. SW1 . . . . .4G 17 (4E 100)
Ormonde Ri. IG9: Buck H 1F 37
Ormonde Rd. SW14 . . . . .3J 115
Ormonde Ter. NW8 . . . . .1D 82
Ormond Ho. N16 . . . . .2D 66
Ormond M. WC1 . . . . .4F 7 (4J 83)
Ormond Rd. N19 . . . . .1J 65
TW10: Rich 5D 114
Ormond Yd. SW1 . . . . .4B 12 (1G 101)
Ormrod Ct. W11 . . . . .6G 81
(off Westbourne Pk. Rd.)
Ormsby SM2: Sutt 7K 165
Ormsby Gdns. UB6: G'frd 2G 77
Ormsby Lodge W4 . . . . .3A 98
Ormsby Pl. N16 . . . . .3F 67
Ormsby Point SE18 . . . . .4F 107
(off Vincent Rd.)
Ormsby St. E2 . . . . .2F 85
Ormside St. SE15 . . . . .6J 103
Ornan Rd. NW3 . . . . .5C 64
Orpen Ho. SW5 . . . . .4J 99
(off Trebovir Rd.)

Orpen Wlk. N16 3E 66
Orpheus St. SE5 1D 120
ORPINGTON 2J 173
Orpington Gdns. N18 3K 33
Orpington Mans. N21 1G 33
Orpington Rd. BR7: Chst 3J 161
N21 1G 33
Orpwood Cl. TW12: Hamp 6D 130
Orsett M. W2 6K 81
(not continuous)
Orsett St. SE11 5H 19 (5K 101)
Orsett Ter. IG8: Wfd G 7F 37
W2 6K 81
Orsman Rd. N1 1E 84
Orton Gro. EN1: Enf 1B 24
Orton St. E1 1G 103
Orville Rd. SW11 2B 118
Orwell Cl. RM13: Rain 5K 91
UB3: Hayes 7G 75
Orwell Ct. *E8* *1G 85*
(off Pownall Rd.)
N5 4C 66
SW17 *3B 136*
(off Grosvenor Way)
Orwell Rd. E13 2A 88
Osbaldeston Rd. N16 2G 67
Osberton Rd. SE12 5J 123
Osbert St. SW1 4C 18 (4H 101)
Osborn Cl. E8 1G 85
Osborne Av. TW19: Stanw 1A 128
Osborne Cl. BR3: Beck 4A 158
EN4: Cockf 3J 21
TW13: Hanw 5B 130
Osborne Ct. E10 7D 50
W5 5E 78
Osborne Gdns. CR7: Thor H 2C 156
Osborne Gro. E17 4B 50
N4 1A 66
Osborne Ho. *E16* *1J 105*
(off Wesley Av.)
Osborne M. E17 4B 50
Osborne Pl. SM1: Sutt 5B 166
Osborne Rd. CR7: Thor H 2C 156
DA17: Belv 5F 109
E7 5K 69
E9 6B 68
E10 2D 68
EN3: Enf H 2F 25
IG9: Buck H 1E 36
KT2: King T 7E 132
KT12: Walt T 7J 147
N4 1A 66
N13 3F 33
NW2 6D 62
RM9: Dag 5F 73
TW3: Houn 3D 112
UB1: S'hall 6G 77
W3 3H 97
Osborne Sq. RM9: Dag 4F 73
Osborne Ter. *SW17* *5D 136*
(off Church La.)
Osborne Way KT9: Chess 5F 163
Osborn Gdns. NW7 7A 30
Osborn La. SE23 7A 122
Osborn St. E1 6K 9 (5F 85)
Osborn Ter. SE3 4H 123
Osbourne Ct. HA2: Harr 4F 41
Osbourne Ho. IG8: Wfd G 7K 37
TW2: Twick 2G 131
Oscar Faber Pl. N1 7E 66
Oscar St. SE8 2C 122
(not continuous)
Oseney Cres. NW5 5G 65
Osgood Av. BR6: Chels 5K 173
Osgood Gdns. BR6: Chels 5K 173
OSIDGE 1A 32
Osidge La. N14 1K 31
Osier Ct. *E1* *4K 85*
(off Osier St.)
RM7: Rom 6K 55
TW8: Bford *6E 96*
(off Ealing Rd.)
Osier Cres. N10 1D 46
Osier La. SE10 3H 105
Osier M. W4 6A 98
Osiers Ct. *KT1: King T* *1D 150*
(off Steadfast Rd.)
Osiers Est., The SW18 4J 117
Osiers Rd. SW18 4J 117
Osier St. E1 4J 85
Osier Way CR4: Mitc 5D 154
E10 3D 68
Oslac Rd. SE6 5D 140
Oslo Ct. *NW8* *2C 82*
(off Prince Albert Rd.)
Oslo Ho. *SE5* *2C 120*
(off Carew St.)
Oslo Sq. SE16 3A 104
Osman Cl. N15 6D 48
Osmani School Sports Cen. 5G 85
Osman Rd. N9 3B 34
W6 3E 98
Osmington Ho. *SW8* *7K 101*
(off Dorset Rd.)
Osmond Cl. HA2: Harr 2G 59
Osmond Gdns. SM6: Wall 5G 167
Osmund St. W12 5B 80
Osnaburgh St. NW1 4K 5 (4F 83)
(Euston Rd.)
NW1 2K 5
(Robert St.)
Osnaburgh Ter. NW1 3K 5 (4F 83)
Osney Ho. SE2 2D 108
Osney Wlk. SM5: Cars 6B 154
Osprey NW9 1B 44
Osprey Cl. BR2: Brom 1C 172
E6 5C 88
E11 4J 51
E17 7F 35
SM1: Sutt 5H 165
UB7: W Dray 2A 92
Osprey Ct. BR3: Beck 7C 140
E1 *3K 15*
(off Star Pl.)
Osprey Est. SE16 4A 104
Osprey Ho. *E14* *7A 86*
(off Victory Pl.)
SE1 *5H 103*
(off Lynton Rd.)
Osprey M. EN3: Pond E 5D 24
Ospringe Cl. SE20 7J 139
Ospringe Ct. SE9 6H 125
Ospringe Ho. *SE1* *6K 13*
(off Wootton St.)
Ospringe Rd. NW5 4G 65
Osram Ct. W6 3E 98
Osram Rd. HA9: Wemb 3D 60
Osric Path N1 2E 84
Ossian M. N4 7K 47
Ossian Rd. N4 7K 47
Ossie Garvin Rdbt.
UB4: Yead 7K 75
Ossington Bldgs. W1 5G 5 (5E 82)
Ossington Cl. W2 7J 81
Ossington St. W2 7J 81
Ossory Rd. SE1 6G 103
Ossulston St. NW1 1D 6 (2H 83)
Ossulton Pl. N2 3A 46
Ossulton Way N2 4A 46
Ostade Rd. SW2 7K 119
Ostell Cres. EN3: Enf L 1H 25
Ostend Pl. SE1 4C 102
Osten M. SW7 3K 99
OSTERLEY 7H 95
Osterley Av. TW7: Isle 7H 95
Osterley Cl. BR5: St P 1K 161
Osterley Ct. TW7: Isle 1H 113
UB5: N'olt *3A 76*
(off Canberra Dr.)
Osterley Cres. TW7: Isle 1J 113
Osterley Gdns. CR7: Thor H 2C 156
UB2: S'hall 2G 95
Osterley Ho. *E14* *6D 86*
(off Girauld St.)
Osterley La. TW7: Isle 4G 95
UB2: S'hall 5E 94
(not continuous)
Osterley Lodge *TW7: Isle* *7J 95*
(off Church Rd.)
Osterley Pk. 6G 95
Osterley Pk. House 6G 95
Osterley Pk. Rd. UB2: S'hall 3D 94
Osterley Pk. Vw. Rd. W7 2J 95
Osterley Rd. N16 4E 66
TW7: Isle 7J 95
Osterley Sports Club 3G 95
Osterley Views UB2: S'hall 1G 95
Oster Ter. E17 5K 49
Ostlers Dr. TW15: Ashf 5E 128
Ostliffe Rd. N13 5H 33
Oswald Bldg. SW8 6F 101
Oswald Rd. UB1: S'hall 1C 94
Oswald's Mead E9 4A 68
Oswald St. E5 3K 67
Oswald Ter. NW2 3E 62
Osward CR0: Sels 7B 170
Osward Pl. N9 2C 34
Osward Rd. SW17 2D 136
Oswell Ho. *E1* *1H 103*
(off Farthing Flds.)
Oswin St. SE11 4B 102
Oswyth Rd. SE5 2E 120
Otford Cl. BR1: Brom 3E 160
DA5: Bexl 6H 127
SE20 1J 157
Otford Cres. SE4 6B 122
Otford Ho. *SE1* *7F 15*
(off Staple St.)
SE15 *6J 103*
(off Lovelinch Cl.)
Othello Cl. SE11 5K 19 (5B 102)
Otho Ct. TW8: Bford 7D 96
Otis St. E3 3E 86
Otley App. IG2: Ilf 6F 53
Otley Dr. IG2: Ilf 5F 53
Otley Ho. N5 3A 66
Otley Rd. E16 6A 88
Otley Ter. E5 3K 67
Ottawa Gdns. RM10: Dag 7K 73
Ottaway Ct. E5 3G 67
Ottaway St. E5 3G 67
Otterbourne Rd.
CR0: C'don 2C 168
E4 3A 36
Otterburn Gdns. TW7: Isle 7A 96
Otterburn Ho. *SE5* *7C 102*
(off Sultan St.)
Otterburn St. SW17 6D 136
Otter Cl. E15 1E 86
Otterden Cl. BR6: Orp 3J 173
Otterden St. SE6 4C 140
Otterfield Rd. UB7: Yiew 7A 74
Otter Rd. UB6: G'frd 4G 77
Otto Cl. SE26 3H 139
Otto St. SE17 6B 102
Otway Gdns. WD23: Bush 1D 26
Oulton Cl. E5 2J 67
SE28 6C 90
Oulton Cres. IG11: Bark 5K 71
Oulton Rd. N15 5D 48
Ouseley Rd. SW12 1D 136
Outer Circ. NW1 1D 4 & 1J 5 (2C 82)
Outgate Rd. NW10 7B 62
Outram Pl. N1 1J 83
Outram Rd. CR0: C'don 2F 169
E6 1C 88
N22 1H 47
Outwich St. EC3 7H 9
Outwood Ho. *SW2* *7K 119*
(off Deepdene Gdns.)
Oval, The DA15: Sidc 7A 126
E2 2H 85
Oval Ct. HA8: Edg 7D 28
Oval Cricket Ground, The 7H 19 (6K 101)
Oval Ho. *CR0: C'don* *1E 168*
(off Oval Rd.)
Oval House Theatre *7J 19*
(off Kennington Oval)
Oval Mans. SE11 7H 19 (6K 101)
Oval Pl. SW8 7K 101
Oval Rd. CR0: C'don 2D 168
NW1 1F 83
Oval Rd. Nth. RM10: Dag 1H 91
Oval Rd. Sth. RM10: Dag 2H 91
Oval Way SE11 6H 19 (5K 101)
Ovanna M. N1 6E 66
Overbrae BR3: Beck 6C 140
Overbrook Wlk. HA8: Edg 7B 28
(not continuous)
Overbury Av. BR3: Beck 3D 158
Overbury Rd. N15 6D 48
Overbury St. E5 4K 67
Overcliff Rd. SE13 3C 122
Overcourt Cl. DA15: Sidc 6B 126
Overdale Av. KT3: N Mald 2J 151
Overdale Rd. W5 3C 96
Overdown Rd. SE6 4C 140
Overhill Rd. SE22 7G 121
Overhill Way BR3: Beck 5F 159
Overlea Rd. E5 7G 49
Overmead DA15: Sidc 7H 125
Oversley Ho. *W2* *5J 81*
(off Alfred Rd.)
Overstand Cl. BR3: Beck 5C 158
Overstone Gdns. CR0: C'don 7B 158
Overstone Ho. *E14* *6C 86*
(off E. India Dock Rd.)
Overstone Rd. W6 3E 98
Overstrand Mans. SW11 1D 118
Overton Cl. NW10 6J 61
TW7: Isle 1K 113
Overton Ct. E11 7J 51
SM2: Sutt 7J 165
Overton Dr. E11 7J 51
RM6: Chad H 7C 54
Overton Ho. *SW15* *7B 116*
(off Tangley Gro.)
Overton Rd. E10 1A 68
N14 5D 22
SE2 3C 108
SM2: Sutt 6J 165
SW9 2A 120
Overton Rd. E. SE2 3D 108
Overton's Yd. CR0: C'don 3C 168
Overy Ho. SE1 7A 14 (2B 102)
Ovesdon Av. HA2: Harr 1D 58
Ovett Cl. SE19 6E 138
Ovex Cl. E14 2E 104
Ovington Ct. *SW3* *2D 16*
(off Brompton Rd.)
Ovington Gdns. SW3 2D 16 (3C 100)
Ovington M. SW3 2D 16
Ovington Sq. SW3 2D 16 (3C 100)
Ovington St. SW3 3D 16 (4C 100)
Owen Cl. CR0: C'don 6D 156
SE28 1C 108
UB5: N'olt 6C 58
(Arnold Rd.)
UB5: N'olt 3K 75
(Attlee Rd.)
Owen Gdns. IG8: Wfd G 6H 37
Owen Ho. TW1: Twick 7B 114
TW14: Felt 7J 111
Owenite St. SE2 4B 108
Owen Mans. *W14* *6G 99*
(off Queen's Club Gdns.)
Owen Rd. N13 5H 33
UB4: Yead 3K 75
Owens M. E11 2G 69
Owen's Row EC1 1A 8 (3B 84)
Owen St. EC1 1A 8 (2B 84)
Owens Way SE23 7A 122
Owen Wlk. SE20 1G 157
Owen Way NW10 6J 61
Owgan Cl. SE5 7D 102
Oxberry Av. SW6 2G 117
Oxendon St. SW1 3C 12 (7H 83)
Oxenford St. SE15 3F 121

Oxenham Ho. *SE8* 6C *104*
  (off Benbow St.)
Oxenholme *NW1* 1A *6*
  (off Hampstead Rd.)
Oxenpark Av. HA9: Wemb 7E *42*
Oxestall's Rd. SE8 . . . . .5A *104*
Oxford & Cambridge Mans. *NW1* 6D *4*
  (off Old Marylebone Rd.)
Oxford Av. N14 . . . . .1B *32*
  NW10 . . . . .3D *80*
  SW20 . . . . .2G *153*
  TW5: Hest 5E *94*
  UB3: Harl .7H *93*
Oxford Cir. W1 . . . . .1A *12*
Oxford Cir. Av. W1 . . . . . . .1A *12* (6G *83*)
Oxford Cir. CR4: Mitc 3G *155*
  N9 . . . . .2C *34*
  TW15: Ashf 7E *128*
Oxford Ct. EC4 . . . . .2E *14*
  TW13: Hanw 4B *130*
  W3 . . . . .6G *79*
  W4 . . . . .5H *97*
  W7 . . . . .5K *77*
  (off Copley Cl.)
  W9 . . . . .5J *81*
  (off Elmfield Way)
Oxford Cres. KT3: N Mald 6K *151*
Oxford Dr. HA4: Ruis 2A *58*
  SE1 . . . . .5G *15* (1E *102*)
Oxford Gdns. N20 . . . . .1G *31*
  N21 . . . . .7H *23*
  W4 . . . . .5G *97*
  W10 . . . . .6E *80*
Oxford Ga. W6 . . . . .4F *99*
Oxford M. DA5: Bexl 7G *127*
Oxford Pl. *NW10* 3K *61*
  (off Press Rd.)
Oxford Rd. DA14: Sidc 5B *144*
  E15 . . . . .6F *69*
  (not continuous)
  EN3: Pond E 5C *24*
  HA1: Harr .6G *41*
  HA3: W'stone 3K *41*
  IG1: Ilf 5G *71*
  IG8: Wfd G 5G *37*
  N4 . . . . .1A *66*
  N9 . . . . .2C *34*
  NW6 . . . . .2J *81*
  SE19 . . . . .6D *138*
  SM5: Cars 6C *166*
  SM6: Wall 5G *167*
  SW15 . . . . .4G *117*
  TW11: Tedd 5H *131*
  W5 . . . . .7D *78*
Oxford Rd. Nth. W4 . . . . .5H *97*
Oxford Rd. Sth. W4 . . . . .5G *97*
Oxford Sq. W2 . . . . .1D *10* (6C *82*)
Oxford St. W1 . . . . .1G *11* (6E *82*)
Oxford Wlk. UB1: S'hall 1D *94*
Oxford Way TW13: Hanw 4B *130*
Oxgate Cen. NW2 . . . . .2D *62*
Oxgate Ct. NW2 . . . . .2C *62*
Oxgate Ct. Pde. NW2 . . . . .2C *62*
Oxgate Gdns. NW2 . . . . .3D *62*
Oxgate La. NW2 . . . . .2D *62*
Oxgate Pde. NW2 . . . . .2C *62*
Oxhawth Cres. BR2: Brom 5E *160*
Oxhey La. HA3: Hat E 5A *26*
  HA5: Hat E 5A *26*
Oxleas E6 . . . . .6F *89*
Oxleas Cl. DA16: Well 2H *125*
Oxleay Rd. HA2: Harr 1E *58*
Oxleigh Cl. KT3: N Mald 5A *152*
Oxley Cl. SE1 . . . . .5F *103*
Oxleys Rd. NW2 . . . . .3D *62*
Oxlip Cl. CR0: C'don 1K *169*
Oxlow La. RM9: Dag 4F *73*
  RM10: Dag 4F *73*
Oxonian St. SE22 . . . . .4F *121*
Oxo Tower Wharf SE1 . . . . .3K *13* (7A *84*)
Oxted Cl. CR4: Mitc 3B *154*
Oxtoby Way SW16 . . . . .1H *155*

Oxygen, The E16 . . . . .7J *87*
Oystercatcher Cl. E16 . . . . .6K *87*
Oyster Ct. *SE17* 4C *102*
  (off Crampton St.)
Oystergate Wlk. EC4 . . . . .3E *14*
Oyster Row E1 . . . . .6J *85*
Oyster Wharf SW11 . . . . .2B *118*
Ozolins Way E16 . . . . .6J *87*

P

Pablo Neruda Cl. SE24 . . . . .4B *120*
Pace Pl. E1 . . . . .6H *85*
Pacific Cl. TW14: Felt 1H *129*
Pacific Ho. *E1* 4K *85*
  (off Ernest St.)
Pacific Rd. E16 . . . . .6J *87*
Pacific Wharf SE16 . . . . .1K *103*
Packenham Ho. *E2* 1K *9*
  (off Wellington Row)
Packham Ct. KT4: Wor Pk 3E *164*
Packington Sq. N1 . . . . .1C *84*
Packington St. N1 . . . . .1B *84*
Packmores Rd. SE9 . . . . .5H *125*
Padbury *SE17* 5E *102*
  (off Bagshot St.)
Padbury Cl. TW14: Bedf 1F *129*
Padbury Ct. E2 . . . . .2K *9* (3F *85*)
Padbury Ho. *NW8* 3D *4*
  (off Tresham Cres.)
Padbury Oaks UB7: Lford 4C *174*
Padcroft Rd. UB7: Yiew 1A *92*
Paddenswick Rd. W6 . . . . .3C *98*
PADDINGTON 7A *4* (6B *82*)
Paddington Bowling & Sports Club 4K *81*
Paddington Cl. UB4: Yead 4B *76*
Paddington Ct. W7 . . . . .5K *77*
  (off Copley Cl.)
Paddington Grn. W2 . . . . .5A *4* (5B *82*)
Paddington St. W1 . . . . .5G *5* (5E *82*)
Paddock, The N10 . . . . .3E *46*
  NW9 . . . . .5G *43*
  UB10: Ick .4D *56*
Paddock Cl. BR6: Farnb 4F *173*
  KT4: Wor Pk 1A *164*
  SE3 . . . . .2J *123*
  SE26 . . . . .4K *139*
  UB5: N'olt .2E *76*
Paddock Gdns. SE19 . . . . .6E *138*
Paddock Lodge *EN1: Enf* 5K *23*
  (off Village Rd.)
Paddock Mobile Home Pk.
  BR2: Kes .7C *172*
Paddock Pas. *SE19* 6E *138*
  (off Paddock Gdns.)
Paddock Rd. DA6: Bex 4E *126*
  HA4: Ruis .3B *58*
  NW2 . . . . .3C *62*
Paddocks, The CR0: Addtn 6C *170*
  EN4: Cockf 3J *21*
  HA9: Wemb 2H *61*
  W5 . . . . .3D *96*
  (off Popes Dr.)
Paddocks Cl. HA2: Harr 4F *59*
Paddocks Grn. NW9 . . . . .1H *61*
Paddock Way BR7: Chst 7H *143*
  SW15 . . . . .7E *116*
Padelford La. HA7: Stan 2F *27*
Padfield Cl. HA9: Wemb 3F *61*
Padfield Rd. SE5 . . . . .3C *120*
Padley Cl. KT9: Chess 5F *163*
Padnall Cl. RM6: Chad H 3D *54*
Padnall Rd. RM6: Chad H 3D *54*
Padstone Ho. *E3* 3D *86*
  (off Talwin St.)
Padstow Cl. BR6: Chels 4K *173*
Padstow Ho. E14 . . . . .7B *86*
  (off Three Colt St.)
Padstow Rd. EN2: Enf 1G *23*
Padstow Wlk. TW14: Felt 1H *129*
Padua Rd. SE20 . . . . .1J *157*

Pagden St. SW8 . . . . .1F *119*
Pageant Av. NW9 . . . . .1K *43*
Pageant Cres. SE16 . . . . .1A *104*
Pageantmaster Ct. EC4 . . . . .1A *14*
Pageant Wlk. CR0: C'don 3E *168*
Page Av. HA9: Wemb 3J *61*
Page Cl. HA3: Kenton 6F *43*
  RM9: Dag .5E *72*
  TW12: Hamp 6C *130*
Page Ct. NW7 . . . . .7J *29*
Page Cres. CR0: Wadd 5B *168*
Page Grn. Rd. N15 . . . . .5G *49*
Page Grn. Ter. N15 . . . . .5F *49*
Page Heath La. BR1: Brom 3B *160*
Page Heath Vs. BR1: Brom 3B *160*
Page High N22 . . . . .2A *48*
  (off Lymington Av.)
Page Ho. SE10 . . . . .6E *104*
  (off Welland St.)
Pagehurst Rd. CR0: C'don 7H *157*
Page Mdw. NW7 . . . . .7J *29*
Page Rd. TW14: Bedf 6F *111*
Pages Hill N10 . . . . .2E *46*
Pages La. N10 . . . . .2E *46*
Page St. NW7 . . . . .1C *44*
  SW1 . . . . .3D *18* (4H *101*)
Page's Wlk. SE1 . . . . .4E *102*
Pages Yd. W4 . . . . .6B *98*
Paget Av. SM1: Sutt 3B *166*
Paget Cl. TW12: Ham H 4H *131*
Paget Gdns. BR7: Chst 1F *161*
Paget Ho. E2 .2J *85*
  (off Bishop's Way)
Paget La. TW7: Isle 3H *113*
Paget Pl. KT2: King T 6J *133*
  KT7: T Ditt 1A *162*
Paget Ri. SE18 . . . . .6E *106*
Paget Rd. IG1: Ilf 4F *71*
  N16 . . . . .1D *66*
  UB10: Hil .4C *74*
Paget St. EC1 . . . . .1A *8* (3B *84*)
Paget Ter. SE18 . . . . .6F *107*
Pagham Ho. *W10* 4E *80*
  (off Sutton Way)
Pagin Ho. N15 . . . . .5E *48*
  (off Braemar Rd.)
Pagitts Gro. EN4: Had W 1E *20*
Pagnell St. SE14 . . . . .7B *104*
Pagoda Av. TW9: Rich 3F *115*
Pagoda Gdns. SE3 . . . . .2F *123*
Pagoda Gro. SE27 . . . . .2C *138*
Paignton Rd. HA4: Ruis 3J *57*
  N15 . . . . .6E *48*
Paines Cl. HA5: Pinn 3C *40*
Paines La. HA5: Pinn 1C *40*
Pain's Cl. CR4: Mitc 2F *155*
Painsthorpe Rd. N16 . . . . .3E *66*
Painswick Ct. *SE15* 7F *103*
  (off Daniel Gdns.)
Painted Hall
  Greenwich .6F *105*
Painters M. SE16 . . . . .4G *103*
Painters Rd. IG2: Ilf 3K *53*
Paisley Rd. N22 . . . . .1B *48*
  SM5: Cars 1B *166*
Paisley Ter. SM5: Cars 7B *154*
Pakeman Ho. *SE1* 6B *14*
  (off Surrey Row)
Pakeman St. N7 . . . . .3K *65*
Pakenham Cl. SW12 . . . . .1E *136*
Pakenham St. WC1 . . . . .2H *7* (3K *83*)
Pakington Ho. *SW9* 2J *119*
  (off Stockwell Gdns. Est.)
Palace Av. W8 . . . . .2K *99*
Palace Bingo Club 4C *102*
  (within Elephant & Castle Shop. Cen.)
Palace Cl. E9 .6B *68*
Palace Ct. BR1: Brom 1K *159*
  (off Palace Gro.)
  HA3: Kenton 6E *42*
  NW3 . . . . .5K *63*
  W2 . . . . .7K *81*

Palace Ct. Gdns. N10 . . . . .3G *47*
Palace Exchange EN2: Enf 4J *23*
Palace Gdns. IG9: Buck H 1G *37*
Palace Gdns. M. W8 . . . . .1K *99*
Palace Gdns. Shop. Cen.
  EN2: Enf 4J *23*
Palace Gdns. Ter. W8 . . . . .1J *99*
Palace Ga. W8 . . . . .2A *100*
Palace Gates M. *N8* 4J *47*
  (off The Campsbourne)
Palace Gates Rd. N22 . . . . .1H *47*
Palace Grn. CR0: Sels 7B *170*
  W8 . . . . .1K *99*
Palace Gro. BR1: Brom 1K *159*
Palace Heath M. W8 . . . . .7F *139*
Palace Ice Rink, The 2H *47*
Palace Mans. KT1: King T 4D *150*
  (off Palace Rd.)
  W14 . . . . .4G *99*
  (off Hammersmith Rd.)
Palace M. E17 . . . . .4B *50*
  EN2: Enf 3J *23*
  SW1 . . . . .4H *17*
  SW6 . . . . .7H *99*
Palace Pde. E17 . . . . .4B *50*
Palace Pl. SW1 . . . . .1A *18* (3G *101*)
Palace Pl. Mans. *W8* 2K *99*
  (off Kensington Ct.)
Palace Rd. BR1: Brom 1K *159*
  HA4: Ruis .4C *58*
  KT1: King T 4D *150*
  KT8: E Mos 3G *149*
  N8 . . . . .5H *47*
  (not continuous)
  N11 . . . . .7D *32*
  SE19 . . . . .7F *139*
  SW2 . . . . .1K *137*
Palace Sq. SE19 . . . . .7F *139*
Palace St. SW1 . . . . .1A *18* (3G *101*)
Palace Superbowl 4C *102*
  (within Elephant & Castle Shop. Cen.)
Palace Theatre
  Soho 1D *12*
  (off Shaftesbury Av.)
Palace Vw. BR1: Brom 3K *159*
  (not continuous)
  CR0: C'don 4B *170*
  SE12 . . . . .2J *141*
Palace Vw. Rd. E4 . . . . .5J *35*
Palace Wharf W6 . . . . .7E *98*
  (off Rainville Rd.)
Palamos Rd. E10 . . . . .1C *68*
Palatine Av. N16 . . . . .4E *66*
Palatine Rd. N16 . . . . .4E *66*
Palazzo Apartments *N1* 7E *66*
  (off Ardleigh Rd.)
Palemead Cl. SW6 . . . . .1F *117*
Palermo Rd. NW10 . . . . .2C *80*
Palestine Gro. SW19 . . . . .1B *154*
Palestra Ho. *SE1* 5A *14*
  (off Blackfriars Rd.)
Palewell Comn. Dr. SW14 . . . . .5K *115*
Palewell Pk. SW14 . . . . .5K *115*
Palfrey Pl. SW8 . . . . .7K *101*
Palgrave Av. UB1: S'hall 7E *76*
Palgrave Gdns. NW1 . . . . .3D *4* (4C *82*)
Palgrave Ho. SE5 . . . . .7C *102*
  (off Wyndham Est.)
  TW2: Whitt 7G *113*
Palgrave Rd. W12 . . . . .3B *98*
Palissy St. E2 . . . . .2J *9* (3F *85*)
  (not continuous)
Palladino Ho. SW17 . . . . .5C *136*
  (off Laurel Cl.)
Palladio Ct. SW18 . . . . .6K *117*
  (off Mapleton Cres.)
Palladium Ct. E8 . . . . .7F *67*
  (off Queensbridge Rd.)
Pallant Ho. *SE1* 3D *102*
  (off Tabard St.)
Pallant Way BR6: Farnb 3E *172*
Pallet Way SE18 . . . . .1C *124*

Palliser Ct.—Park Farm Ct.

Palliser Ct. *W14* *5G 99*
(off Palliser Rd.)
Palliser Ho. *E1* *4K 85*
(off Ernest St.)
SE10 . . . . . *6F 105*
(off Trafalgar Rd.)
Palliser Rd. W14 . . . . . 5G **99**
Pallister Ter. SW15 . . . . . 3B **134**
Pall Mall SW1 . . . . . 5B **12** (1G **101**)
Pall Mall E. SW1 . . . . . 4D **12** (1H **101**)
Pall Mall Pl. SW1 . . . . . 5B **12**
Palmar Cres. DA7: Bex 3G **127**
Palmar Rd. DA7: Bex 2G **127**
Palm Av. DA14: Sidc 6D **144**
Palm Cl. E10 . . . . . 3D **68**
Palm Ct. *SE15* *7F 103*
(off Garnies Cl.)
Palmeira Rd. DA7: Bex 3D **126**
Palmer Av. SM3: Cheam 4E **164**
Palmer Cl. BR4: W W'ck 3F **171**
TW5: Hest 1E **112**
UB5: N'olt 6C **58**
Palmer Cres. KT1: King T 3E **150**
Palmer Dr. BR1: Brom 4F **161**
Palmer Gdns. EN5: Barn 5A **20**
Palmer Pl. N7 . . . . . 5A **66**
Palmer Rd. E13 . . . . . 4K **87**
RM8: Dag 1D **72**
Palmer's Ct. *N11* *5B 32*
(off Palmer's Rd.)
PALMERS GREEN **3F 33**
Palmers Gro. KT8: W Mole 4E **148**
Palmers La. EN1: Enf 1C **24**
EN3: Enf H 1C **24**
Palmers Pas. *SW14* *3J 115*
(off Lit. St Leonard's)
Palmers Rd. E2 . . . . . 2K **85**
N11 . . . . . 5B **32**
SW14 . . . . . 3J **115**
SW16 . . . . . 2K **155**
Palmerston Cen. HA3: W'stone 3K **41**
Palmerston Ct. *E3* *2K 85*
(off Old Ford Rd.)
IG9: Buck H 1F **37**
KT6: Surb 7D **150**
Palmerston Cres. N13 . . . . . 5E **32**
SE18 . . . . . 6G **107**
Palmerston Gro. SW19 . . . . . 7J **135**
Palmerston Ho. *SE1* *7J 13*
(off Westminster Bri. Rd.)
W8 . . . . . *1J 99*
(off Kensington Pl.)
Palmerston Mans. *W14* *6G 99*
(off Queen's Club Gdns.)
Palmerston Rd. BR6: Farnb 4G **173**
CR0: C'don 5D **156**
E7 . . . . . 6K **69**
E17 . . . . . 3B **50**
HA3: W'stone 3J **41**
(not continuous)
IG9: Buck H 2E **36**
N22 . . . . . 7E **32**
NW6 . . . . . 7H **63**
(not continuous)
SM1: Sutt 5A **166**
SM5: Cars 4D **166**
SW14 . . . . . 4J **115**
SW19 . . . . . 7J **135**
TW2: Twick 6J **113**
TW3: Houn 1G **113**
W3 . . . . . 3J **97**
Palmerston Way SW8 . . . . . 7F **101**
Palmer St. SW1 . . . . . 1C **18** (3H **101**)
(not continuous)
Palm Gro. W5 . . . . . 3E **96**
Palm Rd. RM7: Rom 5J **55**
Palm Tree Ho. *SE14* *7K 103*
(off Barlborough St.)
Palyn Ho. *EC1* *2D 8*
(off Ironmonger Row)
Pamela Ct. N12 . . . . . 6E **30**
Pamela Gdns. HA5: Eastc 5K **39**
Pamela Ho. *E8* *1F 85*
(off Haggerston Rd.)
Pamela Wlk. *E8* *1G 85*
(off Marlborough Av.)
Pampisford Rd. CR8: Purl 7B **168**
Pams Way KT19: Ewe 5K **163**
Panama Ho. *E1* *5K 85*
(off Beaumont Sq.)
Pancras La. EC4 . . . . . 1E **14** (6C **84**)
Pancras Rd. NW1 . . . . . 1E **6** (2H **83**)
Pancras Way E3 . . . . . 2C **86**
Pandangle Ho. *E8* *1F 85*
(off Kingsland Rd.)
Pandian Way NW1 . . . . . 6H **65**
Pandora Rd. NW6 . . . . . 6J **63**
Panfield M. IG2: Ilf 6E **52**
Panfield Rd. SE2 . . . . . 3A **108**
Pangbourne *NW1* *2A 6*
(off Stanhope St.)
Pangbourne Av. W10 . . . . . 5E **80**
Pangbourne Dr.
HA7: Stan 5J **27**
Panhard Pl. UB1: S'hall 7F **77**
Pank Av. EN5: New Bar 5F **21**
Pankhurst Av. E16 . . . . . 1K **105**
Pankhurst Cl. SE14 . . . . . 7K **103**
TW7: Isle 3K **113**
Pankhurst Ho. W12 . . . . . 6D **80**
Pankhurst Rd. KT12: Walt T 7A **148**
Panmuir Rd. SW20 . . . . . 1D **152**
Panmure Cl. N5 . . . . . 4B **66**
Panmure Ct. *UB1: S'hall* *6G 77*
(off Osborne Rd.)
Panmure Rd. SE26 . . . . . 3H **139**
Pannells Ct. TW5: Hest 6E **94**
Panorama Ct. N6 . . . . . 6G **47**
Pan Peninsula Sq. E14 . . . . . 2D **104**
Pansy Gdns. W12 . . . . . 7C **80**
Panther Dr. NW10 . . . . . 5K **61**
Pantiles, The BR1: Brom 3C **160**
DA7: Bex 7F **109**
NW11 . . . . . 5H **45**
WD23: B Hea 1C **26**
Pantiles Cl. N13 . . . . . 5G **33**
Panton Cl. CR0: C'don 1B **168**
Panton St. SW1 . . . . . 3C **12** (7H **83**)
Panyer All. *EC1* *7C 8*
(off Newgate St.)
Paper Bldgs. EC4 . . . . . 2K **13**
Papermill Cl. SM5: Cars 4E **166**
Papermill Pl. *E17* *2A 50*
(off St Andrew's Rd.)
Papillons Wlk. SE3 . . . . . 2J **123**
Papworth Gdns. N7 . . . . . 5K **65**
Papworth Way SW2 . . . . . 7A **120**
Parade, The CR0: C'don 6J **155**
KT2: King T *2E 150*
(off London Rd.)
KT4: Wor Pk 4B **164**
N4 . . . . . 1A **66**
SE4 . . . . . *2B 122*
(off Up. Brockley Rd.)
SE26 . . . . . *3H 139*
(off Wells Pk. Rd.)
SM1: Sutt 3H **165**
SM5: Cars *5D 166*
(off Beynon Rd.)
SW11 . . . . . 7D **100**
TW12: Ham H 5H **131**
TW16: Sun 7H **129**
UB6: G'frd 5B **60**
Parade Mans. NW4 . . . . . 5D **44**
Parade M. SE27 . . . . . 2B **138**
Paradise Pk. E5 . . . . . 3K **67**
Paradise Pas. N7 . . . . . 5A **66**
Paradise Path SE28 . . . . . 1A **108**
Paradise Pl. SE18 . . . . . 4C **106**
Paradise Rd. SW4 . . . . . 2J **119**
TW9: Rich 5D **114**
Paradise Row E2 . . . . . 3H **85**
Paradise St. SE16 . . . . . 2H **103**
Paradise Wlk. SW3 . . . . . 7F **17** (6D **100**)
Paragon *TW8: Bford* *5C 96*
(off Boston Pk. Rd.)
Paragon, The SE3 . . . . . 2H **123**
Paragon Cl. E16 . . . . . 6J **87**
Paragon Gro. KT5: Surb 6F **151**
Paragon M. SE1 . . . . . 4D **102**
Paragon Pl. KT5: Surb 6F **151**
SE3 . . . . . 2H **123**
Paragon Rd. E9 . . . . . 6J **67**
Paramount Bldg. *EC1* *3A 8*
(off St John St.)
Paramount Ct. WC1 . . . . . 4B **6**
Parbury Ri. KT9: Chess 6E **162**
Parbury Rd. SE23 . . . . . 6A **122**
Parchmore Rd. CR7: Thor H 2B **156**
Parchmore Way
CR7: Thor H 2B **156**
Pardoe Rd. E10 . . . . . 7D **50**
Pardoner Ho. *SE1* *3D 102*
(off Pardoner St.)
Pardoner St. SE1 . . . . . 7F **15** (3D **102**)
(not continuous)
Pardon St. EC1 . . . . . 3B **8** (4B **84**)
Parent Shop. Mall *E18* *2J 51*
(off Marlborough Rd.)
Parfett St. E1 . . . . . 5G **85**
(not continuous)
Parfitt Cl. NW3 . . . . . 1A **64**
Parfrey St. W6 . . . . . 6E **98**
Pargraves Ct. HA9: Wemb 2G **61**
Parham Dr. IG2: Ilf 6F **53**
Parham Way N10 . . . . . 2G **47**
Paris Gdn. SE1 . . . . . 4A **14** (1B **102**)
Parish Ct. KT6: Surb 5E **150**
Parish Ga. Dr. DA15: Sidc 6J **125**
Parish La. SE20 . . . . . 6K **139**
Parish M. SE20 . . . . . 7K **139**
Paris Ho. *E2* *2H 85*
(off Old Bethnal Grn. Rd.)
Parish Wharf Pl. SE18 . . . . . 4C **106**
Park & Ride
Bromley **6K 159**
Cumberland Gate . . . . . **2E 10 (7D 82)**
Kingston Upon Thames **7C 162**
Park, The DA14: Sidc 5A **144**
HA1: Harr 1J **59**
N6 . . . . . 6E **46**
NW11 . . . . . 1K **63**
SE23 . . . . . 1J **139**
SM5: Cars 5D **166**
W5 . . . . . 1D **96**
Park App. DA16: Well 4B **126**
SE16 . . . . . 3H **103**
Park Av. BR1: Brom 6H **141**
BR4: W W'ck 2E **170**
BR6: Chels 2K **173**
BR6: Farnb 3D **172**
CR4: Mitc 7F **137**
E6 . . . . . 1E **88**
E15 . . . . . 6G **69**
EN1: Enf 5J **23**
HA4: Ruis 6F **39**
IG1: Ilf 1E **70**
IG8: Wfd G 5E **36**
IG11: Bark 6G **71**
N3 . . . . . 1K **45**
N13 . . . . . 3F **33**
N18 . . . . . 4B **34**
N22 . . . . . 2J **47**
NW2 . . . . . 5D **62**
NW10 . . . . . 2F **79**
(Brent Cres., not continuous)
NW10 . . . . . 5D **62**
(Park Av. Nth.)
NW11 . . . . . 1K **63**
SM5: Cars 6E **166**
SW14 . . . . . 4K **115**
TW3: Houn 6F **113**
TW17: Shep 3G **147**
UB1: S'hall 2D **94**
Park Av. E. KT17: Ewe 6C **164**
Park Av. M. CR4: Mitc 7F **137**
Park Av. Nth. N8 . . . . . 3H **47**
NW10 . . . . . 5D **62**
Park Av. Rd. N17 . . . . . 7C **34**
Park Av. Sth. N8 . . . . . 4H **47**
Park Av. W. KT17: Ewe 6C **164**
Park Central Bldg. E3 . . . . . 2C **86**
Park Chase HA9: Wemb 4F **61**
Park Cl. E9 . . . . . 1J **85**
HA3: Hrw W 1J **41**
KT2: King T 1G **151**
N12 . . . . . 3G **31**
NW2 . . . . . 3D **62**
NW10 . . . . . 3F **79**
SM5: Cars 6D **166**
SW1 . . . . . 7E **10** (2D **100**)
TW3: Houn 5G **113**
TW12: Hamp 1G **149**
W4 . . . . . 6K **97**
W14 . . . . . 3H **99**
Park Club, The **1A 98**
Park Ct. *CR2: S Croy* *5C 168*
(off Warham Rd.)
E4 . . . . . 2K **35**
E17 . . . . . 5D **50**
HA3: Kenton 7E **42**
HA9: Wemb 5E **60**
KT1: Ham W 1C **150**
KT3: N Mald 4K **151**
N11 . . . . . 7C **32**
N17 . . . . . 7B **34**
SE21 . . . . . 3C **138**
SE26 . . . . . 6H **139**
SM6: Wall 5J **167**
SW11 . . . . . 1F **119**
UB8: Uxb 1A **74**
W6 . . . . . 4C **98**
Park Cres. DA8: Erith 6J **109**
EN2: Enf 4J **23**
HA3: Hrw W 1J **41**
N3 . . . . . 7F **31**
TW2: Twick 1H **131**
W1 . . . . . 4J **5** (4F **83**)
Park Cres. M. E. W1 . . . . . 4K **5** (4F **83**)
Park Cres. M. W. W1 . . . . . 4J **5** (4F **83**)
Park Cres. Rd. DA8: Erith 6K **109**
Park Cft. HA8: Edg 1J **43**
Parkcroft Rd. SE12 . . . . . 7H **123**
Parkdale N11 . . . . . 6C **32**
Parkdale Cres. KT4: Wor Pk 3K **163**
Parkdale Rd. SE18 . . . . . 5J **107**
Park Dr. HA2: Harr 7E **40**
HA3: Hrw W 6C **26**
N21 . . . . . 6H **23**
NW11 . . . . . 1K **63**
RM1: Rom 4K **55**
RM10: Dag 3J **73**
SE7 . . . . . 6C **106**
SW14 . . . . . 5K **115**
W3 . . . . . 3G **97**
Park Dwellings NW3 . . . . . 5D **64**
Park E. Bldg. *E3* *2C 86*
(off Fairfield Rd.)
Park End BR1: Brom 1H **159**
NW3 . . . . . 4C **64**
Parker Cl. E16 . . . . . 1C **106**
SM5: Cars 6D **166**
Parker Ct. *N1* *1C 84*
(off Basire St.)
Parker Ho. *E14* *2C 104*
(off Admirals Way)
Parker M. WC2 . . . . . 7F **7** (6J **83**)
Parke Rd. SW13 . . . . . 1C **116**
TW16: Sun 4J **147**
Parker Rd. CR0: C'don 4C **168**
Parkers Rd. N2 . . . . . 1C **46**
Parkers Row SE1 . . . . . 7K **15** (2G **103**)
Parker St. E16 . . . . . 1C **106**
WC2 . . . . . 7F **7** (6J **83**)
Park Farm Cl.
HA5: Eastc 5K **39**
N2 . . . . . 3A **46**
Park Farm Ct. UB3: Hayes 7G **75**

A-Z London 351

Park Farm Rd.—Park Sq. W.

Park Farm Rd. BR1: Brom 1B **160**
KT2: King T 7E **132**
Parkfield TW7: Isle 1J **113**
Parkfield Av. HA2: Harr 2G **41**
SW14 4A **116**
TW13: Felt 3J **129**
UB5: N'olt 2B **76**
UB10: Hil 3D **74**
Parkfield Cl. HA8: Edg 6C **28**
UB5: N'olt 2C **76**
Parkfield Ct. *SE14* *1B* ***122***
(off Parkfield Rd.)
Parkfield Cres. HA2: Harr 2G **41**
HA4: Ruis 2C **58**
TW13: Felt 3J **129**
Parkfield Dr. UB5: N'olt 2B **76**
Parkfield Gdns. HA2: Harr 3F **41**
Parkfield Ho. HA2: Harr 1F **41**
Parkfield Ind. Est. SW11 2E **118**
Parkfield Pde. TW13: Felt 3J **129**
Parkfield Rd. HA2: Harr 3G **59**
NW10 7D **62**
SE14 1B **122**
TW13: Felt 3J **129**
UB5: N'olt 2C **76**
UB10: Ick 2D **56**
Parkfields CR0: C'don 1B **170**
SW15 4E **116**
Parkfields Av. NW9 1K **61**
SW20 1D **152**
Parkfields Cl. SM5: Cars 4E **166**
Parkfields Rd. KT2: King T 5F **133**
Parkfield St. N1 2A **84**
Parkfield Way BR2: Brom 6D **160**
Park Gdns. DA8: Erith 4K **109**
E10 1C **68**
KT2: King T 5F **133**
NW9 3H **43**
Park Ga. N2 3B **46**
N21 7E **22**
W5 5D **78**
Parkgate *N1* *1D* ***84***
(off Southgate Rd.)
SE3 3H **123**
Parkgate Av. EN4: Had W 1F **21**
Parkgate Cl. KT2: King T 6H **133**
Park Ga. Ct. TW12: Ham H 6G **131**
Parkgate Cres. EN4: Had W 1F **21**
Parkgate Gdns. SW14 5K **115**
Parkgate M. N6 7G **47**
Parkgate Rd. SM6: Wall 5E **166**
SW11 7C **100**
Park Gates HA2: Harr 4E **58**
Park Gro. BR1: Brom 1K **159**
DA7: Bex 4J **127**
E15 1J **87**
HA8: Edg 5A **28**
N11 7C **32**
Park Gro. Rd. E11 2G **69**
Park Hall *SE10* *7F* ***105***
(off Crooms Hill)
Park Hall Rd. SE21 3C **138**
Parkhall Rd. N2 4C **46**
Park Hall Trad. Est. SE21 3C **138**
Parkham Ct. BR2: Brom 2G **159**
Parkham St. SW11 1C **118**
Park Hgts. Ct. *E14* *6B* ***86***
(off Wharf La.)
Park Hill BR1: Brom 4C **160**
SE23 2H **139**
SM5: Cars 6C **166**
SW4 5H **119**
TW10: Rich 6F **115**
W5 5D **78**
Park Hill Cl. SM5: Cars 5C **166**
Park Hill Ct. SW17 3D **136**
Park Hill M. CR2: S Croy 5D **168**
Park Hill Ri. CR0: C'don 2E **168**
Park Hill Rd. BR2: Brom 2G **159**
CR0: C'don 2E **168**
DA14: Sidc 3H **143**
(not continuous)
Park Hill Rd. DA15: Sidc 3H **143**
SM6: Wall 7F **167**
Parkhill Rd. DA5: Bexl 7F **127**
E4 1K **35**
NW3 5D **64**
Parkhill Wlk. NW3 5D **64**
Parkholme Rd. E8 6F **67**
Park Ho. *E9* *7J* ***67***
(off Shore Rd.)
N21 7E **22**
SE5 *1D* ***120***
(off Camberwell Grn.)
W1 1G **11**
W1 *6E* ***82***
(off Oxford St.)
Park Ho. Gdns. TW1: Twick 5C **114**
Park Ho. Pas. N6 7E **46**
Parkhouse St. SE5 7D **102**
Parkhurst Ct. N7 4J **65**
Parkhurst Gdns. DA5: Bexl 7G **127**
Parkhurst Rd. DA5: Bexl 7G **127**
E12 4E **70**
E17 4A **50**
N7 4J **65**
N11 5K **31**
N17 2G **49**
N22 6E **32**
SM1: Sutt 4B **166**
Parkinson Ct. *N1* *2F* ***9***
(off Charles Sq. Est.)
Parkinson Ho. *E9* *7J* ***67***
(off Frampton Pk. Rd.)
SW1 *5C* ***18***
(off Tachbrook St.)
Parkland Ct. *E15* *5G* ***69***
(off Maryland Pk.)
W14 *2G* ***99***
(off Holland Pk. Av.)
Parkland Gdns. SW19 1F **135**
Parkland Gro. TW15: Ashf 3C **128**
Parkland Mead BR1: Brom 3F **161**
Parkland M. BR7: Chst 7H **143**
Parkland Rd. IG8: Wfd G 7E **36**
N22 2K **47**
TW15: Ashf 4C **128**
Parklands KT5: Surb 5F **151**
N6 7F **47**
Parklands Cl. EN4: Had W 1G **21**
IG2: Ilf 7G **53**
SW14 5J **115**
Parklands Ct. TW5: Hest 2B **112**
Parklands Dr. N3 3G **45**
Parklands Gro. TW7: Isle 1K **113**
Parklands Pde. *TW5: Hest* *2B* ***112***
(off Parklands Ct.)
Parklands Rd. SW16 5F **137**
Parklands Way KT4: Wor Pk 2A **164**
Parkland Walk Local Nature Reserve 7J **47**
Park La. CR0: C'don 3D **168**
E15 1F **87**
HA2: Harr 3F **59**
HA7: Stan 3F **27**
HA9: Wemb 5E **60**
N9 3K **33**
N17 7A **34**
(not continuous)
RM6: Chad H 6D **54**
SM3: Cheam 6G **165**
SM5: Cars 4E **166**
SM6: Wall 5E **166**
TW5: Cran 7J **93**
TW9: Rich 4D **114**
TW11: Tedd 6K **131**
UB4: Hayes 5G **75**
W1 2F **11** (7D **82**)
Park La. Cl. N17 7B **34**
Park La. Mans. *CR0: C'don* *3D* ***168***
(off Edridge Rd.)
PARK LANGLEY 4E **158**
Parklea Cl. NW9 1A **44**
Park Lee Ct. N16 7E **48**
Parkleigh Rd. SW19 2K **153**
Parkleys TW10: Ham 4D **132**
Parkleys Pde. TW10: Ham 4D **132**
Park Lodge NW8 7B **64**
W14 *3H* ***99***
(off Kensington High St.)
Park Lodge Av. UB7: W Dray 2B **92**
Park Lofts *SW2* *5J* ***119***
(off Lyham Rd.)
Park Lorne *NW8* *2D* ***4***
(off Park Rd.)
Park Mnr. *SM2: Sutt* *7A* ***166***
(off Christchurch Pk.)
Park Mans. NW4 5D **44**
NW8 *2C* ***82***
(off Allitsen Rd.)
SW1 *7E* ***10***
(off Knightsbridge)
SW8 7F **19** (6J **101**)
SW11 *1D* ***118***
(off Prince of Wales Dr.)
Park Mead DA15: Sidc 5B **126**
HA2: Harr 3F **59**
Parkmead SW15 6D **116**
Parkmead Gdns. NW7 6G **29**
Park M. BR7: Chst 6F **143**
N8 6J **47**
SE10 5H **105**
SE24 7C **120**
TW19: Stanw 7B **110**
W10 2G **81**
Parkmore Cl. IG8: Wfd G 4D **36**
Park Pde. NW10 2B **80**
UB3: Hayes 6G **75**
W3 3G **97**
Park Piazza SE13 6F **123**
Park Pl. *BR1: Brom* *1K* ***159***
(off Park Rd.)
E14 1C **104**
HA9: Wemb 4F **61**
N1 *7D* ***66***
(off Downham Rd.)
SW1 5A **12** (1G **101**)
TW12: Ham H 6G **131**
W3 4G **97**
W5 1D **96**
Park Pl. Dr. W3 3G **97**
Park Pl. Vs. W2 5A **4** (5A **82**)
Park Ridings N8 3A **48**
Park Ri. HA3: Hrw W 1J **41**
SE23 1A **140**
Park Ri. Rd. SE23 1A **140**
Park Rd. BR1: Brom 1K **159**
BR3: Beck 7B **140**
BR7: Chst 6F **143**
E6 1A **88**
E10 1C **68**
E12 1K **69**
E15 1J **87**
E17 5B **50**
EN4: E Barn 4G **21**
EN5: Barn 4C **20**
HA0: Wemb 6E **60**
IG1: Ilf 3H **71**
KT1: Ham W 1C **150**
KT2: King T 5F **133**
KT3: N Mald 4K **151**
KT5: Surb 6F **151**
KT8: E Mos 4G **149**
N2 3B **46**
N8 4G **47**
N11 7C **32**
N14 1C **32**
N15 4B **48**
N18 4B **34**
NW1 2D **4** (3C **82**)
NW4 7C **44**
NW8 2D **4** (3C **82**)
NW9 7K **43**
NW10 1A **80**
SE25 4E **156**
SM3: Cheam 6G **165**
Park Rd. SM6: Wall 5F **167**
(Clifton Rd.)
SM6: Wall 2F **167**
(Elmwood Cl.)
SW19 6B **136**
TW1: Twick 6C **114**
TW3: Houn 5F **113**
TW7: Isle 1B **114**
TW10: Rich 6F **115**
TW11: Tedd 6K **131**
TW12: Ham H 4F **131**
TW13: Hanw 4B **130**
TW15: Ashf 5D **128**
TW16: Sun 7K **129**
UB4: Hayes 5G **75**
UB8: Uxb 1A **74**
W4 7J **97**
W7 7K **77**
Park Rd. E. UB10: Uxb 2A **74**
W3 2H **97**
Park Rd. Ho. KT2: King T 7G **133**
Park Road Leisure Cen. 5H **47**
Park Rd. Nth. W3 2H **97**
W4 5K **97**
Park Row SE10 6F **105**
SW2 6A **120**
PARK ROYAL 3H **79**
Park Royal NW10 3G **79**
PARK ROYAL JUNC. 1G **79**
Park Royal Metro Cen. NW10 4H **79**
Park Royal Rd. NW10 3J **79**
W3 3J **79**
Park St James *NW8* *1D* ***82***
(off St James's Ter. M.)
Parkshot TW9: Rich 4D **114**
Park Side NW2 3C **62**
Parkside DA14: Sidc 2B **144**
IG9: Buck H 2E **36**
N3 1K **45**
NW7 6H **29**
SE3 7H **105**
SM3: Cheam 6G **165**
SW1 6F **11**
SW19 3F **135**
TW12: Ham H 5H **131**
UB3: Hayes 7G **75**
W3 1A **98**
W5 7E **78**
Parkside Av. BR1: Brom 4C **160**
DA7: Bex 2K **127**
RM1: Rom 3K **55**
SW19 5F **135**
Parkside Bus. Est. SE8 6A **104**
(Blackhorse Rd.)
SE8 6A **104**
(Rolt St.)
Parkside Cl. SE20 7J **139**
Parkside Ct. *E11* *6J* ***51***
(off Wanstead Pl.)
N22 6E **32**
Parkside Cres. KT5: Surb 6J **151**
N7 3A **66**
Parkside Cross DA7: Bex 2K **127**
Parkside Dr. HA8: Edg 3B **28**
Parkside Est. E9 1J **85**
Parkside Gdns. EN4: E Barn 1J **31**
SW19 4F **135**
Parkside Ho. RM10: Dag 3J **73**
Parkside Lodge DA17: Belv 5J **109**
Parkside Rd. DA17: Belv 4H **109**
SW11 1E **118**
TW3: Houn 5F **113**
Parkside Ter. *BR6: Farnb* *3F* ***173***
(off Willow Wlk.)
N18 4J **33**
Parkside Way HA2: Harr 4F **41**
Parks Info. Cen. 1C **100**
Park Sth. *SW11* *1E* ***118***
(off Austin Rd.)
Park Sq. E. NW1 3J **5** (4F **83**)
Park Sq. M. NW1 4J **5** (4E **82**)
Park Sq. W. NW1 3J **5** (4F **83**)

Parkstead Rd. SW15 ....5C 116
Park Steps W2 ....2D 10
Parkstone Av. N18 ....6A 34
Parkstone Rd. E17 ....3E 50
SE15 ....2G 121
Park St. CR0: C'don 2C 168
SE1 ....4C 14 (1C 102)
TW11: Tedd 6J 131
W1 ....2G 11 (7E 82)
Park Ter. EN3: Enf H 1F 25
KT4: Wor Pk 1C 164
SM5: Cars 3C 166
Parkthorne Cl. HA2: Harr 6F 41
Parkthorne Dr. HA2: Harr 6E 40
Parkthorne Rd. SW12 ....7H 119
Park Towers W1 ....5J 11
(off Brick St.)
Park Vw. HA5: Hat E 1D 40
HA9: Wemb 5H 61
KT3: N Mald 3B 152
N5 ....4C 66
N21 ....7E 22
RM6: Chad H 6D 54
SE8 ....5K 103
(off Trundleys Rd.)
UB7: Yiew 7A 74
W3 ....5J 79
Parkview DA18: Erith 3D 108
UB6: G'frd 3A 78
(off Perivale La.)
Park View Academy Sports Cen. 4C 48
Park Vw. Apartments SE16 ....3H 103
(off Banyard Rd.)
Parkview Cl. SM5: Cars 7D 166
Park Vw. Ct. N12 ....4H 31
SE20 ....1H 157
Parkview Ct. HA3: Hrw W 7D 26
IG2: Ilf 6J 53
SW6 ....2G 117
SW18 ....6J 117
Park Vw. Cres. N11 ....4A 32
Parkview Cres.
KT4: Wor Pk 7E 152
Park Vw. Dr. CR4: Mitc 2B 154
Park Vw. Est. E2 ....2K 85
Park Vw. Gdns. IG4: Ilf 4D 52
N22 ....1A 48
NW4 ....5E 44
Park Vw. Ho. E4 ....5H 35
SE24 ....6B 120
(off Hurst St.)
Parkview Ho. N9 ....7C 24
Park Vw. Mans. N4 ....6B 48
Park Vw. M. SW9 ....2K 119
Park Vw. Rd. DA16: Well 3C 126
N3 ....1K 45
N17 ....3G 49
NW10 ....4B 62
UB1: S'hall 1E 94
UB8: Hil 6B 74
W5 ....5E 78
Parkview Rd. CR0: C'don 1G 169
SE9 ....1F 143
Park Village E. NW1 ....1K 5 (2F 83)
Park Village W. NW1 ....2F 83
Park Vs. RM6: Chad H 6D 54
Parkville Rd. SW6 ....7H 99
Park Vista SE10 ....6F 105
Park Wlk. EN4: Cockf 3G 21
IG1: Ilf 2F 71
(in The Exchange)
N6 ....7E 46
SE10 ....7F 105
SW10 ....7A 16 (6A 100)
Park Way EN2: Enf 2F 23
HA4: Ruis 1J 57
HA8: Edg 1H 43
KT8: W Mole 3F 149
N20 ....4J 31
NW11 ....5G 45
TW14: Felt 7K 111
W3 ....3G 97
Parkway DA18: Erith 3E 108
IG3: Ilf 3K 71
IG8: Wfd G 5F 37
N14 ....2D 32
NW1 ....1F 83
SW20 ....4F 153
UB10: Hil 7C 56
Parkway, The TW4: Cran 2K 111
TW5: Cran 5J 93
UB2: S'hall 5J 93
UB3: Hayes 3K 93
UB4: Yead 3K 93
UB5: N'olt 3B 76
Park Way Ct. HA4: Ruis 1H 57
Parkway Cres. E15 ....5E 68
Parkway Trad. Est. TW5: Hest 6A 94
Park W. W2 ....7D 4
Park W. Bldg. E3 ....2C 86
Park W. Pl. W2 ....7D 4 (6C 82)
Park Wharf SE8 ....5A 104
(off Evelyn St.)
Parkwood BR3: Beck 7C 140
N20 ....3K 31
NW8 ....1D 82
(off St Edmund's Ter.)
Parkwood Av. KT10: Esh 7G 149
Parkwood Flats N20 ....3J 31
Parkwood Gro. TW16: Sun 3J 147
Parkwood M. N6 ....6F 47
Parkwood Rd. DA5: Bexl 7F 127
SW19 ....5H 135
TW7: Isle 1K 113
Parliament Ct. E1 ....6H 9
Parliament Hill 3D 64
Parliament Hill NW3 ....4C 64
Parliament Hill Fields 3E 64
Parliament Hill Lido 4E 64
Parliament Hill Mans. NW5 ....4E 64
Parliament M. SW14 ....2J 115
Parliament Sq. SW1 ....7E 12 (2J 101)
Parliament St. SW1 ....6E 12 (2J 101)
Parliament Vw. SE1 ....3G 19 (4K 101)
Parma Cres. SW11 ....4D 118
Parmiter Ind. Est. E2 ....2H 85
(off Parmiter St.)
Parmiter St. E2 ....2H 85
Parmoor Ct. EC1 ....3C 8
Parndon Ho. IG10: Lough 1H 37
Parnell Cl. HA8: Edg 4C 28
W12 ....3D 98
Parnell Ho. WC1 ....6D 6 (5H 83)
Parnell Rd. E3 ....1B 86
Parnell Way HA7: Stan 1B 42
Parnham Cl. BR1: Brom 3F 161
Parnham St. E14 ....6A 86
(not continuous)
Parolles Rd. N19 ....1G 65
Paroma Rd. DA17: Belv 4G 109
Parr Cl. N9 ....4C 34
N18 ....4C 34
Parr Ct. N1 ....2D 84
(off New North Rd.)
TW13: Hanw 4A 130
Parr Ho. E16 ....1K 105
(off Beaulieu Av.)
Parrington Ho. SW4 ....6H 119
Parr Rd. E6 ....1B 88
HA7: Stan 1D 42
Parrs Cl. CR2: Sande 7D 168
Parrs Pl. TW12: Hamp 7E 130
Parr St. N1 ....2D 84
Parry Av. E6 ....6D 88
Parry Cl. KT17: Ewe 7D 164
Parry Ho. E1 ....1H 103
(off Green Bank)
Parry Pl. SE18 ....4F 107
Parry Rd. SE25 ....3E 156
W10 ....3G 81
Parry St. SW8 ....7F 19 (6J 101)
Parsifal Rd. NW6 ....5J 63
Parsley Gdns. CR0: C'don 1K 169
Parsloes Av. RM9: Dag 4D 72
Parsonage Cl. UB3: Hayes 6H 75
Parsonage Gdns. EN2: Enf 2H 23
Parsonage La. DA14: Sidc 4F 145
EN1: Enf 2H 23
EN2: Enf 2H 23
Parsonage Manorway
DA17: Belv 6G 109
Parsonage St. E14 ....4E 104
Parsons Cl. SM1: Sutt 3K 165
Parson's Cres. HA8: Edg 3B 28
PARSONS GREEN 2H 117
Parson's Grn. SW6 ....1J 117
Parson's Grn. La. SW6 ....1J 117
Parson's Gro. HA8: Edg 3B 28
Parsons Hill SE18 ....3E 106
(off Powis St.)
Parsons Ho. W2 ....4A 4
Parsons Lodge NW6 ....7K 63
(off Priory Rd.)
Parsons Mead CR0: C'don 1B 168
KT8: E Mos 3G 149
Parson's Rd. E13 ....2A 88
Parson St. NW4 ....4E 44
Parthenia Rd. SW6 ....1J 117
Partingdale La. NW7 ....5A 30
Partington Cl. N19 ....1H 65
Partridge Cl. E16 ....5B 88
EN5: Barn 6A 20
HA7: Stan 4K 27
WD23: Bush 1B 26
Partridge Ct. EC1 ....3A 8
Partridge Dr. BR6: Farnb 3G 173
Partridge Grn. SE9 ....3E 142
Partridge Ho. E3 ....2B 86
(off Stafford Rd.)
Partridge Rd. DA14: Sidc 3J 143
TW12: Hamp 6D 130
Partridge Sq. E6 ....5C 88
Partridge Way N22 ....1J 47
Pasadena Cl. UB3: Hayes 2J 93
Pasadena Cl. Trad. Est. UB3: Hayes 2K 93
Pascall Ho. SE17 ....6C 102
(off Draco St.)
Pascal M. SE19 ....7G 139
Pascal St. SW8 ....7H 101
Pascoe Rd. SE13 ....5F 123
Pasley Cl. SE17 ....5B 102
Pasquier Rd. E17 ....3A 50
Passage, The TW9: Rich 5E 114
Passey Pl. SE9 ....6D 124
Passfield Dr. E14 ....5D 86
Passfield Hall WC1 ....3D 6
(off Endsleigh Pl.)
Passfield Path SE28 ....7B 90
Passfields SE6 ....3D 140
W14 ....5H 99
(off Star St.)
Passing All. EC1 ....4B 8
Passingham Ho. TW5: Hest 6E 94
Passmore Edwards Ho. N11 ....6C 32
Passmore Gdns. N11 ....6C 32
Passmore House E2 ....1F 85
(off Kingsland Rd.)
Passmore St. SW1 ....5G 17 (5E 100)
Pasteur Cl. NW9 ....2A 44
Pasteur Ct. HA1: Harr 1B 60
Pasteur Gdns. N18 ....5G 33
Paston Cl. E5 ....3K 67
SM6: Wall 3G 167
Paston Cres. SE12 ....7K 123
Pastor Ct. N6 ....6G 47
Pastor St. SE11 ....4B 102
Pasture Cl. HA0: Wemb 3B 60
Pasture Rd. HA0: Wemb 2B 60
RM9: Dag 4F 73
SE6 ....1H 141
Pastures, The N20 ....1C 30
Pastures Mead UB10: Hil 6C 56
Pastures Path E11 ....1H 69
Patcham Ter. SW8 ....1F 119
Patch Cl. UB10: Uxb 1B 74
Patching Way UB4: Yead 5C 76
Patent Ho. E14 ....5D 86
(off Morris Rd.)
Paternoster La. EC4 ....1B 14 (6B 84)
Paternoster Row EC4 ....1C 14 (6C 84)
Paternoster Sq. EC4 ....1B 14 (6B 84)
Paterson Ct. EC1 ....2E 8
Pater St. W8 ....3J 99
Pates Mnr. Dr. TW14: Bedf 7F 111
Path, The SW19 ....1K 153
Pathfield Rd. SW16 ....6H 137
Patience Rd. SW11 ....2C 118
Patio Cl. SW4 ....6H 119
Patmore Est. SW8 ....1G 119
Patmore Ho. N16 ....5E 66
Patmore St. SW8 ....1G 119
Patmos Lodge SW9 ....1B 120
(off Elliott Rd.)
Patmos Rd. SW9 ....7B 102
Paton Cl. E3 ....3C 86
Paton Ho. SW9 ....2K 119
(off Stockwell Rd.)
Paton St. EC1 ....2C 8 (3C 84)
Patricia Ct. BR7: Chst 1H 161
DA16: Well 7B 108
Patrick Coman Ho. EC1 ....2A 8
(off St John St.)
Patrick Connolly Gdns. E3 ....3D 86
Patrick Ct. SE1 ....7B 14
(off Webber St.)
Patrick Pas. SW11 ....2C 118
Patrick Rd. E13 ....3A 88
Patriot Sq. E2 ....2H 85
Patrol Pl. SE6 ....6D 122
Pat Shaw Ho. E1 ....4K 85
(off Globe Rd.)
Patshull Pl. NW5 ....6G 65
Patshull Rd. NW5 ....6G 65
Patten All. TW10: Rich 5D 114
Pattenden Rd. SE6 ....1B 140
Patten Ho. N4 ....1C 66
Patten Rd. SW18 ....7C 118
Patterdale NW1 ....2K 5
(off Osnaburgh St.)
Patterdale Cl.BR1: Brom 6H 141
Patterdale Rd. SE15 ....7J 103
Pattern Ho. EC1 ....3A 8 (4B 84)
Patterson Ct. SE19 ....7F 139
Patterson Rd. SE19 ....6F 139
Pattina Wlk. SE16 ....1A 104
(off Silver Wlk.)
Pattison Ho. E1 ....6K 85
(off Wellesley St.)
SE1 ....6D 14
(off Redcross Way)
Pattison Rd. NW2 ....3J 63
Pattison Wlk. SE18 ....5G 107
Paul Byrne Ho. N2 ....3A 46
Paul Cl. E15 ....7G 69
Paul Ct. N18 ....4B 34
(off Fairfield Rd.)
RM7: Rom 5J 55
Paul Daisley Ct. NW6 ....7G 63
(off Christchurch Av.)
Paulet Rd. SE5 ....2B 120
Paulet Way NW10 ....7A 62
Paul Gdns. CR0: C'don 2F 169
Paulhan Rd. HA3: Kenton 4D 42
Paul Ho. W10 ....4G 81
(off Ladbroke Gro.)
Paulin Dr. N21 ....7F 23
Pauline Cres. TW2: Whitt 1G 131
Pauline Ho. E1 ....5G 85
(off Old Montague St.)
Paul Julius Cl. E14 ....7F 87
Paul Robeson Cl. E6 ....3E 88
Paul Robeson Ho. WC1 ....1H 7
(off Penton Ri.)
Paul Robeson Theatre, The 3F 113
(off High St.)
Paul St. E15 ....1G 87
EC2 ....4F 9 (4D 84)
Paul's Wlk. EC4 ....2B 14 (7C 84)

Paultons Ho. SW3 . . . . . 7B 16
(off King's Rd.)
Paultons Sq. SW3 . . . . . 7B 16 (6B 100)
Paultons St. SW3 . . . . . 6B 100
Pauntley St. N19 . . . . . 1G 65
Pavan Ct. E2 . . . . . 3J 85
(off Sceptre Rd.)
Paved Ct. TW9: Rich 5D 114
Paveley Ct. NW7 . . . . . 7B 30
(off Langstone Way)
Paveley Dr. SW11 . . . . . 7C 100
Paveley Ho. N1 . . . . . 2K 83
(off Priory Grn. Est.)
Paveley St. NW8 . . . . . 2C 4 (3C 82)
Pavement, The E11 . . . . . 1E 68
(off Hainault Rd.)
SW4 . . . . . 4G 119
TW7: Isle 3A 114
(off South St.)
W5 . . . . . 3E 96
Pavement M. RM6: Chad H 7D 54
Pavement Sq. CR0: C'don 1G 169
Pavet Cl. RM10: Dag 6H 73
Pavilion NW8 . . . . . 2B 4 (3B 82)
Pavilion, The SW8 . . . . . 7H 101
Pavilion Ct. NW6 . . . . . 3J 81
(off Stafford Rd.)
Pavilion La. BR3: Beck 6B 140
Pavilion Leisure Cen., The 2J 159
Pavilion Lodge HA2: Harr 1H 59
Pavilion M. N3 . . . . . 3J 45
Pavilion Pde. W12 . . . . . 6E 80
(off Wood La.)
Pavilion Rd. IG1: Ilf 7D 52
SW1 . . . . . 7F 11 (3D 100)
Pavilion Sports & Fitness Club, The
. . . . . 3G 149
Pavilion Sq. SW17 . . . . . 3D 136
Pavilion St. SW1 . . . . . 2F 17 (3D 100)
Pavilion Ter. IG2: Ilf 5J 53
W12 . . . . . 6E 80
(off Wood La.)
Pavilion Way HA4: Ruis 2A 58
HA8: Edg 7C 28
Pavillion Ho. SE16 . . . . . 2K 103
(off Water Gdns. Sq.)
Pavillion M. N4 . . . . . 2K 65
(off Tollington Pl.)
Pawleyne Cl. SE20 . . . . . 7J 139
Pawsey Cl. E13 . . . . . 1K 87
Pawsons Rd. CR0: C'don 6C 156
Paxfold HA7: Stan 5J 27
Paxford Rd. HA0: Wemb 2B 60
Paxton Cl. KT12: Walt T 7A 148
TW9: Kew 2F 115
Paxton Ct. CR4: Mitc 2D 154
(off Armfield Cres.)
SE12 . . . . . 3A 142
SE26 . . . . . 4A 140
(off Adamsrill Rd.)
Paxton Ho. SE17 . . . . . 5D 102
(off Morecambe St.)
Paxton Pl. SE27 . . . . . 4E 138
Paxton Rd. BR1: Brom 7J 141
N17 . . . . . 7A 34
SE23 . . . . . 3A 140
W4 . . . . . 6A 98
Paxton Ter. SW1 . . . . . 7K 17 (6F 101)
Paymal Ho. E1 . . . . . 5J 85
(off Stepney Way)
Payne Cl. IG11: Bark 7J 71
Payne Ho. N1 . . . . . 1K 83
(off Barnsbury Est.)
Paynell Ct. SE3 . . . . . 3G 123
Payne Rd. E3 . . . . . 2D 86
Paynesfield Av. SW14 . . . . . 3K 115
Paynesfield Rd. WD23: B Hea 1E 26
Payne St. SE8 . . . . . 7B 104
Paynes Wlk. W6 . . . . . 6G 99
Payzes Gdns. IG8: Wfd G 6C 36
Peaberry Ct. NW4 . . . . . 3C 44
Peabody Av. SW1 . . . . . 5J 17 (5F 101)
Peabody Bldgs. E1 . . . . . 2K 15
EC1 . . . . . 4D 8
(off Roscoe St.)
SW3 . . . . . 7C 16
Peabody Cl. CR0: C'don 1J 169
SE10 . . . . . 1D 122
SW1 . . . . . 7K 17 (5F 101)
Peabody Cotts. N17 . . . . . 1E 48
Peabody Ct. EC1 . . . . . 4D 8
(off Roscoe St.)
SE5 . . . . . 1D 120
(off Kimpton Rd.)
Peabody Est. E1 . . . . . 7K 85
(off Brodlove La.)
E2 . . . . . 2H 85
(off Minerva St.)
EC1 . . . . . 4D 8
(off Dufferin St., not continuous)
EC1 . . . . . 4K 7
(off Farringdon La.)
N1 . . . . . 1C 84
SE1 . . . . . 5K 13 (1A 102)
(Duchy St.)
SE1 . . . . . 6D 14
(Marshalsea Rd.)
SE1 . . . . . 5C 14 (1C 102)
(Southwark St.)
SE5 . . . . . 1D 120
(off Camberwell Grn.)
SE24 . . . . . 7B 120
SW1 . . . . . 3B 18
SW3 . . . . . 7D 16 (6C 100)
SW6 . . . . . 6J 99
(off Lillie Rd.)
SW11 . . . . . 4C 118
W6 . . . . . 5E 98
W10 . . . . . 5E 80
Peabody Hill SE21 . . . . . 1B 138
Peabody Sq. SE1 . . . . . 7A 14 (2B 102)
(not continuous)
Peabody Ter. EC1 . . . . . 4K 7
(off Farringdon La.)
Peabody Twr. EC1 . . . . . 4D 8
(off Golden La.)
Peabody Trust SE17 . . . . . 4D 102
Peabody Yd. N1 . . . . . 1C 84
Peace Cl. N14 . . . . . 5A 22
SE25 . . . . . 4E 156
UB6: G'frd 1H 77
Peace Ct. SE1 . . . . . 5G 103
(off Harmony Pl.)
Peace Gro. HA9: Wemb 3H 61
Peace St. SE18 . . . . . 6E 106
Peaches Cl. SM2: Cheam 7G 165
Peachey La. UB8: Cowl 5A 74
Peach Gro. E11 . . . . . 3F 69
Peach Rd. TW13: Felt 1J 129
W10 . . . . . 3F 81
Peach Tree Av. UB7: Yiew 6B 74
Peachum Rd. SE3 . . . . . 6H 105
Peachwalk M. E3 . . . . . 2K 85
Peachy Cl. HA8: Edg 6B 28
Peacock Av. TW14: Bedf 1F 129
Peacock Cl. E4 . . . . . 7G 35
NW7 . . . . . 5B 30
RM8: Dag 1C 72
Peacock Ho. SE5 . . . . . 1E 120
(off St Giles Rd.)
Peacock Ind. Est. N17 . . . . . 7A 34
Peacock Pl. N1 . . . . . 6A 66
Peacock St. SE17 . . . . . 4B 102
Peacock Theatre 1G 13
(off Portugal St.)
Peacock Wlk. E16 . . . . . 6K 87
(off Mortlake Rd.)
N6 . . . . . 7F 47
Peacock Yd. SE17 . . . . . 5B 102
(off Iliffe St.)
Peak, The SE26 . . . . . 3J 139
Peaketon Av. IG4: Ilf 4B 52
Peak Hill SE26 . . . . . 4J 139
Peak Hill Av. SE26 . . . . . 4J 139
Peak Hill Gdns. SE26 . . . . . 4J 139
Peak Ho. N4 . . . . . 1C 66
(off Woodberry Down Est.)
Peal Gdns. W13 . . . . . 3A 78
Peall Rd. CR0: C'don 6K 155
Peall Rd. Ind. Est.
CR0: C'don 6K 155
Pearce Cl. CR4: Mitc 2E 154
Pearcefield Av. SE23 . . . . . 1J 139
Pearce Ho. SW1 . . . . . 4D 18
(off Causton St.)
Pear Cl. NW9 . . . . . 4K 43
SE14 . . . . . 7A 104
Pear Ct. SE15 . . . . . 7F 103
(off Thruxton Way)
Pearcroft Rd. E11 . . . . . 2F 69
Peardon St. SW8 . . . . . 2F 119
Peareswood Gdns. HA7: Stan 1D 42
Pearfield Rd. SE23 . . . . . 3A 140
Pearing Cl. KT4: Wor Pk 2F 165
Pearl Cl. E6 . . . . . 6E 88
NW2 . . . . . 7F 45
Pearl Rd. E17 . . . . . 3C 50
Pearl St. E1 . . . . . 1H 103
Pearmain Cl. TW17: Shep 5D 146
Pearman St. SE1 . . . . . 1K 19 (3A 102)
Pear Pl. SE1 . . . . . 6J 13 (2A 102)
Pear Rd. E11 . . . . . 3F 69
Pears Av. TW17: Shep 3G 147
Pearscroft Ct. SW6 . . . . . 1K 117
Pearscroft Rd. SW6 . . . . . 1K 117
Pearse St. SE15 . . . . . 6E 102
Pearson Cl. EN5: New Bar 3E 20
SE5 . . . . . 1C 120
(off Camberwell New Rd.)
Pearson M. SW4 . . . . . 3H 119
(off Edgeley Rd.)
Pearson's Av. SE14 . . . . . 1C 122
Pearson St. E2 . . . . . 2F 85
Pearson Way CR4: Mitc 1E 154
Pears Rd. TW3: Houn 3G 113
Peartree SE26 . . . . . 5A 140
Pear Tree Av. UB7: Yiew 6B 74
Peartree Av. SW17 . . . . . 3A 136
Pear Tree Cl. BR2: Brom 5B 160
CR4: Mitc 2C 154
E2 . . . . . 1F 85
KT9: Chess 5G 163
Peartree Cl. DA8: Erith 1K 127
Pear Tree Ct. E18 . . . . . 1K 51
EC1 . . . . . 4K 7 (4A 84)
Peartree Gdns. RM7: Mawney 2H 55
RM8: Dag 4B 72
Pear Tree Ho. SE4 . . . . . 3B 122
Peartree La. E1 . . . . . 7J 85
Pear Tree Rd. TW15: Ashf 5E 128
Peartree Rd. EN1: Enf 3K 23
Peartrees UB7: Yiew 7A 74
Pear Tree St. EC1 . . . . . 3B 8 (4C 84)
Peartree Way SE10 . . . . . 4J 105
Peary Ho. NW10 . . . . . 7K 61
Peary Pl. E2 . . . . . 3J 85
Peasmead Ter. E4 . . . . . 4K 35
Peatfield Cl. DA15: Sidc 3J 143
Pebble Way W3 . . . . . 1H 97
(off Steyne Rd.)
Pebworth Rd. HA1: Harr 2A 60
Peckarmans Wood SE26 . . . . . 3G 139
Peckett Sq. N5 . . . . . 4C 66
Peckford Pl. SW9 . . . . . 2A 120
PECKHAM 1G 121
Peckham Gro. SE15 . . . . . 7E 102
Peckham High St. SE15 . . . . . 1G 121
Peckham Hill St. SE15 . . . . . 7G 103
Peckham Pk. Rd. SE15 . . . . . 7G 103
Peckham Pulse Health & Leisure Cen.
. . . . . 1G 121
Peckham Rd. SE5 . . . . . 1E 120
SE15 . . . . . 1E 120
Peckham Rye SE15 . . . . . 3G 121
SE22 . . . . . 4G 121
Peckham Sq. SE15 . . . . . 1G 121
Pecks Yd. E1 . . . . . 5J 9
(off Hanbury St.)
Peckwater St. NW5 . . . . . 5G 65
Pedlar's Wlk. N7 . . . . . 5K 65
Pedley Rd. RM8: Dag 1C 72
Pedley St. E1 . . . . . 4K 9 (4G 85)
Pedro St. E5 . . . . . 3K 67
Pedworth Gdns. SE16 . . . . . 4J 103
Peebles Ct. UB1: S'hall 6G 77
(off Haldane Rd.)
Peebles Ho. NW6 . . . . . 2K 81
(off Carlton Va.)
Peek Cres. SW19 . . . . . 5F 135
Peel Cl. E4 . . . . . 2J 35
N9 . . . . . 3B 34
Peel Dr. IG5: Ilf 3C 52
NW9 . . . . . 3B 44
Peel Gro. E2 . . . . . 2J 85
Peel Pas. W8 . . . . . 1J 99
Peel Pl. IG5: Ilf 2C 52
SE9 . . . . . 1D 124
Peel Pct. NW6 . . . . . 2J 81
Peel Rd. BR6: Farnb 5G 173
E18 . . . . . 1H 51
HA3: W'stone 3K 41
(not continuous)
HA9: Wemb 3D 60
Peel St. W8 . . . . . 1J 99
Peel Way UB8: Hil 5A 74
Peerglow Est. EN3: Pond E 5C 24
Peerless St. EC1 . . . . . 2E 8 (3D 84)
Pegamoid Rd. N18 . . . . . 3D 34
Pegasus Cl. N16 . . . . . 4D 66
Pegasus Ct. KT1: King T 3D 150
N21 . . . . . 7H 23
NW10 . . . . . 3D 80
(off Trenmar Gdns.)
TW8: Bford 5F 97
W3 . . . . . 6J 79
(off Horn La.)
Pegasus Ho. E1 . . . . . 4K 85
(off Beaumont Sq.)
E13 . . . . . 3K 87
Pegasus Pl. SE11 . . . . . 7J 19 (6A 102)
SW6 . . . . . 1J 117
Pegasus Rd. CR0: Wadd 6A 168
Pegasus Way N11 . . . . . 6A 32
Peggotty Way UB8: Hil 6D 74
Pegg Rd. TW5: Hest 7B 94
Pegley Gdns. SE12 . . . . . 2J 141
Pegwell St. SE18 . . . . . 7J 107
Pekin Cl. E14 . . . . . 6C 86
(off Pekin St.)
Pekin St. E14 . . . . . 6C 86
Pelabon Ho. TW1: Twick 6D 114
(off Clevedon Rd.)
Peldon Ct. TW9: Rich 4F 115
Peldon Pas. TW10: Rich 4F 115
Peldon Wlk. N1 . . . . . 1B 84
(off Popham St.)
Pelgrave Ct. TW11: Ham W 7B 132
Pelham Av. IG11: Bark 1K 89
Pelham Cl. SE5 . . . . . 3E 120
Pelham Cotts. DA5: Bexl 1H 145
Pelham Ct. DA14: Sidc 3A 144
SW3 . . . . . 4C 16
(off Fulham Rd.)
Pelham Cres. SW7 . . . . . 4C 16 (4C 100)
Pelham Ho. SW1 . . . . . 2D 18
(off Gt. Peter St.)
W14 . . . . . 4H 99
(off Mornington Av.)
Pelham Pl. SW7 . . . . . 4C 16 (4C 100)
W13 . . . . . 4K 77
Pelham Rd. BR3: Beck 2J 157
DA7: Bex 3G 127
E18 . . . . . 3K 51
IG1: Ilf 2H 71
N15 . . . . . 4F 49
N22 . . . . . 2A 48
SW19 . . . . . 7J 135
Pelham St. SW7 . . . . . 3B 16 (4B 100)

Pelican Est. SE15 .... 1F 121
Pelican Ho. SE5 .... 1F 121
SE8 .... 4B 104
Pelican Pas. E1 .... 4J 85
Pelican Wlk. SW9 .... 4B 120
Pelican Wharf E1 .... 1J 103
(off Wapping Wall)
Pelier St. SE17 .... 6C 102
Pelinore Rd. SE6 .... 2G 141
Pella Ho. SE11 .... 5H 19 (5K 101)
Pellant Rd. SW6 .... 7G 99
Pellatt Gro. N22 .... 1A 48
Pellatt Rd. HA9: Wemb 2D 60
SE22 .... 5F 121
Pellerin Rd. N16 .... 5E 66
Pellew Ho. E1 .... 4H 85
(off Somerford St.)
Pellings Cl. BR2: Brom 3G 159
Pelling St. E14 .... 6C 86
Pellipar Cl. N13 .... 3F 33
Pellipar Gdns. SE18 .... 5D 106
Pellipar Rd. SE18 .... 5D 106
Pellow Cl. EN5: Barn 6C 20
Pelly Rd. E13 .... 1J 87
(not continuous)
Pelter St. E2 .... 1J 9 (3F 85)
Pelton Rd. SE10 .... 5G 105
Pembar Av. E17 .... 3A 50
Pemberley Chase KT19: Ewe 5H 163
Pemberley Cl. KT19: Ewe 5H 163
Pemberley Ho. KT19: Ewe 5H 163
(off Pemberley Chase)
Pember Rd. NW10 .... 3F 81
Pemberton Cl. TW19: Stanw 1A 128
Pemberton Ct. E1 .... 3K 85
(off Portelet Rd.)
EN1: Enf 3K 23
Pemberton Gdns. N19 .... 3G 65
RM6: Chad H 5E 54
Pemberton Ho. SE26 .... 4G 139
(off High Level Dr.)
Pemberton Pl. E8 .... 7H 67
Pemberton Rd. KT8: E Mos 4G 149
N4 .... 5A 48
Pemberton Row EC4 .... 7K 7 (6A 84)
Pemberton Ter. N19 .... 3G 65
Pembridge Av. TW2: Whitt 1D 130
Pembridge Cres. W11 .... 7J 81
Pembridge Gdns. W2 .... 7J 81
Pembridge M. W11 .... 7J 81
Pembridge Pl. SW15 .... 5J 117
W2 .... 7J 81
Pembridge Rd. W11 .... 7J 81
Pembridge Sq. W2 .... 7J 81
Pembridge Studios W11 .... 7J 81
(off Pembridge Vs.)
Pembridge Vs. W2 .... 7J 81
W11 .... 7J 81
Pembroke W14 .... 4H 99
(off Mornington Av.)
Pembroke Av. EN1: Enf 1C 24
HA3: Kenton 3A 42
HA5: Pinn 1B 58
KT5: Surb 5H 151
N1 .... 1J 83
Pembroke Bldgs. NW10 .... 3C 80
Pembroke Bus. Cen.
BR8: Swan 7K 145
Pembroke Cen., The HA4: Ruis 1H 57
Pembroke Cl. SW1 .... 7H 11 (2E 100)
Pembroke Cotts. W8 .... 3J 99
(off Pembroke Sq.)
Pembroke Ct. W7 .... 6K 77
(off Copley Cl.)
W8 .... 3J 99
(off Sth. Edwardes Sq.)
Pembroke Gdns. HA4: Ruis 1H 57
RM10: Dag 3H 73
W8 .... 4H 99
Pembroke Gdns. Cl. W8 .... 3J 99
Pembroke Hall NW4 .... 3E 44
(off Mulberry Cl.)
Pembroke Ho. SW1 .... 2G 17
(off Chesham Ho.)
W2 .... 6K 81
(off Hallfield Est.)
W3 .... 2J 97
(off Park Rd. E.)
Pembroke Lodge HA7: Stan 6J 27
Pembroke Mans. NW6 .... 6A 64
(off Canfield Gdns.)
Pembroke M. E3 .... 3A 86
N10 .... 1E 46
W8 .... 3J 99
Pembroke Pde. DA8: Erith 5J 109
Pembroke Pl. HA8: Edg 7B 28
TW7: Isle 2J 113
W8 .... 3J 99
Pembroke Rd. BR1: Brom 2A 160
CR4: Mitc 2E 154
DA8: Erith 5J 109
E6 .... 5D 88
E17 .... 5D 50
HA4: Ruis 1G 57
HA9: Wemb 3D 60
IG3: Ilf 1K 71
N8 .... 4J 47
N10 .... 1E 46
N13 .... 3H 33
N15 .... 5F 49
SE25 .... 4E 156
UB6: G'frd 4F 77
W8 .... 4H 99
Pembroke Sq. W8 .... 3J 99
Pembroke St. N1 .... 7J 65
(not continuous)
Pembroke Studios W8 .... 3H 99
Pembroke Ter. NW8 .... 1B 82
(off Queen's Ter.)
Pembroke Vs. TW9: Rich 4D 114
W8 .... 4J 99
Pembroke Wlk. W8 .... 4J 99
Pembroke Way UB3: Harl 3E 92
Pembrook M. SW11 .... 4B 118
Pembry Cl. SW9 .... 1A 120
Pembury Av. KT4: Wor Pk 1C 164
Pembury Cl. BR2: Hayes 7H 159
E5 .... 5H 67
Pembury Ct. UB3: Harl 6F 93
Pembury Cres. DA14: Sidc 2E 144
Pembury Pl. E5 .... 5H 67
Pembury Rd. DA7: Bex 7E 108
E5 .... 5H 67
N17 .... 1F 49
SE25 .... 4G 157
Pemdevon Rd. CR0: C'don 7A 156
Pemell Cl. E1 .... 4J 85
Pemell Ho. E1 .... 4J 85
(off Pemell Cl.)
Pemerich Cl. UB3: Harl 5H 93
Pempath Pl. HA9: Wemb 2D 60
Penally Pl. N1 .... 1D 84
Penang Ho. E1 .... 1H 103
(off Prusom St.)
Penang St. E1 .... 1H 103
Penard Rd. UB2: S'hall 3F 95
Penart Ct. SM2: Sutt 7A 166
Penarth Cen. SE15 .... 6J 103
Penarth St. SE15 .... 6J 103
Penberth Rd. SE6 .... 2E 140
Penbury Rd. UB2: S'hall 4D 94
Pencombe M. W11 .... 7H 81
Pencraig Way SE15 .... 6H 103
Pendall Cl. EN4: E Barn 4H 21
Penda Rd. DA8: Erith 7H 109
Pendarves Rd. SW20 .... 1E 152
Penda's Mead E9 .... 4A 68
Pendell Av. UB3: Harl 7H 93
Pendennis Ho. SE8 .... 4A 104
Pendennis Rd. N17 .... 3D 48
SW16 .... 4J 137
Penderel Rd. TW3: Houn 5E 112
Penderry Ri. SE6 .... 2F 141
Penderyn Way N7 .... 4H 65
Pendlebury Ct. KT5: Surb 4E 150
(off Cranes Pk.)
Pendle Ct. UB10: Hil 1D 74
Pendle Ho. SE26 .... 3G 139
Pendle Rd. SW16 .... 6F 137
Pendlestone Rd. E17 .... 5D 50
Pendlewood Cl. W5 .... 5C 78
Pendley Ho. E2 .... 1G 85
(off Whiston Rd.)
Pendolino Way NW10 .... 7G 61
Pendragon Rd. BR1: Brom 3H 141
Pendragon Wlk. NW9 .... 6A 44
Pendrell Ho. WC2 .... 1D 12
(off New Compton St.)
Pendrell Rd. SE4 .... 2A 122
Pendrell St. SE18 .... 6H 107
Pendula Dr. UB4: Yead 4B 76
Pendulum M. E8 .... 5F 67
Penerley Rd. SE6 .... 1D 140
Penfield Lodge W9 .... 5J 81
(off Admiral Wlk.)
Penfields Ho. N7 .... 6J 65
(off York Way Est.)
Penfold Cl. CR0: Wadd 3A 168
Penfold La. DA5: Bexl 2D 144
(Cotleigh Av.)
DA5: Bexl 1D 144
(Stansted Cres.)
Penfold Pl. NW1 .... 5C 4 (5C 82)
Penfold Rd. N9 .... 1E 34
Penfold St. NW1 .... 4B 4 (4B 82)
NW8 .... 4B 4 (4B 82)
Penford Gdns. SE9 .... 3B 124
Penford St. SE5 .... 2B 120
Pengarth Rd. DA5: Bexl 5D 126
PENGE 7J 139
Penge Ho. SW11 .... 3B 118
Penge La. SE20 .... 7J 139
Pengelly Apartments E14 .... 5D 104
(off Bartlett M.)
Penge Rd. E13 .... 1A 88
SE20 .... 3G 157
SE25 .... 3G 157
Penhale Cl. BR6: Chels 4K 173
Penhall Rd. SE7 .... 4B 106
Penhill Rd. DA5: Bexl 6C 126
Penhurst Mans. SW6 .... 1H 117
(off Rostrevor Rd.)
Penhurst Pl. SE1 .... 1H 19
Penhurst Rd. IG6: Ilf 1F 53
Penifather La. UB6: G'frd 3H 77
Peninsula Apartments W2 .... 6C 4
(off Praed St.)
Peninsula Ct. E14 .... 3D 104
(off E. Ferry Rd.)
N1 .... 1C 84
(off Basire St.)
Peninsula Hgts. SE1 .... 5F 19 (5J 101)
Peninsular Cl. TW14: Felt 6F 111
Peninsular Pk. SE7 .... 4J 105
Peninsular Pk. Rd. SE7 .... 4J 105
Peninsula Sq. SE10 .... 2G 105
Penistone Rd. SW16 .... 7J 137
Penketh Dr. HA1: Harr 3H 59
Penley Ct. WC2 .... 2H 13 (7K 83)
Penmayne Ho. SE11 .... 5K 19
(off Kennings Way)
Penmon Rd. SE2 .... 3A 108
Pennack Rd. SE15 .... 6F 103
Penn Almshouses SE10 .... 1E 122
(off Greenwich Sth. St.)
Pennant M. W8 .... 4K 99
Pennant Ter. E17 .... 2B 50
Pennard Mans. W12 .... 2E 98
(off Goldhawk Rd.)
Pennard Rd. W12 .... 2E 98
Pennards, The TW16: Sun 3A 148
Penn Cl. HA3: Kenton 4C 42
UB6: G'frd 2F 77
Penn Ct. NW9 .... 3K 43
Penner Cl. SW19 .... 2G 135
Penners Gdns. KT6: Surb 7E 150
Pennethorne Cl. E9 .... 1J 85
Pennethorne Ho. SW11 .... 3B 118
Pennethorne Rd. SE15 .... 7H 103
Penn Gdns. BR7: Chst 2F 161
RM5: Col R 1G 55
Penn Ho. NW8 .... 4C 4
(off Mallory St.)
Pennine Dr. NW2 .... 2F 63
Pennine Ho. N9 .... 3B 34
(off Plevna Rd.)
Pennine La. NW2 .... 2G 63
Pennine Pde. NW2 .... 2G 63
Pennine Way DA7: Bex 1K 127
UB3: Harl 7F 93
Pennington Cl. SE27 .... 4D 138
Pennington Ct. SE16 .... 1A 104
Pennington Dr. N21 .... 5D 22
Pennington Lodge KT5: Surb 5E 150
(off Cranes Dr.)
Pennington St. E1 .... 7H 85
Pennington Way SE12 .... 2K 141
Penniston Cl. N17 .... 2C 48
Penniwell Cl. HA8: Edg 4A 28
Penn La. DA5: Bexl 5D 126
(not continuous)
Penn Rd. N7 .... 5J 65
Penn St. N1 .... 1D 84
Pennycroft CR0: Sels 7A 170
Pennyfather La. EN2: Enf 3H 23
Pennyfields E14 .... 7C 86
(not continuous)
Pennyford Ct. NW8 .... 3A 4
(off St John's Wood Rd.)
Penny La. TW17: Shep 7G 147
Penny M. SW12 .... 7F 119
Pennymoor Wlk. W9 .... 4H 81
(off Fernhead Rd.)
Penny Rd. NW10 .... 3H 79
Penny Royal SM6: Wall 6H 167
Pennyroyal Av. E6 .... 6E 88
Penpoll Rd. E8 .... 6H 67
Penpool La. DA16: Well 3B 126
Penrhyn Av. E17 .... 1B 50
Penrhyn Cres. E17 .... 1C 50
SW14 .... 4J 115
Penrhyn Gdns. KT1: King T 4D 150
Penrhyn Gro. E17 .... 1C 50
Penrhyn Rd. KT1: King T 4E 150
Penrith Cl. BR3: Beck 1D 158
SW15 .... 5G 117
UB8: Uxb 7A 56
Penrith Pl. SE27 .... 2B 138
Penrith Rd. CR7: Thor H 2C 156
KT3: N Mald 4K 151
N15 .... 5D 48
Penrith St. SW16 .... 6G 137
Penrose Gro. SE17 .... 5C 102
Penrose Ho. N21 .... 5E 22
SE17 .... 5C 102
Penrose St. SE17 .... 5C 102
Penryn Ho. SE11 .... 5B 102
(off Seaton Cl.)
Penryn St. NW1 .... 2H 83
Penry St. SE1 .... 4E 102
Pensbury Pl. SW8 .... 2G 119
Pensbury St. SW8 .... 2G 119
Pensford Av. TW9: Kew 2G 115
Penshurst NW5 .... 6E 64
Penshurst Av. DA15: Sidc 6A 126
Penshurst Gdns. HA8: Edg 5C 28
Penshurst Grn. BR2: Brom 5H 159
Penshurst Ho. SE15 .... 6J 103
(off Lovelinch Cl.)
Penshurst Rd.
CR7: Thor H 5B 156
DA7: Bex 1F 127
E9 .... 7K 67
N17 .... 7A 34
Penshurst Wlk. BR2: Brom 5H 159
Penshurst Way SM2: Sutt 7J 165
Pensilver Cl. EN4: E Barn 4H 21
Penstemon Cl. N3 .... 6D 30

Penstock Footpath N8 . . . . .3K 47
 N22 . . . . .3K 47
Pentagram Yd. W11 . . . . .6J 81
                               (off Needham Rd.)
Pentavia Retail Pk. NW7 . . . . .7G 29
Pentelow Gdns.
 TW14: Felt 6J 111
Pentire Rd. E17 . . . . .1F 51
Pentland Av. HA8: Edg 2C 28
 TW17: Shep 5C 146
Pentland Cl. N9 . . . . .2D 34
 NW11 . . . . .2G 63
Pentland Gdns. SW18 . . . . .6A 118
Pentland Pl. UB5: N'olt 1C 76
Pentland Rd. NW6 . . . . .3J 81
Pentlands Cl. CR4: Mitc 3F 155
Pentland St. SW18 . . . . .6A 118
Pentland Way UB10: Ick 3E 56
Pentlow St. SW15 . . . . .3E 116
Pentlow Way IG9: Buck H 1H 37
Pentney Rd. E4 . . . . .1A 36
 SW12 . . . . .1G 137
 SW19 . . . . .1G 153
Penton Gro. N1 . . . . .2A 84
Penton Ho. N1 . . . . .2A 84
                             (off Pentonville Rd.)
 SE2 . . . . .1D 108
Penton Pl. SE17 . . . . .5B 102
Penton Ri. WC1 . . . . .1H 7 (3K 83)
Penton St. N1 . . . . .2A 84
PENTONVILLE 2K 83
Pentonville Rd. N1 . . . . .1F 7 (2J 83)
Pentrich Av. EN1: Enf 1B 24
Pentridge St. SE15 . . . . .7F 103
Pentyre Av. N18 . . . . .5J 33
Penwerris Av. TW7: Isle 7G 95
Penwerris Ct. TW5: Hest 7G 95
Penwith Rd. SW18 . . . . .2J 135
Penwood Ct. HA5: Pinn 4D 40
Penwood Ho. SW15 . . . . .6B 116
Penwortham Ct. N22 . . . . .2A 48
                                    (off Mayes Rd.)
Penwortham Rd. SW16 . . . . .6F 137
Penylan Pl. HA8: Edg 7B 28
Penywern Rd. SW5 . . . . .5J 99
Penzance Pl. W11 . . . . .1G 99
Penzance St. W11 . . . . .1G 99
Peony Ct. IG8: Wfd G 7B 36
 SW10 . . . . .7A 16 (6A 100)
Peony Gdns. W12 . . . . .7C 80
Peperfield WC1 . . . . .2G 7
                                    (off Cromer St.)
Pepler Ho. W10 . . . . .4G 81
                              (off Wornington Rd.)
Pepler M. SE5 . . . . .5F 103
Peploe Rd. NW6 . . . . .2F 81
Peplow Cl. UB7: Yiew 1A 92
Pepper Cl. E6 . . . . .5D 88
Peppercorn Cl. CR7: Thor H 2D 156
Peppermint Sq.
 SE13 . . . . .5C 122
Peppermint Cl. CR0: C'don 7J 155
Peppermint Pl. E11 . . . . .3G 69
Pepper St. E14 . . . . .3D 104
 SE1 . . . . .6C 14 (2C 102)
Peppie Cl. N16 . . . . .2E 66
Pepys Cl. UB10: Ick 4D 56
Pepys Cres. E16 . . . . .1J 105
 EN5: Barn 5A 20
Pepys Ho. E2 .3J 85
                                    (off Kirkwall Pl.)
Pepys Ri. BR6: Orp 1K 173
Pepys Rd. SE14 . . . . .1K 121
 SW20 . . . . .1E 152
Pepys St. EC3 . . . . .2H 15 (7E 84)
Perceval Av. NW3 . . . . .5C 64
Perceval Ct. UB5: N'olt 5C 58
Perceval Ho. W5 . . . . .7C 78
Percheron Cl. TW7: Isle 3K 113
Perch St. E8 .4F 67
Percival Cl. N17 . . . . .7A 34
Percival Gdns. RM6: Chad H 6C 54

Percival Rd. BR6: Farnb 2F 173
 EN1: Enf .4A 24
 SW14 . . . . .4J 115
 TW13: Felt 2H 129
Percival St. EC1 . . . . .3A 8 (4B 84)
Percival Way KT19: Ewe 4K 163
Percy Av. TW15: Ashf 5C 128
Percy Bilton Ct TW5: Hest 1F 113
                                 (off Skinners La.)
Percy Bryant Rd. TW16: Sun 7G 129
Percy Bush Rd. UB7: W Dray 3B 92
Percy Cir. WC1 . . . . .1H 7 (3K 83)
Percy Gdns. EN3: Pond E 5E 24
 KT4: Wor Pk 1K 163
 TW7: Isle 3A 114
 UB4: Hayes 3G 75
Percy Laurie Ho. SW15 . . . . .4F 117
                                    (off Nursery Cl.)
Percy M. N1 . . . . .6C 6
Percy Pas. W1 . . . . .6C 6
Percy Rd. CR4: Mitc 7E 154
 DA7: Bex 2E 126
 E11 . . . . .7G 51
 E16 . . . . .5G 87
 IG3: Ilf 7A 54
 N12 . . . . .5F 31
 N21 . . . . .7H 23
 RM7: Mawney 3H 55
 SE20 . . . . .1K 157
 SE25 . . . . .5G 157
 TW2: Whitt 1F 131
 TW7: Isle 4A 114
 TW12: Hamp 7E 130
 W12 . . . . .2C 98
Percy St. W1 . . . . .6C 6 (5H 83)
Percy Ter. BR1: Brom 3F 161
Percy Way TW2: Whitt 1G 131
Percy Yd. WC1 . . . . .1H 7 (3K 83)
Peregrine Cl. NW10 . . . . .5K 61
Peregrine Ct. DA16: Well 1K 125
 SE8 . . . . .6C 104
                                  (off Edward St.)
 SW16 . . . . .4K 137
Peregrine Gdns. CR0: C'don 2A 170
Peregrine Ho. EC1 . . . . .1B 8
Peregrine Rd. N17 . . . . .7H 33
 IG8: Sun 2H 147
Peregrine Way SW19 . . . . .7E 134
Perham Rd. W14 . . . . .5G 99
Peridot St. E6 . . . . .5C 88
Perifield SE21 . . . . .1C 138
Perimeade Rd. UB6: G'frd 2C 78
Periton Rd. SE9 . . . . .4B 124
PERIVALE 1C 78
Perivale Gdns. W13 . . . . .4B 78
Perivale Grange UB6: G'frd 3A 78
Perivale La. UB6: G'frd 3A 78
Perivale Lodge UB6: G'frd 3A 78
                                   (off Perivale La.)
Perivale New Bus. Cen. UB6: G'frd 2C 78
Perivale Pk. UB6: G'frd 2B 78
Perivale Pk. Athletics Track 3J 77
Perivale Wood Local Nature Reserve
 . . . . .1K 77
Periwood Cres. UB6: G'frd 1A 78
Perkin Cl. HA0: Wemb 5B 60
 TW3: Houn 4E 112
Perkins Ct. TW15: Ashf 5B 128
Perkins Ho. E14 . . . . .5B 86
                                  (off Wallwood St.)
Perkin's Rents SW1 . . . . . . .2C 18 (3H 101)
Perkins Rd. IG2: Ilf 5H 53
Perkins Sq. SE1 . . . . .4D 14 (1C 102)
Perks Cl. SE3 . . . . .3G 123
Perley Ho. E3 .5B 86
                               (off Weatherley Cl.)
Perpins Rd. SE9 . . . . .6J 125
Perran Rd. SW2 . . . . .1B 138
Perran Wlk. TW8: Bford 5E 96
Perren St. NW5 . . . . .6F 65
Perrers Rd. W6 . . . . .4D 98
Perrin Cl. TW15: Ashf 5B 128

Perrin Ct. TW15: Ashf 4C 128
Perring Est. E3 . . . . .5C 86
                                      (off Gale St.)
Perrin Ho. NW6 . . . . .3J 81
Perrin Rd. HA0: Wemb 4B 60
Perrin's Ct. NW3 . . . . .4A 64
Perrin's La. NW3 . . . . .4A 64
Perrin's Wlk. NW3 . . . . .4A 64
Perronet Ho. SE1 . . . . .3B 102
                                  (off Princess St.)
Perrott St. SE18 . . . . .4G 107
Perry Av. W3 .6K 79
Perry Cl. RM13: Rain 2K 91
 UB8: Hil .6D 74
Perry Ct. E14 . . . . .5C 104
                                (off Maritime Quay)
 KT1: King T 2E 150
                                  (off London Rd.)
 N15 . . . . .6E 48
Perryfield Way NW9 . . . . .6B 44
 TW10: Ham 3B 132
Perry Gdns. N9 . . . . .3J 33
Perry Gth. UB5: N'olt 1A 76
Perry Hall Rd. BR6: St M Cry 6K 161
Perry Hill SE6 . . . . .3B 140
Perry Ho. RM13: Rain 2K 91
Perry How KT4: Wor Pk 1B 164
Perry Lodge E12 . . . . .1B 70
Perryman Ho. IG11: Bark 1G 89
                            (off The Shaftesburys)
Perrymans Farm Rd. IG2: Ilf 6H 53
Perry Mead EN2: Enf 2G 23
Perrymead St. SW6 . . . . .1J 117
Perryn Ct. TW1: Twick 6A 114
Perryn Ho. W3 . . . . .7A 80
Perryn Rd. SE16 . . . . .3H 103
 W3 . . . . .1K 97
Perry Ri. SE23 . . . . .3A 140
Perry Rd. RM9: Dag 5F 91
Perry's Pl. W1 . . . . .7C 6 (6H 83)
Perry St. BR7: Chst 6H 143
 DA1: Cray 4K 127
Perry St. Gdns. BR7: Chst 6J 143
Perry St. Shaw BR7: Chst 7J 143
Perry Va. SE23 . . . . .2J 139
Persant Rd. SE6 . . . . .2G 141
Perseverance Pl. SW9 . . . . .7A 102
 TW9: Rich 4E 114
Perseverance Works
 E2 . . . . .1H 9
                                (off Kingsland Rd.)
Pershore Cl. IG2: Ilf 5F 53
Pershore Gro. SM5: Cars 6B 154
Pershore Ho. W13 . . . . .1A 96
                                (off Singapore Rd.)
Pert Cl. N10 . . . . .7A 32
Perth Av. NW9 . . . . .7K 43
 UB4: Yead 4A 76
Perth Cl. SE5 . . . . .4D 120
 SW20 . . . . .2B 152
 UB5: N'olt 5E 58
Perth Ho. N1 .7K 65
                                (off Bemerton Est.)
Perth Rd. BR3: Beck 2E 158
 E10 . . . . .1A 68
 E13 . . . . .2K 87
 IG2: Ilf 6E 52
 IG11: Bark 2H 89
 N4 . . . . .1A 66
 N22 . . . . .1B 48
Perth Ter. IG2: Ilf 7G 53
Perwell Av. HA2: Harr 1D 58
Perystreete SE23 . . . . .2J 139
Petavel Rd. TW11: Tedd 6J 131
Peter Av. NW10 . . . . .7D 62
Peter Best Ho. E1 . . . . .6H 85
                                  (off Nelson St.)
Peterboat Cl. SE10 . . . . .4G 105
Peterborough Ct. EC4 . . . . .1K 13 (6A 84)
Peterborough Gdns.
 IG1: Ilf 7C 52
Peterborough M. SW6 . . . . .2J 117

Peterborough Rd. E10 . . . . .5E 50
 HA1: Harr 1J 59
 SM5: Cars 6C 154
 SW6 . . . . .2J 117
Peterborough Vs. SW6 . . . . .1K 117
Peter Butler Ho. SE1 . . . . .7K 15
                                (off Wolseley St.)
Peterchurch Ho. SE15 . . . . .6F 103
                           (off Commercial Way)
Petergate SW11 . . . . .4A 118
Peter Harrison Planetarium 7F 105
Peterhead Ct. UB1: S'hall 6G 77
                                  (off Osborne Rd.)
Peter Heathfield Ho. E15 . . . . .1F 87
                                      (off Wise Rd.)
Peter Hills Ho. SE16 . . . . .4G 103
                                  (off Alexis St.)
Peter Ho. SW8 . . . . .7J 101
                              (off Luscombe Way)
Peter James Bus. Cen. UB3: Hayes 2J 93
Peter James Ent. Cen. NW10 . . . . .3J 79
Peter Kennedy Ct. CR0: C'don 6B 158
Peterley Bus. Cen. E2 . . . . .2H 85
Peter Lyell Cl. HA4: Ruis 2K 57
Peter May Cen., The 7K 35
Peter Pan Statue 4A 10 (1B 100)
Peters Cl. DA16: Well 2J 125
 HA7: Stan 6J 27
 RM8: Dag 1D 72
Peters Ct. W2 .6K 81
                                (off Porchester Rd.)
Petersfield Cl. N18 . . . . .5H 33
Petersfield Ri. SW15 . . . . .1D 134
Petersfield Rd. W3 . . . . .2J 97
PETERSHAM 1E 132
Petersham Cl. SM1: Sutt 5J 165
 TW10: Ham 2D 132
Petersham Dr. BR5: St P 2K 161
Petersham Gdns. BR5: St P 2K 161
Petersham Ho. SW7 . . . . .3A 16
                               (off Kendrick M.)
Petersham La. SW7 . . . . .3A 100
Petersham M. SW7 . . . . .3A 100
Petersham Pl. SW7 . . . . .3A 100
Petersham Rd. TW10: Rich, Ham 6D 114
Petersham Ter. CR0: Bedd 3J 167
                               (off Richmond Grn.)
Peter's Hill EC4 . . . . .2C 14 (7C 84)
Peter Shore Ct. E1 . . . . .5K 85
                               (off Beaumont Sq.)
Peter's La. EC1 . . . . .5B 8 (5B 84)
                                    (not continuous)
Peter's Path SE26 . . . . .4H 139
Peterstone Rd. SE2 . . . . .2B 108
Peterstow Cl. SW19 . . . . .2G 135
Peter St. W1 . . . . .2C 12 (7H 83)
Peterwood Pk. CR0: Wadd 2K 167
Peterwood Way CR0: Wadd 2K 167
Petherton Ct. HA1: Harr 6K 41
                                   (off Gayton Rd.)
 NW10 . . . . .1F 81
                                  (off Tiverton Rd.)
Petherton Ho. N4 . . . . .1C 66
                           (off Woodberry Down Est.)
Petherton Rd. N5 . . . . .5C 66
Petiver Cl. E9 .7J 67
Petley Rd. W6 . . . . .6F 99
Peto Pl. NW1 . . . . .3K 5 (4F 83)
Peto St. Nth. E16 . . . . .6H 87
Petrie Cl. NW2 . . . . .6G 63
Petrie Ho. SE18 . . . . .6E 106
                                (off Woolwich Comn.)
Petrie Mus. of Egyptian Archaeology . . .4C 6
Petros Gdns. NW3 . . . . .6A 64
Pettacre Cl. SE28 . . . . .3G 107
Petticoat La. E1 . . . . .6J 9 (5E 84)
Petticoat Lane Market 7J 9
                                (off Middlesex St.)
Petticoat Sq. E1 . . . . .7J 9 (6F 85)
Petticoat Twr. E1 . . . . .7J 9
Pettits Cl. RM1: Rom 2K 55
Pettits La. Nth. RM1: Rom 1K 55

Pettits Pl.—Pincott Rd.

Pettits Pl. RM10: Dag 5G 73
Pettits Rd. RM10: Dag 5G 73
Pettiward Cl. SW15 4E 116
Pettley Gdns. RM7: Rom 5K 55
Pettman Cres. SE28 3H 107
Pettsgrove Av. HA0: Wemb 5C 60
Pett's Hill UB5: N'olt 5F 59
Petts La. TW17: Shep 4C 146
Pett St. SE18 4C 106
PETTS WOOD 5G 161
Petts Wood Rd. BR5: Pet W 5G 161
Petty France SW1 1B 18 (3G 101)
Petty Wales EC3 3H 15 (7E 84)
Petworth Cl. UB5: N'olt 7D 58
Petworth Gdns. SW20 3D 152
UB10: Hil 1E 74
Petworth Rd. DA6: Bex 5G 127
N12 5H 31
Petworth St. SW11 1C 118
Petyt Pl. SW3 6C 100
Petyward SW3 4D 16 (4C 100)
Pevensey Av. EN1: Enf 2K 23
N11 5C 32
Pevensey Cl. TW7: Isle 7G 95
Pevensey Ct. SW16 3A 138
W3 2H 97
Pevensey Ho. E1 5K 85 (off Ben Jonson Rd.)
Pevensey Rd. E7 4H 69
SW17 4B 136
TW13: Felt 1C 130
Peverel E6 6E 88
Peverel Ho. RM10: Dag 2G 73
Peveret Cl. N11 5A 32
Peveril Dr. TW11: Tedd 5H 131
Peveril Ho. SE1 3D 102 (off Rephidim St.)
Pewsey Cl. E4 5H 35
Peyton Pl. SE10 7E 104
Pharamond NW2 6F 63
Pharaoh Cl. CR4: Mitc 7D 154
Pheasant Cl. E16 6K 87
Pheasantry Ho. SW3 5D 16 (off Jubilee Pl.)
Pheasantry Welcome Cen., The 1K 149
Phelp St. SE17 6D 102
Phelps Way UB3: Harl 4H 93
Phene St. SW3 7D 16 (6C 100)
Pheonix Point SE28 1C 108
Philadelphia Ct. SW10 7A 100 (off Uverdale Rd.)
Philbeach Gdns. SW5 5J 99
Phil Brown Pl. SW8 3F 119 (off Daley Thompson Way)
Philchurch Pl. E1 6G 85
Philia Ho. NW1 7G 65 (off Farrier St.)
Philimore Cl. SE18 5J 107
Philip Av. RM7: Rush G 1K 73
Philip Cl. RM7: Rush G 1K 73
Philip Ct. W2 5A 4 (off Hall Pl.)
Philip Gdns. CR0: C'don 2B 170
Philip Ho. NW6 1K 81 (off Mortimer Pl.)
Philip Jones Ct. N4 1K 65
Philip La. N15 4D 48
Philip Mole Ho. W9 4J 81 (off Chippenham Rd.)
Philipot Path SE9 6D 124
Philippa Gdns. SE9 5B 124
Philip Rd. TW18: Staines 6A 128
Philips Cl. SM5: Cars 1E 166
Philip Sq. SW8 2F 119
Philip St. E13 4J 87
Philip Wlk. SE15 3G 121 (not continuous)
Phillimore Ct. W8 2J 99 (off Kensington High St.)
Phillimore Gdns. NW10 1E 80
W8 2J 99
Phillimore Gdns. Cl. W8 3J 99
Phillimore Pl. W8 2J 99
Phillimore Ter. W8 3J 99 (off Allen St.)
Phillimore Wlk. W8 3J 99
Phillip Ho. E1 6K 9 (off Heneage St.)
Phillipp St. N1 1E 84
Phillips Ct. HA8: Edg 6B 28
Philpot La. EC3 2G 15 (7E 84)
Philpot Path IG1: Ilf 3G 71
Philpots Cl. UB7: Yiew 7A 74
Philpot Sq. SW6 3K 117
Philpot St. E1 6H 85
Phineas Pett Rd. SE9 3C 124
Phipps Bri. Rd. CR4: Mitc 2A 154
SW19 2A 154
Phipps Hatch La. EN2: Enf 1H 23
Phipps Ho. SE7 5K 105 (off Woolwich Rd.)
W12 7D 80 (off White City Est.)
Phipp's M. SW1 2K 17 (off Buckingham Pal. Rd.)
Phipp St. EC2 3G 9 (4E 84)
Phoebeth Rd. SE4 5C 122
Phoebe Wlk. E16 6K 87
Phoenix Av. SE10 2G 105
Phoenix Bus. Cen. E3 5C 86
Phoenix Cen. 7J 167
Phoenix Cinema 4C 46
Phoenix Cl. BR4: W W'ck 2F 171
E8 1F 85
E17 2B 50
W12 7D 80
Phoenix Ct. CR2: S Croy 5F 169
E1 4H 85 (off Buckhurst St.)
E4 3J 35
E14 4C 104
KT3: N Mald 3B 152
NW1 1D 6 (off Purchese St.)
SE14 6A 104 (off Chipley St.)
TW4: Houn 5B 112
TW8: Bford 5E 96
TW13: Felt 4G 129
Phoenix Dr. BR2: Kes 4B 172
Phoenix Hgts. E. E14 2C 104 (off Byng St.)
Phoenix Hgts. W. E14 2C 104 (off Mastmaker Ct.)
Phoenix Ho. SM1: Sutt 4K 165
Phoenix Ind. Est. HA1: Harr 4K 41
Phoenix Lodge Mans. W6 4F 99 (off Brook Grn.)
Phoenix Pk. NW2 2C 62
Phoenix Pl. WC1 3H 7 (4K 83)
Phoenix Rd. NW1 1C 6 (3H 83)
SE20 6J 139
Phoenix Sports and Fitness Cen. 7C 80
Phoenix St. WC2 1D 12 (6H 83)
Phoenix Theatre 1D 12 (off Charing Cross Rd.)
Phoenix Trad. Est. UB6: G'frd 1C 78
Phoenix Trad. Pk. TW8: Bford 5D 96
Phoenix Way SW18 5A 118
TW5: Hest 6B 94
Phoenix Wharf E1 1H 103 (off Wapping High St.)
Phoenix Wharf Rd. SE1 7K 15
Phoenix Yd. WC1 2H 7
Photographers Gallery 1A 12 (off Ramillies St.)
Phyllis Av. KT3: N Mald 5D 152
Phyllis Hodges Ho. NW1 1C 6 (off Aldenham St.)
Phyllis Ho. CR0: Wadd 4B 168 (off Ashley La.)
Physic Pl. SW3 7E 16 (6D 100)
Piano Works IG11: Bark 7G 71 (off Ripple Rd.)
Piazza, The UB8: Uxb 7A 56
WC2 2F 13 (not continuous)
Picardy Ho. EN2: Enf 1H 23
Picardy Manorway DA17: Belv 3H 109
Picardy Rd. DA17: Belv 5G 109
Picardy St. DA17: Belv 3G 109
Piccadilly W1 5K 11 (1F 101)
Piccadilly Arc. SW1 4A 12
Piccadilly Circus 3C 12 (7H 83)
Piccadilly Cir. W1 3C 12 (7H 83)
Piccadilly Ct. N7 6K 65 (off Caledonian Rd.)
Piccadilly Pl. W1 3B 12
Piccadilly Theatre 2B 12 (off Denman St.)
Pickard Cl. N14 1C 32
Pickard St. EC1 1B 8 (3B 84)
Pickering Av. E6 2E 88
Pickering Cl. E9 7K 67
Pickering Gdns. CR0: C'don 6F 157
N11 6K 31
Pickering Ho. W2 6A 82 (off Hallfield Est.)
W5 4C 96 (off Windmill Rd.)
Pickering M. W2 6K 81
Pickering Pl. SW1 5B 12
Pickering Rd. IG11: Bark 6G 71
Pickering St. N1 1B 84
Pickets Cl. WD23: B Hea 1C 26
Pickets St. SW12 7F 119
Pickett Cft. HA7: Stan 1D 42
Picketts Lock La. N9 2D 34
Picketts Lock La. Ind. Est. N9 2F 35
Picketts Ter. SE22 5G 121
Pickford Cl. DA7: Bex 2E 126
Pickford La. DA7: Bex 2E 126
Pickford Rd. DA7: Bex 3E 126
Pickfords Wharf N1 2C 84
SE1 4E 14 (1D 102)
Pickhurst Grn. BR2: Hayes 7H 159
Pickhurst La. BR2: Hayes 5G 159
BR4: W W'ck 5G 159
Pickhurst Mead BR2: Hayes 7H 159
Pickhurst Pk. BR2: Brom 5G 159
Pickhurst Ri. BR4: W W'ck 7E 158
Pickwick Cl. TW4: Houn 5C 112
Pickwick Ct. SE9 1C 142
Pickwick Ho. SE16 2G 103 (off George Row)
W11 1F 99 (off St Ann's Rd.)
Pickwick M. N18 4K 33
Pickwick Pl. HA1: Harr 7J 41
Pickwick Rd. SE21 7D 120
Pickwick St. SE1 7C 14 (2C 102)
Pickwick Way BR7: Chst 6G 143
Pickworth Cl. SW8 7J 101
Picton Pl. KT6: Surb 1G 163
W1 1H 11 (6E 82)
Picton St. SE5 7D 102
Picture Ho. SW16 2J 137
Pied Bull Ct. WC1 5J 83 (off Bury Pl.)
Pied Bull Yd. N1 1B 84 (off Theberton St.)
WC1 6E 6
Piedmont Rd. SE18 5H 107 (not continuous)
PIELD HEATH 4B 74
Pield Heath Av. UB8: Hil 4C 74
Pield Heath Rd. UB8: Cowl, Hil 4A 74
Pierce Campion Ct. E17 3B 50
Pier Head E1 1H 103 (not continuous)
Pierhead Wharf E1 1H 103 (off Wapping High St.)
Pier Ho. SW3 7D 16 (6C 100)
Pieris Ho. TW13: Felt 2J 129 (off High St.)
Piermont Grn. SE22 5H 121
Piermont Pl. BR1: Brom 2C 160
Piermont Rd. SE22 5H 121
Pier Pde. E16 1E 106 (off Pier Rd.)
Pierpoint Bldg. E14 2B 104
Pierrepoint Rd. W3 7H 79
Pierrepont Arc. N1 2B 84 (off Islington High St.)
Pierrepont Row N1 2B 84 (off Camden Pas.)
Pier Rd. E16 2D 106
TW14: Felt 5K 111
Pier St. E14 4E 104 (not continuous)
Pier Ter. SW18 4K 117
Pier Wlk. SE10 2G 105
Pier Way SE28 2G 107
Pietra Lara Bldg. EC1 3C 8 (off Pear Tree St.)
Pigeon La. TW12: Hamp 4E 130
Piggott Ho. E2 2K 85 (off Sewardstone Rd.)
Pigott St. E14 6C 86
Pike Cl. BR1: Brom 5K 141
UB10: Uxb 1B 74
Pikemans Ct. SW5 4J 99 (off W. Cromwell Rd.)
Pike Rd. NW7 4E 28
Pike's End HA5: Eastc 4K 39
Pikestone Cl. UB4: Yead 4C 76
Pikethorne SE23 2K 139
Pilgrimage St. SE1 7E 14 (2D 102)
Pilgrim Cl. SM4: Mord 7K 153
Pilgrim Hill SE27 4C 138
Pilgrim Ho. SE1 3D 102 (off Tabard St.)
SE16 2J 103 (off Brunel Rd.)
Pilgrims Cloisters SE5 7E 102 (off Sedgmoor Pl.)
Pilgrims Cl. N13 4E 32
UB5: N'olt 5G 59
Pilgrims Cnr. NW6 2J 81 (off Chichester Rd.)
Pilgrims Ct. EN1: Enf 2J 23
Pilgrim's La. NW3 4B 64
Pilgrims M. E14 7G 87
Pilgrim's Pl. NW3 4B 64
Pilgrims Ri. EN4: E Barn 5H 21
Pilgrim St. EC4 1A 14 (6B 84)
Pilgrims Way CR2: S Croy 6F 169
E6 1C 88
HA9: Wemb 1H 61
N19 1H 65
Pilkington Rd. BR6: Farnb 3G 173
SE15 2H 121
Pillfold Ho. SE11 4K 101 (off Old Paradise St.)
Pillions La. UB4: Hayes 4F 75
Pilot Cl. SE8 6B 104
Pilot Ind. Cen. NW10 4K 79
Pilsdon Cl. SW19 1F 135
Pilton Est., The CR0: C'don 2B 168
Pilton Pl. SE17 5C 102
Pimento Ct. W5 3D 96
PIMLICO 6B 18 (5G 101)
Pimlico Ho. SW1 5J 17 (off Ebury Bri. Rd.)
Pimlico Rd. SW1 5G 17 (5E 100)
Pimlico Wlk. N1 1G 9
Pinchbeck Rd. BR6: Chels 6K 173
Pinchin & Johnsons Yd. E1 7G 85 (off Pinchin St.)
Pinchin St. E1 7G 85
Pincombe Ho. SE17 5D 102 (off Orb St.)
Pincott Pl. SE4 3K 121
Pincott Rd. DA6: Bex 5G 127
SW19 7A 136

Pindar St. EC2 . . . . .5G 9 (5E 84)
Pindock M. W9 . . . . .4K 81
Pineapple Ct. SW1 . . . . .1B 18
Pine Av. BR4: W W'ck 1D 170
    E15 . . . . .5F 69
Pine Cl. E10 . . . . .2D 68
    HA7: Stan 4G 27
    N14 . . . . .7B 22
    N19 . . . . .2G 65
    SE20 . . . . .1J 157
Pine Coombe CR0: C'don 4K 169
Pine Ct. N21 . . . . .5E 22
    UB5: N'olt 4C 76
Pinecrest Gdns. BR6: Farnb 4F 173
Pinecroft Ct. DA16: Well 7A 108
Pinecroft Cres. EN5: Barn 4B 20
Pinedene SE15 . . . . .1H 121
Pinefield Cl. E14 . . . . .7C 86
Pine Gdns. HA4: Ruis 1K 57
    KT5: Surb 6G 151
Pine Glade BR6: Farnb 4D 172
Pine Gro. N4 . . . . .2J 65
    N20 . . . . .1C 30
    SW19 . . . . .5H 135
Pine Ho. E3 . . . . .1A 86
                    (off Barge La.)
    SE16 . . . . .2J 103
                   (off Ainsty Est.)
    W10 . . . . .4G 81
                   (off Droop St.)
Pinehurst Ct. W11 . . . . .6H 81
             (off Colville Gdns.)
Pinehurst Wlk. BR6: Orp 1H 173
Pinemartin Cl. NW2 . . . . .3E 62
Pine M. NW10 .2F 81
             (off Clifford Gdns.)
Pine Pl. UB4: Hayes 4H 75
Pine Ridge SM5: Cars 7E 166
Pineridge Ct. EN5: Barn 4A 20
Pine Rd. N11 . . . . .2K 31
    NW2 . . . . .4E 62
Pines, The UB6: Wfd G 3C 36
    KT9: Chess 3E 162
    N14 . . . . .5B 22
    SE19 . . . . .6B 138
    TW16: Sun .3J 147
Pines Rd. BR1: Brom 2C 160
Pine St. EC1 . . . . .3K 7 (4A 84)
Pine Tree Cl. TW5: Cran 1K 111
Pine Tree Ho. SE14 . . . . .7K 103
             (off Reaston St.)
Pine Tree Lodge BR2: Brom 4H 159
Pine Trees Dr. UB10: Ick 4A 56
Pinetree Way SE13 . . . . .3D 122
Pineview Ct. E4 . . . . .1K 35
Pine Wlk. KT5: Surb 6G 151
Pine Wood TW16: Sun 1J 147
Pinewood Av. DA15: Sidc 1J 143
    HA5: Hat E .6A 26
    UB8: Hil 6B 74
Pinewood Cl. BR6: Orp 1H 173
    CR0: C'don 3A 170
    HA5: Hat E .6A 26
Pinewood Ct. EN2: Enf 3G 23
    SW4 . . . . .6H 119
Pinewood Dr. BR6: Orp 5J 173
Pinewood Gro. W5 . . . . .6C 78
Pinewood Lodge W23: B Hea 1C 26
Pinewood Pl. DA2: Dart 2K 145
             (not continuous)
    KT19: Ewe .4K 163
Pinewood Rd. BR2: Brom 4J 159
    SE2 . . . . .6D 108
    TW13: Felt 3K 129
Pinfold Rd. SW16 . . . . .4J 137
Pinglestone Cl. UB7: Harm 7A 92
Pinkcoat Cl. TW13: Felt 3K 129
Pinkerton Pl. SW16 . . . . .4H 137
Pinkham Mans. W4 . . . . .5G 97
Pinkham Way N11 . . . . .7K 31
Pinkwell Av. UB3: Harl 4F 93
Pinkwell La. UB3: Harl 4E 92

Pinley Gdns. RM9: Dag 1B 90
Pinnace Ho. E14 . . . . .3E 104
           (off Manchester Rd.)
Pinnacle Hill DA7: Bex 4H 127
Pinnacle Hill Nth. DA7: Bex 4H 127
Pinnacle Ho. NW9 . . . . .2B 44
             (off Heritage Av.)
Pinnacle Pl. HA7: Stan 4G 27
Pinnacle Way E14 . . . . .6A 86
          (off Commercial Rd.)
Pinnata Cl. EN2: Enf 1H 23
Pinnell Rd. SE9 . . . . .4B 124
PINNER 4C 40
Pinner Ct. HA5: Pinn 4E 40
    NW8 . . . . .3A 4
PINNER GREEN 2A 40
Pinner Grn. HA5: Pinn 2A 40
Pinner Gro. HA5: Pinn 4C 40
Pinner Hill HA5: Pinn 1E 40
Pinner Hill Farm HA5: Pinn 1K 39
Pinner Hill Rd. HA5: Pinn 1K 39
Pinner Pk. 1E 40
Pinner Pk. HA5: Pinn 2E 40
Pinner Pk. Av. HA2: Harr 3F 41
Pinner Pk. Gdns. HA2: Harr 2G 41
Pinner Rd. HA1: Harr 4E 40
    HA2: Harr 4E 40
    HA5: Pinn 1H 39
                    (High St.)
    HA5: Pinn 4D 40
                  (Nower Hill)
    HA6: Nwood, Pinn 1H 39
Pinners Pas. EC2 . . . . .7F 9
             (off Austin Friars)
Pinner Vw. HA1: Harr 6G 41
    HA2: Harr 4G 41
PINNERWOOD PARK 1A 40
Pinn Way HA4: Ruis 7F 39
Pintail Cl. E6 . . . . .5C 88
Pintail Ct. SE8 . . . . .6B 104
                 (off Pilot Cl.)
Pintail Rd. IG8: Wfd G 7E 36
Pintail Way UB4: Yead 5B 76
Pinter Ho. SW9 . . . . .2J 119
           (off Grantham Rd.)
Pinto Way SE3 . . . . .4K 123
Pioneer Cen., The SE15 . . . . .1J 121
Pioneer Cl. E14 . . . . .5D 86
Pioneer Ho. WC1 . . . . .1G 7
            (off Britannia St.)
Pioneer Point IG1: Ilf 3F 71
Pioneers Ind. Pk. CR0: Bedd 1J 167
Pioneer St. SE15 . . . . .1G 121
Pioneer Way W12 . . . . .6D 80
              (off Brook Grn.)
Piper Building, The SW6 . . . . .3K 117
Piper Cl. N7 . . . . .5K 65
Piper Rd. KT1: King T 3G 151
Piper's Gdns. CR0: C'don 7A 158
Pipers Grn. NW9 . . . . .5J 43
Pipers Grn. La. HA8: Edg 3K 27
Pipers Ho. SE10 . . . . .5F 105
           (off Collington St.)
Piper Way IG1: Ilf 1H 71
Pipewell Rd. SM5: Cars 6C 154
Pippenhall SE9 . . . . .6F 125
Pippin Cl. CR0: C'don 1B 170
    NW2 . . . . .3C 62
Pippin Ct. SW8 . . . . .7G 19
            (off Vauxhall Gro.)
Pippin Ho. W10 . . . . .7F 81
            (off Freston Rd.)
Pippins Cl. UB7: W Dray 3A 92
Pippins Ct. TW15: Ashf 6D 128
Piquet Rd. SE20 . . . . .2J 157
Pirbright Cres. CR0: New Ad 6E 170
Pirbright Rd. SW18 . . . . .1H 135
Pirie Cl. SE5 . . . . .3D 120
Pirie St. E16 . . . . .1K 105
Pirin Cl. E4 . . . . .4G 35
Pitcairn Cl. RM7: Mawney 4G 55
Pitcairn Ho. E9 .7J 67
Pitcairn Rd. CR4: Mitc 7D 136

Pitcairn's Path HA2: Harr 3G 59
Pitchford St. E15 . . . . .7F 69
Pitfield Cres. SE28 . . . . .1A 108
Pitfield Est. N1 . . . . .1G 9 (3E 84)
Pitfield St. N1 . . . . .1G 9 (3E 84)
Pitfield Way EN3: Enf H 1D 24
    NW10 . . . . .6J 61
Pitfold Cl. SE12 . . . . .6J 123
Pitfold Rd. SE12 . . . . .6J 123
Pitlake CR0: C'don 2B 168
Pitlochry Ho. SE27 . . . . .2B 138
           (off Elmcourt Rd.)
Pitman Ho. SE8 . . . . .1C 122
Pitman St. SE5 . . . . .7C 102
Pitmaston Ho. SE13 . . . . .2E 122
           (off Lewisham Rd.)
Pitsea Pl. E1 . . . . .6K 85
Pitsea St. E1 . . . . .6K 85
Pitshanger La. W5 . . . . .4B 78
Pitt Cres. SW19 . . . . .4K 135
Pittman Gdns. IG1: Ilf 5G 71
Pitt Rd. BR6: Farnb 4G 173
    CR0: C'don 5C 156
    CR7: Thor H 5C 156
    HA2: Harr 2G 59
Pitt's Head M. W1 . . . . .5H 11 (1E 100)
Pittsmead Av. BR2: Hayes 7J 159
Pitt St. W8 . . . . .2J 99
Pittville Gdns. SE25 . . . . .3G 157
Pixfield Ct. BR2: Brom 2H 159
          (off Beckenham La.)
Pixley St. E14 . . . . .6B 86
Pixton Way CR0: Sels 7A 170
Place, The 3H 83
Place Farm Av. BR6: Orp 1H 173
Plaisterers Highwalk EC2 . . . . .6C 8
           (off London Wall)
PLAISTOW
    BR1 . . . . .7J 141
    E13 . . . . .2K 87
Plaistow Gro. BR1: Brom 7K 141
    E15 . . . . .1H 87
Plaistow La. BR1: Brom 7J 141
             (not continuous)
Plaistow Pk. Rd. E13 . . . . .2K 87
             (not continuous)
Plaistow Rd. E15 . . . . .1H 87
Plaistow Wharf E16 . . . . .2J 105
Plane Ho. BR2: Brom 2G 159
Plane St. SE26 . . . . .3H 139
Planetarium
    Greenwich 7F 105
    W6 . . . . .4F 99
Planetree Cl. W6 . . . . .5G 99
            (off Brook Grn.)
Plane Tree Cres. TW13: Felt 3K 129
Plane Tree Ho. SE8 . . . . .6A 104
                 (off Etta St.)
    W8 . . . . .2H 99
        (off Duchess of Bedford's Wlk.)
Plane Tree Wlk. N2 . . . . .3C 46
    SE19 . . . . .6E 138
Plantagenet Cl. KT4: Wor Pk 4K 163
Plantagenet Gdns. RM6: Chad H 7D 54
Plantagenet Ho. SE18 . . . . .3D 106
                (off Leda Rd.)
Plantagenet Pl. RM6: Chad H 7D 54
Plantagenet Rd. EN5: New Bar 4F 21
Plantain Gdns. E11 . . . . .3F 69
           (off Hollydown Way)
Plantain Pl. SE1 . . . . .6E 14 (2D 102)
Plantation, The SE3 . . . . .2J 123
Plantation Cl. SW4 . . . . .5J 119
Plantation La. EC3 . . . . .2G 15
Plantation Pl. EC3 . . . . .2G 15
Plantation Wharf SW11 . . . . .3A 118
Plantree Path E17 . . . . .4C 50
            (off Selborne Rd.)
Plasel Ct. E13 .1K 87
            (off Pawsey Cl.)
PLASHET 6C 70
Plashet Gro. E6 . . . . .1A 88
Plashet Rd. E13 . . . . .1J 87

Plassy Rd. SE6 . . . . .7D 122
Plate Ho. E14 .5D 104
          (off Burrells Wharf Sq.)
Platina St. EC2 .3F 9
Platinum Ct. E1 . . . . .4J 85
            (off Cephas Av.)
Platinum M. N15 . . . . .5F 49
Plato Rd. SW2 . . . . .4J 119
Platt, The SW15 . . . . .3F 117
Platt Halls NW9 . . . . .2B 44
Platt's Eyot TW12: Hamp 2E 148
Platt's La. NW3 . . . . .4J 63
Platts Rd. EN3: Enf H 1D 24
Platt St. NW1 .2H 83
Plawsfield Rd. BR3: Beck 1K 157
Plaxdale Ho. SE17 . . . . .4E 102
           (off Beckway St.)
Plaxtol Cl. BR1: Brom 1A 160
Plaxtol Rd. DA8: Erith 7G 109
Plaxton Ct. E11 . . . . .3H 69
Playfair Ho. E14 . . . . .6C 86
           (off Saracen St.)
Playfair Mans. W14 . . . . .6G 99
        (off Queen's Club Gdns.)
Playfair St. W6 .5E 98
Playfield Av. RM5: Col R 1J 55
Playfield Cres. SE22 . . . . .5F 121
Playfield Rd. HA8: Edg 2J 43
Playford Rd. N4 . . . . .2K 65
             (not continuous)
Playgreen Way SE6 . . . . .3C 140
Playground Cl. BR3: Beck 2K 157
Playhouse, The 7H 147
          (off Hepworth Way)
Playhouse Ct. SE1 . . . . .6C 14
          (off Southwark Bri. Rd.)
Playhouse Theatre 4F 13
        (off Northumberland Av.)
Playhouse Yd. EC4 . . . . .1A 14 (6B 84)
Plaza Bus. Cen. EN3: Brim 2G 25
Plaza Hgts. E10 . . . . .3E 68
Plaza Pde. HA0: Wemb 6E 60
              (off Ealing Rd.)
    NW6 . . . . .2K 81
Plaza Shop. Cen., The W1 . . .7B 6 (6G 83)
Plaza Wlk. NW9 . . . . .3J 43
Pleasance, The SW15 . . . . .4D 116
             (not continuous)
Pleasance Rd. SW15 . . . . .5D 116
Pleasance Theatre 6J 65
          (off Carpenters M.)
Pleasant Gro. CR0: C'don 3B 170
Pleasant Pl. HA2: Harr 2H 59
    N1 . . . . .7B 66
Pleasant Row NW1 . . . . .1F 83
Pleasant Vw. Pl. BR6: Farnb 5F 173
Pleasant Way HA0: Wemb 2C 78
Plender Ct. NW1 . . . . .1G 83
              (off College Pl.)
Plender St. NW1 . . . . .1G 83
Pleshey Rd. N7 . . . . .4H 65
Plesman Way SM6: Wall 7J 167
Plessey Bldg. E14 . . . . .6C 86
               (off Dod St.)
Plevna Cres. N15 . . . . .6E 48
Plevna Rd. N9 .3B 34
    TW12: Hamp 1F 149
Plevna St. E14 . . . . .3E 104
Pleydell Av. SE19 . . . . .7F 139
    W6 . . . . .4B 98
Pleydell Cl. EC4 . . . . .1K 13
           (off Lombard La.)
Pleydell Est. EC1 . . . . .2D 8
Pleydell Gdns. SE19 . . . . .6E 138
           (off Anerley Hill)
Pleydell St. EC4 . . . . .1K 13
Plimley Pl. W12 . . . . .2F 99
        (off Shepherd's Bush Pl.)
Plimsoll Cl. E14 . . . . .6D 86
Plimsoll Rd. N4 . . . . .3A 66
Plough Ct. EC3 . . . . .2F 15 (7D 84)
Plough Farm Cl. HA4: Ruis 6F 39

Plough La. CR8: Purl 7J 167
SE22 6F 121
SM6: Bedd 4J 167
SW17 5K 135
SW19 5K 135
TW11: Tedd 5A 132
Plough La. Cl. SM6: Bedd 5J 167
Ploughmans Cl. NW1 1H 83
Ploughmans End TW7: Isle 5H 113
Ploughmans Wlk. *N2* *2A 46*
(off Long La.)
Plough M. SW11 4B 118
Plough Pl. EC4 7K 7 (6A 84)
Plough Rd. KT19: Ewe 7K 163
SW11 3B 118
Plough St. E1 7K 9 (6F 85)
Plough Ter. SW11 4B 118
Plough Way SE16 4K 103
Plough Yd. EC2 4H 9 (4E 84)
Plover Ho. *SW9* *7A 102*
(off Brixton Rd.)
Plover Way SE16 3A 104
UB4: Yead 6B 76
Plowden Bldgs. EC4 2J 13
Plowman Cl. N18 5J 33
Plowman Way RM8: Dag 1C 72
Plumber's Row E1 5G 85
Plumbridge St. SE10 1E 122
Plum Cl. TW13: Felt 1J 129
Plume Ho. *SE10* *6D 104*
(off Creek Rd.)
Plum Gth. TW8: Bford 4D 96
Plum La. SE18 7F 107
Plummer La. CR4: Mitc 2D 154
Plummer Rd. SW4 7H 119
Plumpton Cl. UB5: N'olt 6E 58
Plumpton Way SM5: Cars 3C 166
PLUMSTEAD 4J 107
PLUMSTEAD COMMON 6G 107
Plumstead Comn. Rd. SE18 6F 107
Plumstead High St. SE18 4H 107
Plumstead Leisure Cen. 5K 107
Plumstead Rd. SE18 4F 107
Plumtree Cl. RM10: Dag 6H 73
SM6: Wall 7H 167
Plumtree Ct. EC4 7A 8 (6B 84)
Plymen Ho. KT8: W Mole 5E 148
Plymouth Ct. *KT5: Surb* *4E 150*
(off Cranes Pk. Av.)
Plymouth Ho. *IG11: Bark* *7A 72*
(off Margaret Bondfield Av.)
SE10 *1D 122*
(off Devonshire Dr.)
Plymouth Rd. BR1: Brom 1K 159
E16 5J 87
Plymouth Ter. *NW2* *6E 62*
(off Glengall Rd.)
Plymouth Wharf E14 4F 105
Plympton Av. NW6 7H 63
Plympton Cl. DA17: Belv 3E 108
Plympton Pl. NW8 4C 4 (4C 82)
Plympton Rd. NW6 7H 63
Plympton St. NW8 4C 4 (4C 82)
Plymstock Rd. DA16: Well 7C 108
PM Gallery & House 1D 96
Pocklington Cl. NW9 2A 44
W12 *3C 98*
(off Ashchurch Pk. Vs.)
Pocklington Ct. SW15 1C 134
Pocklington Lodge W12 3C 98
Pocock Av. UB7: W Dray 3B 92
Pocock St. SE1 6A 14 (2B 102)
Podmore Rd. SW18 4A 118
Poets Ct. SE25 4G 157
W3 1J 97
Poet's Rd. N5 5D 66
Poets Way HA1: Harr 4J 41
Point, The *E17* *4C 50*
(off Tower M.)
HA4: Ruis 4J 57
W2 6A 4
Pointalls Cl. N3 2A 46
Point Cl. SE10 1E 122
Pointer Cl. SE28 6D 90
Pointers Cl. E14 5D 104
Pointers Cotts. TW10: Ham 2C 132
Point Hill SE10 7E 104
Point Pl. HA9: Wemb 7H 61
Point Pleasant SW18 4J 117
Point Ter. *E7* *5K 69*
(off Claremont Rd.)
Point West SW7 4K 99
Point Wharf TW8: Bford 7E 96
Point Wharf La. TW8: Bford 7D 96
Poland St. W1 1B 12 (6G 83)
Polar Pk. UB7: Harm 7B 92
Polebrook Rd. SE3 3A 124
Pole Cat All. BR2: Hayes 2H 171
Polecroft La. SE6 2B 140
Polehamptons, The TW12: Hamp 7G 131
Pole Hill Rd. E4 7K 25
UB4: Hayes 2E 74
UB10: Hil 4D 74
Polesden Gdns. SW20 2D 152
Polesworth Ho. *W2* *5J 81*
(off Alfred Rd.)
Polesworth Rd. RM9: Dag 7D 72
Police Sta. La. WD23: Bush 1A 26
POLISH WAR MEMORIAL 7A 58
Polka Theatre for Children 6K 135
Pollard Cl. E16 7J 87
N7 4K 65
Pollard Ho. KT4: Wor Pk 4E 164
N1 *1G 7*
(off Northdown St.)
SE16 *3F 103*
(off Spa Rd.)
Pollard Rd. N20 2H 31
SM4: Mord 5B 154
Pollard Row E2 3G 85
Pollards Cres. SW16 3J 155
Pollards Hill E. SW16 3K 155
Pollards Hill Nth. SW16 3J 155
Pollards Hill Sth. SW16 3J 155
Pollards Hill W. SW16 3K 155
Pollard St. E2 3G 85
Pollards Wood Rd. SW16 3J 155
Pollard Wlk. DA14: Sidc 6C 144
Pollen St. W1 1A 12 (6G 83)
Pollitt Dr. NW8 3B 4 (4B 82)
Pollock Ho. *W10* *4G 81*
(off Kensal Rd.)
Pollock's Toy Mus. 5B 6 (5G 83)
Polperro Cl. BR6: St M Cry 6K 161
Polperro Ho. *W2* *5J 81*
(off Westbourne Pk. Rd.)
Polperro M. SE11 3K 19 (4B 102)
Polsted Rd. SE6 7B 122
Polthorne Est. *SE18* *4H 107*
(off Polthorne Gro.)
Polthorne Gro. SE18 4G 107
Polworth Rd. SW16 5J 137
Polychrome Ct. *SE1* *7A 14*
(off Waterloo Rd.)
Polygon, The *NW8* *1B 82*
(off Avenue Rd.)
SW4 4G 119
Polygon Bus. Cen. SL3: Poyle 5A 174
Polygon Rd. NW1 1C 6 (2H 83)
Polytechnic St. SE18 4E 106
Pomell Way E1 7K 9 (6F 85)
Pomeroy Cl. TW1: Twick 4B 114
Pomeroy Ho. *E2* *2K 85*
(off St James's Av.)
W11 *6G 81*
(off Lancaster Rd.)
Pomeroy St. SE14 7J 103
Pomfret Rd. SE5 3B 120
Pomoja La. N19 2J 65
Pomona Ho. *SE8* *4A 104*
(off Evelyn St.)
Pond Cl. N12 6H 31
SE3 2J 123
Pond Cott. La. BR4: W W'ck 1C 170
Pond Cotts. SE21 1E 138
PONDERS END 5D 24
Ponders End Ind. Est. EN3: Pond E 5F 25
Ponder St. N7 7K 65
Pond Farm Est. E5 3J 67
Pondfield Ho. SE27 5C 138
Pondfield Rd. BR2: Hayes 1G 171
BR6: Farnb 3F 173
RM10: Dag 5H 73
Pond Grn. HA4: Ruis 2G 57
Pond Hill Gdns. SM3: Cheam 6G 165
Pond Ho. HA7: Stan 6G 27
SW3 4C 16 (4C 100)
Pond Lees Cl. RM10: Dag 7K 73
Pond Mead SE21 6D 120
Pond Path BR7: Chst 6F 143
Pond Pl. SW3 4C 16 (4C 100)
Pond Rd. E15 2G 87
SE3 2H 123
Pondside Av. KT4: Wor Pk 1E 164
Pondside Cl. UB3: Harl 6F 93
Pond Sq. N6 1E 64
Pond St. NW3 5C 64
Pond Way TW11: Tedd 6C 132
Pondwood Ri. BR6: Orp 7J 161
Ponler St. E1 6H 85
Ponsard Rd. NW10 3D 80
Ponsford St. E9 6J 67
Ponsonby Ho. *E2* *2J 85*
(off Bishop's Way, not continuous)
Ponsonby Pl. SW1 5D 18 (5H 101)
Ponsonby Rd. SW15 7D 116
Ponsonby Ter. SW1 5D 18 (5H 101)
Pontefract Ct. *UB5: N'olt* *5F 59*
(off Newmarket Av.)
Pontefract Rd. BR1: Brom 5H 141
Ponton Rd. SW8 7D 18 (7H 101)
Pont St. SW1 2E 16 (3D 100)
Pont St. M. SW1 2E 16 (3D 100)
Pontypool Pl. SE1 6A 14 (2B 102)
Pooja Ct. *NW1* *7G 65*
(off Agar Gro.)
Pool Cl. BR3: Beck 5C 140
KT8: W Mole 5D 148
Pool Ct. SE6 2C 140
Poole Cl. HA4: Ruis 2G 57
Poole Ct. *N1* *7E 66*
(off St Peter's Way)
TW4: Houn 2C 112
Poole Ct. Rd. TW4: Houn 2C 112
Poole Ho. SE11 2H 19
POOL END 5C 146
Pool End Cl. TW17: Shep 5C 146
Poole Rd. E9 6K 67
KT19: Ewe 6K 163
Pooles Bldgs. WC1 4J 7
Pooles Cotts. TW10: Ham 2D 132
Pooles La. RM9: Dag 2E 90
SW10 7A 100
Pooles Pk. N4 2A 66
Poole St. N1 1D 84
Poole Way UB4: Hayes 3G 75
Pooley Dr. SW14 3J 115
Pooley Ho. E1 3K 85
E18 1J 51
Pool Ho. *NW8* *5C 4*
(off Penfold St.)
Poolmans St. SE16 2K 103
Pool Rd. HA1: Harr 7H 41
KT8: W Mole 5D 148
Poolsford Rd. NW9 4A 44
Pools on the Pk. 4D 114
Poonah St. E1 6J 85
Pope Cl. SW19 6B 136
TW14: Felt 1H 129
Pope Ho. *SE5* *7D 102*
(off Elmington Est.)
SE16 *4H 103*
(off Manor Est.)
Pope Rd. BR2: Brom 5B 160
Popes Av. TW2: Twick 2J 131
Popes Ct. TW2: Twick 2J 131
Popes Dr. N3 1J 45
Popes Gro. CR0: C'don 3B 170
TW1: Twick 2K 131
TW2: Twick 2K 131
Pope's Head All. EC3 1F 15 (6D 84)
Popes La. W5 3D 96
Pope's Rd. SW9 3A 120
Pope St. SE1 7H 15 (2E 102)
Popham Cl. TW13: Hanw 3D 130
Popham Gdns. TW9: Rich 3G 115
Popham Rd. N1 1C 84
Popham St. N1 1B 84
(not continuous)
Pop in Commercial Cen.
HA9: Wemb 5H 61
Popinjays Row *SM3: Cheam* *5F 165*
(off Netley Cl.)
POPLAR 7D 86
Poplar Av. BR6: Farnb 2F 173
CR4: Mitc 1D 154
UB2: S'hall 3F 95
UB7: Yiew 7B 74
Poplar Bath St. E14 6D 86
Poplar Bus. Pk. E14 7E 86
Poplar Cl. E9 5B 68
HA5: Pinn 1B 40
SL3: Poyle 4A 174
Poplar Ct. SW19 5J 135
TW1: Twick 6C 114
UB5: N'olt 2A 76
Poplar Cres. KT19: Ewe 6J 163
Poplar Farm Cl. KT19: Ewe 6J 163
Poplar Gdns. KT3: N Mald 2K 151
SE28 7C 90
Poplar Gro. HA9: Wemb 3J 61
KT3: N Mald 2K 151
N11 6K 31
W6 2E 98
Poplar High St. E14 7D 86
Poplar Ho. *SE4* *4B 122*
(off Wickham Rd.)
SE16 *2K 103*
(off Woodland Cres.)
Poplar M. W12 1E 98
Poplar Mt. DA17: Belv 4H 109
Poplar Pl. SE28 7C 90
UB3: Hayes 7J 75
W2 7K 81
Poplar Rd. E12 2C 70
KT6: Surb 3B 162
SE24 4C 120
SM3: Sutt 1H 165
SW19 2J 153
TW15: Ashf 5E 128
Poplar Rd. Sth. SW19 3J 153
Poplars, The N14 5A 22
Poplars Av. NW2 6E 62
Poplars Cl. HA4: Ruis 1G 57
Poplars Rd. E17 6D 50
Poplar St. RM7: Rom 4J 55
Poplar Vw. HA9: Wemb 2D 60
Poplar Wlk. CR0: C'don 2C 168
SE24 3C 120
(not continuous)
Poplar Way IG6: Ilf 4G 53
TW13: Felt 3J 129
Poppins Ct. EC4 1A 14 (6B 84)
Poppleton Rd. E11 6G 51
Poppy Cl. DA17: Belv 3H 109
EN5: New Bar 6F 21
SM6: Wall 1E 166
UB5: N'olt 6D 58
Poppy La. CR0: C'don 7J 157
Porchester Cl. SE5 4C 120
Porchester Ct. *W2* *7K 81*
(off Porchester Gdns.)
Porchester Gdns. W2 7K 81
Porchester Gdns. M. W2 6K 81
Porchester Ga. *W2* *7K 81*
(off Bayswater Rd.)
Porchester Ho. *E1* *6H 85*
(off Philpot St.)

Porchester Leisure Cen. 6K 81
Porchester Mead BR3: Beck 6D 140
Porchester Pl. W2 . . . . .1D 10 (6C 82)
Porchester Rd. KT1: King T 2H 151
W2 . . . . .6K 81
Porchester Sq. W2 . . . . .6K 81
Porchester Sq. M. W2 . . . . .6K 81
Porchester Ter. W2 . . . . .7A 82
Porchester Ter. Nth. W2 . . . . .6K 81
Porchester Wlk. W2 . . . . .6K 81
                        (off Porchester Ter. Nth.)
Porch Way N20 . . . . .3J 31
Porcupine Cl. SE9 . . . . .2C 142
Porden Rd. SW2 . . . . .4K 119
Porlock Av. HA2: Harr 1G 59
Porlock Ho. SE26 . . . . .3G 139
Porlock Rd. EN1: Enf 7A 24
Porlock St. SE1 . . . . .6F 15 (2D 102)
Porrington Cl. BR7: Chst 1D 160
Porson Cl. SE13 . . . . .3D 122
Portal Cl. HA4: Ruis 4J 57
                        (not continuous)
SE27 .3A 138
UB10: Uxb 7A 56
Portal Way W3 . . . . .5K 79
Portbury Cl. SE15 . . . . .1G 121
Port Cres. E13 . . . . .4K 87
Portcullis Ho. SW1 . . . . .7E 12
Portcullis Lodge Rd.
EN1: Enf 3J 23
Port E. Apartments E14 . . . . .7C 86
                        (off Hertsmere Rd.)
Portelet Ct. N1 . . . . .1E 84
                        (off De Beauvoir Est.)
Portelet Rd. E1 . . . . .3K 85
Porten Ho's. W14 . . . . .3G 99
                        (off Porten Rd.)
Porten Rd. W14 . . . . .3G 99
Porter Rd. E6 . . . . .6D 88
Porters & Walters Almshouses
N22 . . . . .7E 32
                        (off Nightingale Rd.)
Porters Av. RM8: Dag 6B 72
RM9: Dag 6B 72
Porters Lodge, The SW10 . . . . .7A 100
                        (off Coleridge Gdns.)
Porter Sq. N19 . . . . .1J 65
Porter St. SE1 . . . . .4D 14 (1C 102)
W1 . . . . .5F 5 (5D 82)
Porters Wlk. E1 . . . . .7H 85
                        (off Tobacco Dock)
Porters Way N12 . . . . .6H 31
UB7: W Dray 3B 92
Porteus Rd. W2 . . . . .5A 4 (5A 82)
Portgate Cl. W9 . . . . .4H 81
Porthallow Cl. BR6: Chels 4K 173
Porthcawe Rd. SE26 . . . . .4A 140
Porthkerry Av. DA16: Well 4A 126
Port Ho. E14 . . . . .5D 104
                        (off Burrells Wharf Sq.)
Portia Ct. IG11: Bark 7A 72
SE11 .5B 102
                        (off Opal St.)
Portia Way E3 . . . . .4B 86
Porticos, The SW3 . . . . .7A 16
Portinscale Rd. SW15 . . . . .5G 117
Portishead Ho. W2 . . . . .5J 81
                        (off Westbourne Pk. Rd.)
Portland Av. DA15: Sidc 6A 126
KT3: N Mald 7D 152
N16 . . . . .7F 49
Portland Cl. KT4: Wor Pk 7D 152
RM6: Chad H 6E 54
Portland Commercial Est.
IG11: Bark 2C 90
Portland Cotts. CRO: Bedd 7H 155
Portland Ct. N1 . . . . .7E 14
                        (off St Peter's Way)
SE1 . . . . .7E 14
                        (off Gt. Dover St.)
SE14 .6A 104
                        (off Whitcher Cl.)

Portland Cres. HA7: Stan 2D 42
SE9 .2C 142
TW13: Felt 4F 129
UB6: G'frd 4F 77
Portland Dr. EN2: Enf 1K 23
Portland Gdns. N4 . . . . .6B 48
RM6: Chad H 5D 54
Portland Gro. SW8 . . . . .1K 119
Portland Ho. SW1 . . . . .1A 18
Portland Mans. W14 . . . . .3G 99
                        (off Addison Bri. Pl.)
Portland M. W1 . . . . .1B 12 (6G 83)
Portland Pl. SE25 . . . . .4G 157
                        (off Sth. Norwood Hill)
W1 . . . . .4J 5 (5F 83)
Portland Ri. N4 . . . . .1B 66
                        (not continuous)
Portland Rd. BR1: Brom 4A 142
CR4: Mitc 2C 154
KT1: King T 3E 150
N15 . . . . .4F 49
SE9 .2C 142
SE25 .4G 157
TW15: Ashf 3A 128
UB2: S'hall 3D 94
UB4: Hayes 3G 75
W11 . . . . .7G 81
Portland Sq. E1 . . . . .1H 103
Portland St. SE17 . . . . .5D 102
Portland Ter. HA8: Edg 7B 28
TW9: Rich 4D 114
Portland Wlk. SE17 . . . . .6D 102
Portman Av. SW14 . . . . .3K 115
Portman Cl. DA5: Bexl 1K 145
DA7: Bex 3E 126
W1 . . . . .7F 5 (6D 82)
Portman Dr. IG8: Wfd G 2B 52
Portman Gdns. NW9 . . . . .2K 43
UB10: Hil 7C 56
Portman Ga. NW1 . . . . . . .4D 4 (4C 82)
Portman Mans. W1 . . . . .5F 5
                        (off Chiltern St.)
Portman M. Sth. W1 . . . . .1G 11 (6E 82)
Portman Pl. E2 . . . . .3J 85
Portman Rd. KT1: King T 2F 151
Portman Sq. W1 . . . . . . .7G 5 (6E 82)
Portman St. W1 . . . . .1G 11 (6E 82)
Portman Towers W1 . . . . .7F 5 (6D 82)
Portmeadow Wlk. SE2 . . . . .2D 108
Portmeers Cl. E17 . . . . .6B 50
Portnall Ho. W9 . . . . .3H 81
                        (off Portnall Rd.)
Portnall Rd. W9 . . . . .2H 81
Portnoi Cl. RM1: Rom 2K 55
Portobello Ct. Est. W11 . . . . .6H 81
Portobello M. W11 . . . . .7J 81
Portobello Rd. W10 . . . . .5G 81
W11 . . . . .6H 81
Portobello Road Market 7H 81
                        (off Portobello Rd.)
Port of London Authority Bldg.
EC3 . . . . .7E 84
                        (off Trinity Sq.)
Porton Ct. KT6: Surb 6C 150
Portpool La. EC1 . . . . .5J 7 (5A 84)
Portree Cl. N22 . . . . .7E 32
Portree St. E14 . . . . .6F 87
Portrush Cl. UB1: S'hall 6D 76
                        (off Whitecote Rd.)
Portsdown HA8: Edg 5B 28
Portsdown Av. NW11 . . . . .6H 45
Portsdown M. NW11 . . . . .6H 45
Portsea Hall W2 . . . . .1D 10
                        (off Portsea Pl.)
Portsea M. W2 . . . . .1D 10
Portsea Pl. W2 . . . . .1D 10 (6C 82)
Portslade Rd. SW8 . . . . .2G 119
Portsmouth Av. KT7: T Ditt 7A 150
Portsmouth M. E16 . . . . .1K 105
Portsmouth Rd. KT1: King T 7A 150
KT6: Surb 7A 150
KT7: T Ditt 7A 150

Portsmouth Rd. KT10: Esh 1A 162
SW15 .7D 116
Portsmouth St. WC2 . . . . .1G 13 (6K 83)
Portsoken St. E1 . . . . .2J 15 (7F 85)
Portswood Pl. SW15 . . . . .6B 116
Portugal Gdns. TW2: Twick 2G 131
Portugal St. WC2 . . . . . . .1G 13 (6K 83)
Portway E15 . . . . .1H 87
Portway Gdns. SE18 . . . . .7B 106
Pory Ho. SE11 . . . . .4H 19 (4K 101)
Poseidon Ct. E14 . . . . .4C 104
                        (off Homer Dr.)
POSK 4C 98
                        (off King St.)
Postern, The EC2 . . . . .6D 8
Postern Grn. EN2: Enf 2F 23
Post La. TW2: Twick 1H 131
Postmasters Lodge HA5: Pinn 7C 40
Postmill Cl. CRO: C'don 3J 169
Post Office All. W4 . . . . .6H 97
                        (off Thames Rd.)
Post Office App. E7 . . . . .5K 69
Post Office Ct. EC3 . . . . .1F 15
                        (off King William St.)
Post Office Way SW8 . . . . .7H 101
Post Rd. UB2: S'hall 3F 95
Postway M. IG1: Ilf 3F 71
                        (not continuous)
Potier St. SE1 . . . . .3D 102
Potter Cl. CR4: Mitc 2F 155
SE15 .7E 102
Potteries, The EN5: Barn 5D 20
Potterne Cl. SW19 . . . . .7F 117
Potters Cl. CRO: C'don 1A 170
Potters Ct. SM1: Sutt 6H 165
                        (off Rosebery Rd.)
Potters Fld. EN1: Enf 4K 23
Potters Flds. SE1 . . . . . . .5H 15 (1E 102)
Potters Gro. KT3: N Mald 4J 151
Potters Hgts. Cl. HA5: Pinn 1K 39
Potters La. EN5: New Bar 4D 20
SW16 .6H 137
Potters Lodge E14 . . . . .5E 104
                        (off Manchester Rd.)
Potters Rd. EN5: New Bar 4E 20
SW6 .2A 118
Potter St. HA5: Pinn 1K 39
HA6: Nwood 1J 39
Potter St. Hill HA5: Pinn 1K 39
Pottery Cl. SE25 . . . . .3G 157
Pottery La. W11 . . . . .1G 99
Pottery Rd. DA5: Bexl 2J 145
TW8: Bford 6E 96
Pottery St. SE16 . . . . .2H 103
Pott St. E2 .3H 85
Poulett Gdns. TW1: Twick 1A 132
Poulett Rd. E6 . . . . .2D 88
Poulters Wood BR2: Kes 5B 172
Poulton Av. SM1: Sutt 3B 166
Poulton Cl. E8 . . . . .6H 67
Poulton Ho. W3 . . . . .5K 79
                        (off Victoria Rd.)
Poultry EC2 . . . . .1E 14 (6D 84)
Pound Cl. BR6: Orp 2H 173
KT6: Surb 1C 162
Pound Ct. Dr. BR6: Orp 2H 173
Pound Farm Cl. KT10: Esh 7G 149
Pound Grn. DA5: Bexl 7G 127
Pound La. NW10 . . . . .6C 62
Pound Pk. Rd. SE7 . . . . .4B 106
Pound Pl. SE9 . . . . .6E 124
Pound St. SM5: Cars 5D 166
Pound Way BR7: Chst 7G 143
Pountney Rd. SW11 . . . . .3E 118
POVEREST 4K 161
Poverest Rd. BR5: St M Cry 5K 161
Povey Ho. SE17 . . . . .4E 102
                        (off Beckway St.)
Powder Mill La. TW2: Whitt 7D 112
Powell Cl. HA8: Edg 6A 28
KT9: Chess 5D 162

Powell Ct. CR2: S Croy 4B 168
                        (off Bramley Hill)
E17 . . . . .3D 50
Powell Gdns. RM10: Dag 4G 73
Powell Ho. W2 . . . . .2A 10
                        (off Gloucester Ter.)
Powell Rd. E5 . . . . .3H 67
IG9: Buck H 1F 37
Powell's Wlk. W4 . . . . .6A 98
Powergate Bus. Pk. NW10 . . . . .3K 79
Powerleague Soccer Cen.
Barking 3G 89
Catford 1C 140
Colney Hatch 7K 31
Ilford 1K 53
Mill Hill 7J 29
Norbury 1J 155
Purley 6K 167
Tottenham 6C 34
Power Rd. W4 . . . . .4G 97
Powers Ct. TW1: Twick 7D 114
Powerscroft Rd. DA14: Sidc 6C 144
                        (not continuous)
E5 . . . . .4J 67
Powis Ct. W11 . . . . .6H 81
                        (off Powis Gdns.)
WD23: B Hea 1C 26
                        (off Rutherford Way)
Powis Gdns. NW11 . . . . .7H 45
W11 . . . . .6H 81
Powis Ho. WC2 . . . . .7F 7
                        (off Macklin St.)
Powis M. W11 . . . . .6H 81
Powis Pl. WC1 . . . . .4F 7 (4J 83)
Powis Rd. E3 . . . . .3D 86
Powis Sq. W11 . . . . .6H 81
                        (not continuous)
Powis St. SE18 . . . . .3E 106
Powis Ter. W11 . . . . .6H 81
Powlesland Ct. E1 . . . . .6A 86
                        (off White Horse Rd.)
Powlett Ho. NW1 . . . . .6F 65
                        (off Powlett Pl.)
Powlett Pl. NW1 . . . . .7E 64
Pownall Gdns. TW3: Houn 4F 113
Pownall Rd. E8 . . . . .1F 85
TW3: Houn 4F 113
Pownsett Ter. IG1: Ilf 5G 71
Powster Rd. BR1: Brom 5J 141
Powys Cl. DA7: Bex 6D 108
Powys Ct. N11 . . . . .5D 32
Powys La. N13 . . . . .4D 32
N14 . . . . .4D 32
POYLE 5A 174
Poyle Ind. Est. SL3: Poyle 6A 174
Poyle New Cotts. SL3: Poyle 5A 174
Poyle Technical Cen. SL3: Poyle . . .5A 174
Poyle Trad. Est. SL3: Poyle 6A 174
Poynders Ct. SW4 . . . . .6G 119
Poynders Gdns. SW4 . . . . .7G 119
Poynders Rd. SW4 . . . . .6G 119
Poynings, The SL0: Rich P 1A 174
Poynings Rd. N19 . . . . .3G 65
Poynings Way N12 . . . . .5D 30
Poyntell Cres. BR7: Chst 1H 161
Poynter Ct. UB5: N'olt 2B 76
                        (off Gallery Gdns.)
Poynter Ho. NW8 . . . . .3A 4
                        (off Fisherton St.)
W11 . . . . .1F 99
                        (off Queensdale Cres.)
Poynter Rd. EN1: Enf 5B 24
Poynton Rd. N17 . . . . .2G 49
Poyntz Rd. SW11 . . . . .2D 118
Poyser St. E2 . . . . .2H 85
Praed M. W2 . . . . .7B 4 (6B 82)
Praed St. W2 . . . . .1A 10 (6B 82)
Pragel St. E13 . . . . .2A 88
Pragnell Rd. SE12 . . . . .2K 141
Prague Pl. SW2 . . . . .5J 119
Prah Rd. N4 . . . . .2A 66
Prairie St. SW8 . . . . .2E 118

Pratt M. NW1	1G 83
Pratts Pas. KT1: King T	2E 150
Pratt St. NW1	1G 83
Pratt Wlk. SE11	3H 19 (4K 101)
Prayle Gro. NW2	1F 63
Preachers Ct. EC1	5B 8

(off Charterhouse Sq.)

Prebend Gdns. W4	4B 98
W6	4B 98

(not continuous)

Prebend Mans. W4	4B 98

(off Chiswick High Rd.)

Prebend St. N1	1C 84
Precinct, The N1	1C 84

(not continuous)

Precinct Rd. UB3: Hayes	7J 75
Precincts, The SM4: Mord	6J 153
Premier Cinema	2G 121
Premier Cnr. W9	2H 81
Premier Ct. EN3: Enf W	1D 24
Premiere Pl. E14	7C 86
Premier Ho. N1	7B 66

(off Waterloo Ter.)

Premier Pk. NW10	1H 79

(not continuous)

Premier Pk. Rd. NW10	2H 79
Premier Pl. SW15	4G 117
Prendergast Rd. SE3	3G 123
Prentice Ct. SW19	5H 135
Prentis Rd. SW16	4H 137
Prentiss Ct. SE7	4B 106
Presburg Rd. KT3: N Mald	5A 152
Presburg St. E5	3K 67
Prescelly Pl. HA8: Edg	1F 43
Prescot St. E1	2K 15 (7F 85)
Prescott Av. BR5: Pet W	6F 161
Prescott Cl. SW16	7J 137
Prescott Ho. SE17	6B 102

(off Hillingdon St.)

Prescott Pl. SW4	3H 119
Presentation M. SW2	2K 137
Preshaw Cres. CR4: Mitc	3C 154
President Dr. E1	1H 103
President Ho. EC1	2B 8 (3B 84)
President Quay E1	4K 15
President St. EC1	1C 8
Prespa Cl. N9	2D 34
Press Ct. SE1	5G 103
Press Ho. NW10	3K 61
Press Rd. NW10	3K 61
Prestage Way E14	7E 86
Prestbury Rd. E7	7A 70
Prestbury Sq. SE9	4D 142
Prested Rd. SW11	4C 118
Prestige Way NW4	5E 44
PRESTON	1E 60
Preston Av. E4	6A 36
Preston Cl. SE1	4E 102
TW2: Twick	3J 131
Preston Ct. DA14: Sidc	4K 143

(off The Crescent)

EN5: New Bar	4F 21
Preston Dr. DA7: Bex	1D 126
E11	5A 52
KT19: Ewe	6A 164
Preston Gdns. IG1: Ilf	6C 52
NW10	6B 62
Preston Hill HA3: Kenton	7E 42
Preston Ho. RM10: Dag	3G 73

(off Uvedale Rd.)

SE1	4E 102

(off Preston Cl.)

SE1	7J 15

(off St Saviour's Est.)

Preston Pl. NW2	6C 62
TW10: Rich	5E 114
Preston Rd. E11	6G 51
HA3: Kenton	1E 60
HA9: Wemb	1E 60
SE19	6B 138
SW20	7B 134
TW17: Shep	5C 146

Prestons Rd. BR2: Hayes	3J 171
E14	7E 86
Preston St. E2	2K 85
Preston Waye HA3: Kenton	1E 60
Prestwich Ter. SW4	5G 119
Prestwick Cl. UB2: S'hall	5C 94
Prestwick Ct. UB1: S'hall	7G 77

(off Baird Av.)

Prestwood Av. HA3: Kenton	4B 42
Prestwood Cl. HA3: Kenton	4B 42
SE18	6A 108
Prestwood Gdns. CR0: C'don	7C 156
Prestwood Ho. SE16	3H 103

(off Drummond Rd.)

Prestwood St. N1	1D 8 (2C 84)
Pretoria Av. E17	4A 50
Pretoria Cres. E4	1K 35
Pretoria Rd. E4	1K 35
E11	1F 69
E16	4H 87
IG1: Ilf	5F 71
N17	7A 34
RM7: Rom	4J 55
SW16	6F 137
Pretoria Rd. Nth. N18	6A 34
Prevost Rd. N11	2K 31
Priam Ho. E2	2H 85

(off Old Bethnal Grn. Rd.)

Price Cl. SW17	3D 136
Price Ho. N1	1C 84

(off Britannia Row)

Price Rd. CR0: Wadd	5B 168
Price's Ct. SW11	3B 118
Price's M. N1	1K 83
Price's St. SE1	5B 14 (1B 102)
Price Way TW12: Hamp	6C 130
Prichard Cl. N7	6K 65
Prichard Ho. SE11	4J 19

(off Kennington Rd.)

Pricklers Hill EN5: New Bar	6E 20
Prickley Wood BR2: Hayes	1H 171
Priddy's Yd. CR0: C'don	2C 168
Prideaux Pl. W3	7K 79
WC1	1H 7 (3K 83)
Prideaux Rd. SW9	3J 119
Pridham Rd. CR7: Thor H	4D 156
Priestfield Rd. SE23	3A 140
Priestlands Pk. Rd.	
DA15: Sidc	3K 143
Priestley Cl. N16	7F 49
Priestley Gdns.	
RM6: Chad H	6B 54
Priestley Ho. EC1	3D 8

(off Old St.)

HA9: Wemb	3J 61

(off Barnhill Rd.)

Priestley Rd. CR4: Mitc	2E 154
Priestley Way E17	3K 49
NW2	1C 62
Priestman Point E3	3D 86

(off Rainhill Way)

Priest Pk. Av. HA2: Harr	2E 58
Priests Av. RM1: Rom	2K 55
Priests Bri. SW14	3A 116
SW15	3A 116
Priest's Ct. EC2	7C 8
Prima Rd. SW9	7A 102
Prime Meridian Line	7F 105
Primeplace M. CR7: Thor H	2C 156
Primezone M. N8	6J 47
Primrose Av. EN2: Enf	1J 23
RM6: Chad H	7B 54
Primrose Cl. E3	2C 86
HA2: Harr	3D 58
N3	2K 45
SE6	5E 140
SM6: Wall	7F 155
Primrose Ct. NW8	2D 82

(off Prince Albert Rd.)

SW12	7H 119

Primrose Gdns. HA4: Ruis	5A 58
NW3	6C 64
WD23: Bush	1A 26
PRIMROSE HILL	1E 82
Primrose Hill EC4	1K 13 (6A 84)
Primrose Hill Ct. NW3	7D 64
Primrose Hill Rd. NW3	7D 64
Primrose Hill Studios NW1	1E 82
Primrose Ho. SE15	1G 121

(off Peckham Hill St.)

Primrose La. CR0: C'don	1J 169
Primrose Mans. SW11	1E 118
Primrose M. NW1	7D 64

(off Sharpleshall St.)

SE3	7J 105
Primrose Pl. TW7: Isle	2K 113
Primrose Rd. E10	1D 68
E18	2K 51
Primrose Sq. E9	7J 67
Primrose St. EC2	5G 9 (5E 84)
Primrose Wlk. KT17: Ewe	7B 164
SE14	7A 104
Primrose Way HA0: Wemb	2D 78
Primula St. W12	6C 80
Prince Albert Ct. NW8	1D 82

(off Prince Albert Rd.)

TW16: Sun	7G 129
Prince Albert Rd. NW1	1C 4 (3C 82)
NW8	1C 4 (3C 82)
Prince Arthur M. NW3	4A 64
Prince Arthur Rd. NW3	5A 64
Prince Charles Cinema	2D 12
Prince Charles Dr. NW4	7E 44
Prince Charles Rd. SE3	2H 123
Prince Charles Way SM6: Wall	3F 167
Prince Consort Dr. BR7: Chst	1H 161
Prince Consort Rd. SW7	1A 16 (3A 100)
Princedale Rd. W11	1G 99
Prince Edward Mans. W2	7J 81

(off Moscow Rd.)

Prince Edward Rd. E9	6B 68
Prince Edward Theatre	1D 12

(off Old Compton St.)

Prince George Av. N14	5C 22
Prince George Rd. N16	4E 66
Prince George's Av. SW20	2E 152
Prince George's Rd. SW19	1B 154
Prince Henry Rd. SE7	7B 106
Prince Imperial Rd. BR7: Chst	1F 161
SE18	1D 124
Prince John Rd. SE9	5C 124
Princelet St. E1	5K 9 (5F 85)
Prince of Orange Ct. SE16	2J 103

(off Lower Rd.)

Prince of Orange La. SE10	7E 104
Prince of Wales Cl. NW4	4D 44
Prince of Wales Dr. SW8	7F 101
SW11	1C 118
Prince of Wales Mans. SW11	1E 118
Prince of Wales Pas. NW1	2A 6
Prince of Wales Rd. E16	6A 88
NW5	6E 64
SE3	2H 123
SM1: Sutt	2B 166
Prince of Wales Ter. W4	5A 98
W8	2K 99
Prince of Wales Theatre	3C 12

(off Coventry St.)

Prince Regent Ct. NW8	2C 82

(off Avenue Rd.)

SE16	7A 86

(off Edward Sq.)

Prince Regent La. E13	3K 87
E16	3K 87
Prince Regent M. NW1	2A 6
Prince Regent Rd. TW3: Houn	3F 113
Prince Rd. SE25	5E 156
Prince Rupert Rd. SE9	4D 124
Princes Arc. SW1	4B 12
Princes Av. BR5: Pet W	5J 161
IG8: Wfd G	4E 36
KT6: Surb	1G 163

Princes Av. N3	1J 45
N10	3F 47
N13	5F 33
N22	1H 47
NW9	4G 43
SM5: Cars	7D 166
UB6: G'frd	6F 77

(not continuous)

Princes Cir. WC2	7E 6 (6J 83)
Princes Cl. DA14: Sidc	3D 144
HA8: Edg	5B 28
N4	1B 66
NW9	4G 43
SW4	3G 119
TW11: Tedd	4H 131
Princes Club	2D 128
Princes Ct. HA9: Wemb	5E 60
SE16	3B 104
SW3	5D 16

(off Brompton Rd.)

Princes Ct. Bus. Cen. E1	7H 85
Princes Dr. HA1: Harr	3J 41
Princes Gdns. SW7	1B 16 (3B 100)
W3	5G 79
W5	4C 78
Prince's Ga. SW7	7B 10 (2B 100)

(not continuous)

Prince's Ga. SW7	7B 10 (2B 100)
Prince's Ga. M. SW7	1B 16 (3B 100)
Princes Ho. W11	7H 81
Princes La. HA4: Ruis	1G 57
N10	3F 47
Princes M. TW3: Houn	4E 112
W2	7K 81
W6	5D 98

(off Down Pl.)

Princes Pde. NW11	6G 45

(off Golders Grn. Rd.)

Princes Pk. Av. NW11	6G 45
UB3: Hayes	7F 75
Princes Pk. Circ. UB3: Hayes	7F 75
Princes Pk. Cl. UB3: Hayes	7F 75
Princes Pk. La. UB3: Hayes	7F 75
Princes Pk. Pde. UB3: Hayes	7F 75
Princes Pl. SW1	4B 12
W11	1G 99
Prince's Plain BR2: Brom	7C 160
Prince's Ri. SE13	2E 122
Princes Riverside Rd. SE16	1K 103
Prince's Rd. IG6: Ilf	4H 53
IG9: Buck H	2F 37
KT2: King T	7G 133
N18	4D 34
SE20	6K 139
SW14	3K 115
SW19	6J 135
TW9: Kew	1F 115
TW10: Rich	5F 115
TW11: Tedd	4H 131
TW13: Felt	2H 129
TW15: Ashf	5B 128
W13	1B 96
Princessa Ct. EN2: Enf	5J 23
Princess Alice Ho. W10	4E 80
Princess Alice Way SE28	2H 107
Princess Av. HA9: Wemb	2E 60
Princess Ct. SE28	6D 90

(off Horace Rd.)

N6	7G 47
NW6	6K 63

(off Compayne Gdns.)

W1	6E 4

(off Bryanston Pl.)

W2	7K 81

(off Queensway)

Princess Cres. N4	2B 66
Princess Ct. SE7	7C 104

(off Hales St.)

Princess Louise Bldg. SE8	7C 104

(off Hales St.)

Princess Louise Cl. W2	5B 4 (5B 82)
Princess Mary Ho. SW1	3D 18

(off Vincent St.)

Princess May Rd.—Pulton Pl.

Princess May Rd. N16 . . . . 4E **66**
Princess M. KT1: King T 3F **151**
NW3 . . . . 5B **64**
Princess of Wales Memorial Fountain
. . . . 6B **10** (2B **100**)
Princess Pde. BR6: Farnb 3E **172**
RM10: Dag 2G **91**
Princess Pk. Mnr. N11 . . . . 5K **31**
Princes Sq. W2 . . . . 7K **81**
(not continuous)
Princess Rd. CR0: C'don 6C **156**
NW1 . . . . 1E **82**
NW6 . . . . 2J **81**
Princess St. SE1 . . . . 3B **102**
Princes St. DA7: Bex 3F **127**
EC2 . . . . 1E **14** (6D **84**)
N17 . . . . 6K **33**
SM1: Sutt 4B **166**
TW9: Rich 4E **114**
W1 . . . . 1K **11** (6F **83**)
Princes Ter. E13 . . . . 1K **87**
Prince's Twr. *SE16* *2J* ***103***
(off Elephant La.)
Prince St. SE8 . . . . 6B **104**
Princes Way BR4: W W'ck 4H **171**
CR0: Wadd 5K **167**
HA4: Ruis 4C **58**
IG9: Buck H 2F **37**
SW19 . . . . 7F **117**
W3 . . . . 3G **97**
Prince's Yd. W11 . . . . 1G **99**
Princethorpe Ho. *W2* *5K* ***81***
(off Woodchester Sq.)
Princethorpe Rd. SE26 . . . . 4K **139**
Princeton Ct. SW15 . . . . 3F **117**
Princeton M. KT2: King T 1G **151**
Princeton St. WC1 . . . . 6G **7** (5K **83**)
Prince William Ct. *TW15: Ashf* *5B* ***128***
(off Clarendon Rd.)
Principal Sq. E9 . . . . 5K **67**
Pringle Gdns. SW16 . . . . 4G **137**
(not continuous)
Printers Inn Ct. EC4 . . . . 6A **84**
Printers M. E3 . . . . 1A **86**
Printer St. EC4 . . . . 7K **7** (6A **84**)
Printing Ho. La. UB3: Hayes 2G **93**
Printing Ho. Yd. E2 . . . . 1H **9** (3E **84**)
Printon Ho. *E14* *5B* ***86***
(off Wallwood St.)
Print Village SE15 . . . . 2F **121**
Printwork Apartments *SE1* *7G* ***15***
(off Long La.)
Priolo Rd. SE7 . . . . 5A **106**
Prior Av. SM2: Sutt 7C **166**
Prior Bolton St. N1 . . . . 6B **66**
Prioress Ho. *E3* *3D* ***86***
(off Bromley High St.)
Prioress Rd. SE27 . . . . 3B **138**
Prioress St. SE1 . . . . 3E **102**
Prior Rd. IG1: Ilf 3E **70**
Priors Cft. E17 . . . . 2A **50**
Priors Farm La. UB5: N'olt 6C **58**
Priors Fld. UB5: N'olt 6C **58**
Priors Gdns. HA4: Ruis 5A **58**
Priors Mead EN1: Enf 1K **23**
Prior St. SE10 . . . . 7E **104**
Priors Wood KT10: Hin W 2A **162**
Priory, The CR0: Wadd 4A **168**
N8 . . . . 4H **47**
SE3 . . . . 4H **123**
Priory Apartments, The SE6 . . . . 1D **140**
Priory Av. BR5: Pet W 6H **161**
E4 . . . . 3G **35**
E17 . . . . 5C **50**
HA0: Wemb 4K **59**
N8 . . . . 4H **47**
SM3: Cheam 4F **165**
W4 . . . . 4A **98**
Priory Cl. BR3: Beck 3A **158**
BR7: Chst 1D **160**
E4 . . . . 3G **35**
E18 . . . . 1J **51**
Priory Cl. HA0: Wemb 4K **59**
HA4: Ruis 1H **57**
HA7: Stan 3E **26**
N3 . . . . 1H **45**
N14 . . . . 5A **22**
N20 . . . . 1C **30**
SW19 . . . . 1K **153**
TW12: Hamp 1D **148**
TW16: Sun 7J **129**
UB3: Hayes 7K **75**
Priory Ct. E6 . . . . 1A **88**
E9 . . . . 5K **67**
E17 . . . . 2B **50**
EC4 . . . . *1B* ***14***
(off Pilgrim St.)
HA0: Wemb 2E **78**
KT1: King T *3E* ***150***
(off Denmark Rd.)
KT17: Ewe 7B **164**
SM3: Cheam 4G **165**
SW8 . . . . 1H **119**
TW3: Houn 3F **113**
WD23: Bush *1B* ***26***
(off Sparrows Herne)
Priory Ct. Est. E17 . . . . 2B **50**
Priory Cres. HA0: Wemb 3A **60**
SE19 . . . . 7C **138**
SM3: Cheam 4F **165**
Priory Dr. HA7: Stan 3E **26**
SE2 . . . . 5D **108**
Priory Fld. Dr. HA8: Edg 4C **28**
Priory Gdns. HA0: Wemb 4A **60**
N6 . . . . 6F **47**
NW10 . . . . 3E **78**
SE25 . . . . 4F **157**
SW13 . . . . 3B **116**
TW12: Hamp 7D **130**
TW15: Ashf 5F **129**
W4 . . . . 4A **98**
W5 . . . . 3E **78**
Priory Grange *N2* *3D* ***46***
(off Fortis Grn.)
Priory Grn. Est. N1 . . . . 2K **83**
Priory Gro. EN5: Barn 5D **20**
SW8 . . . . 1J **119**
Priory Hgts. *N1* *2K* ***83***
(off Wynford Rd.)
Priory Hill HA0: Wemb 4A **60**
Priory Ho. *E1* *5J* ***9***
(off Folgate St.)
EC1 . . . . *3A* ***8***
(off Sans Wlk.)
SW1 . . . . *5C* ***18***
(off Rampayne St.)
Priory La. KT8: W Mole 4F **149**
SW15 . . . . 6A **116**
Priory Leas SE9 . . . . 1C **142**
Priory Lodge *W4* *5G* ***97***
(off Kew Bri. Ct.)
Priory Mans. *SW10* *5A* ***100***
(off Drayton Gdns.)
Priory M. SW8 . . . . 1J **119**
Priory Pk. SE3 . . . . 3H **123**
Priory Pk. Rd. HA0: Wemb 4A **60**
NW6 . . . . 1H **81**
Priory Retail Pk. SW19 . . . . 7B **136**
Priory Rd. CR0: C'don 7A **156**
E6 . . . . 1B **88**
IG11: Bark 7H **71**
KT9: Chess 3E **162**
N8 . . . . 4G **47**
NW6 . . . . 1K **81**
SM3: Cheam 4F **165**
SW19 . . . . 7B **136**
TW3: Houn 5G **113**
TW9: Kew 6G **97**
TW12: Hamp 7D **130**
W4 . . . . 3K **97**
Priory St. E3 . . . . 3D **86**
Priory Ter. NW6 . . . . 1K **81**
TW16: Sun 7J **129**
Priory Vw. WD23: B Hea 1D **26**
Priory Vs. *N11* *6J* ***31***
(off Colney Hatch La.)
Priory Wlk. SW10 . . . . 5A **100**
Priory Way HA2: Harr 4F **41**
UB2: S'hall 3B **94**
UB7: Harm 6A **92**
Priscilla Cl. N15 . . . . 5C **48**
Pritchard Ho. *E2* *2H* ***85***
(off Ada Pl.)
Pritchard's Rd. E2 . . . . 1G **85**
Priter Rd. SE16 . . . . 3G **103**
Priter Rd. Hostel *SE16* *3G* ***103***
(off Dockley Rd.)
Priter Way SE16 . . . . 3G **103**
Private Rd. EN1: Enf 5J **23**
Probert Rd. SW2 . . . . 5A **120**
Probyn Ho. *SW1* *3D* ***18***
(off Page St.)
Probyn Rd. SW2 . . . . 2B **138**
Procter Ho. *SE1* *5G* ***103***
(off Avondale Sq.)
SE5 . . . . *7D* ***102***
(off Picton St.)
Procter St. WC1 . . . . 6G **7** (5K **83**)
Proctor Cl. CR4: Mitc 1E **154**
Proctors Cl. TW14: Felt 1J **129**
Progress Bus. Pk. CR0: Wadd 2K **167**
Progress Cen., The EN3: Pond E 3E **24**
Progress Way CR0: Wadd 2K **167**
EN1: Enf 5B **24**
N22 . . . . 1A **48**
Project Pk. E3 . . . . 4F **87**
Prologis Pk. CR0: Bedd 7H **155**
E16 . . . . 4F **87**
TW4: Houn 4A **112**
Promenade, The HA8: Edg 5B **28**
W4 . . . . 2A **116**
Promenade App. Rd. W4 . . . . 7A **98**
Pronto Trad. Est. UB3: Hayes 5G **75**
Prospect Cl. DA17: Belv 4G **109**
HA4: Ruis 7B **40**
SE26 . . . . 4H **139**
TW3: Houn 1D **112**
Prospect Cotts. SW18 . . . . 4J **117**
Prospect Cres. TW2: Whitt 6G **113**
Prospect Hill E17 . . . . 4D **50**
Prospect Ho. *E17* *3E* ***50***
(off Prospect Hill)
N1 . . . . *2A* ***84***
(off Donegal St.)
SE1 . . . . *3B* ***102***
(off Gaywood St.)
SE16 . . . . *3G* ***103***
(off Frean St.)
SW19 . . . . *1B* ***154***
(off Chapter Way)
W10 . . . . *6F* ***81***
(off Bridge Cl.)
Prospect Pl. BR2: Brom 3K **159**
CR2: S Croy 6C **168**
E1 . . . . 1J **103**
(not continuous)
N2 . . . . 4B **46**
N7 . . . . 4J **65**
N17 . . . . 7K **33**
NW2 . . . . 3H **63**
NW3 . . . . 4A **64**
RM5: Col R 2J **55**
SE8 . . . . *6B* ***104***
(off Evelyn St.)
SW20 . . . . 7D **134**
W4 . . . . 5K **97**
Prospect Quay *SW18* *4J* ***117***
(off Lightermans Wlk.)
Prospect Ring N2 . . . . 3B **46**
Prospect Rd. EN5: New Bar 4D **20**
IG8: Wfd G 6F **37**
KT6: Surb 6C **150**
NW2 . . . . 3H **63**
Prospect St. SE16 . . . . 3H **103**
Prospect Va. SE18 . . . . 4C **106**
Prospect Wharf E1 . . . . 7J **85**
Prospero Ho. *E1* *7F* ***85***
(off Portsoken St.)
Prospero Rd. N19 . . . . 1H **65**
Protea Cl. E16 . . . . 4H **87**
Protheroe Ho. N17 . . . . 3F **49**
Prothero Gdns. NW4 . . . . 5D **44**
Prothero Ho. *NW10* *7K* ***61***
(off Ayres Cres.)
Prothero Rd. SW6 . . . . 7G **99**
Proud Ho. *E1* *6H* ***85***
(off Amazon St.)
Prout Gro. NW10 . . . . 4A **62**
Prout Rd. E5 . . . . 3H **67**
Provence St. N1 . . . . 2C **84**
Providence Av. HA2: Harr 1E **58**
Providence Cl. E9 . . . . 1K **85**
Providence Ct. W1 . . . . 2H **11** (7E **82**)
Providence Ho. *E14* *6B* ***86***
(off Three Colt St.)
Providence La. UB3: Harl 7F **93**
Providence Pl. N1 . . . . 1B **84**
RM5: Col R 1F **55**
Providence Rd. UB7: Yiew 1A **92**
Providence Row *N1* *2K* ***83***
(off Pentonville Rd.)
Providence Row Cl. E2 . . . . 3H **85**
Providence Sq. SE1 . . . . 6K **15** (2G **103**)
Providence Twr. *SE16* *2G* ***103***
(off Bermondsey Wall W.)
Providence Yd. *E2* *1K* ***9***
(off Ezra St.)
Provident Ind. Est. UB3: Hayes 2J **93**
Provost Ct. *NW3* *6D* ***64***
(off Eton Rd.)
Provost Est. N1 . . . . 1E **8**
Provost Rd. NW3 . . . . 7D **64**
Provost St. N1 . . . . 1E **8** (2D **84**)
Prowse Av. WD23: B Hea 1B **26**
Prowse Pl. NW1 . . . . 7G **65**
Proyers Path HA1: Harr 7B **42**
Prudence La. BR6: Farnb 4E **172**
Pruden Cl. N14 . . . . 2B **32**
Prudent Pas. EC2 . . . . 7D **8**
Prusom's Island *E1* *1J* ***103***
(off Wapping High St.)
Prusom St. E1 . . . . 1H **103**
Pryors, The NW3 . . . . 3B **64**
Pucknells Cl. BR8: Swan 7J **145**
Pudding La. EC3 . . . . 3F **15** (7D **84**)
Pudding Mill La. E15 . . . . 1D **86**
Puddle Dock EC4 . . . . 2A **14** (7B **84**)
(not continuous)
Puffin Cl. BR3: Beck 5K **157**
IG11: Bark 3B **90**
Pugin Ct. *N1* *7A* ***66***
(off Liverpool Rd.)
Pulborough Rd. SW18 . . . . 7H **117**
Pulborough Way TW4: Houn 4A **112**
Pulford Rd. N15 . . . . 6D **48**
Pulham Av. N2 . . . . 4A **46**
Pulham Ho. *SW8* *7K* ***101***
(off Dorset Rd.)
Pullen's Bldgs. *SE17* *5B* ***102***
(off Iliffe St.)
Puller Rd. EN5: Barn 2B **20**
Pulleyns Av. E6 . . . . 3C **88**
Pullman Ct. SW2 . . . . 1J **137**
Pullman Gdns. SW15 . . . . 6E **116**
Pullman M. SE12 . . . . 3K **141**
Pullman Pl. SE9 . . . . 5C **124**
Pulross Rd. SW9 . . . . 3K **119**
Pulse Apartments *NW6* *5K* ***63***
(off Lymington Rd.)
Pulteney Cl. E3 . . . . 1B **86**
TW7: Isle 3A **114**
Pulteney Gdns. E18 . . . . 3K **51**
Pulteney Rd. E18 . . . . 3K **51**
Pulteney Ter. N1 . . . . 1K **83**
(not continuous)
Pulton Ho. *SE4* *4A* ***122***
(off Turnham Rd.)
Pulton Pl. SW6 . . . . 7J **99**

Puma Ct.—Queensberry Ho.

Puma Ct. E1 . . . . 5J **9** (5F **85**)
Pump All. TW8: Bford 7D **96**
Pump Cl. UB5: N'olt 2E **76**
Pump Ct. EC4 . . . . 1J **13** (6A **84**)
Pumphandle Path *N2* *2B* ***46***
(off Oak La.)
Pumphouse, The N8 . . . . 4K **47**
Pump Ho. Cl. BR2: Brom 2G **159**
SE16 . . . . 2J **103**
Pumphouse Educational Mus., The 1A **104**
Pump House Gallery, The 7E **100**
Pump Ho. M. *E1* *7G* ***85***
(off Hooper St.)
Pump House Steam & Transport Mus. 6A **50**
Pumping Ho. *E14* *7F* ***87***
(off Naval Row)
Pumping Sta. Rd. W4 . . . . 7A **98**
Pump La. SE14 . . . . 7J **103**
UB3: Hayes 2J **93**
Pump Pail Nth. CR0: C'don 3C **168**
Pump Pail Sth. CR0: C'don 3C **168**
Punchard Cres. EN3: Enf L 1J **25**
Punderson's Gdns. E2 . . . . 3H **85**
Purbeck Av. KT3: N Mald 6B **152**
Purbeck Dr. NW2 . . . . 2F **63**
Purbeck Ho. *SW8* *7K* ***101***
(off Bolney St.)
Purbrook Est. SE1 . . . . 7H **15** (2E **102**)
Purbrook St. SE1 . . . . 7H **15** (3E **102**)
Purcell Cres. SW6 . . . . 7F **99**
(not continuous)
Purcell Ho. EN1: Enf 1B **24**
SW10 . . . . *6B* ***100***
(off Milman's St.)
Purcell Mans. *W14* *6G* ***99***
(off Queen's Club Gdns.)
Purcell M. NW10 . . . . 7A **62**
Purcell Rd. UB6: G'frd 5F **77**
Purcell Room *4H* ***13***
(off Belvedere Rd.)
Purcells Av. HA8: Edg 5B **28**
Purcell St. N1 . . . . 2E **84**
Purchese St. NW1 . . . . 1D **6** (2H **83**)
Purday Ho. *W10* *3G* ***81***
(off Bruckner St.)
Purdon Ho. *SE15* *1G* ***121***
(off Oliver Goldsmith Est.)
Purdy Ct. KT4: Wor Pk 2C **164**
Purdy St. E3 . . . . 4D **86**
Purelake M. *SE13* *3F* ***123***
(off Marischal Rd.)
Purkis Cl. UB8: Hil 7E **74**
Purland Cl. RM8: Dag 1F **73**
Purland Rd. SE28 . . . . 2K **107**
(not continuous)
Purleigh Av. IG8: Wfd G 6H **37**
Purley Av. NW2 . . . . 2G **63**
Purley Cl. IG5: Ilf 2E **52**
Purley Pl. N1 . . . . 7B **66**
Purley Rd. CR2: S Croy 7D **168**
N9 . . . . 3K **33**
Purley Vw. Ter. *CR2: S Croy* *7D* ***168***
(off Sanderstead Rd.)
Purley Way CR0: C'don, Wadd 7K **155**
Purley Way Cen., The CR0: Wadd 2A **168**
Purley Way Cres. CR0: C'don 7K **155**
Purneys Rd. SE9 . . . . 4B **124**
Purrett Rd. SE18 . . . . 5K **107**
Purser Ho. *SW2* *6A* ***120***
(off Tulse Hill)
Pursers Cross Rd. SW6 . . . . 1H **117**
(not continuous)
Pursewardens Cl. W13 . . . . 1C **96**
Pursley Rd. NW7 . . . . 7J **29**
Purves Rd. NW10 . . . . 3D **80**
Purvis Ho. CR0: C'don 7D **156**
Pusey Ho. *E14* *6C* ***86***
(off Saracen St.)
Puteaux Ho. *E2* *2K* ***85***
(off Mace St.)
PUTNEY 4F **117**
Putney Arts Theatre 4F **117**
Putney Bri. SW15 . . . . 3G **117**
Putney Bri. App. SW6 . . . . 3G **117**
Putney Bri. Rd. SW15 . . . . 4G **117**
SW18 . . . . 4G **117**
Putney Comn. SW15 . . . . 3E **116**
Putney Exchange Shop. Cen.
SW15 . . . . 4F **117**
Putney Gdns. RM6: Chad H 5B **54**
PUTNEY HEATH 6E **116**
Putney Heath SW15 . . . . 7D **116**
Putney Heath La. SW15 . . . . 6F **117**
Putney High St. SW15 . . . . 4F **117**
Putney Hill SW15 . . . . 7F **117**
(not continuous)
Putney Leisure Cen. 4E **116**
Putney Pk. Av. SW15 . . . . 4C **116**
Putney Pk. La. SW15 . . . . 4D **116**
(not continuous)
PUTNEY VALE 3C **134**
Putney Va. Crematorium SW19 . . . . 2D **134**
Putney Wharf SW15 . . . . 3G **117**
Pycroft Way N9 . . . . 4A **34**
Pyecombe Cnr. N12 . . . . 4C **30**
Pylbrook Rd. SM1: Sutt 3J **165**
Pylon Way CR0: Bedd 1J **167**
Pym Cl. EN4: E Barn 5G **21**
Pymers Mead SE21 . . . . 1C **138**
Pymmes Brook Dr. EN4: E Barn 4H **21**
Pymmes Brook Ho. N10 . . . . 7K **31**
Pymmes Cl. N13 . . . . 5E **32**
N17 . . . . 1H **49**
Pymmes Gdns. Nth. N9 . . . . 3A **34**
Pymmes Gdns. Sth. N9 . . . . 3A **34**
Pymmes Grn. Rd. N11 . . . . 4A **32**
Pymmes Rd. N13 . . . . 6D **32**
Pynchester Cl. UB10: Ick 2C **56**
Pyne Rd. KT6: Surb 1G **163**
Pynfolds SE16 . . . . 2H **103**
Pynham Cl. SE2 . . . . 3B **108**
Pynnacles Cl. HA7: Stan 5G **27**
Pynnersmead SE24 . . . . 5C **120**
Pyramid Ct. *KT1: King T* *2F* ***151***
(off Cambridge Rd.)
Pyramid Ho. TW4: Houn 2C **112**
Pyrford Ho. SW9 . . . . 4B **120**
Pyrland Rd. N5 . . . . 5D **66**
TW10: Rich 6F **115**
Pyrmont Gro. SE27 . . . . 3B **138**
Pyrmont Rd. W4 . . . . 6G **97**
Pytchley Cres. SE19 . . . . 6C **138**
Pytchley Rd. SE22 . . . . 3E **120**

Q

Q Bldg., The *E15* *6G* ***69***
(off The Grove)
Quad Ct. *SE1* *3E* ***102***
(off Grigg's Pl.)
Quadrangle, The E15 . . . . 6G **69**
SE24 . . . . 5C **120**
SW6 . . . . 7G **99**
SW10 . . . . 1A **118**
W2 . . . . 7C **4** (6C **82**)
W12 . . . . *6D* ***80***
(off Du Cane Rd.)
Quadrangle Cl. SE1 . . . . 4E **102**
Quadrangle M. HA7: Stan 7H **27**
Quadrant, The DA7: Bex 7D **108**
HA2: Harr 3H **41**
HA8: Edg 6B **28**
NW4 . . . . 4E **44**
SM2: Sutt 6A **166**
SW20 . . . . 1G **153**
TW9: Rich 4D **114**
W10 . . . . 3F **81**
Quadrant Arc. W1 . . . . 3B **12**
Quadrant Bus. Cen. NW6 . . . . 1G **81**
Quadrant Cl. NW4 . . . . 5D **44**
Quadrant Ct. HA9: Wemb 4G **61**
Quadrant Gro. NW5 . . . . 5D **64**
Quadrant Ho. SE1 . . . . 4A **14**
Quadrant Rd.
CR7: Thor H 4B **156**
TW9: Rich 4D **114**
Quad Rd. HA9: Wemb 3D **60**
Quaggy Wlk. SE3 . . . . 4J **123**
Quain Mans. *W14* *6G* ***99***
(off Queen's Club Gdns.)
Quainton St. NW10 . . . . 3K **61**
Quaker Ct. *E1* *4J* ***9***
(off Quaker St.)
EC1 . . . . 3E **8**
Quaker La. UB2: S'hall 3E **94**
Quakers Course NW9 . . . . 1B **44**
Quakers La. TW7: Isle 7A **96**
(not continuous)
Quakers Pl. E7 . . . . 5B **70**
Quaker St. E1 . . . . 4J **9** (4F **85**)
Quakers Wlk. N21 . . . . 5J **23**
Quality Ct. WC2 . . . . 7J **7**
Quantock Cl. UB3: Harl 7F **93**
Quantock Dr. KT4: Wor Pk 2E **164**
Quantock Gdns. NW2 . . . . 2F **63**
Quantock Ho. N16 . . . . 1F **67**
Quantock M. SE15 . . . . 2G **121**
Quantum Ct. *E1* *5J* ***9***
(off King David La.)
Quarles Pk. Rd. RM6: Chad H 6B **54**
Quarrendon St. SW6 . . . . 2J **117**
Quarr Rd. SM5: Cars 6B **154**
Quarry Pk. Rd. SM1: Sutt 6H **165**
Quarry Ri. SM1: Sutt 6H **165**
Quarry Rd. SW18 . . . . 6A **118**
Quarterdeck, The E14 . . . . 2C **104**
Quartz Ho. HA2: Harr 1E **58**
Quastel Ho. *SE1* *7E* ***14***
(off Long La.)
Quatre Ports E4 . . . . 5A **36**
Quay Ho. *E14* *2C* ***104***
(off Admirals Way)
Quayside Cotts. *E1* *4K* ***15***
(off Mews St.)
Quayside Ct. *SE16* *1K* ***103***
(off Abbotshade Rd.)
Quayside Ho. E14 . . . . 1B **104**
W10 . . . . 4G **81**
Quayside Wlk. *KT1: King T* *2D* ***150***
(off Wadbrook St.)
Quay Vw. Apartments *E14* *3C* ***104***
(off Arden Cres.)
Quebec M. W1 . . . . 1F **11** (6D **82**)
Quebec Rd. IG1: Ilf 7F **53**
IG2: Ilf 7F **53**
UB4: Yead 6A **76**
Quebec Way SE16 . . . . 2K **103**
Quebec Way Ind. Est. SE16 . . . . 2A **104**
(not continuous)
Quebec Wharf *E8* *1E* ***84***
(off Kingsland Rd.)
E14 . . . . 6C **86**
Quedgeley Ct. *SE15* *6F* ***103***
(off Ebley Cl.)
Queen Adelaide Ct. SE20 . . . . 6J **139**
Queen Adelaide Rd. SE20 . . . . 6J **139**
Queen Alexandra Mans. *WC1* *2E* ***6***
(off Bidborough St.)
Queen Alexandra's Ct. SW19 . . . . 5H **135**
Queen Anne Av. BR2: Brom 3H **159**
Queen Anne Ho. *E16* *1J* ***105***
(off Hardy Av.)
Queen Anne M. W1 . . . . 6K **5** (5F **83**)
Queen Anne Rd. E9 . . . . 6K **67**
Queen Anne's Cl. TW2: Twick 3H **131**
Queen Anne's Ct. *SE10* *5F* ***105***
(off Park Row)
Queen Anne's Gdns. CR4: Mitc 3D **154**
EN1: Enf 6K **23**
W4 . . . . 3A **98**
W5 . . . . 2E **96**
Queen Anne's Ga. DA7: Bex 3D **126**
SW1 . . . . 7C **12** (2H **101**)
Queen Anne's Gro. EN1: Enf 7J **23**
W4 . . . . 3A **98**
W5 . . . . 2E **96**
Queen Anne's Pl. EN1: Enf 6K **23**
Queen Annes Sq. *SE1* *4G* ***103***
(off Monnow Rd.)
Queen Anne St. W1 . . . . 7J **5** (6F **83**)
Queen Anne's Wlk. WC1 . . . . 4F **7**
Queen Anne Ter. *E1* *7H* ***85***
(off Sovereign Cl.)
Queenborough Gdns. BR7: Chst 6H **143**
IG2: Ilf 4E **52**
Queen Caroline St. W6 . . . . 5E **98**
(not continuous)
Queen Catherine Ho. *SW6* *7K* ***99***
(off Wandon Rd.)
Queen Charlotte's Cottage 2D **114**
Queen Ct. *WC1* *4F* ***7***
(off Queen Sq.)
Queen Elizabeth Bldgs. EC4 . . . . 2J **13**
Queen Elizabeth Ct. EN5: Barn 3D **20**
Queen Elizabeth Gdns. SM4: Mord . . . 4J **153**
Queen Elizabeth Hall 4H **13** (1K **101**)
Queen Elizabeth Ho. SW12 . . . . 7E **118**
Queen Elizabeth II Conference Cen. 7D **12** (2H **101**)
Queen Elizabeth Rd. E17 . . . . 3A **50**
KT2: King T 2F **151**
Queen Elizabeth's Cl. N16 . . . . 2D **66**
Queen Elizabeth's Coll. SE10 . . . . 7E **104**
Queen Elizabeth's Dr. CR0: New Ad . . . 7F **171**
N14 . . . . 1D **32**
Queen Elizabeth's Hunting Lodge 1C **36**
Queen Elizabeth Sports Cen. 4C **20**
Queen Elizabeth Stadium 2A **24**
Queen Elizabeth St. SE1 . . . . . 6J **15** (2E **102**)
Queen Elizabeth's Wlk. N16 . . . . 1D **66**
SM6: Bedd *4H* ***167***
(off Croydon Rd.)
SM6: Bedd 4H **167**
(Evelyn Way)
Queen Elizabeth Wlk. SW13 . . . . 1C **116**
Queenhithe EC4 . . . . 2D **14** (7C **84**)
Queen Isabella Way *EC1* *7B* ***8***
(off King Edward St.)
Queen Margaret Flats *E2* *3H* ***85***
(off St Jude's Rd.)
Queen Margaret's Gro. N1 . . . . 5E **66**
Queen Mary Av. E18 . . . . 1J **51**
SM4: Mord 5F **153**
Queen Mary Cl. KT6: Surb 3G **163**
Queen Mary Ct. TW19: Stanw 1A **128**
Queen Mary Ho. *E16* *1K* ***105***
(off Wesley Av.)
E18 . . . . 1K **51**
Queen Mary Rd. SE19 . . . . 6B **138**
TW17: Shep 2E **146**
Queen Mary's Av. SM5: Cars 7D **166**
Queen Marys Bldgs. *SW1* *3B* ***18***
(off Stillington St.)
Queen Mary's Ct. *SE10* *6F* ***105***
(off Park Row)
Queen Mary's Ho. SW15 . . . . 6C **116**
Queen Mary University of London
Charterhouse Square . . . 4B **8** (4B **84**)
Lincoln's Inn Fields Campus . . . *7G* ***7***
(off Remnant St.)
Mile End Campus 4A **86**
West Smithfield Campus *6B* ***8***
(off Giltspur St.)
Queen Mother Sports Cen., The 3A **18**
Queen of Denmark Ct. SE16 . . . . 3B **104**
Queens Acre SM3: Cheam 7F **165**
Queens Av. HA7: Stan 3C **42**
IG8: Wfd G 5E **36**
N3 . . . . 7F **31**
N10 . . . . 3E **46**
N20 . . . . 2G **31**
N21 . . . . 1G **33**
TW13: Hanw 4A **130**
UB6: G'frd 6F **77**
Queensberry Ho. TW9: Rich 5C **114**

A-Z London 363

Queensberry M. W. SW7 ... 3A 16 (4B 100)
Queensberry Pl. E12 ... 5B 70
SW7 ... 3A 16 (4B 100)
TW9: Rich ... 5D 114
(off Friars La.)
Queensberry Way SW7 ... 3A 16 (4B 100)
Queensborough Ct. *N3 ... 4H 45*
(off Tillingbourne Gdns.)
Queensborough M. W2 ... 7A 82
Queensborough Pas. *W2 ... 7A 82*
(off Queensborough M.)
Queensborough Studios *W2 ... 7A 82*
(off Queensborough M.)
Queensborough Ter. W2 ... 7K 81
Queensbridge Ct. *E2 ... 1F 85*
(off Queensbridge Rd.)
Queensbridge Pk. TW7: Isle ... 5J 113
Queensbridge Rd. E2 ... 6F 67
E8 ... 6F 67
Queensbridge Sports & Community Cen. ... 7F 67
QUEENSBURY ... 3E 42
Queensbury Circ. Pde. HA3: Kenton ... 3E 42
Queensbury Rd. HA0: Wemb ... 2F 79
NW9 ... 7K 43
Queensbury Sta. Pde. HA8: Edg ... 3F 43
Queensbury St. N1 ... 7C 66
Queen's Chapel of the Savoy, The ... 3G 13
(off Savoy Hill)
Queen's Cir. SW8 ... 7F 101
Queens Cl. HA8: Edg ... 5B 28
SM6: Wall ... 5F 167
Queen's Club Gdns. W14 ... 6G 99
Queen's Club, The (Tennis Courts) ... 5G 99
Queens Club Ter. *W14 ... 6H 99*
(off Normand Rd.)
Queens Ct. *CR2: S Croy ... 5C 168*
(off Warham Rd.)
CR7: Thor H ... 5A 156
E11 ... 7G 51
HA3: Kenton ... 2B 42
IG9: Buck H ... 2G 37
NW6 ... 5K 63
NW8 ... 2B 82
(off Queen's Ter.)
NW11 ... 5H 45
SE23 ... 2J 139
TW10: Rich ... 6F 115
W2 ... 7K 81
(off Queensway)
Queenscourt HA9: Wemb ... 4E 60
Queen's Cres. NW5 ... 6E 64
TW10: Rich ... 5F 115
Queenscroft Rd. SE9 ... 5B 124
Queensdale Cres. W11 ... 1F 99
(not continuous)
Queensdale Pl. W11 ... 1G 99
Queensdale Rd. W11 ... 1F 99
Queensdale Wlk. W11 ... 1G 99
Queensdown Rd. E5 ... 4H 67
Queens Dr. E10 ... 7C 50
KT5: Surb ... 7G 151
KT7: T Ditt ... 6A 150
N4 ... 2B 66
W3 ... 6F 79
W5 ... 6F 79
Queen's Elm Pde. *SW3 ... 5B 16*
(off Old Church St.)
Queen's Elm Sq. SW3 ... 6B 16 (5B 100)
Queensferry Wlk. N17 ... 4H 49
Queensfield Ct. SM3: Cheam ... 4E 164
Queen's Gallery ... 7K 11 (2F 101)
Queen's Gdns. NW4 ... 5E 44
RM13: Rain ... 2K 91
TW5: Hest ... 1C 112
W2 ... 7A 82
W5 ... 4C 78
Queen's Ga. SW7 ... 7A 10 (2A 100)
Queensgate Ct. N12 ... 5E 30
Queens Ga. Gdns. BR7: Chst ... 1H 161
SW7 ... 3A 100
SW15 ... 4D 116
Queensgate Ho. *E3 ... 2B 86*
(off Hereford Rd.)
Queen's Ga. M. SW7 ... 3A 100
Queen's Ga. Pl. SW7 ... 3A 100
Queensgate Pl. NW6 ... 7J 63
Queen's Ga. Pl. M. SW7 ... 2A 16 (3A 100)
Queen's Ga. Ter. SW7 ... 1A 16 (3A 100)
Queens Ga. Vs. E9 ... 7A 68
Queen's Gro. NW8 ... 1B 82
Queens Gro. Rd. E4 ... 1A 36
Queen's Gro. Studios NW8 ... 1B 82
Queen's Head Pas. EC4 ... 7C 8 (6C 84)
Queen's Head St. N1 ... 1B 84
Queen's Head Yd. SE1 ... 5E 14
Queen's House, The ... 6F 105
(within National Maritime Mus.)
Queens Ho. *SE17 ... 6D 102*
(off Merrow St.)
SW8 ... 7J 101
(off Sth. Lambeth Rd.)
TW11: Tedd ... 6K 131
W2 ... 7K 81
(off Queensway)
Queen's Ice Bowl ... 7K 81
Queen's Keep TW1: Twick ... 6C 114
Queensland Av. N18 ... 6H 33
SW19 ... 1K 153
Queensland Cl. E17 ... 2B 50
Queensland Ho. *E16 ... 1E 106*
(off Rymill St.)
Queensland Rd. N7 ... 4A 66
Queens La. N10 ... 3F 47
Queen's Mans. *W6 ... 4F 99*
(off Brook Grn.)
Queen's Mkt. E13 ... 1A 88
Queens Mead HA8: Edg ... 6A 28
Queensmead NW8 ... 1B 82
Queen's Mead Rd. BR2: Brom ... 2H 159
Queensmead Sports Cen. ... 4B 58
Queensmere Cl. SW19 ... 2F 135
Queensmere Ct. SW13 ... 7B 98
Queensmere Rd. SW19 ... 2F 135
Queen's M. W2 ... 7K 81
Queensmill Rd. SW6 ... 7F 99
Queens Pde. N8 ... 4B 48
N11 ... 5J 31
(off Friern Barnet Rd.)
NW2 ... 6E 62
(off Willesden La.)
NW4 ... 5E 44
(off Queens Rd.)
W5 ... 6F 79
Queen's Pde. Cl. N11 ... 5J 31
Queens Pk. Ct. W10 ... 3F 81
Queen's Pk. Gdns. TW13: Felt ... 3H 129
Queen's Pk. Rangers FC ... 1D 98
Queens Pas. BR7: Chst ... 6F 143
Queens Pl. SM4: Mord ... 4J 153
Queen's Prom. KT1: King T, Surb ... 4D 150
Queen Sq. WC1 ... 4F 7 (4J 83)
Queen Sq. Pl. WC1 ... 4F 7
Queen's Quay *EC4 ... 2C 14*
(off Up. Thames St.)
Queens Reach KT1: King T ... 2D 150
KT8: E Mos ... 4J 149
Queens Ride SW13 ... 3C 116
SW15 ... 3C 116
Queens Ri. TW10: Rich ... 6F 115
Queens Rd. BR1: Brom ... 2J 159
BR3: Beck ... 2A 158
BR7: Chst ... 6F 143
CR0: C'don ... 6B 156
CR4: Mitc ... 3B 154
DA16: Well ... 2B 126
E11 ... 7F 51
E13 ... 1K 87
E17 ... 6B 50
EN1: Enf ... 4K 23
EN5: Barn ... 3A 20
IG9: Buck H ... 2E 36
IG11: Bark ... 6G 71
KT2: King T ... 7G 133
Queens Rd. KT3: N Mald ... 4B 152
KT7: T Ditt ... 5K 149
N3 ... 1A 46
N9 ... 3C 34
N11 ... 7D 32
NW4 ... 5E 44
SE14 ... 1H 121
SE15 ... 1H 121
SM4: Mord ... 4J 153
SM6: Wall ... 5F 167
SW14 ... 3K 115
SW19 ... 6H 135
TW1: Twick ... 1A 132
TW3: Houn ... 3F 113
TW10: Rich ... 7F 115
TW11: Tedd ... 6K 131
TW12: Ham H ... 4F 131
TW13: Felt ... 1K 129
UB2: S'hall ... 2B 94
UB3: Hayes ... 6G 75
UB7: W Dray ... 2B 92
W5 ... 6E 78
Queens Rd. Est. EN5: Barn ... 3A 20
Queens Rd. W. E13 ... 2J 87
Queen's Row SE17 ... 6D 102
Queens St. TW15: Ashf ... 4B 128
Queens Ter. E1 ... 4J 85
E13 ... 1K 87
KT7: T Ditt ... 6A 150
(off Queens Dr.)
NW8 ... 1B 82
TW7: Isle ... 4A 114
Queen's Ter. Cotts. W7 ... 2J 95
Queen's Theatre
Westminster ... 2C 12
(off Shaftesbury Av.)
Queensthorpe M. SE26 ... 4K 139
Queensthorpe Rd. SE26 ... 4K 139
Queenstown M. SW8 ... 2F 119
Queenstown Rd. SW8 ... 7J 17 (6F 101)
Queen St. CR0: C'don ... 4C 168
DA7: Bex ... 3F 127
EC4 ... 2D 14 (7C 84)
(not continuous)
N17 ... 6K 33
RM7: Rom ... 6K 55
W1 ... 4J 11 (1F 101)
Queen St. Pl. EC4 ... 2D 14 (7C 84)
Queensville Rd. SW12 ... 7H 119
Queens Wlk. E4 ... 1A 36
HA1: Harr ... 4J 41
HA4: Ruis ... 2A 58
N5 ... 5B 66
NW9 ... 2J 61
SW1 ... 5A 12 (1G 101)
TW15: Ashf ... 4A 128
W5 ... 4C 78
Queen's Wlk., The SE1 ... 3K 13 (7A 84)
(Oxo Tower Wharf)
SE1 ... 4F 15 (1E 102)
(Tooley St.)
SE1 ... 4H 13 (1K 101)
(Waterloo Rd.)
Queens Wlk. Ter. HA4: Ruis ... 3A 58
Queens Way NW4 ... 5E 44
TW13: Hanw ... 4A 130
Queensway BR4: W W'ck ... 3G 171
BR5: Pet W ... 5G 161
CR0: Wadd ... 6K 167
EN3: Pond E ... 4C 24
TW16: Sun ... 2K 147
W2 ... 6K 81
Queensway Bus. Cen.
EN3: Pond E ... 4C 24
Queensway Ind. Est. EN3: Pond E ... 4D 24
Queenswell Av. N20 ... 3H 31
Queens Wharf W6 ... 5E 98
Queenswood Av. CR7: Thor H ... 5A 156
E17 ... 1E 50
SM6: Bedd ... 4H 167
TW3: Houn ... 2D 112
TW12: Hamp ... 6F 131
Queenswood Ct. SE27 ... 4D 138
SW4 ... 5J 119
Queenswood Gdns. E11 ... 1K 69
Queenswood Pk. N3 ... 2G 45
Queens Wood Rd. N10 ... 6F 47
Queenswood Rd. DA15: Sidc ... 5K 125
SE23 ... 3K 139
Queen's Yd. WC1 ... 4B 6 (5G 83)
QUEEN VICTORIA ... 3E 164
Queen Victoria Av. HA0: Wemb ... 7D 60
Queen Victoria Memorial ... 7A 12 (2G 101)
Queen Victoria Seaman's Rest *E14 ... 6D 86*
(off E. India Dock Rd.)
Queen Victoria St. EC4 ... 2A 14 (7B 84)
Queen Victoria Ter. *E1 ... 7H 85*
(off Sovereign Cl.)
Quemerford Rd. N7 ... 5K 65
Quendon Ho. *W10 ... 4E 80*
(off Sutton Way)
Quenington Ct. SE15 ... 6F 103
Quentin Ho. *SE1 ... 6A 14*
(off Chaplin Cl.)
SE1 ... 7K 13
(off Gray St.)
Quentin Pl. SE13 ... 3G 123
Quentin Rd. SE13 ... 3G 123
Quernmore Cl. BR1: Brom ... 6J 141
Quernmore Rd. BR1: Brom ... 6J 141
N4 ... 6A 48
Querrin St. SW6 ... 2A 118
Quest, The *W11 ... 7G 81*
(off Clarendon Rd.)
Quested Ct. *E8 ... 5H 67*
(off Brett Rd.)
Questors Theatre, The ... 7C 78
Quex Ct. *NW6 ... 1K 81*
(off West End La.)
Quex M. NW6 ... 1J 81
Quex Rd. NW6 ... 1J 81
Quiberon Ct. TW16: Sun ... 3J 147
Quick Rd. W4 ... 5A 98
Quicks Rd. SW19 ... 7K 135
Quick St. N1 ... 2B 84
Quick St. M. N1 ... 2B 84
Quickswood NW3 ... 7C 64
Quiet Nook BR2: Hayes ... 3B 172
Quill Ho. *E2 ... 3K 9*
(off Cheshire St.)
Quill La. SW15 ... 4F 117
Quill St. N4 ... 3A 66
W5 ... 3E 78
Quilp St. SE1 ... 6C 14 (2C 102)
(not continuous)
Quilter St. E2 ... 1K 9 (3G 85)
SE18 ... 5K 107
Quilting Ct. *SE16 ... 2K 103*
(off Garter Way)
Quince Ho. *SE13 ... 2D 122*
(off Quince Rd.)
Quince Rd. SE13 ... 2D 122
Quinnell Cl. SE18 ... 5K 107
Quinta Dr. EN5: Barn ... 5A 20
Quintet, The KT12: Walt T ... 7J 147
Quintin Av. SW20 ... 1H 153
Quintin Cl. HA5: Eastc ... 4K 39
Quinton Cl. BR3: Beck ... 3E 158
SM6: Wall ... 4F 167
TW5: Cran ... 7K 93
Quinton Ho. *SW8 ... 7J 101*
(off Wyvil Rd.)
Quinton Rd. KT7: T Ditt ... 1A 162
Quinton St. SW18 ... 2A 136
Quixley St. E14 ... 7F 87
Quilters Pl. SE9 ... 1G 143
Quorn Rd. SE22 ... 4E 120

R

Rabbit Row W8 ... 1J 99
Rabbits Rd. E12 ... 4C 70
Rabournmead Dr. UB5: N'olt ... 5C 58

Raby Rd. KT3: N Mald 4K **151**
Raby St. E14 . . . . 6A **86**
Raccoon Way TW4: Houn 2A **112**
Rachel Cl. IG6: Ilf 3H **53**
Racine *SE5* *1E* ***120***
(off Sceaux Gdns.)
Rackham Cl. DA16: Well 2B **126**
Rackham M. SW16 . . . . 6G **137**
Rackstraw Ho. NW3 . . . . 7D **64**
Racton Rd. SW6 . . . . 6J **99**
RADA
Chenies St. 5C **6**
Gower St. *5H* ***83***
(off Gower St.)
Radbourne Av. W5 . . . . 4C **96**
Radbourne Cl. E5 . . . . 4K **67**
Radbourne Ct. HA3: Kenton 6B **42**
Radbourne Cres. E17 . . . . 2F **51**
Radbourne Rd. SW12 . . . . 7G **119**
Radcliffe Av. EN2: Enf 1H **23**
NW10 . . . . 2C **80**
Radcliffe Gdns. SM5: Cars 7C **166**
Radcliffe Ho. *SE16* *4H* ***103***
(off Anchor St.)
Radcliffe M. TW12: Ham H 5G **131**
Radcliffe Path SW8 . . . . 2F **119**
Radcliffe Rd. CR0: C'don 2F **169**
HA3: W'stone 2A **42**
N21 . . . . 1G **33**
SE1 . . . . 3E **102**
Radcliffe Sq. SW15 . . . . 6F **117**
Radcliffe Way UB5: N'olt 3B **76**
Radcot Point SE23 . . . . 3K **139**
Radcot St. SE11 . . . . 6K **19** (5A **102**)
Raddington Rd. W10 . . . . 5G **81**
Raddon Twr. *E8* *6F* ***67***
(off Roseberry St.)
Radfield Way DA15: Sidc 7H **125**
Radford Ct. *SE15* *7H* ***103***
(off Old Kent Rd.)
Radford Est. NW10 . . . . 3A **80**
Radford Ho. *E14* *5D* ***86***
(off St Leonard's Rd.)
N7 . . . . 5K **65**
Radford Rd. SE13 . . . . 6E **122**
Radford Way IG11: Bark 3K **89**
Radipole Rd. SW6 . . . . 1H **117**
Radisson Ct. *SE1* *7G* ***15***
(off Long La.)
Radius Apartments *N1* *1G* ***7***
(off Caledonian Rd.)
Radius Pk. TW14: Felt 4H **111**
Radland Rd. E16 . . . . 6H **87**
Radlet Av. SE26 . . . . 3H **139**
Radlett Cl. E7 . . . . 6H **69**
Radlett Pl. NW8 . . . . 1C **82**
Radley Av. IG3: Bark, Ilf 4A **72**
Radley Cl. TW14: Felt 1H **129**
Radley Ct. SE16 . . . . 2K **103**
Radley Gdns. HA3: Kenton 4E **42**
Radley Ho. *NW1* *3E* ***4***
(off Gloucester Pl.)
SE2 . . . . *2D* ***108***
(off Wolvercote Rd.)
Radley M. W8 . . . . 3J **99**
Radley Rd. N17 . . . . 2E **48**
Radley's La. E18 . . . . 2J **51**
Radleys Mead
RM10: Dag 6H **73**
Radley Sq. E5 . . . . 2J **67**
Radley Ter. *E16* *5H* ***87***
(off Hermit Rd.)
Radlix Rd. E10 . . . . 1C **68**
Radnor Av. DA16: Well 5B **126**
HA1: Harr 5J **41**
Radnor Cl. BR7: Chst 6J **143**
CR4: Mitc 4J **155**
Radnor Ct. HA3: Hrw W 1K **41**
W7 . . . . *6K* ***77***
(off Copley Cl.)
Radnor Cres. IG4: Ilf 5D **52**
SE18 . . . . 7A **108**
Radnor Gdns. EN1: Enf 1K **23**
TW1: Twick 2K **131**
Radnor Gro. UB10: Hil 2C **74**
Radnor Ho. *EC1* *2D* ***8***
(off Bath St.)
SW16 . . . . 2K **155**
Radnor Lodge *W2* *1B* ***10***
(off Sussex Pl.)
Radnor M. W2 . . . . 1B **10** (6B **82**)
Radnor Pl. W2 . . . . 1C **10** (6C **82**)
Radnor Rd. HA1: Harr 5H **41**
NW6 . . . . 1G **81**
SE15 . . . . 7G **103**
TW1: Twick 1K **131**
Radnor St. EC1 . . . . 2D **8** (3C **84**)
Radnor Ter. SM2: Sutt 7J **165**
W14 . . . . 4H **99**
Radnor Wlk. CR0: C'don 6A **158**
E14 . . . . *4C* ***104***
(off Barnsdale Av.)
SW3 . . . . 6D **16** (5C **100**)
Radnor Way NW10 . . . . 4H **79**
Radstock Av. HA3: Kenton 3A **42**
Radstock Cl. N11 . . . . 6K **31**
Radstock St. SW11 . . . . 7C **100**
(not continuous)
Radway Ho. *W2* *5J* ***81***
(off Alfred Rd.)
Raeburn Av. KT5: Surb 1H **163**
Raeburn Cl.
KT1: Ham W 7D **132**
NW11 . . . . 6A **46**
Raeburn Ho. *UB5: N'olt* *2B* ***76***
(off Academy Gdns.)
Raeburn Rd. DA15: Sidc 6J **125**
HA8: Edg 1G **43**
UB4: Hayes 2F **75**
Raeburn St. SW2 . . . . 4J **119**
Raffles Ct. HA8: Edg 4A **28**
Raffles Ho. NW4 . . . . 4D **44**
Rafford Way BR1: Brom 2K **159**
RAF Mus. Hendon 2C **44**
RAF NORTHOLT AERODROME 6H **57**
Ragged School Mus. 5A **86**
Raggleswood BR7: Chst 1E **160**
Raglan Cl. TW4: Houn 5D **112**
Raglan Ct. CR2: S Croy 5B **168**
HA9: Wemb 4F **61**
SE12 . . . . 5J **123**
Raglan Rd. BR2: Brom 4A **160**
DA17: Belv 4F **109**
E17 . . . . 5E **50**
EN1: Enf 7A **24**
SE18 . . . . 5G **107**
Raglan St. NW5 . . . . 6F **65**
Raglan Ter. HA2: Harr 4F **59**
Raglan Way UB5: N'olt 6G **59**
Ragley Cl. W3 . . . . 2J **97**
Ragwort Ct. SE26 . . . . 5H **139**
Raider Cl. RM7: Mawney 1G **55**
Railey M. NW5 . . . . 5G **65**
Railshead Rd. TW1: Isle 4B **114**
TW7: Isle 4B **114**
Railton Rd. SE24 . . . . 4A **120**
Railway App. HA3: Harr 4K **41**
N4 . . . . 6A **48**
RM7: Rush G 6K **55**
SE1 . . . . 5F **15** (1D **102**)
SM6: Wall 5F **167**
TW1: Twick 7A **114**
Railway Arches *E1* *6K* ***85***
(off Barnardo St.)
E1 . . . . *7H* ***85***
(off Chapman St.)
E2 . . . . *1J* ***9***
(off Cremer St.)
E2 . . . . *1F* ***85***
(off Laburnum St.)
E3 . . . . *4B* ***86***
(off Cantrell Rd.)
E8 . . . . *7H* ***67***
(off Mentmore Ter.)
Railway Arches E16 . . . . 1J **105**
W6 . . . . 3E **98**
W12 . . . . *2E* ***98***
(off Shepherd's Bush Mkt.)
Railway Av. SE16 . . . . 2J **103**
(not continuous)
Railway Children Wlk.
BR1: Brom 2J **141**
SE12 . . . . 2J **141**
Railway Cotts. *E15* *2G* ***87***
(off Baker's Row)
SW19 . . . . 4K **135**
W6 . . . . *2E* ***98***
(off Sulgrave Rd.)
Railway Fields Local Nature Reserve
. . . . 6B **48**
Railway Gro. SE14 . . . . 7B **104**
Railway M. W10 . . . . 6G **81**
Railway Pas. TW11: Tedd 6A **132**
Railway Pl. DA17: Belv 3G **109**
Railway Ri. SE22 . . . . 4E **120**
Railway Rd. TW11: Tedd 4J **131**
Railway Side SW13 . . . . 3A **116**
(not continuous)
Railway St. N1 . . . . 2J **83**
RM6: Chad H 7C **54**
Railway Ter. E17 . . . . 1E **50**
SE13 . . . . 5D **122**
TW13: Felt 1J **129**
Rainborough Cl. NW10 . . . . 6J **61**
Rainbow Av. E14 . . . . 5D **104**
Rainbow Ct. *SE14* *6A* ***104***
(off Chipley St.)
Rainbow Ind. Est. SW20 . . . . 2D **152**
UB7: Yiew 7A **74**
Rainbow Quay SE16 . . . . 3A **104**
Rainbow St. SE5 . . . . 7E **102**
Rainbow Theatre 2A **66**
Raine Gdns. IG8: Wfd G 4D **36**
Raines Est. Ct. N16 . . . . 2F **67**
Raine St. E1 . . . . 1H **103**
Rainham Cl. SE9 . . . . 6J **125**
SW11 . . . . 6C **118**
Rainham Ho. *NW1* *1G* ***83***
(off Bayham Pl.)
Rainham Rd. NW10 . . . . 3E **80**
Rainham Rd. Nth. RM10: Dag 2G **73**
Rainham Rd. Sth. RM10: Dag 4H **73**
Rainhill Way E3 . . . . 3C **86**
(not continuous)
Rainsborough Av. SE8 . . . . 4A **104**
Rainsford Cl. HA7: Stan 5H **27**
Rainsford Rd. NW10 . . . . 3G **79**
Rainsford St. W2 . . . . 7C **4** (6C **82**)
Rainton Rd. SE7 . . . . 5J **105**
Rainville Rd. W6 . . . . 6E **98**
Raisins Hill HA5: Eastc 3A **40**
Raith Av. N14 . . . . 3C **32**
Raleana Rd. E14 . . . . 1E **104**
Raleigh Av. SM6: Bedd 4H **167**
UB4: Yead 5K **75**
Raleigh Cl. HA4: Ruis 2H **57**
HA5: Pinn 7B **40**
NW4 . . . . 5E **44**
Raleigh Ct. BR3: Beck 1D **158**
SE8 . . . . *5A* ***104***
(off Evelyn St.)
SE16 . . . . *1K* ***103***
(off Clarence M.)
SM6: Wall 6F **167**
W12 . . . . *2E* ***98***
(off Scott's Rd.)
W13 . . . . 5B **78**
Raleigh Dr. KT5: Surb 1J **163**
N20 . . . . 3H **31**
Raleigh Gdns. CR4: Mitc 3D **154**
(not continuous)
SW2 . . . . 6K **119**
Raleigh Ho. *BR1: Brom* *1J* ***159***
(off Hammelton Rd.)
E14 . . . . *2D* ***104***
(off Admirals Way)
Raleigh Ho. *SW1* *7C* ***18***
(off Dolphin Sq.)
Raleigh M. BR6: Chels 5K **173**
N1 . . . . *1B* ***84***
(off Packington St.)
Raleigh Rd. EN2: Enf 4J **23**
N2 . . . . 2C **46**
N8 . . . . 4A **48**
SE20 . . . . 7K **139**
TW9: Rich 3F **115**
TW13: Felt 3H **129**
UB2: S'hall 5C **94**
Raleigh St. N1 . . . . 1B **84**
Raleigh Way N14 . . . . 1C **32**
TW13: Hanw 5A **130**
Rale La. E4 . . . . 1A **36**
Ralph Brook Ct. *N1* *1F* ***9***
(off Chart St.)
Ralph Ct. *W2* *6K* ***81***
(off Queensway)
Ralph Perring Ct. BR3: Beck 4C **158**
Ralston St. SW3 . . . . 6E **16** (5D **100**)
Ramac Ind. Est. SE7 . . . . 4K **105**
Rama Cl. SW16 . . . . 7J **137**
Rama Ct. HA1: Harr 2J **59**
Ramac Way SE7 . . . . 4K **105**
Rama La. SE19 . . . . 7F **139**
Ramar Ho. *E1* *5G* ***85***
(off Hanbury St.)
Rambler Cl. SW16 . . . . 4G **137**
Rame Cl. SW17 . . . . 5E **136**
Ramilles Cl. SW2 . . . . 6J **119**
Ramillies Pl. W1 . . . . 1A **12** (6G **83**)
Ramillies Rd. DA15: Sidc 6B **126**
NW7 . . . . 2F **29**
W4 . . . . 4K **97**
Ramillies St. W1 . . . . 1A **12** (6G **83**)
Ramones Ter. *CR4: Mitc* *4J* ***155***
(off Yorkshire Rd.)
Rampart St. E1 . . . . 6H **85**
Ram Pas. KT1: King T 2D **150**
Rampayne St. SW1 . . . . 5C **18** (5H **101**)
Ram Pl. E9 . . . . 6J **67**
Rampton Cl. E4 . . . . 3H **35**
Ramsay Ho. *NW8* *2C* ***82***
(off Townshend Est.)
Ramsay M. SW3 . . . . 7C **16** (6C **100**)
Ramsay Rd. E7 . . . . 4G **69**
W3 . . . . 3J **97**
Ramscroft Cl. N9 . . . . 7K **23**
Ramsdale Rd. SW17 . . . . 5E **136**
Ramsden Dr. RM5: Col R 1G **55**
Ramsden Rd. DA8: Erith 7K **109**
N11 . . . . 5J **31**
SW12 . . . . 6E **118**
Ramsey Cl. NW9 . . . . 6B **44**
UB6: G'frd 5H **59**
Ramsey Ct. *CR0: C'don* *2B* ***168***
(off Church St.)
Ramsey Ho. SW9 . . . . 7A **102**
Ramsey Rd. CR7: Thor H 6K **155**
Ramsey St. E2 . . . . 4G **85**
Ramsey Wlk. N1 . . . . 6D **66**
Ramsey Way N14 . . . . 7B **22**
Ramsfort Ho. *SE16* *4H* ***103***
(off Camilla Rd.)
Ramsgate Cl. E16 . . . . 1K **105**
Ramsgate St. E8 . . . . 6F **67**
Ramsgill App. IG2: Ilf 4K **53**
Ramsgill Dr. IG2: Ilf 5K **53**
Rams Gro. RM6: Chad H 4E **54**
Ram St. SW18 . . . . 5K **117**
Ramulis Dr. UB4: Yead 4B **76**
Ramuswood Av. BR6: Chels 5J **173**
Rancliffe Gdns. SE9 . . . . 4C **124**
Rancliffe Rd. E6 . . . . 2C **88**
Randall Av. NW2 . . . . 2A **62**
Randall Cl. DA8: Erith 6J **109**
SW11 . . . . 1C **118**
Randall Ct. NW7 . . . . 7H **29**
Randall Pl. SE10 . . . . 7E **104**
Randall Rd. SE11 . . . . 4G **19** (5K **101**)

Randall Row SE11 . . . . 4G **19** (4K **101**)
Randalls Rents *SE16* *3B 104*
(off Gulliver St.)
Randell's Rd. N1 . . . . 1J **83**
Randisbourne Gdns. SE6 . . . . 3D **140**
Randle Rd. TW10: Ham 4C **132**
Randlesdown Rd. SE6 . . . . 4C **140**
(not continuous)
Randolph App. E16 . . . . 6A **88**
Randolph Av. W9 . . . . 4A **4** (2K **81**)
Randolph Cl. DA7: Bex 3J **127**
KT2: King T 5J **133**
Randolph Cres. W9 . . . . 4A **82**
Randolph Gdns. NW6 . . . . 2K **81**
Randolph Gro. RM6: Chad H 5C **54**
Randolph M. W9 . . . . 4A **82**
Randolph Rd. BR2: Brom 1D **172**
E17 . . . . 5D **50**
UB1: S'hall 2D **94**
W9 . . . . 4A **82**
Randolph St. NW1 . . . . 7G **65**
Randon Cl. HA2: Harr 2F **41**
Ranelagh Av. SW6 . . . . 3H **117**
SW13 . . . . 2C **116**
Ranelagh Bri. W2 . . . . 5K **81**
Ranelagh Cl. HA8: Edg 4B **28**
Ranelagh Cotts. *SW1* *5H 17*
(off Ranelagh Gro.)
Ranelagh Dr. HA8: Edg 4B **28**
TW1: Twick 4B **114**
Ranelagh Gdns. E11 . . . . 5A **52**
IG1: Ilf 1D **70**
SW6 . . . . 3G **117**
(not continuous)
W4 . . . . 7J **97**
W6 . . . . 4B **98**
Ranelagh Gdns. Mans. *SW6* *3G 117*
(off Ranelagh Gdns.)
Ranelagh Gro. SW1 . . . . 5H **17** (5E **100**)
Ranelagh Ho. *SW3* *5E 16*
(off Elystan Pl.)
Ranelagh M. W5 . . . . 2D **96**
Ranelagh Pl. KT3: N Mald 5A **152**
Ranelagh Rd. E6 . . . . 1E **88**
E11 . . . . 4G **69**
E15 . . . . 2G **87**
HA0: Wemb 6D **60**
N17 . . . . 3E **48**
N22 . . . . 1K **47**
NW10 . . . . 2B **80**
SW1 . . . . 6B **18** (5G **101**)
UB1: S'hall 1B **94**
W5 . . . . 2D **96**
Ranfurly Rd. SM1: Sutt 2J **165**
Rangbourne Ho. N7 . . . . 5J **65**
Rangefield Rd. BR1: Brom 5G **141**
Rangemoor Rd. N15 . . . . 5F **49**
Ranger's House 1F **123**
Ranger's Rd. E4 . . . . 1B **36**
Rangers Sq. SE10 . . . . 1F **123**
Range Way TW17: Shep 7C **146**
Rangeworth Pl. DA15: Sidc 3K **143**
Rangoon St. EC3 . . . . 1J **15**
Rankin Cl. NW9 . . . . 3A **44**
Rankine Ho. *SE1* *3C 102*
(off Bath Ter.)
Ranleigh Gdns. DA7: Bex 7F **109**
Ranmere St. SW12 . . . . 1F **137**
Ranmoor Cl. HA1: Harr 4H **41**
Ranmoor Gdns. HA1: Harr 4H **41**
Ranmore Av. CR0: C'don 3F **169**
Ranmore Path BR5: St M Cry 4K **161**
Ranmore Rd. SM2: Cheam 7F **165**
Rannoch Cl. HA8: Edg 2C **28**
Rannoch Rd. W6 . . . . 6E **98**
Rannock Av. NW9 . . . . 7K **43**
Ransome's Dock Bus. Cen.
SW11 . . . . 7C **100**
Ransom Rd. SE7 . . . . 4A **106**
Ranston St. NW1 . . . . 5C **4** (5C **82**)
Ranulf Rd. NW2 . . . . 4H **63**
Ranwell Cl. E3 . . . . 1B **86**
Ranwell Ho. *E3* *1B 86*
(off Ranwell Cl.)
Ranworth Rd. N9 . . . . 2D **34**
Ranyard Cl. KT9: Chess 3F **163**
Raphael Cl. KT1: King T 4D **150**
Raphael Ct. *SE16* *5H 103*
(off Stubbs Dr.)
Raphael Dr. KT7: T Ditt 7K **149**
Raphael St. SW7 . . . . 7E **10** (2D **100**)
Rapley Ho. *E2* *2K 9*
(off Turin St.)
Raquel Ct. *SE1* *6G 15*
(off Snowfields)
Rashleigh Ct. SW8 . . . . 2F **119**
Rashleigh Ho. *WC1* *2E 6*
(off Thanet St.)
Rashleigh St. *SW8* *2F 119*
(off Peardon St.)
Rasper Rd. N20 . . . . 2F **31**
Rastell Av. SW2 . . . . 2H **137**
RATCLIFF 5A **86**
Ratcliffe Cl. SE12 . . . . 7J **123**
Ratcliffe Ct. *SE1* *7D 14*
(off Gt. Dover St.)
Ratcliffe Cross St. E1 . . . . 6K **85**
Ratcliffe Ho. *E14* *6A 86*
(off Barnes St.)
Ratcliffe La. E14 . . . . 6A **86**
Ratcliffe Orchard E1 . . . . 7K **85**
Ratcliff Rd. E7 . . . . 5A **70**
Rathbone Ho. *E16* *6H 87*
(off Rathbone St.)
NW6 . . . . 1J **81**
Rathbone Mkt. E16 . . . . 5H **87**
Rathbone Pl. W1 . . . . 6C **6** (5H **83**)
Rathbone Sq. CR0: C'don 4C **168**
Rathbone St. E16 . . . . 5H **87**
W1 . . . . 6B **6** (5G **83**)
Rathcoole Av. N8 . . . . 5K **47**
Rathcoole Gdns. N8 . . . . 5K **47**
Rathfern Rd. SE6 . . . . 1B **140**
Rathgar Av. W13 . . . . 1B **96**
Rathgar Cl. N3 . . . . 2H **45**
Rathgar Rd. SW9 . . . . 3B **120**
Rathmell Dr. SW4 . . . . 6H **119**
Rathmore Rd. SE7 . . . . 5K **105**
Rathnew Ct. *E2* *3K 85*
(off Meath Cres.)
Rattray Ct. SE6 . . . . 2H **141**
Rattray Rd. SW2 . . . . 4A **120**
Raul Rd. SE15 . . . . 2G **121**
Raveley St. NW5 . . . . 4G **65**
(not continuous)
Raven Cl. NW9 . . . . 2A **44**
Ravendale Rd. TW16: Sun 2H **147**
Ravenet St. SW11 . . . . 1F **119**
(not continuous)
Ravenfield Rd. SW17 . . . . 3D **136**
Ravenhill Rd. E13 . . . . 2A **88**
Raven Ho. *SE16* *4K 103*
(off Tawny Way)
Ravenings Pde. IG3: Ilf 1A **72**
Ravenna Rd. SW15 . . . . 5F **117**
Ravenor Ct. UB6: G'frd 4F **77**
Ravenor Pk. Rd. UB6: G'frd 3F **77**
Raven Rd. E18 . . . . 2A **52**
Raven Row E1 . . . . 5H **85**
Raven's Ait 5D **150**
Ravensbourne Av.
BR2: Brom 7F **141**
TW19: Stanw 1A **128**
Ravensbourne Ct. SE6 . . . . 7C **122**
Ravensbourne Gdns. IG5: Ilf 1E **52**
W13 . . . . 5B **78**
Ravensbourne Ho. BR1: Brom 5F **141**
NW8 . . . . *5C 4*
(off Broadley St.)
Ravensbourne Mans. *SE8* *6C 104*
(off Berthon St.)
Ravensbourne Pk. SE6 . . . . 7C **122**
Ravensbourne Pk. Cres. SE6 . . . . 7B **122**
Ravensbourne Pl. SE13 . . . . 2D **122**
Ravensbourne Rd. BR1: Brom 3J **159**
SE6 . . . . 7B **122**
TW1: Twick 6C **114**
Ravensbourne Ter.
TW19: Stanw 1A **128**
Ravensbury Av. SM4: Mord 5A **154**
Ravensbury Ct. *CR4: Mitc* *4B 154*
(off Ravensbury Gro.)
Ravensbury Gro. CR4: Mitc 4B **154**
Ravensbury La. CR4: Mitc 4B **154**
Ravensbury Path CR4: Mitc 4B **154**
Ravensbury Rd. BR5: St P 3K **161**
SW18 . . . . 2J **135**
Ravensbury Ter. SW18 . . . . 2K **135**
Ravenscar *NW1* *1G 83*
(off Bayham St.)
Ravenscar Rd. BR1: Brom 4G **141**
KT6: Surb 2F **163**
Ravens Cl. BR2: Brom 2H **159**
EN1: Enf 2K **23**
KT6: Surb 6D **150**
Ravens Ct. *KT1: King T* *5D 150*
(off Uxbridge Rd.)
Ravenscourt TW16: Sun 1H **147**
Ravenscourt Av. W6 . . . . 4C **98**
Ravenscourt Cl. HA4: Ruis 7E **38**
Ravenscourt Gdns. W6 . . . . 4C **98**
Ravenscourt Pk. EN5: Barn 4A **20**
W6 . . . . 3C **98**
Ravenscourt Pk. Mans. *W6* *3D 98*
(off Paddenswick Rd.)
Ravenscourt Pl. W6 . . . . 4D **98**
Ravenscourt Rd. W6 . . . . 4D **98**
(not continuous)
Ravenscourt Sq. W6 . . . . 3C **98**
Ravenscraig Rd. N11 . . . . 4B **32**
Ravenscroft Av. HA9: Wemb 1E **60**
NW11 . . . . 7H **45**
(not continuous)
Ravenscroft Cl. E16 . . . . 5J **87**
Ravenscroft Cotts. EN5: New Bar 4D **20**
Ravenscroft Cres. SE9 . . . . 3D **142**
Ravenscroft Pk. *E2* *3F 85*
(off Baroness Rd.)
EN5: Barn 3A **20**
Ravenscroft Rd. BR3: Beck 2J **157**
E16 . . . . 5J **87**
W4 . . . . 4J **97**
Ravenscroft School Sports Cen. 7C **20**
Ravenscroft St. E2 . . . . 1K **9** (2F **85**)
Ravensdale Av. N12 . . . . 4F **31**
Ravensdale Gdns. SE19 . . . . 7D **138**
TW4: Houn 3C **112**
Ravensdale Ind. Est. N16 . . . . 6G **49**
Ravensdale Mans. *N8* *6J 47*
(off Haringey Pk.)
Ravensdale Rd. N16 . . . . 7F **49**
TW4: Houn 3C **112**
Ravensdon St. SE11 . . . . 6K **19** (5A **102**)
Ravensfield Cl. RM9: Dag 4D **72**
Ravensfield Gdns. KT19: Ewe 5A **164**
Ravenshaw St. NW6 . . . . 5H **63**
Ravenshill BR7: Chst 1F **161**
Ravenshurst Av. NW4 . . . . 4E **44**
Ravenside *KT1: King T* *5D 150*
(off Portsmouth Rd.)
Ravenside Cl. N18 . . . . 5E **34**
Ravenside Retail Pk. N18 . . . . 5E **34**
Ravenslea Rd. SW12 . . . . 7D **118**
Ravensleigh Gdns. BR1: Brom 5K **141**
Ravensmead Rd. BR2: Brom 7F **141**
Ravensmede Way W4 . . . . 4B **98**
Ravens M. SE12 . . . . 5J **123**
Ravenstone SE17 . . . . 5E **102**
Ravenstone Rd. N8 . . . . 3A **48**
NW9 . . . . 6B **44**
Ravenstone St. SW12 . . . . 1E **136**
Ravens Way SE12 . . . . 5J **123**
Ravenswood DA5: Bexl 1E **144**
Ravenswood Av. BR4: W W'ck 1E **170**
KT6: Surb 2F **163**
Ravenswood Ct. KT2: King T 6H **133**
Ravenswood Cres. BR4: W W'ck 1E **170**
HA2: Harr 2D **58**
Ravenswood Gdns. TW7: Isle 1J **113**
Ravenswood Ind. Est.
E17 . . . . 4E **50**
Ravenswood Rd. CR0: Wadd 3B **168**
E17 . . . . 4E **50**
SW12 . . . . 7F **119**
Ravensworth Ct. *SW6* *7J 99*
(off Fulham Rd.)
Ravensworth Rd. NW10 . . . . 3D **80**
SE9 . . . . 3D **142**
Raven Wharf *SE1* *6J 15*
(off Lafone St.)
Ravey St. EC2 . . . . 3G **9** (4E **84**)
Ravine Gro. SE18 . . . . 6J **107**
Rav Pinter Cl. N16 . . . . 7E **48**
Rawalpindi Ho. E16 . . . . 4H **87**
Rawchester Cl. SW18 . . . . 1H **135**
Rawlings Cl. BR3: Beck 5E **158**
BR6: Chels 5K **173**
Rawlings Cres. HA9: Wemb 3H **61**
Rawlings St. SW3 . . . . 3E **16** (4D **100**)
Rawlins Cl. CR2: Sels 7A **170**
N3 . . . . 3G **45**
Rawlinson Ct. NW2 . . . . 7E **44**
Rawlinson Ho. *SE13* *4F 123*
(off Mercator Rd.)
Rawlinson Point *E16* *5H 87*
(off Fox Rd.)
Rawnsley Av. CR4: Mitc 5B **154**
Rawreth Wlk. *N1* *1C 84*
(off Basire St.)
Rawson St. SW11 . . . . 1E **118**
(not continuous)
Rawsthorne Cl. E16 . . . . 1D **106**
Rawsthorne Ct. TW4: Houn 4D **112**
Rawstone Wlk. E13 . . . . 2J **87**
Rawstorne Pl. EC1 . . . . 1A **8** (3B **84**)
Rawstorne St. EC1 . . . . 1A **8** (3B **84**)
(not continuous)
Raybell Ct. TW7: Isle 2K **113**
Rayburne Ct. IG9: Buck H 1F **37**
W14 . . . . 3G **99**
Ray Cl. KT9: Chess 6C **162**
Raydean Rd. EN5: New Bar 5E **20**
Raydons Gdns. RM9: Dag 4E **72**
Raydons Rd. RM9: Dag 5E **72**
Raydon St. N19 . . . . 2F **65**
Rayfield Cl. BR2: Brom 6C **160**
Rayford Av. SE12 . . . . 7H **123**
Ray Gdns. HA7: Stan 5G **27**
IG11: Bark 2A **90**
Ray Gunter Ho. *SE17* *5B 102*
(off Marsland Cl.)
Ray Ho. *N1* *1E 84*
(off Colville Est.)
W10 . . . . *6F 81*
(off Cambridge Gdns.)
Rayleas Cl. SE18 . . . . 1F **125**
Rayleigh Av. TW11: Tedd 6J **131**
Rayleigh Cl. N13 . . . . 3J **33**
Rayleigh Ct. KT1: King T 2G **151**
N22 . . . . 1C **48**
Rayleigh Ri. CR2: S Croy 6E **168**
Rayleigh Rd. E16 . . . . 1K **105**
IG8: Wfd G 6F **37**
N13 . . . . 3H **33**
SW19 . . . . 1H **153**
Ray Lodge Rd. IG8: Wfd G 6F **37**
Ray Massey Way *E6* *1C 88*
(off High St. Nth.)
Raymead Av. CR7: Thor H 5A **156**
Raymead Pas. *CR7: Thor H* *5A 156*
(off Raymead Av.)
Raymede Towers *W10* *5F 81*
(off Treverton St.)
Raymere Gdns. SE18 . . . . 7H **107**
Raymond Av. E18 . . . . 3H **51**
W13 . . . . 3A **96**
Raymond Bldgs. WC1 . . . . 5H **7** (5K **83**)
Raymond Chadburn Ho. E7 . . . . 4K **69**

Raymond Cl. SE26 . . . . .5J 139
  SL3: Poyle 4A 174
Raymond Ct. N10 . . . . .7A 32
Raymond Postgate Ct. SE28 . . . . .7B 90
Raymond Rd. BR3: Beck 4A 158
  E13 .1A 88
  IG2: Ilf 7H 53
  SW19 . . . . .6H 135
Raymond Way KT10: Clay 6A 162
Raymouth Rd. SE16 . . . . .4H 103
Raynald Ho. SW16 . . . . .3J 137
Rayne Cl. E18 . . . . .4H 51
Rayne Ho. SW12 . . . . .6E 118
  W9 . . . . .4J 81
    (off Delaware Rd.)
Rayner Ct. W12 . . . . .2E 98
    (off Bamborough Gdns.)
Rayners Cl. HA0: Wemb 5D 60
Rayners Cres. UB5: N'olt 3K 75
Rayners Gdns. UB5: N'olt 2K 75
RAYNERS LANE 1D 58
Rayners La. HA2: Harr 1E 58
  HA5: Harr, Pinn 5D 40
Rayners Rd. SW15 . . . . .5G 117
Rayner Towers E10 . . . . .7C 50
    (off Albany Rd.)
Raynes Av. E11 . . . . .7A 52
RAYNES PARK 4E 152
Raynes Pk. Bri. SW20 . . . . .2E 152
Raynes Pk. School Sports Cen. . . .3D 152
Raynham W2 . . . . .7D 4
    (off Norfolk Cres.)
Raynham Av. N18 . . . . .6B 34
Raynham Ho. E1 . . . . .4K 85
    (off Harpley Sq.)
Raynham Rd. N18 . . . . .5B 34
  W6 . . . . .4D 98
Raynham Ter. N18 . . . . .5B 34
Raynor Cl. UB1: S'hall 1D 94
Raynor Pl. N1 .7C 66
Raynton Cl. HA2: Harr 1C 58
  UB4: Hayes 4H 75
Raynton Dr. UB4: Hayes 4H 75
Ray Rd. KT8: W Mole 5F 149
Rays Av. N18 .4D 34
Rays Rd. BR4: W W'ck 7E 158
  N18 . . . . .4D 34
Ray St. EC1 . . . . .4K 7 (4A 84)
Ray St. Bri. EC1 . . . . .4K 7
Ray Wlk. N7 . . . . .2K 65
Raywood Cl. UB3: Harl 7E 92
Razia M. E12 .5D 70
Reachview Cl. NW1 . . . . .7G 65
Read Cl. KT7: T Ditt 7A 150
Read Ct. E17 .6C 50
Reade Cl. W3 .3J 97
    (off Stanley Rd.)
Reader Ho. SE5 . . . . .1C 120
    (off Badsworth Rd.)
Read Ho. SE11 . . . . .7J 19
Reading Cl. SE22 . . . . .6G 121
Reading Ho. SE15 . . . . .6G 103
    (off Friary Est.)
  W2 . . . . .6A 82
    (off Hallfield Est.)
Reading La. E8 . . . . .6H 67
Reading Rd. SM1: Sutt 5A 166
  UB5: N'olt 5F 59
Reading Way NW7 . . . . .5A 30
Readman Ct. SE20 . . . . .1H 157
Reads Cl. IG1: Ilf 3F 71
Ream Apartments SE23 . . . . .2J 139
    (off Clyde Ter.)
Reapers Cl. NW1 . . . . .1H 83
Reapers Way TW7: Isle 5H 113
Reardon Cl. N21 . . . . .2G 33
Reardon Ho. E1 . . . . .1H 103
    (off Reardon St.)
Reardon Path E1 . . . . .1H 103
    (not continuous)
Reardon St. E1 . . . . .1H 103
Reaston St. SE14 . . . . .7K 103

Rebecca Cl. DA14: Sidc 4B 144
Rebecca Ho. E3 . . . . .4B 86
    (off Brokesley St.)
Reckitt Rd. W4 . . . . .5A 98
Record St. SE15 . . . . .6J 103
Recovery St. SW17 . . . . .5C 136
Recreation Av. RM7: Rom 5J 55
Recreation Rd. BR2: Brom 2H 159
  DA15: Sidc 3J 143
  SE26 . . . . .4K 139
  UB2: S'hall 4C 94
Recreation Way CR4: Mitc 3H 155
Rector St. N1 .1C 84
Rectory Bus. Cen.
  DA14: Sidc 4B 144
Rectory Chambers SW3 . . . . .6C 100
    (off Old Church St.)
Rectory Cl. DA14: Sidc 4B 144
  E4 . . . . .3H 35
  HA7: Stan 5G 27
  KT6: Surb 1C 162
  N3 . . . . .1H 45
  SW20 . . . . .3E 152
  TW17: Shep 3C 146
Rectory Ct. E18 . . . . .1H 51
  SM6: Wall 4G 167
  TW13: Felt 4A 130
Rectory Cres. E11 . . . . .6A 52
    (not continuous)
Rectory Farm Rd. EN2: Enf 1E 22
Rectory Field 7K 105
Rectory Fld. Cres. SE7 . . . . .7A 106
Rectory Gdns. BR3: Beck 1C 158
    (off Rectory Rd.)
  N8 . . . . .4J 47
  SW4 .3G 119
  UB5: N'olt 1D 76
Rectory Grn. BR3: Beck 1B 158
Rectory Gro. CR0: C'don 2B 168
  SW4 .3G 119
  TW12: Hamp 4D 130
Rectory La. DA14: Sidc 4B 144
  HA7: Stan 5G 27
  HA8: Edg 6B 28
  KT6: Surb 1B 162
  SM6: Wall 4G 167
  SW17 . . . . .6E 136
Rectory Orchard SW19 . . . . .4G 135
Rectory Pk. Av. UB5: N'olt 3D 76
Rectory Pl. SE18 . . . . .4E 106
Rectory Rd. BR2: Kes 7B 172
  BR3: Beck 1C 158
  E12 . . . . .5D 70
  E17 . . . . .4D 50
  N16 . . . . .2F 67
  RM10: Dag 6H 73
  SM1: Sutt 3J 165
  SW13 . . . . .2C 116
  TW4: Cran 2A 112
  UB2: S'hall 3D 94
  UB3: Hayes 6J 75
  W3 . . . . .1H 97
Rectory Sq. E1 . . . . .5K 85
Rectory Way UB10: Ick 2D 56
Reculver Ho. SE15 . . . . .6J 103
    (off Lovelinch Cl.)
Reculver M. N18 . . . . .4B 34
Reculver Rd. SE16 . . . . .5K 103
Red Anchor Cl. SW3 . . . . .6B 100
Redan Pl. W2 .6K 81
Redan St. W14 . . . . .3F 99
Redan Ter. SE5 . . . . .2B 120
Red Barracks Rd. SE18 . . . . .4D 106
Redberry Gro. SE26 . . . . .3J 139
Redbourne Av. N3 . . . . .1J 45
Redbourne Dr. SE28 . . . . .6D 90
    (not continuous)
Redbourne Ho. E14 . . . . .6B 86
    (off Norbiton Rd.)
Redbourn Ho. W10 . . . . .4E 80
    (off Sutton Way)
REDBRIDGE .6C 52

Redbridge Ent. Cen. IG1: Ilf 2G 71
Redbridge FC 4H 53
Redbridge Foyer IG1: Ilf 2G 71
    (off Hainault St.)
Redbridge Gdns. SE5 . . . . .7E 102
Redbridge Ho. E16 . . . . .7F 89
    (off University Way)
Redbridge La. E. IG4: Ilf 6B 52
Redbridge La. W. E11 . . . . .6K 51
REDBRIDGE RDBT. 6B 52
Redbridge Sports & Leisure Cen. . .1H 53
Redburn Ind. Est. EN3: Pond E 6E 24
Redburn St. SW3 . . . . .7E 16 (6D 100)
Redcar Cl. UB5: N'olt 5F 59
Redcar St. SE5 . . . . .7C 102
Redcastle Cl. E1 . . . . .7J 85
Red Cedars Rd. BR6: Orp 7J 161
Redchurch St. E2 . . . . .3J 9 (4F 85)
Redcliffe Cl. SW5 . . . . .5K 99
    (off Old Brompton Rd.)
Redcliffe Ct. E5 . . . . .3H 67
    (off Napoleon Rd.)
Redcliffe Gdns. IG1: Ilf 1E 70
  SW10 . . . . .5K 99
  W4 . . . . .7H 97
Redcliffe M. SW10 . . . . .5K 99
Redcliffe Pl. SW10 . . . . .6A 100
Redcliffe Rd. SW10 . . . . .5A 100
Redcliffe Sq. SW10 . . . . .5K 99
Redcliffe St. SW10 . . . . .6K 99
Redclose Av. SM4: Mord 5J 153
Redclyffe Rd. E6 . . . . .1A 88
Redclyf Ho. E1 . . . . .4J 85
    (off Cephas St.)
Redcourt CR0: C'don 3E 168
Red Cow La. EC1 . . . . .3C 8 (4C 84)
Redcroft Rd. UB1: S'hall 7G 77
Red Cross Cotts. SE1 . . . . .2C 102
    (off Ayres St.)
Redcross Way SE1 . . . . . . .6D 14 (2C 102)
Redding Ho. SE18 . . . . .3C 106
Reddings, The NW7 . . . . .3G 29
Reddings Cl. NW7 . . . . .4G 29
Reddins Rd. SE15 . . . . .6G 103
Reddons Rd. BR3: Beck 7A 140
Redenham Ho. SW15 . . . . .7C 116
    (off Ellisfield Dr.)
Rede Pl. W2 . . . . .6J 81
Redesdale Gdns. TW7: Isle 7A 96
Redesdale St. SW3 . . . . . . .7D 16 (6C 100)
Redfern Av. TW4: Houn 7E 112
Redfern Ho. E13 . . . . .1H 87
    (off Redriffe Rd.)
  NW8 .1B 82
    (off Dorman Way)
Redfern Rd. NW10 . . . . .7A 62
  SE6 . . . . .7E 122
Redfield La. SW5 . . . . .4J 99
Redfield M. SW5 . . . . .4K 99
Redford Av. CR7: Thor H 4K 155
  SM6: Wall 6J 167
Redford Cl. TW13: Felt 2H 129
Redford Wlk. N1 . . . . .1C 84
    (off Popham St.)
Redgate Dr. BR2: Hayes 2K 171
Redgate Ter. SW15 . . . . .6F 117
Redgrave Cl. CR0: C'don 6F 157
Redgrave Rd. SW15 . . . . .3F 117
Redgrave Ter. E2 . . . . .3J 85
    (off Derbyshire St.)
Red Hill BR7: Chst 5F 143
Redhill Ct. SW2 . . . . .2A 138
Redhill Dr. HA8: Edg 2H 43
Redhill St. NW1 . . . . .1K 5 (2F 83)
Red House 4E 126
Red Ho. SE20 . . . . .7H 139
    (off Anerley Pk.)
Red Ho. La. DA6: Bex 4D 126
Redhouse Rd. CR0: C'don 6H 155
Red Ho. Sq. N1 . . . . .6C 66
Redif Ho. RM10: Dag 4H 73
Redington Gdns. NW3 . . . . .4K 63

Redington Ho. N1 . . . . .2K 83
    (off Priory Grn. Est.)
Redington Rd. NW3 . . . . .3K 63
Redknap Ho. TW10: Ham 3C 132
Redland Gdns. KT8: W Mole 4D 148
Redlands N15 . . . . .4D 48
  TW11: Tedd 6A 132
Redlands, The BR3: Beck 2D 158
Redlands Cl. BR1: Brom 7H 141
Redlands Ct. BR1: Brom 7H 141
  EN3: Enf H 1F 25
Redlands Way SW2 . . . . .7K 119
Red La. KT10: Clay 6A 162
Redleaf Cl. DA17: Belv 6G 109
Redleaves Av. TW15: Ashf 6D 128
Redlees Cl. TW7: Isle 4A 114
Red Leys UB8: Uxb 7A 56
Red Lion Bus. Pk. KT6: Surb 3F 163
Red Lion Cl. SE17 . . . . .6D 102
    (off Red Lion Row)
Red Lion Ct. EC4 . . . . .1K 13 (6A 84)
  SE1 . . . . .4D 14 (1C 102)
Red Lion Hill N2 . . . . .2B 46
    (not continuous)
Red Lion La. SE18 . . . . .7E 106
Red Lion Pde. HA5: Pinn 3C 40
Red Lion Pl. SE18 . . . . .1E 124
Red Lion Rd. KT6: Surb 2F 163
Red Lion Row SE17 . . . . .6C 102
Red Lion Sq. SW18 . . . . .5J 117
  WC1 . . . . .6G 7 (5K 83)
Red Lion St. TW9: Rich 5D 114
  WC1 . . . . .5G 7 (5K 83)
Red Lion Yd. W1 . . . . .4H 11
Red Lodge BR4: W W'ck 1E 170
Red Lodge Cres. DA5: Bexl 3K 145
Red Lodge Rd. BR4: W W'ck 1E 170
  DA5: Bexl 3K 145
Redlynch Ct. W14 . . . . .2G 99
    (off Addison Cres.)
Redlynch Ho. SW9 . . . . .1A 120
    (off Gosling Way)
Redman Cl. UB5: N'olt 2A 76
Redman Ho. EC1 . . . . .5J 7
    (off Bourne Est.)
  SE1 . . . . .7D 14
    (off Borough High St.)
Redman's Rd. E1 . . . . .5J 85
Redmead La. E1 . . . . .1G 103
Redmead Rd. UB3: Harl 4G 93
Redmill Ho. E1 . . . . .4H 85
    (off Headlam St.)
Redmond Ho. N1 . . . . .1K 83
    (off Barnsbury Est.)
Redmore Rd. W6 . . . . .4D 98
Red Oak Cl. BR6: Farnb 3F 173
Redo Ho. E12 . . . . .5E 70
    (off Dore Av.)
Red Path E9 . . . . .6A 68
Red Pl. W1 . . . . .2G 11 (7E 82)
Redpoll Way DA18: Erith 3D 108
Red Post Hill SE21 . . . . .4D 120
  SE24 . . . . .4D 120
Red Post Ho. E6 . . . . .7B 70
Redriffe Rd. E13 . . . . .1H 87
Redriff Est. SE16 . . . . .3B 104
Redriff Rd. RM7: Mawney 2H 55
  SE16 . . . . .4K 103
Redroofs Cl. BR3: Beck 1D 158
Redrose Trad. Cen. EN4: E Barn . . .5G 21
RED ROVER .4C 116
Redrup Ho. SE14 . . . . .6K 103
    (off John Williams Cl.)
Redruth Cl. N22 . . . . .7E 32
Redruth Gdns. KT10: Clay 7A 162
Redruth Ho. SM2: Sutt 7K 165
Redruth Rd. E9 . . . . .1J 85
Redsan Cl. CR2: S Croy 7D 168
Redshank Ho. SE1 . . . . .5F 103
    (off Avocet Cl.)
Red Sq. N16 . . . . .3D 66
Redstart Cl. E6 . . . . .5C 88
  SE14 .7A 104

Redstart Mans.—Repository Rd.

Redstart Mans. IG1: Ilf 3E 70
(off Mill Rd.)
Redston Rd. N8 4H 47
Redvers Rd. N22 2A 48
Redvers St. N1 1H 9 (3E 84)
Redwald Rd. E5 4K 67
Redway Dr. TW2: Whitt 7G 113
Redwing Ct. SE1 7D 14
(off Swan St.)
Redwing M. SE5 2C 120
Redwing Path SE28 2H 107
Redwing Rd. SM6: Wall 7J 167
Redwood Cl. DA15: Sidc 1A 144
E3 2C 86
IG9: Buck H 2E 36
N14 7C 22
SE16 1A 104
UB10: Hil 2D 74
Redwood Ct. KT6: Surb 7D 150
N19 7H 47
NW6 7G 63
UB5: N'olt 3C 76
Redwood Est. TW5: Cran 6K 93
Redwood Gdns. E4 6J 25
Redwood Gro. W5 3B 96
Redwood Mans. W8 3K 99
(off Chantry Sq.)
Redwood M. SW4 3F 119
TW15: Ashf 7F 129
(off Staines Rd. W.)
Redwoods SW15 1C 134
Redwood Wlk. KT6: Surb 1D 162
Redwood Way EN5: Barn 5A 20
Reece M. SW7 3A 16 (4B 100)
Reed Av. BR6: Orp 3J 173
Reed Cl. E16 5J 87
SE12 5J 123
Reede Gdns. RM10: Dag 5H 73
Reede Rd. RM10: Dag 6G 73
Reede Way RM10: Dag 6H 73
Reedham Cl. N17 4H 49
Reedham St. SE15 2G 121
Reedholm Vs. N16 4D 66
Reed Pl. SW4 4H 119
Reed Rd. N17 2F 49
Reedsfield Cl. TW15: Ashf 3D 128
Reedsfield Rd. TW15: Ashf 4D 128
Reed's Pl. NW1 7G 65
Reedworth St. SE11 4K 19 (4A 102)
Reef Ho. E14 3E 104
(off Manchester St.)
Reenglass Rd. HA7: Stan 4J 27
Rees Dr. HA7: Stan 4K 27
Rees Gdns. CR0: C'don 6F 157
Reesland Cl. E12 6E 70
Rees St. N1 1C 84
Reets Farm Cl. NW9 6A 44
Reeves Av. NW9 7K 43
Reeves Cnr. CR0: C'don 2B 168
Reeves Ho. SE1 7J 13
(off Baylis Rd.)
Reeves M. W1 3G 11 (7E 82)
Reeves Rd. E3 4D 86
SE18 6F 107
Reflection, The E16 2F 107
(off Woolwich Mnr. Way)
Reflection Ho. E2 4G 85
(off Cheshire St.)
Reflex Apartments BR2: Brom 4K 159
(off Wheeler Pl.)
Reform Row N17 2F 49
Reform St. SW11 2D 118
Regal Bldg. W10 3F 81
Regal Cl. E1 5G 85
W5 5D 78
Regal Ct. CR4: Mitc 3D 154
N18 5A 34
NW6 2H 81
(off Malvern Rd.)
SW6 7J 99
(off Dawes Rd.)
Regal Cres. SM6: Wall 3F 167
Regal Dr. N11 5A 32
Regal Ho. IG2: Ilf 6H 53
Regal Ho., The SW6 2A 118
Regal La. NW1 1E 82
Regal Pl. E3 3B 86
SW6 7K 99
Regal Row SE15 1J 121
Regal Way HA3: Kenton 6E 42
Regan Ho. N18 6A 34
Regan Way N1 1G 9 (2E 84)
Regatta Ho. TW11: Tedd 4A 132
Regatta Point E14 2C 104
(off Westferry Rd.)
TW8: Bford 6F 97
Regency Cl. TW12: Hamp 5D 130
W5 6E 78
Regency Ct. E3 2B 86
(off Norman Gro.)
E9 1J 85
(off Park Cl.)
E18 2J 51
EN1: Enf 5J 23
SM1: Sutt 4A 166
TW11: Tedd 6B 132
Regency Cres. NW4 2F 45
Regency Dr. HA4: Ruis 1G 57
Regency Gdns.
KT12: Walt T 7A 148
Regency Ho. E16 1J 105
(off Pepys Cres.)
N3 2H 45
SW1 3D 18
(off Regency St.)
SW6 1A 118
Regency Lawn NW5 3F 65
Regency Lodge IG9: Buck H 2G 37
NW3 7B 64
(off Adelaide Rd.)
Regency M. BR3: Beck 7E 140
NW10 6C 62
SW9 7B 102
TW7: Isle 5J 113
Regency Pde. NW3 7B 64
(off Finchley Rd.)
Regency Pl. SW1 3D 18 (4H 101)
Regency St. NW10 4A 80
SW1 3D 18 (4H 101)
Regency Ter. SW7 5A 16
(off Fulham Rd.)
Regency Wlk. CR0: C'don 6B 158
TW10: Rich 5E 114
(off Grosvenor Av.)
TW10: Rich 5E 114
(off The Vineyard)
Regency Way DA6: Bex 3D 126
Regeneration Rd. SE16 4K 103
Regent Av. UB10: Hil 7D 56
Regent Bus. Cen.
UB3: Hayes 2K 93
Regent Cl. HA3: Kenton 6E 42
N12 5F 31
TW4: Cran 1K 111
Regent Ct. N3 7E 30
N20 2G 31
NW6 7H 63
(off Cavendish Rd.)
NW8 2C 4
W8 3K 99
(off Wright's La.)
Regent Gdns. IG3: Ilf 7A 54
Regent Ho. W14 4G 99
(off Windsor Way)
Regent Pde. SM2: Sutt 6A 166
Regent Pl. CR0: C'don 1F 169
SW19 5A 136
W1 2B 12 (7G 83)
Regent Rd. KT5: Surb 5F 151
SE24 6B 120
Regents Av. N13 5F 33
Regent's Bri. Gdns. SW8 7J 101
Regents Canal Ho. E14 6A 86
(off Commercial Rd.)
Regents Cl. CR2: S Croy 6E 168
HA8: Edg 4K 27
UB4: Hayes 5H 75
Regents College 3F 5
Regents Ct. BR1: Brom 7H 141
E8 1F 85
(off Pownall Rd.)
HA5: Pinn 2B 40
KT2: King T 1E 150
(off Sopwith Way)
Regents Dr. BR2: Kes 5B 172
IG8: Wfd G 6K 37
Regents Ga. Ho. E14 7A 86
(off Horseferry Rd.)
Regents M. NW8 2A 82
REGENT'S PARK 2K 5 (3F 83)
Regent's Pk. 1F 5 (2D 82)
Regent's Pk. Barracks 1K 5
Regents Pk. Est. NW1 1A 6
Regent's Pk. Gdns. M. NW1 1D 82
Regent's Pk. Ho. NW8 2D 4
(off Park Rd.)
Regent's Pk. Open Air Theatre
2G 5 (3E 82)
Regents Pk. Rd. N3 3H 45
NW1 7D 64
(not continuous)
Regent's Pk. Ter. NW1 1F 83
Regents Pl. NW1 3K 5 (4F 83)
SE3 2J 123
Regents Plaza NW6 2K 81
(off Kilburn High Rd.)
Regent Sq. DA17: Belv 4H 109
E3 3D 86
WC1 2F 7 (3J 83)
Regent's Row E8 1G 85
Regent St. NW10 3F 81
SW1 3C 12 (7H 83)
W1 7K 5 (6F 83)
W4 5G 97
Regents Wharf E2 1H 85
(off Wharf Pl.)
N1 2K 83
Regina Cl. EN5: Barn 3A 20
Regina Ho. SE20 1K 157
Reginald Pl. SE8 7C 104
(off Deptford High St.)
Reginald Rd. E7 7J 69
HA6: Nwood 1H 39
SE8 7C 104
Reginald Sorenson Ho. E11 7F 51
Reginald Sq. SE8 7C 104
Regina Point SE16 3J 103
Regina Rd. N4 1K 65
SE25 3G 157
UB2: S'hall 4C 94
W13 1A 96
Regina Ter. W13 1B 96
Regis Ct. CR4: Mitc 1C 154
N8 4K 47
NW1 5E 4
(off Melcombe Pl.)
Regis Ho. W1 5H 5
(off Beaumont St.)
Regis Pl. SW2 4K 119
Regis Rd. NW5 5F 65
Regnart Bldgs. NW1 3B 6
Regnas Ho. E15 6H 69
(off Carnarvon Rd.)
Regnolruf Ct. KT12: Walt T 7J 147
Reid Cl. HA5: Eastc 4J 39
UB3: Hayes 6G 75
Reidhaven Rd. SE18 4J 107
Reigate Av. SM1: Sutt 1J 165
Reigate Rd. BR1: Brom 3H 141
IG3: Ilf 2K 71
Reigate Way SM6: Wall 5J 167
Reighton Rd. E5 3G 67
Reindeer Cl. E13 1J 87
Reinickendorf Av. SE9 6G 125
Reis Pl. N15 4F 49
(off Blenheim Ri.)
Reizel Cl. N16 1F 67
Relay Rd. W12 1E 98
Relf Rd. SE15 3G 121
Reliance Arc. SW9 4A 120
Reliance Sq. EC2 3H 9 (4E 84)
Relko Gdns. SM1: Sutt 5B 166
Relton M. SW7 1D 16 (3C 100)
Rembrandt Cl. E14 3F 105
SW1 4G 17
Rembrandt Ct. KT19: Ewe 6B 164
SE16 5H 103
(off Stubbs Dr.)
Rembrandt Rd. HA8: Edg 2G 43
SE13 4G 123
Remembrance Rd. E7 4B 70
Remington Rd. E6 6C 88
N15 6D 48
Remington St. N1 1B 8 (2B 84)
Remnant St. WC2 7G 7 (6K 83)
Remsted Ho. NW6 1K 81
(off Mortimer Cres.)
Remus Bldg., The EC1 2K 7
(off Hardwick St.)
Remus Rd. E3 7C 68
Renaissance Ct. SM1: Sutt 1A 166
TW3: Houn 3G 113
Renaissance Wlk. SE10 3H 105
(off Teal St.)
Renbold Ho. SE10 1E 122
(off Blissett St.)
Rendalls HA1: Harr 1J 59
(off Grove Hill)
Rendle Cl. CR0: C'don 5F 157
Rendle Ho. W10 4G 81
(off Wornington Rd.)
Rendlesham Rd. E5 4G 67
EN2: Enf 1G 23
Renforth St. SE16 3J 103
Renfree Way TW17: Shep 7C 146
Renfrew Cl. E6 7E 88
Renfrew Ct. TW4: Houn 2C 112
Renfrew Ho. E17 2B 50
NW6 2K 81
(off Carlton Va.)
Renfrew Rd. KT2: King T 7H 133
SE11 3K 19 (4B 102)
TW4: Houn 2B 112
Renmuir St. SW17 6D 136
Rennell St. SE13 3E 122
Rennels Way TW7: Isle 2J 113
Renness Rd. E17 3A 50
Rennets Cl. SE9 5J 125
Rennets Wood Rd. SE9 5H 125
Rennie Cotts. E1 4J 85
(off Pemell Cl.)
Rennie Ct. EN3: Enf L 1H 25
SE1 4A 14
Rennie Est. SE16 4H 103
Rennie Ho. SE1 3C 102
(off Bath Ter.)
Rennie St. SE1 4A 14 (1B 102)
(not continuous)
Renoir Cinema
Brunswick Square 4J 83
Renoir Ct. SE16 5H 103
(off Stubbs Dr.)
Renovation, The E16 2F 107
(off Woolwich Mnr. Way)
Renown Cl. CR0: C'don 1B 168
RM7: Mawney 1G 55
Rensburg Rd. E17 5K 49
Renshaw Cl. DA17: Belv 6F 109
Renters Av. NW4 6E 44
Renton Cl. SW2 6K 119
Renwick Ind. Est.
IG11: Bark 2B 90
Renwick Rd. IG11: Bark 4B 90
Repens Way UB4: Yead 4B 76
Rephidim St. SE1 3E 102
Replingham Rd. SW18 1H 135
Reporton Rd. SW6 7G 99
Repository Rd. SE18 6D 106

Repton Av. HA0: Wemb 4C 60
UB3: Harl 4F 93
Repton Cl. SM5: Cars 5C 166
Repton Ct. BR3: Beck 1D 158
IG5: Ilf 1D 52
Repton Gro. IG5: Ilf 1D 52
Repton Ho. SW1 . . . . .4B 18
(off Charlwood St.)
REPTON PARK 7K 37
Repton Rd. BR6: Chels 3K 173
HA3: Kenton 4F 43
Repton St. E14 . . . . .6A 86
Repulse Cl. RM5: Col R 1G 55
Reservoir Cl. CR7: Thor H 3D 156
Reservoir Rd. HA4: Ruis 4E 38
N14 . . . . .5B 22
SE4 . . . . .2A 122
Reservoir Studios E1 . . . . .6K 85
(off Cable St.)
Resham Cl. UB2: S'hall 3A 94
Resolution Wlk. SE18 . . . . .3D 106
Resolution Way SE8 . . . . .7C 104
(off Deptford High St.)
Restell Cl. SE3 . . . . .6G 105
Restmor Way SM6: Wall 2E 166
Reston Pl. SW7 . . . . .2A 100
Restons Cres. SE9 . . . . .6H 125
Restoration Sq. SW11 . . . . .1B 118
Restormel Cl. TW3: Houn 5E 112
Restormel Ho. SE11 . . . . .4J 19
Retcar Pl. N19 . . . . .2F 65
Retford St. N1 . . . . .1H 9 (2E 84)
Retingham Way E4 . . . . .2J 35
Retlas Ct. HA1: Harr 7J 41
Retreat, The CR7: Thor H 4D 156
HA2: Harr 7E 40
KT4: Wor Pk 2D 164
KT5: Surb 6F 151
NW9 . . . . .5K 43
SW14 . . . . .3A 116
Retreat Cl. HA3: Kenton 5C 42
Retreat Ho. E9 . . . . .6J 67
Retreat Pl. E9 . . . . .6J 67
Retreat Rd. TW9: Rich 5D 114
Reubens Ct. W4 . . . . .5H 97
(off Chaseley Dr.)
Reunion Row E1 . . . . .7H 85
Reuters Plaza E14 . . . . .1D 104
(off The Sth. Colonnade)
Reveley Sq. SE16 . . . . .2A 104
Revell Ri. SE18 . . . . .6K 107
Revell Rd. KT1: King T 2H 151
SM1: Sutt 6H 165
Revelon Rd. SE4 . . . . .4A 122
Revelstoke Rd. SW18 . . . . .2H 135
Reventlow Rd. SE9 . . . . .1G 143
Reverdy Rd. SE1 . . . . .4G 103
Reverend Cl. HA2: Harr 3F 59
Revesby Rd. SM5: Cars 6B 154
Review Lodge RM10: Dag 1H 91
Review Rd. NW2 . . . . .2B 62
RM10: Dag 1H 91
Rewell St. SW6 . . . . .7A 100
Rewley Rd. SM5: Cars 6B 154
Rex Av. TW15: Ashf 6C 128
Rex Pl. W1 . . . . .3H 11 (7E 82)
Reydon Av. E11 . . . . .5A 52
Reynard Cl. BR1: Brom 3E 160
SE4 . . . . .3A 122
Reynard Dr. SE19 . . . . .7F 139
Reynard Mills Trad. Est. TW8: Bford . . .5C 96
Reynard Pl. SE14 . . . . .6A 104
Reynardson Rd. N17 . . . . .7H 33
Reynolah Gdns. SE7 . . . . .5K 105
Reynolds Av. E12 . . . . .5E 70
KT9: Chess 7E 162
RM6: Chad H 7C 54
Reynolds Cl. NW11 . . . . .7K 45
SM5: Cars 1D 166
SW19 . . . . .1B 154
Reynolds Dr. RM6: Chad H 3D 54
Reynolds Dr. HA8: Edg 3F 43

Reynolds Ho. E2 . . . . .2J 85
(off Approach Rd.)
NW8 . . . . .2B 82
(off Wellington Rd.)
SW1 . . . . .4D 18
(off Erasmus St.)
Reynolds Pl. SE3 . . . . .7K 105
TW10: Rich 6F 115
Reynolds Rd. KT3: N Mald 7K 151
SE15 . . . . .4J 121
UB4: Yead 4A 76
W4 . . . . .3J 97
Reynolds Sports Cen. 2G 97
Reynolds Way CR0: C'don 4E 168
Rheidol M. N1 . . . . .2C 84
Rheidol Ter. N1 . . . . .1C 84
Rheingold Way SM6: Wall 7J 167
Rhein Ho. N8 . . . . .3J 47
(off Campsfield Rd.)
Rheola Cl. N17 . . . . .1F 49
Rhoda St. E2 . . . . .3K 9 (4F 85)
Rhodes Av. N22 . . . . .1G 47
Rhodes Ho. N1 . . . . .1E 8
(off Provost Est.)
Rhodesia Rd. E11 . . . . .2F 69
SW9 . . . . .2J 119
Rhodes Moorhouse Ct.
SM4: Mord 6J 153
Rhodes St. N7 . . . . .5K 65
Rhodeswell Rd. E14 . . . . .5A 86
Rhodrons Av. KT9: Chess 5E 162
Rhondda Gro. E3 . . . . .3A 86
Rhyl Rd. UB6: G'frd 2K 77
Rhyl St. NW5 . . . . .6E 64
Rhys Av. N11 . . . . .7C 32
Rialto Rd. CR4: Mitc 2E 154
Ribble Cl. IG8: Wfd G 6F 37
Ribblesdale Av. N11 . . . . .6K 31
UB5: N'olt 6F 59
Ribblesdale Ho. NW6 . . . . .1J 81
(off Kilburn Va.)
Ribblesdale Rd. N8 . . . . .4K 47
SW16 . . . . .6F 137
Ribbon Dance M. SE5 . . . . .1D 120
Ribchester Av. UB6: G'frd 3K 77
Ribston Cl. BR2: Brom 1D 172
Ricardo Path SE28 . . . . .1C 108
Ricardo St. E14 . . . . .6D 86
Ricards Rd. SW19 . . . . .5H 135
Riccall Ct. NW9 . . . . .1A 44
(off Pageant Av.)
Rice Pde. BR5: Pet W 5H 161
Riceyman Ho. WC1 . . . . .2J 7
(off Lloyd Baker St.)
Richard Anderson Ct. SE14 . . . . .7K 103
(off Monson Rd.)
Richard Burbidge Mans. SW13 . . . . .6E 98
(off Brasenose Dr.)
Richard Burton Ct. IG9: Buck H 2F 37
(off Palmerston Rd.)
Richard Challoner Sports Cen. 7K 151
Richard Cl. SE18 . . . . .4C 106
Richard Fell Ho. E12 . . . . .4E 70
(off Walton Rd.)
Richard Fielden Ho. E1 . . . . .3A 86
Richard Ho. SE16 . . . . .4J 103
(off Silwood St.)
Richard Ho. Dr. E16 . . . . .6B 88
Richard Neale Ho. E1 . . . . .7H 85
(off Cornwall St.)
Richard Neve Ho. SE18 . . . . .4J 107
(off Plumstead High St.)
Richard Robert Residence, The E15 . . .6F 69
(off Salway Rd.)
Richards Av. RM7: Rom 6J 55
Richards Cl. HA1: Harr 5A 42
UB3: Harl 6F 93
UB10: Hil 1C 74
WD23: Bush 1C 26
Richards Fld. KT19: Ewe 7K 163
Richard Sharples Ct. SM2: Sutt 7A 166
Richardson Cl. E8 . . . . .1F 85

Richardson Ct. SW4 . . . . .2J 119
(off Studley Rd.)
Richardson Gdns. RM10: Dag 6H 73
Richardson Rd. E15 . . . . .2G 87
Richardson's M. W1 . . . . .4A 6
Richards Pl. E17 . . . . .3C 50
SW3 . . . . .3D 16 (4C 100)
Richard St. E1 . . . . .6H 85
Richbell WC1 . . . . .5F 7
(off Boswell St.)
Richbell Pl. WC1 . . . . .5G 7 (5K 83)
Richborne Ter. SW8 . . . . .7K 101
Richborough Ho. SE15 . . . . .6J 103
(off Sharratt St.)
Richborough Rd. NW2 . . . . .4G 63
Richbourne Ct. W1 . . . . .7D 4
(off Harrowby St.)
Richens Cl. TW3: Houn 2H 113
Riches Rd. IG1: Ilf 2G 71
Richfield Rd. WD23: Bush 1B 26
Richford Ga. W6 . . . . .3E 98
Richford Rd. E15 . . . . .1H 87
Richford St. W6 . . . . .2E 98
Rich Ind. Est. SE1 . . . . .3E 102
SE15 . . . . .6H 103
Richland Ho. SE15 . . . . .1G 121
(off Goldsmith Rd.)
Richlands Av. KT17: Ewe 4C 164
Rich La. SW5 . . . . .5K 99
Richman Ho. SE8 . . . . .58 104
(off Grove St.)
RICHMOND 5D 114
Richmond Av. E4 . . . . .5A 36
N1 . . . . .1K 83
NW10 . . . . .6E 62
SW20 . . . . .1G 153
TW14: Felt 6G 111
UB10: Hil 6D 56
Richmond Bri. TW1: Twick 6D 114
Richmond Bldgs. W1 . . . . . . .1C 12 (6H 83)
RICHMOND CIRCUS 4E 114
Richmond Cl. E17 . . . . .6B 50
Richmond Cotts. W14 . . . . .4G 99
(off Hammersmith Rd.)
Richmond Ct. CR4: Mitc 3B 154
E8 . . . . .7H 67
(off Mare St.)
HA9: Wemb 3F 61
N11 . . . . .6K 31
(off Pickering Gdns.)
NW6 . . . . .7F 63
(off Willesden La.)
SW1 . . . . .7F 11
(off Sloane St.)
W14 . . . . .4G 99
(off Hammersmith Rd.)
Richmond Cres. E4 . . . . .5A 36
N1 . . . . .1K 83
N9 . . . . .1B 34
Richmond Cricket Club 5E 114
(off Kew Rd.)
Richmond Dr. IG8: Wfd G 7K 37
TW17: Shep 6F 147
Richmond Gdns. HA3: Hrw W 7E 26
NW4 . . . . .5C 44
Richmond Gro. KT5: Surb 6F 151
N1 . . . . .7B 66
(not continuous)
Richmond Hill TW10: Rich 6E 114
Richmond Hill Ct. TW10: Rich 6E 114
Richmond Ho. NW1 . . . . .1K 5
(off Park Village E.)
SE17 . . . . .5D 102
(off Portland St.)
Richmond Mans. SW5 . . . . .5K 99
(off Old Brompton Rd.)
TW1: Twick 6D 114
Richmond M. TW11: Tedd 5K 131
W1 . . . . .1C 12 (6H 83)
Richmond Pde. TW1: Twick 6C 114
(off Richmond Rd.)

Richmond Pk. 1G 133
Richmond Pk. Rd. KT2: King T 1E 150
SW14 . . . . .5J 115
Richmond Pl. SE18 . . . . .4G 107
Richmond Rd. CR0: Bedd 3J 167
CR7: Thor H 3B 156
E4 . . . . .1A 36
E7 . . . . .5K 69
(not continuous)
E8 . . . . .7F 67
E11 . . . . .2F 69
EN5: New Bar 5E 20
IG1: Ilf 3G 71
KT2: King T 5D 132
N2 . . . . .2A 46
N11 . . . . .6D 32
N15 . . . . .6E 48
SW20 . . . . .1D 152
TW1: Twick 7B 114
TW7: Isle 3A 114
W5 . . . . .2E 96
Richmond RUFC 3D 114
(off Kew Foot Rd.)
Richmond St. E13 . . . . .2J 87
Richmond Ter. SW1 . . . . . . .6E 12 (2J 101)
Richmond
The American International University
in London
Richmond Hill Campus 7E 114
Kensington Campus -
Ansdell St. 3K 99
St Albans Gro. 3K 99
Young St. 2K 99
Richmond Theatre 4D 114
Richmond Way E11 . . . . .2J 69
W12 . . . . .2F 99
W14 . . . . .2F 99
Richmount Gdns. SE3 . . . . .3J 123
Rich St. E14 . . . . .7B 86
Rickard Cl. NW4 . . . . .4D 44
SW2 . . . . .1A 138
Rickards Cl. KT6: Surb 2E 162
Rickett St. SW6 . . . . .6J 99
Rickman Ho. E1 . . . . .3J 85
(off Rickman St.)
Rickman St. E1 . . . . .4J 85
Rickmansworth Rd. HA5: Pinn 2K 39
HA6: Nwood 1F 39
Rick Roberts Way E15 . . . . .1E 86
Rickthorne Rd. N19 . . . . .2J 65
Rickyard Path SE9 . . . . .4C 124
Riddell Ct. SE5 . . . . .5F 103
(off Albany Rd.)
Ridding La. UB6: G'frd 5K 59
Riddons Rd. SE12 . . . . .3A 142
Ride, The EN3: Pond E 3D 24
TW8: Bford 5B 96
Rideout St. SE18 . . . . .4D 106
Rider Cl. DA15: Sidc 6J 125
Rideway Dr. W3 . . . . .3G 97
Ridgdale St. E3 . . . . .2D 86
Ridge, The BR6: Orp 2H 173
DA5: Bexl 7F 127
EN5: Barn 5C 20
KT5: Surb 5G 151
TW2: Whitt 7H 113
Ridge Av. N21 . . . . .7H 23
Ridgebrook Rd. SE3 . . . . .3B 124
Ridge Cl. NW4 . . . . .2F 45
NW9 . . . . .4K 43
SE28 . . . . .2H 107
Ridge Ct. SE22 . . . . .7G 121
Ridge Crest EN2: Enf 1E 22
Ridgecroft Cl. DA5: Bexl 1J 145
Ridge Hill NW11 . . . . .1G 63
Ridgemead Cl. N14 . . . . .2D 32
Ridgemont Gdns. HA8: Edg 4D 28
Ridgemount Av. CR0: C'don 1K 169
Ridgemount Cl. SE20 . . . . .7H 139
Ridgemount Gdns. EN2: Enf 3G 23
Ridge Rd. CR4: Mitc 7F 137
N8 . . . . .6K 47

Ridge Rd. N21 . . . 1H **33**
NW2 . . . 3H **63**
SM3: Sutt . . . 1G **165**
Ridges Yd. CR0: C'don . . . 3B **168**
Ridgeview Cl. EN5: Barn . . . 6A **20**
Ridgeview Rd. N20 . . . 3E **30**
Ridge Way SE19 . . . 6E **138**
TW13: Hanw . . . 3C **130**
Ridgeway BR2: Hayes . . . 2J **171**
IG8: Wfd G . . . 4F **37**
TW10: Rich . . . 6E **114**
Ridgeway, The CR0: Wadd . . . 3K **167**
E4 . . . 2J **35**
EN2: Enf . . . 1E **22**
HA2: Harr . . . 5D **40**
(not continuous)
HA3: Kenton . . . 6C **42**
HA4: Ruis . . . 7J **39**
HA7: Stan . . . 6H **27**
KT12: Walt T . . . 7H **147**
N3 . . . 7E **30**
N11 . . . 4J **31**
N14 . . . 2D **32**
NW7 . . . 3H **29**
NW9 . . . 4K **43**
NW11 . . . 7G **45**
W3 . . . 3G **97**
Ridgeway Av. EN4: E Barn . . . 6J **21**
Ridgeway Cres. BR6: Orp . . . 3J **173**
Ridgeway Cres. Gdns.
BR6: Orp . . . 2J **173**
Ridgeway Dr. BR1: Brom . . . 4K **141**
Ridgeway E. DA15: Sidc . . . 5K **125**
Ridgeway Gdns. IG4: Ilf . . . 5C **52**
N6 . . . 7G **47**
Ridgeway Rd. TW7: Isle . . . 7J **95**
Ridgeway Rd. Nth. TW7: Isle . . . 6J **95**
Ridgeway Wlk. *UB5: N'olt* . . . *6C 58*
(off Cowings Mead)
Ridgeway W. DA15: Sidc . . . 5J **125**
Ridgewell Cl. N1 . . . 1C **84**
RM10: Dag . . . 1H **91**
SE26 . . . 4B **140**
Ridgmount Gdns. WC1 . . . 5C **6** (5H **83**)
Ridgmount Pl. WC1 . . . 5C **6** (5H **83**)
Ridgmount Rd. SW18 . . . 5K **117**
Ridgmount St. WC1 . . . 5C **6** (5H **83**)
Ridgway SW19 . . . 7E **134**
Ridgway, The SM2: Sutt . . . 7B **166**
Ridgway Ct. SW19 . . . 6F **135**
Ridgway Gdns. SW19 . . . 7F **135**
Ridgway Pl. SW19 . . . 6G **135**
Ridgway Rd. SW9 . . . 3B **120**
Ridgwell Rd. E16 . . . 5A **88**
Riding, The NW11 . . . 7H **45**
Riding Ho. St. W1 . . . 6K **5** (5F **83**)
Ridings, The E11 . . . 5J **51**
EN4: E Barn . . . 7G **21**
KT5: Surb . . . 5G **151**
KT17: Ewe . . . 7B **164**
TW16: Sun . . . 1J **147**
W5 . . . 4F **79**
Ridings Av. N21 . . . 4G **23**
Ridings Cl. N6 . . . 7G **47**
Ridler Rd. EN1: Enf . . . 1K **23**
Ridley Av. W13 . . . 3B **96**
Ridley Cl. IG11: Bark . . . 7K **71**
Ridley Ct. SW16 . . . 6J **137**
Ridley Ho. *SW1* . . . *2D 18*
(off Monck St.)
Ridley Rd. BR2: Brom . . . 3H **159**
DA16: Well . . . 1B **126**
E7 . . . 4A **70**
E8 . . . 5F **67**
NW10 . . . 2C **80**
SW19 . . . 7K **135**
Ridsdale Rd. SE20 . . . 1H **157**
Riefield Rd. SE9 . . . 4G **125**
Riesco Dr. CR0: C'don . . . 6J **169**
Riffel Rd. NW2 . . . 5E **62**
Rifle Ct. SE11 . . . 7K **19** (6A **102**)
Rifle St. E14 . . . 5D **86**

Riga Ho. *E1* . . . *5K 85*
(off Shandy St.)
Riga M. E1 . . . 7K **9**
Rigault Rd. SW6 . . . 2G **117**
Rigby Cl. CR0: Wadd . . . 3A **168**
Rigby La. UB3: Hayes . . . 2E **92**
Rigby M. IG1: Ilf . . . 2E **70**
Rigden St. E14 . . . 6D **86**
Rigeley Rd. NW10 . . . 3C **80**
Rigg App. E10 . . . 1K **67**
Rigge Pl. SW4 . . . 4H **119**
Riggindale Rd. SW16 . . . 5H **137**
Riley Ho. *E3* . . . *4C 86*
(off Ireton St.)
SW10 . . . *7B 100*
(off Riley St.)
Riley Rd. EN3: Enf W . . . 1D **24**
SE1 . . . 7H **15** (3F **103**)
Riley St. SW10 . . . 6B **100**
Rill Ct. *IG11: Bark* . . . *2G 89*
(off Spring Pl.)
Rill Ho. *SE5* . . . *7D 102*
(off Harris St.)
Rima Ho. *SW3* . . . *7A 16*
(off Callow St.)
Rinaldo Rd. SW12 . . . 7F **119**
Ring, The SW7 . . . 7B **10** (2B **100**)
W2 . . . 2C **10** (7B **82**)
Ring Cl. BR1: Brom . . . 7K **141**
Ring Ct. *SE1* . . . *2B 102*
(off The Cut)
Ringcroft St. N7 . . . 5A **66**
Ringers Ct. *BR1: Brom* . . . *3J 159*
(off Ringers Rd.)
Ringers Rd. BR1: Brom . . . 3J **159**
Ringford Rd. SW18 . . . 5H **117**
Ring Ho. *E1* . . . *7J 85*
(off Sage St.)
Ringles Ct. E6 . . . 1D **88**
Ringlet Cl. E16 . . . 5K **87**
Ringlewell Cl. EN1: Enf . . . 2C **24**
Ringmer Av. SW6 . . . 1G **117**
Ringmer Gdns. N19 . . . 2J **65**
Ringmer Pl. N21 . . . 5J **23**
Ringmer Way BR1: Brom . . . 5C **160**
Ringmore Ri. SE23 . . . 7H **121**
Ring Rd. W12 . . . 1E **98**
Ringsfield Ho. *SE17* . . . *5C 102*
(off Bronti Cl.)
Ringside Ct. SE28 . . . 1C **108**
(not continuous)
Ringslade Rd. N22 . . . 2K **47**
Ringstead Rd. SE6 . . . 7D **122**
SM1: Sutt . . . 4B **166**
Ring Way N11 . . . 6B **32**
Ringway UB2: S'hall . . . 5B **94**
Ringwold Cl. BR3: Beck . . . 7A **140**
Ringwood Av. CR0: C'don . . . 7J **155**
N2 . . . 2D **46**
Ringwood Cl. HA5: Pinn . . . 3A **40**
Ringwood Gdns. E14 . . . 4C **104**
SW15 . . . 1C **134**
Ringwood Rd. E17 . . . 6B **50**
Ringwood Way N21 . . . 1G **33**
TW12: Ham H . . . 4E **130**
Rio Cinema
Dalston . . . *5E 66*
(off Kingsland High St.)
Ripley Bldgs. *SE1* . . . *6B 14*
(off Rushworth St.)
Ripley Cl. BR1: Brom . . . 5D **160**
CR0: New Ad . . . 6E **170**
Ripley Ct. CR4: Mitc . . . 2B **154**
Ripley Gdns. SM1: Sutt . . . 4A **166**
(not continuous)
SW14 . . . 3K **115**
Ripley Ho. *SW1* . . . *7A 18*
(off Churchill Gdns.)
Ripley M. E11 . . . 6G **51**
Ripley Rd. DA17: Belv . . . 4G **109**
E16 . . . 6A **88**
EN2: Enf . . . 1H **23**

Ripley Rd. IG3: Ilf . . . 2K **71**
TW12: Hamp . . . 7E **130**
Ripley Vs. W5 . . . 6C **78**
Ripon Cl. UB5: N'olt . . . 5E **58**
Ripon Ct. *N11* . . . *6K 31*
(off Ribblesdale Av.)
Ripon Gdns. IG1: Ilf . . . 6C **52**
KT9: Chess . . . 5D **162**
Ripon Rd. N9 . . . 7C **24**
N17 . . . 3D **48**
SE18 . . . 6F **107**
Rippersley Rd. DA16: Well . . . 1A **126**
Ripple Nature Reserve, The . . . **3B 90**
Ripple Rd. IG11: Bark, Dag . . . 7G **71**
RM9: Dag . . . 1B **90**
RIPPLESIDE . . . **1B 90**
Rippleside Commercial Est.
IG11: Bark . . . 2C **90**
Ripplevale Gro. N1 . . . 7K **65**
Rippolson Rd. SE18 . . . 5K **107**
Ripston Rd. TW15: Ashf . . . 5F **129**
Risborough *SE17* . . . *4C 102*
(off Deacon Way)
Risborough Cl. N10 . . . 3F **47**
Risborough Dr. KT4: Wor Pk . . . 7C **152**
Risborough Ho. *NW8* . . . *3D 4*
(off Mallory St.)
Risborough St. SE1 . . . 6B **14** (2B **102**)
Risdon Ho. *SE16* . . . *2J 103*
(off Risdon St.)
Risdon St. SE16 . . . 3J **103**
Rise, The DA5: Bexl . . . 7C **126**
E11 . . . 5J **51**
HA0: Wemb . . . 5A **60**
HA8: Edg . . . 5C **28**
IG9: Buck H . . . 1G **37**
N13 . . . 4F **33**
NW7 . . . 6G **29**
NW10 . . . 4K **61**
UB6: G'frd . . . 5A **60**
UB10: Hil . . . 2B **74**
Risedale Rd. DA7: Bex . . . 3J **127**
Riseholme Ct. E9 . . . 6B **68**
Riseldine Rd. SE23 . . . 6A **122**
RISE PARK . . . **2K 55**
Rise Pk. Pde. RM1: Rom . . . 2K **55**
Risinghill St. N1 . . . 2K **83**
Risingholme Cl. HA3: Hrw W . . . 1J **41**
WD23: Bush . . . 1A **26**
Risingholme Rd. HA3: Hrw W . . . 2J **41**
Risings, The E17 . . . 4F **51**
Rising Sun Ct. EC1 . . . 5B **8**
Risley Av. N17 . . . 1C **48**
Rita Rd. SW8 . . . 6J **101**
Ritches Rd. N15 . . . 5C **48**
Ritchie Ho. *E14* . . . *6F 87*
(off Blair St.)
N19 . . . 1H **65**
SE16 . . . *3J 103*
(off Howland Est.)
Ritchie Rd. CR0: C'don . . . 6H **157**
Ritchie St. N1 . . . 2A **84**
Ritchings Av. E17 . . . 4A **50**
Ritherdon Rd. SW17 . . . 2E **136**
Ritson Ho. *N1* . . . *1K 83*
(off Barnsbury Est.)
Ritson Rd. E8 . . . 6G **67**
Ritter St. SE18 . . . 6E **106**
Ritz Pde. W5 . . . 4F **79**
Ritzy Picturehouse . . . *4A 120*
(off Coldharbour La.)
Riva Bingo
Streatham Hill . . . **1J 137**
Rivaz Pl. E9 . . . 6J **67**
Riven Ct. *W2* . . . *6K 81*
(off Inverness Ter.)
Rivenhall Gdns. E18 . . . 4H **51**
River App. HA8: Edg . . . 1J **43**
RIVER ASH ESTATE . . . **7H 147**
River Ash Est. TW17: Shep . . . 6H **147**
River Av. KT7: T Ditt . . . 7A **150**
N13 . . . 3G **33**

River Av. Ind. Est. N13 . . . 5F **33**
River Bank KT7: T Ditt . . . 5K **149**
KT8: E Mos . . . 3J **149**
N21 . . . 7H **23**
TW12: Hamp . . . 3E **148**
Riverbank Rd. BR1: Brom . . . 3J **141**
Riverbank Way TW8: Bford . . . 6C **96**
River Barge Cl. E14 . . . 2E **104**
River Brent Bus. Pk. W7 . . . 3J **95**
River Cl. E11 . . . 6A **52**
HA4: Ruis . . . 6H **39**
UB2: S'hall . . . 2G **95**
River Ct. *KT6: Surb* . . . *5D 150*
(off Portsmouth Rd.)
SE1 . . . 3A **14** (7B **84**)
TW17: Shep . . . 7E **146**
Rivercourt Rd. W6 . . . 4D **98**
River Crane Way *TW13: Hanw* . . . *2D 130*
(off Watermill Way)
Riverdale SE13 . . . 4E **122**
Riverdale Cl. IG11: Bark . . . 4B **90**
Riverdale Ct. N21 . . . 5J **23**
Riverdale Dr. SW18 . . . 1K **135**
Riverdale Gdns. TW1: Twick . . . 6C **114**
Riverdale Rd. DA5: Bexl . . . 7F **127**
DA8: Erith . . . 5H **109**
SE18 . . . 5K **107**
TW1: Twick . . . 6C **114**
TW13: Hanw . . . 4C **130**
Riverdale Shop. Cen. SE13 . . . 3E **122**
Riverdene HA8: Edg . . . 3D **28**
Riverdene Rd. IG1: Ilf . . . 3E **70**
Riverfleet *WC1* . . . *1F 7*
(off Birkenhead St.)
Riverford Ho. *W2* . . . *5J 81*
(off Westbourne Pk. Rd.)
River Front EN1: Enf . . . 3K **23**
River Gdns. SM5: Cars . . . 2E **166**
TW14: Felt . . . 5K **111**
River Gdns. Bus. Cen. TW14: Felt . . . 5K **111**
River Gro. Pk. BR3: Beck . . . 1B **158**
Riverhead Cl. E17 . . . 2K **49**
River Hgts. N17 . . . 1F **49**
Riverhill KT4: Wor Pk . . . 2K **163**
Riverhill M. KT4: Wor Pk . . . 3K **163**
Riverhill Mobile Home Pl.
KT4: Wor Pk . . . 2K **163**
Riverholme Dr. KT19: Ewe . . . 7K **163**
Riverhope Mans. SE18 . . . 3C **106**
River Ho. SE26 . . . 3H **139**
Riverhouse Barn . . . **7H 147**
River La. TW10: Ham . . . 7D **114**
Riverleigh Ct. E4 . . . 5G **35**
River Lodge *SW1* . . . *7B 18*
(off Grosvenor Rd.)
Rivermead KT1: King T . . . 5D **150**
KT8: E Mos . . . 3G **149**
Rivermead Cl. TW11: Tedd . . . 5B **132**
Rivermead Ct. SW6 . . . 3H **117**
Rivermead Ho. E9 . . . 5A **68**
TW16: Sun . . . *3A 148*
(off Thames St.)
Rivermead Rd. N18 . . . 6E **34**
River Meads Av. TW2: Twick . . . 3E **130**
River Mt. KT12: Walt T . . . 7H **147**
Rivernook Cl. KT12: Walt T . . . 5A **148**
River Pk. Gdns. BR2: Brom . . . 7F **141**
River Pk. Rd. N22 . . . 2K **47**
River Pl. N1 . . . 7C **66**
River Reach TW11: Tedd . . . 5C **132**
River Rd. IG9: Buck H . . . 1H **37**
IG11: Bark . . . 2J **89**
River Rd. Bus. Pk. IG11: Bark . . . 3K **89**
Riversdale Gdns. N22 . . . 1A **48**
Riversdale Rd. KT7: T Ditt . . . 5A **150**
N5 . . . 3B **66**
RM5: Col R . . . 1H **55**
Riversfield Rd. EN1: Enf . . . 3K **23**
Rivers Ho. *TW7: Isle* . . . *4B 114*
(off Richmond Rd.)
TW8: Bford . . . *5G 97*
(off Aitman Dr.)

Riverside E3 1C 86
NW4 7D 44
SE7 3K 105
SW11 7C 100
TW1: Twick 1B 132
TW9: Rich 5D 114
TW10: Rich 5D 114
TW16: Sun 3B 148
TW17: Shep 7G 147
W6 6E 98
WC1 *1F 7*
(*off Birkenhead St.*)
Riverside, The KT8: E Mos 3H 149
Riverside Apartments N13 5E 32
Riverside Arts Cen. 3A 148
Riverside Av. KT8: E Mos 5H 149
Riverside Bus. Cen.
SW18 1K 135
Riverside Bus. Pk. SW19 1A 154
Riverside Cl. E5 1J 67
KT1: King T 4D 150
RM1: Rom 4K 55
RM7: Rom 4K 55
SM6: Wall 3F 167
W7 4J 77
Riverside Cotts. IG11: Bark 2H 89
Riverside Ct. E4 6H 25
SE3 4H 123
SW8 7D 18 (6H 101)
TW7: Isle *2K 113*
(*off Woodlands Rd.*)
TW14: Felt 7G 111
Riverside Dr. CR4: Mitc 5C 154
NW11 6G 45
TW10: Ham 3B 132
W4 7K 97
Riverside Gdns. EN2: Enf 2H 23
HA0: Wemb 2E 78
N3 3G 45
W6 5D 98
Riverside Ho. *N1* *7C 66*
(*off Canonbury St.*)
Riverside Ind. Est. EN3: Pond E 6F 25
IG11: Bark 3A 90
Riverside Mans. *E1* *1J 103*
(*off Milk Yd.*)
Riverside M. CR0: Bedd 3J 167
Riverside Pl. N11 3B 32
TW19: Stanw 6A 110
Riverside Rd. DA14: Sidc 3E 144
E15 2E 86
N15 6G 49
SW17 4K 135
TW19: Stanw 5A 110
(not continuous)
Riverside Studios 5E 98
Riverside Twr. *SW6* *2A 118*
(*off The Boulevard*)
Riverside Vs. KT6: Surb 6C 150
Riverside Wlk. BR4: W W'ck 1D 170
EN5: Barn 6A 20
(not continuous)
KT1: King T 3D 150
N12 6D 30
(not continuous)
N20 3E 30
SE10 3G 105
(Morden Wharf Rd.)
SE10 2F 105
(Tunnel Av.)
SW6 3G 117
TW7: Isle 3J 113
W4 *6B 98*
(*off Chiswick Wharf*)
Riverside Wharf E3 1C 86
Riverside Works IG11: Bark 7F 71
Riverside Yd. SW17 4A 136
Riverstone Cl. HA2: Harr 1H 59
Riverstone Ct. KT2: King T 1F 151
River St. EC1 1J 7 (3A 84)
River Ter. W6 5E 98
WC2 3G 13
River Thames Vis. Cen. *5D 114*
(*within Mus. of Richmond*)
Riverton Cl. W9 3H 81
River Vw. EN2: Enf 3H 23
Riverview Ct. E14 3B 104
River Vw. Gdns. TW1: Twick 2K 131
Riverview Gdns. SW13 6D 98
Riverview Gro. W4 6H 97
River Vw. Hgts. *SE16* *2G 103*
(*off Bermondsey Wall W.*)
Riverview Pk. SE6 2C 140
Riverview Rd. KT19: Ewe 4J 163
W4 7H 97
Riverview Wlk. SE6 3B 140
River Wlk. E4 7K 35
KT12: Walt T 6J 147
SW6 2A 118
W6 7E 98
Riverwalk Ho. *SW1* *5J 101*
(*off Millbank*)
River Wlk. Rd. EN3: Brim 3G 25
River Way KT19: Ewe 5K 163
SE10 3H 105
TW2: Twick 2F 131
Riverway N13 5F 33
River Wharf Bus. Pk. DA17: Belv 1K 109
Riverwood La. BR7: Chst 1H 161
Rivet Ho. *SE1* *5F 103*
(*off Cooper's Rd.*)
Rivington Av. IG8: Wfd G 2B 52
Rivington Ct. NW10 1C 80
RM10: Dag 6H 73
Rivington Cres. NW7 7G 29
Rivington Pl. EC2 2H 9 (3E 84)
Rivington St. EC2 2G 9 (3E 84)
Rivington Wlk. E8 1G 85
Rivulet Rd. N17 7H 33
Rixon Ho. SE18 6F 107
Rixon St. N7 3A 66
Rixsen Rd. E12 5C 70
Roach Rd. E3 7C 68
Roads Pl. N19 2J 65
Roan Ind. Est. *CR4: Mitc* *1D 154*
(*off Lavender Av.*)
Roan St. SE10 6E 104
Robarts Cl. HA5: Eastc 5K 39
Robbins Hall EN3: Pond E 6E 24
Robb Rd. HA7: Stan 6F 27
Robert Adam St. W1 7G 5 (6E 82)
Roberta St. E2 3G 85
Robert Bell Ho. *SE16* *4G 103*
(*off Rouel Rd.*)
Robert Burns Ho. *N17* *7C 34*
(*off Northumberland Pk.*)
Robert Burns M. SE24 5B 120
Robert Cl. *IG11: Bark* *6G 71*
(*off Tanner St.*)
W9 4A 4 (4A 82)
Robert Ct. SE15 2G 121
Robert Dashwood Way
SE17 4C 102
Robert Gentry Ho. *W14* *5G 99*
(*off Gledstanes Rd.*)
Robert Jones Ho. *SE16* *4G 103*
(*off Rouel Rd.*)
Robert Keen Cl. SE15 1G 121
Robert Lowe Cl. SE14 7K 103
Robert Morton Ho. NW8 7A 64
Roberton Dr. BR1: Brom 1A 160
Robert Owen Ho. *E2* *1K 9*
(*off Baroness Rd.*)
N22 *1A 48*
(*off Progress Way*)
SW6 1F 117
Robert Runcie Ct. SW2 4K 119
Roberts All. W5 2D 96
Robertsbridge Rd. SM5: Cars 1A 166
Roberts Cl. CR7: Thor H 3D 156
SE9 1H 143
SE16 2K 103
SM3: Cheam 7F 165
UB7: Yiew 1A 92
Roberts Ct. KT9: Chess 5D 162
N1 *1B 84*
(*off Essex Rd.*)
NW10 6A 62
SE20 *1J 157*
(*off Maple Rd.*)
Roberts M. BR6: Orp 1K 173
SW1 1G 17 (3E 100)
Robertson Gro. SW17 5C 136
Robertson St. SW8 3F 119
Roberts Pl. EC1 3K 7 (4A 84)
RM10: Dag 6G 73
Roberts Rd. DA17: Belv 5G 109
E17 1D 50
NW7 6B 30
Robert St. CR0: C'don 3C 168
E16 1F 107
NW1 2K 5 (3F 83)
SE18 5H 107
(not continuous)
WC2 3F 13 (7J 83)
Robert Sutton Ho. *E1* *6J 85*
(*off Tarling St.*)
Robeson St. E3 5B 86
Robina Cl. DA6: Bex 4D 126
HA6: Nwood 1H 39
Robin Cl. NW7 3F 29
RM5: Col R 1K 55
TW12: Hamp 5C 130
Robin Ct. E14 2E 104
SE16 4G 103
SM6: Wall 5G 167
Robin Cres. E6 5B 88
Robin Gro. HA3: Kenton 6F 43
N6 2E 64
TW8: Bford 6C 96
Robin Hill Dr. BR7: Chst 6C 142
ROBIN HOOD 3A 134
Robinhood Cl. CR4: Mitc 3G 155
Robin Hood Ct. *EC4* *7K 7*
(*off Shoe La.*)
Robin Hood Dr. HA3: Hrw W 7E 26
Robin Hood Gdns. *E14* *7E 86*
(*off Woolmore St., not continuous*)
Robin Hood Grn. BR5: St M Cry 5K 161
Robin Hood La. DA6: Bex 5E 126
E14 7E 86
SM1: Sutt 5J 165
SW15 3A 134
Robinhood La. CR4: Mitc 3G 155
Robin Hood Rd. SW19 5C 134
Robin Hood Way SW15 3A 134
SW20 3A 134
UB6: G'frd 6K 59
Robin Ho. *NW8* *2C 82*
(*off Newcourt St.*)
Robin Howard Dance Theatre *2D 6*
(*in The Place*)
Robinia Cl. *SE20* *1G 157*
(*off Sycamore Gro.*)
Robinia Cres. E10 2D 68
Robin La. NW4 3F 45
Robins Ct. BR3: Beck 2F 159
CR2: S Croy *4E 168*
(*off Birdhurst Rd.*)
SE12 3A 142
Robinscroft M. SE10 1E 122
Robins Gro. BR4: W W'ck 3J 171
Robinson Cl. E11 3G 69
EN2: Enf 3H 23
Robinson Ct. CR7: Thor H 6B 156
N1 *1B 84*
(*off St Mary's Path*)
TW9: Rich 4F 115
Robinson Cres. WD23: B Hea 1B 26
Robinson Ho. *E14* *5C 86*
(*off Selsey St.*)
W10 *6F 81*
(*off Bramley Rd.*)
Robinson Rd. E2 2J 85
RM10: Dag 4G 73
SW17 6C 136
Robinson's Cl. W13 5A 78
Robinson St. SW3 7E 16 (6D 100)
Robinswood M. N5 5B 66
Robinwood Gro. UB8: Hil 4B 74
Robinwood Pl. SW15 4K 133
Rob Pasco La. RM9: Dag 3E 90
Robsart St. SW9 2K 119
Robson Av. NW10 7C 62
Robson Cl. E6 6C 88
EN2: Enf 2G 23
Robson Rd. SE27 3B 138
Roby Ho. *EC1* *3C 8*
(*off Mitchell St.*)
Roca Ct. E11 5J 51
Rocastle Rd. SE4 5A 122
Roch Av. HA8: Edg 2F 43
Rochdale Rd. E17 7C 50
SE2 5B 108
Rochdale Way SE8 7C 104
(not continuous)
Roche Ho. *E14* *7B 86*
(*off Beccles St.*)
Rochelle Cl. SW11 4B 118
Rochelle St. E2 2J 9 (3F 85)
(not continuous)
Rochemont Wlk. *E8* *1G 85*
(*off Pownell Rd.*)
Roche Rd. SW16 1K 155
Rochester Av. BR1: Brom 2K 159
E13 1A 88
TW13: Felt 2H 129
Rochester Cl. DA15: Sidc 6B 126
EN1: Enf 1K 23
SW16 7J 137
Rochester Ct. *E2* *4H 85*
(*off Wilmot St.*)
NW1 *7G 65*
(*off Rochester Sq.*)
Rochester Dr. DA5: Bexl 6F 127
HA5: Pinn 5B 40
Rochester Gdns. CR0: C'don 3E 168
IG1: Ilf 7D 52
Rochester Ho. *SE1* *7F 15*
(*off Manciple St.*)
SE15 *6J 103*
(*off Sharratt St.*)
Rochester M. NW1 7G 65
W5 4C 96
Rochester Pde. TW13: Felt 2J 129
Rochester Pl. NW1 6G 65
Rochester Rd. HA6: Nwood 3H 39
NW1 6G 65
SM5: Cars 4D 166
Rochester Row SW1 3B 18 (4G 101)
Rochester Sq. NW1 7G 65
Rochester St. SW1 2C 18 (3H 101)
Rochester Ter. NW1 6G 65
Rochester Wlk. SE1 4E 14 (1D 102)
Rochester Way DA1: Dart 7K 127
SE3 1K 123
SE9 2A 124
Rochester Way Relief Rd. SE3 1K 123
SE9 4A 124
Roche Wlk. SM5: Cars 6B 154
Rochford *N17* *2E 48*
(*off Griffin Rd.*)
Rochford Av. RM6: Chad H 5C 54
Rochford Cl. E6 2B 88
Rochford Wlk. E8 7G 67
Rochford Way CR0: C'don 6J 155
Rochfort Ho. SE8 5B 104
Rock Av. SW14 3K 115
Rockbourne M. SE23 1K 139
Rockbourne Rd. SE23 1K 139
Rock Circus *3C 12*
(*in Trocadero Cen.*)
Rock Cl. CR4: Mitc 2B 154
Rockell's Pl. SE22 6H 121
Rockfield Ho. *NW4* *4F 45*
(*off Belle Vue Est.*)
SE10 *6E 104*
(*off Welland St.*)

Rockford Av.—Rookfield Av.

Rockford Av. UB6: G'frd 2A **78**
Rock Gdns. RM10: Dag 5H **73**
Rock Gro. Way SE16 4G **103**
(not continuous)
Rockhall Rd. NW2 4F **63**
Rockhall Way NW2 3F **63**
Rockhampton Cl. SE27 4A **138**
Rockhampton Rd. CR2: S Croy 6E **168**
SE27 4A **138**
Rock Hill SE26 4F **139**
(not continuous)
Rockingham Cl. SW15 4B **116**
Rockingham St. SE1 3C **102**
Rockland Rd. SW15 4G **117**
Rocklands Dr. HA7: Stan 2B **42**
Rockley Ct. *W14* *2F 99*
(off Rockley Rd.)
Rockley Rd. W14 2F **99**
Rockmount Rd. SE18 5K **107**
SE19 6D **138**
Rocks La. SW13 1C **116**
Rock St. N4 2A **66**
Rockware Av. UB6: G'frd 1H **77**
Rockware Av. Bus. Cen. UB6: G'frd 1H **77**
Rockwell Gdns. SE19 5E **138**
Rockwell Rd. RM10: Dag 5H **73**
Rockwood Pl. W12 2E **98**
Rocliffe St. N1 2B **84**
Rocombe Cres. SE23 7J **121**
Rocque Ho. *SW6* *7H 99*
(off Estcourt Rd.)
Rocque La. SE3 3H **123**
Rodale Mans. SW18 6K **117**
Rodborough Ct. *W9* *4J 81*
(off Hermes Cl.)
Rodborough Rd. NW11 1J **63**
Rodd Est. TW17: Shep 5E **146**
Roden Ct. N6 7H **47**
Roden Gdns. CR0: C'don 6E **156**
Rodenhurst Rd. SW4 6G **119**
Roden St. IG1: Ilf 3E **70**
N7 3K **65**
Roden Way *IG1: Ilf* *3E 70*
(off Roden St.)
Roderick Ho. *SE16* *4J 103*
(off Raymouth Rd.)
Roderick Rd. NW3 4D **64**
Rodgers Ho. *SW4* *7H 119*
(off Clapham Pk. Est.)
Rodin Ct. *N1* *1B 84*
(off Essex Rd.)
Roding Av. IG8: Wfd G 6H **37**
Roding Ho. *N1* *1A 84*
(off Barnsbury Est.)
Roding La. IG7: Chig 2K **37**
IG9: Buck H 1G **37**
Roding La. Nth. IG8: Wfd G 6H **37**
Roding La. Sth. IG4: Ilf, Wfd G 4B **52**
(not continuous)
IG8: Wfd G 4B **52**
Roding M. E1 1G **103**
Roding Rd. E5 4K **67**
E6 5F **89**
Rodings, The IG8: Wfd G 6F **37**
Rodings Row *EN5: Barn* *4B 20*
(off Leecroft Rd.)
Roding Trad. Est. IG11: Bark 7F **71**
Roding Valley Meadows Nature Reserve 1K **37**
Roding Vw. IG9: Buck H 1G **37**
Rodmarton St. W1 6F **5** (5D **82**)
Rodmell *WC1* *2F 7*
(off Regent Sq.)
Rodmell Cl. UB4: Yead 4C **76**
Rodmell Slope N12 5C **30**
Rodmere St. SE10 5G **105**
Rodmill La. SW2 7J **119**
Rodney Cl. CR0: C'don 1B **168**
HA5: Pinn 7C **40**
KT3: N Mald 5A **152**
Rodney Ct. EN5: Barn 3C **20**
W9 3A **4** (4A **82**)
Rodney Gdns. BR4: W W'ck 4J **171**
HA5: Eastc 5K **39**
Rodney Ho. *E14* *4D 104*
(off Cahir St.)
N1 *2K 83*
(off Donegal St.)
Rodney Ho. *SW1* *6B 18*
(off Dolphin Sq.)
W11 *7J 81*
(off Pembridge Cres.)
Rodney Pl. E17 2A **50**
SE17 4C **102**
SW19 1A **154**
Rodney Point *SE16* *2B 104*
(off Rotherhithe St.)
Rodney Rd. CR4: Mitc 3C **154**
E11 4K **51**
KT3: N Mald 5A **152**
SE17 4C **102**
(not continuous)
TW2: Whitt 6E **112**
Rodney St. N1 1H **7** (2K **83**)
Rodney Way RM7: Mawney 1H **55**
SL3: Poyle 4A **174**
Rodway Rd. BR1: Brom 1K **159**
SW15 7C **116**
Rodwell Cl. HA4: Ruis 1A **58**
Rodwell Pl. HA8: Edg 6B **28**
Rodwell Rd. SE22 6F **121**
Roe NW9 7G **29**
Roebourne Way E16 1E **106**
Roebuck Cl. N17 6A **34**
TW13: Felt 4K **129**
Roebuck Hgts. IG9: Buck H 1F **37**
Roebuck La. IG9: Buck H 1F **37**
Roebuck Rd. KT9: Chess 5G **163**
Roedean Av. EN3: Enf H 1D **24**
Roedean Cl. EN3: Enf H 1D **24**
Roedean Cres. SW15 6A **116**
Roe End NW9 4J **43**
ROE GREEN 5J **43**
Roe Grn. NW9 5J **43**
ROEHAMPTON 7C **116**
Roehampton Cl. SW15 4C **116**
Roehampton Dr. BR7: Chst 6G **143**
Roehampton Ga. SW15 6A **116**
Roehampton High St. SW15 7C **116**
ROEHAMPTON LANE 1D **134**
Roehampton La. SW15 4C **116**
Roehampton Sport & Fitness Cen. 7C **116**
Roehampton University 6B **116**
Roehampton Va. SW15 3B **134**
Roe La. NW9 4H **43**
Roe Way SM6: Wall 6J **167**
Roffey St. E14 2E **104**
Rogate Ho. E5 3G **67**
Roger Bannister Sports Cen., The 6B **26**
Roger Dowley Ct. E2 2J **85**
Roger Harriss Almshouses *E15* *1H 87*
(off Gift La.)
Roger Reede's Almshouses
RM1: Rom 4K **55**
Rogers Ct. *E14* *7C 86*
(off Premiere Pl.)
Rogers Est. E2 3J **85**
(not continuous)
Rogers Gdns. RM10: Dag 5G **73**
Rogers Ho. RM10: Dag 3G **73**
SW1 *3D 18*
(off Page St.)
Rogers Rd. E16 6H **87**
RM10: Dag 5G **73**
SW17 4B **136**
Rogers Ruff HA6: Nwood 1E **38**
Roger St. WC1 4H **7** (4K **83**)
Rogers Wlk. N12 3E **30**
Rohere Ho. EC1 1C **8** (3C **84**)
Rojack Rd. SE23 1K **139**
Rokeby Gdns. IG8: Wfd G 1J **51**
Rokeby Ho. *SW12* *7F 119*
(off Lochinvar St.)
Rokeby Ho. *WC1* *4G 7*
(off Millman M.)
Rokeby Pl. SW20 7D **134**
Rokeby Rd. HA1: Harr 3H **41**
SE4 2B **122**
Rokeby St. E15 1F **87**
Rokell Ho. *BR3: Beck* *5D 140*
(off Beckenham Hill Rd.)
Roker Pk. Av. UB10: Ick 4A **56**
Rokesby Cl. DA16: Well 2H **125**
Rokesby Pl. HA0: Wemb 5D **60**
Rokesly Av. N8 5J **47**
Roland Gdns. SW7 5A **16** (5A **100**)
Roland Ho. *SW7* *5A 16*
(off Old Brompton Rd.)
Roland Mans. *SW7* *5A 100*
(off Old Brompton Rd.)
Roland M. E1 5K **85**
Roland Rd. E17 4F **51**
Roland Way KT4: Wor Pk 2B **164**
SE17 5D **102**
SW7 5A **16** (5A **100**)
Roles Gro. RM6: Chad H 4D **54**
Rolfe Cl. EN4: E Barn 4H **21**
Rolinsden Way BR2: Kes 5B **172**
Rolland Ho. W7 5J **77**
Rollesby Rd. KT9: Chess 6G **163**
Rollesby Way SE28 6C **90**
Rolleston Av. BR5: Pet W 6F **161**
Rolleston Cl. BR5: Pet W 7F **161**
Rolleston Rd. CR2: S Croy 7D **168**
Roll Gdns. IG2: Ilf 5E **52**
Rollins St. SE15 6J **103**
Rollit Cres. TW3: Houn 5E **112**
Rollit St. N7 5A **66**
Rolls Bldgs. EC4 7J **7** (6A **84**)
Rollscourt Av. SE24 5C **120**
Rolls Pk. Av. E4 5H **35**
Rolls Pk. Rd. E4 5J **35**
Rolls Pas. EC4 7J **7**
Rolls Rd. SE1 5F **103**
Rolls Royce Cl. SM6: Wall 7J **167**
Rolt St. SE8 6A **104**
(not continuous)
Rolvenden Gdns. BR1: Brom 7B **142**
Rolvenden Pl. N17 1G **49**
Roman Cl. RM13: Rain 2K **91**
TW14: Felt 5A **112**
W3 2H **97**
Roman Ct. N7 6K **65**
Romanfield Rd. SW2 7K **119**
Roman Ho. EC2 6D **8**
RM13: Rain 2K **91**
Romanhurst Av. BR2: Brom 4G **159**
Romanhurst Gdns. BR2: Brom 4G **159**
Roman Ind. Est. CR0: C'don 7E **156**
Roman Ri. SE19 6D **138**
Roman Rd. E2 3J **85**
E3 2A **86**
E6 4B **88**
IG1: Ilf 6F **71**
N10 7A **32**
NW2 3E **62**
W4 4A **98**
Roman Sq. SE28 1A **108**
Roman Way CR0: C'don 2B **168**
EN1: Enf 5A **24**
N7 6K **65**
SE15 7J **103**
Roman Way Ind. Est. *N7* *7K 65*
(off Roman Way)
Romany Gdns. E17 1A **50**
SM3: Sutt 7J **153**
Romany Ri. BR5: Farnb 1G **173**
Roma Read Cl. SW15 7D **116**
Roma Rd. E17 3A **50**
Romayne Ho. SW4 3H **119**
Romberg Rd. SW17 3E **136**
Romborough Gdns. SE13 5E **122**
Romborough Way SE13 5E **122**
Romero Cl. SW9 3K **119**
Romero Sq. SE3 4A **124**
Romeyn Rd. SW16 3K **137**
ROMFORD 5K **55**
Romford Rd. E7 6G **69**
E12 5A **70**
E15 6G **69**
RM5: Col R 1E **54**
Romford Stadium (Greyhound) 6J **55**
Romford St. E1 5G **85**
Romilly Ho. *W11* *7G 81*
(off Wilsham St.)
Romilly Rd. N4 2B **66**
Romilly St. W1 2D **12** (7H **83**)
Romily Ct. SW6 2H **117**
Rommany Rd. SE27 4D **138**
(not continuous)
Romney Cl. HA2: Harr 7E **40**
KT9: Chess 4E **162**
N17 1H **49**
NW11 1A **64**
SE14 7J **103**
TW15: Ashf 5E **128**
Romney Ct. NW3 6C **64**
W12 *2F 99*
(off Shepherd's Bush Grn.)
Romney Dr. BR1: Brom 7B **142**
HA2: Harr 7E **40**
Romney Gdns. DA7: Bex 1F **127**
Romney Ho. *SW1* *2E 18*
(off Marsham St.)
Romney M. W1 5G **5** (5E **82**)
Romney Pde. UB4: Hayes 2F **75**
Romney Rd. KT3: N Mald 6K **151**
SE10 6F **105**
UB4: Hayes 2F **75**
Romney Row *NW2* *2F 63*
(off Brent Ter.)
Romney St. SW1 2E **18** (3J **101**)
Romola Rd. SE24 1B **138**
Romsey Cl. BR6: Farnb 4F **173**
Romsey Gdns. RM9: Dag 1D **90**
Romsey Rd. RM9: Dag 1D **90**
W13 7A **78**
Romside Pl. RM7: Rom 4K **55**
Romulus Ct. TW8: Bford 7D **96**
Ronald Av. E15 3G **87**
Ronald Buckingham Ct. *SE16* *2J 103*
(off Kenning St.)
Ronald Cl. BR3: Beck 4B **158**
Ronald Ct. EN5: New Bar 3E **20**
Ronald Ho. SE3 4A **124**
Ronaldshay N4 7A **48**
Ronalds Rd. BR1: Brom 1J **159**
N5 5A **66**
(not continuous)
Ronaldstone Rd. DA15: Sidc 6J **125**
Ronald St. E1 6J **85**
Rona Rd. NW3 4E **64**
Ronart St. HA3: W'stone 3K **41**
Rona Wlk. *N1* *6D 66*
(off Ramsey Wlk.)
Rondel Ct. DA5: Bexl 6E **126**
Rondu Rd. NW2 5G **63**
Ronelean Rd. KT6: Surb 2F **163**
Ron Grn. Ct. DA8: Erith 6K **109**
Ron Leighton Way E6 1C **88**
Ronnie La. E12 4E **70**
Ron Todd Cl. RM10: Dag 1G **91**
Ronver Rd. SE12 1H **141**
Rood La. EC3 2G **15** (7E **84**)
Roof Ter. Apartments, The *EC1* *4B 8*
(off Gt. Sutton St.)
Rookby Ct. N21 2G **33**
Rook Cl. HA9: Wemb 3H **61**
Rookeries Cl. TW13: Felt 3K **129**
Rookery Cl. NW9 5B **44**
Rookery Cres. RM10: Dag 7H **73**
Rookery Dr. BR7: Chst 1E **160**
Rookery La. BR2: Brom 6B **160**
Rookery Rd. SW4 4G **119**
Rookery Way NW9 5B **44**
Rooke Way SE10 5H **105**
Rookfield Av. N10 4G **47**

Rookfield Cl.—Rossall Cres.

Rookfield Cl. N10 4G 47
Rooksmead Rd. TW16: Sun 2H 147
Rooks Ter. UB7: W Dray 2A 92
Rookstone Rd. SW17 5D 136
Rook Wlk. E6 6B 88
Rookwood Av. KT3: N Mald 4C 152
SM6: Bedd 4H 167
Rookwood Gdns. E4 2C 36
Rookwood Ho. IG11: Bark 2H 89
Rookwood Rd. N16 7F 49
Roosevelt Memorial 2H 11 (7E 82)
Roosevelt Way RM10: Dag 6K 73
Rootes Dr. W10 5F 81
Ropemaker Rd. SE16 2A 104
Ropemaker's Flds. E14 7B 86
Ropemaker St. EC2 5E 8 (5D 84)
Roper La. SE1 7H 15 (2E 102)
Ropers Av. E4 5J 35
Ropers Orchard *SW3* *6C 100*
(off Danvers St.)
Roper St. SE9 5D 124
Ropers Wlk. SW2 7A 120
Roper Way CR4: Mitc 2E 154
Ropery Bus. Pk. SE7 4A 106
Ropery St. E3 4B 86
Rope St. SE16 4A 104
Rope Wlk. TW16: Sun 3A 148
Rope Wlk. Gdns. E1 6G 85
Ropewalk M. *E8* *7G 67*
(off Middleton Rd.)
Ropeworks, The IG11: Bark 1G 89
Rope Yd. Rails SE18 3F 107
Ropley St. E2 2G 85
Rosa Alba M. N5 4C 66
Rosa Av. TW15: Ashf 4C 128
Rosalind Ct. *IG11: Bark* *7A 72*
(off Meadow Rd.)
Rosalind Ho. *N1* *2E 84*
(off Arden Ho.)
Rosaline Rd. SW6 7G 99
Rosaline Ter. *SW6* *7G 99*
(off Rosaline Rd.)
Rosamond St. SE26 3H 139
Rosamund Cl. CR2: S Croy 4D 168
Rosamun St. UB2: S'hall 4C 94
Rosa Parks Ho. *SE17* *4C 102*
(off Munton Rd.)
Rosary Cl. TW3: Houn 2C 112
Rosary Gdns. SW7 4A 100
TW15: Ashf 4D 128
Rosaville Rd. SW6 7H 99
Roscoe St. EC1 4D 8 (4C 84)
(not continuous)
Roscoe St. Est. EC1 4D 8 (4C 84)
Roscoff Cl. HA8: Edg 1J 43
Roseacre Cl. SM1: Sutt 2A 166
TW17: Shep 5C 146
W13 5B 78
Roseacre Rd. DA16: Well 3B 126
Rose All. *EC2* *6H 9*
(off Bishopsgate)
SE1 4D 14 (1C 102)
Rose & Crown Ct. EC2 7D 8
Rose & Crown Pas.
TW7: Isle 1A 114
Rose & Crown Yd. SW1 4B 12 (1G 101)
Roseary Cl. UB7: W Dray 4A 92
Rose Av. CR4: Mitc 1D 154
E18 2K 51
SM4: Mord 5A 154
Rosebank SE20 7H 139
SW6 7E 98
(not continuous)
W3 6K 79
Rosebank Av. HA0: Wemb 4K 59
Rosebank Cl. N12 5H 31
TW11: Tedd 6A 132
Rosebank Gdns. E3 2B 86
W3 6K 79
Rosebank Gro. E17 3B 50
Rosebank Rd. E17 6D 50
W7 2J 95
Rosebank Vs. E17 4C 50
Rosebank Wlk. NW1 7H 65
SE18 4C 106
Rosebank Way W3 6K 79
Rose Bates Dr. NW9 4G 43
Rosebay Ho. *E3* *5C 86*
(off Hawgood St.)
Roseberry Gdns. BR6: Orp 3J 173
N4 6B 48
Roseberry Pl. E8 6F 67
Roseberry St. SE16 4H 103
Rosebery Av. CR7: Thor H 2C 156
DA15: Sidc 7J 125
E12 6C 70
EC1 4J 7 (4A 84)
HA2: Harr 4C 58
KT3: N Mald 2B 152
N17 2G 49
Rosebery Cl. SM4: Mord 6F 153
Rosebery Ct. *EC1* *4J 7*
(off Rosebery Av.)
W1 *4J 11*
(off Charles St.)
Rosebery Gdns. N8 5J 47
SM1: Sutt 4K 165
W13 6A 78
Rosebery Ho. *E2* *2J 85*
(off Sewardstone Rd.)
Rosebery Ind. Pk. N17 2H 49
Rosebery M. N10 2G 47
Rosebery Rd. KT1: King T 2H 151
N10 2G 47
SM1: Sutt 6H 165
SW2 6J 119
TW3: Houn 5G 113
WD23: Bush 1A 26
Rosebery Sq. EC1 4J 7
KT1: King T 2H 151
Rosebine Av. TW2: Twick 7H 113
Rosebury Rd. SW6 2K 117
Rosebury Sq. IG8: Wfd G 7K 37
Rosebury Va. HA4: Ruis 2J 57
Rose Bush Ct. NW3 5D 64
Rose Ct. E1 6K 9
E8 *7F 67*
(off Richmond Rd.)
HA0: Wemb *2E 78*
(off Vicars Bri. Cl.)
HA2: Harr 2G 59
N1 *1B 84*
(off Collin's Yd.)
SE8 4K 103
Rosecourt Rd. CR0: C'don 6K 155
Rosecroft N14 2D 32
Rosecroft Av. NW3 3J 63
Rosecroft Gdns. NW2 3C 62
TW2: Twick 1H 131
Rosecroft Rd. UB1: S'hall 4E 76
Rosecroft Wlk. HA0: Wemb 5D 60
HA5: Pinn 5B 40
Rose Dale BR6: Farnb 2F 173
Rosedale Av. UB3: Hayes 5F 75
Rosedale Cl. HA7: Stan 6G 27
SE2 3B 108
W7 2K 95
Rosedale Ct. HA1: Harr 4K 59
N5 4B 66
Rosedale Dr. RM9: Dag 7B 72
Rosedale Gdns. RM9: Dag 7B 72
Rosedale Ho. N16 1D 66
Rosedale Pl. CR0: C'don 7K 157
Rosedale Rd. E7 5A 70
KT17: Ewe 5C 164
RM1: Rom 2J 55
RM9: Dag 7B 72
TW9: Rich 3E 114
Rosedale Ter. *W6* *3D 98*
(off Dalling Rd.)
Rosedene NW6 1F 81
(not continuous)
Rosedene Av. CR0: C'don 7J 155
SM4: Mord 5J 153
Rosedene Av. SW16 3K 137
UB6: G'frd 3E 76
Rosedene Ct. HA4: Ruis 1G 57
Rosedene Gdns. IG2: Ilf 4E 52
Rosedene Ter. E10 2D 68
Rosedew Rd. W6 6F 99
Rose End KT4: Wor Pk 1F 165
Rosefield Cl. SM5: Cars 5C 166
Rosefield Gdns. E14 7C 86
Roseford Ct. *W12* *2F 99*
(off Shepherd's Bush Grn.)
Rose Gdn. Cl. HA8: Edg 6K 27
Rose Gdns. TW13: Felt 2J 129
UB1: S'hall 4E 76
W5 3D 96
Rosegate Ho. *E3* *2B 86*
(off Hereford Rd.)
Rose Glen NW9 4K 43
RM7: Rush G 1K 73
Rosehart M. W11 6J 81
Rose Hatch Av. RM6: Chad H 3D 54
Roseheath Rd. TW4: Houn 5D 112
ROSEHILL 7A 154
Rose Hill SM1: Sutt 2K 165
Rosehill KT10: Clay 6A 162
TW12: Hamp 1E 148
Rosehill Av. SM1: Sutt 1A 166
Rosehill Ct. *SM4: Mord* *7A 154*
(off St Helier Av.)
Rosehill Ct. Pde. *SM4: Mord* *7A 154*
(off St Helier Av.)
Rosehill Gdns. SM1: Sutt 2K 165
UB6: G'frd 5K 59
Rose Hill Pk. W.
SM1: Sutt 1A 166
Rosehill Rd. SW18 6A 118
ROSE HILL RDBT. 7A 154
Rose Joan M. NW6 4J 63
Rosekey Ct. *SE8* *7B 104*
(off Baildon St.)
Roseland Cl. N17 7J 33
Rose La. RM6: Chad H 3D 54
Rose Lawn WD23: B Hea 1B 26
Roseleigh Av. N5 4B 66
Roseleigh Cl. TW1: Twick 6D 114
Rosemary Av. EN2: Enf 1K 23
KT8: W Mole 3E 148
N2 4K 45
N3 2K 45
N9 1C 34
TW4: Houn 2B 112
Rosemary Branch Theatre *1D 84*
(off Rosemary St.)
Rosemary Cl. CR0: C'don 6J 155
UB8: Hil 5C 74
Rosemary Ct. *SE8* *6B 104*
(off Dorking Cl.)
Rosemary Dr. E14 6F 87
IG4: Ilf 5B 52
Rosemary Gdns.
KT9: Chess 4E 162
RM8: Dag 1F 73
SW14 3J 115
Rosemary Ho. *N1* *1D 84*
(off Branch Pl.)
NW10 *1D 80*
(off Uffington Rd.)
Rosemary La. SW14 3J 115
Rosemary Rd. DA16: Well 1K 125
SE15 7F 103
SW17 3A 136
Rosemary St. N1 1D 84
Rosemead NW9 7B 44
Rosemead Av. CR4: Mitc 3G 155
HA9: Wemb 5E 60
TW13: Felt 2H 129
Rose M. N18 4C 34
Rosemont Av. N12 6F 31
Rosemont Ct. *W3* *1H 97*
(off Rosemont Rd.)
Rosemont Rd. HA0: Wemb 1E 78
KT3: N Mald 3J 151
Rosemont Rd. NW3 6A 64
TW10: Rich 6E 114
W3 7H 79
Rosemoor Ho. *W13* *1A 96*
(off Broadway)
Rosemoor St. SW3 4E 16 (4D 100)
Rosemount *SM6: Wall* *6G 167*
(off Clarendon Rd.)
Rosemount Cl. IG8: Wfd G 6J 37
Rosemount Dr. BR1: Brom 4D 160
Rosemount Point SE23 3K 139
Rosemount Rd. W13 6A 78
Rosenau Cres. SW11 1D 118
Rosenau Rd. SW11 1C 118
Rosendale Rd. SE21 7C 120
SE24 7C 120
Roseneath Av. N21 1G 33
Roseneath Pl. *SW16* *4K 137*
(off Curtis Fld. Rd.)
Roseneath Rd. SW11 6E 118
Roseneath Wlk. EN1: Enf 4K 23
Rosen's Wlk. HA8: Edg 3C 28
Rosenthal Rd. SE6 6D 122
Rosenthorpe Rd. SE15 5K 121
Rose Pk. Cl. UB4: Yead 5A 76
Rosepark Ct. IG5: Ilf 2D 52
Roserton St. E14 2E 104
Rosery, The CR0: C'don 6K 157
Roses, The IG8: Wfd G 7C 36
Rose Sq. SW3 5B 16 (5B 100)
Rose St. EC4 7B 8 (6B 84)
WC2 2E 12 (7J 83)
(not continuous)
Rose Theatre
Bexley 1B 144
Kingston 2D 150
Rosethorn Cl. SW12 7H 119
Rose Tree M. IG8: Wfd G 6H 37
Rosetre Pl. TW12: Hamp 7E 130
Rosetta Cl. *SW8* *7J 101*
(off Kenchester Cl.)
Rosetta Ct. SE19 7E 138
Rosetti Ter. *RM8: Dag* *4B 72*
(off Marlborough Rd.)
Roseveare Rd. SE12 4A 142
Roseville *N21* *1F 33*
(off The Green)
Roseville Av. TW3: Houn 5E 112
Roseville Rd. UB3: Harl 5J 93
Rosevine Rd. SW20 1E 152
Rose Wlk. BR4: W W'ck 2E 170
KT5: Surb 5H 151
Rose Way HA8: Edg 4D 28
SE12 5J 123
Roseway SE21 6D 120
Rosewell Cl. SE20 7H 139
Rosewood KT7: T Ditt 2A 162
Rosewood Av. UB6: G'frd 5A 60
Rosewood Cl. DA14: Sidc 3C 144
Rosewood Ct. BR1: Brom 1A 160
E11 4F 69
KT2: King T 7G 133
RM6: Chad H 5C 54
Rosewood Dr. TW17: Shep 5B 146
Rosewood Gdns. SE13 2E 122
Rosewood Gro. SM1: Sutt 2A 166
Rosewood Ho. SW8 7G 19
Rosewood Sq. W12 6C 80
Rosher Cl. E15 7F 69
Roshni Ho. SW17 6C 136
Rosina St. E9 6K 67
Roskell Rd. SW15 3F 117
Roslin Ho. *E1* *7K 85*
(off Brodlove La.)
Roslin Rd. W3 3H 97
Roslin Way BR1: Brom 5J 141
Roslyn Cl. CR4: Mitc 2B 154
Roslyn Rd. N15 5D 48
Rosmead Rd. W11 7G 81
Rosoman Pl. EC1 3K 7 (4A 84)
Rosoman St. EC1 2K 7 (3A 84)
Rossall Cres. NW10 3F 79

Ross Apartments—Roxwell

Ross Apartments *E16* 7J *87*
(off Seagull La.)
Ross Av. RM8: Dag 2F **73**
Ross Cl. HA3: Hrw W 7B **26**
UB3: Harl 4F **93**
UB5: N'olt 4H **59**
Ross Ct. *E5* 4H *67*
(off Napoleon Rd.)
NW9 3A **44**
SW15 7F **117**
W13 5B *78*
(off Cleveland Rd.)
Rosscourt Mans. *SW1* 1A *18*
(off Buckingham Pal. Rd.)
Rossdale SM1: Sutt 5C **166**
Rossdale Dr. N9 6D **24**
NW9 1J **61**
Rossdale Rd. SW15 4E **116**
Rosse Gdns. SE13 6F **123**
Rosse M. SE3 1K **123**
Rossendale St. E5 2H **67**
Rossendale Way NW1 7G **65**
Rossetti Ct. *WC1* 5C *6*
(off Ridgmount Pl.)
Rossetti Gdn. Mans. SW3 7E **16**
Rossetti Ho. *SW1* 4D *18*
(off Erasmus St.)
Rossetti M. NW8 1B **82**
Rossetti Rd. SE16 5H **103**
Rossetti Studios *SW3* 7D *16*
(off Flood St.)
Ross Haven Pl. HA6: Nwood 1H **39**
Ross Ho. *E1* 1H *103*
(off Prusom St.)
Rossignol Gdns. SM5: Cars 2E **166**
Rossindel Rd. TW3: Houn 5E **112**
Rossington Cl. EN1: Enf 1C **24**
Rossington St. E5 2G **67**
Rossiter Cl. SE19 7C **138**
Rossiter Flds. EN5: Barn 6B **20**
Rossiter Gro. SW9 3A **120**
Rossiter Rd. SW12 1F **137**
Rossland Cl. DA6: Bex 5H **127**
Rosslyn Av. E4 2C **36**
EN4: E Barn 6H **21**
RM8: Dag 7F **55**
SW13 3A **116**
TW14: Felt 6J **111**
Rosslyn Cl. BR4: W W'ck 3H **171**
TW16: Sun 6G **129**
UB3: Hayes 5F **75**
Rosslyn Cres. HA1: Harr 4K **41**
HA9: Wemb 4E **60**
Rosslyn Gdns. *HA9: Wemb* 3E *60*
(off Rosslyn Cres.)
Rosslyn Hill NW3 4B **64**
Rosslyn Mans. *NW6* 7A *64*
(off Goldhurst Ter.)
Rosslyn M. NW3 4B **64**
Rosslyn Pk. M. NW3 5B **64**
Rosslyn Rd. E17 4E **50**
IG11: Bark 7H **71**
TW1: Twick 6C **114**
Rossmore Cl. EN3: Pond E 4E **24**
NW1 4D *4*
(off Rossmore Rd.)
Rossmore Ct. NW1 3E **4** (4D **82**)
Rossmore Rd. NW1 4D **4** (4C **82**)
Ross Pde. SM6: Wall 6F **167**
Ross Rd. SE25 3D **156**
SM6: Wall 5G **167**
TW2: Whitt 1F **131**
Ross Wlk. SE27 4D **138**
Ross Way SE9 3C **124**
Rosswood Gdns. SM6: Wall 6G **167**
Rostella Rd. SW17 4B **136**
Rostrevor Av. N15 6F **49**
Rostrevor Gdns. UB2: S'hall 5C **94**
UB3: Hayes 1G **93**
Rostrevor Mans. *SW6* 1H *117*
(off Rostrevor Rd.)
Rostrevor M. SW6 1H **117**
Rostrevor Rd. SW6 1H **117**
SW19 5J **135**
Rotary St. SE1 7A **14** (3B **102**)
Rothay *NW1* 1K *5*
(off Albany St.)
Rothbury Cotts. SE10 4G **105**
Rothbury Gdns. TW7: Isle 7A **96**
Rothbury Rd. E9 7B **68**
Rothbury Wlk. N17 7B **34**
Rotheley Ho. *E9* 7J *67*
(off Balcorne St.)
Rotherfield Ct. *N1* 7D *66*
(off Rotherfield St., not continuous)
Rotherfield Rd. SM5: Cars 4E **166**
Rotherfield St. N1 7C **66**
Rotherham Wlk. SE1 5A **14**
Rotherhill Av. SW16 6H **137**
ROTHERHITHE 2J **103**
Rotherhithe Bus. Est. SE16 4H **103**
Rotherhithe New Rd. SE16 5H **103**
Rotherhithe Old Rd. SE16 4K **103**
Rotherhithe St. SE16 2J **103**
Rotherhithe Tunnel SE16 1K **103**
Rother Ho. SE15 4H **121**
Rotherwick Hill W5 4F **79**
Rotherwick Ho. *E1* 7G *85*
(off Thomas More St.)
Rotherwick Rd. NW11 7J **45**
Rotherwood Cl. SW20 1G **153**
Rotherwood Rd. SW15 3F **117**
Rothery St. *N1* 1B *84*
(off St Marys Path)
Rothery Ter. *SW9* 7B *102*
(off Foxley Rd.)
Rothesay Av. SW20 2G **153**
TW10: Rich 4H **115**
UB6: G'frd 6G **59**
(not continuous)
Rothesay Ct. *SE6* 2H *141*
(off Cumberland Pl.)
SE11 7J **19**
SE12 3K **141**
Rothesay Rd. SE25 4D **156**
Rothley Ct. *NW8* 3A *4*
(off St John's Wood Rd.)
Rothsay Rd. E7 7A **70**
Rothsay St. SE1 3E **102**
Rothsay Wlk. *E14* 4C *104*
(off Charnwood Gdns.)
Rothschild Rd. W4 4J **97**
Rothschild St. SE27 4B **138**
Roth Wlk. N7 2K **65**
Rothwell Ct. HA1: Harr 5K **41**
Rothwell Gdns. RM9: Dag 7C **72**
Rothwell Ho. TW5: Hest 6E **94**
Rothwell Rd. RM9: Dag 1C **90**
Rothwell St. NW1 1D **82**
Rotten Row NW3 1A **64**
SW1 6B **10** (2B **100**)
SW7 6B **10** (2B **100**)
Rotterdam Dr. E14 3E **104**
Rotunda, The *RM7: Rom* 5K *55*
(off Yew Tree Gdns.)
Rotunda Cen., The 2E **150**
Rotunda Ct. *BR1: Brom* 5K *141*
(off Burnt Ash La.)
Rouel Rd. SE16 3G **103**
(Dockley Rd.)
SE16 4G **103**
(Southwark Pk. Rd.)
Rougemont Av. SM4: Mord 6J **153**
Roundabout Ho. HA6: Nwood 1J **39**
Roundacre SW19 2F **135**
Roundaway Rd. IG5: Ilf 1D **52**
Roundel Cl. SE4 4B **122**
Round Gro. CR0: C'don 7K **157**
Roundhay Cl. SE23 2K **139**
Roundhedge Way EN2: Enf 1E **22**
Round Hill SE26 2J **139**
(not continuous)
Roundhill Dr. EN2: Enf 4E **22**
Roundhouse, The 7E **64**
ROUNDSHAW 7J **167**
Roundtable Rd. BR1: Brom 3H **141**
Roundtree Rd. HA0: Wemb 5B **60**
Roundway, The KT10: Clay 6A **162**
N17 1C **48**
Roundways HA4: Ruis 3H **57**
Roundwood BR7: Chst 2F **161**
Roundwood Av.
UB11: Stock P 1E **92**
Roundwood Cl. HA4: Ruis 7F **39**
Roundwood Ct. E2 3K **85**
Roundwood Rd. NW10 6B **62**
Rounton Rd. E3 4C **86**
Roupell Ho. *KT2: King T* 7F *133*
(off Florence Rd.)
Roupell Rd. SW2 1K **137**
Roupell St. SE1 5K **13** (1A **102**)
Rousden St. NW1 7G **65**
Rouse Gdns. SE21 4E **138**
Rous Rd. IG9: Buck H 1H **37**
Routemaster Cl. E13 3K **87**
Routh Ct. TW14: Bedf 1F **129**
Routh Rd. SW18 7C **118**
Routh St. E6 5D **88**
Rover Ho. *N1* 1E *84*
(off Mill Row)
Rowallan Rd. SW6 7G **99**
Rowallen Pde. RM8: Dag 1C **72**
Rowan N10 2F **47**
Rowan Av. E4 6G **35**
Rowan Cl. HA0: Wemb 3A **60**
HA7: Stan 6E **26**
IG1: Ilf 5H **71**
KT3: N Mald 2A **152**
SW16 1G **155**
W5 2E **96**
Rowan Ct. *E13* 2K *87*
(off High St.)
SE15 7F *103*
(off Garnies Cl.)
SW11 6D **118**
Rowan Cres. SW16 1G **155**
Rowan Dr. NW9 3C **44**
Rowan Gdns. CR0: C'don 3F **169**
Rowan Ho. BR2: Brom 2G **159**
DA14: Sidc 3K **143**
E3 1B *86*
(off Hornbeam Sq.)
IG1: Ilf 5H **71**
SE16 2K *103*
(off Woodland Cres.)
Rowan Lodge *W8* 3K *99*
(off Chantry Sq.)
Rowan Pl. UB3: Hayes 7H **75**
Rowan Rd. DA7: Bex 3E **126**
N2 1C **46**
SW16 2G **155**
TW8: Bford 7B **96**
UB7: W Dray 4A **92**
W6 4F **99**
Rowans, The N13 3G **33**
TW16: Sun 5H **129**
Rowans Complex 2A **66**
Rowan Ter. W6 4F **99**
Rowantree Cl. N21 1J **33**
Rowantree Rd. EN2: Enf 2G **23**
N21 1J **33**
Rowan Wlk. BR2: Brom 3D **172**
EN5: New Bar 5E **20**
N2 5A **46**
N19 2G **65**
W10 4G **81**
Rowan Way RM6: Chad H 3C **54**
Rowanwood Av. DA15: Sidc 1A **144**
Rowanwood M. EN2: Enf 2G **23**
Rowben Cl. N20 1E **30**
Rowberry Cl. SW6 7E **98**
Rowcross St. SE1 5F **103**
Rowdell Rd. UB5: N'olt 1E **76**
Rowden Pde. *E4* 6H *35*
(off Chingford Rd.)
Rowden Pk. Gdns. E4 7H **35**
Rowden Rd. BR3: Beck 1A **158**
E4 6J **35**
KT19: Ewe 4H **163**
Rowditch La. SW11 2E **118**
Rowdon Av. NW10 7D **62**
Rowdown Cres. CR0: New Ad 7F **171**
Rowdowns Rd. RM9: Dag 1F **91**
Rowe Gdns. IG11: Bark 2K **89**
Rowe Ho. E9 6J **67**
Rowe La. E9 5J **67**
Rowena Cres. SW11 2C **118**
Rowenhurst Mans. *NW6* 6A *64*
(off Canfield Gdns.)
Rowe Wlk. HA2: Harr 3E **58**
Rowfant Rd. SW17 1E **136**
Rowhill Rd. E5 4H **67**
Rowington Cl. W2 5K **81**
Rowland Av. HA3: Kenton 3C **42**
Rowland Ct. E16 4H **87**
Rowland Gro. SE26 3H **139**
(not continuous)
Rowland Hill Almshouses
TW15: Ashf 5C *128*
(off Feltham Hill Rd.)
Rowland Hill Av. N17 7H **33**
Rowland Hill Ho. SE1 6A **14** (2B **102**)
Rowland Hill St. NW3 5C **64**
Rowlands Av. HA5: Hat E 5A **26**
Rowlands Cl. N6 6E **46**
NW7 7H **29**
Rowlands Rd. RM8: Dag 2F **73**
Rowland Way SW19 1K **153**
TW15: Ashf 7F **129**
Rowley Av. DA15: Sidc 7B **126**
Rowley Cl. HA0: Wemb 7F **61**
Rowley Ct. *EN1: Enf* 5K *23*
(off Wellington Rd.)
Rowley Gdns. N4 7C **48**
Rowley Ho. *SE8* 5C *104*
(off Watergate St.)
Rowley Ind. Pk. W3 3H **97**
Rowley Rd. N15 5C **48**
Rowley Way NW8 1K **81**
Rowlheys Pl. UB7: W Dray 3A **92**
Rowlls Rd. KT1: King T 3F **151**
Rowney Gdns. RM9: Dag 6C **72**
Rowney Rd. RM9: Dag 6B **72**
Rowntree Clifford Cl.
E13 4J **87**
Rowntree Cl. NW6 6J **63**
Rowntree Path SE28 1B **108**
Rowntree Rd. TW2: Twick 1J **131**
Rowse Cl. E15 1E **86**
Rowsley Av. NW4 3E **44**
Rowstock Gdns. N7 5H **65**
Rowton Rd. SE18 7G **107**
Roxborough Av. HA1: Harr 7H **41**
TW7: Isle 7K **95**
Roxborough Hgts. *HA1: Harr* 6J *41*
(off College Rd.)
Roxborough Pk. HA1: Harr 7J **41**
Roxborough Rd. HA1: Harr 5H **41**
Roxbourne Cl. UB5: N'olt 6B **58**
Roxbourne Pk. Miniature Railway 2B **58**
Roxburghe Mans. *W8* 2K *99*
(off Kensington Ct.)
Roxburgh Rd. SE27 5B **138**
Roxburn Way HA4: Ruis 3H **57**
Roxby Pl. SW6 6J **99**
ROXETH 2H **59**
Roxeth Ct. TW15: Ashf 5C **128**
Roxeth Grn. Av. HA2: Harr 3F **59**
UB5: N'olt 5E **58**
Roxeth Gro. HA2: Harr 4F **59**
Roxeth Hill HA2: Harr 2H **59**
Roxford Cl. TW17: Shep 5G **147**
Roxford Ho. *E3* 4D *86*
(off Devas St.)
Roxley Rd. SE13 6D **122**
Roxton Gdns. CR0: Addtn 5C **170**
Roxwell *NW1* 6F *65*
(off Hartland Rd.)

Roxwell Rd. IG11: Bark 2A 90
  W12 ....2C 98
Roxwell Trad. Pk. E10 ....7A 50
Roxwell Way IG8: Wfd G 7F 37
Roxy Av. RM6: Chad H 7C 54
Royal Academy of Arts
  Burlington House 3A 12 (7G 83)
Royal Academy of Music Mus. 4H 5
Royal Air Force Memorial 1J 101
Royal Albert Hall 7A 10 (2B 100)
Royal Albert Rdbt. E16 ....7C 88
  (off Royal Albert Way)
Royal Albert Way E16 ....7B 88
Royal Arc. W1 ....3A 12
Royal Archer SE14 ....7K 103
  (off Egmont St.)
ROYAL ARSENAL WEST 3F 107
Royal Av. KT4: Wor Pk 2A 164
  SW3 ....5E 16 (5D 100)
Royal Av. Ho. SW3 ....5E 16
  (off Royal Av.)
Royal Belgrave Ho. SW1 ....4K 17
  (off Hugh St.)
Royal Botanic Gdns. 1E 114
Royal Brass Foundry 3F 107
Royal Carriage M. SE18 ....3F 107
Royal Ceremonial Dress Collection, The
.........1K 99
  (in Kensington Palace)
Royal Cir. SE27 ....3A 138
Royal Cl. BR6: Farnb 4F 173
  IG3: Ilf 7A 54
  KT4: Wor Pk 2A 164
  N16 ....1E 66
  SE8 ....6B 104
  SW19 ....3F 135
  UB8: Hil 6B 74
Royal College of Art 7A 10 (2B 100)
Royal College of Music 1A 6 (3B 100)
Royal College of Obstetricians &
  Gynaecologists 3E 4 (4D 82)
Royal College of Physicians 3J 5
Royal College of Surgeons 7H 7
Royal Coll. St. NW1 ....7G 65
Royal Connaught Apartments E16 ....1B 106
  (off Connaught Rd.)
Royal Ct. EC3 ....1F 15
  (off Cornhill)
  EN1: Enf 6K 23
  HA4: Ruis 6J 39
  SE9 ....1D 142
  SE16 ....3B 104
Royal Courts of Justice 1H 13
Royal Court Theatre 4G 17
  (off Sloane Sq.)
Royal Cres. HA4: Ruis 4C 58
  IG2: Ilf 6H 53
  W11 ....1F 99
Royal Cres. M. W11 ....1F 99
Royal Docks Rd. E6 ....6F 89
  IG11: Bark 6F 89
Royal Dr. N11 ....5K 31
Royal Duchess M. SW12 ....7F 119
Royale Leisure Pk. W3 ....4G 79
Royal Exchange 1F 15 (6D 84)
Royal Exchange Av. EC3 ....1F 15
Royal Exchange Bldgs. EC3 ....1F 15
Royal Festival Hall 5H 13 (1K 101)
Royal Fusiliers Mus. ....
  (in The Tower of London)
Royal Gdns. W7 ....3A 96
Royal Geographical Society 7A 10
Royal Herbert Pavilions SE18 ....1D 124
Royal Hill SE10 ....7E 104
Royal Hill Ct. SE10 ....7E 104
  (off Greenwich High St.)
Royal Holloway University of London ...5D 6
Royal Hospital Chelsea Mus.
.........6G 17 (5E 100)
Royal Hospital Rd. SW3 ....7E 16 (6D 100)
Royal Institution Faraday Mus.
.........3A 12 (7G 83)

Royal La. UB7: Yiew 5B 74
  UB8: Hil 5B 74
Royal London Bldgs. SE15 ......6H 103
  (off Old Kent Rd.)
Royal London Est., The N17 ......6C 34
Royal London Hospital Archives & Mus.
.........5H 85
  (off Newark St.)
Royal London Ind. Est. NW10 .....2K 79
Royal Mews, The 1K 17 (2F 101)
Royal M. KT8: E Mos 3J 149
  SW1 .....1K 17 (3F 101)
Royal Mid Surrey Golf Course 3D 114
Royal Mint Ct. EC3 .....3K 15 (7F 85)
Royal Mint Pl. E1 .....2K 15 (7G 85)
Royal Mint St. E1 .....2K 15 (7F 85)
Royal Naval Pl. SE14 ....7B 104
Royal Oak Ct. N1 ....1G 9
  (off Pitfield St.)
Royal Oak M. TW11: Tedd 5A 132
Royal Oak Pl. SE22 ....6H 121
Royal Oak Rd. DA6: Bex 5F 127
  (not continuous)
  E8 ....6H 67
Royal Oak Yd. SE1 ....7G 15 (2E 102)
Royal Observatory Greenwich 7G 105
Royal Opera Arc. SW1 ....4C 12 (1H 101)
Royal Opera House 1F 13 (6J 83)
Royal Orchard Cl. SW18 ....7G 117
Royal Pde. BR7: Chst 7G 143
  RM10: Dag 6H 73
  SE3 ....2H 123
  SW6 ....7G 99
  TW9: Kew 1G 115
  W5 ....3E 78
Royal Pde. M. BR7: Chst 7G 143
  (off Royal Pde.)
  SE3 ....2H 123
Royal Pl. SE10 ....7E 104
Royal Quarter KT2: King T 1E 150
Royal Quay Rd. E16 ....7F 89
Royal Rd. DA14: Sidc 3D 144
  E16 ....6B 88
  SE17 ....6B 102
  TW11: Tedd 5H 131
Royal Route HA9: Wemb 4F 61
Royal St. SE1 .....1H 19 (3K 101)
Royal Twr. Lodge E1 ....3K 15
  (off Cartwright St.)
Royalty Mans. W1 ....1C 12
  (off Meard St.)
Royalty M. W1 .....1C 12 (6H 83)
Royalty Studios W11 ....6G 81
  (off Lancaster Rd.)
Royal Veterinary College
  Camden Town 1H 83
Royal Victoria Docks Watersports Cen.
.........7J 87
Royal Victoria Patriotic Bldg.
  SW18 ....6B 118
Royal Victoria Pl. E16 ....1K 105
Royal Victoria Sq. E16 ....7K 87
Royal Victor Pl. E3 ....2K 85
Royal Wlk. SM6: Wall 2F 167
Royal Westminster Lodge SW1 ....3C 18
  (off Elverton St.)
Roycraft Av. IG11: Bark 2K 89
Roycroft Cl. E18 ....1K 51
  SW2 ....1A 138
Roydene Rd. SE18 ....6J 107
Roydon Cl. IG10: Lough 1H 37
  SW11 ....2D 118
  (off Battersea Pk. Rd.)
Roy Gdns. IG2: Ilf 4J 53
Roy Gro. TW12: Hamp 6F 131
Royle Bldg. N1 ....2C 84
  (off Wenlock Rd.)
Royle Cres. W13 ....4A 78
Royley Ho. EC1 ....3D 8
  (off Whitecross St.)

Roymount Ct. TW2: Twick 3J 131
Roy Rd. HA6: Nwood 1H 39
Roy Sq. E14 ....7A 86
Royston Av. E4 ....4H 35
  SM1: Sutt 3B 166
  SM6: Bedd 4H 167
Royston Cl. KT12: Walt T 7J 147
  TW5: Cran 1K 111
Royston Ct. E13 ....1J 87
  (off Stopford Rd.)
  SE24 ....6C 120
  TW9: Kew 1F 115
  W8 ....1J 99
  (off Kensington Chu. St.)
Royston Gdns. IG1: Ilf 6B 52
Royston Ho. N11 ....4J 31
  SE15 ....6H 103
  (off Friary Est.)
Royston Pde. IG1: Ilf 6B 52
Royston Pk. Rd. HA5: Hat E 5A 26
Royston Rd. SE20 ....1K 157
  TW10: Rich 5E 114
Roystons, The KT5: Surb 5H 151
Royston St. E2 ....2J 85
Rozel Cl. N1 ....1E 84
Rozel Rd. SW4 ....3G 119
Rozel Ter. CRO: C'don 2C 168
  (off Church Rd.)
RQ33 SW18 ....4J 117
Rubastic Rd. UB2: S'hall 3A 94
Rubens Gdns. SE22 ....7G 121
  (off Lordship La.)
Rubens Pl. SW4 ....4J 119
Rubens Rd. UB5: N'olt 2A 76
Rubens St. SE6 ....2B 140
Ruby Rd. E17 ....3C 50
Ruby St. NW10 ....7K 61
  SE15 ....6H 103
Ruby Triangle SE15 ....6H 103
Ruby Way NW9 ....1B 44
Ruckholt Cl. E10 ....3D 68
Ruckholt Rd. E10 ....4C 68
Rucklidge Av. NW10 ....2B 80
Rucklidge Pas. NW10 ....2B 80
  (off Rucklidge Av.)
Rudall Cres. NW3 ....4B 64
Rudbeck Ho. SE15 ....7G 103
  (off Peckham Pk. Rd.)
Ruddington Cl. E5 ....4A 68
Ruddock Cl. HA8: Edg 7D 28
Ruddstreet Cl. SE18 ....4F 107
Ruddy Way NW7 ....6G 29
Rudge Ho. SE16 ....3G 103
  (off Jamaica Rd.)
Rudgwick Cl. SE18 ....4C 106
  (off Woodville St., not continuous)
Rudgwick Ter. NW8 ....1C 82
Rudland Rd. DA7: Bex 3H 127
Rudloe Rd. SW12 ....7G 119
Rudolf Pl. SW8 .....7F 19 (6J 101)
Rudolph Rd. E13 ....2H 87
  NW6 ....2J 81
Rudstone Ho. E3 ....3D 86
  (off Bromley High St.)
Rudyard Ct. SE1 ....2D 102
  (off Kipling St.)
Rudyard Gro. NW7 ....6D 28
Ruegg Ho. SE18 ....6E 106
  (off Woolwich Comn.)
Ruffetts, The CR2: Sels 7H 169
Ruffetts Cl. CR2: Sels 7H 169
Ruffle Cl. UB7: W Dray 2A 92
Rufford Cl. HA3: Kenton 6A 42
Rufford St. N1 ....1J 83
Rufford St. M. N1 ....7J 65
Rufford Twr. W3 ....1H 97
Rufforth Cl. NW9 ....1A 44
  (off Pageant Av.)
Rufus Bus. Cen. SW18 ....2K 135
Rufus Cl. HA4: Ruis 3C 58
Rufus Ho. SE1 ....7K 15
  (off St Saviour's Est.)

Rufus St. N1 .....2G 9 (3E 84)
Rugby Av. HA0: Wemb 5B 60
  N9 ....1A 34
  UB6: G'frd 6H 59
Rugby Cl. HA1: Harr 4J 41
Rugby Gdns. RM9: Dag 6C 72
  (off Bishop King's Rd.)
Rugby Rd. NW9 ....4H 43
  RM9: Dag 7B 72
  TW1: Twick 5J 113
  W4 ....2A 98
Rugby St. WC1 .....4G 7 (4K 83)
Rugg St. E14 ....7C 86
Rugless Ho. E14 ....2E 104
  (off E. Ferry Rd.)
Rugmere NW1 ....7E 64
  (off Ferdinand St.)
RUISLIP 1G 57
Ruislip Cl. UB6: G'frd 4F 77
RUISLIP COMMON 4E 38
Ruislip Ct. HA4: Ruis 2H 57
RUISLIP GARDENS 3J 57
Ruislip Lido Railway
  Eleanor's Station 3G 39
  Haste Hill Station 3G 39
  Lakeside Station 4F 39
  Woody Bay Station 5F 39
RUISLIP MANOR 2J 57
Ruislip Rd. UB1: S'hall 2B 76
  UB5: N'olt 1A 76
  UB6: G'frd 3E 76
Ruislip Rd. E. UB6: G'frd 4H 77
  W7 ....4H 77
  W13 ....4H 77
Ruislip St. SW17 ....4D 136
Ruislip Woodlands Cen. 4F 39
Ruislip Wood National Nature Reserve
.........3E 38
Rumball Ho. SE5 ....7E 102
  (off Harris St.)
Rumbold Rd. SW6 ....7K 99
Rum Cl. E1 ....7J 85
Rumford Ho. SE1 ....3C 102
  (off Tiverton St.)
Rumney Ct. UB5: N'olt 2B 76
  (off Parkfield Dr.)
Rumsey Cl. TW12: Hamp 6D 130
Rumsey M. N4 ....3B 66
Rumsey Rd. SW9 ....3K 119
Runacres Ct. SE17 ....5C 102
Runbury Circ. NW9 ....2K 61
Runcorn Cl. N17 ....4H 49
Runcorn Pl. W11 ....7G 81
Rundell Cres. NW4 ....5D 44
Rundell Twr. SW8 ....1K 119
Runes Ct. CR4: Mitc 4B 154
Runnel Ct. IG11: Bark 2A 90
  (off Spring Pl.)
Runnelfield HA1: Harr 3J 59
Running Horse Yd.
  TW8: Bford 6E 96
Runnymede SW19 ....1A 154
Runnymede Cl. TW2: Whitt 6F 113
Runnymede Ct. SM6: Wall 6F 167
  SW15 ....1C 134
Runnymede Cres. SW16 ....1H 155
Runnymede Gdns. TW2: Whitt 6F 113
  UB6: G'frd 2J 77
Runnymede Ho. E9 ....4A 68
Runnymede Rd. TW2: Whitt 6F 113
Runway, The HA4: Ruis 5K 57
Runway Cl. NW9 ....2B 44
Rupack St. SE16 ....2J 103
Rupert Av. HA9: Wemb 5E 60
Rupert Ct. KT8: W Mole 4E 148
  (off St Peters Rd.)
  W1 .....2C 12 (7H 83)
Rupert Gdns. SW9 ....2B 120
Rupert Ho. SE11 .....4K 19 (4A 102)
  SW5 ....1J 99
  (off Nevern Sq.)

Rupert Rd. N19 ... 3H 65
(not continuous)
NW6 ... 2H 81
W4 ... 3A 98
Rupert St. W1 ... 2C 12 (7H 83)
Rural Way SW16 ... 7F 137
Rusbridge Cl. E8 ... 5G 67
Ruscoe Rd. E16 ... 6H 87
Ruscombe *NW1* ... *1F 83*
(off Delancey St.)
Ruscombe Way TW14: Felt ... 7H 111
Rush, The *SW20* ... *1H 153*
(off Watery La.)
Rusham Rd. SW12 ... 6D 118
Rushbridge Cl. CR0: C'don ... 6C 156
Rushbrook Cres. E17 ... 1B 50
Rushbrook Rd. SE9 ... 2G 143
Rushbury Ct. TW12: Hamp ... 1E 148
Rush Comn. M. SW2 ... 7K 119
(Cotherstone Rd.)
SW2 ... 7J 119
(New Pk. Rd.)
Rushcroft Rd. E4 ... 7J 35
SW2 ... 4A 120
Rushcutters Ct. *SE16* ... *4A 104*
(off Boat Lifter Way)
Rushden Cl. SE19 ... 7D 138
Rushdene SE2 ... 3D 108
Rushdene Av. EN4: E Barn ... 7H 21
Rushdene Cl. UB5: N'olt ... 2A 76
Rushdene Cres. UB5: N'olt ... 2K 75
Rushdene Rd. HA5: Eastc ... 6B 40
Rushden Gdns. IG5: Ilf ... 2E 52
NW7 ... 6K 29
Rushen Wlk. SM5: Cars ... 1B 166
Rushett Cl. KT7: T Ditt ... 1B 162
Rushett Rd. KT7: T Ditt ... 7B 150
Rushey Cl. KT3: N Mald ... 4K 151
Rushey Grn. SE6 ... 7D 122
Rushey Hill EN2: Enf ... 4E 22
Rushey Mead SE4 ... 5C 122
Rushford Rd. SE4 ... 6B 122
RUSH GREEN ... 1K 73
Rush Grn. Gdns. RM7: Rush G ... 1J 73
Rush Grn. Rd. RM7: Rush G ... 1H 73
Rushgrove Av. NW9 ... 5A 44
Rushgrove Ct. NW9 ... 5A 44
Rushgrove Pde. NW9 ... 5A 44
Rushgrove St. SE18 ... 4D 106
Rush Hill M. *SW11* ... *3E 118*
(off Rush Hill Rd.)
Rush Hill Rd. SW11 ... 3E 118
Rushley Cl. BR2: Kes ... 4B 172
Rushmead E2 ... 3H 85
TW10: Ham ... 3B 132
Rushmead Cl. CR0: C'don ... 4F 169
HA8: Edg ... 2C 28
Rushmere Ct. KT4: Wor Pk ... 2C 164
Rushmere Pl. SW19 ... 5F 135
Rushmon Pl. SM3: Cheam ... 6G 165
Rushmon Vs. KT3: N Mald ... 4B 152
Rushmoor Cl. HA5: Eastc ... 4K 39
Rushmore Cl. BR1: Brom ... 3C 160
Rushmore Cres. E5 ... 4K 67
Rushmore Ho. SW15 ... 7C 116
W14 ... *3G 99*
(off Russell Rd.)
Rushmore Rd. E5 ... 4J 67
(not continuous)
Rusholme Av. RM10: Dag ... 3G 73
Rusholme Gro. SE19 ... 5E 138
Rusholme Rd. SW15 ... 6F 117
Rushout Av. HA3: Kenton ... 6B 42
Rushton Ho. SW8 ... 2H 119
Rushton St. N1 ... 2D 84
Rushworth St. SE1 ... 6B 14 (2B 102)
Rushy Mdw. La. SM5: Cars ... 2C 166
Ruskin Av. DA16: Well ... 2A 126
E12 ... 6C 70
TW9: Kew ... 7G 97
TW14: Felt ... 6H 111
Ruskin Cl. NW11 ... 6K 45
Ruskin Ct. N21 ... 7E 22
SE5 ... *3D 120*
(off Champion Hill)
Ruskin Dr. BR6: Orp ... 3J 173
DA16: Well ... 3A 126
KT4: Wor Pk ... 2D 164
Ruskin Gdns. HA3: Kenton ... 5F 43
W5 ... 4D 78
Ruskin Gro. DA16: Well ... 2A 126
Ruskin Ho. *CR2: S Croy* ... *5D 168*
(off Selsdon Rd.)
SW1 ... *4D 18*
(off Herrick St.)
Ruskin Mans. *W14* ... *6G 99*
(off Queen's Club Gdns.)
Ruskin Pde. *CR2: S Croy* ... *5D 168*
(off Selsdon Rd.)
Ruskin Pk. Ho. SE5 ... 3D 120
Ruskin Rd. CR0: C'don ... 2B 168
DA17: Belv ... 4G 109
N17 ... 1F 49
SM5: Cars ... 5D 166
TW7: Isle ... 3K 113
UB1: S'hall ... 7C 76
Ruskin Wlk. BR2: Brom ... 6D 160
N9 ... 2B 34
SE24 ... 5C 120
Ruskin Way SW19 ... 1B 154
Rusland Av. BR6: Orp ... 3H 173
Rusland Hgts. HA1: Harr ... 4J 41
Rusland Pk. Rd. HA1: Harr ... 4J 41
Rusper Cl. HA7: Stan ... 4H 27
NW2 ... 3E 62
Rusper Ct. *SW9* ... *2J 119*
(off Clapham Rd.)
Rusper Rd. N17 ... 3C 48
N22 ... 2B 48
RM9: Dag ... 6C 72
Russell Av. N22 ... 2A 48
Russell Chambers *WC1* ... *6F 7*
(off Bury Pl.)
Russell Cl. BR3: Beck ... 3D 158
DA7: Bex ... 4G 127
HA4: Ruis ... 2A 58
NW10 ... 7J 61
SE7 ... 7A 106
W4 ... 6B 98
Russell Ct. E10 ... 7D 50
EN5: New Bar ... 4F 21
N14 ... 6C 22
SE15 ... *2H 121*
(off Heaton Rd.)
SM6: Wall ... *5G 167*
(off Ross Rd.)
SW1 ... 5B 12
SW16 ... 5K 137
WC1 ... 4E 6
Russell Flint Ho. *E16* ... *1K 105*
(off Pankhurst Av.)
Russell Gdns. IG2: Ilf ... 7H 53
N20 ... 2H 31
NW11 ... 6G 45
TW10: Ham ... 2C 132
UB7: Sip ... 5C 92
W14 ... 3G 99
Russell Gdns. M. W14 ... 2G 99
Russell Gro. NW7 ... 5F 29
SW9 ... 7A 102
Russell Ho. *E14* ... *6C 86*
(off Saracen St.)
SW1 ... *5A 18*
(off Cambridge St.)
Russell Kerr Cl. W4 ... 7J 97
Russell La. N20 ... 2H 31
Russell Lodge E4 ... 2K 35
SE1 ... *3D 102*
(off Spurgeon St.)
Russell Mans. *WC1* ... *5F 7*
(off Southampton Row)
Russell Mead HA3: Hrw W ... 1K 41
Russell Pde. *NW11* ... *6G 45*
(off Golders Grn. Rd.)
Russell Pl. NW3 ... 5C 64
SE16 ... 3A 104
SM2: Sutt ... 7K 165
Russell Rd. CR4: Mitc ... 3C 154
E4 ... 4G 35
E10 ... 6D 50
E16 ... 6J 87
E17 ... 3B 50
EN1: Enf ... 1A 24
IG9: Buck H ... 1E 36
KT12: Walt T ... 6J 147
N8 ... 6H 47
N13 ... 6E 32
N15 ... 5E 48
N20 ... 2H 31
NW9 ... 6B 44
SW19 ... 7J 135
TW2: Twick ... 6K 113
TW17: Shep ... 7E 146
UB5: N'olt ... 5G 59
W14 ... 3G 99
Russell's Footpath SW16 ... 5J 137
Russell Sq. WC1 ... 4E 6 (5J 83)
Russell Sq. Mans. *WC1* ... *5F 7*
(off Southampton Row)
Russell St. WC2 ... 2F 13 (7J 83)
Russell's Wharf Flats W10 ... 4H 81
Russell Wlk. TW10: Rich ... 6F 115
Russell Way SM1: Sutt ... 5K 165
Russell Yd. SW15 ... 4G 117
Russet Av. TW17: Shep ... 3G 147
Russet Cl. UB10: Hil ... 4E 74
Russet Cres. N7 ... 5K 65
Russet Dr. CR0: C'don ... 1A 170
Russets Cl. E4 ... 4A 36
Russett Way SE13 ... 2D 122
Russia Dock Rd. SE16 ... 1A 104
Russia La. E2 ... 2J 85
Russia Row EC2 ... 1D 14 (6C 84)
Russia Wlk. SE16 ... 2A 104
Russington Rd. TW17: Shep ... 6F 147
Rusthall Av. W4 ... 4K 97
Rusthall Cl. CR0: C'don ... 6J 157
Rustic Av. SW16 ... 7F 137
Rustic Pl. HA0: Wemb ... 4D 60
Rustic Wlk. *E16* ... *6K 87*
(off Lambert Rd.)
Rustington Wlk. SM4: Mord ... 7H 153
Ruston Av. KT5: Surb ... 7H 151
Ruston Gdns. N14 ... 6K 21
Ruston M. W11 ... 6G 81
Ruston Rd. SE18 ... 3C 106
Ruston St. E3 ... 1B 86
Rust Sq. SE5 ... 7D 102
Rutford Rd. SW16 ... 5J 137
Ruth Cl. HA7: Stan ... 4F 43
Ruth Ct. E3 ... 2A 86
Rutherford Cl. SM2: Sutt ... 6B 166
UB8: Hil ... 4B 74
Rutherford Ho. *E1* ... *4H 85*
(off Brady St.)
HA9: Wemb ... *3J 61*
(off Barnhill Rd.)
Rutherford St. SW1 ... 3C 18 (4H 101)
Rutherford Twr. UB1: S'hall ... 6F 77
Rutherford Way
HA9: Wemb ... 4G 61
WD23: B Hea ... 1C 26
Rutherglen Rd. SE2 ... 6A 108
Rutherwyke Cl. KT17: Ewe ... 6C 164
Ruth Ho. *W10* ... *4G 81*
(off Kensal Rd.)
Ruthin Cl. NW9 ... 6A 44
Ruthin Rd. SE3 ... 6J 105
Ruthven St. E9 ... 1K 85
Rutland Av. DA15: Sidc ... 7A 126
Rutland Cl. DA5: Bexl ... 2D 144
KT9: Chess ... 6F 163
SW14 ... 3H 115
SW19 ... 7C 136
Rutland Ct. BR7: Chst ... 1E 160
EN3: Pond E ... 5C 24
Rutland Ct. *KT1: King T* ... *4D 150*
(off Palace Rd.)
SE5 ... 4D 120
SE9 ... 2G 143
SW7 ... 7D 10
W3 ... 6G 79
Rutland Dr. SM4: Mord ... 6H 153
TW10: Ham ... 1D 132
Rutland Gdns. CR0: C'don ... 4E 168
N4 ... 6B 48
RM8: Dag ... 5C 72
SW7 ... 7D 10 (2C 100)
W13 ... 5A 78
Rutland Gdns. M. SW7 ... 7D 10 (2C 100)
Rutland Ga. BR2: Brom ... 4H 159
DA17: Belv ... 5H 109
SW7 ... 7D 10 (2C 100)
Rutland Ga. M. SW7 ... 7C 10
Rutland Gro. W6 ... 5D 98
Rutland Ho. *UB5: N'olt* ... *6E 58*
(off The Farmlands)
W8 ... *3K 99*
(off Marloes Rd.)
Rutland M. NW8 ... 1K 81
Rutland M. E. SW7 ... 1C 16
Rutland M. Sth. SW7 ... 1C 16
Rutland M. W. SW7 ... 1C 16
Rutland Pk. NW2 ... 6E 62
SE6 ... 2B 140
Rutland Pk. Gdns. *NW2* ... *6E 62*
(off Rutland Pk.)
Rutland Pk. Mans. NW2 ... 6E 62
Rutland Pl. EC1 ... 5B 8 (4B 84)
WD23: B Hea ... 1C 26
Rutland Rd. E7 ... 7B 70
E9 ... 1K 85
E11 ... 5K 51
E17 ... 6C 50
HA1: Harr ... 6G 41
IG1: Ilf ... 3F 71
SW19 ... 7C 136
TW2: Twick ... 2H 131
UB1: S'hall ... 5E 76
UB3: Harl ... 4F 93
Rutland St. SW7 ... 1D 16 (3C 100)
Rutland Wlk. SE6 ... 2B 140
Rutley Cl. SE17 ... 6B 102
Rutlish Rd. SW19 ... 1J 153
Rutter Gdns. CR4: Mitc ... 4A 154
Rutters Cl. UB7: W Dray ... 2C 92
Rutts, The WD23: B Hea ... 1C 26
Rutt's Ter. SE14 ... 1K 121
Ruvigny Gdns. SW15 ... 3F 117
Ruxbury Ct. TW15: Ashf ... 3A 128
RUXLEY ... 7E 144
Ruxley Cl. DA14: Sidc ... 6D 144
KT19: Ewe ... 5H 163
Ruxley Cnr. Ind. Est.
DA14: Sidc ... 6D 144
Ruxley Ct. KT19: Ewe ... 5J 163
Ruxley Cres. KT10: Clay ... 6B 146
Ruxley Gdns. TW17: Shep ... 5E 146
Ruxley La. KT19: Ewe ... 6H 163
Ruxley M. KT19: Ewe ... 5H 163
Ruxley Ridge KT10: Clay ... 7A 162
Ruxley Towers KT10: Clay ... 7A 162
Ryalls Ct. N20 ... 3J 31
Ryan Cl. HA4: Ruis ... 1K 57
SE3 ... 4A 124
Ryan Ct. RM7: Rom ... 6J 55
SW16 ... 7J 137
Ryan Dr. TW8: Bford ... 6A 96
Ryarsh Cres. BR6: Orp ... 4J 173
Rycott Path SE22 ... 7G 121
Rycroft Way N17 ... 3F 49
Ryculff Sq. SE3 ... 2H 123
Rydal Cl. NW4 ... 1G 45
Rydal Ct. HA8: Edg ... 5A 28
HA9: Wemb ... 7F 43
Rydal Cres. UB6: G'frd ... 3B 78
Rydal Dr. BR4: W W'ck ... 2G 171
DA7: Bex ... 1G 127

Rydal Gdns. HA9: Wemb 1C 60
NW9 5A 44
SW15 5A 134
TW3: Houn 6F 113
Rydal Mt. BR2: Brom 4H 159
Rydal Rd. SW16 4H 137
Rydal Water NW1 2A 6 (3G 83)
Rydal Way EN3: Pond E 6D 24
HA4: Ruis 4A 58
Ryde Ho. *NW6* *1J 81*
(off Priory Pk. Rd.)
Rydens Ho. SE9 3A 142
Rydens Rd. KT12: Walt T 7C 148
Ryde Pl. TW1: Twick 6D 114
Ryder Av. E10 7D 50
Ryder Cl. BR1: Brom 5K 141
Ryder Ct. E10 2D 68
SW1 4B 12
Ryder Dr. SE16 5H 103
Ryder Ho. *E1* *4J 85*
(off Colebert Av.)
Ryder M. E9 5J 67
Ryder's Ter. NW8 2A 82
Ryder St. SW1 4B 12 (1G 101)
Ryder Yd. SW1 4B 12 (1G 101)
Ryde Va. Rd. SW12 2G 137
Rydon M. SW19 7E 134
Rydons Cl. SE9 3C 124
Rydon St. N1 1C 84
Rydston Cl. N7 7J 65
Rye, The N14 7C 22
Rye Cl. DA5: Bexl 6H 127
Ryecotes Mead SE21 1E 138
Ryecroft Av. IG5: Ilf 2F 53
TW2: Whitt 7F 113
Ryecroft Rd. BR5: Pet W 6H 161
SE13 5E 122
SW16 6A 138
Ryecroft St. SW6 1K 117
Ryedale SE22 6H 121
Ryefield Av. UB10: Hil 7D 56
Ryefield Ct. HA6: Nwood 2J 39
Ryefield Cres. HA6: Nwood 2J 39
Ryefield Pde. *HA6: Nwood* *2J 39*
(off Joel St.)
Ryefield Path SW15 1C 134
Ryefield Rd. SE19 6C 138
Ryegates *SE15* *2H 121*
(off Caulfield Rd.)
Rye Hill Pk. SE15 4J 121
Rye Ho. *SE16* *2J 103*
(off Swan Rd.)
SW1 *5J 17*
(off Ebury Bri. Rd.)
Ryeland Cl. UB7: Yiew 6A 74
Ryelands Cres. SE12 6A 124
Rye La. SE15 1G 121
Rye Pas. SE15 3G 121
Rye Rd. SE15 4K 121
Rye Wlk. SW15 5F 117
Rye Way HA8: Edg 6A 28
Ryfold Rd. SW19 3J 135
Ryhope Rd. N11 4A 32
Ryland Cl. TW13: Felt 4H 129
Rylandes Rd. NW2 3C 62
Ryland Rd. NW5 6F 65
Rylett Cres. W12 2B 98
Rylett Rd. W12 2B 98
Rylston Rd. N13 3J 33
SW6 6H 99
Rymer Rd. CR0: C'don 7E 156
Rymer St. SE24 6B 120
Rymill St. E16 1E 106
Rysbrack St. SW3 1E 16 (3D 100)
Rythe Cl. KT9: Chess 7C 162
Rythe Ct. KT7: T Ditt 7A 150

S

Saatchi Gallery 5F 17 (5D 100)
Sabah Ct. TW15: Ashf 4C 128
Sabbarton St. E16 6H 87
Sabella Ct. E3 2B 86
Sabine Rd. SW11 3D 118
Sable Cl. TW4: Houn 3A 112
Sable St. N1 7B 66
Sach Rd. E5 2H 67
Sackville Av. BR2: Hayes 1J 171
Sackville Cl. HA2: Harr 3H 59
Sackville Gdns. IG1: Ilf 1D 70
Sackville Ho. SW16 3J 137
Sackville Rd. SM2: Sutt 7J 165
Sackville St. W1 3B 12 (7G 83)
Saddlebrook Pk. TW16: Sun 7G 129
Saddlers Cl. HA5: Hat E 6A 26
Saddlers M. HA0: Wemb 4K 59
KT1: Ham W 1C 150
SW8 1J 119
Saddlescombe Way N12 5D 30
Saddle Yd. W1 4J 11 (1F 101)
Sadler Cl. CR4: Mitc 2D 154
Sadler Ho. *E3* *3D 86*
(off Bromley High St.)
EC1 *1K 7*
(off Spa Grn. Est.)
Sadlers Ga. M. SW15 3E 116
Sadlers Ride KT8: W Mole 2G 149
Sadler's Wells Theatre 1K 7 (3A 84)
Safara Ho. *SE5* *1E 120*
(off Dalwood St.)
Saffron Av. E14 7F 87
Saffron Cl. CR0: C'don 6J 155
NW11 6H 45
Saffron Ct. *E15* *5G 69*
(off Maryland Pk.)
TW14: Bedf 7E 110
Saffron Hill EC1 5K 7 (5A 84)
Saffron Ho. SM2: Sutt 7K 165
TW9: Kew 1H 115
Saffron M. SW19 7G 135
Saffron Rd. RM5: Col R 2K 55
Saffron St. EC1 5K 7 (5A 84)
Saffron Way KT6: Surb 1D 162
Saffron Wharf *SE1* *6K 15*
(off Shad Thames)
Sage Cl. E6 5D 88
Sage M. SE22 5F 121
Sage St. E1 7J 85
Sage Way WC1 2G 7
Sage Yd. KT6: Surb 1F 163
Sahara Ct. UB1: S'hall 7C 76
Saigasso Cl. E16 6B 88
Sailacre Ho. *SE10* *5H 105*
(off Woolwich Rd.)
Sail Ct. *E14* *7F 87*
(off Newport Av.)
Sailmakers Ct. SW6 3A 118
Sail St. SE11 3H 19 (4K 101)
Saimet *NW9* *7G 29*
(off Wiggins Mead)
Sainfoin Rd. SW17 2E 136
Sainsbury Rd. SE19 5E 138
Sainsbury Wing *3D 12*
(in National Gallery)
St Agatha's Dr. KT2: King T 6F 133
St Agatha's Gro. SM5: Cars 1D 166
St Agnes Cl. E9 1J 85
St Agnes Ho. *E3* *2C 86*
(off Ordell Rd.)
St Agnes Pl. SE11 7K 19 (6A 102)
St Agnes Well EC1 3F 9
St Aidans Ct. IG11: Bark 2B 90
St Aidan's Rd. SE22 6H 121
W13 2B 96
St Albans Av. E6 3D 88
TW13: Hanw 5B 130
W4 4K 97
St Albans Cl. NW11 1J 63
St Albans Ct. EC2 6D 8
St Alban's Cres. IG8: Wfd G 7D 36
N22 1A 48
St Albans Farm TW4: Houn 5A 112
St Alban's Gdns. TW11: Tedd 5A 132
St Alban's Gro. SM5: Cars 7C 154
W8 3K 99
St Alban's La. NW11 1J 63
St Albans Mans. *W8* *3K 99*
(off Kensington Ct. Pl.)
St Alban's Pl. N1 1B 84
St Albans Rd.
EN5: Barn 1A 20
IG3: Ilf 1K 71
IG8: Wfd G 7D 36
KT2: King T 6E 132
NW5 3E 64
NW10 1A 80
SM1: Sutt 4H 165
St Alban's St. SW1 3C 12 (7H 83)
St Albans Studios *W8* *3K 99*
(off St Albans Gro.)
St Albans Ter. W6 6G 99
St Albans Vs. NW5 3E 64
St Alfege Pas. SE10 6E 104
St Alfege Rd. SE7 6B 106
St Alphage Ct. NW9 3K 43
St Alphage Gdn. EC2 6D 8 (5C 84)
St Alphage Highwalk EC2 6D 8
St Alphage Ho. EC2 6E 8
St Alphage Wlk. HA8: Edg 2J 43
St Alphege Rd. N9 7D 24
St Alphonsus Rd. SW4 4G 119
St Amunds Cl. SE6 4C 140
St Andrew's Av. HA0: Wemb 4A 60
St Andrews Chambers *W1* *6B 6*
(off Wells St.)
St Andrews Cl. HA4: Ruis 2B 58
HA7: Stan 2C 42
KT7: T Ditt 1B 162
N12 4F 31
NW2 3D 62
SE16 5H 103
SE28 6D 90
SW19 6K 135
TW7: Isle 1J 113
TW17: Shep 4F 147
St Andrews Ct. E17 2A 50
SM1: Sutt 3C 166
SW18 2A 136
St Andrews Dr. HA7: Stan 1C 42
St Andrew's Gro. N16 1D 66
St Andrew's Hill EC4 2B 14 (7B 84)
(not continuous)
St Andrews Ho. *SE16* *3H 103*
(off Southwark Pk. Rd.)
St Andrews Mans. *W1* *6G 5*
(off Dorset St.)
W14 *6G 99*
(off St Andrews Rd.)
St Andrews M. N16 1E 66
SE3 7J 105
SW12 1H 137
St Andrew's Pl. NW1 3K 5 (4F 83)
St Andrews Rd. CR0: C'don 4C 168
DA14: Sidc 3D 144
E11 6G 51
E12 2C 70
E13 3K 87
E17 2K 49
EN1: Enf 3J 23
IG1: Ilf 7D 52
KT6: Surb 6D 150
N9 7D 24
NW9 1K 61
NW10 6D 62
NW11 6H 45
RM7: Rom 6K 55
SM5: Cars 3C 166
UB10: Uxb 1A 74
W3 7A 80
W7 2J 95
W14 6G 99
St Andrews Sq. KT6: Surb 6D 150
W11 6G 81
St Andrew's Twr. *UB1: S'hall* *7G 77*
(off Baird Av.)
St Andrew St. EC4 6K 7 (5A 84)
St Andrews Way E3 4D 86
St Andrew's Wharf SE1 2F 103
St Anna Rd. EN5: Barn 5A 20
St Anne's Cl. N6 3E 64
St Anne's Ct. BR4: W W'ck 4G 171
NW6 1G 81
W1 1C 12 (6H 83)
St Anne's Flats *NW1* *1C 6*
(off Doric Way)
St Anne's Gdns. NW10 3F 79
St Anne's Pas. E14 6B 86
St Anne's Rd. E11 2F 69
HA0: Wemb 5D 60
St Anne's Row E14 6B 86
St Anne's Trad. Est. *E14* *6B 86*
(off St Anne's Row)
St Anne St. E14 6B 86
St Ann's IG11: Bark 1G 89
St Ann's Ct. NW4 3D 44
St Ann's Cres. SW18 6K 117
St Ann's Gdns. NW5 6E 64
St Ann's Hill SW18 5K 117
St Ann's Ho. *WC1* *2J 7*
(off Margery St.)
St Ann's La. SW1 2D 18 (3H 101)
St Ann's Pk. Rd. SW18 6A 118
St Ann's Pas. SW13 3A 116
St Ann's Rd. HA1: Harr 6J 41
IG11: Bark 1G 89
N9 2A 34
N15 5B 48
SW13 2B 116
W11 7F 81
St Ann's Shop. Cen. HA1: Harr 6J 41
St Ann's St. SW1 1D 18 (3H 101)
St Ann's Ter. NW8 2B 82
St Ann's Vs. W11 1F 99
St Ann's Way CR2: S Croy 6B 168
St Anselms Ct. SW16 5J 137
St Anselm's Pl. W1 2J 11 (7F 83)
St Anselm's Rd. UB3: Hayes 2H 93
St Anthony's Av. IG8: Wfd G 6F 37
St Anthony's Cl. E1 1G 103
E9 *6B 68*
(off Wallis Rd.)
SW17 2C 136
St Anthony's Ct. BR6: Farnb 2F 173
SW17 2E 136
St Anthony's Flats *NW1* *2H 83*
(off Aldenham St.)
St Anthony's Way TW14: Felt 4H 111
St Antony's Rd. E7 7K 69
St Arvan's Cl. CR0: C'don 3E 168
St Asaph Rd. SE4 3K 121
St Aubins Ct. N1 1D 84
St Aubyn's Av. SW19 5H 135
TW3: Houn 5E 112
St Aubyn's Cl. BR6: Orp 3K 173
St Aubyn's Gdns. BR6: Orp 2K 173
St Aubyn's Rd. SE19 6F 139
St Audrey Av. DA7: Bex 2G 127
St Augustine's Av. BR2: Brom 5C 160
CR2: S Croy 6C 168
HA9: Wemb 3E 60
W5 2E 78
St Augustine's Ct. *SE1* *5H 103*
(off Lynton Rd.)
St Augustine's Ho. *NW1* *1C 6*
(off Werrington St.)
St Augustine's Mans. *SW1* *4B 18*
(off Bloomburg St.)
St Augustine's Path N5 4C 66
St Augustine's Rd. DA17: Belv 4F 109
NW1 7H 65
St Austell Cl. HA8: Edg 2F 43
St Austell Rd. SE13 2E 122
St Awdry's Rd. IG11: Bark 7H 71
St Awdry's Wlk. IG11: Bark 7G 71
St Barnabas Cl. BR3: Beck 2E 158
SE22 5E 120
St Barnabas Ct. HA3: Hrw W 1G 41

St Barnabas Gdns. KT8: W Mole 5E 148
St Barnabas M. SW1 . . . . .5H 17
  SW1 . . . . .5E 100
    (off St Barnabas St.)
St Barnabas Rd. CR4: Mitc 7E 136
  E17 . . . . .6C 50
  IG8: Wfd G 1K 51
  SM1: Sutt .3B 166
St Barnabas St. SW1 . . . . . .5H 17 (5E 100)
St Barnabas Ter. E9 . . . . .5K 67
St Barnabas Vs. SW1 . . . . .1J 119
St Bartholomew's Cl. SE26 . . . . .4H 139
St Bartholomew's Ct. E6 . . . . .2C 88
    (off St Bartholomew's Rd.)
St Bartholomew's Hospital Mus. 6B 8
St Bartholomew's Rd. E6 . . . . .2D 88
St Benedict's Cl. SW17 . . . . .5E 136
St Benet's Cl. SW17 . . . . .2C 136
St Benet's Gro. SM5: Cars 7A 154
St Benet's Pl. EC3 . . . . .2F 15 (7D 84)
St Bernards CR0: C'don 3E 168
St Bernard's Cl. SE27 . . . . .4D 138
St Bernards Ho. E14 . . . . .3E 104
    (off Galbraith St.)
St Bernard's Rd. E6 . . . . .1B 88
St Blaise Av. BR1: Brom 2K 159
St Botolph Row EC3 . . . . . .1J 15 (6F 85)
St Botolphs E1 . . . . .7J 9
    (off St Botolph St.)
St Botolph St. EC3 . . . . .7J 9 (6F 85)
St Brelades Cl. N1 . . . . .1E 84
St Bride's Av. EC4 . . . . .1A 14
  HA8: Edg .1F 43
St Brides Cl. DA18: Erith 2D 108
St Bride's Crypt Mus. 1A 14
    (off Fleet St.)
St Bride's Ho. E3 . . . . .2C 86
    (off Ordell Rd.)
St Bride's Pas. EC4 . . . . .1A 14
St Bride St. EC4 . . . . .7A 8 (6B 84)
St Catherine's Apartments E3 . . . . . . .3D 86
    (off Bow Rd.)
St Catherines Cl. KT9: Chess 6D 162
  SW17 . . . . .2C 136
St Catherines Ct. TW13: Felt 1J 129
  W4 . . . . .3A 98
St Catherine's Dr. SE14 . . . . .2K 121
St Catherine's Farm Ct. HA4: Ruis 6E 38
St Catherines M. SW3 . . . . .3E 16 (4D 100)
St Catherine's Rd. E4 . . . . .2H 35
  HA4: Ruis .6E 39
St Cecelia's Pl. SE3 . . . . .5J 105
St Cecilia's Cl. SM3: Sutt 1G 165
St Chads Cl. KT6: Surb 7C 150
St Chads Gdns. RM6: Chad H 7E 54
St Chad's Pl. WC1 . . . . .1F 7 (3J 83)
St Chad's Rd. RM6: Chad H 7E 54
St Chad's St. WC1 . . . . .1F 7 (3J 83)
    (not continuous)
St Charles Pl. W10 . . . . .5G 81
St Charles Sq. W10 . . . . .5F 81
St Chloe's Ho. E3 . . . . .2C 86
    (off Ordell Rd.)
St Christopher Rd. UB8: Cowl 6A 74
St Christopher's Cl. TW7: Isle 1J 113
St Christophers Dr. UB3: Hayes 7K 75
St Christopher's Gdns.
  CR7: Thor H 3A 156
St Christopher's Ho. NW1 . . . . .2G 83
    (off Bridgeway St.)
St Christopher's M. SM6: Wall 5G 167
St Christopher's Pl. W1 . . . . .1H 5 (6E 82)
St Clair Cl. IG5: Ilf 2D 52
St Clair Dr. KT4: Wor Pk 3D 164
St Clair Ho. E3 . . . . .3B 86
    (off British St.)
St Clair Rd. E13 . . . . .2K 87
St Clair's Rd. CR0: C'don 2E 168
St Clare Bus. Pk. TW12: Ham H 6G 131
St Clare St. EC3 . . . . .1J 15 (6F 85)
St Clements Ct. EC4 . . . . .2F 15
  N7 . . . . .6K 65

St Clements Ct. SE14 . . . . .6K 103
    (off Myers La.)
  W11 . . . . .7F 81
    (off Stoneleigh St.)
St Clement's Hgts. SE26 . . . . .3G 139
St Clements Ho. E1 . . . . .6J 9
    (off Leyden St.)
St Clement's La. WC2 . . . . .1G 13 (6K 83)
St Clements Mans. SW6 . . . . .6F 99
    (off Lillie Rd.)
St Clements St. N7 . . . . .6A 66
St Clements Yd. SE22 . . . . .4F 121
St Cloud Rd. SE27 . . . . .4C 138
St Columbas Ho. E17 . . . . .4D 50
St Columb's Ho. W10 . . . . .5G 81
    (off Blagrove Rd.)
St Crispin's Cl. NW3 . . . . .4C 64
  UB1: S'hall 6D 76
St Cross St. EC1 . . . . .5K 7 (5A 84)
St Cuthberts Rd. N13 . . . . .6F 33
  NW2 . . . . .6H 63
St Cyprian's St. SW17 . . . . .4D 136
St Daniel Ct. BR3: Beck 7C 140
    (off Brackley Rd.)
St Davids Cl. BR4: W W'ck 7D 158
  HA9: Wemb 3J 61
  SE16 . . . . .5H 103
    (off Masters Dr.)
St Davids Cl. BR1: Brom 3F 161
  E17 . . . . .3E 50
  TW15: Ashf 2B 128
St David's Dr. HA8: Edg 1F 43
St Davids M. E3 . . . . .3A 86
    (off Morgan St.)
  E18 . . . . .1J 51
St David's Pl. NW4 . . . . .7D 44
St Davids Sq. E14 . . . . .5D 104
St Denis Rd. SE27 . . . . .4D 138
St Dionis Rd. E12 . . . . .3C 70
  SW6 . . . . .2H 117
St Domingo Ho. SE18 . . . . .3D 106
    (off Leda Rd.)
St Donatt's Rd. SE14 . . . . .1B 122
ST DUNSTAN'S 6H 165
St Dunstan's All. EC3 . . . . .2G 15
St Dunstans Av. W3 . . . . .7K 79
St Dunstan's Cl. UB3: Harl 5H 93
St Dunstan's Ct. EC4 . . . . . .1K 13 (6A 84)
St Dunstans Gdns. W3 . . . . .7K 79
St Dunstans Hill EC3 . . . . . .3G 15 (7E 84)
  SM1: Sutt .5G 165
St Dunstans La. BR3: Beck 7C 140
  EC3 . . . . .3G 15 (7E 84)
St Dunstans M. E1 . . . . .5A 86
    (off White Horse Rd.)
St Dunstans Rd. E7 . . . . .6K 69
  SE25 . . . . .4F 157
  TW4: Cran 2K 111
    (not continuous)
  TW13: Felt 3H 129
  W6 . . . . .5F 99
  W7 . . . . .2J 95
St Edmund's Av. HA4: Ruis 6F 39
St Edmunds Cl. DA18: Erith 2D 108
  NW8 . . . . .1D 82
  SW17 . . . . .2C 136
St Edmund's Ct. NW8 . . . . .1D 82
    (off St Edmund's Ter.)
St Edmunds Dr. HA7: Stan 1A 42
St Edmund's La. TW2: Whitt 7F 113
St Edmund's Rd. IG1: Ilf 6D 52
  N9 . . . . .7B 24
St Edmunds Sq. SW13 . . . . .6E 98
St Edmund's Ter. NW8 . . . . .1C 82
St Edward's Cl. NW11 . . . . .6J 45
St Edwards Ct. NW11 . . . . .6J 45
St Edwards Way RM1: Rom 5K 55
St Egberts Way E4 . . . . .1K 35
St Elmo Rd. W12 . . . . .1B 98
    (not continuous)
St Elmos Rd. SE16 . . . . .2A 104
St Erkenwald M. IG11: Bark 1H 89

St Erkenwald Rd. IG11: Bark 1H 89
St Ermin's Hill SW1 . . . . .1C 18
St Ervan's Rd. W10 . . . . .5H 81
St Eugene Ct. NW6 . . . . .1G 81
    (off Salusbury Rd.)
St Faith's Cl. EN2: Enf 1H 23
St Faith's Rd. SE21 . . . . .1B 138
St Fidelis Rd. DA8: Erith 4K 109
St Fillans Rd. SE6 . . . . .1E 140
St Francis Cl. BR5: Pet W 6J 161
St Francis' Ho. NW1 . . . . .2H 83
    (off Bridgeway St.)
St Francis Pl. SW12 . . . . .6F 119
St Francis Rd. DA8: Erith 4K 109
  SE22 . . . . .4E 120
St Francis Way IG1: Ilf 4H 71
St Frideswide's M. E14 . . . . .6E 86
St Gabriel's Cl. E11 . . . . .2K 69
  E14 . . . . .5D 86
St Gabriels Ct. N11 . . . . .7C 32
St Gabriels Mnr. SE5 . . . . .1B 120
    (off Cormont Rd.)
St Gabriels Rd. NW2 . . . . .5F 63
St George's Av. E7 . . . . .7K 69
  N7 . . . . .4H 65
  NW9 . . . . .4K 43
  UB1: S'hall 7D 76
  W5 . . . . .2D 96
St George's Bldgs. SE1 . . . . .3B 102
    (off St George's Rd.)
St George's Cathedral 1K 5
    (off Redhill St.)
St George's Cir. SE1 . . . . . .7A 14 (3B 102)
St Georges Cl. HA0: Wemb 3A 60
  NW11 . . . . .6H 45
  SE28 . . . . .6D 90
  SW8 . . . . .1G 119
St Georges Ct. E6 . . . . .4D 88
  E17 . . . . .5F 51
  EC4 . . . . .7A 8 (6B 84)
  HA3: Kenton 6A 42
    (off Kenton Rd.)
  SE1 . . . . .3B 102
    (off Garden Row)
  SW1 . . . . .1D 18
    (off St George's Dr.)
  SW3 . . . . .3C 16
    (off Brompton Rd.)
  SW7 . . . . .3A 100
  SW15 . . . . .4H 117
St George's Dr. SW1 . . . . . .4K 17 (4F 101)
  UB10: Ick .3B 56
ST GEORGE'S FIELD 7C 82
St George's Flds. W2 . . . . . .1D 10 (6C 82)
St George's Gdns. KT6: Surb 2H 163
St George's Gro. SW17 . . . . .3B 136
St Georges Ho. NW1 . . . . .2H 83
    (off Bridgeway St.)
  SW11 . . . . .1E 118
    (off Charlotte Despard Av.)
St Georges Ind. Est. KT2: King T 5D 132
  N22 . . . . .7G 33
St George's Mans. SW1 . . . . .5D 18
    (off Causton St.)
St George's M. NW1 . . . . .7D 64
  SE1 . . . . .1K 19
  SE8 . . . . .4B 104
St Georges Pde. SE6 . . . . .2B 140
St George's Path SE4 . . . . .4C 122
    (off Adelaide Av.)
St George's Pl. TW1: Twick 1A 132
St George's Pools 7H 85
St Georges RC Cathedral 1K 19 (3A 102)
St Georges Rd. BR1: Brom 2D 160
  BR3: Beck 1D 158
  BR5: Pet W 6H 161
  CR4: Mitc .3F 155
  DA14: Sidc 6D 144
  E7 . . . . .7K 69
  E10 . . . . .3E 68
  EN1: Enf 1A 24

St Georges Rd. IG1: Ilf 7D 52
  KT2: King T 7G 133
  N13 . . . . .3E 32
  NW11 . . . . .6H 45
  RM9: Dag .5E 72
  SE1 . . . . .1K 19 (3A 102)
  SM6: Wall .5F 167
  SW19 . . . . .7H 135
    (not continuous)
  TW1: Twick 5B 114
  TW9: Rich .3F 115
  TW13: Hanw 4B 130
  W4 . . . . .2K 97
  W7 . . . . .1K 95
St George's Rd. W.
  BR1: Brom 1C 160
St George's Shop. & Leisure Cen.
  HA1: Harr .6J 41
St Georges Sq. E7 . . . . .7K 69
  E14 . . . . .7A 86
  KT3: N Mald 3A 152
  SE8 . . . . .4B 104
    (not continuous)
  SW1 . . . . .5C 18 (5H 101)
St George's Sq. M.
  SW1 . . . . .6C 18 (5H 101)
St George's Ter. E6 . . . . .3C 88
    (off Masterman Rd.)
  NW1 . . . . .7D 64
  SE15 . . . . .7G 103
    (off Peckham Hill St.)
St George's Theatre 4H 65
St George St. W1 . . . . .1K 11 (7F 83)
St Georges Wlk. CR0: C'don 3C 168
St George's Way SE15 . . . . .6E 102
St George's Wharf SE1 . . . . .6K 15
    (off Shad Thames)
St George Wharf SW8 . . . . . .7E 18 (6J 101)
St Gerards Cl. SW4 . . . . .5G 119
St German's Pl. SE3 . . . . .1J 123
St German's Rd. SE23 . . . . .1A 140
St Giles Av. RM10: Dag 7H 73
  UB10: Ick .4E 56
St Giles Cir. W1 . . . . .7D 6 (6H 83)
St Giles Cl. BR6: Farnb 5H 173
  RM10: Dag 7H 73
  TW5: Hest .7C 94
St Giles High St. WC2 . . . . . .7D 6 (6H 83)
St Giles Ho. EN5: New Bar 4F 21
  SE5 . . . . .1E 120
St Giles Pas. WC2 . . . . .1D 12
St Giles Rd. SE5 . . . . .7E 102
St Giles Ter. EC2 . . . . .6D 8
    (off Wood St.)
St Giles Twr. SE5 . . . . .1E 120
    (off Gables Cl.)
St Gilles Ho. E2 . . . . .2K 85
    (off Mace St.)
St Gothard Rd. SE27 . . . . .4D 138
    (not continuous)
St Gregory Cl. HA4: Ruis 4A 58
St Helena Ho. WC1 . . . . .2J 7
    (off Margery St.)
St Helena Rd. SE16 . . . . .4K 103
St Helena St. WC1 . . . . .2J 7 (3A 84)
St Helens KT7: T Ditt 7K 149
St Helens Cl. UB8: Cowl 5A 74
St Helen's Cres. SW16 . . . . .1K 155
St Helen's Gdns. W10 . . . . .5F 81
St Helens Pl. E10 . . . . .7A 50
  EC3 . . . . .7G 9 (6E 84)
St Helen's Rd. DA18: Erith 2D 108
  IG1: Ilf 6D 52
  SW16 . . . . .1K 155
  W13 . . . . .1B 96
ST HELIER 7C 154
St Helier Av. SM4: Mord 7C 154
St Helier Ct. N1 . . . . .1E 84
    (off De Beauvoir Est.)
  SE16 . . . . .2K 103
    (off Poolmans St.)
St Helier's Av. TW3: Houn 5E 112

St Helier's Rd. E10 6E **50**
St Hilary's Ct. BR1: Brom 3F **161**
St Hilda's Av. TW15: Ashf 5A **128**
St Hilda's Cl. NW6 7F **63**
SW17 2C **136**
St Hilda's Rd. SW13 6D **98**
St Hilda's Wharf *E1* *1J* ***103***
(off Wapping High St.)
St Hubert's Ho. *E14* *3C* ***104***
(off Janet St.)
St Hughes Cl. SW17 2C **136**
St Hugh's Rd. SE20 1H **157**
St Ivian Ct. N10 2E **46**
St James SE14 1A **122**
St James Apartments
E17 *5A* ***50***
(off Pretoria Av.)
St James Av. N20 3H **31**
SM1: Sutt 5J **165**
W13 1A **96**
St James Cl. EN4: E Barn 4G **21**
HA4: Ruis 2A **58**
KT3: N Mald 5B **152**
N20 3H **31**
SE18 5G **107**
St James Ct. CR0: C'don 7B **156**
E2 *3G* ***85***
(off Bethnal Grn. Rd.)
E12 2A **70**
SE3 1K **123**
SW1 1B **18** (3G **101**)
St James Gdns. HA0: Wemb 7D **60**
RM6: Chad H 4B **54**
St James Ga. IG9: Buck H 1F **37**
St James Gro. SW11 2D **118**
St James Hall *N1* *1C* ***84***
(off Prebend St.)
St James Ind. M. SE1 5G **103**
St James Mans. *NW6* *7J* ***63***
(off West End La.)
SE1 *1J* ***19***
(off Kennington Rd.)
St James M. E14 3E **104**
E17 *5A* ***50***
(off St James's St.)
St James Residences *W1* *2C* ***12***
(off Brewer St.)
St James Rd. CR4: Mitc 7E **136**
E15 5H **69**
KT6: Surb 6D **150**
N9 2C **34**
SM1: Sutt 5J **165**
SM5: Cars 3C **166**
ST JAMES'S 4B 12 (1H 101)
St James's App. EC2 4G **9** (4E **84**)
St James's Av. BR3: Beck 3A **158**
E2 2J **85**
TW12: Ham H 5G **131**
St James's Chambers *SW1* *4B* ***12***
(off Jermyn St.)
St James's Cl. *NW8* *1D* ***82***
(off St James's Ter. M.)
SW17 2D **136**
St James's Cotts. TW9: Rich 5D **114**
St James's Ct. HA1: Harr 6A **42**
KT1: King T 3E **150**
N18 *5B* ***34***
(off Fore St.)
St James's Cres. SW9 3A **120**
St James's Dr. SW12 1D **136**
SW17 1D **136**
St James's Gdns. W11 1G **99**
(not continuous)
St James's Ho. *SE1* *4G* ***103***
(off Strathnairn St.)
St James's La. N10 4F **47**
St James's Mkt. SW1 3C **12** (7H **83**)
St James's Palace 6B **12** (2G **101**)
St James's Pk. 6C **12** (2H **101**)
St James's Pk. CR0: C'don 7C **156**
St James's Pas. EC3 1H **15**
St James's Pl. SW1 5A **12** (1G **101**)
St James's Rd. CR0: C'don 7B **156**
KT1: King T 2D **150**
SE1 6G **103**
SE16 3G **103**
TW12: Ham H 5F **131**
St James's Sq. SW1 4B **12** (1G **101**)
St James's St. E17 5A **50**
SW1 4A **12** (1G **101**)
St James's Ter. *NW8* *1D* ***82***
(off Prince Albert Rd.)
St James's Ter. M. NW8 1D **82**
St James St. W6 5E **98**
St James's Wlk. EC1 3A **8** (4B **84**)
St James Ter. SW12 1E **136**
St James Way DA14: Sidc 5E **144**
St Jeromes Gro. UB3: Hayes 6E **74**
St Joan's Rd. N9 2A **34**
St John Fisher Rd. DA18: Erith 3D **108**
ST JOHNS 2C 122
St John's Av. N11 5J **31**
NW10 1B **80**
SW15 5F **117**
St Johns Chu. Rd. E9 5J **67**
St Johns Cl. HA9: Wemb 5E **60**
N14 6B **22**
N20 *3F* ***31***
(off Rasper Rd.)
SW6 7J **99**
St John's Cotts. SE20 7J **139**
St John's Ct. DA8: Erith 4K **109**
E1 *1H* ***103***
(off Scandrett St.)
HA1: Harr 6K **41**
HA6: Nwood *1G* ***39***
(off Murray Rd.)
IG9: Buck H 1E **36**
KT1: King T *4E* ***150***
(off Beaufort Rd.)
N4 2B **66**
N5 4B **66**
SE13 2E **122**
TW7: Isle 2K **113**
W6 *4D* ***98***
(off Glenthorne Rd.)
St John's Cres. SW9 3A **120**
St Johns Dr. SW18 1K **135**
St John's Est. N1 2D **84**
SE1 6J **15**
St John's Gdns. W11 7G **81**
St John's Gate 4A 8
St John's Gro. N19 2G **65**
SW13 2B **116**
TW9: Rich 4E **114**
St John's Hill SW11 5B **118**
St John's Hill Gro. SW11 4B **118**
St Johns Ho. *E14* *4E* ***104***
(off Pier St.)
SE17 *6D* ***102***
(off Lytham St.)
St John's La. EC1 4A **8** (4B **84**)
St John's Lodge *NW3* *7C* ***64***
(off King Henry's Rd.)
St John's Mans. *EC1* *1A* ***8***
(off St John St.)
St John's M. KT1: Ham W 2C **150**
W11 6J **81**
St Johns Pde. *DA14: Sidc* *4A* ***144***
(off Sidcup High St.)
W13 1B **96**
St John's Pk. SE3 7H **105**
St John's Pk. Mans. N19 3G **65**
St John's Pas. SW19 6G **135**
St John's Path EC1 4A **8**
St Johns Pathway SE23 1J **139**
St John's Pl. EC1 4A **8** (4B **84**)
St John's Rd. BR5: Pet W 6H **161**
CR0: C'don 3B **168**
DA8: Erith 5K **109**
DA14: Sidc 4B **144**
DA16: Well 3B **126**
E4 4J **35**
E6 1C **88**
St John's Rd. E16 6J **87**
E17 2D **50**
HA1: Harr 6K **41**
HA9: Wemb 4D **60**
IG2: Ilf 7H **53**
IG11: Bark 1J **89**
KT1: Ham W 2C **150**
KT3: N Mald 3J **151**
KT8: E Mos 4H **149**
N15 6E **48**
NW11 6H **45**
SE20 6J **139**
SM1: Sutt 2K **165**
SM5: Cars 3C **166**
SW11 4C **118**
SW19 7G **135**
TW7: Isle 2K **113**
TW9: Rich 4E **114**
TW13: Hanw 4C **130**
UB2: S'hall 3C **94**
St John's Sq. EC1 4A **8** (4B **84**)
St John's Ter. E7 6K **69**
SE18 6G **107**
SW15 *3A* ***134***
(off Kingston Va.)
W10 4F **81**
St John St. EC1 1K **7** (2A **84**)
St John's Va. SE8 2C **122**
St John's Vs. *N11* *5J* ***31***
(off Friern Barnet Rd.)
N19 2H **65**
W8 *3K* ***99***
(off St Mary's Pl.)
St John's Way N19 2G **65**
ST JOHN'S WOOD 1A 4 (2B 82)
St John's Wood Ct. NW8 2B **4**
St John's Wood High St. NW8 1C **4** (2B **82**)
St John's Wood Pk. NW8 1B **82**
St John's Wood Rd. NW8 3A **4** (4B **82**)
St John's Wood Ter. NW8 2B **82**
St John's Yd. N17 7A **34**
St Josephs Almshouses *W6* *4F* ***99***
(off Brook Grn.)
St Joseph's Cl. BR6: Orp 4K **173**
W10 5G **81**
St Joseph's College Sports Cen. 6B 138
St Joseph's Cotts. *SW3* *4E* ***16***
(off Cadagon St.)
St Josephs Ct. SE7 6K **105**
St Joseph's Dr. UB1: S'hall 1C **94**
St Joseph's Flats *NW1* *1C* ***6***
(off Drummond Cres.)
St Joseph's Gro. NW4 4D **44**
St Joseph's Ho. *W6* *4F* ***99***
(off Brook Grn.)
St Joseph's Rd. N9 7C **24**
St Joseph's St. SW8 1F **119**
St Joseph's Va. SE3 3F **123**
St Judes Ct. IG8: Wfd G 7H **37**
St Jude's Rd. E2 2H **85**
St Jude St. N16 5E **66**
St Julian's Cl. SW16 4A **138**
St Julian's Farm Rd. SE27 4A **138**
St Julian's Rd. NW6 1J **81**
St Katharine Docks 3K 15
St Katharine's Pct. NW1 2F **83**
St Katharine's Way E1 4K **15** (1F **103**)
(not continuous)
St Katharine's Yacht Haven *1F* ***103***
(off St Katharine's Way)
St Katherine's Rd. DA18: Erith 2D **108**
St Katherine's Row EC3 2H **15**
St Katherines Wlk. *W11* *1F* ***99***
(off St Ann's Rd.)
St Keverne Rd. SE9 4C **142**
St Kilda Rd. BR6: Orp 1K **173**
W13 1A **96**
St Kilda's Rd. HA1: Harr 6J **41**
N16 1D **66**
St Kitts Ter. SE19 5E **138**
St Laurence Cl. NW6 1F **81**
St Lawrence Bus. Cen. TW13: Felt 2K **129**
St Lawrence Cl. HA8: Edg 7A **28**
St Lawrence Cotts. *E14* *1E* ***104***
(off St Lawrence St.)
St Lawrence Ct. N1 7D **66**
St Lawrence Dr. HA5: Eastc 5K **39**
St Lawrence Ho. *SE1* *7H* ***15***
(off Purbrook St.)
St Lawrence St. E14 1E **104**
St Lawrence Ter. W10 5G **81**
St Lawrence Way SW9 1A **120**
St Leger Ct. *NW6* *7F* ***63***
(off Coverdale Rd.)
St Leonard M. *N1* *2E* ***84***
(off Hoxton St.)
St Leonard's Av. E4 6A **36**
HA3: Kenton 5C **42**
St Leonard's Cl. DA16: Well 3A **126**
St Leonards Ct. N1 1F **9**
SW14 3J **115**
St Leonard's Gdns. IG1: Ilf 5G **71**
TW5: Hest 7C **94**
St Leonard's Ri. BR6: Orp 4J **173**
St Leonard's Rd. CR0: Wadd 3B **168**
E14 5D **86**
(not continuous)
KT6: Surb 5D **150**
KT7: T Ditt 6A **150**
KT10: Clay 6A **162**
NW10 4K **79**
SW14 3H **115**
W13 7C **78**
(not continuous)
St Leonards Sq. KT6: Surb 5D **150**
NW5 6E **64**
St Leonard's St. E3 3D **86**
St Leonard's Ter. SW3 6E **16** (5D **100**)
St Leonard's Wlk. SW16 7K **137**
St Loo Av. SW3 7D **16** (6C **100**)
St Loo Ct. *SW3* *7D* ***16***
(off St Loo Av.)
St Louis Rd. SE27 4D **138**
St Loy's Rd. N17 2E **48**
St Lucia Dr. E15 1H **87**
St Luke Cl. UB8: Cowl 6A **74**
ST LUKE'S 3D 8 (4C 84)
St Luke's Av. EN2: Enf 1J **23**
IG1: Ilf 5F **71**
SW4 4H **119**
St Luke's Cl. EC1 3D **8** (4C **84**)
SE25 6H **157**
St Lukes Ct. *E10* *7D* ***50***
(off Capworth St.)
W11 *6H* ***81***
(off St Luke's Rd.)
St Luke's Est. EC1 2E **8** (3D **84**)
St Luke's M. W11 6H **81**
St Luke's Pas. KT2: King T 1F **151**
St Luke's Path IG1: Ilf 5F **71**
St Luke's Rd. UB10: Uxb 7A **56**
W11 5H **81**
St Luke's Sq. E16 6H **87**
St Luke's St. SW3 5D **16** (5C **100**)
St Luke's Yd. W9 2H **81**
(not continuous)
St Malo Av. N9 3D **34**
ST MARGARETS 6B 114
St Margarets IG11: Bark 1H **89**
KT2: King T 5J **133**
St Margarets Av. DA15: Sidc 3H **143**
HA2: Harr 3G **59**
N15 4B **48**
N20 1F **31**
SM3: Cheam 3G **165**
TW15: Ashf 5D **128**
UB8: Hil 4C **74**
St Margarets Bus. Cen. TW1: Twick 6B **114**
St Margarets Cl. EC2 6D **84**
St Margarets Ct. HA8: Edg 5C **28**
N11 4K **31**
SE1 5D **14** (1C **102**)
SW15 4D **116**
St Margaret's Cres. SW15 5D **116**

St Margaret's Dr. TW1: Twick 5B 114
St Margaret's Gro. E11 3H 69
SE18 6G 107
TW1: Twick 6A 114
St Margaret's Ho. NW1 1C 6
(off Polygon Rd.)
St Margaret's La. W8 3K 99
St Margaret's M. KT2: King T 5J 133
St Margaret's Pas. SE13 3G 123
(not continuous)
St Margarets Path SE18 5G 107
St Margarets Rd. E12 2A 70
HA4: Ruis 6F 39
HA8: Edg 5C 28
N17 3E 48
NW10 3E 80
SE4 4B 122
(not continuous)
TW1: Twick 6B 114
TW7: Isle 4B 114
W7 2J 95
ST MARGARETS RDBT. 6B 114
St Margaret's Sports Cen. 1A 26
St Margaret's Ter. SE18 5G 107
St Margaret St. SW1 7E 12 (2J 101)
St Marks Cl. EN5: New Bar 3E 20
HA1: Harr 7B 42
SE10 7E 104
SW6 1J 117
St Marks Ct. NW8 2A 82
(off Abercorn Pl.)
W7 2J 95
(off Lwr. Boston Rd.)
St Mark's Cres. NW1 1E 82
St Mark's Ga. E9 7B 68
St Mark's Gro. SW10 7K 99
St Mark's Hill KT6: Surb 6E 150
St Marks Ho. SE17 6D 102
(off Lytham St.)
St Marks Ind. Est. E16 1B 106
St Mark's Pl. RM10: Dag 6G 73
SW19 6H 135
W11 6G 81
St Mark's Ri. E8 5F 67
St Marks Rd. BR2: Brom 3J 159
CR4: Mitc 2D 154
EN1: Enf 6A 24
SE25 4G 157
TW11: Tedd 7B 132
W5 1E 96
W7 2J 95
W10 5F 81
W11 6G 81
St Mark's Sq. NW1 1E 82
St Mark St. E1 1K 15 (6F 85)
St Mark's Vs. N4 2K 65
(off Moray Rd.)
St Martin Cl. UB8: Cowl 6A 74
St Martin-in-the-Fields Church 3E 12
(off St Martin's Pl.)
St Martin's Almshouses NW1 1G 83
St Martin's App. HA4: Ruis 7G 39
St Martin's Av. E6 2B 88
St Martin's Cl. DA18: Erith 2D 108
EN1: Enf 1C 24
NW1 1G 83
St Martins Ct. EC4 7C 8
(off Paternoster Row)
N1 1E 84
(off De Beauvoir Est.)
WC2 2E 12 (7J 83)
St Martins Est. SW2 1A 138
St Martin's Ho. NW1 1C 6
(off Polygon Rd.)
St Martin's La. BR3: Beck 5D 158
WC2 2E 12 (7J 83)
St Martin's Le-Grand EC1 7C 8 (6C 84)
St Martin's Pl. WC2 3E 12 (7J 83)
St Martin's Rd. N9 2C 34
SW9 2K 119
St Martin's St. WC2 3D 12 (7H 83)
(not continuous)
St Martin's Theatre 2E 12
(off West St.)
St Martins Way SW17 3A 136
St Mary Abbot's Ct. W14 3H 99
(off Warwick Gdns.)
St Mary Abbot's Pl. W8 3H 99
St Mary Abbot's Ter. W14 3H 99
St Mary at Hill EC3 3G 15 (7E 84)
St Mary Av. SM6: Wall 3E 166
St Mary Axe EC3 1G 15 (6E 84)
St Marychurch St. SE16 2J 103
St Mary Graces Ct. E1 3K 15 (7F 85)
St Marylebone Cl. NW10 1A 80
St Marylebone Crematorium N2 3K 45
St Mary le-Park Ct. SW11 7C 100
(off Parkgate Rd.)
St Mary Newington Cl. SE17 5E 102
(off Surrey Sq.)
St Mary Rd. E17 4C 50
St Mary's IG11: Bark 1H 89
St Mary's App. E12 5D 70
St Mary's Av. BR2: Brom 3G 159
E11 7K 51
N3 2G 45
TW11: Tedd 6K 131
St Mary's Av. Central UB2: S'hall 4F 95
St Mary's Av. Nth. UB2: S'hall 4F 95
St Mary's Av. Sth. UB2: S'hall 4F 95
St Mary's Cl. KT9: Chess 7F 163
KT17: Ewe 7B 164
N17 1G 49
TW16: Sun 4J 147
St Mary's Copse KT4: Wor Pk 2A 164
St Mary's Ct. E3 3D 86
(off Bow Rd.)
E6 4D 88
SE7 7B 106
SM6: Wall 4G 167
W5 2D 96
W6 3B 98
St Mary's Cres. NW4 3D 44
TW7: Isle 7H 95
UB3: Hayes 7H 75
St Mary's Dr. TW14: Bedf 7E 110
St Mary's Est. SE16 2J 103
(off St Marychurch St.)
St Mary's Flats NW1 1C 6
(off Drummond Cres.)
St Mary's Gdns. SE11 3K 19 (4A 102)
St Mary's Ga. W8 3K 99
St Mary's Grn. N2 2A 46
St Mary's Gro. N1 6B 66
SW13 3D 116
TW9: Rich 4F 115
W4 6H 97
St Mary's Ho. N1 1B 84
(off St Mary's Path)
St Mary's Mans. W2 5A 4 (5B 82)
St Marys M. NW6 7K 63
TW10: Ham 2C 132
St Mary's Path E1 6G 85
(off White Church La.)
N1 1B 84
St Mary's Pl. SE9 6D 124
W5 2D 96
W8 3K 99
St Marys Rd. DA5: Bexl 1J 145
E10 3E 68
E13 2K 87
EN4: E Barn 7J 21
IG1: Ilf 2G 71
KT4: Wor Pk 2A 164
KT6: Surb 7C 150
(St Chads Cl.)
KT6: Surb 6D 150
(Victoria Rd.)
KT8: E Mos 5H 149
N8 4J 47
N9 1C 34
(not continuous)
NW10 1A 80
NW11 7G 45
St Marys Rd. SE15 1J 121
SE25 3E 156
SW19 5G 135
UB3: Hayes 7H 75
W5 2D 96
St Mary's Sq. W2 5A 4 (5B 82)
W5 2D 96
St Mary's Ter. W2 5A 4 (5B 82)
St Mary's Twr. EC1 4D 8
(off Fortune St.)
St Mary St. SE18 4D 106
St Mary's University College 3K 131
St Mary's University College Sports Cen. 4K 131
St Mary's Vw. HA3: Kenton 5C 42
St Mary's Wlk. SE11 3K 19 (4A 102)
UB3: Hayes 7H 75
St Mary's Way IG7: Chig 5K 37
St Matthew Cl. UB8: Cowl 6A 74
St Matthew's Av. KT6: Surb 1E 162
St Matthews Ct. E10 7D 50
N10 2E 46
SE1 3C 102
(off Meadow Row)
TW15: Ashf 4C 128
(off Feltham Rd.)
St Matthew's Dr. BR1: Brom 3D 160
St Matthews Ho. SE17 6D 102
(off Phelp St.)
St Matthew's Lodge NW1 2G 83
(off Oakley Sq.)
St Matthew's Rd. SW2 4K 119
W5 1E 96
St Matthew's Row E2 3G 85
St Matthew St. SW1 2C 18 (3H 101)
St Matthias Cl. NW9 5B 44
St Maur Rd. SW6 1H 117
St Mellion Cl. SE28 6D 90
St Merryn Cl. SE18 7H 107
St Merryn Ct. BR3: Beck 7C 140
St Michael's All. EC3 1F 15 (6D 84)
St Michael's Av. HA9: Wemb 6G 61
N9 7D 24
St Michaels Cl. BR1: Brom 3C 160
DA18: Erith 2D 108
E16 5B 88
KT4: Wor Pk 2B 164
N3 2H 45
N12 5H 31
St Michaels Ct. CR0: C'don 1C 168
(off Station Rd.)
E14 5E 86
(off St Leonard's Rd.)
SE1 7D 14
(off Trinity St.)
St Michael's Cres. HA5: Pinn 6C 40
St Michael's Flats NW1 1C 6
(off Aldenham St.)
St Michael's Gdns. W10 5G 81
St Michaels M. SW1 4G 17 (4E 100)
St Michael's Ri. DA16: Well 1B 126
St Michael's Rd. CR0: C'don 1C 168
DA16: Well 3B 126
NW2 4E 62
SM6: Wall 6G 167
SW9 2K 119
TW15: Ashf 5C 128
St Michael's St. W2 7B 4 (6B 82)
St Michaels Ter. N6 1E 64
(off South Gro.)
N22 1J 47
St Mildred's Ct. EC2 1E 14 (6D 84)
St Mildreds Rd. SE6 7G 123
SE12 7G 123
St Mirren Ct. EN5: New Bar 5F 21
St Nicholas Cen. SM1: Sutt 5K 165
St Nicholas Cl. UB8: Cowl 6A 74
St Nicholas Ct. KT1: King T 4E 150
(off Surbiton Rd.)
St Nicholas Dr. TW17: Shep 7C 146
St Nicholas' Flats NW1 1C 6
(off Werrington St.)
St Nicholas Glebe SW17 5E 136
St Nicholas Ho. SE8 6C 104
(off Deptford Grn.)
SE18 7C 106
(off Shrapnel Cl.)
St Nicholas M. KT7: T Ditt 6K 149
St Nicholas Rd. KT7: T Ditt 6K 149
SE18 5K 107
SM1: Sutt 5K 165
St Nicholas St. SE8 1B 122
St Nicholas Way SM1: Sutt 4K 165
St Nicolas La. BR7: Chst 1C 160
St Ninian's Ct. N20 3J 31
St Norbert Grn. SE4 4A 122
St Norbert Rd. SE4 5K 121
St Olaf Ho. SE1 4F 15
St Olaf's Rd. SW6 7G 99
St Olaf Stairs SE1 4F 15
St Olave's Ct. EC2 1E 14 (6D 84)
St Olave's Est. SE1 6H 15 (2E 102)
St Olave's Gdns. SE11 3J 19 (4A 102)
St Olaves Ho. SE11 3J 19
(off Walnut Tree Wlk.)
St Olave's Mans. SE11 3J 19
St Olave's Rd. E6 1E 88
St Olaves Wlk. SW16 2G 155
St Olav's Sq. SE16 2J 103
St Onge Pde. EN1: Enf 3J 23
(off Southbury Rd.)
St Oswald's Pl. SE11 6G 19 (5K 101)
St Oswald's Rd. SW16 1B 156
St Oswalds Studios SW6 6J 99
(off Sedlescombe Rd.)
St Oswulf St. SW1 4D 18 (4H 101)
St Owen Ho. SE1 3E 102
(off St Saviour's Est.)
ST PANCRAS 2F 7 (3J 83)
St Pancras Commercial Cen. NW1 1G 83
(off Pratt St.)
St Pancras Ct. N2 2B 46
St Pancras Way NW1 7G 65
St Patrick's Ct. IG8: Wfd G 7B 36
St Paul Cl. UB8: Cowl 5A 74
St Paulinus Ct. DA1: Cray 4K 127
(off Manor Rd.)
St Paul's All. EC4 1B 14
(off St Paul's Chyd.)
St Paul's Av. HA3: Kenton 4F 43
NW2 6D 62
SE16 1K 103
St Paul's Bldgs. EC1 3B 8
(off Dallington St.)
St Paul's Cathedral 1B 14 (6C 84)
St Paul's Chyd. EC4 1B 14 (6B 84)
St Pauls Cl. KT9: Chess 4D 162
SE7 5B 106
SM5: Cars 1C 166
TW3: Houn 2C 112
TW15: Ashf 5E 128
UB3: Harl 5F 93
W5 2F 97
St Pauls Ct. SW4 5H 119
TW4: Houn 3C 112
St Pauls Courtyard SE8 7C 104
(off Crossfield St.)
ST PAUL'S CRAY 2K 161
St Paul's Cray Rd. BR7: Chst 1H 161
St Paul's Cres. NW1 7H 65
(not continuous)
St Paul's Dr. E15 5F 69
St Paul's M. NW1 7H 65
St Paul's Pl. N1 6D 66
St Paul's Ri. N13 6G 33
St Paul's Rd. CR7: Thor H 3C 156
DA8: Erith 7J 109
IG11: Bark 1G 89
N1 6B 66
N17 7B 34
TW8: Bford 6D 96
TW9: Rich 3F 115
St Paul's Shrubbery N1 6D 66
St Paul's Sq. BR2: Brom 2H 159

St Paul's Studios *W14* 5G 99
(*off Talgarth Rd.*)
St Pauls Ter. SE17 6B 102
St Paul St. N1 1C 84
(not continuous)
St Pauls Vw. Apartments *EC1* 2J 7
(*off Amwell St.*)
St Paul's Wlk. KT2: King T 7G 133
St Paul's Way E3 5B 86
N3 7E 30
St Paul's Wood Hill BR5: St P 2J 161
St Peter Claver Ct. *BR3: Beck* 1D 158
(*off Albemarle Rd.*)
St Peter's All. *EC3* 1F 15
(*off Gracechurch St.*)
St Peters Av. E2 2G 85
E17 4G 51
N2 7H 31
N18 4B 34
St Petersburgh M. W2 7K 81
St Petersburgh Pl. W2 7K 81
St Peter's Cen. *E1* 1H 103
(*off Reardon St.*)
St Peter's Chu. Ct. *N1* 1B 84
(*off St Peter's St.*)
St Peters Cl. BR7: Chst 7H 143
E2 2G 85
HA4: Ruis 2B 58
IG2: Ilf 4J 53
SW17 2C 136
WD23: B Hea 1C 26
St Peters Ct. KT8: W Mole 4E 148
NW4 5E 44
SE12 5H 123
WC1 2F 7
(*off Seaford St.*)
St Peter's Gdns. SE27 3A 138
St Peter's Gro. W6 4C 98
St Peters Ho. SE17 6D 102
WC1 2F 7
(*off Regent Sq.*)
St Peters M. N8 5A 48
St Peter's Path E17 3G 51
St Peters Pl. W9 4K 81
St Peters Rd. CR0: C'don 4D 168
KT1: King T 2G 151
KT8: W Mole 4E 148
N4 5B 48
N9 1C 34
TW1: Twick 5B 114
UB1: S'hall 5E 76
UB8: Cowl 5A 74
W6 5C 98
St Peter's Sq. E2 2G 85
W6 4B 98
St Peter's St. CR2: S Croy 5D 168
N1 1B 84
St Peter's St. M. *N1* 2B 84
(*off St Peters St.*)
St Peter's Ter. SW6 7H 99
St Peter's Vs. W6 4C 98
St Peters Way N1 7E 66
UB3: Harl 5F 93
W5 5D 78
St Peter's Wharf W4 5C 98
St Philip Ho. *WC1* 2J 7
(*off Lloyd Baker St.*)
St Philips Av. KT4: Wor Pk 2D 164
N2 7H 31
St Philip's Ga. KT4: Wor Pk 2D 164
St Philip Sq. SW8 2F 119
St Philips Rd. E8 6G 67
KT6: Surb 6D 150
St Philip St. SW8 2F 119
St Philip's Way N1 1C 84
St Quentin Ho. SW18 6B 118
St Quentin Rd. DA16: Well 3K 125
St Quintin Av. W10 5E 80
St Quintin Gdns. W10 5E 80
St Quintin Rd. E13 3K 87
St Raphael's Way NW10 5J 61
St Regis Cl. N10 2F 47
St Regis Hgts. NW3 3K 63
St Richard's Ho. *NW1* 1C 6
(*off Eversholt St.*)
St Ronan's Cl. EN4: Had W 1G 21
St Ronan's Cres. IG8: Wfd G 7D 36
St Rule St. SW8 2G 119
St Saviours Ct. HA1: Harr 5J 41
N22 2H 47
St Saviour's Est. SE1 7J 15 (2F 103)
St Saviour's Rd. CR0: C'don 6B 156
SW2 5K 119
St Saviour's Wharf *SE1* 6K 15
(*off Mill St.*)
SE1 6K 15
(*off Shad Thames*)
Saints Cl. SE27 4B 138
Saints Dr. E7 5B 70
St Silas Pl. NW5 6E 64
St Simon's Av. SW15 5E 116
Saints M. CR4: Mitc 3C 154
St Stephen's Av. E17 5E 50
W12 1D 98
(not continuous)
W13 6B 78
St Stephens Cl. E17 5D 50
NW5 5D 64
(*off Malden Rd.*)
NW8 1C 82
UB1: S'hall 5E 76
St Stephens Ct. *EN1: Enf* 6K 23
(*off Park Av.*)
N8 6K 47
W13 6B 78
St Stephen's Cres. CR7: Thor H 3A 156
W2 6J 81
St Stephen's Gdns. SW15 5H 117
TW1: Twick 6C 114
W2 6J 81
(not continuous)
St Stephens Gro. SE13 3E 122
St Stephens Ho. *SE17* 6D 102
(*off Lytham St.*)
St Stephen's M. W2 5J 81
St Stephens Pde. E7 7A 70
St Stephen's Pas. TW1: Twick 6C 114
St Stephen's Rd. E3 1A 86
E6 7A 70
E17 5D 50
EN5: Barn 5A 20
TW3: Houn 6E 112
UB7: Yiew 1A 92
W13 6B 78
St Stephen's Row EC4 1E 14
St Stephen's Ter. SW8 7K 101
St Stephen's Wlk. *SW7* 4A 100
(*off Southwell Gdns.*)
St Swithins La. EC4 2E 14 (7D 84)
St Swithun's Rd. SE13 6F 123
St Theresa's Cl. E9 4C 68
St Theresa's Rd. TW14: Felt 4H 111
St Thomas Cl. KT6: Surb 1F 163
St Thomas Ct. DA5: Bexl 7G 127
E10 7D 50
(*off Lake Rd.*)
HA5: Pinn 1C 40
NW1 7G 65
(*off Wrotham Rd.*)
St Thomas Dr. BR5: Farnb 1G 173
HA5: Pinn 1C 40
St Thomas Gdns. IG1: Ilf 6G 71
St Thomas Ho. *E1* 6K 85
(*off W. Arbour St.*)
St Thomas M. SW18 5J 117
St Thomas Rd. DA17: Belv 2J 109
E16 6J 87
N14 7C 22
W4 6J 97
St Thomas's Gdns. NW5 6E 64
St Thomas's Pl. E9 7J 67
St Thomas's Rd. N4 2A 66
NW10 1A 80
St Thomas's Sq. E9 7J 67
St Thomas St. SE1 5F 15 (1D 102)
St Thomas's Way SW6 7H 99
St Timothys M. BR1: Brom 1K 159
St Ursula Gro. HA5: Pinn 5B 40
St Ursula Rd. UB1: S'hall 6E 76
St Vincent Cl. SE27 5B 138
St Vincent De Paul Ho. *E1* 5J 85
(*off Jubilee St.*)
St Vincent Ho. *SE1* 3F 103
(*off St Saviour's Est.*)
St Vincent Rd. TW2: Whitt 6G 113
St Vincent's La. NW7 4K 29
St Vincent St. W1 6H 5 (5E 82)
St Wilfrid's Cl. EN4: E Barn 5H 21
St Wilfrid's Rd. EN4: E Barn 5G 21
St Williams Ct. N1 7J 65
St Winefride's Av. E12 5D 70
St Winifred's Rd. TW11: Tedd 6B 132
Sakura Dr. N22 1H 47
Sala Ho. SE3 4K 123
Salamanca Pl. SE1 4G 19 (4K 101)
Salamanca Sq. *SE1* 4G 19
(*off Salamanca Pl.*)
Salamanca St. SE1 4G 19 (4K 101)
SE11 4G 19 (4K 101)
Salamander Cl. KT2: King T 5C 132
Salamander Quay KT1: Ham W 1D 150
Salcombe Dr. RM6: Chad H 6F 55
SM4: Mord 1F 165
Salcombe Gdns. NW7 6K 29
Salcombe Rd. E17 7B 50
N16 5E 66
TW15: Ashf 3A 128
Salcombe Vs. TW10: Rich 5E 114
Salcombe Way HA4: Ruis 2J 57
UB4: Hayes 3F 75
Salcott Rd. CR0: Bedd 3J 167
SW11 5C 118
Salehurst Cl. HA3: Kenton 5E 42
Salehurst Rd. SE4 6B 122
Salem Pl. CR0: C'don 3C 168
Salem Rd. W2 7K 81
Salento Cl. N3 7D 30
Sale Pl. W2 6C 4 (5C 82)
Sale St. E2 4G 85
Salford Ho. *E14* 4E 104
(*off Seyssel St.*)
Salford Rd. SW2 1H 137
Salhouse Cl. SE28 6C 90
Salisbury Av. IG11: Bark 7H 71
N3 3H 45
SM1: Sutt 6H 165
Salisbury Cl. KT4: Wor Pk 3B 164
SE17 4D 102
Salisbury Ct. EC4 1A 14 (6B 84)
EN2: Enf 4J 23
(*off London Rd.*)
HA8: Edg 4A 28
SE16 3G 103
(*off Stork's Rd.*)
SM5: Cars 5D 166
UB5: N'olt 5F 59
(*off Newmarket Av.*)
Salisbury Gdns. IG9: Buck H 2G 37
SW19 7G 135
Salisbury Hall Gdns. E4 6H 35
Salisbury Ho. *E14* 6D 86
(*off Hobday St.*)
EC2 6F 9
(*off London Wall*)
HA7: Stan 6F 27
N1 1B 84
(*off St Mary's Path*)
SM6: Wall 5F 167
SW1 5D 18
(*off Drummond Ga.*)
SW9 7A 102
(*off Cranmer Rd.*)
Salisbury Mans. N15 5B 48
Salisbury M. SW6 7H 99
Salisbury Pas. *SW6* 7H 99
(*off Dawes Rd.*)
Salisbury Pavement *SW6* 7H 99
(*off Dawes Rd.*)
Salisbury Pl. SW9 7B 102
W1 5E 4 (5D 82)
Salisbury Prom. N8 5B 48
Salisbury Rd. BR2: Brom 5C 160
DA5: Bexl 1G 145
E4 3H 35
E7 6J 69
E10 2E 68
E12 5B 70
E17 5E 50
EN5: Barn 3B 20
HA1: Harr 5H 41
HA5: Eastc 4J 39
IG3: Ilf 2J 71
KT3: N Mald 3K 151
KT4: Wor Pk 4K 163
N4 5B 48
N22 1B 48
RM10: Dag 6H 73
SE25 6G 157
SM5: Cars 6D 166
SW19 7G 135
TW4: Houn 3A 112
TW6: H'row A 6E 110
(not continuous)
TW9: Rich 4E 114
TW13: Felt 1A 130
UB2: S'hall 4C 94
W13 2B 96
Salisbury Sq. EC4 1K 13 (6A 84)
Salisbury St. NW8 4C 4 (4C 82)
W3 2J 97
Salisbury Ter. SE15 3J 121
Salisbury Wlk. N19 2G 65
Salix Cl. TW16: Sun 7K 129
Salix Ct. N3 6D 30
Salliesfield TW2: Whitt 6H 113
Sally Murray Cl. E12 4E 70
Salmen Rd. E13 2H 87
Salmond Cl. HA7: Stan 6F 27
Salmon La. E14 6A 86
Salmon M. NW6 5J 63
Salmon Rd. DA17: Belv 5G 109
Salmons Rd. KT9: Chess 6E 162
N9 1B 34
Salmon St. E14 6B 86
NW9 1H 61
Salomons Rd. E13 5A 88
Salop Rd. E17 6K 49
Saltash Cl. SM1: Sutt 4H 165
Saltash Rd. DA16: Well 1C 126
IG6: Ilf 1H 53
Saltcoats Rd. W4 2A 98
Saltcroft Cl. HA9: Wemb 1H 61
Saltdene N4 1K 65
Salter Cl. HA2: Harr 4D 58
Salterford Rd. SW17 6E 136
Saltern Ct. *IG11: Bark* 3B 90
(*off Galleons Dr.*)
Salter Rd. SE16 1K 103
Salters Ct. EC4 1D 14
Salter's Hall Ct. EC4 2E 14
Salter's Hill SE19 5D 138
Salters Rd. E17 4F 51
W10 4F 81
Salters Row *N1* 6D 66
(*off Tilney Gdns.*)
Salter St. E14 7B 86
NW10 3C 80
Salterton Rd. N7 3K 65
Salt Hill Cl. UB8: Uxb 5A 56
Saltley Cl. E6 6C 88
Salton Cl. N3 2J 45
Saltoun Rd. SW2 4A 120
Saltram Cl. N15 4F 49
Saltram Cres. W9 3H 81
Saltwell St. E14 7C 86
Saltwood Gro. SE17 5D 102
Saltwood Ho. *SE15* 6J 103
(*off Lovelinch Cl.*)

Salusbury Rd. NW6 . . . 1G 81
Salutation Rd. SE10 . . . 4G 105
Salvador SW17 . . . 5D 136
Salvia Gdns. UB6: G'frd . . . 2A 78
Salvin Rd. SW15 . . . 3F 117
Salway Cl. IG8: Wfd G . . . 7D 36
Salway Pl. E15 . . . 6F 69
Salway Rd. E15 . . . 6F 69
Samantha Cl. E17 . . . 7B 50
Sam Bartram Cl. SE7 . . . 5A 106
Sambrook Ho. *E1* . . . *5J 85*
(off Jubilee St.)
SE11 . . . 4J 19
Sambruck M. SE6 . . . 1D 140
Samels Ct. W6 . . . 5C 98
Samford Ho. *N1* . . . *1A 84*
(off Barnsbury Est.)
Samford St. NW8 . . . 4C 4 (4B 82)
Samira Cl. E17 . . . 6C 50
Sam Manners Ho. *SE10* . . . *5G 105*
(off Tuskar St.)
Sam March Ho. *E14* . . . *6F 87*
(off Blair St.)
Sammi Ct. CR7: Thor H . . . 4C 156
Samos Rd. SE20 . . . 2H 157
Sampson Av. EN5: Barn . . . 5A 20
Sampson Cl. DA17: Belv . . . 3D 108
Sampson Ct. TW17: Shep . . . 5E 146
Sampson Ho. SE1 . . . 4A 14 (1B 102)
Sampson St. E1 . . . 1G 103
Samsbrooke Ct. EN1: Enf . . . 6K 23
Samson St. E13 . . . 2A 88
Samuda Est. E14 . . . 3E 104
Samuel Cl. E8 . . . 1F 85
HA7: Stan . . . 2F 27
SE14 . . . 6K 103
SE18 . . . 4C 106
Samuel Ct. *N1* . . . *2G 9*
(off Pitfield St.)
Samuel Gray Gdns. KT2: King T . . . 1D 150
Samuel Ho. *E8* . . . *1F 85*
(off Clarissa St.)
Samuel Johnson Cl. SW16 . . . 4K 137
Samuel Jones Ind. Est. SE15 . . . 7E 102
Samuel Lewis Bldgs. N1 . . . 6A 66
Samuel Lewis Trust Dwellings *E8* . . . *5G 67*
(off Amhurst Rd.)
N16 . . . 6D 48
SW3 . . . 4C 16 (4C 100)
SW6 . . . *7J 99*
(off Vanston Pl.)
W14 . . . *4H 99*
(off Lisgar Ter.)
Samuel Lewis Trust Est. *SE5* . . . *1C 120*
(off Warner Rd.)
Samuel Richardson Ho. *W14* . . . *4H 99*
(off North End Cres.)
Samuel's Cl. W6 . . . 4E 98
Samuel St. SE15 . . . 7F 103
SE18 . . . 4D 106
Sanchia Ct. *E2* . . . *3G 85*
(off Wellington Row)
Sancroft Cl. NW2 . . . 3D 62
Sancroft Ho. SE11 . . . 5H 19
Sancroft Rd. HA3: W'stone . . . 2K 41
Sancroft St. SE11 . . . 5H 19 (5K 101)
Sanctuary, The DA5: Bexl . . . 6D 126
SM4: Mord . . . 6J 153
SW1 . . . 1D 18
Sanctuary M. E8 . . . 6F 67
Sanctuary Rd. TW6: H'row A . . . 6C 110
Sanctuary St. SE1 . . . 6D 14 (2C 102)
Sandale Cl. N16 . . . 3D 66
Sandall Cl. W5 . . . 4E 78
Sandall Ho. E3 . . . 2A 86
Sandall Rd. NW5 . . . 6G 65
W5 . . . 4E 78
Sandal Rd. KT3: N Mald . . . 5K 151
N18 . . . 5B 34
Sandal St. E15 . . . 1G 87
Sandalwood Cl. E1 . . . 4A 86
Sandalwood Dr. HA4: Ruis . . . 7E 38
Sandalwood Ho. DA15: Sidc . . . 2K 143
Sandalwood Mans. *W8* . . . *3K 99*
(off Stone Hall Gdns.)
Sandalwood Rd. TW13: Felt . . . 3K 129
Sandbach Pl. SE18 . . . 4G 107
Sandbanks TW14: Felt . . . 1G 129
Sandbourne *NW8* . . . *1K 81*
(off Abbey Rd.)
W11 . . . *6J 81*
(off Dartmouth Cl.)
Sandbourne Av. SW19 . . . 2K 153
Sandbourne Rd. SE4 . . . 2A 122
Sandbrook Cl. NW7 . . . 6E 28
Sandbrook Rd. N16 . . . 3E 66
Sandby Grn. SE9 . . . 3C 124
Sandby Ho. NW6 . . . 1J 81
Sandcliff Rd. DA8: Erith . . . 4K 109
Sandcroft Cl. N13 . . . 6G 33
Sandell's Av. TW15: Ashf . . . 4E 128
Sandell St. SE1 . . . 6J 13 (2A 102)
Sanderling Ct. *SE8* . . . *6B 104*
(off Abinger Gro.)
SE28 . . . 7C 90
Sanderling Lodge *E1* . . . *3K 15*
(off Star Pl.)
Sanders Cl. TW12: Ham H . . . 5G 131
Sanders Ho. *WC1* . . . *1J 7*
(off Gt. Percy St.)
Sanders La. NW7 . . . 7K 29
(Bittacy Ri.)
NW7 . . . 7A 30
(Grants Cl.)
Sanderson Cl. NW5 . . . 4F 65
Sanderson Ho. *SE8* . . . *5B 104*
(off Grove St.)
Sanderson Sq. BR1: Brom . . . 3E 160
Sanderstead Av. NW2 . . . 2G 63
Sanderstead Cl. SW12 . . . 7G 119
Sanderstead Rd.
CR2: Sande, S Croy . . . 7D 168
E10 . . . 1A 68
Sanders Way N19 . . . 1H 65
Sandfield *WC1* . . . *2F 7*
(off Cromer St.)
Sandfield Gdns. CR7: Thor H . . . 3B 156
Sandfield Pas. CR7: Thor H . . . 3C 156
Sandfield Pl. CR7: Thor H . . . 3C 156
Sandfield Rd. CR7: Thor H . . . 3B 156
Sandford Av. N22 . . . 1C 48
Sandford Cl. E6 . . . 4D 88
Sandford Ct. EN5: New Bar . . . 3E 20
N16 . . . 1E 66
Sandford Rd. BR2: Brom . . . 3J 159
DA7: Bex . . . 4E 126
E6 . . . 3C 88
Sandford Row SE17 . . . 5D 102
Sandford St. SW6 . . . 7K 99
Sandgate Cl. RM7: Rush G . . . 7J 55
Sandgate Ho. E5 . . . 5H 67
W5 . . . 5C 78
Sandgate La. SW18 . . . 1C 136
Sandgate Rd. DA16: Well . . . 7C 108
Sandgate St. SE15 . . . 6H 103
Sandgate Trad. Est. *SE15* . . . *6H 103*
(off Sandgate St.)
Sandham Ct. SW4 . . . 1J 119
Sandham Point *SE18* . . . *4F 107*
(off Vincent Rd.)
Sandhills SM6: Bedd . . . 4H 167
Sandhills, The *SW10* . . . *7A 16*
(off Limerston St.)
Sandhills Mdw. TW17: Shep . . . 7E 146
Sandhurst Av. HA2: Harr . . . 6F 41
KT5: Surb . . . 7H 151
Sandhurst Cl. CR2: Sande . . . 7E 168
NW9 . . . 3G 43
Sandhurst Ct. SW2 . . . 4J 119
Sandhurst Dr. IG3: Bark, Ilf . . . 4K 71
Sandhurst Ho. *E1* . . . *5J 85*
(off Wolsy St.)
Sandhurst Mkt. *SE6* . . . *1E 140*
(off Sandhurst Rd.)
Sandhurst Rd. BR6: Chels . . . 3K 173
DA5: Bexl . . . 5D 126
DA15: Sidc . . . 3K 143
N9 . . . 6D 24
NW9 . . . 3G 43
SE6 . . . 1F 141
Sandhurst Way CR2: Sande . . . 7E 168
Sandifer Dr. NW2 . . . 3F 63
Sandiford Rd. SM3: Sutt . . . 2H 165
Sandiland Cres. BR2: Hayes . . . 2H 171
Sandilands CR0: C'don . . . 2G 169
Sandilands Rd. SW6 . . . 1K 117
Sandison St. SE15 . . . 3G 121
Sandland St. WC1 . . . 6H 7 (5K 83)
Sandling Ri. SE9 . . . 3E 142
Sandlings, The N22 . . . 2A 48
Sandlings Cl. SE15 . . . 2H 121
Sandmartin Way SM6: Wall . . . 1E 166
Sandmere Rd. SW4 . . . 4J 119
Sandon Cl. KT10: Esh . . . 7H 149
Sandover Ho. *SE16* . . . *3G 103*
(off Spa Rd.)
Sandow Cres. UB3: Hayes . . . 3H 93
Sandown Av. RM10: Dag . . . 6J 73
Sandown Cl. TW5: Cran . . . 1J 111
Sandown Ct. HA7: Stan . . . 5H 27
RM10: Dag . . . *6J 73*
(off Sandown Av.)
SE26 . . . 3H 139
SM2: Sutt . . . 7K 165
Sandown Dr. SM5: Cars . . . 7E 166
Sandown Rd. SE25 . . . 5H 157
Sandown Way UB5: N'olt . . . 6C 58
Sandpiper Cl. E17 . . . 7E 34
SE16 . . . 2B 104
Sandpiper Ct. *E1* . . . *7G 85*
(off Thomas More St.)
E14 . . . *3E 104*
(off New Union Cl.)
SE8 . . . *6C 104*
(off Edward Pl.)
Sandpiper Rd. SM1: Sutt . . . 5H 165
Sandpiper Ter. IG5: Ilf . . . 3F 53
Sandpit Pl. SE7 . . . 5C 106
Sandpit Rd. BR1: Brom . . . 5G 141
Sandpits Rd. CR0: C'don . . . 4K 169
TW10: Ham . . . 2D 132
Sandra Cl. N22 . . . 1C 48
TW3: Houn . . . 5F 113
Sandra Ct. CR4: Mitc . . . 6D 136
Sandra Ho. KT8: E Mos . . . 5H 149
Sandridge Cl. HA1: Harr . . . 4J 41
Sandridge St. N19 . . . 2G 65
Sandringham Av. SW20 . . . 1G 153
Sandringham Bldgs. *SE17* . . . *4D 102*
(off Balfour St.)
Sandringham Cl. EN1: Enf . . . 2K 23
IG6: Ilf . . . 3G 53
SW19 . . . 1F 135
Sandringham Ct. DA15: Sidc . . . 6K 125
KT2: King T . . . *1E 150*
(off Skerne Wlk.)
SE16 . . . *1K 103*
(off King & Queen Wharf)
UB10: Hil . . . 4E 74
W1 . . . *1B 12*
(off Dufour's Pl.)
W9 . . . *3A 82*
(off Maida Va.)
Sandringham Cres. HA2: Harr . . . 2E 58
Sandringham Dr. DA2: Dart . . . 2K 145
DA16: Well . . . 2J 125
TW15: Ashf . . . 4A 128
Sandringham Flats *WC2* . . . *2D 12*
(off Charing Cross Rd.)
Sandringham Gdns. IG6: Ilf . . . 3G 53
KT8: W Mole . . . 4E 148
N8 . . . 6J 47
N12 . . . 6G 31
TW5: Cran . . . 1J 111
Sandringham Ho. *W14* . . . *4G 99*
(off Windsor Way)
Sandringham M. TW12: Hamp . . . 1D 148
W5 . . . 7D 78
Sandringham Rd. BR1: Brom . . . 5J 141
CR7: Thor H . . . 5C 156
E7 . . . 5A 70
E8 . . . 5F 67
E10 . . . 6F 51
IG11: Bark . . . 5K 71
KT4: Wor Pk . . . 3C 164
N22 . . . 3C 48
NW2 . . . 6D 62
NW11 . . . 7G 45
TW6: H'row A . . . 5A 110
UB5: N'olt . . . 7E 58
Sandrock Pl. CR0: C'don . . . 4K 169
Sandrock Rd. SE13 . . . 3C 122
SANDS END . . . 1A 118
Sand's End La. SW6 . . . 1K 117
Sandstone La. E16 . . . 7K 87
Sandstone Pl. N19 . . . 2F 65
Sandstone Rd. SE12 . . . 2K 141
Sands Way IG8: Wfd G . . . 6J 37
Sandtoft Rd. SE7 . . . 6K 105
Sandwell Cres. NW6 . . . 6J 63
Sandwich Ho. *SE16* . . . *2J 103*
(off Swan Rd.)
WC1 . . . *2E 6*
(off Sandwich St.)
Sandwich St. WC1 . . . 2E 6 (3J 83)
Sandwick Cl. NW7 . . . 7H 29
Sandy Bury BR6: Orp . . . 3H 173
Sandycombe Rd. TW9: Kew, Rich . . . 3F 115
TW14: Felt . . . 1J 129
Sandycoombe Rd. TW1: Twick . . . 6C 114
Sandycroft SE2 . . . 6A 108
Sandy Dr. TW14: Felt . . . 1G 129
Sandy Hill Av. SE18 . . . 5F 107
Sandy Hill Rd. SE18 . . . 5F 107
SM6: Wall . . . 7G 167
Sandyhill Rd. IG1: Ilf . . . 4F 71
Sandy La. BR5: St P . . . 7D 144
BR6: Orp . . . 7K 161
CR4: Mitc . . . 1E 154
(not continuous)
DA14: Sidc . . . 7D 144
HA3: Kenton . . . 6F 43
KT1: Ham W . . . 7A 132
KT12: Walt T . . . 6K 147
SM2: Cheam . . . 7G 165
SM6: Wall . . . 6H 167
TW10: Ham . . . 2C 132
TW11: Ham W, Tedd . . . 7A 132
Sandy La. Nth. SM6: Wall . . . 6H 167
Sandy La. Sth. SM6: Wall . . . 7G 167
Sandymount Av. HA7: Stan . . . 5H 27
Sandy Ridge BR7: Chst . . . 6E 142
Sandy Rd. NW3 . . . 2K 63
NW11 . . . 2K 63
Sandys Row E1 . . . 6H 9 (5E 84)
Sandy Way CR0: C'don . . . 3B 170
KT12: Walt T . . . 7H 147
Sanford La. N16 . . . 3F 67
Sanford St. SE14 . . . 6A 104
Sanford Ter. N16 . . . 3F 67
Sanford Wlk. N16 . . . 2F 67
SE14 . . . 6A 104
Sangam Cl. UB2: S'hall . . . 3C 94
Sanger Av. KT9: Chess . . . 5E 162
Sangley Rd. SE6 . . . 7D 122
SE25 . . . 4E 156
Sangora Rd. SW11 . . . 4B 118
Sankey Ho. *E2* . . . *2J 85*
(off St James's Av.)
Sansom Rd. E11 . . . 2H 69
Sansom St. SE5 . . . 1D 120
Sans Wlk. EC1 . . . 3K 7 (4A 84)
Santley Ho. SE1 . . . 7K 13 (2A 102)
Santley St. SW4 . . . 4K 119
Santos Rd. SW18 . . . 5J 117
Santway, The HA7: Stan . . . 5D 26
Sapcote Trad. Cen. NW10 . . . 6B 62
Saperton Wlk. SE11 . . . 3H 19

Saphora Cl. BR6: Farnb 5H 173
Sapperton Ct. EC1 3C 8
Sapperton Ho. *W2* *5J 81*
(off Westbourne Pk. Rd.)
Sapphire Cl. E6 6E 88
RM8: Dag 1C 72
Sapphire Ct. *E1* *7G 85*
(off Cable St.)
Sapphire Rd. NW10 7J 61
SE8 4A 104
Saprano Ct. *E15* *1H 87*
(off Plaistow Rd.)
Saracen Cl. CR0: C'don 6D 156
Saracens Head Yd. EC3 1J 15
Saracen St. E14 6C 86
Sarah Ct. UB5: N'olt 1D 76
Sarah Ho. *E1* *6H 85*
(off Commercial Rd.)
Sarah Swift Ho. *SE1* *6F 15*
(off Kipling St.)
Sara La. Ct. *N1* *2E 84*
(off Stanway St.)
Saratoga Rd. E5 4J 67
Sara Turnbull Ho. SE18 4D 106
Sardinia St. WC2 1G 13 (6K 83)
Sarita Cl. HA3: Hrw W 2H 41
Sarjant Path *SW19* *2F 135*
(off Blincoe Cl.)
Sarjeant Ct. *BR4: W W'ck* *2F 171*
(off Bencurtis Pk.)
Sark Cl. TW5: Hest 7E 94
Sark Ho. EN3: Enf W 1E 24
Sark Twr. SE28 2G 107
Sark Wlk. E16 6K 87
Sarnes Ct. *N11* *4A 32*
(off Oakleigh Rd. Sth.)
Sarnesfield Ho. *SE15* *6H 103*
(off Pencraig Way)
Sarnesfield Rd. EN2: Enf 4J 23
Sarratt Ho. *W10* *5E 80*
(off Sutton Way)
Sarre Rd. NW2 5H 63
Sarsen Av. TW3: Houn 2E 112
Sarsfeld Rd. SW12 2D 136
Sarsfield Rd. UB6: G'frd 2B 78
Sartor Rd. SE15 4K 121
Sarum Ho. *W11* *7H 81*
(off Portobello Rd.)
Sarum Ter. E3 4B 86
Sassoon NW9 1B 44
Satanita Cl. E16 6B 88
Satchell Mead NW9 1B 44
Satchwell Rd. E2 2K 9 (3G 85)
Satchwell St. E2 2K 9 (3G 85)
Sattar M. N16 3D 66
Saturn Ho. *E3* *1C 86*
(off Garrison Rd.)
Saul Ct. SE15 6F 103
Sauls Grn. E11 3G 69
Saunders Cl. *E14* *7B 86*
(off Limehouse C'way.)
IG1: Ilf 1H 71
Saunders Ho. *SE16* *2K 103*
(off Quebec Way)
Saunders Ness Rd. E14 5E 104
Saunders Rd. SE18 5K 107
UB10: Uxb 7B 56
Saunders St. SE11 3J 19 (4A 102)
Saunders Way SE28 7B 90
Saunderton Rd. HA0: Wemb 5B 60
Saunton Av. UB3: Harl 7H 93
Saunton Ct. *UB1: S'hall* *7G 77*
(off Haldane Rd.)
Savage Gdns. E6 6D 88
EC3 2H 15 (7E 84)
(not continuous)
Savannah Cl. SE15 7F 103
Savera Cl. UB2: S'hall 3A 94
Savernake Ct. HA7: Stan 6G 27
Savernake Ho. N4 7C 48
Savernake Rd. N9 6B 24
NW3 4D 64
Savery Dr. KT6: Surb 7B 150
Savile Cl. KT3: N Mald 5A 152
KT7: T Ditt 7K 149
Savile Gdns. CR0: C'don 2F 169
Savile Row W1 2A 12 (7G 83)
Saville Cres.
TW15: Ashf 6F 129
Saville Rd. E16 1C 106
RM6: Chad H 6F 55
TW1: Twick 1K 131
W4 3K 97
Saville Row BR2: Hayes 1H 171
EN3: Enf H 2E 24
Savill Gdns. SW20 3C 152
Savill Ho. *E16* *1F 107*
(off Robert St.)
SW4 6H 119
Savill Row IG8: Wfd G 6C 36
Savin Lodge *SM2: Sutt* *7A 166*
(off Walnut M.)
Savona Cl. SW19 7F 135
Savona Ho. *SW8* *7G 101*
(off Savona St.)
Savona St. SW8 7G 101
Savoy Av. UB3: Harl 5G 93
Savoy Bldgs. WC2 3G 13
SAVOY CIRCUS 7B 80
Savoy Cl. E15 1G 87
HA8: Edg 5B 28
Savoy Ct. HA2: Harr 5F 41
NW3 3A 64
SW5 *4J 99*
(off Cromwell Rd.)
WC2 3F 13 (7K 83)
Savoy Hill WC2 3G 13 (7K 83)
Savoy M. SW9 3J 119
Savoy Pde. EN1: Enf 3K 23
Savoy Pl. W12 1F 99
WC2 3F 13 (7J 83)
Savoy Row WC2 2G 13
Savoy Steps WC2 3G 13
Savoy St. WC2 3G 13 (7K 83)
Savoy Theatre *3F 13*
(off Strand)
Savoy Way WC2 3G 13
Sawbill Cl. UB4: Yead 5B 76
Sawkins Cl. SW19 2G 135
Sawley Rd. W12 1C 98
Sawmill Yd. E3 1A 86
Sawtry Cl. SM5: Cars 7C 154
Sawyer Cl. N9 2B 34
Sawyer Ct. NW10 7K 61
Sawyers Cl. RM10: Dag 6J 73
Sawyer's Hill TW10: Rich 7F 115
Sawyers Lawn W13 6A 78
Sawyer St. SE1 6C 14 (2C 102)
Saxby Rd. SW2 7J 119
Saxham Rd. IG11: Bark 2J 89
Saxlingham Rd. E4 3A 36
Saxon Av. TW13: Hanw 2C 130
Saxonbury Av. TW16: Sun 3K 147
Saxonbury Cl. CR4: Mitc 3B 154
Saxonbury Ct. N7 5J 65
Saxonbury Gdns. KT6: Surb 1C 162
Saxon Bus. Cen. SW19 2A 154
Saxon Chase N8 6K 47
Saxon Cl. E17 7C 50
KT6: Surb 6D 150
UB8: Hil 5B 74
Saxon Dr. W3 6G 79
Saxonfield Cl. SW2 7K 119
Saxon Gdns. UB1: S'hall 7C 76
Saxon Hall *W2* *7K 81*
(off Palace Ct.)
Saxon Ho. *E1* *6K 9*
(off Thrawl St.)
KT1: King T 4F 151
TW13: Hanw 2D 130
Saxon Lea Ct. *E3* *2B 86*
(off Saxon Rd.)
Saxon Lodge *CR0: C'don* *1C 168*
(off Tavistock Rd.)
Saxon Rd. BR1: Brom 7H 141
E3 2B 86
E6 4D 88
HA9: Wemb 3J 61
IG1: Ilf 6F 71
KT2: King T 1E 150
N22 1B 48
SE25 5D 156
TW15: Ashf 6F 129
UB1: S'hall 7C 76
Saxon Ter. SE6 2B 140
Saxon Wlk. DA14: Sidc 6C 144
Saxon Way N14 6C 22
UB7: Harm 2D 174
Saxon Way Ind. Est. UB7: Harm 2D 174
Saxony Pde. UB3: Hayes 5E 74
Saxton Cl. SE13 3F 123
Sayers Ho. *N2* *2B 46*
(off The Grange)
Sayer's Wlk. TW10: Rich 7F 115
Sayesbury La. N18 5B 34
Sayes Ct. SE8 6B 104
Sayes Ct. St. SE8 6B 104
Scadbury Pk. (Nature Reserve) 7K 143
Scads Hill Cl. BR6: Pet W 6K 161
Scafell *NW1* *1A 6*
(off Stanhope St.)
Scala St. W1 5B 6 (5G 83)
Scales Rd. N17 3F 49
Scampston M. W10 6F 81
Scandrett St. E1 1H 103
Scarab Cl. E16 7H 87
Scarba Wlk. *N1* *6D 66*
(off Essex Rd.)
N1 *6D 66*
(off Marquess Rd.)
Scarborough Rd. E11 1F 69
N4 7A 48
N9 7D 24
TW6: H'row A 6E 110
Scarborough St. E1 1K 15 (6F 85)
Scarbrook Rd. CR0: C'don 3C 168
Scarle Rd. HA0: Wemb 6D 60
Scarlet Rd. SE6 3G 141
Scarlette Mnr. Way SW2 7A 120
Scarsbrook Rd. SE3 3B 124
Scarsdale Pl. W8 3K 99
Scarsdale Rd. HA2: Harr 3G 59
Scarsdale Studios *W8* *3J 99*
(off Stratford Rd.)
Scarsdale Vs. W8 3J 99
Scarth Rd. SW13 3B 116
Scawen Cl. SM5: Cars 4E 166
Scawen Rd. SE8 5A 104
Scawfell St. E2 2F 85
Sceaux Gdns. SE5 1E 120
Sceptre Ct. *EC3* *3K 15*
(off Tower Hill)
Sceptre Ho. *E1* *4J 85*
(off Malcolm Rd.)
Sceptre Rd. E2 3J 85
Sceynes Link N12 4D 30
Schafer Ho. NW1 2A 6 (3G 83)
Schiller International University 5J 13
Schofield Wlk. SE3 7J 105
Scholars Cl. EN5: Barn 4B 20
Scholars Ho. *NW6* *1J 81*
(off Glengall Rd.)
Scholars Pl. N16 3E 66
Scholars Rd. E4 1A 36
SW12 1G 137
Scholefield Rd. N19 2H 65
Scholey Ho. SW11 3C 118
Schomberg Ho. *SW1* *3D 18*
(off Page St.)
Schonfeld Sq. N16 2D 66
School All. TW1: Twick 1A 132
School App. E2 1H 9
Schoolbank Rd. SE10 3H 105
Schoolbell M. E3 2A 86
School Ho. *SE1* *4E 102*
(off Page's Wlk.)
School Ho. La. TW11: Tedd 7B 132
Schoolhouse La. E1 7K 85
Schoolhouse Yd. SE18 5F 107
School La. DA16: Well 3B 126
HA5: Pinn 4C 40
KT1: Ham W 1C 150
KT6: Surb 1F 163
TW17: Shep 6D 146
WD23: Bush 1A 26
School Pas. KT1: King T 2F 151
UB1: S'hall 7D 76
School Rd. BR7: Chst 1G 161
E12 4D 70
KT1: Ham W 1C 150
KT8: E Mos 4H 149
NW10 4K 79
RM10: Dag 1G 91
TW3: Houn 3G 113
TW12: Ham H 6G 131
TW15: Ashf 6D 128
UB7: Harm 2E 174
School Rd. Av. TW12: Ham H 6G 131
SCHOOL ROAD JUNC. 7D 128
School Sq. SE10 3H 105
School Wlk. TW16: Sun 4H 147
School Way N12 6G 31
RM8: Dag 3C 72
(not continuous)
Schooner Cl. E14 3F 105
IG11: Bark 3B 90
SE16 2K 103
Schubert Rd. SW15 5H 117
Science Mus. 2B 16 (3B 100)
Sclater St. E1 3J 9 (4F 85)
Scoble Pl. N16 4F 67
Scoles Cres. SW2 1B 138
Scoop, The 5H 15 (1E 102)
Scope Way KT1: King T 4E 150
Score Complex, The 3D 68
Scoresby St. SE1 5A 14 (1B 102)
Scorton Av. UB6: G'frd 2A 78
Scorton Ho. *N1* *2E 84*
(off Whitmore Est.)
Scotch Comn. W13 5A 78
SCOTCH HOUSE 2D 100
Scoter Cl. IG8: Wfd G 7E 36
Scoter Ct. *SE8* *6B 104*
(off Abinger Gro.)
Scot Gro. HA5: Pinn 1B 40
Scotia Bldg. *E1* *7K 85*
(off Jardine Rd.)
Scotia Ct. *SE16* *2J 103*
(off Canada Est.)
Scotia Rd. SW2 7A 120
Scotland Grn. N17 2F 49
Scotland Grn. Rd. EN3: Pond E 5E 24
Scotland Grn. Rd. Nth.
EN3: Pond E 4E 24
Scotland Pl. SW1 5E 12 (1J 101)
Scotland Rd. IG9: Buck H 1F 37
Scotney Cl. BR6: Farnb 4E 172
Scotney Ho. E9 6J 67
Scots Cl. TW19: Stanw 1A 128
Scotsdale Cl. BR5: Pet W 4J 161
SM3: Cheam 7G 165
Scotsdale Rd. SE12 5K 123
Scotson Ho. SE11 4J 19
Scotswood St. EC1 3K 7 (4A 84)
Scotswood Wlk. N17 7B 34
Scott Av. SW15 6G 117
Scott Cl. KT19: Ewe 5J 163
SW16 1K 155
UB7: W Dray 4B 92
Scott Ct. W3 2K 97
Scott Cres. HA2: Harr 1F 59
Scott Ellis Gdns. NW8 2A 4 (3B 82)
Scottes La. RM8: Dag 1D 72
Scott Farm Cl. KT7: T Ditt 1B 162
Scott Gdns. TW5: Hest 7B 94
Scott Ho. DA17: Belv 5F 109
E13 *2J 87*
(off Queens Rd. W.)

Scott Ho.—Selworthy Cl.

Scott Ho. *E14* . . . 2C **104**
(off Admirals Way)
N7 . . . 6K **65**
(off Caledonian Rd.)
N18 . . . 5B **34**
(off Woolmer Rd.)
NW8 . . . 4C **4**
(off Broadley St.)
NW10 . . . 7K **61**
(off Stonebridge Pk.)
SE8 . . . 5B **104**
(off Grove St.)
Scott Lidgett Cres. SE16 . . . 2G **103**
Scott Rd. HA8: Edg . . . 2H **43**
Scott Russell Pl. E14 . . . 5D **104**
Scotts Av. BR2: Brom . . . 2F **159**
TW16: Sun . . . 7G **129**
Scotts Ct. *W12* . . . 2E **98**
(off Scott's Rd.)
Scotts Dr. TW12: Hamp . . . 7F **131**
Scotts Farm Rd. KT19: Ewe . . . 6J **163**
Scott's La. BR2: Brom . . . 3F **159**
Scotts Pas. SE18 . . . 4F **107**
Scotts Rd. BR1: Brom . . . 7J **141**
E10 . . . 1E **68**
UB2: S'hall . . . 3A **94**
W12 . . . 2D **98**
Scott's Sufferance Wharf SE1 . . . 7K **15**
Scotts Ter. SE9 . . . 2C **142**
Scott St. E1 . . . 4H **85**
Scotts Way TW16: Sun . . . 7G **129**
Scott's Yd. EC4 . . . 2E **14** (7D **84**)
Scott Trimmer Way TW3: Houn . . . 2C **112**
Scottwell Dr. NW9 . . . 5B **44**
Scoulding Ho. *E14* . . . 3C **104**
(off Mellish St.)
Scoulding Rd. E16 . . . 6J **87**
Scouler St. E14 . . . 7E **86**
Scout App. NW10 . . . 4A **62**
Scout La. SW4 . . . 3G **119**
Scout Pk. . . . 7C **32**
Scout Way NW7 . . . 4E **28**
Scovell Cres. SE1 . . . 7C **14**
Scovell Rd. SE1 . . . 7C **14** (2C **102**)
Scrattons Ter. IG11: Bark . . . 2D **90**
Screen on Baker Street (Cinema) . . . *5F 5*
(off Baker St.)
Screen on the Green (Cinema) . . . *1B 84*
(off Upper St.)
Screen on the Hill (Cinema)
Belsize Pk. . . . 5C **64**
Scriven Ct. E8 . . . 1F **85**
Scriven St. E8 . . . 1F **85**
Scrooby St. SE6 . . . 6D **122**
Scrope Ho. *EC1* . . . 5J **7**
(off Bourne Est.)
Scrubs La. NW10 . . . 3C **80**
W10 . . . 3C **80**
Scrutton Cl. SW12 . . . 7H **119**
Scrutton St. EC2 . . . 4G **9** (4E **84**)
Scudamore La. NW9 . . . 4J **43**
Scutari Rd. SE22 . . . 5J **121**
Scylla Cres. TW6: H'row A . . . 7D **110**
(not continuous)
Scylla Rd. SE15 . . . 3G **121**
(not continuous)
TW6: H'row A . . . 6D **110**
Seabright St. E2 . . . 3H **85**
Seabrook Dr. BR4: W W'ck . . . 2G **171**
Seabrook Gdns. RM7: Rush G . . . 7G **55**
Seabrook Rd. RM8: Dag . . . 3D **72**
Seaburn Cl. RM13: Rain . . . 2K **91**
Seacole Cl. W3 . . . 6K **79**
Seacole Ct. *N21* . . . 5E **22**
(off Pennington Dr.)
Sea Containers Ho. SE1 . . . 3K **13**
Seacon Twr. E14 . . . 2B **104**
Seacourt Rd. SE2 . . . 2D **108**
Seafield Rd. N11 . . . 4C **32**
Seaford Cl. HA4: Ruis . . . 1F **57**
Seaford Ho. *SE16* . . . 2J **103**
(off Swan Rd.)
Seaford Rd. E17 . . . 3D **50**
EN1: Enf . . . 4K **23**
N15 . . . 5D **48**
TW6: H'row A . . . 5A **110**
W13 . . . 1B **96**
Seaford St. WC1 . . . 2F **7** (3J **83**)
Seaforth Av. KT3: N Mald . . . 5D **152**
Seaforth Cres. N5 . . . 5C **66**
Seaforth Gdns. IG8: Wfd G . . . 5F **37**
KT19: Ewe . . . 4B **164**
N21 . . . 7E **22**
Seaforth Pl. SW1 . . . 1B **18**
Seagrave Cl. E1 . . . 5K **85**
Seagrave Lodge *SW6* . . . 6J **99**
(off Seagrave Rd.)
Seagrave Rd. SW6 . . . 6J **99**
Seagry Rd. E11 . . . 7J **51**
Seagull Cl. IG11: Bark . . . 3A **90**
Seagull La. E16 . . . 7J **87**
Seahorse Sailing Club . . . 2K **61**
Sealand Rd. TW6: H'row A . . . 6C **110**
Sealand Wlk. UB5: N'olt . . . 3B **76**
Seal Ho. *SE1* . . . 7F **15**
(off Weston St.)
Sea Life London Aquarium
. . . 6G **13** (2K **101**)
Seal St. E8 . . . 4F **67**
Searle Ho. *SW11* . . . 1E **118**
(off Macduff Rd.)
Searles Cl. SW11 . . . 7C **100**
Searles Dr. E6 . . . 5F **89**
Searles Rd. SE1 . . . 4D **102**
Searson Ho. *SE17* . . . 4B **102**
(off Canterbury Pl.)
Sears St. SE5 . . . 7D **102**
Seasalter Ho. *SW9* . . . 1A **120**
(off Gosling Way)
Seasons Cl. W7 . . . 1K **95**
Seasprite Cl. UB5: N'olt . . . 3B **76**
Seaton Av. IG3: Ilf . . . 5K **71**
Seaton Cl. E13 . . . 4J **87**
SE11 . . . 5K **19** (5A **102**)
SW15 . . . 1D **134**
TW2: Whitt . . . 6H **113**
Seaton Dr. TW15: Ashf . . . 2A **128**
Seaton Gdns. HA4: Ruis . . . 3H **57**
Seaton Point E5 . . . 4G **67**
Seaton Rd. CR4: Mitc . . . 2C **154**
DA16: Well . . . 7C **108**
HA0: Wemb . . . 2E **78**
TW2: Whitt . . . 6G **113**
UB3: Harl . . . 4F **93**
Seaton Sq. NW7 . . . 7A **30**
Seaton St. N18 . . . 5B **34**
Seawell Ct. *IG11: Bark* . . . 2G **89**
(off Dock Rd.)
Sebastian Ct. IG11: Bark . . . 1K **89**
Sebastian Ho. *N1* . . . 1G **9**
(off Hoxton St.)
Sebastian St. EC1 . . . 2B **8** (3B **84**)
Sebastopol Rd. N9 . . . 4B **34**
Sebbon St. N1 . . . 7B **66**
Sebergham Gro. NW7 . . . 7H **29**
Sebert Rd. E7 . . . 5K **69**
Sebright Ho. *E2* . . . 2G **85**
(off Coate St.)
Sebright Pas. E2 . . . 2G **85**
Sebright Rd. EN5: Barn . . . 2A **20**
Secker Cres. HA3: Hrw W . . . 1G **41**
Secker Ho. *SW9* . . . 2B **120**
(off Loughborough Est.)
Secker St. SE1 . . . 5J **13** (1A **102**)
Secombe Theatre . . . 5K **165**
Second Av. E12 . . . 4C **70**
E13 . . . 3J **87**
E17 . . . 5C **50**
EN1: Enf . . . 5A **24**
HA9: Wemb . . . 2D **60**
KT12: Walt T . . . 6K **147**
N18 . . . 4D **34**
NW4 . . . 4F **45**
RM6: Chad H . . . 5C **54**
Second Av. RM10: Dag . . . 1H **91**
SW14 . . . 3A **116**
UB3: Hayes . . . 1H **93**
W3 . . . 1B **98**
W10 . . . 4G **81**
Second Cl. KT8: W Mole . . . 4G **149**
Second Cross Rd. TW2: Twick . . . 2J **131**
Second Way HA9: Wemb . . . 4H **61**
Sedan Way SE17 . . . 5E **102**
Sedcombe Cl. DA14: Sidc . . . 4B **144**
Sedcote Rd. EN3: Pond E . . . 5D **24**
Sedding St. SW1 . . . 3G **17** (4E **100**)
Sedding Studios *SW1* . . . 3G **17**
(off Sedding St.)
Seddon Highwalk *EC2* . . . 5C **8**
(off Aldersgate St.)
Seddon Ho. EC2 . . . 5C **8**
Seddon Rd. SM4: Mord . . . 5B **154**
Seddon St. WC1 . . . 2H **7** (3K **83**)
Sedgebrook Rd. SE3 . . . 2B **124**
Sedgecombe Av. HA3: Kenton . . . 5C **42**
Sedgefield Ct. *UB5: N'olt* . . . 5F **59**
(off Newmarket Av.)
Sedgeford Rd. W12 . . . 1B **98**
Sedgehill Rd. SE6 . . . 4C **140**
Sedgemere Av. N2 . . . 3A **46**
Sedgemere Rd. SE2 . . . 3C **108**
Sedgemoor Dr. RM10: Dag . . . 4G **73**
Sedge Rd. N17 . . . 7D **34**
Sedgeway SE6 . . . 1H **141**
Sedgewick Av. UB10: Hil . . . 7D **56**
Sedgewood Cl. BR2: Hayes . . . 7H **159**
Sedgmoor Pl. SE5 . . . 7E **102**
Sedgwick Ho. *E3* . . . 5C **86**
(off Gale St.)
Sedgwick Rd. E10 . . . 2E **68**
Sedgwick St. E9 . . . 5K **67**
Sedleigh Rd. SW18 . . . 6H **117**
Sedlescombe Rd. SW6 . . . 6J **99**
Sedley Cl. EN1: Enf . . . 1C **24**
Sedley Ct. SE26 . . . 2H **139**
Sedley Ho. *SE11* . . . 5H **19**
(off Newburn St.)
Sedley Pl. W1 . . . 1J **11** (6F **83**)
Sedum Cl. NW9 . . . 5H **43**
Seeley Dr. SE21 . . . 4E **138**
Seelig Av. NW9 . . . 7C **44**
Seely Rd. SW17 . . . 6E **136**
Seetha Ho. *IG1: Ilf* . . . 2H **71**
(off High Rd.)
Seething La. EC3 . . . 2H **15** (7E **84**)
SEETHING WELLS . . . 6C **150**
Seething Wells La. KT6: Surb . . . 6C **150**
Sefton Av. HA3: Hrw W . . . 2H **41**
NW7 . . . 5E **28**
Sefton Cl. BR5: St M Cry . . . 4K **161**
Sefton Ct. EN2: Enf . . . 2G **23**
TW3: Houn . . . 1F **113**
Sefton Rd. BR5: St M Cry . . . 4K **161**
CR0: C'don . . . 1G **169**
Sefton St. SW15 . . . 3E **116**
Segal Cl. SE23 . . . 7A **122**
Sekforde St. EC1 . . . 4A **8** (4B **84**)
Sekhon Ter. TW13: Hanw . . . 3E **130**
Selah Dr. BR8: Swan . . . 7J **145**
Selan Gdns. UB4: Yead . . . 5K **75**
Selbie Av. NW10 . . . 5B **62**
Selborne Av. DA5: Bexl . . . 1E **144**
E12 . . . 4E **70**
Selborne Gdns. NW4 . . . 4C **44**
UB6: G'frd . . . 1A **78**
Selborne Rd. CR0: C'don . . . 3E **168**
DA14: Sidc . . . 4B **144**
E17 . . . 5B **50**
IG1: Ilf . . . 2E **70**
KT3: N Mald . . . 2A **152**
N14 . . . 3D **32**
N22 . . . 1K **47**
SE5 . . . 2D **120**
Selborne Wlk. E17 . . . 5B **50**
Selborne Wlk. Shop. Cen. E17 . . . 4B **50**
Selbourne Av. KT6: Surb . . . 2F **163**
Selbourne Ho. SE1 . . . 7E **14**
Selby Cen., The . . . 6K **33**
Selby Chase HA4: Ruis . . . 2K **57**
Selby Cl. BR7: Chst . . . 6E **142**
E6 . . . 5C **88**
KT9: Chess . . . 7E **162**
Selby Gdns. UB1: S'hall . . . 4E **76**
Selby Grn. SM5: Cars . . . 7C **154**
Selby Rd. E11 . . . 3G **69**
E13 . . . 5K **87**
N17 . . . 7K **33**
SE20 . . . 2G **157**
SM5: Cars . . . 7C **154**
TW15: Ashf . . . 6E **128**
W5 . . . 4B **78**
Selby Sq. *W10* . . . 3G **81**
(off Dowland St.)
Selby St. E1 . . . 4G **85**
Selcroft Ho. *SE10* . . . 5H **105**
(off Glenister Rd.)
Selden Ho. *SE15* . . . 2J **121**
(off Selden Rd.)
Selden Rd. SE15 . . . 2J **121**
Selden Wlk. N7 . . . 2K **65**
Seldon Ho. *SW1* . . . 6A **18**
(off Churchill Gdns.)
SW8 . . . 7G **101**
(off Stewart's Rd.)
Selfridges . . . 1G **11**
SELHURST . . . 6E **156**
Selhurst Cl. SW19 . . . 1F **135**
Selhurst New Rd. SE25 . . . 6E **156**
Selhurst Pk. . . . 4E **156**
Selhurst Pl. SE25: C'don, Lon . . . 6E **156**
Selhurst Rd. N9 . . . 3J **33**
SE25 . . . 6E **156**
Selig Ct. *NW11* . . . 7G **45**
(off Golders Grn. Rd.)
Selina Ho. *NW8* . . . 3B **4**
(off Frampton St.)
Selinas La. RM8: Dag . . . 7E **54**
Selkirk Ho. *N1* . . . 1K **83**
(off Bingfield St.)
Selkirk Rd. SW17 . . . 4C **136**
TW2: Twick . . . 2G **131**
Sellers Hall Cl. N3 . . . 7D **30**
Sellincourt Rd. SW17 . . . 5C **136**
Sellindge Cl. BR3: Beck . . . 7B **140**
Sellons Av. NW10 . . . 1B **80**
Sellwood Dr. EN5: Barn . . . 5A **20**
Selma Ho. *W12* . . . 6D **80**
(off Du Cane Rd.)
Selman Ho. E9 . . . 6A **68**
SELSDON . . . 7J **169**
Selsdon Av. CR2: S Croy . . . 6D **168**
Selsdon Cl. KT6: Surb . . . 5E **150**
RM5: Col R . . . 1J **55**
Selsdon Pk. Rd. CR0: Sels . . . 7K **169**
CR2: Sels . . . 7K **169**
Selsdon Rd. CR2: S Croy . . . 5D **168**
E11 . . . 7J **51**
E13 . . . 1A **88**
NW2 . . . 2B **62**
SE27 . . . 3A **138**
Selsdon Way E14 . . . 3D **104**
Selsea Pl. N16 . . . 5E **66**
Selsey *WC1* . . . 2F **7**
(off Tavistock Pl.)
Selsey Cres. DA16: Well . . . 1D **126**
Selsey St. E14 . . . 5C **86**
Selvage La. NW7 . . . 5E **28**
Selway Cl. HA5: Eastc . . . 4K **39**
Selway Ho. *SW8* . . . 1J **119**
(off Sth. Lambeth Rd.)
Selwood Pl. SW7 . . . 5A **16** (5B **100**)
Selwood Rd.
CR0: C'don . . . 2H **169**
KT9: Chess . . . 4D **162**
SM3: Sutt . . . 1H **165**
Selwoods SW2 . . . 7A **120**
Selwood Ter. SW7 . . . 5A **16** (5B **100**)
Selworthy Cl. E11 . . . 5J **51**

Selworthy Ho. SW11 . . . 1B 118
(off Battersea Church Rd.)
Selworthy Rd. SE6 . . . 3B 140
Selwyn Av. E4 . . . 6K 35
IG3: Ilf . . . 6K 53
TW9: Rich . . . 3E 114
Selwyn Cl. TW4: Houn . . . 4C 112
Selwyn Ct. E17 . . . 5C 50
(off Yunus Khan Cl.)
HA8: Edg . . . 7C 28
HA9: Wemb . . . 3J 61
SE3 . . . 3H 123
TW10: Rich . . . 5F 115
(off Church Rd.)
Selwyn Cres. DA16: Well . . . 3B 126
Selwyn Rd. E3 . . . 2B 86
E13 . . . 1K 87
KT3: N Mald . . . 5K 151
NW10 . . . 7A 62
Semley Ga. E9 . . . 6B 68
Semley Ho. SW1 . . . 4J 17
(off Semley Pl.)
Semley Pl. SW1 . . . 4H 17 (4E 100)
Semley Rd. SW16 . . . 2J 155
Senate St. SE15 . . . 2J 121
Senators Lodge E3 . . . 2A 86
(off Roman Rd.)
Senator Wlk. SE28 . . . 3H 107
Sendall Ct. SW11 . . . 3B 118
(off Winstanley Rd.)
Seneca Rd. CR7: Thor H . . . 4C 156
Sener Ct. CR2: S Croy . . . 6C 168
Senga Rd. SM6: Wall . . . 1E 166
Senhouse Rd. SM3: Cheam . . . 3F 165
Senior St. W2 . . . 5K 81
Senlac Rd. SE12 . . . 1K 141
Sennen Rd. EN1: Enf . . . 7A 24
Sennen Wlk. SE9 . . . 3C 142
Senrab St. E1 . . . 6K 85
Sentamu Cl. SE24 . . . 1B 138
Sentinel Cl. UB5: N'olt . . . 4C 76
Sentinel Sq. NW4 . . . 4E 44
September Ct. UB1: S'hall . . . 1F 95
(off Dormer's Wells La.)
UB8: Uxb . . . 2A 74
September Way HA7: Stan . . . 6G 27
Septimus Pl. EN1: Enf . . . 5B 24
Sequoia Cl. WD23: B Hea . . . 1C 26
Sequoia Gdns. BR6: Orp . . . 7K 161
Sequoia Pk. HA5: Hat E . . . 6A 26
Seraph Ct. EC1 . . . 1C 8
(off Moreland St.)
Serbin Cl. E10 . . . 7E 50
Serenaders Rd. SW9 . . . 2A 120
Serenity Apartments E17 . . . 5D 50
Seren Pk. Gdns. SE3 . . . 6G 105
Sergeant Ind. Est. SW18 . . . 6K 117
Serica Ct. SE10 . . . 7E 104
Serjeants Inn EC4 . . . 1K 13 (6A 84)
Serlby Ct. W14 . . . 3H 99
(off Somerset Sq.)
Serle St. WC2 . . . 7H 7 (6K 83)
Sermon La. EC4 . . . 1C 14
Serpentine, The . . . 5D 10 (1C 100)
Serpentine Ct. SE16 . . . 2K 103
(off Christopher Cl.)
Serpentine Gallery . . . 6A 10 (2B 100)
Serpentine Rd. W2 . . . 5C 10 (1C 100)
Serviden Dr. BR1: Brom . . . 1B 160
Servite Ho. BR3: Beck . . . 1B 158
KT4: Wor Pk . . . 2B 164
(off The Avenue)
N14 . . . 5A 22
(off Bramley Rd.)
Servius Ct. TW8: Bford . . . 7D 96
Setchell Rd. SE1 . . . 4F 103
Setchell Way SE1 . . . 4F 103
Seth St. SE16 . . . 2J 103
Seton Gdns. RM9: Dag . . . 7C 72
Settle Point E13 . . . 2J 87
(off London Rd.)
Settle Rd. E13 . . . 2J 87
Settlers Ct. E14 . . . 7F 87
Settles St. E1 . . . 5G 85
Settrington Rd. SW6 . . . 2K 117
Seven Acres SM5: Cars . . . 2C 166
Seven Dials WC2 . . . 1E 12 (6J 83)
Seven Dials Ct. WC2 . . . 1E 12
(off Shorts Gdns.)
Sevenex Pde. HA9: Wemb . . . 5E 60
Seven Islands Leisure Cen. . . . 3J 103
SEVEN KINGS . . . 1J 71
Seven Kings Rd. IG3: Ilf . . . 1J 71
Seven Kings Way KT2: King T . . . 1E 150
Sevenoaks Cl. DA7: Bex . . . 4H 127
Sevenoaks Ct. HA6: Nwood . . . 1E 38
Sevenoaks Rd. BR6: Chels, Orp . . . 5K 173
BR6: Prat B . . . 7K 173
SE4 . . . 6A 122
Sevenoaks Way BR5: St P . . . 7C 144
DA14: Sidc . . . 7C 144
Sevenseas Rd.
TW6: H'row A . . . 6E 110
SEVEN SISTERS . . . 5F 49
Seven Sisters Rd. N4 . . . 2A 66
N7 . . . 3K 65
N15 . . . 7C 48
Seven Stars Cnr. W6 . . . 3C 98
W12 . . . 3C 98
Seven Stars Yd. E1 . . . 5K 9
Seventh Av. E12 . . . 4D 70
UB3: Hayes . . . 1J 93
Sevenways Pde. IG2: Ilf . . . 5E 52
Severnake Cl. E14 . . . 4C 104
Severn Av. W10 . . . 3G 81
Severn Ct. KT2: King T . . . 1D 150
(off John Williams Cl.)
Severn Dr. KT10: Hin W . . . 2A 162
Severn Way NW10 . . . 5B 62
Severus Rd. SW11 . . . 4C 118
Seville Ho. E1 . . . 1G 103
(off Hellings St.)
Seville M. N1 . . . 7E 66
Seville St. SW1 . . . 7F 11 (2D 100)
Sevington Rd. NW4 . . . 6D 44
Sevington St. W9 . . . 4K 81
Seward Rd. BR3: Beck . . . 2K 157
W7 . . . 2A 96
SEWARDSTONE . . . 1K 25
Sewardstone Gdns. E4 . . . 5J 25
Sewardstone Rd. E2 . . . 2J 85
E4 . . . 7J 25
Seward St. EC1 . . . 3B 8 (3B 84)
Sewdley St. E5 . . . 3K 67
Sewell Rd. SE2 . . . 3A 108
Sewell St. E13 . . . 3J 87
Sextant Av. E14 . . . 4F 105
Sexton Ct. E14 . . . 7F 87
(off Newport Av.)
Sextons Ho. SE10 . . . 6E 104
(off Bardsley La.)
Seymer Rd. RM1: Rom . . . 3K 55
Seymore M. SE14 . . . 7B 104
(off New Cross Rd.)
Seymour Av. KT17: Ewe . . . 7E 164
N17 . . . 2G 49
SM4: Mord . . . 7F 153
Seymour Cl. HA5: Hat E . . . 1D 40
KT8: E Mos . . . 5G 149
Seymour Ct. E4 . . . 2C 36
KT1: Ham W . . . 1D 150
(off Seymour Rd.)
N10 . . . 2E 46
N21 . . . 6E 22
NW2 . . . 2D 62
Seymour Dr. BR2: Brom . . . 1D 172
Seymour Gdns. HA4: Ruis . . . 1B 58
IG1: Ilf . . . 1D 70
KT5: Surb . . . 5F 151
SE4 . . . 3A 122
TW1: Twick . . . 7B 114
TW13: Hanw . . . 4A 130
Seymour Ho. E16 . . . 1J 105
(off De Quincey M.)
Seymour Ho. NW1 . . . 1D 6
(off Churchway)
SM2: Sutt . . . 6K 165
(off Mulgrave Rd.)
WC1 . . . 3E 6
(off Tavistock Pl.)
Seymour Leisure Cen. . . . 6E 4 (5D 82)
Seymour M. W1 . . . 7G 5 (6E 82)
Seymour Pl. SE25 . . . 4H 157
W1 . . . 6E 4 (5D 82)
Seymour Rd. CR4: Mitc . . . 7E 154
E4 . . . 1J 35
E6 . . . 2B 88
E10 . . . 1B 68
KT1: Ham W . . . 1D 150
KT8: W Mole, E Mos . . . 5G 149
N3 . . . 7E 30
N8 . . . 5A 48
N9 . . . 2C 34
SM5: Cars . . . 5E 166
SW18 . . . 7H 117
SW19 . . . 3F 135
TW12: Ham H . . . 5G 131
W4 . . . 4J 97
Seymour St. SE18 . . . 3G 107
W1 . . . 1E 10 (6D 82)
W2 . . . 1E 10 (6D 82)
Seymour Ter. SE20 . . . 1H 157
Seymour Vs. SE20 . . . 1H 157
Seymour Wlk. SW10 . . . 6A 100
Seymour Way TW16: Sun . . . 7H 129
Seyssel St. E14 . . . 4E 104
Shaa Rd. W3 . . . 7K 79
Shabana Rd. W12 . . . 1D 98
Shacklegate La. TW11: Tedd . . . 4J 131
Shackleton Cl. SE23 . . . 2H 139
Shackleton Ct. E14 . . . 5C 104
(off Maritime Quay)
TW19: Stanw . . . 6A 110
(off Whitley Cl.)
W12 . . . 2D 98
(off Scott's Rd.)
Shackleton Ho. E1 . . . 1J 103
(off Prusom St.)
NW10 . . . 7K 61
Shackleton Rd. UB1: S'hall . . . 7D 76
SHACKLEWELL . . . 4F 67
Shacklewell Grn. E8 . . . 4F 67
Shacklewell Ho. E8 . . . 4F 67
Shacklewell La. E8 . . . 5F 67
Shacklewell Rd. N16 . . . 4F 67
Shacklewell Row E8 . . . 4F 67
Shacklewell St. E2 . . . 2K 9 (3F 85)
Shadbolt Av. E4 . . . 5F 35
Shadbolt Cl. KT4: Wor Pk . . . 2B 164
Shad Thames SE1 . . . 5J 15 (1F 103)
SHADWELL . . . 7H 85
Shadwell Ct. UB5: N'olt . . . 2D 76
Shadwell Dr. UB5: N'olt . . . 3D 76
Shadwell Gdns. E1 . . . 7J 85
Shadwell Pierhead E1 . . . 7J 85
Shadwell Pl. E1 . . . 7J 85
(off Sutton St.)
Shady Bush Cl. WD23: Bush . . . 1B 26
Shaef Way TW11: Tedd . . . 7A 132
Shafter Rd. RM10: Dag . . . 6J 73
Shaftesbury Av. EN3: Enf H . . . 2E 24
EN5: New Bar . . . 4F 21
HA2: Harr . . . 1F 59
HA3: Kenton . . . 5D 42
TW14: Felt . . . 6J 111
UB2: S'hall . . . 4E 94
W1 . . . 3C 12 (7H 83)
WC1 . . . 7E 6 (6J 83)
WC2 . . . 7E 6 (6J 83)
Shaftesbury Cen. W10 . . . 4F 81
(off Barlby Rd.)
Shaftesbury Circ. HA2: Harr . . . 1G 59
Shaftesbury Ct. E6 . . . 6E 88
(off Sapphire Cl.)
N1 . . . 2D 84
(off Shaftesbury St.)
Shaftesbury Ct. SE1 . . . 3D 102
(off Alderney M.)
SE5 . . . 4D 120
SW6 . . . 1K 117
(off Maltings Pl.)
SW16 . . . 3H 137
Shaftesbury Cres. TW18: Staines . . . 7A 128
Shaftesbury Gdns. NW10 . . . 4A 80
Shaftesbury Lodge E14 . . . 6D 86
(off Upper Nth. St.)
Shaftesbury M. SW4 . . . 5G 119
W8 . . . 3J 99
Shaftesbury Pde. HA2: Harr . . . 1G 59
Shaftesbury Pl. EC2 . . . 6C 8
(off Aldersgate St.)
W14 . . . 4H 99
(off Warwick Rd.)
Shaftesbury Point E13 . . . 2J 87
(off High St.)
Shaftesbury Rd. BR3: Beck . . . 2B 158
E4 . . . 1A 36
E7 . . . 7A 70
E10 . . . 1C 68
E17 . . . 6D 50
N18 . . . 6K 33
N19 . . . 1J 65
SM5: Cars . . . 7B 154
TW9: Rich . . . 3E 114
Shaftesburys, The IG11: Bark . . . 2G 89
Shaftesbury St. N1 . . . 2C 84
(not continuous)
Shaftesbury Theatre . . . 7E 6
(off Shaftesbury Av.)
Shaftesbury Vs. W8 . . . 3J 99
(off Allen St.)
Shaftesbury Way TW2: Twick . . . 3H 131
Shaftesbury Waye UB4: Yead . . . 5A 76
Shafto M. SW1 . . . 2F 17 (3D 100)
Shafton M. E9 . . . 1K 85
Shafton Rd. E9 . . . 1K 85
Shafts Ct. EC3 . . . 1G 15 (6E 84)
Shahjalal Ho. E2 . . . 2G 85
(off Pritchards Rd.)
Shakespeare Av. N11 . . . 5B 32
NW10 . . . 1K 79
TW14: Felt . . . 6J 111
UB4: Hayes, Yead . . . 6J 75
(not continuous)
Shakespeare Cl. HA3: Kenton . . . 7G 43
Shakespeare Ct. EN5: New Bar . . . 3E 20
HA3: Kenton . . . 6F 43
NW6 . . . 7A 64
(off Fairfax Rd.)
Shakespeare Cres. E12 . . . 6D 70
Shakespeare Dr. HA3: Kenton . . . 6F 43
Shakespeare Gdns. N2 . . . 4D 46
Shakespeare Ho. E9 . . . 7J 67
(off Lyme Gro.)
N14 . . . 2C 32
Shakespeare Rd. DA7: Bex . . . 1E 126
E17 . . . 2K 49
N3 . . . 1J 45
NW7 . . . 4G 29
NW10 . . . 1K 79
SE24 . . . 5B 120
W3 . . . 1J 97
W7 . . . 7K 77
Shakespeare's Globe & Exhibition
. . . 4C 14 (1C 102)
Shakespeare Twr. EC2 . . . 5D 8
Shakespeare Way TW13: Hanw . . . 4A 130
Shakspeare M. N16 . . . 4E 66
Shakspeare Wlk. N16 . . . 4E 66
Shalbourne Sq. E9 . . . 6B 68
Shalcomb St. SW10 . . . 6A 100
Shalden Ho. SW15 . . . 6B 116
Shaldon Dr. HA4: Ruis . . . 3A 58
SM4: Mord . . . 5G 153
Shaldon Rd. HA8: Edg . . . 2F 43
Shalfleet Dr. W10 . . . 7F 81
Shalford Cl. BR6: Farnb . . . 4G 173
Shalford Ct. N1 . . . 2B 84

Shalford Ho. SE1 . . . 3D 102
Shalimar Gdns. W3 . . . 7J 79
Shalimar Rd. W3 . . . 7J 79
Shallons Rd. SE9 . . . 4F 143
Shalstone Rd. SW14 . . . 3H 115
Shalston Vs. KT6: Surb . . . 6F 151
Shamrock Ho. *SE26* . . . *4G 139*
(off Talisman Sq.)
Shamrock Rd. CR0: C'don . . . 6K 155
Shamrock St. SW4 . . . 3H 119
Shamrock Way N14 . . . 1A 32
Shandon Rd. SW4 . . . 6G 119
Shand St. SE1 . . . 6H 15 (2E 102)
Shandy St. E1 . . . 5K 85
Shan Ho. WC1 . . . 4G 7
Shanklin Ho. E17 . . . 2B 50
Shanklin Rd. N8 . . . 5H 47
N15 . . . 4G 49
Shannon Cl. NW2 . . . 3F 63
UB2: S'hall . . . 5B 94
Shannon Commercial Cen.
KT3: N Mald . . . 4C 152
SHANNON CORNER . . . 4C 152
Shannon Cnr. Retail Pk.
KT3: N Mald . . . 4C 152
Shannon Ct. *CR0: C'don* . . . *1C 168*
(off Tavistock Rd.)
N16 . . . 3E 66
SE15 . . . *7F 103*
(off Garnies Cl.)
Shannon Gro. SW9 . . . 4K 119
Shannon M. SE3 . . . 4H 123
Shannon Pl. NW8 . . . 2C 82
Shannon Way BR3: Beck . . . 6D 140
Shanti Ct. SW18 . . . 1J 135
Shap Cres. SM5: Cars . . . 1D 166
Shapland Way N13 . . . 5E 32
Shapwick Cl. N11 . . . 5J 31
Shard, The SE1 . . . 5F 15
Shardcroft Av. SE24 . . . 5B 120
Shardeloes Rd. SE14 . . . 2B 122
Shard's Sq. SE15 . . . 6G 103
Sharland Cl. CR7: Thor H . . . 6A 156
Sharman Ct. DA14: Sidc . . . 4A 144
Sharnbrooke Cl. DA16: Well . . . 3C 126
Sharnbrook Ho. W14 . . . 6J 99
Sharon Cl. KT6: Surb . . . 1C 162
Sharon Ct. *CR2: S Croy* . . . *5C 168*
(off Warham Rd.)
Sharon Gdns. E9 . . . 1J 85
Sharon Rd. EN3: Enf H . . . 2F 25
W4 . . . 5K 97
Sharpe Cl. W7 . . . 5K 77
Sharp Ho. SW8 . . . 3F 119
TW1: Twick . . . 6D 114
Sharpleshall St. NW1 . . . 7D 64
Sharpness Cl. UB4: Yead . . . 5C 76
Sharpness Ct. *SE15* . . . *7F 103*
(off Daniel Gdns.)
Sharp's La. HA4: Ruis . . . 7F 39
Sharratt St. SE15 . . . 6J 103
Sharsted St. SE17 . . . 5B 102
Sharvel La. UB5: N'olt . . . 1J 75
Sharwood *WC1* . . . *1H 7*
(off Penton Ri.)
Shaver's Pl. SW1 . . . 3C 12
Shaw Av. IG11: Bark . . . 2E 90
Shawbrooke Rd. SE9 . . . 5A 124
Shawbury Cl. NW9 . . . 1A 44
Shawbury Rd. SE22 . . . 5F 121
Shaw Cl. SE28 . . . 1B 108
WD23: B Hea . . . 2D 26
Shaw Ct. SM4: Mord . . . 7A 154
W3 . . . *3J 97*
(off All Saints Rd.)
Shaw Cres. E14 . . . 6A 86
Shaw Dr. KT12: Walt T . . . 7A 148
Shawfield Ct. UB7: W Dray . . . 3A 92
Shawfield Pk. BR1: Brom . . . 2B 160
Shawfield St. SW3 . . . 6D 16 (5C 100)
Shawford Ct. SW15 . . . 7C 116
Shawford Rd. KT19: Ewe . . . 6K 163
Shaw Gdns. IG11: Bark . . . 2E 90
Shaw Ho. DA17: Belv . . . 5F 109
E16 . . . *1E 106*
(off Claremont St.)
Shaw Path BR1: Brom . . . 3H 141
Shaw Rd. BR1: Brom . . . 3H 141
EN3: Enf H . . . 1E 24
SE22 . . . 4E 120
Shaws Cotts. SE23 . . . 3A 140
Shaws Path *KT1: Ham W* . . . *1C 150*
(off Bennett Cl.)
Shaw Sq. E17 . . . 1A 50
Shaw Theatre . . . 2D 6 (3H 83)
Shaw Way SM6: Wall . . . 7J 167
Shead Ct. *E1* . . . *6H 85*
(off James Voller Way)
Shearing Dr. SM5: Cars . . . 7A 154
Shearling Way N7 . . . 6J 65
Shearman Rd. SE3 . . . 4H 123
SHEARS, THE . . . 7G 129
Shears Ct. TW16: Sun . . . 7G 129
Shears Way TW16: Sun . . . 1G 147
Shearwater Cl. IG11: Bark . . . 3A 90
Shearwater Ct. *E1* . . . *3K 15*
(off Star Pl.)
SE8 . . . *6B 104*
(off Abinger Gro.)
Shearwater Rd. SM1: Sutt . . . 5H 165
Shearwater Way UB4: Yead . . . 6B 76
Sheath Cotts. *KT7: T Ditt* . . . *6B 150*
(off Ferry Rd.)
Sheaveshill Av. NW9 . . . 4A 44
Sheaveshill Ct. NW9 . . . 4K 43
Sheaveshill Pde. *NW9* . . . *4A 44*
(off Sheaveshill Av.)
Sheba Ct. *N17* . . . *6B 34*
(off Altair Cl.)
Sheba Pl. E1 . . . 4K 9 (4F 85)
Sheen Comn. Dr.
TW10: Rich . . . 4G 115
Sheen Ct. TW10: Rich . . . 4G 115
Sheen Ct. Rd. TW10: Rich . . . 4G 115
Sheendale Rd. TW9: Rich . . . 4F 115
Sheenewood SE26 . . . 4H 139
Sheen Ga. Gdns. SW14 . . . 4J 115
Sheengate Mans. SW14 . . . 4K 115
Sheen Gro. N1 . . . 1A 84
Sheen La. SW14 . . . 5J 115
Sheen Pk. TW9: Rich . . . 4F 115
Sheen Rd. BR5: St M Cry . . . 4K 161
TW9: Rich . . . 5E 114
TW10: Rich . . . 5E 114
Sheen Sports & Fitness Cen. . . . 4A 116
Sheen Way SM6: Wall . . . 5K 167
Sheen Wood SW14 . . . 5J 115
Sheepcote Cl. TW5: Cran . . . 7J 93
Sheepcote La. SW11 . . . 2D 118
Sheepcote Rd. HA1: Harr . . . 6K 41
Sheepcotes Rd. RM6: Chad H . . . 4E 54
Sheephouse Way KT3: N Mald . . . 1K 163
Sheep La. E8 . . . 1H 85
Sheep Wlk. TW17: Shep . . . 7B 146
Sheep Wlk. M. SW19 . . . 6F 135
Sheerness M. E16 . . . 2F 107
Sheerwater Rd. E16 . . . 5B 88
Sheffield Rd. TW6: H'row A . . . 6E 110
Sheffield Sq. E3 . . . 3B 86
Sheffield St. WC2 . . . 1G 13 (6K 83)
Sheffield Ter. W8 . . . 1J 99
Sheffield Way
TW6: H'row A . . . 5F 111
Shelbourne Cl. HA5: Pinn . . . 3D 40
Shelbourne Pl. BR3: Beck . . . 7B 140
Shelbourne Rd. N17 . . . 2H 49
Shelburne Dr. TW4: Houn . . . 6E 112
Shelburne Rd. N7 . . . 4K 65
Shelbury Cl. DA14: Sidc . . . 3A 144
Shelbury Rd. SE22 . . . 5H 121
Sheldon Av. IG5: Ilf . . . 2F 53
N6 . . . 7C 46
Sheldon Cl. SE12 . . . 5K 123
SE20 . . . 1H 157
Sheldon Ct. EN5: New Bar . . . 4E 20
RM7: Rush G . . . *6K 55*
(off Union Rd.)
SW8 . . . *7J 101*
(off Lansdowne Grn.)
Sheldon Ho. *N1* . . . *1E 84*
(off Kingsland Rd.)
Sheldon Pl. E2 . . . 2G 85
(not continuous)
Sheldon Rd. DA7: Bex . . . 1F 127
N18 . . . 4K 33
NW2 . . . 4F 63
RM9: Dag . . . 7E 72
Sheldon Sq. W2 . . . 6A 4 (5A 82)
Sheldon St. CR0: C'don . . . 3C 168
Sheldrake Cl. E16 . . . 1D 106
Sheldrake Ct. *E6* . . . *2C 88*
(off St Bartholomew's Rd.)
Sheldrake Ho. *SE16* . . . *4K 103*
(off Tawny Way)
Sheldrake Pl. W8 . . . 2J 99
Sheldrick Cl. SW19 . . . 2B 154
Shelduck Cl. E15 . . . 5H 69
Shelduck Ct. *SE8* . . . *6B 104*
(off Pilot Cl.)
Sheldwich Ter. BR2: Brom . . . 6C 160
Shelford KT1: King T . . . 2G 151
Shelford Pl. N16 . . . 3D 66
Shelford Ri. SE19 . . . 7F 139
Shelford Rd. EN5: Barn . . . 6A 20
Shelgate Rd. SW11 . . . 5C 118
Shell Cen. SE1 . . . 5H 13 (2K 101)
Shell Cl. BR2: Brom . . . 6C 160
Shellduck Cl. NW9 . . . 2A 44
Shelley *N8* . . . *3J 47*
(off Boyton Rd.)
Shelley Av. E12 . . . 6C 70
UB6: G'frd . . . 3H 77
Shelley Cl. BR6: Orp . . . 3J 173
HA8: Edg . . . 4B 28
SE15 . . . 2H 121
UB4: Hayes . . . 5J 75
UB6: G'frd . . . 3H 77
Shelley Ct. *E10* . . . *7D 50*
(off Skelton's La.)
E11 . . . *4K 51*
(off Makepeace Rd.)
N19 . . . 1K 65
SW3 . . . *7F 17*
(off Tite St.)
Shelley Cres. TW5: Hest . . . 1B 112
UB1: S'hall . . . 6D 76
Shelley Dr. DA16: Well . . . 1J 125
Shelley Gdns. HA0: Wemb . . . 2C 60
Shelley Ho. *E2* . . . *3J 85*
(off Cornwall Av.)
N16 . . . 4E 66
SE17 . . . *5C 102*
(off Browning St.)
SW1 . . . *7B 18*
(off Churchill Gdns.)
Shelley Lodge EN2: Enf . . . 1J 23
Shelley Rd. NW10 . . . 1K 79
Shelley Way SW19 . . . 5B 136
Shellness Rd. E5 . . . 5H 67
Shell Rd. SE13 . . . 3D 122
Shellwood Rd. SW11 . . . 2D 118
Shelmerdine Cl. E3 . . . 5C 86
Shelson Av. TW13: Felt . . . 3H 129
Shelton Rd. SW19 . . . 1J 153
Shelton St. WC2 . . . 1E 12 (6J 83)
(not continuous)
Shene Ho. *EC1* . . . *5J 7*
(off Bourne Est.)
Shenfield Ho. *SE18* . . . *1B 124*
(off Portway Gdns.)
Shenfield Rd. IG8: Wfd G . . . 7E 36
Shenfield St. N1 . . . 1H 9 (2E 84)
(not continuous)
Shenley Av. HA4: Ruis . . . 2H 57
Shenley Rd. SE5 . . . 1E 120
TW5: Hest . . . 1C 112
Shenstone W13 . . . 1C 96
Shenstone Cl. DA1: Cray . . . 4K 127
Shenstone Ho. SW16 . . . 5G 137
Shepherd Cl. TW13: Hanw . . . 4C 130
Shepherdess Pl. N1 . . . 1D 8 (3C 84)
Shepherdess Wlk. N1 . . . 1D 8 (2C 84)
Shepherd Ho. *E14* . . . *6D 86*
(off Annabel Cl.)
E16 . . . *7F 89*
(off University Way)
Shepherd Mkt. W1 . . . 4J 11 (1F 101)
SHEPHERD'S BUSH . . . 2E 98
Shepherd's Bush Empire Theatre . . . 2E 98
Shepherd's Bush Grn. W12 . . . 2E 98
Shepherd's Bush Mkt. W12 . . . 2E 98
(not continuous)
Shepherd's Bush Pl. W12 . . . 2F 99
Shepherd's Bush Rd. W6 . . . 4E 98
Shepherds Cl. BR6: Orp . . . 3K 173
HA7: Stan . . . 5F 27
(not continuous)
N6 . . . 6F 47
RM6: Chad H . . . 5D 54
TW17: Shep . . . 6D 146
W1 . . . *2G 11*
(off Lees Pl.)
Shepherds Ct. *W12* . . . *2F 99*
(off Shepherd's Bush Grn.)
Shepherds Grn. BR7: Chst . . . 7H 143
Shepherd's Hill N6 . . . 6F 47
Shepherds La. E9 . . . 6K 67
SE28 . . . 1J 107
Shepherds Leas SE9 . . . 4G 125
Shepherds Path *NW3* . . . *5B 64*
(off Lyndhurst Rd.)
UB5: N'olt . . . *6C 58*
(off Arnold Rd.)
Shepherds Pl. W1 . . . 2G 11 (7E 82)
Shepherd St. W1 . . . 5J 11 (1F 101)
Shepherds Wlk. NW2 . . . 2C 62
NW3 . . . 5B 64
WD23: B Hea . . . 2C 26
Shepherds Way CR2: Sels . . . 7K 169
Shepiston La. UB3: Harl . . . 4D 92
Shepley Cl. SM5: Cars . . . 3E 166
Sheppard Cl. EN1: Enf . . . 1C 24
KT1: King T . . . 4E 150
Sheppard Dr. SE16 . . . 5H 103
Sheppard Ho. *E2* . . . *2G 85*
(off Warner Pl.)
SW2 . . . 1A 138
Sheppards Coll. *BR1: Brom* . . . *1J 159*
(off London Rd.)
Sheppard St. E16 . . . 4H 87
SHEPPERTON . . . 6D 146
Shepperton Bus. Pk. TW17: Shep . . . 5E 146
Shepperton Ct. TW17: Shep . . . 6D 146
Shepperton Ct. Dr. TW17: Shep . . . 5D 146
Shepperton Film Studios . . . 3B 146
SHEPPERTON GREEN . . . 4C 146
Shepperton Marina TW17: Shep . . . 6G 147
Shepperton Rd. BR5: Pet W . . . 6G 161
N1 . . . 1C 84
TW18: Lale, Shep . . . 4A 146
Sheppey Gdns. RM9: Dag . . . 7C 72
Sheppey Rd. RM9: Dag . . . 7B 72
Shepton Ho's. *E2* . . . *3J 85*
(off Welwyn St.)
Sherard Ct. N7 . . . 3J 65
Sherard Ho. *E9* . . . *7J 67*
(off Frampton Pk. Rd.)
Sherard Rd. SE9 . . . 5C 124
Sheraton Bus. Cen. UB6: G'frd . . . 2B 78
Sheraton Ho. *SW1* . . . *7K 17*
(off Churchill Gdns.)
Sheraton St. W1 . . . 1C 12 (6H 83)
Sherborne *NW1* . . . *7H 65*
(off Agar Gro.)
Sherborne Av. EN3: Enf H . . . 2D 24
UB2: S'hall . . . 4E 94
Sherborne Cl. SL3: Poyle . . . 4A 174
UB4: Yead . . . 6A 76

Sherborne Cres. SM5: Cars 7C **154**
Sherborne Gdns. NW9 . . . . . 3G **43**
W13 . . . . . 5B **78**
Sherborne Ho. SW1 . . . . . 5F **101**
*SW8 . . . . . 7K **101***
(off Bolney St.)
Sherborne La. EC4 . . . . . 2E **14** (7D **84**)
Sherborne Rd. BR5: St M Cry 4K **161**
KT9: Chess 5E **162**
SM3: Sutt 2J **165**
TW14: Bedf 1F **129**
(not continuous)
Sherborne St. N1 . . . . . 1D **84**
Sherboro Rd. N15 . . . . . 6F **49**
Sherbourne Ct. SM2: Sutt 6A **166**
*SW5 . . . . . 4K **99***
(off Cromwell Rd.)
Sherbourne Gdns. TW17: Shep 7G **147**
Sherbourne Pl. HA7: Stan 6F **27**
Sherbrooke Cl. DA6: Bex 4G **127**
Sherbrooke Ho. *E2 . . . . . 2J **85***
(off Bonner Rd.)
*SW1 . . . . . 3H **101***
(off Monck St.)
Sherbrooke Rd. SW6 . . . . . 7G **99**
Sherbrooke Ter. *SW6 . . . . . 7G **99***
(off Sherbrook Rd.)
Sherbrooke Way KT4: Wor Pk 7D **152**
Sherbrook Gdns. N21 . . . . . 7G **23**
Shere Cl. KT9: Chess 5D **162**
Sheredan Rd. E4 . . . . . 5A **36**
Shere Ho. SE1 . . . . . 7E **14**
Shere Rd. IG2: Ilf 5E **52**
Sherfield Cl. KT3: N Mald 4H **151**
Sherfield Gdns. SW15 . . . . . 6B **116**
Sherfield M. UB3: Hayes 6G **75**
Sheridan Bldgs. *WC2 . . . . . 1F **13***
(off Martlett Ct.)
Sheridan Cl. UB10: Hil 4E **74**
Sheridan Ct. *CR0: C'don 4E **168***
(off Coombe Rd.)
HA1: Harr 6H **41**
*NW6 . . . . . 7A **64***
(off Belsize Rd.)
*SW5 . . . . . 4K **99***
(off Barkston Gdns.)
TW4: Houn 5C **112**
UB5: N'olt 5F **59**
*W7 . . . . . 7K **77***
(off Milton Rd.)
Sheridan Cres. BR7: Chst 2F **161**
Sheridan Gdns. HA3: Kenton 6D **42**
Sheridan Hgts. *E1 . . . . . 6H **85***
(off Watney St.)
Sheridan Ho. *SE11 . . . . . 4K **19***
(off Wincott St.)
Sheridan Lodge *BR2: Brom 4A **160***
(off Homesdale Rd.)
Sheridan M. E11 . . . . . 6K **51**
Sheridan Pl. BR1: Brom 2B **160**
SW13 . . . . . 3B **116**
Sheridan Rd. DA7: Bex 3E **126**
DA17: Belv 4G **109**
E7 . . . . . 3H **69**
E12 . . . . . 5C **70**
SW19 . . . . . 1H **153**
TW10: Ham 3C **132**
Sheridan Ter. UB5: N'olt 5F **59**
Sheridan Wlk. NW11 . . . . . 6J **45**
SM5: Cars 5D **166**
Sheridan Way BR3: Beck 1B **158**
Sheriden Pl. HA1: Harr 7J **41**
TW12: Hamp 1F **149**
Sheringham NW8 . . . . . 1B **82**
Sheringham Av. E12 . . . . . 4D **70**
N14 . . . . . 5C **22**
RM7: Rom 6J **55**
TW2: Whitt 1D **130**
TW13: Felt 3J **129**
Sheringham Ct. *TW13: Felt 3J **129***
(off Sheringham Av.)
UB3: Hayes 2H **93**
Sheringham Dr. IG11: Bark 5K **71**
Sheringham Ho. NW1 . . . . . 5C **4**
Sheringham Rd. N7 . . . . . 6K **65**
SE20 . . . . . 3J **157**
Sheringham Twr.
UB1: S'hall 7F **77**
Sherington Av. HA5: Hat E 7A **26**
Sherington Rd. SE7 . . . . . 6K **105**
Sherland Rd. TW1: Twick 1K **131**
Sherleys Ct. HA4: Ruis 2G **57**
Sherlies Av. BR6: Orp 2J **173**
Sherlock Ct. *NW8 . . . . . 1B **82***
(off Dorman Way)
Sherlock Holmes Mus. 4F **5**
Sherlock M. W1 . . . . . 5G **5** (5E **82**)
Sherman Gdns. RM6: Chad H 6C **54**
Sherman Ho. *E14 . . . . . 6E **86***
(off Dee St.)
*UB3: Harl 3E **92***
(off Nine Acres Cl.)
Sherman Rd. BR1: Brom 1J **159**
Shernhall St. E17 . . . . . 3E **50**
Sherrard Rd. E7 . . . . . 6A **70**
E12 . . . . . 6A **70**
Sherrards Way EN5: Barn 5D **20**
Sherren Ho. E1 . . . . . 4J **85**
Sherrick Grn. Rd. NW10 . . . . . 5D **62**
Sherriff Ct. *NW6 . . . . . 6J **63***
(off Sherriff Rd.)
Sherriff Rd. NW6 . . . . . 6J **63**
Sherringham Av. N17 . . . . . 2G **49**
Sherrin Rd. E10 . . . . . 4D **68**
Sherrock Gdns. NW4 . . . . . 4D **44**
Sherry M. IG11: Bark 7H **71**
Sherston Ct. *SE1 . . . . . 4B **102***
(off Newington Butts)
WC1 . . . . . 2J **7**
Sherwin Ho. SE11 . . . . . 7J **19**
Sherwin Rd. SE14 . . . . . 1K **121**
Sherwood KT6: Surb 2D **162**
NW6 . . . . . 7G **63**
Sherwood Av. E18 . . . . . 3K **51**
HA4: Ruis 6G **39**
SW16 . . . . . 7H **137**
UB4: Yead 4K **75**
UB6: G'frd 6J **59**
Sherwood Cl. DA5: Bexl 6C **126**
E17 . . . . . 2B **50**
SW13 . . . . . 3D **116**
W13 . . . . . 1B **96**
Sherwood Ct. *CR2: S Croy 5C **168***
(off Nottingham Rd.)
HA2: Harr 2F **59**
SW11 . . . . . 3A **118**
*W1 . . . . . 6E **4***
(off Bryanston Pl.)
Sherwood Gdns. E14 . . . . . 4C **104**
IG11: Bark 7H **71**
SE16 . . . . . 5G **103**
Sherwood Pk. Av. DA15: Sidc 7A **126**
Sherwood Pk. Rd. CR4: Mitc 4G **155**
SM1: Sutt 5J **165**
Sherwood Rd. CR0: C'don 7H **157**
DA16: Well 2J **125**
HA2: Harr 2G **59**
IG6: Ilf 4H **53**
NW4 . . . . . 3E **44**
SW19 . . . . . 7H **135**
TW12: Ham H 5G **131**
Sherwood St. N20 . . . . . 3G **31**
W1 . . . . . 2B **12** (7G **83**)
Sherwood Ter. N20 . . . . . 3G **31**
Sherwood Way BR4: W W'ck 2E **170**
Shetland Rd. E3 . . . . . 2B **86**
TW6: H'row A 6E **110**
Shield Dr. TW8: Bford 6A **96**
Shieldhall St. SE2 . . . . . 4C **108**
Shield Rd. TW15: Ashf 4E **128**
Shifford Path SE23 . . . . . 3K **139**
Shillaker Ct. W3 . . . . . 1B **98**
Shillibeer Pl. W1 . . . . . 6D **4**
Shillingford Cl. NW7 . . . . . 7A **30**
Shillingford Ho. *E3 . . . . . 3D **86***
(off Talwin St.)
Shillingford St. N1 . . . . . 7B **66**
Shilling Pl. W7 . . . . . 2A **96**
Shillingshaw Lodge *E16 . . . . . 6J **87***
(off Butchers Rd.)
Shillingstone Ho. *W14 . . . . . 3G **99***
(off Russell Rd.)
Shinfield St. W12 . . . . . 6E **80**
Shinglewell Rd. DA8: Erith 7G **109**
Shinners Cl. SE25 . . . . . 5G **157**
Ship All. W4 . . . . . 6G **97**
Ship & Mermaid Row SE1 . . . 6F **15** (2D **102**)
Shipka Rd. SW12 . . . . . 1F **137**
Shiplake Ho. *E2 . . . . . 2J **9***
(off Arnold Cir.)
Ship La. SW14 . . . . . 3J **115**
Shipman Rd. E16 . . . . . 6K **87**
SE23 . . . . . 2K **139**
Ship St. SE8 . . . . . 1C **122**
Ship Tavern Pas. EC3 . . . . . 2G **15** (7E **84**)
Shipton Cl. RM8: Dag 3D **72**
Shipton Ho. *E2 . . . . . 1K **9***
(off Shipton St.)
Shipton Rd. UB10: Ick 4B **56**
Shipton St. E2 . . . . . 1K **9** (2F **85**)
Shipwright Rd. SE16 . . . . . 2A **104**
Shipwright Yd. SE1 . . . . . 5G **15** (1E **102**)
Ship Yd. E14 . . . . . 5D **104**
Shirburn Cl. SE23 . . . . . 7J **121**
Shirebrook Rd. SE3 . . . . . 3B **124**
Shire Ct. DA18: Erith 3D **108**
KT17: Ewe 7B **164**
Shirehall Cl. NW4 . . . . . 6F **45**
Shirehall Gdns. NW4 . . . . . 6F **45**
Shirehall La. NW4 . . . . . 6F **45**
Shirehall Pk. NW4 . . . . . 5F **45**
Shire Horse Way TW7: Isle 3K **113**
Shire Ho. *E3 . . . . . 3D **86***
(off Talwin St.)
Shire La. BR2: Kes 7C **172**
BR6: Chels, Downe 7F **173**
(not continuous)
Shire M. TW2: Whitt 6G **113**
Shire Pl. SW18 . . . . . 7A **118**
TW8: Bford 7D **96**
Shires, The TW10: Ham 4E **132**
Shirland M. W9 . . . . . 3H **81**
Shirland Rd. W9 . . . . . 3H **81**
Shirlbutt St. E14 . . . . . 7D **86**
SHIRLEY 2J **169**
Shirley Av. CR0: C'don 1J **169**
DA5: Bexl 7D **126**
SM1: Sutt 4B **166**
Shirley Chu. Rd. CR0: C'don 3K **169**
Shirley Cl. E17 . . . . . 5D **50**
TW3: Houn 5G **113**
Shirley Ct. SW16 . . . . . 7J **137**
Shirley Cres. BR3: Beck 4A **158**
Shirley Dr. TW3: Houn 5G **113**
Shirley Gdns. IG11: Bark 6J **71**
W7 . . . . . 1K **95**
Shirley Gro. N9 . . . . . 7D **24**
SW11 . . . . . 3E **118**
Shirley Hgts. SM6: Wall 7G **167**
Shirley Hills Rd. CR0: C'don 5J **169**
Shirley Ho. *SE5 . . . . . 7D **102***
(off Picton St.)
Shirley Ho. Dr. SE7 . . . . . 7A **106**
SHIRLEY OAKS 1K **169**
Shirley Oaks Rd. CR0: C'don 1K **169**
Shirley Pk. CR0: C'don 2J **169**
Shirley Pk. Rd. CR0: C'don 1H **169**
Shirley Rd. CR0: C'don 7H **157**
DA15: Sidc 3J **143**
E15 . . . . . 7G **69**
EN2: Enf 3H **23**
SM6: Wall 7G **167**
W4 . . . . . 2K **97**
Shirley Sherwood Gallery of
Botanical Art, The 2F **115**
Shirley St. E16 . . . . . 6H **87**
Shirley Way CR0: C'don 3A **170**
Shirley Windmill 3J **169**
Shirlock Rd. NW3 . . . . . 4D **64**
Shirwell Cl. NW7 . . . . . 7A **30**
Shobden Rd. N17 . . . . . 1D **48**
Shobroke Cl. NW2 . . . . . 3E **62**
Shoebury Rd. E6 . . . . . 7D **70**
Shoelands Ct. NW9 . . . . . 3K **43**
Shoe La. EC4 . . . . . 7K **7** (6A **84**)
Sholto Rd. TW6: H'row A 5B **110**
Shona Ho. E13 . . . . . 5A **88**
Shooters Av. HA3: Kenton 4C **42**
SHOOTERS HILL 1E **124**
Shooters Hill DA16: Well 1D **124**
SE18 . . . . . 1D **124**
Shooters Hill Rd. SE3 . . . . . 1F **123**
SE10 . . . . . 1F **123**
SE18 . . . . . 1F **123**
Shooters Rd. EN2: Enf 1G **23**
Shoot Up Hill NW2 . . . . . 5G **63**
Shopping Hall, The E6 . . . . . 1C **88**
Shore Bus. Cen. E9 . . . . . 7J **67**
Shore Cl. TW12: Hamp 6C **130**
TW14: Felt 7J **111**
Shorediche Cl. UB10: Ick 3B **56**
SHOREDITCH 1G **9** (3E **84**)
Shoreditch Ct. *E8 . . . . . 7F **67***
(off Queensbridge Rd.)
Shoreditch High St. E1 . . . . . 4H **9** (4E **84**)
Shoreditch Ho. N1 . . . . . 2F **9**
Shore Gro. TW13: Hanw 2D **130**
Shoreham Cl. CR0: C'don 6J **157**
DA5: Bexl 1D **144**
SW18 . . . . . 5K **117**
Shoreham Rd. E. TW6: H'row A 5A **110**
Shoreham Rd. W. TW6: H'row A 5A **110**
Shoreham Way BR2: Hayes 6J **159**
Shore Ho. SW8 . . . . . 3F **119**
Shore M. *E9 . . . . . 7J **67***
(off Shore Rd.)
Shore Pl. E9 . . . . . 7J **67**
Shore Point IG9: Buck H 2E **36**
Shore Rd. E9 . . . . . 7J **67**
Shore Way *SW9 . . . . . 2A **120***
(off Crowhurst Cl.)
Shorncliffe Rd. SE1 . . . . . 5F **103**
Shorndean St. SE6 . . . . . 1E **140**
Shorne Cl. DA15: Sidc 6B **126**
Shornefield Cl. BR1: Brom 3E **160**
Shornells Way SE2 . . . . . 4C **108**
Shorrold's Rd. SW6 . . . . . 7H **99**
Shortcroft Rd. KT17: Ewe 7B **164**
Shortcrofts Rd. RM9: Dag 6F **73**
Shorter St. E1 . . . . . 2K **15** (7F **85**)
Shortgate N12 . . . . . 4C **30**
Short Hedges TW3: Houn 1E **112**
Short Hill HA1: Harr 1J **59**
SHORTLANDS 2G **159**
Shortlands UB3: Harl 6F **93**
W6 . . . . . 4F **99**
Shortlands Cl. DA17: Belv 3F **109**
N18 . . . . . 3J **33**
Shortlands Gdns. BR2: Brom 2G **159**
Shortlands Gro. BR2: Brom 3F **159**
Shortlands Rd. BR2: Brom 3F **159**
E10 . . . . . 7D **50**
KT2: King T 7F **133**
Short La. TW19: Stanw 7B **110**
Short Path SE18 . . . . . 6F **107**
Short Rd. E11 . . . . . 2G **69**
TW6: H'row A 6A **110**
W4 . . . . . 6A **98**
Shorts Cft. NW9 . . . . . 4H **43**
Shorts Gdns. WC2 . . . . . 1E **12** (6J **83**)
Shorts Rd. SM5: Cars 4C **166**
Short St. *NW4 . . . . . 4E **44***
(off Foster St.)
SE1 . . . . . 6K **13** (2A **102**)
Short Wall E15 . . . . . 3E **86**
Short Way N12 . . . . . 6H **31**
SE9 . . . . . 3C **124**
TW2: Whitt 7G **113**

Shotfield SM6: Wall 6F **167**
Shott Cl. SM1: Sutt 5A **166**
Shottendane Rd. SW6 . . . . .1J **117**
Shottery Cl. SE9 . . . . .3D **142**
Shottfield Av. SW14 . . . . .4A **116**
Shottsford *W2* *6J 81*
(off Talbot Rd.)
Shoulder of Mutton All. E14 . . . . . . .7A **86**
Shouldham St. W1 . . . . . .6D **4** (5C **82**)
Showcase Cinema
Barking 3H **89**
Wood Green 2A **48**
Showers Way UB3: Hayes 1J **93**
Shrapnel Cl. SE18 . . . . .7C **106**
Shrapnel Rd. SE9 . . . . .3D **124**
Shrewsbury Av. HA3: Kenton 4E **42**
SW14 . . . . .4J **115**
Shrewsbury Cl. KT6: Surb 2E **162**
Shrewsbury Ct. EC1 . . . . .4D **8**
Shrewsbury Ho. SW3 . . . . .7C **16**
SW8 . . . . .7H **19**
Shrewsbury La. SE18 . . . . .1F **125**
Shrewsbury M. *W2* *5J 81*
(off Chepstow Rd.)
Shrewsbury Rd. BR3: Beck 3A **158**
E7 . . . . .5B **70**
N11 . . . . .6B **32**
NW10 . . . . .1K **79**
SM5: Cars 6C **154**
TW6: H'row A 6E **110**
(not continuous)
W2 . . . .*6J 81*
Shrewsbury St. W10 . . . . .4E **80**
Shrewsbury Wlk. TW7: Isle 3A **114**
Shrewton Rd. SW17 . . . . .7D **136**
Shri Swaminarayan Mandir
London 7G **103**
Shroffold Rd. BR1: Brom 4G **141**
Shropshire Cl. CR4: Mitc 4J **155**
Shropshire Ct. *W7* *6K 77*
(off Copley Cl.)
Shropshire Ho. *N18* *5C 34*
(off Cavendish Cl.)
Shropshire Pl. WC1 . . . . . . .4C **6** (4G **83**)
Shropshire Rd. N22 . . . . .7E **32**
Shroton St. NW1 . . . . .5D **4** (5C **82**)
Shrubberies, The E18 . . . . .2J **51**
Shrubbery, The E11 . . . . .5K **51**
KT6: Surb 1E **162**
Shrubbery Cl. N1 . . . . .1C **84**
Shrubbery Gdns. N21 . . . . .7G **23**
Shrubbery Rd. N9 . . . . .3B **34**
SW16 . . . . .4J **137**
UB1: S'hall 1D **94**
Shrubland Gro. KT4: Wor Pk 3E **164**
Shrubland Rd. E8 . . . . .1F **85**
E10 . . . . .7C **50**
E17 . . . . .5C **50**
Shrublands Av. CR0: C'don 3D **170**
Shrublands Cl. N20 . . . . .1G **31**
SE26 . . . . .3J **139**
Shrubsall Cl. SE9 . . . . .1C **142**
Shuna Wlk. N1 . . . . .6D **66**
Shurland Av. EN4: E Barn 6G **21**
Shurland Gdns. SE15 . . . . .7F **103**
Shurlock Dr. BR6: Farnb 4G **173**
Shuters Sq. W14 . . . . .5H **99**
Shuttle Cl. DA15: Sidc 7K **125**
Shuttlemead DA5: Bexl 7F **127**
Shuttle St. E1 . . . . .4G **85**
Shuttleworth Rd. SW11 . . . . .2C **118**
Siamese M. N3 . . . . .1J **45**
Siani M. N8 . . . . .4B **48**
Sibella Rd. SW4 . . . . .2H **119**
Sibley Cl. BR1: Brom 5C **160**
DA6: Bex 5E **126**
Sibley Ct. BR2: Brom 2F **159**
UB8: Hil 5E **74**
Sibley Gro. E12 . . . . .7C **70**
Sibthorpe Rd. SE12 . . . . .6K **123**
Sibthorp Rd. CR4: Mitc 2D **154**
Sibton Rd. SM5: Cars 7C **154**

Sicilian Av. WC1 . . . . .6F **7**
Sickle Cnr. RM9: Dag 4H **91**
Sidbury St. SW6 . . . . .1G **117**
SIDCUP 4A **144**
Sidcup By-Pass
BR5: Sidc, St P, Swan . . .6A **144**
BR7: Chst, Sidc 3H **143**
DA14: Sidc 6A **144**
Sidcup High St. DA14: Sidc 4A **144**
Sidcup Hill DA14: Sidc 4B **144**
Sidcup Hill Gdns. DA14: Sidc 5C **144**
Sidcup Leisure Cen. 2A **144**
Sidcup Place .5A **144**
Sidcup Pl. DA14: Sidc 5A **144**
Sidcup Rd. SE9 . . . . .1D **142**
SE12 . . . . .6A **124**
Sidcup Technical Cen. DA14: Sidc . . .6D **144**
Siddeley Dr. TW4: Houn 3C **112**
Siddeley Rd. E17 . . . . .2E **50**
Siddons La. NW1 . . . . .4F **5** (4D **82**)
Siddons Rd. CR0: Wadd 3A **168**
N17 . . . . .1G **49**
SE23 . . . . .2A **140**
Side Rd. E17 .5B **50**
Sidewood Rd. SE9 . . . . .1H **143**
Sidford Ho. SE1 . . . . .2H **19**
Sidford Pl. SE1 . . . . .2H **19** (3A **102**)
Sidgwick Ho. *SW9* *2K 119*
(off Stockwell Rd.)
Sidi Ct. N15 . . . . .3B **48**
Sidings, The E11 . . . . .1E **68**
Sidings Apartments, The E16 . . . . . .2E **106**
Sidings M. N7 . . . . .3A **66**
Sidlaw Ho. N16 . . . . .1F **67**
Sidmouth Av. TW7: Isle 2J **113**
Sidmouth Dr. HA4: Ruis 3J **57**
Sidmouth Ho. *SE15* *7G 103*
(off Lindsey Est.)
W1 . . . .*7D 4*
(off Cato St.)
Sidmouth M. WC1 . . . . .2G **7**
Sidmouth Pde. NW2 . . . . .7E **62**
Sidmouth Rd. DA16: Well 7C **108**
E10 . . . . .3E **68**
NW2 . . . . .7E **62**
Sidmouth St. WC1 . . . . .2F **7** (3K **83**)
Sidney Av. N13 . . . . .5E **32**
Sidney Boyd Ct. NW6 . . . . .7J **63**
Sidney Elson Way E6 . . . . .2E **88**
Sidney Est. E1 . . . . .6J **85**
(Bromhead St.)
E1 .5J **85**
(Lindley St.)
Sidney Gdns. TW8: Bford 6D **96**
Sidney Godley (VC) Ho. *E2* *3J 85*
(off Digby St.)
Sidney Gro. EC1 . . . . .1A **8** (2B **84**)
Sidney Ho. *E2* *2K 85*
(off Old Ford Rd.)
Sidney Miller Ct. *W3* *1H 97*
(off Crown St.)
Sidney Rd. BR3: Beck 2A **158**
E7 . . . . .3J **69**
HA2: Harr 3G **41**
KT12: Walt T 7J **147**
N22 . . . . .7E **32**
SE25 . . . . .5G **157**
SW9 . . . . .2K **119**
TW1: Twick 6A **114**
Sidney Sq. E1 . . . . .5J **85**
Sidney St. E1 .5H **85**
(not continuous)
Sidney Webb Ho. *SE1* *3D 102*
(off Gt. Dover St.)
Sidworth St. E8 . . . . .7H **67**
Siebert Rd. SE3 . . . . .6J **105**
Siege Ho. *E1* *6H 85*
(off Sidney St.)
Siemens Rd. SE18 . . . . .3B **106**
Sienna SE28 .3A **108**
Sienna Cl. KT9: Chess 6D **162**
Sienna Ter. NW2 . . . . .2C **62**

Sierra Dr. RM9: Dag 2H **91**
Sigdon Pas. E8 . . . . .5G **67**
Sigdon Rd. E8 . . . . .5G **67**
Sigers, The HA5: Eastc 6K **39**
Sigmund Freud Statue 6B **64**
Signal Ho. *SE8* *7H 67*
(off Martello Ter.)
SE1 . . . .*7C 14*
(off Pickwick St.)
Signmakers Yd. *NW1* *1F 83*
(off Delancey St.)
Sigrist Sq. KT2: King T 1E **150**
Sikorski Mus. 7B **10** (2B **100**)
Silbury Av. CR4: Mitc 1C **154**
Silbury Ho. SE26 . . . . .3G **139**
Silbury St. N1 . . . . .1E **8** (3D **84**)
Silchester Ct. CR7: Thor H 4A **156**
TW15: Ashf 2A **128**
Silchester Rd. W10 . . . . .6F **81**
Silecroft Rd. DA7: Bex 1G **127**
Silesia Bldgs. E8 . . . . .7H **67**
Silex St. SE1 . . . . .7B **14** (2B **102**)
Silk Cl. SE12 .5J **123**
Silk Cl. *E2* *3G 85*
(off Squirries St.)
Silkfield Rd. NW9 . . . . .5A **44**
Silk Ho. NW9 .3K **43**
Silkin M. SE15 . . . . .7G **103**
Silk M. SE11 .5K **19**
Silk Mills Pas. SE13 . . . . .2D **122**
Silk Mills Path SE13 . . . . .2E **122**
(not continuous)
Silk Mills Sq. E3 . . . . .6B **68**
Silks Ct. E11 .1H **69**
Silkstream Pde. HA8: Edg 1J **43**
Silkstream Rd. HA8: Edg 1J **43**
Silk St. EC2 . . . . .5D **8** (5C **84**)
Sillitoe Ho. N1 . . . . .1D **84**
(off Colville Est.)
Silsoe Ho. NW1 . . . . .2F **83**
Silsoe Rd. N22 . . . . .2K **47**
Silverbeck Way TW19: Stan M 7B **174**
Silver Birch Av. E4 . . . . .5G **35**
Silver Birch Cl. DA2: Dart 4K **145**
N11 . . . . .6K **31**
SE6 . . . . .3B **140**
SE28 . . . . .1A **108**
UB10: Ick 4A **56**
Silver Birch Gdns. E6 . . . . .4D **88**
Silverbirch Wlk. NW5 . . . . .6E **64**
Silverburn Ho. *SW9* *1B 120*
(off Lothian Rd.)
Silvercliffe Gdns. EN4: E Barn 4H **21**
Silver Cl. HA3: Hrw W 7C **26**
SE14 . . . . .7A **104**
Silver Cres. W4 . . . . .4H **97**
Silverdale EN2: Enf 4D **22**
NW1 . . . .*1A 6*
(off Hampstead Rd.)
SE26 . . . . .4J **139**
Silverdale Av. IG2: Ilf 5J **53**
Silverdale Cen., The HA0: Wemb . . .1F **79**
Silverdale Cl. SM1: Sutt 4H **165**
UB5: N'olt 5D **58**
W7 . . . . .1J **95**
Silverdale Ct. EC1 . . . . .3B **8**
Silverdale Dr. SE9 . . . . .2E **142**
TW16: Sun 2K **147**
Silverdale Factory Cen. UB3: Hayes . .3J **93**
Silverdale Gdns. UB3: Hayes 2J **93**
Silverdale Ind. Est. UB3: Hayes 2J **93**
Silverdale Rd. BR5: Pet W 4G **161**
DA7: Bex 2H **127**
E4 . . . . .6A **36**
UB3: Hayes 2H **93**
Silverdene *N12* *6E 30*
(off Thyra Gro.)
Silvergate KT19: Ewe 5J **163**
Silverhall St. TW7: Isle 3A **114**
Silverholme Cl. HA3: Kenton 7E **42**
Silver Jubilee Way TW4: Cran 2K **111**
Silverland St. E16 . . . . .1D **106**

Silver La. BR4: W W'ck 2F **171**
Silverleigh Rd. CR7: Thor H 4K **155**
Silver Mead E18 . . . . .1J **51**
Silvermere Dr. N18 . . . . .6E **34**
Silvermere Rd. SE6 . . . . .7D **122**
Silver Pl. W1 . . . . .2B **12** (6G **83**)
Silver Rd. SE13 . . . . .3D **122**
W12 .7F **81**
Silvers IG9: Buck H 1F **37**
(off Palmerston Rd.)
Silver Spring Cl. DA8: Erith 6H **109**
Silverston Way HA7: Stan 2C **27**
Silver St. EN1: Enf 3J **23**
N18 . . . . .4J **33**
Silverthorn *NW8* *1K 81*
(off Abbey Rd.)
Silverthorne Loft Apartments *SE5* . . .*6D 102*
(off Albany Rd.)
Silverthorne Rd. SW8 . . . . .2F **119**
Silverthorn Gdns. E4 . . . . .2H **35**
Silverton Rd. W6 . . . . .6F **99**
SILVERTOWN 1A **106**
Silvertown Viaduct E16 . . . . .6H **87**
Silvertown Way E16 . . . . .6G **87**
Silvertree La. UB6: G'frd 3H **77**
Silver Wlk. SE16 . . . . .1A **104**
Silver Way RM7: Mawney 3H **55**
UB10: Hil 2D **74**
Silver Wing Ind. Est. CR0: Wadd . . .6K **167**
Silverwood Cl. BR3: Beck 7C **140**
CR0: Sels 7B **170**
HA6: Nwood 1E **38**
Silvester Ho. *E1* *6H 85*
(off Varden St.)
E2 . . . .*3J 85*
(off Sceptre Rd.)
W11 . . . .*6H 81*
(off Basing St.)
Silvester Rd. SE22 . . . . .5F **121**
Silvester St. SE1 . . . . .7E **14** (2D **102**)
Silvocea Way E14 . . . . .6E **87**
Silwood Est. SE16 . . . . .4J **103**
Silwood St. *SE16* *4J 103*
(off Rotherhithe New Rd.)
Simla Cl. *N7* *7J 65*
(off Brewery Rd.)
Simla Ho. *SE1* *7F 15*
(off Kipling Est.)
Simmonds Ct. *SW5* *4K 99*
(off Earl's Ct. Gdns.)
Simmons Cl. KT9: Chess 6C **162**
N20 . . . . .2H **31**
Simmons Dr. RM8: Dag 3E **72**
Simmons La. E4 . . . . .2A **36**
Simmons Rd. SE18 . . . . .5F **107**
Simmons Way N20 . . . . .2H **31**
Simms Cl. SM5: Cars 2C **166**
Simms Gdns. N2 . . . . .2A **46**
Simms Rd. SE1 . . . . .4G **103**
Simnel Rd. SE12 . . . . .7K **123**
Simon Cl. W11 . . . . .7H **81**
Simon Ct. *W9* *3J 81*
(off Saltram Cres.)
Simonds Rd. E10 . . . . .2C **68**
Simone Cl. BR1: Brom 1B **160**
Simone Ct. SE26 . . . . .3J **139**
Simon Peter Ct. EN2: Enf 2G **23**
Simons Ct. N16 . . . . .2F **67**
Simons Wlk. E15 . . . . .5F **69**
Simpson Cl. CR0: C'don 5C **156**
N21 . . . . .5D **22**
Simpson Dr. W3 . . . . .6K **79**
Simpson Ho. NW8 . . . . .2D **4** (4C **82**)
SE11 . . . . .6G **19** (5K **101**)
Simpson Rd. TW4: Houn 6D **112**
TW10: Ham 4C **132**
Simpsons Rd. BR2: Brom 3J **159**
E14 . . . . .7D **86**
Simpson St. SW11 . . . . .2C **118**
Simpson Way KT6: Surb 6C **150**
Simrose Ct. SW18 . . . . .5J **117**
Sims Wlk. SE3 . . . . .4H **123**

Sinclair Ct.—Solarium Ct.

Sinclair Ct. CR0: C'don 2E 168
Sinclair Dr. SM2: Sutt 7K 165
Sinclair Gdns. W14 . . . . . 2F 99
Sinclair Gro. NW11 . . . . . 6F 45
Sinclair Ho. *WC1* *2E 6*
(off Sandwich St.)
Sinclair Mans. *W12* *2F 99*
(off Richmond Way)
Sinclair Pl. SE4 . . . . . 6C 122
Sinclair Rd. E4 . . . . . 5G 35
W14 . . . . . 2F 99
Sinclairs Ho. *E3* *2B 86*
(off St Stephen's Rd.)
Sinclare Cl. EN1: Enf 1A 24
Singapore Rd. W13 . . . . . 1A 96
Singer M. *SW4* *2J 119*
(off Union Rd.)
Singer St. EC2 . . . . . 2F 9 (3D 84)
Singleton Cl. CR0: C'don 7C 156
SW17 . . . . . 7D 136
Singleton Rd. RM9: Dag 5F 73
Singleton Scarp N12 . . . . . 5D 30
Sinnott Rd. E17 . . . . . 1K 49
Siobhan Davis Dance Studios *3B 102*
(off St George's Rd.)
Sion Ct. TW1: Twick 1B 132
Sion Rd. TW1: Twick 1B 132
Sippets Ct. IG1: Ilf 1H 71
SIPSON 6C 92
Sipson Cl. UB7: Sip 6C 92
Sipson La. UB3: Harl 6C 92
UB7: Sip 6C 92
Sipson Rd. UB7: Sip, W Dray 3B 92
(not continuous)
Sipson Way UB7: Sip 7C 92
Sir Abraham Dawes Cotts.
SW15 . . . . . 4G 117
Sir Alexander Cl. W3 . . . . . 1B 98
Sir Alexander Rd. W3 . . . . . 1B 98
Sir Christopher France Ho. E1 . . . . . 3A 86
Sir Cyril Black Way SW19 . . . . . 7J 135
Sirdar Rd. CR4: Mitc 6E 136
N22 . . . . . 3B 48
W11 . . . . . 7F 81
Sirinham Point SW8 . . . . . 7H 19
Sirius Bldg. *E1* *7K 85*
(off Jardine Rd.)
Sir James Black Ho. *SE5* *2D 120*
(off Coldharbour La.)
Sir John Kirk Cl. SE5 . . . . . 7C 102
Sir John Lyon Ho. *EC4* *2C 14*
(off High Timber St.)
Sir John Morden Wlk. SE3 . . . . . 2J 123
Sir John Soane's Mus. 7G 7 (6K 83)
Sir Nicholas Garrow Ho. *W10* *4G 81*
(off Kensal Rd.)
Sir Oswald Stoll Foundation, The
SW6 . . . . . *7K 99*
(off Fulham Rd.)
Sir Oswald Stoll Mans. *SW6* *7K 99*
(off Fulham Rd.)
Sirus SW11 . . . . . 2D 118
Sir William Powell's Almshouses
SW6 . . . . . 2G 117
Sise La. EC4 . . . . . 1E 14 (6D 84)
Siskin Ho. *SE16* *4K 103*
(off Tawny Way)
Sisley Rd. IG11: Bark 1J 89
Sispara Gdns. SW18 . . . . . 6H 117
Sissinghurst Cl. BR1: Brom 5G 141
Sissinghurst Ho. *SE15* *6J 103*
(off Sharratt St.)
Sissinghurst Rd. CR0: C'don 7G 157
Sissulu Ct. E6 . . . . . 1A 88
Sister Mabel's Way SE15 . . . . . 7G 103
Sisters Av. SW11 . . . . . 3D 118
Sistova Rd. SW12 . . . . . 1F 137
Sisulu Pl. SW9 . . . . . 3A 120
Sitarey Ct. W12 . . . . . 1D 98
Sittingbourne Av. EN1: Enf 6J 23
Sitwell Gro. HA7: Stan 5E 26
Siverst Cl. UB5: N'olt 6F 59
Sivill Ho. *E2* *1K 9*
(off Columbia Rd.)
Siviter Way RM10: Dag 7H 73
Siward Rd. BR2: Brom 3K 159
N17 . . . . . 1D 48
SW17 . . . . . 3A 136
Six Acres Est. N4 . . . . . 2K 65
Six Bridges Ind. Est. SE1 . . . . . 5G 103
Sixpenny Ct. IG11: Bark 6G 71
Sixth Av. E12 . . . . . 4D 70
UB3: Hayes 1H 93
W10 . . . . . 3G 81
Sixth Cross Rd. TW2: Twick 3G 131
Skardu Rd. NW2 . . . . . 5G 63
Skeena Hill SW18 . . . . . 7G 117
Skeffington Rd. E6 . . . . . 1D 88
Skeffington St. SE18 . . . . . 3G 107
Skeggs Ho. *E14* *3E 104*
(off Glengall St.)
Skegness Ho. *N7* *7K 65*
(off Sutterton St.)
Skelbrook St. SW18 . . . . . 2A 136
Skelgill Rd. SW15 . . . . . 4H 117
Skelley Rd. E15 . . . . . 7H 69
Skelton Cl. E8 . . . . . 6F 67
Skelton Rd. E7 . . . . . 6J 69
Skelton's La. E10 . . . . . 7D 50
Skelwith Rd. W6 . . . . . 6E 98
Skenfrith Ho. *SE15* *6H 103*
(off Commercial Way)
Skerne Rd. KT2: King T 1D 150
Skerne Wlk. KT2: King T 1D 150
Sketchley Gdns. SE16 . . . . . 5K 103
Sketty Rd. EN1: Enf 3A 24
Skiers St. E15 . . . . . 1G 87
Skiffington Cl. SW2 . . . . . 1A 138
Skillen Lodge HA5: Pinn 1B 40
Skinner Pl. SW1 . . . . . 4G 17
Skinners La. EC4 . . . . . 2D 14 (7C 84)
TW5: Hest 1F 113
Skinner's Row SE10 . . . . . 1D 122
Skinner St. EC1 . . . . . 2A 8 (3A 84)
Skip La. UB9: Hare 1A 56
Skipper Ct. IG11: Bark 1G 89
Skipsea Ho. SW18 . . . . . 6C 118
Skipsey Av. E6 . . . . . 3D 88
Skipton Cl. N11 . . . . . 6K 31
Skipton Dr. UB3: Harl 3E 92
Skipton Ho. SE4 . . . . . 4A 122
Skipwith Ho. *EC1* *5J 7*
(off Bourne Est.)
Skipworth Rd. E9 . . . . . 1J 85
Skua Ct. *SE8* *6B 104*
(off Dorking Cl.)
Skylark Ct. *SE1* *7D 14*
(off Swan St.)
Skyline Ct. *CR0: C'don* *3D 168*
(off Park La.)
SE1 . . . . . 3F 103
Skyline Plaza Bldg. *E1* *6G 85*
(off Commercial Rd.)
Skylines E14 . . . . . 2E 104
Skylines Village E14 . . . . . 2E 104
Sky Peals Rd. IG8: Wfd G 7A 36
Skyport Dr. UB7: Harm 3E 174
Skyvan Cl. TW6: H'row A 5E 110
Skyview Apartments *CR0: C'don* *2C 168*
(off Park St.)
Skyway 14 SL3: Poyle 6A 174
Slade, The SE18 . . . . . 6J 107
Sladebrook Rd. SE3 . . . . . 3B 124
Slade Ct. EN5: New Bar 3E 20
Sladedale Rd. SE18 . . . . . 5J 107
Slade Ho. TW4: Houn 6D 112
Sladen Pl. E5 . . . . . 4H 67
Slades Cl. EN2: Enf 3F 23
Slades Dr. BR7: Chst 3G 143
Slades Gdns. EN2: Enf 2F 23
Slades Hill EN2: Enf 3F 23
Slades Ri. EN2: Enf 3F 23
Slade Twr. *E10* *2C 68*
(off Leyton Grange Est.)
Slade Wlk. SE17 . . . . . 6B 102
Slade Way CR4: Mitc 1E 154
Slagrove Pl. SE13 . . . . . 5C 122
Slaidburn St. SW10 . . . . . 6A 100
Slaithwaite Rd. SE13 . . . . . 4E 122
Slaney Ct. NW10 . . . . . 7E 62
Slaney Pl. N7 . . . . . 5A 66
Slater Cl. SE18 . . . . . 5E 106
Slatter NW9 . . . . . 7G 29
Slattery Rd. TW13: Felt 1B 130
Sleaford Ind. Est. SW8 . . . . . 7G 101
Sleaford St. SW8 . . . . . 7G 101
Sleat Ho. *E3* *2B 86*
(off Saxon Rd.)
Sledmere Ct. TW14: Bedf 1G 129
Sleigh Ho. *E2* *3J 85*
(off Bacton St.)
Slievemore Cl. SW4 . . . . . 3H 119
Sligo Ho. *E1* *4K 85*
(off Beaumont Gro.)
Slindon Ct. N16 . . . . . 3F 67
Slingsby Pl. WC2 . . . . . 2E 12 (7J 83)
Slippers Pl. SE16 . . . . . 3H 103
Slipway Ho. *E14* *5D 104*
(off Burrells Wharf Sq.)
Sloane Av. SW3 . . . . . 4D 16 (4C 100)
Sloane Av. Mans.
SW3 . . . . . 4E 16 (4D 100)
Sloane Ct. TW7: Isle 1J 113
Sloane Ct. E. SW3 . . . . . 5G 17 (5E 100)
Sloane Ct. W.SW3 . . . . . 5G 17 (5E 100)
Sloane Gdns. BR6: Farnb 3G 173
SW1 . . . . . 4G 17 (4E 100)
Sloane Ga. Mans. *SW1* *3G 17*
(off D'Oyley St.)
Sloane Ho. *E9* *7J 67*
(off Loddiges Rd.)
Sloane M. N8 . . . . . 5J 47
Sloane Sq. SW1 . . . . . 4G 17 (4E 100)
Sloane St. SW1 . . . . . 7F 11 (2D 100)
Sloane Ter. SW1 . . . . . 3G 17 (4E 100)
Sloane Ter. Mans. *SW1* *3G 17*
(off Sloane Ter.)
Sloane Wlk. CR0: C'don 6B 158
Slocum Cl. SE28 . . . . . 7C 90
Slough La. NW9 . . . . . 5J 43
Sly St. E1 . . . . . 6H 85
Smaldon Cl. UB7: W Dray 3C 92
Smallberry Av. TW7: Isle 2K 113
Smallbrook M. W2 . . . . . 1A 10 (6B 82)
Smalley Cl. N16 . . . . . 3F 67
Smalley Rd. Est. *N16* *3F 67*
(off Smalley Cl.)
Smallwood Rd. SW17 . . . . . 4B 136
Smarden Cl. DA17: Belv 5G 109
Smarden Gro. SE9 . . . . . 4D 142
Smart's Pl. N18 . . . . . 5B 34
WC2 . . . . . 7F 7 (6J 83)
Smart St. E2 . . . . . 3K 85
Smead Way SE13 . . . . . 3D 122
Smeaton Cl. KT9: Chess 6D 162
Smeaton Ct. SE1 . . . . . 3C 102
Smeaton Rd. IG8: Wfd G 5J 37
SW18 . . . . . 7J 117
Smeaton St. E1 . . . . . 1H 103
Smedley St. SW4 . . . . . 2H 119
Smeed Rd. E3 . . . . . 7C 68
Smikle Ct. *SE14* *1K 121*
(off Hatcham Pk. M.)
Smiles Pl. SE13 . . . . . 2E 122
Smith Cl. SE16 . . . . . 1K 103
Smithfield (Central Markets) 6A 8
Smithfield St. EC1 . . . . . 6A 8 (5B 84)
Smith Hill TW8: Bford 6E 96
Smithies Rd. SE2 . . . . . 4B 108
Smith's Ct. W1 . . . . . 2B 12
Smithson Rd. N17 . . . . . 1D 48
Smiths Point *E13* *1J 87*
(off Brooks Rd.)
Smith Sq. SW1 . . . . . 2E 18 (3J 101)
Smith St. KT5: Surb 6F 151
SW3 . . . . . 5E 16 (5D 100)
Smiths Yd. *CR0: C'don* *3C 168*
(off St George's Wlk.)
SW18 . . . . . 2A 136
Smith Ter. SW3 . . . . . 6E 16 (5D 100)
Smithwood Cl. SW19 . . . . . 1G 135
Smithy St. E1 . . . . . 5J 85
Smock Wlk. CR0: C'don 6C 156
Smokehouse Yd. *EC1* *5B 8*
(off St John St.)
Smoothfield Ct. TW3: Houn 4E 112
Smugglers Way SW18 . . . . . 4K 117
Smyrk's Rd. SE17 . . . . . 5E 102
Smyrna Mans. *NW6* *7J 63*
(off Smyrna Rd.)
Smyrna Rd. NW6 . . . . . 7J 63
Smythe Cl. N9 . . . . . 3B 34
Smythe St. E14 . . . . . 7D 86
Snag La. BR6: Prat B 7K 173
Snakes La. N14 . . . . . 3A 22
Snakes La. E.
IG8: Buck H, Wfd G 6F 37
Snakes La. W. IG8: Wfd G 5D 36
Snakey La. TW13: Felt 4J 129
SNARESBROOK 5J 51
Snaresbrook Dr. HA7: Stan 4J 27
Snaresbrook Hall E18 . . . . . 4J 51
Snaresbrook Ho. E18 . . . . . 4H 51
Snaresbrook Rd. E11 . . . . . 4G 51
Snarsgate St. W10 . . . . . 5E 80
Sneath Av. NW11 . . . . . 7H 45
Snells Pk. N18 . . . . . 6A 34
Sneyd Rd. NW2 . . . . . 4E 62
Snowberry Cl. E15 . . . . . 4F 69
Snowbury Rd. SW6 . . . . . 2K 117
Snowden Av. UB10: Hil 2D 74
Snowden St. EC2 . . . . . 4G 9 (4E 84)
Snowdon Aviary *1D 82*
(in London Zoo)
Snowdon Cres. UB3: Harl 3E 92
Snowdon Dr. NW9 . . . . . 6A 44
Snowdon Rd. TW6: H'row A 6E 110
Snowdown Cl. SE20 . . . . . 1J 157
Snowdrop Cl. TW12: Hamp 6E 130
Snow Hill EC1 . . . . . 6A 8 (5B 84)
Snow Hill Ct. EC1 . . . . . 7B 8 (6B 84)
Snowman Ho. NW6 . . . . . 1K 81
Snowsfields SE1 . . . . . 6F 15 (2D 102)
Snowshill Rd. E12 . . . . . 5C 70
Snowy Fielder Waye TW7: Isle 2B 114
Soames Pl. EN4: Had W 2E 20
Soames St. SE15 . . . . . 3F 121
Soames Wlk. KT3: N Mald 1A 152
Soane Cl. W5 . . . . . 2D 96
Soane Ct. *NW1* *7G 65*
(off St Pancras Way)
Soane Ho. *SE17* *5D 102*
(off Roland Way)
Soap Ho. La. TW8: Bford 7E 96
Sobell Leisure Cen. 3K 65
Sobraon Ho. *KT2: King T* *7F 133*
(off Elm Rd.)
Socket La. BR2: Hayes 6K 159
Soda Studios *E8* *1F 85*
(off Kingsland Rd.)
SOHO 1C 12 (6G 83)
Soho Sq. W1 . . . . . 7C 6 (6H 83)
Soho St. W1 . . . . . 7C 6 (6H 83)
Soho Theatre & Writers Cen. 1C 12
(off Dean St.)
Sojourner Truth Cl. E8 . . . . . 6H 67
Sola Ct. *CR0: C'don* *1D 168*
(off Sydenham Rd.)
Solander Gdns. *E1* *7H 85*
(off Cable St.)
E1 . . . . . 7J 85
(The Highway)
Solar Ct. N3 . . . . . 7E 30
SE16 . . . . . *2G 103*
(off Chambers St.)
Solar Ho. E6 . . . . . 5E 88
Solarium Ct. *SE1* *4F 103*
(off Alscot Rd.)

A-Z London 389

Soldene Ct.—Southern Row

Soldene Ct. N7 5K 65
(off George's Rd.)
Solebay St. E1 4A 86
Solent Ct. SW16 2K 155
Solent Ho. E1 5A 86
(off Ben Jonson Rd.)
Solent Ri. E13 3J 87
Solent Rd. NW6 5J 63
Soley M. WC1 1J 7 (3A 84)
Solna Av. SW15 5E 116
Solna Rd. N21 1J 33
Solomon Av. N9 4B 34
Solomons Ct. N12 7F 31
Solomon's Pas. SE15 4H 121
Solon New Rd. SW4 4J 119
Solon New Rd. Est. SW4 4J 119
Solon Rd. SW2 4J 119
Solway Cl. E8 6F 67
(off Queensbridge Rd.)
TW4: Houn 3C 112
Solway Ho. E1 4K 85
(off Ernest St.)
Solway Rd. N22 1B 48
SE22 4G 121
Somaford Gro. EN4: E Barn 6G 21
Somali Rd. NW2 5H 63
Sombourne Ho. SW15 7C 116
(off Fontley Way)
Somerby Rd. IG11: Bark 7H 71
Somercoates Cl. EN4: Cockf 3H 21
Somer Ct. SW6 6J 99
(off Anselm Rd.)
Somerfield Rd. N4 2B 66
(not continuous)
Somerfield St. SE16 5K 103
Somerford Cl. HA5: Eastc 4J 39
Somerford Gro. N16 4F 67
N17 7B 34
(not continuous)
Somerford Gro. Est. N16 4F 67
Somerford St. E1 4H 85
Somerford Way SE16 2A 104
Somerhill Av. DA15: Sidc 7B 126
Somerhill Rd. DA16: Well 2B 126
Somerleyton Pas. SW9 4B 120
Somerleyton Rd. SW9 4A 120
Somersby Gdns. IG4: Ilf 5D 52
Somers Cl. NW1 2H 83
Somers Cres. W2 1C 10 (6C 82)
Somerset Av. DA16: Well 5K 125
KT9: Chess 4D 162
SW20 2D 152
Somerset Cl. IG8: Wfd G 1J 51
KT3: N Mald 6A 152
KT4: Wor Pk 4E 164
N17 2D 48
Somerset Ct. IG9: Buck H 2F 37
NW1 1C 6 (2H 83)
W7 6K 77
(off Copley Cl.)
Somerset Est. SW11 1B 118
Somerset Gdns. HA0: Wemb 5C 60
N6 7E 46
N17 7K 33
SE13 2D 122
SW16 3K 155
TW11: Tedd 5J 131
Somerset Hall N17 7K 33
Somerset House 2G 13 (7K 83)
Somerset Ho. SW19 3F 135
Somerset Lodge TW8: Bford 6D 96
Somerset Rd. E17 5C 50
EN5: New Bar 5E 20
HA1: Harr 5G 41
KT1: King T 2F 151
N17 3F 49
N18 5A 34
NW4 4E 44
SW19 3F 135
TW8: Bford 6C 96
TW11: Tedd 5J 131
UB1: S'hall 5D 76
Somerset Rd. W4 3K 97
W13 1B 96
Somerset Sq. W14 2G 99
Somerset Waye TW5: Hest 6C 94
Somersham Rd. DA7: Bex 2E 126
Somers Pl. SW2 7K 119
Somers Rd. E17 4B 50
SW2 6K 119
SOMERS TOWN 1C 6 (2H 83)
Somers Town Community Sports Cen. 2H 83
Somerton Av. TW9: Rich 3H 115
Somerton Ho. WC1 2D 6
Somerton Rd. NW2 3F 63
SE15 4H 121
Somertrees Av. SE12 2K 141
Somervell Rd. HA2: Harr 5D 58
Somerville Av. SW13 6D 98
Somerville Cl. SW9 1K 119
Somerville Point SE16 2B 104
Somerville Rd. RM6: Chad H 6C 54
SE20 7K 139
Sonderburg Rd. N7 2K 65
Sondes St. SE17 6D 102
Sonesta Apartments SE15 1H 121
Songhurst Cl. CR0: C'don 6K 155
Sonia Ct. HA1: Harr 6K 41
HA8: Edg 7A 28
Sonia Gdns. N12 4F 31
NW10 4B 62
TW5: Hest 7E 94
Sonning Gdns. TW12: Hamp 6C 130
Sonning Ho. E2 2J 9
(off Swanfield St.)
Sonning Rd. SE25 6G 157
Sontan Ct. TW2: Twick 1H 131
Soper Cl. E4 5G 35
SE23 1K 139
Soper M. EN3: Enf L 1H 25
Sophia Cl. N7 6K 65
Sophia Ho. W6 5E 98
(off Queen Caroline St.)
Sophia Rd. E10 1D 68
E16 6K 87
Sophia Sq. SE16 7A 86
(off Sovereign Cres.)
Soprano Way KT6: Surb 3B 162
Sopwith NW9 7G 29
Sopwith Av. KT9: Chess 5E 162
Sopwith Cl. KT2: King T 5F 133
Sopwith Rd. TW5: Hest 7A 94
Sopwith Way KT2: King T 1E 150
SW8 7J 17 (7F 101)
Sorbus Ct. EN2: Enf 2G 23
Sorensen Ct. E10 2D 68
(off Leyton Grange Est.)
Sorrel Cl. SE28 1A 108
Sorrel Gdns. E6 5C 88
Sorrel La. E14 6F 87
Sorrell Cl. SE14 7A 104
SW9 2A 120
Sorrento Rd. SM1: Sutt 3J 165
Sotheby Rd. N5 3B 66
Sotheran Cl. E8 1G 85
Sotherby Lodge E2 2J 85
(off Sewardstone Rd.)
Sotheron Rd. SW6 7K 99
Soudan Rd. SW11 1D 118
Souldern Rd. W14 3F 99
Sth. Access Rd. E17 7A 50
Southacre W2 1C 10
(off Hyde Pk. Cres.)
Southacre Way HA5: Pinn 1A 40
SOUTH ACTON 2J 97
Sth. Africa Rd. W12 1D 98
SOUTHALL 1D 94
Southall Ct. UB1: S'hall 7D 76
Southall Ent. Cen. UB2: S'hall 2E 94
SOUTHALL GREEN 3C 94
Southall La. TW5: Cran 6K 93
UB2: S'hall 6K 93
Southall Pl. SE1 7E 14 (2D 102)
Southall Sports Cen. 1C 94
Southam Ho. W10 4G 81
(off Southam St.)
Southampton Bldgs. WC2 6J 7 (5A 84)
Southampton Gdns. CR4: Mitc 5J 155
Southampton M. E16 1K 105
Southampton Pl. WC1 6F 7 (5J 83)
Southampton Rd. NW5 5D 64
Southampton Rd. E. TW6: H'row A 6B 110
Southampton Rd. W. TW6: H'row A 6A 110
(not continuous)
Southampton Row WC1 5F 7 (5J 83)
Southampton St. WC2 2F 13 (7J 83)
Southampton Way SE5 7D 102
Southam St. W10 4G 81
Sth. Audley St. W1 3H 11 (7E 82)
South Av. E4 7J 25
N2 4K 45
NW10 4E 80
SM5: Cars 7E 166
TW9: Kew 2G 115
UB1: S'hall 7D 76
South Av. Gdns. UB1: S'hall 7D 76
South Bank KT6: Surb 6E 150
Southbank KT7: T Ditt 7B 150
Sth. Bank Bus. Cen. SW8 7D 18 (6H 101)
Southbank Bus. Cen. SW11 1D 118
Southbank Cen. 4H 13 (1K 101)
Sth. Bank Ter. KT6: Surb 6E 150
SOUTH BARNET 1K 31
SOUTH BEDDINGTON 6H 167
Sth. Birkbeck Rd. E11 3F 69
Sth. Black Lion La. W6 5C 98
South Block SE1 7G 13
(off Belvedere Rd.)
Sth. Bolton Gdns. SW5 5K 99
SOUTHBOROUGH
BR2 5D 160
KT6 1E 162
Southborough Cl. KT6: Surb 1D 162
Southborough Ho. SE17 5E 102
(off Kinglake Est.)
Southborough La. BR2: Brom 5C 160
Southborough Rd. BR1: Brom 3C 160
E9 1K 85
KT6: Surb 1E 162
Sth. Boundary Rd. E12 3D 70
Southbourne BR2: Hayes 7J 159
Southbourne Av. NW9 2J 43
Southbourne Cl. HA5: Pinn 7C 40
Southbourne Ct. NW9 2J 43
Southbourne Cres. NW4 4G 45
Southbourne Gdns. HA4: Ruis 1K 57
IG1: Ilf 5G 71
SE12 5K 123
Sth. Branch Av. NW10 4E 80
Southbridge Pl. CR0: C'don 4C 168
Southbridge Rd. CR0: C'don 4C 168
Southbridge Way UB2: S'hall 2C 94
SOUTH BROMLEY 7E 86
Southbrook M. SE12 6H 123
Southbrook Rd. SE12 6H 123
SW16 1J 155
Southbury NW8 1A 82
(off Loudoun Rd.)
Southbury Av. EN1: Enf 4B 24
Southbury Leisure Cen. 3B 24
Southbury Rd. EN1: Enf 3K 23
EN3: Pond E 3A 24
Sth. Carriage Dr. SW1 7B 10 (2B 100)
SW7 7B 10 (2B 100)
SOUTH CHINGFORD 5G 35
Southchurch Ct. E6 2D 88
(off High St. Sth.)
Southchurch Rd. E6 2D 88
Sth. Circular Rd. SW15 4C 116
South City Ct. SE15 7E 102
South Cl. DA6: Bex 4D 126
EN5: Barn 3C 20
HA5: Pinn 7D 40
N6 6F 47
RM10: Dag 1G 91
South Cl. SM4: Mord 6J 153
TW2: Twick 3E 130
UB7: W Dray 3B 92
Sth. Colonnade, The E14 1C 104
(not continuous)
Southcombe St. W14 4G 99
South Comn. Rd. UB8: Uxb 6A 56
Southcote Av. KT5: Surb 7H 151
TW13: Felt 2H 129
Southcote Ri. HA4: Ruis 7F 39
Southcote Rd. E17 5K 49
N19 4G 65
SE25 5H 157
Southcott Ho. E3 3D 86
(off Devons Rd.)
W9 4A 82
(off Clarendon Gdns.)
Southcott M. NW8 2C 82
Southcott Rd. TW11: Ham W 1B 150
Sth. Countess Rd. E17 3B 50
South Cres. E16 4F 87
WC1 6C 6 (5H 83)
Sth. Crescent M. WC1 4J 83
Southcroft Av. BR4: W W'ck 2E 170
DA16: Well 3J 125
Southcroft Rd. BR6: Orp 3J 173
SW16 6E 136
SW17 6E 136
Sth. Cross Rd. IG6: Ilf 5G 53
Sth. Croxted Rd. SE21 3D 138
SOUTH CROYDON 5D 168
South Croydon Sports Club 5E 168
Southdean Gdns. SW19 2H 135
South Dene NW7 3E 28
Southdene Ct. N11 3A 32
Southdown Av. W7 3A 96
Southdown Cres. HA2: Harr 1G 59
IG2: Ilf 5J 53
Southdown Dr. SW20 7F 135
Southdown Rd. SM5: Cars 7E 166
SW20 1F 153
South Dr. BR6: Orp 5J 173
E12 3C 70
HA4: Ruis 1G 57
Sth. Ealing Rd. W5 2D 96
Sth. Eastern Av. N9 3A 34
Sth. Eaton Pl. SW1 3H 17 (4E 100)
Sth. Eden Pk. Rd. BR3: Beck 6D 158
Sth. Edwardes Sq. W8 3H 99
SOUTHEND 4F 141
South End CR0: C'don 4C 168
W8 3K 99
South End Cl. NW3 4C 64
Southend Cl. SE9 6F 125
Southend Cres. SE9 6F 125
South End Grn. NW3 4C 64
Southend La. SE6 4B 140
SE26 4B 140
South End Rd. NW3 4C 64
Southend Rd. BR3: Beck 1C 158
E4 5F 35
E6 7D 70
E17 1D 50
E18 1J 51
IG8: Wfd G 2A 52
South End Row W8 3K 99
Southern Av. SE25 3F 157
TW14: Felt 1J 129
Southern Cotts. TW19: Stan M 7B 174
Southerngate Way SE14 7A 104
Southern Gro. E3 3B 86
Southern Perimeter Rd.
TW6: H'row A 7C 174
(Stanwell Moor Rd.)
TW6: H'row A 5E 110 & 5A 110
(Swindon Rd.)
TW19: Stanw 5A 110
(not continuous)
Southern Pl. HA1: Harr 4K 59
Southern Rd. E13 2K 87
N2 4D 46
Southern Row W10 4G 81

Southern St. N1 . . . . .2K 83
Southern Way RM7: Rom 6G 55
   SE10 . . . . .4H 105
Southernwood Retail Pk. SE1 . . . . .5F 103
Southerton Rd. W6 . . . . .4E 98
South Esk Rd. E7 . . . . .6A 70
Southey Ho. SE17 . . . . .5C 102
                                    (off Browning St.)
Southey M. E16 . . . . .1J 105
Southey Rd. N15 . . . . .5E 48
   SW9 . . . . .1A 120
   SW19 . . . . .7J 135
Southey St. SE20 . . . . .7K 139
Southfield EN5: Barn 6A 20
Southfield Cl. UB8: Hil 4C 74
Southfield Cotts. W7 . . . . .2K 95
Southfield Ct. E11 . . . . .3H 69
Southfield Gdns. TW1: Twick 4K 131
Southfield Pk. HA2: Harr 4F 41
Southfield Rd. BR7: Chst 3K 161
   EN3: Pond E 6C 24
   N17 . . . . .2E 48
   W4 . . . . .2K 97
SOUTHFIELDS 1H 135
Southfields KT8: E Mos 6J 149
   NW4 . . . . .3D 44
Southfields Av. TW15: Ashf 6D 128
Southfields Ct. SM1: Sutt 2J 165
Southfields M. SW18 . . . . .6J 117
Southfields Pas. SW18 . . . . .6J 117
Southfields Rd. SW18 . . . . .6J 117
Southfleet NW5 . . . . .6E 64
Southfleet Rd. BR6: Orp 2G 173
South Gdns. HA9: Wemb 2G 61
   SW19 . . . . .7B 136
SOUTHGATE .1C 32
Southgate Av. TW13: Felt 4F 129
Southgate Cir. N14 . . . . .1C 32
Southgate Ct. N1 . . . . .7D 66
                                    (off Downham Rd.)
Southgate Gro. N1 . . . . .7D 66
Southgate Leisure Cen. 7C 22
South Ga. Rd. E12 . . . . .3B 70
Southgate Rd. N1 . . . . .1D 84
Sth. Gipsy Rd. DA16: Well 3D 126
Sth. Glade, The DA5: Bexl 1F 145
South Grn. NW9 . . . . .1A 44
South Gro. E17 . . . . .5B 50
   N6 . . . . .1E 64
   N15 . . . . .5D 48
South Gro. Ho. N6 . . . . .1E 64
SOUTH HACKNEY 1K 85
SOUTH HAMPSTEAD 7A 64
SOUTH HARROW 3G 59
Sth. Harrow Ind. Est. HA2: Harr 2G 59
South Hill BR7: Chst 6D 142
   HA6: Nwood 1G 39
South Hill Av. HA1: Harr 3G 59
   HA2: Harr .3G 59
South Hill Gro. HA1: Harr 4J 59
South Hill Pk. NW3 . . . . .4C 64
South Hill Pk. Gdns. NW3 . . . . .3C 64
South Hill Rd. BR2: Brom 3G 159
Southholme Cl. SE19 . . . . .1E 156
SOUTH HORNCHURCH 2K 91
Southill Ct. BR2: Brom 5H 159
Southill La. HA5: Eastc 4K 39
Southill Rd. BR7: Chst 7C 142
Southill St. E14 . . . . .6D 86
Sth. Island Pl. SW9 . . . . .7K 101
SOUTH KENSINGTON 4B 100
Sth. Kensington Sta. Arc. SW7 . . . . .3B 16
                                    (off Pelham St.)
SOUTH LAMBETH 7J 101
Sth. Lambeth Pl. SW8 . . . . .7F 19 (6J 101)
Sth. Lambeth Rd. SW8 . . . .7F 19 (6J 101)
Southland Rd. SE18 . . . . .6A 108
Southlands Av. BR6: Orp 4H 173
Southlands Dr. SW19 . . . . .2F 135
Southlands Gro. BR1: Brom 3C 160
Southlands Rd. BR1: Brom 5A 160
   BR2: Brom 5A 160

Southland Way TW3: Houn 5H 113
South La. KT1: King T 3D 150
                                    (not continuous)
   KT3: N Mald 4K 151
South La. W. KT3: N Mald 4K 151
South Lodge E16 . . . . .1K 105
                                    (off Audley Dr.)
   NW8 . . . . .1A 4 (2B 82)
   SW7 . . . . .7D 10
                                    (off Knightsbridge)
   TW2: Whitt 6G 113
Sth. Lodge Av. CR4: Mitc 4J 155
Sth. Lodge Cres. EN2: Enf 4C 22
                                    (not continuous)
Sth. Lodge Dr. N14 . . . . .4C 22
Sth. London Crematorium
   CR4: Mitc .2G 155
South London Gallery 1E 120
South London Theatre 3B 138
                                    (off Norwood High St.)
South Mall N9 . . . . .3B 34
                                    (off Plevna Rd.)
   SW18 . . . . .6K 117
South Mead KT19: Ewe 7B 164
   NW9 . . . . .1B 44
Southmead Gdns.
   TW11: Tedd 6A 132
Southmead Rd. SW19 . . . . .1G 135
Sth. Molton La. W1 . . . . . .1J 11 (6F 83)
Sth. Molton Rd. E16 . . . . .6J 87
Sth. Molton St. W1 . . . . . .1J 11 (6F 83)
Southmoor Way E9 . . . . .6B 68
South Mt. N20 . . . . .2F 31
                                    (off High Rd.)
SOUTH NORWOOD 4F 157
South Norwood Country Pk. 4J 157
South Norwood Country Pk. Vis. Cen.
   . . . . .4H 157
Sth. Norwood Hill SE25 . . . . .1E 156
South Norwood Pools & Fitness Cen.
   . . . . .5H 157
South Oak Rd. SW16 . . . . .4K 137
Southold Ri. SE9 . . . . .3D 142
Southolm St. SW11 . . . . .1F 119
Southover BR1: Brom 5J 141
   N12 . . . . .3D 30
South Pde. HA8: Edg 2G 43
   SM6: Wall .6G 167
   SW3 . . . . .5B 16 (5B 100)
   W4 . . . . .4K 97
South Pk. Ct. BR3: Beck 7C 140
South Pk. Cres. IG1: Ilf 3H 71
   SE6 . . . . .1G 141
South Pk. Dr. IG3: Ilf 2J 71
   IG11: Bark .5J 71
South Pk. Gro. KT3: N Mald 4J 151
South Pk. Hill Rd. CR2: S Croy 5D 168
South Pk. M. SW6 . . . . .3K 117
South Pk. Rd. IG1: Ilf 3H 71
   SW19 . . . . .6J 135
South Pk. Ter. IG1: Ilf 3J 71
South Pk. Vs. IG3: Ilf 4J 71
South Pk. Way HA4: Ruis 6A 58
South Pl. EC2 . . . . .5F 9 (5D 84)
   EN3: Pond E 5D 24
   KT5: Surb .7F 151
South Pl. M. EC2 . . . . .6F 9 (5D 84)
Southport Rd. SE18 . . . . .4H 107
Sth. Quay Plaza E14 . . . . .2D 104
Sth. Quay Sq. E14 . . . . .2D 104
Southridge Pl. SW20 . . . . .7F 135
South Ri. SM5: Cars 7C 166
   W2 . . . . .2D 10
South Ri. Way SE18 . . . . .5H 107
South Rd. HA1: Harr 1A 60
   HA8: Edg 1H 43
   N9 . . . . .1B 34
   RM6: Chad H 5C 54
                                    (Dunmow Cl.)
   RM6: Chad H 6E 54
                                    (Mill La.)
   SE23 . . . . .2K 139

South Rd. SW19 . . . . .6A 136
   TW2: Twick 3H 131
   TW5: Hest .6A 94
   TW12: Hamp 6C 130
   TW13: Hanw 5B 130
   UB1: S'hall .2D 94
   UB7: W Dray 3C 92
   W5 . . . . .4D 96
South Row SE3 . . . . .2H 123
SOUTH RUISLIP 4A 58
Southsea Rd. KT1: King T 4E 150
South Sea St. SE16 . . . . .3B 104
South Side N15 . . . . .4F 49
   W6 . . . . .3B 98
Southside N7 .4H 65
Southside Comn. SW19 . . . . .6E 134
Southside House 6E 134
Southside Ind. Est. SW8 . . . . .1G 119
                                    (off Havelock Ter.)
Southside Shop. Cen. SW18 . . . . . . .6K 117
Southspring DA15: Sidc 7H 125
South Sq. NW11 . . . . .6K 45
   WC1 . . . . .6J 7 (5A 84)
South Stand N5 . . . . .4B 66
South St. BR1: Brom 2J 159
   EN3: Pond E 5D 24
   RM1: Rom .5K 55
   RM13: Rain 2J 91
   TW7: Isle 3A 114
   W1 . . . . .4H 11 (1E 100)
Sth. Tenter St. E1 . . . . . . .2K 15 (7F 85)
   SW7 . . . . .3C 16 (4C 100)
SOUTH TOTTENHAM 5F 49
South Vale HA1: Harr 4J 59
   SE19 . . . . .6E 138
Southvale Rd. SE3 . . . . .2G 123
South Vw. BR1: Brom 2A 160
   SW19 . . . . .6F 135
Southview Av. NW10 . . . . .5B 62
South Vw. Cl. DA5: Bexl 6F 127
Southview Cl. SW17 . . . . .5E 136
South Vw. Ct. SE19 . . . . .7C 138
Southview Cres. IG2: Ilf 6F 53
South Vw. Dr. E18 . . . . .3K 51
Southview Gdns. SM6: Wall 7G 167
Southview Pde. RM13: Rain 3K 91
South Vw. Rd. HA5: Pinn 1K 39
   N8 . . . . .3H 47
Southview Rd. BR1: Brom 4F 141
South Vs. NW1 . . . . .6H 65
Southville SW8 . . . . .1H 119
Southville Cl. KT19: Ewe 7K 163
   TW14: Bedf, Felt 1G 129
Southville Cres. TW14: Felt 1G 129
Southville Rd. KT7: T Ditt 7A 150
   TW14: Felt 1G 129
South Wlk. BR4: W W'ck 3G 171
   UB3: Hayes .5F 75
SOUTHWARK 5A 14 (1B 102)
Southwark Bri. SE1 . . . . . . .3D 14 (7C 84)
Southwark Bri. Bus. Cen. SE1 . . . . . . .5D 14
                                    (off Southwark Bri. Rd.)
Southwark Bri. Rd. SE1 . . . . .3B 102
Southwark Cathedral 4E 14 (1D 102)
Southwark Pk. Est. SE16 . . . . .3H 103
Southwark Pk. Rd. SE16 . . . . .4F 103
Southwark Pk. Sports Cen. Track 4J 103
Southwark Pk. Sports Complex 4J 103
Southwark Pl. BR1: Brom 3D 160
Southwark Playhouse 5G 15
                                    (off Shipwright Yd.)
Southwark St. SE1 . . . . . .4A 14 (1B 102)
Southwater Cl. BR3: Beck 7D 140
   E14 . . . . .6B 86
South Way BR2: Hayes 7J 159
   CRO: C'don 3A 170
   HA2: Harr .4E 40
South Way HA9: Wemb 5G 61
   N9 . . . . .2D 34
   N11 . . . . .6B 32

Southway N20 . . . . .2D 30
   NW11 . . . . .6K 45
   SM6: Wall .4G 167
   SW20 . . . . .5E 152
Southway Cl. W12 . . . . .2D 98
Southwell Av. UB5: N'olt 6E 58
Southwell Gdns. SW7 . . . . .4A 100
Southwell Gro. Rd. E11 . . . . .2G 69
Southwell Ho. SE16 . . . . .4H 103
                                    (off Anchor St.)
Southwell Rd. CRO: C'don 6A 156
   HA3: Kenton 6D 42
   SE5 . . . . .3C 120
Sth. Western Rd. TW1: Twick 6A 114
South W. India Dock Entrance E14 . .2E 104
South W. Middlesex Crematorium
   TW13: Felt 1C 130
Southwest Rd. E11 . . . . .1F 69
Sth. Wharf Rd. W2 . . . . . . .7A 4 (6B 82)
Southwick M. W2 . . . . .7B 4 (6B 82)
Southwick Pl. W2 . . . . . . .1C 10 (6C 82)
Southwick St. W2 . . . . . . .7C 4 (6C 82)
Southwick Yd. W2 . . . . .1C 10
SOUTH WIMBLEDON 5K 135
Southwold Dr. IG11: Bark 5A 72
Southwold Mans. W9 . . . . .3J 81
                                    (off Widley Rd.)
Southwold Rd. DA5: Bexl 6H 127
   E5 . . . . .2H 67
Southwood Av. KT2: King T 1J 151
   N6 . . . . .7F 47
Southwood Cl. BR1: Brom 4D 160
   KT4: Wor Pk 1F 165
Southwood Ct. EC1 . . . . .2A 8
                                    (off Wynyatt St.)
   NW11 . . . . .5K 45
Southwood Dr. KT5: Surb 7J 151
SOUTH WOODFORD 2J 51
Sth. Woodford to Barking Relief Rd.
   E11 . . . . .5B 52
   E12 . . . . .4E 70
   IG1: Ilf 5B 52
   IG4: Ilf 5B 52
Southwood Gdns. IG2: Ilf 4F 53
   KT10: Hin W 3A 162
Southwood Hall N6 . . . . .6F 47
Southwood Hgts. N6 . . . . .7F 47
Southwood Ho. W11 . . . . .7G 81
                                    (off Avondale Pk. Rd.)
Southwood La. N6 . . . . .7E 46
Southwood Lawn Rd. N6 . . . . .7E 46
Southwood Mans. N6 . . . . .6E 46
                                    (off Southwood La.)
Southwood Pk. N6 . . . . .7E 46
Southwood Rd. SE9 . . . . .2F 143
   SE28 . . . . .1B 108
Southwood Smith Ho. E2 . . . . .3H 85
                                    (off Florida St.)
Southwood Smith St. N1 . . . . .1B 84
Sth. Worple Av. SW14 . . . . .3A 116
Sth. Worple Way SW14 . . . . .3K 115
Southwyck Ho. SW9 . . . . .4B 120
Soval Cl. HA6: Nwood 1F 39
Sovereign Bus. Cen.
   EN3: Brim .3G 25
Sovereign Cl. E1 . . . . .7H 85
   HA4: Ruis .1G 57
   W5 . . . . .5C 78
Sovereign Ct. CR2: S Croy 5C 168
                                    (off Warham Rd.)
   HA6: Nwood 1J 39
   KT8: W Mole 4D 148
   TW3: Houn 3E 112
   W8 . . . . .3K 99
                                    (off Wright's La.)
Sovereign Cres. SE16 . . . . .7A 86
Sovereign Gro. HA0: Wemb 3D 60
Sovereign Ho. E1 . . . . .4H 85
                                    (off Cambridge Heath Rd.)
   SE18 . . . . .3D 106
                                    (off Leda Rd.)
   TW15: Ashf 4A 128

Sovereign M. E2 . . . . .2F 85
  EN4: Cockf 3J 21
Sovereign Pk. NW10 . . . . .4H 79
Sovereign Pk. Trad. Est.
  NW10 .4H 79
Sovereign Pl. HA1: Harr 5K 41
Sovereign Rd. IG11: Bark 3C 90
Sowerby Cl. SE9 . . . . .5D 124
Spa at Beckenham, The 1B 158
Space Arts Cen., The 4C 104
  (off Westferry Rd.)
Space Bus. Pk. NW10 . . . . .3H 79
Space Waye TW14: Felt 5J 111
Spa Cl. SE25 . . . . .1E 156
Spa Cl. SE16 . . . . .3G 103
  SW16 .4K 137
Spafield St. EC1 . . . . .3J 7 (4A 84)
Spa Grn. Est. EC1 . . . . .1K 7 (3B 84)
Spa Hill SE19 . . . . .1D 156
Spalding Cl. HA8: Edg 7F 29
Spalding Ho. SE4 . . . . .4A 122
Spalding Rd. NW4 . . . . .7E 44
  SW17 .5F 137
Spanby Rd. E3 . . . . .4C 86
Spaniards Cl. NW11 . . . . .1B 64
Spaniards End NW3 . . . . .1A 64
Spaniards Rd. NW3 . . . . .2A 64
Spanish Pl. W1 . . . . .7H 5 (6E 82)
Spanish Rd. SW18 . . . . .5A 118
Spanswick Lodge N15 . . . . .4B 48
Sparkbridge Rd. HA1: Harr 4J 41
Sparkes Cl. BR2: Brom 4K 159
Sparkes Cotts. SW1 . . . . .4G 17
Sparke Ter. E16 . . . . .6H 87
  (off Clarkson Rd.)
Sparkford Gdns. N11 . . . . .5K 31
Sparkford Ho. SW11 . . . . .1B 118
  (off Battersea Church Rd.)
Sparks Cl. RM8: Dag 2D 72
  TW12: Hamp 6C 130
  W3 . . . . .6K 79
Spa Rd. SE16 . . . . .3F 103
Sparrick's Row SE1 . . . . . . .6F 15 (2D 102)
Sparrow Cl. TW12: Hamp 6C 130
Sparrow Dr. BR5: Farnb 1G 173
Sparrow Ho. E1 . . . . .4J 85
  (off Cephas Av.)
Sparrows Herne WD23: Bush 1A 26
Sparrows La. SE9 . . . . .7G 125
Sparrows Way WD23: Bush 1B 26
Sparsholt Cl. IG11: Bark 1J 89
  (off St John's Rd.)
Sparsholt Rd. IG11: Bark 1J 89
  N19 . . . . .1K 65
Spartan Cl. SM6: Wall 7J 167
Sparta St. SE10 . . . . .1E 122
Speakers' Corner 2F 11 (7D 82)
Speakers Ct. CR0: C'don 1D 168
  (off Arica Rd.)
Speakman Ho. SE4 . . . . .3A 122
  (off Arica Rd.)
Spearman Ho. E14 . . . . .6C 86
  (off Upper Nth. St.)
Spearman St. SE18 . . . . .6E 106
Spear M. W5 . . . . .4J 99
Spearpoint Gdns. IG2: Ilf 5K 53
Spears Rd. N19 . . . . .1J 65
Speart La. TW5: Hest 7C 94
Spectacle Works E13 . . . . .3A 88
Spectrum Pl. SE17 . . . . .6D 102
  (off Lytham St.)
Spectrum Twr. IG1: Ilf 2G 71
  (off Hainault St.)
Spedan Cl. NW3 . . . . .3A 64
Speechly M. E8 . . . . .5F 67
Speedbird Way UB7: Harm 3C 174
Speed Highwalk EC2 . . . . .5D 8
  (off Silk St.)

Speed Ho. EC2 . . . . .5D 8
Speedway Ind. Est. UB3: Hayes 2F 93
Speedwell Ho. N12 . . . . .4E 30
Speedwell St. SE8 . . . . .7C 104
Speedy Pl. WC1 . . . . .2E 6
Speer Rd. KT7: T Ditt 6K 149
Speirs Cl. KT3: N Mald 6B 152
Speke Hill SE9 . . . . .3D 142
Speke Rd. CR7: Thor H 2D 156
Speke's Monument 4A 10 (1A 100)
Speldhurst Cl. BR2: Brom 5H 159
Speldhurst Rd. E9 . . . . .7K 67
  W4 . . . . .3K 97
Spellbrook Wlk. N1 . . . . .1C 84
Spelman Ho. E1 . . . . .6K 9
  (off Spelman St.)
Spelman St. E1 . . . . .5J 9 (5G 85)
  (not continuous)
Spelthorne Gro. TW16: Sun 7H 129
Spelthorne La. TW15: Ashf 1E 146
Spence Cl. SE16 . . . . .2B 104
Spencer Av. N13 . . . . .6E 32
  UB4: Hayes 5J 75
Spencer Cl. BR6: Orp 2J 173
  IG8: Wfd G 5F 37
  N3 . . . . .2J 45
  NW10 .3F 79
Spencer Ct. BR6: Farnb 5G 173
  NW8 . . . . .2A 82
  (off Marlborough Pl.)
  SW20 .1D 152
Spencer Courtyard N3 . . . . .2H 45
  (off Regents Pk. Rd.)
Spencer Dr. N2 . . . . .6A 46
Spencer Gdns. SE9 . . . . .5D 124
  SW14 .5J 115
Spencer Hill SW19 . . . . .6G 135
Spencer Hill Rd. SW19 . . . . .7G 135
Spencer House 5A 12
Spencer Ho. NW4 . . . . .5D 44
Spencer Mans. W14 . . . . .6G 99
  (off Queen's Club Gdns.)
Spencer M. SW8 . . . . .1K 119
  (off Lansdowne Way)
  W6 . . . . .6G 99
SPENCER PARK 5B 118
Spencer Pk. KT8: E Mos 5G 149
  SW18 .5B 118
Spencer Pl. CR0: C'don 7D 156
  N1 . . . . .7B 66
Spencer Ri. NW5 . . . . .4F 65
Spencer Rd. BR1: Brom 7H 141
  CR2: S Croy 5E 168
  CR4: Mitc 3E 154
  (Commonside E.)
  CR4: Mitc 7E 154
  (Wood St.)
  E6 . . . . .1B 88
  E17 . . . . .2E 50
  HA0: Wemb 2C 60
  HA3: W'stone 2J 41
  IG3: Ilf .1K 71
  KT8: E Mos 4G 149
  N8 . . . . .5K 47
  (not continuous)
  N11 . . . . .4A 32
  N17 . . . . .1G 49
  RM13: Rain 3K 91
  SW18 .4B 118
  SW20 .1D 152
  TW2: Twick 3J 131
  TW7: Isle 1G 113
  W3 . . . . .1J 97
  W4 . . . . .1J 97
Spencer St. EC1 . . . . .2A 8 (3B 84)
  UB2: S'hall 2B 94
Spencer Wlk. NW3 . . . . .4A 64
  (off Perrin's Ct.)
  NW3 . . . . .4B 64
  (Hampstead High St.)
  SW15 .4F 117
Spencer Way E1 . . . . .6H 85

Spenlow Ho. SE16 . . . . .3G 103
  (off Jamaica Rd.)
Spenser Gro. N16 . . . . .5E 66
Spenser M. SE21 . . . . .2D 138
Spenser Rd. SE24 . . . . .5B 120
Spenser St. SW1 . . . . .1B 18 (3G 101)
Spens Ho. WC1 . . . . .4G 7
  (off Long Yd.)
Spensley Wlk. N16 . . . . .3D 66
Speranza St. SE18 . . . . .5K 107
Sperling Rd. N17 . . . . .2E 48
Spert St. E14 . . . . .7A 86
Speyside N14 . . . . .6B 22
Spey St. E14 . . . . .5E 86
Spey Way RM1: Rom 1K 55
Spezia Rd. NW10 . . . . .2C 80
Sphere, The E16 . . . . .6H 87
  (off Hallsville Rd.)
Spice Cl. E1 . . . . .7G 85
Spice Quay Hgts. SE1 . . . . . .5K 15 (1F 103)
Spicer Cl. KT12: Walt T 6A 148
  SW9 . . . . .2B 120
Spicer Ct. EN1: Enf 3K 23
Spice's Yd. CR0: C'don 4C 168
Spigurnell Rd. N17 . . . . .1D 48
Spikes Bri. Rd. UB1: S'hall 6C 76
Spindle Cl. SE18 . . . . .3C 106
Spindlewood Gdns.
  CR0: C'don 4E 168
Spindrift Av. E14 . . . . .4C 104
Spinel Cl. SE18 . . . . .5K 107
Spinnaker Cl. IG11: Bark 3B 90
Spinnaker Ct. KT1: Ham W 1D 150
  (off Becketts Pl.)
Spinnaker Ho. E14 . . . . .2C 104
  (off Byng St.)
Spinnells Rd. HA2: Harr 1D 58
Spinney, The DA14: Sidc 5E 144
  EN5: New Bar 2E 20
  HA0: Wemb 3A 60
  HA7: Stan 4K 27
  N21 . . . . .7F 23
  SM3: Cheam 4E 164
  SW13 .7D 98
  SW16 .3G 137
  TW16: Sun 1J 147
Spinney Cl. BR3: Beck 4D 158
  KT3: N Mald 5A 152
  KT4: Wor Pk 2B 164
  UB7: Yiew 7A 74
Spinney Dr. TW14: Bedf 7E 110
Spinney Gdns. RM9: Dag 5E 72
  SE19 . . . . .5F 139
Spinney Oak BR1: Brom 2C 160
Spinneys, The BR1: Brom 2D 160
Spire Ct. BR3: Beck 2D 158
  (off Crescent Rd.)
Spire Ho. W2 . . . . .7A 82
  (off Lancaster Ga.)
Spires Shop. Cen., The EN5: Barn . .3B 20
Spirit Quay E1 . . . . .1G 103
SPITALFIELDS 5J 9 (5F 85)
Spitalfields City Farm 4G 85
Spital Sq. E1 . . . . .5H 9 (5E 84)
Spital St. E1 . . . . .5K 9 (5G 85)
Spital Yd. E1 . . . . .5H 9 (5E 84)
Spitfire Bus. Pk. CR0: Wadd 6A 168
Spitfire Est., The TW5: Cran 5A 94
Spitfire Rd. SM6: Wall 7J 167
  TW6: H'row A 6E 110
Spitfire Way TW5: Cran 5A 94
Splendour Wlk. SE16 . . . . .5J 103
  (off Verney Rd.)
Spode Ho. SE11 . . . . .2J 19
Spode Wlk. NW6 . . . . .5K 63
Spondon Rd. N15 . . . . .4G 49
Spoonbill Way UB4: Yead 5B 76
Spooner Ho. TW5: Hest 6E 94
Spooners M. W3 . . . . .1K 97
Spooner Wlk. SM6: Wall 5J 167
Sporle Rd. Ct. SW11 . . . . .3B 118
Sportsbank St. SE6 . . . . .7E 122

Sportsman Pl. E2 . . . . .1G 85
Spottiswood Ct. CR0: C'don 6C 156
  (off Harry Cl.)
Spottons Gro. N17 . . . . .1C 48
Spout Hill CR0: Addtn 5C 170
Spout La. TW19: Stan M 7B 174
Spout La. Nth. TW19: Stan M 7C 174
Spratt Hall Rd. E11 . . . . .6J 51
Spray La. TW2: Whitt 6J 113
Spray St. SE18 . . . . .4F 107
Spreighton Rd. KT8: W Mole 4F 149
Spriggs Ho. N1 . . . . .7B 66
  (off Canonbury Rd.)
Sprimont Pl. SW3 . . . . .5E 16 (5D 100)
Springall St. SE15 . . . . .7H 103
Springalls Wharf SE16 . . . . .2G 103
  (off Bermondsey Wall W.)
Springbank N21 . . . . .6E 22
Springbank Rd. SE13 . . . . .6F 123
Springbank Wlk. NW1 . . . . .7H 65
Springbourne Ct. BR3: Beck 1E 158
  (not continuous)
Spring Bri. M. W5 . . . . .7D 78
Spring Bri. Rd. W5 . . . . .7D 78
Spring Cl. EN5: Barn 5A 20
  RM8: Dag 1D 72
Springclose La. SM3: Cheam 6G 165
Spring Cnr. TW13: Felt 3J 129
Spring Cotts. KT6: Surb 5D 150
Spring Ct. KT17: Ewe 7B 164
  NW6 . . . . .6H 63
  W7 . . . . .7H 77
Spring Ct. Rd. EN2: Enf 1F 23
Springcroft Av. N2 . . . . .4D 46
Springdale M. N16 . . . . .4D 66
Springdale Rd. N16 . . . . .4D 66
Spring Dr. HA5: Eastc 6J 39
Springett Ho. SW2 . . . . .5A 120
  (off St Matthews Rd.)
Springfield E5 . . . . .1H 67
  SE25 . . . . .3G 157
  WD23: B Hea 1C 26
Springfield Av. N10 . . . . .3G 47
  SW20 .3H 153
  TW12: Hamp 6F 131
Springfield Cl. HA7: Stan 3F 27
  N12 . . . . .5E 30
Springfield Ct. IG1: Ilf 5F 71
  KT1: King T 3E 150
  (off Springfield Rd.)
  NW3 . . . . .7C 64
  (off Eton Av.)
  SM6: Wall 5F 167
Springfield Dr. IG2: Ilf 5G 53
Springfield Gdns. BR1: Brom 4D 160
  BR4: W W'ck 2D 170
  E5 . . . . .1H 67
  HA4: Ruis 1K 57
  IG8: Wfd G 7F 37
  NW9 . . . . .5K 43
Springfield Gro. SE7 . . . . .6A 106
  TW16: Sun 1H 147
Springfield La. NW6 . . . . .1K 81
Springfield Mt. NW9 . . . . .5A 44
Springfield Pde. M.
  N13 . . . . .4F 33
Springfield Pl. KT3: N Mald 4J 151
Springfield Ri. SE26 . . . . .3H 139
Springfield Rd. BR1: Brom 4D 160
  CR7: Thor H 1C 156
  DA7: Bex 4H 127
  DA16: Well 3B 126
  E4 . . . . .1B 36
  E6 . . . . .7D 70
  E15 . . . . .3G 87
  E17 . . . . .6B 50
  HA1: Harr 6J 41
  KT1: King T 3E 150
  N11 . . . . .5A 32
  N15 . . . . .4G 49
  NW8 . . . . .1A 82
  SE26 . . . . .5H 139

Springfield Rd. SM6: Wall 5F **167**
SW19 .....5H **135**
TW2: Whitt 1E **130**
TW11: Tedd 5A **132**
TW15: Ashf 5B **128**
UB4: Yead 1A **94**
W7 .....1J **95**
Springfields *EN5: New Bar* *5E 20*
(off Somerset Rd.)
Springfield Wlk. *BR6: Orp* *1H 173*
(off Place Farm Av.)
NW6 .....1K **81**
Spring Gdns. IG8: Wfd G 7F **37**
KT8: W Mole 5F **149**
N5 .....5C **66**
RM7: Rom 5J **55**
SM6: Wall 5G **167**
SW1 .....4D **12** (1H **101**)
(not continuous)
Spring Gdns. Bus. Pk. RM7: Rom 6J **55**
SPRING GROVE 1J **113**
Spring Gro. CR4: Mitc 1E **154**
SE19 .....7F **139**
TW12: Hamp 1F **149**
W4 .....5G **97**
W7 .....7J **77**
Spring Gro. Cres. TW3: Houn 1G **113**
Spring Gro. Rd. TW3: Houn, Isle 1F **113**
TW7: Isle 1F **113**
TW10: Rich 5F **115**
Spring Health Leisure Club
Richmond *4D 114*
(in Pools on the Pk.)
Spring Hill E5 .....7G **49**
SE26 .....4J **139**
Springhill Cl. SE5 .....3D **120**
Spring Ho. WC1 .....2J **7**
Springhurst Cl. CR0: C'don 4B **170**
Spring Lake HA7: Stan 4G **27**
Spring La. E5 .....7H **49**
N10 .....3E **46**
SE25 .....6H **157**
Spring M. KT17: Ewe 7B **164**
TW9: Rich *4E 114*
(off Rosedale Rd.)
W1 .....5F **5** (5D **82**)
SPRING PARK 3C **170**
Spring Pk. Av. CR0: C'don 2K **169**
Spring Pk. Dr. N4 .....1C **66**
Springpark Dr. BR3: Beck 3E **158**
Spring Pk. Rd. CR0: C'don 2K **169**
Spring Pas. SW15 .....3F **117**
Spring Path NW3 .....5B **64**
Spring Pl. IG11: Bark 2G **89**
N3 .....3J **45**
NW5 .....5F **65**
Springpond Rd. RM9: Dag 5E **72**
Springrice Rd. SE13 .....6F **123**
Spring Rd. TW13: Felt 3H **129**
Spring Shaw Rd. BR5: St P 7A **144**
Spring St. W2 .....1A **10** (6B **82**)
Spring Ter. TW9: Rich 5E **114**
Spring Tide Cl. SE15 .....1H **121**
Spring Va. DA7: Bex 4H **127**
Springvale Av. TW8: Bford 5D **96**
Spring Va. Ter. W14 .....3F **99**
Spring Villa Pk. HA8: Edg 7B **28**
Spring Villa Rd. HA8: Edg 7B **28**
Spring Wlk. E1 .....5G **85**
Springwater WC1 .....5G **7**
Springwater Cl. SE18 .....1E **124**
Springway HA1: Harr 7H **41**
Springwell Av. NW10 .....1B **80**
Springwell Cl. SW16 .....4K **137**
Springwell Rd. SW16 .....4A **138**
TW4: Houn 2B **112**
TW5: Hest 2B **112**
Springwood Cl. E3 .....2C **86**
Springwood Ct. CR2: S Croy 4E **168**
Springwood Cres. HA8: Edg 2C **28**
Sproggit Ind. Est. TW19: Stanw 6B **110**
Sprowston M. E7 .....6J **69**
Sprowston Rd. E7 .....5J **69**
Spruce Ct. W5 .....3E **96**
Sprucedale Gdns. CR0: C'don 4K **169**
Spruce Hills Rd. E17 .....2E **50**
Spruce Ho. *SE16* *2K 103*
(off Woodland Cres.)
Spruce Pk. BR2: Brom 4H **159**
Sprules Rd. SE4 .....2A **122**
Spurfield KT8: W Mole 3F **149**
Spurgeon Av. SE19 .....1D **156**
Spurgeon Rd. SE19 .....1D **156**
Spurgeon St. SE1 .....3D **102**
Spurling Rd. RM9: Dag 6F **73**
SE22 .....4F **121**
Spurrell Av. DA5: Bexl 4K **145**
Spur Rd. BR6: Orp 2K **173**
HA8: Edg 4K **27**
N15 .....4D **48**
SE1 .....6J **13** (2A **102**)
SW1 .....7A **12** (2G **101**)
TW7: Isle 7A **96**
TW14: Felt 4K **111**
Spurstowe Rd. E8 .....6H **67**
Spurstowe Ter. E8 .....5G **67**
Spurway Pde. *IG2: Ilf* *5D 52*
(off Woodford Av.)
Square, The E10 .....3E **68**
IG1: Ilf 7E **52**
IG8: Wfd G 5D **36**
SM5: Cars 5E **166**
TW9: Rich 5D **114**
UB7: Lford 4C **174**
UB11: Stock P 1F **93**
W6 .....5E **98**
Square of Fame *4G 61*
(off Arena Sq.)
Square Rigger Row SW11 .....3A **118**
Squarey St. SW17 .....3A **136**
Squire Gdns. *NW8* *2A 4*
(off Grove End Rd.)
Squires, The RM7: Rom 6J **55**
Squire's Bri. Rd. TW17: Shep 4B **146**
Squires Ct. SW4 .....1J **119**
SW19 .....4J **135**
Squires La. N3 .....2K **45**
Squires Mt. NW3 .....3B **64**
Squire's Rd. TW17: Shep 4B **146**
Squires Wlk. TW15: Ashf 7F **129**
(not continuous)
Squires Way DA2: Dart 4K **145**
Squires Wood Dr. BR7: Chst 7C **142**
Squirrel Cl. TW4: Houn 3A **112**
Squirrel M. W13 .....7K **77**
Squirrels, The HA5: Pinn 3D **40**
SE13 .....3F **123**
Squirrels Cl. BR6: Orp 1J **173**
N12 .....4F **31**
UB10: Hil 7C **56**
Squirrels Ct. *KT4: Wor Pk* *2B 164*
(off The Avenue)
Squirrels Drey *BR2: Brom* *2G 159*
(off Park Hill Rd.)
Squirrels Grn. KT4: Wor Pk 2B **164**
Squirrel's La. IG9: Buck H 3G **37**
Squirrels Trad. Est., The
UB3: Hayes 3H **93**
Squirries St. E2 .....3G **85**
SS Robin 7C **86**
Stable Cl. KT2: King T 6F **133**
UB5: N'olt 2E **76**
Stable Ct. SM6: Wall 3E **166**
Stable M. NW5 .....6F **65**
SE6 .....1G **141**
TW1: Twick 1K **131**
Stables, The IG9: Buck H 1F **37**
Stables End BR6: Farnb 3G **173**
Stables Gallery & Arts Cen. 3C **62**
Stables Lodge *E8* *7H 67*
(off Mare St.)
Stables Market, The 7F **65**
Stables M. SE27 .....5C **138**
Stables Way SE11 .....5J **19** (5A **102**)
Stables Yd. SW18 .....6J **117**
Stable Wlk. N2 .....1B **46**
Stable Way W10 .....6E **80**
Stable Yd. SW1 .....6A **12**
SW15 .....3E **116**
Stableyard, The SW9 .....2K **119**
Stableyard M. TW11: Tedd 6K **131**
Stable Yd. Rd. SW1 .....6B **12** (2G **101**)
(not continuous)
Staburn Ct. HA8: Edg 2J **43**
Stacey Av. N18 .....4D **34**
Stacey Cl. E10 .....5F **51**
Stacey St. N7 .....3A **66**
WC2 .....1D **12** (6H **83**)
Stack Ho. *SW1* *4H 17*
(off Cundy St.)
Stackhouse St. SW3 .....1E **16**
Stacy Path SE5 .....7E **102**
Staddon Cl. BR3: Beck 4A **158**
Stadium Bus. Cen. HA9: Wemb 3H **61**
Stadium Retail Pk. HA9: Wemb 3G **61**
Stadium Rd. SE18 .....7C **106**
Stadium Rd. E. NW4 .....7D **44**
Stadium St. SW10 .....7A **100**
Stadium Way HA9: Wemb 4F **61**
Staffa Rd. E10 .....1A **68**
Stafford Cl. E17 .....6B **50**
(not continuous)
N14 .....5B **22**
NW6 .....3J **81**
SM3: Cheam 6G **165**
Stafford Ct. DA5: Bexl 7F **127**
SW8 .....7J **101**
W7 .....*6K 77*
(off Copley Cl.)
W8 .....3J **99**
Stafford Cripps Ho. *E2* *3J 85*
(off Globe Rd.)
SW6 .....*6H 99*
(off Clem Attlee Ct.)
Stafford Cross Bus. Pk. CR0: Wadd 5K **167**
Stafford Gdns. CR0: Wadd 5K **167**
Stafford Ho. *SE1* *5F 103*
(off Cooper's Rd.)
Stafford Mans. *SW1* *1A 18*
(off Stafford Pl.)
SW4 .....4J **119**
SW11 .....*7D 100*
(off Albert Bri. Rd.)
W14 .....*3F 99*
(off Haarlem Rd.)
Stafford Pl. SW1 .....1A **18** (3G **101**)
TW10: Rich 7F **115**
Stafford Rd. CR0: Wadd 4A **168**
DA14: Sidc 4J **143**
E3 .....2B **86**
E7 .....7A **70**
HA3: Hrw W 7B **26**
HA4: Ruis 4H **57**
KT3: N Mald 3J **151**
NW6 .....3J **81**
SM6: Wall 6G **167**
Staffordshire St. SE15 .....1G **121**
Stafford St. W1 .....4A **12** (1G **101**)
Stafford Ter. W8 .....3J **99**
Staff St. EC1 .....2F **9** (3D **84**)
Stag Cl. HA8: Edg 2H **43**
Stag Ct. *KT2: King T* *1G 151*
(off Coombe Rd.)
STAG LANE **2B 134**
Stag La. HA8: Edg 2H **43**
IG9: Buck H 2E **36**
NW9 .....2H **43**
SW15 .....3B **134**
Stags Way TW7: Isle 6K **95**
Stainbank Rd. CR4: Mitc 3F **155**
Stainby Cl. UB7: W Dray 3A **92**
Stainby Rd. N15 .....4F **49**
Stainer Ho. SE3 .....4A **124**
Stainer St. SE1 .....5F **15** (1D **102**)
Staines Av. SM3: Cheam 2F **165**
Staines By-Pass TW15: Ashf 5A **128**
Staines Rd. IG1: Ilf 5G **71**
TW2: Twick 3E **130**
TW3: Houn 7F **111**
TW4: Houn 7F **111**
TW14: Bedf, Felt 1C **128**
(not continuous)
Staines Rd. E. TW16: Sun 7J **129**
Staines Rd. W. TW15: Ashf 6D **128**
TW16: Sun 6D **128**
Staines Wlk. DA14: Sidc 6C **144**
Stainford Cl. TW15: Ashf 5F **129**
Stainforth Rd. E17 .....4C **50**
IG2: Ilf 7H **53**
Staining La. EC2 .....7D **8** (6C **84**)
Stainmore Cl. BR7: Chst 1H **161**
Stainsbury St. E2 .....2J **85**
Stainsby Rd. E14 .....6C **86**
Stainton Rd. EN3: Enf H 1D **24**
SE6 .....6F **123**
Stalbridge Flats *W1* *1H 11*
(off Lumley St.)
Stalbridge Ho. *NW1* *1A 6*
(off Harrington St.)
Stalbridge St. NW1 .....5D **4** (5C **82**)
Stalham St. SE16 .....3H **103**
Stalham Way IG6: Ilf 1F **53**
Stambourne Way BR4: W W'ck 2E **170**
SE19 .....7E **138**
Stambourne Woodland Wlk. SE19 .....7E **138**
Stamford Bridge 7K **99**
Stamford Bri. Studios *SW6* *7K 99*
(off Wandon Rd.)
Stamford Brook Arches W6 .....4C **98**
Stamford Brook Av. W6 .....3B **98**
Stamford Brook Gdns. W6 .....3B **98**
Stamford Brook Mans. *W6* *4B 98*
(off Goldhawk Rd.)
Stamford Brook Rd. W6 .....3B **98**
Stamford Bldgs. *SW8* *7J 101*
(off Meadow Pl.)
Stamford Cl. HA3: Hrw W 7D **26**
N15 .....4G **49**
NW3 .....*3A 64*
(off Heath St.)
UB1: S'hall 7E **76**
Stamford Cotts. *SW10* *7K 99*
(off Billing St.)
Stamford Ct. HA8: Edg 4A **28**
W6 .....4C **98**
Stamford Dr. BR2: Brom 4H **159**
Stamford Gdns. RM9: Dag 7C **72**
Stamford Ga. SW6 .....7K **99**
Stamford Gro. E. N16 .....1G **67**
Stamford Gro. W. N16 .....1G **67**
STAMFORD HILL 1F **67**
Stamford Hill N16 .....2F **67**
Stamford Lodge N16 .....7F **49**
Stamford Rd. E6 .....1C **88**
N1 .....7E **66**
N15 .....5G **49**
RM9: Dag 1B **90**
Stamford St. SE1 .....5J **13** (1A **102**)
Stamp Pl. E2 .....1J **9** (2F **85**)
Stanard Cl. N16 .....7E **48**
Stanborough Cl. TW12: Hamp 6D **130**
Stanborough Pas. E8 .....6F **67**
Stanborough Rd. TW3: Houn 3H **113**
Stanbridge Pl. N21 .....2G **33**
Stanbridge Rd. SW15 .....3E **116**
Stanbrook Rd. SE2 .....2B **108**
Stanbury Ct. NW3 .....6D **64**
Stanbury Rd. SE15 .....2H **121**
(not continuous)
Stancroft NW9 .....5A **44**
Standale Gro. HA4: Ruis 5E **38**
Standard Ind. Est. E16 .....2D **106**
Standard Pl. EC2 .....2H **9**
Standard Rd. DA6: Bex 4E **126**
DA17: Belv 5G **109**
NW10 .....4J **79**
TW4: Houn 3C **112**
Standen Rd. SW18 .....7H **117**

Standfield Gdns.—Station App.

Standfield Gdns. RM10: Dag 6G **73**
Standfield Rd. RM10: Dag 5G **73**
Standish Ho. *SE3* *4K 123*
(off Elford Cl.)
W6 . . . . *4C 98*
(off St Peter's Gro.)
Standish Rd. W6 . . . . 4C **98**
Standlake Point SE23 . . . . 3K **139**
Stane Cl. SW19 . . . . 7K **135**
Stane Gro. SW9 . . . . 2J **119**
Stanesgate Ho. *SE15* *7G 103*
(off Friary Est.)
Stane Way SE18 . . . . 7B **106**
Stanfield Ho. *NW8* *3B 4*
(off Frampton St.)
UB5: N'olt *2B 76*
(off Academy Gdns.)
Stanfield Rd. E3 . . . . 2A **86**
Stanford Cl. HA4: Ruis 6E **38**
IG8: Wfd G 5H **37**
RM7: Rom 6H **55**
TW12: Hamp 6D **130**
Stanford Ct. SW6 . . . . 1K **117**
W8 . . . . *3K 99*
(off Cornwall Gdns.)
Stanford Ho. IG11: Bark 2B **90**
Stanford M. E8 . . . . 5G **67**
Stanford Pl. SE17 . . . . 4E **102**
Stanford Rd. N11 . . . . 5J **31**
SW16 . . . . 2H **155**
W8 . . . . 3K **99**
Stanford St. SW1 . . . . 4C **18** (4H **101**)
Stanford Way SW16 . . . . 2H **155**
Stangate SE1 . . . . 1H **19**
Stangate Gdns. HA7: Stan 4G **27**
Stangate Lodge N21 . . . . 6E **22**
Stanger Rd. SE25 . . . . 4G **157**
Stanhill Cotts. DA2: Dart 7K **145**
Stanhope Av. BR2: Hayes 1H **171**
HA3: Hrw W 1H **41**
N3 . . . . 3H **45**
Stanhope Cl. SE16 . . . . 2K **103**
Stanhope Gdns. IG1: Ilf 1D **70**
N4 . . . . 6B **48**
N6 . . . . 6F **47**
NW7 . . . . 5G **29**
RM8: Dag 3F **73**
SW7 . . . . 3A **16** (4A **100**)
Stanhope Ga. W1 . . . . 5H **11** (1E **100**)
Stanhope Gro. BR3: Beck 5B **158**
Stanhope Ho. *N11* *4A 32*
(off Coppies Gro.)
SE8 . . . . *7B 104*
(off Adolphus St.)
Stanhope M. E. SW7 . . . . . . 3A **16** (4A **100**)
Stanhope M. Sth. SW7 . . . . 4A **100**
Stanhope M. W. SW7 . . . . 4A **100**
Stanhope Pde. NW1 . . . . 1A **6** (3G **83**)
Stanhope Pk. Rd. UB6: G'frd 4G **77**
Stanhope Pl. W2 . . . . 1E **10** (7D **82**)
Stanhope Rd. CR0: C'don 3E **168**
DA7: Bex 2E **126**
DA15: Sidc 4A **144**
E17 . . . . 5D **50**
EN5: Barn 6A **20**
N6 . . . . 6G **47**
N12 . . . . 5F **31**
RM8: Dag 2F **73**
SM5: Cars 7E **166**
UB6: G'frd 5G **77**
Stanhope Row W1 . . . . 5J **11** (1F **101**)
Stanhope St. NW1 . . . . 1A **6** (2G **83**)
Stanhope Ter. TW2: Twick 7K **113**
W2 . . . . 2B **10** (7B **82**)
Stanier Cl. W14 . . . . 5H **99**
Stanier Ho. *SW6* *1A 118*
(off Station Ct.)
Stanlake M. W12 . . . . 1E **98**
Stanlake Rd. W12 . . . . 1E **98**
Stanlake Vs. W12 . . . . 1E **98**
Stanley Av. BR3: Beck 2E **158**
HA0: Wemb 7E **60**
Stanley Av. IG11: Bark 2K **89**
KT3: N Mald 5C **152**
RM8: Dag 1F **73**
UB6: G'frd 1G **77**
Stanley Bri. Studios *SW6* *7K 99*
(off King's Rd.)
Stanley Cl. HA0: Wemb 7E **60**
SE9 . . . . 1G **143**
SW8 . . . . 6K **101**
Stanley Cohen Ho. *EC1* *4C 8*
(off Golden La.)
Stanley Ct. SM2: Sutt 7K **165**
SM5: Cars 7E **166**
W5 . . . . 5C **78**
Stanley Cres. W11 . . . . 7H **81**
Stanleycroft Cl. TW7: Isle 1J **113**
Stanley Gdns. CR4: Mitc 6E **136**
NW2 . . . . 5E **62**
SM6: Wall 6G **167**
W3 . . . . 2A **98**
W11 . . . . 7H **81**
Stanley Gdns. M. *W11* *7H 81*
(off Kensington Pk. Rd.)
Stanley Gdns. Rd. TW11: Tedd 5J **131**
Stanley Gro. CR0: C'don 6A **156**
SW8 . . . . 2E **118**
Stanley Holloway Ct.
E16 . . . . *6J 87*
(off Coolfin Rd.)
Stanley Ho. *E14* *6C 86*
(off Saracen St.)
SW10 . . . . *7A 100*
(off Coleridge Gdns.)
Stanley Mans. *SW10* *7A 16*
(off Park Wlk.)
Stanley M. *SW10* *7A 100*
(off Coleridge Gdns.)
Stanley Pk. Dr. HA0: Wemb 1F **79**
Stanley Pk. Rd. SM5: Cars 7C **166**
SM6: Wall 6F **167**
Stanley Picker Gallery *3E 150*
(off Springfield Rd.)
Stanley Rd. BR2: Brom 4K **159**
BR6: Orp 1K **173**
CR0: C'don 7A **156**
CR4: Mitc 7E **136**
DA14: Sidc 3A **144**
E4 . . . . 1A **36**
E10 . . . . 6D **50**
E12 . . . . 5C **70**
E18 . . . . 1H **51**
EN1: Enf 3K **23**
HA2: Harr 2G **59**
HA6: Nwood 1J **39**
HA9: Wemb 6F **61**
IG1: Ilf 2H **71**
N2 . . . . 3B **46**
N9 . . . . 1A **34**
N10 . . . . 7A **32**
N11 . . . . 6C **32**
N15 . . . . 4B **48**
NW9 . . . . 7C **44**
SM2: Sutt 6K **165**
SM4: Mord 4J **153**
SM5: Cars 7E **166**
SW14 . . . . 4H **115**
SW19 . . . . 6J **135**
TW2: Twick 3H **131**
TW3: Houn 4G **113**
TW11: Tedd 4J **131**
TW15: Ashf 5A **128**
UB1: S'hall 7C **76**
W3 . . . . 3J **97**
Stanley Sq. SM5: Cars 7D **166**
Stanley St. SE8 . . . . 7B **104**
Stanley Studios *SW10* *7A 16*
(off Fulham Rd.)
Stanley Ter. DA6: Bex 4G **127**
N19 . . . . 2J **65**
Stanliffe Ho. E14 . . . . 3C **104**
Stanmer St. SW11 . . . . 1C **118**
STANMORE 5G **27**
Stanmore Common Local Nature Reserve
. . . . 2E **26**
Stanmore Country Pk. &
Local Nature Reserve 3H **27**
Stanmore Gdns. SM1: Sutt 3A **166**
TW9: Rich 3F **115**
Stanmore Hill HA7: Stan 3F **27**
Stanmore Lodge HA7: Stan 4G **27**
Stanmore Pl. NW1 . . . . 1F **83**
Stanmore Rd. DA17: Belv 4J **109**
E11 . . . . 1H **69**
N15 . . . . 4B **48**
TW9: Rich 3F **115**
Stanmore St. N1 . . . . 1K **83**
Stanmore Ter. BR3: Beck 2C **158**
Stannard Cotts. *E1* *4J 85*
(off Fox Cl.)
Stannard Ct. SE6 . . . . 1D **140**
Stannard M. *E8* *6G 67*
(off Stannard Rd.)
Stannard Rd. E8 . . . . 6G **67**
Stannary Pl. SE11 . . . . 6K **19** (5A **102**)
Stannary St. SE11 . . . . 7K **19** (6A **102**)
Stannet Way SM6: Wall 4G **167**
Stansbury Sq. W10 . . . . 3G **81**
Stansfeld Ho. *SE1* *4F 103*
(off Longfield Est.)
Stansfeld Rd. E6 . . . . 5B **88**
E16 . . . . 5B **88**
Stansfield Rd. SW9 . . . . 3K **119**
TW4: Cran 2K **111**
Stansgate Rd. RM10: Dag 2G **73**
Stanstead *WC1* *2F 7*
(off Tavistock Pl.)
Stanstead Cl. BR2: Brom 5H **159**
Stanstead Gro. SE6 . . . . 1B **140**
Stanstead Ho. *E3* *4E 86*
(off Devas St.)
Stanstead Mnr. SM1: Sutt 6J **165**
Stanstead Rd. E11 . . . . 5K **51**
SE6 . . . . 1A **140**
SE23 . . . . 1K **139**
Stansted Cres. DA5: Bexl 1D **144**
Stansted Rd. TW6: H'row A 6B **110**
Stanswood Gdns. SE5 . . . . 7E **102**
Stanthorpe Cl. SW16 . . . . 5J **137**
Stanthorpe Rd. SW16 . . . . 5J **137**
Stanton Av. TW11: Tedd 6J **131**
Stanton Cl. KT4: Wor Pk 1F **165**
KT19: Ewe 5H **163**
Stanton Ct. *CR2: S Croy* *5E 168*
(off Birdhurst Ri.)
Stanton Ho. *SE10* *6E 104*
(off Thames St.)
SE16 . . . . *2B 104*
(off Rotherhithe St.)
Stanton Rd. CR0: C'don 7C **156**
SE26 . . . . 4B **140**
SW13 . . . . 2B **116**
SW20 . . . . 1F **153**
Stanton Sq. SE26 . . . . 4B **140**
Stanton Way SE26 . . . . 4B **140**
Stanway Ct. N1 . . . . 2E **84**
(not continuous)
Stanway Gdns. HA8: Edg 5D **28**
W3 . . . . 1G **97**
Stanway St. N1 . . . . 2E **84**
STANWELL 6A **110**
Stanwell Cl. TW19: Stanw 6A **110**
STANWELL MOOR 7B **174**
Stanwell Moor Rd. UB7: Lford 7C **174**
Stanwell Rd. TW14: Bedf 7D **110**
TW15: Ashf 2A **128**
Stanwick Rd. W14 . . . . 4H **99**
Stanworth Ct. TW5: Hest 7D **94**
Stanworth St. SE1 . . . . 7J **15** (3F **103**)
Stanyhurst SE23 . . . . 1A **140**
Stapenhill Rd. HA0: Wemb 3B **60**
Staple Cl. DA5: Bexl 3K **145**
Staplefield Cl. SW2 . . . . 1J **137**
Stapleford *N17* *2E 48*
(off Willan Rd.)
Stapleford Av. IG2: Ilf 5J **53**
Stapleford Cl. E4 . . . . 3K **35**
KT1: King T 2G **151**
SW19 . . . . 7G **117**
Stapleford Rd. HA0: Wemb 7D **60**
Stapleford Way IG11: Bark 3B **90**
Staplehurst Rd. SE13 . . . . 5F **123**
SM5: Cars 7C **166**
Staple Inn WC1 . . . . 6J **7**
Staple Inn Bldgs. WC1 . . . . 6J **7** (5A **84**)
Staples Cl. SE16 . . . . 1A **104**
STAPLES CORNER **1D 62**
Staples Cnr. Bus. Pk. NW2 . . . . 1D **62**
Staples Cnr. Retail Pk. NW2 . . . . 1D **62**
Staples Ho. *E6* *6E 88*
(off Savage Gdns.)
Staple St. SE1 . . . . 7F **15** (2D **102**)
Stapleton Gdns. CR0: Wadd 5A **168**
Stapleton Hall Rd. N4 . . . . 1K **65**
Stapleton Ho. *E2* *3H 85*
(off Ellsworth St.)
Stapleton Rd. BR6: Orp 4K **173**
DA7: Bex 7F **109**
SW17 . . . . 3E **136**
Stapleton Vs. *N16* *4E 66*
(off Wordsworth Rd.)
Stapley Rd. DA17: Belv 5G **109**
Stapylton Rd. EN5: Barn 3B **20**
Star All. EC3 . . . . 2H **15**
Star & Garter Hill TW10: Rich 1E **132**
Starboard Way E14 . . . . 3C **104**
Starbuck Cl. SE9 . . . . 7E **124**
Star Bus. Cen. RM13: Rain 5K **91**
Starch Ho. La. IG6: Ilf 2H **53**
Star Cl. EN3: Pond E 6D **24**
Starcross St. NW1 . . . . 2B **6** (3G **83**)
Starfield Rd. W12 . . . . 2C **98**
Star Hill DA1: Cray 5K **127**
Star La. E16 . . . . 4G **87**
Starlight Way TW6: H'row A 5E **110**
Starling Cl. CR0: C'don 6A **158**
HA5: Pinn 3A **40**
IG9: Buck H 1D **36**
Starling Ho. *NW8* *2C 82*
(off Charlbert St.)
Starling Wlk. TW12: Hamp 5C **130**
Starmans Cl. RM9: Dag 1E **90**
Star Path *UB5: N'olt* *2E 76*
(off Brabazon Rd.)
Star Pl. E1 . . . . 3K **15** (7F **85**)
Star Rd. TW7: Isle 2H **113**
UB10: Hil 4E **74**
W14 . . . . 6H **99**
Star St. W2 . . . . 7B **4** (6C **82**)
Starts Cl. BR6: Farnb 3E **172**
Starts Hill Av. BR6: Farnb 4F **173**
Starts Hill Rd. BR6: Farnb 3E **172**
Starveall Cl. UB7: W Dray 3B **92**
Star Wharf *NW1* *1G 83*
(off St Pancras Way)
Star Yd. WC2 . . . . 7J **7** (6A **84**)
State Farm Av. BR6: Farnb 4F **173**
Staten Bldg. *E3* *2C 86*
(off Fairfield Rd.)
Staten Gdns. TW1: Twick 1K **131**
Statham Gro. N16 . . . . 4D **66**
N18 . . . . 5K **33**
Statham Ho. *SW8* *1G 119*
(off Wadhurst Rd.)
Station App. *BR1: Brom* *3J 159*
(off High St.)
BR2: Hayes 1J **171**
BR3: Beck 1C **158**
BR4: W W'ck 7E **158**
BR6: Orp 2K **173**
BR7: Chst 6C **142**
(Elmstead La.)
BR7: Chst 1E **160**
(Vale Rd.)
CR0: C'don *2D 168*
(off Dingwall Rd.)
CR2: Sande 7D **168**

Station App.—Sterry Cres.

Station App. DA5: Bexl 1G **145**
DA7: Bex 2J **127**
(Barnehurst Rd.)
DA7: Bex 2E **126**
(Pickford La.)
DA16: Well 2A **126**
E4 6A **36**
E7 4K **69**
E11 5J **51**
E17 5C **50**
(not continuous)
E18 2K **51**
EN5: New Bar 4F **21**
HA0: Wemb 6B **60**
HA1: Harr 7J **41**
HA4: Ruis 5K **57**
(Mahlon Av.)
HA4: Ruis 1G **57**
(Pembroke Rd.)
HA5: Pinn 3C **40**
IG8: Wfd G 6E **36**
IG9: Buck H 4G **37**
KT1: King T 1G **151**
KT4: Wor Pk 1C **164**
KT17: Ewe 7B **164**
KT19: Ewe 5C **164**
N11 5A **32**
N12 4E **30**
N16 *2F* ***67***
(off Stamford Hill)
NW1 4F **5** (4D **82**)
NW10 3B **80**
NW11 7F **45**
SE3 3K **123**
SE9 2G **143**
(Bercta Rd.)
SE9 1D **142**
(Crossmead)
SE12 *6J* ***123***
(off Burnt Ash Hill)
SE26 4J **139**
SM2: Cheam 7G **165**
SM5: Cars 4D **166**
SW6 3G **117**
SW14 3J **115**
SW16 6H **137**
(Estreham Rd.)
SW16 5H **137**
(Gleneagle Rd.)
SW20 2D **152**
TW8: Bford *6C* ***96***
(off Sidney Gdns.)
TW9: Kew 1G **115**
TW12: Hamp 1E **148**
TW15: Ashf 4B **128**
TW16: Sun 1J **147**
TW17: Shep 5E **146**
UB3: Hayes 3H **93**
UB6: G'frd 7G **59**
UB7: Yiew 1A **92**
W7 1J **95**
Station App. Nth. DA15: Sidc 2A **144**
Station App. Rd. SE1 7H **13** (2A **102**)
W4 7J **97**
Station App. Sth. *DA15: Sidc* *2A* ***144***
(off Jubilee Way, not continuous)
Station Arc. *W1* *4K* ***5***
(off Gt. Portland St.)
Station Av. KT3: N Mald 3A **152**
KT19: Ewe 7A **164**
SW9 3B **120**
TW9: Kew 1G **115**
Station Bldgs. *KT1: King T* *2E* ***150***
(off Fife Rd.)
Station Chambers *E6* *7C* ***70***
(off High St. Nth.)
Station Cl. N3 1J **45**
N12 4E **30**
TW12: Hamp 1F **149**
Station Cotts. BR6: Orp 2K **173**
Station Ct. N15 5F **49**
SW6 1A **118**
Station Cres. HA0: Wemb 6B **60**
N15 4D **48**
SE3 5J **105**
TW15: Ashf 3A **128**
Stationer's Hall Ct.
EC4 1B **14** (6B **84**)
Station Est. BR3: Beck 3K **157**
E18 2K **51**
Station Est. Rd. TW14: Felt 1K **129**
Station Garage M. SW16 6H **137**
Station Gdns. W4 7J **97**
Station Gro. HA0: Wemb 6E **60**
Station Hill BR2: Hayes 2J **171**
Station Ho. M. N9 4B **34**
Station Pde. *DA7: Bex* *2E* ***126***
(off Pickford La.)
DA15: Sidc 2A **144**
E6 7C **70**
E11 5J **51**
E13 *1A* ***88***
(off Green St.)
EN4: Cockf 4K **21**
HA2: Harr 4F **59**
HA3: Kenton 2A **42**
HA4: Ruis 2F **57**
HA8: Edg 7K **27**
IG9: Buck H 4G **37**
IG11: Bark 7G **71**
N14 1C **32**
NW2 6E **62**
RM9: Dag 6G **73**
SM2: Sutt *6A* ***166***
(off High St.)
SW12 1E **136**
TW9: Kew 1G **115**
TW14: Felt 1K **129**
TW15: Ashf 4B **128**
UB5: N'olt 7E **58**
(Court Farm Rd.)
UB5: N'olt 4F **59**
(Halsbury Rd. W.)
W3 6G **79**
W4 7J **97**
W5 1F **97**
Station Pas. E18 2K **51**
SE15 1J **121**
Station Path *E8* *6H* ***67***
(off Graham Rd.)
SW6 3H **117**
Station Pl. N4 2A **66**
Station Ri. SE27 2B **138**
Station Rd. BR1: Brom 1J **159**
BR2: Brom 2G **159**
BR4: W W'ck 1E **170**
BR6: Orp 2K **173**
CR0: C'don 1C **168**
DA7: Bex 3E **126**
DA15: Sidc 2A **144**
DA17: Belv 3G **109**
E4 1A **36**
E7 4J **69**
E12 4C **70**
E17 6A **50**
EN5: New Bar 5E **20**
HA1: Harr 4K **41**
HA2: Harr 5F **41**
HA8: Edg 6B **28**
IG1: Ilf 3F **71**
IG6: Ilf 3H **53**
KT1: Ham W 1C **150**
KT2: King T 1G **151**
KT3: N Mald 5D **152**
KT7: T Ditt 7K **149**
KT9: Chess 5E **162**
N3 1J **45**
N11 5A **32**
N17 3G **49**
N19 3G **65**
N21 1G **33**
N22 2J **47**
NW4 6C **44**
NW7 6F **29**
Station Rd. NW10 2B **80**
RM6: Chad H, Dag 7D **54**
SE13 3E **122**
SE20 6J **139**
SE25 4F **157**
SM5: Cars 4D **166**
SW13 2B **116**
SW19 1A **154**
TW1: Twick 1K **131**
TW3: Houn 4F **113**
TW11: Tedd 6A **132**
TW12: Hamp 1E **148**
TW15: Ashf 4B **128**
TW16: Sun 7J **129**
TW17: Shep 5E **146**
UB3: Harl, Hayes 4G **93**
UB7: W Dray 2A **92**
W5 6F **79**
W7 1J **95**
Station Rd. Nth. DA17: Belv 3H **109**
Station Sq. BR5: Pet W 5G **161**
Station St. E15 7F **69**
E16 1F **107**
Station Ter. NW10 2F **81**
SE5 1C **120**
Station Ter. M. SE3 5J **105**
Station Vw. UB6: G'frd 1H **77**
Station Wlk. *IG1: Ilf* *2F* ***71***
(in The Exchange)
Station Way IG9: Buck H 4F **37**
SE15 2G **121**
SM3: Cheam 6G **165**
Station Yd. TW1: Twick 7A **114**
Staton Ct. *E10* *7D* ***50***
(off Kings Cl.)
Staunton Ho. *SE17* *4E* ***102***
(off Tatum St.)
Staunton Rd. KT2: King T 6E **132**
Staunton St. SE8 6B **104**
Stave Hill Ecological Pk. 2A **104**
Staveley *NW1* *1A* ***6***
(off Varndell St.)
Staveley Cl. E9 5J **67**
N7 4J **65**
SE15 1H **121**
Staveley Ct. E11 5J **51**
Staveley Gdns. W4 1K **115**
Staveley Rd. TW15: Ashf 6F **129**
W4 6J **97**
Stavers Ho. *E3* *2B* ***86***
(off Tredegar Rd.)
Staverton Rd. NW2 7E **62**
Stave Yd. Rd. SE16 1A **104**
Stavordale Lodge *W14* *3H* ***99***
(off Melbury Rd.)
Stavordale Rd. N5 4B **66**
SM5: Cars 7A **154**
Stayner's Rd. E1 4K **85**
Stayton Rd. SM1: Sutt 3J **165**
Steadfast Rd. KT1: King T 1D **150**
Steadman Ct. *EC1* *3D* ***8***
(off Old St.)
Steadman Ho. *RM10: Dag* *3G* ***73***
(off Uvedale Rd.)
Stead St. SE17 4D **102**
Steam Farm La. TW14: Felt 4H **111**
Stean St. E8 1F **85**
Stebbing Ho. *W11* *1F* ***99***
(off Queensdale Cres.)
Stebbing Way IG11: Bark 2A **90**
Stebondale St. E14 4E **104**
Stedham Pl. WC1 7E **6**
Stedman Cl. DA5: Bexl 3K **145**
UB10: Ick 3C **56**
Steedman St. SE17 4C **102**
Steeds Rd. N10 1D **46**
Steele Ct. TW11: Tedd 7C **132**
Steele Ho. *E15* *2G* ***87***
(off Eve Rd.)
Steele Rd. E11 4G **69**
N17 3E **48**
NW10 2J **79**
Steele Rd. TW7: Isle 4A **114**
W4 3J **97**
Steele's M. Nth. NW3 6D **64**
Steele's M. Sth. NW3 6D **64**
Steele's Rd. NW3 6D **64**
Steele's Studios NW3 6D **64**
Steele Wlk. DA8: Erith 7H **109**
Steel's La. E1 6J **85**
Steelyard Pas. EC4 3E **14**
Steen Way SE22 5E **120**
Steep Cl. BR6: Chels 6K **173**
Steep Hill CR0: C'don 4E **168**
SW16 3H **137**
Steeple Cl. SW6 2G **117**
SW19 5G **135**
Steeple Ct. E1 4H **85**
Steeplestone Cl. N18 5H **33**
Steeple Wlk. *N1* *1C* ***84***
(off New Nth. Rd.)
Steerforth St. SW18 2A **136**
Steering Cl. N9 1D **34**
Steers Mead CR4: Mitc 1D **154**
Steers Way SE16 2A **104**
Stelfox Ho. *WC1* *1H* ***7***
(off Penton Ri.)
Stella Cl. UB8: Hil 5D **74**
Stellar Ho. N17 6A **34**
Stella Rd. SW17 6D **136**
Stelling Rd. DA8: Erith 7K **109**
Stellman Cl. E5 3G **67**
Stembridge Rd. SE20 2H **157**
Stephan Cl. E8 1G **85**
Stephen Cl. BR6: Orp 3J **173**
Stephendale Rd. SW6 3K **117**
Stephen Fox Ho. *W4* *5A* ***98***
(off Chiswick La.)
Stephen M. W1 6C **6** (5H **83**)
Stephen Pl. SW4 3G **119**
Stephen Rd. DA7: Bex 3J **127**
Stephens Ct. E16 4H **87**
SE4 3A **122**
Stephens Lodge *N12* *3F* ***31***
(off Woodside La.)
Stephenson Cl. DA16: Well 2A **126**
E3 3D **86**
Stephenson Ct. *SM2: Cheam* *7G* ***165***
(off Station App.)
Stephenson Ho. SE1 3C **102**
Stephenson Rd. E17 5A **50**
TW2: Whitt 7E **112**
W7 6K **77**
Stephenson St. E16 4G **87**
NW10 3A **80**
Stephenson Way NW1 3B **6** (4G **83**)
Stephen's Rd. E15 1G **87**
Stephen St. W1 6C **6** (5H **83**)
STEPNEY 5K **85**
Stepney C'way. E1 6K **85**
Stepney City Apartments E1 5J **85**
Stepney Cl. CR4: Mitc 1E **154**
Stepney Grn. E1 5J **85**
Stepney Grn. Ct. *E1* *5K* ***85***
(off Stepney Grn.)
Stepney High St. E1 5K **85**
Stepney Way E1 5H **85**
Stepping Stones Farm 5K **85**
Sterling Av. HA8: Edg 4A **28**
Sterling Cl. NW10 7C **62**
Sterling Gdns. SE14 6A **104**
Sterling Ho. SE3 4K **123**
Sterling Ind. Est. RM10: Dag 4H **73**
Sterling Pl. W5 4E **96**
Sterling Rd. EN2: Enf 1J **23**
Sterling St. SW7 1D **16** (3C **100**)
Sterling Way N18 4J **33**
Sternberg Cen., The 3J **45**
Stern Cl. IG11: Bark 2C **90**
Sterndale Rd. W14 3F **99**
Sterne St. W12 2F **99**
Sternhall La. SE15 3G **121**
Sternhold Av. SW2 2H **137**
Sterry Cres. RM10: Dag 5G **73**

Sterry Dr. KT7: T Ditt 6J 149
  KT19: Ewe 4A 164
Sterry Gdns. RM10: Dag 6G 73
Sterry Rd. IG11: Bark 1K 89
  RM10: Dag 4G 73
Sterry St. SE1 .....7E 14 (2D 102)
Steucers La. SE23 .....1A 140
Stevannie Ct. DA17: Belv 5F 109
Steve Biko La. SE6 .....4C 140
Steve Biko Lodge E13 .....2J 87
(off London Rd.)
Steve Biko Rd. N7 .....3A 66
Steve Biko Way TW3: Houn 3E 112
Stevedale Rd. DA16: Well 2C 126
Stevedore St. E1 .....1H 103
Stevenage Rd. E6 .....6E 70
  SW6 .....7F 99
Stevens Av. E9 .....6J 67
Stevens Cl. BR3: Beck 6C 140
  DA5: Bexl 4K 145
  HA5: Eastc 5A 40
  TW12: Hamp 6D 130
Stevens Grn. WD23: B Hea 1B 26
Stevens La. KT10: Clay 7A 162
Stevenson Cl. EN5: New Bar 7G 21
Stevenson Cres. SE16 .....5G 103
Stevenson Ho. NW8 .....1A 82
(off Boundary Rd.)
Stevens Rd. RM8: Dag 2C 72
Stevens St. SE1 .....7H 15 (3E 102)
Steventon Rd. W12 .....7B 80
Stewards Holte Wlk.
  N11 .....4A 32
Steward St. E1 .....6H 9 (5E 84)
Stewart Av. TW17: Shep 4C 146
Stewart Cl. BR7: Chst 5F 143
  NW9 .....6J 43
  TW12: Hamp 6C 130
Stewart Ho. KT1: King T 3F 151
Stewart Quay UB3: Hayes 2G 93
Stewart Rainbird Ho. E12 .....5E 70
(off Parkhurst Rd.)
Stewart Rd. E15 .....4F 69
Stewartsby Cl. N18 .....5H 33
Stewart's Gro. SW3 .....5B 16 (5B 100)
Stewart's Rd. SW8 .....7G 101
Stewart St. E14 .....2E 104
Stew La. EC4 .....2C 14 (7C 84)
Steyne Ho. W3 .....1J 97
(off Narrow St.)
Steyne Rd. W3 .....1H 97
Steyning Gro. SE9 .....4D 142
Steynings Way N12 .....5D 30
Steyning Way TW4: Houn 4A 112
Steynton Av. DA5: Bexl 2D 144
Stibbington Ho. NW1 .....2G 83
(off Cranleigh St.)
Stickland Rd. DA17: Belv 4G 109
Stickleton Cl. UB6: G'frd 3F 77
Stifford Ho. E1 .....5J 85
(off Stepney Way)
Stilecroft Gdns. HA0: Wemb 3B 60
Stile Hall Gdns. W4 .....5G 97
Stile Hall Mans. W4 .....5G 97
(off Wellesley Rd.)
Stile Hall Pde. W4 .....5G 97
Stileman Ho. E3 .....5B 86
(off Ackroyd Dr.)
Stile Path TW16: Sun 3J 147
Stiles Cl. BR2: Brom 6D 160
  DA8: Erith 5H 109
Stillingfleet Rd. SW13 .....6C 98
Stillington St. SW1 .....3B 18 (4G 101)
Stillness Rd. SE23 .....6A 122
Stilwell Dr. UB8: Hil 4B 74
Stilwell Rdbt. UB8: Hil 7C 74
Stipularis Dr. UB4: Yead 4B 76
Stirling Av. HA5: Pinn 1B 58
  SM6: Wall 7J 167
  TW17: Shep 3G 147
Stirling Cl. DA14: Sidc 4J 143
  SW16 .....1H 155

Stirling Ct. EC1 .....3A 8
(off St John St.)
  W13 .....7B 78
Stirling Gro. TW3: Houn 2G 113
Stirling Ho. SE18 .....5F 107
Stirling Rd. E13 .....2K 87
  E17 .....3A 50
  HA3: W'stone 3K 41
  N17 .....1G 49
  N22 .....1B 48
  SW9 .....2J 119
  TW2: Whitt 7E 112
  TW6: H'row A 6B 110
  UB3: Hayes 7K 75
  W3 .....3H 97
Stirling Rd. Path E17 .....3A 50
Stirling Wlk. KT5: Surb 6H 151
Stirling Way CR0: Bedd 7J 155
Stiven Cres. HA2: Harr 3D 58
Stockbeck NW1 .....1B 6
(off Ampthill Est.)
Stockbury Rd. CR0: C'don 6J 157
Stockdale Rd. RM8: Dag 2F 73
Stockdove Way UB6: G'frd 3K 77
Stocker Gdns. RM9: Dag 7C 72
Stockfield Rd. SW16 .....3K 137
Stockford Av. NW7 .....7A 30
Stockholm Ho. E1 .....7G 85
(off Swedenborg Gdns.)
Stockholm Rd. SE16 .....5J 103
Stockholm Way E1 .....1G 103
Stockhurst Cl. SW15 .....2E 116
Stockingswater La. EN3: Brim 2G 25
Stockland Rd. RM7: Rom 6K 55
Stockleigh Hall NW8 .....2C 82
(off Prince Albert Rd.)
Stockley Cl. UB7: W Dray 2D 92
Stockley Country Pk. 7C 74
Stockley Farm Rd. UB7: W Dray 3D 92
STOCKLEY PARK 1D 92
Stockley Rd. UB7: W Dray 4D 92
  UB8: Hil 6C 74
  UB11: Stock P 6C 74
Stock Orchard Cres. N7 .....5K 65
Stock Orchard St. N7 .....5K 65
Stockport Rd. SW16 .....1H 155
Stocksfield Rd. E17 .....3E 50
Stocks Pl. E14 .....7B 86
  UB10: Hil 1C 74
Stock St. E13 .....2J 87
Stockton Cl. EN5: New Bar 4F 21
Stockton Ct. SW1 .....2C 18
(off Rochester Row)
Stockton Gdns. N17 .....7H 33
  NW7 .....3F 29
Stockton Ho. E2 .....3H 85
(off Ellsworth St.)
  HA2: Harr 1E 58
Stockton Rd. N17 .....7H 33
  N18 .....6B 34
STOCKWELL 2K 119
Stockwell Av. SW9 .....3K 119
Stockwell Cl. BR1: Brom 2K 159
  HA8: Edg 2J 43
Stockwell Gdns. SW9 .....1K 119
Stockwell Gdns. Est. SW9 .....2J 119
Stockwell Grn. SW9 .....2K 119
Stockwell Grn. Ct. SW9 .....2K 119
Stockwell La. SW9 .....2K 119
Stockwell M. SW9 .....2K 119
Stockwell Pk. Cres. SW9 .....2K 119
Stockwell Pk. Est. SW9 .....2K 119
Stockwell Pk. Rd. SW9 .....1K 119
Stockwell Pk. Wlk. SW9 .....3A 120
Stockwell Rd. SW9 .....2K 119
Stockwell St. SE10 .....6E 104
Stockwell Ter. SW9 .....1K 119
Stodart Rd. SE20 .....1J 157
Stoddart Ho. SW8 .....7H 19 (6K 101)
Stodmarsh Ho. SW9 .....1A 120
(off Cowley Rd.)
Stofield Gdns. SE9 .....3B 142

Stoford Cl. SW19 .....7G 117
Stokenchurch St. SW6 .....1K 117
STOKE NEWINGTON 3F 67
Stoke Newington Chu. St. N16 .....3D 66
Stoke Newington Comn. N16 .....2F 67
Stoke Newington High St. N16 .....3F 67
Stoke Newington Rd. N16 .....5F 67
Stoke Pl. NW10 .....3B 80
Stoke Rd. KT2: King T 7J 133
Stokesby Rd. KT9: Chess 6F 163
Stokes Cotts. IG6: Ilf 1G 53
Stokes Ct. N2 .....4C 46
Stokesley St. W12 .....6B 80
Stokes Rd. CR0: C'don 6K 157
  E6 .....4C 88
Stokley Ct. N8 .....4J 47
Stoll Cl. NW2 .....3E 62
Stoms Path SE6 .....5C 140
(off Maroons Way)
Stonard Rd. N13 .....3F 33
  RM8: Dag 5B 72
Stondon Pk. SE23 .....6A 122
Stondon Wlk. E6 .....2B 88
Stonebanks KT12: Walt T 7J 147
STONEBRIDGE 1K 79
Stonebridge Cen. N15 .....5F 49
Stonebridge Pk. NW10 .....7K 61
Stonebridge Rd. N15 .....5F 49
Stonebridge Shop. Cen. NW10 .....1K 79
Stonebridge Way HA9: Wemb 6H 61
Stone Bldgs. WC2 .....6H 7
Stonechat Sq. E6 .....5C 88
Stone Cl. RM8: Dag 2F 73
  SW4 .....2G 119
  UB7: Yiew 1B 92
Stonecot Cl. SM3: Sutt 1G 165
Stonecot Hill SM3: Sutt 1G 165
Stone Cres. TW14: Felt 7H 111
Stonecroft Rd. DA8: Erith 7J 109
Stonecroft Way CR0: C'don 7J 155
Stonecrop Cl. NW9 .....3K 43
Stonecutter St. EC4 .....7A 8 (6B 84)
Stonefield N4 .....2K 65
Stonefield Cl. DA7: Bex 3G 127
  HA4: Ruis 5C 58
Stonefield Mans. N1 .....1A 84
(off Cloudesley St.)
Stonefield St. N1 .....1A 84
Stonefield Way HA4: Ruis 4C 58
  SE7 .....7B 106
STONEGROVE 4A 28
Stonegrove HA8: Edg 4K 27
Stone Gro. Ct. HA8: Edg 5A 28
Stonegrove Gdns. HA8: Edg 5K 27
Stone Hall W8 .....3K 99
(off Stone Hall Gdns.)
Stonehall Av. IG1: Ilf 6C 52
Stone Hall Gdns. W8 .....3K 99
Stone Hall Pl. W8 .....3K 99
Stone Hall Rd. N21 .....7E 22
Stoneham Rd. N11 .....5B 32
Stonehill Bus. Pk. N18 .....6F 35
Stonehill Cl. SW14 .....5K 115
STONEHILL GREEN 7J 145
Stonehill Rd. SW14 .....5J 115
  W4 .....5G 97
Stonehills Ct. SE21 .....3E 138
Stonehill Woods Pk. DA14: Sidc 6H 145
Stonehorse Rd. EN3: Pond E 5D 24
Stonehouse NW1 .....1G 83
(off Plender St.)
Stone Ho. Ct. EC3 .....6H 9
Stonehouse Ho. W2 .....5J 81
(off Westbourne Pk. Rd.)
Stone Lake Ind. Pk. SE7 .....4A 106
Stone Lake Retail Pk. SE7 .....4A 106
STONELEIGH 5C 164
Stoneleigh Av. EN1: Enf 1C 24
  KT4: Wor Pk 4C 164
Stoneleigh B'way. KT17: Ewe 5C 164
Stoneleigh Cl. IG5: Ilf 3C 52

Stoneleigh Cres. KT19: Ewe 5B 164
Stoneleigh M. E3 .....2A 86
Stoneleigh Pk. Av. CR0: C'don 6K 157
Stoneleigh Pk. Rd. KT19: Ewe 6B 164
Stoneleigh Pl. W11 .....7F 81
Stoneleigh Rd. BR1: Brom 3F 161
  IG5: Ilf 3C 52
  N17 .....3F 49
  SM5: Cars 7C 154
Stoneleigh St. W11 .....7F 81
Stoneleigh Ter. N19 .....2F 65
Stonell's Rd. SW11 .....6D 118
Stonemason Cl. SE1 .....7C 14
(off Borough Rd.)
Stonemasons Cl. N15 .....4D 48
Stonenest St. N4 .....1K 65
Stone Pk. Av. BR3: Beck 4C 158
Stone Pl. KT4: Wor Pk 2C 164
Stone Rd. BR2: Brom 5H 159
Stones End St. SE1 .....7C 14 (2C 102)
Stonewall E6 .....5E 88
Stonewold Ct. W5 .....6D 78
Stoney All. SE18 .....2E 124
Stoneyard La. E14 .....7D 86
Stoneycroft Cl. SE12 .....7H 123
Stoneycroft Rd. IG8: Wfd G 6H 37
Stoneydeep TW11: Tedd 4A 132
Stoneydown E17 .....4A 50
Stoneydown Av. E17 .....4A 50
Stoneydown Ho. E17 .....4A 50
(off Blackhorse Rd.)
Stoneyfields Gdns. HA8: Edg 4E 28
Stoneyfields La. HA8: Edg 5D 28
Stoney La. E1 .....7H 9 (6F 85)
  SE19 .....6E 139
Stoney St. SE1 .....4E 14 (1D 102)
Stonhouse St. SW4 .....4H 119
Stonor Rd. W14 .....4H 99
Stonycroft Cl. EN3: Enf H 2F 25
Stopes St. SE15 .....7F 103
Stopford Rd. E13 .....1J 87
  SE17 .....5B 102
Stopher Ho. SE1 .....7B 14
(off Webber St.)
Storehouse M. E14 .....7C 86
Store Rd. E16 .....2E 106
Storers Quay E14 .....4F 105
Store St. E15 .....5F 69
  WC1 .....6C 6 (5H 83)
Storey Ct. NW8 .....2A 4
Storey Ho. E14 .....7D 86
(off Cottage St.)
Storey Rd. E17 .....4B 50
  N6 .....6D 46
Storey's Ga. SW1 .....7D 12 (2H 101)
Storey St. E16 .....1E 106
Stories M. SE5 .....2E 120
Stories Rd. SE5 .....3E 120
Stork Rd. E7 .....6H 69
Storksmead Rd. HA8: Edg 7F 29
Stork's Rd. SE16 .....3G 103
Stormont Lawn Tennis & Squash Club
.....5D 46
Stormont Rd. N6 .....7D 46
  SW11 .....3E 118
Stormont Way KT9: Chess 5C 162
Stormount Dr. UB3: Harl 2E 92
Storrington WC1 .....2F 7
(off Regent Sq.)
Storrington Rd. CR0: C'don 1F 169
Story St. N1 .....7K 65
Stothard Ho. E1 .....4J 85
(off Amiel St.)
Stothard Pl. E1 .....5H 9 (5E 84)
Stothard St. E1 .....4J 85
Stott Cl. SW18 .....6B 118
Stoughton Av. SM3: Cheam 5F 165
Stoughton Cl. SE11 .....4H 19 (4K 101)
  SW15 .....1C 134
Stour Av. UB2: S'hall 3E 94
Stourcliffe Cl. W1 .....1E 10 (6D 82)
Stourcliffe St. W1 .....1E 10 (6D 82)

Stour Cl. BR2: Kes 4A 172
Stourhead Cl. SW19 ....7F 117
Stourhead Gdns. SW20 ....3C 152
Stourhead Ho. *SW1* *5C 18*
(off Tachbrook St.)
Stour Rd. E3 ....7C 68
RM10: Dag 2G 73
Stourton Av.
TW13: Hanw 4D 130
Stowage SE8 ....6C 104
Stow Cres. E17 ....7F 35
Stowe Cres. HA4: Ruis 6D 38
Stowe Gdns. N9 ....1A 34
Stowe Ho. NW11 ....6A 46
Stowell Ho. *N8* *4J 47*
(off Pembroke Rd.)
Stowe Pl. N15 ....3E 48
Stowe Rd. W12 ....2D 98
Stowting Rd. BR6: Orp 4J 173
Stox Mead HA3: Hrw W 1H 41
Stracey Rd. E7 ....4J 69
NW10 ....1K 79
Strachan Pl. SW19 ....6E 134
Stradbroke Dr. IG7: Chig 6K 37
Stradbroke Gro. IG5: Ilf 3C 52
IG9: Buck H 1G 37
Stradbroke Pk. IG7: Chig 6K 37
Stradbroke Rd. N5 ....4C 66
Stradbrook Cl. HA2: Harr 3D 58
Stradella Rd. SE24 ....6C 120
Strafford Av. IG5: Ilf 2E 52
Strafford Ho. *SE8* *5B 104*
(off Grove St.)
Strafford Rd. EN5: Barn 3B 20
TW1: Twick 7A 114
TW3: Houn 3D 112
W3 ....2J 97
Strafford St. E14 ....2C 104
Strahan Rd. E3 ....3A 86
Straight, The UB1: S'hall 2B 94
Straightsmouth SE10 ....7E 104
Strait Rd. E6 ....7C 88
Strakers Rd. SE15 ....4H 121
Strale Ho. *N1* *1E 84*
(off Whitmore Est.)
Strand WC2 ....3F 13 (7J 83)
Strand Ct. SE18 ....5J 107
Strand Dr. TW9: Kew 7H 97
Strandfield Cl. SE18 ....5J 107
Strand Ho. SE28 ....1H 107
SW18 ....4A 118
Strand La. WC2 ....2H 13 (7K 83)
STRAND ON THE GREEN 6G 97
Strand on the Grn. W4 ....6G 97
Strand Pl. N18 ....4K 33
Strand School App. W4 ....6G 97
Strand Theatre *2G 13*
(off Aldwych)
Strang Ho. N1 ....1C 84
Strangways Ter. W14 ....3H 99
Stranraer Way N1 ....7J 65
Strasburg Rd. SW11 ....1E 118
Strata Ct. KT12: Walt T 7H 147
Stratfield Pk. Cl. N21 ....7G 23
STRATFORD 7F 69
Stratford Av. UB10: Hil 2B 74
Stratford Cen., The E15 ....7F 69
Stratford Circus (Performing Arts Cen.)
....6F 69
Stratford City Shop. Cen.
E15 ....6E 68
Stratford Cl. IG11: Bark 7A 72
RM10: Dag 7J 73
Stratford Ct. KT3: N Mald 4K 151
Stratford Gro. SW15 ....4F 117
Stratford Ho. Av. BR1: Brom 3C 160
STRATFORD NEW TOWN 6F 69
Stratford Office Village, The
E15 ....*7G 69*
(off Romford Rd.)
Stratford Picture House 6F 69
Stratford Pl. W1 ....1J 11 (6F 83)
Stratford Rd. CR7: Thor H 4A 156
E13 ....1H 87
(not continuous)
NW4 ....4F 45
TW6: H'row A 6D 110
UB2: S'hall 4C 94
UB4: Yead 4K 75
W8 ....3J 99
Stratford Shop. Cen. *E15* *7F 69*
(off The Stratford Cen.)
Stratford Studios W8 ....3J 99
Stratford Vs. NW1 ....7G 65
Stratham Ct. *N19* *3J 65*
(off Alexander Rd.)
Strathan Cl. SW18 ....6G 117
Strathaven Rd. SE12 ....6K 123
Strathblaine Rd. SW11 ....5B 118
Strathbrook Rd. SW16 ....7K 137
Strathcona Rd. HA9: Wemb 2D 60
Strathdale SW16 ....5K 137
Strathdon Dr. SW17 ....3B 136
Strathearn Av. TW2: Whitt 1F 131
UB3: Harl 7H 93
Strathearn Ho. *W2* *2C 10*
(off Streathern Pl.)
Strathearn Pl. W2 ....1C 10 (6C 82)
Strathearn Rd. SM1: Sutt 5J 165
SW19 ....5J 135
Stratheden Pde. SE3 ....7J 105
Stratheden Rd. SE3 ....1J 123
Strathfield Gdns. IG11: Bark 6H 71
Strathleven Rd. SW2 ....5J 119
Strathmore Ct. *NW8* *1C 4*
(off Park Rd.)
Strathmore Gdns. HA8: Edg 2H 43
N3 ....1K 45
W8 ....1J 99
Strathmore Rd. CR0: C'don 7D 156
SW19 ....3J 135
TW11: Tedd 4J 131
Strathnairn St. SE1 ....4G 103
Strathray Gdns. NW3 ....6C 64
Strath Ter. SW11 ....4C 118
Strathville Rd. SW18 ....2J 135
(not continuous)
Strathyre Av. SW16 ....3A 156
Stratton Cl. DA7: Bex 3E 126
HA8: Edg 6A 28
SW19 ....2J 153
TW3: Houn 1E 112
Stratton Ct. *HA5: Hat E* *1D 40*
(off Devonshire Rd.)
N1 ....*7E 66*
(off Hertford Rd.)
Strattondale St. E14 ....3E 104
Stratton Dr. IG11: Bark 5J 71
Stratton Gdns. UB1: S'hall 6D 76
Stratton Ho. *HA8: Edg* *4A 28*
(off Lacey Dr.)
Stratton Rd. DA7: Bex 3E 126
SW19 ....2J 153
TW16: Sun 2H 147
Stratton St. W1 ....4K 11 (1F 101)
Strauss Rd. W4 ....2K 97
Strawberry Flds. BR6: Farnb 5F 173
STRAWBERRY HILL 3K 131
Strawberry Hill TW1: Twick 3K 131
Strawberry Hill Cl.
TW1: Twick 3K 131
Strawberry Hill House 3K 131
Strawberry Hill Rd.
TW1: Twick 3K 131
Strawberry La. SM5: Cars 3E 166
Strawberry Ter. N10 ....1D 46
Strawberry Va. N2 ....1B 46
TW1: Twick 3A 132
(not continuous)
Streakes Fld. Rd. NW2 ....2C 62
Streamdale SE2 ....6B 108
Stream La. HA8: Edg 5C 28
Streamline Ct. *SE22* *1G 139*
(off Streamline M.)
Streamline M. SE22 ....1G 139
Streamside Cl. BR2: Brom 4J 159
N9 ....1A 34
Stream Way DA17: Belv 6G 109
Streatfeild Av. E6 ....1D 88
Streatfield Rd. HA3: Kenton 3C 42
STREATHAM 5J 137
Streatham Cl. SW16 ....2J 137
STREATHAM COMMON 6H 137
Streatham Comn. Nth. SW16 ....5J 137
Streatham Comn. Sth. SW16 ....6J 137
Streatham Ct. SW16 ....3J 137
Streatham High Rd. SW16 ....4J 137
STREATHAM HILL 2J 137
Streatham Hill SW2 ....2J 137
Streatham Ice Arena 5H 137
Streatham Kart Raceway 5H 137
Streatham Leisure Cen. 5H 137
STREATHAM PARK 5G 137
Streatham Pl. SW2 ....7J 119
Streatham Rd. CR4: Mitc 1E 154
SW16 ....1E 154
Streatham St. WC1 ....7E 6 (6J 83)
STREATHAM VALE 7G 137
Streatham Va. SW16 ....1G 155
Streathbourne Rd. SW17 ....2E 136
Streatley Pl. NW3 ....4A 64
Streatley Rd. NW6 ....7H 63
Streeters La. SM6: Bedd 3H 167
Streetfield M. SE3 ....3J 123
Streimer Rd. E15 ....2E 86
Strelley Way W3 ....7A 80
Stretton Mans. SE8 ....5C 104
Stretton Rd. CR0: C'don 7E 156
TW10: Ham 2C 132
Strickland Ct. SE15 ....3G 121
Strickland Ho. *E2* *2K 9*
(off Chambord St.)
Strickland Row SW18 ....7B 118
Strickland St. SE8 ....2C 122
Strickland Way BR6: Orp 4K 173
Stride Rd. E13 ....2H 87
Strimon Cl. N9 ....2D 34
Stringer Ho. *N1* *1E 84*
(off Whitmore Est.)
Strode Cl. N10 ....7K 31
Strode Rd. E7 ....4J 69
N17 ....2E 48
NW10 ....6C 62
SW6 ....7G 99
Strome Ho. *NW6* *2K 81*
(off Carlton Va.)
Strone Rd. E7 ....6A 70
E12 ....6A 70
Strone Way UB4: Yead 4C 76
Strongbow Cres. SE9 ....5D 124
Strongbow Rd. SE9 ....5D 124
Strongbridge Cl. HA2: Harr 1E 58
Stronsa Rd. W12 ....2B 98
Strood Av. RM7: Rush G 1K 73
Strood Ho. *SE1* *7F 15*
(off Staple St.)
Stroud Cres. SW15 ....3C 134
Stroudes Cl. KT4: Wor Pk 7A 152
Stroud Fld. UB5: N'olt 6C 58
Stroud Ga. HA2: Harr 4F 59
STROUD GREEN 7K 47
Stroud Grn. Gdns. CR0: C'don 7J 157
Stroud Grn. Rd. N4 ....1K 65
Stroud Grn. Way CR0: C'don 7H 157
Stroudley Ho. SW8 ....1G 119
Stroudley Wlk. E3 ....3D 86
Stroud Rd. SE25 ....6G 157
SW19 ....3J 135
Stroud's Cl. RM6: Chad H 5B 54
Stroud Way TW15: Ashf 6D 128
Strouts Pl. E2 ....1J 9 (3F 85)
Strudwick Ct. *SW4* *1J 119*
(off Binfield Rd.)
Strutton Ct. *SW1* *2C 18*
(off Strutton Ground)
Strutton Ground SW1 ....1C 18 (3H 101)
Strype St. E1 ....6J 9 (5F 85)
Stuart Av. BR2: Hayes 1J 171
HA2: Harr 3D 58
KT12: Walt T 7K 147
NW9 ....7C 44
W5 ....2F 97
Stuart Cl. UB10: Hil 6C 56
Stuart Ct. *CR0: C'don* *3B 168*
(off St John's Rd.)
Stuart Cres. CR0: C'don 3B 170
N22 ....1K 47
UB3: Hayes 6E 74
Stuart Evans Cl. DA16: Well 3C 126
Stuart Gro. TW11: Tedd 5J 131
Stuart Ho. *E16* *1K 105*
(off Beaulieu Av.)
W14 ....*4G 99*
(off Windsor Way)
Stuart Mantle Way DA8: Erith 7K 109
Stuart Mill Ho. *N1* *1G 7*
(off Killick St.)
Stuart Pl. CR4: Mitc 1D 154
Stuart Rd. CR7: Thor H 4C 156
DA16: Well 1B 126
EN4: E Barn 7H 21
HA3: W'stone 3K 41
IG11: Bark 7K 71
NW6 ....3J 81
SE15 ....4J 121
SW19 ....3J 135
TW10: Ham 2B 132
W3 ....1J 97
Stuart Twr. *W9* *3A 82*
(off Maida Va.)
Stubbs Cl. NW9 ....5J 43
Stubbs Ct. *W4* *5H 97*
(off Chaseley Dr.)
Stubbs Dr. SE16 ....5H 103
Stubbs Ho. *E2* *3K 85*
(off Bonner St.)
SW1 ....*4D 18*
(off Erasmus St.)
Stubbs M. *RM8: Dag* *4B 72*
(off Marlborough Rd.)
Stubbs Point E13 ....4J 87
Stubbs Way SW19 ....1B 154
Stucley Pl. NW1 ....7F 65
Stucley Rd. TW5: Hest 7G 95
Studdridge St. SW6 ....2J 117
(not continuous)
Studd St. N1 ....1B 84
Studholme Ct. NW3 ....4J 63
Studholme St. SE15 ....7H 103
Studio Arts & Media Cen., The 1A 158
Studio Ct. N15 ....4E 48
Studio La. W5 ....1D 96
Studio M. NW4 ....4E 44
Studio Pl. SW1 ....7F 11
Studio Plaza KT12: Walt T 7J 147
Studios, The *SW4* *4G 119*
(off Crescent La.)
W8 ....*1J 99*
(off Edge St.)
Studios Rd. TW17: Shep 3B 146
Studio Theatre 4E 166
Studland *SE17* *5D 102*
(off Portland St.)
Studland Cl. DA15: Sidc 3K 143
Studland Ho. *E14* *6A 86*
(off Aston St.)
Studland Rd. KT2: King T 6E 132
SE26 ....5K 139
W7 ....6H 77
Studland St. W6 ....4D 98
Studley Av. E4 ....7A 36
Studley Cl. E5 ....5A 68
Studley Ct. DA14: Sidc 5B 144
E14 ....*7F 87*
(off Jamestown Way)
Studley Dr. IG4: Ilf 6B 52
Studley Est. SW4 ....1J 119
Studley Grange Rd. W7 ....2J 95

Studley Rd. E7 6K 69
RM9: Dag 7D 72
SW4 1J 119
Stukeley Rd. E7 7K 69
Stukeley St. WC2 7F 7 (6J 83)
Stumps Hill La. BR3: Beck 6C 140
Stunell Ho. *SE14* *6K 103*
(off John Williams Cl.)
Sturdee Ho. *E2* *2G 85*
(off Horatio St.)
Sturdy Ho. *E3* *2A 86*
(off Gernon Rd.)
Sturdy Rd. SE15 2H 121
Sturge Av. E17 2D 50
Sturgeon Rd. SE17 5C 102
Sturges Fld. BR7: Chst 6H 143
Sturgess Av. NW4 7D 44
Sturge St. SE1 6C 14 (2C 102)
Sturmer Way N7 5K 65
Sturminster *NW1* *7H 65*
(off Agar Gro.)
Sturminster Cl. UB4: Yead 6A 76
Sturminster Ho. *SW8* *7K 101*
(off Dorset Rd.)
Sturrock Cl. N15 4D 48
Sturry St. E14 6D 86
Sturt St. N1 1D 8 (2C 84)
Stutfield St. E1 6G 85
Stuttle Ho. *E1* *4K 9*
(off Buxton St.)
Styles Gdns. SW9 3B 120
Styles Ho. SE1 6A 14
Styles Way BR3: Beck 4E 158
Stylus Ho. E1 6J 85
Success Ho. *SE1* *5F 103*
(off Cooper's Rd.)
Sudbourne Rd. SW2 5J 119
Sudbrooke Rd. SW12 6D 118
Sudbrook Gdns. TW10: Ham 3D 132
Sudbrook La. TW10: Ham 1E 132
SUDBURY 5B 60
Sudbury E6 5E 88
Sudbury Av. HA0: Wemb 3C 60
Sudbury Cl. RM6: Chad H 5B 54
Sudbury Ct. *SW8* *1H 119*
(off Allen Edwards Dr.)
Sudbury Ct. Dr. HA1: Harr 3K 59
Sudbury Ct. Rd. HA1: Harr 3K 59
Sudbury Cres. BR1: Brom 6J 141
HA0: Wemb 5B 60
Sudbury Cft. HA0: Wemb 4K 59
Sudbury Gdns. CR0: C'don 4E 168
Sudbury Hgts. Av. UB6: G'frd 5K 59
Sudbury Hill HA1: Harr 2J 59
Sudbury Hill Cl. HA0: Wemb 4K 59
Sudbury Ho. SW18 5K 117
Sudbury Rd. IG11: Bark 5K 71
Sudeley St. N1 2B 84
Sudlow Rd. SW18 5J 117
Sudrey St. SE1 7C 14 (2C 102)
Suez Av. UB6: G'frd 2K 77
Suez Rd. EN3: Brim 4F 25
SUFFIELD HATCH 4K 35
Suffield Ho. *SE17* *5B 102*
(off Berryfield Rd.)
Suffield Rd. E4 3J 35
N15 5F 49
SE20 2J 157
Suffolk Ct. E10 7C 50
IG3: Ilf 6J 53
RM6: Chad H 6C 54
Suffolk Ho. *CR0: C'don* *2D 168*
(off George St.)
SE20 *1K 157*
(off Croydon Rd.)
Suffolk La. EC4 2E 14 (7D 84)
Suffolk Pk. Rd. E17 4A 50
Suffolk Pl. SW1 4D 12 (1H 101)
Suffolk Rd. DA14: Sidc 6C 144
E13 3J 87
EN3: Pond E 5C 24
HA2: Harr 6D 40
Suffolk Rd. IG3: Ilf 6J 53
IG11: Bark 7H 71
KT4: Wor Pk 2B 164
N15 5D 48
NW10 7A 62
RM10: Dag 5J 73
SE25 4F 157
SW13 7B 98
Suffolk St. E7 4J 69
SW1 3D 12 (7H 83)
Sugar Bakers Ct. EC3 1H 15
Sugar Ho. *E1* *1K 15*
(off Leman St.)
Sugar Ho. La. E15 2E 86
Sugar Loaf Wlk. E2 3J 85
Sugar Quay EC3 3H 15
Sugar Quay Wlk. EC3 3H 15 (7E 84)
Sugden Rd. KT7: T Ditt 1B 162
SW11 3E 118
Sugden Way IG11: Bark 2K 89
Sulby Ho. *SE4* *4A 122*
(off Turnham Rd.)
Sulgrave Gdns. W6 2E 98
Sulgrave Rd. W6 3E 98
Sulina Rd. SW2 7J 119
Sulivan Ct. SW6 2J 117
Sulivan Ent. Cen. SW6 3K 117
Sulivan Rd. SW6 3J 117
Sulkin Ho. *E2* *3K 85*
(off Knottisford St.)
Sullivan Av. E16 5B 88
Sullivan Cl. KT8: W Mole 3F 149
SW11 3C 118
UB4: Yead 5A 76
Sullivan Ct. N16 7F 49
SW5 *4J 99*
(off Earls Ct. Rd.)
Sullivan Cres. UB9: Hare 2A 38
Sullivan Ho. *SE11* *4H 19*
(off Vauxhall St.)
SW1 *7K 17*
(off Churchill Gdns.)
Sullivan Rd. SE11 3K 19 (4A 102)
Sullivans Reach KT12: Walt T 7H 147
Sultan Rd. E11 4K 51
Sultan St. BR3: Beck 2K 157
SE5 7C 102
Sultan Ter. N22 2A 48
Sumatra Rd. NW6 5J 63
Sumburgh Rd. SW12 6E 118
Sumeria Ct. *SE16* *4J 103*
(off Rotherhithe New Rd.)
Summer Av. KT8: E Mos 5J 149
Summercourt Rd. E1 6J 85
Summer Crossing KT7: T Ditt 5J 149
Summerene Cl. SW16 7G 137
Summerfield *BR1: Brom* *1K 159*
(off Freelands Rd.)
Summerfield Av. NW6 2G 81
Summerfield La. KT6: Surb 2D 162
Summerfield Rd. W5 4B 78
Summerfields Av. N12 6H 31
Summerfield St. SE12 7H 123
Summer Gdns. KT8: E Mos 5J 149
Summer Gro. BR4: W W'ck 2G 171
Summer Hill BR7: Chst 2E 160
Summerhill Cl. BR6: Orp 3J 173
Summerhill Gro. EN1: Enf 6K 23
Summerhill Rd. N15 4D 48
Summerhill Vs. *BR7: Chst* *1E 160*
(off Susan Wood)
Summerhill Way CR4: Mitc 1E 154
Summerhouse Av. TW5: Hest 1C 112
Summerhouse Dr. DA2: Dart 4K 145
DA5: Bexl, Dart 4K 145
Summerhouse La. UB7: Harm 2E 174
Summerhouse Rd. N16 2E 66
Summerland Gdns. N10 3F 47
Summerland Grange N10 3F 47
Summerlands Av. W3 7J 79
Summerlands Lodge BR6: Farnb 4E 172
Summerlee Av. N2 4D 46
Summerlee Gdns. N2 4D 46
Summerley St. SW18 2K 135
Summer Rd. KT7: T Ditt 5J 149
KT8: E Mos 5H 149
(not continuous)
Summersby Rd. N6 6F 47
Summers Cl. HA9: Wemb 1H 61
SM2: Sutt 7J 165
Summerskill Cl. SE15 3H 121
Summerskille Cl. N9 3C 34
Summers La. N12 7G 31
Summers Row N12 6H 31
Summers St. EC1 4J 7 (4A 84)
SUMMERSTOWN 3A 136
Summerstown SW17 3A 136
Summerton Way SE28 6D 90
Summer Trees TW16: Sun 1K 147
Summerville Gdns. SM1: Sutt 6H 165
Summerwood Rd. TW7: Isle 5K 113
Summit Av. NW9 5K 43
Summit Bus. Pk. TW16: Sun 7J 129
Summit Cl. HA8: Edg 7B 28
N14 2B 32
NW9 4K 43
Summit Ct. NW2 5G 63
Summit Dr. IG8: Wfd G 2B 52
Summit Est. N16 7G 49
Summit Rd. E17 4D 50
UB5: N'olt 7E 58
Summit Way N14 2A 32
SE19 7E 138
Sumner Av. SE15 1F 121
Sumner Bldgs. SE1 4C 14
Sumner Cl. BR6: Farnb 4G 173
Sumner Ct. SW8 7J 101
Sumner Est. SE15 7F 103
Sumner Gdns. CR0: C'don 1A 168
Sumner Ho. *E3* *5D 86*
(off Watts Gro.)
Sumner Pl. SW7 4B 16 (4B 100)
Sumner Pl. M. SW7 4B 16 (4B 100)
Sumner Rd. CR0: C'don 1A 168
HA1: Harr 7G 41
SE15 6F 103
Sumner Rd. Sth. CR0: C'don 1A 168
Sumner St. SE1 4B 14 (1B 102)
Sumpter Cl. NW3 6A 64
Sun All. TW9: Rich 4E 114
Sunbeam Cres. W10 4E 80
Sunbeam Rd. NW10 4J 79
SUNBURY 3A 148
Sunbury Av. NW7 5E 28
SW14 4K 115
Sunbury Av. Pas. SW14 4A 116
Sunbury Bus. Cen. TW16: Sun 1H 147
Sunbury Cl. KT12: Walt T 6J 147
SUNBURY COMMON 7H 129
Sunbury Ct. EN5: Barn 4B 20
Sunbury Ct. Island TW16: Sun 3B 148
Sunbury Ct. M. TW16: Sun 2B 148
Sunbury Ct. Rd. TW16: Sun 2A 148
Sunbury Cres. TW13: Felt 4H 129
SUNBURY CROSS 7J 129
Sunbury Cross Cen. TW16: Sun 7H 129
Sunbury Embroidery Gallery, The 3K 147
Sunbury Gdns. NW7 5E 28
Sunbury Ho. *E2* *2J 9*
(off Swanfield St.)
SE14 *6K 103*
(off Myers La.)
TW16: Sun *1G 147*
(off Brooklands Cl.)
Sunbury La. KT12: Walt T 6J 147
SW11 1B 118
(not continuous)
Sunbury Leisure Cen. 1H 147
Sunburylock Ait KT12: Walt T 4K 147
Sunbury Pk. Walled Garden 3K 147
Sunbury Rd. SM3: Cheam 3F 165
TW13: Felt 3H 129
Sunbury St. SE18 3D 106
Sunbury Way TW13: Hanw 5A 130
Sunbury Workshops *E2* *2J 9*
(off Swanfield St.)
Sun Ct. EC3 1F 15
Suncroft Pl. SE26 3J 139
Sundeala Cl. *TW16: Sun* *7J 129*
(off Hanworth Rd.)
Sunderland Ct. SE22 7G 121
TW19: Stanw *6A 110*
(off Whitley Cl.)
Sunderland Ho. *W2* *5J 81*
(off Westbourne Pk. Rd.)
Sunderland Mt. SE23 2K 139
Sunderland Point E16 1G 107
Sunderland Rd. SE23 1K 139
W5 3D 96
Sunderland Ter. W2 6K 81
Sunderland Way E12 2B 70
Sundew Av. W12 7C 80
Sundew Cl. W12 7C 80
Sundew Ct. *HA0: Wemb* *2E 78*
(off Elmore Cl.)
Sundial Av. SE25 3F 157
Sundial Ct. *EC1* *5E 8*
(off Chiswell St.)
Sundorne Rd. SE7 5A 106
Sundown Rd. TW15: Ashf 5E 128
Sundra Wlk. E1 4K 85
SUNDRIDGE 6K 141
Sundridge Av. BR1: Brom 1B 160
BR7: Chst 1B 160
DA16: Well 2H 125
Sundridge Ho. *E9* *7K 67*
(off Church Cres.)
Sundridge Pde. BR1: Brom 7K 141
SUNDRIDGE PARK 7K 141
Sundridge Pk. Manor Conference Cen.
6B 142
Sundridge Pl. CR0: C'don 1G 169
Sundridge Rd. CR0: C'don 7F 157
Sunfields Pl. SE3 7K 105
Sunflower Ct. NW2 2H 63
Sungate Cotts. RM5: Col R 1F 55
SUN-IN-THE-SANDS 7K 105
Sunken Rd. CR0: C'don 5J 169
Sunkist Way SM6: Wall 7J 167
Sunland Av. DA6: Bex 4E 126
Sun La. SE3 7K 105
Sunleigh Rd. HA0: Wemb 1E 78
Sunley Gdns. UB6: G'frd 1A 78
Sun Life Trad. Est. TW14: Felt 3J 111
Sunlight Cl. SW19 6A 136
Sunlight Sq. E2 3H 85
Sunmead Rd. TW16: Sun 3J 147
Sunna Gdns. TW16: Sun 2K 147
Sunna Lodge TW16: Sun 7H 129
Sunniholme Ct. *CR2: S Croy* *5C 168*
(off Warham Rd.)
Sunningdale N14 5C 32
W13 *5B 78*
(off Hardwick Grn.)
Sunningdale Av. HA4: Ruis 1A 58
IG11: Bark 1H 89
TW13: Hanw 2C 130
W3 7A 80
Sunningdale Cl. E6 3D 88
HA7: Stan 6F 27
KT6: Surb 2E 162
SE16 5H 103
SE28 6E 90
Sunningdale Ct. *TW7: Isle* *6H 113*
(off Whitton Dene)
UB1: S'hall *6G 77*
(off Fleming Rd.)
Sunningdale Gdns. NW9 5J 43
W8 *3J 99*
(off Stratford Rd.)
Sunningdale Lodge *HA8: Edg* *5A 28*
(off Stonegrove)
Sunningdale Rd. BR1: Brom 4C 160
SM1: Sutt 3H 165
Sunningfields Cres. NW4 2D 44
Sunningfields Rd. NW4 3D 44

Sunninghill Ct. W3 . . . 2J 97
Sunninghill Rd. SE13 . . . 2D 122
Sunny Bank SE25 . . . 3G 157
Sunny Cres. NW10 . . . 7J 61
Sunnycroft Rd. SE25 . . . 3G 157
TW3: Houn . . . 2F 113
UB1: S'hall . . . 5E 76
Sunnydale BR6: Farnb . . . 2E 172
Sunnydale Gdns. NW7 . . . 6E 28
Sunnydale Rd. SE12 . . . 5K 123
Sunnydene Av. E4 . . . 5A 36
HA4: Ruis . . . 1J 57
Sunnydene Gdns. HA0: Wemb . . . 6C 60
Sunnydene St. SE26 . . . 4A 140
Sunnyfield NW7 . . . 4G 29
Sunnyfield Rd. BR7: Chst . . . 3K 161
Sunny Gdns. Pde. NW4 . . . 2D 44
Sunny Gdns. Rd. NW4 . . . 2D 44
Sunny Hill NW4 . . . 3D 44
Sunnyhill Cl. E5 . . . 4A 68
Sunnyhill Rd. SW16 . . . 4J 137
Sunnyhurst Cl. SM1: Sutt . . . 3J 165
Sunnymead Av. CR4: Mitc . . . 3H 155
Sunnymead Rd. NW9 . . . 7K 43
SW15 . . . 5D 116
Sunnymede Av. KT19: Ewe . . . 7A 164
Sunnymede Dr. IG2: Ilf . . . 5F 53
IG6: Ilf . . . 5F 53
Sunny Nook Gdns.
CR2: S Croy . . . 6D 168
Sunny Pl. NW4 . . . 4E 44
Sunny Rd., The EN3: Enf H . . . 1E 24
Sunnyside KT12: Walt T . . . 5A 148
NW2 . . . 3H 63
SE6 . . . 7B 122
(off Blythe Hill)
SW19 . . . 6G 135
Sunnyside Dr. E4 . . . 7K 25
Sunnyside Ho's. *NW2 . . . 3H 63*
(off Sunnyside)
Sunnyside Pas. SW19 . . . 6G 135
Sunnyside Pl. SW19 . . . 6G 135
Sunnyside Rd. E10 . . . 1C 68
IG1: Ilf . . . 3G 71
N19 . . . 7H 47
TW11: Tedd . . . 4H 131
W5 . . . 1D 96
Sunnyside Rd. E. N9 . . . 3B 34
Sunnyside Rd. Nth. N9 . . . 3A 34
Sunnyside Rd. Sth. N9 . . . 3A 34
Sunnyside Ter. NW9 . . . 3K 43
Sunny Vw. NW9 . . . 5K 43
Sunny Way N12 . . . 7H 31
Sun Pas. *SE16 . . . 3G 103*
(off Old Jamaica Rd.)
Sunray Av. BR2: Brom . . . 6C 160
KT5: Surb . . . 2H 163
SE24 . . . 4D 120
Sunrise Cl. TW13: Hanw . . . 3D 130
Sunrise Vw. NW7 . . . 6G 29
Sun Rd. W14 . . . 5H 99
Sunset Av. E4 . . . 1J 35
IG8: Wfd G . . . 4C 36
Sunset Ct. IG8: Wfd G . . . 7F 37
Sunset Gdns. SE25 . . . 2F 157
Sunset Lodge *NW10 . . . 7E 62*
(off Hanover Rd.)
Sunset Rd. SE5 . . . 4C 120
SE28 . . . 1A 108
SW19 . . . 5D 134
Sunset Vw. EN5: Barn . . . 2B 20
Sunshine Way CR4: Mitc . . . 2D 154
Sun St. EC2 . . . 5F 9 (5D 84)
(Finsbury Sq.)
EC2 . . . 5G 9 (5E 84)
(Primrose St.)
Sun St. Pas. EC2 . . . 6G 9 (5E 84)
Sun Wlk. E1 . . . 3K 15 (7F 85)
Sunwell Cl. SE15 . . . 1H 121
Sun Wharf *SE8 . . . 7D 104*
(off Creekside)
Superior Dr. BR6: Chels . . . 6K 173
Supreme Court . . . *7E 12*
(off Parliament Sq.)
SURBITON . . . 6D 150
Surbiton Ct. KT6: Surb . . . 6C 150
Surbiton Cres. KT1: King T . . . 4E 150
Surbiton Fitness and Wellbeing Cen.
. . . 6C 150
Surbiton Hall Cl. KT1: King T . . . 4E 150
Surbiton Hill Pk. KT5: Surb . . . 5F 151
Surbiton Hill Rd. KT6: Surb . . . 4E 150
Surbiton Pde. KT6: Surb . . . 6E 150
Surbiton Raceway . . . 3K 163
Surbiton Rd. KT1: King T . . . 4D 150
Surlingham Cl. SE28 . . . 7D 90
Surma Cl. E1 . . . 4H 85
Surmans Cl. RM9: Dag . . . 1C 90
Surrendale Pl. W9 . . . 4J 81
Surrey Canal Rd. SE14 . . . 6J 103
SE15 . . . 6J 103
Surrey Cl. N3 . . . 3G 45
Surrey County Cricket Club
. . . 7H 19 (6K 101)
Surrey Cres. W4 . . . 5G 97
Surrey Docks Farm . . . 2B 104
Surrey Docks Watersports Cen. . . . 3A 104
Surrey Gdns. N4 . . . 6C 48
Surrey Gro. SE17 . . . 5E 102
SM1: Sutt . . . 3B 166
Surrey Ho. *SE16 . . . 1K 103*
(off Rotherhithe St.)
Surrey La. SW11 . . . 1C 118
Surrey La. Est. SW11 . . . 1C 118
Surrey M. SE27 . . . 4E 138
Surrey Mt. SE23 . . . 1H 139
Surrey Quays Rd. SE16 . . . 3J 103
Surrey Quays Shop. Cen. SE16 . . . 3K 103
Surrey Rd. BR4: W W'ck . . . 1D 170
HA1: Harr . . . 5G 41
IG11: Bark . . . 7J 71
RM10: Dag . . . 5H 73
SE15 . . . 5K 121
Surrey Row SE1 . . . 6A 14 (2B 102)
Surrey Sq. SE17 . . . 5E 102
Surrey Steps *WC2 . . . 2H 13*
(off Surrey St.)
Surrey St. CR0: C'don . . . 2C 168
E13 . . . 3K 87
WC2 . . . 2H 13 (7K 83)
Surrey Ter. SE17 . . . 5E 102
Surrey Water Rd. SE16 . . . 1K 103
Surridge Ct. *SW9 . . . 2J 119*
(off Clapham Rd.)
Surridge Gdns. SE19 . . . 6D 138
Surr St. N7 . . . 5J 65
Sury Basin KT2: King T . . . 1E 150
Susan Cl. RM7: Mawney . . . 3J 55
Susan Constant Ct. *E14 . . . 7F 87*
(off Newport Av.)
Susan Lawrence Ho. *E3 . . . 2A 86*
(off Zealand Rd.)
E12 . . . 4E 70
(off Walton Rd.)
Susannah St. E14 . . . 6D 86
Susan Rd. SE3 . . . 2K 123
Susan Wood BR7: Chst . . . 1E 160
Sussex Av. TW7: Isle . . . 3J 113
Sussex Cl. IG4: Ilf . . . 5D 52
KT3: N Mald . . . 4A 152
N19 . . . 2J 65
TW1: Twick . . . 6B 114
Sussex Ct. *SE10 . . . 6E 104*
(off Roan St.)
W2 . . . 1A 10
(off Spring St.)
Sussex Cres. UB5: N'olt . . . 6E 58
Sussex Gdns. KT9: Chess . . . 6D 162
N4 . . . 5C 48
N6 . . . 5D 46
W2 . . . 2A 10 (7B 82)
Sussex Ga. N6 . . . 5D 46
Sussex Ho. *NW1 . . . 2H 83*
(off Chalton St.)
Sussex Lodge *W2 . . . 1B 10*
(off Sussex Pl.)
Sussex Mans. SW7 . . . 4A 16
WC2 . . . 2F 13
(off Maiden La.)
Sussex M. SE6 . . . 7C 122
Sussex M. E. W2 . . . 1B 10
Sussex M. W. W2 . . . 2B 10 (7B 82)
Sussex Pl. KT3: N Mald . . . 4A 152
NW1 . . . 3E 4 (4D 82)
W2 . . . 1B 10 (6B 82)
W6 . . . 5E 98
Sussex Ring N12 . . . 5D 30
Sussex Rd. BR4: W W'ck . . . 1D 170
CR2: S Croy . . . 6D 168
CR4: Mitc . . . 5J 155
DA8: Erith . . . 7H 109
DA14: Sidc . . . 5B 144
E6 . . . 1E 88
HA1: Harr . . . 5G 41
KT3: N Mald . . . 4A 152
SM5: Cars . . . 6D 166
UB2: S'hall . . . 3B 94
UB10: Ick . . . 4E 56
Sussex Sq. W2 . . . 2B 10 (7B 82)
Sussex St. E13 . . . 3K 87
SW1 . . . 6K 17 (5F 101)
Sussex Ter. *SE20 . . . 7J 139*
(off Graveney Gro.)
Sussex Way EN4: Cockf . . . 5A 22
N7 . . . 2J 65
N19 . . . 1H 65
(not continuous)
Sutcliffe Cl. NW11 . . . 5K 45
Sutcliffe Ho. UB3: Hayes . . . 6J 75
Sutcliffe Pk. Athletics Track . . . 5A 124
Sutcliffe Rd. DA16: Well . . . 2C 126
SE18 . . . 6J 107
Sutherland Av. BR5: St M Cry . . . 6K 161
DA16: Well . . . 4J 125
TW16: Sun . . . 2H 147
UB3: Hayes . . . 4J 93
W9 . . . 4J 81
W13 . . . 6B 78
Sutherland Cl. EN5: Barn . . . 4B 20
Sutherland Ct. N16 . . . 3D 66
NW9 . . . 5H 43
W9 . . . 4J 81
(off Marylands Rd.)
Sutherland Dr. SW19 . . . 1B 154
Sutherland Gdns. KT4: Wor Pk . . . 1D 164
SW14 . . . 3A 116
TW16: Sun . . . 2H 147
Sutherland Gro. SW18 . . . 6G 117
TW11: Tedd . . . 5J 131
Sutherland Ho. IG8: Wfd G . . . 7K 37
W8 . . . 3K 99
Sutherland Pl. W2 . . . 6J 81
Sutherland Rd. CR0: C'don . . . 7A 156
DA17: Belv . . . 3G 109
E3 . . . 2B 86
E17 . . . 2K 49
EN3: Pond E . . . 6E 24
N9 . . . 1C 34
N17 . . . 7B 34
UB1: S'hall . . . 6D 76
W4 . . . 6A 98
W13 . . . 6A 78
Sutherland Rd. Path E17 . . . 3K 49
Sutherland Row SW1 . . . 5K 17 (5F 101)
Sutherland Sq. SE17 . . . 5C 102
Sutherland St. SW1 . . . 5J 17 (5F 101)
Sutherland Wlk. SE17 . . . 5C 102
Sutlej Rd. SE7 . . . 7A 106
Sutterton St. N7 . . . 6K 65
SUTTON . . . 5K 165
Sutton Arena Leisure Cen. . . . 7A 154
Sutton Cl. BR3: Beck . . . 1D 158
HA5: Eastc . . . 5J 39
IG10: Lough . . . 1H 37
W4 . . . 6J 97
(off Sutton La. Sth.)
Sutton Comn. Rd. SM1: Sutt . . . 7H 153
SM3: Sutt . . . 7H 153
Sutton Ct. KT8: W Mole . . . 5D 148
SE19 . . . 7F 139
SM2: Sutt . . . 6A 166
W4 . . . 6J 97
W5 . . . 1E 96
Sutton Ct. Rd. E13 . . . 3A 88
SM1: Sutt . . . 6A 166
UB10: Hil . . . 1D 74
W4 . . . 7J 97
Sutton Cres. EN5: Barn . . . 5A 20
Sutton Dene TW3: Houn . . . 1F 113
Sutton Ecology Cen. . . . 4D 166
Sutton Est. EC1 . . . 2F 9
W10 . . . 5E 80
Sutton Est., The N1 . . . 7B 66
SW3 . . . 5D 16 (5C 100)
Sutton Gdns. CR0: C'don . . . 5F 157
IG11: Bark . . . 1J 89
Sutton Grn. *IG11: Bark . . . 1J 89*
(off Sutton Rd.)
Sutton Gro. SM1: Sutt . . . 4B 166
Sutton Hall Rd. TW5: Hest . . . 7E 94
Sutton Hgts. SM2: Sutt . . . 7B 166
Sutton Junior Tennis Cen. . . . 1K 165
Sutton La. *EC1 . . . 4B 8*
(off Gt. Sutton St.)
TW3: Houn . . . 3D 112
Sutton La. Nth. W4 . . . 5J 97
Sutton La. Sth. W4 . . . 6J 97
Sutton Pde. *NW4 . . . 4E 44*
(off Church Rd.)
Sutton Pk. Rd. SM1: Sutt . . . 6K 165
Sutton Pl. E9 . . . 5J 67
Sutton Rd. E13 . . . 4H 87
E17 . . . 1K 49
IG11: Bark . . . 2J 89
N10 . . . 1E 46
TW5: Hest . . . 1E 112
Sutton Row W1 . . . 7D 6 (6H 83)
Suttons Bus. Pk. RM13: Rain . . . 3K 91
Sutton Sq. E9 . . . 5J 67
TW5: Hest . . . 1D 112
Sutton St. E1 . . . 7J 85
Sutton Superbowl . . . 5K 165
Sutton's Way EC1 . . . 4D 8
Sutton United FC . . . 4J 165
Sutton Wlk. SE1 . . . 5H 13 (1K 101)
Sutton Way TW5: Hest . . . 1D 112
W10 . . . 4E 80
SW1 Gallery . . . 1A 18 (3G 101)
Swaby Rd. SW18 . . . 1A 136
Swaffam Ct. RM6: Chad H . . . 6C 54
Swaffham Way N22 . . . 7G 33
Swaffield Rd. SW18 . . . 7K 117
Swain Cl. SW16 . . . 6F 137
Swain Rd. CR7: Thor H . . . 5C 156
Swains Cl. UB7: W Dray . . . 2A 92
Swains La. N6 . . . 1E 64
Swainson Rd. W3 . . . 2B 98
Swains Rd. SW17 . . . 7D 136
Swain St. NW8 . . . 3C 4 (4C 82)
Swakeleys Dr. UB10: Ick . . . 4C 56
Swakeleys Rd. UB10: Ick . . . 4A 56
SWAKELEYS RDBT. . . . 4A 56
Swalecliffe Rd. DA17: Belv . . . 5H 109
Swaledale Cl. N11 . . . 6K 31
Swallands Rd. SE6 . . . 3C 140
(not continuous)
Swallow Cl. DA8: Erith . . . 1K 127
SE14 . . . 1K 121
WD23: Bush . . . 1B 26
Swallow Ct. HA4: Ruis . . . 1A 58
IG2: Ilf . . . 5F 53
SE1 . . . 7D 14
(off Swan St.)
SE12 . . . 7J 123
W9 . . . 5J 81
(off Admiral Wlk.)
Swallow Dr. NW10 . . . 6K 61
UB5: N'olt . . . 2E 76

Swallowfield *NW1* *2K 5*
(off Munster Sq.)
Swallowfield Rd. SE7 5K **105**
Swallowfield Way UB3: Hayes 2F **93**
Swallow Gdns. SW16 5H **137**
Swallow Ho. *NW8* *2C 82*
(off Allitsen Rd.)
Swallow Pk. KT6: Surb 3F **163**
Swallow Pas. *W1* *1K 11*
(off Swallow Pl.)
Swallow Pl. W1 1K **11** (6F **83**)
Swallow St. E6 5C **88**
W1 3B **12** (7G **83**)
SWAN, THE **2E 170**
Swanage Ct. *N1* *7E 66*
(off Hertford Rd.)
Swanage Ho. *SW8* *7K 101*
(off Dorset Rd.)
Swanage Rd. E4 7K **35**
SW18 6A **118**
Swanage Waye UB4: Yead 6A **76**
Swan & Pike Rd.
EN3: Enf L 1H **25**
Swan App. E6 5C **88**
Swanbourne *SE17* *4C 102*
(off Wansey St.)
Swanbourne Ho. *NW8* *3C 4*
(off Capland St.)
Swanbridge Rd. DA7: Bex 1G **127**
Swan Cen., The SW17 3K **135**
Swan Cl. CR0: C'don 7E **156**
E17 1A **50**
TW13: Hanw 4C **130**
Swan Ct. *E1* *3K 15*
(off Star Pl.)
E14 *6B 86*
(off Agnes St.)
HA4: Ruis 7F **39**
SW3 6D **16** (5C **100**)
SW6 *7J 99*
(off Fulham Rd.)
TW7: Isle *3B 114*
(off Swan St.)
Swandon Way SW18 5K **117**
Swan Dr. NW9 2A **44**
Swanfield St. E2 2J **9** (3F **85**)
Swan Ho. *E15* *7F 69*
(off The Broadway)
EN3: Pond E 5D **24**
N1 *7D 66*
(off Oakley Rd.)
Swan Island TW1: Twick 3A **132**
Swan La. EC4 3F **15** (7D **84**)
N20 3F **31**
Swanley Ho. *SE17* *5E 102*
(off Kinglake Est.)
Swanley Rd. DA16: Well 1C **126**
Swan Mead SE1 3E **102**
Swan M. CR4: Mitc 1D **154**
RM7: Mawney 4H **55**
SW6 1H **117**
SW9 2K **119**
Swann Ct. *TW7: Isle* *3A 114*
(off South St.)
Swanne Ho. *SE10* *7E 104*
(off Gloucester Cir.)
Swan Pas. E1 3K **15**
Swan Path KT1: King T 3F **151**
Swan Pl. SW13 2B **116**
Swan Rd. SE16 2J **103**
SE18 3B **106**
TW13: Hanw 5C **130**
UB1: S'hall 6F **77**
UB7: W Dray 2A **92**
Swanscombe Ho. *W11* *1F 99*
(off St Ann's Rd.)
Swanscombe Point *E16* *5H 87*
(off Clarkson Rd.)
Swanscombe Rd. W4 5A **98**
W11 1F **99**
Swansea Ct. *E16* *1F 107*
(off Fishguard Way)
Swansea Rd. EN3: Pond E 4D **24**
TW14: Felt 6E **110**
Swansland Gdns. E17 1A **50**
Swansmere Cl. KT12: Walt T 7A **148**
Swan St. SE1 7D **14** (3C **102**)
TW7: Isle 3B **114**
Swanton Gdns. SW19 1F **135**
Swanton Rd. DA8: Erith 7G **109**
Swan Wlk. SW3 7E **16** (6D **100**)
TW17: Shep 7G **147**
Swan Way EN3: Enf H 2E **24**
Swanwick Cl. SW15 7B **116**
Swan Yd. N1 6B **66**
Sward Rd. BR5: St M Cry 6K **161**
Swathling Ho. *SW15* *6B 116*
(off Tunworth Cres.)
Swaton Rd. E3 4C **86**
Swaylands Rd. DA17: Belv 6G **109**
Swaythling Cl. N18 4C **34**
Swedeland Ct. E1 6H **9**
Swedenborg Gdns. E1 7H **85**
Sweden Ga. SE16 3A **104**
Swedish Quays SE16 3A **104**
(not continuous)
Sweeney Cres. SE1 7K **15** (2F **103**)
Sweet Briar Grn. N9 3A **34**
Sweet Briar Gro. N9 3A **34**
Sweet Briar Wlk. N18 4A **34**
Sweetcroft La. UB10: Hil 7B **56**
Sweetland Ct. RM8: Dag 6B **72**
Sweetmans Av. HA5: Pinn 3B **40**
Sweets Way N20 2G **31**
Swell Ct. E17 6C **50**
Swetenham Wlk. SE18 5G **107**
Swete St. E13 2J **87**
Sweyn Pl. SE3 2J **123**
Swift Cen. CR0: Wadd 7K **167**
Swift Cl. E17 7F **35**
HA2: Harr 2F **59**
SE28 7B **90**
UB3: Hayes 6H **75**
Swift Ct. SM2: Sutt 7K **165**
Swift Ho. *E3* *1B 86*
(off Old Ford Rd.)
Swift Lodge *W9* *5J 81*
(off Admiral Wlk.)
Swift Rd. TW13: Hanw 3C **130**
UB2: S'hall 3E **94**
Swiftsden Way BR1: Brom 6G **141**
Swift St. SW6 1H **117**
Swinbrook Rd. W10 5G **81**
Swinburne Ct. *SE5* *4D 120*
(off Basingdon Way)
Swinburne Cres. CR0: C'don 6J **157**
Swinburne Ho. *E2* *3J 85*
(off Roman Rd.)
Swinburne Rd. SW15 4C **116**
Swinderby Rd. HA0: Wemb 6E **60**
Swindon Cl. IG3: Ilf 2J **71**
Swindon Rd. TW6: H'row A 5E **110**
Swindon St. W12 1D **98**
Swinfield Cl. TW13: Hanw 3C **130**
Swinford Gdns. SW9 3B **120**
Swingate La. SE18 6J **107**
Swingfield Ho. *E9* *1J 85*
(off Templecombe Rd.)
Swinley Ho. *NW1* *1K 5*
(off Redhill St.)
Swinnerton St. E9 5A **68**
Swinson Ho. N11 5B **32**
Swinton Cl. HA9: Wemb 1H **61**
Swinton Pl. WC1 1G **7** (3K **83**)
Swinton St. WC1 1G **7** (3K **83**)
Swires Shaw BR2: Kes 4B **172**
Swiss Cen. W1 3C **12**
SWISS COTTAGE **7B 64**
Swiss Cottage Sports Cen. 7B 64
Swiss Ct. WC2 3D **12**
Swiss Ter. NW6 7B **64**
Switch Ho. E14 7F **87**
Swithland Gdns. SE9 4E **142**
Swyncombe Av. W5 4B **96**
Swynford Gdns. NW4 4C **44**
Sybil M. N4 6B **48**
Sybil Phoenix Cl. SE8 5K **103**
Sybil Thorndike Casson Ho.
SW5 *5J 99*
(off Kramer M.)
Sybourn St. E17 7B **50**
Sycamore Av. DA15: Sidc 6K **125**
E3 1B **86**
UB3: Hayes 7G **75**
W5 3D **96**
Sycamore Cl. CR2: S Croy 5E **168**
E16 4G **87**
EN4: E Barn 6G **21**
HA8: Edg 4D **28**
N9 4B **34**
SE9 2C **142**
SM5: Cars 4D **166**
TW13: Felt 3J **129**
UB5: N'olt 1C **76**
UB7: Yiew 7B **74**
W3 1A **98**
Sycamore Ct. *DA8: Erith* *5K 109*
(off Sandcliff Rd.)
E7 6J **69**
KT3: N Mald 3A **152**
NW6 *1J 81*
(off Bransdale Cl.)
SE1 *7G 15*
(off Royal Oak Yd.)
TW4: Houn 4C **112**
Sycamore Gdns. CR4: Mitc 2B **154**
N15 4F **49**
W6 2D **98**
Sycamore Gro. KT3: N Mald 3K **151**
NW9 7J **43**
SE6 6E **122**
SE20 1G **157**
Sycamore Hill N11 6K **31**
Sycamore Ho. BR2: Brom 2G **159**
IG9: Buck H 2G **37**
N2 *2B 46*
(off The Grange)
SE16 *2K 103*
(off Woodland Cres.)
W6 2D **98**
Sycamore Lodge BR6: Orp 2K **173**
TW16: Sun 7H **129**
W8 *3K 99*
(off Stone Hall Pl.)
Sycamore M. *DA8: Erith* *5K 109*
(off St John's Rd.)
SW4 3G **119**
Sycamore Path *E17* *6D 50*
(off Poplars Rd.)
Sycamore Pl. BR1: Brom 3E **160**
Sycamore Rd. SW19 6E **134**
Sycamore St. EC1 4C **8** (4C **84**)
Sycamore Wlk. IG6: Ilf 4G **53**
W10 4G **81**
Sycamore Way CR7: Thor H 5A **156**
TW11: Tedd 6C **132**
Sydcote SE21 1C **138**
SYDENHAM 4J **139**
Sydenham Av. N21 5E **22**
SE26 5H **139**
Sydenham Cotts. SE12 2A **142**
Sydenham Ct. *CR0: C'don* *1D 168*
(off Sydenham Rd.)
Sydenham Hill SE23 1H **139**
SE26 4F **139**
Sydenham Hill Wood &
Cox's Walk Nature Reserve
2G 139
Sydenham Pk. SE26 3J **139**
Sydenham Pk. Mans. *SE26* *3J 139*
(off Sydenham Pk.)
Sydenham Pk. Rd. SE26 3J **139**
Sydenham Pl. SE27 3B **138**
Sydenham Ri. SE23 2H **139**
Sydenham Rd. CR0: C'don 1C **168**
SE26 5K **139**
Sydmons Ct. SE23 7J **121**
Sydner M. N16 4F **67**
Sydner Rd. N16 4F **67**
Sydney Chapman Way
EN5: Barn 2C **20**
Sydney Cl. SW3 4B **16** (4B **100**)
Sydney Ct. UB4: Yead 4A **76**
Sydney Cres. TW15: Ashf 6D **128**
Sydney Gro. NW4 5E **44**
Sydney M. SW3 4B **16** (4B **100**)
Sydney Pl. SW7 4B **16** (4B **100**)
Sydney Rd. DA6: Bex 4D **126**
DA14: Sidc 4J **143**
E11 6K **51**
EN2: Enf 4J **23**
IG6: Ilf 2G **53**
IG8: Wfd G 4D **36**
N8 4A **48**
N10 1E **46**
SE2 3C **108**
SM1: Sutt 4J **165**
SW20 2F **153**
TW9: Rich 4E **114**
TW11: Tedd 5K **131**
TW14: Felt 1J **129**
W13 1A **96**
Sydney Russell Leisure Cen. 5E 72
Sydney St. SW3 5C **16** (5C **100**)
Sylvana Cl. UB10: Hil 1B **74**
Sylvan Av. N3 2J **45**
N22 7E **32**
NW7 6F **29**
RM6: Chad H 6F **55**
Sylvan Ct. N12 3E **30**
NW6 *1K 81*
(off Abbey Rd.)
Sylvan Est. SE19 1F **157**
Sylvan Gdns. KT6: Surb 7D **150**
Sylvan Gro. NW2 4F **63**
SE15 6H **103**
Sylvan Hill SE19 1E **156**
Sylvan Rd. E7 6K **69**
E11 5J **51**
E17 5C **50**
IG1: Ilf 2G **71**
SE19 1F **157**
Sylvan Ter. *SE15* *6H 103*
(off Sylvan Gro.)
Sylvan Wlk. BR1: Brom 3D **160**
Sylvan Way BR4: W W'ck 4G **171**
RM8: Dag 4B **72**
Sylverdale Rd. CR0: C'don 3B **168**
Sylvester Av. BR7: Chst 6D **142**
Sylvester Path E8 6H **67**
Sylvester Rd. E8 6H **67**
E17 7B **50**
HA0: Wemb 5C **60**
N2 2A **46**
Sylvestrian Leisure Cen. 4G 51
Sylvestrus Cl. KT1: King T 1G **151**
Sylvia Ct. HA9: Wemb 7H **61**
N1 *2D 84*
(off Wenlock St.)
Sylvia Gdns. HA9: Wemb 7H **61**
Sylvia Pankhurst Ho.
RM10: Dag *3G 73*
(off Wythenshawe Rd.)
Symes M. NW1 2G **83**
Symington Ho. *SE1* *3D 102*
(off Deverell St.)
Symington M. E9 5K **67**
Symister M. N1 2G **9**
Symons Cl. SE15 2J **121**
Symons St. SW3 4F **17** (4D **100**)
Symphony Cl. HA8: Edg 7C **28**
Symphony M. W10 3G **81**
Syon Ct. E11 5K **51**
Syon Ga. Way TW8: Bford 7A **96**
Syon House 1C 114
Syon La. TW7: Isle 6J **95**
Syon Lodge SE12 7J **123**
Syon Pk. 1B 114

Syon Pk. Gdns.—Tate Britain

Syon Pk. Gdns. TW7: Isle ... 7K 95
Syringa Ho. SE4 ... 3B 122

T

Tabard Ct. E14 ... 6E 86
(off Lodore St.)
Tabard Gdn. Est. SE1 ... 7E 14 (3D 102)
Tabard Ho. SE1 ... 7F 15
(off Manciple St.)
Tabard St. SE1 ... 6D 14 (2D 102)
Tabard Theatre ... 4A 98
Tabernacle Av. E13 ... 4J 87
Tabernacle St. EC2 ... 4F 9 (4D 84)
Tableer Av. SW4 ... 5G 119
Tabley Rd. N7 ... 4J 65
Tabor Ct. SM3: Cheam ... 6G 165
Tabor Gdns. SM3: Cheam ... 6H 165
Tabor Gro. SW19 ... 7H 135
Tabor Rd. W6 ... 3D 98
Tachbrook Est. SW1 ... 6C 18 (5H 101)
Tachbrook M. SW1 ... 3A 18 (4G 101)
Tachbrook Rd. TW14: Felt ... 7H 111
UB2: S'hall ... 4B 94
UB7: W Dray ... 1A 92
Tachbrook St. SW1 ... 4B 18 (4G 101)
Tack M. SE4 ... 3C 122
Tadema Ho. NW8 ... 4B 4
Tadema Rd. SW10 ... 7A 100
Tadlow KT1: King T ... 3G 151
(off Washington Rd.)
Tadmor Cl. TW16: Sun ... 4H 147
Tadmor St. W12 ... 1F 99
Tadworth Av. KT3: N Mald ... 4B 152
Tadworth Ho. SE1 ... 7A 14
Tadworth Rd. NW2 ... 2C 62
Taeping St. E14 ... 4D 104
Taff Ho. KT2: King T ... 1D 150
(off Henry Macaulay Av.)
Taffrail Ho. E14 ... 5D 104
(off Burrells Wharf Sq.)
Taffy's How CR4: Mitc ... 3C 154
Taft Way E3 ... 3D 86
Taggs Ho. KT1: King T ... 2D 150
(off Wadbrook St.)
Taggs Island TW12: Hamp ... 2H 149
Tagwright Ho. N1 ... 1E 8
(off Nile St.)
Tailor Ho. WC1 ... 4F 7
(off Colonnade)
Tailworth St. E1 ... 6K 9
(off Chicksand St.)
Tait Ct. E3 ... 1A 86
(off St Stephen's Rd.)
SW8 ... 1J 119
(off Lansdowne Grn.)
Tait Ho. SE1 ... 5K 13
(off Greet St.)
Tait Rd. CR0: C'don ... 7E 156
Tait Rd. Ind. Est. CR0: C'don ... 7E 156
(off Tait Rd.)
Tait St. E1 ... 6H 85
Takeley Cl. RM5: Col R ... 2K 55
Takhar M. SW11 ... 2C 118
Talacre Community Sports Cen. ... 6E 64
Talacre Rd. NW5 ... 6E 64
Talbot Av. N2 ... 3B 46
Talbot Cl. N15 ... 4F 49
Talbot Ct. EC3 ... 2F 15
NW9 ... 3K 61
Talbot Cres. NW4 ... 5C 44
Talbot Gdns. IG3: Ilf ... 2A 72
Talbot Gro. Ho. W11 ... 6G 81
(off Lancaster Rd.)
Talbot Ho. E14 ... 6D 86
(off Girauld St.)
N7 ... 3A 66
Talbot Pl. SE3 ... 2G 123
Talbot Rd. CR7: Thor H ... 4D 156
E6 ... 2E 88
E7 ... 4J 69
Talbot Rd. HA0: Wemb ... 6D 60
HA3: W'stone ... 2K 41
N6 ... 6E 46
N15 ... 4F 49
N22 ... 2G 47
RM9: Dag ... 6F 73
SE22 ... 4E 120
SM5: Cars ... 5E 166
TW2: Twick ... 1J 131
TW7: Isle ... 4A 114
TW15: Ashf ... 5A 128
UB2: S'hall ... 4C 94
W2 ... 6H 81
W11 ... 6H 81
(not continuous)
W13 ... 1A 96
Talbot Sq. W2 ... 1B 10 (6B 82)
Talbot Wlk. NW10 ... 6A 62
W11 ... 6G 81
(off St Mark's Rd.)
Talbot Yd. SE1 ... 5E 14 (1D 102)
Talcott Path SW2 ... 1A 138
Talehangers Cl. DA6: Bex ... 4D 126
(not continuous)
Talfourd Pl. SE15 ... 1F 121
Talfourd Rd. SE15 ... 1F 121
Talgarth Mans. W14 ... 5G 99
(off Talgarth Rd.)
Talgarth Rd. W6 ... 5F 99
W14 ... 5F 99
Talgarth Wlk. NW9 ... 5A 44
Talia Ho. E14 ... 3E 104
(off Manchester Rd.)
Talina Cen. SW6 ... 1A 118
Talisman Cl. IG3: Ilf ... 1B 72
Talisman Sq. SE26 ... 4G 139
Talisman Way HA9: Wemb ... 3F 61
Tallack Cl. HA3: Hrw W ... 7D 26
Tallack Rd. E10 ... 1B 68
Tall Elms Cl. BR2: Brom ... 5H 159
Talleyrand Ho. SE5 ... 2C 120
(off Lilford Rd.)
Tallis Cl. E16 ... 6K 87
Tallis Gro. SE7 ... 6K 105
Tallis St. EC4 ... 2K 13 (7A 84)
Tallis Vw. NW10 ... 6K 61
Tallow Cl. RM9: Dag ... 7D 72
Tallow Rd. TW8: Bford ... 6C 96
Tall Trees SW16 ... 3K 155
Talma Gdns. TW2: Twick ... 6J 113
Talmage Cl. SE23 ... 7J 121
Talman Gro. HA7: Stan ... 6J 27
Talma Rd. SW2 ... 4A 120
Talwin St. E3 ... 3D 86
Tamar Cl. E3 ... 1B 86
Tamar Ho. E14 ... 2E 104
(off Plevna St.)
SE11 ... 5K 19
(off Kennington La.)
Tamarind Ct. SE1 ... 6K 15
W8 ... 3K 99
(off Stone Hall Gdns.)
Tamarind Ho. SE15 ... 7G 103
(off Reddins Rd.)
Tamarind Yd. E1 ... 1G 103
(off Kennet St.)
Tamarisk Sq. W12 ... 7B 80
Tamar Sq. IG8: Wfd G ... 6E 36
Tamar St. SE7 ... 3C 106
Tamar Way N17 ... 3F 49
Tamesis Gdns. KT4: Wor Pk ... 2A 164
Tamian Ind. Est. TW4: Houn ... 4A 112
Tamian Way TW4: Houn ... 4A 112
Tamworth N7 ... 6J 65
(off Market Est.)
Tamworth Av. IG8: Wfd G ... 6B 36
Tamworth La. CR4: Mitc ... 2F 155
Tamworth Pk. CR4: Mitc ... 4F 155
Tamworth Pl. CR0: C'don ... 2C 168
Tamworth Rd. CR0: C'don ... 2B 168
Tamworth St. SW6 ... 6J 99
Tamworth Vs. CR4: Mitc ... 4F 155
Tancred Rd. N4 ... 6B 48
Tandem Cen. SW19 ... 1B 154
Tandem Way SW19 ... 1B 154
Tandridge Dr. BR6: Orp ... 1H 173
Tandridge Pl. BR6: Orp ... 1H 173
Tanfield Av. NW2 ... 4B 62
Tanfield Rd. CR0: C'don ... 4C 168
Tangerine Ho. SE1 ... 7F 15
(off Long La.)
Tangier Rd. TW10: Rich ... 4G 115
Tangleberry Cl. BR1: Brom ... 4D 160
Tangle Tree Cl. N3 ... 2K 45
Tanglewood Cl. CR0: C'don ... 3J 169
HA7: Stan ... 2D 26
UB10: Hil ... 4C 74
Tanglewood Way TW13: Felt ... 3K 129
Tangley Gro. SW15 ... 6B 116
Tangley Pk. Rd. TW12: Hamp ... 6D 130
Tanglyn Av. TW17: Shep ... 5D 146
Tangmere N17 ... 2D 48
(off Willan Rd.)
WC1 ... 2G 7
(off Sidmouth St.)
Tangmere Gdns. UB5: N'olt ... 2A 76
(not continuous)
Tangmere Gro. KT2: King T ... 5D 132
Tangmere Way NW9 ... 2A 44
Tanhouse Fld. NW5 ... 5H 65
(off Torriano Av.)
Tanhurst Ho. SW2 ... 7K 119
(off Redlands Way)
Tanhurst Wlk. SE2 ... 3D 108
(off Alsike Rd.)
Tankerton Ho's. WC1 ... 2F 7
(off Tankerton St.)
Tankerton Rd. KT6: Surb ... 2F 163
Tankerton St. WC1 ... 2F 7 (3J 83)
Tankerton Ter. CR0: C'don ... 6K 155
Tankerville Ct. TW3: Houn ... 3G 113
Tankerville Rd. SW16 ... 7H 137
Tankridge Rd. NW2 ... 2D 62
Tanner Ho. SE1 ... 7H 15
(off Tanner St.)
Tanneries, The E1 ... 4J 85
(off Cephas Av.)
Tanner Point E13 ... 1J 87
(off Pelly Rd.)
Tanners Cl. KT12: Walt T ... 6K 147
Tanners End La. N18 ... 4K 33
Tanner's Hill SE8 ... 1B 122
Tanners La. IG6: Ilf ... 3G 53
Tanner St. IG11: Bark ... 6G 71
SE1 ... 7H 15 (2E 102)
Tanners Yd. E2 ... 2H 85
(off Treadway St.)
Tannery, The SE1 ... 2E 102
(off Black Swan Yd.)
Tannery Cl. BR3: Beck ... 5K 157
RM10: Dag ... 3H 73
Tannery Ho. E1 ... 5G 85
(off Deal St.)
Tannington Ter. N5 ... 3B 66
Tannoy Sq. SE27 ... 4D 138
Tannsfeld Rd. SE26 ... 5K 139
Tansley Cl. N7 ... 5H 65
Tanswell St. SE1 ... 7J 13 (2A 102)
Tansy Cl. E6 ... 6E 88
Tantallon Rd. SW12 ... 1E 136
Tant Av. E16 ... 6H 87
Tantony Gro. RM6: Chad H ... 3D 54
Tanworth Gdns. HA5: Pinn ... 2K 39
Tanyard Ho. TW8: Bford ... 7C 96
(off High St.)
Tanyard La. DA5: Bexl ... 7G 127
Tanza Rd. NW3 ... 4D 64
Tapestry Cl. SM2: Sutt ... 7K 165
Tapley Ho. SE1 ... 7K 15
(off Wolseley St.)
Taplow NW3 ... 7B 64
SE17 ... 5D 102
(off Thurlow St.)
Taplow Ct. CR4: Mitc ... 4C 154
Taplow Ho. E2 ... 2J 9
(off Palissy St.)
Taplow Rd. N13 ... 4H 33
Taplow St. N1 ... 1D 8 (2C 84)
Tappesfield Rd. SE15 ... 3J 121
Tapping Cl. KT2: King T ... 7G 133
Tapp St. E1 ... 4H 85
Tapster St. EN5: Barn ... 3C 20
Tara Arts Cen. ... 1A 136
Tara Ct. BR3: Beck ... 2D 158
Tara Ho. E14 ... 4C 104
(off Deptford Ferry Rd.)
Tara M. N8 ... 6J 47
Taransay Wlk. N1 ... 6D 66
Taranto Ho. E1 ... 5K 85
(off Master's St.)
Tarbert M. N15 ... 5E 48
Tarbert Rd. SE22 ... 5E 120
Tarbert Wlk. E1 ... 7J 85
Target Cl. TW14: Felt ... 6G 111
Target Ho. W13 ... 1B 96
(off Sherwood Cl.)
TARGET RDBT. ... 1D 76
Tariff Cres. SE8 ... 4B 104
Tariff Rd. N17 ... 6B 34
Tarleton Ct. N22 ... 2A 48
Tarleton Gdns. SE23 ... 2H 139
Tarling Cl. DA14: Sidc ... 3B 144
Tarling Rd. E16 ... 6H 87
N2 ... 2A 46
Tarling St. E1 ... 6H 85
Tarling St. Est. E1 ... 6J 85
Tarmac Way UB7: Harm ... 3C 174
Tarnbank EN2: Enf ... 5D 22
Tarnbrook Ct. SW1 ... 4G 17
(off Whittaker St.)
Tarns, The NW1 ... 1A 6
(off Varndell St.)
Tarn St. SE1 ... 3C 102
Tarnwood Pk. SE9 ... 7D 124
Tarplett Ho. SE14 ... 6K 103
(off John Williams Cl.)
Tarquin Ho. SE26 ... 4G 139
(off High Level Dr.)
Tarragon Cl. SE14 ... 7A 104
Tarragon Ct. IG1: Ilf ... 2J 71
Tarragon Gro. SE26 ... 6K 139
Tarranbrae NW6 ... 7G 63
Tarrant Ho. E2 ... 3J 85
(off Roman Rd.)
W14 ... 3G 99
(off Russell Rd.)
Tarrant Pl. W1 ... 6E 4 (5D 82)
Tarrington Cl. SW16 ... 3H 137
Tartan Ho. E14 ... 6E 86
(off Dee St.)
Tarver Rd. SE17 ... 5B 102
Tarves Way SE10 ... 7D 104
(not continuous)
Tash Pl. N11 ... 5A 32
Tasker Cl. UB3: Harl ... 7E 92
Tasker Ho. E14 ... 5B 86
(off Wallwood St.)
IG11: Bark ... 2H 89
Tasker Lodge W8 ... 2J 99
(off Campden Hill)
Tasker Rd. NW3 ... 5D 64
Tasman Ct. E14 ... 4D 104
(off Westferry Rd.)
TW16: Sun ... 7G 129
Tasman Ho. E1 ... 1H 103
(off Clegg St.)
Tasmania Ter. N18 ... 6H 33
Tasman Rd. SW9 ... 3J 119
Tasman Wlk. E16 ... 6B 88
Tasso Rd. W6 ... 6G 99
Tasso Yd. W6 ... 6G 99
(off Tasso Rd.)
Tatam Rd. NW10 ... 7K 61
Tatchbury Ho. SW15 ... 6B 116
(off Tunworth Cres.)
Tate Britain ... 4E 18 (4J 101)

Tate Ho.—Temple Yd.

Tate Ho. *E2* 2K 85
(off Mace St.)
Tate Modern 4B 14 (1B 102)
Tate Rd. E16 .... 1D 106
(not continuous)
SM1: Sutt 5J 165
Tatham Pl. NW8 .... 2B 82
Tatnell Rd. SE23 .... 6A 122
Tatsfield Ho. *SE1* 7F 15
(off Pardoner St.)
Tattersall Cl. SE9 .... 5C 124
Tatton Cl. SM6: Wall 1E 166
Tatton Cres. N16 .... 7F 49
Tatum St. SE17 .... 4D 102
Tauheed Cl. N4 .... 2C 66
Taunton Av. SW20 .... 2D 152
TW3: Houn 2G 113
Taunton Cl. DA7: Bex 2K 127
SM3: Sutt 1J 165
Taunton Dr. EN2: Enf 3F 23
N2 .... 2A 46
Taunton Ho. *W2* 6A 82
(off Hallfield Est.)
Taunton M. NW1 .... 4E 4 (4D 82)
Taunton Pl. NW1 .... 3E 4 (4D 82)
Taunton Rd. SE12 .... 5G 123
UB6: G'frd 1F 77
Taunton Way HA7: Stan 2E 42
Tavern Cl. SM5: Cars 7C 154
Tavern Ct. *SE1* 3C 102
(off New Kent Rd.)
Taverners Cl. W11 .... 1G 99
Taverners Ct. *E3* 3A 86
(off Grove Rd.)
Taverner Sq. N5 .... 4C 66
Taverners Way E4 .... 1B 36
Tavern La. SW9 .... 2A 120
Tavern Quay SE16 .... 4A 104
Tavistock Av. E17 .... 3K 49
NW7 .... 7A 30
UB6: G'frd 2A 78
Tavistock Cl. N16 .... 5E 66
TW18: Staines 7A 128
Tavistock Ct. *CR0: C'don* 1D 168
(off Tavistock Rd.)
WC1 .... 3D 6
(off Tavistock Sq.)
WC2 .... 2F 13
(off Tavistock St.)
Tavistock Cres. CR4: Mitc 4J 155
W11 .... 5H 81
(not continuous)
Tavistock Gdns. IG3: Ilf 4J 71
Tavistock Ga. CR0: C'don 1D 168
Tavistock Gro. CR0: C'don 7D 156
Tavistock Ho. IG8: Wfd G 6K 37
WC1 .... 3D 6 (4H 83)
Tavistock M. *N19* 3J 65
(off Tavistock Ter.)
W11 .... 6H 81
Tavistock Pl. N14 .... 6A 22
WC1 .... 3E 6 (4J 83)
Tavistock Rd. BR2: Brom 4H 159
CR0: C'don 1D 168
DA16: Well 1C 126
E7 .... 4H 69
E15 .... 6H 69
E18 .... 3J 51
HA8: Edg 1G 43
N4 .... 6D 48
NW10 .... 2B 80
SM5: Cars 1B 166
UB7: Yiew 1A 92
UB10: Ick 5F 57
W11 .... 6H 81
(not continuous)
Tavistock Sq. WC1 .... 3D 6 (4H 83)
Tavistock St. WC2 .... 2F 13 (7J 83)
Tavistock Ter. N19 .... 3H 65
Tavistock Twr. SE16 .... 3A 104
Tavistock Wlk. SM5: Cars 1B 166
Taviton St. WC1 .... 3C 6 (4H 83)
Tavy Bri. SE2 .... 2C 108
Tavy Cl. SE11 .... 5K 19
Tawney Rd. SE28 .... 7B 90
Tawny Cl. TW13: Felt 3J 129
W13 .... 1B 96
Tawny Way SE16 .... 4K 103
Tayben Av. TW2: Twick 6J 113
Taybridge Rd. SW11 .... 3E 118
Tay Bldgs. SE1 .... 7G 15
Tayburn Cl. E14 .... 6E 86
Tay Ct. *E2* 3K 85
(off Meath Cres.)
SE1 .... 3E 102
(off Decima St.)
Tayfield Cl. UB10: Ick 3F 57
Tay Ho. *E3* 2B 86
(off St Stephen's Rd.)
Tayler Ct. NW8 .... 1B 82
Taylor Av. TW9: Kew 2H 115
Taylor Cl. BR6: Orp 4K 173
N17 .... 7B 34
SE8 .... 6B 104
TW3: Houn 1G 113
TW12: Ham H 5G 131
Taylor Ct. *SE20* 2J 157
(off Elmers End Rd.)
Taylor Ho. *E14* 7C 86
(off Storehouse M.)
Taylor Rd. CR4: Mitc 7C 136
SM6: Wall 5F 167
Taylors Bldgs. SE18 .... 4F 107
Taylors Cl. DA14: Sidc 3K 143
Taylors Ct. TW13: Felt 2J 129
Taylors Grn. W3 .... 6A 80
Taylors La. EN5: Barn 1C 20
SE26 .... 4H 139
Taylorsmead NW7 .... 5H 29
Taymount Grange SE23 .... 2J 139
Taymount Ri. SE23 .... 2J 139
Tayport Cl. N1 .... 7J 65
Tayside Ct. SE5 .... 4D 120
Tayside Dr. HA8: Edg 3C 28
Taywood Rd. UB5: N'olt 4D 76
Teak Cl. SE16 .... 1A 104
Tealby Ct. *N7* 5K 65
(off George's Rd.)
Teal Cl. E16 .... 5B 88
Teal Ct. *E1* 3K 15
(off Star Pl.)
NW10 .... 6K 61
SE8 .... 6B 104
(off Taylor Cl.)
SM6: Wall 5G 167
Teal Dr. HA6: Nwood 1E 38
Teale St. E2 .... 2G 85
Tealing Dr. KT19: Ewe 4K 163
Teal Pl. SM1: Sutt 5H 165
Teal St. SE10 .... 3H 105
Teamsport Karting 4E 34
Teasel Cl. CR0: C'don 1K 169
Teasel Cres. SE28 .... 1J 107
Teasel Way E15 .... 3G 87
Teather St. *SE5* 7E 102
(off Southampton Way)
Tea Trade Wharf *SE1* 6K 15
(off Shad Thames)
Tebworth Rd. N17 .... 7A 34
Technology Pk., The NW9 .... 3A 44
Teck Cl. TW7: Isle 2A 114
Tedder Cl. HA4: Ruis 5J 57
KT9: Chess 5C 162
UB10: Uxb 7B 56
Tedder Rd. CR2: Sels 7J 169
TEDDINGTON 5A 132
Teddington Bus. Pk.
TW11: Tedd 6K 131
(off Station Rd.)
Teddington Lock TW11: Tedd 4B 132
Teddington Pk. TW11: Tedd 5K 131
Teddington Pk. Rd. TW11: Tedd 4K 131
Teddington Pool & Fitness Cen. 5A 132
Teddington Sports Cen. 6D 132
Teddy Bear Mus. 6K 135
(within Polka Theatre for Children)
Ted Hennem Ho. RM10: Dag 3H 73
Ted Roberts Ho. *E2* 2H 85
(off Parmiter St.)
Tedworth Gdns. SW3 .... 6E 16 (5D 100)
Tedworth Sq. SW3 .... 6E 16 (5D 100)
Tee, The W3 .... 6A 80
Tees Av. UB6: G'frd 2J 77
Tees Ct. *W7* 6H 77
(off Hanway Rd.)
Teesdale Av. TW7: Isle 1A 114
Teesdale Cl. E2 .... 2G 85
Teesdale Gdns. SE25 .... 2E 156
TW7: Isle 1A 114
Teesdale Rd. E11 .... 6H 51
Teesdale St. E2 .... 2H 85
Teesdale Yd. *E2* 2H 85
(off Teesdale St.)
Teeswater Ct. DA18: Erith 3D 108
Teevan Cl. CR0: C'don 7G 157
Teevan Rd. CR0: C'don 1G 169
Teignmouth Cl. HA8: Edg 2F 43
SW4 .... 4H 119
Teignmouth Gdns. UB6: G'frd 2A 78
Teignmouth Pde. UB6: G'frd 2A 78
Teignmouth Rd. DA16: Well 2C 126
NW2 .... 5F 63
Telcote Way HA4: Ruis 7A 40
Telegraph Hill NW3 .... 3K 63
Telegraph La. KT10: Clay 4A 162
Telegraph M. IG3: Ilf 1A 72
Telegraph Pas. *SE1* 1A 102
(off New Pk. Rd.)
SW2 .... 7J 119
(off New Pk. Rd.)
Telegraph Path BR7: Chst 5F 143
Telegraph Pl. E14 .... 4D 104
Telegraph Quarters *SE10* 5F 105
(off Park Row)
Telegraph Rd. SW15 .... 7D 116
Telegraph St. EC2 .... 7E 8 (6D 84)
Telemann Sq. SE3 .... 4K 123
Telephone Pl. SW6 .... 6H 99
Telfer Cl. W3 .... 2J 97
Telfer Ho. EC1 .... 2B 8
Telferscot Rd. SW12 .... 1H 137
Telford Av. SW2 .... 1H 137
Telford Cl. E17 .... 7A 50
SE19 .... 6F 139
Telford Dr. KT12: Walt T 7A 148
Telford Ho. *SE1* 3C 102
(off Tiverton St.)
W10 .... 5G 81
(off Portobello Rd.)
Telford Rd. N11 .... 5B 32
NW9 .... 6C 44
SE9 .... 2H 143
TW2: Whitt 7E 112
UB1: S'hall 7F 77
W10 .... 5G 81
Telfords Yd. E1 .... 7G 85
Telford Ter. SW1 .... 7A 18 (6G 101)
Telford Way UB4: Yead 5C 76
W3 .... 5A 80
Telham Rd. E6 .... 2E 88
Tell Gro. SE22 .... 4F 121
Tellson Av. SE18 .... 1B 124
Telscombe Cl. BR6: Orp 2J 173
Temair Ho. *SE10* 7D 104
(off Tarves Way)
Temeraire Pl. TW8: Bford 5F 97
Temeraire St. SE16 .... 2J 103
Tempelhof Av. NW2 .... 7E 44
NW4 .... 7E 44
Temperley Rd. SW12 .... 7E 118
Templar Ct. NW8 .... 2A 4
RM7: Mawney 4H 55
Templar Dr. SE28 .... 6D 90
Templar Ho. HA2: Harr 2G 59
NW2 .... 6H 63
RM13: Rain 2K 91
Templar Pl. TW12: Hamp 7E 130
Templars Av. NW11 .... 6H 45
Templars Cres. N3 .... 2J 45
Templars Dr. HA3: Hrw W 6C 26
Templars Ho. *E16* 7F 89
(off University Way)
Templar St. SE5 .... 2B 120
Temple Av. CR0: C'don 2B 170
EC4 .... 2K 13 (7A 84)
N20 .... 7G 21
RM8: Dag 1G 73
Temple Bar 1J 13
Temple Bar Gate 1B 14
(off Paternoster Sq.)
Temple Chambers EC4 .... 2K 13
Temple Cl. E11 .... 7G 51
N3 .... 2H 45
SE28 .... 3G 107
Templecombe Rd. E9 .... 1J 85
Templecombe Way SM4: Mord 5G 153
Temple Ct. *E1* 5K 85
(off Rectory Sq.)
SW8 .... 7J 101
(off Thorncroft St.)
Templecroft TW15: Ashf 6F 129
Temple Dwellings *E2* 2H 85
(off Temple St.)
TEMPLE FORTUNE 5H 45
Temple Fortune Hill NW11 .... 5J 45
Temple Fortune La. NW11 .... 6H 45
Temple Fortune Pde. NW11 .... 5H 45
Temple Gdns. EC4 .... 2J 13
N21 .... 2G 33
NW11 .... 6H 45
RM8: Dag 3D 72
Temple Gro. EN2: Enf 2G 23
NW11 .... 6J 45
Temple Hall Ct. E4 .... 2A 36
Temple La. EC4 .... 1K 13 (6A 84)
Templeman Rd. W7 .... 5K 77
Temple Mead Cl.
HA7: Stan 6G 27
Templemead Cl. W3 .... 6A 80
Templemead Ho. E9 .... 4A 68
Temple Mill La. E10 .... 4D 68
E15 .... 4E 68
TEMPLE MILLS 4D 68
Temple of Mithras (remains) 1E 14
(off Queen Victoria St.)
Temple Pde. *EN5: New Bar* 7G 21
(off Netherlands Rd.)
Temple Pk. UB8: Hil 3C 74
Temple Pl. WC2 .... 2H 13 (7K 83)
Temple Rd. CR0: C'don 4D 168
E6 .... 1C 88
N8 .... 4K 47
NW2 .... 4E 62
TW3: Houn 4F 113
TW9: Rich 2F 115
W4 .... 3J 97
W5 .... 3D 96
Temple Sheen SW14 .... 4J 115
Temple Sheen Rd. SW14 .... 4H 115
Temple St. E2 .... 2H 85
Temple Ter. *N22* 2A 48
(off Vincent Rd.)
Templeton Av. E4 .... 4H 35
Templeton Cl. N15 .... 6D 48
N16 .... 5E 66
SE19 .... 1D 156
Templeton Ct. EN3: Enf W 1D 24
Templeton Pl. SW5 .... 4J 99
Templeton Rd. N4 .... 6D 48
Temple Way SM1: Sutt 3B 166
Temple West M. SE11 .... 3B 102
Templewood W13 .... 5B 78
Templewood Av. NW3 .... 3K 63
Templewood Gdns. NW3 .... 3K 63
Templewood Point *NW2* 2H 63
(off Granville Rd.)
Temple Yd. *E2* 2H 85
(off Temple St.)

Tempo Ho. UB5: N'olt 3B 76
Tempsford Cl. EN2: Enf 4H 23
Tempsford Cl. HA1: Harr 6K 41
Tempus Ct. E18 . . . . .1J 51
Tempus Wharf SE16 . . . . .2G 103
   (off Bermondsey Wall W.)
Temsford Cl. HA2: Harr 2G 41
Tenbury Cl. E7 . . . . .5B 70
Tenbury Ct. SW2 . . . . .1H 137
Tenby Av. HA3: Kenton 2B 42
Tenby Cl. N15 . . . . .4F 49
   RM6: Chad H 6E 54
Tenby Ct. E17 . . . . .5A 50
Tenby Gdns. UB5: N'olt 6E 58
Tenby Ho. UB3: Harl 3E 92
   W2 .6A 82
   (off Hallfield Est.)
Tenby Mans. W1 . . . . .5H 5
   (off Nottingham St.)
Tenby Rd. DA16: Well 1D 126
   E17 . . . . .5A 50
   EN3: Pond E 4D 24
   HA8: Edg 1F 43
   RM6: Chad H 6E 54
Tench St. E1 . . . . .1H 103
Tenda Rd. SE16 . . . . .4H 103
Tendring Way RM6: Chad H 5C 54
Tenham Av. SW2 . . . . .1H 137
Tenison Ct. W1 . . . . .2A 12 (7G 83)
Tenison Way SE1 . . . . .5J 13
   SE1 . . . . .1A 102
   (off York Rd.)
Tenniel Cl. W2 . . . . .7A 82
Tennis Cl. La. KT8: E Mos 3K 149
Tennison Rd. SE25 . . . . .4F 157
Tennis St. SE1 . . . . .6E 14 (2D 102)
Tenniswood Rd. EN1: Enf 1K 23
Tennyson N8 . . . . .3J 47
   (off Boyton Cl.)
Tennyson Av. E11 . . . . .7J 51
   E12 . . . . .7C 70
   KT3: N Mald 5D 152
   NW9 . . . . .3J 43
   TW1: Twick 1K 131
Tennyson Cl. DA16: Well 1J 125
   EN3: Pond E 5E 24
   TW14: Felt 6H 111
Tennyson Ct. SW6 . . . . .1A 118
   (off Imperial Rd.)
Tennyson Ho. DA17: Belv 5F 109
   SE17 . . . . .5C 102
   (off Browning St.)
Tennyson Mans. SW1 . . . . .5J 17
   (off Sutherland St.)
   SW3 . . . . .7C 16
   (off Lordship Pl.)
   W14 . . . . .6H 99
   (off Queen's Club Gdns.)
Tennyson Rd. E10 . . . . .1D 68
   E15 . . . . .7G 69
   E17 . . . . .6B 50
   NW6 . . . . .1H 81
   NW7 . . . . .5H 29
   SE20 . . . . .7K 139
   SW19 . . . . .6A 136
   TW3: Houn 2G 113
   TW15: Ashf 5A 128
   W7 .7K 77
Tennyson St. SW8 . . . . .2F 119
Tenpin
   Acton 4G 79
   Bexleyheath 4F 127
   Croydon 2K 167
   Feltham 2K 129
   Kingston upon Thames 2E 150
   (in The Rotunda Cen.)
Tensing Ct. TW19: Stanw 1A 128
Tensing Rd. UB2: S'hall 3E 94
Tentelow La. UB2: S'hall 5E 94
Tenterden Cl. NW4 . . . . .3F 45
   SE9 . . . . .4D 142
Tenterden Dr. NW4 . . . . .3F 45

Tenterden Gdns. CR0: C'don 7G 157
   NW4 . . . . .3F 45
Tenterden Gro. NW4 . . . . .3F 45
Tenterden Ho. SE17 . . . . .5E 102
   (off Surrey Gro.)
Tenterden Rd. CR0: C'don 7G 157
   N17 . . . . .7A 34
   RM8: Dag 2F 73
Tenterden St. W1 . . . . . .1K 11 (6F 83)
Tenter Ground E1 . . . . . . .6J 9 (5F 85)
Tenter Pas. E1 . . . . .1K 15
   (off Nth. Tenter St.)
Tent Peg La. BR5: Pet W 5G 161
Tent St. E1 . . . . .4H 85
Tequila Wharf E14 . . . . .6A 86
Tera 40 UB6: G'frd 7G 59
Terborch Way SE22 . . . . .5E 120
Teredo St. SE16 . . . . .3K 103
Terence Ct. DA17: Belv 6F 109
   (off Stream Way)
Terence McMillan Stadium 4A 88
Terence Messenger Twr. E10 . . . . .2D 68
   (off Alpine Rd.)
Teresa M. E17 . . . . .4C 50
Teresa Wlk. N10 . . . . .5F 47
Terling Cl. E11 . . . . .3H 69
Terling Ho. W10 . . . . .5E 80
   (off Sutton Way)
Terling Rd. RM8: Dag 2G 73
Terling Wlk. N1 . . . . .1C 84
   (off Popham St.)
Terminal 4 Rdbt. TW6: H'row A . . .6E 110
Terminal 5 Rdbt. TW6: H'row A . . .5C 174
Terminal Ho. HA7: Stan 5J 27
Terminus Pl. SW1 . . . . . .2K 17 (3F 101)
Terrace, The E2 . . . . .3J 85
   (off Old Ford Rd.)
   E4 .3B 36
   (off Newgate St.)
   EC4 . . . . .1K 13
   IG8: Wfd G 6D 36
   N3 .2H 45
   NW6 . . . . .1J 81
   SE8 . . . . .4B 104
   (off Longshore)
   SE23 . . . . .7A 122
   SW13 . . . . .2A 116
Terrace Apartments N5 . . . . .5A 66
Terrace Av. NW10 . . . . .4E 80
Terrace Gdns. SW13 . . . . .2B 116
Terrace Hill CR0: C'don 3B 168
   (off Hanover St.)
Terrace La. TW10: Rich 6E 114
Terrace Rd. E9 . . . . .7J 67
   E13 . . . . .2J 87
   KT12: Walt T 7J 147
Terraces, The NW8 . . . . .2B 82
   (off Queen's Ter.)
Terrace Wlk. RM9: Dag 5E 72
   SW11 . . . . .7H 17 (6E 100)
Terrano Ho. TW9: Kew 7H 97
Terrapin Rd. SW17 . . . . .3F 137
Terretts Pl. N1 . . . . .7B 66
   (off Upper St.)
Terrick Rd. N22 . . . . .1J 47
Terrick St. W12 . . . . .6D 80
Terrilands HA5: Pinn 3D 40
Territorial Ho. SE11 . . . . .4K 19
Terront Rd. N15 . . . . .4C 48
Tersha St. TW9: Rich 4F 115
Tessa Sanderson Pl. SW8 . . . . . . .3F 119
   (off Daley Thompson Way)
Tessa Sanderson Way UB6: G'frd .5H 59
Testerton Rd. W11 . . . . .7F 81
   (off Hurstway Rd.)
Testerton Wlk. W11 . . . . .7F 81
Testwood Ct. W7 . . . . .7J 77
Tetbury Pl. N1 . . . . .1B 84
Tetcott Rd. SW10 . . . . .7A 100
   (not continuous)
Tetherdown N10 . . . . .3E 46
Tetty Way BR1: Brom 2J 159

Tevatree Ho. SE1 . . . . .5G 103
   (off Avondale Sq.)
Teversham La. SW8 . . . . .1J 119
Teviot Cl. DA16: Well 1B 126
Teviot Est. E14 . . . . .5D 86
Teviot St. E14 . . . . .5E 86
Tewkesbury Av. HA5: Pinn 5C 40
   SE23 . . . . .1H 139
Tewkesbury Cl. EN4: E Barn 4G 21
   N15 . . . . .6D 48
Tewkesbury Gdns. NW9 . . . . .3H 43
Tewkesbury Rd. N15 . . . . .6D 48
   SM5: Cars 1B 166
   W13 . . . . .1A 96
Tewkesbury Ter. N11 . . . . .6B 32
Tewson Rd. SE18 . . . . .5J 107
Teynham Av. EN1: Enf 6J 23
Teynham Ct. BR3: Beck 3D 158
Teynham Grn. BR2: Brom 5J 159
Teynton Ter. N17 . . . . .1C 48
Thackeray Av. N17 . . . . .2G 49
Thackeray Cl. SW19 . . . . .7F 135
   TW7: Isle 2A 114
   UB8: Hil 6D 74
Thackeray Ct. NW6 . . . . .7A 64
   (off Fairfax Rd.)
   SW3 . . . . .5E 16
   (off Elystan Pl.)
   W5 .6F 79
   (off Hanger Va. La.)
   W14 . . . . .3G 99
   (off Blythe Rd.)
Thackeray Dr. RM6: Chad H 7A 54
Thackeray Ho. WC1 . . . . .3E 6
Thackeray Lodge TW14: Bedf 6F 111
Thackeray M. E8 . . . . .6G 67
Thackeray Rd. E6 . . . . .2B 88
   SW8 . . . . .2F 119
Thackeray St. W8 . . . . .3K 99
Thackery Ct. EC1 . . . . .5A 8
   (off Turnmill St.)
Thackrah Cl. N2 . . . . .2A 46
   (off Simms Gdns.)
Thakeham Cl. SE26 . . . . .4H 139
Thalia Cl. SE10 . . . . .6F 105
Thalia Ct. E8 . . . . .7F 67
   (off Albion Dr.)
Thame Rd. SE16 . . . . .2K 103
Thames Av. KT4: Wor Pk 1E 164
   RM9: Dag, Rain 4H 91
   SW10 . . . . .1A 118
   UB6: G'frd 2K 77
Thames Bank SW14 . . . . .2J 115
Thamesbank Pl. SE28 . . . . .6C 90
Thames Barrier Ind. Area SE18 . . .3B 106
   (off Faraday Way)
Thames Barrier Info. Cen. 3B 106
Thames Barrier Pk. 2A 106
Thamesbrook SW3 . . . . .6C 16
Thames Circ. E14 . . . . .4C 104
Thames Cl. TW12: Hamp 2F 149
Thames Cotts. KT7: T Ditt 6B 150
Thames Ct. KT8: W Mole 2F 149
   SE15 . . . . .7F 103
   (off Daniel Gdns.)
   W7 .6J 77
   (off Hanway Rd.)
Thames Cres. W4 . . . . .7A 98
THAMES DITTON 6A 150
Thames Ditton Miniature Railway . .1A 162
Thames Dr. HA4: Ruis 8E 38
Thames Exchange Bldg. EC4 . . . . .3D 14
Thames Eyot TW1: Twick 1A 132
Thamesfield Ct. TW17: Shep 7E 146
Thamesfield M. TW17: Shep 7E 145
Thamesgate Cl. TW10: Ham 4B 132
Thames Gateway RM9: Dag 2F 91
   RM13: Avel, Rain, Wenn 2F 91
Thames Gateway Pk. RM9: Dag . . .3F 91
Thames Haven KT6: Surb 5D 150
Thames Hgts. SE1 . . . . .6J 15
   (off Gainsford St.)

Thameshill Av. RM5: Col R 2J 55
Thames Ho. EC4 . . . . .2D 14
   (off Queen St. Pl.)
   KT1: King T 4D 150
   (off Surbiton Rd.)
   SW1 . . . . .3E 18
   (off Millbank)
Thameside KT8: W Mole 3F 149
   TW11: Tedd 7D 132
Thameside Ind. Est. E16 . . . . .2B 106
Thameside Pk. KT1: Ham W 1D 150
Thameside Wlk. SE28 . . . . .6A 90
Thames Innovation Cen.
   DA18: Erith 2F 109
Thames Lock KT12: Walt T 3A 148
THAMESMEAD 1B 108
Thamesmead KT12: Walt T 6J 147
THAMESMEAD CENTRAL 1A 108
THAMESMEAD EAST 2G 109
THAMESMEAD NORTH 6D 90
Thames Mdw. KT8: W Mole 2E 148
   TW17: Shep 7F 147
THAMESMEAD SOUTH 2D 108
THAMESMEAD SOUTH EAST 2K 107
THAMESMEAD SOUTH WEST 2K 107
THAMESMEAD WEST 3G 107
Thamesmere Dr. SE28 . . . . .7A 90
Thamesmere Leisure Cen. 7A 90
Thames Path SW15 . . . . .1G 105
Thames Pl. SW15 . . . . .3F 117
   (not continuous)
Thames Point SW6 . . . . .2A 118
Thamespoint TW11: Tedd 7D 132
Thames Quay E14 . . . . .2D 104
   SW10 . . . . .1A 118
   (off Chelsea Harbour)
Thames Reach SE28 . . . . .2J 107
   W6 .6E 98
   (off Rainville Rd.)
Thames Rd. E16 . . . . .1B 106
   IG11: Bark 3K 89
   W4 .6G 97
Thames Rd. Ind. Est. E16 . . . . . . .2B 106
Thames Side KT1: King T 1D 150
   KT7: T Ditt 6B 150
Thames St. KT1: King T 2D 150
   (not continuous)
   KT12: Walt T 7H 147
   SE10 . . . . .6D 104
   TW12: Hamp 1F 149
   TW16: Sun 4J 147
Thames Tunnel Mills SE16 . . . . . . .2J 103
Thamesvale Cl. TW3: Houn 3E 112
Thames Valley University,
   Ealing Campus -
     Grove House 1D 96
     Spesom House 7C 78
     St Marys Road 1D 96
     Vestry Hall 2D 96
     (off Ranelagh Rd.)
     Walpole House 7D 78
     Paragon Campus 5C 96
     (off Boston Mnr. Rd.)
Thamesview Bus. Cen. RM13: Rain . .5K 91
Thamesview Ho's. KT12: Walt T . . .6J 147
Thames Vw. Lodge IG11: Bark 3J 89
Thames Village W4 . . . . .1J 115
Thames Wlk. KT12: Walt T 7J 147
   (off Mnr. Rd.)
   SW11 . . . . .7C 100
Thames Wharf Studios W6 . . . . . . .6E 98
   (off Rainville Rd.)
Thanescroft Gdns. CR0: C'don 3E 168
Thanet Cl. W3 . . . . .6G 79
Thanet Dr. BR2: Kes 3B 172
Thanet Ho. CR0: C'don 4C 168
   (off Coombe Rd.)
   WC1 . . . . .2E 6
   (off Thanet St.)
Thanet Lodge NW2 . . . . .6G 63
   (off Mapesbury Rd.)
Thanet Pl. CR0: C'don 4C 168

Thanet Rd.—Thorn Ter.

Thanet Rd. DA5: Bexl 7G **127**
Thanet St. WC1 . . . . .2E **6** (3J **83**)
Thanet Wharf *SE8* *6D* ***104***
(off Copperas St.)
Thane Vs. N7 . . . . .3K **65**
Thane Works N7 . . . . .3K **65**
Thanington Ct. SE9 . . . . .6J **125**
Thant Cl. E10 . . . . .3D **68**
Tharp Rd. SM6: Wall 5H **167**
Thatcham Ct. N20 . . . . .7F **21**
Thatcham Gdns. N20 . . . . .7F **21**
Thatcher Cl. UB7: W Dray 2A **92**
Thatchers Way TW7: Isle 5H **113**
Thatches Gro. RM6: Chad H 4E **54**
Thavie's Inn EC4 . . . . .7K **7** (6A **84**)
Thaxted Ct. *N1* *1F* ***9***
(off Murray Gro.)
Thaxted Ho. RM10: Dag 7H **73**
SE16 . . . .*4J* ***103***
(off Abbeyfield Est.)
Thaxted Pl. SW20 . . . . .7F **135**
Thaxted Rd. IG9: Buck H 1H **37**
SE9 . . . . .3G **143**
Thaxton Rd. W14 . . . . .6H **99**
Thayers Farm Rd. BR3: Beck 1A **158**
Thayer St. W1 . . . . .6H **5** (6E **82**)
The . . . .
Names prefixed with 'The'
for example 'The Acacias'
are indexed under the main
name such as 'Acacias, The'
Theatre Bldg. *E3* *3C* ***86***
(off Paton Cl.)
Theatrerites **2K 135**
Theatre Royal
Stratford **7F 69**
Theatre Sq. E15 . . . . .6F **69**
Theatre St. SW11 . . . . .3D **118**
Theatre Vw. Apartments *SE1* *2B* ***102***
(off Short St.)
Theatro Technis ***1G 83***
(off Crowndale Rd.)
Theatro Twr. SE8 . . . . .6C **104**
Theberton St. N1 . . . . .1A **84**
Theed St. SE1 . . . . .5K **13** (1A **102**)
Thelbridge Ho. *E3* *3D* ***86***
(off Bruce Rd.)
Thelma Gdns. SE3 . . . . .1B **124**
Thelma Gro. TW11: Tedd 6A **132**
Theobald Cres. HA3: Hrw W 1G **41**
Theobald Rd. CR0: C'don 2B **168**
E17 . . . . .7B **50**
Theobalds Av. N12 . . . . .4F **31**
Theobalds Ct. N4 . . . . .3C **66**
Theobald's Rd. WC1 . . . . .5G **7** (5K **83**)
Theobald St. SE1 . . . . .3D **102**
Theodora Way HA5: Eastc 3H **39**
Theodore Ct. SE13 . . . . .6F **123**
Theodore Rd. SE13 . . . . .6F **123**
Therapia La. CR0: Bedd 7H **155**
CR0: C'don 6J **155**
Therapia Rd. SE22 . . . . .6J **121**
Theresa Rd. W6 . . . . .4C **98**
Therfield Ct. N4 . . . . .2C **66**
Thermopylae Ga. E14 . . . . .4D **104**
Theseus Wlk. N1 . . . . .1B **8**
Thesiger Rd. SE20 . . . . .7K **139**
Thessaly Ho. *SW8* *7G* ***101***
(off Thessaly Rd.)
Thessaly Rd. SW8 . . . . .7G **101**
(not continuous)
Thesus Ho. *E14* *6E* ***86***
(off Blair St.)
Thetford Cl. N13 . . . . .6G **33**
Thetford Gdns. RM9: Dag 7E **72**
Thetford Ho. *SE1* *7J* ***15***
(off St Saviour's Est.)
Thetford Rd. KT3: N Mald 6K **151**
RM9: Dag 7D **72**
TW15: Ashf 4A **128**
Thetis Ter. TW9: Kew 6G **97**
Theydon Gro. IG8: Wfd G 6F **37**
Theydon Rd. E5 . . . . .2J **67**
Theydon St. E17 . . . . .7B **50**
Thicket, The UB7: Yiew 6A **74**
Thicket Cres. SM1: Sutt 4A **166**
Thicket Gro. RM9: Dag 6C **72**
SE20 . . . . .7G **139**
Thicket Rd. SE20 . . . . .7G **139**
SM1: Sutt 4A **166**
Third Av. E12 . . . . .4C **70**
E13 . . . . .3J **87**
E17 . . . . .5C **50**
EN1: Enf 5A **24**
HA9: Wemb 2D **60**
RM6: Chad H 6C **54**
RM10: Dag 1H **91**
UB3: Hayes 1H **93**
W3 . . . . .1B **98**
W10 . . . . .3G **81**
Third Cl. KT8: W Mole 4G **149**
Third Cross Rd. TW2: Twick 2H **131**
Third Way HA9: Wemb 4H **61**
Thirleby Rd. HA8: Edg 1K **43**
SW1 . . . . .2B **18** (3G **101**)
Thirlestane Ct. N10 . . . . .2E **46**
Thirlmere *NW1* *1K* ***5***
(off Cumberland Mkt.)
Thirlmere Av. UB6: G'frd 3C **78**
Thirlmere Gdns. HA9: Wemb 1C **60**
Thirlmere Ho. *N16* *4D* ***66***
(off Howard Rd.)
TW7: Isle 5K **113**
Thirlmere Ri. BR1: Brom 6H **141**
Thirlmere Rd. DA7: Bex 1J **127**
N10 . . . . .1F **47**
SW16 .4H **137**
Thirsk Cl. UB5: N'olt 6E **58**
Thirsk Rd. CR4: Mitc 7E **136**
SE25 . . . . .4D **156**
SW11 . . . . .3E **118**
Thirza Ho. *E1* *6J* ***85***
(off Devonport St.)
Thistlebrook SE2 . . . . .3C **108**
Thistlebrook Ind. Est. SE2 . . . . .3C **108**
Thistlecroft Gdns. HA7: Stan 1D **42**
Thistledene KT7: T Ditt 6J **149**
Thistledene Av. HA2: Harr 3C **58**
Thistlefield Cl. DA5: Bexl 1D **144**
Thistle Gro. SW10 . . . . .6A **16** (5A **100**)
Thistle Ho. *E14* *6E* ***86***
(off Dee St.)
Thistlemead BR7: Chst 2F **161**
Thistlewaite Rd. E5 . . . . .3H **67**
Thistlewood Cl. N7 . . . . .2K **65**
Thistleworth Cl. TW7: Isle 7H **95**
Thistleworth Marina *TW7: Isle* *4B* ***114***
(off Railshead Rd.)
Thistley Cl. N12 . . . . .6H **31**
Thistley Ct. SE8 . . . . .6D **104**
Thomas A Beckett Cl. HA0: Wemb 4K **59**
Thomas Baines Rd. SW11 . . . . .3B **118**
Thomas Burt Ho. *E2* *3H* ***85***
(off Canrobert St.)
Thomas Cribb M. E6 . . . . .6E **88**
Thomas Darby Ct. *W11* *6G* ***81***
(off Lancaster Rd.)
Thomas Dean Rd. SE26 . . . . .4B **140**
Thomas Dinwiddy Rd. SE12 . . . . .2K **141**
Thomas Doyle St. SE1 . . . . . .7A **14** (3B **102**)
Thomas England Ho. *RM7: Rom* *6K* ***55***
(off Waterloo Gdns.)
Thomas Frye Ct. *E15* *2D* ***86***
(off High St.)
Thomas Fyre Dr. E3 . . . . .2C **86**
Thomas Hardy Ho. N22 . . . . .7E **32**
Thomas Hewlett Ho. HA1: Harr 4J **59**
Thomas Hollywood Ho. *E2* *2J* ***85***
(off Approach Rd.)
Thomas Ho. SM2: Sutt 7K **165**
Thomas Jacomb Pl. E17 . . . . .4B **50**
Thomas Joseph Ho. *SE4* *5K* ***121***
(off St Norbert Rd.)
Thomas La. SE6 . . . . .7C **122**
Thomas Lodge E17 . . . . .5D **50**
Thomas More Highwalk *EC2* *6C* ***8***
(off Aldersgate St.)
Thomas More Ho. EC2 . . . . .6C **8**
HA4: Ruis 1G **57**
Thomas More Sq. E1 . . . . .7G **85**
Thomas More St. E1 . . . . .7G **85**
Thomas More Way N2 . . . . .3A **46**
Thomas Neal's Cen. WC2 . . . . .1E **12** (6J **83**)
Thomas Nth. Ter. *E16* *5H* ***87***
(off Barking Rd.)
Thomas Pl. W8 . . . . .3K **99**
Thomas Rd. E14 . . . . .6B **86**
Thomas Rd. Ind. Est. E14 . . . . .5C **86**
Thomas Spencer Hall of Residence
SE18 . . . .*4E* ***106***
(off Depot Rd.)
Thomas St. SE18 . . . . .4F **107**
Thomas Turner Path *CR0: C'don* *2C* ***168***
(off George St.)
Thomas Wall Cl. SM1: Sutt 5K **165**
Thomas Watson Cott. Homes
EN5: Barn *4B* ***20***
(off Leecroft Rd.)
Thompson Av. TW9: Rich 3G **115**
Thompson Cl. IG1: Ilf 2G **71**
SM3: Sutt 1J **165**
Thompson Ho. *SE14* *6K* ***103***
(off John Williams Cl.)
W10 . . . .*4G* ***81***
(off Wornington Rd.)
Thompson Rd. RM9: Dag 3F **73**
SE22 . . . . .6F **121**
TW3: Houn 4F **113**
UB10: Uxb 1A **74**
Thompson's Av. SE5 . . . . .7C **102**
Thomson Cres. CR0: C'don 1A **168**
Thomson Ho. *E14* *6C* ***86***
(off Saracen St.)
SE17 . . . .*4E* ***102***
(off Tatum St.)
SW1 . . . . .6D **18**
UB1: S'hall *7C* ***76***
(off The Broadway)
Thomson Rd. HA3: W'stone 3J **41**
Thorburn Ho. *SW1* *7F* ***11***
(off Kinnerton St.)
Thorburn Sq. SE1 . . . . .4G **103**
Thorburn Way SW19 . . . . .1B **154**
Thoresby St. N1 . . . . .1D **8** (3C **84**)
Thorkhill Gdns. KT7: T Ditt 1A **162**
Thorkhill Rd. KT7: T Ditt 1A **162**
Thornaby Gdns. N18 . . . . .6B **34**
Thornaby Ho. *E2* *3H* ***85***
(off Canrobert St.)
Thorn Av. WD23: B Hea 1B **26**
Thornbill Ho. *SE15* *7G* ***103***
(off Bird in Bush Rd.)
Thornbury *NW4* *4D* ***44***
(off Prince of Wales Cl.)
Thornbury Av. TW7: Isle 7H **95**
Thornbury Cl. N16 . . . . .5E **66**
NW7 . . . . .7A **30**
Thornbury Ct. *CR2: S Croy* *5D* ***168***
(off Blunt Rd.)
TW7: Isle 7J **95**
W11 . . . .*7J* ***81***
(off Chepstow Vs.)
Thornbury Lodge EN2: Enf 3G **23**
Thornbury Rd. SW2 . . . . .6J **119**
TW7: Isle 7H **95**
Thornbury Sq. N6 . . . . .1G **65**
Thornby Rd. E5 . . . . .3J **67**
Thorncliffe Rd. SW2 . . . . .6J **119**
UB2: S'hall 5D **94**
Thorn Cl. BR2: Brom 6E **160**
UB5: N'olt 3D **76**
Thorncombe Rd. SE22 . . . . .5E **120**
Thorncroft Rd. SM1: Sutt 5K **165**
Thorncroft St. SW8 . . . . .7J **101**
Thorndean St. SW18 . . . . .2A **136**
Thorndene SE28 . . . . .7B **90**
Thorndene Av. N11 . . . . .1K **31**
Thorndike Av. UB5: N'olt 1B **76**
Thorndike Cl. SW10 . . . . .7A **100**
Thorndike Ho. *SW1* *5C* ***18***
(off Vauxhall Bri. Rd.)
Thorndike Rd. N1 . . . . .6D **66**
Thorndike St. SW1 . . . . .4C **18** (4H **101**)
Thorndon Cl. BR5: St P 2K **161**
Thorndon Gdns. KT19: Ewe 5A **164**
Thorndon Rd. BR5: St P 2K **161**
Thorne Cl. DA8: Erith 6H **109**
E11 . . . . .4F **69**
E16 . . . . .6J **87**
KT10: Clay 7A **162**
TW15: Ashf 7E **128**
Thorne Ho. *E2* *3J* ***85***
(off Roman Rd.)
E14 . . . .*3E* ***104***
(off Launch St.)
Thorneloe Gdns. CR0: Wadd 5A **168**
Thorne Pas. SW13 . . . . .2A **116**
Thorne Rd. SW8 . . . . .7J **101**
Thornes Cl. BR3: Beck 3E **158**
Thorne St. SW13 . . . . .3A **116**
Thornet Wood Rd. BR1: Brom 3E **160**
Thornewill Ho. *E1* *7J* ***85***
(off Cable St.)
Thorney Ct. *W8* *2A* ***100***
(off Palace Ga.)
Thorney Cres. SW11 . . . . .7B **100**
Thorneycroft Cl. KT12: Walt T 6A **148**
Thorney Hedge Rd. W4 . . . . .4H **97**
Thorney St. SW1 . . . . .3E **18** (4J **101**)
Thornfield Av. NW7 . . . . .1G **45**
Thornfield Ct. NW7 . . . . .1G **45**
Thornfield Ho. *E14* *7C* ***86***
(off Rosefield Gdns.)
Thornfield Pde. *NW7* *7B* ***30***
(off Holders Hill Rd.)
Thornfield Rd. W12 . . . . .2D **98**
(not continuous)
Thornford Rd. SE13 . . . . .5E **122**
Thorngate Rd. W9 . . . . .4J **81**
Thorngrove Rd. E13 . . . . .1K **87**
Thornham Gro. E15 . . . . .5F **69**
Thornham Ind. Est. E15 . . . . .5F **69**
Thornham St. SE10 . . . . .6D **104**
Thornhaugh M. WC1 . . . . .4D **6** (4H **83**)
Thornhaugh St. WC1 . . . . .4D **6** (4H **83**)
Thornhill Av. KT6: Surb 2E **162**
SE18 . . . . .7J **107**
Thornhill Bri. *N1* *2K* ***83***
(off Caledonian Rd.)
Thornhill Bri. Wharf N1 . . . . .1K **83**
Thornhill Cres. N1 . . . . .7K **65**
Thornhill Gdns. E10 . . . . .2D **68**
IG11: Bark 7J **71**
Thornhill Gro. N1 . . . . .7K **65**
Thornhill Ho. *W4* *5A* ***98***
(off Wood St.)
Thornhill Ho's. N1 . . . . .7A **66**
Thornhill M. SW15 . . . . .4H **117**
Thornhill Rd. CR0: C'don 7C **156**
E10 . . . . .2D **68**
KT6: Surb 2E **162**
N1 . . . . .7A **66**
UB10: Ick 4B **56**
Thornhill Sq. N1 . . . . .7K **65**
Thornhill Way TW17: Shep 5C **146**
Thornicroft Ho. *SW9* *2K* ***119***
(off Stockwell Rd.)
Thornlaw Rd. SE27 . . . . .4A **138**
Thornley Cl. N17 . . . . .7B **34**
Thornley Dr. HA2: Harr 2F **59**
Thornley Pl. SE10 . . . . .5G **105**
Thornsbeach Rd. SE6 . . . . .1E **140**
Thornsett Pl. SE20 . . . . .2H **157**
Thornsett Rd. SE20 . . . . .2H **157**
SW18 .1K **135**
Thornsett Ter. *SE20* *2H* ***157***
(off Croydon Rd.)
Thorn Ter. SE15 . . . . .3J **121**

Thornton Av. CR0: C'don 6K **155**
SW2 1H **137**
UB7: W Dray 3B **92**
W4 4A **98**
Thornton Cl. UB7: W Dray 3B **92**
Thornton Dene BR3: Beck 2C **158**
Thornton Gdns. SW12 1H **137**
Thornton Health Leisure Cen. 4C **156**
THORNTON HEATH 4C **156**
THORNTON HEATH POND **5A 156**
Thornton Hill SW19 7G **135**
Thornton Ho. *SE17 4E **102***
(off Townsend St.)
Thornton Pl. W1 5F **5** (5D **82**)
Thornton Rd. BR1: Brom 5J **141**
CR0: C'don 7K **155**
CR7: Thor H 7K **155**
DA17: Belv 4H **109**
E11 2F **69**
EN5: Barn 3B **20**
IG1: Ilf 4F **71**
N18 3D **34**
SM5: Cars 1B **166**
SW12 7H **119**
SW14 4K **115**
SW19 6F **135**
Thornton Rd. E. SW19 6F **135**
Thornton Rd. Ind. Est. CR0: C'don 6K **155**
Thornton Row CR7: Thor H 5A **156**
Thornton's Farm Av. RM7: Rush G 1J **73**
Thornton St. SW9 2A **120**
Thornton Way NW11 5K **45**
Thorntree Ct. W5 5E **78**
Thorntree Rd. SE7 5B **106**
Thornville Gro. CR4: Mitc 2B **154**
Thornville St. SE8 1C **122**
Thornwell Ct. *W7 2J **95***
(off Lwr. Boston Rd.)
Thornwood Cl. E18 2K **51**
Thornwood Gdns. W8 2J **99**
Thornwood Ho. IG9: Buck H 1H **37**
Thornwood Lodge *W8 2J **99***
(off Thornwood Gdns.)
Thornwood Rd. SE13 5G **123**
Thornycroft Ho. *W4 5A **98***
(off Fraser St.)
Thorogood Gdns. E15 5G **69**
Thorogood Way RM13: Rain 1K **91**
Thorold Ho. *SE1 6C **14***
(off Pepper St.)
Thorold Rd. IG1: Ilf 2F **71**
N22 7D **32**
Thorparch Rd. SW8 1H **119**
Thorpebank Rd. W12 1C **98**
Thorpe Cl. BR6: Orp 2J **173**
SE26 4K **139**
W10 6G **81**
Thorpe Ct. EN2: Enf 3G **23**
Thorpe Cres. E17 2B **50**
Thorpedale Gdns. IG2: Ilf 4E **52**
IG6: Ilf 4E **52**
Thorpedale Rd. N4 2J **65**
Thorpe Hall Rd. E17 1E **50**
Thorpe Ho. *N1 1K **83***
(off Barnsbury Est.)
Thorpe Rd. E6 1D **88**
E7 4H **69**
E17 2E **50**
IG11: Bark 7H **71**
KT2: King T 7E **132**
N15 6E **48**
Thorpewood Av. SE26 2H **139**
Thorpland Av. UB10: Ick 3E **56**
Thorsden Way SE19 5E **138**
Thorverton Rd. NW2 3G **63**
Thoydon Rd. E3 2A **86**
Thrale Rd. SW16 4G **137**
Thrale St. SE1 5D **14** (1C **102**)
Thrasher Cl. E8 1F **85**
Thrawl St. E1 6K **9** (5F **85**)
Thrayle Ho. *SW9 3K **119***
(off Benedict Rd.)

Threadgold Ho. *N1 6D **66***
(off Dovercourt Est.)
Threadneedle St. EC2 1F **15** (6D **84**)
Threadneedle Wlk. EC2 1F **15**
Three Barrels Wlk. *EC4 3D **14***
(off Queenhithe)
Three Bridges Bus. Cen. UB2: S'hall 2G **95**
Three Bridges Path *KT1: King T 3E **150***
(off Bellvue Rd.)
Three Colt Cnr. E2 3K **9**
Three Colts La. E2 4H **85**
Three Colt St. E14 6B **86**
Three Corners DA7: Bex 2H **127**
Three Cranes Wlk. EC4 3D **14**
Three Cups Yd. WC1 6H **7**
Three Kings Yd. W1 2J **11** (7F **83**)
Three Mdws. M. HA3: Hrw W 1K **41**
Three Mill La. E3 3E **86**
(not continuous)
Three Mills Studios E3 3E **86**
Three Nun Ct. *EC2 7D **8***
(off Aldermanbury)
Three Oak La. SE1 6J **15** (2F **103**)
Three Oaks Cl. UB10: Ick 3B **56**
Three Quays EC3 3H **15**
Three Quays Wlk.
EC3 3H **15** (7E **84**)
Threshers Pl. W11 7G **81**
Thriffwood SE26 3J **139**
Thrigby Rd. KT9: Chess 6F **163**
Thring Ho. *SW9 2K **119***
(off Stockwell Rd.)
Throckmorten Rd. E16 6K **87**
Throgmorton Av. EC2 7F **9** (6D **84**)
(not continuous)
Throgmorton St. EC2 7F **9** (6D **84**)
Throwley Cl. SE2 3C **108**
(not continuous)
Throwley Rd. SM1: Sutt 5K **165**
Throwley Way SM1: Sutt 4K **165**
Thrupp Cl. CR4: Mitc 2F **155**
Thrush Grn. HA2: Harr 4E **40**
Thrush St. SE17 5C **102**
Thurbarn Rd. SE6 5D **140**
Thurland Ho. *SE16 4H **103***
(off Camilla Rd.)
Thurland Rd. SE16 3G **103**
Thurlby Cl. HA1: Harr 6A **42**
IG8: Wfd G 5J **37**
Thurlby Cft. *NW4 3E **44***
(off Mulberry Cl.)
Thurlby Rd. HA0: Wemb 6D **60**
SE27 4A **138**
Thurleigh Av. SW12 6E **118**
Thurleigh Ct. SW12 6E **118**
Thurleigh Rd. SW12 7D **118**
Thurleston Av. SM4: Mord 5G **153**
Thurlestone Av. IG3: Bark, Ilf 4K **71**
N12 6J **31**
Thurlestone Cl. TW17: Shep 6E **146**
Thurlestone Ct. *UB1: S'hall 6F **77***
(off Howard Rd.)
Thurlestone Pde. *TW17: Shep 6E **146***
(off High St.)
Thurlestone Rd. SE27 3A **138**
Thurloe Cl. SW7 3C **16** (4C **100**)
Thurloe Ct. *SW3 4C **16***
(off Fulham Ct.)
Thurloe Pl. SW7 3B **16** (4B **100**)
Thurloe Pl. M. SW7 3B **16**
Thurloe Sq. SW7 3C **16** (4C **100**)
Thurloe St. SW7 3B **16** (4B **100**)
Thurlow Cl. E4 6K **35**
Thurlow Gdns. HA0: Wemb 5D **60**
Thurlow Hill SE21 1C **138**
Thurlow Ho. SW16 3J **137**
Thurlow Pk. Rd. SE21 2B **138**
Thurlow Rd. NW3 5B **64**
W7 2A **96**
Thurlow St. SE17 5D **102**
(not continuous)
Thurlow Ter. NW5 5E **64**

Thurlow Wlk. SE17 5E **102**
(not continuous)
Thurlstone Rd. HA4: Ruis 3J **57**
Thurnby Ct. TW2: Twick 3J **131**
Thurnscoe *NW1 1G **83***
(off Pratt St.)
Thursland Rd. DA14: Sidc 5E **144**
Thursley Cres. CR0: New Ad 7E **170**
Thursley Gdns. SW19 2F **135**
Thursley Ho. *SW2 7K **119***
(off Holmewood Gdns.)
Thursley Rd. SE9 3D **142**
Thurso Ho. NW6 2K **81**
Thurso St. SW17 4B **136**
Thurstan Dwellings *WC2 7F **7***
(off Newton St.)
Thurstan Rd. SW20 7D **134**
Thurston Ho. BR3: Beck 6D **140**
*N1 1K **83***
(off Carnegie St.)
Thurston Ind. Est. SE13 3D **122**
Thurston Rd. SE13 2D **122**
UB1: S'hall 6D **76**
Thurtle Rd. E2 1F **85**
Thwaite Cl. DA8: Erith 6J **109**
Thyer Cl. BR6: Farnb 4G **173**
Thyme Cl. SE3 3A **124**
Thyme Ct. NW7 1G **45**
Thyra Gro. N12 6E **30**
Tibbatt's Rd. E3 4D **86**
Tibbenham Pl. SE6 2C **140**
Tibbenham Wlk. E13 2H **87**
Tibberton Sq. N1 1C **84**
Tibbet's Cl. SW19 1F **135**
TIBBET'S CORNER **7F 117**
Tibbet's Ride SW15 7F **117**
Tiber Cl. E3 1C **86**
Tiber Gdns. N1 1J **83**
Ticehurst Cl. BR5: St P 7A **144**
Ticehurst Rd. SE23 2A **140**
Tickford Cl. SE2 2C **108**
Tickford Ho. NW8 2C **4** (3C **82**)
Tidal Basin Rd. E16 7H **87**
(not continuous)
Tidbury Ct. *SW8 7G **101***
(off Stewart's Rd.)
Tide Cl. CR4: Mitc 1E **154**
Tideham Ho. SE28 1H **107**
Tidelea Twr. SE28 2G **107**
Tidenham Gdns. CR0: C'don 3E **168**
Tideside Ct. SE18 3C **106**
Tideslea Path SE28 1H **107**
Tideswell Rd. CR0: C'don 3C **170**
SW15 4E **116**
Tideway Cl. TW10: Ham 4B **132**
Tideway Ct. SE16 1K **103**
Tideway Ho. *E14 2C **104***
(off Strafford St.)
Tideway Ind. Est. SW8 6G **101**
Tideway Wlk. SW8 7B **18** (6G **101**)
Tidey St. E3 5C **86**
Tidford Rd. DA16: Well 2K **125**
Tidlock Ho. SE28 2H **107**
Tidworth Rd. E3 4C **86**
Tiepigs La. BR2: Hayes 2G **171**
BR4: W W'ck 2G **171**
Tierney Ct. CR0: C'don 2E **168**
Tierney Rd. SW2 1J **137**
Tiffany Hgts. SW18 7J **117**
Tiffin School Sports Hall 2F **151**
Tiffins Girls Community Sports Cen.
6E **132**
Tiger Ho. *WC1 2D **6***
(off Burton St.)
Tiger La. BR2: Brom 4K **159**
Tiger Way E5 4H **67**
Tigris Cl. N9 2D **34**
Tilbrook Rd. SE3 3A **124**
Tilbury Cl. HA5: Hat E 1D **40**
SE15 7F **103**
Tilbury Ho. *SE14 6K **103***
(off Myers La.)

Tilbury Rd. E6 2D **88**
E10 7E **50**
Tildesley Rd. SW15 6E **116**
Tile Farm Rd. BR6: Orp 3H **173**
Tilehurst NW1 2K **5**
Tilehurst Point SE2 2C **108**
(not continuous)
Tilehurst Rd. SM3: Cheam 5G **165**
SW18 1B **136**
Tile Kiln La. DA5: Bexl 2J **145**
N6 1F **65**
N13 5H **33**
UB9: Hare 7D **38**
Tile Kiln Studios N6 7G **47**
Tile Yd. E14 6B **86**
Tileyard Rd. N7 7J **65**
Tilford Av. CR0: New Ad 7E **170**
Tilford Gdns. SW19 1F **135**
Tilford Ho. *SW2 7K **119***
(off Holmewood Gdns.)
Tilia Cl. SM1: Sutt 5H **165**
Tilia Rd. E5 4H **67**
Tilia Wlk. SW9 4B **120**
Tiller Ho. *N1 1E **84***
(off Whitmore Est.)
Tiller Leisure Cen., The 3C **104**
Tiller Rd. E14 3C **104**
Tillett Cl. NW10 6J **61**
Tillett Sq. SE16 2A **104**
Tillet Way E2 3G **85**
Tilley Rd. TW13: Felt 1J **129**
Tillingbourne Gdns. N3 3H **45**
Tillingbourne Grn.
BR5: St M Cry 4K **161** & 5K **161**
Tillingbourne Way N3 4H **45**
Tillingham Way N12 4D **30**
Tilling Rd. NW2 1E **62**
Tillings Cl. SE5 1C **120**
Tilling Way HA9: Wemb 2D **60**
Tillman St. E1 6H **85**
Tilloch St. N1 7K **65**
Tillotson Ct. *SW8 7H **101***
(off Wandsworth Rd.)
Tillotson Rd. HA3: Hrw W 7A **26**
IG1: Ilf 7E **52**
N9 2A **34**
Tilney Ct. EC1 3D **8** (4C **84**)
IG9: Buck H 2D **36**
Tilney Dr. IG9: Buck H 2D **36**
Tilney Gdns. N1 6D **66**
Tilney Rd. RM9: Dag 6F **73**
(not continuous)
UB2: S'hall 4A **94**
Tilney St. W1 4H **11** (1E **100**)
Tilson Cl. SE5 7E **102**
Tilson Gdns. SW2 7J **119**
Tilson Ho. SW2 7J **119**
Tilson Rd. N17 1G **49**
Tilston Cl. E11 3H **69**
Tiltman Pl. N7 3K **65**
Tilton St. SW6 6G **99**
Tiltwood, The W3 7J **79**
Tilt Yd. App. SE9 6D **124**
Timber Cl. BR7: Chst 2E **160**
Timbercroft KT19: Ewe 4A **164**
Timbercroft La. SE18 6J **107**
Timberdene NW4 2F **45**
Timberdene Av. IG6: Ilf 1G **53**
Timberland Cl. SE15 7G **103**
Timberland Rd. E1 6H **85**
Timberley Ct. DA14: Sidc 5K **143**
Timber Mill Way SW4 3H **119**
Timber Pond Rd. SE16 1K **103**
Timbers, The SM3: Cheam 6G **165**
Timberslip Dr. SM6: Wall 7H **167**
Timber St. EC1 3C **8** (4C **84**)
Timber Wharf E2 1F **85**
Timberwharf Rd. N16 6G **49**
Timber Wharves Est. *E14 4C **104***
(off Copeland Dr.)
Timber Yd., The *N1 2H **9***
(off Drysdale St.)

Timbrell Pl. SE16 . . . . .1B 104
Time Sq. E8 .5F 67
Times Sq. E1 . . . . .6G 85
   SM1: Sutt 5K 165
Timms Cl. BR1: Brom 4D 160
Timor Ho. E1 . . . . .4A 86
   (off Duckett St.)
Timothy Cl. DA6: Bex 5E 126
   SW4 .5G 119
Timothy Ho. DA18: Erith 2E 108
   (off Kale Rd.)
Timothy Pl. KT8: W Mole 5D 148
Timperley Ct. SW19 . . . . .1G 135
Timsbury Wlk. SW15 . . . . .1C 134
Tina Ct. SE6 . . . . .7B 122
Tindal St. SW9 . . . . .1B 120
Tinderbox All. SW14 . . . . .3K 115
Tinniswood Cl. N5 . . . . .5A 66
Tinsley Cl. SE25 . . . . .3H 157
Tinsley Rd. E1 . . . . .5J 85
Tintagel Ct. EC1 . . . . .3A 8
   (off St John St.)
Tintagel Cres. SE22 . . . . .4F 121
Tintagel Dr. HA7: Stan 4J 27
Tintagel Gdns. SE22 . . . . .4F 121
Tintern Av. NW9 . . . . .3H 43
Tintern Cl. SW15 . . . . .5G 117
   SW19 . . . . .6A 136
Tintern Gdns. N14 . . . . .7D 22
Tintern Ho. NW1 . . . . .1K 5
   (off Augustus St.)
   SW1 . . . . .4J 17
   (off Abbots Mnr.)
Tintern Path NW9 . . . . .6A 44
   (off Fryent Gro.)
Tintern Rd. N22 . . . . .1C 48
   SM5: Cars 1B 166
Tintern St. SW4 . . . . .4J 119
Tintern Way HA2: Harr 1F 59
Tinto Rd. E16 . . . . .4J 87
Tinworth St. SE11 . . . . . .5F 19 (5J 101)
Tippett Ct. E6 . . . . .2D 88
Tippetts Cl. EN2: Enf 1H 23
Tipthorpe Rd. SW11 . . . . .3E 118
Tipton Dr. CR0: C'don 4E 168
Tiptree NW1 . . . . .7F 65
   (off Castlehaven Rd.)
Tiptree Cl. E4 . . . . .3K 35
Tiptree Cres. IG5: Ilf 2E 52
Tiptree Dr. EN2: Enf 4J 23
Tiptree Rd. HA4: Ruis 4K 57
Tirlemont Rd. CR2: S Croy 7C 168
Tirrell Rd. CR0: C'don 6C 156
Tisbury Ct. W1 . . . . .2C 12
Tisbury Rd. SW16 . . . . .2J 155
Tisdall Ho. SE17 . . . . .4D 102
   (off Catesby St.)
Tisdall Pl. SE17 . . . . .4D 102
Tissington Ct. SE16 . . . . .4J 103
Titan Bus. Est. SE8 . . . . .7C 104
   (off Ffinch St.)
Titan Ct. TW8: Bford 5F 97
Titchborne Row W2 . . . . .1D 10 (6C 82)
Titchfield Rd. NW8 . . . . .1C 82
   SM5: Cars 1B 166
Titchfield Wlk. SM5: Cars 7B 154
Titchwell Rd. SW18 . . . . .1B 136
Tite St. SW3 . . . . .6E 16 (5D 100)
Tithe Barn Cl. KT2: King T 1F 151
Tithe Barn Way UB5: N'olt 2K 75
Tithe Cl. KT12: Walt T 6K 147
   NW7 . . . . .1C 44
   UB4: Hayes 5H 75
Tithe Farm Av. HA2: Harr 3E 58
Tithe Farm Cl. HA2: Harr 3E 58
Tithe Wlk. NW7 . . . . .1C 44
Titian Av. WD23: B Hea 1D 26
Titley Cl. E4 . . . . .5H 35
Titmus Av. SE28 . . . . .7B 90
Titmuss St. W12 . . . . .2E 98

Tivendale N8 . . . . .3J 47
Tiverton Av. IG5: Ilf 3E 52
Tiverton Cl. CR0: C'don 7F 157
Tiverton Dr. SE9 . . . . .1G 143
Tiverton Ho. EN3: Enf H 3E 24
Tiverton Rd. HA0: Wemb 2E 78
   HA4: Ruis 3J 57
   HA8: Edg 2F 43
   N15 . . . . .6D 48
   N18 . . . . .5K 33
   NW10 . . . . .1F 81
   TW3: Houn 2G 113
Tiverton St. SE1 . . . . .3C 102
Tiverton Way KT9: Chess 5D 162
   NW7 . . . . .7A 30
Tivoli Ct. SE16 . . . . .1B 104
Tivoli Gdns. SE18 . . . . .4C 106
   (not continuous)
Tivoli Rd. N8 . . . . .5J 47
   SE27 .5C 138
   TW4: Houn 4C 112
Toad La. TW4: Houn 4D 112
Tobacco Dock E1 . . . . .7H 85
Tobacco Quay E1 . . . . .7H 85
Tobago St. E14 . . . . .2C 104
Tobin Cl. NW3 . . . . .7C 64
Toby Cl. N9 . . . . .7D 24
   (off Tramway Av.)
Toby La. E1 . . . . .4A 86
Toby Way KT5: Surb 2H 163
Todber Ho. W14 . . . . .3G 99
   (off Russell Rd.)
Todd Ho. N2 . . . . .2B 46
   (off The Grange)
Todds Wlk. N7 . . . . .2K 65
Todhunter Ter. EN5: New Bar 4D 20
Tokenhouse Yd. EC2 . . . . .7E 8 (6D 84)
Token Yd. SW15 . . . . .4G 117
TOKYNGTON 6H 61
Tokyngton Av. HA9: Wemb 6G 61
Toland Sq. SW15 . . . . .5C 116
Tolcairn Ct. DA17: Belv 5G 109
Tolcarne Dr. HA5: Eastc 2J 39
Tolchurch W11 . . . . .6H 81
   (off Dartmouth Cl.)
Toley Av. HA9: Wemb 7E 42
Tolhurst Dr. W10 . . . . .3G 81
Tollard Ho. W14 . . . . .3G 99
Toll Bar Cl. SM2: Sutt 7K 165
Tollbridge Cl. W10 . . . . .4G 81
Tollesbury Gdns. IG6: Ilf 3H 53
Tollet St. E1 . . . . .4K 85
Tollgate Ct. CR2: S Croy 5D 168
Tollgate Dr. SE21 . . . . .2E 138
   UB4: Yead 7B 76
Tollgate Gdns. NW6 . . . . .2K 81
Tollgate Ho. NW6 . . . . .2K 81
   (off Tollgate Gdns.)
Tollgate Lodge BR7: Chst 1E 160
   (off Caveside Cl.)
Tollgate Rd. E6 . . . . .5A 88
   E16 . . . . .5A 88
Tollgate Sq. E6 . . . . .5D 88
Tollhouse Way N19 . . . . .2G 65
Tollington Pk. N4 . . . . .2K 65
Tollington Pl. N4 . . . . .2K 65
Tollington Rd. N7 . . . . .4K 65
Tollington Way N7 . . . . .3J 65
Tolmers Sq. NW1 . . . . .3B 6 (4G 83)
   (not continuous)
Tolpaide Ho. SE11 . . . . .4J 19
Tolpuddle Av. E13 . . . . .1A 88
Tolpuddle St. N1 . . . . .2A 84
Tolsford Rd. E5 . . . . .5A 68
Tolson Rd. TW7: Isle 3A 114
Tolverne Rd. SW20 . . . . .1E 152
TOLWORTH 2H 163
Tolworth B'way. KT6: Surb 1H 163
Tolworth Cl. KT6: Surb 1H 163
Tolworth Gdns. RM6: Chad H 5D 54
TOLWORTH JUNC. (TOBY JUG) . . .2H 163
Tolworth Pde. RM6: Chad H 5E 54

Tolworth Pk. Rd. KT6: Surb 2F 163
Tolworth Recreation Cen. 3F 163
Tolworth Ri. Nth. KT5: Surb 1H 163
Tolworth Ri. Sth. KT5: Surb 2H 163
Tolworth Rd. KT6: Surb 2E 162
Tolworth Twr. KT6: Surb 2F 163
Tomahawk Gdns. UB5: N'olt 3B 76
Tom Coombs Cl. SE9 . . . . .4C 124
Tom Cribb Rd. SE28 . . . . .3G 107
Tom Groves Cl. E15 . . . . .5F 69
Tom Hood Cl. E15 . . . . .5F 69
Tom Jenkinson Rd. E16 . . . . .1J 105
Tomkyns Ho. SE11 . . . . .3J 19
Tomline Ho. SE1 . . . . .5C 14
   (off Union St.)
Tomlins All. TW1: Twick 1A 132
Tomlin's Gro. E3 . . . . .3C 86
Tomlinson Cl. E2 . . . . .2K 9 (3F 85)
   W4 . . . . .5H 97
Tomlins Orchard IG11: Bark 1G 89
Tomlins Ter. E14 . . . . .6A 86
Tomlins Wlk. N7 . . . . .2K 65
Tom Mann Cl. IG11: Bark 1J 89
Tom Nolan Cl. E15 . . . . .2G 87
Tom Oakman Cen. E4 . . . . .2A 36
Tompion Ho. EC1 . . . . .3B 8
   (off Percival St.)
Tompion St. EC1 . . . . .2A 8 (3B 84)
   (not continuous)
Tom Smith Cl. SE10 . . . . .6G 105
Tomson Ho. SE1 . . . . .7J 15
   (off St Saviour's Est.)
Tomswood Ct. IG6: Ilf 1G 53
Tomswood Hill IG6: Ilf . . . . .6K 37 & 1F 53
Tomswood Rd. IG7: Chig 6K 37
Tom Williams Ho. SW6 . . . . .6H 99
   (off Clem Attlee Ct.)
Tonbridge Cres. HA3: Kenton 4E 42
Tonbridge Ho's. WC1 . . . . .2E 6
   (off Tonbridge St., not continuous)
Tonbridge Rd. KT8: W Mole 4D 148
Tonbridge St. WC1 . . . . . .1E 6 (3J 83)
Tonbridge Wlk. WC1 . . . . .1E 6
   (off Tonbridge St.)
Toneborough NW8 . . . . .1K 81
   (off Abbey Rd.)
Tonfield Rd. SM3: Sutt 1H 165
Tonge Cl. BR3: Beck 5C 158
Tonsley Hill SW18 . . . . .5K 117
Tonsley Pl. SW18 . . . . .5K 117
Tonsley Rd. SW18 . . . . .5K 117
Tonsley St. SW18 . . . . .5K 117
Tonstall Rd. CR4: Mitc 2E 154
Tony Cannell M. E3 . . . . .3B 86
Tony Law Ho. SE20 . . . . .1H 157
Tooke Cl. HA5: Pinn 1C 40
Tookey Cl. HA3: Kenton 7F 43
Took's Ct. EC4 . . . . .7J 7 (6A 84)
Tooley St. SE1 . . . . .4F 15 (1D 102)
Toomy Cen. E16 . . . . .1K 105
   (off Evelyn Rd.)
Toorack Rd. HA3: Hrw W 2H 41
TOOTING 5C 136
Tooting & Mitcham United FC 5C 154
TOOTING BEC 3D 136
Tooting Bec Gdns. SW16 . . . . .4H 137
   (not continuous)
Tooting Bec Lido 4G 137
Tooting Bec Rd. SW16 . . . . .3E 136
   SW17 .3E 136
Tooting B'way. SW17 . . . . .5C 136
TOOTING GRAVENEY 6D 136
Tooting Gro. SW17 . . . . .5C 136
Tooting High St. SW17 . . . . .6C 136
Tooting Leisure Cen. 4B 136
Tooting Mkt. SW17 . . . . .4D 136
Tootswood Rd. BR2: Brom 5G 159
Topaz W2 . . . . .6B 4
Topaz Ct. E11 . . . . .1G 69
Topaz Wlk. NW2 . . . . .7F 45
Topcliffe Dr. BR6: Farnb 4H 173
Topham Ho. SE10 . . . . .7E 104
   (off Prior St.)

Topham Sq. N17 . . . . .1C 48
Topham St. EC1 . . . . .3J 7 (4A 84)
Top Ho. Ri. E4 . . . . .7K 25
Topiary Sq. TW9: Rich 3F 115
Topley St. SE9 . . . . .4A 124
Topmast Point E14 . . . . .2C 104
Top Pk. BR3: Beck 5G 159
Topp Wlk. NW2 . . . . .2E 62
Topsfield Cl. N8 . . . . .5H 47
Topsfield Pde. N8 . . . . .5J 47
   (off Tottenham La.)
Topsfield Rd. N8 . . . . .5J 47
Topsham Rd. SW17 . . . . .3D 136
Tora Ct. IG9: Buck H 2F 37
Torbay Cl. NW1 . . . . .7F 65
Torbay Mans. NW6 . . . . .1H 81
   (off Willesden La.)
Torbay Rd. HA2: Harr 2C 58
   NW6 . . . . .7H 63
Torbay St. NW1 . . . . .7F 65
Torbitt Way IG2: Ilf 5K 53
Torbridge Cl. HA8: Edg 7K 27
Torbrook Cl. DA5: Bexl 6E 126
Tor Ct. W8 . . . . .2J 99
Torcross Dr. SE23 . . . . .2J 139
Torcross Rd. HA4: Ruis 3K 57
Tor Gdns. W8 . . . . .2J 99
Tor Gro. SE28 . . . . .1J 107
Tor Ho. N6 . . . . .6F 47
Tormead Cl. SM1: Sutt 6J 165
Tormount Rd. SE18 . . . . .6J 107
Tornay Ho. E9 . . . . .7J 67
   N1 . . . . .2K 83
   (off Priory Grn. Est.)
Toronto Av. E12 . . . . .4D 70
Toronto Ho. SE16 . . . . .2K 103
Toronto Rd. IG1: Ilf 1F 71
Torquay Gdns. IG4: Ilf 4B 52
Torquay St. W2 . . . . .5K 81
Torrance Cl. SE7 . . . . .6B 106
Torrens Ct. SE5 . . . . .3D 120
Torrens Rd. E15 . . . . .6H 69
   SW2 . . . . .5K 119
Torrens Sq. E15 . . . . .6H 69
Torrens St. EC1 . . . . .2A 84
Torres Sq. E14 . . . . .5C 104
Torre Wlk. SM5: Cars 1C 166
Torrey Dr. SW9 . . . . .2A 120
Torriano Av. NW5 . . . . .5H 65
Torriano Cotts. NW5 . . . . .5G 65
Torriano M. NW5 . . . . .5G 65
Torridge Gdns. SE15 . . . . .4J 121
Torridge Rd. CR7: Thor H 5B 156
Torridon Ho. NW6 . . . . .2K 81
   (off Randolph Gdns.)
Torridon Rd. SE6 . . . . .7F 123
   SE13 .7F 123
Torrington Av. N12 . . . . .5G 31
Torrington Cl. N12 . . . . .4G 31
Torrington Ct. SE26 . . . . .5G 139
   (off Crystal Pal. Pk. Rd.)
Torrington Dr. HA2: Harr 4F 59
Torrington Gdns. N11 . . . . .6B 32
   UB6: G'frd 1C 78
Torrington Gro. N12 . . . . .5H 31
Torrington Pk. N12 . . . . .5F 31
Torrington Pl. E1 . . . . .1G 103
   WC1 . . . . .5C 6 (5H 83)
Torrington Rd. E18 . . . . .3J 51
   HA4: Ruis 3J 57
   RM8: Dag 1F 73
   UB6: G'frd 1C 78
Torrington Sq. CR0: C'don 7D 156
   WC1 . . . . .4D 6 (4H 83)
Torrington Way SM4: Mord 6J 153
Tor Rd. DA16: Well 1C 126
Torr Rd. SE20 . . . . .7K 139
Tortington Ho. SE15 . . . . .7G 103
   (off Friary Est.)
Torver Rd. HA1: Harr 4J 41
Torver Way BR6: Orp 3H 173
Torwood Rd. SW15 . . . . .5C 116

Tothill Ho. *SW1* 3D *18*
(off Page St.)
Tothill St. SW1 . . . . .7D 12 (2H *101*)
Totnes Rd. DA16: Well 7B *108*
Totnes Vs. *N11* 5B *32*
(off Telford Rd.)
Totnes Wlk. N2 . . . . .4B *46*
Tottan Ter. E1 . . . . .6K *85*
Tottenhall *NW1* 7E *64*
(off Ferdinand St.)
Tottenhall Rd. N13 . . . . .6F *33*
TOTTENHAM 1F 49
Tottenham Community Sports Cen. . .1F 49
Tottenham Ct. Rd. W1 . . . .4B 6 (4G *83*)
Tottenham Ent. Cen. N17 . . . . .2F 49
Tottenham Grn. E. N15 . . . . .4F 49
Tottenham Green Leisure Cen. 4F 49
TOTTENHAM HALE 2G 49
TOTTENHAM HALE GYRATORY 4G 49
Tottenham Hale Retail Pk. N15 . . .4G 49
Tottenham Hotspur FC 7B 34
Tottenham La. N8 . . . . .6J 47
Tottenham M. W1 . . . . . . .5B 6 (5G *83*)
Tottenham Rd. N1 . . . . .6E 66
Tottenham St. W1 . . . . . .6B 6 (5G *83*)
Totterdown St. SW17 . . . . .4D 136
TOTTERIDGE 1C 30
Totteridge Comn. N20 . . . . .2H 29
Totteridge Fields Local Nature Reserve
. . . . .1H 29
Totteridge Grn. N20 . . . . .2D 30
Totteridge Ho. *SW11* 2B *118*
(off Yelverton Rd.)
Totteridge La. N20 . . . . .2D 30
Totteridge Village N20 . . . . .1B 30
Totternhoe Cl. HA3: Kenton 5C 42
Totton Rd. CR7: Thor H 3A 156
Touchard Ho. N1 . . . . .2F 9
Toulmin St. SE1 . . . . . . .7C 14 (2C *102*)
Toulon St. SE5 . . . . .7C 102
Toulouse Ct. *SE16* 5H *103*
(off Rossetti Rd.)
Tounson Ct. *SW1* 4D *18*
(off Montaigne Cl.)
Tourist Info. Cen.
Bexley 6J 127
Bexleyheath 4G 127
City of London 1C 14 (6C 84)
Greenwich 6E 104
Hammersmith 4E 98
Harrow 4J 41
Heathrow Central 3D 110
Hounslow 3F 113
Kingston upon Thames 2D 150
Leicester Square 3D 12 (7H 83)
Lewisham 4E 122
London - Heathrow Airport
Terminal 1 . . . . .2D 110
Terminal 3 . . . . .3C 110
Regent Street 4C 12
Richmond 5D 114
Twickenham 1B 132
Victoria Station 2K 17
Tournay Rd. SW6 . . . . .7H 99
Tours Pas. SW11 . . . . .4A 118
Toussaint Wlk. SE16 . . . . .3G 103
Tovil Cl. SE20 . . . . .2H 157
Tovy Ho. *SE1* 5G *103*
(off Avondale Sq.)
Towcester Rd. E3 . . . . .4D *86*
Tower 42 . . . . .7G 9 (6E 84)
Tower Bri. SE1 . . . . .5J 15 (1F 103)
Tower Bri. App. E1 . . . . .4J 15 (1F *103*)
Tower Bri. Bus. Complex
SE16 . . . . .3G 103
Tower Bri. Bus. Sq. SE16 . . . . . . .4H 103
Tower Bridge Exhibition 4J 15
Tower Bri. M. HA1: Harr 4B 42
Tower Bri. Plaza SE1 . . . .5J 15 (1F *103*)
Tower Bri. Rd. SE1 . . . .7H 15 (3E *102*)
Tower Bri. Sq. SE1 . . . . .6J 15
Tower Bri. Wharf E1 . . . . .5K 15 (1G *103*)

Tower Bldgs. *E1* 1H *103*
(off Brewhouse La.)
Tower Cl. BR6: Orp 2K 173
NW3 .5B 64
SE20 . . . . .7H 139
Tower Ct. E5 . . . . .7F 49
N1 . . . . .7C *66*
(off Canonbury St.)
NW8 .2C *82*
(off Mackennal St.)
WC2 .1E 12
Tower Gdns. KT10: Clay 7A 162
Tower Gdns. Rd. N17 . . . . .1C 48
Towergate *SE1* 4E *102*
(off Page's Wlk.)
Towergate Cl. UB8: Uxb 5A 56
Towergate Ho. *E3* 2B *86*
(off Ordell Rd.)
Tower Gym 2A 34
Tower Hamlets Rd. E7 . . . . .4H 69
E17 .3C 50
TOWER HILL 7F 85
Tower Hill EC3 . . . . .3H 15 (7E 84)
Tower Hill Ter. EC3 . . . . .3H 15
Tower Ho. *E1* 5G *85*
(off Fieldgate St.)
Tower La. HA9: Wemb 3D 60
Tower Mans. *SE1* 5F *103*
(off Grange Rd.)
Tower M. E5 . . . . .4A 68
E17 .4C 50
Tower Mill Rd. SE15 . . . . .7E 102
Tower of London, The 3J 15 (7F 85)
Tower of London Welcome Cen.
. . . . .3H 15 (7E 84)
Tower Pl. EC3 . . . . .3H 15 (7E 84)
Tower Pl. E. *EC3* 3H 15
(off Lwr. Thames St.)
Tower Pl. W. *EC3* 3H 15
(off Lwr. Thames St.)
Tower Point EN2: Enf 4J 23
Tower Ri. TW9: Rich 3E 114
Tower Rd. BR6: Orp 2K 173
DA7: Bex 4G 127
DA17: Belv 4J 109
NW10 . . . . .7C 62
TW1: Twick 3K 131
Tower Royal EC4 . . . . . . .2E 14 (7D 84)
Towers Av. UB10: Hil 3E 74
Towers Bus. Pk. *HA9:* Wemb 4J *61*
(off Carey Way)
Towers Ct. UB10: Hil 3E 74
Towers Pl. TW9: Rich 5E 114
Towers Rd. HA5: Pinn 1C 40
UB1: S'hall 4E 76
Tower St. WC2 . . . . .1E 12 (6J 83)
Tower Ter. N22 . . . . .2K 47
Tower Vw. CR0: C'don 7A 158
WD23: B Hea 1D 26
Tower Wlk. *SE1* 4E *102*
(off Aberdour St.)
Tower Wharf *SE1* 6J *15*
(off Tooley St.)
Tower Workshops SE1 . . . . .7J 15
SE1 .2F *103*
(off Riley Rd.)
Tower Yd. TW10: Rich 5F 115
Towfield Ct. TW13: Hanw 2D 130
Towfield Rd. TW13: Hanw 2D 130
Town, The EN2: Enf 3J 23
Towncourt Cres. BR5: Pet W 5G 161
Towncourt La. BR5: Pet W 6H 161
Town Cl. Path N4 . . . . .1C 66
Town End Pde. *KT1:* King T 3D *150*
(off High St.)
Towney Mead UB5: N'olt 2D 76
Towney Mead Ct. UB5: N'olt 2D 76
Townfield Rd. UB3: Hayes 1H 93
Townfield Sq. UB3: Hayes 7H 75
Town Fld. Way TW7: Isle 2A 114
Town Hall App. Rd. N15 . . . . .4F 49
Town Hall Av. W4 . . . . .5K 97

Town Hall Rd. SW11 . . . . .3D 118
Town Hall Wlk. *N16* 4D *66*
(off Albion Rd.)
Townholm Cres. W7 . . . . .3K 95
Town La. TW19: Stanw 1A 128
(not continuous)
Townley Ct. E15 . . . . .6H 69
Townley Rd. DA6: Bex 5F 127
SE22 . . . . .5E 120
Townley St. SE17 . . . . .5D 102
(not continuous)
Townmead Bus. Cen. SW6 . . . . . . .3A 118
Town Mdw. TW8: Bford 6D 96
Town Mdw. Rd. TW8: Bford 7D 96
Townmead Rd. SW6 . . . . .3K 117
TW9: Kew 2H 115
Town Quay IG11: Bark 1F 89
Town Quay Wharf IG11: Bark 1F 89
Town Rd. N9 . . . . .2C 34
Townsend Av. N14 . . . . .4C 32
Townsend Ho. *SE1* 4G *103*
(off Strathnairn St.)
Townsend Ind. Est. NW10 . . . . .2J 79
Townsend La. NW9 . . . . .7K 43
Townsend M. SW18 . . . . .2A 136
Townsend Rd. N15 . . . . .5F 49
TW15: Ashf 5A 128
UB1: S'hall 1C 94
Townsend St. SE17 . . . . .4E 102
Townsend Way HA6: Nwood 1H 39
Townsend Yd. N6 . . . . .1F 65
Townshend Cl. DA14: Sidc 6B 144
Townshend Ct. *NW8* 2C *82*
(off Townshend Rd.)
Townshend Est. NW8 . . . . .2C 82
Townshend Rd. BR7: Chst 5F 143
NW8 .1C 82
(not continuous)
TW9: Rich 4F 115
Townshend Ter. TW9: Rich 4F 115
Towns Ho. SW4 . . . . .3H 119
Townson Av. UB5: N'olt 2J 75
Townson Way UB5: N'olt 2J 75
Town Sq. *IG11:* Bark 1G *89*
(off Clockhouse Av.)
TW7: Isle 3B *114*
(off Swan St.)
Town Tree Rd. TW15: Ashf 5C 128
Town Wharf TW7: Isle 3B 114
Towpath KT12: Walt T 5J 147
TW17: Shep 7B 146
Towpath, The SW10 . . . . .1B 118
Towpath Rd. N18 . . . . .6E 34
Towpath Wlk. E9 . . . . .5B 68
Towpath Way CR0: C'don 6F 157
Towton Rd. SE27 . . . . .2C 138
Toynbee Cl. BR7: Chst 4F 143
Toynbee Rd. SW20 . . . . .1G 153
Toynbee St. E1 . . . . . . .6J 9 (5F 85)
Toynbee Studios 7K 9
Toyne Way N6 . . . . .6D 46
Tracey Av. NW2 . . . . .5E 62
Tracy Ct. HA7: Stan 7H 27
Tracy Ho. *E3* 3B *86*
(off Mile End Rd.)
Trade Cl. N13 . . . . .4F 33
Trader Rd. E6 . . . . .6F 89
Tradescant Ho. *E9* 7J *67*
(off Frampton Pk. Rd.)
Tradescant Rd. SW8 . . . . .7J 101
Tradewind Hgts. *SE16* 1K *103*
(off Rotherhithe St.)
Tradewinds Ct. E1 . . . . .7G 85
Trading Est. Rd. NW10 . . . . .4J 79
Trafalgar Av. KT4: Wor Pk 1F 165
N17 .6K 33
SE15 . . . . .5F 103
Trafalgar Bus. Cen.
IG11: Bark 4K 89
Trafalgar Chambers *SW3* 5B *16*
(off South Pde.)
Trafalgar Cl. SE16 . . . . .3A 104

Trafalgar Ct. *E1* 1J *103*
(off Wapping Wall)
Trafalgar Gdns. E1 . . . . .5K *85*
W8 . . . . .3K 99
Trafalgar Gro. SE10 . . . . .6F 105
Trafalgar Ho. *SE17* 5C *102*
(off Bronti Cl.)
Trafalgar M. E9 . . . . .6B 68
Trafalgar Pl. E11 . . . . .4J 51
N18 .5B 34
Trafalgar Point *N1* 7D *66*
(off Downham Rd.)
Trafalgar Rd. SE10 . . . . .6F 105
SW19 . . . . .7K 135
TW2: Twick 2H 131
Trafalgar Square 4E 12 (1J 101)
Trafalgar Sq. WC2 . . . . . .4D 12 (1H 101)
(not continuous)
Trafalgar St. SE17 . . . . .5D 102
Trafalgar Studios 4E 12
(off Whitehall)
Trafalgar Ter. HA1: Harr 1J 59
Trafalgar Trad. Est. EN3: Brim 4F 25
Trafalgar Way CR0: Wadd 2A 168
E14 .1E 104
Trafford Ho. *N1* 2D *84*
(off Cranston Est.)
Trafford Rd. CR7: Thor H 5K 155
Trafford Way BR3: Beck 6C 140
Traherne Lodge TW11: Tedd 5K 131
Trahorn Cl. E1 . . . . .4H 85
Traitors' Gate 4J 15
Tralee Ct. *SE16* 5H *103*
(off Masters Dr.)
Tram Cl. *SE24* 3B *120*
(off Milkwood Rd.)
Tramlink, The SW19 . . . . .2A 154
Tramsheds, The CR0: Bedd 7H 155
Tramway Av. E15 . . . . .7G 69
N9 . . . . .7C 24
Tramway Cl. SE20 . . . . .1J 157
Tramway Ct. E1 . . . . .5A *86*
Tramway Path CR4: Mitc 4C 154
(not continuous)
Tranley M. *NW3* 4C *64*
(off Fleet Rd.)
Tranmere Ct. SM2: Sutt 7A 166
Tranmere Rd. N9 . . . . .7A 24
SW18 . . . . .2A 136
TW2: Whitt 7F 113
Tranquil Pas. *SE3* 2H *123*
(off Montpelier Va.)
Tranquil Va. SE3 . . . . .2G 123
Transenna Works *N1* 6B *66*
(off Laycock St.)
Transept St. NW1 . . . . . . .6D 4 (5C 82)
Transmere Cl. BR5: Pet W 6G 161
Transmere Rd. BR5: Pet W 6G 161
Transom Cl. SE16 . . . . .4A 104
Transom Sq. E14 . . . . .5D 104
Transport Av. TW8: Bford 5A 96
Tranton Rd. SE16 . . . . .3G 103
Trappes Ho. SE16 . . . . .4H *103*
(off Camilla Rd.)
Traps La. KT3: N Mald 1A 152
Traq Motor Racing 6F 155
Travellers Way TW4: Cran 2A 112
Travers Cl. E17 . . . . .1K 49
Travers Ho. *SE10* 6E *105*
(off Trafalgar Gro.)
Travers Rd. N7 . . . . .3A 66
Travis Ho. SE10 . . . . .1E 122
Treacy Cl. WD23: B Hea 2B 26
Treadgold Ho. *W11* 7F *81*
(off Bomore Rd.)
Treadgold St. W11 . . . . .7F 81
Treadway St. E2 . . . . .2H 85
Treasury Cl. SM6: Wall 5H 167
Treasury Pas. SW1 . . . . .6E 12
Treaty Cen. TW3: Houn 3F 113
Treaty St. N1 . . . . .1K 83
Trebeck St. W1 . . . . .4J 11 (1F 101)

Trebovir Rd. SW5 5J 99
Treby St. E3 4B 86
Trecastle Way N7 4H 65
Tredegar Ho. *E3* *3C 86*
(*off Bow Rd.*)
Tredegar M. E3 3B 86
Tredegar Rd. E3 2B 86
N11 7C 32
Tredegar Sq. E3 3B 86
Tredegar Ter. E3 3B 86
Trederwen Rd. E8 1G 85
Tredown Rd. SE26 5J 139
Tredwell Cl. BR2: Brom 4C 160
SW2 2K 137
Tredwell Rd. SE27 4B 138
Tree Cl. TW10: Ham 1D 132
Treen Av. SW13 3B 116
Tree Rd. E16 6A 88
Treeside Cl. UB7: W Dray 4A 92
Tree Top M. RM10: Dag 6K 73
Treetops Cl. SE2 5E 108
Treeview Cl. SE19 1E 156
Treewall Gdns. BR1: Brom 4K 141
Trefgarne Rd. RM10: Dag 2G 73
Trefil Wlk. N7 4J 65
Trefoil Ho. *DA18: Erith* *2E 108*
(*off Kale Rd.*)
Trefoil Rd. SW18 5A 118
Trefusis Ct. TW5: Cran 1K 111
Tregaron Av. N8 6J 47
Tregaron Gdns. KT3: N Mald 4A 152
Tregarvon Rd. SW11 4E 118
Tregenna Av. HA2: Harr 4E 58
Tregenna Cl. N14 5B 22
Tregenna Ct. HA2: Harr 4E 58
Tregony Rd. BR6: Chels 4K 173
Trego Rd. E9 7C 68
Tregothnan Rd. SW9 3J 119
Tregunter Rd. SW10 6K 99
Trehearn Rd. IG6: Ilf 1H 53
Treherne Ct. SW9 1B 120
SW17 4E 136
Trehern Rd. SW14 3K 115
Trehurst St. E5 5A 68
Trelawney Est. E9 6J 67
Trelawney Ho. *SE1* *5C 14*
(*off Union St.*)
Trelawney Rd. IG6: Ilf 1H 53
Trelawn Rd. E10 3E 68
SW2 5A 120
Trelawny Cl. E17 4D 50
Trellick Twr. *W10* *4H 81*
(*off Golborne Rd.*)
Trellis Ho. SW19 7A 136
Trellis Sq. E3 3B 86
Treloar Gdns. SE19 6D 138
Tremadoc Rd. SW4 4H 119
Tremaine Cl. SE4 2C 122
Tremaine Rd. SE20 2H 157
Trematon Ho. *SE11* *5K 19*
(*off Kennings Way*)
Trematon Pl. TW11: Tedd 7C 132
Tremlett Gro. N19 3G 65
Trenance Gdns. IG3: Ilf 3A 72
Trenchard Av. HA4: Ruis 4K 57
Trenchard Cl. HA7: Stan 6F 27
NW9 1A 44
Trenchard Ct. NW4 5C 44
SM4: Mord 6J 153
Trenchard St. SE10 5F 105
Trenchold St. SW8 6J 101
Trendell Ho. *E14* *6C 86*
(*off Dod St.*)
Trenear Cl. BR6: Chels 4K 173
Trenholme Cl. SE20 7H 139
Trenholme Rd. SE20 7H 139
Trenholme Ter. SE20 7H 139
Trenmar Gdns. NW10 3D 80
Trent Av. W5 3C 96
Trent Ct. *CR2: S Croy* *5C 168*
(*off Nottingham Rd.*)
Trent Gdns. N14 6A 22
Trentham Ho. W3 5K 79
Trentham St. SW18 1J 135
Trent Ho. KT2: King T 1D 150
SE15 4J 121
TRENT PARK 2A 22
Trent Pk. (Country Pk.) 1A 22
Trent Pk. Sports Cen. 3A 22
Trent Rd. IG9: Buck H 1E 36
SW2 5K 119
Trent Way KT4: Wor Pk 3E 164
UB4: Hayes 2G 75
Trentwood Side EN2: Enf 3E 22
Treport St. SW18 7K 117
Tresco Cl. BR1: Brom 6G 141
Trescoe Gdns. HA2: Harr 7C 40
Tresco Gdns. IG3: Ilf 2A 72
Tresco Ho. SE11 5J 19
Tresco Rd. SE15 4H 121
Tresham Cres. NW8 3D 4 (4C 82)
Tresham Ho. *WC1* *5G 7*
(*off Red Lion Sq.*)
Tresham Rd. IG11: Bark 7K 71
Tresham Wlk. E9 5J 67
Tresidder Ho. SW4 7H 119
Tresilian Av. N21 5E 22
Tressell Cl. N1 7B 66
Tressillian Cres. SE4 3C 122
Tressillian Rd. SE4 4B 122
Tress Pl. SE1 4A 14
Trestis Cl. UB4: Yead 4B 76
Treswell Rd. RM9: Dag 1E 90
Tretawn Gdns. NW7 4F 29
Tretawn Pk. NW7 4F 29
Trevanion Rd. W14 4G 99
Treve Av. HA1: Harr 7H 41
Trevelyan Av. E12 4D 70
Trevelyan Ct. KT3: N Mald 7A 152
Trevelyan Cres. HA3: Kenton 7D 42
Trevelyan Gdns. NW10 1E 80
Trevelyan Ho. *E2* *3K 85*
(*off Morpeth St.*)
SE5 *7B 102*
(*off John Ruskin St.*)
Trevelyan Rd. E15 4H 69
SW17 5C 136
Trevenna Ho. *SE23* *3K 139*
(*off Dacres Rd.*)
Trevera Ct. EN3: Pond E 4F 25
Treveris St. SE1 5B 14 (1B 102)
Treverton St. W10 4F 81
Treverton Towers *W10* *5F 81*
(*off Treverton St.*)
Treves Cl. N21 5E 22
Treves Ho. *E1* *4G 85*
(*off Vallance Rd.*)
Treville St. SW15 7D 116
Treviso Rd. SE23 2K 139
Trevithick Cl. TW14: Felt 1H 129
Trevithick Ho. *SE16* *4H 103*
(*off Rennie Est.*)
Trevithick St. SE8 6C 104
Trevone Gdns. HA5: Pinn 6C 40
Trevor Cl. BR2: Hayes 7H 159
EN4: E Barn 6G 21
HA3: Hrw W 7E 26
TW7: Isle 5K 113
UB5: N'olt 2A 76
Trevor Cres. HA4: Ruis 4H 57
Trevor Gdns. HA4: Ruis 4J 57
HA8: Edg 1K 43
UB5: N'olt 2A 76
Trevor Pl. SW7 7D 10 (2C 100)
Trevor Rd. HA8: Edg 1K 43
IG8: Wfd G 7D 36
SW19 7G 135
UB3: Hayes 2G 93
Trevor Sq. SW7 7E 10 (2D 100)
Trevor St. SW7 7D 10 (2C 100)
Trevor Wlk. *SW7* *7E 10*
(*off Lancelot Pl.*)
SW7 *7D 10*
(*off Trevor Pl., not continuous*)
Trevose Ho. *SE11* *5H 19*
(*off Orsett St.*)
Trevose Rd. E17 1F 51
Trewenna Dr. KT9: Chess 5D 162
Trewince Rd. SW20 1E 152
Trewint St. SW18 2A 136
Trewsbury Ho. SE2 1D 108
Trewsbury Rd. SE26 5K 139
Tria Apartments *E2* *3G 85*
(*off Durant St.*)
Triandra Way UB4: Yead 5B 76
Triangle, The *DA15: Sidc* *7A 126*
(*off Burnt Oak La.*)
E8 1H 85
EC1 3B 8
IG11: Bark 6G 71
KT1: King T 2H 151
N13 4E 32
Triangle Bus. Cen., The NW10 3B 80
Triangle Cen. UB1: S'hall 1H 95
Triangle Ct. E16 5B 88
SE1 *5D 14*
(*off Redcross Way*)
Triangle Est. *SE11* *6J 19*
(*off Kennington La.*)
SE11 *5A 102*
(*off Kennington Rd.*)
Triangle Ho. *SE1* *6J 15*
(*off Three Oak La.*)
Triangle Pas. EN4: E Barn 4F 21
Triangle Pl. SW4 4H 119
Triangle Rd. E8 1H 85
Triangle Way W3 3G 97
Tribeca Apartments *E1* *6K 9*
(*off Henage St.*)
Trickett Ho. SM2: Sutt 7K 165
Tricorn Ho. SE28 1J 107
Tricycle Cinema, The 7H 63
Tricycle Theatre, The 7H 63
Trident Bus. Cen. SW17 5D 136
Trident Gdns. UB5: N'olt 3B 76
Trident Ho. *E14* *6E 86*
(*off Blair St.*)
SE28 1H 107
TW19: Stanw *7A 110*
(*off Clare Rd.*)
Trident Pl. *SW3* *7B 16*
(*off Old Church St.*)
Trident St. SE16 4K 103
Trident Way UB2: S'hall 3K 93
Trig La. EC4 2C 14 (7C 84)
Trigon Rd. SW8 7K 101
Trilby Rd. SE23 2K 139
Trillo Ct. IG2: Ilf 7J 53
Trimdon NW1 1G 83
Trimmer Wlk. TW8: Bford 6E 96
Trim St. SE14 6B 104
Trinder Gdns. N19 1J 65
Trinder M. TW11: Tedd 5A 132
Trinder Rd. EN5: Barn 5A 20
N19 1J 65
Tring Av. HA9: Wemb 6G 61
UB1: S'hall 6D 76
W5 1F 97
Tring Cl. IG2: Ilf 5H 53
Tring Ct. TW1: Twick 4A 132
Trinidad Gdns. RM10: Dag 7K 73
Trinidad Ho. *E14* *7B 86*
(*off Gill St.*)
Trinidad St. E14 7B 86
Trinity Av. EN1: Enf 6A 24
N2 3B 46
Trinity Buoy Wharf *E14* *7G 87*
(*off Orchard Pl.*)
Trinity Chu. Pas. SW13 6D 98
Trinity Chu. Rd. SW13 6D 98
Trinity Chu. Sq. SE1 7D 14 (3C 102)
Trinity Cl. BR2: Brom 1C 172
CR2: Sande 7E 168
E8 6F 67
E11 2G 69
NW3 4B 64
Trinity Cl. SE13 4F 123
SW4 4G 119
TW4: Houn 4C 112
Trinity College of Music 6E 104
Trinity Cotts. TW9: Rich 3F 115
Trinity Ct. CR0: C'don 2C 168
EN2: Enf 2H 23
N1 *1E 84*
(*off Downham Rd.*)
NW2 5E 62
SE7 4B 106
SE8 *5A 104*
(*off Evelyn St.*)
SE25 6E 156
SE26 3J 139
SW9 3K 119
W2 *6A 82*
(*off Gloucester Ter.*)
W9 *3H 81*
(*off Croxley Rd.*)
WC1 3G 7
Trinity Cres. SW17 2D 136
Trinity Dr. UB8: Hil 5E 74
Trinity Gdns. E16 5H 87
(not continuous)
SW9 4K 119
Trinity Grn. E1 4J 85
Trinity Gro. SE10 1E 122
Trinity Hospital (Almshouses)
SE10 5F 105
Trinity Ho. EC3 2J 15
SE1 *3C 102*
(*off Bath Ter.*)
Trinity M. *E1* *5J 85*
(*off Redman's Rd.*)
SE20 1H 157
W10 6F 81
Trinity Pk. E4 6G 35
Trinity Path SE23 3J 139
Trinity Pl. DA6: Bex 4F 127
EC3 2J 15 (7F 85)
Trinity Ri. SW2 1A 138
Trinity Rd. IG6: Ilf 3G 53
N2 3B 46
N22 7D 32
(not continuous)
SW17 4A 118
SW18 4A 118
SW19 6J 135
TW9: Rich 3F 115
UB1: S'hall 1C 94
Trinity Sq. EC3 3H 15 (7E 84)
Trinity St. E16 5H 87
EN2: Enf 2H 23
SE1 7D 14 (2C 102)
(not continuous)
Trinity Twr. *E1* *7G 85*
(*off Vaughan Way*)
Trinity Wlk. NW3 6A 64
Trinity Way E4 6G 35
W3 7A 80
Trio Pl. SE1 7D 14 (2C 102)
Tristan Ct. *SE8* *6B 104*
(*off Dorking Cl.*)
Tristan Sq. SE3 3G 123
Tristram Cl. E17 3F 51
Tristram Dr. N9 3B 34
Tristram Rd. BR1: Brom 4H 141
Triton Ho. *E14* *4D 104*
(*off Cahir St.*)
Triton Sq. NW1 3A 6 (4G 83)
Triton St. NW1 3A 6 (4G 83)
Tritton Av. CR0: Bedd 4J 167
Tritton Rd. SE21 3D 138
Triumph Cl. UB3: Harl 1E 110
Triumph Ho. IG11: Bark 3A 90
Triumph Rd. E6 6D 88
Triumph Trad. Est. N17 6B 34
Trocadero Cen. 2C 12 (7H 83)
Trocette Mans. *SE1* *3E 102*
(*off Bermondsey St.*)
Trojan Ct. NW6 7G 63

Trojan Ind. Est. NW10 6B 62
Trojan Way CR0: Wadd 3K 167
Troon Cl. SE16 5H 103
SE28 6D 90
Troon Ho. *E1* *6A 86*
(off White Horse Rd.)
Troon St. E1 6A 86
Tropical Ct. *W10* *3F 81*
(off Kilburn La.)
Tropical Forest, The 7C 96
Trosley Rd. DA17: Belv 6G 109
Trossachs Rd. SE22 5E 120
Trothy Rd. SE1 4G 103
Trotman Ho. *SE14* *1J 121*
(off Pomeroy St.)
Trott Rd. N10 7J 31
Trott St. SW11 1C 118
Trotwood Ho. *SE16* *2H 103*
(off Wilson Gro.)
Troughton Rd. SE7 5K 105
Troutbeck NW1 2K 5
Troutbeck Rd. SE14 1A 122
Trout Rd. UB7: Yiew 7A 74
Trouville Rd. SW4 6G 119
Trowbridge Rd. E9 6B 68
Trowlock Av. TW11: Tedd 6C 132
Trowlock Island TW11: Tedd 6D 132
Trowlock Way TW11: Tedd 6D 132
Troy Ct. SE18 4F 107
W8 *3J 99*
(off Kensington High St.)
Troy Ind. Est. HA1: Harr 5K 41
Troy Rd. SE19 6D 138
Troy Town SE15 3G 121
Trubshaw Rd. UB2: S'hall 3F 95
True Lovers Ct. HA6: Nwood 1F 39
Trueman Cl. HA8: Edg 7C 28
Truesdale Rd. E6 6D 88
Trulock Ct. N17 7B 34
Trulock Rd. N17 7B 34
Trumans Rd. N16 5F 67
Trumble Gdns. CR7: Thor H 4C 156
Trumpers Way W7 3J 95
Trumpington Rd. E7 4H 69
Trump St. EC2 1D 14 (6C 84)
Trundle Ho. *SE1* *2C 102*
(off Trundle St.)
Trundlers Way WD23: B Hea 1D 26
Trundle St. SE1 6C 14 (2C 102)
Trundleys Rd. SE8 5K 103
Trundley's Ter. SE8 4K 103
Truro Gdns. IG1: Ilf 7C 52
Truro Ho. HA5: Hat E 1D 40
W2 *5J 81*
(off Westbourne Pk. Rd.)
Truro Rd. E17 4B 50
N22 7D 32
Truro St. NW5 6E 64
Truro Way UB4: Hayes 3G 75
Truslove Rd. SE27 5A 138
Trussley Rd. W6 3E 98
Trust Wlk. SE21 1B 138
Tryfan Cl. IG4: Ilf 5B 52
Tryon Cres. E9 1J 85
Tryon St. SW3 5E 16 (5D 100)
Trystings Cl. KT10: Clay 6A 162
Tuam Rd. SE18 6H 107
Tubbenden Cl. BR6: Orp 3J 173
Tubbenden Dr. BR6: Orp 4H 173
Tubbenden La. BR6: Orp 4H 173
Tubbenden La. Sth. BR6: Farnb 5H 173
Tubbs Rd. NW10 2B 80
Tucklow Wlk. SW15 7B 116
Tudor Av. KT4: Wor Pk 3D 164
TW12: Hamp 6E 130
Tudor Cl. BR7: Chst 1D 160
HA5: Eastc 5J 39
IG7: Chig 4K 37
IG8: Wfd G 5E 36
KT9: Chess 5E 162
N6 7G 47
NW3 5C 64
Tudor Cl. NW7 6H 29
NW9 2J 61
SM3: Cheam 5F 165
SM6: Wall 7G 167
SW2 6K 119
TW12: Ham H 5G 131
TW15: Ashf 4A 128
Tudor Ct. DA14: Sidc 3A 144
E17 7B 50
N1 6E 66
N22 7D 32
SE9 4C 124
SE16 *1K 103*
(off Princes Riverside Rd.)
TW11: Tedd 6K 131
TW13: Hanw 4A 130
TW19: Stanw 6A 110
W3 2G 97
Tudor Ct. Nth. HA9: Wemb 5G 61
Tudor Ct. Sth. HA9: Wemb 5G 61
Tudor Cres. EN2: Enf 1H 23
Tudor Dr. KT2: King T 5D 132
SM4: Mord 6F 153
Tudor Ent. Pk. HA1: Harr 3K 59
HA3: W'stone 3H 41
Tudor Est. NW10 2H 79
Tudor Gdns. BR4: W W'ck 3E 170
HA3: Hrw W 2H 41
NW9 2J 61
SW13 3A 116
TW1: Twick 1K 131
W3 5G 79
Tudor Gro. E9 7J 67
Tudor Ho. E9 7J 67
E16 *1K 105*
(off Wesley Av.)
HA5: Pinn *2A 40*
(off Pinner Hill Rd.)
W14 *4F 99*
(off Windsor Way)
Tudor M. E17 4B 50
Tudor Pde. RM6: Chad H 7D 54
SE9 4C 124
Tudor Pl. CR4: Mitc 7C 136
SE19 7F 139
Tudor Rd. BR3: Beck 3E 158
E4 6J 35
E6 1A 88
E9 1H 85
EN5: New Bar 3D 20
HA3: Hrw W, W'stone 2H 41
HA5: Pinn 2A 40
IG11: Bark 1K 89
KT2: King T 7G 133
N9 7C 24
SE19 7F 139
SE25 5H 157
TW3: Houn 4H 113
TW12: Hamp 7E 130
TW15: Ashf 6F 129
UB1: S'hall 7C 76
UB3: Hayes 6F 75
Tudor Sq. UB3: Hayes 5F 75
Tudor Stacks SE24 4C 120
Tudor St. EC4 2K 13 (7A 84)
Tudor Wlk. DA5: Bexl 6E 126
Tudor Way BR5: Pet W 6H 161
N14 1C 32
UB10: Hil 6C 56
W3 2G 97
Tudor Well Cl. HA7: Stan 5G 27
Tudor Works UB4: Yead 1A 94
Tudway Rd. SE3 3K 123
Tufnell Ct. *E3* *1B 86*
(off Old Ford Rd.)
TUFNELL PARK 4G 65
Tufnell Pk. Rd. N7 4G 65
N19 4G 65
Tufton Ct. *SW1* *2E 18*
(off Tufton St.)
Tufton Gdns. KT8: W Mole 2F 149
Tufton Rd. E4 4H 35
Tufton St. SW1 1E 18 (3J 101)
Tugboat St. SE28 2J 107
Tugela Rd. CR0: C'don 6D 156
Tugela St. SE6 2B 140
Tugmutton Cl. BR6: Farnb 4F 173
Tulip Cl. CR0: C'don 1K 169
E6 5D 88
TW12: Hamp 6D 130
UB2: S'hall 2G 95
Tulip Gdns. E4 3A 36
IG1: Ilf 6F 71
Tullis Ho. *E9* *7J 67*
(off Frampton Pk. Rd.)
Tull St. CR4: Mitc 7D 154
Tulse Cl. BR3: Beck 3E 158
TULSE HILL 1B 138
Tulse Hill SW2 6A 120
Tulse Hill Est. SW2 6A 120
Tulse Ho. SW2 6A 120
Tulsemere Rd. SE27 2C 138
Tumbling Bay KT12: Walt T 6J 147
Tummons Gdns. SE25 2E 156
Tump Ho. SE28 1J 107
Tunbridge Ho. EC1 1K 7
Tuncombe Rd. N18 4K 33
Tunis Rd. W12 1E 98
Tunley Grn. E14 5B 86
Tunley Rd. NW10 1A 80
SW17 1E 136
Tunmarsh La. E13 3K 87
Tunnan Leys E6 6E 88
Tunnel App. E14 7A 86
SE10 2G 105
SE16 2J 103
Tunnel Av. SE10 2F 105
(not continuous)
Tunnel Av. Trad. Est. SE10 2F 105
Tunnel Gdns. N11 7B 32
Tunnel Link Rd. TW6: H'row A 5C 110
Tunnel Rd. SE16 2J 103
Tunnel Rd. E. TW6: H'row A 1D 110
Tunnel Rd. W.
TW6: H'row A 1C 110
Tunstall Cl. BR6: Orp 4J 173
Tunstall Rd. CR0: C'don 1E 168
SW9 4K 119
Tunstall Wlk. TW8: Bford 6E 96
Tunstock Way DA17: Belv 3E 108
Tunworth Cl. NW9 6J 43
Tunworth Cres. SW15 6B 116
Tun Yd. *SW8* *2F 119*
(off Peardon St.)
Tupelo Rd. E10 2D 68
Tupman Ho. *SE16* *2G 103*
(off Scott Lidgett Cres.)
Tuppy St. SE28 3G 107
Turenne Cl. SW18 4A 118
Turin Rd. N9 7D 24
Turin St. E2 2K 9 (3G 85)
Turkey Oak Cl. SE19 1E 156
Turks Boatyard
KT1: King T 1D 150
Turks Cl. UB8: Hil 3C 74
Turk's Head Yd. EC1 5A 8 (5B 84)
Turk's Row SW3 5F 17 (5D 100)
Turle Rd. N4 2K 65
SW16 2J 155
Turlewray Cl. N4 1K 65
Turley Cl. E15 1G 87
Turnagain La. EC4 7A 8
Turnage Rd. RM8: Dag 1E 72
Turnant Rd. N17 1C 48
Turnberry Cl. NW4 2F 45
SE16 5H 103
Turnberry Quay E14 3D 104
Turnberry Way BR6: Orp 1H 173
Turnbull Ho. N1 1B 84
Turnbury Cl. SE28 6D 90
Turnchapel M. SW4 3F 119
Turner Av. CR4: Mitc 1D 154
N15 4E 48
TW2: Twick 3G 131
Turner Cl. HA0: Wemb 6D 60
NW11 6K 45
SW9 7B 102
UB4: Hayes 2E 74
Turner Ct. *SE16* *2J 103*
(off Albion St.)
Turner Cres. CR0: C'don 6C 156
Turner Dr. NW11 6K 45
Turner Ho. *E14* *2C 104*
(off Cassilis Rd.)
NW6 *5A 64*
(off Dresden Cl.)
NW8 *2C 82*
(off Townshend Est.)
SW1 *4D 18*
(off Herrick St.)
TW1: Twick *6D 114*
(off Clevedon Rd.)
Turner M. SM2: Sutt 7K 165
Turner Pl. SW11 5C 118
Turner Rd. E17 3E 50
HA8: Edg 2E 42
KT3: N Mald 7K 151
Turners Cl. N20 3J 31
Turners Ct. N15 5D 48
Turners Mdw. Way
BR3: Beck 1B 158
Turners Rd. E3 5B 86
Turner St. E1 5H 85
E16 6H 87
Turners Way CR0: Wadd 2A 168
Turners Wood NW11 7A 46
Turneville Rd. W14 6H 99
Turney Rd. SE21 7C 120
TURNHAM GREEN 4A 98
Turnham Grn. Ter. W4 4A 98
Turnham Grn. Ter. M.
W4 4A 98
Turnham Rd. SE4 5A 122
Turnmill St. EC1 4A 8 (4B 84)
Turnour Ho. *E1* *6H 85*
(off Walburgh St.)
Turnpike Cl. SE8 7B 104
Turnpike Ct. DA6: Bex 4D 126
Turnpike Ho. EC1 2B 8 (3B 84)
Turnpike La. N8 4K 47
SM1: Sutt 5A 166
UB10: Uxb 3A 74
Turnpike Link CR0: C'don 2E 168
Turnpike M. *N8* *3A 48*
(off Turnpike La.)
Turnpike Pde. *N15* *3B 48*
(off Green Lanes)
Turnpike Way TW7: Isle 1A 114
Turnpin La. SE10 6E 104
Turnstone Cl. E13 3J 87
NW9 2A 44
UB10: Ick 5D 56
Turnstone Ho. *E1* *3K 15*
(off Star Pl.)
Turpentine La. SW1 5K 17 (5F 101)
Turpin Cl. E1 7K 85
Turpington Cl. BR2: Brom 6C 160
Turpington La. BR2: Brom 7C 160
Turpin Ho. SW11 1F 119
Turpin Rd. TW14: Felt 6H 111
Turpin's La. IG8: Wfd G 5J 37
Turpins Yd. NW2 5F 63
SE10 7E 104
Turpin Way N19 2H 65
SM6: Wall 7F 167
Turquand St. SE17 4C 102
Turret Gro. SW4 3G 119
Turton Rd. HA0: Wemb 5E 60
Turville Ho. *NW8* *3C 4*
(off Grendon St.)
Turville St. E2 3J 9 (4F 85)
Tuscan Ho. *E2* *3J 85*
(off Knottisford St.)
Tuscan Rd. SE18 5H 107
Tuscany Ho. E17 2B 50
IG3: Ilf 6A 54

Tuskar St. SE10 . . . . .6G 105
Tustin Est. SE15 . . . . .6J 103
Tuttlebee La. IG9: Buck H 2D 36
Tuttle Ho. SW1 . . . . .6C 18
(off Aylesford St.)
Tweed Ct. W7 . . . . .6J 77
(off Hanway Rd.)
Tweeddale Gro. UB10: Ick 3E 56
Tweeddale Rd. SM5: Cars 1B 166
Tweed Glen RM1: Rom 1K 55
Tweed Grn. RM1: Rom 1K 55
Tweed Ho. E14 . . . . .4E 86
(off Teviot St.)
Tweedmouth Rd. E13 . . . . .2K 87
Tweed Way RM1: Rom 1K 55
Tweedy Cl. EN1: Enf 5A 24
Tweedy Rd. BR1: Brom 1J 159
Tweezer's All. WC2 . . . . .2J 13
Twelve Acre Ho. E12 . . . . .3E 70
(off Grantham Rd.)
Twelvetrees Bus. Pk. E3 . . . . .4F 87
Twelvetrees Cres. E3 . . . . .4E 86
(not continuous)
E16 . . . . .4E 86
Twentyman Cl. IG8: Wfd G 5D 36
TWICKENHAM 1A 132
Twickenham Bri. TW1: Twick 5C 114
Twickenham Cl. CR0: Bedd 3K 167
Twickenham Gdns.
HA3: Hrw W 7D 26
UB6: G'frd 5A 60
Twickenham Rd. E11 . . . . .2E 68
TW7: Isle 5A 114
TW9: Rich 4C 114
TW11: Tedd 4A 132
(not continuous)
TW13: Hanw 3D 130
Twickenham Stadium 6J 113
Twickenham Stoop, The 7J 113
Twickenham Trad. Est.
TW1: Twick 6K 113
Twig Folly Cl. E2 . . . . .2K 85
Twigg Cl. DA8: Erith 7K 109
Twilley St. SW18 . . . . .7K 117
Twin Bridges Bus. Pk.
CR2: S Croy 6D 168
Twine Cl. IG11: Bark 3B 90
Twine Ct. E1 . . . . .7J 85
Twineham Grn. N12 . . . . .4D 30
Twine Ter. E3 . . . . .4B 86
(off Ropery St.)
Twining Av. TW2: Twick 3G 131
Twin Tumps Way SE28 . . . . .7A 90
Twisden Rd. NW5 . . . . .4F 65
Twitten Gro. BR1: Brom 3D 160
Twybridge Way NW10 . . . . .7J 61
Twycross M. SE10 . . . . .5G 105
Twyford Abbey Rd. NW10 . . . . .3F 79
Twyford Av. N2 . . . . .3D 46
W3 . . . . .7G 79
Twyford Ct. HA0: Wemb 2E 78
(off Vicars Bri. Cl.)
N10 . . . . .3E 46
Twyford Cres. W3 . . . . .1G 97
Twyford Ho. N5 . . . . .3B 66
N15 . . . . .6E 48
(off Chisley Rd.)
Twyford Pl. WC2 . . . . .7G 7 (6K 83)
Twyford Rd. HA2: Harr 1F 59
IG1: Ilf 5G 71
SM5: Cars 1B 166
Twyford Sports Cen. 1H 97
Twyford St. N1 . . . . .1K 83
Twynholm Mans. SW6 . . . . .7G 99
(off Lillie Rd.)
Tyas Rd. E16 . . . . .4H 87
Tybenham Rd. SW19 . . . . .3J 153
Tyberry Rd. EN3: Enf H 3C 24
Tyburn Ho. NW8 . . . . .4B 82
(off Fisherton St.)
NW8 . . . . .3B 4
(off Fisherton St.)

Tyburn La. HA1: Harr 7K 41
Tyburn Tree (site of) 1F 11
Tyburn Way W1 . . . . .2F 11 (7D 82)
Tye La. BR6: Farnb 5G 173
Tyers Est. SE1 . . . . .6G 15
Tyers Ga. SE1 . . . . .7G 15 (2E 102)
Tyers St. SE11 . . . . .6G 19 (5K 101)
Tyers Ter. SE11 . . . . .6G 19 (5K 101)
Tyeshurst Cl. SE2 . . . . .5E 108
Tylecroft Rd. SW16 . . . . .2J 155
Tylehurst Gdns. IG1: Ilf 5G 71
Tyler Cl. DA8: Erith 7H 109
E2 . . . . .2F 85
Tyler Rd. UB2: S'hall 3F 95
Tylers Ct. E17 . . . . .4C 50
(off Westbury Rd.)
HA0: Wemb 2E 78
W1 . . . . .1C 12
Tylers Ga. HA3: Kenton 6E 42
Tylers Path SM5: Cars 4D 166
Tyler St. SE10 . . . . .5G 105
(not continuous)
Tylney Av. SE19 . . . . .5F 139
(not continuous)
Tylney Ho. E1 . . . . .6H 85
(off Nelson St.)
Tylney Rd. BR1: Brom 2B 160
E7 . . . . .4A 70
Tynamara KT1: King T 4D 150
(off Portsmouth Rd.)
Tynan Cl. TW14: Felt 1J 129
Tyndale Ct. E14 . . . . .5D 104
(off Transom Sq.)
Tyndale Ho. N1 . . . . .7B 66
(off Tyndale La.)
Tyndale La. N1 . . . . .7B 66
Tyndale Mans. N1 . . . . .7B 66
(off Upper St.)
Tyndale Ter. N1 . . . . .7B 66
Tyndall Gdns. E10 . . . . .2E 68
Tyndall Rd. DA16: Well 3K 125
E10 . . . . .2E 68
Tyne St. W7 . . . . .6J 77
(off Hanway Rd.)
Tyneham Cl. SW11 . . . . .3E 118
Tyneham Rd. SW11 . . . . .2E 118
Tyne Ho. KT2: King T 1D 150
Tynemouth Cl. E6 . . . . .6F 89
Tynemouth Dr. EN1: Enf 1B 24
Tynemouth Rd.
CR4: Mitc 7E 136
N15 . . . . .4F 49
SE18 . . . . .5J 107
Tynemouth St. SW6 . . . . .2A 118
Tyne St. E1 . . . . .7K 9 (6F 85)
Tynsdale Rd. NW10 . . . . .7A 62
Tynwald Ho. SE26 . . . . .3G 139
Type St. E2 . . . . .2K 85
Typhoon Way SM6: Wall 7J 167
Tyrawley Rd. SW6 . . . . .1K 117
Tyre La. NW9 . . . . .4A 44
Tyrell Cl. HA1: Harr 4J 59
Tyrell Ct. SM5: Cars 4D 166
Tyrell Ho. BR3: Beck 5D 140
(off Beckenham Hill Rd.)
Tyrols Rd. SE23 . . . . .1K 139
Tyrone Rd. E6 . . . . .2D 88
Tyron Way DA14: Sidc 4J 143
Tyrrell Av. DA16: Well 5A 126
Tyrrell Ho. SW1 . . . . .7B 18
(off Churchill Gdns.)
Tyrrell Rd. SE22 . . . . .4G 121
Tyrrell Sq. CR4: Mitc 1C 154
Tyrrel Way NW9 . . . . .7B 44
Tyrwhitt Rd. SE4 . . . . .3C 122
Tysoe St. EC1 . . . . .2K 7 (3A 84)
Tyson Gdns. SE23 . . . . .7J 121
Tyson Rd. SE23 . . . . .7J 121
Tyssen Pas. E8 . . . . .6F 67
Tyssen Rd. N16 . . . . .3F 67
Tyssen St. E8 . . . . .6F 67
N1 . . . . .2E 84

Tytherton E2 . . . . .2J 85
(off Cyprus St.)
Tytherton Rd. N19 . . . . .3H 65

U

Uamvar St. E14 . . . . .5D 86
Uber E17 . . . . .4B 50
Uckfield Gro. CR4: Mitc 7E 136
Udall St. SW1 . . . . .4B 18 (4G 101)
Udimore Ho. W10 . . . . .5E 80
(off Sutton Way)
Udney Pk. Rd. TW11: Tedd 6A 132
Uffington Rd. NW10 . . . . .1C 80
SE27 . . . . .4A 138
Ufford Cl. HA3: Hrw W 7A 26
Ufford Rd. HA3: Hrw W 7A 26
Ufford St. SE1 . . . . .6K 13 (2A 102)
Ufton Cl. UB5: N'olt 3B 76
Ufton Gro. N1 . . . . .7D 66
Ufton Rd. N1 . . . . .7D 66
(not continuous)
Uhura Sq. N16 . . . . .3E 66
Ujima Ct. SW16 . . . . .4J 137
Ullathorne Rd. SW16 . . . . .4G 137
Ulleswater Rd. N14 . . . . .3D 32
Ullin St. E14 . . . . .5E 86
Ullswater E18 . . . . .2J 51
Ullswater Cl. BR1: Brom 7G 141
SW15 . . . . .4K 133
UB4: Hayes 2G 75
Ullswater Ct. HA2: Harr 7E 40
Ullswater Cres. SW15 . . . . .4K 133
Ullswater Ho. SE15 . . . . .6J 103
(off Hillbeck Cl.)
Ullswater Rd. SE27 . . . . .2B 138
SW13 . . . . .7C 98
Ulster Gdns. N13 . . . . .4H 33
Ulster Pl. NW1 . . . . .4J 5 (4F 83)
Ulster Ter. NW1 . . . . .3H 5 (4F 83)
Ulundi Rd. SE3 . . . . .6G 105
Ulva Rd. SW15 . . . . .5F 117
Ulverscroft Rd. SE22 . . . . .5F 121
Ulverstone Rd. SE27 . . . . .2B 138
Ulverston Rd. E17 . . . . .2F 51
Ulysses Rd. NW6 . . . . .5H 63
Umberston St. E1 . . . . .6G 85
Umbria St. SW15 . . . . .6C 116
Umfreville Rd. N4 . . . . .6B 48
Undercliff Rd. SE13 . . . . .3C 122
UNDERHILL 5D 20
Underhill EN5: Barn 5D 20
Underhill Cl. EN5: Barn 5C 20
Underhill Ho. E14 . . . . .5C 86
(off Burgess St.)
Underhill Pas. NW1 . . . . .1F 83
(off Camden High St.)
Underhill Rd. SE22 . . . . .5G 121
Underhill Stadium 5D 20
Underhill St. NW1 . . . . .1F 83
Underne Av. N14 . . . . .2A 32
Undershaft EC3 . . . . .1G 15 (6E 84)
Undershaw Rd.
BR1: Brom 3H 141
Underwood CR0: New Ad 5E 170
Underwood, The SE9 . . . . .2D 142
Underwood Ct. E10 . . . . .1D 68
(off Leyton Grange Est.)
Underwood Ho. KT8: W Mole 5E 148
(off Approach Rd.)
W6 . . . . .3D 98
(off Sycamore Gdns.)
Underwood Rd. E1 . . . . .4G 85
E4 . . . . .5J 35
IG8: Wfd G 7F 37
Underwood Row N1 . . . . .1D 8 (3C 84)
Underwood St. N1 . . . . .1D 8 (3C 84)
Undine Rd. E14 . . . . .4D 104
Undine St. SW17 . . . . .5D 136
Uneeda Dr. UB6: G'frd 1H 77

Unicorn Bldg. E1 . . . . .7K 85
(off Jardine Rd.)
Unicorn Theatre 1E 102
Unicorn Works N17 . . . . .7D 34
Union Cl. E11 . . . . .4F 69
Union Cotts. E15 . . . . .7G 69
Union Ct. EC2 . . . . .7G 9
SW4 . . . . .2J 119
TW9: Rich 5E 114
W9 . . . . .5J 81
(off Elmfield Way)
Union Dr. E1 . . . . .4A 86
Union Gro. SW8 . . . . .2H 119
Union M. SW9 . . . . .2J 119
Union Pk. SE10 . . . . .5H 105
(off Calvert Rd.)
Union Rd. BR2: Brom 5B 160
CR0: C'don 7C 156
HA0: Wemb 6E 60
N11 . . . . .6C 32
RM7: Rush G 6K 55
SW4 . . . . .2H 119
SW8 . . . . .2H 119
UB5: N'olt 2E 76
Union Sq. N1 . . . . .1C 84
Union St. EN5: Barn 3B 20
KT1: King T 2D 150
SE1 . . . . .5A 14 (1B 102)
Union Theatre 5B 14
Union Wlk. E2 . . . . .1H 9 (3E 84)
Union Wharf N1 . . . . .1C 84
(Arlington Av.)
N1 . . . . .2C 84
(off Wenlock Rd.)
UB7: Yiew 1A 92
(off Bentinck Rd.)
Union Yd. W1 . . . . .1K 11 (6F 83)
Unitair Cen. TW14: Bedf 6E 110
United Ho. SE16 . . . . .2J 103
(off Brunel Rd.)
Unit Workshops E1 . . . . .6G 85
(off Adler St.)
Unity Cl. CR0: New Ad 7D 170
NW10 . . . . .6C 62
SE19 . . . . .5C 138
Unity Ct. SE1 . . . . .5F 103
(off Fortune Pl.)
Unity M. NW1 . . . . .2H 83
Unity Ter. HA2: Harr 1F 59
Unity Trad. Est. IG8: Wfd G 2B 52
Unity Way SE18 . . . . .3B 106
Unity Wharf SE1 . . . . .6K 15
(off Mill St.)
Universal Ho. UB1: S'hall 7C 76
University Cl. NW7 . . . . .7G 29
University College London
Art Collections 3C 6
Bloomsbury Campus . . .3C 6 (4H 83)
Department of
Geological Sciences Collection
. . . . .4C 6
(off Gower St.)
Institute of Neurology 4F 7
(off Queen Sq.)
Slade School of Fine Art 3C 6
(off Gower St.)
Windeyer Institute 5B 6 (5G 83)
University Gdns. DA5: Bexl 7F 127
University of East London
Docklands Campus 7E 88
Duncan House 1F 87
Stratford Campus 6G 69
University of Greenwich
Avery Hill Campus 6G 125
Greenwich Campus -
King William Wlk. 6F 105
Maritime Greenwich Campus
. . . . .6E 104
University of London
Birkbeck College 5D 6 (5H 83)
Heythrop College 3K 99
(off Kensington Sq.)

University of London—Vale, The

University of London
Institute of Education &
Institute of Advanced Legal Studies
. . . 4D 6 (4H 83)
School of Hygiene & Tropical Medicine
. . . 5D 6
School of Oriental & African Studies
. . . 4D 6
Senate House . . . 5D 6 (5H 83)
Warburg Institute . . . 4D 6 (4H 83)
University of London Observatory . . . 6G 29
University of North London
Hornsey Rd. . . . 4A 66
Ladbrooke House . . . 5C 66
North London Campus -
Spring House . . . 6A 66
University of the Arts London
Chelsea College of Art & Design
. . . 5D 18 (5H 101)
London College of Fashion
. . . 4C 8 (7J 67)
Wimbledon College of Art . . . *1G 153*
(off Merton Hall Rd.)
Camberwell College of Arts -
Peckham Rd. . . . 1E 120
Wilson Rd. . . . 1E 120
University of Westminster
Cavendish Campus-
Bolsover St. . . . 5K 5 (5F 83)
Hanson St. . . . 5A 6 (5G 83)
Lit. Titchfield St. . . . 6A 6
Harrow Campus . . . 7A 42
Marylebone Campus . . . 5G 5 (5E 82)
Regent Campus -
Regent St. . . . 7K 5
Wells St. . . . 7B 6
University of Westminster Sports Cen.
. . . 7A 42
University Pl. DA8: Erith . . . 7J **109**
University Rd. SW19 . . . 6B **136**
University St. WC1 . . . 4B **6** (4G **83**)
University Way E16 . . . 7E **88**
Unwin Av. TW14: Felt . . . 5F **111**
Unwin Cl. SE15 . . . 6G **103**
Unwin Mans. *W14* . . . *6H* ***99***
(off Queen's Club Gdns.)
Unwin Rd. SW7 . . . 1A **16** (3B **100**)
TW7: Isle . . . 3J **113**
Upbrook M. W2 . . . 1A **10** (6A **82**)
Upcerne Rd. SW10 . . . 7A **100**
Upchurch Cl. SE20 . . . 7H **139**
Upcott Ho. *E3* . . . *3D* ***86***
(off Bruce Rd.)
E9 . . . *7J* ***67***
(off Frampton Pk. Rd.)
Upcroft Av. HA8: Edg . . . 5D **28**
Updale Rd. DA14: Sidc . . . 4K **143**
Upfield CR0: C'don . . . 3H **169**
Upfield Rd. W7 . . . 5K **77**
Upgrove Mnr. Way SW2 . . . 7A **120**
Uphall Rd. IG1: Ilf . . . 5F **71**
Upham Pk. Rd. W4 . . . 4A **98**
Uphill *BR2: Brom* . . . *4H* ***159***
(off Westmoreland Rd.)
Uphill Dr. NW7 . . . 5F **29**
NW9 . . . 5J **43**
Uphill Gro. NW7 . . . 4F **29**
Uphill Rd. NW7 . . . 4F **29**
Upland M. SE22 . . . 5G **121**
Upland Rd. CR2: S Croy . . . 5D **168**
DA7: Bex . . . 3F **127**
E13 . . . 4J **87**
SE22 . . . 5G **121**
SM2: Sutt . . . 7B **166**
Uplands BR3: Beck . . . 2C **158**
Uplands, The HA4: Ruis . . . 1J **57**
Uplands Av. E17 . . . 2K **49**
Uplands Bus. Pk. E17 . . . 3K **49**
Uplands Cl. SE18 . . . 5F **107**
SW14 . . . 5H **115**
Uplands Ct. *N21* . . . *7F* ***23***
(off The Green)
Uplands End IG8: Wfd G . . . 7H **37**
Uplands Pk. Rd. EN2: Enf . . . 2F **23**
Uplands Rd. EN4: E Barn . . . 1K **31**
IG8: Wfd G . . . 7H **37**
N8 . . . 5K **47**
RM6: Chad H . . . 3D **54**
Uplands Way N21 . . . 5F **23**
Upnall Ho. SE15 . . . 6J **103**
Upney La. IG11: Bark . . . 6J **71**
Upnor Way SE17 . . . 5E **102**
Uppark Dr. IG2: Ilf . . . 6G **53**
Up. Abbey Rd. DA17: Belv . . . 4F **109**
Up. Addison Gdns. W14 . . . 2G **99**
Up. Bank St. E14 . . . 1D **104**
(not continuous)
Up. Bardsey Wlk. *N1* . . . *6C* ***66***
(off Douglas Rd. Nth.)
Up. Belgrave St. SW1 . . . 1H **17** (3E **100**)
Up. Berenger Wlk. *SW10* . . . *7B* ***100***
(off Berenger Wlk.)
Up. Berkeley St. W1 . . . 1E **10** (6D **82**)
Up. Beulah Hill SE19 . . . 1E **156**
Up. Blantyre Wlk. *SW10* . . . *7B* ***100***
(off Blantyre Wlk.)
Up. Brighton Rd. KT6: Surb . . . 6D **150**
Up. Brockley Rd. SE4 . . . 3B **122**
(not continuous)
Up. Brook St. W1 . . . 2G **11** (7E **82**)
Upper Butts TW8: Bford . . . 6C **96**
Up. Caldy Wlk. *N1* . . . *6C* ***66***
(off Caldy Wlk.)
Up. Camelford Wlk. *W11* . . . *6G* ***81***
(off Cambourne M.)
W11 . . . *6G* ***81***
(off St Mark's Rd.)
Up. Cavendish Av. N3 . . . 3J **45**
Up. Cheyne Row SW3 . . . 7C **16** (6C **100**)
UPPER CLAPTON . . . 2H 67
Up. Clapton Rd. E5 . . . 1H **67**
Up. Clarendon Wlk. *W11* . . . *6G* ***81***
(off Clarendon Rd.)
Up. Dartrey Wlk. *SW10* . . . *7A* ***100***
(off Whistler Wlk.)
Up. Dengie Wlk. *N1* . . . *1C* ***84***
(off Baddow Wlk.)
UPPER EDMONTON . . . 5B 34
UPPER ELMERS END . . . 5B 158
Up. Elmers End Rd. BR3: Beck . . . 4A **158**
Up. Farm Rd. KT8: W Mole . . . 4D **148**
Upper Feilde *W1* . . . *2G* ***11***
(off Park St.)
Upper Fosters *NW4* . . . *4E* ***44***
(off New Brent St.)
Up. Green E. CR4: Mitc . . . 3D **154**
Up. Green W. CR4: Mitc . . . 2D **154**
(not continuous)
Up. Grosvenor St. W1 . . . 3G **11** (7E **82**)
Up. Grotto Rd. TW1: Twick . . . 2K **131**
Upper Ground SE1 . . . 4J **13** (1A **102**)
Upper Gro. SE25 . . . 4E **156**
Up. Grove Rd. DA17: Belv . . . 6F **109**
Up. Gulland Wlk. *N1* . . . *7C* ***66***
(off Church Rd.)
UPPER HALLIFORD . . . 4G 147
Up. Halliford By-Pass TW17: Shep . . . 5G **147**
Up. Halliford Grn. TW17: Shep . . . 4G **147**
Up. Halliford Rd. TW17: Shep . . . 3G **147**
Up. Hampstead Wlk. NW3 . . . 4A **64**
Up. Ham Rd. KT2: King T . . . 4D **132**
TW10: Ham . . . 4D **132**
Up. Handa Wlk. *N1* . . . *6D* ***66***
(off Handa Wlk.)
Up. Hawkwell Wlk. *N1* . . . *1C* ***84***
(off Maldon Cl.)
UPPER HOLLOWAY . . . 2G 65
Up. Holly Hill Rd. DA17: Belv . . . 5H **109**
Up. James St. W1 . . . 2B **12** (7G **83**)
Up. John St. W1 . . . 2B **12** (7G **83**)
Up. Lismore Wlk. *N1* . . . *6C* ***66***
(off Clephane Rd.)
Upper Lodge *W8* . . . *1K* ***99***
(off Palace Grn.)
Up. Lodge M. TW12: Ham H . . . 6H **131**
Upper Mall W6 . . . 5C **98**
(not continuous)
Upper Marsh SE1 . . . 1H **19** (3K **101**)
Up. Montagu St. W1 . . . 5E **4** (5D **82**)
Up. Mulgrave Rd. SM2: Cheam . . . 7G **165**
Upper Nth. St. E14 . . . 5C **86**
UPPER NORWOOD . . . 1E 156
Up. Park Rd. BR1: Brom . . . 1K **159**
DA17: Belv . . . 4H **109**
KT2: King T . . . 6G **133**
N11 . . . 5A **32**
NW3 . . . 5D **64**
Up. Phillimore Gdns. W8 . . . 2J **99**
Up. Ramsey Wlk. *N1* . . . *6D* ***66***
(off Ramsey Wlk.)
Up. Rawreth Wlk. *N1* . . . *1C* ***84***
(off Basire St.)
Up. Richmond Rd. SW15 . . . 4B **116**
Up. Richmond Rd. W. SW14 . . . 4G **115**
TW10: Rich . . . 4G **115**
Upper Rd. E13 . . . 3J **87**
SM6: Wall . . . 5H **167**
UPPER RUXLEY . . . 7G 145
Up. St Martin's La. WC2 . . . 2E **12** (7J **83**)
Up. Selsdon Rd.
CR2: Sande, Sels . . . 7F **169**
Up. Sheridan Rd. DA17: Belv . . . 4G **109**
UPPER SHIRLEY . . . 4K 169
Up. Shirley Rd. CR0: C'don . . . 2J **169**
Upper Sq. TW7: Isle . . . 3A **114**
Upper St. N1 . . . 2A **84**
Up. Sunbury Rd. TW12: Hamp . . . 1C **148**
Up. Sutton La. TW5: Hest . . . 7E **94**
UPPER SYDENHAM . . . 3H 139
Up. Tachbrook St. SW1 . . . 3B **18** (4G **101**)
Up. Talbot Wlk. *W11* . . . *6G* ***81***
(off Talbot Wlk.)
Up. Teddington Rd.
KT1: Ham W . . . 7C **132**
Upper Ter. NW3 . . . 3A **64**
Up. Thames St. EC4 . . . 2B **14** (7B **84**)
Up. Tollington Pk. N4 . . . 1A **66**
(not continuous)
Upperton Rd. DA14: Sidc . . . 5K **143**
Upperton Rd. E. E13 . . . 3A **88**
Upperton Rd. W. E13 . . . 3A **88**
UPPER TOOTING . . . 4D 136
Up. Tooting Pk. SW17 . . . 2D **136**
Up. Tooting Rd. SW17 . . . 4D **136**
Up. Town Rd. UB6: G'frd . . . 4F **77**
Up. Tulse Hill SW2 . . . 7K **119**
Up. Vernon Rd. SM1: Sutt . . . 5B **166**
UPPER WALTHAMSTOW . . . 4F 51
Up. Walthamstow Rd. E17 . . . 4E **50**
Up. Whistler Wlk. *SW10* . . . *7A* ***100***
(off Worlds End Est.)
Up. Wickham La.
DA16: Well . . . 7B **108**
Up. Wimpole St. W1 . . . 5H **5** (5E **82**)
Up. Woburn Pl. WC1 . . . 2D **6** (3H **83**)
Uppingham Av. HA7: Stan . . . 1B **42**
Upsdell Av. N13 . . . 6F **33**
Upshire Ho. E17 . . . 2B **50**
Upstall St. SE5 . . . 1B **120**
UPTON
DA6 . . . 5D 126
E7 . . . 7J 69
Upton Av. E7 . . . 7J **69**
Upton Cl. DA5: Bexl . . . 6F **127**
NW2 . . . 3G **63**
Upton Ct. *SE20* . . . *7J* ***139***
(off Blean Gro.)
Upton Dene SM2: Sutt . . . 7K **165**
Upton Gdns. HA3: Kenton . . . 5B **42**
Upton Hgts. E7 . . . 7J **69**
Upton La. E7 . . . 7J **69**
Upton Lodge E7 . . . 6J **69**
Upton Lodge Cl. WD23: Bush . . . 1B **26**
UPTON PARK . . . 1B 88
Upton Pk. . . . 2A 88
Upton Pk. Boleyn Cinema . . . 2B 88
Upton Pk. Rd. E7 . . . 7K **69**
Upton Rd. CR7: Thor H . . . 2D **156**
DA5: Bexl . . . 4E **126**
DA6: Bex . . . 4E **126**
N18 . . . 5B **34**
SE18 . . . 6G **107**
TW3: Houn . . . 3E **112**
Upton Rd. Sth. DA5: Bexl . . . 6F **127**
Upton Vs. DA6: Bex . . . 4E **126**
Upway N12 . . . 6H **31**
Upwey Ho. N1 . . . 1E **84**
Upwood Rd. SE12 . . . 6J **123**
SW16 . . . 1J **155**
Urban M. N4 . . . 6B **48**
Urdang, The *EC1* . . . *3A* ***84***
(off Rosebery Av.)
Urlwin St. SE5 . . . 6C **102**
Urlwin Wlk. SW9 . . . 1A **120**
Urmston Dr. SW19 . . . 1G **135**
Urmston Ho. *E14* . . . *4E* ***104***
(off Seyssel St.)
Urquhart Ct. BR3: Beck . . . 7B **140**
Ursula Gould Way E14 . . . 5C **86**
Ursula Lodges DA14: Sidc . . . 5B **144**
Ursula M. N4 . . . 1C **66**
Ursula St. SW11 . . . 1C **118**
Urswick Gdns. RM9: Dag . . . 7E **72**
Urswick Rd. E9 . . . 5J **67**
RM9: Dag . . . 7D **72**
Usborne M. SW8 . . . 7K **101**
Usher Hall *NW4* . . . *4D* ***44***
(off The Burroughs)
Usher Rd. E3 . . . 1B **86**
Usk Rd. SW11 . . . 4A **118**
Usk St. E2 . . . 3K **85**
Utah Bldg. *SE10* . . . *1D* ***122***
(off Deal's Gateway)
Utopia Village NW1 . . . 7E **64**
Uvedale Rd. EN2: Enf . . . 5J **23**
RM10: Dag . . . 3G **73**
Uverdale Rd. SW10 . . . 7A **100**
UXBRIDGE . . . 1A 74
Uxbridge Ct. *KT1: King T* . . . *5D* ***150***
(off Uxbridge Rd.)
Uxbridge Lido . . . 6A 56
Uxbridge Rd. HA3: Hrw W . . . 7A **26**
HA5: Hat E, Pinn . . . 2A **40**
HA7: Stan . . . 7A **26**
KT1: King T . . . 4D **150**
TW12: Hamp, Ham H . . . 4E **130**
TW13: Felt . . . 2A **130**
UB1: S'hall . . . 1E **94**
UB4: Hayes, Yead . . . 5G **75**
UB10: Hil . . . 3C **74**
W3 . . . 7E **78**
W7 . . . 1K **95**
W12 . . . 1C **98**
W13 . . . 1B **96**
Uxbridge Rd. Retail Pk.
UB4: Yead . . . 7A **76**
Uxbridge St. W8 . . . 1J **99**
Uxendon Cres. HA9: Wemb . . . 1E **60**
Uxendon Hill HA9: Wemb . . . 1F **61**

V

Vaine Ho. E9 . . . 6A **68**
Vaizeys Wharf SE7 . . . 3K **105**
Valance Av. E4 . . . 1B **36**
Valan Leas BR2: Brom . . . 3G **159**
Vale, The CR0: C'don . . . 2K **169**
HA4: Ruis . . . 4A **58**
IG8: Wfd G . . . 7D **36**
N10 . . . 1E **46**
N14 . . . 7C **22**
NW11 . . . 3F **63**
SW3 . . . 7A **16** (6B **100**)
TW5: Hest . . . 6C **94**
TW14: Felt . . . 6K **111**
TW16: Sun . . . 6J **129**
W3 . . . 1K **97**

A-Z London 411

Vale Cl.—Vere Ct.

Vale Cl. BR6: Farnb .4E 172
N2 .3D 46
TW1: Twick .3A 132
W9 .3A 82
Vale Cotts. SW15 .3A 134
Vale Ct. EN5: New Bar .4E 20
W3 .1B 98
W9 .3A 82
Vale Cres. SW15 .4A 134
Vale Cft. HA5: Pinn .5C 40
Vale Dr. EN5: Barn .4C 20
Vale End SE22 .4F 121
Vale Est., The W3 .1A 98
Vale Farm Sports Cen. .4B 60
Vale Gro. N4 .7C 48
W3 .2K 97
Vale La. W3 .5G 79
Vale Lodge SE23 .2J 139
Valence Av. RM8: Dag .1D 72
Valence Cir. RM8: Dag .3D 72
Valence House Mus. .3E 72
Valence Rd. DA8: Erith .7K 109
Valence Wood Rd. RM8: Dag .3D 72
Valencia Rd. HA7: Stan .4H 27
Valentia Pl. SW9 .4A 120
Valentine Av. DA5: Bexl .2E 144
Valentine Ct. SE23 .2K 139
(not continuous)
Valentine Ho. E3 .1B 86
(off Garrison Rd.)
Valentine Pl. SE1 .6A 14 (2B 102)
Valentine Rd. E9 .6K 67
HA2: Harr .3F 59
Valentine Row SE1 .7A 14 (2B 102)
Valentines Mansion & Gardens .7E 52
Valentines Rd. IG1: Ilf .1F 71
Valentine's Way RM7: Rush G .2K 73
VALE OF HEALTH .3A 64
Vale of Health NW3 .3B 64
Vale Pde. SW15 .3A 134
Valerian Wlk. N11 .2K 31
Valerian Way E15 .3G 87
Valerie Ct. SM2: Sutt .7K 165
WD23: Bush .1B 26
Vale Ri. NW11 .1H 63
Vale Rd. BR1: Brom .1E 160
CR4: Mitc .3H 155
E7 .6K 69
KT4: Wor Pk .3B 164
KT19: Ewe .4B 164
N4 .7C 48
SM1: Sutt .4K 165
Vale Rd. Nth. KT6: Surb .2E 162
Vale Rd. Sth. KT6: Surb .2E 162
Vale Row N5 .3B 66
Vale Royal N7 .7J 65
Vale Royal Ho. WC2 .2D 12
(off Charing Cross Rd.)
Valery Pl. TW12: Hamp .7E 130
Valeside Ct. EN5: New Bar .4E 20
Vale St. SE27 .3D 138
Valeswood Rd. BR1: Brom .5H 141
Vale Ter. N4 .6C 48
Valetta Gro. E13 .2J 87
Valetta Rd. W3 .2A 98
Valette Ct. N10 .4F 47
(off St James's La.)
Valette Ho. E9 .6J 67
Valette St. E9 .6J 67
Valiant Cl. RM7: Mawney .2H 55
UB5: N'olt .3B 76
Valiant Ho. E14 .2E 104
(off Plevna St.)
SE7 .5A 106
Valiant Path NW9 .1A 44
(not continuous)
Valiant Way E6 .5D 88
Vallance Rd. E1 .3G 85
E2 .3G 85
N22 .2G 47
Vallentin Rd. E17 .4E 50
Valley, The .5A 106
Valley Av. N12 .4G 31
Valley Cl. HA5: Pinn .2K 39
Valley Dr. NW9 .6G 43
Valleyfield Rd. SW16 .5K 137
Valley Flds. Cres. EN2: Enf .2F 23
Valley Gdns. HA0: Wemb .7F 61
SW19 .7B 136
Valley Gro. SE7 .5A 106
Valley Leisure Pk. CR0: Wadd .1J 167
Valleylink Est. EN3: Pond E .6F 25
Valley M. TW1: Twick .2K 131
Valley Point Ind. Est.
CR0: Bedd .7J 155
Valley Rd. BR2: Brom .2G 159
BR5: St P .7B 144
DA8: Erith .4J 109
DA17: Belv .4H 109
SW16 .5K 137
UB10: Uxb .2A 74
Valley Side E4 .2H 35
SE7 .5B 106
Valley Side Pde. E4 .2H 35
Valley Vw. EN5: Barn .6B 20
Valley Wlk. CR0: C'don .2J 169
Valliere Rd. NW10 .3C 80
Valliers Wood Rd. DA15: Sidc .1J 143
Vallis Way KT9: Chess .4D 162
W13 .5A 78
Val McKenzie Av. N7 .3A 66
Valmar Rd. SE5 .1C 120
Valmar Trad. Est. SE5 .1C 120
Valnay St. SW17 .5D 136
Valognes Av. E17 .1A 50
Valois Ho. SE1 .3F 103
(off St Saviour's Est.)
Valonia Gdns. SW18 .6H 117
Vambery Rd. SE18 .6G 107
V&A Mus. of Childhood .3J 85
Vanbrough Cres. UB5: N'olt .1A 76
Vanbrugh Castle SE10 .6G 105
(off Maze Hill)
Vanbrugh Cl. E16 .5B 88
Vanbrugh Ct. SE11 .4K 19
Vanbrugh Dr. KT12: Walt T .7A 148
Vanbrugh Flds. SE3 .6H 105
Vanbrugh Hill SE3 .5H 105
SE10 .5H 105
Vanbrugh Ho. E9 .7J 67
(off Loddiges Rd.)
Vanbrugh M. KT12: Walt T .7A 148
Vanbrugh Pk. SE3 .7H 105
Vanbrugh Pk. Rd. SE3 .7H 105
Vanbrugh Pk. Rd. W.
SE3 .7H 105
Vanbrugh Rd. W4 .3K 97
Vanbrugh Ter. SE3 .1H 123
Vanburgh Cl. BR6: Orp .1J 173
Vanburgh Ho. E1 .5J 9
(off Folgate St.)
Vancouver Cl. BR6: Chels .4K 173
Vancouver Ho. E1 .1H 103
(off Reardon Path)
Vancouver Mans. HA8: Edg .1H 43
Vancouver Rd. HA8: Edg .1H 43
SE23 .2A 140
TW10: Ham .4C 132
UB4: Yead .4K 75
Vanderbilt Rd. SW18 .1K 135
Vanderbilt Vs. W12 .2F 99
(off Sterne St.)
Vanderville Gdns. N2 .2B 46
Vandome Cl. E16 .6K 87
Vandon Ct. SW1 .1B 18
(off Petty France)
Vandon Pas. SW1 .1B 18 (3G 101)
Vandon St. SW1 .1B 18 (3G 101)
Van Dyck Av. KT3: N Mald .7K 151
Vandyke Cl. SW15 .7F 117
Vandyke Cross SE9 .5C 124
Vandy St. EC2 .4G 9 (4E 84)
Vane Cl. HA3: Kenton .6F 43
NW3 .5B 64
Vanessa Cl. DA17: Belv .5G 109
Vanessa Way DA5: Bexl .3K 145
Vane St. SW1 .3B 18 (4G 101)
Vange Ho. W10 .5E 80
(off Sutton Way)
Van Gogh Cl. TW7: Isle .3A 114
Van Gogh Ct. E14 .3F 105
Vanguard NW9 .7F 29
Vanguard Bldg. E14 .2B 104
Vanguard Cl. CR0: C'don .1B 168
E16 .5J 87
RM7: Mawney .2G 55
Vanguard Ct. SE5 .1E 120
Vanguard Ho. E8 .7H 67
Vanguard St. SE8 .1C 122
Vanguard Way SM6: Wall .7J 167
TW6: H'row A .2G 111
Vanilla & Sesame Ct.
SE1 .6K 15
(off Curlew St.)
SE1 .2F 103
(off Curlew St.)
Vanneck Sq. SW15 .5C 116
Vanoc Gdns. BR1: Brom .4J 141
Vanquish Cl. TW2: Whitt .7E 112
Vansittart Rd. E7 .4H 69
Vansittart St. SE14 .7A 104
Vanston Pl. SW6 .7J 99
Vantage Bldg.
UB3: Hayes .3H 93
(off Station App.)
Vantage Ct. UB3: Harl .7G 93
Vantage M. E14 .1E 104
(off Coldharbour)
Vantage Pl. TW14: Felt .6J 111
W8 .3J 99
Vantage Point EN5: Barn .4C 20
(off Victors Way)
Vantage W. TW8: Bford .4F 97
Vantrey Ho. SE11 .4J 19
Vant Rd. SW17 .5D 136
Varcoe Rd. SE16 .5H 103
Vardens Rd. SW11 .4B 118
Varden St. E1 .6H 85
Vardon Cl. W3 .6K 79
Vardon Ho. SE10 .1E 122
Varley Dr. TW1: Isle .4B 114
Varley Ho. NW6 .1J 81
SE1 .3C 102
(off New Kent Rd.)
Varley Pde. NW9 .4A 44
Varley Rd. E16 .6K 87
Varley Way CR4: Mitc .2B 154
Varna Rd. SW6 .7G 99
TW12: Hamp .1F 149
Varndell St. NW1 .1A 6 (3G 83)
Varnishers Yd. N1 .1F 7
(off York Way)
Varsity Dr. TW1: Twick .5J 113
Varsity Row SW14 .2J 115
Vartry Rd. N15 .6D 48
Vascroft Est. NW10 .4H 79
Vassall Ho. E3 .3A 86
(off Antill Rd.)
Vassall Rd. SW9 .7A 102
Vat Ho. SW8 .7J 101
(off Rita Rd.)
Vauban Est. SE16 .3F 103
Vauban St. SE16 .3F 103
Vaudeville Ct. N4 .2A 66
Vaudeville Theatre .3F 13
(off Strand)
Vaughan Almshouses TW15: Ashf .5D 128
(off Feltham Hill Rd.)
Vaughan Av. NW4 .5C 44
W6 .4B 98
Vaughan Cl. TW12: Hamp .6C 130
Vaughan Est. E2 .1J 9
Vaughan Gdns. IG1: Ilf .7D 52
Vaughan Ho. SE1 .6A 14
(off Blackfriars Rd.)
SW4 .7G 119
Vaughan Rd. DA16: Well .2K 125
E15 .6H 69
HA1: Harr .6G 41
KT7: T Ditt .7B 150
SE5 .2C 120
Vaughan St. SE16 .2B 104
Vaughan Way E1 .7G 85
Vaughan Williams Cl. SE8 .7C 104
VAUXHALL .5H 19 (6J 101)
Vauxhall Bri. SW1 .6E 18 (5J 101)
Vauxhall Bri. Rd. SW1 .2A 18 (3G 101)
Vauxhall City Farm .6G 19
VAUXHALL CROSS .6F 19 (5J 101)
Vauxhall Distribution Pk.
SW8 .7C 18 (6H 101)
Vauxhall Gdns. CR2: S Croy .6C 168
Vauxhall Gro. SW8 .7G 19 (6K 101)
Vauxhall St. SE11 .5H 19 (5K 101)
Vauxhall Wlk. SE11 .5G 19 (5K 101)
Vawdrey Cl. E1 .4J 85
Veals Mead CR4: Mitc .1C 154
Vectis Gdns. SW17 .6F 137
Vectis Rd. SW17 .6F 137
Veda Rd. SE13 .4C 122
Vega Rd. WD23: Bush .1B 26
Veitch Cl. TW14: Felt .7H 111
Veldene Way HA2: Harr .3D 58
Velde Way SE22 .5E 120
Velletri Ho. E2 .2K 85
(off Mace St.)
Vellum Ct. E17 .3A 50
Vellum Dr. SM5: Cars .3E 166
Venables Cl. RM10: Dag .4H 73
Venables St. NW8 .5B 4 (4B 82)
Vencourt Pl. W6 .4C 98
Venetian Rd. SE5 .2C 120
Venetia Rd. N4 .6B 48
W5 .2D 96
Venice Ct. SE5 .7C 102
(off Bowyer St.)
Venice Wlk. W2 .5A 82
Venner Rd. SE26 .6J 139
(not continuous)
Venners Cl. DA7: Bex .2K 127
Venn Ho. N1 .1K 83
(off Barnsbury Est.)
Venn St. SW4 .4G 119
Ventnor Av. HA7: Stan .1B 42
Ventnor Dr. N20 .3E 30
Ventnor Gdns. IG11: Bark .6J 71
Ventnor Rd. SE14 .7K 103
SM2: Sutt .7K 165
Venture Cl. DA5: Bexl .7E 126
Venture Ct. SE1 .7H 15
(off Bermondsey St.)
SE12 .7J 123
Venture Ho. W10 .6F 81
(off Bridge Cl.)
Venue St. E14 .5E 86
Venus Ho. E3 .1C 86
(off Garrison Rd.)
E14 .4C 104
(off Westferry Rd.)
Venus M. CR4: Mitc .3C 154
Venus Rd. SE18 .3D 106
Vera Av. N21 .5F 23
Vera Ct. E3 .3D 86
(off Grace Pl.)
Vera Lynn Cl. E7 .4J 69
Vera Rd. SW6 .1G 117
Verbena Cl. E16 .4H 87
UB7: W Dray .1E 174
Verbena Gdns. W6 .5C 98
Verdant Ct. SE6 .7G 123
(off Verdant La.)
Verdant La. SE6 .7G 123
Verdayne Av. CR0: C'don .2K 169
Verdi Cres. W10 .2G 81
Verdun Rd. SE18 .6A 108
SW13 .6C 98
Vere Ct. W2 .6K 81
(off Westbourne Gdns.)

Vereker Dr. TW16: Sun 3J 147
Vereker Rd. W14 ....5G 99
Vere St. W1 ....1J 11 (6F 83)
Veridion Way DA18: Erith 2F 109
Veritas Ho. DA15: Sidc 2A 144
(off Station Rd.)
Verity Cl. W11 ....7G 81
Verity Ho. E3 ....3B 86
(off Merchant St.)
Vermeer Ct. E14 ....3F 105
Vermeer Gdns. SE15 ....4J 121
Vermont Cl. EN2: Enf 4G 23
Vermont Ho. E17 ....2B 50
Vermont Rd. SE19 ....6D 138
SM1: Sutt 3K 165
SW18 ....6K 117
Verne Ct. W3 ....3J 97
(off Vincent Rd.)
Verney Gdns. RM9: Dag 4E 72
Verney Ho. NW8 ....3B 4
Verney Rd. RM9: Dag 4E 72
(not continuous)
SE16 ....6G 103
Verney St. NW10 ....3K 61
Verney Way SE16 ....5H 103
Vernham Rd. SE18 ....6G 107
Vernon Av. E12 ....4D 70
IG8: Wfd G 7E 36
SW20 ....2F 153
Vernon Cl. KT19: Ewe 6J 163
TW19: Stanw 1A 128
Vernon Ct. HA7: Stan 1B 42
NW2 ....3H 63
W5 ....7C 78
Vernon Cres. EN4: E Barn 6K 21
Vernon Dr. HA7: Stan 1A 42
Vernon Ho. SE11 ....6H 19
WC1 ....6F 7
(off Vernon Pl.)
Vernon Mans. W14 ....6H 99
(off Queen's Club Mans.)
Vernon M. E17 ....5B 50
W14 ....4G 99
Vernon Pl. WC1 ....6F 7 (5J 83)
Vernon Ri. UB6: G'frd 5H 59
WC1 ....1H 7 (3K 83)
Vernon Rd. E3 ....2B 86
E11 ....1G 69
E15 ....7G 69
E17 ....5B 50
IG3: Ilf 1K 71
N8 ....3A 48
SM1: Sutt 5A 166
SW14 ....3K 115
TW13: Felt 2H 129
Vernon Sq. WC1 ....1H 7 (3K 83)
Vernon St. W14 ....4G 99
Vernon Yd. W11 ....7H 81
Veroan Rd. DA7: Bex 2E 126
Verona Ct. SE14 ....6K 103
(off Myers La.)
TW15: Ashf 4D 128
W4 ....5A 98
Verona Dr. KT6: Surb 2E 162
Verona Rd. E7 ....7J 69
Veronica Gdns. SW16 ....1G 155
Veronica Ho. E3 ....3D 86
(off Talwin St.)
SE4 ....3B 122
Veronica Rd. SW17 ....2F 137
Veronique Gdns. IG6: Ilf 5G 53
Verran Rd. SW12 ....7F 119
Versailles Rd. SE20 ....7G 139
Verulam Av. E17 ....6B 50
Verulam Bldgs. WC1 ....5H 7
Verulam Ct. NW9 ....7C 44
UB1: S'hall 6G 77
(off Haldane Rd.)
Verulam Ho. W6 ....2E 98
(off Hammersmith Gro.)
Verulam Rd. UB6: G'frd 4E 76
Verulam St. WC1 ....5J 7 (5A 84)

Vervian Ho. SE15 ....7G 103
(off Reddins Rd.)
Verwood Dr. EN4: Cockf 3J 21
Verwood Ho. SW8 ....7K 101
(off Cobbett St.)
Verwood Lodge E14 ....3F 105
(off Manchester Rd.)
Verwood Rd. HA2: Harr 2G 41
Veryan Ct. N8 ....5H 47
Vesage Ct. EC1 ....6K 7
Vesey Path E14 ....6D 86
Vespan Rd. W12 ....2C 98
Vesta Ct. SE1 ....7G 15
Vesta Ho. E3 ....1C 86
(off Garrison Rd.)
Vesta Rd. SE4 ....2A 122
Vestris Rd. SE23 ....2K 139
Vestry Ct. SW1 ....2D 18
(off Monck St.)
Vestry House Mus. 4D 50
Vestry M. SE5 ....1E 120
Vestry Rd. E17 ....4D 50
SE5 ....1E 120
Vestry St. N1 ....1E 8 (3D 84)
Vevey St. SE6 ....2B 140
Veysey Gdns. RM10: Dag 3G 73
Viaduct, The E18 ....2J 51
HA0: Wemb 1E 78
N10 ....4F 47
Viaduct Bldgs. EC1 ....6K 7 (5A 84)
Viaduct Pl. E2 ....3H 85
Viaduct Rd. N2 ....2B 46
Viaduct St. E2 ....3H 85
Vian St. SE13 ....3D 122
Viant Ho. NW10 ....7K 61
(off Fawood Av.)
Vibart Gdns. SW2 ....7K 119
Vibart Wlk. N1 ....1J 83
(off Outram Pl.)
Vibeca Apartments E1 ....6K 9
(off Chicksands St.)
Vibia Cl. TW19: Stanw 7A 110
Vicarage Av. SE3 ....7J 105
Vicarage Cl. DA8: Erith 6J 109
HA4: Ruis 7F 39
KT4: Wor Pk 1A 164
UB5: N'olt 7D 58
Vicarage Ct. BR3: Beck 3A 158
IG1: Ilf 5F 71
TW14: Bedf 7E 110
W8 ....2K 99
Vicarage Cres. SW11 ....1B 118
Vicarage Dr. BR3: Beck 1C 158
IG11: Bark 7G 71
SW14 ....5K 115
Vicarage Farm Ct. TW5: Hest 7D 94
Vicarage Farm Rd. TW3: Houn 2C 112
TW5: Hest 1C 112
Vicarage Flds. KT12: Walt T 6A 148
Vicarage Fld. Shop. Cen.
IG11: Bark 7G 71
Vicarage Gdns. CR4: Mitc 3C 154
SW14 ....5J 115
W8 ....1J 99
Vicarage Ga. W8 ....1K 99
Vicarage Gro. SE5 ....1D 120
Vicarage Ho. KT1: King T 2F 151
(off Cambridge Rd.)
Vicarage La. E6 ....3D 88
E15 ....7G 69
IG1: Ilf 1H 71
KT17: Ewe 7C 164
(not continuous)
Vicarage M. NW9 ....2K 61
Vicarage Pde. N15 ....4C 48
Vicarage Pk. SE18 ....5G 107
Vicarage Path N8 ....7J 47
Vicarage Rd. CR0: Wadd 3A 168
DA5: Bexl 1H 145
E10 ....7C 50
E15 ....7H 69
IG8: Wfd G 7H 37

Vicarage Rd. KT1: Ham W 1C 150
KT1: King T 2D 150
N17 ....1G 49
NW4 ....6C 44
RM10: Dag 7H 73
SE18 ....5G 107
(not continuous)
SM1: Sutt 3K 165
SW14 ....5J 115
TW2: Twick 2J 131
TW2: Whitt 6G 113
TW11: Tedd 5A 132
TW16: Sun 5H 129
Vicarage Wlk.
KT12: Walt T 7J 147
SW11 ....1B 118
Vicarage Way HA2: Harr 7E 40
NW10 ....3K 61
Vicars Bri. Cl.
HA0: Wemb 2E 78
Vicars Cl. E9 ....1J 85
E15 ....1J 87
EN1: Enf 2K 23
Vicar's Hill SE13 ....4D 122
Vicars Moor La. N21 ....7F 23
Vicars Oak Rd. SE19 ....6E 138
Vicar's Rd. NW5 ....5E 64
Vicars Wlk. RM8: Dag 3B 72
Vicentia Quay SW11 ....3A 118
Viceroy Cl. N2 ....4C 46
(off East End Rd.)
Viceroy Ct. CR0: C'don 1D 168
NW8 ....2C 82
(off Prince Albert Rd.)
Viceroy Pde. N2 ....4C 46
(off High Rd.)
Viceroy Rd. SW8 ....1J 119
Vicinity Ho. E14 ....7C 86
(off Storehouse M.)
Vic Johnson Ho. E3 ....1B 86
(off Armagh Rd.)
Vickers Cl. SM6: Wall 7K 167
Vickers Ct. SE20 ....7K 139
TW19: Stanw 6A 110
(off Whitley Cl.)
Vickers Rd. DA8: Erith 5K 109
Vickers Way TW4: Houn 5C 112
Vickery Ct. EC1 ....3D 8
(off Mitchell St.)
Vickery's Wharf E14 ....6C 86
Victor Cazalet Ho. N1 ....1B 84
(off Gaskin St.)
Victor Gro. HA0: Wemb 7E 60
Victor Ho. SE7 ....6A 106
(off Victoria St.)
Victoria & Albert Mus. 2B 16 (3B 100)
Victoria Arc. SW1 ....2K 17
(off Victoria St.)
Victoria Av. E6 ....6H 9 (5E 84)
EC2 ....6H 9 (5E 84)
EN4: E Barn 4G 21
HA9: Wemb 6H 61
KT6: Surb 6D 150
KT8: W Mole 3F 149
N3 ....1H 45
SM6: Wall 3E 166
TW3: Houn 5E 112
UB10: Hil 6D 56
Victoria Bldgs. E8 ....1H 85
(off Mare St.)
Victoria Chambers EC2 ....3G 9
(off Paul St.)
Victoria Cl. EN4: E Barn 4G 21
HA1: Harr 6K 41
KT8: W Mole 3E 148
SE22 ....5G 121
UB3: Hayes 6F 75
Victoria Colonnade WC1 ....6F 7
(off Southampton Row)
Victoria Cotts. E1 ....5G 85
(off Deal St.)
Victoria Cotts. N10 ....2E 46
TW9: Kew 1F 115

Victoria Ct. E18 ....3K 51
HA9: Wemb 6G 61
SE1 ....4E 102
(off Hendre Rd.)
SE26 ....6J 139
W3 ....2G 97
Victoria Cres. N15 ....5E 48
SE19 ....6E 138
SW19 ....7H 135
Victoria Dock Rd. E16 ....6H 87
Victoria Dr. SW19 ....7F 117
Victoria Emb. EC4 ....6F 13 (7K 83)
SW1 ....6F 13 (2J 101)
WC2 ....6F 13 (2J 101)
Victoria Gdns. TW5: Hest 1C 112
W11 ....1J 99
Victoria Gro. N12 ....5G 31
W8 ....3A 100
Victoria Gro. M. W2 ....7J 81
Victoria Hall E16 ....1J 105
(off Wesley Av., not continuous)
Victoria Ho. E6 ....6E 88
HA8: Edg 6C 28
SW1 ....5J 17
(off Ebury Bri. Rd.)
SW1 ....3B 18
(off Francis St.)
SW8 ....7J 101
(off Sth. Lambeth Rd.)
Victoria Ind. Est. W3 ....5A 80
Victoria La. EN5: Barn 4C 20
UB3: Harl 5F 93
Victoria Mans. NW10 ....7D 62
SW8 ....7J 101
(off Sth. Lambeth Rd.)
W14 ....6H 99
(off Queen's Club Mans.)
Victoria M. E8 ....6G 67
NW6 ....1J 81
SW4 ....4F 119
SW18 ....1A 136
Victoria Mills Studios E15 ....1F 87
Victorian Gro. N16 ....4E 66
Victorian Hgts. SW8 ....2F 119
(off Thackeray Rd.)
Victorian Rd. N16 ....3E 66
Victoria Palace Theatre 2A 18
(off Victoria St.)
Victoria Pde. TW9: Kew 1G 115
(off Sandycombe Rd.)
Victoria Pk. 1K 85
Victoria Pk. Ct. E9 ....7J 67
(off Well St.)
Victoria Pk. Ind. Cen. E9 ....7C 68
(off Rothbury Rd.)
Victoria Pk. Rd. E9 ....1J 85
Victoria Pk. Sq. E2 ....3J 85
Victoria Pas. NW8 ....3B 4
Victoria Pl. TW9: Rich 5D 114
Victoria Pl. Shop. Cen. SW1 ....3K 17
(off Victoria St.)
Victoria Point E13 ....2J 87
(off Victoria Rd.)
Victoria Retail Pk. HA4: Ruis 5B 58
Victoria Ri. NW6 ....7A 64
(off Hilgrove Rd.)
SW4 ....3F 119
Victoria Rd. BR2: Brom 5B 160
BR7: Chst 5E 142
CR4: Mitc 7C 136
DA6: Bex 4G 127
DA8: Erith 6K 109
(not continuous)
DA15: Sidc 3K 143
E4 ....1B 36
E11 ....4G 69
E13 ....2J 87
E17 ....2E 50
E18 ....2K 51
EN4: E Barn 4G 21
HA4: Ruis 1J 57
IG9: Buck H 2G 37
IG11: Bark 6F 71

Victoria Rd. KT1: King T 2F **151**
KT6: Surb 6D **150**
N4 . . . . . 7K **47**
N9 . . . . . 4A **34**
N15 . . . . . 4G **49**
N18 . . . . . 4A **34**
N22 . . . . . 1G **47**
NW4 . . . . . 4E **44**
NW6 . . . . . 2H **81**
NW7 . . . . . 5G **29**
NW10 . . . . . 5K **79**
RM10: Dag 5H **73**
SM1: Sutt 5B **166**
SW14 . . . . . 3K **115**
TW1: Twick 7B **114**
TW11: Tedd 6A **132**
TW13: Felt 1K **129**
UB2: S'hall 3D **94**
W3 . . . . . 5K **79**
W5 . . . . . 5B **78**
W8 . . . . . 3A **100**
WD23: Bush 1A **26**
Victoria Sq. SW1 . . . . . 1K **17** (3F **101**)
Victoria St. DA17: Belv 5F **109**
E15 . . . . . 7G **69**
SW1 . . . . . 2K **17** (3G **101**)
Victoria Ter. HA1: Harr 1J **59**
N4 . . . . . 1A **66**
NW10 . . . . . 4B **80**
W5 . . . . . 1D **96**
Victoria Vs. TW9: Rich 3F **115**
Victoria Way HA4: Ruis 5B **58**
SE7 . . . . . 5K **105**
Victoria Wharf *E2* *2K **85***
(off Palmers Rd.)
E14 . . . . . 7A **86**
SE8 . . . . . *5B **104***
(off Dragoon Rd.)
Victoria Works NW2 . . . . . 2D **62**
Victoria Yd. E1 . . . . . 6G **85**
Victor Rd. HA2: Harr 3G **41**
NW10 . . . . . 3D **80**
SE20 . . . . . 7K **139**
TW11: Tedd 4J **131**
Victors Dr. TW12: Hamp 6C **130**
Victors Way EN5: Barn 3C **20**
Victor Vs. N9 . . . . . 3J **33**
Victor Wlk. NW9 . . . . . 2A **44**
Victor Wharf *SE1* *4E **14***
(off Clink St.)
Victory Av. SM4: Mord 5A **154**
Victory Bus. Cen. TW7: Isle 4K **113**
Victory Cl. TW19: Stanw 1A **128**
Victory Ct. IG11: Bark 4B **90**
W9 . . . . . *4J **81***
(off Hermes Cl.)
Victory M. UB2: S'hall 3C **94**
Victory Pk. HA9: Wemb 3D **60**
Victory Pl. E14 . . . . . 7A **86**
SE17 . . . . . 4D **102**
SE19 . . . . . 7E **138**
Victory Rd. E11 . . . . . 4J **51**
SW19 . . . . . 7A **136**
Victory Rd. M. *SW19* *7A **136***
(off Victory Rd.)
Victory Wlk. SE8 . . . . . 1C **122**
Victory Way RM7: Mawney 2H **55**
SE16 . . . . . 2A **104**
TW5: Cran 5A **94**
Video Ct. N4 . . . . . 7K **47**
Vidler Cl. KT9: Chess 6C **162**
Vienna Cl. IG5: Ilf 2B **52**
View, The SE2 . . . . . 5E **108**
View Cl. HA1: Harr 4H **41**
N6 . . . . . 7D **46**
View Ct. SE12 . . . . . 3A **142**
View Cres. N8 . . . . . 5H **47**
Viewfield Cl. HA3: Kenton 7E **42**
Viewfield Rd. DA5: Bexl 1C **144**
SW18 . . . . . 6H **117**
Viewland Rd. SE18 . . . . . 5K **107**
View Rd. N6 . . . . . 7D **46**
Viga Rd. N21 . . . . . 6F **23**
Vigilant Cl. SE26 . . . . . 4G **139**
Vignoles Rd. RM7: Rush G 7G **55**
Vigo St. W1 . . . . . 3A **12** (7G **83**)
Viking Bus. Cen.
RM7: Rush G 7J **55**
Viking Cl. E3 . . . . . 2A **86**
Viking Ct. SW6 . . . . . 6J **99**
Viking Gdns. E6 . . . . . 4C **88**
Viking Ho. *SE5* *2C **120***
(off Denmark Rd.)
SE18 . . . . . *4C **106***
(off Pett St.)
Viking Pl. E10 . . . . . 1B **68**
Viking Rd. UB1: S'hall 7C **76**
Viking Way DA8: Erith 3J **109**
Villacourt Rd. SE18 . . . . . 7A **108**
Village, The NW3 . . . . . 2A **64**
SE7 . . . . . 6A **106**
Village Arc. E4 . . . . . 1A **36**
Village Cl. E4 . . . . . 5K **35**
NW3 . . . . . *5B **64***
(off Belsize La.)
Village Ct. *E17* *5D **50***
(off Eden Rd.)
SE3 . . . . . *3G **123***
(off Hurren Cl.)
Village Ga. TW17: Shep 5D **146**
Village Hgts. IG8: Wfd G 5C **36**
Village M. NW9 . . . . . 2K **61**
Village Mt. *NW3* *4A **64***
(off Perrins Ct.)
Village Pk. Cl. EN1: Enf 6K **23**
Village Rd. EN1: Enf 5K **23**
N3 . . . . . 2G **45**
Village Row SM2: Sutt 7J **165**
Village Way BR3: Beck 2C **158**
HA5: Pinn 7C **40**
IG6: Ilf 4G **53**
NW10 . . . . . 4K **61**
SE21 . . . . . 6D **120**
TW15: Ashf 4B **128**
Village Way E. HA2: Harr 7E **40**
Villa Rd. SW9 . . . . . 3A **120**
Villas on the Heath NW3 . . . . . 3A **64**
Villas Rd. SE18 . . . . . 5G **107**
Villa St. SE17 . . . . . 5D **102**
Villa Wlk *SE17* *5D **102***
(off Villa St.)
Villiers Av. KT5: Surb 5F **151**
TW2: Whitt 1D **130**
Villiers Cl. E10 . . . . . 2C **68**
KT5: Surb 4F **151**
Villiers Ct. *SW11* *1C **118***
(off Battersea Bri. Rd.)
Villiers Gro. SM2: Cheam 7F **165**
Villiers M. NW2 . . . . . 6C **62**
Villiers Path KT6: Surb 5E **150**
Villiers Rd. BR3: Beck 2K **157**
KT1: King T 4F **151**
NW2 . . . . . 6C **62**
TW7: Isle 2J **113**
UB1: S'hall 1D **94**
Villiers St. WC2 . . . . . 3E **12** (1J **101**)
Vimy Cl. TW4: Houn 5D **112**
Vincam Cl. TW2: Whitt 7E **112**
Vince Ct. N1 . . . . . 2F **9** (3D **84**)
Vincennes Est. SE27 . . . . . 4D **138**
Vincent Av. KT5: Surb 2J **163**
Vincent Cl. BR2: Brom 4K **159**
DA15: Sidc 1J **143**
EN5: New Bar 3E **20**
SE16 . . . . . 2A **104**
UB7: Sip 6C **92**
Vincent Ct. HA6: Nwood 1H **39**
N4 . . . . . 1J **65**
NW4 . . . . . 4F **45**
SW9 . . . . . 1K **119**
W1 . . . . . *7E **4***
(off Seymour Pl.)
Vincent Dr. TW17: Shep 3G **147**
UB10: Uxb 1B **74**
Vincent Gdns. NW2 . . . . . 3B **62**
Vincent Ho. *SW1* *3D **18***
(off Regency St.)
SW1 . . . . . *4C **18***
(off Vincent Sq.)
Vincent M. E3 . . . . . 2C **86**
Vincent Rd. CR0: C'don 7E **156**
E4 . . . . . 6A **36**
HA0: Wemb 7F **61**
KT1: King T 3G **151**
N15 . . . . . 4C **48**
N22 . . . . . 2A **48**
RM9: Dag 7E **72**
SE18 . . . . . 4F **107**
TW4: Houn 2B **112**
TW7: Isle 1H **113**
W3 . . . . . 3J **97**
Vincent Row TW12: Ham H 6G **131**
Vincents Path *UB5: N'olt* *6C **58***
(off Arnold Rd.)
Vincent Sq. N22 . . . . . 2A **48**
SW1 . . . . . 3C **18** (4H **101**)
Vincent Sq. Mans. *SW1* *3B **18***
(off Walcott St.)
Vincent St. E16 . . . . . 5H **87**
SW1 . . . . . 3C **18** (4H **101**)
Vincent Ter. N1 . . . . . 2B **84**
Vince St. EC1 . . . . . 2F **9** (3D **84**)
Vine Cl. E5 . . . . . 4G **67**
KT5: Surb 6F **151**
SM1: Sutt 3A **166**
TW19: Stan M 7B **174**
UB7: W Dray 4C **92**
Vine Cotts. *E1* *6J **85***
(off Sidney Sq.)
W7 . . . . . 1J **95**
Vine Ct. E1 . . . . . 5G **85**
HA3: Kenton 6E **42**
Vinegar All. E17 . . . . . 4D **50**
Vine Gdns. IG1: Ilf 5G **71**
Vinegar St. E1 . . . . . 1H **103**
Vinegar Yd. SE1 . . . . . 6G **15** (2E **102**)
Vine Gro. UB10: Hil 7C **56**
Vine Hill EC1 . . . . . 4J **7** (4A **84**)
Vine La. SE1 . . . . . 5H **15** (1E **102**)
UB10: Hil 1B **74**
Vine Pl. TW3: Houn 4F **113**
W5 . . . . . *1E **96***
(off St Mark's Rd.)
Viner Cl. KT12: Walt T 6A **148**
Vineries, The EN1: Enf 3K **23**
N14 . . . . . 6B **22**
SE6 . . . . . 1C **140**
Vineries Bank NW7 . . . . . 5J **29**
Vineries Cl. RM9: Dag 6F **73**
UB7: Sip 6C **92**
Vine Rd. BR6: Chels 6K **173**
E15 . . . . . 7H **69**
KT8: E Mos 4G **149**
SW13 . . . . . 3B **116**
Vinery Row W6 . . . . . 3D **98**
Vines Av. N3 . . . . . 1K **45**
Vine Sq. *W14* *5H **99***
(off Star Rd.)
Vine St. EC3 . . . . . 1J **15** (6F **85**)
RM7: Rom 4J **55**
W1 . . . . . 3B **12** (7G **83**)
Vine St. Bri. EC1 . . . . . 4K **7** (4A **84**)
Vine Yd. SE1 . . . . . 6D **14**
Vineyard, The TW10: Rich 5E **114**
Vineyard Av. NW7 . . . . . 7B **30**
Vineyard Cl. KT1: King T 3F **151**
SE6 . . . . . 1C **140**
Vineyard Gro. N3 . . . . . 1K **45**
Vineyard Hill Rd. SW19 . . . . . 4H **135**
Vineyard M. TW10: Rich 5E **114**
Vineyard Pas. TW10: Rich 5E **114**
Vineyard Path *SW14* *3K **115***
(off Church Path)
SW14 . . . . . 3K **115**
(Sheen La.)
Vineyard Rd. TW13: Felt 3J **129**
Vineyard Row KT1: Ham W 1C **150**
Vineyards, The *TW13: Felt* *3J **129***
(off High St.)
TW16: Sun 3J **147**
Vineyard Wlk. EC1 . . . . . 3J **7** (4A **84**)
Viney Bank CR0: Sels 7B **170**
Viney Rd. SE13 . . . . . 3D **122**
Vining St. SW9 . . . . . 4A **120**
Vinlake Av. UB10: Ick 3B **56**
Vinopolis 4D 14 (1C 102)
Vinson Cl. BR6: Orp 1K **173**
Vinson Ho. *N1* *2D **84***
(off Cranston Est.)
Vintage M. E4 . . . . . 4H **35**
Vinter Ct. TW17: Shep 5C **146**
Vintner's Ct. EC4 . . . . . 3D **14** (7C **84**)
Vintner's Pl. EC4 . . . . . 3D **14**
Vintry M. E17 . . . . . 4C **50**
Viola Av. SE2 . . . . . 4B **108**
TW14: Felt 6A **112**
TW19: Stanw 1A **128**
Viola Sq. W12 . . . . . 7B **80**
Violet Av. EN2: Enf 1J **23**
UB8: Hil 5B **74**
Violet Cl. E16 . . . . . 4G **87**
SE8 . . . . . 6B **104**
SM3: Sutt 1G **165**
SM6: Wall 1E **166**
Violet Gdns. CR0: Wadd 5B **168**
Violet Hill NW8 . . . . . 2A **82**
Violet Hill Ho. *NW8* *2A **82***
(off Violet Hill)
Violet La. CR0: Wadd 6B **168**
Violet Rd. E3 . . . . . 4D **86**
E17 . . . . . 6C **50**
E18 . . . . . 2K **51**
Violet St. E2 . . . . . 4H **85**
VIP Trading Est. SE7 . . . . . 4A **106**
Virgil Pl. W1 . . . . . 6E **4** (5D **82**)
Virgil St. SE1 . . . . . 1H **19** (3K **101**)
Virgin Active Health Club
Barbican *5C 8*
(off Aldersgate St.)
Bromley 4B 160
Cricklewood 3G 63
Crouch End *5J 47*
(off Topsfield Pde.)
Croydon 3C 168
Ealing *7D 78*
(within Ealing Broadway Cen.)
Hammersmith *4F 99*
(off Hammersmith Rd.)
Hendon 5E 44
Holloway 3J 65
Islington *1A 8*
(off Owen St.)
Mayfair 2G 11 (6E 82)
Mill Hill East 7B 30
Moorgate 4E 8 (4D 84)
Notting Hill 6G 81
Putney 4G 117
South Wimbledon 6A 136
Stockley Pk. 7E 74
Sunbury 1J 147
Wandsworth 5J 117
West London 1A 98
Virginia Cl. BR2: Brom 3G **159**
KT3: N Mald 4J **151**
RM5: Col R 1J **55**
Virginia Ct. *SE16* *2K **103***
(off Eleanor Cl.)
WC1 . . . . . *3D **6***
(off Burton St.)
Virginia Gdns. IG6: Ilf 2G **53**
Virginia Ho. *E14* *7E **86***
(off Newby Pl.)
TW11: Tedd 5B **132**
Virginia Rd. CR7: Thor H 1B **156**
E2 . . . . . 2J **9** (3F **85**)
Virginia St. E1 . . . . . 7G **85**
Virginia Wlk. SW2 . . . . . 6K **119**
Viridian Apartments SW8 . . . . . 7G **101**

Visage NW3 . . . 7B 64
(off Winchester Rd.)
Viscount Cl. N11 . . . 6A 32
Viscount Ct. W2 . . . 6J 81
(off Pembridge Vs.)
Viscount Dr. E6 . . . 5D 88
Viscount Gro. UB5: N'olt . . . 3B 76
Viscount Rd. TW19: Stanw . . . 1A 128
Viscount St. EC1 . . . 4C 8 (4C 84)
Viscount Way TW6: H'row A . . . 4G 111
Vision 20 IG1: Ilf . . . 2G 71
Vista, The DA14: Sidc . . . 5K 143
SE9 . . . 6B 124
Vista Av. EN3: Enf H . . . 2E 24
Vista Bldg. E3 . . . 3B 86
(off Bow Rd.)
SE18 . . . 4E 106
Vista Dr. IG4: Ilf . . . 5B 52
Vista Ho. N4 . . . 2A 66
SW19 . . . 1B 154
(off Chapter Way)
Vista Way HA3: Kenton . . . 6E 42
Vitae Apartments W6 . . . 3C 98
Vittoria Ho. N1 . . . 1K 83
(off High Rd.)
Viveash Cl. UB3: Hayes . . . 3H 93
Vivian Av. HA9: Wemb . . . 5G 61
NW4 . . . 5D 44
Vivian Comma Cl. N4 . . . 3B 66
Vivian Ct. N12 . . . 5E 30
W9 . . . 2K 81
Vivian Gdns. HA9: Wemb . . . 5G 61
Vivian Mans. NW4 . . . 5D 44
(off Vivian Av.)
Vivian Rd. E3 . . . 2A 86
Vivian Sq. SE15 . . . 3H 121
Vivian Way N2 . . . 5B 46
Vivien Cl. KT9: Chess . . . 7E 162
Vivienne Cl. TW1: Twick . . . 6D 114
Vixen M. E8 . . . 7F 67
(off Haggerston Rd.)
Voce Rd. SE18 . . . 7H 107
Voewood Cl. KT3: N Mald . . . 6B 152
Vogans Mill SE1 . . . 6K 15 (2F 103)
Vogler Ho. E1 . . . 7J 85
(off Cable St.)
Vogue Ct. BR1: Brom . . . 1K 159
Vollasky Ho. E1 . . . 5K 9
(off Daplyn St.)
Volta Cl. N9 . . . 3D 34
Voltaire Rd. SW4 . . . 3H 119
Voltaire Way UB3: Hayes . . . 7G 75
Volt Av. NW10 . . . 3A 80
Volta Way CR0: Wadd . . . 1K 167
Voluntary Pl. E11 . . . 6J 51
Vorley Rd. N19 . . . 2G 65
Voss Ct. SW16 . . . 6J 137
Voss St. E2 . . . 3G 85
Voyager Bus. Est. SE16 . . . 3G 103
(off Spa Rd.)
Voyagers Cl. SE28 . . . 6C 90
Voysey Cl. N3 . . . 3G 45
Vue Cinema
Croydon, High Street . . . 3C 168
Croydon, Purley Way . . . 1K 167
Dagenham . . . 1E 90
Fallow Corner . . . 7G 31
Finchley Road . . . 6A 64
(in O2 Cen.)
Fulham Broadway . . . 7J 99
Harrow . . . 6J 41
(in St George's Shop. & Leisure Cen.)
Islington . . . 2A 84
Leicester Square . . . 2D 12
(off Cranbourn St.)
Romford . . . 6K 55
Royale Leisure Pk. . . . 4G 79
Shepherds Bush . . . 2F 99
The O2 . . . 1G 105
(in The O2)
Westfield . . . 1E 98
Vulcan Cl. E6 . . . 6E 88
Vulcan Ga. EN2: Enf . . . 2F 23
Vulcan Rd. SE4 . . . 2B 122
Vulcan Sq. E14 . . . 4D 104
Vulcan Ter. SE4 . . . 2B 122
Vulcan Way N7 . . . 6K 65
SM6: Wall . . . 7J 167
Vulcan Wharf E15 . . . 2D 86
(off Cook's Rd.)
Vyne, The DA7: Bex . . . 3H 127
Vyner Rd. W3 . . . 7K 79
Vyner St. E2 . . . 1H 85
Vyners Way UB10: Ick . . . 5C 56

W

Wadbrook St. KT1: King T . . . 2D 150
Wadding St. SE17 . . . 4D 102
Waddington Cl. EN1: Enf . . . 4K 23
Waddington Rd. E15 . . . 5F 69
Waddington St. E15 . . . 6F 69
Waddington Way SE19 . . . 7C 138
WADDON . . . 3A 168
Waddon Cl. CR0: Wadd . . . 3A 168
Waddon Ct. Rd. CR0: Wadd . . . 3A 168
Waddon Marsh Way CR0: Wadd . . . 1K 167
Waddon New Rd. CR0: C'don . . . 3B 168
Waddon Pk. Av. CR0: Wadd . . . 4A 168
Waddon Rd. CR0: C'don, Wadd . . . 3A 168
Waddon Way CR0: Wadd . . . 6A 168
Wade Ct. N10 . . . 7A 32
Wade Ho. EN1: Enf . . . 5J 23
SE1 . . . 7K 15
(off Parkers Row)
Wades Gro. N21 . . . 7F 23
Wades Hill N21 . . . 6F 23
Wades La. TW11: Tedd . . . 5A 132
Wades M. N21 . . . 7F 23
Wadeson St. E2 . . . 2H 85
Wade's Pl. E14 . . . 7D 86
Wadeville Av. RM6: Chad H . . . 6E 54
Wadeville Cl. DA17: Belv . . . 5G 109
Wadham Av. E17 . . . 7J 35
Wadham Cl. TW17: Shep . . . 7E 146
Wadham Gdns. NW3 . . . 1C 82
UB6: G'frd . . . 6H 59
Wadham Ho. N18 . . . 5A 34
Wadham Rd. E17 . . . 7J 35
SW15 . . . 4G 117
Wadhurst Cl. SE20 . . . 2H 157
Wadhurst Rd. SW8 . . . 1G 119
W4 . . . 3K 97
Wadley Rd. E11 . . . 7G 51
Wadsworth Bus. Cen. UB6: G'frd . . . 2C 78
Wadsworth Cl. EN3: Pond E . . . 5E 24
UB6: G'frd . . . 2C 78
Wadsworth Rd. UB6: G'frd . . . 2B 78
Wager St. E3 . . . 4B 86
WAGGONERS RDBT. . . . 1K 111
Waggon La. N17 . . . 6B 34
Waggon M. N14 . . . 1B 32
Waghorn Rd. E13 . . . 1A 88
HA3: Kenton . . . 3D 42
Waghorn St. SE15 . . . 3G 121
Wagner M. KT6: Surb . . . 5E 150
(off Avenue Elmers)
Wagner St. SE15 . . . 7J 103
Wagstaff Gdns. RM9: Dag . . . 7C 72
Wagtail Cl. EN1: Enf . . . 1C 24
NW9 . . . 2A 44
Wagtail Rd. TW6: H'row A . . . 5C 174
Wagtail Wlk. BR3: Beck . . . 5E 158
Waight's Ct. KT2: King T . . . 1E 150
Wainfleet Av. RM5: Col R . . . 2J 55
Wainford Cl. SW19 . . . 1F 135
Wainwright Gro. TW7: Isle . . . 4H 113
Wainwright Ho. E1 . . . 1J 103
(off Garnet St.)
Waite Davies Rd. SE12 . . . 7H 123
Waite St. SE15 . . . 6F 103
Waithman St. EC4 . . . 1A 14
(off Black Friars La.)
Wakefield Ct. SE26 . . . 6J 139
Wakefield Gdns. IG1: Ilf . . . 6C 52
SE19 . . . 7E 138
Wakefield Ho. SE15 . . . 1G 121
Wakefield M. WC1 . . . 2F 7 (3J 83)
Wakefield Rd. N11 . . . 5C 32
N15 . . . 5F 49
TW10: Rich . . . 5D 114
Wakefield St. E6 . . . 1B 88
N18 . . . 5B 34
WC1 . . . 2F 7 (3J 83)
Wakeford Cl. DA5: Bexl . . . 1D 144
(not continuous)
SW4 . . . 5G 119
Wakehams Hill HA5: Pinn . . . 3D 40
Wakeham St. N1 . . . 6D 66
Wakehurst Rd. SW11 . . . 5C 118
Wakeling Cl. HA0: Wemb . . . 3B 60
Wakeling Rd. W7 . . . 5K 77
Wakeling St. E14 . . . 6A 86
Wakelin Ho. N1 . . . 7B 66
(off Sebbon St.)
SE23 . . . 7A 122
(off Brockley Pk.)
Wakelin Rd. E15 . . . 2G 87
Wakeman Ho. NW10 . . . 3F 81
(off Wakeman Rd.)
Wakeman Rd. NW10 . . . 3E 80
Wakemans Hill Av. NW9 . . . 5K 43
Wakering Rd. IG11: Bark . . . 7G 71
Wakerley Cl. E6 . . . 6D 88
Wakley St. EC1 . . . 1A 8 (3B 84)
Walberswick St. SW8 . . . 7J 101
Walbrook EC4 . . . 2E 14 (7D 84)
(not continuous)
Walbrook Ct. N1 . . . 2E 84
(off Hemsworth St.)
Walbrook Ho. N9 . . . 2D 34
(off Huntingdon Rd.)
Walbrook Wharf EC4 . . . 3D 14
(off Cousin La.)
Walburgh St. E1 . . . 6H 85
Walcorde Av. SE17 . . . 4C 102
Walcot Gdns. SE11 . . . 3J 19
Walcot Rd. EN3: Brim . . . 2G 25
Walcot Sq. SE11 . . . 3K 19 (4A 102)
Walcott St. SW1 . . . 3B 18 (4G 101)
Waldair Ct. E16 . . . 2F 107
Waldeck Gro. SE27 . . . 3B 138
Waldeck Rd. N15 . . . 4B 48
SW14 . . . 3J 115
W4 . . . 6G 97
W13 . . . 6B 78
Waldeck Ter. SW14 . . . 3J 115
(off Waldeck Rd.)
Waldegrave Ct. IG11: Bark . . . 1H 89
Waldegrave Gdns.
TW1: Twick . . . 2K 131
Waldegrave Pk. TW1: Twick . . . 4K 131
Waldegrave Rd. BR1: Brom . . . 4C 160
N8 . . . 3A 48
RM8: Dag . . . 2C 72
SE19 . . . 7F 139
TW1: Twick . . . 4K 131
TW11: Tedd . . . 4K 131
W5 . . . 7F 79
Waldegrove CR0: C'don . . . 3F 169
Waldemar Av. SW6 . . . 1G 117
W13 . . . 1C 96
Waldemar Rd. SW19 . . . 5J 135
Walden Av. BR7: Chst . . . 4D 142
N13 . . . 4H 33
RM13: Rain . . . 2K 91
Walden Cl. DA17: Belv . . . 5F 109
Walden Ct. SW8 . . . 1H 119
Walden Gdns. CR7: Thor H . . . 3K 155
Walden Ho. SW1 . . . 4H 17
(off Pimlico Rd.)
SW11 . . . 1E 118
(off Dagnall St.)
Walden Pde. BR7: Chst . . . 6D 142
(not continuous)
Walden Rd. BR7: Chst . . . 6D 142
N17 . . . 1D 48
Waldenshaw Rd. SE23 . . . 1J 139
Walden St. E1 . . . 6H 85
(not continuous)
Walden Way NW7 . . . 6A 30
Waldo Cl. SW4 . . . 5G 119
Waldo Ho. NW10 . . . 3D 80
(off Waldo Rd.)
Waldo Ind. Est. BR1: Brom . . . 3B 160
Waldo Pl. CR4: Mitc . . . 7C 136
Waldorf Cl. CR2: S Croy . . . 7B 168
Waldo Rd. BR1: Brom . . . 3B 160
NW10 . . . 3C 80
(not continuous)
Waldram Cres. SE23 . . . 1J 139
Waldram Pk. Rd. SE23 . . . 1K 139
Waldram Pl. SE23 . . . 1J 139
Waldrist Way DA18: Erith . . . 3F 109
Waldron Gdns. BR2: Brom . . . 3F 159
Waldronhyrst CR2: S Croy . . . 4B 168
Waldron M. SW3 . . . 7B 16 (6B 100)
Waldron Rd. HA1: Harr . . . 1J 59
HA2: Harr . . . 1J 59
SW18 . . . 3A 136
Waldrons, The CR0: C'don . . . 4B 168
Waldron's Path CR2: S Croy . . . 4C 168
Waldrons Yd. HA2: Harr . . . 2H 59
Waldstock Rd. SE28 . . . 7A 90
Waleran Cl. HA7: Stan . . . 5E 26
Walerand Rd. SE13 . . . 2E 122
Waleran Flats SE1 . . . 4E 102
Wales Av. SM5: Cars . . . 5C 166
Wales Cl. SE15 . . . 6H 103
Wales Farm Rd. W3 . . . 5K 79
Waleton Acres SM6: Wall . . . 6G 167
Waley St. E1 . . . 5A 86
Walfield Av. N20 . . . 7E 20
Walford Ho. E1 . . . 6G 85
Walford Rd. N16 . . . 4E 66
Walfrey Gdns. RM9: Dag . . . 7E 72
WALHAM GREEN . . . 1J 117
Walham Grn. Ct. SW6 . . . 7K 99
(off Waterford Rd.)
Walham Gro. SW6 . . . 7J 99
Walham Ri. SW19 . . . 6G 135
Walham Yd. SW6 . . . 7J 99
Walk, The N13 . . . 3F 33
(off Fox La.)
TW16: Sun . . . 7H 129
Walkato Lodge IG9: Buck H . . . 1F 37
Walkden Rd. BR7: Chst . . . 5E 142
Walker Cl. CR0: New Ad . . . 7E 170
N11 . . . 4B 32
SE18 . . . 4G 107
TW12: Hamp . . . 6D 130
TW14: Felt . . . 7H 111
W7 . . . 1J 95
Walker Ho. NW1 . . . 1C 6 (2H 83)
SE16 . . . 3B 104
(off Redriff Est.)
Walker M. SW2 . . . 5A 120
Walker's Ct. W1 . . . 2C 12
Walkerscroft Mead SE21 . . . 1C 138
Walkers Lodge E14 . . . 2E 104
(off Manchester Rd.)
Walkers Pl. SW15 . . . 4G 117
Walkinshaw Ct. N1 . . . 7C 66
(off Rotherfield St.)
Walks, The N2 . . . 3B 46
Walkynscroft SE15 . . . 2H 121
(off Caulfield Rd.)
Wallace Cl. SE28 . . . 7D 90
TW17: Shep . . . 4F 147
UB10: Uxb . . . 2A 74
Wallace Collection . . . 7H 5 (6E 82)
Wallace Ct. NW1 . . . 6D 4
(off Old Marylebone Rd.)
Wallace Cres. SM5: Cars . . . 5D 166
Wallace Ho. N7 . . . 6K 65
(off Caledonian Rd.)
Wallace Rd. N1 . . . 6C 66

Wallace Way N19 . . . . .2H 65
(off St John's Way)
RM1: Rom 1K 55
Wallasey Cres. UB10: Ick 2C 56
Wallbrook Bus. Cen.
TW4: Houn 3K 111
Wallbutton Rd. SE4 . . . . .2A 122
Wallcote Av. NW2 . . . . .1F 63
Wall Ct. N4 . . . . .1K 65
(off Stroud Grn. Rd.)
Walled Gdn. Cl. BR3: Beck 4D 158
WALLEND .1E 88
Wall End Cl. E6 . . . . .1E 88
(off Wall End Rd.)
Wall End Rd. E6 . . . . .7E 70
Waller Dr. HA6: Nwood 2J 39
Waller Rd. SE14 . . . . .1K 121
Wallers Cl. IG8: Wfd G 6J 37
RM9: Dag 1E 90
Waller Way SE10 . . . . .7D 104
Wallflower St. W12 . . . . .7B 80
Wallgrave Rd. SW5 . . . . .4K 99
Wallingford Av. W10 . . . . .5F 81
WALLINGTON 6F 167
Wallington Cl. HA4: Ruis 6E 38
Wallington Cnr. SM6: Wall 4F 167
(off Manor Rd. Nth.)
Wallington Ct. SM6: Wall 6F 167
(off Stanley Pk. Rd.)
WALLINGTON GREEN 4F 167
Wallington Rd. IG3: Ilf 7K 53
Wallington Sq. SM6: Wall 6F 167
Wallis All. SE1 . . . . .6D 14
Wallis Cl. SW11 . . . . .3B 118
Wallis Ho. HA4: Ruis 1F 57
SE14 . . . . .1A 122
TW8: Bford 5E 96
Wallis M. N8 . . . . .3A 48
(off Courcy Rd.)
Wallis Rd. E9 . . . . .6B 68
TW6: H'row A 5C 174
UB1: S'hall 6F 77
Wallis's Cotts. SW2 . . . . .7J 119
Wallman Pl. N22 . . . . .1K 47
Wallorton Gdns. SW14 . . . . .4K 115
Wallside EC2 . . . . .6D 8
Wall St. N1 . . . . .6D 66
Wallwood Rd. E11 . . . . .7F 51
Wallwood St. E14 . . . . .5B 86
Walmar Cl. EN4: Had W 1G 21
Walmer Cl. BR6: Farnb 4H 173
E4 .2J 35
RM7: Mawney 2H 55
Walmer Ct. KT5: Surb 5E 150
(off Cranes Pk.)
Walmer Gdns. W13 . . . . .2A 96
Walmer Ho. W10 . . . . .6F 81
(off Bramley Rd.)
Walmer Pl. W1 . . . . .5E 4
Walmer Rd. W10 . . . . .6E 80
W11 .7G 81
Walmer St. W1 . . . . .5E 4 (5D 82)
Walmer Ter. SE18 . . . . .4G 107
Walmgate Rd. UB6: G'frd 1B 78
Walmington Fold N12 . . . . .6D 30
Walm La. NW2 . . . . .6E 62
Walney Wlk. N1 . . . . .6C 66
Walnut Av. UB7: W Dray 3C 92
Walnut Cl. IG6: Ilf 4G 53
SE8 . . . . .6B 104
SM5: Cars 5D 166
UB3: Hayes 7G 75
Walnut Ct. E17 . . . . .4E 50
W5 .2E 96
W8 .3K 99
(off St Mary's Ga.)
Walnut Flds.
KT17: Ewe 7B 164
Walnut Gdns. E15 . . . . .5G 69
Walnut Gro. EN1: Enf 5J 23
Walnut Ho. E3 . . . . .1B 86
(off Barge La.)

Walnut M. N22 . . . . .3A 48
(off High Rd.)
SM2: Sutt 7A 166
Walnut Rd. E10 . . . . .2C 68
Walnut Tree Av. CR4: Mitc 3C 154
(off Dearn Gdns.)
Walnut Tree Cl. BR7: Chst 1H 161
SW13 . . . . .1B 116
TW17: Shep 3E 146
UB10: Ick 4A 56
Walnut Tree Cotts.
SW19 . . . . .5G 135
Walnut Tree Ho. SW10 . . . . .6K 99
(off Tregunter Rd.)
Walnut Tree Rd. RM8: Dag 2E 72
SE10 . . . . .5G 105
(not continuous)
TW5: Hest 6D 94
TW8: Bford 6E 96
TW17: Shep 2E 146
Walnut Tree Wlk.
SE11 . . . . .3J 19 (4A 102)
Walnut Way HA4: Ruis 6A 58
IG9: Buck H 3G 37
Walpole Av. TW9: Kew 2F 115
Walpole Cl. W13 . . . . .2C 96
Walpole Ct. NW6 . . . . .7A 64
(off Fairfax Rd.)
TW2: Twick 2J 131
W14 .3F 99
(off Blythe Rd.)
Walpole Cres. TW11: Tedd 5K 131
Walpole Gdns. TW2: Twick 2J 131
W4 .5J 97
Walpole Ho. KT8: W Mole 5E 148
(off Approach Rd.)
SE1 .7J 13
(off Westminster Bri. Rd.)
Walpole Lodge W13 . . . . .1C 96
Walpole M. NW8 . . . . .1B 82
SW19 . . . . .6B 136
Walpole Pl. SE18 . . . . .4F 107
TW11: Tedd 5K 131
Walpole Rd. BR2: Brom 5B 160
CR0: C'don 2D 168
E6 .7A 70
E17 . . . . .4A 50
E18 . . . . .1H 51
KT6: Surb 7E 150
N17 . . . . .2C 48
(not continuous)
SW19 . . . . .6B 136
TW2: Twick 2J 131
TW11: Tedd 5K 131
Walpole St. SW3 . . . . . . .5E 16 (5D 100)
Walrond Av. HA9: Wemb 5E 60
Walsham Cl. N16 . . . . .1G 67
SE28 . . . . .7D 90
Walsham Ho. SE14 . . . . .2K 121
SE17 . . . . .5D 102
(off Blackwood St.)
Walsham Rd. SE14 . . . . .2K 121
TW14: Felt 7K 111
Walsingham NW8 . . . . .1B 82
Walsingham Gdns.
KT19: Ewe 4A 164
Walsingham Lodge SW13 . . . . .1C 116
Walsingham Mans. SW6 . . . . .7K 99
(off Fulham Rd.)
Walsingham Pk. BR7: Chst 2H 161
Walsingham Pl. SW4 . . . . .6E 118
Walsingham Rd. CR4: Mitc 5D 154
E5 .3G 67
EN2: Enf 4J 23
W13 . . . . .1A 96
Walsingham Wlk. DA17: Belv 6G 109
Walston Ho. SW1 . . . . .5C 18
(off Aylesford St.)
Walter Besant Ho. E1 . . . . .3K 85
(off Bancroft Rd.)
Walter Ct. W3 . . . . .6J 79
(off Lynton Ter.)

Walter Grn. Ho. SE15 . . . . .1J 121
(off Lausanne Rd.)
Walter Ho. SW10 . . . . .7B 100
(off Riley St.)
Walter Hurford Pde. E12 . . . . .4E 70
(off Grantham Rd.)
Walter Langley Ct. SE16 . . . . .2J 103
(off Brunel Rd.)
Walter Rodney Cl. E6 . . . . .6D 70
Walter Savil Twr. E17 . . . . .6C 50
(off Colchester Rd.)
Walters Cl. SE17 . . . . .4D 102
(off Brandon St.)
UB3: Hayes 2H 93
Walters Ho. SE17 . . . . .6B 102
(off Otto St.)
Walter Sickert Hall N1 . . . . .1C 8
(off Graham St.)
Walters Rd. EN3: Pond E 4D 24
SE25 . . . . .4E 156
Walter St. E2 . . . . .3K 85
KT2: King T 1E 150
Walters Way SE23 . . . . .6K 121
Walter Ter. E1 . . . . .6K 85
Walterton Rd. W9 . . . . .4H 81
Walter Wlk. HA8: Edg 6D 28
Waltham Av. NW9 . . . . .6G 43
UB3: Harl 3E 92
Waltham Dr. HA8: Edg 2G 43
Waltham Forest Pool & Track 2D 50
Waltham Forest Theatre 2C 50
Waltham Ho. NW8 . . . . .1A 82
Waltham Pk. Way E17 . . . . .1C 50
Waltham Rd. IG8: Wfd G 6H 37
SM5: Cars 7B 154
UB2: S'hall 3C 94
WALTHAMSTOW 3C 50
Walthamstow Av. E4 . . . . .6G 35
Walthamstow Bus. Cen. E17 . . . . . . .2E 50
Walthamstow Marsh Nature Reserve
. . . . .7H 49
Walthamstow Stadium 7J 35
Waltham Way E4 . . . . .3G 35
Waltheof Av. N17 . . . . .1D 48
Waltheof Gdns. N17 . . . . .1D 48
Walton Av. HA2: Harr 5D 58
HA9: Wemb 3H 61
KT3: N Mald 4B 152
SM3: Cheam 3H 165
Walton Bri. TW17: Shep 7G 147
Walton Bri. Rd. TW17: Shep 7G 147
Walton Cl. E5 . . . . .3K 67
(off Orient Way)
HA1: Harr 4H 41
NW2 . . . . .2D 62
SW8 .7J 101
Walton Ct. CR2: S Croy 5C 168
(off Warham Rd.)
EN5: New Bar 5F 21
NW6 . . . . .7A 64
(off Fairfax Rd.)
Walton Cft. HA1: Harr 4J 59
Walton Dr. HA1: Harr 4H 41
NW10 . . . . .6K 61
Walton Gdns. HA9: Wemb 2E 60
TW13: Felt 4H 129
W3 .5H 79
Walton Grn. CR0: New Ad 7D 170
Walton Ho. E2 . . . . .4K 9
(off Montclare St.)
E17 . . . . .3D 50
NW1 . . . . .4F 83
(off Longford St.)
SW1 . . . . .2E 16
(off Walton St.)
Walton La. KT13: Weyb . . . .7F 147 & 7G 147
TW17: Shep 7F 147
Walton on Thames Camping & Cvn. Site
KT12: Walt T 7E 148
Walton Pl. SW3 . . . . .1E 16 (3D 100)

Walton Rd. DA14: Sidc 2C 144
E12 . . . . .4E 70
(not continuous)
E13 . . . . .2A 88
HA1: Harr 4H 41
KT8: W Mole, E Mos 4D 148
KT12: Walt T 5A 148
N15 . . . . .4F 49
RM5: Col R 1F 55
Walton St. EN2: Enf 1J 23
SW3 . . . . .3D 16 (4C 100)
Walton Vs. N1 . . . . .7E 66
(off Downham Rd.)
Walton Way CR4: Mitc 4G 155
W3 .5H 79
Walt Whitman Cl. SE24 . . . . .4B 120
WALWORTH 5C 102
Walworth Pl. SE17 . . . . .5C 102
Walworth Rd. SE1 . . . . .4C 102
SE17 . . . . .4C 102
Walwyn Av. BR1: Brom 3B 160
Wanborough Dr. SW15 . . . . .1D 134
Wanderer Dr. IG11: Bark 3C 90
Wandle Bank CR0: Bedd 3J 167
SW19 . . . . .7B 136
Wandle Cl. CR0: Bedd 3J 167
KT19: Ewe 4J 163
Wandle Ct. Gdns. CR0: Bedd 3J 167
Wandle Ho. BR1: Brom 5F 141
NW8 .5C 4
(off Penfold St.)
Wandle Industrial Mus.
(within The Vestry Hall Annexe)
. . . . .3D 154
Wandle Meadow Nature Pk. 5A 136
Wandle Pk. Trad. Est., The
CR0: C'don 1B 168
Wandle Recreation Cen. 6K 117
Wandle Rd. CR0: Bedd 3J 167
CR0: C'don 3C 168
SM4: Mord 4A 154
SM6: Wall 3F 167
SW17 . . . . .2C 136
Wandle Side CR0: Wadd 3K 167
SM6: Wall 3F 167
Wandle Technology Pk. CR4: Mitc . . .7D 154
Wandle Trad. Est. CR4: Mitc 7D 154
Wandle Way CR4: Mitc 5D 154
SW18 . . . . .1K 135
Wandon Rd. SW6 . . . . .7K 99
(not continuous)
Wandsdown Pl. SW6 . . . . .7K 99
WANDSWORTH 5K 117
Wandsworth Bri. SW6 . . . . .3K 117
Wandsworth Bri. Rd. SW6 . . . . .1K 117
WANDSWORTH COMMON 1D 136
Wandsworth Comn. W. Side SW18 . .5A 118
WANDSWORTH GYRATORY 5K 117
Wandsworth High St. SW18 . . . . . . .5J 117
Wandsworth Plain SW18 . . . . .5K 117
Wandsworth Rd. SW8 . . . .7E 18 (3F 119)
Wangey Rd. RM6: Chad H 7D 54
Wangford Ho. SW9 . . . . .4B 120
(off Loughborough Pk.)
Wanless Rd. SE24 . . . . .3C 120
Wanley Rd. SE5 . . . . .4D 120
Wanlip Rd. E13 . . . . .4K 87
Wannock Gdns. IG6: Ilf 1F 53
Wansbeck Ct. EN2: Enf 3G 23
(off Waverley Rd.)
Wansbeck Rd. E9 . . . . .7B 68
Wansey St. SE17 . . . . .4C 102
Wansford Rd. IG8: Wfd G 1A 52
WANSTEAD 6K 51
Wanstead Cl. BR1: Brom 2A 160
Wanstead Gdns. IG4: Ilf 6B 52
Wanstead La. IG1: Ilf 6B 52
Wanstead Leisure Cen. 6A 52
Wanstead Pk. Av. E12 . . . . .1B 70
Wanstead Pk. Rd. IG1: Ilf 6B 52
Wanstead Pl. E11 . . . . .6J 51
Wanstead Rd. BR1: Brom 2A 160

Wansunt Rd. DA5: Bexl 1J 145
Wantage Rd. SE12 5H 123
Wantz Rd. RM10: Dag 4H 73
WAPPING 1H 103
Wapping Dock St. E1 1H 103
Wapping High St. E1 1G 103
Wapping La. E1 7H 85
Wapping Wall E1 1J 103
Warbank La. KT2: King T 7B 134
Warbeck Rd. W12 2D 98
Warberry Rd. N22 1K 47
Warboys App. KT2: King T 6H 133
Warboys Cres. E4 5K 35
Warboys Rd. KT2: King T 6H 133
Warburton Cl. HA3: Hrw W 6C 26
N1 6E 66
(off Culford Rd.)
Warburton Ct. HA4: Ruis 2J 57
Warburton Ho. E8 1H 85
(off Warburton St.)
Warburton Rd. E8 1H 85
TW2: Whitt 1F 131
Warburton St. E8 1H 85
Warburton Ter. E17 2D 50
Wardalls Gro. SE14 7J 103
Wardalls Ho. SE8 6B 104
(off Staunton St.)
Ward Cl. CR2: S Croy 6E 168
DA8: Erith 6K 109
Wardell Cl. NW7 7F 29
Wardell Fld. NW9 1A 44
Wardell Ho. SE10 6E 104
(off Welland St.)
Warden Av. HA2: Harr 1D 58
Warden Rd. NW5 6E 64
Wardens Fld. Cl. BR6: Chels 6J 173
Wardens Gro. SE1 5C 14 (1C 102)
Wardle St. E9 5K 67
Wardley St. SW18 7K 117
Wardo Av. SW6 1G 117
Wardour M. W1 1B 12
Wardour St. W1 7B 6 (6G 83)
Ward Point SE11 4J 19 (4A 102)
Ward Rd. E15 1F 87
N19 3G 65
SW19 1A 154
Wardrobe, The TW9: Rich 5D 114
(off Old Palace Yd.)
Wardrobe Pl. EC4 1B 14
Wardrobe Ter. EC4 2B 14
Wards Rd. IG2: Ilf 7H 53
Wards Wharf App. E16 1B 106
Ware Ct. HA8: Edg 4K 27
SM1: Sutt 4H 165
Wareham Cl. TW3: Houn 4F 113
Wareham Ct. N1 7E 66
(off Hertford Rd.)
Wareham Ho. SW8 7K 101
Warehouse Theatre 2D 168
Warehouse Way E16 7K 87
Waremead Rd. IG2: Ilf 5F 53
Warepoint Dr. SE28 2H 107
Warfield Rd. NW10 3F 81
TW12: Hamp 1F 149
TW14: Felt 7G 111
Warfield Yd. NW10 3F 81
(off Warfield Rd.)
Wargrave Av. N15 6F 49
Wargrave Ho. E2 2J 9
(off Navarre St.)
Wargrave Rd. HA2: Harr 3G 59
Warham Rd. CR2: S Croy 5B 168
HA3: W'stone 2K 41
N4 5A 48
Warham St. SE5 7B 102
Waring & Gillow Est. W3 4G 79
Waring Cl. BR6: Chels 6K 173
Waring Dr. BR6: Chels 6K 173
Waring Rd. DA14: Sidc 6C 144
Waring St. SE27 4C 138
Warkworth Gdns. TW7: Isle 7A 96
Warkworth Rd. N17 7J 33
Warland Rd. SE18 7H 107
Warley Av. RM8: Dag 7F 55
UB4: Hayes 6J 75
Warley Cl. E10 1B 68
Warley Rd. IG5: Ilf 1E 52
IG8: Wfd G 7E 36
N9 2D 34
UB4: Hayes 6J 75
Warley St. E2 3K 85
Warlingham Ct. SE13 6E 122
Warlingham Rd. CR7: Thor H 4B 156
Warlock Rd. W9 4H 81
Warlters Cl. N7 4J 65
Warlters Rd. N7 4J 65
Warltersville Mans. N19 7J 47
Warltersville Rd. N19 7J 47
Warmington Cl. E5 3K 67
Warmington Rd. SE24 6C 120
Warmington St. E13 4J 87
Warminster Gdns. SE25 2G 157
Warminster Rd. SE25 2F 157
Warminster Sq. SE25 2G 157
Warminster Way CR4: Mitc 1F 155
Warmsworth NW1 1G 83
(off Pratt St.)
Warmwell Av. NW9 1A 44
Warndon St. SE16 4K 103
Warneford Rd. HA3: Kenton 3D 42
TW6: H'row A 5C 174
Warneford St. E9 1H 85
Warne Pl. DA15: Sidc 6B 126
Warner Av. SM3: Cheam 2G 165
Warner Cl. E15 5G 69
NW9 7B 44
TW12: Hamp 5D 130
UB3: Harl 7F 93
Warner Ho. BR3: Beck 6D 140
NW8 3A 82
SE13 2D 122
(off Russett Way)
Warner Pl. E2 2G 85
Warner Rd. BR1: Brom 7H 141
E17 4A 50
N8 4H 47
SE5 1C 120
Warners Cl. IG8: Wfd G 5D 36
Warners La. KT2: King T 4D 132
Warners Path IG8: Wfd G 5D 36
Warner St. EC1 4J 7 (4A 84)
Warner Ter. E14 5D 86
(off Broomfield St.)
Warner Yd. EC1 4J 7
Warnford Ct. EC2 7F 9
(off Throgmorton Av.)
Warnford Ho. SW15 6A 116
(off Tunworth Cres.)
Warnford Ind. Est. UB3: Hayes 2G 93
Warnford Rd. BR6: Chels 5K 173
Warnham WC1 2G 7
(off Sidmouth St.)
Warnham Ct. Rd. SM5: Cars 7D 166
Warnham Ho. SW2 7K 119
(off Up. Tulse Hill)
Warnham Rd. N12 5H 31
Warple M. W3 2A 98
Warple Way W3 2A 98
(not continuous)
Warren, The E12 4C 70
KT4: Wor Pk 4K 163
SE7 6A 106
TW5: Hest 7D 94
UB4: Hayes 6J 75
Warren Av. BR1: Brom 7G 141
BR6: Chels 5K 173
CR2: Sels 7K 169
E10 3E 68
TW10: Rich 4H 115
Warren Cl. DA6: Bex 5G 127
HA9: Wemb 2D 60
N9 7E 24
SE21 7C 120
UB4: Yead 5A 76
Warren Ct. BR3: Beck 7C 140
CR0: C'don 1E 168
N17 3G 49
(off High Cross Rd.)
NW1 3B 6
(off Warren St.)
W5 5C 78
Warren Cres. N9 7A 24
Warren Cutting KT2: King T 7K 133
Warrender Rd. N19 3G 65
Warrender Way HA4: Ruis 7J 39
Warren Dr. HA4: Ruis 7B 40
UB6: G'frd 4F 77
Warren Dr., The E11 7A 52
Warren Dr. Nth. KT5: Surb 1H 163
Warren Dr. Sth. KT5: Surb 1J 163
Warren Farm Cotts.
RM6: Chad H 4F 55
Warren Farm Sports Cen. 3H 95
Warren Flds. HA7: Stan 4H 27
Warren Footpath TW1: Twick 1C 132
Warren Gdns. BR6: Chels 5K 173
E15 5F 69
Warren Ho. E3 3D 86
(off Bromley High St.)
N17 3G 49
(off High Cross Rd.)
W14 4H 99
(off Beckford Cl.)
Warren La. HA7: Stan 2F 27
SE18 3F 107
Warren La. Ga. SE18 3F 107
Warren M. W1 4A 6 (4G 83)
Warren Pk. KT2: King T 6J 133
Warren Pk. Rd. SM1: Sutt 6B 166
Warren Pl. E1 6K 85
(off Pitsea St.)
Warren Pond Rd. E4 1C 36
Warren Ri. KT3: N Mald 1K 151
Warren Rd. BR2: Hayes 2J 171
BR6: Chels 5K 173
CR0: C'don 1E 168
DA6: Bex 5G 127
DA14: Sidc 3C 144
E4 2K 35
E10 3E 68
E11 6A 52
IG6: Ilf 5H 53
KT2: King T 6J 133
NW2 2B 62
SW19 6C 136
TW2: Whitt 6G 113
TW15: Ashf 7G 129
UB10: Ick 4A 56
WD23: B Hea 1B 26
Warren Sports Cen. 5F 55
Warrens Shawe La. HA8: Edg 2C 28
Warren St. W1 4A 6 (4G 83)
Warren Ter. RM6: Chad H 4D 54
Warren Wlk. SE7 6A 106
Warren Way HA8: Edg 2H 43
Warren Wood Cl. BR2: Hayes 2H 171
Warriner Dr. N9 3B 34
Warriner Gdns. SW11 1D 118
Warrington Ct. CR0: Wadd 3B 168
(off Warrington Rd.)
Warrington Cres. W9 4A 82
Warrington Gdns. W9 4A 82
(not continuous)
Warrington Rd. CR0: Wadd 3B 168
HA1: Harr 5J 41
RM8: Dag 2D 72
TW10: Rich 5D 114
Warrington Sq. RM8: Dag 2D 72
Warrior Cl. SE28 1H 107
Warrior Ct. SW9 3B 120
(off Coldharbour Rd.)
Warrior Sq. E12 4E 70
Warsaw Cl. HA4: Ruis 6K 57
Warspite Ho. E14 4D 104
(off Cahir St.)
Warspite Rd. SE18 3C 106
Warton Ct. E1 7K 85
(off Cable St.)
Warton Rd. E15 1E 86
Warwall E6 6F 89
Warwark Ct. KT6: Surb 2E 162
Warwick W14 4H 99
(off Kensington Village)
Warwick Av. HA2: Harr 4D 58
HA8: Edg 3C 28
W2 4A 82
W9 4K 81
Warwick Bldg. SW8 6F 101
Warwick Chambers W8 3J 99
(off Pater St.)
Warwick Cl. DA5: Bexl 7F 127
EN4: E Barn 5G 21
TW12: Hamp 7G 131
W8 3H 99
(off Kensington High St.)
WD23: B Hea 1D 26
Warwick Ct. BR2: Brom 2G 159
EC4 1B 14
(off Warwick La.)
EN5: New Bar 5E 20
(off Station Rd.)
HA3: W'stone 3J 41
N11 6C 32
UB5: N'olt 5E 58
(off Newmarket Av.)
W7 6K 77
(off Copley Cl.)
WC1 6H 7 (5K 83)
Warwick Cres. UB4: Hayes 4H 75
W2 5A 82
Warwick Dene W5 1E 96
Warwick Dr. SW15 3D 116
Warwick Est. W2 5K 81
Warwick Gdns. CR7: Thor H 3A 156
EN5: Barn 1C 20
IG1: Ilf 1F 71
KT7: T Ditt 5K 149
N4 5C 48
W14 3H 99
Warwick Gro. E5 1H 67
KT5: Surb 7F 151
Warwick Ho. E16 1J 105
(off Wesley Av.)
KT2: King T 1E 150
(off Acre Rd.)
SW9 2A 120
Warwick Ho. St. SW1 4D 12 (1H 101)
Warwick La. EC4 7B 8 (6B 84)
Warwick Lodge TW2: Twick 3F 131
Warwick Mans. SW5 4J 99
(off Cromwell Cres.)
Warwick Pde. HA3: Kenton 2B 42
Warwick Pas. EC4 7B 8
(off Old Bailey)
Warwick Pl. KT7: T Ditt 6A 150
W5 2D 96
W9 5A 82
Warwick Pl. Nth. SW1 4A 18 (4G 101)
Warwick Rd. CR7: Thor H 3A 156
DA14: Sidc 5B 144
DA16: Well 3C 126
E4 5H 35
E11 5K 51
E12 5C 70
E15 6H 69
E17 1B 50
EN5: New Bar 4E 20
KT1: Ham W 1C 150
KT3: N Mald 3J 151
KT7: T Ditt 5K 149
N11 6C 32
N18 4K 33
SE20 3H 157
SM1: Sutt 4A 166
SW5 4H 99
TW2: Twick 1J 131
TW4: Houn 3K 111
TW6: H'row A 5C 174

Warwick Rd. TW15: Ashf 5A **128**
UB2: S'hall 3D **94**
UB7: W Dray 2A **92**
W5 2D **96**
W14 4H **99**
Warwick Row SW1 1K **17** (3F **101**)
Warwickshire Path SE8 7B **104**
Warwickshire Rd. N16 4E **66**
Warwick Sq. EC4 7B **8** (6B **84**)
SW1 5A **18** (5G **101**)
(not continuous)
Warwick Sq. M. SW1 4A **18** (4G **101**)
Warwick St. W1 2B **12** (7G **83**)
Warwick Ter. *E17* *5F* ***51***
(off Lea Bri. Rd.)
SE18 6H **107**
Warwick Way SW1 5J **17** (5F **101**)
Warwick Yd. EC1 4D **8** (4C **84**)
Wasdale *NW1* *3F* ***83***
(off Cumberland Mkt.)
Washbourne Ct. *N9* *2B* ***34***
(off Acton Cl.)
Washington Av. E12 4D **70**
Washington Bldg. *SE10* *1D* ***122***
(off Deal's Gateway)
Washington Cl. E3 3D **86**
Washington Ho. E17 2B **50**
SW3 *7E* ***10***
(off Basil St.)
Washington Rd. E6 7A **70**
E18 2H **51**
KT1: King T 2G **151**
KT4: Wor Pk 2D **164**
SW13 7C **98**
TW6: H'row A 6D **174**
Wasp Rd. *TW6: H'row A* *5C* ***174***
(off Welland Rd.)
Wastdale Rd. SE23 1K **139**
Watch, The N12 4F **31**
Watchfield Ct. W4 5J **97**
Watcombe Cotts. TW9: Kew 6G **97**
Watcombe Pl. SE25 5H **157**
Watcombe Rd. SE25 5H **157**
Waterbank Rd. SE6 3D **140**
Waterbeach Rd. RM9: Dag 6C **72**
Water Brook La. NW4 5E **44**
Watercress Pl. N1 7E **66**
Waterdale Rd. SE2 6A **108**
Waterden Ct. W11 1G **99**
Waterer Ho. SE6 4E **140**
Waterer Ri. SM6: Wall 6H **167**
Waterfall Cl. N14 3B **32**
Waterfall Cotts. SW19 6B **136**
Waterfall Rd. N11 4A **32**
N14 4A **32**
SW19 6B **136**
Waterfall Ter. SW17 6C **136**
Waterfall Wlk. N14 1A **32**
Waterfield Cl. DA17: Belv 3G **109**
SE28 1B **108**
Waterfield Gdns. SE25 4D **156**
Waterford Ho. *W11* *7H* ***81***
(off Kensington Pk. Rd.)
Waterford Rd. SW6 7K **99**
(not continuous)
Waterford Way NW10 5D **62**
Waterfront W6 6E **98**
Waterfront Ho. *E5* *2J* ***67***
(off Harry Zeital Way)
Waterfront Leisure Cen.
Woolwich 3E **106**
Waterfront M. N1 2C **84**
Waterfront Studios Bus. Cen. *E16* *1J* ***105***
(off Dock Rd.)
Water Gdns. HA7: Stan 6G **27**
Water Gdns., The W2 7D **4** (6C **82**)
Watergardens, The KT2: King T 6J **133**
Water Gdns. Sq. SE16 2K **103**
Watergate EC4 2A **14** (7B **84**)
Watergate St. SE8 6C **104**
Watergate Wlk. WC2 4F **13** (1J **101**)
Waterhall Av. E4 4B **36**
Waterhall Cl. E17 1K **49**
Waterhead *NW1* *1A* ***6***
(off Varndell St.)
Waterhouse Cl. E16 5B **88**
NW3 5B **64**
W6 4F **99**
Waterhouse Sq. EC1 6J **7** (5A **84**)
Wateridge Cl. E14 3C **104**
Water La. DA14: Sidc 2F **145**
E15 6G **69**
EC3 3H **15** (7E **84**)
IG3: Ilf 3J **71**
KT1: King T 1D **150**
N9 1C **34**
NW1 7F **65**
SE14 7J **103**
TW1: Twick 1A **132**
TW9: Rich 5D **114**
Water Lily Cl. UB2: S'hall 2G **95**
Waterloo Bri. WC2 3G **13** (7K **83**)
Waterloo Cl. E9 5J **67**
TW14: Felt 1H **129**
Waterloo Gdns. E2 2J **85**
N1 7B **66**
RM7: Rom 6K **55**
Waterloo Pas. NW6 7H **63**
Waterloo Pl. *SM5: Cars* *3D* ***166***
(off Wrythe La.)
SW1 4C **12** (1H **101**)
TW9: Rich 4E **114**
Waterloo Rd. E6 7A **70**
E7 5H **69**
E10 7C **50**
IG6: Ilf 2G **53**
NW2 1C **62**
RM7: Rom, Rush G 6K **55**
SE1 4H **13** (1K **101**)
SM1: Sutt 5B **166**
Waterloo Ter. N1 7B **66**
Waterlow Ct. NW11 7K **45**
Waterlow Pk. Cen. 1F **65**
Waterlow Rd. N19 1G **65**
Waterman Bldg. E14 2B **104**
Watermans Art Cen., Cinema & Theatre
6E **96**
Watermans Cl. KT2: King T 7E **132**
Watermans Ct. *TW8: Bford* *6D* ***96***
(off High St.)
Watermans M. W5 7E **78**
Waterman's Quay SW6 2A **118**
Waterman St. SW15 3F **117**
Watermans Wlk. SE16 2A **104**
Waterman Way E1 1H **103**
Watermark Ct. *RM6: Chad H* *6B* ***54***
(off Quarles Pk. Rd.)
Watermead TW14: Felt 1G **129**
Watermead Ho. E9 5A **68**
Watermead La. SM5: Cars 7D **154**
Watermead Lodge *SE16* *1K* ***103***
(off Princes Riverside Rd.)
Watermeadow La. SW6 2A **118**
Watermead Rd. SE6 4E **140**
Watermead Way N17 3H **49**
Watermen's Sq. SE20 7J **139**
Water M. SE15 4J **121**
Watermill Bus. Cen.
EN3: Brim 2G **25**
Watermill Cl. TW10: Ham 3C **132**
Water Mill Ho. TW13: Hanw 2E **130**
Watermill La. N18 5K **33**
Watermill Way SW19 1A **154**
TW13: Hanw 2D **130**
Watermint Quay N16 7G **49**
Water Rd. HA0: Wemb 1F **79**
Water's Edge *SW6* *1E* ***116***
(off Palemead Cl.)
Watersedge KT19: Ewe 4J **163**
Watersfield Way HA8: Edg 7J **27**
Waters Gdns. RM10: Dag 5G **73**
Waterside BR3: Beck 1B **158**
E17 6J **49**
N1 2C **84**
Waterside UB7: Harm 3D **174**
W2 6A **4**
Waterside Av. *BR3: Beck* *5E* ***158***
(off Adamson Way)
Waterside Bus. Cen. TW7: Isle 4B **114**
Waterside Cl. E3 1B **86**
IG11: Bark 4A **72**
KT6: Surb 2E **162**
SE16 2G **103**
SE28 1K **107**
UB5: N'olt 3D **76**
Waterside Ct. *SM5: Cars* *3E* ***166***
(off Millpond Pl.)
Waterside Dr. KT12: Walt T 5J **147**
Waterside Pl. NW1 1E **82**
Waterside Point SW11 7C **100**
Waterside Rd. UB2: S'hall 3E **94**
Waterside Twr. *SW6* *2A* ***118***
(off The Boulevard)
Waterside Trad. Cen. W7 3J **95**
Waterside Way SW17 4A **136**
Watersmeet Way SE28 6C **90**
Waterson St. E2 1H **9** (3E **84**)
Waters Pl. SW15 2E **116**
Watersplash Cl. KT1: King T 3E **150**
Watersplash La. TW5: Cran 5K **93**
UB3: Harl 4J **93**
Watersplash Rd. TW17: Shep 5C **146**
Waters Rd. KT1: King T 2H **151**
SE6 3G **141**
Waters Sq. KT1: King T 3H **151**
Water St. WC2 2J **13**
Water Twr. Cl. UB8: Uxb 5A **56**
Water Twr. Hill CR0: C'don 4D **168**
Water Twr. Pl. N1 1A **84**
Waterview Cl. DA6: Bex 5D **126**
Waterview Ho. *E14* *5A* ***86***
(off Carr St.)
Waterway Av. SE13 3D **122**
Waterway Pk. UB3: Hayes 2E **92**
Waterways Bus. Cen. EN3: Enf L 1G **25**
Waterweave W2 6B **4**
WATERWORKS CORNER **1G 51**
Waterworks La. E5 2K **67**
Waterworks Nature Reserve & Golf Cen.
2A **68**
Waterworks Rd. SW2 6K **119**
Waterworks Vis. Cen. 2A **68**
Watery La. DA14: Sidc 6B **144**
SW20 2H **153**
UB3: Harl 5F **93**
(not continuous)
UB5: N'olt 2A **76**
Wates Way CR4: Mitc 6D **154**
Wateville Rd. N17 1C **48**
Watford By-Pass HA8: Edg 1G **27**
Watford Cl. SW11 1C **118**
Watford Rd. E16 5J **87**
HA0: Wemb 2A **60**
HA1: Harr 7A **42**
Watford Way NW4 4C **44**
NW7 4F **29**
Watkin Rd. HA9: Wemb 3H **61**
Watkins Cl. HA6: Nwood 1H **39**
Watkins Ho. *E14* *2E* ***104***
(off Manchester Rd.)
Watkinson Rd. N7 6K **65**
WATLING 7E **28**
Watling Av. HA8: Edg 1J **43**
Watling Ct. EC4 1D **14**
Watling Farm Cl.
HA7: Stan 1H **27**
Watling Gdns. NW2 6G **63**
Watling Ga. NW9 4A **44**
Watling Ho. *SE1* *4C* ***102***
(off New Kent Rd.)
Watlings Cl. CR0: C'don 6A **158**
Watling St. DA1: Cray 5K **127**
DA6: Bex 4H **127**
EC4 1D **14** (6C **84**)
SE15 6E **102**
Watlington Gro. SE26 5A **140**
Watney Cotts. SW14 3J **115**
Watney Mkt. E1 6H **85**
Watney Rd. SW14 3J **115**
Watney's Rd. CR4: Mitc 5H **155**
Watney St. E1 6H **85**
Watson Av. E6 7E **70**
SM3: Cheam 2G **165**
Watson Cl. N16 5D **66**
SW19 6C **136**
Watsons Ho. *N1* *1E* ***84***
(off Nuttall St.)
Watson's M. W1 6D **4** (5C **82**)
Watsons Rd. N22 1K **47**
Watsons St. SE8 7C **104**
Watson St. E13 2K **87**
Wattisfield Rd. E5 3J **67**
Watts Cl. N15 5E **48**
Wattsdown Cl. E13 1J **87**
Watts Gro. E3 5C **86**
Watts Ho. *W10* *5G* ***81***
(off Wornington Rd.)
Watts La. BR7: Chst 1F **161**
TW11: Tedd 5A **132**
Watts Point *E13* *1J* ***87***
(off Brooks Rd.)
Watts Rd. KT7: T Ditt 7A **150**
Watts St. E1 1H **103**
SE15 1F **121**
Wat Tyler Ho. *N8* *3J* ***47***
(off Boyton Rd.)
Wat Tyler Rd. SE3 2E **122**
SE10 2E **122**
Wauthier Cl. N13 5G **33**
Wavel Ct. *CR0: C'don* *5D* ***168***
(off Hurst Rd.)
E1 *1J* ***103***
(off Garnet St.)
Wavelengths Leisure Pool 7C **104**
Wavell Dr. DA15: Sidc 6J **125**
Wavel M. N8 4H **47**
NW6 7K **63**
Wavel Pl. SE26 4F **139**
Wavendon Av. W4 5K **97**
Waveney Av. SE15 4H **121**
Waveney Cl. E1 1G **103**
Waveney Ho. SE15 4H **121**
Waverley Av. E4 4G **35**
E17 3F **51**
HA9: Wemb 5F **61**
KT5: Surb 6H **151**
SM1: Sutt 2K **165**
TW2: Whitt 1D **130**
Waverley Cl. BR2: Brom 5B **160**
E18 1A **52**
KT8: W Mole 5E **148**
UB3: Harl 4F **93**
Waverley Ct. EN2: Enf 3G **23**
NW3 6D **64**
NW6 7G **63**
SE26 5J **139**
Waverley Cres. SE18 5H **107**
Waverley Gdns. E6 5C **88**
HA6: Nwood 1J **39**
IG6: Ilf 2G **53**
IG11: Bark 2J **89**
NW10 2F **79**
Waverley Gro. N3 3F **45**
Waverley Ind. Est.
HA1: Harr 3H **41**
Waverley Pl. N4 2B **66**
NW8 2B **82**
Waverley Rd. E17 3E **50**
E18 1A **52**
EN2: Enf 3G **23**
HA2: Harr 2C **58**
KT17: Ewe 5D **164**
N8 6J **47**
N17 7C **34**
SE18 5G **107**
SE25 4H **157**
UB1: S'hall 7E **76**
Waverley Vs. N17 2F **49**

Waverley Way—Wellington Gro.

Waverley Way SM5: Cars 6C 166
Waverton Ho. E3 1B 86
Waverton Rd. SW18 7A 118
Waverton St. W1 4J 11 (1E 100)
Wavertree Ct. SW2 1J 137
Wavertree Rd. E18 2J 51
SW2 1K 137
Waxham NW3 5D 64
Waxlow Cres. UB1: S'hall 6E 76
Waxlow Ho. UB4: Yead 5B 76
Waxlow Rd. NW10 2J 79
Waxlow Way UB5: N'olt 4D 76
Waxwell Cl. HA5: Pinn 2B 40
Waxwell Farm Ho. HA5: Pinn 2B 40
Waxwell La. HA5: Pinn 2B 40
Wayborne Gro. HA4: Ruis 6E 38
Waye Av. TW5: Cran 1J 111
Wayfarer Rd. TW6: H'row A 5C 174
UB5: N'olt 3B 76
Wayfield Link SE9 6H 125
Wayford St. SW11 2C 118
Wayland Av. E8 5G 67
Wayland Ho. *SW9 2A 120*
(off Robsart St.)
Waylands UB3: Hayes 5F 75
Waylands Mead BR3: Beck 1D 158
Waylett Ho. SE11 6J 19
Waylett Pl. HA0: Wemb 4D 60
SE27 3B 138
Wayman Ct. E8 6H 67
Wayne Cl. BR6: Orp 3K 173
Wayne Kirkum Way NW6 5H 63
Waynflete Av. CR0: Wadd 3B 168
Waynflete Ho. *SE1 5C 14*
(off Union St.)
Waynflete Sq. W10 7F 81
Waynflete St. SW18 2A 136
Wayside CR0: New Ad 6D 170
NW11 1G 63
SW14 5J 115
Wayside Cl. N14 6B 22
Wayside Commercial Est.
IG11: Bark 1K 89
Wayside Ct. HA9: Wemb 3G 61
TW1: Twick 6C 114
Wayside Gdns. RM10: Dag 5G 73
Wayside Gro. SE9 4D 142
Wayside M. IG2: Ilf 5E 52
Weald, The BR7: Chst 6D 142
Weald Cl. BR2: Brom 2C 172
SE16 5H 103
Wealden Ho. *E3 3D 86*
(off Talwin St.)
Weald La. HA3: Hrw W 2H 41
Weald Ri. HA3: Hrw W 7E 26
Weald Rd. UB10: Hil 2C 74
Weald Sq. E5 2G 67
WEALDSTONE 3J 41
Wealdstone Rd. SM3: Sutt 2H 165
Weald Way RM7: Rom 6H 55
UB4: Hayes 3G 75
Wealdwood Gdns. HA5: Hat E 6A 26
Weale Rd. E4 3A 36
Weall Ct. HA5: Pinn 4C 40
Weardale Gdns. EN2: Enf 1J 23
Weardale Rd. SE13 4F 123
Wearmouth Ho. *E3 5B 86*
(off Joseph St.)
Wear Pl. E2 3H 85
(not continuous)
Wearside Rd. SE13 4D 122
Weatherbury *W2 6J 81*
(off Talbot Rd.)
Weatherbury Ho. *N19 3H 65*
(off Wedmore St.)
Weatherley Cl. E3 5B 86
Weaver Cl. CR0: C'don 4F 169
E6 7F 89
Weaver Ho. *E1 4G 85*
(off Pedley St.)
Weavers Almshouses *E11 6H 51*
(off Cambridge Rd.)
Weavers Cl. TW7: Isle 4J 113
Weavers Ho. *E11 6J 51*
(off New Wanstead)
Weavers La. SE1 5H 15 (1E 102)
Weavers Ter. *SW6 6J 99*
(off Micklethwaite Rd.)
Weaver St. E1 4G 85
Weavers Way NW1 1H 83
Weaver Wlk. SE27 4C 138
Webb Cl. W10 4E 80
Webb Ct. *SE28 7B 90*
(off Attlee Rd.)
Webber Ho. *IG11: Bark 7G 71*
(off North St.)
Webber Row SE1 1K 19 (3A 102)
(not continuous)
Webber St. SE1 6K 13 (2A 102)
Webb Est. E5 7G 49
Webb Gdns. E13 4J 87
Webb Ho. *RM10: Dag 3G 73*
(off Kershaw Rd.)
SW8 7H 101
TW13: Hanw 3C 130
Webb Pl. NW10 3B 80
Webb Rd. SE3 6H 105
Webbscroft Rd. RM10: Dag 4H 73
Webbs Rd. SW11 4D 118
UB4: Yead 3K 75
Webb St. SE1 3E 102
Webheath NW6 7H 63
(not continuous)
Webster Gdns. W5 1D 96
Webster Rd. E11 3E 68
SE16 3G 103
Weddell Ho. *E1 4K 85*
(off Duckett St.)
Wedderburn Ho. *SW1 5G 17*
(off Lwr. Sloane St.)
Wedderburn Rd. IG11: Bark 1J 89
NW3 5B 64
Wedgewood Ct. *BR2: Brom 3H 159*
(off Cumberland Rd.)
DA5: Bexl 7G 127
Wedgewood Ho. *SW1 6K 17*
(off Churchill Gdns.)
Wedgewood M. W1 1D 12 (6H 83)
Wedgwood Ho. *E2 3K 85*
(off Warley St.)
SE11 2J 19
Wedgwood Wlk. *NW6 5K 63*
(off Dresden Cl.)
Wedgwood Way SE19 7C 138
Wedlake St. W10 4G 81
Wedmore Av. IG5: Ilf 1E 52
Wedmore Gdns. N19 2H 65
Wedmore M. N19 3H 65
Wedmore Rd. UB6: G'frd 3H 77
Wedmore St. N19 3H 65
Weech Rd. NW6 4J 63
Weedington Rd. NW5 5E 64
Weedon Ho. W12 6C 80
Weekley Sq. SW11 3B 118
Weigall Rd. SE12 5J 123
Weighhouse St. W1 1H 11 (6E 82)
Weightman Ho. SE16 3G 103
Weighton M. SE20 2H 157
Weighton Rd. HA3: Hrw W 1H 41
SE20 2H 157
Weihurst Ct. SM1: Sutt 5C 166
Weihurst Gdns. SM1: Sutt 5B 166
Weimar St. SW15 3G 117
Weirdale Av. N20 2J 31
Weir Hall Av. N18 6J 33
Weir Hall Gdns. N18 5J 33
Weir Hall Rd. N17 6J 33
N18 5J 33
Weir Rd. DA5: Bexl 7H 127
KT12: Walt T 6J 147
SW12 7G 119
SW19 3K 135
Weir's Pas. NW1 1D 6 (3H 83)
Weiss Rd. SW15 3F 117
Welbeck Av. BR1: Brom 4J 141
DA15: Sidc 1A 144
UB4: Yead 4K 75
Welbeck Cl. KT3: N Mald 5B 152
KT17: Ewe 7C 164
N12 5G 31
Welbeck Ct. *W14 4H 99*
(off Addison Bri. Pl.)
Welbeck Ho. *W1 7J 5*
(off Welbeck St.)
Welbeck Rd. E6 3B 88
EN4: E Barn 6H 21
HA2: Harr 1F 59
SM1: Sutt 2B 166
SM5: Cars 2B 166
Welbeck St. W1 6H 5 (5E 82)
Welbeck Vs. N21 2H 33
Welbeck Wlk.
SM5: Cars 1B 166
Welbeck Way W1 7J 5 (6F 83)
Welbury Ct. *E8 7E 66*
(off Kingsland Rd.)
Welby Ho. N19 7H 47
Welby St. SE5 1B 120
Welch Pl. HA5: Pinn 1A 40
Welcome Ct. *E17 7C 50*
(off Saxon Cl.)
Weldon Cl. HA4: Ruis 6K 57
Weldon Ct. N21 5E 22
Weldon Dr. KT8: W Mole 4D 148
Weld Pl. N11 5A 32
(not continuous)
Welfare Rd. E15 7G 69
Welford Cl. E5 3K 67
Welford Ct. *NW1 7F 65*
(off Castlehaven Rd.)
SW8 2G 119
W9 5J 81
(off Elmfield Way)
Welford Ho. UB5: N'olt 4D 76
Welford Pl. SW19 4G 135
Welham Rd. SW16 5E 136
SW17 5E 136
Welhouse Rd. SM5: Cars 1C 166
Wellacre Rd. HA3: Kenton 6B 42
Wellan Cl. DA15: Sidc 5B 126
Welland Ct. *SE6 2B 140*
(off Oakham Cl.)
Welland Gdns. UB6: G'frd 2K 77
Welland Ho. SE15 4J 121
Welland M. E1 1G 103
Welland Rd. TW6: H'row A 5C 174
Wellands Cl. BR1: Brom 2D 160
Welland St. SE10 6E 104
Well App. EN5: Barn 5A 20
Wellbrook Rd. BR6: Farnb 4E 172
Wellby Cl. N9 1B 34
Wellby Ct. E13 1A 88
Well Cl. HA4: Ruis 3C 58
SW16 4K 137
Wellclose Sq. E1 7G 85
(not continuous)
Wellclose St. E1 7G 85
Wellcome Collection 3C 6
Wellcome Mus., The *7H 7*
(within Royal College of Surgeons)
Well Cott. Cl. E11 6A 52
Well Ct. EC4 1D 14 (6C 84)
(not continuous)
Welldon Ct. HA1: Harr 5J 41
Welldon Cres. HA1: Harr 5J 41
Weller Ct. *W11 1H 99*
(off Ladbroke Rd.)
Weller Ho. *SE16 2G 103*
(off George Row)
Weller M. BR2: Brom 4K 159
EN2: Enf 1F 23
Weller St. SE1 6C 14 (2C 102)
Welles Ct. *E14 7C 86*
(off Premiere Pl.)
Wellesley Av. W6 3D 98
Wellesley Cl. SE7 5A 106
Wellesley Ct. NW2 2C 62
SE1 3C 102
SM3: Sutt 1G 165
W9 3A 82
Wellesley Ct. Rd. CR0: C'don 2D 168
Wellesley Cres. TW2: Twick 2J 131
Wellesley Gro. CR0: C'don 2D 168
Wellesley Ho. *NW1 2D 6*
(off Wellesley Pl.)
SW1 5J 17
(off Ebury Bri. Rd.)
Wellesley Mans. *W14 5H 99*
(off Edith Vs.)
Wellesley Pde. TW2: Twick 3J 131
Wellesley Pk. M. EN2: Enf 2G 23
Wellesley Pas. CR0: C'don 2C 168
Wellesley Pl. NW1 2C 6 (3H 83)
NW5 5E 64
Wellesley Rd. CR0: C'don 1C 168
E11 5J 51
E17 6C 50
HA1: Harr 5J 41
IG1: Ilf 2F 71
N22 2A 48
NW5 5E 64
SM2: Sutt 6A 166
(not continuous)
TW2: Twick 3H 131
W4 5G 97
Wellesley St. E1 5K 85
Wellesley Ter. N1 1D 8 (3C 84)
Wellfield Av. N10 3F 47
Wellfield Rd. SW16 4J 137
Wellfield Wlk. SW16 4K 137
Wellfit St. SE24 3B 120
Wellgarth UB6: G'frd 6B 60
Wellgarth Rd. NW11 1K 63
Well Gro. N20 1F 31
Well Hall Pde. SE9 4D 124
Well Hall Rd. SE9 3C 124
WELL HALL RDBT. 4C 124
Wellhouse La. EN5: Barn 4A 20
Wellhouse Rd. BR3: Beck 4C 158
Wellhurst Cl. BR6: Chels 7K 173
WELLING 3B 126
Welling High St.
DA16: Well 3B 126
Wellings Ho. UB3: Hayes 1K 93
Wellington N8 4J 47
(not continuous)
Wellington Arch 6H 11 (2E 100)
Wellington Av. DA15: Sidc 6A 126
E4 2H 35
HA5: Hat E 1D 40
KT4: Wor Pk 3E 164
N9 3C 34
N15 6F 49
TW3: Houn 5E 112
Wellington Bldgs. *E3 3C 86*
(off Wellington Way)
SW1 6H 17 (5E 100)
Wellington Cl. KT12: Walt T 7H 147
RM10: Dag 7J 73
SE14 1K 121
W11 6J 81
Wellington Ct. *HA5: Hat E 1D 40*
(off Wellington Rd.)
NW8 2B 82
(off Wellington Rd.)
SW1 7E 10
(off Knightsbridge)
SW6 1K 117
(off Maltings Pl.)
TW12: Ham H 5H 131
TW15: Ashf 5A 128
TW19: Stanw 7A 110
Wellington Cres.
KT3: N Mald 3J 151
Wellington Dr. RM10: Dag 7J 73
Wellington Gdns. SE7 6A 106
TW2: Twick 4H 131
Wellington Gro. SE10 7F 105

Wellington Ho. *E16* 1J **105**
(off Pepys Cres.)
NW3 . . . . . 6D **64**
(off Eton Rd.)
SE17 . . . . . 6C **102**
(off Arnside St.)
UB5: N'olt 7E **58**
(off The Farmlands)
W5 . . . . . 3E **78**
Wellington Mans. E10 . . . . . 1C **68**
SE7 . . . . . 5A **106**
(off Wellington Gdns.)
W14 . . . . . 6H **99**
(off Queen's Club Mans.)
Wellington M. *N7* 6K **65**
(off Roman Way)
SE7 . . . . . 6A **106**
SE22 . . . . . 4G **121**
SW16 . . . . . 3H **137**
Wellington Monument 6H **11**
Wellington Mus. 6H **11** (2E **100**)
Wellington Pde.
DA15: Sidc 5A **126**
Wellington Pk. Est. NW2 . . . . . 2C **62**
Wellington Pas. E11 . . . . . 5J **51**
Wellington Pl. N2 . . . . . 5C **46**
NW8 . . . . . 1B **4** (3B **82**)
Wellington Rd. BR2: Brom 4A **160**
CR0: C'don 7B **156**
DA5: Bexl 5D **126**
DA17: Belv 5F **109**
E6 . . . . . 1D **88**
E7 . . . . . 4H **69**
E10 . . . . . 1A **68**
E11 . . . . . 5J **51**
E17 . . . . . 4A **50**
EN1: Enf 5K **23**
HA3: W'stone 3J **41**
HA5: Hat E 1D **40**
NW8 . . . . . 1B **4** (2B **82**)
NW10 . . . . . 3F **81**
SW19 . . . . . 2J **135**
TW2: Twick 5H **131**
TW6: H'row A 5D **174**
(off Wallis Rd.)
TW6: H'row A 6D **174**
(off Warwick Rd.)
TW12: Ham H 5H **131**
TW14: Felt 5G **111**
TW15: Ashf 5A **128**
W5 . . . . . 3C **96**
Wellington Rd. Nth. TW4: Houn 3D **112**
Wellington Rd. Sth.
TW4: Houn 4D **112**
Wellington Row E2 . . . . . 1K **9** (3F **85**)
Wellington Sq. N1 . . . . . 1J **83**
SW3 . . . . . 5E **16** (5D **100**)
Wellington St. IG11: Bark 1G **89**
SE18 . . . . . 4E **106**
WC2 . . . . . 2G **13** (7K **83**)
Wellington Ter. E1 . . . . . 1H **103**
HA1: Harr 1H **59**
N8 . . . . . 3A **48**
(off Turnpike La.)
W2 . . . . . 7J **81**
Wellington Way E3 . . . . . 3C **86**
Welling United FC (Park View Road)
. . . . . 3C **126**
Welling Way DA16: Well 3G **125**
SE9 . . . . . 3G **125**
Well La. SW14 . . . . . 5J **115**
Wellmeadow Rd. SE6 . . . . . 7G **123**
SE13 . . . . . 6G **123**
(not continuous)
W7 . . . . . 4A **96**
Wellow Wlk. SM5: Cars 1B **166**
Well Pl. NW3 . . . . . 3B **64**
Well Rd. EN5: Barn 5A **20**
NW3 . . . . . 3B **64**
Wells, The N14 . . . . . 7C **22**
Wells Cl. CR2: S Croy 5E **168**
UB5: N'olt 3A **76**
Wells Ct. BR2: Brom 2F **159**
NW6 . . . . . 2J **81**
(off Cambridge Av.)
Wells Dr. NW9 . . . . . 1K **61**
Wells Gdns. IG1: Ilf 7C **52**
RM10: Dag 5H **73**
Wells Ho. *BR1: Brom* 5K **141**
(off Pike Cl.)
EC1 . . . . . 1K **7**
(off Spa Grn. Est.)
IG11: Bark 7A **72**
(off Margaret Bondfield Av.)
SE16 . . . . . 3J **103**
(off Howland Est.)
W5 . . . . . 1D **96**
(off Grove Rd.)
W10 . . . . . 4G **81**
(off Wornington Rd.)
Wells Ho. Rd. NW10 . . . . . 5A **80**
Wellside Cl. EN5: Barn 4A **20**
Wellside Gdns. SW14 . . . . . 4J **115**
Wells M. W1 . . . . . 6B **6** (5G **83**)
Wellsmoor Gdns. BR1: Brom 3E **160**
Wells Pk. Rd. SE26 . . . . . 3G **139**
Wells Path UB4: Hayes 3G **75**
Wells Pl. SW18 . . . . . 7A **118**
Wellspring Cres. HA9: Wemb 3H **61**
Wells Ri. NW8 . . . . . 1D **82**
Wells Rd. BR1: Brom 2D **160**
W12 . . . . . 2E **98**
Wells Sq. WC1 . . . . . 2G **7** (3K **83**)
Wells St. W1 . . . . . 6A **6** (5G **83**)
Wellstead Av. N9 . . . . . 7E **24**
Wellstead Rd. E6 . . . . . 2E **88**
Wells Ter. N4 . . . . . 2A **66**
Well St. E9 . . . . . 7J **67**
E15 . . . . . 6G **69**
Wells Way SE5 . . . . . 6D **102**
SW7 . . . . . 1A **16** (3B **100**)
Wells Yd. N7 . . . . . 5A **66**
Well Wlk. NW3 . . . . . 4B **64**
Wellwood Rd. IG3: Ilf 1A **72**
Welmar M. *SW4* 5H **119**
(off Clapham Pk. Rd.)
Welsby Ct. W5 . . . . . 5C **78**
Welsford St. SE1 . . . . . 4G **103**
(not continuous)
Welsh Cl. E13 . . . . . 3J **87**
Welsh Harp Nature Reserve 1A **62**
Welsh Ho. *E1* 1H **103**
(off Wapping La.)
Welshpool Ho. *E8* 1G **85**
(off Welshpool St.)
Welshpool St. E8 . . . . . 1G **85**
(not continuous)
Welshside *NW9* 6A **44**
(off Ruthin Cl.)
Welshside Wlk. NW9 . . . . . 6A **44**
Welstead Ho. *E1* 6H **85**
(off Cannon St. Rd.)
Welstead Way W4 . . . . . 4B **98**
Weltje Rd. W6 . . . . . 4C **98**
Welton Ct. SE5 . . . . . 1E **120**
Welton Ho. *E1* 5K **85**
(off Stepney Way)
Welton Rd. SE18 . . . . . 7J **107**
Welwyn Av. TW14: Felt 6H **111**
Welwyn St. E2 . . . . . 3J **85**
Welwyn Way UB4: Hayes 4G **75**
WEMBLEY 5E **60**
Wembley Arena 4G **61**
Wembley Commercial Cen.
HA9: Wemb 2D **60**
Wembley Hill Rd. HA9: Wemb 3F **61**
WEMBLEY PARK 4G **61**
Wembley Pk. Blvd. HA9: Wemb 4G **61**
Wembley Pk. Bus. Cen. HA9: Wemb . . . 4H **61**
Wembley Pk. Dr. HA9: Wemb 4F **61**
Wembley Retail Pk. HA9: Wemb 4H **61**
Wembley Rd. TW12: Hamp 1E **148**
Wembley Sailing Club 2K **61**
Wembley Stadium 4G **61**
Wembley Stadium Ind. Est.
HA9: Wemb 4H **61**
Wembley Way HA9: Wemb 6H **61**
Wemborough Rd. HA7: Stan 1B **42**
Wembury M. N6 . . . . . 7G **47**
Wembury Rd. N6 . . . . . 7F **47**
Wemyss Rd. SE3 . . . . . 2H **123**
Wendela Ct. HA1: Harr 2J **59**
Wendell Rd. W12 . . . . . 3B **98**
Wenderholme *CR2: S Croy* 5D **168**
(off South Pk. Hill Rd.)
Wendle Ct. SW8 . . . . . 7E **18** (6J **101**)
Wendle Sq. SW11 . . . . . 1C **118**
Wendling NW5 . . . . . 5D **64**
Wendling Rd. SM1: Sutt 1B **166**
Wendon St. E3 . . . . . 1B **86**
Wendover SE17 . . . . . 5E **102**
(not continuous)
Wendover Cl. UB4: Yead 4C **76**
Wendover Ct. *BR2: Brom* 3K **159**
(off Wendover Rd.)
NW2 . . . . . 3J **63**
NW10 . . . . . 4H **79**
W1 . . . . . 6G **5**
(off Chiltern St.)
Wendover Dr. KT3: N Mald 6B **152**
Wendover Ho. *W1* 6G **5**
(off Chiltern St.)
Wendover Rd. BR2: Brom 4K **159**
NW10 . . . . . 2B **80**
SE9 . . . . . 3B **124**
Wendover Way DA16: Well 5A **126**
Wendy Cl. EN1: Enf 6A **24**
Wendy Way HA0: Wemb 1E **78**
Wenham Ho. SW8 . . . . . 7G **101**
Wenlake Ho. *EC1* 3C **8**
(off Old St.)
Wenlock Barn Est. *N1* 2D **84**
(off Wenlock St.)
Wenlock Ct. N1 . . . . . 1F **9** (2D **84**)
Wenlock Gdns. NW4 . . . . . 4D **44**
Wenlock Rd. HA8: Edg 7C **28**
N1 . . . . . 1D **8** (2C **84**)
Wenlock St. N1 . . . . . 1D **8** (2C **84**)
Wennington Rd. E3 . . . . . 2K **85**
Wensdale Ho. E5 . . . . . 2G **67**
Wensley Av. IG8: Wfd G 7C **36**
Wensley Cl. N11 . . . . . 6K **31**
SE9 . . . . . 6D **124**
Wensleydale Av. IG5: Ilf 2C **52**
Wensleydale Gdns.
TW12: Hamp 7F **131**
Wensleydale Pas. TW12: Hamp 1E **148**
Wensleydale Rd. TW12: Hamp 6E **130**
Wensley Rd. N18 . . . . . 6C **34**
Wentland Cl. SE6 . . . . . 2F **141**
Wentland Rd. SE6 . . . . . 2F **141**
Wentway Ct. *W13* 4K **77**
(off Ruislip Rd. E.)
Wentworth Av. N3 . . . . . 7D **30**
Wentworth Cl. BR2: Hayes 2J **171**
BR6: Farnb 5J **173**
KT6: Surb 2D **162**
N3 . . . . . 7E **30**
SE28 . . . . . 6D **90**
SM4: Mord 7J **153**
TW15: Ashf 4D **128**
Wentworth Ct. SW1 . . . . . 6J **17**
SW1 . . . . . 5F **101**
SW18 . . . . . 6K **117**
(off Garratt La.)
TW2: Twick 3J **131**
W6 . . . . . 6G **99**
(off Paynes Wlk.)
Wentworth Cres. SE15 . . . . . 7G **103**
UB3: Harl 3F **93**
Wentworth Dr. HA5: Eastc 5J **39**
Wentworth Dwellings *E1* 7J **9**
(off Wentworth St.)
Wentworth Flds. UB4: Hayes 2F **75**
Wentworth Gdns. N13 . . . . . 3G **33**
Wentworth Hill HA9: Wemb 1F **61**
Wentworth M. E3 . . . . . 4A **86**
W3 . . . . . 6A **80**
Wentworth Pk. N3 . . . . . 7D **30**
Wentworth Pl. HA7: Stan 6G **27**
Wentworth Rd. CR0: C'don 7A **156**
E12 . . . . . 4B **70**
EN5: Barn 3A **20**
NW11 . . . . . 6H **45**
UB2: S'hall 4A **94**
Wentworth St. E1 . . . . . 7J **9** (6F **85**)
Wentworth Way HA5: Pinn 4C **40**
Wenvoe Av. DA7: Bex 2H **127**
Wepham Cl. UB4: Yead 5B **76**
Wernbrook St. SE18 . . . . . 6G **107**
Werndee Rd. SE25 . . . . . 4G **157**
Werneth Hall Rd. IG5: Ilf 3D **52**
Werrington St. NW1 . . . . . 1B **6** (2G **83**)
Werter Rd. SW15 . . . . . 4G **117**
Wesleyan Pl. NW5 . . . . . 4F **65**
Wesley Apartments SW8 . . . . . 1H **119**
Wesley Av. E16 . . . . . 1J **105**
NW10 . . . . . 3K **79**
TW3: Houn 2C **112**
Wesley Cl. HA2: Harr 2G **59**
N7 . . . . . 2K **65**
SE17 . . . . . 4B **102**
Wesley Ct. SE16 . . . . . 3H **103**
Wesley Rd. E10 . . . . . 7E **50**
N2 . . . . . 1C **46**
NW10 . . . . . 1J **79**
UB3: Hayes 7J **75**
Wesley's Chapel & Mus. of Methodism
. . . . . 3F **9** (4D **84**)
Wesley's House 3F **9** (4D **84**)
Wesley Sq. W11 . . . . . 6G **81**
Wesley St. W1 . . . . . 6H **5** (5E **82**)
Wessex Av. SW19 . . . . . 3J **153**
Wessex Cl. IG3: Ilf 6J **53**
KT1: King T 1H **151**
Wessex Ct. BR3: Beck 1A **158**
EN5: Barn 4A **20**
HA9: Wemb 2F **61**
TW19: Stanw 6A **110**
Wessex Dr. HA5: Hat E 1C **40**
Wessex Gdns. NW11 . . . . . 1G **63**
Wessex Ho. SE1 . . . . . 5F **103**
Wessex La. UB6: G'frd 3H **77**
Wessex St. E2 . . . . . 3J **85**
Wessex Wlk. DA2: Dart 2K **145**
Wessex Way NW11 . . . . . 1G **63**
Wesson Mead *SE5* 7C **102**
(off Camberwell Rd.)
West 12 W12 . . . . . 2F **99**
Westacott UB4: Hayes 5G **75**
Westacott Cl. N19 . . . . . 1H **65**
West Acre HA2: Harr 2J **59**
WEST ACTON 6G **79**
West App. BR5: Pet W 5G **161**
W. Arbour St. E1 . . . . . 6K **85**
West Av. E17 . . . . . 4D **50**
HA5: Pinn 6D **40**
N2 . . . . . 4K **45**
N3 . . . . . 6D **30**
NW4 . . . . . 5F **45**
SM6: Wall 5J **167**
UB1: S'hall 7D **76**
UB3: Hayes 7H **75**
West Av. Rd. E17 . . . . . 4C **50**
West Bank EN2: Enf 2H **23**
IG11: Bark 1F **89**
N16 . . . . . 7E **48**
Westbank Rd. TW12: Ham H 6G **131**
WEST BARNES 5D **152**
W. Barnes La. KT3: N Mald 4D **152**
SW20 . . . . . 3D **152**
WEST BECKTON 6B **88**
WEST BEDFONT 6B **110**
Westbeech Rd. N22 . . . . . 3A **48**
Westbere Dr. HA7: Stan 5J **27**
Westbere Rd. NW2 . . . . . 4G **63**
West Block *SE1* 7H **13**
(off York Rd.)

Westbourne Av. SM3: Cheam 2G 165
W3 ....6K 79
Westbourne Bri. W2 ....5A 82
Westbourne Cl. UB4: Yead 4A 76
Westbourne Ct. W2 ....5A 82
Westbourne Cres. W2 ....2A 10 (7B 82)
Westbourne Cres. M. W2 ....2A 10
Westbourne Dr. SE23 ....2K 139
Westbourne Gdns. W2 ....6K 81
WESTBOURNE GREEN 6H 81
Westbourne Gro. W2 ....6J 81
W11 ....7H 81
Westbourne Gro. M. W11 ....6J 81
Westbourne Gro. Ter. W2 ....6K 81
Westbourne Ho. *SW1* *5J 17*
(off Ebury Bri. Rd.)
TW5: Hest 6E 94
Westbourne Pde. UB10: Hil 4D 74
Westbourne Pk. Pas. W2 ....5J 81
(not continuous)
Westbourne Pk. Rd. W2 ....5J 81
W11 ....6G 81
Westbourne Pk. Vs. W2 ....5J 81
Westbourne Pl. N9 ....3C 34
Westbourne Rd. CR0: C'don 6F 157
DA7: Bex 7D 108
N7 ....6K 65
SE26 ....6K 139
TW13: Felt 3H 129
UB8: Hil 4D 74
Westbourne St. W2 ....2A 10 (7B 82)
Westbourne Ter. *SE23* *2K 139*
(off Westbourne Dr.)
W2 ....1A 10 (6A 82)
Westbourne Ter. M. W2 ....6A 82
Westbourne Ter. Rd. W2 ....5K 81
Westbourne Ter. Rd. Bri.
W2 ....*5A 82*
(off Westbourne Ter. Rd.)
Westbridge Cl. W12 ....2C 98
Westbridge Ho. *SW11* *1C 118*
(off Westbridge Rd.)
Westbridge Rd. SW11 ....1B 118
WEST BROMPTON 6A 100
Westbrook Av. TW12: Hamp 7D 130
Westbrook Cl. EN4: Cockf 3G 21
Westbrook Cres. EN4: Cockf 3G 21
Westbrooke Cres. DA16: Well 3C 126
Westbrooke Rd. DA15: Sidc 2H 143
DA16: Well 3B 126
Westbrook Ho. *E2* *3J 85*
(off Victoria Pk. Sq.)
Westbrook Rd. CR7: Thor H 1D 156
SE3 ....1K 123
TW5: Hest 7D 94
Westbrook Sq. EN4: Cockf 3G 21
Westbury Av. HA0: Wemb 7E 60
N22 ....3B 48
UB1: S'hall 4E 76
Westbury Cl. HA4: Ruis 7J 39
TW17: Shep 6D 146
Westbury Ct. *IG11: Bark* *1H 89*
(off Ripple Rd.)
Westbury Gro. N12 ....6D 30
Westbury Ho. E17 ....4B 50
W11 ....*5J 81*
(off Aldridge Rd. Vs.)
Westbury La. IG9: Buck H 2E 36
Westbury Lodge Cl. HA5: Pinn 3B 40
Westbury Pde. *SW12* *6F 119*
(off Balham Hill)
Westbury Pl. TW8: Bford 6D 96
Westbury Rd. BR1: Brom 1B 160
BR3: Beck 3A 158
CR0: C'don 6D 156
E7 ....6K 69
E17 ....4B 50
HA0: Wemb 7E 60
IG1: Ilf 2E 70
IG9: Buck H 2F 37
IG11: Bark 1H 89
KT3: N Mald 4K 151
Westbury Rd. N11 ....6D 32
N12 ....6D 30
SE20 ....1K 157
TW13: Felt 1B 130
W5 ....6E 78
Westbury Ter. E7 ....6K 69
Westbush Ct. *W12* *2D 98*
(off Goldhawk M.)
W. Carriage Dr. W2 ....3C 10 (7C 82)
(North Ride)
W2 ....6B 10 (2B 100)
(The Ring)
W. Carriage Ho. SE18 ....3F 107
W. Central St. WC1 ....7E 6 (6J 83)
West Cen. Av. NW10 ....4D 80
West Chantry HA3: Hrw W 1F 41
Westchester Dr. NW4 ....3F 45
Westcliffe Apartments W2 ....6B 4 (5B 82)
West Cl. EN4: Cockf 4K 21
HA9: Wemb 1F 61
N9 ....3A 34
TW12: Hamp 6C 130
TW15: Ashf 4A 128
UB6: G'frd 2G 77
Westcombe Av. CR0: C'don 7J 155
Westcombe Ct. SE3 ....7H 105
Westcombe Dr. EN5: Barn 5D 20
Westcombe Hill SE3 ....7J 105
Westcombe Lodge Dr. UB4: Hayes 5G 75
Westcombe Pk. Rd. SE3 ....6G 105
West Comn. Rd. BR2: Hayes, Kes 1J 171
UB8: Uxb 5A 56
Westcoombe Av. SW20 ....1B 152
Westcote Ri. HA4: Ruis 7E 38
Westcote Rd. SW16 ....5G 137
West Cotts. NW6 ....5J 63
Westcott Cl. BR1: Brom 5D 160
CR0: New Ad 7D 170
N15 ....6F 49
Westcott Cres. W7 ....6J 77
Westcott Ho. E14 ....7C 86
Westcott Rd. SE17 ....6B 102
West Ct. E17 ....4C 50
HA0: Wemb 2C 60
TW7: Isle 7G 95
Westcroft Cl. EN3: Enf W 1D 24
NW2 ....4G 63
Westcroft Est. NW2 ....4G 63
Westcroft Gdns. SM4: Mord 3H 153
Westcroft Leisure Cen. 4E 166
Westcroft Rd. SM5: Cars 4E 166
SM6: Wall 4E 166
Westcroft Sq. W6 ....4C 98
Westcroft Way NW2 ....4G 63
W. Cromwell Rd. SW5 ....5H 99
W14 ....5H 99
W. Cross Cen. TW8: Bford 6A 96
W. Cross Route W10 ....7F 81
W11 ....7F 81
W12 ....7F 81
W. Cross Way TW8: Bford 6B 96
Westdale Pas. SE18 ....6F 107
Westdale Rd. SE18 ....6F 107
Westdean Av. SE12 ....1K 141
Westdean Cl. SW18 ....6K 117
West Dene SM3: Cheam 6G 165
Westdown Rd. E15 ....4E 68
SE6 ....7C 122
WEST DRAYTON 2A 92
W. Drayton Pk. Av. UB7: W Dray 3A 92
W. Drayton Rd. UB8: Hil 6D 74
West Dr. HA3: Hrw W 6C 26
SM2: Cheam 7F 165
SW16 ....4G 137
West Dr. Gdns. HA3: Hrw W 6C 26
WEST DULWICH 2D 138
WEST EALING 1B 96
W. Ealing Bus. Cen. W13 ....7A 78
W. Eaton Pl. SW1 ....3G 17 (4E 100)
W. Eaton Pl. M. SW1 ....2G 17
W. Ella Rd. NW10 ....7A 62
WEST END 2B 76
West End Av. E10 ....5F 51
HA5: Pinn 4B 40
West End Cl. NW10 ....7J 61
West End Ct. HA5: Pinn 4B 40
NW6 ....7K 63
West End Gdns. UB5: N'olt 2A 76
West End La. EN5: Barn 4A 20
HA5: Pinn 3B 40
NW6 ....5J 63
(not continuous)
UB3: Harl 7E 92
West End Quay W2 ....6B 4
West End Reach W2 ....6B 4
W2 ....*5C 82*
(off Harbet Rd.)
West End Rd. HA4: Ruis 2G 57
UB1: S'hall 1C 94
UB5: N'olt 7A 58
Westerdale Rd. SE10 ....5J 105
Westerfield Rd. N15 ....5F 49
Westergate W5 ....5E 78
Westergate Ho. *KT1: King T* *4D 150*
(off Portsmouth Rd.)
Westergate Rd. SE2: Belv, Lon 6E 108
Westerham *NW1* *1G 83*
(off Bayham St.)
Westerham Av. N9 ....3J 33
Westerham Dr. DA15: Sidc 6B 126
Westerham Ho. *SE1* *3D 102*
(off Law St.)
Westerham Lodge *BR3: Beck* *7C 140*
(off Park Rd.)
Westerham Rd. BR2: Kes 6B 172
E10 ....7D 50
Westerley Cres. SE26 ....5B 140
Westerley Ware *TW9: Kew* *6G 97*
(off Kew Grn.)
Western Av. HA4: Ruis 4A 56
NW11 ....6F 45
RM10: Dag 6J 73
UB5: N'olt 7A 58
UB6: G'frd 2H 77
UB10: Hil 4A 56
W3 ....4F 79
W5 ....4F 79
Western Av. Bus. Pk. W3 ....4H 79
Western Beach Apartments E16 ....7J 87
Western Ct. N3 ....6D 30
NW6 ....2H 81
W3 ....6K 79
Western Courtyard *EC2* *7H 9*
(off Cutlers Gdns.)
Western Dr. TW17: Shep 6F 147
Western Gdns. W5 ....7G 79
Western Gateway E16 ....7J 87
Western Intl. Mkt. UB2: S'hall 4K 93
Western La. SW12 ....7E 118
Western Mans. *EN5: New Bar* *5E 20*
(off Great Nth. Rd.)
Western M. W9 ....4H 81
Western Pde. EN5: New Bar 5D 20
Western Perimeter Rd.
TW6: H'row A, Lford 5C 174
Western Pl. SE16 ....2J 103
Western Rd. CR4: Mitc 1B 154
E13 ....2A 88
E17 ....5E 50
N2 ....4D 46
N22 ....2K 47
NW10 ....4J 79
SM1: Sutt 5J 165
SW9 ....3A 120
SW19 ....1B 154
UB2: S'hall 4A 94
W5 ....7D 78
Western Ter. *W6* *5C 98*
(off Chiswick Mall)
Western Vw. UB3: Hayes 2H 93
Westernville Gdns. IG2: Ilf 7G 53
Western Way EN5: Barn 6D 20
SE28 ....3H 107
WEST EWELL 7K 163
Westferry Cir. E14 ....1B 104
Westferry Rd. E14 ....7B 86
Westfield W12 ....1E 98
Westfield Cl. EN3: Enf H 3F 25
NW9 ....3J 43
SM1: Sutt 4H 165
SW10 ....7A 100
Westfield Ct. *KT6: Surb* *5D 150*
(off Portsmouth Rd)
NW10 ....*3F 81*
(off Chamberlayne Rd.)
Westfield Dr. HA3: Kenton 4D 42
Westfield Gdns. HA3: Kenton 4D 42
RM6: Chad H 6C 54
Westfield Ho. *SE16* *4K 103*
(off Rotherhithe New Rd.)
SW10 ....*7B 100*
(off Cremorne Est.)
SW18 ....1K 135
Westfield La. HA3: Kenton 5D 42
(not continuous)
Westfield Pk. HA5: Hat E 1D 40
Westfield Pk. Dr. IG8: Wfd G 6H 37
Westfield Rd. BR3: Beck 2B 158
CR0: C'don 2B 168
CR4: Mitc 2C 154
DA7: Bex 3J 127
KT6: Surb 5D 150
KT12: Walt T 7C 148
NW7 ....3E 28
RM9: Dag 4E 72
SM1: Sutt 4H 165
W13 ....1A 96
Westfields SW13 ....3B 116
Westfields Av. SW13 ....3A 116
Westfields Rd. W3 ....5H 79
Westfield Stratford City Shop. Cen.
E15 ....6E 68
Westfield St. SE18 ....3B 106
Westfield Way E1 ....3A 86
HA4: Ruis 3G 57
West Gdn. Pl. W2 ....1D 10 (6C 82)
West Gdns. E1 ....7H 85
SW17 ....6C 136
Westgate W5 ....3E 78
Westgate Apartments *E16* *7J 87*
(off Western Gateway)
Westgate Cen., The *E8* *1H 85*
(off Bocking St.)
Westgate Ct. *SE12* *1J 141*
(off Burnt Ash Hill)
SW9 ....*3A 120*
(off Canterbury Cres.)
Westgate Est. TW14: Bedf 1D 128
Westgate Ho. TW7: Isle 2H 113
Westgate M. *W10* *4G 81*
(off West Row)
Westgate Rd. BR3: Beck 1E 158
SE25 ....4H 157
Westgate St. E8 ....1H 85
Westgate Ter. SW10 ....6K 99
Westglade Ct. HA3: Kenton 5D 42
WEST GREEN 4B 48
West Grn. Pl. UB6: G'frd 1H 77
West Grn. Rd. N15 ....4B 48
West Gro. IG8: Wfd G 6F 37
SE10 ....1E 122
Westgrove La. SE10 ....1E 122
W. Halkin St. SW1 ....1G 17 (3E 100)
West Hallowes SE9 ....1B 142
W. Hall Rd. TW9: Kew 1H 115
WEST HAM 1H 87
W. Ham La. E15 ....7F 69
(not continuous)
WEST HAMPSTEAD 6K 63
W. Hampstead M. NW6 ....6K 63
West Ham United FC 2A 88
W. Harding St. EC4 ....7K 7 (6A 84)
WEST HARROW 7G 41
W. Hatch Mnr. HA4: Ruis 1H 57
Westhay Gdns. SW14 ....5H 115
WEST HEATH 6D 108

W. Heath Av.—W. Warwick Pl.

W. Heath Av. NW11 1J **63**
W. Heath Cl. NW3 3J **63**
W. Heath Ct. NW11 1J **63**
W. Heath Dr. NW11 1J **63**
W. Heath Gdns. NW3 2J **63**
W. Heath Rd. NW3 2J **63**
SE2 6C **108**
WEST HENDON 7C **44**
W. Hendon B'way. NW9 6B **44**
WEST HILL 6H **117**
West Hill CR2: Sande 7E **168**
HA2: Harr 2J **59**
HA9: Wemb 1F **61**
SW15 7F **117**
SW18 7F **117**
W. Hill Ct. N6 3E **64**
Westhill Ct. *W11* *7H 81*
(off Denbigh Rd.)
W. Hill Pk. N6 2D **64**
(not continuous)
W. Hill Rd. SW18 6H **117**
W. Hill Way N20 1E **30**
Westholm NW11 4K **45**
West Holme DA8: Erith 1J **127**
Westholme BR6: Orp 7J **161**
Westholme Gdns. HA4: Ruis 1J **57**
Westhope Ho. *E2* *4G 85*
(off Derbyshire St.)
Westhorne Av. SE9 7J **123**
SE12 7J **123**
Westhorpe Gdns. NW4 3E **44**
Westhorpe Rd. SW15 3E **116**
West Ho. IG11: Bark 6F **71**
West Ho. Cl. SW19 1G **135**
West Ho. Cotts. HA5: Pinn 4B **40**
Westhurst Dr. BR7: Chst 5F **143**
W. India Av. E14 1C **104**
W. India Dock Rd. E14 7B **86**
W. India Ho. *E14* *7C 86*
(off W. India Dock Rd.)
W. Kensington Ct. *W14* *5H 99*
(off Edith Vs.)
W. Kensington Mans. *W14* *5H 99*
(off Beaumont Cres.)
WEST KILBURN 3H **81**
Westlake *SE16* *4J 103*
(off Rotherhithe New Rd.)
Westlake Cl. N13 3F **33**
UB4: Yead 4C **76**
Westlake Rd. HA9: Wemb 2D **60**
Westland Cl. TW19: Stanw 6A **110**
Westland Ct. *UB5: N'olt* *3B 76*
(off Seasprite Cl.)
Westland Dr. BR2: Hayes 2H **171**
Westland Ho. *E16* *1E 106*
(off Rymill St.)
Westland Pl. N1 1E **8** (3D **84**)
Westlands Cl. UB3: Harl 4J **93**
Westlands Ct. KT8: E Mos 4H **149**
Westlands Ter. SW12 6G **119**
West La. SE16 2H **103**
Westlea Rd. W7 3A **96**
Westleigh Av. SW15 5D **116**
Westleigh Ct. *CR2: S Croy* *4E 168*
(off Birdhurst Rd.)
E11 5J **51**
Westleigh Dr. BR1: Brom 1C **160**
Westleigh Gdns. HA8: Edg 1G **43**
West Links HA0: Wemb 3D **78**
Westlinton Cl. NW7 6C **30**
West Lodge *E16* *1J 105*
(off Britannia Ga.)
W. Lodge Av. W3 1G **97**
W. Lodge Ct. W3 1G **97**
W. London Crematorium NW10 4D **80**
Westmacott Dr. TW14: Felt 1H **129**
Westmacott Ho. *NW8* *4B 4*
(off Hatton St.)
West Mall *W8* *1J 99*
(off Kensington Mall)
Westmark Point *SW15* *1D 134*
(off Norley Va.)
West Mead HA4: Ruis 4A **58**
KT19: Ewe 6A **164**
Westmead SW15 6D **116**
Westmead Cnr. SM5: Cars 4C **166**
Westmead Ho. SM1: Sutt 4B **166**
Westmead Rd. SM1: Sutt 4B **166**
Westmere Dr. NW7 3E **28**
W. Mersea Cl. E16 1K **105**
West M. N17 7C **34**
SW1 4A **18**
WESTMINSTER 7E **12** (2J **101**)
Westminster Abbey 7E 12 (3H 101)
Westminster Abbey Chapter House *1E 18*
(in Westminster Abbey)
Westminster Abbey Mus. *1E 18*
(in Westminster Abbey)
Westminster Abbey Pyx Chamber *1E 18*
(in Westminster Abbey)
Westminster Av. CR7: Thor H 2B **156**
Westminster Boating Base & Pier
7C 18 (6H 101)
Westminster Bri. SW1 7F **13** (2J **101**)
Westminster Bri. Ho. *SE1* *7A 14*
(off Lambeth Rd.)
Westminster Bri. Rd. SE1 7G **13** (2K **101**)
Westminster Bus. Sq.
SE11 7H **19**
Westminster Cl. IG6: Ilf 2H **53**
TW11: Tedd 5A **132**
TW14: Felt 1J **129**
Westminster Ct. *E11* *6K 51*
(off Cambridge Pk.)
NW8 *4A 4*
(off Aberdeen Pl.)
SE16 *1K 103*
(off King & Queen Wharf)
Westminster Dr. N13 5D **32**
Westminster Gdns. E4 1B **36**
IG6: Ilf 2G **53**
IG11: Bark 2J **89**
SW1 *3E 18*
(off Marsham St.)
Westminster Hall 7E 12
Westminster Ho. HA3: Hrw W 7E **26**
Westminster Ind. Est. SE18 3B **106**
Westminster Kingsway College
2C 12 (7G 83)
Westminster Mans. *SW1* *2D 18*
(off Gt. Smith St.)
Westminster Pal. Gdns. SW1 2C **18**
Westminster RC Cathedral
2A 18 (3G 101)
Westminster Rd. N9 1C **34**
SM1: Sutt 2B **166**
W7 1J **95**
Westminster Theatre *3G 101*
(off Palace St.)
Westmoat Cl. BR3: Beck 7E **140**
WEST MOLESEY 4E **148**
Westmoor Gdns. EN3: Enf H 2E **24**
Westmoor Rd. EN3: Enf H 2E **24**
Westmoor St. SE7 3A **106**
Westmore Ct. SW15 5G **117**
Westmoreland Av. DA16: Well 3J **125**
Westmoreland Dr. SM2: Sutt 7K **165**
Westmoreland Ho. *E16* *1J 105*
(off Gatcombe Rd.)
Westmoreland Pl. BR1: Brom 3J **159**
SW1 6K **17** (5F **101**)
W5 5D **78**
Westmoreland Rd. BR2: Brom 5G **159**
NW9 3F **43**
SE17 6D **102**
(not continuous)
SW13 1B **116**
Westmoreland St. W1 6H **5** (5E **82**)
Westmoreland Ter. SE20 7H **139**
SW1 6K **17** (5F **101**)
Westmoreland Wlk. SE17 6D **102**
(not continuous)
Westmorland Cl. E12 2B **70**
TW1: Twick 6B **114**
Westmorland Ct. KT6: Surb 7D **150**
Westmorland Rd. E17 6C **50**
HA1: Harr 5F **41**
Westmorland Sq. *CR4: Mitc* *5J 155*
(off Westmorland Way)
Westmorland Way CR4: Mitc 4H **155**
Westmount Ct. W5 6F **79**
Westmount Rd. SE9 2D **124**
WEST NORWOOD 4C **138**
West Norwood Crematorium
SE27 3C **138**
West Oak BR3: Beck 1F **159**
Westoe Rd. N9 2C **34**
Weston Av. KT7: T Ditt 7J **149**
KT8: W Mole 3C **148**
Westonbirt Ct. *SE15* *6F 103*
(off Ebley Cl.)
Weston Ct. *KT1: King T* *3E 150*
(off Grove Cres.)
N4 3C **66**
N20 *7F 21*
(off Farnham Cl.)
Weston Dr. HA7: Stan 1B **42**
West One Ho. *W1* *6A 6*
(off Wells St.)
Westone Mans. *IG11: Bark* *7K 71*
(off Upney La.)
West One Shop. Cen. W1 1H **11**
Weston Gdns. TW7: Isle 1J **113**
WESTON GREEN 7J **149**
Weston Grn. KT7: T Ditt 7J **149**
RM9: Dag 4F **73**
Weston Grn. Rd.
KT7: T Ditt 7J **149**
KT10: Esh 7J **149**
Weston Gro. BR1: Brom 1H **159**
Weston Ho. *E9* *1J 85*
(off King Edward's Rd.)
NW6 7G **63**
Weston Pk. KT1: King T 2E **150**
KT7: T Ditt 7J **149**
N8 6J **47**
Weston Ri. WC1 1H **7** (3K **83**)
Weston Rd. BR1: Brom 7H **141**
EN2: Enf 2J **23**
RM9: Dag 4E **72**
W4 3J **97**
Weston St. SE1 7F **15** (2E **102**)
(not continuous)
Weston Wlk. E8 7H **67**
Westover Hill NW3 2J **63**
Westover Rd. SW18 7A **118**
Westow Hill SE19 6E **138**
Westow St. SE19 6E **138**
West Pk. SE9 2C **142**
West Pk. Av. TW9: Kew 1G **115**
West Pk. Cl. RM6: Chad H 5D **54**
TW5: Hest 6D **94**
West Pk. Rd. TW9: Kew 1G **115**
UB2: S'hall 1G **95**
West Parkside SE10 2G **105**
West Pl. SW19 5E **134**
West Point *E14* *7B 86*
(off Grenade St.)
SE1 5G **103**
Westpoint Apartments N8 3K **47**
W. Point Cl. *TW4: Houn* *3D 112*
(off Grosvenor Rd.)
Westpoint Trad. Est. W3 5H **79**
Westpole Av. EN4: Cockf 4K **21**
Westport Ct. UB4: Yead 4A **76**
Westport Rd. E13 4K **87**
Westport St. E1 6K **85**
W. Poultry Av. EC1 6A **8** (5B **84**)
West Quarters W12 6C **80**
West Quay SW10 1A **118**
W. Quay Dr. UB4: Yead 5C **76**
West Quay Wlk. E14 3D **104**
West Ramp TW6: H'row A 1C **110**
West Reservoir Cen. 1C 66
W. Ridge Gdns. UB6: G'frd 2G **77**
West Ri. W2 2D **10**
West Rd. E15 1H **87**
EN4: E Barn 1K **31**
KT2: King T 1J **151**
N2 2B **46**
N17 6C **34**
RM6: Chad H 6D **54**
RM7: Rush G 7K **55**
SE1 6H **13** (2K **101**)
SW3 6F **17** (5D **100**)
SW4 5H **119**
TW14: Bedf 6F **111**
UB7: W Dray 3B **92**
W5 5E **78**
Westrovia Ct. *SW1* *4C 18*
(off Moreton St.)
SW1 *5H 101*
(off Moreton St.)
West Row W10 4G **81**
Westrow SW15 6E **116**
Westrow Dr. IG11: Bark 5A **72**
Westrow Gdns. IG3: Ilf 2K **71**
WEST RUISLIP 2E **56**
W. Ruislip Ct. *HA4: Ruis* *2F 57*
(off Ickenham Rd.)
W. Sheen Va. TW9: Rich 4F **115**
Westside N2 3D **46**
NW4 2D **44**
Westside Apartments *IG1: Ilf* *3E 70*
(off Roden St.)
W. Side Comn. SW19 5E **134**
W. Side Ct. *TW16: Sun* *7G 129*
(off Scotts Av.)
Westside Ct. *W9* *4J 81*
(off Elgin Av.)
West Smithfield EC1 6A **8** (5B **84**)
West Sq. E10 7D **50**
SE11 2K **19** (3B **102**)
West Stand N5 3B **66**
West St. BR1: Brom 1J **159**
CR0: C'don 4C **168**
DA7: Bex 3F **127**
DA8: Erith 4K **109**
E2 2H **85**
E11 3G **69**
E17 5D **50**
HA1: Harr 1H **59**
SM1: Sutt 5K **165**
SM5: Cars 3D **166**
TW8: Bford 6C **96**
WC2 1D **12** (6H **83**)
West St. La. SM5: Cars 4D **166**
(not continuous)
West St. Pl. *CR0: C'don* *4C 168*
(off West St.)
W. Temple Sheen SW14 5H **115**
W. Tenter St. E1 1K **15** (6F **85**)
West Ter. DA15: Sidc 1J **143**
W. Thamesmead Bus. Pk.
SE28 3J **107**
(not continuous)
West Twr. *E14* *2D 104*
(off Pan Peninsula Sq.)
West Towers HA5: Pinn 5B **40**
Westvale M. W3 2A **98**
West Vw. NW4 4E **44**
TW14: Bedf 7E **110**
Westview W7 6J **77**
Westview Cl. NW10 5B **62**
W10 6E **80**
Westview Ct. N20 1F **31**
Westview Cres. N9 7K **23**
Westview Dr. IG8: Wfd G 2B **52**
Westville Rd. KT7: T Ditt 1A **162**
W12 2C **98**
West Wlk. EN4: E Barn 7K **21**
NW9 1A **44**
UB3: Hayes 1J **93**
W5 5E **78**
Westward Rd. E4 5G **35**
(not continuous)
Westward Way HA3: Kenton 6E **42**
W. Warwick Pl. SW1 4A **18** (4G **101**)

422 A-Z London

West Way BR4: W W'ck . . . 6F 159
BR5: Pet W . . . 5H 161
CR0: C'don . . . 2A 170
HA4: Ruis . . . 1H 57
HA5: Pinn . . . 4B 40
HA8: Edg . . . 6C 28
NW10 . . . 3K 61
TW5: Hest . . . 1D 112
TW17: Shep . . . 6F 147
Westway N18 . . . 4J 33
SW20 . . . 3D 152
UB6: G'frd . . . 1J 77
W2 . . . 6A 4 (5H 81)
W10 . . . 5H 81
W12 . . . 7B 80
Westway Cl. SW20 . . . 3D 152
Westway Ct. UB5: N'olt . . . 1E 76
Westway Est. W3 . . . 5A 80
West Way Gdns. CR0: C'don . . . 2K 169
Westway Lodge W9 . . . 5J 81
(off Amberley Rd.)
West Ways HA6: Nwood . . . 2J 39
Westways KT19: Ewe . . . 4B 164
Westway Sports Cen. . . . 6F 81
Westway Travellers Site W12 . . . 7F 81
(off Stable Way)
Westwell M. SW16 . . . 6J 137
Westwell Rd. SW16 . . . 6J 137
Westwell Rd. App. SW16 . . . 6J 137
Westwick KT1: King T . . . 2G 151
(off Chesterton Ter.)
Westwick Gdns. TW4: Cran . . . 2K 111
W14 . . . 2F 99
WEST WICKHAM . . . 1E 170
West Wickham Leisure Cen. . . . 1E 170
West Winter Garden . . . 1D 104
(off Bank St.)
Westwood Av. HA2: Harr . . . 4F 59
SE19 . . . 1C 156
Westwood Bus. Cen. NW10 . . . 4A 80
Westwood Cl. BR1: Brom . . . 2B 160
HA4: Ruis . . . 6D 38
Westwood Ct. EN1: Enf . . . 6K 23
(off Village Rd.)
HA0: Wemb . . . 4B 60
UB6: G'frd . . . 5H 59
Westwood Gdns. SW13 . . . 3B 116
Westwood Hill SE26 . . . 5G 139
Westwood Ho. W12 . . . 1E 98
(off Wood La.)
Westwood La. DA15: Sidc . . . 5A 126
DA16: Well . . . 3K 125
Westwood M. E3 . . . 3C 86
(off Addington Rd.)
Westwood Pk. SE23 . . . 7H 121
Westwood Pk. Trad. Est. W3 . . . 5H 79
Westwood Pl. SE26 . . . 4G 139
Westwood Rd. E16 . . . 1K 105
IG3: Ilf . . . 1K 71
SW13 . . . 3B 116
West Woodside DA5: Bexl . . . 7E 126
Wetheral Dr. HA7: Stan . . . 1B 42
Wetherby Cl. UB5: N'olt . . . 6F 59
Wetherby Gdns. SW5 . . . 4A 100
Wetherby Mans. SW5 . . . 5K 99
(off Earls Ct. Sq.)
Wetherby M. SW5 . . . 5K 99
Wetherby Pl. SW7 . . . 4A 100
Wetherby Rd. EN2: Enf . . . 1H 23
Wetherby Way KT9: Chess . . . 7E 162
Wetherden St. E17 . . . 7B 50
Wetherell Rd. E9 . . . 1K 85
Wetherill Rd. N10 . . . 1E 46
Wetland Cen., The . . . 1D 116
Wevco Wharf SE15 . . . 6H 103
Wevell Ho. N6 . . . 7E 46
(off Hillcrest)
Wexford Ho. E1 . . . 5J 85
(off Sidney St.)
Wexford Rd. SW12 . . . 7D 118
Weybourne St. SW18 . . . 2A 136
Weybridge Ct. SE16 . . . 5H 103
Weybridge Point SW11 . . . 2D 118
Weybridge Rd. CR7: Thor H . . . 4A 156
Wey Ct. KT19: Ewe . . . 4J 163
Weydown Cl. SW19 . . . 1G 135
Weyhill Rd. E1 . . . 6G 85
Wey Ho. NW8 . . . 4B 4
(off Church St. Est.)
Weylands Cl. KT12: Walt T . . . 7D 148
Weylond Rd. RM8: Dag . . . 3F 73
Weyman Rd. SE3 . . . 1A 124
Weymarks, The N17 . . . 6J 33
Weymouth Av. NW7 . . . 5F 29
W5 . . . 3C 96
Weymouth Cl. E6 . . . 6F 89
Weymouth Ct. E2 . . . 2F 85
(off Weymouth Ter.)
SM2: Sutt . . . 7J 165
Weymouth Ho. BR2: Brom . . . 2H 159
(off Beckenham La.)
SW8 . . . 7K 101
(off Bolney St.)
Weymouth M. W1 . . . 5J 5 (5F 83)
Weymouth Rd. UB4: Hayes . . . 3G 75
Weymouth St. W1 . . . 6H 5 (5E 82)
Weymouth Ter. E2 . . . 1K 9 (2F 85)
Weymouth Vs. N4 . . . 2K 65
(off Moray Rd.)
Weymouth Wlk. HA7: Stan . . . 6F 27
Whadcoat St. N4 . . . 2A 66
Whalebone Av. RM6: Chad H . . . 6F 55
Whalebone Ct. EC2 . . . 7E 8
Whalebone Gro. RM6: Chad H . . . 6F 55
Whalebone La. E15 . . . 7G 69
Whalebone La. Nth.
RM6: Chad H, Col R . . . 1E 54
Whalebone La. Sth.
RM6: Chad H, Dag . . . 7F 55
RM8: Dag . . . 7F 55
Whales Yd. E15 . . . 7G 69
(off W. Ham La.)
Wharf, The EC3 . . . 4H 15 (1F 103)
Wharfdale Cl. N11 . . . 6K 31
Wharfdale Rd. N1 . . . 2J 83
Wharfedale Ct. E5 . . . 4K 67
Wharfedale Gdns. CR7: Thor H . . . 4K 155
Wharfedale Ho. NW6 . . . 1K 81
(off Kilburn Va.)
Wharfedale St. SW10 . . . 5K 99
Wharfedale Yd. N1 . . . 2J 83
(off Wharfedale Rd.)
Wharf La. E14 . . . 6B 86
TW1: Twick . . . 1A 132
Wharf Pl. E2 . . . 1H 85
Wharf Rd. EN3: Pond E . . . 6F 25
N1 . . . 1C 8 (2C 84)
(Baldwin Ter.)
N1 . . . 1J 83
(Camley St.)
Wharf Rd. Ind. Est. EN3: Pond E . . . 6F 25
Wharfside Point Nth. E14 . . . 7E 86
(off Poplar High St.)
Wharfside Point Sth. E14 . . . 7E 86
Wharfside Rd. E16 . . . 5G 87
Wharf St. E16 . . . 5G 87
Wharf Vw. Ct. E14 . . . 6E 86
(off Blair St.)
Wharncliffe Dr. UB1: S'hall . . . 1H 95
Wharncliffe Gdns. SE25 . . . 2E 156
Wharncliffe Rd. SE25 . . . 2E 156
Wharton Cl. NW10 . . . 6A 62
Wharton Cotts. WC1 . . . 2J 7 (3A 84)
Wharton Ho. SE1 . . . 7J 15
(off St Saviour's Est.)
Wharton Rd. BR1: Brom . . . 1K 159
Wharton St. WC1 . . . 2H 7 (3K 83)
Whatcott's Yd. N16 . . . 4E 66
Whateley Rd. SE20 . . . 7K 139
SE22 . . . 5F 121
Whatley Av. SW20 . . . 3F 153
Whatman Ho. E14 . . . 6B 86
(off Wallwood St.)
Whatman Rd. SE23 . . . 7K 121
Wheatcroft Ct. SM1: Sutt . . . 1K 165
(off Cleeve Way)
Wheatfield Ho. NW6 . . . 3J 81
(off Kilburn Pk. Rd.)
Wheatfields E6 . . . 6F 89
EN3: Enf H . . . 1F 25
Wheatfield Way KT1: King T . . . 2E 150
Wheathill Ho. SE20 . . . 2H 157
(off Croydon Rd.)
Wheathill Rd. SE20 . . . 3H 157
Wheatland Ho. SE22 . . . 3E 120
Wheatlands TW5: Hest . . . 6E 94
Wheatlands Rd. SW17 . . . 3E 136
Wheatley Cl. NW4 . . . 2C 44
Wheatley Ct. E3 . . . 3D 86
(off Bruce Rd.)
Wheatley Cres. UB3: Hayes . . . 7J 75
Wheatley Gdns. N9 . . . 2K 33
Wheatley Ho. SW15 . . . 7C 116
(off Ellisfield Dr)
Wheatley Mans. IG11: Bark . . . 7A 72
(off Lansbury Av.)
Wheatley Rd. TW7: Isle . . . 3K 113
Wheatley's Eyot TW16: Sun . . . 5J 147
Wheatley St. W1 . . . 6H 5 (5E 82)
Wheat Sheaf Cl. E14 . . . 4D 104
Wheatsheaf Cl. UB5: N'olt . . . 5C 58
Wheatsheaf La. SW6 . . . 7E 98
SW8 . . . 7J 101
Wheatsheaf Ter. SW6 . . . 7H 99
Wheatstone Cl. CR4: Mitc . . . 1C 154
Wheatstone Ho. SE1 . . . 3C 102
(off County St.)
W10 . . . 5G 81
(off Telford Rd.)
Wheatstone Rd. DA8: Erith . . . 5K 109
W10 . . . 5G 81
Wheeler Cl. IG8: Wfd G . . . 6J 37
Wheeler Gdns. N1 . . . 1J 83
(off Outram Pl.)
Wheeler Pl. BR2: Brom . . . 4K 159
Wheelers Cross IG11: Bark . . . 2H 89
Wheelers Dr. HA4: Ruis . . . 6E 38
Wheeler's St. SM1: Sutt . . . 3J 165
Wheel Farm Dr. RM10: Dag . . . 3J 73
Wheel Ho. E14 . . . 5D 104
(off Burrells Wharf Sq.)
Wheelock Cl. DA8: Erith . . . 7H 109
Wheelwright St. N7 . . . 7K 65
Whelan Way SM6: Bedd . . . 3H 167
Wheler Ho. E1 . . . 4J 9
(off Quaker St.)
Whellock Rd. W4 . . . 3A 98
Whenman Av. DA5: Bexl . . . 2J 145
Whernside Cl. SE28 . . . 7C 90
WHETSTONE . . . 2F 31
Whetstone Cl. N20 . . . 2G 31
Whetstone Pk. WC2 . . . 7G 7 (6K 83)
Whetstone Rd. SE3 . . . 2A 124
Whewell Rd. N19 . . . 2J 65
Whidborne Bldgs. WC1 . . . 2F 7
(off Whidborne St.)
Whidborne Cl. SE8 . . . 2C 122
Whidborne St. WC1 . . . 2F 7 (3J 83)
(not continuous)
Whimbrel Cl. SE28 . . . 7C 90
Whimbrel Way UB4: Yead . . . 5B 76
Whinchat Rd. SE28 . . . 3H 107
Whinfell Cl. SW16 . . . 5H 137
Whinyates Rd. SE9 . . . 3C 124
Whippendell Way BR5: St P . . . 7B 144
Whippingham Ho. E3 . . . 3B 86
(off Merchant St.)
Whipps Cross E17 . . . 5F 51
Whipps Cross Ho. E17 . . . 5F 51
(off Wood St.)
Whipps Cross Rd. E11 . . . 5F 51
(not continuous)
Whiskin St. EC1 . . . 2A 8 (3B 84)
Whisperwood Cl.
HA3: Hrw W . . . 1J 41
Whistler Gdns. HA8: Edg . . . 2F 43
Whistler M. RM8: Dag . . . 5B 72
(off Fitzstephen Rd.)
SE15 . . . 7F 103
Whistlers Av. SW11 . . . 7B 100
Whistler St. N5 . . . 5B 66
Whistler Twr. SW10 . . . 7A 100
(off Worlds End Est.)
Whistler Wlk. SW10 . . . 7B 100
Whiston Ho. N1 . . . 7B 66
(off Richmond Gro.)
Whiston Rd. E2 . . . 2F 85
Whitacre M. SE11 . . . 6K 19 (5A 102)
Whitakers Lodge EN2: Enf . . . 1J 23
Whitbread Cl. N17 . . . 1G 49
Whitbread Rd. SE4 . . . 4A 122
Whitburn Rd. SE13 . . . 4D 122
Whitby Av. NW10 . . . 3H 79
Whitby Ct. N7 . . . 4J 65
Whitby Gdns. NW9 . . . 3G 43
SM1: Sutt . . . 2B 166
Whitby Ho. NW8 . . . 1A 82
(off Boundary Rd.)
Whitby Pde. HA4: Ruis . . . 2A 58
Whitby Rd. HA2: Harr . . . 3G 59
HA4: Ruis . . . 3K 57
SE18 . . . 4D 106
SM1: Sutt . . . 2B 166
Whitby St. E1 . . . 3J 9 (4F 85)
(not continuous)
Whitcher Cl. SE14 . . . 6A 104
Whitcher Pl. NW1 . . . 6G 65
Whitchurch Av. HA8: Edg . . . 7A 28
Whitchurch Cl. HA8: Edg . . . 6A 28
Whitchurch Gdns. HA8: Edg . . . 6A 28
Whitchurch Ho. W10 . . . 6F 81
(off Kingsdown Cl.)
Whitchurch La. HA8: Edg . . . 7J 27
Whitchurch Pde. HA8: Edg . . . 7B 28
Whitchurch Rd. W11 . . . 7F 81
Whitcomb Ct. WC2 . . . 3D 12
Whitcombe M. TW9: Kew . . . 1H 115
Whitcomb St. WC2 . . . 3D 12 (7H 83)
Whitcome M. TW9: Kew . . . 1H 115
Whiteadder Way E14 . . . 4D 104
Whitear Wlk. E15 . . . 6F 69
Whitebarn La. RM10: Dag . . . 1G 91
Whitebeam Av. BR2: Brom . . . 7E 160
Whitebeam Cl. SW9 . . . 7K 101
White Bear Pl. NW3 . . . 4B 64
White Bear Yd. EC1 . . . 4J 7
(off Clerkenwell Rd.)
White Bri. Av. CR4: Mitc . . . 3B 154
Whitebridge Cl. TW14: Felt . . . 6H 111
White Butts Rd. HA4: Ruis . . . 3B 58
WHITECHAPEL . . . 5G 85
Whitechapel Art Gallery . . . 7K 9 (6F 85)
Whitechapel High St. E1 . . . 7K 9 (6F 85)
Whitechapel Rd. E1 . . . 7K 9 (5G 85)
Whitechapel Sports Cen. . . . 5H 85
White Church La. E1 . . . 7K 9 (6G 85)
White Church Pas. E1 . . . 7K 9
(off White Church La.)
WHITE CITY . . . 7D 80
WHITE CITY . . . 6E 80
White City Cl. W12 . . . 7E 80
White City Est. W12 . . . 7D 80
White City Rd. W12 . . . 7E 80
White Conduit St. N1 . . . 2A 84
Whitecote Rd. UB1: S'hall . . . 6G 77
Whitecroft Cl. BR3: Beck . . . 4F 159
Whitecroft Way BR3: Beck . . . 5E 158
Whitecross Pl. EC2 . . . 5F 9 (5D 84)
Whitecross St. EC1 . . . 3D 8 (4C 84)
Whitefield Av. NW2 . . . 1E 62
Whitefield Cl. SW15 . . . 6G 117
Whitefoot La. BR1: Brom . . . 4E 140
(not continuous)
Whitefoot Ter. BR1: Brom . . . 3H 141
Whitefriars Av. HA3: W'stone . . . 2J 41
Whitefriars Ct. N12 . . . 5G 31
Whitefriars Dr. HA3: Hrw W . . . 2H 41
Whitefriars St. EC4 . . . 1K 13 (6A 84)

Whitefriars Trad. Est.—Widmore Green

Whitefriars Trad. Est. HA3: W'stone . . . 3H 41
White Gables Ct. CR2: S Croy . . . 5E 168
White Gdns. RM10: Dag . . . 6G 73
Whitegate Gdns. HA3: Hrw W . . . 7E 26
White Gates KT7: T Ditt . . . 7A 150
Whitehall . . . 6G 165
Whitehall SW1 . . . 5E 12 (1J 101)
Whitehall Ct. SW1 . . . 5E 12 (1J 101)
(not continuous)
Whitehall Cres. KT9: Chess . . . 5D 162
Whitehall Gdns. E4 . . . 1B 36
SW1 . . . 5E 12
W3 . . . 1G 97
W4 . . . 6H 97
Whitehall La. IG9: Buck H . . . 2D 36
Whitehall Lodge N10 . . . 2E 46
Whitehall Pk. N19 . . . 1G 65
Whitehall Pk. Rd. W4 . . . 6H 97
Whitehall Pl. E7 . . . 5J 69
SM6: Wall . . . 4F 167
SW1 . . . 5E 12 (1J 101)
Whitehall Rd. BR2: Brom . . . 5B 160
CR7: Thor H . . . 5A 156
E4 . . . 2B 36
HA1: Harr . . . 7J 41
IG8: Wfd G . . . 2B 36
W7 . . . 2A 96
Whitehall St. N17 . . . 7A 34
White Hart Av. SE18 . . . 4K 107
SE28 . . . 4K 107
White Hart Cl. UB3: Harl . . . 6F 93
White Hart Ct. EC2 . . . 6G 9
White Hart Lane . . . 7B 34
White Hart La. N17 . . . 7H 33
N22 . . . 1K 47
NW10 . . . 6B 62
RM7: Col R, Mawney . . . 1G 55
SW13 . . . 3A 116
White Hart Lane Community Sports Cen. . . . 7G 33
White Hart Rd. SE18 . . . 4J 107
White Hart Rdbt. UB5: N'olt . . . 2B 76
White Hart School Sports Cen. . . . 7G 33
White Hart Slip BR1: Brom . . . 2J 159
White Hart St. EC4 . . . 7B 8 (6B 84)
SE11 . . . 5K 19 (5A 102)
White Hart Triangle SE28 . . . 2K 107
White Hart Triangle Bus. Pk. SE28 . . . 2A 108
White Hart Yd. SE1 . . . 5E 14 (1D 102)
Whitehaven Cl. BR2: Brom . . . 4J 159
Whitehaven St. NW8 . . . 4C 4 (4C 82)
Whitehead Cl. N18 . . . 5J 33
SW18 . . . 7A 118
Whiteheads Gro. SW3 . . . 4D 16 (4C 100)
White Heart Av. UB8: Hil . . . 5E 74
Whiteheath Av. HA4: Ruis . . . 7E 38
White Heather Ho. WC1 . . . 2F 7
(off Cromer St.)
White Heron M. TW11: Tedd . . . 6K 131
White Horse All. EC1 . . . 5A 8
White Horse Hill BR7: Chst . . . 4E 142
White Horse La. E1 . . . 4K 85
Whitehorse La. SE25 . . . 4D 156
Whitehorse M. SE1 . . . 1K 19 (3A 102)
White Horse Rd. E1 . . . 5A 86
(not continuous)
E6 . . . 3D 88
Whitehorse Rd. CR0: C'don . . . 7C 156
CR7: Thor H . . . 7C 156
White Horse St. W1 . . . 5K 11 (1F 101)
White Horse Yd. EC2 . . . 7E 8 (6D 84)
White Ho. SW4 . . . 7H 119
(off Clapham Pk. Est.)
SW11 . . . 1B 118
White House, The NW1 . . . 3K 5
Whitehouse Apartments SE1 . . . 1K 101
White Ho. Ct. N14 . . . 2D 32
White Ho. Dr. HA7: Stan . . . 4H 27
IG8: Wfd G . . . 6C 36
Whitehouse Est. E10 . . . 6E 50
White Ho. La. EN2: Enf . . . 1H 23
Whitehouse Way N14 . . . 2A 32
Whitehurst Dr. N18 . . . 5E 34
White Kennett St. E1 . . . 7H 9 (6F 85)
Whitelands Cres. SW18 . . . 7G 117
Whitelands Ho. SW3 . . . 5F 17
(off Cheltenham Ter.)
Whiteledges W13 . . . 6C 78
Whitelegg Rd. E13 . . . 2H 87
Whiteley Rd. SE19 . . . 5D 138
Whiteleys Cen. (Shop. Cen.)
W2 . . . 6K 81
Whiteleys Pde. UB10: Hil . . . 4D 74
Whiteley's Way TW13: Hanw . . . 3E 130
White Lion Ct. EC3 . . . 1G 15
SE15 . . . 6J 103
TW7: Isle . . . 3B 114
White Lion Hill EC4 . . . 2B 14 (7B 84)
White Lion St. N1 . . . 2A 84
White Lodge SE19 . . . 7B 138
W5 . . . 5C 78
White Lodge Cl. N2 . . . 6B 46
SM2: Sutt . . . 7A 166
TW7: Isle . . . 2A 114
White Lodge Ct. TW16: Sun . . . 1A 148
White Lyon Ct. EC2 . . . 5C 8
Whiteoak Ct. BR7: Chst . . . 6E 142
White Oak Dr. BR3: Beck . . . 2E 158
White Oak Gdns. DA15: Sidc . . . 7K 125
Whiteoaks La. UB6: G'frd . . . 3H 77
White Orchards HA7: Stan . . . 5F 27
N20 . . . 1C 30
White Post La. E9 . . . 7C 68
White Post St. SE15 . . . 7J 103
White Rd. E15 . . . 7G 69
Whiterose Trad. Est. EN4: E Barn . . . 5G 21
(off Margaret Rd.)
Whites Av. IG2: Ilf . . . 6J 53
White's Grounds SE1 . . . 7H 15 (2E 102)
White's Grounds Est. SE1 . . . 6H 15
White's Mdw. BR1: Brom . . . 4E 160
White's Row E1 . . . 6J 9 (5F 85)
Whites Sq. SW4 . . . 4H 119
Whitestile Rd. TW8: Bford . . . 5C 96
Whitestone La. NW3 . . . 3A 64
Whitestone Wlk. NW3 . . . 3A 64
Whitestone Way CR0: Wadd . . . 2A 168
White St. UB1: S'hall . . . 2B 94
White Swan M. W4 . . . 5A 98
Whitethorn Av. UB7: Yiew . . . 7A 74
Whitethorn Gdns. CR0: C'don . . . 2H 169
EN2: Enf . . . 5J 23
Whitethorn Ho. E1 . . . 1J 103
(off Prusom St.)
Whitethorn Pas. E3 . . . 4C 86
(off Whitethorn St.)
Whitethorn Pl. UB7: Yiew . . . 1B 92
Whitethorn St. E3 . . . 5C 86
White Twr. Way E1 . . . 5A 86
Whitewebbs Way BR5: St P . . . 1K 161
Whitfield Ct. IG1: Ilf . . . 7D 52
Whitfield Ho. NW8 . . . 4C 4
(off Salisbury St.)
Whitfield Pl. W1 . . . 4A 6
Whitfield Rd. DA7: Bex . . . 7F 109
E6 . . . 7A 70
SE3 . . . 1F 123
Whitfield St. W1 . . . 4A 6 (4G 83)
Whitford Gdns. CR4: Mitc . . . 3D 154
Whitgift Av. CR2: S Croy . . . 5B 168
Whitgift Cen. CR0: C'don . . . 2C 168
Whitgift Ct. CR2: S Croy . . . 5C 168
(off Nottingham Rd.)
Whitgift Ho. SE11 . . . 3G 19 (4K 101)
SW11 . . . 1C 118
Whitgift Sq. CR0: C'don . . . 2C 168
Whitgift St. CR0: C'don . . . 3C 168
SE11 . . . 3G 19 (4K 101)
Whiting Av. IG11: Bark . . . 7F 71
Whitings IG2: Ilf . . . 5J 53
Whitings Rd. EN5: Barn . . . 5A 20
Whitings Way E6 . . . 5E 88
Whitland Rd. SM5: Cars . . . 1B 166
Whitley Cl. TW19: Stanw . . . 6A 110
Whitley Ho. SW1 . . . 7B 18
(off Churchill Gdns.)
Whitley Rd. N17 . . . 2E 48
Whitlock Dr. SW19 . . . 7G 117
Whitman Ho. E2 . . . 3J 85
(off Cornwall Av.)
Whitman Rd. E3 . . . 4A 86
Whitmead Cl. CR2: S Croy . . . 6E 168
Whitmore Cl. N11 . . . 5A 32
Whitmore Est. N1 . . . 1E 84
Whitmore Gdns. NW10 . . . 2E 80
Whitmore Ho. N1 . . . 1E 84
(off Whitmore Est.)
Whitmore Rd. BR3: Beck . . . 3B 158
HA1: Harr . . . 7G 41
N1 . . . 1E 84
Whitmore Sports Cen. . . . 7G 41
Whitnell Way SW15 . . . 5E 116
(not continuous)
Whitney Av. IG4: Ilf . . . 4B 52
Whitney Rd. E10 . . . 7D 50
Whitney Wlk. DA14: Sidc . . . 6E 144
Whitstable Cl. BR3: Beck . . . 1B 158
HA4: Ruis . . . 2G 57
Whitstable Ho. W10 . . . 6F 81
(off Silchester Rd.)
Whitstable Pl. CR0: C'don . . . 4C 168
Whitstone La. BR3: Beck . . . 5D 158
Whittaker Av. TW9: Rich . . . 5D 114
Whittaker Pl. TW9: Rich . . . 5D 114
(off Whittaker Av.)
Whittaker Rd. E6 . . . 7A 70
SM3: Sutt . . . 3H 165
Whittaker St. SW1 . . . 4G 17 (4E 100)
Whittaker Way SE1 . . . 4G 103
Whitta Rd. E12 . . . 4B 70
Whittell Gdns. SE26 . . . 3J 139
Whittingham N17 . . . 7C 34
Whittingham Ct. W4 . . . 7A 98
Whittingstall Rd. SW6 . . . 1H 117
Whittington Av. EC3 . . . 1G 15 (6E 84)
UB4: Hayes . . . 5H 75
Whittington Ct. N2 . . . 5D 46
Whittington M. N12 . . . 4F 31
Whittington Rd. N22 . . . 7D 32
Whittington Way HA5: Pinn . . . 5C 40
Whittlebury Cl. SM5: Cars . . . 7D 166
Whittle Cl. E17 . . . 6A 50
UB1: S'hall . . . 6F 77
Whittle Rd. TW5: Hest . . . 7A 94
TW6: H'row A . . . 6C 174
UB2: S'hall . . . 2F 95
Whittlesea Cl. HA3: Hrw W . . . 7B 26
Whittlesea Path HA3: Hrw W . . . 1G 41
Whittlesea Rd. HA3: Hrw W . . . 7B 26
Whittlesey St. SE1 . . . 5J 13 (1A 102)
WHITTON . . . 7G 113
Whitton NW3 . . . 7D 64
Whitton Av. E. UB6: G'frd . . . 5J 59
Whitton Av. W. UB5: N'olt . . . 5F 59
UB6: G'frd . . . 5F 59
Whitton Cl. UB6: G'frd . . . 6B 60
Whitton Dene TW3: Houn, Isle . . . 5G 113
TW7: Isle . . . 6H 113
Whitton Dr. UB6: G'frd . . . 6A 60
Whitton Mnr. Rd. TW7: Isle . . . 6G 113
Whitton Rd. TW1: Twick . . . 6K 113
TW2: Twick . . . 6J 113
TW3: Houn . . . 4F 113
WHITTON ROAD RDBT. . . . 6K 113
Whitton Sports & Fitness Cen. . . . 2F 131
Whitton Wlk. E3 . . . 3C 86
Whitton Waye TW3: Houn . . . 6E 112
Whitwell Rd. E13 . . . 3J 87
Whitworth Ho. SE1 . . . 3C 102
Whitworth Rd. SE18 . . . 7E 106
SE25 . . . 3E 156
Whitworth St. SE10 . . . 5G 105
Whorlton Rd. SE15 . . . 3H 121
Whychcote Point NW2 . . . 1E 62
(off Whitefield Av.)
Whymark Av. N22 . . . 3A 48
Whytecroft TW5: Hest . . . 7B 94
Whyte M. SM3: Cheam . . . 7G 165
Whyteville Rd. E7 . . . 6K 69
Whytlaw Ho. E3 . . . 5B 86
(off Baythorne St.)
Wickersley Rd. SW11 . . . 2E 118
Wickers Oake SE19 . . . 4F 139
Wicker St. E1 . . . 6H 85
Wicket, The CR0: Addtn . . . 5C 170
Wicket Rd. UB6: G'frd . . . 3A 78
Wickets, The TW15: Ashf . . . 4A 128
Wickfield Apartments E15 . . . 6F 69
(off Grove Cres. Rd.)
Wickfield Ho. SE16 . . . 2H 103
(off Wilson Gro.)
Wickford Ho. E1 . . . 4J 85
(off Wickford St.)
Wickford St. E1 . . . 4J 85
Wickford Way E17 . . . 4K 49
Wickham Av. CR0: C'don . . . 2A 170
SM3: Cheam . . . 5E 164
Wickham Chase BR4: W W'ck . . . 1F 171
Wickham Cl. E1 . . . 5J 85
EN3: Enf H . . . 3C 24
KT3: N Mald . . . 6B 152
Wickham Ct. KT5: Surb . . . 5F 151
(off Cranes Pk.)
Wickham Ct. Rd. BR4: W W'ck . . . 2E 170
Wickham Cres. BR4: W W'ck . . . 2E 170
Wickham Gdns. SE4 . . . 3B 122
Wickham Ho. N1 . . . 1E 84
(off New Era Est.)
Wickham La. DA16: Well . . . 5A 108
SE2 . . . 5A 108
Wickham M. SE4 . . . 2B 122
Wickham Rd. BR3: Beck . . . 2D 158
CR0: C'don . . . 2K 169
E4 . . . 7K 35
HA3: Hrw W . . . 2H 41
SE4 . . . 4B 122
Wickham St. DA16: Well . . . 2J 125
SE11 . . . 5G 19 (5K 101)
Wickham Theatre Cen. . . . 2F 171
Wickham Way BR3: Beck . . . 4E 158
Wick Ho. KT1: Ham W . . . 1D 150
(off Station Rd.)
Wick La. E3 . . . 1C 86
Wickliffe Av. N3 . . . 2G 45
Wickliffe Gdns. HA9: Wemb . . . 2H 61
Wicklow Ho. N16 . . . 1F 67
Wicklow St. WC1 . . . 1G 7 (3K 83)
Wick M. E9 . . . 6A 68
Wick Rd. E9 . . . 6K 67
TW11: Tedd . . . 7B 132
Wicks Cl. SE9 . . . 4B 142
Wick Sq. E9 . . . 6B 68
Wicksteed Cl. DA5: Bexl . . . 3K 145
Wicksteed Ho. SE1 . . . 3C 102
TW8: Bford . . . 5F 97
Wickway Ct. SE15 . . . 6F 103
(off Cator St.)
Wickwood St. SE5 . . . 2B 120
Widdecombe Av. HA2: Harr . . . 2C 58
Widdenham Rd. N7 . . . 4K 65
Widdin St. E15 . . . 7G 69
Widecombe Gdns. IG4: Ilf . . . 4C 52
Widecombe Rd. SE9 . . . 3C 142
Widecombe Way N2 . . . 5B 46
Widegate St. E1 . . . 6H 9 (5E 84)
Widenham Cl. HA5: Eastc . . . 5A 40
Wide Way CR4: Mitc . . . 3H 155
Widewing Cl. TW11: Tedd . . . 7B 132
Widford NW1 . . . 6F 65
(off Lewis St.)
Widford Ho. N1 . . . 2B 84
(off Colebrooke Rd.)
Widgeon Cl. E16 . . . 6K 87
Widgeon Rd. TW6: H'row A . . . 5C 174
Widley Rd. W9 . . . 3J 81
Widmer Ct. TW3: Houn . . . 2C 112
WIDMORE . . . 3A 160
WIDMORE GREEN . . . 2B 160

Widmore Lodge Rd.—Willow Ct.

Widmore Lodge Rd. BR1: Brom 2B 160
Widmore Rd. BR1: Brom 2J 159
UB8: Hil 4D 74
Wigan Ho. E5 1H 67
Wigeon Path SE28 3H 107
Wigeon Way UB4: Yead 6C 76
Wiggins La. TW10: Ham 2C 132
Wiggins Mead NW9 7G 29
Wigginton Av. HA9: Wemb 6H 61
Wight Ho. *KT1: King T* *3D 150*
(off Portsmouth Rd.)
Wightman Rd. N4 4A 48
N8 4A 48
Wighton M. TW7: Isle 2J 113
Wigley Rd. TW13: Felt 2B 130
Wigmore Ct. *W13* *1A 96*
(off Singapore Rd.)
Wigmore Hall 7J 5
Wigmore Pl. W1 7J 5 (6F 83)
Wigmore Rd. SM5: Cars 2B 166
Wigmore St. W1 7H 5 (6E 82)
Wigmore Wlk. SM5: Cars 2B 166
Wigram Ho. *E14* *7D 86*
(off Wade's Pl.)
Wigram Rd. E11 6A 52
Wigram Sq. E17 3E 50
Wigston Cl. N18 5K 33
Wigston Rd. E13 4K 87
Wigton Gdns. HA7: Stan 1E 42
Wigton Pl. SE11 6K 19 (5A 102)
Wigton Rd. E17 1B 50
Wilberforce Ct. BR2: Kes 7B 172
HA8: Edg *4A 28*
(off King's Dr.)
Wilberforce M. SW4 4H 119
Wilberforce Rd. N4 2B 66
NW9 6C 44
Wilberforce Wlk. E15 5G 69
Wilberforce Way SW19 6F 135
Wilbraham Ho. *SW8* *7J 101*
(off Wandsworth Rd.)
Wilbraham Mans. *SW1* *3G 17*
(off Wilbraham Pl.)
Wilbraham Pl. SW1 3F 17 (4D 100)
Wilbrahams Almshouses
EN5: Barn 2C 20
Wilbury Way N18 5J 33
Wilby M. W11 1H 99
Wilcox Cl. SW8 7J 101
(not continuous)
Wilcox Gdns. TW17: Shep 3A 146
Wilcox Ho. *E3* *5B 86*
(off Ackroyd Dr.)
Wilcox Pl. SW1 2B 18 (3G 101)
Wilcox Rd. SM1: Sutt 4K 165
SW8 7J 101
TW11: Tedd 4H 131
Wildberry Cl. W7 4A 96
Wildcat Rd. TW6: H'row A 6C 174
Wild Ct. WC2 1G 13 (6K 83)
(not continuous)
Wildcroft Gdns. HA8: Edg 6J 27
Wildcroft Mnr. SW15 7E 116
Wildcroft Rd. SW15 7E 116
Wilde Cl. E8 1G 85
Wilde Ho. *W2* *2A 10*
(off Gloucester Ter.)
Wilde Pl. N13 6G 33
SW18 7B 118
Wilder Cl. HA4: Ruis 1K 57
Wilderness, The
KT8: W Mole, E Mos 5G 149
TW12: Ham H 4F 131
Wilderness Island Nature Reserve 2E 166
Wilderness Local Nature Reserve, The
6E 100
Wilderness M. SW4 4F 119
Wilderness Rd. BR7: Chst 7F 143
Wilde Rd. DA8: Erith 7H 109
Wilderton Rd. N16 7E 48
Wildfell Rd. SE6 7D 122
Wild Goose Dr. SE14 1J 121
Wild Hatch NW11 6J 45
Wild's Rents SE1 7G 15 (3E 102)
Wild St. WC2 1F 13 (6J 83)
Wildwood Cl. SE12 7H 123
Wildwood Gro. NW3 1A 64
Wildwood Ri. NW11 1A 64
Wildwood Rd. NW11 6K 45
Wildwood Ter. NW3 1A 64
Wilford Cl. EN2: Enf 3J 23
Wilford Rd. CR0: C'don 6C 156
Wilfred Ct. *N15* *5D 48*
(off South Gro.)
Wilfred Owen Cl. SW19 6A 136
Wilfred St. SW1 1A 18 (3G 101)
Wilfrid Gdns. W3 5J 79
Wilkes Rd. TW8: Bford 6E 96
Wilkes St. E1 5K 9 (5F 85)
Wilkie Ho. *SW1* *5D 18*
(off Cureton St.)
Wilkins Cl. CR4: Mitc 1C 154
UB3: Harl 5H 93
Wilkins Ho. *SW1* *7A 18*
(off Churchill Gdns.)
Wilkinson Cl. UB10: Hil 1D 74
Wilkinson Ct. SW17 4B 136
Wilkinson Gdns. SE25 1E 156
Wilkinson Ho. *N1* *2D 84*
(off Cranston Est.)
Wilkinson Rd. E16 6A 88
Wilkinson St. SW8 7K 101
Wilkinson Way W4 2K 97
Wilkin St. NW5 6E 64
Wilkin St. M. NW5 6F 65
Wilks Gdns. CR0: C'don 1A 170
Wilks Pl. N1 2E 84
Willan Rd. N17 2D 48
Willan Wall E16 7H 87
Willard St. SW8 3F 119
Willcocks Cl. KT9: Chess 3E 162
Willcott Rd. W3 1H 97
Will Crooks Gdns. SE9 4A 124
Willenfield Rd. NW10 2J 79
Willenhall Av. EN5: New Bar 6F 21
Willenhall Ct. EN5: New Bar 6F 21
Willenhall Dr. UB3: Hayes 7G 75
Willenhall Rd. SE18 5F 107
Willersley Av. BR6: Orp 3H 173
DA15: Sidc 1K 143
Willersley Cl. DA15: Sidc 1K 143
WILLESDEN 6C 62
Willesden Belle Vue Cinema *6D 62*
(off High Rd.)
WILLESDEN GREEN 6E 62
Willesden La. NW2 6E 62
NW6 6E 62
Willesden Section Ho.
NW2 *6F 63*
(off Willesden La.)
Willesden Sports Cen. 1D 80
Willesden Sports Stadium 1D 80
Willes Rd. NW5 6F 65
Willett Cl. BR5: Pet W 6J 161
UB5: N'olt 3A 76
Willett Ho. *E13* *2K 87*
(off Queens Rd. W.)
Willett Pl. CR7: Thor H 5A 156
Willett Rd. CR7: Thor H 5A 156
Willett Way BR5: Pet W 5H 161
William IV St. WC2 3E 12 (7J 83)
William Allen Ho. HA8: Edg 7A 28
William Ash Cl. RM9: Dag 6B 72
William Banfield Ho. *SW6* *2H 117*
(off Munster Rd.)
William Barefoot Dr. SE9 4E 142
William Blake Ho. SW11 1C 118
William Bonney Est. SW4 4H 119
William Booth Rd. SE20 1G 157
William Carey Way HA1: Harr 6J 41
William Caslon Ho. *E2* *2H 85*
(off Patriot Sq.)
William Channing Ho. *E2* *3H 85*
(off Canrobert St.)
William Cl. N2 3B 46
RM5: Col R 1J 55
SE13 3E 122
UB2: S'hall 2G 95
William Cobbett Ho. *W8* *3K 99*
(off Scarsdale Pl.)
William Ct. *SW16* *7K 137*
(off Streatham High Rd.)
W5 5C 78
William Covell Cl. EN2: Enf 1E 22
William Dr. HA7: Stan 6F 27
William Dromey Ct. NW6 7H 63
William Dunbar Ho. *NW6* *2H 81*
(off Albert Rd.)
William Dyce M. SW16 4H 137
William Ellis Way *SE16* *3G 103*
(off St James's Rd.)
William Evans Ho. *SE8* *4K 103*
(off Haddonfield)
William Farm La. SW15 3D 116
William Fenn Ho. *E2* *1K 9*
(off Shipton Rd.)
William Foster La. DA16: Well 2A 126
William Gdns. SW15 5D 116
William Gibbs Ct. *SW1* *2C 18*
(off Old Pye St.)
William Gunn Ho. NW3 5C 64
William Guy Gdns. E3 3D 86
William Harvey Ho. *SW19* *1G 135*
(off Whitlock Dr.)
William Henry Wlk. SW8 7C 18 (6H 101)
William Hunt Mans. SW13 6E 98
William Margrie Cl. SE15 2G 121
William M. SW1 7F 11 (2D 100)
William Morley Cl. E6 1B 88
William Morris Cl. E17 3B 50
William Morris Gallery 3C 50
William Morris Ho. W6 6F 99
William Morris Way SW6 3A 118
William Perkin Ct. UB6: G'frd 6J 59
William Pike Ho. *RM7: Rom* *6K 55*
(off Waterloo Gdns.)
William Pl. E3 2B 86
William Rathbone Ho. *E2* *3H 85*
(off Florida St.)
William Rd. NW1 2A 6 (3G 83)
SM1: Sutt 5A 166
SW19 7G 135
William Rushbrooke Ho. *SE16* *4G 103*
(off Rouel Rd.)
Williams Av. E17 1B 50
William Saville Ho. *NW6* *2H 81*
(off Denmark Rd.)
William's Bldgs. E2 4J 85
Williams Cl. N8 6H 47
SW6 7G 99
Williams Dr. TW3: Houn 4E 112
Williams Gro. KT6: Surb 6C 150
N22 1A 48
Williams Ho. *E3* *3C 86*
(off Alfred St.)
E9 *1H 85*
(off King Edward's Rd.)
NW2 *3E 62*
(off Stoll Cl.)
SW1 *4D 18*
(off Regency St.)
Williams La. SM4: Mord 5A 154
SW14 3J 115
William Smith Ho. *DA17: Belv* *3G 109*
(off Ambrooke Rd.)
E3 *3C 86*
(off Ireton St.)
Williamson Cl. SE10 5H 105
Williamson Ct. SE17 5C 102
Williamson Rd. N4 6B 48
Williamson St. N7 4J 65
William Sq. *SE16* *7A 86*
(off Sovereign Cres.)
Williams Rd. UB2: S'hall 4C 94
W13 1A 96
Williams Ter. CR0: Wadd 6A 168
William St. E10 6D 50
IG11: Bark 7G 71
N17 7A 34
SM5: Cars 3C 166
SW1 7F 11 (2D 100)
Williams Way DA2: Dart 2K 145
William White Ct. *E13* *1A 88*
(off Green St.)
William Wood Ho. *SE26* *3J 139*
(off Shrublands Cl.)
Willifield Way NW11 4H 45
Willingale Cl. IG8: Wfd G 6F 37
Willingdon Rd. N22 2B 48
Willingham Cl. NW5 5G 65
Willingham Ter. NW5 5G 65
Willingham Way KT1: King T 3G 151
Willington Ct. E5 3A 68
Willington Rd. SW9 3J 119
Willis Av. SM2: Sutt 6C 166
Willis Ct. BR4: W W'ck 2F 171
CR7: Thor H 6A 156
Willis Ho. *E14* *7D 86*
(off Hale St.)
Willis Rd. CR0: C'don 7C 156
DA8: Erith 4J 109
E15 2H 87
Willis St. E14 6D 86
Willis Yd. N14 7C 22
Will Miles Ct. SW19 7A 136
Willmore End SW19 1K 153
Willoughby Av. CR0: Bedd 4K 167
Willoughby Dr. RM13: Rain 7K 73
Willoughby Gro. N17 7C 34
Willoughby Highwalk *EC2* *6E 8*
(off Moor La.)
Willoughby Ho. *E1* *1H 103*
(off Reardon Path)
EC2 5E 8
Willoughby La. N17 6C 34
Willoughby M. N17 7C 34
SW4 *4F 119*
(off Cedars M.)
Willoughby Pk. Rd. N17 7C 34
Willoughby Pas. *E14* *1C 104*
(off W. India Av.)
Willoughby Rd. KT2: King T 1F 151
N8 3A 48
NW3 4B 64
TW1: Twick 5C 114
(not continuous)
Willoughbys, The SW14 3A 116
Willoughby St. WC1 6E 6
Willoughby Way SE7 4K 105
Willow Av. DA15: Sidc 6A 126
SW13 2B 116
UB7: Yiew 7B 74
Willow Bank SW6 3G 117
TW10: Ham 3B 132
Willowbank KT7: T Ditt 1A 162
Willowbay Cl. EN5: Barn 6A 20
Willow Bri. Rd. N1 6C 66
(not continuous)
Willowbrook TW12: Ham H 5F 131
Willowbrook Est. SE15 7G 103
Willow Brook Rd. SE15 7F 103
Willowbrook Rd. TW19: Stanw 2A 128
UB2: S'hall 3E 94
Willow Bus. Pk. SE26 3J 139
Willow Cl. BR2: Brom 5D 160
DA5: Bexl 6F 127
IG9: Buck H 3G 37
SE6 1H 141
TW8: Bford 6C 96
Willow Cotts. TW9: Kew 6G 97
TW13: Hanw 3C 130
Willow Ct. *E11* *2G 69*
(off Trinity Cl.)
EC2 3G 9 (4E 84)
HA3: Hrw W 1K 41
HA8: Edg 4K 27
N12 4E 30
NW6 7G 63

Willow Ct.—Winchester Ho.

Willow Ct. *SM6: Wall* 7F 167
(off Willow Rd.)
TW16: Sun 7G 129
(off Staines Rd. W.)
W4 7A 98
(off Corney Reach Way)
W9 5J 81
(off Admiral Wlk.)
Willowcourt Av. HA3: Kenton 5B 42
Willow Dene HA5: Pinn 2B 40
WD23: B Hea 1D 26
Willowdene N6 7D 46
SE15 7H 103
Willowdene Cl. TW2: Whitt 7G 113
Willowdene Ct. *N20* 7F 21
(off High Rd.)
Willow Dr. EN5: Barn 4B 20
Willow End KT6: Surb 1E 162
N20 2D 30
Willowfields Cl. SE18 5J 107
Willow Gdns. HA4: Ruis 2H 57
TW3: Houn 1E 112
Willow Grange DA14: Sidc 3B 144
Willow Grn. NW9 1A 44
Willow Gro. BR7: Chst 6E 142
E13 2J 87
HA4: Ruis 2H 57
Willowhayne Ct. *KT12: Walt T* 7K 147
(off Willowhayne Dr.)
Willowhayne Dr. KT12: Walt T 7K 147
Willowhayne Gdns.
KT4: Wor Pk 3E 164
Willow Ho. BR2: Brom 2G 159
SE1 4F 103
(off Curtis St.)
W10 4F 81
(off Maple Wlk.)
Willow La. CR4: Mitc 5D 154
SE18 4D 106
Willow La. Bus. Pk. CR4: Mitc 6D 154
Willow La. Ind. Est. CR4: Mitc 6D 154
Willow Lodge RM7: Rom 5K 55
SW6 1F 117
TW16: Sun 7H 129
(off Forest Dr.)
Willowmead Cl. W5 4D 78
Willow Mt. CR0: C'don 3E 168
Willow Pl. SW1 3B 18 (4G 101)
Willow Rd. E12 3D 70
EN1: Enf 3K 23
KT3: N Mald 4J 151
NW3 4B 64
RM6: Chad H 6E 54
SL3: Poyle 5A 174
SM6: Wall 7F 167
W5 2E 96
Willows, The BR3: Beck 1C 158
E6 7D 70
SE1 4E 102
(off Willow Wlk.)
Willows Av. SM4: Mord 5K 153
Willows Cl. HA5: Pinn 2A 40
Willowside Ct. EN2: Enf 3G 23
Willows Ter. *NW10* 2B 80
(off Rucklidge Av.)
Willow St. E4 1A 36
EC2 3G 9 (4E 84)
RM7: Rom 4J 55
Willow Tree Cl. E3 1B 86
SW18 1K 135
UB4: Yead 4A 76
UB5: N'olt 6D 58
Willowtree Cl. UB10: Ick 3E 56
Willow Tree Ct. DA14: Sidc 5A 144
HA0: Wemb 5D 60
Willow Tree La. UB4: Yead 4A 76
Willow Tree Rdbt. UB4: Yead 5B 76
Willow Tree Wlk. BR1: Brom 1K 159
Willowtree Way CR7: Thor H 1A 156
Willow Va. BR7: Chst 6F 143
W12 1C 98
Willow Vw. SW19 1B 154
Willow Wlk. BR6: Farnb 3F 173
E17 5B 50
IG1: Ilf 2F 71
N2 2B 46
N15 4B 48
N21 6E 22
SE1 3E 102
SM3: Sutt 3H 165
Willow Way HA0: Wemb 3A 60
KT19: Ewe 6K 163
N3 7E 30
SE26 3J 139
TW2: Twick 2F 131
TW16: Sun 4J 147
W11 7F 81
Willow Wood Cres. SE25 6E 156
Willow Wren Wharf UB2: S'hall 4K 93
Willrose Cres. SE2 5B 108
Willsbridge Ct. SE15 6E 102
Wills Cres. TW3: Houn 6F 113
Wills Gro. NW7 5H 29
(not continuous)
Will Wyatt Ct. *N1* 2E 84
(off Pitfield St.)
Wilman Gro. E8 7G 67
Wilmar Cl. UB4: Hayes 4F 75
Wilmar Gdns. BR4: W W'ck 1D 170
Wilmcote Ho. *W2* 5K 81
(off Woodchester Sq.)
Wilment Ct. NW2 3E 62
Wilmer Cl. KT2: King T 5F 133
Wilmer Cres. KT2: King T 5F 133
Wilmer Gdns. N1 1E 84
(not continuous)
Wilmer Ho. *E3* 2A 86
(off Daling Way)
Wilmer Lea Cl. E15 7E 68
Wilmer Pl. N16 2F 67
Wilmers Ct. *NW10* 1K 79
(off Lawrence Av.)
Wilmer Way N14 5C 32
Wilmington Av. W4 7K 97
Wilmington Ct. SW16 7J 137
Wilmington Gdns. IG11: Bark 6H 71
Wilmington Sq. WC1 2J 7 (3A 84)
(not continuous)
Wilmington St. WC1 2J 7 (3A 84)
Wilmot Cl. N2 2A 46
SE15 7G 103
Wilmot Pl. *NW1* 7G 65
(off St Pancras Way)
NW1 7G 65
(Rochester Rd.)
W7 1J 95
Wilmot Rd. E10 2D 68
N17 3D 48
SM5: Cars 5D 166
Wilmot St. E2 4H 85
Wilmount St. SE18 4F 107
Wilna Rd. SW18 7A 118
Wilsham St. W11 1F 99
Wilshaw Cl. NW4 3C 44
Wilshaw Ho. SE8 7C 104
Wilshaw St. SE14 1C 122
Wilsmere Dr. HA3: Hrw W 7D 26
UB5: N'olt 6C 58
Wilson Av. CR4: Mitc 7C 136
Wilson Cl. CR2: S Croy 5D 168
HA9: Wemb 7F 43
Wilson Ct. *RM7: Rush G* 6K 55
(off Union Rd.)
SE28 3G 107
Wilson Dr. HA9: Wemb 7F 43
Wilson Gdns. HA1: Harr 7G 41
Wilson Gro. SE16 2H 103
Wilson Ho. *NW6* 7A 64
(off Goldhurst Ter.)
Wilson Rd. E6 3B 88
IG1: Ilf 7D 52
KT9: Chess 6F 163
SE5 1E 120
Wilson's Av. N17 2F 49
Wilson's Pl. E14 6B 86
Wilson's Rd. W6 5F 99
Wilson St. E17 5E 50
EC2 5F 9 (5D 84)
N21 7F 23
Wilson Wlk. *W4* 4B 98
(off Prebend Gdns.)
W6 4B 98
(off Prebend Gdns.)
Wilstone Cl. UB4: Yead 4C 76
Wiltern Ct. NW2 6G 63
Wilthorne Gdns. RM10: Dag 7H 73
Wilton Av. W4 5A 98
Wilton Cl. UB7: Harm 2E 174
Wilton Ct. *E1* 6H 85
(off Cavell St.)
Wilton Cres. SW1 7G 11 (2E 100)
SW19 7H 135
Wilton Dr. RM5: Col R 1J 55
Wilton Est. E8 6G 67
Wilton Gdns. KT8: W Mole 3E 148
Wilton Gro. KT3: N Mald 6B 152
SW19 1H 153
Wilton Ho. *CR2: S Croy* 5C 168
(off Nottingham Rd.)
Wilton M. E8 6H 67
SW1 1H 17 (3E 100)
Wilton Pde. TW13: Felt 2J 129
Wilton Pl. HA1: Harr 6K 41
SW1 7G 11 (2E 100)
Wilton Plaza *SW1* 3A 18
(off Wilton Rd.)
SW1 4G 101
(off Wilton Rd.)
Wilton Rd. EN4: Cockf 4J 21
N10 2E 46
SE2 4C 108
SW1 2A 18 (3F 101)
SW19 7C 136
TW4: Houn 3B 112
Wilton Row SW1 7G 11 (2E 100)
Wiltons Music Hall 7G 85
(off Graces All.)
Wilton Sq. N1 1D 84
Wilton St. SW1 1J 17 (3F 101)
Wilton Ter. SW1 1G 17 (3E 100)
Wilton Vs. *N1* 1D 84
(off Wilton Sq.)
Wilton Way E8 6G 67
Wiltshire Cl. NW7 5G 29
SW3 3E 16 (4D 100)
Wiltshire Ct. CR2: S Croy 5C 168
IG1: Ilf 6G 71
N4 1K 65
(off Marquis Rd.)
Wiltshire Gdns. N4 6C 48
TW2: Twick 1G 131
Wiltshire La. HA5: Eastc 3H 39
Wiltshire Rd. BR6: Orp 7K 161
CR7: Thor H 3A 156
SW9 3A 120
Wiltshire Row N1 1D 84
Wilverley Cres. KT3: N Mald 6A 152
Wimbart Rd. SW2 7K 119
WIMBLEDON 6G 135
Wimbledon
All England Lawn Tennis &
Croquet Club 4G 135
Wimbledon Bri. SW19 6H 135
Wimbledon Cl. SW20 7F 135
Wimbledon Common 4C 134
Wimbledon Hill Rd. SW19 6G 135
Wimbledon Lawn Tennis Mus. 3G 135
Wimbledon Leisure Cen. 6K 135
Wimbledon Mus. of Local History 6G 135
WIMBLEDON PARK 3J 135
Wimbledon Pk. Athletics Track 2H 135
Wimbledon Pk. Ct. SW19 1H 135
Wimbledon Pk. Rd. SW18 2G 135
SW19 2G 135
Wimbledon Pk. Sailing Club 2H 135
Wimbledon Pk. Side SW19 3F 135
Wimbledon Rd. SW17 4A 136
Wimbledon Stadium Bus. Cen.
SW17 3K 135
Wimbledon Stadium (Greyhound) 4A 136
Wimbledon Theatre 7J 135
Wimbledon Windmill Mus. 2D 134
Wimbolt St. E2 3G 85
Wimborne Av. BR5: St P 4K 161
BR7: Chst 4K 161
UB2: S'hall 4E 94
UB4: Yead 6K 75
Wimborne Cl. IG9: Buck H 2E 36
KT4: Wor Pk 1E 164
SE12 5H 123
Wimborne Ct. SW12 3G 137
UB5: N'olt 6E 58
Wimborne Dr. HA5: Pinn 7B 40
NW9 3G 43
Wimborne Gdns. W13 5B 78
Wimborne Ho. *E16* 7H 87
(off Victoria Dock Rd.)
NW1 4D 4
(off Harewood Av.)
SW8 7K 101
(off Dorset Rd.)
SW12 3G 137
Wimborne Rd. N9 2B 34
N17 2E 48
Wimborne Way BR3: Beck 3K 157
Wimbourne Ct. *N1* 2D 84
(off Wimbourne St.)
Wimbourne St. N1 2D 84
Wimpole Cl. BR2: Brom 4A 160
KT1: King T 2F 151
Wimpole M. W1 5J 5 (5F 83)
Wimpole Rd. UB7: Yiew 1A 92
Wimpole St. W1 6J 5 (5F 83)
Wimshurst Cl. CR0: Wadd 1J 167
Winans Wlk. SW9 2A 120
Winant Ho. *E14* 7D 86
(off Simpson's Rd.)
Wincanton Ct. *N11* 6K 31
(off Martock Gdns.)
Wincanton Cres. UB5: N'olt 5E 58
Wincanton Gdns. IG6: Ilf 3F 53
Wincanton Rd. SW18 7H 117
Winchcombe Rd. SM5: Cars 7B 154
Winchcomb Gdns. SE9 3B 124
Winchelsea Av. DA7: Bex 7F 109
Winchelsea Cl. SW15 5F 117
Winchelsea Ho. *SE16* 2J 103
(off Swan Rd.)
Winchelsea Rd. E7 3J 69
N17 3E 48
NW10 1K 79
Winchelsey Ri. CR2: S Croy 6F 169
Winchendon Rd. SW6 1H 117
TW11: Tedd 4H 131
Winchester Av. NW6 1G 81
NW9 3G 43
TW5: Hest 6D 94
Winchester Bldgs. *SE1* 2C 102
(off Copperfield St.)
Winchester Cl. BR2: Brom 3H 159
E6 6D 88
EN1: Enf 5K 23
KT2: King T 7H 133
SE17 4B 102
SL3: Poyle 4A 174
Winchester Ct. *W8* 2J 99
(off Vicarage Ga.)
Winchester Dr. HA5: Pinn 5B 40
Winchester Ho. *E3* 3B 86
(off Hamlets Way)
IG11: Bark 7A 72
(off Margaret Bondfield Av.)
SE18 7B 106
(off Portway Gdns.)
SW3 7B 16
SW9 7A 102
W2 6A 82
(off Hallfield Est.)

Winchester M. KT4: Wor Pk 2F **165**
NW3 7B 64
(off Winchester Rd.)
Winchester Pk. BR2: Brom 3H **159**
Winchester Pl. E8 5F **67**
N6 1F **65**
Winchester Rd. BR2: Brom 3H **159**
DA7: Bex 2D **126**
E4 7K **35**
HA3: Kenton 4E **42**
HA6: Nwood 2H **39**
IG1: Ilf 3H **71**
KT12: Walt T 7J **147**
N6 7F **47**
N9 1A **34**
NW3 7B **64**
TW1: Twick 6B **114**
TW13: Hanw 3D **130**
UB3: Harl 7G **93**
Winchester Sq. SE1 4E **14**
Winchester St. SW1 5K **17** (5F **101**)
W3 1J **97**
Winchester Wlk. SE1 4E **14** (1D **102**)
Winchester Wharf *SE1 4E 14*
(off Clink St.)
Winchet Wlk. CR0: C'don 6J **157**
Winchfield Cl. HA3: Kenton 6C **42**
Winchfield Ho. SW15 6B **116**
Winchfield Rd. SE26 5A **140**
Winch Ho. *E14 3D 104*
(off Tiller Rd.)
SW10 7A 100
(off King's Rd.)
Winchilsea Cres. KT8: W Mole 2G **149**
Winchilsea Ho. *NW8 2B 4*
(off St John's Wood Rd.)
WINCHMORE HILL 7F **23**
Winchmore Hill Rd. N14 1C **32**
N21 1C **32**
Winchmore Vs. *N21 7E 22*
(off Winchmore Hill Rd.)
Winchstone Cl. TW17: Shep 4B **146**
Winckley Cl. HA3: Kenton 5F **43**
Winckworth Ct. *N1 2F 9*
(off Brunswick Pl.)
Wincott Pde. *SE11 3K 19*
(off Wincott St.)
Wincott St. SE11 4K **19** (4A **102**)
Wincrofts Dr. SE9 4H **125**
Windall Cl. SE19 1G **157**
Windborough Rd. SM5: Cars 7E **166**
Windermere *NW1 2K 5*
(off Albany St.)
Windermere Av. HA4: Ruis 7A **40**
HA9: Kenton, Wemb 7C **42**
N3 3J **45**
NW6 1G **81**
SW19 3K **153**
Windermere Cl. BR6: Farnb 3F **173**
TW14: Felt 1H **129**
TW19: Stanw 1A **128**
Windermere Ct. HA9: Wemb 7C **42**
SM5: Cars 3E **166**
SW13 6B **98**
Windermere Gdns. IG4: Ilf 5C **52**
Windermere Gro. HA9: Wemb 1C **60**
Windermere Hall HA8: Edg 5A **28**
Windermere Ho. E3 4B **86**
EN5: New Bar 4E **20**
TW7: Isle 5K **113**
Windermere Point *SE15 7J 103*
(off Old Kent Rd.)
Windermere Rd.
BR4: W W'ck 2G **171**
CR0: C'don 1F **169**
DA7: Bex 2J **127**
N10 1F **47**
N19 2G **65**
SW15 4A **134**
SW16 1G **155**
UB1: S'hall 5D **76**
W5 3C **96**
Windermere Way UB7: Yiew 1A **92**
Winders Rd. SW11 2C **118**
(not continuous)
Windfield Cl. SE26 4K **139**
Windham Rd. TW9: Rich 3F **115**
Winding Way RM8: Dag 3C **72**
Windlass Pl. SE8 4A **104**
Windlesham Gro. SW19 1F **135**
Windley Cl. SE23 2J **139**
Windmill *WC1 5G 7*
(off New North St.)
Windmill Av. UB2: S'hall 1G **95**
Windmill Bri. Ho.
CR0: C'don 1E 168
(off Freemasons Rd.)
Windmill Bus. Village TW16: Sun 1G **147**
Windmill Cl. KT6: Surb 1C **162**
SE1 4G 103
(off Beatrice Rd.)
SE13 2E **122**
TW16: Sun 7G **129**
Windmill Ct. HA4: Ruis 1J **57**
NW2 6G **63**
W5 4C 96
(off Windmill Rd.)
Windmill Dr. BR2: Kes 4A **172**
NW2 3G **63**
SW4 5F **119**
Windmill Gdns. EN2: Enf 3F **23**
Windmill Grn. *TW17: Shep 7G 147*
(off Walton La.)
Windmill Gro. CR0: C'don 6C **156**
Windmill Hill EN2: Enf 3G **23**
HA4: Ruis 7H **39**
NW3 3A **64**
Windmill Ho. E14 4C **104**
SE1 5K 13
(off Windmill Wlk.)
Windmill La. E15 6F **69**
KT6: Surb 6B **150**
TW7: Isle 1G **95**
UB2: S'hall 1G **95**
UB6: G'frd 6G **77**
WD23: B Hea 1D **26**
Windmill M. W4 4A **98**
Windmill Pas. W4 4A **98**
Windmill Pl. Bus. Cen.
UB2: S'hall 1G **95**
Windmill Ri. KT2: King T 7H **133**
Windmill Rd. CR0: C'don 7C **156**
CR4: Mitc 5G **155**
N18 4J **33**
SW18 6B **118**
SW19 2D **134**
TW8: Bford 4C **96**
TW12: Ham H 5F **131**
TW16: Sun 1G **147**
W4 4A **98**
W5 4C **96**
Windmill Rd. W. TW16: Sun 2G **147**
Windmill Row SE11 6J **19** (5A **102**)
Windmill St. W1 6C **6** (5H **83**)
(not continuous)
WD23: B Hea 1D **26**
Windmill Ter. TW17: Shep 7G **147**
Windmill Wlk. SE1 5K **13** (1A **102**)
Windmill Way HA4: Ruis 1H **57**
Windmore Cl. HA0: Wemb 5A **60**
Windrose Cl. SE16 2K **103**
Windrush KT3: N Mald 4H **151**
SE28 1B **108**
Windrush Cl. E8 7G **67**
N17 1E **48**
SW11 4B **118**
UB10: Ick 4B **56**
W4 1J **115**
Windrush Ho. *NW8 5B 4*
(off Church St. Est.)
Windrush La. SE23 3K **139**
Windrush Rd. NW10 1K **79**
Windsock Cl. SE16 4B **104**
Windsock Way TW6: H'row A 5C **174**
Windsor Av. E17 2A **50**
HA8: Edg 4C **28**
KT3: N Mald 5J **151**
KT8: W Mole 3E **148**
SM3: Cheam 3G **165**
SW19 1A **154**
UB10: Hil 1D **74**
Windsor Cen., The *N1 1B 84*
(off Windsor St.)
Windsor Cl. BR7: Chst 5F **143**
HA2: Harr 3E **58**
HA6: Nwood 2J **39**
N3 2G **45**
SE27 4C **138**
TW6: H'row A 6D 174
(off Whittle Rd.)
TW8: Bford 6B **96**
Windsor Cotts. *SE14 7B 104*
(off Amersham Gro.)
Windsor Ct. *E3 2C 86*
(off Mostyn Gro.)
HA5: Pinn 3B **40**
KT1: King T 4D 150
(off Palace Rd.)
N11 5J **31**
N14 7B **22**
NW3 4J **63**
NW11 6G 45
(off Golders Grn. Rd.)
SE16 7K 85
(off King & Queen Wharf)
SW3 5D 16
(off Jubilee Pl.)
SW11 2B **118**
TW16: Sun 7J **129**
W2 7K 81
(off Moscow Rd.)
W10 6F 81
(off Bramley Rd.)
WD23: Bush 1B 26
(off Catsey La.)
Windsor Cres. HA2: Harr 3E **58**
HA9: Wemb 3H **61**
Windsor Dr. BR6: Chels 6K **173**
EN4: E Barn 6J **21**
Windsor Gdns. CR0: Bedd 3J **167**
UB3: Harl 3F **93**
W9 5J **81**
Windsor Gro. SE27 4C **138**
Windsor Hall *E16 1K 105*
(off Wesley Av.)
Windsor Ho. *E2 3K 85*
(off Knottisford St.)
N1 2C **84**
NW1 1K **5**
NW2 6G 63
(off Chatsworth Rd.)
UB5: N'olt 6E 58
(off The Farmlands)
Windsor M. SE6 1E **140**
SE23 1A **140**
SW18 7A 118
(off Wilna Rd.)
Windsor Pk. Rd. UB3: Harl 7H **93**
Windsor Pl. SW1 3B **18** (3G **101**)
Windsor Rd. CR7: Thor H 2B **156**
DA6: Bex 4E **126**
E4 4J **35**
E7 5K **69**
E10 2D **68**
E11 1J **69**
EN5: Barn 6A **20**
HA3: Hrw W 1G **41**
IG1: Ilf 4F **71**
KT2: King T 7E **132**
KT4: Wor Pk 2C **164**
N3 2G **45**
N7 3J **65**
N13 3F **33**
N17 2G **49**
NW2 6D **62**
RM8: Dag 3E **72**
Windsor Rd. TW4: Cran 2K **111**
TW9: Kew 2F **115**
TW11: Tedd 5H **131**
TW16: Sun 6J **129**
UB2: S'hall 3D **94**
W5 7E **78**
(not continuous)
Windsors, The IG9: Buck H 2H **37**
Windsor St. N1 1B **84**
Windsor Ter. N1 1D **8** (3C **84**)
Windsor Wlk. SE5 2D **120**
Windsor Way W14 4F **99**
Windsor Wharf E9 5B **68**
Windspoint Dr. SE15 6H **103**
Windus Rd. N16 1F **67**
Windus Wlk. N16 1F **67**
Windward Ct. *E16 7F 89*
(off Gallions Rd.)
Windy Ridge BR1: Brom 1C **160**
Windy Ridge Cl. SW19 5F **135**
Wine Cl. E1 7J **85**
(not continuous)
Wine Office Ct. EC4 7K **7** (6A **84**)
EC4 1K 13
(off Fleet St.)
Winery La. KT1: King T 3F **151**
Winey Cl. KT9: Chess 7C **162**
Winford Ct. SE15 1H **121**
Winford Ho. E3 7B **68**
Winford Pde. *UB1: S'hall 6F 77*
(off Marconi Way)
Winforton St. SE10 1E **122**
Winfrith Rd. SW18 7A **118**
Wingate Cres. CR0: C'don 6J **155**
Wingate Ho. *E3 3D 86*
(off Bruce Rd.)
Wingate Rd. DA14: Sidc 6C **144**
IG1: Ilf 5F **71**
W6 3D **98**
Wingate Sq. SW4 3G **119**
Wingate Trad. Est. N17 7A **34**
Wingfield Ct. DA15: Sidc 2K **143**
E14 7F 87
(off John Smith M.)
Wingfield Ho. *E2 2J 9*
(off Virginia Rd.)
NW6 2K 81
(off Tollgate Gdns.)
Wingfield M. SE15 3G **121**
Wingfield Rd. E15 4G **69**
E17 5D **50**
KT2: King T 6F **133**
Wingfield St. SE15 3G **121**
Wingfield Way HA4: Ruis 5K **57**
Wingford Rd. SW2 6J **119**
Wingmore Rd. SE24 3C **120**
Wingrad Ho. *E1 5J 85*
(off Jubilee St.)
Wingrave SE17 4D **102**
Wingrave Rd. W6 6E **98**
Wingreen *NW8 1K 81*
(off Abbey Rd.)
Wingrove E4 7H **25**
Wingrove Ct. RM7: Rom 5J **55**
Wingrove Rd. SE6 2G **141**
Wings Cl. SM1: Sutt 4J **165**
Wings Rd. *TW6: H'row A 6C 174*
(off Whittle Rd.)
Wing Yip Bus. Cen. NW2 2D **62**
Winicotte Ho. *W2 5B 4*
(off Paddington Grn.)
Winifred Pl. N12 5F **31**
Winifred Rd. DA8: Erith 5K **109**
RM8: Dag 2E **72**
SW19 1J **153**
TW12: Ham H 4E **130**
Winifred St. E16 1D **106**
Winifred Ter. *E13 2J 87*
(off Upper Rd.)
EN1: Enf 7A **24**
Winkfield Rd. E13 2K **87**
N22 1A **48**

Winkley Ct. HA2: Harr 3E **58**
N10 *4F* ***47***
(off St James's La.)
Winkley St. E2 2H **85**
Winkworth Cotts. *E1* *4J* ***85***
(off Cephas St.)
Winlaton Rd. BR1: Brom 4F **141**
Winmill Rd. RM8: Dag 3F **73**
Winnett St. W1 2C **12** (7H **83**)
Winningales Ct. IG5: Ilf 2C **52**
Winnings Wlk. UB5: N'olt 6C **58**
Winnington Cl. N2 6B **46**
Winnington Ho. *SE5* *7C* ***102***
(off Wyndham Est.)
W10 *4G* ***81***
(off Southern Row)
Winnington Rd. N2 6B **46**
Winnipeg Dr. BR6: Chels 6K **173**
Winnock Rd. UB7: Yiew 1A **92**
Winn Rd. SE12 1J **141**
Winns Av. E17 3B **50**
Winns Comn. Rd. SE18 6J **107**
Winns M. N15 4E **48**
Winns Ter. E17 3C **50**
Winsbeach E17 2F **51**
Winscombe Cres. W5 4D **78**
Winscombe St. N19 2F **65**
Winscombe Way HA7: Stan 5F **27**
Winsford Rd. SE6 3B **140**
Winsford Ter. N18 5J **33**
Winsham Gro. SW11 5E **118**
Winsham Ho. *NW1* *1D* ***6***
(off Churchway)
Winslade Rd. SW2 5J **119**
Winslade Way SE6 7D **122**
Winsland M. W2 7A **4** (6B **82**)
Winsland St. W2 7A **4** (6B **82**)
Winsley St. W1 7B **6** (6G **83**)
Winslow SE17 5E **102**
Winslow Cl. HA5: Eastc 6K **39**
NW10 3A **62**
Winslow Gro. E4 2B **36**
Winslow Rd. W6 6E **98**
Winslow Way TW13: Hanw 3B **130**
Winsmoor Ct. EN2: Enf 3G **23**
WINSOR PARK 5F **89**
Winsor Ter. E6 5E **88**
Winstanley Est. SW11 3B **118**
Winstanley Rd. SW11 3B **118**
(not continuous)
Winstead Gdns. RM10: Dag 5J **73**
Winston Av. NW9 7A **44**
Winston Churchill's Britain at War Experience 5G **15**
Winston Cl. HA3: Hrw W 6E **26**
RM7: Mawney 4H **55**
Winston Ct. *BR1: Brom* *1K* ***159***
(off Widmore Rd.)
HA3: Hrw W 7A **26**
Winston Ho. *W13* *2A* ***96***
(off Balfour Rd.)
WC1 3D **6**
Winston Rd. N16 4D **66**
Winston Wlk. W4 3K **97**
Winston Way IG1: Ilf 3F **71**
Winter Av. E6 1C **88**
Winterborne Av. BR6: Orp 3H **173**
Winterbourne Ho. *W11* *7G* ***81***
(off Portland Rd.)
Winterbourne Rd. CR7: Thor H 4A **156**
RM8: Dag 2C **72**
SE6 1B **140**
Winter Box Wlk. TW10: Rich 5F **115**
Winterbrook Rd. SE24 6C **120**
Winterburn Cl. N11 6K **31**
Winterfold Cl. SW19 2G **135**
Winter Gdns. TW11: Tedd 4A **132**
Wintergreen Cl. E6 5C **88**
Winterleys *NW6* *2H* ***81***
(off Denmark Rd.)
Winter Lodge *SE16* *5G* ***103***
(off Fern Wlk.)
Winter's Ct. E4 3J **35**
Winterslow Ho. *SE5* *2C* ***120***
(off Flaxman Rd.)
Winters Rd. KT7: T Ditt 7B **150**
Winterstoke Gdns. NW7 5H **29**
Winterstoke Rd. SE6 1B **140**
Winterton Ct. *KT1: Ham W* *1D* ***150***
(off Lwr. Teddington Rd.)
SE20 2G **157**
Winterton Ho. *E1* *6J* ***85***
(off Deancross St.)
Winterton Pl. SW10 7A **16** (6A **100**)
Winterwell Rd. SW2 5J **119**
Winthorpe Rd. SW15 4G **117**
Winthrop Ho. *W12* *7D* ***80***
(off White City Est.)
Winthrop St. E1 5H **85**
Winthrop Wlk. *HA9: Wemb* *3E* ***60***
(off Everard Way)
Winton Av. N11 7B **32**
Winton Cl. N9 7E **24**
Winton Ct. *N1* *2K* ***83***
(off Calshot St.)
Winton Gdns. HA8: Edg 7A **28**
Winton Rd. BR6: Farnb 4F **173**
Winton Way SW16 5A **138**
Wireworks Ct. *SE1* *7C* ***14***
(off Gt. Sufolk St.)
Wirrall Ho. SE26 3G **139**
Wirral Wood Cl.
BR7: Chst 6E **142**
Wirra Rd. *TW6: H'row A* *5C* ***174***
(off Wayfarer Rd.)
Wisbeach Rd. CR0: C'don 5D **156**
Wisbech *N4* *1K* ***65***
(off Lorne Rd.)
Wisborough Rd. CR2: Sande 7F **169**
Wisden Ho. SW8 7H **19** (6K **101**)
Wisdom Ct. *TW7: Isle* *3A* ***114***
(off South St.)
Wisdons Cl. RM10: Dag 1H **73**
Wise La. NW7 5H **29**
UB7: W Dray 4A **92**
Wiseman Rd. E10 2C **68**
Wise Rd. E15 1F **87**
Wiseton Rd. SW17 1C **136**
Wishart Rd. SE3 2B **124**
Wishaw Wlk. N13 6D **32**
Wisley Ho. *SW1* *5C* ***18***
(off Rampayne St.)
Wisley Rd. BR5: St P 7A **144**
SW11 5E **118**
Wistaria Cl. BR6: Farnb 2F **173**
Wisteria Apartments *E9* *6J* ***67***
(off Chatham Pl.)
Wisteria Cl. IG1: Ilf 5F **71**
NW7 6G **29**
Wisteria Gdns. IG8: Wfd G 5D **36**
Wisteria Rd. SE13 4F **123**
Wistow Ho. *E2* *1G* ***85***
(off Whiston Rd.)
Witanhurst La. N6 1E **64**
Witan St. E2 3H **85**
Witchwood Ho. *SW9* *3A* ***120***
(off Gresham Rd.)
Witham Ct. E10 3D **68**
SW17 3D **136**
Witham Rd. RM10: Dag 5G **73**
SE20 3J **157**
TW7: Isle 1H **113**
W13 1A **96**
Witherby Cl. CR0: C'don 5E **168**
Witherington Rd. N5 5A **66**
Withers Cl. KT9: Chess 6C **162**
Withers Mead NW9 1B **44**
Withers Pl. EC1 3D **8** (4C **84**)
Witherston Way SE9 2E **142**
Withycombe Rd. SW19 7F **117**
Withy Ho. *E1* *4K* ***85***
(off Globe Rd.)
Withy La. HA4: Ruis 5E **38**
Withy Mead E4 3A **36**
Witley Ct. WC1 4E **6**
Witley Cres. CR0: New Ad 6E **170**
Witley Gdns. UB2: S'hall 4D **94**
Witley Ho. SW2 7J **119**
Witley Ind. Est. UB2: S'hall 4D **94**
Witley Point *SW15* *1D* ***134***
(off Wanborough Dr.)
Witley Rd. N19 2G **65**
Witney Cl. UB10: Ick 4B **56**
Witney Path SE23 3K **139**
Wittenham Way E4 3A **36**
Wittering Cl. KT2: King T 5D **132**
Wittersham Rd. BR1: Brom 5H **141**
Witts Ho. *KT1: King T* *3F* ***151***
(off Winery La.)
Wivenhoe Cl. SE15 3H **121**
Wivenhoe Ct. TW3: Houn 4D **112**
Wivenhoe Rd. IG11: Bark 2A **90**
Wiverton Rd. SE26 6J **139**
Wixom Ho. SE3 4A **124**
Wix Rd. RM9: Dag 1D **90**
Wix's La. SW4 3F **119**
Woburn *W13* *5B* ***78***
(off Clivedon Ct.)
Woburn Cl. SE28 6D **90**
SW19 6A **136**
Woburn Ct. CR0: C'don 1C **168**
E18 2J **51**
SE16 *5H* ***103***
(off Masters Dr.)
WC1 *4E* ***6***
(off Bernard St.)
Woburn Mans. *WC1* *5C* ***6***
(off Torrington Pl.)
Woburn M. WC1 4D **6** (4H **83**)
Woburn Pl. WC1 4E **6** (4J **83**)
Woburn Rd. CR0: C'don 1C **168**
SM5: Cars 1C **166**
Woburn Sq. WC1 4D **6** (4H **83**)
(not continuous)
Woburn Twr. *UB5: N'olt* *3B* ***76***
(off Broomcroft Av.)
Woburn Wlk. WC1 2D **6** (3H **83**)
Wodeham Gdns. E1 5G **85**
Wodehouse Av. SE5 1F **121**
Wodehouse Ct. *W3* *3J* ***97***
(off Vincent Rd.)
Woffington Cl. KT1: Ham W 1C **150**
Woking Cl. SW15 4B **116**
Wolcot Ho. *NW1* *1B* ***6***
(off Aldenham St.)
Woldham Pl. BR2: Brom 4A **160**
Woldham Rd. BR2: Brom 4A **160**
Wolds Dr. BR6: Farnb 4E **172**
Wolfe Cl. BR2: Hayes 6J **159**
UB4: Yead 3K **75**
Wolfe Cres. SE7 5B **106**
SE16 2K **103**
Wolfe Ho. *W12* *7D* ***80***
(off White City Est.)
Wolferton Rd. E12 4D **70**
Wolffe Gdns. E15 6H **69**
Wolfington Rd. SE27 4B **138**
Wolfram Cl. SE13 5G **123**
Wolftencroft Cl. SW11 3C **118**
Wollaston Cl. SE1 4C **102**
Wollaton Ho. *N1* *2A* ***84***
(off Batchelor St.)
Wollett Ct. *NW1* *7G* ***65***
(off St Pancras Way)
Wolmer Cl. HA8: Edg 4B **28**
Wolmer Gdns. HA8: Edg 3B **28**
Wolseley Av. SW19 2J **135**
Wolseley Gdns. W4 6H **97**
Wolseley Rd. CR4: Mitc 7E **154**
E7 7K **69**
HA3: W'stone 3J **41**
N8 6H **47**
N22 1K **47**
RM7: Rush G 7K **55**
W4 4J **97**
Wolseley St. SE1 7K **15** (2G **103**)
Wolsey Av. E6 3E **88**
E17 3B **50**
KT7: T Ditt 5K **149**
Wolsey Cl. KT2: King T 1H **151**
KT4: Wor Pk 4C **164**
SW20 7D **134**
TW3: Houn 4G **113**
UB2: S'hall 3G **95**
Wolsey Ct. NW6 7A **64**
SW11 *1C* ***118***
(off Westbridge Rd.)
Wolsey Cres. CR0: New Ad 7E **170**
SM4: Mord 7G **153**
Wolsey Dr. KT2: King T 5E **132**
KT12: Walt T 7B **148**
Wolsey Gro. HA8: Edg 7E **28**
Wolsey M. BR6: Chels 5K **173**
NW5 6G **65**
Wolsey Rd. EN1: Enf 2C **24**
KT8: E Mos 4H **149**
N1 5D **66**
TW12: Ham H 6F **131**
TW15: Ashf 4A **128**
TW16: Sun 7H **129**
Wolsey St. E1 5J **85**
Wolsey Way KT9: Chess 5G **163**
Wolsternholme HA7: Stan 5G **27**
Wolstonbury N12 5D **30**
Wolvercote Rd. SE2 2D **108**
Wolverley St. E2 3H **85**
Wolverton SE17 5E **102**
(not continuous)
Wolverton Av. KT2: King T 1G **151**
Wolverton Gdns. W5 7F **79**
W6 4F **99**
Wolverton Rd. HA7: Stan 6G **27**
Wolverton Way N14 5B **22**
Wolves La. N13 7F **33**
N22 7F **33**
Womersley Rd. N8 6K **47**
Wonersh Way SM2: Cheam 7F **165**
Wonford Cl. KT2: King T 1A **152**
Wontner Cl. N1 7C **66**
Wontner Rd. SW17 2D **136**
Wooburn Cl. UB8: Hil 4D **74**
Woodall Av. EN3: Pond E 6E **24**
Woodall Cl. E14 7D **86**
KT9: Chess 7C **162**
Woodall Rd. EN3: Pond E 6E **24**
Woodbank Rd. BR1: Brom 3H **141**
Woodbastwick Rd. SE26 5K **139**
Woodberry Av. HA2: Harr 4F **41**
N21 2F **33**
Woodberry Cl. NW7 7A **30**
TW16: Sun 6J **129**
Woodberry Cres. N10 3F **47**
Woodberry Down N4 7C **48**
Woodberry Down Est. N4 1C **66**
(Spring Pk. Dr.)
N4 7C **48**
(Woodberry Gro.)
Woodberry Gdns. N12 6F **31**
Woodberry Gro. DA5: Bexl 3K **145**
N4 7C **48**
N12 6F **31**
Woodberry Way E4 7K **25**
N12 6F **31**
Woodbine Cl. TW2: Twick 2H **131**
Woodbine Gro. EN2: Enf 1J **23**
SE20 7H **139**
Woodbine La. KT4: Wor Pk 3D **164**
Woodbine Pl. E11 6J **51**
Woodbine Rd. DA15: Sidc 1J **143**
Woodbines Av. KT1: King T 3D **150**
Woodbine Ter. E9 6J **67**
Woodborough Rd. SW15 4D **116**
Woodbourne Av. SW16 3H **137**
Woodbourne Cl. SW16 3J **137**
Woodbourne Gdns. SM6: Wall 7F **167**
Woodbridge Cl. N7 2K **65**
NW2 3C **62**
Woodbridge Ct. IG8: Wfd G 7H **37**

Woodbridge Ho. E11 1H **69**
Woodbridge Rd. IG11: Bark 5K **71**
Woodbridge St. EC1 3A **8** (4B **84**)
(not continuous)
Woodbridge Ter. RM6: Chad H 6B **54**
Woodbrook Rd. SE2 6A **108**
Woodburn Cl. NW4 5F **45**
Woodbury Cl. CR0: C'don 2F **169**
E11 4K **51**
Woodbury Gdns. BR1: Brom 3K **141**
Woodbury Ho. SE26 3G **139**
Woodbury Pk. Rd. W13 4B **78**
Woodbury Rd. E17 4D **50**
Woodbury St. SW17 5C **136**
Woodchester Ho. *E14* *3D **104***
(off Selsdon Way)
Woodchester Sq. W2 5K **81**
Woodchurch Cl. DA14: Sidc 3H **143**
Woodchurch Dr. BR1: Brom 7B **142**
Woodchurch Rd. NW6 7J **63**
Wood Cl. E2 4G **85**
HA1: Harr 7H **41**
NW9 7K **43**
Woodclyffe Dr. BR7: Chst 2E **160**
Woodcock Ct. HA3: Kenton 7E **42**
Woodcock Dell Av. HA3: Kenton 7D **42**
Woodcock Hill HA3: Kenton 5C **42**
Woodcock Ho. *E14* *5C **86***
(off Burgess St.)
Woodcock Rd. TW6: H'row A 7C **174**
Woodcocks E16 5A **88**
Woodcombe Cres. SE23 1J **139**
Woodcote Av. CR7: Thor H 4B **156**
NW7 6K **29**
SM6: Wall 7F **167**
Woodcote Cl. EN3: Pond E 6D **24**
KT2: King T 5F **133**
Woodcote Dr. BR6: Orp 1H **173**
Woodcote Grn. SM6: Wall 7G **167**
Woodcote Ho. *SE8* *6B **104***
(off Prince St.)
Woodcote M. SM6: Wall 6F **167**
Woodcote Pl. SE27 5B **138**
Woodcote Rd. E11 7J **51**
SM6: Wall 6F **167**
Woodcote Vs. *SE27* *5C **138***
(off Woodcote Pl.)
Wood Crest *SM2: Sutt* *7A **166***
(off Christchurch Pk.)
Woodcroft N21 1F **33**
SE9 3D **142**
UB6: G'frd 6A **60**
Woodcroft Av. HA7: Stan 1A **42**
NW7 6F **29**
Woodcroft Cres. UB10: Hil 1D **74**
Woodcroft M. SE8 4A **104**
Woodcroft Rd. CR7: Thor H 5B **156**
Wood Dr. BR7: Chst 6C **142**
Woodedge Cl. E4 1C **36**
WOOD END
UB4 5H **75**
UB5 5G **59**
Wood End UB3: Hayes 6G **75**
Wood End, The SM6: Wall 7F **167**
Woodend SE19 6C **138**
SM1: Sutt 2A **166**
Wood End Av. HA2: Harr 4F **59**
Wood End Cl. UB5: N'olt 5H **59**
Wood End Gdns. UB5: N'olt 5G **59**
Woodend Gdns. EN2: Enf 4D **22**
WOOD END GREEN 5F **75**
Wood End Grn. Rd. UB3: Hayes 5F **75**
Wood End La. UB5: N'olt 6F **59**
(not continuous)
Wood End Rd. HA1: Harr 4H **59**
Woodend Rd. E17 2E **50**
Wood End Way UB5: N'olt 5G **59**
Wooder Gdns. E7 4J **69**
Wooderson Cl. SE25 4E **156**
Woodfall Av. EN5: Barn 5C **20**
Woodfall Rd. N4 2A **66**
Woodfall St. SW3 6E **16** (5D **100**)
Woodfarrs SE5 4D **120**
Wood Fld. NW3 5D **64**
Woodfield Av. HA0: Wemb 3C **60**
NW9 4A **44**
SM5: Cars 6E **166**
SW16 3H **137**
W5 4C **78**
Woodfield Cl. EN1: Enf 4K **23**
SE19 7C **138**
Woodfield Cres. W5 4C **78**
Woodfield Dr. EN4: E Barn 1K **31**
Woodfield Gdns. KT3: N Mald 5B **152**
Woodfield Gro. SW16 3H **137**
Woodfield Ho. *SE23* *3K **139***
(off Dacres Rd.)
Woodfield La. SW16 3H **137**
Woodfield Pl. W9 4H **81**
Woodfield Ri. WD23: Bush 1C **26**
Woodfield Rd. TW4: Cran 2K **111**
W5 4C **78**
W9 5H **81**
Woodfield Way N11 7C **32**
WOODFORD 6F **37**
Woodford Av. IG2: Ilf 5D **52**
IG4: Ilf, Wfd G 3B **52**
WOODFORD BRIDGE 6H **37**
Woodford Bri. Rd. IG4: Ilf 3B **52**
Woodford Ct. *W12* *2F **99***
(off Shepherd's Bush Grn.)
Woodford Cres. HA5: Pinn 2K **39**
Woodforde Ct. UB3: Harl 5F **93**
WOODFORD GREEN 6D **36**
Woodford Grn. IG8: Wfd G 7C **36**
Woodford Green Athletics Club 6H **37**
Woodford Hall Path E18 1H **51**
Woodford Ho. E18 4J **51**
Woodford New Rd. E17 4G **51**
E18 1G **51**
IG8: Wfd G 1G **51**
Woodford Pl. HA9: Wemb 1E **60**
Woodford Rd. E7 3K **69**
E18 4J **51**
WOODFORD SIDE 5C **36**
Woodford Trad. Est.
IG8: Wfd G 2B **52**
WOODFORD WELLS 3E **36**
Woodgate Av. KT9: Chess 5D **162**
Woodgate Dr. SW16 7H **137**
Woodger Rd. W12 2E **98**
Woodget Cl. E6 6C **88**
Woodgrange Av. EN1: Enf 6B **24**
HA3: Kenton 5C **42**
N12 6G **31**
W5 1G **97**
Woodgrange Cl. HA3: Kenton 5D **42**
Woodgrange Gdns. EN1: Enf 6B **24**
Woodgrange Ho. *W5* *1F **97***
(off Woodgrange Av.)
Woodgrange Mans. HA3: Kenton 5D **42**
Woodgrange Rd. E7 5K **69**
Woodgrange Ter. EN1: Enf 6B **24**
WOOD GREEN 2K **47**
Wood Grn. Hall *N22* *2K **47***
(off Station Rd.)
Wood Green Shop. City N22 2A **48**
Woodhall *NW1* *2A **6***
(off Robert St.)
Woodhall Av. HA5: Pinn 1C **40**
SE21 3F **139**
Woodhall Cl. UB8: Uxb 5A **56**
Woodhall Dr. HA5: Pinn 1B **40**
SE21 3F **139**
Woodhall Ga. HA5: Pinn 1B **40**
Woodhall Ho. SW18 6B **118**
Woodham Ct. E18 4H **51**
Woodham Rd. SE6 3E **140**
Woodhatch Cl. E6 5C **88**
Woodhaven Gdns. IG6: Ilf 4G **53**
Woodhayes Rd. SW19 7E **134**
Woodhead Dr. BR6: Orp 3J **173**
Woodheyes Rd. NW10 5K **61**
Woodhill SE18 4C **106**
Woodhill Cres. HA3: Kenton 6D **42**
Wood Ho. *NW6* *2H **81***
(off Albert Rd.)
Woodhouse Av. UB6: G'frd 2K **77**
Woodhouse Cl. SE22 4G **121**
UB3: Harl 3G **93**
UB6: G'frd 1K **77**
Woodhouse Gro. E12 6C **70**
Woodhouse Rd. E11 3H **69**
N12 6G **31**
Woodhurst Av.
BR5: Pet W 6G **161**
Woodhurst Rd. SE2 5A **108**
W3 7J **79**
Woodington Cl. SE9 6E **124**
Woodknoll Dr. BR7: Chst 1D **160**
Woodland App. UB6: G'frd 6A **60**
Woodland Av. E12 3C **70**
Woodland Cl. IG8: Wfd G 3E **36**
KT19: Ewe 6A **164**
NW9 6J **43**
SE19 6E **138**
UB10: Ick 2D **56**
Woodland Ct. *E11* *6J **51***
(off New Wanstead)
Woodland Cres. SE10 6G **105**
SE16 2K **103**
Woodland Gdns. N10 5F **47**
TW7: Isle 3J **113**
Woodland Gro. SE10 5G **105**
Woodland Hill SE19 6E **138**
Woodland M. SW16 3J **137**
Woodland Ri. N10 4F **47**
UB6: G'frd 6A **60**
Woodland Rd. CR7: Thor H 4A **156**
E4 1K **35**
N11 5A **32**
SE19 5E **138**
WOODLANDS 3J **113**
Woodlands BR2: Brom 4H **159**
DA6: Bex 5H **127**
HA2: Harr 4E **40**
NW11 5G **45**
SW20 4E **152**
Woodlands, The HA1: Harr 2J **59**
HA7: Stan 5G **27**
N5 4C **66**
N12 6F **31**
N14 1A **32**
SE13 7F **123**
SE19 7C **138**
SM6: Wall 7F **167**
TW7: Isle 2K **113**
Woodlands Av. DA15: Sidc 1J **143**
E11 1K **69**
HA4: Ruis 7A **40**
KT3: N Mald 1J **151**
KT4: Wor Pk 2B **164**
N3 7F **31**
RM6: Chad H 6E **54**
W3 1H **97**
Woodlands Cl. BR1: Brom 2D **160**
KT10: Clay 7A **162**
NW11 5G **45**
Woodlands Ct. BR1: Brom 1H **159**
HA1: Harr 5K **41**
NW10 *1F **81***
(off Wrentham Av.)
SE23 7H **121**
Woodlands Dr. HA7: Stan 6E **26**
TW16: Sun 2A **148**
Woodlands Gdns. E17 4G **51**
Woodlands Ga. *SW15* *5H **117***
(off Woodlands Way)
Woodlands Gro. TW7: Isle 2J **113**
Woodlands Hgts. *SE3* *6H **105***
(off Vanburgh Hill)
Woodlands Pde. TW15: Ashf 6E **128**
Woodlands Pk. DA5: Bexl 4K **145**
Woodlands Pk. Rd. N15 5B **48**
SE10 6G **105**
(not continuous)
Woodlands Rd. BR1: Brom 2C **160**
BR6: Chels 6K **173**
DA7: Bex 3E **126**
E11 2G **69**
E17 3E **50**
EN2: Enf 1J **23**
HA1: Harr 5K **41**
IG1: Ilf 3G **71**
KT6: Surb 7D **150**
N9 1D **34**
SW13 3B **116**
TW7: Isle 3H **113**
UB1: S'hall 1B **94**
Woodlands St. SE13 7F **123**
Woodland St. E8 6F **67**
Woodlands Way SW15 5H **117**
Woodland Ter. SE7 4C **106**
Woodland Wlk. BR1: Brom 4F **141**
(not continuous)
KT19: Ewe 6G **163**
NW3 5C **64**
SE10 5G **105**
Woodland Way BR4: W W'ck 4D **170**
BR5: Pet W 4G **161**
CR0: C'don 1A **170**
CR4: Mitc 7E **136**
IG8: Wfd G 3E **36**
KT5: Surb 2H **163**
N21 2F **33**
NW7 6G **29**
SE2 4D **108**
SM4: Mord 4H **153**
Wood La. HA4: Ruis 1F **57**
HA7: Stan 3F **27**
IG8: Wfd G 4C **36**
N6 6F **47**
NW9 7K **43**
RM8: Dag 4C **72**
RM9: Dag 4C **72**
RM10: Dag 2G **73**
TW7: Isle 6J **95**
W12 6E **80**
Wood Lane Sports Cen. 1H **73**
Woodlawn Cl. SW15 5H **117**
Woodlawn Cres. TW2: Whitt 2F **131**
Woodlawn Dr. TW13: Felt 2B **130**
Woodlawn Rd. SW6 7F **99**
Woodlawns KT19: Ewe 7K **163**
Woodlea Dr. BR2: Brom 5G **159**
Woodlea Rd. N16 3E **66**
Woodleigh E18 1J **51**
Woodleigh Av. N12 6H **31**
Woodleigh Gdns. SW16 3J **137**
Woodley Cl. SW17 7D **136**
Woodley La. SM5: Cars 3C **166**
Wood Lodge Gdns. BR1: Brom 7C **142**
Wood Lodge La. BR4: W W'ck 3E **170**
Woodman M. TW9: Kew 1H **115**
Woodman Pde. *E16* *1E **106***
(off Woodman St.)
Woodmans Gro. NW10 5B **62**
Woodman's M. W12 5D **80**
Woodmansterne Rd. SM5: Cars 7C **166**
SW16 7G **137**
Woodman St. E16 1E **106**
Wood Martyn Ct. *BR6: Orp* *2K **173***
(off Orchard Gro.)
Wood Mead N17 6B **34**
Woodmere SE9 1D **142**
Woodmere Av. CR0: C'don 7J **157**
Woodmere Cl. CR0: C'don 7K **157**
SW11 3E **118**
Woodmere Ct. N14 7A **22**
Woodmere Gdns. CR0: C'don 7K **157**
Woodmere Way BR3: Beck 5F **159**
Woodmill Rd. E5 2J **67**
Woodnook Rd. SW16 5F **137**
Woodpecker Cl. HA3: Hrw W 1K **41**
N9 6C **24**
WD23: Bush 1B **26**
Woodpecker M. *SE13* *4F **123***
(off Freshfield Cl.)

Woodpecker Mt. CR0: Sels 7A 170
Woodpecker Rd. SE14 . . . . 6A 104
  SE28 . . . . 7C 90
Wood Point E16 . . . . 5J 87
  (off Fife Rd.)
Woodquest Av. SE24 . . . . 5C 120
Wood Retreat SE18 . . . . 7H 107
Wood Ride BR5: Pet W 4H 161
  EN4: Had W 1G 21
Woodridge Cl. EN2: Enf 1F 23
Woodridings Av. HA5: Hat E 1D 40
Woodridings Cl. HA5: Hat E 1C 40
Woodridings Ct. N22 . . . . 1H 47
Woodriffe Rd. E11 . . . . 7F 51
Wood Ri. HA5: Eastc 5J 39
Wood Rd. NW10 . . . . 7J 61
  TW17: Shep 4C 146
Woodrow SE18 . . . . 4D 106
Woodrow Av. UB4: Hayes 5H 75
Woodrow Cl. UB6: G'frd 7B 60
Woodrow Ct. N17 . . . . 7C 34
Woodrush Cl. SE14 . . . . 7A 104
Woodrush Way RM6: Chad H 4D 54
Woods, The UB10: Ick 4D 56
Wood's Bldgs. E1 . . . . 5H 85
  (off Winthrop St.)
Woodseer St. E1 . . . . 5K 9 (5F 85)
Woodsford SE17 . . . . 5D 102
  (off Portland St.)
Woodsford Sq. W14 . . . . 2G 99
Woodshire Rd. RM10: Dag 3H 73
Woods Ho. SW1 . . . . 6J 17
  SW1 . . . . 5F 101
  SW8 . . . . 1G 119
  (off Wadhurst Rd.)
WOODSIDE 6G 157
Wood Side NW11 . . . . 5J 45
Woodside IG9: Buck H 2F 37
  N10 . . . . 3E 46
  SW19 . . . . 6H 135
Woodside Av. BR7: Chst 5G 143
  HA0: Wemb 1E 78
  KT10: Esh 7J 149
  N6 . . . . 5D 46
  N10 . . . . 5D 46
  N12 . . . . 4E 30
  SE25 . . . . 6H 157
Woodside Cl. DA7: Bex 4K 127
  HA0: Wemb 1E 78
  HA4: Ruis 6F 39
  HA7: Stan 5G 27
  KT5: Surb 7J 151
Woodside Ct. E12 . . . . 1A 70
  N12 . . . . 4E 30
  RM7: Mawney 4G 55
  W5 . . . . 1E 96
Woodside Ct. Rd. CR0: C'don 7G 157
Woodside Cres. DA15: Sidc 3J 143
Woodside Dr. DA2: Dart 4K 145
Woodside End HA0: Wemb 1E 78
Woodside Gdns. E4 . . . . 6J 35
  N17 . . . . 2E 48
Woodside Grange Rd. N12 . . . . 4E 30
Woodside Grn. SE25 . . . . 6G 157
  (not continuous)
Woodside Gro. N12 . . . . 3F 31
Woodside Ho. SW19 . . . . 6H 135
Woodside La. DA5: Bexl 6D 126
  N12 . . . . 3F 31
Woodside M. SE22 . . . . 5F 121
Woodside Pde. DA15: Sidc 3J 143
WOODSIDE PARK 4D 30
Woodside Pk. SE25 . . . . 6H 157
Woodside Pk. Av. E17 . . . . 4F 51
Woodside Pk. Rd. N12 . . . . 4E 30
Woodside Pl. HA0: Wemb 1E 78
Woodside Rd. BR1: Brom 5C 160
  DA7: Bex 4K 127
  DA15: Sidc 3J 143
  E13 . . . . 4A 88
  IG8: Wfd G 4D 36
  KT2: King T 7E 132

Woodside Rd. KT3: N Mald 2K 151
  N22 . . . . 7E 32
  SE25 . . . . 6H 157
  SM1: Sutt 3A 166
Woodside Way CR0: C'don 6J 157
  CR4: Mitc 1F 155
Woods M. W1 . . . . 2G 11 (7E 82)
Woodsome Rd. NW5 . . . . 3E 64
Woods Pl. SE1 . . . . 3E 102
Woodspring Rd. SW19 . . . . 2G 135
Woods Rd. SE15 . . . . 1H 121
Woodstar Ho. SE15 . . . . 7G 103
  (off Reddins Rd.)
Woodstead Gro. HA8: Edg 6K 27
WOODSTOCK, THE 7H 153
Woodstock Av. NW11 . . . . 7G 45
  SM3: Sutt 7H 153
  TW7: Isle 5A 114
  UB1: S'hall 3D 76
  W13 . . . . 3A 96
Woodstock Cl. DA5: Bexl 7F 127
  HA7: Stan 2E 42
Woodstock Ct. SE11 . . . . . . 5H 19 (5K 101)
  SE12 . . . . 6J 123
Woodstock Cres. N9 . . . . 6C 24
Woodstock Dr. UB10: Ick 4A 56
Woodstock Gdns. BR3: Beck 1D 158
  IG3: Ilf 2A 72
  UB4: Hayes 5H 75
Woodstock Grange W5 . . . . 1E 96
Woodstock Gro. W12 . . . . 2F 99
Woodstock La. KT9: Chess 4B 162
Woodstock La. Nth. KT6: Surb 2C 162
Woodstock La. Sth. KT9: Chess . . . 5B 162
  KT10: Clay 5B 162
Woodstock M. W1 . . . . 6H 5
Woodstock Ri. SM3: Sutt 7H 153
Woodstock Rd. CR0: C'don 3D 168
  E7 . . . . 7A 70
  E17 . . . . 2F 51
  HA0: Wemb 1F 79
  N4 . . . . 1A 66
  NW11 . . . . 7H 45
  SM5: Cars 5E 166
  W4 . . . . 4A 98
Woodstock St. W1 . . . . 1J 11 (6F 83)
Woodstock Studios W12 . . . . 2F 99
  (off Woodstock Gro.)
Woodstock Ter. E14 . . . . 7D 86
Woodstock Way CR4: Mitc 2F 155
Woodstone Av. KT17: Ewe 5C 164
WOOD STREET 3E 50
Wood St. CR4: Mitc 7E 154
  E17 . . . . 3E 50
  EC2 . . . . 7D 8 (6C 84)
  (not continuous)
  EN5: Barn 4A 20
  KT1: King T 2D 150
  W4 . . . . 5A 98
Woodsyre SE26 . . . . 4F 139
Wood Ter. NW2 . . . . 3D 62
Woodthorpe Rd. SW15 . . . . 4D 116
  TW15: Ashf 5A 128
Woodtree Cl. NW4 . . . . 2F 45
Wood Va. N10 . . . . 5G 47
  SE23 . . . . 1H 139
Woodvale Av. SE25 . . . . 3F 157
Woodvale Ct. BR1: Brom 1K 159
  (off Widmore Rd.)
Wood Va. Est. SE23 . . . . 7J 121
Woodvale Wlk. SE27 . . . . 5C 138
Woodvale Way NW11 . . . . 3F 63
Woodview Av. E4 . . . . 4K 35
Woodview Cl. BR6: Farnb 2G 173
  N4 . . . . 7B 48
  SW15 . . . . 4K 133
Woodville SE3 . . . . 7K 105
Woodville, The W5 . . . . 6D 78
  (off Woodville Rd.)
Woodville Cl. SE12 . . . . 5J 123
  TW11: Tedd 4A 132

Woodville Ct. N14 . . . . 5B 22
  SE10 . . . . 1E 122
  (off Blissett St.)
  SE19 . . . . 1F 157
Woodville Gdns. HA4: Ruis 7E 38
  IG6: Ilf 3F 53
  KT6: Surb 7D 150
  NW11 . . . . 7F 45
  W5 . . . . 6E 78
Woodville Gro. DA16: Well 3A 126
Woodville Ho. SE1 . . . . 3F 103
  (off St Saviour's Est.)
Woodville Rd. CR7: Thor H 4C 156
  E11 . . . . 1H 69
  E17 . . . . 4B 50
  E18 . . . . 2K 51
  EN5: New Bar 3E 20
  N16 . . . . 5E 66
  NW6 . . . . 2H 81
  NW11 . . . . 7F 45
  SM4: Mord 4J 153
  TW10: Ham 3B 132
  W5 . . . . 6D 78
Woodville St. SE18 . . . . 4C 106
Woodward Av. NW4 . . . . 5C 44
Woodward Cl. KT10: Clay 6A 162
Woodwarde Rd. SE22 . . . . 6E 120
Woodward Gdns. HA7: Stan 7E 26
  RM9: Dag 7C 72
Woodward Rd. RM9: Dag 7B 72
Woodward's Footpath TW2: Whitt . . 6G 113
Wood Way BR6: Farnb 2E 172
Woodway Cres. HA1: Harr 6A 42
Woodwell St. SW18 . . . . 5A 118
Wood Wharf SE10 . . . . 6D 104
Wood Wharf Bus. Pk. E14 . . . . 1D 104
  (not continuous)
Woodyard Cl. NW5 . . . . 5E 64
Woodyard La. SE21 . . . . 7E 120
Woodyates Rd. SE12 . . . . 6J 123
Woody Bay Station
  Ruislip Lido Railway 5F 39
Woolacombe Rd. SE3 . . . . 1A 124
Woolacombe Way UB3: Harl 4G 93
Woolcombes Ct. SE16 . . . . 1K 103
  (off Princes Riverside Rd.)
Wooldridge Cl. TW14: Bedf 1E 128
Wooler St. SE17 . . . . 5D 102
Woolf Cl. SE28 . . . . 1B 108
Woolf Ct. W3 . . . . 3J 97
  (off Vincent Rd.)
Woolf M. WC1 . . . . 3D 6
  (off Burton Pl.)
Woolford Cl. SE5 . . . . 2C 120
  (off Coldharbour La.)
Woolgar M. N16 . . . . 5E 66
  (off Gillett St.)
Woollaston Rd. N4 . . . . 6B 48
Woolley Ho. SW9 . . . . 3B 120
  (off Loughborough Rd.)
Woollon Ho. E1 . . . . 6J 85
  (off Clark St.)
Woolmead Av. NW9 . . . . 7C 44
Woolmer Gdns. N18 . . . . 6B 34
Woolmer Rd. N18 . . . . 5B 34
Woolmore St. E14 . . . . 7E 86
Woolneigh St. SW6 . . . . 3K 117
Woolridge Way E9 . . . . 7J 67
Wool Rd. SW20 . . . . 6D 134
Woolstaplers Way SE16 . . . . 3G 103
Woolston Cl. E17 . . . . 2K 49
Woolstone Ho. E2 . . . . 1G 85
  (off Whiston Rd.)
Woolstone Rd. SE23 . . . . 2A 140
WOOLWICH 3E 106
Woolwich Chu. St. SE18 . . . . 3C 106
Woolwich Comn. SE18 . . . . 6E 106
Woolwich Dockyard Ind. Est.
  SE18 . . . . 3C 106
Woolwich High St. SE18 . . . . 3E 106
Woolwich Ho. UB3: Harl 3E 92
  (off Nine Acres Cl.)

Woolwich Mnr. Way E6 . . . . 4D 88
  E16 . . . . 2F 107
Woolwich New Rd. SE18 . . . . 5E 106
Woolwich Rd. DA6: Bex 4G 127
  (not continuous)
  DA7: Bex 3G 127
  DA17: Belv 5F 109
  SE2 . . . . 6D 108
  SE7 . . . . 5H 105
  SE10 . . . . 5H 105
Woolwich Trad. Pk. SE28 . . . . 3H 107
Wooster Gdns. E14 . . . . 6F 87
Wooster M. HA2: Harr 3G 41
Wooster Pl. SE1 . . . . 4D 102
  (off Searles Rd.)
Wootton Gro. N3 . . . . 1J 45
Wootton St. SE1 . . . . 5K 13 (1A 102)
Worbeck Rd. SE20 . . . . 2H 157
Worcester Av. N17 . . . . 7B 34
Worcester Cl. CR0: C'don 2C 170
  CR4: Mitc 2E 154
  NW2 . . . . 3D 62
Worcester Ct. HA1: Harr 3J 41
  KT4: Wor Pk 3A 164
  N12 . . . . 5E 30
  W7 . . . . 6K 77
  (off Copley Cl.)
  W9 . . . . 5J 81
  (off Elmfield Way)
Worcester Cres. IG8: Wfd G 5E 36
  NW7 . . . . 3F 29
Worcester Dr. TW15: Ashf 5D 128
  W4 . . . . 2A 98
Worcester Gdns. IG1: Ilf 7C 52
  KT4: Wor Pk 3A 164
  SW11 . . . . 5D 118
  (off Grandison Rd.)
  UB6: G'frd 6H 59
Worcester Ho. SE11 . . . . 2J 19
  (off Kennington Rd.)
  SW9 . . . . 7A 102
  (off Cranmer Rd.)
  W2 . . . . 6A 82
  (off Hallfield Est.)
Worcester M. NW6 . . . . 6K 63
WORCESTER PARK 1C 164
Worcester Pk. Rd. KT4: Wor Pk . . . 3K 163
Worcester Rd. E12 . . . . 4D 70
  E17 . . . . 2K 49
  SM2: Sutt 7J 165
  SW19 . . . . 5H 135
Worcesters Av. EN1: Enf 1B 24
Wordsworth Av. E12 . . . . 7C 70
  E18 . . . . 3H 51
  UB6: G'frd 3H 77
Wordsworth Ct. HA1: Harr 7J 41
Wordsworth Dr. SM3: Cheam 4E 164
Wordsworth Ho. NW6 . . . . 3J 81
  (off Stafford Rd.)
  SE18 . . . . 6E 106
  (off Woolwich Comn.)
Wordsworth Mans. W14 . . . . 6H 99
  (off Queens Club Gdns.)
Wordsworth Pde. N8 . . . . 4B 48
Wordsworth Pl. NW5 . . . . 5D 64
Wordsworth Rd. DA16: Well 1J 125
  N16 . . . . 4E 66
  SE1 . . . . 4F 103
  SE20 . . . . 7K 139
  SM6: Wall 6G 167
  TW12: Hamp 4D 130
Wordsworth Wlk. NW11 . . . . 4J 45
Wordsworth Way UB7: W Dray 4A 92
Worfield St. SW11 . . . . 7C 100
Worgan St. SE11 . . . . 5G 19 (5K 101)
  SE16 . . . . 4K 103
Worland Rd. E15 . . . . 7G 69
World Bus. Cen. TW6: H'row A 1E 110
World of Golf at Sidcup 3G 143
World of Golf Driving Range
  New Malden 3C 152
World Rugby Mus. 6J 113

WORLD'S END 3E 22
Worlds End Est. SW10 . . . . .7B 100
Worlds End La. BR6: Chels 6K 173
  EN2: Enf 5E 22
  N21 . . . . .5E 22
World's End Pas. SW10 . . . . .7B 100
  (off Worlds End Est.)
World's End Pl. SW10 . . . . .7B 100
  (off Worlds End Est.)
Worleys Dr. BR6: Orp 4H 173
Worlidge St. W6 . . . . .5E 98
Worlingham Rd. SE22 . . . . .4F 121
Wormholt Rd. W12 . . . . .7C 80
Wormwood Scrubs Pk. &
  Local Nature Reserve 5B 80
Wormwood St. EC2 . . . . . . .7G 9 (6E 84)
Wornington Rd. W10 . . . . .4G 81
  (not continuous)
Woronzow Rd. NW8 . . . . .1B 82
Worple Av. SW19 . . . . .7F 135
  TW7: Isle 5A 114
Worple Cl. HA2: Harr 1D 58
Worple Rd. SW19 . . . . .2E 152
  SW20 .2E 152
  TW7: Isle 4A 114
Worple Rd. M. SW19 . . . . .6H 135
Worple St. SW14 . . . . .3K 115
Worple Way HA2: Harr 1D 58
  TW10: Rich 5E 114
Worship St. EC2 . . . . . . .4F 9 (4D 84)
Worslade Rd. SW17 . . . . .4B 136
Worsley Bri. Rd. BR3: Beck 7C 140
  SE26 . . . . .4B 140
Worsley Grange BR7: Chst 6G 143
Worsley Gro. E5 . . . . .4G 67
Worsley Ho. SE23 . . . . .2J 139
Worsley Rd. E11 . . . . .4G 69
Worsopp Dr. SW4 . . . . .5G 119
Worth Cl. BR6: Orp 4J 173
Worthfield Cl. KT19: Ewe 7K 163
Worth Gro. SE17 . . . . .5C 102
Worthing Cl. E15 . . . . .1G 87
Worthing Rd. TW5: Hest 6D 94
Worthington Cl. CR4: Mitc 4F 155
Worthington Ho. EC1 . . . . .1K 7
  (off Myddelton Pas.)
Worthington Rd. KT6: Surb 1F 163
Wortley Rd. CR0: C'don 7A 156
  E6 . . . . .7B 70
Worton Ct. TW7: Isle 4J 113
Worton Gdns. TW7: Isle 2H 113
Worton Hall Ind. Est.
  TW7: Isle 4J 113
Worton Rd. TW7: Isle 4H 113
Worton Way TW3: Houn 2H 113
  TW7: Houn, Isle 2H 113
Wotton Ct. E14 . . . . .7F 87
  (off Jamestown Way)
Wotton Rd. NW2 . . . . .3E 62
  SE8 . . . . .6B 104
Wouldham Rd. E16 . . . . .6H 87
Wragby Rd. E11 . . . . .3G 69
Wrampling Pl. N9 . . . . .1B 34
Wrangthorn Wlk. CR0: Wadd 4A 168
Wray Av. IG5: Ilf 3E 52
Wrayburn Ho. SE16 . . . . .2G 103
  (off Llewellyn St.)
Wray Cres. N4 . . . . .2J 65
Wrayfield Rd. SM3: Cheam 3F 165
Wray Rd. SM2: Cheam 7H 165
Wraysbury Cl. TW4: Houn 5C 112
Wrays Way HA5: Hayes 4G 75
Wrekin Rd. SE18 . . . . .7G 107
Wren Av. NW2 . . . . .4E 62
  UB2: S'hall 4D 94
Wren Cl. E16 . . . . .6H 87
  N9 . . . . .1E 34
  TW6: H'row A 6C 174
Wren Ct. CR0: C'don 4D 168
  (off Coombe Rd.)
Wren Cres. WD23: Bush 1B 26
Wren Gdns. RM9: Dag 5D 72

Wren Ho. E3 . . . . .2A 86
  (off Gernon Rd.)
  KT1: Ham W 2D 150
  (off High St.)
  SW1 . . . . .6C 18
  (off Aylesford St.)
Wren Landing E14 . . . . .1C 104
Wrenn Ho. SW13 . . . . .6E 98
Wren Path SE28 . . . . .3H 107
Wren Rd. DA14: Sidc 4C 144
  RM9: Dag 5D 72
  SE5 . . . . .1D 120
Wren's Av. TW15: Ashf 4E 128
Wren's Pk. Ho. E5 . . . . .2H 67
Wren St. WC1 . . . . .3H 7 (4K 83)
Wrentham Av. NW10 . . . . .2F 81
Wrenthorpe Rd. BR1: Brom 4G 141
Wren Vw. N6 . . . . .7G 47
Wrenwood Way HA5: Eastc 4K 39
Wrestlers Cl. EC3 . . . . .7G 9
Wrexham Rd. E3 . . . . .2C 86
Wricklemarsh Rd. SE3 . . . . .2K 123
  (not continuous)
Wrigglesworth St. SE14 . . . . .7K 103
Wright Cl. SE13 . . . . .4F 123
Wright Gdns. TW17: Shep 5C 146
Wright Rd. N1 . . . . .6E 66
  TW5: Hest 7A 94
Wrights All. SW19 . . . . .6E 134
Wrights Cl. RM10: Dag 4H 73
Wrights Grn. SW4 . . . . .4H 119
Wright's La. W8 . . . . .3K 99
Wrights Pl. NW10 . . . . .6J 61
Wrights Rd. E3 . . . . .2B 86
  (not continuous)
  SE25 . . . . .3E 156
Wrights Row SM6: Wall 4F 167
Wrights Wlk. SW14 . . . . .3K 115
Wright Way TW6: H'row A 5C 174
Wrigley Cl. E4 . . . . .5A 36
Writtle Ho. NW9 . . . . .2B 44
Wrotham Ho. BR3: Beck 7B 140
  (off Sellindge Cl.)
  SE1 . . . . .3D 102
  (off Law St.)
Wrotham Rd. DA16: Well 1C 126
  EN5: Barn 2B 20
  NW1 . . . . .7G 65
  W13 . . . . .1C 96
Wrottesley Rd. NW10 . . . . .2C 80
  SE18 . . . . .6G 107
Wroughton Rd. SW11 . . . . .5D 118
Wroughton Ter. NW4 . . . . .4D 44
Wroxall Rd. RM9: Dag 6C 72
Wroxham Gdns. N11 . . . . .7C 32
Wroxham Rd. SE28 . . . . .7D 90
Wroxham Way IG6: Ilf 1F 53
Wroxton Rd. SE15 . . . . .2J 121
WRYTHE, THE 3D 166
Wrythe Grn. SM5: Cars 3D 166
Wrythe Grn. Rd.
  SM5: Cars 3D 166
Wrythe La. SM5: Cars 1A 166
Wulfstan St. W12 . . . . .5B 80
Wyatt Cl. SE16 . . . . .2B 104
  TW13: Felt 1B 130
  UB4: Hayes 5J 75
  WD23: Bush 1C 26
Wyatt Ct. HA0: Wemb 7E 60
Wyatt Dr. SW13 . . . . .6D 98
Wyatt Ho. NW8 . . . . .4B 4
  (off Frampton St.)
  SE3 . . . . .2H 123
  TW1: Twick 6D 114
Wyatt Pk. Rd. SW2 . . . . .2J 137
Wyatt Point SE28 . . . . .2G 107
Wyatt Rd. E7 . . . . .6J 69
  N5 . . . . .3C 66
Wyatts La. E17 . . . . .3E 50
Wybert St. NW1 . . . . .3A 6 (4G 83)
Wyborne Ho. NW10 . . . . .7J 61
Wyborne Way NW10 . . . . .7J 61

Wyburn Av. EN5: Barn 3C 20
Wychcombe Studios NW3 . . . . .6D 64
Wyche Gro. CR2: S Croy 7D 168
Wych Elm Cl. KT2: King T 7F 133
Wych Elm Lodge BR1: Brom 7H 141
Wych Elm Pas. KT2: King T 7F 133
Wycherley Cl. SE3 . . . . .7H 105
Wycherley Cres. EN5: New Bar 6E 20
Wychwood Av. CR7: Thor H 3C 156
  HA8: Edg 6J 27
Wychwood Cl. HA8: Edg 6J 27
  TW16: Sun 6J 129
Wychwood End N6 . . . . .7G 47
Wychwood Gdns. IG5: Ilf 4D 52
Wychwood Way SE19 . . . . .6D 138
Wyclif Cl. EC1 . . . . .2A 8
  (off Wyclif St.)
Wycliffe Cl. DA16: Well 1K 125
Wycliffe Rd. SW11 . . . . .2E 118
  SW19 .6K 135
Wyclif St. EC1 . . . . .2A 8 (3B 84)
Wycombe Gdns. NW11 . . . . .2J 63
Wycombe Ho. NW8 . . . . .3C 4
  (off Grendon St.)
Wycombe Pl. SW18 . . . . .6A 118
Wycombe Rd. HA0: Wemb 1G 79
  IG2: Ilf 5D 52
  N17 . . . . .1G 49
Wycombe Sq. W8 . . . . .1H 99
Wydehurst Rd. CR0: C'don 7G 157
Wydell Cl. SM4: Mord 6F 153
Wydeville Mnr. Rd. SE12 . . . . .4K 141
Wye Cl. BR6: Orp 7K 161
  HA4: Ruis 6E 38
  TW15: Ashf 4D 128
Wye Ct. W13 . . . . .5B 78
  (off Malvern Way)
Wyemead Cres. E4 . . . . .2B 36
Wye St. SW11 . . . . .2B 118
Wyevale Cl. HA5: Eastc 3J 39
Wyfields IG5: Ilf 1F 53
Wyfold Ho. SE2 . . . . .2D 108
  (off Wolvercote Rd.)
Wyfold Rd. SW6 . . . . .7G 99
Wyhill Wlk. RM10: Dag 6J 73
Wyke Cl. TW7: Isle 6K 95
Wyke Gdns. W7 . . . . .3A 96
Wykeham Av. RM9: Dag 6C 72
Wykeham Cl. UB7: Sip 6C 92
Wykeham Ct. NW4 . . . . .5E 44
  (off Wykeham Rd.)
Wykeham Grn. RM9: Dag 6C 72
Wykeham Hill HA9: Wemb 1F 61
Wykeham Ho. SE1 . . . . .5C 14
  (off Union St.)
Wykeham Ri. N20 . . . . .1B 30
Wykeham Rd. HA3: Kenton 4B 42
  NW4 . . . . .4E 44
Wyke Rd. E3 . . . . .7C 68
  SW20 .2E 152
Wylchin Cl. HA5: Eastc 3H 39
Wyldes Cl. NW11 . . . . .1A 64
Wyldfield Gdns. N9 . . . . .2A 34
Wyld Way HA9: Wemb 6H 61
Wyleu St. SE23 . . . . .7A 122
Wylie Rd. UB2: S'hall 3E 94
Wyllen Cl. E1 . . . . .4J 85
Wymans Way E7 . . . . .4A 70
Wymering Mans. W9 . . . . .3J 81
  (off Wymering Rd.)
Wymering Rd. W9 . . . . .3J 81
Wymondham Ct. NW8 . . . . .1B 82
  (off Queensmead)
Wymond St. SW15 . . . . .3E 116
Wynan Rd. E14 . . . . .5D 104
Wynash Gdns. SM5: Cars 5C 166
Wynaud Ct. N22 . . . . .6E 32
Wyncham Av. DA15: Sidc 1J 143
Wyncham Ho. DA15: Sidc 2A 144
  (off Longlands Rd.)
Wynchgate HA3: Hrw W 7D 26
  N14 . . . . .1C 32

Wynchgate N21 . . . . .1C 32
  UB5: N'olt 5C 58
Wyncroft Cl. BR1: Brom 3D 160
Wyndale Av. NW9 . . . . .6G 43
Wyndcliff Rd. SE7 . . . . .6K 105
Wyndcroft Cl. EN2: Enf 3G 23
Wyndham Cl. BR6: Farnb 1G 173
  SM2: Sutt 7J 165
Wyndham Ct. W7 . . . . .4A 96
Wyndham Cres. N19 . . . . .3G 65
  TW4: Houn 6E 112
Wyndham Deedes Ho. E2 . . . . .2G 85
  (off Hackney Rd.)
Wyndham Est. SE5 . . . . .7C 102
Wyndham Ho. E14 . . . . .2D 104
  (off Marsh Wall)
  SW1 . . . . .4G 17
  (off Sloane Sq.)
Wyndham M. W1 . . . . .6E 4 (5D 82)
Wyndham Pl. W1 . . . . .6E 4 (5D 82)
Wyndham Rd. E6 . . . . .7B 70
  EN4: E Barn 1J 31
  KT2: King T 7F 133
  (not continuous)
  SE5 . . . . .7C 102
  W13 . . . . .3B 96
Wyndhams Ct. E8 . . . . .7F 67
  (off Celandine Dr.)
Wyndham's Theatre 2E 12
  (off Charing Cross Rd.)
Wyndham St. W1 . . . . .5E 4 (5D 82)
Wyndham Yd. W1 . . . . .6E 4 (5D 82)
Wyndhurst Cl. CR2: S Croy 7B 168
Wyneham Rd. SE24 . . . . .5D 120
Wynell Rd. SE23 . . . . .3K 139
Wynford Pl. DA17: Belv 6G 109
Wynford Rd. N1 . . . . .2K 83
Wynford Way SE9 . . . . .3D 142
Wynlie Gdns. HA5: Pinn 2K 39
Wynn Bri. Cl. IG8: Wfd G 1B 52
Wynndale Rd. E18 . . . . .1K 51
Wynne Rd. SW9 . . . . .2A 120
Wynn's Av. DA15: Sidc 5K 125
Wynnstay Gdns. W8 . . . . .3J 99
Wynter St. SW11 . . . . .4A 118
Wynton Gdns. SE25 . . . . .5F 157
Wynton Pl. W3 . . . . .6H 79
Wynyard Ho. SE11 . . . . .5H 19
Wynyard Ter. SE11 . . . . . . .5H 19 (5K 101)
Wynyatt St. EC1 . . . . .2A 8 (3B 84)
Wyre Gro. HA8: Edg 3C 28
  UB3: Harl 4J 93
Wyresdale Cres. UB6: G'frd 3K 77
Wyteleaf Cl. HA4: Ruis 6E 38
Wytham Ho. NW8 . . . . .4B 4
  (off Church St. Est.)
Wythburn Ct. W1 . . . . .7E 4
  (off Wythburn Pl.)
Wythburn Pl. W1 . . . . .1E 10 (6D 82)
Wythenshawe Rd. RM10: Dag 3G 73
Wythens Wlk. SE9 . . . . .6F 125
Wythes Cl. BR1: Brom 2D 160
Wythes Rd. E16 . . . . .1C 106
Wythfield Rd. SE9 . . . . .6D 124
Wyvenhoe Rd. HA2: Harr 4G 59
Wyvern Est. KT3: N Mald 4C 152
Wyvil Rd. SW8 . . . . .7J 101
Wyvis St. E14 . . . . .5D 86

X

Xylon Ho. KT4: Wor Pk 2D 164

Y

Yabsley St. E14 . . . . .1E 104
Yaldham Ho. SE1 . . . . .4G 17
  (off Massinger St.)
Yalding Rd. SE16 . . . . .3G 103
Yale Cl. TW4: Houn 5D 112

Yale Ct. NW6 .5K 63
Yarborough Rd. W19 . . . . .1B 154
Yard, The N1 . . . . .1F 7
(off Caledonian Rd.)
Yardley Cl. E4 .5J 25
Yardley Ct. SM3: Cheam 4E 164
Yardley La. E4 .5J 25
Yardley St. WC1 . . . . .2J 7 (3A 84)
(not continuous)
Yarlington Ct. N11 . . . . .5K 31
(off Sparkford Gdns.)
Yarmouth Cres. N17 . . . . .5H 49
Yarmouth Pl. W1 . . . . .5J 11 (1F 101)
Yarnfield Sq. SE15 . . . . .1G 121
Yarnton Way DA18: Belv, Erith 3F 109
SE2: Erith, Lon 2C 108
Yarrell Mans. W14 . . . . .6H 99
(off Queen's Club Mans.)
Yarrow Cres. E6 . . . . .5C 88
Yarrow Ho. E14 . . . . .3E 104
(off Stewart St.)
W10 . . . . .5E 80
(off Sutton Way)
Yateley St. SE18 . . . . .3B 106
Yates Ct. NW2 . . . . .6F 63
(off Willesden La.)
Yates Ho. E2 . . . . .3G 85
(off Roberta St.)
Yatton Ho. W10 . . . . .5E 80
(off Sutton Way)

YEADING 4A 76
Yeading Av. HA2: Harr 2C 58
Yeading Brook Meadows Nature Reserve
. . . . .4J 75
Yeading Ct. UB4: Yead 4A 76
Yeading Fork UB4: Yead 5A 76
Yeading Gdns. UB4: Yead 5K 75
Yeading Ho. UB4: Yead 5B 76
Yeading La. UB4: Yead 6K 75
UB5: N'olt 6K 75
Yeading Wlk. HA2: Harr 5D 40
Yeadon Ho. W10 . . . . .5E 80
(off Sutton Way)
Yeames Cl. W13 . . . . .6A 78
Yearby Ho. W10 . . . . .4E 80
(off Sutton Way)
Yeate St. N1 .7D 66
Yeatman Rd. N6 . . . . .6D 46
Yeats Cl. NW10 . . . . .5A 62
SE13 . . . . .2F 123
W7 . . . . .7K 77
Yeend Cl. KT8: W Mole 4E 148
Yeldham Ho. W6 . . . . .5F 99
(off Yeldham Rd.)
Yeldham Rd. W6 . . . . .5F 99
Yeldham Vs. W6 . . . . .5F 99
(off Yeldham Rd.)
Yellowhammer Ct. NW9 . . . . .2A 44
(off Eagle Dr.)
Yelverton Lodge TW1: Twick 7C 114
(off Richmond Rd.)
Yelverton Rd. SW11 . . . . .2B 118
Ye Market CR2: S Croy 5D 168
(off Selsdon Rd.)
Yenston Cl. SM4: Mord 6J 153
Yeoman Cl. E6 . . . . .7F 89
SE27 . . . . .3B 138
Yeoman Ct. TW5: Hest 7D 94
Yeoman Dr. TW19: Stanw 1A 128
Yeoman Rd. UB5: N'olt 7C 58
Yeomans Acre HA4: Ruis 6J 39
Yeomans M. TW7: Isle 6H 113
Yeoman's Row SW3 . . . . . .2D 16 (3C 100)
Yeoman St. SE8 . . . . .4A 104
Yeomans Way EN3: Enf H 2D 24
Yeoman's Yd. E1 . . . . .2K 15

Yeo St. E3 . . . . .5D 86
Yeovil Cl. BR6: Orp 2J 173
Yeovil Ho. W10 . . . . .4E 80
(off Sutton Way)
Yeovilton Pl. KT2: King T 5C 132
Yerbury Rd. N19 . . . . .3H 65
(not continuous)
Yester Dr. BR7: Chst 7C 142
Yester Pk. BR7: Chst 7D 142
Yester Rd. BR7: Chst 7C 142
Yetev Lev Cl. E5 . . . . .1G 67
Yew Av. UB7: Yiew 7A 74
Yew Cl. IG9: Buck H 2G 37
Yewdale Cl. BR1: Brom 6G 141
Yewfield Rd. NW10 . . . . .6B 62
Yew Gro. NW2 . . . . .4F 63
Yew Ho. SE16 . . . . .2K 103
(off Woodland Cres.)
Yews, The TW15: Ashf 4D 128
Yew Tree Cl. DA16: Well 1A 126
KT4: Wor Pk 1A 164
N21 . . . . .7F 23
SE13 . . . . .3E 122
Yewtree Cl. HA2: Harr 4F 41
N22 . . . . .1G 47
Yew Tree Ct. NW11 . . . . .5H 45
(off Bridge La.)
SM2: Sutt 7A 166
(off Walnut M.)
Yew Tree Gdns. RM6: Chad H 5E 54
RM7: Rom 5K 55
Yew Tree Lodge HA5: Eastc 6J 39
RM7: Rom 5K 55
(off Yew Tree Gdns.)
SW16 . . . . .4G 137
Yew Tree Rd. BR3: Beck 3B 158
UB10: Uxb 1B 74
W12 . . . . .7B 80
Yew Trees TW17: Shep 4B 146
Yew Tree Wlk. TW4: Houn 5D 112
Yew Tree Way CR0: Sels 7B 170
(not continuous)
Yew Wlk. HA1: Harr . . . .≠. .1J 59
YIEWSLEY 1A 92
Yiewsley Ct. UB7: Yiew 1A 92
Yiewsley Swimming Pool 7A 74
YMCA Hawker Cen.
(Health & Fitness) 5D 132
Yoakley Rd. N16 . . . . .2E 66
Yoga Way KT4: Wor Pk 2C 164
Yoke Cl. N7 .6J 65
Yolande Gdns. SE9 . . . . .5C 124
Yonge Pk. N4 . . . . .3A 66
York Av. DA15: Sidc 2J 143
HA7: Stan 1B 42
SE17 . . . . .5C 102
SW14 . . . . .5J 115
UB3: Hayes 5E 74
W7 . . . . .1J 95
York Bri. NW1 . . . . .3G 5 (4E 82)
York Bldgs. WC2 . . . . .3F 13 (7J 83)
York Cl. E6 . . . . .6D 88
SE5 . . . . .2C 120
(off Lilford Rd.)
SM4: Mord 4K 153
TW18: Staines 6A 128
W7 . . . . .1J 95
York Ct. N14 . . . . .3D 32
York Ga. N14 . . . . .7D 22
NW1 . . . . .4G 5 (4E 82)
York Gro. SE15 . . . . .1J 121
York Hall Leisure Cen. 2H 85
York Hill SE27 . . . . .3B 138
York Ho. E16 . . . . .1J 105
(off De Quincey M.)
EN2: Enf 1J 23

York Ho. HA9: Wemb 4G 61
KT2: King T 7F 133
(off Elm Rd.)
SE1 . . . . .2H 19 (3K 101)
SW3 . . . . .5F 17
W1 .5E 4
(off York St.)
W8 . . . . .2K 99
(off York Ho. Pl.)
York Ho. Pl. W8 . . . . .2K 99
Yorkland Av. DA16: Well 3K 125
Yorkley Ho. W10 . . . . .4E 80
(off Sutton Way)
York Mans. SE17 . . . . .5C 102
(off Browning St.)
SW5 . . . . .5K 99
(off Earls Ct. Rd.)
SW11 . . . . .1E 118
(off Prince of Wales Dr.)
W1 . . . . .5G 5
(off Chiltern St.)
York M. IG1: Ilf 3E 70
NW5 . . . . .5F 65
York Pde. NW9 . . . . .6C 44
(off W. Hendon B'way.)
TW8: Bford 5D 96
York Pas. W8 . . . . .2K 99
(off York Ho. Pl.)
York Pl. IG1: Ilf 2E 70
RM10: Dag 6J 73
SW11 . . . . .3B 118
WC2 . . . . .3F 13
York Pl. Mans. W1 . . . . .5F 5
(off Baker St.)
York Ri. BR6: Orp 2J 173
NW5 . . . . .3C 64
York Rd. CR0: C'don 7A 156
E4 . . . . .4H 35
E7 . . . . .6J 69
E10 . . . . .3E 68
E17 . . . . .5K 49
EN5: New Bar 5F 21
HA6: Nwood 2J 39
IG1: Ilf 3E 70
KT2: King T 7F 133
N11 . . . . .6C 32
N18 . . . . .6C 34
N21 . . . . .7J 23
RM13: Rain 7K 73
SE1 . . . . .6H 13 (2K 101)
SM1: Sutt 6J 165
SM2: Sutt 6J 165
SW11 . . . . .4A 118
SW18 . . . . .4A 118
SW19 . . . . .6A 136
TW3: Houn 3F 113
TW8: Bford 5D 96
TW10: Rich 5F 115
TW11: Tedd 4J 131
W3 . . . . .6J 79
W5 . . . . .3C 96
York Rd. Bus. Cen.
SW11 . . . . .2B 118
Yorkshire Cl. N16 . . . . .3E 66
Yorkshire Gdns. N18 . . . . .5C 34
YORKSHIRE GREY 5B 124
Yorkshire Grey Pl. NW3 . . . . .4A 64
Yorkshire Grey Yd. WC1 . . . . .6G 7
Yorkshire Rd. CR4: Mitc 5J 155
E14 . . . . .6A 86
York Sq. E14 . . . . .6A 86
York St. CR4: Mitc 7E 154
TW1: Twick 1A 132
W1 . . . . .6E 4 (5D 82)
York St. Chambers W1 . . . . .6E 4
(off York St.)

York Ter. DA8: Erith 1J 127
EN2: Enf 1H 23
York Ter. E. NW1 . . . . .4H 5 (4E 82)
York Ter. W. NW1 . . . . .4G 5 (4E 82)
Yorkton St. E2 . . . . .2G 85
York Way KT9: Chess 7E 162
N1 . . . . .1F 7 (6J 65)
N7 . . . . .6H 65
N20 . . . . .3J 31
TW13: Hanw 3D 130
(not continuous)
York Way Ct. N1 . . . . .1J 83
(not continuous)
York Way Est. N7 . . . . .6J 65
Young Cl. NW6 . . . . .7G 63
Youngmans Cl. EN2: Enf 1H 23
Young Rd. E16 . . . . .6A 88
Youngs Bldgs. EC1 . . . . .3D 8
Youngs Ct. SW11 . . . . .1E 118
Youngs Rd. IG2: Ilf 5H 53
Young St. W8 . . . . .2K 99
Young Vic Theatre, The 6K 13
Youth Court
Balham 2E 136
Yoxall Ho. W10 . . . . .4E 80
(off Sutton Way)
Yoxford Ct. RM6: Chad H 5B 54
Yoxley App. IG2: Ilf 6G 53
Yoxley Dr. IG2: Ilf 6G 53
Yukon Rd. SW12 . . . . .7F 119
Yunus Khan Cl. E17 . . . . .5C 50
Yvon Ho. SW11 . . . . .1E 118
(off Alexandra Av.)

Z

Zachary Ct. SW1 . . . . .4H 101
(off Vincent St.)
Zahra Ho. NW10 . . . . .4E 80
(off Harrow Rd.)
Zambezie Dr. N9 . . . . .3D 34
Zampa Rd. SE16 . . . . .5J 103
Zander Ct. E2 . . . . .3G 85
Zangwill Ho. NW6 . . . . .2H 81
(off Carlton Vale)
Zangwill Rd. SE3 . . . . .1B 124
Zapotec Ho. SE8 . . . . .4K 103
(off Chilton Gro.)
Zealand Av. UB7: Harm 3E 174
Zealand Ho. SE5 . . . . .2C 120
(off Denmark Rd.)
SE18 . . . . .4C 106
Zealand Rd. E3 . . . . .2A 86
Zenith Lodge N3 . . . . .7E 30
Zennor Rd. SW12 . . . . .1G 137
Zennor Rd. Ind. Est. SW12 . . . . .1G 137
Zenobia Mans. W14 . . . . .6H 99
(off Queen's Club Mans.)
Zenoria St. SE22 . . . . .4F 121
Zermatt Rd. CR7: Thor H 4C 156
Zetland Ho. W8 . . . . .3K 99
(off Marloes Rd.)
Zetland St. E14 . . . . .5D 86
Zinc Building, The SE13 . . . . .4G 123
Zion Ho. E1 . . . . .6J 85
(off Jubilee St.)
Zion Pl. CR7: Thor H 4D 156
Zion Rd. CR7: Thor H 4D 156
Zoar St. SE1 . . . . .4C 14 (1C 102)
Zodiac Ct. CR0: C'don 1B 168
Zodiac Ho. E3 . . . . .4C 86
(off Wellington Way)
Zoffany St. N19 . . . . .2H 65
Zoroastrian Ho. NW6 . . . . .6K 63
(off Compayne Gdns.)

HOSPITALS, TREATMENT CENTRES, WALK-IN CENTRES and HOSPICES covered by this atlas.

N.B. Where it is not possible to name these facilities on the map, the reference given is for the road in which they are situated.

ASHFORD HOSPITAL 2A **128**
London Road
ASHFORD
TW15 3AA
Tel: 01784 884488

BARKING HOSPITAL 7K **71**
Upney Lane
BARKING
IG11 9LX
Tel: 0845 130 4204

BARNES HOSPITAL 3A **116**
South Worple Way
LONDON
SW14 8SU
Tel: 020 88784981

BARNET HOSPITAL 4A **20**
Wellhouse Lane
BARNET
EN5 3DJ
Tel: 0845 111 4000

BECKENHAM BEACON 2B **158**
379 Croydon Road
BECKENHAM
BR3 3QL
Tel: 01689 863000

BECKTON CYGNET HOSPITAL 6E **88**
23 Tunnan Leys
LONDON
E6 6ZB
Tel: 0207 5112299

BELVEDERE HOUSE (DAY) HOSPITAL 1C **80**
341 Harlesden Road
LONDON
NW10 3RX
Tel: 020 8459 3562

BELVEDERE PRIVATE HOSPITAL 5C **108**
Knee Hill
LONDON
SE2 0GD
Tel: 020 8310 8866

BETHLEM ROYAL HOSPITAL 7C **158**
Monks Orchard Road
BECKENHAM
BR3 3BX
Tel: 020 32286000

BLACKHEATH BMI HOSPITAL 3H **123**
40-42 Lee Terrace
LONDON
SE3 9UD
Tel: 020 8318 7722

BUSHEY SPIRE HOSPITAL 1E **26**
Heathbourne Road
Bushey Heath
BUSHEY
WD23 1RD
Tel: 0845 603 9090

CAMDEN MEWS DAY HOSPITAL .7G **65**
1-5 Camden Mews
LONDON
NW1 9DB
Tel: 020 3317 4740

CASSEL HOSPITAL 4D **132**
1 Ham Common
RICHMOND
TW10 7JF
Tel: 020 84832 900

CASUALTY PLUS WALK-IN CENTRE (BRENTFORD) 5C **96**
1010 Great West Road
BRENTFORD
TW8 9BA
Tel: 0208 8380 6202

CAVELL BMI HOSPITAL, THE 2F **23**
Cavell Drive
ENFIELD
EN2 7PR
Tel: 020 8366 2122

CENTRAL MIDDLESEX HOSPITAL .3J **79**
Acton Lane
LONDON
NW10 7NS
Tel: 020 8965 5733

CHARING CROSS HOSPITAL 6F **99**
Fulham Palace Road
LONDON
W6 8RF
Tel: 020 8846 1234

CHASE FARM HOSPITAL 1F **23**
127 The Ridgeway
ENFIELD
EN2 8JL
Tel: 0845 111 4000

CHELSEA & WESTMINSTER HOSPITAL 6A **100**
369 Fulham Road
LONDON
SW10 9NH
Tel: 020 8746 8000

CHILDREN'S HOSPITAL, THE (LEWISHAM) 5D **122**
Lewisham University Hospital
Lewisham High Street
LONDON
SE13 6LH
Tel: 020 8333 3000

CHURCHILL LONDON CLINIC 1K **19** (3A **102**)
22 Barkham Terrace
LONDON
SE1 7PW
Tel: 020 7928 5633

CLAYPONDS HOSPITAL 4E **96**
Sterling Place
LONDON
W5 4RN
Tel: 020 8560 4011

CLEMENTINE CHURCHILL BMI HOSPITAL, THE 3K **59**
Sudbury Hill
HARROW
HA1 3RX
Tel: 020 8872 3872

CROMWELL BUPA HOSPITAL 4K **99**
162-174 Cromwell Road
LONDON
SW5 0TU
Tel: 020 7460 2000

DEMELZA HOSPICE CARE FOR CHILDREN 6D **124**
Wensley Close
LONDON
SE9 5AB
Tel: 0208 859776

DULWICH COMMUNITY HOSPITAL 4E **120**
East Dulwich Grove
LONDON
SE22 8PT
Tel: 020 3299 6257

EALING CYGNET HOSPITAL 5E **78**
22 Corfton Road
LONDON
W5 2HT
Tel: 0208 9916699

EALING HOSPITAL 2H **95**
Uxbridge Road
SOUTHALL
UB1 3HW
Tel: 020 8967 5000

EAST HAM CARE CENTRE & DAY HOSPITAL 7B **70**
Shrewsbury Road
LONDON
E7 8QP
Tel: 0208 475 2005

EASTMAN DENTAL HOSPITAL & DENTAL INSTITUTE
. . . . .3G **7** (4K **83**)
256 Gray's Inn Road
LONDON
WC1X 8LD
Tel: 020 7915 1000

EDGWARE COMMUNITY HOSPITAL 7C **28**
Burnt Oak Broadway
EDGWARE
HA8 0AD
Tel: 020 8952 2381

ELIZABETH GARRETT ANDERSON & OBSTETRIC HOSPITAL
...............................4B **6** (4G **83**)
Huntley Street
LONDON
WC1E 6DH
Tel: 0845 155 5000

ERITH & DISTRICT HOSPITAL 6K **109**
Park Crescent
ERITH
DA8 3EE
Tel: 020 8308 3131

EVELINA CHILDREN'S HOSPITAL 1G **19** (3K **101**)
St Thomas' Hospital
Lambeth Palace Road
LONDON
SE1 7EH
Tel: 020 7188 7188

FINCHLEY MEMORIAL HOSPITAL 7F **31**
Granville Road
LONDON
N12 0JE
Tel: 020 8349 7500

FITZROY SQUARE BMI HOSPITAL 4A **6** (4G **83**)
14 Fitzroy Square
LONDON
W1T 6AH
Tel: 020 7388 4954

GARDEN BMI HOSPITAL, THE 3E **44**
46-50 Sunny Gardens Road
LONDON
NW4 1RP
Tel: 020 8457 4500

GATEWAY SURGICAL CENTRE 4B **88**
Cherry Tree Way
LONDON
E13 8SL
Tel: 0207 055 5550

GOODMAYES HOSPITAL 5A **54**
Barley Lane
ILFORD
IG3 8XJ
Tel: 0844 600 1200

GORDON HOSPITAL......................4C **18** (4H **101**)
Bloomburg Street
LONDON
SW1V 2RH
Tel: 020 8746 8733

GREAT ORMOND STREET HOSPITAL FOR CHILDREN
...............................4F **7** (4J **83**)
Great Ormond Street
LONDON
WC1N 3JH
Tel: 020 7405 9200

GREENWICH & BEXLEY COTTAGE HOSPICE 5C **108**
185 Bostall Hill
LONDON
SE2 0GB
Tel: 020 8312 2244

GUY'S HOSPITAL 5F **15** (1D **102**)
Great Maze Pond
LONDON
SE1 9RT
Tel: 020 7188 7188

GUY'S NUFFIELD HOUSE 6E **14** (2D **102**)
Guy's Hospital
Newcomen Street
LONDON
SE1 1YR
Tel: 020 7188 5292

HAMMERSMITH HOSPITAL 6C **80**
Du Cane Road
LONDON
W12 0HS
Tel: 020 8383 1000

HARLEY STREET CLINIC 5J **5** (5F **83**)
35 Weymouth Street
LONDON
W1G 8BJ
Tel: 020 7935 7700

HARLINGTON HOSPICE (REG HOPKINS DAY CARE HOSPICE)
...............................5F **93**
St Peters Way
HAYES
UB3 5AB
Tel: 020 8759 0453

HARRIS HOSPISCARE 4K **173**
Tregony Road
ORPINGTON
BR6 9XA
Tel: 01689 825755

HARROW CYGNET HOSPITAL 2J **59**
London Road
HARROW
HA1 3JL
Tel: 020 8966 7000

HAVEN HOUSE FOUNDATION (HOSPICE) 6C **36**
High Road
WOODFORD GREEN
IG8 9LB
Tel: 020 8505 9944

HAYES GROVE PRIORY HOSPITAL 2J **171**
Prestons Road
Hayes
BROMLEY
BR2 7AS
Tel: 020 8462 7722

HEART HOSPITAL, THE 6H **5** (5E **82**)
16-18 Westmoreland Street
LONDON
W1G 8PH
Tel: 020 7573 8888

HEATHVIEW DAY CENTRE 6C **108**
Lodge Hill
LONDON
SE2 0AY
Tel: 020 8319 7166

HIGHGATE HOSPITAL 6D **46**
17 View Road
LONDON
N6 4DJ
Tel: 020 8341 4182

HIGHGATE MENTAL HEALTH CENTRE 2F **65**
Dartmouth Park Hill
LONDON
N19 5NX
Tel: 020 7561 4090

HILLINGDON HOSPITAL 5B **74**
Pield Heath Road
UXBRIDGE
UB8 3NN
Tel: 01895 238282

HOLLY HOUSE HOSPITAL 2E **36**
High Road
BUCKHURST HILL
IG9 5HX
Tel: 020 8505 3311

HOMERTON UNIVERSITY HOSPITAL 5K **67**
Homerton Row
LONDON
E9 6SR
Tel: 020 8510 5555

HOSPITAL FOR TROPICAL DISEASES 4B **6** (4G **83**)
Mortimer Market,
Capper Street
LONDON
WC1E 6JD
Tel: 0845 155 5000

HOSPITAL OF ST JOHN & ST ELIZABETH 2B **82**
60 Grove End Road
LONDON
NW8 9NH
Tel: 020 7806 4000

JOHN HOWARD CENTRE 5A **68**
12 Kenworthy Road
LONDON
E9 5TD
Tel: 020 8919 8447

KING EDWARD VII'S HOSPITAL SISTER AGNES
...............................5H **5** (5E **82**)
5-10 Beaumont Street
LONDON
W1G 6AA
Tel: 020 7486 4411

KING GEORGE HOSPITAL 5A **54**
Barley Lane
ILFORD
IG3 8YB
Tel: 0845 130 4204

KING'S COLLEGE HOSPITAL 2D **120**
Denmark Hill
LONDON
SE5 9RS
Tel: 0203 299 9000

KING'S OAK BMI HOSPITAL 1F **23**
The Ridgeway
ENFIELD
EN2 8SD
Tel: 020 8370 9500

KINGSTON HOSPITAL 1H **151**
Galsworthy Road
KINGSTON UPON THAMES
KT2 7QB
Tel: 020 8546 7711

LAMBETH HOSPITAL 3K **119**
108 Landor Road
LONDON
SW9 9NT
Tel: 020 32286000

LATIMER DAY HOSPITAL 5A **6** (5G **83**)
40 Hanson Street
LONDON
W1W 6UL
Tel: 020 7612 1620

LEWISHAM UNIVERSITY HOSPITAL 5D **122**
Lewisham High Street
LONDON
SE13 6LH
Tel: 020 8333 3000

LISTER HOSPITAL, THE 6J **17** (5F **101**)
Chelsea Bridge Road
LONDON
SW1W 8RH
Tel: 020 7730 7733

LONDON BRIDGE HOSPITAL 4F **15** (1D **102**)
27 Tooley Street
LONDON
SE1 2PR
Tel: 020 7407 3100

LONDON CHEST HOSPITAL 2J **85**
Bonner Road
LONDON
E2 9JX
Tel: 020 7377 7000

LONDON CLINIC, THE 4H **5** (4E **82**)
20 Devonshire Place
LONDON
W1G 6BW
Tel: 020 7935 4444

LONDON INDEPENDENT BMI HOSPITAL 5K **85**
1 Beaumont Square
LONDON
E1 4NL
Tel: 020 7780 2400

LONDON WELBECK HOSPITAL 6J **5** (5F **83**)
27 Welbeck Street
LONDON
W1G 8EN
Tel: 020 7224 2242

MARGARET CENTRE (HOSPICE) 6G **51**
Whipps Cross University Hospital
Whipps Cross Road
LONDON
E11 1NR
Tel: 020 8535 6604

MARIE CURIE HOSPICE, HAMPSTEAD 5B **64**
11 Lyndhurst Gardens
LONDON
NW3 5NS
Tel: 020 7853 3400

MAUDSLEY HOSPITAL, THE 2D **120**
Denmark Hill
LONDON
SE5 8AZ
Tel: 020 32286000

MAYDAY UNIVERSITY HOSPITAL 6B **156**
530 London Road
THORNTON HEATH
CR7 7YE
Tel: 020 8401 3000

MEADOW HOUSE HOSPICE 2H **95**
Ealing Hospital
Uxbridge Road
SOUTHALL
UB1 3HW
Tel: 020 8967 5179

MEMORIAL HOSPITAL 2E **124**
Shooters Hill
LONDON
SE18 3RZ
Tel: 020 8836 8500

MILDMAY HOSPITAL 2J **9** (3F **85**)
Austin Street
LONDON
E2 7NA
Tel: 020 7613 6300

MILE END HOSPITAL 4K **85**
Bancroft Road
LONDON
E1 4DG
Tel: 020 7377 7000

MOLESEY HOSPITAL 5E **148**
High Street
WEST MOLESEY
KT8 2LU
Tel: 020 8941 4481

MOORFIELDS EYE HOSPITAL 2E **8** (3D **84**)
162 City Road
LONDON
EC1V 2PD
Tel: 020 7253 3411

NATIONAL HOSPITAL FOR
NEUROLOGY & NEUROSURGERY, THE
.................................4F **7** (4J **83**)
Queen Square
LONDON
WC1N 3BG
Tel: 0845 155 5000

NELSON HOSPITAL 2H **153**
Kingston Road
LONDON
SW20 8DB
Tel: 020 8296 3795

NEWHAM CENTRE FOR MENTAL HEALTH 4B **88**
Cherry Tree Way
Glen Road
LONDON
E13 8SH
Tel: 0207 5404380

NEWHAM UNIVERSITY HOSPITAL 4A **88**
Glen Road
LONDON
E13 8SL
Tel: 020 7476 4000

NEW VICTORIA HOSPITAL 1A **152**
184 Coombe Lane West
KINGSTON UPON THAMES
KT2 7EG
Tel: 020 8949 9000

NHS WALK-IN CENTRE (ASHFORD) 2A **128**
Ashford Hospital
London Road
ASHFORD
TW15 3AA
Tel: 01784 884000

NHS WALK-IN CENTRE (BROAD STREET) 1G **91**
Broad Street Centre
Morland Road
DAGENHAM
RM10 9HU
Tel: 020 8596 4400

NHS WALK-IN CENTRE (CANARY WHARF) 2C **104**
30 Marsh Wall
LONDON
E14 9TP
Tel: 020 7517 3300

NHS WALK-IN CENTRE (CHARING CROSS) 5F **99**
Charing Cross Hospital
Fulham Palace Road
LONDON
W6 8RF
Tel: 020 8383 0904

NHS WALK-IN CENTRE (CROYDON) 3C **168**
45 High Street
CROYDON
CR0 1QD
Tel: 020 8666 0555

NHS WALK-IN CENTRE (EDGWARE) 7C **28**
Edgware Community Hospital
Burnt Oak Broadway
EDGWARE
HA8 0AD
Tel: 020 8732 6459

NHS WALK-IN CENTRE (FINCHLEY) 7F **31**
Finchley Memorial Hospital
Granville Road
LONDON
N12 0JE
Tel: 020 8349 7471

NHS WALK-IN CENTRE (HACKNEY) 5K **67**
Homerton University Hospital
Homerton Row
LONDON
E9 6SR
Tel: 020 8510 5342

NHS WALK-IN CENTRE (LIVERPOOL STREET)
. . . . .5H **9** (5E **84**)
Exchange Arcade
Bishopsgate
LONDON
EC2M 3WA
Tel: 0845 880 1242

NHS WALK-IN CENTRE (NEW CROSS) 7A **104**
40 Goodwood Road
LONDON
SE14 6BL
Tel: 020 7206 3100

NHS WALK-IN CENTRE (NEWHAM) 4A **88**
Newham University Hospital
Glen Road
LONDON
E13 8SH
Tel: 020 7363 9200

NHS WALK-IN CENTRE
(NORTH MIDDLESEX UNIVERSITY HOSPITAL)
. . . . .5K **33**
North Middlesex University Hospital
Sterling Way
LONDON
N18 1QX
Tel: 020 8887 2680

NHS WALK-IN CENTRE (PARSONS GREEN) 1J **117**
5-7 Parsons Green
LONDON
SW6 4UL
Tel: 020 8846 6758

NHS WALK-IN CENTRE (SOHO) 1C **12** (6H **83**)
1 Frith Street
LONDON
W1D 3HZ
Tel: 020 7534 6500

NHS WALK-IN CENTRE (TEDDINGTON) 6J **131**
Teddington Memorial Hospital
Hampton Road
TEDDINGTON
TW11 0JL
Tel: 020 8714 4004

NHS WALK-IN CENTRE
(TOLLGATE LODGE PRIMARY CARE CENTRE)
. . . . .1F **67**
57 Stamford Hill
LONDON
N16 5SR
Tel: 020 7689 3140

NHS WALK-IN CENTRE (TOOTING) 5C **136**
St George's Hospital
Blackshaw Road
LONDON
SW17 0QT
Tel: 020 8700 0505

NHS WALK-IN CENTRE (UPNEY LANE) 6K **71**
132 Upney Lane
BARKING
IG11 9YD
Tel: 020 8924 6262

NHS WALK-IN CENTRE (VICTORIA) 1C **18** (3H **101**)
63 Buckingham Gate
LONDON
SW1E 6AS
Tel: 020 7340 1190

NHS WALK-IN CENTRE (WEMBLEY) 6D **60**
Wembley Centre for Health & Care
116 Chaplin Road
WEMBLEY
HA0 4UZ
Tel: 0208 795 6000

NHS WALK-IN CENTRE (WHIPPS CROSS HOSPITAL) . . .5F **51**
Whipps Cross University Hospital
Whipps Cross Road
LONDON
E11 1NR
Tel: 020 8539 5522

NHS WALK-IN CENTRE (WHITECHAPEL) 5H **85**
Royal London Hospital
174 Whitechapel Road
LONDON
E1 1BZ
Tel: 020 7943 1333

NHS WALK-IN CENTRE (WHITTINGTON) 2G **65**
Whittington Hospital
Highgate Hill
LONDON
N19 5NF
Tel: 020 7272 3070

NIGHTINGALE CAPIO HOSPITAL 5D **4** (5C **82**)
11-19 Lisson Grove
LONDON
NW1 6SH
Tel: 020 7535 7700

NORTH EAST LONDON NHS TREATMENT CENTRE 5A **54**
Within King George Hospital
ILFORD
IG3 8YB
Tel: 0845 052 4175

NORTH LONDON CLINIC 2B **34**
15 Church Street
LONDON
N9 9DY
Tel: 020 8956 1234

NORTH LONDON HOSPICE 3F **31**
47 Woodside Avenue
LONDON
N12 8TT
Tel: 020 8343 8841

NORTH LONDON PRIORY HOSPITAL 1D **32**
The Bourne
Southgate
LONDON
N14 6RA
Tel: 020 8882 8191

NORTH MIDDLESEX UNIVERSITY HOSPITAL 5K **33**
Sterling Way
LONDON
N18 1QX
Tel: 020 8887 2000

NORTHWICK PARK HOSPITAL 7A **42**
Watford Road
HARROW
HA1 3UJ
Tel: 020 8864 3232

ORPINGTON HOSPITAL 4K **173**
Sevenoaks Road
ORPINGTON
BR6 9JU
Tel: 01689 863000

PARK ROYAL CENTRE (FOR MENTAL HEALTH) 2J **79**
Central Way
LONDON
NW10 7NS
Tel: 020 8955 4400

PARKSIDE HOSPITAL 3F **135**
53 Parkside
LONDON
SW19 5NX
Tel: 020 8971 8000

PEMBRIDGE PALLIATIVE CARE CENTRE 5F **81**
St Charles Hospital
Exmoor Street
LONDON
W10 6DZ
Tel: 020 8962 4410 / 4411

PLAISTOW DAY HOSPITAL 2A **88**
Samson Street
LONDON
E13 9EH
Tel: 020 8586 6200

PORTLAND HOSPITAL FOR WOMEN & CHILDREN
. . . . .4K **5** (4F **83**)
205-209 Great Portland Street
LONDON
W1W 5AH
Tel: 020 7580 4400

PRINCESS GRACE HOSPITAL 4G **5** (4E **82**)
42-52 Nottingham Place
LONDON
W1U 5NY
Tel: 020 7486 1234

PRINCESS GRACE HOSPITAL (OUTPATIENTS)
. . . . .5H **5** (5E **82**)
30 Devonshire Street
LONDON
W1G 6PU
Tel: 020 7908 3602

PRINCESS ROYAL UNIVERSITY HOSPITAL 3E **172**
Farnborough Common
ORPINGTON
BR6 8ND
Tel: 01689 863000

QUEEN CHARLOTTE'S & CHELSEA HOSPITAL 6C **80**
Du Cane Road
LONDON
W12 0HS
Tel: 020 8383 1111

QUEEN ELIZABETH HOSPITAL 7C **106**
Stadium Road
LONDON
SE18 4QH
Tel: 020 8836 6000

QUEEN MARY'S HOSPITAL 5A **144**
Frognal Avenue
SIDCUP
DA14 6LT
Tel: 020 8302 2678

QUEEN MARY'S HOSPITAL FOR CHILDREN
. . . . .1A **166**
Wrythe Lane
CARSHALTON
SM5 1AA
Tel: 020 8296 2000

QUEEN MARY'S HOSPITAL, ROEHAMPTON
. . . . .6C **116**
Roehampton Lane
LONDON
SW15 5PN
Tel: 020 8487 6000

QUEEN MARY'S HOUSE 3A **64**
23 East Heath Road
LONDON
NW3 1DU
Tel: 020 7431 5508

QUEEN'S HOSPITAL 7K **55**
Rom Valley Way
ROMFORD
RM7 0AG
Tel: 0845 130 4204

RICHARD DESMOND CHILDREN'S EYE CENTRE
. . . . .2E **8** (3D **84**)
Moorfields Eye Hospital
162 City Road
LONDON
EC1V 2PD
Tel: 020 7253 3411

RICHARD HOUSE CHILDREN'S HOSPICE 7B **88**
Richard House Drive
LONDON
E16 3RG
Tel: 020 7511 0222

RICHMOND ROYAL HOSPITAL .3E **114**
Kew Foot Road
RICHMOND
TW9 2TE
Tel: 020 8940 3331

RODING SPIRE HOSPITAL 3B **52**
Roding Lane South
ILFORD
IG4 5PZ
Tel: 020 8551 1100

ROEHAMPTON HUNTERCOMBE HOSPITAL 7C **116**
Holybourne Avenue
LONDON
SW15 4JL
Tel: 020 8780 6155

ROEHAMPTON PRIORY HOSPITAL 4B **116**
Priory Lane
LONDON
SW15 5JJ
Tel: 020 8876 8261

ROYAL BROMPTON HOSPITAL 5C **16** (5C **100**)
Sydney Street
LONDON
SW3 6NP
Tel: 020 7352 8121

ROYAL BROMPTON HOSPITAL (OUTPATIENTS)
. . . . .5B **16** (5B **100**)
Fulham Road
LONDON
SW3 6HP
Tel: 020 7352 8121

ROYAL FREE HOSPITAL, THE .5C **64**
Pond Street
LONDON
NW3 2QG
Tel: 020 7794 0500

ROYAL HOSPITAL FOR NEURO-DISABILITY 6G **117**
West Hill
LONDON
SW15 3SW
Tel: 020 8780 4500

ROYAL LONDON HOMOEOPATHIC HOSPITAL 5F **7** (5J **83**)
Great Ormond Street
LONDON
WC1N 3HR
Tel: 0845 155 5000

ROYAL LONDON HOSPITAL, THE 5H **85**
Whitechapel Road
LONDON
E1 1BB
Tel: 020 7377 7000

ROYAL MARSDEN HOSPITAL (FULHAM), THE
. . . . .5B **16** (5B **100**)
Fulham Road
LONDON
SW3 6JJ
Tel: 020 7352 8171

ROYAL NATIONAL ORTHOPAEDIC HOSPITAL 2G **27**
Brockley Hill
STANMORE
HA7 4LP
Tel: 020 8954 2300

ROYAL NATIONAL ORTHOPAEDIC HOSPITAL
(CENTRAL LONDON OUTPATIENT DEPT.)
. . . . .4K **5** (4F **83**)
45-51 Bolsover Street
LONDON
W1W 5AQ
Tel: 020 7387 5070

ROYAL NATIONAL THROAT, NOSE & EAR HOSPITAL
. . . . .1G **7** (3K **83**)
330 Gray's Inn Road
LONDON
WC1X 8DA
Tel: 020 7915 1300

ST ANN'S HOSPITAL 5C **48**
St Ann's Road
LONDON
N15 3TH
Tel: 020 8442 6000

ST ANTHONY'S HOSPITAL 1F **165**
London Road
SUTTON
SM3 9DW
Tel: 020 8337 6691

ST BARTHOLOMEW'S HOSPITAL
. . . . .6B **8** (5B **84**)
West Smithfield
LONDON
EC1A 7BE
Tel: 020 7377 7000

ST BERNARD'S HOSPITAL 2H **95**
Uxbridge Road
SOUTHALL
UB1 3EU
Tel: 020 8967 5000

ST CHARLES HOSPITAL 5F **81**
Exmoor Street
LONDON
W10 6DZ
Tel: 020 8206 7000

ST CHRISTOPHER'S HOSPICE 5J **139**
51-59 Lawrie Park Road
LONDON
SE26 6DZ
Tel: 020 8768 4500

ST GEORGE'S HOSPITAL (TOOTING) 5C **136**
Blackshaw Road
LONDON
SW17 0QT
Tel: 020 8672 1255

ST HELIER HOSPITAL 1A **166**
Wrythe Lane
CARSHALTON
SM5 1AA
Tel: 020 8296 2000

ST JOHN'S HOSPICE 1A **4** (2B **82**)
Hospital of St John & St Elizabeth
60 Grove End Road
LONDON
NW8 9NH
Tel: 020 7806 4040

ST JOSEPH'S HOSPICE 1H **85**
Mare Street
LONDON
E8 4SA
Tel: 020 8525 6000

ST LUKE'S HOSPICE 5D **42**
Kenton Road
HARROW
HA3 0YG
Tel: 020 8382 8000

ST LUKE'S WOODSIDE HOSPITAL 4E **46**
Woodside Avenue
LONDON
N10 3HU
Tel: 020 8219 1823

ST MARK'S HOSPITAL 7B **42**
Watford Road
HARROW
HA1 3UJ
Tel: 020 8864 3232

ST MARY'S HOSPITAL 7B **4** (6B **82**)
Praed Street
LONDON
W2 1NY
Tel: 020 7886 6666

ST MICHAEL'S PRIMARY CARE CENTRE 1J **23**
Gater Drive
ENFIELD
EN2 0JL
Tel: 020 8375 2894

ST PANCRAS HOSPITAL 1H **83**
4 St Pancras Way
LONDON
NW1 0PE
Tel: 020 7530 3500

ST RAPHAEL'S HOSPICE 2F **165**
London Road
SUTTON
SM3 9DX
Tel: 020 8335 4575

ST THOMAS' HOSPITAL...............1G **19** (3K **101**)
Westminster Bridge Road
LONDON
SE1 7EH
Tel: 020 7188 7188

SHIRLEY OAKS BMI HOSPITAL 7J **157**
Poppy Lane
CROYDON
CR9 8AB
Tel: 020 8655 5500

SHOOTING STAR HOUSE, CHILDREN'S HOSPICE 6D **130**
The Avenue
HAMPTON
TW12 3RA
Tel: 020 8783 2000

SLOANE BMI HOSPITAL 1F **159**
125 Albemarle Road
BECKENHAM
BR3 5HS
Tel: 020 8466 4000

SPRINGFIELD UNIVERSITY HOSPITAL 3C **136**
61 Glenburnie Road
LONDON
SW17 7DJ
Tel: 020 8682 6000

SURBITON HOSPITAL 6E **150**
Ewell Road
SURBITON
KT6 6EZ
Tel: 020 8399 7111

TEDDINGTON MEMORIAL HOSPITAL 6J **131**
Hampton Road
TEDDINGTON
TW11 0JL
Tel: 020 8714 4000

THORPE COOMBE HOSPITAL 3E **50**
714 Forest Road
LONDON
E17 3HP
Tel: 020 8520 8971

TOLWORTH HOSPITAL 2G **163**
Red Lion Road
SURBITON
KT6 7QU
Tel: 020 8390 0102

TRINITY HOSPICE 4F **119**
30 Clapham Common North Side
LONDON
SW4 0RN
Tel: 020 7787 1000

UNIVERSITY COLLEGE HOSPITAL 3B **6** (4G **83**)
235 Euston Road
LONDON
NW1 2BU
Tel: 0845 155 5000

UPTON CENTRE 4E **126**
14 Upton Road
BEXLEYHEATH
DA6 8LQ
Tel: 020 8301 7900

WELLINGTON HOSPITAL, THE 1B **4** (3B **82**)
8a Wellington Place
LONDON
NW8 9LE
Tel: 020 7586 5959

WESTERN EYE HOSPITAL 5E **4** (5D **82**)
171 Marylebone Road
LONDON
NW1 5QH
Tel: 020 7886 6666

WEST MIDDLESEX UNIVERSITY HOSPITAL 2A **114**
Twickenham Road
ISLEWORTH
TW7 6AF
Tel: 020 8560 2121

WHIPPS CROSS UNIVERSITY HOSPITAL 5F **51**
Whipps Cross Road
LONDON
E11 1NR
Tel: 020 8539 5522

WHITTINGTON HOSPITAL 2G **65**
Highgate Hill
LONDON
N19 5NF
Tel: 020 7272 3070

WILLESDEN CENTRE FOR HEALTH & CARE 7C **62**
Robson Avenue
LONDON
NW10 3RY
Tel: 020 8438 7000

WOODBURY UNIT 6G **51**
178 James Lane
LONDON
E11 1NU
Tel: 020 8535 6478

RAIL, CROYDON TRAMLINK, DOCKLANDS LIGHT RAILWAY, RIVERBUS, UNDERGROUND AND OVERGROUND STATIONS

with their map square reference

A

Abbey Road (DLR) 2G 87
Abbey Wood (Rail) 3C 108
Acton Central (Overground) 1K 97
Acton Main Line (Rail) 6J 79
Acton Town (Underground) 2G 97
Addington Village Stop (Tramlink) 6C 170
Addiscombe Stop (Tramlink) 1G 169
Albany Park (Rail) 2D 144
Aldgate (Underground) 1J 15 (6F 85)
Aldgate East (Underground) 7K 9 (6F 85)
Alexandra Palace (Rail) 2J 47
All Saints (DLR) 7D 86
Alperton (Underground) 1D 78
Anerley (Rail & Overground) 1H 157
Angel (Underground) 2A 84
Angel Road (Rail) 5D 34
Archway (Underground) 2G 65
Arena Stop (Tramlink) 5J 157
Arnos Grove (Underground) 5B 32
Arsenal (Underground) 3A 66
Ashford (Rail) 4B 128
Avenue Road Stop (Tramlink) 2K 157

B

Baker Street (Underground) 4F 5 (4D 82)
Balham (Rail & Underground) 1F 137
Bank (Underground & DLR) 1E 14 (6D 84)
Bankside Pier (Riverbus) 3C 14 (7C 84)
Barbican (Underground) 5C 8 (5C 84)
Barking (Rail, Underground & Overground) ...7G 71
Barkingside (Underground) 3H 53
Barnehurst (Rail) 2J 127
Barnes (Rail) 3C 116
Barnes Bridge (Rail) 2B 116
Barons Court (Underground) 5G 99
Battersea Park (Rail) 7F 101
Bayswater (Underground) 7K 81
Beckenham Hill (Rail) 5E 140
Beckenham Junction (Rail & Tramlink) 1C 158
Beckenham Road Stop (Tramlink) 1A 158
Beckton (DLR) 5E 88
Beckton Park (DLR) 7D 88
Becontree (Underground) 6D 72
Beddington Lane Stop (Tramlink) 6G 155
Belgrave Walk Stop (Tramlink) 4B 154
Bellingham (Rail) 3D 140
Belsize Park (Underground) 5C 64
Belvedere (Rail) 3H 109
Bermondsey (Underground) 3G 103
Berrylands (Rail) 4H 151
Bethnal Green (Rail) 4H 85
Bethnal Green (Underground) 3J 85
Bexley (Rail) 1G 145
Bexleyheath (Rail) 2E 126
Bickley (Rail) 3C 160
Birkbeck (Rail & Tramlink) 3J 157
Blackfriars (Rail & Underground) 2A 14 (7B 84)
Blackfriars Millennium Pier (Riverbus) .2A 14 (7A 84)
Blackheath (Rail) 3H 123
Blackhorse Lane Stop (Tramlink) 7G 157
Blackhorse Road (Underground & Overground) ..4K 49
Blackwall (DLR) 7E 86
Bond Street (Underground) 1J 11 (6F 83)
Borough (Underground) 7D 14 (2C 102)
Boston Manor (Underground) 4A 96
Bounds Green (Underground) 6C 32
Bow Church (DLR) 3C 86

Bowes Park (Rail) 7D 32
Bow Road (Underground) 3C 86
Brent Cross (Underground) 7F 45
Brentford (Rail) 6C 96
Brimsdown (Rail) 3F 25
Brixton (Rail & Underground) 4A 120
Brockley (Rail & Overground) 3A 122
Bromley-by-Bow (Underground) 3D 86
Bromley North (Rail) 1J 159
Bromley South (Rail) 3J 159
Brondesbury (Overground) 7H 63
Brondesbury Park (Overground) 1G 81
Bruce Grove (Rail) 2F 49
Buckhurst Hill (Underground) 2G 37
Burnt Oak (Underground) 1J 43
Bush Hill Park (Rail) 6A 24

C

Cadogan Pier (Riverbus) 7D 16 (6C 100)
Caledonian Road & Barnsbury (Overground) 7K 65
Caledonian Road (Underground) 6K 65
Cambridge Heath (Rail) 2H 85
Camden Road (Overground) 7G 65
Camden Town (Underground) 1F 83
Canada Water (Overground & Underground) ...2J 103
Canary Wharf (DLR & Underground) 1C 104
Canary Wharf Pier (Riverbus) 1B 104
Canning Town (Underground & DLR) 6G 87
Cannon Street (Rail & Underground) ...2E 14 (7D 84)
Canonbury (Overground) 5C 66
Canons Park (Underground) 7K 27
Carshalton (Rail) 4D 166
Carshalton Beeches (Rail) 6D 166
Castle Bar Park (Rail) 5A 78
Catford (Rail) 7C 122
Catford Bridge (Rail) 7C 122
Centrale Stop (Tramlink) 2C 168
Chadwell Heath (Rail) 7D 54
Chalk Farm (Underground) 7E 64
Chancery Lane (Underground) 6J 7 (5A 84)
Charing Cross (Rail & Underground) ...4E 12 (1J 101)
Charlton (Rail) 5A 106
Cheam (Rail) 7G 165
Chelsea Harbour Pier (Riverbus) 1B 118
Chessington North (Rail) 5E 162
Chessington South (Rail) 7D 162
Chigwell (Underground) 3K 37
Chingford (Rail) 1B 36
Chislehurst (Rail) 2E 160
Chiswick (Rail) 7J 97
Chiswick Park (Underground) 4J 97
Church Street Stop (Tramlink) 2C 168
City Thameslink (Rail) 7A 8 (6B 84)
Clapham Common (Underground) 4G 119
Clapham High Street (Rail) 3H 119
Clapham Junction (Rail & Overground) 3C 118
Clapham North (Underground) 3J 119
Clapham South (Underground) 6F 119
Clapton (Rail) 2H 67
Clock House (Rail) 1A 158
Cockfosters (Underground) 4K 21
Colindale (Underground) 3A 44
Colliers Wood (Underground) 7B 136
Coombe Lane Stop (Tramlink) 5J 169
Covent Garden (Underground) 2F 13 (7J 83)
Cricklewood (Rail) 4F 63
Crofton Park (Rail) 5B 122
Crossharbour (DLR & Underground) 3D 104
Crouch Hill (Overground) 7K 47
Crystal Palace (Rail & Overground) 6G 139

Custom House for ExCeL (DLR) 7K 87
Cutty Sark for Maritime Greenwich (DLR) ...6E 104
Cyprus (DLR) 7E 88

D

Dagenham Dock (Rail) 2F 91
Dagenham East (Underground) 5J 73
Dagenham Heathway (Underground) 6F 73
Dalston Junction (Overground) 6F 67
Dalston Kingsland (Overground) 5E 66
Denmark Hill (Rail) 2D 120
Deptford (Rail) 7C 104
Deptford Bridge (DLR) 1C 122
Devons Road (DLR) 4D 86
Dollis Hill (Underground) 5C 62
Drayton Green (Rail) 6K 77
Drayton Park (Rail) 4A 66
Dundonald Road Stop (Tramlink) 7H 135

E

Ealing Broadway (Rail & Underground) 7D 78
Ealing Common (Underground) 1F 97
Earl's Court (Underground) 4K 99
Earlsfield (Rail) 1A 136
East Acton (Underground) 6B 80
Eastcote (Underground) 7A 40
East Croydon (Rail & Tramlink) 2D 168
East Dulwich (Rail) 4E 120
East Finchley (Underground) 4C 46
East Ham (Underground) 7C 70
East India (DLR) 7F 87
East Putney (Underground) 5G 117
Eden Park (Rail) 5C 158
Edgware (Underground) 6C 28
Edgware Road (Underground) 5C 4 (5C 82)
Edmonton Green (Rail) 2B 34
Elephant & Castle (Rail & Underground) 4C 102
Elmers End (Rail & Tramlink) 4K 157
Elmstead Woods (Rail) 6C 142
Eltham (Rail) 5D 124
Elverson Road (DLR) 2D 122
Embankment (Underground) 4F 13 (1J 101)
Embankment Pier (Riverbus) 4G 13 (1J 101)
Enfield Chase (Rail) 3H 23
Enfield Town (Rail) 3K 23
Erith (Rail) 5K 109
Essex Road (Rail) 7C 66
Euston (Rail, Underground & Overground)
....2C 6 (3G 83)
Euston Square (Underground) 3B 6 (4G 83)
Ewell West (Rail) 7A 164

F

Fairlop (Underground) 1H 53
Falconwood (Rail) 4H 125
Farringdon (Rail & Underground) 5A 8 (5B 84)
Feltham (Rail) 1K 129
Fenchurch Street (Rail) 2J 15 (7F 85)
Festival Pier (Riverbus) 4G 13 (1K 101)
Fieldway Stop (Tramlink) 7D 170
Finchley Central (Underground) 1J 45
Finchley Road (Underground) 6A 64
Finchley Road & Frognal (Overground) 5A 64
Finsbury Park (Rail & Underground) 2A 66
Forest Gate (Rail) 5J 69
Forest Hill (Rail & Overground) 2J 139

Fulham Broadway (Underground) 7J 99
Fulwell (Rail) 4H 131

G

Gallions Reach (DLR) 7F 89
Gants Hill (Underground) 6E 52
George Street Stop (Tramlink) 2C 168
Gipsy Hill (Rail) 5E 138
Gloucester Road (Underground) 4A 100
Golders Green (Underground) 1J 63
Goldhawk Road (Underground) 2E 98
Goodge Street (Underground) 5C 6 (5H 83)
Goodmayes (Rail) 1A 72
Gordon Hill (Rail) 1G 23
Gospel Oak (Overground) 4E 64
Grange Park (Rail) 5G 23
Gravel Hill Stop (Tramlink) 6A 170
Great Portland Street (Underground) 4K 5 (4F 83)
Greenford (Rail & Underground) 1H 77
Greenland Pier (Riverbus) 3B 104
Green Park (Underground) 4K 11 (1G 101)
Greenwich (Rail & DLR) 7D 104
Greenwich Pier (Riverbus) 5E 104
Grove Park (Rail) 3K 141
Gunnersbury (Underground & Overground) 5H 97

H

Hackbridge (Rail) 2F 167
Hackney Central (Overground) 6H 67
Hackney Downs (Rail) 5H 67
Hackney Wick (Overground) 6C 68
Hadley Wood (Rail) 1F 21
Haggerston (Overground) 1F 85
Hammersmith (Underground) 4E 98
Hampstead (Underground) 4A 64
Hampstead Heath (Overground) 4C 64
Hampton (Rail) 1E 148
Hampton Court (Rail) 4J 149
Hampton Wick (Rail) 1C 150
Hanger Lane (Underground) 3E 78
Hanwell (Rail) 7J 77
Harlesden (Overground & Underground) 2K 79
Harringay Green Lanes (Overground) 6B 48
Harringay (Rail) 6A 48
Harrington Road Stop (Tramlink) 3J 157
Harrow-on-the-Hill (Rail & Underground) 6J 41
Harrow & Wealdstone (Rail, Underground & Overground)
.............4J 41
Hatch End (Overground) 1E 40
Hatton Cross (Underground) 4H 111
Haydons Road (Rail) 5A 136
Hayes (Rail) 1J 171
Hayes & Harlington (Rail) 3H 93
Headstone Lane (Overground) 1F 41
Heathrow
    Central (Underground) 3C 110
    Terminals 1, 2 & 3 (Underground) 3D 110
    Terminal 4 (Underground) 6E 110
    Terminal 4 (Underground) 5E 110
    Terminal 5 (Rail &Underground) 6D 174
Hendon (Rail) 6C 44
Hendon Central (Underground) 5D 44
Herne Hill (Rail) 6B 120
Heron Quays (DLR) 1C 104
Highams Park (Rail) 6A 36
High Barnet (Underground) 4D 20
Highbury & Islington (Underground) 6B 66
Highgate (Underground) 6F 47
High Street Kensington (Underground) 2K 99
Hillingdon (Underground) 5D 56
Hilton Docklands Pier (Riverbus) 1B 104
Hither Green (Rail) 6G 123
Holborn (Underground) 6G 7 (6K 83)
Holland Park (Underground) 1H 99
Holloway Road (Underground) 5K 65
Homerton (Overground) 6K 67
Honor Oak Park (Rail & Overground) 6K 121
Hornsey (Rail) 4K 47

Hounslow (Rail) 5F 113
Hounslow Central (Underground) 3F 113
Hounslow East (Underground) 2G 113
Hounslow West (Underground) 2C 112
Hoxton (Overground) 1J 9 (2F 85)
Hyde Park Corner (Underground) 6H 11 (2E 100)

I

Ickenham (Underground) 4E 56
Ikea Ampere Way Stop (Tramlink) 7K 155
Ilford (Rail) 3E 70
Imperial Wharf (Rail & Overground) 1A 118
Island Gardens (DLR) 5E 104
Isleworth (Rail) 2K 113

K

Kempton Park (Rail) 7K 129
Kennington (Underground) 5B 102
Kensal Green (Rail, Underground & Overground) 3E 80
Kensal Rise (Overground) 2F 81
Kensington Olympia (Rail, Underground & Overground)
.............3G 99
Kent House (Rail) 1A 158
Kentish Town (Rail & Underground) 5G 65
Kentish Town West (Overground) 6F 65
Kenton (Overground & Underground) 6B 42
Kew Bridge (Rail) 5F 97
Kew Gardens (Underground & Overground) 1G 115
Kidbrooke (Rail) 3K 123
Kilburn (Underground) 6H 63
Kilburn High Road (Overground) 1K 81
Kilburn Park (Underground) 2J 81
King George V (DLR) 1E 106
Kingsbury (Underground) 5G 43
King's Cross (Rail & Underground) 1F 7 (2J 83)
King's Cross St Pancras (Underground) 1E 6 (3J 83)
Kingston (Rail) 1E 150
Knightsbridge (Underground) 7F 11 (2D 100)

L

Ladbroke Grove (Underground) 6G 81
Ladywell (Rail) 5D 122
Lambeth North (Underground) 1J 19 (3A 102)
Lancaster Gate (Underground) 2A 10 (7B 82)
Langdon Park (DLR) 6D 86
Latimer Road (Underground) 7F 81
Lebanon Road Stop (Tramlink) 2E 168
Lee (Rail) 6J 123
Leicester Square (Underground) 2D 12 (7J 83)
Lewisham (Rail & DLR) 3E 122
Leyton (Underground) 3E 68
Leyton Midland Road (Overground) 7E 50
Leytonstone (Underground) 1G 69
Leytonstone High Road (Overground) 2G 69
Limehouse (Rail & DLR) 6A 86
Liverpool Street (Rail & Underground) 6G 9 (5E 84)
Lloyd Park Stop (Tramlink) 4F 169
London Bridge (Rail & Underground) 5F 15 (1D 102)
London Bridge City Pier (Riverbus) 4F 15 (1E 102)
London City Airport (DLR) 1C 106
London Eye Millennium Pier (Riverbus) 6G 13 (2K 101)
London Fields (Rail) 7H 67
Loughborough Junction (Rail) 3B 120
Lower Sydenham (Rail) 5B 140

M

Maida Vale (Underground) 3K 81
Malden Manor (Rail) 7A 152
Manor House (Underground) 7C 48
Manor Park (Rail) 4B 70
Mansion House (Underground) 2D 14 (7C 84)
Marble Arch (Underground) 1F 11 (6D 82)
Maryland (Rail) 6G 69
Marylebone (Rail & Underground) 4E 4 (4D 82)

Masthouse Terrace Pier (Riverbus) 5C 104
Maze Hill (Rail) 6G 105
Merton Park Stop (Tramlink) 1J 153
Mile End (Underground) 4B 86
Millbank Millennium Pier(Riverbus) 4F 19 (4J 101)
Mill Hill Broadway (Rail) 6F 29
Mill Hill East (Underground) 7B 30
Mitcham Eastfields (Rail) 2E 154
Mitcham Junction (Rail & Tramlink) 5E 154
Mitcham Stop (Tramlink) 4C 154
Monument (Underground) 2F 15 (7D 84)
Moorgate (Rail & Underground) 6E 8 (5D 84)
Morden (Underground) 3K 153
Morden Road Stop (Tramlink) 2K 153
Morden South (Rail) 5J 153
Mornington Crescent (Underground) 2G 83
Mortlake (Rail) 3J 115
Motspur Park (Rail) 5D 152
Mottingham (Rail) 1D 142
Mudchute (DLR) 4D 104

N

Neasden (Underground) 5A 62
New Barnet (Rail) 5G 21
New Beckenham (Rail) 7B 140
Newbury Park (Underground) 6H 53
New Cross (Rail & Overground) 7B 104
New Cross Gate (Rail & Overground) 1A 122
New Eltham (Rail) 1F 143
New Malden (Rail) 3A 152
New Southgate (Rail) 5A 32
Norbiton (Rail) 1G 151
Norbury (Rail) 1K 155
North Acton (Underground) 5K 79
North Dulwich (Rail) 5D 120
North Ealing (Underground) 6F 79
Northfields (Underground) 3C 96
North Greenwich (Underground) 2G 105
North Harrow (Underground) 5F 41
Northolt (Underground) 6E 58
Northolt Park (Underground) 4F 59
North Sheen (Rail) 4G 115
Northumberland Park (Rail) 7C 34
North Wembley (Overground & Underground) 3D 60
Northwick Park (Underground) 7B 42
Northwood (Underground) 2J 39
Norwood Junction (Rail & Overground) 4G 157
Notting Hill Gate (Underground) 1J 99
Nunhead (Rail) 2J 121

O

Oakleigh Park (Rail) 7G 21
Oakwood (Underground) 5B 22
Old Street (Rail & Underground) 2F 9 (4D 84)
Orpington (Rail) 2J 173
Osterley (Underground) 7H 95
Oval (Underground) 6A 102
Oxford Circus (Underground) 1A 12 (6G 83)

P

Paddington (Rail & Underground) 7A 4 (6B 82)
Palmers Green (Rail) 4E 32
Park Royal (Underground) 4G 79
Parsons Green (Underground) 1J 117
Peckham Rye (Rail) 2G 121
Penge East (Rail) 6J 139
Penge West (Rail & Overground) 6H 139
Perivale (Underground) 2A 78
Petts Wood (Rail) 5G 161
Phipps Bridge Stop (Tramlink) 3B 154
Piccadilly Circus (Underground) 3C 12 (7H 83)
Pimlico (Underground) 5C 18 (5H 101)
Pinner (Underground) 4C 40
Plaistow (Underground) 2H 87
Plumstead (Rail) 4H 107
Ponders End (Rail) 5F 25

Pontoon Dock (DLR) .1A 106
Poplar (DLR) 7D 86
Preston Road (Underground) 1E 60
Prince Regent (DLR) .7A 88
Pudding Mill Lane (DLR) 1D 86
Putney (Rail) 4G 117
Putney Bridge (Underground) 3H 117
Putney Pier (Riverbus) 3G 117

Q

Queen Elizabeth II Pier (Riverbus) 1H 105
Queensbury (Underground) 3F 43
Queen's Park (Underground & Overground) 2H 81
Queens Road , Peckham (Rail) 1J 121
Queenstown Road, Battersea (Rail) 1F 119
Queensway (Underground) 7K 81

R

Ravensbourne (Rail) .7F 141
Ravenscourt Park (Underground) 4D 98
Rayners Lane (Underground) 7D 40
Raynes Park (Rail) 2E 152
Rectory Road (Rail) 3F 67
Redbridge (Underground) 6B 52
Reeves Corner Stop (Tramlink) 2B 168
Regent's Park (Underground) 4J 5 (4F 83)
Richmond (Rail, Underground & Overground) 4E 114
Roding Valley (Underground) 4G 37
Rotherhithe (Overground) 2J 103
Royal Albert (DLR) 7C 88
Royal Arsenal Woolwich Pier (Riverbus) 3F 107
Royal Oak (Underground) 5K 81
Royal Victoria (DLR) .7J 87
Ruislip (Underground) 1G 57
Ruislip Gardens (Underground) 4J 57
Ruislip Manor (Underground) 1J 57
Russell Square (Underground) 4E 6 (4J 83)

S

St Helier (Rail) 6J 153
St James's Park (Underground) 1C 18 (2H 101)
St James Street (Rail) 5A 50
St Johns (Rail) 2C 122
St John's Wood (Underground) 2B 82
St Katharine's Pier (Riverbus) 4K 15 (1F 103)
St Margarets (Rail) 6B 114
St Pancras International (Rail) 1E 6 (3J 83)
St Paul's (Underground) 7C 8 (6C 84)
Sanderstead (Rail) 7D 168
Sandilands Stop (Tramlink) 2F 169
Selhurst (Rail) 5E 156
Seven Kings (Rail) 1J 71
Seven Sisters (Rail & Underground) 5E 48
Shadwell (Overground & DLR) 7H 85
Shepherd's Bush (Underground & Overground) . . .2F 99
Shepherd's Bush Market (Underground) 1E 98
Shepperton (Rail) 5E 146
Shoreditch High Street (Overground) 3J 9 (4F 85)
Shortlands (Rail) 2G 159
Sidcup (Rail) 2A 144
Silver Street (Rail) 4A 34
Sloane Square (Underground) 4G 17 (4E 100)
Snaresbrook (Underground) 5J 51
South Acton (Overground) 3J 97
Southall (Rail) 2D 94
South Bermondsey (Rail) 5J 103
Southbury (Rail) 4C 24
South Croydon (Rail) 5D 168
South Ealing (Underground) 3D 96
Southfields (Underground) 1H 135
Southgate (Underground) 1C 32
South Greenford (Rail) 3J 77
South Hampstead (Overground) 7A 64

South Harrow (Underground) 3G 59
South Kensington (Underground) 3B 16 (4B 100)
South Kenton (Overground & Underground) 1C 60
South Merton (Rail) .3H 153
South Quay (DLR) 2D 104
South Ruislip (Rail & Underground) 5A 58
South Tottenham (Overground) 5F 49
Southwark (Underground) 5A 14 (1B 102)
South Wimbledon (Underground) 7K 135
South Woodford (Underground) 2K 51
Stamford Brook (Underground) 4B 98
Stamford Hill (Rail) 7E 48
Stanmore (Underground) 4J 27
Star Lane (DLR) 4G 87
Stepney Green (Underground) 4K 85
Stockwell (Underground) 1J 119
Stoke Newington (Rail) 2F 67
Stonebridge Park (Underground & Overground) . . .7H 61
Stoneleigh (Rail) 5C 164
Stratford (Overground, Underground & DLR) 7F 69
Stratford High Street (DLR) 1F 87
Stratford International (Rail & DLR) 6E 68
Strawberry Hill (Rail) 3K 131
Streatham (Rail) 5H 137
Streatham Common (Rail) 6H 137
Streatham Hill (Rail) .2J 137
Sudbury & Harrow Road (Rail) 5B 60
Sudbury Hill (Underground) 4J 59
Sudbury Hill Harrow (Rail) 4J 59
Sudbury Town (Underground) 6B 60
Sunbury (Rail) 1J 147
Sundridge Park (Rail) 7K 141
Surbiton (Rail) 6E 150
Surrey Quays (Overground) 4K 103
Sutton (Rail) 6A 166
Sutton Common (Rail) 2K 165
Swiss Cottage (Underground) 7B 64
Sydenham (Rail & Overground) 4J 139
Sydenham Hill (Rail) .3F 139
Syon Lane (Rail) 7A 96

T

Teddington (Rail) 6A 132
Temple (Underground) 2J 13 (7K 83)
Thames Ditton (Rail) .7K 149
Therapia Lane Stop (Tramlink) 7J 155
Thornton Heath (Rail) 4C 156
Tolworth (Rail) 2H 163
Tooting (Rail) 6D 136
Tooting Bec (Underground) 3E 136
Tooting Broadway (Underground) 5C 136
Tottenham Court Road (Underground) 7D 6 (6H 83)
Tottenham Hale (Rail & Underground) 3H 49
Totteridge & Whetstone (Underground) 2F 31
Tower Gateway (DLR) 2J 15 (7F 85)
Tower Hill (Underground) 2J 15 (7F 85)
Tower Millennium Pier (Riverbus) 4H 15 (1E 102)
Tufnell Park (Underground) 4G 65
Tulse Hill (Rail) 2B 138
Turnham Green (Underground) 4A 98
Turnpike Lane (Underground) 3B 48
Twickenham (Rail) 7A 114

U

Upney (Underground) 7K 71
Upper Halliford (Rail) 2G 147
Upper Holloway (Overground) 2H 65
Upton Park (Underground) 1A 88

V

Vauxhall (Rail & Underground) 6F 19 (5J 101)
Victoria (Coach) 4J 17 (4F 101)
Victoria (Rail & Underground) 3K 17 (4F 101)

W

Waddon (Rail) 4A 168
Waddon Marsh Stop (Tramlink) 2A 168
Wallington (Rail) 6F 167
Walthamstow Central (Rail & Underground) 5C 50
Walthamstow Queens Road (Overground) 5C 50
Wandle Park Stop (Tramlink) 2A 168
Wandsworth Common (Rail) 1D 136
Wandsworth Riverside Quarter Pier (Riverbus) . . .4J 117
Wandsworth Road (Rail) 2G 119
Wandsworth Town (Rail) 4K 117
Wanstead (Underground) 6K 51
Wanstead Park (Overground) 4K 69
Wapping (Overground) 1J 103
Warren Street (Underground) 3A 6 (4G 83)
Warwick Avenue (Underground) 4A 82
Waterloo (Rail & Underground) 6J 13 (2A 102)
Waterloo East (Rail) 5K 13 (1A 102)
Wellesley Road Stop (Tramlink) 2D 168
Welling (Rail) 2A 126
Wembley Central (Overground & Underground) . . .5E 60
Wembley Park (Underground) 3G 61
Wembley Stadium (Rail) 5F 61
West Acton (Underground) 6G 79
Westbourne Park (Underground) 5H 81
West Brompton (Rail, Underground & Overground) . .5J 99
Westcombe Park (Rail) 5J 105
West Croydon (Rail, Overground & Tramlink) 1C 168
West Drayton (Rail) 1A 92
West Dulwich (Rail) .2D 138
West Ealing (Rail) 7B 78
Westferry (DLR) 7C 86
West Finchley (Underground) 6E 30
West Ham (DLR) 3G 87
West Ham (Rail & Underground) 3G 87
West Hampstead (Underground & Overground) . . .6J 63
West Hampstead Thameslink (Rail) 6J 63
West Harrow (Underground) 6G 41
West India Quay (DLR) 7C 86
West Kensington (Underground) 5H 99
Westminster (Underground) 7F 13 (2J 101)
Westminster Millennium Pier (Riverbus) . . .6F 13 (2J 101)
West Norwood (Rail) .4B 138
West Ruislip (Rail & Underground) 2E 56
West Silvertown (DLR) 1J 105
West Sutton (Rail) 4J 165
West Wickham (Rail) .7E 158
Whitechapel (Underground & Overground) 5H 85
White City (Underground) 7E 80
White Hart Lane (Rail) 7A 34
Whitton (Rail) 7G 113
Willesden Green (Underground) 6E 62
Willesden Junction (Rail, Underground & Overground)
. . . . .3B 80
Wimbledon (Rail, Underground & Tramlink) 6H 135
Wimbledon Chase (Rail) 2G 153
Wimbledon Park (Underground) 3J 135
Winchmore Hill (Rail) 7G 23
Woodford (Underground) 6E 36
Woodgrange Park (Overground) 5B 70
Wood Green (Underground) 2A 48
Wood Lane (Underground) 7E 80
Woodside Park (Underground) 4E 30
Woodside Stop (Tramlink) 6H 157
Wood Street Walthamstow (Rail) 4F 51
Woolwich Arsenal (Rail & DLR) 4F 107
Woolwich Dockyard (Rail) 4D 106
Worcester Park (Rail) 1C 164

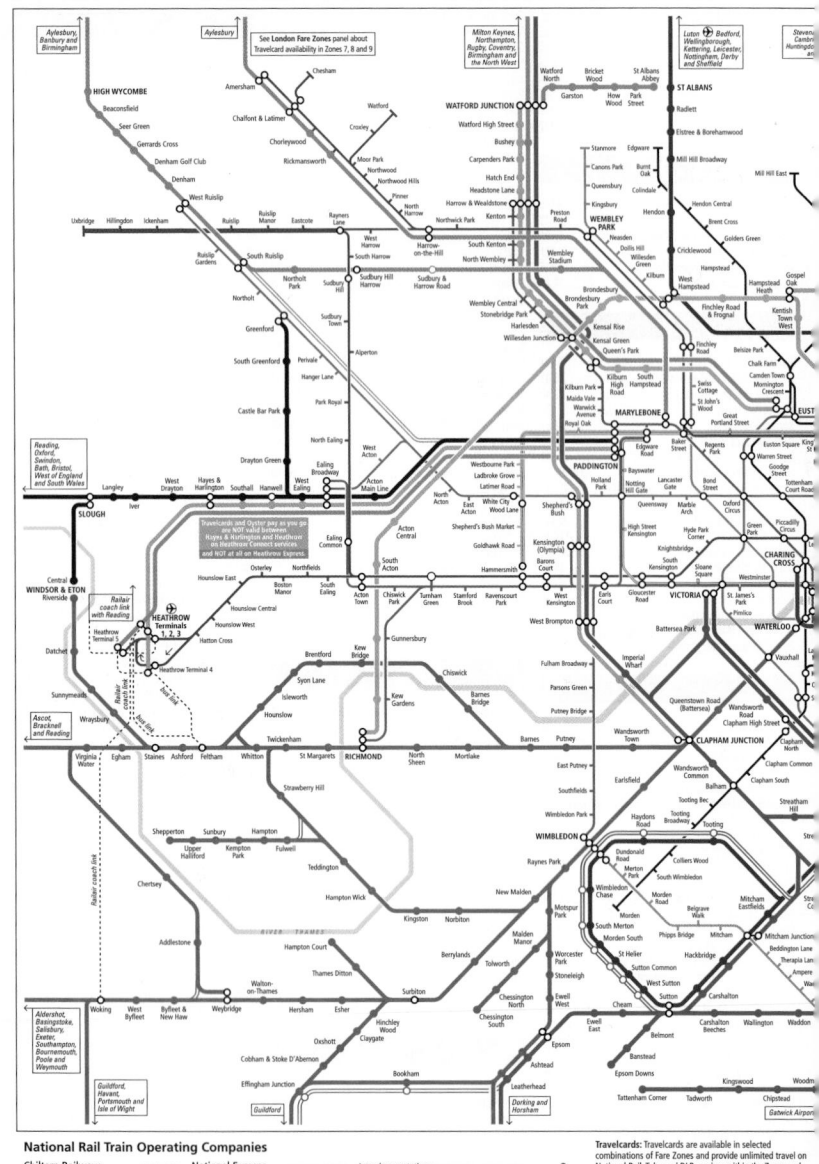

National Rail Train Operating Companies

Chiltern Railways	National Express East Anglia
c2c	Southern
First Capital Connect	Southeastern
First Great Western	Southeastern high-speed
London Midland	South West Trains
London Overground (managed under contract by TfL)	Peak hour or limited service routes and/or stations (in Train Company colours)

Interchange stations .... ○
Bus and coach links .... – – – – –

AIRPORT SERVICES:
Heathrow Connect ....
Heathrow Express ....
Stations with Airport links .... ✈
Heathrow Connect is jointly operated by First Group and BAA;
Heathrow Express is operated by BAA.

Travelcards: Travelcards are available in selected combinations of Fare Zones and provide unlimited travel on National Rail, Tube and DLR services within the Zones and on the day(s) for which they are valid. Any valid Travelcard can be used on most London Buses, and when valid for travel in Zone(s) 3, 4, 5 or 6 can be used throughout the London Tramlink network.

Note 1: Travelcards are NOT valid at all on Heathrow Express, or on Heathrow Connect services between Hayes & Harlington and Heathrow.

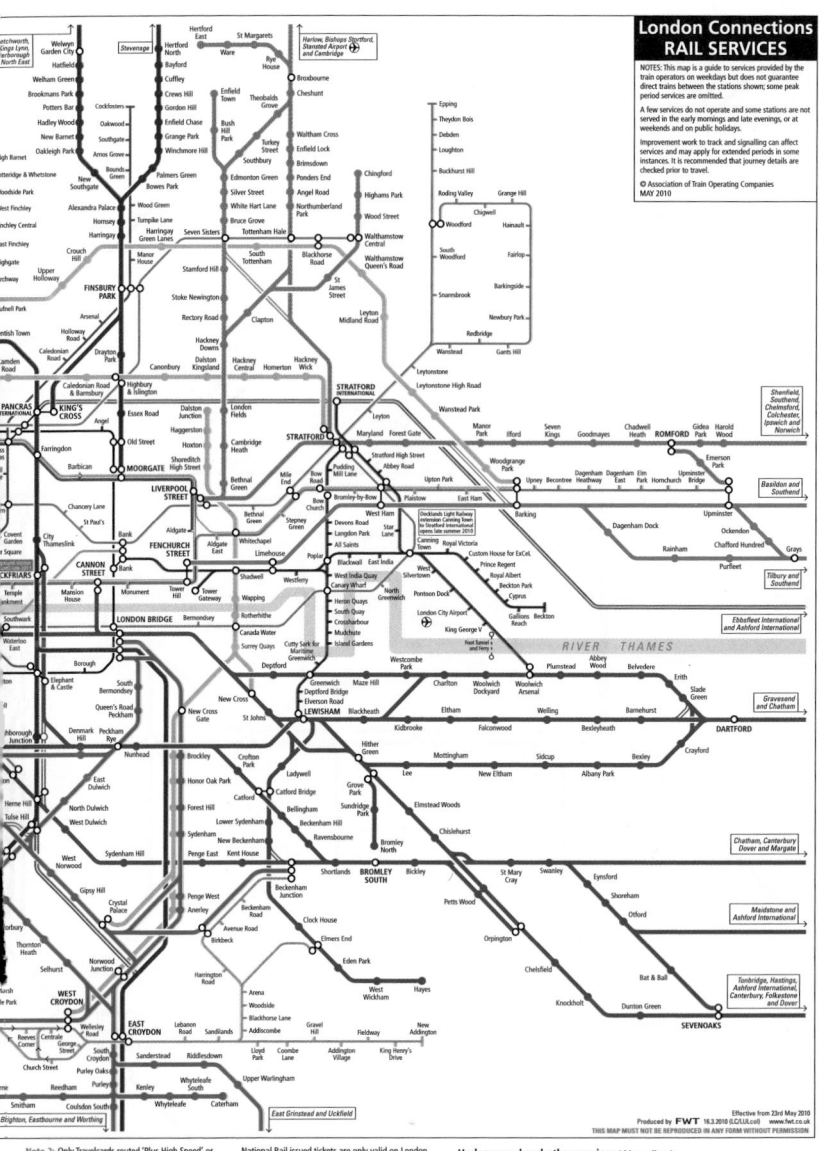

London Connections
RAIL SERVICES

NOTES: This map is a guide to services provided by the train operators on weekdays but does not guarantee direct trains between the stations shown; some peak period services are omitted.

A few services do not operate and some stations are not served in the early mornings and late evenings, or at weekends and on public holidays.

Improvement work to track and signalling can affect services and may apply for extended periods in some instances. It is recommended that journey details are checked prior to travel.

© Association of Train Operating Companies
MAY 2010

Effective from 23rd May 2010
Produced by FWT 16.3.2010 (LCZ/LUL.col)   www.fwt.co.uk
THIS MAP MUST NOT BE REPRODUCED IN ANY FORM WITHOUT PERMISSION

Note 2: Only Travelcards routed 'Plus High Speed' or 'Any Permitted + HS' are valid on Southeastern high speed services

Day single or return tickets: Ticket prices for journeys between stations within the Fare Zones are determined by the Zones travelled in and through. Different prices apply for journeys wholly between London Overground stations and those that include or permit travel on Tube and/or DLR services.

National Rail issued tickets are only valid on London Tramlink services when issued to or from 'TRAMLINK'.

Tickets between any two National Rail stations which have the 'f' symbol shown in the 'Route' section on the ticket, are valid 'Via London' and include the cost of transfer between London Mainline terminals and other designated interchanges by Tube, DLR, or National Rail services via City Thameslink.

Underground and other services (thinner lines)

Bakerloo Line
Central Line
Circle Line
District Line
Hammersmith & City Line
Jubilee Line
Metropolitan Line

Northern Line
Piccadilly Line
Victoria Line
Waterloo & City Line

Docklands Light Railway
London Tramlink

443

Chesham
Chalfont & Latimer
Amersham
Chorleywood
Rickmansworth
Watford
Croxley
Moor Park
Northwood
Northwood Hills
Pinner
North Harrow
Harrow-on-the-Hill
West Harrow
Northwick Park
West Ruislip
Hillingdon
Uxbridge
Ickenham
Ruislip
Ruislip Manor
Eastcote
Rayners Lane
Ruislip Gardens
South Ruislip
South Harrow
Northolt
Sudbury Hill
Greenford
Sudbury Town
Alperton
Perivale
Hanger Lane
Park Royal
North Ealing
Ealing Broadway
West Acton
North Acton
East Acton
White City
Wood Lane
Ealing Common
Acton Central
South Acton
Acton Town
South Ealing
Northfields
Boston Manor
Osterley
Hounslow East
Hounslow Central
Hounslow West
Hatton Cross
Heathrow Terminals 1, 2, 3
Heathrow Terminal 4
Heathrow Terminal 5
Chiswick Park
Turnham Green
Stamford Brook
Ravenscourt Park
Gunnersbury
Kew Gardens
Richmond
Watford Junction
Watford High Street
Bushey
Carpenders Park
Hatch End
Headstone Lane
Harrow & Wealdstone
Kenton
Preston Road
South Kenton
North Wembley
Wembley Central
Stonebridge Park
Harlesden
Willesden Junction
Wembley Park
Kensal Rise
Brondesbury Park
Brondesbury
Kensal Green
Queen's Park
Kilburn High Road
South Hampstead
Kilburn Park
Maida Vale
Warwick Avenue
Royal Oak
Westbourne Park
Paddington
Edgware Road
Marylebone
Ladbroke Grove
Latimer Road
Shepherd's Bush
Shepherd's Bush Market
Goldhawk Road
Hammersmith
Kensington (Olympia)
Barons Court
West Kensington
Earl's Court
West Brompton
Fulham Broadway
Parsons Green
Putney Bridge
East Putney
Southfields
Wimbledon Park
Wimbledon
Imperial Wharf
Clapham Junction
River Thames
Stanmore
Canons Park
Queensbury
Kingsbury
Neasden
Dollis Hill
Willesden Green
Kilburn
West Hampstead
Finchley Road
Swiss Cottage
St. John's Wood
Edgware
Burnt Oak
Colindale
Hendon Central
Brent Cross
Golders Green
Hampstead
Hampstead Heath
Finchley Road & Frognal
Belsize Park
Chalk Farm
Mornington Crescent
Baker Street
Great Portland Street
Euston
Warren Street
Regent's Park
Goodge Street
Bayswater
Notting Hill Gate
Lancaster Gate
Bond Street
Oxford Circus
Holland Park
Queensway
Marble Arch
Tottenham Court Road
High Street Kensington
Green Park
Hyde Park Corner
Piccadilly Circus
Knightsbridge
Gloucester Road
Sloane Square
St. James's Park
South Kensington
Victoria
Westminster
Waterloo
Pimlico
Vauxhall
Kennington
Oval
Stockwell
Clapham North
Clapham Common
Clapham South
Balham
Tooting Bec
Tooting Broadway
Colliers Wood
South Wimbledon
Morden
Bakerloo
Central
Circle
District
Hammersmith & City
Jubilee
Metropolitan
Northern
Piccadilly
Victoria
Waterloo & City
DLR
London Overground
Blackfriars Station closed
Interchange stations
Step-free access from the platform to the street
National Rail
Riverboat services
Tramlink
Airport
MAYOR OF LONDON
Website
tfl.gov.uk
© Transport for London
Reg. user No. 09/1555/P
Improvement works may affect

High Barnet
Totteridge & Whetstone
ll East
Woodside Park
West Finchley
Finchley Central
East Finchley
Highgate
Gospel
Oak
Archway
Tufnell Park

Cockfosters
Oakwood
Southgate
Arnos Grove
Bounds Green
Wood Green
Turnpike Lane
Crouch
Hill
Manor House
Upper Holloway

Harringay
Green Lanes
South
Tottenham
Blackhorse
Road

Theydon Bois
Debden
Loughton
Buckhurst Hill

Epping

Roding
Valley
Chigwell
Grange Hill
Hainault
Fairlop
Barkingside
Newbury Park

Woodford

South
Woodford

Kentish
wn West
Kentish
Town
Holloway Road
Caledonian Road
Camden
Road
Camden
Road &
Barnsbury
King's Cross
St. Pancras

Arsenal
Finsbury Park
Highbury &
Islington
Canonbury
Dalston
Kingsland
Dalston Junction

Seven Sisters
Tottenham
Hale
Walthamstow
Central
Walthamstow
Queen's Road
Snaresbrook
Leytonstone
Leyton
Midland Road
Hackney Central
Stratford
Leyton

Upminster
Upminster Bridge
Hornchurch
Elm Park
Dagenham East
Dagenham Heathway
Becontree
Upney
Barking
East Ham
Upton Park
Plaistow
West Ham

Wanstead
Gants
Hill
Leytonstone
High Road
Wanstead
Park
Woodgrange Park

Angel
ton
are
Farringdon
Barbican
Moorgate
Chancery
Lane
St. Paul's
Covent Garden
Bank
er
Mansion
House
Blackfriars
Temple
bankment

Old Street
Liverpool
Street
Shoreditch
High Street
Aldgate
East
Aldgate
Monument
Tower
Hill
Tower
Gateway
Wapping
Rotherhithe
London
Bridge
Canada
Water
Bermondsey
Surrey Quays

Haggerston
Hoxton
Bethnal
Green
Stepney Green
Whitechapel
Shadwell
Limehouse

Homerton
Mile End
Bow Road
Bow
Church
Devons Road
Langdon Park
All Saints
Westferry
Poplar
Blackwall
West India
Quay
Canary Wharf
Heron Quays
South Quay
Crossharbour
Mudchute
Island Gardens

Hackney
Wick
Pudding
Mill Lane
Bromley-
by-Bow

East
India
Canning Town

North
Greenwich

Royal Victoria
Custom House for ExCeL
Prince Regent
Royal Albert
Beckton Park
Cyprus
Gallions
Reach
Beckton
London City Airport
King George V

West
Silvertown
Pontoon Dock

Woolwich
Arsenal

uthwark
Southwark
beth
h
Borough
Elephant & Castle

New Cross Gate
Brockley
Honor Oak Park
Forest Hill
Sydenham
Crystal Palace

New Cross
Penge West
Anerley
Norwood Junction
West Croydon

Cutty Sark
for Maritime Greenwich
Greenwich
Deptford Bridge
Elverson Road
Lewisham

River Thames

09/1555/P

nformation
22 1234

urney, please check before you travel
Version A TfL 02.2010
Correct at time of going to print

445

Transport for London

UNDERGROUND

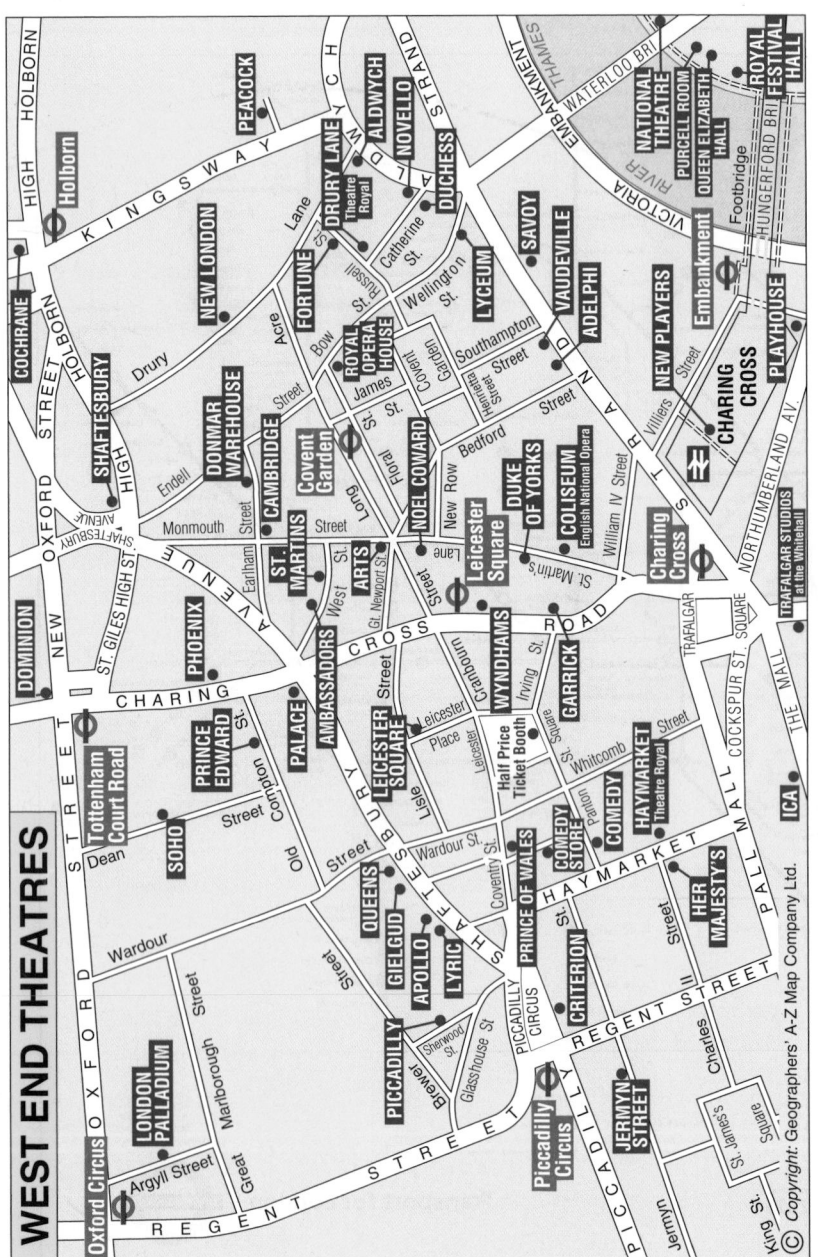

WEST END THEATRES

446